IN SIX VOLUMES, CAREFULLY REVISED AND CORRECTED

MATTHEW HENRY'S COMMENTARY

ON THE WHOLE BIBLE

WHEREIN EACH CHAPTER IS SUMMED UP IN ITS CONTENTS: THE SACRED TEXT INSERTED AT LARGE IN DISTINCT PARAGRAPHS; EACH PARAGRAPH REDUCED TO ITS PROPER HEADS: THE SENSE GIVEN, AND LARGELY ILLUSTRATED

WITH

PRACTICAL REMARKS AND OBSERVATIONS

VOL. VI.—ACTS TO REVELATION

World Bible Publishers
Iowa Falls, Iowa

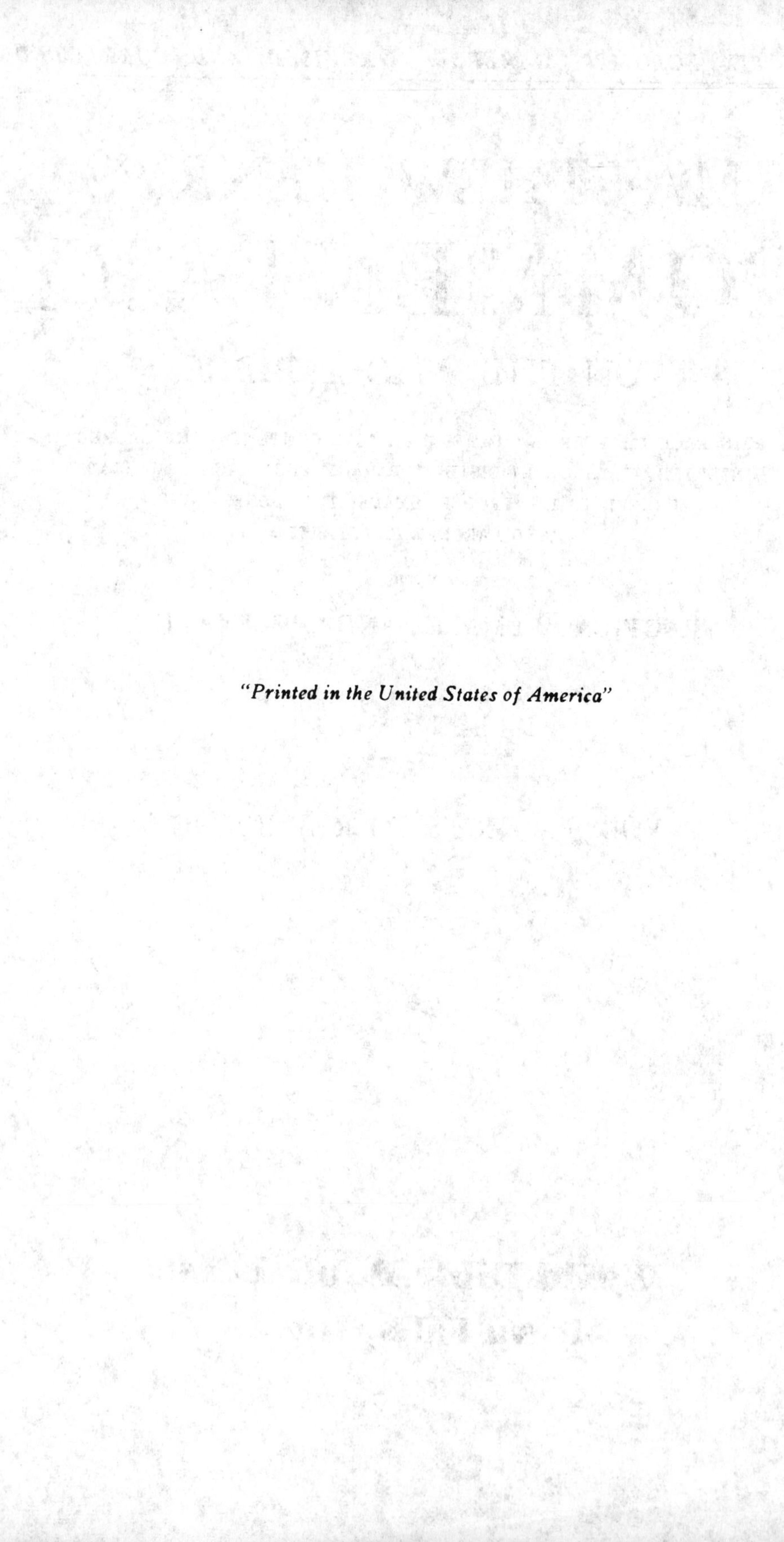

"Printed in the United States of America"

PREFACE.

AFTER much expectation, and many enquiries, the last volume of the late reverend Mr. Henry's Exposition now appears in the world. The common disadvantages that attend posthumous productions will doubtless be discerned in this; but we hope, though there are diversities of gifts, there will be found to be the same spirit. Some of the relations and hearers of that excellent person have been at the pains of transcribing the notes they took in short-hand of this part of the holy scripture, when expounded by him in his family or in the congregation; they have furnished us with very good materials for the finishing of this great work, and we doubt not but that the ministers who have been concerned in it have made that use of those assistances which may entitle this composure to the honour of Mr. Henry's name; and, if so, they can very willingly conceal their own.

The New Testament may be very properly divided into two parts, the one *historical* the other *epistolary*. It is the exposition of the latter we now recommend, and shall offer some thoughts on the epistolary way of writing in general, and then proceed to observe the divine authority of these epistles, together with the style, matter, method, and design of them, leaving what might be said concerning the several inspired penmen to the prefaces appertaining to the particular epistles.

As to the epistolary way of writing, it may be sufficient to observe that it has usually three properties:—It may in some things be more *difficult* to be understood, but then it is very *profitable*, and very *pleasant*; these will be found to be the properties of these sacred letters. We shall meet with things not easy to be understood, especially in some parts of them, where we cannot so well discover the particular occasions on which they were written or the questions or matters of fact to which they refer; but this is abundantly compensated by the profit which will accrue to those that read them with due attention. They will find the strongest reasoning, the most moving expostulations, and warm and pressing exhortations, mixed with seasonable cautions and reproofs, which are all admirably fitted to impress the mind with suitable sentiments and affections. And how much solid pleasure and delight must this afford to persons of a serious and religious spirit, especially when they wisely and faithfully apply to themselves what they find to suit their case! Thus they will appear to be as truly written to them as if their names were superscribed on them. It is natural for us to be very much pleased in perusing a wise and kind letter, full of instruction and comfort, sent to us by an absent friend: how then should we prize this part of holy scripture, when we consider herein that our God and Saviour has written these letters *to us*, in which we have the great things of his law and gospel, the things that belong to our peace! By these means not only the holy apostles, *being dead, yet speak*, but the Lord of the prophets and apostles continues to speak and write to us; and while we read them with proper affections, and follow them with suitable petitions and thanksgivings, a blessed correspondence and intercourse will be kept up between heaven and us, while we are yet sojourners in the earth.

But it is the divine inspiration and authority of these epistles we are especially concerned to know; and it is of the last importance that in this our minds be fully established. And we have strong and clear evidence that these epistles were written by the apostles of our Lord Jesus, and that they (like the prophets of the Old Testament) spoke and wrote *as they were moved by the Holy Ghost*. These epistles have in all ages of the church been received by Christians as a part of those holy scriptures that are *given by inspiration of God, and are profitable for doctrine, for reproof, for correction, and for instruction in righteousness, and are able to make us wise to salvation through faith which is in Jesus Christ;* they are part of that perpetual universal rule of faith and life which contains doctrines and revelations we are bound to believe with a divine faith, as coming from the God of truth, and duties to be practised by us in obedience to the will of God, *acknowledging that the things written therein are the commandments of God*, 1 Cor. xiv. 37. And, for the same reasons that lead us to acknowledge the other parts of the Bible to be the word of God, we must own these to be so too. If there is good reason (as indeed there is) to believe that the books of Moses were written by inspiration of God, there is the same reason to believe that the writings of the prophets were also from God, because the law and the prophets speak the same things, and such things as none but the Holy Ghost could teach; and, if we must with a divine faith believe the Old Testament to be a revelation from God, we cannot with any good reason question the divine authority of the New, when we consider how exactly the histories of the one agree with the prophecies of the other, and how the dark types and shadows of the law are illustrated and accomplished in the gospel. Nor can any person who pretends to believe the divine authority of the historical part of the New Testament, containing the Gospels and the Acts, with good reason question the equal authority of the epistolary part; for the subject-matter of all these epistles, as well as of the sermons of the apostles, is the *word of God* (Rom. x. 17; 1 Thess. ii. 13; Col. i. 25), and the *gospel of God* (Rom. xv. 16; 2 Cor. xi. 7), and the *gospel of Christ*, 2 Cor. ii. 12. We *are built upon the foundation of the apostles and prophets, Jesus Christ himself being the chief corner-stone;* and, as Moses wrote of Christ, so did all the prophets, for the Spirit of Christ in them did testify of him. And the apostles confirmed what Christ himself began to teach, *God also bearing them witness with signs, and wonders, and divers miracles, and gifts of the Holy Ghost, according to his will*, Heb. ii. 3, 4. The manifestation of God in the flesh, and the things *he began both to do and teach until the day in which he was taken up*, together with his sufferings unto death, and his resurrection (which things are declared to us, and are firmly to be believed, and strictly regarded by us), do give us an ample account of the way of life and salvation by Jesus Christ; but still it was the will of our blessed Lord that his apostles should not only publish his gospel to all the world, but also that, after his resurrection, they should declare some things more plainly concerning him than he thought fit to do while he was here on earth, for which end he promised to send his Holy Spirit *to teach them all things, to bring all things to their remembrance which he had spoken unto them*, John xiv. 26. For he told them (John xvi. 12, 13), *I have many things to say unto you, but you cannot bear them now; but when he, the Spirit of truth, is come, he shall lead you into all truth, and shall show you things to come.* Accordingly we find there was a wonderful effusion of the Holy Spirit upon the apostles (who in these epistles are called the *servants, ambassadors, and ministers* of Christ, *and stewards of the mysteries of God*), under whose infallible guidance they preached the gospel, and declared the whole counsel of God, and that with amazing courage and success, Satan every where falling down before them like lightning from heaven. That in preaching the gospel they were under the influence of the infallible Spirit is undeniable, from the miraculous gifts and powers they received for their work, particularly that gift of tongues so necessary for the publication of the gospel throughout the world to nations of different languages; nor must we omit that mighty power that accompanied the word preached, bringing multitudes to the obedience of faith, notwithstanding all opposition from earth and hell, and the potent lusts in the hearts of those who were *turned from idols to serve the living God, and to wait for his Son from heaven, whom he raised from the dead, even Jesus, that delivered us from the wrath to come*. Now that they were under the same mighty influence in writing these epistles as in preaching cannot be denied. Such infallible assistance seems to be as needful at least to direct their writing as their preaching, considering that these epistles were written to keep in memory those things that had been delivered by word of mouth (2 Pet. i. 15), and to rectify the mistakes that might arise about some expressions that had been used in preaching (2 Thess. ii. 2), and were to remain as a standing rule and record to which believers were to appeal, for defending the truth and discovering error, and a proper means to transmit the truths of the gospel to posterity, even to the end of time. Besides, the writers of these epistles have declared that what they wrote was from God: now they must know whether they had the special assistance of the divine Spirit or no, in their writing as well as preaching; and they in all things appear to have been men of such probity that they would not dare to say they had the Spirit of God when they had it not, or if they so much as doubted whether they had it or not; yea, they are careful, when they speak their own private opinion, or only under some common influence, to tell the world that not the *Lord*, but *they*, spoke those things, but that in the rest it was not they but the Lord, 1 Cor. vii. 10, 12, &c. And the apostle Paul makes the acknowledgment of this their inspiration to be a test to try those that pretended to be prophets or spiritual: *Let them* (says he) *acknowledge that the things I write unto you are the commandments of the Lord*, 1 Cor. xiv. 37. And the apostle Peter gives this as the reason of his writing, that those he wrote to *might after his decease have those things always in remembrance* (2 Pet. i. 15), which afterwards he calls the *commandment of the apostles of the Lord* (*ch.* iii. 1, 2), and so of the Lord himself. And the apostle John declareth (1 John iv. 6), *We are of God; he that knoweth God heareth us; he that is not of God heareth not us; by this we know the Spirit of truth, and the spirit of error.*

As to the style of these epistles, though it be necessary we should believe a divine influence superintending the several writers of them, yet it is not easy to explain the manner of it, nor to determine whether and in what particulars the words they wrote were dictated to them by the Holy Spirit, as mere *amanuenses*, or how far their own memories, and reasoning faculties, and other natural or acquired endowments, were employed under the inspection of the Spirit. We must believe that these holy men spoke and wrote *as they were moved by the Holy Ghost*, that he put them on and assisted them in this work. It is very probable that sometimes he not only suggested the very thoughts in their minds, but put words into their mouths, and always infallibly guided them into all truth, both when they expounded the scriptures of the Old Testament and when they gave rules for our faith and practice in the gospel church state. And yet perhaps it may be allowed, without any diminution to the authority of these epistles, that the penmen of them made some use of their own reasoning powers and different endowments in their manner of writing, as well as of their different sorts of chirography; and that by this we are to account for that difference of style which has been observed between the writings of Paul, who was brought up at the feet of Gamaliel, and those of Peter and John, who were fishermen. The like difference may be discerned between the style of the prophet Isaiah, who was educated in a court, and that of Amos, who was one of the herdsmen of Tekoa. However, the best way to understand these scriptures aright is not to criticise too nicely upon the words and phrases, but to attend carefully to the drift and design of these inspired writers in them.

The *subject-matter* of these epistles is entirely conformable to the rest of the scriptures. In them we find frequent reference to some passages of the Old Testament, and explanations of them: in the epistle to the Hebrews we have the best exposition of the Levitical law. Indeed the New Testament refers to, and in a manner builds upon, the Old, showing the accomplishment of all the ancient promises and prophecies concerning the Messiah, and explains all the antiquated types and *shadows of the good things that were then to come*. But, besides these references to the preceding part of holy writ, in some of these epistles there are contained prophecies, either wholly new or at least more largely and plainly revealed, as that in the *Revelation* concerning the rise, reign, and fall of antichrist, of which great apostasy we have some account in 2 Thess. ii. 3, 4, and in 1 Tim. iv. 1—3. And in these epistles we have several of the great doctrines of the gospel more fully discussed than elsewhere, particularly the doctrine of original sin, of the sin that dwells in the regenerate, and of justification by the righteousness of Christ, of the abolishing of the Jewish rites and ceremonies, of the true nature and design of the seals of the new covenant, the obligations they bring us under, and their perpetual use in the Christian church.

The general method of these epistles is such as best serves the end or design of them, which is indeed the end of the whole scripture—practical godliness, out of a principle of divine love, a good conscience, and faith unfeigned. Accordingly most of the epistles begin with the great doctrines of the gospel, the articles of the Christian faith, which, when received, work by love, purify the conscience, and produce evangelical obedience; and, after these principles have been laid down, practical conclusions are drawn and urged from them. In taking this method there is a regard paid to the nature and faculties of the soul of man (where the understanding is to lead the way, the will, affections, and executive powers, to follow after), and to the nature of religion in general, which is a reasonable service. We are not to be determined by superstitious fancies, nor by blind passions, but by a sound judgment and good understanding in the mind and will of God By this we are taught how necessary it is that faith and practice, truth and holiness, be joined together, that the performance of moral duties will never be acceptable to God, nor available to our own salvation, without the belief of the truth, since those who make shipwreck of the faith seldom maintain a good conscience, and the most solemn profession of the faith will never save those that *hold the truth in unrighteousness.*

The particular occasions upon which these epistles were written do not so evidently appear in them all as in some. The first to the Corinthians seems to have taken its rise from the unhappy divisions that so early rose in the churches of Christ, through the emulation of the ministers and personal affections of the people; but it does not confine itself to that subject. That to the Galatians seems directed chiefly against those judaizing teachers that went about to draw the Gentile converts away from the simplicity of the gospel in doctrine and worship. The epistle to the Hebrews is manifestly calculated to wean the converted Jews from those Mosaical rites and ceremonies for which they retained too great a fondness, and to reconcile them to the abolition of that economy. Those epistles that are directed to particular persons more evidently carry their design in them, which he that runs may read. But this is certain, none of these epistles are of private interpretation. Most of the psalms and of the prophecies of the Old Testament were penned or pronounced on particular occasions, and yet they are of standing and universal use, and very instructive even to us upon whom the ends of the world have come. And so are those epistles that seem to have been most limited in the rise and occasion of them. There will always be need enough to warn Christians against uncharitable divisions, against corrupting the faith and worship of the gospel; and, whenever the case is the same, these epistles are as certainly directed to such churches and persons as if they had been inscribed to them.

These general observations, we suppose, may be sufficient to introduce the reader into the book itself; let us now take a short view of the whole work, of which this posthumous piece is the conclusion. It is now about fourteen years since the first part of this exposition of the Bible was made public. In five years' time the Old Testament was finished in four volumes. The first volume of the New Testament was longer in hand; for though the ever-memorable author was always fully employed in the ordinary work of his ministry, yet those last years of his life, in which he drew up the exposition upon the historical part of the New Testament, were less at his own command than any other had been. His removal to Hackney, his almost continual preaching from day to day, his journeys to Chester, and the necessity of more frequent visits to his friends in and about London, together with a gradual sensible decay of health, will more than excuse the three years' time that passed before that was finished. And under such difficulties none but a man of his holy zeal, unwearied industry, and great sagacity, could have gone through such a service in that space of time. He lived not to see that volume published, though left by him ready for the press. The church of God was suddenly deprived of one of the most useful ministers of the age. We have been gathering up the fragments of those feasts with which he used to entertain his family and friends, in his delightful work of opening the scriptures. What remains is that we recommend the whole of this work to the acceptance and blessing of our God and Saviour, to whose honour and interest it was from the first directed and devoted. We need not be very solicitous about the acceptance it may meet with in the world: what has been before published has been received and read with great pleasure and advantage by the most serious experienced Christians in Great Britain and Ireland; and the many loud calls there have been for the publishing of this supplement, and reprinting the whole, leave us no room to doubt but that it will meet with a hearty welcome. Though it must be acknowledged that we live in an age which, by feeding upon ashes and the wind, has very much lost the relish of every thing that is spiritual and evangelical, yet we persuade ourselves there will still be found many who, *by reason of use, have their senses exercised to discern both good and evil.* Those that may think the expository notes too long, especially for family worship, may easily relieve themselves, either by reading a less part of the chapter at one time, or by abridging the annotations, and perusing the rest when they have more leisure; for, though it must be owned they are somewhat copious, yet we are persuaded that those who peruse them seriously will find nothing in them superfluous or impertinent; and, if any where some things in the comment do not seem to flow so naturally and necessarily from the text, we believe when they are well considered and compared it will appear they come under the analogy and general reason of the subject, and truly belong to it. If there be any that think this exposition of the Bible is too plain and familiar, that it wants the beauties of oratory and the strength of criticism, we only wish that they will read it over again with due attention, and we are pretty confident they will find the style natural, clear, and comprehensive; and we think they will hardly be able to produce one valuable criticism out of the most learned commentators but they will have it in this exposition, though couched in plain terms, and not brought in as of a critical nature. No man was more happy than Mr. Henry in that useful talent of making dark things plain, while too many, that value themselves upon their criticising faculty, affect rather to make plain things dark.

But we leave this great and good work to speak for itself, and doubt not but it will grow in its use and esteem, and will, through the blessing of God, help to revive and promote family religion and scriptural knowledge, and support the credit of scripture commentaries, though couched in human expressions. These have been always accounted the great treasures of the church, and, when done with judgment, have been so far from lessening the authority of the Bible that they have greatly promoted its honour and usefulness.

The following are the ministers by whom the Exposition on the Epistolary writings, and the Revelation, was completed, as given by J. B. Williams, Esq., LL.D., F.S.A., in his *Memoirs of the Life, Character, and Writings, of the Rev. Matthew Henry*, 8vo. p. 308.

Romans	Mr. [afterwards Dr.] John Evans.
1 Corinthians	Mr. Simon Browne.
2 Corinthians	Mr. Daniel Mayo.
Galatians	Mr. Joshua Bayes.
Ephesians	Mr. Samuel Rosewell.
Philippians Colossians	Mr. [afterwards Dr.] William Harris.
1 Thessalonians 2 Thessalonians	Mr. Daniel Mayo.
1 Timothy 2 Timothy	Mr. Benjamin Andrews Atkinson.
Titus Philemon	Mr. Jeremiah Smith.
Hebrews	Mr. William Tong.
James	Dr. S. Wright.
1 Peter	Mr. Zech. Merrill.
2 Peter	Mr. Joseph Hill.
1, 2, and 3 John	Mr. John Reynolds, of Shrewsbury
Jude	Mr. John Billingsley.
Revelations	Mr. William Tong.

AN

EXPOSITION,

WITH PRACTICAL OBSERVATIONS,

OF THE

ACTS OF THE APOSTLES.

We have with an abundant satisfaction seen the foundation of our holy religion laid in the history of our blessed Saviour, its great author, which was related and left upon record by four several inspired writers, who all agree in this sacred truth, and the incontestable proofs of it, that *Jesus is the Christ, the Son of the living God*. Upon this rock the Christian church is built. How it began to be built upon this rock comes next to be related in this book which we have now before us, and of this we have the testimony only of *one witness;* for the matters of fact concerning Christ were much more necessary to be fully related and attested than those concerning the apostles. Had Infinite Wisdom seen fit, we might have had as many books of the Acts of the Apostles as we have gospels, nay, as we might have had gospels: but, for fear of over-burdening the world (John xxi. 25), we have sufficient to answer the end, if we will but make use of it.

The history of this book (which was always received as a part of the sacred canon) may be considered,

I. As looking back to the preceding gospels, giving light to them, and greatly assisting our faith in them. The promises there made we here find made good, particularly the great promises of the descent of the Holy Ghost, and his wonderful operations, both *on* the apostles (whom here in a few days we find quite other men than what the gospels left them; no longer weak-headed and weak-hearted, but able to say that which then they were not able to bear (John xvi. 12) and bold as lions to face those hardships at the thought of which they then trembled as lambs), and also with the apostles, making the word mighty to the *pulling down of* Satan's *strong holds,* which had been before comparatively preached in vain. The commission there granted to the apostles we here find executed, and the powers there lodged in them we here find exerted in miracles wrought on the bodies of people—miracles of mercy, restoring sick bodies to health and dead bodies to life—miracles of judgment, striking rebels blind or dead; and much greater miracles wrought on the minds of people, in conferring spiritual gifts upon them, both of understanding and utterance; and this in pursuance of Christ's purposes, and in performance of his promises, which we had in the gospels. The proofs of Christ's resurrection with which the gospels closed are here abundantly corroborated, not only by the constant and undaunted testimony of those that conversed with him after he arose (who had all deserted him, and one of them denied him, and would not otherwise have been rallied again but by his resurrection, but must have been irretrievably dispersed, and yet by that were enabled to own him more resolutely than ever, in defiance of bonds and deaths), but by the working of the Spirit with that testimony for the conversion of multitudes to the faith of Christ, according to the word of Christ, that his resurrection, the sign of the prophet Jonas, which was reserved to the last, should be the most convincing proof of his divine mission. Christ had told his disciples that they should be his witnesses, and this book brings them in witnessing for him,—that they should be *fishers of men,* and here we have them enclosing multitudes in the gospel-net,—that they should be the *lights of the world,* and here we have the world enlightened by them; but that day-spring from on high the first appearing of which we there discerned we here find shining more and more. The *corn of wheat,* which there fell to the ground, here springs up and bears much fruit; the *grain of mustard-seed* there is here a *great tree;* and *the kingdom of heaven,* which was then *at hand,* is here set up. Christ's predictions of the virulent persecutions which the preachers of the gospel should be afflicted with (though one could not have imagined that a doctrine so well worthy of all acceptation should meet with so much opposition) we here find abundantly fulfilled, and also the assurances he gave them of extraordinary supports and comforts under their sufferings. Thus, as the latter part of the history of the Old Testament verifies the promises made to the fathers of the former part (as appears by that famous and solemn acknowledgment of Solomon's, which runs like a receipt in full, 1 Kings viii. 56, *There has not failed one word of all his good promises which he promised by the hand of Moses his servant*), so this latter part of the history of the New Testament exactly answers to the word of Christ in the former part of it: and thus they mutually confirm and illustrate each other.

II. As looking forward to the following epistles, which are an explication of the gospels, which open the mysteries of Christ's death and resurrection, the history of which we had in the gospels. This book introduces them and is a key to them, as the history of David is to David's psalms. We are members of the Christian church, that *tabernacle of God among men*, and it is our honour and privilege that we are so. Now this book gives us an account of the framing and rearing of that tabernacle. The four gospels showed us how the foundation of that house was laid; this shows us how the superstructure began to be raised, 1. Among the Jews and Samaritans, which we have an account of in the former part of this book. 2. Among the Gentiles, which we have an account of in the latter part: from thence, and downward to our own day, we find the Christian church subsisting in a visible profession of faith in Christ, as the Son of God and Saviour of the world, made by his baptized disciples, incorporated into religious societies, statedly meeting in religious assemblies, attending on the apostles' doctrine, and joining in prayers and the breaking of bread, under the guidance and presidency of men that gave themselves to prayer and the ministry of the word, and in a spiritual communion with all in every place that do likewise. Such a body as this there is now in the world, which we belong to: and, to our great satisfaction and honour, in this book we find the rise and origin of it, vastly different from the Jewish church, and erected upon its ruins; but undeniably appearing to be of God, and not of man. With what confidence and comfort may we proceed in, and adhere to, our Christian profession, as far as we find it agrees with this *pattern in the mount*, to which we ought religiously to conform and confine ourselves!

Two things more are to be observed concerning this book:—(1.) The penman of it. It was written by Luke, who wrote the third of the four gospels, which bears his name; and who (as the learned Dr. Whitby shows) was, very probably, one of the seventy disciples, whose commission (Luke x. 1, &c.) was little inferior to that of the twelve apostles. This Luke was very much a companion of Paul in his services and sufferings. *Only Luke is with me*, 2 Tim. iv. 11. We may know by his style in the latter part of this book when and where he was with him, for then he writes, We did so and so, as *ch.* xvi. 10; xx. 6; and thenceforward to the end of the book. He was with Paul in his dangerous voyage to Rome, when he was carried thither a prisoner, was with him when from his prison there he wrote his epistles to the Colossians and Philemon, in both which he is named. And it should seem that St. Luke wrote this history when he was with St. Paul at Rome, during his imprisonment there, and was assistant to him; for the history concludes with St. Paul's preaching there in his *own hired house*. (2.) The title of it: *The Acts of the Apostles; of the holy Apostles*, so the Greek copies generally read it, and so they are called, Rev. xviii. 20, *Rejoice over her you holy apostles*. One copy inscribes it, *The Acts of the Apostles by Luke the Evangelist*. [1.] It is the history of the apostles; yet there is in it the history of Stephen, Barnabas, and some other apostolical men, who, though not of the twelve, were endued with the same Spirit, and employed in the same work; and, of those that were apostles, it is the history of Peter and Paul only that is here recorded (and Paul was now of the twelve), Peter the apostle of the circumcision, and Paul the apostle of the Gentiles, Gal. ii. 7. But this suffices as a specimen of what the rest did in other places, pursuant to their commission, for there were none of them idle; and as we are to think what is related in the gospels concerning Christ sufficient, because Infinite Wisdom thought so, the same we are to think here concerning what is related of the apostles and their labours; for what more is told us from tradition of the labours and sufferings of the apostles, and the churches they planted, is altogether doubtful and uncertain, and what I think we cannot build upon with any satisfaction at all. This is *gold, silver*, and *precious stones*, built upon the *foundation*: that is *wood, hay, and stubble*. [2.] It is called their *acts*, or *doings*; *Gesta apostolorum*; so some. Πράξεις—their practices of the lessons their Master had taught them. The apostles where active men; and though the wonders they did were by the word, yet they are fitly called *their acts*; they spoke, or rather the Spirit by them *spoke, and it was done*. The history is filled with their sermons and their sufferings; yet so much did they labour in their preaching, and so voluntarily did they expose themselves to sufferings, and such were their achievements by both, that they may very well be called their *acts*.

CHAP. I.

The inspired historian begins his narrative of the Acts of the Apostles, I. With a reference to, and a brief recapitulation of, his gospel, or history of the life of Christ, inscribing this, as he had done that, to his friend Theophilus, ver. 1, 2. II. With a summary of the proofs of Christ's resurrection, his conference with his disciples, and the instructions he gave them during the forty days of his continuance on earth, ver. 3—5. III. With a particular narrative of Christ's ascension into heaven, his disciples' discourse with him before he ascended, and the angels' discourse with them after he ascended, ver. 6—11. IV. With a general idea of the embryo of the Christian church, and its state from Christ's ascension to the pouring out of the Spirit, ver. 12—14. V. With a particular account of the filling up of the vacancy that was made in the sacred college by the death of Judas, by the electing of Matthias in his room, ver. 15—26.

THE former treatise have I made,
O Theophilus, of all that Jesus
began both to do and teach, 2 Until
the day in which he was taken up,
after that he through the Holy Ghost
had given commandments unto the
apostles whom he had chosen: 3 To
whom also he showed himself alive
after his passion by many infallible
proofs, being seen of them forty days,
and speaking of the things pertaining
to the kingdom of God: 4 And, being
assembled together with *them*,
commanded them that they should
not depart from Jerusalem, but wait
for the promise of the Father, which,
saith he, ye have heard of me. 5

For John truly baptized with water; but ye shall be baptized with the Holy Ghost not many days hence.

In these verses, I. Theophilus is put in mind, and we in him, of St. Luke's gospel, which it will be of use for us to cast an eye upon before we enter upon the study of this book, that we may not only see how this begins where that breaks off, but that, *as in water face answers to face,* so do the acts of the apostles to the acts of their Master, the acts of his grace.

1. His patron, to whom he dedicates this book (I should rather say his *pupil,* for he designs, in dedicating it to him, to instruct and direct him, and not to crave his countenance or protection), is Theophilus, *v.* 1. In the epistle dedicatory before his gospel, he had called him *most excellent Theophilus;* here he calls him no more than *O Theophilus;* not that he had lost his excellency, nor that it was diminished and become less illustrious; but perhaps he had now quitted his place, whatever it was, for the sake of which that title was given him,—or he was now grown into years, and despised such titles of respect more than he had done,—or Luke was grown more intimate with him, and therefore could address him with the more freedom. It was usual with the ancients, both Christian and heathen writers, thus to inscribe their writings to some particular persons. But the directing some of the books of the scripture so is an intimation to each of us to receive them as if directed to us in particular, to us by name; for *whatsoever things were written aforetime were written for our learning.*

2. His gospel is here called *the former treatise which he had made,* which he had an eye to in writing this, intending this for a continuation and confirmation of that, τὸν πρῶτον λόγον—*the former word.* What is written of the gospel is the word as truly as what was spoken; nay, we now know no unwritten word that we are to give credit to, but as it agrees with that which is written. He made the former treatise, and now is divinely inspired to make this, for Christ's scholars must *go on towards perfection,* Heb. vi. 1. And therefore their guides must help them on, must *still teach the people knowledge* (Eccl. xii. 9), and not think that their former labours, though ever so good, will excuse them from further labours; but they should rather be quickened and encouraged by them, as St. Luke here, who, because he had laid the foundation in a former treatise, will build upon it in this. Let not this therefore drive out that; let not new sermons and new books make us forget old ones, but put us in mind of them, and help us to improve them.

3. The contents of his gospel were *that, all that, which Jesus began both to do and teach;* and the same is the subject of the writings of the other three evangelists. Observe, (1.) Christ both did and taught. The doctrine he taught was confirmed by the miraculous works he did, which proved him *a teacher come from God* (John iii. 2); and the duties he taught were copied out in the holy gracious works he did, for he hath *left us an example,* and that such as proves him a *teacher come from God* too, for *by their fruits you shall know them.* Those are the best ministers that both do and teach, whose lives are a constant sermon. (2.) *He began both to do and teach;* he laid the foundation of all that was to be taught and done in the Christian church. His apostles were to carry on and continue what he began, and to do and teach the same things. Christ set them in, and then left them to go on, but sent his Spirit to empower them both to do and teach. It is a comfort to those who are endeavouring to carry on the work of the gospel that Christ himself began it. The great salvation *at the first began to be spoken by the Lord,* Heb. ii. 3. (3.) The four evangelists, and Luke particularly, have handed down to us *all that Jesus began both to do and to teach;* not all the particulars—the world could not have contained them; but all the heads, samples of all, so many, and in such variety, that by them we may judge of the rest. We have the beginnings of his doctrine (Matt. iv. 17), and the beginnings of his miracles, John ii. 11. Luke had spoken, had treated, of all Christ's sayings and doings, had given us a general idea of them, though he had not recorded each in particular.

4. The period of the evangelical story is fixed *to the day in which he was taken up, v.* 2. Then it was that he left this world, and his bodily presence was no more in it. St. Mark's gospel concludes with *the Lord's being received up into heaven* (Mark xvi. 19). and so does St. Luke's, Luke xxiv. 51. Christ continued doing and teaching to the last, *till he was taken up* to the other work he had to do within the veil.

II. The truth of Christ's resurrection is maintained and evidenced, *v.* 3. That part of what was related in *the former treatise* was so material that it was necessary to be upon all occasions repeated. The great evidence of his resurrection was that *he showed himself alive to his apostles;* being alive, he showed himself so, and *he was seen of them.* They were honest men, and one may depend upon their testimony; but the question is whether they were not imposed upon, as many a well-meaning man is. No, they were not; for, 1. The proofs were infallible, τεκμήρια—*plain indications,* both that he was *alive* (he walked and talked with them, he ate and drank with them) and that *it was he himself, and not another;* for he showed them again and again the marks of *the wounds in his hands, and feet, and side,* which was the utmost proof the thing was capable of or required. 2. They were many, and often repeated: *He was seen by them forty days,* not constantly residing with them, but frequently appearing to them, and bringing them by degrees to be fully satisfied concerning it, so that all their sorrow for his departure was done away by it. Christ's staying upon earth so long after he had entered upon his state of exaltation and glory, to confirm the faith of his disciples and comfort their hearts, was such an instance of condescension and compassion to believers as may fully assure us *that we have a high priest that is touched with the feeling of our infirmities.*

III. A general hint given of the instructions he furnished his disciples with, now that he was about to leave them, and they, since *he breathed on them* and *opened their understandings,* were better able to receive them. 1. He instructed them concerning the work they were to do: *He gave commandments to the apostles whom he had chosen.* Note, Christ's choice is always attended with his charge. Those whom he elected into the apostleship expected he should give them preferments, instead of which *he gave them commandments.* When *he took his journey, and gave authority to his servants, and to every one his work* (Mark xiii. 34), *he gave them commandments through the Holy Ghost,* which he was himself filled with as Mediator, and which he had breathed into them. In giving them the Holy Ghost, he gave them his commandments; for the Comforter will be a commander; and his office was *to bring to their remembrance what Christ had said. He charged those that were apostles by the Holy Ghost;* so the words are placed. It was their receiving the Holy Ghost that sealed their commission, John xx. 22. He was not taken up till after he had given them their charge, and so finished his work. 2. He instructed them concerning the doctrine they were to preach: *He spoke to them of the things pertaining to the kingdom of God.* He had given them a general idea of that kingdom, and the certain time it should be set up in the world (in his parable, Mark xiii.), but here he instructed them more in the nature of it, as a kingdom of grace in this world and of glory in the other, and opened to them that covenant which is the great charter by which it is incorporated. Now this was intended, (1.) To prepare them to receive the Holy Ghost, and to go through that which they were designed for. He tells them in secret what they must tell the world; and they shall find that the Spirit of truth, when he comes, will say the same. (2.) To be one of the proofs of Christ's resurrection; so it comes in here; the disciples, to whom *he showed himself alive,* knew that it was he, not only by what he showed them, but by what he said to them. None but he could speak thus clearly, thus fully, *of the things pertaining to the kingdom of God.* He did not entertain them with discourses of politics or the kingdoms of men, of philosophy or the kingdom of nature, but pure divinity and the kingdom of grace, the things which most nearly concerned them, and those to whom they were sent.

IV. A particular assurance given them that they should now shortly receive the Holy Ghost, with orders given them to expect it (*v.* 4, 5), he *being assembled together with them,* probably in the interview at the mountain in Galilee which he had appointed before his death; for there is mention of their *coming together again* (*v.* 6), to attend his ascension. Though he had now ordered them to Galilee, yet they must not think to continue there; no, they must return to Jerusalem, and not depart thence. Observe,

1. The command he gives them to wait. This was to raise their expectations of something great; and something very great they had reason to expect from their exalted Redeemer. (1.) They must wait till the time appointed, which is now *not many days hence.* Those that by faith hope promised mercies will come must with patience wait till they do come, according *to the time, the set time.* And when *the time draws nigh,* as now it did, we must, as Daniel, look earnestly for it, Dan. ix. 3. (2.) They must wait in the place appointed, *in Jerusalem,* for there the Spirit must be first poured out, because Christ was to be as *king upon the holy hill of Zion;* and because *the word of the Lord must go forth from Jerusalem;* this must be the mother-church. There Christ was put to shame, and therefore there he will have this honour done him, and this favour is done to Jerusalem to teach us to forgive our enemies and persecutors. The apostles were more exposed to danger at Jerusalem than they would have been in Galilee; but we may cheerfully trust God with our safety, when we keep in the way of our duty. The apostles were now to put on a public character, and therefore must venture in a public station. Jerusalem was the fittest candlestick for those lights to be set up in.

2. The assurance he gives them that they shall not wait in vain.

(1.) The blessing designed them shall come, and they shall find it was worth waiting for: *You shall be baptized with the Holy Ghost;* that is, [1.] "The Holy Ghost shall be poured out upon you more plentifully than ever." They had already been breathed upon with the Holy Ghost (John xx. 22), and they had found the benefit of it; but now they shall have larger measures of his gifts, graces, and comforts, and *be baptized with them,* in which there seems to be an allusion to those Old-Testament promises of the pouring out of the Spirit, Joel ii. 28; Isa. xliv. 3; xxxii. 15. [2.] "You shall be cleansed and purified by the Holy Ghost," as the priests were baptized and washed with water, when they were consecrated to the sacred function: "They had the sign; you shall have the thing signified. You shall be sanctified by the truth, as the Spirit shall lead you more and more into it, and have your consciences purged by the witness of the Spirit, that you may serve the living God in the apostleship." [3.] "You shall hereby be more effectually than ever engaged to your Master, and to his guidance, as Israel was *baptized unto Moses in the cloud, and in the sea;* you shall be tied so fast to Christ that you shall never, for fear of any sufferings, forsake him again, as once you did."

(2.) Now this gift of the Holy Ghost he speaks of,

[1.] As *the promise of the Father, which they had heard of him,* and might therefore depend upon. *First,* The Spirit was given by promise, and it was at this time the great promise, as that of the Messiah was before (Luke i. 72), and that of eternal life is now, 1 John ii. 25. Temporal good things are given by Providence, but the Spirit and spiritual blessings are given by promise, Gal. iii. 18. The Spirit of God is not given as the spirit of men is given us, and formed within us, by a course of nature (Zech. xii. 1), but by the word of God. 1. That the gift may be the more valuable, Christ thought the promise of the Spirit a legacy worth leaving to his church. 2. That it may be the more sure, and that the heirs of promise may be confident of the immutability of God's counsel herein. 3. That it may be of grace, peculiar grace, and may be received by faith, laying hold on the promise, and depending upon it. As Christ, so the Spirit, is received by faith. *Secondly,* It was *the promise of the Father,* 1. Of Christ's Father. Christ, as Mediator, had an eye to God as his Father, fathering his design, and owning it all along. 2. Of our Father, who, if he give us *the adoption of sons,* will certainly give us *the Spirit of adoption,* Gal. iv. 5, 6. He will give the Spirit, as *the Father of lights,* as *the Father of spirits,* and as *the Father of mercies;* it is *the promise of the Father. Thirdly,* This promise of the Father they had heard from Christ many a time, especially in the farewell sermon he preached to them a little before he died, wherein he assured them, again and again, that *the Comforter* should come. This confirms the promise of God, and encourages us to depend upon it, that we have heard it from Jesus Christ; *for in him all the promises of God are yea, and amen.* "You have heard it from me; and I will make it good."

[2.] As the prediction of John Baptist; for so far back Christ here directs them to look (*v.* 5): "You have not only heard it from me, but you had it from John; when he turned you over to me, he said (Matt. iii. 11), *I indeed baptize you with water, but he that comes after me shall baptize you with the Holy Ghost.*" It is a great honour that Christ now does to John, not only to quote his words, but to make this great gift of the Spirit, now at hand, to be the accomplishment of them. Thus *he confirmeth the word of his servants, his messengers,* Isa. xliv. 26. But Christ can do more than any of his ministers. It is an honour to them to be employed in dispensing the means of grace, but it is his prerogative to give *the Spirit of grace. He shall baptize you with the Holy Ghost,* shall teach you by his Spirit, and give his Spirit to make intercession in you, which is more than the best ministers preaching with us.

(3.) Now this gift of the Holy Ghost thus promised, thus prophesied of, thus waited for, is that which we find the apostles received in the next chapter, for in that this promise had its full accomplishment; this was it *that should come,* and *we look for no other;* for it is here promised to be given *not many days hence.* He does not tell them how many, because they must keep every day in a frame fit to receive it. Other scriptures speak of *the gift of the Holy Ghost* to ordinary believers; this speaks of that particular power which, by the Holy Ghost, the first preachers of the gospel, and planters of the church, were endued with, enabling them infallibly to relate to that age, and record to posterity, the doctrine of Christ, and the proofs of it; so that by virtue of this promise, and the performance of it, we receive the New Testament as of divine inspiration, and venture our souls upon it.

6 When they therefore were come
together, they asked of him, saying,
Lord, wilt thou at this time restore
again the kingdom to Israel? 7 And
he said unto them, It is not for you
to know the times or the seasons,
which the Father hath put in his own
power. 8 But ye shall receive power,
after that the Holy Ghost is come
upon you: and ye shall be witnesses
unto me both in Jerusalem, and in
all Judæa, and in Samaria, and unto
the uttermost part of the earth. 9
And when he had spoken these things,
while they beheld, he was taken up;
and a cloud received him out of their
sight. 10 And while they looked
stedfastly toward heaven as he went
up, behold, two men stood by them
in white apparel; 11 Which also said,
Ye men of Galilee, why stand ye
gazing up into heaven? this same Jesus, which is taken up from you into
heaven, shall so come in like manner
as ye have seen him go into heaven.

In Jerusalem Christ, by his angel, had appointed his disciples to meet him in Galilee; there he appointed them to meet him in Jerusalem again, such a day. Thus he would try their obedience, and it was found ready and cheerful; *they came together,* as he appointed them, to be *the witnesses* of his ascension, of which we have here an account. Observe,

I. The question they asked him at this interview. *They came together* to him, as those that had consulted one another about it, and concurred in the question *nemine contradicente—unanimously;* they came in a body, and put it to him as the sense of the house, *Lord, wilt thou at this time restore again the kingdom to Israel?* Two ways this may be taken:—

1. "Surely thou wilt not at all restore it to the present rulers of Israel, the chief priests and the elders, that put thee to death, and, to compass that design, tamely gave up the kingdom to Cæsar, and owned themselves his subjects. What! Shall those that hate and persecute thee and us be trusted with power? *This be far from thee.*" Or rather,

2. "Surely thou wilt now restore it to the Jewish nation, as far as it will submit to thee as their king." Now two things were amiss in this question:—

(1.) Their expectation of the thing itself. They thought Christ would *restore the kingdom to Israel,* that is, that he would make the nation of the Jews as great and considerable among the nations as it was *in the days of David and Solomon, of Asa and Jehoshaphat;* that, as Shiloh, he would *restore the sceptre to Judah, and the lawgiver;* whereas Christ came to set up his own kingdom, and that a kingdom of heaven, not to *restore the kingdom to Israel,* an earthly kingdom. See here, [1.] How apt even good men are to place the happiness of the church too much in external pomp and power; as if Israel could not be glorious unless the kingdom were restored to it, nor Christ's disciples honoured unless they were peers of the realm; whereas we are told to expect the cross in this world, and to wait for the kingdom in the other world. [2.] How apt we are to retain what we have imbibed, and how hard it is to get over the prejudices of education. The disciples, having sucked in this notion with their milk that the Messiah was to be a temporal prince, were long before they could be brought to have any idea of his kingdom as spiritual. [3.] How naturally we are biassed in favour of our own people. They thought God would have no kingdom in the world unless it were *restored to Israel;* whereas the kingdoms of this world were to become his, in whom he would be glorified, whether Israel should sink or swim. [4.] How apt we are to misunderstand scripture—to understand that literally which is spoken figuratively, and to expound scripture by our schemes, whereas we ought to form our schemes by the scriptures. But, *when the Spirit shall be poured out from on high,* our mistakes will be rectified, as the apostles' soon after were.

(2.) Their enquiry concerning the time of it: "*Lord, wilt thou* do it *at this time?* Now that thou hast called us together is it for this purpose, that proper measures may be concerted for the restoring of the kingdom to Israel? Surely there cannot be a more favourable juncture than this." Now herein they missed their mark, [1.] That they were inquisitive into that which their Master had never directed nor encouraged them to enquire into. [2.] That they were impatient for the setting up of that kingdom in which they promised themselves so great a share, and would anticipate the divine counsels. Christ had told them that they should *sit on thrones* (Luke xxii. 30), and now nothing will serve them but they must be in the throne immediately, and cannot stay the time; whereas *he that believeth doth not make haste,* but is satisfied that God's time is the best time.

II. The check which Christ gave to this question, like that which he had a little before given to Peter's enquiry concerning John, *What is that to thee? v.* 7, *It is not for you to know the times and seasons.* He does not contradict their expectation that the kingdom would be restored to Israel, because that mistake would soon be rectified by the pouring out of the Spirit, after which they never had any more thoughts of the temporal kingdom; and also because there is a sense of the expectation which is true, the setting up of the gospel kingdom in the world; and their mistake of the promise shall not make it of no effect; but he checks their enquiry after the time.

1. The knowledge of this is not allowed to them: *It is not for you to know,* and therefore it is not for you to ask. (1.) Christ is now parting from them, and parts in love; and yet he gives them this rebuke, which is intended for a caution to his church in all ages, to take heed of splitting upon the rock which was fatal to our first parents—an inordinate desire of forbidden knowledge, and intruding into things which we have not seen because God has not shown them. *Nescire velle quæ magister maximus docere non vult, erudita inscitia est—It is folly to covet to be wise above what is written, and wisdom to be content to be no wiser.* (2.) Christ had given his disciples a great deal of knowledge above others (*to you it is given to know the mysteries of the kingdom of God*), and had promised them his Spirit, to teach them more; now, lest they should be puffed up with the abundance of the revelations, he here lets them understand that there were some things which it was not for them to know. We shall see how little reason we have to be proud of our knowledge when we consider how many things we are ignorant of. (3.) Christ had given his disciples instructions sufficient for the discharge of their duty, both before his death and since his resurrection, and in this knowledge he will have them to be satisfied; for it is enough for a Christian, in whom vain curiosity is a corrupt humour, to be mortified, and not

gratified. (4.) Christ had himself told his disciples *the things pertaining to the kingdom of God,* and had promised that the Spirit should *show them things to come* concerning it, John xvi. 13. He had likewise given them *signs of the times,* which it was their duty to observe, and a sin to overlook, Matt. xxiv. 33; xvi. 3. But they must not expect nor desire to know either all the particulars of future events or the exact times of them. It is good for us to be kept in the dark, and left at uncertainty concerning *the times and moments* (as Dr. Hammond reads it) of future events concerning the church, as well as concerning ourselves,—concerning all the periods of time and the final period of it, as well as concerning the period of our own time.

Prudens futuri temporis exitum
Caliginosa nocte premit Deus—

But Jove, in goodness ever wise,
Hath hid, in clouds of thickest night,
All that in future prospect lies
Beyond the ken of mortal sight.—Hor.

As to the times and seasons of the year, we know, in general, there will be summer and winter counterchanged, but we know not particularly which day will be fair or which foul, either in summer or in winter; so, as to our affairs in this world, when it is a summer-time of prosperity, that we may not be secure, we are told there will come a winter-time of trouble; and in that winter, that we may not despond and despair, we are assured that summer will return; but what this or that particular *day will bring forth* we cannot tell, but must accommodate ourselves to it, whatever it is, and make the best of it.

2. The knowledge of it is reserved to God as his prerogative; it is what *the Father hath put in his own power;* it is hid with him. None besides can reveal the times and seasons to come. *Known unto God are all his works,* but not to us, *ch.* xv. 18. It is in his power, and in his only, *to declare the end from the beginning;* and by this he proves himself to be God, Isa. xlvi. 10. "And though he did think fit sometimes to let the Old-Testament prophets know the times and the seasons (as of the Israelites' bondage in Egypt four hundred years, and in Babylon seventy years), yet he has not thought fit to let you know the times and seasons, no not just how long it shall be before Jerusalem be destroyed, though you be so well assured of the thing itself. He hath not said that he will not give you to know something more than you do of the times and seasons;" he did so afterwards *to his servant John;* "but he has put it in his own power to do it or not, as he thinks fit;" and what is in that New-Testament prophecy discovered concerning the times and the seasons is so dark, and hard to be understood, that, when we come to apply it, it concerns us to remember this word, that it is not for us to be positive in determining the times and the seasons. Buxtorf mentions a saying of the rabbin concerning the coming of the Messiah: *Rumpatur spiritus eorum qui supputant tempora—Perish the men who calculate the time.*

III. He appoints them their work, and with authority assures them of an ability to go on with it, and of success in it. "*It is not for you to know the times and the seasons* — this would do you no good; but know this (*v.* 8) that you shall receive a spiritual *power,* by the *descent of the Holy Ghost upon you,* and shall not receive it in vain, for *you shall be witnesses unto me* and my glory; and your testimony shall not be in vain, for it shall be received here in Jerusalem, in the country about, and all the world over," *v.* 8. If Christ make us serviceable to his honour in our own day and generation, let this be enough for us, and let not us perplex ourselves about times and seasons to come. Christ here tells them,

1. That their work should be honourable and glorious: *You shall be witnesses unto me.* (1.) They shall proclaim him king, and publish those truths to the world by which his kingdom should be set up, and he would rule. They must openly and solemnly preach his gospel to the world. (2.) They shall prove this, shall confirm their testimony, not as witnesses do, with an oath, but with the divine seal of miracles and supernatural gifts: *You shall be martyrs to me,* or *my martyrs,* as some copies read it; for they attested the truth of the gospel with their sufferings, even unto death.

2. That their power for this work should be sufficient. They had not strength of their own for it, nor wisdom nor courage enough; they were naturally of *the weak and foolish things of the world;* they durst not appear as witnesses for Christ upon his trial, neither as yet were they able. "*But you shall receive the power of the Holy Ghost coming upon you*" (so it may be read), "shall be animated and actuated by a better spirit than your own; you shall have power to preach the gospel, and to prove it out of the scriptures of the Old Testament" (which, when they were *filled with the Holy Ghost,* they did to admiration, *ch.* xviii. 28), "and to confirm it both by miracles and by sufferings." Note, Christ's witnesses shall receive power for that work to which he calls them; those whom he employs in his service he will qualify for it, and will bear them out in it.

3. That their influence should be great and very extensive: "*You shall be witnesses* for Christ, and shall carry his cause," (1.) "*In Jerusalem;* there you must begin, and many there will receive your testimony; and those that do not will be left inexcusable." (2. "Your light shall thence shine throughout all Judea, where before you have laboured in vain." (3.) "Thence you shall proceed *to Samaria,* though at your first mission you were forbidden to preach in *any of the cities of the Samaritans.*" (4.) "Your use-

fulness shall reach *to the uttermost part of the earth*, and you shall be blessings to the whole world."

IV. Having left these instructions with them, he leaves them (*v.* 9): *When he had spoken these things*, and had said all that he had to say, *he blessed them* (so we were told, Luke xxiv. 50); and *while they beheld him*, and had their eye fixed upon him, receiving his blessing, *he was* gradually *taken up, and a cloud received him out of their sight*. We have here Christ's ascending on high; not fetched away, as Elijah was, with *a chariot of fire and horses of fire*, but rising to heaven, as he rose from the grave, purely by his own power, his body being now, as the bodies of the saints will be at the resurrection, a spiritual body, and raised in power and incorruption. Observe, 1. He began his ascension in the sight of his disciples, even *while they beheld*. They did not see him come up out of the grave, because they might see him after he had risen, which would be satisfaction enough; but they saw him go up towards heaven, and had actually their eye upon him with so much care and earnestness of mind that they could not be deceived. It is probable that he did not fly swiftly up, but moved upwards gently, for the further satisfaction of his disciples. 2. He *vanished out of their sight, in a cloud*, either a thick cloud, for God said that he would *dwell in the thick darkness;* or a bright cloud, to signify the splendour of his glorious body. It was a bright cloud that overshadowed him in his transfiguration, and most probably this was so, Matt. xvii. 5. This *cloud received him*, it is probable, when he had gone about as far from the earth as the clouds generally are; yet it was not such a spreading cloud as we commonly see, but such as just served to enclose him. Now he *made the clouds his chariot*, Ps. civ. 3. God had often come down in a cloud; now he went up in one. Dr. Hammond thinks that the clouds receiving him here were the angels receiving him; for the appearance of angels is ordinarily described by a cloud, comparing Exod. xxv. 22 with Lev. xvi. 2. By the clouds there is a sort of communication kept up between the upper and lower world; in them the vapours are sent up from the earth, and the dews sent down from heaven. Fitly therefore does he ascend in a cloud who is *the Mediator between God and man*, by whom God's mercies come down upon us and our prayers come up to him. This was the last that was seen of him. The eyes of a great many witnesses followed him into the cloud; and, if we would know what became of him then, we may find (Dan. vii. 13), *That one like the Son of man came with the clouds of heaven, and came to the Ancient of days, and they brought him* in the clouds as he came *near before him*.

V. The disciples, when he had gone out of their sight, yet still continued *looking up stedfastly to heaven* (*v.* 10), and this longer than it was fit they should; and why so? 1. Perhaps they hoped that Christ would presently come back to them again, to restore the kingdom to Israel, and were loth to believe they should now part with him for good and all; so much did they still dote upon his bodily presence, though he had told them that *it was expedient for them that he should go away*. Or, they looked after him, as doubting whether he might not be dropped, as *the sons of the prophets* thought concerning Elijah (2 Kings ii. 16), and so they might have him again. 2. Perhaps they expected to see some change in the visible heavens now upon Christ's ascension, that either *the sun should be ashamed or the moon confounded* (Isa. xxiv. 23), as being out-shone by his lustre; or, rather, that they should show some sign of joy and triumph; or perhaps they promised themselves a sight of the glory of the invisible heavens, upon their opening to receive him. Christ had told them that hereafter they should *see heaven opened* (John i. 51), and why should not they expect it now?

VI. Two angels appeared to them, and delivered them a seasonable message from God. There was a world of angels ready to receive our Redeemer, now that he made his public entry into *the Jerusalem above:* we may suppose these two loth to be absent then; yet, to show how much Christ had at heart the concerns of his church on earth, he sent back to his disciples two of those that came to meet him, who appear as *two men in white apparel*, bright and glittering; for they know, according to the duty of their place, that they are really serving Christ when they are ministering to his servants on earth. Now we are told what the angels said to them, 1. To check their curiosity: *You men of Galilee, why stand you gazing up into heaven?* He calls them *men of Galilee*, to put them in mind of *the rock out of which they were hewn*. Christ had put a great honour upon them, in making them his ambassadors; but they must remember that they are men, earthen vessels, and men of Galilee, illiterate men, looked upon with disdain. Now, say they, "*Why stand you here*, like Galileans, rude and unpolished men, *gazing up into heaven?* What would you see? You have seen all that you were called together to see, and why do you look any further? *Why stand you gazing*, as men frightened and perplexed, as men astonished and at their wits' end?" Christ's disciples should never stand at a gaze, because they have a sure rule to go by, and a sure foundation to build upon. 2. To confirm their faith concerning Christ's second coming. Their Master had often told them of this, and the angels are sent at this time seasonably to put them in mind of it: *"This same Jesus, who is taken up from you into heaven,* and whom you are looking thus long after, wishing you had him with you again, is not gone for ever; for there is a day appointed in which he *will come in like manner thence, as you have seen him go thither,* and you must not expect him back till that appointed day." (1.) "*This same Jesus* shall come again in his own person, clothed with a glorious body; *this same Jesus,* who came once *to put away sin by the sacrifice of himself, will appear a second time without sin* (Heb. ix. 26, 28), who came once in disgrace to be judged, will come again in glory to judge. *The same Jesus* who has given you your charge will come again to call you to an account how you have performed your trust; *he, and not another,*" Job xix. 27. (2.) "He *shall come in like manner.* He is gone away in a *cloud,* and *attended with angels;* and, *behold, he comes in the clouds, and with him an innumerable company of angels!* He is *gone up with a shout and with the sound of a trumpet* (Ps. xlvii. 5), and he will *descend from heaven with a shout and with the trump of God,* 1 Thess. iv. 16. You have now lost the sight of him in the clouds and in the air; and *whither he is gone you cannot follow him now,* but shall then, when you shall *be caught up in the clouds, to meet the Lord in the air.*" When we stand gazing and trifling, the consideration of our Master's second coming should quicken and awaken us; and, when we stand gazing and trembling, the consideration of it should comfort and encourage us.

12 Then returned they unto Jerusalem from the mount called Olivet,
which is from Jerusalem a sabbath
day's journey. 13 And when they
were come in, they went up into an
upper room, where abode both Peter,
and James, and John, and Andrew,
Philip, and Thomas, Bartholomew,
and Matthew, James *the son* of Al-
phæus, and Simon Zelotes, and Judas
the brother of James. 14 These all
continued with one accord in prayer
and supplication, with the women,
and Mary the mother of Jesus, and
with his brethren.

We are here told, I. Whence Christ ascended—*from the mount of Olives* (*v.* 12), from that part of it where the town of Bethany stood, Luke xxiv. 50. There he began his sufferings (Luke xxii. 39), and therefore there he rolled away the reproach of them by his glorious ascension, and thus showed that his passion and his ascension had the same reference and tendency. Thus would he enter upon his kingdom in the sight of Jerusalem, and of those undutiful ungrateful citizens of his that would not have him to reign over them. It was prophesied of him (Zech. xiv. 4), *That his feet should stand upon the mount of Olives, which is before Jerusalem,* should stand last there; and presently it follows, *The mount of Olives shall cleave in two. From the mount of Olives he* ascended who is *the good olive-tree,* whence we receive *the unction,* Zech. iv. 12; Rom. xi. 24. This mount is here said to be near Jerusalem, *a sabbath day's journey* from it, that is, a little way; no further than devout people used to walk out on a sabbath evening, after the public worship was over, for meditation. Some reckon it a thousand paces, others two thousand cubits; some seven furlongs, others eight. Bethany indeed was *fifteen furlongs from Jerusalem* (John xi. 18), but that part of the mount of Olives which was next to Jerusalem, whence Christ began to ride in triumph, was but seven or eight furlongs off. The Chaldee paraphrast on Ruth i. says, *We are commanded to keep the sabbaths and the holy days, so as not to go above two thousand cubits,* which they build upon Josh. iii. 4, where, in their march through Jordan, the space between them and the ark was to be *two thousand cubits.* God had not then thus limited them, but they limited themselves; and thus far it is a rule to us, not to journey on the sabbath any more than in order to the sabbath work; and as far as is necessary to this we are not only allowed, but enjoined, 2 Kings iv. 23.

II. Whither the disciples returned: They came to Jerusalem, according to their Master's appointment, though there they were in the midst of enemies; but it should seem that though immediately after Christ's resurrection they were watched, and were *in fear of the Jews,* yet after it was known that they were gone into Galilee no notice was taken of their return to Jerusalem, nor any further search made for them. God can find out hiding-places for his people in the midst of their enemies, and so influence Saul that he shall not seek for David any more. At Jerusalem they *went up into an upper room, and there abode;* not that they all lodged and dieted together in one room, but there they assembled every day, and spent time together in religious exercises, in expectation of the descent of the Spirit. Divers conjectures the learned have about this upper room. Some think it was one of the upper rooms in the temple; but it cannot be thought that the chief priests, who had the letting of these rooms, would suffer Christ's disciples constantly to reside in any of them. It was said indeed, by the same historian, that *they were continually in the temple* (Luke xxiv. 53), but that was *in the courts of the temple, at the hours of prayer,* where they could not be hindered from attending; but, it should seem, this upper room was in a private house. Mr. Gregory, of Oxford, is of this opinion, and quotes a Syriac scholiast upon this place, who says that it was *the same upper room in which they had eaten the passover;* and though that was called *ἀνῶγεον,* this *ὑπερῷον,* both may signify the same. "Whether," says he, "it was in the house of St. John the evangelist, as Euodius delivered, or that of Mary the mother of John Mark, as others have collected, cannot be certain." Notes, *ch.* xiii.

III. Who the disciples were, that kept together. The eleven apostles are here named (*v.* 13), so is Mary the mother of our Lord (*v.* 14), and it is the last time that ever any mention is made of her in the scriptures. There were others that are here said to be the brethren of our Lord, *his kinsmen according to the flesh;* and, to make up *the hundred and twenty* spoken of (*v.* 15), we may suppose that all or most of *the seventy disciples* were with them, that were associates with the apostles, and were employed as evangelists.

IV. How they spent their time: *They all continued with one accord in prayer and supplication.* Observe, 1. *They prayed, and made supplication.* All God's people are praying people, and *give themselves to prayer.* It was now a time of trouble and danger with the disciples of Christ; they were as sheep in the midst of wolves; and, *Is any afflicted? Let him pray;* this will silence cares and fears. They had new work before them, great work, and, before they entered upon it, *they were instant in prayer to God* for his presence with them in it. Before they were first sent forth Christ spent time in prayer for them, and now they spent time in prayer for themselves. They were waiting for the descent of the Spirit upon them, and therefore abounded thus in prayer. The Spirit descended upon our Saviour when he was praying, Luke iii. 21. Those are in the best frame to receive spiritual blessings that are in a praying frame. Christ had promised now shortly to send the Holy Ghost; now this promise was not to supersede prayer, but to quicken and encourage it. God will be enquired of for promised mercies, and the nearer the performance seems to be the more earnest we should be in prayer for it. 2. *They continued in prayer,* spent much time in it, more than ordinary, prayed frequently, and were long in prayer. They never missed an hour of prayer; they resolved to persevere herein till the Holy Ghost came, according to the promise, *to pray, and not to faint.* It is said (Luke xxiv. 53), *They were praising and blessing God;* here, *They continued in prayer and supplication;* for as praise for the promise is a decent way of begging for the performance, and praise for former mercy of begging further mercy, so, in seeking to God, we give him the glory of the mercy and grace which we have found in him. 3. They did this *with one accord.* This intimates that they were together in holy love, and that there was no quarrel nor discord among them; and those who so keep *the unity of the Spirit in the bond of peace* are best prepared to receive the *comforts of the Holy Ghost.* It also intimates their worthy concurrence in the supplications that were made; though but one spoke, they all prayed, and if, when *two agree to ask, it shall be done for them,* much more when many agree in the same petition. See Matt. xviii. 19.

15 And in those days Peter stood
up in the midst of the disciples, and
said, (the number of the names together were about a hundred and
twenty,) 16 Men *and* brethren, this
scripture must needs have been fulfilled, which the Holy Ghost by the
mouth of David spake before concerning Judas, which was guide to them
that took Jesus. 17 For he was
numbered with us, and had obtained
part of this ministry. 18 Now this
man purchased a field with the reward of iniquity; and falling headlong
he burst asunder in the midst, and all
his bowels gushed out. 19 and it
was known unto all the dwellers at
Jerusalem; insomuch as that field is
called in their proper tongue, Aceldama, that is to say, The field of
blood. 20 For it is written in the
book of Psalms, Let his habitation be
desolate, and let no man dwell therein: and his bishopric let another
take. 21 Wherefore of these men
which have companied with us all
the time that the Lord Jesus went in
and out among us, 22 Beginning
from the baptism of John, unto that
same day that he was taken up from
us, must one be ordained to be a witness with us of his resurrection. 23
And they appointed two, Joseph
called Barsabas, who was surnamed
Justus, and Matthias. 24 And they
prayed, and said, Thou, Lord, which
knowest the hearts of all *men,* show
whether of these two thou hast
chosen, 25 That he may take part of
this ministry and apostleship, from
which Judas by transgression fell, that
he might go to his own place. 26
And they gave forth their lots; and
the lot fell upon Matthias; and he
was numbered with the eleven apostles.

The sin of Judas was not only his shame and ruin, but it made a vacancy in the college of the apostles. They were ordained twelve, with an eye *to the twelve tribes of Israel,* descended from the twelve patriarchs; they were *the twelve stars* that make up the church's crown (Rev. xii. 1), and for them *twelve thrones* were designated, Matt. xix. 28.

Now being twelve when they were learners, if they were but eleven when they were to be teachers, it would occasion every one to enquire what had become of the twelfth, and so revive the remembrance of the scandal of their society; and therefore care was taken, before the descent of the Spirit, to fill up the vacancy, of the doing of which we now have an account, our Lord Jesus, probably, having given directions about it, among other things which he spoke *pertaining to the kingdom of God.* Observe,

I. The persons concerned in this affair. 1. The house consisted of *about a hundred and twenty.* This was *the number of the names,* that is, the persons; some think the men only, distinguished from the women. Dr. Lightfoot reckons that *the eleven apostles, the seventy disciples,* and about thirty-nine more, all of Christ's own kindred, country, and concourse, made up this *one hundred and twenty,* and that these were a sort of synod, or congregation of ministers, a standing presbytery (*ch.* iv. 23), *to whom none of the rest durst join themselves* (*ch.* v. 13), and that they continued together till the persecution at Stephen's death dispersed them all but the apostles (*ch.* viii. 1); but he thinks that besides these there were many hundreds in Jerusalem, if not thousands, at this time, that believed; and we have indeed read of many that *believed on him there, but durst not confess him,* and therefore I cannot think, as he does, that they were now formed into distinct congregations, for the preaching of the word and other acts of worship; nor that there was any thing of this till after the pouring out of the Spirit, and the conversions recorded in the following chapter. Here was the beginning of the Christian church: this hundred and twenty was the grain of mustard-seed that grew into a tree, the leaven that leavened the whole lump. 2. The speaker was Peter, who had been, and still was, the most forward man; and therefore notice is taken of his forwardness and zeal, to show that he had perfectly recovered the ground he lost by his denying his Master, and, Peter being designed to be the apostle of the circumcision, while the sacred story stays among the Jews, he is still brought in, as afterwards, when it comes to speak of the Gentiles, it keeps to the story of Paul.

II. The proposal which Peter made for the choice of another apostle. He *stood up in the midst of the disciples, v.* 15. He did not sit down, as one that gave laws, or had any supremacy over the rest, but stood up, as one that had only a motion to make, in which he paid a deference to his brethren, standing up when he spoke to them. Now in his speech we may observe,

1. The account he gives of the vacancy made by the death of Judas, in which he is very particular, and, as became one that Christ had breathed upon, takes notice of the fulfilling of the scriptures in it. Here is,

(1.) The power to which Judas had been advanced (*v.* 17): *He was numbered with us, and had obtained part of this ministry* which we are invested with. Note, Many are numbered with the saints in this world that will not be found among them in the day of separation between the precious and the vile. What will it avail us to be added to the number of Christians, if we partake not of the spirit and nature of Christians? Judas's having obtained part of this ministry was but an aggravation of his sin and ruin, as it will be of theirs who *prophesied in Christ's name,* and yet were *workers of iniquity.*

(2.) The sin of Judas, notwithstanding his advancement to this honour. He was *guide to those that took Jesus,* not only informed Christ's persecutors where they might find him (which they might have done effectually though he had kept out of sight), but he had the impudence to appear openly at the head of the party that seized him. He went before them to the place, and, as if he had been proud of the honour, gave the word of command: *That same is he, hold him fast.* Note, Ringleaders in sin are the worst of sinners, especially if those that by their office should have been guides to the friends of Christ are guides to his enemies.

(3.) The ruin of Judas by this sin. Perceiving the chief priests to seek the life of Christ and his disciples, he thought to save his by going over to them, and not only so, but to get an estate under them, of which his wages for his service, he hoped, would be but an earnest; but see what came of it. [1.] He lost his money shamefully enough (*v.* 18): *He purchased a field* with the *thirty pieces of silver,* which were the *reward of his iniquity.* He did not purchase the field, but the wages of his unrighteousness did, and it is very elegantly expressed thus, in derision of his projects to enrich himself by this bargain. He thought to have purchased a field for himself, as Gehazi did with what he got from Naaman by a lie (see 2 Kings v. 26), but it proved the purchase of a field to bury strangers in; and what was he or any of his the better for this? It was to him an unrighteous mammon, it deceived him; and the reward of his iniquity was the *stumbling-block of his iniquity.* [2.] He lost his life more shamefully. We were told (Matt. xxvii. 5) that he *went away* in despair, and was suffocated (so the word signifies there, and no more); here it is added (as latter historians add to those who went before) that, being strangled, or choked with grief and horror, he *fell headlong,* fell *on his face* (so Dr. Hammond), and partly with the swelling of his own breast, and partly with the violence of the fall, he *burst asunder in the midst,* so that *all his bowels tumbled out.* If, when the devil was cast out of a child, he *tore him, threw him down,* and *rent him,* and almost killed him (as we find Mark ix. 26;

Luke ix. 42), no wonder if, when he had full possession of Judas, he threw him headlong, and burst him. The suffocation of him, which Matthew relates, would make him swell till he burst, which Peter relates. He burst asunder *with a great noise* (so Dr. Edwards), which was heard by the neighbours, and so, as it follows, it came *to be known* (*v.* 19): *His bowels gushed out;* Luke writes like a physician, understanding all the entrails of the middle and lower ventricle. Bowelling is part of the punishment of traitors. Justly do those bowels gush out that were shut up against the Lord Jesus. And perhaps Christ had an eye to the fate of Judas, when he said of the wicked servant that he would *cut him in sunder*, Matt. xxiv. 51.

(4.) The public notice that was taken of this: *It was known to all the dwellers in Jerusalem.* It was, as it were, put into the newspapers, and was all the talk of the town, as a remarkable judgment of God upon him that betrayed his Master, *v.* 19. It was not only discoursed of among the disciples, but it was in every body's mouth, and nobody disputed the truth of the fact. *It was known,* that is, it was known to be true, incontestably so. Now one would think this should have awakened those to repentance that had had any hand in the death of Christ when they saw him that had the first hand thus made an example. But their hearts were hardened, and, as to those of them that were to be softened, it must be done by the word, and the Spirit working with it. Here is one proof of the notoriety of the thing mentioned, that the field which was purchased with Judas's money was called *Aceldama—the field of blood,* because it was bought with the *price of blood,* which perpetuated the infamy not only of him that sold that innocent precious blood, but of those that bought it too. Look how they will answer it, when God shall make inquisition for blood.

(5.) The fulfilling of the scriptures in this, which had spoken so plainly of it, *that it must needs be fulfilled, v.* 16. Let none be surprised nor stumble at it, that this should be the exit of one of the twelve, for David had not only foretold his sin (which Christ had taken notice of, John xiii. 18, from Ps. xli. 9, He that *eateth bread with me* hath *lifted up the heel against me),* but had also foretold, [1.] His punishment (Ps. lxix. 25): *Let his habitation be desolate.* This Psalm refers to the Messiah. Mention is made but two or three verses before of their giving him gall and vinegar, and therefore the following predictions of the destruction of David's enemies must be applied to the enemies of Christ, and particularly to Judas. Perhaps he had some habitation of his own at Jerusalem, which, upon this, every body was afraid to live in, and so it became desolate. This prediction signifies the same with that of Bildad concerning the wicked man, that his *confidence shall be rooted out of his tabernacle, and shall bring him to the king of terrors: it shall dwell in his tabernacle, because it is none of his; brimstone shall be scattered upon his habitation,* Job xviii. 14, 15. [2.] The substitution of another in his room. His *bishopric,* or *his office* (for so the word signifies in general) *shall another take,* which is quoted from Ps. cix. 8. With this quotation Peter very aptly introduces the following proposal. Note, We are not to think the worse of any office that God has instituted (whether magistracy or ministry) either for the wickedness of any that are in that office or for the ignominious punishment of that wickedness; nor will God suffer any purpose of his to be frustrated, any commission of his to be vacated, or any work of his to be undone, for the miscarriages of those that are entrusted therewith. *The unbelief of man shall not make the promise of God of no effect.* Judas is hanged, but his bishopric is not lost. It is said of *his habitation,* that *no man shall dwell therein,* there he shall have no heir; but it is not said so of his bishopric, there he shall not want a successor. It is with the officers of the church as with the members of it, if the *natural branches* be *broken off,* others shall be *grafted in,* Rom xi. 17. Christ's cause shall never be lost for want of witnesses.

2. The motion he makes for the choice of another apostle, *v.* 21, 22. Here observe, (1.) How the person must be qualified that must fill up the vacancy. It must be one of *these men,* these seventy disciples, *that have companied with us,* that have constantly attended us, *all the time that the Lord Jesus went in and out among us,* preaching and working miracles for three years and a half, *beginning from the baptism of John,* from which the gospel of Christ commenced, *unto that same day that he was taken up from us.* Those that have been diligent, faithful, and constant, in the discharge of their duty in a lower station, are fittest to be preferred to a higher; those that have been faithful in a little shall be entrusted with more. And none should be employed as ministers of Christ, preachers of his gospel, and rulers in his church, but those that are well acquainted with his doctrine and doings, from first to last. None shall be an apostle but one that has companied with the apostles, and that continually; not that has visited them now and then, but been intimately conversant with them. (2.) To what work he is called that must fill up the vacancy: He must be *a witness with us of his resurrection.* By this it appears that others of the disciples were with the eleven when Christ appeared to them, else they could not have been *witnesses with them,* as competent witnesses as they, of his resurrection. The great thing which the apostles were to attest to the world was Christ's resurrection, for this was the great proof of his being the Messiah, and the

foundation of our hope in him. See what the apostles were ordained to, not to a secular dignity and dominion, but to preach Christ, and the power of his resurrection.

III. The nomination of the person that was to succeed Judas in his office as an apostle.

1. Two, who were known to have been Christ's constant attendants, and men of great integrity, were set up as candidates for the place (*v.* 23): *They appointed two;* not the *eleven,* they did not take upon them to determine who should be put up, but the *hundred and twenty,* for to them Peter spoke, and not to the eleven. The two they nominated were *Joseph* and *Matthias,* of neither of whom do we read elsewhere, except this Joseph be the same with that *Jesus who is called Justus,* of whom Paul speaks (Col. iv. 11), and who is said to be *of the circumcision,* a native Jew, as this was, and who was a *fellow-worker with Paul in the kingdom of God* and a comfort to him; and then it is observable that, though he came short of being an apostle, he did not therefore quit the ministry, but was very useful in a lower station; for, *Are all apostles? Are all prophets?* Some think this Joseph is he that is called *Joses* (Mark vi. 3), the *brother of James the less* (Mark xv. 40), and was called *Joses the just,* as he was called *James the just.* Some confound this with that Joses mentioned Acts iv. 36. But that was of Cyprus, this of Galilee; and, it should seem, to distinguish them, that was called *Barnabas—a son of consolation;* this *Barsabas—a son of the oath.* These two were both of them such worthy men, and so well qualified for the office, that they could not tell which of them was the fitter, but all agreed it must be one of these two. They did not propose themselves nor strive for the place, but humbly sat still, and were appointed to it.

2. They applied to God by prayer for direction, not which of the seventy, for none of the rest could stand in competition with these in the opinion of all present, but *which of these two? v.* 24, 25. (1.) They appeal to God as the searcher of hearts: "*Thou, Lord, who knowest the hearts of all men,* which we do not, and better than they know their own." Observe, When an apostle was to be chosen, he must be chosen by his heart, and the temper and disposition of that. Yet Jesus, who knew all men's hearts, for wise and holy ends chose Judas to be one of the twelve. It is comfortable to us, in our prayers for the welfare of the church and its ministers, that the God to whom we pray *knows the hearts of all men,* and has them not only under his eye, but in his hand, and turns them which way soever he will, can make them fit for his purpose, if he do not find them so, by giving them another spirit. (2.) They desire to know which of these God had chosen: *Lord, show us this,* and we are satisfied. It is fit that God should choose his own servants; and so far as he in any way by the disposals of his providence or the gifts of his Spirit, shows whom he hath chosen, or what he hath chosen, for us, we ought to comply with him. (3.) They are ready to receive him as a brother whom God hath chosen; for they are not contriving to have so much the more dignity themselves, by keeping out another, but desire to have one to *take part of this ministry and apostleship,* to join with them in the work and share with them in the honour, *from which Judas by transgression fell,* threw himself, by deserting and betraying his Master, *from the place* of an apostle, of which he was unworthy, that he might go *to his own place,* the place of a traitor, the fittest place for him, not only to the gibbet, but to hell—this was his own place. Note, Those that betray Christ, as they fall from the dignity of relation to him, so they fall into all misery. It is said of Balaam (Num. xxiv. 25) that he *went to his own place,* that is, says one of the rabbin, *he went to hell.* Dr. Whitby quotes Ignatius saying, There is appointed to every man ἴδιος τόπος—*a proper place,* which imports the same with that of God's rendering to every man according to his works. And our Saviour had said that Judas's own place should be such that *it had been better for him that he had never been born* (Matt. xxvi. 24)—his misery such as to be worse than not being. Judas had been a hypocrite, and hell is the proper place of such; other sinners, as inmates, have their portion with them, Matt. xxiv. 51. (4.) The doubt was determined by lot (*v.* 26), which is an appeal to God, and lawful to be used for determining matters not otherwise determinable, provided it be done in a solemn religious manner, and with prayer, the prayer of faith; for *the lot is cast into the lap, but the whole disposal thereof is of the Lord,* Prov. xvi. 33. Matthias was not ordained by the imposition of hands, as presbyters were, for he was chosen by lot, which was the act of God; and therefore, as he must be baptized, so he must be ordained, by the Holy Ghost, as they all were not many days after. Thus the number of the apostles was made up, as afterwards, when James, another of the twelve, was martyred, Paul was made an apostle.

CHAP. II.

Between the promise of the Messiah (even the latest of those promises) and his coming many ages intervened; but between the promise of the Spirit and his coming there were but a few days; and during those days the apostles, though they had received orders to preach the gospel to every creature, and to begin at Jerusalem, yet lay perfectly wind-bound, incognito—concealed, and not offering to preach. But in this chapter the north wind and the south wind awake, and then they awake, and we have them in the pulpit presently. Here is, I. The descent of the Spirit upon the apostles, and those that were with them, on the day of pentecost, ver. 1—4. II. The various speculations which this occasioned among the people that were now met in Jerusalem from all parts, ver. 5—13. III. The sermon which Peter preached to them hereupon, wherein he shows that this pouring out of the Spirit was the accomplishment of an Old-Testament promise (ver. 14—21), that it was a confirmation of Christ's being the Messiah, which was already proved by his resurrection (ver. 22—32), and that it was a fruit and evidence of his ascension into heaven, ver. 33—36. IV. The good effect of this sermon in the conversion of many to the faith of Christ, and their addition to the church, ver. 37—41. V. The eminent piety and charity of

these primitive Christians, and the manifest tokens of God's presence with them, and power in them, ver. 42—47.

AND when the day of Pentecost
was fully come, they were all
with one accord in one place. 2 And
suddenly there came a sound from
heaven as of a rushing mighty wind,
and it filled all the house where they
were sitting. 3 And there appeared
unto them cloven tongues like as of
fire, and it sat upon each of them. 4 And
they were all filled with the Holy Ghost,
and began to speak with other tongues,
as the Spirit gave them utterance.

We have here an account of the descent of the Holy Ghost upon the disciples of Christ. Observe,

I. When, and where, this was done, which are particularly noted, for the greater certainty of the thing.

1. It was *when the day of pentecost was fully come,* in which there seems to be a reference to the manner of the expression in the institution of this feast, where it is said (Lev. xxiii. 15), *You shall count unto you seven sabbaths complete,* from the day of the offering of the first-fruits, which was the next day but one after the passover, the sixteenth day of the month Abib, which was the day that Christ arose. This day was *fully come,* that is, the night preceding, with a part of the day, was fully past. (1.) The Holy Ghost came down at the time of a solemn feast, because there was then a great concourse of people to Jerusalem from all parts of the country, and the proselytes from other countries, which would make it the more public, and the fame of it to be spread the sooner and further, which would contribute much to the propagating of the gospel into all nations. Thus now, as before at the passover, the Jewish feasts served to toll the bell for gospel services and entertainments. (2.) This feast of pentecost was kept in remembrance of the giving of the law upon mount Sinai, whence the incorporating of the Jewish church was to be dated, which Dr. Lightfoot reckons to be just one thousand four hundred and forty-seven years before this. Fitly, therefore, is the Holy Ghost given at that feast, in fire and in tongues, for the promulgation of the evangelical law, not as that to one nation, but to every creature. (3.) This feast of pentecost happened on the *first day of the week,* which was an additional honour put on that day, and a confirmation of it to be the Christian sabbath, *the day which the Lord hath made,* to be a standing memorial in his church of those two great blessings—the resurrection of Christ, and the pouring out of the Spirit, both on that day of the week. This serves not only to justify us in observing that day under the style and title of *the Lord's day,* but to direct us in the sanctifying of it to give God praise particularly for those two great blessings; every Lord's day in the year, I think, there should be a full and particular notice taken in our prayers and praises of these two, as there is by some churches of the one once a year, upon Easter-day, and of the other once a year, upon Whit-sunday. Oh! that we may do it with suitable affections!

2. It was when *they were all with one accord in one place.* What place it was we are not told particularly, whether in the temple, where they attended at public times (Luke xxiv. 53), or whether in their own upper room, where they met at other times. But it was at Jerusalem, because this had been the place which God chose, to put his name there, and the prophecy was that thence the word of the Lord should go forth to all nations, Isa. ii. 3. It was now the place of the general rendezvous of all devout people: here God had promised to meet them and bless them; here therefore he meets them with this blessing of blessings. Though Jerusalem had done the utmost dishonour imaginable to Christ, yet he did this honour to Jerusalem, to teach us not to fall out with places, nor conceive prejudices against them; for God has his remnant in all places; he had this in Jerusalem. Here the disciples were in one place, and they were not as yet so many but that one place, and no large one, would hold them all. And here they were *with one accord.* We cannot forget how often, while their Master was with them, there were *strifes among them, who should be the greatest;* but now all these strifes were at an end, we hear no more of them. What they had received already of the Holy Ghost, when Christ breathed on them, had in a good measure rectified the mistakes upon which those contests were grounded, and had disposed them to holy love. They had prayed more together of late than usual (*ch.* i. 14), and this made them love one another better. By his grace he thus prepared them for the gift of the Holy Ghost; for that blessed dove comes not where there is noise and clamour, but moves upon the face of the still waters, not the rugged ones. Would we have the Spirit *poured out upon us from on high?* Let us be all of one accord, and, notwithstanding variety of sentiments and interests, as no doubt there was among those disciples, let us agree to love one another; for, where *brethren dwell together in unity,* there it is that *the Lord commands his blessing.*

II. How, and in what manner, the Holy Ghost came upon them. We often read in the Old Testament of God's coming down in a cloud; as when he took possession first of the tabernacle, and afterwards of the temple, which intimates the darkness of that dispensation. And Christ went up to heaven in a cloud, to intimate how much we are kept in the dark concerning the upper world. But the Holy Ghost did not descend in a cloud; for he was to dispel and scatter the clouds that overspread men's minds, and to bring light into the world.

1. Here is an audible summons given them to awaken their expectations of something great, *v.* 2. It is here said, (1.) That it came *suddenly*, did not rise gradually, as common winds do, but was at the height immediately. It came sooner than they expected, and startled even those that were now together waiting, and probably employed in some religious exercises. (2.) It was *a sound from heaven*, like a thunder-clap, Rev. vi. 1. God is said to *bring the winds out of his treasuries* (Ps. cxxxv. 7), and *to gather them in his hands*, Prov. xxx. 4. From him this sound came, like the voice of one crying, *Prepare ye the way of the Lord.* (3.) It was the sound of a wind, for the way of the Spirit is like that of the wind (John iii. 8), *thou hearest the sound thereof, but canst not tell whence it comes nor whither it goes.* When the Spirit of life is to enter into the dry bones, the prophet is told to *prophecy unto the wind: Come from the four winds, O breath*, Ezek. xxxvii. 9. And though it was not *in the wind* that the Lord came to Elijah, yet this prepared him to receive his discovery of himself in the *still small voice*, 1 Kings xix. 11, 12. *God's way is in the whirlwind and the storm* (Nah. i. 3), and out of the whirlwind he spoke to Job. (4.) It was a *rushing mighty wind;* it was strong and violent, and came not only with a great noise, but with great force, as if it would bear down all before it. This was to signify the powerful influences and operations of the Spirit of God upon the minds of men, and thereby upon the world, that they should be *mighty through God, to the casting down of imaginations.* (5.) *It filled* not only the room, but *all the house where they were sitting.* Probably it alarmed the whole city, but, to show that it was supernatural, presently fixed upon that particular house: as some think the wind that was sent to arrest Jonah affected only the ship that he was in (Jon. i. 4), and as the wise men's star stood over the house where the child was. This would direct the people who observed it whither to go to enquire the meaning of it. This wind filling the house would strike an awe upon the disciples, and help to put them into a very serious, reverent, and composed frame, for the receiving of the Holy Ghost. Thus the convictions of the Spirit make way for his comforts; and the rough blasts of that blessed wind prepare the soul for its soft and gentle gales.

2. Here is a visible sign of the gift they were to receive. They saw *cloven tongues, like as of fire* (*v.* 3), and *it sat*—ἐκάθισέ, not *they* sat, those cloven tongues, but he, that is the Spirit (signified thereby), rested upon each of them, as he is said to rest upon the prophets of old. Or, as Dr. Hammond describes it, "There was an appearance of something like flaming fire lighting on every one of them, which divided asunder, and so formed the resemblance of tongues, with that part of them that was next their heads divided or cloven." The flame of a candle is somewhat like a tongue; and there is a meteor which naturalists call *ignis lambens—a gentle flams*, not a devouring fire; such was this. Observe,

(1.) There was an outward sensible sign, for the confirming of the faith of the disciples themselves, and for the convincing of others. Thus the prophets of old had frequently their first mission confirmed by signs, that all Israel might know them to be established prophets.

(2.) The sign given was fire, that John Baptist's saying concerning Christ might be fulfilled, *He shall baptize you with the Holy Ghost and with fire ;* with the Holy Ghost as with fire. They were now, in the feast of pentecost, celebrating the memorial of the giving of the law upon mount Sinai; and as that was given in fire, and therefore is called a fiery law, so is the gospel. Ezekiel's mission was confirmed by a vision of *burning coals of fire* (*ch.* i. 13), and Isaiah's by *a coal of fire* touching his lips, *ch.* vi. 7. The Spirit, like fire, melts the heart, separates and burns up the dross, and kindles pious and devout affections in the soul, in which, as in the fire upon the altar, the spiritual sacrifices are offered up. This is that fire which Christ came to send upon the earth. Luke xii. 49.

(3.) This fire appeared in cloven tongues. The operations of the Spirit were many; that of speaking with divers tongues was one, and was singled out to be the first indication of the gift of the Holy Ghost, and to that this sign had a reference. [1.] They were tongues; for from the Spirit we have the word of God, and by him Christ would speak to the world, and he gave the Spirit to the disciples, not only to endue them with knowledge, but to endue them with a power to publish and proclaim to the world what they knew; for *the dispensation of the Spirit is given to every man to profit withal.* [2.] These tongues were cloven, to signify that God would hereby divide unto all nations the knowledge of his grace, as he is said to have divided to them by his providence the light of the heavenly bodies, Deut. iv. 19. The tongues were divided, and yet they still continued all of one accord; for there may be a sincere unity of affections where yet there is a diversity of expression. Dr. Lightfoot observes that the dividing of tongues at Babel was the casting off of the heathen; for, when they had lost the language in which alone God was spoken of and preached, they utterly lost the knowledge of God and religion, and fell into idolatry. But now, after above two thousand years, God, by another dividing of tongues, restores the knowledge of himself to the nations.

(4.) This fire sat upon them for some time, to denote the constant residence of the Holy Ghost with them. The prophetic gifts of old were conferred sparingly and but at some times, but the disciples of Christ had the gifts of the Spirit always with them, though the sign, we may suppose, soon disappeared. Whether these flames of fire passed from one to another, or whether there were as many flames as there were persons, is not certain. But they must be strong and bright flames that would be visible in the day-light, as it now was, for the day was fully come.

III. What was the immediate effect of this? 1. *They were all filled with the Holy Ghost*, more plentifully and powerfully than they were before. They were filled with the graces of the Spirit, and were more than ever under his sanctifying influences—were now holy, and heavenly, and spiritual, more weaned from this world and better acquainted with the other. They were more filled with the comforts of the Spirit, rejoiced more than ever in the love of Christ and the hope of heaven, and in it all their griefs and fears were swallowed up. They were also, for the proof of this, filled with the gifts of the Holy Ghost, which are especially meant here; they were endued with miraculous powers for the furtherance of the gospel. It seems evident to me that not only the twelve apostles, but all the hundred and twenty disciples were *filled with the Holy Ghost* alike at this time—all the seventy disciples, who were apostolic men, and employed in the same work, and all the rest too that were to preach the gospel; for it is said expressly (Eph. iv. 8, 11), *When Christ ascended on high* (which refers to this, *v.* 33), *he gave gifts unto men,* not only *some apostles* (such were the twelve), but *some prophets* and *some evangelists* (such were many of the seventy disciples, itinerant preachers), and some *pastors and teachers* settled in particular churches, as we may suppose some of these afterwards were. The *all* here must refer to the *all* that were together, *v.* 1; *ch.* i. 14, 15. 2. *They began to speak with other tongues*, besides their native language, though they had never learned any other. They spoke not matters of common conversation, but the word of God, and the praises of his name, *as the Spirit gave them utterance*, or gave them to speak ἀποφθέγγεσθαι—*apophthegms*, substantial and weighty sayings, worthy to be had in remembrance. It is probable that it was not only one that was enabled to speak one language, and another another (as it was with the several families that were dispersed from Babel), but that every one was enabled to speak divers languages, as he should have occasion to use them. And we may suppose that they understood not only themselves but one another too, which the builders of Babel did not, Gen. xi. 7. They did not speak here and there a word of another tongue, or stammer out some broken sentences, but spoke it as readily, properly, and elegantly, as if it had been their mother-tongue; for whatever was produced by miracle was the best of the kind. They spoke not from any previous thought or meditation, but *as the Spirit gave them utterance;* he furnished them with the matter as well as the language. Now this was, (1.) A very great miracle; it was a miracle upon the mind (and so had most of the nature of a gospel miracle), for in the mind words are framed. They had not only never learned these languages, but had never learned any foreign tongue, which might have facilitated these; nay, for aught that appears, they had never so much as heard these languages spoken, nor had any idea of them. They were neither scholars nor travellers, nor had had any opportunity of learning languages either by books or conversation. Peter indeed was forward enough to speak in his own tongue, but the rest of them were no spokesmen, nor were they quick of apprehension; yet now not only *the heart of the rash understands knowledge, but the tongue of the stammerers is ready to speak eloquently*, Isa. xxxii. 4. When Moses complained, *I am slow of speech*, God said, *I will be with thy mouth*, and *Aaron shall be thy spokesman.* But he did more for these messengers of his: he that made man's mouth new-made theirs. (2.) A very proper, needful, and serviceable miracle. The language the disciples spoke was Syriac, a dialect of the Hebrew; so that it was necessary that they should be endued with the gift, for the understanding both of the original Hebrew of the Old Testament, in which it was written, and of the original Greek of the New Testament, in which it was to be written. But this was not all; they were commissioned to *preach the gospel to every creature, to disciple all nations.* But here is an insuperable difficulty at the threshold. How shall they master the several languages so as to speak intelligibly to all nations? It will be the work of a man's life to learn their languages. And therefore, to prove that Christ could give authority to preach to the nations, he gives ability to preach to them in their own language. And it should seem that this was the accomplishment of that promise which Christ made to his disciples (John xiv 12), *Greater works than these shall you do.* For this may well be reckoned, all things considered, a greater work than the miraculous cures Christ wrought. Christ himself did not speak with other tongues, nor did he enable his disciples to do so while he was with them: but it was the first effect of the *pouring out of the Spirit* upon them. And archbishop Tillotson thinks it probable that if the conversion of infidels to Christianity were now sincerely and vigorously attempted, by men of honest minds, God would extraordinarily countenance such an attempt with all fitting assistance, as he did the first publication of the gospel.

5 And there were dwelling at Jerusalem Jews, devout men, out of every nation under heaven. 6 Now when this was noised abroad, the

multitude came together, and were
confounded, because that every man
heard them speak in his own language. 7 And they were all amazed,
and marvelled, saying one to another,
Behold, are not all these which speak
Galilæans? 8 And how hear we
every man in our own tongue, wherein we were born? 9 Parthians and
Medes, and Elamites, and the dwellers in Mesopotamia, and in Judæa,
and Cappadocia, in Pontus, and Asia,
10 Phrygia, and Pamphylia, in Egypt,
and in the parts of Libya about Cyrene, and strangers of Rome, Jews
and proselytes, 11 Cretes and Arabians, we do hear them speak in our
tongues the wonderful works of God.
12 And they were all amazed, and
were in doubt saying one to another,
What meaneth this? 13 Others
mocking said, These men are full of
new wine.

We have here an account of the public notice that was taken of this extraordinary gift with which the disciples were all on a sudden endued. Observe,

I. The great concourse of people that there was now at Jerusalem, it should seem more than was usual at the feast of pentecost. *There were dwelling* or abiding *at Jerusalem* Jews that were *devout men*, disposed to religion, and that had the fear of God before their eyes (so the word properly signifies), some of them *proselytes of righteousness*, that were circumcised, and admitted members of the Jewish church, others only *proselytes of the gate*, that forsook idolatry, and gave up themselves to the worship of the true God, but not to the ceremonial law; some of those that were at Jerusalem now, *out of every nation under heaven*, whither the Jews were dispersed, or whence proselytes were come. The expression is hyperbolical, denoting that there were some from most of the then known parts of the world; as much as ever Tyre was, or London is, the rendezvous of trading people from all parts, Jerusalem at that time was of religious people from all parts. Now, 1. We may here see what were some of those countries whence those strangers came (*v.* 9—11), some from the eastern countries, as the *Parthians, Medes, Elamites, and dwellers in Mesopotamia*, the posterity of Shem; thence we come in order to Judea, which ought to be mentioned, because, though the language of those in Judea was the same with that which the disciples spoke, yet, before, they spoke it with the north-country tone and dialect (*Thou art a Galilean, and thy speech betrays thee*), but now they spoke it as correctly as the inhabitants of Judea themselves did. Next come the inhabitants of Cappadocia, Pontus, and that country about Propontis which was particularly called *Asia*, and these were the countries in which those strangers were scattered to whom St. Peter writes. 1 Pet. i. 1. Next come the dwellers in *Phrygia and Pamphylia*, which lay westward, the posterity of Japhet, as were also the *strangers of Rome*; there were some also that dwelt in the southern parts of *Egypt, in the parts of Libya about Cyrene*; there were also some from the island of Crete, and some from the deserts of Arabia; but they were all either Jews originally, dispersed into those countries; or *proselytes* to the Jewish religion, but natives of those countries. Dr. Whitby observes that the Jewish writers about this time, as Philo and Josephus, speak of the Jews as *dwelling every where through the whole earth*; and that *there is not a people upon earth among whom some Jews do not inhabit*. 2. We may enquire what brought all those Jews and proselytes together to Jerusalem as this time? not to make a transient visit thither to the feast of pentecost, for they are said to dwell there. They took lodgings there, because there was at this time a general expectation of the appearing of the Messiah; for Daniel's weeks had just now expired, the sceptre had departed from Judah, and it was then generally thought that *the kingdom of God would immediately appear*, Luke xix. 11. This brought those who were most zealous and devout to Jerusalem, to sojourn there, that they might have an early share in the kingdom of the Messiah and the blessings of that kingdom.

II. The amazement with which these strangers were seized when they heard the disciples speak in their own tongues. It should seem, the disciples spoke in various languages before the people of those languages came to them; for it is intimated (*v.* 6) that the spreading of the report of this abroad was that which *brought the multitude together*, especially those of different countries, who seem to have been more affected with this work of wonder than the inhabitants of Jerusalem themselves.

1. They observe that the speakers are all Galileans, that know no other than their mother tongue (*v.* 7); they are despicable men, from whom nothing learned nor polite is to be expected. God chose the weak and foolish things of the world to confound the wise and mighty. Christ was thought to be a Galilean, and his disciples really were so, unlearned and ignorant men.

2. They acknowledge that they spoke intelligibly and readily their own language (which they were the most competent judges of), so correctly and fluently that none of their own countrymen could speak it better: *We hear every man in our own tongue wherein we were born* (*v.* 8), that is, we hear one or other of them speak our native language

The Parthians hear one of them speak their language, the Medes hear another of them speak theirs; and so of the rest; *v.* 11, *We do hear them speak in our tongues the wonderful works of God.* Their respective languages were not only unknown at Jerusalem, but probably despised and undervalued, and therefore it was not only a surprise, but a pleasing surprise, to them to hear the language of their own country spoken, as it naturally is to those that are strangers in a strange land. (1.) The things they heard the apostles discourse of were the *wonderful works of God, μεγαλεῖα τοῦ Θεοῦ—Magnalia Dei, the great things of God.* It is probable that the apostles spoke of Christ, and redemption by him, and the grace of the gospel; and these are indeed the *great things of God,* which will be for ever *marvellous in our eyes.* (2.) They heard them both praise God for these great things and instruct the people concerning these things, *in their own tongue,* according as they perceived the language of their hearers, or those that enquired of them, to be. Now though, perhaps, by dwelling some time at Jerusalem, they were got to be so much masters of the Jewish language that they could have understood the meaning of the disciples if they had spoken that language, yet, [1.] This was more strange, and helped to convince their judgment, that this doctrine was of God; for *tongues were for a sign* to those that believed not, 1 Cor. xiv. 22. [2.] It was more kind, and helped to engage their affections, as it was a plain indication of the favour intended to the Gentiles, and that the knowledge and worship of God should no longer be confined to the Jews, but the partition-wall should be broken down; and this is to us a plain intimation of the mind and will of God, that the sacred records of God's wonderful works should be preserved by all nations *in their own tongue;* that the scriptures should be read, and public worship performed, in the vulgar languages of the nations.

3. They wonder at it, and look upon it as an astonishing thing (*v.* 12): *They were all amazed,* they were in an *ecstacy,* so the word is; and they were in doubt what the meaning of it was, and whether it was to introduce the kingdom of the Messiah, which they were big with the expectation of; they asked themselves and one another *τί ἂν θέλοι τοῦτο εἶναι;—Quid hoc sibi vult?—What is the tendency of this?* Surely it is to dignify, and so to distinguish, these men as messengers from heaven; and therefore, like Moses at the bush, they will *turn aside, and see this great sight.*

III. The scorn which some made of it who were natives of Judea and Jerusalem, probably the scribes and Pharisees, and chief priests, who always resisted the Holy Ghost; they said, *These men are full of new wine,* or *sweet wine;* they have drunk too much this festival-time, *v.* 13. Not that they were so absurd as to think that wine in the head would enable men to speak languages which they never learned; but these, being native Jews, knew not, as the others did, that what was spoken was really the languages of other nations, and therefore took it to be gibberish and nonsense, such as drunkards, those *fools in Israel,* sometimes talk. As when they resolved not to believe the finger of the Spirit in Christ's miracles, they turned it off with this, "He casteth out devils by compact with the prince of the devils;" so, when they resolved not to believe the voice of the Spirit in the apostles' preaching, they turned it off with this, *These men are full of new wine.* And, if they called the Master of the house a wine-bibber, no marvel if they so call those of his household.

14 But Peter, standing up with
the eleven, lifted up his voice, and
said unto them, Ye men of Judæa,
and all *ye* that dwell at Jerusalem, be
this known unto you, and hearken to
my words: 15 For these are not
drunken, as ye suppose, seeing it is
but the third hour of the day. 16
But this is that which was spoken by
the prophet Joel; 17 And it shall
come to pass in the last days, saith
God, I will pour out of my Spirit
upon all flesh: and your sons and
your daughters shall prophesy, and
your young men shall see visions, and
your old men shall dream dreams:
18 And on my servants and on my
handmaidens I will pour out in those
days of my Spirit; and they shall
prophesy: 19 And I will show wonders in heaven above, and signs in
the earth beneath; blood, and fire,
and vapour of smoke 20 The sun
shall be turned into darkness, and the
moon into blood, before that great
and notable day of the Lord come:
21 And it shall come to pass, *that*
whosoever shall call on the name of
the Lord shall be saved. 22 Ye men
of Israel, hear these words; Jesus of
Nazareth, a man approved of God
among you by miracles and wonders
and signs, which God did by him in
the midst of you, as ye yourselves
also know: 23 Him, being delivered
by the determinate counsel and foreknowledge of God, ye have taken,
and by wicked hands have crucified
and slain: 24 Whom God hath raised

up, having loosed the pains of death:
because it was not possible that he
should be holden of it. 25 For David speaketh concerning him, I foresaw the Lord always before my face,
for he is on my right hand, that I
should not be moved: 26 Therefore
did my heart rejoice, and my tongue
was glad; moreover also my flesh
shall rest in hope: 27 Because thou
wilt not leave my soul in hell, neither
wilt thou suffer thine Holy One to see
corruption. 28 Thou hast made
known to me the ways of life; thou
shalt make me full of joy with thy
countenance. 29 Men *and* brethren,
let me freely speak unto you of the
patriarch David, that he is both dead
and buried, and his sepulchre is with
us unto this day. 30 Therefore being a prophet, and knowing that God
had sworn with an oath to him, that
of the fruit of his loins, according to
the flesh, he would raise up Christ to
sit on his throne; 31 He seeing this
before spake of the resurrection of
Christ, that his soul was not left in
hell, neither his flesh did see corruption. 32 This Jesus hath God raised
up, whereof we all are witnesses. 33
Therefore being by the right hand of
God exalted, and having received of
the Father the promise of the Holy
Ghost, he hath shed forth this, which
ye now see and hear. 34 For David
is not ascended into the heavens:
but he saith himself, The LORD said
unto my Lord. Sit thou on my right
hand, 35 Until I make thy foes thy
footstool. 36 Therefore let all the
house of Israel know assuredly, that
God hath made that same Jesus,
whom ye have crucified, both Lord
and Christ.

We have here the first-fruits of the Spirit in the sermon which Peter preached immediately, directed, not to those of other nations in a strange language (we are not told what answer he gave to those that were amazed, and said, *What meaneth this?*) but to the Jews in the vulgar language, even to those that mocked; for he begins with the notice of that (*v.* 15), and addresses his discourse (*v.* 14) *to the men of Judea and the inhabitants of Jerusalem;* but we have reason enough to think that the other disciples continued to speak to those who understood them (and therefore flocked about them), in the languages of their respective countries, *the wonderful works of God.* And it was not by Peter's preaching only, but that of all, or most, of the rest of the hundred and twenty, *that three thousand souls were* that day converted, and added to the church; but Peter's sermon only is recorded, to be an evidence for him that he was thoroughly recovered from his fall, and thoroughly restored to the divine favour. He that had sneakingly denied Christ now as courageously confesses him. Observe,

I. His introduction or preface, wherein he craves the attention of the auditory, or demands it rather: *Peter stood up* (*v.* 14), to show that he was not drunk, *with the eleven,* who concurred with him in what he said, and probably in their turns spoke likewise to the same purport; those that were of greatest authority stood up to speak to the scoffing Jews, and to confront those who contradicted and blasphemed, but left the seventy disciples to speak to the willing proselytes from other nations, who were not so prejudiced, in their own language. Thus among Christ's ministers, some of greater gifts are called out to instruct those that oppose themselves, to take hold of sword and spear; others of meaner abilities are employed in instructing those that resign themselves, and to be vine-dressers and husbandmen. *Peter lifted up his voice,* as one that was both well assured of and much affected with what he said, and was neither afraid nor ashamed to own it. He applied himself to *the men of Judea,* ἄνδρες Ἰουδαῖοι*—the men that were Jews;* so it should be read; "and you especially *that dwell at Jerusalem,* who were accessory to the death of Jesus, *be this known unto you,* which you did not know before, and which you are concerned to know now, *and hearken to my words,* who would draw you to Christ, and not to the words of the scribes and Pharisees, that would draw you from him. My Master is gone, whose words you have often heard in vain, and shall hear no more as you have done, but he speaks to you by us; hearken now to our words."

II. His answer to their blasphemous calumny (*v.* 15): "*These men are not drunken, as you suppose.* These disciples of Christ, that now *speak with other tongues,* speak good sense, and know what they say, and so do those they speak to, who are led by their discourses into the knowledge of *the wonderful works of God.* You cannot think they are drunk, for *it is but the third hour of the day,*" nine of the clock in the morning; and before this time, on the sabbaths and solemn feasts, the Jews did not eat nor drink: nay, ordinarily, *those that are drunk are drunk in the night,* and not in the morning; those are besotted drunkards indeed who, *when they awake,* immediately *seek it yet again,* Prov. xxiii 35.

III. His account of the miraculous effusion of the Spirit, which is designed to awaken them all to embrace the faith of Christ, and to join themselves to his church. Two things he resolves it into:—that it was the fulfilling of the scripture, and the fruit of Christ's resurrection and ascension, and consequently the proof of both.

1. That it was the accomplishment of the prophecies of the Old Testament which related to the kingdom of the Messiah, and therefore an evidence that this kingdom is come, and the other predictions of it are fulfilled. He specifies one, that of *the prophet Joel, ch.* ii. 28. It is observable that though Peter *was filled with the Holy Ghost, and spoke with tongues as the Spirit gave him utterance,* yet he did not set aside the scriptures, nor think himself above them; nay, much of his discourse is quotation out of the Old Testament, to which he appeals, and with which he proves what he says. Christ's scholars never learn above their Bible; and the Spirit is given not to supersede the scriptures, but to enable us to understand and improve the scriptures. Observe,

(1.) The text itself that Peter quotes, *v.* 17—21. It refers to *the last days,* the times of the gospel, which are called *the last days* because the dispensation of God's kingdom among men, which the gospel sets up, is the last dispensation of divine grace, and we are to look for no other than the continuation of this to the end of time. Or, *in the last days,* that is, a great while after the ceasing of prophecy in the Old-Testament church. Or, in the days immediately preceding the destruction of the Jewish nation, in the last days of that people, just before *that great and notable day of the Lord* spoken of, *v.* 20. "It was prophesied of and promised, and therefore you ought to expect it, and not to be surprised at it; to desire it, and bid it welcome, and not to dispute it, as not worth taking notice of." The apostle quotes the whole paragraph, for it is good to take scripture entire; now it was foretold,

[1.] That there should be a more plentiful and extensive effusion of the Spirit of grace from on high than had ever yet been. The prophets of the Old Testament had been *filled with the Holy Ghost,* and it was said of the people of Israel *that God gave them his good Spirit to instruct them,* Neh. ix. 20. But now *the Spirit shall be poured out,* not only upon the Jews, but *upon all flesh,* Gentiles as well as Jews, though yet Peter himself did not understand it so, as appears, *ch.* xi. 17. Or, *upon all flesh,* that is, upon some of all ranks and conditions of men. The Jewish doctors taught that the Spirit came only upon wise and rich men, and such as were of the seed of Israel; but God will not tie himself to their rules.

[2.] That the Spirit should be in them a Spirit of prophecy; by the Spirit they should be enabled to foretel things to come, and to *preach the gospel to every creature.* This power shall be given without distinction of sex—not only *your sons,* but *your daughters shall prophesy;* without distinction of age—both *your young men and your old men shall see visions, and dream dreams,* and in them receive divine revelations, to be communicated to the church; and without distinction of outward condition—even the *servants and handmaids* shall receive of *the Spirit, and shall prophesy* (*v.* 18); or, in general, men and women, whom God calls his servants and his handmaids. In the beginning of the age of prophecy in the Old Testament there were *schools of the prophets,* and, before that, *the Spirit of prophecy* came upon *the elders of Israel* that were appointed to the government; but now the Spirit shall be poured out upon persons of inferior rank, and such as were not brought up in the schools of the prophets, for the kingdom of the Messiah is to be purely spiritual. The mention of *the daughters* (*v.* 17) and *the handmaidens* (*v.* 18) would make one think that *the women* who were taken notice of (*ch.* i. 14) received the extraordinary gifts of the Holy Ghost, as well as the men. Philip, the evangelist, had *four daughters who did prophesy* (*ch.* xxi. 9), and St. Paul, finding abundance of the gifts both of tongues and prophecy in the church of Corinth, saw it needful to prohibit women's use of those gifts in public, 1 Cor. xiv. 26, 34.

[3.] That one great thing which they should prophesy of should be the judgment that was coming upon the Jewish nation, for this was the chief thing that Christ himself had foretold (Matt. xxiv.) at his entrance into Jerusalem (Luke xix. 41), and when he was going to die (Luke xxiii. 29); and these judgments were to be brought upon them to punish them for their contempt of the gospel, and their opposition to it, though it came to them thus proved. Those that would not submit to the power of God's grace, in this wonderful effusion of his Spirit, should fall and lie under the pourings out of the vials of his wrath. Those shall break that will not bend. *First,* The destruction of Jerusalem, which was about forty years after Christ's death, is here called *that great and notable day of the Lord,* because it put a final period to the Mosaic economy; the Levitical priesthood and the ceremonial law were thereby for ever abolished and done away. The desolation itself was such as was never brought upon any place or nation, either before or since. It was *the day of the Lord,* for it was the day of his vengeance upon that people for crucifying Christ, and persecuting his ministers; it was *the year of recompences for that controversy;* yea, and for all the blood of the saints and martyrs, *from the blood of righteous Abel,* Matt. xxiii. 35. It was a little day of judgment; it was a *notable day:* in Joel it is called a *terrible day,* for so it was to men on earth; but here ἐπιφανῆ (after the Septuagint), *a glorious, illustrious* day, for so it was to Christ in heaven; it was the epiphany, his appearing, so he himself spoke of it, Matt. xxiv. 30. The destruction of the Jews was the deliverance of the Christians, who were hated and persecuted by them; and therefore that day was often spoken of by the prophets of that time, for the encouragement of suffering Christians, *that the Lord was at hand, the coming of the Lord drew nigh, the Judge stood before the door,* James v. 8, 9. *Secondly,* The terrible presages of that destruction are here foretold: *There shall be wonders in heaven above, the sun turned into darkness and the moon into blood; and signs* too *in the earth beneath, blood and fire.* Josephus, in his preface to his history of the wars of the Jews, speaks of the signs and prodigies that preceded them, terrible thunders, lightnings, and earthquakes; there was a fiery comet that hung over the city for a year, and a flaming sword was seen pointing down upon it; a light shone upon the temple and the altar at midnight, as if it had been noonday. Dr. Lightfoot gives another sense of these presages: *The blood of the Son of God, the fire of the Holy Ghost* now appearing, the vapour of the smoke in which Christ ascended, *the sun darkened, and the moon made blood,* at the time of Christ's passion, were all loud warnings given to that unbelieving people to prepare for the judgments coming upon them. Or, it may be applied, and very fitly, to the previous judgments themselves by which that desolation was brought on. *The blood* points at the wars of the Jews with the neighbouring nations, with the Samaritans, Syrians, and Greeks, in which abundance of blood was shed, as there was also in their civil wars, and the struggles of the *seditious* (as they called them), which were very bloody; there was no peace to him that went out nor to him that came in. *The fire and vapour of smoke,* here foretold, literally came to pass in the burning of their cities, and towns, and synagogues, and temple at last. And this turning of *the sun into darkness, and the moon into blood,* bespeaks the dissolution of their government, civil and sacred, and the extinguishing of all their lights. *Thirdly,* The signal preservation of the Lord's people is here promised (*v.* 21): *Whosoever shall call upon the name of the Lord Jesus* (which is the description of a true Christian, 1 Cor. i. 2) *shall be saved,* shall escape that judgment which shall be a type and earnest of everlasting salvation. In the destruction of Jerusalem by the Chaldeans, there was a remnant sealed to be hid in *the day of the Lord's anger;* and in the destruction by the Romans not one Christian perished. Those that distinguish themselves by singular piety shall be distinguished by special preservation. And observe, the saved remnant are described by this, that they are a praying people: *they call on the name of the Lord,* which intimates that they are not saved by any merit or righteousness of their own, but purely by the favour of God, which must be sued out by prayer. It is *the name of the Lord* which *they call upon* that is *their strong tower.*

(2.) The application of this prophecy to the present event (*v.* 16): *This is that which was spoken by the prophet Joel;* it is the accomplishment of that, it is the full accomplishment of it. This is that effusion of the Spirit upon all flesh which should come, and we are to look for no other, no more than we are to look for another Messiah; for as our Messiah ever lives in heaven, reigning and interceding for his church on earth, so this Spirit of grace, the Advocate, or Comforter, that was given now, according to the promise, will, according to the same promise, continue with the church on earth to the end, and will work all its works in it and for it, and every member of it, ordinary and extraordinary, by means of the scriptures and the ministry.

2. That it was the gift of Christ, and the product and proof of his resurrection and ascension. From this *gift of the Holy Ghost,* he takes occasion to preach unto them Jesus; and this part of his sermon he introduces with another solemn preface (*v.* 22): "*You men of Israel, hear these words.* It is a mercy that you are within hearing of them, and it is your duty to give heed to them." Words concerning Christ should be acceptable words to the men of Israel. Here is,

(1.) An abstract of the history of the life of Christ, *v.* 22. He calls him *Jesus of Nazareth,* because by that name he was generally known, but (which was sufficient to roll away that reproach) he was *a man approved of God among you,* censured and condemned by men, but approved of God: God testified his approbation of his doctrine by the power he gave him to work miracles: *a man marked out by God,* so Dr. Hammond reads it; "signalized and made remarkable among you that now hear me. He was sent to you, set up, a glorious light in your land; you yourselves are witnesses how he became famous by *miracles, wonders, and signs,* works above the power of nature, out of its ordinary course, and contrary to it, *which God did by him;* that is, which he did by that divine power with which he was clothed, and in which God plainly went along with him; *for no man could do such works unless God were with him.*" See what a stress Peter lays upon Christ's miracles. [1.] The matter of fact was not to be denied: "They were done *in the midst of you,* in the midst of your country, your city, your solemn assemblies, *as you yourselves also know.* You have been eye-witnesses of his miracles; I appeal to yourselves whether you have any thing to object against them or can offer any thing to disprove them." [2.] The inference from them cannot be disputed; the reasoning is as strong as the evidence; if he did those miracles, certainly God approved him, *declared him to be*, what he declared himself to be, *the Son of God* and *the Saviour of the world;* for the God of truth would never set his seal to a lie.

(2.) An account of his death and sufferings which they were witness of also but a few weeks ago; and this was the greatest miracle of all, that a man approved of God should thus seem to be abandoned of him; and a man thus approved among the people, and in the midst of them, should be thus abandoned by them too. But both these mysteries are here explained (*v.* 23), and his death considered, [1.] As God's act; and in him it was an act of wonderful grace and wisdom. He *delivered him to death;* not only permitted him to be put to death, but gave him up, devoted him: this is explained Rom. viii. 32, *He delivered him up for us all.* And yet he was approved of God, and there was nothing in this that signified the disapproving of him; for it was done by *the determinate counsel and foreknowledge of God,* in infinite wisdom, and for holy ends, which Christ himself concurred in, and in the means leading to them. Thus divine justice must be satisfied, sinners saved, God and man brought together again, and Christ himself glorified. It was not only according to the will of God, but according *to the counsel of his will,* that he suffered and died; according to an eternal counsel, which could not be altered. This reconciled him to the cross: *Father, thy will be done;* and *Father, glorify thy name;* let thy purpose take effect, and let the great end of it be attained. [2.] As the people's act; and in them it was an act of prodigious sin and folly; it was fighting against God to persecute one whom he approved as the darling of heaven; and fighting against their own mercies to persecute one that was the greatest blessing of this earth. Neither God's designing it from eternity, nor his bringing good out of it to eternity, would in the least excuse their sin; for it was their voluntary act and deed, from a principle morally evil, and therefore "they were *wicked hands with which you have crucified and slain* him." It is probable that some of those were here present who had cried. *Crucify him, crucify him,* or had been otherwise aiding and abetting in the murder; and Peter knew it. However, it was justly looked upon as a national act, because done both by the vote of the great council and by the voice of the great crowd. It is a rule, *Refertur ad universos quod publice fit per majorem partem—That which is done publicly by the greater part we attribute to all.* He charges it particularly on them as parts of the nation on which it would be visited, the more effectually to bring them to faith and repentance, because that was the only way to distinguish themselves from the guilty and discharge themselves from the guilt.

(3.) An attestation of his resurrection, which effectually wiped away the reproach of his death (*v.* 24): *Whom God raised up;* the same that delivered him *to death* delivers him *from death,* and thereby gave a higher approbation of him than he had done by any other of *the signs and wonders wrought by him,* or by all put together. This therefore he insists most largely upon.

[1.] He describes his resurrection: God *loosed the pains of death, because it was impossible that he should be holden of it;* ὠδῖνας*—the sorrows of death;* the word is used for *travailing pains,* and some think it signifies *the trouble and agony* of his soul, in which *it was exceedingly sorrowful, even to the death;* from *these pains and sorrows of soul, this travail of soul, the Father loosed him,* when at his death he said, *It is finished.* Thus Dr. Godwin understands it: "Those terrors which made Heman's soul lie like *the slain* (Ps. lxxxviii. 5, 15) had hold of Christ; but he was too strong for them, and broke through them; this was *the resurrection of his soul* (and it is a great thing to bring a soul *out of the depths* of spiritual agonies); this was not leaving his soul in hell; as that which follows, *that he should not see corruption,* speaks of the resurrection of his body; and both together make up the great resurrection." Dr. Lightfoot gives another sense of this: "Having *dissolved the pains of death,* in reference to all that believe in him, God raised up Christ, and by his resurrection *broke all the power of death,* and destroyed its pangs upon his own people. He *has abolished death,* has altered the property of it, and, because *it was not possible that he should be* long *holden of it, it is not possible that they should be* for ever holden." But most refer this to the resurrection of Christ's body. And death (says Mr. Baxter), as a separation between soul and body, is by privation a penal state, though not dolorous by positive evil. But Dr. Hammond shows that the Septuagint, and from them the apostle here, uses the word for *cords* and *bands* (as Ps. xviii. 4), to which the metaphor of loosing and being held best agrees. Christ was imprisoned for our debt, was thrown into the bands of death; but, divine justice being satisfied, it was not possible he should be detained there, either by right or by force; for he had life in himself, and in his own power, and had conquered the prince of death.

[2.] He attests the truth of his resurrection (*v.* 32): *God hath raised him up, whereof we all are witnesses*—we apostles, and others our companions, that were intimately acquainted with him before his death, were intimately conversant with him after his resurrection, *did eat and drink with him.* They *received power,* by *the descent of the Holy Ghost upon them,* on purpose that they might be skilful, faithful, and courageous witnesses of this thing, notwithstanding their being charged by his enemies as having stolen him away.

[3.] He showed it to be the fulfilling of the scripture, and, because the scripture had said that he must rise again before he saw corruption, therefore *it was impossible that he should be holden* by *death* and *the grave; for David speaks* of his being raised, so it comes in, *v.* 25. The scripture he refers to is that of David (Ps. xvi. 8—11), which, though in part applicable to David as a saint, yet refers chiefly to Jesus Christ, of whom David was a type. Here is,

First, The text quoted at large (*v.* 25—28), for it was all fulfilled in him, and shows us, 1. The constant regard that our Lord Jesus had to his Father in his whole undertaking: *I foresaw the Lord before me continually.* He set before him his Father's glory as his end in all—*for he saw* that his sufferings would redound abundantly to the honour of God, and would issue in his own joy; these were *set before him,* and these he had an eye to, in all he did and suffered; and with the prospect of these he was borne up and carried on, John xiii. 31, 32; xvii. 4, 5. 2. The assurance he had of his Father's presence and power going along with him: "*He is on my right hand,* the hand of action, strengthening, guiding, and upholding that, *that I should not be moved,* nor driven off from my undertaking, notwithstanding the hardships I must undergo." This was an article of the covenant of redemption (Ps. lxxxix. 21), *With him my hand shall be established, my arm also shall strengthen him;* and therefore he is confident the work shall not miscarry in his hand. If God be at our right hand we shall not be moved. 3. The cheerfulness with which our Lord Jesus went on in his work, notwithstanding the sorrows he was to pass through: "Being satisfied *that I shall not be moved,* but the good pleasure of the Lord shall prosper in my hand, therefore *doth my heart rejoice, and my tongue is glad,* and the thought of my sorrow is as nothing to me." Note, It was a constant pleasure to our Lord Jesus to look *to the end of his work,* and to be sure that the issue would be glorious; so well pleased is he with his undertaking that it does his heart good to think how the issue would answer the design. *He rejoiced in spirit,* Luke x. 21. *My tongue was glad.* In the psalm it is, *My glory rejoiceth;* which intimates that our tongue is our glory, the faculty of speaking is an honour to us, and never more so than when it is employed in praising God. Christ's *tongue was glad,* for when he was just entering upon his sufferings, in the close of his last supper, he *sang a hymn.* 4. The pleasing prospect he had of the happy issue of his death and sufferings; it was this that carried him, not only with courage, but with cheerfulness, through them; he was putting off the body, but *my flesh shall rest;* the grave shall be to the body, while it lies there, a bed of repose, and hope shall give it a sweet repose; *it shall rest in hope,* ὅτι, *that thou wilt not leave my soul in hell;* what follows is the matter of his hope, or assurance rather, (1.) That the soul shall not continue in a state of separation from the body; for, besides that this is some uneasiness to a human soul made for its body, it would be the continuance of death's triumph over him who was in truth a conqueror over death: "*Thou wilt not leave my soul in hell*" (in *hades,* in *the invisible state,* so *hades* properly signifies); "but, though thou suffer it for a time to remove thither, and to remain there, yet thou wilt remand it; *thou wilt not leave it* there, as thou dost the souls of other men." (2.) That the body shall lie but a little while in the grave: *Thou wilt not suffer thy Holy One to see corruption;* the body shall not continue dead so long as to begin to putrefy or become noisome; and therefore it must return to life on or before the third day after its death. Christ was God's *Holy One,* sanctified and set apart to his service in the work of redemption; he must die, for he must be *consecrated by his own blood;* but he must *not see corruption,* for his death was to be unto God *of a sweet smelling savour.* This was typified by the law concerning the sacrifice, *that no part of the flesh of the sacrifice which was to be eaten should be kept till the third day,* for fear it should see corruption and begin to putrefy, Lev. vii. 15—18. (3.) That his death and sufferings should be, not to him only, but to all his, an inlet to a blessed immortality: "*Thou hast made known to me the ways of life,* and by me made them known to the world, and laid them open." When *the Father gave to the Son to have life in himself, a power to lay down his life and to take it again,* then he showed him *the way of life,* both to and fro; *the gates of death were open to him and the doors of the shadow of death* (Job xxxviii. 17), to pass and repass through them, as his occasion led him, for man's redemption. (4.) That all his sorrows and sufferings should end in perfect and perpetual felicity: *Thou shalt make me full of joy with thy countenance.* The reward set before him was *joy,* a *fulness of joy,* and that in God's *countenance,* in the countenance he gave to his undertaking, and to all those, for his sake, that should believe in him. The smiles with which the Father received him, when, at his ascension, he was *brought to the Ancient of days,* filled him *with joy unspeakable,* and that is *the joy of our Lord,* into which all his shall enter, and in which they shall be for ever happy.

Secondly, The comment upon this text, especially so much of it as relates to the resurrection of Christ. He addresses himself to them with a title of respect, *Men and brethren, v.* 29. "You are men, and therefore should be ruled by reason; you are brethren, and therefore should take kindly what is said to you by one who, being nearly related to you, is heartily concerned for you, and wishes you well. Now, give me leave *freely to speak to you concerning the patriarch*

David, and let it be no offence to you if I tell you that David cannot be understood here as speaking of himself, but of the Christ to come." David is here called a patriarch, because he was the father of the royal family, and a man of great note and eminency in his generation, and whose name and memory were justly very precious. Now when we read that psalm of his, we must consider, 1. That he could not say *that of himself*, for *he died, and was buried, and his sepulchre remained in Jerusalem till now*, when Peter spoke this, and his bones and ashes in it. Nobody ever pretended that he had risen, and therefore he could never say of himself that he *should not see corruption;* for it was plain he did see corruption. St. Paul urges this, *ch.* xiii. 35—37. Though he *was a man after God's own heart, yet he went the way of all the earth*, as he saith himself (1 Kings ii. 2), both in death and burial. 2. Therefore certainly he spoke *it as a prophet*, with an eye to the Messiah, whose sufferings the prophets testified beforehand, and with them *the glory that should follow;* so did David in that psalm, as Peter here plainly shows. (1.) David knew that the Messiah should descend from his loins (*v.* 30), *that God had sworn to him, that of the fruit of his loins, according to the flesh, he would raise up Christ to sit on his throne.* He promised him a Son, *the throne of whose kingdom should be established for ever*, 2 Sam. vii. 12. And it is said (Ps. cxxxii. 11), *God swore it in truth unto David.* When our Lord Jesus was born, it was promised *that the Lord God would give him the throne of his father David*, Luke i. 32. And all Israel knew that the Messiah was to be the Son of David, that is, that, *according to the flesh*, he should be so by his human nature; for otherwise, *according to the spirit*, and by his divine nature, he was *to be David's Lord*, not his son. God having sworn to David that the Messiah, promised to his fathers, should be his son and successor, the fruit of his loins, and heir to his throne, he kept this in view, in penning his psalms. (2.) Christ being *the fruit of his loins*, and consequently in his loins when he penned that psalm (as Levi is said to be in Abraham's loins when he paid *tithes to Melchizedek*), if what he says, as in his own person, be not applicable to himself (as it is plain that it is not), we must conclude it points to that son of his that was then in his loins, in whom his family and kingdom were to have their perfection and perpetuity; and therefore, when he says that *his soul should not be left in its separate state, nor his flesh see corruption*, without doubt he must be understood to speak of the resurrection of Christ, *v.* 31. And as *Christ died*, so *he rose again, according to the scriptures;* and *that he did so we are witnesses.* (3.) Here is a glance at his ascension too. As David did not rise from the dead, so neither did he *ascend into the heavens*, bodily, as Christ did, *v.* 34. And further, to prove that when he spoke of the resurrection he meant it of Christ, he observes that when in another psalm he speaks of the next step of his exaltation he plainly shows that he spoke of another person, and such another as was his Lord (Ps cx. 1): "*The Lord said unto my Lord*, when he had raised him from the dead, *Sit thou at my right hand*, in the highest dignity and dominion there; be thou entrusted with the administration of the kingdom both of providence and grace; *sit there* as king, *until I make thy foes* either thy friends or *thy footstool*," *v.* 35. Christ rose from the grave to rise higher, and therefore it must be of his resurrection that David spoke, and not his own, in the 16th Psalm; for there was no occasion for him to rise out of his grave who was not to ascend to heaven.

(4.) The application of this discourse concerning the death, resurrection, and ascension of Christ.

[1.] This explains the meaning of the present wonderful effusion of the Spirit in those extraordinary gifts. Some of the people had asked (*v.* 12), *What meaneth this?* I will tell you the meaning of it, says Peter. *This Jesus being exalted to the right hand of God*, so some read it, to sit there; *exalted by the right hand of God*, so we read it, by his power and authority—it comes all to one; and *having received of the Father*, to whom he has ascended, *the promise of the Holy Ghost*, he hath given what he received (Ps. lxviii. 18), and *hath shed forth this which you now see and hear;* for the Holy Ghost was to be given when Jesus was glorified, and not before, John vii. 39. You see and hear us speak with tongues that we never learned; probably there was an observable change in the air of their countenances, which they saw, as well as heard the change of their voice and language; now this is from the Holy Ghost, whose coming is an evidence that Jesus is exalted, and he has *received this gift from the Father*, to confer it upon the church, which plainly bespeaks him to be the Mediator, or middle person between God and the church. *The gift of the Holy Ghost* was, *First*, A performance of divine promises already made; here it is called *the promise of the Holy Ghost;* many *exceedingly great and precious promises* the divine power has given us, but this is *the promise*, by way of eminency, as that of the Messiah had been, and this is the promise that includes all the rest; hence God's giving *the Holy Spirit to those that ask him* (Luke xi. 13) is his giving them all *good things*, Matt. vii. 11. Christ received *the promise of the Holy Ghost*, that is, the promised gift of the Holy Ghost, and has given it to us; for all *the promises are yea and amen in him. Secondly*, It was a pledge of all divine favours further intended; what you now see and hear is but an earnest of greater things.

[2.] This proves what you are all bound to believe, that Christ Jesus is the true Messiah and Saviour of the world; this he closes his sermon with, as *the conclusion of the whole matter,* the *quod erat demonstrandum—the truth to be demonstrated* (*v.* 36): *Therefore let all the house of Israel know assuredly* that this truth has now received its full confirmation, and we our full commission to publish it, *That God has made that same Jesus whom you have crucified both Lord and Christ.* They were charged to *tell no man that he was Jesus the Christ* till after his resurrection (Matt. xvi. 20; xvii 9); but now it must be *proclaimed on the housetops, to all the house of Israel; he that hath ears to hear, let him hear it.* It is not proposed as probable, but deposed as certain: *Let them know it assuredly,* and know that it is their duty to receive it as *a faithful saying, First,* That God has glorified him *whom they have crucified.* This aggravates their wickedness, that they crucified one whom God designed to glorify, and put him to death as a deceiver who had given such pregnant proofs of his divine mission; and it magnifies the wisdom and power of God that though they crucified him, and thought thereby to have put him under an indelible mark of infamy, yet God had glorified him, and the indignities they had done him served as a foil to his lustre. *Secondly,* That he has glorified him to such a degree as to make him *both Lord and Christ:* these signify the same; he is *Lord of all,* and he is not a usurper, but is *Christ, anointed* to be so. He is *one Lord to the Gentiles,* who had had lords many; and *to the Jews he is Messiah,* which includes all his offices. He is *the king Messiah,* as the Chaldee paraphrast calls him; or, as the angel to Daniel, *Messiah the prince,* Dan. ix. 25. This is the great truth of the gospel which we are to believe, *that that same Jesus,* the very same *that was crucified at Jerusalem,* is he to whom we owe allegiance, and from whom we are to expect protection, as *Lord and Christ.*

37 Now when they heard *this,* they
were pricked in their heart, and said
unto Peter and to the rest of the
apostles, Men *and* brethren, what
shall we do? 38 Then Peter said
unto them, Repent, and be baptized
every one of you in the name of Jesus Christ for the remission of sins,
and ye shall receive the gift of the
Holy Ghost. 39 For the promise is
unto you, and to your children, and
to all that are afar off, *even* as many
as the Lord our God shall call. 40
And with many other words did he
testify and exhort, saying, Save yourselves from this untoward generation.
41 Then they that gladly received
his word were baptized: and the
same day there were added *unto them*
about three thousand souls.

We have seen the wonderful effect of the pouring out of the Spirit, in its influence upon the preachers of the gospel. Peter, in all his life, never spoke at the rate that he had done now, with such fulness, perspicuity, and power. We are now to see another blessed fruit of the pouring out of the Spirit in its influence upon the hearers of the gospel. From the first delivery of that divine message, it appeared that there was a divine power going along with it, and *it was mighty, through God,* to do wonders: thousands were immediately brought by it to the *obedience of faith;* it was *the rod of God's strength sent out of Zion,* Ps. cx. 2, 3. We have here the first-fruits of that vast harvest of souls which by it were gathered in to Jesus Christ. Come and see, in these verses, the exalted Redeemer riding forth, in these chariots of salvation, *conquering and to conquer,* Rev. vi. 2.

In these verses we find the word of God the means of beginning and carrying on a good work of grace in the hearts of many, *the Spirit of the Lord working by it.* Let us see the method of it.

I. They were startled, and convinced, and put upon a serious enquiry, *v.* 37. *When they heard,* or *having heard,* having patiently heard Peter out, and not given him the interruption they had been used to give to Christ in his discourses (this was one good point gained, that they were become attentive to the word), *they were pricked to the heart,* or *in the heart,* and, under a deep concern and perplexity, applied themselves to the preachers with this question, *What shall we do?* It was very strange that such impressions should be made upon such hard hearts all of a sudden. They were Jews, bred up in the opinion of the sufficiency of their religion to save them, had lately seen this Jesus crucified in weakness and disgrace, and were told by their rulers that he was a deceiver. Peter had charged them with having a hand, a *wicked hand,* in his death, which was likely to have exasperated them against him; yet, when they heard this plain scriptural sermon, they were much affected with it.

1. It put them in pain: *They were pricked in their hearts.* We read of those that were *cut to the heart* with indignation at the preacher (*ch.* vii. 54), but these were *pricked to the heart* with indignation at themselves for having been accessory to the death of Christ. Peter, charging it upon them, awakened their consciences, touched them to the quick, and the reflection they now made upon it was as *a sword in their bones,* it pierced them as they had pierced Christ. Note, Sinners, when their eyes are opened, cannot but be *pricked to the heart* for sin, cannot but experience an inward uneasiness; this is having

the *heart rent* (Joel ii. 13), *a broken and contrite heart,* Ps. li. 17. Those that are truly sorry for their sins, and ashamed of them, and afraid of the consequences of them, are *pricked to the heart.* A prick in the heart is mortal, and under those commotions (says Paul) I died, Rom. vii. 9. "All my good opinion of myself and confidence in myself failed me."

2. It put them upon enquiry. *Out of the abundance of the heart,* thus pricked, *the mouth spoke.* Observe,

(1.) To whom they thus addressed themselves: *To Peter and to the rest of the apostles,* some to one and some to another; to them they opened their case; by them they had been convinced, and therefore by them they expect to be counselled and comforted. They do not appeal from them to the scribes and Pharisees, to justify them against the apostles' charge, but apply to them, as owning the charge, and referring the case to them. They call them *men* and *brethren,* as Peter had called them (*v.* 29): it is a style of friendship and love, rather than a title of honour: "You are men, look upon us with humanity; you are brethren, look upon us with brotherly love." Note, Ministers are spiritual physicians; they should be advised with by those whose consciences are wounded; and it is good for people to be free and familiar with those ministers, as men and their brethren, who deal for their souls as for their own.

(2.) What the address is: *What shall we do?* [1.] They speak as men at a stand, that did not know what to do; in a perfect surprise: "*Is that Jesus* whom we have crucified both *Lord and Christ?* Then what will become of us who crucified him? We are all undone!" Note, No way of being happy but by seeing ourselves miserable. When we find ourselves in danger of being lost for ever, there is hope of our being made for ever, and not till then. [2.] They speak as men at a point, that were resolved to do any thing they should be directed to immediately; they are not for taking time to consider, nor for adjourning the prosecution of their convictions to a more convenient season, but desire now to be told what they must do to escape the misery they were liable to. Note, Those that are convinced of sin would gladly know the way to peace and pardon, *ch.* ix. 6; xvi. 30.

II. Peter and the other apostles direct them in short what they must do, and what in so doing they might expect, *v.* 38, 39. Sinners convinced must be encouraged; and that which is broken must be bound up (Ezek. xxxiv. 16); they must be told that though their case is sad it is not desperate, there is hope for them.

1. He here shows them the course they must take. (1.) *Repent;* this is a plank after shipwreck. "Let the sense of this horrid guilt which you have brought upon yourselves by putting Christ to death awaken you to a penitent reflection upon all your other sins (as the demand of some one great debt brings to light all the debts of a poor bankrupt) and to bitter remorse and sorrow for them." This was the same duty that John the Baptist and Christ had preached, and now that the Spirit is poured out it is still insisted on: "*Repent, repent;* change your mind, change your way; admit an after-thought." (2.) *Be baptized every one of you in the name of Jesus Christ;* that is, "firmly believe the doctrine of Christ, and submit to his grace and government; and make an open solemn profession of this, and come under an engagement to abide by it, by submitting to the ordinance of baptism; be proselyted to Christ and to his holy religion, and renounce your infidelity." They must be baptized *in the name of Jesus Christ.* They did believe in the Father and the Holy Ghost speaking by the prophets; but they must also believe in the name of Jesus, that he is the Christ, the Messias promised to the fathers. "Take Jesus for your king, and by baptism swear allegiance to him; take him for your prophet, and hear him; take him for your priest, to make atonement for you," which seems peculiarly intended here; for they must be baptized *in his name* for the *remission of sins* upon the score of his righteousness. (3.) This is pressed upon each particular person: *Every one of you.* "Even those of you that have been the greatest sinners, if they repent and believe, are welcome to be baptized; and those who think they have been the greatest saints have yet need to repent, and believe, and be baptized. There is grace enough in Christ for every one of you, be you ever so many, and grace suited to the case of every one. Israel of old were baptized unto Moses in the camp, the whole body of the Israelites together, when they passed *through the cloud* and *the sea* (1 Cor. x. 1, 2), for the covenant of peculiarity was national; but now *every one of you* distinctly must be *baptized in the name of the Lord Jesus,* and transact for himself in this great affair." See Col. i. 28.

2. He gives them encouragement to take this course:—(1.) "It shall be for *the remission of sins.* Repent of your sin, and it shall not be your ruin; be baptized into the faith of Christ, and in truth you shall be justified, which you could never be by the law of Moses. Aim at this, and depend upon Christ for it, and this you shall have. As the cup in the Lord's supper is the New Testament in the blood of Christ for the remission of sins, so baptism is in the name of Christ for the remission of sins. Be washed, and you shall be washed." (2.) "You shall *receive the gift of the Holy Ghost* as well as we; for it is designed for a general blessing: some of you shall receive these external gifts, and each of you, if you be sincere in your faith and repentance, shall receive his internal graces and comforts, shall be *sealed with the Holy Spirit of promise.*" Note, All that receive the remission of sins *receive the gift of the Holy Ghost.* All that

are justified are sanctified. (3.) "Your children shall still have, as they have had, an interest in the covenant, and a title to the external seal of it. Come over to Christ, to receive those inestimable benefits; for the promise of the remission of sins, and the gift of the Holy Ghost, is *to you and to your children*," *v.* 39. It was very express (Isa. xliv. 3): *I will pour my Spirit upon thy seed.* And (Isa. lix. 21), *My Spirit and my word shall not depart from thy seed, and thy seed's seed.* When God took Abraham into covenant, he said, *I will be a God to thee, and to thy seed* (Gen. xvii. 7); and, accordingly, every Israelite had his son circumcised at eight days old. Now it is proper for an Israelite, when he is by baptism to come into a new dispensation of this covenant, to ask, "What must be done with my children? Must they be thrown out, or taken in with me? "Taken in" (says Peter) "by all means; for the promise, that great promise of God's being to you a God, is as much to you and to your children now as ever it was." (4.) "Though the promise is still extended to your children as it has been, yet it is not, as it has been, confined to you and them, but the benefit of it is *designed* for *all that are afar off;*" we may add, *and their children,* for the blessing of Abraham comes upon the Gentiles, through Jesus Christ, Gal. iii. 14. The promise had long pertained to the Israelites (Rom. ix. 4); but now it is sent to *those that are afar off,* the remotest nations of the Gentiles, and *every one* of them too, *all that are afar off.* To this general the following limitation must refer, *even as many of them,* as many particular persons in each nation, *as the Lord our God shall call* effectually into the fellowship of Jesus Christ. Note, God can make his call to reach those that are ever so far off, and none come but those whom he calls.

III. These directions are followed with a needful caution (*v.* 40): *With many other words,* to the same purport, *did he testify* gospel truths, and exhort to gospel duties; now that the word began to work he followed it; he had said much in a little (*v.* 38, 39), and that which, one would think, included all, and yet he had more to say. When we have heard those words which have done our souls good, we cannot but wish to hear more, to hear many more such words. Among other things he said (and it should seem inculcated it), *Save yourselves from this untoward generation. Be you free* from them. The unbelieving Jews were an untoward generation, perverse and obstinate; they walked contrary to God and man (1 Thess. ii. 15), wedded to sin and marked for ruin. Now as to them, 1. "Give diligence to save yourselves from their ruin, that you may not be involved in that, and may *escape all those things*" (as the Christians did): "*Repent, and be baptized;* and then you shall not be sharers in destruction with those with whom you have been sharers in sin." *O gather not my soul with sinners.* 2. "In order to this continue not with them in their sin, persist not with them in infidelity. *Save yourselves,* that is, separate yourselves, distinguish yourselves, from this *untoward generation. Be not rebellious like this rebellious house;* partake not with them in their sins, that you share not with them in their plagues." Note, To separate ourselves from wicked people is the only way to save ourselves from them; though we hereby expose ourselves to their rage and enmity, we really save ourselves from them; for, if we consider whither they are hastening, we shall see it is better to have the trouble of swimming against their stream than the danger of being carried down their stream. Those that repent of their sins, and give up themselves to Jesus Christ, must evidence their sincerity by breaking off all intimate society with wicked people. *Depart from me, ye evil doers,* is the language of one that determines to keep *the commandments of his God,* Ps. cxix. 115. We must *save ourselves* from them, which denotes avoiding them with dread and holy fear, as we would save ourselves from an enemy that seeks to destroy us, or from a house infected with the plague.

IV. Here is the happy success and issue of this, *v.* 41. The Spirit wrought with the word, and wrought wonders by it. These same persons that had many of them been eye-witnesses of the death of Christ, and the prodigies that attended it, and were not wrought upon by them, were yet wrought upon by the preaching of the word, for it is this that is the *power of God unto salvation.* 1. They received the word; and *then* only the word does us good, when we do receive it, embrace it, and bid it welcome. They admitted the conviction of it, and accepted the offers of it. 2. They gladly received it. Herod *heard* the word gladly, but these gladly *received* it, were not only glad that they had it to receive, but glad that by the grace of God they were enabled to receive it, though it would be a humbling changing word to them, and would expose them to the enmity of their countrymen. 3. They were baptized; believing with the heart, they made confession with the mouth, and enrolled themselves among the disciples of Christ by that sacred rite and ceremony which he had instituted. And though Peter had said, "Be baptized in the name of *the Lord Jesus*" (because the doctrine of Christ was the present truth), yet we have reason to think that, in baptizing them, the whole form Christ prescribed was used, *in the name of the Father, the Son, and the Holy Ghost.* Note, Those that receive the Christian covenant ought to receive the Christian baptism. 4. Hereby there were added to the disciples to the number of about *three thousand souls that same day.* All those that had received the Holy Ghost had their tongues at work to preach, and their hands at work to baptize; for it was time to be busy, when such a harvest was to be gathered in. The conversion of these three thousand with these words was a *greater work* than the feeding of four or five thousand with a few loaves. Now Israel began to multiply after the death of our Joseph. They are said to be *three thousand souls* (which word is generally used for persons when women and children are included with men, as Gen. xiv. 21, *margin, Give me the souls;* Gen. xlvi. 27, *seventy souls*), which intimates that those that were here baptized were not so many men, but so many heads of families as, with their children and servants baptized, might make up *three thousand souls.* These were *added to them.* Note, Those who are joined to Christ are added to the disciples of Christ, and join with them. When we take God for our God, we must take his people to be our people.

42 And they continued stedfastly
in the apostles' doctrine and fellowship, and in breaking of bread, and in
prayers. 43 And fear came upon
every soul: and many wonders and
signs were done by the apostles. 44
And all that believed were together,
and had all things common; 45 And
sold their possessions and goods, and
parted them to all *men*, as every man
had need. 46 And they, continuing
daily with one accord in the temple,
and breaking bread from house to
house, did eat their meat with gladness and singleness of heart, 47
Praising God, and having favour with
all the people. And the Lord added
to the church daily such as should be
saved.

We often speak of the primitive church, and appeal to it, and to the history of it; in these verses we have the history of the *truly primitive church,* of the *first days* of it, its state of infancy indeed, but, like that, the state of its greatest *innocence.*

I. They kept close to holy ordinances, and abounded in all instances of piety and devotion, for Christianity, admitted in the power of it, will dispose the soul to communion with God in all those ways wherein he has appointed us to meet him and promised to meet us.

1. They were diligent and constant in their attendance upon the *preaching of the word.* They *continued in the apostles' doctrine,* and never disowned nor deserted it; or, as it may be read, *they continued constant to the apostles' teaching* or *instruction;* by *baptism* they were discipled to be taught, and they were willing to be taught. Note, Those who have given up their names to Christ must make conscience of hearing his word; for thereby we give honour to him, and build up ourselves in our most holy faith.

2. They kept up the *communion of saints.* They continued *in fellowship* (*v.* 42), and *continued daily with one accord in the temple, v.* 46. They not only had a mutual affection to each other, but a great deal of mutual conversation with each other; they were much together. When they withdrew from *the untoward* generation, they did not turn hermits, but were very intimate with one another, and took all occasions to meet; wherever you saw one disciple, you would see more, like *birds of a feather.* See how these Christians love one another. They were concerned for one another, sympathized with one another, and heartily espoused one another's interests. They had fellowship with one another in religious worship. They met *in the temple:* there was their rendezvous; for joint-fellowship with God is the best fellowship we can have with one another, 1 John i. 3. Observe, (1.) They were daily in the temple, not only on the days of the sabbaths and solemn feasts, but on other days, every day. Worshipping God is to be our daily work, and, where there is opportunity, the oftener it is done publicly the better. God loves the gates of Zion, and so must we. (2.) They were *with one accord;* not only no discord nor strife, but a great deal of holy love among them; and they heartily joined in their public services. Though they met with the Jews in the courts of the temple, yet the Christians kept together by themselves, and were unanimous in their separate devotions.

3. They frequently joined in the ordinance of the Lord's supper. They continued *in the breaking of bread,* in celebrating that memorial of their Master's death, as those that were not ashamed to own their relation to, and their dependence upon, Christ and him crucified. They could not forget the death of Christ, yet they kept up this memorial of it, and made it their constant practice, because it was an institution of Christ, to be transmitted to the succeeding ages of the church. They broke bread *from house to house; κατ' οἰκον—house by house;* they did not think fit to celebrate the eucharist in the temple, for that was peculiar to the Christian institutes, and therefore they administered that ordinance in private houses, choosing such houses of the converted Christians as were convenient, to which the neighbours resorted; and they went from one to another of these little synagogues or domestic chapels, houses that had churches in them, and there celebrated the eucharist with those that usually met there to worship God.

4. They continued *in prayers. After* the Spirit was poured out, as well as before, while they were waiting for him, they continued instant in prayer; for prayer will never be superseded till it comes to be swallowed up in everlasting praise. *Breaking of bread* comes in between the *word* and *prayer,* for

it has reference to both, and is a help to both. The Lord's supper is a sermon to the eye, and a confirmation of God's word to us; and it is an encouragement to our prayers, and a solemn expression of the ascent of our souls to God.

5. They abounded in thanksgiving; were continually *praising God, v.* 47. This should have a part in every prayer, and not be crowded into a corner. Those that have received the gift of the Holy Ghost will be much in praise.

II. They were loving one to another, and very kind; their charity was as eminent as their piety, and their joining together in holy ordinances knit their hearts to each other, and very much endeared them to one another.

1. They had frequent meetings for Christian converse (*v.* 44): *All that believed were together;* not all those thousands in one place (this was impracticable); but, as Dr. Lightfoot explains it, they kept together in several companies or congregations, according as their languages, nations, or other associations, brought them and kept them together. And thus joining together, because it was apart from those that believed not, and because it was in the same profession and practice of the duties of religion, they are said to be together, ἐπὶ τὸ αὐτὸ. They associated together, and so both expressed and increased their mutual love.

2. They had *all things common;* perhaps they had common tables (as the Spartans of old), for familiarity, temperance and freedom of conversation; they *ate together*, that those who had much might have the less, and so be kept from the temptations of abundance; and they who had little might have the more, and so be kept from the temptations of want and poverty. Or, There was such a concern for one another, and such a readiness to help one another as there was occasion, that it might be said, They had *all things common,* according to the law of friendship; one wanted not what another had; for he might have it for the asking.

3. They were very cheerful, and very generous in the use of what they had. Besides the religion that was in their sacred feasts, (their *breaking bread from house to house)* a great deal of it appeared in their common meals; they did *eat their meat with gladness and singleness of heart.* They brought the comforts of *God's table* along with them to *their own,* which had two good effects upon them:—(1.) It made them very pleasant, and enlarged their hearts with holy joy; they did eat their bread with joy, and *drank their wine with a merry heart,* as knowing that *God now accepted their works.* None have such cause to be cheerful as good Christians have; it is a pity but that they should always have hearts to be so. (2.) It made them very liberal to their poor brethren, and enlarged their hearts in charity. They did *eat their meat with singleness of heart,* ἐν ἀφελότητι καρδίας—*with liberality of heart;* so some: they did not eat their morsels alone, but bade the poor welcome to their table, not grudgingly, but with all the hearty freedom imaginable. Note, It becomes Christians to be open-hearted and open-handed, and in every good work to sow plentifully, as those on whom God hath sown plentifully, and who hope to reap so.

4. They raised a fund for charity (*v.* 45): They *sold their possessions and goods;* some sold their lands and houses, others their stocks and the furniture of their houses, and *parted* the money to their brethren, *as every man had need.* This was to destroy, not property (as Mr. Baxter says), but selfishness. Herein, probably, they had an eye to the command which Christ gave to the rich man, as a test of his sincerity, *Sell that thou hast, and give to the poor.* Not that this was intended for an example to be a constant binding rule, as if all Christians in all places and ages were bound to sell their estates, and give away the money in charity. For St. Paul's epistles, after this, often speak of the distinction of rich and poor, and Christ hath said that *the poor we always have with us,* and shall have, and the rich must be always doing them good out of the rents, issues, and profits, of their estates, which they disable themselves to do, if they sell them, and give all away at once. But here the case was extraordinary (1.) They were under no obligation of a divine command to do this, as appears by what Peter said to Ananias (*ch.* v. 4): *Was it not in thine own power?* But it was a very commendable instance of their raisedness above the world, their contempt of it, their assurance of another world, their love to their brethren, their compassion to the poor, and their great zeal for the encouraging of Christianity, and the nursing of it in its infancy. The apostles left all to follow Christ, and were to give themselves wholly to the word and prayer, and something must be done for their maintenance; so that this extraordinary liberality was like that of Israel in the wilderness towards the building of the tabernacle, which needed to be restrained, Exod. xxxvi. 5, 6. Our rule is, to give according as God has blessed us; yet, in such an extraordinary case as this, those are to be praised who give *beyond their power,* 2 Cor. viii. 3. (2.) They were Jews that did this, and those who believed Christ must believe that the Jewish nation would shortly be destroyed, and an end put to the possession of estates and goods in it, and, in the belief of this, they sold them for the present service of Christ and his church.

III. God owned them, and gave them signal tokens of his presence with them (*v.* 43): *Many wonders and signs were done by the apostles* of divers sorts, which confirmed their doctrine, and incontestably proved that it was from God. Those that could work miracles could have maintained themselves and the poor that were among them miraculously, as Christ fed thousands with a little food; but it was as much for the glory of God that it should be done by a miracle of grace (inclining people to sell their estates, to do it) as if it had been done by a miracle in nature.

But the Lord's giving them power to work miracles was not all he did for them; he *added to the church daily*. The word in their mouths *did wonders*, and God blessed their endeavours for the increase of the number of believers. Note, It is God's work to add souls to the church; and it is a great comfort both to ministers and Christians to see it.

IV. The people were influenced by it; those that were without, the standers by, that were spectators. 1. They *feared them*, and had a veneration for them (*v.* 43): *Fear came upon every soul*, that is, upon very many who saw the *wonders* and *signs* done by the apostles, and were afraid lest their not being respected as they should be would bring desolation upon their nation. The common people stood in awe of them, as Herod feared John. Though they had nothing of external pomp to command external respect, as the *scribes' long robes* gained them the *greetings in the market-places*, yet they had abundance of spiritual gifts that were truly honourable, which possessed men with an inward reverence for them. Fear came upon *every soul;* the *souls* of people were strangely influenced by their awful preaching and living. 2. They *favoured them*. Though we have reason to think there were those that despised them and hated them (we are sure the Pharisees and chief priests did), yet far the greater part of the common people had a kindness for them—they *had favour with all the people*. Christ was so violently run upon and run down by a *packed mob*, which cried, *Crucify him, crucify him*, that one would think his doctrine and followers were never likely to have an interest in the common people any more. And yet here we find them *in favour with them all*, by which it appears that their prosecuting Christ was a sort of force put upon them by the artifices of the priests; now they returned to their wits, to their right mind. Note, Undissembled piety and charity will command respect; and cheerfulness in serving God will recommend religion to those that are without. Some read it, *They had charity to all the people*—χάριν ἔχοντες πρὸς ὅλον τὸν λαὸν· they did not confine their charity to those of their own community, but it was *catholic* and *extensive;* and this recommended them very much. 3. They *fell over* to them. Some or other were daily coming in, though not so many as the first day; and they were such as *should be saved*. Note, Those that God has designed for eternal salvation shall one time or other be effectually brought to Christ: and those that are brought to Christ are *added to the church* in a holy covenant by baptism, and in holy communion by other ordinances.

CHAP. III.

In this chapter we have a miracle and a sermon: the miracle wrought to make way for the sermon, to confirm the doctrine that was to be preached, and to make way for it into the minds of the people; and then the sermon to explain the miracle, and to sow the ground which by it was broken up. I. The miracle was the healing of a man that was lame from his birth, with a word speaking (ver. 1—8), and the impression which this made upon the people, ver. 9—11. II. The scope of the sermon which was preached hereupon was to bring people to Christ, to repent of their sin in crucifying him (ver. 12—19), to believe in him now that he was glorified, and to comply with the Father's design in glorifying him, ver. 20—26. The former part of the discourse opens the wound, the latter applies the remedy.

NOW Peter and John went up
together into the temple at the
hour of prayer, *being* the ninth *hour*.
2 And a certain man lame from his
mother's womb was carried, whom
they laid daily at the gate of the temple which is called Beautiful, to ask
alms of them that entered into the
temple; 3 Who seeing Peter and
John about to go into the temple
asked an alms. 4 And Peter, fastening his eyes upon him with John,
said, Look on us. 5 And he gave
heed unto them, expecting to receive
something of them. 6 Then Peter
said, Silver and gold have I none;
but such as I have give I thee: In
the name of Jesus Christ of Nazareth
rise up and walk. 7 And he took
him by the right hand, and lifted *him*
up: and immediately his feet and
ankle bones received strength. 8 And
he leaping up stood, and walked, and
entered with them into the temple,
walking, and leaping, and praising
God. 9 And all the people saw him
walking and praising God: 10 And
they knew that it was he which sat
for alms at the Beautiful gate of the
temple: and they were filled with
wonder and amazement at that which
had happened unto him. 11 And as
the lame man which was healed held
Peter and John, all the people ran
together unto them in the porch that
is called Solomon's, greatly wondering.

We were told in general (*ch.* ii. 43) that *many signs and wonders were done by the apostles*, which are not written in this book; but here we have one given us for an instance. As they wrought miracles, not upon every body as every body had occasion for them, but as the Holy Spirit gave direction, so as to answer the end of their commission; so all the miracles they did work are not written in this book, but such only are recorded as the Holy Ghost thought fit, to answer the end of this sacred history.

I. The persons by whose ministry this miracle was wrought were Peter and John, two principal men among the apostles; they were so in Christ's time, one speaker of the house for the most part, the other favourite of the Master; and they continue so. When, upon the conversion of thousands, the church was divided into several societies, perhaps Peter and John presided in that which Luke associated with, and therefore he is more particular in recording what they said and did, as afterwards what Paul said and did when he attended him, both the one and the other being designed for specimens of what the other apostles did.

Peter and John had each of them a brother among the twelve, with whom they were coupled when they were sent out; yet now they seem to be knit together more closely than either of them to his brother, for the bond of friendship is sometimes stronger than that of relation: *there is a friend that sticks closer than a brother.* Peter and John seem to have hȧd a peculiar intimacy after Christ's resurrection more than before, John xx. 2. The reason of which (if I may have liberty to conjecture) might be this, that John, a disciple made up of love, was more compassionate to Peter upon his fall and repentance, and more tender of him in his *bitter weeping* for his sin, than any other of the apostles were, and more solicitous to restore him in the *spirit of meekness,* which made him very dear to Peter ever after; and it was good evidence of Peter's acceptance with God, upon his repentance, that Christ's favourite was made his bosom friend. David prayed, after his fall, *Let those that fear thee turn unto me,* Ps. cxix. 79.

II. The time and place are here set down. 1. It was in *the temple,* whither *Peter and John went up together,* because it was the place of concourse; there were the shoals of fish among which the net of the gospel was to be cast, especially during the days of pentecost, within the compass of which we may suppose this to have happened. Note, It is good to go up to the temple, to attend on public ordinances; and it is comfortable to go up together to the temple: *I was glad when they said unto me, Let us go.* The best society is society in worshipping God. 2. It was *at the hour of prayer,* one of the hours of public worship commonly appointed and observed among the Jews. Time and place are two necessary circumstances of every action, which must be determined by consent, as is most convenient for edification. With reference to public worship, there must be a house of prayer and an hour of prayer: the ninth hour, that is, three o'clock in the afternoon, was one of the hours of prayer among the Jews; nine in the morning and twelve at noon were the other two. See Ps. lv. 17; Dan. vi. 10. It is of use for private Christians so far to have their hours of prayer as may serve, though not to bind, yet to remind, conscience: *every thing is beautiful in its season.*

III. The patient on whom this miraculous cure was wrought is here described, *v.* 2. He was a poor lame beggar at the temple gate. 1. He was a cripple, not by accident, but born so; he was *lame from his mother's womb,* as it should seem, by a paralytic distemper, which weakened his limbs; for it is said in the description of his cure (*v.* 7), *His feet and ankle bones received strength.* Some such piteous cases now and then there are, which we ought to be affected with and look upon with compassion, and which are designed to show us what we all are by nature spiritually: *without strength,* lame from our birth, unable to work or walk in God's service. 2. He was a beggar. Being unable to work for his living, he must live upon alms; such are God's poor. He was *laid daily* by his friends at *one of the gates of the temple,* a miserable spectacle, unable to do any thing for himself but to *ask alms of those that entered into the temple* or came out There was a concourse, — a concourse of devout good people, from whom charity might be expected, and a concourse of such people when it might be hoped they were in the best frame; and there he was laid. Those that need, and cannot work, must not be ashamed to beg. He would not have been laid there, and laid there daily, if he had not been used to meet with supplies, daily supplies there. Note, Our prayers and our alms should go together; Cornelius's did, *ch.* x. 4. Objects of charity should be in a particular manner welcome to us when we go up to the temple to pray; it is a pity that common beggars at church doors should any of them be of such a character as to discourage charity; but they ought not always to be overlooked: some there are surely that merit regard, and better feed ten drones, yea, and some wasps, than let one bee starve. The gate of the temple at which he was laid is here named: it was called *Beautiful,* for the extraordinary splendour and magnificence of it. Dr. Lightfoot observes that this was the gate that led out of the court of the Gentiles into that of the Jews, and he supposes that the cripple would beg only of the Jews, as disdaining to ask any thing of the Gentiles. But Dr. Whitby takes it to be at the first entrance into the temple, and beautified sumptuously, as became the frontispiece of that place where the divine Majesty vouchsafed to dwell; and it was no diminution to the beauty of this gate that a poor man lay there begging. 3. He begged of Peter and John (*v.* 3), begged an alms; this was the utmost he expected from them, who had the reputation of being charitable men, and who, though they had not much, yet did good with what they had. It was not many weeks ago that the blind and the lame came to Christ in the temple, and were healed there, Matt. xxi. 14. And why might not he have asked more than an alms, if he knew that Peter and John were Christ's messengers, and preached and wrought miracles in his name? But he had that done for him which he looked not for; he *asked an alms,* and had a cure.

IV. We have here the method of the cure.

1. His expectations were raised. Peter, instead of turning his eyes from him, as many do from objects of charity, turned his eyes to him, nay, he *fastened his eyes upon him,* that his eye might affect his heart with compassion towards him, *v.* 4. John did so too, for they were both guided by one and the same Spirit, and concurred in this miracle; they said, *Look on us.* Our eye must be ever towards the Lord (the eye of our mind), and, in token of this, the eye of the body may properly be fixed on those whom he employs as the ministers of his grace. This man needed not to be bidden twice to look on the apostles; for he justly thought this gave him cause to expect that he should *receive something from them,* and therefore he *gave heed to them, v.* 5. Note, We must come to God both to attend on his word and to apply ourselves to him in prayer, with hearts fixed and expectations raised. We must look up to heaven and expect to receive benefit by that which God speaks thence, and an answer of peace to the prayers sent up thither. *I will direct my prayer unto thee, and will look up.*

2. His expectation of an alms was disappointed. *Peter said, "Silver and gold have I none,* and therefore none to give thee;" yet he intimated that if he had had any he would have given him an alms, not brass, but silver or gold. Note, (1.) It is not often that Christ's friends and favourites have abundance of the wealth of this world. The apostles were very poor, had but just enough for themselves, and no overplus. Peter and John had abundance of money laid at their feet, but this was appropriated to the maintenance of the poor of the church, and they would not convert any of it to their own use, nor dispose of it otherwise than according to the intention of the donors. Public trusts ought to be strictly and faithfully observed. (2.) Many who are well inclined to works of charity are yet not in a capacity of doing any thing considerable, while others, who have wherewithal to do much, have not a heart to do any thing.

3. His expectations, notwithstanding, were quite outdone. Peter had no money to give him; but, (1.) He had that which was better, such an interest in heaven, such a power from heaven, as to be able to cure his disease. Note, Those who are poor in the world may yet be rich, very rich, in spiritual gifts, graces, and comforts; certainly there is that which we are capable of possessing which is infinitely better than silver and gold; the merchandise and gain of it are better, Job xxviii. 12, &c.; Prov. iii. 14, &c. (2.) He gave him that which was better—the cure of his disease, which he would gladly have given a great deal of silver and gold for, if he had had it, and the cure could have been so obtained. This would enable him to work for his living, so that he would not need to beg any more; nay, he would *have to give to those that needed,* and it *is more blessed to give than to receive.* A miraculous cure would be a greater instance of God's favour, and would put a greater honour upon him, than thousands of gold and silver could. Observe, When Peter had no silver and gold to give, yet (says he) *such as I have I give thee.* Note, Those may be, and ought to be, otherwise charitable and helpful to the poor, who have not wherewithal to give in charity; those who have not silver and gold have their limbs and senses, and with these may be serviceable to the blind, and lame, and sick, and if they be not, as there is occasion, neither would they give to them if they had silver and gold. *As every one hath received the gift, so let him minister it.* Let us now see how the cure was wrought. [1.] Christ *sent his word, and healed him* (Ps. cvii. 20); for healing grace is given by the word of Christ; this is the vehicle of the healing virtue derived from Christ. Christ spoke cures by himself; the apostles spoke them in his name. Peter bids a lame man *rise up and walk,* which would have been a banter upon him if he had not premised *in the name of Jesus Christ of Nazareth:* "I say it by warrant from him, and it shall be done by power from him, and all the glory and praise of it shall be ascribed to him." He calls Christ *Jesus of Nazareth,* which was a name of reproach, to intimate that the indignities done him on earth served but as a foil to his glories now that he was in heaven. "Give him what name you will, call him if you will in scorn Jesus of Nazareth, in that name you shall see wonders done; for, because he humbled himself, thus highly was he exalted." He bids the cripple *rise up and walk,* which does not prove that he had power in himself to do it, but that if he attempt to rise and walk, and, in a sense of his own impotency, depend upon a divine power to enable him to do it, he shall be enabled; and by rising and walking he must evidence that that power has wrought upon him; and then let him take the comfort, and let God have the praise. Thus it is in the healing of our souls, which are spiritually impotent. [2.] Peter lent his hand, and helped him (*v.* 7): *He took him by the right hand,* in the same name in which he had spoken to him to arise and walk, *and lifted him up.* Not that this could contribute any thing to his cure; but it was a sign, plainly intimating the help he should receive from God, if he exerted himself as he was bidden. When God by his word commands us to

rise, and walk in the way of his commandments, if we mix faith with that word, and lay our souls under the power of it, he will give his Spirit to take us by the hand, and lift us up. If we set ourselves to do what we can, God has promised his grace to enable us to do what we cannot; and by that promise we partake of a new nature, and that grace shall not be in vain; it was not here: *His feet and ankle-bones received strength,* which they had not done if he had not attempted to rise, and been helped up; he does his part, and Peter does his, and yet it is Christ that does all: it is he that puts strength into him. As the bread was multiplied in the breaking, and the water turned into wine in the pouring out, so strength was given to the cripple's feet in his stirring them and using them.

V. Here is the impression which this cure made upon the patient himself, which we may best conceive of if we put our soul into his soul's stead. 1. He leaped up, in obedience to the command, *Arise.* He found in himself such a degree of strength in his feet and ankle-bones that he did not steal up gently, with fear and trembling, as weak people do when they begin to recover strength; but he started up, as one refreshed with sleep, boldly, and with great agility, and as one that questioned not his own strength. The incomes of strength were sudden, and he was no less sudden in showing them. He leaped, as one glad to quit the bed or pad of straw on which he had lain so long lame. 2. He stood, and walked. He stood without either leaning or trembling, stood straight up, and walked without a staff. He trod strongly, and moved steadily; and this was to manifest the cure, and that it was a thorough cure. Note, Those who have had experience of the working of divine grace upon them should evidence what they have experienced. Has God put strength into us? Let us stand before him in the exercises of devotion; let us walk before him in all the instances of a religious conversation. Let us stand up resolutely for him, and walk cheerfully with him, and both in strength derived and received from him. 3. He *held Peter and John, v.* 11. We need not ask why he held them. I believe he scarcely knew himself: but it was in a transport of joy that he embraced them as the best benefactors he had ever met with, and hung upon them to a degree of rudeness; he would not let them go forward, but would have them stay with him, while he published to all about him what God had done for him by them. Thus he testified his affection to them; he held them, and would not let them go. Some suggest that he clung to them for fear lest, if they should leave him, his lameness should return. Those whom God hath healed love those whom he made instruments of their healing, and see the need of their further help. 4. He *entered with them into the temple.* His strong affection to them held them; but it could not hold them so fast as to keep them out of the temple, whither they were going to preach Christ. We should never suffer ourselves to be diverted by the most affectionate kindnesses of our friends from going in the way of our duty. But, if they will not stay with him, he is resolved to go with them, and the rather because they are going into the temple, whence he had been so long kept by his weakness and his begging: like the impotent man whom Christ cured, he was presently found in the temple, John v. 14. He went into the temple, not only to offer up his praises and thanksgivings to God, but to hear more from the apostles of that Jesus in whose name he had been healed. Those that have experienced the power of Christ should earnestly desire to grow in their acquaintance with Christ. 5. He was there *walking, and leaping, and praising God.* Note, The strength God has given us, both in mind and body, should be made use of to his praise, and we should study how to honour him with it. Those that are healed in his name must walk up and down in his name and in his strength, Zech. x. 12. This man, as soon as he could leap, leaped for joy in God, and praised him. Here was that scripture fulfilled (Isa. xxxv. 6): *Then shall the lame man leap as a hart.* Now that this man was newly cured he was in this excess of joy and thankfulness. All true converts walk and praise God; but perhaps young converts leap more in his praises.

VI. How the people that were eye-witnesses of this miracle were influenced by it we are next told. 1. They were entirely satisfied in the truth of the miracle, and had nothing to object against it. *They knew it was he that sat begging at the beautiful gate of the temple, v.* 10. He had sat there so long that they all knew him; and for this reason he was chosen to be the vessel of this mercy. Now they were not so perverse as to make any doubt whether he was the same man, as the Pharisees had questioned concerning the blind man that Christ cured, John ix. 9, 18. They now saw him *walking, and praising God* (*v.* 9), and perhaps took notice of a change in his mind; for he was now as loud in praising God as he had before been in begging relief. The best evidence that it was a complete cure was that he praised God for it. Mercies are then perfected, when they are sanctified. 2. They were astonished at it: They were *filled with wonder and amazement* (*v.* 10); *greatly wondering, v* 11. They were in an *ecstasy.* There seems to have been this effect of the pouring out of the Spirit, that the people, at least those in Jerusalem, were much more affected with the miracles the apostles wrought than they had been with those of the same kind that had been wrought by

Christ himself; and this was in order to the miracles answering their end. 3. They gathered about Peter and John: *All the people ran together unto them in Solomon's porch:* some only to gratify their curiosity with the sight of men that had such power; others with a desire to hear them preach, concluding that their doctrine must needs be of divine origin, which thus had a divine ratification. They flocked to them in Solomon's porch, a part of the court of the Gentiles, where Solomon had built the outer porch of the temple; or, some cloisters or piazzas which Herod had erected upon the same foundation upon which Solomon had built the stately porch that bore his name, Herod being ambitious herein to be a second Solomon. Here the people met, to see this great sight.

12 And when Peter saw *it*, he answered unto the people, Ye men of
Israel, why marvel ye at this? or
why look ye so earnestly on us, as
though by our own power or holiness
we had made this man to walk? 13
The God of Abraham, and of Isaac,
and of Jacob, the God of our fathers,
hath glorified his Son Jesus; whom
ye delivered up, and denied him in
the presence of Pilate, when he was
determined to let *him* go. 14 But
ye denied the Holy One and the Just,
and desired a murderer to be granted
unto you; 15 And killed the Prince
of life, whom God hath raised from
the dead; whereof we are witnesses.
16 And his name through faith in his
name hath made this man strong,
whom ye see and know: yea, the
faith which is by him hath given him
this perfect soundness in the presence
of you all. 17 And now, brethren,
I wot that through ignorance ye did
it, as *did* also your rulers. 18 But
those things, which God before had
showed by the mouth of all his prophets, that Christ should suffer, he
hath so fulfilled. 19 Repent ye therefore, and be converted, that your
sins may be blotted out, when the
times of refreshing shall come from
the presence of the Lord; 20 And he
shall send Jesus Christ, which before
was preached unto you: 21 Whom
the heaven must receive until the
times of restitution of all things, which
God hath spoken by the mouth of all
his holy prophets since the world began. 22 For Moses truly said unto
the fathers, A prophet shall the Lord
your God raise up unto you of your
brethren, like unto me; him shall ye
hear in all things whatsoever he shall
say unto you. 23 And it shall come
to pass, *that* every soul, which will
not hear that prophet, shall be destroyed from among the people. 24
Yea, and all the prophets from Samuel and those that follow after, as
many as have spoken, have likewise
foretold of these days. 25 Ye are
the children of the prophets, and of
the covenant which God made with
our fathers, saying unto Abraham,
And in thy seed shall all the kindreds
of the earth be blessed. 26 Unto
you first God, having raised up his
Son Jesus, sent him to bless you, in
turning away every one of you from
his iniquities.

We have here the sermon which Peter preached after he had cured the lame man. *When Peter saw it.* 1. When he saw the people got together in a crowd, he took that opportunity to preach Christ to them, especially the temple being the place of their concourse, and Solomon's porch there: let them come and hear a more excellent wisdom than Solomon's, for, behold, a greater than Solomon is here preached. 2. When he saw the people affected with the miracle, and filled with admiration, then he sowed the gospel seed in the ground which was thus broken up, and prepared to receive it. 3. When he saw the people ready to adore him and John, he stepped in immediately, and diverted their respect from them, that it might be directed to Christ only; to this *he answered* presently, as Paul and Barnabas at Lystra. See *ch.* xiv. 14, 15. In the sermon,

I. He humbly disclaims the honour of the miracle as not due to them, who were only the ministers of Christ, or instruments in his hand for the doing of it. The doctrines they preached were not of their own invention, nor were the seals of it their own, but his whose the doctrines were. He addresses himself to them as *men of Israel*, men to whom pertained, not only the law and the promises, but the gospel and the performances, and who were nearly interested in the present dispensation. Two things he asks them:—1. Why they were so surprised at the miracle itself: *Why marvel you at this?* It was indeed marvellous, and they justly wondered at it, but it was no more than what Christ had done many a time, and they had not duly regarded it, nor been affected with it. It was but a little before that Christ had *raised Lazarus from the dead;* and why should this then seem so strange? Note, Stupid people think that strange now which might have been familiar to them if it had not been their own fault. Christ had lately risen from the dead himself; why did they not marvel at this? why were they not convinced by this? 2. Why they gave so much of the praise of it to them, who were only the instruments of it: *Why look you so earnestly on us?* (1.) It was certain that they *had made this man to walk*, by which it appeared that the apostles not only were sent of God, but were sent to be blessings to the world, benefactors to mankind, and were sent to heal sick and distempered souls, that were spiritually lame and impotent, to set broken bones, and make them rejoice. (2.) Yet they did not do it by any *power or holiness of their own.* It was not done by any might of their own, any skill they had in physic or surgery, nor any virtue in their word: the power they did it by was wholly derived from Christ. Nor was it done by any merit of their own; the power which Christ gave them to do it they had not deserved: it was not by their own holiness; for, as they were weak things, so they were foolish things, that Christ chose to employ; Peter was a sinful man. What holiness had Judas? Yet he wrought miracles in Christ's name. What holiness any of them had it was wrought in them, and they could not pretend to merit by it. (3.) It was the people's fault that they attributed it to their power and holiness, and accordingly looked at them. Note, The instruments of God's favour to us, though they must be respected, must not be idolized; we must take heed of reckoning that to be done by the instrument which God is the author of. (4.) It was the praise of Peter and John that they would not take the honour of this miracle to themselves, but carefully transmitted it to Christ. Useful men must see to it that they be very humble. *Not unto us, O Lord, not unto us, but to thy name give glory.* Every crown must be cast at the feet of Christ; *not I, but the grace of God with me.*

II. He preaches Christ to them; this was his business, that he might lead them into obedience to Christ.

1. He preaches Christ, as the true Messiah promised to the fathers (*v.* 13); for, (1.) He is Jesus the Son of God; though they had lately condemned Christ as a blasphemer for saying that he was the Son of God, yet Peter avows it: he is *his Son Jesus;* to him dear as a Son; to us, *Jesus*, a Saviour. (2.) God hath glorified him, in raising him up to be king, priest, and prophet, of his church; he glorified him in his life and in his death, as well as in his resurrection and ascension. (3.) He hath glorified him as *the God of our fathers*, whom he names with respect (for they were great names with the men of Israel, and justly), *the God of Abraham, of Isaac, and of Jacob.* God sent him into the world, pursuant to the promises made to those patriarchs, *that in their seed the families of the earth should be blessed*, and the covenant made with them, *that God would be a God to them, and their seed.* The apostles call the patriarchs their fathers, and God the God of those patriarchs from whom the Jews were descended, to intimate to them that they had no evil design upon the Jewish nation (that they should look upon them with a jealous eye), but had a value and concern for it, and were hereby well-wishers to it; and the gospel they preached was the revelation of the mind and will of the God of Abraham. See *ch.* xxvi. 7, 22; Luke i. 72, 73.

2. He charges them flatly and plainly with the murder of this Jesus, as he had done before. (1.) "*You delivered him up* to your chief priests and elders, the representative body of the nation; and you of the common people were influenced by them to clamour against him, as if he had been a public grievance." (2.) "*You denied him,* and you disowned him, would not have him then to be your king, could not look upon him as the Messiah, because he came not in external pomp and power; *you denied him in the presence of Pilate*, renounced all the expectations of your church, in the presence of the Roman governor, who justly laughed at you for it; *you denied him against the face of Pilate*" (so Dr. Hammond), "in defiance of his reasonings with you" *(Pilate had determined to let him go,* but the people opposed it, and overruled him). "You were worse than Pilate, for he would have released him, if you had let him follow his own judgment. *You denied the holy One and the Just,* who had approved himself so, and all the malice of his persecutors could not disprove it." The holiness and justice of the Lord Jesus, which are something more than his innocency, were a great aggravation of the sin of those that put him to death. (3.) "*You desired a murderer to be released*, and Christ crucified; as if Barabbas had deserved better at your hands than the Lord Jesus, than which a greater affront could not be put upon him." (4.) *You killed the prince of life.* Observe the antithesis: "You preserved *a murderer*, a destroyer of life; and destroyed the Saviour, *the author of life. You killed* him who was sent to be to you *the prince of life,* and so not only forsook, but rebelled against your own mercies. You did an ungrateful thing, in taking away his life who would have been your life You did a foolish thing to think you could conquer *the prince of life,* who has life in himself, and would soon resume the life he resigned."

3. He attests his resurrection as before, *ch.* ii. 32. "You thought *the prince of life* might be deprived of his life, as any other prince might be deprived of his dignity and dominion, but you found yourselves mistaken, for *God raised him from the dead;* so that in putting him to death you fought against God, and were baffled. *God raised him from*

the dead, and thereby ratified his demands, and confirmed his doctrine, and rolled away all the reproach of his sufferings, and *for the truth of his resurrection we are all witnesses.*"

4. He ascribes the cure of this impotent man to the power of Christ (*v.* 16): *His name, through faith in his name,* in that discovery which he hath made of himself, *has made this man strong.* He repeats it again, *The faith which is by him hath given him this soundness.* Here, (1.) He appeals to themselves concerning the truth of the miracle; the man on whom it was wrought is one *whom you see, and know, and have known;* he was not acquainted with Peter and John before, so that there was no room to suspect a compact between them: "You know him to have been a cripple from a child. The miracle was wrought publicly, *in the presence of you all;* not in a corner, but in the gate of the temple; you saw in what manner it was done, so that there could be no juggle in it; you had liberty to examine it immediately, and may yet. The cure is complete; it is a *perfect soundness;* you see the man walks and leaps, as one that has no remainder either of weakness or pain." (2.) He acquaints them with the power by which it was wrought. [1.] It is done by the name of Christ, not merely by naming it as a spell or charm, but it is done by us as professors and teachers of his name, by virtue of a commission and instructions we have received from him, and a power which he has invested us with, that name which Christ has above every name; his authority, his command has done it; as writs run in the king's name, though it is an inferior officer that executes them. [2.] The power of Christ is fetched in *through faith in his name,* a confidence in him, a dependence on him, a believing application to him, and expectation from him, even *that faith which is, δι' αὐτοῦ—by him,* which is of his working; *it is not of ourselves, it is the gift of Christ;* and it is for his sake, that he may have the glory of it; for he is both *the author and finisher of our faith.* Dr. Lightfoot suggests that faith is twice named in this verse, because of the apostles' faith in doing this miracle and the cripple's faith in receiving it; but I suppose it relates chiefly, if not only, to the former. Those that wrought this miracle by faith derived power from Christ to work it, and therefore returned all the glory to him. By this true and just account of the miracle, Peter both confirmed the great gospel truth they were to preach to the world—that Jesus Christ is the fountain of all power and grace, and the great healer and Saviour—and recommended the great gospel duty of faith in him as the only way of receiving benefit by him. It explains likewise the great gospel mystery of our salvation by Christ; it is his name that justifies us, that glorious name of his, *The Lord our righteousness;* but we, in particular, are justified by that name, through faith in it, applying it to ourselves. Thus does Peter preach unto them Jesus, and him crucified, as a faithful friend of the bridegroom, to whose service and honour he devoted all his interest.

III. He encourages them to hope that, though they had been guilty of putting Christ to death, yet they might find mercy; he does all he can to convince them, yet is careful not to drive them to despair. The guilt was very great, but, 1. He mollifies their crime by a candid imputation of it to their ignorance. Perhaps he perceived by the countenance of his hearers that they were struck with great horror when he told them that they had *killed the prince of life,* and were ready either to sink down or to fly off, and therefore he saw it needful to mitigate the rigour of the charge by calling them *brethren;* and well might he call them so, for he had been himself a brother with them in this iniquity: he had *denied the holy One and the Just,* and sworn that he did not know him; he did it by surprise; "and, for your parts, *I know that through ignorance you did it, as did also your rulers,*" *v.* 17. This was the language of Peter's charity, and teaches us to make the best of those whom we desire to make better. Peter had searched the wound to the bottom, and now he begins to think of healing it up, in order to which it is necessary to beget in them a good opinion of their physician; and could any thing be more winning than this? That which bears him out in it is that he has the example of his Master's praying for his crucifiers, and pleading in their behalf that they knew not what they did. And it is said of the rulers that *if they had known they would not have crucified the Lord of glory.* See 1 Cor. ii. 8. Perhaps some of the rulers, and of the people, did therein rebel against the light and the convictions of their own consciences, and did it through malice; but the generality went down the stream, and did it through ignorance; as Paul persecuted the church, *ignorantly, and in unbelief,* 1 Tim. i. 13. 2. He mollifies the effects of their crime—the death of *the prince of life;* this sounds very dreadful, but it was *according to the scriptures* (*v.* 18), the predictions of which, though they did not necessitate their sin, yet did necessitate his sufferings; so he himself saith: *Thus it is written, and thus it behoved Christ to suffer. You did it through ignorance* may be taken in this sense: "You fulfilled the scripture, and did not know it; *God,* by your hands, *hath fulfilled what he showed by the mouth of all his prophets, that Christ should suffer;* this was his design in delivering him up to you, but you had views of your own, and were altogether ignorant of this design; *you meant not so, neither did your heart think so.* God was fulfilling the scripture when you were gratifying your own passions." Observe, It was not only determined in the secret counsel of God, but declared to the world many ages before, *by the mouth* and pen *of the prophets, that Christ should suffer,* in order to the accomplishment of his undertaking; and it was God himself that *showed* it by them, who will see that his words be made good; what he showed he fulfilled, he so fulfilled as he had shown, punctually and exactly, without any variation. Now, though this is no extenuation at all of their sin in hating and persecuting Christ *to the death* (this still appears exceedingly sinful), yet it was an encouragement to them to repent, and hope for mercy upon their repentance; not only because in general God's gracious designs were carried on by it (and thus it agrees with the encouragement Joseph gave to his brethren, when they thought their offence against him almost unpardonable: *Fear not,* saith he, *you thought evil against me, but God meant it unto good,* Gen. l. 15, 20), but because in particular the death and sufferings of Christ were for *the remission of sins,* and the ground of that display of mercy for which he now encouraged them to hope.

IV. He exhorts them all to turn Christians, and assures them it would be unspeakably for their advantage to do so; it would be the making of them for ever. This is the application of his sermon.

1. He tells them what they must believe. (1.) They must believe that Jesus Christ is the promised seed, that seed in which God had told Abraham *all the kindreds of the earth should be blessed, v.* 25. This refers to that promise made to Abraham (Gen. xii. 3), which promise was long ere it was fulfilled, but now at length had its accomplishment in this *Jesus,* who was of *the seed of Abraham, according to the flesh,* and *in him all the families of the earth are blessed,* and not the families of Israel only; all have some benefits by him, and some have all benefits. (2.) They must believe that Jesus Christ is a prophet, *that prophet like unto Moses* whom God had promised to *raise up to them from among their brethren, v.* 22. This refers to that promise, Deut. xviii. 18. Christ is a prophet, for by him God speaks unto us; in him all divine revelation centres, and by him it is handed to us; he is a *prophet like unto Moses,* a favourite of Heaven; more intimately acquainted with the divine counsel, and more familiarly conversed with, than any other prophet. He was a deliverer of his people out of bondage, and their guide through the wilderness, like Moses; a prince and a lawgiver, like Moses; the builder of the true tabernacle, as Moses was of the typical one. Moses was *faithful as a servant,* Christ *as a Son.* Moses was murmured against by Israel, defied by Pharaoh, yet God owned him, and ratified his commission. Moses was a pattern of meekness and patience, so is Christ. Moses died by *the word of the Lord,* so did Christ. *There was no prophet like unto Moses* (Num. xii. 6, 7; Deut. xxxiv. 10), but a greater than Moses is here where Christ is. He is a prophet of God's raising up, for he took not this honour of himself, but was called of God to it. He was raised up unto Israel in the first place. He executed this office in his own person among them only. They had the first offer of divine grace made to them; and therefore he was *raised up from among them—of them, as concerning the flesh, Christ came,* which, as it was a great honour done to them, so it was both an obligation upon them and an encouragement to them to embrace him. If he come to his own, one would think, they should receive him. The Old-Testament church was blessed with many prophets, with schools of prophets, for many ages with a constant succession of prophets (which is here taken notice of, from *Samuel, and those that follow after, v.* 24, for from Samuel the prophetic era commenced); but, these servants being abused, last of all God sent them his Son, who had been in his bosom. (3.) They must believe *that times of refreshing will come from the presence of the Lord* (*v.* 19), and that they will be *the times of the restitution of all things, v.* 21. There is a future state, another life after this; those times will come from the presence of the Lord, from his glorious appearance at that day, his coming at the end of time. The absence of the Lord occasions many of the securities of sinners and the distrusts of saints; but his presence is hastening on, which will for ever silence both. *Behold, the Judge standeth before the door.* The presence of the Lord will introduce, [1.] *The restitution of all things* (*v.* 21); *the new heavens, and the new earth,* which will be the product of the dissolution of all things (Rev. xxi. 1), the renovation of the whole creation, which is that which it grieves after, as its present burden under the sin of man is that which it groans under. Some understand this of a state on this side the end of time; but it is rather to be understood of that *end of all things which God hath spoken of by the mouth of all his holy prophets since the world began;* for this is that which *Enoch, the seventh from Adam, prophesied of* (Jude 14), and the temporal judgments which the other prophets foretold were typical of that which the apostle calls *the eternal judgment.* This is more clearly and plainly revealed in the New Testament than it had been before, and all that receive the gospel have an expectation of it. [2.] With this will come *the times of refreshing* (*v.* 19), of consolation to the Lord's people, like a cool shade to those *that have borne the burden and heat of the day.* All Christians look for *a rest that remains for the people of God,* after the travails and toils of their present state, and, with the prospect of this, they are borne up under their present sufferings and carried on in their present services. The refreshing that then *comes from the presence of the Lord* will continue eternally in the presence of the Lord

2. He tells them what they must do. (1.) They must *repent,* must bethink themselves of what they have done amiss, must return to their right mind, admit a second thought, and submit to the convictions of it; they must begin anew. Peter, who had himself denied Christ, repented, and he would have them to do so too. (2.) They must *be converted,* must face about, and direct both their faces and steps the contrary way to what they had been; they must *return to the Lord their God,* from whom they had revolted. It is not enough to repent of sin, but we must be converted from it, and not return to it again. They must not only exchange the profession of Judaism for that of Christianity, but the power and dominion of a carnal, worldly, sensual mind, for that of holy, heavenly, and divine principles and affections. (3.) They must hear Christ, the great prophet: "*Him shall you hear in all things whatsoever he shall say unto you.* Attend his dictates, receive his doctrine, submit to his government. Hear him with a divine faith, as prophets should be heard, that come with a divine commission. *Him shall you hear,* and to him shall you subscribe with an implicit faith and obedience. *Hear him in all things;* let his laws govern all your actions, and his counsels determine all your submissions. Whenever he has a mouth to speak, you must have an ear to hear. Whatever he saith to you, though ever so displeasing to flesh and blood, bid it welcome." *Speak, Lord, for thy servant hears.* A good reason is here given why we should be observant of, and obedient to, the word of Christ; for it is at our peril if we turn a deaf ear to his call and a stiff neck to his yoke (*v.* 23): *Every soul that will not hear that prophet,* and be directed by what he saith, *shall be destroyed from among the people.* The destruction of the city and nation, by war and famine, was threatened for slighting the prophets of the Old Testament; but the destruction of the soul, a spiritual and eternal destruction, is threatened for slighting Christ, *this great prophet.* Those that will not be advised by the Saviour can expect no other than to fall into the hands of the destroyer.

3. He tells them what they might expect.

(1.) That they should have the pardon of their sins; this is always spoken of as the great privilege of all those that embrace the gospel (*v.* 19): *Repent, and be converted, that your sins may be blotted out.* This implies, [1.] That the remission of sin is the blotting of it out, as a cloud is blotted out by the beams of the sun (Isa. xliv. 22), as a debt is crossed and blotted out when it is remitted. It intimates that when God forgives sin he remembers it no more against the sinner; it is forgotten, as that which is blotted out; all the bitter things written against the sinner (Job xiii. 26) are wiped out as it were with a sponge; it is the cancelling of a bond, the vacating of a judgment. [2.] That we cannot expect our sins should be pardoned unless we repent of them, and turn from them to God. Though Christ has died to purchase the remission of sin, yet, that we may have the benefit of that purchase in the forgiveness of our sins, we must repent, and be converted: if no repentance, no remission. [3.] Hopes of the pardon of sin upon repentance should be a powerful inducement to us to repent. *Repent, that your sins may be blotted out:* and that repentance is evangelical which flows from an apprehension of the mercy of God in Christ, and the hopes of pardon. This was the first and great argument, *Repent, for the kingdom of heaven is at hand.* [4.] The most comfortable fruit of the forgiveness of our sins will be *when the times of refreshing shall come;* if our sins be forgiven us, we have now reason to be of good cheer; but the comfort will be complete when the pardon shall be allowed in open court, and our justification published *before angels and men*—when *whom he has justified, them he glorifies,* Rom. viii. 30. As *now we are the sons of God* (1 John iii. 2), so now we have our sins blotted out; *but it doth not yet appear what* are the blessed fruits of it, till *the times of refreshing shall come.* During these times of toil and conflict (doubts and fears within, troubles and dangers without) we cannot have that full satisfaction of our pardon, and in it, that we shall have when the refreshing times come, which shall wipe away all tears.

(2.) That they should have the comfort of Christ's coming (*v.* 20, 21): "*He shall send Jesus Christ,* the same Jesus, the very same *that before was preached unto you;* for you must not expect another dispensation, another gospel, but the continuance and completion of this; you must not expect another prophet like unto Jesus, as Moses bade you expect another like unto him; for, though *the heavens must receive him till the times of the restitution of all things;* yet, if you *repent and be converted,* you shall find no want of him; some way or other he shall be seen of you." [1.] We must not expect Christ's personal presence with us in this world; for the heavens, which received him out of the sight of the disciples, must retain him till the end of time. To that seat of the blessed his bodily presence is confined, and will be to the end of time, the accomplishment of all things (so it may be read); and therefore those dishonour him, and deceive themselves, who dream of his corporal presence in the eucharist. It is agreeable to a state of trial and probation that the glorified Redeemer should be out of sight, because we must live by that faith in him which is *the evidence of things not seen;* because he must be *believed on in the world,* he must be *received up into glory.* Dr. Hammond reads it, *Who must receive the heavens,* that is, who must *receive the glory and power of the upper world; he must reign till all be made subject to him,* 1 Cor. xv. 25; Ps. lxxv. 2. [2.] Yet it is promised that he shall be sent to all that repent and are converted (*v.* 20): "*He shall send Jesus Christ, who was preached to you* by his disciples, both before and since his resurrection, and is, and will be, all in all to them." *First,* "You shall have his spiritual presence. He that is sent into the world shall be sent to you; you shall have the comfort of his being sent; he shall be sent among you in his gospel, which shall be his tabernacle, his chariot of war." *Secondly,* "*He shall send Jesus Christ* to destroy Jerusalem, and the nation of unbelieving Jews, that are enemies to Christ and Christianity, and to deliver his ministers and people from them, and give them peace in the profession of the gospel, and that shall be a time of refreshing, in which you shall share." *Then had the churches rest;* so Dr. Hammond. *Thirdly,* "The sending of Christ to judge the world, at the end of time, will be a blessing to you; you shall then *lift up your heads with joy, knowing that your redemption draws nigh.*" It seems to refer to this, for till then *the heavens must receive him, v.* 21. As God's counsels from eternity, so his predictions from the beginning of time, had a reference to the transactions of the last day, when *the mystery of God shall be finished, as he had declared to his servants the prophets,* Rev. x. 7. The institution of all things in the church had an eye to the restitution of all things at the end of time.

4. He tells them what ground they had to expect these things, if they were converted to Christ. Though they had denied him, and put him to death, yet they might hope to find favour through him, upon the account of their being Israelites. For,

(1.) As Israelites, they had the monopoly of the grace of the Old Testament; they were, above any other, God's favourite nation, and the favours God bestowed upon them were such as had a reference to the Messiah, and his kingdom: *You are the children of the prophets, and of the covenant.* A double privilege. [1.] They were *the children,* that is, the disciples, *of the prophets,* as children at school; *not sons of the prophets,* in the sense that we read of such in the Old Testament, from Samuel and downward, who were, or are, trained up to be *endued with the spirit of prophecy;* but you are of that people from among whom prophets were raised up, and to whom prophets were sent. It is spoken of as a great favour to Israel *that God raised up of their sons for prophets,* Amos ii. 11. All the inspired writers, both of the Old and New Testament, were of *the seed of Abraham;* and it was their honour and advantage *that unto them were committed the oracles of God,* Rom. iii. 2. Their government was constituted by prophecy, that is, by divine revelation; and by it their affairs were for many ages very much managed. See Hos. xii. 13. *By a prophet the Lord brought Israel out of Egypt, and by a prophet was he preserved.* Those of the latter ages of the church, when prophecy had ceased, might yet be fitly called *the children of the prophets,* because they heard, though they did not know, *the voices of the prophets, which were read in their synagogues every sabbath day, ch.* xiii. 27. Now this should quicken them to embrace Christ, and they might hope to be accepted of him; for their own prophets had foretold *that this grace should be brought unto them at the revelation of Jesus Christ* (1 Pet. i. 13), and therefore ought not to be neglected by them, nor should be denied to them. Those that are blessed with prophets and prophecy (as all are that have the scriptures) are concerned not to receive the grace of God therein in vain. We may apply it particularly to ministers' children, who, if they plead their parentage effectually with themselves, as an inducement to be faithful and forward in religion, may comfortably plead it with God, and hope *that the children of God's servants shall continue.* [2.] They were *the children,* that is, the heirs, *of the covenant which God made with our Fathers,* as children in the family. God's covenant was made *with Abraham and his seed,* and they were *that seed* with whom the *covenant was made,* and on whom *the blessings of the covenant were entailed:* "The promise of the Messiah was made to you, and therefore if you forsake not your own mercies, and do not by an obstinate infidelity put a bar in your own door, you may hope it shall be made good to you." That promise here mentioned, as the principal article of the covenant, *In thy seed shall all the kindreds of the earth be blessed,* though referring principally to Christ (Gal. iii. 16), yet may include the church also, which is his body, all believers, that are the spiritual seed of Abraham. *All the kindreds of the earth were blessed* in having a church for Christ among them; and those that were *the seed of Abraham according to the flesh* stood fairest for this privilege. If all the kindreds of the earth were to be blessed in Christ, much more that kindred, *his kinsmen according to the flesh.*

(2.) As Israelites, they had the first offer of the grace of the New Testament. Because *they were the children of the prophets and the covenant,* therefore to them the Redeemer was first sent, which was an encouragement to them to hope that if they did repent, and were converted, he should be yet further sent for their comfort (*v.* 20): *He shall send Jesus Christ,* for to you first he hath sent him, *v.* 26. *Unto you first,* you Jews, though not to you only, *God, having raised up his Son Jesus,* appointed and authorized him *to be a prince and a Saviour,* and, in confirmation of this, *raised him from the dead, sent him to bless you,* to make a tender of his blessing to you, especially that great blessing of *turning every one of you from his iniquities;* and therefore it concerns you to receive this blessing, and turn from your iniquities, and you may be encouraged to hope that you shall. [1.] We are here told whence Christ had his mission: *God raised up his Son Jesus, and sent him.* God raised him up when he constituted him a prophet, owned him by a voice from heaven, and filled him with his Spirit without measure, and then sent him; for to this end he raised him up, that he might be his commissioner to treat of peace. He sent him to bear witness of the truth, sent him to seek and save lost souls, sent him against his enemies, to conquer them. Some refer *the raising of him up to the resurrection,* which was the first step towards his exaltation; this was, as it were, the renewing of his commission; and though, having raised him up, he seemed presently to take him from us, yet he did really send him afresh to us in his gospel and Spirit. [2.] To whom he was sent: "*Unto you first.* You of the seed of Abraham, you that are *the children of the prophets, and of the covenant,* to you is the tender made of gospel grace." The personal ministry of Christ, as that of the prophets, was confined to the Jews; he was not then *sent but to the lost sheep of the house of Israel,* and he forbade the disciples he then sent forth to go any further. After his resurrection, he was to be preached indeed to all nations, but they must *begin at Jerusalem,* Luke xxiv. 47. And, when they went to other nations, they first preached to the Jews they found therein. They were the first-born, and, as such, had the privilege of the first offer. So far were they from being excluded for their putting Christ to death, that, when he is risen, he is first sent to them, and they are primarily intended to have benefit by his death. [3.] On what errand he was sent: "*He is sent to you first, to bless you;* this is his primary errand, not to condemn you, as you deserve, but to justify you, if you will accept of the justification offered you, in the way wherein it is offered; but he that sends him first to bless you, if you refuse and reject that blessing, will send him to curse you with a curse," Mal. iv. 6. Note, *First,* Christ's errand into the world was to bless us, to bring a blessing with him, for *the Sun of righteousness rose with healing under his wings;* and, when he left the world, he left a blessing behind him, for he was *parted from the disciples as he blessed them,* Luke xxiv. 51. He sent his Spirit to be the great blessing, the blessing of blessings, Isa. xliv. 3. It is by Christ that God sends blessings to us, and through him only we can expect to receive them. *Secondly,* The great blessing wherewith Christ came to bless us was the turning of us away from our iniquities, the saving of us from our sins (Matt. i. 21), to turn us from sin, that we may be qualified to receive all other blessings. Sin is that to which naturally we cleave; the design of divine grace is to turn us from it, nay, to turn us against it, that we may not only forsake it, but hate it. The gospel has a direct tendency to do this, not only as it requires us, every one of us, to turn from our iniquities, but as it promises us grace to enable us to do so. "Therefore, do your part; *repent, and be converted,* because Christ is ready to do his, *in turning you from your iniquities,* and so blessing you."

CHAP. IV.

In going over the last two chapters, where we met with so many good things that the apostles did, I wondered what was become of the scribes and Pharisees, and chief priests, that they did not appear to contradict and oppose them, as they had used to treat Christ himself; surely they were so confounded at first with the pouring out of the Spirit that they were for a time struck dumb! But I find we have not lost them; their forces rally again, and here we have an encounter between them and the apostles; for from the beginning the gospel met with opposition. Here, I. Peter and John are taken up, upon a warrant from the priests, and committed to jail, ver. 1—4. II. They are examined by a committee of the great sanhedrim, ver. 5—7. III. They bravely avow what they have done, and preach Christ to their persecutors, ver. 8—12. IV. Their persecutors, being unable to answer them, enjoin them silence, threatening them if they go on to preach the gospel, and so dismiss them, ver. 13—22. V. They apply to God by prayer, for the further operations of that grace which they had already experienced, ver. 23—30. VI. God owns them, both outwardly and inwardly, by manifest tokens of his presence with them, ver. 31—33. VII. The believers had their hearts knit together in holy love, and enlarged their charity to the poor, and the church flourished more than ever, to the glory of Christ, ver. 33—37.

AND as they spake unto the people,
the priests, and the captain of
the temple, and the Sadducees, came
upon them, 2 Being grieved that
they taught the people, and preached
through Jesus the resurrection from the
dead. 3 And they laid hands on
them, and put *them* in hold unto the
next day: for it was now eventide.
4 Howbeit many of them which heard
the word believed; and the number
of the men was about five thousand.

We have here the interests of the kingdom of heaven successfully carried on, and the powers of darkness appearing against them to put a stop to them. Let Christ's servants be ever so resolute, Satan's agents will be spiteful; and therefore, let Satan's agents be ever so spiteful, Christ's servants ought to be resolute.

I. The apostles, Peter and John, went on in their work, and did not labour in vain. The Spirit enabled the ministers to do their part, and the people theirs.

1. The preachers faithfully deliver the doctrine of Christ: *They spoke unto the people,* to all that were within hearing, *v.* 1. What they said concerned them all, and they spoke it openly and publicly. *They taught the people,* still *taught the people knowledge;* taught those that as yet did not believe, for their conviction and conversion; and taught those that did believe, for their comfort and establishment. *They preached through Jesus the resurrection from the dead.* The doctrine of the resurrection of the dead, (1.) Was verified in Jesus; this they proved, that

Jesus Christ had risen from the dead, as the first, the chief, that should rise from the dead, *ch.* xxvi. 23. They preached the resurrection of Christ as their warrant for what they did. Or, (2.) It is secured by him to all believers. The resurrection of the dead includes all the happiness of the future state. This *they preached through Jesus Christ,* attainable through him (Phil. iii. 10, 11), and through him only. They meddled not with matters of state, but kept to their business, and preached to the people heaven as their end and Christ as their way. See *ch.* xvii. 18.

2. The hearers cheerfully receive it (*v.* 4): *Many of those who heard the word believed;* not all—perhaps not the most, yet many, *to the number of about five thousand,* over and above the three thousand we read of before. See how the gospel got ground, and it was the effect of the pouring out of the Spirit. Though the preachers were persecuted, the word prevailed; for sometimes the church's suffering days have been her growing days: the days of her infancy were so.

II. The chief priests and their party now made head against them, and did what they could to crush them; their hands were tied awhile, but their hearts were not in the least changed. Now here observe, 1. Who they were that appeared against the apostles. They were *the priests;* you may be sure, in the first place, they were always sworn enemies to Christ and his gospel; they were as jealous for their priesthood as Cæsar for his monarchy, and would not bear one they thought their rival now, when he was preached as a priest, as much as when he himself preached as a prophet. With them was joined *the captain of the temple,* who, it is supposed, was a Roman officer, governor of the garrison placed in the tower of Antonia, for the guard of the temple: so that still here were both Jews and Gentiles confederate against Christ. *The Sadducees* also, who denied *the being of spirits* and *the future state,* were zealous against them. "One would wonder" (saith Mr. Baxter) "what should make such brutists as the Sadducees were to be such furious silencers and persecutors. If there is no life to come, what harm can other men's hopes of it do them? But in depraved souls all faculties are vitiated. A blind man has a malignant heart and a cruel hand, to this day." 2. How they stood affected to the apostles' preaching: *They were grieved that they taught the people, v.* 2. It grieved them, both that the gospel doctrine was preached (was so preached, so publicly, so boldly), and that the people were so ready to hear it. They thought, when they had put Christ to such an ignominious death, his disciples would ever after be ashamed and afraid to own him, and the people would have invincible prejudices against his doctrine; and now it vexed them to see themselves disappointed, and that his gospel got ground, instead of losing it. *The wicked shall see it, and be grieved,* Ps. cxii. 10. They were grieved at that which they should have rejoiced in, at that which angels rejoice in. Miserable is their case to whom the glory of Christ's kingdom is a grief; for, since the glory of that kingdom is everlasting, it follows of course that their grief will be everlasting too. It grieved them that the apostles *preached through Jesus the resurrection from the dead.* The Sadducees were grieved that the resurrection from the dead was preached; for they opposed that doctrine, and could not bear to hear of a future state, to hear it so well attested. The chief priests were grieved that they preached the resurrection of the dead through Jesus, that he should have the honour of it; and, though they professed to believe the resurrection of the dead against the Sadducees, yet they would rather give up that important article than have it preached and proved to be through Jesus. 3. How far they proceeded against the apostles (*v.* 3): *They laid hands on them* (that is, their servants and officers did at their command), and *put them in hold,* committed them to the custody of the proper officer until the next day; they could not examine them now, for it was even-tide, and yet would defer it no longer than *till next day.* See how God trains up his servants for sufferings by degrees, and by less trials prepares them for greater; now they resist unto bonds only, but afterwards to blood.

5 And it came to pass on the morrow, that their rulers, and elders, and
scribes, 6 And Annas the high priest,
and Caiaphas, and John, and Alexander, and as many as were of the kindred of the high priest, were gathered
together at Jerusalem. 7 And when
they had set them in the midst, they
asked, By what power, or by what
name, have ye done this? 8 Then
Peter, filled with the Holy Ghost,
said unto them, Ye rulers of the
people, and elders of Israel, 9 If we
this day be examined of the good
deed done to the impotent man, by
what means he is made whole; 10 Be
it known unto you all, and to all the
people of Israel, that by the name of Jesus Christ of Nazareth, whom ye crucified, whom God raised from the dead,
even by him doth this man stand here
before you whole. 11 This is the stone
which was set at nought of you builders, which is become the head of the
corner. 12 Neither is there salvation
in any other: for there is none other
name under heaven given among men,

whereby we must be saved. 13 Now when they saw the boldness of Peter and John, and perceived that they were unlearned and ignorant men, they marvelled; and they took knowledge of them, that they had been with Jesus. 14 And beholding the man which was healed standing with them, they could say nothing against it.

We have here the trial of Peter and John before the judges of the ecclesiastical court, for preaching a sermon concerning Jesus Christ, and working a miracle in his name. This is charged upon them as a crime, which was the best service they could do to God or men.

I. Here is the court set. An extraordinary court, it should seem, was called on purpose upon this occasion. Observe, 1. The time when the court sat (*v.* 5)—*on the morrow;* not in the night, as when Christ was to be tried before them, for they seem not to have been so hot upon this prosecution as they were upon that; it was well if they began to relent. But they adjourned it to the morrow, and no longer; for they were impatient to get them silenced, and would lose no time. 2. The place where—in Jerusalem (*v.* 6); there it was that he told his disciples they must expect to suffer hard things, as he had done before them in that place. This seems to come in here as an aggravation of their sin, that in Jerusalem, where there were so many that looked for redemption before it came, yet there were more that would not look upon it when it did come. How is that faithful city become a harlot! See Matt. xxiii. 37. It was in the foresight of Jerusalem's standing in her own light that Christ beheld the city, and wept over it. 3. The judges of the court. (1.) Their general character: they were *rulers, elders,* and *scribes, v.* 5. The scribes were men of learning, who came to dispute with the apostles, and hoped to confute them. The rulers and elders were men in power, who, if they could not answer them, thought they could find some cause or other to silence them. If the gospel of Christ had not been of God, it could not have made its way, for it had both the learning and power of the world against it, both the colleges of the scribes and the courts of the elders. (2.) The names of some of them, who were most considerable. Here were Annas and Caiaphas, ringleaders in this persecution; Annas the president of the sanhedrim, and Caiaphas the high priest (though Annas is here called so) and *father of the house of judgment.* It should seem that Annas and Caiaphas executed the high priest's office alternately, year for year. These two were most active against Christ; then Caiaphas was high priest, now Annas was; however they were both equally malignant against Christ and his gospel. John is supposed to be the son of Annas; and Alexander is mentioned by Josephus as a man that made a figure at that time. There were others likewise that were *of the kindred of the high priest,* who having dependence on him, and expectations from him, would be sure to say as he said, and vote with him against the apostles. Great relations, and not good, have been a snare to many.

II. The prisoners are arraigned, *v.* 7. 1. They are brought to the bar; they *set them in the midst,* for the sanhedrim sat in a circle, and those who had any thing to do in the court stood or sat in the midst of them (Luke ii. 46), so Dr. Lightfoot. Thus the scripture was fulfilled, *The assembly of the wicked has enclosed me,* Ps. xxii. 16. *They compassed me about like bees,* Ps. cxviii. 12. They were seated on every side. 2. The question they asked them was, "*By what power, or by what name, have you done this?* By what authority do you these things?" (the same question that they had asked their Master, Matt. xxi. 23): "Who commissioned you to preach such a doctrine as this, and empowered you to work such a miracle as this? You have no warrant nor license from us, and therefore are accountable to us whence you have your warrant." Some think this question was grounded upon a fond cônceit that the very naming of some names might do wonders, as *ch.* xix. 13. The Jewish exorcists made use of the name of Jesus. Now they would know what name they made use of in their cure, and consequently what name they set themselves to advance in their preaching. They knew very well that they preached Jesus, and the resurrection of the dead, and the healing of the sick, through Jesus (*v.* 2), yet they asked them, to tease them, and try if they could get any thing out of them that looked criminal.

III. The plea they put in, the design of which was not so much to clear and secure themselves as to advance the name and honour of their Master, who had told them that their being brought before governors and kings would give them an opportunity of preaching the gospel to those to whom otherwise they could not have had access, and it should be *a testimony against them.* Mark xiii. 19. Observe,

1. By whom this plea was drawn up: it was dictated by the Holy Ghost, who fitted Peter more than before for this occasion. The apostles, with a holy negligence of their own preservation, set themselves to preach Christ as he had directed them to do in such a case, and then Christ made good to them his promise, that the Holy Ghost should *give them in that same hour what they should speak.* Christ's faithful advocates shall never want instructions, Mark xiii. 11.

2. To whom it was given in: Peter, who is still the chief speaker, addresses himself to

the judges of the court, as the *rulers of the people, and elders of* Israel; for the wickedness of those in power does not divest them of their power, but the consideration of the power they are entrusted with should prevail to divest them of their wickedness. "You are rulers and elders, and should know more than others of the signs of the times, and not oppose that which you are bound by the duty of your place to embrace and advance, that is, the kingdom of the Messiah; you are rulers and elders of Israel, God's people, and if you mislead them, and cause them to err, you will have a great deal to answer for."

3. What the plea is: it is a solemn declaration,

(1.) That what they did was in the name of Jesus Christ, which was a direct answer to the question the court asked them (*v.* 9, 10): "*If we this day be examined*, be called to an account as criminals, so the word signifies, for *a good deed* (as any one will own it to be) *done to the impotent man,*—if this be the ground of the commitment, this the matter of the indictment,—if we are put to the question, *by what means*, or by whom, *he is made whole,* we have an answer ready, and it is the same we gave to the people (*ch.* iii. 16), we will repeat it to you, as that which we will stand by. *Be it known to you all* who pretend to be ignorant of this matter, and not to you only, but *to all the people of Israel*, for they are all concerned to know it, *that by the name of Jesus Christ*, that precious, powerful, prevailing name, that name above every name, even by him whom you in contempt called Jesus of Nazareth, *whom you crucified*, both rulers and people, and *whom God hath raised from the dead* and advanced to the highest dignity and dominion, *even by him doth this man stand here before you whole*, a monument of the power of the Lord Jesus." Here, [1.] He justifies what he and his colleague had done in curing the lame man. It was a *good deed;* it was a kindness to the man that had begged, but could not work for his living; a kindness to the temple, and to those that went in to worship, who were now freed from the noise and clamour of this common beggar. "Now, if we be reckoned with for this good deed, we have no reason to be ashamed, 1 Pet. ii. 20; *ch.* iv. 14, 16. Let those be ashamed who bring us into trouble for it." Note, It is no new thing for good men to suffer ill for doing well. *Bene agere et male pati vere Christianum est—To do well and to suffer punishment is the Christian's lot.* [2.] He transfers all the praise and glory of this good deed to Jesus Christ. "It is by him, and not by any power of ours, that this man is cured." The apostles seek not to raise an interest for themselves, nor to recommend themselves by this miracle to the good opinion of the court; but, "Let the Lord alone be exalted, no matter what becomes of us." [3.] He charges it upon the judges themselves, that they had been the murderers of this Jesus: "It is he *whom you crucified*, look how you will answer it;" in order to the bringing of them to believe in Christ (for he aims at no less than this) he endeavours to convince them of sin, of that sin which, one would think, of all others, was most likely to startle conscience—their putting Christ to death. Let them take it how they will, Peter will miss no occasion to tell them of it. [4.] He attests the resurrection of Christ as the strongest testimony for him, and against his persecutors: "*They crucified him*, but God *raised him from the dead;* they took away his life, but God gave it to him again, and your further opposition to his interest will speed no better." He tells them that God raised him from the dead, and they could not for shame answer him with that foolish suggestion which they palmed upon the people, that *his disciples came by night and stole him away*. [5.] He preaches this to all the bystanders, to be by them repeated to all their neighbours, and commands all manner of persons, from the highest to the lowest, to take notice of it at their peril: "*Be it known to you all* that are here present, and it shall be made known to *all the people of Israel,* wherever they are dispersed, in spite of all your endeavours to stifle and suppress the notice of it: as the Lord God of gods knows, so Israel shall know, all Israel shall know, that wonders are wrought in the name of Jesus, not by repeating it as a charm, but believing in it as a divine revelation of grace and good-will to men.

(2.) That the name of this Jesus, by the authority of which they acted, is that name alone by which we can be saved. He passes from this particular instance to show that it is not a particular sect or party that is designed to be set up by the doctrine they preached, and the miracle they wrought, which people might either join with or keep off from at their pleasure, as it was with the sects of the philosophers and those among the Jews; but that it is a sacred and divine institution that is hereby ratified and confirmed, and which all people are highly concerned to submit to and come into the measures of. It is not an indifferent thing, but of absolute necessity, that people believe in this name, and call upon it. [1.] We are obliged to it in duty to God, and in compliance with his designs (*v.* 11): "*This is the stone which was set at nought of you builders*, you that are *the rulers of the people, and the elders of Israel*, that should be the builders of the church, that pretend to be so, for the church is God's building. Here was a stone offered you, to be put in the chief place of the building, to be the main pillar on which the fabric might entirely rest; but you set it at nought, rejected it, would not make use of it, but threw it by as good for nothing but to make a stepping-stone of; but this stone is *now become the head of the corner;* God has raised up this Jesus whom you rejected, and, by setting him at his right hand, has made him both the corner stone and the head stone, the centre of unity and the fountain of power." Probably St. Peter here chose to make use of this quotation because Christ had himself made use of it, in answer to the demand of the chief priests and the elders concerning his authority, not long before this, Matt. xxi. 42. Scripture is a tried weapon in our spiritual conflicts: let us therefore stick to it. [2.] We are obliged to it for our own interest. We are undone if we do not take shelter in this name, and make it our refuge and strong tower; for we cannot be saved but by Jesus Christ, and, if we be not eternally saved, we are eternally undone (*v.* 12): *Neither is there salvation in any other.* As there is no other name by which diseased bodies can be cured, so there is no other by which sinful souls can be saved. "By him, and him only, by receiving and embracing his doctrine, salvation must now be hoped for by all. For there is no other religion in the world, no, not that delivered by Moses, by which salvation can be had for those that do not now come into this, at the preaching of it." So Dr. Hammond. Observe here, *First,* Our salvation is our chief concern, and that which ought to lie nearest to our hearts—our rescue from wrath and the curse, and our restoration to God's favour and blessing. *Secondly,* Our salvation is not in ourselves, nor can be obtained by any merit or strength of our own; we can destroy ourselves, but we cannot save ourselves. *Thirdly,* There are among men many names that pretend to be saving names, but really are not so; many institutions in religion that pretend to settle a reconciliation and correspondence between God and man, but cannot do it. *Fourthly,* It is only by Christ and his name that those favours can be expected from God which are necessary to our salvation, and that our services can be accepted with God. This is the honour of Christ's name, that it is the only name whereby we must be saved, the only name we have to plead in all our addresses to God. This name is *given.* God has appointed it, and it is an inestimable benefit freely conferred upon us. It is given *under heaven.* Christ has not only a great name in heaven, but a great name under heaven; for he has all power both in the upper and in the lower world. It is given *among men,* who need salvation, men who are ready to perish. We may be saved by his name, that name of his, *The Lord our righteousness;* and we cannot be saved by any other. How far those may find favour with God who have not the knowledge of Christ, nor any actual faith in him, yet live up to the light they have, it is not our business to determine. But this we know, that whatever saving favour such may receive it is upon the account of Christ, and for his sake only; so that still *there is no salvation in any other. I have surnamed thee, though thou hast not known me,* Isa. xlv. 4.

IV. The stand that the court was put to in the prosecution, by this plea, *v.* 13, 14. Now was fulfilled that promise Christ made, that he would give them *a mouth and wisdom, such as all their adversaries should not be able to gainsay nor resist.*

1. They could not deny the cure of the lame man to be both a good deed and a miracle. He was there standing with Peter and John, ready to attest the cure, if there were occasion, and they had *nothing to say against it* (*v.* 14), either to disprove it or to disparage it. It was well that it was not the sabbath day, else they would have had that to say against it.

2. They could not, with all their pomp and power, face down Peter and John. This was a miracle not inferior to the cure of the lame man, considering both what cruel bloody enemies these priests had been to the name of Christ (enough to make any one tremble that appeared for him), and considering what cowardly faint-hearted advocates those disciples had lately been for him, Peter particularly, who denied him for fear of a silly maid; yet now they see *the boldness of Peter and John, v.* 13. Probably there was something extraordinary and very surprising in their looks; they appeared not only undaunted by the rulers, but daring and daunting to them; they had something majestic in their foreheads, sparkling in their eyes, and commanding, if not terrifying, in their voice. They *set their faces like a flint,* as the prophet, Isa. l. 7; Ezek. iii. 9. The courage of Christ's faithful confessors has often been the confusion of their cruel persecutors. Now, (1.) We are here told what increased their wonder: They *perceived that they were unlearned and ignorant men.* They enquired either of the apostles or themselves or of others, and found that they were of mean extraction, born in Galilee, that they were bred fishermen, and had no learned education, had never been at any university, were not brought up at the feet of any of the rabbin, had never been conversant in courts, camps, or colleges; nay, perhaps, talk to them at this time upon any point in natural philosophy, mathematics, or politics, and you will find they know nothing of the matter; and yet speak to them of the Messiah and his kingdom, and they speak with so much clearness, evidence, and assurance, so pertinently and so fluently, and are so ready in the scriptures of the Old Testament relating to it, that the most learned judge upon the bench is not able to answer them, nor to enter the lists with them. They were *ignorant men—ἰδιῶται, private men,* men that had not any public character nor employment; and therefore they wondered they should have such high pretensions. They were *idiots* (so the word signifies): they looked upon them with as much contempt as if they had been *mere naturals,* and expected no more from them, which made them wonder to see what freedom they took. (2.) We are told what

made their wonder in a great measure to cease: they *took knowledge of them that they had been with Jesus;* they, themselves, it is probable, had seen them with him in the temple, and now recollected that they had seen them; or some of their servants or those about them informed them of it, for they would not be thought themselves to have taken notice of such inferior people. But when they understood that *they had been with Jesus,* had been conversant with him, attendant on him, and trained up under him, they knew what to impute their boldness to; nay, their boldness in divine things was enough to show with whom they had had their education. Note, Those that *have been with Jesus,* in converse and communion with him, have been attending on his word, praying in his name, and celebrating the memorials of his death and resurrection, should conduct themselves, in every thing, so that those who converse with them may *take knowledge of them that they have been with Jesus;* and this makes them so holy, and heavenly, and spiritual, and cheerful; this has raised them so much above this world, and filled them with another. One may know that they have been in the mount by the shining of their faces.

15 But when they had commanded
them to go aside out of the council,
they conferred among themselves,
16 Saying, What shall we do to these
men? for that indeed a notable miracle hath been done by them *is* manifest to them that dwell in Jerusalem; and we cannot deny *it.* 17 But
that it spread no further among the
people, let us straitly threaten them,
that they speak henceforth to no man
in this name. 18 And they called
them, and commanded them not to
speak at all nor teach in the name of
Jesus. 19 But Peter and John answered and said unto them, Whether
it be right in the sight of God to
hearken unto you more than unto
God, judge ye. 20 For we cannot
but speak the things which we have
seen and heard. 21 So when they
had further threatened them, they
let them go, finding nothing how they
might punish them, because of the
people: for all *men* glorified God for
that which was done. 22 For the
man was above forty years old, on
whom this miracle of healing was
showed.

We have here the issue of the trial of Peter and John before the council. They came off now with flying colours, because they must be trained up to sufferings by degrees, and by less trials be prepared for greater. They now but *run with the footmen;* hereafter we shall have them *contending with horses,* Jer. xii. 5.

I. Here is the consultation and resolution of the court about this matter, and their proceeding thereupon.

1. The prisoners were ordered to withdraw (*v.* 15): They *commanded them to go aside out of the council,* willing enough to get clear of them (they spoke so home to their consciences), and not willing they should hear the acknowledgments that were extorted from them; but, though they might not hear them, we have them here upon record. The designs of Christ's enemies are carried on in close cabals, and they dig deep, as if they would hide their counsels from the Lord.

2. A debate arose upon this matter: *They conferred among themselves;* every one is desired to speak his mind freely, and to give advice upon this important affair. *Now the scripture was fulfilled* that the rulers would *take counsel together against the Lord, and against his anointed,* Ps. ii. 2. The question proposed was, *What shall we do to these men? v.* 16. If they would have yielded to the convincing commanding power of truth, it had been easy to say what they should do to these men. They should have placed them at the head of their council, and received their doctrine, and been baptized by them in the name of the Lord Jesus, and joined in fellowship with them. But, when men will not be persuaded to do what they should do, it is no marvel that they are ever and anon at a loss what to do. The truths of Christ, if men would but entertain them as they should, would give them no manner of trouble or uneasiness; but, if they *hold them* or imprison them *in unrighteousness* (Rom. i. 18), they will find them a burdensome stone that they will not know what to do with, Zech. xii. 3.

3. They came at last to a resolution, in two things:—

(1.) That it was not safe to punish the apostles for what they had done. Very willingly would they have done it, but they had not courage to do it, because the people espoused their cause, and cried up the miracle; and they stood now in as much awe of them as they had done formerly, when they durst not lay hands on Christ *for fear of the people.* By this it appears that the outcry of the mob against our Saviour was a forced or managed thing, the stream soon returned to its former channel. Now they could not find how they might punish Peter and John, what colour they might have for it, *because of the people.* They knew it would be an unrighteous thing to punish them, and therefore should have been restrained from it by the fear of God; but they considered it only as a dangerous thing, and therefore were held in from it only by the fear of *the people.* For, [1.] The people were convinced of the truth of the miracle; it was a ***notable miracle, γνωστὸν σημεῖον—a known miracle;*** it was known that they did it in Christ's name, and that Christ himself had often done the like before. This was a known instance of the power of Christ, and a proof of his doctrine. That it was a great miracle, and wrought for the confirmation of the doctrine they preached (for it was a sign), was *manifest to all that dwelt in Jerusalem:* it was an opinion universally received, and, the miracle being wrought at the gate of the temple, universal notice was taken of it; and they themselves, with all the craftiness and all the effrontery they had, *could not deny it* to be a true miracle; every body would have hooted at them if they had. They could easily deny it to their own consciences, but not to the world. The proofs of the gospel were undeniable. [2.] They went further, and were not only convinced of the truth of the miracle, but all men *glorified God for that which was done.* Even those that were not persuaded by it to believe in Christ were yet so affected with it, as a mercy to a poor man and an honour to their country, that they could not but give praise to God for it; even natural religion taught them to do this. And, if the priests had punished Peter and John for that for which all men glorified God, they would have lost all their interest in the people, and been abandoned as enemies both to God and man. Thus therefore their wrath shall be made to praise God, and the remainder thereof shall be restrained.

(2.) That it was nevertheless necessary to silence them for the future, *v.* 17, 18. They could not prove that they had said or done any thing amiss, and yet they must no more say nor do what they have done. All their care is that the doctrine of Christ *spread no further among the people;* as if that healing institution were a plague begun, the contagion of which must be stopped. See how the malice of hell fights against the counsels of heaven; God will have the knowledge of Christ to spread all the world over, but the chief priests would have it spread no further, which he that sits in heaven laughs at. Now, to prevent the further spreading of this doctrine, [1.] They charge the apostles never to preach it any more. Be it enacted by their authority (which they think every Israelite is bound in conscience to submit to) that *no man speak at all nor teach in the name of Jesus, v.* 18. We do not find that they give them any reason why the doctrine of Christ must be suppressed; they cannot say it is false or dangerous, or of any ill tendency, and they are ashamed to own the true reason, that it testifies against their hypocrisy and wickedness, and shocks their tyranny. But, *Stat pro ratione voluntas—They can assign no reason but their will.* "We strictly charge and command you, not only that you do not preach this doctrine publicly, but that you *speak henceforth to no man,* not to any particular person privately, *in this name," v.* 17. There is not a greater service done to the devil's kingdom than the silencing of faithful ministers, and putting those under a bushel that are the lights of the world. [2.] They threaten them if they do, strictly threaten them: it is at their peril. This court will reckon itself highly affronted if they do, and they shall fall under its displeasure. Christ had not only charged them to preach the gospel to every creature, but had promised to bear them out in it, and reward them for it. Now these priests not only forbid the preaching of the gospel, but threaten to punish it as a heinous crime; but those who know how to put a just value upon Christ's promises know how to put a just contempt upon the world's threatenings, though they be threatenings of slaughter that it breathes out, *ch.* ix. 1.

II. Here is the courageous resolution of the prisoners to go on in their work, notwithstanding the resolutions of this court, and their declaration of this resolution, *v.* 19, 20. Peter and John needed not confer together, to know one another's minds (for they were both actuated by one and the same Spirit), but agree presently in the same sentiments, and jointly put in the answer: "*Whether it be right in the sight of God,* to whom both you and we are accountable, *to hearken unto you more than unto God,* we appeal to yourselves, *judge you; for we cannot forbear speaking* to every body *the things which we have seen and heard,* and are ourselves full of, and are charged to publish." The prudence of the serpent would have directed them to be silent, and, though they could not with a good conscience promise that they would not preach the gospel any more, yet they needed not tell the rulers that they would But the boldness of the lion directed them thus to set both the authority and the malignity of their persecutors at defiance. They do, in effect, tell them that they are resolved to go on in preaching, and justify themselves in it with two things:—1. The command of God: "You charge us not to preach the gospel; he has charged us to preach it, has committed it to us as a trust, requiring us upon our allegiance faithfully to dispense it; now whom must we obey, God or you?" Here they appeal to one of the *communes notitiæ—to a settled and acknowledged maxim* in the law of nature, that if men's commands and God's interfere God's commands must take place. It is a rule in the common law of England that if any statute be made contrary to the law of God it is null and void. Nothing can be more absurd than to hearken unto weak and fallible men, that are fellow-creatures and fellow-subjects, more than unto a God that is infinitely wise and holy, our Creator and sovereign Lord, and the Judge to whom we are all accountable. The case is so plain, so uncontroverted and self-evident, that we will venture to leave it to yourselves to judge of it, though you are biassed and prejudiced. Can you think it *right in the sight of God* to break a divine command in obedience to a human injunction? That is right indeed which is *right in the sight of God;* for his judgment, we are sure, is according to truth, and therefore by that we ought to govern ourselves. 2. The convictions of their consciences. Even if they had not had such an express command from heaven to preach the doctrine of Christ, yet they *could not but speak,* and speak publicly, *those things which they had seen and heard.* Like Elihu, they were *full of this matter,* and *the Spirit within them constrained them,* they must speak, that they might be refreshed, Job xxxii. 18, 20. (1.) They felt the influence of it upon themselves, what a blessed change it had wrought upon them, had brought them into a new world, and therefore they could not but speak of it: and those speak the doctrine of Christ best that have felt the power of it, and tasted the sweetness of it, and have themselves been deeply affected with it; it is as a *fire in their bones,* Jer. xx. 9. (2.) They knew the importance of it to others. They look with concern upon perishing souls, and know that they cannot escape eternal ruin but by Jesus Christ, and therefore will be faithful to them in giving them warning, and showing them the right way. They are things *which we have seen and heard,* and therefore are fully assured of ourselves: and things which we only have seen and heard, and therefore, if we do not publish them, who will? Who can? *Knowing the* favour, as well as the *terror of the Lord, we persuade men; for the love of Christ* and the love of souls constrain us, 2 Cor. v. 11, 14.

III. Here is the discharge of the prisoners (*v.* 21): *They further threatened them,* and thought they frightened them, and then *let them go.* There were many whom they terrified into an obedience to their unrighteous decrees; they knew how to keep men in awe with their excommunication (John ix. 22), and thought they could have the same influence upon the apostles that they had upon other men; but they were deceived, for they had been with Jesus. They threatened them, and that was all they did now: when they had done this they *let them go,* 1. Because they durst not contradict the people, who *glorified God for that which was done,* and would have been ready (at least they thought so) to pull them out of their seats, if they had punished the apostles for doing it. As rulers by the ordinance of God are made a terror and restraint to wicked people, so people are sometimes by the providence of God made a terror and restraint to wicked rulers. 2. Because they could not contradict the miracle: *For* (*v.* 22) *the man was above forty years old on whom this miracle of healing was shown.* And therefore, (1.) The miracle was so much the greater, he having been lame *from his mother's womb, ch.* iii. 2. The older he grew the more inveterate the disease was, and the more hardly cured. If those that are grown into years, and have been long accustomed to evil, are cured of their spiritual impotency to good, and thereby of their evil customs, the power of divine grace is therein so much the more magnified. (2.) The truth of it was so much the better attested; for *the man being above forty years old,* he was able, like the blind man whom Christ healed, when he was asked, to *speak for himself,* John ix. 21

23 And being let go, they went to
their own company, and reported all
that the chief priests and elders had
said unto them. 24 And when they
heard that, they lifted up their voice
to God with one accord, and said,
Lord, thou *art* God, which hast
made heaven, and earth, and the sea,
and all that in them is: 25 Who by
the mouth of thy servant David hast
said, Why did the heathen rage, and
the people imagine vain things? 26
The kings of the earth stood up, and
the rulers were gathered together
against the Lord, and against his
Christ. 27 For of a truth against
thy holy child Jesus, whom thou
hast anointed, both Herod, and Pontius Pilate, with the Gentiles, and
the people of Israel, were gathered together, 28 For to do whatsoever
thy hand and thy counsel determined
before to be done. 29 And now,
Lord, behold their threatenings: and
grant unto thy servants, that with all
boldness they may speak thy word,
30 By stretching forth thine hand to
heal; and that signs and wonders
may be done by the name of thy holy
child Jesus. 31 And when they had
prayed, the place was shaken where
they were assembled together; and
they were all filled with the Holy
Ghost, and they spake the word of
God with boldness.

We hear no more at present of the chief priests, what they did when they had dismissed Peter and John, but are to attend those *two witnesses.* And here we have,

I. Their return to their brethren, the apostles and ministers, and perhaps some private Christians (*v.* 23): *Being let go, they went to their own company,* who perhaps at this time were met together in pain for them, and praying for them; as *ch.* xii. 12. As soon as ever they were at liberty, they went to their old friends, and returned to their church-fellowship. 1. Though God had highly honoured them, in calling them out to be his witnesses, and enabling them to acquit themselves so well, yet they were not puffed up with the honour done them, nor thought themselves thereby exalted above their brethren, but *went to their own company.* No advancement in gifts or usefulness should make us think ourselves above either the duties or the privileges of the communion of saints. 2. Though their enemies had severely threatened them, and endeavoured to break their knot, and frighten them from the work they were jointly engaged in, yet they *went to their own company,* and feared not the wrath of their rulers. They might have had comfort, if, being let go, they had retired to their closets, and spent some time in devotion there. But they were men in a public station, and must seek not so much their own personal satisfaction as the public good. Christ's followers do best in company, provided it be in their own company.

II. The account they gave them of what had passed: They *reported all that the chief priests and elders had said to them,* adding, no doubt, what they were enabled by the grace of God to reply to them, and how their trial issued. They related it to them, 1. That they might know what to expect both from men and from God in the progress of their work. From men they might expect every thing that was terrifying, but from God every thing that was encouraging; men would do their utmost to run them down, but God would take effectual care to bear them up. Thus the brethren in the Lord would wax confident through their bonds, and their experiences, as Phil. i. 14. 2. That they might have it recorded in the history of the church, for the benefit of posterity, particularly for the confirmation of our faith touching the resurrection of Christ. The silence of an adversary, in some cases, is next door to the consent and testimony of an adversary. These apostles told the chief priests to their faces that God had *raised up Jesus from the dead,* and, though they were a body of them together, they had not the confidence to deny it, but, in the silliest and most sneaking manner imaginable, bade the apostles not to tell any body of it. 3. That they might now join with them in prayers and praises; and by such a concert as this God would be the more glorified, and the church the more edified. We should therefore communicate to our brethren the providences of God that relate to us, and our experience of his presence with us, that they may assist us in our acknowledgment of God therein.

III. Their address to God upon this occasion: *When they heard* of the impotent malice of the priests, and the potent courage of the sufferers, they called their company together and went to prayer: *They lifted up their voice to God with one accord, v.* 24. Not that it can be supposed that they all said the same words at the same time (though it was possible they might, being all inspired by one and the same Spirit), but one in the name of the rest *lifted up his voice to God* and the rest joined with him, ὁμοθυμαδὸν—*with one mind* (so the word signifies); their hearts went along with him, and so, though but one spoke, they all prayed; one lifted up his voice, and, in concurrence with him, they all lifted up their hearts, which was, in effect, lifting up their voice to God; for thoughts are as words to God. *Moses cried unto God,* when we find not a word said. Now in this solemn address to God we have,

1. Their adoration of God as the Creator of the world (*v.* 24): With *one mind,* and so, in effect, with *one mouth,* they *glorified God,* Rom. xv. 6. They *said,* " *O Lord, thou art God,* God alone; Δέσποτα, thou art *our Master and sovereign Ruler* " (so the word signifies), "thou art God; God, and not man; God, and not the work of men's hands; the Creator of all, and not the creature of men's fancies. Thou art the God *who hast made heaven, and earth, and the sea,* the upper and lower world, and all the creatures that are in both." Thus we Christians distinguish ourselves from the heathen, that, while they worship gods which they have made, we are worshipping the God that made us and all the world. And it is very proper to begin our prayers, as well as our creed, with the acknowledgment of this, that God is the *Father almighty, Maker of heaven and earth, and of all things visible and invisible.* Though the apostles were at this time full of the mystery of the world's redemption, yet they did not forget nor overlook the history of the world's creation; for the Christian religion was intended to confirm and improve, not to eclipse nor jostle out, the truths and dictates of natural religion. It is a great encouragement to God's servants, both in doing work and suffering work, that they serve the God that made all things, and therefore has the disposal of their times, and all events concerning them, and is able to strengthen them under all their difficulties. And, if we give him the glory of this, we may take the comfort of it.

2. Their reconciling themselves to the present dispensations of Providence, by reflecting upon those scriptures in the Old Testament which foretold that the kingdom of the Messiah would meet with such opposition as this at the first setting of it up in the world, *v.* 25, 26. God, who *made heaven and earth,* cannot meet with any [effectual] opposition to his designs, since none dare [at least, can prevailingly] dispute or contest with him. Yea, thus it was written, *thus he spoke by the mouth,* thus he wrote by the pen, *of his servant David,* who, as appears by this, was the penman of the second psalm, and therefore, most probably, of the first, and other psalms that are not ascribed to any other, though they have not his name in the title. Let it not therefore be a surprise to them, nor any discouragement to any in embracing their doctrine, for the *scripture must*

be fulfilled. It was foretold, Ps. ii. 1, 2, (1.) That the heathen would rage at Christ and his kingdom, and be angry at the attempts to set it up, because that would be the pulling down of the gods of the heathen, and giving a check to the wickedness of the heathen. (2.) That the people would imagine all the things that could be against it, to silence the teachers of it, to discountenance the subjects of it, and to crush all the interests of it. If they prove vain things in the issue, no thanks to those who imagined them. (3.) That the kings of the earth, particularly, would stand up in opposition to the kingdom of Christ, as if they were jealous (though there is no occasion for their being so) that it would interfere with their powers, and intrench upon their prerogatives. The kings of the earth that are most favoured and honoured by divine Providence, and should do most for God, are strangers and enemies to divine grace, and do most against God. (4.) That the rulers would gather together against God and Christ; not only monarchs, that have the power in their single persons, but where the power is in many rulers, councils, and senates, they *gather together*, to consult and decree *against the Lord and against his Christ*—against both natural and revealed religion. What is done against Christ, God takes as done against himself. Christianity was not only destitute of the advantage of the countenance and support of kings and rulers (it had neither their power nor their purses), but it was opposed and fought against by them, and they combined to run it down and yet it made its way.

3. Their representation of the present accomplishment of those predictions in the enmity and malice of the rulers against Christ. What was foretold we see fulfilled, *v.* 27, 28. It is *of a truth*—it is certainly so, it is too plain to be denied, and in it appears the truth of the prediction that Herod and Pilate, the two Roman governors, with the Gentiles (the Roman soldiers under their command), and with the *people of Israel* (the rulers of the Jews and the mob that is under their influence), were *gathered together* in a confederacy *against thy holy child Jesus whom thou hast anointed.* Some copies add another circumstance, *ἐν τῇ πόλει σου ταύτῃ*—*in this thy holy city*, where, above any place, he should have been welcomed. But herein they do *that which thy hand and thy counsel determined before to be done.* See here, (1.) The wise and holy designs God had concerning Christ. He is here called the *child Jesus,* as he was called (Luke ii. 27, 43) in his infancy, to intimate that even in his exalted state he is not ashamed of his condescensions for us, and that he continues meek and lowly in heart. In the height of his glory he is the *Lamb of God,* and the *child Jesus.* But he is the *holy child Jesus* (so he was called, Luke i. 35, *that holy thing),* and *thy* holy child; the word signifies both a son and a servant: *παῖδά σου.* He was the Son of God; and yet in the work of redemption he acted as his Father's servant (Isa. xlii. 1), *My servant whom I uphold.* It was he whom God anointed, both qualified for the undertaking and called to it; and thence he was called the Lord's Christ, *v.* 26. And this comes in as a reason why they set themselves with so much rage and violence against him, because God had anointed him, and they were resolved not to resign, much less to submit to him. David was envied by Saul, because he was the Lord's anointed. And the Philistines came up to seek David when they heard he was anointed, 2 Sam. v. 17. Now the God that anointed Christ determined what should be done to him, pursuant to that anointing. He was anointed to be a Saviour, and therefore it was determined he should be a sacrifice to make atonement for sin. He must die—therefore he must be slain; yet not by his own hands—therefore God wisely determined before by what hands it should be done. It must be by the hands of those who will treat him as a criminal and malefactor, and therefore it cannot be done by the hands either of angels or of good men; he must therefore be *delivered into the hands of sinners* as Job was, *ch* xvi. 11. And as David was delivered to Shimei to be *made a curse* (2 Sam. xvi. 11): *The Lord has bidden him. God's hand and his counsel determined it*—his will, and his wisdom. God's *hand,* which properly denotes his executive power, is here put for his purpose and decree, because with him saying and doing are not two things, as they are with us. His hand and his counsel always agree; for *whatsoever the Lord pleased that did he.* Dr. Hammond makes this phrase of *God's hand determining it* to be an allusion to the high priest's casting lots upon the two goats on the day of atonement (Lev. xvi. 8), in which he lifted up the hand that he happened to have the lot for the Lord in, and that goat on which it fell was immediately sacrificed; and the disposal of this lot was from the Lord, Prov. xvi. 33. Thus God's hand determined what should be done, that Christ should be the sacrifice slain. Or, if I may offer a conjecture, when God's hand is here said to determine, it may be meant, not of God's acting hand, but his writing hand, as Job. xiii. 26, *Thou writest bitter things against us;* and God's decree is said to be *that which is written in the scriptures of truth* (Dan. x. 21), and *in the volume of the book it was written of Christ,* Ps. xl. 7. It was *God's hand* that wrote it, his hand according to his counsel. The commission was given under his hand. (2.) The wicked and unholy instruments that were employed in the executing of this design, though they *meant not so, neither did their hearts think so.* Herod and Pilate, Gentiles and Jews, who had been at variance with each other, united against Christ. And God's serving his own purposes by what they did was no excuse at all

for their malice and wickedness in the doing of it, any more than God's making the blood of the martyrs the seed of the church extenuated the guilt of their bloody persecutors. Sin is not the less evil for God's bringing good out of it, but he is by this the more glorified, and will appear to be so when the mystery of God shall be finished.

4. Their petition with reference to the case at this time. The enemies *were gathered together against Christ,* and then no wonder that they were so against his ministers: *the disciple is not better than his Master,* nor must expect better treatment; but, being thus insulted, they pray,

(1.) That God would take cognizance of the malice of their enemies: *Now, Lord, behold their threatenings, v.* 29. Behold them, as thou art said to behold them in the psalm before quoted (Ps. ii. 4), when they thought *to break his bands asunder, and cast away his cords from them; he that sits in heaven laughs at them, and has them in derision;* and *then the virgin, the daughter of Zion, may despise* the impotent menaces even of *the great king, the king of Assyria,* Isa. xxxvii. 22. And *now, Lord; τὰ νῦν·* there is an emphasis upon the *now,* to intimate that then is God's time to appear for his people, when the power of their enemies is most daring and threatening. They do not dictate to God what he shall do, but refer themselves to him, like *Hezekiah* (Isa. xxxvii. 17): "*Open thine eyes, O Lord, and see;* thou knowest what they say, *thou beholdest mischief and spite* (Ps. x. 14); to thee we appeal, *behold their threatenings,* and either tie their hands or turn their hearts; make their wrath, as far as it is let loose, to praise thee, and the remainder thereof do thou restrain," Ps. lxxvi. 10. It is a comfort to us that if we be unjustly threatened, and bear it patiently, we may make ourselves easy by spreading the case before the Lord, and leaving it with him.

(2.) That God, by his grace, would keep up their spirits, and animate them to go on cheerfully with their work: *Grant unto thy servants that with all boldness they may speak thy word,* though the priests and rulers have enjoined them silence. Note, In threatening times, our care should not be so much that troubles may be prevented as that we may be enabled to go on with cheerfulness and resolution in our work and duty, whatever troubles we may meet with. Their prayer is not, "*Lord, behold their threatenings,* and frighten them, and stop their mouths, and fill their faces with shame;" but, "*Behold their threatenings,* and animate us, open our mouths and fill our hearts with courage." They do not pray, "Lord, give us a fair opportunity to retire from our work, now that it is become dangerous;" but, "Lord, give us grace to go on in our work, and not to be afraid of the face of man." Observe, [1.] Those that are sent on God's errands ought to deliver their message with boldness, with all boldness, with all liberty of speech, *not shunning to declare the whole counsel of God,* whoever is offended; not doubting of what they say, nor of being borne out in saying it. [2.] God is to be sought unto for an ability to speak his word with boldness, and those that desire divine aids and encouragements may depend upon them, and ought to go forth and go on *in the strength of the Lord God* [3.] The threatenings of our enemies, that are designed to weaken our hands and drive us off from our work, should rather stir us up to so much the more courage and resolution in our work. Are they daring that fight against Christ? For shame, let not us be sneaking that are for him.

(3.) That God would still give them power to work miracles for the confirmation of the doctrine they preached, which, by *the cure of the lame man,* they found to contribute very much to their success, and would contribute abundantly to their further progress: *Lord, grant us boldness, by stretching forth thy hand to heal.* Note, Nothing emboldens faithful ministers more in their work than the tokens of God's presence with them, and a divine power going along with them. They pray, [1.] That God would *stretch forth his hand to heal* both the bodies and souls of men; else in vain do *they stretch forth their hands,* either in preaching (Isa. lxv. 2), or in curing, *ch.* ix. 17. [2.] *That signs and wonders might be done by the name of the holy child Jesus,* which would be convincing to the people, and confounding to the enemies. Christ had promised them a power to work miracles, for the proof of their commission (Mark xvi. 17, 18); yet they must pray for it; and, though they had it, must pray for the continuance of it. Christ himself must ask, and it shall be given him. Observe, It is the honour of Christ that they aim at in this request, that the wonders might be done by the name of Jesus, the holy child Jesus, and his name shall have all the glory.

IV. The gracious answer God gave to this address, not in word, but in power. 1. God gave them a sign of the acceptance of their prayers (*v.* 31): *When they had prayed* (perhaps many of them prayed successively, one by one, according to the rule (1 Cor. xiv. 31), and when they had concluded the work of the day, *the place was shaken where they were assembled together;* there was a *strong mighty wind,* such as that when the Spirit was poured out upon them (*ch.* ii. 1, 2), *which shook the house,* which was now their house of prayer. This shaking of the place was designed to strike an awe upon them, to awaken and raise their expectations, and to give them a sensible token that God was with them of a truth: and perhaps it was to put them in mind of that prophecy (Hag. ii. 7), *I will shake all nations, and will fill this house with glory.* This was to show them what reason they had to fear God more, and then they would fear man less. He that shook this place could make the hearts of those who threatened his servants thus to tremble, for he *cuts off the spirit of princes, and is terrible to the kings of the earth.* The place was shaken, that their faith might be established and unshaken. 2. God gave them greater degrees of his Spirit, which was what they prayed for. Their prayer, without doubt, was accepted, for it was answered: *They were all filled with the Holy Ghost,* more than ever; by which they were not only encouraged, but enabled to speak the word of God with boldness, and not to be afraid of the proud and haughty looks of men. The Holy Ghost taught them not only *what* to speak, but *how* to speak. Those that were endued habitually with the powers of the Holy Ghost had yet occasion for fresh supplies of the Spirit, according as the various occurrences of their service were. They were *filled with the Holy Ghost* at the bar (*v.* 8), and now *filled with the Holy Ghost* in the pulpit, which teaches us to live in an actual dependence upon the grace of God, according as the duty of every day requires; we need to be *anointed with fresh oil* upon every fresh occasion. As in the providence of God, so in the grace of God, we not only in general *live, and have our being,* but *move* in every particular action, *ch.* xvii. 28. We have here an instance of the performance of that promise, *that God will give the Holy Spirit to those that ask him* (Luke xi. 13), for it was in answer to prayer that *they were filled with the Holy Ghost:* and we have also an example of the improvement of that gift, which is required of all on whom it is bestowed; have it and use it, use it and have more of it. When *they were filled with the Holy Ghost, they spoke the word with all boldness;* for *the ministration of the Spirit is given to every man, to profit withal.* Talents must be traded with, not buried. When they find *the Lord God help them* by his Spirit, they know they shall *not be confounded,* Isa. l. 7.

32 And the multitude of them that
believed were of one heart and of one
soul: neither said any *of them* that
aught of the things which he possessed was his own; but they had all
things common. 33 And with great
power gave the apostles witness of the
resurrection of the Lord Jesus: and
great grace was upon them all. 34 Neither was there any among them that
lacked: for as many as were possessors of lands or houses sold them,
and brought the prices of the things
that were sold, 35 And laid *them*
down at the apostles' feet: and distribution was made unto every man
according as he had need. 36 And
Joses, who by the apostles was surnamed Barnabas, (which is, being interpreted, The son of consolation,) a
Levite, *and* of the country of Cyprus,
37 Having land, sold *it,* and brought
the money, and laid *it* at the apostles'
feet.

We have a general idea given us in these verses, and it is a very beautiful one, of the spirit and state of this truly primitive church; it is *conspectus sæculi—a view of that age* of infancy and innocence.

I. The disciples loved one another dearly. Behold, how good and how pleasant it was to see how *the multitude of those that believed were of one heart, and of one soul* (*v.* 32), and there was no such thing as discord nor division among them. Observe here, 1. There were multitudes that believed; even in Jerusalem, where the malignant influence of the chief priests was most strong, *there were three thousand* converted on one day, and *five thousand* on another, and, besides these, *there were added to the church daily;* and no doubt they were all baptized, and made profession of the faith; for the same Spirit that endued the apostles with courage to preach the faith of Christ endued them with courage to confess it. Note, The increase of the church is the glory of it, and the multitude of those that believe, more than their quality. Now the church shines, and her light is come, when souls thus fly like a cloud into her bosom, and *like doves to their windows,* Isa. lx. 1, 8. 2. They *were all of one heart, and of one soul.* Though there were many, very many, of different ages, tempers, and conditions, in the world, who perhaps, before they believed, were perfect strangers to one another, yet, when they met in Christ, they were as intimately acquainted as if they had known one another many years. Perhaps they had been of different sects among the Jews, before their conversion, or had had discords upon civil accounts; but now these were all forgotten and laid aside, and they were unanimous in the faith of Christ, and, being all *joined to the Lord, they were joined to one another in holy love.* This was the blessed fruit of Christ's dying precept to his disciples, to *love one another,* and his dying prayer for them, *that they all might be one.* We have reason to think they divided themselves into several congregations, or worshipping assemblies, according as their dwellings were, under their respective ministers; and yet this occasioned no jealousy or uneasiness; for *they were all of one heart, and one soul,* notwithstanding; and loved those of other congregations as truly as those of their own. Thus it was then, and we may not despair of seeing it so again, *when the Spirit shall be poured out upon us from on high.*

II. The ministers went on in their work

with great vigour and success (*v.* 33): *With great power gave the apostles witness of the resurrection of the Lord Jesus.* The doctrine they preached was, the resurrection of Christ: a matter of fact, which served not only for the confirmation of the truth of Christ's holy religion, but being duly explained and illustrated, with the proper inferences from it, served for a summary of all the duties, privileges, and comforts of Christians. The resurrection of Christ, rightly understood and improved, will let us into the great mysteries of religion. By the great power wherewith the apostles attested the resurrection may be meant, 1. The great vigour, spirit, and courage, with which they published and avowed this doctrine; they did it not softly and diffidently, but with liveliness and resolution, as those that were themselves abundantly satisfied of the truth of it, and earnestly desired that others should be so too. Or, 2. The miracles which they wrought to confirm their doctrine. With works of great power, they *gave witness to the resurrection of Christ,* God himself, in them, *bearing witness* too.

III. The beauty of the Lord our God shone upon them, and all their performances: *Great grace was upon them all,* not only all the apostles, but all the believers, *χάρις μεγάλη*—*grace* that had something *great* in it (magnificent and very extraordinary) *was upon them all.* 1. Christ poured out abundance of *grace upon them,* such as qualified them for great services, by enduing them with *great power;* it came *upon them* from on high, from above. 2. There were evident fruits of this grace in all they said and did, such as put an honour upon them, and recommended them to the favour of God, as being in his sight *of great price.* 3. Some think it includes the favour they were in with the people. Every one saw a beauty and excellency in them, and respected them.

IV. They were very liberal to the poor, and dead to this world. This was as great an evidence of the grace of God in them as any other, and recommended them as much to the esteem of the people.

1. They insisted not upon property, which even children seem to have a sense of and a jealousy for, and which worldly people triumph in, as Laban (Gen. xxxi. 43): *All that thou seest is mine;* and Nabal (1 Sam. xxv. 11): *My bread and my water.* These believers were so taken up with the hopes of an inheritance in the other world that this was as nothing to them. *No man said that aught of the things which he possessed was his own, v.* 32. They did not take away property, but they were indifferent to it. They did not call what they had their own, in a way of pride and vainglory, boasting of it, or trusting in it. They did not call it their own, because they had, in affection, forsaken all for Christ, and were continually expecting to be stripped of all for their adherence to him. They did not say that aught was their own; for we can call nothing our own but sin. What we have in the world is more God's than our own; we have it from him, must use it for him, and are accountable for it to him. *No man said that what he had was his own, ἴδιον—his peculiar;* for he was *ready to distribute, willing to communicate,* and desired not to eat his morsel alone, but what he had to spare from himself and family his poor neighbours were welcome to. Those that had estates were not solicitous to lay up, but very willing to lay out, and would straiten themselves to help their brethren. No marvel that *they were of one heart and soul,* when they sat so loose to the wealth of this world; for *meum—mine,* and *tuum—thine,* are the great makebates. Men's holding their own, and grasping at more than their own, are the rise of wars and fightings.

2. They abounded in charity, so that, in effect, *they had all things common;* for (*v.* 34) *there was not any among them that lacked,* but care was taken for their supply. Those that had been maintained upon the public charity were probably excluded when they turned Christians, and therefore it was fit that the church should take care of them. As there were many poor that received the gospel, so there were some rich that were able to maintain them, and the grace of God made them willing. Those *that gather much have nothing over,* because what they have over they have for those who gather little, that they may have no lack, 2 Cor. viii. 14, 15. The gospel hath laid *all things common,* not so that the poor are allowed to rob the rich, but so that the rich are appointed to relieve the poor.

3. They did many of them sell their estates, to raise a fund for charity: *As many as had possession of lands or houses sold them, v.* 34. Dr. Lightfoot computes that this was the year of jubilee in the Jewish nation, the fiftieth year (the twenty-eighth since they settled in Canaan fourteen hundred years ago), so that, what was sold that year being not to return till the next jubilee, lands then took a good price, and so the sale of those lands would raise the more money. Now,

(1.) We are here told what they did with the money that was so raised: They *laid it at the apostles' feet*—they left it to them to be disposed of as they thought fit; probably they had their support from it; for whence else could they have it? Observe, The apostles would have it laid at their feet, in token of their holy contempt of the wealth of the world; they thought it fitter it should be laid at their feet than lodged in their hands or in their bosoms. Being laid there, it was not hoarded up, but *distribution was made,* by proper persons, *unto every man according as he had need.* Great care ought to be taken in the distribution of public charity, [1.] That it be given to such as have need; such as are not able to procure a competent maintenance for themselves, through age, infancy, sickness, or bodily disability, or incapacity of mind, want either of ingenuity or activity, cross providences, losses, oppressions, or a numerous charge. Those who upon any of these accounts, or any other, have real need, and have not relations of their own to help them—but, above all, those that are reduced to want for well doing, and for *the testimony of a good conscience,* ought to be taken care of, and provided for, and, with such a prudent application of what is given, as may be most for their benefit. [2.] That it be given *to every man* for whom it is intended, *according as he has need,* without partiality or respect of persons. It is a rule in dispensing charity, as well as in administering justice, *ut parium par sit ratio—that those who are equally needy and equally deserving should be equally helped,* and that the charity should be suited and adapted to the necessity, as the word is.

(2.) Here is one particular person mentioned that was remarkable for this generous charity: it was *Barnabas,* afterwards Paul's colleague. Observe, [1.] The account here given concerning him, *v.* 36. His name was *Joses;* he was of *the tribe of Levi,* for there were Levites among the Jews of the dispersion, who, it is probable, presided in their synagogue-worship, and, according to the duty of that tribe, *taught them the good knowledge of the Lord.* He was born in Cyprus, a great way off from Jerusalem, his parents, though Jews, having a settlement there. Notice is taken of the apostles' changing his name after he associated with them. It is probable that he was one of the seventy disciples, and, as he increased in gifts and graces, grew eminent, and was respected by the apostles, who, in token of their value for him, gave him a name, *Barnabas—the son of prophecy* (so it properly signifies), he being endued with extraordinary gifts of prophecy. But the Hellenist Jews (saith Grotius) called *praying* παράκλησις, and therefore by that word it is rendered here: *A son of exhortation* (so some), one that had an excellent faculty of healing and persuading; we have an instance of it, *ch.* xi. 22—24. *A son of consolation* (so we read it); one that did himself walk very much in *the comforts of the Holy Ghost*—a cheerful Christian, and this enlarged his heart in charity to the poor; or one that was eminent for comforting the Lord's people, and speaking peace to wounded troubled consciences; he had an admirable facility that way. There were two among the apostles that were called *Boanerges—sons of thunder* (Mark iii. 17); but here was a *son of consolation* with them. Each had his several gift. Neither must censure the other, but both ease one another; let the one search the wound, and then let the other heal it and bind it up. [2.] Here is an account of his charity, and great generosity to the public fund. This is particularly taken notice of, because of the eminency of his services afterwards in the church of God, especially in carrying the gospel to the Gentiles; and, that this might not appear to come from any ill-will to his own nation, we have here his benevolence to the Jewish converts. Or perhaps this is mentioned because it was a leading card, and an example to others: *He having land,* whether in Cyprus, where he was born, or in Judea, where he now lived, or elsewhere, is not certain, but *he sold it,* not to buy elsewhere to advantage, but, as a Levite indeed, who knew he had the Lord God of Israel for his inheritance, he despised earthly inheritances, would be encumbered no more with them, but *brought the money, and laid it at the apostles' feet,* to be given in charity. Thus, as one that was designed to be a preacher of the gospel, he disentangled himself from the affairs of this life: and he lost nothing upon the balance of the account, by laying the purchase-money at the apostles' feet, when he himself was, in effect, numbered among the apostles, by that word of the Holy Ghost, *Separate me Barnabas and Saul for the work whereunto I have called them, ch.* xiii. 2. Thus, for the respect he showed to the apostles as apostles, he had an apostle's reward.

CHAP. V.

In this chapter we have, I. The sin and punishment of Ananias and Sapphira, who, for lying to the Holy Ghost, were struck dead at the word of Peter, ver. 1—11. II. The flourishing state of the church, in the power that went along with the preaching of the gospel, ver. 12—16. III. The imprisonment of the apostles, and their miraculous discharge out of prison, with fresh orders to go on to preach the gospel, which they did, to the great vexation of their persecutors, ver. 17—26. IV. Their arraignment before the great sanhedrim, and their justification of themselves in what they did, ver. 27—33. V. Gamaliel's counsel concerning them, that they should not persecute them, but let them alone, and see what would come of it, and their concurrence, for the present, with this advice, in the dismission of the apostles with no more than a scourging, ver. 34—40. VI. The apostles' cheerful progress in their work notwithstanding the prohibition laid upon them and the indignity done them, ver. 41, 42.

BUT a certain man named Ananias,
with Sapphira his wife, sold a
possession, 2 And kept back *part*
of the price, his wife also being
privy *to it,* and brought a certain
part, and laid *it* at the apostles' feet.
3 But Peter said, Ananias, why hath
Satan filled thine heart to lie to the
Holy Ghost, and to keep back *part*
of the price of the land? 4 Whiles
it remained, was it not thine own?
and after it was sold, was it not in
thine own power? why hast thou
conceived this thing in thine heart?
thou hast not lied unto men, but unto God. 5 And Ananias hearing
these words fell down, and gave up
the ghost: and great fear came on all
them that heard these things. 6 And
the young men arose, wound him up,
and carried *him* out, and buried *him.*

7 And it was about the space of three
hours after, when his wife, not knowing what was done, came in. 8 And
Peter answered unto her, Tell me
whether ye sold the land for so much?
And she said, Yea, for so much. 9
Then Peter said unto her, How is it
that ye have agreed together to tempt
the Spirit of the Lord? behold, the
feet of them which have buried thy
husband *are* at the door, and shall
carry thee out. 10 Then fell she
down straightway at his feet, and
yielded up the ghost: and the young
men came in, and found her dead,
and, carrying *her* forth, buried *her* by
her husband. 11 And great fear
came upon all the church, and upon
as many as heard these things.

The chapter begins with a melancholy *but,* which puts a stop to the pleasant and agreeable prospect of things which we had in the foregoing chapters; as every man, so every church, in its best state has its *but.* 1. The disciples were very holy, and heavenly, and seemed to be all exceedingly good; *but* there were hypocrites among them, whose *hearts were not right in the sight of God,* who, when they were baptized, and took upon them *the form of godliness, denied the power of godliness,* and stopped short of that. There is a mixture of bad with good in the best societies on this side heaven; tares will grow among the wheat until the harvest. 2. It was the praise of the disciples that they came up to that perfection which Christ recommended to the rich young man—they *sold what they had, and gave to the poor; but* even that proved a cloak and cover of hypocrisy which was thought the greatest proof and evidence of sincerity. 3. The signs and wonders which the apostles wrought were hitherto miracles of mercy; *but* now comes in a miracle of judgment, and here is an instance of severity following the instances of goodness, that God may be both loved and feared. Observe here,

I. The sin of Ananias and Sapphira his wife. It is good to see husband and wife joining together in that which is good, but to be confederate in evil is to be like Adam and Eve, when they agreed to eat the forbidden fruit, and were one in their disobedience. Now their sin was, 1. That they were ambitious of being thought eminent disciples, and of the first rank, when really they were not true disciples; they would pass for some of the most fruitful trees in Christ's vineyard, when really the root of the matter was not found in them. They *sold a possession, and brought the money* (as Barnabas did) *to the apostles' feet,* that they might not seem to be behind the very chief of believers, but might be applauded and cried up, and stand so much the fairer for preferment in the church, which perhaps they thought would shortly shine in secular pomp and grandeur. Note, It is possible that hypocrites may deny themselves in one thing, but then it is to serve themselves in another; they may forego their secular advantage in one instance, with a prospect of finding their account in something else. Ananias and Sapphira would take upon them a profession of Christianity, *and make a fair show in the flesh* with it, and so would mock God, and deceive others, when they knew they could not go through with the Christian profession. It was commendable, and so far it was right, in that rich young man, that he would not pretend to follow Christ, when, if it should come to a pinch, he knew he could not come up to his terms, *but he went away sorrowful.* Ananias and Sapphira pretended they could come up to the terms, that they might have the credit of being disciples, when really they could not, and so were a discredit to discipleship. Note, It is often of fatal consequence for people to go a greater length in profession than their inward principle will admit of. 2. That they were covetous of the wealth of the world, and distrustful of God and his providence: *They sold their land,* and perhaps then, in a pang of zeal, designed no other than to dedicate the whole of the purchase-money to pious uses, and made a vow, or at least conceived a full purpose, to do so; but, when the money was received, their heart failed them, and *they kept back part of the price* (*v.* 2), because they loved the money, and thought it was too much to part with at once, and to trust in the apostles' hands, and because they knew not but they might want it themselves; though now all things were common, yet it would not be so long, and what should they do in a time of need, if they should leave themselves nothing to take to? They could not take God's word that they should be provided for, but thought they would play a wiser part than the rest had done, and lay up for a rainy day. Thus they thought to serve both God and mammon—God, by bringing part of the money to the apostles' feet, and mammon, by keeping the other part in their own pockets; as if there were not an all-sufficiency in God to make up the whole to them, except they retained some in their own hands by way of caution-money. Their hearts were divided, so *they were found faulty,* Hos. x. 2. They *halted between two;* if they had been thorough-paced worldlings, they would not have sold their possession; and, if they had been thorough-paced Christians, they would not have detained part of the price. 3. That they thought to deceive the apostles, and make them believe they brought the whole purchase-money, when really it was but a part. They came with as good an assurance, and as great a show of piety and devotion, as any of them, and *laid the money at the apostles' feet,* as if it were their all. They dissembled with God and his Spirit, with Christ and his church and ministers; and this was their sin.

II. The indictment of Ananias, which proved both his condemnation and execution for this sin. When he brought the money, and expected to be commended and encouraged, as others were, Peter took him to task about it. He, without any enquiry or examination of witnesses concerning it, charges him peremptorily with the crime, and aggravates it, and lays a load upon him for it, showing it to him in its own colour, *v.* 3, 4. The Spirit of God in Peter not only discovered the fact without any information (when perhaps no man in the world knew it but the man and his wife themselves), but likewise discerned the principle of reigning infidelity in the heart of Ananias, which was at the bottom of it, and therefore proceeded against him so suddenly. Had it been a sin of infirmity, through the surprise of a temptation, Peter would have taken Ananias aside, and have bidden him go home, and fetch the rest of the money, and repent of his folly in attempting to put this cheat upon them; but he knew *that his heart was fully set in him to do this evil,* and therefore allowed him not space to repent. He here showed him,

1. The origin of his sin: *Satan filled his heart;* he not only suggested it to him, and put it into his head, but hurried him on with resolution to do it. Whatever is contrary to the good Spirit proceeds from the evil spirit, and those hearts are filled by Satan in which worldliness reigns, and has the ascendant. Some think that Ananias was one of those that had received the Holy Ghost, and was filled with his gifts, but, having provoked the Spirit to withdraw from him, now *Satan filled his heart;* as, *when the Spirit of the Lord departed from Saul, an evil spirit from God troubled him.* Satan is a lying spirit; he was so in the mouth of Ahab's prophets, and so he was in the mouth of Ananias, and by this made it appear that he filled his heart.

2. The sin itself: *He lied to the Holy Ghost;* a sin of such a heinous nature that he could not have been guilty of it if Satan had not filled his heart.

(1.) The phrase which we render *lying to the Holy Ghost,* *ψεύσασθαί σε τὸ πνεῦμα τὸ ἅγιον*, some read, *to belie the Holy Ghost,* which may be taken two ways: [1.] That he belied the Holy Ghost in himself; so Dr. Lightfoot takes it, and supposes that Ananias was not an ordinary believer, but a minister, and one that had received the gift of the Holy Ghost with the hundred and twenty (for mention is made of him immediately after Barnabas); yet he durst thus, by dissembling, belie and shame that gift. Or thus; Those who had sold their estates, and laid the money at the apostles' feet, did it by the special impulse of the Holy Ghost, enabling them to do an act so very great and generous; and Ananias pretended that he was moved by the Holy Ghost to do what he did, as others were; whereas it appeared by his baseness that he was not under the influence of the good Spirit at all; for, had it been his work, it would have been perfect. [2.] That he belied the Holy Ghost in the apostles, to whom he brought the money; he misrepresented the Spirit they were actuated by, either by a suspicion that they would not faithfully distribute what they were entrusted with (which was a base suggestion, as if they were false to the trust reposed in them), or by an assurance that they could not discover the fraud. He belied the Holy Ghost when by what he did he would have it thought that those who are endued with the gifts of the Holy Ghost might as easily be imposed upon as other men; like Gehazi, whom his master convicted of his error by that word, *Went not my heart with thee?* 2 Kings v. 26. It is charged upon the house of Israel and Judah, when, like Ananias here, they dealt very treacherously, that they belied the Lord, *saying, It is not he,* Jer. v. 11, 12. Thus Ananias thought the apostles were altogether such as himself, and this was belying the Holy Ghost in them, as if he were not in them a discerner of spirits, whereas they had all the gifts of the Spirit in them, which to others were divided severally. See 1 Cor. xii. 8—11. Those that pretend to an inspiration of the Spirit, in imposing upon the church their own fancies, either in opinion or practice—that say they are moved from above when they are carried on by their pride, covetousness, or affectation of dominion, belie the Holy Ghost.

(2.) But we read it, *to lie unto the Holy Ghost,* which reading is countenanced by *v.* 4, *Thou hast not lied unto men, but unto God.* [1.] Ananias told a lie, a deliberate lie, and with a purpose to deceive; he told Peter that he had sold a possession (house or lands) and this was the purchase-money. Perhaps he expressed himself in words that were capable of a double meaning, used some equivocations about it, which he thought might palliate the matter a little, and save him from the guilt of a downright lie: or perhaps he said nothing; but it was all one, he did as the rest did who brought the whole price, and would be thought to do so, and expected the praise those had that did so, and the same privilege and access to the common stock as they had; and therefore it was an implicit protestation that he brought the whole price, as they did; and this was a lie, for he kept back part. Note, Many are brought to gross lying by reigning pride, and affectation of the applause of men, particularly in works of charity to the poor. That therefore we may not be found boasting of a false gift given to us, or given by us (Prov xxv. 14), we must not boast even of a true gift, which is the meaning of our Saviour's caution in works of charity, *Let not thy left hand know what thy right hand doeth.* Those that boast of good works they never did, or promise good works they never do, or make the good works they do more or better than really they are, come under the guilt of Ananias's lie, which it concerns us all to dread the thought of. [2.] He told this lie *to the Holy Ghost.* It was not so much to the apostles as to the Holy Ghost in them that the money was brought, and that was said which was said, *v.* 4, *Thou hast not lied unto men* (not to men only, not to men chiefly, though the apostles be but men), *but thou hast lied unto God.* Hence it is justly inferred that the Holy Ghost is God; for he that lieth to the Holy Ghost lieth to God. "Those that lied to the apostles, actuated and acting by the Spirit of God, are said to lie to God, because the apostles acted by the power and authority of God, whence it follows (as Dr. Whitby well observes) that the power and authority of the Spirit must be the power and authority of God." And, as he further argues, "Ananias is said to lie to God, because he lied to that Spirit in the apostles which enabled them to discern the secrets of men's hearts and actions, which being the property of God alone, he that lies to him must therefore lie to God, because he lies to one who has the incommunicable property of God, and consequently the divine essence."

3. The aggravations of the sin (*v.* 4): *While it remained, was it not thine own? And, after it was sold, was it not in thine own power?* Which may be understood two ways:—(1.) "Thou wast under no temptation *to keep back part of the price;* before it was sold it was thy own, and not mortgaged nor encumbered, nor any way engaged for debt; and when it was sold it was in thy own power to dispose of the money at thy pleasure; so that thou mightest as well have brought the whole as a part. Thou hadst no debts to pay, perhaps no children to provide for; so that thou wast not under the influence of any particular inducement to keep back part of the price. Thou wast a transgressor without a cause." Or, (2.) "Thou wast under no necessity of selling thy land at all, nor bringing any of the money to the apostles' feet. Thou mightest have kept the money, if thou hadst pleased, and the land too, and never have pretended to this piece of perfection." This rule of charity the apostle gives, that people be not pressed, and that it be not urged as of necessity, because God loves a cheerful giver (2 Cor. ix. 7), and Philemon must do a good work, *not as it were of necessity, but willingly,* Philem. 14. As it is better not to vow than to vow and not to pay, so better had it been for him not to have sold his land at all than thus to keep back part of the price; not to have pretended to do the good work than thus to do it by the halves. "*When it was sold, it was in thine own power;* but it was not so when it was vowed: thou hadst then opened thy mouth to the Lord, and couldst not go back. Thus, in giving our hearts to God, we are not admitted to divide them. Satan, like the mother whose own the child was not, would take up with a half; but God will have all or none.

4. All this guilt, thus aggravated, is charged upon him: *Why hast thou conceived this thing in thine heart?* Observe, Though Satan filled his heart to do it, yet he is said to have conceived it in his own heart, which shows that we cannot extenuate our sins by laying the fault of them upon the devil; he tempts, but he cannot force; it is of *our own lusts that we are drawn away and enticed.* The evil thing, whatever it is, that is said or done, the sinner has conceived it in his own heart; and therefore, *if thou scornest, thou alone shalt bear it.* The close of the charge is very high, but very just: *Thou hast not lied unto men, but unto God.* What emphasis does the prophet lay upon that of Ahaz, *not wearying men only, but wearying my God also!* Isa. vii. 13. And Moses upon that of Israel, *Your murmurings are not against us, but against the Lord!* Exod. xvi. 8. So here, Thou mightest have imposed upon us, who are men like thyself; but, *be not deceived, God is not mocked.* If we think to put a cheat upon God, we shall prove in the end to have put a fatal cheat upon our own souls.

III. The death and burial of Ananias, *v.* 5, 6.

1. He died upon the spot: *Ananias, hearing these words, was speechless,* in the same sense that he was who was charged with intruding into the wedding feast without a wedding garment: he had nothing to say for himself; but this was not all: he was struck speechless with a witness, for he was struck dead: *He fell down, and gave up the ghost.* It does not appear whether Peter designed and expected that this would follow upon what he said to him; it is probable that he did, for to Sapphira his wife Peter particularly spoke death, *v.* 9. Some think that an angel struck him, that he died, as Herod, *ch.* xii. 23. Or, his own conscience smote him with such horror and amazement at the sense of his guilt, that he sunk and died away under the load of it. And perhaps, when he was convicted of lying to the Holy Ghost, he remembered the unpardonableness of *the blasphemy against the Holy Ghost,* which struck him like a dagger to the heart. See the power of the word of God in the mouth of the apostles. As it was to some *a savour of life unto life,* so it was to others *a savour of death unto death.* As there are those whom the gospel justifies, so there are those whom it condemns. This punishment of Ananias may seem severe, but we are sure it was just. (1.) It was designed to maintain the honour of the Holy Ghost as now lately poured out upon the apostles, in order to the setting up of the gospel kingdom. It was a great affront

which Ananias put upon the Holy Ghost, as if he could be imposed upon: and it had a direct tendency to invalidate the apostles' testimony; for, if they could not by the Spirit discover this fraud, how could they by this Spirit discover the deep things of God, which they were to reveal to the children of men? It was therefore necessary that the credit of the apostles' gifts and powers should be supported, though it was at this expense. (2.) It was designed to deter others from the like presumptions, now at the beginning of this dispensation. Simon Magus afterwards was not thus punished, nor Elymas; but Ananias was made an example now at first, that, with the sensible proofs given what a comfortable thing it is to receive the Spirit, there might be also sensible proofs given what a dangerous thing it is to resist the Spirit, and do despite to him. How severely was the worshipping of the golden calf punished, and the gathering of sticks on the sabbath-day, when the laws of the second and fourth commandments were now newly given! So was the offering of strange fire by Nadab and Abihu, and the mutiny of Korah and his company, when the fire from heaven was now newly given, and the authority of Moses and Aaron now newly established. The doing of this by the ministry of Peter, who himself with a lie denied his Master but a little while ago, intimates that it was not the resentment of a wrong done to himself; for then he, who had himself been faulty, would have had charity for those that offended; and he, who himself had repented and been forgiven, would have forgiven this affront, and endeavoured to bring this offender to repentance; but it was the act of the Spirit of God in Peter: to him the indignity was done, and by him the punishment was inflicted.

2. He was buried immediately, for this was the manner of the Jews (*v.* 6): *The young men*, who it is probable were appointed to that office in the church of burying the dead, as among the Romans the *libitinarii* and *pollinctores;* or the young men that attended the apostles, and waited on them, they *wound up* the dead body in grave-clothes, *carried it out* of the city, and *buried it* decently, though he died in sin, and by an immediate stroke of divine vengeance.

IV. The reckoning with Sapphira, the wife of Ananias, who perhaps was first in the transgression, and tempted her husband to eat this forbidden fruit. *She came in* to the place where the apostles were, which, as it should seem, was Solomon's porch, for there we find them (*v.* 12), a part of the temple where Christ used to walk, John x. 23. *She came in about three hours after*, expecting to share in the thanks of the house for her coming in, and consenting to the sale of the land, of which perhaps she was entitled to her dower or thirds; for *she knew not what had been done.* It was strange that nobody ran to tell her of the sudden death of her husband, that she might keep away; perhaps some one did, and she was not at home; and so when she came to present herself before the apostles, as a benefactor to the fund, she met with a breach instead of a blessing.

1. She was found guilty of sharing with her husband in his sin, by a question that Peter asked her (*v.* 8): *Tell me whether you sold the land for so much?* naming the sum which Ananias had brought and laid at the apostles' feet. "Was this all you received for the sale of the land, and had you no more for it?" "No," saith she, "we had no more, but that was every farthing we received." Ananias and his wife agreed to tell the same story, and the bargain being private, and by consent kept to themselves, nobody could disprove them, and therefore they thought they might safely stand in the lie, and should gain credit to it. It is sad to see those relations who should quicken one another to that which is good harden one another in that which is evil.

2. Sentence was passed upon her, that she should partake in her husband's doom, *v.* 9.

(1.) Her sin is opened: *How is it that you have agreed together to tempt the Spirit of the Lord?* Before he passes sentence, he makes her to know her abominations, and shows her the evil of her sin. Observe, [1.] That they tempted the Spirit of the Lord; as Israel tempted God in the desert, when they said, *Is the Lord among us, or is he not?* after they had seen so many miraculous proofs of his power; and not only his presence, but his presidency, when they said, *Can God furnish a table?* So here, "Can the Spirit in the apostles discover this fraud? Can they discern that this is but a part of the price, when we tell them it is the whole?" *Can he judge through this dark cloud?* Job xxii. 13. They saw that the apostles had the gift of tongues; but had they the gift of discerning spirits? . Those that presume upon security and impunity in sin tempt the Spirit of God; they tempt God as if he were altogether such a one as themselves. [2.] That they agreed together to do it, making the bond of their relation to each other (which by the divine institution is a sacred tie) to become a bond of iniquity. It is hard to say which is worse between yoke-fellows and other relations—a discord in good or concord in evil. It seems to intimate that their agreeing together to do it was a further tempting of the Spirit; as if, when they had engaged to keep one another's counsel in this matter, even the Spirit of the Lord himself could not discover them. Thus they *digged deep to hide their counsel from the Lord*, but were made to know it is in vain. "How is it that you are thus infatuated? What strange stupidity has seized you, that you would venture to make trial of that which is past dispute? How is it that you, who are baptized Christians, do not understand yourselves better? How durst you run so great a risk?

(2.) Her doom is read: *Behold, the feet of those who have buried thy husband are at the door* (perhaps he heard them coming, or knew that they could not be long): *and* they *shall carry thee out.* As Adam and Eve, who agreed to eat the forbidden fruit, were turned together out of paradise, so Ananias and Sapphira, who agreed to tempt the Spirit of the Lord, were together chased out of the world.

3. The sentence executed itself. There needed no executioner, a killing power went along with Peter's word, as sometimes a healing power did; for the God in whose name he spoke *kills and makes alive;* and *out of his mouth* (and Peter was now his mouth) *both evil and good proceed* (*v.* 10): *Then fell she down straightway at his feet.* Some sinners God makes quick work with, while others he bears long with; for which difference, doubtless, there are good reasons; but he is not accountable to us for them. She heard not till now that her husband was dead, the notice of which, with the discovery of her sin, and the sentence of death passed upon her, struck her as a thunderbolt and took her away as with a whirlwind. And many instances there are of sudden deaths which are not to be looked upon as the punishment of some gross sin, like this. We must not think that all who die suddenly are sinners above others; perhaps it is in favour to them, that they have a quick passage: however, it is forewarning to all to be always ready. But here it is plain that it was in judgment. Some put the question concerning the eternal state of Ananias and Sapphira, and incline to think that the destruction of the flesh was that *the spirit might be saved in the day of the Lord Jesus.* And I should go in with that charitable opinion if there had been any space given them to repent, as there was to the incestuous Corinthian. But secret things belong not to us. It is said, *She fell down at Peter's feet;* there, where she should have laid the whole price and did not, she was herself laid, as it were to make up the deficiency. The *young men* that had the care of funerals coming in *found her dead;* and it is not said, *They wound her up,* as they did Ananias, but, *They carried her out* as she was, *and buried her by her husband;* and probably an inscription was set over their graves, intimating that they were joint-monuments of divine wrath against those that lie to the Holy Ghost. Some ask whether the apostles kept the money which they did bring, and concerning which they lied? I am apt to think they did; they had not the superstition of those who said, *It is not lawful for us to put it into the treasury:* for unto the pure all things are pure. What they brought was not polluted to those to whom they brought it; but what they kept back was polluted to those that kept it back. Use was made of the censers of Korah's mutineers.

V. The impression that this made upon the people. Notice is taken of this in the midst of the story (*v.* 5): *Great fear came upon all that heard these things,* that heard what Peter said, and saw what followed; or upon all that heard the story of it; for, no doubt, it was all the talk of the city. And again (*v.* 11), *Great fear came upon all the church, and upon as many as heard these things.* 1. Those that had joined themselves to the church were thereby struck with an awe of God and of his judgments, and with a greater veneration for this dispensation of the Spirit which they were now under. It was not a damp or check to their holy joy, but it taught them to be serious in it, and to rejoice with trembling. All that laid their money at the apostles' feet after this were afraid of keeping back any part of the price. 2. All that heard it were put into a consternation by it, and were ready to say, *Who is able to stand before this holy Lord God* and his Spirit in the apostles? As 1 Sam. vi. 20.

12 And by the hands of the apostles were many signs and wonders
wrought among the people; (and
they were all with one accord in Solomon's porch. 13 And of the rest
durst no man join himself to them;
but the people magnified them. 14
And believers were the more added
to the Lord, multitudes both of men
and women.) 15 Insomuch that
they brought forth the sick into the
streets, and laid *them* on beds and
couches, that at the least the shadow
of Peter passing by might overshadow
some of them. 16 There came also
a multitude *out* of the cities round
about unto Jerusalem, bringing sick
folks, and them which were vexed
with unclean spirits: and they were
healed every one.

We have here an account of the progress of the gospel, notwithstanding this terrible judgment inflicted upon two hypocrites.

I. Here is a general account of the miracles which the apostles wrought (*v.* 12): *By the hands of the apostles were many signs and wonders wrought among the people,* many miracles of mercy for one of judgment. Now the gospel power returned to its proper channel, which is that of mercy and grace. God had come out of his place to punish, but now returns to his place, to his mercy-seat again. The miracles they wrought proved their divine mission. They were not a few, but many, of divers kinds and often repeated; they were signs and wonders, such wonders as were confessedly signs of a divine presence and power. They were not done in a corner, but among the people, who were at liberty to enquire into them, and, if there had been any fraud or collusion in them, would have discovered it.

II. We are here told what were the effects of these miracles which the apostles wrought.

1. The church was hereby kept together, and confirmed in its adherence both to the apostles and to one another: *They* of the church *were all with one accord in Solomon's porch.* (1.) They met in the temple, in the open place that was called Solomon's porch. It was strange that the rulers of the temple suffered them to keep their meeting there. But God inclined their hearts to tolerate them there awhile, for the more convenient spreading of the gospel; and those who permitted buyers and sellers could not for shame prohibit such preachers and healers there. They all met in public worship; so early was the institution of religious assemblies observed in the church, which must by no means be forsaken or let fall, for in them a profession of religion is kept up. (2.) They were there with one accord, unanimous in their doctrine, worship, and discipline; and there was no discontent nor murmuring about the death of Ananias and Sapphira, as there was against Moses and Aaron about the death of Korah and his company: *You have killed the people of the Lord,* Num. xvi. 41. The separation of hypocrites, by distinguishing judgments, should make the sincere cleave so much the closer to each other and to the gospel ministry.

2. It gained the apostles, who were the prime ministers in Christ's kingdom, very great respect. (1.) The other ministers kept their distance: *Of the rest* of their company *durst no man join himself to them,* as their equal or an associate with them; though others of them were endued with the Holy Ghost, and spoke with tongues, yet none of them at this time did such signs and wonders as the apostles did: and therefore they acknowledged their superiority, and in every thing yielded to them. (2.) All *the people magnified them,* and had them in great veneration, spoke of them with respect, and represented them as the favourites of Heaven, and unspeakable blessings to this earth. Though the chief priests vilified them, and did all they could to make them contemptible, this did not hinder the people from magnifying them, who saw the thing in a true light. Observe, The apostles were far from magnifying themselves; they transmitted the glory of all they did very carefully and faithfully to Christ, and yet the people magnified them; for those that humble themselves shall be exalted, and those honoured that honour God only.

3. The church increased in number (*v.* 14): *Believers were the more added to the Lord,* and no doubt joined themselves to the church, when they saw that God was in it of a truth, even *multitudes both of men and women.* They were so far from being deterred by the example that was made of Ananias and Sapphira that they were rather invited by it into a society that kept such a strict discipline. Observe, (1.) Believers are added to the Lord Jesus, joined to him, and so joined to his mystical body, from which nothing can separate us and cut us off, but that which separates us and cuts us off from Christ. Many have been brought to the Lord, and yet there is room for others to be added to him, added to the number of those that are united to him; and additions will still be making till the mystery of God shall be finished, and the number of the elect accomplished. (2.) Notice is taken of the conversion of *women* as well as *men;* more notice than generally was in the Jewish church, in which they neither received the sign of circumcision nor were obliged to attend the solemn feasts; and the *court of the women* was one of the outer courts of the temple. But, as among those that followed Christ while he was upon earth, so among those that believed on him after he went to heaven, great notice was taken of the good women.

4. The apostles had abundance of patients, and gained abundance of reputation both to themselves and their doctrine by the cure of them all, *v.* 15, 16. So many *signs and wonders were wrought by the apostles* that all manner of people put in for the benefit of them, both in city and country, and had it. (1.) In the city: They *brought forth their sick into the streets;* for it is probable that the priests would not suffer them to bring them into the temple to Solomon's porch, and the apostles had not leisure to go to the houses of them all. And they *laid them on beds and couches* (because they were so weak that they could neither go nor stand), *that at the least the shadow of Peter, passing by, might overshadow some of them,* though it could not reach them all; and, it should seem, it had the desired effect, as the woman's touch of the hem of Christ's garment had; and in this, among other things, that word of Christ was fulfilled, *Greater works than these shall you do.* God expresses his care of his people, by his being their *shade on their right hand;* and the benign influences of Christ as a king are compared to the *shadow of a great rock.* Peter comes between them and the sun, and so heals them, cuts them off from a dependence upon creature sufficiency as insufficient, that they may expect help only from that Spirit of grace with whom he was filled. And, if such miracles were wrought by Peter's shadow, we have reason to think they were so by the other apostles, as by the handkerchiefs from Paul's body (*ch.* xix. 12), no doubt both being with an actual intention in the minds of the apostles thus to heal; so that it is absurd to infer hence a healing virtue in the relics of saints that are dead and gone; we read not of any cured by the relics of Christ himself, after he was gone, as certainly we should if there had been any such thing. (2.) In the country towns: Multitudes came to Jerusalem from *the ci-*

ties round about, bringing sick folks that were afflicted in body, and *those that were vexed with unclean spirits,* that were troubled in mind, and they were *healed every one;* distempered bodies and distempered minds were set to rights. Thus opportunity was given to the apostles, both to convince people's judgments by these miracles of the heavenly origin of the doctrine they preached, and also to engage people's affections both to them and it, by giving them a specimen of its beneficial tendency to the welfare of this lower world.

17 Then the high priest rose up, and
all they that were with him, (which is
the sect of the Sadducees,) and were
filled with indignation, 18 And laid
their hands on the apostles, and put
them in the common prison. 19 But
the angel of the Lord by night opened
the prison doors, and brought them
forth, and said, 20 Go, stand and
speak in the temple to the people all
the words of this life. 21 And when
they heard *that,* they entered into
the temple early in the morning, and
taught. But the high priest came,
and they that were with him, and
called the council together, and all
the senate of the children of Israel,
and sent to the prison to have them
brought. 22 But when the officers
came, and found them not in the prison, they returned, and told, 23
Saying, The prison truly found we
shut with all safety, and the keepers
standing without before the doors:
but when we had opened, we found
no man within. 24 Now when the
high priest and the captain of the
temple and the chief priests heard
these things, they doubted of them
whereunto this would grow. 25 Then
came one and told them, saying, Behold, the men whom ye put in prison
are standing in the temple, and teaching the people.

Never did any good work go on with any hope of success, but it met with opposition; those that are bent to do mischief cannot be reconciled to those who make it their business to do good. Satan, the destroyer of mankind, ever was, and will be, an adversary to those who are the benefactors of mankind; and it would have been strange if the apostles had gone on thus teaching and healing and had had no check. In these verses we have the malice of hell and the grace of heaven struggling about them, the one to drive them off from this good work, the other to animate them in it,

I. The priests were enraged at them, and shut them up in prison, *v.* 17, 18. Observe, 1. Who their enemies and persecutors were. The high priest was the ringleader, Annas or Caiaphas, who saw their wealth and dignity, their power and tyranny, that is, their all, at stake, and inevitably lost, if the spiritual and heavenly doctrine of Christ should get ground and prevail among the people. Those that were most forward to join with the high priest herein were the *sect of the Sadducees,* who had a particular enmity to the gospel of Christ, because it confirmed and established the doctrine of the invisible world, the resurrection of the dead, and the future state, which they denied. It is not strange if men of no religion be bigoted in their opposition to true and pure religion. 2. How they were affected towards them, ill affected, and exasperated to the last degree. When they heard and saw what flocking there was to the apostles, and how considerable they were become, they *rose up* in a passion, as men that could no longer bear it, and were resolved to make head against it, being *filled with indignation* at the apostles for preaching the doctrine of Christ, and curing the sick,—at the people for hearing them, and bringing the sick to them to be cured,—and at themselves and their own party for suffering this matter to go so far, and not knocking it on the head at first. Thus are the enemies of Christ and his gospel a torment to themselves. *Envy slays the silly one.* 3. How they proceeded against them (*v.* 18): *They laid their hands on them,* perhaps their own hands (so low did their malice make them stoop), or, rather, the hands of their officers, and *put them in the common prison,* among the worst of malefactors. Hereby they designed, (1.) To put a restraint upon them; though they could not lay any thing criminal to their charge worthy of death or of bonds, yet while they had them in prison they kept them from going on in their work, and this they reckoned a good point gained. Thus early were the ambassadors of Christ in bonds. (2.) To put a terror upon them, and so to drive them off from their work. The last time they had them before them, they only threatened them (*ch.* iv. 21); but now, finding that this did not do, they imprisoned them, to make them afraid of them. (3.) To put a disgrace upon them, and therefore they chose to clap them up in the common prison, that, being thus vilified, the people might not, as they had done, magnify them. Satan has carried on his design against the gospel very much by making the preachers and professors of it appear despicable.

II. God sent his angel to release them out of prison, and to renew their commission to preach the gospel. The powers of darkness fight against them, but the Father of lights fights for them, and sends an angel of light to plead their cause. The Lord will never desert his witnesses, his advocates, but will certainly stand by them, and bear them out.

1. The apostles are discharged, legally discharged, from their imprisonment (*v.* 19): *The angel of the Lord by night*, in spite of all the locks and bars that were upon them, *opened the prison doors*, and, in spite of all the vigilance and resolution of the keepers that *stood without before the doors, brought forth* the prisoners (see *v.* 23), gave them authority to go out without crime, and led them through all opposition. This deliverance is not so particularly related as that of Peter (*ch.* xii. 7, &c.); but the miracle here was the very same. Note, There is no prison so dark, so strong, but God can both visit his people in it, and, if he pleases, fetch them out of it. This discharge of the apostles out of prison by an angel was a resemblance of Christ's resurrection, and his discharge out of the prison of the grave, and would help to confirm the apostles' preaching of it.

2. They are charged, and legally charged, to go on with their work, so as thereby to be discharged from the prohibition which the high priest laid them under; the angel bade them, *Go, stand, and speak in the temple to the people all the words of this life*, *v.* 20. When they were miraculously set at liberty, they must not think it was that they might save their lives by making their escape out of the hands of their enemies. No; it was that they might go on with their work with so much the more boldness. Recoveries from sickness, releases out of trouble, are granted us, and are to be looked upon by us as granted, not that we may enjoy the comforts of our life, but that God may be honoured with the services of our life. *Let my soul live, and it shall praise thee*, Ps. cxix. 175. *Bring my soul out of prison* (as the apostles here), *that I may praise thy name*, Ps. cxlii. 7. See Isa. xxxviii. 22. Now in this charge given them, observe, (1.) Where they must preach: *Speak in the temple.* One would think, though they might not quit their work, yet it had been prudent to go on with it in a more private place, where it would give less offence to the priests than in the temple, and so would the less expose them. No; "Speak in the temple, for this is the place of concourse, this is your Father's house, and it is not to be as yet quite left desolate." It is not for the preachers of Christ's gospel to retire into corners, as long as they can have any opportunity of preaching in the great congregation. (2.) To whom they must preach: "*Speak to the people;* not to the princes and rulers, for they will not hearken; but to the people, who are willing and desirous to be taught, and whose souls are as precious to Christ, and ought to be so to you, as the souls of the greatest. Speak to the people, to all in general, for all are concerned." (3.) How they must preach: *Go, stand, and speak*, which intimates, not only that they must speak publicly, stand up and speak, that all may hear; but that they must speak boldly and resolutely: *Stand and speak;* that is, "Speak it as those that resolve to stand to it, to live and die by it." (4.) What they must speak: *All the words of this life. This life* which you have been speaking of among yourselves, referring perhaps to the conferences concerning heaven which they had among themselves for their own and one another's encouragement in prison: "Go, and preach the same to the world, that others may be comforted with the same comforts with which you yourselves are comforted of God." Or, "of this life which the Sadducees deny, and therefore persecute you; preach this, though you know it is this that they have indignation at." Or, "of this life emphatically; this heavenly, divine life, in comparison with which the present earthly life does not deserve the name." Or, "*these words of life*, the very same you have preached, these words which the Holy Ghost puts into your mouth." Note, The words of the gospel are the words of life, quickening words; they are spirit, and they are life; *words whereby we may be saved*—that is the same with this here, *ch.* xi. 14. The gospel is the word of this life, for it secures to us the privileges of our way as well as those of our home, and the promises of the life that now is as well as of that to come. And yet even spiritual and eternal life are brought so much to light in the gospel that they may be called *this life;* for the word is nigh thee. Note, The gospel is concerning matters of life and death, and ministers must preach it and people hear it accordingly. They must speak *all the words of this life*, and not conceal any for fear of offending, or in hope of ingratiating themselves with their rulers. Christ's witnesses are sworn to speak the whole truth.

III. They went on with their work (*v.* 21): *When they heard this*, when they heard that it was the will of God that they should continue to preach in the temple, they *returned to Solomon's porch*, *v.* 12. 1. It was a great satisfaction to them to have these fresh orders. Perhaps they began to question whether, if they had their liberty, they should preach as publicly in the temple as they had done, because they had been told, when they were *persecuted in one city, to flee to another.* But, now that the angel ordered them to go preach in the temple, their way was plain, and they ventured without any difficulty, entered into the temple, and feared not the face of man. Note, If we may but be satisfied concerning our duty, our business is to keep close to this, and then we may cheerfully trust God with our safety. (2.) They set themselves immediately to execute them, without dispute or delay. They *entered into the temple early in the morning* (as soon as the gates were opened, and people began to come together there), and taught them the gospel of the kingdom: and did not at all fear what man could do unto them. The case here was extraordinary: the whole treasure of the gospel is lodged in their hands; if they be silent now the springs are shut up, and the whole work falls to the ground and is made to cease, which is not the case of ordinary ministers, who therefore are not by this example bound to throw themselves into the mouth of danger; and yet when God gives opportunity of doing good, though we be under the restraint and terror of human powers, we should venture far rather than let go such an opportunity.

IV. The high priest and his party went on with their prosecution, *v.* 21. They, supposing they had the apostles sure enough, *called the council together,* a great and extraordinary council, for they summoned *all the senate of the children of Israel.* See here,

1. How they were prepared, and how big with expectation, to crush the gospel of Christ and the preachers of it, for they raised the whole posse. The last time they had the apostles in custody they convened them only before a committee of those that were of the kindred of the high priest, who were obliged to act cautiously; but now, that they might proceed further and with more assurance, they called together, *πᾶσαν τὴν γερουσίαν—all the eldership,* that is (says Dr. Lightfoot), all the three courts or benches of judges in Jerusalem, not only the great sanhedrim, consisting of seventy elders, but the other two judicatories that were erected one in the outer-court gate of the temple, the other in the inner or beautiful gate, consisting of twenty-three judges each; so that, if there was a full appearance, here were one hundred and sixteen judges. Thus God ordered it, that the confusion of the enemies, and the apostles' testimony against them, might be more public, and that those might hear the gospel who would not hear it otherwise than from the bar. Howbeit, the high priest *meant not so, neither did his heart think so;* but it was in his heart to rally all his forces against the apostles, and by a universal consent to cut them all off at once.

2. How they were disappointed, and had their faces filled with shame: *He that sits in heaven laughs at them,* and so may we too, to see how gravely the court is set; and we may suppose the high priest makes a solemn speech to them, setting forth the occasion of their coming together—that a very dangerous faction was now lately raised at Jerusalem, by the preaching of the doctrine of Jesus, which it was needful, for the preservation of their church (which never was in such danger as now), speedily and effectually to suppress—that it was now in the power of their hands to do it, for he had the ringleaders of the faction now in the common prison, to be proceeded against, if they would but agree to it, with the utmost severity. An officer is, in order hereunto, despatched immediately to fetch the prisoners to the bar. But see how they are baffled. (1.) The officers come, and tell them that they are not to be found in the prison, *v.* 22, 23. The last time they were forthcoming when they were called for, *ch.* iv. 7. But now they were gone, and the report which the officers make is, "*The prison-doors truly found we shut with all safety*" (nothing had been done to weaken them); "*the keepers* had not been wanting to their duty; we found them *standing without before the doors,* and knowing nothing to the contrary but that the prisoners were all safe: but when we went in *we found no man* therein, that is, none of the men we were sent to fetch." It is probable that they found the common prisoners there. Which way the angel fetched them, whether by some back way, or opening the door and fastening it closely again (the keepers all the while asleep), we are not told; however it was, they were gone. The Lord knows, though we do not, how to deliver the godly out of temptation, and how to loose those that are in bonds for his name's sake, and he will do it, as here, when he has occasion for them. Now think how confused the court looked, when the officers made this return upon their order (*v.* 24): *When the high priest, and the captain of the temple,* and the *chief priests, heard these things,* they were all at a plunge, and looked one upon another, *doubting what this thing should be.* They were extremely perplexed, were at their wits' end, having never been so disappointed in all their lives of any thing they were so sure of. It occasioned various speculations, some suggesting that they were conjured out of the prison, and made their escape by magic arts; others that the keepers had played tricks with them, knowing how many friends these prisoners had, that were so much the darlings of the people. Some feared that, having made such a wonderful escape, they would be the more followed; others that, though perhaps they had frightened them from Jerusalem, they should hear of them again in some part or other of the country, where they would do yet more mischief, and it would be yet more out of their power to stop the spreading of the infection; and now they begin to fear that instead of curing the ill they have made it worse. Note, Those often distress and embarrass themselves that think to distress and embarrass the cause of Christ. (2.) Their doubt is, in part, determined; and yet their vexation is increased by another messenger, who brings them word that their prisoners are preaching in the temple (*v.* 25): "*Behold, the men whom you put in prison,* and have sent for to your bar, *are now* hard by you here, *standing in the temple,* under your nose and in defiance of you, *teaching the people.*" Prisoners, that have broken prison, usually abscond, for fear of being retaken; but these prisoners, that

here made their escape, dare to show their faces even where their persecutors have the greatest influence. Now this confounded them more than any thing. Common malefactors may have art enough to break prison; but those are uncommon ones that have courage enough to avow it when they have so done.

26 Then went the captain with the
officers, and brought them without
violence: for they feared the people,
lest they should have been stoned.
27 And when they had brought them,
they set *them* before the council: and
the high priest asked them, 28 Saying, Did not we straitly command
you that ye should not teach in this
name? and, behold, ye have filled
Jerusalem with your doctrine, and
intend to bring this man's blood
upon us. 29 Then Peter and the
other apostles answered and said, We
ought to obey God rather than men.
30 The God of our fathers raised up
Jesus, whom ye slew and hanged on
a tree. 31 Him hath God exalted
with his right hand *to be* a Prince
and a Saviour, for to give repentance
to Israel, and forgiveness of sins. 32
And we are his witnesses of these
things; and *so is* also the Holy
Ghost, whom God hath given to
them that obey him. 33 When they
heard *that*, they were cut *to the heart*,
and took counsel to slay them. 34
Then stood there up one in the council, a Pharisee, named Gamaliel, a
doctor of the law, had in reputation
among all the people, and commanded
to put the apostles forth a little
space; 35 And said unto them, Ye
men of Israel, take heed to yourselves what ye intend to do as touching these men. 36 For before these
days rose up Theudas, boasting himself to be somebody; to whom a
number of men, about four hundred,
joined themselves: who was slain;
and all, as many as obeyed him, were
scattered, and brought to nought. 37
After this man rose up Judas of Galilee in the days of the taxing, and
drew away much people after him:
he also perished; and all, *even* as
many as obeyed him, were dispersed.
38 And now I say unto you, Refrain
from these men, and let them alone:
for if this counsel or this work be of
men, it will come to nought: 39 But
if it be of God, ye cannot overthrow
it; lest haply ye be found even to
fight against God. 40 And to him
they agreed: and when they had
called the apostles, and beaten *them*,
they commanded that they should
not speak in the name of Jesus, and
let them go. 41 And they departed
from the presence of the council, rejoicing that they were counted worthy
to suffer shame for his name. 42
And daily in the temple, and in every
house, they ceased not to teach and
preach Jesus Christ.

We are not told what it was that the apostles preached to the people; no doubt it was according to the direction of the angel—*the words of this life;* but what passed between them and the council we have here an account of; for in their sufferings there appeared more of a divine power and energy than even in their preaching. Now here we have,

I. The seizing of the apostles a second time. We may think, if God designed this, "Why were they rescued from their first imprisonment?" But this was designed to humble the pride, and check the fury, of their persecutors; and now he would show that they were discharged, not because they feared a trial, for they were ready to surrender themselves and make their appearance before the greatest of their enemies. 1. They brought them without violence, with all the respect and tenderness that could be: did not pull them out of the pulpit, nor bind them, nor drag them along, but accosted them respectfully; and one would think they had reason to do so, in reverence to the temple, that holy place, and for fear of the apostles, lest they should strike them, as they did Ananias, or call for fire from heaven upon them, as Elias did; but all that restrained their violence was their fear of the people, who had such a veneration for the apostles that they would have stoned the officers if they had offered them any abuse. 2. Yet they brought them to those who, they knew, were violent against them, and were resolved to take violent courses with them (*v.* 27): They *brought them, to set them before the council,* as delinquents. Thus the powers that should have been a terror to evil works and workers became so to the good.

II. Their examination. Being brought before this august assembly, the high priest, as the mouth of the court, told them what it was they had to lay to their charge, *v.* 28. 1. That they had disobeyed the commands of authority, and would not submit to the injunctions and prohibitions given them (*v.* 28), "*Did not we,* by virtue of our authority, strictly charge and command you, upon pain of our highest displeasure, *that you should not teach in this name?* But you have disobeyed our commands, and gone on to preach not only without our licence, but against our express order." Thus those who make void the commandments of God are commonly very strict in binding on their own commandments, and insisting upon their own power: *Did not we command you?* Yes, they did; but did not Peter at the same time tell them that God's authority was superior to theirs, and his commands must take place of theirs? And they had forgotten this. 2. That they had spread false doctrine among the people, or at least a singular doctrine, which was not allowed by the Jewish church, nor agreed with what was delivered from Moses's chair. "*You have filled Jerusalem with your doctrine,* and thereby have disturbed the public peace, and drawn people from the public establishment." Some take this for a haughty scornful word: "This silly senseless doctrine of yours, that is not worth taking notice of, you have made such a noise with, that even Jerusalem, the great and holy city, is become full of it, and it is all the talk of the town." They are angry that men, whom they look upon as despicable, should make themselves thus considerable. 3. That they had a malicious design against the government, and aimed to stir up the people against it, by representing it as wicked and tyrannical, and as having made itself justly odious both to God and man: "*You intend to bring this man's blood,* the guilt of it before God, the shame of it before men, *upon us.*" Thus they charge them not only with contumacy and contempt of the court, but with sedition and faction, and a plot both to set the people against them, for having persecuted even to death not only so innocent but so good and great a man as this Jesus, and also the Romans, for having drawn them into it. See here how those who with a great deal of presumption will do an evil thing yet cannot bear to hear of it afterwards, nor to have it charged upon them. When they were in the heat of the persecution they could cry daringly enough, "*His blood be upon us and upon our children;* let us bear the blame for ever." But now that they have time for a cooler thought they take it as a great affront to have his blood laid at their door. Thus are they convicted and condemned by their own consciences, and dread lying under that guilt in which they were not afraid to involve themselves.

III. Their answer to the charge exhibited against them: *Peter and the other apostles* all spoke to the same purport; whether severally examined, or answering jointly, they spoke as one and the same Spirit gave them utterance, depending upon the promise their Master had made them, that, when they were brought before councils, it should be *given them in that same hour what they should speak,* and courage to speak it.

1. They justified themselves in their disobedience to the commands of the great sanhedrim, great as it was (*v.* 29): *We ought to obey God rather than men.* They do not plead the power they had to work miracles (this spoke sufficiently for them, and therefore they humbly decline mentioning it themselves), but they appeal to a maxim universally owned, which even natural conscience subscribes to, and which comes home to their case. God had commanded them to teach in the name of Christ, and therefore they ought to do it, though the chief priests forbade them. Note, Those rulers set up in opposition to God, and have a great deal to answer for, who punish men for disobedience to them in that which is their duty to God.

2. They justified themselves in doing what they could to fill Jerusalem with the doctrine of Christ, though, in preaching him up, they did indeed reflect upon those that maliciously ran him down, and if they thereby bring his blood upon them they may thank themselves. It is charged upon them as a crime that they preached Christ and his gospel. "Now," say they, "we will tell you who this Christ is, and what his gospel is, and then do you judge whether we ought not to preach it; nay, and we shall take this opportunity to preach it to you, *whether you will hear, or whether you will forbear.*"

(1.) The chief priests are told to their faces the indignities they did to this Jesus: "*You slew him and hanged him on a tree,* you cannot deny it." The apostles, instead of making an excuse, or begging their pardon, for bringing the guilt of this man's blood upon them, repeat the charge, and stand to it: "It was you that slew him; it was your act and deed." Note, People's being unwilling to hear of their faults is no good reason why they should not be faithfully told of them. It is a common excuse made for not reproving sin that the times will not bear it. But those whose office it is to reprove must not be awed by this; the times must bear it, and shall bear it. *Cry aloud and spare not;* cry aloud and fear not.

(2.) They are told also what honours God put upon this Jesus, and then let them judge who was in the right, the persecutors of his doctrine or the preachers of it. He calls God the *God of our fathers,* not only *ours,* but *yours,* to show that in preaching Christ they did not preach a new god, nor entice people to come and worship other gods; nor did they set up an institution contrary to that of Moses and the prophets, but they adhered to the God of the Jewish fathers; and that name of Christ which they preached answered the promises made to the fathers, and the covenant God entered into with them, and the types and figures of the law he gave them. The God of *Abraham, Isaac,* and *Jacob,* is the *God and Father of our Lord Jesus Christ;* see what honour he did him. [1.] He *raised him up;* he qualified him for, and called him to, his great undertaking, It seems to refer to the promise God made by Moses, *A prophet shall the Lord your God raise up unto you.* God raised him up out of obscurity, and made him great. Or, it may be meant of his raising him up from the grave: "You put him to death, but God has restored him to life, so that God and you are manifestly contesting about this Jesus; and which must we side with?" [2.] He *exalted him with his right hand,* ὕψωσε—*hath lifted him up.* "You loaded him with disgrace, but God has crowned him with honour; and ought we not to honour him whom God honours?" God has *exalted him,* τῇ δεξιᾷ αὐτοῦ—*with his right hand,* that is, by his power put forth; Christ is said to *live by the power of God.* Or, to his right hand, to sit there, to rest there, to rule there. "He has invested him with the highest dignity, and entrusted him with the highest authority, and therefore we must teach in his name, for God has *given him a name above every name.*" [3.] "He has appointed him to be *a prince and a Saviour,* and therefore we ought to preach in his name, and to publish the laws of his government as he is a prince, and the offers of his grace as he is a Saviour." Observe, There is no having Christ to be our Saviour, unless we be willing to take him for our prince. We cannot expect to be redeemed and healed by him, unless we give up ourselves to be ruled by him. The judges of old were saviours. Christ's ruling is in order to his saving, and faith takes an entire Christ, that came, not to save us in our sins, but to save us from our sins. [4.] He is appointed, as a prince and a Saviour, to *give repentance to Israel and remission of sins.* Therefore they must preach in his name to the people of Israel, for his favours were designed primarily and principally for them; and none that truly loved their country could be against this. Why should the rulers and elders of Israel oppose one who came with no less a blessing to Israel than repentance and pardon? Had he been exalted to give deliverance to Israel from the Roman yoke, and dominion over the neighbouring nations, the chief priests would have welcomed him with all their hearts. But repentance and remission of sins are blessings they neither value nor see their need of, and therefore they can by no means admit his doctrine. Observe here, *First,* Repentance and remission go together; wherever repentance is wrought, remission is without fail granted, and the favour is given to all those to whom is given the qualification for it. On the other hand, no remission without repentance; none are freed from the guilt and punishment of sin but those that are freed from the power and dominion of sin, that are turned from it and turned against it. *Secondly,* It is Jesus Christ that gives, and is authorized to give, both repentance and remission. Whatsoever is required in the gospel-covenant is promised. Are we appointed to repent? Christ is appointed to give repentance, by his Spirit working with the word, to awaken the conscience, to work contrition for sin, and an effectual change in the heart and life. The new heart is his work, and the broken spirit a sacrifice of his providing; and, when he has given repentance, if he should not give remission he would *forsake the work of his own hands.* See how necessary it is that we repent, and that we apply ourselves to Christ by faith for his grace to work repentance in us. [5.] All this is well attested, *First,* by the apostles themselves; they are ready to testify upon oath, if required, that they saw him alive after his resurrection, and saw him ascend into heaven; and also that they experienced the power of his grace upon their hearts, raising them up to that which was far above their natural capacities: "*We are his witnesses,* appointed by him to publish this to the world; and if we should be silent, as you would have us, we should betray a trust, and be false to it." When a cause is trying, witnesses, of all men, ought not to be silenced, for the issue of the cause depends on their testimony. *Secondly,* By the Spirit of God: "We are witnesses, competent ones, and whose testimony is sufficient before any human judicature." But this is not all: *The Holy Ghost is witness,* a witness from heaven; for God hath given his gifts and graces to those that obey Christ. Therefore we must preach in this name, because for this end the Holy Ghost is given us, whose operations we cannot stifle. Note, The giving of the Holy Ghost to obedient believers, not only to bring them to the obedience of faith, but to make them eminently useful therein, is a very strong proof of the truth of Christianity. God gave the Holy Ghost by his Son and in his name (John xiv. 26), and in answer to his prayer (John xiv. 16), nay, it was Christ that sent him from the Father (John xv. 26; xvi. 7), and this proves the glory to which the Father has exalted him. The great work of the Spirit being not only to justify Christ (1 Tim. iii. 16), but to glorify him, and all his gifts having a direct tendency to exalt his name, prove that his doctrine is divine. else it would not be carried on thus by divine power. And, *Lastly,* The giving of the Holy Ghost to those that obey Christ, both for their assistance in their obedience and as a present recompence for their obedience, is a plain evidence that it is the will of God that Christ should be obeyed; "judge then whether we ought to obey you in opposition to him."

IV. The impression which the apostles' defence of themselves made upon the court. It was contrary to what one would have expected from men that pretended to reason, learning, and sanctity. Surely such fair reasoning could not but clear the prisoners, and convert the judges. No, instead of yielding to it, they raged against it, and were filled, 1. With indignation at what the apostles said: They were *cut to the heart*, angry to see their own sin set in order before them; stark mad to find that the gospel of Christ had so much to say for itself, and consequently was likely to get ground. When a sermon was preached to the people to this purport, they were *pricked to the heart*, in remorse and godly sorrow, *ch.* ii. 37. These here were *cut to the heart* with rage and indignation. Thus the same gospel is to some a savour of life unto life, to others of death unto death. The enemies of the gospel not only deprive themselves of its comforts, but fill themselves with terrors, and are their own tormentors. 2. With malice against the apostles themselves. Since they see they cannot stop their mouths any other way than by stopping their breath, they *take counsel to slay them*, hoping that so they shall *cause the work to cease*. While the apostles went on in the service of Christ, with a holy security and serenity of mind, perfectly composed, and in a sweet enjoyment of themselves, their persecutors went on in their opposition to Christ, with a constant perplexity and perturbation of mind, and vexation to themselves.

V. The grave advice which Gamaliel, a leading man in the council, gave upon this occasion, the scope of which was to moderate the fury of these bigots, and check the violence of the prosecution. This Gamaliel is here said to be a *Pharisee* by his profession and sect, and by office a *doctor of the law*, one that studied the scriptures of the Old Testament, read lectures upon the sacred authors, and trained up pupils in the knowledge of them. Paul was brought up at his feet (*ch.* xxii. 3), and tradition says that so were Stephen and Barnabas. Some say he was the son of that Simeon that took up Christ in his arms, when he was presented in the temple, and grandson of the famous Hillel. He is here said to be *in reputation among all the people* for his wisdom and conduct, it appearing by this passage that he was a moderate man, and not apt to go in with furious measures. Men of temper and charity are justly had in reputation, for checking the incendiaries that otherwise would set the world on fire. Now observe here,

1. The necessary caution he gives to the council, with reference to the case before them: *He commanded to put the apostles forth a little while*, that he might speak the more freely, and be the more freely answered (it was fit that the prisoners should withdraw when their case was to be debated); and then put the house in mind of the importance of this matter, which in their heat they were not capable of considering as they ought: *You men of Israel*, saith he, *take heed to yourselves*, consider what you do, or *intend to do, as touching these men*, *v.* 35. It is not a common case, and therefore should not be hastily determined. He calls them *men of Israel*, to enforce this caution: "You are men, that should be governed by reason, be not then as *the horse and the mule that have no understanding;* you are men of Israel, that should be governed by revelation, be not then as strangers and heathens, that have no regard to God and his word. *Take heed to yourselves* now that you are angry with these men, lest you *meddle to your own hurt*." Note, The persecutors of God's people had best look to themselves, lest they fall into the pit which they dig. We have need to be cautious whom we give trouble to, lest we be found making the hearts of the righteous sad.

2. The cases he cites, to pave the way to his opinion. Two instances he gives of factious seditious men (such as they would have the apostles thought to be), whose attempts came to nothing of themselves; whence he infers that if these men were indeed such as they represented them their cause would sink with its own weight, and Providence would infatuate and defeat them, and then they needed not persecute them.

(1.) There was one *Theudas*, that made a mighty noise for awhile, as one sent of God, *boasting himself to be somebody*, *some great one* (so the word is), either a teacher or a prince, with a divine commission to effect some great revolution in the church or in the state; and he observes here (*v.* 36) concerning him, [1.] How far he prevailed: "*A number of men, about four hundred* in all, joined themselves to him, that knew not what to do with themselves, or hoped to better themselves; and they seemed then a formidable body." [2.] How soon his pretensions were all dashed: "When *he was slain*" (probably in war) "there needed no more ado, *all, as many as obeyed him, were scattered*, and melted away like snow before the sun. Now compare that case with this. You have slain Jesus, the ringleader of this faction; you have taken him off. Now if he was, as you say he was, an impostor and pretender, his death, like that of Theudas, will be the death of his cause, and the final dispersion of his followers." From what has been we may infer what will be in a like case; the smiting of the shepherd will be the scattering of the sheep: and, if the God of peace had not *brought again from the dead that great Shepherd*, the dispersion of the sheep, at his death, had been total and final.

(2.) The case was the same with *Judas of Galilee*, *v.* 37. Observe, [1.] The attempt he made. It is said to be *after this*, which some read, *besides this*, or, Let me mention, *after this*,—supposing that Judas's insurrection was long before that of Theudas; for it was *in the time of the taxation*, namely, that at our Saviour's birth (Luke ii. 1), and that of Theudas, whom Josephus speaks of, that mutinied, in the time of *Cuspius Fadus;* but this was in the days of Claudius Cæsar, some years after Gamaliel spoke this, and therefore could not be the same. It is not easy to determine particularly when these events happened, nor whether this taxing was the same with that at our Saviour's birth or one of a later date. Some think this Judas of Galilee was the same with Judas Gaulonites, whom Josephus speaks of, others not. It is probable that they were cases which lately happened, and were fresh in memory. This *Judas drew away much people after him,* who gave credit to his pretensions. But, [2.] Here is the defeat of his attempt, and that without any interposal of the great sanhedrim, or any decree of theirs against him (it did not need it); *he also perished, and all, even as many as obeyed him,* or were persuaded by him, were dispersed. Many have foolishly thrown away their lives, and brought others into the same snares, by a jealousy for their liberties, *in the days of the taxing,* who had better have been content, when Providence had so determined, *to serve the king of Babylon.*

3. His opinion upon the whole matter.

(1.) That they should not persecute the apostles (*v.* 38): *Now I say unto you,* τὰ νῦν—*for the present,* as the matter now stands, my advice is, "*Refrain from these men;* neither punish them for what they have done nor restrain them for the future. Connive at them; let them take their course; *let not our hand be upon them.*" It is uncertain whether he spoke this out of policy, for fear of offending either the people or the Romans and making further mischief. The apostles did not attempt any thing by outward force. The weapons of their warfare were not carnal; and therefore why should any outward force be used against them? Or, whether he was under any present convictions, at least of the probability of the truth of the Christian doctrine, and thought it deserved better treatment, at least a fair trial. Or, whether it was only the language of a mild quiet spirit, that was against persecution for conscience' sake. Or, whether God put this word into his mouth beyond his own intention, for the deliverance of the apostles at this time. We are sure there was an overruling Providence in it, that the servants of Christ might not only come off, but come off honourably.

(2.) That they should refer this matter to Providence: "Wait the issue, and see what it will come to. *If it be of men, it will come to nought* of itself; *if of God, it will stand,* in spite of all your powers and policies." That which is apparently wicked and immoral must be suppressed, else the magistrate bears the sword in vain; but that which has a show of good, and it is doubtful whether it be of God or men, it is best to let it alone, and let it take its fate, not to use any external force for the suppressing of it. Christ rules by the power of truth, not of the sword. What Christ asked concerning John's baptism, *Was it from heaven or of men?* was a question proper to be asked concerning the apostles' doctrine and baptism, which followed Christ, as John Baptist's went before him. Now they, having owned, concerning the former, that they could not tell whether it was from heaven or of men, ought not to be too confident concerning the latter. But, take it which way you will, it is a reason why they should not be persecuted. [1.] "If this *counsel, and this work,* this forming of a society, and incorporating it in the name of Jesus, *be of men, it will come to nothing.* If it be the counsel and work of foolish crack-brained men that know not what they do, let them alone awhile, and they will run themselves out of breath, and *their folly will be manifest before all men,* and they will make themselves ridiculous. If it be the counsel and work of politic and designing men, who under colour of religion are setting up a secular interest, let them alone awhile, and they will throw off the mask, and their knavery will be manifest to all men, and they will make themselves odious; Providence will never countenance it. *It will come to nothing* in a little time; and, if so, your persecuting and opposing it is very needless; there is no occasion for giving yourselves so much trouble, and bringing such an odium upon yourselves, to kill that which, if you give it a little time, will die of itself. The unnecessary use of power is an abuse of it. But," [2.] "If it should prove (and as wise men as you have been mistaken) *that this counsel and this work is of God,* that these preachers have their commissions and instructions from him, that they are as truly his messengers to the world as the Old-Testament prophets were, then what do you think of persecuting them, of this attempt of yours (*v.* 33) *to slay them?* You must conclude it to be," *First,* "A fruitless attempt against them: *If it be of God, you cannot overthrow it;* for *there is no wisdom nor counsel against the Lord; he that sits in heaven laughs at you.*" It may be the comfort of all who are sincerely on God's side, who have a single eye to his will as their rule and his glory as their end, that whatsoever is of God cannot be overthrown totally and finally, though it may be very vigorously opposed; it may be run upon, but cannot be run down. *Secondly,* "A dangerous attempt to yourselves. Pray let it alone, *lest haply you be found even to fight against God;* and I need not tell you who will come off by the worse in that contest." *Woe unto him that strives with his Maker;* for he will not only be overcome as an impotent enemy, but severely reckoned with as a rebel and traitor against his rightful prince. Those that hate and abuse God's faithful people, that restrain and silence his faithful ministers, fight against God, for he takes what is done against them as done against himself. *Whoso touches them, touches the apple of his eye.* Well, this was the advice of Gamaliel: we wish it were duly considered by those that persecute for conscience' sake, for it was a good thought, and natural enough, though we are uncertain what the man was. The tradition of the Jewish writers is that, for all this, he lived and died an inveterate enemy to Christ and his gospel; and though (now at least) he was not for persecuting the followers of Christ, yet he was the man who composed that prayer which the Jews use to this day for the extirpating of Christians and Christianity. On the contrary, the tradition of the Papists is that he turned Christian, and became an eminent patron of Christianity and a follower of Paul, who had formerly sat at his feet. If it had been so, it is very probable that we should have heard of him somewhere in the *Acts* or *Epistles.*

VI. The determination of the council upon the whole matter, *v.* 40. 1. Thus far they agreed with Gamaliel that they let fall the design of putting the apostles to death. They saw a great deal of reason in what Gamaliel said, and, for the present, it gave some check to their fury, and a remainder of their wrath was restrained by it. 2. Yet they could not forbear giving some vent to their rage (so outrageous was it) contrary to the convictions of their judgments and consciences; for, though they were advised to let them alone, yet, (1.) *They beat them,* scourged them as malefactors, stripped them, and whipped them, as they used to do in the synagogues, and notice is taken (*v.* 41) of the ignominy of it. Thus they thought to make them ashamed of preaching, and the people ashamed of hearing them; as Pilate scourged our Saviour to expose him, when yet he declared he found no fault in him. (2.) *They commanded them that they should not speak* any more *in the name of Jesus,* that, if they could find no other fault with their preaching, they might have this ground to reproach it, that it was against law, and not only without the permission, but against the express order of their superiors.

VII. The wonderful courage and constancy of the apostles in the midst of all these injuries and indignities done them. When they were dismissed *they departed from the council,* and we do not find one word they said by way of reflection upon the court and the unjust treatment given them. *When they were reviled they reviled not again; and when they suffered they threatened not; but committed their cause to him* to whom Gamaliel had referred it, even *to a God who judgeth righteously.* All their business was to preserve the possession of their own souls, and to make full proof of their ministry, notwithstanding the opposition given them; and both these they did to admiration.

1. They bore their sufferings with an invincible cheerfulness (*v.* 41): When *they went out,* perhaps with the marks of the lashes given them on their arms and hands appearing, hissed at by the servants and rabble, it may be, or public notice given of the infamous punishment they had undergone, instead of being ashamed of Christ, and their relation to him, *they rejoiced that they were counted worthy to suffer shame for his name.* They were men, and men in reputation, that had never done any thing to make themselves vile, and therefore could not but have a sense of the shame they suffered, which, it should seem, was more grievous to them than the smart, as it usually is to ingenuous minds; but they considered that it was for the name of Christ that they were thus abused, because they belonged to him and served his interest, and their sufferings should be made to contribute to the further advancement of his name; and therefore, (1.) They reckoned it an honour, looked upon it *that they were counted worthy to suffer shame,* κατηξιώθησαν ἀτιμασθῆναι—*that they were honoured to be dishonoured for Christ.* Reproach for Christ is true preferment, as it makes us conformable to his pattern and serviceable to his interest. (2.) They rejoiced in it, remembering what their Master had said to them at their first setting out (Matt. v. 11, 12): *When men shall revile you, and persecute you, rejoice and be exceedingly glad.* They rejoiced, not only though they suffered shame (their troubles did not diminish their joy), but *that they suffered shame;* their troubles increased their joy, and added to it. If we suffer ill for doing well, provided we suffer it well, and as we should, we ought to rejoice in that grace which enables us so to do.

2. They went on in their work with indefatigable diligence (*v.* 42): They were punished for preaching, and were commanded *not to preach,* and *yet they ceased not to teach and preach;* they omitted no opportunity, nor abated any thing of their zeal or forwardness. Observe, (1.) When they preached—*daily;* not only on sabbath days, or on Lord's days, but every day, as duly as the day came, without intermitting any day, as their Master did (Matt. xxvi. 55, Luke xix. 47), not fearing that they should either kill themselves or cloy their hearers. (2.) Where they preached—both publicly *in the temple,* and privately *in every house;* in promiscuous assemblies, to which all resorted, and in the select assemblies of Christians for special ordinances. They did not think that either one would excuse them from the other, for the word must be *preached in season and out of season.* Though in the temple they were more exposed, and under the eye of their enemies, yet they did not confine themselves to their little oratories in their own houses, but ventured into the post of danger; and though they had the liberty of the temple, a consecrated place, yet they made no difficulty of preaching in houses, in every house, even the poorest cottage. They visited the families of those that were under their charge, and gave particular instructions to them ac-

cording as their case required, even to the children and servants. (3.) What was the subject matter of their preaching: *They preached Jesus Christ;* they preached concerning him; and this was not all, they preached him up, they proposed him to those who heard them, *to be their prince and Saviour.* They did *not preach themselves, but Christ,* as faithful friends to the bridegroom, making it their business to advance his interest. This was the preaching that gave most offence to the priests, who were willing they should preach any thing but Christ; but they would not alter their subject to please them. It ought to be the constant business of gospel ministers to preach Christ; *Christ, and him crucified; Christ, and him glorified;* nothing besides this but what is reducible to it.

CHAP. VI.

In this chapter we have, I. The discontent that was among the disciples about the distribution of the public charity, ver. 1. II. The election and ordination of seven men, who should take care of that matter, and ease the apostles of the burden, ver. 2—6. III. The increase of the church, by the addition of many to it, ver. 7. IV. A particular account of Stephen, one of the seven. 1. His great activity for Christ, ver. 8. 2. The opposition he met with from the enemies of Christianity, and his disputes with them, ver. 9, 10. 3. The convening of him before the great sanhedrim, and the crimes laid to his charge, ver. 11—14. 4. God's owning him upon his trial, ver. 15.

AND in those days, when the
number of the disciples was
multiplied, there arose a murmuring
of the Grecians against the Hebrews,
because their widows were neglected
in the daily ministration. 2 Then
the twelve called the multitude of the
disciples *unto them,* and said, It is
not reason that we should leave the
word of God, and serve tables. 3
Wherefore, brethren, look ye out
among you seven men of honest report, full of the Holy Ghost and wisdom, whom we may appoint over
this business. 4 But we will give
ourselves continually to prayer, and
to the ministry of the word. 5 And
the saying pleased the whole multitude: and they chose Stephen, a
man full of faith and of the Holy
Ghost, and Philip, and Prochorus,
and Nicanor, and Timon, and Par-
menas, and Nicolas a proselyte of
Antioch: 6 Whom they set before
the apostles: and when they had
prayed, they laid *their* hands on
them. 7 And the word of God increased; and the number of the disciples multiplied in Jerusalem greatly;
and a great company of the priests
were obedient to the faith.

Having seen the church's struggles with her enemies, and triumphed with her in her victories, we now come to take a view of the administration of her affairs at home; and here we have,

I. An unhappy disagreement among some of the church-members, which might have been of ill consequence, but was prudently accommodated and taken up in time (*v.* 1): *When the number of the disciples* (for so Christians were at first called, learners of Christ) *was multiplied* to many thousands in Jerusalem, *there arose a murmuring.*

1. It does our hearts good to find *that the number of the disciples is multiplied,* as, no doubt, it vexed *the priests and Sadducees* to the heart to see it. The opposition that the preaching of the gospel met with, instead of checking its progress, contributed to the success of it; and this infant Christian church, like the infant Jewish church in Egypt, *the more it was afflicted, the more it multiplied.* The preachers were beaten, threatened, and abused, and yet the people received their doctrine, invited, no doubt, thereto by their wonderful patience and cheerfulness under their trials, which convinced men that they were borne up and carried on by a better spirit than their own.

2. Yet it casts a damp upon us to find that the multiplying of the disciples proves an occasion of discord. Hitherto *they were all with one accord.* This had been often taken notice of to their honour; but now that they were multiplied they began to murmur; as in the old world, *when men began to multiply, they corrupted themselves. Thou hast multiplied the nation, and not increased their joy,* Isa. ix. 3. When Abraham and Lot increased their families, *there was a strife between their herdsmen;* so it was here: *There arose a murmuring,* not an open falling out, but a secret heart-burning.

(1.) The complainants were *the Grecians,* or Hellenists, *against the Hebrews*—the Jews that were scattered in Greece, and other parts, who ordinarily spoke the Greek tongue, and read the Old Testament in the Greek version, and not the original Hebrew, many of whom being at Jerusalem at the feast embraced the faith of Christ, and were added to the church, and so continued there. These complained against the Hebrews, the native Jews, that used the original Hebrew of the Old Testament. Some of each of these became Christians, and, it seems, their joint-embracing of the faith of Christ did not prevail, as it ought to have done, to extinguish the little jealousies they had one of another before their conversion, but they retained somewhat of that old leaven; not understanding, or not remembering, *that in Christ Jesus there is neither Greek nor Jew,* no distinction of Hebrew and Hellenist, but all are alike welcome to Christ, and should be, for his sake, dear to one another.

(2.) The complaint of these Grecians was *that their widows were neglected in the daily administration,* that is, in the distribution of the public charity, and the Hebrew widows had more care taken of them. Observe, The first contention in the Christian church was about a money-matter; but it is a pity *that the little things of this world* should be make-bates among those that profess to be taken up with *the great things of another world*. A great deal of money was gathered for the relief of the poor, but, as often happens in such cases, it was impossible to please every body in the laying of it out. *The apostles, at whose feet it was laid,* did their best to dispose of it so as to answer the intentions of the donors, and no doubt designed to do it with the utmost impartiality, and were far from respecting the Hebrews more than the Grecians; and yet here they are complained to, and tacitly complained of, *that the Grecian widows were neglected;* though they were as real objects of charity, yet they had not so much allowed them, or not to so many, or not so duly paid them, as the Hebrews. Now, [1.] Perhaps this complaint was groundless and unjust, and there was no cause for it; but those who, upon any account, lie under disadvantages (as the Grecian Jews did, in comparison with those that were Hebrews of the Hebrews) are apt to be jealous that they are slighted when really they are not so; and it is the common fault of poor people that, instead of being thankful for what is given them, they are querulous and clamorous, and apt to find fault that more is not given them, or that more is given to others than to them; and there are envy and covetousness, those roots of bitterness, to be found among the poor as well as among the rich, notwithstanding the humbling providences they are under, and should accommodate themselves to. But, [2.] We will suppose there might be some occasion for their complaint. *First,* Some suggest that though their other poor were well provided for, yet their widows were neglected, because the managers governed themselves by an ancient rule which the Hebrews observed, *that a widow was to be maintained by her husband's children.* See 1 Tim. v. 4. But, *Secondly,* I take it that the widows are here put for all the poor, because many of those that were in the church-book, and received alms, were widows, who were well provided for by the industry of their husbands while they lived, but were reduced to straits when they were gone. As those that have the administration of public justice ought in a particular manner to protect widows from injury (Isa. i. 17; Luke xviii. 3); so those that have the administration of public charity ought in a particular manner to provide for widows what is necessary. See 1 Tim. v. 3. And observe, The widows here, and the other poor, had a daily ministration; perhaps they wanted forecast, and could not save for hereafter, and therefore the managers of the fund, in kindness to them, gave them day by day their daily bread; they lived from hand to mouth. Now, it seems, the Grecian widows were, comparatively, neglected. Perhaps those that disposed of the money considered that there was more brought into the fund by the rich Hebrews than by the rich Grecians, who had not estates to sell, as the Hebrews had, and therefore the poor Grecians should have less out of the fund; this, though there was some tolerable reason for it, they thought hard and unfair. Note, In the best-ordered church in the world there will be something amiss, some mal-administration or other, some grievances, or at least some complaints; those are the best that have the least and the fewest.

II. The happy accommodating of this matter, and the expedient pitched upon for the taking away of the cause of this murmuring. The apostles had hitherto the directing of the matter. Applications were made to them, and appeals in cases of grievances. They were obliged to employ persons under them, who did not take all the care they might have taken, nor were so well fortified as they should have been against temptations to partiality; and therefore some persons must be chosen to manage this matter who have more leisure to attend to it than the apostles had, and were better qualified for the trust than those whom the apostles employed were. Now observe,

1. How the method was proposed by the apostles: They *called the multitude of the disciples unto them,* the heads of the congregations of Christians in Jerusalem, the principal leading men. The twelve themselves would not determine any thing without them, for *in multitude of counsellors there is safety;* and in an affair of this nature those might be best able to advise who were more conversant in the affairs of this life than the apostles were.

(1.) The apostles urge that they could by no means admit so great a diversion, as this would be, from their great work (*v.* 2): *It is not reasonable that we should leave the word of God and serve tables.* The receiving and paying of money was serving tables, too like *the tables of the money-changers in the temple.* This was foreign to the business which the apostles were called to. They were *to preach the word of God;* and though they had not such occasion to study for what they preached as we have (it being *given in that same hour what they should speak*), yet they thought that was work enough for a whole man, and to employ all their thoughts, and cares, and time, though one man of them was more than ten of us, *than ten thousand.* If they serve tables, they must, in some measure, *leave the word of God;* they could not attend their preaching work so closely as they ought. *Pectora nostra duas non admittentia curas—These minds of ours admit not of two distinct anxious employments.* Though this serving of tables was for pious uses, and serving the charity of rich Christians and the necessity of poor Christians, and in both serving Christ, yet the apostles would not take so much time from their preaching as this would require. They will no more be drawn from their preaching by the money laid at their feet than they will be driven from it by the stripes laid on their backs. While the number of the disciples was small, the apostles might manage this matter without making it any considerable interruption to their main business; but, now that their number was increased, they could not do it. *It is not reason, οὐκ ἀρεστόν ἐστιν—it is not fit,* or commendable, that we should neglect the business of feeding souls with the bread of life, to attend the business of relieving the bodies of the poor. Note, Preaching the gospel is the best work, and the most proper and needful that a minister can be employed in, and that which he must give himself wholly to (1 Tim. iv. 15), which that he may do, he must not entangle himself in the affairs of this life (2 Tim. ii. 4), no, not in the outward business of the house of God, Neh. xi. 16.

(2.) They therefore desire *that seven men* might be chosen, well qualified for the purpose, whose business it should be *to serve tables, διακονεῖν τραπέζαις—to be deacons to the tables, v.* 2. The business must be minded, must be better minded than it had been, and than the apostles could mind it; and therefore proper persons must be chosen, who, though they might be occasionally employed in the word, and prayer, were not so entirely devoted to it as the apostles were; and these must take care of the church's stock—must review, and pay, and keep accounts—must *buy those things which they had need of against the feast* (John xiii. 29), and attend to all those things which are necessary *in ordine ad spiritualia—in order to spiritual exercises,* that every thing might be done decently and in order, and no person nor thing neglected. Now,

[1.] The persons must be duly qualified. The people are to choose, and the apostles to ordain; but the people have no authority to choose, nor the apostles to ordain, men utterly unfit for the office: *Look out seven men;* so many they thought might suffice for the present, more might be added afterwards if there were occasion. These must be, *First, Of honest report,* men free from scandal, that were looked upon by their neighbours as men of integrity, and faithful men, well attested, as men that might be trusted, not under a blemish for any vice, but, on the contrary, well spoken of for every thing that is virtuous and praiseworthy; *μαρτυρουμένους —men that can produce good testimonials* concerning their conversation. Note, Those that are employed in any office in the church ought to be men of honest report, of a blameless, nay, of an admirable character, which is requisite not only to the credit of their office, but to the due discharge of it. *Secondly,* They must be *full of the Holy Ghost,* must be filled with those gifts and graces of the Holy Ghost which were necessary to the right management of this trust. They must not only be honest men, but they must be men of ability and men of courage; such as were to be made judges in Israel (Exod. xviii. 21), *able men, fearing God; men of truth, and hating covetousness;* and hereby appearing to be *full of the Holy Ghost. Thirdly,* They must be *full of wisdom.* It was not enough that they were honest, good men, but they must be discreet, judicious men, that could not be imposed upon, and would order things for the best, and with consideration: *full of the Holy Ghost, and wisdom,* that is, of the Holy Ghost as a Spirit of wisdom. We find the word of wisdom given by the Spirit, as distinct from the word of knowledge by the same Spirit, 1 Cor. xii. 8. Those must be full of wisdom who are entrusted with public money, that it may be disposed of, not only with fidelity, but with frugality.

[2.] The people must nominate the persons: "*Look you out among yourselves seven men;* consider among yourselves who are the fittest for such a trust, and whom you can with the most satisfaction confide in." They might be presumed to know better, or at least were fitter to enquire, what character men had, than the apostles; and therefore they are entrusted with the choice.

[3.] The apostles will ordain them to the service, will give them their charge, that they may know what they have to do and make conscience of doing it, and give them their authority, that the persons concerned may know whom they are to apply to, and submit to, in affairs of that nature: *Men, whom we may appoint.* In many editions of our English Bibles there has been an error of the press here; for they have read it, *whom ye may appoint,* as if the power were in the people; whereas it was certainly in the apostles: *whom we may appoint over this business,* to take care of it, and to see that there be neither waste nor want.

(3.) The apostles engage to addict themselves wholly to their work as ministers, and the more closely if they can but get fairly quit of this troublesome office (*v.* 4): *We will give ourselves continually to prayer, and to the ministry of the word.* See here, [1.] What are the two great gospel ordinances—*the word, and prayer;* by these two communion between God and his people is kept up and maintained; by the word he speaks to them, and by prayer they speak to him; and these have a mutual reference to each other. By these two the kingdom of Christ must be advanced, and additions made to it; we must *prophesy upon the dry bones,* and *then pray for a spirit of life* from God *to enter into them.* By the word and prayer other ordinances are sanctified to us, and sacraments have their efficacy. [2.] What is the great business of gospel ministers—to give themselves continually to prayer, and to the ministry of the word; they must still be either fitting and furnishing themselves for those services, or employing themselves in them; either publicly or privately; in the stated times, or out of them. They must be God's mouth to the people in the ministry of the word, and the people's mouth to God in prayer. In order to the conviction and conversion of sinners, and the edification and consolation of saints, we must not only offer up our prayers for them, but we must minister the word to them, seconding our prayers with our endeavours, in the use of appointed means. Nor must we only minister the word to them, but we must pray for them, that it may be effectual; for God's grace can do all without our preaching, but our preaching can do nothing without God's grace. The apostles were endued with extraordinary gifts of the Holy Ghost, tongues and miracles; and yet that to which they gave themselves continually was preaching and praying, by which they might edify the church: and those ministers, without doubt, are the successors of the apostles (not in the plenitude of the apostolical power—those are daring usurpers who pretend to this, but in the best and most excellent of the apostolical works) who give themselves continually to prayer, and to the ministry of the word; and such Christ will always be with, *even to the end of the world.*

2. How this proposal was agreed to, and presently put in execution, by the disciples. It was not imposed upon them by an absolute power, though they might have been bold in Christ to do this (Philem. 8), but proposed, as that which was highly convenient, and *then the saying pleased the whole multitude, v.* 5. It pleased them to see the apostles so willing to have themselves discharged from intermeddling in secular affairs, and to transmit them to others; it pleased them to hear that they would give themselves to the word and prayer; and therefore they neither disputed the matter nor deferred the execution of it.

(1.) They pitched upon the persons. It is not probable that they all cast their eye upon the same men. Every one had his friend, whom he thought well of. But the majority of votes fell upon the persons here named; and the rest both of the candidates and the electors acquiesced, and made no disturbance, as the members of societies in such cases ought to do. An apostle, who was an extraordinary officer, was chosen by lot, which is more immediately the act of God; but the overseers of the poor were chosen by the suffrage of the people, in which yet a regard is to be had to the providence of God, who has all men's hearts and tongues in his hand. We have a list of the persons chosen. Some think they were such as were before of the seventy disciples; but this is not likely, for they were ordained by Christ himself, long since, *to preach the gospel;* and there was no more reason that they should leave the word of God to serve tables than that the apostles should. It is therefore more probable that they were of those that were converted since the pouring out of the Spirit; for it was promised to all that would be baptized that they should *receive the gift of the Holy Ghost;* and the gift, according to that promise, is that fulness of the Holy Ghost which was required in those that were to be chosen to this service. We may further conjecture, concerning these seven, [1.] That they were such as had sold their estates, and brought the money into the common stock; for, *cæteris paribus—other things being equal,* those were fittest to be entrusted with the distribution of it who had been most generous in the contribution to it. [2.] That these seven were all of the Grecian or Hellenist Jews, for they have all Greek names, and this would be most likely *to silence the murmurings of the Grecians* (which occasioned this institution), to have the trust lodged in those that were foreigners, like themselves, who would be sure not to neglect them. *Nicolas,* it is plain, was one of them, for he was *a proselyte of Antioch;* and some think the manner of expression intimates that they were all proselytes of Jerusalem, as he was of Antioch. The first named is *Stephen,* the glory of these *septemviri, a man full of faith and of the Holy Ghost;* he had a strong faith in the doctrine of Christ, and was full of it above most; *full of fidelity, full of courage* (so some), for he was *full of the Holy Ghost,* of his gifts and graces. He was an extraordinary man, and excelled in every thing that was good; his name signifies *a crown. Philip* is put next, because he, having *used this office of a deacon well, thereby obtained a good degree,* and was afterwards ordained to the office of an evangelist, a companion and assistant to the apostles, for so he is expressly called, *ch.* xxi. 8. Compare Eph. iv. 11. And his preaching and baptizing (which we read of *ch.* viii. 12) were certainly not as a deacon (for it is plain that that office was *serving tables,* in opposition *to the ministry of the word),* but as an evangelist; and, when he was preferred to that office, we have reason to think he quitted this office, as incompatible with that. As for *Stephen,* nothing we find done by him proves him to be a preacher of the gospel; for he only disputes in the schools, and pleads for his life at the bar, *v.* 9, and *ch.* vii. 2. The last named is *Nicolas,* who, some say, afterwards degenerated (as the Judas among these seven) and was the founder of *the sect of the Nicolaitans* which we read of (Rev. ii. 6, 15), and which Christ there says, once and again, was a thing he hated. But some of the ancients clear him from this charge, and tell us that, though that vile impure sect denominated themselves from him, yet it was unjustly, and because he only insisted much upon it *that those that had wives should be as though they had none,* thence they wickedly inferred *that those that had wives should have them in common,* which therefore Tertullian, when he speaks of the community of goods, particularly excepts: *Omnia indiscreta apud nos, præter uxores—All things are common among us, except our wives.*—Apol. cap. 39.

(2.) The apostles appointed them to this work of serving tables for the present, *v.* 6. The people presented them to the apostles, who approved their choice, and ordained them. [1.] They prayed with them, and for them, that God would give them more and more of the Holy Ghost and of wisdom—that he would qualify them for the service to which they were called, and own them in it, and make them thereby a blessing to the church, and particularly to the poor of the flock. All that are employed in the service of the church ought to be committed to the conduct of the divine grace by the prayers of the church. [2.] *They laid their hands on them,* that is, *they blessed them in the name of the Lord,* for laying on hands was used in blessing; so *Jacob blessed both the sons of Joseph;* and, without controversy, *the less is blessed of the greater* (Heb. vii. 7); the deacons are blessed by the apostles, and the overseers of the poor by the pastors of the congregation. Having by prayer implored a blessing upon them, they did by the laying on of hands assure them that the blessing was conferred in answer to the prayer; and this was giving them authority to execute that office, and laying an obligation upon the people to be observant of them therein.

III. The advancement of the church hereupon. When things were thus put into good order in the church (grievances were redressed and discontents silenced) then religion got ground, *v.* 7. 1. *The word of God increased.* Now that the apostles resolved to stick more closely than ever to their preaching, it spread the gospel further, and brought it home with the more power. Ministers disentangling themselves from secular employments, and addicting themselves entirely and vigorously to their work, will contribute very much, as a means, to the success of the gospel. The word of God is said to increase as the seed sown increases when it comes up again thirty, sixty, a hundred fold. 2. Christians became numerous: *The number of the disciples multiplied in Jerusalem greatly.* When Christ was upon earth, his ministry had least success in Jerusalem; yet now that city affords most converts. God has his remnant even in the worst of places. 3. *A great company of the priests were obedient to the faith. Then* is the word and grace of God greatly magnified when those are wrought upon by it that were least likely, as the priests here, who either had opposed it, or at least were linked in with those that had. The priests, whose preferments arose from the law of Moses, were yet willing to let them go for the gospel of Christ; and, it should seem, they came *in a body:* many of them agreed together, for the keeping up of one another's credit, and the strengthening of one another's hands, to join at once in giving up their names to Christ: πολὺς ὄχλος—*a great crowd of priests* were by the grace of God helped over their prejudices, and *were obedient to the faith,* so their conversion is described. (1.) They embraced the doctrine of the gospel; their understandings were captivated to the power of the truths of Christ, and every opposing objecting thought brought into obedience to him, 2 Cor. x. 4, 5. The gospel is said to be *made known for the obedience of faith,* Rom. xvi. 26. Faith is an act of obedience, for this is God's commandment, *that we believe,* 1 John iii. 23. (2.) They evinced the sincerity of their believing the gospel of Christ by a cheerful compliance with all the rules and precepts of the gospel. The design of the gospel is to refine and reform our hearts and lives; faith gives law to us, and we must be obedient to it.

8 And Stephen, full of faith and
power, did great wonders and miracles among the people. 9 Then
there arose certain of the synagogue,
which is called *the synagogue* of the
Libertines, and Cyrenians, and Alexandrians, and of them of Cilicia and
of Asia, disputing with Stephen. 10
And they were not able to resist the
wisdom and the spirit by which he
spake. 11 Then they suborned men,
which said, We have heard him speak
blasphemous words against Moses,
and *against* God. 12 And they
stirred up the people, and the elders,
and the scribes, and came upon *him,*
and caught him, and brought *him* to
the council, 13 And set up false
witnesses, which said, This man
ceaseth not to speak blasphemous
words against this holy place, and the
law: 14 For we have heard him
say, that this Jesus of Nazareth shall
destroy this place, and shall change
the customs which Moses delivered
us. 15 And all that sat in the
council, looking stedfastly on him,
saw his face as it had been the face
of an angel.

Stephen, no doubt was diligent and faithful in the discharge of his office as distributor of the church's charity, and laid out himself to put that affair in a good method, which he did to universal satisfaction; and though it appears here that he was a man of uncommon gifts, and fitted for a higher station, yet, being called to that office, he did not think it below him to do the duty of it. And, being faithful in a little, he was entrusted with more; and, though we do not find him propagating the gospel by preaching and baptizing, yet we find him here called out to very honourable services, and owned in them.

I. He proved the truth of the gospel, by working miracles in Christ's name, *v.* 8. 1. He was *full of faith and power*, that is, of a strong faith, by which he was enabled to do great things. Those that are full of faith are full of power, because by faith the power of God is engaged for us. His faith did so fill him that it left no room for unbelief and made room for the influences of divine grace, so that, as the prophet speaks, he was *full of power by the Spirit of the Lord of hosts,* Mic. iii. 8. By faith we are emptied of self, and so are filled with Christ, who is the *wisdom of God and the power of God.* 2. Being so *he did great wonders and miracles among the people,* openly, and in the sight of all; for Christ's miracles feared not the strictest scrutiny. It is not strange that Stephen, though he was not a preacher by office, did these great wonders, for we find that these were distinct gifts of the Spirit, and divided severally, for *to one was given the working of miracles, and to another prophecy,* 1 Cor. xii. 10, 11. And *these signs followed* not only those that preached, but those that believed. Mark xvi. 17.

II. He pleaded the cause of Christianity against those that opposed it, and argued against it (*v.* 9, 10); he served the interests of religion as a disputant, in the high places of the field, while others were serving them as vinedressers and husbandmen.

1. We are here told who were his opponents, *v.* 9. They were Jews, but Hellenist Jews, Jews of the dispersion, who seem to have been more zealous for their religion than the native Jews; it was with difficulty that they retained the practice and profession of it in the country where they lived, where they were as speckled birds, and not without great expense and toil that they kept up their attendance at Jerusalem, and this made them more active sticklers for Judaism than those were whose profession of their religion was cheap and easy. They were *of the synagogue which is called the synagogue of the Libertines;* the Romans called those *Liberti,* or *Libertini,* who either, being foreigners, were naturalized, or, being slaves by birth, were manumitted, or made freemen. Some think that these Libertines were such of the Jews as had obtained the Roman freedom, as Paul had (*ch.* xxii. 27, 28); and it is probable that he was the most forward man of this synagogue of the Libertines in disputing with Stephen, and engaged others in the dispute, for we find him busy in the stoning of Stephen, and consenting to his death. There were others that belonged to the synagogue of the Cyrenians and Alexandrians, of which synagogue the Jewish writers speak; and others that belonged to their synagogue who were of Cilicia and Asia; and if Paul, as a freeman of Rome, did not belong to the synagogue of the Libertines, he belonged to this, as a native of Tarsus, a city of Cilicia: it is probable that he might be a member of both. The Jews that were born in other countries, and had concerns in them, had frequent occasion, not only to resort to, but to reside in, Jerusalem. Each nation had its synagogue, as in London there are French, and Dutch, and Danish churches: and those synagogues were the schools to which the Jews of those nations sent their youth to be educated in the Jewish learning. Now those that were tutors and professors in these synagogues, seeing the gospel grow, and the rulers conniving at the growth of it, and fearing what would be the consequence of it to the Jewish religion, which they were jealous for, being confident of the goodness of their cause, and their own sufficiency to manage it, would undertake to run down Christianity by force of argument. It was a fair and rational way of dealing with it, and what religion is always ready to admit. *Produce your cause, saith the Lord, bring forth your strong reasons,* Isa. xli. 21. But why did they dispute with Stephen? And why not with the apostles themselves? (1.) Some think because they despised the apostles as *unlearned and ignorant men,* whom they thought it below them to engage with; but Stephen was bred a scholar, and they thought it their honour to meddle with their match. (2.) Others think it was because they stood in awe of the apostles, and could not be so free and familiar with them as they could be with Stephen, who was in an inferior office. (3.) Perhaps, they having given a public challenge, Stephen was chosen and appointed by the disciples to be their champion; for it was not meet that the apostles should leave the preaching of the word of God to engage in controversy. Stephen, who was only a deacon in the church, and a very sharp young man, of bright parts, and better qualified to deal with wrangling disputants than the apostles themselves, was appointed to this service. Some historians say that Stephen had been bred up at the feet of Gamaliel, and that Saul and the rest of them set upon him as a deserter, and with a particular fury made him their mark. (4.) It is probable that they disputed with Stephen because he was zealous to argue with them and convince them, and this was the service to which God had called him.

2. We are here told how he carried the point in this dispute (*v.* 10): *They were not able to resist the wisdom and the Spirit by which he spoke.* They could neither support their own arguments nor answer his. He proved by such irresistible arguments that Jesus is the Christ, and delivered himself with so much clearness and fulness that they had nothing to object against what he said; though they were not convinced, yet they were confounded. It is not said, They were not able

to resist him, but, They were not able to resist the *wisdom and the Spirit by which he spoke,* that Spirit of wisdom which spoke by him. Now was fulfilled that promise, *I will give you a mouth and wisdom which all your adversaries shall not be able to gainsay nor resist,* Luke xxi. 15. They thought they had only disputed with Stephen, and could make their part good with him; but they were disputing with the Spirit of God in him, for whom they were an unequal match.

III. At length, he sealed it with his blood; so we shall find he did in the next chapter; here we have some steps taken by his enemies towards it. When they could not answer his arguments as a disputant, they prosecuted him as a criminal, and suborned witnesses against him, to swear blasphemy upon him. "On such terms (saith Mr. Baxter here) do we dispute with malignant men. And it is next to a miracle of providence that no greater number of religious persons have been murdered in the world, by the way of purjury and pretence of law, when so many thousands hate them who make no conscience of false oaths." They suborned men, that is, instructed them what to say, and then hired them to swear it. They were the more enraged against him because he had proved them to be in the wrong, and shown them the right way; for which they ought to have given him their best thanks. *Was he therefore become their enemy, because he told them the truth,* and proved it to be so? Now let us observe here,

1. How with all possible art and industry they incensed both the government and the mob against him, that, if they could not prevail by the one, they might by the other (*v.* 12): *They stirred up the people* against him, that, if the sanhedrim should still think fit (according to Gamaliel's advice) to let him alone, yet they might run him down by a popular rage and tumult; they also found means to stir up the elders and scribes against him, that, if the people should countenance and protect him, they might prevail by authority. Thus they doubted not but to gain their point, when they had two strings to their bow.

2. How they got him to the bar: *They came upon him,* when he little thought of it, *and caught him and brought him to the council.* They came upon him in a body, and flew upon him as a lion upon his prey; so the word signifies. By their rude and violent treatment of him, they would represent him, both to the people and to the government, as a dangerous man, that would either flee from justice if he were not watched, or fight with it if he were not put under a force. Having caught him, they brought him triumphantly into the council, and, as it should seem, so hastily that he had none of his friends with him. They had found, when they brought many together, that they emboldened one another, and strengthened one another's hands; and therefore they will try how to deal with them singly.

3. How they were prepared with evidence ready to produce against him. They were resolved that they would not be run a-ground, as they were when they brought our Saviour upon his trial, and then had to seek for witnesses. These were got ready beforehand, and were instructed to make oath that they had *heard him speak blasphemous words against Moses and against God* (*v.* 11)—against this *holy place and the law* (*v.* 13); for they heard him say what Jesus would do to their place and their customs, *v.* 14. It is probable that he had said something to that purport; and yet those who swore it against him are called *false witnesses,* because, though there was something of truth in their testimony, yet they put a wrong and malicious construction upon what he had said, and perverted it. Observe,

(1.) What was the general charge exhibited against him—that he *spoke blasphemous words;* and, to aggravate the matter, "He *ceases not to speak blasphemous words;* it is his common talk, his discourse in all companies; wheresoever he comes, he makes it his business to instil his notions into all he converses with." It intimates likewise something of contumacy and contempt of admonition. "He has been warned against it, and yet ceases not to talk at this rate." Blasphemy is justly reckoned a heinous crime (to speak contemptibly and reproachfully of God our Maker), and therefore Stephen's persecutors would be thought to have a deep concern upon them for the honour of God's name, and to do this in a jealousy for that. As it was with the confessors and martyrs of the Old Testament, so it was with those of the New—their brethren that hated them, and cast them out, said, *Let the Lord be glorified;* and pretended they did him service in it. He is said to have spoken blasphemous words *against Moses and against God.* Thus far they were right, that those who blaspheme Moses (if they meant the writings of Moses, which were given by inspiration of God) blaspheme God himself. Those that speak reproachfully of the scriptures, and ridicule them, reflect upon God himself, and do despite to him. His great intention is to *magnify the law and make it honourable;* those therefore that vilify the law, and make it contemptible, blaspheme his name; for he has *magnified his word above all his name.* But did Stephen blaspheme Moses? By no means, he was far from it. Christ, and the preachers of his gospel, never said any thing that looked like blaspheming Moses; they always quoted his writings with respect, appealed to them, and said no other things than what Moses said should come; very unjustly therefore is Stephen indicted for blaspheming Moses. But,

(2.) Let us see how this charge is supported and made out; why, truly, when the thing was to be proved, all they can charge him with is that *that he hath spoken blasphemous words against this holy place and the law;* and this must be deemed and taken as blasphemy against Moses and against God himself. Thus does the charge dwindle when it comes to the evidence. [1.] He is charged with blaspheming *this holy place.* Some understand this of the city of Jerusalem, which was the holy city, and which they had a mighty jealousy for. But it is rather meant of the temple, that holy house. Christ was condemned as a blasphemer for words which were thought to reflect upon the temple, which they seemed concerned for the honour of, even when they by their wickedness had profaned it. [2.] He is charged with blaspheming *the law,* of which they *made their boast,* and in which they put their trust, when through *breaking the law they dishonoured God,* Rom. ii. 23. Well, but how can they make this out? Why, here the charge dwindles again; for all they can accuse him of is that *they had* themselves *heard him say* (but how it came in, or what explication he gave of it, they think not themselves bound to give account) that this *Jesus of Nazareth,* who was so much talked of, *shall destroy this place, and change the customs which Moses delivered to us.* He could not be charged with having said any thing to the disparagement either of the temple or of the law. The priests had themselves profaned the temple, by making it not only a house of merchandise, but a den of thieves; yet they would be thought zealous for the honour of it, against one that had never said any thing amiss of it, but had attended it more as a house of prayer, according to the true intention of it, than they had. Nor had he ever reproached the law as they had. But, *First,* He had said, *Jesus of Nazareth shall destroy this place,* destroy the temple, destroy Jerusalem. It is probable that he might say so; and what blasphemy was it against the holy place to say that it should not be perpetual any more than Shiloh was, and that the just and holy God would not continue the privileges of his sanctuary to those that abused them? Had not the prophets given the same warning to their fathers of the destruction of that holy place by the Chaldeans? Nay, when the temple was first built, had not God himself given the same warning: *This house, which is high, shall be an astonishment,* 2 Chron. vii. 21. And is he a blasphemer, then, who tells them that Jesus of Nazareth, if they continue their opposition to him, will bring a just destruction upon their place and nation, and they may thank themselves? Those wickedly abuse their profession of religion who, under colour of that, call the reproofs given them for their disagreeable conversations blasphemous reflections upon their religion. *Secondly,* He had said, *This Jesus shall change the customs which Moses delivered to us.* And it was expected that in the days of the Messiah they should be changed, and that the shadows should be done away when the substance was come; yet this was no essential change of the law, but the perfecting of it. *Christ came, not to destroy,* but to fulfil, the law; and, if he changed some customs that Moses delivered, it was to introduce and establish those that were much better; and if the Jewish church had not obstinately refused to come into this new establishment, and adhered to the ceremonial law, for aught I know *their place* had not been destroyed; so that for putting them into a certain way to prevent their destruction, and for giving them certain notice of their destruction if they did not take that way, he is accused as a blasphemer.

IV. We are here told how God owned him when he was brought before the council, and made it to appear that he stood by him (*v.* 15); *All that sat in the council,* the priests, scribes, and elders, *looking stedfastly on him,* being a stranger, and one they had not yet had before them, *saw his face as it had been the face of an angel.* It is usual for judges to observe the countenance of the prisoner, which sometimes is an indication either of guilt or innocence. Now Stephen appeared at the bar with the countenance *as of an angel.* 1. Perhaps it intimates no more than that he had an extraordinarily pleasant, cheerful countenance, and there was not in it the least sign either of fear for himself or anger at his persecutors. He looked as if he had never been better pleased in his life than he was now when he was called out to bear his testimony to the gospel of Christ, thus publicly, and stood fair for the crown of martyrdom. Such an undisturbed serenity, such an undaunted courage, and such an unaccountable mixture of mildness and majesty, there was in his countenance, that every one said he looked like an angel; enough surely to convince the Sadducees that there are angels, when they saw before their eyes an incarnate angel. 2. It should rather seem that there was a miraculous splendour and brightness upon his countenance, like that of our Saviour when he was transfigured—or, at least, that of Moses when he came down from the mount—God designing thereby to put honour upon his faithful witness and confusion upon his persecutors and judges, whose sin would be highly aggravated, and would be indeed a rebellion against the light, if, notwithstanding this, they proceeded against him. Whether he himself knew that the skin of his face shone or no we are not told; but *all that sat in the council saw it,* and probably took notice of it to one another, and an arrant shame it was that when they saw, and could not but see by it that he was owned of God, they did not call him from standing at the bar to sit in the chief seat upon the bench. Wisdom and holiness make a man's face to shine, and yet these will not secure men from the greatest indignities; and no wonder, when the shining of Stephen's face could not be his protection; though it had been easy to prove that if he had been guilty of putting any dishonour upon Moses God would not thus have put Moses's honour upon him.

CHAP. VII.

When our Lord Jesus called his apostles out to be employed in services and sufferings for him, he told them that yet the last should be first, and the first last, which was remarkably fulfilled in St. Stephen and St. Paul, who were both of them late converts, in comparison of the apostles, and yet got the start of them both in services and sufferings; for God, in conferring honours and favours, often crosses hands. In this chapter we have the martyrdom of Stephen, the first martyr of the Christian church, who led the van in that noble army. And therefore his sufferings and death are more largely related than those of any other, for direction and encouragement to all those who are called out to resist unto blood, as he did. Here is, I. His defence of himself before the council, in answer to the matters and things he stood charged with, the scope of which is to show that it was no blasphemy against God, nor any injury at all to the glory of his name, to say that the temple should be destroyed and the customs of the ceremonial law changed. And, 1. He shows this by going over the history of the Old Testament, and observing that God never intended to confine his favours to that place, or that ceremonial law; and that they had no reason to expect he should, for the people of the Jews had always been a provoking people, and had forfeited the privileges of their peculiarity: nay, that that holy place and that law were but figures of good things to come, and it was no disparagement at all to them to say that they must give place to better things, ver. 1—50. And then, 2. He applies this to those that prosecuted him, and sat in judgment upon him, sharply reproving them for their wickedness, by which they had brought upon themselves the ruin of their place and nation, and then could not bear to hear of it, ver. 51—53. II. The putting of him to death by stoning him, and his patient, cheerful, pious submission to it, ver. 54—60.

THEN said the high priest, Are
these things so? 2 And he said,
Men, brethren, and fathers, hearken;
The God of glory appeared unto our
father Abraham, when he was in Mesopotamia,
before he dwelt in Charran,
3 And said unto him, Get thee
out of thy country, and from thy kindred,
and come into the land which
I shall show thee. 4 Then came he
out of the land of the Chaldæans,
and dwelt in Charran: and from
thence, when his father was dead, he
removed him into this land, wherein
ye now dwell. 5 And he gave him
none inheritance in it, no, not *so
much as* to set his foot on: yet he
promised that he would give it to
him for a possession, and to his
seed after him, when *as yet* he had
no child. 6 And God spake on
this wise, That his seed should sojourn
in a strange land; and that
they should bring them into bondage
and entreat *them* evil four hundred
years. 7 And the nation to whom
they shall be in bondage will I judge,
said God: and after that shall they
come forth, and serve me in this
place. 8 And he gave him the covenant
of circumcision: and so *Abraham*
begat Isaac, and circumcised
him the eighth day; and Isaac *begat*
Jacob; and Jacob *begat* the twelve
patriarchs. 9 And the patriarchs,
moved with envy, sold Joseph into
Egypt: but God was with him, 10
And delivered him out of all his
afflictions, and gave him favour and
wisdom in the sight of Pharaoh king
of Egypt; and he made him governor
over Egypt and all his house. 11
Now there came a dearth over all the
land of Egypt and Chanaan, and
great affliction: and our fathers found
no sustenance. 12 But when Jacob
heard that there was corn in Egypt,
he sent out our fathers first. 13 And
at the second *time* Joseph was made
known to his brethren; and Joseph's
kindred was made known unto Pharaoh.
14 Then sent Joseph, and
called his father Jacob to *him*, and
all his kindred, threescore and fifteen
souls. 15 So Jacob went down into
Egypt, and died, he, and our fathers,
16 And were carried over into Sychem,
and laid in the sepulchre that Abraham
bought for a sum of money of the
sons of Emmor *the father* of Sychem.

Stephen is now at the bar before the great council of the nation, indicted for blasphemy: what the witnesses swore against him we had an account of in the foregoing chapter, that he spoke blasphemous words against Moses and God; for he spoke against this holy place and the law. Now here,

I. The high priest calls upon him to answer for himself, *v.* 1. He was president, and, as such, the mouth of the court, and therefore he saith, "You, the prisoner at the bar, you hear what is sworn against you; what do you say to it? *Are these things so?* Have you ever spoken any words to this purport? If you have, will you recant them, or will you stand to them? *Guilty or not guilty?* This carried a show of fairness, and yet seems to have been spoken with an air of haughtiness; and thus far he seems to have prejudged the cause, that, if it were so, that he had spoken such and such words, he shall certainly be adjudged a blasphemer, whatever he may offer in justification or explanation of them.

II. He begins his defence, and it is long; but it should seem by his breaking off abruptly, just when he came to the main point (*v.* 50), that it would have been much longer if his enemies would have given him leave to say all he had to say. In general we may observe,

1. That in this discourse he appears to be

a man ready and mighty in the scriptures, and thereby thoroughly furnished for every good word and work. He can relate scripture stories, and such as were very pertinent to his purpose, off-hand without looking in his Bible. He was *filled with the Holy Ghost,* not so much to reveal to him new things, or open to him the secret counsels and decrees of God concerning the Jewish nation, with them to convict these gainsayers; no, but to bring to his remembrance the scriptures of the Old Testament, and to teach him how to make use of them for their conviction. Those that are full of the Holy Ghost will be full of the scripture, as Stephen was.

2. That he quotes the scriptures according to the Septuagint translation, by which it appears he was one of the Hellenist Jews, who used that version in their synagogues. His following this, occasions divers variations from the Hebrew original in this discourse, which the judges of the court did not correct, because they knew how he was led into them; nor is it any derogation to the authority of that Spirit by which he spoke, for the variations are not material. We have a maxim, *Apices juris non sunt jura—Mere points of law are not law itself.* These verses carry on this his compendium of church history to the end of the book of Genesis. Observe,

(1.) His preface: *Men, brethren, and fathers, hearken.* He gives them, though not flattering titles, yet civil and respectful ones, signifying his expectation of fair treatment with them; from men he hopes to be treated with humanity, and he hopes that brethren and fathers will use him in a fatherly brotherly way. They are ready to look upon him as an apostate from the Jewish church, and an enemy to them. But, to make way for their conviction to the contrary, he addresses himself to them as *men, brethren, and fathers,* resolving to look on himself as one of them, though they would not so look on him. He craves their attention: *Hearken;* though he was about to tell them what they already knew, yet he begs them to hearken to it, because, though they knew it all, yet they would not without a very close application of mind know how to apply it to the case before them

(2.) His entrance upon the discourse, which (whatever it may seem to those that read it carelessly) is far from being a long ramble only to amuse the hearers, and give them a diversion by telling them an old story. No; it is all pertinent and *ad rem—to the purpose,* to show them that God had not his heart so much upon that holy place and the law as they had; but, as he had a church in the world many ages before that holy place was founded and the ceremonial law given, so he would have when they should both have had their period.

[1.] He begins with the call of Abraham out of Ur of the Chaldees, by which he was set apart for God to be the trustee of the promise, and the father of the Old-Testament church. This we had an account of (Gen. xii. 1, &c.), and it is referred to, Neh. ix. 7, 8. His native country was an idolatrous country, it was Mesopotamia, (*v.* 2), *the land of the Chaldeans* (*v.* 4); thence God brought him at two removes, not too far at once, dealing tenderly with him; he first brought him out of the land of the Chaldeans to Charran, or Haran, a place midway between that and Canaan (Gen. xi. 31), and thence five years after, when his father was dead, he *removed him into* the land of *Canaan, wherein you now dwell.* It should seem, the first time that God spoke to Abraham, he appeared in some visible display of the divine presence, as the *God of glory* (*v.* 2), to settle a correspondence with him: and then afterwards he kept up that correspondence, and spoke to him from time to time as there was occasion, without repeating his visible appearances as the God of glory.

First, From this call of Abraham we may observe, 1. That in all our ways we must acknowledge God, and attend the directions of his providence, as of the pillar of cloud and fire. It is not said, Abraham removed, but, *God removed him into this land wherein you now dwell,* and he did but follow his Leader. 2. Those whom God takes into covenant with himself he distinguishes from the children of this world; they are effectually called out of the state, out of the land, of their nativity; they must sit loose to the world, and live above it and every thing in it, even that in it which is most dear to them, and must trust God to make it up to them in another and better country, that is, the heavenly, which he will show them. God's chosen must follow him with an implicit faith and obedience.

Secondly, But let us see what this is to Stephen's case. 1. They had charged him as a blasphemer of God, and an apostate from the church; therefore he shows that he is a son of Abraham, and values himself upon his being able to say, *Our father Abraham,* and that he is a faithful worshipper of the God of Abraham, whom therefore he here calls *the God of glory.* He also shows that he owns divine revelation, and that particularly by which the Jewish church was founded and incorporated. 2. They were proud of their being circumcised; and therefore he shows that Abraham was taken under God's guidance, and into communion with him, before he was circumcised, for that was not till *v.* 8. With this argument Paul proves that Abraham was justified by faith, because he was justified when he was in uncircumcision: and so here. 3. They had a mighty jealousy for this holy place, which may be meant of the whole land of Canaan; for it was called the *holy land, Immanuel's land*; and the destruction of the holy house inferred that of the holy land. "Now," says Stephen, "you need not be so proud of it; for," (1.) "You came originally out of *Ur of the Chaldees*, where *your fathers served other gods* (Josh. xxiv. 2), and you were not the first planters of this country. Look therefore *unto the rock whence you were hewn, and the hole of the pit out of which you were digged;*" that is, as it follows there, "*look unto Abraham your father*, for *I called him alone* (Isa. li. 1, 2)—think of the meanness of your beginnings, and how you are entirely indebted to divine grace, and then you will see boasting to be for ever excluded. It was God that *raised up the righteous man from the* east, *and called him to his foot*, Isa. xli. 2. But, if his seed degenerate, let them know that God can destroy this holy place, and raise up to himself another people, for he is not a debtor to them." (2.) "God appeared in his glory to Abraham a great way off in Mesopotamia, before he came near Canaan, nay, before he dwelt in Charran; so that you must not think God's visits are confined to *this land;* no; he that brought the seed of the church from a country so far east can, if he pleases, carry the fruit of it to another country as far west." (3.) "God made no haste to bring him into this land, but let him linger some years by the way, which shows that God has not his heart so much upon this land as you have yours, neither is his honour, nor the happiness of his people, bound up in it. It is therefore neither blasphemy nor treason to say, It shall be destroyed,"

[2.] The unsettled state of Abraham and his seed for many ages after he was called out of Ur of the Chaldees. God did indeed promise that he would *give it to him for a possession, and to his seed after him, v.* 5. But, *First, As yet he had no child,* nor any by Sarah for many years after. *Secondly,* He himself was but a stranger and a sojourner in that land, and God *gave him no inheritance in it, no, not so much as to set his foot on;* but there he was as in a strange country, where he was always upon the remove, and could call nothing his own. *Thirdly,* His posterity did not come to the possession of it for a long time: *After four hundred years* they shall come *and serve me in this place,* and not till then, *v.* 7. Nay, *Fourthly,* They must undergo a great deal of hardship and difficulty before they shall be put into the possession of that land: they shall be brought into bondage, and ill treated in a strange land: and this, not as the punishment of any particular sin, as their wandering in the wilderness was, for we never find any such account given of their bondage in Egypt; but so God had appointed, and it must be. And *at the end of four hundred years,* reckoning from the birth of Isaac, *that nation to whom they shall be in bondage will I judge, saith God.* Now this teaches us, 1. That *known unto God are all his works* beforehand. When Abraham had neither inheritance nor heir, yet he was told he should have both, the one a land of promise, and the other a child of promise; and therefore both had, and received, by faith. 2. That God's promises, though they are slow, are sure in the operation of them; they will be fulfilled in the season of them, though perhaps not so soon as we expect. 3. That though the people of God may be in distress and trouble for a time, yet God will at length both rescue them and reckon with those that do oppress them; for, *verily there is a God that judgeth in the earth.*

But let us see how this serves Stephen's purpose. 1. The Jewish nation, for the honour of which they were so jealous, was very inconsiderable in its beginnings; as their common father Abraham was fetched out of obscurity in Ur of the Chaldees, so their tribes, and the heads of them, were fetched out of servitude in Egypt, when they were the *fewest of all people,* Deut. vii. 7. And what need is there of so much ado, as if their ruin, when they bring it upon themselves by sin, must be the ruin of the world, and of all God's interest in it? No; he that brought them out of Egypt can bring them into it again, as he threatened (Deut. xxviii. 68), and yet be no loser, while he can out of stones raise up children unto Abraham. 2. The slow steps by which the promise made to Abraham advanced towards the performance, and the many seeming contradictions here taken notice of, plainly show that it had a spiritual meaning, and that the land principally intended to be conveyed and secured by it was the *better country, that is, the heavenly;* as the apostle shows from this very argument that the patriarchs *sojourned in the land of promise, as in a strange country,* thence inferring that *they looked for a city that had foundations,* Heb. xi. 9, 10. It was therefore no blasphemy to say, *Jesus shall destroy this place,* when at the same time we say, "He shall lead us to the heavenly Canaan, and put us in possession of that, of which the earthly Canaan was but a type and figure."

[3.] The building up of the family of Abraham, with the entail of divine grace upon it, and the disposals of divine Providence concerning it, which take up the rest of the book of Genesis.

First, God engaged to be a God to Abraham and his seed; and, in token of this, appointed that he and his male seed should be circumcised, Gen. xvii. 9, 10. He *gave him the covenant of circumcision,* that is, the covenant of which circumcision was the seal; and accordingly, when Abraham had a son born, he *circumcised him the eighth day* (*v.* 8), by which he was both bound by the divine law and interested in the divine promise; for circumcision had reference to both, being a seal of the covenant both on God's part—I will be to thee *a God all-sufficient* and on man's part—*Walk before me, and be thou perfect.* And then when effectual care was thus taken for the securing of Abraham's seed, to be a *seed to serve the Lord,* they began to multiply: *Isaac begat Jacob, and Jacob the twelve patriarchs,* or roots of the respective tribes.

Secondly, Joseph, the darling and blessing of his father's house, was abused by his brethren; they *envied him* because of his dreams, and *sold him into Egypt.* Thus early did the children of Israel begin to grudge those among them that were eminent and outshone others, of which their enmity to Christ, who, like Joseph, was a *Nazarite among his brethren,* was a great instance.

Thirdly, God owned Joseph in his troubles, and was with him (Gen. xxxix. 2, 21), by the influence of his Spirit, both on his mind, giving him comfort, and on the minds of those he was concerned with, giving him favour in their eyes. And thus at length he *delivered him out of his afflictions,* and Pharaoh made him the second man in the kingdom, Ps. cv. 20—22. And thus he not only arrived at great preferment among the Egyptians, but became the *shepherd and stone of Israel,* Gen. xlix. 24.

Fourthly, Jacob was compelled to go down into Egypt, by a famine which forced him out of Canaan, *a dearth* (which was a *great affliction),* to that degree that *our fathers found no sustenance* in Canaan, *v.* 11. That *fruitful land was turned into barrenness.* But, hearing that there was *corn in Egypt* (treasured up by the wisdom of his own son), he *sent out our fathers first* to fetch corn, *v.* 12. And the *second time* that they went, Joseph, who at first made himself strange to them, made himself known to them, and it was notified to Pharaoh that they were Joseph's kindred and had a dependence upon him (*v.* 13), whereupon, with Pharaoh's leave, *Joseph sent for his father Jacob to him into Egypt,* with *all his kindred and family,* to the number of *seventy-five souls,* to be subsisted there, *v.* 14. In Genesis they are said to be *seventy souls,* Gen. xlvi. 27. But the Septuagint there makes them seventy-five, and Stephen or Luke follows that version, as Luke iii. 36, where Cainan is inserted, which is not in the Hebrew text, but in the Septuagint. Some, by excluding Joseph and his sons, who were in Egypt before (which reduces the number to sixty-four), and adding the sons of the eleven patriarchs, make the number seventy-five.

Fifthly, Jacob and his sons died in Egypt (*v.* 15), but were carried over to be buried in Canaan, *v.* 16. A very considerable difficulty occurs here: it is said, *They were carried over into Sychem,* whereas Jacob was buried not in Sychem, but near Hebron, in the cave of Machpelah, where Abraham and Isaac were buried, Gen. l. 13. Joseph's bones indeed were buried in Sychem (Josh. xxiv. 32), and it seems by this (though it is not mentioned in the story) that the bones of all the other patriarchs were carried with his, each of them giving the same commandment concerning them that he had done; and of them this must be understood, not of Jacob himself. But then the sepulchre in Sychem was bought by Jacob (Gen. xxxiii. 19), and by this it is described, Josh. xxiv. 32. How then is it here said to be bought by Abraham? Dr. Whitby's solution of this is very sufficient. He supplies it thus: *Jacob went down into Egypt and died, he and our fathers;* and *(our fathers) were carried over into Sychem; and he,* that is, *Jacob,* was laid *in the sepulchre that Abraham bought for a sum of money,* Gen. xxiii. 16. (Or, they were laid there, that is, Abraham, Isaac, and Jacob.) *And they,* namely, the other patriarchs, were *buried in the sepulchre bought of the sons of Emmor, the father of Sychem.*

Let us now see what this is to Stephen's purpose. 1. He still reminds them of the mean beginning of the Jewish nation, as a check to their priding themselves in the glories of that nation; and that it was by a miracle of mercy that they were raised up out of nothing to what they were, from so small a number to be so great a nation; but, if they answer not the intention of their being so raised, they can expect no other than to be destroyed. The prophets frequently put them in mind of the bringing of them out of Egypt, as an aggravation of their contempt of the law of God, and here it is urged upon them as an aggravation of their contempt of the gospel of Christ. 2. He reminds them likewise of the wickedness of those that were the patriarchs of their tribes, in envying their brother Joseph, and selling him into Egypt; and the same spirit was still working in them towards Christ and his ministers. 3. Their holy land, which they doted so much upon, their fathers were long kept out of the possession of, and met with dearth and great affliction in it; and therefore let them not think it strange if, after it has been so long polluted with sin, it be at length destroyed. 4. The faith of the patriarchs in desiring to be buried in the land of Canaan plainly showed that they had an eye to the heavenly country, to which it was the design of this Jesus to lead them.

17 But when the time of the promise drew nigh, which God had sworn to Abraham, the people grew and multiplied in Egypt, 18 Till another king arose, which knew not Joseph. 19 The same dealt subtilly with our kindred, and evil entreated our fathers, so that they cast out their young children, to the end they might not live. 20 In which time Moses was born, and was exceeding fair, and nourished up in his father's

house three months: 21 And when
he was cast out, Pharaoh's daughter
took him up, and nourished him for
her own son. 22 And Moses was
learned in all the wisdom of the
Egyptians, and was mighty in words
and in deeds. 23 And when he was
full forty years old, it came into his
heart to visit his brethren the children of Israel. 24 And seeing one
of them suffer wrong, he defended
him, and avenged him that was oppressed, and smote the Egyptian:
25 For he supposed his brethren
would have understood how that God
by his hand would deliver them: but
they understood not. 26 And the
next day he showed himself unto
them as they strove, and would have
set them at one again, saying, Sirs,
ye are brethren; why do ye wrong
one to another? 27 But he that
did his neighbour wrong thrust him
away, saying, Who made thee a ruler
and a judge over us? 28 Wilt thou
kill me, as thou didst the Egyptian
yesterday? 29 Then fled Moses at
this saying, and was a stranger in the
land of Madian, where he begat two
sons.

Stephen here goes on to relate,

I. The wonderful increase of the people of Israel in Egypt; it was by a wonder of providence that in a little time they advanced from a family into a nation. 1. It was *when the time of the promise drew nigh*—the time when they were to be formed into a people. During the first two hundred and fifteen years after the promise made to Abraham, the children of the covenant were increased but to seventy; but in the latter two hundred and fifteen years they increased to six hundred thousand fighting men. The motion of providence is sometimes quickest when it comes nearest the centre. Let us not be discouraged at the slowness of the proceedings towards the accomplishment of God's promises; God knows how to redeem the time that seems to have been lost, and, *when the year of the redeemed is at hand,* can do a double work in a single day. 2. It was *in Egypt,* where they were oppressed, and ruled with rigour; when their lives were made so bitter to them that, one would think, they should have wished to be written childless, yet they married, in faith that God in due time would visit them; and God *blessed them,* who thus honoured him, saying, *Be fruitful, and multiply.* Suffering times have often been growing times with the church.

II. The extreme hardships which they underwent there, *v.* 18, 19. When the Egyptians observed them to increase in number they increased their burdens, in which Stephen observes three things:—1. Their base ingratitude: They were oppressed by *another king that knew not Joseph,* that is, did not consider the good service that Joseph had done to that nation; for, if he had, he would not have made so ill a requital to his relations and family. Those that injure good people are very ungrateful, for they are the blessings of the age and place they live in. 2. Their hellish craft and policy: *They dealt subtly with our kindred. Come on,* said they, *let us deal wisely,* thinking thereby to secure themselves, but it proved dealing foolishly, for they did but treasure up wrath by it. Those are in a great mistake who think they deal wisely for themselves when they deal deceitfully or unmercifully with their brethren. 3. Their barbarous and inhuman cruelty. That they might effectually extirpate them, *they cast out their young children, to the end they might not live.* The killing of their infant seed seemed a very likely way to crush an infant nation. Now Stephen seems to observe this to them, not only that they might further see how mean their beginnings were, fitly represented (perhaps with an eye to the exposing of the young children in Egypt) by the forlorn state of a helpless, out-cast infant (Ezek. xvi. 4), and how much they were indebted to God for his care of them, which they had forfeited, and made themselves unworthy of: but also that they might consider that what they were now doing against the Christian church in its infancy was as impious and unjust, and would be in the issue as fruitless and ineffectual, as that was which the Egyptians did against the Jewish church in its infancy. "You think you deal subtly in your ill treatment of us, and, in persecuting young converts, you do as they did in casting out the young children; but you will find it is to no purpose, in spite of your malice Christ's disciples will *increase and multiply.*

III. The raising up of *Moses to be their deliverer.* Stephen was charged with having spoken blasphemous words against Moses, in answer to which charge he here speaks very honourably of him. 1. Moses was born when the persecution of Israel was at the hottest, especially in that most cruel instance of it, the murdering of the new-born children: *At that time, Moses was born* (*v.* 20), and was himself in danger, as soon as he came into the world (as our Saviour also was at Bethlehem) of falling a sacrifice to that bloody edict. God is preparing for his people's deliverance, when their way is darkest, and their distress deepest. 2. *He was exceedingly fair;* his face began to shine as soon as he was born, as a happy presage of the honour God designed to put upon him; he was ἀστεῖος τῷ Θεῷ—*fair towards God;* he was sanctified from the womb, and this made him beautiful in God's eyes; for it is the beauty of holiness that is in God's sight of great price. 3. He was wonderfully preserved in his infancy, first, by the care of his tender parents, who *nourished him three months in their own house,* as long as they durst; and then by a favourable providence that threw him *into the arms of Pharaoh's daughter, who took him up, and nourished him as her own son* (*v.* 21); for those whom God designs to make special use of he will take special care of. And did he thus protect the child Moses? Much more will he secure the interests of his holy child Jesus (as he is called *ch.* iv. 27) from *the enemies that are gathered together against him.* 4. He became a great scholar (*v.* 22): *He was learned in all the wisdom of the Egyptians,* who were then famed for all manner of polite literature, particularly philosophy, astronomy, and (which perhaps helped to lead them to idolatry) hieroglyphics. Moses, having his education at court, had opportunity of improving himself by the best books, tutors, and conversation, in all the arts and sciences, and had a genius for them. Only we have reason to think that he had not so far forgotten the God of his fathers as to acquaint himself with the unlawful studies and practices of the magicians of Egypt, any further than was necessary to the confuting of them. 5. He became a prime minister of state in Egypt. This seems to be meant by his being *mighty in words and deeds.* Though he had not a ready way of expressing himself, but stammered, yet he spoke admirably good sense, and every thing he said commanded assent, and carried its own evidence and force of reason along with it; and, in business, none went on with such courage, and conduct, and success. Thus was he prepared, by human helps, for those services, which, after all, he could not be thoroughly furnished for without divine illumination. Now, by all this, Stephen will make it appear that, notwithstanding the malicious insinuations of his persecutors, he had as high and honourable thoughts of Moses as they had.

IV. The attempts which Moses made to deliver Israel, which they spurned, and would not close in with. This Stephen insists much upon, and it serves for a key to this story (Exod. ii. 11—15), as does also that other construction which is put upon it by the apostle, Heb. xi. 24—26. There it is represented as an act of holy self-denial, here as a designed prelude to, or entrance upon, the public service he was to be called out to (*v.* 23): *When he was full forty years old,* in the prime of his time for preferment in the court of Egypt, *it came into his heart* (for God put it there) *to visit his brethren the children of Israel,* and to see which way he might do them any service; and he showed himself as a public person, with a public character. 1. As Israel's saviour. This he gave a specimen of in avenging an oppressed Israelite, and killing the Egyptian that abused him (*v.* 24). *Seeing one of his brethren suffer wrong,* he was moved with compassion towards the sufferer, and a just indignation at the wrong-doer, as men in public stations should be, and *he avenged him that was oppressed, and smote the Egyptian,* which, if he had been only a private person, he could not lawfully have done; but he knew that his commission from heaven would bear him out, and *he supposed that his brethren* (who could not but have some knowledge of the promise made to Abraham, *that the nation that should oppress them God would judge) would have understood that God by his hand would deliver them;* for he could not have had either presence of mind or strength of body to do what he did, if he had not been clothed with such a divine power as evinced a divine authority. If they had but understood the signs of the times, they might have taken this for the dawning of the day of their deliverance; *but they understood not,* they did not take this, as it was designed, for the setting up of a standard, and sounding of a trumpet, to proclaim Moses *their deliverer.* 2. As Israel's judge. This he gave a specimen of, *the* very *next day,* in offering to accommodate matters between two contending Hebrews, wherein he plainly assumed a public character (*v.* 26): *He showed himself to them as they strove,* and, putting on an air of majesty and authority, *he would have set them at one again,* and as their prince have determined the controversy between them, *saying, Sirs, you are brethren,* by birth and profession of religion; *why do you wrong one to another?* For he observed that (as in most strifes) there was a fault on both sides; and therefore, in order to peace and friendship, there must be a mutual remission and condescension. When Moses was to be Israel's deliverer out of Egypt, he slew the Egyptians, and so delivered Israel out of their hands; but, when he was to be Israel's judge and lawgiver, he ruled them with the golden sceptre, not the iron rod; he did not kill and slay them when they strove, but gave them excellent laws and statutes, and decided upon their complaints and appeals made to him, Exod. xviii. 16. *But* the contending Israelite that was most in *the wrong thrust him away* (*v.* 27), would not bear the reproof, though a just and gentle one, but was ready to fly in his face, with, *Who made thee a ruler and a judge over us?* Proud and litigious spirits are impatient of check and control. Rather would these Israelites have their bodies ruled with rigour by their task-masters than be delivered, and have their minds ruled with reason, by their deliverer. The wrong-doer was so enraged at the reproof given him that he upbraided Moses with the service he had done to their nation in killing the Egyptian, which, if they had pleased, would have been the earnest of further and greater service: *Wilt thou kill me as thou didst the Egyptian yesterday?* v. 28, charging that upon him as his crime, and threatening to accuse him for it, which was the hanging out of the flag of defiance to the Egyptians, and the banner of love and deliverance to Israel. Hereupon *Moses fled into the land of Midian,* and made no further attempt to deliver Israel till forty years after; he settled as a stranger in Midian, married, and had two sons, by Jethro's daughter, *v.* 29.

Now let us see how this serves Stephen's purpose. 1. They charged him with blaspheming Moses, in answer to which he retorts upon them the indignities which their fathers did to Moses, which they ought to be ashamed of, and humbled for, instead of picking quarrels thus, under pretence of zeal for the honour of Moses, with one that had as great a veneration for him as any of them had. 2. They persecuted him for disputing in defence of Christ and his gospel, in opposition to which they set up Moses and his law: "But," saith he, "you had best take heed," (1.) "Lest you hereby do as your fathers did, refuse and reject one *whom God has raised up to be to you a prince and a Saviour;* you may understand, if you will not wilfully shut your eyes against the light, that God will, by this Jesus, deliver you out of a worse slavery than that in Egypt; take heed then of thrusting him away, but receive him as a ruler and a judge over you." (2.) "Lest you hereby fare as your fathers fared, who for this were very justly left to die in their slavery, for the deliverance came not till forty years after. This will be the issue of it, you put away the gospel from you, and it will be *sent to the Gentiles;* you will not have Christ, and you shall not have him, so shall your doom be." Matt. xxiii. 38, 39.

30 And when forty years were expired, there appeared to him in the
wilderness of mount Sina an angel of
the Lord in a flame of fire in a bush.
31 When Moses saw *it*, he wondered
at the sight: and as he drew near to
behold *it*, the voice of the Lord came
unto him, 32 *Saying*, I *am* the
God of thy fathers, the God of
Abraham, and the God of Isaac, and
the God of Jacob. Then Moses
trembled, and durst not behold. 33
Then said the Lord to him, Put off
thy shoes from thy feet: for the
place where thou standest is holy
ground. 34 I have seen, I have
seen the affliction of my people which
is in Egypt, and I have heard their
groaning, and am come down to deliver them. And now come, I will
send thee into Egypt. 35 This
Moses whom they refused, saying,
Who made thee a ruler and a judge?
the same did God send *to be* a ruler
and a deliverer by the hand of the
angel which appeared to him in the
bush. 36 He brought them out,
after that he had showed wonders
and signs in the land of Egypt, and
in the Red sea, and in the wilderness
forty years. 37 This is that Moses,
which said unto the children of Israel,
A prophet shall the Lord your God
raise up unto you of your brethren,
like unto me; him shall ye hear.
38 This is he, that was in the church
in the wilderness with the angel
which spake to him in the mount
Sina, and *with* our fathers: who received the lively oracles to give unto
us: 39 To whom our fathers would
not obey, but thrust *him* from them,
and in their hearts turned back again
into Egypt, 40 Saying unto Aaron,
Make us gods to go before us: for
as for this Moses, which brought us
out of the land of Egypt, we wot not
what is become of him. 41 And they
made a calf in those days, and offered
sacrifice unto the idol, and rejoiced
in the works of their own hands.

Stephen here proceeds in his story of Moses; and let any one judge whether these are the words of one that was a blasphemer of Moses or no; nothing could be spoken more honourably of him. Here is,

I. The vision which he saw of the glory of God at the bush (*v.* 30): *When forty years had expired* (during all which time Moses was buried alive in Midian, and was now grown old, and one would think past service), that it might appear that all his performances were products of a divine power and promise (as it appeared that Isaac was a child of promise by his being born of parents stricken in years), now, at eighty years old, he enters upon that post of honour to which he was born, in recompence for his self-denial at forty years old. Observe, 1. Where God appeared to him: *In the wilderness of Mount Sinai, v.* 30. And, when he appeared to him there, that was holy ground (*v.* 33), which Stephen takes notice of, as a check to those who prided themselves in the temple, that holy place, as if there were no communion to be had with God but there; whereas God met Moses, and manifested himself to him, in a remote obscure place in the wilderness of Sinai. They deceive themselves if they think God is confined to places; he can bring his people into a wilderness, and there speak comfortably to them. 2. How he appeared to him: *In a flame of fire* (for our God is a consuming fire), and yet *the bush*, in which this fire was, though combustible matter, *was not consumed*, which, as it represented the state of Israel in Egypt (where, though they were in the fire of affliction, yet they were not consumed), so perhaps it may be looked upon as a type of Christ's incarnation, and the union between the divine and human nature: God, manifested in the flesh, was as the flame of fire manifested in the bush. 3. How Moses was affected with this: (1.) *He wondered at the sight*, *v.* 31. It was a phenomenon with the solution of which all his Egyptian learning could not furnish him. He had the curiosity at first to pry into it: *I will turn aside now, and see this great sight;* but the nearer he drew the more he was struck with amazement; and, (2.) *He trembled, and durst not behold*, durst not look stedfastly upon it; for he was soon aware that it was not a fiery meteor, but *the angel of the Lord;* and no other than *the Angel of the covenant*, the Son of God himself. This set him a trembling. Stephen was accused for blaspheming Moses and God (*ch.* vi. 11), as if Moses had been a little god; but by this it appears that he was a *man, subject to like passions as we are*, and particularly that of fear, upon any appearance of the divine majesty and glory.

II. The declaration which he heard of the covenant of God (*v.* 32): *The voice of the Lord came to him;* for faith comes by hearing; and this was it: *I am the God of thy fathers, the God of Abraham, the God of Isaac, and the God of Jacob;* and therefore, 1. "I am the same that I was." The covenant God made with Abraham some ages ago was, *I will be to thee a God*, a God all-sufficient. "Now," saith God, "that covenant is still in full force; it is not cancelled nor forgotten, but I am, as I was, the God of Abraham, and now I will make it to appear so;" for all the favours, all the honours God put upon Israel, were founded upon this covenant with Abraham, and flowed from it. 2. "I will be the same that I am." For if the death of Abraham, Isaac, and Jacob, cannot break the covenant-relation between God and them (as byt his it appears it cannot), then nothing else can: and then he will be a God, (1.) To their souls, which are now separated from their bodies. Our Saviour by this proves the future state, Matt. xxii. 31, 32. Abraham is dead, and yet God is still his God, therefore Abraham is still alive. God never did that for him in this world which would answer the true intent and full extent of that promise, that he would be the God of Abraham; and therefore it must be done for him in the other world. Now this is that life and immortality which are brought to light by the gospel, for the full conviction of the Sadducees, who denied it. Those therefore who stood up in defence of the gospel, and endeavoured to propagate it, were so far from blaspheming Moses that they did the greatest honour imaginable to Moses, and that glorious discovery which God made of himself to him at the bush. (2.) To their seed. God, in declaring himself thus the God of their fathers, intimated his kindness to their seed, that they should be *beloved for the fathers' sakes*, Rom. xi. 28; Deut. vii. 8. Now the preachers of the gospel preached up this covenant, *the promise made of God unto the fathers; unto which promise* those of *the twelve tribes* that did continue *serving God hoped to come*, *ch.* xxvi. 6, 7. And shall they, under colour of supporting the holy place and the law, oppose the covenant which was made with Abraham and his seed, his spiritual seed, before the law was given, and long before the holy place was built? Since God's glory must be for ever advanced, and our glorying for ever silenced, God will have our salvation to be by promise, and not by the law; the Jews therefore who persecuted the Christians, under pretence that they blasphemed the law, did themselves blaspheme the promise, and forsook all their own mercies that were contained in it.

III. The commission which God gave him to deliver Israel out of Egypt. The Jews set up Moses in competition with Christ, and accused Stephen as a blasphemer because he did not do so too. But Stephen here shows that Moses was an eminent type of Christ, as he was Israel's deliverer. When God had declared himself the God of Abraham he proceeded, 1. To order Moses into a reverent posture: "*Put off thy shoes from thy feet.* Enter not upon sacred things with low, and cold, and common thoughts. *Keep thy foot*, Eccl. v. 1. Be not hasty and rash in thy approaches to God; tread softly." 2. To order Moses into a very eminent service. When he is ready to receive commands, he shall have commission. He is commissioned to demand leave from Pharaoh for Israel to go out of his land, and to enforce that demand, *v.* 34. Observe, (1.) The notice God took both of their sufferings and of their sense of their sufferings: *I have seen, I have seen their affliction, and have heard their groaning.* God has a compassionate regard to the troubles of his church, and the groans of his persecuted people; and their deliverance takes rise from his pity. (2.) The determination he fixed to redeem them by the hand of Moses: *I am come down to deliver them.* It should seem, though God is present in all places, yet he uses that expression here of coming down to deliver them because that deliverance was typical of what Christ did, when, *for us men, and for our salvation, he came down from heaven; he that ascended first descended.* Moses is the man that must be employed: *Come, and I will send thee into Egypt:* and, if God send him, he will own him and give him success.

IV. His acting in pursuance of this commission, wherein he was a figure of the Messiah. And Stephen takes notice here again of the slights they had put upon him, the affronts they had given him, and their refusal to have him to reign over them, as tending very much to magnify his agency in their deliverance. 1. God put honour upon him whom they put contempt upon (*v.* 35): *This Moses whom they refused* (whose kind offers and good offices they rejected with scorn, *saying, Who made thee a ruler and a judge? Thou takest too much upon thee, thou son of Levi,* Num. xvi. 3), this same Moses *did God send to be a ruler, and a deliverer, by the hand of the angel which appeared to him in the bush.* It may be understood either that God sent to him by the hand of the angel, or that by the hand of the angel going along with him he became a complete deliverer. Now, by this example, Stephen would intimate to the council *that this Jesus whom they now refused,* as their fathers did Moses, *saying, Who made thee a prophet and a king? Who gave thee this authority?* even this same has God advanced *to be a prince and a Saviour, a ruler and a deliverer;* as the apostles had told them awhile ago (*ch.* v. 30, 31), *that the stone which the builders refused was become the head-stone in the corner, ch.* iv. 11. 2. God showed favour to them by him, and he was very forward to serve them, though they had thrust him away. God might justly have refused them his service, and he might justly have declined it; but it is all forgotten: they are not so much as upbraided with it, *v.* 36. *He brought them out,* notwithstanding, *after he had shown wonders and signs in the land of Egypt* (which were afterwards continued for the completing of their deliverance, according as the case called for them) *in the Red Sea, and in the wilderness forty years.* So far is he from blaspheming Moses that he admires him as a glorious instrument in the hand of God for the forming of the Old-Testament church. But it does not at all derogate from his just honour to say that he was but an instrument, and that he is outshone by this Jesus, whom he encourages these Jews yet to close with, and to come into his interest, not fearing but that then they should be received into his favour, and receive benefit by him, as the people of Israel were delivered by Moses, though they had once refused him.

V. His prophecy of Christ and his grace, *v.* 37. He not only was a type of Christ (many were so that perhaps had not an actual foresight of his day), but Moses spoke of him (*v.* 37): *This is that Moses who said unto the children of Israel, A prophet shall the Lord your God raise up unto you of your brethren.* This is spoken of as one of the greatest honours God put upon him (nay, as that which exceeded all the rest), that by him he gave notice to the children of Israel of the great prophet that should come into the world, raised their expectation of him, and required them to receive him. When his bringing them out of Egypt is spoken of it is with an emphasis of honour, *This is that Moses,* Exod. vi. 26. And so it is here, *This is that Moses.* Now this is very full to Stephen's purpose; in asserting that Jesus should change the customs of the ceremonial law, he was so far from blaspheming Moses that really he did him the greatest honour imaginable, by showing how the prophecy of Moses was accomplished, which was so clear, that, as Christ told them himself, *If they had believed Moses, they would have believed him,* John v. 46. 1. Moses, in God's name, told them that, in the fulness of time, they should have a prophet raised up among them, one of their own nation, that should be like unto him (Deut. xviii. 15, 18),—a ruler and a deliverer, a judge and a lawgiver, like him,—who should therefore have authority to change the customs that he had delivered, and to bring in a better hope, as *the Mediator of a better testament.* 2. He charged them to hear that prophet, to receive his dictates, to admit the change he would make in their customs, and to submit to him in every thing; "and this will be the greatest honour you can do to Moses and to his law, who said, *Hear you him;* and came to be a witness to the repetition of this charge by *a voice from heaven,* at the transfiguration of Christ, and by his silence gave consent to it," Matt. xvii. 5.

VI. The eminent services which Moses continued to do to the people of Israel, after he had been instrumental to bring them out of Egypt, *v.* 38. And herein also he was a type of Christ, who yet so far exceeds him that it is no blasphemy to say, "He has authority to change the customs that Moses delivered." It was the honour of Moses, 1. That *he was in the church in the wilderness;* he presided in all the affairs of it for forty years, was king in Jeshurun, Deut. xxxiii. 5. The camp of Israel is here called *the church in the wilderness;* for it was a sacred society, incorporated by a divine charter under a divine government, and blessed with divine revelation. The church in the wilderness was a church, though it was not yet perfectly formed, as it was to be when they came to Canaan, *but every man did that which was right in his own eyes,* Deut. xii. 8, 9. It was the honour of Moses that he was in that church, and many a time it had been destroyed if Moses had not been in it to intercede for it. But Christ is the president and guide of a more excellent and glorious church than that in the wilderness was, and is more in it, as the life and soul of it, than Moses could be in that. 2. That *he was with the angel that spoke to him in the mount Sinai, and with our fathers*—was with him in the holy mount twice forty days, with the angel of the covenant, Michael, our prince. Moses was immediately conversant with God, but never lay in his bosom as Christ did from eternity. Or these words may be taken thus: *Moses was in the church in the wilderness,* but it was *with the angel that spoke to him in mount Sinai,* that is, at the burning bush; for that was said to be at mount Sinai (*v.* 30); that angel went before him, and was guide to him, else he could not have been a guide to Israel; of this God speaks (Exod. xxiii. 20), *I send an angel before thee,* and Exod. xxxiii. 2. And see Num. xx. 16. He was in the church with the angel, without whom he could have done no service to the church; but Christ is himself that angel which was with the church in the wilderness, and therefore has an authority above Moses. 3. That *he received the lively oracles to give unto them;* not only the ten commandments, but the other instructions which *the Lord spoke unto Moses, saying, Speak them to the children of Israel.* (1.) The words of God are *oracles,* certain and infallible, and of unquestionable authority and obligation; they are to be consulted as oracles, and by them all controversies must be determined. (2.) They are *lively oracles,* for they are the oracles of the living God, not of the dumb and dead idols of the heathens: the word that God speaks is spirit and life; not that the law of Moses could give life, but it showed the way to life: *If thou wilt enter into life, keep the commandments.* (3.) Moses received them from God, and delivered nothing as an oracle to the people but what *he had first received from God.* (4.) The lively oracles which he received from God he faithfully gave to the people, to be observed and preserved. It was the principal privilege of the Jews that *to them were committed the oracles of God;* and it was by the hand of Moses that they were committed. As Moses gave them not that bread, so neither did he give them that law from heaven (John vi. 32), but God gave it to them; and he that gave them those customs by his servant Moses might, no doubt, when he pleased, change the customs by his Son Jesus, who received more lively oracles to give unto us than Moses did.

VII. The contempt that was, after this, and notwithstanding this, put upon him by the people. Those that charged Stephen with speaking against Moses would do well to answer what their own ancestors had done, and they tread in their ancestors' steps. 1. *They would not obey him, but thrust him from them, v.* 39. They murmured at him, mutinied against him, refused to obey his orders, and sometimes were ready to stone him. Moses did indeed give them an excellent law, but by this it appeared that *it could not make the comers thereunto perfect* (Heb. x. 1), for *in their hearts they turned back again into Egypt,* and preferred their garlic and onions there before the manna they had under the guidance of Moses, or the milk and honey they hoped for in Canaan. Observe, Their secret disaffection to Moses, with their inclination to Egyptianism, if I may so call it. This was, in effect, turning back to Egypt; it was doing it in heart. Many that pretend to be going forward towards Canaan, by keeping up a show and profession of religion, are, at the same time, in their hearts turning back to Egypt, like Lot's wife to Sodom, and will be dealt with as deserters, for it is the heart that God looks at. Now, if the customs that Moses delivered to them could not prevail to change them, wonder not that Christ comes to change the customs, and to introduce a more spiritual way of worship. 2. *They made a golden calf* instead of him, which, besides the affront that was thereby offered to God, was a great indignity to Moses: for it was upon this consideration that they made the calf, because "*as for this Moses, who brought us out of the land of Egypt, we know not what is become of him;* therefore make us gods of gold;" as if a calf were sufficient to supply the want of Moses, and as capable of going before them into the promised land. *So they made a calf in those days* when the law was given them, *and offered sacrifices unto the idol, and rejoiced in the work of their own hands.* So proud were they of their new god that when they had *sat down to eat and drink, they rose up to play!* By all this it appears that there was a great deal which the law could not do, *in that it was weak through the flesh;* it was therefore necessary that this law should be perfected by a better hand, and he was no blasphemer against Moses who said that Christ had done it.

42 Then God turned, and gave
them up to worship the host of
heaven; as it is written in the book
of the prophets, O ye house of Israel,
have ye offered to me slain beasts
and sacrifices *by the space of* forty
years in the wilderness? 43 Yea,
ye took up the tabernacle of Moloch,
and the star of your god Remphan,
figures which ye made to worship
them: and I will carry you away beyond Babylon: 44 Our fathers had
the tabernacle of witness in the wilderness, as he had appointed, speaking unto Moses, that he should make
it according to the fashion that he
had seen. 45 Which also our fathers that came after brought in with
Jesus into the possession of the
Gentiles, whom God drove out before the face of our fathers, unto the
days of David; 46 Who found favour before God, and desired to find
a tabernacle for the God of Jacob.
47 But Solomon built him a house.
48 Howbeit the most High dwelleth

not in temples made with hands; as saith the prophet, 49 Heaven *is* my throne, and earth *is* my footstool: what house will ye build me? saith the Lord: or what *is* the place of my rest? 50 Hath not my hand made all these things?

Two things we have in these verses:—

I. Stephen upbraids them with the idolatry of their fathers, which God gave them up to, as a punishment for their early forsaking him in worshipping the golden calf; and this was the saddest punishment of all for that sin, as it was of the idolatry of the Gentile world *that God gave them up to a reprobate mind.* When *Israel was joined to idols,* joined to the golden calf, and not long after to Baal-peor, God said, *Let them alone;* let them go on (*v.* 42): *Then God turned, and gave them up to worship the host of heaven.* He particularly cautioned them not to do it, at their peril, and gave them reasons why they should not; but, when they were bent upon it, *he gave them up to their own hearts' lust,* withdrew his restraining grace, and then they walked in their own counsels, and were so scandalously mad upon their idols as never any people were. Compare Deut. iv. 19 with Jer. viii. 2. For this he quotes a passage out of Amos v. 25. For it would be less invidious to tell them their own [character and doom] from an Old-Testament prophet, who upbraids them,

1. For not sacrificing to their own God in the wilderness (*v.* 42): *Have you offered to me slain beasts, and sacrifices, by the space of forty years in the wilderness?* No; during all that time sacrifices to God were intermitted; they did not so much as keep the passover after the second year. It was God's condescension to them that he did not insist upon it during their unsettled state; but then let them consider how ill they requited him in offering sacrifices to idols, when God dispensed with their offering them to him. This is also a check to their zeal for the customs that Moses delivered to them, and their fear of having them changed by *this Jesus,* that immediately after they were delivered these customs were for forty years together disused as needless things.

2. For sacrificing to other gods after they came to Canaan (*v.* 43): *You took up the tabernacle of Moloch.* Moloch was the idol of the children of Ammon, to which they barbarously offered their own children in sacrifice, which they could not do without great terror and grief to themselves and their families; yet this unnatural idolatry they arrived at, when *God gave them up to worship the host of heaven.* See 2 Chron. xxviii. 3. It was surely the strongest delusion that ever people were given up to, and the greatest instance of the power of Satan in the children of disobedience, and therefore it is here spoken of emphatically: *Yea, you took up the tabernacle of Moloch,* you submitted even to that, and to the worship of *the star of your god Remphan.* Some think Remphan signifies *the moon,* as Moloch does *the sun;* others take it for *Saturn,* for that planet is called *Remphan* in the Syriac and Persian languages. The Septuagint puts it for *Chiun,* as being a name more commonly known. They had images representing the star, like the silver shrines for Diana, here called *the figures which they made to worship.* Dr. Lightfoot thinks they had figures representing the whole starry firmament, with all the constellations, and the planets, and these are called *Remphan*—"the high representation," like the celestial globe: a poor thing to make an idol of, and yet better than a golden calf! Now for this it is threatened, *I will carry you away beyond Babylon.* In Amos it is *beyond Damascus,* meaning *to Babylon, the land of the north.* But Stephen changes it, with an eye to the captivity of the ten tribes, who were *carried away beyond Babylon, by the river of Gozan, and in the cities of the Medes,* 2 Kings xvii. 6. Let it not therefore seem strange to them to hear of the destruction of this place, for they had heard of it many a time from the prophets of the Old Testament, who were not therefore accused as blasphemers by any but the wicked rulers. It was observed, in the debate on Jeremiah's case, that Micah was not called to an account though he prophesied, saying, *Zion shall be ploughed as a field,* Jer. xxvi. 18, 19.

II. He gives an answer particularly to the charge exhibited against him relating to the temple, *that he spoke blasphemous words against that holy place, v.* 44—50. He was accused for saying that Jesus would destroy this holy place: "And what if I did say so?" (saith Stephen) "the glory of the holy God is not bound up in the glory of this holy place, but that may be preserved untouched, though this be laid in the dust;" for, 1. "It was not till our fathers came into the wilderness, in their way to Canaan, that they had any fixed place of worship; and yet the patriarchs, many ages before, worshipped God acceptably at the altars they had adjoining to their own tents *in the open air—sub dio;* and he that was worshipped without a holy place in the first, and best, and purest ages of the Old-Testament church, may and will be so when this holy place is destroyed, without any diminution to his glory." 2. The holy place was at first but a tabernacle, mean and movable, showing itself to be short-lived, and not designed to continue always. Why might not this holy place, though built of stones, be decently brought to its end, and give place to its betters, as well as that though framed of curtains? As it was no dishonour, but an honour to God, that the tabernacle gave way to the temple, so it is now that the material temple gives way to the spiritual one, and so it will be when, at last, the spiritual temple shall give way to the eternal one. 3. That tabernacle was *a tabernacle of witness*, or of testimony, *a figure for the time then present* (Heb. ix. 9), *a figure of good things to come, of the true tabernacle which the Lord pitched, and not men*, Heb. viii. 2. This was the glory both of the tabernacle and temple, that they were erected for a testimony of that temple of God which in the latter days should be opened in heaven (Rev. xi. 19), and of Christ's tabernacling on earth (as the word is, John i. 14), and of the temple of his body. 4. That tabernacle was framed just as God appointed, and *according to the fashion which Moses saw in the mount*, which plainly intimates that it had reference to good things to come. Its rise being heavenly, its meaning and tendency were so; and therefore it was no diminution at all to its glory to say that this temple made with hands should be destroyed, in order to the building of *another made without hands*, which was Christ's crime (Mark xiv. 58), and Stephen's. 5. That tabernacle was pitched first in the wilderness; it was not a native of this land of yours (to which you think it must for ever be confined), but was brought in in the next age, by our fathers, who came after those who first erected it, into the possession of the Gentiles, into the land of Canaan, which had long been in the possession of the devoted nations *whom God drove out before the face of our fathers*. And why may not God set up his spiritual temple, as he had done the material tabernacle, in those countries that were now the possession of the Gentiles? That tabernacle was brought in by those who came *with Jesus*, that is, *Joshua*. And I think, for distinction sake, and to prevent mistakes, it ought to be so read, both here and Heb. iv. 8. Yet in naming *Joshua* here, which in Greek is *Jesus*, there may be a tacit intimation that as the Old-Testament Joshua brought in that typical tabernacle, so the New-Testament Joshua should bring in the true tabernacle into the possession of the Gentiles. 6. That tabernacle continued for many ages, *even to the days of David*, above four hundred years, before there was any thought of building a temple, *v.* 45. David, having *found favour before God*, did indeed desire this further favour, to have leave to build God a house, to be a constant settled tabernacle, or dwelling-place, for the Shechinah, or the tokens of the presence of the God of Jacob, *v.* 46. Those who have found favour with God should show themselves forward to advance the interests of his kingdom among men. 7. God had his heart so little upon a temple, or such a holy place as they were so jealous for, that, when David desired to build one, he was forbidden to do it; God was in no haste for one, as he told David (2 Sam. vii. 7), and therefore it was not he, but his son Solomon, some years after, that built him a house. David had all that sweet communion with God in public worship which we read of in his Psalms before there was any temple built. 8. God often declared that temples made with hands were not his delight, nor could add any thing to the perfection of his rest and joy. Solomon, when he dedicated the temple, acknowledged that God *dwelleth not in temples made with hands;* he has not need of them, is not benefited by them, cannot be confined to them. The whole world is his temple, in which he is every where present, and fills it with his glory; and what occasion has he for a temple then to manifest himself in? Indeed the pretended deities of the heathen needed temples made with hands, for they were gods made with hands (*v.* 41), and had no other place to manifest themselves in than in their own temples; but the one only true and living God needs no temple, for *the heaven is his throne*, in which he rests, *and the earth is his footstool*, over which he rules (*v.* 49, 50), and therefore, *What house will you build me*, comparable to this which I have already? *Or, what is the place of my rest?* What need have I of a house, either to repose myself in or to show myself? *Hath not my hand made all these things?* And *these show his eternal power and Godhead* (Rom. i. 20); they so show themselves to all mankind that those who worship other gods are without excuse. And as the world is thus God's temple, wherein he is manifested, so it is God's temple in which he will be worshipped. As the earth is full of his glory, and is therefore his temple (Isa. vi. 3), so the earth is, or shall be, full of his praise (Hab. iii. 3), *and all the ends of the earth shall fear him* (Ps. lxvii. 7), and upon this account it is his temple. It was therefore no reflection at all upon this holy place, however they might take it, to say *that Jesus should destroy this temple*, and set up another, into which all nations should be admitted, *ch.* xv. 16, 17. And it would not seem strange to those who considered that scripture which Stephen here quotes (Isa. lxvi. 1—3), which, as it expressed God's comparative contempt of the external part of his service, so it plainly foretold the rejection of the unbelieving Jews, and the welcome of the Gentiles that were of a contrite spirit into the church.

51 Ye stiffnecked and uncircumcised in heart and ears, ye do always resist the Holy Ghost: as your fathers *did*, so *do* ye.
52 Which of the prophets have not your fathers persecuted? and they have slain them which showed before of the coming of the Just One; of whom ye have been now the betrayers and murderers:
53 Who have received the law by the disposition of angels, and have not kept *it*.

Stephen was going on in his discourse (as it should seem by the thread of it) to show that, as the temple, so the temple-service must come to an end, and it would be the glory of both to give way to that worship of the Father in spirit and in truth which was to be established in the kingdom of the Messiah, stripped of the pompous ceremonies of the old law, and so he was going to apply all this which he had said more closely to his present purpose; but he perceived they could not bear it. They could patiently hear the history of the Old Testament told (it was a piece of learning which they themselves dealt much in); but if Stephen go about to tell them that their power and tyranny must come down, and that the church must be governed by a spirit of holiness and love, and heavenly-mindedness, they will not so much as give him the hearing. It is probable that he perceived this, and that they were going to silence him; and therefore he breaks off abruptly in the midst of his discourse, and by that spirit of wisdom, courage, and power, wherewith he was filled, he sharply rebuked his persecutors, and exposed their true character; for, if they will not admit the testimony of the gospel to them, it shall become a testimony against them.

I. They, like their fathers, were stubborn and wilful, and would not be wrought upon by the various methods God took to reclaim and reform them; they were like their fathers, inflexible both to the word of God and to his providences. 1. They were *stiff-necked* (*v.* 51), and would not submit their necks to the sweet and easy yoke of God's government, nor draw in it, but were *like a bullock unaccustomed to the yoke;* or they would not bow their heads, no, not to God himself, would not do obeisance to him, would not humble themselves before him. The stiff neck is the same with the hard heart, obstinate and contumacious, and that will not yield—the general character of the Jewish nation, Exod. xxxii. 9; xxxiii. 3, 5; xxxiv. 9; Deut. ix. 6, 13; xxxi. 27; Ezek ii. 4. 2. They were *uncircumcised in heart and ears;* their hearts and ears were not devoted and given up to God, as the body of the people were in profession by the sign of circumcision: "In name and show you are circumcised Jews, but in heart and ears you are still uncircumcised heathens, and pay no more deference to the authority of your God than they do, Jer. ix. 26. You are under the power of unmortified lusts and corruptions, which stop your ears to the voice of God, and harden your hearts to that which is both most commanding and most affecting." They had not that *circumcision made without hands, in putting off the body of the sins of the flesh,* Col. ii. 11.

II. They, like their fathers, were not only not influenced by the methods God took to reform them, but they were enraged and incensed against them: *You do always resist the Holy Ghost.* 1. They resisted the Holy Ghost speaking to them by the prophets, whom they opposed and contradicted, hated and ridiculed; this seems especially meant here, by the following explication, *Which of the prophets have not your fathers persecuted?* In persecuting and silencing those that spoke by the inspiration of the Holy Ghost they resisted the Holy Ghost. Their fathers resisted the Holy Ghost in the prophets that God raised up to them, and so did they in Christ's apostles and ministers, who spoke by the same Spirit, and had greater measures of his gifts than the prophets of the Old Testament had, and yet were more resisted. 2. They resisted the Holy Ghost striving with them by their own consciences, and would not comply with the convictions and dictates of them. God's Spirit strove with them as with the old world, but in vain; they resisted him, took part with their corruptions against their convictions, and rebelled against the light. There is that in our sinful hearts that always resists the Holy Ghost, a flesh that lusts against the Spirit, and wars against his motions; but in the hearts of God's elect, when the fulness of time comes, this resistance is overcome and overpowered, and after a struggle the throne of Christ is set up in the soul, and every thought that had exalted itself against it is brought into captivity to it, 2 Cor. x. 4, 5. That grace therefore which effects this change might more fitly be called *victorious* grace than *irresistible.*

III. They, like their fathers, persecuted and slew those whom God sent unto them to call them to duty, and make them offers of mercy. 1. Their fathers had been the cruel and constant persecutors of the Old-Testament prophets (*v.* 52): *Which of the prophets have not your fathers persecuted?* More or less, one time or other, they had a blow at them all. With regard even to those that lived in the best reigns, when the princes did not persecute them, there was a malignant party in the nation that mocked at them and abused them, and most of them were at last, either by colour of law or popular fury, put to death; and that which aggravated the sin of persecuting the prophets was, that the business of the prophets they were so spiteful at was to *show before of the coming of the just One,* to give notice of God's kind intentions towards that people, to send the Messiah among them in the fulness of time. Those that were the messengers of such glad tidings should have been courted and caressed, and have had the preferments of the best of benefactors; but, instead of this, they had the treatment of the worst of malefactors. 2. They had been the *betrayers and murderers of the just One* himself, as Peter had told them, *ch.* iii. 14, 15; v. 30. They had hired Judas to betray him, and had in a manner forced Pilate to condemn him; and therefore it is charged upon them that they were his betrayers and murderers. Thus they were the genuine seed of those who slew the prophets that foretold his coming, which, by slaying him, they showed they would have done if they had lived then; and thus, as our Saviour had told them, they brought upon themselves the guilt of the blood of all the prophets. To which of the prophets would those have shown any respect who had no regard to the Son of God himself?

IV. They, like their fathers, put contempt upon divine revelation, and would not be guided and governed by it; and this was the aggravation of their sin, that God had given, as to their fathers his law, so to them his gospel, in vain. 1. Their fathers received the law, and did not observe it, *v.* 53. God wrote to them the great things of his law, after he had first spoken them to them; and yet they were counted by them as a strange or foreign thing, which they were no way concerned in. The law is said to be *received by the disposition of angels,* because angels were employed in the solemnity of giving the law, in the thunderings and lightnings, and the sound of the trumpet. It is said to be *ordained by angels* (Gal. iii. 19), God is said to come *with ten thousand* of his saints to give the law (Deut. xxxiii. 2), and it was a *word spoken by angels,* Heb. ii. 2. This put an honour both upon the law and the Lawgiver, and should increase our veneration for both. But those that thus received the law yet kept it not, but by making the golden calf broke it immediately in a capital instance. 2. They received the gospel now, by the disposition, not of angels, but of the Holy Ghost,—not with the sound of a trumpet, but, which was more strange, in the gift of tongues, and yet they did not embrace it. They would not yield to the plainest demonstrations, any more than their fathers before them did, for they were resolved not to comply with God either in his law or in his gospel.

We have reason to think Stephen had a great deal more to say, and would have said it if they would have suffered him; but they were wicked and unreasonable men with whom he had to do, that could no more hear reason than they could speak it.

54 When they heard these things,
they were cut to the heart, and they
gnashed on him with *their* teeth. 55
But he, being full of the Holy Ghost,
looked up stedfastly into heaven, and
saw the glory of God, and Jesus
standing on the right hand of God,
56 And said, Behold, I see the
heavens opened, and the Son of man
standing on the right hand of God.
57 Then they cried out with a loud
voice, and stopped their ears, and
ran upon him with one accord, 58
And cast *him* out of the city, and
stoned *him:* and the witnesses laid
down their clothes at a young man's
feet, whose name was Saul. 59 And
they stoned Stephen, calling upon
God, and saying, Lord Jesus, receive
my spirit. 60 And he kneeled down,
and cried with a loud voice, Lord,
lay not this sin to their charge. And
when he had said this, he fell asleep.

We have here the death of the first martyr of the Christian church, and there is in this story a lively instance of the outrage and fury of the persecutors (such as we may expect to meet with if we are called out to suffer for Christ), and of the courage and comfort of the persecuted, that are thus called out. Here is hell in its fire and darkness, and heaven in its light and brightness; and these serve as foils to set off each other. It is not here said that the votes of the council were taken upon his case, and that by the majority he was found guilty, and then condemned and ordered to be stoned to death, according to the law, as a blasphemer; but, it is likely, so it was, and that it was not by the violence of the people, without order of the council, that he was put to death; for here is the usual ceremony of regular executions—he was cast out of the city, and the hands of the witnesses were first upon him.

Let us observe here the wonderful discomposure of the spirits of his enemies and persecutors, and the wonderful composure of his spirit.

I. See the strength of corruption in the persecutors of Stephen—malice in perfection, hell itself broken loose, men become incarnate devils, and the serpent's seed spitting their venom.

1. *When they heard these things they were cut to the heart* (*v.* 54), διεπρίοντο, the same word that is used Heb. xi. 37, and translated *they were sawn asunder.* They were put to as much torture in their minds as ever the martyrs were put to in their bodies. They were filled with indignation at the unanswerable arguments that Stephen urged for their conviction, and that they could find nothing to say against them. They were not pricked to the heart with sorrow, as those were *ch.* ii. 37, but cut to the heart with rage and fury, as they themselves were, *ch.* v. 33. Stephen rebuked them sharply, as Paul expresses it (Tit. i. 13), ἀποτόμως—*cuttingly,* for they were cut to the heart by the reproof. Note, Rejecters of the gospel and opposers of it are really tormentors to themselves. Enmity to God is a heart-cutting thing; faith and love are heart-healing. When they heard how he that *looked like an angel* before he began his discourse talked like an angel, like a messenger from heaven, before he concluded it, they were *like a wild bull in a net, full of the fury of the Lord* (Isa. li. 20), despairing to run down

a cause so bravely pleaded, and yet resolved not to yield to it.

2. They *gnashed upon him with their teeth.* This denotes,(1.) Great malice and rage against him. Job complained of his enemy that he *gnashed upon him with his teeth,* Job xvi. 9. The language of this was, *Oh that we had of his flesh to eat!* Job xxxi. 31. They *grinned at him,* as dogs at those they are enraged at; and therefore Paul, cautioning against those of the circumcision, says, *Beware of dogs,* Phil. iii. 2. Enmity at the saints turns men into brute beasts. (2.) Great vexation within themselves; they fretted to see in him such manifest tokens of a divine power and presence, and it vexed them to the heart. The *wicked shall see it and be grieved, he shall gnash with his teeth and melt away,* Ps. cxii. 10. Gnashing with the teeth is often used to express the horror and torments of the damned. Those that have the malice of hell cannot but have with it some of the pains of hell.

3. *They cried out with a loud voice* (*v.* 57), to irritate and excite one another, and to drown the noise of the clamours of their own and one another's consciences; when he said, *I see heaven opened,* they cried with a loud voice, that he might not be heard to speak. Note, It is very common for a righteous cause, particularly the righteous cause of Christ's religion, to be attempted to be run down by noise and clamour; what is wanting in reason is made up in tumult, and *the cry of him that ruleth among fools, while the words of the wise are heard in quiet.* They cried with a loud voice, as soldiers when they are going to engage in battle, mustering up all their spirit and vigour for this desperate encounter.

4. They *stopped their ears,* that they might not hear their own noisiness; or perhaps under pretence that they could not bear to hear his blasphemies. As Caiaphas rent his clothes when Christ said, *Hereafter you shall see the Son of man coming in glory* (Matt. xxvi. 64, 65), so here these *stopped their ears* when Stephen said, *I now see the Son of man standing in glory,* both pretending that what was spoken was not to be heard with patience. Their stopping their ears was, (1.) A manifest specimen of their wilful obstinacy; they were resolved they would not hear what had a tendency to convince them, which was what the prophets often complained of: they were *like the deaf adder, that will not hear the voice of the charmer,* Ps. lviii. 4, 5. (2.) It was a fatal omen of that judicial hardness to which God would give them up. They stopped their ears, and then God, in a way of righteous judgment, stopped them. This was the work that was now in doing with the unbelieving Jews: *Make the heart of this people fat, and their ears heavy;* thus was Stephen's character of them answered, *You uncircumcised in heart and ears.*

5. They *ran upon him with one accord*—the people and the elders of the people, judges, prosecutors, witnesses, and spectators, they all flew upon him, as beasts upon their prey. See how violent they were, and in what haste—they ran upon him, though there was no danger of his outrunning them; and see how unanimous they were in this evil thing—they ran upon him *with one accord,* one and all, hoping thereby to terrify him, and put him into confusion, envying him his composure and comfort in soul, with which he wonderfully enjoyed himself in the midst of this hurry; they did all they could to ruffle him.

6. They *cast him out of the city, and stoned him,* as if he were not worthy to live in Jerusalem; nay, not worthy to live in this world, pretending herein to execute the law of Moses (Lev. xxiv. 16), *He that blasphemeth the name of the Lord shall surely be put to death, all the congregation shall certainly stone him.* And thus they had put Christ to death, when this same court had found him guilty of blasphemy, but that, for his greater ignominy, they were desirous he should be crucified, and God overruled it for the fulfilling of the scripture. The fury with which they managed the execution is intimated in this: they cast him out of the city, as if they could not bear the sight of him; they treated him as an anathema, as the offscouring of all things. The witnesses against him were the leaders in the execution, according to the law (Deut. xvii. 7), *The hands of the witnesses shall be first upon him, to put him to death,* and particularly in the case of blasphemy, Lev. xxiv. 14; Deut. xiii. 9. Thus they were to confirm their testimony. Now, the stoning of a man being a laborious piece of work, the witnesses took off their upper garments, that they might not hang in their way, *and they laid them down at a young man's feet, whose name was Saul,* now a pleased spectator of this tragedy. It is the first time we find mention of his name; we shall know it and love it better when we find it changed to *Paul,* and him changed from a persecutor into a preacher. This little instance of his agency in Stephen's death he afterwards reflected upon with regret (*ch.* xxii. 20): *I kept the raiment of those that slew him.*

II. See the strength of grace in Stephen, and the wonderful instances of God's favour to him, and working in him. As his persecutors were full of Satan, so was he *full of the Holy Ghost,* fuller than ordinary, anointed with fresh oil for the combat, that, as the day, so might the strength be. Upon this account those are *blessed who are persecuted for righteousness' sake,* that *the Spirit of God and of glory rests upon them,* 1 Pet. iv. 14. When he was chosen to public service, he was described to be a man *full of the Holy Ghost* (*ch.* vi. 5), and now he is called out to martyrdom he has still the same character. Note, Those that are full of the Holy Ghost are fit for any thing, either to act for Christ or to suffer for him. And those whom God calls out to difficult services for his name he will qualify for those services, and carry comfortably through them, by filling them with the Holy Ghost, that, as their afflictions for Christ abound, their consolation in him may yet more abound, and then *none of these things move them.* Now here we have a remarkable communion between this blessed martyr and the blessed Jesus in this critical moment. When the followers of Christ are for his sake *killed all the day long, and accounted as s eep for the slaughter,* does this separate them from the love of Christ? Does he love them the less? Do they love him the less? No, by no means; and so it appears by this narrative, in which we may observe,

1. Christ's gracious manifestation of himself to Stephen, both for his comfort and for his honour, in the midst of his sufferings. When they were cut to the heart, and gnashed upon him with their teeth, ready to eat him up, then he had a view of the glory of Christ sufficient to fill him with joy unspeakable, which was intended not only for his encouragement, but for the support and comfort of all God's suffering servants in all ages.

(1.) He, *being full of the Holy Ghost, looked up stedfastly into heaven, v.* 55. [1.] Thus he looked above the power and fury of his persecutors, and did as it were despise them, and laugh them to scorn, as the daughter of Zion, Isa. xxxvii. 22. They had their eyes fixed upon him, full of malice and cruelty; but he looked up to heaven, and never minded them, was so taken up with the eternal life now in prospect that he seemed to have no manner of concern for the natural life now at stake. Instead of looking about him, to see either which way he was in danger or which way he might make his escape, he looks up to heaven; thence only comes his help, and thitherward his way is still open; though they compass him about on every side, they cannot interrupt his intercourse with heaven. Note, A believing regard to God and the upper world will be of great use to us, to set us above the fear of man; for as far as we are under the influence of that fear we *forget the Lord our Maker,* Isa. li. 13. [2.] Thus he directed his sufferings to the glory of God, to the honour of Christ, and did as it were appeal to heaven concerning them (Lord, for thy sake I suffer this) and express his earnest expectation that Christ should be magnified in his body. Now that he was ready to be offered he looks up stedfastly to heaven, as one willing to offer himself. [3.] Thus he lifted up his soul with his eyes to God in the heavens, in pious ejaculations, calling upon God for wisdom and grace to carry him through this trial in a right manner. God has promised that he will be with his servants whom he calls out to suffer for him; but he will for this be sought unto. He is nigh unto them, but it is *in that for which they call upon him. Is any afflicted? Let him pray.* [4.] Thus he breathed after the heavenly country, to which he saw the fury of his persecutors would presently send him. It is good for dying saints to look up stedfastly to heaven: "Yonder is the place whither death will carry my better part, and then, *O death! where is thy sting?"* [5.] Thus he made it to appear that he was full of the Holy Ghost; for, wherever the Spirit of grace dwells, and works, and reigns, he directs the eye of the soul upward. Those that are full of the Holy Ghost will look up stedfastly to heaven, for there their heart is. [6.] Thus he put himself into a posture to receive the following manifestation of the divine glory and grace. If we expect to hear from heaven, we must look up stedfastly to heaven.

(2.) He saw the glory of God (*v.* 55); for *he saw,* in order to this, *the heavens opened, v.* 56. Some think his eyes were strengthened, and the sight of them so raised above its natural pitch, by a supernatural power, that he saw into the third heavens, though at so vast a distance, as Moses's sight was enlarged to see the whole land of Canaan Others think it was a representation of the glory of God set before his eyes, as, before, Isaiah and Ezekiel; heaven did as it were come down to him, as Rev. xxi. 2. The heavens were opened, to give him a view of the happiness he was going to, that he might, in prospect of it, go cheerfully through death, so great a death. Would we by faith look up stedfastly, we might see the heavens opened by the mediation of Christ, the veil being rent, and a new and living way laid open for us into the holiest. The heaven is opened for the settling of a correspondence between God and men, that his favours and blessings may come down to us, and our prayers and praises may go up to him. We may also see the glory of God, as far as he has revealed it in his word, and the sight of this will carry us through all the terrors of sufferings and death.

(3.) He *saw Jesus standing on the right hand of God* (*v.* 55), *the Son of man,* so it is *v.* 56. Jesus, being the Son of man, having taken our nature with him to heaven, and being there clothed with a body, might be seen with bodily eyes, and so Stephen saw him. When the Old-Testament prophets saw the glory of God it was attended with angels. The Shechinah or divine presence in Isaiah's vision was attended with seraphim, in Ezekiel's vision with cherubim, both signifying the angels, the ministers of God's providence. But here no mention is made of the angels, though they surround the throne and the Lamb; instead of them Stephen sees Jesus at the right hand of God, the great Mediator of God's grace, from whom more glory redounds to God than from all the ministration of the holy angels. The glory of God shines brightest in the face of Jesus Christ; for there shines the glory of his grace, which is the most illustrious instance of his glory. God appears more glorious with Jesus standing at his right hand than with millions of angels about him. Now, [1.] Here is a proof of the exaltation of Christ to the Father's right hand; the apostles saw him ascend, but they did not see him sit down, *A cloud received him out of their sight*. We are told that he sat down on the right hand of God; but was he ever seen there? Yes, Stephen saw him there, and was abundantly satisfied with the sight. He saw Jesus at the right hand of God, denoting both his transcendant dignity and his sovereign dominion, his uncontrollable ability and his universal agency; whatever God's right hand gives to us, or receives from us, or does concerning us, it is by him; for he is his right hand. [2.] He is usually said to *sit* there; but Stephen sees him *standing* there, as one more than ordinarily concerned at present for his suffering servant; he stood up as a judge to plead his cause against his persecutors; he is *raised up out of his holy habitation* (Zech. ii. 13), *comes out of his place to punish*, Isa. xxvi. 21. He stands ready to receive him and crown him, and in the mean time to give him a prospect of the joy set before him. [3.] This was intended for the encouragement of Stephen. He sees Christ is for him, and then no matter who is against him. When our Lord Jesus was in his agony an angel appeared to him, strengthening him; but Stephen had Christ himself appearing to him. Note, Nothing so comfortable to dying saints, nor so animating to suffering saints, as to see Jesus at the right hand of God; and, blessed be God, by faith we may see him there.

(4.) He told those about him what he saw (*v.* 56): *Behold, I see the heavens opened.* That which was a cordial to him ought to have been a conviction to them, and a caution to them to take heed of proceeding against one upon whom heaven thus smiled; and therefore what he saw he declared, let them make what use they pleased of it. If some were exasperated by it, others perhaps might be wrought upon to consider this Jesus whom they persecuted, and to believe in him.

2. Stephen's pious addresses to Jesus Christ. The manifestation of God's glory to him did not set him above praying, but rather set him upon it: *They stoned Stephen, calling upon God, v.* 59. Though he called upon God, and by that showed himself to be a trueborn Israelite, yet they proceeded to stone him, not considering how dangerous it is to fight against those who have an interest in heaven. Though they stoned him, yet he called upon God; nay, therefore he called upon him. Note, It is the comfort of those who are unjustly hated and persecuted by men that they have a God to go to, a God all-sufficient to call upon. Men stop their ears, as they did here (*v.* 57), but God does not. Stephen was now cast out of the city, but he was not cast out from his God. He was now taking his leave of the world, and therefore calls upon God; for we must do this as long as we live. Note, It is good to die praying; then we need help—strength we never had, to do a work we never did—and how can we fetch in that help and strength but by prayer? Two short prayers Stephen offered up to God in his dying moments, and in them as it were breathed out his soul:—

(1.) Here is a prayer for himself: *Lord Jesus, receive my spirit.* Thus Christ had himself resigned his spirit immediately into the hands of the Father. We are here taught to resign ours into the hands of Christ as Mediator, by him to be recommended to the Father. Stephen saw Jesus standing at the Father's right hand, and he thus calls to him: "Blessed Jesus, do that for me now which thou standest there to do for all thine, receive my departing spirit into thy hand." Observe, [1.] The soul is the man, and our great concern, living and dying, must be about our souls. Stephen's body was to be miserably broken and shattered, and overwhelmed with a shower of stones, the earthly house of this tabernacle violently beaten down and abused; but, however it goes with that, "Lord," saith he, "let my spirit be safe; let it go well with my poor soul." Thus, while we live, our care should be that though the body be starved or stripped the soul may be fed and clothed, though the body lie in pain the soul may dwell at ease; and, when we die, that though the body be thrown by as a despised broken vessel, and a vessel in which there is no pleasure, yet the soul may be presented a vessel of honour, that God may be the strength of the heart and its portion, though the flesh fail. [2.] Our Lord Jesus is God, to whom we are to seek, and in whom we are to confide and comfort ourselves living and dying. Stephen here prays to Christ, and so must we; for it is the will of God that all men should thus *honour the Son, even as they honour the Father.* It is Christ we are to commit ourselves to, who alone is able to keep what we commit to him against that day; it is necessary that we have an eye to Christ when we come to die, for there is no venturing into another world but under his conduct, no living comforts in dying moments but what are fetched from him. [3.] Christ's receiving our spirits at death is the great thing we are to be careful about, and to comfort ourselves with. We ought to be in care about this while we live, that Christ may receive our spirits when we die; for, if he reject and disown them, whither will they betake themselves? How can they escape being a prey to the roaring lion? To him therefore we must commit them daily, to be ruled and sanctified, and made meet for heaven, and then, and not otherwise, he will receive them. And, if this has been our care while we live, it may be our comfort when we come to die, that we shall be received into everlasting habitations.

(2.) Here is a prayer for his persecutors, *v.* 60.

[1.] The circumstances of this prayer are observable; for it seems to have been offered up with something more of solemnity than the former. *First,* He *knelt down,* which was an expression of his humility in prayer. *Secondly,* He *cried with a loud voice,* which was an expression of his importunity. But why should he thus show more humility and importunity in this request than in the former? Why, none could doubt of his being in good earnest in his prayers for himself, and therefore there he needed not to use such outward expressions of it; but in his prayer for his enemies, because that is so much against the grain of corrupt nature, it was requisite he should give proofs of his being in earnest.

[2.] The prayer itself: *Lord, lay not this sin to their charge.* Herein he followed the example of his dying Master, who prayed thus for his persecutors, *Father, forgive them;* and set an example to all following sufferers in the cause of Christ thus to pray for those that persecute them. Prayer may preach. This did so to those who stoned Stephen, and he knelt down that they might take notice he was going to pray, and cried with a loud voice that they might take notice of what he said, and might learn, *First,* That what they did was a sin, a great sin, which, if divine mercy and grace did not prevent, would be laid to their charge, to their everlasting confusion. *Secondly,* That, notwithstanding their malice and fury against him, he was in charity with them, and was so far from desiring that God would avenge his death upon them that it was his hearty prayer to God that it might not in any degree be laid to their charge. A sad reckoning there would be for it. If they did not repent, it would certainly be laid to their charge; but he, for his part, did not desire the woeful day. Let them take notice of this, and, when their thoughts were cool, surely they would not easily forgive themselves for putting him to death who could so easily forgive them. *The blood-thirsty hate the upright, but the just seek his soul,* Prov. xxix. 10. *Thirdly,* That, though the sin was very heinous, yet they must not despair of the pardon of it upon their repentance. If they would lay it to their hearts, God would not lay it to their charge. "Do you think," saith St. Austin, "that Paul heard Stephen pray this prayer? It is likely he did and ridiculed it then *(audivit subsannans, sed irrisit—he heard with scorn),* but afterwards he had the benefit of it, and fared the better for it."

3. His expiring with this: *When he had said this, he fell asleep;* or, as he was saying this, the blow came that was mortal. Note, Death is but a sleep to good people; not the sleep of the soul (Stephen had given that up into Christ's hand), but the sleep of the body; it is its rest from all its griefs and toils; it is perfect ease from toil and pain. Stephen died as much in a hurry as ever any man did, and yet, when he died, he fell asleep. He applied himself to his dying work with as much composure of mind as if he had been going to sleep; it was but closing his eyes, and dying. Observe, He fell asleep when he was praying for his persecutors; it is expressed as if he thought he could not die in peace till he had done this. It contributes very much to our dying comfortably to die in charity with all men; we are then found of Christ in peace; let not the sun of life go down upon our wrath. He fell asleep; the vulgar Latin adds, *in the Lord,* in the embraces of his love. If he thus sleep, he shall do well; he shall awake again in the morning of the resurrection.

CHAP. VIII.

In this chapter we have an account of the persecutions of the Christians, and the propagating of Christianity thereby. It was strange, but very true, that the disciples of Christ the more they were afflicted the more they multiplied. I. Here is the church suffering; upon the occasion of putting Stephen to death a very sharp storm arose, which forced many from Jerusalem, ver. 1—3. II. Here is the church spreading by the ministry of Philip and others that were dispersed upon that occasion. We have here, 1. The gospel brought to Samaria, preached there (ver. 4, 5), embraced there (ver. 6—8), even by Simon Magus (ver. 9—13); the gift of the Holy Ghost conferred upon some of the believing Samaritans by the imposition of the hands of Peter and John (ver. 14—17); and the severe rebuke given by Peter to Simon Magus for offering money for a power to bestow that gift, ver. 18—25. 2. The gospel sent to Ethiopia, by the eunuch, a person of quality of that country. He is returning home in his chariot from Jerusalem, ver. 26—28. Philip is sent to him, and in his chariot preaches Christ to him (ver. 29—35), baptizes him upon his profession of the Christian faith (ver. 36—38), and then leaves him, ver. 39, 40. Thus in different ways and methods the gospel was dispersed among the nations, and, one way or other, "Have they not all heard?"

AND Saul was consenting unto
his death. And at that time
there was a great persecution against
the church which was at Jerusalem;
and they were all scattered abroad
throughout the regions of Judæa and
Samaria, except the apostles. 2 And
devout men carried Stephen *to his
burial,* and made great lamentation
over him. 3 As for Saul, he made
havock of the church, entering into
every house, and haling men and
women committed *them* to prison.

In these verses we have,

I. Something more concerning Stephen and his death; how people stood affected to it—variously, as generally in such cases, according to men's different sentiments of things. Christ had said to his disciples, when he was parting with them (John xvi. 20), *You shall weep and lament, but the world shall rejoice.* Accordingly here is, 1. Stephen's death rejoiced in by one—by many, no doubt, but by one in particular, and that was Saul, who was afterwards called Paul; he was *consenting to his death,* συνευδοκῶν—*he consented to it with delight* (so the word signifies); he was pleased with it. He fed his eyes with this bloody spectacle, in hopes it would put a stop to the growth of Christianity. We have reason to think that Paul ordered Luke to insert this, for shame to himself, and glory to free grace. Thus he owns himself guilty of the blood of Stephen, and aggravates it with this, that he did not do it with regret and reluctancy, but with delight and a full satisfaction, like those who not only *do such things, but have pleasure in those that do them.* 2. Stephen's death bewailed by others (*v.* 2)—*devout men,* which some understand of those that were properly so called, *proselytes,* one of whom Stephen himself probably was. Or, it may be taken more largely; some of the church that were more devout and zealous than the rest went and gathered up the poor crushed and broken remains, to which they gave a decent interment, probably in the *field of blood,* which was bought some time ago to bury strangers in. They buried him solemnly, and made great lamentation over him. Though his death was of great advantage to himself, and great service to the church, yet they bewailed it as a general loss, so well qualified was he for the service, and so likely to be useful both as a deacon and as a disputant. It is a bad symptom if, when such men are taken away, it is not laid to heart. Those devout men paid these their last respects to Stephen, (1.) To show that they were not ashamed of the cause for which he suffered, nor afraid of the wrath of those that were enemies to it; for, though they now triumph, the cause is a righteous cause, and will be at last a victorious one. (2.) To show the great value and esteem they had for this faithful servant of Jesus Christ, this first martyr for the gospel, whose memory shall always be precious to them, notwithstanding the ignominy of his death. They study to do honour to him upon whom God put honour. (3.) To testify their belief and hope of the *resurrection of the dead, and the life of the world to come.*

II. An account of this persecution of the church, which begins upon the martyrdom of Stephen. When the fury of the Jews ran with such violence, and to such a height, against Stephen, it could not quickly either stop itself or spend itself. The bloody are often in scripture called *blood-thirsty;* for when they have tasted blood they thirst for more. One would have thought Stephen's dying prayers and dying comforts should have overcome them, and melted them into a better opinion of Christians and Christianity; but it seems they did not: the persecution goes on; for they were more exasperated when they saw they could prevail nothing, and, as if they hoped to be too hard for God himself, they resolve to follow their blow; and perhaps, because they were none of them struck dead upon the place for stoning Stephen, their hearts were the more fully set in them to do evil. Perhaps the disciples were also the more emboldened to dispute against them as Stephen did, seeing how triumphantly he finished his course, which would provoke them so much the more. Observe,

1. Against whom this persecution was raised: It was *against the church in Jerusalem,* which is no sooner planted than it is persecuted, as Christ often intimated that tribulation and persecution would arise *because of the word.* And Christ had particularly foretold that Jerusalem would soon be made too hot for his followers, for that city had been famous for killing the prophets and stoning those that were sent to it, Matt. xxiii. 37. It should seem that in this persecution many were put to death, for Paul owns that at this time he persecuted this way *unto the death* (*ch.* xxi. 4), and (*ch.* xxvi. 10) that *when they were put to death he gave his voice against them.*

2. Who was an active man in it; none so zealous, so busy, as Saul, a young Pharisee, *v.* 3. As for Saul (who had been twice mentioned before, and now again for a notorious persecutor) *he made havoc of the church;* he did all he could to lay it waste and ruin it; he cared not what mischief he did to the disciples of Christ, nor knew when to stop. He aimed at no less than the cutting off of the gospel Israel, that the name of it should be no more in remembrance, Ps. lxxxiii. 4. He was the fittest tool the chief priests could find out to serve their purposes; he was informer-general against the disciples, a messenger of the great council to be employed in searching for meetings, and seizing all that were suspected to favour that way. Saul was bred a scholar, a gentleman, and yet did not think it below him to be employed in the vilest work of that kind. (1.) He *entered into every house,* making no difficulty of breaking open doors, night or day, and having a force attending him for that purpose. He entered into every house where they used to hold their meetings, or every house that had any Christians in it, or was thought to have. No man could be secure in his own house, though it was his castle. (2.) He haled, with the utmost contempt and cruelty, both men and women, dragged them along the streets, without any regard to the tenderness of the weaker sex; he stooped so low as to take cognizance of the meanest that were leavened with the gospel, so extremely bigoted was he. (3.) He committed them to prison, in order to their being tried and put to death, unless they would renounce Christ; and some, we find, were compelled by him to blaspheme, *ch.* xxvi. 11.

3. What was the effect of this persecution: *They were all scattered abroad* (*v.* 1), not all the believers, but all the preachers, who were principally struck at, and against whom warrants were issued out to take them up. They, remembering our Master's rule *(when they persecute you in one city, flee to another)*, dis-

persed themselves by agreement *throughout the regions of Judea* and of Samaria; not so much for fear of sufferings (for Judea and Samaria were not so far off from Jerusalem but that, if they made a public appearance there, as they determined to do, their persecutors' power would soon reach them there), but because they looked upon this as an intimation of Providence to them to scatter. Their work was pretty well done in Jerusalem, and now it was time to think of the necessities of other places; for their Master had told them that they must be his witnesses in Jerusalem first, and then *in all Judea and in Samaria,* and then *to the uttermost part of the earth* (*ch.* i. 8), and this method they observe. Though persecution may not drive us off from our work, yet it may send us, as a hint of Providence, to work elsewhere. The preachers were all scattered *except the apostles,* who, probably, were directed by the Spirit to continue at Jerusalem yet for some time, they being, by the special providence of God, screened from the storm, and by the special grace of God enabled to face the storm. They tarried at Jerusalem, that they might be ready to go where their assistance was most needed by the other preachers that were sent to break the ice; as Christ ordered his disciples to go to those places where he himself designed to go, Luke x. 1. The apostles continued longer together at Jerusalem than one would have thought, considering the command and commission given them, to *go into all the world,* and to *disciple all nations.* See *ch.* xv. 6; Gal. i. 17. But what was done by the evangelists whom they sent forth was reckoned as done by them.

4 Therefore they that were scattered abroad went every where preaching the word. 5 Then Philip went
down to the city of Samaria, and
preached Christ unto them. 6 And
the people with one accord gave heed
unto those things which Philip spake,
hearing and seeing the miracles which
he did. 7 For unclean spirits, crying with loud voice, came out of
many that were possessed *with them:*
and many taken with palsies, and
that were lame, were healed. 8 And
there was great joy in that city. 9
But there was a certain man, called
Simon, which beforetime in the same
city used sorcery, and bewitched the
people of Samaria, giving out that
himself was some great one: 10 To
whom they all gave heed, from the
least to the greatest, saying, This
man is the great power of God. 11
And to him they had regard, because
that of long time he had bewitched
them with sorceries. 12 But when
they believed Philip preaching the
things concerning the kingdom of
God, and the name of Jesus Christ,
they were baptized, both men and
women. 13 Then Simon himself
believed also: and when he was baptized, he continued with Philip, and
wondered, beholding the miracles and
signs which were done.

Samson's riddle is here again unriddled: *Out of the eater comes forth meat, and out of the strong sweetness.* The persecution that was designed to extirpate the church was by the overruling providence of God made an occasion of the enlargement of it. Christ had said, *I am come to send fire on the earth;* and they thought, by scattering those who were kindled with that fire, to have put it out, but instead of this they did but help to spread it.

I. Here is a general account of what was done by them all (*v.* 4): *They went every where, preaching the word.* They did not go to hide themselves for fear of suffering, no, nor to show themselves as proud of their sufferings; but they went up and down to scatter the knowledge of Christ in every place where they were scattered. They went every where, into the way of the Gentiles, and the cities of the Samaritans, which before they were forbidden to go into, Matt. x. 5. They did not keep together in a body, though this might have been a strength to them; but they scattered into all parts, not to take their ease, but to find out work. They went *evangelizing* the world, preaching the word of the gospel; it was this which filled them, and which they endeavoured to fill the country with, those of them that were preachers in their preaching, and others in their common converse. They were now in a country where they were no strangers, for Christ and his disciples had conversed much in the regions of Judea; so that they had a foundation laid there for them to build upon; and it would be requisite to let the people there know what that doctrine which Jesus had preached there some time ago was come to, and that it was not lost and forgotten, as perhaps they were made to believe.

II. A particular account of what was done by Philip. We shall hear of the progress and success of others of them afterwards (*ch.* xi. 19), but here must attend the motions of Philip, not Philip the apostle, but Philip the deacon, who was chosen and ordained to serve tables, but having *used the office of a deacon well he purchased to himself a good degree, and great boldness in the faith,* 1 Tim. iii. 13. Stephen was advanced to the degree of a martyr, Philip to the degree of an evangelist, which when he entered upon, being obliged by it to *give himself to the word and prayer*, he was, no doubt, discharged from the office of a deacon; for how could he serve tables at Jerusalem, which by that office he was obliged to do, when he was preaching in Samaria? And it is probable that two others were chosen in the room of Stephen and Philip. Now observe,

1. What wonderful success Philip had in his preaching, and what reception he met with.

(1.) The place he chose was the city of Samaria, the head city of Samaria, the metropolis of that country, which stood where the city of Samaria had formerly stood, of the building of which we read, 1 Kings xvi. 24, now called *Sebaste*. Some think it was the same with Sychem or Sychar, that city of Samaria where Christ was, John iv. 5. Many of that city then believed in Christ, though he did no miracle among them (*v.* 39, 41), and now Philip, three years after, carries on the work then begun. The Jews would have no dealings with the Samaritans; but Christ sent his gospel to slay all enmities, and particularly that between the Jews and the Samaritans, by making them one in his church.

(2.) The doctrine he preached was Christ; for he determined to know nothing else. He *preached Christ to them; he proclaimed Christ to them* (so the word signifies), as a king, when he comes to the crown, is proclaimed throughout his dominions. The Samaritans had an expectation of the Messiah's coming, as appears by John iv. 25. Now Philip tells them that he is come, and that the Samaritans are welcome to him. Ministers' business is to preach Christ—Christ, and him crucified—Christ, and him glorified.

(3.) The proofs he produced for the confirmation of his doctrine were miracles, *v.* 6. To convince them that he had his commission from heaven (and therefore not only they might venture upon what he said, but they were bound to yield to it), he shows them this broad seal of heaven annexed to it, which the God of truth would never put to a lie. The miracles were undeniable; they heard and saw the miracles which he did. They heard the commanding words he spoke, and saw the amazing effects of them immediately; that he spoke, and it was done. And the nature of the miracles was such as suited the intention of his commission, and gave light and lustre to it. [1.] He was sent to break the power of Satan; and, in token of this, unclean spirits, being charged in the name of the Lord Jesus to remove, *came out of many that were possessed with them, v.* 7. As far as the gospel prevails, Satan is forced to quit his hold of men and his interest in them, and then those are restored to themselves, and to their right mind again, who, while he kept possession, were distracted. Wherever the gospel gains the admission and submission it ought to have, evil spirits are dislodged, and particularly *unclean spirits,* all inclinations to the lusts of the flesh, which war against the soul; for God has called us from uncleanness to holiness, 1 Thess. iv. 7. This was signified by the casting of these unclean spirits out of the bodies of people, who, it is here said, came out *crying with a loud voice,* which signifies that they came out with great reluctancy, and sorely against their wills, but were forced to acknowledge themselves overcome by a superior power, Mark i. 26; iii. 11; ix. 26. [2.] He was sent to heal the minds of men, to cure a distempered world, and to put it into a good state of health; and, in token of this, *many that were taken with palsies, and that were lame, were healed.* Those distempers are specified that were most difficult to be cured by the course of nature (that the miraculous cure might be the more illustrious), and those that were most expressive of the disease of sin and that moral impotency which the souls of men labour under as to the service of God. The grace of God in the gospel is designed for the healing of those that are spiritually lame and paralytic, and cannot help themselves, Rom. v. 6.

(4.) The acceptance which Philip's doctrine, thus proved, met with in Samaria (*v.* 6): *The people with one accord gave heed to those things which Philip spoke,* induced thereto by the miracles which served at first to gain attention, and so by degrees to gain assent. There then begin to be some hopes of people when they begin to take notice of what is said to them concerning the things of their souls and eternity—when they begin to give heed to the word of God, as those that are well pleased to hear it, desirous to understand and remember it, and that look upon themselves as concerned in it. The common people gave heed to Philip, οἱ ὄχλοι—*a multitude of them,* not here and there one, but with one accord; they were all of a mind, that it was fit the doctrine of the gospel should be enquired into, and an impartial hearing given to it.

(5.) The satisfaction they had in attending on, and attending to, Philip's preaching, and the success it had with many of them (*v.* 8): *There was great joy in that city;* for (*v.* 12) *they believed Philip, and were baptized* into the faith of Christ, the generality of them, *both men and women.* Observe, [1.] Philip preached *the things concerning the kingdom of God*, the constitution of that kingdom, the laws and ordinances of it, the liberties and privileges of it, and the obligations we are all under to be the loyal subjects of that kingdom; and he preached the name of Jesus Christ, as king of that kingdom—his *name, which is above every name.* He preached it up in its commanding power and influence—all that by which he has made himself known. [2.] The people not only gave heed to what he said, but at length believed it, were fully convinced that it was of God and not of men, and gave up themselves to the direction and government of it. As to this mountain, on which they had hitherto worshipped God, and placed a great deal of religion in it, they were now as much weaned from it as ever they had been wedded to it, and become *the true worshippers, who worship the Father in spirit and in truth,* and in the name of Christ, the true temple, John iv. 20—23. [3.] When they believed, without scruple (though they were Samaritans) and without delay *they were baptized,* openly professed the Christian faith, promised to adhere to it, and then, by washing them with water, were solemnly admitted into the communion of the Christian church, and owned as brethren by the disciples. *Men* only were capable of being admitted into the Jewish church by circumcision; but, to show that *in Jesus Christ there is neither male nor female* (Gal. iii. 28), but both are alike welcome to him, the initiating ordinance is such as women are capable of, for they are numbered with God's spiritual Israel, though not with Israel according to the flesh, Num. i. 2. And hence it is easily gathered that women are to be admitted to the Lord's supper, though it does not appear that there were any among those to whom it was first administered. [4.] This occasioned great joy; each one rejoiced for himself, as he in the parable who *found the treasure hid in the field;* and they all rejoiced for the benefit hereby brought to their city, and that it came without opposition, which it would scarcely have done if Samaria had been within the jurisdiction of the chief priests. Note, The bringing of the gospel to any place is just matter of joy, of great joy, to that place. Hence the spreading of the gospel in the world is often prophesied of in the Old Testament as the diffusing of joy among the nations: *Let the nations be glad and sing for joy,* Ps. lxvii. 4; 1 Thes. i. 6. The gospel of Christ does not make men melancholy, but fills them with joy, if it be received as it should be; for it is *glad tidings of great joy to all people,* Luke ii. 10.

2. What there was in particular at this city of Samaria that made the success of the gospel there more than ordinarily wonderful.

(1.) That Simon Magus had been busy there, and had gained a great interest among the people, and *yet they believed the things that Philip spoke.* To unlearn that which is bad proves many times a harder task than to learn that which is good. These Samaritans, though they were not idolaters as the Gentiles, nor prejudiced against the gospel by traditions received from their fathers, yet had of late been drawn to follow Simon, a conjurer (for so *Magus* signifies) who made a mighty noise among them, and had strangely *bewitched them.* We are told,

[1.] How strong the delusion of Satan was by which they were brought into the interests of this great deceiver. He had been for some time, nay, for a *long time, in this city, using sorceries;* perhaps he came there by the instigation of the devil, soon after our Saviour had been there, to undo what he had been doing there; for it was always Satan's way to crush a good work in its bud and infancy, 2 Cor. xi. 3; 1 Thes. iii. 5. Now,

First, Simon assumed to himself that which was considerable: *He gave out that he himself was some great one,* and would have all people to believe so and to pay him respect accordingly; and then, as to every thing else, they might do as they pleased. He had no design to reform their lives, nor improve their worship and devotion, only to make them believe that he was, *τὶς μέγας—some divine person.* Justin Martyr says that he would be worshipped as *πρῶτον θεὸν—the chief god.* He gave out himself to be *the Son of God, the Messiah,* so some think; or to be an angel, or a prophet. Perhaps he was uncertain within himself what title of honour to pretend to; but he would be thought *some great one.* Pride, ambition, and an affectation of grandeur, have always been the cause of abundance of mischief both to the world and to the church.

Secondly, The people ascribed to him what he pleased. 1. *They all gave heed to him, from the least to the greatest,* both young and old, both poor and rich, both governors and governed. *To him they had regard* (*v.* 10,11), and perhaps the more because the time fixed for the coming of the Messiah had now expired, which had raised a general expectation of the appearing of some great one about this time. Probably he was a native of their country, and therefore they embraced him the more cheerfully, that by giving honour to him they might reflect it upon themselves. 2. They said of him, *This man is the great power of God—the power of God, that great power* (so it might be read), that power which made the world. See how ignorant inconsiderate people mistake that which is done by the power of Satan, as if it were done by the power of God. Thus, in the Gentile world, devils pass for deities; and in the antichristian kingdom *all the world wonders after a beast,* to whom the dragon gives his power, and *who opens his mouth in blasphemy against God,* Rev. xiii. 2—5. 3. They were brought to it by his sorceries: *He bewitched the people of Samaria* (*v.* 9), *bewitched them with sorceries* (*v.* 11), that is, either, (1.) By his magic arts *he bewitched the minds of the people,* at least some of them, who drew in others. Satan, by God's permission, filled their hearts to follow Simon. *O foolish Galatians,* saith Paul, *who hath bewitched you?* Gal. iii. 1. These people are said to be bewitched by Simon, because they were so strangely infatuated to believe a lie. Or, (2.) By his magic arts he did *many signs and lying wonders,* which seemed to be miracles, but really were not so: like those of the magicians of Egypt, and those of *the man of sin,* 2 Thess. ii. 9. When they knew no better, they were influenced by his sorceries; but, when they were acquainted with Philip's real miracles, they saw plainly that the one was real and the other a sham, and that there was as much difference as between Aaron's rod and those of the magicians. *What is the chaff to the wheat?* Jer. xxiii. 28.

Thus, notwithstanding the influence Simon Magus had had upon them, and the unwillingness there generally is in people to own themselves in an error, and to retract it, yet, when they saw the difference between Simon and Philip, they quitted Simon, gave heed no longer to him, but to Philip: and thus you see,

[2.] How strong the power of Divine grace is, by which they were brought to Christ, who is truth itself, and was, as I may say, the great undeceiver. By that grace working with the word those that had been led captive by Satan *were brought into obedience to Christ.* Where Satan, as a *strong man armed,* kept possession of the palace, and thought himself safe, Christ, as a *stronger than he,* dispossessed him, and *divided the spoil; led captivity captive,* and made those the trophies of his victory whom the devil had triumphed over. Let us not despair of the worst, when even those whom Simon Magus had bewitched were brought to believe.

(2.) Here is another thing yet more wonderful, that Simon Magus himself became a convert to the faith of Christ, in show and profession, for a time. *Is Saul also among the prophets?* Yes (*v.* 13), *Simon himself believed also.* He was convinced that Philip preached a true doctrine, because he saw it confirmed by real miracles, of which he was the better able to judge because he was conscious to himself of the trick of his own pretended ones. [1.] The present conviction went so far that *he was baptized,* was admitted, as other believers were, into the church by baptism; and we have no reason to think that Philip did amiss in baptizing him, no, nor in baptizing him quickly. Though he had been a very wicked man, a sorcerer, a pretender to divine honours, yet, upon his solemn profession of repentance for his sin and faith in Jesus Christ, he was baptized. For, as great wickedness before conversion keeps not true penitents from the benefits of God's grace, so neither should it keep professing ones from church-fellowship. Prodigals, when they return, must be joyfully welcomed home, though we cannot be sure but that they will play the prodigal again. Nay, though he was now but a hypocrite, and really in *the gall of bitterness and bond of iniquity* all this while, and would soon have been found to be so if he had been tried awhile, yet Philip baptized him; for it is God's prerogative to know the heart. The church and its ministers must go by a judgment of charity, as far as there is room for it. It is a maxim in the law, *Donec contrarium patet, semper præsumitur meliori parti—We must hope the best as long as we can.* And it is a maxim in the discipline of the church, *De secretis non judicat ecclesia—The secrets of the heart God only judges.* [2.] The present conviction lasted so long that he continued with Philip. Though afterwards he apostatized from Christianity, yet not quickly. He courted Philip's acquaintance and now he that had given out himself to be some great one is content to sit at the feet of a preacher of the gospel. Even bad men, very bad, may sometimes be in a good frame, very good; and those whose hearts still go after their covetousness may possibly not only come before God as his people come, but continue with them. [3.] The present conviction was wrought and kept up by the miracles; he wondered to see himself so far outdone in signs and miracles. Many wonder at the proofs of divine truths who never experience the power of them.

14 Now when the apostles which
were at Jerusalem heard that Samaria
had received the word of God, they
sent unto them Peter and John: 15
Who, when they were come down,
prayed for them, that they might receive the Holy Ghost: 16 (For as
yet he was fallen upon none of them:
only they were baptized in the name
of the Lord Jesus.) 17 Then laid
they *their* hands on them, and they
received the Holy Ghost. 18 And
when Simon saw that through laying
on of the apostles' hands the Holy
Ghost was given, he offered them
money, 19 Saying, Give me also
this power, that on whomsoever I
lay hands, he may receive the Holy
Ghost. 20 But Peter said unto
him, Thy money perish with thee,
because thou hast thought that the
gift of God may be purchased with
money. 21 Thou hast neither part
nor lot in this matter: for thy heart
is not right in the right of God. 22
Repent therefore of this thy wickedness, and pray God, if perhaps the
thought of thine heart may be forgiven thee. 23 For I perceive that
thou art in the gall of bitterness, and
in the bond of iniquity. 24 Then
answered Simon, and said, Pray ye
to the Lord for me, that none of
these things which ye have spoken
come upon me. 25 And they, when
they had testified and preached the
word of the Lord, returned to Jerusalem, and preached the gospel in
many villages of the Samaritans.

God had wonderfully owned Philip in his work as an evangelist at Samaria, but he could do no more than an evangelist; there were some peculiar powers reserved to the apostles, for the keeping up of the dignity of their office, and here we have an account of what was done by two of them there—*Peter and John.* The twelve kept together at Jerusalem (*v.* 1), and thither these good tidings were brought them *that Samaria had received the word of God* (*v.* 14), that a great harvest of souls was gathered, and was likely to be gathered in to Christ there. The word of God was not only preached to them, but received by them; they bade it welcome, admitted the light of it, and submitted to the power of it: *When they heard it, they sent unto them Peter and John.* If Peter had been, as some say he was, the prince of the apostles, he would have sent some of them, or, if he had seen cause, would have gone himself of his own accord; but he was so far from this that he submitted to an order of the house, and, as a servant to the body, went whither they sent him. Two apostles were sent, the two most eminent, to Samaria, 1. To encourage Philip, to assist him, and strengthen his hands. Ministers in a higher station, and that excel in gifts and graces, should contrive how they may be helpful to those in a lower sphere, and contribute to their comfort and usefulness. 2. To carry on the good work that was begun among the people, and, with those heavenly graces that had enriched them, to confer upon them spiritual gifts. Now observe,

I. How they advanced and improved those of them that were sincere. It is said (*v.* 16), *The Holy Ghost was as yet fallen upon none of them,* in those extraordinary powers which were conveyed by the descent of the Spirit upon the day of pentecost. They were none of them endued with the gift of tongues, which seems then to have been the most usual immediate effect of the pouring out of the Spirit. See *ch.* x. 45, 46. This was both an eminent sign to those that believed not, and of excellent service to those that did. This, and other such gifts, they had not, *only they were baptized in the name of the Lord Jesus,* and so engaged in him and interested in him, which was necessary to salvation, and in this they had joy and satisfaction (*v.* 8), though they could not speak with tongues. Those that are indeed given up to Christ, and have experienced the sanctifying influences and operations of the Spirit of grace, have great reason to be thankful, and no reason to complain, though they have not those gifts that are for ornament, and would make them bright. But it is intended that they should go on to the perfection of the present dispensation, for the greater honour of the gospel. We have reason to think that Philip had received these gifts of the Holy Ghost himself, but had not a power to confer them; the apostles must come to do this; and they did it not upon all that were baptized, but upon some of them, and, it should seem, such as were designed for some office in the church, or at least to be eminent active members of it; and upon some of them *one gift of the Holy Ghost,* and upon others *another.* See 1 Cor. xii. 4, 8; xiv. 26. Now in order to this, 1. *The apostles prayed for them, v.* 15. The Spirit is given, not to ourselves only (Luke xi. 13), but to others also, in answer to prayer: *I will put my Spirit within you* (Ezek. xxxvi. 27), *but I will for this be enquired of, v.* 37. We may take encouragement from this example in praying to God to give the renewing graces of the Holy Ghost to those whose spiritual welfare we are concerned for—for our children, for our friends, for our ministers. We should pray, and pray earnestly, *that they may receive the Holy Ghost;* for this includes all blessings. 2. They laid their hands on them, to signify that their prayers were answered, and *that the gift of the Holy Ghost was conferred upon them;* for, upon the use of this sign, *they received the Holy Ghost, and spoke with tongues.* The laying on of hands was anciently used in blessing, by those who blessed with authority. Thus the apostles blessed these new converts, ordained some to be ministers, and confirmed others in their Christianity. We cannot now, nor can any, thus give the Holy Ghost by the laying on of hands; but this may intimate to us that those whom we pray for we should use our endeavours with.

II. How they discovered and discarded him that was a hypocrite among them, and this was Simon Magus; for they knew how to *separate between the precious and the vile.* Now observe here,

1. The wicked proposal that Simon made, by which his hypocrisy was discovered (*v.* 18, 19): *When he saw that through laying on of the apostles' hands the Holy Ghost was given* (which should have confirmed his faith in the doctrine of Christ, and increased his veneration for the apostles), it gave him a notion of Christianity as no other than an exalted piece of sorcery, in which he thought himself capable of being equal to the apostles, and therefore *offered them money, saying, Give me also this power.* He does not desire them to lay their hands on him, that he might receive the Holy Ghost himself (for he did not foresee that any thing was to be got by that), but that they would convey to him a power to bestow the gift upon others. He was ambitious to have the honour of an apostle, but not at all solicitous to have the spirit and disposition of a Christian. He was more desirous to gain honour to himself than to do good to others. Now, in making this motion, (1.) He put a great affront upon the apostles, as if they were mercenary men, would do any thing for money, and loved it as well as he did; whereas they had left what they had, for Christ, so far were they

from aiming to make it more. (2.) He put a great affront upon Christianity, as if the miracles that were wrought for the proof of it were done by magic arts, only of a different nature from what he himself had practised formerly. (3.) He showed that, like Balaam, he aimed at the rewards of divination; for he would not have offered money for this power if he had not hoped to get money by it. (4.) He showed that he had a very high conceit of himself, and that he had never his heart truly humbled. Such a wretch as he had been before his baptism should have asked, like the prodigal, to be made as one of the hired servants. But, as soon as he is admitted into the family, no less a place will serve him than to be one of the stewards of the household, and to be entrusted with a power which Philip himself had not, but the apostles only.

2. The just rejection of his proposal, and the cutting reproof Peter gave him for it, *v.* 20—23.

(1.) Peter shows him his crime (*v.* 20): *Thou hast thought that the gift of God may be purchased with money;* and thus, [1.] He had overvalued the wealth of this world, as if it were an equivalent for any thing, and as if, because, as Solomon saith, *it answers all things*, relating to the life that now is, it would answer all things relating to the other life, and would purchase the pardon of sin, the gift of the Holy Ghost, and eternal life. [2.] He had undervalued the gift of the Holy Ghost and put it upon a level with the common gifts of nature and providence. He thought the power of an apostle might as well be had for a good fee as the advice of a physician or a lawyer, which was the greatest despite that could be done to the Spirit of grace. All the buying and selling of pardons and indulgences in the church of Rome is the product of this same wicked *thought, that the gift of God may be purchased with money*, when the offer of divine grace so expressly runs, *without money and without price.*

(2.) He shows him his character, which is inferred from his crime. From every thing that a man says or does amiss we cannot infer that he is a hypocrite in the profession he makes of religion; but this of Simon's was such a fundamental error as could by no means consist with a state of grace; his offering money (and that got by sorcery too) was an incontestable evidence that he was yet under the power of a worldly and carnal mind, and was yet that *natural man which receiveth not the things of the Spirit of God, neither can he know them.* And therefore Peter tells him plainly, [1.] That his heart was *not right in the sight of God, v.* 21. "Though thou professest to believe, and art baptized, yet thou art not sincere." We are as our hearts are; if they be not right, we are wrong; and they are open in the sight of God, who knows them, judges them, and judges of us by them. Our hearts are that which they are in the sight of God, who cannot be deceived; and if they be not right in his sight, whatever our pretensions be, our religion is vain, and will stand us in no stead: our great concern is to approve ourselves to him in our integrity, for otherwise we cheat ourselves into our own ruin. Some refer this particularly to the proposal he made; what he asked is denied him, because his *heart is not right in the sight of God* in asking it. He does not aim at the glory of God nor the honour of Christ in it, but to make a hand of it for himself; he *asks, and has not, because he asks amiss; that he may consume it upon his lusts*, and be still thought some great one. [2.] That he is *in the gall of bitterness, and in the bond of iniquity: I perceive that thou art* so, *v.* 23. This is plain dealing, and plain dealing is best when we are dealing about souls and eternity. Simon had got a great name among the people, and of late a good name too among God's people, and yet Peter here gives him a black character. Note, It is possible for a man to continue under the power of sin, and yet to put on a form of godliness. *I perceive it*, saith Peter. It was not so much by the spirit of discerning, with which Peter was endued, that he perceived this, as by Simon's discovery of it in the proposal he made. Note, The disguises of hypocrites many times are soon seen through; the nature of the wolf shows itself notwithstanding the cover of the sheep's clothing. Now the character here given of Simon is really the character of all wicked people. *First*, They are *in the gall of bitterness*—odious to God, as that which is bitter as gall is to us. Sin is an abominable thing, which the Lord hates, and sinners are by it made abominable to him; they are vicious in their own nature. Indwelling sin is *a root of bitterness*, that *bears gall and wormwood*, Deut. xxix. 18. The faculties are corrupted, and the mind embittered against all good, Heb. xii. 15. It intimates likewise the pernicious consequences of sin; the *end is bitter as wormwood. Secondly*, They are *in the bond of iniquity*—bound over to the judgment of God by the guilt of sin, and bound under the dominion of Satan by the power of sin; led captive by him at his will, and it is a sore bondage, like that in Egypt, making the life bitter.

(3.) He reads him his doom in two things:—

[1.] He shall sink with his worldly wealth, which he overvalued: *Thy money perish with thee. First*, Hereby Peter rejects his offer with the utmost disdain and indignation: "Dost thou think thou canst bribe us to betray our trust, and to put the power we are entrusted with into such unworthy hands? Away with thee and thy money too; we will have nothing to do with either. *Get thee behind me, Satan.*" When we are tempted with money to do an evil thing, we should see what a perishing thing money is, and scorn to be biassed by it. It is the character of the upright man that he shakes his hands from holding, from touching bribes, Isa. xxxiii. 15. *Secondly,* He warns him of his danger of utter destruction if he continued in this mind: "Thy money will perish and thou wilt lose it, and all that thou canst purchase with it. As *meats for the belly and the belly for meats* (1 Cor. vi. 13), so goods for money and money for goods, *but God shall destroy both it and them*—they perish in the using; but this is not the worst of it: *thou wilt perish with it, and it with thee;* and it will be an aggravation of thy ruin, and a heavy load upon thy perishing soul, that thou hadst money, which might have been made to turn to a good account (Luke xvi. 9), which might have been laid at the apostles' feet, as a charity, and would have been accepted, but was thrust into their hands as a bribe, and was rejected. *Son, remember this.*"

[2.] He shall come short of the spiritual blessings which he undervalued (*v.* 21): "*Thou hast neither part nor lot in this matter;* thou hast nothing to do with the gifts of the Holy Ghost, thou dost not understand them, thou art excluded from them, hast put a bar in thine own door; thou canst not receive the Holy Ghost thyself, nor power to confer the Holy Ghost upon others, for *thy heart is not right in the sight of God,* if thou thinkest that Christianity is a trade to live by in this world, and therefore *thou hast no part nor lot* in the eternal life in the other world which the gospel offers. Note, *First,* There are many who profess the Christian religion, and yet have *no part nor lot in the matter, no part in Christ* (John xiii. 8), *no lot in the heavenly Canaan. Secondly,* They are those whose *hearts are not right in the sight of God,* are not animated by a right spirit, nor guided by a right rule, nor directed to the right end.

(4.) He gives him good counsel, notwithstanding, *v.* 22. Though he was angry with him, yet he did not abandon him; and, though he would have him see his case to be very bad, yet he would not have him think it desperate; *yet now there is hope in Israel.* Observe,

[1.] What it is that he advises him to: He must do his first works. *First,* He must *repent,*—must see his error and retract it,—must change his mind and way,—must be humbled and ashamed for what he has done. His repentance must be particular: "Repent of this, own thyself guilty in this, and be sorry for it." He must lay a load upon himself for it, must not extenuate it, by calling it a mistake, or misguided zeal, but must aggravate it by calling it *wickedness,* his wickedness, the fruit of his own corruption. Those that have said and done amiss must, as far as they can, unsay it and undo it again by repentance. *Secondly,* He must *pray* to God, must pray that God would give him repentance, and pardon upon repentance. Penitents must pray, which implies a desire towards God, and a confidence in Christ. Simon Magus, as great a man as he thinks himself, shall not be courted into the apostles' communion (how much soever some would think it a reputation to them) upon any other terms than those upon which other sinners are admitted—repentance and prayer.

[2.] What encouragement he gives him to do this: *If perhaps the thought of thy heart,* this wicked thought of thine, *may be forgiven thee.* Note, *First,* There may be a great deal of wickedness in the thought of the heart, its false notions, and corrupt affections, and wicked projects, which must be repented of, or we are undone. *Secondly,* The thought of the heart, though ever so wicked, shall be forgiven, upon our repentance, and not laid to our charge. When Peter here puts a *perhaps* upon it, the doubt is of the sincerity of his repentance, not of his pardon if his repentance be sincere. *If indeed the thought of thy heart may be forgiven,* so it may be read. Or it intimates that the greatness of his sin might justly make the pardon doubtful, though the promise of the gospel had put the matter out of doubt, in case he did truly repent: like that (Lam. iii. 29), *If so be there may be hope.*

[3.] Simon's request to them to pray for him, *v.* 24. He was startled and put into confusion by that which Peter said, finding that resented thus which he thought would have been embraced with both arms; and he cries out, *Pray you to the Lord for me, that none of the things which you have spoken come upon me.* Here was, *First,* Something well—that he was affected with the reproof given him, and terrified by the character given of him, enough to make the stoutest heart to tremble; and, this being so, he begged the prayers of the apostles for him, wishing to have an interest in them, who, he believed, had a good interest in heaven. *Secondly,* Something wanting. He begged of them to pray for him, but did not pray for himself, as he ought to have done; and, in desiring them to pray for him, his concern is more that the judgments he had made himself liable to might be prevented than that his corruptions might be mortified, and his heart, by divine grace, be made right in the sight of God; like Pharaoh, who would have Moses entreat the Lord for him, that he would take away this death only, not that he would take away this sin, this hardness of heart, Exod. viii. 8; x. 17. Some think that Peter had denounced some particular judgments against him, as against Ananias and Sapphira, which, upon this submission of his, at the apostle's intercession, were prevented; or, from what is related, he might infer that some token of God's wrath would fall upon him, which he thus dreaded and deprecated.

Lastly, Here is the return of the apostles to Jerusalem, when they had finished the business they came about; for as yet they were not to disperse; but, though they came hither to do that work which was peculiar to them as apostles, yet, opportunity offering itself, they applied themselves to that which was common to all gospel ministers. 1. There, in the city of Samaria, they were preachers: *They testified the word of the Lord,* solemnly attested the truth of the gospel, and confirmed what the other ministers preached. They did not pretend to bring them any thing new, though they were apostles, but bore their testimony to the word of the Lord as they had received it. 2. In their road home they were itinerant preachers; as they passed through many villages of the Samaritans they preached the gospel. Though the congregations there were not so considerable as those in the cities, either for number or figure, yet their souls were as precious, and the apostles did not think it below them to preach the gospel to them. God has a regard to the inhabitants of his villages in Israel (Judg. v. 11), and so should we.

26 And the angel of the Lord
spake unto Philip, saying, Arise, and
go toward the south unto the way
that goeth down from Jerusalem unto
Gaza, which is desert. 27 And he
arose and went: and, behold, a man
of Ethiopia, a eunuch of great authority under Candace queen of the
Ethiopians, who had the charge of
all her treasure, and had come to Jerusalem for to worship, 28 Was
returning, and sitting in his chariot
read Esaias the prophet. 29 Then
the Spirit said unto Philip, Go near,
and join thyself to this chariot. 30
And Philip ran thither to *him*, and
heard him read the prophet Esaias,
and said, Understandest thou what
thou readest? 31 And he said, How
can I, except some man should guide
me? And he desired Philip that he
would come up and sit with him. 32
The place of the scripture which he
read was this, He was led as a sheep
to the slaughter; and like a lamb
dumb before his shearer, so opened
he not his mouth: 33 In his humiliation his judgment was taken
away: and who shall declare his
generation? for his life is taken from
the earth. 34 And the eunuch answered Philip, and said, I pray thee,
of whom speaketh the prophet this?
of himself, or of some other man?
35 Then Philip opened his mouth,
and began at the same scripture, and
preached unto him Jesus. 36 And
as they went on *their* way, they came
unto a certain water: and the eunuch
said, See, *here is* water; what doth
hinder me to be baptized? 37 And
Philip said, If thou believest with all
thine heart, thou mayest. And he
answered and said, I believe that
Jesus Christ is the Son of God. 38
And he commanded the chariot to
stand still: and they went down both
into the water, both Philip and the
eunuch; and he baptized him. 39
And when they were come up out of
the water, the Spirit of the Lord
caught away Philip, that the eunuch
saw him no more: and he went on
his way rejoicing. 40 But Philip
was found at Azotus: and passing
through he preached in all the cities,
till he came to Cæsarea.

We have here the story of the conversion of an Ethiopian eunuch to the faith of Christ, by whom, we have reason to think, the knowledge of Christ was sent into that country where he lived, and that scripture fulfilled, *Ethiopia shall soon stretch out her hands* (one of the first of the nations) *unto God,* Ps. lxviii. 31.

I. Philip the evangelist is directed into the road where he would meet with this Ethiopian, *v.* 26. When the churches in Samaria were settled, and had ministers appointed them, the apostles went back to Jerusalem; but Philip stays, expecting to be employed in breaking up fresh ground in the country. And here we have, 1. Direction given him by an angel (probably in a dream or vision of the night) what course to steer: *Arise, and go towards the south.* Though angels were not employed to preach the gospel, they were often employed in carrying messages to ministers for advice and encouragement, as *ch.* v. 19. We cannot now expect such guides in our way; but doubtless there is a special providence of God conversant about the removes and settlements of ministers, and one way or other he will direct those who sincerely desire to follow him into that way in which he will own them: *he will guide them with his eye.* Philip must *go southward, to the way that leads from Jerusalem to Gaza,* through the desert or wilderness of Judah. He would never have thought of going thither, into a desert, into a common road through the desert; small probability of finding work there! Yet thither he is sent, according to our Saviour's parable, foretelling the call of the Gentiles, *Go you into the highways, and the hedges,* Matt. xxii. 9. Sometimes God opens a door of opportunity to his ministers in places very unlikely. 2. His obedience to this direction (*v.* 27): *He arose and went,* without objecting, or so much as asking, "What business have I there?" Or, "What likelihood is there of doing good there?" *He went out, not knowing whither he went;* or whom he was to meet.

II. An account is given of this eunuch (*v.* 27), who and what he was, on whom this distinguishing favour was bestowed. 1. He was a foreigner, *a man of Ethiopia.* There were two Ethiopias, one in Arabia, but that lay east from Canaan; it should seem this was Ethiopia in Africa, which lay south, beyond Egypt, a great way off from Jerusalem; for *in Christ those that were afar off were made nigh,* according to the promise, *that the ends of the earth should see the great salvation.* The Ethiopians were looked upon as the meanest and most despicable of the nations, blackamoors, as if nature had stigmatized them; yet the gospel is sent to them, and divine grace looks upon them, *though they are black, though the sun has looked upon them.* 2. He was a person of quality, a great man in his own country, *a eunuch,* not in body, but in office—lord chamberlain or steward of the household; and either by the dignity of his place or by his personal character, which commanded respect, he was *of great authority,* and bore a mighty sway *under Candace queen of the Ethiopians,* who probably was successor to the queen of Sheba, who is called *the queen of the south,* that country being governed by queens, to whom *Candace* was a common name, as *Pharaoh* to the kings of Egypt. He *had the charge of all her treasure;* so great a trust did she repose in him. *Not many mighty, not many noble, are called;* but some are. 3. He was a proselyte to the Jewish religion, for *he came to Jerusalem to worship.* Some think that he was a proselyte of righteousness, who was circumcised, and kept the feasts; others that he was only a proselyte of the gate, a Gentile, but who had renounced idolatry, and worshipped the God of Israel occasionally in the court of the Gentiles; but, if so, then Peter was not the first that preached the gospel to the Gentiles, as he says he was. Some think that there were remains of the knowledge of the true God in this country, ever since the queen of Sheba's time; and probably the ancestor of this eunuch was one of her attendants, who transmitted to his posterity what he learned at Jerusalem.

III. Philip and the eunuch are brought together into a close conversation; and now Philip shall know the meaning of his being sent into a desert, for there he meets with a chariot, that shall serve for a synagogue, and one man, the conversion of whom shall be in effect, for aught he knows, the conversion of a whole nation.

1. Philip is ordered to fall into company with this traveller that is going home from Jerusalem towards Gaza, thinking he has done all the business of his journey, when the great business which the overruling providence of God designed in it was yet undone. He had been at Jerusalem, where the apostles were preaching the Christian faith, and multitudes professing it, and yet there he had taken no notice of it, and made no enquiries after it—nay, it should seem, had slighted it, and turned his back upon it; yet the grace of God pursues him, overtakes him in the desert, and there overcomes him. Thus God is often *found of those that sought him not,* Isa. lxv. 1. Philip has this order, not by an angel, as before, but by the Spirit whispering it in his ear (*v.* 29): "*Go near, and join thyself to this chariot;* go so near as that the gentleman may take notice of thee." We should study to do good to those we light in company with upon the road: thus the lips of the righteous may feed many. We should not be so shy of all strangers as some affect to be. Of those of whom we know nothing else we know this, that they have souls.

2. He finds him reading in his Bible, as he sat in his chariot (*v.* 28): He *ran to him, and heard him read;* he read out, for the benefit of those that were with him, *v.* 30. He not only relieved the tediousness of the journey, but redeemed time by reading, not philosophy, history, nor politics, much less a romance or a play, but the scriptures, *the book of Esaias;* that book Christ read in (Luke iv. 17) and the eunuch here, which should recommend it particularly to our reading. Perhaps the eunuch was now reading over again those portions of scripture which he had heard read and expounded at Jerusalem, that he might recollect what he had heard. Note, (1.) It is the duty of every one of us to converse much with the holy scriptures. (2.) Persons of quality should abound more than others in the exercises of piety, because their example will influence many, and they have their time more at command. (3.) It is wisdom for men of business to redeem time for holy duties; time is precious, and it is the best husbandry in the world to gather up the fragments of time, that none be lost, to fill up every minute with something that will turn to a good account. (4.) When we are returning from public worship we should use means in private for the keeping up of the good affections there kindled, and the preserving of the good impressions there made, 1 Chron. xxix. 18. (5.) Those that are diligent in searching the scriptures are in a fair way to improve in knowledge; for *to him that hath shall be given.*

3. He puts a fair question to him: *Understandest thou what thou readest?* Not

by way of reproach, but with design to offer him his service. Note, What we read and hear of the word of God it highly concerns us to understand, especially what we read and hear concerning Christ; and therefore we should often ask ourselves whether we understand it or no: *Have you understood all these things?* Matt. xiii. 51. And have you understood them aright? We cannot profit by the scriptures unless we do in some measure understand them, 1 Cor. xiv. 16, 17. And, blessed be God, what is necessary to salvation is easy to be understood.

4. The eunuch in a sense of his need of assistance, desires Philip's company (*v.* 31): "*How can I understand,* says he, *except some one guide me?* Therefore pray come up, and sit with me." (1.) He speaks as one that had very low thoughts of himself, and his own capacity and attainments. He was so far from taking it as an affront to be asked whether he understood what he read, though Philip was a stranger, on foot, and probably looked mean (which many a less man would have done, and have called him an impertinent fellow, and bid him go about his business, what was it to him?) that he takes the question kindly, makes a very modest reply, *How can I?* We have reason to think he was an intelligent man, and as well acquainted with the meaning of scripture as most were, and yet he modestly confesses his weakness. Note, Those that would learn must see their need to be taught. The prophet must first own that he knows not what these are, and then the angel will tell him, Zech. iv. 13. (2.) He speaks as one very desirous to be taught, to have some one to guide him. Observe, He read the scripture, though there were many things in it which he did not understand. Though there are many things in the scriptures which are *dark and hard to be understood,* nay, which are often misunderstood, yet we must not therefore throw them by, but study them for the sake of those things that are easy, which is the likeliest way to come by degrees to the understanding of those things that are difficult: for knowledge and grace grow gradually. (3.) He invited Philip to *come up and sit with him;* not as Jehu took Jonadab into his chariot, to come and see his zeal for the Lord of hosts (2 Kings x. 16), but rather, "Come, see my ignorance, and instruct me." He will gladly do Philip the honour to take him into the coach with him, if Philip will do him the favour to expound a portion of scripture to him. Note, In order to our right understanding of the scripture, it is requisite we should have some one to guide us; some good books, and some good men, but, above all, the Spirit of grace, to lead us into all truth.

IV. The portion of scripture which the eunuch recited, with some hints of Philip's discourse upon it. The preachers of the gospel had a very good handle to take hold of those by who were conversant with the scriptures of the Old Testament and received them, especially when they found them actually engaged in the study of them, as the eunuch was here.

1. The chapter he was reading was the fifty-third of Isaiah, two verses of which are here quoted (*v.* 32, 33), part of the seventh and eighth verses; they are set down according to the Septuagint version, which in some things differs from the original Hebrew. Grotius thinks the eunuch read it in the Hebrew, but that Luke takes the Septuagint translation, as readier to the language in which he wrote; and he supposes that the eunuch had learned from the many Jews that were in Ethiopia both their religion and language. But, considering that the Septuagint version was made in Egypt, which was the next country adjoining to Ethiopia, and lay between it and Jerusalem, I rather think that translation was most familiar to him: it appears by Isa. xx. 4 that there was much communication between those two nations—Egypt and Ethiopia. The greatest variation from the Hebrew is that what in the original is, *He was taken from prison and from judgment* (hurried with the utmost violence and precipitation from one judgment-seat to another; or, *From force and from judgment he was taken away;* that is, It was from the fury of the people, and their continual clamours, and the judgment of Pilate thereupon, that he was taken away), is here read, *In his humiliation his judgment was taken away.* He appeared so mean and despicable in their eyes that they denied him common justice, and against all the rules of equity, to the benefit of which every man is entitled, they declared him innocent, and yet condemned him to die; nothing criminal can be proved upon him, but he is down, and down with him. Thus *in his humiliation his judgment was taken away;* so, the sense is much the same with that of the Hebrew. So that these verses foretold concerning the Messiah, (1.) That he should die, should be *led to the slaughter,* as sheep that were offered in sacrifice—that his life should be taken from among men, taken from the earth. With what little reason then was the death of Christ a stumbling-block to the unbelieving Jews, when it was so plainly foretold by their own prophets, and was so necessary to the accomplishment of his undertaking! Then is the offence of the cross ceased. (2.) That he should die wrongfully, should die by violence, should be hurried out of his life, and *his judgment shall be taken away*—no justice done to him; for he must be *cut off, but not for himself.* (3.) That he should die patiently. Like *a lamb dumb before the shearer,* nay, and before the butcher too, *so he opened not his mouth.* Never was there such an example of patience as our Lord Jesus was in his sufferings; when he was accused, when he was abused, he was silent, *reviled not*

again, threatened not. (4.) That yet he should live for ever, to ages which cannot be numbered; for so I understand those words, *Who shall declare his generation?* The Hebrew word properly signifies *the duration of one life,* Eccl. i. 4. Now who can conceive or express how long he shall continue, notwithstanding this; *for his life is taken* only *from the earth;* in heaven he shall live to endless and innumerable ages, as it follows in Isa. liii. 10, *He shall prolong his days.*

2. The eunuch's question upon this is, *Of whom speaketh the prophet this? v.* 34. He does not desire Philip to give him some critical remarks upon the words and phrases, and the idioms of the language, but to acquaint him with the general scope and design of the prophecy, to furnish him with a key, in the use of which he might, by comparing one thing with another, be led into the meaning of the particular passage. Prophecies had usually in them something of obscurity, till they were explained by the accomplishment of them, as this now was. It is a material question he asks, and a very sensible one: "Does the prophet speak this of himself, in expectation of being used, being misused, as the other prophets were? or does he speak it *of some other man,* in his own age, or in some age to come?" Though the modern Jews will not allow it to be spoken of the Messiah, yet their ancient doctors did so interpret it; and perhaps the eunuch knew this, and did partly understand it so himself, only he proposed this question, to draw on discourse with Philip; for the way to improve in learning is to consult the learned. As *they must enquire the law at the mouth of the priests* (Mal. ii. 7), so they must enquire the gospel, especially that part of the treasure which is hid in the field of the Old Testament, at the mouth of the ministers of Christ. The way to receive good instructions is to ask good questions.

3. Philip takes this fair occasion given him to open to him the great mystery of the gospel concerning *Jesus Christ, and him crucified.* He *began at this scripture,* took this for his text (as Christ did another passage of the same prophecy, Luke iv. 21), and *preached unto him Jesus, v.* 35. This is all the account given us of Philip's sermon, because it was the same in effect with Peter's sermons, which we have had before. The business of gospel ministers is to preach Jesus, and this is the preaching that is likely to do good. It is probable that Philip had now occasion for his gift of tongues, that he might preach Christ to this Ethiopian in the language of his own country. And here we have an instance of speaking of the things of God, and speaking of them to good purpose, not only as we *sit in the house,* but *as we walk by the way,* according to that rule, Deut. vi. 7.

V. The eunuch is baptized in the name of Christ, *v.* 36—38. It is probable that the eunuch had heard at Jerusalem of the doctrine of Christ, so that it was not altogether new to him. But, if he had, what could that do towards this speedy conquest that was made of his heart for Christ. It was a powerful working of the Spirit with and by Philip's preaching that gained the point. Now here we have,

1. The modest proposal which the eunuch made of himself for baptism (*v.* 36): *As they went on their way,* discoursing of Christ, the eunuch asking more questions and Philip answering them to his satisfaction, they *came unto a certain water,* a well, river, or pond, the sight of which made the eunuch think of being baptized. Thus God, by hints of providence which seem casual, sometimes puts his people in mind of their duty, of which otherwise perhaps they would not have thought. The eunuch knew not how little a while Philip might be with him, nor where he might afterwards enquire for him. He could not expect his travelling with him to his next stage, and therefore, if Philip think fit, he will take the present convenience which offers itself of being baptized: "*See, here is water,* which perhaps we may not meet with a great while again; *what doth hinder me to be baptized?* Canst thou show any cause why I should not be admitted a disciple and follower of Christ by baptism?" Observe, (1.) He does not demand baptism, does not say, "Here is water and here I am resolved I will be baptized;" for, if Philip have any thing to offer to the contrary, he is willing to waive it for the present. If he think him not fit to be baptized, or if there be any thing in the institution of the ordinance which will not admit such a speedy administration of it, he will not insist upon it. The most forward zeal must submit to order and rule. But, (2.) He does desire it, and, unless Philip can show cause why not, he desires it now, and is not willing to defer it. Note, In the solemn dedicating and devoting of ourselves to God, it is good to make haste, and not to delay; for the present time is the best time, Ps. cxix. 60. Those who have received the thing signified by baptism should not put off receiving the sign. The eunuch feared lest the good affections now working in him should cool and abate, and therefore was willing immediately to bind his soul with the baptismal bonds unto the Lord, that he might bring the matter to an issue.

2. The fair declaration which Philip made him of the terms upon which he might have the privilege of baptism (*v.* 37): "*If thou believest with all thy heart, thou mayest;* that is, If thou believest this doctrine which I have preached to thee concerning Jesus, if thou receivest the record God has given concerning him, and set to thy seal that it is true." He must believe with all his heart, for with the heart man believeth, not with the head only, by an assent to gospel truths in the understanding; but with the heart, by a consent of the will to gospel terms. "If thou do in-

deed believe with all thy heart, thou art by that united to Christ, and, if thou give proofs and evidences that thou dost so, thou mayest by baptism be joined to the church."

3. The confession of faith which the eunuch made in order to his being baptized. It is very short, but it is comprehensive and much to the purpose, and what was sufficient: *I believe that Jesus Christ is the Son of God.* He was before a worshipper of the true God, so that all he had to do now was to *receive Christ Jesus the Lord.* (1.) He believes that Jesus is *the Christ,* the true Messiah promised, the *anointed One.* (2.) That Christ is *Jesus —a Saviour,* the only Saviour of his people from their sins. And, (3.) That this Jesus Christ is the *Son of God,* that he has a divine nature, as the Son is of the same nature with the Father; and that, being the Son of God, he is the *heir of all things.* This is the principal peculiar doctrine of Christianity, and whosoever believe this with all their hearts, and confess it, they and their seed are to be baptized.

4. The baptizing of him hereupon. The eunuch ordered his coachman to stop, *commanded the chariot to stand still.* It was the best baiting place he ever met with in any of his journeys. *They went down both into the water,* for they had no convenient vessels with them, being upon a journey, wherewith to take up water, and must therefore go down into it; not that they stripped off their clothes, and went naked into the water, but, going barefoot according to the custom, they went perhaps up to the ankles or mid-leg into the water, and Philip sprinkled water upon him, according to the prophecy which this eunuch had probably but just now read, for it was but a few verses before those which Philip found him upon, and was very apposite to his case (Isa. lii. 15): *So shall he sprinkle many nations, kings* and great men *shall shut their mouths at him,* shall submit to him, and acquiesce in him, *for that which had not* before *been told them shall they see, and that which they had not heard shall they consider.* Observe, Though Philip had very lately been deceived in Simon Magus, and had admitted him to baptism, though he afterwards appeared to be no true convert, yet he did not therefore scruple to baptize the eunuch upon his profession of faith immediately, without putting him upon a longer trial than usual. If some hypocrites crowd into the church, who afterwards prove a grief and scandal to us, yet we must not therefore make the door of admission any straiter than Christ has made it; they shall answer for their apostasy, and not we.

VI. Philip and the eunuch are separated presently; and this is as surprising as the other parts of the story. One would have expected that the eunuch should either have staid with Philip, or have taken him along with him into his own country, and, there being so many ministers in those parts, he might be spared, and it would be worth while: but God ordered otherwise. As soon as they had *come up out of the water,* before the eunuch went into his chariot again, *the Spirit of the Lord caught away Philip* (*v.* 39), and did not give him time to make an exhortation to the eunuch, as usual after baptism, which it is probable the one intended and the other expected. But his sudden departure was sufficient to make up the want of that exhortation, for it seems to have been miraculous, and that he was *caught up* in the air in the eunuch's sight, and so carried out of his sight; and the working of this miracle upon Philip was a confirmation of his doctrine, as much as the working of a miracle by him would have been. He was *caught away, and the eunuch saw him no more,* but, having lost his minister, returned to the use of his Bible again. Now here we are told,

1. How the eunuch was disposed: He *went on his way rejoicing.* He pursued his journey. Business called him home, and he must hasten to it; for it was no way inconsistent with his Christianity, which places no sanctity nor perfection in men's being hermits or recluses, but is a religion which men may and ought to carry about with them into the affairs of this life. But he went on rejoicing; so far was he from reflecting upon this sudden revolution and change, or advancement rather, in his religion, with any regret, that his second thoughts confirmed him abundantly in it, and he went on, *rejoicing with joy unspeakable and full of glory;* he was never better pleased in all his life. He rejoiced, (1.) That he himself was joined to Christ and had an interest in him. And, (2.) That he had these good tidings to bring to his countrymen, and a prospect of bringing them also, by virtue of his interest among them, into fellowship with Christ; for he returned, not only a Christian, but a minister. Some copies read this verse thus: *And, when they were come up out of the water, the Holy Spirit fell upon the eunuch* (without the ceremony of the apostle's imposition of hands), *but the angel of the Lord caught away Philip.*

2. How Philip was disposed of (*v.* 40): *He was found at Azotus* or *Ashdod,* formerly a city of the Philistines; there the angel or Spirit of the Lord dropped him, which was about thirty miles from Gaza, whither the eunuch was going, and where Dr. Lightfoot thinks he took ship, and went by sea into his own country. But Philip, wherever he was, would not be idle. *Passing through, he preached in all the cities* till he came to Cesarea, and there he settled, and, for aught that appears, had his principal residence ever after; for at Cesarea we find him in a house of his own, *ch.* xxi. 8. He that had been faithful in working for Christ as an itinerant at length gains a settlement.

CHAP. IX.

In this chapter we have, I. The famous story of St. Paul's conversion from being an outrageous persecutor of the gospel of Christ to be an illustrious professor and preacher of it. 1. How he was first awakened and wrought upon by an appearance of Christ himself to him as he was going upon an errand of persecution to Damascus: and what a condition he was in while he lay under the power of those convictions and terrors, ver. 1—9. 2. How he was baptized by Ananias, by immediate directions from heaven, ver. 10—19. 3. How he immediately commenced doctor, and preached the faith of Christ, and proved what he preached, ver. 20—22. 4. How he was persecuted, and narrowly escaped with his life, ver. 23—25. 5. How he was admitted among the brethren at Jerusalem: how he preached, and was persecuted there, ver. 26—30. 6. The rest and quietness which the churches enjoyed for some time after this, ver. 31. II. The cure wrought by Peter on Eneas, who had long been laid up with a palsy, ver. 32—35. III. The raising of Tabitha from death to life, at the prayer of Peter, ver. 36—43.

AND Saul, yet breathing out threatenings and slaughter against the
disciples of the Lord, went unto the
high priest, 2 And desired of him
letters to Damascus to the synagogues, that if he found any of this
way, whether they were men or women, he might bring them bound
unto Jerusalem. 3 And as he journeyed, he came near Damascus: and
suddenly there shined round about
him a light from heaven: 4 And he
fell to the earth, and heard a voice
saying unto him, Saul, Saul, why
persecutest thou me? 5 And he
said, Who art thou, Lord? And the
Lord said, I am Jesus whom thou
persecutest: *it is* hard for thee to
kick against the pricks. 6 And he
trembling and astonished said, Lord,
what wilt thou have me to do? And
the Lord *said* unto him, Arise, and
go into the city, and it shall be told
thee what thou must do. 7 And
the men which journeyed with him
stood speechless, hearing a voice, but
seeing no man. 8 And Saul arose
from the earth; and when his eyes
were opened, he saw no man: but
they led him by the hand, and
brought *him* into Damascus. 9 And
he was three days without sight, and
neither did eat nor drink.

We found mention made of Saul twice or thrice in the story of Stephen, for the sacred penman longed to come to his story; and now we are come to it, not quite taking leave of Peter, but from henceforward being mostly taken up with Paul the apostle of the Gentiles, as Peter was of the circumcision. His name in Hebrew was *Saul—desired,* though as remarkably little in stature as his namesake king Saul was tall and stately; one of the ancients calls him, *Homo tricubitalis—but four feet and a half in height;* his Roman name which he went by among the citizens of Rome was *Paul—little.* He was born in Tarsus, a city of Cilicia, a free city of the Romans, and himself a freeman of that city. His father and mother were both native Jews; therefore he calls himself a *Hebrew of the Hebrews;* he was of the tribe of Benjamin, which adhered to Judah. His education was in the schools of Tarsus first, which was a little Athens for learning; there he acquainted himself with the philosophy and poetry of the Greeks. Thence he was sent to the university at Jerusalem, to study divinity and the Jewish law. His tutor was Gamaliel, an eminent Pharisee. He had extraordinary natural parts, and improved mightily in learning. He had likewise a handicraft trade (being bred to tent-making), which was common with those among the Jews who were bred scholars (as Dr. Lightfoot saith), for the earning of their maintenance, and the avoiding of idleness. This is the young man on whom the grace of God wrought this mighty change here recorded, about a year after the ascension of Christ, or little more. We are here told,

I. How bad he was, how very bad, before his conversion; just before he was an inveterate enemy to Christianity, did his utmost to root it out, by persecuting all that embraced it. In other respects he was well enough, as *touching the righteousness which is of the law, blameless,* a man of no ill morals, but a blasphemer of Christ, a persecutor of Christians, and injurious to both, 1 Tim. i. 13. And so ill informed was his conscience that he thought he ought to do what he did against the name of Christ (*ch.* xxvi. 9) and that he did God service in it, as was foretold, John xvi. 2. Here we have,

1. His general enmity and rage against the Christian religion (*v.* 1): He *yet breathed out threatenings and slaughter against the disciples of the Lord.* The persons persecuted were the disciples of the Lord; because they were so, under that character he hated and persecuted them. The matter of the persecution was threatenings and slaughter. There is persecution in threatenings (*ch.* iv. 17, 21); they terrify and break the spirit: and though we say, Threatened folks live long, yet those whom Saul threatened, if he prevailed not thereby to frighten them from Christ, he slew them, he persecuted them to death, *ch.* xxii. 4. His breathing out threatenings and slaughter intimates that it was natural to him, and his constant business. He even breathed in this as in his element. He breathed it out with heat and vehemence; his very breath, like that of some venomous creatures, was pestilential. He breathed death to the Christians, wherever he came; he puffed at them in his pride (Ps. xii. 4, 5), spit his venom at them in his rage. Saul yet breathing thus intimates, (1.) That he still persisted in it; not satisfied with the blood of those he had slain, he still cries, *Give, give.* (2.) That he should shortly be of another mind; as yet he breathes out threatenings and slaughter, but he has not long to live such a life as this, that breath will be stopped shortly.

2. His particular design upon the Christians at Damascus; thither was the gospel now lately carried by those that fled from the persecution at Stephen's death, and thought to be safe and quiet there, and were connived at by those in power there: but Saul cannot be easy if he knows a Christian is quiet; and therefore, hearing that the Christians in Damascus were so, he resolves to give them disturbance. In order to this, he applies to the high priest for a commission (*v.* 1) to go to Damascus, *v.* 2. The high priest needed not to be stirred up to persecute the Christians, he was forward enough of himself to do it; but it seems the young persecutor drove more furiously than the old one. Leaders in sin are the worst of sinners; and the proselytes which the scribes and Pharisees make often prove seven times more the children of hell than themselves. He saith (*ch.* xxii. 5) that this commission was had from the whole estate of the elders: and proud enough this furious bigot was to have a commission directed to him, with the seal of the great sanhedrim affixed to it. Now the commission was to empower him to enquire among the synagogues, or congregations, of the Jews that were at Damascus, whether there were any that belonged to them that inclined to favour this new sect or heresy, that believed in Christ; and if he found any such, whether men or women, to bring them up prisoners to Jerusalem, to be proceeded against according to law by the great council there. Observe, (1.) The Christians are here said to be *those of this way; those of the way,* so it is in the original. Perhaps the Christians sometimes called themselves so, from Christ *the Way;* or, because they looked on themselves as but in the way, and not yet at home; or, the enemies thus represented it as a way by itself, a by-way, a party, a faction. (2.) The high priest and sanhedrim claimed a power over the Jews in all countries, and had a deference paid to their authority in matters of religion, by all their synagogues, even those that were not of the jurisdiction of the civil government of the Jewish nation. And such a sovereignty the Roman pontiff now claims as the Jewish pontiff then did, though he has not so much to show for it. (3.) By this commission, all that worshipped God in the way that they called heresy, though agreeing exactly with the original institutes even of the Jewish church, whether they were men or women, were to be prosecuted. Even the weaker sex, who in a case of this nature might deserve excuse, or at least compassion, shall find neither with Saul any more than they do with the popish persecutors. (4.) He was ordered to bring them all bound to Jerusalem as criminals of the first magnitude, which, as it would be the more likely to terrify them, so it would be to magnify Saul, as having the command of the forces that were to carry them up, and opportunity of breathing out threatenings and slaughter. Thus was Saul employed when the grace of God wrought that great change in him. Let not us then despair of renewing grace for the conversion of the greatest sinners, nor let such despair of the pardoning mercy of God for the greatest sin; for Paul himself obtained mercy, that he might be a monument, 1 Tim. i. 13.

II. How suddenly and strangely a blessed change was wrought in him, not in the use of any ordinary means, but by miracles. The conversion of Paul is one of the wonders of the church. Here is,

1. The place and time of it: *As he journeyed, he came near to Damascus;* and there Christ met with him.

(1.) He was in the way, travelling upon his journey; not in the temple, nor in the synagogue, nor in the meeting of the Christians, but by the way. The work of conversion is not tied to the church, though ordinarily public administrations are made use of. Some are reclaimed in slumberings on the bed (Job xxxiii. 15—17), and some in travelling upon the road alone: Thoughts are as free, and there is as good an opportunity of communing with our own hearts there, as upon the bed; and there the Spirit may set in with us, for that wind blows where it listeth. Some observe that Saul was spoken to abroad in the open air that there might be no suspicion of imposture, nor of a trick put upon him in it.

(2.) He was near Damascus, almost at his journey's end, ready to enter the city, the chief city of Syria. Some observe that he who was to be the apostle of the Gentiles was converted to the faith of Christ in a Gentile country. Damascus had been infamous for persecuting God's people formerly—they threshed Gilead with threshing instruments of iron (Amos i. 3), and now it was likely to be so again.

(3.) He was in a wicked way, pursuing his design against the Christians at Damascus, and pleasing himself with the thought that he should devour this new-born child of Christianity there. Note, Sometimes the grace of God works upon sinners when they are at the worst, and hotly engaged in the most desperate sinful pursuits, which is much for the glory both of God's pity and of his power.

(4.) The cruel edict and decree he had with him drew near to be put in execution; and now it was happily prevented, which may be considered, [1.] As a great kindness to the poor saints at Damascus, who had notice of his coming, as appears by what Ananias said (*v.* 13, 14), and were apprehensive of their danger from him, and trembled as poor lambs at the approach of a ravening wolf; Saul's conversion was their security for the present. Christ has many ways of delivering the godly out of temptation, and sometimes does it by a change wrought in their persecutors, either restraining their wrathful spirits (Ps. lxxvi,

10) and mollifying them for a time, as the Old-Testament Saul, who relented towards David more than once (1 Sam. xxiv. 16; xxvi. 21), or renewing their spirits, and fixing upon them durable impressions, as upon the New-Testament Saul here. [2.] It was also a very great mercy to Saul himself to be hindered from executing his wicked design, in which if he had now proceeded, perhaps it had been the filling up of the measure of his iniquity. Note, It is to be valued as a signal token of the divine favour if God, either by the inward operations of his grace or the outward occurrences of his providence, prevent us from prosecuting and executing a sinful purpose, 1 Sam. xxv. 32.

2. The appearance of Christ to him in his glory. Here it is only said that there *shone round about him a light from heaven;* but it appears from what follows (*v.* 17) that the Lord Jesus was in this light, and appeared to him by the way. He saw that just One (*ch.* xxii. 14), and see *ch.* xxvi. 13. Whether he saw him at a distance, as Stephen saw him, in the heavens, or nearer in the air, is not certain. It is not inconsistent with what is said of the heavens receiving Christ till the end of time (*ch.* iii. 21) to suppose that he did, upon such an extraordinary occasion as this, make a personal visit, but a very short one, to this lower world; it was necessary to Paul's being an apostle that he should see the Lord, and so he did, 1 Cor. ix. 1; xv. 8. (1.) This light shone upon him *suddenly*—ἐξαίφνης, when Paul never thought of any such thing, and without any previous warning. Christ's manifestations of himself to poor souls are many times sudden and very surprising, and he anticipates them with the blessings of his goodness. This the disciples that Christ called to himself found. *Or ever I was aware,* Cant. vi. 12. (2.) It was a light from heaven, the fountain of light, from the God of heaven, the Father of lights. It was a light above the brightness of the sun (*ch.* xxvi. 13), for it was visible at mid-day, and outshone the sun in his meridian strength and lustre, Isa. xxiv. 23. (3.) It shone *round about him,* not in his face only, but on every side of him; let him turn which way he will, he finds himself surrounded with the discoveries of it. And this was designed not only to startle him, and awaken his attention (for well may he expect to hear when he is thus made to see something very extraordinary), but to signify the enlightening of his understanding with the knowledge of Christ. The devil comes to the soul in darkness; by this he gets and keeps possession of it. But Christ comes to the soul in light, for he is himself the light of the world, bright and glorious in himself, beneficial and gracious to us, as light. The first thing in this new creation, as in that of the world, is light, 2 Cor. iv. 6. Hence all Christians are said to be *children of the light and of the day,* Eph. v. 8.

3. The arresting of Saul, and his detachment: *He fell to the earth, v.* 4. Some think that he was on foot, and that this light, which perhaps was accompanied with a thunder-clap, so terrified him that he could not keep his feet, but fell upon his face, usually a posture of adoration, but here of astonishment. It is probable that he was mounted, as Balaam, when he went to curse Israel, and perhaps better mounted than he; for Saul was now in a public post, was in haste, and the journey was long, so that it is not likely he should travel on foot. The sudden light would frighten the beast he rode on, and make it throw him; and it was God's good providence that his body got no hurt by the fall: but angels had a particular charge concerning him, to keep all his bones, so that not one of them was broken. It appears (*ch.* xxvi. 14) that all that were with him fell to the earth as well as he, but the design was upon him. This may be considered, (1.) As the effect of Christ's appearing to him, and of the light which shone round about him. Note, Christ's manifestations of himself to poor souls are humbling; they lay them very low, in mean thoughts of themselves, and a humble submission to the will of God. Now *mine eyes see thee,* saith Job, *I abhor myself. I saw the Lord,* saith Isaiah, *sitting upon a throne, and I said, Woe is me, for I am undone.* (2.) As a step towards this intended advancement. He is designed not only to be a Christian, but to be a minister, an apostle, a great apostle, and therefore he must thus be cast down. Note, Those whom Christ designs for the greatest honours are commonly first laid low. Those who are designed to excel in knowledge and grace are commonly laid low first, in a sense of their own ignorance and sinfulness. Those whom God will employ are first struck with a sense of their unworthiness to be employed.

4. The arraigning of Saul. Being by the fall taken into custody, and as it were set to the bar, he heard a voice saying to him (and it was distinguishing, to him only, for though those that were with him heard a sound (*v.* 7) yet they knew not the words, *ch.* xxii. 9), *Saul, Saul, why persecutest thou me?* Observe here,

(1.) Saul not only saw a light from heaven, but heard a voice from heaven; wherever the glory of God was seen, the word of God was heard (Exod. xx. 18); and to Moses (Num. vii. 89); and to the prophets. God's manifestations of himself were never dumb shows, for he magnifies his word above all his name, and what was seen was alway designed to make way for what was said. Saul heard a voice. Note, Faith comes by hearing; hence the Spirit is said to be received by the hearing of faith, Gal. iii. 2. The voice he heard was the voice of Christ. When he *saw that just One, he heard the voice of his mouth, ch.* xxii. 14. Note, The word we hear is likely to profit us when we hear it as the voice of Christ, 1 Thess. ii. 13. *It is the voice of my beloved;* no voice but his can reach the heart. Seeing and hearing are the two learning senses; Christ here, by both these doors, entered into Saul's heart.

(2.) What he heard was very awakening. [1.] He was called by his name, and that doubled: *Saul, Saul.* Some think, in calling him Saul, he hints at that great persecutor of David whose name he bore. He was indeed a second Saul, and such an enemy to the Son of David as the other was to David. Calling him by his name intimates the particular regard that Christ had to him: *I have surnamed thee, though thou hast not known me,* Isa. xlv. 4. See Exod. xxxiii. 12. His calling him by name brought the conviction home to his conscience, and put it past dispute to whom the voice spoke this. Note, What God speaks in general is then likely to do us good when we apply it to ourselves, and insert our own names into the precepts and promises which are expressed generally, as if God spoke to us by name, and when he saith, *Ho, every one,* he had said, *Ho, such a one: Samuel, Samuel; Saul, Saul.* The doubling of it, *Saul, Saul,* intimates, *First,* The deep sleep that Saul was in; he needed to be called again and again, as Jer. xxii. 29, *O earth, earth, earth. Secondly,* The tender concern that the blessed Jesus had for him, and for his recovery. He speaks as one in earnest; it is like *Martha, Martha* (Luke x. 41), or *Simon, Simon* (Luke xxii. 31), or *O Jerusalem, Jerusalem,* Matt. xxiii. 37. He speaks to him as to one in imminent danger, at the pit's brink, and just ready to drop in: "*Saul, Saul,* dost thou know whither thou art going, or what thou art doing?"

[2.] The charge exhibited against him is, *Why persecutest thou me?* Observe here, *First,* Before Saul was made a saint, he was made to see himself a sinner, a great sinner, a sinner against Christ. Now he was made to see that evil in himself which he never saw before; sin revived and he died. Note, A humbling conviction of sin is the first step towards a saving conversion from sin. *Secondly,* He is convinced of one particular sin, which he was most notoriously guilty of, and had justified himself in, and thereby way is made for his conviction of all the rest. *Thirdly,* The sin he is convinced of is persecution: *Why persecutest thou me?* It is a very affectionate expostulation, enough to melt a heart of stone. Observe, 1. The person sinning: "It is thou; thou, that art not one of the ignorant, rude, unthinking crowd, that will run down any thing they hear put into an ill name, but thou that hast had a liberal learned education, hast good parts and accomplishments, hast the knowledge of the scriptures, which, if duly considered, would show thee the folly of it. It is worse in thee than in another." 2. The person sinned against: "It is I, who never did thee any harm, who came from heaven to earth to do thee good, who was not long since crucified for thee; and was not that enough, but must I afresh be crucified by thee?" 3. The kind and continuance of the sin. It was persecution, and he was at this time engaged in it: "Not only thou hast persecuted, but thou persecutest, thou persistest in it." He was not at this time haling any to prison, nor killing them; but this was the errand he came upon to Damascus; he was now projecting it, and pleasing himself with the thought of it. Note, Those that are designing mischief are, in God's account, doing mischief. 4. The question put to him upon it: "Why dost thou do it?" (1.) It is complaining language. "Why dealest thou thus unjustly, thus unkindly, with my disciples?" Christ never complained so much of those who persecuted him in his own person as he did here of those who persecuted him in his followers. He complains of it as it was Saul's sin: "Why art thou such an enemy to thyself, to thy God?" Note, The sins of sinners are a very grievous burden to the Lord Jesus. He is grieved for them (Mark iii. 5), he is pressed under them, Amos ii. 13. (2.) It is convincing language: "Why dost thou thus? Canst thou give any good reason for it?" Note, It is good for us often to ask ourselves why we do so and so, that we may discern what an unreasonable thing sin is: and of all sins none so unreasonable, so unaccountable, as the sin of persecuting the disciples of Christ, especially when it is discovered to be, as certainly it is, persecuting Christ. Those have no knowledge who eat up God's people, Ps. xiv. 4. *Why persecutest thou me?* He thought he was persecuting only a company of poor, weak, silly people, that were an offence and eye-sore to the Pharisees, little imagining that it was one in heaven that he was all this while insulting; for surely, if he had known, he would not have persecuted the Lord of glory. Note, Those who persecute the saints persecute Christ himself, and he takes what is done against them as done against himself, and accordingly will be the judgment in the great day, Matt. xxv. 45.

5. Saul's question upon his indictment, and the reply to it, *v.* 5.

(1.) He makes enquiry concerning Christ: *Who art thou, Lord?* He gives no direct answer to the charge preferred against him, being convicted by his own conscience, and self-condemned. If God contend with us for our sins, we are not able to answer for one of a thousand, especially such a one as the sin of persecution. Convictions of sin, when they are set home with power upon the conscience, will silence all excuses and self-justifications. *Though I were righteous, yet would I not answer.* But he desires to know who is his judge; the compellation is respectful: *Lord.* He who had been a blasphemer of Christ's name now speaks to him as his Lord. The question is proper: *Who art thou?* This implies his present unacquaintedness with Christ; he knew not his voice as his own sheep do, but he desired to be acquainted with him; he is convinced by this light which encloses him that it is one from heaven that speaks to him, and he has a veneration for every thing that appears to him to come from heaven; and therefore, *Lord, who art thou? What is thy name?* Judg. xiii. 17; Gen. xxxii. 29. Note, There is some hope of people when they begin to enquire after Jesus Christ.

(2.) He has an answer immediately, in which we have,

[1.] Christ's gracious revelation of himself to him. He is always ready to answer the serious enquiries of those who covet an acquaintance with him: *I am Jesus whom thou persecutest.* The name of Jesus was not unknown to him; his heart had risen against it many a time, and gladly would he bury it in oblivion. He knew it was the name that he persecuted, but little did he think to hear it from heaven, or from the midst of such a glory as now shone round about him. Note, Christ brings souls into fellowship with himself by manifesting himself to them. He said, *First, I am Jesus, a Saviour; I am Jesus of Nazareth,* so it is, *ch.* xxii. 8. Saul used to call him so when he blasphemed him: "I am that very Jesus whom thou usedst to call in scorn *Jesus of Nazareth.*" And he would show that now that he is in his glory he is not ashamed of his humiliation. *Secondly,* "*I am that Jesus whom thou persecutest,* and therefore it will be at thy peril if thou persist in this wicked course." There is nothing more effectual to awaken and humble the soul than to see sin to be against Christ, an affront to him, and a contradiction to his designs.

[2.] His gentle reproof of him: *It is hard for thee to kick against the pricks,* or *goads*—to spurn at the spur. It is hard, it is in itself an absurd and evil thing, and will be of fatal consequence to him that does it. Those kick at the goad that stifle and smother the convictions of conscience, that rebel against God's truths and laws, that quarrel with his providences, and that persecute and oppose his ministers, because they reprove them, and their words are as goads and as nails. Those that revolt more and more when they are stricken by the word or rod of God, that are enraged at reproofs and fly in the face of their reprovers, kick against the pricks and will have a great deal to answer for.

6. His surrender of himself to the Lord Jesus at length, *v.* 6. See here,

(1.) The frame and temper he was in, when Christ had been dealing with him. [1.] He trembled, as one in a great fright. Note, Strong convictions, set home by the blessed Spirit, will make an awakened soul to tremble. How can those choose but tremble that are made to see the eternal God provoked against them, the whole creation at war with them, and their own souls upon the brink of ruin! [2.] He was astonished, was filled with amazement, as one brought into a new world, that knew not where he was. Note, The convincing, converting, work of Christ is astonishing to the awakened soul, and fills it with admiration. "What is this that God has done with me, and what will he do?"

(2.) His address to Jesus Christ, when he was in this frame: *Lord, what wilt thou have me to do?* This may be taken, [1.] As a serious request for Christ's teachings: "Lord, I see I have hitherto been out of the way; thou hast shown me my error, set me to rights; thou hast discovered sin to me, discover to me the way to pardon and peace." It is like that, *Men and brethren, what must we do?* Note, A serious desire to be instructed by Christ in the way of salvation is an evidence of a good work begun in the soul. Or, [2.] As a sincere resignation of himself to the direction and government of the Lord Jesus. This was the first word that grace spoke in Paul, and with this began a spiritual life: Lord Jesus, *What wilt thou have me to do?* Did not he know what he had to do? Had he not his commission in his pocket? And what had he to do but to execute it? No, he had done enough of this work already, and resolves now to change his master, and employ himself better. Now it is not, What will the high priest and the elders have me to do? What will my own wicked appetites and passions have me to do? But, *What wilt thou have me to do?* The great change in conversion is wrought upon the will, and consists in the resignation of that to the will of Christ.

(3.) The general direction Christ gave him, in answer to this: *Arise, go into the city of Damascus,* which thou art now near to, *and it shall be told thee what thou must do.* It is encouragement enough to have further instruction promised him, but, [1.] He must not have it yet; it shall be told him shortly what he must do, but, for the present, he must pause upon what has been said to him, and improve that. Let him consider awhile what he has done in persecuting Christ, and be deeply humbled for that, and then he shall be told what he has further to do. [2.] He must not have it in this way, by a voice from heaven, for it is plain that he cannot bear it; he trembles, and is astonished. He shall be told therefore what he must do by a man like himself, whose terror shall not make him afraid, nor his hand be heavy upon him, which Israel desired at mount Sinai. Or, it is an intimation that Christ would take some other time to manifest himself further to him, when he was more composed, and this fright pretty well over. Christ manifests himself to his people by degrees; and both what he does and would he have them to do, though they know not now, they shall know hereafter.

7. How far his fellow travellers were affected with this, and what impression it made upon them. They fell to the earth, as he did, but rose without being bidden, which he did not, but lay still till it was said to him, *Arise;* for he lay under a heavier load than any of them did; but when they were up, (1.) *They stood speechless*, as men in confusion, and that was all, *v.* 7. They were going on the same wicked errand that Paul was, and perhaps, to the best of their power, were as spiteful as he; yet we do not find that any of them were converted, though they saw the light, and were struck down and struck dumb by it. No external means will of themselves work a change in the soul, without the Spirit and grace of God, which distinguish between some and others; among these that journeyed together, one is taken, and the others left. *They stood speechless;* none of them said, *Who art thou, Lord?* or, *What wilt thou have me to do?* as Paul did, but none of God's children are born dumb. (2.) *They heard a voice, but saw no man;* they heard Paul speak, but saw not him to whom he spoke, nor heard distinctly what was said to him: which reconciles it with what is said of this matter, *ch.* xxii. 9, where it is said, *They saw the light and were afraid* (which they might do and yet see no man in the light, as Paul did), and *that they heard not the voice of him that spoke to Paul,* so as to understand what he said, though they did hear a confused noise. Thus those who came hither to be the instruments of Paul's rage against the church serve for witnesses of the power of God over him.

8. What condition Saul was in after this, *v.* 8, 9. (1.) *He arose from the earth,* when Christ commanded him, but probably not without help, the vision had made him so faint and weak, I will not say like Belshazzar, when the joints of his loins were loosed and his knees smote one against another, but like Daniel, when upon the sight of a vision no strength remained in him, Dan. x. 16—17. (2.) *When his eyes were opened,* he found that his sight was gone, and *he saw no man,* none of the men that were with him, and began now to be busy about him. It was not so much this glaring light that, *by dazzling his eyes, had dimmed them—Nimium sensibile lædit sensum;* for then those with him would have lost their sight too; but it was a sight of Christ, whom the rest saw not, that had this effect upon him. Thus a believing sight of the glory of God in the face of Christ dazzles the eyes to all things here below. Christ, in order to the further discovery of himself and his gospel to Paul, took him off from the sight of other things, which he must look off, that he may look unto Jesus, and to him only. (3.) *They led him by the hand into Damascus;* whether to a public house, or to some friend's house, is not certain; but thus he who thought to have led the disciples of Christ prisoners and captives to Jerusalem was himself led a prisoner and a captive to Christ into Damascus. He was thus taught what need he had of the grace of Christ to lead his soul (being naturally blind and apt to mistake) into all truth. (4.) He lay *without sight,* and without food, *neither did eat nor drink for three days, v.* 9. I do not think, as some do, that now he had his rapture into the third heavens, which he speaks of, 2 Cor. xii. So far from this that we have reason to think he was all this time rather in the belly of hell, suffering God's terrors for his sins, which were now set in order before him: he was in the dark concerning his own spiritual state, and was so wounded in spirit for sin that he could relish neither meat nor drink.

10 And there was a certain disciple at Damascus, named Ananias;
and to him said the Lord in a vision,
Ananias. And he said, Behold, I *am*
here, Lord. 11 And the Lord *said*
unto him, Arise, and go into the
street which is called Straight, and
enquire in the house of Judas for *one*
called Saul, of Tarsus: for, behold,
he prayeth, 12 And hath seen in a
vision a man named Ananias coming
in, and putting *his* hand on him, that
he might receive his sight. 13 Then
Ananias answered, Lord, I have
heard by many of this man, how
much evil he hath done to thy saints
at Jerusalem: 14 And here he hath
authority from the chief priests to
bind all that call on thy name. 15
But the Lord said unto him, Go thy
way: for he is a chosen vessel unto
me, to bear my name before the
Gentiles, and kings, and the children
of Israel: 16 For I will show him
how great things he must suffer for
my name's sake. 17 And Ananias
went his way, and entered into the
house; and putting his hands on
him said, Brother Saul, the Lord,
even Jesus, that appeared unto thee
in the way as thou camest, hath sent
me, that thou mightest receive thy
sight, and be filled with the Holy
Ghost. 18 And immediately there
fell from his eyes as it had been
scales: and he received sight forthwith, and arose, and was baptized.
19 And when he had received meat
he was strengthened. Then was
Saul certain days with the disciples

which were at Damascus. 20 And
straightway he preached Christ in
the synagogues, that he is the Son of
God. 21 But all that heard *him*
were amazed, and said; Is not this
he that destroyed them which called
on this name in Jerusalem, and came
hither for that intent, that he might
bring them bound unto the chief
priests? 22 But Saul increased the
more in strength, and confounded
the Jews which dwelt at Damascus,
proving that this is very Christ.

As for God, his work is perfect; if he begin, he will make an end: a good work was begun in Saul, when he was brought to Christ's feet, in that word, *Lord, what wilt thou have me to do?* And never did Christ leave any that were brought to that. Though Saul was sadly mortified when he lay three days blind, yet he was not abandoned. Christ here takes care of the work of his own hands. He that hath torn will heal—that hath smitten will bind up—that hath convinced will comfort.

I. Ananias is here ordered to go and look after him, to heal and help him; for he that causeth grief will have compassion.

1. The person employed is *Ananias, a certain disciple at Damascus,* not lately driven thither from Jerusalem, but a native of Damascus; for it is said (*ch.* xxii. 12) *that he had a good report of all the Jews who dwelt there, as a devout man according to the law;* he had lately embraced the gospel, and given up his name to Christ, and, as it should seem, officiated as a minister, at least *pro hac vice—on this occasion,* though it does not appear that he was apostolically ordained. But why were not some of the apostles from Jerusalem sent for upon this great occasion, or Philip the evangelist, who had lately baptized the eunuch, and might have been fetched hither by the Spirit in a little time? Surely, because Christ would employ variety of hands in eminent services, that the honours might not be monopolized nor engrossed by a few,—because he would put work into the hands, and thereby put honour upon the heads, of those that were mean and obscure, to encourage them,—and because he would direct us to make much of the ministers that are where our lot is cast, if they have obtained mercy to be faithful, though they are not of the most eminent.

2. The direction given him is to go and enquire at such a house, probably an inn, for one *Saul of Tarsus.* Christ, in a vision, called to Ananias by name, *v.* 10. It is probable it was not the first time that he had heard the words of God, and seen the visions of the Almighty; for, without terror or confusion, he readily answers, "*Behold I am here, Lord,* ready to go wherever thou sendest me, and to do whatever thou biddest me." *Go then,* saith Christ, *into the street which is called Straight, and enquire in the house of Judas* (where strangers used to lodge) *for one called Saul of Tarsus.* Note, Christ very well knows where to find out those that are his, in their distresses: when their relations, it may be, know not what is become of them, they have a friend in heaven, that knows in what street, in what house, nay, and which is more, in what frame they are: he knows their souls in adversity.

3. Two reasons are given him why he must go and enquire for this stranger, and offer him his service:—

(1.) Because he prays, and his coming to him must answer his prayer. This is a reason, [1.] Why Ananias needed not to be afraid of him, as we find he was, *v.* 13, 14. There is no question, saith Christ, but he is a true convert, *for behold he prayeth. Behold* denotes the certainty of it: "Assure thyself it is so; go and see." Christ was so pleased to find Paul praying that he must have others to take notice of it: *Rejoice with me, for I have found the sheep which I had lost.* It denotes also the strangeness of it: "Behold, and wonder, that he who but the other day breathed nothing but threatenings and slaughter, now breathes nothing but prayer." But was it such a strange thing for Saul to pray? Was he not a Pharisee? and have we not reason to think he did, as the rest of them did, make long prayers in the synagogues and the corners of the streets? Yes; but now he began to pray after another manner than he had done; then he said his prayers, now he prayed them. Note, Regenerating grace evermore sets people on praying; you may as soon find a living man without breath as a living Christian without prayer; if breathless, lifeless; and so, if prayerless, graceless. [2.] As a reason why Ananias must go to him with all speed. It is no time to linger, *for behold he prayeth:* if the child cry, the tender nurse will hasten to it with the breast. Saul here, like Ephraim, is bemoaning himself, as a bullock unaccustomed to the yoke, and kicking against the goad. "Oh! go to him quickly, and tell him he is a dear son, a pleasant child, and *since I spoke against him,* for persecuting me, *I do earnestly remember him still.*" Jer. xxxi. 18—20. Observe what condition Saul was now in. He was under conviction of sin, trembling and astonished; the setting of sin in order before us should drive us to prayer. He was under a bodily affliction, blind and sick; and, *Is any afflicted? Let him pray.* Christ had promised him that it should be further told him what he should do (*v.* 6), and he prays that one may be sent to him to instruct him. Note, What God has promised we must pray for; he will for this be enquired of, and particularly for divine instruction.

(2.) Because he hath seen in a vision such a man coming to him, to restore him to his sight; and Ananias's coming to him must answer his dream, for it was of God (*v.* 12): *He hath seen in a vision a man named Ananias,* and just such a man as thou art, *coming in* seasonably for his relief, *and putting his hand on him that he might receive his sight.* Now this vision which Paul had may be considered, [1.] As an immediate answer to his prayer, and the keeping up of that communion with God which he had entered into by prayer. He had, in prayer, spread the misery of his own case before God, and God presently manifests himself and the kind intentions of his grace to him; and it is very encouraging to know God's thoughts to us-ward. [2.] As designed to raise his expectations, and to make Ananias's coming more welcome to him. He would readily receive him as a messenger from God when he was told beforehand, in vision, that one of that name would come to him. See what a great thing it is to bring a spiritual physician and his patient together: here were two visions in order to it. When God, in his providence, does it without visions, brings a messenger to the afflicted soul, an interpreter, one among a thousand, to show unto man his uprightness, it must be acknowledged with thankfulness to his praise.

II. Ananias objects against going to him, and the Lord answers the objection. See how condescendingly the Lord admits his servant to reason with him.

1. Ananias pleads that this Saul was a notorious persecutor of the disciples of Christ, *v.* 13, 14. (1.) He had been so at Jerusalem: "*Lord, I have heard by many of this man,* what a malicious enemy he is to the gospel of Christ: all those that were scattered upon the late persecution, many of whom are come to Damascus, tell *how much evil he hath done to thy saints in Jerusalem,* that he was the most virulent, violent persecutor of all, and a ringleader in the mischief—what havoc he has made in the church: there was no man they were more afraid of, no, not the high priest himself, than of Saul; nay," (2.) "His errand to Damascus at this time is to persecute us Christians: *Here he has authority from the chief priests to bind all that call on thy name,* to treat the worshippers of Christ as the worst of criminals." Now, why does Ananias object this. Not, "Therefore I do not owe him so much service. Why should I do him a kindness who has done and designed us so much unkindness?" No, Christ has taught us another lesson, to render good for evil, and pray for our persecutors; but if he be such a persecutor of Christians, [1.] Will it be safe for Ananias to go to him? Will he not throw himself like a lamb into the mouth of a lion? And, if he thus bring himself into trouble, he will be blamed for his indiscretion. [2.] Will it be to any purpose to go to him? Can such a hard heart ever be softened, or such an Ethiopian ever change his skin?

2. Christ overrules the objection (*v.* 15, 16): "Do not tell me how bad he has been, I know it very well; but go thy way with all speed, and give him all the help thou canst, *for he is a chosen vessel,* or instrument, unto me; I design to put confidence in him, and then thou needest not fear him." He was a vessel in which the gospel-treasure should be lodged, in order to the conveyance of it to many; an earthen vessel (2 Cor. iv. 7), but a chosen vessel. The vessel God uses he himself chooses; and it is fit he should himself have the choosing of the instruments he employs (John xv. 16): *You have not chosen me, but I have chosen you.* He is a vessel of honour, and must not be neglected in his present forlorn condition, nor thrown away as a despised broken vessel, or a vessel in which there is no pleasure. He is designed, (1.) For eminent services: *He is to bear my name before the Gentiles,* is to be the apostle of the Gentiles, and to carry the gospel to heathen nations. Christ's name is the standard to which souls must be gathered, and under which they must be enlisted, and Saul must be a standard-bearer. He must bear Christ's name, must bear witness to it before kings, king Agrippa and Cæsar himself; nay, he must bear it before the children of Israel, though there were so many hands already at work about them. (2.) For eminent sufferings (*v.* 16): *I will show him how great things he must suffer for my name's sake.* He that has been a persecutor shall be himself persecuted. Christ's showing him this intimates either his bringing him to these trials (as Ps. lx. 3), *Thou hast shown thy people hard things,* or his giving notice of them beforehand, that they might be no surprise to him. Note, Those that bear Christ's name must expect to bear the cross for his name; and those that do most for Christ are often called out to suffer most for him. Saul must suffer great things. This, one would think, was a cold comfort for a young convert; but it is only like telling a soldier of a bold and brave spirit, when he is enlisted, that he shall take the field, and enter upon action, shortly. Saul's sufferings for Christ shall redound so much to the honour of Christ and the service of the church, shall be so balanced with spiritual comforts and recompensed with eternal glories, that it is no discouragement to him to be told how great things he must suffer for Christ's name's sake.

III. Ananias presently goes on Christ's errand to Saul, and with good effect. He had started an objection against going to him, but, when an answer was given to it, he dropped it, and did not insist upon it. When difficulties are removed, what have we to do but to go on with our work, and not hang upon an objection?

1. Ananias delivered his message to Saul, *v.* 17. Probably he found him in bed, and applied to him as a patient. (1.) *He put his hands on him.* It was promised, as one of

the signs that should follow those that believe, that they should lay hands on the sick, and they should recover (Mark xvi. 18), and it was for that intent that he put his hands on him. Saul came to lay violent hands upon the disciples at Damascus, but here a disciple lays a helping healing hand upon him. *The bloodthirsty hate the upright, but the just seek his soul.* (2.) He called him *brother*, because he was made a partaker of the grace of God, though not yet baptized; and his readiness to own him as a brother intimated to him God's readiness to own him as a son, though he had been a blasphemer of God and a persecutor of his children. (3.) He produces his commission from the same hand that had laid hold on him by the way, and now had him in custody. "That *same Jesus that appeared unto thee in the way as thou camest*, and convinced thee of thy sin in persecuting him, has now sent me to thee to comfort thee." *Una eademque manus vulnus opemque tulit*—*The hand that wounded heals.* His light struck thee blind, but he *hath sent me to thee that thou mightest receive thy sight;* for the design was not to blind thine eyes, but to dazzle them, that thou mightest see things by another light: he that then put clay upon thine eyes hath sent me to wash them, that they may be cured." Ananias might deliver his message to Saul very appositely in the prophet's words (Hos. vi. 1, 2): *Come and turn to the Lord, for he hath torn and he will heal thee; he hath smitten, and he will bind thee up; now after two days he will revive thee, and the third day he will raise thee up, and thou shalt live in his sight.* Corrosives shall be no more applied, but lenitives. (4.) He assures him that he shall not only have his sight restored, but be filled with the Holy Ghost: he must himself be an apostle, and must in nothing come behind the chief of the apostles, and therefore must receive the Holy Ghost immediately, and not, as others did, by the interposition of the apostles; and Ananias's putting his hands upon him before he was baptized was for the conferring of the Holy Ghost.

2. Ananias saw the good issue of his mission. (1.) In Christ's favour to Saul. At the word of Ananias, Saul was discharged from his confinement by the restoring of his sight; for Christ's commission to open the prison to those that were bound (Isa. lxi. 1) is explained by the giving of sight to the blind, Luke iv. 18; Isai. xlii. 7. Christ's commission is to open the blind eyes, and to bring out the prisoners from the prison. Saul is delivered from the spirit of bondage by his receiving sight (*v.* 18), which was signified by the falling of scales from his eyes; and this immediately, and forthwith: the cure was sudden, to show that it was miraculous. This signified the recovering of him, [1.] From the darkness of his unconverted state. When he persecuted the church of God, and walked in the spirit and way of the Pharisees, he was blind; he saw not the meaning either of the law or of the gospel, Rom. vii. 9. Christ often told the Pharisees that they were blind, and could not make them sensible of it; they said, *We see*, John ix. 41. Saul is saved from his Pharisaical blindness, by being made sensible of it. Note, Converting grace opens the eyes of the soul, and makes the scales to fall from them (*ch.* xxvi. 18), to open men's eyes, and turn them from darkness to light: this was what Saul was sent among the Gentiles to do, by the preaching of the gospel, and therefore must first experience it in himself. [2.] From the darkness of his present terrors, under the apprehension of guilt upon his conscience, and the wrath of God against him. This filled him with confusion, during those three days he sat in darkness, like Jonah for three days in the belly of hell; but now the scales fell from his eyes, the cloud was scattered, and the Sun of righteousness rose upon his soul, with healing under his wings. (2.) In Saul's subjection to Christ: He was baptized, and thereby submitted to the government of Christ, and cast himself upon the grace of Christ. Thus he was entered into Christ's school, hired into his family, enlisted under his banner, and joined himself to him for better for worse. The point was gained: it is settled; Saul is now a disciple of Christ, not only ceases to oppose him, but devotes himself entirely to his service and honour.

IV. The good work that was begun in Saul is carried on wonderfully; this new-born Christian, though he seemed *as one born out of due time*, yet presently comes to maturity.

1. He received his bodily strength, *v.* 19. He had continued three days fasting, which, with the mighty weight that was all that time upon his spirits, had made him very weak; but, *when he had received meat, he was strengthened*, *v.* 19. The Lord is for the body, and therefore care must be taken of it, to keep it in good plight, that it may be fit to serve the soul in God's service, and that Christ may be magnified in it, Phil. i. 20

2. He associated with the disciples that were at Damascus, fell in with them, conversed with them, went to their meetings, and joined in communion with them. He had lately *breathed out threatenings and slaughter against them*, but now breathes love and affection to them. Now *the wolf dwells with the lamb*, and *the leopard lies down with the kid*, Isa. xi. 6. Note, Those that take God for their God take his people for their people. Saul associated with the disciples, because now he saw an amiableness and excellency in them, because he loved them, and found that he improved in knowledge and grace by conversing with them; and thus he made profession of his Christian faith, and openly declared himself a disciple of Christ, by associating with those that were his disciples.

3 *He preached Christ in the synagogues, v.* 20. To this he had an extraordinary call, and for it an extraordinary qualification, God having immediately revealed his Son to him and in him, that he might preach him, Gal. i. 15, 16. He was so full of Christ himself, that *the Spirit within him constrained him* to preach him to others, and, like Elihu, *to speak that he might be refreshed,* Job xxxii. 20. Observe, (1.) Where he preached—in the synagogues of the Jews, for they were to have the first offer made them. The synagogues were their places of concourse; there he met with them together, and there they used to preach against Christ and to punish his disciples, by the same token that Paul himself *had punished them oft in every synagogue* (*ch.* xxvi. 11), and therefore there he would face the enemies of Christ where they were most daring, and openly profess Christianity where he had most opposed it. (2.) What he preached: *He preached Christ.* When he began to be a preacher, he fixed this for his principle, which he stuck to ever after: *We preach not ourselves, but Christ Jesus our Lord;* nothing but Christ, and him crucified. He preached concerning Christ, *that he is the Son of God,* his beloved Son, in whom he is well pleased, and with us in him, and not otherwise. (3.) How people were affected with it (*v.* 21): *All that heard him were amazed, and said, "Is not this he that destroyed those who called on this name in Jerusalem,* and now does he call on this name himself, and persuade others to call upon it, and strengthen the hands of those that do?" *Quantum mutatus ab illo!—Oh how changed! Is Saul also among the prophets?* Nay, did he not come hither for that intent, to seize all the Christians he could find, and *bring them bound to the chief priests?* Yes, he did. Who would have thought then that he would ever preach Christ as he does? Doubtless this was looked upon by many as a great confirmation of the truth of Christianity, that one who had been such a notorious persecutor of it came, on a sudden, to be such an intelligent, strenuous, and capacious preacher of it. This miracle upon the mind of such a man outshone the miracles upon men's bodies; and giving a man such another heart was more than giving men to speak with other tongues.

4. He confuted and confounded those that opposed the doctrine of Christ, *v.* 22. He signalized himself, not only in the pulpit, but in the schools, and showed himself supernaturally enabled, not only to preach the truth, but to maintain and defend it when he had preached it. (1.) He increased in strength. He became more intimately acquainted with the gospel of Christ, and his pious affections grew more strong. He grew more bold and daring and resolute in defence of the gospel: *He increased the more* for the reflections that were cast upon him (*v.* 21), in which his new friends upbraided him as having been a persecutor, and his old friends upbraided him as being now a turncoat; but Saul, instead of being discouraged by the various remarks made upon his conversion, was thereby so much the more emboldened, finding he had enough at hand wherewith to answer the worst they could say to him. (2.) He ran down his antagonists, and *confounded the Jews who dwelt in Damascus;* he silenced them, and shamed them—answered their objections to the satisfaction of all indifferent persons, and pressed them with arguments which they could make no reply to. In all his discourses with the Jews he was still *proving that this Jesus is very Christ, is the Christ, the anointed of God, the true Messiah promised to the fathers.* He was proving it, *συμβιβάζων—affirming it and confirming it,* teaching with persuasion. And we have reason to think he was instrumental in converting many to the faith of Christ, and building up the church at Damascus, which he went thither to make havoc of. Thus *out of the eater came forth meat, and out of the strong sweetness.*

23 And after that many days were
fulfilled, the Jews took counsel to
kill him: 24 But their laying await
was known of Saul. And they
watched the gates day and night to
kill him. 25 Then the disciples took
him by night, and let *him* down by
the wall in a basket. 26 And when
Saul was come to Jerusalem, he assayed to join himself to the disciples:
but they were all afraid of him, and
believed not that he was a disciple.
27 But Barnabas took him, and
brought *him* to the apostles, and declared unto them how he had seen
the Lord in the way, and that he
had spoken to him, and how he had
preached boldly at Damascus in the
name of Jesus. 28 And he was with
them coming in and going out at Jerusalem. 29 And he spake boldly
in the name of the Lord Jesus, and
disputed against the Grecians: but
they went about to slay him. 30
Which when the brethren knew, they
brought him down to Cæsarea, and
sent him forth to Tarsus. 31 Then
had the churches rest throughout all
Judæa and Galilee and Samaria, and
were edified; and walking in the
fear of the Lord, and in the comfort
of the Holy Ghost, were multiplied.

Luke here makes no mention of Paul's journey into Arabia, which he tells us himself was immediately after his conversion, Gal. i.

16 17. As soon as God *had revealed his Son in him, that he might preach him, he went not up to Jerusalem,* to receive instructions from the apostles (as any other convert would have done, that was designed for the ministry), but he went to Arabia, where there was new ground to break up, and where he would have opportunity of teaching, but not of learning; thence he returned to Damascus, and there, three years after his conversion, this happened, which is here recorded.

I. He met with difficulties at Damascus, and had a narrow escape of being killed there. Observe, 1. What his danger was (*v.* 23): *The Jews took counsel to kill him,* being more enraged at him than at any other of the preachers of the gospel, not only because he was more lively and zealous in his preaching than any of them, and more successful, but because he had been such a remarkable deserter, and his being a Christian was a testimony against them. It is said (*v.* 24), *The Jews watched the gates day and night to kill him;* they incensed the governor against him, as a dangerous man, who therefore kept the city with a guard to apprehend him, at his going out or coming in, 2 Cor. xi. 32. Now Christ showed Paul *what great things he must suffer for his name* (*v.* 16), when here was presently the government in arms against him, which was a great thing, and, as all his other sufferings afterwards, helped to make him considerable. Saul was no sooner a Christian than a preacher, no sooner a preacher than a sufferer; so quickly did he rise to the summit of his preferment. Note, Where God gives great grace he commonly exercises it with great trials. 2. How he was delivered. (1.) The design against him was discovered: *Their lying in wait was known of Saul,* by some intelligence, whether from heaven or from men we are not told. (2.) The disciples contrived to help him away—hid him, it is likely, by day; and in the night, the gates being watched, that he could not get away through them, *they let him down by the wall, in a basket,* as he himself relates it (2 Cor. xi. 33), *so he escaped out of their hands.* This story, as it shows us that when we enter into the way of God we must look for temptation, and prepare accordingly, so it shows us *that the Lord knows how to deliver the godly out of temptation, and will with the temptation also make a way to escape, that we may* not be by it deterred nor driven from the way of God.

II. He met with difficulties at Jerusalem the first time he went thither, *v.* 26. He came to Jerusalem. This is thought to be that journey to Jerusalem of which he himself speaks (Gal. i. 18): *After three years I went up to Jerusalem,* saith he, *to see Peter, and abode with him fifteen days.* But I rather incline to think that this was a journey before that, because *his coming in* and *going out, his preaching and disputing* (*v.* 28, 29), seem to be more than would consist with his fifteen days' stay (for that was no more) and to require a longer time; and, besides, now he came a stranger, but then he came, ἱστορῆσαι Πέτρον—*to confer with Peter,* as one he was intimate with; however, it might possibly be the same. Now observe,

1. How shy his friends were of him (*v.* 26): *When he came to Jerusalem,* he did not go to the chief priests and the Pharisees (he had taken his leave of them long since), but *he assayed to join himself to the disciples.* Wherever he came, he owned himself one of that despised persecuted people, and associated with them. They were now in his eyes *the excellent ones of the earth, in whom was all his delight.* He desired to be acquainted with them, and to be admitted into communion with them; but they looked strange upon him, shut the door against him, and would not go about any of their religious exercises if he were by, for *they were afraid of him.* Now might Paul be tempted to think himself in an ill case, when the Jews had abandoned and persecuted him, and the Christians would not receive and entertain him. Thus does he fall into divers temptations, and needs the armour of righteousness, as we all do, both on the right hand and on the left, that we may not be discouraged either by the unjust treatment of our enemies or the unkind treatment of our friends. (1.) See what was the cause of their jealousy of him: *They believed not that he was a disciple,* but that he only pretended to be so, and came among them as a spy or an informer. They knew what a bitter persecutor he had been, with what fury he went to Damascus some time ago; they had heard nothing of him since, and therefore thought he was but a wolf in sheep's clothing. The disciples of Christ had need to be cautious whom they admit into communion with them. *Believe not every spirit.* There is need of the wisdom of the serpent, to keep the mean between the extremes of suspicion on the one hand and credulity on the other; yet methinks it is safer to err on the charitable side, because it is an adjudged case that it is better the tares should be found among the wheat than that the wheat should any of it be rooted up and thrown out of the field. (2.) See how it was removed (*v.* 27): *Barnabas took him to the apostles* themselves, who were not so scrupulous as the inferior disciples, *to whom he first assayed to join himself, and he declared to them,* [1.] What Christ had done for him: *He had shown himself to him in the way* and spoken to him; and what he said. [2.] What he had since done for Christ: *He had preached boldly at Damascus in the name of Jesus.* How Barnabas came to know this, more than the rest of them, we are not told; whether he had himself been at Damascus, or had had letters thence, or discoursed with some of that city, by which he came to the knowledge of this; or whether he had formerly been acquainted with Paul in the Grecian synagogues, or at the feet of Gamaliel, and had such an account

of his conversion from himself as he saw cause enough to give credit to: but so it was that, being satisfied himself, he gave satisfaction to the apostles concerning him, he having brought no testimonials from the disciples at Damascus, thinking *he needed not, as some others, epistles of commendation,* 2 Cor. iii. 1. Note, The introducing of a young convert into the communion of the faithful is a very good work, and one which, as we have opportunity, we should be ready to do.

2. How sharp his enemies were upon him. (1.) He was admitted into the communion of the disciples, which was no little provocation to his enemies. It vexed the unbelieving Jews to see Saul a trophy of Christ's victory, and a captive to his grace, who had been such a champion for their cause—to see him *coming in, and going out, with the apostles* (*v.* 28), and to hear them glorying in him, or rather glorifying God in him. (2.) He appeared vigorous in the cause of Christ, and this was yet more provoking to them (*v.* 29): *He spoke boldly in the name of the Lord Jesus.* Note, Those that speak for Christ have reason to speak boldly; for they have a good cause, and speak for one who will at last speak for himself and them too. The Grecians, or Hellenist Jews, were most offended at him, because he had been one of them; and they drew him into a dispute, in which, no doubt, he was too hard for them, as he had been for the Jews at Damascus. One of the martyrs said, Though she could not dispute for Christ, she could die for Christ; but Paul could do both. Now the Lord Jesus divided the spoils of the strong man armed in Saul. For that same natural quickness and fervour of spirit which, while he was in ignorance and unbelief, made him a furious bigoted persecutor of the faith, made him a most zealous courageous defender of the faith. (3.) This brought him into peril of his life, with which he narrowly escaped: *The Grecians,* when they found they could not deal with him in disputation, contrived to silence him another way; *they went about to slay him,* as they did Stephen when *they could not resist the Spirit by which he spoke, ch.* vi. 10. That is a bad cause that has recourse to persecution for its last argument. But notice was given of this conspiracy too, and effectual care taken to secure this young champion (*v.* 30): *When the brethren knew* what was designed against him *they brought him down to Cesarea.* They remembered how the putting of Stephen to death, upon his disputing with the Grecians, had been the beginning of a sore persecution; and therefore were afraid of having such a vein opened again, and hastened Paul out of the way. He that flies may fight again. He that fled from Jerusalem might do service at Tarsus, the place of his nativity; and thither they desired him by all means to go, hoping he might there go on in his work with more safety than at Jerusalem. Yet it was also by direction from heaven that he left Jerusalem at this time, as he tells us himself (*ch.* xxii. 17, 18), that Christ now appeared to him, and ordered him to *go quickly out of Jerusalem,* for he must be sent *to the Gentiles, v.* 15. Those by whom God has work to do shall be protected from all the designs of their enemies against them till it be done. Christ's witnesses cannot be slain till they have *finished their testimony.*

III. The churches had now a comfortable gleam of liberty and peace (*v.* 31): *Then had the churches rest. Then,* when Saul was converted, so some; when that persecutor was taken off, those were quiet whom he used to irritate, and then those were quiet whom he used to molest. Or, *then,* when he had gone from Jerusalem, the fury of the Grecian Jews was a little abated, and they were the more willing to bear with the other preachers now that Saul had gone out of the way. Observe,

1. *The churches had rest.* After a storm comes a calm. Though we are always to expect troublesome times, yet we may expect that they shall not last always. This was a breathing-time allowed them, to prepare them for the next encounter. The churches that were already planted were mostly in Judea, Galilee, and Samaria, within the limits of the holy land. There were the first Christian churches, where Christ had himself laid the foundation.

2. They made a good use of this lucid interval. Instead of growing secure and wanton in the day of their prosperity, they abounded more in their duty, and made a good use of their tranquillity. (1.) They *were edified,* were built up in their most holy faith; the more free and constant enjoyment they had of the means of knowledge and grace, the more they increased in knowledge and grace. (2.) They *walked in the fear of the Lord*—were more exemplary themselves for a holy heavenly conversation. They so lived that all who conversed with them might say, Surely the fear of God reigns in those people. (3.) They *walked in the comfort of the Holy Ghost*—were not only faithful, but cheerful, in religion; they stuck to the ways of the Lord, and sang in those ways. *The comfort of the Holy Ghost* was their consolation, and that which they made their chief joy. They had recourse to the comfort of the Holy Ghost, and lived upon that, not only in days of trouble and affliction, but in days of rest and prosperity. The comforts of the earth, when they had the most free and full enjoyment of them, could not content them without the comfort of the Holy Ghost. Observe the connection of these two: when they walked *in the fear of the Lord,* then they walked *in the comfort of the Holy Ghost.* Those are most likely to walk cheerfully that walk circumspectly.

3. God blessed it to them for their increase in number: They *were multiplied.* Sometimes the church multiplies the more for its being afflicted, as Israel in Egypt; yet if it

were always so, the saints of the Most High would be worn out. At other times its rest contributes to its growth, as it enlarges the opportunity of ministers, and invites those in who at first are afraid of suffering. Or, *then*, when *they walked in the fear of God and his comforts, they were multiplied.* Thus those that will not be won by the word may be won by the conversation of professors.

32 And it came to pass, as Peter
passed throughout all *quarters*, he
came down also to the saints which
dwelt at Lydda. 33 And there he
found a certain man named Æneas,
which had kept his bed eight years,
and was sick of the palsy. 34 And
Peter said unto him, Æneas, Jesus
Christ maketh thee whole: arise, and
make thy bed. And he arose immediately. 35 And all that dwelt at
Lydda and Saron saw him, and turned
to the Lord.

Here we have, I. The visit Peter made to the churches that were newly planted by the dispersed preachers, *v.* 32. 1. He *passed through all quarters.* As an apostle, he was not to be the resident pastor of any one church, but the itinerant visitor of many churches, to confirm the doctrine of inferior preachers, to confer *the Holy Ghost on those that believed*, and to ordain ministers. He passed *διὰ πάντων—among them all*, who pertained to the churches of Judea, Galilee, and Samaria, mentioned in the foregoing chapter. He was, like his Master, always upon the remove, and *went about doing good;* but still his head-quarters were at Jerusalem, for there we shall find him imprisoned, *ch.* xii. 2. *He came to the saints at Lydda.* This seems to be the same with *Lod*, a city in the tribe of Benjamin, mentioned 1 Chron. viii. 12; Ezra ii. 33. The Christians are called *saints*, not only some particular eminent ones, as saint Peter and saint Paul, but every sincere professor of the faith of Christ. These are the saints on the earth, Ps. xvi. 3.

II. The cure Peter wrought on *Eneas*, a man that had been bedridden eight years, *v.* 33. 1. His case was very deplorable: *He was sick of the palsy*, a dumb palsy, perhaps a dead palsy. The disease was extreme, for *he kept his bed;* it was inveterate, for he kept his bed *eight years;* and we may suppose that both he himself and all about him despaired of relief for him, and concluded upon no other than that he must still keep his bed till he removed to his grave. Christ chose such patients as this, whose disease was incurable in a course of nature, to show how desperate the case of fallen mankind was when he undertook their cure. When we were without strength, as this poor man, *he sent his word to heal us.* 2. His cure was very admirable, *v.* 34. (1.) Peter interested Christ in his case, and engaged him for his relief: *Eneas, Jesus Christ maketh thee whole.* Peter does not pretend to do it himself by any power of his own, but declares it to be Christ's act and deed, directs him to look up to Christ for help, and assures him of an *immediate* cure—not, "He *will* make thee," but, "He *does* make thee, whole;" and a *perfect* cure—not, "He makes thee *easy*," but "He makes thee *whole*." He does not express himself by way of prayer to Christ that he would make him whole, but as one having authority from Christ, and that knew his mind, he declares him made whole. (2.) He ordered him to bestir himself, to exert himself: "*Arise and make thy bed*, that all may see thou art thoroughly cured." Let none say that because it is Christ that by the power of his grace works all our works in us therefore we have no work, no duty, to do; for, though Jesus Christ makes thee whole, yet thou must arise and make use of the power he gives thee: "*Arise, and make thy bed*, to be to thee no longer a bed of sickness, but a bed of rest." (3.) Power went along with this word: he arose immediately, and no doubt very willingly made his own bed.

III. The good influence this had upon many (*v.* 35): *All that dwelt at Lydda and Saron saw him, and turned to the Lord.* We can scarcely think that every individual person in those countries took cognizance of the miracle, and was wrought upon by it; but many, the generality of the people in the town of Lydda and in the country of Saron, or Sharon, a fruitful plain or valley, of which it was foretold, *Sharon shall be a fold of flocks*, Isa. lxv. 10. 1. They all made enquiry into the truth of the miracle, did not overlook it, but saw him that was healed, and saw that it was a miraculous cure that was wrought upon him by the power of Christ, in his name, and with a design to confirm and ratify that doctrine of Christ which was now preached to the world. 2. They all submitted to the convincing proof and evidence there was in this of the divine origin of the Christian doctrine, and *turned to the Lord*, to the Lord Jesus. They turned from Judaism to Christianity; they embraced the doctrine of Christ, and submitted to his ordinances, and turned themselves over to him to be ruled and taught and saved by him.

36 Now there was at Joppa a certain disciple named Tabitha, which
by interpretation is called Dorcas:
this woman was full of good works,
and almsdeeds which she did. 37
And it came to pass in those days,
that she was sick, and died: whom
when they had washed, they laid *her*
in an upper chamber. 38 And forasmuch as Lydda was nigh to Joppa,
and the disciples had heard that

Peter was there, they sent unto him
two men, desiring *him* that he would
not delay to come to them. 39 Then
Peter arose and went with them.
When he was come, they brought
him into the upper chamber: and all
the widows stood by him weeping,
and showing the coats and garments
which Dorcas made, while she was
with them. 40 But Peter put them
all forth, and kneeled down, and
prayed; and turning *him* to the body
said, Tabitha, arise. And she opened
her eyes: and when she saw Peter,
she sat up. 41 And he gave her *his*
hand, and lifted her up, and when he
had called the saints and widows,
presented her alive. 42 And it was
known throughout all Joppa; and
many believed in the Lord. 43 And
it came to pass, that he tarried many
days in Joppa with one Simon a
tanner.

Here we have another miracle wrought by Peter, for the confirming of the gospel, and which exceeded the former—the raising of Tabitha to life when she had been for some time dead. Here is,

I. The life, and death, and character of Tabitha, on whom this miracle was wrought, *v.* 36, 37. 1. She lived at Joppa, a sea-port town in the tribe of Dan, where Jonah took shipping to go to Tarshish, now called *Japho.* 2. Her name was *Tabitha*, a Hebrew name, the Greek for which is *Dorcas*, both signifying a *doe*, or *hind*, or *deer*, a pleasant creature. *Naphtali is* compared to *a hind let loose, giving goodly words;* and the wife to the kind and tender husband is as the loving *hind*, and as the pleasant *roe*, Prov. v. 19. 3. She was a disciple, one that had embraced the faith of Christ and was baptized; and not only so, but was eminent above many for works of charity. She showed her faith by her works, her good works, which she was full of, that is, in which she abounded. Her head was full of cares and contrivances which way she should do good. She *devised liberal things*, Isa. xxxii. 8. Her hands were full of good employment; she made a business of doing good, was never idle, having learned to *maintain good works* (Tit. iii. 8), to keep up a constant course and method of them. She was *full of good works*, as a tree that is full of fruit. Many are full of good words, who are empty and barren in good works; but Tabitha was a great doer, no great talker: *Non magna loquimur, sed vivimus—We do not talk great things, but we live them.* Among other good works, she was remarkable for her *alms-deeds which she did*, not only her works of piety, which are good works and the fruits of faith, but works of charity and beneficence, flowing from love to her neighbour and a holy contempt of this world. Observe, She is commended not only for the alms which she gave, but for the alms-deeds which she did. Those that have not estates wherewith to give in charity may yet be able to do in charity, working with their hands, or walking with their feet, for the benefit of the poor. And those who will not do a charitable deed, whatever they may pretend, if they were rich would not bestow a charitable gift. She was full of alms-deeds, *ὧν ἐποίει—which she made;* there is an emphasis upon her *doing* them, because what her hand found to do of this kind she did with all her might, and persevered in. They were alms-deeds, not which she purposed and designed and said she would do, but which she did; not which she began to do, but which she did, which she went through with, which she performed the doing of, 2 Cor. viii. 11; ix. 7. This is the life and character of a certain disciple, and should be of all the disciples of Christ; for, if we thus bear much fruit, then are we his disciples indeed, John xv. 8. 4. She was removed in the midst of her usefulness (*v.* 37): *In those days she fell sick, and died.* It is promised to those who consider the poor, not that they shall never be sick, but that the Lord will *strengthen them upon the bed of languishing*, at least with strength in their souls, and so will *make all their bed in their sickness*, will make it easy, Ps. xli. 1, 3. They cannot hope that they shall never die (*merciful men are taken away*, and merciful women too, witness Tabitha), but they may hope that they shall *find mercy of the Lord in that day*, 2 Tim. i. 18. 5. Her friends and those about her did not presently bury her, as usual, because they were in hopes Peter would come and raise her to life again; but they *washed the dead body*, according to the custom, which, it is said, was with warm water, which, if there were any life remaining in the body, would recover it; so that this was done to show that she was really and truly dead. They tried all the usual methods to bring her to life, and could not. *Conclamatum est—the last cry was uttered.* They *laid her out* in her grave-clothes *in an upper chamber*, which Dr. Lightfoot thinks was probably the public meeting-room for the believers of that town; and they laid the body there, that Peter, if he would come, might raise her to life the more solemnly in that place.

II. The request which her Christian friends sent to Peter to come to them with all speed, not to attend the funeral, but, if it might be, to prevent it, *v.* 38. Lydda, where Peter now was, was nigh to Joppa, and the disciples at Joppa had heard that Peter was there, and that he had raised Eneas from a bed of languishing; and therefore they *sent him two men,* to make the message the more solemn and respectful, *desiring him that he would not delay to come to them;* not telling him the occasion, lest he should modestly decline coming upon so great an errand as to raise the dead: if they can but get him to them, they will leave it to him. Their friend was dead, and it was too late to send for a physician, but not too late to send for Peter. *Post mortem medicus—a physician after death,* is an absurdity, but not *Post mortem apostolus—an apostle after death.*

III. The posture in which he found the survivors, when he came to them (*v.* 39): *Peter arose and went with them.* Though they did not tell him what they wanted him for, yet he was willing to go along with them, believing it was upon some good account or other that he was sent for. Let not faithful ministers grudge to be at every body's beck, as far as they have ability, when the great apostle *made himself the servant of all,* 1 Cor. ix. 19. He found the corpse laid in the upper chamber, and attended by widows, probably such as were in the communion of the church, poor widows; there they were,

1. Commending the deceased—a good work, when there was that in them which was truly commendable, and worthy of imitation, and when it is done modestly and soberly, and without flattery of the survivors or any sinister intention, but purely for the glory of God and the exciting of others to that which is virtuous and praiseworthy. The commendation of Tabitha was like her own virtues, not in word, but in deed. Here were no encomiums of her in orations, nor poems inscribed to her memory; but *the widows showed the coats and garments which she made* for them, and bestowed upon them *while she was with them.* It was the comfort of Job, while he lived, that the loins of the poor blessed him, because they were warmed with the fleece of his sheep, Job xxxi. 20. And here it was the credit of Tabitha, when she was dead, that the backs of the widows praised her for the garments which she made them. And those are certainly best praised *whose own works praise them in the gates,* whether the words of others do or no. It is much more honourable to clothe a company of decrepit widows with needful clothing for night and day, who will pray for their benefactors when they do not see them, than to clothe a company of lazy footmen with rich liveries, who perhaps behind their backs will curse those that clothe them (Eccl. vii. 21); and it is what all that are wise and good will take a greater pleasure in, for goodness is true greatness, and will pass better in the account shortly. Observe, (1.) Into what channel Tabitha turned much of her charity. Doubtless there were other instances of her almsdeeds which she did, but this was now produced; she did, as it should seem with her own hands, *make coats and garments* for poor widows, who perhaps with their own labour could make a shift to get their bread, but could not earn enough to buy clothes. And this is an excellent piece of charity, *If thou seest the naked, that thou cover him* (Isa. lviii. 7), and not think it enough to say, *Be ye warmed,* James ii. 15, 16. (2.) What a grateful sense the poor had of her kindness: *They showed the coats,* not ashamed to own that they were indebted to her for the clothes on their backs. Those are horribly ungrateful indeed who have kindness shown them and will not make at least an acknowledgment of it, by showing the kindness that is done them, as these widows here did. Those who receive alms are not obliged so industriously to conceal it, as those are who give alms. When the poor reflect upon the rich as uncharitable and unmerciful, they ought to reflect upon themselves, and consider whether they are not unthankful and ungrateful Their showing the coats and garments which Dorcas made tended to the praise not only of her charity, but of her industry, according to the character of the virtuous woman, that she *lays her hands to the spindle,* or at least to the needle, and then *stretches out her hand to the poor,* and *reaches forth her hands to the needy,* of what she has worked; and, when God and the poor have thus had their due, *she makes herself coverings of tapestry* and *her* own *clothing is silk and purple,* Prov. xxxi. 19—22.

2. They were here lamenting the loss of her: The widows stood by Peter, weeping. When the merciful are taken away, it should be laid to heart, especially by those to whom they have been in a particular manner merciful. They need not weep for her; she is taken from the evil to come, *she rests from her labours and her works follow her,* besides those she leaves behind her: but they weep for themselves and for their children, who will soon find the want of such a good woman, that has not left her fellow. Observe, They take notice of what good Dorcas did *while she was with them;* but now she is gone from them, and this is their grief. Those that are charitable will find that the *poor they have always with them;* but it is well if those that are poor find that they have always the charitable with them. We must make a good use of the lights that yet a little while are with us, because they will not be always with us, will not be long with us: and when they are gone we shall think what they did when they were with us. It should seem, the widows wept before Peter, as an inducement to him, if he could do any thing, to have compassion on them and help them, and restore one to them that used to have compassion on them. When charitable people are dead, there is no praying them to life again; but, when they are sick, this piece of gratitude is owing them, to pray for their recovery, that, if it be the will of God, those may be spared to live who can ill be spared to die.

IV. The manner in which she was raised to

life 1 Privately: She was laid in the upper room where they used to have their public meetings, and, it should seem, there was great crowding about the dead body, in expectation of what would be done; *but Peter put them all forth,* all the weeping widows, all but some few relations of the family, or perhaps the heads of the church, to join with him in prayer; as Christ did, Matt. ix. 25. Thus Peter declined every thing that looked like vainglory and ostentation; they came to see, but he did not come to be seen. He put them all forth, that he might with the more freedom pour out his soul before God in prayer upon this occasion, and not be disturbed with their noisy and clamorous lamentations. 2. By prayer. In his healing Eneas there was an implied prayer, but in this greater work he addressed himself to God by solemn prayer, as Christ when he raised Lazarus; but Christ's prayer was with the authority of a Son, who *quickens whom he will;* Peter's with the submission of a servant, who is under direction, and therefore he *knelt down and prayed.* 3. By the word, a quickening word, a word which is spirit and life: *He turned to the body,* which intimates that when he prayed he turned from it; lest the sight of it should discourage his faith, he looked another way, to teach us, like Abraham, *against hope, to believe in hope,* and overlook the difficulties that lie in the way, *not considering the body as now dead,* lest we should *stagger at the promise,* Rom. iv. 19, 20. But, when he had prayed, he *turned to the body,* and spoke in his Master's name, according to his example: *"Tabitha, arise;* return to life again." Power went along with this word, and she came to life, *opened her eyes* which death had closed. Thus, in the raising of dead souls to spiritual life, the first sign of life is the opening of the eyes of the mind, *ch.* xxvi. 18. When she saw Peter, she sat up, to show that she was really and truly alive; and (*v.* 41) *he gave her his hand and lifted her up,* not as if she laboured under any remaining weakness, but thus he would as it were welcome her to life again, and give her the right hand of fellowship among the living, from whom she had been cut off. And, *lastly,* he *called the saints and widows,* who were all in sorrow for her death, and *presented her alive* to them, to their great comfort, particularly of the widows, who laid her death much to heart (*v.* 41); to them he presented her, as Elijah (1 Kings xvii. 23), and Elisha (2 Kings iv. 36), and Christ (Luke vii. 15), presented the dead sons alive to their mothers. The greatest joy and satisfaction are expressed by life from the dead.

V. The good effect of this miracle. 1. Many were by it convinced of the truth of the gospel, that it was from heaven, and not of men, and believed in the Lord, *v.* 42. The thing was *known throughout all Joppa;* it would be in every body's mouth quickly, and, it being a town of seafaring men, the notice of it would be the sooner carried thence to other countries, and though some never minded it many were wrought upon by it. This was the design of miracles, to confirm a divine revelation. 2. Peter was hereby induced to continue some time in this city, *v.* 43. Finding that a door of opportunity was opened for him there, he tarried there many days, till he was sent thence, and sent for thence upon business to another place. He tarried not in the house of Tabitha, though she was rich, lest he should seem to seek his own glory; but he took up his lodgings with one Simon a tanner, an ordinary tradesman, which is an instance of his condescension and humility: and hereby he has taught us not to *mind high things, but to condescend to those of low estate,* Rom. xii. 16. And, though Peter might seem to be buried in obscurity here in the house of a poor tanner by the sea-side, yet hence God fetched him to a noble piece of service, which is recorded in the next chapter; for *those that humble themselves shall be exalted.*

CHAP. X.

It is a turn very new and remarkable which the story of this chapter gives to the Acts of the apostles; hitherto, both at Jerusalem and every where else where the ministers of Christ came, they preached the gospel only to the Jews, or those Greeks that were circumcised and proselyted to the Jews' religion; but now, "Lo, we turn to the Gentiles;" and to them the door of faith is here opened: good news indeed to us sinners of the Gentiles. The apostle Peter is the man that is first employed to admit uncircumcised Gentiles into the Christian church; and Cornelius, a Roman centurion or colonel, is the first that with his family and friends is so admitted. Now here we are told, I. How Cornelius was directed by a vision to send for Peter, and did send for him accordingly, ver. 1—8. II. How Peter was directed by a vision to go to Cornelius, though he was a Gentile, without making any scruple of it, and did go accordingly, ver. 9—23. III. The happy interview between Peter and Cornelius at Cesarea, ver. 24—33. IV. The sermon Peter preached in the house of Cornelius to him and to his friends, ver. 34—43. V. The baptizing of Cornelius and his friends with the Holy Ghost first, and then with water, ver. 44—48.

THERE was a certain man in
Cæsarea called Cornelius, a centurion of the band called the Italian
band, 2 A devout *man,* and one
that feared God with all his house,
which gave much alms to the people,
and prayed to God alway. 3 He
saw in a vision evidently about the
ninth hour of the day an angel of
God coming in to him, and saying unto him, Cornelius. 4 And
when he looked on him, he was
afraid, and said, What is it, Lord?
And he said unto him, Thy prayers
and thine alms are come up for a
memorial before God. 5 And now
send men to Joppa, and call for *one*
Simon, whose surname is Peter: 6
He lodgeth with one Simon a tanner,
whose house is by the sea side: he
shall tell thee what thou oughtest to
do. 7 And when the angel which
spake unto Cornelius was departed,

he called two of his household servants, and a devout soldier of them that waited on him continually; 8
And when he had declared all *these* things unto them, he sent them to Joppa.

The bringing of the gospel to the Gentiles, and the bringing of those who had been strangers and foreigners to be fellow-citizens with the saints, and of the household of God, were such a mystery to the apostles themselves, and such a surprise (Eph. iii. 3, 6), that it concerns us carefully to observe all the circumstances of the beginning of this great work, this part of the *mystery of godliness—Christ preached to the Gentiles, and believed on in the world,* 1 Tim. iii. 16. It is not unlikely that some Gentiles might before now have stepped into a synagogue of the Jews, and heard the gospel preached; but the gospel was never yet designedly preached to the Gentiles, nor any of them baptized—Cornelius was the first; and here we have,

I. An account given us of this Cornelius, who and what he was, who was the first-born of the Gentiles to Christ. We are here told that he was a great man and a good man—two characters that seldom meet, but here they did; and where they do meet they put a lustre upon each other: goodness makes greatness truly valuable, and greatness makes goodness much more serviceable. 1. Cornelius was an officer of the army, *v.* 1. He was at present quartered in Cesarea, a strong city, lately re-edified and fortified by Herod the Great, and called *Cesarea* in honour of Augustus Cæsar. It lay upon the sea-shore, very convenient for the keeping up of a correspondence between Rome and its conquests in those parts. The Roman governor or proconsul ordinarily resided here, *ch.* xxiii. 23, 24; xxv. 6. Here there was a band, or cohort, or regiment, of the Roman army, which probably was the governor's life-guard, and is here called *the Italian band,* because, that they might be the more sure of their fidelity, they were all native Romans, or Italians. Cornelius had a command in this part of the army. His name, *Cornelius,* was much used among the Romans, among some of the most ancient and noble families. He was an officer of considerable rank and figure, a centurion. We read of one of that rank in our Saviour's time, of whom he gave a great commendation, Matt. viii. 10. When a Gentile must be pitched upon to receive the gospel first, it is not a Gentile philosopher, much less a Gentile priest (who are bigoted to their notions and worship, and prejudiced against the gospel of Christ), but a Gentile soldier, who is a man of more free thought; and he that truly is so, when the Christian doctrine is fairly set before him, cannot but receive it and bid it welcome. Fishermen, unlearned and ignorant men, were the first of the Jewish converts, but not so of the Gentiles; for the world shall know that the gospel has that in it which may recommend it to men of polite learning and a liberal education, as we have reason to think this centurion was. Let not soldiers and officers of the army plead that their employment frees them from the restraints which some others are under, and, giving them an opportunity of living more at large, may excuse them if they be not religious; for here was an officer of the army that embraced Christianity, and yet was neither turned out of his place nor turned himself out. And, *lastly,* it was a mortification to the Jews that not only the Gentiles were taken into the church, but that the first who was taken in was an officer of the Roman army, which was to them *the abomination of desolation.* 2. He was, according to the measure of the light he had, a religious man. It is a very good character that is given of him, *v.* 2. He was no idolater, no worshipper of false gods or images, nor allowed himself in any of those immoralities to which the greater part of the Gentile world were given up, to punish them for their idolatry. (1.) He was possessed with a principle of regard to the true and living God. He was *a devout man and one that feared God.* He believed in one God, the Creator of heaven and earth, and had a reverence for his glory and authority, and a dread of offending him by sin; and, though he was a soldier, it was no diminution to the credit of his valour to tremble before God. (2.) He kept up religion in his family. He *feared God with all his house.* He would not admit any idolaters under his roof, but took care that not himself only, but all his, should serve the Lord. Every good man will do what he can that those about him may be good too. (3.) He was a very charitable man: He *gave much alms to the people,* the people of the Jews, notwithstanding the singularities of their religion. Though he was a Gentile, he was willing to contribute to the relief of one that was a real object of charity, without asking what religion he was of. (4.) He was much in prayer: He *prayed to God always.* He kept up stated times for prayer, and was constant to them. Note, Wherever the fear of God rules in the heart, it will appear both in works of charity and of piety, and neither will excuse us from the other.

II. The orders given him from heaven, by the ministry of an angel, to send for Peter to come to him, which he would never have done if he had not been thus directed to do it. Observe,

1. How, and in what way, these orders were given him. He had a vision, in which an angel delivered them to him. It was about the *ninth hour of the day,* at three of the clock in the afternoon, which is with us an hour of business and conversation; but then, because it was in the temple the time of offering the evening sacrifice, it was made by

devout people an *hour of prayer,* to intimate that all our prayers are to be offered up in the virtue of the great sacrifice. Cornelius was now at prayer: so he tells us himself, *v.* 30. Now here we are told, (1.) That an angel of God *came in to him.* By the brightness of his countenance, and the manner of his coming in, he knew him to be something more than a man, and therefore nothing less than an angel, an express from heaven. (2.) That he *saw him evidently* with his bodily eyes, not in a dream presented to his imagination, but in a vision presented to his sight; for his greater satisfaction, it carried its own evidence along with it. (3.) That he called him by his name, *Cornelius,* to intimate the particular notice God took of him. (4.) That this put Cornelius for the present into some confusion (*v.* 4): *When he looked on him he was afraid.* The wisest and best men have been struck with fear upon the appearance of any extraordinary messenger from heaven; and justly, for sinful man knows that he has no reason to expect any good tidings thence. And therefore Cornelius cries, "*What is it, Lord?* What is the matter?" This he speaks as one afraid of something amiss, and longing to be eased of that fear, by knowing the truth; or as one desirous to know the mind of God, and ready to comply with it, as Joshua: *What saith my Lord unto his servant?* And Samuel: *Speak, for thy servant heareth.*

2. What the message was that was delivered to him.

(1.) He is assured that God accepts him in walking according to the light he had (*v.* 4): *Thy prayers and thine alms are come up for a memorial before God.* Observe, Prayers and alms must go together. We must follow our prayers with alms; for the fast that God hath chosen is to *draw out the soul to the hungry,* Isa. lviii. 6, 7. It is not enough to pray that what we have may be sanctified to us, but we must *give alms of such things as we have;* and then, behold, all things are clean to us, Luke xi. 41. And we must follow our alms with our prayers that God would graciously accept them, and that they may be blessed to those to whom they are given. Cornelius prayed, and gave alms, not as the Pharisees, *to be seen of men,* but in sincerity, as unto God; and he is here told that they were *come up for a memorial before God.* They were upon record in heaven, in the book of remembrance that is written there for all that fear God, and shall be remembered to his advantage: "Thy prayers shall be answered, and thine alms recompensed." The sacrifices under the law are said to be *for a memorial.* See Lev. ii. 9, 16; v. 12; vi. 15. And prayers and alms are our spiritual offerings, which God is pleased to take cognizance of, and have regard to. The divine revelation communicated to the Jews, as far as the Gentiles were concerned in it, not only as it directed and improved the light and law of nature, but as it promised a Messiah to come, Cornelius believed and submitted to. What he did he did in that faith, and was accepted of God in it; for the Gentiles, to whom the law of Moses came, were not obliged to become circumcised Jews, as those to whom the gospel of Christ comes are to become baptized Christians.

(2.) He is appointed to enquire after a further discovery of divine grace, now lately made to the world, *v.* 5, 6. He must *send* forthwith *to Joppa, and enquire for one Simon Peter; he lodgeth at the house of one Simon a tanner; his house is by the sea side,* and, if he be sent for, he will come; and *when he comes he shall tell thee what thou oughtest to do,* in answer to thy question, *What is it, Lord?* Now here are two things very surprising, and worthy our consideration:—[1.] Cornelius prays and gives alms in the fear of God, is religious himself and keeps up religion in his family, and all this so as to be accepted of God in it, and yet there is something further that he ought to do—he ought to embrace the Christian religion, now that God has established it among men. Not, He may do it if he pleases; it will be an improvement and entertainment to him. But, He must do it; it is indispensably necessary to his acceptance with God for the future, though he has been accepted in his services hitherto. He that believed the promise of the Messiah must now believe the performance of that promise. Now that God has given a further record concerning his Son than what had been given in the Old-Testament prophecies he requires that we receive this when it is brought to us; and now neither our prayers nor our alms can come up for a memorial before God unless we believe in Jesus Christ, for it is that further which we ought to do. *This is his commandment, that we believe.* Prayers and alms are accepted from those that believe that the Lord is God, and have not opportunity of knowing more; but, from those to whom it is preached that Jesus is Christ, it is necessary to the acceptance of their persons, prayers, and alms, that they believe this, and rest upon him alone for acceptance. [2.] Cornelius has now an angel from heaven talking to him, and yet he must not receive the gospel of Christ from this angel, nor be told by him what he ought to do, but all that the angel has to say is, "Send for Peter, and he shall tell thee." As the former observation puts a mighty honour upon the gospel, so does this upon the gospel ministry: it was not to the highest of angels, but to those who were less than the least of all saints, that this grace was given, *to preach among the Gentiles the unsearchable riches of Christ* (Eph. iii. 8), that the excellency of the power might be of God, and the dignity of an institution of Christ supported; for *unto the angels hath he not put in subjection the world to come* (Heb.

ii. 5), but to the Son of man as the sovereign, and the sons of men as his agents and ministers of state, whose *terrors shall not make us afraid, nor their hand be heavy upon us,* as this angel's now was to Cornelius. And as it was an honour to the apostle that he must preach that which an angel might not, so it was a further honour that an angel was despatched on purpose from heaven to order him to be sent for. To bring a faithful minister and a willing people together is a work worthy of an angel, and what therefore the greatest of men should be glad to be employed in.

III. His immediate obedience to these orders, *v.* 7, 8. He sent with all speed to Joppa, to fetch Peter to him. Had he himself only been concerned, he would have gone to Joppa to him. But he had a family, and kinsmen, and friends (*v.* 24), a little congregation of them, that could not go with him to Joppa, and therefore he sends for Peter. Observe, 1. When he sent: As soon as ever the *angel which spoke unto him had departed,* without dispute or delay, he was obedient to the heavenly vision. He perceived, by what the angel said, he was to have some further work prescribed him, and he longed to have it told him. He made haste, and delayed not, to do this commandment. In any affair wherein our souls are concerned it is good for us not to lose time. 2. Whom he sent: *Two of his household servants,* who all feared God, *and a devout soldier,* one of those *that waited on him continually.* Observe, a devout centurion had devout soldiers. A little devotion commonly goes a great way with soldiers, but there would be more of it in the soldiers if there were but more of it in the commanders. Officers in an army, that have such a great power over the soldiers, as we find the centurion had (Matt. viii. 9), have a great opportunity of promoting religion, at least of restraining vice and profaneness, in those under their command, if they would but improve it. Observe, When this centurion had to choose some of his soldiers to attend his person, and to be always about him, he pitched upon such of them as were devout; they shall be preferred and countenanced, to encourage others to be so. He went by David's rule (Ps. ci. 6), *Mine eye shall be upon the faithful in the land, that they may dwell with me.* 3. What instructions he gave them (*v.* 8): *He declared all these things unto them,* told them of the vision he had, and the orders given him to send for Peter, because Peter's coming was a thing in which they were concerned, for they had souls to save as well as he. Therefore he does not only tell them where to find Peter (which he might have thought it enough to do—the *servant knows not what his Lord doeth),* but he tells them on what errand he was to come, that they might importune him.

9 On the morrow, as they went
on their journey, and drew nigh unto
the city, Peter went up upon the
housetop to pray about the sixth
hour: 10 And he became very hungry, and would have eaten: but while
they made ready, he fell into a trance,
11 And saw heaven opened, and a
certain vessel descending unto him,
as it had been a great sheet knit at
the four corners, and let down to the
earth: 12 Wherein were all manner
of fourfooted beasts of the earth, and
wild beasts, and creeping things, and
fowls of the air. 13 And there came
a voice to him, Rise, Peter; kill, and
eat. 14 But Peter said, Not so,
Lord; for I have never eaten any
thing that is common or unclean. 15
And the voice *spake* unto him again
the second time, What God hath
cleansed, *that* call not thou common.
16 This was done thrice: and the
vessel was received up again into
heaven. 17 Now while Peter doubted
in himself what this vision which he
had seen should mean, behold, the men
which were sent from Cornelius had
made enquiry for Simon's house, and
stood before the gate, 18 And called,
and asked whether Simon, which was
surnamed Peter, were lodged there.

Cornelius had received positive orders from heaven to send for Peter, whom otherwise he had not heard of, or at least not heeded; but here is another difficulty that lies in the way of bringing them together—the question is whether Peter will come to Cornelius when he is sent for; not as if he thought it below him to come at a beck, or as if he were afraid to preach his doctrine to a polite man as Cornelius was: but it sticks at a point of conscience. Cornelius is a very worthy man, and has many good qualities, but he is a Gentile, he is not circumcised; and, because God in his law had forbidden his people to associate with idolatrous nations, they would not keep company with any but those of their own religion, though they were ever so deserving, and they carried the matter so far that they made even the involuntary touch of a Gentile to contract a ceremonial pollution, John xviii. 28. Peter had not got over this stingy bigoted notion of his countrymen, and therefore will be shy of coming to Cornelius. Now, to remove this difficulty, he has a vision here, to prepare him to receive the message sent him by Cornelius, as Ananias had to prepare him to go to Paul. The scriptures of the Old Testament had spoken plainly of the bringing in of the Gentiles into the church.

Christ had given plain intimations of it when he ordered them to *teach all nations;* and yet even Peter himself, who knew so much of his Master's mind, could not understand it, till it was here revealed by vision, *that the Gentiles should be fellow-heirs,* Eph. iii. 6. Now here observe,

I. The circumstances of this vision.

1. It was when the messengers sent from Cornelius were now *nigh the city, v.* 9. Peter knew nothing of their approach, and they knew nothing of his praying; but he that knew both him and them was preparing things for the interview, and facilitating the end of their negociation. To all God's purposes *there is a time,* a proper time; and he is pleased often to bring things to the minds of his ministers, which they had not thought of, just then when they have occasion to use them.

2. It was when *Peter went up upon the house-top to pray,* about noon. (1.) Peter was much in prayer, much in secret prayer, though he had a great deal of public work upon his hands. (2.) He prayed *about the sixth hour,* according to David's example, who, not only *morning and evening,* but *at noon,* addressed himself to God by prayer, Ps. lv. 17. From morning to night we should think to be too long to be without meat; yet who thinks it is too long to be without prayer? (3.) He prayed *upon the house-top;* thither he retired for privacy, where he could neither hear nor be heard, and so might avoid both distraction and ostentation. There, upon the roof of the house, he had a full view of the heavens, which might assist his pious adoration of the God he prayed to; and there he had also a full view of the city and country, which might assist his pious compassion of the people he prayed for. (4.) He had this vision immediately after he had prayed, as an answer to his prayer for the spreading of the gospel, and because the ascent of the heart to God in prayer is an excellent preparative to receive the discoveries of the divine grace and favour.

3. It was when he became *very hungry,* and was waiting for his dinner (*v.* 10); probably he had not that day eaten before, though doubtless he had prayed before; and now *he would have eaten,* ἤθελε γεύσασθαι—*he would have tasted,* which intimates his great moderation and temperance in eating. When he was very hungry, yet he would be content with a little, with a taste, and would not *fly upon the spoil.* Now this hunger was a proper inlet to the vision about meats, as Christ's hunger in the wilderness was to Satan's temptation to turn stones into bread.

II. The vision itself, which was not so plain as that to Cornelius, but more figurative and enigmatical, to make the deeper impression. 1. He *fell into a trance or ecstasy,* not of terror, but of contemplation, with which he was so entirely swallowed up as not only not to be regardful, but not to be sensible, of external things. He quite lost himself to this world, and so had his mind entirely free for converse with divine things; as Adam in innocency, when the deep sleep fell upon him. The more clear we get of the world, the more near we get to heaven: whether Peter was now *in the body or out of the body* he could not himself tell, much less can we, 2 Cor. xii. 2, 3. See Gen. xv. 12; Acts xxii. 17. 2. He *saw heaven opened,* that he might be sure that his authority to go to Cornelius was indeed from heaven—that it was a divine light which altered his sentiments, and a divine power which gave him his commission. The opening of the heavens signified the opening of a mystery that had been hid, Rom. xvi. 25. 3. He saw *a great sheet full of all manner of living creatures, which descended from heaven, and was let down to him to the earth,* that is, to the roof of the house where he now was. Here were not only beasts of the earth, but fowls of the air, which might have flown away, laid at his feet; and not only tame beasts, but wild. Here were no fishes of the sea, because there were none of them in particular unclean, but whatever had fins and scales was allowed to be eaten. Some make this sheet, thus filled, to represent the church of Christ. It comes down from heaven, from heaven opened, not only to send it down (Rev. xxi. 2), but to receive souls sent up from it. It is knit at the four corners, to receive those from all parts of the world that are willing to be added to it; and to retain and keep those safe that are taken into it, that they may not fall out; and in this we find some of all countries, nations, and languages, without any distinction of Greek or Jew, or any disadvantage put upon Barbarian or Scythian, Col. iii. 11. The net of the gospel encloses all, both bad and good, those that before were clean and unclean. Or it may be applied to the bounty of the divine Providence, which, antecedently to the prohibitions of the ceremonial law, had given to man a liberty to use all the creatures, to which by the cancelling of that law we are now restored. By this vision we are taught to see all the benefit and service we have from the inferior creatures coming down to us from heaven; it is the gift of God who made them, made them fit for us, and then gave to man a right to them, and dominion over them. Lord, what is man that he should be thus magnified! Ps. viii. 4—8. How should it double our comfort in the creatures, and our obligations to serve God in the use of them, to see them thus let down to us out of heaven! 4. He was ordered by a voice from heaven to make use of this plenty and variety which God had sent him (*v.* 13): "*Rise, Peter, kill and eat:* without putting any difference between clean and unclean, take which thou hast most mind to." The distinction of meats which the law made was intended to put a difference between Jew and

Gentile, that it might be difficult to them to dine and sup with a Gentile, because they would have that set before them which they were not allowed to eat; and now the taking off of that prohibition was a plain allowance to converse with the Gentiles, and to be free and familiar with them. Now they might fare as they fared, and therefore might eat with them, and be fellow-commoners with them. 5. He stuck to his principles, and would by no means hearken to the motion, though he was hungry (*v.* 14): *Not so, Lord.* Though hunger will break through stone walls, God's laws should be to us a stronger fence than stone walls, and not so easily broken through. And he will adhere to God's laws, though he has a countermand by a voice from heaven, not knowing at first but that *Kill, and eat,* was a command of trial whether he would adhere to the more sure word, the written law; and if so his answer had been very good, *Not so, Lord.* Temptations to eat forbidden fruit must not be parleyed with, but peremptorily rejected; we must startle at the thought of it: *Not so, Lord.* The reason he gives is, "*For I have never eaten any thing that is common or unclean;* hitherto I have kept my integrity in this matter, and will still keep it." If God, by his grace, has preserved us from gross sin unto this day, we should use this as an argument with ourselves to abstain *from all appearance of evil.* So strict were the pious Jews in this matter, that the seven brethren, those glorious martyrs under Antiochus, choose rather to be tortured to death in the most cruel manner that ever was than to eat swine's flesh, because it was forbidden by the law. No wonder then that Peter says it with so much pleasure, that his conscience could witness for him that he had never gratified his appetite with any forbidden food. 6. God, by a second voice from heaven, proclaimed the repeal of the law in this case (*v.* 15): *What God hath cleansed, that call thou not common.* He that made the law might alter it when he pleased, and reduce the matter to its first state. God had, for reasons suited to the Old-Testament dispensation, restrained the Jews from eating such and such meats, to which, while that dispensation lasted, they were obliged in conscience to submit; but he has now, for reasons suited to the New-Testament dispensation, taken off that restraint, and set the matter at large—has cleansed that which was before polluted to us, and we ought to make use of, and *stand fast in, the liberty wherewith Christ has made us free,* and not call that common or unclean which God has now declared clean. Note, We ought to welcome it as a great mercy that by the gospel of Christ we are freed from the distinction of meats, which was made by the law of Moses, and that now *every creature of God is good, and nothing to be refused;* not so much because hereby we gain the use of swine's flesh, hares, rabbits, and other pleasant and wholesome food for our bodies, but chiefly because conscience is hereby freed from a yoke in things of this nature, *that we might serve God without fear.* Though the gospel has made duties which were not so by the law of nature, yet it has not, like the law of Moses, made sins that were not so. Those who command to abstain from some kinds of meat at some times of the year, and place religion in it, call that common which God hath cleansed, and in that error, more than in any truth, are the successors of Peter. 7. *This was done thrice, v.* 16. The sheet was drawn up a little way, and let down again the second time, and so the third time, with the same call to him, to kill, and eat, and the same reason, that what God hath cleansed we must not call common; but whether Peter's refusal was repeated the second and third time is not certain; surely it was not, when his objection had the first time received such a satisfactory answer. The trebling of Peter's vision, like the doubling of Pharaoh's dream, was to show that *the thing was certain,* and engage him to take so much the more notice of it. The instructions given us in the things of God, whether by the ear in the preaching of the word, or by the eye in sacraments, need to be often repeated; *precept must be upon precept, and line upon line.* But at last *the vessel was received up into heaven.* Those who make this vessel to represent the church, including both Jews and Gentiles, as this did both clean and unclean creatures, make this very aptly to signify the admission of the believing Gentiles into the church, and into heaven too, into the Jerusalem above. Christ *has opened the kingdom of heaven to all believers,* and there we shall find, besides *those that are sealed out of all the tribes of Israel,* an *innumerable company out of every nation* (Rev. vii. 9); but they are such as God has cleansed.

III. The providence which very opportunely explained this vision, and gave Peter to understand the intention of it, *v.* 17, 18. 1. What Christ did, Peter knew not just then (John xiii. 7): *He doubted within himself what this vision which he had seen should mean.* He had no reason to doubt the truth of it, that it was a heavenly vision; all his doubt was concerning the meaning of it. Note, Christ reveals himself to his people by degrees, and not all at once; and leaves them to doubt awhile, to ruminate upon a thing, and debate it to and fro in their own minds, before he clears it up to them. 2. Yet he was made to know presently, for *the men who were sent from Cornelius* were just now come to *the house,* and were at *the gate enquiring whether Peter lodged there;* and by their errand it will appear what was the meaning of this vision. Note, God knows what services are before us, and therefore how to prepare us; and we then better know the meaning of what he has taught us when we find what occasion we have to make use of it.

19 While Peter thought on the
vision, the Spirit said unto him, Behold, three men seek thee. 20 Arise,
therefore, and get thee down, and go
with them, doubting nothing: for I
have sent them. 21 Then Peter
went down to the men which were
sent unto him from Cornelius; and
said, Behold, I am he whom ye seek:
what *is* the cause wherefore ye are
come? 22 And they said, Cornelius the centurion, a just man, and
one that feareth God, and of good
report among all the nation of the
Jews, was warned from God by a
holy angel to send for thee into his
house, and to hear words of thee.
23 Then called he them in, and
lodged *them.* And on the morrow
Peter went away with them, and certain brethren from Joppa accompanied him. 24 And the morrow
after they entered into Cæsarea. And
Cornelius waited for them, and had
called together his kinsmen and near
friends. 25 And as Peter was coming
in, Cornelius met him, and fell down
at his feet, and worshipped *him.* 26
But Peter took him up, saying, Stand
up; I myself also am a man. 27
And as he talked with him, he went
in, and found many that were come
together. 28 And he said unto them,
Ye know how that it is an unlawful
thing for a man that is a Jew to keep
company, or come unto one of another nation; but God hath showed
me that I should not call any man
common or unclean. 29 Therefore
came I *unto you* without gainsaying,
as soon as I was sent for: I ask
therefore for what intent ye have
sent for me? 30 And Cornelius said,
Four days ago I was fasting until this
hour; and at the ninth hour I prayed
in my house, and, behold, a man
stood before me in bright clothing,
31 And said, Cornelius, thy prayer is
heard, and thine alms are had in remembrance in the sight of God. 32
Send therefore to Joppa, and call hither Simon, whose surname is Peter;
he is lodged in the house of *one* Simon
a tanner by the sea side: who, when
he cometh, shall speak unto thee.
33 Immediately therefore I sent to
thee; and thou hast well done that
thou art come. Now therefore are
we all here present before God, to
hear all things that are commanded
thee of God.

We have here the meeting between Peter the apostle, and Cornelius the centurion. Though Paul was designed to be the apostle of the Gentiles, and to gather in the harvest among them, and Peter to be the apostle of the circumcision, yet it is ordered that Peter shall break the ice, and reap the first-fruits of the Gentiles, that the believing Jews, who retained too much of the old leaven of ill-will to the Gentiles, might be the better reconciled to their admission into the church, when they were first brought in by their own apostle, which Peter urges against those that would have imposed circumcision upon the Gentile converts (*ch.* xv. 7), *You know that God made choice among us that the Gentiles by my mouth should hear the word of the gospel.* Now here,

I. Peter is directed by the Spirit to go along with Cornelius's messengers (*v.* 19, 20), and this is the exposition of the vision; now the riddle is unriddled: *While Peter thought on the vision;* he was musing upon it, and then it was opened to him. Note, Those that would be taught the things of God must think on those things; those that would understand the scriptures must meditate in them day and night. He was at a loss about it, and then had it explained, which encourages us, when we know not what to do, to have our eyes up unto God for direction. Observe, 1. Whence he had the direction. The Spirit said to him what he should do. It was not spoken to him by an angel, but spoken in him by the Spirit, secretly whispering it in his ear as it were, as God spoke to Samuel (1 Sam. ix. 15), or impressing it powerfully upon his mind, so that he knew it to be a divine afflatus or inspiration, according to the promise, John xvi. 13. 2. What the direction was. (1.) He is told, before any of the servants could come up to tell him, that three men below want to speak with him (*v.* 19), and he must arise from his musings, leave off thinking of the vision, and go down to them, *v.* 20. Those that are searching into the meaning of the words of God, and the visions of the Almighty, should not be always poring, no, nor always praying, but should sometimes look abroad, look about them, and they may meet with that which will be of use to them in their enquiries; for the scripture is in the fulfilling every day. (2.) He is ordered to *go along with the messengers to Cornelius,* though he was a Gentile, *doubting nothing.* He must not only go, but go cheerfully, without reluctance or hesitation, or any scruple concerning the lawfulness of it; not doubting whether he might go, no, nor whether he ought to go; for it was his duty.

"Go with them, for I have sent them; and I will bear thee out in going along with them, however thou mayest be censured for it." Note, When we see our call clear to any service, we should not suffer ourselves to be perplexed with doubts and scruples concerning it arising from former prejudices or prepossessions, or a fear of men's censure. *Let every man be fully persuaded in his own mind, and prove his own work.*

II. He receives both them and their message: *He went down to them, v.* 21. So far was he from going out of the way, or refusing to be spoken with, as one that was shy of them, or making them tarry, as one that took state upon him, that he went to them himself, told them he was the person they were enquiring for. And, 1. He favourably receives their message; with abundance of openness and condescension he asks what their business is, what they have to say to him: *What is the cause wherefore you are come?* and they tell him their errand (*v.* 22): "*Cornelius,* an officer of the Roman army, a very honest gentleman, and one who has more religion than most of his neighbours, *who fears God above many* (Neh. vii. 2), who, though he is not a Jew himself, has carried it so well that he is *of good report among all the people of the Jews*—they will all give him a good word, for a conscientious, sober, charitable man, so that it will be no discredit to thee to be seen in his company—he *was warned from God,*" *ἐχρηματίσθη*—"*he had an oracle from God,* sent to him by an angel" (and the lively oracles of the law of Moses were given by the disposition of angels), "by which he was ordered to send for thee to his house (where he is expecting thee, and ready to bid thee welcome), *and to hear words of thee:* they know not what words, but they are such as he may hear from thee, and not from any one else so well." *Faith comes by hearing.* When Peter repeats this, he tells us more fully, they are *words whereby thou and all thy house shall be saved, ch.* xi. 14. "Come to him, for an angel bade him send for thee: come to him, for he is ready to hear and receive the saving words thou hast to bring to him." 2. He kindly entertained the messengers (*v.* 23): *He called them in, and lodged them.* He did not bid them go and refresh and repose themselves in an inn at their own charge, but was himself at the charge of entertaining them in his own quarters. What was getting ready for him (*v.* 10) they should be welcome to share in; he little thought what company he should have when he bespoke his dinner, but God foresaw it. Note, It becomes Christians and ministers to be hospitable, and ready, according as their ability is, and there is occasion for it, *to entertain strangers.* Peter lodged them, though they were Gentiles, to show how readily he complied with the design of the vision in eating with Gentiles; for he immediately took them to eat with him. Though they were two of them servants, and the other a common soldier, yet Peter thought it not below him to take them into his house. Probably he did it that he might have some talk with them about Cornelius and his family; for the apostles, though they had instructions from the Spirit, yet made use of other information, as they had occasion for it.

III. He *went with them* to Cornelius, whom he found ready to receive and entertain him. 1. Peter, when he went with them, was *accompanied by certain brethren from Joppa,* where he now was, *v.* 23. Six of them went along with him, as we find, *ch.* xi. 12. Either Peter desired their company, that they might be witnesses of his proceeding cautiously with reference to the Gentiles, and of the good ground on which he went, and therefore he invited them (*ch.* xi. 12), or they offered their service to attend him, and desired they might have the honour and happiness of being his fellow-travellers. This was one way in which the primitive Christians very much showed their respect to their ministers: they accompanied them in their journeys, to keep them in countenance, to be their guard, and, as there was occasion, to minister to them; with a further prospect not only of doing them service, but of being edified by their converse. It is a pity that those who have skill and will to do good to others by their discourse should want an opportunity for it by travelling alone. 2. Cornelius, when he was ready to receive him, *had got some friends together of Cesarea.* It seems, it was above a day's journey, nearly two, from Joppa to Cesarea; for it was *the day after* they set out that *they entered into Cesarea* (*v.* 24), and the afternoon of that day, *v.* 30. It is probable that they travelled on foot; the apostles generally did so. Now when they came into the house of Cornelius Peter found, (1.) That he was expected, and this was an encouragement to him. *Cornelius waited for them,* and such a guest was worth waiting for; nor can I blame him if he waited with some impatience, longing to know what that mighty thing was which an angel bade him expect to hear from Peter. (2.) That he was expected by many, and this was a further encouragement to him. As Peter brought some with him to partake of the spiritual gift he had now to dispense, so *Cornelius had called together,* not only his own family, but *kinsmen and near friends,* to partake with him of the heavenly instructions he expected from Peter, which would give Peter a larger opportunity of doing good. Note, We should not covet to eat our spiritual morsels alone, Job xxxi. 17. It ought to be both given and taken as a piece of kindness and respect to our kindred and friends to invite them to join with us in religious exercises, to go with us to hear a sermon. What Cornelius ought to do he thought his kinsmen and friends ought to do too; and therefore let them come and hear it at the first hand, that it may be no surprise to them to see him change upon it.

IV. Here is the first interview between Peter and Cornelius, in which we have, 1. The profound and indeed undue respect and honour which Cornelius paid to Peter (*v.* 25): *He met him as he was coming in,* and instead of taking him in his arms, and embracing him as a friend, which would have been very acceptable to Peter, *he fell down at his feet, and worshipped him;* some think, as a prince and a great man, according to the usage of the eastern countries; others think, as an incarnate deity, or as if he took him to be the Messiah himself. His worshipping a man was indeed culpable; but, considering his present ignorance, it was excusable, nay, and it was an evidence of something in him that was very commendable—and that was a great veneration for divine and heavenly things: no wonder if, till he was better informed, he took him to be the Messiah, and therefore worshipped him, whom he was ordered to send for by an angel from heaven. But the worshipping of his pretended successor, who is not only a man, but a sinful man, the man of sin himself, is altogether inexcusable, and such an absurdity as would be incredible if we were not told before that all *the world would worship the beast,* Rev. xiii. 4. 2. Peter's modest and indeed just and pious refusal of this honour that was done him (*v.* 26): *He took him up* into his arms, with his own hands (though time was when he little thought he should ever either receive so much respect from or show so much affection to an uncircumcised Gentile), *saying,* "*Stand up, I myself also am a man,* and therefore not to be worshipped thus." The good angels of the churches, like the good angels of heaven, cannot bear to have the least of that honour shown to them which is due to God only. *See thou do it not,* saith the angel to John (Rev. xix. 10; xxii. 9), and in like manner the apostle to Cornelius. How careful was Paul *that no man should think of him above what he saw in him!* 2 Cor. xii. 6. Christ's faithful servants could better bear to be vilified than to be deified. Peter did not entertain a surmise that his great respect for him, though excessive, might contribute to the success of his preaching, and therefore if he will be deceived let him be deceived; no, let him know that Peter is a man, that *the treasure is in earthen vessels,* that he may value the treasure for its own sake.

V. The account which Peter and Cornelius give to each other, and to the company, of the hand of Heaven in bringing them together: *As he talked with him—συνομιλῶν αὐτω, he went in, v.* 27. Peter went in, talking familiarly with Cornelius, endeavouring, by the freedom of his converse with him, to take off something of that dread which he seemed to have of him; and, when he came in, *he found many that were come together,* more than he expected, which added solemnity, as well as opportunity of doing good, to this service. Now,

1. Peter declares the direction God gave to him to come to those Gentiles, *v.* 28, 29. They knew it had never been allowed by the Jews, but always looked upon as an *unlawful thing, ἀθέμιτόν—an abomination, for a man that is a Jew,* a native Jew as I am, *to keep company or come unto one of another nation,* a stranger, an uncircumcised Gentile. It was not made so by the law of God, but by the decree of their wise men, which they looked upon to be no less binding. They did not forbid them to converse or traffic with Gentiles in the street or shop, or upon the exchange, but to eat with them. Even in Joseph's time, the Egyptians and Hebrews could not eat together, Gen. xliii. 32. The three children *would not defile themselves with the king's meat,* Dan. i. 8. They might not come into the house of a Gentile, for they looked upon it to be ceremonially polluted. Thus scornfully did the Jews look upon the Gentiles, who were not behindhand with them in contempt, as appears by many passages in the Latin poets. "*But now,*" saith Peter, "*God hath shown me,* by a vision, *that I should not call any man common or unclean,* nor refuse to converse with any man for the sake of his country." Peter, who had taught his new converts to *save themselves from the untoward generation of wicked men* (*ch* ii. 40), is now himself taught to join himself with the towardly generation of devout Gentiles. Ceremonial characters were abolished, that more regard might be had to moral ones. Peter thought it necessary to let them know how he came to change his mind in this matter, and that it was by a divine revelation, lest he should be upbraided with it as having used lightness. God having thus taken down the partition-wall, (1.) He assures them of his readiness to do them all the good offices he could; that, when he kept at a distance, it was not out of any personal disgust to them, but only because he wanted leave from heaven, and, having now received permission, he was at their service: "*Therefore came I unto you without gainsaying, as soon as I was sent for,* ready to preach the same gospel to you that I have preached to the Jews." The disciples of Christ could not but have some notion of the preaching of the gospel to the Gentiles, but they imagined it must be only to those Gentiles that were first proselyted to the Jewish religion, which mistake Peter acknowledges was not rectified. (2.) He enquires wherein he might be serviceable to them: "*I ask, therefore, for what intent you have sent for me?* What do you expect from me, or what business have you with me?" Note, Those that desire the help of God's ministers ought to look well to it that they propose right ends to themselves in it, and do it with a good intention.

2. Cornelius declares the directions God gave to him to send for Peter, and that it was purely in obedience to those directions

that he had sent for him. Then we are right in our aims, in sending for and attending on a gospel-ministry, when we do it with a regard to the divine appointment instituting that ordinance and requiring us to make use of it. Now,

(1.) Cornelius gives an account of the angel's appearing to him, and ordering him to send for Peter; not as glorying in it, but as that which warranted his expectation of a message from heaven by Peter. [1.] He tells how this vision found him employed (*v.* 30): *Four days ago I was fasting until this hour,* this hour of the day that it is now when Peter came, about the middle of the afternoon. By this it appears that religious fasting, in order to the greater seriousness and solemnity of praying, was used by devout people who were not Jews; *the king of Nineveh proclaimed a fast,* Jonah iii. 5. Some give these words another sense: *From four days ago I have been fasting until this hour;* as if he had eaten no meat, or at least no meal, from that time to this. But it comes in as an introduction to the story of the vision; and therefore the former must be the meaning. *He was at the ninth hour praying in his house,* not in the synagogue, but at home. *I will that men pray* wherever they dwell. His praying in his house intimates that it was not a secret prayer in his closet, but in a more public room of his house, with his family about him; and perhaps after prayer he retired, and had this vision. Observe, *At the ninth hour of the day,* three of the clock in the afternoon, most people were travelling or trading, working in the fields, visiting their friends, taking their pleasure, or taking a nap after dinner; yet then Cornelius was at his devotions, which shows how much he made religion his business; and then it was that he had this message from heaven. Those that would hear comfortably from God must be much in speaking to him. [2.] He describes the messenger that brought him this message from heaven: *There stood a man before me in bright clothing,* as Christ's was when he was transfigured, and that of the two angels who appeared at Christ's resurrection (Luke xxiv. 4), and at his ascension (*ch.* i. 10), showing their relation to the world of light. [3.] He repeats the message that was sent to him (*v.* 31, 32), just as we had it, *v.* 4—6. Only here it is said, *Thy prayer is heard.* We are not told what his prayer was; but if this message was an answer to it, and it should seem it was, we may suppose that finding the deficiency of natural light, and that it left him at a loss how to obtain the pardon of his sin and the favour of God, he prayed that God would make some further discoveries of himself and of the way of salvation to him. "Well," saith the angel, "*send for Peter,* and he shall give thee such a discovery."

(2.) He declares his own and his friends' readiness to receive the message Peter had to deliver (*v.* 33): *Immediately therefore I sent to thee,* as I was directed, *and thou hast well done that thou hast come* to us, though we are Gentiles. Note, Faithful ministers do well to come to people that are willing and desirous to receive instruction from them; to come when they are sent for; it is as good a deed as they can do. Well, Peter is come to do his part; but will they do theirs? Yes. "Thou art here prepared to speak, and we are here prepared to hear," 1 Sam. iii. 9, 10. Observe, [1.] Their religious attendance upon the word: "*We are all here present before God;* we are here in a religious manner, are here as worshippers" (they thus compose themselves into a serious solemn frame of spirit): "*therefore,* because thou art come to us by such a warrant, on such an errand, because we have such a price in our hand as we never had before and perhaps may never have again, we are ready now at this time of worship, here in this place of worship" (though it was in a private house): "*we are present, πάρεσμεν—we are at the business,* and are ready to come at a call." If we would have God's special presence at an ordinance, we must be there with a special presence, an ordinance presence: *Here I am.* "*We are all present,* all that were invited; we, and all that belong to us; we, and all that is within us." The whole of the man must be present; not the body here, and the heart, with the fool's eyes, in the ends of the earth. But that which makes it indeed a religious attendance is, *We are present before God.* In holy ordinances we present ourselves unto the Lord, and we must be as before him, as those that see his eye upon us. [2.] The intention of this attendance: "*We are present to hear all things that are commanded thee of God,* and given thee in charge to be delivered to us." Observe, *First,* Peter was there to preach all things that were commanded him of God; for, as he had an ample commission to preach the gospel, so he had full instructions what to preach. *Secondly,* They were ready to hear, not whatever he pleased to say, but what he was commanded of God to say. The truths of Christ were not communicated to the apostles to be published or stifled as they thought fit, but entrusted with them to be published to the world. "We are ready to hear *all,* to come at the beginning of the service and stay to the end, and be attentive all the while, else how can we hear all? We are desirous to hear all that thou art commissioned to preach, though it be ever so displeasing to flesh and blood, and ever so contrary to our former notions or present secular interests. We are ready to hear all, and therefore let nothing be kept back that is profitable for us."

34 Then Peter opened *his* mouth,
and said, Of a truth I perceive that
God is no respecter of persons: 35

But in every nation he that feareth
him, and worketh righteousness, is
accepted with him. 36 The word
which *God* sent unto the children of
Israel, preaching peace by Jesus
Christ (he is Lord of all): 37 That
word, *I say,* ye know, which was
published throughout all Judæa, and
began from Galilee, after the baptism
which John preached; 38 How God
anointed Jesus of Nazareth with the
Holy Ghost and with power: who
went about doing good, and healing
all that were oppressed of the devil;
for God was with him. 39 And we
are witnesses of all things which he
did both in the land of the Jews, and
in Jerusalem; whom they slew and
hanged on a tree: 40 Him God
raised up the third day, and showed
him openly; 41 Not to all the
people, but unto witnesses chosen
before of God, *even* to us, who did
eat and drink with him after he rose
from the dead. 42 And he commanded us to preach unto the people,
and to testify that it is he which was
ordained of God *to be* the Judge of
quick and dead. 43 To him give all
the prophets witness, that through
his name whosoever believeth in him
shall receive remission of sins.

We have here Peter's sermon preached to Cornelius and his friends: that is, an abstract or summary of it; for we have reason to think that he did with many other words testify and exhort to this purport. It is intimated that he expressed himself with a great deal of solemnity and gravity, but with freedom and copiousness, in that phrase, *he opened his mouth, and spoke, v.* 34. *O ye Corinthians, our mouth is open to you,* saith Paul, 2 Cor. vi. 11. "You shall find us communicative, if we but find you inquisitive." Hitherto the mouths of the apostles had been shut to the uncircumcised Gentiles, they had nothing to say to them; but now God gave unto them, as he did to Ezekiel, *the opening of the mouth.* This excellent sermon of Peter's is admirably suited to the circumstances of those to whom he preached it; for it was a new sermon.

I. Because they were Gentiles to whom he preached. He shows that, notwithstanding this, they were interested in the gospel of Christ, which he had to preach, and entitled to the benefit of it, upon an equal footing with the Jews. It was necessary that this should be cleared, or else with what comfort could either he preach or they hear? He therefore lays down this as an undoubted principle, *that God is no respecter of persons; doth not know favour in judgment,* as the Hebrew phrase is; which magistrates are forbidden to do (Deut. i. 17; xvi. 19; Prov. xxiv. 23), and are blamed for doing, Ps. lxxxii. 2. And it is often said of God that he doth not respect persons, Deut. x. 17; 2 Chron. xix. 7; Job xxxiv. 19; Rom. ii. 11; Col. iii. 25; 1 Pet. i. 17. He doth not give judgment in favour of a man for the sake of any external advantage foreign to the merits of the cause. God never perverts judgment upon personal regards and considerations, nor countenances a wicked man in a wicked thing for the sake of his beauty, or stature, his country, parentage, relations, wealth, or honour in the world. God, as a benefactor, gives favours arbitrarily and by sovereignty (Deut. vii. 7, 8; ix. 5, 6; Matt. xx. 10); but he does not, as a judge, so give sentence; *but in every nation,* and under every denomination, *he that fears God and works righteousness is accepted of him, v.* 35. The case is plainly thus:—

1. God never did, nor ever will, justify and save a wicked Jew that lived and died impenitent, though he was *of the seed of Abraham,* and a *Hebrew of the Hebrews,* and had all the honour and advantages that attended circumcision. He does and will render *indignation and wrath, tribulation and anguish, upon every soul of man that doeth evil;* and *of the Jew first,* whose privileges and professions, instead of screening him from the judgment of God, will but aggravate his guilt and condemnation. See Rom. ii. 3, 8, 9, 17. Though God has favoured the Jews, above other nations, with the dignities of visible church-membership, yet he will not therefore accept of any particular persons of that dignity, if they allow themselves in immoralities contradictory to their profession; and particularly in persecution, which was now, more than any other, the national sin of the Jews.

2. He never did, nor ever will, reject or refuse an honest Gentile, who, though he has not the privileges and advantages that the Jews have, yet, like Cornelius, fears God, and worships him, and works righteousness, that is, is just and charitable towards all men, who lives up to the light he has, both in a sincere devotion and in a regular conversation. Whatever nation he is of, though ever so far remote from kindred to the seed of Abraham, though ever so despicable, nay, though in ever so ill a name, that shall be no prejudice to him. God judges of men by their hearts, not by their country or parentage; and, wherever he finds an upright man, he will be found an upright God, Ps. xviii. 25. Observe, *Fearing God, and working righteousness,* must go together; for, as righteousness towards men is a branch of

true religion, so religion towards God is a branch of universal righteousness. Godliness and honesty must go together, and neither will excuse for the want of the other. But, where these are predominant, no doubt is to be made of acceptance with God. Not that any man, since the fall, can obtain the favour of God otherwise than through the mediation of Jesus Christ, and by the grace of God in him; but those that have not the knowledge of him, and therefore cannot have an explicit regard to him, may yet receive grace from God for his sake, *to fear God and to work righteousness;* and wherever God gives grace to do so, as he did to Cornelius, he will, through Christ, accept the work of his own hands. Now, (1.) This was always a truth, before Peter perceived it, *that God respecteth no man's person;* it was the fixed rule of judgment from the beginning: *If thou doest well, shalt thou not be accepted? And, if not well, sin,* and the punishment of it, *lie at the door,* Gen. iv. 7. God will not ask in the great day what country men were of, but what they were, what they did, and how they stood affected towards him and towards their neighbours; and, if men's personal characters received neither advantage nor disadvantage from the great difference that existed between Jews and Gentiles, much less from any less difference of sentiments and practices that may happen to be among Christians themselves, as those *about meats and days,* Rom. xiv. It is certain *the kingdom of God is not meat and drink, but righteousness, and peace, and joy in the Holy Ghost;* and he that in these things serveth Christ is accepted of God, and ought to be approved of men; for dare we reject those whom God doth not? (2.) Yet now it was made more clear than it had been; this great truth had been darkened by the covenant of peculiarity made with Israel, and the badges of distinction put upon them; the ceremonial law was a wall of partition between them and other nations; it is true that in it *God favoured that nation* (Rom. iii. 1, 2; ix. 4), and thence particular persons among them were ready to infer that they were sure of God's acceptance, though they lived as they listed, and that no Gentile could possibly be accepted of God. God had said a great deal by the prophets to prevent and rectify this mistake, but now at length he doth it effectually, by abolishing the covenant of peculiarity, repealing the ceremonial law, and so setting the matter at large, and placing both Jew and Gentile upon the same level before God; and Peter is here made to perceive it, by comparing the vision which he had with that which Cornelius had. Now *in Christ Jesus,* it is plain, *neither circumcision availeth any thing, nor uncircumcision,* Gal. v. 6; Col. iii. 11.

II. Because they were Gentiles inhabiting a place within the confines of the land of Israel, he refers them to what they themselves could not but know concerning the life and doctrine, the preaching and miracles, the death and sufferings of our Lord Jesus: for these were things the report of which spread into every corner of the nation, *v.* 37, &c. It facilitates the work of ministers, when they deal with such as have some knowledge of the things of God, to which they may appeal, and on which they may build.

1. They knew in general, *the word,* that is, the gospel, *which God sent to the children of Israel: That word, I say, you know, v.* 37. Though the Gentiles were not admitted to hear it (Christ and his disciples were *not sent but to the lost sheep of the house of Israel),* yet they could not but hear of it: it was all the talk both of city and country. We are often told in the gospels how the fame of Christ went into all parts of Canaan, when he was on earth, as afterwards the fame of his gospel went into all parts of the world, Rom. x. 18. That word, that divine word, that word of power and grace, *you know.* (1.) What the purport of this word was. God by it *published the glad tidings of peace by Jesus Christ,* so it should be read—*εὐαγγελιζόμενος εἰρήνην.* It is God himself that proclaims *peace,* who justly might have proclaimed war. He lets the world of mankind know that he is willing to be at peace with them through Jesus Christ; in him he was *reconciling the world to himself.* (2.) To whom it was sent—to the children of Israel, in the first place. The prime offer is made to them; this all their neighbours heard of, and were ready to envy them those advantages of the gospel, more than they ever envied them those of their law. *Then said they among the heathen, The Lord hath done great things for them,* Ps. cxxvi. 2.

2. They knew the several matters of fact relating to this word of the gospel sent to Israel. (1.) They knew the baptism of repentance which John preached by way of introduction to it, and in which the gospel first began, Mark i. 1. They knew what an extraordinary man John was, and what a direct tendency his preaching had to *prepare the way of the Lord.* They knew what great flocking there was to his baptism, what an interest he had, and what he did. (2.) They knew that immediately after John's baptism the gospel of Christ, that word of *peace, was published throughout all Judea,* and that it took its rise from Galilee. The twelve apostles, and seventy disciples, and our Master himself, published these glad tidings in all parts of the land; so that we may suppose there was not a town or village in all the land of Canaan but had had the gospel preached in it. (3.) They knew that Jesus of Nazareth, when he was here upon earth, *went about doing good.* They knew what a benefactor he was to that nation, both to the souls and the bodies of men; how he made it his business to do good to all, and never did hurt to any. He was not idle, but still doing; not

selfish, but doing good; did not confine himself to one place, nor wait till people came to him to seek his help, but went to them, went about from place to place, and wherever he came he was doing good. Hereby he showed *that he was sent of God, who is good and does good;* and does good because he is good: and who hereby *left not himself without witness* to the world, *in that he did good, ch.* xiv. 17. And in this he hath set us an example of indefatigable industry in serving God and our generation; for we came into the world that we might do all the good we can in it; and therein, like Christ, we must always abide and abound. (4.) They knew more particularly that he *healed all that were oppressed of the devil,* and helped them from under his oppressing power. By this it appeared not only that he was sent of God, as it was a kindness to men, but that he was sent to *destroy the works of the devil;* for thus he obtained many a victory over him. (5.) They knew that the Jews put him to death; they *slew* him by *hanging him on a tree.* When Peter preached to the Jews, he said *whom you slew;* but now that he preached to the Gentiles it is whom *they* slew; they, to whom he had done and designed so much good. All this they knew; but lest they should think it was only a report, and was magnified, as reports usually are, more than the truth, Peter, for himself and the rest of the apostles, attested it (*v.* 39): *We are witnesses,* eye-witnesses, of *all things which he did;* and ear-witnesses of the doctrine which he preached, *both in the land of the Jews and in Jerusalem,* in city and country.

3. They did know, or might know, by all this, that he had a commission from heaven to preach and act as he did. This he still harps upon in his discourse, and takes all occasions to hint it to them. Let them know, (1.) That this Jesus *is Lord of all;* it comes in in a parenthesis, but is the principal proposition intended to be proved, that Jesus Christ, by whom peace is made between God and man, *is Lord of all;* not only as *God over all blessed for evermore,* but as Mediator, *all power both in heaven and on earth* is put into his hand, and all judgment committed to him. He is Lord of angels; they are all his humble servants. He is Lord of the powers of darkness, for he hath triumphed over them. He is king of nations, has a power over all flesh. He is king of saints, all the children of God are his scholars, his subjects, his soldiers. (2.) That *God anointed him with the Holy Ghost and with power;* he was both authorized and enabled to do what he did by a divine anointing, whence he was called *Christ—the Messiah, the anointed One.* The Holy Ghost descended upon him at his baptism, and he was full of power both in preaching and working miracles, which was the seal of a divine mission. (3.) That *God was with him, v.* 38. His works were wrought in God. God not only sent him, but was present with him all along, owned him, stood by him, and carried him on in all his services and sufferings. Note, Those whom God anoints he will accompany; he will himself be with those to whom he has given his Spirit.

III. Because they had had no more certain information concerning this Jesus, Peter declares to them his resurrection from the dead, and the proofs of it, that they might not think that when he was slain there was an end of him. Probably, they had heard at Cesarea some talk of his having risen from the dead; but the talk of it was soon silenced by that vile suggestion of the Jews, that *his disciples came by night and stole him away.* And therefore Peter insists upon this as the main support of that word which preacheth peace by Jesus Christ. 1. The power by which he arose is incontestably divine (*v.* 40): *Him God raised up the third day,* which not only disproved all the calumnies and accusations he was laid under by men, but effectually proved God's acceptance of the satisfaction he made for the sin of man by the blood of his cross. He did not break prison, but had a legal discharge. *God raised him up.* 2. The proofs of his resurrection were incontestably clear; for God *showed him openly. He gave him to be made manifest—ἔδωκεν αὐτὸν ἐμφανῆ γενέσθαι,* to be visible, evidently so; so he appears, as that it appears beyond contradiction to be him, and not another. It was such a showing of him as amounted to a demonstration of the truth of his resurrection. He showed him not publicly indeed (it was not open in this sense), but evidently; *not to all the people,* who had been the witnesses of his death. By resisting all the evidences he had given them of his divine mission in his miracles, they had forfeited the favour of being eye-witnesses of this great proof of it. Those who immediately forged and promoted that lie of his being stolen away were justly given up to strong delusions to believe it, and not suffered to be undeceived by his being shown to all the people; and so much the greater shall be the blessedness of those *who have not seen, and yet have believed—Nec ille se in vulgus edixit, ne impii errore, liberarentur; ut et fides non præmio mediocri destinato difficultate constaret—He showed not himself to the people at large, lest the impious among them should have been forthwith loosed from their error, and that faith, the reward of which is so ample, might be exercised with a degree of difficulty.*—Tertul. Apol. cap. 11. But, though all the people did not see him, a sufficient number saw him to attest the truth of his resurrection. The testator's declaring his last will and testament needs not to be before all the people; it is enough that it be done before a competent number of credible witnesses; so the resurrection of Christ was proved before sufficient witnesses. (1.) They were not so by chance, but they were *chosen before of God* to be witnesses of it, and, in order to this, had their education under the Lord Jesus, and intimate converse with him, that, having known him so intimately before, they might the better be assured it was he. (2.) They had not a sudden and transient view of him, but a great deal of free conversation with him: *They did eat and drink with him after he rose from the dead.* This implies that they saw him eat and drink, witness their dining with him at the sea of Tiberias, and the two disciples supping with him at Emmaus; and this proved that he had a true and real body. But this was not all; they saw him without any terror or consternation, which might have rendered them incompetent witnesses, for they saw him so frequently, and he conversed with them so familiarly, that *they did eat and drink with him.* It is brought as a proof of the clear view which the nobles of Israel had of the glory of God (Exod. xxiv. 11), that *they saw God, and did eat and drink.*

IV. He concludes with an inference from all this, that therefore that which they all ought to do was to believe in this Jesus: he was sent to tell Cornelius what he must do, and it is this; his praying and his giving alms were very well, but one thing he lacked, he must believe in Christ. Observe,

1. Why he must believe in him. Faith has reference to a testimony, and the Christian faith is *built upon the foundation of the apostles and prophets,* it is built upon the testimony given by them. (1.) By the apostles. Peter as foreman speaks for the rest, that *God commanded them,* and gave them in charge, to *preach to the people, and to testify* concerning Christ; so that their testimony was not only credible, but authentic, and what we may venture upon. Their testimony is God's testimony; and they are his witnesses to the world. They do not only say it as matter of news, but testify it as matter of record, by which men must be judged. (2.) By the prophets of the Old Testament, whose testimony beforehand, not only concerning his sufferings, but concerning the design and intention of them, very much corroborates the apostles' testimony concerning them (*v.* 43): *To him give all the prophets witness.* We have reason to think that Cornelius and his friends were no strangers to the writings of the prophets. Out of the mouth of these two clouds of witnesses, so exactly agreeing, *this word is established.*

2. What they must believe concerning him. (1.) That we are all accountable to Christ as our Judge; this the apostles were commanded to testify to the world, that this Jesus is *ordained of God to be the Judge of the quick and dead, v.* 42. He is empowered to prescribe the terms of salvation, that rule by which we must be judged, to give laws both to *quick and dead,* both to Jew and Gentile; and he is appointed to determine the everlasting condition of all the children of men at the great day, of those that shall be found alive and of those that shall be raised from the dead. He hath assured us of this, *in that he hath raised him from the dead* (*ch.* xvii. 31), so that it is the great concern of every one of us, in the belief of this, to seek his favour, and to make him our friend. (2.) That if we believe in him we shall all be justified by him as our righteousness, *v.* 43. The prophets, when they spoke of the death of Christ, did witness this, *that through his name,* for his sake, and upon the account of his merit, *whosoever believeth in him,* Jew or Gentile, *shall receive remission of sins.* This is the great thing we need, without which we are undone, and which the convinced conscience is most inquisitive after, which the carnal Jews promised themselves from their ceremonial sacrifices and purifications, yea, and the heathen too from their atonements, but all in vain; it is to be had only through the name of Christ, and only by those that believe in his name; and those that do so may be assured of it; their sins shall be pardoned, and there shall be no condemnation to them. And the remission of sins lays a foundation for all other favours and blessings, by taking that out of the way which hinders them. If sin be pardoned, all is well, and shall end everlastingly well.

44 While Peter yet spake these
words, the Holy Ghost fell on all
them which heard the word. 45
And they of the circumcision which
believed were astonished, as many as
came with Peter, because that on the
Gentiles also was poured out the gift
of the Holy Ghost. 46 For they
heard them speak with tongues, and
magnify God. Then answered Peter,
47 Can any man forbid water, that
these should not be baptized, which
have received the Holy Ghost as well
as we? 48 And he commanded them
to be baptized in the name of the
Lord. Then prayed they him to
tarry certain days.

We have here the issue and effect of Peter's sermon to Cornelius and his friends. He did not labour in vain among them, but they were all brought home to Christ. Here we have,

I. God's owning Peter's word, by conferring the Holy Ghost upon the hearers of it, and immediately upon the hearing of it (*v.* 44): *While Peter was yet speaking these words,* and perhaps designed to say more, he was happily superseded by visible indications that *the Holy Ghost,* even in his miraculous gifts and powers, *fell on all those who heard the word,* even as he did on the apostles at first; so Peter saith, *ch.* xi. 15. Therefore some think it was with a rushing mighty wind, and in cloven tongues, as that was. Observe, 1. When the Holy Ghost fell upon them—while Peter was preaching. Thus God bore witness to what he said, and accompanied it with a divine power. Thus were the *signs of an apostle wrought among them,* 2 Cor. xii. 12. Though Peter could not give the Holy Ghost, yet the Holy Ghost being given along with the word of Peter, by this it appeared he was sent of God. The Holy Ghost fell upon others after they were baptized, for their confirmation; but upon these Gentiles before they were baptized: as Abraham was justified by faith, being yet in uncircumcision, to show that God is not tied to a method, nor confines himself to external signs. The Holy Ghost fell upon those that were neither circumcised nor baptized; for *it is the Spirit that quickeneth, the flesh profiteth nothing.* 2. How it appeared that the Holy Ghost had fallen upon them (*v.* 46): *They spoke with tongues* which they never learned, perhaps the Hebrew, the holy tongue; as the preachers were enabled to speak the vulgar tongues, that they might communicate the doctrine of Christ to the hearers, so, probably, the hearers were immediately taught the sacred tongue, that they might examine the proofs which the preachers produced out of the Old Testament in the original. Or their being enabled to speak with tongues intimated that they were all designed for ministers, and by this first descent of the Spirit upon them were qualified to preach the gospel to others, which they did but now receive themselves. But, observe, when they spoke with tongues, they *magnified God,* they spoke of Christ and the benefits of redemption, which Peter had been preaching to the glory of God. Thus did they on whom the Holy Ghost first descended, *ch.* ii. 11. Note, Whatever gift we are endued with, we ought to honour God with it, and particularly the gift of speaking, and all the improvements of it. 3. What impression it made upon the believing Jews that were present (*v.* 45): *Those of the circumcision who believed were astonished*—those six that came along with Peter; it surprised them exceedingly, and perhaps gave them some uneasiness, because *upon the Gentiles also was poured out the gift of the Holy Ghost,* which they thought had been appropriated to their own nation. Had they understood the scriptures of the Old Testament, which pointed at this, it would not have been such an astonishment to them; but by our mistaken notions of things we create difficulties to ourselves in the methods of divine providence and grace.

II. Peter's owning God's work in baptizing those on whom the Holy Ghost fell. Observe, 1. Though they had received the Holy Ghost, yet it was requisite they should be baptized; though God is not tied to instituted ordinances, we are; and no extraordinary gifts set us above them, but rather oblige us so much the more to conform to them. Some in our days would have argued "These are baptized with the *Holy Ghost* and therefore what need have they to be baptized with *water?* It is below them." No; it is not below them, while water-baptism is an ordinance of Christ, and the door of admission into the visible church, and a seal of the new covenant. 2. Though they were Gentiles, yet, having received the Holy Ghost, they might be admitted to baptism (*v.* 47): *Can any man,* though ever so rigid a Jew, *forbid water, that these should not be baptized, who have received the Holy Ghost as well as we?* The argument is conclusive; can we deny the sign to those who have received the thing signified? Are not those on whom God has bestowed the grace of the covenant plainly entitled to the seals of the covenant? Surely those that have *received the Spirit as well as we* ought to receive baptism as well as we; for it becomes us to follow God's indications, and to take those into communion with us whom he hath taken into communion with himself. God hath promised to pour his Spirit upon the seed of the faithful, upon their offspring; and who then can forbid water, that they should not be baptized, who have *received the promise of the Holy Ghost as well as we?* Now it appears why the Spirit was given them before they were baptized—because otherwise Peter could not have persuaded himself to baptize them, any more than to have preached to them, if he had not been ordered to do it by a vision; at least he could not have avoided the censure of *those of the circumcision that believed.* Thus is there one unusual step of divine grace taken after another to bring the Gentiles into the church. How well is it for us that the grace of a good God is so much more extensive than the charity of some good men! 3. Peter did not baptize them himself, but *commanded them to be baptized, v.* 48. It is probable that some of the brethren who came with him did it by his order, and that he declined it for the same reason that Paul did—lest those that were baptized by him should think the better of themselves for it. or he should seem to *have baptized in his own name,* 1 Cor. i. 15. The apostles received the commission to *go and disciple all nations by baptism.* But it was to prayer and the ministry of the word that they were to *give* themselves. And Paul says that he was sent, *not to baptize but to preach,* which was the more noble and excellent work. The business of baptizing was therefore ordinarily devolved upon the inferior ministers; these acted by the orders of the apostles, who might therefore be said to do it. *Qui per alterum facit, per seipsum facere dicitur—What a man does by another, he may be said to do by himself.*

III. Their owning both Peter's word and God's work in their desire for further advantage by Peter's ministry: *They prayed him to tarry certain days.* They could not press him to reside constantly among them—they knew that he had work to do in other places, and that for the present he was expected at Jerusalem; yet they were not willing he should go away immediately, but earnestly begged he would stay for some time among them, that they might be further instructed by him in the things pertaining to the kingdom of God. Note, 1. Those who have some acquaintance with Christ cannot but covet more. 2. Even those that have received the Holy Ghost must see their need of the ministry of the word.

CHAP. XI.

In this chapter we have, I. Peter's necessary vindication of what he did in receiving Cornelius and his friends into the church, from the censure he lay under for it among the brethren, and their acquiescence in it, ver. 1—18. II. The good success of the gospel at Antioch, and the parts adjacent, ver. 19—21. III. The carrying on of the good work that was begun at Antioch, by the ministry of Barnabas first, and afterwards of Paul in conjunction with him, and the lasting name of Christian first given to the disciples there, ver. 22—26. IV. A prediction of an approaching famine, and the contribution that was made among the Gentile converts for the relief of the poor saints in Judea, upon that occasion, ver. 27—30.

AND the apostles and brethren
that were in Judæa heard that
the Gentiles had also received the
word of God. 2 And when Peter
was come up to Jerusalem, they that
were of the circumcision contended
with him, 3 Saying, Thou wentest
in to men uncircumcised, and didst
eat with them. 4 But Peter rehearsed *the matter* from the beginning, and expounded *it* by order unto
them, saying, 5 I was in the city of
Joppa praying: and in a trance I saw
a vision, A certain vessel descend, as
it had been a great sheet, let down
from heaven by four corners; and it
came even to me: 6 Upon the
which when I had fastened mine
eyes, I considered, and saw fourfooted
beasts of the earth, and wild beasts,
and creeping things, and fowls of the
air. 7 And I heard a voice saying
unto me, Arise, Peter; slay and eat.
8 But I said, Not so, Lord: for nothing common or unclean hath at any
time entered into my mouth. 9 But
the voice answered me again from
heaven, What God hath cleansed,
that call not thou common. 10 And
this was done three times: and all
were drawn up again into heaven.
11 And, behold, immediately there
were three men already come unto
the house where I was, sent from
Cæsarea unto me. 12 And the spirit
bade me go with them, nothing
doubting. Moreover these six brethren accompanied me, and we entered into the man's house: 13 And
he showed us how he had seen an
angel in his house, which stood and
said unto him, Send men to Joppa,
and call for Simon, whose surname is
Peter; 14 Who shall tell thee words,
whereby thou and all thy house shall
be saved. 15 And as I began to speak,
the Holy Ghost fell on them, as on
us at the beginning. 16 Then remembered I the word of the Lord,
how that he said, John indeed baptized with water; but ye shall be
baptized with the Holy Ghost. 17
Forasmuch then as God gave them
the like gift as *he did* unto us, who
believed on the Lord Jesus Christ;
what was I, that I could withstand
God? 18 When they heard these
things, they held their peace, and
glorified God, saying, Then hath God
also to the Gentiles granted repentance unto life.

The preaching of the gospel to Cornelius was a thing which we poor sinners of the Gentiles have reason to reflect upon with a great deal of joy and thankfulness; for it was the bringing of light to us who sat in darkness. Now it being so great a surprize to the believing as well as the unbelieving Jews, it is worth while to enquire how it was received, and what comments were made upon it. And here we find,

I. Intelligence was presently brought of it to the church in Jerusalem, and thereabouts; for Cesarea was not so far from Jerusalem but that they might presently hear of it. Some for good-will, and some for ill-will, would spread the report of it; so that before he himself had returned to Jerusalem *the apostles and* the *brethren* there and *in Judea heard that the Gentiles also had received the word of God,* that is, the gospel of Christ, which is not only a word of God, but the word of God; for it is the summary and centre of all divine revelation. They received Christ; *for his name is called the Word of God,* Rev. xix. 13. Not only that the Jews who were dispersed into the Gentile countries, and the Gentiles who were proselyted to the Jewish religion, but that the Gentiles also themselves, with whom it had hitherto been thought unlawful to hold common conversation, were taken into church-communion, that they had *received the word of God.* That is, 1. That the word of God was preached to them, which was a greater honour put upon them than they expected. Yet I wonder this should seem strange to those who were themselves commissioned to *preach the gospel to every creature.* But thus often are the prejudices of pride and bigotry held fast against the clearest discoveries of divine truth. 2. That it was entertained and submitted to by them, which was a better work wrought upon them than they expected. It is likely they had got a notion that if the gospel were preached to the Gentiles it would be to no purpose, because the proofs of the gospel were fetched so much out of the Old Testament, which the Gentiles did not receive: they looked upon them as not inclined to religion, nor likely to receive the impressions of it; and therefore were surprized to hear that they had received the word of the Lord. Note, We are too apt to despair of doing good to those who yet, when they are tried, prove very tractable.

II. That offence was taken at it by the believing Jews (*v.* 2, 3): *When Peter had himself come up to Jerusalem, those that were of the circumcision,* those Jewish converts that still retained a veneration for circumcision, *contended with him.* They charged it upon him as a crime that he *went in to men uncircumcised, and did eat with them;* and thereby they think he has stained, if not forfeited, the honour of his apostleship, and ought to come under the censure of the church: so far were they from looking upon him as infallible, or as the supreme head of the church that all were accountable to, and he to none. See here, 1. How much it is the bane and damage of the church, to monopolize it, and to exclude those from it, and from the benefit of the means of grace, that are not in every thing as we are. There are narrow souls that are for engrossing the riches of the church, as there are that would engross the riches of the world, and would be *placed alone in the midst of the earth.* These men were of Jonah's mind, who, in a jealousy for his people, was angry that the Ninevites received the word of God, and justified himself in it. 2. Christ's ministers must not think it strange if they be censured and quarrelled with, not only by their professed enemies, but by their professing friends; not only for their follies and infirmities, but for their good actions seasonably and well done; but, if we have proved our own work, we may have rejoicing in ourselves, as Peter had, whatever reflections we may have from our brethren. Those that are zealous and courageous in the service of Christ must expect to be censured by those who, under pretence of being cautious, are cold and indifferent. Those who are of catholic, generous, charitable principles, must expect to be censured by such as are conceited and strait-laced, who say, *Stand by thyself, I am holier than thou.*

III. Peter gave such a full and fair account of the matter of fact as was sufficient, without any further argument or apology, both to justify him, and to satisfy them (*v.* 4): *He rehearsed the matter from the beginning,* and laid it before them in order, and then could appeal to themselves whether he had done amiss; for it appeared all along God's own work, and not his.

1. He takes it for granted that if they had rightly understood how the matter was they would not have contended with him, but rather have concurred with him, and commended him. And it is a good reason why we should be moderate in our censures, and sparing of them, because if we rightly understood that which we are so forward to run down perhaps we should see cause to run in with it. When we see others do that which looks suspicious, instead of contending with them, we should enquire of them what ground they went upon; and, if we have not an opportunity to do that, should ourselves put the best construction upon it that it will bear, and *judge nothing before the time.*

2. He is very willing to stand right in their opinion, and takes pains to give them satisfaction. He does not insist upon his being the chief of the apostles, for he was far from the thought of that supremacy which his pretended successors claim. Nor does he think it enough to tell them that he is satisfied himself in the grounds he went upon, and they need not trouble themselves about it; but he is ready to *give a reason of the hope that is in him* concerning the Gentiles, and why he had receded from his former sentiments, which were the same with theirs. It is a debt we owe both to ourselves and to our brethren to set those actions of ours in a true light which at first looked ill and gave offence, that we may remove stumbling-blocks out of our brethren's way. Let us now see what Peter pleads in his own defence.

(1.) That he was instructed by a vision no longer to keep up the distinctions which were made by the ceremonial law; he relates the vision (*v.* 5, 6), as we had it before, *ch.* x. 9, &c. The sheet which was there said to be *let down to the earth* he here says came *even to him,* which circumstance intimates that it was particularly designed for instruction to him. We should thus see all God's discoveries of himself, which he has made to the children of men, coming even to us, applying them by faith to ourselves. Another circumstance here added is that when the sheet *came to him he fastened his eyes upon it, and considered it, v.* 6. If we would be led into the knowledge of divine things, we must fix our minds upon them, and consider them. He tells them what orders he had to eat of all sorts of meat without distinction, asking no questions for conscience'sake, *v.* 7. It was not till after the flood (as it should seem) that man was allowed to eat flesh at all, Gen. ix. 3. That allowance was afterwards limited by the ceremonial law; but now the restrictions were taken off, and the matter set at large again. It was not the design of Christ to abridge us in the use of our creature-comforts by any other law than that of sobriety and temperance, and preferring the meat that endures to eternal life before that which perishes. He pleads that he was as averse to the thoughts of conversing with Gentiles, or eating of their dainties, as they could be, and therefore refused the liberty given him: *Not so, Lord; for nothing common or unclean has at any time entered into my mouth, v.* 8. But he was told from heaven that the case was now altered, that God had cleansed those persons and things which were before polluted; and therefore that he must no longer call them common, nor look upon them as unfit to be meddled with by the peculiar people (*v.* 9); so that he was not to be blamed for changing his thoughts, when God had changed the thing. In things of this nature we must act according to our present light; yet must not be so wedded to our opinion concerning them as to be prejudiced against further discoveries, when the matter may either be otherwise or appear otherwise; and God may reveal even this unto us, Phil. iii. 15. And, that they might be sure he was not deceived in it, he tells them it was done three times (*v.* 10), the same command given, to kill and eat, and the same reason, because that which God hath cleansed is not to be called common, repeated a second and third time. And, further to confirm him that it was a divine vision, the things he saw did not vanish away into the air, but *were drawn up again into heaven,* whence they were let down.

(2.) That he was particularly directed by the Spirit to go along with the messengers that Cornelius sent. And, that it might appear that the vision was designed to satisfy him in this matter, he observes to them the time when the messengers came—immediately after he had that vision; yet, lest this should not be sufficient to clear his way, the Spirit bade him *go with the men* that were then sent from Cesarea to him, *nothing doubting* (*v.* 11, 12); though they were Gentiles he went to, and went with, yet he must make no scruple of going along with them.

(3.) That he took some of his brethren along with him, who were of the circumcision, that they might be satisfied as well as he; and these he had brought up from Joppa, to witness for him with what caution he proceeded, foreseeing the offence that would be taken at it. He did not act separately, but with advice; not rashly, but upon due deliberation.

(4.) That Cornelius had a vision too, by which he was directed to send for Peter (*v.* 13): *He showed us how he had seen an angel in his house,* that bade him *send to Joppa for one Simon, whose surname is Peter.* See how good it is for those that have communion with God, and keep up a correspondence with heaven, to compare notes, and communicate their experiences to each other; for hereby they may strengthen one another's faith: Peter is the more confirmed in the truth of his vision by Cornelius's, and Cornelius by Peter's. Here is something added in what the angel said to Cornelius; before it was, *Send for Peter, and he shall speak to thee, he shall tell thee what thou oughtest to do* (*ch.* x. 6, 32); but here it is, "*He shall tell thee words whereby thou and thy house shall be saved* (*v.* 14), and therefore it is of vast concern to thee, and will be of unspeakable advantage, to send for him." Note, [1.] The words of the gospel are words whereby we may be saved, eternally saved; not merely by hearing them and reading them, but by believing and obeying them. They set the salvation before us, and show us what it is; they open the way of salvation to us, and, if we follow the method prescribed us by them, we shall certainly be saved from wrath and the curse, and be for ever happy. [2.] Those that embrace the gospel of Christ will have salvation brought by it to their families: "*Thou and all thy house shall be saved;* thou and thy children shall be taken into covenant, and have the means of salvation; thy house shall be as welcome to the benefit of the salvation, upon their believing, as thou thyself, even the meanest servant thou hast. *This day is salvation come to this house,*" Luke xix. 9. Hitherto salvation was of the Jews (John iv. 22), but now salvation is brought to the Gentiles as much as ever it was with the Jews; the promises, privileges, and means of it are conveyed to all nations as amply and fully, to all intents and purposes, as ever it had been appropriated to the Jewish nation.

(5). That which put the matter past all dispute was the descent of the Holy Ghost upon the Gentile hearers; this completed the evidence that it was the will of God that he should take the Gentiles into communion. [1.] The fact was plain and undeniable (*v.* 15): "*As I began to speak*" (and perhaps he felt some secret reluctance in his own breast, doubting whether he was in the right to preach to the uncircumcised), "presently *the Holy Ghost fell on them* in as visible signs *as on us at the beginning,* in which there could be no fallacy." Thus God attested what was done, and declared his approbation of it; that preaching is certainly right with which the Holy Ghost is given. The apostle supposes this, when he thus argues with the Galatians: *Received you the Spirit by the works of the law, or by the hearing of faith?* Gal. iii. 2. [2.] Peter was hereby put in mind of a saying of his Master's, when he was leaving them (*ch.* i. 5): *John baptized with water; but you shall be baptized with the Holy Ghost, v.* 16. This plainly intimated, *First,* That the Holy Ghost was the gift of Christ, and the product and performance of his promise, that great promise which he left with them when he went to heaven. It was therefore without doubt from him that this gift came; and the filling of them with the Holy Ghost was his act and deed. As it was promised by his mouth, so it was performed by his hand, and was a token of his favour. *Secondly,* That the gift of the Holy Ghost was a kind of baptism. Those that received it were baptized with it in a more excellent manner than any of those that even the Baptist himself baptized with water. [3.] Comparing that promise, so worded, with this gift just now conferred, when the question was started, whether these persons should be baptized or no, he concluded that the question was determined by Christ himself (*v.* 17): "*Forasmuch then as God gave them the like gift as he did to us*—gave it to us as *believing in the Lord Jesus Christ,* and to them upon their believing in him—*What was I, that I could withstand God?* Could I refuse to baptize them with water, whom God had baptized with the Holy Ghost? Could I deny the sign to those on whom he had conferred the thing signified? *But, as for me, who was I?* What! able to forbid God? Did it become me to control the divine will, or to oppose the counsels of Heaven?" Note, Those who hinder the conversion of souls withstand God; and those take too much upon them who contrive how to exclude from their communion those whom God has taken into communion with himself.

IV. This account which Peter gave of the matter satisfied them, and all was well. Thus, when the two tribes and a half gave an account to Phinehas and the princes of Israel of the true intent and meaning of their building themselves an altar on the banks of Jordan, the controversy was dropped, and it pleased them that it was so, Josh. xxii. 30. Some people, when they have fastened a censure upon a person, will stick to it, though afterwards it appear ever so plainly to be unjust and groundless. It was not so here; for these brethren, though they were of the circumcision, and their bias went the other way, yet, when they heard this, 1. They let fall their censures: they held their peace, and said no more against what Peter had done; they laid their hand upon their mouth, because now they perceived that God did it. Now those who prided themselves in their dignities as Jews began to see that God was staining their pride, by letting in the Gentiles to share, and to share equally, with them. And now that prophecy was fulfilled, *Thou shalt no more be haughty because of my holy mountain,* Zeph. iii. 11. 2. They turned them into praises. They not only held their peace from quarrelling with Peter, but opened their mouths to glorify God for what he had done by and with Peter's ministry; they were thankful that their mistake was rectified, and that God had shown more mercy to the poor Gentiles than they were inclined to show them, saying, *Then hath God also to the Gentiles granted repentance unto life!* He hath granted them not only the means of repentance, in opening a door of entrance for his ministers among them, but the grace of repentance, in having given them his Holy Spirit, who, wherever he comes to be a Comforter, first convinces, and gives a sight of sin and sorrow for it, and then a sight of Christ and joy in him. Note, (1.) Repentance, if it be true, is unto life. It is to spiritual life; all that truly repent of their sins evidence it by living a new life, a holy, heavenly, and divine life. Those that by repentance die unto sin thenceforward live unto God; and then, and not till then, we begin to live indeed, and it shall be to eternal life. All true penitents shall live, that is, they shall be restored to the favour of God, which is life, which is better than life; they shall be comforted with the assurance of the pardon of their sins, and shall have the earnest of eternal life, and at length the fruition of it. (2.) Repentance is God's gift; it is not only his free grace that accepts it, but his mighty grace that works it in us, that *takes away the heart of stone, and gives us a heart of flesh. The sacrifice of God is a broken spirit;* it is he that provides himself this lamb. (3.) Wherever God designs to give life he gives repentance; for this is a necessary preparative for the comforts of a sealed pardon and a settled peace in this world, and for the seeing and enjoying of God in the other world. (4.) It is a great comfort to us that God has exalted his Son Jesus, not only to *give repentance to Israel, and the remission of sins* (*ch.* v. 31), but to the Gentiles also.

19 Now they which were scattered
abroad upon the persecution that
arose about Stephen travelled as far
as Phenice, and Cyprus, and Antioch,
preaching the word to none but unto
the Jews only. 20 And some of
them were men of Cyprus and Cyrene, which, when they were come to
Antioch, spake unto the Grecians,
preaching the Lord Jesus. 21 And
the hand of the Lord was with them:
and a great number believed, and
turned unto the Lord. 22 Then
tidings of these things came unto the
ears of the church which was in Jerusalem: and they sent forth Barnabas, that he should go as far as Antioch. 23 Who, when he came, and
had seen the grace of God, was glad,
and exhorted them all, that with purpose of heart they would cleave unto
the Lord. 24 For he was a good
man, and full of the Holy Ghost and
of faith: and much people was added
unto the Lord. 25 Then departed
Barnabas to Tarsus, for to seek Saul:
26 And when he had found him, he

brought him unto Antioch. And it came to pass, that a whole year they assembled themselves with the church, and taught much people. And the disciples were called Christians first in Antioch.

We have here an account of the planting and watering of a church at Antioch, the chief city of Syria, reckoned afterwards the third most considerable city of the empire, only Rome and Alexandria being preferred before it, next to whose patriarch that of Antioch took place. It stood where Hamath or Riblah did, which we read of in the Old Testament. It is suggested that Luke, the penman of this history, as well as Theophilus, to whom he dedicates it, was of Antioch, which may be the reason why he takes more particular notice of the success of the gospel at Antioch, as also because there it was that Paul began to be famous, towards the story of whom he is hastening. Now concerning the church at Antioch observe,

I. The first preachers of the gospel there were such as were dispersed from Jerusalem by persecution, that persecution which arose five or six years years ago (as some compute), at the time of Stephen's death (*v.* 19): *They travelled as far as Phenice* and other places *preaching the word.* God suffered them to be persecuted, that thereby they might be dispersed in the world, sown as seed to God, in order to their bringing forth much fruit. Thus what was intended for the hurt of the church was made to work for its good; as Jacob's curse of the tribe of Levi *(I will divide them in Jacob, and scatter them in Israel)* was turned into a blessing. The enemies designed to scatter and lose them, Christ designed to scatter and use them. Thus the wrath of man is made to praise God. Observe,

1. Those that *fled from persecution* did not flee from their work; though for the time they declined suffering, yet they did not decline service; nay, they threw themselves into a larger field of opportunity than before. Those that persecuted the preachers of the gospel hoped thereby to prevent their carrying it to the Gentile world; but it proved that they did but hasten it the sooner. *Howbeit, they meant not so, neither did their heart think so.* Those that were persecuted in one city fled to another; but they carried their religion along with them, not only that they might take the comfort of it themselves, but that they might communicate it to others, thus showing that when they got out of the way it was not because they were afraid of suffering, but because they were willing to reserve themselves for further service.

2. They pressed forward in their work, finding that the *good pleasure of the Lord prospered in their hands.* When they had preached successfully in Judea, Samaria, and Galilee, they got out of the borders of the land of Canaan, and travelled into Phœnicia, into the island of Cyprus, and into Syria. Though the further they travelled the more they exposed themselves, yet they travelled on; *plus ultra—further still,* was their motto; grudging no pains, and dreading no perils, in carrying on so good a work, and serving so good a Master.

3. They *preached the word to none but to the Jews only* who were dispersed in all those parts, and had synagogues of their own, in which they met with them by themselves, and preached to them. They did not yet understand that the Gentiles were to be fellow-heirs, and of the same body; but left the Gentiles either to turn Jews, and so come into the church, or else remain as they were.

4. They particularly applied themselves to the Hellenist Jews, here called the Grecians, that were at Antioch. Many of the preachers were natives of Judea and Jerusalem; but some of them were by birth of Cyprus and Cyrene, as Barnabas himself (*ch.* iv. 36), and Simon (Mark xv. 21), but had their education in Jerusalem; and these, being themselves Grecian Jews, had a particular concern for those of their own denomination and distinction, and applied themselves closely to them at Antioch. Dr. Lightfoot says that they were there called *Hellenists,* or *Grecians,* because they were Jews of the corporation or enfranchisement of the city; for Antioch was a Syrogrecian city. To them they preached the Lord Jesus. This was the constant subject of their preaching; what else should the ministers of Christ preach, but Christ—Christ, and him crucified—Christ, and him glorified?

5. They had wonderful success in their preaching, *v.* 21. (1.) Their preaching was accompanied with a divine power: *The hand of the Lord was with them,* which some understand of the power they were endued with to work miracles for the confirming of their doctrine; in these the Lord *was working with them, for he confirmed the word with signs following* (Mark xvi. 20); in these God *bore them witness,* Heb. ii. 4. But I rather understand it of the power of divine grace working on the hearts of the hearers, and opening them, as Lydia's heart was opened, because many saw the miracles who were not converted; but when by the Spirit the understanding was enlightened, and the will bowed to the gospel of Christ, that was a day of power, in which volunteers were enlisted under the banner of the Lord Jesus, Ps. cx. 3. *The hand of the Lord was with them,* to bring that home to the hearts and consciences of men which they could but speak to the outward ear. Then the word of the Lord gains its end, when the hand of the Lord goes along with it, to write it in their heart. Then people are brought to believe the report of the gospel, when with it the *arm of the Lord is revealed* (Isa. liii. 1), when God *teaches with a strong hand,* Isa. viii. 11. These were

not apostles, but ordinary ministers, yet they had the hand of the Lord with them, and did wonders. (2.) Abundance of good was done: *A great number believed, and turned unto the Lord*—many more than could have been expected, considering the outward disadvantages they laboured under: some of all sorts of people were wrought upon, and brought into obedience to Christ. Observe, What the change was. [1.] They believed; they were convinced of the truth of the gospel, and subscribed to the record God had given in it concerning his Son. [2.] The effect and evidence of this was that they *turned unto the Lord.* They could not be said to turn from the service of idols, for they were Jews, worshippers of the true God only; but they turned from a confidence in the righteousness of the law, to rely only upon the righteousness of Christ, the righteousness which is by faith; they turned from a loose, careless, carnal way of living, to live a holy, heavenly, spiritual, and divine life; they turned from worshipping God in show and ceremony, to worship him *in spirit and in truth.* They turned to the Lord Jesus, and he became all in all with them. This was the work of conversion wrought upon them, and it must be wrought upon every one of us. It was the fruit of their faith. All that sincerely believe will turn to the Lord; for, whatever we profess or pretend, we do not really believe the gospel if we do not cordially embrace Christ offered to us in the gospel.

II. The good work thus begun at Antioch was carried on to great perfection; and the church, thus founded, grew to be a flourishing one, by the ministry of Barnabas and Saul, who built upon the foundation which the other preachers had laid, and *entered into their labours,* John iv. 37, 38.

1. The church at Jerusalem sent Barnabas thither, to nurse this new-born church, and to strengthen the hands both of preachers and people, and put a reputation upon the cause of Christ there.

(1.) They heard the good news, that the gospel was received at Antioch, *v.* 22. The apostles there were inquisitive how the work went on in the countries about; and, it is likely, kept up a correspondence with all parts where preachers were, so that *tidings of these things,* of the great numbers that were converted at Antioch, soon *came to the ears of the church that was in Jerusalem.* Those that are in the most eminent stations in the church ought to concern themselves for those in a lower sphere.

(2.) They despatched Barnabas to them with all speed; they desired him to go, and assist and encourage these hopeful beginnings. They *sent him forth* as an envoy from them, and a representative of their whole body, to congratulate them upon the success of the gospel among them, as matter of rejoicing both to preachers and hearers, and with both they rejoiced. He must go *as far as Antioch.* It was a great way, but, far as it was, he was willing to undertake the journey for a public service. It is probable that Barnabas had a particular genius for work of this kind, was active and conversable, loved to be in motion, and delighted in doing good abroad as much as others in doing good at home, was as much of Zebulun's spirit, who rejoiced *in his going out,* as others are of Issachar's, who rejoiced *in his tent;* and, his talent lying this way, he was fittest to be employed in this work. God gives various gifts for various services.

(3.) Barnabas was wonderfully pleased to find that the gospel got ground, and that some of his countrymen, men of Cyprus (of which country he was, *ch.* iv. 36) were instrumental in it (*v.* 23): *When he came, and had seen the grace of God,* the tokens of God's good-will to the people of Antioch and the evidences of his good work among them, *he was glad.* He took time to make his observations, and not only in their public worship, but in their common conversations and in their families, he saw the grace of God among them. Where the grace of God is it will be seen, as the *tree is known by its fruits;* and, where it is seen, it ought to be owned. What we see which is good in any we must call God's grace in them, and give that grace the glory of it; and we ought ourselves to take the comfort of it, and make it the matter of our rejoicing. We must be glad to see the grace of God in others, and the more when we see it where we did not expect it.

(4.) He did what he could to fix them, to confirm those in the faith who were converted to the faith. He *exhorted them*—*παρεκάλει.* It is the same word with that by which the name of Barnabas is interpreted (*ch.* iv. 36), *υἱὸς παρακλήσεως*—*a son of exhortation;* his talent lay that way, and he traded with it; let him that *exhorteth attend to exhortation,* Rom. xii. 8. Or, being *a son of consolation* (for so we render the word), he *comforted or encouraged them with purpose of heart to cleave to the Lord.* The more he rejoiced in the beginning of the good work among them, the more earnest he was with them to proceed according to these good beginnings. Those we have comfort in we should exhort. Barnabas was glad for what he saw of the grace of God among them, and therefore was the more earnest with them to persevere. [1.] To *cleave to the Lord.* Note, Those that have *turned to the Lord* are concerned to *cleave unto the Lord,* not to fall off from following him, not to flag and tire in following him. To cleave to the Lord Jesus is to live a life of dependence upon him and devotedness to him: not only to hold him fast, but to hold fast by him, to *be strong in the Lord and in the power of his might.* [2.] To cleave to him with purpose of heart, with an intelligent, firm, and deliberate resolution, founded upon good grounds, and fixed upon that foundation, Ps. cviii. 1. It is to bind our souls with a bond to be the Lord's, and to say as Ruth, *Entreat me not to leave* him, or to return from following after him.

(5.) Herein he gave a proof of his good character (*v.* 24): *He was a good man, and full of the Holy Ghost, and of faith*, and approved himself so upon this occasion. [1.] He showed himself to be a man of a very sweet, affable, courteous disposition, that had himself the art of obliging, and could teach others. He was not only a righteous man, but a *good man*, a good-tempered man. Ministers that are so recommend themselves and their doctrine very much to the good opinion of those that are without. He was a good man, that is, a charitable man; so he had approved himself, when he sold an estate, and gave the money to the poor, *ch.* iv. 37. [2.] By this it appeared that he was richly endued with the gifts and graces of the Spirit. The goodness of his natural disposition would not have qualified him for this service if he had not been *full of the Holy Ghost, and so full of power by the Spirit of the Lord.* [3.] He was full of faith, full of the Christian faith himself, and therefore desirous to propagate it among others; full of the grace of faith, and full of the fruits of that faith that works by love. He was *sound in the faith,* and therefore pressed them to be so.

(6.) He was instrumental to do good, by bringing in those that were without, as well as by building up those that were within: *Much people were added to the Lord,* and thereby added to the *church;* many were turned to the Lord before, yet more are to be turned; it is *done as thou hast commanded, and yet there is room.*

2. Barnabas went to fetch Saul, to join with him in the work of the gospel at Antioch. The last news we heard of him was that, when his life was sought at Jerusalem, he was sent away to Tarsus, the city where he was born, and, it should seem, he continued there ever since, doing good, no doubt. But now Barnabas takes a journey to Tarsus on purpose to see what had become of him, to tell him what a door of opportunity was opened at Antioch, and to desire him to come and spend some time with him there, *v.* 25, 26. And here also it appears that Barnabas was a good sort of a man in two things:—(1.) That he would take so much pains to bring an active useful man out of obscurity. It was he that introduced Saul to the disciples at Jerusalem, when they were shy of him; and it was he that brought him out of the corner into which he was driven, into a more public station. It is a very good work to fetch a candle from under a bushel, and to set it in a candlestick. (2.) That he would bring in Saul at Antioch, who, being a *chief speaker* (*ch.* xiv. 12), and probably a more popular preacher, would be likely to eclipse him there, by outshining him; but Barnabas is very willing to be eclipsed when it is for the public service. If God by his grace inclines us to do what good we can, according to the ability we have, we ought to rejoice if others that have also larger capacities have larger opportunities, and do more good than we can do. Barnabas brought Saul to Antioch, though it might be the lessening of himself, to teach us to seek the things of Christ more than our own things.

3. We are here further told,

(1.) What service was now done to the church at Antioch. Paul and Barnabas continued there a whole year, presiding in their religious assemblies, and preaching the gospel, *v.* 26. Observe, [1.] The church frequently assembled. The religious assemblies of Christians are appointed by Christ for his honour, and the comfort and benefit of his disciples. God's people of old frequently came together, *at the door of the tabernacle of the congregation;* places of meeting are now multiplied, but they must come together, though it be with difficulty and peril. [2.] Ministers were the masters of those assemblies, and held those courts in Christ's name to which all that hold by, from, and under him, owe suit and service. [3.] *Teaching the people* is one part of the work of ministers, when they preside in religious assemblies. They are not only to be the people's mouth to God in prayer and praise, but God's mouth to the people in opening the scriptures, and teaching out of them the good knowledge of the Lord. [4.] It is a great encouragement to ministers when they have opportunity of teaching much people, of casting the net of the gospel where there is a large shoal of fish, in hopes that the more may be enclosed. [5.] Preaching is not only for the conviction and conversion of those that are without, but for the instruction and edification of those that are within. A constituted church must have its teachers.

(2.) What honour was now put upon the church *at Antioch: There the disciples were first called Christians;* it is probable they called themselves so, incorporated themselves by that title, whether by some solemn act of the church or ministers, or whether this name insensibly obtained there by its being frequently used in their praying and preaching, we are not told; but it should seem that two such great men as Paul and Barnabas continuing there so long, being exceedingly followed, and meeting with no opposition, Christian assemblies made a greater figure there than any where, and became more considerable, which was the reason of their being called *Christians* first there, which, if there were to be a mother-church to rule over all other churches, would give Antioch a better title to the honour than Rome can pretend to. Hitherto those who gave up their names to Christ were called *disciples, learners, scholars,* trained up under him, in order to their being employed by him; but henceforward they were called *Christians*. [1.] Thus the reproachful names which their enemies had hitherto branded them with would, perhaps, be superseded and disused. They called them *Nazarenes* (*ch*. 24, 5), *the men of that way, that by-way*, which had no name; and thus they prejudiced people against them. To remove the prejudice, they gave themselves a name which their enemies could not but say was proper. [2.] Thus those who before their conversion had been distinguished by the names of Jews and Gentiles might after their conversion be called by one and the same name, which would help them to forget their former dividing names, and prevent their bringing their former marks of distinction, and with them the seeds of contention, into the church. Let not one say, "I was a *Jew;*" nor the other, "I was a *Gentile;*" when both the one and the other must now say, "I am a *Christian*." [3.] Thus they studied to do honour to their Master, and showed that they were not ashamed to own their relation to him, but gloried in it; as the scholars of Plato called themselves *Platonists*, and so the scholars of other great men. They took their denomination not from the name of his person, *Jesus*, but of his office, *Christ—anointed*, so putting their creed into their names, *that Jesus is the Christ;* and they were willing all the world should know that this is the truth they will live and die by. Their enemies will turn this name to their reproach, and impute it to them as their crime, but they will glory in it: *If this be to be vile, I will be yet more vile*. [4.] Thus they now owned their dependence upon Christ, and their receivings from him; not only that they believed in him who is *the anointed*, but that through him they themselves had *the anointing*, 1 John ii. 20, 27. And God is said to have *anointed us in Christ*, 2 Cor. i. 21. [5.] Thus they laid upon themselves, and all that should ever profess that name, a strong and lasting obligation to submit to the laws of Christ, to follow the example of Christ, and to devote themselves entirely to the honour of Christ—*to be to him for a name and a praise*. Are we Christians? Then we ought to think, and speak, and act, in every thing as becomes Christians, and to do nothing to the reproach of that worthy name by which we are called; that that may not be said to us which Alexander said to a soldier of his own name that was noted for a coward, *Aut nomen, aut mores muta—Either change thy name or mend thy manners*. And as we must look upon ourselves as Christians, and carry ourselves accordingly, so we must look upon others as Christians, and carry ourselves towards them accordingly. A Christian, though not in every thing of our mind, should be loved and respected for his sake whose name he bears, because he belongs to Christ. [6.] Thus *the scripture was fulfilled*, for so it was written (Isa. lxii. 2) concerning the gospel-church, *Thou shalt be called by a new name, which the mouth of the Lord shall name*. And it is said to the corrupt and degenerate church of the Jews, *The Lord God shall slay thee, and call his servants by another name*, Isa. lxv. 15.

27 And in these days came prophets from Jerusalem unto Antioch.
28 And there stood up one of them named Agabus, and signified by the spirit that there should be great dearth throughout all the world: which came to pass in the days of Claudius Cæsar.
29 Then the disciples, every man according to his ability, determined to send relief unto the brethren which dwelt in Judæa:
30 Which also they did, and sent it to the elders by the hands of Barnabas and Saul.

When our Lord Jesus *ascended on high he gave gifts unto men*, not only *apostles and evangelists, but prophets*, who were enabled by the Spirit to foresee and foretel things to come, which not only served for a confirmation of the truth of Christianity (for all that these prophets foretold came to pass, which proved that *they were sent of God*, Deut. xviii. 22; Jer. xxviii. 9), but was also of great use to the church, and served very much for its guidance. Now here we have,

I. A visit which some of these prophets made to Antioch (*v*. 27): *In these days*, during that year that Barnabas and Saul lived at Antioch, there *came prophets from Jerusalem to Antioch:* we are not told how many, nor is it certain whether these were any of those prophets that we afterwards find *in the church at Antioch, ch*. xiii. 1. 1. They came from Jerusalem, probably because they were not now so much regarded there as they had been; they saw their work in a manner done there, and therefore thought it time to be gone. Jerusalem had been infamous for *killing the prophets* and abusing them, and therefore is now justly deprived of these prophets. 2. They came to Antioch, because they heard of the flourishing state of that church, and there they hoped they might be of some service. Thus should *every one as he hath received the gift minister the same*. Barnabas came to exhort them, and they, having received the exhortation well, now have prophets sent them *to show them things to come*, as Christ had promised, John xvi. 13. Those that are faithful in their little shall be entrusted with more. The best understanding of scripture-predictions is to be got in the way of obedience to scripture-instructions.

II. A particular prediction of a famine approaching, delivered by one of these prophets, his name *Agabus;* we read of him again prophesying Paul's imprisonment, *ch*. xxi. 10, 11. Here he stood up, probably in one of their public assemblies, and prophesied, *v.* 28. Observe, 1. Whence he had his prophecy. What he said was not of himself, nor a fancy of his own, nor an astronomical prediction, nor a conjecture upon the present workings of second causes, but *he signified it by the Spirit, the Spirit of prophecy, that there should be* a famine; as Joseph, by the Spirit enabling him, understood Pharaoh's dreams, foretold the famine in Egypt, and Elijah the famine in Israel in Ahab's time. Thus God revealed his secrets to his servants the prophets. 2. What the prophecy was: *There should be great dearth throughout all the world,* by unseasonable weather, that corn should be scarce and dear, so that many of the poor should perish for want of bread. This should be not in one particular country, but *through all the world,* that is, all the Roman empire, which they in their pride, like Alexander before them, called *the world.* Christ had foretold in general *that there should be famines* (Matt. xxiv. 7; Mark xiii. 8; Luke xxi. 11); but Agabus foretels one very remarkable famine now at hand. 3. The accomplishment of it: *It came to pass in the days of Claudius Cesar;* it began in the second year of his reign, and continued to the fourth, if not longer. Several of the Roman historians make mention of it, as does also Josephus. God sent them the bread of life, and they rejected it, loathed the plenty of that manna; and therefore God justly broke the staff of bread, and punished them with famine; and herein he was righteous. They were barren, and did not bring forth to God, and therefore God made the earth barren to them.

III. The good use they made of this prediction. When they were told of a famine at hand, they did not do as the Egyptians, hoard up corn for themselves; but, as became Christians, laid by for charity to relieve others, which is the best preparative for our own sufferings and want. It is promised to those that *consider the poor that God will preserve them, and keep them alive, and they shall be blessed upon the earth,* Ps. xli. 1, 2. And *those who show mercy, and give to the poor, shall not be ashamed in the evil time, but in the days of famine they shall be satisfied,* Ps. xxxvii. 19, 21. The best provision we can lay up against a dear time is to lay up an interest in these promises, by doing good, and communicating, Luke xii. 33. Many give it as a reason why they should be sparing, but the scripture gives it as a reason why we should be liberal, *to seven, and also to eight,* because *we know not what evil shall be upon the earth,* Eccl. xi. 2. Observe,

1. What they determined—that *every man, according to his ability,* should *send relief to the brethren that dwelt in Judea, v.* 29. (1.) The persons that were recommended to them as objects of charity were *the brethren that dwelt in Judea.* Though we must, as we have opportunity, *do good to all men,* yet we must have a special regard *to the household of faith,* Gal. vi. 10. No poor must be neglected, but God's poor most particularly regarded. The care which every particular church ought to take of their own poor we were taught by the early instance of that in the church at Jerusalem, where the ministration was so constant *that none lacked, ch.* iv. 34. But the communion of saints in that instance is here extended further, and provision is made by the church at Antioch for the relief of the poor in Judea, whom they call their brethren. It seems it was the custom of the Jews of the dispersion to send money to those Jews who dwelt in Judea, for the relief of the poor that were among them, and to make collections for that purpose (Tully speaks of such a thing in his time, *Orat. pro Flacco),* which supposes there were many poor in Judea, more than in other countries, so that the rich among them were not able to bear the charge of keeping them from starving; either because their land had become *barren,* though it had been a fruitful land, *for the iniquity of those that dwelt therein,* or because they had no traffic with other nations. Now we may suppose that the greatest part of those who turned Christians in that country were the poor (Matt. xi. 5, *The poor are evangelized),* and also that when the poor turned Christians they were put out of the poor's book, and cut off from their shares in the public charity; and it were easy to foresee that if there came a famine it would go very hard with them; and, if any of them should perish for want, it would be a great reproach to the Christian profession; and therefore this early care was taken, upon notice of this famine coming, to send them a stock beforehand, lest, if it should be deferred till the famine came, it should be too late. (2.) The agreement there was among the disciples about it, that *every man* should contribute, *according to his ability,* to this good work. The Jews abroad, in other countries, grew rich by trade, and many of the rich Jews became Christians, whose abundance ought to be *a supply to the want of their poor brethren* that were at a great distance; for the case of such ought to be considered, and not theirs only that live among us. Charitable people are traders with what God has given them, and the merchants find their account in sending effects to countries that lie very remote; and so should we in giving alms to those afar off that need them, which therefore we should be forward to do when we are called to it. *Every man determined to send* something, more or less, *according to his ability,* what he could spare from the support of himself and his family, and *according as God had prospered him.* What may be said to be *according to our ability* we must judge for ourselves, but must be careful *that we judge righteous judgment.*

2. What they did—they did as they de-

termined (*v.* 30). *Which also they did.* They not only talked of it, but they did it. Many a good motion of that kind is made and commended, but is not prosecuted, and so comes to nothing. But this was pursued, the collection was made, and was so considerable that they thought it worth while *to send Barnabas and Saul to Jerusalem,* to carry it *to the elders* there, though they would want their labours in the mean time at Antioch. They sent it, (1.) *To the elders,* the presbyters, the ministers or pastors, *of the churches in Judea,* to be by them distributed according to the necessity of the receivers, as it had been contributed according to the ability of the givers. (2.) It was sent *by Barnabas and Saul,* who perhaps wanted an occasion to go to Jerusalem, and therefore were willing to take this. Josephus tells us that at this time king Irates sent his charity to the chief men of Jerusalem, for the poor of that country; and Helena, queen of the Adiabeni, being now at Jerusalem, and hearing of many that died of famine there, and in the country about, sent for provisions from Cyprus and Alexandria, and distributed them among the people; so says Dr. Lightfoot, who also computes, by the date of Paul's rapture, "fourteen years before he wrote the second Epistle to the Corinthians" (2 Cor. xii. 1, 2), that it was in this journey of his *to Jerusalem, with these alms and offerings,* that he had his *trance* in the temple (which he speaks of, *ch.* xxii. 17), and in that *trance was rapt up into the third heaven;* and then it was that Christ told him he would send him thence *unto the Gentiles,* which accordingly he did as soon as ever he came back to Antioch. It is no disparagement, in an extraordinary case, for ministers of the gospel to be messengers of the church's charity, though to undertake the constant care of that matter would ordinarily be too great a diversion from more needful work *to those who have given themselves to prayer and the ministry of the word.*

CHAP. XII.

In this chapter we have the story, I. Of the martyrdom of James the apostle, and the imprisonment of Peter by Herod Agrippa, who now reigned as king in Judea, ver. 1—4. II. The miraculous deliverance of Peter out of prison by the ministry of an angel, in answer to the prayers of the church for him, ver. 5—19. III. The cutting off of Herod in the height of his pride by the stroke of an angel, the minister of God's justice (ver. 20—23); and this was done while Barnabas and Saul were at Jerusalem, upon the errand that the church of Antioch sent them on, to carry their charity; and therefore in the close we have an account of their return to Antioch, ver. 24, 25.

NOW about that time Herod the king stretched forth *his* hands to vex certain of the church.
2 And he killed James the brother of John with the sword.
3 And because he saw it pleased the Jews, he proceeded further to take Peter also. (Then were the days of unleavened bread.)
4 And when he had apprehended him, he put *him* in prison, and delivered *him* to four quaternions of soldiers to keep him; intending after Easter to bring him forth to the people.

Ever since the conversion of Paul, we have heard no more of the agency of the priests in persecuting the saints at Jerusalem; perhaps that wonderful change wrought upon him, and the disappointment it gave to their design upon the Christians at Damascus, had somewhat mollified them, and brought them under the check of Gamaliel's advice—to *let those men alone,* and see what would be the issue; but here the storm arises from another point. The civil power, not now, as usual (for aught that appears) stirred up by the ecclesiastics, acts by itself in the persecution. But Herod, though originally of an Edomite family, yet seems to have been a proselyte to the Jewish religion; for Josephus says he was zealous for the Mosaic rites, a bigot for the ceremonies. He was not only (as Herod Antipas was) tetrarch of Galilee, but had also the government of Judea committed to him by Claudius the emperor, and resided most at Jerusalem, where he was at this time. Three things we are here told he did:—

I. He *stretched forth his hands to vex certain of the church, v.* 1. His stretching forth his hands to it intimates that his hands had been tied up by the restraints which perhaps his own conscience held him under in this matter; but now he broke through them, and stretched forth his hands deliberately, and of malice prepense. *Herod laid hands upon some of the church to afflict them,* so some read it; he employed his officers to seize them, and take them into custody, in order to their being prosecuted. See how he advances gradually. 1. He began with some of the members of the church, certain of them that were of less note and figure; played first at small game, but afterwards flew at the apostles themselves. His spite was at the church, and, with regard to those he gave trouble to, it was not upon any other account, but because they belonged to the church, and so belonged to Christ. 2. He began with vexing them only, or afflicting them, imprisoning them, fining them, spoiling their houses and goods, and other ways molesting them; but afterwards he proceeded to greater instances of cruelty. Christ's suffering servants are thus trained up by less troubles for greater, *that tribulation may work patience, and patience experience.*

II. *He killed James the brother of John with the sword, v.* 2. We are here to consider, 1. Who the martyr was: it was *James the brother of John;* so called to distinguish him from the other James the brother of Joses. This was called *Jacobus major—James the greater;* that, *minor—the less.* This who was here crowned with martyrdom was one of the first three of Christ's disciples, one of those that were *the witnesses of his transfiguration and agony,* whereby he was prepared for martyrdom; he was one of those whom Christ called *Boanerges—Sons of thunder;* and perhaps by his powerful awakening preaching he had provoked Herod, or those about him, as John Baptist did the other Herod, and that was the occasion of his coming into this trouble. He was one of those sons of Zebedee whom Christ told *that they should drink of the cup that he was to drink of, and be baptized with the baptism that he was to be baptized with,* Matt. xx. 23. And now those words of Christ were made good in him; but it was in order to his sitting at Christ's right hand; for *if we suffer with him, we shall reign with him.* He was one of the twelve who were commissioned *to disciple all nations;* and to take him off now, before he had removed from Jerusalem, was like Cain's killing Abel when the world was to be peopled, and one man was then more than many at another time. To kill an apostle now was killing he knew not how many. But why would God permit it? If *the blood of his saints,* much more the blood of apostles, *is precious in his eyes,* and therefore, we may be sure, is not shed but upon a valuable consideration. Perhaps God intended hereby to awaken the rest of the apostles to disperse themselves among the nations, and not to nestle any longer at Jerusalem. Or it was to show that though the apostles were appointed *to plant the gospel in the world,* yet if they were taken off God could do his work without them, and would do it. The apostle died a martyr, to show the rest of them what they must expect, that they might prepare accordingly. The tradition that they have in the Romish church, that this James had been before this in Spain, and had planted the gospel there, is altogether groundless; nor is there any certainty of it, or good authority for it. 2. What kind of death he suffered: he was slain *with the sword,* that is, his head was *cut off with a sword,* which was looked upon by the Romans to be a more disgraceful way of being beheaded than with an axe; so Lorinus. Beheading was not ordinarily used among the Jews; but, when kings gave verbal orders for private and sudden executions, this manner of death was used, as most expeditious; and it is probable that this Herod killed James, as the other Herod killed John Baptist, privately *in the prison.* It is strange that we have not a more full and particular account of the martyrdom of this great apostle, as we had of Stephen. But even this short mention of the thing is sufficient to let us know that the first preachers of the gospel were so well assured of the truth of it that they sealed it with their blood, and thereby have encouraged us, if at any time we are called to it, *to resist unto blood too.* The Old-Testament martyrs were *slain with the sword* (Heb. xi. 37), and Christ *came not to send peace, but a sword* (Matt. x. 34), in preparation for which we must arm ourselves *with the sword of the Spirit,* which is the word of God, and then we need not fear *what* the sword of *men can do unto us.*

III. He imprisoned Peter, of whom he had heard most, as making the greatest figure among the apostles and whom therefore he would be proud of the honour of taking off. Observe here, 1. When he had beheaded James, *he proceeded further,* he added, *to take Peter also.* Note, Blood to the bloodthirsty does but make them more so, and the way of persecution, as of other sins, is downhill; when men are in it, they cannot easily stop themselves; when they are in they find they must on. *Male facta male factis tegere ne perpluant—One evil deed is covered with another, so that there is no passage through them.* Those that take one bold step in a sinful way give Satan advantage against them to tempt them to take another, and provoke God to leave them to themselves, to go from bad to worse. It is therefore our wisdom to take heed of the beginnings of sin. 2. He did this *because he saw it pleased the Jews.* Observe, The Jews made themselves guilty of the blood of James by showing themselves well pleased with it afterwards, though they had not excited Herod to it. There are accessaries *ex post facto—after the fact;* and those will be reckoned with as persecutors who take pleasure in others' persecuting, who delight to see good men ill used, and cry, *Aha, so would we have it,* or at least secretly approve of it. For bloody persecutors, when they perceive themselves applauded for that which every one ought to cry shame upon them for, are encouraged to go on, and have their hands strengthened and their hearts hardened, and the checks of their own consciences smothered; nay, it is as strong a temptation to them to do the like as it was here to Herod, *because he saw it pleased the Jews.* Though he had no reason to fear displeasing them if he did not, as Pilate condemned Christ, yet he hoped to please them by doing it, and so to make an interest among them, and make amends for displeasing them in something else. Note, Those make themselves an easy prey to Satan who make it their business to please men. 3. Notice is taken of the time when Herod laid hold on Peter: *Then were the days of unleavened bread.* It was at the feast of the passover, when their celebrating the memorial of their typical deliverance should have led them to the acceptance of their spiritual deliverance; instead of this, they, under pretence of zeal for the law, were most violently fighting against it, and, in *the days of unleavened bread,* were most soured and embittered *with the old leaven of malice and wickedness.* At the passover, when *the Jews came from all parts to Jerusalem to keep the feast,* they irritated one another against the Christians and Christianity, and were then more violent than at other times. 4. Here is an account of Peter's imprisonment (*v.* 4): *When he* had laid hands on him, and, it is likely, examined him, *he put him in prison,* into the inner prison; some say, into the same prison into which he and the other apostles were cast some years before, and were rescued out of it by an angel, *ch.* v. 18. He was *delivered to four quaternions of soldiers,* that is, to sixteen, who were to be a guard upon him, four at a time, that he should not make his escape, nor be rescued by his friends. Thus they thought they had him fast. 5. Herod's design was, *after Easter, to bring him forth unto the people.* (1.) He would make a spectacle of him. Probably he had put James to death privately, which the people had complained of, not because it was an unjust thing to put a man to death without giving him a public hearing, but because it deprived them of the satisfaction of seeing him executed; and therefore Herod, now he knows their minds, will gratify them with the sight of Peter in bonds, of Peter upon the block, that they may feed their eyes with such a pleasing spectacle. And very ambitious surely he was to please the people who was willing thus to please them! (2.) He would do this *after Easter,* *μετὰ τὸ πάσχα*—*after the passover,* certainly so it ought to be read, for it is the same word that is always so rendered; and to insinuate the introducing of a gospel-feast, instead of the passover, when we have nothing in the New Testament of such a thing, is to mingle Judaism with our Christianity. Herod would not condemn him till the passover was over, some think, for fear lest he should have such an interest among the people that they should demand the release of him, according to the custom of the feast: or, after the hurry of the feast was over, and the town was empty, he would entertain them with Peter's public trial and execution. Thus was the plot laid, and both Herod and the people long to have the feast over, that they may gratify themselves with this barbarous entertainment.

5 Peter therefore was kept in
prison: but prayer was made without
ceasing of the church unto God for
him. 6 And when Herod would
have brought him forth, the same
night Peter was sleeping between
two soldiers, bound with two chains:
and the keepers before the door kept
the prison. 7 And, behold, the angel
of the Lord came upon *him,* and a
light shined in the prison: and he
smote Peter on the side, and raised
him up, saying, Arise up quickly.
And his chains fell off from *his*
hands. 8 And the angel said unto
him, Gird thyself, and bind on thy
sandals. And so he did. And he
saith unto him, Cast thy garment
about thee, and follow me. 9 And
he went out, and followed him; and
wist not that it was true which was
done by the angel; but thought he
saw a vision. 10 When they were
past the first and the second ward,
they came unto the iron gate that
leadeth unto the city; which opened
to them of his own accord: and they
went out, and passed on through one
street; and forthwith the angel departed from him. 11 And when
Peter was come to himself, he said,
Now I know of a surety, that the
Lord hath sent his angel, and hath
delivered me out of the hand of
Herod, and *from* all the expectation
of the people of the Jews. 12 And
when he had considered *the thing,*
he came to the house of Mary the
mother of John, whose surname was
Mark; where many were gathered
together praying. 13 And as Peter
knocked at the door of the gate, a
damsel came to hearken, named
Rhoda. 14 And when she knew
Peter's voice, she opened not the
gate for gladness, but ran in, and
told how Peter stood before the gate.
15 And they said unto her, Thou art
mad. But she constantly affirmed
that it was even so. Then said they,
It is his angel. 16 But Peter continued knocking: and when they had
opened *the door,* and saw him, they
were astonished. 17 But he, beckoning unto them with the hand to
hold their peace, declared unto them
how the Lord had brought him out
of the prison. And he said, Go show
these things unto James, and to the
brethren. And he departed, and
went into another place. 18 Now
as soon as it was day, there was no
small stir among the soldiers, what
was become of Peter. 19 And when
Herod had sought for him, and
found him not, he examined the
keepers, and commanded that *they*
should be put to death. And he
went down from Judæa to Cæsarea,
and *there* abode.

We have here an account of Peter's deliverance out of prison, by which the design of Herod against him was defeated, and his life preserved for further service, and a stop given to this bloody torrent. Now,

I. One thing that magnified his deliverance was that it was a signal answer to prayer (*v.* 5): *Peter was kept in prison* with a great deal of care, so that it was altogether impossible, either by force or by stealth, to get him out. *But prayer was made without ceasing of the church unto God for him,* for prayers and tears are the church's arms; therewith she fights, not only against her enemies, but for her friends: and to these means they have recourse. 1. The delay of Peter's trial gave them time for prayer. It is probable that James was hurried off so suddenly and so privately that they had not time to pray for him, God so ordering it that they should not have space to pray, when he designed they should not have the thing they prayed for. James must be offered upon the sacrifice and service of their faith, and therefore prayer for him is restrained and prevented; but Peter must be continued to them, and therefore prayer for him is stirred up, and time is given them for it, by Herod's putting off the prosecution. *Howbeit, he meant not so, neither did his heart think so.* 2. They were very particular in their prayers for him, that it would please God, some way or other, to defeat Herod's purpose, and to snatch the lamb out of the jaws of the lion. The death of James alarmed them to a greater fervency in their prayer for Peter; for, if they be broken thus with breach upon breach, they fear that the enemy will make a full end. Stephen is not, and James is not, and will they take Peter also? All these things are against them; this will be sorrow upon sorrow, Phil. ii. 27. Note, Though the death and sufferings of Christ's ministers may be made greatly to serve the interests of Christ's kingdom, yet it is the duty and concern of the church earnestly to pray for their life, liberty, and tranquillity; and sometimes Providence orders it that they are brought into imminent danger, to stir up prayer for them. 3. *Prayer was made without ceasing;* it was, προσευχὴ ἐκτενὴς—*fervent prayer.* It is the word that is used concerning Christ's praying in his agony *more earnestly;* it is *the fervent prayer of the righteous man, that* is effectual, and *availeth much.* Some think it denotes the constancy and continuance of their prayers; so we take it: *They prayed without ceasing.* It was an extended prayer; they prayed for his release in their public assemblies (private ones, perhaps, *for fear of the Jews);* then they went home, and prayed for it in their families; then retired into their closets, and prayed for it there; so *they prayed without ceasing:* or first one knot of them, and then another, and then a third, kept a day of prayer, or rather a night of prayer, for him, *v.* 12. Note, Times of public distress and danger should be praying times with the church; we must pray always, but then especially.

II. Another thing that magnified his deliverance was that *when the king's commandment and decree drew near to be put in execution,* then his deliverance was wrought, as Esth. ix. 1, 2. Let us observe when his deliverance came. 1. It was the very night before Herod designed to bring him forth, which made it to be so much the greater consolation to his friends and confusion to his enemies. It is probable some who had an interest in Herod, or those about him, had been improving it to get a discharge for Peter, but in vain; Herod resolves he shall die. And now they despair of prevailing in this way, for to-morrow is *the day set for the bringing of him forth;* and, it is likely, they will make as quick work with him as with his Master; and now God opened a door of escape for him. Note, God's time to help is when things are brought to the last extremity, when there is none shut up nor left (Deut. xxxii. 36), and for this reason it has been said, "The worse the better." When Isaac is bound upon the altar, and the knife in the hand, and the hand stretched out to slay him, then *Jehovah-jireh, the Lord will provide.* 2. It was when he was *fast bound with two chains, between two soldiers;* so that if he offer to stir he wakes them; and, besides this, though the prison-doors, no doubt, were locked and bolted, yet, to make sure work, *the keepers before the door kept the prison,* that no one might so much as attempt to rescue him. Never could the art of man do more to secure a prisoner. Herod, no doubt, said, as Pilate (Matt. xxvii. 65), *Make it as sure as you can.* When men will think to be too hard for God, God will make it appear that he is too hard for them. 3. It was when he was *sleeping between the soldiers,* fast asleep; (1.) Not terrified with his danger, though it was very imminent, and there was no visible way for his escape. There was but a step between him and death, and yet he could lay himself down in peace, and sleep—sleep in the midst of his enemies—sleep when, it may be, they were awake, having a good cause that he suffered for, and a good conscience that he suffered with, and being assured that God would issue his trial that way that should be most for his glory. Having *committed his cause to him that judgeth righteously, his soul dwells at ease;* and even in prison, between two soldiers, God gives him sleep, as he doth to his beloved. (2.) Not expecting his deliverance. He did not keep awake, looking to the right hand, or to the left, for relief, but lay asleep, and was perfectly surprised with his deliverance. Thus the church (Ps. cxxvi. 1): *We were like those that dream.*

III. It also magnified his deliverance very much that an *angel was sent from heaven* on purpose to rescue him, which made his escape both practicable and warrantable. This angel brought him a legal discharge, and enabled him to make use of it.

1. *The angel of the Lord came upon him;*

ἐπέστη—stood over him. He seemed as one abandoned by men, yet not forgotten of his God; *the Lord thinketh upon him.* Gates and guards kept all his friends from him, but could not keep the angels of God from him: and *they invisibly encamp round about those that fear God, to deliver them* (Ps. xxxiv. 7), *and therefore they need not fear, though a host of enemies encamp against them,* Ps. xxvii. 3. Wherever the people of God are, and however surrounded, they have a way open heavenward, nor can any thing intercept their intercourse with God.

2. *A light shone in the prison.* Though it is a dark place, and in the night, Peter shall see his way clear. Some observe that we do not find in the Old Testament that where angels appeared *the light shone round about them;* for that was a dark dispensation, and the glory of angels was then veiled. But in the New Testament, when mention is made of the appearing of the angels, notice is taken of the light that they appeared in; for it is by the gospel that the upper world is brought to light. The soldiers to whom Peter was chained were either struck into a deep sleep for the present (as Saul and his soldiers were when David carried off his spear and cruise of water), or, if they were awake, the appearance of the angel made them to *shake, and to become as dead men,* as it was with the guard set on Christ's sepulchre.

3. The angel awoke Peter, by giving him *a blow on his side,* a gentle touch, enough to rouse him out of his sleep, though so fast asleep that the light that shone upon him did not awaken him. When good people slumber in a time of danger, and are not awakened by the light of the word, and the discoveries it gives them, let them expect to be smitten on the side by some sharp affliction; better be raised up so than left asleep. The language of this stroke was, *Arise up quickly;* not as if the angel feared coming short by his delay, but Peter must not be indulged in it. When David hears *the sound of the going on the tops of the mulberry trees, then he must rise up quickly, and bestir himself.*

4. *His chains fell off from his hands.* It seems they had handcuffed him, to make him sure, but *God loosed his bands;* and, if they fall off from his hands, it is as well as if he had the strength of Samson to break them like threads of tow. Tradition makes a mighty rout about these chains, and tells a formal story that one of the soldiers kept them for a sacred relic, and they were long after presented to Eudoxia the empress, and I know not what miracles are said to have been wrought by them; and the Romish church keeps a feast on the first of August yearly in remembrance of Peter's chains, *Festum vinculorum Petri—The feast of Peter's chains;* whereas this was at the passover. Surely they are thus fond of Peter's chains in hopes with them to enslave the world!

5. He was ordered to dress himself immediately, and follow the angel; and he did so, *v.* 8, 9. When Peter was awake he knew not what to do but as the angel directed him. (1.) He must *gird himself;* for those that slept in their clothes ungirded themselves, so that they had nothing to do, when they got up, but to fasten their girdles. (2.) He *must bind on his sandals,* that he might be fit to walk. Those whose bonds are loosed by the power of divine grace must have *their feet shod with the preparation of the gospel of peace.* (3.) He must *cast his garments about him,* and come away as he was, and follow the angel; and he might go with a great deal of courage and cheerfulness who had a messenger from heaven for his guide and guard. He *went out, and followed him.* Those who are delivered out of a spiritual imprisonment must follow their deliverer, as Israel when they went out of the house of bondage did; they *went out, not knowing whither they went,* but whom they followed. Now it is said, when Peter went out after the angel, *he knew not that it was true which was done by the angel,* that it was really matter of fact, *but thought he saw a vision;* and, if he did, it was not the first he had seen: but by this it appears that a heavenly vision was so plain, and carried so much of its own evidence along with it, that it was difficult to distinguish between what was done in fact and what was done in vision. *When the Lord brought back the captivity of his people we were like those that dream,* Ps. cxxvi. 1. Peter was so; he thought the news was too good to be true.

6. He was led safely by the angel out of danger, *v.* 10. Guards were kept at one pass and at another, which they were to make their way through when they were out of the prison, and they did so without any opposition; nay, for aught that appears, without any discovery: either their eyes were closed, or their hands were tied, or their hearts failed them; so it was that the angel and Peter safely *passed the first and second ward.* Those watchmen represented the watchmen of the Jewish church, on whom God had *poured out a spirit of slumber, eyes that they should not see and ears that they should not hear,* Rom. xi. 8. His *watchmen are blind, sleeping, lying down, and loving to slumber.* But still there is an iron gate, after all, that will stop them, and, if the guards can but recover themselves, there they may recover their prisoner, as Pharaoh hoped to retake Israel at the Red Sea. However, up to that gate they march, and, like the Red Sea before Israel, it *opened to them.* They did not so much as put a hand to it, but it opened *of its own accord,* by an invisible power; and thus was fulfilled in the letter what was figuratively promised to Cyrus (Isa. xlv. 1, 2): *I will open before him the two-leaved gates, will break in pieces the gates of brass, and cut in sunder the bars of iron.* And probably the iron gate shut again of itself, that none of the guards might pursue Peter. Note, When God will work

salvation for his people, no difficulties in their way are insuperable; but even gates of iron are made to open of their own accord. This iron gate led him into the city out of the castle or tower; whether within the gates of the city or without is not certain, so that, when they were through this, they were got into the street. This deliverance of Peter represents to us our redemption by Christ, which is often spoken of as the setting of prisoners free, not only the proclaiming of liberty to the captives, but the *bringing of them out of the prison-house.* The application of the redemption in the conversion of souls is the *sending forth of the prisoners, by the blood of the covenant, out of the pit wherein is no water,* Zech. ix. 11. The grace of God, like this angel of the Lord, brings light first into the prison, by the opening of the understanding, smites the sleeping sinner on the side by the awakening of the conscience, causes the chains to fall off from the hands by the renewing of the will, and then gives the word of command, *Gird thyself, and follow me.* Difficulties are to be passed through, and the opposition of Satan and his instruments, a first and second ward, an untoward generation, from which we are concerned to save ourselves; and we shall be saved by the grace of God, if we put ourselves under the divine conduct. And at length the iron gate shall be opened to us, to enter into the New Jerusalem, where we shall be perfectly freed from all the marks of our captivity, and brought into the *glorious liberty of the children of God.*

7. When this was done, *the angel departed from him,* and left him to himself. He was out of danger from his enemies, and needed no guard. He knew where he was, and how to find out his friends, and needed no guide, and therefore his heavenly guard and guide bids him farewell. Note, Miracles are not to be expected when ordinary means are to be used. When Peter has now no more wards to pass, nor iron gates to get through, he needs only the ordinary invisible ministration of the angels, who encamp round about those that fear God, and deliver them.

IV. Having seen how his deliverance was magnified, we are next to see how it was manifested both to himself and others, and how, being made great, it was made known. We are here told,

1. How Peter came to himself, and so came himself to the knowledge of it, *v.* 11. So many strange and surprising things coming together upon a man just awoke out of sleep put him for the present into some confusion; so that he knew not where he was, nor what he did, nor whether it was fancy or fact; but at length Peter *came to himself,* was thoroughly awake, and found that it was not a dream, but a real thing: "*Now I know of a surety,* now I know ἀληθῶς—*truly,* now I know that it is truth, and not an illusion of the fancy. Now I am well satisfied concerning it *that the Lord Jesus hath sent his angel,* for angels are subject to him and go on his errands, and by him *hath delivered me out of the hands of Herod,* who thought he had me fast, and so hath disappointed *all the expectation of the people of the Jews,* who doubted not to see Peter cut off the next day, and hoped it was the one neck of Christianity, in which it would all be struck off at one blow." For this reason it was a cause of great expectation, among not only the common people, but the great people of the Jews. Peter, when he recollected himself, *perceived of a truth* what great things God had done for him, which at first he could not believe for joy. Thus souls who are delivered out of a spiritual bondage are not at first aware what God has wrought in them. Many have the truth of grace that want the evidence of it. They are questioning whether there be indeed this change wrought in them, or whether they have not been all this while in a dream. But *when the Comforter comes, whom the Father will send* sooner or later, he will let them know of a surety what a blessed change is wrought in them, and what a happy state they are brought into.

2. How Peter came to his friends, and brought the knowledge of it to them. Here is a particular account of this, and it is very interesting.

(1.) He *considered the thing* (*v.* 12), considered how imminent his danger was, how great his deliverance; and now what has he to do? What improvement must he make of this deliverance? What must he do next? God's providence leaves room for the use of our prudence; and, though he has undertaken to perform and perfect what he has begun, yet he expects we should consider the thing.

(2.) He went directly to a friend's house, which, it is likely, lay near to the place where he was; it was the house of Mary, a sister of Barnabas, and mother of John Mark, whose house, it should seem, was frequently made use of for the private meeting of the disciples, either because it was large, and would hold many, or because it lay obscure, or because she was more forward than others were to open her doors to them; and, no doubt, it was, like the house of Obededom, blessed for the ark's sake. A church in the house makes it a little sanctuary.

(3.) There he found *many* that were *gathered together praying,* at the dead time of the night, praying for Peter, who was the next day to come upon his trial, that God would find out some way or other for his deliverance. Observe, [1.] They continued in prayer, in token of their importunity; they did not think it enough once to have presented his case to God, but they did it again and again. Thus *men ought always to pray, and not to faint.* As long as we are kept waiting for a mercy we must continue praying for it. [2.] It should seem that now when the affair came near to a crisis, and the very next day was fixed for the determining of it, they were more fervent in prayer than before; and it was a good sign that God intended to deliver Peter when he thus stirred up a spirit of prayer for his deliverance, for he never *said to the seed of Jacob, Seek ye my face in vain.* [3.] They gathered together for prayer on this occasion; though this would make them obnoxious to the government if they were discovered, yet they know what an encouragement Christ gave to joint-prayer, Matt. xviii. 19, 20. And it was always the practice of God's praying people to unite their forces in prayer, as 2 Chron. xx. 4; Esth. iv. 16. [4.] They were many that were got together for this work, as many perhaps as the room would hold; and first one prayed, and then another, of those who gave themselves to the word and prayer, the rest joining with them; or, if they had not ministers among them, no doubt but there were many private Christians that knew how to pray, and to pray pertinently, and to continue long in prayer when the affections of those who joined were so stirred as to keep pace with them upon such an occasion. This was in the night, when others were asleep, which was an instance both of their prudence and of their zeal. Note, It is good for Christians to have private meetings for prayer, especially in times of distress, and not to let fall nor forsake such assemblies. [5.] Peter came to them when they were thus employed, which was an immediate present answer to their prayer. It was as if God should say, "You are praying that Peter may be restored to you; now here he is." *While they are yet speaking, I will hear,* Isa. lxv. 24. Thus the angel was sent with an answer of peace to Daniel's prayer, *while he was praying,* Dan ix. 20, 21. *Ask, and it shall be given.*

(4.) He knocked at the gate, and had much ado to get them to let him in (*v.* 13—16): *Peter knocked at the door of the gate,* designing by it to awaken them out of their sleep, and, for aught that appears, not knowing that he disturbed them in their devotions. Yet, if his friends were permitted to speak with him in private in the prison, it is possible he might know of this appointment, and it was this which he recollected and considered when he determined to go to that house, where he knew he should find many of his friends together. Now when he knocked there, [1.] A *damsel came to hearken;* not to open the door till she knew who was there, a friend or a foe, and what their business was, fearing informers. Whether this damsel was one of the family or one of the church, whether a servant or a daughter, does not appear; it should seem, by her being named, that she was of note among the Christians, and more zealously affected to the better part than most of her age. [2.] She knew Peter's voice, having often heard him pray, and preach, and discourse, with a great deal of pleasure. But, instead of letting him in immediately out of the cold, *she opened not the gate for gladness.* Thus sometimes, in a transport of affection to our friends, we do that which is unkind. In an ecstasy of joy she forgets herself, and *opened not the gate.* [3.] She ran in, and probably went up to an upper room where they were together, and told them that Peter was certainly at the gate, though she had not courage enough to open the gate, for fear she should be deceived, and it should be the enemy. But, when she spoke of Peter's being there, they said, "*Thou art mad;* it is impossible it should be he, for he is in prison." Sometimes that which we most earnestly wish for we are most backward to believe, because we are afraid of imposing upon ourselves, as the disciples, who, when Christ had risen, *believed not for joy.* However, she stood to it that it was he. Then said they, *It is his angel, v.* 15. *First,* "It is a *messenger* from him, that makes use of his name;" so some take it; ἄγγελος often signifies no more than *a messenger.* It is used of John's messengers (Luke vii. 24, 27), of Christ's, Luke ix. 52. When the damsel was confident it was Peter, because she knew his voice, they thought it was because he that stood at the door had called himself Peter, and therefore offer this solution of the difficulty, "It is one that comes with an errand from him, and thou didst mistake as if it had been he himself." Dr. Hammond thinks this the easiest way of understanding it. *Secondly,* "It is his *guardian angel,* or some other angel that has assumed his shape and voice, and stands at the gate in his resemblance." Some think that they supposed his angel to appear as a presage of his death approaching; and this agrees with a notion which the vulgar have, that sometimes before persons have died *their ward has been seen,* that is, some spirit exactly in their likeness for countenance and dress, when they themselves have been at the same time in some other place; they call it their *ward,* that is, their angel, who is their guard. If so, they concluded this an ill omen, that their prayers were denied, and that the language of the apparition was, "Let it suffice you, Peter must die, say no more of that matter." And, if we understand it so, it only proves that they had then such an opinion of a man's *ward* being seen a little before his death, but does not prove that there is such a thing. Others think they took this to be an angel from heaven, sent to bring them a grant to their prayers. But why should they imagine that angel to assume the voice and shape of Peter, when we find not any thing like it in the appearance of angels? Perhaps they herein spoke the language of the Jews, who had a fond conceit that every good man has a particular tutelar angel, that has the charge of him, and sometimes personates him. The heathen called it a *good genius,* that attended a man; but, since no other scripture speaks of such a thing, this alone is too weak to bear the weight of such a doctrine. We are sure that the angels are *ministering spirits* for the good of *the heirs of salvation*, that they have a *charge concerning them*, and *pitch their tents round about them;* and we need not be solicitous that every particular saint should have his guardian angel, when we are assured he has a guard of angels.

(5.) At length they let him in (*v.* 16): *He continued knocking* though they delayed to open to him, and at last they admitted him. The iron gate which opposed his enlargement opened of itself, without so much as once knocking at it; but the door of his friend's house that was to welcome him does not open of its own accord, but must be knocked at, long knocked at; lest Peter should be puffed up by the honours which the angel did him, he meets with this mortification, by a seeming slight which his friends put upon him. But, *when they saw him, they were astonished,* were filled with wonder and joy in him, as much as they were but just now with sorrow and fear concerning him. It was both surprising and pleasing to them in the highest degree.

(6.) Peter gave them an account of his deliverance. When he came to the company that were gathered together with so much zeal to pray for him, they gathered about him with no less zeal to congratulate him on his deliverance; and herein they were so noisy that when Peter himself begged them to consider what peril he was yet in, if they should be overheard, he could not make them hear him, but was forced to *beckon to them with the hand to hold their peace,* and had much ado thereby to command silence, while *he declared unto them how the Lord Jesus had* by an angel *brought him out of prison;* and it is very likely, having found them praying for his deliverance, he did not part with them till he and they had together solemnly given thanks to God for his enlargement; or, if he could not stay to do it, it is probable they staid together to do it; for what is won by prayer must be worn with praise; and God must always have the glory of that which we have the comfort of. When David declares *what God had done for his soul,* he blesses God who had not turned away his prayer, Ps. lxvi. 16, 20.

(7.) Peter sent the account to others of his friends: *Go, show these things to James, and to the brethren with him,* who perhaps were met together in another place at the same time, upon the same errand to the throne of grace, which is one way of keeping up the communion of saints and wrestling with God in prayer—acting in concert, though at a distance, like Esther and Mordecai. He would have James and his company to know of his deliverance, not only that they might be eased of their pain and delivered from their fears concerning Peter, but that they might return thanks to God with him and for him. Observe, Though Herod had slain one James with the sword, yet here was another James, and that in Jerusalem too, that stood up in his room to preside among the brethren there; for, when God has work to do, he will never want instruments to do it with.

(8.) Peter had nothing more to do for the present than to shift for his own safety, which he did accordingly: He *departed, and went into another place more obscure,* and therefore more safe. He knew the town very well, and knew where to find a place that would be a shelter to him. Note, Even the Christian law of self-denial and suffering for Christ has not abrogated and repealed the natural law of self-preservation, and care for our own safety, as far as God gives an opportunity of providing for it by lawful means.

V. Having seen the triumph of Peter's friends in his deliverance, let us next observe the confusion of his enemies thereupon, which was so much the greater because people's expectation was so much raised of the putting of him to death. 1. The guards were in the utmost consternation upon it, for they knew how highly penal it was to them to let a prisoner escape that they had charge of (*v.* 18): *As soon as it was day,* and they found the prisoner gone, there was *no small stir or strife,* as some read it, *among the soldiers, what had become of Peter;* he is gone, and nobody knows how or which way. They thought themselves as sure as could be of him but last night; yet now the bird is flown, and they can hear no tale nor tidings of him. This set them together by the ears; one says, "It was your fault;" the other, "Nay, but it was yours;" having no other way to clear themselves, but by accusing one another. With us, if but a prisoner for debt escape, the sheriff must answer for the debt. Thus have the persecutors of the gospel of Christ been often filled with vexation to see its cause conquering, notwithstanding the opposition they have given to it. 2. Houses were searched in vain for the rescued prisoner (*v.* 19): *Herod sought for him, and found him not.* Who can find whom God hath hidden? Baruch and Jeremiah are safe, though searched for, because *the Lord has hidden them,* Jer. xxxvi. 26. In times of public danger, all believers have God for *their hiding-place,* which is such a secret, that there the ignorant world cannot find them; such a strength, that the impotent world cannot reach them. 3. The keepers were reckoned with for a permissive escape: *Herod examined the keepers,* and finding that they could give no satisfactory account how Peter got away, *he commanded that they should be put to death,* according to the Roman law, and that 1 Kings xx. 39, *If by any means he be missing, then shall thy life go for his life.* It is probable that these keepers had been more severe with Peter than they needed to be (as the jailor, *ch.* xvi. 24), and had been abusive to him, and to others that had been their prisoners upon the like account; and now justly are they put to death for that which was not their fault, and by him too that had set them to work to *vex the church.* When the wicked are thus snared in the work of their own hands, the Lord is known by the judgments which he executes. Or, if they had not thus made themselves obnoxious to the justice of God, and it be thought hard that innocent men should suffer thus for that which was purely the act of God, we may easily admit the conjectures of some, that though they were *commanded to be put to death,* to please the Jews, who were sadly disappointed by Peter's escape, yet they were not executed; but Herod's death, immediately after, prevented it. 4. Herod himself retired upon it: *He went down from Judea to Cesarea, and there abode.* He was vexed to the heart, as a lion disappointed of his prey; and the more because he had so much raised the *expectation of the people of the Jews* concerning Peter, had told them how he would very shortly gratify them with the sight of Peter's head in a charger, which would oblige them as much as John Baptist's did Herodias; it made him ashamed to be robbed of this boasting, and to see himself, notwithstanding his confidence, disabled to make his words good. This is such a mortification to his proud spirit that he cannot bear to stay in Judea, but away he goes to Cesarea. Josephus mentions this coming of Herod to Cesarea, at the end of the third year of his reign over all Judea (*Antiquit.* xix. 7), and says, he came thither to solemnize the plays that were kept there, by a vast concourse of the nobility and gentry of the kingdom, for the health of Cæsar, and in honour of him.

20 And Herod was highly displeased with them of Tyre and Sidon:
but they came with one accord to
him, and, having made Blastus the
king's chamberlain their friend, desired peace; because their country
was nourished by the king's *country.*
21 And upon a set day Herod, arrayed in royal apparel, sat upon his
throne, and made an oration unto
them. 22 And the people gave a
shout, *saying, It is* the voice of a
god, and not of a man. 23 And
immediately the angel of the Lord
smote him, because he gave not God
the glory: and he was eaten of
worms, and gave up the ghost. 24
But the word of God grew and multiplied. 25 And Barnabas and Saul
returned from Jerusalem, when they
had fulfilled *their* ministry, and took
with them John, whose surname
was Mark.

In these verses we have,

I. The death of Herod. God reckoned with him, not only for his putting James to death, but for his design and endeavour to put Peter to death; for sinners will be called to an account, not only for the wickedness of their deeds, but for the wickedness of their endeavours (Ps. xxviii. 4), for the mischief they have done and the mischief they would have done. It was but a little while that Herod lived after this. Some sinners God makes quick work with. Observe,

1. How the measure of his iniquity was filled up: it was *pride* that did it; it is this that commonly goes more immediately *before destruction,* and a *haughty spirit before a fall.* Nebuchadnezzar had been a very bloody man, and a great persecutor; but the word that was in the king's mouth when the judgments of God fell upon him was a proud word: *Is not this great Babylon that I have built?* Dan. iv. 30, 31. It is the glory of God to *look on every one that is proud, and bring him low,* Job xl. 12. The instance of it here is very remarkable, and shows how God *resists the proud*

(1.) The men of Tyre and Sidon had, it seems, offended Herod. Those cities were now under the Roman yoke, and they had been guilty of some misdemeanours which Herod highly resented, and was resolved they should feel his resentment. Some very small matter would serve such a proud imperious man as Herod was for a provocation, where he was disposed to pick a quarrel. He was highly displeased with this people, and they must be made to know that his wrath was as the *roaring of a lion, as messengers of death.*

(2.) The offenders truckled, being convinced, if not that they had done amiss, yet that it was in vain to contend with such a potent adversary, who, right or wrong, would be too hard for them; they submitted and were willing upon any terms to *make peace with him.* Observe, [1.] The reason why they were desirous to have the matter accommodated: *Because their country was nourished by the king's country.* Tyre and Sidon were trading cities, and had little land belonging to them, but were always supplied with corn from the land of Canaan; *Judah and Israel traded in their market, with wheat, and honey, and oil,* Ezek. xxvii. 17. Now if Herod should make a law to prohibit the exportation of corn to Tyre and Sidon (which they knew not but a man so revengeful as he might soon do, not caring how many were famished by it), their country would be undone; so that it was their interest to keep in with him. And is it not then our wisdom to make our peace with God, and humble ourselves before him, who have a much more constant and necessary dependence upon him than one country can have upon another? for *in him we live, and move, and have our being.* [2.] The method they took to prevent a rupture: *They made Blastus the king's chamberlain their friend*, probably with bribes and good presents; that is usually the way for men to make courtiers their friends. And it is the hard fate of princes that they must have not only their affairs, but their affections too, governed by such mercenary tools; yet such men as Herod, that will not be governed by reason, had better be so governed than by pride and passion. Blastus had Herod's ear, and has the art of mollifying his resentments; and a time is fixed for the ambassadors of Tyre and Sidon to come and make a public submission, to beg his majesty's pardon, throw themselves upon his clemency, and promise never again to offend in the like manner; and that which will thus feed his pride shall serve to cool his passion.

(3.) Herod appeared in all the pomp and grandeur he had: He was *arrayed in his royal apparel* (*v.* 21), *and sat upon his throne.* Josephus gives an account of this splendid appearance which Herod made upon this occasion.—*Antiquit.* lib. xix. cap. 7. He says that Herod at this time wore a robe of cloth of silver, so richly woven, and framed with such art, that when the sun shone it reflected the light with such a lustre as dazzled the eyes of the spectators, and struck an awe upon them. Foolish people value men by their outward appearance; and no better are those who value themselves by the esteem of such, who court it, and recommend themselves to it as Herod did, who thought to make up the want of a royal heart with his *royal apparel; and sat upon his throne*, as if that gave him a privilege to trample upon all about him as his footstool.

(4.) He made a speech to the men of Tyre and Sidon, a fine oration, in which, probably, after he had aggravated their fault, and commended their submission, he concluded with an assurance that he would pass by their offence and receive them into his favour again —proud enough that he had it in his power *whom he would to keep alive*, as well as *whom he would to slay;* and probably he kept them in suspense as to what their doom should be, till he made this oration to them, that the act of grace might come to them with the more pleasing surprise.

(5.) The people applauded him, the people that had a dependence upon him, and had benefit by his favour, they *gave a shout;* and this was what they shouted, *It is the voice of a god, and not of a man*, *v.* 22. God is great and good, and they thought such was Herod's greatness in his apparel and throne, and such his goodness in forgiving them, that he was worthy to be called no less than a god; and perhaps his speech was delivered with such an air of majesty, and a mixture of clemency with it, as affected the auditors thus. Or, it may be, it was not from any real impression made upon their minds, or any high or good thoughts they had indeed conceived of him; but, how meanly soever they thought of him, they were resolved thus to curry favour with him, and strengthen the new-made peace between him and them. Thus great men are made an easy prey to flatterers if they lend an ear to them, and encourage them. Grotius here observes that, though magistrates are called *gods* (Ps. lxxxii. 1), yet *kings or monarchs, that is, single persons, are not, lest countenance should thereby be given to the Gentiles, who gave divine honours to their kings alive and dead, as here; but they are a college of senators, or a bench of judges, that are called gods.—In collegio toto senatorum non idem erat periculi; itaque eos, non autem reges, invenimus dictos elohim.* Those that live by sense vilify God, as if he were *altogether such a one as themselves*, and deify men, as if they were gods; having *their persons in admiration, because of advantage.* This is not only a great affront to God, giving that glory to others which is due to him alone, but a great injury to those who are thus flattered, as it makes them forget themselves, and so puffs them up with pride that they are in the utmost danger possible of falling into the condemnation of the devil.

(6.) These undue praises he took to himself, pleased himself with them, and prided himself in them; and this was his sin. We do not find that he had given any private orders to his confidants to begin such a shout, or to put those words into the mouths of the people, nor that he returned them thanks for the compliment and undertook to answer their opinion of him. But his fault was that he said nothing, did not rebuke their flattery, nor disown the title they had given him, nor *give God the glory* (*v.* 23); but he took it to himself, was very willing it should terminate in himself, and that he should be thought a god and have divine honours paid him. *Si populus vult decipi, decipiatur—If the people will be deceived, let them.* And it was worse in him who was a Jew, and professed to believe in one God only, than it was in the heathen emperors, who had gods many and lords many.

2. How his iniquity was punished: *Immediately* (*v.* 23) *the angel of the Lord smote him* (by the order of Christ, for to him all judgment is committed), *because he gave not God the glory* (for God is jealous for his own honour, and will be glorified upon those whom he is not glorified by); and *he was eaten of worms* above ground, *and gave up the ghost.* Now he was reckoned with for vexing the church of Christ, killing James, imprisoning Peter, and all the other mischiefs he had done. Observe in the destruction of Herod,

(1.) It was no less than an angel that was the agent—*the angel of the Lord*, that angel that was ordered and commissioned to do it, or that angel that used to be employed in works of this nature, the destroying angel: or *the angel*, that is, that angel that delivered Peter in the former part of the chapter—that angel smote Herod. For those ministering spirits are the ministers either of divine justice or of divine mercy, as God is pleased to employ them. The angel smote him with a sore disease just at that instant when he was strutting at the applauses of the people, and adoring his own shadow. Thus the king of Tyre said in his pride, *I am a god, I sit in the seat of God; and set his heart as the heart of God;* but he shall be *a man, and no God,* a weak mortal man, *in the hand of him that slayeth him* (Ezek. xxviii. 2—9), so Herod here. Potent princes must know, not only that God is omnipotent, but that angels too are greater in power and might than they. The angel *smote him, because he gave not the glory to God;* angels are jealous for God's honour, and as soon as ever they have commission are ready to smite those that usurp his prerogatives, and rob God of his honour.

(2.) It was no more than a worm that was the instrument of Herod's destruction: He was *eaten of worms,* γενόμενος σκωληκόβρωτος—*he became worm-eaten,* so it must be read; rotten he was, and he became like a piece of rotten wood. The body in the grave is destroyed by worms, but Herod's body putrefied while he was yet alive, and bred the worms which began to feed upon it betimes; so Antiochus, that great persecutor, died. See here, [1.] What vile bodies those are which we carry about with us; they carry about with them the seeds of their own dissolution, by which they will soon be destroyed whenever God does but speak the word. Surprising discoveries have of late been made by microscopes of the multitude of worms that there are in human bodies, and how much they contribute to the diseases of them, which is a good reason why we should not be proud of our bodies, or of any of their accomplishments, and why we should not pamper our bodies, for this is but feeding the worms, and feeding them for the worms. [2.] See what weak and contemptible creatures God can make the instruments of his justice, when he pleases. Pharaoh is plagued with lice and flies, Ephraim consumed as with a moth, and Herod eaten with worms. [3.] See how God delights not only to bring down proud men, but to bring them down in such a way as is most mortifying, and pours most contempt upon them. Herod is not only destroyed, but destroyed by worms, that the pride of his glory may be effectually stained. This story of the death of Herod is particularly related by Josephus, a Jew, *Antiquit.* lib. xix. cap. 7, thus: "That Herod came down to Cesarea, to celebrate a festival in honour of Cæsar; that the second day of the festival he went in the morning to the theatre, clothed with that splendid robe mentioned before; that his flatterers saluted him as a god, begged that he would be propitious to them; that hitherto they had reverenced him as a man, but now they would confess to be in him something more excellent than a mortal nature. That he did not refuse nor correct this impious flattery (so the historian expresses it); but, presently after, looking up, he saw an owl perched over his head, and was at the same instant seized with a most violent pain in his bowels, and gripes in his belly, which were exquisite from the very first; that he turned his eyes upon his friends, and said to this purpose: 'Now I, whom you called a god, and therefore immortal, must be proved a man, and mortal.' That his torture continued without intermission, or the least abatement, and then he died in the fifty-fourth year of his age, when he had been king seven years."

II. The progress of the gospel after this. 1. *The word of God grew and multiplied,* as seed sown, which comes up with a great increase, thirty, sixty, a hundred fold; wherever the gospel was preached, multitudes embraced it, and were added to the church by it, *v.* 24. After the death of James, the word of God grew; for the church, the more it was afflicted, the more it multiplied, like Israel in Egypt. The courage and comfort of the martyrs, and God's owning them, did more to invite people to Christianity, than their sufferings did to deter them from it. After the death of Herod the word of God gained ground. When such a persecutor was taken off by a dreadful judgment, many were thereby convinced that the cause of Christianity was doubtless the cause of Christ, and therefore embraced it. 2. Barnabas and Saul returned to Antioch as soon as they had despatched the business they were sent upon: *When they had fulfilled their ministry,* had paid in their money to the proper persons, and taken care about the due distribution of it to those for whom it was collected, they *returned from Jerusalem.* Though they had a great many friends there, yet at present their work lay at Antioch; and where our business is there we should be, and no longer from it than is requisite. When a minister is called abroad upon any service, when he has fulfilled that ministry, he ought to remember that he has work to do at home, which wants him there and calls him thither. Barnabas and Saul, when they went to *Antioch, took with them John, whose surname was Mark,* at whose mother's house they had that meeting for prayer which we read of *v.* 12. She was sister to Barnabas. It is probable that Barnabas lodged there, and perhaps Paul with him, while they were at Jerusalem, and it was that that occasioned the meeting there at that time (for wherever Paul was he would have some good work doing), and their intimacy in that family while they were at Jerusalem occasioned their taking a son of that family with them when they returned, to be trained up under them, and employed by them, in the service of the gospel. Educating young men for the ministry, and entering them into it, is a very good work for elder ministers to take care of, and of good service to the rising generation.

CHAP. XIII.

We have not yet met with any thing concerning the spreading of the gospel to the Gentiles which bears any proportion to the largeness of that commission, "Go, and disciple all nations." The door was opened in the baptizing of Cornelius and his friends; but since then we had the gospel preached to the Jews only, ch. xi. 19. It should seem as if the light which began to shine upon the Gentile world had withdrawn itself. But here in this chapter that work, that great good work, is revived in the midst of the years; and though the Jews shall still have the first offer of the gospel made to them, yet, upon their refusal, the Gentiles shall have their share of the offer of it. Here is, I. The solemn ordination of Barnabas and Saul, by divine direction, to the ministry, to the great work of spreading the gospel among the nations about (and it is probable that other apostles or apostolical men dispersed themselves by order from Christ, upon the same errand, ver. 1—3). II. Their preaching the gospel in Cyprus, and the opposition they met with there from Elymas the sorcerer, ver. 4—13. III. The heads of a sermon which Paul preached to the Jews at Antioch in Pisidia, in their synagogue, which is given us as a specimen of what they usually preached to the Jews, and the method they took with them, ver. 14—41. IV. The preaching of the gospel to the Gentiles at their request, and upon the Jews' refusal of it, wherein the apostles justified themselves against the displeasure which the Jews conceived at it, and God owned them, ver. 42—49. V. The trouble which the infidel Jews gave to the apostles, which obliged them to remove to another place (ver. 50—52), so that the design of this chapter is to show how cautiously, how gradually, and with what good reason the apostles carried the gospel into the Gentile world, and admitted the Gentiles into the church, which was so great an offence to the Jews, and which Paul is so industrious to justify in his epistles.

NOW there were in the church that was at Antioch certain prophets and teachers; as Barnabas, and Simeon that was called Niger, and Lucius of Cyrene, and Manaen, which had been brought up with Herod the tetrarch, and Saul.
2 As they ministered to the Lord, and fasted, the Holy Ghost said, Separate me Barnabas and Saul for the work whereunto I have called them.
3 And when they had fasted and prayed, and laid *their* hands on them, they sent *them* away.

We have here a divine warrant and commission to Barnabas and Saul to go and preach the gospel among the Gentiles, and their ordination to that service by the imposition of hands, with fasting and prayer.

I. Here is an account of the present state of the church at Antioch, which was planted *ch.* xi. 20.

1. How well furnished it was with good ministers; there were there *certain prophets and teachers* (*v.* 1), men that were eminent for gifts, graces, and usefulness. Christ, when he *ascended on high*, gave *some prophets and some teachers* (Eph. iv. 11); these were both. Agabus seems to have been a prophet and not a teacher, and many were teachers who were not prophets; but those here mentioned were at times divinely inspired, and had instructions immediately from heaven upon special occasions, which gave them the title of prophets; and withal they were stated teachers of the church in their religious assemblies, expounded the scriptures, and opened the doctrine of Christ with suitable applications. These were the prophets, and scribes, or teachers, which Christ promised to send (Matt. xxiii. 34), such as were every way qualified for the service of the Christian church. Antioch was a great city, and the Christians there were many, so that they could not all meet in one place; it was therefore requisite they should have many teachers, to preside in their respective assemblies, and to deliver God's mind to them. Barnabas is first named, probably because he was the eldest, and Saul last, probably because he was the youngest; but afterwards the last became first, and Saul more eminent in the church. Three others are mentioned. (1.) *Simeon*, or Simon, who for distinction-sake was called *Niger*, *Simon the Black*, from the colour of his hair; like him that with us was surnamed the Black Prince. (2.) *Lucius* of Cyrene, who some think (and Dr. Lightfoot inclines to it) was the same with this Luke that wrote the Acts, originally a Cyrenian, and educated in the Cyrenian college or synagogue at Jerusalem, and there first receiving the gospel. (3.) *Manaen*, a person of some quality, as it should seem, for he was *brought up with Herod the tetrarch*, either nursed of the same milk, or bred at the same school, or pupil to the same tutor, or rather one that was his constant colleague and companion—that in every part of his education was his comrade and intimate, which gave him a fair prospect of preferment at court, and yet for Christ's sake he quitted all the hopes of it; like Moses, who, *when he had come to years, refused to be called the son of Pharaoh's daughter*. Had he joined in with Herod, with whom he was brought up, he might have had Blastus's place, and have been his chamberlain; but it is better to be fellow-sufferer with a saint than fellow-persecutor with a tetrarch.

2. How well employed they were (*v.* 2): *They ministered to the Lord, and fasted.* Observe, (1.) Diligent faithful teachers do truly minister unto the Lord. Those that instruct Christians serve Christ; they really do him honour, and carry on the interest of his kingdom. Those that minister to the church in praying and preaching (both which are included here), *minister unto the Lord*, for they are the church's servants for Christ's sake; to him they must have an eye in their ministrations, and from him they shall have their recompence. (2.) Ministering to the Lord, in one way or other, ought to be the stated business of churches and their teachers; to this work time ought to be set apart, nay, it is set apart, and in this work we ought to spend some part of every day. What have we to do as Christians and ministers but to *serve the Lord Christ?* Col. iii. 24; Rom. xiv. 18. (3.) Religious *fasting* is of use in our ministering to the Lord, both as a sign of our humiliation and a means of our mortification. Though it was not so much practised by the disciples of Christ, *while the bridegroom was with them*, as it was by the disciples of John and of the Pharisees; yet, after the bridegroom was taken away, they abounded in it, as those that had well learned to deny themselves and to endure hardness.

II. The orders given by the Holy Ghost for the setting apart of Barnabas and Saul, while they were engaged in public exercises, the ministers of the several congregations in the city joining in one solemn fast or day of prayer: The *Holy Ghost said,* either by a voice from heaven, or by a strong impulse on the minds of those of them that were prophets, *Separate me Barnabas and Saul for the work whereunto I have called them.* He does not specify the work, but refers to a former call of which they themselves knew the meaning, whether others did or no: as for Saul, he was particularly told that he must *bear Christ's name to the Gentiles* (*ch.* ix. 15), that *he must be sent to the Gentiles* (*ch.* xxii. 21); the matter was settled between them at Jerusalem before this, that as Peter, James, and John laid out themselves among those of the circumcision, so Paul and Barnabas should *go to the heathen,* Gal. ii. 7—9. Barnabas, it is likely, knew himself designed for this service as well as Paul. Yet they would not thrust themselves into this harvest, though it appeared plenteous, till they received their orders from the Lord of the harvest: *Thrust in thy sickle for the harvest is ripe,* Rev. xiv. 15. The orders were, *Separate me Barnabas and Saul.* Observe here, 1. Christ by his Spirit has the nomination of his ministers; for it is by the Spirit of Christ that they are qualified in some measure for his services, inclined to it, and taken off from other cares inconsistent with it. There are some whom the Holy Ghost has separated for the service of Christ, has distinguished from others as men that are offered and that willingly offer themselves to the temple service; and concerning them directions are given to those who are competent judges of the sufficiency of the abilities and the sincerity of the inclination: *Separate* them. 2. Christ's ministers are separated to him and to the Holy Ghost: *Separate them to me;* they are to be employed in Christ's work and under the Spirit's guidance, to the glory of God the Father. 3. All that are separated to Christ as his ministers are separated to work; Christ keeps no servants to be idle. *If any man desires the office of a bishop, he desires a good work;* that is what he is separated to, *to labour in the word and doctrine.* They are separated to take pains, not to take state. 4. The work of Christ's ministers, to which they are to be separated, is work that is already settled, and that which all Christ's ministers hitherto have been called to, and which they themselves have first been, by an external call, directed to and have chosen.

III. Their ordination, pursuant to these orders: not to the ministry in general (Barnabas and Saul had both of them been ministers long before this), but to a particular service in the ministry, which had something peculiar in it, and which required a fresh commission, which commission God saw fit at this time to transmit by the hands of *these prophets and teachers,* for the giving of this direction to the church, that teachers should ordain teachers (for prophets we are not now any longer to expect), and that those who have the dispensing of the oracles of Christ committed to them should, for the benefit of posterity, *commit the same to faithful men, who shall be able also to teach others,* 2 Tim. ii. 2. So here, Simeon, and Lucius, and Manaen, faithful teachers at this time in the church of Antioch, *when they had fasted and prayed, laid their hands on Barnabas and Saul, and sent them away* (*v.* 3), according to the directions received. Observe, 1. They prayed for them. When good men are going forth about good work, they ought to be solemnly and particularly prayed for, especially by their brethren that are their fellow-labourers and fellow-soldiers. 2. They joined fasting with their prayers, as they did in their other ministrations, *v.* 3. Christ has taught us this by his abstaining from sleep (a night-fast, if I may so call it) the night before he sent forth his apostles, that he might spend it in prayer. 3. They laid their hands on them. Hereby, (1.) They gave them their manumission, dismission, or discharge from the present service they were engaged in, in the church of Antioch, acknowledging that they went off not only fairly and with consent, but honourably and with a good report. (2.) They implored a blessing upon them in their present undertaking, begged that God would be with them, and give them success; and, in order to this, that *they might be filled with the Holy Ghost* in their work. This very thing is explained *ch.* xiv. 26, where it is said, concerning Paul and Barnabas, that from *Antioch they had been recommended to the grace of God for the work which they fulfilled.* As it was an instance of the humility of Barnabas and Saul that they submitted to the imposition of the hands of those that were their equals, or rather their inferiors; so it was of the good disposition of the other teachers that they did not envy Barnabas and Saul the honour to which they were preferred, but cheerfully committed it to them, with hearty prayers for them; and *they sent them away* with all expedition, out of a concern for those countries where they were to break up fallow ground.

4 So they, being sent forth by the
Holy Ghost, departed unto Seleucia;
and from thence they sailed to Cyprus. 5 And when they were at Salamis, they preached the word of
God in the synagogues of the Jews:
and they had also John to *their* minister. 6 And when they had gone
through the isle unto Paphos, they
found a certain sorcerer, a false prophet, a Jew, whose name *was* Bar-
jesus: 7 Which was with the de-

puty of the country, Sergius Paulus,
a prudent man; who called for Barnabas and Saul, and desired to hear
the word of God. 8 But Elymas
the sorcerer (for so is his name by
interpretation) withstood them, seeking to turn away the deputy from
the faith. 9 Then Saul, (who also *is*
called Paul,) filled with the Holy
Ghost, set his eyes on him, 10
And said, O full of all subtilty and
all mischief, *thou* child of the devil,
thou enemy of all righteousness, wilt
thou not cease to pervert the right
ways of the Lord? 11 And now,
behold, the hand of the Lord *is* upon
thee, and thou shalt be blind, not
seeing the sun for a season. And
immediately there fell on him a mist
and a darkness; and he went about
seeking some to lead him by the
hand. 12 Then the deputy, when
he saw what was done, believed,
being astonished at the doctrine of
the Lord. 13 Now when Paul and
his company loosed from Paphos,
they came to Perga in Pamphylia:
and John departing from them returned to Jerusalem.

In these verses we have,

I. A general account of the coming of Barnabas and Saul to the famous island of Cyprus; and perhaps thitherward they steered their course because Barnabas was a native of that country (*ch.* iv. 36), and he was willing they should have the first-fruits of his labours, pursuant to his new commission. Observe, 1. Their being sent forth by the Holy Ghost was the great thing that encouraged them in this undertaking, *v.* 4. If the Holy Ghost send them forth, he will go along with them, strengthen them, carry them on in their work, and give them success; and then they fear no colours, but can cheerfully venture upon a stormy sea from Antioch, which was now to them a quiet harbour. 2. They came to Seleucia, the sea-port town opposite to Cyprus, thence crossed the sea to Cyprus, and in that island the first city they came to was Salamis, a city on the east side of the island (*v.* 5); and, when they had sown good seed there, *thence they* went onward *through the isle* (*v.* 6) till they came to Paphos, which lay on the western coast. 3. *They preached the word of God* wherever they came, *in the synagogues of the Jews;* so far were they from excluding them that they gave them the preference, and so left those among them who believed not inexcusable; *they would have gathered them, but they would not.* They did not act clandestinely, nor preach the Messiah to others unknown to them, but laid their doctrine open to the censure of the rulers of their synagogues, who might, if they had any thing to say, object against it. Nor would they have acted separately, but in concert with them, if they had not driven them out from them, and from their synagogues. 4. *They had John for their minister;* not their servant in common things, but their assistant in the things of God, either to prepare their way in places where they designed to come or to carry on their work in places where they had begun it, or to converse familiarly with those to whom they preached publicly, and explain things to them; and such a one might be many ways of use to them, especially in a strange country.

II. A particular account of their encounter with *Elymas the sorcerer,* whom they met with at Paphos, where the governor resided; a place famous for a temple built to Venus there, thence called *Paphian Venus;* and therefore there was more than ordinary need that *the Son of God* should there *be manifested to destroy the works of the devil.*

1. There the *deputy,* a Gentile, *Sergius Paulus* by name, encouraged the apostles, and was willing to hear their message. He was governor *of the country,* under the Roman emperor; proconsul or proprætor, such a one as we should call *lord lieutenant of the island.* He had the character of *a prudent man,* an intelligent, considerate man, that was ruled by reason, not passion nor prejudice, which appeared by this, that, having a character of Barnabas and Saul, he sent for them, *and desired to hear the word of God.* Note, When that which we hear has a tendency to lead us to God, it is prudence to desire to hear more of it. Those are wise people, however they may be ranked among the foolish of this world, who are inquisitive after the mind and will of God. Though he was a great man, and a man in authority, and the preachers of the gospel were men that made no figure, yet, if they have a message from God, let him know what it is, and, if it appear to be so, he is ready to receive it.

2. There Elymas, a Jew, a *sorcerer,* opposed them, and did all he could to obstruct their progress. This justified the apostles in *turning to the Gentiles,* that this Jew was so malignant against them.

(1.) This Elymas was a pretender *to the gift of prophecy, a sorcerer, a false-prophet*—one that would be taken for a divine, because he was skilled in the arts of divination; he was a conjurer, and took on him to tell people their fortune, and to discover things lost, and probably was in league with the devil for this purpose; *his name was Bar-jesus—the son of Joshua;* it signifies *the son of salvation;* but the Syriac calls him, *Bar-shoma—the son of pride; filius inflationis—the son of inflation.*

(2.) He was hanging on at court, *was with the deputy* of the country. It does not appear that the deputy called for him, as he did for Barnabas and Saul; but he thrust himself upon him, aiming, no doubt, to make a hand of him, and get money by him.

(3.) He made it his business to withstand Barnabas and Saul, as the magicians of Egypt, in Pharaoh's court, *withstood* Moses and Aaron, 2 Tim. iii. 8. He set up himself to be a messenger from heaven, and denied that they were. And *thus he sought to turn away the deputy from the faith* (*v.* 8), to keep him from receiving the gospel, which he saw him inclined to do. Note, Satan is in a special manner busy with great men and men of power, to keep them from being religious; because he knows that their example, whether good or bad, will have an influence upon many. And those who are in any way instrumental to prejudice people against the truths and ways of Christ are doing the devil's work.

(4.) Saul (who is here for the first time called Paul) fell upon him for this with a holy indignation. *Saul, who is also called Paul, v.* 9. Saul was his name as he was a Hebrew, and of the tribe of Benjamin; Paul was his name as he was a citizen of Rome. Hitherto we have had him mostly conversant among the Jews, and therefore called by his Jewish name; but now, when he is sent forth among the Gentiles, he is called by his Roman name, to put somewhat of a reputation upon him in the Roman cities, Paulus being a very common name among them. But some think he was never called Paul till now that he was instrumental in the conversion of Sergius Paulus to the faith of Christ, and that he took the name Paulus as a memorial of this victory obtained by the gospel of Christ, as among the Romans he that had conquered a country took his denomination from it, as *Germanicus, Britannicus, Africanus;* or rather, Sergius Paulus himself gave him the name Paulus in token of his favour and respect to him, as Vespasian gave his name Flavius to Josephus the Jew. Now of Paul it is said,

[1.] That he was *filled with the Holy Ghost* upon this occasion, filled with a holy zeal against a professed enemy of Christ, which was one of the graces of the Holy Ghost—*a spirit of burning;* filled with power to denounce the wrath of God against him, which was one of the gifts of the Holy Ghost—*a spirit of judgment.* He felt a more than ordinary fervour in his mind, as the prophet did when he was *full of power by the Spirit of the Lord* (Mic. iii. 8), and another prophet when *his face was made harder than flint* (Ezek. iii. 9), and another when his *mouth was made like a sharp sword,* Isa. xlix. 2. What Paul said did not come from any personal resentment, but from the strong impressions which the Holy Ghost made upon his spirit.

[2.] He *set his eyes upon him,* to face him down, and to show a holy boldness, in opposition to his wicked impudence. He set his eyes upon him, as an indication that the eye of the heart-searching God was upon him, and saw through and through him; nay, *that the face of the Lord was against him,* Ps. xxxiv. 16. He fixed his eyes upon him, to see if he could discern in his countenance any marks of remorse for what he had done; for, if he could have discerned the least sign of this, it would have prevented the ensuing doom.

[3.] He gave him his true character, not in passion, but by the Holy Ghost, who knows men better than they know themselves, *v.* 10. He describes him to be, *First,* An agent for hell; and such there have been upon this earth (the seat of the war between *the seed of the woman and of the serpent*) ever since Cain *who was of that wicked one,* an incarnate devil, *slew his brother,* for no other reason than because *his own works were evil and his brother's righteous.* This Elymas, though called *Bar-jesus—a son of Jesus,* was really a *child of the devil,* bore his image, did his lusts, and served his interests, John viii. 44. In two things he resembled the devil as a child does his father:—1. In craftiness. *The serpent was more subtle than any beast of the field* (Gen. iii. 1), and Elymas, though void of all wisdom, was *full of all subtlety,* expert in all the arts of deceiving men and imposing upon them. 2. In malice. He was *full of all mischief*—a spiteful ill-conditioned man, and a sworn implacable enemy to God and goodness. Note, A fulness of subtlety and mischief together make a man indeed a child of the devil. *Secondly,* An adversary to heaven. If he be a child of the devil, it follows of course that he is *an enemy to all righteousness,* for the devil is so. Note, Those that are enemies to the doctrine of Christ are enemies to all righteousness, for in it all righteousness is summed up and fulfilled.

[4.] He charged upon him his present crime, and expostulated with him upon it: "*Wilt thou not cease to pervert the right ways of the Lord,* to misrepresent them, to put false colours upon them, and so to discourage people from entering into them, and walking in them?" Note, *First,* The ways of the Lord are right: they are all so, they are perfectly so. The ways of the Lord Jesus are right, the only right ways to heaven and happiness. *Secondly,* There are those who pervert these right ways, who not only wander out of these ways themselves (as Elihu's penitent, who owns, *I have perverted that which was right, and it profited me not),* but mislead others, and suggest to them unjust prejudices against these ways: as if the doctrine of Christ were uncertain and precarious, the laws of Christ unreasonable and impracticable, and the service of Christ unpleasant and unprofitable, which is an unjust perverting of the right ways of the Lord, and making them seem crooked ways. *Thirdly,* Those who pervert the right ways of the Lord are commonly so hardened in it that, though the equity of those ways be set before them by the most powerful and commanding evidence, yet they will not cease to do it. *Etsi suaseris, non persuaseris—You may advise, but you will never persuade;* they will have it their own way; *they have loved strangers, and after them they will go.*

[5.] He denounced the judgment of God upon him, in a present blindness (*v.* 11): "*And now, behold, the hand of the Lord is upon thee,* a righteous hand. God is now about to lay hands on thee, and make thee his prisoner, for thou art taken in arms against him; *thou shalt be blind, not seeing the sun for a season.* This was designed both for the proof of his crime, as it was a miracle wrought to confirm the right ways of the Lord, and consequently to show the wickedness of him who would not cease to pervert them, as also for the punishment of his crime. It was a suitable punishment; he shut his eyes, the eyes of his mind, against the light of the gospel, and therefore justly were the eyes of his body shut against the light of the sun; he sought to blind the deputy (as an agent for *the god of this world, who blindeth the minds of those that believe not, lest the light of the gospel should shine unto them,* 2 Cor. iv. 4), and therefore is himself struck blind. Yet it was a moderate punishment: he was only struck blind, when he might most justly have been struck dead; and it was only *for a season;* if he will repent, and give glory to God, by making confession, his sight shall be restored; nay, it should seem, though he do not, yet his sight shall be restored, to try if he will be led to repentance either by the judgments of God or by his mercies.

[6.] This judgment was immediately executed: *There fell on him a mist and a darkness,* as on the Sodomites when they persecuted Lot, and on the Syrians when they persecuted Elisha. This silenced him presently, filled him with confusion, and was an effectual confutation of all he said against the doctrine of Christ. Let not him any more pretend to be a guide to the deputy's conscience who is himself struck blind. It was also an earnest to him of a much sorer punishment if he repent not; for he is one of those *wandering stars to whom is reserved the blackness of darkness for ever,* Jude 13. Elymas did himself proclaim the truth of the miracle, when *he went about seeking some to lead him by the hand;* and where now is all his skill in sorcery, upon which he had so much valued himself, when he can neither find his way himself nor find a friend that will be so kind as to lead him!

3. Notwithstanding all the endeavours of Elymas *to turn away the deputy from the faith,* he was brought to believe, and this miracle, wrought upon the magician himself (like *the boils of Egypt,* which *were upon the magicians, so that they could not stand before Moses,* Exod. ix. 11), contributed to it. The deputy was a very sensible man, and observed something uncommon, and which intimated its divine original, (1.) In Paul's preaching: he was *astonished at the doctrine of the Lord,* the Lord Christ,—the doctrine that *is from him,* the discoveries he has made of the Father,—the doctrine that *is concerning him,* his person, natures, offices, undertaking. Note, The doctrine of Christ has a great deal in it that is astonishing; and the more we know of it the more reason we shall see to wonder and stand amazed at it. (2.) In this miracle: *When he saw what was done,* and how much Paul's power transcended that of the magician, and how plainly Elymas was baffled and confounded, he believed. It is not said that he was baptized, and so made a complete convert, but it is probable that he was. Paul would not do his business by the halves; *as for God, his work is perfect.* When he became a Christian, he neither laid down his government, nor was turned out of it, but we may suppose, as a Christian magistrate, by his influence helped very much to propagate Christianity in that island. The tradition of the Romish church, which has taken care to find bishoprics for all the eminent converts we read of in *the Acts,* has made this Sergius Paulus bishop of Narbon in France, left there by Paul in his journey to Spain.

III. Their departure from the island of Cyprus. It is probable that they did a great deal more there than is recorded, where an account is given only of that which was extraordinary—the conversion of the deputy. When they had done what they had to do, 1. They quitted the country, and *went to Perga.* Those that went were *Paul and his company,* which, it is probable, was increased in Cyprus, many being desirous to accompany him. Ἀναχθέντες οἱ περὶ τὸν Παῦλον—*Those that were about Paul loosed from Paphos,* which supposes that he went too; but such an affection had his new friends for him that they were always about him, and by their good will would be never from him. 2. Then John *Mark quitted them, and returned to Jerusalem,* without the consent of Paul and Barnabas; either he did not like the work, or he wanted to go and see his mother. It was his fault, and we shall hear of it again.

14 But when they departed from
Perga, they came to Antioch in Pisidia, and went into the synagogue
on the sabbath day, and sat down.
15 And after the reading of the law
and the prophets the rulers of the
synagogue sent unto them, saying,
Ye men *and* brethren, if ye have any

word of exhortation for the people,
say on. 16 Then Paul stood up,
and beckoning with *his* hand said,
Men of Israel, and ye that fear God,
give audience. 17 The God of this
people of Israel chose our fathers,
and exalted the people when they
dwelt as strangers in the land of
Egypt, and with a high arm brought
he them out of it. 18 And about
the time of forty years suffered he
their manners in the wilderness. 19
And when he had destroyed seven
nations in the land of Chanaan, he
divided their land to them by lot.
20 And after that he gave *unto them*
judges about the space of four hundred and fifty years, until Samuel
the prophet. 21 And afterward
they desired a king: and God gave
unto them Saul the son of Cis, a
man of the tribe of Benjamin, by the
space of forty years. 22 And when
he had removed him, he raised up
unto them David to be their king;
to whom also he gave testimony,
and said, I have found David the
son of Jesse, a man after mine own
heart, which shall fulfil all my will.
23 Of this man's seed hath God according to *his* promise raised unto
Israel a Saviour, Jesus: 23 When
John had first preached before his
coming the baptism of repentance to
all the people of Israel. 25 And as
John fulfilled his course, he said,
Whom think ye that I am? I am
not *he*. But, behold, there cometh
one after me, whose shoes of *his* feet
I am not worthy to loose. 26 Men
and brethren, children of the stock
of Abraham, and whosoever among
you feareth God, to you is the word
of this salvation sent. 27 For they
that dwell at Jerusalem, and their
rulers, because they knew him not,
nor yet the voices of the prophets
which are read every sabbath day,
they have fulfilled *them* in condemning *him*. 28 And though they found
no cause of death *in him*, yet desired
they Pilate that he should be slain.
29 And when they had fulfilled all
that was written of him, they took
him down from the tree, and laid
him in a sepulchre. 30 But God
raised him from the dead: 31 And
he was seen many days of them
which came up with him from Galilee to Jerusalem, who are his witnesses unto the people. 32 And we
declare unto you glad tidings, how
that the promise which was made
unto the fathers, 33 God hath fulfilled the same unto us their children,
in that he hath raised up Jesus
again; as it is also written in the
second psalm, Thou art my Son, this
day have I begotten thee. 34 And
as concerning that he raised him up
from the dead, *now* no more to return to corruption, he said on this
wise, I will give you the sure mercies
of David. 35 Wherefore he saith
also in another *psalm*, Thou shalt
not suffer thine Holy One to see
corruption. 36 For David, after he
had served his own generation by
the will of God, fell on sleep, and
was laid unto his fathers, and saw
corruption: 37 But he, whom God
raised again, saw no corruption. 38
Be it known unto you therefore, men
and brethren, that through this man
is preached unto you the forgiveness
of sins: 39 And by him all that
believe are justified from all things,
from which ye could not be justified
by the law of Moses. 40 Beware
therefore, lest that come upon you,
which is spoken of in the prophets;
41 Behold, ye despisers, and wonder,
and perish: for I work a work in
your days, a work which ye shall in
no wise believe, though a man declare it unto you.

Perga in Pamphylia was a noted place, especially for a temple there erected to the goddess Diana, yet nothing at all is related of what Paul and Barnabas did there, only that *thither they came* (*v.* 13), and *thence they departed*, *v.* 14. But the history of the apostles' travels, as that of Christ's, passes by many things worthy to have been recorded, because, *if all had been written, the world could not have contained the books.* But the next place we find them in is another Antioch, said to be in Pisidia, to distinguish it from that Antioch in Syria from which they were sent out. Pisidia was a province of the Lesser Asia, bordering upon Pamphylia; this Antioch, it is likely, was the metropolis of it. Abundance of Jews lived there, and to them *the gospel was to be first preached;* and Paul's sermon to them is what we have in these verses, which, it is likely, is the substance of what was preached by the apostles generally to the Jews in all places; for in dealing with them the proper way was to show them how the New Testament, which they would have them to receive, exactly agreed with the Old Testament, which they not only received, but were zealous for. We have here,

I. The appearance which Paul and Barnabas made in a religious assembly of the Jews at Antioch, *v.* 14. Though they had lately had such good success with a Roman deputy, yet, *when they came to Antioch,* they did not enquire for the chief magistrate, nor make their court to him, but they applied to the Jews, which is a further proof of their good affection to them and their desire of their welfare. 1. They observed their time of worship, *on the sabbath day,* the Jewish sabbath. *The first day of the week* they observed among themselves as a Christian sabbath; but, if they will meet the Jews, it must be on the seventh-day sabbath, which therefore, upon such occasions, they did as yet sometimes observe. For, though it was by the death of Christ that the ceremonial law died, yet it was in the ruins of Jerusalem that it was to be buried; and therefore, though the morality of the fourth commandment was entirely transferred to the Christian sabbath, yet it was not incongruous to join with the Jews in their sabbath sanctification. 2. They met them in their place of worship, *in the synagogue.* Note, Sabbath days should be kept holy in solemn assemblies; they are instituted chiefly for public worship. *The sabbath day is a holy convocation,* and for that reason *no servile work must be done therein.* Paul and Barnabas were strangers; but, wherever we come, we must enquire out God's faithful worshippers, and join with them (as these apostles here did), as those that desire to keep up a communion with all saints; though they were strangers, yet they were admitted into the synagogue, and to sit down there. Care should be taken in places of public worship that strangers be accommodated, even the poorest; for, of those of whom we know nothing else, we know this, that they have precious souls, for which our charity binds us to be concerned.

II. The invitation given them to preach. 1. The usual service of the synagogue was performed (*v.* 15): *The law and the prophets were read,* a portion of each, the lessons for the day. Note, When we come together to worship God, we must do it not only by prayer and praise, but by the reading and hearing of the word of God; hereby we *give him the glory due to his name,* as our Lord and Lawgiver. 2. When that was done, they were asked by *the rulers of the synagogue* to give them a sermon (*v.* 15): They sent a messenger to them with the respectful message, *Men and brethren, if you have any word of exhortation for the people, say on.* It is probable that the rulers of the synagogue had met with them, and been in private conversation with them before; and, if they had not an affection to the gospel, yet they had at least the curiosity to hear Paul preach; and therefore not only gave him permission, but begged the favour of him that he would speak a *word of exhortation to the people.* Note, (1.) The bare reading of the scriptures in the public assemblies is not sufficient, but they should be expounded, and the people exhorted out of them. This is spreading the net, and assisting people in doing that which is necessary to the making of the word profitable to them—that is, the applying of it to themselves. (2.) Those that preside, and have power, in public assemblies, should provide for a word of exhortation to the people, whenever they come together. (3.) Sometimes a word of exhortation from a strange minister may be of great use to the people, provided he be well approved. It is likely Paul did *often preach in the synagogue,* when he was not thus invited to it by the rulers of the synagogues; for he often preached *with much contention,* 1 Thess. ii. 2. But these were more noble, more generous, than the rulers of the synagogues generally were.

III. The sermon Paul preached in the synagogue of the Jews, at the invitation of the rulers of the synagogue. He gladly embraced the opportunity given him to preach Christ to his countrymen the Jews. He did not object to them that he was a stranger, and that it was none of his business; nor object to himself, that he might get ill-will by preaching Christ among the Jews; but *stood up,* as one prepared and determined to speak, *and beckoned with his hand,* to excite and prepare them to hear. He waved his hand as an orator, not only desiring silence and attention, but endeavouring to move affection, and to show himself in earnest. Perhaps, upon the moving of them *to give an exhortation to the people,* there were those in the synagogue that were ready to mutiny against the rulers, and opposed the toleration of Paul's preaching, and that occasioned some tumult and commotion, which Paul endeavoured to quiet by that decent motion of his hand; as also by his modest desire of a patient impartial hearing: "*Men of Israel,* that are *Jews* by birth, *and you that fear God,* that are proselyted to the Jewish religion, *give audience;* let me beg your attention a little, for I have something to say to you which concerns your everlasting peace, and would not say it in vain." Now this excellent sermon is recorded, to show that those who preached the gospel to the Gentiles did it not till they had first used their utmost endeavours with the Jews, to persuade them to come in and take the benefit of it; and that they had no prejudice at all against the Jewish nation, nor any desire *that they should perish, but rather that they should turn and live.* Every thing is touched in this sermon that might be proper either to convince the judgment or insinuate into the affections of the Jews, to prevail with them to receive and embrace Christ as the promised Messiah.

1. He owns them to be God's favourite people, whom he had taken into special relation to himself, and for whom he had done great things. Probably *the Jews of the dispersion*, that lived in other countries, being more in danger of mingling with the nations, were more jealous of their peculiarity than those that lived in their own land were; and therefore Paul is here very careful to take notice of it, to their honour.

(1.) That *the God of the whole earth* was, in a particular manner, *the God of this people Israel*, a God *in covenant with them,* and that he had given them a revelation of his mind and will, such as he *had not given to any other nation or people;* so that hereby they were distinguished from, and dignified above, all their neighbours, having peculiar precepts to be governed by, and peculiar promises to depend upon.

(2.) That he had *chosen their fathers* to be his friends: Abraham was called *the friend of God;* to be his prophets, by whom he would reveal his mind to his church, and to be the trustees of his covenant with the church. He puts them in mind of this, to let them know that the reason why God favoured them, though undeserving, and ill deserving, was because he would adhere to the choice he had made of *their fathers*, Deut. vii. 7, 8. *They were beloved* purely *for the fathers' sakes,* Rom. xi. 28.

(3.) That he had *exalted that people,* and put a great deal of honour upon them, had advanced them into a people, and raised them from nothing, *when they dwelt as strangers in the land of Egypt*, and had nothing in them to recommend them to the divine favour. They ought to remember this, and to infer hence that God was no debtor to them; for it was *ex mero motu—out of his mere good pleasure,* and not upon a valuable consideration, that they had the grant of the divine favour; and therefore it was revocable at pleasure; and God did them no wrong if he at length plucked up the hedge of their peculiarity. But they were debtors to him, and obliged to receive such further discoveries as he should make of his will, and to admit such further additions as he should make to his church.

(4.) That he had *with a high hand brought them out of Egypt,* where they were not only strangers, but captives, had delivered them at the expense of a great many miracles, both of mercy to them and judgment on their oppressors (*signs and wonders,* Deut. iv. 34), and at the expense of a great many lives, *all the first-born of Egypt, Pharaoh, and all his host, in the Red Sea; I gave Egypt for thy ransom, gave men for thee.* Isa. xliii. 3, 4.

(5.) That *he had suffered their manners forty years in the wilderness, v.* 18 Ἐτροποφόρησεν. Some think it should be read, ἐτροφοφόρησεν—*he educated them,* because this is the word the Septuagint use concerning the fatherly care God took of that people, Deut. i. 31. Both may be included; for, [1.] God made a great deal of provision for them for forty years in the wilderness: miracles were their daily bread, and kept them from starving: *They lacked not any thing.* [2.] He exercised a great deal of patience with them. They were a provoking, murmuring, unbelieving people; and yet he bore with them, did not deal with them as they deserved, but suffered his anger many a time to be turned away by the prayer and intercession of Moses. So many years as we have each of us lived in this world, we must own that God has thus been as a tender father to us, has supplied our wants, has *fed us all our life long unto this day,* has been indulgent to us, a God of pardons (as he was to Israel, Neh. ix. 17), and *not extreme to mark what we have done amiss;* we have tried his patience, and yet not tired it. Let not the Jews insist too much upon the privileges of their peculiarity, for they have forfeited them a thousand times.

(6.) That he had put them in possession of the land of Canaan (*v.* 19): *When he had destroyed seven nations in the land of Canaan,* that were doomed to be rooted out to make room for them, *he divided their land to them by lot,* and put them in possession of it. This was a signal favour of God to them, and he owns that hereby a great honour was put upon them, from which he would not in the least derogate.

(7.) That he had raised up men, inspirited from heaven, to deliver them out of the hands of those that invaded their rights, and oppressed them after their settlement in Canaan, *v.* 20, 21. [1.] He *gave them judges,* men qualified for public service, and, by an immediate impulse upon their spirits, called to it, *pro re nata—as the occasion required.* Though they were a provoking people, and were never in servitude but their sin brought them to it, yet upon their petition a deliverer was raised up. The critics find some difficulty in computing *these four hundred and fifty years.* From the *deliverance out of Egypt* to David's expulsion of *the Jebusites from the strong-hold of Zion,* which completed the casting out of the heathen nations, *was four hundred and fifty years;* and most of that time they were under judges. Others thus: The government of the judges, from the death of Joshua to the death of Eli, was just *three hundred and thirty-nine years,* but it is said to be [ὡς] as it were *four hundred and fifty years,* because the years of their servitude to the several nations that oppressed them, though really they were included in the years of the judges, are yet mentioned in the history as if they had been distinct from them. Now these, all put together, make *one hundred and eleven years*, which, added to the *three hundred and thirty nine*, make them *four hundred and fifty;* as so many, though not really so many. [2.] He governed them by a *prophet, Samuel*, a man divinely inspired to preside in their affairs. [3.] He *afterwards* at their request *set a king over them* (*v.* 21), *Saul, the son of Cis.* Samuel's government and his lasted *forty years*, which was a kind of transition from the theocracy to the kingly government. [4.] At last, he made David their king, *v.* 22. *When God had removed Saul*, for his mal-administration, *he raised up unto them David to be their king*, and made *a covenant of royalty with him, and with his seed.* When he had removed one king, he did not leave them as sheep without a shepherd, but soon raised up another, raised him up from a mean and low estate, *raised him up on high*, 2 Sam. xxiii. 1. He quotes the testimony God gave concerning him, *First*, That his choice was divine: *I have found David*, Ps. lxxxix. 20. God himself pitched upon him. Finding implies seeking; as if God had ransacked all the families of Israel to find a man fit for his purpose, and this was he. *Secondly*, That his character was divine: *A man after my own heart*, such a one as I would have, one on whom the image of God is stamped, and therefore one in whom God is well pleased and whom he approves. This character was given of him before he was first anointed, 1 Sam. xiii. 14. *The Lord hath sought out a man after his own heart*, such a one as he would have. *Thirdly*, That his conduct was divine, and under divine direction: *He shall fulfil all my will.* He shall desire and endeavour to do the will of God, and shall be enabled to do it, and employed in the doing of it, and go through with it. Now all this seems to show not only the special favour of God to the people of Israel (with the acknowledgment of which the apostle is very willing to oblige them) but the further favours of another nature which he designed them, and which were now, by the preaching of the gospel, offered to them. Their deliverance out of Egypt, and settlement in Canaan, *were types and figures of good things to come.* The changes of their government showed that it *made nothing perfect*, and therefore must give way to the spiritual kingdom of the Messiah, which was now in the setting up, and which, if they would admit it and submit to it, would be *the glory of their people Israel;* and therefore they needed not conceive any jealousy at all of the preaching of the gospel, as if it tended in the least to damage the true excellences of the Jewish church.

2. He gives them a full account of our Lord Jesus, passing from David to the Son of David, and shows that this Jesus is his promised Seed (*v.* 23): *Of this man's seed*, from that *root of Jesse*, from that *man after God's own heart, hath God, according to his promise, raised unto Israel a Saviour—Jesus*, who carries salvation in his name.

(1.) How welcome should the preaching of the gospel of Christ be to the Jews, and how should they embrace it, as *well worthy of all acceptation*, when it brought them the tidings, [1.] Of a Saviour, to deliver *them out of the hands of their enemies*, as the judges of old, who were therefore called *saviours;* but this *a Saviour* to do that for them which, it appears by the history, those could not do—*to save them from their sins*, their worst enemies. [2.] A Saviour of God's raising up, that has his commission from heaven. [3.] Raised up *to be a Saviour unto Israel*, to them in the first place: *He was sent to bless them;* so far was the gospel from designing the rejection of Israel, that it designed the gathering of them. [4.] Raised up *of the seed of David*, that ancient royal family, which the people of Israel gloried so much in, and which at this time, to the great disgrace of the whole nation, was buried in obscurity. It ought to be a great satisfaction to them *that God had raised up this horn of salvation for them in the house of his servant David*, Luke i. 69. [5.] Raised up *according to his promise*, the promise to David (Ps. cxxxii. 11), the promise to the Old-Testament church in the latter times of it: *I will raise unto David a righteous branch*, Jer. xxiii. 5. This promise was it *to which the twelve tribes hoped to come* (*ch.* xxvi. 7); why then should they entertain it so coldly, now that it was brought to them? Now,

(2.) Concerning this Jesus, he tells them,

[1.] That John the Baptist was his harbinger and forerunner, that great man whom all acknowledged to be a prophet. Let them not say that the Messiah's coming was a surprise upon them, and that this might excuse them if they took time to consider whether they should entertain him or no; for they had sufficient warning by John, who *preached before his coming*, *v.* 24. Two things he did:—*First*, He made way for his entrance, by preaching *the baptism of repentance*, not to a few select disciples, but *to all the people of Israel.* He showed them their sins, *warned them of the wrath to come, called them to repentance*, and *to bring forth fruits meet for repentance*, and bound those to this who were willing to be bound by the solemn rite or sign of baptism; and by this he *made ready a people prepared for the Lord Jesus*, to whom his grace would be acceptable when they were thus brought to know themselves. *Secondly*, He gave notice of his approach (*v.* 25): *As he fulfilled his course*, when he was going on vigorously in his work, and had had wonderful success in it, and an established interest: "Now," saith he to those that attended his ministry, "*Whom think you that I am?* What notions have you of me, what expectations from me? You may be thinking that I am *the Messiah*, whom you expect; but you are mistaken, *I am not he* (see John i. 20), but he is at the door; *behold, there cometh one* immediately *after me,* who will so far exceed me upon all accounts, *that I am not worthy* to be employed in the meanest office about him, no, not to help him on and off with his shoes—*whose shoes of his feet I am not worthy to loose,* and you may guess who that must be."

[2.] That the rulers and people of the Jews, who should have welcomed him, and been his willing, forward, faithful subjects, were his persecutors and murderers. When the apostles preach Christ as *the Saviour,* they are so far from concealing his ignominious death, and drawing a veil over it, that they always *preach Christ crucified,* yea, and (though this added much to the reproach of his sufferings) crucified by his own people, by *those that dwelt in Jerusalem,* the holy city—the royal city, and *their rulers, v.* 27. *First,* Their sin was *that though they found no cause of death in him,* could not prove him, no, nor had any colour to suspect him, guilty of any crime (the judge himself that tried him, when he had heard all they could say against him, declared he *found no fault with him), yet they desired Pilate that he might be slain* (*v.* 28), and presented their address against Christ with such fury and outrage that they compelled Pilate to crucify him, not only contrary to his inclination, but contrary to his conscience; they condemned him *to so great a death,* though they could not convict him of the least sin. Paul cannot charge this upon his hearers, as Peter did (*ch.* ii. 23): *You have with wicked hands crucified and slain him;* for these, though Jews, were far enough off; but he charges it upon the Jews at Jerusalem and the rulers, to show what little reason those Jews of the dispersion had to be so jealous for the honour of their nation as they were, when it had brought upon itself such a load and stain of guilt as this, and how justly they might have been cut off from all benefit by the Messiah, who had thus abused him, and yet they were not; but, notwithstanding all this, the preaching of this gospel shall begin at Jerusalem. *Secondly,* The reason of this was because *they knew him not, v.* 27. They knew not who he was, nor what errand he came into the world upon; for, *if they had known, they would not have crucified the Lord of glory.* Christ owned this in extenuation of their crime: *They know not what they do;* and so did Peter: *I wot that through ignorance you did this; ch.* iii. 17. It was also because they knew not the voice of the prophets though they heard them read every sabbath day. They did not understand nor consider that it was foretold that the Messiah should suffer, or else they would never have been the instruments of his suffering. Note, Many that read the prophets do not know the voice of the prophets, do not understand the meaning of the scriptures; they have the sound of the gospel in their ears, but not the sense of it in their heads, nor the savour of it in their hearts. And *therefore* men do not know Christ, nor know how to carry it towards him, because they do not know the voice of the prophets, who *testified beforehand concerning Christ. Thirdly,* God overruled them, for the accomplishment of the prophecies of the Old-Testament: *Because they knew not the voice of the prophets,* which warned them not to touch God's Anointed, *they fulfilled them in condemning him;* for so it was written that *Messiah the prince shall be cut off, but not for himself.* Note, It is possible that men may be fulfilling scripture prophecies, even when they are breaking scripture precepts, particularly in the persecution of the church, as in the persecution of Christ. And this justifies the reason which is sometimes given for the obscurity of scripture prophecies, that, if they were too plain and obvious, the accomplishment of them would thereby be prevented. So Paul saith here, *Because they knew not the voice of the prophets,* therefore *they have fulfilled them,* which implies that if they had understood them they would not have fulfilled them. *Fourthly,* All that was foretold concerning the sufferings of the Messiah was fulfilled in Christ (*v.* 29): *When they had fulfilled all* the rest *that was written of him,* even to the giving of him vinegar to drink in his thirst, then they fulfilled what was foretold concerning his being buried. They *took him down from the tree, and laid him in a sepulchre.* This is taken notice of here as that which made his resurrection the more illustrious. Christ was separated from this world, as those that are buried have nothing more to do with this world, nor this world with them; and therefore our complete separation from sin is represented by our being *buried with Christ.* And a good Christian will be willing to be buried alive with Christ. They laid him in a sepulchre, and thought they had him fast.

[3.] That he *rose again from the dead,* and saw no corruption. This was the great truth that was to be preached; for it is the main pillar, by which the whole fabric of the gospel is supported, and therefore he insists largely upon this, and shows,

First, That he rose by consent. When he was imprisoned in the grave for our debt, he did not break prison, but had a fair and legal discharge from the arrest he was under (*v.* 30): *God raised him from the dead,* sent an angel on purpose to roll away the stone from the prison-door, returned to him the spirit which at his death he had committed into the hands of his Father, and quickened him by the Holy Ghost. His enemies laid him in a sepulchre, with design he should always lay there; but God said, *No;* and it was soon seen whose purpose should stand, his or theirs.

Secondly, That there was sufficient proof of his having risen (*v.* 31): *He was seen many days,* in divers places, upon divers occasions, by those that were most intimately acquainted with him; for they *came up with him from Galilee to Jerusalem,* were his constant attendants, and *they are his witnesses unto the people.* They were appointed to be so, have attested the thing many a time, and are ready to attest it, though they were to die for the same. Paul says nothing of his own seeing him (which he mentions 1 Cor. xv. 8), because it was in a vision, which was more convincing to himself than it could be when produced to others.

Thirdly, That the resurrection of Christ was the performance of the promise made to the patriarchs; it was not only true news, but good news: "In declaring this, we *declare unto you glad tidings* (*v.* 32, 33), which should be in a particular manner acceptable to you Jews. So far are we from designing to put any slur upon you, or do you any wrong, that the doctrine we preach, if you receive it aright, and understand it, brings you the greatest honour and satisfaction imaginable; for it is in the resurrection of Christ that *the promise which was made to your fathers is fulfilled to you.*" He acknowledges it to be the dignity of the Jewish nation that *to them pertained the promises* (Rom ix. 4), that they were the heirs of the promise, as they were the children of the patriarchs to whom the promises were first made. The great promise of the Old Testament was that of the Messiah, *in whom all the families of the earth should be blessed,* and not the family of Abraham only; though it was to be the peculiar honour of that family that he should be raised up of it, yet it was to be the common benefit of all families that he should be raised up to them. Note, 1. God hath *raised up Jesus,* advanced him, and exalted him; *raised* him *again* (so we read it), meaning *from the dead.* We may take in both senses. God raised up Jesus to be a prophet at his baptism, to be a priest to make atonement at his death, and to be a king to rule over all at his ascension; and *his raising him up from the dead* was the confirmation and ratification of all these commissions, and proved him raised of God to these offices. 2. This is the fulfilling of the promises made to the fathers, the promise of sending the Messiah, and of all those benefits and blessings which were to be had with him and by him: "This is he that should come, and in him you have all that God promised in the Messiah, though not all that you promised yourselves." Paul puts himself into the number of the Jews, to whom the promise was fulfilled: *To us their children.* Now, if those who preached the gospel brought them *these glad tidings,* instead of looking upon them as enemies to their nation, they ought to caress them as their best friends, and embrace their doctrine with both arms; for if they valued the promise so much, and themselves by it, much more the performance. And the preaching of the gospel to the Gentiles, which was the great thing that the Jews found themselves aggrieved at, was so far from infringing the promise made to them that the promise itself, that *all the families of the earth* should be blessed in the Messiah, could not otherwise be accomplished.

Fourthly, That the resurrection of Christ was the great proof of his being the Son of God, and confirms what was written in the second Psalm (thus ancient was the order in which the Psalms are now placed), *Thou art my Son, this day have I begotten thee.* That the resurrection of Christ from the dead was designed to evidence and evince this is plain from that of the apostle (Rom. i. 4): *He was delared to be the Son of God with power, by the resurrection from the dead.* When he was first raised up out of obscurity, God declared concerning him by a voice from heaven, *This is my beloved Son* (Matt. iii. 17), which has a plain reference to that in the second Psalm, *Thou art my Son.* Abundance of truth there is couched in those words: that this Jesus was *begotten of the Father before all worlds*—was *the brightness of his glory and the express image of his person,* as the son is of the father's,—that he was the λόγος, the *eternal thought of the eternal mind,*—that he was conceived by the power of the Holy Ghost in the womb of the virgin; for upon this account, also, *that holy thing was called the Son of God* (Luke i. 35), that he was God's agent in creating and governing the world, and in redeeming it and reconciling it to himself, and *faithful as a son in his own house,* and as such was *heir of all things.* Now all this, which was declared at Christ's baptism and again at his transfiguration, was undeniably proved by his resurrection. The decree which was so long before declared was then confirmed; and the reason why it was impossible he should be held by the bands of death was because he was the Son of God, and consequently had *life in himself,* which he could not lay down but with a design to resume it. When his eternal generation is spoken of, it is not improper to say, *This day have I begotten thee;* for *from everlasting to everlasting* is with God as it were one and the same eternal day. Yet it may also be accommodated to his resurrection, in a subordinate sense, "This day have I made it to appear that I have begotten thee, and this day have I begotten all that are given to thee;" for it is said (1 Pet. i. 3) that *the God and Father of our Lord Jesus Christ,* as our God and Father, *hath begotten us again to a lively hope, by the resurrection of Jesus Christ from the dead.*

Fifthly, That his being raised the third day, so as not to see corruption, and to a heavenly life, so as no more to return to corruption, that is, to the state of the dead, as others did who were raised to life, further confirms his being the Messiah promised.

a. He rose to die no more; so it is expressed, Rom. vi. 9: *As concerning that he raised him up from the dead, now no more to*

return to corruption, that is, to the grave, which is called *corruption,* Job xvii. 14. Lazarus came out of the grave with his grave-clothes on, because he was to use them again; but Christ, having no more occasion for them, left them behind. Now this was the fulfilling of that scripture (Isa. lv. 3), *I will give you the sure mercies of David; τὰ ὅσια Δαβὶδ τὰ πιστά—the holy things of David, the faithful things;* for in the promise made to David, and in him to Christ, great stress is laid upon the faithfulness of God (Ps. lxxxix. 1, 2, 5, 24, 33), and upon the oath God had sworn *by his holiness,* Ps. lxxxix. 35. Now this makes them sure mercies indeed that he who is entrusted with the dispensing of them has risen to die no more; so that he ever lives to see his own will executed, and the blessings he hath purchased for us given out to us. As, if Christ had died and had not risen again, so if he had risen to die again, we had come short of the sure mercies, or at least could not have been sure of them.

b. He rose so soon after he was dead that his body did not see corruption; for it is not till the third day that the body begins to change. Now this was promised to David; it was one of *the sure mercies of David,* for it was said to him in Ps. xvi. 10, *Neither wilt thou suffer thy Holy One to see corruption,* ***v.*** 35. God had promised to David that he would raise up the Messiah of his seed, who should therefore be a man, but should not, like other men, see corruption. This promise could not have its accomplishment in David, but looked forward to Christ.

(*a.*) It could not be accomplished in David himself (*v.* 36), for *David, after he had served his own generation, by the will of God,* who raised him up to be what he was, *fell asleep, and was laid to his fathers, and saw corruption.* Here we have a short account of the life, death, and burial, of the patriarch David, and his continuance under the power of death. [*a.*] His life: *He served his own generation, by the will of God,* before he slept the sleep of death. David was a useful good man; he did good in the world *by the will of God.* He made God's precepts his rule; he *served his own generation* so as therein to serve God; he so *served* and *pleased men (as whatever the king did pleased the people,* 2 Sam. iii. 36), as still to keep himself the faithful servant of God. See Gal. i. 10. He served the good of men, but did not serve the will of men. Or, by the will of God's providence so ordering it, qualifying him for, and calling him to, a public station, he *served his own generation;* for every creature is that to us which God makes it to be. David was a great blessing to the age wherein he lived; he was the *servant* of his generation: many are the curse, and plague, and burden of their generation. Even those that are in a lower and narrower sphere must look upon it that they live to *serve their generation;* and those that will do good in the world must make themselves *servants of all,* 1 Cor. ix. 19. We were not born for ourselves, but are members of communities, to which we must study to be serviceable. Yet here is the difference between David and Christ, that David was to serve only his own generation, that generation in which he lived, and therefore when he had done what he had to do, and written what he had to write, he died, and continued in the grave; but Christ (not by his writings or words upon record only as David, but by his personal agency) was to serve *all* generations, must ever live to reign over the house of Jacob, not as David, for forty years, but for all ages, as long as the sun and moon endure, Ps. lxxxix. 29, 36, 37. His throne must be as the days of heaven, and all generations must be blessed in him, Ps. lxxii. 17. [*b.*] His death: *He fell asleep.* Death is a sleep, a quiet rest, to those who, while they lived, laboured in the service of God and their generation. Observe, He did not fall asleep till he had served his generation, till he had done the work for which God raised him up. God's servants have their work assigned them; and, when they have *accomplished as a hireling their day,* then, and not till then, they are called to rest. God's witnesses never die till they have finished their testimony; and then *the sleep,* the death, *of the labouring man will be sweet.* David was not permitted to build the temple, and therefore when he had made preparation for it, which was the service he was designed to, he fell asleep, and left the work to Solomon. [*c.*] His burial: *He was laid to his fathers.* Though he was buried in *the city of David* (1 Kings ii. 10), and not in the sepulchre of Jesse his father in Bethlehem, yet he might be said to be *laid to his fathers;* for the grave, in general, is the habitation of our fathers, of those that are gone before us, Ps. xlix. 19. [*d.*] His continuance in the grave: *He saw corruption.* We are sure he did not rise again; this Peter insists upon when he freely speaks of the patriarch David (*ch.* ii. 29): *He is both dead and buried, and his sepulchre is with us unto this day.* He saw corruption, and therefore that promise could not have its accomplishment in him. But,

(*b.*) It was accomplished in the Lord Jesus (*v.* 37): *He whom God raised again saw no corruption;* for it was in him that the sure mercies were to be reserved for us. He rose the third day, and therefore did not see corruption then; and he rose to die no more, and therefore never did. Of him therefore the promise must be understood, and no other.

c. Having given them this account of the Lord Jesus, he comes to make application of it.

(*a.*) In the midst of his discourse, to engage their attention, he had told his hearers that they were concerned in all this (*v.* 26): "*To you is the word of this salvation sent,* to you first. If you by your unbelief make it a word of rejection to you, you may thank yourselves; but it is sent to you for a word of salvation; if it be not so, it is your own fault." Let them not peevishly argue that because it was sent to the Gentiles, who had no communion with them, therefore it was not sent to them; for to them it was sent in the first place. "*To you men* this is sent, and not to the angels that sinned. To you living men, and not to the congregation of the dead and damned, whose day of grace is over." He therefore speaks to them with tenderness and respect: You are *men and brethren;* and so we are to look upon all those that stand fair with us for the great salvation as having the word of salvation sent to them. Those to whom he does by warrant from heaven here bring the *word of salvation* are, [*a.*] The native Jews, Hebrews of the Hebrews, as Paul himself was: *Children of the stock of Abraham,* though a degenerate race, yet to you is this word of salvation sent; nay, it is therefore sent to you, to save you from your sins." It is an advantage to be of a good stock; for, though salvation does not always follow the children of godly parents, yet the word of salvation does: *Abraham will command his children and his household after him.* [*b.*] The proselytes, the Gentiles by birth, that were in some degree brought over to the Jews' religion: "*Whosoever among you that feareth God.* You that have a sense of natural religion, and have subjected yourselves to the laws of that, and taken hold of the comforts of that, *to you is the word of this salvation sent;* you need the further discoveries and directions of revealed religion, are prepared for them, and will bid them welcome, and therefore shall certainly be welcome to take the benefit of them."

(*b.*) In the close of his discourse he applies what he had said concerning Christ to his hearers. He had told them a long story concerning *this Jesus;* now they would be ready to ask, What is all this to us? And he tells them plainly what it is to them.

[*a.*] It will be their unspeakable advantage if they embrace Jesus Christ, and believe this word of salvation. It will relieve them where their greatest danger lies; and that is from the guilt of their sins: "*Be it known unto you therefore, men and brethren*—we are warranted to proclaim it to you, and you are called to take notice of it." He did not stand up to preach before them, but to preach to them, and not without hopes of prevailing with them; for they are men, reasonable creatures, and capable of being argued with; they are *brethren,* spoken to, and dealt with, by men like themselves; not only of the same nature, but of the same nation. It is proper for the preachers of the gospel to call their hearers brethren, as speaking familiarly to them, and with an affectionate concern for their welfare, and as being equally interested with them in the gospel they preach. Let all that hear the gospel of Christ know these two things:—1*st,* That it is an act of indemnity granted by the King of kings to the children of men, who stand attainted at his bar of treason against his crown and dignity; and it is for and in consideration of the mediation of Christ between God and man that this act of grace is passed and proclaimed (*v.* 38): "*Through this man,* who died and rose again, *is preached unto you the forgiveness of sins.* We have to tell you, in God's name, that your sins, though many and great, may be forgiven, and how it is come about that they may be so, without any injury to God's honour, and how you may obtain the forgiveness of your sins. We are to preach repentance for the remission of sins, and divine grace giving both *repentance and remission of sins.* The remission of sins is *through this man.* By his merit it was purchased, in his name it is offered, and by his authority it is bestowed; and therefore you are concerned to be acquainted with him, and interested in him. We preach to you *the forgiveness of sins.* That is the salvation we bring you, the word of God; and therefore you ought to bid us welcome and look upon us as your friends, and messengers of good tidings." 2*ndly,* That it does that for us which the law of Moses could not do. The Jews were jealous for the law, and because it prescribed expiatory and pacificatory sacrifices, and a great variety of purifications, fancied they might be justified by it before God. "No," saith Paul, "be it known to you that it is by Christ only that *those who believe in him,* and none else, are *justified from all things,* from all the guilt and stain of sin, *from which you could not be justified by the law of Moses*" (*v.* 39); therefore they ought to entertain and embrace the gospel, and not to adhere to the law in opposition to it, because the gospel is perfective, not destructive, of the law. Note, 1. The great concern of sinners is to be justified, to be acquitted from guilt and accepted as righteous in God's sight. 2. Those who are truly justified are acquitted from all their guilt; for if any be left charged upon the sinner he is undone. 3. It was impossible for a sinner to be justified by the law of Moses. Not by his moral law, for we have all broken it, and are transgressing it daily, so that instead of justifying us it condemns us. Not by his remedial law, for it was not possible that the *blood of bulls and goats should take away sin,* should satisfy God's offended justice, or pacify the sinner's wounded conscience. It was but a ritual and typical institution. See Heb. ix. 9; x. 1, 4. 4. By Jesus Christ we obtain a complete justification; for by him a complete atonement was made for sin. We are justified, not only by him as our Judge, but by him as our righteousness, *the Lord our righteousness.* 5. All that believe in Christist, that rely upon him and give up themselves to be ruled by him, are justified by him, and none but they. 6. What the law *could not do* for us, *in that it was weak,* that the gospel of Christ does; and therefore it was folly, out of a jealousy for the law of Moses and the honour of that institution, to conceive a jealousy of the gospel of Christ and the designs of that more perfect institution.

[*b.*] It is at their utmost peril if they reject the gospel of Christ, and turn their backs upon the offer now made them (*v,* 40, 41): "*Beware therefore;* you have a fair invitation given you, look to yourselves, lest you either neglect or oppose it." Note, Those to whom the gospel is preached must see themselves upon their trial and good behaviour, and are concerned to beware lest they be found refusers of the grace offered. "Beware lest you not only come short of the blessings and benefits spoken of in the prophets as coming upon those that believe, but fall under the doom spoken of in the prophets as coming upon those that persist in unbelief: *lest that come upon you which is spoken of.*" Note, The threatenings are warnings; what we are told will come upon impenitent sinners is designed to awaken us to beware lest it should come upon us. Now the prophecy referred to we have Hab. i. 5, where the destruction of the Jewish nation by the Chaldeans is foretold as an incredible unparalleled destruction; and this is here applied to the destruction that was coming upon that nation by the Romans, for their rejecting the gospel of Christ. The apostle follows the Septuagint translation, which reads, *Behold, you despisers* (for, *behold, you among the heathen);* because it made the text more apposite to his purpose. 1*st,* "Take heed lest the guilt come upon you which was spoken of in the prophets—the guilt of despising the gospel and the tenders of it, and despising the Gentiles that were advanced to partake of it. Beware lest it be said to you, *Behold, you despisers.*" Note, It is the ruin of many that they despise religion, they look upon it as a thing below them, and are not willing to stoop to it. 2*ndly,* "Take heed lest the judgment come upon you which was spoken of in the prophets: that *you shall wonder and perish,* that is, wonderfully perish; your perdition shall be amazing to yourselves and all about you." Those that will not wonder and be saved shall wonder and perish. Those that enjoyed the privileges of the church, and flattered themselves with a conceit that these would save them, will wonder when they find their vain presumption overruled and that their privileges do but make their condemnation the more intolerable. Let the unbelieving Jews expect that God will *work a work in their days which you shall in no wise believe, though a man declare it unto you.* This may be understood as a prediction, either, 1. Of their sin, that they should be incredulous, that that great work of God, the redemption of the world by Christ, though it should be in the most solemn manner declared unto them, yet they would *in no wise believe it,* Isa. liii. 1, *Who hath believed our report?* Though it was of God's working, to whom nothing is impossible, and of his declaring, who cannot lie, yet they would not give credit to it. Those that had the honour and advantage to have this work wrought in their days had not the grace to believe it. Or, 2. Of their destruction. The dissolving of the Jewish polity, the taking of the kingdom of God from them and giving it to the Gentiles, the destruction of their holy house and city, and the dispersion of their people, was a work which one would not have believed should have ever been done, considering how much they had been the favourites of Heaven. The calamities that were brought upon them were such as were never before brought upon any people, Matt. xxiv. 21. It was said of their destruction by the Chaldeans, and it was true of their last destruction, *All the inhabitants of the world would not have believed that the enemy would have entered into the gates of Jerusalem as they did,* Lam. iv. 12. Thus is there a *strange punishment to the workers of iniquity,* especially to the despisers of Christ, Job xxxi. 3.

42 And when the Jews were gone
out of the synagogue, the Gentiles
besought that these words might be
preached to them the next sabbath.
43 Now when the congregation was
broken up, many of the Jews and
religious proselytes followed Paul
and Barnabas: who, speaking to
them, persuaded them to continue in
the grace of God. 44 And the next
sabbath day came almost the whole
city together to hear the word of
God. 45 But when the Jews saw
the multitudes, they were filled with
envy, and spake against those things
which were spoken by Paul, contradicting and blaspheming. 46 Then
Paul and Barnabas waxed bold, and
said, It was necessary that the word
of God should first have been spoken
to you: but seeing ye put it from
you, and judge yourselves unworthy
of everlasting life, lo, we turn to the
Gentiles. 47 For so hath the Lord
commanded us, *saying,* I have set
thee to be a light of the Gentiles,
that thou shouldest be for salvation
unto the ends of the earth. 48 And
when the Gentiles heard this, they
were glad, and glorified the word of
the Lord: and as many as were or-

dained to eternal life believed. 49
And the word of the Lord was published throughout all the region. 50
But the Jews stirred up the devout
and honourable women, and the
chief men of the city, and raised persecution against Paul and Barnabas,
and expelled them out of their coasts,
51 But they shook off the dust of
their feet against them, and came
unto Iconium. 52 And the disciples
were filled with joy, and with the
Holy Ghost.

The design of this story being to vindicate the apostles, especially Paul (as he doth himself at large, Rom. xi.), from the reflections of the Jews upon him for preaching the gospel to the Gentiles, it is here observed that he proceeded therein with all the caution imaginable, and upon due consideration, of which we have here an instance.

I. There were some of the Jews that were so incensed against the preaching of the gospel, not to the Gentiles, but to themselves, that they would not bear to hear it, but *went out of the synagogue* while Paul was preaching (*v.* 42), in contempt of him and his doctrine, and to the disturbance of the congregation. It is probable they whispered among themselves, exciting one another to it, and did it by consent. Now this bespoke, 1. An open infidelity, as plain a profession of unbelief as coming to hear the gospel is of faith. They thus publicly avowed their contempt of Christ and of his doctrine and law, were not ashamed, neither could they blush; and they thus endeavoured to beget prejudices in the minds of others against the gospel; they went out to draw others to follow their pernicious ways. 2. An obstinate infidelity. They went out of the synagogue, not only to show that they did not believe the gospel, but because they were resolved they would not, and therefore got out of the hearing of those things that had a tendency to convince them. They stopped their ears like the deaf adder. Justly therefore was the gospel taken from them, when they first took themselves from it, and turned themselves out of the church before they were turned out of it. For it is certainly true that God never leaves any till they first leave him.

II. The Gentiles were as willing to hear the gospel as those rude and ill-conditioned Jews were to get out of the hearing of it: *They besought that these words*, or words to this effect, *might be preached to them the next sabbath;* in *the week between*, so some take it; on the second and fifth days of the week, which in some synagogues were their lecture days. But it appears (*v.* 44) that it was the next sabbath day that they came together. They begged, 1. That the same offer might be made to them that was made to the Jews. Paul in this sermon had brought the word of salvation to the Jews and proselytes, but had taken no notice of the Gentiles; and therefore they begged that forgiveness of sins through Christ might be preached to them, as it was to the Jews. The Jews' leavings, nay, loathings, were their longings. This justifies Paul in his preaching to them, that he was invited to it, as Peter was sent for to Cornelius. Who could refuse to break the bread of life to those who begged so hard for it, and to give that to the poor at the door which the children at the table threw under their feet? 2. That the same instructions might be given to them. They had heard the doctrine of Christ, but did not understand it at the first hearing, nor could they remember all that they had heard, and therefore they begged it might be preached to them again. Note, It is good to have the word of Christ repeated to us. What we have heard we should desire to hear again, that it may take deep root in us, and the nail that is driven may be clenched and be *as a nail in a sure place.* To hear *the same things* should not be grievous, because it is safe, Phil. iii. 1. It aggravates the bad disposition of the Jews that the Gentiles desired to hear that often which they were not willing to hear once; and commends the good disposition of the Gentiles that they did not follow the bad example which the Jews set them.

III. There were some, nay, there were many, both of Jews and proselytes, that were wrought upon by the preaching of the gospel. Those who aggravated the matter of the Jews' rejection by the preaching of the gospel, cried out, as is usual in such cases, "They have cast away, and cast off, all the people of God." "Nay," says Paul, "it is not so; for abundance of the Jews have embraced Christ, and are taken in;" himself for one, Rom. xi. 1, 5. So it was here: *Many of the Jews and religious proselytes followed Paul and Barnabas,* and received further instructions and encouragement from them. 1. They submitted to the grace of God, and were admitted to the benefit and comfort of it, which is implied in their being exhorted to continue in it. They *followed Paul and Barnabas;* they became their disciples, or rather the disciples of Christ, whose agents they were. Those that join themselves to Christ will join themselves to his ministers, and follow them. And Paul and Barnabas, though they were sent to the Gentiles, yet bade those of the Jews welcome that were willing to come under their instructions, such hearty well-wishers were they to all the Jews and their friends, if they pleased. 2. They were exhorted and encouraged to persevere herein: *Paul and Barnabas, speaking to them* with all the freedom and friendship imaginable, *persuaded them to continue in the grace of God,* to hold fast that which they had received, to continue in their belief of the gospel of grace, their dependence upon the Spirit of grace, and their attendance upon the means of grace. And the grace of God shall not be wanting to those who thus continue in it.

IV. There was a cheerful attendance upon the preaching of the gospel the *next sabbath day* (*v.* 44): *Almost the whole city* (the generality of whom were Gentiles) *came together to hear the word of God.* 1. It is probable that Paul and Barnabas were not idle in the week-days, but took all opportunities in the week between (as some think the Gentiles desired) to bring them acquainted with Christ, and to raise their expectations from him. They did a great deal of service to the gospel in private discourse and conversation, as well as in their public sermons. Wisdom cried in the chief places of concourse, and the opening of the gates, as well as in the synagogues, Prov. i. 20, 21. 2. This brought a vast concourse of people to the synagogue on the sabbath day. Some came out of curiosity, the thing being new; others longing to see what the Jews would do upon the second tender of the gospel to them; and many who had heard something of the word of God came to hear more, and to hear it, *not as the word of men but as the word of God,* by which we must be ruled and judged. Now this justified Paul in preaching to the Gentiles, that he met with the most encouraging auditors among them. There *the fields were white to the harvest,* and therefore why should he not there put in his sickle?

V. The Jews were enraged at this; and not only would not receive the gospel themselves, but were filled with indignation at those that crowded after it (*v.* 45): *When the Jews saw the multitudes,* and considered what an encouragement it was to Paul to go on in his work when he saw the people thus flying like doves to their windows, and what probability there was that among these multitudes some would be, without doubt, wrought upon, and probably the greater part, to embrace Christ — this *filled them with envy.* 1. They grudged the interest the apostles had in the people, were vexed to see the synagogne so full when they were going to preach. This was the same spirit that worked in the Pharisees towards Christ; they were cut to the heart when they saw *the whole world go after him.* When the kingdom of heaven was opened they not only would not go in themselves, but were angry with those that did. 2. They opposed the doctrine the apostles preached: *They spoke against those things that were spoken by Paul,* cavilled at them, started objections againt them, finding some fault or other with every thing he said, *contradicting and blaspheming;* ἀντέλεγον ἀντιλέγοντες—*contradicting, they contradicted.* They did it with the utmost spite and rage imaginable: they persisted in their contradiction, and nothing would silence them. they contradicted for contradiction-sake, and denied that which was most evident; and, when they could find no colour of objection, they broke out into ill language against Christ and his gospel, blaspheming him and it. From the language of the carnal man that receives not the things of the Spirit of God, and therefore contradicts them, they proceed to the language of incarnate devils, and blaspheme them. Commonly those who begin with contradicting end with blaspheming.

VI. The apostles hereupon solemnly and openly declare themselves discharged from their obligations to the Jews, and at liberty to bring the word of salvation to the Gentiles, even by the tacit consent of the Jews themselves. Never let the Jew lay the fault of the carrying of the kingdom of God to the Gentiles upon the apostles, for that complaint of theirs is for ever silenced by their own act and deed, for what they did here is for ever a bar to it. "Tender and refusal (we say) are good payment in law." The Jews had the tender of the gospel, and did refuse it, and therefore ought not to say any thing against the Gentiles having it. In declaring this, it is said (*v.* 46), *Paul and Barnabas waxed bold,* more bold than they had been while they were shy of looking favourably upon the Gentiles, for fear of giving offence to the Jews, and laying a stumbling-block in their way. Note, There is a time for the preachers of the gospel to show as much of the boldness of the lion as of the wisdom of the serpent and the harmlessness of the dove. When the adversaries of Christ's cause begin to be daring, it is not for its advocates to be timid. While there is any hope of working upon those that oppose themselves they must be *instructed with meekness* (2 Tim. ii. 25); but, when that method has long been tried in vain, we must wax bold, and tell them what will be the issue of their opposition. The impudence of the enemies of the gospel, instead of frightening, should rather embolden its friends; for they are sure that they have a good cause, and they know in whom they have trusted to bear them out. Now Paul and Barnabas, having made the Jews a fair offer of gospel grace, here give them fair notice of their bringing it to the Gentiles, *if by any means* (as Paul says Rom. xi. 14) *they might provoke them to emulation.* 1. They own that the Jews were entitled to the first offer: "*It was necessary that the word of God should first have been spoken to you,* to whom the promise was made, to you *of the lost sheep of the house of Israel,* to whom Christ reckoned himself first sent." And his charge to the preachers of his gospel to *begin at Jerusalem* (Luke xxiv. 47) was a tacit direction to all that went into other countries to begin with the Jews, *to whom pertained the giving of the law,* and therefore the preaching of the gospel. *Let the children first be served,* Mark vii. 27. 2. They charge them with the refusal of it: *You put it from you;* you will not accept of it; nay, you will not so much as bear the offer of it, but take it as an affront to you." If men put the gospel from them, God justly takes it from them; why should manna be given to those that loathe it and call it *light bread*, or the privileges of the gospel forced on those that put them away, and say, *We have no part in David?* Herein they *judge themselves unworthy of everlasting life.* In one sense we must all judge ourselves unworthy of everlasting life, for there is nothing in us, nor done by us, by which we can pretend to merit it, and we must be made sensible of this; but here the meaning is, "You discover, or make it to appear, that you are not meet for eternal life; you throw away all your claims and give up your pretensions to it; since you will not take it from his hands, into whose hand the Father has given it, *κρίνετε, you do,* in effect, *pass this judgment* upon yourselves, and *out of your own mouth you shall be judged;* you will not have it by Christ, by whom alone it is to be had, and so shall your doom be, you shall not have it at all." 3. Upon this they ground their preaching the gospel to the uncircumcised: "Since you will not accept eternal life as it is offered, our way is plain, *Lo, we turn to the Gentiles.* If one will not, another will. If those that were first invited to the wedding-feast will not come, we must invite out of the highways and hedges those that will, for *the wedding must be furnished with guests.* If he that is next of kin will not do the kinsman's part, he must not complain that another will," Ruth iv. 4. 4. They justify themselves in this by a divine warrant (*v.* 47): "*For so hath the Lord commanded us;* the Lord Jesus gave us directions to witness to him in Jerusalem and Judea first, and after that *to the utmost part of the earth,* to preach the gospel to *every creature,* to *disciple all nations.*" This is according to what was foretold in the Old-Testament. When the Messiah, in the prospect of the Jews' infidelity, was ready to say, *I have laboured in vain,* he was told, to is satisfaction, that though *Israel were not gathered,* yet *he should be glorious,* that his blood should not be shed in vain, nor his purchase made in vain, nor his doctrine preached in vain, nor his Spirit sent in vain,—"For *I have set thee,* not only raised thee up, but established thee, to be *a light of the Gentiles,* not only a shining light for a time, but a standing light, set thee for a light, *that thou shouldst be for salvation unto the ends of the earth.*" Note, (1.) Christ is not only the Saviour, but the salvation, is himself our righteousness, and life, and strength. (2.) Wherever Christ is designed to be salvation, he is set up to be a light; he enlightens the understanding, and so saves the soul. (3.) He is, and is to be, light and salvation to the Gentiles, to the ends of the earth. Those of every nation shall be welcome to him, some of every nation have heard of him (Rom. x. 18), and all nations shall at length become his kingdom. This prophecy has had its accomplishment in part in the setting up of the kingdom of Christ in this island of ours, which lies, as it were, in the *ends of the earth,* a corner of the world, and shall be accomplished more and more when the time comes for the *bringing in of the fulness of the Gentiles.*

VII. The Gentiles cheerfully embraced that which the Jews scornfully rejected, *v.* 48, 49. Never was land lost for want of heirs; *through the fall of the Jews, salvation is come to the Gentiles:* the *casting off of them was the reconciling of the world, and the diminishing of them the riches of the Gentiles;* so the apostle shows at large, Rom. xi. 11, 12, 15. The Jews, the natural branches, were broken off, and the Gentiles, that were branches of the wild olive, were thereupon grafted in, *v.* 17, 19. Now here we are told how the Gentiles welcomed this happy turn in their favour.

1. They took the comfort of it: *When they heard this they were glad.* It was good news to them that they might have admission into covenant and communion with God by a clearer, nearer, and better way than submitting to the ceremonial law, and being proselyted to the Jewish religion,—that the partition-wall was taken down and they were as welcome to the benefits of the Messiah's kingdom as the Jews themselves, and might share in their promise, without coming under their yoke. This was indeed *glad tidings of great joy to all people.* Note, Our being put into a possibility of salvation, and a capacity for it, ought to be the matter of our rejoicing; when the Gentiles did but hear that the offers of grace should be made them, the word of grace preached to them, and the means of grace afforded them, *they were glad.* "Now there is some hope for us." Many grieve under doubts whether they have an interest in Christ or no, when they should be rejoicing that they have an interest in him; the golden sceptre is held out to them, and they are invited to come and touch the top of it.

2. They gave God the praise of it: *They glorified the word of the Lord;* that is, Christ (so some), the essential Word; they entertained a profound veneration for him, and expressed the high thoughts they had of him. Or, rather, *the gospel;* the more they knew of it, the more they admired it. Oh! what a light, what a power, what a treasure, does this gospel bring along with it! How excellent are its truths, its precepts, its promises! How far transcending all other institutions! How plainly divine and heavenly is its origin! Thus they *glorified the word of the Lord,* and it is this which he has himself *magnified above all his name* (Ps. cxxxviii. 2), and will *magnify* and *make honourable,* Isa. xlii. 21. They glorified the word of the Lord, (1.) Because now the knowledge of it was diffused, and not confined to the Jews only. Note, It is the glory of the word of the Lord that the

further it spreads the brighter it shines, which shows it to be not like the light of the candle, but like that of the sun when he goes forth in his strength. (2.) Because now the knowledge of it was brought to them. Note, Those speak best of the honour of the word of the Lord that speak experimentally, that have themselves been subdued by its power, and comforted by its sweetness.

3. Many of them became, not only professors of the Christian faith, but sincerely obedient to the faith: *As many as were ordained to eternal life believed.* God by his Spirit wrought true faith in those for whom he had in his councils from everlasting designed a happiness to everlasting. (1.) Those believed to whom God gave grace to believe, whom by a secret and mighty operation he brought into subjection to the gospel of Christ, and made willing in the day of his power. Those came to Christ whom the Father drew, and to whom the Spirit made the gospel call effectual. It is called *the faith of the operation of God* (Col. ii. 12), and is said to be *wrought by the same power that raised up Christ*, Eph. i. 19, 20. (2.) God gave this grace to believe to all those among them who were ordained to eternal life (for *whom he had predestinated, them he also called*, Rom. viii. 30); or, *as many as were disposed to eternal life*, as many as had a concern about their eternal state, and aimed to make sure of eternal life, believed in Christ, in whom God hath treasured up that life (1 John v. 11), and who is the only way to it; and it was the grace of God that wrought it in them. Thus all those captives, and those only, took the benefit of Cyrus's proclamation, *whose spirit God had raised up to build the house of the Lord which is in Jerusalem*, Ezra i. 5. Those will be brought to believe in Christ that by his grace are well disposed to eternal life, and make this their aim.

4. When they believed they did what they could to spread the knowledge of Christ and his gospel among their neighbours (*v.* 49): *And the word of the Lord was published throughout all the region.* When it was received with so much satisfaction in the chief city, it soon spread into all parts of the country. Those new converts were themselves ready to communicate to others that which they were so full of themselves. *The Lord gave the word, and then great was the company of those that published it*, Ps. lxviii. 11. Those that have become acquainted with Christ themselves will do what they can to bring others acquainted with him. Those in great and rich cities that have received the gospel should not think to engross it, as if, like learning and philosophy, it were only to be the entertainment of the more polite and elevated part of mankind, but should do what they can to get it published in the country among the ordinary sort of people, the poor and unlearned, who have souls to be saved as well as they.

VIII. Paul and Barnabas, having sown the seeds of a Christian church there, quitted the place, and went to do the like elsewhere. We read not any thing of their working miracles here, to confirm their doctrine, and to convince people of the truth of it; for, though God then did ordinarily make use of that method of conviction, yet he could, when he pleased, do his work without it; and begetting faith by the immediate influence of his Spirit was itself the greatest miracle to those in whom it was wrought. Yet, it is probable that they did work miracles, for we find they did in the next place they came to, *ch.* xiv. 3. Now here we are told,

1. How *the unbelieving Jews* expelled the apostles out of that country. They first turned their back upon them, and then *lifted up the heel against them* (*v.* 50): *They raised persecution against Paul and Barnabas,* excited the mob to persecute them in *their* way by insulting their persons as they went along the streets; excited the magistrates to persecute them in *their* way, by imprisoning and punishing them. When *they could not resist the wisdom and spirit wherewith they spoke,* they had recourse to these brutish methods, the last refuge of an obstinate infidelity. Satan and his agents are most exasperated against the preachers of the gospel when they see them go on successfully, and therefore then will be sure to raise persecution against them. Thus it has been the common lot of the best men in the world to suffer ill for doing well, to be persecuted instead of being preferred for the good services they have done to mankind. Observe, (1.) What method the Jews took to give them trouble: *They stired up the devout and honourable women* against them. They could not make any considerable interest themselves, but they applied to some ladies of quality in the city, that were well affected to the Jewish religion, and were proselytes of the gate, therefore called *devout women.* These, according to the genius of their sex, were zealous in their way, and bigoted; and it was easy, by false stories and misrepresentations, to incense them against the gospel of Christ, as if it had been destructive of all religion, of which really it is perfective. It is good to see honourable women devout, and well affected to religious worship: the less they have to do in the world, the more they should do for their souls, and the more time they should spend in communion with God; but it is sad when, under colour of devotion to God, they conceive an enmity to Christ, as those here mentioned. What! women persecutors! Can they forget the tenderness and compassion of their sex? What! honourable women! Can they thus stain their honour, and disgrace themselves, and do so mean a thing? But, which is strangest of all, devout women! Will they kill Christ's servants, and think therein they do God service? Let those

therefore that have zeal see that it be according to knowledge. By these devout and honourable women they stirred up likewise *the chief men of the city*, the magistrates and the rulers, who had power in their hands and set them against the apostles, and they had so little consideration as to suffer themselves to be made the tools of this ill-natured party, who *would neither go into the kingdom of heaven themselves nor suffer those who were entering to go in.* (2.) How far they carried it, so far that *they expelled them out of their coasts;* they banished them, ordered them to be carried, as we say, from constable to constable, till they were forced out of their jurisdi tion; so that it was not by fear, but downright violence, that they were driven out. This was one method which the overruling providence of God took to keep the first planters of the church from staying too long at a place; as Matt. x. 23, *When they persecute you in one city flee to another*, that thus you may the sooner *go over the cities of Israel.* This was likewise a method God took to make those that were well disposed the more warmly affected towards the apostles; for it is natural to us to pity those that are persecuted, to think the better of those that suffer when we know they suffer unjustly, and to be the more ready to help them. The expelling of the apostles out of their coasts made people inquisitive what evil they had done, and perhaps raised them more friends than conniving at them in their coasts would have done.

2. How the apostles abandoned and rejected the unbelieving Jews (*v.* 51): *They shook off the dust of their feet against them.* When they went out of the city they used this ceremony in the sight of those that sat in the gate; or, when they went out of the borders of their country, in the sight of those that were sent to see the country rid of them. Hereby, (1.) They declared that they would have no more to do with them, would take nothing that was theirs; for *they sought not theirs, but them.* Dust they are, and let them keep their dust to themselves, it shall not cleave to them. (2.) They expressed their detestation of their infidelity, and that, though they were Jews by birth, yet, having rejected the gospel of Christ, they were in their eyes no better than heathen and profane. As Jews and Gentiles, if they believe, are equally acceptable to God and good men; so, if they do not, they are equally abominable. (3.) Thus they set them at defiance, and expressed their contempt of them and their malice, which they looked upon as impotent. It was as much as to say, "Do your worst, we do not fear you; we know whom we serve and whom we have trusted." (4.) Thus they left a testimony behind them that they had had a fair offer made them of the grace of the gospel, which shall be proved against them in the day of judgment. This dust will prove that the preachers of the gospel had been among them, but were expelled by them. Thus Christ had ordered them to do, and for this reason, Matt. x. 14; Luke ix. 5. When *they left them, they came to Iconium*, not so much for safety, as for work.

3. What frame they left the new converts in *at Antioch* (*v.* 52): *The disciples*, when they saw with what courage and cheerfulness Paul and Barnabas not only bore the indignities that were done them, but went on with their work notwithstanding, they were in like manner inspirited. (1.) They were very cheerful. One would have expected that when Paul and Barnabas were expelled out of their coasts, and perhaps forbidden to return upon pain of death, the disciples would have been full of grief and full of fear, looking for no other than that, if the planters of Christianity go, the plantation would soon come to nothing; or that it would be their turn next to be banished the country, and to them it would be more grievous, for it was their own. But no; *they were filled with joy* in Christ, had such a satisfactory assurance of Christ's carrying on and perfecting his own work in them and among them, and that either he would screen them from trouble or bear them up under it, that all their fears were swallowed up in their believing joys. (2.) They were courageous, wonderfully animated with a holy resolution to cleave to Christ, whatever difficulties they met with. This seems especially to be meant by *their being filled with the Holy Ghost*, for the same expression is used of Peter's boldness (*ch.* iv. 8), and Stephen's (*ch.* vii. 55), and Paul's, *ch.* xiii. 9. The more we relish the comforts and encouragements we meet with in the power of godliness, and the fuller our hearts are of them, the better prepared we are to face the difficulties we meet with in the profession of godliness.

CHAP. XIV.

We have, in this chapter, a further account of the progress of the gospel, by the ministry of Paul and Barnabas among the Gentiles; it goes on conquering and to conquer, yet meeting with opposition, as before, among the unbelieving Jews. Here is, I. Their successful preaching of the gospel for some time at Iconium, and their being driven thence by the violence of their persecutors, both Jews and Gentiles, and forced into the neighbouring countries, ver. 1—7. II. Their healing a lame man at Lystra, and the profound veneration which the people conceived of them thereupon, which they had much ado to keep from running into an extreme, ver. 8—18. III. The outrage of the people against Paul, at the instigation of the Jews, the effect of which was that they stoned him, as they thought, to death; but he was wonderfully restored to life, ver. 19, 20. IV. The visit which Paul and Barnabas made to the churches which they had planted, to confirm them, and put them into order, ver. 21—23. V. They return to Antioch, whence they were sent forth; the good they did by the way, and the report they made to the church of Antioch of their expedition, and, if I may so say, of the campaign they had made, ver. 24—28.

AND it came to pass in Iconium,
that they went both together
into the synagogue of the Jews, and
so spake, that a great multitude both
of the Jews and also of the Greeks
believed. 2 But the unbelieving
Jews stirred up the Gentiles, and
made their minds evil affected against
the brethren. 3 Long time therefore

abode they speaking boldly in the Lord, which gave testimony unto the word of his grace, and granted signs and wonders to be done by their hands.
4 But the multitude of the city was divided: and part held with the Jews, and part with the apostles.
5 And when there was an assault made both of the Gentiles, and also of the Jews with their rulers, to use *them* despitefully, and to stone them,
6 They were ware of *it*, and fled unto Lystra and Derbe, cities of Lycaonia, and unto the region that lieth round about:
7 And there they preached the gospel.

In these verses we have,

I. The preaching of the gospel in Iconium, whither the apostles were forced to retire from Antioch. As the blood of the martyrs has been the seed of the church, so the banishment of the confessors has helped to scatter that seed. Observe, 1. How they made the first offer of the gospel *to the Jews in their synagogues;* thither they went, not only as to a place of meeting, but as to a place of meeting with them, to whom, wherever they came, they were to apply themselves in the first place. Though the Jews at Antioch had used them barbarously, yet they did not therefore decline preaching the gospel to the Jews at Iconium, who perhaps might be better disposed. Let not those of any denomination be condemned in the gross, nor some suffer for others' faults; but let us do good to those who have done evil to us. Though *the blood-thirsty hate the upright, yet the just seek their soul* (Prov. xxix. 10), seek the salvation of it. 2. How the apostles concurred herein. Notice is taken of this, that *they went both together into the synagogue,* to testify their unanimity and mutual affection, that people might say, *See how they love one another,* and might think the better of Christianity, and that they might strengthen one another's hands and confirm one another's testimony, and *out of the mouth of two witnesses every word might be established.* They did not go one one day and another another, nor one go at the beginning and the other some time after; but they went in both together.

II. The success of their preaching there: *They so spoke that a great multitude,* some hundreds perhaps, if not thousands, *both of the Jews and also of the Greeks,* that is the Gentiles, *believed.* Observe here, 1. That the gospel was now preached to Jews and Gentiles together, and those of each denomination that believed came together into the church. In the close of the foregoing chapter it was preached first to the Jews, and some of them believed, and then to the Gentiles, and some of them believed; but here they are put together, being put upon the same level. The Jews have not so lost their preference as to be thrown behind, only the Gentiles are brought to stand upon even terms with them; *both are reconciled to God in one body* (Ephes. ii. 16), and both together admitted into the church without distinction. 2. There seems to have been something remarkable in the manner of the apostles' preaching here, which contributed to their success: *They so spoke that a great multitude believed*—so plainly, so convincingly, with such an evidence and *demonstration of the Spirit,* and *with such power;* they so spoke, so warmly, so affectionately, and with such a manifest concern for the souls of men, that one might perceive they were not only convinced, but filled, with the things they spoke of, and that what they spoke came from the heart and therefore was likely to reach to the heart; they so spoke, so earnestly and so seriously, so boldly and courageously, that those who heard them could not but say that *God was with them of a truth.* Yet the success was not to be attributed to the manner of their preaching, but to the Spirit of God, who made use of that means.

III. The opposition that their preaching met with there, and the trouble that was created them; lest they should be puffed up with the multitude of their converts, there was given them this thorn in the flesh. 1. Unbelieving Jews were the first spring of their trouble here, as elsewhere (*v.* 2): they *stirred up the Gentiles.* The influence which the gospel had upon many of the Gentiles, and their embracing it, as it provoked some of the Jews to a holy jealousy and stirred them up to receive the gospel too (Rom. xi. 14), so it provoked others of them to a wicked jealousy, and exasperated them against the gospel. Thus as good instructions, so good examples, which to some are a savour of life unto life, to others are a savour of death unto death. See 2 Cor. ii. 15, 16. 2. Disaffected Gentiles, irritated by the unbelieving Jews, were likely to be the instruments of their trouble. The Jews, by false suggestions, which they were continually buzzing in the ears of the Gentiles, made *their minds evil affected against the brethren,* whom of themselves they were inclined to think favourably of. They not only took occasion in all companies, as it came in their way, but made it their business to go purposely to such as they had any acquaintance with, and said all that their wit or malice could invent to beget in them not only a mean but an ill opinion of Christianity, telling them how destructive it would certainly be to their pagan theology and worship; and, for their parts, they would rather be Gentiles than Christians. Thus they soured and embittered their spirits against both the converters and the converted. *The old serpent* did, by their poisonous tongues, infuse his venom against *the seed of the woman* into the minds of these Gentiles, and this was a *root of bitterness in them, bearing gall and wormwood.* It is no wonder if those who are ill affected towards good people wish ill to them, speak ill of them, and contrive ill against them; it is all owing to ill will. 'Εκάκωσαν, *they molested* and vexed the minds of the Gentiles (so some of the critics take it); they were continually teasing them with their impertinent solicitations. The tools of persecutors have a dog's life, set on continually.

IV. Their continuance in their work there, notwithstanding this opposition, and God's owning them in it, *v.* 3. We have here, 1. The apostles working for Christ, faithfully and diligently, according to the trust committed to them. Because the minds of *the Gentiles were evil affected against them,* one would think that therefore they should have withdrawn and hastened out of the way, or, if they had preached, should have preached cautiously, for fear of giving further provocation to those who were already enough enraged. No; on the contrary, therefore *they abode there a long time, speaking boldly in the Lord.* The more they perceived the spite and rancour of the town against the new converts, the more they were animated to go on in their work, and the more needful they saw it to continue among them, *to confirm them in the faith, and to comfort them. They spoke boldly,* and were not afraid of giving offence to the unbelieving Jews. What God said to the prophet, with reference to the unbelieving Jews in his day, was now made good to the apostles: *I have made thy face strong against their faces,* Ezek. iii. 7—9. But observe what it was that animated them: *They spoke boldly in the Lord,* in his strength, and trusting in him to bear them out; not depending upon any thing in themselves. *They were strong in the Lord, and in the power of his might.* 2. Christ working with the apostles, according to his promise, *Lo, I am with you always.* When they went on in his name and strength, he failed not to give testimony to the word of his grace. Note, (1.) The gospel is a word of grace, the assurance of God's good will to us and the means of his good work in us. It is the word of Christ's grace, for it is in him alone that we find favour with God. (2.) Christ himself has attested this word of grace, who is *the Amen, the faithful witness;* he has assured us that it is the word of God, and that we may venture our souls upon it. As it was said in general concerning the first preachers of the gospel that they had *the Lord working with them, and confirming the word by signs following* (Mark xvi. 20), so it is said particularly concerning the apostles here *that the Lord confirmed their testimony, in granting signs and wonders to be done by their hands*—in the miracles they wrought in the kingdom of nature—as well as the wonders done by their word, in the greater miracles wrought on men's minds by the power of divine grace. The Lord was with them, while they were with him, and abundance of good was done.

V. The division which this occasioned in the city (*v.* 4): *The multitude of the city was divided* into two parties, and both active and vigorous. Among the rulers and persons of rank, and among the common people, there were some that held with the unbelieving Jews, and others that held with the apostles. Barnabas is here reckoned an apostle, though not one of the twelve, nor called in the extraordinary manner that Paul was, because set apart by special designation of *the Holy Ghost to the service of the Gentiles.* It seems, this business of the preaching of the gospel was so universally taken notice of with concern that every person, even of *the multitude of the city,* was either for it or against it; none stood neuter. "Either for us or for our adversaries, for God or Baal, for Christ or Beelzebub." 1. We may here see the meaning of Christ's prediction that he *came not to send peace upon earth, but rather division,* Luke xii. 51—53. If all would have given in unanimously into his measures, there would have been universal concord; and, could men have agreed in this, there would have been no dangerous discord nor disagreement in other things; but, disagreeing here, the breach was wide as the sea. Yet the apostles must not be blamed for coming to Iconium, although before they came the city was united, and now it was divided; for it is better that part of the city go to heaven than all to hell. 2. We may here take the measures of our expectations; let us not think it strange if the preaching of the gospel occasion division, nor be offended at it; it is better to be reproached and persecuted as dividers for swimming against the stream than yield ourselves to be carried down the stream that leads to destruction. Let us hold with the apostles, and not fear those that hold with the Jews.

VI. The attempt made upon the apostles by their enemies. Their evil affection against them broke out at length into violent outrages, *v.* 5. Observe, 1. Who the plotters were: *Both the Gentiles and the Jews, with their rulers.* The Gentiles and Jews were at enmity with one another, and yet united against Christians, like Herod and Pilate, Sadducees and Pharisees, against Christ; and like *Gebal and Ammon and Amalek, of old,* against Israel. If the church's enemies can thus unite for its destruction, shall not its friends, laying aside all personal feuds, unite for its preservation? 2. What the plot was. Having now got *the rulers* on their side, they doubted not but to carry their point, and their design was *to use the apostles despitefully,* to expose them to disgrace, and then *to stone them,* to put them to death; and thus they hoped to sink their cause. They aimed to take away both their reputation and their life, and this was all they had to lose which men could take from them, for they had neither lands nor goods.

VII. The deliverance of the apostles out of the hands of those *wicked and unreasonable men, v.* 6, 7. They got away, upon notice given them of the design against them, or the beginning of the attempt upon them, of which they were soon aware, and they made an honourable retreat (for it was not an inglorious flight) to *Lystra and Derbe;* and there, 1. They found safety. Their persecutors in Iconium were for the present satisfied that they were thrust out of their borders, and pursued them no further. God has shelters for his people in a storm; nay, he is, and will be, himself their hiding place. 2. They found work, and this was what they went for. When the door of opportunity was shut against them at Iconium, it was opened at *Lystra* and *Derbe.* To these cities they went, and there, and *in the region that lieth round about, they preached the gospel.* In times of persecution ministers may see cause to quit the spot, when yet they do not quit the work.

8 And there sat a certain man at
Lystra, impotent in his feet, being a
cripple from his mother's womb, who
never had walked: 9 The same
heard Paul speak: who stedfastly
beholding him, and perceiving that
he had faith to be healed, 10 Said
with a loud voice, Stand upright on
thy feet. And he leaped and walked.
11 And when the people saw what
Paul had done, they lifted up their
voices, saying in the speech of Lycaonia, The gods are come down to us
in the likeness of men. 12 And
they called Barnabas, Jupiter; and
Paul, Mercurius, because he was the
chief speaker. 13 Then the priest of
Jupiter, which was before their city,
brought oxen and garlands unto the
gates, and would have done sacrifice
with the people. 14 *Which* when
the apostles, Barnabas and Paul,
heard *of*, they rent their clothes, and
ran in among the people, crying out,
15 And saying, Sirs, why do ye these
things? We also are men of like passions with you, and preach unto you
that ye should turn from these vanities unto the living God, which made
heaven, and earth, and the sea, and
all things that are therein: 16 Who
in times past suffered all nations to
walk in their own ways. 17 Nevertheless he left not himself without
witness, in that he did good, and
gave us rain from heaven, and fruitful seasons, filling our hearts with
food and gladness. 18 And with
these sayings scarce restrained they
the people, that they had not done
sacrifice unto them.

In these verses we have,

I. A miraculous cure wrought by Paul at Lystra upon a cripple that had been lame from his birth, such a one as was miraculously cured by Peter and John, *ch.* iii. 2. That introduced the gospel among the Jews, this among the Gentiles; both that and this were designed to represent the impotency of all the children of men in spiritual things: they are lame from their birth, till the grace of God puts strength into them; for it was when we were yet *without strength* that *Christ died for the ungodly,* Rom. v. 6. Observe here, 1. The deplorable case of the poor cripple (*v.* 8): He was *impotent in his feet, disabled* (so the word is) to such a degree that it was impossible he should set his foot to the ground, to lay any stress upon it. It was well known that he had been so *from his mother's womb,* and that he *never had walked,* nor could *stand up.* We should take occasion hence to thank God for the use of our limbs; and those who are deprived of it may observe that their case is not singular. 2. The expectation that was raised in him of a cure (*v.* 9): He heard Paul preach, and, it is likely, was much affected with what he heard, believed that the message was from heaven, and that the messengers, having their commission thence, had a divine power going along with them, and were therefore able to cure him of his lameness. This Paul was aware of, by the spirit of discerning that he had, and perhaps the aspect of his countenance did in part witness for him: *Paul perceived that he had faith to be healed;* desired it, hoped for it, had such a thing in his thoughts, which it does not appear that the lame man Peter healed had, for he expected no more than an *alms.* There *was not found such great faith in Israel* as was among the Gentiles, Matt. viii. 10. 3. The cure wrought: *Paul, perceiving that he had faith to be healed,* brought *the word and healed him,* Ps. cvii. 20. Note, God will not disappoint the desires that are of his own kindling, nor the hopes of his own raising. Paul spoke to him *with a loud voice,* either because he was at some distance, or to show that the true miracles, wrought by the power of Christ, were far unlike the lying wonders wrought by deceivers, *that peeped, and muttered, and whispered,* Isa. viii. 19. God saith, *I have not spoken in secret, in a dark place of the earth,* Isa. xlv. 19. Paul spoke to him with a loud voice, that the people about might take notice, and have their expectations raised of the effect. It does not appear that this cripple was a beggar; it is said (*v.* 8) *that he sat,* not that he sat begging. But we may imagine how melancholy it was to him to see other people walking about him, and himself disabled; and therefore how welcome Paul's word was to him, "*Stand upright on thy feet;* help thyself, and God shall help thee; try whether thou hast strength, and thou shalt find that thou hast." Some copies read it, *I say unto thee, in the name of the Lord Jesus Christ, Stand upright on thy feet.* It is certain that this is implied, and very probably was expressed, by Paul, and *power went along with this word;* for presently *he leaped and walked,* leaped up from the place where he sat, and not only *stood upright,* but to show that he was perfectly cured, and that immediately, he walked to and fro before them all. Herein the scripture was fulfilled, that when *the wilderness of the Gentile world is made to blossom as the rose then shall the lame man leap as a hart,* Isa. xxxv. 1, 6. Those that by the grace of God are cured of their spiritual lameness must show it by leaping with a holy exultation and walking in a holy conversation.

II. The impression which this cure made upon the people: they were amazed at it, had never seen nor heard the like, and fell into an ecstacy of wonder. Paul and Barnabas were strangers, exiles, refugees, in their country; every thing concurred to make them mean and despicable: yet the working of this one miracle was enough to make them in the eyes of this people truly great and honourable, though the multitude of Christ's miracles could not screen him from the utmost contempt among the Jews. We find here, 1. The people take them for gods (*v.* 11): *They lifted up their voices* with an air of triumph, saying in their own language (for it was the common people that said it), *in the speech of Lycaonia,* which was a dialect of the Greek, *The gods are come down to us in the likeness of men.* They imagined that Paul and Barnabas had dropped down to them out of the clouds, and that they were some divine powers, no less than gods, though in the likeness of men. This notion of the thing agreed well enough with the pagan theology, and the fabulous account they had of the visits which their gods made to this lower world; and proud enough they were to think that they should have a visit made to them. They carried this notion so far here that they pretended to tell which of their gods they were, according to the ideas their poets had given them of the gods (*v.* 12): *They called Barnabas Jupiter;* for, if they will have him to be a god, it is as easy to make him the prince of their gods as not. It is probable that he was the senior, and the more portly comely man, that had something of majesty in his countenance. And *Paul they called Mercury,* who was the messenger of the gods, that was sent on their errands; for Paul, though he had not the appearance that Barnabas had, was *the chief speaker,* and had a greater command of language, and perhaps appeared to have something mercurial in his temper and genius. *Jupiter* used to take *Mercury* along with him, they said, and, if he make a visit to their city, they will suppose he does so now. 2. The priest thereupon prepares *to do sacrifice to them, v.* 13. The temple of Jupiter was, it seems, before the gate of their city, as its protector and guardian; and the priest of that idol and temple, hearing the people cry out thus, took the hint presently, and thought it was time for him to bestir himself to do his duty: many a costly sacrifice he had offered to the image of Jupiter, but if Jupiter be among them *himself—in propria persona,* it concerns him to do him the utmost honours imaginable; and the people are ready to join with him in it. See how easily vain minds are carried away with a popular outcry. If the crowd give a shout, Here is Jupiter, the priest of Jupiter takes the first hint, and offers his service immediately. When Christ, the Son of God, came down, and appeared in the likeness of men, and did many, very many miracles, yet they were so far from doing sacrifice to him that they made nim a sacrifice to their pride and malice: *He was in the world, and the world knew him not; he came to his own, and his own received him not;* but Paul and Barnabas, upon the working of one miracle, are immediately deified. The same power of the god of this world which prejudices the carnal mind against truth makes errors and mistakes to find easy admission; and both ways his turn is served. They *brought oxen,* to be sacrificed *to them, and garlands,* with which to crown the sacrifices. These garlands were made up of flowers and ribbons; and they gilded the horns of the oxen they sacrificed.

Victimæ ad supplicium saginantur, hostiæ ad pœnam coronantur.

So beasts for sacrifice do feed,
First to be crown'd, and then to bleed.

So Octavius in Minutius Felix.

III. Paul and Barnabas protest against this undue respect paid them, and with much ado prevent it. Many of the heathen emperors called themselves *gods,* and took a pride in having divine honours paid them: but Christ's ministers, though real benefactors to mankind, while these tyrants only pretended to be so, refused those honours when they were tendered. Whose successor therefore he is who *sits in the temple of God,* and shows *that he is god* (2 Thess. ii. 4), and who is adored as *our lord god,* the pope, it is easy to say. Observe,

1. The holy indignation which Paul and Barnabas conceived at this: *When they heard this, they rent their clothes.* We do not find that they rent their clothes when the people vilified them, and spoke of stoning them; they could bear this without disturbance: but when they deified them, and spoke of worshipping them, they could not bear it, but rent their clothes, as being more concerned for God's honour than their own.

2. The pains they took to prevent it. They did not connive at it, nor say, "If people will be deceived, let them be deceived," much less suggest to themselves and one another that it might contribute both to the safety of their persons and the success of their ministry if they suffered the people to continue in this mistake, and so they might make a good hand of an ill thing. No, God's truth needs not the service of man's lie. Christ had put honour enough upon them in making them apostles, they needed not assume either the honour of princes or the honour of gods; they appeared with much more magnificent titles when they were called *the ambassadors of Christ,* and *the stewards of the mysteries of God,* than when they were called Jupiter and Mercury. Let us see how they prevented it.

(1.) *They ran in among the people,* as soon as they heard of it, and would not so much as stay awhile to see what the people would do. Their running in, like servants, among the people, showed that they were far from looking upon themselves as gods, or taking state upon them; they did not stand still, expecting honours to be done them, but plainly declined them by thrusting themselves into the crowd. They ran in, as men in earnest, with as much concern as Aaron *ran in between the living and the dead,* when the plague was begun.

(2.) They reasoned with them, *crying out,* that all might hear, "*Sirs, why do you these things?* Why do you go about to make gods of us? It is the most absurd thing you can do; for,

[1.] "Our nature will not admit it: *We also are men of like passions with you*" ὁμοιοπαθεῖς: it is the same word that is used concerning Elias, Jam. v. 17, where we render it, *subject to like passions as we are.* "We are men, and therefore you wrong yourselves if you expect that from us which is to be had in God only; and you wrong God if you give that honour to us, or to any other man, which is to be given to God only. We not only have such bodies as you see, but *are of like passions with you,* have *hearts fashioned like as other men* (Ps. xxxiii. 15); for, *as in water face answers to face, so doth the heart of man to man,* Prov. xxvii. 19. We are naturally subject to the same infirmities of the human nature, and liable to the same calamities of the human life; not only men, but sinful men and suffering men, and therefore will not be deified.

[2.] "Our doctrine is directly against it. Must we be added to the number of your gods whose business it is to abolish the gods you have? *We preach unto you that you should turn from these vanities unto the living God.* If we should suffer this, we should confirm you in that which it is our business to convert you from:" and so they take this occasion to show them how just and necessary it was that they should *turn to God from idols,* 1 Thess. i. 9. When they preached to the Jews, who hated idolatry, they had nothing to do but to preach the grace of God in Christ, and needed not, as the prophets in dealing with their fathers, to preach against idolatry: but, when they had to do with the Gentiles, they must rectify their mistakes in natural religion, and bring them off from the gross corruptions of that. See here what they preached to the Gentiles.

First, That the gods which they and their fathers worshipped, and all the ceremonies of their worship of them, were *vanities,* idle things, unreasonable, unprofitable, which no rational account could be given of, nor any real advantage gained from. Idols are often called vanities in the Old Testament, Deut. xxxii. 21; 1 Kings x. 13; Jer. xiv. 22. *An idol is nothing in the world* (1 Cor. viii. 4): it is not at all what it is pretended to be, it is a cheat, it is a counterfeit; it deceives those that trust to it and expect relief from it. Therefore *turn from these vanities,* turn from them with abhorrence and detestation, as Ephraim did (Hos. xiv. 8): "*What have I to do any more with idols?* I will never again be thus imposed upon."

Secondly, That the God to whom they would have them *turn* is *the living God.* They had hitherto worshipped dead images, that were utterly unable to help them (Isa. lxiv. 9), or (as they now attempted) dying men, that would soon be disabled to help them; but now they are persuaded to worship a living God, who has life in himself, and life for us, and lives for evermore.

Thirdly, That this God is the creator of the world, the fountain of all being and power: "He *made heaven and earth, and the sea, and all things therein,* even those things which you worship as gods, so that he *is the God* of your gods. You worship gods which you made, the creatures of your own fancy, and the work of your own hands. We call you to worship *the God that made you and all the world;* worship the true God, and cheat not yourselves with pretenders; worship the Sovereign Lord of all, and disparage not yourselves in bowing down to his creatures and subjects."

Fourthly, That the world owed it to his patience that he had not destroyed them long ere this for their idolatry (*v.* 16): *In times past,* for many ages, unto this day, he *suffered all nations to walk in their own ways.* These idolaters, that were called from the service of other gods, might think, "Have we not served these gods hitherto, and our fathers before us, time out of mind; and why may we not as well go on to serve them still?"—No, your serving them was a trial of God's patience, and it was a miracle of mercy that you were not cut off for it. But, though he did not destroy you for it while you were in ignorance, and knew no better (*ch.* xvii. 30) yet now that he has sent his gospel into the world, and by it has made a clear discovery o himself and his will to *all nations,* and not to the Jews only, if you still continue in your idolatry he will not bear with you as he has done. All the nations that had not the benefit of divine revelation, that is, all but the Jews, *he suffered to walk in their own ways,* for they had nothing to check them, or control them, but their own consciences, their own thoughts (Rom. ii. 15), no scriptures, no prophets; and then they were the more excusable if they mistook their way: but now that God has sent a revelation into the world which is to be published to *all nations* the case is altered. We may understand it as a judgment upon all nations that *God suffered them to walk in their own ways, gave them up to their own hearts' lusts;* but now the time is come when *the veil of the covering spread over all nations should be taken off* (Isa. xxv. 7), and now you will no longer be excused in these vanities, but must turn from them. Note, 1. God's patience with us hitherto should *lead us to repentance,* and not encourage us to presume upon the continuance of it, while we continue to provoke him. 2. Our having done ill while we were in ignorance will not bear us out in doing ill when we are better taught.

Fifthly, That even when they were not under the direction and correction of the word of God, yet they might have known, and should have known, to do better by the works of God, *v.* 17. Though the Gentiles had not the *statutes and judgments* that the Jews had to witness for God against all pretenders, no tables of testimony or tabernacle of testimony, yet *he left not himself without witness;* besides *the witness* for God within them (the dictates of natural conscience), they had *witnesses* for God round about them—the bounty of common providence. Their having no scriptures did in part excuse them, and therefore God did not destroy them for their idolatry, as he did the Jewish nation. This however did not wholly excuse them, but that notwithstanding this they were highly criminal and deeply guilty before God; for there were other *witnesses* for God, sufficient to inform them that he and he only is to be worshipped, and that to him they owed all their services from whom they received all their comforts, and therefore that they were guilty of the highest injustice and ingratitude imaginable, in alienating them from him. God, having *not left himself without witness,* has not left us without a guide, and so has left us without excuse; for whatever is a witness for God is a witness against us, if we give that glory to any other which is due to him only. 1. The bounties of common providence witness to us that there is a God, for they are all dispensed wisely and with design. The *rain and fruitful seasons* could not come by chance, nor *are there any of the vanities of the heathen that can give rain,* neither *can the heavens* of themselves *give showers,* Jer. xiv. 22. All the powers of nature witness to us a sovereign power in the God of nature, from whom they are derived, and on whom they depend. It is not the heaven that gives us rain, but God that gives us rain from heaven, he is the Father of the rain, Job xxxviii. 28. 2. The benefits we have by these bounties witness to us that we ought to make our acknowledgments not to the creatures who are made serviceable to us, but to the Creator who makes them so. *He left not himself without witness, in that he did good.* God seems to reckon the instances of his *goodness* to be more pregnant, cogent proofs of his title to our homage and adoration than the evidences of his *greatness;* for his goodness is his glory. *The earth is full of his goodness; his tender mercies are over all his works;* and therefore *they praise him,* Ps. cxlv. 9, 10. God does us good, in preserving to us his air to breathe in, his ground to go upon, the light of his sun to see by; but, because the most sensible instance of the goodness of Providence to each of us in particular is that of the daily provision made by it of meat and drink for us, the apostle chooses to insist upon that, and shows how God does us good, (1.) In preparing it for us, and that by a long train of causes which depend upon him as the first cause: *The heavens hear the earth; the earth hears the corn, and wine, and oil; and they hear Jezreel.* Hos. ii. 21, 22. He does us good in giving us rain from heaven,—rain for us to drink, for if there were no rain there would be no springs of water and we should soon die for thirst,—rain for our land to drink, for our meat as well as drink we have from the rain; in giving us this, he *gives us fruitful seasons. If the heavens be as iron, the earth* will soon *be as brass,* Lev. xxvi. 19. *This is the river of God* which *greatly enriches the earth,* and by *it God prepares us corn,* Ps. lxv. 9—13. Of all the common operations of providence, the heathen chose to form their notion of the supreme God by that which bespeaks terror, and is proper to strike an awe of him upon us, and this was *the thunder;* and therefore they called Jupiter *the thunderer,* and represented him with a thunderbolt in his hand; and it appears by Ps. xxix. 3 that this ought not to be overlooked; but the apostle here, to engage us to worship God, sets before us his beneficence, that we may have good thoughts of him in every thing wherein we have to do with him—may love him and delight in him, as one that does good, does good to us, does good to all, in giving *rain from heaven and fruitful seasons;* and if at any time rain be withheld, or the seasons be unfruitful, we may thank ourselves; it is our sin *that turns away these good things from us* which were coming to us, and stops the current of God's favours. (2.) In giving us the comforts of it. It is he *that fills our hearts with food and gladness.* God *is rich in mercy to all* (Rom. x. 12): *he gives us richly all things to enjoy* (1 Tim. vi. 17), is not only a benefactor, but a bountiful one; not only *gives us the things we need,* but *gives us to enjoy them* (Eccl. ii. 24): *He fills our hearts with food,* that is, he gives us food to our hearts' content, or according to our hearts' desire; not merely for necessity, but plenty, dainty, and variety. Even those nations that had lost the knowledge of him, and worshipped other gods, yet he *filled their houses, filled their mouths, filled their bellies* (Job xxii. 18; Ps. xvii. 14) *with good things.* The Gentiles that *lived without God in the world,* yet lived upon God, which Christ urges as a reason why we should *do good to those that hate us,* Matt. v. 44, 45. Those heathen had *their hearts filled with food;* this was their felicity and satisfaction, they desired no more; but *these things will not fill the soul* (Ezek. vii. 19), nor will those that know how to value their own souls be satisfied with them; but the apostles put themselves in as sharers in the divine beneficence. We must all own that God fills our hearts with food and gladness; not only *food,* that we may live, but *gladness,* that we may live cheerfully; to him we owe it that we do not *all our days eat in sorrow.* Note, We must thank God, not only for our food, but for our gladness—that he gives us leave to be cheerful, cause to be cheerful, and hearts to be cheerful. And, if *our hearts be filled with food and gladness,* they ought to be filled with love and thankfulness, and enlarged in duty and obedience, Deut. viii. 10; xxviii. 47.

Lastly, The success of this prohibition which the apostles gave to *the people* (*v.* 18): By *these sayings,* with much ado, they *restrained the people from doing sacrifice to them,* so strongly were these idolaters set upon their idolatry. It was not enough for the apostles to refuse to be deified (this would be construed only a pang of modesty), but they resented it, they showed the people the evil of it, and all little enough, for they could *scarcely* restrain them from it, and some of them were ready to blame the priest, that he did not go on with his business notwithstanding. We may see here what gave rise to the pagan idolatry; it was terminating those regards in the instruments of our comfort which should have passed through them to the Author. Paul and Barnabas had cured a cripple, and therefore the people deified them, instead of glorifying God for giving them such power, which should make us very cautious that we do not give that honour to another, or take it to ourselves, which is due to God only.

19 And there came thither *certain*
Jews from Antioch and Iconium, who
persuaded the people, and, having
stoned Paul, drew *him* out of the
city, supposing he had been dead.
20 Howbeit, as the disciples stood
round about him, he rose up, and
came into the city: and the next
day he departed with Barnabas to
Derbe. 21 And when they had
preached the gospel to that city, and
had taught many, they returned again
to Lystra, and *to* Iconium, and Antioch.
22 Confirming the souls of
the disciples, *and* exhorting them to
continue in the faith, and that we
must through much tribulation enter
into the kingdom of God. 23 And
when they had ordained them elders
in every church, and had prayed with
fasting, they commended them to the
Lord, on whom they believed. 24
And after they had passed throughout
Pisidia, they came to Pamphylia.
25 And when they had preached the
word in Perga, they went down into
Attalia: 26 And thence sailed to
Antioch, from whence they had been
recommended to the grace of God for
the work which they fulfilled. 27
And when they were come, and had
gathered the church together, they
rehearsed all that God had done with
them, and how he had opened the
door of faith unto the Gentiles. 28
And there they abode long time with
the disciples.

We have here a further account of the services and sufferings of Paul and Barnabas.

I. How Paul was stoned and left for dead, but miraculously came to himself again, *v.* 19, 20. They fell upon Paul rather than Barnabas, because Paul, being the chief speaker, galled and vexed them more than Barnabas did. Now observe here, 1. How the people were incensed against Paul; not by any injury they pretended he had done them (if they took it for an affront that he would not let them misplace divine honours upon him, when they considered themselves they would easily forgive him that wrong), but *there came certain Jews from Antioch,* hearing, it is likely, and vexed to hear, what respect was shown to Paul and Barnabas at Lystra; and they incensed the people against them, as factious, seditious, dangerous persons, not fit to be harboured. See how restless the rage of the Jews was against the gospel of Christ; they could not bear that it should have footing any where. 2. To what degree they were incensed by these barbarous Jews: they were irritated to such a degree that the mob rose and *stoned Paul,* not by a judicial sentence, but in a popular tumult; they threw stones at him, with which they knocked him down, and then *drew him out of the city,* as one not fit to live in it, or drew him out upon a sledge, or in a cart, to bury him, *supposing he had been dead.* So strong is the bias of the corrupt and carnal heart to that which is evil, even in contrary extremes, that, as it is with great difficulty that men are restrained from evil on one side, so it is with great ease that they are persuaded to evil on the other side. See how fickle and mutable the minds of carnal worldly people are, that do not know and consider things. Those that but the other day would have treated the apostles as more than men now treat them as worse than brutes, as the worst of men, as the worst of malefactors. To-day *Hosanna,* to-morrow *Crucify;* to-day sacrificed to, to-morrow sacrificed. We have an instance of a change the other way, *ch.* xxviii. *This man is a murderer, v.* 4; no doubt *he is a god, v.* 6. Popular breath turns like the wind. If Paul would have been Mercury, he might have been enthroned, nay, he might have been enshrined; but, if he will be a faithful minister of Christ, he shall be stoned, and thrown out of the city. Thus those who easily submit to strong delusions hate to receive the truth in the love of it. 3. How he was delivered by the power of God: When he was *drawn out of the city, the disciples stood round about him, v.* 20. It seems there were some here at Lystra that became disciples, that found the mean between deifying the apostles and rejecting them; and even these new converts had courage to own Paul when he was thus run down, though they had reason enough to fear that the same that stoned him would stone them for owning him. They stood round about him, as a guard to him against the further outrage of the people—stood about him to see whether he were alive or dead; and all of a sudden *he rose up.* Though he was not dead, yet he was ill crushed and bruised, no doubt, and fainted away; he was in a *deliquium,* so that it was not without a miracle that he came so soon to himself, and was so well as to be able to go into the city. Note, God's faithful servants, though they may be brought within a step of death, and may be looked upon as dead both by friends and enemies, shall not die as long as he has work for them to do. They *are cast down, but not destroyed,* 2 Cor. iv. 9.

II. How they went on with their work, notwithstanding the opposition they met with. All the stones they threw at Paul could not beat him off from his work: They *drew him out of the city* (*v.* 19), but, as one that set them at defiance, he *came into the city* again, to show that he did not fear them; *none* even *of these things move him.* However, their being persecuted here is a known indication to them to seek for opportunities of usefulness elsewhere, and therefore for the present they quit Lystra.

1. They went to break up and sow fresh ground at *Derbe.* Thither the next day *Paul and Barnabas departed,* a city not far off; there they preached the gospel, there they *taught many, v.* 21. And it should seem that Timothy was of that city, and was one of the disciples that now attended Paul, had met him at Antioch and accompanied him in all this circuit; for, with reference to this story, Paul tells him how fully *he had known the afflictions he endured at Antioch, Iconium, and Lystra,* 2 Tim. iii. 10, 11. Nothing is recorded that happened at Derbe.

2. They returned, and went over their work again, watering what they had sown; and, having staid as long as they thought fit at Derbe, they came back to Lystra, to Iconium, and Antioch, the cities where they had preached, *v.* 21. Now, as we have had a very instructive account of the methods they took in laying the foundation, and beginning the good work, so here we have the like of their building upon that foundation, and carrying on that good work. Let us see what they did,

(1.) They *confirmed the souls of the disciples;* that is, they inculcated that upon them which was proper to confirm them, *v.* 22. Young converts are apt to waver, and a little thing shocks them. Their old acquaintances beg they will not leave them. Those that they look upon to be wiser than themselves set before them the absurdity, indecency, and danger, of a change. They were allured, by the prospect of preferment, to stick to the traditions of their fathers; they are frightened with the danger of swimming against the stream. All this tempts them to think of making a retreat in time; but the apostles come and tell them that *this is the true grace of God wherein they stand,* and therefore they must stand to it that there is no danger like that of losing their part in Christ, no advantage like that of keeping their hold of him; that, whatever their trials may be, they shall have strength from Christ to pass through them; and, whatever their losses may be, they shall be abundantly recompensed. And this *confirms the souls of the disciples;* it fortifies their pious resolutions, in the strength of Christ, to adhere to Christ whatever it may cost them. Note, [1.] Those that are converted need to be confirmed; those that are planted need to be rooted. Ministers' work is to establish saints as well as to awaken sinners. *Non minor est virtus quam quærere parta tueri—To retain is sometimes as difficult as to acquire.* Those that were instructed in the truth must know the certainty of the things in which they have been instructed; and those that are resolved must be fixed in their resolutions. [2.] True confirmation is confirmation of the soul; it is not binding the body by severe penalties on apostates, but binding the soul. The best ministers can do this only by pressing those things which are proper to bind the soul; it is the grace of God, and nothing less, that can effectually *confirm the souls of the disciples,* and prevent their apostasy.

(2.) *They exhorted them to continue in the*

faith; or, as it may be read, *they encouraged them.* They told them it was both their duty and interest to persevere; to abide in the belief of Christ's being the Son of God, and the Saviour of the world. Note, Those that are in the faith are concerned to *continue in the faith,* notwithstanding all the temptations they may be under to desert it, from the smiles or frowns of this world. And it is requisite that they should often be exhorted to do so. Those that are continually surrounded with temptations to apostasy have need to be continually attended with pressing exhortations to perseverance.

(3.) That which they insisted most upon was *that we must through much tribulation enter into the kingdom of God.* Not only *they* must, but *we* must; it must be counted upon that all who will go to heaven must expect tribulation and persecution in their way thither. But is this the way to *confirm the souls of the disciples,* and to engage them to *continue in the faith?* One would think it would rather shock them, and make them weary. No, as the matter is fairly stated and taken entire, it will help to confirm them, and fix them for Christ. It is true they will meet with tribulation, with much tribulation; that is the worst of it: but then, [1.] It is so appointed. They must undergo it, there is no remedy, the matter is already fixed, and cannot be altered. He that has the sovereign disposal of us has determined it to be our lot that all that *will live godly in Christ Jesus should suffer persecution;* and he that has the sovereign command over us has determined this to be our duty, that all that will be Christ's disciples must *take up their cross.* When we gave up our names to Jesus Christ it was what we agreed to; when we sat down and counted the cost, if we reckoned aright, it was what we counted upon; so that if *tribulation and persecution arise because of the word* it is but what we had notice of before, it must be so: *he performeth the thing that is appointed for us.* The matter is fixed unalterably; and *shall the rock be* for us *rem ved out of its place?* [2.] It is the lot of the leaders in Christ's army, as well as of the soldiers. It is not only *you,* but *we,* that (if it be thought a hardship) are subject to it; therefore, as your own sufferings must not be a stumbling-block to you, so neither must ours; see 1 Thess. iii. 3. *Let none be moved by our afflictions, for you yourselves know that we are appointed thereunto.* As Christ did not put the apostles upon any harder service than what he underwent before them, so neither did the apostles put the ordinary Christians. [3.] It is true we must count upon *much tribulation,* but this is encouraging, that we shall get through it; we shall not be lost and perish in it. It is a Red Sea, but the Lord has opened a way through it, for *the redeemed of the Lord to pass over.* We must go down to trouble, but we shall come up again. [4.] We shall not only get through it, but get through it *into the kingdom of God;* and the joy and glory of the end will make abundant amends for all the difficulties and hardships we may meet with in the way. It is true *we must go by the cross,* but it is as true that if we keep in the way, and do not turn aside nor turn back, we shall *go to the crown,* and the believing prospect of this will make the tribulation easy and pleasant.

(4.) *They ordained them elders,* or presbyters, *in every church.* Now at this second visit they settled them in some order, formed them into religious societies under the guidance of a settled ministry, and settled that distinction between those that are taught in the word and those that teach. [1.] Every church had its governors or presidents, whose office it was to pray with the members of the church, and to preach to them in their solemn assemblies, to administer all gospel ordinances to them, and to take the oversight of them, *to instruct the ignorant, warn the unruly, comfort the feeble-minded, and convince gainsayers.* It is requisite that every particular church should have one or more such to preside in it. [2.] Those governors were then elders, that had in their qualification the wisdom and gravity of seniors, and had in their commission the authority and command of seniors: not to make new laws (this is the prerogative of the Prince, the great Lawgiver; the government of the church is an absolute monarchy, and the legislative power entirely in Christ), but to see to the observance and execution of the laws Christ has made; and so far they are to be obeyed and submitted to. [3.] These elders were *ordained.* The qualifications of such as were proposed or proposed themselves (whether the apostles or the people put them up) were judged of by the apostles, as most fit to judge; and they, having *devoted* themselves, were solemnly set *apart* to the work of the ministry, and bound to it. [4.] These elders were ordained to them, to the disciples, to their service, for their good. Those that are in the faith have need to be built up in it, and have need of the elders' help therein—the *pastors and teachers,* who are *to edify the body of Christ.*

(5.) *By prayer* joined with *fasting* they *commended them to the Lord,* to the Lord Jesus, *on whom they believed.* Note, [1.] Even when persons are brought to believe, and that sincerely, yet ministers' care concerning them is not over; there is need of watching over them still, instructing and admonishing them still; there is still that lacking in their faith which needs to be perfected. [2.] The ministers that take most care of those that believe must after all commend them to the Lord, and put them under the protection and guidance of his grace: *Lord, keep them through thine own name.* To his custody they must commit themselves, and their ministers must commit them. [3.] It is by prayer that they must be commended to the Lord. Christ, in his prayer (John xvii.), commended his disciples to his Father: *Thine they were, and thou gavest them to me. Father, keep them.* [4.] It is a great encouragement to us, in commending the disciples to the Lord, that we can say, "It is he in whom they believed; we commit to him those who have committed themselves to him, and who know they have *believed in one who is able to keep what they* and we have *committed to him against* that day," 2 Tim. i. 12. [5.] It is good to join fasting with prayer, in token of our humiliation for sin, and in order to add vigour to our prayers. [6.] When we are parting with our friends, the best farewell is to commend them to the Lord, and to leave them with him.

3. They went on preaching the gospel in other places where they had been, but, as it should seem, had not made so many converts as that now at their return they could form them into churches; therefore thither they came to pursue and carry on conversion-work. From Antioch they *passed through Pisidia,* the province in which that Antioch stood; thence they came into the province of *Pamphylia,* the head-city of which was *Perga,* where they had been before (*ch.* xiii. 13), and came thither again to *preach the word* (*v.* 25), making a second offer, to see if they were now better disposed than they were before to receive the gospel. What success they had there we are not told, but that thence they *went down to Attalia,* a city of Pamphylia, on the sea-coast. They staid not long at a place, but wherever they came endeavoured to lay a foundation which might afterwards be built upon, and to sow the seeds which would in time produce a great increase. Now Christ's parables were explained, in which he compared the kingdom of heaven to a little leaven, which in time leavened the whole lump,—to a grain of mustard-seed, which, though very inconsiderable at first, grew to a great tree,—and to the seed which a man sowed in his ground, and it sprung up he knew not how.

III. How they at length came back to Antioch in Syria, whence they had been sent forth upon this expedition. From Attalia they came by sea to Antioch, *v.* 26. And we are here told,

1. Why they came thither: because *thence they had been recommended to the grace of God,* and such a value did they put upon a solemn recommendation to the grace of God, though they had themselves a great interest in heaven, that they never thought they could show respect enough to those who had so recommended them. The brethren having recommended them to the grace of God, for the work *which they fulfilled,* now that they had fulfilled it they thought they owed them an account of it, that they might help them by their praises, as they had been helped by their prayers.

2. What account they gave them of their negociation (*v.* 27): They *gathered the church together.* It is probable that there were more Christians at Antioch than ordinarily met, or could meet, in one place, but on this occasion they called together the *leading men* of them; as the heads of the tribes are often called the *congregation* of Israel, so the ministers and principal members of the church at Antioch are called the *church.* Or perhaps as many of the people as the place would hold came together on this occasion. Or some met at one time, or in one place, and others at another. But when they had called them together, they gave them an account of two things:—(1.) Of the tokens they had had of the divine presence with them in their labours: *They rehearsed all that God had done with them.* They did not tell what *they* had done (this would have savoured of vain-glory), but what God had done with them and by them. Note, The praise of all the little good we do at any time must be ascribed to God; for it is he that not only worketh in us both to will and to do, but then worketh with us to make what we do successful. God's grace can do any thing without ministers' preaching; but ministers' preaching, even Paul's, can do nothing without God's grace; and the operations of that grace must be acknowledged in the efficacy of the word. (2.) Of the fruit of their labours among the heathen. They told how *God had opened the door of faith unto the Gentiles;* had not only ordered them to be invited to the gospel feast, but had inclined the hearts of many of them to accept the invitation. Note, [1.] There is no entering into the kingdom of Christ but by the door of faith; we must firmly believe in Christ, or we have no part in him. [2.] It is God that opens the door of faith, that opens to us the truths we are to believe, opens our hearts to receive them, and makes this a wide door, and an effectual, into the church of Christ. [3.] We have reason to be thankful that God has *opened the door of faith to the Gentiles,* has both sent them his gospel, which is *made known to all nations for the obedience of faith* (Rom. xvi. 26), and has also given them hearts to entertain the gospel. Thus the gospel was spread, and it shone more and more, and none was able to shut this door which God had opened; not all the powers of hell and earth.

3. How they disposed of themselves for the present: *There they abode a long time with the disciples* (*v.* 28), longer than perhaps at first they intended, not because they *feared their enemies,* but because they *loved their friends,* and were loth to part from them.

CHAP. XV.

Hitherto we have, with a great deal of pleasure, attended the apostles in their glorious travels for the propagating of the gospel in foreign parts, have seen the bounds of the church enlarged by the accession both of Jews and Gentiles to it; and thanks be to that God who always caused them to triumph. We left them, in the close of the foregoing chapter, reposing themselves at Antioch, and edifying the church there with the rehearsal of their experiences, and it is a pity they should ever be otherwise employed; but in this chapter we find other work (not so pleasant) cut out for them. The Christians and ministers are engaged in controversy, and those that should have been now busied in enlarging the dominions of the church have as much as they can do to compose the divisions of it; when they should have been making war upon the devil's kingdom they have much ado to keep the peace in Christ's kingdom. Yet this occurrence and the record of it are of great use to the church, both for warning to us to expect such unhappy discords among Christians, and direction to us what method to take for accommodating them. Here is, I. A controversy raised at Antioch by the judaizing teachers, who would have the believing Gentiles brought under the yoke of circumcision and the ceremonial law, ver. 1, 2. II. A consultation held with the church at Jerusalem about this matter, and the sending of delegates thither for that purpose, which occasioned the starting of the same question there, ver. 3—5. III. An account of what passed in the synod that was convened upon this occasion ver. 6. What Peter said, ver. 7—11. What Paul and Barnabas discoursed of, ver. 12. And, lastly, what James proposed for the settling of this matter, ver. 13—21. IV. The result of this debate, and the circular letter that was written to the Gentile converts, directing them how to govern themselves with respect to Jews, ver. 22—29. V. The delivering of this determination to the church at Antioch, and the satisfaction it gave them, ver. 30—35. VI. A second expedition designed by Paul and Barnabas to preach to the Gentiles, in which they quarrelled about their assistant, and separated upon it, one steering one course and the other another, ver. 36—41.

AND certain men which came
down from Judæa taught the
brethren, *and said*, Except ye be circumcised after the manner of Moses,
ye cannot be saved. 2 When therefore Paul and Barnabas had no small
dissension and disputation with them,
they determined that Paul and Barnabas, and certain other of them,
should go up to Jerusalem unto the
apostles and elders about this question. 3 And being brought on their
way by the church, they passed
through Phenice, and Samaria, declaring the conversion of the Gentiles: and they caused great joy unto
all the brethren. 4 And when they
were come to Jerusalem, they were
received of the church, and *of* the
apostles and elders, and they declared
all things that God had done with
them. 5 But there rose up certain
of the sect of the Pharisees which believed, saying, That it was needful to
circumcise them, and to command
them to keep the law of Moses.

Even when things go on very smoothly and pleasantly in a state or in a church, it is folly to be secure, and to think the mountain stands strong and cannot be moved; some uneasiness or other will arise, which is not foreseen, cannot be prevented, but must be prepared for. If ever there was a heaven upon earth, surely it was in the church at Antioch at this time, when there were so many excellent ministers there, and blessed Paul among them, building up that church in her most holy faith. But here we have their peace disturbed, and differences arising. Here is,

I. A new doctrine started among them, which occasioned this division, obliging the Gentile converts to submit to circumcision and the ceremonial law, *v.* 1. Many that had been proselytes to the Jewish religion became Christians; and they would have such as were proselyted to the Christian religion to become Jews.

1. The persons that urged this were *certain men who came down from Judea;* some think such as had been of the Pharisees (*v* 5), or perhaps of those priests who were *obedient to the faith, ch.* vi. 7. They came from Judea, pretending perhaps to be sent by the apostles at Jerusalem, at least to be countenanced by them. Having a design to spread their notions, they came to Antioch, because that was the head-quarters of those that preached to the Gentiles, and the rendezvous of the Gentile converts; and, if they could but make an interest there, this leaven would soon be diffused to all the churches of the Gentiles. They insinuated themselves into an acquaintance with the brethren, pretended to be very glad that they had embraced the Christian faith, and congratulated them on their conversion; but tell them that *yet one thing they lack,* they must be circumcised. Note, Those that are ever so well taught have need to stand upon their guard that they be not untaught again, or ill taught.

2. The position they laid down, the thesis they gave, was this, that except the Gentiles who turned Christians were *circumcised after the manner of Moses,* and thereby bound themselves to all the observances of the ceremonial law, *they could not be saved.* As to this, (1.) Many of the Jews who embraced the faith of Christ, yet continued very *zealous for the law, ch.* xxi. 20. They knew it was from God and its authority was sacred, valued it for its antiquity, had been bred up in the observance of it, and it is probable had been often devoutly affected in their attendance on these observances; they therefore kept them up after they were by baptism admitted into the Christian church, kept up the distinction of meats, and used the ceremonial purifyings from ceremonial pollutions, attended the temple service, and celebrated the feasts of the Jews. Herein they were connived at, because the prejudices of education are not to be overcome all at once, and in a few years the mistake would be effectually rectified by the destruction of the temple and the total dissolution of the Jewish church, by which the observance of the Mosaic ritual would become utterly impracticable. But it did not suffice them that they were herein indulged themselves, they must have the Gentile converts brought under the same obligations. Note, There is a strange proneness in us to make our own opinion and practice a rule and a law to every body else, to judge of all about us by our standard, and to conclude that because we do well all do wrong that do not just as we do. (2.) Those Jews who believed that Christ was the Messiah, as they could not get clear of their affection to the law, so they could not get

clear of the notions they had of the Messiah, that he should set up a temporal kingdom in favour of the Jewish nation, should make this illustrious and victorious; it was a disappointment to them that there was as yet nothing done towards this in the way they expected. But now that they hear the doctrine of Christ is received among the Gentiles, and his kingdom begins to be set up in the midst of them, if they can but persuade those that embrace Christ to embrace the law of Moses too they hope their point will be gained, the Jewish nation will be made as considerable as they can wish, though in another way; and "Therefore by all means let the brethren be pressed to be *circumcised and keep the law,* and then with our religion our dominion will be extended, and we shall in a little time be able to shake off the Roman yoke; and not only so, but to put it on the necks of our neighbours, and so shall have such a kingdom of the Messiah as we promised ourselves." Note, It is no wonder if those who have wrong notions of the kingdom of Christ take wrong measures for the advancement of it, and such as really tend to the destruction of it, as these do. (3.) The controversy about the circumcising of the Gentile proselytes had been on foot among the Jews long before this. This is observed by Dr. Whitby out of Josephus. —*Antiquit.* lib. xx. cap. 2. "That when Izates, the son of Helen queen of Adiabene, embraced the Jews' religion, Ananias declared he might do it without circumcision; but Eleazar maintained that it was a great impiety to remain uncircumcised." And when two eminent Gentiles fled to Josephus (as he relates in the history of his own life) "the zealots among the Jews were urgent for their circumcision; but Josephus dissuaded them from insisting upon it." Such has been the difference in all ages between bigotry and moderation. (4.) It is observable what a mighty stress they laid upon it; they do not only say, "*You ought to be circumcised after the manner of Moses,* and it will be good service to the kingdom of the Messiah if you be; it will best accommodate matters between you and the Jewish converts, and we shall take it very kindly if you will, and shall converse the more familiarly with you;" but, "*Except you be circumcised you cannot be saved.* If you be not herein of our mind and way, you will never go to heaven, and therefore of course you must go to hell." Note, It is common for proud impostors to enforce their own inventions under pain of damnation; and to tell people that unless they believe just as they would have them believe, and do just as they would have them do, they cannot be saved, it is impossible they should; not only their case is hazardous, but it is desperate. Thus the Jews tell their brethren that except they be of their church, and come into their communion, and conform to the ceremonies of their worship, though otherwise good men and believers in Christ, yet they cannot be saved; salvation itself cannot save them. None are in Christ but those that are within their pale. We ought to see ourselves well warranted by the word of God before we say, "Except you do so and so, you cannot be saved."

II. The opposition which Paul and Barnabas gave to this schismatical notion, which engrossed salvation to the Jews, now that Christ had opened the door of salvation to the Gentiles (*v.* 2): *They had no small dissension and disputation with them.* They would by no means yield to this doctrine, but appeared and argued publicly against it. 1. As faithful servants of Christ, they would not see his truths betrayed. They knew that Christ came to free us from the yoke of the ceremonial law, and to take down that wall of partition between Jews and Gentiles and unite them both in himself; and therefore could not bear to hear of circumcising the Gentile converts, when their instructions were only to baptize them. The Jews would unite with the Gentiles, that is, they would have them to conform in every thing to their rites, and then, and not till then, they will look upon them as their brethren; and no thanks to them. But, this not being the way in which Christ designed to unite them, it is not to be admitted. 2. As spiritual fathers to the Gentile converts, they would not see their liberties encroached upon. They had told the Gentiles that if they believed in Jesus Christ they should be saved; and now to be told that this was not enough to save them, except they were circumcised and kept the law of Moses, this was such a discouragement to them at setting out, and would be such a stumbling-block in their way, as might almost tempt them to think of returning into Egypt again; and therefore the apostles set themselves against it.

III. The expedient pitched upon for preventing the mischief of this dangerous notion, and silencing those that vented it, as well as quieting the minds of the people with reference to it. They determined that Paul and Barnabas, and some others of their number, should *go to Jerusalem to the apostles and elders,* concerning this doubt. Not that the church at Antioch had any doubt concerning it: they knew the liberty wherewith Christ had made them free; but they sent the case to Jerusalem, 1. Because those who taught this doctrine came from Jerusalem, and pretended to have directions from the apostles there to urge circumcision upon the Gentile converts; it was therefore very proper to send to Jerusalem about it, to know if they had any such direction from the church there. And it was soon found to be all wrong, which yet pretended to be of apostolical right. It was true that these *went out from them* (*v* 24), but they never had any such orders from them. 2. Because those who were taught this doctrine would be the better confirmed in their opposition to it, and in the less danger of being shocked and disturbed by it, if they were sure that *the apostles and elders at Jerusalem* (which was the Christian church that of all others retained the most affection to the law of Moses) were against it; and, if they could but have this under their hands, it would be the likeliest means to silence and shame these incendiaries, who had pretended to have it from them. 3. Because the apostles at Jerusalem were fittest to be consulted in a point not yet fully settled; and being most eminent for an infallible spirit, peculiar to them as apostles, their decision would be likely to end the controversy. It was owing to the subtlety and malice of the great enemy of the church's peace (as it appears by Paul's frequent complaints of these *judaizing teachers,* these *false apostles,* these *deceitful workers,* these *enemies of the cross of Christ),* that it had not this effect.

IV. Their journey to Jerusalem upon this errand, *v.* 3. Where we find, 1. That they were honoured at parting: *They were brought on their way by the church,* which was then much used as a token of respect to useful men, and is directed to be done *after a godly sort,* 3 John 6. Thus the church showed their favour to those who witnessed against these encroachments on the liberties of the Gentile converts, and stood up for them. 2. That they did good as they went along. They were men that would not lose time, and therefore visited the churches by the way; they passed through Phenice and Samaria, and as they went *declared the conversion of the Gentiles,* and what wonderful success the gospel had had among them, which *caused great joy to all the brethren.* Note, The progress of the gospel is and ought to be a matter of great joy. *All the brethren,* the faithful brethren in Christ's family, rejoice when more are born into the family; for the family will be never the poorer for the multitude of its children. In Christ and heaven there is portion enough, and inheritance enough for them all.

V. Their hearty welcome at Jerusalem, *v.* 4. 1. The good entertainment their friends gave them: They were *received of the church, and of the apostles and elders,* were embraced as brethren, and had audience as messengers of the church at Antioch; they received them with all possible expressions of love and friendship. 2. The good entertainment they gave their friends: They *declared all things that God had done with them,* gave them an account of the success of their ministry among the Gentiles, not what they had done, but *what God had done with them,* what he had by his grace in them enabled them to do, and what he had by his grace in their hearers enabled them to receive. As they went they had planted, as they came back they had watered; but in both they were ready to own it was God that gave the increase. Note, It is a great honour to be employed for God, to be workers for him; for those that are so have him a worker with them, and he must have all the glory.

VI. The opposition they met with from the same party at Jerusalem, *v.* 5. When Barnabas and Paul gave an account of the multitude of the Gentiles, and of the great harvest of souls gathered in to Christ there, and all about them congratulated them upon it, *there rose up certain of the sect of the Pharisees,* who received the tidings very coldly, and, though they believed in Christ, yet were not satisfied in the admission of these converts, but thought it was needful to circumcise them. Observe here, 1. That those who have been most prejudiced against the gospel yet have been captivated by it; so mighty has it been through God to the pulling down of strong-holds. When Christ was here upon earth, few or none of the rulers and of the Pharisees believed on him; but now there are those of the sect of the Pharisees who believed, and many of them, we hope, in sincerity. 2. That it is very hard for men suddenly to get clear of their prejudices: those that had been Pharisees, even after they became Christians, retained some of the old leaven. All did not so, witness Paul, but some did; and they had such a jealousy for the ceremonial law, and such a dislike of the Gentiles, that they could not admit the Gentiles into communion with them, unless they would be circumcised, and thereby engage themselves to keep the law of Moses. This was, in their opinion, needful; and for their parts they would not converse with them unless they submitted to it.

6 And the apostles and elders
came together for to consider of this
matter. 7 And when there had been
much disputing, Peter rose up, and
said unto them, Men *and* brethren,
ye know how that a good while ago
God made choice among us, that the
Gentiles by my mouth should hear
the word of the gospel and believe.
8 And God, which knoweth the
hearts, bare them witness, giving them
the Holy Ghost, even as *he did* unto
us; 9 And put no difference between us and them, purifying their
hearts by faith. 10 Now therefore
why tempt ye God, to put a yoke
upon the neck of the disciples, which
neither our fathers nor we were able
to bear? 11 But we believe that
through the grace of the Lord Jesus
Christ we shall be saved, even as
they. 12 Then all the multitude
kept silence, and gave audience to

Barnabas and Paul, declaring what miracles and wonders God had wrought
among the Gentiles by them. 13 And
after they had held their peace, James
answered, saying, Men *and* brethren,
hearken unto me: 14 Simeon hath
declared how God at the first did
visit the Gentiles, to take out of
them a people for his name. 15
And to this agree the words of the
prophets; as it is written, 16 After
this I will return, and will build again
the tabernacle of David, which is
fallen down; and I will build again
the ruins thereof, and I will set it
up: 17 That the residue of men
might seek after the Lord, and all
the Gentiles, upon whom my name
is called, saith the Lord, who doeth
all these things. 18 Known unto
God are all his works from the beginning of the world. 19 Wherefore
my sentence is, that we trouble not
them, which from among the Gentiles are turned to God: 20 But
that we write unto them, that they
abstain from pollutions of idols, and
from fornication, and *from* things
strangled, and *from* blood. 21 For
Moses of old time hath in every city
them that preach him, being read in
the synagogues every sabbath day.

We have here a council called, not by writ, but by consent, on this occasion (*v.* 6): *The apostles and presbyters came together, to consider of this matter.* They did not give their judgment separately, but came together to do it, that they might hear one another's sense in this matter; for in the multitude of counsellors there is safety and satisfaction. They did not give their judgment rashly, but considered of this matter. Though they were clear concerning it in their own minds, yet they would take time to consider of it, and to hear what might be said by the adverse party. Nor did the apostles give their judgment concerning it without the elders, the inferior ministers, to whom they thus condescended, and on whom they thus put an honour. Those that are most eminent in gifts and graces, and are in the most exalted stations in the church, ought to show respect to their juniors and inferiors; for, though *days should speak,* yet *there is a spirit in man,* Job xxxii. 7, 8. Here is a direction to the pastors of the churches, when difficulties arise, to come together in solemn meetings for mutual advice and encouragement, that they may know one another's mind, and strengthen one another's hands, and may act in concert. Now here we have,

I. Peter's speech in this synod. He did not in the least pretend to any primacy or headship in this synod. He was not master of this assembly, nor so much as chairman or moderator, *pro hac vice—on this occasion;* for we do not find that either he spoke first, to open the synod *(there having been much disputing* before he *rose up),* nor that he spoke last, to sum up the cause and collect the suffrages; but he was a faithful, prudent, zealous member of this assembly, and offered that which was very much to the purpose, and which would come better from him than from another, because he had himself been the first that preached the gospel to the Gentiles. *There had been much disputing, pro and con,* upon this question, and liberty of speech allowed, as ought to be in such cases; those of the sect of the Pharisees were some of them present, and allowed to say what they could in defence of those of their opinion at Antioch, which probably was answered by some of the elders; such questions ought to be fairly disputed before they are decided. When both sides had been heard, *Peter rose up,* and addressed himself to the assembly, *Men and brethren,* as did James afterwards, *v.* 13. And here,

1. He put them in mind of the call and commission he had some time ago *to preach the gospel to the Gentiles;* he wondered there should be any difficulty made of a matter already settled: *You know that ἀφ' ἡμερῶν ἀρχάιων—from the beginning of the days* of the gospel, many years ago, *God made choice* among us apostles of one to preach the gospel to the Gentiles, and I was the person chosen, *that the Gentiles by my mouth should hear the word, and believe, v.* 7. You know I was questioned about it and cleared myself to universal satisfaction; every body rejoiced that *God had granted to the Gentiles repentance unto life,* and nobody said a word of circumcising them, nor was there any thought of such a thing. See *ch.* xi. 18. Why should the Gentiles who hear the word of the gospel by Paul's mouth be compelled to submit to circumcision, any more than those that heard it by my mouth? Or why should the terms of their admission now be made harder than they were then?"

2. He puts them in mind how remarkably God owned him in preaching to the Gentiles, and gave testimony to their sincerity in embracing the Christian faith (*v.* 8): *God, who knows the hearts,* and therefore is able to judge infallibly of men, *bore them witness* that they were his indeed, by *giving them the Holy Ghost;* not only the graces and comforts, but the extraordinary miraculous gifts of the Holy Ghost, *even as he did unto us* apostles." See *ch.* xi. 15—17. Note, *The Lord knows those that are his,* for he knows men's hearts; and we are as our hearts are. Those to whom God *gives the Holy Ghost.*

he thereby *bears witness* to that they are his; hence we are said to be *sealed* with that Holy Spirit of promise—*marked* for God. God had bidden the Gentiles welcome to the privilege of communion with him, without requiring them to be circumcised and to keep the law; and therefore shall not we admit them into communion with us but upon those terms? "God has *put no difference between us and them* (*v.* 9); they, though Gentiles, are as welcome to the grace of Christ and the throne of grace as we Jews are; why then should we set them at a distance, as if we were holier than they?" Isa. lxv. 5. Note, We ought not to make any conditions of our brethren's acceptance with us but such as God has made the conditions of their acceptance with him, Rom. xiv. 3. Now the Gentiles were fitted for communion with God, in *having their hearts purified by faith,* and that faith God's own work in them; and therefore why should we think them unfit for communion with us, unless they will submit to the ceremonial purifying enjoined by the law to us? Note, (1.) *By faith the heart is purified;* we are not only justified, and conscience purified, but the work of sanctification is begun and carried on. (2.) Those that have their hearts purified by faith are therein made so nearly to resemble one another, that, whatever difference there may be between them, no account is to be made of it; for the faith of all the saints is alike precious, and has like precious effects (2 Peter i. 1), and those that by it are united to Christ are so to look upon themselves as joined to one another as that all distinctions, even that between Jew and Gentile, are merged and swallowed up in it.

3. He sharply reproves those teachers (some of whom, it is likely, were present) who went about to bring the Gentiles under the obligation of the law of Moses, *v.* 10. The thing is so plain that he cannot forbear speaking of it with some warmth: "*Now therefore,* since God has owned them for his, *why tempt you God to put a yoke upon the neck of the disciples,* of the believing Gentiles and their children" (for circumcision was a yoke upon their infant seed, who are here reckoned among the disciples), "*a yoke which neither our fathers nor we were able to bear?* Here he shows that in this attempt, (1.) They offered a very great affront to God: "You tempt him, by calling that in question which he has already settled and determined by no less an indication than that of the gift of the Holy Ghost; you do, in effect, ask, 'Did he know what he did? Or was he in earnest in it? Or will he abide by his own act?' Will you try whether God, who designed the ceremonial law for the people of the Jews only, will now, in its last ages, bring the Gentiles too under the obligation of it, to gratify you?" Those tempt God who prescribe to him, and say that people cannot be saved but upon such and such terms, which God never appointed; as if the God of salvation must come into their measures. (2.) They offered a very great wrong to the disciples: Christ came to proclaim *liberty to the captives,* and they go about to enslave those whom he has made free. See Neh. v. 8. The ceremonial law was a heavy yoke; they and their fathers found it difficult to be borne, so numerous, so various, so pompous, were the institutions of it. The distinction of meats was a heavy yoke, not only as it rendered conversation less pleasant, but as it embarrassed conscience with endless scruples. The ado that was made about even the unavoidable touch of a grave or a dead body, the pollution contracted by it, and the many rules about purifying from that pollution, were a heavy burden. This yoke Christ came to ease us of, and called those that were *weary and heavy laden* under it to come and take his yoke upon them, his easy yoke. Now for these teachers to go about to lay that yoke upon the neck of the Gentiles from which he came to free even the Jews was the greatest injury imaginable to them.

4. Whereas the Jewish teachers had urged that circumcision was necessary to salvation, Peter shows it was so far from being so that both Jews and Gentiles were to be saved purely *through the grace of our Lord Jesus Christ,* and in no other way (*v.* 11): *We believe to be saved through that grace* only; *πιστεύομεν σωθῆναι—We hope to be saved;* or, *We believe unto salvation in the same manner as they—καθ' ὃν τρόπον κἀκεῖνοι.* "We that are circumcised believe to salvation, and so do those that are uncircumcised; and, as our circumcision will be no advantage to us, so their uncircumcision will be no disadvantage to them; for we must depend upon the grace of Christ for salvation, and must apply that grace by faith, as well as they. There is not one way of salvation for the Jews and another for the Gentiles; *neither circumcision avails any thing nor uncircumcision* (that is neither here nor there), *but faith which works by love,* Gal. v. 6. Why should we burden them with the law of Moses, as necessary to their salvation, when it is not that, but the gospel of Christ, that is necessary both to our salvation and theirs?"

II. An account of what Barnabas and Paul said in this synod, which did not need to be related, for they only gave in a narrative of what was recorded in the foregoing chapters, *what miracles and wonders God had wrought among the Gentiles by them, v.* 12. This they had given in to the church *at Antioch* (*ch.* xiv. 27), *to their brethren by the way* (*ch.* xv. 3), and now again to the synod; and it was very proper to be given in here. That which was contended for was that the Gentiles ought to submit to the law of Moses; now, in opposition to this, Paul and Barnabas undertake to show, by a plain relation of matters of fact, that God owned the preaching of the pure gospel to them without the law, and therefore to press the law upon them now was to undo what God had done. Observe, 1. What account they gave; they declared, or opened in order, and with all the magnifying and affecting circumstances, what glorious miracles, what signs and wonders, *God had wrought among the Gentiles by them,* what confirmation he had given to their preaching by miracles wrought in the kingdom of nature, and what success he had given to it by miracles wrought in the kingdom of grace. Thus God had honoured these apostles whom the Jewish teachers condemned, and had thus honoured the Gentiles whom they contemned. What need had they of any other advocate when God himself pleaded their cause? The conversion of the Gentiles was itself a wonder, all things considered, no less than a miracle. Now if *they received the Holy Ghost by the hearing of faith,* why should they be embarrassed with *the works of the law?* See Gal iii. 2. 2. What attention was given to them: *All the multitude* (who, though they had not votes, yet came together to hear what was said) *kept silence, and gave audience to Paul and Barnabas;* it should seem they took more notice of their narrative than they did of all the arguments that were offered. As in natural philosophy and medicine nothing is so satisfactory as experiments, and in law nothing is so satisfactory as cases adjudged, so in the things of God the best explication of the word of grace is the accounts given of the operations of the Spirit of grace; to these the multitude will with silence give audience. Those that fear God will most readily hear those that can tell them *what God has done for their souls,* or by their means, Ps. lxvi. 16.

III. The speech which James made to the synod. He did not interrupt Paul and Barnabas, though, it is likely, he had before heard their narrative, but let them go on with it, for the edification of the company, and that they might have it from the first and best hand; but, *after they had held their peace,* then James stood up. *You may all prophesy one by one,* 1 Cor. xiv. 31. God is the God of order. He let Paul and Barnabas say what they had to say, and then he made the application of it. The hearing of variety of ministers may be of use when one truth does not drive out, but clench, another.

1. He addresses himself respectfully to those present: "*Men and brethren, hearken unto me.* You are men, and therefore, it is to be hoped, will hear reason; you are my brethren, and therefore will hear me with candour. We are all brethren, and equally concerned in this cause that nothing be done to the dishonour of Christ and the uneasiness of Christians."

2. He refers to what Peter had said concerning the conversion of the Gentiles (*v.* 14): "*Simeon*" (that is, Simon Peter) "*hath declared,* and opened the matter to you—*how God at the first did visit the Gentiles,* in Cornelius and his friends, who were the first-fruits of the Gentiles—how, when the gospel began first to spread, presently the Gentiles were invited to come and take the benefit of it;" and James observes here, (1.) That the *grace of God* was the origin of it; it was God *that visited the Gentiles;* and it was a kind visit. Had they been left to themselves, they would never have visited him, but the acquaintance began on his part; he not only *visited and redeemed his people,* but visited and redeemed those that were *lo ammi—not a people.* (2.) That the glory of God was the end of it: it was *to take out of them a people for his name,* who should glorify him, and in whom he would be glorified. As of old he took the Jews, so now the Gentiles, *to be to him for a name, and for a praise, and for a glory,* Jer. xiii. 11. Let all the people of God remember that therefore they are thus dignified in God, that God may be glorified in them.

3. He confirms this with a quotation out of the Old Testament: he could not prove the calling of the Gentiles by a vision, as Peter could, nor by miracles wrought by his hand, as Paul and Barnabas could, but he would prove that it was foretold in the Old Testament, and therefore it must be fulfilled, *v.* 15. *To this agree the words of the prophets;* most of the Old-Testament prophets spoke more or less of the calling in of the Gentiles, even Moses himself, Rom. x. 19. It was the general expectation of the pious Jews that the Messiah should be *a light to enlighten the Gentiles* (Luke ii. 32): but James waives the more illustrious prophecies of this, and pitches upon one that seemed more obscure: *It is written,* Amos ix. 11, 12, where is foretold, (1.) The setting up of the kingdom of the Messiah (*v.* 16): *I will raise up the tabernacle of David, that is fallen.* The covenant was made with David and his seed; but the house and family of David are here called his *tabernacle,* because David in his beginning was a shepherd, and dwelt in tents, and his house, that had been as a stately palace, had become a mean and despicable tabernacle, reduced in a manner to its small beginning. This tabernacle was ruined and *fallen down;* there had not been for many ages a king of the house of David; *the sceptre had departed from Judah,* the royal family was sunk and buried in obscurity, and, as it should seem, not enquired after. But God *will return, and will build it again,* raise it out of its ruins, a phœnix out of its ashes; and this was now lately fulfilled, when our Lord Jesus was raised out of that family, had *the throne of his father David given him,* with a promise *that he should reign over the house of Jacob for ever,* Luke i. 32, 33. And, when *the tabernacle of David* was thus rebuilt in Christ, all the rest of it was, not many years after, wholly extirpated and cut off, as was also the nation of the Jews itself, and all their genealogies were

lost. The church of Christ may be called the tabernacle of David. This may sometimes be brought very low, and may seem to be in ruins, but it shall be built again, its withering interests shall revive; it is *cast down, but not destroyed:* even dry bones are made to live. (2.) The bringing in of the Gentiles as the effect and consequence of this (*v.* 17): *That the residue of men might seek after the Lord;* not the Jews only, who thought they had the monopoly of the tabernacle of David, but *the residue of men,* such as had hitherto been left out of the pale of the visible church; they must now, upon this re-edifying of the tabernacle of David, be brought *to seek after the Lord,* and to enquire how they may obtain his favour. When David's tabernacle is set up, they *shall seek the Lord their God,* and *David their king,* Hos. iii. 5; Jer. xxx. 9. *Then Israel shall possess the remnant of Edom* (so it is in the Hebrew); but the Jews called all the Gentiles *Edomites,* and therefore the Septuagint leave out the particular mention of Edom, and read it just as it is here, *that the residue of men might seek* (James here adds, *after the Lord), and all the Gentiles,* or heathen, *upon whom my name is called.* The Jews were for many ages so peculiarly favoured that the residue of men seemed neglected; but now God will have an eye to them, and his name shall be called upon by the Gentiles; his name shall be declared and published among them, and they shall be brought both to know his name and to call upon it: they shall call themselves the people of God, and he shall call them so; and thus, by consent of both parties, *his name is called upon them.* This promise we may depend upon the fulfilling of in its season; and now it begins to be fulfilled, for it is added, *saith the Lord, who doeth this; who doeth all these things* (so the Seventy); and the apostle here: *he saith it who doeth it,* who therefore said it because he was determined to do it; and who therefore does it because he hath said it; for though with us saying and doing are two things they are not so with God. The uniting of *Jews and Gentiles in one body,* and all those things that were done in order to it, which were here foretold, were, [1.] What God did: *This was the Lord's doing,* whatever instruments were employed in it: and, [2.] It was what God delighted in, and was well pleased with; for he is the God of the Gentiles, as well as the Jews, and it is his honour *to be rich in mercy to all that call upon him.*

4. He resolves it into the purpose and counsel of God (v. 18): *Known unto God are all his works from the beginning of the world.* He not only foretold the calling of the Gentiles many ages ago by the prophets (and therefore it ought not to be a surprise or stumbling-block to us), but he foresaw and foreordained it in his eternal counsels, which are unquestionably wise and unalterably firm. It is an excellent maxim here laid down concerning all God's works, both of providence and grace, in the natural and spiritual kingdom, that they were all *known unto him from the beginning of the world,* from the time he first began to work, which supposes his knowing them (as other scriptures speak) *from before the foundation of the world,* and therefore from all eternity. Note, Whatever God does, he did before design and determine to do; for he works all, not only according to his will, but *according to the counsel of his will:* he not only *does whatever he determined* (Ps. cxxxv. 6), which is more than we can do (our purposes are frequently broken off, and our measures broken), but he *determined whatever he does.* Whatever he may say, to prove us, *he himself knows what he will do.* We know not our works beforehand, but must *do as occasion shall serve,* 1 Sam. x. 7. What we shall do in such or such a case we cannot tell till it comes to the setting to; but *known unto God are all his works;* in the volume of his book (called *the scriptures of truth,* Dan. x. 21) they are all written in order, without any erasure or interlining (Ps. xl. 7); and all God's works will, in the day of review, be found to agree exactly with his counsels, without the least error or variation. We are poor short-sighted creatures; the wisest men can see but a little way before them, and not at all with any certainty; but this is our comfort, that, whatever uncertainty we are at, there is an infallible certainty in the divine prescience: *known unto God are all his works.*

5. He gives his advice what was to be done in the present case, as the matter now stood with reference *to the Gentiles* (*v.* 19): *My sentence is; ἐγὼ κρίνω—I give it as my opinion,* or judgment; not as having authority over the rest, but as being an adviser with them. Now his advice is,

(1.) That circumcision and the observance of the ceremonial law be by no means imposed upon the Gentile converts; no, not so much as recommended nor mentioned to them. "There are many from among the Gentiles that are turned to God in Christ, and we hope there will be many more. Now I am clearly for using them with all possible tenderness, and putting no manner of hardship or discouragement upon them," *μὴ παρενοχλεῖν—"not to give them any molestation nor disturbance,* nor suggest any thing to them that may be disquieting, or raise scruples in their minds, or perplex them." Note, Great care must be taken not to discourage nor disquiet young converts with matters of *doubtful disputation.* Let the essentials of religion, which an awakened conscience will readily receive, be first impressed deeply upon them, and these will satisfy them and make them easy; and let not things foreign and circumstantial be urged upon them, which will but trouble them. *The kingdom of God,* in which they are to be trained up, *is not meat and drink,* neither the opposition nor the imposition of indifferent things, which will but trouble them; *but it is righteousness, and peace, and joy in the Holy Ghost,* which we are sure will trouble nobody.

(2.) That yet it would be well that in some things, which gave most offence to the Jews, the Gentiles should comply with them. Because they must not humour them so far as to be circumcised, and keep the whole law, it does not therefore follow that they must act in a continual contradiction to them, and study how to provoke them. It will please the Jews (and, if a little thing will oblige them, better do so than cross them) if the Gentile converts abstain, [1.] *From pollutions of idols, and from fornication,* which are two bad things, and always to be abstained from; but writing to them particularly and expressly to abstain from them (because in these things the Jews were jealous of the Gentile converts, lest they should transgress) would very much gratify the Jews; not but that the apostles, both in preaching and writing to the Gentiles that embraced Christianity, were careful to warn against, *First, Pollutions of idols,* that they should have no manner of fellowship with idolaters in their idolatrous worships, and particularly not in the feasts they held upon their sacrifices. See 1 Cor. x. 14, &c.; 2 Cor. vi. 14, &c. *Secondly, Fornication, and all manner of uncleanness.* How large, how pressing, is Paul in his cautions against this sin! 1 Cor. vi. 9—15; Eph. v. 3, &c. But the Jews, who were willing to think the worst of those they did not like, suggested that these were things in which the Gentiles, even after conversion, allowed themselves, and the apostle of the Gentiles connived at it. Now, to obviate this suggestion, and to leave no room for this calumny, James advises that, besides the private admonitions which were given them by their ministers, they should be publicly warned *to abstain from pollutions of idols and from fornication*—that herein they should be very circumspect, and should avoid all appearances of these two evils, which would be in so particular a manner offensive to the Jews. [2.] *From things strangled, and from blood,* which, though not evil in themselves, as the other two, nor designed to be always abstained from, as those were, had been forbidden by *the precepts of Noah* (Gen. ix. 4), before the giving of the law of Moses; and the Jews had a great dislike to them, and to all those that took a liberty to use them; and therefore, to avoid giving offence, let the Gentile converts abridge themselves of their liberty herein, 1 Cor. viii. 9, 13. Thus we must *become all things to all men.*

6. He gives a reason for his advice—that great respect ought to be shown to the Jews, for they have been so long accustomed to the solemn injunctions of the ceremonial law that they must be borne with, if they cannot presently come off from them (*v.* 21): *For Moses hath of old those that preach him in every city,* his writings (a considerable part of which is the ceremonial law) *being read in the synagogues every sabbath day.* "You cannot blame them if they have a great veneration for the law of Moses; for besides that they are very sure God spoke by Moses," (1.) "Moses is continually preached to them, and they are called upon *to remember the law of Moses,*" Mal. iv. 4. Note, Even that word of God which is written to us should also be preached: those that have the scriptures have still need of ministers to help them to understand and apply the scriptures. (2.) "His writings are read in a solemn religious manner, *in their synagogues,* and on *the sabbath day,* in the place and at the time of their meetings for the worship of God; so that from their childhood they have been trained up in a regard to the law of Moses; the observance of it is a part of their religion." (3.) "This has been done *of old time;* they have received from their fathers an honour for Moses; they have antiquity for it." (4.) "This has been done *in every city,* wherever there are any Jews, so that none of them can be ignorant what stress that law laid upon these things: and therefore, though the gospel has set us free from these things, yet they cannot be blamed if they are loth to part with them, and cannot of a sudden be persuaded to look upon those things as needless and indifferent which they, and their fathers before them, had been so long taught, and taught of God too, to place religion in. We must therefore give them time, must meet them half-way; they must be borne with awhile, and brought on gradually, and we must comply with them as far as we can without betraying our gospel liberty." Thus does this apostle show the spirit of a moderator, that is, a spirit of moderation, being careful to give no offence either to Jew or Gentile, and contriving, as much as may be, to please both sides and provoke neither. Note, We are not to think it strange if people be wedded to customs which they have had transmitted to them from their fathers, and which they have been educated in an opinion of as sacred; and therefore allowances must be made in such cases, and not rigour used.

22 Then pleased it the apostles
and elders, with the whole church,
to send chosen men of their own
company to Antioch with Paul and
Barnabas; *namely,* Judas surnamed
Barsabas, and Silas, chief men among
the brethren: 23 And they wrote
letters by them after this manner;
The apostles and elders and brethren
send greeting unto the brethren which
are of the Gentiles in Antioch and

Syria and Cilicia: 24 Forasmuch
as we have heard, that certain which
went out from us have troubled you
with words, subverting your souls,
saying, *Ye must* be circumcised, and
keep the law: to whom we gave no
such commandment: 25 It seemed
good unto us, being assembled with
one accord, to send chosen men unto
you with our beloved Barnabas and
Paul, 26 Men that have hazarded
their lives for the name of our Lord
Jesus Christ. 27 We have sent
therefore Judas and Silas, who shall
also tell *you* the same things by
mouth. 28 For it seemed good to
the Holy Ghost, and to us, to lay
upon you no greater burden than
these necessary things; 29 That ye
abstain from meats offered to idols,
and from blood, and from things
strangled, and from fornication: from
which if ye keep yourselves, ye shall
do well. Fare ye well. 30 So when
they were dismissed, they came to
Antioch: and when they had gathered the multitude together, they
delivered the epistle: 31 *Which*
when they had read, they rejoiced
for the consolation. 32 And Judas
and Silas, being prophets also themselves, exhorted the brethren with
many words, and confirmed *them.*
33 And after they had tarried *there*
a space, they were let go in peace
from the brethren unto the apostles.
34 Notwithstanding it pleased Silas
to abide there still. 35 Paul also
and Barnabas continued in Antioch,
teaching and preaching the word of
the Lord, with many others also.

We have here the result of the consultation that was held at Jerusalem about the imposing of the ceremonial law upon the Gentiles. Much more, it is likely, was said about it than is here recorded; but at length it was brought to a head, and the advice which James gave was universally approved and agreed to *nemine contradicente—unanimously;* and letters were accordingly sent by messengers of their own to the Gentile converts, acquainting them with their sentiments in this matter, which would be a great confirmation to them against the false teachers. Now observe here,

I. The choice of the delegates that were to be sent with Paul and Barnabas on this errand; not as if they had any suspicion of the fidelity of these great men, and could not trust them with their letters, nor as if they thought that those to whom they sent them would suspect them to have altered any thing in their letter; no, their charity thought no such evil concerning men of such tried integrity; but,

1. They thought fit *to send men of their own company to Antioch, with Paul and Barnabas, v.* 22. This was agreed to by *the apostles and elders, with the whole church,* who, it is likely, undertook to bear their charges, 1 Cor. ix. 7. They sent these messengers, (1.) To show their respect to the church at Antioch, as a sister-church, though a younger sister, and that they looked upon it as upon the same level with them; as also that they were desirous further to know their state. (2.) To encourage Paul and Barnabas, and to make their journey home the more pleasant (for it is likely they travelled on foot) by sending such excellent men to bear them company; *amicus pro vehiculo—a friend instead of a carriage.* (3.) To put a reputation upon the letters they carried, that it might appear a solemn embassy, and so much the more regard might be paid to the message, which was likely to meet with opposition from some. (4.) To keep up *the communion of saints,* and cultivate an acquaintance between churches and ministers that were at a distance from each other, and to show *that, though they were many, yet they were one.*

2. Those they sent were not inferior persons, who might serve to carry the letters, and attest the receipt of them from the apostles; but *they were chosen men, and chief men among the brethren,* men of eminent gifts, graces, and usefulness; for these are the things which denominate men chief among the brethren, and qualify them to be the messengers of the churches. They are here named: *Judas,* who was called *Barsabas* (probably the brother of that Joseph who was called *Barsabas,* that was a candidate for the apostleship, *ch.* i. 23), *and Silas.* The character which these men had in the church at Jerusalem would have some influence upon those that came from Judea, as those false teachers did, and engage them to pay the more deference to the message that was sent by them.

II. The drawing up of the letters, circular letters, that were to be sent to the churches, to notify the sense of the synod in this matter.

1. Here is a very condescending obliging preamble to this decree, *v.* 23. There is nothing in it haughty or assuming, but, (1.) That which intimates the humility of the apostles, that they join *the elders and brethren* in commission with them, the ministers, the ordinary Christians, whom they had advised with in this case, as they used to do in other cases. Though never men were so qualified as they were for a monarchical power and

authority in the church, nor had such a commission as they had, yet their decrees run not, "We, the apostles, Christ's vicars upon earth, and pastors of all the pastors of the churches" (as the pope styles himself), "and sole judges in all matters of faith;" but *the apostles, and elders, and brethren,* agree in their orders. Herein they remembered the instructions their Master gave them (Matt. xxiii. 8): *Be not you called Rabbi; for you are all brethren.* (2.) That which bespeaks their respect to the churches they wrote to; they *send* to them *greeting,* wish them health and happiness and joy, and call them *brethren of the Gentiles,* thereby owning their admission into the church, and giving them the right hand of fellowship: "You are our brethren, though Gentiles; for we meet in Christ, *the first born among many brethren,* in God our common Father." Now that *the Gentiles are fellow-heirs and of the same body,* they are to be countenanced and encouraged, and called brethren.

2. Here is a just and severe rebuke to the judaizing teachers (*v.* 24): "*We have heard that certain who went out from us have troubled you with words,* and we are very much concerned to hear it; now this is to let them know that those who preached this doctrine were false teachers, both as they produced a false commission and as they taught a false doctrine." (1.) They did a great deal of wrong to the apostles and ministers at Jerusalem, in pretending that they had instructions from them to impose the ceremonial law upon the Gentiles, when there was no colour for such a pretension. "They *went out from us* indeed—they were such as belonged to our church, of which, when they had a mind to travel, we gave them perhaps a testimonial; but, as for their urging the law of Moses upon you, we *gave* them *no such commandment,* nor had we ever thought of such a thing, nor given them the least occasion to use our names in it." It is no new thing for apostolical authority to be pleaded in defence of those doctrines and practices for which yet the apostles gave neither command nor encouragement. (2.) They did a great deal of wrong to the Gentile converts, in saying, *You must be circumcised, and must keep the law.* [1.] It perplexed them: "*They have troubled you with words,* have occasioned disturbance and disquietment to you. You depended upon those who told you, *If you believe in the Lord Jesus Christ you shall be saved;* and now you are startled by those that tell you *you must keep the law of Moses or you cannot be saved,* by which you see yourselves drawn into a snare. They trouble you with words—words, and nothing else—mere words—sound, but no substance." How has the church been troubled with words, by the pride of men that loved to hear themselves talk! [2.] It endangered them; they *subverted* their souls, put them into disorder, and pulled down that which had been built up. They took them off from pursuing pure Christianity, and minding the business of that, by filling their heads with the necessity of circumcision, and the law of Moses, which were nothing to the purpose.

3. Here is an honourable testimony given of the messengers by whom these letters were sent.

(1.) Of Paul and Barnabas, whom these judaizing teachers had opposed and censured as having done their work by the halves, because they had brought the Gentile converts to Christianity only, and not to Judaism. Let them say what they will of these men, [1.] "They are men that are dear to us; they are *our beloved Barnabas and Paul*—men whom we have a value for, a kindness for, a concern for." Sometimes it is good for those that are of eminence to express their esteem, not only for the despised truth of Christ, but for the despised preachers and defenders of that truth, to encourage them, and weaken the hands of their opposers. [2.] "They are men that have signalized themselves in the service of Christ, and therefore have deserved well of all the churches: they are men *that have hazarded their lives for the name of our Lord Jesus Christ* (*v.* 26), and therefore are worthy of double honour, and cannot be suspected of having sought any secular advantage to themselves; for they have ventured their all for Christ, have engaged in the most dangerous services, as good soldiers of Christ, and not only in laborious services." It is not likely that such faithful confessors should be unfaithful preachers. Those that urged circumcision did it to avoid persecution (Gal. vi. 12, 13); those that opposed it knew they thereby exposed themselves to persecution; and which of these were most likely to be in the right?

(2.) Of Judas and Silas: *They are chosen men* (*v.* 25), and they are men that have heard our debates, and are perfectly apprized of the matter, and will *tell you the same things by mouth," v.* 27. What is of use to us it is good to have both in writing and by word of mouth, that we may have the advantage both of reading and of hearing it. The apostles refer them to the bearers for a further account of their judgment and their reasons, and the bearers will refer them to their letters for the certainty of the determination.

4. Here is the direction given what to require from the Gentile converts, where observe,

(1.) The matter of the injunction, which is according to the advice given by James, that, to avoid giving offence to the Jews, [1.] They should never eat any thing that they knew had been offered in sacrifice to an idol, but look upon it as, though clean in itself, yet thereby polluted to them. This prohibition was afterwards in part taken off, for they were allowed to eat whatever was sold in the shambles, or set before them at their friend's table, though it had been offered to idols, except when there was danger of giving offence by it, that is, of giving occasion either to a weak Christian to think the worse of our Christianity, or to a wicked heathen to think the better of his idolatry; and in these cases it is *good to forbear,* 1 Cor. x. 25, &c. This to us is an antiquated case. [2.] *That they should not eat blood,* nor drink it; but avoid every thing that looked cruel and barbarous in that ceremony which had been of so long standing. [3.] *That they should not eat any thing that was strangled,* or died of itself, or had not the blood let out. [4.] That they should be very strict in censuring those that *were guilty of fornication,* or marrying within the degrees prohibited by the Levitical law, which, some think, is principally intended here. See 1 Cor. v. 1. Dr. Hammond states this matter thus: The judaizing teachers would have the Gentile converts to submit to all that those submitted to whom they called the proselytes of righteousness, *to be circumcised and keep the whole law;* but the apostles required no more of them than what was required of the proselytes of the gate, which was to observe *the seven precepts of the sons of Noah,* which, he thinks, are here refered to. But the only ground of this decree being in complaisance to the rigid Jews that had embraced the Christian faith, and, except in that one case of scandal, all meats being pronounced free and indifferent to all Christians as soon as the reason of the decree ceased, which, at furthest, was after the destruction of Jerusalem, the obligation of it ceased likewise. "These things are in a particular manner offensive to the Jews, and therefore do not disoblige them herein for the present; in a little time the Jews will incorporate with the Gentiles, and then the danger is over."

(2.) The manner in which it is worded. [1.] They express themselves with something of authority, that what they wrote might be received with respect, and deference paid to it: *It seemed good to the Holy Ghost, and to us,* that is, to us under the guidance of the Holy Ghost, and by direction from him: not only the apostles, but others, were endued with spiritual gifts extraordinary, and knew more of the mind of God than any since those gifts ceased can pretend to; their infallibility gave an incontestable authority to their decrees, and they would not order any thing because *it seemed good to them,* but that they knew it first *seemed good to the Holy Ghost.* Or it refers to what the Holy Ghost had determined in this matter formerly. When the Holy Ghost descended upon the apostles, he endued them with the gift of tongues, in order to their preaching the gospel to the Gentiles, which was a plain indication of God's purpose to call them in. When the Holy Ghost descended upon Cornelius and his friends, upon Peter's preaching, it was plain that Christ designed the taking down of the Jewish pale, within which they fancied the Spirit had been enclosed. [2.] They express themselves with abundance of tenderness and fatherly concern. *First,* They are afraid of burdening them: We will *lay upon you no greater burden.* So far were they from delighting to impose upon them that they dreaded nothing so much as imposing too far upon them, so as to discourage them at their setting out. *Secondly,* They impose upon them *no other than necessary things.* "The avoiding of *fornication* is necessary to all Christians at all times; the avoiding of *things strangled,* and of *blood,* and of *things offered to idols,* is necessary at this time, for the keeping up of a good understanding between you and the Jews, and the preventing of offence;" and as long as it continues necessary for that end, and no longer, it is enjoined. Note, Church-rulers should impose only necessary things, things which Christ has made our duty, which have a real tendency to the edification of the church, and, as here, to the uniting of good Christians. If they impose things only to show their own authority, and to try people's obedience, they forget that they have not authority to make new laws, but only to see that the laws of Christ be duly executed, and to enforce the observance of them. *Thirdly,* They enforce their order with a commendation of those that shall comply with it, rather than with the condemnation of those that shall transgress it. They do not conclude, "From which if you do not keep yourselves, you shall be an anathema, you shall be cast out of the church, and accursed," according to the style of after-councils, and particularly that of Trent; but, "*From which if you keep yourselves,* as we do not question but you will, *you will do well;* it will be for the glory of God, the furtherance of the gospel, the strengthening of the hands of your brethren, and your own credit and comfort." It is all sweetness and love and good humour, such as became the followers of him who, when he called us to take his yoke upon us, assured us we should find him *meek and lowly in heart.* The difference of the style of the true apostles from that of the false is very observable. Those that were for imposing the ceremonial laws were positive and imperious: *Except you keep it, you cannot be saved* (*v.* 1), you are excommunicated *ipso facto—at once, and delivered to Satan.* The apostles of Christ, who only recommend necessary things, are mild and gentle: "*From which if you keep yourselves, you will do well,* and as becomes you. *Fare ye well;* we are hearty well-wishers to your honour and peace."

III. The delivering of the letters, and how the messengers disposed of themselves.

1. *When they were dismissed,* had had their audience of leave of the apostles (it is probable that they were dismissed with prayer, and a solemn blessing in the name of the Lord, and with instructions and encouragements in their work), *they then came to An-*

tioch; they staid no longer at Jerusalem than till their business was done, and then came back, and perhaps were met at their return by those that brought them on their way at their setting out; for those that have taken pains in public service ought to be countenanced and encouraged.

2. As soon as they came to Antioch, *they gathered the multitude together, and delivered the epistle to them* (*v.* 30, 31), that they might all know what it was that was forbidden them, and might observe these orders, which would be no difficulty for them to do, most of them having been, before their conversion to Christ, proselytes of the gate, who had laid themselves under these restrictions already. But this was not all; it was that they might know that *no more* than this was forbidden them, that it was no longer a sin to eat swine's flesh, no longer a pollution to touch a grave or a dead body.

3. The people were wonderfully pleased with the orders that came from Jerusalem (*v.* 31): *They rejoiced for the consolation;* and a great consolation it was to the multitude, (1.) That they were confirmed in their freedom from the yoke of the ceremonial law, and were not burdened with that, as those upstart teachers would have had them to be. It was a comfort to them to hear that the carnal ordinances were no longer imposed on them, which perplexed the conscience, but could not purify nor pacify it. (2.) That those who troubled their minds with an attempt to force circumcision upon them were hereby for the present silenced and put to confusion, the fraud of their pretensions to an apostolical warrant being now discovered. (3.) That the Gentiles were hereby encouraged to receive the gospel, and those that had received it to adhere to it. (4.) That the peace of the church was hereby restored, and that removed which threatened a division. All this was consolation which they rejoiced in, and blessed God for.

4. They got the strange ministers that came from Jerusalem to give them each a sermon, and more, *v.* 32. Judas and Silas, *being prophets also themselves,* endued with the Holy Ghost, and called to the work, and being likewise entrusted by the apostles to deliver some things relating to this matter by word of mouth, *exhorted the brethren with many words,* and *confirmed them.* Even those that had the constant preaching of Paul and Barnabas, yet were glad of the help of Judas and Silas; the diversity of the gifts of ministers is of use to the church. Observe what is the work of ministers with those that are in Christ. (1.) To confirm them, by bringing them to see more reason both for their faith in Christ and their obedience to him; to confirm their choice of Christ and their resolutions for Christ. (2.) To exhort them to perseverance, and to the particular duties required of them: to quicken them to that which is good, and direct them in it. They comforted the brethren (so it may be rendered), and this would contribute to the confirming of them; for the joy of the Lord will be our strength. They exhorted them with many words; they used a very great copiousness and variety of expression. One word would affect one, and another another; and therefore, though what they had to say might have been summed up in a few words, yet it was for the edification of the church that they used *many words, διὰ λόγου πολλοῦ—with much speech, much reasoning; precept must be upon precept.*

5. The dismission of the Jerusalem ministers, *v.* 33. When they had *spent some time among them* (so it might be read), ποιήσαντες χρόνον—*having made some stay,* and having made it to good purpose, not having trifled away time, but having filled it up, they were let go in peace from the brethren at Antioch, to the apostles at Jerusalem, with all possible expressions of kindness and respect; they thanked them for their coming and pains, and the good service they had done, wished them their health and a good journey home, and committed them to the custody of the peace of God.

6. The continuance of Silas, notwithstanding, together with Paul and Barnabas, at Antioch. (1.) Silas, when it came to the setting to, would not go back with Judas to Jerusalem, but let him go home by himself, and chose rather to *abide still at Antioch, v.* 34. And we have no reason at all to blame him for it, though we know not the reason that moved him to it. I am apt to think the congregations at Antioch were both more large and more lively than those at Jerusalem, and that this tempted him to stay there, and he did well: so did Judas, who, notwithstanding this, returned to his post of service at Jerusalem. (2.) Paul and Barnabas, though their work lay chiefly among the Gentiles, yet continued for some time in Antioch, being pleased with the society of the ministers and people there, which, it should seem by divers passages, was more than ordinarily inviting. They continued there, not to take their pleasure, but *teaching and preaching the word of God.* Antioch, being the chief city of Syria, it is probable there was a great resort of Gentiles thither from all parts upon one account or other, as there was of Jews to Jerusalem; so that in preaching there they did in effect preach to many nations, for they preached to those who would carry the report of what they preached to many nations, and thereby prepare them for the apostles' coming in person to preach to them. And thus they were not only not idle at Antioch, but were serving their main intention. (3.) There were *many others also* there, labouring at the same oar. The multitude of workmen in Christ's vineyard does not give us a writ of ease. Even where there are many others labouring in the word and doctrine, yet there may be opportunity for us; the zeal and

usefulness of others should excite us, not lay us asleep.

36 And some days after Paul said
unto Barnabas, Let us go again and
visit our brethren in every city where
we have preached the word of the
Lord, *and see* how they do. 37 And
Barnabas determined to take with
them John, whose surname was
Mark. 38 But Paul thought not
good to take him with them, who
departed from them from Pamphylia,
and went not with them to the work.
39 And the contention was so sharp
between them, that they departed
asunder one from the other: and so
Barnabas took Mark, and sailed unto
Cyprus; 40 And Paul chose Silas,
and departed, being recommended
by the brethren unto the grace of
God. 41 And he went through
Syria and Cilicia, confirming the
churches.

We have seen one unhappy difference among the brethren, which was of a public nature, brought to a good issue; but here we have a private quarrel between two ministers, no less men than Paul and Barnabas, not compromised indeed, yet ending well.

I. Here is a good proposal Paul made to Barnabas to go and review their work among the Gentiles and renew it, to take a circuit among the churches they had planted, and see what progress the gospel made among them. Antioch was now a safe and quiet harbour for them: they had there no adversary nor evil occurrent; but Paul remembered that they only put in there to refit and refresh themselves, and therefore begins now to think of putting to sea again; and, having been in winter quarters long enough, he is for taking the field again, and making another campaign, in a vigorous prosecution of this holy war against Satan's kingdom. Paul remembered that the work appointed him was afar off among the Gentiles, and therefore he is here meditating a second expedition among them to do the same work, though to encounter the same difficulties; and this *some days after*, for his active spirit could not bear to be long out of work; no, nor his bold and daring spirit to be long out of danger. Observe, 1. To whom he makes this proposal—to Barnabas, his old friend and fellow-labourer; he invites his company and help in this work. We have need one of another, and may be in many ways serviceable one to another; and therefore should be forward both to borrow and lend assistance. Two are better than one. Every soldier has his comrade. 2. For whom the visit is designed: "Let us not presently begin new work, nor break up new ground; but let us take a view of the fields we have sown. *Come, and let us get up early to the vineyards, let us see if the vine flourish*, Cant. vii. 12. *Let us go again and visit our brethren in every city where we have preached the word of the Lord.*" Observe, He calls all the Christians brethren, and not ministers only; for, *Have we not all one Father?* He has a concern for them in *every city*, even where the brethren were fewest and poorest, and most persecuted and despised; yet let us visit them. Wherever we have *preached the word of the Lord*, let us go and water the seed sown. Note, Those that have preached the gospel should visit those to whom they have preached it. As we must look after our praying, and hear what answer God gives to that; so we must look after our preaching, and see what success that has. Faithful ministers cannot but have a particular tender concern for those to whom they have preached the gospel, that they may not bestow upon them labour in vain. See 1 Thess. iii. 5, 6. 3. What was intended in this visit: "Let us *see how they do*," πῶς ἔχουσι—*how it is with them.* It was not merely a compliment that he designed, nor did he take such a journey with a bare *How do you do?* No, he would visit them that he might acquaint himself with their case, and impart unto them such spiritual gifts as were suited to it; as the physician visits his recovering patient, that he may prescribe what is proper for the perfecting of his cure, and the preventing of a relapse. Let us see how they do, that is, (1.) What spirit they are of, how they stand affected, and how they behave themselves; it is probable that they frequently heard from them, "But let us go and see them; let us go and see whether they hold fast what we preached to them, and live up to it, that we may endeavour to reduce them if we find them wandering, to confirm them if we find them wavering, and to comfort them if we find them steady." (2.) What state they are in, whether the churches have rest and liberty, or whether they are not in trouble or distress, that we may rejoice with them if they rejoice, and caution them against security, and may weep with them if they weep, and comfort them under the cross, and may know the better how to pray for them.

II. The disagreement between Paul and Barnabas about an assistant; it was convenient to have a young man with them that should attend on them and minister to them, and be a witness of their *doctrine, manner of life, and patience*, and that should be fitted and trained up for further service, by being occasionally employed in the present service. Now, 1. Barnabas would have his nephew John, whose surname was Mark, to go along with them, *v.* 37. He determined to take him, because he was his relation, and, it is likely, was brought up under him, and he had a kindness for him, and was solicitous for his welfare. We should suspect ourselves of partiality, and guard against it in preferring our relations. 2. Paul opposed it (*v.* 38): *He thought not good to take him with them, οὐκ ἠξίου—he did not think him worthy* of the honour, nor fit for the service, who had *departed from them,* clandestinely as it should seem, without their knowledge, or wilfully, without their consent, from Pamphylia (*ch.* xiii. 13), and *went not with them to the work,* because he was either lazy and would not take the pains that must be taken, or cowardly and would not run the hazard. He run his colours just as they were going to engage. It is probable that he promised very fair now that he would not do so again. But Paul thought it was not fit he should be thus honoured who had forfeited his reputation, nor thus employed who had betrayed his trust; at least, not till he had been longer tried. If a man deceive me once, it is his fault; but, if twice, it is my own, for trusting him. Solomon saith, *Confidence in an unfaithful man in time of trouble is like a broken tooth, and a foot out of joint,* which will hardly be used again, Prov. xxv. 19.

III. The issue of this disagreement: it came to such a height that they separated upon it. The contention, the *paroxysm* (so the word is), the fit of passion which this threw them both into, was so sharp that they *departed asunder one from the other.* Barnabas was peremptory that he would not go with Paul unless they took John Mark with them; Paul was as peremptory that he would not go if John did go with them. Neither would yield, and therefore there is no remedy but they must part. Now here is that which is very humbling, and just matter of lamentation, and yet very instructive. For we see, 1. That the best of men are but men, *subject to like passions* as we are, as these two good men had expressly owned concerning themselves (*ch.* xiv. 15), and now it appeared too true. I doubt there was (as usually there is in such contentions) a *fault on both sides;* perhaps Paul was too severe upon the young man, and did not allow his fault the extenuation it was capable of, did not consider what a useful woman his mother was in Jerusalem (*ch.* xii. 12), nor make the allowances he might have made to Barnabas's natural affection. But it was Barnabas's fault that he took this into consideration, in a case wherein the interest of Christ's kingdom was concerned, and indulged it too much. And they were certainly both in fault to be hot as to let the contention be sharp (it is to be feared they gave one another some hard words), as also to be so stiff as each to stick resolutely to his opinion, and neither to yield. It is a pity that they did not refer the matter to a third person, or that some friend did not interpose to prevent its coming to an open rupture. Is there never a wise man among them to interpose his good offices, and to accommodate the matter, and to put them in mind of the Canaanite and the Perizzite that were *now in the land,* and that not only Jews and heathens, but the false brethren among themselves, would warm their hands at the flames of the contention between Paul and Barnabas? We must own it was their infirmity, and is recorded for our admonition; not that we must make use of it to excuse our own intemperate heats and passions, or to rebate the edge of our sorrow and shame for them; we must not say, "What if I was in a passion, were not Paul and Barnabas so?" No; but it must check our censures of others, and moderate them. If good men are soon put into a passion, we must make the best of it, it was the infirmity once of two of the best men that ever the world had. Repentance teaches us to be severe in reflections upon ourselves; but charity teaches us to be candid in our reflections upon others. It is only Christ's example that is a copy without a blot. 2. That we are not to think it strange if there be differences among wise and good men; we were told before that such offences would come, and here is an instance of it. Even those that are united to one and the same Jesus, and sanctified by one and the same Spirit, have different apprehensions, different opinions, different views, and different sentiments in points of prudence. It will be so while we are in this state of darkness and imperfection; we shall never be all of a mind till we come to heaven, where light and love are perfect. That is *charity* which *never fails.* 3. That these differences often prevail so far as to occasion separations. Paul and Barnabas, who were not separated by the persecutions of the unbelieving Jews, nor the impositions of the believing Jews, were yet separated by an unhappy disagreement between themselves. O the mischief that even the poor and weak remainders of pride and passion, that are found even in good men, do in the world, do in the church! No wonder the consequences are so fatal where they reign.

IV. The good that was brought out of this evil—meat out of the eater, and sweetness out of the strong. It was strange that even the sufferings of the apostles (as Phil. i. 12), but much more strange that even the quarrels of the apostles, should tend to the *furtherance of the gospel of Christ;* yet so it proved here. God would not permit such things to be, if he knew not how to make them to serve his own purposes. 1. More places are hereby visited. Barnabas went one way; he sailed to Cyprus (*v.* 39), that famous island where they began their work (*ch.* xiii. 4), and which was *his own country, ch.* iv. 36. Paul went another way into Cilicia, which was *his own country, ch.* xxi. 39. Each seems to be influenced by his affection to his native soil, as usual *(Nescio quâ natale solum dulcedine cunctos ducit—There is something that attaches us all to our native soil),* and yet God served his own purposes by it, for the diffusing of gospel light. 2. More hands are hereby employed in the ministry of the gospel among the Gentiles; for, (1.) John Mark, who had been an unfaithful hand, is not rejected, but is again made use of, against Paul's mind, and, for aught we know, proves a very useful and successful hand, though many think it was not the same with that Mark that wrote the gospel, and founded the church at Alexandria, and whom Peter calls his son, 1 Pet. v. 13. (2.) Silas who was a new hand, and never yet employed in that work, nor intended to be, but to return to the service of the church at Jerusalem, had not God changed his mind (*v.* 33, 34), he is brought in, and engaged in that noble work.

V. We may further observe, 1. That the church at Antioch seem to countenance Paul in what he did. Barnabas sailed with his nephew to Cyprus, and no notice was taken of him, nor a *bene discessit—a recommendation* given him. Note, Those that in their service of the church are swayed by private affections and regards forfeit public honours and respect. But, when Paul departed, he was *recommended by the brethren to the grace of God.* They thought he was in the right in refusing to make use of John Mark, and could not but blame Barnabas for insisting upon it, though he was one who had deserved well of the church (*ch.* xi. 22) before they knew Paul; and therefore they prayed publicly for Paul, and for the success of his ministry, encouraged him to go on in his work, and, though they could do nothing themselves to further him, they transferred the matter to the grace of God, leaving it to that grace both to work upon him and to work with him. Note, Those are happy at all times, and especially in times of disagreement and contention, who are enabled so to carry themselves as not to forfeit their interest in the love and prayers of good people. 2. That yet Paul afterwards seems to have had, though not upon second thoughts, yet upon further trial, a better opinion of John Mark than now he had; for he writes to Timothy (2 Tim. iv. 11), *Take Mark and bring him with thee, for he is profitable to me for the ministry;* and he writes to the Colossians concerning Marcus, sister's son to Barnabas, that *if he came to them* they should *receive him,* bid him welcome, and employ him (Col. iv. 10), which teaches us, (1.) That even those whom we justly condemn we should condemn moderately, and with a great deal of temper, because we know not but afterwards we may see cause to think better of them, and both to make use of them and make friendship with them, and we should so regulate our resentments that if it should prove so we may not afterwards be ashamed of them. (2.) That even those whom we have justly condemned, if afterwards they prove more faithful, we should cheerfully receive, forgive and forget, and put a confidence in, and, as there is occasion, give a good word to. 3. That Paul, though he wanted his old friend and companion in the kingdom and patience of Jesus Christ, yet went on cheerfully in his work (*v.* 41): *He went through Syria and Cilicia,* countries which lay next to Antioch, *confirming the churches.* Though we change our colleagues, we do not change our principal president. And observe, Ministers are well employed, and ought to think themselves so, and be satisfied, when they are made use of in confirming those that believe, as well as in converting those that believe not.

CHAP. XVI.

It is some rebuke to Barnabas that after he left Paul we hear no more of him, of what he did or suffered for Christ. But Paul, as he was recommended by the brethren to the grace of God, so his services for Christ after this are largely recorded; we are to attend him in this chapter from place to place, wherever he came doing good, either watering or planting, beginning new work or improving what was done. Here is, I. The beginning of his acquaintance with Timothy, and taking him to be his assistant, ver. 1—3. II. The visit he made to the churches for their establishment, ver. 4, 5. III. His call to Macedonia (after a restraint he had been under from going to some other places), and his coming to Philippi, the chief city of Macedonia, with his entertainment there, ver. 6—13. IV. The conversion of Lydia there, ver. 14, 15. V. The casting of an evil spirit out of a damsel, ver. 16—18. VI. The accusing and abusing of Paul and Silas for it, their imprisonment, and the indignities done them, ver. 19—24. VII. The miraculous conversion of the jailer to the faith of Christ, ver. 25—34. VIII. The honourable discharge of Paul and Silas by the magistrates, ver. 35—40.

THEN came he to Derbe and
Lystra: and, behold, a certain
disciple was there, named Timotheus,
the son of a certain woman, which
was a Jewess, and believed; but his
father *was* a Greek: 2 Which was
well reported of by the brethren that
were at Lystra and Iconium. 3 Him
would Paul have to go forth with
him; and took and circumcised him
because of the Jews which were in
those quarters: for they knew all
that his father was a Greek. 4 And
as they went through the cities, they
delivered them the decrees for to
keep, that were ordained of the
apostles and elders which were at
Jerusalem. 5 And so were the
churches established in the faith, and
increased in number daily.

Paul was a spiritual father, and as such a one we have him here adopting Timothy, and taking care of the education of many others who had been begotten to Christ by his ministry: and in all he appears to have been a wise and tender father. Here is,

I. His taking Timothy into his acquaintance and under his tuition. One thing designed in the book of the Acts is to help us to understand Paul's epistles, two of which are directed to Timothy; it was therefore necessary that in the history of Paul we should have some account concerning him. And we are here accordingly told, 1. That he was a disciple, one that belonged to Christ, and was baptized, probably in his infancy, when his mother became a believer, as Lydia's household was baptized upon her believing, *v.* 15. Him, that was a disciple of Christ, Paul took to be his disciple, that he might further train him up in the knowledge and faith of Christ; he took him to be brought up for Christ. 2. That his mother was a Jewess originally, *but believed in Christ;* her name was *Eunice,* his grandmother's name was *Lois.* Paul speaks of them both with great respect, as women of eminent virtue and piety, and commends them especially for their unfeigned faith (2 Tim. i. 5), their sincerely embracing and adhering to the doctrine of Christ. 3. That his father was a Greek, a Gentile. The marriage of a Jewish woman to a Gentile husband (though some would make a difference) was prohibited as much as the marriage of a Jewish man to a Gentile wife, Deut. vii. 3. Thou shalt no more *give thy daughter to his son than take his daughter to thy son;* yet this seems to have been limited to the nations that lived among them in Canaan, whom they were most in danger of infection from. Now because his father was a Greek he was not circumcised: for the entail of the covenant and the seal of it, as of other entails in that nation, went by the father, not by the mother; so that his father being no Jew he was not obliged to circumcision, nor entitled to it, unless when he grew up he did himself desire it. But, observe, though his mother could not prevail to have him circumcised in his infancy, because his father was of another mind and way, yet she educated him in the fear of God, that though he wanted the sign of the covenant he might not want the thing signified. 4. That he had gained a very good character among the Christians: he was *well reported of by the brethren* that were at Lystra and Iconium; he had not only an unblemished reputation, and was free from scandal, but he had a bright reputation, and great encomiums were given of him, as an extraordinary young man, and one from whom great things were expected. Not only those in the place where he was born, but those in the neighbouring cities, admired him, and spoke honourably of him. He had a name for good things with good people. 5. That Paul would have him *to go forth with him,* to accompany him, to give attendance on him, to receive instruction from him, and to join with him in the work of the gospel—to preach for him when there was occasion, and to be left behind in places where he had planted churches. Paul had a great love for him, not only because he was an ingenious young man, and one of great parts, but because he was a serious young man, and one of devout affections: for Paul was always *mindful of his tears,* 2 Tim. i. 4. 6. That Paul took him and circumcised him, or ordered it to be done. This was strange. Had not Paul opposed those with all his might that were for imposing circumcision upon the Gentile converts? Had he not at this time the decrees of the council at Jerusalem with him, which witnessed against it? He had, and yet circumcised Timothy, not, as those teachers designed in imposing circumcision, to oblige him to keep the ceremonial law, but only to render his conversation and ministry passable, and, if it might be, acceptable among the Jews that abounded in those quarters. He knew Timothy was a man likely to do a great deal of good among them, being admirably qualified for the ministry, if they were not invincibly prejudiced against him; and therefore, that they might not shun him as one unclean, because uncircumcised, he took him and *circumcised him.* Thus *to the Jews he became as a Jew, that he might gain the Jews,* and *all things to all men, that he might gain some.* He was against those who made circumcision necessary to salvation, but used it himself when it was conducive to edification; nor was he rigid in opposing it, as they were in imposing it. Thus, though he went not in this instance according to the letter of the decree, he went according to the spirit of it, which was a spirit of tenderness towards the Jews, and willingness to bring them off gradually from their prejudices. Paul made no difficulty of taking Timothy to be his companion, though he was uncircumcised; but the Jews would not hear him if he were, and therefore Paul will humour them herein. It is probable that it was at this time that Paul laid his hands on Timothy, for the conferring of the gift of the Holy Ghost upon him, 2 Tim. i. 6.

II. His confirming the churches which he had planted (*v.* 4, 5): *He went through the cities* where he had *preached the word of the Lord,* as he intended (*ch.* xv. 36), to enquire into their state. And we are told,

1. That they delivered to them copies of the decrees of the Jerusalem synod, to be a direction to them in the government of themselves, and that they might have wherewith to answer the judaizing teachers, and to justify themselves in adhering to the *liberty with which Christ had made them free.* All the churches were concerned in that decree, and therefore it was requisite they should all have it well attested. Though Paul had for a particular reason circumcised Timothy, yet he would not have that drawn into a precedent; and therefore he *delivered the decrees* to the churches, to be religiously observed; for they must abide by the rule, and not be drawn from it by a particular example.

2. That this was of very good service to them. (1.) The churches were hereby *established in the faith, v.* 5. They were confirmed particularly in their opinion against the imposing of the ceremonial law upon the Gentiles; the great assurance and heat wherewith the judaizing teachers pressed the necessity of circumcision, and the plausible arguments they produced for it, had shocked them, so that they began to waver concerning it. But when they saw the testimony, not

only of the apostles and elders, but of the Holy Ghost in them, against it, they were established, and did not longer waver about it. Note, Testimonies to truth, though they may not prevail to convince those that oppose it, may be of very good use to establish those that are in doubt concerning it, and to fix them. Nay, the design of this decree being to set aside the ceremonial law, and the carnal ordinances of that, they were by it established in the Christian faith in general, and were the more firmly assured that it was of God, because it set up a spiritual way of serving God, as more suited to the nature both of God and man; and, besides, that spirit of tenderness and condescension which appeared in these letters plainly showed that the apostles and elders were herein under the guidance of him who is love itself. (2.) They *increased in number daily*. The imposing of the yoke of the ceremonial law upon their converts was enough to frighten people from them. If they had been disposed to turn Jews, they could have done that long since, before the apostles came among them; but, if they cannot be interested in the Christian privileges without submitting to the Jews' yoke, they will be as they are. But, if they find there is no danger of their being so enslaved, they are ready to embrace Christianity, and join themselves to the church. And thus the church *increased in numbers daily;* not a day passed but some or other gave up their names to Christ. And it is a joy to those who heartily wish well to the honour of Christ, and the welfare of the church and the souls of men, to see such an increase.

6 Now when they had gone
throughout Phrygia and the region
of Galatia, and were forbidden of the
Holy Ghost to preach the word in
Asia, 7 After they were come to
Mysia, they assayed to go into
Bithynia: but the Spirit suffered
them not. 8 And they passing by
Mysia came down to Troas. 9 And
a vision appeared to Paul in the
night; There stood a man of Macedonia, and prayed him, saying, Come
over into Macedonia, and help us.
10 And after he had seen the vision,
immediately we endeavoured to go
into Macedonia, assuredly gathering
that the Lord had called us for to
preach the gospel unto them. 11
Therefore loosing from Troas, we
came with a straight course to Samothracia, and the next *day* to Neapolis; 12 And from thence to Philippi, which is the chief city of that
part of Macedonia, *and* a colony: and
we were in that city abiding certain
days. 13 And on the sabbath we
went out of the city by a river side,
where prayer was wont to be made;
and we sat down, and spake unto the
women which resorted *thither*. 14
And a certain woman named Lydia,
a seller of purple, of the city of Thyatira, which worshipped God, heard
us: whose heart the Lord opened,
that she attended unto the things
which were spoken of Paul. 15 And
when she was baptized, and her household, she besought *us*, saying, If ye
have judged me to be faithful to the
Lord, come into my house, and abide
there. And she constrained us.

In these verses we have,

I. Paul's travels up and down to do good. 1. He and Silas his colleague went throughout Phrygia and the region of Galatia, where, it should seem, the gospel was already planted, but whether by Paul's hand or no is not mentioned; it is likely it was, for in his epistle to the Galatians he speaks of his *preaching the gospel to them at the first*, and how very acceptable he was among them, Gal. iv.13—15. And it appears by that epistle that the judaizing teachers had then done a great deal of mischief to these churches of Galatia, had prejudiced them against Paul and drawn them from the gospel of Christ, for which he there severely reproves them. But probably that was a great while after this. 2. They were forbidden at this time to preach the gospel in Asia (the country properly so called), because it did not need, other hands being at work there; or because the people were not yet prepared to receive it, as they were afterwards (*ch.* xix. 10), when *all those that dwelt in Asia heard the word of the Lord;* or, as Dr. Lightfoot suggests, because at this time Christ would employ Paul in a piece of new work, which was to preach the gospel to a Roman colony at Philippi, for hitherto the Gentiles to whom he had preached were Greeks. The Romans were more particularly hated by the Jews than other Gentiles; their armies were the *abomination of desolation;* and therefore there is this among other things extraordinary in his call thither that he is forbidden to preach the gospel in Asia and other places, in order to his preaching it there, which is an intimation that the light of the gospel would in aftertimes be directed more westward than eastward. It was the Holy Ghost that forbade them, either by secret whispers in the minds of both of them, which, when they came to compare notes, they found to be the same, and to come from the same Spirit; or by some prophets who spoke to them from the

Spirit. The removals of ministers, and the dispensing of the means of grace by them, are in a particular manner under a divine guidance and direction. We find an Old-Testament minister forbidden to preach at all (Ezek. iii. 26): *Thou shalt be dumb.* But these New-Testament ministers are only forbidden to preach in one place, while they are directed to another where there is more need. 3. They would have gone into Bithynia, but were not permitted: *the Spirit suffered them not, v.* 7. They came to Mysia, and, as it should seem, preached the gospel there; for though it was a very mean contemptible country, even to a proverb (*Mysorum ultimus*, in Cicero, is *a most despicable man*), yet the apostles disdained not to visit it, owning themselves debtors both *to the wise and to the unwise*, Rom. i. 14. In Bithynia was the city of Nice, where the first general council was held against the Arians; into these countries Peter sent his epistle (1 Pet. i. 1); and there were flourishing churches here, for, though they had not the gospel sent them now, they had it in their turn, not long after. Observe, Though their judgment and inclination were to go into Bithynia, yet, having then extraordinary ways of knowing the mind of God, they were overruled by them, contrary to their own mind. We must now follow providence, and submit to the guidance of that pillar of cloud and fire; and, if this *suffer us not* to do what we assay to do, we ought to acquiesce, and believe it for the best. *The Spirit of Jesus* suffered them not; so many ancient copies read it. The servants of the Lord Jesus ought to be always under the check and conduct of the *Spirit of the Lord Jesus*, by whom he governs men's minds. 4. They *passed by Mysia*, or passed *through it* (so some), sowing good seed, we may suppose, as they went along; and they came down to Troas, the city of Troy, so much talked of, or the country thereabouts, which took its denomination from it. Here a church was planted; for here we find one in being, *ch.* xx. 6, 7, and probably planted at this time, and in a little time. It should seem that at Troas Luke fell in with Paul, and joined himself to his company; for henceforward, for the most part, when he speaks of Paul's journeys, he puts himself into the number of his retinue, *we* went, *v.* 10.

II. Paul's particular call to Macedonia, that is, to Philippi, the chief city, inhabited mostly by Romans, as appears, *v.* 21. Here we have,

1. The vision Paul had, *v.* 9. Paul had many visions, sometimes to encourage, sometimes, as here, to direct him in his work. An angel appeared to him, to intimate to him that it was the will of Christ he should go to Macedonia. Let him not be discouraged by the embargo laid upon him once and again, by which his designs were crossed; for, though he shall not go where he has a mind to go, he shall go where God has work for him to do. Now observe, (1.) The person Paul saw. There stood by him *a man of Macedonia*, who by his habit or dialect seemed so to Paul, or who told him he was so. The angel, some think, assumed the shape of such a man; or, as others think, impressed upon Paul's fancy, when between asleep and awake, the image of such a man: he dreamt he saw such a one. Christ would have Paul directed to Macedonia, not as the apostles were at other times, by a messenger from heaven, to send him thither, but by a messenger thence to call him thither, because in this way he would afterwards ordinarily direct the motions of his ministers, by inclining the hearts of those who needed them to invite them. Paul shall be called to Macedonia by a man of Macedonia, and by him speaking in the name of the rest. Some make this man to be the tutelar angel of Macedonia, supposing angels to have charge of particular places as well as persons, and that so much is intimated Dan. x. 20, where we read of the *princes of Persia and Grecia*, that seem to have been angels. But there is no certainty of this. There was presented either to Paul's eyes or to his mind a man of Macedonia. The angel must not preach the gospel himself to the Macedonians, but must bring Paul to them. Nor must he by the authority of an angel order him to go, but in the person of a Macedonian court him to come. A man of Macedonia, not a magistrate of the country, much less a priest (Paul was not accustomed to receive invitations from such) but an ordinary inhabitant of that country, a plain man, that carried in his countenance marks of probity and seriousness, that did not come to banter Paul nor trifle with him, but in good earnest and with all earnestness to importune his assistance. (2.) The invitation given him. This honest Macedonian *prayed him, saying, Come over into Macedonia, and help us;* that is, "Come and preach the gospel to us; let us have the benefit of thy labours." [1.] "*Thou hast helped many;* we have heard of those in this and the other country to whom thou hast been very useful; and why may we not put in for a share? O come and help us." The benefits others have received from the gospel should quicken our enquiries, our further enquiries, after it. [2.] "It is thy business, and it is thy delight, to help poor souls; thou art a physician for the sick, that art to be ready at the call of every patient; O come and help us." [3.] "We have need of thy help, as much as any people; we in Macedonia are as ignorant and as careless in religion as any people in the world are, are as idolatrous and as vicious as any, and as ingenious and industrious to ruin ourselves as any; and therefore, O come, come with all speed among us. *If thou canst do any thing, have compassion on us, and help us.*" [4.] "Those few among us that have any sense of divine things, and any con-

cern for their own souls and the souls of others, have done what can be done, by the help of natural light; I have done my part for one. We have carried the matter as far as it will go, to persuade our neighbours to fear and worship God, but we can do little good among them. *O come come, thou over, and help us.* The gospel thou preachest has arguments and powers beyond those we have yet been furnished with." [5.] "Do not only help us with thy prayers here: this will not do; thou must come over and help us." Note, People have great need of help for their souls, and it is their duty to look out for it and invite those among them that can help them.

2. The interpretation made of the vision (*v.* 10): They *gathered assuredly from this that the Lord had called them to preach the gospel* there; and they were ready to go wherever God directed. Note, We may sometimes infer a call of God from a call of man. If a man of Macedonia says, *Come and help us,* Paul thence gathers assuredly that God says, Go and help them. Ministers may go on with great cheerfulness and courage in their work when they perceive Christ calling them, not only to preach the gospel, but to preach it at this time, in this place, to this people.

III. Paul's voyage to Macedonia hereupon: He *was not disobedient to the heavenly vision,* but followed this divine direction much more cheerfully, and with more satisfaction, than he would have followed any contrivance or inclination of his own. 1. Thitherward he turned his thoughts. Now that he knows the mind of God in the matter he is determined, for this is all he wanted; now he thinks no more of Asia, nor Bithynia, but *immediately we endeavoured to go into Macedonia.* Paul only had the vision, but he communicated it to his companions, and they all, upon the credit of this, resolved for Macedonia. As Paul will follow Christ, so all his will follow him, or rather follow Christ with him. They are getting things in readiness for this expedition immediately, without delay. Note, God's calls must be complied with immediately. As our obedience must not be disputed, so it must not be deferred; do it to-day, lest thy heart be hardened. Observe, They could not immediately go into Macedonia; but they immediately endeavoured to go. If we cannot be so quick as we would be in our performances, yet we may be in our endeavours, and this shall be accepted. 2. Thitherward he steered his course. They *set sail* by the first shipping and with the first fair wind *from Troas;* for they may be sure they have done what they had to do there when God calls them to another place. They *came with a straight course,* a prosperous voyage, *to Samothracia;* the *next day they came to Neapolis,* a city on the confines of Thrace and Macedonia; and at last they landed at *Philippi,* a city so called from Philip king of Macedon, the father of Alexander the Great; it is said (*v.* 12) to be, (1.) *The chief city of that part of Macedonia;* or, as some read it, *the first city,* the first they came to when they came from Troas. As an army that lands in a country of which they design to make themselves masters begin with the reduction of the first place they come to, so did Paul and his assistants: they began with the first city, because, if the gospel were received there, it would the more easily spread thence all the country over. (2.) It was a colony. The Romans not only had a garrison, but the inhabitants of the city were Romans, the magistrates at least, and the governing part. There were the greatest numbers and variety of people, and therefore the most likelihood of doing good

IV. The cold entertainment which Paul and his companions met with at Philippi. One would have expected that having such a particular call from God thither they would have had a joyful welcome there, as Peter had with Cornelius when the angel sent him thither. Where was the man of Macedonia that begged Paul to come thither with all speed? Why did not he stir up his countrymen, some of them at least, to go and meet him? Why was not Paul introduced with solemnity, and the keys of the city put into his hand? Here is nothing like this; for, 1. It is a good while before any notice at all is taken of him: *We were in that city abiding certain days,* probably at a public house and at their own charge, for they had no friend to invite them so much as to a meal's meat, till Lydia welcomed them. They had made all the haste they could thither, but, now that they are there, they are almost tempted to think they might as well have staid where they were. But so it was ordered for their trial whether they could bear the pain of silence and lying by, when this was their lot. Those eminent and useful men are not fit to live in this world that know not how to be slighted and overlooked. Let not ministers think it strange if they be first strongly invited to a place, and then looked shyly upon when they come. 2. When they have an opportunity of preaching it is in an obscure place, and to a mean and small auditory, *v.* 13. There was no synagogue of the Jews there, for aught that appears, to be a door of entrance to them, and they never went to the idol-temples of the Gentiles, to preach to the auditories there; but here, upon enquiry, they found out a little meeting of good women, *that were proselytes of the gate,* who would be thankful to them if they would give them a sermon. The place of this meeting is out of the city; there it was connived at, but would not be suffered any where within the walls. It was a place *where prayer was wont to be made; προσευχή—where an oratory or house of prayer was* (so some), a chapel, or smaller synagogue. But I rather take it, as we read it, where prayer was appointed or accustomed to be. Those that worshipped the true God, and would not worship idols, met there to pray together, and, according to the description of the most ancient and universal devotion, *to call upon the name of the Lord.* Each of them prayed apart every day; this was always the practice of those that worshipped God: but, besides this, *they came together on the sabbath day.* Though they were but a few and discountenanced by the town, though their meeting was at some distance, though, for aught that appears, there were none but women, yet a solemn assembly the worshippers of God must have, if by any means it be possible, on the sabbath day. When we cannot do as we would we must do as we can; if we have not synagogues, we must be thankful for more private places, and resort to them, *not forsaking the assembling of ourselves together,* according as our opportunities are. This place is said to be *by a river side,* which perhaps was chosen, as befriending contemplation. Idolaters are said *to take their lot among the smooth stones of the stream,* Isa. lvii. 6. But these proselytes had in their eye, perhaps, the example of those prophets who had their visions, one by the *river of Chebar* (Ezek. i. 1), another by *the great river Hiddekel,* Dan. x. 4. Thither Paul and Silas and Luke went, and *sat down,* to instruct the congregation, that they might the better pray with them. They *spoke unto the women who resorted thither,* encouraged them in practising according to the light they had, and led them on further to the knowledge of Christ.

V. The conversion of *Lydia,* who probably was the first that was wrought upon there to believe in Christ, though not the last. In this story of *the Acts,* we have not only the conversion of places recorded, but of many particular persons; for such is the worth of souls that the reducing of one to God is a great matter. Nor have we only the conversions that were effected by miracle, as Paul's, but some that were brought about by the ordinary methods of grace, as Lydia's here. Observe,

1. Who this convert was that there is such particular notice taken of. Four things are recorded of her:—

(1.) Her name, *Lydia.* It is an honour to her to have her name recorded here in the book of God, so that *wherever the scriptures are read there shall this be told concerning her.* Note, The names of the saints are precious with God, and should be so with us; we cannot have our names recorded in the Bible, but, if God open our hearts, we shall find them *written in the book of life,* and this is better (Phil. iv. 3) and more *to be rejoiced in,* Luke x. 20.

(2.) Her calling. She was *a seller of purple,* either of purple dye or of purple cloth or silk. Observe, [1.] She had a calling, an honest calling, which the historian takes notice of to her praise; she was none of those women that the apostle speaks of (1 Tim. v. 13), *who learn to be idle, and not only idle, &c.* [2.] It was a mean calling. She was *a seller of purple,* not a wearer of purple, few such are called. The notice here taken of this is an intimation to those who are employed in honest callings, if they be honest in the management of them, not to be ashamed of them. [3.] Though she had a calling to mind, yet she was a worshipper of God, and found time to improve advantages for her soul. The business of our particular callings may be made to consist very well with the business of religion, and therefore it will not excuse us from religious exercises alone, and in our families, or in solemn assemblies, to say, We have shops to look after, and a trade to mind; for have we not also a God to serve and a soul to look after? Religion does not call us from our business in the world, but directs us in it. Every thing in its time and place.

(3.) The place she was of—*of the city of Thyatira,* which was a great way from Philippi; there she was born and bred, but either married at Philippi, or brought by her trade to settle there. The providence of God, as it always appoints, so it often removes, *the bounds of our habitation,* and sometimes makes the change of our outward condition or place of our abode wonderfully subservient to the designs of his grace concerning our salvation. Providence brings Lydia to Philippi, to be under Paul's ministry, and there, where she met with it, she made a good use of it; so should we improve opportunities.

(4.) Her religion before the Lord opened her heart. [1.] She worshipped God according to the knowledge she had; she was one of the devout women. Sometimes the grace of God wrought upon those who, before their conversion, were very wicked and vile, publicans and harlots; *such were some of you,* 1 Cor. vi. 11. But sometimes it fastened upon those who were of a good character, who had some good in them, as the eunuch, Cornelius, and Lydia. Note, It is not enough to be worshippers of God, but we must be believers in Jesus Christ, for there is no coming to God as a Father, but by him as Mediator. But those who worshipped God according to the light they had stood fair for the discoveries of Christ, and his grace to them; for *to him that has shall be given:* and to them Christ would be welcome; for those that know what it is to worship God see their need of Christ, and know what use to make of his mediation. [2.] She heard the apostles. Here, where prayer was made, when there was an opportunity, *the word was preached;* for hearing the word of God is a part of religious worship, and how can we expect God should hear our prayers if we will not hearken to his word? Those that worshipped God according to the light they had looked out for further light; we must improve *the day of small things,* but must not rest in it.

2. What the work was that was wrought upon her: *Whose heart the Lord opened.* Ob-

serve here, (1.) The author of this work: it was *the Lord,*—the Lord Christ, to whom this judgment is committed,—the Spirit of the Lord, who is the sanctifier. Note, Conversion-work is God's work; it is he *that works in us both to will and to do;* not as if we had nothing to do, but of ourselves, without God's grace, we can do nothing; nor as if God were in the least chargeable with the ruin of those that perish, but the salvation of those that are saved must be wholly ascribed to him. (2.) The seat of this work; it is in the heart that the change is made, it is to the heart that this blessed turn is given; it was the heart of Lydia that was wrought upon. Conversion-work is heart-work; it is a *renewing of the heart, the inward man, the spirit of the mind.* (3.) The nature of the work; she had not only her heart touched, but her heart opened. An unconverted soul is shut up, and fortified against Christ, *straitly shut up,* as Jericho against Joshua, Josh. vi. 1. Christ, in dealing with the soul, knocks at the door that is shut against him (Rev. iii. 20); and, when a sinner is effectually persuaded to embrace Christ, *then the heart is opened for the King of glory to come in*—the understanding is opened to receive the divine light, the will opened to receive the divine law, and the affections opened to receive the divine love. When the heart is thus opened to Christ, the ear is opened to his word, the lips opened in prayer, the hand opened in charity, and the steps enlarged in all manner of gospel obedience.

3. What were the effects of this work on the heart. (1.) She took great notice of the word of God. Her heart was so *opened that she attended to the things that were spoken by Paul;* she not only gave attendance on Paul's preaching, but gave attention to it; *she applied to herself* (so some read it) *the things that were spoken by Paul;* and then only the word does us good, and makes an abiding impression upon us, when we apply it to ourselves. Now this was an evidence of the opening of her heart, and was the fruit of it; wherever the heart is opened by the grace of God, it will appear by a diligent attendance on, and attention to, the word of God, both for Christ's sake, whose word it is, and for our own sakes, who are so nearly interested in it. (2.) She gave up her name to Jesus Christ, and took upon her the profession of his holy religion: *She was baptized,* and by this solemn rite was admitted a member of the church of Christ; and with her *her household* also was baptized, those of them that were infants in her right, for if *the root be holy so are the branches,* and those that were grown up by her influence and authority. She and her household were baptized by the same rule that Abraham and his household were circumcised, because the seal of the covenant belongs to the covenanters and their seed. (3.) She was very kind to the ministers, and very desirous to be further instructed by them in *the things pertaining to the kingdom of God: She besought us saying, "If you have judged me to be faithful to the Lord,* if you take me to be a sincere Christian, manifest your confidence in me by this, *come into my house, and abide there."* Thus she desired an opportunity, [1.] To testify her gratitude to those who had been the instruments of divine grace in this blessed change that was wrought upon her. When her heart was open to Christ, her house was open to his ministers for his sake, and they were welcome to the best entertainment she had, which she did not think too good for those of whose spiritual things she had reaped so plentifully. Nay, they are not only welcome to her house, but she is extremely pressing and importunate with them: *She constrained us;* which intimates that Paul was very backward and unwilling to go, because he was afraid of being burdensome to the families of the young converts, and would study *to make the gospel of Christ without charge* (1 Cor. ix. 18; Acts xx. 34), that those who were without might have no occasion given them to reproach the preachers of the gospel as designing, self-seeking men, and that those who were within might have no occasion to complain of the expenses of their religion: but Lydia will have no nay; she will not believe that they take her to be a sincere Christian unless they will oblige her herein; like Abraham inviting the angels (Gen. xviii. 3), *If now I have found favour in thy sight, pass not away from thy servant.* [2.] She desired an opportunity of receiving further instruction. If she might but have them for awhile in her family, she might hear them daily (Prov. viii. 34), and not merely on sabbath days at the meeting. In her own house she might not only hear them, but ask them questions; and she might have them to pray with her daily, and to bless her household. Those that know something of Christ cannot but desire to know more, and seek opportunities of increasing their acquaintance with his gospel.

16 And it came to pass, as we
went to prayer, a certain damsel possessed with a spirit of divination met
us, which brought her masters much
gain by soothsaying: 17 The same
followed Paul and us, and cried, saying, These men are the servants of
the most high God, which show unto
us the way of salvation. 18 And this
did she many days. But Paul, being
grieved, turned and said to the spirit,
I command thee in the name of Jesus
Christ to come out of her. And he
came out the same hour. 19 And
when her masters saw that the hope
of their gains was gone, they caught

Paul and Silas, and drew *them* into
the marketplace unto the rulers, 20
And brought them to the magistrates, saying, These men, being Jews, do exceedingly trouble our
city, 21 And teach customs, which
are not lawful for us to receive, neither to observe, being Romans.
22 And the multitude rose up together against them: and the magistrates rent off their clothes, and commanded to beat *them.* 23 And
when they had laid many stripes upon them, they cast *them* into prison, charging the jailor to keep them safely: 24 Who, having received such a charge, thrust them into the inner prison, and made their feet fast in the stocks.

Paul and his companions, though they were for some time buried in obscurity at Philippi, yet now begin to be taken notice of.

I. *A damsel that had a spirit of divination* caused them to be taken notice of, by proclaiming them to be the servants of God. Observe,

1. The account that is given of this damsel: She was *pythonissa, possessed with* such *a spirit of divination* as that damsel was by whom the oracles of Apollo at Delphos were delivered; she was actuated by an evil spirit, that dictated ambiguous answers to those who consulted her, which served to gratify their vain desire of knowing things to come, but often deceived them. In those times of ignorance, infidelity, and idolatry, the devil, by the divine permission, thus led men captive at his will; and he could not have gained such adoration from them as he had, if he had not pretended to give oracles to them, for by both his usurpation is maintained as the god of this world. This damsel *brought her masters much gain by soothsaying;* many came to consult this witch for the discovery of robberies, the finding of things lost, and especially to be told their fortune, and none came but with the rewards of divination in their hands, according to the quality of the person and the importance of the case. Probably there were many that were thus kept for fortune-tellers, but, it should seem, this was more in repute than any of them; for, while others brought some gain, this *brought much gain to her masters,* being consulted more than any other.

2. The testimony which this damsel gave to Paul and his companions: She *met them* in the street, as they were going to prayer, to the house of prayer, or rather to the work of prayer there, *v.* 16. They went thither publicly, every body knew whither they were going, and what they were going to do. If what she did was likely to be any distraction to them, or a hindrance in their work, it is observable how subtle Satan is, that great tempter, in taking the opportunity to give us diversion when we are going about any religious exercises, to ruffle us and to put us out of temper when we need to be most composed. When she met with them she followed them, crying, "*These men,* how contemptible soever they look and are looked upon, are great men, for they *are the servants of the most high God,* and men that should be very welcome to us, for *they show unto us the way of salvation,* both the salvation that will be our happiness, and the way to it that will be our holiness."

Now, (1.) This witness is true; it is a comprehensive encomium on the faithful preachers of the gospel, and makes their feet beautiful, Rom. x. 15. Though they are *men subject to like passions as we are,* and *earthen vessels,* yet, [1.] "They are *the servants of the most high God;* they attend on him, are employed by him, and are devoted to his honour, as servants; they come to us on his errands, the message they bring is from him, and they serve the purposes and interests of his kingdom. The gods we Gentiles worship are inferior beings, therefore not gods, but these men belong to the supreme *Numen, to the most high God,* who is over all men, over all gods, who made us all, and to whom we are all accountable. They are his servants, and therefore it is our duty to respect them, and hearken to them for their Master's sake, and it is at our peril if we affront them." [2.] "They *show unto us the way of salvation.*" Even the heathen had some notion of the miserable deplorable state of mankind, and their need of salvation, and it was what they made some enquiries after. "Now," saith she, "these are the men that show us what we have in vain sought for in our superstitious profitless application to our priests and oracles." Note, God has, in the gospel of his Son, plainly shown us the way of salvation, has told us what we must do that we may be delivered from the misery to which by sin we have exposed ourselves.

But, (2.) How came this testimony from the mouth of one that had a spirit of divination? Is Satan divided against himself? Will he cry up those whose business it is to pull him down? We may take it either, [1.] As extorted from this spirit of divination for the honour of the gospel by the power of God; as the devil was forced to say of Christ (Mark i. 24): *I know thee who thou art, the Holy One of God.* The truth is sometimes magnified by the confession of its adversaries, in which they are witnesses against themselves. Christ would have this testimony of the damsel to rise up in judgment against those at Philippi who slighted and persecuted the apostles; though the gospel needed no such testimony, yet it shall serve to add to their commendation that the damsel whom they looked upon as an oracle in other things proclaimed the apostles God's servants. Or, [2.] As designed by the evil spirit, that subtle serpent, to the dishonour of the gospel; some think she designed hereby to gain credit to herself and her prophecies, and so to increase her master's profit by pretending to be in the interest of the apostles, who, she thought, had a growing reputation, or to curry favour with Paul, that he might not separate her and her familiar. Others think that Satan, who can transform himself into an angel of light, and can say any thing to serve a turn, designed hereby to disgrace the apostles; as if these divines were of the same fraternity with their diviners, because they were witnessed to by them, and then the people might as well adhere to those they had been used to. Those that were most likely to receive the apostles' doctrine were such as were prejudiced against these spirits of divination, and therefore would, by this testimony, be prejudiced against the gospel; and, as for those who regarded these diviners, the devil thought himself sure of them.

II. Christ caused them to be taken notice of, by giving them power to cast the devil out of this damsel. She continued *many days* clamouring thus (*v.* 18); and, it should seem, Paul took no notice of her, not knowing but it might be ordered of God for the service of his cause, that she should thus witness concerning his ministers; but finding perhaps that it did them a prejudice, rather than any service, he soon silenced her, by casting the devil out of her. 1. He was *grieved.* It troubled him to see the damsel made an instrument of Satan to deceive people, and to see the people imposed upon by her divinations. It was a disturbance to him to hear a sacred truth so profaned, and good words come out of such a wicked mouth with such an evil design. Perhaps they were spoken in an ironical bantering way, as ridiculing the apostles' pretensions, and mocking them, as when Christ's persecutors complimented him with *Hail, king of the Jews;* and then justly might Paul be grieved, as any good man's heart would be, to hear any good truth of God bawled out in the streets in a canting jeering way. 2. He *commanded the evil spirit to come out of her. He turned* with a holy indignation, angry both at the flatteries and at the reproaches of *the unclean spirit, and said, I command thee in the name of Jesus Christ to come out of her;* and by this he will show *that these men are the servants of the living God*, and are able to prove themselves so, without her testimony: her silence shall demonstrate it more than her speaking could do. Thus Paul shows *the way of salvation* indeed, that it is by breaking *the power of Satan, and chaining him up, that he may not deceive the world* (Rev. xx. 3), and that this salvation is to be obtained *in the name of Jesus Christ* only, as in his name the devil was now cast out and by no other. It was a great blessing to the country when Christ by a word cast the devil out of those in whom he frightened people and molested them, *so that no man might pass by that way* (Matt. viii. 28); but it was a much greater kindness to the country when Paul now, in Christ's name, cast the devil out of one who deceived people and imposed upon their credulity. Power went along with the word of Christ, before which Satan could not stand, but was forced to quit his hold, and in this case it was a strong hold: *He came out the same hour.*

III. The masters of the damsel that was dispossessed caused them to be taken notice of, by bringing them before the magistrates for doing it, and laying it to their charge as their crime. The preachers of the gospel would never have had an opportunity of speaking to the magistrates if they had not been brought before them as evil doers. Observe here,

1. That which provoked them was, that, the damsel being restored to herself, *her masters saw that the hope of their gain was gone, v.* 19. See here what evil *the love of money is the root of!* If the preaching of the gospel ruin the craft of the silversmiths (*ch.* xix. 24), much more the craft of the soothsayers; and therefore here is a great outcry raised, when Satan's power to deceive is broken: the priests hated the gospel because it turned men from the blind service of dumb idols, and so the hope of their gains was gone. The power of Christ, which appeared in dispossessing the woman, and the great kindness done to her in delivering her out of Satan's hand, made no impression upon them when they apprehended that they should hereby lose money.

2. The course they took with them was to incense the higher powers against them, as men fit to be punished: *They caught them* as they went along, and, with the utmost fury and violence, *dragged them into the marketplace,* where public justice was administered. (1.) They brought them *to the rulers,* their justices of peace, to do by them as men taken into the hands of the law, the *duumviri.* (2.) From them they hurried them *to the magistrates,* the prætors or governors of the city, *τοῖς στρατηγοῖς—the officers of the army,* so the word signifies; but it is taken in general for the judges or chief rulers: to them they brought their complaint.

3. The charge they exhibited against them was that they were the troublers of the land, *v.* 20. They take it for granted that these men are Jews, a nation at this time as much an *abomination to the Romans* as they had long ago been to the Egyptians. Piteous was the case of the apostles, when it was turned to their reproach that they were Jews, and yet the Jews were their most violent persecutors! (1.) The general charge against them is *that they troubled the city,* sowed discord, and disturbed the public peace, and occasioned riots and tumults, than which nothing

could be more false and unjust, as was Ahab's character of Elijah (1 Kings xviii. 17): *Art thou he that troubleth Israel?* If they troubled the city, it was but like the angel's troubling the water of Bethesda's pool, in order to healing—shaking, in order to a happy settlement. Thus those that rouse the sluggards are exclaimed against for troubling them. (2.) The proof of this charge is their teaching customs not proper to be admitted by a Roman colony, *v.* 21. The Romans were always very jealous of innovations in religion. Right or wrong, they would adhere to that, how vain soever, which they had received by tradition from their fathers. No foreign nor upstart deity must be allowed, without the approbation of the senate; the gods of their country must be their gods, true or false. This was one of the laws of the twelve tables. *Hath a nation changed their gods?* It incensed them against the apostles that they taught a religion destructive of polytheism and idolatry, and preached to them to turn from those vanities. This the Romans could not bear: "If this grow upon us, in a little while we shall lose our religion."

IV. The magistrates, by their proceedings against them, caused them to be taken notice of.

1. By countenancing the persecution they raised the mob upon them (*v.* 22): *The multitude rose up together against them,* and were ready to pull them to pieces. It has been the artifice of Satan to make God's ministers and people odious to the commonalty, by representing them as dangerous men, who aimed at the destruction of the constitution and the changing of the customs, when really there has been no ground for such an imputation.

2. By going on to an execution they further represented them as the vilest malefactors: *They rent off their clothes,* with rage and fury, not having patience till they were taken off, in order to their being scourged. This the apostle refers to when he speaks of *their being shamefully treated at Philippi,* 1 Thess. ii. 2. The magistrates commanded that they should be whipped as vagabonds, by the lictors or beadles who attended the prætors, and carried rods with them for that purpose; this was one of those three times that Paul was beaten with rods, according to the Roman usage, which was not under the compassionate limitation of the number of stripes not to exceed forty, which was provided by the Jewish law. It is here said that *they laid many stripes upon them* (*v.* 23), without counting how many, because they seemed vile unto them, Deut. xxv. 3. Now, one would think, this might have satiated their cruelty; if they must be whipped, surely they must be discharged. No, they are imprisoned, and it is probable the present purpose was to try them for their lives, and put them to death; else why should there be such care taken to prevent their escape? (1.) The judges made their commitment very strict: They *charged the jailer to keep them safely,* and have a very watchful eye upon them, as if they were dangerous men, that either would venture to break prison themselves or were in confederacy with those that would attempt to rescue them. Thus they endeavoured to render them odious, that they might justify themselves in the base usage they had given them. (2.) The jailer made their confinement very severe (*v.* 24): *Having received such a charge,* though he might have kept them safely enough in the outer prison, yet *he thrust them into the inner prison.* He was sensible that the magistrates had a great indignation against these men, and were inclined to be severe with them, and therefore he thought to ingratiate himself with them, by exerting his power likewise against them to the uttermost. When magistrates are cruel, it is no wonder that the officers under them are so too. *He put them into the inner prison,* the dungeon, into which none were usually put but condemned malefactors, dark at noon-day, damp and cold, dirty, it is likely, and every way offensive, like that into which Jeremiah was let down (Jer. xxxviii. 6); and, as if this were not enough, *he made their feet fast in the stocks.* Perhaps, having heard a report of the escape of *the preachers of the gospel out of prison, when the doors were fast barred* (*ch.* v. 19; xii. 9), he thought he would be wiser than other jailers had been, and therefore would effectually secure them by fastening them in the stocks; and they were not the first of God's messengers that had their feet in the stocks; Jeremiah was so treated, and publicly too, in *the high-gate of Benjamin* (Jer. xx. 2); Joseph had his *feet hurt with fetters,* Ps. cv. 18. Oh what hard usage have God's servants met with, as in the former days, so in the latter times! Witness the Book of Martyrs, martyrs in queen Mary's time.

25 And at midnight Paul and
Silas prayed, and sang praises unto
God: and the prisoners heard them.
26 And suddenly there was a great
earthquake, so that the foundations
of the prison were shaken: and immediately all the doors were opened,
and every one's bands were loosed.
27 And the keeper of the prison
awaking out of his sleep, and seeing
the prison doors open, he drew out
his sword, and would have killed
himself, supposing that the prisoners
had been fled. 28 But Paul cried
with a loud voice, saying, Do thyself
no harm: for we are all here. 29
Then he called for a light, and sprang
in, and came trembling, and fell

down before Paul and Silas, 30
And brought them out, and said,
Sirs, what must I do to be saved?
31 And they said, Believe on the
Lord Jesus Christ, and thou shalt
be saved, and thy house. 32 And
they spake unto him the word of the
Lord, and to all that were in his
house. 33 And he took them the
same hour of the night, and washed
their stripes; and was baptized, he
and all his, straightway. 34 And
when he had brought them into his
house, he set meat before them, and
rejoiced, believing in God with all
his house.

We have here the designs of the persecutors of Paul and Silas baffled and broken.

I. The persecutors designed to dishearten and discourage the preachers of the gospel, and to make them sick of the cause and weary of their work; but here we find them both hearty and heartened.

1. They were themselves hearty, wonderfully hearty; never were poor prisoners so truly cheerful, nor so far from laying their hard usage to heart. Let us consider what their case was. The prætors among the Romans had rods carried before them, and axes bound upon them, the *fasces* and *secures*. Now they had felt the smart of the rods, *the ploughers had ploughed upon their backs, and made long furrows.* The many stripes they had laid upon them were very sore, and one might have expected to hear them complaining of them, of the rawness and soreness of their backs and shoulders. Yet this was not all; they had reason to fear the axes next. Their Master was first scourged and then crucified; and they might expect the same. In the mean time they were in the inner prison, their feet in the stocks, which, some think, not only held them, but hurt them; and yet, *at midnight*, when they should have been trying, if possible, to get a little rest, they *prayed and sang praises to God.* (1.) They prayed together, prayed to God to support them and comfort them in their afflictions, to visit them, as he did Joseph in the prison, and to be with them,—prayed that their consolations in Christ might abound, as their afflictions for him did,—prayed that even their bonds and stripes might turn to the furtherance of the gospel,—prayed for their persecutors, that God would forgive them and turn their hearts. This was not at an hour of prayer, but at midnight; it was not in a house of prayer, but in a dungeon; yet it was seasonable to pray, and the prayer was acceptable. As in the dark, so out of the depths, we may cry unto God. No place, no time, amiss for prayer, if the heart be lifted up to God. Those that are companions in suffering should join in prayer. *Is any afflicted? Let him pray.* No trouble, how grievous soever, should indispose us for prayer. (2.) *They sang praises to God.* They praised God; for we must *in every thing give thanks.* We never want matter for praise, if we do not want a heart. And what should put the heart of a child of God out of tune for this duty if a dungeon and a pair of stocks will not do it? They praised God that they were counted worthy to suffer shame for his name, and that they were so wonderfully supported and borne up under their sufferings, and felt divine consolations so sweet, so strong, in their souls. Nay, *they not only praised God, but they sang praises to him,* in some psalm, or hymn, or spiritual song, either one of David's, or some modern composition, or one of their own, as *the Spirit gave them utterance.* As our rule is that the afflicted should pray, and therefore, being in affliction, they prayed; so our rule is that the merry should sing psalms (James v. 13), and therefore, being merry in their affliction, *merry after a godly sort, they sang psalms.* This proves that the singing of psalms is a gospel ordinance, and ought to be used by all good Christians; and that it is instituted, not only for the expressing of their joys in a day of triumph, but for the balancing and relieving of their sorrows in a day of trouble. It was at midnight that they sang psalms, according to the example of the sweet psalmist of Israel (Ps. cxix. 62): *At midnight will I rise to give thanks unto thee.* (3.) Notice is here taken of the circumstance that *the prisoners heard them.* If the prisoners did not hear them pray, yet *they heard them sing praises.* [1.] It intimates how hearty they were in singing praises to God; they sang so loud that, though they were in the dungeon, they were heard all the prison over; nay, so loud that they woke the prisoners: for we may suppose, being at midnight, they were all asleep. We should sing psalms with all our heart. The saints are called upon to sing aloud upon their beds, Ps. cxlix. 5. But gospel grace carries the matter further, and gives us an example of those that sang aloud in the prison, in the stocks. [2.] Though they knew the prisoners would hear them, yet they sang aloud, as those that were not ashamed of their Master, nor of his service. Shall those that would sing psalms in their families plead, in excuse for their omission of the duty, that they are afraid their neighbours should hear them, when those that sing profane songs roar them out, and care not who hears them? [3.] The prisoners were made to hear the prison-songs of Paul and Silas, that they might be prepared for the miraculous favour shown to them all for the sake of Paul and Silas, when *the prison-doors were thrown open.* By this extraordinary comfort with which they were filled it was published that he whom they preached was *the consolation of Israel.* Let the prisoners that mean to oppose him hear

and tremble before him; let those that are faithful to him hear and triumph, and take of the comfort that is spoken to the prisoners of hope, Zech. ix. 12.

2. God heartened them wonderfully by his signal appearances for them, *v.* 26. (1.) There was immediately a great earthquake; how far it extended we are not told, but it was such a violent shock in this place *that the very foundations of the prison were shaken.* While the prisoners were hearkening to the midnight devotions of Paul and Silas, and perhaps laughing at them and making a jest of them, this earthquake would strike a terror upon them, and convince them that those men were the favourites of Heaven, and such as God owned. We had *the house of prayer shaken,* in answer to prayer, and as a token of God's acceptance of it, *ch.* iv. 31. Here *the prison shaken.* The Lord was in these earthquakes, to show his resentment of the indignities done to his servants, to testify to those whose confidence is in the earth the weakness and instability of that in which they confide, and to teach people *that, though the earth be moved, yet they need not fear.* (2.) The prison-doors were thrown open, and the prisoners' fetters were knocked off: *Every man's bands were loosed.* Perhaps the prisoners, when they heard Paul and Silas pray and sing psalms, admired them, and spoke honourably of them, and said what the damsel had said of them, Surely, *these men are the servants of the living God.* To recompense them for, and confirm them in, their good opinion of them, they share in the miracle, and have *their bands loosed;* as afterwards God gave to Paul all *those that were in the ship with him* (*ch.* xxvii. 24), so now he gave him all those that were in the prison with him. God hereby signified to these prisoners, as Grotius observes, that the apostles, in preaching the gospel, were public blessings to mankind, as they *proclaimed liberty to the captives, and the opening of the prison-doors to those that were bound,* Isa. lxi. 1. *Et per eos solvi animorum vincula—and as by them the bonds of souls were unloosed.*

II. The persecutors designed to stop the progress of the gospel, that no more might embrace it; thus they hoped to ruin the meeting by the river side, that no more hearts should be opened there; but here we find converts made in the prison, that house turned into a meeting, the trophies of the gospel's victories erected there, and the jailer, their own servant, become a servant of Christ. It is probable that some of the prisoners, if not all, were converted; surely the miracle wrought on their bodies, in loosing their bands, was wrought on their souls too. See Job xxxvi. 8.—10; Ps. cvii. 14, 15. But it is only the conversion of the jailer that is recorded.

1. He is afraid he shall lose his life, and Paul makes him easy as to this care, *v.* 27, 28. (1.) He *awoke out of his sleep.* It is probable that the shock of the earthquake woke him, and the opening of the prison-doors, and the prisoners' expressions of joy and amazement, when in the dark they found their bands loosed, and called to tell one another what they felt: this was enough to awaken the jailer, whose place required that he should not be hard to wake. This waking him out of his sleep signified the awakening of his conscience out of its spiritual slumber. The call of the gospel is, *Awake, thou that sleepest* (Eph. v. 14), like that of Jonah, i. 6. (2.) He saw the prison-doors open, and supposed, as well he might, that the prisoners had fled; and then what would become of him? He knew the Roman law in that case, and it was executed not long ago upon the keepers out of whose hands Peter escaped, *ch.* xii. 19. It was according to that of the prophet, 1 Kings xx. 39, 42, *Keep this man; if he be missing, thy life shall go for his life.* The Roman lawyers after this, in their readings upon the law, *De custodia reorum—The custody of criminals* (which appoints that the keeper should undergo the same punishment that should have been inflicted on the prisoner if he let him escape), take care to except an escape by miracle. (3.) In his fright *he drew his sword,* and was going *to kill himself,* to prevent a more terrible death, an expected one, a pompous ignominious death, which he knew he was liable to for letting his prisoners escape and not looking better to them; and the extraordinarily strict charge which the magistrates gave him concerning Paul and Silas made him conclude they would be very severe upon him if they were gone. The philosophers generally allowed self-murder. Seneca prescribes it as the last remedy which those that are in distress may have recourse to. The Stoics, notwithstanding their pretended conquest of the passions, yielded thus far to them. And the Epicureans, who indulged the pleasures of sense, to avoid its pains chose rather to put an end to it. This jailer thought there was no harm in anticipating his own death; but Christianity proves itself to be of God by this, that it keeps us to the law of our creation—revives, enforces, and establishes it, obliges us to be just to our own lives, and teaches us cheerfully to resign them to our graces, but courageously to hold them out against our corruptions. (4.) Paul stopped him from his proceeding against himself (*v.* 28): He *cried with a loud voice,* not only to make him hear, but to make him heed, *saying, Do not practise any evil to thyself; Do thyself no harm.* All the cautions of the word of God against sin, and all appearances of it and approaches to it, have this tendency, "*Do thyself no harm.* Man, woman, do not wrong thyself, nor ruin thyself; hurt not thyself, and then none else can hurt thee; do not sin, for nothing else can hurt thee." Even as to the body, we are cautioned against those sins which do harm to it, and

are taught not to *hate our own flesh, but to nourish and cherish it.* The jailer needs not fear being called to an account for the escape of his prisoners, for *they are all here.* It was strange that some of them did not slip away, when the prison-doors were opened, and they were loosed from their bands; but their amazement held them fast, and, being sensible it was by the prayers of Paul and Silas that they were loosed, they would not stir unless they stirred; and God showed his power in binding their spirits, as much as in loosing their feet.

2. He is afraid he shall lose his soul, and Paul makes him easy as to this care too. One concern leads him to another, and a much greater; and, being hindered from hastening himself out of this world, he begins to think, if he had pursued his intention, whither death would have brought him, and what would have become of him on the other side death—a very proper thought for such as have been snatched as a brand out of the fire, when there was but a step between them and death. Perhaps the heinousness of the sin he was running into helped to alarm him.

(1.) Whatever was the cause, he was put into a great consternation. The Spirit of God, that was sent to convince, in order to his being a Comforter, struck a terror upon him, and startled him. Whether he took care to shut the prison-doors again we are not told. Perhaps he forgot this as the woman of Samaria, when Christ had impressed convictions on her conscience, *left her water-pot* and forgot her errand to the well; for *he called for a light* with all speed, and *sprang in* to the inner prison, *and came trembling to Paul and Silas.* Those that have sin set in order before them, and are made to know their abominations, cannot but tremble at the apprehension of their misery and danger. This jailer, when he was thus made to tremble, could not apply to a more proper person than to Paul, for it had once been his own case; he had been once a persecutor of good men, as this jailer was—had cast them into prison, as he kept them—and when, like him, he was made sensible of it, *he trembled, and was astonished;* and therefore he was able to speak the more feelingly to the jailer.

(2.) In this consternation, he applied to Paul and Silas for relief. Observe, [1.] How reverent and respectful his address to them is: *He called for a light,* because they were in the dark, and that they might see what a fright he was in; *he fell down before them,* as one amazed at the badness of his own condition, and ready to sink under the load of his terror because of it; he fell down before them, as one that had upon his spirit an awe of them, and of the image of God upon them, and of their commission from God. It is probable that he had heard what the damsel said of them, that they were *the servants of the living God, who showed to them the way of salvation,* and as such he thus expressed his veneration for them. He fell down before them, to beg their pardon, as a penitent, for the indignities he had done them, and to beg their advice, as a supplicant, what he should do. He gave them a title of respect, *Sirs, κύριοι—lords, masters;* just now it was, *Rogues* and *villains,* and he was their master; but now, *Sirs, lords,* and they are his masters. Converting grace changes people's language of and to good people and good ministers; and, to such as are thoroughly convinced of sin, the very feet of those that bring tidings of Christ are beautiful; yea, though they are disgracefully fastened in the stocks. [2.] How serious his enquiry is: *What must I do to be saved? First,* His salvation is now his great concern, and lies nearest his heart, which before was the furthest thing from his thoughts. Not, What shall I do to be preferred, to be rich and great in the world? but, *What shall I do to be saved? Secondly,* He does not enquire concerning others, what they must do; but concerning himself, "What must I do?" It is his own precious soul that he is in care about: Let others do as they please; tell me what I must do, what course I must take." *Thirdly,* He is convinced that something must be done, and done by him too, in order to his salvation; that it is not a thing of course, a thing that will do itself, but a thing about which we must strive, wrestle, and take pains. He asks not, "What may be done for me?" but, "What shall I do, that, being *now in fear and trembling,* I may *work out my salvation?*" as Paul speaks in his epistle to the church at Philippi, of which this jailer was, perhaps with respect to his trembling enquiry here, intimating that he must not only ask after salvation (as he had done), but *work out his salvation with* a holy *trembling,* Phil ii. 12. *Fourthly,* He is willing to do any thing: "Tell me what I must do, and I am here ready to do it. Sirs, put me into any way, if it be but the right way, and a sure way; though narrow, and thorny, and uphill, yet I will walk in it." Note, Those who are thoroughly convinced of sin, and truly concerned about their salvation, will surrender at discretion to Jesus Christ, will give him a blank to write what he pleases, will be glad to have Christ upon his own terms, Christ upon any terms. *Fifthly,* He is inquisitive what he should do, is desirous to know what he should do, and asks those that were likely to tell him. *If you will enquire, enquire ye,* Isa. xxi. 12. Those that set their faces Zionward must ask the way thither, Jer. l. 5. We cannot know it of ourselves, but God has made it known to us by his word, has appointed his ministers to assist us in consulting the scriptures, and has promised *to give his Holy Spirit to those that ask him,* to be their guide in the way of salvation. *Sixthly,* He *brought them out,* to put this question to them, that their answer might not be by duress or compulsion, but that they might prescribe to him, though he was their keeper, with the same liberty as they did to others. He brings them out of the dungeon, in hopes they will bring him out of a much worse.

(3.) They very readily directed him what he must do, *v.* 31. They were always ready to answer such enquiries; though they are cold, and sore, and sleepy, they do not adjourn this cause to a more convenient time and place, do not bid him come to them the next sabbath at their meeting-place by the river side, and they will tell him, but they strike while the iron is hot, take him now when he is in a good mind, lest the conviction should wear off. Now that God begins to work, it is time for them to set in as *workers together with God.* They do not upbraid him with his rude and ill carriage towards them, and his going beyond his warrant; all this is forgiven and forgotten, and they are as glad to show him the way to heaven as the best friend they have. They did not triumph over him, though he trembled; they gave him the same directions they did to others, *Believe in the Lord Jesus Christ.* One would think they should have said, "Repent of thy abusing us, in the first place." No, that is overlooked and easily passed by, if he will but believe in Christ. This is an example to ministers to encourage penitents, to meet those that are coming to Christ and take them by the hand, not to be hard upon any for unkindness done to them, but to seek Christ's honour more than their own. Here is the sum of the whole gospel, the covenant of grace in a few words: *Believe in the Lord Jesus Christ, and thou shalt be saved, and thy house.* Here is, [1.] The happiness promised: "*Thou shalt be saved;* not only rescued from eternal ruin, but brought to eternal life and blessedness. Though thou art a *poor man,* an under-jailer or turnkey, mean and of low condition in the world, yet this shall be no bar to thy salvation. Though a great sinner, though a persecutor, yet thy heinous transgressions shall be all forgiven through the merits of Christ; and thy hard embittered heart shall be softened and sweetened by the grace of Christ, and thus thou shalt neither die for thy crime nor die of thy disease." [2.] The condition required: *Believe in the Lord Jesus Christ.* We must admit the record that God hath given in his gospel concerning his Son, and assent to it as faithful, and well *worthy of all acceptation.* We must approve the method God has taken of reconciling the world to himself by a Mediator; and accept of Christ as he is offered to us, and give up ourselves to be ruled and taught and saved by him. This is the only way and a sure way to salvation. No other way of salvation than by Christ, and no other way of our being saved by Christ than by believing in him; and no danger of coming short if we take this way, for it is the way that God has appointed, and he is faithful that has promised. It is the gospel that is to be preached to every creature, *He that believes shall be saved.* [3.] The extension of this to his family: *Thou shalt be saved, and thy house;* that is, "God will be in Christ a God to thee and to thy seed, as he was to Abraham. Believe, and salvation shall *come to thy house,* as Luke xix. 9. Those of thy house that are infants shall be admitted into the visible church with thee, and thereby put into a fair way for salvation; those that are grown up shall have the means of salvation brought to them, and, be they ever so many, let them believe in Jesus Christ and they shall be saved; they are all welcome to Christ upon the same terms."

(4.) They proceeded to instruct him and his family in the doctrine of Christ (*v.* 32): They *spoke unto him the word of the Lord.* He was, for aught that appears, an utter stranger to Christ, and therefore it is requisite he should be told who this Jesus is, that he may believe in him, John ix. 36. And, the substance of the matter lying in a little compass, they soon told him enough to make his being baptized a reasonable service. Christ's ministers should have the word of the Lord so ready to them, and so richly dwelling in them, as to be able to give instructions offhand to any that desire to hear and receive them, for their direction in the way of salvation. They spoke the word not only to him, but to *all that were in his house.* Masters of families should take care that all under their charge partake of the means of knowledge and grace, and that the word of the Lord be spoken to them; for the souls of the poorest servants are as precious as those of their masters, and are bought with the same price.

(5.) The jailer and his family were immediately baptized, and thereby took upon them the profession of Christianity, submitted to its laws, and were admitted to its privileges, upon their declaring solemnly, as the eunuch did, that they believed that *Jesus Christ is the Son of God:* He was *baptized, he and all his, straightway.* Neither he nor any of his family desired time to consider whether they should come into baptismal bonds or no; nor did Paul and Silas desire time to try their sincerity and to consider whether they should baptize them or no. But the Spirit of grace worked such a strong faith in them, all on a sudden, as superseded further debate; and Paul and Silas knew by the Spirit that it was a work of God that was wrought in them: so that there was no occasion for demur. This therefore will not justify such precipitation in ordinary cases.

(6.) The jailer was hereupon very respectful to Paul and Silas, as one that knew not how to make amends for the injury he had done to them, much less for the kindness he had received from them: He *took them the same hour of the night,* would not let them lie a minute longer in the inner prison; but, [1.] He *washed their stripes,* to cool them, and abate the smart of them; to clean them from the blood which the stripes had fetched. It is probable that he bathed them with some healing liquor, as the good Samaritan helped the wounded man by *pouring in oil and wine.* [2.] He *brought them into his house,* bade them welcome to the best room he had, and prepared his best bed for them. Now nothing was thought good enough for them, as before nothing bad enough. [3.] He *set meat before them,* such as his house would afford, and they were welcome to it, by which he expressed the welcome which his soul gave to the gospel. They had spoken to him the word of the Lord, had broken the bread of life to him and his family; and he, having reaped so plentifully of their spiritual things, thought it was but reasonable that they should reap of his carnal things, 1 Cor. ix. 11. What have we houses and tables for but as we have opportunity to serve God and his people with them?

(7.) The voice of rejoicing with that of salvation was heard in the jailer's house; never was such a truly merry night kept there before: *He rejoiced, believing in God, with all his house.* There was none in his house that refused to be baptized, and so made a jar in the harmony; but they were unanimous in embracing the gospel, which added much to the joy. Or it may be read, *He, believing in God, rejoiced all the house over; πανοικὶ*—he went to every apartment, expressing his joy. Observe, [1.] His believing in Christ is called believing *in God,* which intimates that Christ is God, and that the design of the gospel is so far from being to draw us from God (saying, *Go serve other gods,* Deut. xiii. 2) that it has a direct tendency to bring us to God. [2.] His faith produced joy. Those that by faith have given up themselves to God in Christ as theirs have a great deal of reason to rejoice. The eunuch, when he was converted, *went on his way rejoicing;* and here the jailer rejoiced. The conversion of the nations is spoken of in the Old Testament as their rejoicing, Ps. lxvii. 4; xcvi. 11. For, *believing, we rejoice with joy unspeakable, and full of glory.* Believing in Christ is rejoicing in Christ. [3.] He signified his joy to all about him. Out of the abundance of the joy in his heart, his mouth spoke to the glory of God, and their encouragement who believed in God too. Those who have themselves tasted the comforts of religion should do what they can to bring others to the taste of them. One cheerful Christian should make many.

35 And when it was day, the magistrates sent the serjeants, saying,
Let those men go. 36 And the
keeper of the prison told this saying
to Paul, The magistrates have sent
to let you go: now therefore depart,
and go in peace. 37 But Paul said
unto them, They have beaten us
openly uncondemned, being Romans,
and have cast *us* into prison; and
now do they thrust us out privily?
nay verily; but let them come themselves and fetch us out. 38 And the
serjeants told these words unto the
magistrates: and they feared, when
they heard that they were Romans.
39 And they came and besought
them, and brought *them* out, and desired *them* to depart out of the city.
40 And they went out of the prison,
and entered into *the house of* Lydia:
and when they had seen the brethren,
they comforted them, and departed.

In these verses we have,

I. Orders sent for the discharge of Paul and Silas out of prison *v.* 35, 36. 1. The magistrates that had so basely abused them the day before gave the orders; and their doing it so early, *as soon as it was day,* intimates that either they were sensible the terrific earthquake they felt at midnight was intended to plead the cause of their prisoners, or their consciences had smitten them for what they had done and made them very uneasy. While the persecuted were singing in the stocks, the persecutors were full of tossings to and fro upon their beds, through anguish of mind, complaining more of the lashes of their consciences than the prisoners did of the lashes on their backs, and more in haste to give them a discharge than they were to petition for one. Now God caused his servants to be *pitied of those that had carried them captives,* Ps. cvi. 46. The magistrates sent *sergeants, ῥαβδοῦχους—those that had the rods,* the vergers, the tipstaves, the beadles, those that had been employed in beating them, that they might go and ask them forgiveness. The order was, *Let those men go.* It is probable that they designed further mischief to them, but God turned their hearts, and, as he had made their wrath hitherto to praise him, so the remainder thereof he did restrain, Ps. lxxvi. 10. 2. The jailer brought them the news (*v.* 36): *The magistrates have sent to let you go.* Some think the jailer had betimes transmitted an account to the magistrates of what had passed in his house that night, and so had obtained this order for the discharge of his prisoners: *Now therefore depart.* Not that he was desirous to part with them as his guests, but as his prisoners; they shall still be welcome to his house, but he is glad they are at liberty from his stocks. God could by his grace as easily have converted the magistrates as the jailer, and have brought them to faith and baptism; but God hath *chosen the poor of this world*, James ii. 5.

II. Paul's insisting upon the breach of privilege which the magistrates had been guilty of, *v.* 37. Paul said to the sergeants, "*They have beaten us openly, uncondemned, being Romans, and have cast us into prison* against all law and justice, and *now do they thrust us out privily*, and think to make us amends with this for the injury done us? *Nay verily; but let them come themselves and fetch us out*, and own that they have done us wrong." It is probable that the magistrates had some intimation that they were Romans, and were made sensible that their fury had carried them further than the law would bear them out; and that this was the reason why they gave orders for their discharge. Now observe,

1. Paul did not plead this before he was beaten, though it is probable that it might have prevented it, lest he should seem to be afraid of suffering for the truth which he had preached. Tully, in one of his orations, against Verres, tells of one Ganius, who was ordered by Verres to be beaten in Sicily, that all the while he was under the lash he cried out nothing but *Civis Romanus sum—I am a citizen of Rome;* Paul did not do so; he had nobler things than this to comfort himself with in his affliction.

2. He did plead it afterwards, to put an honour upon his sufferings and upon the cause he suffered for, to let the world know that the preachers of the gospel were not such despicable men as they were commonly looked upon to be, and that they merited better treatment. He did it likewise to mollify the magistrates towards the Christians at Philippi, and to gain better treatment for them, and beget in the people a better opinion of the Christian religion, when they saw that Paul had a fair advantage against their magistrates, might have brought his action against them and had them called to an account for what they had done, and yet did not take the advantage, which was very much to the honour of that worthy name by which he was called. Now here,

(1.) Paul lets them know how many ways they had run themselves into a premunire, and that he had law enough to know it. [1.] They had *beaten* those that were Romans; some think that Silas was a Roman citizen as well as Paul; others that this does not necessarily follow. Paul was a citizen, and Silas was his companion. Now both the *lex Porcia* and the *lex Sempronia* did expressly forbid *liberum corpus Romani civis, virgis aut aliis verberibus cædi—the free body of a Roman citizen to be beaten with rods or otherwise.* Roman historians give instances of cities that had their charters taken from them for indignities done to Roman citizens; we shall afterwards find Paul making use of this plea, *ch.* xxii. 25, 26. To tell them they had beaten those who were the messengers of Christ and the favourites of Heaven would have had no influence upon them; but to tell them they have abused Roman citizens will put them into a fright: so common is it for people to be more afraid of Cæsar's wrath than of Christ's. He that affronts a Roman, a gentleman, a nobleman, though ignorantly, and through mistake, thinks himself concerned to cry *Peccavi—I have done wrong*, and make his submission; but he that persecutes a Christian because he belongs to Christ stands to it, and thinks he may do it securely, though God hath said, *He that toucheth them toucheth the apple of my eye*, and Christ has warned us of the danger of *offending his little ones.* [2.] They had beaten them *uncondemned; indicta causa—without a fair hearing*, had not calmly examined what was said against them, much less enquired what they had to say for themselves. It is a universal rule of justice, *Causâ cognitâ possunt multi absolvi, incognitâ nemo condemnari potest—Many may be acquitted in consequence of having had a hearing, while without a hearing no one can be condemned.* Christ's servants would not have been abused as they have been if they and their cause might but have had an impartial trial. [3.] It was an aggravation of this that they had done it openly, which, as it was so much the greater disgrace to the sufferers, so it was the bolder defiance to justice and the law. [4.] They had *cast them into prison*, without showing any cause of their commitment, and in an arbitrary manner, by a verbal order. [5.] They now *thrust them out privily;* they had not indeed the impudence to stand by what they had done, but yet had not the honesty to own themselves in a fault.

(2.) He insists upon it that they should make them an acknowledgment of their error, and give them a public discharge, to make it the more honourable, as they had done them a public disgrace, which made that the more disgraceful: "*Let them come themselves, and fetch us out*, and give a testimony to our innocency, and that we have done nothing worthy of stripes or of bonds." It was not a point of honour that Paul stood thus sitffly upon, but a point of justice, and not to himself so much as to his cause: "Let them come and stop the clamours of the people, by confessing that we are not the troublers of the city."

III. The magistrates' submission, and the reversing of the judgment given against Paul and Silas, *v.* 38, 39. 1. The magistrates were frightened when they were told (though it may be they knew it before) that Paul was a Roman. They feared when they heard it, lest some of his friends should inform the government of what they had done, and they should fare the worse for it. The proceedings of persecutors have often been illegal, even by the law of nations, and often inhuman, against the law of nature, but always sinful, and against God's law. 2. They *came and besought them* not to take advantage of the law against them, but to overlook the illegality of what they had done and say no more of it: they *brought them out* of the prison, owning that they were wrongfully put into it, and desired them that they would peaceably and quietly *depart out of the city.* Thus Pharaoh and his servants, who had set God and Moses at defiance, came to Moses, and *bowed down themselves to him, saying, Get thee out,* Exod. xi. 8. God can make the enemies of his people ashamed of their envy and enmity to them, Isa. xxvi. 11. Jerusalem is sometimes made a burdensome stone to those that heave at it, which they would gladly get clear of, Zech. xii. 3. Yet, if the repentance of these magistrates had been sincere, they would not have desired them to depart out of their city (as the Gadarenes desired to be rid of Christ), but would have courted their stay, and begged of them to continue in their city, to show them the way of salvation. But many are convinced that Christianity is not to be persecuted who yet are not convinced that it ought to be embraced, or at least are not persuaded to embrace it. They are compelled to do honour to Christ and his servants, *to worship before their feet, and to know that he has loved them* (Rev. iii. 9), and yet do not go so far as to have benefit by Christ, or to come in for a share in his love.

IV. The departure of Paul and Silas from Philippi, *v.* 40. They went out of the prison when they were legally discharged, and not till then, though they were illegally committed, and then, 1. They took leave of their friends: they *went to the house of Lydia,* where probably the disciples had met to pray for them, and there they *saw the brethren,* or visited them at their respective habitations (which was soon done, they were so few); and they *comforted them,* by telling them (saith an ancient Greek commentary) what God had done for them, and how he had owned them in the prison. They encouraged them to keep close to Christ, and hold fast the profession of their faith, whatever difficulties they might meet with, assuring them that all would then end well, everlastingly well. Young converts should have a great deal said to them to comfort them, for *the joy of the Lord will be* very much *their strength.* 2. They quitted the town: *They departed.* I wonder they should do so; for, now that they had had such an honourable discharge from their imprisonment, surely they might have gone on at least for some time in their work without danger; but I suppose they went away upon that principle of their Master's (Mark i. 38). *Let us go into the next towns, that I may preach there also, for therefore came I forth.* Paul and Silas had an extraordinary call to Philippi; and yet, when they have come thither, they see little of the fruit of their labours, and are soon driven thence. Yet they did not come in vain. Though the beginnings here were *small, the latter end greatly increased;* now they laid the foundation of a church at Philippi, which became very eminent, had its bishops and deacons, and people that were more generous to Paul than any other church, as appears by his epistle to the Philippians, *ch.* i. 1; iv. 25. Let not ministers be discouraged, though they see not the fruit of their labours presently; the seed sown seems to be lost under the clods, but it shall come up again in a plentiful harvest in due time.

CHAP. XVII.

We have here a further account of the travels of Paul, and his services and sufferings for Christ. He was not like a candle upon a table, that gives light only to one room, but like the sun that goes its circuit to give light to many. He was called into Macedonia, a large kingdom, ch. xvi. 9. He began with Philippi, because it was the first city he came to; but he must not confine himself to this. We have him here, I. Preaching and persecuted at Thessalonica, another city of Macedonia, ver. 1—9. II. Preaching at Berea, where he met with an encouraging auditory, but was driven thence also by persecution, ver. 10—15. III. Disputing at Athens, the famous university of Greece (ver. 16—21), and the account he gave of natural religion, for the conviction of those that were addicted to polytheism and idolatry, and to lead them to the Christian religion (ver. 22—31), together with the success of this sermon, ver. 32—34.

NOW when they had passed
through Amphipolis and Apollonia, they came to Thessalonica,
where was a synagogue of the Jews;
2 And Paul, as his manner was,
went in unto them, and three sabbath days reasoned with them out of
the scriptures, 3 Opening and al-
leging, that Christ must needs have
suffered, and risen again from the
dead; and that this Jesus, whom I
preach unto you, is Christ. 4 And
some of them believed, and consorted
with Paul and Silas; and of the devout Greeks a great multitude, and
of the chief women not a few. 5
But the Jews which believed not,
moved with envy, took unto them certain lewd fellows of the baser sort, and
gathered a company, and set all the
city on an uproar, and assaulted the
house of Jason, and sought to bring
them out to the people. 6 And when
they found them not, they drew
Jason and certain brethren unto the
rulers of the city, crying, These that
have turned the world upside down
are come hither also; 7 Whom
Jason hath received: and these all
do contrary to the decrees of Cæsar,
saying that there is another king, *one*
Jesus. 8 And they troubled the
people and the rulers of the city,
when they heard these things. 9 And
when they had taken security of Jason,
and of the other, they let them go.

Paul's two epistles to the Thessalonians, the first two he wrote by inspiration, give such a shining character of that church, that we cannot but be glad here in the history to meet with an account of the first founding of the church there.

I. Here is Paul's coming to Thessalonica, which was the chief city of this country, called at this day *Salonech*, in the Turkish dominions. Observe, 1. Paul went on with his work, notwithstanding the ill usage he had met with at Philippi; he did not fail, nor was discouraged. He takes notice of this in his first epistle to the church here (1 Thess. ii. 2): *After we were shamefully treated at Philippi, yet we were bold in our God to speak unto you the gospel of God.* The opposition and persecution that he met with made him the more resolute. None of these things moved him; he could never have held out, and held on, as he did, if he had not been animated by a spirit of power from on high. 2. He did but *pass through Amphipolis and Apollonia*, the former a city near Philippi, the latter near Thessalonica; doubtless he was under divine direction, and was told by the Spirit (who, as the wind, bloweth where he listeth) what places he should pass through, and what he should rest in. Apollonia was a city of Illyricum, which, some think, illustrates that of Paul, that he had preached the gospel *from Jerusalem, and round about unto Illyricum* (Rom. xv. 19), that is, to the borders of Illyricum where he now was; and we may suppose though he is said only to *pass through* these cities, yet that he staid so long in them as to publish the gospel there, and to prepare the way for the entrance of other ministers among them, whom he would afterwards send.

II. His preaching to the Jews first, in their synagogue at Thessalonica. He found a synagogue of the Jews there (*v.* 1), which intimates that one reason why he passed through those other cities mentioned, and did not continue long in them, was because there were no synagogues in them. But, finding one in Thessalonica, by it he made his entry. 1. It was always his manner to begin with the Jews, to make them the first offer of the gospel, and not to turn to the Gentiles till they had refused it, that their mouths might be stopped from clamouring against him because he preached to the Gentiles; for if they received the gospel they would cheerfully embrace the new converts; if they refused it, they might thank themselves if the apostles carried it to those that would bid it welcome. That command of beginning at Jerusalem was justly construed as a direction, wherever they came, to begin with the Jews. 2. He met them in their synagogue on the sabbath day, in their place and at their time of meeting, and thus he would pay respect to both. Sabbaths and solemn assemblies are always very precious to those to whom Christ is precious, Ps. lxxxiv. 10. It is good being in the house of the Lord on his day. This was Christ's manner, and Paul's manner, and has been the manner of all the saints, the *good old way* which they have walked in. 3. He *reasoned with them out of the scriptures.* They agreed with him to receive the scriptures of the Old Testament: so far they were of a mind. But they received the scripture, and therefore thought they had reason to reject Christ; Paul received the scripture, and therefore saw great reason to embrace Christ. It was therefore requisite, in order to their conviction, that he should, by reasoning with them, the Spirit setting in with him, convince them that his inferences from the scripture were right and theirs were wrong. Note, The preaching of the gospel should be both scriptural preaching and rational; such Paul's was, for he *reasoned out of the scriptures:* we must take the scriptures for our foundation, our oracle, and touchstone, and then reason out of them and upon them, and against those who, though they pretend zeal for the scriptures, as the Jews did, yet wrest them to their own destruction. Reason must not be set up in competition with the scripture, but it must be made use of in explaining and applying the scripture. 4. He continued to do this *three sabbath days* successively. If he could not convince them the first sabbath, he would try the second and the third; for *precept must be upon precept, and line upon line.* God waits for sinners' conversion, and so must his ministers; all the labourers come not into the vineyard at the first hour, nor at the first call, nor are wrought upon so suddenly as the jailer. 5. The drift and scope of his preaching and arguing was to prove that *Jesus is the Christ;* this was that which he opened and alleged, *v.* 3. He first explained his thesis, and opened the terms, and then alleged it, and laid it down, as that which he would abide by, and which he summoned them in God's name to subscribe to. Paul had an admirable method of discourse; and showed he was himself both well apprized of the doctrine he preached and thoroughly understood it, and that he was fully assured of the truth of it, and therefore he opened it like one that knew it, and alleged it like one that believed it. He showed them, (1.) That it was necessary the Messiah should *suffer, and die, and rise again,* that the Old-Testament prophecies concerning the Messiah made it necessary he should. The great objection which the Jews made against Jesus being the Messiah was his ignominious death and sufferings. The *cross of Christ was to the Jews a stumbling-block,* because it did by no means agree with the idea they had framed of the Messiah; but Paul here alleges and makes it out undeniably, not only that it was possible he might be the Messiah, though he suffered, but that, being the Messiah, it was necessary he should suffer. He could not be made perfect but by sufferings; for, if he had not died, he could not have risen again from the dead. This was what Christ himself insisted upon (Luke xxiv. 26): *Ought not Christ to have suffered these things, and to enter into his glory?* And again (*v.* 46): *Thus it is written, and* therefore *thus it behoved Christ to suffer, and to rise from the dead.* He must needs have suffered for us, because he could not otherwise purchase redemption for us; and he must needs have risen again because he could not otherwise apply the redemption to us. (2.) That Jesus is the Messiah: "*This Jesus whom I preach unto you,* and call upon you to believe in, *is Christ,* is the Christ, is the anointed of the Lord, is he that should come, and you are to look for no other; for God has both by his word and by his works (the two ways of his speaking to the children of men), by the scriptures and by miracles, and the gift of the Spirit to make both effectual, borne witness to him." Note, [1.] Gospel ministers should preach Jesus; he must be their principal subject; their business is to bring people acquainted with him. [2.] That which we are to preach concerning Jesus is that he is Christ; and therefore we may hope to be saved by him and are bound to be ruled by him.

III. The success of his preaching there, *v.* 4. 1. Some of the Jews believed, notwithstanding their rooted prejudices against Christ and his gospel, and they *consorted with Paul and Silas:* they not only associated with them as friends and companions, but they gave up themselves to their direction, as their spiritual guides; they put themselves into their possession as an inheritance into the possession of the right owner, so the word signifies; they first *gave themselves to the Lord,* and then to them *by the will of God,* 2 Cor. viii. 5. They adhered to Paul and Silas, and attended them wherever they went. Note, Those that believe in Jesus Christ come into communion with his faithful ministers, and associate with them. 2. Many more of the devout Greeks, and of the chief women, embraced the gospel. These were proselytes of the gate, the *godly among the Gentiles* (so the Jews called them), such as, though they did not submit to the law of Moses, yet renounced idolatry and immorality, worshipped the true God only, and did no man any wrong. These were ὁι σεβόμενοι Ἕλληνες—*the worshipping Gentiles;* as in America they call those of the natives that are converted to the faith of Christ the *praying Indians.* These were admitted to join with the Jews in their synagogue-worship. Of these *a great multitude believed,* more of them than of the thorough-paced Jews, who were wedded to the ceremonial law. And not a few of the chief women of the city, that were devout and had a sense of religion, embraced Christianity. Particular notice is taken of this, for an example to the ladies, the chief women, and an encouragement to them to employ themselves in the exercises of devotion and to submit themselves to the commanding power of Christ's holy religion, in all the instances of it; for this intimates how acceptable it will be to God, what an honour to Christ, and what great influence it may have upon many, besides the advantages of it to their own souls. No mention is here made of their preaching the gospel to the Gentile idolaters at Thessalonica, and yet it is certain that they did, and that great numbers were converted; nay, it should seem that of the Gentile converts that church was chiefly composed, though notice is not taken of them here; for Paul writes to the Christians there as having *turned to God from idols* (1 Thess. i. 9), and that at the first entering in of the apostles among them.

IV. The trouble that was given to Paul and Silas at Thessalonica. Wherever they preached, they were sure to be persecuted; bonds and afflictions awaited them in every city. Observe,

1. Who were the authors of their trouble: the *Jews who believed not, who were moved with envy, v.* 5. The Jews were in all places the most inveterate enemies to the Christians, especially to those Jews that turned Christians, against whom they had a particular spleen, as deserters. Now see what that division was which Christ came to send upon earth; some of the Jews believed the gospel and pitied and prayed for those that did not; while those that did not envied and hated those that did. St. Paul in his epistle to this church takes notice of the rage and enmity of the Jews against the preachers of the gospel, as their measure-filling sin. 1 Thess. ii. 15, 16.

2. Who were the instruments of the trouble: the Jews made use of *certain lewd persons of the baser sort,* whom they picked up and got together, and who must undertake to give the sense of the city against the apostles. All wise and sober people looked upon them with respect, and valued them, and none would appear against them but such as were the scum of the city, a company of vile men, that were given to all manner of wickedness. Tertullian pleads this with those that opposed Christianity, that the enemies of it were generally the worst of men: *Tales semper nobis insecutores, injusti, impii, turpes, quos, et ipsi damnare consuestis—Our persecutors are invariably unjust, impious, infamous, whom you yourselves have been accustomed to condemn.*—Apologia, cap. 5. It is the honour of religion that those who hate it are generally the *lewd fellows of the baser sort,* that are lost to all sense of justice and virtue.

3. In what method they proceeded against them. (1.) They *set the city in an uproar,* made a noise to put people in a fright, and then every body ran to see what the matter was; they began a riot, and then the mob was up presently. See who are the troublers

of Israel—not the faithful preachers of the gospel, but the enemies of it. See how the devil carries on his designs; he sets cities in an uproar, sets souls in an uproar, and then fishes in troubled waters (2.) They *assaulted the house of Jason,* where the apostles lodged, with a design *to bring them out to the people,* whom they had incensed and enraged against them, and by whom they hoped to see them pulled to pieces. The proceedings here were altogether illegal; if Jason's house must be searched, it ought to be done by the proper officers, and not without a warrant: "A man's house," the law says, "is his castle," and for them in a tumultuous manner to assault a man's house, to put him and his family in fear, was but to show to what outrages men are carried by a spirit of persecution. If men have offended, magistrates are appointed to enquire into the offence, and to judge of it; but to make the rabble judges and executioners too (as these Jews designed to do) was to make truth fall in the street, to set servants on horseback, and leave princes to walk as servants on the earth—to depose equity, and enthrone fury. (3.) When they could not get the apostles into their hands (whom they would have punished as vagabonds, and incensed the people against as strangers that came to spy out the land, and devour its strength, and eat the bread out of their mouths), then they fall upon an honest citizen of their own, who entertained the apostles in his house, his name *Jason,* a converted Jew, and drew him out with some others of the brethren to the rulers of the city. The apostles were advised to withdraw, for they were more obnoxious, *Currenti cede furori—Retire before the torrent.* But their friends were willing to expose themselves, being better able to weather this storm. *For a good man,* for such good men as the apostles were, *some would even dare to die.* (4.) They accused them to the rulers, and represented them as dangerous persons, not fit to be tolerated; the crime charged upon Jason is receiving and harbouring the apostles (*v.* 7), countenancing them and promoting their interest. And what was the apostles' crime, that it should be no less than misprision of treason to give them lodging? Two very black characters are here given them, enough to make them odious to the people and obnoxious to the magistrates, if they had been just:—[1.] That they were enemies to the public peace, and threw every thing into disorder wherever they came: *Those that have turned the world upside down are come hither also.* In one sense it is true that wherever the gospel comes in its power to any place, to any soul, it works such a change there, gives such a wide change to the stream, so directly contrary to what it was, that it may be said to turn the world upside down in that place, in that soul. The love of the world is rooted out of the heart, and the way of the world contradicted in the life; so that the world is turned upside down there. But in the sense in which they meant it it is utterly false: they would have it thought that the preachers of the gospel were incendiaries and mischief makers wherever they came, that they sowed discord among relations, set neighbours together by the ears, obstructed commerce, and inverted all order and regularity. Because they persuaded people to turn from vice to virtue, from idols to the living and true God, from malice and envy to love and peace, they are charged with turning the world upside down, when it was only the kingdom of the devil in the world that they thus overturned. Their enemies *set the city in an uproar,* and then laid the blame upon them; as Nero set Rome on fire, and then charged it upon the Christians. If Christ's faithful ministers, even those that are most quiet in the land, be thus invidiously misrepresented and miscalled, let them not think it strange nor be exasperated by it; we are not better than Paul and Silas, who were thus abused. The accusers cry out, "They are *come hither also;* they have been doing all the mischief they could in other places, and now they have brought the infection hither; it is therefore time for us to bestir ourselves, and make head against them." [2.] That they were enemies to the established government, and disaffected to that, and their principles and practices were destructive to monarchy and inconsistent with the constitution of the state (*v.* 7): They all *do contrary to the decrees of Cæsar;* not to any particular decree, for there was as yet no law of the empire against Christianity, but contrary to Cæsar's power in general to make decrees; for they say, *There is another king, one Jesus,* not only a king of the Jews, as our Saviour was himself charged before Pilate, but *Lord of all;* so Peter called him in the first sermon he preached to the Gentiles, *ch.* x. 36. It is true the Roman government, both while it was a commonwealth and after it came into the Cæsars' hands, was very jealous of any governor under their dominion taking upon him the title of king, and there was an express law against it. But Christ's *kingdom was not of this world.* His followers said indeed, Jesus is a king, but not an earthly king, not a rival with Cæsar, nor his ordinances interfering with the decrees of Cæsar, but who had made it a law of his kingdom to *render unto Cæsar the things that are Cæsar's.* There was nothing in the doctrine of Christ that tended to the dethroning of princes, nor the depriving them of any of their prerogatives. The Jews knew this very well, and it was against their consciences that they brought such a charge against the apostles; and of all people it ill became the Jews to do it, who hated Cæsar and his government, and sought the ruin of him and it, and who expected a Messiah that should be a temporal prince, and overturn the thrones of kingdoms, and were therefore opposing our Lord Jesus because he did not appear under that character. Thus those have been most spiteful in representing God's faithful people as enemies to Cæsar, and hurtful to kings and provinces, who have been themselves setting up *imperium in imperio—a kingdom within a kingdom,* a power not only in competition with Cæsar's but superior to it, that of the papal supremacy.

4. The great uneasiness which this gave to the city (*v.* 8): *They troubled the people and the rulers of the city, when they heard these things.* They had no ill opinion of the apostles or their doctrine, could not apprehend any danger to the state from them, and therefore were willing to connive at them; but, if they be represented to them by the prosecutors as enemies to Cæsar, they will be obliged to take cognizance of them, and to suppress them, for fear of the government, and this troubled them. Claudius, who then held the reins of government, is represented by Suetonius as a man very jealous of the least commotion and timorous to the last degree, which obliged the rulers under him to be watchful against every thing that looked dangerous, or gave the least cause of suspicion; and therefore it troubled them to be brought under a necessity of disturbing good men.

5. The issue of this troublesome affair. The magistrates had no mind to prosecute the Christians. Care was taken to secure the apostles; they absconded, and fled, and kept out of their hands; so that nothing was to be done but to discharge Jason and his friends upon bail, *v.* 9. The magistrates here were not so easily incensed against the apostles as the magistrates at Philippi were, but were more considerate and of better temper; so they *took security of Jason and the other,* bound them to their good behaviour; and perhaps they gave bond for Paul and Silas, that they should be forthcoming when they were called for, if any thing should afterwards appear against them. Among the persecutors of Christianity, as there have been instances of the madness and rage of brutes, so there have been likewise of the prudence and temper of men; moderation has been a virtue.

10 And the brethren immediately
sent away Paul and Silas by night
unto Berea: who coming *thither*
went into the synagogue of the Jews.
11 These were more noble than those
in Thessalonica, in that they received
the word with all readiness of mind,
and searched the scriptures daily,
whether those things were so. 12
Therefore many of them believed;
also of honourable women which
were Greeks, and of men, not a few.
13 But when the Jews of Thessalonica had knowledge that the word
of God was preached of Paul at
Berea, they came thither also, and
stirred up the people. 14 And then
immediately the brethren sent away
Paul to go as it were to the sea: but
Silas and Timotheus abode there
still. 15 And they that conducted
Paul brought him unto Athens: and
receiving a commandment unto Silas
and Timotheus for to come to him
with all speed, they departed.

In these verses we have,

I. Paul and Silas removing to Berea, and employed in preaching the gospel there, *v.* 10. They had proceeded so far at Thessalonica that the foundations of a church were laid, and others were raised up to carry on the work that was begun, against whom the rulers and people were not so much prejudiced as they were against Paul and Silas; and therefore when the storm rose they withdrew, taking this as an indication to them that they must quit that place for the present. That command of Christ to his disciples, *When they persecute you in one city flee to another,* intends their flight to be not so much for their own safety ("flee to another, to hide there") as for the carrying on of their work ("flee to another, to preach there"), as appears by the reason given—*You shall not have gone over the cities of Israel till the Son of man come,* Matt. x. 23. Thus out of the eater came forth meat, and the devil was outshot in his own bow; he thought by persecuting the apostles to stop the progress of the gospel, but it was so overruled as to be made to further it. See here, 1. The care that the brethren took of Paul and Silas, when they perceived how the plot was laid against them: They *immediately sent them away by night,* incognito, *to Berea.* This could be no surprise to the young converts; *For when we were with you* (saith Paul to them, 1 Thess, iii. 4), when we came first among you, *we told you that we should suffer tribulation, even as it came to pass, and you know.* It should seem that Paul and Silas would willingly have staid, and faced the storm, if the brethren would have let them; but they would rather be deprived of the apostles' help than expose their lives, which, it should seem, were dearer to their friends than to themselves. They *sent them away by night,* under the covert of that, as if they had been evil doers. 2. The constancy of Paul and Silas in their work. Though they fled from Thessalonica, they did not flee from the service of Christ. When *they came to Berea, they went into the synagogue of the Jews,* and made their public appearance there. Though the Jews at Thessalonica had been their spiteful enemies, and, for aught they knew, the Jews at Berea would be so too, yet they did not therefore decline paying their respect to the Jews, either in revenge for the injuries they had received or for fear of what they might receive. If others will not do their duty to us, yet we ought to do ours to them.

II. The good character of the Jews in Berea (*v.* 11): *These were more noble than those in Thessalonica.* The Jews in the synagogue at Berea were better disposed to receive the gospel than the Jews in the synagogue at Thessalonica; they were not so bigoted and prejudiced against it, not so peevish and ill-natured; they *were more noble, εὐγενέστεροι—better bred.*

1. They had a freer thought, and lay more open to conviction, were willing to hear reason, and admit the force of it, and to subscribe to that which appeared to them to be truth, though it was contrary to their former sentiments. This was more noble.

2. They had a better temper, were not so sour, and morose, and ill-conditioned towards all that were not of their mind. As they were ready to come into a unity with those that by the power of truth they were brought to concur with, so they continued in charity with those that they saw cause to differ from. This was more noble. They neither prejudged the cause, nor were moved with envy at the managers of it, as the Jews at Thessalonica were, but very generously gave both it and them a fair hearing, without passion or partiality; for, (1.) *They received the word with all readiness of mind;* they were very willing to hear it, presently apprehended the meaning of it, and did not shut their eyes against the light. *They attended to the things that were spoken by Paul,* as Lydia did, and were very well pleased to hear them. They did not pick quarrels with the word, nor find fault, nor seek occasion against the preachers of it; but bade it welcome, and put a candid construction upon every thing that was said. Herein *they were more noble than the Jews in Thessalonica,* but walked in the same spirit, and in the same steps, with the Gentiles there, of whom it is said *that they received the word with joy of the Holy Ghost,* and *turned to God from idols,* 1 Thess. i. 6—9. This was true nobility. The Jews gloried much in their being Abraham's seed, thought themselves well-born and that they could not be better born. But they are here told who among them were the most noble and the best-bred men—those that were most disposed to receive the gospel, and had the high and conceited thoughts in them subdued, and *brought into obedience to Christ.* These were the most noble, and, if I may so say, the most gentleman-like men. *Nobilitas sola est atque unica virtus—Virtue and piety are true nobility,* true honour; and, without these, *Stemmata quid prosunt?—What are pedigrees and pompous titles worth?* (2.) *They searched the scriptures daily whether those things were so.* Their readiness of mind to receive the word was not such as that they took things upon trust, swallowed them upon an implicit faith: no; but since Paul reasoned out of the scriptures, and referred them to the Old Testament for the proof of what he said, they had recourse to their Bibles, turned to the places to which he referred them, read the context, considered the scope and drift of them, compared them with other places of scripture, examined whether Paul's inferences from them were natural and genuine and his arguments upon them cogent, and determined accordingly. Observe, [1.] The doctrine of Christ does not fear a scrutiny. We that are advocates for his cause desire no more than that people will not say, *These things are not so,* till they have first, without prejudice and partiality, examined whether they be so or no. [2.] The New Testament is to be examined by the Old. The Jews received the Old Testament, and those that did so, if they considered things aright, could not but see cause sufficient to receive the New, because in it they see all the prophecies and promises of the Old fully and exactly accomplished. [3.] Those that read and receive the scriptures must *search them* (John v. 39), must study them, and take pains in considering them, both that they may find out the truth contained in them, and may not mistake the sense of them and so run into error, or remain in it; and that they may find out the whole truth contained in them, and may not rest in a superficial knowledge, in the outward court of the scriptures, but may have an intimate acquaintance with the mind of God revealed in them. [4.] Searching the scriptures must be our daily work. Those that heard *the word in the synagogue on the sabbath day* did not think this enough, but were searching it every day in the week, that they might improve what they had heard the sabbath before, and prepare for what they were to hear the sabbath after. [5.] Those are truly noble, and are in a fair way to be more and more so, that make the scriptures their oracle and touchstone, and consult them accordingly. Those that rightly study the scriptures, and *meditate therein day and night,* have their minds filled with noble thoughts, fixed to noble principles, and formed for noble aims and designs. *These are more noble.*

III. The good effect of the preaching of the gospel at Berea: it had the desired success; the people's hearts being prepared, a great deal of work was done suddenly, *v.* 12. 1. Of the Jews there were many that believed. At Thessalonica there were only *some of them that believed* (*v.* 4), but at Berea, where they heard with unprejudiced minds, many believed, many more Jews than at Thessalonica. Note, God gives grace to those whom he first inclines to make a diligent use of the means of grace, and particularly to search the scriptures. 2. Of the Greeks likewise, the Gentiles, many believed, both of *the honourable women,* the ladies of quality, *and of men not a few*, men of the first rank, as should seem by their being mentioned with the honourable women. The wives first embraced the gospel, and then they persuaded their husbands to embrace it. *For what knowest thou, O wife, but thou shalt save thy husband?* 1 Cor. vii. 16.

IV. The persecution that was raised against Paul and Silas at Berea, which forced Paul thence. 1. *The Jews at Thessalonica* were the mischief-makers at *Berea.* They *had notice that the word of God was preached at Berea* (for envy and jealousy bring quick intelligence), and likewise that the Jews there were not so inveterately set against it as they were. They came thither also, to turn the world upside down there, *and they stirred up the people,* and incensed them against the preachers of the gospel; as if they had such a commission from the prince of darkness to go from place to place to oppose the gospel as the apostles had to go from place to place to preach it. Thus we read before that the Jews of Antioch and Iconium came to Lystra on purpose to incense the people against the apostles, *ch.* xiv. 19. See how restless Satan's agents are in their opposition to the gospel of Christ and the salvation of the souls of men. This is an instance of the enmity that is in the serpent's seed against the seed of the woman; and we must not think it strange if persecutors at home extend their rage to stir up persecution abroad. 2. This occasioned Paul's removal to Athens. By seeking to extinguish this divine fire which Christ had already kindled, they did but spread it the further and the faster; so long Paul staid at Berea, and such success he had there, that there were brethren there, and sensible active men too, which appeared by the care they took of Paul, *v.* 14. They were aware of the coming of the persecuting Jews from Thessalonica, and that they were busy in irritating the people against Paul; and, fearing what it would come to, they lost no time, but *immediately sent Paul away,* against whom they were most prejudiced and enraged, hoping that this would pacify them, while they retained Silas and Timothy there still, who, now that Paul had broken the ice, might be sufficient to carry on the work without exposing him. They *sent Paul to go even to the sea,* so some; *to go as it were to the sea,* so we read it; *ὡς ἐπὶ τὴν ϑάλασσαν.* He went out from Berea, in that road which went to the sea, that the Jews, if they enquired after him, might think he had gone to a great distance; but he went by land to Athens, in which there was no culpable dissimulation at all. *Those that conducted Paul* (as his guides and guards, he being both a stranger in the country and one that had many enemies) *brought him to Athens.* The Spirit of God, influencing his spirit, directed him to that famous city,—famous of old for its power and dominion, when the Athenian commonwealth coped with the Spartan,—famous afterwards for learning; it was the rendezvous of scholars. Those who wanted learning went thither to get it, because those that had learning went thither to show it. It was a great university, much resorted to from all parts, and therefore, for the better diffusing of gospel light, Paul is sent thither, and is not ashamed nor afraid to show his face among the philosophers there, and there to preach Christ crucified, though he knew it would be as much foolishness to the Greeks as it was to the Jews a stumbling-block. 3. He ordered *Silas and Timothy to come to him to Athens,* when he found there was a prospect of doing good there; or because, there being none there that he knew, he was solitary and melancholy without them. Yet it should seem that, great as was the haste he was in for them, he ordered Timothy to go about by Thessalonica, to bring him an account of the affairs of that church; for he says (1 Thess. iii. 1, 2), *We thought it good to be left at Athens alone, and sent Timotheus to establish you.*

16 Now while Paul waited for
them at Athens, his spirit was stirred
in him, when he saw the city wholly
given to idolatry. 17 Therefore disputed he in the synagogue with the
Jews, and with the devout persons,
and in the market daily with them
that met with him. 18 Then certain philosophers of the Epicureans,
and of the Stoics, encountered him.
And some said, What will this babbler say? other some, He seemeth to
be a setter forth of strange gods: because he preached unto them Jesus,
and the resurrection. 19 And they
took him, and brought him unto
Areopagus, saying, May we know
what this new doctrine, whereof thou
speakest, *is*? 20 For thou bringest
certain strange things to our ears:
we would know therefore what these
things mean. 21 (For all the Athenians and strangers which were there
spent their time in nothing else, but
either to tell, or to hear some new
thing.)

A scholar that has acquaintance, and is in love, with the learning of the ancients, would think he should be very happy if he were where Paul now was, at Athens, in the midst of the various sects of philosophers, and would have a great many curious questions to ask them, for the explication of the remains we have of the Athenian learning; but Paul, though bred a scholar, and an ingenious active man, does not make this any of his business at Athens. He has other work to mind: it is not the improving of himself in their philosophy that he aims at, he has learned to call it a vain thing, and is above it (Col. ii. 8); his business is, in God's name, to correct their disorders in religion, and *to turn them from the service of idols,* and of Satan in them, to the *service of the true and living God* in Christ.

I. Here is the impression which the abominable ignorance and superstition of the Athenians made upon Paul's spirit, *v.* 16. Observe, 1. The account here given of that city: it was *wholly given to idolatry.* This agrees with the account which the heathen writers give of it, that there were more idols in Athens than there were in all Greece besides put together, and that they had twice as many sacred feasts as others had. Whatever strange gods were recommended to them, they admitted them, and allowed them a temple and an altar, *so that they had almost as many gods as men—facilius possis deum quam hominem invenire.* And this city, after the empire became Christian, continued incurably addicted to idolatry, and all the pious edicts of the Christian emperors could not root it out, till, by the irruption of the Goths, that city was in so particular a manner laid waste that there are now scarcely any remains of it. It is observable that there, where human learning most flourished, idolatry most abounded, and the most absurd and ridiculous idolatry, which confirms that of the apostle, that when *they professed themselves to be wise they became fools* (Rom. i. 22), and, in the business of religion, were of all other the most *vain in their imaginations. The world by wisdom knew not God,* 1 Cor. i. 21. They might have reasoned against polytheism and idolatry; but, it seems, the greatest pretenders to reason were the greatest slaves to idols: so necessary was it to the re-establishing even of natural religion that there should be a divine revelation, and that centering in Christ. 2. The disturbance which the sight of this gave to Paul. Paul was not willing to appear publicly till Silas and Timothy came to him, that out of the mouth of two or three witnesses the word might be established; but in the mean time *his spirit was stirred within him.* He was filled with concern for the glory of God, which he saw given to idols, and with compassion to the souls of men, which he saw thus enslaved to Satan, *and led captive by him at his will.* He beheld these transgressors, and was grieved; and horror took hold of him. He had a holy indignation at the heathen priests, that led the people such an endless trace of idolatry, and at their philosophers, that knew better, and yet never said a word against it, but themselves went down the stream.

II. The testimony that he bore against their idolatry, and his endeavours to bring them to the knowledge of the truth. He did not, as Witsius observes, in the heat of his zeal break into the temples, pull down their images, demolish their altars, or fly in the face of their priests; nor did he run about the streets crying, "You are all the bond-slaves of the devil," though it was too true; but he observed decorum, and kept himself within due bounds, doing that only which became a prudent man. 1. He *went to the synagogue of the Jews,* who, though enemies to Christianity, were free from idolatry, and joined with them in that among them which was good, and took the opportunity given him there of disputing for Christ, *v.* 17. He discoursed *with the Jews,* reasoned fairly with them, and put it to them what reason they could give why, since they expected the Messiah, they would not receive Jesus. There he met with the devout persons that had forsaken the idol temples, but rested in the Jews' synagogue, and he talked with these to lead them on to the Christian church, to which the Jews' synagogue was but as a porch. 2. He entered into conversation with all that came in his way about matters of religion: *In the market—ἐν τῇ ἀγορᾷ,* in the exchange, or place of commerce, *he disputed daily,* as he had occasion, *with those that met with him,* or that he happened to fall into company with, that were heathen, and never came to the Jews' synagogue. The zealous advocates for the cause of Christ will be ready to plead it in all companies, as occasion offers. The ministers of Christ must not think it enough to speak a good word for Christ once a week, but should be daily speaking honourably of him to such as meet with them.

III. The enquiries which some of the philosophers made concerning Paul's doctrine. Observe,

1. Who they were that encountered him, that entered into discourse with him, and opposed him: *He disputed with all that met him, in the places of concourse,* or rather of discourse. Most took no notice of him, slighted him, and never minded a word he said; but there were some of the philosophers that thought him worth making remarks upon, and they were those whose principles were most directly contrary to Christianity. (1.) *The Epicureans,* who *thought God altogether such a one as themselves,* an idle inactive being, that minded nothing, nor put any difference between good and evil. They would not own, either that God made the world or that he governs it; nor that man needs to make any conscience of what he says or does, having no punishment to fear nor rewards to hope for, all which loose atheistical notions Christianity is levelled against. The Epicureans indulged themselves in all the pleasures of sense, and placed their happiness in them, in what Christ has taught us in the first place to deny ourselves. (2.) *The Stoics,* who thought themselves altogether as good as God, and indulged themselves as much in the pride of life as the Epicureans did in the lusts of the flesh and of the eye; they made

their virtuous man to be no way inferior to God himself, nay to be superior. *Esse aliquid quo sapiens antecedat Deum—There is that in which a wise man excels God,* so Seneca: to which Christianity is directly opposite, as it teaches us to deny ourselves and abase ourselves, and to come off from all confidence in ourselves, that Christ may be all in all.

2. What their different sentiments were of him; such there were as there were of Christ, *v.* 18. (1.) *Some called him a babbler,* and thought he spoke, without any design, whatever came uppermost, as men of crazed imaginations do: *What will this babbler say?* ὁ σπερμολόγος οὗτος—*this scatterer of words,* that goes about, throwing here one idle word or story and there another, without any intendment or signification; or, *this picker up of seeds.* Some of the critics tell us that the term is used for *a little sort of bird,* that is worth nothing at all, either for the spit or for the cage, *that picks up the seeds that lie uncovered, either in the field or by the way-side, and hops here and there for that purpose—Avicula parva quæ semina in triviis dispersa colligere solet;* such a pitiful contemptible animal they took Paul to be, or supposed he went from place to place venting his notions to get money, a penny here and another there, as that bird picks up here and there a grain. They looked upon him as an idle fellow, and regarded him, as we say, no more than a ballad-singer. (2.) *Others* called him *a setter forth of strange gods,* and thought he spoke with design to make himself considerable by that means. And, if he had strange gods to set forth, he could not bring them to a better market than to Athens. He did not, as many did, directly set forth new gods, nor avowedly; but they thought he seemed to do so, *because he preached unto them Jesus, and the resurrection.* From his first coming among them he ever and anon harped upon these two strings, which are indeed the principal doctrines of Christianity—Christ and a future state—Christ our way, and heaven our end; and, though he did not call these gods, yet they thought he meant to make them so. Τὸν Ἰησοῦν καὶ τὴν ἀνάστασιν, "Jesus they took for a new god, and *anastasis,* the resurrection, for a new goddess." Thus they lost the benefit of the Christian doctrine by dressing it up in a pagan dialect, as if believing in Jesus, and looking for the resurrection, were the worshipping of new demons.

3. The proposal they made to give him a free, full, fair, and public hearing, *v.* 19, 20. They had heard some broken pieces of his doctrine, and are willing to have a more perfect knowledge of it. (1.) They look upon it as strange and surprising, and very different from the philosophy that had for many ages been taught and professed at Athens. "It is a new doctrine, which we do not understand the drift and design of. *Thou bringest certain strange things to our ears,* which we never heard of before, and know not what to make of now." By this it should seem that, among all the learned books they had, they either had not, or heeded not, the books of Moses and the prophets, else the doctrine of Christ would not have been so perfectly new and strange to them. There was but one book in the world that was of divine inspiration, and that was the only book they were strangers to, which, if they would have given a due regard to it, would, in its very first page, have determined that great controversy among them about the origin of the universe. (2.) They desired to know more of it, only because it was new and strange: "*May we know what this new doctrine is?* Or, is it (like the mysteries of the gods) to be kept as a profound secret? If it may be, we would gladly know, and desire thee to tell us, *what these things mean,* that we may be able to pass a judgment upon them." This was a fair proposal; it was fit they should know what this doctrine was before they embraced it; and they were so fair as not to condemn it till they had had some account of it. (3.) The place they brought him to, in order to this public declaration of his doctrine; it was *to Areopagus,* the same word that is translated (*v.* 22) *Mars' Hill;* it was the town-house, or guildhall of their city, where the magistrates met upon public business, and the courts of justice were kept; and it was as the theatre in the university, or the schools, where learned men met to communicate their notions. The court of justice which sat here was famous for its equity, which drew appeals to it from all parts; if any denied a God, he was liable to the censure of this court. Diagoras was by them put to death, as a contemner of the gods; nor might any new God be admitted without their approbation. Hither they brought Paul to be tried, not as a criminal but as a candidate.

4. The general character of the people of that city given upon this occasion (*v.* 21): *All the Athenians,* that is natives of the place, and strangers who sojourned there for their improvement, *spent their time in nothing else but either to tell or to hear some new thing,* which comes in as the reason why they were inquisitive concerning Paul's doctrine, not because it was *good,* but because it was *new.* It is a very sorry character which is here given of these people, yet many transcribe it. (1.) They were all for conversation. St. Paul exhorts his pupil to *give attendance to reading and meditation* (1 Tim. iv. 13, 15), but these people despised those old-fashioned ways of getting knowledge, and preferred that of telling and hearing. It is true that good company is of great use to a man, and will polish one that has laid a good foundation in study; but that knowledge will be very flashy and superficial which is got by conversation only. (2.) They affected novelty; they were for *telling and hearing some new thing.* They were for new schemes and new notions in

philosophy, new forms and plans of government in politics, and, in religion, for new gods that came newly up (Deut. xxxii. 17), new demons, new-fashioned images and altars (2 Kings xvi. 10); they were given to change. Demosthenes, an orator of their own, had charged this upon them long before, in one of his Philippics, that their common question in the markets, or wherever they met, was ἐί τὶ λὲ εται νεωτερον—*whether there was any news.* (3.) They meddled in other people's business, and were inquisitive concerning that, and never minded their own. Tattlers are always *busy bodies,* 1 Tim. v. 13. (4.) *They spent their time in nothing else,* and a very uncomfortable account those must needs have to make of their time who thus spend it. Time is precious, and we are concerned to be good husbands of it, because eternity depends upon it, and it is hastening apace into eternity, but abundance of it is wasted in unprofitable converse. To tell or hear the new occurrences of providence concerning the public in our own or other nations, and concerning our neighbours and friends, is of good use now and then; but to set up for news-mongers, and to spend our time in nothing else, is to lose that which is very precious for the gain of that which is worth little.

22 Then Paul stood in the midst
of Mars' hill, and said, *Ye* men of
Athens, I perceive that in all things
ye are too superstitious. 23 For as
I passed by, and beheld your devotions, I found an altar with this
inscription, TO THE UNKNOWN
GOD. Whom therefore ye ignorantly worship, him declare I unto
you. 24 God that made the world
and all things therein, seeing that he
is Lord of heaven and earth, dwelleth
not in temples made with hands;
25 Neither is worshipped with men's
hands, as though he needed any
thing, seeing he giveth to all life,
and breath, and all things; 26 And
hath made of one blood all nations
of men for to dwell on all the face of
the earth, and hath determined the
times before appointed, and the
bounds of their habitation; 27 That
they should seek the Lord, if haply
they might feel after him, and find
him, though he be not far from every
one of us: 28 For in him we live,
and move, and have our being; as
certain also of your own poets have
said, For we are also his offspring.
29 Forasmuch then as we are the
offspring of God, we ought not to
think that the Godhead is like unto
gold, or silver, or stone, graven by
art and man's device. 30 And the
times of this ignorance God winked
at; but now commandeth all men
every where to repent: 31 Because
he hath appointed a day, in the
which he will judge the world in
righteousness by *that* man whom he
hath ordained; *whereof* he hath given
assurance unto all *men,* in that he
hath raised him from the dead.

We have here St. Paul's sermon at Athens. Divers sermons we have had, which the apostles preached to the Jews, or such Gentiles as had an acquaintance with and veneration for the Old Testament, and were worshippers of the true and living God; and all they had to do with them was to open and allege *that Jesus is the Christ;* but here we have a sermon to heathens, that worshipped false gods, and were without the true God in the world, and to them the scope of their discourse was quite different from what it was to the other. In the former case their business was to lead their hearers by prophecies and miracles to the knowledge of the Redeemer, and faith in him; in the latter it was to lead them by the common works of providence to the knowledge of the Creator, and the worship of him. One discourse of this kind we had before to the rude idolaters of Lystra that deified the apostles (*ch.* xiv. 15); this recorded here is to the more polite and refined idolaters at Athens, and an admirable discourse it is, and every way suited to his auditory and the design he had upon them.

I. He lays down this, as the scope of his discourse, that he aimed to bring them to *the knowledge of the only living and true God,* as the sole and proper object of their adoration. He is here obliged to lay the foundation, and to instruct them in the first principle of all religion, that there is a God, and that God is but one. When he preached against the gods they worshipped, he had no design to draw them to atheism, but to the service of the true Deity. Socrates, who had exposed the pagan idolatry, was indicted in this very court, and condemned, not only because he did not esteem those to be gods whom the city esteemed to be so, but because he introduced new demons; and this was the charge against Paul. Now he tacitly owns the former part of the charge, but guards against the latter, by declaring that he does not introduce any new gods, but reduce them *to the knowledge of one God, the Ancient of days.* Now,

1. He shows them that they needed to be instructed herein; for they had lost the knowledge of the true God that made them,

in the worship of false gods that they had made *(Deos qui rogat ille facit—He who worships the gods makes them)*: *I perceive that in all things you are too superstitious.* The crime he charges upon them is giving that glory to others which is due to God only, that they feared and worshipped demons, spirits that they supposed inhabited the images to which they directed their worship. "It is time for you to be told that *there is but one God* who are multiplying deities above any of your neighbours, and mingle your idolatries with all your affairs. *You are in all things too superstitious*—*δεισιδαιμονέστεροι*, you easily admit every thing that comes under a show of religion, but it is that which corrupts it more and more; I bring you that which will reform it." Their neighbours praised them for this as a pious people, but Paul condemns them for it. Yet it is observable how he mollifies the charge, does not aggravate it, to provoke them. He uses a word which among them was taken in a good sense: *You are every way more than ordinarily religious,* so some read it; *you are very devout in your way.* Or, if it be taken in a bad sense, it is mitigated: "You are as it were (ὡς) more superstitious than you need be;" and he says no more than what he himself perceived; *θεωρῶ—I see it, I observe it.* They charged Paul with setting forth new demons: "Nay," says he, "you have demons enough already; I will not add to the number of them."

2. He shows them that they themselves had given a fair occasion for the declaring of this one true God to them, by *setting up an altar, To the unknown God,* which intimated an acknowledgment that there was a God who was yet to them *an unknown God;* and it is sad to think that at Athens, a place which was supposed to have the monopoly of wisdom, the true God was an unknown God, the only God that was unknown. "Now you ought to bid Paul welcome, for this is the God whom he comes to make known to you, the God whom you tacitly complain that you are ignorant of." There, where we are sensible we are defective and come short, just there, the gospel takes us up, and carries us on.

(1.) Various conjectures the learned have concerning this *altar dedicated to the unknown God.* [1.] Some think the meaning is, *To the God whose honour it is to be unknown,* and that they intended the God of the Jews, whose name is ineffable, and whose nature is unsearchable. It is probable they had heard from the Jews, and from the writings of the Old Testament, of the God of Israel, who had proved himself to be above all gods, but was *a God hiding himself,* Isa. xlv. 15. The heathen called the Jews' God, *Deus incertus, incertum Mosis Numen—an uncertain God, the uncertain Deity of Moses,* and the God without name. Now *this God,* says Paul, *this God, who cannot by searching be found out to perfection, I now declare unto you.* [2.] Others think the meaning is, *To the God whom it is our unhappiness not to know,* which intimates that they would think it their happiness to know him. Some tell us that upon occasion of a plague that raged at Athens, when they had sacrificed to all their gods one after another for the staying of the plague, they were advised to let some sheep go where they pleased, and, where they lay down, to build an altar, *τῷ προσήκοντι Θεῷ—to the proper God, or the God to whom that affair of staying the pestilence did belong;* and, because they knew not how to call him, they inscribed it, *To the unknown God.* Others, from some of the best historians of Athens, tell us they had many altars inscribed, *To the gods of Asia, Europe, and Africa—To the unknown God:* and some of the neighbouring countries used to swear *by the God that was unknown at Athens;* so Lucian.

(2.) Observe, how modestly Paul mentions this. That he might not be thought a spy, nor one that had intruded himself more than became a stranger into the knowledge of their mysteries, he tells them that he observed it *as he passed by, and saw their devotions,* or *their sacred things.* It was public, and he could not forbear seeing it, and it was proper enough to make his remarks upon the religion of the place; and observe how prudently and ingeniously he takes occasion from this to bring in his discourse of the true God. [1.] He tells them that the God he preached to them was one that they did already worship, and therefore he was not a setter forth of new or strange gods: "As you have a dependence upon him, so he has had some kind of homage from you." [2.] He was one whom they ignorantly worshipped, which was a reproach to them, who were famous all the world over for their knowledge. "Now," says he, "I come to take away *that reproach,* that you may worship him understandingly whom now you worship ignorantly; and it cannot but be acceptable to have your blind devotion turned into a reasonable service, that you may not worship *you know not what.*"

II. He confirms his doctrine of one living and true God, by his works of creation and providence: "The God whom I declare unto you to be the sole object of your devotion, and call you to the worship of, is *the God that made the world* and governs it; and, by the visible proofs of these, you may be led to this invisible Being, and be convinced of his *eternal power and Godhead.*" The Gentiles in general, and the Athenians particularly, in their devotions were governed, not by their philosophers, many of whom spoke clearly and excellently well of one supreme *Numen,* of his infinite perfections and universal agency and dominion (witness the writings of Plato, and long after of Cicero); but by their poets, and their idle fictions. Homer's works were the Bible of the pagan theology, or demonology rather, not Plato's; and the philosophers tamely submitted to this, rested in their speculations, disputed them among themselves, and taught them to their scholars, but never made the use they ought to have made of them in opposition to idolatry; so little certainty were they at concerning them, and so little impression did these things make upon them! Nay, they ran themselves into the superstition of their country, and thought they ought to do so. *Eamus ad communem errorem—Let us embrace the common error.* Now Paul here sets himself, in the first place, to reform the philosophy of the Athenians (he corrects the mistakes of that), and to give them right notions of *the one only living and true God,* and then to carry the matter further than they ever attempted for the reforming of their worship, and the bringing them off from their polytheism and idolatry. Observe what glorious things Paul here says of that God whom he served, and would have them to serve.

1. *He is the God that made the world, and all things therein; the Father almighty, the Creator of heaven and earth.* This was admitted by many of the philosophers; but those of Aristotle's school denied it, and maintained "that the world was from eternity, and every thing always was what now it is." Those of the school of Epicurus fancied "that the world was made by a fortuitous concourse of atoms, which, having been in perpetual motion, at length accidently jumped into this frame." Against both these Paul here maintains that God by the operations of an infinite power, according to the contrivance of an infinite wisdom, in the beginning of time made the world and all things therein, the origin of which was owing, not as they fancied to an eternal matter, but to an eternal mind.

2. He is therefore *Lord of heaven and earth,* that is, he is the rightful owner, proprietor, and possessor, of all the beings, powers, and riches of the upper and lower world, material and immaterial, visible and invisible. This follows from his making heaven and earth. If he created all, without doubt he has the disposing of all: and, where he gives being, he has an indisputable right to give law.

3. He is, in a particular manner, the Creator of men, of all men (*v.* 26): *He made of one blood all nations of men.* He made the first man, he makes every man, is the former of every man's body and the Father of every man's spirit. He has made the nations of men, not only all men in the nations, but as nations in their political capacity; he is their founder, and disposed them into communities for their mutual preservation and benefit. He made them all of one blood, of one and the same nature; *he fashions their heart alike.* Descended from one and the same common ancestor, in Adam they are all akin, so they are in Noah, that hereby they might be engaged in mutual affection and assistance, as fellow-creatures and brethren. *Have we not all one Father? Hath not one God created us?* Mal. ii. 10. *He hath made them to dwell on all the face of the earth,* which, as a bountiful benefactor, *he has given,* with all its fulness, *to the children of men.* He made them not to live in one place, but to be dispersed over all the earth; one nation therefore ought not to look with contempt upon another, as the Greeks did upon all other nations; for those on all the face of the earth are of the same blood. The Athenians boasted that they sprung out of their own earth, were *aborigines,* and nothing akin by blood to any other nation, which proud conceit of themselves the apostle here takes down.

4. That he is the great benefactor of the whole creation (*v.* 25): *He giveth to all life, and breath, and all things.* He not only *breathed into the first man the breath of life,* but still breathes it into every man. He gave us these souls; he formed the spirit of man within him. He not only gave us our life and breath, when he brought us into being, but he is continually giving them to us; his providence is a continued creation; he *holds our souls in life;* every moment our breath goes forth, but he graciously gives it us again the next moment; it is not only *his air that we breathe in, but it is in his hand that our breath is,* Dan. v. 23. He *gives to all the children of men their life and breath;* for as the meanest of the children of men live upon him, and receive from him, so the greatest, the wisest philosophers and mightiest potentates, cannot live without him. *He gives to all,* not only to all the children of men, but to the inferior creatures, to all animals, *every thing wherein is the breath of life* (Gen. vi. 17); they have their life and breath from him, and where he gives life and breath he gives all things, all other things needful for the support of life. *The earth is full of his goodness,* Ps. civ. 24, 27.

5. That he is the sovereign disposer of all the affairs of the children of men, according to the counsel of his will (*v.* 26): *He hath determined the times before appointed, and the bounds of their habitation.* See here, (1.) The sovereignty of God's disposal concerning us: he *hath determined* every event, ὁρίσας, the matter is fixed; the disposals of Providence are incontestable and must not be disputed, unchangeable and cannot be altered. (2.) The wisdom of his disposals; he hath *determined* what was *before appointed.* The determinations of the Eternal Mind are not sudden resolves, but the counterparts of an eternal counsel, the copies of divine decrees. *He performeth the thing that is appointed for me,* Job xxiii. 14. *Whatever comes forth from God was before all worlds hid in God.* (3.) The things about which his providence is conversant; these are time and place: the times and places of our living in this world are determined and appointed by the God that made us. [1.] *He has determined the*

times that are concerning us. Times to us seem changeable, but God has fixed them. *Our times are in his hand,* to lengthen or shorten, embitter or sweeten, as he pleases. He has appointed and determined the time of our coming into the world, and the time of our continuance in the world; our time to be born, and our time to die (Eccl. iii. 1, 2), and all that little that lies between them—the time of all our concernments in this world. Whether they be prosperous times or calamitous times, it is he that has determined them; and on him we must depend, with reference to the times that are yet before us. [2.] He has also *determined and appointed the bounds of our habitation.* He that *appointed the earth to be a habitation for the children of men* has appointed to the children of men a distinction of habitations upon the earth, has instituted such a thing as property, to which he has set bounds to keep us from trespassing one upon another. The particular habitations in which our lot is cast, the place of our nativity and of our settlement, are of God's determining and appointing, which is a reason why we should accommodate ourselves to the habitations we are in, and make the best of that which is.

6. That *he is not far from every one of us, v.* 27. He is every where present, not only is *at our right hand, but has possessed our reins* (Ps. cxxxix. 13), has his eye upon us at all times, and knows us better than we know ourselves. Idolaters made images of God, that they might have him with them in those images, the absurdity of which the apostle here shows; for he is an infinite Spirit, *that is not far from any of us,* and never the nearer, but in one sense the further off from us, for our pretending to realize or presentiate him to ourselves by any image. He is nigh unto us, both to receive the homage we render him and to give the mercies we ask of him, wherever we are, though near no altar, image, or temple. The Lord of all, as *he is rich* (Rom. x. 12), so *he is nigh* (Deut. iv. 7), *to all that call upon him.* He that wills us to *pray every where,* assures us that he is no where far from us; whatever country, nation, or profession we are of, whatever our rank and condition in the world are, be we in a palace or in a cottage, in a crowd or in a corner, in a city or in a desert, in the depths of the sea or afar off upon the sea, this is certain, *God is not far from every one of us.*

7. That *in him we live, and move, and have our being, v.* 28. We have a necessary and constant dependence upon his providence, as the streams have upon the spring, and the beams upon the sun. (1.) *In him we live;* that is, the continuance of our lives is owing to him and the constant influence of his providence; *he is our life, and the length of our days.* It is not only owing to his patience and pity that our forfeited lives are not cut off, but it is owing to his power, and goodness, and fatherly care, that our frail lives are prolonged. There needs not a positive act of his wrath to destroy us; if he suspend the positive acts of his goodness, we die of ourselves. (2.) *In him we move;* it is by the uninterrupted concourse of his providence that our souls move in their outgoings and operations, that our thoughts run to and fro about a thousand subjects, and our affections run out towards their proper objects. It is likewise by him that our souls move our bodies; we cannot stir a hand, or foot, or a tongue, but by him, who, as he is the first cause, so he is the first mover. (3.) *In him we have our being;* not only from him we had it at first, but in him we have it still; to his continued care and goodness we owe it, not only that we have a being and are not sunk into nonentity, but that we have our being, have this being, were and still are of such a noble rank of beings, capable of knowing and enjoying God; and are not thrust into the meanness of brutes, nor the misery of devils.

8. That upon the whole matter we are *God's offspring;* he is *our Father that begat us* (Deut. xxxii. 6, 18), and he hath *nourished and brought us up as children,* Isa. i. 2. The confession of an adversary in such a case is always looked upon to be of use as *argumentum ad hominem—an argument to the man,* and therefore the apostle here quotes a saying of one of the Greek poets, Aratus, a native of Cilicia, Paul's countryman, who, in his *Phenomena,* in the begining of his book, speaking of the heathen *Jupiter,* that is, in the poetical dialect, the supreme *God,* says this of him, *τοῦ γὰρ καὶ γένος ἐσμεν—for we are also his offspring.* And he might have quoted other poets to the purpose of what he was speaking, that *in God we live and move:—*

> Spiritus intus alit, totamque infusa per artus
> Mens agitat molem.
> This active mind, infus'd through all the space,
> Unites and mingles with the mighty mass.—*Virgil,* Æneid vi
>
> Est Deus in nobis, agitante calescimus illo.
> 'Tis the Divinity that warms our hearts.—*Ovid,* Fast. vi.
>
> Jupiter est quodcunque vides,
> Quocunque moveris.
> Where'er you look, where'er you rove
> The spacious scene is full of Jove.—*Lucan,* lib. ii.

But he chooses this of Aratus, as having much in a little. By this it appears not only that Paul was himself a scholar, but that human learning is both ornamental and serviceable to a gospel minister, especially for the convincing of those that are without; for it enables him to beat them at their own weapons, and to cut off Goliath's head with his own sword. How can the adversaries of truth be beaten out of their strong-holds by those that do not know them? It may likewise shame God's professing people, who forget their relation to God, and walk contrary to it, that a heathen poet could say of God, *We are his offspring,* formed by him, formed for him, more the care of his providence than ever any children were the care of their parents; and therefore are obliged to obey his commands, and acquiesce in his disposals, and *to be unto him for a name and a praise.* Since in him and upon him we live, we ought to live to him; since in him we move, we ought to move towards him; and since in him we have our being, and from him we receive all the supports and comforts of our being, we ought to consecrate our being to him, and to apply to him for a new being, a better being, an eternal well-being.

III. From all these great truths concerning God, he infers the absurdity of their idolatry, as the prophets of old had done. If this be so, 1. Then God cannot be represented by an image. If we are *the offspring of God*, as we are spirits in flesh, then certainly he who is *the Father of our spirits* (and they are the principal part of us, and that part of us by which we are denominated God's offspring) is himself a Spirit, and we ought not to think that the Godhead is *like unto gold, or silver, or stone, graven by art and man's device, v.* 29. We wrong God, and put an affront upon him, if we think so. God honoured man in making his soul after his own likeness; but man dishonours God if he makes him after the likeness of his body. The Godhead is spiritual, infinite, immaterial, incomprehensible, and therefore it is a very false and unjust conception which an image gives us of God, be the matter ever so rich, *gold or silver;* be the shape ever so curious, and be it ever so well *graven by art or man's device*, its countenance, posture, or dress, ever so significant, it is a teacher of lies. 2. Then *he dwells not in temples made with hands, v.* 24. He is not invited to any temple men can build for him, nor confined to any. A temple brings him never the nearer to us, nor keeps him ever the longer among us. A temple is convenient for us to come together in to worship God; but God needs not any place of rest or residence, nor the magnificence and splendour of any structure, to add to the glory of his appearance. A pious, upright heart, *a temple not made with hands*, but by *the Spirit of God*, is that which *he dwells in*, and *delights to dwell in.* See 1 Kings viii. 27; Isa. lxvi. 1, 2. 3. Then he is *not worshipped*, *θεραπεύεται*, he is *not served*, or *ministered unto, with men's hands, as though he needed any thing, v.* 25. He that made all, and maintains all, cannot be benefited by any of our services, nor needs them. If we receive and derive all from him, he is all-sufficient, and therefore cannot but be self-sufficient, and independent. What need can God have of our services, or what benefit can he have by them, when he has all perfection in himself, and we have nothing that is good but what we have from him? The philosophers, indeed, were sensible of this truth, that God has no need of us or our services; but the vulgar heathen built temples and offered sacrifices to their gods, with an opinion that they needed houses and food. See Job xxxv. 5—8; Ps. l. 8, &c. 4. Then it concerns us all to enquire after God (*v.* 27): *That they should seek the Lord,* that is, fear and worship him in a right manner. Therefore God has kept the children of men in a constant dependence upon him for life and all the comforts of life, that he might keep them under constant obligations to him. We have plain indications of God's presence among us, his presidency over us, the care of his providence concerning us, and his bounty to us, that we might be put upon enquiring, *Where is God our Maker, who giveth songs in the night, who teacheth us more than the beasts of the earth, and maketh us wiser than the fowls of heaven?* Job xxxv. 10, 11. Nothing, one would think, should be more powerful with us to convince us that there is a God, and to engage us to seek his honour and glory in our services, and to seek our happiness in his favour and love, than the consideration of our own nature, especially the noble powers and faculties of our own souls. If we reflect upon these, and contemplate these, we may perceive both our relation and obligation to a God above us. Yet so dark is this discovery, in comparison with that by divine revelation, and so unapt are we to receive it, that those who have no other could but *haply feel after God* and *find him.* (1.) It was very uncertain whether they could by this searching *find out God;* it is but a peradventure: *if haply* they might. (2.) If they did find out something of God, yet it was but some confused notions of him; they did but feel after him, as men in the dark, or blind men, who lay hold on a thing that comes in their way, but know not whether it be that which they are in quest of or no. It is a very confused notion which this poet of theirs has of the relation between God and man, and very general, that *we are his offspring:* as was also that of their philosophers. Pythagoras said, Θεῖον γένος ἐστι βροτοῖος—*Men have a sort of a divine nature.* And Heraclitus *(apud Lucian)* being asked, *What are men?* answered, Θεοὶ θνητόι—*Mortal gods;* and, *What are the gods?* answered, ἄθάνατοι ἄνθρωποι—*Immortal men.* And Pindar saith *(Nemean, Ode* 6), Ἑν ἀνδρῶν ἓν θεων γένος—*God and man are near a-kin.* It is true that by the knowledge of ourselves we may be led to the knowledge of God, but it is a very confused knowledge. This is but feeling after him. We have therefore reason to be thankful that by the gospel of Christ we have notices given us of God much clearer than we could have by the light of nature; we do not now feel after him, but *with open face behold, as in a glass, the glory of God.*

IV. He proceeds to call them all to repent of their idolatries, and to turn from them, *v.* 30, 31. This is the practical part of Paul's sermon before the university; having declared God to them (*v.* 23), he properly presses upon them *repentance towards God,* and would also have taught them *faith towards our Lord Jesus Christ,* if they had had the patience to hear him. Having shown them the absurdity of their worshipping other gods, he persuades them to go on no longer in that foolish way of worship, but to return from it to the living and true God. Observe,

1. The conduct of God towards the Gentile world before the gospel came among them: *The times of this ignorance God winked at.* (1.) They were times of great ignorance. Human learning flourished more than ever in the Gentile world just before Christ's time; but in the things of God they were grossly ignorant. Those are ignorant indeed who either know not God or worship him ignorantly; idolatry was owing to ignorance. (2.) These times of ignorance God winked at. Understand it, [1.] As an act of divine justice. God despised or neglected these times of ignorance, and did not send them his gospel, as now he does. It was very provoking to him to see his glory thus given to another; and he detested and hated these times. So some take it. Or rather, [2.] As an act of divine patience and forbearance. He winked at these times; he did not restrain them from these idolatries by sending prophets to them, as he did to Israel; he did not punish them in their idolatries, as he did Israel; but gave them the gifts of his providence, *ch.* xiv. 16, 17. *These things thou hast done, and I kept silence,* Ps. l. 21. He did not give them such calls and motives to repentance as he does now. He *let them alone.* Because they did not improve the light they had, but were willingly ignorant, he did not send them greater lights. Or, he was not quick and severe with them, but was long-suffering towards them, because they did it ignorantly, 1 Tim. i. 13.

2. The charge God gave to the Gentile world by the gospel, which he now sent among them: *He now commandeth all men every where to repent*—to change their mind and their way, to be ashamed of their folly and to act more wisely, to break off the worship of idols and bind themselves to the worship of the true God. Nay, it is to turn with sorrow and shame from every sin, and with cheerfulness and resolution to every duty. (1.) This is God's command. It had been a great favour if he had only told us that there was room left for repentance, and we might be admitted to it; but he goes further, he interposes his own authority for our good, and has made that our duty which is our privilege. (2.) It is his command to *all men, every where,*—to men, and not to angels, that need it not,—to men, and not to devils, that are excluded the benefit of it,—to all men in all places; all men have made work for repentance, and have cause enough to repent, and all men are invited to repent, and shall have the benefit of it. The apostles are commissioned to preach this every where. The prophets were sent to command the Jews to repent; but the apostles were sent to preach *repentance and remission of sins to all nations.* (3.) Now in gospel times it is more earnestly commanded, because more encouraged than it had been formerly. Now the way of remission is more opened than it had been, and the promise more fully confirmed; and therefore now he expects we should all repent. "Now repent; now at length, now in time, repent; for you have too long gone on in sin. Now in time repent, for it will be too late shortly."

3. The great reason to enforce this command, taken from the judgment to come. God commands us to repent, *because he hath appointed a day in which he will judge the world in righteousness* (*v.* 31), and has now under the gospel made a clearer discovery of a state of retribution in the other world than ever before. Observe, (1.) The God that made the world will judge it; he that gave the children of men their being and faculties will call them to an account for the use they have made of them, and recompense them accordingly, whether the body served the soul in serving God or the soul was a drudge to the body in making provision for the flesh; and *every man shall receive according to the things done in the body,* 2 Cor. v. 10. The God that now governs the world will judge it, will reward the faithful friends of his government and punish the rebels. (2.) There is a day appointed for this general review of all that men have done in time, and a final determination of their state for eternity. The day is fixed in the counsel of God, and cannot be altered; but it is hid there, and cannot be known. A day of decision, a day of recompence, a day that will put a final period to all the days of time. (3.) The world will be judged in righteousness; for God is not unrighteous, who taketh vengeance; far be it from him that he should do iniquity. His knowledge of all men's characters and actions is infallibly true, and therefore his sentence upon them incontestably just. And, as there will be no appeal from it, so there will be no exception against it. (4.) God will judge the world *by that man whom he hath ordained,* who can be no other than the Lord Jesus, to whom all judgment is committed. By him God made the world, by him he redeemed it, by him he governs it, and by him he will judge it. (5.) God's raising Christ from the dead is the great proof of his being appointed and ordained the Judge of quick and dead. His doing him that honour evidenced his designing him this honour. His raising him from the dead was the beginning of his exaltation, his judging the world will be the perfection of it; and he that begins will make an end. God hath *given assurance unto all men,* sufficient ground for their faith to build upon, both that there is a judgment to come and that Christ will be their Judge; the matter is not left doubtful, but is of unquestionable certainty. Let all his enemies be assured of it, and tremble before him; let all his friends be assured of it, and triumph in him. (6.)

The consideration of the judgment to come, and of the great hand Christ will have in that judgment, should engage us all to repent of our sins and turn from them to God. This is the only way to make the Judge our friend in that day, which will be a terrible day to all who live and die impenitent; but true penitents will then *lift up their heads with joy, knowing that their redemption draws nigh.*

32 And when they heard of the resurrection of the dead, some mocked:
and others said, We will hear thee
again of this *matter.* 33 So Paul
departed from among them. 34
Howbeit certain men clave unto him,
and believed: among the which *was*
Dionysius the Areopagite, and a
woman named Damaris, and others
with them.

We have here a short account of the issue of Paul's preaching at Athens.

I. Few were the better: the gospel had as little success at Athens as any where; for the pride of the philosophers there, as of the Pharisees at Jerusalem, prejudiced them against the gospel of Christ. 1. Some ridiculed Paul and his preaching. They heard him patiently till he came to speak of the resurrection of the dead (*v.* 32), and then some of them began to hiss him: they *mocked.* What he had said before was somewhat like what they had sometimes heard in their own schools, and some notion they had of a resurrection, as it signifies a future state; but, if he speak of a *resurrection of the dead,* though it be of the resurrection of Christ himself, it is altogether incredible to them, and they cannot bear so much as to hear of it, as being contrary to a principle of their philosophy: *A privatione ad habitum non datur regressus—Life when once lost is irrecoverable.* They had deified their heroes after their death, but never thought of their being raised from the dead, and therefore they could by no means reconcile themselves to this doctrine of Christ's being raised from the dead; how can this be? This great doctrine, which is the saints' joy, is their jest; when it was but mentioned to them they mocked, and made a laughing matter of it. We are not to think it strange if sacred truths of the greatest certainty and importance are made the scorn of profane wits. 2. Others were willing to take time to consider of it; they said, *We will hear thee again of this matter.* They would not at present comply with what Paul said, nor oppose it; but *we will hear thee again of this matter,* of the resurrection of the dead. It should seem, they overlooked what was plain and uncontroverted, and shifted off the application and the improvement of that, by starting objections against what was disputable, and would admit a debate. Thus many lose the benefit of the practical doctrine of Christianity, by wading beyond their depth into controversy, or, rather, by objecting against that which has some difficulty in it; whereas, if any man were disposed and determined to *do the will of God,* as far as it is discovered to him, he should *know of the doctrine of Christ,* that it is *of God, and not of man,* John vii. 17. Those that would not yield to the present convictions of the word thought to get clear of them, as Felix did, by putting them off to another opportunity; they will hear of it again some time or other, but they know not when; and thus the devil cozens them of all their time, by cozening them of the present time. 3. Paul thereupon left them for the present to consider of it (*v.* 33): *He departed from amongst them,* as seeing little likelihood of doing any good with them at this time; but, it is likely, with a promise to those that were willing to hear him again that he would meet them whenever they pleased.

II. Yet there were some that were wrought upon, *v.* 34. If some would not, others would. 1. There were certain men that adhered to him, and believed. When he departed from amongst them, they would not part with him so; wherever he went, they would follow him, with a resolution to adhere to the doctrine he preached, which they believed. 2. Two are particularly named; one was an eminent man, *Dionysius the Areopagite,* one of that high court or great council that sat in Areopagus, or Mars' Hill—a judge, a senator, one of those before whom Paul was summoned to appear; his judge becomes his convert. The account which the ancients give of this Dionysius is that he was bred at Athens, had studied astrology in Egypt, where he took notice of the miraculous eclipse at our Saviour's passion,—that, returning to Athens, he became a senator, disputed with Paul, and was by him converted from his error and idolatry; and, being by him thoroughly instructed, was made the first bishop of Athens. So *Eusebius,* lib. v. cap. 4, lib. iv. cap. 22. The *woman named Damaris* was, as some think, the wife of Dionysius; but, rather, some other person of quality; and, though there was not so great a harvest gathered in at Athens as there was at other places, yet, these few being wrought upon there, Paul had no reason to say he had *laboured in vain.*

CHAP. XVIII.

In this chapter we have, I. Paul's coming to Corinth, his private converse with Aquila and Priscilla, and his public reasonings with the Jews, from whom, when they rejected him, he turned to the Gentiles, ver. 1—6. II. The great success of his ministry there, and the encouragement Christ gave him in a vision to continue his labours there, in hopes of further success, ver. 7—11. III. The molestations which after some time he met with there from the Jews, which he got pretty well through by the coldness of Gallio, the Roman governor, in the cause, ver. 12—17. IV. The progress Paul made through many countries, after he had continued long at Corinth, for the edifying and watering of the churches which he had founded and planted, in which circuit he made a short visit to Jerusalem, ver. 18—23. V. An account of Apollo's improvement in knowledge, and of his usefulness in the church, ver. 24—28.

AFTER these things Paul departed from Athens, and came

to Corinth; 2 And found a certain
Jew named Aquila, born in Pontus,
lately come from Italy, with his wife
Priscilla; (because that Claudius had
commanded all Jews to depart from
Rome:) and came unto them. 3
And because he was of the same
craft, he abode with them, and
wrought: for by their occupation
they were tentmakers. 4 And he
reasoned in the synagogue every
sabbath, and persuaded the Jews and
the Greeks. 5 And when Silas and
Timotheus were come from Macedonia, Paul was pressed in the spirit,
and testified to the Jews *that* Jesus
was Christ. 6 And when they opposed themselves, and blasphemed,
he shook *his* raiment, and said unto
them, Your blood *be* upon your own
heads; I *am* clean: from henceforth
I will go unto the Gentiles.

We do not find that Paul was much persecuted at Athens, nor that he was driven thence by any ill usage, as he was from those places where the Jews had or could make any interest; but his reception at Athens being cold, and little prospect of doing good there, he departed from Athens, leaving the care of those there who believed with Dionysius; and thence he came to Corinth, where he was now instrumental in planting a church that became on many accounts considerable. Corinth was the chief city of Achaia, now a province of the empire, a rich and splendid city. *Non cuivis homini contingit adire Corinthum—It is not permitted every man to see Corinth.* The country thereabouts at this day is called *the Morea.* Now here we have,

I. Paul working for his living, *v.* 2, 3. 1. Though he was bred a scholar, yet he was master of a handicraft trade. He was a tentmaker, an upholsterer; he made tents for the use of soldiers and shepherds, of cloth or stuff, or (as some say tents were then generally made) of leather or skins, as the outer covering of the tabernacle. Hence to live in tents was to live *sub pellibus—under skins.* Dr. Lightfoot shows that it was the custom of the Jews to bring up their children to some trade, yea, though they gave them learning or estates. Rabbi Judah says, "He that teaches not his son a trade is as if he taught him to be a thief." And another says, "He that has a trade in his hand is as a vineyard that is fenced." An honest trade, by which a man may get his bread, is not to be looked upon by any with contempt. Paul, though a Pharisee, and bred up at the feet of Gamaliel, yet, having in his youth learned to make tents, did not by disuse lose the art. 2. Though he was entitled to a maintenance from the churches he had planted, and from the people to whom he preached, yet he worked at his calling to get bread, which is more to his praise who did not ask for supplies than to theirs who did not supply him unasked, knowing what straits he was reduced to. See how humble Paul was, and wonder that so great a man could stoop so low; but he had learned condescension of his Master, who came not to be ministered to, but to minister. See how industrious he was, and how willing to take pains. He that had so much excellent work to do with his mind, yet, when there was occasion, did not think it below him to work with his hands. Even those that are redeemed from the curse of the law are not exempt from that sentence, *In the sweat of thy face thou shalt eat bread.* See how careful Paul was to recommend his ministry, and to prevent prejudices against it, even the most unjust and unreasonable; he therefore maintained himself with his own labour that he might not make the gospel of Christ *burdensome,* 2 Cor. xi. 7, &c.; 2 Thess. iii. 8, 9. 3. Though we may suppose he was master of his trade, yet he did not disdain to work at journey-work: He *wrought with Aquila and Priscilla,* who *were of that calling,* so that he got no more than day-wages, a bare subsistence. Poor tradesmen must be thankful if their callings bring them in a maintenance for themselves and their families, though they cannot do as the rich merchants that raise estates by their callings. 4. Though he was himself a great apostle, yet he chose to work with Aquila and Priscilla, because he found them to be very intelligent in the things of God, as appears afterwards (*v.* 26), and he owns that they had been his *helpers in Christ Jesus,* Rom. xvi. 3. This is an example to those who are going to service to seek for those services in which they may have the best help for their souls. Choose to work with those that are likely to be helpers in Christ Jesus. It is good to be in company and to have conversation with those that will further us in the knowledge of Christ, and to put ourselves under the influence of such as are resolved that they will serve the Lord. Concerning this Aquila we are here told, (1.) That he was a Jew, but born in Pontus, *v.* 2. Many of the Jews of the dispersion were seated in that country, as appears 1 Pet. i. 1. (2.) That he was lately come from Italy to Corinth. It seems he often changed his habitation; this is not the world we can propose ourselves a settlement in. (3.) That the reason of his leaving Italy was because by a late edict of the emperor Claudius Cæsar all Jews were banished from Rome; for the Jews were generally hated, and every occasion was taken to put hardship and disgrace upon them. God's heritage was as a *speckled bird, the birds round about were against her,* Jer. xii. 9. Aquila, though a Christian, was banished because he had been a Jew; and the Gentiles had such confused notions of the thing that they could not distinguish between a Jew and a Christian. Suetonius, in the life of Claudius, speaks of this decree in the ninth year of his reign, and says, The reason was because the Jews were *a turbulent people—assiduo tumultuantes;* and that it was *impulsore Christo—upon the account of Christ;* some zealous for him, others bitter against him, which occasioned great heats, such as gave umbrage to the government, and provoked the emperor, who was a timorous jealous man, to order them all to be gone. If Jews persecute Christians, it is not strange if heathens persecute them both.

II. We have here Paul preaching to the Jews, and dealing with them to bring them to the faith of Christ, both the native *Jews and the Greeks,* that is, those that were more or less proselyted to the Jewish religion, and frequented their meetings.

1. He *reasoned with them in the synagogue* publicly *every sabbath.* See in what way the apostles propagated the gospel, not by force and violence, by fire and sword, not by demanding an implicit consent, but by fair arguing; they drew with the cords of a man, gave a reason for what they said, and gave a liberty to object against it, having satisfactory answers ready. God invites us to come and reason with him (Isa. i. 18), and challenges sinners to *produce their cause,* and *bring forth their strong reasons,* Isa. xli. 21. Paul was a rational as well as a scriptural preacher.

2. *He persuaded them—ἔπειθέ.* It denotes, (1.) The urgency of his preaching. He did not only dispute argumentatively with them, but he followed his arguments with affectionate persuasions, begging of them for God's sake, for their own soul's sake, for their children's sake, not to refuse the offer of salvation made to them. Or, (2.) The good effect of his preaching. He persuaded them, that is, he prevailed with them; so some understand it. *In sententiam suam adducebat—He brought them over to his own opinion.* Some of them were convinced by his reasonings, and yielded to Christ.

3. He was yet more earnest in this matter when his fellow-labourers, his seconds, came up with him (*v.* 5): *When Silas and Timothy had come from Macedonia,* and had brought him good tidings from the churches there, and were ready to assist him here, and strengthened his hands, then Paul was more than before *pressed in spirit,* which made him more than ever pressing in his preaching. He was grieved for the obstinacy and infidelity of his countrymen the Jews, was more intent than ever upon their conversion, and the *love of Christ constrained him* to it (2 Cor. v. 14); it is the word that is used here, it *pressed him in spirit* to it. And, being thus pressed, he *testified to the Jews* with all possible solemnity and seriousness, as that which he was perfectly well assured of himself, and attested to them as a *faithful saying, and worthy of all acceptation, that Jesus is the Christ,* the Messiah promised to the fathers and expected by them.

III. We have him here abandoning the unbelieving Jews, and turning from them to the Gentiles, as he had done in other places, *v.* 6.

1. Many of the Jews, and indeed the most of them, persisted in their contradiction to the gospel of Christ, and would not yield to the strongest reasonings nor the most winning persuasions; they *opposed themselves* and *blasphemed;* they *set themselves in battle array* (so the word signifies) against the gospel; they joined hand in hand to stop the progress of it. They resolved they would not believe it themselves, and would do all they could to keep others from believing it. They could not argue against it, but what was wanting in reason they made up in ill language: they *blasphemed,* spoke reproachfully of Christ, and in him of God himself, as Rev. xiii. 5, 6. To justify their infidelity, they broke out into downright blasphemy.

2. Paul hereupon declared himself discharged from them, and left them to perish in their unbelief. He that was *pressed in spirit* to *testify to them* (*v.* 5), when they opposed that testimony, and persisted in their opposition, was pressed in spirit to testify against them (*v.* 6), and his zeal herein also he showed by a sign: he *shook his raiment,* shaking off the dust from it (as before they *shook off the dust from their feet, ch.* xiii. 51), for a testimony against them. Thus he cleared himself from them, but threatened the judgments of God against them. As Pilate by washing his hands signified the devolving of the guilt of Christ's blood from himself upon the Jews, so Paul by shaking his raiment signified what he said, if possible to affect them with it. (1.) He had done his part, and was clean from the blood of their souls; he had, like a faithful watchman, given them warning, and thereby had *delivered his soul,* though he could not prevail to deliver theirs. He had tried all methods to work upon them, but all in vain, so that if they perish in their unbelief their blood is not to be required at his hands; here, and *ch.* xx. 26, he plainly refers to Ezek. xxxiii. 8, 9. It is very comfortable to a minister to have the testimony of his conscience for him, that he has faithfully discharged his trust by warning sinners. (2.) They would certainly perish if they persisted in their unbelief, and the blame would lie wholly upon themselves: "Your *blood be upon your own heads,* you will be your own destroyers, your nation will be ruined in this world, and particular persons will be ruined in the other world, and *you alone shall bear it.*" If any thing would frighten them at last into a compliance with the gospel, surely this would.

3. Having given them over, yet he does not give over his work. Though Israel be not gathered, Christ and his gospel shall be glorious: *Henceforth I will go unto the Gentiles;* and the Jews cannot complain, for they had the first offer, and a fair one, made to them. The guests that were first invited will not come, and the provision must not be lost; guests must be had therefore *from the highways and the hedges.* "We *would have gathered* the Jews (Matt. xxiii. 37), would have *healed them* (Jer. li. 9), and they would not; but Christ must not be a head without a body, nor a foundation without a building, and therefore, if they will not, we must try whether others will." Thus the fall and diminishing of the Jews became the riches of the Gentiles; and Paul said this to their faces, not only because it was what he could justify, but to *provoke them to jealousy,* Rom. xi. 12, 14.

7 And he departed thence, and
entered into a certain *man's* house,
named Justus, *one* that worshipped
God, whose house joined hard to the
synagogue. 8 And Crispus, the
chief ruler of the synagogue, believed
on the Lord with all his house; and
many of the Corinthians hearing, believed, and were baptized. 9 Then
spake the Lord to Paul in the night
by a vision, Be not afraid, but speak,
and hold not thy peace: 10 For I
am with thee, and no man shall set
on thee to hurt thee: for I have
much people in this city. 11 And
he continued *there* a year and six
months, teaching the word of God
among them.

Here we are told,

I. That Paul changed his quarters. Christ directed his disciples, when he sent them forth, not to *go from house to house* (Luke x. 7), but there might be occasion to do it, as Paul did here. He departed out of the synagogue, being driven out by the perverseness of the unbelieving Jews, and he *entered into a certain man's house, named Justus, v.* 7. It should seem, he went to this man's house, not to lodge, for he continued with Aquila and Priscilla, but to preach. When the Jews would not let him go on peaceably with his work in their meeting, this honest man opened his doors to him, and told him he should be welcome to preach there; and Paul accepted the proposal. It was not the first time that God's ark had taken up its lodging in a private house. When Paul could not have liberty to preach in the synagogue, he preached in a house, without any disparagement to his doctrine. But observe the account of this man and his house. 1. The man was next door to a Jew; he was one that *worshipped God;* he was not an idolater, though he was a Gentile, but was a worshipper of the God of Israel, and him only, as Cornelius. That Paul might give the less offence to the Jews, though he had abandoned them, he set up his meeting in this man's house. Even when he was under a necessity of breaking off from them to turn to the Gentiles, yet he would study to oblige them. 2. The house was next door to the synagogue, it *joined close to it,* which some perhaps might interpret as done with design to draw people from the synagogue to the meeting; but I rather think it was done in charity, to show that he would come as near to them as he could, and was ready to return to them if they were but willing to receive his message, and would not contradict and blaspheme as they had done.

II. That Paul presently saw the good fruit of his labours, both among Jews and Gentiles. 1. *Crispus* a Jew, an eminent one, the *chief ruler of the synagogue, believed on the Lord Jesus, with all his house, v.* 8. It was for the honour of the gospel that there were some rulers, and persons of the first rank both in church and state, that embraced it. This would leave the Jews inexcusable, that the ruler of their synagogue, who may be supposed to have excelled the rest in knowledge of the scriptures and zeal for their religion, believed the gospel, and yet they opposed and blasphemed it. Not only he, but his house, believed, and, probably, were baptized with him by Paul, 1 Cor. i. 14 2. Many of the Corinthians, who were Gentiles (and some of them persons of bad character, as appears, 1 Cor. vi. 11, *such were some of you), hearing, believed, and were baptized.* First, they heard, for *faith comes by hearing.* Some perhaps came to hear Paul under some convictions of conscience that the way they were in was not right; but it is probable that the most came only for curiosity, because it was a new doctrine that was preached; but, hearing, *they believed,* by the power of God working upon them; and, *believing,* they were *baptized,* and so fixed for Christ, took upon them the profession of Christianity, and became entitled to the privileges of Christians.

III. That Paul was encouraged by a vision to go on with his work at Corinth (*v.* 9): *The Lord Jesus spoke to Paul in the night by a vision;* when he was musing on his work, *communing with his own heart upon his bed,* and considering whether he should continue here or no, what method he should take here, and what probability there was of doing good, then Christ appeared very seasonably to him, and *in the multitude of his thoughts within him* delighted his soul with divine consolations. 1. He renewed his commission and charge to preach the gospel: "*Be not afraid of the Jews;* though they are very outrageous, and perhaps the more enraged by the conversion of the chief ruler of their synagogue. Be not afraid of the magistrates of the city, for they have no power against thee but what is given them from above. It is the cause of heaven thou art pleading, do it boldly. *Be not afraid of their words, nor dismayed at their looks;* but *speak, and hold not thy peace;* let slip no opportunity of speaking to them; *cry aloud, spare not.* Do not hold thy peace from speaking for fear of them, nor hold thy peace in speaking" (if I may so say); "do not speak shyly and with caution, but plainly and fully and with courage. Speak out; use all the liberty of spirit that becomes an ambassador for Christ." 2. He assured him of his presence with him, which was sufficient to animate him, and put life and spirit into him: "*Be not afraid, for I am with thee,* to protect thee, and bear thee out, and to deliver thee from all thy fears; *speak, and hold not thy peace, for I am with thee,* to own what thou sayest, to work with thee, and to confirm the word by signs following." The same promise that ratified the general commission (Matt. xxviii. 19, 20), *Lo, I am with you always,* is here repeated. Those that have Christ with them need not to fear, and ought not to shrink. 3. He gave him a warrant of protection to save him harmless: "*No man shall set on thee to hurt thee;* thou shalt be delivered out of the hands of wicked and unreasonable men and shalt not be driven hence, as thou wast from other places, by persecution." He does not promise that no man should set on him (for the next news we hear is that he is set upon, and *brought to the judgment-seat, v.* 12), but, "*No man shall set on thee to hurt thee;* the remainder of their wrath shall be restrained; thou shalt not be beaten and imprisoned here, as thou wast at Philippi." Paul met with coarser treatment at first than he did afterwards, and was now *comforted according to the time wherein he had been afflicted.* Trials shall not last always, Ps. lxvi. 10—12. Or we may take it more generally: "*No man shall set on thee,* τοῦ κακῶσαί σε—to *do evil* to thee; whatever trouble they may give thee, there is no real evil in it. They may kill thee, but they cannot hurt thee; for *I am with thee,*" Ps. xxiii. 4; Isa. xli. 10. 4. He gave him a prospect of success: "*For I have much people in this city.* Therefore no man shall prevail to obstruct thy work, therefore I will be with thee to own thy work, and therefore do thou go on vigorously and cheerfully in it; for there are many in this city that are to be effectually called by thy ministry, in whom thou shalt *see of the travail of thy soul.*" Λαός ἐςὶ μοι πολὺς—*There is to me a great people here.* The Lord knows those that are his, yea, and those that shall be his; for it is by his work upon them that they become his, and *known unto him are all his works.* "I have them, though they yet know me not, though yet they are led captive by Satan at his will; for the Father has given them to me, to be a seed to serve me; I have them written in the book of life; I have their names down, and of all that were given me I will lose none; I have them, for I am sure to have them;" *whom he did predestinate, those he called. In this city,* though it be a very profane wicked city, full of impurity, and the more so for a temple of Venus there, to which there was a great resort, yet in this heap, that seems to be all chaff, there is wheat; in this ore, that seems to be all dross, there is gold. Let us not despair concerning any place, when even in Corinth Christ had *much people.*

IV. That upon this encouragement he made a long stay there (*v.* 11): He *continued at Corinth a year and six months,* not to take his ease, but to follow his work, *teaching the word of God among them;* and, it being a city flocked to from all parts, he had opportunity there of preaching the gospel to strangers, and sending notice of it thence to other countries. He staid so long, 1. For the bringing in of those that were without. Christ had many people there, and by the power of his grace he could have had them all converted in one month or week, as at the first preaching of the gospel, when thousands were enclosed at one cast of the net; but God works variously. The people Christ has at Corinth must be called in by degrees, some by one sermon, others by another; *we see not yet all things put under Christ.* Let Christ's ministers go on in their duty, though their work be not done all at once; nay, though it be done but a little at a time. 2. For the building up of those that were within. Those that are converted have still need to be *taught the word of God,* and particular need at Corinth to be taught it by Paul himself; for no sooner was the good seed sown in that field than the enemy came and sowed tares, the false apostles, those deceitful workers, of whom Paul in his epistles to the Corinthians complains so much. When the hands of Jewish persecutors were tied, who were professed enemies to the gospel, Paul had a more vexatious trouble created him, and the church more mischievous damage done it, by the tongue of judaizing preachers, who, under colour of the Christian name, undermined the very foundations of Christianity. Soon after Paul came to Corinth, it is supposed, he wrote the first epistle to the Thessalonians, which in order of time was the first of all the epistles he wrote by divine inspiration; and the second epistle to the same church was written not long after. Ministers may be serving Christ, and promoting the great ends of their ministry, by writing good letters, as well as by preaching good sermons.

12 And when Gallio was the deputy of Achaia, the Jews made insurrection with one accord against Paul, and brought him to the judgment seat, 13 Saying, This *fellow*

persuadeth men to worship God contrary to the law. 14 And when Paul
was now about to open *his* mouth,
Gallio said unto the Jews, If it were
a matter of wrong or wicked lewdness, O *ye* Jews, reason would that I
should bear with you: 15 But if it
be a question of words and names,
and *of* your law, look ye *to it;* for I
will be no judge of such *matters.* 16
And he drave them from the judgment seat. 17 Then all the Greeks
took Sosthenes, the chief ruler of the
synagogue, and beat *him* before the
judgment seat. And Gallio cared
for none of those things.

We have here an account of some disturbance given to Paul and his friends at Corinth, but no great harm done, nor much hindrance given to the work of Christ there.

I. Paul is accused by the Jews before the Roman governor, *v.* 12, 13. The governor was *Gallio, deputy of Achaia,* that is, proconsul; for Achaia was a consular province of the empire. This Gallio was elder brother to the famous Seneca; in his youth he was called Novatus, but took the name of Gallio upon his being adopted into the family of Julius Gallio; he is described by Seneca, his brother, to be a man of great ingenuousness and great probity, and a man of wonderful good temper; he was called *Dulcis Gallio—Sweet Gallio,* for his sweet disposition; and is said to have been universally beloved. Now observe, 1. How rudely Paul is apprehended, and brought before Gallio; *The Jews made insurrection with one accord against Paul.* They were the ringleaders of all the mischief against Paul, and they entered into a confederacy to do him a mischief. They were unanimous in it: they came upon him *with one accord;* hand joined in hand to do this wickedness. They did it with violence and fury: *They made an insurrection* to the disturbance of the public peace, and hurried Paul away *to the judgment-seat,* and, for aught that appears, allowed him no time to prepare for his trial. 2. How falsely Paul is accused before Gallio (*v.* 13): *This fellow persuades men to worship God contrary to the law.* They could not charge him with persuading men not to worship God at all, or to worship other gods (Deut. xiii. 2): but only to worship God in a way contrary to the law. The Romans allowed the Jews in their provinces the observance of their own law; and what then? Must those therefore be prosecuted as criminals who worship God in any other way? Does their toleration include a power of imposition? But the charge was unjust; for their own law had in it a promise of a prophet whom God would raise up to them, and him they should hear. Now Paul persuaded them to believe in this prophet, who was come, and to hear him, which was according to the law; for he came not *to destroy the law, but to fulfil it.* The law relating to the temple-service those Jews at Corinth could not observe, because of their distance from Jerusalem, and there was no part of their synagogue-worship which Paul contradicted. Thus when people are taught to worship God in Christ, and to worship him in the Spirit, they are ready to quarrel, as if they were taught to worship him contrary to the law; whereas this is indeed perfective of the law.

II. Gallio, upon the first hearing, or rather without any hearing at all, dismisses the cause, and will not take any cognizance of it, *v.* 14, 15. Paul was going about to make his defence, and to show that he did not teach men to worship God contrary to the law; but the judge, being resolved not to pass any sentence upon this cause, would not give himself the trouble of examining it. Observe,

1. He shows himself very ready to do the part of a judge in any matter that it was proper for him to take cognizance of. He *said to the Jews,* that were the prosecutors, "*If it were a matter of wrong, or wicked lewdness,*—if you could charge the prisoner with theft or fraud, with murder or rapine, or any act of immorality,—I should think myself bound *to bear with you* in your complaints, though they were clamorous and noisy;" for the rudeness of the petitioners was no good reason, if their cause was just, why they should not have justice done them. It is the duty of magistrates to right the injured, and to animadvert upon the injurious; and, if the complaint be not made with all the decorum that might be, yet they should hear it out. But,

2. He will by no means allow them to make a complaint to him of a thing that was not within his jurisdiction (*v.* 15): "*If it be a question of words and names, and of your law, look you to it;* end it among yourselves as you can, but *I will be no judge of such matters;* you shall neither burden my patience with the hearing of it, nor burden my conscience with giving judgment upon it;" and therefore, when they were urgent and pressing to be heard, *he drove them from the judgment-seat* (*v.* 16), and ordered another cause to be called. Now, (1.) Here was something right in Gallio's conduct, and praiseworthy—that he would not pretend to judge of things he did not understand; that he left the Jews to themselves in matters relating to their own religion, but yet would not let them, under pretence of that, run down Paul, and abuse him; or, at least, would not himself be the tool of their malice, to give judgment against him. He looked upon the matter to be not within his jurisdiction, and therefore would not meddle in it. But, (2.) It was certainly wrong to speak so slightly of a law and religion which he might have

known to be of God, and with which he ought to have acquainted himself. In what way God is to be worshipped, whether Jesus be the Messiah, whether the gospel be a divine revelation, were not *questions of words and names,* as he scornfully and profanely called them. They are questions of vast importance, and in which, if he had understood them himself aright, he would have seen himself nearly concerned. He speaks as if he boasted of his ignorance of the scriptures, and took a pride in it; as if it were below him to take notice of the law of God, or make any enquiries concerning it.

III. The abuse done to Sosthenes, and Gallio's unconcernedness in it, *v.* 17. 1. The parties put a great contempt upon the court, when *they took Sosthenes and beat him before the judgment-seat.* Many conjectures there are concerning this matter, because it is uncertain who this Sosthenes was, and who the Greeks were that abused him. It seems most probable that Sosthenes was a Christian, and Paul's particular friend, that appeared for him on this occasion, and probably had taken care of his safety, and conveyed him away, when Gallio dismissed the cause; so that, when they could not light on Paul, they fell foul on him who protected him. It is certain that there was one Sosthenes that was a friend of Paul, and well known at Corinth; it is likely he was a minister, for Paul calls him his brother, and joins him with himself in his first epistle to the church at Corinth (1 Cor. i. 1), as he does Timothy in his second, and it is probable that this was he; he is said to be a *ruler of the synagogue,* either joint-ruler with Crispus (*v.* 8), or a ruler of one synagogue, as Crispus was of another. As for the Greeks that abused him, it is very probable that they were either Hellenist Jews, or Jewish Greeks, those that joined with the Jews in opposing the gospel (*v.* 4, 6), and that the native Jews put them on to do it, thinking it would in them be less offensive. They were so enraged against Paul that they beat Sosthenes; and so enraged against Gallio, because he would not countenance the prosecution, that they beat him before the judgment-seat, whereby they did, in effect, tell him that they cared not for him; if he would not be their executioner, they would be their own judges. 2. The court put no less a contempt upon the cause, and the persons too. But *Gallio cared for none of these things.* If by this be meant that he cared not for the affronts of bad men, it was commendable. While he steadily adhered to the laws and rules of equity, he might despise their contempts; but, if it be meant (as I think it is) that he concerned not himself for the abuses done to good men, it carries his indifference too far, and gives us but an ill character of him. Here is *wickedness* done *in the place of judgment* (which Solomon complains of, Eccl. iii. 16), and nothing done to discountenance and suppress it. Gallio, as a judge, ought to have protected Sosthenes, and restrained and punished the Greeks that assaulted him. For a man to be mobbed in the street or in the market, perhaps, may not be easily helped; but to be so in his court, the judgment-seat, the court sitting and not concerned at it, is an evidence that *truth is fallen in the street, and equity cannot enter;* for *he that departeth from evil maketh himself a prey,* Isa. lix. 14, 15. Those that see and hear of the sufferings of God's people, and have no sympathy with them, nor concern for them, do not pity and pray for them, it being all one to them whether the interests of religion sink or swim, are of the spirit of Gallio here, who, when a good man was abused before his face, *cared for none of these things;* like those that were *at ease in Zion,* and *were not grieved for the affliction of Joseph* (Amos vi. 6), like *the king and Haman, that sat down to drink when the city Shushan was perplexed,* Esth. iii. 15.

18 And Paul *after this* tarried *there* yet a good while, and then took his leave of the brethren, and sailed thence into Syria, and with him Priscilla and Aquila; having shorn *his* head in Cenchrea: for he had a vow. 19 And he came to Ephesus, and left them there: but he himself entered into the synagogue, and reasoned with the Jews. 20 When they desired *him* to tarry longer time with them, he consented not; 21 But bade them farewell, saying, I must by all means keep this feast that cometh in Jerusalem: but I will return again unto you, if God will. And he sailed from Ephesus. 22 And when he had landed at Cæsarea, and gone up, and saluted the church, he went down to Antioch. 23 And after he had spent some time *there,* he departed, and went over *all* the country of Galatia and Phrygia in order, strengthening all the disciples.

We have here Paul in motion, as we have had him at Corinth for some time at rest, but in both busy, very busy, in the service of Christ; if he sat still, if he went about, still it was to do good. Here is,

I. Paul's departure from Corinth, *v.* 18. 1. He did not go away till some time after the trouble he met with there; from other places he had departed when the storm arose, but not from Corinth, because there it had no sooner risen than it fell again. Some tell us that Gallio did privately countenance Paul, and took him into his favour, and that this occasioned a correspondence between Paul and Seneca, Gallio's brother, which some of the ancients speak of. *After this he tarried there yet a good while,* some think, beyond *the year and a half* mentioned *v.* 11. While he found he laboured not in vain, he continued labouring. 2. When he went, he took leave of the brethren solemnly, and with much affection, with suitable comforts and counsels, and prayers at parting, commending what was good, reproving what was otherwise, and giving them necessary cautions against the wiles of the false apostles; and his farewell sermon would leave impressions upon them. 3. He took *with him Priscilla and Aquila,* because they had a mind to accompany him; for they seemed disposed to remove, and not inclined to stay long at a place, a disposition which may arise from a good principle, and have good effects, and therefore ought not to be condemned in others, though it ought to be suspected in ourselves. There was a great friendship contracted between them and Paul, and therefore, when he went, they begged to go along with him. 4. At Cenchrea, which was hard by Corinth, the port where those that went to sea from Corinth took ship, either Paul or Aquila (for the original does not determine which) had his head shaved, to discharge himself from the vow of a Nazarite: *Having shorn his head at Cenchrea; for he had a vow.* Those that lived in Judea were, in such a case, bound to do it at the temple: but those who lived in other countries might do it in other places. The Nazarite's head was to be shaved when either his consecration was accidentally polluted, in which case he must begin again, or *when the days of his separation were fulfilled* (Num. vi. 9; xiii. 18), which, we suppose, was the case here. Some throw it upon Aquila, who was a Jew (*v.* 2), and retained perhaps more of his Judaism than was convenient; but I see no harm in admitting it concerning Paul, for concerning him we must admit the same thing (*ch.* xxi. 24, 26), not only in compliance for a time with the Jews, to whom he *became as a Jew* (1 Cor. ix. 20), *that he might win upon them,* but because the vow of the Nazarites, though ceremonial, and as such ready to vanish away, had yet a great deal of moral and very pious significance, and therefore was fit to die the last of all the Jewish ceremonies. The Nazarites are joined with the prophets (Amos ii. 11), and were very much *the glory of Israel* (Lam. iv. 7), and therefore it is not strange if Paul bound himself for some time with the vow of a Nazarite from wine and strong drink, and from being trimmed, to recommend himself to the Jews; and from this he now discharged himself.

II. Paul's calling *at Ephesus,* which was the metropolis of the Lesser Asia, and a sea-port. 1. *There he left Aquila and Priscilla;* not only because they would be but burdensome to him in his journey, but because they might be serviceable to the interests of the gospel at Ephesus. Paul intended shortly to settle there for some time, and he left Aquila and Priscilla there in the mean time, for the same end as Christ sent his disciples before to every place where he himself would come, to prepare his way. Aquila and Priscilla might, by private conversation, being very intelligent judicious Christians, dispose the minds of many to give Paul, when he should come among them, a favourable reception, and to understand his preaching; therefore he calls them his *helpers in Christ Jesus,* Rom. xvi. 3. 2. There he preached *to the Jews in their synagogue;* though he did but call there in his journey, yet he would not go without giving them a sermon. *He entered into the synagogue,* not as a hearer, but as a preacher, for *there he reasoned with the Jews.* Though he had abandoned the Jews at Corinth, who opposed themselves, and blasphemed, yet he did not, for their sakes, decline the synagogues of the Jews in other places, but still made the first offer of the gospel to them. We must not condemn a whole body or denomination of men, for the sake of some that conduct themselves ill. 3. The Jews at Ephesus were so far from driving Paul away that they courted his stay with them (*v.* 20): *They desired him to tarry longer with them,* to instruct them in the gospel of Christ. These were more noble, and better bred, than those Jews at Corinth, and other places; and it was a sign that God had not quite cast away his people, but had a remnant among them. 4. Paul would not stay with them now: *He consented not; but bade them farewell.* He had further to go; he *must by all means keep this feast at Jerusalem;* not that he thought himself bound in duty to it (he knew the laws of the feasts were no longer binding), but he had business at Jerusalem (whatever it was) which would be best done at the time of the feast, when there was a general rendezvous of all the Jews from all parts; which of the feasts it was we are not told, probably it was the passover, which was the most eminent. 5. He intimated his purpose, after this journey, to come and spend some time at Ephesus, being encouraged by their kind invitation to hope that he should do good among them. It is good to have opportunities in reserve, when one good work is over to have another to apply ourselves to: *I will return again to you,* but he inserts that necessary proviso, *if God will.* Our times are in God's hand; we purpose, but he disposes; and therefore we must make all our promises with submission to the will of God. *If the Lord will, we shall live, and do this or that. I will return again to you, if the Spirit suffer me* (*ch.* xvi. 7); this was included in Paul's case; not only if providence permit, but if God do not otherwise direct my motions.

III. Paul's visit to Jerusalem; a short

visit it was, but it served as a token of respect to that truly mother-church. 1. He came by sea to the port that lay next to Jerusalem. *He sailed from Ephesus* (*v.* 21), *and landed at Cæsarea, v.* 22. He chose to go by sea, for expedition and for safety, and that he might *see the works of the Lord, and his wonders in the deep.* Joppa had been the port for Jerusalem, but Herod having improved Cæsarea, and the port at Joppa being dangerous, that was generally made use of. 2. He went *up, and saluted the church,* by which, I think, is plainly meant the church at Jerusalem, which is emphatically called *the church,* because there the Christian church began, *ch.* xv. 4. Paul thought it requisite to show himself among them, that they might not think his success among the Gentiles had made him think himself either above them or estranged from them, or that the honour God had put upon him made him unmindful of the honour he owed to them. His going to salute the church at Jerusalem intimates, (1.) That it was a very friendly visit that he made them, in pure kindness, to enquire into their state, and to testify his hearty good-will to them. Note, The increase of our new friends should not make us forget our old ones, but it should be a pleasure to good men, and good ministers, to revive former acquaintance. The ministers at Jerusalem were constant residents, Paul was a constant itinerant; but he took care to keep up a good correspondence with them, that they might rejoice with him in his going out, and he might rejoice with them in their tents, and they might both congratulate and wish well to one another's comfort and success. (2.) That it was but a short visit. He went *up, and saluted them,* perhaps *with the holy kiss,* and made no stay among them. It was designed but for a transient interview, and yet Paul undertook this long journey for that. This is not the world we are to be together in. God's people are *the salt of the earth,* dispersed and scattered; yet it is good to see one another sometimes, if it be but to see one another, that we may confirm mutual love, may the better keep up our spiritual communion with one another at a distance, and may long the more for that heavenly Jerusalem in which we hope to be together for ever.

IV. His return through those countries where he had formerly preached the gospel. 1. *He went and spent some time in Antioch,* among his old friends there, whence he was first sent out to preach among the Gentiles, *ch.* xiii. 1. He went down to Antioch, to refresh himself with the sight and conversation of the ministers there; and a very good refreshment it is to a faithful minister to have for awhile the society of his brethren; for, *as iron sharpeneth iron, so doth a man the countenance of his friend.* Paul's coming to Antioch would bring to remembrance the former days, which would furnish him with matter for fresh thanksgiving. 2. *Thence he went over the country of Galatia and Phrygia in order,* where he had preached the gospel, and planted churches, which, though very briefly mentioned (*ch.* xvi. 6), was yet a glorious work, as appears by Gal. iv. 14, 15, where Paul speaks of his preaching the gospel to the Galatians at the first, and their receiving him *as an angel of God.* These country churches (for such they were (Gal. i. 2), and we read not of any city in Galatia where a church was) Paul visited *in order* as they lay, watering what he had been instrumental to plant, and *strengthening all the disciples.* His very coming among them, and owning them, were a great strengthening to them and their ministers. Paul's countenancing them was encouraging them; but that was not all: he preached that to them which strengthened them, which confirmed their faith in Christ, their resolutions for Christ, and their pious affections to him. Disciples need to be strengthened, for they are compassed about with infirmity; ministers must do what they can to strengthen them, to strengthen them all, by directing them to Christ, and bringing them to live upon him, whose strength is perfected in their weakness, and who is himself their strength and song.

24 And a certain Jew named
Apollos, born at Alexandria, an eloquent man, *and* mighty in the scriptures, came to Ephesus. 25 This
man was instructed in the way of
the Lord; and being fervent in the
spirit, he spake and taught diligently
the things of the Lord, knowing only
the baptism of John. 26 And he
began to speak boldly in the synagogue: whom when Aquila and Priscilla had heard, they took him unto
them, and expounded unto him the
way of God more perfectly. 27 And
when he was disposed to pass into
Achaia, the brethren wrote, exhorting
the disciples to receive him: who,
when he was come, helped them
much which had believed through
grace: 28 For he mightily convinced the Jews, *and that* publicly,
showing by the scriptures that Jesus
was Christ.

The sacred history leaves Paul upon his travels, and goes here to meet Apollos at Ephesus, and to give us some account of him, which was necessary to our understanding some passages in Paul's epistles.

I. Here is an account of his character, when he came to Ephesus.

1. He was *a Jew, born at Alexandria* in

Egypt, but of Jewish parents; for there were abundance of Jews in that city, since the dispersion of the people, as it was foretold (Deut. xxviii. 68): *The Lord shall bring thee into Egypt again.* His name was not *Apollo,* the name of one of the heathen gods, but *Apollos,* some think the same with *Apelles,* Rom. xvi. 10.

2. He was a man of excellent good parts, and well fitted for public service. He was *an eloquent man, and mighty in the scriptures* of the Old Testament, in the knowledge of which he was, as a Jew, brought up. (1.) He had a great command of language: he was *an eloquent man;* he was ἀνὴρ λόγιος—*a prudent man,* so some; *a learned man,* so others; *historiarum peritus—a good historian,* which is an excellent qualification for the ministry: he was one that could speak well, so it properly signifies; he was *an oracle of a man;* he was famous for speaking pertinently and closely, fully and fluently, upon any subject. (2.) He had a great command of scripture-language, and this was the eloquence he was remarkable for. He *came to Ephesus,* being *mighty in the scriptures,* so the words are placed; having an excellent faculty of expounding scripture, he came to Ephesus, which was a public place, to trade with that talent, for the honour of God and the good of many. He was not only ready in the scriptures, able to quote texts off-hand, and repeat them, and tell you where to find them (many of the carnal Jews were so, who were therefore said to have the *form of knowledge,* and *the letter of the law);* but he was *mighty in the scriptures.* He understood the sense and meaning of them, he knew how to make use of them and to apply them, how to reason out of the scriptures, and to reason strongly; a convincing, commanding, confirming power went along with all his expositions and applications of the scripture. It is probable he had given proof of his knowledge of the scriptures, and his abilities in them, in many synagogues of the Jews.

3. He *was instructed in the way of the Lord:* that is, he had some acquaintance with the doctrine of Christ, had obtained some general notions of the gospel and the principles of Christianity, *that Jesus is the Christ,* and *that prophet that should come into the world;* the first notice of this would be readily embraced by one that was so mighty in the scripture as Apollos was, and therefore understood *the signs of the times.* He *was instructed,* κατηχημένος—*he was catechised* (so the word is), either by his parents or by ministers; he was taught something of Christ and the way of salvation by him. Those that are to teach others must first be themselves taught the word of the Lord, not only to talk of it, but to walk in it. It is not enough to have our tongues tuned to the word of the Lord, but we must have our feet directed into the way of the Lord.

4. Yet he *knew only the baptism of John;* he was instructed in the gospel of Christ as far as John's ministry would carry him, and no further; he knew *the preparing of the way of the Lord* by *that voice crying in the wilderness,* rather than the way of the Lord itself. We cannot but think he had heard of Christ's death and resurrection, but he was not let into the mystery of them, had not had opportunity of conversing with any of the apostles since the pouring out of the Spirit; or he had himself been baptized *only with the baptism of John,* but was not baptized with the Holy Ghost, as the disciples were at the day of pentecost.

II. We have here the employment and improvement of his gifts at Ephesus; he came thither, seeking opportunities of doing and getting good, and he found both.

1. He there made a very good use of his gifts in public. He came, probably, recommended to the synagogue of the Jews as a fit man to be a teacher there, and according to the light he had, and *the measure of the gift given to him,* he was willing to be employed (*v.* 25): *Being fervent in the Spirit, he spoke and taught diligently the things of the Lord.* Though he had not the miraculous gifts of the Spirit, as the apostles had, he made use of the gifts he had; *for the dispensation of the Spirit,* whatever the measure of it is, *is given to every man to profit withal.* And our Saviour, by a parable, designed to teach his ministers that though they had but one talent they must not bury that. We have seen how Apollos was qualified with a good head and a good tongue: he was *an eloquent man, and mighty in the scriptures;* he had laid in a good stock of useful knowledge, and had an excellent faculty of communicating it. Let us now see what he had further to recommend him as a preacher; and his example is recommended to the imitation of all preachers. (1.) He was a lively affectionate preacher; as he had a good head, so he had a good heart; he was *fervent in Spirit.* He had in him a great deal of divine fire as well as divine light, was burning as well as shining. He was full of zeal for the glory of God, and the salvation of precious souls. This appeared both in his forwardness to preach when he was called to it by *the rulers of the synagogue,* and in his fervency in his preaching. He preached as one in earnest, and that had his heart in his work. What a happy composition was here! Many are fervent in spirit, but are weak in knowledge, in scripture-knowledge—have far to seek for proper words, and are full of improper ones; and, on the other hand, many are eloquent enough, and mighty in the scriptures, and learned, and judicious, but they have no life or fervency. Here was a complete *man of God, thoroughly furnished for his work;* both eloquent and fervent, full both of divine knowledge and of divine affections. (2.) He was an industrious laborious preacher. *He spoke and taught diligently.* He took pains

in his preaching, what he delivered was elaborate; and he did not offer that to God, or to the synagogue, that either cost nothing or cost *him* nothing. He first worked it upon his own heart, and then laboured to impress it on those he preached to: *he taught diligently, ἀκριβῶς—accurately, exactly;* every thing he said was well-weighed. (3.) He was an evangelical preacher. Though he knew only the baptism of John, yet that was the beginning of the gospel of Christ, and to that he kept close; for he taught the things of the Lord, of the Lord Christ, the things that tended to make way for him, and to set him up. The things pertaining to the kingdom of the Messiah were the subjects he chose to insist upon; not the things of the ceremonial law, though those would be pleasing to his Jewish auditors; not the things of the Gentile philosophy, though he could have discoursed very well on those things; but the things of the Lord. (4.) He was a courageous preacher: *He began to speak boldly in the synagogue,* as one who, having put confidence in God, did not fear the face of man; he spoke as one that knew the truth of what he said, and had no doubt of it, and that knew the worth of what he said and was not afraid to suffer for it; *in the synagogue,* where the Jews not only were present, but had power, there he preached the things of God, which he knew they were prejudiced against.

2. He there made a good increase of his gifts in private, not so much in study, as in conversation with *Aquila and Priscilla.* If Paul or some other apostle or evangelist had been at Ephesus, he would have instructed him; but, for want of better help, *Aquila and Priscilla* (who were tent-makers) *expounded to him the way of God more perfectly.* Observe, (1.) Aquila and Priscilla heard him preach in the synagogue. Though in knowledge he was much inferior to them, yet, having excellent gifts for public service, they encouraged his ministry, by a diligent and constant attendance upon it. Thus young ministers, that are hopeful, should be countenanced by grown Christians, for it becomes them to fulfil all righteousness. (2.) Finding him defective in his knowledge of Christianity, *they took him to them,* to lodge in the same house with them, and *expounded to him the way of God,* the way of salvation by Jesus Christ, *more perfectly.* They did not take occasion from what they observed of his deficiency either to despise him themselves, or to disparage him to others; did not call him a young raw preacher, not fit to come into a pulpit, but considered the disadvantages he had laboured under, as knowing only the baptism of John; and, having themselves got great knowledge in the truths of the gospel by their long and intimate conversation with Paul, they communicated what they knew to him, and gave him a clear, distinct, and methodical account of those things which before he had but confused notions of. [1.] See here an instance of that which Christ has promised, that *to him that hath shall be given;* he that has, and uses what he has, shall have more. He that diligently traded with the talent he had doubled it quickly. [2.] See an instance of truly Christian charity in Aquila and Priscilla; they did good according to their ability. Aquila, though a man of great knowledge, yet did not undertake to speak in the synagogue, because he had not such gifts for public work as Apollos had; but he furnished Apollos with matter, and then left him to clothe it with acceptable words. Instructing young Christians and young ministers privately in conversation, who mean well, and perform well, as far as they go, is a piece of very good service, both to them and to the church. [3.] See an instance of great humility in Apollos. He was a very bright young man, of great parts and learning, newly come from the university, a popular preacher, and one mightily cried up and followed; and yet, finding that Aquila and Priscilla were judicious serious Christians, that could speak intelligently and experimentally of the things of God, though they were but mechanics, poor tent-makers, he was glad to receive instructions from them, to be shown by them his defects and mistakes, and to have his mistakes rectified by them, and his deficiencies made up. Young scholars may gain a great deal by converse with old Christians, as young students in the law may by old practitioners. Apollos, though he *was instructed in the way of the Lord,* did not rest in the knowledge he had attained, nor thought he understood Christianity as well as any man (which proud conceited young men are apt to do), but was willing to have it expounded to him more perfectly. Those that know much should covet to know more, and what they know to know it better, pressing forward towards perfection. [4.] Here is an instance of a good woman, though not permitted to speak in the church or in the synagogue, yet doing good with the knowledge God had given her in private converse. Paul will have *the aged women to be teachers of good things* Tit. ii, 3, 4.

III. Here is his preferment to the service of the church of Corinth, which was a larger sphere of usefulness than Ephesus at present was. Paul had set the wheels a-going in Achaia and particularly at Corinth, the county-town. Many were stirred up by his preaching to receive the gospel, and they needed to be confirmed; and many were likewise irritated to oppose the gospel, and they needed to be confuted. Paul was gone, was called away to other work, and now there was a fair occasion in this vacancy for Apollos to set in, who was fitted rather to water than to plant, to build up those that were within than to bring in those that were without. Now here we have,

1. His call to this service, not by a vision,

as Paul was called to Macedonia, no, nor so much as by the invitation of those he was to go to; but, (1.) He himself inclined to go: *He was disposed to pass into Achaia;* having heard of the state of the churches there, he had a mind to try what good he could do among them. Though there were those there who were eminent for spiritual gifts, yet Apollos thought there might be some work for him, and God disposed his mind that way. (2.) His friends encouraged him to go, and approved of his purpose; and, he being a perfect stranger there, they gave him a testimonial or letters of recommendation, exhorting the disciples in Achaia to entertain him and employ him. In this way, among others, the communion of churches is kept up, by the recommending of members and ministers to each other, when ministers, as Apollos here, are disposed to remove. Though those at Ephesus had a great loss of his labours, they did not grudge those in Achaia the benefit of them; but, on the contrary, used their interest in them to introduce him; for the churches of Christ, though they are many, yet they are one.

2. His success in this service, which both ways answered his intention and expectation; for,

(1.) Believers were greatly edified, and those that had received the gospel were very much confirmed: *He helped those much who had believed through grace.* Note, [1.] Those who believe in Christ, it is through grace that they believe; it is *not of themselves, it is God's gift to them;* it is his work in them. [2.] Those who through grace do believe, yet still have need of help; as long as they are here in this world there are remainders of unbelief, and something lacking in their faith to be perfected, and the work of faith to be fulfilled. [3.] Faithful ministers are capable of being in many ways helpful to those who through grace do believe, and it is their business to help them, to help them much; and, when a divine power goes along with them, they will be helpful to them.

(2.) Unbelievers were greatly mortified. Their objections were fully answered, the folly and sophistry of their arguments were discovered, so that they had nothing to say in defence of the opposition they made to the gospel; their mouths were stopped, and their faces filled with shame (*v.* 28): *He mightily convinced the Jews, and that publicly,* before the people; he did it, *εὐτόνως—earnestly,* and with a great deal of vehemence; he took pains to do it; his heart was upon it, as one that was truly desirous both to serve the cause of Christ and to save the souls of men. He did it effectually and to universal satisfaction. He did it *levi negotio—with facility.* The case was so plain, and the arguments were so strong on Christ's side, that it was an easy matter to baffle all that the Jews could say against it. Though they were so fierce, yet their cause was so weak that he made nothing of their opposition. Now that which he aimed to convince them of was *that Jesus is the Christ,* that he is *the Messiah promised to the fathers, who should come,* and they were to look for no other. If the Jews were but convinced of this—that Jesus is Christ, even their own law would teach them to hear him. Note, The business of ministers is to preach Christ: *We preach not ourselves, but Christ Jesus the Lord.* The way he took to convince them was *by the scriptures;* thence he fetched his arguments; for the Jews owned the scriptures to be of divine authority, and it was easy for him, who was mighty in the scriptures, from them to show that Jesus is the Christ. Note, Ministers must be able not only to preach the truth, but to prove it and defend it, and to convince gainsayers with meekness and yet with power, instructing those that oppose themselves; and this is real service to the church.

CHAP. XIX.

We left Paul in his circuit visiting the churches (ch. xviii. 23), but we have not forgotten, nor has he, the promise he made to his friends at Ephesus, to return to them, and make some stay there; now this chapter shows us his performance of that promise, his coming to Ephesus, and his continuance there two years; we are here told, I. How he laboured there in the word and doctrine, how he taught some weak believers that had gone no further than John's baptism (ver. 1—7), how he taught three months in the synagogue of the Jews (ver. 8), and, when he was driven thence, how he taught the Gentiles a long time in a public school (ver. 9, 10), and how he confirmed his doctrine by miracles, ver. 11, 12. II. What was the fruit of his labour, particularly among the conjurors, the worst of sinners: some were confounded, that did but make use of his name (ver. 13—17), but others were converted, that received and embraced his doctrine, ver. 18—20. III. What projects he had of further usefulness (ver. 21, 22), and what trouble at length he met with at Ephesus from the silversmiths, which forced him thence to pursue the measures he had laid; how a mob was raised by Demetrius to cry up Diana (ver. 23—34), and how it was suppressed and dispersed by the town-clerk, ver. 35—41.

AND it came to pass, that, while
Apollos was at Corinth, Paul
having passed through the upper
coasts came to Ephesus: and finding
certain disciples, 2 He said unto
them, Have ye received the Holy
Ghost since ye believed? And they
said unto him, We have not so much
as heard whether there be any Holy
Ghost. 3 And he said unto them,
Unto what then were ye baptized?
And they said, Unto John's baptism.
4 Then said Paul, John verily baptized with the baptism of repentance,
saying unto the people, that they
should believe on him which should
come after him, that is, on Christ
Jesus. 5 When they heard *this,*
they were baptized in the name of
the Lord Jesus. 6 And when Paul
had laid *his* hands upon them, the
Holy Ghost came on them; and they
spake with tongues, and prophesied.
7 And all the men were about twelve.

Ephesus was a city of great note in Asia, famous for a temple built there to Diana, which was one of the wonders of the world: thither *Paul came to preach the gospel while Apollos was at Corinth* (*v.* 1); while he was watering there, Paul was planting here, and grudged not that Apollos entered into his labours and was building upon his foundation, but rejoiced in it, and went on in the new work that was cut out for him at Ephesus with the more cheerfulness and satisfaction, because he knew that such an able minister of the New Testament as Apollos was now at Corinth, carrying on the good work there. Though there were those that made him the head of a party against Paul (1 Cor. i. 12), yet Paul had no jealousy of him, nor any way disliked the affection the people had for him. Paul having gone through the country of Galatia and Phrygia, having *passed through the upper coasts*, Pontus and Bithynia, that lay north, at length *came to Ephesus*, where he had left Aquila and Priscilla, and there found them. At his first coming, he met with some disciples there, who professed faith in Christ as the true Messiah, but were as yet in the first and lowest form in the school of Christ, under his usher John the Baptist. They were in number *about twelve* (*v.* 7); they were much of the standing that Apollos was of when he came to Ephesus (for he *knew only the baptism of John*, *ch.* xviii. 25), but they had not opportunity of being acquainted with Aquila and Priscilla, or had not been so long in Ephesus or were not so willing to receive instruction as Apollos was, otherwise they might have had the way of God expounded to them more perfectly, as Apollos had. Observe here,

I. How Paul catechised them. He was told, probably by Aquila and Priscilla, that they were believers, that they did own Christ, and had given up their names to him; now Paul hereupon takes them under examination.

1. They did believe in the Son of God; but Paul enquires whether they had *received the Holy Ghost*,—whether they believed in the Spirit, whose operations on the minds of men, for conviction, conversion, and comfort, were revealed some time after the doctrine of Jesus being the Christ,—whether they had been acquainted with, and had admitted, this revelation? This was not all; extraordinary gifts of the Holy Ghost were conferred upon the apostles and other disciples presently after Christ's ascension, which was frequently repeated upon occasion; had they participated in these gifts? "*Have you received the Holy Ghost since you believed?* Have you had that seal of the trtuh of Christ's doctrine in yourselves?" We are not now to expect any such extraordinary gifts as they had then. The canon of the New Testament being long since completed and ratified, we depend upon that as the most sure word of prophecy. But there are graces of the Spirit given to all believers, which are as earnests to them, 2 Cor. i. 22; v. 5; Eph. i. 13, 14. Now it concerns us all who profess the Christian faith seriously to enquire whether we have received the Holy Ghost or not. The Holy Ghost is promised to all believers, to all petitioners (Luke xi. 13); but many are deceived in this matter, thinking they have received the Holy Ghost when really they have not. As there are pretenders to the gifts of the Holy Ghost, so there are to his graces and comforts; we should therefore strictly examine ourselves, Have we received the Holy Ghost since we believed? The tree will be known by its fruits. Do we bring forth the fruits of the Spirit? Are we led by the Spirit? Do we walk in the Spirit? Are we under the government of the Spirit?

2. They owned their ignorance in this matter: "*Whether there be a Holy Ghost* is more than we know. That there is a promise of the Holy Ghost we know from the scriptures of the Old Testament, and that this promise will be fulfilled in its season we doubt not; but so much have we been out of the way of intelligence in this matter that we have not so much as heard whether the Holy Ghost be indeed yet given as a Spirit of prophecy." They knew (as Dr. Lightfoot observes) that, according to the tradition of their nation, after the death of Ezra, Haggai, Zechariah, and Malachi, *the Holy Ghost departed from Israel, and went up;* and they professed that they had never heard of his return. They spoke as if they expected it, and wondered they did not hear of it, and were ready to welcome the notice of it. The gospel light, like that of the morning, shone more and more, gradually; not only clearer and clearer, in the discovery of truths not before heard of, but further and further, in the discovery of them to persons that had not before heard of them.

3. Paul enquired how they came to be baptized, if they knew nothing of the Holy Ghost; for, if they were baptized by any of Christ's ministers, they were instructed concerning the Holy Ghost, and were baptized in his name. "Know you not that Jesus being glorified, consequently the Holy Ghost is given? *unto what then were you baptized?* This is strange and unaccountable. What! baptized, and yet know nothing of the Holy Ghost? Surely your baptism was a nullity, if you know nothing of the Holy Ghost; for it is the receiving of the Holy Ghost that is signified and sealed by that washing of regeneration. Ignorance of the Holy Ghost is as inconsistent with a sincere profession of Christianity as ignorance of Christ is." Applying it to ourselves, it intimates that those are baptized to no purpose, and have received the grace of God therein in vain, that do not receive and submit to the Holy Ghost. It is also an enquiry we should often make, not only to whose honour we were born, but into whose service we were baptized, that we may study to answer the ends both of our birth and of our baptism. Let us often consider

unto what we were baptized, that we may live up to our baptism.

4. They own that they were baptized *unto John's baptism*—εἰς τὸ Ἰωάννου βάπτισμα· that is, as I take it, they were baptized in the name of John, not by John himself (he was far enough from any such thought), but by some weak, well-meaning disciple of his, that ignorantly kept up his name as the head of a party, retaining the spirit and notion of those disciples of his that were jealous of the growth of Christ's interest, and complained to him of it, John iii. 26. Some one or more of these, that found themselves much edified by John's baptism of *repentance for the remission of sins*, not thinking that the kingdom of heaven, which he spoke of as at hand, was so very near as it proved, ran away with that notion, rested in what they had, and thought they could not do better than to persuade others to do so too; and so, ignorantly, in a blind zeal for John's doctrine, they baptized here and there one in John's name, or, as it is here expressed, *unto John's baptism*, looking no further themselves, nor directing those that they baptized any further.

5. Paul explains to them the true intent and meaning of John's baptism, as principally referring to Jesus Christ, and so rectifies the mistake of those who had baptized them into the baptism of John, and had not directed them to look any further, but to rest in that. Those that have been left in ignorance, or led into error, by any infelicities of their education, should not therefore be despised nor rejected by those who are more knowing and orthodox, but should be compassionately instructed, and better taught, as these disciples were by Paul. (1.) He owns that John's baptism was a very good thing, as far as it went: *John verily baptized with the baptism of repentance.* By this baptism he required people to be sorry for their sins, and to confess them and turn from them; and to bring any to this is a great point gained. But, (2.) He shows them that John's baptism had a further reference, and he never designed that those he baptized should rest there, but told them that they should believe on him who should come after him, that is, on Christ Jesus,—that his baptism of repentance was designed only to prepare the way of the Lord, and to dispose them to receive and entertain Christ, whom he left them big with expectations of; nay, whom he directed them to: *Behold the Lamb of God.* "John was a great and good man; but he was only the harbinger,—Christ is the Prince. His baptism was the porch which you were to pass through, not the house you were to rest in; and therefore it was all wrong for you to be baptized into the baptism of John."

6. When they were thus shown the error they were led into, they thankfully accepted the discovery, and *were baptized in the name of the Lord Jesus, v.* 5. As for Apollos, of whom it was said (*ch.* xviii. 25) that he *knew the baptism of John*—that he rightly understood the meaning of it when he was baptized with it, though he knew that *only*—yet, when he understood the way of God more perfectly, he was not again baptized, any more than Christ's first disciples that had been baptized with John's baptism and knew it referred to the Messiah at the door (and, with an eye to this, submitted to it), were baptized again. But to these disciples, who received it only with an eye to John and looked no further, as if he were their saviour, it was such a fundamental error as was as fatal to it as it would have been for any to be baptized in the name of Paul (1 Cor. i. 13); and therefore, when they came to understand things better, they desired to be *baptized in the name of the Lord Jesus*, and were so: not by Paul himself, as we have reason to think, but by some of those who attended him. It does not therefore follow hence that there was not an agreement between John's baptism and Christ's, or that they were not for substance the same; much less does it follow that those who have been once baptized *in the name of the Father, Son, and Holy Ghost* (which is the appointed form of Christ's baptism), may be again baptized in the same name; for those that were here baptized *in the name of the Lord Jesus* had never been so baptized before.

II. How Paul conferred the extraordinary gifts of the Holy Ghost upon them, *v.* 6. 1. Paul solemnly *prayed to God* to give them those gifts, signified by his *laying his hands on them*, which was a gesture used in blessing by the patriarchs, especially in conveying the great trust of the promise, as Gen. xlviii. 14. The Spirit being the great promise of the New Testament, the apostles conveyed it by the imposition of hands: "The Lord bless thee with that blessing, that blessing of blessings," Isa. xliv. 3. 2. God granted the thing he prayed for: *The Holy Ghost came upon them* in a surprising overpowering manner, and *they spoke with tongues and prophesied*, as the apostles did and the first Gentile converts, *ch.* x. 44. This was intended to introduce the gospel at Ephesus, and to awaken in the minds of men an expectation of some great things from it; and some think that it was further designed to qualify these twelve men for the work of the ministry, and that these twelve were the elders of Ephesus, to whom Paul committed the care and government of that church. They had the Spirit of prophesy, that they might understand the mysteries of the kingdom of God themselves, and the gift of tongues, that they might preach them to every nation and language. Oh, what a wonderful change was here made on a sudden in these men! those that but just now had *not so much as heard that there was any Holy Ghost* are now themselves filled with the Holy Ghost; for the Spirit, like the wind, blows where and when he listeth.

8 And he went into the syna-

gogue, and spake boldly for the space of three months, disputing and persuading the things concerning the kingdom of God.
9 But when divers were hardened, and believed not, but spake evil of that way before the multitude, he departed from them, and separated the disciples, disputing daily in the school of one Tyrannus.
10 And this continued by the space of two years; so that all they which dwelt in Asia heard the word of the Lord Jesus, both Jews and Greeks.
11 And God wrought special miracles by the hands of Paul:
12 So that from his body were brought unto the sick handkerchiefs or aprons, and the diseases departed from them, and the evil spirits went out of them.

Paul is here very busy at Ephesus to do good.

I. He begins, as usual, in the Jews' synagogue, and makes the first offer of the gospel to them, that he might gather in the *lost sheep of the house of Israel*, who were now scattered upon the mountains. Observe,

1. Where he preached to them: in their synagogue (*v.* 8), as Christ used to do. He went and joined with them in their synagogue-worship, to take off their prejudices against him, and to ingratiate himself with them, while there was any hope of winning upon them. Thus he would bear his testimony to public worship on sabbath days. Where there were no Christian assemblies yet formed, he frequented the Jewish assemblies, while the Jews were not as yet wholly cast off. Paul went into the synagogue, because there he had them together, and had them, it might be hoped, in a good frame.

2. What he preached to them: *The things concerning the kingdom of God* among men, the great things which concerned God's dominion over all men and favour to them, and men's subjection to God and happiness in God. He showed them their obligations to God and interest in him, as the Creator, by which the kingdom of God was set up,—the violation of those obligations, and the forfeiture of that interest, by sin, by which the kingdom of God was pulled down,—and the renewing of those obligations and the restoration of man to that interest again, by the Redeemer, whereby the kingdom of God was again set up. Or, more particularly, *the things concerning the kingdom of the Messiah*, which the Jews were in expectation of, and promised themselves great matters from; he opened the scriptures which spoke concerning this, gave them a right notion of this kingdom, and showeh them their mistakes about it.

3. How he preached to them. (1.) He preached argumentatively: he disputed; gave reasons, scripture-reasons, for what he preached, and answered objections, for the convincing of men's judgments and consciences, that they might not only believe, but might see cause to believe. He preached διαλεγόμενος—*dialogue-wise;* he put questions to them and received their answers, gave them leave to put questions to him and answered them. (2.) He preached affectionately: he persuaded; he used not only logical arguments, to enforce what he said upon their understandings, but rhetorical motives, to impress what he said upon their affections, showing them that the things he preached concerning the kingdom of God were things concerning themselves, which they were nearly concerned in, and therefore ought to concern themselves about, 2 Cor. v. 11, *We persuade men.* Paul was a moving preacher, and was master of the art of persuasion. (3.) He preached undauntedly, and with a holy resolution: he spoke boldly, as one that had not the least doubt of the things he spoke of, nor the least distrust of him he spoke from, nor the least dread of those he spoke to.

4. How long he preached to them: *For the space of three months*, which was a competent time allowed them to consider of it; in that time those among them that belonged to the election of grace were called in, and the rest were left inexcusable. Thus long Paul preached the gospel *with much contention* (1 Thess. ii. 2), yet he *did not fail, nor was discouraged.*

5. What success his preaching had among them. (1.) There were some that were persuaded to believe in Christ; some think this is intimated in the word *persuading*—he prevailed with them. But, (2.) Many continued in their infidelity, and were confirmed in their prejudices against Christianity. When Paul called on them before, and preached only some general things to them, they courted his stay among them (*ch.* xviii. 20); but now that he settled among them, and his word came more closely to their consciences, they were soon weary of him. [1.] They had an invincible aversion to the gospel of Christ themselves: they were *hardened, and believed not;* they were resolved they would not believe, though the truth shone in their faces with ever such a convincing light and evidence. Therefore they believed not, because they were hardened. [2.] They did their utmost to raise and keep up in others an aversion to the gospel; they not only entered not into the kingdom of God themselves, but neither did they suffer those that were entering to go in; for *they spoke evil of that way before the multitude*, to prejudice them against it. Though they could not show any manner of evil in it, yet they said all manner of evil concerning it. These sinners, like the angels that sinned, be-

came Satans, adversaries and devils, false accusers.

II. When he had carried the matter as far as it would go in the synagogue of the Jews, and found that their opposition grew more obstinate, he left the synagogue, because he could not safely, or rather because he could not comfortably and successfully, continue in communion with them. Though their worship was such as he could join in, and they had not silenced him, nor forbidden him to preach among them, yet they drove him from them by their railing at those things which he spoke *concerning the kingdom of God:* they hated to be reformed, hated to be instructed, and therefore *he departed from them.* Here we are sure there was a separation and no schism; for there was a just cause for it and a clear call to it. Now observe,

1. When Paul departed from the Jews he took the disciples with him, and *separated them, to save them from that untoward generation* (according to the charge Peter gave to his new converts, *ch.* ii. 40); lest they should be infected with the poisonous tongues of those blasphemers, he separated those who believed, to be the foundation of a Christian church, now that they were a competent number to be incorporated, that others might attend with them upon the preaching of the gospel, and might, upon their believing, be added to them. When Paul departed there needed no more to separate the disciples; let him go where he will, they will follow him.

2. When Paul separated from the synagogue he set up a meeting of his own, he *disputed daily in the school of one Tyrannus.* He left the synagogue of the Jews, that he might go on with the more freedom in his work; still he disputed for Christ and Christianity, and was ready to answer all opponents whatsoever in defence of them; and he had by this separation a double advantage. (1.) That now his opportunities were more frequent. In the synagogue he could only preach every sabbath day (*ch.* xiii. 42), but now he disputed daily, he set up a lecture every day, and thus redeemed time: those whose business would not permit them to come one day might come another day; and those were welcome who *watched daily at these gates of wisdom, and waited daily at the posts of her doors.* (2.) That now they were more open. To the synagogue of the Jews none might come, nor could come, but Jews or proselytes; Gentiles were excluded; but, when he set up a meeting in the school of Tyrannus, both Jews and Greeks attended his ministry, *v.* 10. Thus, as he describes this gate of opportunity at Ephesus (1 Cor. xvi. 8, 9), *a wide door and an effectual* was *opened to him,* though *there were many adversaries.* Some think this school of Tyrannus was a divinity-school of the Jews, and such a one they commonly had in their great cities besides their synagogue; they called it *Bethmidrash, the house of enquiry,* or of *repetition;* and they went to that on the sabbath day, after they had been in the synagogue. They go *from strength to strength,* from the *house of the sanctuary* to the *house of doctrine.* If this was such a school, it shows that though Paul left the synagogue he left it gradually, and still kept as near it as he could, as he had done, *ch.* xviii. 7. But others think it was a philosophy-school of the Gentiles, belonging to one Tyrannus, or a retiring place (for so the word σχολὴ sometimes signifies) belonging to a principal man or governor of the city; some convenient place it was, which Paul and the disciples had the use of, either for love or money.

3. Here he continued his labours for *two years,* read his lectures and disputed daily. These two years commence from the end of the *three months* which he spent in the synagogue (*v.* 8); after they were ended, he continued for some time in the country about, preaching; therefore he might justly reckon it in all three years, as he does, *ch.* xx. 31.

4. The gospel hereby spread far and near (*v.* 10): *All those that dwelt in Asia heard the word of the Lord Jesus;* not only all that dwelt in Ephesus, but all that dwelt in that large province called *Asia,* of which Ephesus was the head city—*Asia the Less* it was called. There was great resort to Ephesus from all parts of the country, for law, traffic, religion, and education, which gave Paul an opportunity of sending the report of the gospel to all the towns and villages of that country. They all heard the *word of the Lord Jesus.* The gospel is Christ's word, it is a word concerning Christ. This they heard, or at least heard of it. Some of all sects, some out of all parts both in city and country, embraced this gospel, and entertained it, and by them it was communicated to others; and so they all *heard the word of the Lord Jesus,* or might have heard it. Probably Paul sometimes made excursions himself into the country, to preach the gospel, or sent his missionaries or assistants that attended him, and thus the word of the Lord was *heard throughout that region.* Now *those that sat in darkness saw a great light.*

III. God confirmed Paul's doctrine by miracles, which awakened people's enquiries after it, fixed their affection to it, and engaged their belief of it, *v.* 11, 12. I wonder we have not read of any miracle wrought by Paul since the casting of the evil spirit out of the damsel at Philippi; why did he not work miracles at Thessalonica, Berea, and Athens? Or, if he did, why are they not recorded? Was the success of the gospel, without miracles in the kingdom of nature, itself such a miracle in the kingdom of grace, and the divine power which went along with it such a proof of its divine original, that there needed no other? It is certain that at Corinth he wrought many miracles, though

Luke has recorded none, for he tells them (2 Cor. xii. 12) that the signs of his apostleship were among them, *in wonders and mighty deeds.* But here at Ephesus we have a general account of the proofs of this kind which he gave of his divine mission. 1. They were *special miracles*—Δυνάμεις οὐ τυχούσας. God exerted powers that were not according to the common course of nature: *Virtutes non vulgares.* Things were done which could by no means be ascribed either to chance or second causes. Or, they were not only (as all miracles are) *out of the common road*, but they were even uncommon miracles, such miracles as had not been wrought by the hands of any other of the apostles. The opposers of the gospel were so prejudiced that any miracles would not serve their turn; therefore God wrought *virtutes non quaslibet* (so they render it), *something above the common road of miracles.* 2. It was not Paul that wrought them *(What is Paul, and what is Apollos?)* but it was God that *wrought them by the hand of Paul.* He was but the instrument, God was the principal agent.

3. He not only cured the sick that were brought to him, or to whom he was brought, but *from his body were brought to the sick handkerchiefs or aprons;* they got Paul's handkerchiefs, or his aprons, that is, say some, the aprons he wore when he worked at his trade, and the application of them to the sick cured them immediately. Or, they brought the sick people's handkerchiefs, or their girdles, or caps, or head-dresses, and laid them for awhile to Paul's body, and then took them to the sick. The former is more probable. Now was fulfilled that word of Christ to his disciples, *Greater works than these shall you do.* We read of one that was cured by the touch of Christ's garment when it was upon him, and he perceived that *virtue went out of him;* but here were people cured by Paul's garments when they were taken from him. Christ gave his apostles power *against unclean spirits and against all manner of sickness* (Matt. x. 1), and accordingly we find here that those to whom Paul sent relief had it in both those cases: *for the diseases departed from them* and the *evil spirits went out of them,* which were both significant of the great design and blessed effect of the gospel, the healing of spiritual disease, and freeing the souls of men from the power and dominion of Satan.

13 Then certain of the vagabond
Jews, exorcists, took upon them to
call over them which had evil spirits
the name of the Lord Jesus, saying,
We adjure you by Jesus whom Paul
preacheth. 14 And there were seven
sons of *one* Sceva, a Jew, *and* chief
of the priests, which did so. 15 And
the evil spirit answered and said,
Jesus I know, and Paul I know;
but who are ye? 16 And the man
in whom the evil spirit was leaped
on them, and overcame them, and
prevailed against them, so that they
fled out of that house naked and
wounded. 17 And this was known
to all the Jews and Greeks also
dwelling at Ephesus; and fear fell
on them all, and the name of the
Lord Jesus was magnified. 18 And
many that believed came, and confessed, and showed their deeds. 19
Many of them also which used
curious arts brought their books together, and burned them before all
men: and they counted the price of
them, and found *it* fifty thousand
pieces of silver. 20 So mightily grew
the word of God and prevailed.

The preachers of the gospel were sent forth to carry on a war against Satan, and therein Christ went forth *conquering and to conquer.* The casting of evil spirits out of those that were possessed was one instance of Christ's victory over Satan; but, to show in how many ways Christ triumphed over that great enemy, we have here in these verses two remarkable instances of the conquest of Satan, not only in those that were violently possessed by him, but in those that were voluntarily devoted to him.

I. Here is the confusion of some of Satan's servants, some *vagabond Jews,* that were *exorcists,* who made use of Christ's name profanely and wickedly in their diabolical enchantments, but were made to pay dearly for their presumption. Observe,

1. The general character of those who were guilty of this presumption. They were Jews, but *vagabond* Jews, were of the Jewish nation and religion, but went about from town to town to get money by conjuring. They strolled about to tell people their fortunes, and pretended by spells and charms to cure diseases, and bring people to themselves that were melancholy or distracted. They called themselves exorcists, because in doing their tricks they used forms of adjuration, by such and such commanding names. The superstitious Jews, to put a reputation upon these magic arts, wickedly attributed the invention of them to Solomon. So Josephus *(Antiquit.* lib. viii. cap. 2) says that Solomon composed charms by which diseases were cured, and devils driven out so as never to return; and that these operations continued common among the Jews to his time. And Christ seems to refer to this (Matt. xii. 27), *By whom do your children cast them out?*

2. A particular account of some at Ephesus that led this course of life and came thither

in their travels; they were *seven sons of one Sceva, a Jew, and chief of the priests, v.* 14. It is sad to see the house of Jacob thus degenerated, much more the house of Aaron, the family that was in a peculiar manner consecrated to God; it is truly sad to see any of that race in league with Satan. Their father was a chief of the priests, head of one of the twenty-four courses of priests. One would think the temple would find both employment and encouragement enough for the sons of a chief priest, if they had been twice as many. But probably it was a vain, rambling, rakish humour that led them to turn mountebanks, and wander all the world over to cure mad folks.

3. The profaneness they were guilty of: *They took upon them to call over evil spirits the name of the Lord Jesus;* not as those who had a veneration for Christ and a confidence in his name, as we read of some who cast out devils in Christ's name and yet did not follow with his disciples (Luke ix. 49), whom he would not have to be discouraged; but as those who were willing to try all methods to carry on their wicked trade, and, it should seem, had this design:—If the evil spirits should yield to an adjuration in the name of Jesus by those that did not believe in him, they would say it was no confirmation of his doctrine to those that did; for it was all one whether they believed it or no. If they should not yield to it, they would say the name of Christ was not so powerful as the other names they used, to which the devils had often by collusion yielded. They said, *We adjure you by Jesus whom Paul preaches;* not, "whom we believe in, or depend upon, or have any authority from," but *whom Paul preaches;* as if they had said, "We will try what that name will do." The exorcists in the Romish church, who pretend to cast the devil out of melancholy people by spells and charms which they understand not, and which, not having any divine warrant, cannot be used in faith, are the followers of these vagabond Jews.

4. The confusion they were put to in their impious operations. Let them not be deceived, God is not mocked, nor shall the glorious name of Jesus be prostituted to such a vile purpose as this; *what communion hath Christ with Belial?* (1.) The evil spirit gave them a sharp reply (*v.* 15): "*Jesus I know, and Paul I know; but who are you?* I know that Jesus has conquered principalities and powers, and that Paul has authority in his name to cast out devils; but what power have you to command us in his name, or who gave you any such power? What have you to do to declare the power of Jesus, or to take his covenant and commands into your mouths, seeing you hate his instructions?" Ps. l. 16, 17. This was extorted out of the mouth of the evil spirit by the power of God, to gain honour to the gospel, and to put those to shame that made a bad use of Christ's name. Antichristian powers and factions pretend a mighty zeal for Jesus and Paul, and to have authority from them; but, when the matter comes to be looked into, it is a mere worldly secular interest that is to be thus supported; nay, it is an enmity to true religion: *Jesus we know, and Paul we know; but who are you?* (2.) *The man in whom the evil spirit was* gave them a warm reception, fell foul upon them, *leaped upon them* in the height of his frenzy and rage, *overcame them* and all their enchantments, *prevailed against them,* and was every way too hard for them; so that *they fled out of the house,* not only *naked,* but *wounded;* their clothes pulled off their backs, and their heads broken. This is written for a warning to all those who name the name of Christ, but do not depart from iniquity. The same enemy that overcomes them with his temptations will overcome them with his terrors; and their adjuring him in Christ's name to let them alone will be no security to them. If we resist the devil by a true and lively faith in Christ, he will flee from us; but if we think to resist him by the bare using of Christ's name, or any part of his word, as a spell or charm, he will prevail against us.

5. The general notice that was taken of this, and the good impression it made upon many (*v.* 17): *This was known to all the Jews and Greeks also dwelling at Ephesus.* It was the common talk of the town; and the effect of it was, (1.) That men were terrified: *fear fell on them all.* In this instance they saw the malice of the devil whom they served, and the power of Christ whom they opposed; and both were awful considerations. They saw that the name of Christ was not to be trifled with, nor his religion compounded with the pagan superstitions. (2.) That God was glorified; *the name of the Lord Jesus,* by which his faithful servants cast out devils and cured diseases, without any resistance, *was the more magnified;* for now it appeared to be a name above every name.

II. Here is the conversion of others of Satan's servants, with the evidences of their conversion.

1. Those that had been guilty of wicked practices confessed them, *v.* 18. Many that had believed and were baptized, but had not then been so particular as they might have been in the confession of their sins, were so terrified with these instances of the magnifying of the name of Jesus Christ that they came to Paul, or some of the other ministers that were with him, and confessed what evil lives they had led, and what a great deal of secret wickedness their own consciences charged them with, which the world knew not of—secret frauds and secret filthiness; *they showed their deeds,* took shame to themselves and gave glory to God and warning to others. These confessions were not extorted from them, but were voluntary, for the ease of their consciences, upon which the late mi-

racles had struck a terror. Note, Where there is true contrition for sin there will be an ingenuous confession of sin to God in every prayer, and to man whom we have offended when the case requires it.

2. Those that had conversed with wicked books burnt them (*v.* 19): *Many also of those who used curious arts, τὰ περίεργα—impertinent things; multa nihil ad se pertinentia satagentes—busy bodies* (so the word is used, 2 Thess. iii. 11; 1 Tim. v. 13), that traded in the study of magic and divination, in books of judicial astrology, casting nativities, telling fortunes, raising and laying spirits, interpreting dreams, predicting future events, and the like, to which some think are to be added *plays, romances, love-books, and unchaste and immodest poems—histrionica, amatoria, saltatoria.*—Stres. These, having their consciences more awakened than ever to see the evil of those practices in which these books instructed them, *brought their books together, and burnt them before all men.* Ephesus was notorious for the use of these curious arts; hence spells and charms were called *Literæ Ephesiæ.* Here people furnished themselves with all those sorts of books, and, probably, had tutors to instruct them in those *black* arts. It was therefore much for the honour of Christ and his gospel to have such a noble testimony borne against those *curious* arts, in a place where they were so much in vogue. It is taken for granted that they were convinced of the evil of these curious arts, and resolved to deal in them no longer; but they did not think this enough unless they burnt their books. (1.) Thus they showed a holy indignation at the sins they had been guilty of; as the idolaters, when they were brought to repentance, said to their idols, *Get you hence* (Isa. xxx. 22), and cast even those of silver and gold *to the moles and to the bats*, Isa. ii. 20. They thus took a pious revenge on those things that had been the instruments of sin to them, and proclaimed the force of their convictions of the evil of it, and that those very things were now detestable to them, as much as ever they had been delectable. (2.) Thus they showed their resolution never to return to the use of those arts, and the books which related to them, again. They were so fully convinced of the evil and danger of them that they would not throw the books by, within reach of a recal, upon supposition that it was possible they might change their mind; but, being stedfastly resolved never to make use of them, they burnt them. (3.) Thus they put away a temptation to return to them again. Had they kept the books by them, there was danger lest, when the heat of the present conviction was over, they should have the curiosity to look into them, and so be in danger of liking them and loving them again, and therefore they burnt them. Note, Those that truly repent of sin will keep themselves as far as possible from the occasions of it. (4.) Thus they prevented their doing mischief to others. If Judas had been by he would have said, "Sell them, and give the money to the poor;" or, "Buy Bibles and good books with it." But then who could tell into whose hands these dangerous books might fall, and what mischief might be done by them? it was therefore the safest course to commit them all to the flames. Those that are recovered from sin themselves will do all they can to keep others from falling into it, and will be much more afraid of laying an occasion of sin in the way of others. (5.) Thus they showed a contempt of the wealth of this world; for the price of the books was cast up, probably by those that persuaded them not to burn them, and it was found to be *fifty thousand pieces of silver,* which some compute to be fifteen hundred pounds of our money. It is probable that the books were scarce, perhaps prohibited, and therefore dear. Probably they had cost them so much; yet, being the devil's books, though they had been so foolish as to buy them, they did not think this would justify them in being so wicked as to sell them again. (6.) Thus they publicly testified their joy for their conversion from these wicked practices, as Matthew did by the great feast he made when Christ had called him from the receipt of custom. These converts joined together in making this bonfire, and made it before all men. They might have burnt the books privately, every one in his own house, but they chose to do it together, by consent, and to do it at the high cross (as we say), that Christ and his grace in them might be the more magnified, and all about them the more edified.

III. Here is a general account of the progress and success of the gospel in and about Ephesus (*v.* 20): *So mightily grew the word of God, and prevailed.* It is a blessed sight to see the word of God growing and prevailing mightily, as it did here. 1. To see it grow extensively, by the addition of many to the church. When still more and more are wrought upon by the gospel, and wrought up into a conformity to it, then it grows; when those that were least likely to yield to it, and that had been most stiff in their opposition to it, are captivated and brought into obedience to it, then it may be said to *grow mightily.* 2. To see it prevail extensively, by the advancement in knowledge and grace of those that are added to the church; when strong corruptions are mortified, vicious habits changed, evil customs of long standing broken off, and pleasant, gainful, fashionable sins are abandoned, then it prevails mightily; and Christ in it goes on conquering and to conquer.

21 After these things were ended, Paul purposed in the spirit, when he had passed through Macedonia and Achaia, to go to Jerusalem, saying,

After I have been there, I must also
see Rome. 22 So he sent into Macedonia two of them that ministered unto
him, Timotheus and Erastus; but he
himself stayed in Asia for a season.
23 And the same time there arose
no small stir about that way. 24 For
a certain *man* named Demetrius, a
silversmith which made silver shrines
for Diana, brought no small gain
unto the craftsmen; 25 Whom he
called together with the workmen of
like occupation, and said, Sirs, ye know
that by this craft we have our wealth.
26 Moreover ye see and hear, that
not alone at Ephesus, but almost
throughout all Asia, this Paul hath
persuaded and turned away much
people, saying that they be no gods,
which are made with hands: 27 So
that not only this our craft is in
danger to be set at nought; but also
that the temple of the great goddess
Diana should be despised, and her
magnificence should be destroyed,
whom all Asia and the world wor-
shippeth. 28 And when they heard
these sayings, they were full of wrath,
and cried out, saying, Great *is* Diana
of the Ephesians. 29 And the whole
city was filled with confusion: and
having caught Gaius and Aristarchus,
men of Macedonia, Paul's companions
in travel, they rushed with one accord into the theatre. 30 And when
Paul would have entered in unto the
people, the disciples suffered him
not. 31 And certain of the chief of
Asia, which were his friends, sent
unto him, desiring *him* that he would
not adventure himself into the theatre. 32 Some therefore cried one
thing, and some another: for the
assembly was confused; and the
more part knew not wherefore they
were come together. 33 And they
drew Alexander out of the multitude,
the Jews putting him forward. And
Alexander beckoned with the hand,
and would have made his defence
unto the people. 34 But when they
knew that he was a Jew, all with one
voice about the space of two hours
cried out, Great *is* Diana of the
Ephesians. 35 And when the
town clerk had appeased the people,
he said, *Ye* men of Ephesus, what
man is there that knoweth not how
that the city of the Ephesians is
a worshipper of the great goddess
Diana, and of the *image* which
fell down from Jupiter? 36 Seeing
then that these things cannot be
spoken against, ye ought to be
quiet, and to do nothing rashly. 37
For ye have brought hither these
men, which are neither robbers of
churches, nor yet blasphemers of
your goddess. 38 Wherefore if Demetrius, and the craftsmen which are
with him, have a matter against any
man, the law is open, and there are
deputies: let them implead one another. 39 But if ye enquire any
thing concerning other matters, it
shall be determined in a lawful assembly. 40 For we are in danger to
be called in question for this day's
uproar, there being no cause whereby
we may give an account of this concourse. 41 And when he had thus
spoken, he dismissed the assembly.

I. Paul is here brought into some trouble at Ephesus, just when he is forecasting to go thence, and to cut out work for himself elsewhere. See here,

1. How he laid his purpose of going to other places, *v.* 21, 22. He was a man of vast designs for God, and was for making his influences as widely diffusive as might be. Having spent above two years at Ephesus, (1.) He designed a visit to the churches of Macedonia and Achaia, especially of Philippi and Corinth, the chief cities of those provinces, *v.* 21. There he had planted churches, and now is concerned to visit them. He *purposed in the spirit,* either in his own spirit, not communicating his purpose as yet, but keeping it to himself; or by the direction of the Holy Spirit, who was his guide in all his motions, and by whom he was led. He purposed to go and see how the work of God went on in those places, that he might rectify what was amiss and encourage what was good. (2.) Thence he designed to go to Jerusalem, to visit the brethren there, and give an account to them of the prospering of the good pleasure of the Lord in his hand; and thence he intended to go to Rome, to go and *see Rome;* not as if he designed only the gratifying of his curiosity with the sight of that ancient famous city, but because it was an expression people commonly used, that they would go and see Rome, would look about them there, when that which he designed was to see the Christians there, and to do them some service,

Rom. i. 11. The good people at Rome were the glory of the city which he longed for a sight of. Dr. Lightfoot supposes that it was upon the death of the emperor Claudius, who died the second year of Paul's being at Ephesus, that Paul thought of going to Rome, because while he lived the Jews were forbidden Rome, *ch.* xviii. 2. (3.) He sent Timothy and Erastus into Macedonia, to give them notice of the visit he intended them, and to get their collection ready for the poor saints at Jerusalem. Soon after he wrote *the first epistle to the Corinthians,* designing to follow it himself, as appears 1 Cor. iv. 17, 19, *I have sent to you Timotheus ; but I will myself come to you shortly, if the Lord will.* For the present, he staid in Asia, in the country about Ephesus, founding churches.

2. How he was seconded in his purpose, and obliged to pursue it by the troubles which at length he met with at Ephesus. It was strange that he had been quiet there so long; yet it should seem he had met with trouble there not recorded in this story, for in his epistle written at this time he speaks of his having *fought with beasts at Ephesus* (1 Cor. xv. 32), which seems to be meant of his being put to fight with wild beasts in the theatre, according to the barbarous treatment they sometimes gave the Christians. And he speaks of the trouble which came to them in Asia, near Ephesus, when he *despaired of life,* and *received a sentence of death within himself,* 2 Cor. i. 8, 9.

II. But, in the trouble here related, he was worse frightened than hurt. In general, *there arose no small stir about that way, v.* 23. Some historians say that the famous impostor Apollonius Tyanæus, who set up for a rival with Christ, and gave out himself, as Simon Magus, to be *some great one,* was at Ephesus about this time that Paul was there. But it seems the opposition he gave to the gospel was so insignificant that St. Luke did not think it worth taking notice of. The disturbance he gives an account of was of another nature : let us view the particulars of it. Here is,

1. A great complaint against Paul and the other preachers of the gospel for drawing people off from the worship of Diana, and so spoiling the trade of the silversmiths that worked for Diana's temple.

(1.) The complainant is Demetrius, a silversmith, a principal man, it is likely, of the trade, and one that would be thought to understand and consult the interests of it more than others of the company. Whether he worked in other sorts of plate or no we are not told; but the most advantageous branch of his trade was *making silver shrines for Diana, v.* 24. Some think these were medals stamped with the effigies of Diana, or her temple, or both; others think they were representations of the temple, with the image of Diana in it in miniature, all of silver, but so small that people might carry them about with them, as the papists do their crucifixes. Those that came from far to pay their devotions at the temple of Ephesus, when they went home bought these little temples or shrines, to carry home with them, for the gratifying of the curiosity of their friends, and to preserve in their own minds the idea of that stately edifice. See how craftsmen, and crafty men too above the rank of silversmiths, make an advantage to themselves of people's superstition, and serve their worldly ends by it.

(2.) The persons he appeals to are not the magistrates, but the mob ; he called the *craftsmen* together, *with the workmen of like occupation* (a company of mechanics, who had no sense of any thing but their worldly interest), and these he endeavoured to incense against Paul, who would be actuated as little by reason and as much by fury as he could desire.

(3.) His complaint and representation are very full. [1.] He lays it down for a principle that the art and mystery of making silver shrines for the worshippers of Diana was very necessary to be supported and kept up (*v.* 25): "*You know that by this craft we have* not only our subsistence, and our necessary food, but *our wealth.* We grow rich, and raise estates. We live great, and have wherewithal to maintain our pleasures ; and therefore, whatever comes of it, we must not suffer this craft to grow into contempt." Note, It is natural for men to be jealous for that, whether right or wrong, by which they get their wealth ; and many have, for this reason alone, set themselves against the gospel of Christ, because it calls men off from those crafts which are unlawful, how much wealth soever is to be obtained by them. [2.] He charges it upon Paul that he had dissuaded men from worshipping idols. The words, as they are laid in the indictment, are, that he had asserted, *Those are no gods which are made with hands, v.* 26. Could any truth be more plain and self-evident than this, or any reasoning more cogent and convincing than that of the prophets, *The workman made it, therefore it is not God?* The first and most genuine notion we have of God is, that he has his being of himself, and depends upon none ; but that all things have their being from him, and their dependence on him : and then it must follow that those are no gods which are the creatures of men's fancy and the work of men's hands. Yet this must be looked upon as an heretical and atheistical notion, and Paul as a criminal for maintaining it ; not that they could advance any thing against this doctrine itself, but that the consequence of it was that not only at Ephesus, the chief city, but almost throughout all Asia, among the country people, who were their best customers, and whom they thought they were surest of, he had *persuaded and turned away much people* from the worship of Diana ; so that there was not now such a demand for the silver shrines as had been, nor were such good rates given for them.

There are those who will stickle for that which is most grossly absurd and unreasonable, and which carries along with it its own conviction of falsehood, as this does, *that those are gods which are made with hands,* if it have but human laws, and worldly interest and prescription, on its side. [3.] He reminds them of the danger which their trade was in of going to decay. Whatever touches this touches them in a sensible tender part: "If this doctrine gains credit, we are all undone, and may even shut up shop; *this our craft will be set at nought,* will be convicted, and put into an ill name as superstition, and a cheat upon the world, and every body will run it down. *This our part*" (so the word is), "our interest or share of trade and commerce," κινδυνεύει ἡμῖν τὸ μέρος, "will not only come into danger of being lost, but it will bring us into danger, and we shall become not only beggars, but malefactors." [4.] He pretends a mighty zeal for Diana, and a jealousy for her honour: *Not only this our craft is in danger;* if that were all, he would not have you think that he would have spoken with so much warmth, but all his care is lest *the temple of the great goddess Diana should be despised, and her magnificence should be destroyed;* and he would not, for all the world, see the diminution of the honour of that goddess, *whom all Asia and the world worship.* See what the worship of Diana had to plead for itself, and what was the utmost which the most zealous bigots for it had to say in its behalf. *First,* That it had pomp on its side; the magnificence of the temple was the thing that charmed them, the thing that chained them; they could not bear the thoughts of any thing that tended to the diminution, much less to the destruction, of that. *Secondly,* That it had numbers on its side; *All Asia and the world worship* it; and therefore it must needs be the right way of worship, let Paul say what he will to the contrary. Thus, because *all the world wonders after the beast,* therefore *the dragon, the devil, the god of this world, gives him his power, and his seat, and great authority,* Rev. xiii. 2, 3.

2. The popular resentment of this complaint. The charge was managed by a craftsman, and was framed to incense the common people, and it had the desired effect; for on this occasion they showed, (1.) A great displeasure against the gospel and the preachers of it: *They were full of wrath* (*v.* 28), *full of fury and indignation,* so the word signifies. The craftsmen went stark mad when they were told that their trade and their idol were both in danger. (2.) A great jealousy for the honour of their goddess: *They cried out, "Great is Diana of the Ephesians;* and we are resolved to stand by her, and live and die in the defence of her. Are there any that expose her to contempt, or threaten her destruction? Let us alone to deal with them. Let Paul say ever so much to prove that those are no gods which are made with hands, we will abide by it that, whatever becomes of other gods and goddesses, *Great is Diana of the Ephesians.* We must and will stand up for the religion of our country, which we have received by tradition from our fathers." Thus all people *walked every one in the name of his god,* and all thought well of their own; much more should the servants of the true God do so, who can say, *This God is our God for ever and ever.* (3.) A great disorder among themselves (*v.* 29): *The whole city was full of confusion*—the common and natural effect of an intemperate zeal for a false religion; it throws all into confusion, dethrones reason, and enthrones passion; and men run together, not only not knowing one another's minds, but not knowing their own.

3. The proceedings of the mob under the power of these resentments, and how far they were carried.

(1.) They laid hands on some of Paul's companions, and hurried them into the theatre (*v.* 29), some think with design there to make them *fight with beasts,* as Paul had sometimes done; or perhaps they intended only to abuse them, and to make them a spectacle to the crowd. Those whom they seized were *Gaius and Aristarchus,* of both of whom we read elsewhere. *Gaius was of Derbe, ch.* xx. 4. *Aristarchus* is also there spoken of, and Col. iv. 10. They came with Paul *from Macedonia,* and this was their only crime, that they were Paul's companions in travel, both in services and sufferings.

(2.) *Paul,* who had escaped being seized by them, when he perceived his friends in distress for his sake, *would have entered in unto the people,* to sacrifice himself, if there were no other remedy, rather than his friends should suffer upon his account; and it was an evidence of a generous spirit, and that he loved his neighbour as himself.

(3.) He was persuaded from it by the kindness of his friends, who overruled him. [1.] *The disciples suffered him not,* for it better became him to offer it than it would have become them to suffer it. They had reason to say to Paul, as David's servants did to him, when he was for exposing himself in a piece of public service, *Thou art worth ten thousand of us,* 2 Sam. xviii. 3. [2.] Others of his friends interposed, to prevent his throwing himself thus into the mouth of danger. They would treat him much worse than Gaius and Aristarchus, looking upon him as the ringleader of the party; and therefore better let them bear the brunt of the storm than that he should venture into it, *v.* 31. They were *certain of the chief of Asia, the princes of Asia*—Ἀσιαρχαὶ. The critics tell us they were the chief of their priests; or, as others, the chief of their players. Whether they were converts to the Christian faith (and some such there were even of their priests and governors), or whether they were only well-wishers to Paul, as an ingenuous good man, we are not told, only that they were *Paul's friends.* Dr. Lightfoot suggests that they kept up a respect and kindness for him ever since he fought with beasts in their theatre, and were afraid he should be abused so again. Note, It is a friendly part to take more care of the lives and comforts of good men than they do themselves. It would be a very hazardous adventure for Paul to go into the theatre; it was a thousand to one that it would cost him his life; and therefore Paul was overruled by his friends to obey the law of self-preservation, and has taught us to keep out of the way of danger as long as we can without going out of the way of duty. We may be called to lay down our lives, but not to throw away our lives. It would better become Paul to venture into a synagogue than into a theatre.

(4.) The mob was in a perfect confusion (*v.* 32): *Some cried one thing and some another,* according as their fancies and passions, and perhaps the reports they received, led them. Some cried, Down with the Jews; others, Down with Paul; but *the assembly was confused,* as not understanding one another's minds. They contradicted one another, and were ready to fly in one another's faces for it, but they did not understand their own; for the truth was *the greater part knew not wherefore they had come together.* They knew not what began the riot, nor who, much less what business they had there; but, upon such occasions, the greatest part come only to enquire what the matter is: they follow the cry, follow the crowd, increase like a snow-ball, and where there are many there will be more.

(5.) The Jews would have interested themselves in this tumult (in other places they had been the first movers of such riots) but now at Ephesus they had not interest enough to raise the mob, and yet, when it was raised, they had ill-will enough to set in with it (*v.* 33): *They drew Alexander out of the multitude,* called him out to speak on the behalf of the Jews against Paul and his companions: "You have heard what Demetrius and the silversmiths have to say against them, as enemies to their religion; give us leave now to tell you what we have to say against him as an enemy to our religion. " *The Jews put him forward* to do this, encouraged him, and told him they would stand by him and second him; and this they looked upon as necessary in their own defence, and therefore what he designed to say is called his apologizing to the people, not for himself in particular, but for the Jews in general, whom the worshippers of Diana looked upon to be as much their enemies as Paul was. Now they would have them know that they were as much Paul's enemies as they were; and those who are thus careful to distinguish themselves from the servants of Christ now, and are afraid of being taken for them, shall have their doom accordingly in the great day. *Alexander beckoned with the hand,* desiring to be heard against Paul; for it had been strange if a persecution had been carried on against the Christians and there were not Jews at one end or the other of it: if they could not begin the mischief, they would help it forward, and so make themselves partakers of other men's sins. Some think this Alexander had been a Christian, but had apostatized to Judaism, and therefore was drawn out as a proper person to accuse Paul; and that he was that *Alexander the coppersmith* that did Paul so much evil (2 Tim. iv. 14), and whom he had *delivered unto Satan.* 1 Tim. i. 20.

(6.) This occasioned the prosecutors to drop the prosecution of Paul's friends, and to turn it into acclamations in honour of their goddess (*v.* 34): *When they knew that he was a Jew,* and, as such, an enemy to the worship of Diana (for the Jews had now an implacable hatred to idols and idolatry), whatever he had to say for Paul or against him, they were resolved not to hear him, and therefore set the mob a shouting, " *Great is Diana of the Ephesians;* whoever runs her down, be he Jew or Christian, we are resolved to cry her up. *She is Diana of the Ephesians,* our Diana; and it is our honour and happiness to have her temple with us; and she is great, a famous goddess, and universally adored. There are other Dianas, but Diana of the Ephesians is beyond them all, because her temple is more rich and magnificent than any of theirs." This was all the cry for *two hours* together; and it was thought a sufficient confutation of Paul's doctrine, *that those are not gods which are made with hands.* Thus the most sacred truths are often run down with nothing else but noise and clamour and popular fury. It was said of old concerning idolaters that they were *mad upon their idols;* and here is an instance of it. Diana made the Ephesians great, for the town was enriched by the vast concourse of people from all parts to Diana's temple there, and therefore they are concerned by all means possible to keep up her sinking reputation with, *Great is Diana of the Ephesians.*

4. The suppressing and dispersing of these rioters, by the prudence and vigilance of *the town-clerk;* he is called, γραμματεὺς—*the scribe,* or *secretary,* or *recorder;* "the governor of the city," so some; "the register of their games," the Olympic games (so others), whose business it was to preserve the names of the victors and the prizes they won. With much ado he, at length, stilled the noise, so as to be heard, and then made a pacific speech to them, and gave us an instance of that of Solomon, *The words of wise men are heard in quiet more than the cry of him that rules among fools,* as Demetrius did. Eccl. ix. 17.

(1.) He humours them with an acknowledgment that Diana was the celebrated goddess of the Ephesians, *v.* 35. They needed not to be so loud and strenuous in asserting a truth which nobody denied, or could be ignorant of: Every one *knows that the city of the Ephesians is a worshipper of the great goddess Diana;* is νεωκόρος· not only that the inhabitants were worshippers of this goddess, but the city, as a corporation, was, by its charter, entrusted with the worship of Diana, to take care of her temple, and to accommodate those who came thither to do her homage. Ephesus is *the æditua* (they say that is the most proper word), or *the sacrist, of the great goddess Diana.* The city was more the patroness and protectress of Diana than Diana was of the city. Such great care did idolaters take for the keeping up of the worship of gods made with hands, while the worship of the true and living God is neglected, and few nations or cities glory in patronizing and protecting that. The temple of Diana at Ephesus was a very rich and sumptuous structure, but, it should seem, the *image* of Diana in the temple, because they thought it sanctified the temple, was had in greater veneration than the temple, for they persuaded the people that it *fell down from Jupiter,* and therefore was none of the gods that were made with men's hands. See how easily the credulity of superstitious people is imposed upon by the fraud of designing men. Because this image of Diana had been set up time out of mind, and nobody could tell who made it, they made the people believe it fell down from Jupiter. "Now *these things,*" says the town-clerk very gravely (but whether seriously or no, and as one that did himself believe them, may be questioned), "*cannot be spoken against;* they have obtained such universal credit that you need not fear contradiction, it can do you no prejudice." Some take it thus: "Seeing the image of Diana fell down from Jupiter, as we all believe, then what is said against gods made with hands does not at all affect us."

(2.) He cautions them against all violent and tumultuous proceedings, which their religion did not need, nor could receive any real advantage from (*v.* 36): *You ought to be quiet, and to do nothing rashly.* A very good rule this is to be observed at all times, both in private and public affairs; not to be hasty and precipitate in our motions, but to deliberate and take time to consider: not to put ourselves or others into a heat, but to be calm and composed, and always keep reason in the throne and passion under check. This word should be ready to us, to command the peace with, when we ourselves or those about us are growing disorderly: *We ought to be quiet, and to do nothing rashly;* to do nothing in haste, which we may repent of at leisure.

(3.) He wipes off the odium that had been cast upon Paul and his associates, and tells them, they were not the men that they were represented to them to be (*v.* 37): "*You have brought hither these men,* and are ready to pull them to pieces; but have you considered what is their transgression and what is their offence? What can you prove upon them? They are not robbers of churches, you cannot charge them with sacrilege, or the taking away of any dedicated thing. They have offered no violence to Diana's temple or the treasures of it; nor are they *blasphemers of your goddess;* they have not given any opprobrious language to the worshippers of Diana, nor spoken scurrilously of her or her temple. Why should you prosecute those *with all this violence* who, though they are not of your mind, yet do not inveigh with any bitterness against you? Since they are calm, why should you be hot?" It was the idol in the heart that they levelled all their force against, by reason and argument; if they can but get that down, the idol in the temple will fall of course. Those that preach against idolatrous churches have truth on their side, and ought vigorously to maintain it and press it on men's consciences; but let them not be robbers of those churches (*on the prey laid they not their hand,* Est. ix. 15, 16), nor blasphemers of those worships; with meekness instructing, not with passion and foul language reproaching, those that oppose themselves; for God's truth, as it needs not man's lie, so it needs not man's intemperate heat. *The wrath of man worketh not the righteousness of God.*

(4.) He turns them over to the regular methods of the law, which ought always to supersede popular tumults, and in civilized well-governed nations will do so. A great mercy it is to live in a country where provision is made for the keeping of the peace, and the administration of public justice, and the appointing of a remedy for every wrong; and herein we of this nation are as happy as any people. [1.] If the complaint be of a private injury, let them have recourse to the judges and courts of justice, which are kept publicly at stated times. If Demetrius and the company of the silversmiths, that have made all this rout, find themselves aggrieved, or any privilege they are legally entitled to infringed or entrenched upon, let them bring their action, take out a process, and the matter shall be fairly tried, and justice done: *The law is open, and there are deputies;* there is a proconsul and his delegate, whose business it is to hear both sides, and to determine according to equity; and in their determination all parties must acquiesce, and not be their own judges, nor appeal to the people. Note, *The law is good if a man use it lawfully,* as the last remedy both for the discovery of a right disputed and the recovery of a right denied. [2.] If the complaint be of a public grievance, relating to the constitution, it must be redressed, not by a confused rabble, but by a convention of the states (*v.* 39): *If you enquire any thing concerning other matters,* that are of common concern, *it shall be determined in a lawful assembly* of the aldermen and common-council, called together in a regular way by those in authority. Note, Private persons should not intermeddle in public matters, so as to anticipate the counsels of those whose business it is to take cognizance of them; we have enough to do to mind our own business.

(5.) He makes them sensible of the danger they are in, and of the premunire they have run themselves into by this riot (*v.* 40): "It is well if we be not *called in question for this day's uproar,* if we be not complained of at the emperor's court, as a factious and seditious city, and if a *quo warranto* be not brought against us and our charter taken away; for *there is no cause whereby we may give an account of this concourse,* we have nothing to say in excuse of it. We cannot justify ourselves in breaking the peace by saying that others broke it first, and we only acted defensively; we have no colour for any such plea, and therefore let the matter go no further, for it has gone too far already." Note, Most people stand in awe of men's judgment more than of the judgment of God. How well were it if we would thus still the tumult of our disorderly appetites and passions, and check the violence of them, with the consideration of the account we must shortly give to the Judge of heaven and earth for all these disorders! *We are in danger to be called in question for this day's uproar* in our hearts, in our houses; and how shall we answer it, there being no cause, no just cause, or no proportionable one, whereby we may give an account of this concourse, and of this heat and violence? As we must repress the inordinacy of our appetites, so also of our passions, with this, that *for all these things God will bring us into judgment* (Eccl. xi. 9), and we are concerned to manage ourselves *as those that must give account.*

(6.) When he has thus shown them the absurdity of their riotous meeting, and the bad consequences that might follow from it, he advises them to separate with all speed (*v.* 41): he *dismissed the assembly,* ordered the crier perhaps to give notice that all manner of persons should peaceably depart and go about their own business, and they did so. See here, [1.] How the overruling providence of God preserves the public peace, by an unaccountable power over the spirits of men. Thus the world is kept in some order, and men are restrained from being as the fishes of the sea, where the greater devour the less. Considering what an impetuous furious thing, what an ungovernable untameable wild beast the mob is, when it is up, we shall see reason to acknowledge God's goodness that we are not always under the tyranny of it. *He stills the noise of the sea, the noise of her waves, and* (which is no less an instance of his almighty power) *the tumult of the people,* Ps. lxv. 7. [2.] See how many ways God has of protecting his people. Perhaps this town-clerk was no friend at all to Paul, nor to the gospel he preached, yet his human prudence is made to serve the divine purpose. *Many are the troubles of the righteous, but the Lord delivereth them out of them all.*

CHAP. XX.

In this chapter we have, I. Paul's travels up and down about Macedonia, Greece, and Asia, and his coming at length to Troas, ver. 1—6. II. A particular account of his spending one Lord's-day at Troas, and his raising Eutychus to life there, ver. 7—12. III. His progress, or circuit, for the visiting of the churches he had planted, in his way towards Jerusalem, where he designed to be by the next feast of pentecost, ver. 13—16. IV. The farewell sermon he preached to the presbyters at Ephesus, now that he was leaving that country, 17—35. V. The very sorrowful parting between him and them, ver. 36—38. And in all these we find Paul very busy to serve Christ, and to do good to the souls of men, not only in the conversion of heathens, but in the edification of Christians.

AND after the uproar was ceased,
Paul called unto *him* the disciples, and embraced *them,* and departed for to go into Macedonia. 2
And when he had gone over those
parts, and had given them much exhortation, he came into Greece, 3
And *there* abode three months. And
when the Jews laid wait for him, as
he was about to sail into Syria, he
purposed to return through Macedonia. 4 And there accompanied
him into Asia Sopater of Berea; and
of the Thessalonians, Aristarchus and
Secundus; and Gaius of Derbe, and
Timotheus; and of Asia, Tychicus
and Trophymus. 5 These going before tarried for us at Troas. 6 And
we sailed away from Philippi after
the days of unleavened bread, and
came unto them to Troas in five
days; where we abode seven days.

These travels of Paul which are thus briefly related, if all in them had been recorded that was memorable and worthy to be written in letters of gold, *the world would not contain the books that would have been* written; and therefore we have only some general hints of occurrences, which therefore ought to be the more precious. Here is,

I. Paul's departure from Ephesus. He had tarried there longer than he had done at any one place since he had been ordained to the apostleship of the Gentiles; and now it was time to think of removing, for he must *preach in other cities also;* but after this, to the end of the scripture-history of his life (which is all we can depend upon), we never find him breaking up fresh ground again, nor preaching *the gospel where Christ had not been named,* as hitherto he had done (Rom. xv. 20), for in the close of the next chapter we find him made a prisoner, and so continued, and so left, at the end of this book. 1. Paul left Ephesus soon after the uproar had ceased, looking upon the disturbance he met with there to be an indication of Providence to him not to stay there any longer, *v.* 1. His removal might somewhat appease the rage of his adversaries, and gain better quarter for the Christians there. *Currenti cede furori—It is good to lie by in a storm.* Yet some think that before he now left Ephesus he wrote *the first epistle to the Corinthians,* and that his *fighting with beasts at Ephesus,* which he mentions in that epistle, was a figurative description of this uproar; but I rather take that literally. 2. He did not leave them abruptly and in a fright, but took leave of them solemnly: *He called unto him the disciples,* the principal persons of the congregation, *and embraced them, took leave of them* (saith the Syriac) *with the kiss of love,* according to the usage of the primitive church. Loving friends know not how well they love one another till they come to part, and then it appears how near they lay to one another's hearts.

II. His visitation of the Greek churches, which he had planted, and more than once watered, and which appear to have laid very near his heart. 1. He went first *to Macedonia* (*v.* 1), according to his purpose before the uproar (*ch.* xix. 21); there he visited the churches of Philippi and Thessalonica, and *gave them much exhortation, v.* 2. Paul's visits to his friends were preaching visits, and his preaching was large and copious: *He gave them much exhortation;* he had a great deal to say to them, and did not stint himself in time; he exhorted them to many duties, in many cases, and (as some read it) *with many reasonings.* He enforced his exhortation with a great variety of motives and arguments. 2. He staid *three months in Greece* (*v.* 2, 3), that is, *in Achaia,* as some think, for thither also he purposed to go, to Corinth, and thereabouts (*ch.* xix. 21), and, no doubt, there also he gave the disciples much exhortation, to direct and confirm them, and engage them to cleave to the Lord.

III. The altering of his measures; for we cannot always stand to our purposes. Accidents unforeseen put us upon new counsels, which oblige us to purpose with a proviso. 1. *Paul was about to sail into Syria, to Antioch,* whence he was first sent out into the service of the Gentiles, and which therefore in his journeys he generally contrived to take in his way; but he changed his mind, and resolved *to return to Macedonia,* the same way he came. 2. The reason was because the Jews, expecting he would steer that course as usual, had way-laid him, designing to be the death of him; since they could not get him out of the way by stirring up both mobs and magistrates against him, which they had often attempted, they contrived to assassinate him. Some think they *laid wait for him,* to rob him of the money that he was carrying to Jerusalem for the relief of the poor saints there; but, considering how very spiteful the Jews were against him, I suppose they thirsted for his blood more than for his money.

IV. His companions in his travels when he went into Asia; they are here named, *v.* 4. Some of them were ministers, whether they were all so or no is not certain. *Sopater of Berea,* it is likely, is the same with *Sosipater,* who is mentioned Rom. xvi. 21. *Timothy* is reckoned among them, for though Paul, when he departed from Ephesus (*v.* 1), left Timothy there, and afterwards wrote his first epistle to him thither, to direct him as an evangelist how to settle the church there, and in what hands to leave it (see 1 Tim. i. 3; iii. 14, 15), which epistle was intended for direction to Timothy what to do, not only at Ephesus where he now was, but also at other places where he should be in like manner left, or whither he should be sent to reside as an evangelist (and not to him only, but to the other evangelists that attended Paul, and were in like manner employed); yet he soon followed him, and accompanied him, with others here named. Now, one would think, this was no good husbandry, to have all these worthy men accompanying Paul, for there was more need of them where Paul was not than where he was; but so it was ordered, 1. That they might assist him in instructing such as by his preaching were awakened and startled; wherever Paul came, the waters were stirred, and then there was need of many hands to help the cripples in. It was time to strike when the iron was hot. 2. That they might be trained up by him, and fitted for future service, *might fully know his doctrine and manner of life,* 2 Tim. iii. 10. Paul's bodily presence was weak and despicable, and therefore these friends of his accompanied him, to put a reputation upon him, to keep him in countenance, and to intimate to strangers, who would be apt to judge by the sight of the eye, that he had a great deal in him truly valuable, which was not discovered upon the outward appearance.

V. His coming to Troas, where he had appointed a general rendezvous of his friends. 1. They went before, and staid for him at Troas (*v.* 5), designing to go along with him to Jerusalem, as Trophimus particularly did, *ch.* xxi. 29. We should not think it hard to stay awhile for good company in a journey. 2. Paul made the best of his way thither; and, it should seem, Luke was now in company with him; for he says, *We sailed from Philippi* (*v.* 6), and the first time we find him in his company was here at Troas, *ch.* xvi. 11. *The days of unleavened bread* are mentioned only to describe the time, not to intimate that Paul kept the passover after the manner of the Jews; for just about this time he had written in his first epistle to the church at Corinth, and taught, that Christ is our Passover, and a Christian life our feast of unleavened bread (1 Cor. v. 7, 8), and when the substance was come the shadow was done away. He *came to them to Troas,* by sea, *in five days,* and when he was there staid but *seven days.* There is no remedy, but a great deal of time will unavoidably be lost in travelling to and fro, by those who go about doing good, yet it shall not be put upon the score of lost time. Paul thought it worth while to bestow *five days* in going to Troas, though it was but for an opportunity 'of *seven days*' stay there; but he knew, and so should we, how to redeem even journeying time, and make it turn to some good account.

7 And upon the first *day* of the
week, when the disciples came together to break bread, Paul preached
unto them, ready to depart on the
morrow; and continued his speech
until midnight. 8 And there were
many lights in the upper chamber,
where they were gathered together.
9 And there sat in a window a
certain young man named Eutychus,
being fallen into a deep sleep: and
as Paul was long preaching, he sunk
down with sleep, and fell down from
the third loft, and was taken up dead.
10 And Paul went down, and fell on
him, and embracing *him* said, Trouble
not yourselves; for his life is in him.
11 When he therefore was come up
again, and had broken bread, and
eaten, and talked a long while, even
till break of day, so he departed. 12
And they brought the young man
alive, and were not a little comforted.

We have here an account of what passed at Troas the last of the seven days that Paul staid there.

I. There was a solemn religious assembly of the Christians that were there, according to their constant custom, and the custom of all the churches. 1. *The disciples came together, v.* 7. Though they read, and meditated, and prayed, and sung psalms, apart, and thereby kept up their communion with God, yet that was not enough; they must come together to worship God in concert, and so keep up their communion with one another, by mutual countenance and assistance, and testify their spiritual communion with all good Christians. There ought to be stated times for the disciples of Christ to come together; though they cannot all come together in one place, yet as many as can. 2. They *came together upon the first day of the week,* which they called *the Lord's day* (Rev. i. 10), the Christian sabbath, celebrated to the honour of Christ and the Holy Spirit, in remembrance of the resurrection of Christ, and the pouring out of the Spirit, both on the first day of the week. This is here said to be the day when the disciples came together, that is, when it was their practice to come together in all the churches. Note, The first day of the week is to be religiously observed by all the disciples of Christ; and it is a sign between Christ and them, for by this it is known that they are his disciples; and it is to be observed in solemn assemblies, which are, as it were, the courts held in the name of our Lord Jesus, and to his honour, by his ministers, the stewards of his courts, to which all that hold from and under him owe suit and service, and at which they are to make their appearance, as tenants at their Lord's courts, and the first day of the week is appointed to be the court-day. 3. *They were gathered together in an upper chamber* (*v.* 8); they had no temple nor synagogue to meet in, no capacious stately chapel, but met in a private house, in a garret. As they were few, and did not need, so they were poor, and could not build, a large meeting-place; yet they came together, in that despicable inconvenient place. It will be no excuse for our absenting ourselves from religious assemblies that the place of them is not so decent nor so commodious as we would have it to be. 4. They *came together to break bread,* that is, to celebrate the ordinance of the Lord's supper, that one instituted sign of breaking the bread being put for all the rest. *The bread which we break is the communion of the body of Christ,* 1 Cor. x. 16. In the breaking of the bread, not only the breaking of Christ's body for us, to be a sacrifice for our sins, is commemorated, but the breaking of Christ's body to us, to be food and a feast for our souls, is signified. In the primitive times it was the custom of many churches to receive the Lord's supper every Lord's day, celebrating the memorial of Christ's death in the former, with that of his resurrection in the latter; and both in concert, in a solemn assembly, to testify their joint concurrence in the same faith and worship.

II. In this assembly Paul gave them a sermon, a long sermon, a farewell sermon, *v.* 7. 1. He gave them a sermon: he *preached to them.* Though they were disciples already, yet it was very necessary they should have the word of God preached to them, in order to their increase in knowledge and grace. Observe, The preaching of the gospel ought to accompany the sacraments. *Moses read the book of the covenant in the audience of the people, and then sprinkled the blood of the covenant, which the Lord had made with them concerning all these words,* Exod. xxiv. 7, 8. What does the seal signify without a writing? 2. It was a farewell sermon, he being *ready to depart on the morrow.* When he was gone, they might have the same gospel preached, but not as he preached it; and therefore they must make the best use of him that they could while they had him. Farewell sermons are usually in a particular manner affecting both to the preacher and to the hearers. 3. It was a very long sermon: He *continued his speech until midnight;* for he had a great deal to say, and knew not that ever he should have another opportunity of preaching to them. After they had received the Lord's supper, he preached to them the duties they had thereby engaged themselves to, and the comforts they were interested in, and in this he was very large and full and particular. There may be occasion for ministers to preach, not only *in season, but out of season.* We know some that would have reproached Paul for this as a long-winded preacher, that tired his hearers; but they were willing to hear: he saw them so, and therefore continued his speech. He *continued it till midnight;* perhaps they met in the evening for privacy, or in conformity to the example of the disciples who came together on the first Christian sabbath in the evening. It is probable he had preached to them in the morning, and yet thus lengthened out his evening sermon even till midnight; we wish we had the heads of this long sermon, but we may suppose it was for substance the same with his epistles. The meeting being continued till midnight, there were candles set up, *many lights* (*v.* 8), that the hearers might turn to the scriptures Paul quoted, and see *whether these things were so;* and that this might prevent the reproach of their enemies, who said they met in the night for works of darkness.

III. *A young man* in the congregation, that slept at sermon, was killed by a fall *out of the window, but raised to life again;* his name signifies *one that had good fortune—Eutychus, bene fortunatus;* and he answered his name. Observe,

1. The infirmity with which he was overtaken. It is probable his parents brought him, though but a boy, to the assembly, out of a desire to have him well instructed in the things of God by such a preacher as Paul. Parents should bring their children to hear sermons as soon as they can hear with understanding (Neh. viii. 2), even *the little ones,* Deut. xxix. 11. Now this youth was to be blamed, (1.) That he presumptuously *sat in the window,* unglazed perhaps, and so exposed himself; whereas, if he could have been content to sit on the floor, he had been safe. Boys that love to climb, or otherwise endanger themselves, to the grief of their parents, consider not how much it is also an offence to God. (2.) That he slept, nay, he *fell into a deep sleep when Paul was preaching,* which was a sign he did not duly attend to the things that Paul spoke of, though they were weighty things. The particular notice taken of his sleeping makes us willing to hope none of the rest slept, though it was sleeping time and after supper; but this youth fell fast asleep, he was *carried away with it* (so the word is), which intimates that he strove against it, but was overpowered by it, and at last sunk down with sleep.

2. The calamity with which he was seized herein: *He fell down from the third loft, and was taken up dead.* Some think that the hand of Satan was in it, by the divine permission, and that he designed it for a disturbance to this assembly and a reproach to Paul and it. Others think that God designed it for a warning to all people to take heed of sleeping when they are hearing the word preached; and certainly we are to make this use of it. We must look upon it as an evil thing, as a bad sign of our low esteem of the word of God, and a great hindrance to our profiting by it. We must be afraid of it, do what we can to prevent our being sleepy, not compose ourselves to sleep, but get our hearts affected with the word we hear to such a degree as may drive sleep far enough. Let us *watch and pray, that we enter not into this temptation,* and by it into worse. Let the punishment of Eutychus strike an awe upon us, and show us how jealous God is in the matters of his worship: *Be not deceived, God is not mocked.* See how severely God visited an iniquity that seemed little, and but in a youth, and say, *Who is able to stand before this holy Lord God?* Apply to this story that lamentation (Jer. ix. 20, 21), *Hear the word of the Lord, for death is come up into our windows, to cut off the children from without and the young men from the streets.*

3. The miraculous mercy shown him in his recovery *to life again, v.* 10. It gave a present distraction to the assembly, and an interruption to Paul's preaching; but it proved an occasion of that which was a great confirmation to his preaching, and helped to set it home and make it effectual. (1.) *Paul fell on the dead body, and embraced it,* thereby expressing a great compassion to, and an affectionate concern for, this young man, so far was he from saying, "He was well enough served for minding so little what I said!" Such tender spirits as Paul had are much affected with sad accidents of this kind, and are far from judging and censuring those that fall under them, as if those on whom *the tower of Siloam fell were sinners above all that dwelt at Jerusalem; I tell you, nay.* But this was not all; his falling on him and embracing him were in imitation of Elijah (1 Kings xvii. 21), and Elisha (2 Kings iv. 34), in order to the raising of him to life again; not that this could as a means contribute any thing to it, but as a sign it represented the descent of that divine power upon the dead body, for the putting of life into it again, which at the same time he inwardly, earnestly, and in faith prayed for. (2.) He assured them that he had returned to life, and it would appear presently. Various speculations, we may suppose, this ill accident had occasioned in the congregation, but Paul puts an end to them all: "*Trouble not yourselves,* be not in any disorder about it, let it not put you into any hurry, *for his life is in him;* he is not dead, but sleepeth:

lay him awhile upon a bed, and he will come to himself, for he is now alive." Thus, when Christ raised Lazarus, he said, *Father, I thank thee that thou hast heard me.* (3.) He returned to his work immediately after this interruption (*v.* 11): *He came up again* to the meeting, they broke bread together in a love-feast, which usually attended the eucharist, in token of their communion with each other, and for the confirmation of friendship among them; and *they talked a long while, even till break of day.* Paul did not now go on in a continued discourse, as before, but he and his friends fell into a free conversation, the subject of which, no doubt, was good, and to the use of edifying. Christian conference is an excellent means of promoting holiness, comfort, and Christian love. They knew not when they should have Paul's company again, and therefore made the best use they could of it when they had it, and reckoned a night's sleep well lost for that purpose. (4.) Before they parted *they brought the young man alive* into the congregation, every one congratulating him upon his return to life from the dead, and *they were not a little comforted, v.* 12. It was matter of great rejoicing among them, not only to the relations of the young man, but to the whole society, as it not only prevented the reproach that would otherwise have been cast upon them, but contributed very much to the credit of the gospel.

13 And we went before to ship, and sailed unto Assos, there intending to take in Paul: for so had he appointed, minding himself to go afoot.
14 And when he met with us at Assos, we took him in, and came to Mitylene.
15 And we sailed thence, and came the next *day* over against Chios; and the next *day* we arrived at Samos, and tarried at Trogyllium; and the next *day* we came to Miletus.
16 For Paul had determined to sail by Ephesus, because he would not spend the time in Asia: for he hasted, if it were possible for him, to be at Jerusalem the day of Pentecost.

Paul is hastening towards Jerusalem, but strives to do all the good he can by the way, ὡς ἐν παρόδῳ, "as it were by the by." He had called at Troas, and done good there; and now he makes a sort of coasting voyage, the merchants would call it a trading voyage, going from place to place, and no doubt endeavouring to make every place he came to the better for him, as every good man should do.

I. He sent his companions by sea to Assos, but he himself was *minded to go afoot, v.* 13. He had decreed or determined within himself that whatever importunity should be used with him to the contrary, urging either his ease or his credit, or the conveniency of a ship that offered itself, or the company of his friends, he would foot it to Assos: and, if the land-way which Paul took was the shorter way, yet it is taken notice of by the ancients as a rough way (Homer, Iliad 6, and Eustathius upon him, say, it was enough to *kill one* to go *on foot* to Assos.—*Lorin. in locum);* yet that way Paul would take, 1. That he might call on his friends by the way, and do good among them, either converting sinners or edifying saints; and in both he was serving his great Master, and carrying on his great work. Or, 2. That he might be alone, and might have the greater freedom of converse with God and his own heart in solitude. He loved his companions, and delighted in their company, yet he would show hereby that he did not need it, but could enjoy himself alone. Or, 3. That he might inure himself to hardship, and not seem to indulge his ease. Thus he would by voluntary instances of mortification and self-denial *keep under the body, and bring it into subjection,* that he might make his sufferings for Christ, when he was called out to them, the more easy, 2 Tim. ii. 3. We should use ourselves to deny ourselves.

II. At Assos he went on board with his friends. There they *took him in;* for by this time he had enough of his walk, and was willing to betake himself to the other way of travelling; or perhaps he could not go any further by land, but was obliged to go by water. When Christ sent his disciples away by ship, and tarried behind himself, yet he came to them, and they took him in, Mark vi. 45, 51.

III. He made the best of his way to Jerusalem. His ship passed by *Chios* (*v.* 15), touched at *Samos* (these are places of note among the Greek writers, both poets and historians); they tarried awhile at *Trogyllium,* the sea-port next to Samos; *and the next day* they came *to Miletus,* the sea-port that lay next to Ephesus; for (*v.* 16) he had determined not to go to Ephesus at this time, because he could not go thither without being urged by his friends, whose importunity he could not resist, to make some stay with them there; and, because he was resolved not to stay, he would not put himself into a temptation to stay; *for he hasted, if it were possible for him, to be at Jerusalem on the day of pentecost.* He had been at Jerusalem about four or five years ago (*ch.* xviii. 21, 22), and now he was going thither again to pay his continued respects to that church, with which he was careful to keep a good correspondence, that he might not be thought alienated from it by his commission to preach among the Gentiles. He aimed to be there by the feast of pentecost because it was a time of concourse, which would give him an opportunity of propagating the gospel among the Jews and proselytes, who came from all parts to worship at the feast: and the feast of pentecost had been particularly made famous among the Christians by the pouring out of the Spirit. Note, Men of business must fit themselves, and it will contribute to the expediting of it, to set time (with submission to Providence) and strive to keep it, contriving to do that first which we judge to be most needful, and not suffering ourselves to be diverted from it. It is a pleasure to us to be with our friends; it diverts us, nothing more; but we must not by it be diverted from our work. When Paul has a call to Jerusalem, he will not loiter away the time in Asia, though he had more and kinder friends there. This is not the world we are to be together in; we hope to be so in the other world.

17 And from Miletus he sent to
Ephesus, and called the elders of the
church. 18 And when they were
come to him, he said unto them, Ye
know, from the first day that I came
into Asia, after what manner I have
been with you at all seasons, 19
Serving the Lord with all humility of
mind, and with many tears, and
temptations, which befel me by the
lying in wait of the Jews: 20 *And*
how I kept back nothing that was
profitable *unto you*, but have showed
you, and have taught you publicly,
and from house to house, 21 Testifying both to the Jews, and also to
the Greeks, repentance toward God,
and faith toward our Lord Jesus
Christ. 22 And now, behold, I go
bound in the spirit unto Jerusalem,
not knowing the things that shall befal me there: 23 Save that the
Holy Ghost witnesseth in every city,
saying that bonds and afflictions abide
me. 24 But none of these things
move me, neither count I my life
dear unto myself, so that I might
finish my course with joy, and the
ministry, which I have received of
the Lord Jesus, to testify the gospel
of the grace of God. 25 And now,
behold, I know that ye all, among
whom I have gone preaching the
kingdom of God, shall see my face
no more. 26 Wherefore I take you
to record this day, that I *am* pure
from the blood of all *men*. 27 For I
have not shunned to declare unto you
all the counsel of God. 28 Take
heed therefore unto yourselves, and
to all the flock, over the which the
Holy Ghost hath made you overseers,
to feed the church of God, which he
hath purchased with his own blood.
29 For I know this, that after my
departing shall grievous wolves enter
in among you, not sparing the flock.
30 Also of your own selves shall men
arise, speaking perverse things, to
draw away disciples after them. 31
Therefore watch, and remember, that
by the space of three years I ceased
not to warn every one night and day
with tears. 32 And now, brethren,
I commend you to God, and to the
word of his grace, which is able to
build you up, and to give you an inheritance among all them which are
sanctified. 33 I have coveted no
man's silver, or gold, or apparel. 34
Yea, ye yourselves know, that these
hands have ministered unto my necessities, and to them that were with
me. 35 I have showed you all things,
how that so labouring ye ought to
support the weak, and to remember
the words of the Lord Jesus, how he
said, It is more blessed to give than
to receive.

It should seem the ship Paul and his companions were embarked in for Jerusalem attended him on purpose, and staid or moved as he pleased; for when he came to Miletus, he went ashore, and tarried there so long as to send for the elders of Ephesus to come to him thither; for if he had gone up to Ephesus, he could never have got away from them. These elders, or presbyters, some think, were those twelve who received the Holy Ghost by Paul's hands, *ch.* xix. 6. But, besides these, it is probable that Timothy had ordained other elders there for the service of that church, and the country about; these Paul sent for, that he might instruct and encourage them to go on in the work to which they had laid their hands. And what instructions he gave to them they would give to the people under their charge.

It is a very pathetic and practical discourse with which Paul here takes leave of these elders, and has in it much of the excellent spirit of this good man.

I. He appeals to them concerning both his life and doctrine, all the time he had been in and about Ephesus (*v.* 18): "*You know after what manner I have been with you,* and how I have done the work of an apostle among you." He mentions this as a confirmation of his commission and consequently of the doctrine he had preached among them. They all knew him to be a man of a serious, gracious, heavenly spirit, that he was no designing self-seeking man, as seducers are; he could not have been carried on with so much evenness and constancy in his services and sufferings, but by the power of divine grace. The temper of his mind, and the tenour both of his preaching and conversation, were such as plainly proved that God was with him of a truth, and that he was actuated and animated by a better spirit than his own.—He likewise makes this reference to his own conduct as an instruction to them, in whose hands the work was now left, to follow his example: "*You know after what manner I have been with you,* how I have conducted myself as a minister; in like manner be you with those that are committed to your charge when I am gone (Phil. iv.9), *what you have seen in me* that is good *do.*"

1. His spirit and conversation were excellent and exemplary; they knew after what manner he had been among them, and how he had had his conversation towards them, in simplicity and godly sincerity (2 Cor. i. 12), how holily, justly, and unblamably he behaved himself, and how gentle he was towards them, 1 Thess. ii. 7, 10. (1.) He had conducted himself well all along, *from the very first day that he came into Asia*—at all seasons; the manner of his entering in among them was such as nobody could find fault with. He appeared from the first day they knew him to be a man that aimed not only to do well, but to do good, wherever he came. He was a man that was consistent with himself, and all of a piece; take him where you would he was the same at all seasons, he did not turn with the wind nor change with the weather, but was uniform like a die, which, throw it which way you will, lights on a square side. (2.) He had made it his business to serve the Lord, to promote the honour of God and the interest of Christ and his kingdom among them. He never served himself, nor made himself a servant of men, of their lusts and humours, nor was he a time-server; but he made it his business to serve the Lord. In his ministry, in his whole conversation, he proved himself what he wrote himself, Paul *a servant of Jesus Christ,* Rom. i. 1. (3.) He had done his work *with all humility of mind—μετὰ πάσης ταπεινοφροσύνης,* that is, in all works of condescension, modesty, and self-abasement. Though he was one that God had put a great deal of honour upon, and done a great deal of good by, yet he never took state upon him, nor kept people at a distance, but conversed as freely and familiarly with the meanest, for their good, as if he had stood upon a level with them. He was willing to stoop to any service, and to make himself and his labours as cheap as they could desire. Note, Those that would in any office serve the Lord acceptably to him, and profitably to others, must do it with all humility of mind, Matt. xx. 26, 27. (4.) He had always been very tender, affectionate, and compassionate, among them; he had *served the Lord with many tears.* Paul was herein like his Master; often in tears; in his praying, he *wept and made supplication,* Hos. xii. 5. In his preaching, what he had told them before he told them again, *even weeping,* Phil. iii. 18. In his concern for them, though his acquaintance with them was but of a late standing, yet so near did they lie to his heart that he *wept with those that wept,* and mingled his tears with theirs upon every occasion, which was very endearing. (5.) He had struggled with many difficulties among them. He went on in his work in the face of much opposition, *many temptations,* trials of his patience and courage, such discouragements as perhaps were sometimes *temptations* to him, as to Jeremiah in a like case to say, *I will not speak any more in the name of the Lord,* Jer. xx. 8, 9. These befel him *by the lying in wait of the Jews,* who still were plotting some mischief or other against him. Note, Those are the faithful servants of the Lord that continue to serve him in the midst of troubles and perils, that care not what enemies they make, so that they can but approve themselves to their Master, and make him their friend. Paul's tears were owing to his temptations; his afflictions helped to excite his good affections.

2. His preaching was likewise such as it should be, *v.* 20, 21. He came to Ephesus to preach the gospel of Christ among them, and he had been faithful both to them and to him that appointed him. (1.) He was a plain preacher, and one that delivered his message so as to be understood. This is intimated in two words, *I have shown you, and have taught you.* He did not amuse them with nice speculations, nor lead them into, and then lose them in, the clouds of lofty notions and expressions; but he showed them the plain truths of the gospel, which were of the greatest consequence and importance, and taught them as children are taught. "I have shown you the right way to happiness, and taught you to go in it." (2.) He was a powerful preacher, which is intimated in his *testifying* to them; he preached as one upon oath, that was himself fully assured of the truth of what he preached and was desirous to convince them of it and to influence and govern them by it. He preached the gospel, not as a hawker proclaims news in the street (it is all one to him whether it be true or false), but as a conscientious witness gives in his evidence at the bar, with the utmost seriousness and concern. Paul preached the gospel as a testimony to them if they received it, but as a testimony against them if they rejected it. (3.) He was a profitable preacher, one that in all his preaching aimed at doing good to those he preached to; he studied that which was *profitable unto them,* which had a tendency to make them wise and good, wiser and better, to inform their

judgments and reform their hearts and lives. He preached τὰ συμφέροντα, such things as *brought with them* divine light, and heat, and power to their souls. It is not enough not to preach that which is hurtful, which leads into error or hardens in sin, but we must preach that which is profitable. *We do all things, dearly beloved, for your edifying.* Paul aimed to preach not that which was pleasing, but that which was profitable, and to please only in order to profit. God is said to teach his people to profit, Isa. xlviii. 17. Those teach for God that teach people to profit. (4.) He was a painstaking preacher, very industrious and indefatigable in his work; he preached *publicly, and from house to house.* He did not confine himself to a corner when he had opportunity of preaching in the great congregation; nor did he confine himself to the congregation when there was occasion for private and personal instruction. He was neither afraid nor ashamed to preach the gospel publicly, nor did he grudge to bestow his pains privately, among a few, when there was occasion for it. He preached publicly to the flock that came together into the green pastures, and went from house to house to seek those that were weak and had wandered, and did not think that the one would excuse him from the other. Ministers should in their private visits, and as they go from house to house, discourse of those things which they have taught publicly, repeat them, inculcate them, and explain them, if it be needful, asking, *Have you understood all these things?* And, especially, they should help persons to apply the truth to themselves and their own case. (5.) He was a faithful preacher. He not only preached that which was profitable, but he preached every thing that he thought might be profitable, and kept back nothing, though the preaching of it might either cost him more pains or be disobliging to some and expose him to their ill-will. He declined not preaching whatever he thought might be profitable, though it was not fashionable, nor to some acceptable. He did not keep back reproofs, when they were necessary and would be profitable, for fear of offending; nor did he keep back the preaching of the cross, though he knew it was to the Jews a stumbling-block and to the Greeks foolishness, as the Roman missionaries in China lately did. (6.) He was a catholic preacher. He *testified both to the Jews and also to the Greeks.* Though he was born and bred a Jew, and had an entire affection for that nation, and was trained up in their prejudices against the Gentiles, yet he did not therefore confine himself to the Jews and avoid the Gentiles; but preached as readily to them as to the Jews, and conversed as freely with them. And, on the other hand, though he was called to be the apostle of the Gentiles, and the Jews had an implacable enmity against him upon that score, had done him many an ill turn, and here at Ephesus were continually plotting against him, yet he did not therefore abandon them as reprobates, but continued to deal with them for their good. Ministers must preach the gospel with impartiality; for they are ministers of Christ for the universal church. (7.) He was a truly Christian evangelical preacher. He did not preach philosophical notions, or matters of doubtful disputation, nor did he preach politics, or intermeddle at all with affairs of state or the civil government; but he preached faith and repentance, the two great gospel graces, the nature and necessity of them; these he urged upon all occasions. [1.] *Repentance towards God;* that those who by sin had gone away from God, and were going further and further from him into a state of endless separation from him, should by true repentance look towards God, turn towards him, move towards him, and hasten to him. He preached repentance as God's great command (*ch.* xvii. 30), which we must obey—*that men should repent, and turn to God, and do works meet for repentance* (so he explains it, *ch.* xxvi. 20); and he preached it as Christ's gift, in order to the *remission of sins* (*ch.* v. 31), and directed people to look up to him for it. [2.] *Faith towards our Lord Jesus Christ.* We must by repentance look towards God as our end; and by faith towards Christ as our way to God. Sin must by repentance be abandoned and forsaken, and then Christ must by faith be relied on for the pardon of sin. Our repentance towards God is not sufficient, we must have a true faith in Christ as our Redeemer and Saviour, consenting to him as our Lord and our God. For there is no coming to God, as penitent prodigals to a Father, but in the strength and righteousness of Jesus Christ as Mediator.

Such a preacher as this they all knew Paul had been; and, if they will carry on the same work, they must walk in the same spirit, in the same steps.

II. He declares his expectation of sufferings and afflictions in his present journey to Jerusalem, *v.* 22—24. Let them not think that he quitted Asia now for fear of persecution; no, he was so far from running away like a coward from the post of danger that he was now like a hero hastening to the high places of the field, where the battle was likely to be hottest: *Now, behold, I go bound in the spirit to Jerusalem,* which may be understood either, (1.) Of the certain foresight he had of trouble before him. Though he was not yet bound in body, he was bound in spirit; he was in full expectation of trouble, and made it his daily business to prepare for it. He was bound in spirit, as all good Christians are poor in spirit, endeavouring to accommodate themselves to the will of God if they should be reduced to poverty. Or, (2.) Of the strong impulse he was under from the Spirit of God working upon his spirit to go this journey: "*I go bound in the spirit,* that is, firmly resolved to proceed, and well assured that it is by a divine direction and influence that I am so, and not from any humour or design of my own. I go led by the Spirit, and bound to follow him wherever he leads me."

1. He does not know particularly the things that shall befal him at Jerusalem. Whence the trouble shall spring, what shall be the occasion of it, what the circumstances and to what degree it shall arise, God had not thought fit to reveal to him. It is good for us to be kept in the dark concerning future events, that we may be always waiting on God and waiting for him. When we go abroad, it should be with this thought, we know not the things that shall befal us, nor what a day, or a night, or an hour, may bring forth; and therefore must refer ourselves to God, let him do with us as seemeth good in his eyes, and study to stand complete in his whole will.

2. Yet he does know in general that there is a storm before him; for the prophets in every city he passed through told him, by the Holy Ghost, that bonds and afflictions awaited him. Besides the common notice given to all Christians and ministers to expect and prepare for sufferings, Paul had particular intimations of an extraordinary trouble, greater and longer than any he had yet met with, that was now before him.

3. He fixes a brave and heroic resolution to go on with his work, notwithstanding. It was a melancholy peal that was rung in his ears in every city, that *bonds and afflictions did abide him;* it was a hard case for a poor man to labour continually to do good, and to be so ill treated for his pains. Now it is worth while to enquire how he bore it. He was flesh and blood as well as other men; he was so, and yet by the grace of God he was enabled to go on with his work, and to look with a gracious and generous contempt upon all the difficulties and discouragements he met with in it. Let us take it from his own mouth here (*v.* 24), where he speaks not with obstinacy nor ostentation, but with a holy humble resolution: "*None of these things move me;* all my care is to proceed and to persevere in the way of my duty, and to finish well." Paul is here an example,

(1.) Of holy courage and resolution in our work, notwithstanding the difficulties and oppositions we meet with in it; he saw them before him, but he made nothing of them: *None of these things move me; οὐδενὸς λόγον ποιοῦμαι—I make no account of them.* He did not lay these things to heart, Christ and heaven lay there. None of these things moved him. [1.] They did not drive him off from his work; he did not tack about, and go back again, when he saw the storm rise, but went on resolutely, preaching there, where he knew how dearly it would cost him. [2.] They did not deprive him of his comfort, nor make him drive on heavily in his work. In the midst of troubles he was as one unconcerned. In his patience he possessed his soul, and, when he was as sorrowful, yet he was always rejoicing, and in all things more than a conqueror. Those that have their conversation in heaven can look down, not only upon the common troubles of this earth but upon the threatening rage and malice of hell itself, and say that none of these things moved them, as knowing that none of these things can hurt them.

(2.) Of a holy contempt of life, and the continuance and comforts of it: *Neither count I my life dear to myself.* Life is sweet, and is naturally dear to us. *All that a man has will he give for his life;* but all that a man has, and life too, will he give who understands himself aright and his own interest, rather than lose the favour of God and hazard eternal life. Paul was of this mind. Though to an eye of nature life is superlatively valuable, yet to an eye of faith it is comparatively despicable; it is not so dear but it can be cheerfully parted with for Christ. This explains Luke xiv. 26, where we are required to hate our own lives, not in a hasty passion, as Job and Jeremiah, but in a holy submission to the will of God, and a resolution to die for Christ rather than to deny him.

(3.) Of a holy concern to go through with the work of life, which should be much more our care than to secure either the outward comforts of it or the countenance of it. Blessed Paul counts not his life dear in comparison with this, and resolves in the strength of Christ, *non propter vitam vivendi perdere causas—that he never will, to save his life, lose the ends of living.* He is willing to spend his life in labour, to hazard his life in dangerous services, to waste it in toilsome services; nay, to lay down his life in martyrdom, so that he may but answer the great intentions of his birth, of his baptism, and of his ordination to the apostleship. Two things this great and good man is in care about, and if he gain them it is no matter to him what becomes of life:—[1.] That he may be found faithful to the trust reposed in him, that he may *finish the ministry which he has received of the Lord Jesus,* may do the work which he was sent into the world about, or, rather, which he was sent into the church about,—that he may complete the service of his generation, may make full proof of his ministry,—that he may go through the business of it, and others may reap the advantage of it, to the utmost of what was designed,—that he may, as is said of the two witnesses, *finish his testimony* (Rev. xi. 7), and may not do his work by halves. Observe, *First,* The apostleship was a ministry both to Christ and to the souls of men; and those that were called to it considered more the ministry of it than the dignity or dominion of it; and, if the apostles did so, much more ought the pastors and teachers to do so, and to be in the church as those that serve. *Secondly,* This ministry was *received from the Lord Jesus.* He entrusted them with it, and from him they received their charge; for him they do their work, in his name, in his strength; and to him they must give up their account. It was Christ that put them into the ministry (1 Tim. i. 12); it is he that carries them on in their ministry, and from him they have strength to do their service and bear up under the hardships of it. *Thirdly,* The work of this ministry was to *testify the gospel of the grace of God,* to publish it to the world, to prove it, and to recommend it; and, being the gospel of the grace of God, it has enough in it to recommend itself. It is a proof of God's good-will to us, and a means of his good work in us; it shows him gracious towards us, and tends to make us gracious, and so is the gospel of the grace of God. Paul made it the business of his life to testify this, and desired not to live a day longer than he might be instrumental to spread the knowledge and savour and power of this gospel. [2.] That he may finish well. He cares not when the period of his life comes, nor how, be it ever so soon, ever so sudden, ever so sad, as to outward circumstances, so that he may but *finish his course with joy. First,* He looks upon his life as *a course, a race,* so the word is. Our life is *a race set before us,* Heb. xii. 1. This intimates that we have our labours appointed us, for we were not sent into the world to be idle; and our limits appointed us, for we were not sent into the world to be here always, but to pass through the world, nay, to run through it, and it is soon run through; I may add, to *run the gauntlet* through it. *Secondly,* He counts upon the finishing of his course, and speaks of it as sure and near, and that which he had his thoughts continually upon. Dying is the end of our race, when we come off either with honour or shame. *Thirdly,* He is full of care to finish it well, which implies a holy desire of obtaining and a holy fear of coming short. "Oh! that I may but finish my course with joy; and then all will be well, perfectly and eternally well." *Fourthly,* He thinks nothing too much to do, nor too hard to suffer, so that he may but finish well, finish with joy. We must look upon it as the business of our life to provide for a joyful death, that we may not only die safely, but die comfortably.

III. Counting upon it that this was the last time they should see him, he appeals to their consciences concerning his integrity, and demands of them a testimony to it.

1. He tells them that he was now taking his last leave of them (*v.* 25): *I know that you all, among whom I have* been conversant *preaching the kingdom of God,* though you may have letters from me, shall never see my face again. When any of us part with our friends, we may say, and should say, "We know not that ever we shall see one another again: our friends may be removed, or we ourselves may." But Paul here speaks it with assurance, by the Spirit of prophecy, that these Ephesians should *see his face no more;* and we cannot think that he who spoke so doubtfully of that which he was not sure of (*not knowing the things that shall befal me there, v.* 22) would speak this with so much confidence, especially when he foresaw what a trouble it would be to his friends here, unless he had had a special warrant from the Spirit to say it, to whom I think those do wrong who suppose that, notwithstanding this, Paul did afterwards come to Ephesus, and see them again. He would never have said thus solemnly, *Now, behold, I know it,* if he had not known it *for certain.* Not but that he foresaw that he had a great deal of time and work yet before him, but he foresaw that his work would be cut out for him in other places, and in these parts he had no more to do. Here he had for a great while gone about preaching the kingdom of God, preaching down the kingdom of sin and Satan, and preaching up the authority and dominion of God in Christ, preaching the kingdom of glory as the end and the kingdom of grace as the way. Many a time they had been glad to see his face in the pulpit, and saw it *as it had been the face of an angel.* If the feet of these messengers of peace were beautiful upon the mountains, what were their faces? But now they shall see his face no more. Note, We ought often to think of it, that those who now are preaching to us the kingdom of God will shortly be removed and we shall see their faces no more: *the prophets, do they live for ever?* Yet a little while is their light with us; it concerns us therefore to improve it while we have it, that when we shall see their faces no more on earth, yet we may hope to look them in the face with comfort in the great day.

2. He appeals to them concerning the faithful discharge of his ministry among them (*v.* 26): "*Wherefore,* seeing my ministry is at an end with you, it concerns both you and me to reflect, and look back;" and, (1.) He challenges them to prove him unfaithful, or to have said or done any thing by which he had made himself accessory to the ruin of any precious soul: *I am pure from the blood of all men,* the blood of souls. This plainly refers to that of the prophet (Ezek. xxxiii. 6), where the blood of him that perishes by the sword of the enemy is said to be required at the hand of the unfaithful watchman that did not give warning: "You cannot say but I have given warning, and therefore no man's blood can be laid at my door." If a minister has approved himself faithful, he may have this rejoicing in himself, *I am pure from the blood of all men,* and ought to have this testimony from others. (2.) He therefore leaves the blood of those that perish upon their own heads, because they had fair warning given them, but they would not take

it. (3.) He charges these ministers to look to it that they took care and pains, as he had done: "*I am pure from the blood of all men,* see that you keep yourselves so too. *I take you to record this day*"—ἐν τῇ σήμερον ἡμέρα, "I call this day to witness to you:" so Streso. As sometimes the heaven and earth are appealed to, so here this day shall be a witness, this parting day.

3. He proves his own fidelity with this (*v.* 27): *For I have not shunned to declare unto you all the counsel of God.* (1.) He had preached to them nothing but the counsel of God, and had not added any inventions of his own; "it was pure gospel, and nothing else, the will of God concerning your salvation." The gospel is the counsel of God; it is admirably contrived by his wisdom, it is unalterably determined by his will, and it is kindly designed by his grace for our glory, 1 Cor. ii. 7. This counsel of God it is the business of ministers to declare as it is revealed, and not otherwise nor any further. (2.) He had preached to them the whole counsel of God. As he had preached to them the gospel pure, so he had preached it to them entire; he had gone over a body of divinity among them, that, having the truths of the gospel opened to them methodically from first to last in order, they might the better understand them, by seeing them in their several connections with, and dependences upon, one another. (3.) He had not shunned to do it; had not wilfully nor designedly avoided the declaring of any part of the counsel of God. He had not, to save his own pains, declined preaching upon the most difficult parts of the gospel, nor, to save his own credit, declined preaching upon the most plain and easy parts of it; he had not shunned preaching those doctrines which he knew would be provoking to the watchful enemies of Christianity, or displeasing to the careless professors of it, but faithfully took his work before him, whether they would hear or forbear. And thus it was that he kept himself pure from the blood of all men.

IV. He charges them as ministers to be diligent and faithful in their work.

1. He commits the care of the church at Ephesus, that is, the saints, the Christians that were there and thereabouts (Eph. i. 1), to them, who, though doubtless they were so numerous that they could not all meet in one place, but worshipped God in several congregations, under the conduct of several ministers, are yet called here *one flock,* because they not only agreed in one faith, as they did with all Christian churches, but in many instances they kept up communion one with another. To these elders or presbyters the apostle here, upon the actual foresight of his own final leaving them, commits the government of this church, and tells them that not he, but *the Holy Ghost, had made them overseers,* ἐπισκόπους—*bishops of the flock.* "You that are presbyters are bishops of the Holy Ghost's making, that are to take the oversight of this part of the church of God," 1 Pet. v. 1, 2; Tit. i. 5, 7. While Paul was present at Ephesus, he presided in all the affairs of that church, which made the elders loth to part with him; but now this eagle *stirs up the nest, flutters over her young;* now that they begin to be fledged they must learn to fly themselves, and to act without him, for the Holy Ghost had made them overseers. They took not this honour to themselves, nor was it conferred upon them by any prince or potentate, but the Holy Ghost in them qualified them for, and enriched them to, this great undertaking, the *Holy Ghost fell upon them, ch.* xix. 6. The Holy Ghost also directed those that chose, and called, and ordained, them to this work in answer to prayer.

2. He commanded them to mind the work to which they were called. Dignity calls for duty; if the Holy Ghost has made them *overseers of the flock,* that is, shepherds, they must be true to their trust. (1.) They must take heed to themselves in the first place, must have a very jealous eye upon all the motions of their own souls, and upon all they said and did, must walk circumspectly, and know how to behave themselves aright in the house of God, in which they were now advanced to the office of stewards: "You have many eyes upon you, some to take example by you, others to pick quarrels with you, and therefore you ought to *take heed to yourselves.*" Those are not likely to be skilful or faithful keepers of the vineyards of others that do not keep their own. (2.) "*Take heed to the flock,* to all the flock, some to one part of it, others to another, according as your call and opportunity are, but see that no part of it be neglected among you." Ministers must not only take heed to their own souls, but must have a constant regard to the souls of those who are under their charge, as shepherds have to their sheep, that they may receive no damage: "*Take heed to all the flock,* that none of them either of themselves wander from the fold or be seized by the beasts of prey; that none of them be missing, or miscarry, through your neglect." (3.) They must feed the church of God, must do all the parts of the shepherd's office, must lead the sheep of Christ into the green pastures, must lay meat before them, must do what they can to heal those that are distempered and have no appetite to their meat, must feed them with wholesome doctrine, with a tender evangelical discipline, and must see that nothing is wanting that is necessary in order to their being nourished up to eternal life. There is need of pastors, not only to gather the church of God by the bringing in of those that are without, but to *feed* it by building up those that are within. (4.) They must watch (*v.* 31), as shepherds keep watch over their flocks by night, must be awake and watchful, must not give way to spiritual sloth and slumber, but must stir up them-

selves to their business and closely attend it. *Watch thou in all things* (2 Tim. iv. 5), watch against every thing that will be hurtful to the flock, and watch to every thing that will be advantageous to it; improve every opportunity of doing it a kindness.

3. He gives them several good reasons why they should mind the business of their ministry.

(1.) Let them consider the interest of their Master, and his concern for the flock that was committed to their charge, *v.* 28. It is *the church which he has purchased with his own blood.* [1.] "It is his own; you are but his servants to take care of it for him. It is your honour that you are employed for God, who will own you in his service; but then your carelessness and treachery are so much the worse if you neglect your work, for you wrong God and are false to him. From him you received the trust, and to him you must give up your account, and therefore *take heed to yourselves.* And, if it be the church of God, he expects you should show your love to him by feeding his sheep and lambs." [2.] He has purchased it. The world is God's by right of creation, but the church is his by right of redemption, and therefore it ought to be dear to us, for it was dear to him, because it cost him dear, and we cannot better show it than by feeding his sheep and his lambs. [3.] This church of God is what he has purchased; not as Israel of old, when he *gave men for them, and people for their life* (Isa. xliii. 3, 4), but *with his own blood.* This proves that Christ is God, for he is called so here, where yet he is said to purchase the church *with his own blood;* the blood was his as man, yet so close is the union between the divine and human nature that it is here called the blood of God, for it was the blood of him who is God, and his being so put such dignity and worth into it as made it both a valuable ransom of us from evil, and a valuable purchase for us of all good, nay, a purchase of us to Christ, to be to him a peculiar people: *Thine they were, and thou gavest them to me.* In consideration of this, therefore, *feed the church of God,* because it is purchased at so dear a rate. Did Christ lay down his life to purchase it, and shall his ministers be wanting in any care and pains to feed it? Their neglect of its true interest is a contempt of his blood that purchased it.

(2.) Let them consider the danger that the flock was in of being made a prey to its adversaries, *v.* 29, 30. "If the flock be thus precious upon the account of its relation to God, and its redemption by Christ, then you are concerned to take heed both to yourselves and to it." Here are reasons for both. [1.] *Take heed to the flock,* for wolves are abroad, that seek to devour (*v.* 29): *I know this, that after my departure grievous wolves shall enter in among you. First,* Some understand it of persecutors, that will inform against the Christians, and incense the magistrates against them, and will have no compassion on the flock. They thought, because, while Paul was with them, the rage of the Jews was most against him, that, when he had gone out of the country, they would be quiet: "No," says he, "*after my departure* you will find the persecuting spirit still working, therefore take heed to the flock, confirm them in the faith, comfort and encourage them, that they may not either leave Christ for fear of suffering or lose their peace and comfort in their sufferings." Ministers must take a more than ordinary care of the flock in times of persecution. *Secondly,* It is rather to be understood of seducers and false teachers. Probably Paul has an eye to those of the circumcision, who preached up the ceremonial law; these he calls *grievous wolves,* for though they came in sheep's clothing, nay, in shepherds' clothing, they made mischief in the congregations of Christians, sowed discord among them, drew away many from the pure gospel of Christ, and did all they could to blemish and defame those that adhered to it; not sparing the most valuable members of the flock, stirring up those whom they could influence to bite and devour them (Gal. v. 15); therefore they are called dogs (Phil. iii. 2), as here wolves. While Paul was at Ephesus, they kept away, for they durst not face him; but, when he was gone, then they entered in among them, and sowed their tares where he had sown the good seed. "Therefore take heed to the flock, and do all you can to establish them in the truth, and to arm them against the insinuations of the false teachers." [2.] *Take heed to yourselves,* for some shepherds will apostatise (*v.* 30): "*Also of your ownselves,* among the members, nay, perhaps, among the ministers of your own church, among you that I am now speaking to (though I am willing to hope it does not go so far as that), *shall men arise speaking perverse things,* things contrary to the right rule of the gospel, and destructive of the great intentions of it. Nay, they will pervert some sayings of the gospel, and wrest them to make them patronize their errors, 2 Pet. iii. 16. Even those that were well thought of among you, and that you had confidence in, will grow proud, and conceited, and opinionative, and will refine upon the gospel, and will pretend with more nice and curious speculations to advance you to a higher form; but it is to *draw away disciples after them,* to make a party for themselves, that shall admire them, and be led by them, and pin their faith upon their sleeve." Some read it, *to draw away disciples after them*—those that are already disciples of Christ, draw them from him to follow them. "Therefore, take heed to yourselves; when you are told that some of you shall betray the gospel, you are each of you concerned to ask, *Is it I?* and to look well to yourselves. This was there fulfilled in *Phygellus and Hermogenes,* who turned away from Paul and the doctrine he had preached (2 Tim. i. 15), and in *Hymeneus and Philetus,* who *concerning the truth erred, and overthrew the faith of some* (2 Tim. ii. 18), which explains the expression here. But, though there were some such seducers in the church of Ephesus, yet it should seem by Paul's Epistle to that church (wherein we do not find such complaints and reprehensions as we meet with in some other of his epistles) that that church was not so much infested with false teachers, at least not so much infected with their false doctrine, as some other churches were; but its peace and purity were preserved by the blessing of God on the pains and vigilance of these presbyters, to whom the apostle, in the actual foresight and consideration of the rise of heresies and schisms, as well as of his own death, committed the government of this church.

(3.) Let them consider the great pains that Paul had taken in planting this church (*v.* 31): "*Remember that for the space of three years*" (for so long he had been preaching in Ephesus, and the parts adjacent) "*I ceased not to warn every one night and day with tears;* and be not you negligent in building upon that foundation which I was so diligent to lay." [1.] Paul, like a faithful watchman, had warned them, and, by the warnings he gave men of the danger of their continuing in their Judaism and heathenism, he prevailed with them to embrace Christianity. [2.] He warned every one; besides the public warnings he gave in his preaching, he applied himself to particular persons according as he saw their case called for it, which he had something to say peculiar to. [3.] He was constant in giving warning; he *warned night and day;* his time was filled up with his work. In the night, when he should have been reposing himself, he was dealing with those he could not get to speak with in the day about their souls. [4.] He was indefatigable in it; he *ceased not* to warn. Though they were ever so obstinate against his warnings, yet he did not cease to warn, not knowing but that at length they might, by the grace of God, be overcome; though they were ever so pliable to his warnings, yet he did not think this would be a sufficient excuse for him to desist, but still he warned those that were righteous not to turn from their righteousness, as he had warned them when they were wicked to turn from their wickedness, Ezek. iii. 18—21. [5.] He spoke to them about their souls with a great deal of affection and concern: he *warned them with tears.* As he had served the Lord, so he had served them, *with many tears, v.* 19. He warned them with tears of compassion, thereby showing how much he was himself affected with their misery and danger in a sinful state and way, that he might affect them with it. Thus Paul had begun the good work at Ephesus, thus free had he been of his pains; and why then should they be sparing of their pains in carrying it on?

V. He recommends them to divine direction and influence (*v.* 32): "*And now, brethren,* having given you this solemn charge and caution, *I commend you to God.* Now that I have said what I have to say, The Lord be with you; I must leave you, but I leave you in good hands." They were in care what would become of them, how they should go on in their work, break through their difficulties, and what provision would be made for them and their families. In answer to all these perplexities, Paul directs them to look up to God with an eye of faith, and beseeches God to look down on them with an eye of favour.

1. See here to whom he commends them. He calls them brethren, not only as Christians, but as ministers, and thereby encourages them to hope in God, as he had done; for they and he were brethren. (1.) He commends them to God, begs of God to provide for them, to take care of them, and to supply all their needs, and encourages them to cast all their care upon him, with an assurance that he cared for them: "Whatever you want, go to God, let your eye be ever towards him, and your dependence upon him, in all your straits and difficulties; and let this be your comfort, that you have a God to go to, a God all sufficient." *I commend you to God,* that is, to his providence, and to the protection and care of that. It is enough that, from whomsoever we are separated, still we have God nigh unto us, 1 Pet. iv. 19. (2.) He commends them *to the word of his grace,* by which some understand Christ: he is *the word* (John i. 1), *the word of life,* because life is treasured up for us in him (1 John i. 1), and in the same sense he is here called *the word of God's grace,* because *from his fulness we receive grace for grace.* He commends them to Christ, puts them into his hand, as being his servants, whom he would in a particular manner take care of. Paul commends them not only to God and to his providence, but to Christ and his grace, as Christ himself did his disciples when he was leaving them: *You believe in God, believe also in me.* It comes to much the same thing, if by the word of his grace we understand the gospel of Christ, for it is Christ in the word that is nigh unto us for our support and encouragement, and his word is spirit and life: "You will find much relief by acting faith on the providence of God, but much more by acting faith on the promises of the gospel." He commends them to the word of Christ's grace, which he spoke to his disciples when he sent them forth, the commission he gave them, with assurance that he would be with them *always to the end of the world:* "Take hold of that word, and God give you the benefit and comfort of it, and you need no more." He commends them to the word of God's grace, not only as the foundation of their hope and the fountain of their joy, but as the rule of their walking:

"*I commend you to God,* as your Master, whom you are to serve, and I have found him a good Master, *and to the word of his grace,* as cutting you out your work, and by which you are to govern yourselves; observe the precepts of this word, and then live upon the promises of it."

2. See here what he commends them to the word of God's grace for, not so much for a protection from their enemies, or a provision for their families, as for the spiritual blessings which they most needed and ought most to value. They had received the gospel of the grace of God, and were entrusted to preach it. Now he recommends them to that, (1.) For their edification: "*It is able* (the Spirit of grace working with it and by it) *to build you up,* and you may depend upon this, while you keep close to it, and are deriving daily from it. Though you are already furnished with good gifts, yet this is able to build you up; there is that in it with which you need to be better acquainted and more affected." Note, Ministers, in preaching the word of grace, must aim at their own edification as well as at the edification of others. The most advanced Christians, while they are in this world, are capable of growing, and they will find the word of grace to have still more and more in it to contribute to their growth. It is still able to build them up. (2.) For their glorification: *It is able to give you an inheritance among all those who are sanctified.* The word of God's grace gives it, not only as it gives the knowledge of it (for *life and immortality are brought to light by the gospel*), but as it gives the promise of it, the promise of a God *that cannot lie,* and which is *yea and amen in Christ;* and by the word, as the ordinary vehicle, the Spirit of grace is given (*ch.* x. 44), to be the seal of the promise, and the earnest of the eternal life promised; and thus it is the word of God's grace that gives us the inheritance. Note, [1.] Heaven is an inheritance which gives an indefeasible right to all the heirs; it is an inheritance like that of the Israelites in Canaan, which was by promise and yet by lot, but was *sure to all the seed.* [2.] This inheritance is entailed upon and secured to all those, and those only, that are sanctified; for as those cannot be welcome guests to the holy God, or the holy society above, that are unsanctified, so really heaven would be no heaven to them; but *to all that are sanctified,* that are born again, and on whom the image of God is renewed, it is as sure as almighty power and eternal truth can make it. Those therefore that would make out a title to that inheritance must make it sure that they are among the sanctified, are joined to them and incorporated with them, and partake of the same image and nature; for we cannot expect to be among the glorified hereafter unless we be among the sanctified here.

VI. He recommends himself to them as an example of indifference to this world, and to every thing in it, which, if they would walk in the same spirit and in the same steps, they would find to contribute greatly to their easy and comfortable passage through it. He had recommended them to God, and to the word of his grace, for spiritual blessings, which, without doubt, are the best blessings; but what shall they do for food for their families, an agreeable subsistence for themselves, and portions for their children? "As to these," Paul says, "do as I did;" and how was that? He here tells them,

1. That he never aimed at worldly wealth (*v.* 33): "*I have coveted no man's silver, or gold, or apparel;* nor do you, and then you will be easy." There were many in Ephesus, and many of those that had embraced the Christian faith, who were rich, had a great deal of money, and plate, and rich furniture, and wore very good clothes, and made a very good appearance. Now, (1.) Paul was not ambitious to live like them. We may take it in this sense: *I never coveted to have so much silver and gold at command* as I see others have, nor to wear such rich clothes as I see others wear. I neither condemn them nor envy them. I can live comfortably and usefully without living great." The false apostles desired *to make a fair show in the flesh* (Gal. vi. 12), to make a figure in the world; but Paul did not do so. *He knew how to want and how to be abased.* (2.) He was not greedy to receive from them, silver, or gold, or apparel; so far from being always craving that he was not so much as coveting, nor desired them to allow him so and so for his pains among them, but was *content with such things as he had;* he never *made a gain of them,* 2 Cor. xii. 17. He could not only say with Moses (Num. xvi. 15), and with Samuel (1 Sam. xii. 3, 5), *Whose ox have I taken? Or whom have I defrauded?* But, "Whose kindness have I coveted, or asked? Or to whom have I been burdensome?" He protests against desiring a gift, Phil. iv. 17.

2. That he had worked for his living, and taken a great deal of pains to get bread (*v.* 34) "*Yea, you yourselves know,* and have been eye-witnesses of it, *that these hands of mine have ministered to my necessities, and to those that were with me;* you have seen me busy early and late, cutting out tents and making them up;" and, they being commonly made of leather, it was very hard work. Observe, (1.) Paul was sometimes reduced to necessities, and the want of the common supports of life, though he was so great a favourite of Heaven and so great a blessing to this earth. What an unthinking, unkind, and ungrateful world is this, that could let such a man as Paul be poor in it! (2.) He desired no more than to have his necessities supplied; he did not work at his calling to enrich himself, but to maintain himself with food and raiment (3.) When he was to earn his bread, he did it by a manual occupation. Paul had a head

and a tongue that he might have got money by, but they were these hands, saith he, *that ministered to my necessities.* What a pity was it that those hands by the laying on of which the Holy Ghost had been so often conferred, those hands by which God had wrought special miracles, and both these at Ephesus too (*ch.* xix. 6, 11), should there be obliged to lay themselves to the needle and shears, the awl and tacking-end, in tent-making, purely to get bread! Paul puts these presbyters (and others in them) in mind of this, that they may not think it strange if they be thus neglected, and yet to go on in their work, and make the best shift they can to live; the less encouragement they have from men, the more they shall have from God. (4.) He worked not only for himself, but for the support of those also that were with him. This was hard indeed. It had better become them to have worked for him (to maintain him as their tutor) than he for them. But so it is; those that are willing to take the labouring oar will find those about them willing they should have it. If Paul will work for the maintenance of his companions, he is welcome to do it.

3. That even then, when he worked for the supply of his own necessities, yet he spared something out of what he got for the relief of others; for this he here obliges them to do (*v.* 35): "*I have shown you all things,* that is, in all the parts of your duty I have set you your copy and given you a good example, and particularly in this, *that so labouring you ought to support the weak.*" Some understand it of their supporting the faith of weak believers, by removing the prejudices which some conceived against Christianity, as if the preachers of it made a gainful trade of their preaching, and the gospel was only a trick to get money by, and pick people's pockets. "Now, that you may *cut off occasion from those that seek occasion to reproach us,* and so may support the weak among us, you will do well, for the present, to get your livelihood by the labour of your hands, and not to depend upon your ministry." But I rather understand it of their helping to support the sick, and the poor, and those that could not labour, because it agrees with Paul's exhortation (Eph. iv. 28): *Let him labour, working with his hands, that he may have to give to him that needeth.* We must labour in an honest employment, not only that we may be able to live, but that we may be able to give. This might seem a hard saying, and therefore Paul backs it with a saying of our Master's, which he would have them always to remember. These words our Lord Jesus said; it should seem, they were words he often used to his disciples. When he himself did so much good gratis, and bade them do so too (Matt. x. 8, 9), he added this saying, which, though nowhere recorded by the evangelists, yet Paul had by word of mouth from Peter, or some other of the disciples; and an excellent saying it is, and has something of a paradox in it: *It is more blessed to give than to receive.* "It is" (saith Dr. Tillotson) "a particular endearment of this admirable saying of our Saviour's to us, that, being omitted by the evangelists, and in danger of being lost and forgotten, it was thus happily retrieved by St. Paul, and recorded by St. Luke." It is more blessed to give to others than to receive from others; not only more blessed to be rich, and so on the giving hand, than to be poor, and so on the receiving hand (every one will own this); but more blessed to do good with what we have, be it much or little, than to increase it and make it more. The sentiment of the children of this world is contrary to this; they are afraid of giving. "This giving," they say, "undoes us all;" but they are in hope of getting. *Every one for his gain from his quarter,* Isa. lvi. 11. Clear gain is with them the most blessed thing that can be; but Christ tells us, *It is more blessed* (more excellent in itself, an evidence of a more excellent disposition of mind, and the way to a better blessedness at last) *to give than to receive.* It makes us more like to God, who gives to all, and receives from none; and to the Lord Jesus, *who went about doing good.* It is more blessed to give our pains than to receive pay for it, and what we should delight to do if the necessities of ourselves and families would admit it. It is more pleasant to do good to the grateful, but it is more honourable to do good to the ungrateful, for then we have God to be our paymaster, who will reward in the resurrection of the just what has not otherwise been recompensed.

36 And when he had thus spoken,
he kneeled down, and prayed with
them all. 37 And they all wept
sore, and fell on Paul's neck, and
kissed him. 38 Sorrowing most of
all for the words which he spake,
that they should see his face no more.
And they accompanied him unto the
ship.

After the parting sermon that Paul preached to the elders of Ephesus, which was very affecting, we have here the parting prayer and tears, which were yet more affecting; we can scarcely read the account here given of them, and meditate upon them with dry eyes.

I. They parted with prayer (*v.* 36): *And, when he had thus spoken, he kneeled down, and prayed with them all.* And, no doubt, it was a prayer every way suited to the present mournful occasion. He committed them to God in this prayer, prayed that he would not leave them, but continue his presence with them. 1. It was a joint prayer. He not only prayed for them, but prayed with them, *prayed with them all;* that they might put up the same petitions for themselves and one another that he put up to God for them all, and that they might learn what to ask of God for themselves when he was gone. Public prayers are so far from being intended to supersede our own secret prayers, and make them needless, that they are designed to quicken and encourage them, and to direct us in them. When we are alone we should pray over the prayers that our ministers have put up with us. 2. It was a humble reverent prayer. This was expressed by the posture they used: *He kneeled down, and prayed with them,* which is the most proper gesture in prayer, and significant both of adoration and of petition, especially petition for the forgiveness of sin. Paul used it much: *I bow my knees,* Eph. iii. 14. 3. It was a prayer after sermon; and, we may suppose, he prayed over what he had preached. He had committed the care of the church at Ephesus to those elders, and now he prays that God would enable them faithfully to discharge this great trust reposed in them, and would give them those measures of wisdom and grace which it required; he prayed for the flock, and all that belonged to it, *that the great Shepherd of the sheep* would take care of them all, and keep them from being a prey to the grievous wolves. Thus he taught these ministers to pray for those they preached to, *that they might not labour in vain.* 4. It was a parting prayer, which might be likely to leave lasting impressions, as the farewell sermon did. It is good for friends, when they part, to part with prayer, that by praying together just at parting they may be enabled to pray the more feelingly one for another when they are separated, which is one part of our Christian duty, and an improvement of the communion of saints. The Lord watch between us, and watch over us both, when we are absent one from the other, is a good parting prayer (Gen. xxxi. 49), as also that our next meeting may be either nearer heaven or in heaven. Paul here followed the example of Christ, who, when he took leave of his disciples, after he had preached to them, prayed with them all, John xvii. 1.

II. They parted with tears, abundance of tears, and most affectionate embraces, *v.* 37, 38. 1. *They all wept sorely.* We have reason to think that Paul himself began; though he was determined to go, and saw his call clear to other work, yet he was sorry in his heart to leave them, and many a tear it cost him. He that was so often in tears while he was with them (*v.* 19, 31), no doubt shed many at parting, so watering what he had sown among them. But the notice is taken of their tears: *They all wept sorely;* there was not a dry eye among them; and it is probable the affectionate expressions Paul used in prayer set them a weeping. These were tears of love and mutual endearment, like those of Jonathan and David, when they were forced to part, and *wept one with another, until* (as if they wept for strife) *David exceeded,* 1 Sam. xx. 41. 2. *They fell upon Paul's neck, and kissed him,* all, one after another, each bewailing his own loss: "How can I part with this invaluable man, this blessed Paul," says one, "in whom my life is in a manner bound up?"—"Farewell, my dear friend," says another, "a thousand thanks to thee, and ten thousand to God for thee, and for all the pains thou hast taken with me for my good." "And must we part?" says another: "must I lose my spiritual father, nurse, and guide?"—"What will become of us now?" says another, "when we shall no more have him to apply to, and receive direction from? What shall I do, if the Lord take away my master from my head? *My father, my father, the chariots of Israel, and the horsemen thereof.*" Note, Those that are most loving are commonly best beloved. Paul, who was a most affectionate friend himself, had friends that were very affectionate to him. These tears at parting with Paul were a grateful return for all the tears he had shed in preaching to them and praying with them. *He that watereth shall be watered also himself.* 3. That which cut them to the heart thus, and made this place such a *Bochim, such a place of weepers,* was, *that word which Paul spoke, that* he was certain *they should see his face no more.* If he had given them directions to follow him, as he did to those that were his usual companions, or any intimation that he would come hereafter and make them a visit, they could have borne this parting pretty well; but when they are told that they shall see his face no more in this world, that it is a final farewell they are now giving and taking, this makes it a great mourning; it makes the farewell just like a funeral, and puts them into this passion of weeping. There were other things for which they sorrowed—that they should lose the benefit of his public performances, and see him no longer presiding in their assemblies, should have none of his personal counsels and comforts; and, we hope, they sorrowed for their own sin, in not profiting more by his labours while they had him among them, and which had provoked God to order his remove. But that which gave the most sensible accent to their grief was *that they should see his face no more.* When our friends are separated from us by death, this is the consideration with which we raise up our mourning, that we shall see their faces no more; but we complain not of this as those that have no hope, for if our friends died in Christ, and we live to him, they are gone to see God's face, to behold his glory, with the reflection of which their faces shine, and we hope to be with them shortly. Though we shall see their faces no more in this world, we hope to see them again in a better world, and to be there together for ever and with the Lord.

III. They *accompanied him unto the ship,* partly to show their respect for him (they would bring him on his way as far as they could), and partly that they might have a little more of his company and conversation; if it must be the last interview, they will have as much of him as they can, and see the last of him. And we have reason to think that when they came to the water-side, and he was about to go on board, their tears and embraces were repeated; for loth to part bids oft farewell. But this was a comfort to both sides, and soon turned this tide of passion, that the presence of Christ both went with him and staid with them.

CHAP. XXI.

We have, with a great deal of pleasure, attended the apostle in his travels throughout the Gentile nations to preach the gospel, and have seen a great harvest of souls gathered in to Christ; there we have seen likewise what persecutions he endured; yet still out of them all the Lord presently delivered him, 2 Tim. iii. 11. But now we are to attend him to Jerusalem, and there into lasting bonds; the days of his service now seem to be over, and nothing to remain but days of suffering, days of darkness, for they are many. It is a thousand pities that such a workman should be laid aside; yet so it is, and we must not only acquiesce, as his friends then did, saying, "The will of the Lord be done;" but we must believe, and shall find reason to do so, that Paul in the prison, and at the bar, is as truly glorifying God, and serving Christ's interest, as Paul in the pulpit was. In this chapter we have, I. A journal of Paul's voyage from Ephesus to Cæsarea, the next sea-port to Jerusalem, some places he touched at, and his landing there, ver. 1—7. II. The struggles he had with his friends at Cæsarea, who mightily opposed his going up to Jerusalem, but could not prevail, ver. 8—14. III. Paul's journey from Cæsarea to Jerusalem, and the kind entertainment which the Christians there gave him, ver. 15—17. IV. His compliance with the persuasions of the brethren there, who advised him so far to compliment the Jews as to go and purify himself with an offering in the temple, as if he had had a vow, that it might appear he was no such enemy to the Mosaic rites and ceremonies as he was reported to be, ver. 18—26. V. The turning of this very thing against him by the Jews, and the apprehending of him in the temple as a criminal thereupon, ver. 27—30. VI. The narrow escape he had of being pulled to pieces by the rabble, and the taking of him into fair and legal custody by the chief captain, who permitted him to speak for himself to the people, ver. 31—40. And so we have him made a prisoner, and shall never have him otherwise to the end of the history of this book.

AND it came to pass, that after
we were gotten from them,
and had launched, we came with a
straight course unto Coos, and the
day following unto Rhodes, and from
thence unto Patara: 2 And finding
a ship sailing over unto Phenicia, we
went aboard, and set forth. 3 Now
when we had discovered Cyprus, we
left it on the left hand, and sailed
into Syria, and landed at Tyre: for
there the ship was to unlade her
burden. 4 And finding disciples, we
tarried there seven days: who said
to Paul through the Spirit, that he
should not go up to Jerusalem. 5
And when we had accomplished those
days, we departed and went our way;
and they all brought us on our way,
with wives and children, till *we were*
out of the city: and we kneeled
down on the shore, and prayed. 6
And when we had taken our leave
one of another, we took ship; and
they returned home again. 7 And
when we had finished *our* course
from Tyre, we came to Ptolemais,
and saluted the brethren, and abode
with them one day.

We may observe here,

I. How much ado Paul had to get clear from Ephesus, intimated in the first words of the chapter, *after we had gotten from them,* that is, were drawn from them as by violence. It was a force put upon both sides; Paul was loth to leave them, and they were loth to part with him, and yet there was no remedy, but so it must be. When good people are taken away by death, they are, as it were, gotten from their friends here below, who struggled hard to have detained them if possible.

II. What a prosperous voyage they had thence. Without any difficulty, *they came with a straight course,* by direct sailing, *to Coos,* a famous Grecian island,—*the next day to Rhodes,* talked of for the Colossus there,—*thence to Patara,* a famous port, the metropolis of Lycia (*v.* 1); here they very happily *found a ship sailing over into Phenicia,* the very course they were steering, *v.* 2. Providence must be acknowledged when things happen thus opportunely, and we are favoured by some little circumstances that contribute to the expediting of our affairs; and we must say, *It is God that maketh our way perfect.* This ship that was bound for Phenicia (that is, Tyre) they took the convenience of, *went on board, and set sail* for Tyre. In this voyage *they discovered Cyprus,* the island that Barnabas was of, and which he took care of, and therefore Paul did not visit it, but *we left it on the left hand* (*v.* 3), *sailed* upon the coast of *Syria, and* at length *landed at Tyre,* that celebrated mart of the nations, so it had been, but was now reduced; yet something of a trade it had still, *for there the ship was to unlade her burden,* and did so.

III. The halt that Paul made at Tyre; when he had arrived there, he was upon the coast of the land of Israel, and found now that he could compass the remainder of his journey within the time he had fixed.

1. *At Tyre he found disciples,* some that had embraced the gospel, and professed the Christian faith. Observe, Wherever Paul came, he enquired what disciples were there, found them out, and associated with them; for we know what is the usage with birds of a feather. When Christ was upon earth, though he went sometimes into the coast of Tyre, yet he never went thither to preach the gospel there; nor did he think fit to afford to Tyre and Sidon the advantages which Chorazin and Bethsaida had, though he knew that if they had had them they would have made a better improvement of them, Luke x. 13. 14. But, after the enlarging of the gospel-commission, Christ was preached

at Tyre, and had disciples there; and to this, some think, that prophecy concerning Tyre had reference (Isa. xxiii. 18), *Her merchandise and her hire shall be holiness to the Lord.*

2. Paul, *finding those disciples at Tyre, tarried there seven days,* they urging him to stay with them as long as he could. He staid seven days at Troas (*ch.* xx. 6), and here so many days at Tyre, that he might be sure to spend one Lord's day with them, and so might have an opportunity of preaching publicly among them; for it is the desire of good men to do good wherever they come, and where we find disciples we may either benefit them or be benefited by them.

3. The disciples at Tyre were endowed with such gifts that they could by the Spirit foretel the troubles Paul would meet with at Jerusalem; for *the Holy Ghost witnessed it in every city, ch.* xx. 23. Being a thing that would be so much talked of when it came to pass, God saw fit to have it much prophesied of before, that people's faith, instead of being offended, might be confirmed. And withal they were endowed with such graces that foreseeing his troubles, out of love to him and concern for the church, especially the churches of the Gentiles, that could ill spare him,they begged of him *that he would not go up to Jerusalem,* for they hoped the decree was conditional: If he go up, he will come into trouble there; as the prediction to David *that the men of Keilah will deliver him up* (that is, if he *venture himself with them);* and therefore they said to him, *by the Spirit, that he should not go up,* because they concluded it would be most for the glory of God that he should continue at liberty; and it was not at all their fault to think so, and consequently to dissuade him; but it was their mistake, for his trial would be for the glory of God and the furtherance of the gospel, and he knew it; and the importunity that was used with him, to dissuade him from it, renders his pious and truly heroic resolution the more illustrious.

4. The disciples of Tyre, though they were none of Paul's converts, yet showed a very great respect to Paul, whose usefulness in the church they had heard so much of when he departed from Tyre. Though they had had but seven days' acquaintance with him, yet, as if he had been some great man, they all came together, *with their wives and children,* solemnly to take leave of him, to beg his blessing, and to bring him as far on his way as the sea would permit them. Note, (1.) We should pay respect, not only to our own ministers, that are over us in the Lord, and admonish us, and, for their work's sake among us, *esteem them highly in love,* but we must, as there is occasion, testify our love and respect to all the faithful ministers of Christ, both for his sake whose ministers they are, and for their work's sake among others. (2.) We must, in a particular manner, honour those whom God hath singularly honoured, by making them eminently useful in their generation. (3.) It is good to train up children in a respect to good people and good ministers. This was particularly remarkable at Tyre, which we have not met with any where else, that they brought their wives and children to attend Paul, to do him the more honour and to receive benefit by his instructions and prayers; and as angry notice was taken of the children of the idolaters of Bethel, that mocked a prophet, so, no doubt, gracious notice was taken of the children of the disciples at Tyre, that honoured an apostle, as Christ accepted the hosannas of the little children. (4.) We should be good husbands of our opportunities, and make the utmost we can of them for the good of our souls. *They brought Paul on his way,* that they might have so much the more of his company and his prayers. Some refer us to Ps. xlv. 12, as a prediction of this, *The daughter of Tyre shall be there with a gift;* for it is probable that they made some presents to Paul at parting, as usual to our friends that are going to sea, *ch.* xxviii. 10.

5. They parted with prayer, as Paul and the Ephesian elders had done, *ch.* xx. 36. Thus Paul has taught us by example, as well as rule, to pray always, to pray without ceasing. *We kneeled down on the shore and prayed.* Paul prayed for himself, prayed for them, prayed for all the churches; as he was much in prayer so he was mighty in prayer. They prayed upon the shore, that their last farewell might be sanctified and sweetened with prayer. Those that are going to sea should, when they quit the shore, commit themselves to God by prayer, and put themselves under his protection, as those that hope, even when they leave the *terra firma,* to find firm footing for their faith in the providence and promise of God. They kneeled down on the shore, though we may suppose it either stony or dirty, and there prayed. Paul would *that men should pray every where,* and so he did himself; and, where he lifted up his prayer, he bowed his knees. Mr. George Herbert says, *Kneeling never spoiled silk stockings.*

6. They parted at last (*v.* 6): *When we had taken our leave one of another,* with the most affectionate embraces and expressions of love and grief, *we took ship* to be gone, and *they returned home again,* each complaining that this is a parting world. Observe how they disposed of themselves: "We, that had a journey before us, took ship, thankful that we had a ship to carry us; and those, who had no occasions to call them abroad returned home again, thankful that they had a home to go to." *Rejoice Zebulun in thy going out, and Issachar in thy tents.* Paul left his blessing behind him with those that returned home, and those that staid sent their prayers after those that went to sea.

IV. Their arrival at Ptolemais, which was not far from Tyre (*v.* 7): *We came to Ptolemais,* which some think is the same place with

Accho, which we find in the tribe of Asher, Judg. i. 31. Paul begged leave to go ashore there, *to salute the brethren,* to enquire of their state, and to testify his good will to them; though he could not stay long with them, yet he would not pass by them without paying his respects to them, and he *abode with them one day,* perhaps it was a Lord's day; better a short stay than no visit.

8 And the next *day* we that were
of Paul's company departed, and
came into Cæsarea: and we entered
into the house of Philip the evangelist, which was *one* of the seven;
and abode with him. 9 And the
same man had four daughters, virgins,
which did prophesy. 10 And as we
tarried *there* many days, there came
down from Judæa a certain prophet,
named Agabus. 11 And when he
was come unto us, he took Paul's
girdle, and bound his own hands and
feet, and said, Thus saith the Holy
Ghost, So shall the Jews at Jerusalem bind the man that owneth this
girdle, and shall deliver *him* into the
hands of the Gentiles. 12 And
when we heard these things, both
we, and they of that place, besought
him not to go up to Jerusalem. 13
Then Paul answered, What mean ye
to weep and to break mine heart?
for I am ready not to be bound only,
but also to die at Jerusalem for the
name of the Lord Jesus. 14 And
when he would not be persuaded, we
ceased, saying, The will of the Lord
be done.

We have here Paul and his company arrived at length at Cæsarea, where he designed to make some stay, it being the place where the gospel was first preached to the Gentiles, and *the Holy Ghost fell upon them, ch.* x. 1, 44. Now here we are told,

I. Who it was that entertained Paul and his company *at Cæsarea.* He seldom had occasion to go to a public house, but, wherever he came, some friend or other took him in, and bade him welcome. Observe, those that had sailed together parted when the voyage was accomplished, according as their business was. "Those that were concerned in the cargo staid where the ship was *to unlade her burden* (*v.* 3); others, when they came to Ptolemais, went as their occasions led them; but we that were of Paul's company went where he went, and came to Cæsarea." Those that travel together through this world will separate at death, and then it will appear who are of Paul's company and who are not. Now at Cæsarea.

1 They were entertained by Philip the evangelist, whom we left at Cæsarea many years ago, after he had baptized the eunuch (*ch.* viii. 40), and there we now find him again. (1.) He was originally a deacon, one of the seven that were chosen to serve tables, *ch.* vi. 5. (2.) He was now and had long been an evangelist, one that went about to plant and water churches, as the apostles did, and gave himself, as they did, *to the word and prayer;* thus, having *used the office of a deacon well, he purchased to himself a good degree;* and, having been *faithful in a few things, was made ruler over many things.* (3.) He had a house at Cæsarea, fit to entertain Paul and all his company, and he bade him and them very welcome to it: *We entered into the house of Philip the evangelist, and we abode with him.* Thus does it become Christians and ministers, according as their ability is, to *use hospitality one to another, without grudging,* 1 Pet. iv. 9.

2. This Philip *had four maiden daughters, who did prophesy, v.* 9. It intimates that they prophesied of Paul's troubles at Jerusalem, as others had done, and dissuaded him from going; or perhaps they prophesied for his comfort and encouragement, in reference to the difficulties that were before him. Here was a further accomplishment of that prophecy, Joel ii. 28, of such a plentiful pouring out of the Spirit upon all flesh that their *sons and their daughters should prophesy,* that is, foretel things to come.

II. A plain and full prediction of the sufferings of Paul, by a noted prophet, *v.* 10, 11. 1. Paul and his company tarried many days at Cæsarea, perhaps Cornelius was yet living there, and (though Philip lodged them) yet might be many ways kind to them, and induce them to stay there. What cause Paul saw to tarry so long there, and to make so little haste at the latter end of his journey to Jerusalem, when he seemed so much in haste at the beginning of it, we cannot tell; but we are sure he did not stay either there or any where else to be idle; he measured his time by days, and numbered them. 2. *Agabus the prophet came to Cæsarea from Judea;* this was he of whom we read before, who came *from Jerusalem to Antioch,* to foretel a general famine, *ch.* xi. 27, 28. See how God dispenseth his gifts variously. To Paul was given the word of wisdom and knowledge, as an apostle, by the Spirit, and the gifts of healing; to Agabus, and to Philip's daughters, was given prophecy, by the same Spirit—the foretelling of things to come, which came to pass according to the prediction. See 1 Cor. xii. 8, 10. So that that which was the most eminent gift of the Spirit under the Old Testament, the foretelling of things to come, was under the New Testament quite outshone by other gifts, and was bestowed upon those that were of less note in the church. It should seem as if Agabus came on purpose to Cæsarea, to meet Paul with this prophetic intelligence. 3. He foretold Paul's bonds at Jerusalem, (1.) By a sign, as the prophets of old did, Isaiah (*ch.* xx. 3), Jeremiah (*ch.* xiii. 1; xxvii. 2), Ezekiel (*ch.* iv. 1; xii. 3), and many others. *Agabus took Paul's girdle,* when he laid it by, or perhaps took it from about him, and with it *bound* first *his own hands, and then his own feet,* or perhaps bound his hands and feet together; this was designed both to confirm the prophecy (it was as sure to be done as if it were done already) and to affect those about him with it, because that which we see usually makes a greater impression upon us than that which we only hear of. (2.) By an explication of the sign: *Thus saith the Holy Ghost,* the Spirit of prophecy, *So shall the Jews at Jerusalem bind the man that owneth this girdle, and,* as they dealt with his Master (Matt. xx. 18, 19), *shall deliver him into the hands of the Gentiles,* as the Jews in other places had all along endeavoured to do, by accusing him to the Roman governors. Paul had this express warning given him of his troubles, that he might prepare for them, and that when they came they might be no surprise nor terror to him; the general notice given us *that through much tribulation we must enter into the kingdom of God* should be of the same use to us.

III. The great importunity which his friends used with him to dissuade him from going forward to Jerusalem, *v.* 12. "Not only those of that place, but we that were of Paul's company, and among the rest Luke himself, who had heard this often before, and seen Paul's resolution notwithstanding, besought him with tears that he would not go up to Jerusalem, but steer his course some other way." Now, 1. Here appeared a commendable affection to Paul, and a value for him, upon account of his great usefulness in the church. Good men that are very active sometimes need to be dissuaded from overworking themselves, and good men that are very bold need to be dissuaded from exposing themselves too far. *The Lord is for the body,* and so must we be. 2. Yet there was a mixture of infirmity, especially in those of Paul's company, who knew he undertook this journey by divine direction, and had seen with what resolution he had before broken through the like opposition. But we see in them the infirmity incident to us all; when we see trouble at a distance, and have only a general notice of it, we can make light of it; but when it comes near we begin to shrink, and draw back. *Now that it toucheth thee thou art troubled,* Job iv. 5.

IV. The holy bravery and intrepidity with which Paul persisted in his resolution, *v.* 13.

1. He reproves them for dissuading him. Here is a quarrel of love on both sides, and very sincere and strong affections clashing with each other. They love him dearly, and therefore oppose his resolution; he loves them dearly, and therefore chides them for opposing it: *What mean you to weep and to break my heart?* They were an offence to him, as Peter was to Christ, when, in a like case, he said, *Master, spare thyself.* Their weeping about him *broke his heart.* (1.) It was a temptation to him, it shocked him, it began to weaken and slacken his resolution, and caused him to entertain thoughts of tacking about: "I know I am appointed to suffering, and you ought to animate and encourage me, and to say that which will strengthen my heart; but you, with your tears, break my heart, and discourage me. What do you mean by doing thus? Has not our Master told us to take up our cross? And would you have me to avoid mine?" (2.) It was a trouble to him that they should so earnestly press him to that in which he could not gratify them without wronging his conscience. Paul was of a very tender spirit. As he was much in tears himself, so he had a compassionate regard to the tears of his friends; they made a great impression upon him, and would bring him almost to yield to any thing. But now it breaks his heart, when he is under a necessity of denying the request of his weeping friends. It was an unkind kindness, a cruel pity, thus to torment him with their dissuasions, and to add affliction to his grief. When our friends are called out to sufferings, we shall show our love rather by comforting them than by sorrowing for them. But observe, These Christians at Cæsarea, if they could have foreseen the particulars of that event, the general notice of which they received with so much heaviness, would have been better reconciled to it for their own sakes; for, when Paul was made a prisoner at Jerusalem, he was presently sent to Cæsarea, the very place where he now was (*ch.* xxiii. 33), and there he continued at least *two years* (*ch.* xxiv. 27), and he was a prisoner at large, as appears (*ch.* xxiv. 23), orders being given that he should have liberty to go among his friends, and his friends to come to him; so that the church at Cæsarea had much more of Paul's company and help when he was imprisoned than they could have had if he had been at liberty. That which we oppose, as thinking it to operate much against us, may be overruled by the providence of God to work for us, which is a reason why we should follow providence, and not fear it.

2. He repeats his resolution to go forward, notwithstanding: "*What mean you to weep thus? I am ready* to suffer whatever is appointed for me. I am fully determined to go, whatever comes of it, and therefore it is to no purpose for you to oppose it. I am willing to suffer, and therefore why are you unwilling that I should suffer? Am not I nearest myself, and fittest to judge for myself? If the trouble found me unready, it would be a trouble indeed, and you might well weep at the thoughts of it. But, blessed be God, it does not. It is very welcome to me, and therefore should not be such a terror to you. For my part, *I am ready,*" ἑτοίμως ἔχω—*I have myself in a readiness,* as soldiers for

an engagement. "I expect trouble, I count upon it, it will be no surprise to me. I was told at first *what great things I must suffer,*" *ch.* ix. 16. "I am *prepared* for it, by a clear conscience, a firm confidence in God, a holy contempt of the world and the body, a lively faith in Christ, and a joyful hope of eternal life. I can *bid it welcome,* as we do a friend that we look for, and have made preparation for. I can, through grace, not only bear it, but rejoice in it." Now, (1.) See how far his resolution extends: You are told that I must be bound at Jerusalem, and you would have me keep away for fear of this. I tell you, *I am ready not only to be bound, but,* if the will of God be so, *to die at Jerusalem;* not only to lose my liberty, but to lose my life." It is our wisdom to think of the worst that may befal us, and to prepare accordingly, that we may *stand complete in all the will of God.* (2.) See what it is that carries him out thus, that makes him willing to suffer and die: it is *for the name of the Lord Jesus.* All that a man has will he give for his life; but life itself will Paul give for the service and honour of the name of Christ.

V. The patient acquiescence of his friends in his resolution, *v.* 14. 1. They submitted to the wisdom of a good man. They had carried the matter as far as they could with decency; but, "*when he would not be persuaded, we ceased* our importunity. Paul knows best his own mind, and what he has to do, and it becomes us to leave it to himself, and not to censure him for what he does, nor to say he is rash, and wilful, and humoursome, and has a spirit of contradiction, as some people are apt to judge of those that will not do just as they would have them do. No doubt, Paul has a good reason for his resolution, though he sees cause to keep it to himself, and God has gracious ends to serve in confirming him in it." It is good manners not to over-press those in their own affairs that will not be persuaded. 2. They submitted to the will of a good God: *We ceased,* saying, *The will of the Lord be done.* They did not resolve his resolution into his stubbornness, but into his willingness to suffer, and God's will that he should. *Father in heaven, thy will be done,* as it is a rule to our prayers and to our practice, so it is to our patience. This may refer, (1.) To Paul's present firmness; he is inflexible, and unpersuadable, and in this they see the will of the Lord done. "It is he that has wrought this fixed resolution in him, and therefore we acquiesce in it." Note, In the turning of the hearts of our friends or ministers, this way or that way (and it may be quite another way than we could wish), we should eye the hand of God, and submit to that. (2.) To his approaching sufferings: "If there be no remedy, but Paul will run himself into bonds, the will of the Lord Jesus be done. We have done all that we could do on our parts to prevent it, and now we leave it to God, we leave it to Christ, to whom the Father has committed all judgment, and therefore we do, not as we will, but as he will." Note, When we see trouble coming, and particularly that of our ministers' being silenced or removed from us, it becomes us to say, *The will of the Lord be done.* God is wise, and knows how to make all work for good, and therefore "welcome his holy will." Not only, "The will of the Lord must be done, and there is no remedy;" but, "Let the will of the Lord be done, for his will is his wisdom, and he doeth all according to the counsel of it; let him therefore do with us and ours as seemeth good in his eyes." When a trouble is come, this must allay our griefs, that the will of the Lord is done; when we see it coming, this must silence our fears, that the will of the Lord shall be done, to which we must say, *Amen,* let it be done.

15 And after those days we took
up our carriages, and went up to Jerusalem. 16 There went with us
also *certain* of the disciples of Cæsarea, and brought with them one
Mnason of Cyprus, an old disciple,
with whom we should lodge. 17
And when we were come to Jerusalem, the brethren received us gladly.
18 And the *day* following Paul went
in with us unto James; and all the
elders were present. 19 And when
he had saluted them, he declared particularly what things God had wrought
among the Gentiles by his ministry.
20 And when they heard *it,* they glorified the Lord, and said unto him,
Thou seest, brother, how many thousands of Jews there are which believe; and they are all zealous of the
law: 21 And they are informed of
thee, that thou teachest all the Jews
which are among the Gentiles to forsake Moses, saying that they ought
not to circumcise *their* children,
neither to walk after the customs.
22 What is it therefore? the multitude must needs come together: for
they will hear that thou art come.
23 Do therefore this that we say to
thee: We have four man which have
a vow on them; 24 Them take, and
purify thyself with them, and be at
charges with them, that they may
shave *their* heads: and all may know
that those things, whereof they were
informed concerning thee, are no-

thing; but *that* thou thyself also
walkest orderly, and keepest the law.
25 As touching the Gentiles which
believe, we have written *and* concluded that they observe no such
thing, save only that they keep themselves from *things* offered to idols,
and from blood, and from strangled,
and from fornication. 26 Then Paul
took the men, and the next day purifying himself with them entered
into the temple, to signify the accomplishment of the days of purification, until that an offering should
be offered for every one of them.

In these verses we have,

I. Paul's journey to Jerusalem from Cæsarea, and the company that went along with him. 1. They *took up their carriages,* their bag and baggage, and as it should seem, like poor travellers or soldiers, were their own porters; so little had they of change of raiment. *Omnia mea mecum porto —My property is all about me.* Some think they had with them the money that was collected in the churches of Macedonia and Achaia for the poor saints at Jerusalem. If they could have persuaded Paul to go some other way, they would gladly have gone along with him; but if, notwithstanding their dissuasive, he will go to Jerusalem, they do not say, "Let him go by himself then;" but as Thomas, in a like case, when Christ would go into danger at Jerusalem, *Let us go and die with him,* John xi. 16. Their resolution to cleave to Paul was like that of Ittai to cleave to David (2 Sam. xv. 21): *In what place my Lord the king shall be, whether in death or life, there also will thy servant be.* Thus Paul's boldness emboldened them. 2. Certain of the disciples of Cæsarea went along with them. Whether they designed to go however, and took this opportunity of going with so much good company, or whether they went on purpose to see if they could do Paul any service and if possible prevent his trouble, or at least minister to him in it, does not appear. The less while that Paul is likely to enjoy his liberty the more industrious they are to improve every opportunity of conversation with him. Elisha kept close to Elijah when he knew the time was at hand that he should be taken up. 3. They brought with them an honest old gentleman that had a house of his own at Jerusalem, in which he would gladly entertain Paul and his company, *one Mnason of Cyprus* (*v.* 16), *with whom we should lodge.* Such a great concourse of people there was to the feast that it was a hard matter to get lodgings; the public houses would be taken up by those of the better sort, and it was looked upon as a scandalous thing for those that had private houses to let their rooms out at those times, but they must freely accommodate strangers with them. Every one then would choose his friends to be his guests, and Mnason took Paul and his company to be his lodgers; though he had heard what trouble Paul was likely to come into, which might bring those that entertained him into trouble too, yet he shall be welcome to him, whatever comes of it. This Mnason is called an *old disciple*—a disciple *from the beginning;* some think, one of the seventy disciples of Christ, or one of the first converts after the pouring out of the Spirit, or one of the first that was converted by the preaching of the gospel in Cyprus, *ch.* xiii. 4. However it was, it seems he had been long a Christian, and was now in years. Note, It is an honourable thing to be an old disciple of Jesus Christ, to have been enabled by the grace of God to continue long in a course of duty, stedfast in the faith, and growing more and more prudent and experienced to a good old age. And with these old disciples one would choose to lodge; for the multitude of their years will teach wisdom.

II. Paul's welcome at Jerusalem. 1. Many of the brethren there *received him gladly, v.* 17. As soon as they had notice that he was come to town, they went to his lodgings at Mnason's house, and congratulated him on his safe arrival, and told him they were glad to see him, and invited him to their houses, accounting it an honour to be known to one that was such an eminent servant of Christ. Streso observes that the word here used concerning the welcome they gave to the apostles, ἀσμένως ἀποδέχειν, is used concerning the welcome of the apostles' doctrine, *ch.* ii. 41. They *gladly received his word.* We think if we had Paul among us we should gladly receive him; but it is a question whether we should or no if, having his doctrine, we do not gladly receive that. 2. They paid a visit to James and the elders of the church, at a church-meeting (*v.* 18): "*The day following, Paul went in unto James,* and took us with him, that were his companions, to introduce us into acquaintance with the church at Jerusalem." It should seem that James was now the only apostle that was resident at Jerusalem; the rest had dispersed themselves, to preach the gospel in other places. But still they forecasted to have an apostle at Jerusalem, perhaps sometimes one and sometimes another, because there was a great resort thither from all parts. James was now upon the spot, and all the elders or presbyters that were the ordinary pastors of the church, both to preach and govern, were present. Paul saluted them all, paid his respects to them, enquired concerning their welfare, and gave them the right hand of fellowship. He *saluted them,* that is, he wished them all health and happiness, and prayed to God to bless them. The proper signification of salutation is, wishing salvation to you: *salve,* or *salus tibi sit;* like *peace be unto you.* And such mutual salutations, or good wishes, very well become Christians, in token of their love to each other and joint regard to God.

III. The account they had from him of his ministry among the Gentiles, and their satisfaction in it. 1 He gave them a narrative of the success of the gospel in those countries where he had been employed, knowing it would be very acceptable to them to hear of the enlarging of Christ's kingdom: *He declared particularly what things God had wrought among the Gentiles by his ministry, v.* 19. Observe how modestly he speaks, not what things he had wrought (he was but the instrument), but what God had wrought by his ministry. It was *not I, but the grace of God which was with me.* He planted and watered, but God gave the increase. He declared it particularly, that the grace of God might appear the more illustrious in the circumstances of his success. Thus David will tell others what God has done for his soul (Ps. lxvi. 16), as Paul here what God has done by his hand, and both that their friends may help them to be thankful. 2. Hence they took occasion to give praise to God (*v.* 20): *When they heard it, they glorified the Lord.* Paul ascribed it all to God, and to God they gave the praise of it. They did not break out into high encomiums of Paul, but left it to his Master to say to him, *Well done, good and faithful servant;* but they gave glory to the grace of God, which was extended to the Gentiles. Note, The conversion of sinners ought to be the matter of our joy and praise as it is of the angels'. God had honoured Paul more than any of them, in making his usefulness more extensive, yet they did not envy him, nor were they jealous of his growing reputation, but, on the contrary, *glorified the Lord.* And they could not do more to encourage Paul to go on cheerfully in his work than to glorify God for his success in it; for, if God be praised, Paul is pleased.

IV. The request of James and the elders of the church at Jerusalem to Paul, or their advice rather, that he would gratify the believing Jews by showing some compliance with the ceremonial law, and appearing publicly in the temple to offer sacrifice, which was not a thing in itself sinful; for the ceremonial law, though it was by no means to be imposed upon the Gentile converts (as the false teachers would have it, and thereby endeavoured to subvert the gospel), yet it was not become unlawful as yet to those that had been bred up in the observance of it, but were far from expecting justification by it. It was dead, but not buried; dead, but not yet deadly. And, being not sinful, they thought it was a piece of prudence in Paul to conform thus far. Observe the counsel they give to Paul herein, not as having authority over him, but an affection for him.

1. They desired him to take notice of the great numbers there were of the Jewish converts: *Thou seest, brother, how many thousands of the Jews there are who believe.* They called him brother, for they looked upon him as a joint-commissioner with them in gospel-work. Though they were of the circumcision and he the apostle of the Gentiles, though they were conformists and he a nonconformist, yet they were brethren, and owned the relation. Thou hast been in some of our assemblies, and seest how numerous they are: *how many myriads of Jews believe.* The word signifies, not thousands, but *ten thousands.* Even among the Jews, who were most prejudiced against the gospel, yet there were great multitudes that received it; for the grace of God can break down the strongest holds of Satan. The number of the names at first was but one hundred and twenty, yet now many thousands. Let none therefore despise the day of small things; for, though the beginning be small, God can make the latter end greatly to increase. Hereby it appeared that God had not quite cast away his people the Jews, for among them there was a remnant, an election, that obtained (see Rom. xi. 1, 5, 7): *many thousands that believed.* And this account which they could give to Paul of the success of the gospel among the Jews was, no doubt, as grateful to Paul as the account which he gave them of the conversion of the Gentiles was to them; for his heart's desire and prayer to God for the Jews was *that they might be saved.*

2. They informed him of a prevailing infirmity these believing Jews laboured under, of which they could not yet be cured: *They are all zealous of the law.* They believe in Christ as the true Messiah, they rest upon his righteousness and submit to his government; but they know the law of Moses was of God, they have found spiritual benefit in their attendance on the institutions of it, and therefore they can by no means think of parting with it, no, nor of growing cold to it. And perhaps they urged Christ's being *made under the law,* and observing it (which was designed to be our deliverance from the law), as a reason for their continuance under it. This was a great weakness and mistake, to be so fond of the shadows when the substance was come, to keep their necks under a yoke of bondage when Christ had come to make them free. But see, (1.) The power of education and long usage, and especially of a ceremonial law. (2.) The charitable allowance that must be made in consideration of these. These Jews that believed were not therefore disowned and rejected as no Christians because they were for the law, nay, were zealous for it, while it was only in their own practice, and they did not impose it upon others. Their being zealous of the law was capable of a good construction, which charity would put upon it; and it was capable of a good excuse, considering what they were brought up in, and among whom they lived.

3. They gave him to understand that these Jews, who were so zealous of the law, were ill-affected to him, *v.* 21. Paul himself, though as faithful a servant as any Christ ever had, yet could not get the good word of all that belonged to Christ's family: "*They are informed of thee* (and form their opinion of thee accordingly) that thou not only dost not teach the Gentiles to observe the law, as some would have had thee (we have prevailed with them to drop that), but *dost teach all the Jews who are* dispersed *among the Gentiles to forsake Moses, not to circumcise their children nor to walk after the customs* of our nation, which were of divine appointment, so far as they might be observed even among the Gentiles, at a distance from the temple,—not to observe the fasts and feasts of the church, not to wear their phylacteries, nor abstain from unclean meats." Now, (1.) It was true that Paul preached the abrogation of the law of Moses, taught them that it was impossible to be justified by it, and therefore we are not bound up any longer to the observance of it. But, (2.) It was false that he taught them to forsake Moses; for the religion he preached tended not to destroy the law, but to fulfil it. He preached Christ *(the end of the law for righteousness)*, and repentance and faith, in the exercise of which we are to make great use of the law. The Jews among the Gentiles whom Paul taught were so far from forsaking Moses that they never understood him better, nor ever embraced him so heartily as now when they were taught to make use of him as a *schoolmaster to bring them to Christ*. But even the believing Jews, having got this notion of Paul, that he was an enemy to Moses, and perhaps giving too much regard to the unbelieving Jews too, were much exasperated against him. Their ministers, the elders here present, loved and honoured him, and approved of what he did, and called him brother, but the people could hardly be induced to entertain a favourable thought of him; for it is certain the least judicious are the most censorious, the weak-headed are the hot-headed. They could not distinguish upon Paul's doctrine as they ought to have done, and therefore condemned it in the gross, through ignorance.

4. They therefore desired Paul that he would by some public act, now that he had come to Jerusalem, make it to appear that the charge against him was false, and that he did not teach people to forsake Moses and to break the customs of the Jewish church, for he himself retained the use of them.

(1.) They conclude that something of this kind must be done: "*What is it therefore?* What must be done? The *multitude will hear that thou art come* to town." This is an inconvenience that attends men of fame, that their coming and going are taken notice of more than other people's, and will be talked of, by some for good-will and by others for ill-will. "When they hear thou art come, *they must needs come together*, they will expect that we call them together, to advise with them whether we should admit thee to preach among us as a brother or no; or, they will come together of themselves expecting to hear thee." Now something must be done to satisfy them that Paul does not teach the people to forsake Moses, and they think it necessary, [1.] For Paul's sake, that his reputation should be cleared, and that so good a man may not lie under any blemish, nor so useful a man labour under any disadvantage which may obstruct his usefulness. [2.] For the people's sake, that they may not continue prejudiced against so good a man, nor lose the benefit of his ministry by those prejudices. [3.] For their own sake, that since they knew it was their duty to own Paul their doing it might not be turned to their reproach among those that were under their charge.

(2.) They produce a fair opportunity which Paul might take to clear himself: "*Do this that we say unto thee*, take our advice in this case. *We have four men*, Jews who believe, of our own churches, and *they have a vow on them*, a vow of Nazariteship for a certain time; their time has now expired (*v.* 23), and they are to offer their offering according to the law, when they shave the head of their separation, a he-lamb for a burnt-offering, a ewe-lamb for a sin-offering, and a ram for a peace-offering, with other offerings appertinent to them, Num. vi. 13—20. Many used to do this together, when their vow expired about the same time, either for the greater expedition or for the greater solemnity. Now Paul having so far of late complied with the law as to take upon him the vow of a Nazarite, and to signify the expiration of it by shaving his head at Cenchrea (*ch.* xviii. 18), according to the custom of those who lived at a distance from the temple, they desire him but to go a little further, and to join with these four in offering the sacrifices of a Nazarite: "*Purify thyself with them* according to the law; and be willing not only to take that trouble, but to be at charges with them, in buying sacrifices for this solemn occasion, and to join with them in the sacrifice." This, they think, will effectually stop the mouth of calumny, and every one will be convinced that the report was false, that Paul was not the man he was represented to be, did not teach the Jews to forsake Moses, but that he himself, being originally a Jew, walked orderly, and kept the law; and then all would be well.

5. They enter a protestation that this shall be no infringement at all of the decree lately made in favour of the Gentile converts, nor do they intend by this in the least to derogate from the liberty allowed them (*v.* 25): "*As touching the Gentiles* who *believe, we have written and concluded*, and resolve to abide by it, *that they observe no such things;* we would not have them to be bound up by the ceremonial law by any means, but only

that they keep themselves from *things offered to idols, and from blood, and from things strangled, and from fornication;* but let not them be tied to the Jewish sacrifices or purifications, nor any of their rites and ceremonies." They knew how jealous Paul was for the preservation of the liberty of the converted Gentiles, and therefore expressly covenant to abide by that. Thus far is their proposal.

V. Here is Paul's compliance with it. He was willing to gratify them in this matter. Though he would not be persuaded not to go to Jerusalem, yet, when he was there, he was persuaded to do as they there did, *v.* 26. *Then Paul took the men,* as they advised, and the very *next day, purifying himself with them,* and not *with multitude nor tumult,* as he himself pleads (*ch.* xxiv. 18), he *entered into the temple,* as other devout Jews that came upon such errands did, to signify the accomplishment of the days of purification to the priests; desiring the priest would appoint a time when the offering should be offered for every one of them, one for each. Ainsworth, on Num. vi. 18, quotes out of Maimonides a passage which gives some light to this: *If a man say, Upon me be half the oblations of a Nazarite,* or, *Upon me be half the shaving of a Nazarite, then he brings half the offerings by what Nazarite he will, and that Nazarite pays his offering out of that which is his.* So Paul did here; he contributed what he vowed to the offerings of these Nazarites, and some think bound himself to the law of Nazariteship, and to an attendance at the temple with fastings and prayers for seven days, not designing that the offering should be offered till then, which was what he signified to the priest. Now it has been questioned whether James and the elders did well to give Paul this advice, and whether he did well to take it. 1. Some have blamed this occasional conformity of Paul's, as indulging the Jews too much in their adherence to the ceremonial law, and a discouragement of those who stood fast in the liberty wherewith Christ had made them free. Was it not enough for James and the elders of Jerusalem to connive at this mistake in the Jewish converts themselves, but must they wheedle Paul to countenance them in it? Had it not been better, when they had told Paul how zealous the believing Jews were for the law, if they had desired him, whom God had endued with such excellent gifts, to take pains with their people to convince them of their error, and to show them that they were made free from the law by their marriage to Christ? Rom. vii. 4. To urge him to encourage them in it by his example seems to have more in it of fleshly wisdom than of the grace of God. Surely Paul knew what he had to do better than they could teach him. But, 2. Others think the advice was prudent and good, and Paul's following it was justifiable enough, as the case stood. It was Paul's avowed principle, *To the Jews became I as a Jew, that I might gain the Jews,* 1 Cor. ix. 20. He had circumcised Timothy, to please the Jews; though he would not constantly observe the ceremonial law, yet, to gain an opportunity of doing good, and to show how far he could comply, he would occasionally go to the temple and join in the sacrifices there. Those that are weak in the faith are to be borne with, when those that undermine the faith must be opposed. It is true, this compliance of Paul's sped ill to him, for this very thing by which he hoped to pacify the Jews did but provoke them, and bring him into trouble; yet this is not a sufficient ground to go upon in condemning it: Paul might do well, and yet suffer for it. But perhaps the wise God overruled both their advice and Paul's compliance with it to serve a better purpose than was intended; for we have reason to think that when the believing Jews, who had endeavoured by their zeal for the law to recommend themselves to the good opinion of those who believed not, saw how barbarously they used Paul (who endeavoured to oblige them), they were by this more alienated from the ceremonial law than they could have been by the most argumentative or affecting discourses. They saw it was in vain to think of pleasing men that would be pleased with nothing else but the rooting out of Christianity. Integrity and uprightness will be more likely to preserve us than sneaking compliances. And when we consider what a great trouble it must needs be to James and the presbyters, in the reflection upon it, that they had by their advice brought Paul into trouble, it should be a warning to us not to press men to oblige us by doing any thing contrary to their own mind.

27 And when the seven days were
almost ended, the Jews which were
of Asia, when they saw him in the
temple, stirred up all the people, and
laid hands on him, 28 Crying out,
Men of Israel, help: This is the
man, that teacheth all *men* every
where against the people, and the
law, and this place: and further
brought Greeks also into the temple,
and hath polluted this holy place.
29 (For they had seen before with
him in the city Trophimus an Ephesian, whom they supposed that Paul
had brought into the temple.) 30
And all the city was moved, and the
people ran together: and they took
Paul, and drew him out of the temple:
and forthwith the doors were shut.
31 And as they went about to kill
him, tidings came unto the chief
captain of the band, that all Jerusalem was in an uproar. 32 Who

immediately took soldiers and centurions, and ran down unto them:
and when they saw the chief captain
and the soldiers, they left beating of
Paul. 33 Then the chief captain
came near, and took him, and commanded *him* to be bound with two
chains; and demanded who he was,
and what he had done. 34 And
some cried one thing, some another,
among the multitude: and when he
could not know the certainty for the
tumult, he commanded him to be
carried into the castle. 35 And
when he came upon the stairs, so it
was, that he was borne of the soldiers
for the violence of the people. 36
For the multitude of the people followed after, crying, Away with him.
37 And as Paul was to be led into
the castle, he said unto the chief
captain, May I speak unto thee?
Who said, Canst thou speak Greek?
38 Art not thou that Egyptian,
which before these days madest an
uproar, and leddest out into the wilderness four thousand men that were
murderers? 39 But Paul said, I am
a man *which am* a Jew of Tarsus, *a
city* in Cilicia, a citizen of no mean
city: and, I beseech thee, suffer me
to speak unto the people. 40 And
when he had given him licence, Paul
stood on the stairs, and beckoned
with the hand unto the people. And
when there was made a great silence,
he spake unto *them* in the Hebrew
tongue, saying,

We have here Paul brought into a captivity which we are not likely to see the end of; for after this he is either hurried from one bar to another, or lies neglected, first in one prison and then in another, and can neither be tried nor bailed. When we see the beginning of a trouble, we know not either how long it will last or how it will issue.

I. We have here Paul seized, and laid hold on.

1. He was seized in the temple, when he was there attending the days of his purifying, and the solemn services of those days, *v.* 27. Formerly he had been well known in the temple, but now he had been so long in his travels abroad that he had become a stranger there; so that it was not till *the seven days were almost ended* that he was taken notice of by those that had an evil eye towards him. In the temple, where he should have been protected, as in a sanctuary, he was most violently set upon by those who did what they could to have his blood mingled with his sacrifices—in the temple, where he should have been welcomed as one of the greatest ornaments of it that ever had been there since the Lord of the temple left it. The temple, which they themselves pretended such a mighty zeal for, yet did they themselves thus profane. Thus is the church polluted by none more than by popish persecutors, under the colour of the church's name and interest.

2. The informers against him were the Jews of Asia, not those of Jerusalem—the Jews of the dispersion, who knew him best, and who were most exasperated against him. Those who seldom came up to worship at the temple in Jerusalem themselves, but contentedly lived at a distance from it, in pursuit of their private advantages, yet appeared most zealous for the temple, as if thereby they would atone for their habitual neglect of it.

3. The method they took was to raise the mob, and to incense them against him. They did not go to the high priest, or the magistrates of the city, with their charge (probably because they expected not to receive countenance from them), but *they stirred up all the people*, who were at this time more than ever disposed to any thing that was tumultuous and seditious, riotous and outrageous. Those are fittest to be employed against Christ and Christianity that are governed least by reason and most by passion; therefore Paul described the Jewish persecutors to be not only wicked, but absurd unreasonable men.

4. The arguments wherewith they exasperated the people against him were popular, but very false and unjust. They cried out, "*Men of Israel, help.* If you are indeed men of Israel, true-born Jews, that have a concern for your church and your country, now is your time to show it, by helping to seize an enemy to both." Thus *they cried after him as after a thief* (Job xxx. 5), or after a mad dog. Note, The enemies of Christianity, since they could never prove it to be an ill thing, have been always very industrious, right or wrong, to put it into an ill name, and so run it down by outrage and outcry. It had become men of Israel to help Paul, who preached up him who was so much the *glory of his people Israel;* yet here the popular fury will not allow them to be men of Israel, unless they will help against him. This was like, *Stop thief*, or Athaliah's cry, *Treason, treason;* what is wanting in right is made up in noise.

5. They charge upon him both bad doctrine and bad practice, and both against the Mosaic ritual.

(1.) They charge upon him bad doctrine; not only that he holds corrupt opinions himself, but that he vents and publishes them, though not here at Jerusalem, yet in other places, nay in all places, he teaches all men, every where; so artfully is the crime aggravated, as if, because he was an itinerant, he was a ubiquitary: "He spreads to the utmost of his power certain damnable and heretical positions," [1.] Against the people of the Jews. He had taught that Jews and Gentiles stand on the same level before God, *and neither circumcision avails any thing nor uncircumcision;* nay, he had taught against the unbelieving Jews that they were rejected (and therefore had separated from them and their synagogues), and this is interpreted to be speaking against the whole nation, as if no doubt but *they were the people, and wisdom must die with them* (Job xii. 2), whereas God, though he had cast them off, yet had not *cast away his people,* Rom. xi. 1. They were *Lo-ammi, not a people* (Hos. i. 9), and yet pretended to be the only people. Those commonly seem most jealous for the church's name that belong to it in name only. [2.] Against the law. His teaching men to believe the gospel as the end of the law, and the perfection of it, was interpreted his preaching against the law; whereas it was so far from making void the law that it established it, Rom. iii. 31. [3.] Against *this place,* the temple. Because he taught men to pray every where, he was reproached as an enemy to the temple, and perhaps because he sometimes mentioned the destruction of Jerusalem and the temple, and of the Jewish nation, which his Master had foretold. Paul had himself been active in persecuting Stephen, and putting him to death for words spoken *against this holy place,* and now the same thing is laid to his charge. He that was then made use of as the tool is now set up as the butt of Jewish rage and malice.

(2.) They charge upon him bad practices. To confirm their charge against him, as teaching people against this holy place, they charge it upon him that he had himself polluted it, and by an overt-act showed his contempt of it, and a design to make it common. He *has brought Gentiles also into the temple,* into the inner court of the temple, which none that were uncircumcised were admitted, under any pretence, to come into; there was written upon the wall that enclosed this inner court, in Greek and Latin, *It is a capital crime for strangers to enter.*—Joseph. *Antiq.* lib. xv. cap. 14. Paul was himself a Jew, and had right to enter into the court of the Jews. And they, seeing one with him there that joined with him in his devotions, concluded that Trophimus an Ephesian, who was a Gentile, was one of them. Why? Did they see him there? Truly no; but they had seen him with Paul in the streets of the city, which was no crime at all, and therefore they affirm that he was with Paul in the inner court of the temple, which was a heinous crime. They had seen him with him in the city, and therefore they supposed that Paul had brought him with him into the temple, which was utterly false. See here, [1.] Innocency is no fence against calumny and false accusation. It is no new thing for those that mean honestly, and act regularly, to have things laid to their charge which they know not, nor ever thought of. [2.] *Evil men dig up mischief,* and go far to seek proofs of their false accusations, as they did here, who, because they saw a Gentile with Paul in the city, will thence infer that he was with him in the temple. This was a strained innuendo indeed, yet by such unjust and groundless suggestions have wicked men thought to justify themselves in the most barbarous outrages committed upon the *excellent ones of the earth.* [3.] It is common for malicious people to improve that against those that are wise and good with which they thought to have obliged them and ingratiated themselves with them. Paul thought to recommend himself to their good opinion by going into the temple, and thence they take an occasion to accuse him. If he had kept further off them, he had not been so maligned by them. This is the genius of ill-nature; *for my love, they are my adversaries,* Ps. cix. 4; lxix. 10.

II. We have Paul in danger of being pulled in pieces by the rabble. They will not be at the pains to have him before the high priest, or the sanhedrim; that is a roundabout way: the execution shall be of a piece with the prosecution, all unjust and irregular. They cannot prove the crime upon him, and therefore dare not bring him upon a fair trial; nay, so greedily do they thirst after his blood that they have not patience to proceed against him by a due course of law, though they were ever so sure to gain their point; and therefore, as those who neither feared God nor regarded man, they resolved to knock him on the head immediately.

1. All the city was in an uproar, *v.* 30. The people, who though they had little holiness themselves, yet had a mighty veneration for the holy place, when they heard a hue-and-cry from the temple, were up in arms presently, being resolved to stand by that with their lives and fortunes. *All the city was moved,* when they were called to from the temple, *Men of Israel, help,* with as much violence as if the old complaint were revived (Ps. lxxix. 1), *O God, the heathen are come into thine inheritance, thy holy temple have they defiled.* Just such a zeal the Jews here show for God's temple as the Ephesians did for Diana's temple, when Paul was informed against as an enemy to that (*ch.* xix. 29): *The whole city was full of confusion.* But God does not reckon himself at all honoured by those whose zeal for him transports them to such irregularities, and who, while they pretend to act for him, act in such a brutish barbarous manner.

2. They drew Paul out of the temple, and shut the doors between the outer and inner court of the temple, or perhaps the doors of

the outer court. In dragging him furiously out of the temple, (1.) They showed a real detestation of him as one not fit to be suffered in the temple, nor to worship there, nor to be looked upon as a member of the Jewish nation; as if his sacrifice had been an abomination. (2.) They pretended a veneration for the temple; like that of good Jehoiada, who would not have Athaliah to be *slain in the house of the Lord,* 2 Kings xi. 15. See how absurd these wicked men were; they condemned Paul for drawing people from the temple, and yet, when he himself was very devoutly worshipping in the temple, they drew him out of it. The officers of the temple shut the doors, either, [1.] Lest Paul should find means to get back and take hold of the horns of the altar, and so protect himself by that sanctuary from their rage. Or rather, [2.] Lest the crowd should by the running in of more to them be thrust back into the temple, and some outrage should be committed, to the profanation of that holy place. Those that made no conscience of doing so ill a thing as the murdering of a good man for well-doing, yet would be thought to scruple doing it in a holy place, or at a holy time: *Not in the temple,* as *Not on the feast-day.*

3. They went about to kill him (*v.* 31), for they fell a beating him (*v.* 32), resolving to beat him to death by blows without number, a punishment which the Jewish doctors allowed in some cases (not at all to the credit of their nation), and called *the beating of the rebels.* Now was Paul, like a lamb, thrown into a den of lions, and made an easy prey to them, and, no doubt, he was still of the same mind as when he said, *I am ready not only to be bound, but to die at Jerusalem,* to die so great a death.

III. We have here Paul rescued out of the hands of his Jewish enemies by a Roman enemy. 1. Tidings were brought of the tumult, and that the mob was up, *to the chief captain of the band,* the governor of the castle, or, whoever he was, the now commander-in-chief of the Roman forces that were quartered in Jerusalem. Somebody that was concerned not for Paul, but for the public peace and safety, gave this information to the colonel, who had always a jealous and watchful eye upon these tumultuous Jews, and he is the man that must be instrumental to save Paul's life, when never a friend he had was capable of doing him any service. 2. The tribune, or chief captain, got his forces together with all possible expedition, and went to suppress the mob: *He took soldiers* and *centurions,* and *ran down to them.* Now at the feast, as at other such solemn times, the guards were up, and the militia more within cal' than at other times, and so he had them near at hand, and *he ran down unto the multitude;* for at such times delays are dangerous. Sedition must be crushed at first, lest it grow headstrong. 3. The very sight of the Roman general frightened them from beating Paul; for they knew they were doing what they could not justify, and were in danger of being called in question for this day's uproar, as the town-clerk told the Ephesians. They were deterred from that by the power of the Romans from which they ought to have been restrained by the justice of God and the dread of his wrath. Note, God often makes the earth to help the woman (Rev. xii. 16), and those to be a protection to his people who yet have no affection for his people; they have only a compassion for sufferers, and are zealous for the public peace. The shepherd makes use even of his dogs for the defence of his sheep. It is Streso's comparison here. See here how these wicked people were frightened away at the very sight of the chief captain; for the *king that sitteth on the throne of judgment scattereth away all evil with his eyes.* 4. The governor takes him into custody. He rescued him, not out of a concern for him, because he thought him innocent, but out of a concern for justice, because he ought not to be put to death without trial; and because he knew not how dangerous the consequence might be to the Roman government if such tumultuous proceedings were not timely suppressed, nor what such an outrageous people might do if once they knew their own strength: he therefore takes Paul out of the hands of the mob into the hands of the law (*v.* 33): *He took him, and commanded him to be bound with two chains,* that the people might be satisfied he did not intend to discharge him, but to examine him, *for he demanded of* those who were so eager against him *who he was, and what he had done.* This violent taking of him out of the hands of the multitude, though there was all the reason in the world for it, yet they laid to the charge of the chief captain as his crime (*ch.* xxiv. 7): *The chief captain Lysias came with great violence, and took him out of our hands,* which refers to this rescue as appears by comparing *ch.* xxiii. 27, 28, where the chief captain gives an account of it to Felix.

IV. The provision which the chief captain made, with much ado, to bring Paul to speak for himself. One had almost as good enter into a struggle with the winds and the waves, as with such a mob as was here got together; and yet Paul made a shift to get liberty of speech among them.

1. There was no knowing the sense of the people; for when the chief captain enquired concerning Paul, having perhaps never heard of his name before (such strangers were the great ones to the excellent ones of the earth, and affected to be so), *some cried one thing, and some another,* among the multitude; so that it was impossible for the chief captain to know their mind, when really they knew not either one another's mind or their own, when every one pretended to give the sense of the whole body. Those that will hearken to the clamours of the multitude will know nothing for a certainty, any more than the builders of Babel, when their tongues were confounded.

2. There was no quelling the rage and fury of the people; for when *the chief captain commanded that Paul should be carried into the castle,* the tower of Antonia, where the Roman soldiers kept garrison, near the temple, the soldiers themselves had much ado to get him safely thither out of the noise, the people were so violent (*v.* 35): *When he came upon the stairs,* leading up to the castle, the soldiers were forced to take him up in their arms, and carry him (which they might easily do, for he was a little man, and his bodily presence weak), to keep him from the people, who would have pulled him limb from limb if they could. When they could not reach him with their cruel hands, they followed him with their *sharp arrows, even bitter words: They followed, crying, Away with him, v.* 36. See how the most excellent persons and things are often run down by a popular clamour. Christ himself was so, with, *Crucify him, crucify him,* though they could not say what evil he had done. *Take him out of the land of the living* (so the ancients expound it), chase him out of the world.

3. Paul at length begged leave of the chief captain to speak to him (*v.* 37): *As he was to be led into the castle,* with a great deal of calmness and composedness in himself, and a great deal of mildness and deference to those about him, *he said unto the chief captain,* "*May I speak unto thee?* Will it be no offence, nor construed as a breach of rule, if I give thee some account of myself, since my persecutors can give no account of me?" What a humble modest question was this! Paul knew how to speak to the greatest of men, and had many a time spoken to his betters, yet he humbly begs leave to speak to this commander, and will not speak till he has obtained leave: *May I speak unto thee?*

4. The chief captain tells him what notion he had of him: *Canst thou speak Greek?* I am surprised to hear thee speak a learned language; for, *Art not thou that Egyptian who made an uproar?* The Jews made the uproar, and then would have it thought that Paul had given them occasion for it, by beginning first; for probably some of them whispered this in the ear of the chief captain. See what false mistaken notions of good people and good ministers many run away with, and will not be at the pains to have the mistake rectified. It seems, there had lately been an insurrection somewhere in that country, headed by an Egyptian, who took on him to be a prophet. Josephus mentions is story, that "an Egyptian raised a seditious party, promised to show them the fall of *the walls of Jerusalem from the mount of Olives,* and that they should enter the city upon the ruins." The captain here says *that he led out into the wilderness four thousand men that were murderers*—desperadoes, banditti, raparees, cut-throats. What a degeneracy was there in the Jewish nation, when there were found there so many that had such a character, and could be drawn into such an attempt upon the public peace! But Josephus says that "Felix the Roman president went out against them, killed four hundred, and took two hundred prisoners, and the rest were dispersed."—*Antiq.* xx. 6. *De Bello Jud.* ii. 12. And Eusebius speaks of it, *Hist.* ii. 20. It happened in the thirteenth year of Claudius, a little before those days, about three years ago. The ringleader of this rebellion, it seems, had made his escape, and the chief captain concluded that one who lay under so great an odium as Paul seemed to lie under, and against whom there was so great an outcry, could not be a criminal of less figure than this Egyptian. See how good men are exposed to ill-will by mistake.

5. Paul rectifies his mistake concerning him, by informing him particularly what he was; not such a vagabond, a scoundrel, a rake, as that Egyptian, who could give no good account of himself. No: *I am a man who is a Jew* originally, and no Egyptian—a Jew both by nation and religion; *I am of Tarsus, a city of Cilicia,* of honest parents and a liberal education (Tarsus was a university), and, besides that, *a citizen of no mean city.* Whether he means Tarsus or Rome is not certain; they were neither of them mean cities, and he was a freeman of both. Though the chief captain had put him under such an invidious suspicion, that he was that Egyptian, he kept his temper, did not break out into any passionate exclamations against the times he lived in or the men he had to do with, did not render railing for railing, but mildly denied the charge, and owned what he was.

6. He humbly desired a permission from the chief captain, whose prisoner he now was, to speak to the people. He does not demand it as a dèbt, though he might have done so, but sues for it as a favour, which he will be thankful for: *I beseech thee, suffer me to speak to the people.* The chief captain rescued him with no other design than to give him a fair hearing. Now, to show that his cause needs no art to give it a plausible colour, he desires he may have leave immediately to defend himself; for it needed no more than to be set in a true light; nor did he depend only on the goodness of his cause, but upon the goodness and fidelity of his patron, and that promise of his to all his advocates, *that it should be given them in that same hour what they should speak.*

7. He obtained leave to plead his own cause, for he needed not to have counsel assigned him, when the Spirit of the Father was ready to dictate to him, Matt. x. 20. *The chief captain gave him license* (*v.* 40), so that now he could speak with a good grace, and with the more courage; he had, I will not say that favour, but that justice, done him by the chief captain, which he could not obtain from his countrymen the Jews; for they

would not hear him, but the captain would, though it were but to satisfy his curiosity. This licence being obtained, (1.) The people were attentive to hear: *Paul stood on the stairs,* which gave a little man like Zaccheus some advantage, and consequently some boldness, in delivering himself. A sorry pulpit it was, and yet better than none; it served the purpose, though it was not, like Ezra's pulpit of wood, made for the purpose. There he *beckoned with the hand unto the people,* made signs to them to be quiet and to have a little patience, for he had something to say to them; and so far he gained his point that every one cried hush to his neighbour, and there was made a profound silence. Probably the chief captain also intimated his charge to all manner of people to keep silence; if the people were not required to give audience, it was to no purpose at all that Paul was allowed to speak. When the cause of Christ and his gospel is to be pleaded, there ought to be a great silence, that we may *give the more earnest heed,* and all little enough. (2.) Paul addressed himself to speak, well assured that he was serving the interest of Christ's kingdom as truly and effectually as if he had been preaching in the synagogue: he *spoke unto them in the Hebrew tongue,* that is, in their own vulgar tongue, which was the language of their country, to which he hereby owned not only an abiding relation, but an abiding respect.

CHAP. XXII.

In the close of the foregoing chapter we had Paul bound, according to Agabus's prophecy of the hard usage he should receive from the Jews at Jerusalem, yet he had his tongue set at liberty, by the permission the chief captain gave him to speak for himself; and so intent he is upon using that liberty of speech which is allowed him, to the honour of Christ and the service of his interest, that he forgets the bonds he is in, makes no mention of them, but speaks of the great things Christ had done for him with as much ease and cheerfulness as if nothing had been done to ruffle him or put him into disorder. We have here, I. His address to the people, and their attention to it, ver. 1, 2. II. The account he gives of himself. 1. What a bigoted Jew he had been in the beginning of his time, ver. 3—5. 2. How he was miraculously converted and brought over to the faith of Christ, ver. 6—11. 3. How he was confirmed and baptized by the ministry of Ananias, ver. 12—16. 4. How he was afterwards called, by an immediate warrant from heaven, to be the apostle of the Gentiles, ver. 17—21. III. The interruption given him upon this by the rabble, who could not bear to hear any thing said in favour of the Gentiles, and the violent passion they flew into upon it, ver. 22, 23. IV. Paul's second rescue out of the hands of the rabble, and the further course which the chief captain took to find out the true reason of this mighty clamour against Paul, ver. 24, 25. V. Paul's pleading his privilege as a Roman citizen, by which he was exempted from this barbarous method of inquisition, ver. 26—29. VI. The chief captain's removing the cause into the high priest's court, and Paul's appearing there, ver. 30.

MEN, brethren, and fathers, hear
ye my defence *which I make*
now unto you. 2 (And when they
heard that he spake in the Hebrew
tongue to them, they kept the more
silence: and he saith,)

Paul had, in the last verse of the foregoing chapter, gained a great point, by commanding so profound a silence after so loud a clamour. Now here observe,

I. With what an admirable composure and presence of mind he addresses himself to speak. Never was poor man set upon in a more tumultuous manner, nor with more rage and fury; and yet, in what he said, 1. There appears no fright, but his mind is sedate and composed. Thus he makes his own words good, *None of these things move me;* and David's (Ps. iii. 6), *I will not be afraid of ten thousands of people that have set themselves against me round about.* 2. There appears no passion. Though the suggestions against him were all frivolous and unjust, though it would have vexed any man alive to be charged with profaning the temple just then when he was contriving and designing to show his respect to it, yet he breaks out into no angry expressions, but is *led as a lamb to the slaughter.*

II. What respectful titles he gives even to those who thus abused him, and how humbly he craves their attention: "*Men, brethren, and fathers, v.* 1. *To you, O men, I call;* men, that should hear reason, and be ruled by it; men, from whom one may expect humanity. You, *brethren* of the common people; you, *fathers* of the priests." Thus he lets them know that he was one of them, and had not renounced his relation to the Jewish nation, but still had a kindness and concern for it. Note, Though we must not give flattering titles to any, yet we ought to give titles of due respect to all; and those we would do good to we should endeavour not to provoke. Though he was rescued out of their hands, and was taken under the protection of the chief captain, yet he does not fall foul upon them, with, *Hear now, you rebels;* but compliments them with, *Men, brethren, and fathers.* And observe, he does not exhibit a charge against them, does not recriminate, Hear now what I have to say against you, but, Hear now what I have to say for myself: *Hear you my defence;* a just and reasonable request, for every man that is accused has a right to answer for himself, and has not justice done him if his answer be not patiently and impartially heard.

III. The language he spoke in, which recommended what he said to the auditory: *He spoke in the Hebrew tongue,* that is, the vulgar language of the Jews, which, at this time, was not the pure Old-Testament Hebrew, but the Syriac, a dialect of the Hebrew, or rather a corruption of it, as the Italian of the Latin. However, 1. It showed his continued respect to his countrymen, the Jews. Though he had conversed so much with the Gentiles, yet he still retained the Jews' language, and could talk it with ease; by this it appears he is a Jew, *for his speech betrayeth him.* 2. What he said was the more generally understood, for that was the language every body spoke, and therefore to speak in that language was indeed to appeal to the people, by which he might have somewhat to insinuate into their affections; and therefore, *when they heard that he spoke in the Hebrew tongue, they kept the more silence.* How can it be thought people should give any attention to that which is spoken to them in a language they do not understand? The chief captain was surprised to hear him speak Greek (*ch.* xxi. 37), the Jews were surprised to hear him speak Hebrew, and both therefore think the better of him. But how would they have been surprised if they had enquired, as they ought to have done, and had found in what variety of tongues *the Spirit gave him utterance!* 1 Cor. xiv. 18, *I speak with tongues more than you all.* But the truth is, many wise and good men are therefore slighted only because they are not known.

3 I am verily a man *which am* a
Jew, born in Tarsus, *a city* in Cilicia,
yet brought up in this city at the
feet of Gamaliel, *and* taught according to the perfect manner of the law
of the fathers, and was zealous toward God, as ye all are this day. 4
And I persecuted this way unto the
death, binding and delivering into
prisons both men and women. 5
As also the high priest doth bear me
witness, and all the estate of the
elders: from whom also I received
letters unto the brethren, and went
to Damascus, to bring them which
were there bound unto Jerusalem,
for to be punished. 6 And it came
to pass, that, as I made my journey,
and was come nigh unto Damascus
about noon, suddenly there shone
from heaven a great light round
about me. 7 And I fell unto the
ground, and heard a voice saying
unto me, Saul, Saul, why persecutest
thou me? 8 And I answered, Who
art thou, Lord? And he said unto
me, I am Jesus of Nazareth, whom
thou persecutest. 9 And they that
were with me saw indeed the light,
and were afraid; but they heard not
the voice of him that spake to me.
10 And I said, What shall I do,
Lord? And the Lord said unto me,
Arise, and go into Damascus; and
there it shall be told thee of all things
which are appointed for thee to do.
11 And when I could not see for the
glory of that light, being led by the
hand of them that were with me, I
came into Damascus, 12 And one
Ananias, a devout man according to
the law, having a good report of all
the Jews which dwelt *there*, 13
Came unto me, and stood, and said
unto me, Brother Saul, receive thy
sight. And the same hour I looked
up upon him. 14 And he said, The
God of our fathers hath chosen thee,
that thou shouldest know his will,
and see that Just One, and shouldest
hear the voice of his mouth. 15 For
thou shalt be his witness unto all
men of what thou hast seen and
heard. 16 And now why tarriest
thou? arise, and be baptized, and
wash away thy sins, calling on the
name of the Lord. 17 And it came
to pass, that, when I was come again
to Jerusalem, even while I prayed in
the temple, I was in a trance; 18
And saw him saying unto me, Make
haste, and get thee quickly out of
Jerusalem: for they will not receive
thy testimony concerning me. 19
And I said, Lord, they know that I
imprisoned and beat in every synagogue them that believed on thee:
20 And when the blood of thy
martyr Stephen was shed, I also was
standing by, and consenting unto
his death, and kept the raiment of
them that slew him. 21 And he
said unto me, Depart: for I will send
thee far hence unto the Gentiles.

Paul here gives such an account of himself as might serve not only to satisfy the chief captain that he was not that Egyptian he took him to be, but the Jews also that he was not that enemy to their church and nation, to their law and temple, they took him to be, and that what he did in preaching Christ, and particularly in preaching him to the Gentiles, he did by a divine commission. He here gives them to understand,

I. What his extraction and education were. 1. That he was one of their own nation, *of the stock of Israel, of the seed of Abraham, a Hebrew of the Hebrews,* not of any obscure family, or a renegado of some other nation: "No, *I am verily a man who is a Jew,* ἀνὴρ Ἰουδαῖος—*a Jewish man;* I am a man, and therefore ought not to be treated as a beast; a man who is a Jew, not a barbarian; I am a sincere friend to your nation, for I am one of it, and should defile my own nest if I should unjustly derogate from the honour of your law and your temple." 2. That he was born in a creditable reputable place, *in Tarsus, a city of Cilicia,* and was by his birth a freeman of that city. He was not born in servitude, as some of the Jews of the dispersion, it is likely, were; but he was a gentleman born, and perhaps could produce his certificate of his freedom in that ancient and honourable city. This was, indeed, but a small matter to make any boast of, and yet it was needful to be mentioned at this time to those who insolently trampled upon him, as if he were to be ranked with the children of fools, yea, the children of base men, Job xxx. 8. 3. That he had a learned and liberal education. He was not only a Jew, and a gentleman, but a scholar. He *was brought up* in Jerusalem, the principal seat of the Jewish learning, and *at the feet of Gamaliel,* whom they all knew to be an eminent doctor of the Jewish law, of which Paul was designed to be himself a teacher; and therefore he could not be ignorant of their law, nor be thought to slight it because he did not know it. His parents had brought him very young to this city, designing him for a Pharisee; and some think his being brought up at the feet of Gamaliel intimates, not only that he was one of his pupils, but that he was, above any other, diligent and constant in attending his lectures, observant of him, and obsequious to him, in all he said, as *Mary,* that *sat at Jesus' feet, and heard his word.* 4. That he was in his early days a very forward and eminent professor of the Jews' religion; his studies and learning were all directed that way. So far was he from being principled in his youth with any disaffection to the religious usages of the Jews that there was not a young man among them who had a greater and more entire veneration for them than he had, was more strict in observing them himself, or more hot in enforcing them upon others. (1.) He was an intelligent professor of their religion, and had a clear head. He minded his business at Gamaliel's feet, and was there *taught according to the perfect manner of the law of the fathers.* What departures he had made from the law were not owing to any confused or mistaken notions of it, for he understood it to a nicety, *κατὰ ἀκρίβειαν—according to the most accurate and exact method.* He was not trained up in the principles of the latitudinarians, had nothing in him of a Sadducee, but was of that sect that was most studious in the law, kept most close to it, and, to make it more strict than it was, added to it the traditions of the elders, the law of the fathers, the law which was given to them, and which they gave to their children, and so it was handed down to us. Paul had as great a value for antiquity, and tradition, and the authority of the church, as any of them had; and there was never a Jew of them all that understood his religion better than Paul did, or could better give an account of it or a reason for it. (2.) He was an active professor of their religion, and had a warm heart: *I was zealous towards God, as you all are this day.* Many that are very well skilled in the theory of religion are willing to leave the practice of it to others, but Paul was as much a zealot as a rabbi. He was zealous against every thing that the law prohibited, and for every thing that the law enjoined; and this was zeal towards God, because he thought it was for the honour of God and the service of his interests; and here he compliments his hearers with a candid and charitable opinion of them, *that they all were this day zealous towards God; he bears them record* (Rom. x. 2) *that they have a zeal for God, but not according to knowledge.* In hating him, and casting him out, they said, *Let the Lord be glorified* (Isa. lxvi. 5), and, though this did by no means justify their rage, yet it enabled those that prayed, *Father, forgive them,* to plead, as Christ did, *For they know not what they do.* And when Paul owns that he had been zealous for God in the law of Moses, *as they were this day,* he intimates his hope that they might be zealous for God, in Christ, as he was this day.

II. What a fiery furious persecutor he had been of the Christian religion in the beginning of his time, *v.* 4, 5. He mentions this to make it the more plainly and evidently to appear that the change which was wrought upon him, when he was converted to the Christian faith, was purely the effect of a divine power; for he was so far from having any previous inclinations to it, or favourable opinions of it, that immediately before that sudden change was wrought in him he had the utmost antipathy imaginable to Christianity, and was filled with rage against it to the last degree. And perhaps he mentions it to justify God in his present trouble; how unrighteous soever those were that persecuted him, God was righteous, who permitted them to do it, for time was when he was a persecutor; and he may have a further view in it to invite and encourage those people to repent, for he himself had been *a blasphemer, and a persecutor,* and yet obtained mercy. Let us view Paul's picture of himself when he was a persecutor. 1. He hated Christianity with a mortal enmity: *I persecuted this way unto the death,* that is, "Those that walked in this way I aimed, if possible, to be the death of." He *breathed out slaughter against them, ch.* ix. 1. When *they were put to death, he gave his voice against them, ch.* xxvi. 10. Nay, he persecuted not only those that walked in this way, but the way itself, Christianity, which was branded as a by-way, a sect; he aimed to persecute this to the death, to be the ruin of this religion. He *persecuted it to the death,* that is, he could have been willing himself to die in his opposition to Christianity, so some understand it. He would contentedly have lost his life, and would have thought it well laid out, in defence of the laws and traditions of the fathers. 2. He did all he could to frighten people from this way, and out of it, by *binding and delivering into prison both men and women;* he filled the jails with Christians. Now that he himself was bound, he lays a particular stress upon this part of his charge against himself, that he had bound the Christians, and carried them to prison; he likewise reflects upon it with a special regret that he had imprisoned not only the men, but the women, the weaker sex, who ought to be treated with particular tenderness and compassion. 3. He was employed by the great sanhedrim, the high priest, and all the estate of the elders, as an agent for them, in suppressing this new sect; so much had he already signalized himself for his zeal against it, *v.* 5. The high priest can witness for him that he was ready to be employed in any service against the Christians. When they heard that many of the Jews at Damascus had embraced the Christian faith, to deter others from doing the like they resolved to proceed against them with the utmost severity, and could not think of a fitter person to be employed in that business, nor one more likely to go through with it, than Paul. They therefore sent him, and letters by him, to the Jews at Damascus, here called *the brethren,* because they all descended from one common stock, and were of one family in religion too, ordering them to be assisting to Paul in seizing those among them that had turned Christians, and bringing them up prisoners to Jerusalem, in order to their being punished as deserters from the faith and worship of the God of Israel; and so might either be compelled to retract, or be put to death for a terror to others. Thus did Saul make *havoc of the church,* and was in a fair way, if he had gone on awhile, to ruin it, and root it out. "Such a one," says Paul, "I was at first, just such as you now are. I know the heart of a persecutor, and therefore pity you, and pray that you may know the heart of a convert, as God soon made me to do. *And who was I that I could withstand God?*"

III. In what manner he was converted, and made what he now was. It was not from any natural or external causes; he did not change his religion from an affectation of novelty, for he was then as well affected to antiquity as he used to be; nor did it arise from discontent because he was disappointed in his preferment, for he was now, more than ever, in the way of preferment in the Jewish church; much less could it arise from covetousness, or ambition, or any hope of mending his fortune in the world by turning Christian, for it was to expose himself to all manner of disgrace and trouble; nor had he any conversation with the apostles or any other Christians, by whose subtlety and sophistry he might be thought to have been wheedled into this change. No, it was the Lord's doing, and the circumstances of the doing of it were enough to justify him in the change, to all those who believe there is a supernatural power; and none can condemn him for it, without reflecting upon that divine energy by which he was herein overruled. He relates the story of his conversion here very particularly, as we had it before (*ch.* ix), aiming to show that it was purely the act of God. 1. He was as fully bent upon persecuting the Christians just before Christ arrested him as ever. He *made his journey, and was come nigh to Damascus* (*v.* 6), and had no other thought than to execute the cruel design he was sent upon; he was not conscious of the least compassionate relentings towards the poor Christians, but still represented them to himself as heretics, schismatics, and dangerous enemies both to church and state. 2. It was *a light from heaven* that first startled him, *a great light,* which *shone suddenly round about him,* and the Jews knew that God is light, and his angels angels of light, and that such a light as this shining at noon, and therefore exceeding that of the sun, must be from God. Had it shone in upon him into some private room, there might have been a cheat in it, but it shone upon him in the open road, at high noon, and so strongly *that it struck him to the ground* (*v.* 7), and all *that were with him, ch.* xxvi. 14. They could not deny but that surely the Lord was in this light. 3. It was a *voice from heaven* that first begat in him awful thoughts of Jesus Christ, of whom before he had had nothing but hateful spiteful thoughts. The voice called to him by name, to distinguish him from *those that journeyed with him, Saul, Saul, why persecutest thou me?* And when he asked, *Who art thou, Lord?* it was answered, *I am Jesus of Nazareth, whom thou persecutest, v.* 8. By which it appeared that this Jesus of Nazareth, whom they also were now persecuting, was one that spoke from heaven, and they knew it was dangerous resisting one that did so, Heb. xii. 25. 4. Lest it should be objected, "How came this light and voice to work such a change upon him, and not upon those that journeyed with him?" (though, it is very probable, it had a good effect upon them, and that they thereupon became Christians), he observes *that his fellow travellers saw indeed the light, and were afraid* they should be consumed with fire from heaven, their own consciences, perhaps, now telling them that the way they were in was not good, but like Balaam's when he was going to curse Israel, and therefore they might expect to meet an angel with a flaming glittering sword; but, though the light made them afraid, they heard not the voice of him that spoke to Paul, that is, they did not distinctly hear the words. Now faith comes by hearing, and therefore that change was now presently wrought upon him that heard the words, and heard them directed to himself, which was not wrought upon those who only saw the light; and yet it might afterwards be wrought upon them too. 5. He assures them that when he was thus startled he referred himself entirely to a divine guidance; he did not hereupon presently cry out, "Well, I will be a Christian," but, "*What shall I do, Lord?* Let the same voice from heaven that has stopped me in the wrong way guide me into the right way, *v.* 10. Lord, tell me what I shall do, and I will do it." And immediately he had directions to go to Damascus, and there he should hear further from him that now spoke to him: "No more needs to be said from heaven, *there it shall be told thee*, by a man like thyself, in the name of him that now speaks to thee, *all things which are appointed for thee to do*." The extraordinary ways of divine revelation, by visions, and voices, and the appearance of angels, were designed, both in the Old Testament and in the New, only to introduce and establish the ordinary method by the scriptures and a standing ministry, and therefore were generally superseded when these were settled. The angel did not preach to Cornelius himself, but bade him send for Peter; so the voice here tells not Paul what he shall do, but bids him go to Damascus, and there it shall be told him. 6. As a demonstration of the greatness of that light which fastened upon him, he tells them of the immediate effect it had upon his eye-sight (*v.* 11): *I could not see for the glory of that light.* It struck him blind for the present. *Nimium sensibile lædit sensum—Its radiance dazzled him.* Condemned sinners are struck blind, as the Sodomites and Egyptians were, by the power of darkness, and it is a lasting blindness, like that of the unbelieving Jews; but convinced sinners are struck blind, as Paul here was, not by darkness, but by light: they are for the present brought to be at a loss within themselves, but it is in order to their being enlightened, as the putting of clay upon the eyes of the blind man was the designed method of his cure. Those that were with Paul had not the light so directly darted into their faces as Paul had into his, and therefore they were not blinded, as he was; yet, considering the issue, who would not rather have chosen his lot than theirs? They, having their sight, led *Paul by the hand into the city.* Paul, being a Pharisee, was proud of his spiritual eye-sight. The Pharisees said, *Are we blind also?* John ix. 40. Nay, they were confident *that they themselves were guides to the blind,* and *lights to those that were in darkness,* Rom. ii. 19. Now Paul was thus struck with bodily blindness to make him sensible of his spiritual blindness, and his mistake concerning himself, when he was *alive without the law,* Rom. vii. 9.

IV. How he was confirmed in the change he had made, and further directed what he should do, by Ananias who lived at Damascus.

Observe, 1. The character here given of Ananias. He was not a man that was any way prejudiced against the Jewish nation or religion, but was himself *a devout man according to the law;* if not a Jew by birth, yet one that had been proselyted to the Jewish religion, and therefore called a devout man, and thence advanced further to the faith of Christ; and he conducted himself so well that he had a *good report of all the Jews that dwelt at Damascus* This was the first Christian that Paul had any friendly communication with, and it was not likely that he should instil into him any such notions as they suspected him to espouse, injurious to the law or to this holy place.

2. The cure immediately wrought by him upon Paul's eyes, which miracle was to confirm Ananias's mission to Paul, and to ratify all that he should afterwards say to him. He *came to him* (*v.* 13); and, to assure him that he came to him from Christ (the very same who had torn and would heal him, had smitten, but would bind him up, had taken away his sight, but would restore it again, with advantage), he *stood by him, and said, Brother Saul, receive thy sight.* Power went along with this word, and *the same hour,* immediately, he recovered his sight, and *looked up upon him,* ready to receive from him the instructions sent by him.

3. The declaration which Ananias makes to him of the favour, the peculiar favour, which the Lord Jesus designed him above any other.

(1.) In the present manifestation of himself to him (*v.* 14): *The God of our fathers has chosen thee.* This powerful call is the result of a particular choice; his calling God the God of our fathers intimates that Ananias was himself a Jew by birth, that observed the law of the fathers, and lived upon the promise made unto the fathers; and he gives a reason why he said *Brother Saul,* when he speaks of God as the God of our fathers: *This God of our fathers has chosen thee that thou shouldst,* [1.] *Know his will,* the will of his precept that is to be done by thee, the will of his providence that is to be done concerning thee. He hath chosen thee that thou shouldst know it in a more peculiar manner; not of man nor by man, but immediately by *the revelation of Christ,* Gal. i. 1, 12. Those whom God hath chosen he hath chosen to know his will, and to do it. [2.] *That thou shouldst see that Just One, and shouldst hear the voice of his mouth,* and so shouldst know his will immediately from himself. This was what Paul was, in a particular manner, chosen to above others; it was a distinguishing favour, that he should see Christ here upon earth after his ascension into heaven. Stephen saw him *standing at the right hand of God,* but Paul saw him standing at his right hand. This honour none had but Paul. Stephen saw him, but we do not find that he heard the voice of his mouth, as Paul did, who says, *he was last of all seen of me, as of one born out of due time,* 1 Cor. xv. 8. Christ is here called *that Just One;* for he is Jesus Christ the righteous, and suffered wrongfully. Observe, Those whom God has chosen to know his will must have an eye to Christ, and must see him, and hear the voice of his mouth; for it is by him that God has made known his will, his good-will to us, and he has said, *Hear you him.*

(2.) In the after-manifestation of himself by him to others (*v.* 15): "*Thou shalt be his witness,* not only a monument of his grace, as a pillar may be, but a witness *viva voce—by word of mouth;* thou shalt publish his gospel, as that which thou hast experienced the power of, and been delivered into the mould of; *thou shalt be his witness unto all men,* Gentiles as well as Jews, *of what thou hast seen and heard,* now at the very first." And finding Paul so particularly relating the manner of his conversion in his apologies for himself, here and *ch.* xxvi., we have reason to think that he frequently related the same narrative in his preaching for the conversion of others; he told them what God had done for his soul, to encourage them to hope that he would do something for their souls.

4. The counsel and encouragement he gave him to join himself to the Lord Jesus by baptism (*v.* 16): *Arise, and be baptized.* He had in his circumcision been given up to God, but he must now by baptism be given up to God in Christ—must embrace the Christian religion and the privileges of it, in submission to the precepts of it. This must now be done immediately upon his conversion, and so was added to his circumcision: but to the seed of the faithful it comes in the room of it; for it is, as that was to Abraham and his believing seed, *a seal of the righteousness which is by faith.* (1.) The great gospel privilege which by baptism we have sealed to us is the remission of sins: *Be baptized and wash away thy sins;* that is, "Receive the comfort of the pardon of thy sins in and through Jesus Christ and lay hold of his righteousness for that purpose, and receive power against sin for the mortifying of thy corruption;" for our being washed includes our being both justified and sanctified, 1 Cor. vi. 11. Be baptized, and rest not in the sign, but make sure of the thing signified, the putting away of the filth of sin. (2.) The great gospel duty which by our baptism we are bound to is *to call on the name of the Lord, the Lord Jesus;* to acknowledge him to be our Lord and our God, and to apply to him accordingly; to give honour to him, to put all our petitions in his hand. To *call on the name of Jesus Christ our Lord* (Son of David, have mercy on us) is the periphrasis of a Christian, 1 Cor. i. 2. We must *wash away our sins, calling on the name of the Lord;* that is, we must seek for the pardon of our sins in Christ's name, and in dependence on him and his righteousness. In prayer, we must not any longer call God the God of Abraham, but the Father of our Lord Jesus Christ, and in him our Father; in every prayer, our eye must be to Christ. (3.) We must do this quickly. *Why tarriest thou?* Our covenanting with God in Christ is needful work, that must not be deferred. The case is so plain that it is needless to deliberate; and the hazard so great that it is folly to delay. Why should not that be done at the present time that must be done some time, or we are undone?

V. How he was commissioned to go and preach the gospel to the Gentiles. This was the great thing for which they were so angry at him, and therefore it was requisite he should for this, in a special manner, produce a divine warrant; and here he does it. This commission he did not receive presently upon his conversion, for this was *at Jerusalem,* whither he did not go till *three years after,* or more (Gal. i. 18); and whether it was then, or afterwards, that he had this vision here spoken of, we are not certain. But, to reconcile them, if possible, to his preaching the gospel among the Gentiles, he tells them, 1. That he received his orders to do it when he was at prayer, begging of God to appoint him his work and to show him the course he should steer; and (which was a circumstance that would have some weight with those he was now speaking to) he was *at prayer in the temple,* which was to be called *a house of prayer for all people;* not only in which all people should pray, but in which all people should be prayed for. Now as Paul's praying in the temple was an evidence, contrary to their malicious suggestion, that he had a veneration for the temple, though he did not make an idol of it as they did; so God's giving him this commission there in the temple was an evidence that the sending him to the Gentiles would be no prejudice to the temple, unless the Jews by their infidelity made it so. Now it would be a great satisfaction to Paul afterwards, in the execution of this commission, to reflect upon it that he received it when he was at prayer. 2. He received it in a vision. He fell *into a trance* (*v.* 17), his external senses, for the present, locked up; he was in an ecstasy, as when he was *caught up into the third heaven,* and was not at that time sensible whether he was *in the body or out of the body.* In this trance he saw Jesus Christ, not with the eyes of his body, as at his conversion, but represented to the eye of his mind (*v.* 18): *I saw him saying unto me.* Our eye must be upon Christ when we are receiving the law from his mouth; and we must not only hear him speak, but see him speaking to us. 3. Before Christ gave him a commission to go to the Gentiles, he told him it was to no purpose for him to think of doing any good at Jerusalem; so that they must not blame him, but themselves, if he be sent to the Gentiles. Paul came to Jerusalem full of hopes that, by the grace of God, he might be instrumental to bring those to the faith of Christ who had stood it out against the ministry of the other apostles; and perhaps this was what he was now praying for, that he, having had his education at Jerusalem and being well known there, might be employed in gathering the children of Jerusalem to Christ that were not yet gathered, which he thought he had particular advantages for the doing of. But Christ crosses the measures he had laid: "*Make haste,*" says he, "*and get thee quickly out of Jerusalem;*" for, though thou thinkest thyself more likely to work upon them than others, thou wilt find they are more prejudiced against thee than against any other, and therefore *will not receive thy testimony concerning me.*" As God knows before who will receive the gospel, so he knows who will reject it. 4. Paul, notwithstanding this, renewed his petition that he might be employed at Jerusalem, because they knew, better than any did, what he had been before his conversion, and therefore must ascribe so great a change in him to the power of almighty grace, and consequently give the greater regard to his testimony; thus he reasoned, both with himself and with the Lord, and thought he reasoned justly (*v.* 19, 20): "*Lord,*" says he, "*they know* that I was once of their mind, that I was as bitter an enemy as any of them to such as believed on thee, that I irritated the civil power against them, and *imprisoned them,* and turned the edge of the spiritual power against them too, and *beat them in every synagogue.* And therefore they will not impute my preaching Christ to education nor to any prepossession in his favour (as they do that of other ministers), but will the more readily regard what I say because they know I have myself been one of them: particularly in Stephen's case; they know that when he was stoned I was standing by, I was aiding and abetting and *consenting to his death,* and in token of this *kept the clothes of those that stoned him.* Now, "Lord," says he, "if I appear among them, preaching the doctrine that Stephen preached and suffered for, they will no doubt receive my testimony." "No," says Christ to him, "they will not; but will be more exasperated against thee as a deserter from, than against others whom they look upon only as strangers to, their constitution." 5. Paul's petition for a warrant to preach the gospel at Jerusalem is overruled, and he has peremptory orders to go among the Gentiles (*v.* 21): *Depart, for I will send thee far hence, unto the Gentiles.* Note, God often gives gracious answers to the prayers of his people, not in the thing itself that they pray for, but in something better. Abraham prays, *O that Ishmael may live before thee;* and God hears him for Isaac. So Paul here prays that he may be an instrument of converting souls at Jerusalem: "No," says Christ, "but thou shalt be employed among the Gentiles, and *more shall be the children of the desolate than those of the married wife.*" It is God that appoints his labourers both their day and their place, and it is fit they should acquiesce in his appointment, though it may cross their own inclinations. Paul hankers after Jerusalem: to be a preacher there was the summit of his ambition; but Christ designs him greater preferment. He shall not enter into other men's labours (as the other apostles did, John iv. 38), but shall break up new ground, and *preach the gospel where Christ was not named,* Rom. xv. 20. So often does Providence contrive better for us than we for ourselves; to the guidance of that we must therefore refer ourselves. *He shall choose our inheritance for us.* Observe, Paul shall not go to preach among the Gentiles without a commission *I will send thee.* And, if Christ send him, his Spirit will go along with him, he will stand by him, will carry him on, and bear him out, and give him to see the fruit of his labours. Let not Paul set his heart upon Judea and Jerusalem, for he must be sent far hence; his call must be quite another way, and his work of another kind. And it might be a mitigation of the offence of this to the Jews that he did not set up a Gentile church in the neighbouring nations; others did this in their immediate vicinity; he was sent to places at a distance, a vast way off, where what he did could not be thought an annoyance to them.

Now, if they would lay all this together, surely they would see that they had no reason to be angry with Paul for preaching among the Gentiles, or construe it as an act of ill-will to his own nation, for he was compelled to it, contrary to his own mind, by an overruling command from heaven.

22 And they gave him audience
unto this word, and *then* lifted up
their voices, and said, Away with
such a *fellow* from the earth: for it
is not fit that he should live. 23
And as they cried out, and cast off
their clothes, and threw dust into
the air, 24 The chief captain commanded him to be brought into the
castle, and bade that he should be
examined by scourging; that he might
know wherefore they cried so against
him. 25 And as they bound him
with thongs, Paul said unto the centurion that stood by, Is it lawful for
you to scourge a man that is a
Roman, and uncondemned? 26
When the centurion heard *that,* he
went and told the chief captain, saying, Take heed what thou doest: for
this man is a Roman. 27 Then the
chief captain came, and said unto
him, Tell me, art thou a Roman?
He said, Yea. 28 And the chief
captain answered, With a great sum
obtained I this freedom. And Paul
said, But I was *free* born. 29 Then
straightway they departed from him
which should have examined him:
and the chief captain also was afraid

after he knew that he was a Roman, and because he had bound him. 30
On the morrow, because he would have known the certainty wherefore he was accused of the Jews, he loosed him from *his* bands, and commanded the chief priests and all their council to appear, and brought Paul down, and set him before them.

Paul was going on with this account of himself, had shown them his commission to preach among the Gentiles without any peevish reflections upon the Jews, and we may suppose designed next to show how he was afterwards, by a special direction of the Holy Ghost at Antioch, separated to this service, how tender he was of the Jews, how respectful to them and how careful to give them the precedency in all places whither he came, and to unite Jews and Gentiles in one body; and then to show how wonderfully God had owned him, and what good service had been done to the interest of God's kingdom among men in general, without damage to any of the true interests of the Jewish church in particular. But, whatever he designs to say, they resolve he shall say no more to them: *They gave him audience to this word.* Hitherto they had heard him with patience and some attention. But when he speaks of being sent to the Gentiles, though it was what Christ himself said to him, they cannot bear it, not so much as to hear the Gentiles named, such an enmity had they to them, and such a jealousy of them. Upon the mention of this, they have no manner of patience, but forget all rules of decency and equity; thus were they *provoked to jealousy by those that were no people*, Rom. x. 19.

Now here we are told how furious and outrageous the people were against Paul, for mentioning the Gentiles as taken into the cognizance of divine grace, and so justifying his preaching among them.

I. They interrupted him, by lifting up their voice, to put him into confusion, and that nobody might hear a word he said. Galled consciences kick at the least touch; and those who are resolved not to be ruled by reason commonly resolve not to hear it if they can help it. And the spirit of enmity against the gospel of Christ commonly shows itself in silencing the ministers of Christ and his gospel, and stopping their mouths, as the Jews did Paul's here. Their fathers had said to the best of seers, *See not*, Isa. xxx. 10. And so they to the best of speakers, *Speak not. Forbear, wherefore shouldst thou be smitten?* 2 Chron. xxv. 16.

II. They clamoured against him as one that was unworthy of life, much more of liberty. Without weighing the arguments he had urged in his own defence, or offering to make any answer to them, they cried out with a confused noise, "*Away with such a fellow* as this *from the earth*, who pretends to have a commission to preach to the Gentiles; why, *it is not fit that he should live.*" Thus the men that have been the greatest blessings of their age have been represented not only as the burdens of the earth, but the plague of their generation. He that was worthy of the greatest honours of life is condemned as not worthy of life itself. See what different sentiments God and men have of good men, and yet they both agree in this that they are not likely to live long in this world. Paul says of the godly Jews that they were men of *whom the world was not worthy*, Heb. xi. 38. And therefore they must be removed, that the world may be justly punished with the loss of them. The ungodly Jews here say of Paul that it was not fit he should live; and therefore he must be removed, that the world may be eased of the burden of him, as of the two witnesses, Rev. xi. 10.

III. They went stark mad against Paul, and against the chief captain for not killing him immediately at their request, or throwing him as a prey into their teeth, that they might devour him (*v.* 23); as men whose reason was quite lost in passion, they cried out like roaring lions or raging bears, and howled like the evening wolves; they *cast off their clothes* with fury and violence, as much as to say that thus they would tear him if they could but come at him. Or, rather, they thus showed how ready they were to stone him; those that stoned Stephen threw off their clothes, *v.* 20. Or, they *rent their clothes*, as if he had spoken blasphemy; and *threw dust into the air*, in detestation of it; or signifying how ready they were to throw stones at Paul, if the chief captain would have permitted them. But why should we go about to give a reason for these expressions of fury, which they themselves could not account for? All they intended was to make the chief captain sensible how much they were enraged and exasperated at Paul, so that he could not do any thing to gratify them more than to let them have their will against him.

IV. The chief captain took care for his safety, by ordering him to be brought into the castle, *v.* 24. A prison sometimes has been a protection to good men from popular rage. Paul's hour was not yet come, he had not finished his testimony, and therefore God raised up one that took care of him, when none of his friends durst appear on his behalf. *Grant not, O Lord, the desire of the wicked.*

V. He ordered him the torture, to force from him a confession of some flagrant crimes which had provoked the people to such an uncommon violence against him. *He ordered that he should be examined by scourging* (as now in some countries by the rack), that *he might know wherefore they cried so against him.* Herein he did not proceed fairly; he should have singled out some of the clamorous tumultuous complainants, and taken them into the castle as breakers of the peace, and should have examined them, and by scourging too, what they had to lay to the charge of a man that could give so good an account of himself, and did not appear to have done any thing worthy of death or of bonds. It was proper to ask them, but not at all proper to ask Paul, *wherefore they cried so against him.* He could tell that he had given them no just cause to do it; if there were any cause, let them produce it. No man is bound to accuse himself, though he be guilty, much less ought he to be compelled to accuse himself when he is innocent. Surely the chief captain did not know the Jewish nation when he concluded that he must needs have done something very bad whom they cried out against. Had they not just thus cried out against our Lord Jesus, *Crucify him, crucify him,* when they had not one word to say in answer to the judge's question, *Why, what evil has he done?* Is this a fair or just occasion to scourge Paul, that a rude tumultuous mob cry out against him, but cannot tell why or wherefore, and therefore he must be forced to tell?

VI. Paul pleaded his privilege as a Roman citizen, by which he was exempted from all trials and punishments of this nature (*v.* 25): *As they bound him with thongs,* or leathern bands, to the whipping post, as they used to bind the vilest of malefactors in bridewell from whom they would extort a confession, he made no outcry against the injustice of their proceedings against an innocent man, but very mildly let them understand the illegality of their proceedings against him as a citizen of Rome, which he had done once before at Philippi after he had been scourged (*ch.* xvi. 37), but here he makes use of it for prevention. He *said to the centurion that stood by,* "You know the law; pray *is it lawful for you* who are yourselves Romans to *scourge a man that is a Roman, and uncondemned?*" The manner of his speaking plainly intimates what a holy security and serenity of mind this good man enjoyed, not disturbed either with anger or fear in the midst of all those indignities that were done him, and the danger he was in. The Romans had a law (it was called *lex Sempronia),* that if any magistrate did chastise or condemn a freeman of Rome, *indicta causa—without hearing him speak for himself, and deliberating upon the whole of his case,* he should be liable to the sentence of the people, who were very jealous of their liberties. It is indeed the privilege of every man not to have wrong done him, except it be proved he has done wrong; as it is of every Englishman by *Magna Charta* not to be dis-seized of his life or freehold, but by a verdict of twelve men of his peers.

VII. The chief captain was surprised at this, and put into a fright. He had taken Paul to be a vagabond Egyptian, and wondered he could speak Greek (*ch.* xxi. 37), but is much more surprised now he finds that he is as good a gentleman as himself. How many men of great worth and merit are despised because they are not known, are looked upon and treated as the offscouring of all things, when those that count them so, if they knew their true character, would own them to be of the excellent ones of the earth! The chief captain had centurions, under-officers, attending him, *ch.* xxi. 32. One of these reports this matter to the chief captain (*v.* 26): *Take heed what thou doest, for this man is a Roman,* and what indignity is done to him will be construed an offence against the majesty of the Roman people, as they loved to speak. They all knew what a value was put upon this privilege of the Roman citizens. Tully extols it in one of his orations against Verres, *O nomen dulce libertatis, O jus eximium nostræ civitatis! O lex Porcia! O leges Semproniæ; facinus est vincere Romanum civem, scelus verberare—O Liberty! I love thy charming name; and these our Porcian and Sempronian laws, how admirable! It is a crime to bind a Roman citizen, but an unpardonable one to beat him.* "Therefore" (says the centurion) "let us look to ourselves; if this man be a Roman, and we do him any indignity, we shall be in danger to lose our commissions at least." Now, 1. The chief captain would be satisfied of the truth of this from his own mouth (*v.* 27): "*Tell me, art thou a Roman?* Art thou entitled to the privileges of a Roman citizen?" "Yes," says Paul, "*I am;*" and perhaps produced some ticket or instrument which proved it; for otherwise they would scarcely have taken his word. 2. The chief captain very freely compares notes with him upon this matter, and it appears that the privilege Paul had as a Roman citizen was of the two more honourable than the colonel's; for the colonel owns that his was purchased: "I am a freeman of Rome; but *with a great sum obtained I this freedom,* it cost me dear, how came you by it?" "Why truly," says Paul, "*I was free-born.*" Some think he became entitled to this freedom by the place of his birth, as a native of Tarsus, a city privileged by the emperor with the same privileges that Rome itself enjoyed; others rather think it was by his father or grandfather having served in the war between Cæsar and Antony, or some other of the civil wars of Rome, and being for some signal piece of service rewarded with a freedom of the city, and so Paul came to be free-born; and here he pleads it for his own preservation, for which end not only we may but we ought to use all lawful means. 3. This put an immediate stop to Paul's trouble. Those that were appointed to examine him by scourging quitted the spot; they *departed from him* (*v.* 29), lest they should run themselves into a snare. Nay, and the colonel himself, though we may suppose him to have a considerable interest, was afraid when he heard he was a Roman, because, though he had not beaten him, yet he had bound him in order to his being beaten. Thus many are restrained from evil practices by the fear of man who would not be restrained from them by the fear of God. See here the benefit of human laws and magistracy, and what reason we have to be thankful to God for them; for even when they have given no countenance nor special protection to God's people and ministers, yet, by the general support of equity and fair dealing between man and man, they have served to check the rage of wicked and unreasonable illegal men, who otherwise would know no bounds, and to say, *Hitherto it shall come, but no further; here shall its proud waves be stayed.* And therefore this service we owe to all in authority, to pray for them, because this benefit we have reason to expect from them, whether we have it or no, as long as we are quiet and peaceable—to live *quiet and peaceable lives in all godliness and honesty,* 1 Tim. ii. 1, 2. 4. The governor, the next day, brought Paul before the sanhedrim, *v.* 30. He first *loosed him from his bands,* that those might not prejudge his cause, and that he might not be charged with having pinioned a Roman citizen, and then summoned the chief priests and all their council to come together to take cognizance of Paul's case, for he found it to be a matter of religion, and therefore looked upon them to be the most proper judges of it. Gallio in this case discharged Paul; finding it to be a matter of their law, he drove the prosecutors from the judgment-seat (*ch.* xviii. 16), and would not concern himself at all in it: but this Roman, who was a military man, kept Paul in custody, and appealed from the rabble to the general assembly. Now, (1.) We may hope that hereby he intended Paul's safety, as thinking, if he were an innocent and inoffensive man, though the multitude might be incensed against him, yet the chief priests and elders would do him justice, and clear him; for they were, or should be, men of learning and consideration, and their court governed by rules of equity. When the prophet could find no good among the poorer sort of people, he concluded that it was because they *knew not the way of the Lord, nor the judgments of their God,* and promised himself that he should speed better among the great men, as the chief captain here did, but soon found himself disappointed there: these have *altogether broken the yoke, and burst the bonds,* Jer. v. 4, 5. But, (2.) That which he is here said to aim at is the gratifying of his own curiosity: He *would have known the certainty wherefore he was accused of the Jews.* Had he sent for Paul to his own chamber, and talked freely with him, he might soon have learned from him that which would have done more than satisfy his enquiry, and which might have persuaded him to be a Christian. But it is too common for great men to affect to set that at a distance from them which might awaken their consciences, and to desire to have no more of the knowledge of God's ways than may serve them to talk of.

CHAP. XXIII.

The close of the foregoing chapter left Paul in the high priest's court, into which the chief captain (whether to his advantage or no I know not) had removed his cause from the mob; and, if his enemies act there against him with less noise, yet it is with more subtlety. Now here we have, I. Paul's protestation of his own integrity, and of a civil respect to the high priest, however he had upon a sudden spoken warmly to him, and justly, ver. 1—5. II. Paul's prudent contrivance to get himself clear of them, by setting the Pharisees and Sadducees at variance one with another, ver. 6—9. III. The governor's seasonable interposal to rescue him out of their hands likewise, ver. 10. IV. Christ's more comfortable appearing to him, to animate him against those difficulties that lay before him, and to tell him what he must expect, ver. 11. V. A bloody conspiracy of some desperate Jews to kill Paul, and their drawing in the chief priests and the elders to be aiders and abettors with them in it, ver. 12—15. VI. The discovery of this conspiracy to Paul, and by him to the chief captain, who perceived so much of their inveterate malice against Paul that he had reason enough to believe the truth of it, ver. 16—22. VII. The chief captain's care of Paul's safety, by which he prevented the execution of the design; he sent him away immediately under a strong guard from Jerusalem to Cæsarea, which was now the residence of Felix, the Roman governor, and there he safely arrived, ver. 23—35.

AND Paul, earnestly beholding
the council, said, Men *and*
brethren, I have lived in all good
conscience before God until this day.
2 And the high priest Ananias commanded them that stood by him to
smite him on the mouth. 3 Then
said Paul unto him, God shall smite
thee, *thou* whited wall: for sittest
thou to judge me after the law, and
commandest me to be smitten contrary to the law? 4 And they that
stood by said, Revilest thou God's
high priest? 5 Then said Paul, I
wist not, brethren, that he was the
high priest: for it is written, Thou
shalt not speak evil of the ruler of
thy people.

Perhaps when Paul was brought, as he often was (*corpus cum causa—the person and the cause together*), before heathen magistrates and councils, where he and his cause were slighted, because not at all understood, he thought, if he were brought before the sanhedrim at Jerusalem, he should be able to deal with them to some good purpose, and yet we do not find that he works at all upon them. Here we have,

I. Paul's protestation of his own integrity. Whether the chief priest put any question to him, or the chief captain made any representation of his case to the court, we are not told; but Paul appeared here,

1. With a good courage. He was not at all put out of countenance upon his being brought before such an august assembly, for which in his youth he had conceived such a veneration; nor did he fear their calling him to an account about the letters they gave him to Damascus, to persecute the Christians

there, though (for aught we know) this was the first time he had ever seen them since; but *he earnestly beheld the council.* When Stephen was brought before them, they thought to have faced him down, but could not, such was his holy. confidence; they *looked stedfastly on him, and his face was as that of an angel, ch.* vi. 15. Now that Paul was brought before them he thought to have faced them down, but could not, such was their wicked impudence. However, now was fulfilled in him what God promised to Ezekiel (*ch.* iii. 8, 9): *I have made thy face strong against their faces; fear them not, neither be dismayed at their looks.*

2. With a good conscience, and that gave him a good courage.

——Hic murus aheneus esto,
Nil conscire sibi ——————

Be this thy brazen bulwark of defence,
Still to preserve thy conscious innocence.

He said, "*Men and brethren, I have lived in all good conscience before God unto this day.* However I may be reproached, my heart does not reproach me, but witnesses for me." (1.) He had always been a man inclined to religion; he never was a man that lived at large, but always put a difference between moral good and evil; even in his unregenerate state, he was, *as touching the righteousness that was in the law, blameless.* He was no unthinking man, who never considered what he did, no designing man, who cared not what he did, so he could but compass his own ends. (2.) Even when he persecuted the church of God, he thought he ought to do it, and that he did God service in it. Though his conscience was misinformed, yet he acted according to the dictates of it. See *ch.* xxvi. 9. (3.) He seems rather to speak of the time since his conversion, since he left the service of the high priest, and fell under their displeasure for so doing; he does not say, From my beginning until this day; but, "All the time in which you have looked upon me as a deserter, an apostate, and an enemy to your church, even *to this day,* I have *lived in all good conscience before God;* whatever you may think of me, I have in every thing approved myself to God, and lived honestly," Heb. xiii. 18. He had aimed at nothing but to please God and do his duty, in those things for which they were so incensed against him; in all he had done towards the setting up of the kingdom of Christ, and the setting of it up among the Gentiles, he had acted conscientiously. See here the character of an honest man. [1.] He sets God before him, and lives as in his sight, and under his eyes, and with an eye to him. *Walk before me, and be thou upright.* [2.] He makes conscience of what he says and does, and, though he may be under some mistakes, yet, according to the best of his knowledge, he abstains from that which is evil and cleaves to that which is good. [3.] He is universally conscientious; and those that are not so are not at all truly conscientious; is so in *all manner of conversation:* "I have lived in all good conscience; have had my whole conversation under the direction and dominion of conscience." [4.] He continues so, and perseveres in it: "I have lived so *until this day.*" Whatever changes pass over him, he is still the same, strictly conscientious. And those who thus live in all good conscience before God may, like Paul here, *lift up their face without spot;* and, if their hearts condemn them not, may have confidence both towards God and man, as Job had when he *still held fast his integrity,* and Paul himself, whose rejoicing was this, the testimony of his conscience.

II. The outrage of which Ananias the high priest was guilty: he *commanded those that stood by,* the beadles that attended the court, *to smite him on the mouth* (*v.* 2), to give him a dash on the teeth, either with a hand or with a rod. Our Lord Jesus was thus despitefully used in this court, by one of the servants (John xviii. 22), as was foretold, Mic. v. 1, *They shall smite the Judge of Israel upon the cheek.* But here was an order of court for the doing of it, and, it is likely, it was done. 1. The high priest was highly offended at Paul; some think, because he looked so boldly and earnestly at the council, as if he would face them down; others because he did not address himself particularly to him as president, with some title of honour and respect, but spoke freely and familiarly to them all, as men and brethren. His protestation of his integrity was provocation enough to one who was resolved to run him down and make him odious. When he could charge him with no crime, he thought it was crime enough that he asserted his own innocency. 2. In his rage he ordered him to be smitten, so to put disgrace upon him, and to be smitten on the mouth, as having offended with his lips, and in token of his enjoining him silence. This brutish and barbarous method he had recourse to when he *could not answer the wisdom and spirit wherewith he spoke.* Thus Zedekiah smote Micaiah (1 Kings xxii. 24), and Pashur smote Jeremiah (Jer. xx. 2), when they spoke in the name of the Lord. If therefore we see such indignities done to good men, nay, if they be done to us for well doing and well saying, we must not think it strange; Christ will give those the *kisses of his mouth* (Cant. i. 2) who for his sake receive blows on the mouth. And though it may be expected that, as Solomon says, *every man should kiss his lips that giveth a right answer* (Prov. xxiv. 26), yet we often see the contrary.

III. The denunciation of the wrath of God against the high priest for this *wickedness in the place of judgment* (Eccl. iii. 16): it agrees with what follows there, *v.* 17, with which Solomon comforted himself (*I said in my heart, God shall judge the righteous and the wicked): God shall smite thee, thou whited wall, v.* 3. Paul did not speak this in any sinful heat or passion, but in a holy zeal against the high priest's abuse of his power, and with something of a prophetic spirit, not at all with a spirit of revenge. 1. He gives him his due character: *Thou whited wall;* that is, thou hypocrite—a mud-wall, trash and dirt and rubbish underneath, but plastered over, or white-washed. It is the same comparison in effect with that of Christ, when he compares the Pharisees to whited sepulchres, Matt. xxiii. 27. Those that daubed with untempered mortar failed not to daub themselves over with something that made them look not only clean, but gay. 2. He reads him his just doom: "*God shall smite thee,* shall bring upon thee his sore judgments, especially spiritual judgments. Grotius thinks this was fulfilled soon after, in his removal from the office of the high priest, either by death or deprivation, for he finds another in that office a little while after this; probably he was smitten by some sudden stroke of divine vengeance. Jeroboam's hand was withered when it was stretched out against a prophet. 3. He assigns a good reason for that doom: "For *sittest thou* there as president in the supreme judicature of the church, pretending *to judge me after the law,* to convict and condemn me by the law, and yet *commandest me to be smitten* before any crime is proved upon me, which is *contrary to the law?*" No man must be beaten unless he be *worthy to be beaten,* Deut. xxv. 2. It is against all law, human and divine, natural and positive, to hinder a man from making his defence, and to condemn him unheard. When Paul was beaten by the rabble, he could say, *Father, forgive them, they know not what they do;* but it is inexcusable in a high priest that is appointed to judge according to the law.

IV. The offence which was taken at this bold word of Paul's (*v.* 4): *Those that stood by said, Revilest thou God's high priest?* It is a probable conjecture that those who blamed Paul for what he said were believing Jews, who were zealous for the law, and consequently for the honour of the high priest, and therefore took it ill that Paul should thus reflect upon him, and checked him for it. See here then, 1. What a hard game Paul had to play, when his enemies were abusive to him, and his friends were so far from standing by him, and appearing for him, that they were ready to find fault with his management. 2. How apt even the disciples of Christ themselves are to overvalue outward pomp and power. As because the temple had been God's temple, and a magnificent structure, there were those who followed Christ that could not bear to have any thing said that threatened the destruction of it; so because the high priest had been God's high priest, and was a man that made a figure, though he was an inveterate enemy to Christianity, yet these were disgusted at Paul for giving him his due.

V. The excuse that Paul made for what he had said, because he found it was a stumbling-block to his weak brethren, and might prejudice them against him in other things. These Jewish Christians, though weak, yet were brethren, so he calls them here, and, in consideration of that, is almost ready to recal his words; for *who is offended,* saith he, *and I burn not?* 2 Cor. xi. 29. His fixed resolution was rather to abridge himself in the use of his Christian liberty than give offence to a weak brother; rather than do this, he will *eat no flesh while the world stands,* 1 Cor. viii. 13. And so here though he had taken the liberty to tell the high priest his own, yet, when he found it gave offence, he cried *Peccavi—I have done wrong.* He wished he had not done it; and though he did not beg the high priest's pardon, nor excuse it to him, yet he begs their pardon who took offence at it, because this was not a time to inform them better, nor to say what he could say to justify himself. 1. He excuses it with this, that he did not consider when he said it to whom he spoke (*v.* 5): *I wist not, brethren, that he was the high priest*—*οὐκ ᾔδειν.* "I did not just then think of the dignity of his place, or else I would have spoken more respectfully to him." I see not how we can with any probability think that Paul did not know him to be the high priest, for Paul had been seven days in the temple at the time of the feast, where he could not miss of seeing the high priest; and his telling him that *he sat to judge him after the law* shows that he knew who he was; but, says he, I did not consider it. Dr. Whitby puts this sense upon it, that the prophetic impulse that was upon him, and inwardly moved him to say what he did, did not permit him to notice that it was the high priest, lest this law might have restrained him from complying with that impulse; but the Jews acknowledged that prophets might use a liberty in speaking of rulers which others might not, as Isa. i. 10, 23. Or (as he quotes the sense of Grotius and Lightfoot) Paul does not go about to excuse what he had said in the least, but rather to justify it: "I own that God's high priest is not to be reviled, but I do not own this Ananias to be high priest. He is a usurper; he came to the office by bribery and corruption, and the Jewish rabbin say that he who does so is neither a judge nor to be honoured as such." Yet, 2. He takes care that what he had said should not be drawn into a precedent, to the weakening of the obligation of that law in the least: *For it is written,* and it remains a law in full force, *Thou shalt not speak evil of the ruler of thy people.* It is for the public good that the honour of magistracy should be supported, and not suffer for the miscarriages of those who are entrusted with it, and therefore that decorum be observed in speaking both of and to princes and judges. Even in Job's time it was not thought fit to *say to a king, Thou art wicked, or to princes, You are ungodly,* Job xxxiv. 18. Even when we do well, and suffer for it, we must *take it patiently,* 1 Pet. ii. 20. Not as if great men may not hear of their faults, and public grievances be complained of by proper persons and in a decent manner, but there must be a particular tenderness for the honour and reputation of those in authority more than of other people, because the law of God requires a particular reverence to be paid to them, as God's vicegerents; and it is of dangerous consequence to have those any way countenanced who *despise dominions,* and *speak evil of dignities,* Jude viii. *Curse not the king, no not in thy thought,* Eccl. x. 20.

6 But when Paul perceived that
the one part were Sadducees, and the
other Pharisees, he cried out in the
council, Men *and* brethren, I am a
Pharisee, the son of a Pharisee: of
the hope and resurrection of the
dead I am called in question. 7 And
when he had so said, there arose a
dissension between the Pharisees and
the Sadducees: and the multitude
was divided. 8 For the Sadducees
say that there is no resurrection,
neither angel, nor spirit: but the
Pharisees confess both. 9 And there
arose a great cry: and the scribes
that were of the Pharisees' part
arose, and strove, saying, We find no
evil in this man: but if a spirit or an
angel hath spoken to him, let us not
fight against God. 10 And when
there arose a great dissension, the
chief captain, fearing lest Paul should
have been pulled in pieces of them,
commanded the soldiers to go down,
and to take him by force from among
them, and to bring *him* into the
castle. 11 And the night following
the Lord stood by him, and said, Be
of good cheer, Paul: for as thou hast
testified of me in Jerusalem, so must
thou bear witness also at Rome.

Many are the troubles of the righteous, but some way or other *the Lord delivereth them out of them all.* Paul owned he had experienced the truth of this in the persecutions he had undergone among the Gentiles (see 2 Tim. iii. 11): *Out of them all the Lord delivered me.* And now he finds that he who has delivered does and will deliver. He that delivered him in the foregoing chapter from the tumult of the people here delivers him from that of the elders.

I. His own prudence and ingenuity stand him in some stead, and contribute much to his escape. Paul's greatest honour, and that upon which he most valued himself, was that he was a Christian, and an apostle of Christ; and all his other honours he despised and made nothing of, in comparison with this, *counting them but dung, that he might win Christ;* and yet he had sometimes occasion to make use of his other honours, and they did him service. His being a citizen of Rome saved him in the foregoing chapter from his being scourged by the chief captain as a vagabond, and here his being a Pharisee saved him from being condemned by the sanhedrim, as an apostate from the faith and worship of the God of Israel. It will consist very well with our willingness to suffer for Christ to use all lawful methods, nay, and arts too, both to prevent suffering and to extricate ourselves out of it. The honest policy Paul used here for his own preservation was to divide his judges, and to set them at variance one with another about him; and, by incensing one part of them more against him, to engage the contrary part for him.

1. The great council was made up of Sadducees and Pharisees, and Paul perceived it. He knew the characters of many of them ever since he lived among them, and saw those among them whom he knew to be Sadducees, and others whom he knew to be Pharisees (*v.* 6): *One part were Sadducees and the other Pharisees,* and perhaps nearly an equal part. Now these differed very much from one another, and yet they ordinarily agreed well enough to do the business of the council together. (1.) The Pharisees were bigots, zealous for the ceremonies, not only those which God had appointed, but those which were enjoined by the tradition of the elders. They were great sticklers for the authority of the church, and for enforcing obedience to its injunctions, which occasioned many quarrels between them and our Lord Jesus; but at the same time they were very orthodox in the faith of the Jewish church concerning the world of spirits, the resurrection of the dead, and the life of the world to come. (2.) The Sadducees were deists—no friends to the scripture, or divine revelation. The books of Moses they admitted as containing a good history and a good law, but had little regard to the other books of the Old Testament; see Matt. xxii. 23. The account here given of these Sadducees is, [1.] That they *deny the resurrection;* not only the return of the body to life, but a future state of rewards and punishments. They had neither hope of eternal happiness nor dread of eternal misery, nor expectation of any thing on the other side death; and it was upon these principles that they said, *It is in vain to serve God,* and called the proud happy, Mal. iii. 14, 15. [2.] That they denied the existence of angels and

spirits, and allowed of no being but matter. They thought that God himself was corporeal, and had parts and members as we have. When they read of angels in the Old Testament, they supposed them to be messengers that God made and sent on his errands as there was occasion, or that they were impressions on the fancies of those they were sent to, and no real existences—that they were this, or that, or any thing rather than what they were. And, as for the souls of men, they looked upon them to be nothing else but the temperament of the humours of the body, or the animal spirits, but denied their existence in a state of separation from the body, and any difference between the soul of a man and of a beast. These, no doubt, pretended to be free-thinkers, but really thought as meanly, absurdly, and slavishly, as possible. It is strange how men of such corrupt and wicked principles could come into office, and have a place in the great sanhedrim; but many of them were of quality and estate, and they complied with the public establishment, and so got in and kept in. But they were generally stigmatized as heretics, were ranked with the Epicureans, and were prayed against and excluded from eternal life. The prayer which the modern Jews use against Christians, Witsius thinks, was designed by Gamaliel, who made it, against the Sadducees; and that they meant them in their usual imprecation, *Let the name of the wicked rot.* But how degenerate was the character and how miserable the state of the Jewish church, when such profane men as these were among their rulers!

2. In this matter of difference between the Pharisees and Sadducees Paul openly declared himself to be on the Pharisees' side against the Sadducees (*v.* 6): He *cried out,* so as to be heard by all, "*I am a Pharisee,* was bred a Pharisee, nay, I was born one, in effect, for I was the *son of a Pharisee,* my father was one before me, and thus far I am still a Pharisee that I *hope for the resurrection of the dead,* and I may truly say that, if the matter were rightly understood, it would be found that this is it for which I am now *called in question.* When Christ was upon earth the Pharisees set themselves most against him, because he witnessed against their traditions and corrupt glosses upon the law; but, after his ascension, the Sadducees set themselves most against his apostles, because they *preached through Jesus the resurrection of the dead, ch.* iv. 1, 2. And it is said (*ch.* v. 17) that they were *the sect of the Sadducees* that were *filled with indignation* at them, because they preached that life and immortality which is *brought to light by the gospel.* Now here, (1.) Paul owns himself a Pharisee, so far as the Pharisees were in the right. Though as Pharisaism was opposed to Christianity he set himself against it, and against all its traditions that were set up in competition with the law of God or in contradiction to the gospel of Christ, yet, as it was opposed to Sadducism, he adhered to it. We must never think the worse of any truth of God, nor be more shy of owning it, for its being held by men otherwise corrupt. If the Pharisees will hope for the resurrection of the dead, Paul will go along with them in that hope, and be one of them, whether they will or no. (2.) He might truly say that being persecuted, as a Christian, this was the thing he was called in question for. Perhaps he knew that the Sadducees, though they had not such an interest in the common people as the Pharisees had, yet had underhand incensed the mob against him, under pretence of his having preached to the Gentiles, but really because he had preached the hope of the resurrection. However, being called in question for his being a Christian, he might truly say he was called in question for the hope of the resurrection of the dead, as he afterwards pleaded, *ch.* xxiv. 15, and *ch.* xxvi. 6, 7. Though Paul preached against the traditions of the elders (as his Master had done), and therein opposed the Pharisees, yet he valued himself more upon his preaching the resurrection of the dead, and a future state, in which he concurred with the Pharisees.

3. This occasioned a division in the council. It is probable that the high priest sided with the Sadducees (as he had done *ch.* v. 17, and made it to appear by his rage at Paul, *v.* 2), which alarmed the Pharisees so much the more; but so it was, there arose a *dissension between the Pharisees and the Sadducees* (*v.* 7), for this word of Paul's made the Sadducees more warm and the Pharisees more cool in the prosecution of him; so that *the multitude was divided; ἐσχίσθη—there was a schism,* a quarrel among them, and the edge of their zeal began to turn from Paul against one another; nor could they go on to act against him when they could not agree among themselves, or prosecute him for breaking the unity of the church when there was so little among them of the unity of the spirit. All the cry had been against Paul, but now there arose a great cry against one another, *v.* 9. So much did a fierce furious spirit prevail among all orders of the Jews at this time that every thing was done with clamour and noise; and in such a tumultuous manner were the great principles of their religion stickled for, by which they received little service, for *the wrath of man worketh not the righteousness of God.* Gainsayers may be convinced by fair reasoning, but never by a great cry.

4. The Pharisees hereupon (would one think it?) took Paul's part (*v.* 9): *They strove, διεμάχοντο—They fought, saying, We find no evil in this man.* He had conducted himself decently and reverently in the temple, and had attended the service of the church; and, though it was but occasionally, yet it showed

that he was not such an enemy to it as he was said to be. He had spoken very handsomely in his own defence, and given a good account of himself, and had now declared himself orthodox in the great principles of religion, as well as regular and conscientious in his conversation; and therefore they cannot see that he has *done any thing worthy of death or of bonds.* Nay, they go further, "*If a spirit or an angel hath spoken to him* concerning Jesus, and put him upon preaching as he does, though we may not be so far satisfied as to give credit to him, yet we ought to be cautioned not to oppose him, *lest we be found fighting against God;*" as Gamaliel, who was himself a Pharisee, had argued, *ch.* v. 39. Now here, (1.) We may observe, to the honour of the gospel, that it was witnessed to even by its adversaries, and confessions, not only of its innocency, but of its excellency, were extorted sometimes by the power of truth even from those that persecuted it. Pilate found no fault in Christ though he put him to death, nor Festus in Paul though he detained him in bonds; and the Pharisees here supposed it possible that Paul might have a commission sent him from heaven by an angel to do what he did; and yet it should seem, as elders, they after this joined with the high priest in prosecuting him, *ch.* xxiv. 1. They sinned against the knowledge which they not only had, but sometimes owned, as Christ had said of them, *They have both seen and hated both me and my Father*, John xv. 24. Yet, (2.) We will hope that some of them at least did henceforward conceive a better opinion of Paul than they had had, and were favourable to him, having had such a satisfactory account both of his conversation in all good conscience and of his faith touching another world; and then it must be observed to their honour that their zeal for the traditions of the elders, which Paul had departed from, was so far swallowed up in a zeal for the great and fundamental doctrines of religion, to which Paul still adhered, that if he will heartily join with them against the Sadducees, and adhere to the hope of the resurrection of the dead, they will not think his shaking off the ceremonial law to be an evil in him, but charitably hope that he walks according to the light God has given him by some angel or spirit, and are so far from persecuting him that they are ready to patronize and protect him. The persecuting Pharisees of the church of Rome are not of this spirit: for let a man be ever so sincere and zealous for all the articles of the Christian faith, yet, if he lay not his neck under the yoke of their church's authority, they find evil enough in him to persecute him unto the death.

II. The chief captain's care and conduct stand him in more stead; for when he has thrown this bone of contention between the Pharisees and Sadducees (which set them together by the ears, and gained a fair testimony from the Pharisees), yet he is never the nearer, but is in danger of being pulled in pieces by them—the Pharisees pulling to have him set at liberty, and the Sadducees pulling to have him put to death, or thrown to the people, like Daniel into the den of lions; so that the chief captain is forced to come with his soldiers and rescue him, as he had done, *ch.* xxi. 32, and *ch.* xxii. 24. 1. See here Paul's danger. Between his friends and his enemies he had like to have been pulled to pieces, the one hugging him to death, the other crushing him to death, such violences are those liable to that are eminent, and that are become remarkable, as Paul was, who was by some so much beloved and by others so much maligned. 2. His deliverance: *The chief captain ordered his soldiers to go down* from the upper wards, and *to take them by force from among them,* out of that apartment in *the temple* where he had ordered the council to meet, and *to bring him into the castle,* or tower of Antonio; for he saw he could make nothing of them towards the understanding of the merits of his cause.

III. Divine consolations stood him in most stead of all. The chief captain had rescued him out of the hands of cruel men, but still he had him in custody, and what might be the issue he could not tell. The castle was indeed a protection to him, but withal it was a confinement; and, as it was now his preservation from so great a death, it might be his reservation for a greater. We do not find that any of the apostles or elders at Jerusalem came to him; either they had not courage or they had not admission. Perhaps, in the night following, Paul was full of thoughts and cares what should become of him, and how his present troubles might be turned to answer some good purpose. Then did the Lord Jesus make him a kind visit, and, though at midnight, yet a very seasonable one (*v.* 11): *The Lord stood by him,* came to his bed-side, though perhaps it was but a bed of straw, to show him that he was all the day long with him really as sure as he was in the night with him visibly. Note, Whoever is against us, we need not fear if the Lord stand by us; if he undertake our protection, we may set those that seek our ruin at defiance. *The Lord is with those that uphold my soul,* and then nothing can come amiss. 1. Christ bids him have a good heart upon it: "*Be of good cheer, Paul;* be not discouraged; let not what has happened sadden thee, nor let what may yet be before thee frighten thee." Note, It is the will of Christ that his servants who are faithful should be always cheerful. Perhaps Paul, in the reflection, began to be jealous of himself whether he had done well in what he said to the council the day before; but Christ, by his word, satisfies him that God approved of his conduct. Or, perhaps, it troubled him that his friends did not come to him; but Christ's visit did itself speak, though he had not said, *Be of good cheer,*

Paul. 2. It is a strange argument which he makes use of to encourage him: *As thou hast testified of me in Jerusalem, so must thou bear witness also at Rome.* One would think this was but cold comfort: "As thou hast undergone a great deal of trouble for me so thou must undergo a great deal more;" and yet this was designed to encourage him; for hereby he is given to understand, (1.) That he had been serving Christ as a witness for him in what he had hitherto endured. It was for no fault that he was buffeted, and it was not his former persecuting of the church that was now remembered against him, however he might remember it against himself, but he was still going on with his work. (2.) That he had not yet finished his testimony, nor was, by his imprisonment, laid aside as useless, but was only reserved for further service. Nothing disheartened Paul so much as the thought of being taken off from doing service to Christ and good to souls: *Fear not,* says Christ, *I have not done with thee* (3.) Paul seems to have had a particular fancy, and an innocent one, to go to Rome, to preach the gospel there, though it was already preached, and a church planted there; yet, being citizen of Rome, he longed for a journey thither, and had designed it (*ch.* xix. 21): *After I have been at Jerusalem, I must also see Rome.* And he had written to the Romans some time ago *that he longed to see them,* Rom. i. 11. Now he was ready to conclude that this had broken his measures, and he should never see Rome; but even in that Christ tells him he should be gratified, since he desired it for the honour of Christ and to do good.

12 And when it was day, certain
of the Jews banded together, and
bound themselves under a curse,
saying that they would neither eat
nor drink till they had killed Paul.
13 And they were more than forty
which had made this conspiracy. 14
And they came to the chief priests
and elders, and said, We have bound
ourselves under a great curse, that
we will eat nothing until we have
slain Paul. 15 Now therefore ye
with the council signify to the chief
captain that he bring him down unto
you to morrow, as though ye would
enquire something more perfectly
concerning him: and we, or ever he
come near, are ready to kill him.
16 And when Paul's sister's son
heard of their lying in wait, he went
and entered into the castle, and told
Paul. 17 Then Paul called one of
the centurions unto *him,* and said,
Bring this young man unto the chief
captain: for he hath a certain thing
to tell him. 18 So he took him, and
brought *him* to the chief captain, and
said, Paul the prisoner called me
unto *him,* and prayed me to bring
this young man unto thee, who hath
something to say unto thee. 19
Then the chief captain took him by
the hand, and went *with him* aside
privately, and asked *him,* What is that
thou hast to tell me? 20 And he
said, The Jews have agreed to desire
thee that thou wouldest bring down
Paul to morrow into the council, as
though they would enquire somewhat
of him more perfectly. 21 But do
not thou yield unto them: for there
lie in wait for him of them more than
forty men, which have bound themselves with an oath, that they will
neither eat nor drink till they have
killed him: and now are they ready,
looking for a promise from thee. 22
So the chief captain *then* let the
young man depart, and charged *him,*
See thou tell no man that thou hast
showed these things to me. 23 And
he called unto *him* two centurions,
saying, Make ready two hundred
soldiers to go to Cæsarea, and horsemen threescore and ten, and spearmen two hundred, at the third hour
of the night; 24 And provide *them*
beasts, that they may set Paul on,
and bring *him* safe unto Felix the
governor. 25 And he wrote a letter
after this manner: 26 Claudius
Lysias unto the most excellent governor Felix *sendeth* greeting. 27
This man was taken of the Jews, and
should have been killed of them:
then came I with an army, and
rescued him, having understood that
he was a Roman. 28 And when I
would have known the cause wherefore they accused him, I brought him
forth into their council: 29 Whom I
perceived to be accused of questions
of their law, but to have nothing laid
to his charge worthy of death or of
bonds. 30 And when it was told
me how that the Jews laid wait for
the man, I sent straightway to thee,
and gave commandment to his ac-

cusers also to say before thee what
they had against him. Farewell. 31
Then the soldiers, as it was commanded them, took Paul, and brought
him by night to Antipatris. 32 On
the morrow they left the horsemen
to go with him, and returned to the
castle: 33 Who, when they came
to Cæsarea, and delivered the epistle
to the governor, presented Paul also
before him. 34 And when the governor had read *the letter*, he asked
of what province he was. And when
he understood that *he was* of Cilicia;
35 I will hear thee, said he, when
thine accusers are also come. And
he commanded him to be kept in
Herod's judgment hall.

We have here the story of a plot against the life of Paul; how it was laid, how it was discovered, and how it was defeated.

I. How this plot was laid. They found they could gain nothing by popular tumult, or legal process, and therefore have recourse to the barbarous method of assassination; they will come upon him suddenly, and stab him, if they can but get him within their reach. So restless is their malice against this good man that, when one design fails, they will turn another stone. Now observe here,

1. Who they were that formed this conspiracy. They were *certain Jews* that had the utmost degree of indignation against him because he was the apostle of the Gentiles, *v.* 12. *And they were more than forty* that were in the design, *v.* 13. *Lord, how are they increased that trouble me!*

2. When the conspiracy was formed: *When it was day. Satan had filled their hearts* in the night to purpose it, and, as soon as it was day, they got together to prosecute it; answering to the account which the prophet gives of some who *work evil upon their beds, and when the morning is light they practise it,* and are laid under a woe for it, Mic. ii. 1. In the night Christ appeared to Paul to protect him, and, when it was day, here were forty men appearing against him to destroy him; they were not up so soon but Christ was up before them *God shall help her, and that right early,* Ps. xlvi. 5.

3. What the conspiracy was. These men *banded together* in a league, perhaps they called it a *holy* league; they engaged to stand by one another, and every one, to his power, to be aiding and assisting to murder Paul. It was strange that so many could so soon be got together, and that in Jerusalem too, who were so perfectly lost to all sense of humanity and honour as to engage in so bloody a design. Well might the prophet's complaint be renewed concerning Jerusalem (Isa. i. 21): *Righteousness has lodged in it, but now murderers.* What a monstrous idea must these men have formed of Paul, before they could be capable of forming such a monstrous design against him; they must be made to believe that he was the worst of men, an enemy to God and religion, and the curse and plague of his generation; when really his character was the reverse of all this! What laws of truth and justice so sacred, so strong which malice and bigotry will not break through!

4. How firm they made it, as they thought, that none of them might fly off, upon conscience of the horror of the fact, at second thoughts: *They bound themselves under an anathema,* imprecating the heaviest curses upon themselves, their souls, bodies, and families, if they did not kill Paul, and so quickly *that they would not eat nor drink till they had done it.* What a complication of wickedness is here! To design to kill an innocent man, a good man, a useful man, a man that had done them no harm, but was willing to do them all the good he could, was *going in the way of Cain,* and proved them to be of *their father the devil, who was a murderer from the beginning;* yet, as if this had been a small matter, (1.) They bound themselves to it. To incline to do evil, and intend to do it, is bad; but to engage to do it is much worse. This is entering into covenant with the devil; it is swearing allegiance to the prince of darkness; it is leaving no room for repentance; nay, it is bidding defiance to it. (2.) They bound one another to it, and did all they could, not only to secure the damnation of their own souls, but of theirs whom they drew into the association. (3.) They showed a great contempt of the providence of God, and a presumption upon it, in that they bound themselves to do such a thing within so short a time as they could continue fasting, without any proviso or reserve for the disposal of an overruling Providence. When we say, *To-morrow we will do this or that,* be it ever so lawful and good, forasmuch as *we know not what shall be on the morrow,* we must add, *If the Lord will.* But with what face could they insert a proviso for the permission of God's providence when they knew that what they were about was directly against the prohibitions of God's word? (4.) They showed a great contempt of their own souls and bodies; of their own souls in imprecating a curse upon them if they did not proceed in this desperate enterprise (what a woeful dilemma did they throw themselves upon! God certainly meets them with his curse if they do go on in it, and they desire he would if they do not!)—and of their own bodies too (for wilful sinners are the destroyers of both) in tying themselves out from the necessary supports of life till they had accomplished a thing which they could never lawfully do, and perhaps not possibly do. Such language of hell those speak that wish God to damn them, and the devil to take them, if they do not do so and so. *As they love cursing,* so

shall it come unto them. Some think the meaning of this curse was, they would either kill Paul, as an Achan, an accursed thing, a troubler of the camp; or, if they did not do it, they would make themselves accursed before God in his stead. (5.) They showed a most eager desire to compass this matter, and an impatience till it was done: not only like David's enemies, *that were mad against him,* and *sworn against him* (Ps. cii. 8), but like the servants of Job against his enemy: *O that we had of his flesh! we cannot be satisfied,* Job xxxi. 31. Persecutors are said to *eat up God's people as they eat bread;* it is as much a gratification to them as meat to one that is hungry, Ps. xiv. 4.

5. What method they took to bring it about. There is no getting near Paul in the castle. He is there under the particular protection of the government, and is imprisoned, not, as others are, lest he should do harm, but lest he should have harm done him; and therefore the contrivance is that the chief priests and elders must desire the governor of the castle to let Paul come to them to the council-chamber, to be further examined (they have some questions to ask him, or something to say to him), and then, in his passage from the castle to the council, they would put an end to all disputes about Paul by killing him; thus the plot was laid, *v.* 14, 15. Having been all day employed in engaging one another to this wickedness, towards evening they come to the principal members of the great sanhedrim, and, though they might have concealed their mean design and yet might have moved them upon some other pretence to send for Paul, they are so confident of their approbation of this villany, that they are not ashamed nor afraid to own to them *that they have bound themselves under a great curse,* without consulting the priests first whether they might lawfully do it, *that they will eat nothing* the next day *till they have killed Paul.* They design to breakfast the next morning upon his blood. They doubt not but the chief priests will not only countenance them in the design, but will lend them a helping hand, and be their tools to get them an opportunity of killing Paul; nay, and tell a lie for them too, pretending to *the chief captain that they would enquire something more perfectly concerning him,* when they meant no such thing. What a mean, what an ill opinion had they of their priests, when they could apply to them on such an errand as this! And yet, vile as the proposal was which was made to them (for aught that appears), the priests and elders consented to it, and at the first word, without boggling at it in the least, promised to gratify them. Instead of reproving them, as they ought, for their wicked conspiracy, they bolstered them up in it, because it was against Paul whom they hated; and thus they made themselves partakers of the crime as much as if they had been the first in the conspiracy.

II. How the plot was discovered. We do not find that the plotters, though they took an oath of fidelity, took an oath of secrecy, either because they thought it did not need it (they would every one keep his own counsel) or because they thought they could accomplish it, though it should take wind and be known; but Providence so ordered it that it was brought to light, and so as effectually to be brought to nought. See here,

1. How it was discovered to Paul, *v.* 16. There was a youth that was related to Paul, *his sister's son,* whose mother probably lived in Jerusalem; and some how or other, we are not told how, *he heard of their lying in wait,* either overheard them talking of it among themselves, or got intelligence from some that were in the plot: and *he went into the castle,* probably, as he used to do, to attend on his uncle, and bring him what he wanted, which gave him a free access to him, and *he told Paul* what he heard. Note, God has many ways of bringing *to light the hidden works of darkness;* though the contrivers of them *dig deep to hide them from the Lord,* he can make a *bird of the air to carry the voice* (Eccl. x. 20), or the conspirators' own tongues to betray them.

2. How it was discovered to the chief captain by the young man that told it to Paul. This part of the story is related very particularly, perhaps because the penman was an eye-witness of the prudent and successful management of this affair, and remembered it with a great deal of pleasure. (1.) Paul had got a good interest in the officers that attended, by his prudent peaceable deportment. He could call one of the centurions to him, though a centurion was one in authority, that had soldiers under him, and used to call, not to be called to, and he was ready to come at his call (*v.* 17); and he desired that he would introduce this young man to the chief captain, to give in an information of something that concerned the honour of the government. (2.) The centurion very readily gratified him, *v.* 18. He did not send a common soldier with him, but went himself to keep the young man in countenance, to recommend his errand to the chief captain, and to show his respect to Paul: "*Paul the prisoner* (this was his title now) *called me to him, and prayed me to bring this young man to thee;* what his business is I know not, but *he has something to say to thee.*" Note, It is true charity to poor prisoners to act for them as well as to give to them. "*I was sick and in prison,* and you went on an errand for me," will pass as well in the account as, "*I was sick and in prison, and you came unto me,* to visit me, or sent me a token." Those that have acquaintance and interest should be ready to use them for the assistance of those that are in distress. This centurion helped to save Paul's life by this piece of civility, which should engage us to be ready to do the like when there is occasion. *Open*

thy mouth for the dumb, Prov. xxxi. 8. Those that cannot give a good gift to God's prisoners may yet speak a good word for them. (3.) The chief captain received the information with a great deal of condescension and tenderness, *v.* 19. He *took the young man by the hand*, as a friend or father, to encourage him, that he might not be put out of countenance, but might be assured of a favourable audience. The notice that is taken of this circumstance should encourage great men to make themselves easy of access to the meanest, upon any errand which may give them an opportunity of doing good—*to condescend to those of low estate.* This familiarity to which this Roman tribune or colonel admitted Paul's nephew is here upon record to his honour. Let no man think he disparages himself by his humility or charity. He *went with him aside privately*, that none might hear his business, *and asked him*, "*What is it that thou hast to tell me?* Tell me wherein I can be serviceable to Paul." It is probable that the chief captain was the more obliging in this case because he was sensible he had run himself into a premunire in binding Paul, against his privilege as a Roman citizen, which he was willing now to atone for. (4.) The young man delivered his errand to the chief captain very readily and handsomely (*v.* 20, 21). "*The Jews*" (he does not say who, lest he should invidiously reflect upon *the chief priests and the elders*; and his business was to save his uncle's life, not to accuse his enemies) "*have agreed to desire thee that thou wouldest bring down Paul to-morrow into the council*, presuming that, being so short a distance, thou wilt send him without a guard; *but do not thou yield unto them*, we have reason to believe thou wilt not when thou knowest the truth; *for there lie in wait for him of them more than forty men*, who have sworn to be the death of him, *and now are they ready looking for a promise from thee*, but I have happily got the start of them. (5). The captain dismissed the young man with a charge of secrecy: *See that thou tell no man that thou hast shown these things unto me*, *v.* 22. The favours of great men are not always to be boasted of; and those that cannot keep counsel are not fit to be employed in business. If it should be known that the chief captain had this information brought to him, perhaps they would compass and imagine the death of Paul some other way; "therefore keep it private."

III. How the plot was defeated: The chief captain, finding how implacable and inveterate the malice of the Jews was against Paul, how restless they were in their designs to do him a mischief, and how near he was to become himself accessory to it as a minister, resolves to send him away with all speed out of their reach. He received the intelligence with horror and indignation at the baseness and bloody-mindedness of these Jews; and seemed afraid lest, if he should detain Paul in his castle here, under ever so strong a guard, they would find some way or other to compass their end notwithstanding, either beating the guards or burning the castle; and, whatever came of it, he would, if possible, protect Paul, because he looked upon it that he did not deserve such treatment. What a melancholy observation is it, that the Jewish *chief priests*, when they knew of this assassination-plot, should countenance it, and assist in it, while a Roman *chief captain*, purely from a natural sense of justice and humanity, when he knows it, sets himself to baffle it, and puts himself to a greatt deal of trouble to do it effectually!

1. He orders a considerable detachment of the Roman forces under his command to get ready *to go to Cæsarea* with all expedition, and to bring Paul thither *to Felix the governor*, where he might sooner expect to have justice done him than by the great sanhedrim at Jerusalem. I see not but the chief captain might, without any unfaithfulness to the duty of his place, have set Paul at liberty, and given him leave to shift for his own safety, for he was never legally committed to his custody as a criminal, he himself owns *that nothing was laid to his charge worthy of bonds* (*v.* 29), and he ought to have had the same tenderness for his liberty that he had for his life; but he feared that this would have incensed the Jews too much against him. Or perhaps, finding Paul to be a very extraordinary man, he was proud to have him his prisoner, and under his protection; and the mighty parade with which he sent him off intimates as much. *Two centurions*, or captains of the hundreds, are employed in this business, *v.* 23, 24. They must *get ready two hundred soldiers*, probably those under their own command, *to go to Cæsarea;* and with these *seventy horse, and two hundred spearmen* besides, which some think were the *chief captain's* guards; whether they were horse or foot is not certain, most probably foot, as pikemen for the protection of the horse. See how justly God brought the Jewish nation under the Roman yoke, when such a party of the Roman army was necessary to restrain them from the most execrable villanies! There needed not all this force, there needed not any of it, to keep Paul from being rescued by his friends; ten times this force would not have kept him from being rescued by an angel, if it had pleased God to work his deliverance that way, as he had sometimes done; but, (1.) The chief captain designed hereby to expose the Jews, as a headstrong tumultuous people, that would not be kept within the bounds of duty and decency by the ordinary ministers of justice, but needed to be awed by such a train as this; and, hearing how many were in the conspiracy against Paul, he thought less would not serve to defeat their attempt. (2.) God designed hereby to encourage Paul; for, being thus attended, he was not only kept

safely in the hands of his friends, but out of the hands of his enemies. Yet Paul did not desire such a guard, any more than Ezra did (Ezra viii. 22), and for the same reason, because he trusted in God's all-sufficiency; it was owing, however, to the governor's own care. But he was also made considerable; thus his *bonds in Christ* were made manifest all the country over (Phil. i. 13); and, so great an honour having been put upon them before by the prediction of them, it was agreeable enough that they should be thus honourably attended, *that the brethren in the Lord might wax the more confident by his bonds,* when they saw him rather guarded as the patriot of his country than guarded against as the pest of his country, and so great a preacher made so great a prisoner. When his enemies hate him, and I doubt his friends neglect him, then does a Roman tribune patronise him, and carefully provide, [1.] For his ease: *Let them provide beasts, that they may set Paul on.* Had his Jewish persecutors ordered his removal by *habeas corpus* to Cæsarea, they would have made him run on foot, or dragged him thither in a cart, or on a sledge, or have horsed him behind one of the troopers; but the chief captain treats him like a gentleman, though he was his prisoner, and orders him a good horse to ride upon, not at all afraid that he should ride away. Nay, the order being that they should provide, not a beast, but beasts, to set Paul on, we must either suppose that he was allowed so great a piece of state as to have a led horse, or more, that if he did not like one he might take to another; or (as some expositors conjecture) that he had beasts assigned him for his friends and companions, as many as pleased to go along with him, to divert him in his journey, and to minister to him. [2.] For his security. They have a strict charge given them by their commander in chief *to bring him safely to Felix the governor,* to whom he is consigned, and who was supreme in all civil affairs among the Jews, as this chief captain was in military affairs. The Roman historians speak much of this Felix, as a man of mean extraction, but that raised himself by his shifts to be governor of Judea, in the execution of which office, Tacitus, *Hist.* 5, says this of him: *Per omnem sævitiam ac libidinem jus regium servili ingenio exercuit—He used royal power with a servile genius, and in connection with all the varieties of cruelty and lust.* To the judgment of such a man as this is poor Paul turned over; and yet better so than in the hands of *Ananias the high priest!* Now, a prisoner, thus upon his deliverance by course of law, ought to be protected as well as a prince.

2. The chief captain orders, for the greater security of Paul, that he be taken away at *the third hour of the night,* which some understand of three hours after sun-set, that, it being now soon after *the feast of pentecost* (that is, in the midst of summer), they might have the cool of the night to march in. Others understand it of *three hours after midnight, in the third watch, about three in the morning,* that they might have the day before them, and might get out of Jerusalem before Paul's enemies were stirring, and so might prevent any popular tumult, and leave them to roar when they rose, like a lion disappointed of his prey.

3. *He writes a letter to Felix the governor* of this province, by which he discharges himself from any further care about Paul, and leaves the whole matter with Felix. This letter is here inserted *totidem verbis—verbatim, v.* 25. It is probable that Luke the historian had a copy of it by him, having attended Paul in this remove. Now in this epistle we may observe,

(1.) The compliments he passes upon *the governor, v.* 26. He is *the most excellent governor Felix,* this title being given him of course, his excellency, &c. He sends him *greeting,* wishes him all health and prosperity; may he rejoice, may he ever rejoice.

(2.) The just and fair account which he gives him of Paul's case: [1.] That he was one that the Jews had a pique against: *They had taken him,* and would *have killed him;* and perhaps Felix knew the temper of the Jews so well that he did not think much the worse of him for that, *v.* 27. [2.] That he had protected him because he was a Roman: "When they were about to kill him, *I came with an army,* a considerable body of men, *and rescued him;*" which action for a citizen of Rome would recommend him to the Roman governor. [3.] That he could not understand the merits of his cause, nor what it was that made him so odious to the Jews, and obnoxious to their ill-will. He took the proper method to know: he *brought him forth into their council* (*v.* 28), to be examined there, hoping that, either from their complaints or his own confessions, he should learn something of the ground of all this clamour, but he found *that he was accused of questions of their law* (*v.* 29), about *the hope of the resurrection of the dead, v.* 6. This chief captain was a man of sense and honour, and had good principles in him of justice and humanity; and yet see how slightly he speaks of another world, and the great things of that world, as if that were a question, which is of undoubted certainty, and which both sides agreed in, except the Sadducees; and as if that were a question only *of their law,* which is of the utmost concern to all mankind! Or perhaps he refers rather to the question about their rituals than about their doctrinals, and the quarrel he perceived they had with him was for lessening the credit and obligation of their ceremonial law, which he looked upon as a thing not worth speaking of. The Romans allowed the nations they conquered the exercise of their own religion, and never offered to impose theirs upon them; yet, as conservators of the public peace, they would not suffer them, under colour of their religion, to abuse their neighbours. [4.] That thus far he understood that there was *nothing laid to his charge worthy of death or of bonds,* much less proved or made out against him. The Jews had, by their wickedness, made themselves odious to the world, had polluted their own honour and profaned their own crown, had brought disgrace upon their church, their law, and their holy place, and then they cry out against Paul, as having diminished the reputation of them; and was this a crime *worthy of death or of bonds?*

(3.) His referring Paul's case to Felix (*v.* 30): "*When it was told me that the Jews laid wait for the man,* to kill him, without any legal process against him, *I sent straightway to thee,* who art the most proper person to hear the cause, and give judgment upon it, and let *his accusers* go after him, if they please, and *say before thee what they have against him,* for, being bred a soldier, I will never pretend to be a judge, and so *farewell.*"

4. Paul was accordingly conducted to Cæsarea; the soldiers got him safely out of Jerusalem by night, and left the conspirators to consider whether they should eat and drink or no before they had killed Paul; and, if they would not repent of the wickedness of their oath as it was against Paul, they were now at leisure to repent of the rashness of it as it was against themselves; if any of them did starve themselves to death, in consequence of their oath and vexation at their disappointment, they fell unpitied. Paul was conducted to *Antipatris,* which was seventeen miles from Jerusalem, and about the mid-way to Cæsarea, *v.* 31. Thence *the two hundred foot-soldiers,* and *the two hundred spearmen, returned* back to Jerusalem, to their quarters in *the castle;* for, having conducted Paul out of danger, there needed not so strong a guard, but *the horsemen* might serve to bring him to Cæsarea, and would do it with more expedition; this they did, not only to save their own labour, but their master's charge; and it is an example to servants, not only to act obediently according to their masters' orders, but to act prudently, so as may be most for their masters' interest.

5. He was delivered into the hands of Felix, as his prisoner, *v.* 33. The officers *presented the letter,* and *Paul with it, to Felix,* and so discharged themselves of their trust. Paul had never affected acquaintance or society with great men, but with the disciples, wherever he came; yet Providence overrules his sufferings so as by them to give him an opportunity of witnessing to Christ before great men; and so Christ had foretold concerning his disciples, *that they should be brought before rulers and kings for his sake, for a testimony against them,* Mark xiii. 9. *The governor* enquired *of what province* of the empire the prisoner originally was, and was told *that he was a native of Cilicia, v.* 34; and, (1.) He promises him a speedy trial (*v.* 35): "*I will hear thee when thine accusers have come,* and will have an ear open to both sides, as becomes a judge." (2.) He ordered him into custody, that he should *be kept* a prisoner *in Herod's judgment-hall,* in some apartment belonging to that palace which was denominated from Herod the Great, who built it. There he had opportunity of acquainting himself with the great men that attended the governor's court, and, no doubt, he improved what acquaintance he got there to the best purposes.

CHAP. XXIV.

We left Paul a prisoner at Cæsarea, in Herod's judgment-hall, expecting his trial to come on quickly; for in the beginning of his imprisonment his affairs moved very quickly, but afterwards very slowly. In this chapter we have his arraignment and trial before Felix the governor at Cæsarea; here is, I. The appearing of the prosecutors against him, and the setting of the prisoner to the bar, ver. 1, 2. II. The opening of the indictment against him by Tertullus, who was of counsel for the prosecutors, and the aggravating of the charge, with abundance of compliments to the judge, and malice to the prisoner, ver. 2–8. III. The corroborating of the charge by the testimony of the witnesses, or rather the prosecutors themselves, ver. 9. IV. The prisoner's defence, in which, with all due deference to the governor (ver. 10), he denies the charge, and challenges them to prove it (ver. 11–13), owns the truth, and makes an unexceptionable profession of his faith, which he declares was it that they hated him for (ver. 14–16), and gives a more particular account of what had passed from their first seizing him, challenging them to specify any ill they had found in him, ver. 17–21. V. The adjourning of the cause, and the continuing of the prisoner in custody, ver. 22, 23. VI. The private conversation that was between the prisoner and the judge, by which the prisoner hoped to do good to the judge and the judge thought to get money by the prisoner, but both in vain, ver. 24–26. VII. The lengthening out of Paul's imprisonment for two years, till another governor came (ver. 27), where he seems as much neglected as there had been ado about him.

AND after five days Ananias the
high priest descended with the
elders, and *with* a certain orator
named Tertullus, who informed the
governor against Paul. 2 And when
he was called forth, Tertullus began
to accuse *him,* saying, Seeing that by
thee we enjoy great quietness, and
that very worthy deeds are done
unto this nation by thy providence,
3 We accept *it* always, and in all
places, most noble Felix, with all
thankfulness. 4 Notwithstanding,
that I be not further tedious unto
thee, I pray thee that thou wouldest
hear us of thy clemency a few words.
5 For we have found this man *a*
pestilent *fellow,* and a mover of sedition among all the Jews throughout
the world, and a ringleader of the
sect of the Nazarenes: 6 Who also
hath gone about to profane the temple: whom we took, and would have
judged according to our law. 7 But
the chief captain Lysias came *upon*
us, and with great violence took *him*
away out of our hands. 8 Com-

manding his accusers to come unto thee: by examining of whom thyself mayest take knowledge of all these things, whereof we accuse him. 9 And the Jews also assented, saying that these things were so.

We must suppose *that Lysias, the chief captain,* when he had *sent away Paul to Cæsarea,* gave notice to the chief priests, and others that had appeared against Paul, that if they had any thing to accuse him of they must follow him to Cæsarea, and there they would find him, and a judge ready to hear them—thinking, perhaps, they would not have given themselves so much trouble; but what will not malice do?

I. We have here the cause followed against Paul, and it is vigorously carried on. 1. Here is no time lost, for they are ready for a hearing *after five days;* all other business is laid aside immediately, to prosecute Paul; so intent are evil men to do evil! Some reckon *these five days* from Paul's being first seized, and with most probability, for he says here (*v.* 11) *that it was but twelve days since he came up to Jerusalem,* and he had *spent seven in his purifying in the temple,* so that these five must be reckoned from the last of those. 2. Those who had been his judges do themselves appear here as his prosecutors. *Ananias* himself *the high priest,* who had sat to judge him, now stands to inform against him. One would wonder, (1.) That he should thus disparage himself, and forget the dignity of his place. Shall *the high priest* turn informer, and leave all his business in *the temple at Jerusalem,* to go to be called as a prosecutor in *Herod's judgment-hall?* Justly did God make *the priests contemptible and base,* when they made themselves so, Mal. ii. 9. (2.) That he should thus discover himself and his enmity against Paul! If men of the first rank have a malice against any, they think it policy to employ others against them, and to play least in sight themselves, because of the odium that commonly attends it; but Ananias is not ashamed to own himself a sworn enemy to Paul. *The elders* attended him, to signify their concurrence with him, and to invigorate the prosecution; for they could not find any attorneys or solicitors that would follow it with so much violence as they desired. The pains that evil men take in an evil matter, their contrivances, their condescensions, and their unwearied industry, should shame us out of our coldness and backwardness, and our indifference in that which is good.

II. We have here the cause pleaded against Paul. The prosecutors brought *with them a certain orator named Tertullus,* a Roman, skilled in the Roman law and language, and therefore fittest to be employed in a cause before *the Roman governor,* and most likely to gain favour. The high priest, and elders, though they had their own hearts spiteful enough, did not think their own tongues sharp enough, and therefore retained Tertullus, who probably was noted for a satirical wit, to be of counsel for them; and, no doubt, they gave him a good fee, probably out of the treasury of the temple, which they had the command of, it being a cause wherein the church was concerned and which therefore must not be starved. Paul is set to the bar before Felix the governor: *He was called forth, v.* 2. Tertullus's business is, on the behalf of the prosecutors, to open the information against him, and he is a man that will say any thing for his fee; mercenary tongues will do so. No cause so unjust but can find advocates to plead it; and yet we hope many advocates are so just as not knowingly to patronise an unrighteous cause, but Tertullus was none of these: his speech (or at least an abstract of it, for it appears, by Tully's orations, that the Roman lawyers, on such occasions, used to make long harangues) is here reported, and it is made up of flattery and falsehood; it calls evil good, and good evil.

1. One of the worst of men is here applauded as one of the best of benefactors, only because he was the judge. Felix is represented by the historians of his own nation, as well as by Josephus the Jew, as a very bad man, who, depending upon his interest in the court, allowed himself in all manner of wickedness, was a great oppressor, very cruel, and very covetous, patronising and protecting assassins.—Joseph. *Antiq.* lib. xx. cap. 6. And yet Tertullus here, in the name of the high priest and elders, and probably by particular directions from them and according to the instructions of his breviate, compliments him, and extols him to the sky, as if he were so good a magistrate as never was the like: and this comes the worse from the high priest and the elders, because he had given a late instance of his enmity to their order; for Jonathan the high priest, or one of the chief priests, having offended him by too free an invective against the tyranny of his government, he had him murdered by some villains whom he hired for that purpose, and who afterwards did the like for others, as they were hired: *Cujus facinoris quia nemo ultor extitit, invitati hac licentia sicarii multos confodiebant, alios propter privatas inimicitias, alios conducti pecunia, etiam in ipso templo—No one being found to punish such enormous wickedness, the assassins, encouraged by this impunity, stabbed several persons, some from personal malice, some for hire, and that even in the temple itself.* And yet, to engage him to gratify their malice against Paul, and to return them that kindness for their kindness in overlooking all this, they magnify him as the greatest blessing to their church and nation that ever came among them.

(1.) They are very ready to own it (*v.* 2):

"*By thee we,* of the church, *enjoy great quietness,* and we look upon thee as our patron and protector, *and very worthy deeds are done,* from time to time, *to the whole nation of the Jews, by thy providence*—thy wisdom, and care, and vigilance." To give him his due, he had been instrumental to suppress the insurrection of that Egyptian of whom the chief captain spoke (*ch.* xxi. 38); but will the praise of that screen him from the just reproach of his tyranny and oppression afterwards? See here, [1.] The unhappiness of great men, and a great unhappiness it is, to have their services magnified beyond measure, and never to be faithfully told of their faults: and hereby they are hardened and encouraged in evil. [2.] The policy of bad men, by flattering princes in what they do amiss to draw them in to do worse. The bishops of Rome got themselves confirmed in their exorbitant church power, and have been assisted in persecuting the servants of Christ, by flattering and caressing usurpers and tyrants, and so making them the tools of their malice, as the high priest, by his compliments, designed to make Felix here.

(2.) They promise to retain a grateful sense of it (*v.* 3): "*We accept it always, and in all places,* every where and at all times we embrace it, we admire it, *most noble Felix, with all thankfulness.* We will be ready, upon any occasion, to witness for thee, that thou art a wise and good governor, and very serviceable to the country." And, if it had been true that he was such a governor, it had been just that they should thus accept his good offices with all thankfulness. The benefits which we enjoy by government, especially by the administration of wise and good governors, are what we ought to be thankful for, both to God and man. This is part of the honour due to magistrates, to acknowledge the quietness we enjoy under their protection, and the worthy deeds done by their prudence.

(3.) They therefore expect his favour in this cause, *v.* 4. They pretend a great care not to intrench upon his time: We will *not be further tedious to thee;* and yet to be very confident of his patience: *I pray thee that thou wouldest hear us of thy clemency a few words.* All this address is only *ad captandam benevolentiam—to induce him to give countenance to their cause;* and they were so conscious to themselves that it would soon appear to have more malice than matter in it that they found it necessary thus to insinuate themselves into his favour. Every body knew that the high priest and the elders were enemies to the Roman government, and were uneasy under all the marks of that yoke, and therefore, in their hearts, hated Felix; and yet, to gain their ends against Paul, they, by their counsel, show him all this respect, as they did to Pilate and Cæsar when they were persecuting our Saviour. Princes cannot always judge of the affections of their people by their applauses; flattery is one thing, and true loyalty is another.

2. One of the best of men is here accused as one of the worst of malefactors, only because he was the prisoner. After a flourish of flattery, in which you cannot see matter for words, he comes to his business, and it is to inform his excellency concerning the prisoner at the bar; and this part of his discourse is as nauseous for its raillery as the former part is for its flattery. I pity the man, and believe he has no malice against Paul, nor does he think as he speaks in calumniating him, any more than he did in courting Felix; but, as I cannot but be sorry that a man of wit and sense should have such a saleable tongue (as one calls it), so I cannot but be angry at those dignified men that had such malicious hearts as to put such words into his mouth. Two things Tertullus here complains of to Felix, in the name of the high priest and the elders:—

(1.) That the peace of the nation was disturbed by Paul. They could not have baited Christ's disciples if they had not first dressed them up in the skins of wild beasts, nor have given them as they did the vilest of treatment if they had not first represented them as the vilest of men, though the characters they gave of them were absolutely false and there was not the least colour nor foundation for them. Innocence, nay excellence and usefulness, are no fence against calumny, no, nor against the impressions of calumny upon the minds both of magistrates and multitudes to excite their fury and jealousy; for, be the representation ever so unjust, when it is enforced, as here it was, with gravity and pretence of sanctity, and with assurance and noise, something will stick. The old charge against God's prophets was that they were the troublers of the land, and against God's Jerusalem that it was a rebellious city, hurtful to kings and provinces (Ezra iv. 15, 19), and against our Lord Jesus that he perverted the nation, and forbade to give tribute to Cæsar. It is the very same against Paul here; and, though utterly false, is averred with all the confidence imaginable. They do not say, "We suspect him to be a dangerous man, and have taken him up upon that suspicion;" but, as if the thing were past dispute, "*We have found him* to be so; we have often and long found him so;" as if he were a traitor and rebel already convicted. And yet, after all, there is not a word of truth in this representation; but, if Paul's just character be enquired into, it will be found directly the reverse of this.

[1.] Paul was a useful man, and a great blessing to his country, a man of exemplary candour and goodness, obliging to all, and provoking to none; and yet he is here called *a pestilent fellow* (*v.* 5): "*We have found him,* λοιμὸν—*pestem—the plague* of the nation, a walking pestilence, which supposes him to be a man of a turbulent spirit, malicious and ill-natured, and one that threw all things in disorder wherever he came. They would have it thought that he had done more mischief in his time than a plague could do,—that the mischief he did was spreading and infectious, and that he made others as mischievous as himself,—that it was of as fatal consequence as the plague is, killing and destroying, and laying all waste,—that it was as much to be dreaded and guarded against as a plague is. Many a good sermon he had preached, and many a good work he had done, and for these he is called a pestilent fellow.

[2.] Paul was a peace-maker, was a preacher of that gospel which has a direct tendency to *slay all enmities,* and to establish true and lasting peace; he lived peaceably and quietly himself, and taught others to do so too, and yet is here represented as *a mover of sedition among all the Jews throughout all the world.* The Jews were disaffected to the Roman government; those of them that were most bigoted were most so. This Felix knew, and had therefore a watchful eye upon them. Now they would fain make him believe that this Paul was the man that made them so, whereas they themselves were the men that sowed the seeds of faction and sedition among them: and they knew it; and the reason why they hated Christ and his religion was because he did not go about to head them in an opposition to the Romans. The Jews were every where much set against Paul, and stirred up the people to clamour against him; they moved sedition in all places where he came, and then cast the blame unjustly upon him, as if he had been the mover of the sedition; as Nero not long after set Rome on fire, and then said the Christians did it.

[3.] Paul was a man of catholic charity, who did not affect to be singular, but made himself the servant of all for their good; and yet he is here charged as being a *ringleader of the sect of the Nazarenes,* a standard-bearer of that sect, so the word signifies. When Cyprian was condemned to die for being a Christian, this was inserted in his sentence, that he was *auctor iniqui nominis et signifer—The author and standard-bearer of a wicked cause.* Now it was true that Paul was an active leading man in propagating Christianity. But, *First,* It was utterly false that this was a sect; he did not draw people to a party or private opinion, nor did he make his own opinions their rule. True Christianity establishes that which is of common concern to all mankind, publishes good-will to men, and shows us God in Christ reconciling the world to himself, and therefore cannot be thought to take its rise from such narrow opinions and private interests as sects owe their origin to. True Christianity has a direct tendency to the uniting of the children of men, and the gathering of them together in one; and, as far as it obtains its just power and influence upon the minds of men, will make them meek and quiet, and peaceable and loving, and every way easy, acceptable, and profitable one to another, and therefore is far from being a sect, which is supposed to lead to division and to sow discord. True Christianity aims at no worldly benefit or advantage, and therefore must by no means be called a sect. Those that espouse a sect are governed in it by their secular interest, they aim at wealth and honour; but the professors of Christianity are so far from this that they expose themselves thereby to the loss and ruin of all that is dear to them in this world. *Secondly,* It is invidiously called *the sect of the Nazarenes,* by which Christ was represented as of Nazareth, whence no good thing was expected to arise; whereas he was of Bethlehem, where the Messiah was to be born. Yet he was pleased to call himself, *Jesus of Nazareth, ch.* xxii. 8. And the scripture has put an honour on the name, Matt. ii. 23. And therefore, though intended for a reproach, the Christians had no reason to be ashamed of sharing with their Master in it. *Thirdly,* It was false that Paul was the author or standard-bearer of this sect; for he did not draw people to himself, but to Christ—did not preach himself, but Christ Jesus.

[4.] Paul had a veneration for the temple, as it was the place which God had chosen to put his name there, and had lately himself with reverence attended the temple-service; and yet it is here charged upon him that he went about to *profane the temple,* and that he designedly put contempt upon it, and violated the laws of it, *v.* 6. Their proof of this failed; for what they alleged as matter of fact was utterly false, and they knew it, *ch.* xxi. 29.

(2.) That the course of justice against Paul was obstructed by the chief captain. [1.] They pleaded that they *took him, and would have judged him according to their law.* This was false; they did not go about to judge him according to their law, but, contrary to all law and equity, went about to *beat him to death* or to *pull him to pieces,* without hearing what he had to say for himself—went about, under pretence of having him into their court, to throw him into the hands of ruffians that lay in wait to destroy him. Was this judging him according to their law? It is easy for men, when they know what they should have done, to say, this they would have done, when they meant nothing less. [2.] They reflected upon the chief captain as having done them an injury in rescuing Paul out of their hands; whereas he therein not only did him justice, but them the greatest kindness that could be, in preventing the guilt they were bringing upon themselves: *The chief captain Lysias came upon us and with great violence* (but really no more than was necessary) *took him out of our hands, v.* 7. See how persecutors are enraged at their disappointments, which they ought to be thankful for. When David in a heat of passion was going upon a bloody enterprise, he thanked Abigail for stopping him, and God for sending her to do it, so soon did he correct and recover himself. But these cruel men justify themselves, and reckon him their enemy who kept them (as David there speaks) from shedding blood with their own hands. [3.] They referred the matter to Felix and his judgment, yet seeming uneasy that they were under a necessity of doing so, the chief captain having obliged them to it (*v.* 8): "It was he that forced us to give your excellency this trouble, and ourselves too; for," *First,* "He *commanded his accusers to come to thee,* that thou mightest hear the charge, when it might as well have been ended in the inferior court." *Secondly,* "He has left it to thee to examine him, and try what thou canst get out of him, and whether thou canst by his confession come to the knowledge of those things which we lay to his charge."

III. The assent of the Jews to this charge which Tertullus exhibited (*v.* 9): *They confirmed it, saying that those things were so.* 1. Some think this expresses the proof of their charge by witnesses upon oath, that were examined as to the particulars of it, and attested them. And no wonder if, when they had found an orator that would say it, they found witnesses that would swear it, for money. 2. It rather seems to intimate the approbation which the high priest and the elders gave to what Tertullus said. Felix asked them, "Is this your sense, and is it all that you have to say?" And they answered, "Yes it is;" and so they made themselves guilty of all the falsehood that was in his speech. Those that have not the wit and parts to do mischief with that some others have, that cannot make speeches and hold disputes against religion, yet make themselves guilty of the mischiefs others do, by assenting to that which others do, and saying, These things are so, repeating and standing by what is said, to *pervert the right ways of the Lord.* Many that have not learning enough to plead for Baal yet have wickedness enough to vote for Baal.

10 Then Paul, after that the governor had beckoned unto him to
speak, answered, Forasmuch as I
know that thou hast been of many
years a judge unto this nation, I do
the more cheerfully answer for myself: 11 Because that thou mayest
understand, that there are yet but
twelve days since I went up to Jerusalem for to worship. 12 And
they neither found me in the temple
disputing with any man, neither
raising up the people, neither in the
synagogues, nor in the city: 13
Neither can they prove the things
whereof they now accuse me. 14
But this I confess unto thee, that
after the way which they call heresy,
so worship I the God of my fathers,
believing all things which are written
in the law and in the prophets: 15
And have hope toward God, which
they themselves also allow, that there
shall be a resurrection of the dead,
both of the just and unjust. 16 And
herein do I exercise myself, to have
always a conscience void of offence
toward God, and *toward* men. 17
Now after many years I came to
bring alms to my nation, and offerings. 18 Whereupon certain Jews
from Asia found me purified in the
temple, neither with multitude, nor
with tumult. 19 Who ought to have
been here before thee, and object, if
they had ought against me. 20 Or
else let these same *here* say, if they
have found any evil doing in me,
while I stood before the council, 21
Except it be for this one voice, that I
cried standing among them, Touching
the resurrection of the dead I am
called in question by you this day.

We have here Paul's defence of himself, in answer to Tertullus's charge, and there appears in it a great deal of the spirit of wisdom and holiness, and an accomplishment of Christ's promise to his followers that when they were before governors and kings, for his sake, it should be *given them in that same hour what they should speak.* Though Tertullus had said a great many provoking things, yet Paul did not interrupt him, but let him go on to the end of his speech, according to the rules of decency and the method in courts of justice, that the plaintiff be allowed to finish his evidence before the defendant begins his plea. And when he had done, he did not presently fly out into passionate exclamations against the iniquity of the times and the men *(O tempora! O mores!—Oh the degeneracy of the times!)* but he waited for a permission from the judge to speak in his turn, and had it. The *governor beckoned to him to speak, v.* 10. And now he also may have leave to speak out, under the protection of the governor, which was more than he could hitherto obtain. And, when he did speak, he made no reflections at all upon Tertullus, who he knew spoke for his fee, and therefore despised what he said, and levelled his defence against those that employed him. And here,

I. He addressed himself very respectfully to the governor, and with a confidence that he would do him justice. Here are no such flattering compliments as Tertullus soothed him up with, but, which was more truly respectful, a profession that he *answered for himself cheerfully,* and with good assurance *before him,* looking upon him, though not as one that was his friend, yet as one that would be fair and impartial. He thus expresses his expectation that he would be so, to engage him to be so. It was likewise the language of one that was conscious to himself of his own integrity, and whose heart did not reproach him, whoever did. He did not stand trembling at the bar; on the contrary, he was very cheerful when he had one to be his judge that was not a party, but an indifferent person. Nay, when he considers who his judge is, he *answers the more cheerfully;* and why so? He does not say, "Because I know thee to be a judge of inflexible justice and integrity, that hatest bribes, and in giving judgment fearest God, and regardest not man;" for he could not justly say this of him, and therefore would not say it, though it were to gain his favour ever so much; but, *I the more cheerfully answer for myself,* because *I know thou hast been many years a judge to this nation;* and this was very true, and being so, 1. He could say of his own knowledge that there had not formerly been any complaints against Paul. Such clamours as they raised are generally against old offenders; but, though he had long sat judge there, he never had Paul brought before him till now; and therefore he was not so dangerous a criminal as he was represented to be. 2. He was well acquainted with the Jewish nation, and with their temper and spirit. He knew how bigoted they were to their own way, what furious zealots they were against all that did not comply with them, how peevish and perverse they generally were, and therefore would make allowances for that in their accusation of him, and not regard that which he had reason to think came so much from party-malice. Though he did not know him, he knew his prosecutors, and by this might guess what manner of man he was.

II. He denies the facts that he was charged with, upon which their character of him was grounded. *Moving sedition,* and *profaning the temple,* were the crimes for which he stood indicted, crimes which they knew the Roman governors were not accustomed to enquire into, and therefore they hoped that the governor would return him back to them to be judged by their law, and this was all they wished for. But Paul desires that though he would not enquire into the crimes he would protect one that was unjustly charged with them from those whom he knew to be spiteful and ill-natured enough. Now he would have him to understand (and what he said he was ready, if required, to make out by witnesses),

1. That he came up to Jerusalem on purpose to worship God in peace and holiness, so far was he from any design to move sedition among the people, or to profane the temple. He came to keep up his communion with the Jews, not to put any affront upon them.

2. That it was but twelve days since he came up to Jerusalem, and he had been six days a prisoner; he was alone, and it could not be supposed that in so short a time he could do the mischief they charged upon him. And, as for what he had done in other countries, they knew nothing of it but by uncertain report, by which the matter was very unfairly represented.

3. That he had demeaned himself at Jerusalem very quietly and peaceably, and had made no manner of stir. If it had been true (as they alleged) that he was a *mover of sedition among all the Jews,* surely he would have been industrious to make a party at Jerusalem: but he did not do so. He was in the temple, attending the public service there. He was in the synagogues where the law was read and opened. He went about in the city among his relations and friends, and conversed freely in the places of concourse; and he was a man of a great genius and an active spirit, and yet they could not charge him with offering any thing either against the faith or against the peace of the Jewish church. (1.) He had nothing in him of a contradicting spirit, as the movers of sedition have; he had no disposition to quarrel or oppose. They never found him *disputing with any man,* either affronting the learned with captious cavils or perplexing the weak and simple with curious subtleties. He was ready, if asked, to give a reason of his own hope, and to give instruction to others; but he never picked a quarrel with any man about his religion, nor made that the subject of debate, and controversy, and perverse dispute, which ought always to be treated of with humility and reverence, with meekness and love. (2.) He had nothing in him of a turbulent spirit: "They never found me *raising up the people,* by incensing them against their governors in church or state or suggesting to them fears and jealousies concerning public affairs, nor by setting them at variance one with another or sowing discord among them." He behaved as became a Christian and minister, with love and quietness, and due subjection to lawful authority. The weapons of his warfare were not carnal, nor did he ever mention or think of such a thing as taking up arms for the propagating of the gospel or the defence of the preachers of it; though he could have made, perhaps, as strong a party among the common people as his adversaries, yet he never attempted it.

4. That as to what they had charged him with, of moving sedition in other countries, he was wholly innocent, and they could not make good the charge (*v.* 13): *Neither can they prove the things whereof they now accuse me.* Hereby, (1.) He maintains his own in-

nocency; for when he says, They cannot prove it, he means, The matter is not so. He was no enemy to the public peace; he had done no real prejudice, but a great deal of real service, and would gladly have done more, to the nation of the Jews. He was so far from having any antipathy to them that he had the strongest affection imaginable for them, and a most passionate desire for their welfare, Rom. ix. 1—3. (2.) He bemoans his own calamity, that he was accused of those things which could not be proved against him. And it has often been the lot of very worthy good men to be thus injured, to have things laid to their charge which they are at the greatest distance from and abhor the thought of. But, while they are lamenting this calamity, this may be their rejoicing, even the *testimony of their consciences* concerning their integrity. (3.) He shows the iniquity of his prosecutors, who said that which they knew they could not prove, and thereby did him wrong in his name, liberty, and life, and did the judge wrong too, in imposing upon him, and doing what in them lay to pervert his judgment. (4.) He appeals to the equity of his judge, and awakens him to look about him, that he might not be drawn into a snare by the violence of the prosecution. The judge must give sentence *secundum allegata et probata—according to that which is not only alleged but proved,* and therefore must enquire, and make search, and ask diligently, whether the thing be true and certain (Deut. xiii. 14); he cannot otherwise give a right judgment.

III. He gives a fair and just account of himself, which does at once both clear him from crime and likewise intimate what was the true reason of their violence in prosecuting him.

1. He acknowledges himself to be one whom they looked upon as a heretic, and that was the reason of their spleen against him. The chief captain had observed, and the governor now cannot but observe, an uncommon violence and fury in his prosecutors, which they know not what to make of, but, guessing at the crime by the cry, conclude he must needs have been a very bad man only for that reason. Now Paul here unriddles the matter: I confess that *in the way which they call heresy*—or a *sect, so worship I the God of my fathers.* The controversy is in a matter of religion, and such controversies are commonly managed with most fury and violence. Note, It is no new thing for the right way of worshipping God to be called heresy; and for the best of God's servants to be stigmatized and run down as sectaries. The reformed churches are called heretical ones by those who themselves hate to be reformed, and are themselves heretics. Let us therefore never be driven off from any good way by its being put into an ill name; for true and pure Christianity is never the worse, nor to be the worse thought of, for its being called heresy; no, not though it be called so by the high priest and the elders.

2. He vindicates himself from this imputation. They call Paul a heretic, but he is not so; for,

(1.) He *worships the God of his fathers,* and therefore is right in the object of his worship. He does not say, *Let us go after other gods, which we have not known, and let us serve them,* as the false prophet is supposed to do, Deut. xiii. 2. If so, they might justly call his way heresy, a drawing of them aside into a by-path, and a dangerous one; but he worships the God of Abraham, Isaac, and Jacob, not only the God whom they worshipped, but the God who took them into covenant with himself, and was and would be called their God. Paul adheres to that covenant, and sets up no other in opposition to it. The *promise made unto the fathers* Paul preached as *fulfilled to the children* (*ch.* xiii. 32, 33), and so directed both his own devotions and those of others to God, as the *God of their fathers.* He also refers to the practice of all his pious ancestors: *I worship* the same God that all my fathers worshipped. His religion was so far from being chargeable with novelty that it gloried in its antiquity, and in an uninterrupted succession of its professors. Note, It is very comfortable in our worshipping God to have an eye to him as the God of our fathers. Our fathers trusted in him, and were owned by him, and he engaged to be their God, and the God of their seed. He approved himself theirs, and therefore, if we serve him as they did, he will be ours; what an emphasis is laid upon this, *He is my father's God, and I will exalt him!* Exod. xv. 2.

(2.) He *believes all things which are written in the law and the prophets,* and therefore is right in the rule of his worship. His religion is grounded upon, and governed by, the holy scriptures; they are his oracle and touchstone, and he speaks and acts according to them. He receives the scriptures entire, and believes all things that are there written; and he receives them pure, for he says no other things than what are contained in them, as he explains himself, *ch.* xxvi. 22. He sets not up any other rule of faith or practice but the scriptures—not tradition, nor the authority of the church, nor the infallibility of any man or company of men on earth, nor the light within, nor human reason; but divine revelation, as it is in the scripture, is that which he resolves to live and die by, and therefore he is not a heretic.

(3.) He has his eye upon a future state, and is a believing expectant of that, and therefore is right in the end of his worship. Those that turn aside to heresy have a regard to this world, and some secular interest, but Paul aims to make heaven of his religion, and neither more nor less (*v.* 15): "*I have hope towards God,* all my expectation is from him, and therefore all my desire is towards him and all my dependence upon him; my hope is towards God and not towards the world, towards another world and not towards this. I depend upon God and upon his power, that *there shall be a resurrection of the dead* at the end of time, of all, both *the just and unjust;* and the great thing I aim at in my religion is to obtain a joyful and happy resurrection, a share in the resurrection of the just." Observe here, [1.] That there shall be a resurrection of the dead, the dead bodies of men, of all men from the beginning to the end of time. It is certain, not only that the soul does not die with the body, but that the body itself shall live again; we have not only another life to live when our present life is at an end, but there is to be another world, which shall commence when this world is at an end, into which all the children of men must enter at once by a resurrection from the dead, as they entered into this, one after another, by their birth. [2.] It shall be a resurrection *both of the just and of the unjust*, the sanctified and the unsanctified, of those that did well, and to them our Saviour has told us that it will be a *resurrection of life;* and of those that did evil, and to them that it will be a resurrection of condemnation, John v. 29. See Dan. xii. 2. This implies that it will be a resurrection to a final judgment, by which all the children of men will be determined to everlasting happiness or misery in a world of retribution, according to what they were and what they did in this state of probation and preparation. The just shall rise by virtue of their union with Christ as their head; the unjust shall rise by virtue of Christ's dominion over them as their Judge. [3.] God is to be depended upon for the resurrection of the dead: I have *hope towards God*, and in God, that there shall be a resurrection; it shall be effected by the almighty power of God, in performance of the word which God hath spoken; so that those who doubt of it betray their ignorance both of the scriptures and of the power of God, Matt. xxii. 29. [4.] The resurrection of the dead is a fundamental article of our creed, as it was also of that of the Jewish church. It is what *they themselves also allow;* nay, it was the expectation of the ancient patriarchs, witness Job's confession of his faith; but it is more clearly revealed and more fully confirmed by the gospel, and therefore those who believed it should have been thankful to the preachers of the gospel for their explications and proofs of it, instead of opposing them. [5.] In all our religion we ought to have an eye to the other world, and to serve God in all instances with a confidence in him *that there will be a resurrection of the dead,* doing all in preparation for that, and expecting our recompence in that.

(4.) His conversation is of a piece with his devotion (*v.* 16): *And herein do I exercise myself, to have always a conscience void of offence towards God and towards men.* Prophets and their doctrine were to be tried by their fruits. Paul was far from having made shipwreck of a good conscience, and therefore it is not likely he has made shipwreck of the faith, the mystery of which is best held in a pure conscience. This protestation of Paul's is to the same purport with that which he made before the high priest (*ch.* xxiii. 1): *I have lived in all good conscience;* and this was his rejoicing. Observe, [1.] What was Paul's aim and desire: To *have a conscience void of offence.* Either, *First,* "A conscience not offending; not informing me wrong, nor flattering me, nor dealing deceitfully with me, nor in any thing misleading me." Or, *Secondly,* A conscience not offended; it is like Job's resolution, "*My heart shall not reproach me,* that is, I will never give it any occasion to do so. This is what I am ambitious of, to keep upon good terms with my own conscience, that it may have no cause either to question the goodness of my spiritual state or to quarrel with me for any particular action. I am as careful not to offend my conscience as I am not to offend a friend with whom I daily converse; nay, as I am not to offend a magistrate whose authority I am under, and to whom I am accountable; for conscience is God's deputy in my soul." [2.] What was his care and endeavour, in pursuance of this: "*I exercise myself—ἀσκῶ.* I make it my constant business, and govern myself by this intention; I discipline myself, and live by rule" (those that did so were called *ascetics,* from the word here used), "abstain from many a thing which my inclination leads me to, and abound in all the exercises of religion that are most spiritual, with this in my eye, that I may keep peace with my own conscience." [3.] The extent of this care: *First,* To all times: *To have always a conscience void of offence,* always void of gross offence; for though Paul was conscious to himself that he *had not yet attained perfection,* and the evil that he would not do yet he did, yet he was *innocent from the great transgression.* Sins of infirmity are uneasy to conscience, but they do not wound it, and waste it, as presumptuous sins do; and, though offence may be given to conscience, yet care must be taken that it be not an abiding offence, but that by the renewed acts of faith and repentance the matter may be taken up again quickly. This however we must always exercise ourselves in, and, though we come short, we must follow after. *Secondly,* To all things: *Both towards God, and towards man.* His conscientious care extended itself to the whole of his duty, and he was afraid of breaking the law of love either to God or his neighbour. Conscience, like the magistrate, is *custos utriusque tabulæ—the guardian of each table.* We must be very cautious that we do not think, or speak, or do any thing amiss, either against God or man, 2 Cor. viii. 21. [4.] The inducement to it: *Herein, ἐν τούτῳ, for this cause;* so it may be read. "Because I look for the resurrection of the dead and the life of the world to come, therefore I thus exercise myself." The consideration of the future state should engage us to be universally conscientious in our present state.

IV. Having made confession of his faith, he gives a plain and faithful account of his case, and of the wrong done him by his persecutors. Twice he had been rescued by the chief captain out of the hands of the Jews, when they were ready to pull him to pieces, and he challenges them to prove him guilty of any crime either time.

1. In the temple. Here they fell furiously upon him as an enemy to their nation and the temple, *ch.* xxi. 28. But was there any colour for the charge? No, but evidence sufficient against it. (1.) It was very hard to accuse him as an *enemy to their nation,* when after long absence from Jerusalem he came to *bring alms to his nation,* money which (though he had need enough himself of it) he had collected among his friends, for the relief of the poor at Jerusalem. He not only had no malice to that people, but he had a very charitable concern for them, and was ready to do them all good offices; and were they his adversaries for his love? Ps. cix. 4. (2.) It was very hard to accuse him of having profaned the temple when he brought offerings to the temple, and was himself at charges therein (*ch.* xxi. 24), and was found *purifying himself in the temple,* according to the law (*v.* 18), and that in a very quiet decent manner, *neither with multitude nor with tumult.* Though he was a man so much talked of, he was far from coveting to show himself when he came to Jerusalem, or to be crowded after, but went to the temple, as much as was possible, *incognito.* They were Jews from Asia, his enemies, that caused him to be taken notice of; they had no pretence to make a tumult and raise a multitude against him, for he had neither multitude nor tumult for him. And as to what was perhaps suggested to Felix that he had brought Greeks into the temple, contrary to their law, and the governor ought to reckon with him for that, the Romans having stipulated with the nations that submitted to them to preserve them in their religion, he challenges them to prove it (*v.* 19): "Those Jews of Asia ought to have been *here before thee,* that they might have been examined, whether *they had aught against me,* that they would stand by and swear to;" for some that will not scruple to tell a lie have such heavings of conscience that they scruple confirming it with an oath.

2. In the council: "Since the Jews of Asia are not here to prove any thing upon me done amiss in the temple, let *these same* that are *here,* the high priest and the elders, say whether they have *found any evil doing in me,* or whether I was guilty of any misdemeanor *when I stood before the council,* when also they were ready to pull me in pieces, *v.* 20. When I was there, they could not take offence at any thing I said; for all I said was, *Touching the resurrection of the dead I am called in question by you this day* (*v.* 21), which gave no offence to any one but the Sadducees. This I hope was no crime, that I stuck to that which is the faith of the whole Jewish church, excepting those whom they themselves call heretics."

22 And when Felix heard these
things, having more perfect knowledge of *that* way, he deferred them,
and said, When Lysias the chief captain shall come down, I will know the
uttermost of your matter. 23 And
he commanded a centurion to keep Paul, and to let *him* have liberty, and
that he should forbid none of his acquaintance to minister or come unto
him. 24 And after certain days,
when Felix came with his wife Drusilla, which was a Jewess, he sent for
Paul, and heard him concerning the faith in Christ. 25 And as he reasoned of righteousness, temperance,
and judgment to come, Felix trembled, and answered, Go thy way for
this time; when I have a convenient season, I will call for thee. 26 He
hoped also that money should have been given him of Paul, that he might
loose him: wherefore he sent for him the oftener, and communed with him.
27 But after two years Porcius Festus came into Felix' room: and Felix, willing to show the Jews a pleasure, left Paul bound.

We have here the result of Paul's trial before Felix, and what was the consequence of it.

I. Felix adjourned the cause, and took further time to consider of it (*v.* 22): He *had a more perfect knowledge of that way* which the Jews called heresy than the high priest and the elders thought he had. He understood something of the Christian religion; for, living at Cæsarea, where Cornelius, a Roman centurion, was, who was a Christian, from him and others he had got a notion of Christianity, that it was not such an evil thing as it was represented. He himself knew some of that way to be honest good men, and very conscientious, and therefore he put off the prosecutors with an excuse: "*When the chief captain shall come down* hither, *I will know the uttermost of your matter,* or I shall know the truth, whether this Paul did go about to raise sedition or no; you are parties, he is an indifferent person. Either Paul deserves to be punished for raising the tumult, or you do for doing it yourselves and then charging it upon him; and I will hear what he says, and determine accordingly between you." Now, 1. It was a disappointment to the high priest and the elders that Paul was not condemned, or remitted to their judgment, which they wished for and expected. But thus sometimes God restrains the wrath of his people's enemies by the agency, not of their friends, but of such as are strangers to them. And though they be so, if they have but some *knowledge of their way*, they cannot but appear for their protection. 2. It was an injury to Paul that he was not released. Felix ought to have *avenged him of his adversaries*, when he so plainly saw there was nothing but malice in the prosecution, and to have delivered *him out of the hand of the wicked*, according to the duty of a judge, Ps. lxxxii. 4. But he was a judge that neither feared God nor regarded man, and what good could be expected from him? It is a wrong not only to deny justice, but to delay it.

II. He detained the prisoner in custody, and would not take bail for him; else here at Cæsarea Paul had friends enough that would gladly have been his security. Felix thought a man of such a public character as Paul was had many friends, as well as many enemies, and he might have an opportunity of obliging them, or making a hand of them, if he did not presently release him, and yet did show him countenance; and therefore, 1. He continued him a prisoner, commanded a centurion or captain to keep him, *v.* 23. He did not commit him to the common jail, but, being first made an army-prisoner, he shall still be so. 2. Yet he took care he should be *a prisoner at large—in libera custodia;* his keeper must let him have liberty, not bind him nor lock him up, but make his confinement as easy to him as possible; let him have the liberty of the castle, and, perhaps, he means liberty to take the air, or go abroad upon his parole: and Paul was such an honest man that they might take his word for his return. The high priest and the elders grudged him his life, but Felix generously allows him a sort of liberty; for he had not those prejudices against him and his way that they had. He also gave orders that none of his friends should be hindered from coming to him; the centurion must not forbid any of his acquaintances from ministering to him; and a man's prison is as it were his own house if he has but his friends about him.

III. He had frequent conversation with him afterwards in private, once particularly, not long after his public trial, *v.* 24, 25. Observe,

1. With what design *Felix sent for Paul.* He had a mind to have some talk with him *concerning the faith in Christ*, the Christian religion; he had some knowledge of that way, but he desired to have an account of it from Paul, who was so celebrated a preacher of that faith, above the rest. Those that would enlarge their knowledge must discourse with men of their own profession, and those that would be acquainted with any profession should consult those that excel in the knowledge of it; and therefore Felix has a mind to talk with Paul more freely than he could in open court, where he observed Paul upon his guard, *concerning the faith of Christ;* and this only to satisfy his curiosity, or rather the curiosity of *his wife Drusilla, who was a Jewess,* daughter of Herod Agrippa, that was eaten of worms. Being educated in the Jewish religion, she was more inquisitive concerning the Christian religion, which pretended to be the perfection of that, and desired to hear Paul discourse of it. But it was no great matter what religion she was of; for, whatever it was, she was a reproach and scandal to it—a Jewess, but an adulteress; she was another man's wife when Felix took her to be his wife, and she lived with him in whoredom and was noted for an impudent woman, yet she desires to hear *concerning the faith of Christ.* Many are fond of new notions and speculations in religion, and can hear and speak of them with pleasure, who yet hate to come under the power and influence of religion, can be content to have their judgments informed but not their lives reformed.

2. What the account was which Paul gave him of the Christian religion; by the idea he had of it, he expected to be amused with a mystical divinity, but, as Paul represents it to him, he is alarmed with a practical divinity. Paul, being asked *concerning the faith in Christ, reasoned* (for Paul was always a rational preacher) concerning *righteousness, temperance, and judgment to come.* It is probable that he mentioned the peculiar doctrines of Christianity concerning the death and resurrection of the Lord Jesus, and his being *the Mediator between God and man;* but he hastened to his application, in which he designed to come home to the consciences of his hearers.

(1.) He discoursed with clearness and warmth *of righteousness, temperance, and judgment to come:* and here he showed, [1.] That the faith in Christ is designed to enforce upon the children of men the great laws of justice and temperance. *The grace of God teacheth us to live soberly and righteously,* Tit. ii. 12. Justice and temperance were celebrated virtues among the heathen moralists; if the doctrine Paul preaches, which Felix has heard of as proclaiming liberty, will but free him from an obligation to these, he will readily embrace it: "No," says Paul, "it is so far from doing so that it strengthens the obligations of those sacred laws; it binds all under the highest penalties to be *honest in all their dealings*, and to *render to all their due;* to *deny themselves*, and *to keep under the body, and bring it into subjection.*" The world and the flesh being in our baptism renounced, all our pursuits of the world and all our gratifications of the desires of the body are to be under the regulations of religion. *Paul reasoned of righteousness and temperance,* to convince Felix of his unrighteousness and intemperance, of which he had been notoriously guilty, that, seeing the odiousness of them, and his obnoxiousness to the wrath of God for them (Eph. v. 6), he might enquire concerning the faith of Christ, with a resolution to embrace it. [2.] That by the doctrine of Christ is discovered to us the judgment to come, by the sentence of which the everlasting state of all the children of men will be finally and irreversibly determined. Men have their day now, Felix hath his; but God's day is coming, *when every one shall give account of himself to God, the Judge of all.* Paul reasoned concerning this; that is, he showed what reason we have to believe *that there is a judgment to come,* and what reason we have, in consideration thereof, to be religious.

(2.) From this account of the heads of Paul's discourse we may gather, [1.] That Paul in his preaching had no respect to persons, for the word of God, which he preached, has not: he urged the same convictions and instructions upon the Roman governor that he did upon other people. [2.] That Paul in his preaching aimed at the consciences of men, and came close to them, sought not to please their fancy nor to gratify their curiosity, but led them to a sight of their sins and a sense of their duty and interest. [3.] That Paul preferred the serving of Christ, and the saving of souls, before his own safety. He lay at the mercy of Felix, who had power (as Pilate said) *to crucify him* (or, which was as bad, to deliver him back to the Jews), *and he had power to release him.* Now when Paul had his ear, and had him in a good humour, he had a fair opportunity of ingratiating himself with him, and obtaining a release, nay, and of incensing him against his prosecutors: and, on the contrary, if he disobliged him, and put him out of humour, he might do himself a great diskindness by it; but he is wholly negligent of these considerations, and is intent upon doing good, at least discharging his duty. [4.] That Paul was willing to take pains, and run hazards, in his work, even where there was little probability of doing good. Felix and Drusilla were such hardened sinners that it was not at all likely they should be brought to repentance by Paul's preaching, especially under such disadvantages; and yet Paul deals with them as one that did not despair of them. Let the watchman give fair warning, and then they have delivered their own souls, though they should not prevail to deliver the souls they watch for.

3. What impressions Paul's discourse made upon this great but wicked man: *Felix trembled,* ἔμφοβος γενόμενος—*being put into a fright,* or made *a terror to himself, a magor-missabib,* as Pashur, Jer. xx. 3, 4. Paul never trembled before him, but he was made to tremble before Paul. "If this be so, as Paul says, what will become of me in another world? If the unrighteous and intemperate will be condemned in the judgment to come, I am undone, for ever undone, unless I lead a new course of life." We do not find that Drusilla trembled, though she was equally guilty, for she was a Jewess, and depended upon the ceremonial law, which she adhered to the observance of, to justify her; but Felix for the present could fasten upon nothing to pacify his conscience, and therefore trembled. See here, (1.) The power of the word of God, when it comes with commission; it is searching, it is startling, it can strike a terror into the heart of the most proud and daring sinner, by *setting his sins in order before him,* and showing him *the terrors of the Lord.* (2.) The workings of natural conscience; when it is startled and awakened, it fills the soul with horror and amazement at its own deformity and danger. Those that are themselves *the terror of the mighty in the land of the living* have hereby been made a terror to themselves. A prospect of the judgment to come is enough to make the stoutest heart to tremble, as when it comes indeed it will make *the mighty men and the chief captains* to call in vain *to rocks and mountains to shelter them.*

4. How Felix struggled to get clear of these impressions, and to shake off the terror of his convictions; he did by them as he did by Paul's prosecutors (*v.* 25), *he deferred them;* he said, *Go thy way for this time, when I have a convenient season I will call for thee.* (1.) He trembled and that was all. Paul's trembling (*ch.* ix. 6), and the *jailer's* (*ch.* xvi. 29), ended in their conversion, but this of Felix did not. Many are startled by the word of God who are not effectually changed by it. Many are in fear of the consequences of sin, and yet continue in love and league with sin. (2.) He did not fight against his convictions, nor fly in the face of the word or of the preacher of it, to be revenged on them for making his conscience fly in his face; he did not say to Paul, as Amaziah to the prophet, *Forbear, why shouldst thou be smitten?* He did not threaten him with a closer confinement, or with death, for touching him (as John Baptist did Herod) in the sore place. But, (3.) He artfully shifted off his convictions by putting off the prosecution of them to another time. He has nothing to object against what Paul has said; it is weighty and worth considering. But, like a sorry debtor, he begs a day; Paul has spent himself, and has tired him and his lady, and therefore, "*Go thy way for this time*—break off here, business calls me away; but *when I have a convenient season,* and have nothing else to do, *I will call for thee,* and hear what thou hast further to say." Note, [1.] Many lose all the benefit of their convictions for want of striking while the iron is hot. If Felix, now that he trembled, had but asked, as Paul and

the jailer did when they trembled, *What shall I do?* he might have been brought to the faith of Christ, and have been a *Felix* indeed, *happy* for ever; but, by dropping his convictions now, he lost them for ever, and himself with them. [2.] In the affairs of our souls, delays are dangerous; nothing is of more fatal consequence than men's putting off their conversion from time to time. They will repent, and turn to God, but not yet; the matter is adjourned to some more convenient season, when such a business or affair is compassed, when they are so much older; and then convictions cool and wear off, good purposes prove to no purpose, and they are more hardened than ever in their evil way. Felix put off this matter to a more convenient season, but we do not find that this more convenient season ever came; for the devil cozens us of all our time by cozening us of the present time. The present season is, without doubt, the most convenient season. *Behold, now is the accepted time. To-day if you will hear his voice.*

IV. After all, he detained him a prisoner, and left him so, when two years after he was removed from the government, *v.* 26, 27. He was convinced in his conscience that Paul had done *nothing worthy of death or of bonds,* and yet had not the honesty to release him. To little purpose had Paul reasoned with him about righteousness, though he then trembled at the thought of his own iniquity, who could thus persist in such a palpable piece of injustice. But here we are told what principles he was governed by herein; and they were such as make the matter yet much worse. 1. The love of money. He would not release Paul because he hoped to make his market of him, and that at length his friends would make a purse to purchase his liberty, and then he would satisfy his conscience by releasing him when he could withal satisfy his covetousness by it; but he cannot find in his heart to do his duty as a judge, unless he can get money by it: *He hoped that money would have been given him of Paul,* or somebody for him, and then he would have loosed him, and set him at liberty. In hopes of this, he detains him a prisoner, and *sends for him the oftener, and communes with him;* not any more about the faith of Christ (he had had enough of that, and of the judgment to come; Paul must not return to those subjects, nor go on with them), but about his discharge, or ransom rather, out of his present captivity. He cannot for shame ask Paul what he will give him to release him, but he sends for him to feel his pulse, and gives him an opportunity to ask what he would take to release him. And now we see what became of his promise both to Paul and to himself, that he would hear more of Christ at some other convenient season. Here were many seasons convenient enough to have talked that matter through, but nothing is done in it; all his business now is to get money by Paul, not to get the knowledge of Christ by him. Note, It is just with God to say concerning those who trifle with their convictions, and think they can have the grace of God at command when they please, *My Spirit shall no more strive with them.* When men will not hear God's voice *to-day, while it is called to-day,* the heart is commonly *hardened by the deceitfulness of sin.* Paul was but a poor man himself, *silver and gold he had none* to give, to purchase his liberty; but Felix knew there were those who wished well to him who were able to assist him. He having lately collected a great deal of money for the poor saints to relieve them, it might also be expected that the rich saints should contribute some to release him, and I wonder it was not done. Though Paul is to be commended that he would not offer money to Felix, nor beg money of the churches (his great and generous soul disdained both), yet I know not whether his friends are to be commended, nay, whether they can be justified, in not doing it for him. They ought to have solicited the governor as pressingly for him as his enemies did against him: and if a *gift was necessary to make room for them* (as Solomon speaks) and to bring them before great men, they might lawfully have brought it. I ought not to bribe a man to do an unjust thing, but, if he will not do me justice without a fee, it is but doing myself justice to give it to him; and, if they might do it, it was a shame they did not do it. I blush for them, that they would let such an eminent and useful man as Paul lie in the jail, when a little money would have fetched him out, and restored him to his usefulness again. The Christians here at Cæsarea, where he now was, had parted with their tears to prevent his going to the prison (*ch.* xxi. 13), and could they not find in their hearts to part with their money to help him out? Yet there might be a providence of God in it; Paul's bonds must be for the furtherance of the gospel of Christ, and therefore he must continue in bonds. However, this will not excuse Felix, who ought to have released an innocent man, without demanding or accepting any thing for it: the judge that will not do right without a bribe will no doubt do wrong for a bribe. 2. Men-pleasing. Felix was recalled from his government about *two years after this,* and Porcius Festus was put in his place, and one should have expected he would have at least concluded his government with this act of justice, the release of Paul, but he did not; he *left Paul bound,* and the reason here given is because he was *willing to do the Jews a pleasure.* Though he would not deliver him *to death, to please them,* yet he would continue him a prisoner rather than offend them; and he did it in hope hereby to atone for the many offences he had done against them. He did not think Paul had either interest or inclination to complain of him at court, for detaining him so long in custody, against all law and equity; but he was jealous of the high priest and elders, that they would be his accusers to the emperor for the wrongs he had done them, and therefore hopes by gratifying them in this matter to stop their mouths. Thus those who do some base things are tempted to do more to screen themselves and bear them out. If Felix had not injured the Jews, he needed not to have done this to please them; but, when he had done it, it seems he did not gain his point. The Jews, notwithstanding this, accused him to the emperor, and some historians say he was sent bound to Rome by Festus; and, if so, surely his remembering how light he had made of Paul's bonds would help to make his own chain heavy. Those that aim to please God by doing good will have what they aim at; but so will not those that seek to please men by doing evil.

CHAP. XXV.

Some think that Felix was turned out, and Festus succeeded him, quickly after Paul's imprisonment, and that the two years mentioned in the close of the foregoing chapter are to be reckoned from the beginning of Nero's reign; but it seems more natural to compute them from Paul's being delivered into the hands of Felix. However, we have here much the same management of Paul's case as we had in the foregoing chapter; cognizance is here taken of it, I. By Festus the governor; it is brought before him by the Jews, ver. 1—3. The hearing of it is appointed to be, not at Jerusalem, as the Jews desired, out at Cæsarea, ver. 4—6. The Jews appear against Paul and accuse him (ver. 7), but he stands upon his own innocency (ver. 8); and to avoid the removing of the cause to Jerusalem, to which he was pressed to consent, he at length appeals to Cæsar, ver. 9—12. II. By king Agrippa, to whom Festus relates his case (ver. 13—21), and Agrippa desires he might have the hearing of it himself, ver. 22. The court is accordingly set, and Paul brought to the bar (ver. 23), and Festus opens the cause (ver. 24—27), to introduce Paul's defence in the next chapter.

NOW when Festus was come into
the province, after three days he
ascended from Cæsarea to Jerusalem.
2 Then the high priest and the chief
of the Jews informed him against
Paul, and besought him, 3 And desired favour against him, that he
would send for him to Jerusalem,
laying wait in the way to kill him. 4
But Festus answered, that Paul should
be kept at Cæsarea, and that he himself would depart shortly *thither*. 5
Let them therefore, said he, which
among you are able, go down with *me*,
and accuse this man, if there be any
wickedness in him. 6 And when he
had tarried among them more than
ten days, he went down unto Cæsarea; and the next day sitting on the
judgment seat commanded Paul to be
brought. 7 And when he was come,
the Jews which came down from Jerusalem stood round about, and laid
many and grievous complaints against
Paul, which they could not prove.
8 While he answered for himself,
Neither against the law of the Jews,
neither against the temple, nor yet
against Cæsar, have I offended any
thing at all. 9 But Festus, willing
to do the Jews a pleasure, answered
Paul, and said, Wilt thou go up to
Jerusalem, and there be judged of
these things before me? 10 Then
said Paul, I stand at Cæsar's judgment seat, where I ought to be judged: to the Jews have I done no wrong,
as thou very well knowest. 11 For
if I be an offender, or have committed
any thing worthy of death, I refuse
not to die: but if there be none of
these things whereof these accuse me,
no man may deliver me unto them.
I appeal unto Cæsar. 12 Then Festus, when he had conferred with the
council, answered, Hast thou appealed
unto Cæsar? unto Cæsar shalt thou go.

We commonly say, "New lords, new laws, new customs;" but here was a new governor, and yet Paul had the same treatment from him that he had from the former, and no better. Festus, like Felix, is not so just to him as he should have been, for he does not release him; and yet not so unjust to him as the Jews would have had him to be, for he will not condemn him to die, nor expose him to their rage. Here is,

I. The pressing application which the high priest and other Jews used with the governor to persuade him to abandon Paul; for to send him to Jerusalem was in effect to abandon him. 1. See how speedy they were in their applications to Festus concerning Paul. As soon as ever he *had come into the province,* and had taken possession of the government, into which, probably, he was installed at Cæsarea, within *three days he went up to Jerusalem,* to show himself there, and presently the priests were upon him to proceed against Paul. He staid *three days at Cæsarea,* where Paul was a prisoner, and we do not find that in that time Paul made any application to him to release him, though, no doubt, he could have made good friends, that he might hope to have prevailed by, but as soon as ever he comes up to Jerusalem the priests are in all haste to make an interest with him against Paul. See how restless a thing malice is. Paul more patiently bears the lengthening out of his imprisonment than his enemies do the delay of his prosecution even to the death. 2. See how spiteful they were in their application. They *informed the governor against Paul* (*v.* 2) before he was brought upon a fair trial, that so they might, if possible, prejudge the cause with the governor, and make him a party who was to be the judge. But this artifice, though base enough, they could not confide in; for the governor would be sure to hear him himself, and then all their informations against him would fall to the ground; and therefore they form another project much more base, and that is to assassinate Paul before he came upon his trial. These inhuman hellish methods, which all the world profess at least to abhor, have these persecutors recourse to, to gratify their malice against the gospel of Christ, and this too under colour of zeal for Moses. *Tantum religio potuit suadere malorum—Such was their dire religious zeal.* 3. See how specious the pretence was. Now that *the governor was himself at Jerusalem they desired he would send for Paul thither*, and try him there, which would save the prosecutors a great deal of labour, and looked most reasonable, because he was charged with having profaned the temple at Jerusalem, and it is usual for criminals to be tried in the court where the fact was committed; but that which they designed was to way-lay him as he was brought up, and to murder him upon the road, supposing that he would not be brought up under so strong a guard as he was sent down with, or that the officers that were to bring him up might be bribed to give them an opportunity for their wickedness. It is said, *They desired favour against Paul.* The business of prosecutors is to demand justice against one that they suppose to be a criminal, and, if he be not proved so, it is as much justice to acquit him as it is to condemn him if he be. But to desire favour against a prisoner, and from the judge too, who ought to be of counsel for him, is a very impudent thing. The favour ought to be for the prisoner, *in favorem vitæ—to favour his life*, but here they desire it against him. They will take it as a favour if the governor will but condemn Paul, though they can prove no crime upon him.

II. The governor's resolution that Paul shall take his trial at Cæsarea, where he now is, *v.* 4, 5. See how he manages the prosecutors. 1. He will not do them the kindness to send for him to Jerusalem; no, he gave orders *that Paul should be kept at Cæsarea.* It does not appear that he had any suspicion, much less any certain information, of their bloody design to murder him by the way, as the chief captain had when he sent him to Cæsarea (*ch.* xxiii. 30); but perhaps he was not willing so far to oblige the high priest and his party, or he would maintain the honour of his court at Cæsarea and require their attendance there, or he was not willing to be at the trouble or charge of bringing Paul up; whatever was his reason for refusing it, God made use of it as a means of preserving Paul out of the hands of his enemies. Perhaps now they were more careful to keep their conspiracy secret than they had been before, that the discovery of it might not be now, as it was then, the defeat of it. But though God does not, as then, bring it to light, yet he finds another way, as effectual, to bring it to nought, by inclining the heart of the governor, for some other reasons, not to remove Paul to Jerusalem. God is not tied to one method, in working out salvation for his people. He can suffer the designs against them to be concealed, and yet not suffer them to be accomplished; and can make even the carnal policies of great men to serve his gracious purposes. 2. Yet he will do them the justice to hear what they have to say against Paul, if they will go down to Cæsarea, and appear against him there: "*Let those among you who are able*, able in body and purse for such a journey, or able in mind and tongue to manage the prosecution—*let those among you* who are fit to be managers, *go down with me, and accuse this man;* or, those who are competent witnesses, who are able to prove any thing criminal upon him, let them go and give in their evidence, if there be any such wickedness in him as you charge upon him." Festus will not take it for granted, as they desire he should, that there is wickedness in him, till it is proved upon him, and he has been heard in his own defence; but, if he be guilty, it lies upon them to prove him so.

III. Paul's trial before Festus. Festus staid *at Jerusalem about ten days*, and then *went down to Cæsarea*, and the prosecutors, it is likely, in his retinue; for he said they should *go down with him;* and, since they are so eager in the prosecution, he is willing this cause should be first called; and, that they may hasten home, he will despatch it *the next day*. Expedition in administering justice is very commendable, provided more haste be not made than good speed. Now here we have, 1. The court set, and the prisoner called to the bar. Festus *sat in the judgment-seat*, as he used to do when any cause was brought before him that was of consequence, and he *commanded Paul to be brought*, and to make his appearance, *v.* 6. Christ, to encourage his disciples and keep up their spirits under such awful trials of their courage as this was to Paul, promised them that the day should come when they *should sit on thrones, judging the tribes of Israel.* 2. The prosecutors exhibiting their charges against the prisoner (*v.* 7): *The Jews stood round about*, which intimates that they were many. *Lord, how are they increased that trouble me!* It intimates also that they were unanimous, they stood by one another, and resolved to hold together; and that they were intent upon the prosecution, and eager in clamouring against Paul. They *stood round about*, if possible, to frighten the judge into a compliance with their malicious design, or, at least, to frighten the prisoner, and to put him out of countenance; but in vain: he had too just and strong an assurance to be frightened by them. *They compassed me about like bees, but they are quenched as the fire of thorns*, Ps.

cxviii. 12. *When they stood round about him, they brought many and grievous accusations against Paul,* so it should be read. They charged him with high crimes and misdemeanors. The articles of impeachment were many, and contained things of a very heinous nature. They represented him to the court as black and odious as their wit and malice could contrive; but when they had opened the cause as they thought fit, and came to the evidence, there they failed: *they could not prove* what they alleged against him,for it was all false, and the complaints were groundless and unjust. Either the fact was not as they opened it, or there was no fault in it; *they laid to his charge things that he knew not,* nor they neither. It is no new thing for the most excellent ones of the earth to have all manner of evil said against them falsely, not only *in the song of the drunkards,* and upon *the seat of the scornful,* but even *before the judgment-seat.* 3. The prisoner's insisting upon his own vindication, *v.* 8. Whoever reproaches him, his own heart does not, and therefore his own tongue shall not; *though he die, he will not remove his integrity from him.* When it came to his turn to speak *for himself,* he insisted upon his general plea, Not guilty: *Neither against the law of the Jews, nor against the temple, nor yet against Cæsar, have I offended any thing at all.* (1.) He had not violated the law of the Jews, nor taught any doctrine destructive of it. *Did he make void the law by faith? No, he established the law.* Preaching Christ, *the end of the law,* was no offence against the law. (2.) He had not profaned the temple, nor put any contempt at all upon the temple-service; his helping to set up the gospel temple did not at all offend against that temple which was a type of it. (3.) He had not offended against Cæsar, nor his government. By this it appears that now his cause being brought before the government, to curry favour with the governor and that they might seem friends to Cæsar, they had charged him with some instances of disaffection to the present higher powers, which obliged him to purge himself as to that matter, and to protest that he was no enemy to Cæsar, not so much as these were who charged him with being so.

IV. Paul's appeal to the emperor, and the occasion of it. This gave the cause a new turn. Whether he had before designed it, or whether it was a sudden resolve upon the present provocation, does not appear; but God puts it into his heart to do it, for the bringing about of that which he had said to him, *that he must bear witness to Christ at Rome,* for there the emperor's court was, *ch.* xxiii. 11. We have here,

1. The proposal which Festus made to Paul to go and take his trial at Jerusalem, *v.* 9. *Festus* was *willing to do the Jews a pleasure,* inclined to gratify the prosecutors rather than the prisoner, as far as he could go with safety against one that was a citizen of Rome, and therefore asked him whether he would be willing to go up to Jerusalem, and clear himself there, where he had been accused, and where he might have his witnesses ready to vouch for him and confirm what he said. He would not offer to turn him over to the high priest and the sanhedrim, as the Jews would have had him; but, *Wilt thou go thither, and be judged of these things before me?* The president, if he had pleased, might have ordered him thither, but he would not do it without his own consent, which, if he could have wheedled him to give it, would have taken off the odium of it. In suffering times, the prudence of the Lord's people is tried as well as their patience; being sent forth therefore as sheep in the midst of wolves, they have need to be wise as serpents.

2. Paul's refusal to consent to it, and his reasons for it. He knew, if he were removed to Jerusalem, notwithstanding the utmost vigilance of the president, the Jews would find some means or other to be the death of him; and therefore desires to be excused, and pleads, (1.) That, as a citizen of Rome, it was most proper for him to be tried, not only by the president, but in that which was properly his court, which sat at Cæsarea: *I stand at Cæsar's judgment-seat, where I ought to be judged,* in the city which is the metropolis of the province. The court being held in Cæsar's name, and by his authority and commission, before one that was delegated by him, it might well be said to be his judgment seat, as, with us, all writs run in the name of the sovereign, in whose name all courts are held. Paul's owning that he ought to be judged at Cæsar's judgment-seat plainly proves that Christ's ministers are not exempted from the jurisdiction of the civil powers, but ought to be subject to them, as far as they can with a good conscience; and, if they be guilty of a real crime, to submit to their censure; if innocent, yet to submit to their enquiry, and to clear themselves before them. (2.) That, as a member of the Jewish nation, he had done nothing to make himself obnoxious to them: *To the Jews have I done no wrong, as thou very well knowest.* It very well becomes those that are innocent to plead their innocency, and to insist upon it; it is a debt we owe to our own good name, not only not to bear false witness against ourselves, but to maintain our own integrity against those who bear false witness against us. (3.) That he was willing to abide by the rules of the law, and to let that take its course, *v.* 11. If he be guilty of any capital crime that deserves death, he will not offer either to make resistance or to make his escape, will neither flee from justice nor fight with it: "I refuse not to die, but will accept of the punishment of my iniquity." Not that all who have committed any thing worthy of death are obliged to accuse themselves, and offer themselves to justice; but, when they are accused and brought to justice, they ought to submit, and

to say both God and the government are righteous; as it is necessary that some should be made examples. But, if he be innocent, as he protests he is, "*If there be none of these things whereof these accuse me*,—if the prosecution be malicious and they are resolved to have my blood right or wrong,—*no man may deliver me unto them*, no, not the governor himself, without palpable injustice; for it is his business as much to protect the innocent as to punish the guilty;" and he claims his protection.

3. His appealing to court. Since he is continually in danger of the Jews, and one attempt made after another to get him into their hands, *whose tender mercies were cruel*, he flies to the *dernier resort—the last refuge* of oppressed innocency, and takes sanctuary there, since he cannot have justice done him in any other way: "*I appeal unto Cæsar*. Rather than be delivered to the Jews" (which Festus seems inclined to consent to) "let me be delivered to Nero." When David had divers times narrowly escaped the rage of Saul, and concluded he was such a restless enemy that he should *one day perish by his hands*, he came to this resolution, being in a manner compelled to it, *There is nothing better for me than to take shelter in the land of the Philistines*, 1 Sam. xxvii. 1. So Paul here. But it is a hard case that a son of Abraham must be forced to appeal to a Philistine, to a Nero, from those who call themselves the seed of Abraham, and shall be safer in Gath or Rome than in Jerusalem. *How is the faithful city become a harlot!*

V. The judgment given upon the whole matter. Paul is neither released nor condemned. His enemies hoped the cause would be ended in his death; his friends hoped it would be ended in his deliverance; but it proved neither so nor so, they are both disappointed, the thing is left as it was. It is an instance of the slow steps which Providence sometimes takes, not bringing things to an issue so soon as we expect, by which we are often made ashamed both of our hopes and of our fears, and are kept still waiting on God. The cause had before been adjourned to another time, now to another place, to another court, that Paul's *tribulation might work patience*. 1. The president takes advice upon the matter: *He conferred with the council*—μετὰ τοῦ συμβουλίου, not with the council of the Jews (that is called συνέδριον), but with his own counsellors, who were always ready to assist the governor with their advice. *In multitude of counsellors there is safety;* and judges should consult both with themselves and others before they pass sentence. 2. He determines to send him to Rome. Some think Paul meant not an appeal to Cæsar's person, but only to his court, the sentence of which he would abide by, rather than be remitted to the Jew's council, and that Festus might have chosen whether he would have sent him to Rome, or, at least, whether he would have joined issue with him upon the appeal. But it should seem, by what Agrippa said (*ch.* xxvi. 32), that *he might have been set at liberty if he had not appealed to Cæsar*—that, by the course of the Roman law, a Roman citizen might appeal at any time to a superior court, even to the supreme, as causes with us are removed by *certiorari*, and criminals by *habeas corpus*, and as appeals are often made to the house of peers. Festus, therefore, either of choice or of course, comes to this resolution: *Hast thou appealed unto Cæsar? Unto Cæsar thou shalt go.* He found there was something very extraordinary in the case, which he was therefore afraid of giving judgment upon, either one way or other, and the knowledge of which he thought would be an entertainment to the emperor, and therefore he transmitted it to his cognizance. In our judgment before God those that by justifying themselves appeal to the law, to the law they shall go, and it will condemn them; but those that by repentance and faith appeal to the gospel, to the gospel they shall go, and it will save them.

13 And after certain days king
Agrippa and Bernice came unto Cæsarea to salute Festus. 14 And when
they had been there many days, Festus declared Paul's cause unto the
king, saying, There is a certain man
left in bonds by Felix: 15 About
whom, when I was at Jerusalem, the
chief priests and the elders of the
Jews informed *me*, desiring *to have*
judgment against him. 16 To whom
I answered, It is not the manner of
the Romans to deliver any man to
die, before that he which is accused
have the accusers face to face, and
have licence to answer for himself
concerning the crime laid against him.
17 Therefore, when they were come
hither, without any delay on the morrow I sat on the judgment seat, and
commanded the man to be brought
forth. 18 Against whom when the
accusers stood up, they brought none
accusation of such things as I supposed: 19 But had certain questions
against him of their own superstition,
and of one Jesus which was dead,
whom Paul affirmed to be alive. 20
And because I doubted of such manner of questions, I asked *him* whether
he would go to Jerusalem, and there
be judged of these matters. 21 But
when Paul had appealed to be reserved unto the hearing of Augustus, I

commanded him to be kept till I might
send him to Cæsar. 22 Then Agrippa
said unto Festus, I would also hear
the man myself. To morrow, said he,
thou shalt hear him. 23 And on the
morrow, when Agrippa was come, and
Bernice, with great pomp, and was
entered into the place of hearing, with
the chief captains, and principal men
of the city, at Festus' commandment
Paul was brought forth. 24 And
Festus said, King Agrippa, and all
men which are here present with us,
ye see this man, about whom all the
multitude of the Jews have dealt with
me, both of Jerusalem, and *also* here,
crying that he ought not to live any
longer. 25 But when I found that
he had committed nothing worthy of
death, and that he himself hath appealed to Augustus, I have determined
to send him. 26 Of whom I have no
certain thing to write unto my lord.
Wherefore I have brought him forth
before you, and specially before thee,
O king Agrippa, that after examination had, I might have somewhat to
write. 27 For it seemeth to me unreasonable to send a prisoner, and not
withal to signify the crimes *laid* against
him.

We have here the preparation that was made for another hearing of Paul before king Agrippa, not in order to his giving judgment upon him, but in order to his giving advice concerning him, or rather only to gratify his curiosity. Christ had said, concerning his followers, *that they should be brought before governors and kings.* In the former part of this chapter Paul was brought before Festus the governor, here before Agrippa the king, for a testimony to both. Here is,

I. The kind and friendly visit which king Agrippa made to Festus, now upon his coming into the government in that province (*v.* 13): *After certain days, king Agrippa came to Cæsarea.* Here is a royal visit. Kings usually think it enough to send their ambassadors to congratulate their friends, but here was a king that came himself, that made the majesty of a prince yield to the satisfaction of a friend; for personal converse is the most pleasant among friends. Observe,

1. Who the visitants were. (1.) King Agrippa, the son of that Herod (surnamed *Agrippa*) who killed James the apostle, and was himself eaten of worms, and great grandson of Herod the Great, under whom Christ was born. Josephus calls this *Agrippa the younger;* Claudius the emperor made him king of Chalcis, and *tetrarch of Trachonitis and Abylene,* mentioned Luke iii. 1. The Jewish writers speak of him, and (as Dr. Lightfoot tells us) among other things relate this story of him, "That reading the law publicly, in the latter end of the year of release, as was enjoined, the king, when he came to those words (Deut. xvii. 15), *Thou shalt not set a stranger king over thee, who is not of thy brethren,* the tears ran down his cheeks, for he was not of the seed of Israel, which the congregation observing, cried out, Be of good comfort, king Agrippa, thou art our brother; for he was of their religion, though not of their blood." (2.) Bernice came with him. She was his own sister, now a widow, the widow of his uncle Herod, king of Chalcis, after whose death she lived with this brother of hers, who was suspected to be too familiar with her, and, after she was a second time married to Polemon king of Cilicia, she got to be divorced from him, and returned to her brother king Agrippa. Juvenal (*Sat.* 6) speaks of a diamond ring which Agrippa gave to Bernice, his incestuous sister:—

> ——— ——————— ———Berenices
> In digito factus pretiosior; hunc dedit olim
> Barbarus incestæ, dedit hunc Agrippa sorori.
>
> That far-famed gem which on the finger glow'd
> Of Bernice (dearer thence), bestowed
> By an incestuous brother.—Gifford.

And both Tacitus and Suetonius speak of a criminal intimacy afterwards between her and Titus Vespasian. Drusilla, the wife of Felix, was another sister. Such lewd people were the great people generally in those times! *Say not that the former days were better.*

2. What the design of this visit was: they *came to salute Festus,* to give him joy of his new promotion, and to wish him joy in it; they came to compliment him upon his accession to the government, and to keep up a good correspondence with him, that Agrippa, who had the government of Galilee, might act in concert with Festus, who had the government of Judea; but it is probable they came as much to divert themselves as to show respect to him, and to share in the entertainments of his court, and to show their fine clothes, which would do vain people no good if they did not go abroad.

II. The account which Festus gave to king Agrippa of Paul and his case, which he gave.

1. To entertain him, and give him some diversion. It was a very remarkable story, and worth any man's hearing, not only as it was surprising and entertaining, but, if it were truly and fully told, very instructive and edifying; and it would be particularly acceptable to Agrippa, not only because he was a judge, and there were some points of law and practice in it well worth his notice, but much more as he was a Jew, and there were some points of religion in it much more deserving his cognizance.

2. To have his advice. *Festus* was but newly come to be a judge, at least to be a judge in these parts, and therefore was diffident of himself and of his own ability, and willing to have the counsel of those that were older and more experienced, especially in a matter that had so much difficulty in it as Paul's case seemed to have, and therefore he declared it to the king. Let us now see the particular account he gives to king Agrippa concerning Paul, *v.* 14—21.

(1.) He found him a prisoner when he came into the government of this province; and therefore could not of his own knowledge give an account of his cause from the beginning: *There is a certain man left in bonds by Felix;* and therefore, if there were any thing amiss in the first taking of him into custody, Festus is not to answer for that, for he found him in bonds. When *Felix, to do the Jews a pleasure, left Paul bound,* though he knew him to be innocent, he knew not what he did, knew not but he might fall into worse hands than he did fall into, though they were none of the best.

(2.) That the Jewish sanhedrim were extremely set against him: "The *chief priests and the elders informed me* against him as a dangerous man, and not fit to live, and desired he might therefore be condemned to die." These being great pretenders to religion, and therefore to be supposed men of honour and honesty, Festus thinks he ought to give credit to them; but Agrippa knows them better than he does, and therefore Festus desires his advice in this matter.

(3.) That he had insisted upon the Roman law in favour of the prisoner, and would not condemn him unheard (*v.* 16): "*It is not the manner of the Romans,* who herein govern themselves by the law of nature and the fundamental rules of justice, to *deliver any man to die,* to grant him to destruction" (so the word is), "to gratify his enemies with his destruction, *before the accused has the accusers face to face,* to confront their testimony, and have both licence and time given him to answer for himself." He seems to upbraid them as if they reflected upon the Romans and their government in asking such a thing, or expecting that they would condemn a man without trying him: "No," says he, "I would have you to know, whatever you may allow of among yourselves, the Romans allow not of such a piece of injustice among them." *Audi et alteram partem—Hear the other side,* had become a proverb among them. This rule we ought to be governed by in our private censures in common conversation; we must not give men bad characters, nor condemn their words and actions, till we have heard what is to be said in their vindication. See John vii. 51.

(4.) That he had brought him upon his trial, according to the duty of his place, *v.* 17. That he had been expeditious in it, and the prosecutors had no reason to complain of his being dilatory, for *as soon as ever they had come* (and we are sure they lost no time) *without any delay, on the morrow,* he had brought on the cause. He had likewise tried him in the most solemn manner: He *sat on the judgment-seat,* as they used to do in weightier causes, while those that were of small moment they judged *de plano—upon even ground.* He called a great court on purpose for the trial of Paul, that the sentence might be definitive, and the cause ended.

(5.) That he was extremely *disappointed* in the charge they brought against him (*v.* 18, 19): *When the accusers stood up against him,* and opened their indictment, *they brought no accusations of such things as I supposed.*

[1.] He supposed by the eagerness of their prosecution, and their urging it thus upon the Roman governors one after another, *First,* That they had something to accuse him of that was dangerous either to private property or the public peace,—that they would undertake to prove him a robber, or a murderer, or a rebel against the Roman power,—that he had been in arms to head a sedition,—that if he were not that Egyptian who lately made an uproar, and commanded a party of cut-throats, as the chief captain supposed him to be, yet he was one of the same kidney. Such were the outcries against the primitive Christians, so loud, so fierce, that the standers-by, who judged of them by those outcries, could not but conclude them the worst of men; and to represent them so was the design of that clamour, as it was against our Saviour. *Secondly,* That they had something to accuse him of that was cognizable in the Roman courts, and which the governor was properly the judge of, as Gallio expected (*ch.* xviii. 14); otherwise it was absurd and ridiculous to trouble him with it, and really an affront to him.

[2.] But to his great surprise he finds the matter is neither so nor so; they had *certain questions against him,* instead of proofs and evidences against him. The worst they had to say against him was disputable whether it was a crime or no—moot-points, that would bear an endless debate, but had no tendency to fasten any guilt upon him, questions fitter for the schools than for the judgment-seat. And they were questions *of their own superstition,* so he calls their religion; or, rather, so he calls that part of their religion which Paul was charged with doing damage to. The Romans protected their religion according to their law, but not their superstition, nor the tradition of their elders. But the great question, it seems, was *concerning one Jesus that was dead, whom Paul affirmed to be alive.* Some think the superstition he speaks of was the Christian religion, which Paul preached, and that he had the same notion of it that the Athenians had, that it was the introducing of a new demon, even Jesus. See how slightly this Roman speaks of Christ, and of his death and resurrection, and of the great controversy between the Jews and the Christians whether he were the Messiah promised or no, and the great proof of his being the Messiah, his resurrection from the dead, as if it were no more than this, There was one Jesus that was dead, and Paul affirmed he was alive. In many causes issue is joined upon this question, whether such a person that has been long absent be living or dead, and proofs are brought on both sides; and Festus will have it thought that this is a matter of no more moment. Whereas this Jesus, whom he prides himself in being thus ignorant of, as if he were below his notice, is he that *was dead, and is alive, and lives for evermore, and has the keys of hell and of death,* Rev. i. 18. What Paul affirmed concerning Jesus, that he is alive, is a matter of such vast importance that if it be not true we are all undone.

(6.) That therefore he had proposed to Paul that the cause might be adjourned to the Jewish courts, as best able to take cognizance of an affair of this nature (*v.* 20): "*Because I doubted of such manner of questions,* and thought myself unfit to judge of things I did not understand, *I asked him whether he would go to Jerusalem,* appear before the great sanhedrim, *and there be judged of these matters.*" He would not force him to it, but would be glad if Paul would consent to it, that he might not have his conscience burdened with a cause of this nature.

(7.) That Paul had chosen rather to remove his cause to Rome than to Jerusalem, as expecting fairer play from the emperor than from the priests: "He *appealed to be reserved to the hearing of Augustus* (*v.* 21), having no other way to stop proceedings here in this inferior court; and therefore I *commanded him to be kept* a close prisoner *till I might send him to Cæsar,* for I did not see cause to refuse his appeal, but rather was pleased with it."

III. The bringing of him before Agrippa, that he might have the hearing of his cause.

1. The king desired it (*v.* 22): "I thank you for your account of him, but *I would also hear the man myself.*" Agrippa knows more of this matter, of the cause and of the person, than Festus does; he has heard of Paul, and knows of what vast concern this question is, which Festus makes such a jest of, whether Jesus be alive or no. And nothing would oblige him more than to hear Paul. Many great men think it below them to take cognizance of the matters of religion, except they can hear them like themselves in the judgment-seat. Agrippa would not for all the world have gone to a meeting to hear Paul preach, any more than Herod to hear Jesus; and yet they are both glad to have them brought before them, only to satisfy their curiosity. Perhaps Agrippa desired to hear him himself, that he might be in a capacity to do him a kindness, and yet did him none, only put some credit upon him.

2. Festus granted it: *To-morrow thou shalt hear him.* There was a good providence in this, for the encouragement of Paul, who seemed buried alive in his imprisonment, and deprived of all opportunities of doing good. We know not of any of his epistles that bore date from his prison at Cæsarea. What opportunity he had of doing good to his friends that visited him, and perhaps to a little congregation of them that visited him every Lord's-day, was but a low and narrow sphere of usefulness, so that he seemed to be thrown by as a *despised broken vessel, in which there was no pleasure;* but this gives him an opportunity of preaching Christ to a great congregation, and (which is more) to a congregation of great ones. Felix heard him in private concerning the faith of Christ. But Agrippa and Festus agree he shall be heard in public. And we have reason to think that his sermon in the next chapter, though it might not be so instrumental as some other of his sermons for the conversion of souls, redounded as much to the honour Christ and Christianity as any sermon he ever preached in his life.

3. Great preparation was made for it (*v.* 23): *The next day* there was a great appearance *in the place of hearing,* Paul and his cause being much talked of, and the more for their being much talked against.

(1.) Agrippa and Bernice took this opportunity to show themselves in state, and to make a figure, and perhaps for that end desired the occasion, that they might see and be seen; for *they came with great pomp,* richly dressed, with gold and pearls, and costly array; with a great retinue of footmen in rich liveries, which made a splendid show, and dazzled the eyes of the gazing crowd. They came μετὰ πολλῆς φαντασίας—*with great fancy,* so the word is. Note, Great pomp is but great fancy. It neither adds any real excellency, nor gains any real respect, but feeds a vain humour, which wise men would rather mortify than gratify. It is but a show, a dream, a fantastical thing (so the word signifies), superficial, and *it passeth away.* And the pomp of this appearance would put one for ever out of conceit with pomp, when the pomp which Agrippa and Bernice appeared in was, [1.] Stained by their lewd characters, and all the beauty of it sullied, and all virtuous people that knew them could not but contemn them in the midst of all this pomp as vile persons, Ps. xv. 4. [2.] Outshone by the real glory of the poor prisoner at the bar. What was the honour of their fine clothes, compared with that of his wisdom, and grace, and holiness, his courage and constancy in suffering for Christ! His bonds in so good a cause were more glorious than their chains of gold, and his guards than their equipage. Who would be fond of worldly pomp that here sees so bad a woman loaded with it and so good a man loaded with the reverse of it?

(2.) The chief captains and principal men

of the city took this opportunity to pay their respects to Festus and to his guests. It answered the end of a ball at court, it brought the fine folks together in their fine clothes, and served for an entertainment. It is probable that Festus sent Paul notice of it overnight, to be ready for a hearing the next morning before Agrippa. And such confidence had Paul in the promise of Christ, that it should be *given him in that same hour what he should speak*, that he complained not of the short warning, nor was put into confusion by it. I am apt to think that those who were to appear in pomp perplexed themselves more with care about their clothes than Paul, who was to appear as a prisoner, did with care about his cause; for he knew whom he had believed, and who stood by him.

IV. The speech with which Festus introduced the cause, when the court, or rather the audience, was set, which is much to the same purport with the account he had just now given to Agrippa. 1. He addressed himself respectfully to the company: "*King Agrippa, and all men who are here present with us.* He speaks *to all the men*—*πάντες ἄνδρες*, as if he intended a tacit reflection upon Bernice, a woman, for appearing in a meeting of this nature; he does not refer any thing to her judgment nor desire her counsel; but, "*All you that are present that are men* (so the words are placed), I desire you to take cognizance of this matter." The word used is that which signifies men in distinction from women; what had Bernice to do here? 2. He represents the prisoner as one that the Jews had a very great spite against; not only the rulers, but *the multitude of them, both at Jerusalem and here at Cæsarea*, cry out *that he ought not to live any longer*, for they think he has lived too long already, and if he live any longer it will be to do more mischief. They could not charge him with any capital crime, but they wanted to have him out of the way. 3. He confesses the prisoner's innocency; and it was much for the honour of Paul and his bonds that he had such a public acknowledgment as this from the mouth of his judge (*v.* 25): *I found that he had committed nothing worthy of death.* Upon a full hearing of the case, it appeared there was no evidence at all to support the indictment: and therefore, though he was inclinable enough to favour the prosecutors, yet his own conscience brought in Paul *not guilty.* And why did he not discharge him then, for he stood upon his deliverance? Why, truly, because he was so much clamoured against, and he feared the clamour would turn upon himself if he should release him. It is a pity but every man that has a conscience should have courage to act according to it. Or perhaps because there was so much smoke that he concluded there could not but be some fire, which would appear at last, and he would detain him a prisoner in expectation of it. 4. He acquaints them with the present state of the case, that the prisoner had appealed to the emperor himself (whereby he put an honour upon his own cause, as knowing it not unworthy the cognizance of the greatest of men), and that he had admitted his appeal: *I have determined to send him.* And thus the cause now stood. 5. He desires their assistance in examining the matter calmly and impartially, now that there was no danger of their being interrupted, as he had been with the noisiness and outrage of the prosecutors—that he might have at least such an insight into the cause as was necessary to his stating it to the emperor, *v.* 26, 27. (1.) He thought it *unreasonable to send a prisoner*, especially so far as Rome, *and not withal to signify the crimes laid against him*, that the matter might be prepared as much as possible, and put in a readiness for the emperor's determination; for he is supposed to be a man of great business, and therefore every affair must be laid before him in as little compass as possible. (2.) He could not as yet write *any thing certain* concerning Paul; so confused were the informations that were given in against him, and so inconsistent, that Festus could make nothing at all of them. He therefore desired Paul might thus be publicly examined, that he might be advised by them what to write. See what a great deal of trouble and vexation those were put to, and to what delay, nay, and to what hazard, in the administration of public justice, who live at such a distance from Rome, and yet were subject to the emperor of Rome. The same was this nation of ours put to (which is about as far distant from Rome the other way) when it was in ecclesiastical affairs subject to the pope of Rome, and appeals were upon all occasions made to his court; and the same mischiefs, and a thousand worse, would those bring upon us who would again entangle us in that yoke of bondage.

CHAP. XXVI.

We left Paul at the bar, and Festus, and Agrippa, and Bernice, and all the great men of the city of Cæsarea, upon the bench, or about it, waiting to hear what he had to say for himself. Now in this chapter we have, I. The account he gives of himself, in answer to the calumnies of the Jews. And in this, 1. His humble address to king Agrippa, and the compliment he passed upon him, ver. 1—3. 2. His account of his origin, and education, his profession as a Pharisee, and his adherence still to that which was then the main article of his creed, in distinction from the Sadducees, the "resurrection of the dead," however in rituals he had since departed from it, ver. 3—8. 3. Of his zeal against the Christian religion, and the professors of it, in the beginning of his time, ver. 9—11. 4. Of his miraculous conversion to the faith of Christ, ver. 12—16. 5. Of the commission he received from heaven to preach the gospel to the Gentiles, ver. 17, 18. 6. Of his proceedings pursuant to that commission, which had given this mighty offence to the Jews, ver. 19—21. 7. Of the doctrine which he had made it his business to preach to the Gentiles, which was so far from destroying the law and the prophets that it showed the fulfilling of both, ver. 22, 23. II. The remarks that were made upon his apology. 1. Festus thought he never heard a man talk so madly, and slighted him as crazed, ver. 24. In answer to him, he denies the charge, and appeals to king Agrippa, ver. 25—27. 2. King Agrippa, being more closely and particularly dealt with, thinks he never heard a man talk more rationally and convincingly, and owns himself almost his convert (ver. 28), and Paul heartily wishes him so, ver. 29. 3. They all agreed that he was an innocent man, that he ought to be set at liberty, and that it was a pity he was provoked to put a bar in his own door by appealing to Cæsar, ver. 30—32.

THEN Agrippa said unto Paul, Thou art permitted to speak

for thyself. Then Paul stretched
forth the hand, and answered for
himself: 2 I think myself happy,
king Agrippa, because I shall answer
for myself this day before thee touching all the things whereof I am
accused of the Jews: 3 Especially
because I know thee to be expert in
all customs and questions which are
among the Jews: wherefore I beseech thee to hear me patiently. 4
My manner of life from my youth,
which was at the first among mine
own nation at Jerusalem, know all
the Jews; 5 Which knew me from
the beginning, if they would testify,
that after the most straitest sect of
our religion I lived a Pharisee. 6
And now I stand and am judged for
the hope of the promise made of God
unto our fathers: 7 Unto which
promise our twelve tribes, instantly
serving *God* day and night, hope to
come. For which hope's sake, king
Agrippa, I am accused of the Jews.
8 Why should it be thought a thing
incredible with you, that God should
raise the dead? 9 I verily thought
with myself, that I ought to do many
things contrary to the name of Jesus
of Nazareth. 10 Which thing I also
did in Jerusalem: and many of the
saints did I shut up in prison, having
received authority from the chief
priests; and when they were put to
death, I gave my voice against *them.*
11 And I punished them oft in every
synagogue, and compelled *them* to
blaspheme; and being exceedingly
mad against them, I persecuted *them*
even unto strange cities.

Agrippa was the most honourable person in the assembly, having the title of king bestowed upon him, though otherwise having only the power of other governors under the emperor, and, though not here superior, yet senior, to Festus; and therefore, Festus having opened the cause, Agrippa, as the mouth of the court, intimates to Paul a licence given him to *speak for himself, v.* 1. Paul was silent till he had this liberty allowed him; for those are not the most forward to speak that are best prepared to speak and speak best. This was a favour which the Jews would not allow him, or not without difficulty; but Agrippa freely gives it to him. And Paul's cause was so good that he desired no more than to have liberty to speak for himself; he needed no advocate, no Tertullus, to speak for him. Notice is taken of his gesture: He *stretched forth his hand,* as one that was under no consternation at all, but had perfect freedom and command of himself; it also intimates that he was in earnest, and expected their attention while he answered for himself. Observe, He did not insist upon his having appealed to Cæsar as an excuse for being silent, did not say, "I will be examined no more till I come to the emperor himself;" but cheerfully embraced the opportunity of doing honour to the cause he suffered for. If we must be ready to give *a reason of the hope that is in us to every man that asketh us,* much more to every man in authority, 1 Pet. iii. 15. Now in this former part of the speech,

I. Paul addressed himself with a very particular respect to Agrippa, *v.* 2, 3. He answered cheerfully before Felix, because he knew he had been *many years a judge to that nation, ch.* xxiv. 10. But his opinion of Agrippa goes further. Observe, 1. Being accused of the Jews, and having many base things laid to his charge, he is glad he has an opportunity of clearing himself; so far is he from imagining that his being an apostle exempted him from the jurisdiction of the civil powers. Magistracy is an ordinance of God, which we have all benefit by, and therefore must all be subject to. 2. Since he is forced to answer for himself, he is glad it is before king Agrippa, who, being himself a proselyte to the Jewish religion, understood all matters relating to it better than the other Roman governors did: *I know thee to be expert in all customs and questions which are among the Jews.* It seems, Agrippa was a scholar, and had been particularly conversant in the Jewish learning, was expert in the customs of the Jewish religion, and knew the nature of them, and that they were not designed to be either universal or perpetual. He was expert also in the questions that arose upon those customs, in determining which the Jews themselves were not all of a mind. Agrippa was well versed in the scriptures of the Old-Testament, and therefore could make a better judgment upon the controversy between him and the Jews concerning Jesus being the Messiah than another could. It is an encouragement to a preacher to have those to speak to that are intelligent, and can discern things that differ. When Paul says, *Judge you what I say,* yet he *speaks as to wise men,* 1 Cor. x. 15. 3. He therefore begs that he would *hear him patiently,* μακροθύμως—*with long suffering.* Paul designs a long discourse, and begs that Agrippa will hear him out, and not be weary; he designs a plain discourse, and begs that he will hear him with mildness, and not be angry. Paul had some reason to fear that as Agrippa, being a Jew, was well versed in the Jewish customs, and therefore the more competent judge of his cause, so he was soured in some measure with the Jewish leaven, and therefore prejudiced against Paul as the apostle of the Gentiles; he therefore says this to sweeten him: *I beseech thee, hear me patiently.* Surely the least we can expect, when we preach the faith of Christ, is to be heard patiently.

II. He professes that though he was hated and branded as an apostate, yet he still adhered to all that good which he was first educated and trained up in; his religion was always built upon the *promise of God made unto the fathers;* and this he still built upon.

1. See here what his religion was in his youth: His *manner of life* was *well known, v.* 4, 5. He was not indeed born among his own nation, but he was bred among them at Jerusalem. Though he had of late years been conversant with the Gentiles (which had given great offence to the Jews), yet at his setting out in the world he was intimately acquainted with the Jewish nation, and entirely in their interests. His education was neither foreign nor obscure; it was among his own nation at Jerusalem, where religion and learning flourished. All the Jews knew it, all that could remember so long, for Paul made himself remarkable betimes. Those that *knew him from the beginning* could testify for him that he was a Pharisee, that he was not only of the Jewish religion, and an observer of all the ordinances of it, but that he was of the *most strict sect of that religion,* most nice and exact in observing the institutions of it himself, and most rigid and critical in imposing them upon others. He was not only called a Pharisee, but he *lived a Pharisee.* All that knew him knew very well that never any Pharisee conformed more punctually to the rules of his order than he did. Nay, and he was of the better sort of Pharisees; for he was brought up at the feet of Gamaliel, who was an eminent rabbi of the school or house of Hillel, which was in much greater reputation for religion than the school or house of Samai. Now if Paul was a Pharisee, and lived a Pharisee, (1.) Then he was a scholar, a man of learning, and not an ignorant, illiterate, mechanic; the Pharisees knew the law, and were well versed in it, and in the traditional expositions of it. It was a reproach to the other apostles that they had not had an academical education, but were bred fishermen, *ch.* iv. 13. Therefore, that the unbelieving Jews might be left without excuse, here is an apostle raised up that had sat at the feet of their most eminent doctors. (2.) Then he was a moralist, a man of virtue, and not a rake or loose debauched young man. If he lived like a Pharisee, he was no drunkard nor fornicator; and, being a young Pharisee, we may hope he was no extortioner, nor had yet learned the arts which the crafty covetous old Pharisees had of devouring the houses of poor widows; but he was, *as touching the righteousness which is in the law, blameless.* He was not chargeable with any instance of open vice and profaneness; and therefore, as he could not be thought to have deserted his religion because he did not know it (for he was a learned man), so he could not be thought to have deserted it because he did not love it, or was disaffected to the obligations of it, for he was a virtuous man, and not inclined to any immorality. (3.) Then he was orthodox, sound in the faith, and not a deist or sceptic, or a man of corrupt principles that led to infidelity. He was a Pharisee, in opposition to a Sadducee; he received those books of the Old Testament which the Sadducees rejected, believed a world of spirits, the immortality of the soul, the resurrection of the body, and the rewards and punishments of the future state, all which the Sadducees denied. They could not say, He quitted his religion for want of a principle, or for want of a due regard to divine revelation; no, he always had a veneration for the ancient *promise made of God unto the fathers,* and built his hope upon it.

Now though Paul knew very well that all this would not justify him before God, nor make a righteousness for him. yet he knew it was for his reputation among the Jews, and an argument *ad hominem—such as Agrippa would feel,* that he was not such a man as they represented him to be. Though he counted it but loss that he might win Christ, yet he mentioned it when it might serve to honour Christ. He knew very well that all this while he was a stranger to the spiritual nature of the divine law, and to heart-religion, and that except his righteousness exceeded this he should never go to heaven; yet he reflects upon it with some satisfaction that he had not been before his conversion an atheistical, profane, vicious man, but, according to the light he had, had *lived in all good conscience before God.*

2. See here what his religion is. He has not indeed such a zeal for the ceremonial law as he had in his youth. The sacrifices and offerings appointed by that, he thinks, are superseded by the great sacrifice which they typified; ceremonial pollutions and purifications from them he makes no conscience of, and thinks the Levitical priesthood is honourably swallowed up in the priesthood of Christ; but for the main principles of his religion he is as zealous for them as ever, and more so, and resolves to live and die by them.

(1.) His religion is built upon the *promise made of God unto the fathers.* It is built upon divine revelation, which he receives and believes, and ventures his soul upon; it is built upon divine grace, and that grace manifested and conveyed by promise. The promise of God is the guide and ground of his religion, the promise *made to the fathers,* which was more ancient than the ceremonial law, *that covenant which was confirmed before of God in Christ, and which the law, that was not till four hundred and thirty years after, could not disannul,* Gal. iii. 17. Christ and heaven are the two great doctrines of the gospel—that *God has given to us eternal life, and this life is in his Son.* Now these two are the matter of the *promise made unto the fathers.* It may look back as far as the promise made to father Adam, concerning the seed of the woman, and those discoveries of a future state which the first patriarchs acted faith upon, and were saved by that faith; but it respects chiefly the promise made to father Abraham, that *in his seed all the families of the earth should be blessed,* and that *God would be a God to him, and to his seed after him:* the former meaning Christ, the latter heaven; for, if God had not *prepared for them a city,* he would have been ashamed to have called himself *their God.* Heb. xi. 16.

(2.) His religion consists in the hopes of this promise. He places it not, as they did, in meats and drinks, and the observance of carnal ordinances (God had often shown what little account he made of them), but in a believing dependence upon God's grace in the covenant, and upon the promise, which was the great charter by which the church was first incorporated. [1.] He had hope in Christ as the promised seed; he hoped to be blessed in him, to receive the blessing of God and to be truly blessed. [2.] He had hopes of heaven; this is expressly meant, as appears by comparing *ch.* xxiv. 15, *That there shall be a resurrection of the dead.* Paul had no confidence in the flesh, but in Christ; no expectation at all of great things in this world, but of greater things in the other world than any this world can pretend to; he had his eye upon a future state.

(3.) Herein he concurred with all the pious Jews; his faith was not only according to the scripture, but according to the testimony of the church, which was a support to it. Though they set him up as a mark, he was not singular: "*Our twelve tribes,* the body of the Jewish church, *instantly serving God day and night,* hope to *come to this promise,* that is, to the good promised." The people of Israel are called *the twelve tribes,* because so they were at first; and, though we read not of the return of the ten tribes in a body, yet we have reason to think many particular persons, more or less of every tribe, returned to their own land; perhaps, by degrees, the greater part of those that were carried away. Christ speaks of the *twelve tribes,* Matt. xix. 28. Anna was of the tribe of Asher, Luke ii. 36. James directs his epistle to the *twelve tribes scattered abroad,* Jam. i. 1. "Our twelve tribes, which make up the body of our nation, to which I and others belong. Now all the Israelites profess to believe in this promise, both of Christ and heaven, and hope to come to the benefits of them. They all hope for a Messiah to come, and we that are Christians hope in a Messiah already come; so that we all agree to build upon the same promise. They look for the *resurrection of the dead* and *the life of the world to come,* and this is what I look for. Why should I be looked upon as advancing something dangerous and heterodox, or as an apostate from the faith and worship of the Jewish church, when I agree with them in this fundamental article? I hope to come to the same heaven at last that they hope to come to; and, if we expect to meet so happily in our end, why should we fall out so unhappily by the way?" Nay, the Jewish church not only hoped to come to this promise, but, in the hope of it, they *instantly served God day and night.* The temple-service, which consisted in a continual course of religious duties, morning and evening, day and night, from the beginning of the year to the end of it, and was kept up by the priests and Levites, and the *stationary men,* as they called them, who continually attended there to lay their hands upon the public sacrifices, as the representatives of all the twelve tribes, this service was kept up in the profession of faith in the promise of eternal life, and, in expectation of it, *Paul instantly serves God day and night* in the gospel of his Son; the twelve tribes by their representatives do so in the law of Moses, but he and they do it in hope of the same promise: "Therefore they ought not to look upon me as a deserter from their church, so long as I hold by the same promise that they hold by." Much more should Christians, who hope in the same Jesus, for the same heaven, though differing in the modes and ceremonies of worship, hope the best one of another, and live together in holy love. Or it may be meant of particular persons who continued in the communion of the Jewish church, and were very devout in their way, serving God with great intenseness, and a close application of mind, and constant in it, *night and day,* as Anna, who *departed not from the temple, but served God* (it is the same word here used) *in fastings and prayers night and day,* Luke ii. 37. "In this way they hope to come to the promise, and I hope they will." Note, Those only can upon good grounds hope for eternal life that are diligent and constant in the service of God; and the prospect of that eternal life should engage us to diligence and constancy in all religious exercises. We should go on with our work with heaven in our eye. And of those that *instantly serve God day and night,* though not in our way, we ought to judge charitably.

(4.) This was what he was now suffering for—for preaching that doctrine which they themselves, if they did but understand themselves aright, must own: *I am judged for the hope of the promise made unto the fathers.* He stuck to the promise, against the ceremonial law, while his persecutors stuck to the ceremonial law, against the promise: "It is *for this hope's sake, king Agrippa, that I am accused of the Jews*—because I do that which I think myself obliged to do by the hope of this promise." It is common for men to hate and persecute the power of that religion in others which yet they pride themselves in the form of. Paul's hope was what *they themselves also allowed* (*ch.* xxiv. 15), and yet they were thus enraged against him for practising according to that hope. But it was his honour that when he suffered as a Christian he suffered *for the hope of Israel, ch.* xxviii. 20.

(5.) This was what he would persuade all that heard him cordially to embrace (*v.* 8): *Why should it be thought a thing incredible with you that God should raise the dead?* This seems to come in somewhat abruptly; but it is probable Paul said much more than is here recorded, and that he explained the *promise made to the fathers* to be the promise of the resurrection and eternal life, and proved that he was in the right way of pursuing his hope of that happiness because he believed in Christ who had *risen from the dead,* which was a pledge and earnest of that resurrection which the fathers hoped for. Paul is therefore earnest to *know the power of Christ's resurrection,* that by it he might *attain to the resurrection of the dead;* see Phil. iii. 10, 11. Now many of his hearers were Gentiles, most of them perhaps, Festus particularly, and we may suppose, when they heard him speak so much of Christ's resurrection, and of the resurrection from the dead, which the twelve tribes hoped for, that they mocked, as the Athenians did, began to smile at it, and whispered to one another what an absurd thing it was, which occasioned Paul thus to reason with them. *What! is it thought incredible with you that God should raise the dead?* So it may be read. *If it be marvellous in your eyes, should it be marvellous in mine eyes, saith the Lord of hosts?* Zech. viii. 6. If it be above the power of nature, yet it is not above the power of the God of nature. Note, There is no reason why we should think it at all incredible that God should raise the dead. We are not required to believe any thing that is incredible, any thing that implies a contradiction. There are motives of credibility sufficient to carry us through all the doctrines of the Christian religion, and this particularly of the resurrection of the dead. Has not God an infinite almighty power, to which nothing is impossible? Did not he make the world at first out of nothing, with a word's speaking? Did he not form our bodies, form them out of the clay, and breathe into us the breath of life at first? and cannot the same power form them again out of their own clay, and put life into them again? Do we not see a kind of resurrection in nature, at the return of every spring? Has the sun such a force to raise dead plants, and should it seem incredible to us that God should raise dead bodies?

III. He acknowledges that while he continued a Pharisee he was a bitter enemy to Christians and Christianity, and thought he ought to be so, and continued so to the moment that Christ wrought that wonderful change in him. This he mentions,

1. To show that his becoming a Christian and a preacher was not the product and result of any previous disposition or inclination that way, or any gradual advance of thought in favour of the Christian doctrine; he did not reason himself into Christianity by a chain of arguments, but was brought into the highest degree of an assurance of it, immediately from the highest degree of prejudice against it, by which it appeared that he was made a Christian and a preacher by a supernatural power; so that his conversion in such a miraculous way was not only to himself, but to others also, a convincing proof of the truth of Christianity.

2. Perhaps he designs it for such an excuse of his prosecutors as Christ made for his, when he said, *They know not what they do.* Paul himself once thought he did what he ought to do when he persecuted the disciples of Christ, and he charitably thinks they laboured under the like mistake. Observe,

(1.) What a fool he was in his opinion (*v.* 9): He *thought with himself that he ought to do many things,* every thing that lay in his power, *contrary to the name of Jesus of Nazareth,* contrary to his doctrine, his honour, his interest. That name did no harm, yet, because it agreed not with the notion he had of the kingdom of the Messiah, he was for doing all he could against it. He thought he did God good service in persecuting those who called on the name of Jesus Christ. Note, It is possible for those to be confident they are in the right who yet are evidently in the wrong; and for those to think they are doing their duty who are wilfully persisting in the greatest sin. Those that hated their brethren, and cast them out, said, *Let the Lord be glorified,* Isa. lxvi. 5. Under colour and pretext of religion, the most barbarous and inhuman villanies have been not only justified, but sanctified and magnified, John xvi. 2.

(2.) What a fury he was in his practice, *v.* 10, 11. There is not a more violent principle in the world than conscience misinformed. When Paul thought it his duty to do all he could against the name of Christ, he spared no pains nor cost in it. He gives an account of what he did of that kind, and aggravates it as one that was truly penitent for it: *I was a blasphemer, a persecutor,* 1 Tim. i. 13. [1.] He filled the jails with Christians, as if they had been the worst of criminals, designing hereby not only to terrify them, but to make them odious to the people. He was *the devil that cast some of them into prison* (Rev. ii. 10), took them into custody, in order to their being prosecuted. *Many of the saints did I shut up in prison (ch.* xxvi. 10), *both men and women, ch.* viii. 3. [2.] He made himself the tool of the chief priests. Herein from them he *received authority,* as an inferior officer, to put their laws in execution, and proud enough he was to be a man in authority for such a purpose. [3.] He was very officious to vote, unasked for, the putting of Christians to death, particularly Stephen, to whose death Saul was consenting (*ch.* viii. 1), and so made himself *particeps criminis—partaker of the crime.* Perhaps he was, for his great zeal, though young, made a member of the sanhedrim, and there voted for the condemning of Christians to die; or, after they were condemned, he justified what was done, and commended it, and so made himself guilty *ex post facto—after the deed was committed,* as if he had been a judge or jury-man. [4.] He brought them under punishments of an inferior nature, *in the synagogues,* where they were *scourged* as transgressors of the rules of the synagogue. He had a hand in the punishing of many; nay, it should seem the same persons were by his means *often punished,* as he himself was five times, 2 Cor. xi. 24. [5.] He not only punished them for their religion, but, taking a pride in triumphing over men's consciences, he forced them to abjure their religion, by putting them to the torture: "*I compelled them to blaspheme* Christ, and to say he was a deceiver and they were deceived in him—compelled them to deny their Master, and renounce their obligations to him." Nothing will lie heavier upon persecutors than forcing men's consciences, how much soever they may now triumph in the proselytes they have made by their violences. [6.] His rage swelled so against Christians and Christianity that Jerusalem itself was too narrow a stage for it to act upon, but, being *exceedingly mad against them, he persecuted them even to strange cities.* He was mad at them, to see how much they had to say for themselves, notwithstanding all he did against them, mad to see them multiply the more for their being afflicted. He was *exceedingly mad;* the stream of his fury would admit no banks, no bounds, but he was as much a terror to himself as he was to them, so great was his vexation within himself that he could not prevail, as well as his indignation against them. Persecutors are mad men, and some of them *exceedingly mad.* Paul was mad to see that those in other cities were not so outrageous against the Christians, and therefore made himself busy where he had no business, and persecuted the Christians even in strange cities. There is not a more restless principle than malice, especially that which pretends conscience.

This was Paul's character, and this his manner of life in the beginning of his time; and therefore he could not be presumed to be a Christian by education or custom, or to be drawn in by hope of preferment, for all imaginable external objections lay against his being a Christian.

12 Whereupon as I went to Damascus with authority and commission from the chief priests, 13 At
midday, O king, I saw in the way a
light from heaven, above the brightness of the sun, shining round about
me and them which journeyed with
me. 14 And when we were all
fallen to the earth, I heard a voice
speaking unto me, and saying in the
Hebrew tongue, Saul, Saul, why persecutest thou me? *it is* hard for thee
to kick against the pricks. 15 And
I said, Who art thou, Lord? And
he said, I am Jesus whom thou persecutest. 16 But rise, and stand
upon thy feet: for I have appeared
unto thee for this purpose, to make
thee a minister and a witness both of
these things which thou hast seen,
and of those things in the which I
will appear unto thee; 17 Delivering thee from the people, and *from*
the Gentiles, unto whom now I send
thee, 18 To open their eyes, *and*
to turn *them* from darkness to light,
and *from* the power of Satan unto
God, that they may receive forgiveness of sins, and inheritance among
them which are sanctified by faith
that is in me. 19 Whereupon, O
king Agrippa, I was not disobedient
unto the heavenly vision: 20 But
showed first unto them of Damascus,
and at Jerusalem, and throughout all
the coasts of Judæa, and *then* to the
Gentiles, that they should repent and
turn to God, and do works meet for
repentance. 21 For these causes
the Jews caught me in the temple,
and went about to kill *me.* 22 Having therefore obtained help of God, I
continue unto this day, witnessing
both to small and great, saying none
other things than those which the
prophets and Moses did say should
come: 23 That Christ should suffer,
and that he should be the first that
should rise from the dead, and should
show light unto the people, and unto
the Gentiles.

All who believe a God, and have a reverence for his sovereignty, must acknowledge that those who speak and act by his direction, and by warrant from him, are not to be opposed; for that *is fighting against God.* Now Paul here, by a plain and faithful narrative of matters of fact, makes it out to this august assembly that he had an immediate call from heaven to preach the gospel of Christ to the

Gentile world, which was the thing that exasperated the Jews against him. He here shows,

I. That he was made a Christian by a divine power, notwithstanding all his prejudices against that way. He was brought into it on a sudden by the hand of heaven; not compelled to confess Christ by outward force, as he had compelled others to blaspheme him, but by a divine and spiritual energy, by a revelation of Christ from above, both to him and in him: and this when he was in the full career of his sin, going to Damascus, to suppress Christianity by persecuting the Christians there, as hot as ever in the cause, his persecuting fury not in the least spent nor tired, nor was he tempted to give it up by the failing of his friends, for he had at this time as ample an *authority and commission from the chief priests* to persecute Christianity as ever he had, when he was obliged by a superior power to give up that, and accept another commission to preach up Christianity Two things bring about this surprising change, a vision from heaven and a voice from heaven, which conveyed the knowledge of Christ to him by the two learning senses of seeing and hearing.

1. He saw a heavenly vision, the circumstances of which were such that it could not be a *delùsion—deceptio visus,* but it was without doubt a divine appearance. (1.) He *saw a great light, a light from heaven,* such as could not be produced by any art, for it was not in the night, but *at mid day;* it was not in a house where tricks might have been played with him, but it was *in the way,* in the open air; it was such a light as was *above the brightness of the sun,* outshone and eclipsed that (Isa. xxiv. 23), and this could not be the product of Paul's own fancy, for it *shone round about those that journeyed with him:* they were all sensible of their being surrounded with this inundation of light, which made the sun itself to be in their eyes a less light. The force and power of this light appeared in the effects of it; they all fell to the earth upon the sight of it, such a mighty consternation did it put them into; this light was lightning for its force, yet did not pass away as lightning, but continued to shine round about them. In Old-Testament times God commonly manifested himself in the thick darkness, and made that his pavilion, 2 Chron. vi. 1. He spoke to Abraham in a great darkness (Gen. xv. 12), for that was a dispensation of darkness; but now that *life and immortality were brought to light by the gospel* Christ appeared in a great light. In the creation of grace, as of the world, the first thing created is light, 2 Cor. iv. 6. (2.) Christ himself appeared to him (*v.* 16): *I have appeared to thee for this purpose.* Christ was in this light, though those that travelled with Paul saw the light only, and not Christ in the light. It is not every knowledge that will serve to make us Christians, but it must be *the knowledge of Christ.*

2. He heard a heavenly voice, an articulate one, *speaking to him;* it is here said to be *in the Hebrew tongue* (which was not taken notice of before), his native language, the language of his religion, to intimate to him that though he must be sent among the Gentiles, yet he must not forget that he was a Hebrew, nor make himself a stranger to the Hebrew language. In what Christ said to him we may observe, (1.) That he called him by his name, and repeated it *(Saul, Saul),* which would surprise and startle him; and the more because he was now in a strange place, where he thought nobody knew him. (2.) That he convinced him of sin, of that great sin which he was now in the commission of, the sin of persecuting the Christians, and showed him the absurdity of it. (3.) That he interested himself in the sufferings of his followers: *Thou persecutest me* (*v.* 14), and again, It is *Jesus whom thou persecutest, v.* 15. Little did Paul think, when he was trampling upon those that he looked upon as the burdens and blemishes of this earth, that he was insulting one that was so much the glory of heaven. (4.) That he checked him for his wilful resistance of those convictions: *It is hard for thee to kick against the pricks,* or goads, *as a bullock unaccustomed to the yoke.* Paul's spirit at first perhaps began to rise, but he is told it is at his peril, and then he yields. Or, it was spoken by way of caution: "Take heed lest thou resist these convictions, for they are designed to affect thee, not to affront thee." (5.) That, upon his enquiry, Christ made himself known to him. Paul asked (*v.* 15), "*Who art thou, Lord?* Let me know who it is that speaks to me from heaven, that I may answer him accordingly?" And he said, "*I am Jesus;* he whom thou hast despised, and hated, and vilified; I bear that name which thou hast made so odious, and the naming of it criminal." Paul thought Jesus was buried in the earth, and, though stolen out of his own sepulchre, yet laid in some other. All the Jews were taught to say so, and therefore he is amazed to hear him speak from heaven, to see him surrounded with all this glory whom he had loaded with all possible ignominy. This convinced him that the doctrine of Jesus was divine and heavenly, and not only not to be opposed, but to be cordially embraced: *That Jesus is the Messiah,* for he has not only *risen from the dead,* but he has *received from God the Father honour and glory;* and this is enough to make him a Christian immediately, to quit the society of the persecutors, whom the Lord from heaven thus appears against, and to join himself with the society of the persecuted, whom the Lord from heaven thus appears for.

II. That he was made a minister by a divine authority: *That the same Jesus that appeared to him in that glorious light* ordered him *to go and preach the gospel to the Gentiles;* he did not run without sending, nor was he sent by men like himself, but by him whom the Father sent, John xx. 21. What is said of his being an apostle is here joined immediately to that which was said to him by the way, but it appears by *ch.* ix. 15, and xxii. 15, 17, &c., that it was spoken to him afterwards; but he puts the two together for brevity-sake: *Rise, and stand upon thy feet.* Those whom Christ, by the light of his gospel, casts down in humiliation for sin, shall find that it is in order to their rising and standing upon their feet, in spiritual grace, strength, and comfort. If Christ has torn, it is that he may heal; if he has cast down, it is that he may raise up. *Rise then, and shake thyself from the dust* (Isa. lii. 2), help thyself, and Christ shall help thee. He must stand up, for Christ has work for him to do—has an errand, and a very great errand, to send him upon: *I have appeared to thee to make thee a minister.* Christ has the making of his own ministers; they have both their qualifications and their commissions from him. Paul thanks Christ Jesus who put him into the ministry, 1 Tim. i. 12. Christ appeared to him to make him a minister. One way or other, Christ will manifest himself to all those whom he makes his ministers; for how can those preach him who do not know him? And how can those know him to whom he does not by his spirit make himself known? Observe,

1. The office to which Paul is appointed: he is made a minister, to attend on Christ, and act for him, as a witness—to give evidence in his cause, and attest the truth of his doctrine. He must testify *the gospel of the grace of God;* Christ appeared to him that he might appear for Christ before men.

2. The matter of Paul's testimony: he must give an account to the world, (1.) *Of the things which he had seen,* now at this time, must tell people of Christ's manifesting himself to him by the way, and what he said to him. He saw these things that he might publish them, and he did take all occasions to publish them, as here, and before, *ch.* 22. (2.) *Of those things in which he would appear to him.* Christ now settled a correspondence with Paul, which he designed afterwards to keep up, and only told him now that he should hear further from him. Paul at first had but confused notions of the gospel, till Christ appeared to him and gave him fuller instructions. *The gospel he preached he received from Christ* immediately (Gal. i. 12); but he received it gradually, some at one time and some at another, as there was occasion. Christ often appeared to Paul, oftener, it is likely, than is recorded, and still taught him, *that he might still teach the people knowledge.*

3. The spiritual protection he was taken under, while he was thus employed as Christ's witness: all the powers of darkness could not prevail against him till he had finished his testimony (*v.* 17), *delivering thee from the people of the Jews and from the Gentiles.* Note, Christ's witnesses are under his special care, and, though they may fall into the hands of the enemies, yet he will take care to deliver them out of their hands, and he knows how to do it. Christ had shown Paul at this time *what great things he must suffer* (*ch.* ix. 16), and yet tells him here he will *deliver him from the people.* Note, Great sufferings are reconcileable to the promise of the deliverance of God's people, for it is not promised that they shall be kept from trouble, but kept through it; and sometimes God delivers them into the hands of their persecutors that he may have the honour of delivering them out of their hands.

4. The special commission given him to go among the Gentiles, and the errand upon which he is sent to them; it was some years after Paul's conversion before he was *sent to the Gentiles,* or (for aught that appears) knew any thing of his being designed for that purpose (see *ch.* xxii. 21); but at length he is ordered to steer his course that way.

(1.) There is great work to be done among the Gentiles, and Paul must be instrumental in doing it. Two things must be done, which their case calls for the doing of:—[1.] A world that sits in darkness must be enlightened; those must be brought to *know the things that belong to their everlasting peace* who are yet ignorant of them, to know God as their end, and Christ as their way, who as yet know nothing of either. He is *sent to open their eyes, and to turn them from darkness to light.* His preaching shall not only make known to them those things which they had not before heard of, but shall be the vehicle of that divine grace and power by which their understandings shall be enlightened to receive those things, and bid them welcome. Thus he shall open their eyes, which before were shut against the light, and they shall be willing to understand themselves, their own case and interest. Christ opens the heart by opening the eyes, does not lead men blindfold, but gives them to see their own way. He is sent not only to open their eyes for the present, but to keep them open, *to turn them from darkness to light,* that is, from following false and blind guides, their oracles, divinations, and superstitious usages, received by tradition from their fathers, and the corrupt notions and ideas they had of their gods, to follow a divine revelation of unquestionable certainty and truth. This was turning them from darkness to light, from the ways of darkness to those on which the light shines. The great design of the gospel is to instruct the ignorant, and to rectify the mistakes of those who are in error, that things may be set and seen in a true light. [2.] A world that lies in wickedness, in the wicked one, must be sanctified and reformed; it is not enough for them to have their eyes opened, they must have their hearts renewed; not enough to be turned from darkness to light, but they must be turned from the power of Satan unto God, which will follow of course; for Satan rules by the power of darkness, and God by the convincing evidence of light. Sinners are under the power of Satan; idolaters were so in a special manner, they paid their homage to devils. All sinners are under the influence of his temptations, yield themselves captives to him, are at his beck; converting grace turns them from under the dominion of Satan, and brings them into subjection to God, to conform to the rules of his word and comply with the dictates and directions of his Spirit, *translates them out of the kingdom of darkness into the kingdom of his dear Son.* When gracious dispositions are strong in the soul (as corrupt and sinful dispositions had been), it is then turned from the power of Satan unto God.

(2.) There is a great happiness designed for the Gentiles by this work—*that they may receive forgiveness of sins, and inheritance among those who are sanctified;* they are turned from the darkness of sin to the light of holiness, from the slavery of Satan to the service of God; not that God may be a gainer by them, but that they may be gainers by him. [1.] That they may be restored to his favour, which by sin they have forfeited and thrown themselves out of: *That they may receive forgiveness of sins.* They are delivered from the dominion of sin, that they may be saved from that death which is the wages of sin. Not that they may merit forgiveness as a debt or reward, but that they may receive it as a free gift, that they may be qualified to receive the comfort of it. They are persuaded to lay down their arms, and return to their allegiance, that they may have the benefit of the act of indemnity, and may plead it in arrest of the judgment to be given against them. [2.] That they may be happy in the fruition of him; not only that they may have their sins pardoned, but *that they may have an inheritance among those who are sanctified by faith that is in me.* Note, *First,* Heaven is an inheritance, it descends to all the children of God; for, *if children, then heirs. That they may have,* κλῆρον—*a lot* (so it might be read), alluding to the inheritances of Canaan, which were appointed by lot, and that also is the act of God, *the disposal thereof is of the Lord. That they may have a right,* so some read it; not by merit, but purely by grace. *Secondly,* All that are effectually turned from sin to God are not only pardoned, but preferred—have not only their attainder reversed, but a patent of honour given to them, and a grant of a rich inheritance. And the forgiveness of sins makes way for this inheritance, by taking that out of the way which alone hindered. *Thirdly,* All that shall be saved hereafter are sanctified now; those that have the heavenly inheritance must have it in this way, they must be prepared and made meet for it. None can be happy that are not holy; nor shall any be saints in heaven that are not first saints on earth. *Fourthly,* We need no more to make us happy than to have our lot among those that are sanctified, to fare as they fare; this is having our lot among the chosen, for they are chosen to salvation through sanctification. Those who are sanctified shall be glorified. Let us therefore now cast in our lot among them, by coming into the communion of saints, and be willing to take our lot with them, and share with them in their afflictions, which (how grievous soever) our lot with them in the inheritance will abundantly make amends for. *Fifthly,* We are sanctified and saved by faith in Christ. Some refer it to the word next before, *sanctified by faith,* for faith purifies the heart, and applies to the soul those precious promises, and subjects the soul to the influence of that grace, by which we partake of a divine nature Others refer it to the receiving of both pardon and the inheritance; it is by faith accepting the grant: it comes all to one; for it is by faith that we are justified, sanctified, and glorified. *By faith,* τῇ εἰς ἐμέ—*that faith which is in me;* it is emphatically expressed. That faith which not only receives divine revelation in general, but which in a particular manner fastens upon Jesus Christ and his mediation, by which we rely upon Christ as *the Lord our righteousness,* and resign ourselves to him as the Lord our ruler. This is that by which we receive *the remission of sins, the gift of the Holy Ghost, and eternal life.*

III. That he had discharged his ministry, pursuant to his commission, by divine aid, and under divine direction and protection. God, who called him to be an apostle, owned him in his apostolical work, and carried him on in it with enlargement and success.

1. God gave him a heart to comply with the call (*v.* 19): *I was not disobedient to the heavenly vision,* for any one would say he ought to be obedient to it. Heavenly visions have a commanding power over earthly counsels, and it is at our peril if we be disobedient to them; yet if Paul had conferred with flesh and blood, and been swayed by his secular interest, he would have done as Jonah did, gone any where rather than upon this errand; but God *opened his ear, and he was not rebellious.* He accepted the commission, and, having with it received his instructions, he applied himself to act accordingly.

2. God enabled him to go through a great deal of work, though in it he grappled with a great deal of difficulty, *v.* 20. He applied himself to the preaching of the gospel with all vigour. (1.) He began at Damascus, where he was converted, for he resolved to lose no time, *ch.* ix. 20. (2.) When he came to Jerusalem, where he had his education, he there witnessed for Christ, where he had most furiously set himself against him, *ch.* ix. 29. (3.) He preached *throughout all the coasts of Judea,* in the country towns and villages, as Christ had done; he made the first offer of the gospel to the Jews, as Christ had appointed, and did not leave them till

they had wilfully thrust the gospel from them; and then, (4.) He turned to the Gentiles, and laid out himself for the good of their souls, labouring more abundantly than any of the apostles, nay perhaps than all put together.

3. His preaching was all practical. He did not go about to fill people's heads with airy notions, did not amuse them with nice speculations, nor set them together by the ears with matters of doubtful disputation, but he showed them, declared it, demonstrated it, that they ought, (1.) *To repent of their sins,* to be sorry for them and to confess them, and enter into covenant against them; they ought to *bethink themselves,* so the word μετανοεῖν properly signifies; they ought to change their mind and change their way, and undo what they had done amiss. (2.) *To turn to God.* They must not only conceive an antipathy to sin, but they must come into a conformity to God—must not only turn from that which is evil, but turn to that which is good; they must turn to God, in love and affection, and return to God in duty and obedience, and turn and return from the world and the flesh; this is that which is required from the whole revolted degenerate race of mankind, both Jews and Gentiles; ἐπιςρέφειν ἐπὶ τὸν Θεὸν—*to turn back to God, even to him:* to turn to him as our chief good and highest end, as our ruler and portion, turn our eye to him, turn our heart to him, and turn our feet unto his testimonies. (3.) *To do works meet for repentance.* This was what John preached, who was the first gospel preacher, Matt. iii. 8. Those that profess repentance must practise it, must live a life of repentance, must in every thing carry it as becomes penitents. It is not enough to speak penitent words, but we must do works agreeable to those words. As true faith, so true repentance, will work. Now what fault could be found with such preaching as this? Had it not a direct tendency to reform the world, and to redress its grievances, and to revive natural religion?

4. The Jews had no quarrel with him but upon this account, that he did all he could to persuade people to be religious, and to bring them to God by bringing them to Christ (*v.* 21): It was for these causes, and no other, *that the Jews caught me in the temple, and went about to kill me;* and let any one judge whether these were crimes worthy of death or of bonds. He suffered ill, not only for doing well himself, but for doing good to others. They attempted to kill him; it was his precious life that they hunted for, and hated, because it was a useful life; they caught him in the temple worshipping God, and there they set upon him, as if the better place the better deed.

5. He had no help but from heaven; supported and carried on by that, he went on in this great work (*v.* 22): "*Having therefore obtained help of God, I continue unto this day;* ἕςηκα—*I have stood,* my life has been preserved, and my work continued; I have stood my ground, and have not been beaten off; I have stood to what I said, and have not been afraid nor ashamed to persist in it." It was now above twenty years since Paul was converted, and all that time he had been very busy preaching the gospel in the midst of hazards; and what was it that bore him up? Not any strength of his own resolutions, but *having obtained help of God;* for therefore, because the work was so great and he had so much opposition, he could not otherwise have gone on in it, but by help obtained of God. Note, Those who are employed in work for God shall obtain help from God; for he will not be wanting in necessary assistances to his servants. And our continuance to this day must be attributed to help obtained of God; we had sunk, if he had not borne us up—had fallen off, if he had not carried us on; and it must be acknowledged with thankfulness to his praise. Paul mentions it as an evidence that he had his commission from God that from him he had ability to execute it. The preachers of the gospel could never have done, and suffered, and prospered, as they did, if they had not had immediate help from heaven, which they would not have had if it had not been the cause of God that they were now pleading.

6. He preached no doctrine but what agreed with the scriptures of the Old Testament: He *witnessed both to small and great,* to young and old, rich and poor, learned and unlearned, obscure and illustrious, all being concerned in it. It was an evidence of the condescending grace of the gospel that it was witnessed to the meanest, and the poor were welcome to the knowledge of it; and of the incontestable truth and power of it that it was neither afraid nor ashamed to show itself to the greatest. The enemies of Paul objected against him that he preached something more than *that men should repent, and turn to God, and do works meet for repentance.* These indeed were but what the prophets of the Old Testament had preached; but, besides these, he had preached Christ, and his death, and his resurrection, and this was what they quarrelled with him for, as appears by *ch.* xxv. 19, *that he affirmed Jesus to be alive:* "And so I did," says Paul, "and so I do, but therein also I say *no other than that which Moses and the prophets said should come;* and what greater honour can be done to them than to show that what they foretold is accomplished, and in the appointed season too—that what they said should come is come, and at the time they prefixed?" Three things they prophesied, and Paul preached:—(1.) *That Christ should suffer,* that the Messiah should be a *sufferer*—παθητὸς· not only a man, and capable of suffering, but that, as Messiah, he should be

appointed to sufferings; that his ignominious death should be not only consistent with, but pursuant of, his undertaking. The cross of Christ was a stumbling-block to the Jews, and Paul's preaching it was the great thing that exasperated them; but Paul stands to it that, in preaching that, he preached the fulfilling of the Old-Testament predictions, and therefore they ought not only not to be offended at what he preached, but to embrace it, and subscribe to it. (2.) *That he should be the first that should rise from the dead;* not the first in time, but the first in influence—*that he should be the chief of the resurrection, the head, or principal one,* πρῶτος ἐξ ἀναστάσεως, in the same sense that he is called *the first-begotten from the dead* (Rev. i. 5), and *the first-born from the dead,* Col. i. 18. He opened the womb of the grave, as the first-born are said to do, and made way for our resurrection; and he is said *to be the first-fruits of those that slept* (1 Cor. xv. 20), for he sanctified the harvest. He was the first that rose from the dead to die no more; and, to show that the resurrection of all believers is in virtue of his, just when he arose *many dead bodies of saints arose, and went into the holy city,* Matt. xxvii. 52, 53. (3.) *That he should show light unto the people, and to the Gentiles,* to the people of the Jews in the first place, for he was to be *the glory of his people Israel.* To them he showed light by himself, and then to the Gentiles by the ministry of his apostles, for he was *to be a light to enlighten those who sat in darkness.* In this Paul refers to his commission (*v.* 18), *To turn them from darkness to light.* He rose from the dead on purpose that he might show light to the people, that he might give a convincing proof of the truth of his doctrine, and might send it with so much the greater power, both among Jews and Gentiles. This also was foretold by the Old-Testament prophets, *that the Gentiles should be brought to the knowledge of God by the Messiah;* and what was there in all this that the Jews could justly be displeased at?

24 And as he thus spake for himself, Festus said with a loud voice,
Paul, thou art beside thyself; much
learning doth make thee mad. 25
But he said, I am not mad, most
noble Festus; but speak forth the
words of truth and soberness. 26
For the king knoweth of these things,
before whom also I speak freely: for
I am persuaded that none of these
things are hidden from him; for this
thing was not done in a corner. 27
King Agrippa, believest thou the
prophets? I know that thou believest. 28 Then Agrippa said unto
Paul, Almost thou persuadest me to
be a Christian. 29 And Paul said,
I would to God, that not only thou,
but also all that hear me this day,
were both almost, and altogether such
as I am, except these bonds. 30
And when he had thus spoken, the
king rose up, and the governor, and
Bernice, and they that sat with them:
31 And when they were gone aside,
they talked between themselves, saying, This man doeth nothing worthy
of death or of bonds. 32 Then said
Agrippa unto Festus, This man might
have been set at liberty, if he had not
appealed unto Cæsar.

We have reason to think that Paul had a great deal more to say in defence of the gospel he preached, and for the honour of it, and to recommend it to the good opinion of this noble audience; he had just fallen upon that which was the life of the cause—the death and resurrection of Jesus Christ, and here he is in his element; now he warms more than before, his mouth is opened towards them, his heart is enlarged. Lead him but to this subject, and let him have leave to go on, and he will never know when to conclude; for the power of Christ's death, and the fellowship of his sufferings, are with him inexhaustible subjects. It was a thousand pities then that he should be interrupted, as he is here, and that, being permitted to speak for himself (*v.* 1), he should not be permitted to say all he designed. But it was a hardship often put upon him, and is a disappointment to us too, who read his discourse with so much pleasure. But there is no remedy, the court thinks it is time to proceed to give in their judgment upon his case.

I. Festus, the Roman governor, is of opinion that the poor man is crazed, and that Bedlam is the fittest place for him. He is convinced that he is no criminal, no bad man, that should be punished, but he takes him to be a lunatic, a distracted man, that should be pitied, but at the same time should not be heeded, nor a word he says regarded; and thus he thinks he has found out an expedient to excuse himself both from condemning Paul as a prisoner and from believing him as a preacher; for, if he be not *compos mentis—in his senses,* he is not to be either condemned or credited. Now here observe,

1. What it was that Festus said of him (*v.* 24): *He said with a loud voice,* did not whisper it to those that sat next him; if so, it had been the more excusable, but (without consulting Agrippa, to whose judgment he had seemed to pay profound deference, *ch.* xxv. 26), *said aloud,* that he might oblige Paul to break off his discourse, and might divert the auditors from attending to it

"*Paul, thou art beside thyself,* thou talkest like a madman, like one with a heated brain, that knowest not what thou sayest;" yet he does not suppose that a guilty conscience had disturbed his reason, nor that his sufferings, and the rage of his enemies against him, had given any shock to it; but he puts the most candid construction that could be upon his delirium: *Much learning hath made thee mad,* thou hast cracked thy brains with studying. This he speaks, not so much in anger, as in scorn and contempt. He did not understand what Paul said; it was above his capacity, it was all a riddle to him, and therefore he imputes it all to a heated imagination. *Si non vis intelligi, debes negligi—If thou art not willing to be understood, thou oughtest to be neglected.* (1.) He owns Paul to be a scholar, and a man of learning, because he could so readily refer to what Moses and the prophets wrote, books that he was a stranger to; and even this is turned to his reproach. The apostles, who were fishermen, were despised because they had no learning; Paul, who was a university-man, and bred a Pharisee, is despised as having too much learning, more than did him good. Thus the enemies of Christ's ministers will always have something or other to upbraid them with. (2.) He reproaches him as a madman. The prophets of the Old Testament were thus stigmatized, to prejudice people against them by putting them into an ill-name: *Wherefore came this mad fellow unto thee?* said the captains of the prophet, 2 Kings ix. 11; Hos. ix. 7. John Baptist and Christ were represented as having a devil, as being crazed. It is probable that Paul now spoke with more life and earnestness than he did in the beginning of his discourse, and used more gestures that were expressive of his zeal, and therefore Festus put this invidious character upon him, which perhaps never a one in the company but himself thought of. It is not so harmless a suggestion as some make it to say concerning those that are zealous in religion above others that they are crazed.

2. How Paul cleared himself from this invidious imputation, which whether he had ever lain under before is not certain; it should seem, it had been said of him by the false apostles, for he says (2 Cor. v. 13), *If we be beside ourselves,* as they say we are, *it is to God;* but he was never charged with this before *the Roman governor,* and therefore he must say something to this. (1.) He denies the charge, with due respect indeed to the governor, but with justice to himself, protesting that there was neither ground nor colour for it (*v.* 25): "*I am not mad, most noble Festus,* nor ever was, nor any thing like it; the use of my reason, thanks be to God, has been all my days continued to me, and at this time I do not ramble, *but speak the words of truth and soberness,* and know what I say." Observe, Though Festus gave Paul this base and contemptuous usage, not becoming a gentlemen, much less a judge, yet Paul is so far from resenting it, and being provoked by it, that he gives him all possible respect, compliments him with his title of honour, *most noble Festus,* to teach us not to render railing for railing, nor one invidious character for another, but to speak civilly to those who speak slightly of us. It becomes us, upon all occasions, to speak the words of truth and soberness, and then we may despise the unjust censures of men. (2.) He appeals to Agrippa concerning what he spoke (*v.* 26): *For the king knows of these things,* concerning Christ, and his death and resurrection, and the prophecies of the Old Testament, which had their accomplishment therein. He therefore *spoke freely before him,* who knew these were no fancies, but matters of fact, knew something of them, and therefore would be willing to know more: *For I am persuaded that none of these things are hidden from him;* no, not that which he had related concerning his own conversion, and the commission he had received to preach the gospel. Agrippa could not but have heard of it, having been so long conversant among the Jews. *This thing was not done in a corner;* all the country rang of it; and any of the Jews present might have witnessed for him that they had heard it many a time from others, and therefore it was unreasonable to censure him as a distracted man for relating it, much more for speaking of the death and resurrection of Christ, which was so universally spoken of. Peter tells Cornelius and his friends (*ch.* x. 37), *That word you know which was published throughout all Judea* concerning Christ; and therefore Agrippa could not be ignorant of it, and it was a shame for Festus that he was so.

II. Agrippa is so far from thinking him a madman that he thinks he never heard a man argue more strongly, nor talk more to the purpose.

1. Paul applies himself closely to Agrippa's conscience. Some think Festus was displeased at Paul because he kept his eye upon Agrippa, and directed his discourse to him all along, and that therefore he gave him that interruption, *v.* 24. But, if that was the thing that affronted him, Paul regards it not: he will speak to those who understand him, and whom he is likely to fasten something upon, and therefore still addresses *Agrippa;* and, because he had mentioned Moses and the prophets as confirming the gospel he preached, he refers Agrippa to them (*v.* 27): "*King Agrippa, believest thou the prophets?* Dost thou receive the scriptures of the Old Testament as a divine revelation, and admit them as foretelling good things to come?" He does not stay for an answer, but, in compliment to Agrippa, takes it for granted: *I know that thou believest;* for every one knew that Agrippa professed the Jews' religion, as his fathers had done, and therefore both knew the writings of the prophets and gave

credit to them. Note, It is good dealing with those who have acquaintance with the scriptures and believe them; for such one has some hold of.

2. Agrippa owns there was a great deal of reason in what Paul said (*v.* 28): *Almost thou persuadest me to be a Christian.* Some understand this as spoken ironically, and read it thus, *Wouldest thou in so little a time persuade me to be a Christian?* But, taking it so, it is an acknowledgment that Paul spoke very much to the purpose, and that, whatever others thought of it, to his mind there came a convincing power along with what he said: "Paul, thou art too hasty, thou canst not think to make a convert of me all of a sudden." Others take it as spoken seriously, and as a confession that he was in a manner, or within a little, convinced that Christ was the Messiah; for he could not but own, and had many a time thought so within himself, that the prophecies of the Old Testament had had their accomplishment in him; and now that it is urged thus solemnly upon him he is ready to yield to the conviction, he begins to sound a parley, and to think of rendering. He is as near being persuaded to believe in Christ as Felix, when he trembled, was to leave his sins: he sees a great deal of reason for Christianity; the proofs of it, he owns, are strong, and such as he cannot answer; the objections against it trifling, and such as he cannot for shame insist upon; so that if it were not for his obligations to the ceremonial law, and his respect to the religion of his fathers and of his country, or his regard to his dignity as a king and to his secular interests, he would turn Christian immediately. Note, Many are almost persuaded to be religious who are not quite persuaded; they are under strong convictions of their duty, and of the excellency of the ways of God, but yet are overruled by some external inducements, and do not pursue their convictions.

3. Paul, not being allowed time to pursue his argument, concludes with a compliment, or rather a pious wish that all his hearers were Christians, and this wish turned into a prayer: εὐξάιμην ἄν τῷ Θεῷ—*I pray to God for it* (*v.* 29); it was *his heart's desire and prayer to God for them all that they might be saved,* Rom. x. 1. *That not only thou but all that hear me this day* (for he has the same kind design upon them all) *were both almost, and altogether, such as I am, except these bonds.* Hereby, (1.) He professes his resolution to cleave to his religion, as that which he was entirely satisfied in, and determined to live and die by. In wishing that they were all as he was, he does in effect declare against ever being as they were, whether Jews or Gentiles, how much soever it might be to his worldly advantage. He adheres to the instruction God gave to the prophet (Jer. xv. 19), *Let them return unto thee, but return not thou unto them.* 2.) He intimates his satisfaction not only in the truth, but in the benefit and advantage of Christianity; he had so much comfort in it for the present, and was so sure it would end in his eternal happiness, that he could not wish better to the best friend he had in the world than to wish him such a one as he was, a faithful zealous disciple of Jesus Christ. *Let my enemy be as the wicked,* says Job, *ch.* xxvii. 7. Let my friend be as the Christian, says Paul. (3.) He intimates his trouble and concern that Agrippa went no further than being almost such a one as he was, almost a Christian, and not altogether one; for he wishes that he and the rest of them might be not only almost (what good would that do?) but altogether such as he was, sincere thorough-paced Christians. (4.) He intimates that it was the concern, and would be the unspeakable happiness, of every one of them to become *true Christians*—that there is grace enough in Christ for all, be they ever so many—enough for each, be they ever so craving. (5.) He intimates the hearty good-will he bore to them all; he wishes them, [1.] As well as he wished his own soul, that they might be as happy in Christ as he was. [2.] Better than he now was as to his outward condition, for he excepts these bonds; he wishes they might all be comforted Christians as he was, but not persecuted Christians as he was—that they might taste as much as he did of the advantages that attended religion, but not so much of its crosses. They had made light of his imprisonment, and were in no concern for him. Felix detained him in bonds to gratify the Jews. Now this would have tempted many a one to wish them all in his bonds, that they might know what it was to be confined as he was, and then they would know the better how to pity him; but he was so far from this that, when he wished them in bonds to Christ, he desired they might never be in bonds for Christ. Nothing could be said more tenderly nor with a better grace.

III. They all agree that Paul is an innocent man, and is wronged in his prosecution. 1. The court broke up with some precipitation (*v.* 30): *When he had spoken* that obliging word (*v.* 29), which moved them all, the king was afraid, if he were permitted to go on, he would say something yet more moving, which might work upon some of them to appear more in his favour than was convenient, and perhaps might prevail with them to turn Christians. The king himself found his own heart begin to yield, and durst not trust himself to hear more, but, like Felix, dismissed Paul for this time. They ought in justice to have asked the prisoner whether he had any more to say for himself; but they thought he had said enough, and therefore *the king rose up, and the governor, and Bernice, and those that sat with them,* concluding the case was plain, and with this they contented themselves, when Paul had more to say which would have made it plainer. 2. They all concurred in an opinion of Paul's innocency, *v.* 31. The court withdrew to consult of the matter, to know one another's minds upon it, and *they talked among themselves*, all to the same purport, *that this man does nothing worthy of death*—he is not a criminal that deserves to die; nay, he *does nothing worthy of bonds*—he is not a dangerous man, whom it is prudent to confine. After this, Nero made a law for the putting of those to death who professed the Christian religion, but as yet there was no law of that kind among the Romans, and therefore no transgression; and this judgment of theirs is a testimony against that wicked law which Nero made not long after this, that Paul, the most active zealous Christian that ever was, was adjudged, even by those that were no friends to his way, to have *done nothing worthy of death, or of bonds.* Thus was he made manifest in the consciences of those who yet would not receive his doctrine; and the clamours of the hot-headed Jews, who cried out, *Away with him, it is not fit he should live,* were shamed by the moderate counsels of this court. 3. *Agrippa* gave his judgment *that he might have been set at liberty, if he had not himself appealed to Cæsar* (*v.* 32), but by that appeal he had put a bar in his own door. Some think that by the Roman law this was true, that, when a prisoner had appealed to the supreme court, the inferior courts could no more discharge him than they could condemn him; and we suppose the law was so, if the prosecutors joined issue upon the appeal, and consented to it. But it does not appear that in Paul's case the prosecutors did so; he was forced to do it, to screen himself from their fury, when he saw the governor did not take the care he ought to have done for his protection. And therefore others think that Agrippa and Festus, being unwilling to disoblige the Jews by setting him at liberty, made this serve for an excuse of their continuing him in custody, when they themselves knew they might have justified the discharging of him. Agrippa, who was but almost persuaded to be a Christian, proves no better than if he had not been at all persuaded. And now I cannot tell, (1.) Whether Paul repented of his having appealed to Cæsar, and wished he had not done it, blaming himself for it as a rash thing, now he saw that was the only thing that hindered his discharge. He had reason perhaps to reflect upon it with regret, and to charge himself with imprudence and impatience in it, and some distrust of the divine protection. He had better have appealed to God than to Cæsar. It confirms what Solomon says (Eccl. vi. 12), *Who knows what is good for man in this life?* What we think is for our welfare often proves to be a trap; such short-sighted creatures are we, and so ill-advised in leaning, as we do, to our own understanding. Or, (2.) Whether, notwithstanding this, he was satisfied in what he had done, and was easy in his reflections upon it. His appealing to Cæsar was lawful, and what became a Roman citizen, and would help to make his cause considerable; and forasmuch as when he did it it appeared to him, as the case then stood, to be for the best, though afterwards it appeared otherwise, he did not vex himself with any self-reproach in the matter, but believed there was a providence in it, and it would issue well at last. And besides, he was told in a vision that he must *bear witness to Christ at Rome, ch.* xxiii. 11. And it is all one to him whether he goes thither a prisoner or at his liberty; he knows *the counsel of the Lord shall stand*, and says, *Let it stand. The will of the Lord be done*

CHAP. XXVII.

This whole chapter is taken up with an account of Paul's voyage towards Rome, when he was sent thither a prisoner by Festus the governor, upon his appeal to Cæsar. I. The beginning of the voyage was well enough, it was calm and prosperous, ver. 1—8. II. Paul gave them notice of a storm coming, but could not prevail with them to lie by, ver. 9—11. III. As they pursued their voyage, they met with a great deal of tempestuous weather, which reduced them to such extremity that they counted upon nothing but being cast away, ver. 12—20. IV. Paul assured them that though they would not be advised by him to prevent their coming into this danger, yet, by the good providence of God, the should be brought safely through it, and none of them should be lost, ver. 21—26. V. At length they were at midnight thrown upon an island, which proved to be Malta, and then they were in the utmost danger imaginable, but were assisted by Paul's counsel to keep the mariners in the ship, and encouraged by his comforts to eat their meat, and have a good heart on it, ver. 27—36. VI. Their narrow escape with their lives, when they came to shore, when the ship was wrecked, but all the persons wonderfully preserved, ver. 37—44.

AND when it was determined
that we should sail into Italy,
they delivered Paul and certain other
prisoners unto *one* named Julius, a
centurion of Augustus' band. 2 And
entering into a ship of Adramyttium,
we launched, meaning to sail by the
coasts of Asia; *one* Aristarchus, a
Macedonian of Thessalonica, being
with us. 3 And the next *day* we
touched at Sidon. And Julius courteously entreated Paul, and gave *him*
liberty to go unto his friends to refresh himself. 4 And when we had
launched from thence, we sailed under
Cyprus, because the winds were contrary. 5 And when we had sailed
over the sea of Cilicia and Pamphylia,
we came to Myra, *a city* of Lycia.
6 And there the centurion found a
ship of Alexandria sailing into Italy;
and he put us therein. 7 And when
we had sailed slowly many days, and
scarce were come over against Cnidus,
the wind not suffering us, we sailed
under Crete, over against Salmone;
8 And, hardly passing it, came unto
a place which is called The fair
havens; nigh whereunto was the city

of Lasea. 9 Now when much time
was spent, and when sailing was now
dangerous, because the fast was now
already past, Paul admonished *them*,
10 And said unto them, Sirs, I perceive that this voyage will be with
hurt and much damage, not only of
the lading and ship, but also of our
lives. 11 Nevertheless the centurion
believed the master and the owner of
the ship, more than those things
which were spoken by Paul.

It does not appear how long it was after Paul's conference with Agrippa that he was sent away for Rome, pursuant to his appeal to Cæsar; but it is likely they took the first convenience they could hear of to do it; in the mean time Paul is in the midst of his friends at Cæsarea—they comforts to him, and he a blessing to them. But here we are told,

I. How Paul was shipped off for Italy: a long voyage, but there is no remedy. He has appealed to Cæsar, and to Cæsar he must go: *It was determined that we should sail into Italy*, for to Rome they must go by sea; it would have been a vast way about to go by land. Hence, when the Roman conquest of the Jewish nation is foretold, it is said (Num. xxiv. 24), *Ships shall come from Chittim*, that is, *Italy, and shall afflict Eber*, that is, the Hebrews. It was determined by the counsel of God, before it was determined by the counsel of Festus, that Paul should go to Rome; for, whatever man intended, God had work for him to do there. Now here we are told, 1. Whose custody he was committed to—to *one named Julius, a centurion of Augustus's band*, as Cornelius was of the Italian band, or legion, *ch.* x. 1. He had soldiers under him, who were a guard upon Paul, that he might not make his escape, and likewise to protect him, that he might have no mischief done him. 2. What bottom he embarked in: they went on board a ship of Adramyttium (*v.* 2), a sea-port of Africa, whence this ship brought African goods, and, as it should seem, made a coasting voyage for Syria, where those goods came to a good market. 3. What company he had in this voyage, there were some prisoners who were committed to the custody of the same centurion, and who probably had appealed to Cæsar too, or were upon some other account removed to Rome, to be tried there, or to be examined as witnesses against some prisoners there; perhaps some notorious offenders, like Barabbas, who were therefore ordered to be brought before the emperor himself. Paul was linked with these, as Christ with the thieves that were crucified with him, and was obliged to take his lot with them in this voyage; and we find in this chapter (*v.* 42) that for their sakes he had like to have been killed, but for his sake they were preserved. Note, It is no new thing for the innocent to be numbered among the transgressors. But he had also some of his friends with him, Luke particularly, the penman of this book, for he puts himself in all along, *We* sailed into Italy, and, *We* launched, *v.* 2. Aristarchus a Thessalonian is particularly named, as being now in his company. Dr. Lightfoot thinks that Trophimus the Ephesian went off with him, but that he left him sick at Miletum (2 Tim. iv. 20), when he passed by those coasts of Asia mentioned here (*v.* 2), and that there likewise he left Timothy. It was a comfort to Paul to have the society of some of his friends in this tedious voyage, with whom he might converse freely, though he had so much loose profane company about him. Those that go long voyages at sea are commonly necessitated to sojourn, as it were, in Mesech and Kedar, and have need of wisdom, that they may do good to the bad company they are in, may make them better, or at least be made never the worse by them.

II. What course they steered, and what places they touched at, which are particularly recorded for the confirming of the truth of the history to those who lived at that time, and could by their own knowledge tell of their being at such and such a place. 1. They touched at Sidon, not far off from where they went on board; thither they came *the next day*. And that which is observable here is, that *Julius the centurion* was extraordinarily civil to Paul. It is probable that he knew his case, and was one of the *chief captains, or principal men*, that heard him plead his own cause before Agrippa (*ch.* xxv. 23), and was convinced of his innocency, and the injury done him; and therefore, though Paul was committed to him as a prisoner, he treated him as a friend, as a scholar, as a gentleman, and as a man that had an interest in heaven: He *gave him liberty*, while the business of the ship detained it at Sidon, *to go among his friends* there, to *refresh himself;* and it would be a great refreshment to him. Julius herein gives an example to those in power to be respectful to those whom they find worthy of their respect, and in using their power to make a difference. A Joseph, a Paul, are not to be used as common prisoners. God herein encourages those that suffer for him to trust in him; for he can put it into the hearts of those to befriend them from whom they least expect it—can cause them to be pitied, nay, can cause them to be prized and valued, even in the eyes of those that carry them captive, Ps. cvi. 46. And it is likewise an instance of Paul's fidelity. He did not go about to make his escape, which he might have easily done; but, being out upon his parole of honour, he faithfully returns to his imprisonment. If the centurion is so civil as to take his word, he is so just and honest as to keep his word. 2. They thence *sailed under Cyprus*, *v.* 4. If the wind had been fair, they had gone forward by direct sailing, and had left Cyprus on the right hand; but, the wind not favouring them, they were driven to oblique sailing with a side wind, and so compassed the island, in a manner, and left it on the left hand. Sailors must do as they can, when they cannot do as they would, and make the best of their wind, whatever point it is in; so must we all in our passage over the ocean of this world. When the winds are contrary yet we must be getting forward as well as we can. 3. At a port called Myra they changed their ship; that which they were in, it is probable, having business no further, they went on board a vessel of Alexandria bound for Italy, *v.* 5, 6. Alexandria was now the chief city of Egypt, and great trading there was between that city and Italy; from Alexandria they carried corn to Rome, and the East-India goods and Persian which they imported at the Red Sea they exported again to all parts of the Mediterranean, and especially to Italy. And it was a particular favour shown to the Alexandrian ships in the ports of Italy that they were not obliged to strike sail, as other ships were, when they came into port. 4. With much ado they made *The Fair Havens,* a port of the island of Crete, *v.* 7, 8. They *sailed slowly many days,* being becalmed, or having the wind against them. It was a great while before they made the point of Cnidus, a port of Caria, and were forced to sail under Crete, as before under Cyprus; much difficulty they met with in passing by Salmone, a promontory on the eastern shore of the island of Crete. Though the voyage hitherto was not tempestuous, yet it was very tedious. Thus many that are not driven backward in their affairs by cross providences, yet sail slowly, and do not get forward by favourable providences. And many good Christians make this complaint in the concerns of their souls, that they do not rid ground in their way to heaven, but have much ado to keep their ground; they move with many stops and pauses, and lie a great while wind-bound. Observe, The place they came to was called *The Fair Havens.* Travellers say that it is known to this day by the same name, and that it answers the name from the pleasantness of its situation and prospect. And yet, (1.) It was not the harbour they were bound for; it was a fair haven, but it was not their haven. Whatever agreeable circumstances we may be in in this world, we must remember we are not at home, and therefore we must arise and depart; for, though it be a fair haven, it is not the desired haven, Ps. cvii. 30 (2.) It was not a *commodious haven to winter in,* so it is said, *v.* 12. It had a fine prospect, but it lay exposed to the weather. Note, Every fair haven is not a safe haven; nay, there may be most danger where there is most pleasure.

III. What advice Paul gave them with reference to that part of their voyage they had before them—it was to be content to winter where they were, and not to think of stirring till a better season of the year. 1. It was now a bad time for sailing; they had lost a deal of time while they were struggling with contrary winds. Sailing was now dangerous, because *the fast was already past,* that is, the famous yearly fast of the Jews, the day of atonement, which was on the tenth day of the seventh month, *a day to afflict the soul* with fasting; it was about the 20th of our September. That yearly fast was very religiously observed; but (which is strange) we never have any mention made in all the scripture history of the observance of it, unless it be meant here, where it serves only to describe the season of the year. Michaelmas is reckoned by mariners as bad a time of the year to be at sea in as any other; they complain of their Michaelmas-blasts; it was that time now with these distressed voyagers. *The harvest was past, the summer was ended;* they had not only lost time, but lost the opportunity. 2. Paul put them in mind of it, and gave them notice of their danger (*v.* 10): "*I perceive*" (either by notice from God, or by observing their wilful resolution to prosecute the voyage notwithstanding the peril of the season) "that *this voyage will be with hurt and damage;* you that have effects on board are likely to lose them, and it will be a miracle of mercy if our lives be given us for a prey." There were some good men in the ship, and many more bad men: but in things of this nature *all things come alike to all,* and *there is one event to the righteous and to the wicked.* If both be in the same ship, they both are in the same danger. 3. They would not be advised by Paul in this matter, *v.* 11. They thought him impertinent in interposing in an affair of this nature, who did not understand navigation; and the centurion to whom it was referred to determine it, though himself a passenger, yet, being a man in authority, takes upon him to overrule, though he had not been oftener at sea perhaps than Paul, nor was better acquainted with these seas, for Paul had planted the gospel in Crete (Tit. i. 5), and knew the several parts of the island well enough. But the centurion gave more regard to the opinion of the master and owner of the ship than to Paul's; for every man is to be credited in his own profession ordinarily: but such a man as Paul, who was so intimate with Heaven, was rather to be regarded in seafaring matters than the most celebrated sailors. Note, Those know not what dangers they run themselves into who will be governed more by human prudence than by divine revelation. The centurion was very civil to Paul (*v.* 3), and yet would not be governed by his advice. Note, Many will show respect to good ministers that will not take their advice, Ezek. xxxiii. 31.

12 And because the haven was not

commodious to winter in, the more
part advised to depart thence also, if
by any means they might attain to
Phenice, *and there* to winter; *which*
is a haven of Crete, and lieth toward the south west and north west.
13 And when the south wind blew
softly, supposing that they had obtained *their* purpose, loosing *thence*,
they sailed close by Crete. 14 But
not long after there arose against it
a tempestuous wind, called Euroclydon. 15 And when the ship was
caught, and could not bear up into
the wind, we let *her* drive. 16 And
running under a certain island which
is called Clauda, we had much work
to come by the boat: 17 Which
when they had taken up, they used
helps, undergirding the ship; and,
fearing lest they should fall into the
quicksands, strake sail, and so were
driven. 18 And we being exceedingly tossed with a tempest, the next
day they lightened the ship; 19
And the third *day* we cast out with
our own hands the tackling of the
ship. 20 And when neither sun nor
stars in many days appeared, and no
small tempest lay on *us*, all hope
that we should be saved was then
taken away.

In these verses we have,

I. The ship putting to sea again, and pursuing her voyage at first with a promising gale. Observe, 1. What induced them to leave the fair havens: it was because they thought the harbour not *commodious to winter in;* it was pleasant enough in summer, but in the winter they lay bleak. Or perhaps it was upon some other account incommodious; provisions perhaps were scarce and dear there; and they ran upon a mischief to avoid an inconvenience, as we often do. Some of the ship's crew, or of the council that was called to advise in this matter, were for staying there, rather than venturing to sea now that the weather was so uncertain: it is better to be safe in an incommodious harbour than to be lost in a tempestuous sea. But they were outvoted when it was put to the question, and the *greater part advised to depart thence also;* yet they aimed not to go far, but only to another port of the same island, here called *Phenice*, and some think it was so called because the Phenicians frequented it much, the merchants of Tyre and Sidon. It is here described to lie towards the south-west and north-west. Probably the haven was between two promontories or juttings-out of land into the sea, one of which pointed to the north-west and the other to the south-west, by which it was guarded against the east winds. Thus hath the wisdom of the Creator provided for the relief and safety of those who *go down to the sea in ships, and do business in great waters.* In vain had nature provided for us the waters to sail on, if it had not likewise provided for us natural harbours to take shelter in. 2. What encouragement they had at first to pursue their voyage. They set out with a fair wind (*v.* 13), the *south wind blew softly*, upon which they flattered themselves with hope that they should gain their point, and so they sailed close by the coast of Crete and were not afraid of running upon the rocks or quicksands, because the wind blew so gently. Those who put to sea with ever so fair a gale know not what storms they may yet meet with, and therefore must not be secure, nor take it for granted that they have obtained their purpose, when so many accidents may happen to cross their purpose. *Let not him that girdeth on the harness boast as though he had put it off.*

II. The ship in a storm presently, a dreadful storm. They looked at second causes, and took their measures from the favourable hints they gave, and imagined that because the south wind now blew softly it would always blow so; in confidence of this, they ventured to sea, but were soon made sensible of their folly in giving more credit to a smiling wind than to the word of God in Paul's mouth, by which they had fair warning given them of a storm. Observe,

1. What their danger and distress was, (1.) There *arose against them a tempestuous wind*, which was not only contrary to them, and directly in their teeth, so that they could not get forward, but a violent wind, which raised the waves, like that which was sent forth in pursuit of Jonah, though Paul was following God, and going on in his duty, and not as Jonah running away from God and his duty. This wind the sailors called *Euroclydon*, a north-east wind, which upon those seas perhaps was observed to be in a particular manner troublesome and dangerous. It was a sort of whirlwind, for the ship is said to be caught by it, *v.* 15. It was God that commanded this wind to rise, designing to bring glory to himself, and reputation to Paul, out of it; stormy winds being brought *out of his treasuries* (Ps. cxxxv. 7), they *fulfil his word*, Ps. cxlviii. 8. (2.) The ship was *exceedingly tossed* (*v.* 18); it was kicked like a football from wave to wave; its passengers (as it is elegantly described, Ps. cvii. 26, 27) *mount up to the heavens, go down again to the depths, reel to and fro, stagger like a drunken man, and are at their wits' end.* The ship could not possibly *bear up into the wind*, could not make her way in opposition to the wind; and therefore they folded up their sails, which in such a storm would endanger them rather than do them any service, and so

let the ship drive, Not whither it would, but whither it was impelled by the impetuous waves—Non quo voluit, sed quo rapit impetus undæ. Ovid. Trist. It is probable that they were very near the haven of Phenice when this tempest arose, and thought they should presently be in a quiet haven, and were pleasing themselves with the thought of it, and wintering there, and lo, of a sudden, they are in this distress. Let us therefore always rejoice with trembling, and never expect a perfect security, nor a perpetual security, till we come to heaven. (3.) They saw neither sun nor stars for many days. This made the tempest the more terrible, that they were all in the dark; and the use of the loadstone for the direction of sailors not being then found out (so that they had no guide at all, when they could see neither sun nor stars) made the case the more hazardous. Thus melancholy sometimes is the condition of the people of God upon a spiritual account. They *walk in darkness and have no light.* Neither sun nor stars appear; they cannot dwell, nay, they cannot fasten, upon any thing comfortable or encouraging; thus it may be with them, and yet light is sown for them. (4.) They had abundance of winter-weather: *No small tempest*—χειμὼν οὐκ ὀλίγος, cold rain, and snow, and all the rigours of that season of the year, so that they were ready to perish for cold; and all this continued many days. See what hardships those often undergo who are much at sea, besides the hazards of life they run; and yet to get gain there are still those who make nothing of all this; and it is an instance of divine Providence that it disposes some to this employment, notwithstanding the difficulties that attend it, for the keeping up of commerce among the nations, and the isles of the Gentiles particularly; and Zebulun can as heartily rejoice in his going out as Issachar in his tents. Perhaps Christ therefore chose ministers from among seafaring men, because they had been used to endure hardness.

2. What means they used for their own relief: they betook themselves to all the poor shifts (for I can call them no better) that sailors in distress have recourse to. (1.) When they could not make head against the wind, they let the ship run adrift, finding it was to no purpose to ply either the oar or the sail. When it is fruitless to struggle, it is wisdom to yield. (2.) They nevertheless did what they could to avoid the present danger; there was a little island called Clauda, and when they were near that, though they could not pursue their voyage, they took care to prevent their shipwreck, and therefore so ordered their matters that they did not run against the island, but quietly ran under it, *v.* 16. (3.) When they were afraid they should scarcely save the ship, they were busy to save the boat, which they did with much ado. They had *much work to come by the boat* (*v.* 16), but at last they took it up, *v.* 17. This might be of use in any exigence, and therefore they made hard shift to get it into the ship to them. (4.) They used means which were proper enough in those times, when the art of navigation was far short of the perfection it is now come to; they *undergirded the ship, v.* 17. They bound the ship under the bottom of it with strong cables, to keep it from bulging in the extremity of the tempest. (5.) For fear of falling *into the quicksands* they *struck sail,* and then let the ship go as it would. It is strange how a ship will live at sea (so they express it), even in very stormy weather, if it have but sea-room; and, when the sailors cannot make the shore, it is their interest to keep as far off it as they can. (6.) The next day they lightened the ship of its cargo, threw the goods and merchandises overboard (as Jonah's mariners did, *ch.* i. 5), being willing rather to be poor without them than to perish with them. *Skin for skin, and all that a man has, will he give for his life.* See what the wealth of this world is; how much soever it is courted as a blessing, the time may come when it will be a burden, not only too heavy to be carried safe of itself, but heavy enough to sink him that has it. Riches are often *kept by the owners thereof to their hurt* (Eccl. v. 13); and parted with to their good. But see the folly of the children of this world, they can be thus prodigal of their goods when it is for the saving of their lives, and yet how sparing of them in works of piety and charity, and in suffering for Christ, though they are told by eternal Truth itself that those shall be recompensed more than a thousand fold *in the resurrection of the just.* Those went upon a principle of faith who *took joyfully the spoiling of their goods, knowing in themselves that they had in heaven a better and a more enduring substance,* Heb. x. 34. Any man will rather make shipwreck of his goods than of his life; but many will rather make *shipwreck of faith and a good conscience* than of their goods. (7.) The third day they *cast out the tacklings of the ship*—the utensils of it, *Armamenta* (so some render it), as if it were a ship of force. With us it is common to heave the guns over-board in the extremity of a storm; but what heavy artillery they had then which it was necessary to lighten the ship of I do not know; and I question whether it was not then a vulgar error among seamen thus to throw every thing into the sea, even that which would be of great use in a storm, and no great weight.

3. The despair which at last they were brought to (*v.* 20): *All hope that we should be saved was then taken away.* The storm continued, and they saw no symptoms of its abatement; we have known very blustering weather to continue for some weeks. The means they had used were ineffectual, so that they were at their wits' end; and such was the consternation that this melancholy prospect put them into that they had no heart either to eat or drink. They had provision

enough on board (*v.* 38), but such bondage were they under, through fear of death, that they could not admit the supports of life. Why did not Paul, by the power of Christ, and in his name, lay this storm? Why did he not say to the winds and waves, *Peace, be still,* as his Master had done? Surely it was because the apostles wrought miracles for the confirmation of their doctrine, not for the serving of a turn for themselves or their friends.

21 But after long abstinence Paul
stood forth in the midst of them, and
said, Sirs, ye should have hearkened
unto me, and not have loosed from
Crete, and to have gained this harm
and loss. 22 And now I exhort you
to be of good cheer: for there shall
be no loss of *any man's* life among
you, but of the ship. 23 For there
stood by me this night the angel of
God, whose I am, and whom I serve,
24 Saying, Fear not, Paul; thou
must be brought before Cæsar: and,
lo, God hath given thee all them that
sail with thee. 25 Wherefore, sirs,
be of good cheer: for I believe God,
that it shall be even as it was told
me. 26 Howbeit we must be cast
upon a certain island. 27 But when
the fourteenth night was come, as we
were driven up and down in Adria,
about midnight the shipmen deemed
that they drew near to some country; 28 And sounded, and found it
twenty fathoms: and when they had
gone a little further, they sounded
again, and found *it* fifteen fathoms.
29 Then fearing lest we should have
fallen upon rocks, they cast four anchors out of the stern, and wished for
the day. 30 And as the shipmen
were about to flee out of the ship,
when they had let down the boat
into the sea, under colour as though
they would have cast anchors out of
the foreship, 31 Paul said to the
centurion and to the soldiers, Except
these abide in the ship, ye cannot be
saved. 32 Then the soldiers cut off
the ropes of the boat, and let her fall
off. 33 And while the day was
coming on, Paul besought *them* all to
take meat, saying, This day is the
fourteenth day that ye have tarried
and continued fasting, having taken
nothing. 34 Wherefore I pray you
to take *some* meat: for this is for
your health: for there shall not a
hair fall from the head of any of you.
35 And when he had thus spoken,
he took bread and gave thanks to
God in presence of them all: and
when he had broken *it,* he began to
eat. 36 Then were they all of good
cheer, and they also took *some* meat.
37 And we were in all in the ship
two hundred threescore and sixteen
souls. 38 And when they had eaten
enough, they lightened the ship, and
cast out the wheat into the sea. 39
And when it was day, they knew not
the land: but they discovered a certain creek with a shore, into the
which they were minded, if it were
possible, to thrust in the ship. 40
And when they had taken up the
anchors, they committed *themselves*
unto the sea, and loosed the rudder
bands, and hoised up the mainsail to
the wind, and made toward shore.
41 And falling into a place where
two seas met, they ran the ship
aground; and the forepart stuck fast,
and remained unmoveable, but the
hinder part was broken with the violence of the waves. 42 And the
soldiers' counsel was to kill the prisoners, lest any of them should swim
out, and escape. 43 But the centurion, willing to save Paul, kept them
from *their* purpose; and commanded
that they which could swim should
cast *themselves* first *into the sea,* and
get to land: 44 And the rest, some
on boards, and some on *broken pieces*
of the ship. And so it came to pass,
that they escaped all safe to land.

We have here the issue of the distress of Paul and his fellow-travellers; they escaped with their lives and that was all, and that was for Paul's sake. We are here told (*v.* 37) what number there were on board—mariners, merchants, soldiers, prisoners, and other passengers, in all two hundred and seventy-six souls; this is taken notice of to make us the more concerned for them in reading the story, that they were such a considerable number, whose lives were now in the utmost jeopardy, and one Paul among them worth more than all the rest. We left them in despair, giving up themselves for gone. Whether they *called every man on his God,* as Jonah's mariners did, we are not told; it is well if this laudable practice in a storm was not gone out of fashion and made a jest of. However, Paul among these seamen was not, like Jonah among his, the cause of the storm, but the comforter in the storm, and as much a credit to the profession of an apostle as Jonah was a blemish to the character of a prophet. Now here we have,

I. The encouragement Paul gave them, by assuring them, in the name of God, that their lives should all be saved, even when, in human appearance, all hope that they should be saved was taken away. Paul rescued them from their despair first, that they might not die of that, and starve themselves in that, and then they were in a fair way to be rescued from their distress. *After long abstinence*, as if they were resolved not to eat till they knew whether they should live or die, *Paul stood forth in the midst of them.* During the distress hitherto Paul hid himself among them, was one of the crowd, helped with the rest to *throw out the tackling* (*v.* 19), but now he distinguished himself, and, though a prisoner, undertook to be their counsellor and comforter.

1. He reproves them for not taking his advice, which was to stay where they were, in the road of Lasea (*v.* 8): "*You should have hearkened to me and not have loosed from Crete*, where we might have made a shift to winter well enough, and then we should not have *gained this harm and loss*, that is, we should have escaped them. Harm and loss in the world, if sanctified to us, may be truly said to be gain; for if they wean us from present things, and awaken us to think of a future state, we are truly gainers by them. Observe, They did not hearken to Paul when he warned them of their danger, and yet if they will but acknowledge their folly, and repent of it, he will speak comfort and relief to them now that they are in danger, so compassionate is God to those that are in misery, though they bring themselves into it by their own incogitancy, nay, by their own wilfulness, and contempt of admonition. Paul, before administering comfort, will first make them sensible of their sin in not hearkening to him, by upbraiding them with their rashness, and probably, when he tells them of their gaining harm and loss, he reflects upon what they promised themselves by proceeding on their voyage, that they should gain so much time, gain this and the other point: "But," says he, "you have gained nothing but harm and loss; how will you answer it?" That which they are blamed for is their loosing from Crete, where they were safe. Note, Most people bring themselves into inconvenience, because they do not know when they are well off, but gain harm and loss by aiming against advice to better themselves.

2. He assures them that though they should lose the ship yet they should none of them lose their lives: "You see your folly in not being ruled by me:" he does not say, "Now therefore expect to fare accordingly, you may thank yourselves if you be all lost, those that will not be counselled cannot be helped." No, "Yet now there is hope in Israel concerning this thing; your case is sad, but it is not desperate, now, *I exhort you to be of good cheer.*" Thus we say to sinners that are convinced of their sin and folly, and begin to see and bewail their error, "*You should have hearkened unto us*, and should have had nothing to do with sin; yet now we *exhort you to be of good cheer:* though you would not take our advice when we said, *Do not presume*, yet take it now when we say, *Do not despair.*" They had given up the cause, and would use no further means, because *all hope that they should be saved was taken away.* Now Paul quickens them to bestir themselves yet in working for their own safety, by telling them that if they would resume their vigour they should secure their lives. He gives them this assurance when they were brought to the last extremity, for now it would be doubly welcome to them to be told that not a life should be lost when they were ready to conclude they must inevitably be all lost. He tells them, (1.) That they must count upon the loss of the ship. Those who were interested in that and the goods were probably those greater part that were for pushing forward the voyage and running the venture, notwithstanding Paul's admonition, and they are made to pay for their rashness. Their ship shall be wrecked. Many a stately, strong, rich, gallant ship is lost in the mighty waters in a little time; *for vanity of vanities, all is vanity and vexation of spirit.* But, (2.) *Not a life shall be lost.* This would be good news to those that were ready to die for fear of dying, and whose guilty consciences made death look very terrible to them.

3. He tells them what ground he had for this assurance, that it is not a banter upon them, to put them into humour, nor a human conjecture, he has a divine revelation for it, and is as confident of it as that God is true, being fully satisfied that he has his word for it. An angel of God appeared to him in the night, and told him that for his sake they should all be preserved (*v.* 23—25), which would double the mercy of their preservation, that they should have it not only by providence, but by promise, and as a particular favour to Paul. Now observe here,

(1.) The solemn profession Paul makes of relation to God, the God from whom he had this favourable intelligence: It is he *whose I am, and whom I serve.* He looks upon God, [1.] As his rightful owner, who has a sovereign incontestable title to him, and dominion over him: *Whose I am.* Because God made us and not we ourselves, therefore we are not our own but his. His we are by creation, for he made us; by preservation, for he maintains us; by redemption, for he bought us. We are more his than our own

[2.] As his sovereign ruler and master, who, having given him being, has right to give him law: *Whom I serve.* Because his we are, therefore we are bound to serve him, to devote ourselves to his honour and employ ourselves in his work. It is Christ that Paul here has an eye to; he is God, and the angels are his, and go on his errands. Paul often calls himself a *servant of Jesus Christ;* he is his, and him he serves, both as a Christian and as an apostle; he does not say, "Whose *we* are, and whom we serve," for most that were present were strangers to him, but, "Whose *I am,* and whom *I serve,* whatever others do; nay, whom I am now in the actual service of, going to Rome, not as you are, upon worldly business, but to appear as a witness for Christ." Now this he tells the company, that, seeing their relief coming from his God whose he was and whom he served, they might thereby be drawn in to take him for their God, and to serve him likewise; for the same reason Jonah said to his mariners, *I fear the Lord, the God of heaven, who has made the sea and the dry land,* Jonah i. 9.

(2.) The account he gives of the vision he had: *There stood by me this night an angel of God,* a divine messenger who used formerly to bring him messages from heaven; he *stood by him,* visibly appeared to him, probably when he was awake upon his bed. Though he was *afar off upon the sea* (Ps. lxv. 5), *on the uttermost parts of the sea* (Ps. cxxxix. 9), yet this could not intercept his communion with God, nor deprive him of the benefit of divine visits. Thence he can direct a prayer to God, and thither God can direct an angel to him. He knows not where he is himself, yet God's angel knows where to find him out. The *ship is tossed* with winds and waves, hurried to and fro with the utmost violence, and yet the angel finds a way into it. No storms nor tempests can hinder the communications of God's favour to his people, for he is a very present help, a help at hand, even when the *sea roars and is troubled,* Ps. xlvi. 1, 3. We may suppose that Paul, being a prisoner, had not a cabin of his own in the ship, much less a bed in the captain's cabin, but was put down into the hold (any dark or dirty place was thought good enough for him in common with the rest of the prisoners), and yet there the angel of God stood by him. Meanness and poverty set none at a distance from God and his favour. Jacob, when he has no pillow but a stone, no curtains but the clouds, yet has a vision of angels. Paul had this vision but *this last night.* He had himself been assured by a former vision that he should go to Rome (*ch.* xxiii. 11), from which he might infer that he himself should be safe; but he has this fresh vision to assure him of the safety of those with him.

(3.) The encouragements that were given him in the vision, *v.* 14. [1.] He is forbidden to fear. Though all about him are at their wits' end, and lost in despair, yet, *Fear not, Paul;* fear not *their fear, nor be afraid,* Isa. viii. 12. Let the *sinners in Zion be afraid,* but let not the saints be afraid, no, not at sea, in a storm; for *the Lord of hosts is with them,* and their *place of defence shall be the munitions of rocks,* Isa. xxxiii. 14—16. [2.] He is assured that for his part he shall come safely to Rome: *Thou must be brought before Cæsar.* As the rage of the most potent enemies, so the rage of the most stormy sea, cannot prevail against God's witnesses till they have finished their testimony. Paul must be preserved in this danger, for he is reserved for further service. This is comfortable for the faithful servants of God in straits and difficulties, that as long as God has any work for them to do their lives shall be prolonged. [3.] That for his sake all that were in the ship with him should be delivered too from perishing in this storm: *God hath given thee all those that sail with thee.* The angel that was ordered to bring him this message could have singled him out from this wretched crew, and those that were his friends too, and have carried them safely to shore, and have left the rest to perish, because they would not take Paul's counsel. But God chooses rather, by preserving them all for his sake, to show what great blessings good men are to the world, than by delivering him only to show how good men are distinguished from the world. *God has given thee all those that sail with thee,* that is, spares them in answer to thy prayers, or for thy sake. Sometimes good men deliver *neither sons nor daughters, but their own souls only,* Ezek. xiv. 18. But Paul here delivers a whole ship's crew, almost three hundred souls. Note, God often spares wicked people for the sake of the godly; as Zoar for Lot's sake, and as Sodom might have been, if there had been ten righteous persons in it. The good people are hated and persecuted in the world as if they were not worthy to live in it, yet really it is for their sakes that the world stands. If Paul had thrust himself needlessly into bad company, he might justly have been cast away with them, but, God calling him into it, they are preserved with him. And it is intimated that it was a great favour to Paul, and he looked upon it to be so, that others were saved for his sake: *They are given thee.* There is no greater satisfaction to a good man than to know that he is a public blessing.

4. He comforts them with the same comforts wherewith he himself was comforted (*v.* 25): "*Wherefore, Sirs, be of good cheer,* you shall see even this will end well; *for I believe God,* and depend upon his word, *that it shall be even as it was told me.*" He would not require them to give credit to that to which he did not himself give credit; and therefore solemnly professes that he believes it himself, and the belief of it makes him easy: "I doubt not but it shall be as it was

told me." Thus he *staggers not at the promise of God through unbelief. Hath God spoken, and shall he not make it good?* No doubt he can, no doubt he will; for *he is not a man that he should lie.* And shall it be as God hath said? Then be of good cheer, be of good courage. God is ever faithful, and therefore let all that have an interest in his promise be ever cheerful. If with God saying and doing are not two things, then with us believing and enjoying should not.

5. He gives them a sign, telling them particularly what this tempestuous voyage would issue in (*v.* 26): "*We must be cast upon a certain island,* and that will both break the ship and save the passengers; and so the prediction in both respects will be fulfilled." The pilot had quitted his post, the ship was left to run at random, they knew not what latitude they were in, much less how to steer their course, and yet Providence undertakes to bring them to an island that shall be a refuge for them. When the church of God, like this ship, is *tossed with tempests, and not comforted,* when *there is none to guide her of all her sons,* yet God can bring her safely to shore, and will do it.

II. Their coming at length to an anchor upon an unknown shore, *v.* 27—29. 1. They had been a full fortnight in the storm, continually expecting death: *The fourteenth night,* and not sooner, *they came near land;* they were *that night driven up and down in Adria,* not in the Adriatic Gulf on which Venice stands, but in the Adriatic Sea, a part of the Mediterranean, containing both the Sicilian and Ionian seas, and extending to the African shore; in this sea they were tossed, and knew not whereabouts they were. 2. *About midnight the mariners apprehended that they drew near to some shore,* which confirmed what Paul had told them, that they must be driven upon some island. To try whether it was so or no, *they sounded,* in order to their finding the depth of the water, for the water would be shallower as they drew nearer to shore; by the first experiment *they found they drew twenty fathoms deep of water,* and by *the next fifteen fathoms,* which was a demonstration that they were near some shore; God has wisely ordered such a natural notice to sailors in the dark, that they may be cautious. 3. They took the hint, and, fearing rocks near the shore, *they cast anchor, and wished for the day;* they durst not go forward for fear of rocks, and yet would not go back in hope of shelter, but they would wait for the morning, and heartily wished for it; who can blame them when the affair came to a crisis? When they had light, there was no land to be seen; now that there was land near them, they had no light to see it by; no marvel then they wished for day. When those that fear God *walk in darkness, and have no light,* yet let them not say, *The Lord has forsaken us,* or, *Our God has forgotten us;* but let them do as these mariners did, cast anchor, and wish for the day, and be assured that the day will dawn. *Hope is an anchor of the soul, sure and stedfast, entering into that within the veil.* Hold fast by that, think not of putting to sea again, but abide by Christ, and wait till the day break, and the shadows flee away.

III. The defeating of the sailors' attempt to quit the ship; here was a new danger added to their distress, which they narrowly escaped. Observe, 1. The treacherous design of the seamen, and that was to leave the sinking ship, which, though a piece of wisdom in others, yet in those that were entrusted with the care of it was the basest fraud that could be (*v.* 30): *They were about to flee out of the ship,* concluding no other than that when it ran ashore it must be broken all to pieces; having the command of the boat, the project was to get all of them into that, and so save themselves, and leave all the rest to perish. To cover this vile design, they pretended they would *cast anchors out of the fore-ship,* or carry them further off, and in order to this *they let down the boat,* which they had taken in (*v.* 16, 17), and were *going into it,* having agreed among themselves, when they were in to make straight for the shore. The treacherous seamen are like the treacherous shepherd, who flees when he sees the danger coming, and there is most need of his help, John x. 12. Thus true is that of Solomon, *Confidence in an unfaithful man in time of trouble is like a broken tooth or a foot out of joint.* Let us therefore cease from man. Paul had, in God's name, assured them that they should come safely to land, but they will rather trust their own refuge of lies than God's word and truth. 2. Paul's discovery of it, and protestation against it, *v.* 31. They all saw them preparing to go into the boat, but were deceived by the pretence they made; only Paul saw through it, and gave notice to the centurion and the soldiers concerning it, and told them plainly, *Except these abide in the ship, you cannot be saved.* The skill of a mariner is seen in a storm, and, in the distress of the ship, then is the proper time for him to exert himself. Now the greatest difficulty of all was before them, and therefore the seamen were now more necessary than ever yet; it was indeed not by any skill of theirs *that they were brought to land,* for it was quite beyond their skill, but, now that they are near land, they must use their art to bring the ship to it. When God has done that for us which we could not, we must then in his strength help ourselves. Paul speaks humanly, when he says, *You cannot be saved except these abide in the ship;* and he does not at all weaken the assurances he had divinely given that they should infallibly be saved. God, who appointed the end, *that they should be saved,* appointed the means, that they should be saved by the help of these seamen; though, if they had gone off, no doubt God would have made his word good some other way. Paul speaks as a prudent man, not as a prophet, when he says, These are necessary to your preservation. Duty is ours, events are God's; and we do not trust God, but tempt him, when we say, "We put ourselves under his protection," and do not use proper means, such as are within our power, for our own preservation. 3. The effectual defeat of it by the soldiers, *v.* 32. It was no time to stand arguing the case with the seamen, and therefore they made no more ado, *but cut the ropes of the boat,* and, though it might otherwise have done them service in their present distress, they chose rather *to let it fall off,* and lose it, than suffer it to do them this disservice. And now the seamen, being forced to stay in the ship whether they would or no, are forced likewise to work for the safety of the ship as hard as they could, because if the rest perish they must perish with them.

IV. The new life which Paul put into the company, by cheerfully inviting them to take some refreshment, and by the repeated assurances he gave them that they should all of them have their lives given them for a prey. Happy they who had such a one as Paul in their company, who not only had correspondence with Heaven, but was of a hearty lively spirit with those about him, that sharpened the countenance of his friend, as iron sharpens iron. Such a friend in distress, when *without are fightings and within are fears,* is a friend indeed. *Ointment and perfume rejoice the heart; so doth the sweetness of a man's friend by hearty counsel,* Prov. xxvii. 9. Such was Paul's here to his companions in tribulation. The day was coming on: those that wish for the day, let them wait awhile, and they shall have what they wish for. The dawning of the day revived them a little, and then Paul got them together. 1. He chid them for their neglect of themselves, that they had so far given way to fear and despair as to forget or not to mind their food: *This is the fourteenth day that you have tarried, and continued fasting, having taken nothing;* and that is not well, *v.* 33. Not that they had all, or any of them, continued fourteen days without any food, but they had not had any set meal, as they used to have, all that time; they ate very little, next to nothing. Or, "*You have continued fasting,* that is, you have lost your stomach; you have had no appetite at all to your food, nor any relish of it, through prevailing fear and despair." A very disconsolate state is thus expressed (Ps. cii. 4), *I forget to eat my bread.* It is a sin to starve the body, and to deny it its necessary supports; he is an unnatural man indeed *that hateth his own flesh, and does not nourish and cherish it;* and it is a sore evil under the sun to have a sufficiency of the good things of this life, and not to have power to use them, Eccl. vi. 2 If this arise from the sorrow of the world, and from any inordinate fear or trouble, it is so far from excusing it that it is another sin, it is discontent, it is distrust of God, it is all wrong. What folly is it to die for fear of dying! But thus *the sorrow of the world works death,* while joy in God is life and peace in the greatest distresses and dangers. 2. He courts them to their food (*v.* 34): "*Wherefore I pray you to take some meat.* We have a hard struggle before us, must get to shore as well as we can; if our bodies be weak through fasting, we shall not be able to help ourselves." The angel bade Elijah, *Arise and eat,* for otherwise he would find *the journey too great for him,* 1 Kings xix. 7. So Paul will have these people eat, or otherwise the waves will be too hard for them: *I pray you,* παρακαλῶ, "*I exhort you,* if you will be ruled by me, take some nourishment; though you have no appetite to it, though you have fasted away your stomach, yet let reason bring you to it, *for this is for your health,* or rather *your preservation, or safety, at this time;* it is for your salvation, you cannot without nourishment have strength to shift for your lives." As *he that will not labour, let him not eat;* so he that means to labour must eat. Weak and trembling Christians, that give way to doubts and fears about their spiritual state, continue fasting from the Lord's supper, and fasting from divine consolations, and then complain they cannot go on in their spiritual work and warfare; and it is owing to themselves. If they would feed and feast as they ought, upon the provision Christ has made for them, they would be strengthened, and it would be for their souls' health and salvation. 3. He assures them of their preservation: *There shall not a hair fall from the head of any of you.* It is a proverbial expression, denoting a complete indemnity. It is used 1 Kings i. 52; Luke xxi. 18. "You cannot eat for fear of dying; I tell you, you are sure of living, and therefore eat. You will come to shore wet and cold, but sound wind and limb; your hair wet, but not a hair lost." 4. He himself spread their table for them; for none of them had any heart to do it, they were all so dispirited: *When he had thus spoken, he took bread,* fetched it from the ship's stores, to which every one might safely have access when none of them had an appetite. They were not reduced to short allowance, as sailors sometimes are when they are kept longer at sea than they expected by distress of weather; they had plenty, but what good did that do them, when they had no stomach? We have reason to be thankful to God that we have not only food to our appetite, but appetite to our food; that our soul abhors not even dainty meat (Job xxxiii. 20), through sickness or sorrow. 5. He was chaplain to the ship, and they had reason to be proud of their chaplain. *He gave thanks to God in presence of them all*

We have reason to think he had often prayed with Luke and Aristarchus, and what others there were among them that were Christians, that they prayed daily together; but whether he had before this prayed with the whole company promiscuously is not certain. Now *he gave thanks to God, in presence of them all,* that they were alive, and had been preserved hitherto, and that they had a promise that their lives should be preserved in the imminent peril now before them; he gave thanks for the provision they had, and begged a blessing upon it. We must *in every thing give thanks;* and must particularly have an eye to God in receiving our food, for *it is sanctified to us by the word of God and prayer,* and is *to be received with thanksgiving.* Thus the curse is taken off from it, and we obtain a covenant-right to it and a covenant-blessing upon it, 1 Tim. iv. 3—5. And *it is not by bread alone that man lives, but by the word of God,* which must be met with prayer. *He gave thanks in presence of them all,* not only to show that he served a Master he was not ashamed of, but to invite them into his service too. If we crave a blessing upon our meat, and give thanks for it in a right manner, we shall not only keep up a comfortable communion with God ourselves, but credit our profession, and recommend it to the good opinion of others. 6. He set them a good example: *When he had given thanks, he broke the bread* (it was sea-biscuit) and *he began to eat.* Whether they would be encouraged or no, he would; if they would be sullen, and, like froward children, refuse their victuals because they had not every thing to their mind, he would eat his meat, and be thankful. Those that teach others are inexcusable if they do not themselves do as they teach, and the most effectual way of preaching is by example. 7. It had a happy influence upon them all (*v.* 36): *Then were they all of good cheer.* They then ventured to believe the message God sent them by Paul when they plainly perceived that Paul believed it himself, who was in the same common danger with them. Thus God sends good tidings to the perishing world of mankind by those who are of themselves, and in the same common danger with themselves, who are sinners too, and must be saved, if ever they be saved, in the same way in which they persuade others to venture; for it is a common salvation which they bring the tidings of; and it is an encouragement to people to commit themselves to Christ as their Saviour when those who invite them to do so make it to appear that they do so themselves. It is here upon this occasion that the number of the persons is set down, which we took notice of before: *they were in all two hundred threescore and sixteen souls.* See how many may be influenced by the good example of one. *They did all eat,* nay, *they did all eat enough* (*v.* 38), they were satiated with food, or filled with it; *they made a hearty meal.* This explains the meaning of *their fasting before for fourteen days;* not that they did not eat during all that time, but they never had enough all that time, as they had now. 8. They once more lightened the ship, that it might escape the better in the shock it was now to have. They had before thrown *the wares and the tackle overboard,* and now *the wheat,* the victuals and provisions they had; better they should sink the food than that it should sink them. See what good reason our Saviour had to call our bodily food meat that perishes. We may ourselves be under a necessity of throwing that away to save our lives which we had gathered and laid up for the support of our lives. It is probable that the ship was overloaded with the multitude of the passengers (for this comes in just after the account of the number of them) and that this obliged them so often to lighten the ship.

V. Their putting to shore, and the staving of the ship in the adventure. It was about break of day when they ate their meat, and when it was quite day they began to look about them; and here we are told, 1. *That they knew not where they were;* they could not tell what country it was they were now upon the coast of, whether it was Europe, Asia, or Africa, for each had shores washed by the Adriatic Sea. It is probable that these seamen had often sailed this way, and thought they knew every country they came near perfectly well, and yet here they were at a loss. *Let not the wise man then glory in his wisdom,* since it may perhaps fail him thus egregiously even in his own profession. 2. *They observed a creek with a level shore, into which they hoped to thrust the ship, v.* 39. Though they knew not what country it was, nor whether the inhabitants were friends or foes, civil or barbarous, they determined to cast themselves upon their mercy; it was dry land, which would be very welcome to those that had been so long at sea. It was a pity but they had had some help from the shore, a pilot sent them, that knew the coast, who might steer their ship in, or another second ship, to take some of the men on board. Those who live on the sea-coast have often opportunity of succouring those who are in distress at sea, and of saving precious lives, and they ought to do their utmost in order to it, with all readiness and cheerfulness; for it is a great sin, and very provoking to God, *to forbear to deliver those that are driven unto death, and are ready to be slain;* and it will not serve for an excuse to say, *Behold, we knew it not,* when either we did, or might, and should, have *known* it, Prov. xxiv. 11, 12. I have been told there are some, and in our own nation too, who when from the sea-coast they sea a ship in distress and at a loss will, by misguiding fires or otherwise, purposely lead them into danger, that the lives may be lost, and they may have the plunder of the ship. One can scarcely believe that any of the human species can possibly be so wicked, so barbarously inhuman, and can have so much of the devil in them; if there be, *let them know of a truth that they shall have judgment without mercy who have shown no mercy*. 3. They made straight to the shore with wind and tide (*v.* 40): *They took up the anchors, the four anchors which they cast out of the stern*, *v.* 29. Some think that they took pains to weigh them up, hoping they should have use for them again at the shore; others that they did it with such precipitation that they were forced to cut the cables and leave them; the original will admit either. *They then committed themselves to the sea*, the wind standing fair to carry them into the port, and *they loosed the rudder-bands*, which were fastened during the storm for the greater steadiness of the ship, but, now that they were *putting into the port, were loosed*, that the pilot might steer with the greater freedom; *they then hoisted up the main-sail to the wind, and made towards shore.* The original words here used for the *rudder-bands* and the *main-sail* find the critics a great deal of work to accommodate them to the modern terms; but they need not give us any difficulty who are content to know that when they saw the shore they hastened to it as fast as they could, and perhaps made more haste than good speed. And should not a poor soul that has long been struggling with winds and tempests in this world long to put into the safe and quiet haven of everlasting rest? Should it not get clear from all that which fastens it to this earth, and straitens the out-goings of its pious and devout affections heavenward? And should it not hoist up the main-sail of faith to the wind of the Spirit, and so with longing desires make to shore? 4. They made a shift among them *to run the ship aground*, in a shelf or bed of sand, as it should seem, or an isthmus, or neck of land, washed with the sea on both sides, and therefore two seas are said to meet upon it, and *there the forepart stuck fast;* and then, when it had no liberty to play, as a ship has when it rides at anchor, but remained immovable, *the hinder part* would soon be broken of course *by the violence of the waves*. Whether the seamen did not do their part, being angry that they were disappointed in their design to escape, and therefore wilfully ran the ship aground, or whether we may suppose that they did their utmost to save it, but God in his providence overruled, for the fulfilling of Paul's word, *that the ship must be lost* (*v.* 22), I cannot say; but this we are sure of *that God will confirm the word of his servants, and perform the counsel of his messengers*, Isa. xliv. 26. The ship, that had strangely weathered the storm in the vast ocean, where it had room to roll, is dashed to pieces when it sticks fast. Thus if the heart fixes in the world, in love and affection, and adherence to it, it is lost. Satan's temptations beat against it, and it is gone; but, as long as it keeps above the world, though it be tossed with its cares and tumults, there is hope of it. They had the shore in view, and yet suffered shipwreck in the harbour, to teach us never to be secure.

VI. A particular danger that Paul and the rest of the prisoners were in, besides their share in the common calamity, and their deliverance from it. 1. In this critical moment, when every man hung in doubt of his life, *the soldiers advised the killing of the prisoners* that were committed to their custody, and whom they were to give an account of, *lest any of them should swim out and escape*, *v.* 42. There was no great danger of that, for they could not escape far, weak and weary as they were; and, under the eye of so many soldiers that had the charge of them, it was not likely they should attempt it; and if it should so happen, though they might be obnoxious to the law for a permissive escape, yet in such a case as this equity would certainly relieve them. But it was a brutish barbarous motion, and so much the worse that they were thus prodigal of other people's lives when without a miracle of mercy they must lose their own. 2. The centurion, for Paul's sake, quashed this motion presently. Paul, who was his prisoner, had found favour with him, as Joseph with the captain of the guard. Julius, though he despised Paul's advice (*v.* 11), yet afterwards saw a great deal of cause to respect him, and therefore, being *willing to save Paul*, he prevented the execution of that bloody project, and *in favorem vitæ—from a regard to his life*, he kept them from their purpose. It does not appear that they were any of them malefactors convicted, but only suspected, and waiting their trial, and in such a case as this better ten guilty ones should escape than one that was innocent be slain. As God had saved all in the ship for Paul's sake, so here the centurion saves all the prisoners for his sake; such a diffusive good is a good man.

VII. The saving of the lives of all the persons in the ship, by the wonderful providence of God. When the ship broke under them, surely *there was but a step between them and death;* and yet infinite mercy interposed, and that step was not stepped. 1. Some were saved by swimming: *The centurion commanded his soldiers* in the first place, *as many of them as could swim, to get to land* first, and to be ready to receive the prisoners, and prevent their escape. The Romans trained up their youth, among other exercises, to that of swimming, and it was often of service to them in their wars: Julius Cæsar was a famous swimmer. It may be very useful to those who deal much at sea, but otherwise perhaps more lives have been lost by swimming in sport, and learning to swim, than have been saved by swimming for need. 2. The rest with much ado scrambled to the shore, some on boards that they had loose with them in the ship, and others on the *broken pieces of the ship*, every one making the best shift he could for himself and his friends, and the more busy because they were assured their labour should not be in vain; but *so it came to pass* that through the good providence of God none of them miscarried, none of them were by accident turned off, but they *escaped all safely to land*. See here an instance of the special providence of God in the preservation of people's lives, and particularly in the deliverance of many from perils by water, ready to sink, and yet kept from sinking, *the deep from swallowing them up* and *the water-floods from overflowing them*, the storm turned into a calm. They were rescued from the dreaded sea, and brought to the desired haven. *O that men would praise the Lord for his goodness!* Ps. cvii. 30, 31. Here was an instance of the performance of a particular word of promise which God gave, that all the persons in this ship should be saved for Paul's sake. Though there be great difficulty in the way of the promised salvation, yet it shall without fail be accomplished; and even the wreck of the ship may furnish out means for the saving of the lives, and, when all seems to be gone, all proves to be safe, though it be *on boards, and broken pieces of the ship*.

CHAP. XXVIII.

We are the more concerned to take notice of and to improve what is here recorded concerning blessed Paul because, after the story of this chapter, we hear no more of him in the sacred history, though we have a great deal of him yet before us in his epistles. We have attended him through several chapters from one judgment-seat to another, and could at last have taken leave of him with the more pleasure if we had left him at liberty; but in this chapter we are to condole with him, and yet congratulate him. I. We condole with him as a poor shipwrecked passenger, stripped of all; and yet congratulate him, 1. As singularly owned by his God in his distress, preserved himself from receiving hurt by a viper that fastened on his hand (ver. 1—6), and being made an instrument of much good in the island on which they were cast, in healing many that were sick, and particularly the father of Publius, the chief man of the island, ver. 7—9. 2. As much respected by the people there, ver. 10 II. We condole with him as a poor confined prisoner, carried to Rome under the notion of a criminal removed by "habeas corpus" (ver. 11—16), and yet we congratulate him, 1. Upon the respect shown him by the Christians at Rome, who came a great way to meet him, ver. 15. 2. Upon the favour he found with the captain of the guard, into whose custody he was delivered, who suffered him to dwell by himself, and did not put him in the common prison, ver. 16. 3. Upon the free conference he had with the Jews at Rome, both about his own affair (ver. 17—22) and upon the subject of the Christian religion in general (ver. 23), the issue of which was that God was glorified, many were edified, the rest left inexcusable, and the apostles justified in preaching the gospel to the Gentiles, ver. 24—29. 4. Upon the undisturbed liberty he had to preach the gospel to all comers in his own house for two years together, ver. 30, 31.

AND when they were escaped,
then they knew that the island
was called Melita. 2 And the barbarous people showed us no little
kindness: for they kindled a fire,
and received us every one, because of
the present rain, and because of the
cold. 3 And when Paul had gathered
a bundle of sticks, and laid *them* on
the fire, there came a viper out of the
heat, and fastened on his hand. 4
And when the barbarians saw the
venomous beast hang on his hand,
they said among themselves, No
doubt this man is a murderer, whom,
though he hath escaped the sea, yet
vengeance suffereth not to live. 5
And he shook off the beast into the
fire, and felt no harm. 6 Howbeit
they looked when he should have
swollen, or fallen down dead suddenly: but after they had looked a great
while, and saw no harm come to him,
they changed their minds, and said
that he was a god. 7 In the same
quarters were possessions of the chief
man of the island, whose name was
Publius; who received us, and lodged
us three days courteously. 8 And it
came to pass, that the father of Publius lay sick of a fever and of a
bloody flux: to whom Paul entered
in, and prayed, and laid his hands on
him, and healed him. 9 So when
this was done, others also, which had
diseases in the island, came, and were
healed: 10 Who also honoured us
with many honours; and when we
departed, they laded *us* with such
things as were necessary.

What a great variety of places and circumstances do we find Paul in! He was a planet, and not a fixed star. Here we have him in an island to which, in all probability, he had never come if he had not been thrown upon it by a storm; and yet it seems God has work for him to do here. Even stormy winds fulfil God's counsel, and an ill wind indeed it is that blows nobody any good; this ill wind blew good to the island of Melita; for it gave them Paul's company for three months, who was a blessing to every place he came to. This island was called Melita, lying between Sicily and Africa, twenty miles long, and twelve broad; it lies furthest from the continent of any island in the Mediterranean; it is about sixty miles from Sicily. It has been famous since for the knights of Malta, who, when the Turks overran that part of Christendom, made a noble stand, and gave some check to the progress of their arms. Now here we have,

I. The kind reception which the inhabitants of this island gave to the distressed strangers that were shipwrecked on their coast (*v.* 2): *The barbarous people showed us no little kindness.* God had promised that there should be no loss of any man's life; and, *as for God, his work is perfect.* If they had escaped the sea, and when they came ashore had perished for cold or want, it had been all one; therefore Providence continues its care of them, and what benefits we receive by the hand of man must be acknowledged to come from the hand of God; for every creature is that to us, and no more, that he makes it to be, and when he pleases, as he can make enemies to be at peace, so he can make strangers to be friends, friends in need, and those are friends indeed—friends *in adversity*, and that is *the time that a brother is born for*. Observe, 1. The general notice taken of the kindness which the natives of Malta showed to Paul and his company. They are called *barbarous people,* because they did not, in language and customs, conform either to the Greeks or Romans, who looked (superciliously enough) upon all but themselves as barbarians, though otherwise civilized enough, and perhaps in some cases more civil than they. These barbarous people, however they were called so, were full of humanity: They *showed us no little kindness.* So far were they from making a prey of this shipwreck, as many, I fear, who are called Christian people, would have done, that they laid hold of it as an opportunity of showing mercy. *The Samaritan* is a better neighbour to the poor wounded man *than the priest or Levite.* And verily we have not found greater humanity among Greeks, or Romans, or Christians, than among these barbarous people; and it is written for our imitation, that we may hence learn to be compassionate to those that are in distress and misery, and to relieve and succour them to the utmost of our ability, as those *that know we ourselves are also in the body.* We should be ready *to entertain strangers, as Abraham, who sat at his tent door to invite passengers in* (Heb. xiii. 2), but especially strangers in distress, as these were. *Honour all men.* If Providence hath so *appointed the bounds of our habitation* as to give us an opportunity of being frequently serviceable to persons at a loss, we should not place it among the inconveniences of our lot, but the advantages of it; because *it is more blessed to give than to receive.* Who knows but these barbarous people had their lot cast in this island for such a time as this! 2. A particular instance of their kindness: *They kindled a fire,* in some large hall or other, and *they received us every one*—made room for us about the fire, and bade us all welcome, without asking either what country we were of or what religion. In swimming *to the shore,* and coming on *the broken pieces of the ship,* we must suppose that they were sadly wet, that they had not a dry thread on them; and, as if that were not enough, to complete the deluge, waters from above met those from below, and it rained so hard that this would wet them to the skin presently; and *it was a cold rain too,* so that they wanted nothing so much as a good fire (for they had eaten heartily but just before on ship-board), and this they got for them presently, *to warm them, and dry their clothes.* It is sometimes as much a piece of charity to poor families to supply them with fuel as with food or raiment. *Be you warmed,* is as necessary as, *Be you filled.* When in the extremities of bad weather we find ourselves fenced against the rigours of the season, by the accommodations of a warm house, bed, clothes, and a good fire, we should think how many lie exposed *to the present rain, and to the cold,* and pity them, and pray for them, and help them if we can.

II. The further danger that Paul was in by a viper's fastening on his hand, and the unjust construction that the people put upon it. Paul is among strangers, and appears one of the meanest and most contemptible of the company, therefore God distinguishes him, and soon causes him to be taken notice of.

1. When the fire was to be made, and to be made bigger, that so great a company might all have the benefit of it, Paul was as busy as any of them in gathering sticks, *v.* 3. Though he was free from all, and of greater account than any of them, *yet he made himself servant of all.* Paul was an industrious active man, and loved to be doing when any thing was to be done, and never contrived to take his ease. Paul was a humble self-denying man, and would stoop to any thing by which he might be serviceable, even to the gathering of sticks to make a fire of. We should reckon nothing below us but sin, and be willing to condescend to the meanest offices, if there be occasion, for the good of our brethren. The people were ready to help them; yet Paul, wet and cold as he is, will not throw it all upon them, but will help himself. Those that receive benefit by the fire should help to carry fuel to it.

2. The sticks being old dry rubbish, it happened there was a viper among them, that lay as dead till it came to the heat, and then revived, or lay quiet till it felt the fire, and then was provoked, and flew at him that unawares threw it into the fire, and *fastened upon his hand, v.* 3. Serpents and such venomous creatures commonly lie among sticks; hence we read of him *that leans on the wall, and a serpent bites him,* Amos v. 19. It was so common that people were by it frightened from tearing hedges (Eccl. x. 8): *Whoso breaketh a hedge, a serpent shall bite him.* As there is a snake under the green grass, so there is often under the dry leaves. See how many perils human life is exposed to, and what danger we are in from the inferior creatures, which have many of them become enemies to men, since men became rebels to God; and what a mercy it is that we are preserved from them as we are. We often meet with that which is mischievous where we expect that which is beneficial; and many come by hurt when they are honestly employed, and in the way of their duty.

3. The barbarous people concluded that Paul, being a prisoner, was certainly a murderer, who had appealed to Rome, to escape justice in his own country, and that this viper was sent by divine justice to be the avenger of blood; or, if they were not aware that he

was a prisoner, they supposed that he was in his flight; and *when they saw the venomous animal hang on his hand,* which it seems he could not, or would not, immediately throw off, but let it hang, they concluded, "*No doubt this man is a murderer,* has shed innocent blood, and therefore, *though he has escaped the sea, yet* divine *vengeance* pursues him, and fastens upon him now that he is pleasing himself with the thoughts of that escape, and will *not suffer him to live.*" Now in this we may see,

(1.) Some of the discoveries of natural light. They were barbarous people, perhaps had no books nor learning among them, and yet they knew naturally, [1.] That there is a God that governs the world, and a providence that presides in all occurrences, that things do not come to pass by chance, no, not such a thing as this, but by divine direction. [2.] That evil pursues sinners, that there are good works which God will reward and wicked works which he will punish; there is a divine *nemesis—a vengeance,* which sooner or later will reckon for enormous crimes. They believe not only that there is a God, but that this God hath said, *Vengeance is mine, I will repay,* even to death. [3.] That murder is a heinous crime, and which shall not long go unpunished, that *whoso sheds man's blood,* if his blood be not shed by man (by the magistrate, as it ought to be) it shall be shed by the righteous Judge of heaven and earth, who is the avenger of wrong. Those that think they shall go unpunished in any evil way will be judged out of the mouth of these barbarians, who could say, without book, *Woe to the wicked, for it shall be ill with them, for the reward of their hands shall be given them.* Those who, because they have escaped many judgments, are secure, and say, *We shall have peace though we go on,* and have their hearts so much the more *set to do evil because sentence against their evil works is not executed speedily,* may learn from these illiterate people that, though malefactors have escaped the vengeance of the sea, yet there is no outrunning divine justice, *vengeance suffers not to live.* In Job's time you might ask *those that go by the way,* ask the next body you met, and they would tell you that *the wicked is reserved to the day of destruction.*

(2.) Some of the mistakes of natural light, which needed to be rectified by divine revelation. In two things their knowledge was defective:—[1.] That they thought all wicked people were punished in this life; that divine vengeance never suffers great and notorious sinners, such as murderers are, to live long; but that, if *they come up out of the pit, they shall be taken in the snare* (Jer. xlviii. 43, 44), if *they flee from a lion, a bear shall meet them* (Amos v. 19), if they escape being drowned, a viper shall fasten upon them; whereas it is not so. The wicked, even murderers, sometimes *live, become old, yea, are mighty in power;* for the day of vengeance is to come in the other world, *the great day of wrath;* and though some are made examples of in this world, to prove that there is a God and a providence, yet many are left unpunished, to prove that there is a judgment to come. [2.] That they thought all who were remarkably afflicted in this life were wicked people; that a man on whose hand a viper fastens may thence be judged to be a murderer, as if those on whom the tower in Siloam fell must needs be greater sinners than all in Jerusalem. This mistake Job's friends went upon, in their judgment upon his case; but divine revelation sets this matter in a true light—that all things come ordinarily alike to all, that good men are oftentimes greatly afflicted in this life, for the exercise and improvement of their faith and patience.

4. When he shook off the viper from his hand, yet they expected that divine vengeance would ratify the censure they had passed, and *that he would have swollen* and burst, through the force of the poison, or *that he would have fallen down dead suddenly.* See how apt men are, when once they have got an ill opinion of a man, though ever so unjust, to abide by it, and to think that God must necessarily confirm and ratify their peevish sentence. It was well they did not knock him down themselves, when they saw he did not swell and fall down; but so considerate they are as to let Providence work, and to attend the motions of it.

III. Paul's deliverance from the danger, and the undue construction the people put upon this. The viper's fastening on his hand was a trial of his faith; and it was found to praise, and honour, and glory: for, 1. It does not appear that it put him into any fright or confusion at all. He did not shriek or start, nor, as it would be natural for us to do, throw it off with terror and precipitation; for he suffered it to hang on so long that the people had time to take notice of it and to make their remarks upon it. Such a wonderful presence of mind he had, and such a composure, as no man could have upon such a sudden accident, but by the special aids of divine grace, and the actual belief and consideration of that word of Christ concerning his disciples (Mark xvi. 18), *They shall take up serpents.* This it is to have *the heart fixed, trusting in God.* 2. He carelessly *shook off the viper into the fire,* without any difficulty, calling for help, or any means used to loosen its hold; and it is probable that it was consumed in the fire. Thus, in the strength of the grace of Christ, believers shake off the temptations of Satan, with a holy resolution, saying, as Christ did, *Get thee behind me, Satan; the Lord rebuke thee;* and thus they *keep themselves, that the wicked one toucheth them not,* so as to fasten upon them, 1 John v. 18. When we despise the censures and reproaches of men, and look upon them with a holy contempt, having the testimony of conscience for us, then we do, as Paul here, *shake off the viper into the fire.* It does us no harm, except we fret at it, or be deterred by it from our duty, or be provoked to render railing for railing. 3. He was none the worse. Those that thought it would have been his death *looked a great while, but saw no harm at all come to him.* God hereby intended to make him remarkable among these barbarous people, and so to make way for the entertainment of the gospel among them. It is reported that after this no venomous creature would live in that island, any more than in Ireland; but I do not find that the matter of fact is confirmed, though the popish writers speak of it with assurance. 4. They then magnified him as much as before they had vilified him: *They changed their minds, and said that he was a god*—an immortal god; for they thought it impossible that a mortal man should have a viper hang on his hand so long and be never the worse. See the uncertainty of popular opinion, how it turns with the wind, and how apt it is to run into extremes both ways; from *sacrificing to Paul and Barnabas to stoning them;* and here, from condemning him as a murderer to idolizing him as a god.

IV. The miraculous cure of an old gentleman that was ill of a fever, and of others that were otherwise diseased, by Paul. And, with these confirmations of the doctrine of Christ, no doubt there was a faithful publication of it. Observe, 1. The kind entertainment which *Publius, the chief man of the island,* gave to these distressed strangers; he had a considerable estate in the island, and some think was governor, and he *received them and lodged them three days very courteously,* that they might have time to furnish themselves in other places at the best hand. It is happy when God gives a large heart to those to whom he has given a large estate. It became him, who was the chief man of the island, to be most hospitable and generous,—who was the richest man, to be rich in good works. 2. The illness of *the father of Publius:* He *lay sick of a fever and a bloody flux,* which often go together, and, when they do, are commonly fatal. Providence ordered it that he should be ill just at this time, that the cure of him might be a present recompence to Publius for his generosity, and the cure of him by miracle a recompence particularly for his kindness to Paul, whom he received in the name of a prophet, and had this prophet's reward. 3. His cure: Paul took cognizance of his case, and though we do not find he was urged to it, for they had no thought of any such thing, yet he entered in, not as a physician to heal him by medicines, but as an apostle to heal him by miracle; and he prayed to God, in Christ's name, for his cure, and then laid his hands on him, and he was perfectly well in an instant. Though he must needs be in years, yet he recovered his health, and the lengthening out of his life yet longer would be a mercy to him. 4. The cure of many others, who were invited by this cure to apply to Paul. If he can heal diseases so easily, so effectually, he shall soon have patients enough; and he *bade them all welcome,* and sent them away with what they came for. He did not plead that he was a stranger there, thrown accidentally among them, under no obligations to them, and waiting to be gone by the first opportunity, and therefore might be excused from receiving their applications. No, a good man will endeavour to do good wherever the providence of God casts him. Paul reckoned himself a debtor, not only to the Greeks, but to the Barbarians, and thanked God for an opportunity of being useful among them. Nay, he was particularly obliged to these inhabitants of Malta for the seasonable shelter and supply they had afforded him, and hereby he did in effect discharge his quarters, which should encourage us to entertain strangers, for some thereby have entertained angels and some apostles unawares. God will not be behind-hand with any for kindness shown to his people in distress. We have reason to think that Paul with these cures preached the gospel to them, and that, coming thus confirmed and recommended, it was generally embraced among them. And, if so, never were any people so enriched by a shipwreck on their coasts as these Maltese were.

V. The grateful acknowledgment which even these barbarous people made of the kindness Paul had done them, in preaching Christ unto them. They were civil to him, and to the other ministers that were with him, who, it is likely, were assisting to him in preaching among them, *v.* 10. 1. They *honoured us with many honours.* They showed them all possible respect; they saw God honoured them, and therefore they justly thought themselves obliged to honour them, and thought nothing too much by which they might testify the esteem they had for them. Perhaps they made them free of their island by naturalizing them, and admitted them members of their guilds and fraternities. The faithful preachers of the gospel are worthy of a double honour, especially when they succeed in their labours. 2. *When we departed, they loaded us with such things as were necessary;* or, they put on board such things as we had occasion for. Paul could not labour with his hands here, for he had nothing to work upon, and therefore accepted the kindness of the good people of Melita, not as a fee for his cures (freely he had received, and freely he gave), but as the relief of his wants, and theirs that were with him. And, having reaped of their spiritual things, it was but just they should make them those returns, 1 Cor. ix. 11.

11 And after three months we
departed in a ship of Alexandria,
which had wintered in the isle, whose
sign was Castor and Pollux. 12

And landing at Syracuse, we tarried
there three days. 13 And from
thence we fetched a compass, and
came to Rhegium: and after one day
the south wind blew, and we came
the next day to Puteoli: 14 Where
we found brethren, and were desired
to tarry with them seven days: and
so we went toward Rome. 15 And
from thence, when the brethren heard
of us, they came to meet us as far as
Appii forum, and The three taverns:
whom when Paul saw, he thanked
God, and took courage. 16 And
when we came to Rome, the centurion delivered the prisoners to the
captain of the guard: but Paul was
suffered to dwell by himself with a
soldier that kept him.

We have here the progress of Paul's voyage towards Rome, and his arrival there at length. A rough and dangerous voyage he had hitherto had, and narrowly escaped with his life; but after a storm comes a calm: the latter part of his voyage was easy and quiet.

> Per varios casus, per tot discrimina rerum,
> Tendimus ad Latium————————
>
> Through various hazards and events we move
> To Latium.
>
> Tendimus ad cœlum.
> We make for heaven.
>
> ———————— Dabit Deus his quoque finem.
> To these a period will be fixed by Heaven.

We have here,

I. Their leaving Malta. That island was a happy shelter to them, but it was not their home; when they are refreshed they must put to sea again. The difficulties and discouragements we have met with in our Christian course must not hinder us from pressing forward. Notice is here taken, 1. Of the time of their departure: *After three months*, the three winter months. Better lie by, though they lay upon charges, than go forward while the season was dangerous. Paul had warned them against venturing to sea in winter weather, and they would not take the warning; but, now that they had learned it by the difficulties and dangers they had gone through, he needed not to warn them: their learning did them good when they had paid dearly for it. Experience is therefore called the mistress of fools, because those are fools that will not learn till experience has taught them. 2. Of the ship in which they departed. It was in a ship of Alexandria; so was that which was cast away, *ch.* xxvii. 6. This ship had *wintered in that isle*, and was safe. See what different issues there are of men's undertakings in this world. Here were two ships, both of Alexandria, both bound for Italy, both thrown upon the same island, but one is wrecked there and the other is saved. Such occurrences may often be observed. Providence sometimes favours those that deal in the world, and prospers them, that people may be encouraged to set their hands to worldly business; at other times Providence crosses them, that people may be warned not to set their hearts upon it. Events are thus varied, that we may learn both how to want and how to abound. The historian takes notice of the sign of the ship, which probably gave it its name: it was *Castor and Pollux*. Those little foolish pagan deities, which the poets had made to preside over storms and to protect seafaring men, as gods of the sea, were painted or graven upon the fore-part of the ship, and thence the ship took its name. I suppose this is observed for no other reason than for the better ascertaining of the story, that ship being well known by that name and sign by all that dealt between Egypt and Italy. Dr. Lightfoot thinks that Luke mentions this circumstance to intimate the men's superstition, that they hoped they should have better sailing under this badge than they had had before.

II. Their landing in or about Italy, and the pursuing of their journey towards Rome. 1. They landed first at Syracuse in Sicily, the chief city of that island. There they *tarried three days*, probably having some goods to put ashore, or some merchandise to make there; for it seems to have been a trading voyage that this ship made. Paul had now his curiosity gratified with the sight of places he had often heard of and wished to see, particularly Syracuse, a place of great antiquity and note; and yet, it should seem, there were no Christians there. 2. From Syracuse they came to Rhegium, a city in Italy, directly opposite to Messina in Sicily, belonging to the kingdom of Calabria or Naples. There, it seems, they staid one day; and a very formal story the Romish legends tell of Paul's preaching here at this time, and the fish coming to the shore to hear him,—that with a candle he set a stone pillar on fire, and by that miracle convinced the people of the truth of his doctrine, and they were many of them baptized, and he ordained Stephen, one of his companions in this voyage, to be their bishop,—and all this, they tell you, was done in this one day; whereas it does not appear that they did so much as go ashore, but only came to an anchor in the road. 3. From Rhegium they came to Puteoli, a sea-port town not far from Naples, now called *Pozzolana*. The ship of Alexandria was bound for that port, and therefore there Paul, and the rest that were bound for Rome, were put ashore, and went the remainder of their way by land. At Puteoli they *found brethren*, Christians. Who brought the knowledge of Christ hither we are not told, but here it was, so wonderfully did the leaven of the gospel diffuse itself. God has many that serve and worship him in places where we little think he has. And observe, (1.) Though it is probable there were but few brethren in Puteoli, yet Paul found them out; either they heard of him, or he enquired them out, but as it were by instinct they got together. Brethren in Christ should find out one another, and keep up communion with each other, as those of the same country do in a foreign land. (2.) They desired Paul and his companions to *tarry with them seven days*, that is, to forecast to stay at least one Lord's day with them, and to assist them in their public worship that day. They knew not whether ever they should see Paul at Puteoli again, and therefore he must not go without giving them a sermon or two, or more. And Paul was willing to allow them so much of his time; and the centurion under whose command Paul now was, perhaps having himself friends or business at Puteoli, agreed to stay one week there, to oblige Paul. 4. From Puteoli they went forward towards Rome; whether they travelled on foot, or whether they had beasts provided for them to ride on (as *ch.* xxiii. 24), does not appear; but to Rome they must go, and this was their last stage.

III. The meeting which the Christians at Rome gave to Paul. It is probable that notice was sent to them by the Christians at Puteoli, as soon as ever Paul had come thither, how long he intended to stay there, and when he would set forward for Rome, which gave an opportunity for this interview. Observe,

1. The great honour they did to Paul. They had heard much of his fame, what use God had made of him, and what eminent service he had done to the kingdom of Christ in the world, and to what multitudes of souls he had been a spiritual father. They had heard of his sufferings, and how God had owned him in them, and therefore they not only longed to see him, but thought themselves obliged to show him all possible respect, as a glorious advocate for the cause of Christ. He had some time ago written a long epistle to them, and a most excellent one, *the epistle to the Romans*, in which he had not only expressed his great kindness for them, but had given them a great many useful instructions, in return for which they show him this respect. They *went to meet him*, that they might bring him in state, as ambassadors and judges make their public entry, though he was a prisoner. Some of them went as far as *Appii-forum*, which was fifty-one miles from Rome; others to a place called the *Three Taverns*, which was twenty-eight miles (some reckon it thirty-three miles) from Rome. They are to be commended for it, that they were so far from being ashamed of him, or afraid of owning him, because he was a prisoner, that for that very reason they counted him worthy of double honour, and were the more careful to show him respect.

2. The great comfort Paul had in this. Now that he was drawing near to Rome, and perhaps heard at Puteoli what character the emperor Nero now had, and what a tyrant he had of late become, he began to have some melancholy thoughts about his appeal to Cæsar, and the consequences of it. He was drawing near to Rome, where he had never been, where there were few that knew him or that he knew, and what things might befal him here he could not tell; but he began to grow dull upon it, till he met with these good people that came from Rome to show him respect; and *when he saw them*, (1.) He *thanked God*. We may suppose he thanked them for their civility, told them again and again how kindly he took it; but this was not all: he *thanked God*. Note, If our friends be kind to us, it is God that makes them so, that puts it into their hearts, and into the power of their hands, to be so, and we must give him the glory of it. He thanked God, no doubt, for the civility and generosity of the barbarous people at Melita, but much more for the pious care of the Christian people at Rome for him. When he saw so many Christians that were of Rome, he thanked God that the gospel of Christ had had such wonderful success there in the metropolis of the empire. When we go abroad, or but look abroad, into the world, and meet with those, even in strange places, that bear up Christ's name, and fear God, and serve him, we should lift up our hearts to heaven in thanksgiving; blessed be God that there are so many excellent ones on this earth, bad as it is. Paul had thanked God for the Christians at Rome before he had ever seen them, upon the report he had heard concerning them (Rom. i. 8): *I thank my God for you all.* But now that he saw them (and perhaps they appeared more fashionable and genteel people than most he had conversed with, or more grave, serious, and intelligent, than most) *he thanked God.* But this was not all: (2.) He *took courage.* It put new life into him, cheered up his spirits, and banished his melancholy, and now he can enter Rome a prisoner as cheerfully as ever he had entered Jerusalem at liberty. He finds there are those there who love and value him, and whom he may both converse with and consult with as his friends, which will take off much of the tediousness of his imprisonment, and the terror of his appearing before Nero. Note, It is an encouragement to those who are travelling towards heaven to meet with their fellow travellers, who are their *companions in the kingdom and patience of Jesus Christ.* When we see the numerous and serious assemblies of good Christians, we should not only give thanks to God, but take courage to ourselves. And this is a good reason why respect should be shown to good ministers, especially when they are in sufferings, and have contempt put upon them, that it encourages them, and makes both their sufferings and their services more easy. Yet it is observable that though the Christians at Rome were now so respectful to Paul, and he had promised himself so much from their respect, yet they failed him when he most needed them; for he says (2

Tim. iv. 16), *At my first answer, no man stood with me, but all men forsook me.* They could easily take a ride of forty or fifty miles to go and meet Paul, for the pleasantness of the journey; but to venture the displeasure of the emperor and the disobliging of other great men, by appearing in defence of Paul and giving evidence for him, here they desire to be excused; when it comes to this, they will rather ride as far out of town to miss him as now they did to meet him, which is an intimation to us to cease from man, and to encourage ourselves in the Lord our God. The courage we take from his promises will never fail us, when we shall be ashamed of that which we took from men's compliments. *Let God be true, but every man a liar.*

IV. The delivering of Paul into custody at Rome, *v.* 16. He is now come to his journey's end. And, 1. He is still a prisoner. He had longed to see Rome, but, when he comes there, he is delivered, with other prisoners, to the *captain of the guard,* and can see no more of Rome than he will permit him. How many great men had made their entry into Rome, crowned and in triumph, who really were the plagues of their generation! But here a good man makes his entry into Rome, chained and triumphed over as a poor captive, who was really the greatest blessing to his generation. This thought is enough to put one for ever out of conceit with this world. 2. Yet he has some favour shown him. He is a prisoner, but not a close prisoner, not in the common jail: *Paul was suffered to dwell by himself,* in some convenient private lodgings which his friends there provided for him, and a soldier was appointed to be his guard, who, we hope, was civil to him, and let him take all the liberty that could be allowed to a prisoner, for he must be very ill-natured indeed that could be so to such a courteous obliging man as Paul. Paul, being suffered to dwell by himself, could the better enjoy himself, and his friends, and his God, than if he had been lodged with the other prisoners. Note, This may encourage God's prisoners, that he can give them favour in the eyes of those that carry them captive (Ps. cvi. 46), as Joseph in the eyes of his keeper (Gen. xxxix. 21), and Jehoiachin in the eyes of the king of Babylon, 2 Kings xxv. 27, 28. When God does not deliver his people presently out of bondage, yet, if he either make it easy to them or them easy under it, they have reason to be thankful.

17 And it came to pass, that after
three days Paul called the chief of
the Jews together: and when they
were come together, he said unto
them, Men *and* brethren, though I
have committed nothing against the
people, or customs of our fathers,
yet was I delivered prisoner from
Jerusalem into the hands of the
Romans. 18 Who, when they had
examined me, would have let *me* go,
because there was no cause of death
in me. 19 But when the Jews spake
against *it,* I was constrained to appeal unto Cæsar; not that I had
aught to accuse my nation of. 20
For this cause therefore have I called
for you, to see *you,* and to speak
with *you:* because that for the hope
of Israel I am bound with this chain.
21 And they said unto him, We
neither received letters out of Judæa
concerning thee, neither any of the
brethren that came showed or spake
any harm of thee. 22 But we desire
to hear of thee what thou thinkest:
for as concerning this sect, we know
that every where it is spoken against.

Paul, with a great deal of expense and hazard, is brought a prisoner to Rome, and when he has come nobody appears to prosecute him or lay any thing to his charge; but he must call his own cause; and here he represents it to the chief of the Jews at Rome It was not long since, by an edict of Claudius, all the Jews were banished from Rome, and kept out till his death; but, in the five years since then, many Jews had come thither, for the advantage of trade, though it does not appear that they were allowed any synagogue there or place of public worship; but these *chief of the Jews* were those of best figure among them, the most distinguished men of that religion, who had the best estates and interests. *Paul called them together,* being desirous to stand right in their opinion, and that there might be a good understanding between him and them. And here we are told,

I. What he said to them, and what account he gave them of his cause. He speaks respectfully to them, calls them men and brethren, and thereby intimates that he expects to be treated by them both as a man and as a brother, and engages to treat them as such and to tell them nothing but the truth; for *we are members one of another—all we are brethren.* Now, 1. He professes his own innocency, and that he had not given any just occasion to the Jews to bear him such an ill will as generally they did: "I have *committed nothing against the people* of the Jews, have done nothing to the prejudice of their religion or civil liberties, have added no affliction to their present miseries, they know I have not; nor have I committed any thing *against the customs of our fathers,* either by abrogating or by innovating in religion." It is true Paul did not impose the customs of the fathers upon the Gentiles: they were never intended for them. But it is as true that he never opposed them in the Jews, but did himself, when he was among them, conform to them. He never quarrelled with them for practising according to the usages of their own religion, but only for their enmity to the Gentiles, Gal. ii. 12. Paul had the testimony of his conscience for him that he had done his duty to the Jews. 2. He modestly complains of the hard usage he had met with—that, though he had given them no offence, yet *he was delivered prisoner from Jerusalem into the hands of the Romans.* If he had spoken the whole truth in this matter, it would have looked worse than it did upon the Jews, for they would have murdered him without any colour of law or justice if the Romans had not protected him; but, however, they accused him as a criminal, before Felix the governor, and, demanding judgment against him, were, in effect, delivering him prisoner into the hands of the Romans, when he desired no more than a fair and impartial trial by their own law. 3. He declares the judgment of the Roman governors concerning him, *v.* 18. They examined him, enquired into his case, heard what was to be said against him, and what he had to say for himself. The chief captain examined him, so did Felix, and Festus, and Agrippa, and they could find no cause of death in him; nothing appeared to the contrary but that he was an honest, quiet, conscientious, good man, and therefore they would never gratify the Jews with a sentence of death upon him; but, on the contrary, would have let him go, and have let him go on in his work too, and have given him no interruption, for they all heard him and liked his doctrine well enough. It was for the honour of Paul that those who most carefully examined his case acquitted him, and none condemned him but unheard, and such as were prejudiced against him. 4. He pleads the necessity he was under to remove himself and his cause to Rome; and that it was only in his own defence, and not with any design to recriminate, or exhibit a cross bill against the complainants, (*v.* 19): *When the Jews spoke against it,* and entered a caveat against his discharge, designing, if they could not have him condemned to die, yet to have him made a prisoner for life, he was *constrained to appeal unto Cæsar,* finding that the governors, one after another, stood so much in awe of the Jews that they could not discharge him, for fear of making him their enemies, which made it necessary for him to pray the assistance of the higher powers. This was all he aimed at in this appeal; not to accuse his nation, but only to vindicate himself. Every man has a right to plead in his own defence, who yet ought not to find fault with his neighbours. It is an invidious thing to accuse, especially to accuse a nation, such a nation. Paul made intercession for them, but never against them. The Roman government had at this time an ill opinion of the Jewish nation, as factious, turbulent, disaffected, and dangerous; and it had been an easy thing for a man with such a fluent tongue as Paul had, a citizen of Rome, and so injured as he was, to have exasperated the emperor against the Jewish nation. But Paul would not for ever so much do such a thing; he was for making the best of every body, and not making bad worse. 5. He puts his sufferings upon the true footing, and gives them such an account of the reason of them as should engage them not only not to join with his persecutors against him, but to concern themselves for him, and to do what they could on his behalf (*v.* 20): "*For this cause I have called for you,* not to quarrel with you, for I have no design to incense the government against you, but to *see you and speak with you* as my countrymen, and men that I would keep up a correspondence with, because *for the hope of Israel I am bound with this chain.*" He carried the mark of his imprisonment about with him, and probably was chained to the soldier that kept him; and it was, (1.) Because he preached that the Messiah was come, who was the hope of Israel, he whom Israel hoped for. "Do not all the Jews agree in this, that the Messiah will be the glory of his people Israel? And therefore he is to be hoped for, and this Messiah I preach, and prove he is come. They would keep up such a hope of a Messiah yet to come as must end in a despair of him; I preach such a hope in a Messiah already come as must produce a joy in him. (2.) Because he preached that the resurrection of the dead would come. This also was the hope of Israel; so he had called it, *ch.* xxiii. 6; xxiv. 15; xxvi. 6, 7. "They would have you still expect a Messiah that would free you from the Roman yoke, and make you great and prosperous upon earth, and it is this that occupies their thoughts; and they are angry at me for directing their expectations to the great things of another world, and persuading them to embrace a Messiah who will secure those to them, and not external power and grandeur. I am for bringing you to the spiritual and eternal blessedness upon which our fathers by faith had their eye, and this is what they hate me for,—because I would take you off from that which is the cheat of Israel, and will be its shame and ruin, the notion of a temporal Messiah, and lead you to that which is the true and real hope of Israel, and the genuine sense of all the promises made to the fathers, a spiritual kingdom of holiness and love set up in the hearts of men, to be the pledge of, and preparative for, the joyful resurrection of the dead and the life of the world to come."

II. What was their reply. They own, 1. That they had nothing to say in particular against him; nor had any instructions to appear as his prosecutors before the emperor, either by letter or word of mouth (*v.* 21): "*We have neither received letters out of Judea concerning thee* (have no orders to prosecute thee) *nor have any of the brethren* of the Jewish nation that have lately come up to Rome (as many occasions drew the Jews thither now that their nation was a province of that empire) *shown or spoken any harm of thee.*" This was very strange, that that restless and inveterate rage of the Jews which had followed Paul wherever he went should not follow him to Rome, to get him condemned there. Some think they told a lie here, and had orders to prosecute him, but durst not own it, being themselves obnoxious to the emperor's displeasure, who though he had not, like his predecessors, banished them all from Rome, yet gave them no countenance there. But I am apt to think that what they said was true, and Paul now found he had gained the point he aimed at in appealing to Cæsar, which was to remove his cause into a court to which they durst not follow it. This was David's policy, and it was his security (1 Sam. xxvii. 1): *There is nothing better for me than to escape into the land of the Philistines, and Saul shall despair of me, to seek me any more in any coasts of Israel; so shall I escape out of his hands:* and it proved so, *v.* 4. *When Saul heard that David had fled to Gath, he sought no more again for him.* Thus did Paul by his appeal: he fled to Rome, where he was out of their reach; and they said, "Even let him go." 2. That they desired to know particularly concerning the doctrine he preached, and the religion he took so much pains to propagate in the face of so much opposition (*v.* 22): *We desire to hear of thee what thou thinkest*—ἃ φρονεῖς what thy opinions or sentiments are, what are those things which thou art so wise about, and hast such a relish of and such a zeal for; for, though we know little else of Christianity, we know *it is a sect every where spoken against.*" Those who said this scornful spiteful word of the Christian religion were Jews, *the chief of the Jews at Rome,* who boasted of their knowledge (Rom. ii. 17), and yet this was all they knew concerning the Christian religion, that it was a *sect every where spoken against.* They put it into an ill name, and then ran it down. (1.) They looked upon it to be a sect, and this was false. True Christianity establishes that which is of common concern to all mankind, and is not built upon such narrow opinions and private interests as sects commonly owe their original to. It aims at no worldly benefit or advantage as sects do; but all its gains are spiritual and eternal. And, besides, it has a direct tendency to the uniting of the children of men, and not the dividing of them, and setting them at variance, as sects have. (2.) They said it was every where spoken against, and this was too true. All that they conversed with spoke against it, and therefore they concluded every body did: most indeed did. It is, and always has been, the lot of Christ's holy religion to be every where spoken against.

23 And when they had appointed
him a day, there came many to him
into *his* lodging; to whom he expounded and testified the kingdom
of God, persuading them concerning
Jesus, both out of the law of Moses,
and *out of* the prophets, from morning till evening. 24 And some
believed the things which were spoken,
and some believed not. 25 And
when they agreed not among themselves, they departed, after that Paul
had spoken one word, Well spake
the Holy Ghost by Esaias the prophet unto our fathers, 26 Saying,
Go unto this people, and say, Hearing ye shall hear, and shall not
understand; and seeing ye shall see,
and not perceive: 27 For the
heart of this people is waxed gross,
and their ears are dull of hearing, and
their eyes have they closed; lest they
should see with *their* eyes, and hear
with *their* ears, and understand with
their heart, and should be converted,
and I should heal them. 28 Be it
known therefore unto you, that the
salvation of God is sent unto the
Gentiles, and *that* they will hear it.
29 And when he had said these
words, the Jews departed, and had
great reasoning among themselves.

We have here a short account of a long conference which Paul had with the Jews at Rome about the Christian religion. Though they were so far prejudiced against it, because it was every where spoken against, as to call it *a sect,* yet they were willing to give it a hearing, which was more than the Jews at Jerusalem would do. It is probable that these Jews at Rome, being men of larger acquaintance with the world and more general conversation, were more free in their enquiries than the bigoted Jews at Jerusalem were, and would not answer this matter before they heard it.

I. We are here told how Paul managed this conference in defence of the Christian religion. The Jews appointed the time, a day was set for this dispute, that all parties concerned might have sufficient notice, *v.* 23. Those Jews seemed well disposed to receive conviction, and yet it did not prove that they all were so. Now when the day came,

1. There were *many got together to Paul.* Though he was a prisoner, and could not come out to them, yet they were willing to come to him to his lodging. And the confinement he was now under, if duly considered, instead of prejudicing them against

his doctrine, ought to confirm it to them; for it was a sign not only that he believed it, but that he thought it worth suffering for. One would visit such a man as Paul in his prison rather than not have instruction from him. And he made room for them in his lodging, not fearing to give offence to the government, so that he might do good to them.

2. He was very large and full in his discourse with them, seeking their conviction more than his own vindication. (1.) He expounded, or explained, the kingdom of God to them,—showed them the nature of that kingdom and the glorious purposes and designs of it, that it is heavenly and spiritual, seated in the minds of men, and shines not in external pomp, but in purity of heart and life. That which kept the Jews in their unbelief was a misunderstanding of the kingdom of God, as if it came with observation; let but that be expounded to them, and set in a true light, and they will be brought into obedience to it. (2.) He not only expounded the kingdom of God, but he testified it,—plainly declared it to them, and confirmed it by incontestable proofs, that the kingdom of God by the Messiah's administration was come, and was now set up in the world. He attested the extraordinary powers in the kingdom of grace by which it was set up, and the miracles in the kingdom of nature by which it was confirmed. He bore his testimony to it from his own experience of its power and influence upon him, and the manner of his being brought into subjection to it. (3.) He not only expounded and testified the kingdom of God, but he persuaded them, urged it upon their consciences and pressed them with all earnestness to embrace the kingdom of God, and submit to it, and not to persist in an opposition to it. He followed his doctrine (the explication and confirmation of it) with a warm and lively application to his hearers, which is the most proper and profitable method of preaching. (4.) He persuaded them concerning Jesus. The design and tendency of his whole discourse were to bring them to Christ, to convince them of his being the Messiah, and to engage them to believe in him as he is offered in the gospel. He urged upon them, *τὰ περὶ τοῦ Ἰησοῦ—the things concerning Jesus,* the prophecies of him, which he read to them *out of the law of Moses and out of the prophets,* as pointing at the Messiah, and showed how they had all had their accomplishment in this Jesus. They being Jews, he dealt with them out of the scriptures of the Old Testament, and demonstrated that these were so far from making against Christianity that they were the great proofs of it; so that, if we compare the history of the New Testament with the prophecy of the Old, we must conclude that this Jesus is he that should come, and we are to look for no other.

3. He was very long; for he continued his discourse, and it should seem to have been a continued discourse, from *morning till evening;* perhaps it was a discourse eight or ten hours long. The subject was curious—he was full of it—it was of vast importance—he was in good earnest, and his heart was upon it—he knew not when he should have such another opportunity, and therefore, without begging pardon for tiring their patience, he kept them all day; but it is probable that he spent some of the time in prayer with them and for them.

II. What was the effect of this discourse. One would have thought that so good a cause as that of Christianity, and managed by such a skilful hand as Paul's, could not but carry the day, and that all the hearers would have yielded to it presently; but it did not prove so: the child Jesus is set for the fall of some and the rising again of others, a foundation stone to some and a stone of stumbling to others. 1. *They did not agree among themselves, v.* 25. Some of them thought Paul was in the right, others would not admit it. This is that division which Christ came to send, that fire which he came to kindle, Luke xii. 49, 51. Paul preached with a great deal of plainness and clearness, and yet his hearers could not agree about the sense and evidence of what he preached. 2. *Some believed the things that were spoken, and some believed not, v.* 24. There was the disagreement. Such as this has always been the success of the gospel; to some it has been *a savour of life unto life,* to others *a savour of death unto death.* Some are wrought upon by the word, and others hardened; some receive the light, and others shut their eyes against it. So it was among Christ's hearers, and the spectators of his miracles, some believed and some blasphemed. If all had believed, there had been no disagreement; so that all the blame of the division lay upon those who would not believe.

III. The awakening word which Paul said to them at parting. He perceived by what they muttered that there were many among them, and perhaps the greater part, that were obstinate, and would not yield to the conviction of what he said; and they were getting up to be gone, they had had enough of it: "Hold," says Paul, "take one word with you before you go, and consider of it when you come home: what do you think will be the effect of your obstinate infidelity? What will you do in the end hereof? What will it come to?"

1 "You will by the righteous judgment of God be sealed up under unbelief. You harden your own hearts, and God will harden them as he did Pharaoh's; and this is what was prophesied of concerning you. Turn to that scripture (Isa. vi. 9, 10), and read it seriously, and tremble lest the case there described should prove to be your case." As

there are in the Old Testament gospel promises, which will be accomplished in all that believe, so there are gospel threatenings of spiritual judgments, which will be fulfilled in those that believe not; and this is one. It is part of the commission given to Isaiah the prophet; he is sent to make those worse that would not be made better. *Well spoke the Holy Ghost by* Esaias *the prophet unto our fathers.* What was spoken by JEHOVAH is here said to be spoken by the Holy Ghost, which proves that the Holy Ghost is God; and what was spoken to Isaiah is here said to be spoken by him to their fathers, for he was ordered to tell the people what God said to him; and, though what is there said had in it much of terror to the people and of grief to the prophet, yet it is here said to be well spoken. Hezekiah said concerning a message of wrath, *Good is the word of the Lord which thou hast spoken,* Isa. xxxix. 8. And *he that believes not shall be damned* is gospel, as well as, *He that believes shall be saved,* Mark xvi. 16. Or this may be explained by that of our Saviour (Matt. xv. 7), "*Well did Esaias prophesy of you.* The Holy Ghost said to your fathers, that which would be fulfilled in you, *Hearing you shall hear, and shall not understand.*" (1.) "That which was their great sin against God is yours; and that is this, you will not see. You shut your eyes against the most convincing evidence possible, and will not admit the conclusion, though you cannot deny the premises: *Your eyes you have closed,*" *v.* 27. This intimates an obstinate infidelity, and a willing slavery to prejudice. "As your fathers would not see God's hand lifted up against them in his judgments (Isa. xxvi. 11), so you will not see God's hand stretched out to you in gospel grace." It was true of these unbelieving Jews that they were prejudiced against the gospel; they did not see, because they were resolved they would not, and none so blind as those that will not see. They would not prosecute their convictions, and for this reason would not admit them. They have purposely *closed their eyes, lest they should see with their eyes* the great things which belong to their everlasting peace, should see the glory of God, the amiableness of Christ, the deformity of sin, the beauty of holiness, the vanity of this world, and the reality of another. They will not be changed and governed by these truths, and therefore will not receive the evidence of them, *lest they should hear with their ears* that which they are loth to hear, the wrath of God revealed from heaven against them, and the will of God revealed from heaven to them. They stop their ears, like the deaf adder, that *will not hearken to the voice of the charmer, charm he ever so wisely.* Thus their fathers did; they *would not hear,* Zech. vii. 11, 12. And that which they are afraid of in shutting up their eyes and ears, and barricading (as it were) both their learning senses against him that made both the hearing ear and the seeing eye, is, *lest they should understand with their heart, and should be converted, and I should heal them.* They kept their mind in the dark, or at least in a constant confusion and tumult, lest, if they should admit a considerate sober thought, they should understand with their heart how much it is both their duty and their interest to be religious, and so by degrees the truth should be too hard for them, and they should be converted from the evil ways which they take pleasure in, to those exercises to which they have now an aversion. Observe, God's method is to bring people first to see and hear, and so to understand with their hearts, and then to convert them, and bow their wills, and so heal them, which is the regular way of dealing with a rational soul; and therefore Satan prevents the conversion of souls to God by blinding the mind and darkening the understanding, 2 Cor. iv. 4. And the case is very sad when the sinner joins with him herein, and puts out his own eyes. *Ut liberius peccent, libenter ignorant—They plunge into ignorance, that they may sin the more freely.* They are in love with their disease, and are afraid lest God should heal them; like Babylon of old, We would have healed her, and she would not be healed, Jer. li. 9. This was the sin. (2.) "That which was the great judgment of God upon them for this sin is his judgment upon you, and that is, you shall be blind. God will give you up to a judicial infatuation: *Hearing you shall hear*—you shall have the word of God preached to you over and over—*but you shall not understand* it; because you will not give your minds to understand it, God will not give you strength and grace to understand it. *Seeing you shall see*—you shall have abundance of miracles and signs done before your eyes—*but you shall not perceive* the convincing evidence of them. Take heed lest what Moses said to your fathers should be true of you (Deut. xxix. 4), *The Lord has not given you a heart to perceive, and eyes to see, and ears to hear, unto this day;* and what Isaiah said to the men of his generation (Isa. xxix. 10—12), *The Lord has poured out upon you the spirit of deep sleep, and has closed your eyes.*" What with their resisting the grace of God and rebelling against the light, and God's withdrawing and withholding his grace and light from them,—what with their not receiving the love of the truth, and God's giving them up for that to strong delusions, to believe a lie,—what with their wilful and what with their judicial hardness, *the heart of this people is waxed gross, and their ears are dull of hearing.* They are stupid and senseless, and not wrought upon by all that can be said to them. No physic that can be given them operates upon them, nor will reach them, and therefore their disease must be adjudged incurable, and their case desperate. How should those be happy that will not be healed of a disease that makes them miserable? And how should those be healed that will not be converted to the use of the methods of cure? And how should those be converted that will not be convinced either of their disease or of their remedy? And how should those be convinced that *shut their eyes and stop their ears?* Let all that hear the gospel, and do not heed it, tremble at this doom; for, when once they are thus given up to hardness of heart, they are already in the suburbs of hell; for who shall heal them, if God do not?

2. "Your unbelief will justify God in sending the gospel to the Gentile world, which is the thing you look upon with such a jealous eye (*v.* 28): therefore seeing you put the grace of God away from you, and will not submit to the power of divine truth and love, seeing you will not be converted and healed in the methods which divine wisdom has appointed, *therefore be it known unto you that the salvation of God is sent unto the Gentiles,* that salvation which was of the Jews only (John iv. 22), the offer of it is made to them, the means of it afforded to them, and they stand fairer for it than you do; it is sent to them, and they will hear it, and receive it, and be happy in it. Now Paul designs hereby, (1.) To abate their displeasure at the preaching of the gospel to the Gentiles, by showing them the absurdity of it. They were angry that the salvation of God was sent to the Gentiles, and thought it was too great a favour done to them; but, if they thought that salvation of so small a value as not to be worthy of their acceptance, surely they could not grudge it to the Gentiles as too good for them, nor envy them for it. The salvation of God was sent into the world, the Jews had the first offer of it, it was fairly proposed to them, it was earnestly pressed upon them, but they refused it; they would not accept the invitation which was given to them first to the wedding-feast and therefore must thank themselves if other guests be invited. If they will not strike the bargain, nor come up to the terms, they ought not to be angry at those that will. They cannot complain that the Gentiles took it over their heads, or out of their hands, for they had quite taken their hands off it, nay, *they had lifted up the heel against it;* and therefore it is their fault, for *it is through their fall that salvation is come to the Gentiles,* Rom. xi. 11. (2.) To improve their displeasure at the favour done to the Gentiles to their advantage, and to bring good out of that evil; for when he had spoken of this very thing in his epistle to the Romans, the benefit which the Gentiles had by the unbelief and rejection of the Jews, he says, he took notice of it on purpose that he might provoke his dear countrymen the Jews *to a holy emulation, and might save some of them,* Rom. xi. 14. The Jews have rejected the gospel of Christ, and pushed it off to the Gentiles, but it is not yet too late to repent of their refusal, and to accept of the salvation which they did make light of; they may say No, and take it, as the elder brother in the parable, who, when he was bidden to *go work in the vineyard,* first said, *I will not,* and yet *afterwards repented and went,* Matt. xxi. 29. Is the gospel sent to the Gentiles? Let us go after it rather than come short of it. And will they hear it, who are thought to be out of hearing, and have been so long like the idols they worshipped, *that have ears and hear not?* And shall not we hear it, whose privilege it is to have God so nigh to us in all that we call upon him for? Thus he would have them to argue, and to be shamed into the belief of the gospel by the welcome it met with among the Gentiles. And, if it had not that effect upon them, it would aggravate their condemnation, as it did that of the scribes and Pharisees, who, when they saw the publicans and harlots submit to John's baptism, did not afterwards thereupon repent of their folly, *that they might believe him,* Matt. xxi. 32.

IV. The breaking up of the assembly, as it should seem, in some disorder. 1. They turned their backs upon Paul. Those of them that believed not were extremely nettled at that last word which he said, that they should be judicially blinded, and that the light of the gospel should shine among those that sat in darkness. *When Paul had said these words,* he had said enough for them, and *they departed,* perhaps not so much enraged as some others of their nation had been upon the like occasion, but stupid and unconcerned, no more affected, either with those terrible words in the close of his discourse or all the comfortable words he had spoken before, than the seats they sat on. They departed, many of them with a resolution never to hear Paul preach again, nor trouble themselves with further enquiries about this matter. 2. They set their faces one against another; for they had great disputes among themselves. There was not only a quarrel between those who believed and those who believed not, but even among those who believed not there were debates. Those that agreed to depart from Paul, yet agreed not in the reasons why they departed, but had *great reasoning among themselves.* Many have great reasoning who yet do not reason right, can find fault with one another's opinions, and yet not yield to truth. Nor will men's reasoning among themselves convince them, without the grace of God to open their understandings.

30 And Paul dwelt two whole years in his own hired house, and received all that came in unto him,
31 Preaching the kingdom of God, and teaching those things which concern the Lord Jesus Christ, with all confidence, no man forbidding him.

We are here taking our leave of the history

of blessed Paul; and therefore, since God saw it not fit that we should know any more of him, we should carefully take notice of every particular of the circumstances in which we must here leave him.

I. It cannot but be a trouble to us that we must leave him in bonds for Christ, nay, and that we have no prospect given us of his being set at liberty. *Two whole years* of that good man's life are here spent in confinement, and, for aught that appears, he was never enquired after, all that time, by those whose prisoner he was. He appealed to Cæsar, in hope of a speedy discharge from his imprisonment, the governors having signified to his imperial majesty concerning the prisoner *that he had done nothing worthy of death or bonds*, and yet he is detained a prisoner. So little reason have we to trust in men, especially despised prisoners in great men; witness the case of Joseph, whom *the chief butler remembered not, but forgot*, Gen. xl. 23. Yet some think that though it be not mentioned here, yet it was in the former of these two years, and early too in that year, that he was first brought before Nero, and then his bonds in Christ were manifest in Cæsar's court, as he says, Phil. i. 13. And at this first answer it was that *no man stood by him*, 2 Tim. iv. 16. But it seems, instead of being set at liberty upon this appeal, as he expected, he hardly escaped out of the emperor's hands with his life; he calls it a deliverance out of the mouth of the lion, 2 Tim. iv. 17, and his speaking there of his first answer intimates that since that he had a second, in which he had come off better, and yet was not discharged. During these two years' imprisonment he wrote his epistle to the Galatians, then his second epistle to Timothy, then those to the Ephesians, Philippians, Colossians, and to Philemon, in which he mentions several things particularly concerning his imprisonment; and, lastly, his epistle to the Hebrews just after he was set at liberty, as Timothy also was, who, coming to visit him, was upon some account or other made his fellow-prisoner *(with whom*, writes Paul to the Hebrews (xiii. 23), *if he come shortly, I will see you)*, but how or by what means he obtained his liberty we are not told, only that two years he was a prisoner. Tradition says that after his discharge he went from Italy to Spain, thence to Crete, and so with Timothy into Judea, and thence went to visit the churches in Asia, and at length came a second time to Rome, and there was beheaded in the last year of Nero. But Baronius himself owns that there is no certainty of any thing concerning him betwixt his release from this imprisonment and his martyrdom; but it is said by some that Nero, having, when he began to play the tyrant, set himself against the Christians, and persecuted them (and he was the first of the emperors that made a law against them, as Tertullian says, *Apol.* cap. 5), the church at Rome was much weakened by that persecution, and this brought Paul the second time to Rome, to re-establish the church there, and to comfort the souls of the disciples that were left, and so he fell a second time into Nero's hand. And Chrysostom relates that a young woman that was one of Nero's misses (to speak modishly) being converted, by Paul's preaching, to the Christian faith, and so brought off from the lewd course of life she had lived, Nero was incensed against Paul for it, and ordered him first to be imprisoned, and then put to death. But to keep to this short account here given of it, 1. It would grieve one to think that such a useful man as Paul was should be so long in restraint. Two years he was a prisoner under Felix (*ch.* xxiv. 27), and, besides all the time that passed between that and his coming to Rome, he is here two years more a prisoner under Nero. How many churches might Paul have planted, how many cities and nations might he have brought over to Christ, in these five years' time (for so much it was at least), if he had been at liberty! But God is wise, and will show that he is no debtor to the most useful instruments he employs, but can and will carry on his own interest, both without their services and by their sufferings. Even Paul's bonds fell out *to the furtherance of the gospel*, Phil. i. 12—14. 2. Yet even Paul's imprisonment was in some respects a kindness to him, for these *two years he dwelt in his own hired house*, and that was more, for aught I know, than ever he had done before. He had always been accustomed to sojourn in the houses of others, now he has a house of his own—his own while he pays the rent of it; and such a retirement as this would be a refreshment to one who had been all his days an itinerant. He had been accustomed to be always upon the remove, seldom staid long at a place, but now he lived for two years in the same house; so that the bringing of him into this prison was like Christ's call to his disciples *to come into a desert place, and rest awhile*, Mark vi. 31. When he was at liberty, he was in continual fear by reason of *the lying in wait of the Jews* (*ch.* xx. 19), but now his prison was his castle. Thus *out of the eater came forth meat, and out of the strong sweetness.*

II. Yet it is a pleasure to us (for we are sure it was to him) that, though we leave him in bonds for Christ, yet we leave him at work for Christ, and this made his bonds easy that he was not by them bound out from serving God and doing good. His prison becomes a temple, a church, and then it is to him a palace. His hands are tied, but, thanks be to God, his mouth is not stopped; a faithful zealous minister can better bear any hardship than being silenced. Here is Paul a prisoner, and yet a preacher; he is bound, but the word of the Lord is not bound. When he wrote his epistle to the Romans, he said *he longed to see them, that he might impart unto them some spiritual gift* (Rom. i. 11); he was glad *to see some of them* (*v.* 15), but it would not be half his joy unless he could impart to them some spiritual gift, which here he has an opportunity to do, and then he will not complain of his confinement. Observe,

1. To whom he preached: to all that had a mind to hear him, whether Jews or Gentiles. Whether he had liberty to go to other houses to preach does not appear; it is likely not; but whoever would had liberty to come to his house to hear, and they were welcome: *He received all that came to him.* Note, Ministers' doors should be open to such as desire to receive instruction from them, and they should be glad of an opportunity to advise those that are in care about their souls. Paul could not preach in a synagogue, or any public place of meeting that was sumptuous and capacious, but he preached in a poor cottage of his own. Note, When we cannot do what we would in the service of God we must do what we can. Those ministers that have but little hired houses should rather preach in them, if they may be allowed to do that, than be silent. *He received all that came to him,* and was not afraid of the greatest, nor ashamed of the meanest. He was ready to preach on the first day of the week to Christians, on the seventh day to Jews, and to all who would come on any day of the week; and he might hope the better to speed because *they came in unto him,* which supposed a desire to be instructed and a willingness to learn, and where these are it is probable that some good may be done.

2. What he preached. He does not fill their heads with curious speculations, nor with matters of state and politics, but he keeps to his text, minds his business as an apostle. (1.) He is God's ambassador, and therefore *preaches the kingdom of God,* does all he can to preach it up, negociates the affairs of it, in order to the advancing of all its true interests. He meddles not with the affairs of the kingdoms of men; let those treat of them whose work it is. He preaches the kingdom of God among men, and the word of that kingdom; the same that he defended in his public disputes, *testifying the kingdom of God* (*v.* 23), he enforced in his public preaching, as that which, if received aright, will make us all wise and good, wiser and better, which is the end of preaching. (2.) He is an agent for Christ, a friend of the bridegroom, and therefore *teaches those things which concern the Lord Jesus Christ*—the whole history of Christ, his incarnation, doctrine, life, miracles, death, resurrection, ascension; all that relates to the mystery of godliness. Paul stuck still to his principle —to know and preach *nothing but Christ, and him crucified.* Ministers, when in their preaching they are tempted to diverge from that which is their main business, should reduce themselves with this question, What does this concern the Lord Jesus Christ? What tendency has it to bring us to him, and to keep us walking in him? *For we preach not ourselves, but Christ.*

3. With what liberty he preached. (1.) Divine grace gave him a liberty of spirit. He preached *with all confidence,* as one that was himself well assured of the truth of what he preached—that it was what he durst stand by; and of the worth of it—that it was what he durst suffer for. He was *not ashamed of the gospel of Christ.* (2.) Divine Providence gave him a liberty of speech: *No man forbidding him,* giving him any check for what he did or laying any restraint upon him. The Jews that used to forbid him to speak to the Gentiles had no authority here; and the Roman government as yet took no cognizance of the profession of Christianity as a crime. Herein we must acknowledge the hand of God, [1.] Setting bounds to the rage of persecutors; where he does not turn the heart, yet he can tie the hand and bridle the tongue. Nero was a bloody man, and there were many, both Jews and Gentiles, in Rome, that hated Christianity; and yet so it was, unaccountably, that Paul though a prisoner was connived at in preaching the gospel, and it was not construed a breach of the peace. Thus God makes *the wrath of men to praise him, and restrains the remainder of it,* Ps. lxxvi. 10. Though there were so many that had it in their power to forbid Paul's preaching (even the common soldier that kept him might have done it), yet God so ordered it, *that no man did forbid him.* [2.] See God here providing comfort for the relief of the persecuted. Though it was a very low and narrow sphere of opportunity that Paul was here placed in, compared with what he had been in, yet, such as it was, he was not molested nor disturbed in it. Though it was not a wide door that was opened to him, yet it was kept open, and no man was suffered to shut it; and it was to many an effectual door, so that there were saints even in Cæsar's household, Phil. iv. 22. When the city of our solemnities is thus made a quiet habitation at any time, and we are fed from day to day with the bread of life, no man forbidding us, we must give thanks to God for it and prepare for changes, still longing for that holy mountain in which there shall never be any pricking brier nor grieving thorn.

AN

EXPOSITION,

WITH PRACTICAL OBSERVATIONS,

OF THE EPISTLE OF ST. PAUL TO

THE ROMANS.

If we may compare scripture with scripture, and take the opinion of some devout and pious persons, in the Old Testament David's Psalms, and in the New Testament Paul's Epistles, are stars of the first magnitude, that differ from the other stars in glory. The whole scripture is indeed an epistle from heaven to earth: but in it we have upon record several particular epistles, more of Paul's than of any other, for he was the chief of the apostles, and laboured more abundantly than they all. His natural parts, I doubt not, were very pregnant; his apprehension was quick and piercing; his expressions were fluent and copious; his affections, wherever he took, very warm and zealous, and his resolutions no less bold and daring: this made him, before his conversion, a very keen and bitter persecutor; but when the strong man armed was dispossessed, and the stronger than he came to divide the spoil and to sanctify these qualifications, he became the most skilful zealous preacher; never any better fitted to win souls, nor more successful. Fourteen of his epistles we have in the canon of scripture; many more, it is probable, he wrote in the course of his ministry, which might be profitable enough for doctrine, for reproof, &c., but, not being given by inspiration of God, they were not received as canonical scripture, nor handed down to us. Six epistles, said to be Paul's, written to Seneca, and eight of Seneca's to him, are spoken of by some of the ancients [*Sixt. Senens. Biblioth. Sanct.* lib. ii.] and are extant; but, upon the first view, they appear spurious and counterfeit.

This epistle to the Romans is placed first, not because of the priority of its date, but because of the superlative excellency of the epistle, it being one of the longest and fullest of all, and perhaps because of the dignity of the place to which it is written. Chrysostom would have this epistle read over to him twice a week. It is gathered from some passages in the epistle that it was written *Anno Christi* 56, from Corinth, while Paul made a short stay there in his way to Troas, Acts xx. 5, 6. He commendeth to the Romans Phebe, a servant of the church at Cenchrea (*ch.* xvi.), which was a place belonging to Corinth. He calls Gaius his *host*, or the man with whom he lodged (*ch.* xvi. 23), and he was a Corinthian, not the same with Gaius of Derbe, mentioned Acts xx. Paul was now going up to Jerusalem, with the money that was given to the poor saints there; and of that he speaks, *ch.* xv. 26. The great mysteries treated of in this epistle must needs produce in this, as in other writings of Paul, many things dark and hard to be understood, 2 Pet. iii. 16. The method of this (as of several other of the epistles) is observable; the former part of it doctrinal, in the first eleven chapters; the latter part practical, in the last five: to inform the judgment and to reform the life. And the best way to understand the truths explained in the former part is to abide and abound in the practice of the duties prescribed in the latter part; for, if any man will do his will, he shall know of the doctrine, John vii. 17.

I. The doctrinal part of the epistle instructs us,

1. Concerning the way of salvation. (1.) The foundation of it laid in justification, and that not by the Gentiles' works of nature (*ch.* i.), nor by the Jews' works of the law (*ch.* ii. iii.), for both Jews and Gentiles were liable to the curse; but only by faith in Jesus Christ, *ch.* iii. 21, &c., *ch.* iv. *throughout*. (2.) The steps of this salvation are, [1.] Peace with God, *ch.* v. [2.] Sanctification, *ch.* vi. vii. [3.] Glorification, *ch.* viii.

2. Concerning the persons saved, such as belong to the election of grace (*ch.* ix.), Gentiles and Jews, *ch.* x, xi. By this it appears that the subjects he discourses of were such as were then the present truths, as the apostle speaks, 2 Peter i. 12. Two things the Jews then stumbled at—justification by faith without the works of the law, and the admission of the Gentiles into the church; and therefore both these he studied to clear and vindicate.

II. The practical part follows, wherein we find, 1. Several general exhortations proper for all Christians, *ch.* xii. 2. Directions for our behaviour, as members of civil society, *ch.* xiii. 3 Rules for the conduct of Christians to one another, as members of the Christian church, *ch.* xiv. and *ch.* xv. to *v.* 14.

III. As he draws towards a conclusion, he makes an apology for writing to them (*ch.* xv. 14—16), gives them an account of himself and his own affairs (*v.* 17—21), promises them a visit (*v.* 22—29), begs their prayers (*v.* 30—33), sends particular salutations to many friends there (*ch.* xvi. 1—16), warns them against those who caused divisions (*v.* 17—20), adds the salutations of his friends with him (*v.* 21—23), and ends with a benediction to them and a doxology to God, *v.* 24—27.

CHAP. I.

In this chapter we may observe, I. The preface and introduction to the whole epistle, to ver. 16. II. A description of the deplorable condition of the Gentile world, which begins the proof of the doctrine of justification by faith, here laid down at ver. 17. The first is according to the then usual formality of a letter, but intermixed with very excellent and savoury expressions.

PAUL, a servant of Jesus Christ,
called *to be* an apostle, separated
unto the gospel of God, 2 (Which
he had promised afore by his prophets in the holy scriptures,) 3
Concerning his Son Jesus Christ our
Lord, which was made of the seed of
David according to the flesh ; 4
And declared *to be* the Son of God
with power, according to the spirit of
holiness, by the resurrection from the
dead : 5 By whom we have received
grace and apostleship, for obedience
to the faith among all nations, for his
name : 6 Among whom are ye also
the called of Jesus Christ : 7 To all
that be in Rome, beloved of God,
called *to be* saints : Grace to you and
peace from God our Father, and the
Lord Jesus Christ.

In this paragraph we have,

I. The person who writes the epistle described (*v.* 1) : *Paul, a servant of Jesus Christ;* this is his title of honour, which he glories in, not as the Jewish teachers, *Rabbi, Rabbi;* but a servant, a more immediate attendant, a steward in the house. *Called to be an apostle.* Some think he alludes to his old name Saul, which signifies *one called for*, or *enquired after:* Christ sought him to make an apostle of him, Acts ix. 15. He here builds his authority upon his call; he did not run without sending, as the false apostles did; *κλητὸς απόστολος—called an apostle*, as if this were the name he would be called by, though he acknowledged himself not meet to be called so, 1 Cor. xv. 9. *Separated to the gospel of God.* The Pharisees had their name from separation, because they *separated themselves to the study of the law*, and might be called *ἀφωρισμένοι εἰς τὸν νόμον·* such a one Paul had formerly been; but now he had changed his studies, was *ἀφωρισμένος εἰς τὸ Εὐαγγέλιον*, a gospel Pharisee, separated by the counsel of God (Gal. i. 15), *separated from his mother's womb*, by an immediate direction of the Spirit, and a regular ordination according to that direction (Acts xiii. 2, 3), by a dedication of himself to this work. He was an entire devotee to the gospel of God, the gospel which has God for its author, the origin and extraction of it divine and heavenly.

II. Having mentioned the gospel of God, he digresses, to give us an encomium of it.

1. The antiquity of it. It was *promised before* (*v.* 2); it was no novel upstart doctrine, but of ancient standing in the promises and prophecies of the Old Testament, which did all unanimously point at the gospel, the morning-beams that ushered in the sun of righteousness : this not by word of mouth only, but in the scriptures.

2. The subject-matter of it : it is concerning Christ, *v.* 3, 4. The prophets and apostles all bear witness to him; he is the true treasure hid in the field of the scriptures. Observe, When Paul mentions Christ, how he heaps up his names and titles, *his Son Jesus Christ our Lord,* as one that took a pleasure in speaking of him; and, having mentioned him, he cannot go on in his discourse without some expression of love and honour, as here, where in one person he shows us his two distinct natures. (1.) His human nature : *Made of the seed of David* (*v.* 3), that is, born of the virgin Mary, who was of the house of David (Luke i. 27), as was Joseph his supposed father, Luke ii. 4. David is here mentioned, because of the special promises made to him concerning the Messiah, especially his kingly office ; 2 Sam. vii. 12; Ps. cxxxii. 11, compared with Luke i. 32, 33. (2.) His divine nature : *Declared to be the Son of God* (*v.* 4), the Son of God by eternal generation, or, as it is here explained, *according to the Spirit of holiness. According to the flesh,* that is, his human nature, *he was of the seed of David ;* but, *according to the Spirit of holiness*, that is, the divine nature (as he is said to be *quickened by the Spirit,* 1 Pet. iii. 18, compared with 2 Cor. xiii. 4), he is the Son of God. The great proof or demonstration of this is *his resurrection from the dead,* which proved it effectually and undeniably. The sign of the prophet Jonas, Christ's resurrection, was intended for the last conviction, Matt. xii. 39, 40. Those that would not be convinced by that would be convinced by nothing. So that we have here a summary of the gospel doctrine concerning Christ's two natures in one person.

3. The fruit of it (*v.* 5) : *By whom,* that is, by Christ manifested and made known in the gospel, *we (Paul* and the rest of the ministers) *have received grace and apostleship,* that is, the favour to be made apostles, Eph. iii. 8. The apostles were made a spectacle to the world, led a life of toil, and trouble, and hazard, *were killed all the day long,* and yet Paul reckons the apostleship a favour we may justly reckon it a great favour to be employed in any work or service for God, whatever difficulties or dangers we may meet with in it. This apostleship was received *for obedience to the faith,* that is, to bring people to that obedience; as Christ, so his ministers, received that they might give. Paul's was for this obedience *among all nations,* for he was the *apostle of the Gentiles, ch.* xi. 13. Observe the description here given of the Christian profession : it is *obedience to the faith.* It does not consist in a

notional knowledge or a naked assent, much less does it consist in perverse disputings, but in obedience. This obedience to the faith answers the *law of faith*, mentioned *ch.* iii. 27. The act of faith is the obedience of the understanding to God revealing, and the product of that is the obedience of the will to God commanding. To anticipate the ill use which might be made of the doctrine of justification by faith without the works of the law, which he was to explain in the following epistle, he here speaks of Christianity as an obedience. Christ has a yoke. "*Among whom are you, v.* 6. You Romans in this stand upon the same level with other Gentile nations of less fame and wealth ; you are all one in Christ." The gospel salvation is a common salvation, Jude 3. No respect of persons with God. *The called of Jesus Christ;* all those, and those only, are brought to an obedience of the faith that are effectually called of Jesus Christ.

III. The persons to whom it is written (*v.* 7): *To all that are in Rome, beloved of God, called to be saints ;* that is, to all the professing Christians that were in Rome, whether Jews or Gentiles originally, whether high or low, bond or free, learned or unlearned. Rich and poor meet together in Christ Jesus. Here is, 1. The privilege of Christians: They are *beloved of God*, they are members of that body which is beloved, which is God's *Hephzibah*, in which his delight is. We speak of God's love by his bounty and beneficence, and so he hath a common love to all mankind and a peculiar love for true believers; and between these there is a love he hath for all the body of visible Christians. 2. The duty of Christians; and that is to be holy, for hereunto are they called, *called to be saints,* called to salvation through sanctification. Saints, and only saints, are beloved of God with a special and peculiar love. Κλητοῖς ἁγίοις—*called saints,* saints in profession ; it were well if all that are called saints were saints indeed. Those that are called saints should labour to answer to the name; otherwise, though it is an honour and a privilege, yet it will be of little avail at the great day to have been called saints, if we be not really so.

IV. The apostolical benediction (*v.* 7): *Grace to you and peace.* This is one of the tokens in every epistle ; and it hath not only the affection of a good wish, but the authority of a blessing. The priests under the law were to bless the people, and so are gospel ministers, in the name of the Lord. In this usual benediction observe, 1. The favours desired: *Grace and peace.* The Old-Testament salutation was, *Peace be to you ;* but now grace is prefixed—*grace*, that is, the favour of God towards us or the work of God in us ; both are previously requisite to true peace. All gospel blessings are included in these two: *grace and peace. Peace,* that is, all good; peace with God, peace in your own consciences, peace with all that are about you; all these founded in grace. 2. The fountain of those favours, *from God our Father, and the Lord Jesus Christ.* All good comes, (1.) From God as a Father; he hath put himself into that relation to engage and encourage our desires and expectations; we are taught, when we come for grace and peace, to call him our Father. (2.) *From the Lord Jesus Christ,* as Mediator, and the great feoffee in trust for the conveying and securing of these benefits. We have them from his fulness, peace from the fulness of his merit, grace from the fulness of his Spirit.

8 First, I thank my God through
Jesus Christ for you all, that your
faith is spoken of throughout the
whole world. 9 For God is my
witness, whom I serve with my spirit
in the gospel of his Son, that without
ceasing I make mention of you always
in my prayers ; 10 Making request,
if by any means now at length I
might have a prosperous journey by
the will of God to come unto you.
11 For I long to see you, that I may
impart unto you some spiritual gift,
to the end ye may be established ;
12 That is, that I may be comforted
together with you by the mutual
faith both of you and me. 13 Now
I would not have you ignorant,
brethren, that oftentimes I purposed
to come unto you, (but was let
hitherto,) that I might have some
fruit among you also, even as among
other Gentiles. 14 I am debtor
both to the Greeks, and to the Barbarians ; both to the wise, and to the
unwise. 15 So, as much as in me is,
I am ready to preach the gospel to
you that are at Rome also.

We may here observe,

I. His thanksgivings for them (*v.* 8): *First, I thank my God.* It is good to begin every thing with blessing God, to make that *the alpha and omega* of every song, *in every thing to give thanks.—My God.* He speaks this with delight and triumph. In all our thanksgivings, it is good for us to eye God as our God; this makes every mercy sweet, when we can say of God, "He is mine in covenant."—*Through Jesus Christ.* All our duties and performances are pleasing to God only through Jesus Christ, praises as well as prayers.—*For you all.* We must express our love to our friends, not only by praying for them, but by praising God for them. God must have the glory of all the comfort we have in our friends; for every creature is that to us, and no more, which God makes it to be. Many of these Romans Paul had no personal acquaintance with, and yet he could heartily rejoice in their gifts and graces. When some of the Roman Christians met him (Acts xxviii. 15), he thanked God for them, and took courage; but here his true catholic love extends itself further, and he *thanks God for them all;* not only for those among them that were his helpers in Christ, and that bestowed much labour upon him (of whom he speaks *ch.* xvi. 3, 6), but for them all.—*That your faith is spoken of.* Paul travelled up and down from place to place, and, wherever he came, he heard great commendations of the Christians at Rome, which he mentions, not to make them proud, but to quicken them to answer the general character people gave of them, and the general expectation people had from them. The greater reputation a man hath for religion, the more careful he should be to preserve it, because *a little folly spoils him that is in reputation,* Eccl. x. 1.—*Throughout the whole world,* that is, the Roman empire, into which the Roman Christians, upon Claudius's edict to banish all the Jews from Rome, were scattered abroad, but had now returned, and, it seems, left a very good report behind them, wherever they had been, in all the churches. There was this good effect of their sufferings: if they had not been persecuted, they had not been famous. This was indeed a good name, a name for good things with God and good people. As the elders of old, so these Romans, *obtained a good report through faith,* Heb. xi. 2. It is a desirable thing to be famous for faith. The faith of the Roman Christians came to be thus talked of, not only because it was excelling in itself, but because it was eminent and observable in its circumstances. Rome was a city upon a hill, every one took notice of what was done there. Thus those who have many eyes upon them have need to walk circumspectly, for what they do, good or bad, will be spoken of. The church of Rome was then a flourishing church; but since that time how is the gold become dim! How is the most fine gold changed! Rome is not what it was. She was then espoused a *chaste virgin to Christ,* and excelled in beauty; but she has since *degenerated, dealt treacherously, and embraced the bosom of a stranger;* so that (as that good old book, *the Practice of Piety,* makes appear in no less than twenty-six instances) even *the epistle to the Romans* is now an epistle *against* the Romans; little reason has she therefore to boast of her former credit.

II. His prayer for them, *v.* 9. Though a famous flourishing church, yet they had need to be prayed for; they *had not yet attained.* Paul mentions this as an instance of his love to them. One of the greatest kindnesses we can do our friends, and sometimes the only kindness that is in the power of our hands, is, by prayer to recommend them to the loving-kindness of God. From Paul's example here we may learn, 1. Constancy in prayer: *Always without ceasing.* He did himself observe the same rules he gave to others, Eph. vi. 18; 1 Thes. v. 17. Not that Paul did nothing else but pray, but he kept up stated times for the solemn performance of that duty, and those very frequent, and observed without fail. 2. Charity in prayer: *I make mention of you.* Though he had no particular acquaintance with them, nor interest in them, yet he prayed for them; not only for all saints in general, but he made express mention of them. It is not unfit sometimes to be express in our prayers for particular churches and places; not to inform God, but to affect ourselves. We are likely to have the most comfort in those friends that we pray most for. Concerning this he makes a solemn appeal to the searcher of hearts: *For God is my witness.* It was in a weighty matter, and in a thing known only to God and his own heart, that he used this asseveration. It is very comfortable to be able to call God to witness to our sincerity and constancy in the discharge of a duty. God is particularly a witness to our secret prayers, the matter of them, the manner of the performance; then our Father sees in secret, Matt. vi. 6. *God, whom I serve with my spirit.* Those that serve God with their spirits may, with a humble confidence, appeal to him; hypocrites who rest in bodily exercise cannot. His particular prayer, among many other petitions he put up for them, was that he might have an opportunity of paying them a visit (*v.* 10): *Making request, if by any means,* &c. Whatever comfort we desire to find in any creature, we must have recourse to God for it by prayer; for *our times are in his hand,* and all our ways at his disposal. The expressions here used intimate that he was very desirous of such an opportunity: *if by any means;* that he had long and often been disappointed: *now at length;* and yet that he submitted it to the divine Providence: *a prosperous journey by the will of God.* As in our purposes, so in our desires, we must still remember to insert this, *if the Lord will,* James iv. 15. Our journeys are prosperous or otherwise according to the will of God, comfortable or not as he pleases.

III. His great desire to see them, with the reasons of it, *v.* 11—15. He had heard so much of them that he had a great desire to be better acquainted with them. Fruitful Christians are as much the joy as barren professors are the grief of faithful ministers. Accordingly, he *often purposed to come, but was let hitherto* (*v.* 13), for man purposeth, but God disposeth. He was hindered by other business that took him off, by his care of other churches, whose affairs were pressing; and Paul was for doing that first, not which was most pleasant (then he would have gone to Rome), but which was most needful—a good example to ministers, who must not consult their own inclinations so much as the necessity of their people's souls. Paul desired to visit these Romans,

1. That they might be edified (*v.* 11): *That I may impart unto you.* He received, that he might communicate. Never were full breasts so desirous to be drawn out to the sucking infant as Paul's head and heart were to be imparting spiritual gifts, that is, preaching to them. A good sermon is a good gift, so much the better for being a spiritual gift. —*To the end you may be established.* Having commended their flourishing he here expresses his desire of their establishment, that as they grew upward in the branches they might grow downward in the root. The best saints, while they are in such a shaking world as this, have need to be more and more established; and spiritual gifts are of special use for our establishment.

2. That he might be comforted, *v.* 12. What he heard of their flourishing in grace was so much a joy to him that it must needs be much more so to behold it. Paul could take comfort in the fruit of the labours of other ministers.—*By the mutual faith both of you and me,* that is, our mutual faithfulness and fidelity. It is very comfortable when there is a mutual confidence between minister and people, they confiding in him as a faithful minister, and he in them as a faithful people. Or, the mutual work of faith, which is love; they rejoiced in the expressions of one another's love, or communicating their faith one to another. It is very refreshing to Christians to compare notes about their spiritual concerns; thus are they sharpened, *as iron sharpens iron.*—*That I might have some fruit, v.* 13. Their edification would be his advantage, it would be fruit abounding to a good account. Paul minded his work, as one that believed the more good he did the greater would his reward be.

3. That he might discharge his trust as the apostle of the Gentiles (*v.* 14): *I am a debtor.* (1.) His receivings made him a debtor; for they were talents he was entrusted with to trade for his Master's honour. We should think of this when we covet great things, that all our receivings put us in debt; we are but stewards of our Lord's goods. (2.) His office made him a debtor. He was a debtor as he was an apostle; he was called and sent to work, and had engaged to mind it. Paul had improved his talent, and laboured in his work, and done as much good as ever any man did, and yet, in reflection upon it, he still writes himself debtor; for, *when we have done all, we are but unprofitable servants.*—*Debtor to the Greeks, and to the barbarians,* that is, as the following words explain it, *to the wise and to the unwise.* The Greeks fancied themselves to have the monopoly of wisdom, and looked upon all the rest of the world as barbarians, comparatively so; not cultivated with learning and arts as they were. Now Paul was a debtor to both, looked upon himself as obliged to do all the good he could both to the one and to the other. Accordingly, we find him paying his debt, both in his preaching and in his writing, doing good *both to Greeks and barbarians,* and suiting his discourse to the capacity of each. You may observe a difference between his sermon at Lystra among the plain Lycaonians (Acts xiv. 15, &c.) and his sermon at Athens among the polite philosophers, Acts xvii. 22, &c. He delivered both as debtor to each, giving to each their portion. Though a plain preacher, yet, as debtor to the wise, he speaks wisdom among those that are perfect, 1 Cor. ii. 6. For these reasons he was ready, if he had an opportunity, *to preach the gospel at Rome, v.* 15. Though a public plaee, though a perilous place, where Christianity met with a great deal of opposition, yet Paul was ready to run the risk at Rome, if called to it: *I am ready* —*πρόθυμον.* It denotes a great readiness of mind, and that he was very forward to it. What he did was not for filthy lucre, but of a ready mind. It is an excellent thing to be ready to meet every opportunity of doing or getting good.

16 For I am not ashamed of the gospel of Christ: for it is the power of God unto salvation to every one that believeth; to the Jew first, and also to the Greek. 17 For therein is the righteousness of God revealed from faith to faith: as it is written, The just shall live by faith. 18 For the wrath of God is revealed from heaven against all ungodliness and unrighteousness of men, who hold the truth in unrighteousness;

Paul here enters upon a large discourse of justification, in the latter part of this chapter laying down his thesis, and, in order to the proof of it, describing the deplorable condition of the Gentile world. His transition is very handsome, and like an orator: he was ready to preach the gospel at Rome, though a place where the gospel was run down by those that called themselves the wits; *for,* saith he, *I am not ashamed of it, v.* 16. There is a great deal in the gospel which such a man as Paul might be tempted to be ashamed of, especially that he whose gospel it is was a man hanged upon a tree, that the doctrine of it was plain, had little in it to set it off among scholars, the professors of it were mean and despised, and every where spoken against; yet Paul was not ashamed to own it. I reckon him a Christian indeed that is neither ashamed of the gospel nor a shame to it. The reason of this bold profession, taken from the nature and excellency of the gospel, introduces his dissertation.

I. The proposition, *v.* 16, 17. The excellency of the gospel lies in this, that it reveals to us,

1. The salvation of believers as the end: *It is the power of God unto salvation.* Paul is not ashamed of the gospel, how mean and contemptible soever it may appear to a carnal eye; for *the power of God works by it the salvation of all that believe;* it shows us *the way of salvation* (Acts xvi. 17), and is the great charter by which salvation is conveyed and made over to us. But, (1.) *It is through the power of God;* without that power the gospel is but a dead letter; the revelation of the gospel is the revelation of *the arm of the Lord* (Isa. liii. 1), as power went along with the word of Christ to heal diseases. (2.) It is to those, and those only, that believe. Believing interests us in the gospel salvation; to others it is hidden. The medicine prepared will not cure the patient if it be not taken.—*To the Jew first. The lost sheep of the house of Israel* had the first offer made them, both by Christ and his apostles. *You first* (Acts iii. 26), but upon their refusal the apostles turned to the Gentiles, Acts xiii. 46. Jews and Gentiles now stand upon the some level, both equally miserable without a Saviour, and both equally welcome to the Saviour, Col. iii. 11 Such doctrine as this was surprising to the Jews, who had hitherto been the peculiar people, and had looked with scorn upon the Gentile world; but the long-expected Messiah proves *a light to enlighten the Gentiles,* as well as *the glory of his people Israel.*

2. The justification of believers as the way (*v.* 17): *For therein,* that is, in this gospel, which Paul so much triumphs in, *is the righteousness of God revealed.* Our misery and ruin being the product and consequent of our iniquity, that which will show us the way of salvation must needs show us the way of justification, and this the gospel does. The gospel makes known a righteousness. While God is a just and holy God, and we are guilty sinners, it is necessary we should have a righteousness wherein to appear before him; and, blessed be God, there is such a righteousness brought in by Messiah the prince (Dan. ix. 24) and *revealed in the gospel;* a *righteousness,* that is, a gracious method of reconciliation and acceptance, notwithstanding the guilt of our sins. This evangelical righteousness, (1.) Is called the *righteousness of God;* it is of God's appointing, of God's approving and accepting. It is so called to cut off all pretensions to a righteousness resulting from the merit of our own works. It is the righteousness of Christ, who is God, resulting from a satisfaction of infinite value. (2.) It is said to be *from faith to faith,* from the faithfulness of God revealing to the faith of man receiving (so some); from the faith of dependence upon God, and dealing with him immediately, as Adam before the fall, to the faith of dependence upon a Mediator, and so dealing with God (so others); from the first faith, by which we are put into a justified state, to after faith, by which we live, and are continued in that state: and the faith that justifies us is no less than our taking Christ for our Saviour, and becoming true Christians, according to the tenour of the baptismal covenant; from faith engrafting us into Christ, to faith deriving virtue from him as our root: both implied in the next words, *The just shall live by faith. Just by faith,* there is faith justifying us; *live by faith,* there is faith maintaining us; and so *there is a righteousness from faith to faith.* Faith is all in all, both in the beginning and progress of a Christian life. It is not from faith to works, as if faith put us into a justified state, and then works preserved and maintained us in it, but it is all along from faith to faith, as 2 Cor. iii. 18, *from glory to glory;* it is increasing, continuing, persevering faith, faith pressing forward, and getting ground of unbelief. To show that this is no novel upstart doctrine, he quotes for it that famous scripture in the Old Testament, so often mentioned in the New (Hab. ii. 4): *The just shall live by faith.* Being justified by faith he shall live by it both the life of grace and of glory. The prophet there had placed himself upon the watch-tower, expecting some extraordinary discoveries (*v.* 1), and the discovery was of the certainty of the appearance of the promised Messiah in the fulness of time, notwithstanding seeming delays. This is there called *the vision,* by way of eminence, as elsewhere *the promise;* and while that time is coming, as well as when it has come, *the just shall live by faith.* Thus is the evangelical righteousness from faith to faith—from Old-Testament faith in a Christ to come to New-Testament faith in a Christ already come.

II. The proof of this proposition, that both Jews and Gentiles stand in need of a righteousness wherein to appear before God, and that neither the one nor the other have any of their own to plead. Justification must be either by faith or works. It cannot be by works, which he proves at large by describing the works both of Jews and Gentiles; and therefore he concludes it must be by faith, *ch.* iii. 20, 28. The apostle, like a skilful surgeon, before he applies the plaster, searches the wound—endeavours first to convince of guilt and wrath, and then to show the way of salvation. This makes the gospel the more welcome. We must first see the righteousness of God condemning, and then the righteousness of God justifying will appear *worthy of all acceptation.* In general (*v.* 18), *the wrath of God is revealed.* The light of nature and the light of the law reveal the wrath of God from sin to sin. It is well for us that the gospel reveals the justifying righteousness of God from faith to faith. The antithesis is observable. Here is

1. The sinfulness of man described; he reduceth it to two heads, *ungodliness and unrigh-*

teousness; ungodliness against the laws of the first table, unrighteousness against those of the second.

2. The cause of that sinfulness, and that is, *holding the truth in unrighteousness.* Some *communes notitiæ*, some ideas they had of the being of God, and of the difference of good and evil; but they held them in unrighteousness, that is, they knew and professed them in a consistency with their wicked courses. They held the truth as a captive or prisoner, that it should not influence them, as otherwise it would. An unrighteous wicked heart is the dungeon in which many a good truth is detained and buried. *Holding fast the form of sound words in faith and love* is the root of all religion (2 Tim. i. 13), but holding it fast in unrighteousness is the root of all sin.

3. The displeasure of God against it: *The wrath of God is revealed from heaven;* not only in the written word, *which is given by inspiration of God* (the Gentiles had not that), but in the providences of God, his judgments executed upon sinners, which do not spring out of the dust, or fall out by chance, nor are they to be ascribed to second causes, but they are a revelation from heaven. Or *wrath from heaven is revealed;* it is not the wrath of a man like ourselves, *but wrath from heaven,* therefore the more terrible and the more unavoidable.

19 Because that which may be
known of God is manifest in them;
for God hath showed *it* unto them.
20 For the invisible things of him
from the creation of the world are
clearly seen, being understood by the
things that are made, *even* his eternal
power and Godhead; so that they
are without excuse: 21 Because
that, when they knew God, they glorified *him* not as God, neither were
thankful; but became vain in their
imaginations, and their foolish heart
was darkened. 22 Professing themselves to be wise, they became fools,
23 And changed the glory of the
incorruptible God into an image
made like to corruptible man, and to
birds, and four footed beasts, and
creeping things. 24 Wherefore God
also gave them up to uncleanness
through the lusts of their own hearts,
to dishonour their own bodies between themselves: 25 Who changed
the truth of God into a lie, and
worshipped and served the creature
more than the Creator, who is
blessed for ever. Amen. 26 For
this cause God gave them up unto
vile affections: for even their women
did change the natural use into that
which is against nature: 27 And
likewise also the men, leaving the
natural use of the woman, burned in
their lust one toward another; men
with men working that which is unseemly, and receiving in themselves
that recompence of their error which
was meet. 28 And even as they did
not like to retain God in *their* knowledge, God gave them over to a
reprobate mind, to do those things
which are not convenient; 29 Being
filled with all unrighteousness, fornication, wickedness, covetousness,
maliciousness; full of envy, murder,
debate, deceit, malignity; whisperers,
30 Backbiters, haters of God, despiteful, proud, boasters, inventors of
evil things, disobedient to parents,
31 Without understanding, covenant-
breakers, without natural affection,
implacable, unmerciful: 32 Who
knowing the judgment of God, that
they which commit such things are
worthy of death, not only do the
same, but have pleasure in them that
do them.

In this last part of the chapter the apostle applies what he had said particularly to the Gentile world, in which we may observe,

I. The means and helps they had to come to the knowledge of God. Though they had not such a knowledge of his law as Jacob and Israel had (Ps. cxlvii. 20), yet among them *he left not himself without witness* (Acts xiv. 17): *For that which may be known,* &c., *v.* 19. 20. Observe,

1. What discoveries they had: *That which may be known of God is manifest,* ἐν αὐτοῖς—*among them;* that is, there were some even among them that had the knowledge of God, were convinced of the existence of one supreme *Numen.* The philosophy of Pythagoras, Plato, and the Stoics, discovered a great deal of the knowledge of God, as appears by abundance of testimonies. *That which may be known,* which implies that there is a great deal which may not be known. The being of God may be apprehended, but cannot be comprehended. We cannot by searching find him out, Job xi. 7—9. Finite understandings cannot perfectly know an infinite being; but, blessed be God, there is that which may be known, enough to lead us to our chief end, the glorifying and enjoying of him; and these things revealed belong to us and to our children, while secret things are not to be pried into, Deut. xxix. 29.

2. Whence they had these discoveries: *God hath shown it to them.* Those common natural notions which they had of God were imprinted upon their hearts by the God of nature himself, who is the *Father of lights.* This sense of a Deity, and a regard to that Deity, are so connate with the human nature that some think we are to distinguish men from brutes by these rather than by reason.

3. By what way and means these discoveries and notices which they had were confirmed and improved, namely, by the work of creation (*v.* 20): *For the invisible things of God,* &c.

(1.) Observe what they knew: *The invisible things of him, even his eternal power and Godhead.* Though God be not the object of sense, yet he hath discovered and made known himself by those things that are sensible. The power and Godhead of God are invisible things, and yet are clearly seen in their products. He works in secret (Job xxiii. 8, 9; Ps. cxxxix. 15; Eccl. xi. 5), but manifests what he has wrought, and therein makes known his power and Godhead, and others of his attributes which natural light apprehends in the idea of a God. They could not come by natural light to the knowledge of the three persons in the Godhead (though some fancy they have found footsteps of this in Plato's writings), but they did come to the knowledge of the Godhead, at least so much knowledge as was sufficient to have kept them from idolatry. This was that truth which they held in unrighteousness.

(2.) How they knew it: *By the things that are made,* which could not make themselves, nor fall into such an exact order and harmony by any casual hits; and therefore must have been produced by some first cause or intelligent agent, which first cause could be no other than an eternal powerful God. See Ps. xix. 1; Isa. xl. 26; Acts xvii. 24. The workman is known by his work. The variety, multitude, order, beauty, harmony, different nature, and excellent contrivance, of the things that are made, the direction of them to certain ends, and the concurrence of all the parts to the good and beauty of the whole, do abundantly prove a Creator and his eternal power and Godhead. Thus did the light shine in the darkness. And *this from the creation of the world.* Understand it either, [1.] As the topic from which the knowledge of them is drawn. To evince this truth, we have recourse to the great work of creation. And some think this *κτίσις κόσμου, this creature of the world* (as it may be read), is to be understood of man, the *κτίσις κατ' ἐξοχὴν—the most remarkable creature* of the lower world, called *κτίσις*, Mark xvi. 15. The frame and structure of human bodies, and especially the most excellent powers, faculties, and capacities of human souls, do abundantly prove that there is a Creator, and that he is God. Or, [2.] As the date of the discovery. It as old as the creation of the world. In this sense *ἀπὸ κτίσεως κόσμου* is most frequently used in scripture. These notices concerning God are not any modern discoveries, hit upon of late, but ancient truths, which were from the beginning. The way of the acknowledgment of God is a good old way; it was from the beginning. Truth got the start of error.

II. Their gross idolatry, notwithstanding these discoveries that God made to them of himself; described here, *v.* 21—23, 25. We shall the less wonder at the inefficacy of these natural discoveries to prevent the idolatry of the Gentiles if we remember how prone even the Jews, who had scripture light to guide them, were to idolatry; so miserably are the degenerate sons of men plunged in the mire of sense. Observe,

1. The inward cause of their idolatry, *v.* 21, 22. They are therefore without excuse, in that they did know God, and from what they knew might easily infer that it was their duty to worship him, and him only. Though some have greater light and means of knowledge than others, yet all have enough to leave them inexcusable. But the mischief of it was that, (1.) They *glorified him not as God.* Their affections towards him, and their awe and adoration of him, did not keep pace with their knowledge. To glorify him as God is to glorify him only; for there can be but one infinite: but they did not so glorify him, for they set up a multitude of other deities. To glorify him as God is to worship him with spiritual worship; but they made images of him. Not to glorify God as God is in effect not to glorify him at all; to respect him as a creature is not to glorify him, but to dishonour him. (2.) *Neither were they thankful;* not thankful for the favours in general they received from God (insensibleness of God's mercies is at the bottom of our sinful departures from him); not thankful in particular for the discoveries God was pleased to make of himself to them. Those that do not improve the means of knowledge and grace are justly reckoned unthankful for them. (3.) *But they became vain in their imaginations, ἐν τοῖς διαλογισμοῖς—in their reasonings,* in their practical inferences. They had a great deal of knowledge of general truths (*v.* 19), but no prudence to apply them to particular cases. Or, in their notions of God, and the creation of the world, and the origination of mankind, and the chief good; in these things, when they quitted the plain truth, they soon disputed themselves into a thousand vain and foolish fancies. The several opinions and hypotheses of the various sects of philosophers concerning these things were so many vain imaginations. When truth is forsaken, errors multiply *in infinitum—infinitely.* (4.) *And their foolish heart was darkened.* The foolishness and practical wickedness of the heart cloud and darken the intellectual powers and faculties. Nothing tends more to the blinding and perverting of the under-

standing than the corruption and depravedness of the will and affections. (5.) *Professing themselves to be wise, they became fools, v.* 22. This looks black upon the philosophers, the pretenders to wisdom and professors of it. Those that had the most luxuriant fancy, in framing to themselves the idea of a God, fell into the most gross and absurd conceits: and it was the just punishment of their pride and self-conceitedness. It has been observed that the most refined nations, that made the greatest show of wisdom, were the arrantest fools in religion The barbarians adored the sun and moon, which of all others was the most specious idolatry; while the learned Egyptians worshipped an ox and an onion. The Grecians, who excelled them in wisdom, adored diseases and human passions. The Romans, the wisest of all, worshipped the furies. And at this day the poor Americans worship the thunder; while the ingenious Chinese adore the devil. Thus the *world by wisdom knew not God,* 1 Cor. i. 21. As a profession of wisdom is an aggravation of folly, so a proud conceit of wisdom is the cause of a great deal of folly. Hence we read of few philosophers who were converted to Christianity; and Paul's preaching was no where so laughed at and ridiculed as among the learned Athenians, Acts xvii. 18—32. Φάσκοντες εἶναι—*conceiting themselves* to be wise. The plain truth of the being of God would not content them; they thought themselves above that, and so fell into the greatest errors.

2. The outward acts of their idolatry, *v.* 23—25. (1.) Making images of God (*v.* 23), by which, as much as in them lay, they *changed the glory of the incorruptible God.* Compare Ps. cvi. 20; Jer. ii. 11. They ascribed a deity to the most contemptible creatures, and by them represented God. It was the greatest honour God did to man that he made man in the image of God; but it is the greatest dishonour man has done to God that he has made God in the image of man. This was what God so strictly warned the Jews against, Deut. iv. 15, &c. This the apostle shows the folly of in his sermon at Athens, Acts xvii. 29. See Isa. xl. 18, &c.; xliv. 10, &c. This is called (*v.* 25) *changing the truth of God into a lie.* As it did dishonour his glory, so it did misrepresent his being. Idols are called lies, for they belie God, as if he had a body, whereas he is a Spirit, Jer. xxiii. 14; Hos. vii. 1. *Teachers of lies,* Hab. ii. 18. (2.) Giving divine honour to the creature: *Worshipped and served the creature,* παρὰ τὸν κτίσαντα—*besides the Creator.* They did own a supreme *Numen* in their profession, but they did in effect disown him by the worship they paid to the creature; for God will be all or none. Or, *above* the Creator, paying more devout respect to their inferior deities, stars, heroes, demons, thinking the supreme God inaccessible, or above their worship. The sin itself was their worshipping the creature at all; but this is mentioned as an aggravation of the sin, that they worshipped the creature more than the Creator. This was the general wickedness of the Gentile world, and became twisted in with their laws and government; in compliance with which even the wise men among them, who knew and owned a supreme God and were convinced of the nonsense and absurdity of their polytheism and idolatry, yet did as the rest of their neighbours did. *Seneca,* in his book *De Superstitione,* as it is quoted by *Aug. de Civit. Dei,* lib. vi. cap. 10 (for the book itself is lost), after he had largely shown the great folly and impiety of the vulgar religion, in divers instances of it, yet concludes, *Quæ omnia sapiens servabit tanquam legibus jussa, non tanquam diis grata —All which a wise man will observe as established by law, not imagining them grateful to the gods.* And afterwards, *Omnem istam ignobilem deorum turbam, quam longo ævo longa superstitio congessit, sic adorabimus, ut meminerimus cultum ejus magis ad morem quam ad rem pertinere—All this ignoble rout of gods, which ancient superstition has amassed together by long prescription, we will so adore as to remember that the worship of them is rather a compliance with custom than material in itself.* Upon which Augustine observes, *Colebat quod reprehendebat, agebat quod arguebat, quod culpabat adorabat—He worshipped that which he censured, he did that which he had proved wrong, and he adored what he found fault with.* I mention this thus largely because methinks it doth fully explain that of the apostle here (*v.* 18): *Who hold the truth in unrighteousness.* It is observable that upon the mention of the dishonour done to God by the idolatry of the Gentiles the apostle, in the midst of his discourse, expresses himself in an awful adoration of God: *Who is blessed for ever. Amen.* When we see or hear of any contempt cast upon God or his name, we should thence take occasion to think and speak highly and honourably of him. In this, as in other things, the worse others are, the better we should be. *Blessed for ever,* notwithstanding these dishonours done to his name: though there are those that do not glorify him, yet he is glorified, and will be glorified to eternity.

III. The judgments of God upon them for this idolatry; not many temporal judgments (the idolatrous nations were the conquering ruling nations of the world), but spiritual judgments, giving them up to the most brutish and unnatural lusts. Παρέδωκεν αὐτοὺς —*He gave them up;* it is thrice repeated here, *v.* 24, 26, 28. Spiritual judgments are of all judgments the sorest, and to be most dreaded. Observe,

1. By whom they were given up. God gave them up, in a way of righteous judgment, as the just punishment of their idolatry—taking off the bridle of restraining grace—leaving them to themselves—letting

them alone; for his grace is his own, he is debtor to no man, he may give or withhold his grace at pleasure. Whether this giving up be a positive act of God or only privative we leave to the schools to dispute: but this we are sure of that it is no new thing for God to give men up to their own hearts' lusts, to send them strong delusions, to let Satan loose upon them, nay, to lay stumbling-blocks before them. And yet God is not the author of sin, but herein infinitely just and holy; for, though the greatest wickedness follow upon this giving up, the fault of that is to be laid upon the sinner's wicked heart. If the patient be obstinate, and will not submit to the methods prescribed, but wilfully takes and does that which is prejudicial to him, the physician is not to be blamed if he give him up as in a desperate condition; and all the fatal symptoms that follow are not to be imputed to the physician, but to the disease itself and to the folly and wilfulness of the patient.

2. To what they were given up.

(1.) *To uncleanness and vile affections*, *v.* 24, 26, 27. Those that would not entertain the more pure and refined notices of natural light, which tend to preserve the honour of God, justly forfeited those more gross and palpable sentiments which preserve the honour of human nature. *Man being in honour*, and refusing to understand the God that made him, thus becomes worse than the *beasts that perish*, Ps. xlix. 20. Thus one, by the divine permission, becomes the punishment of another; but it is (as it is said here) *through the lusts of their own hearts*—there all the fault is to be laid. Those who dishonoured God were given up to dishonour themselves. A man cannot be delivered up to a greater slavery than to be given up to his own lusts. Such are given over, like the Egyptians (Isa. xix. 4), into the hand of a cruel lord. The particular instances of their uncleanness and vile affections are their unnatural lusts, for which many of the heathen, even of those among them who passed for wise men, as Solon and Zeno, were infamous, against the plainest and most obvious dictates of natural light. The crying iniquity of Sodom and Gomorrah, for which God rained hell from heaven upon them, became not only commonly practised, but avowed, in the pagan nations. Perhaps the apostle especially refers to the abominations that were committed in the worship of their idol-gods, in which the worst of uncleannesses were prescribed for the honour of their gods; dunghill service for dunghill gods: the unclean spirits delight in such ministrations. In the church of Rome, where the pagan idolatries are revived, images worshipped, and saints only substituted in the room of demons, we hear of these same abominations going barefaced, licensed by the pope (*Fox's Acts and Monuments*, vol. i. p. 808), and not only commonly perpetrated, but justified and pleaded for by some of their cardinals: the same spiritual plagues for the same spiritual wickednesses. See what wickedness there is in the nature of man. How abominable and filthy is man! *Lord, what is man?* says David; what a vile creature is he when left to himself! How much are we beholden to the restraining grace of God for the preserving any thing of the honour and decency of the human nature! For, were it not for this, man, who was made but little lower than the angels, would make himself a great deal lower than the devils. This is said to be that *recompence of their error which was meet.* The Judge of all the earth does right, and observes a meetness between the sin and the punishment of it.

(2.) To a reprobate mind in these abominations, *v.* 28.

[1.] They *did not like to retain God in their knowledge.* The blindness of their understandings was caused by the wilful aversion of their wills and affections. They did not retain God in their knowledge, because they did not like it. They would neither know nor do any thing but just what pleased themselves. It is just the temper of carnal hearts; the pleasing of themselves is their highest end. There are many that have God in their knowledge, they cannot help it, the light shines so fully in their faces; but they do not retain him there. They *say to the Almighty, Depart* (Job xxi. 14), and they therefore do not retain God in their knowledge because it thwarts and contradicts their lusts; they do not like it. In their knowledge—*ἐν ἐπιγνώσει.* There is a difference between *γνῶσις* and *ἐπιγνωσις*, the *knowledge* and the *acknowledgment* of God; the pagans knew God, but did not, would not, acknowledge him.

[2.] Answerable to this wilfulness of theirs, in gainsaying the truth, God gave them over to a wilfulness in the grossest sins, here called a *reprobate mind—εἰς ἀδόκιμον νοῦν*, a mind void of all sense and judgment to discern things that differ, so that they could not distinguish their right hand from their left in spiritual things. See whither a course of sin leads, and into what a gulf it plunges the sinner at last; hither fleshly lusts have a direct tendency. *Eyes full of adultery cannot cease from sin*, 2 Pet. ii. 14. This reprobate mind was a blind seared conscience, past feeling, Eph. iv. 19. When the judgment is once reconciled to sin, the man is in the suburbs of hell. At first Pharaoh hardened his heart, but afterwards God hardened Pharaoh's heart. Thus wilful hardness is justly punished with judicial hardness.—*To do those things which are not convenient.* This phrase may seem to bespeak a diminutive evil but here it is expressive of the grossest enormities; things that are not agreeable to men, but contradict the very light and law of nature. And here he subjoins a black list of those unbecoming things which the Gentiles were guilty of, being delivered up to a reprobate mind. No wickedness so heinous, so contrary to the light of nature, to the law of nations, and to all the interests of mankind, but a reprobate mind will comply with it. By the histories of those times, especially the accounts we have of the then prevailing dispositions and practices of the Romans when the ancient virtue of that commonwealth was so degenerated, it appears that these sins here mentioned were then and there reigning national sins. No fewer than twenty-three several sorts of sins and sinners are here specified, *v.* 29—31. Here the devil's seat is; his name is legion, for they are many. It was time to have the gospel preached among them, for the world had need of reformation.

First, Sins against the first table: *Haters of God.* Here is the devil in his own colours, sin appearing sin. Could it be imagined that rational creatures should hate the chief good, and depending creatures abhor the fountain of their being? And yet so it is. Every sin has in it a hatred of God; but some sinners are more open and avowed enemies to him than others, Zech. xi. 8. *Proud men and boasters* cope with God himself, and put those crowns upon their own heads which must be cast before his throne.

Secondly, Sins against the second table. These are especially mentioned, because in these things they had a clearer light. In general here is a charge of unrighteousness. This is put first, for every sin is unrighteousness; it is withholding that which is due, perverting that which is right; it is especially put for second-table sins, doing as we would not be done by. Against the fifth commandment: *Disobedient to parents,* and *without natural affection—ἀστόργους,* that is, parents unkind and cruel to their children. Thus, when duty fails on one side, it commonly fails on the other. Disobedient children are justly punished with unnatural parents; and, on the contrary, unnatural parents with disobedient children. Against the sixth commandment: *Wickedness* (doing mischief for mischief's sake), *maliciousness, envy, murder, debate* (*ἔριδος—contention*), *malignity, despiteful, implacable, unmerciful;* all expressions of that hatred of our brother which is heart-murder. Against the seventh commandment: *Fornication;* he mentions no more, having spoken before of other uncleannesses. Against the eighth commandment: *Unrighteousness, covetousness.* Against the ninth commandment: *Deceit, whisperers, back-biters, covenant-breakers,* lying and slandering. Here are two generals not before mentioned—*inventors of evil things, and without understanding;* wise to do evil, and yet having no knowledge to do good. The more deliberate and politic sinners are in inventing evil things, the greater is their sin: so quick of invention in sin, and yet without understanding (stark fools) in the thoughts of God. Here is enough to humble us all, in the sense of our original corruption; for every heart by nature has in it the seed and spawn of all these sins. In the close he mentions the aggravations of the sins, *v.* 32. 1. They *knew the judgment of God;* that is, (1.) They knew the law. The judgment of God is that which his justice requires, which, because he is just, he judgeth meet to be done. (2.) They knew the penalty; so it is explained here: They knew *that those who commit such things were worthy of death,* eternal death; their own consciences could not but suggest this to them, and yet they ventured upon it. It is a great aggravation of sin when it is committed against knowledge (James iv. 17), especially against the knowledge of the judgment of God. It is daring presumption to run upon the sword's point. It argues the heart much hardened, and very resolutely set upon sin. 2. They *not only do the same, but have pleasure in those that do them.* The violence of some present temptation may hurry a man into the commission of such sins himself in which the vitiated appetite may take a pleasure; but to be pleased with other people's sins is to love sin for sin's sake: it is joining in a confederacy for the devil's kingdom and interest. Συνευδοκοῦσι: they do not only commit sin, but they defend and justify it, and encourage others to do the like. Our own sins are much aggravated by our concurrence with, and complacency in, the sins of others.

Now lay all this together, and then say whether the Gentile world, lying under so much guilt and corruption, could be justified before God by any works of their own.

CHAP. II.

The scope of the first two chapters of this epistle may be gathered from ch. iii. 9, "We have before proved both Jews and Gentiles that they are all under sin." This we have proved upon the Gentiles (chap. i.), now in this chapter he proves it upon the Jews, as appears by ver. 17, "thou art called a Jew." I. He proves in general that Jews and Gentiles stand upon the same level before the justice of God, to ver. 11. II. He shows more particularly what sins the Jews were guilty of, notwithstanding their profession and vain pretensions, ver. 17, to the end.

THEREFORE thou art inexcusable, O man, whosoever thou
art that judgest: for wherein thou
judgest another, thou condemnest
thyself; for thou that judgest doest
the same things. 2 But we are sure
that the judgment of God is according to truth against them which commit such things. 3 And thinkest
thou this, O man, that judgest them
which do such things, and doest the
same, that thou shalt escape the judgment of God? 4 Or despisest thou
the riches of his goodness and forbearance and longsuffering; not
knowing that the goodness of God
leadeth thee to repentance? 5 But
after thy hardness and impenitent
heart treasurest up unto thyself wrath
against the day of wrath and revela-

tion of the righteous judgment of
God; 6 Who will render to every
man according to his deeds: 7 To
them who by patient continuance in
well doing seek for glory and honour
and immortality, eternal life: 8 But
unto them that are contentious, and
do not obey the truth, but obey unrighteousness, indignation, and wrath,
9 Tribulation and anguish, upon every
soul of man that doeth evil, of the
Jew first, and also of the Gentile;
10 But glory, honour, and peace, to
every man that worketh good, to the
Jew first, and also to the Gentile:
11 For there is no respect of persons
with God. 12 For as many as have
sinned without law shall also perish
without law: and as many as have
sinned in the law shall be judged by
the law; 13 (For not the hearers of
the law *are* just before God, but the
doers of the law shall be justified.
14 For when the Gentiles, which
have not the law, do by nature the
things contained in the law, these,
having not the law, are a law unto
themselves: 15 Which show the
work of the law written in their hearts,
their conscience also bearing witness,
and *their* thoughts the mean while
accusing or else excusing one another;)
16 In the day when God shall judge
the secrets of men by Jesus Christ
according to my gospel.

In the former chapter the apostle had represented the state of the Gentile world to be as bad and black as the Jews were ready enough to pronounce it. And now, designing to show that the state of the Jews was very bad too, and their sin in many respects more aggravated, to prepare his way he sets himself in this part of the chapter to show that God would proceed upon equal terms of justice with Jews and Gentiles; and not with such a partial hand as the Jews were apt to think he would use in their favour.

I. He arraigns them for their censoriousness and self-conceit (*v.* 1): *Thou art inexcusable, O man, whosoever thou art that judgest.* As he expresses himself in general terms, the admonition may reach those *many masters* (Jam. iii. 1), of whatever nation or profession they are, that assume to themselves a power to censure, control, and condemn others. But he intends especially the Jews, and to them particularly he applies this general charge (*v.* 21), *Thou who teachest another teachest thou not thyself?* The Jews were generally a proud sort of people, that looked with a great deal of scorn and contempt upon the poor Gentiles, as not worthy to be set with the dogs of their flock; while in the mean time they were themselves as bad and immoral—though not idolaters, as the Gentiles, yet sacrilegious, *v.* 22. *Therefore thou art inexcusable.* If the Gentiles, who had but the light of nature, were inexcusable (*ch.* i. 20), much more the Jews, who had the light of the law, the revealed will of God, and so had greater helps than the Gentiles.

II. He asserts the invariable justice of the divine government *v.* 2, 3. To drive home the conviction, he here shows what a righteous God that is with whom we have to do, and how just in his proceedings. It is usual with the apostle Paul, in his writings, upon mention of some material point, to make large digressions upon it; as here concerning the justice of God (*v.* 2), That the *judgment of God is according to truth,*—according to the eternal rules of justice and equity,—according to the heart, and not according to the outward appearance (1 Sam. xvi. 7),—according to the works, and not with respect to persons, is a doctrine which we are all sure of, for he would not be God if he were not just; but it behoves those especially to consider it who condemn others for those things which they themselves are guilty of, and so, while they practise sin and persist in that practice, think to bribe the divine justice by protesting against sin and exclaiming loudly upon others that are guilty, as if preaching against sin would atone for the guilt of it. But observe how he puts it to the sinner's conscience (*v.* 3): *Thinkest thou this, O man?* O man, a rational creature, a dependent creature, made by God, subject under him, and accountable to him. The case is so plain that we may venture to appeal to the sinner's own thoughts: "Canst thou think that *thou shalt escape the judgment of God?* Can the heart-searching God be imposed upon by formal pretences, the righteous Judge of all so bribed and put off?" The most plausible politic sinners, who acquit themselves before men with the greatest confidence, cannot *escape the judgment of God,* cannot avoid being judged and condemned.

III. He draws up a charge against them (*v.* 4, 5) consisting of two branches:—

1. Slighting the goodness of God (*v.* 4), *the riches of his goodness.* This is especially applicable to the Jews, who had singular tokens of the divine favour. Means are mercies, and the more light we sin against the more love we sin against. Low and mean thoughts of the divine goodness are at the bottom of a great deal of sin. There is in every wilful sin an interpretative contempt of the goodness of God; it is spurning at his bowels, particularly the goodness of his patience, his forbearance and long-suffering, taking occasion thence to be so much the more bold in sin, Eccl. viii. 11. *Not knowing,*

that is, not considering, not knowing practically and with application, that *the goodness of God leadeth thee*, the design of it is to lead thee, *to repentance*. It is not enough for us to know that God's goodness leads to repentance, but we must know that it leads *us—thee* in particular. See here what method God takes to bring sinners to repentance. He leads them, not drives them like beasts, but leads them like rational creatures, allures them (Hos. ii. 14); and it is goodness that leads, bands of love, Hos. xi. 4. Compare Jer. xxxi. 3. The consideration of the goodness of God, his common goodness to all (the goodness of his providence, of his patience, and of his offers), should be effectual to bring us all to repentance; and the reason why so many continue in impenitency is because they do not know and consider this.

2. Provoking the wrath of God, *v.* 5. The rise of this provocation is a *hard and impenitent heart;* and the ruin of sinners is their walking after such a heart, being led by it. To sin is to walk in the way of the heart; and when that is a hard and impenitent heart (contracted hardness by long custom, besides that which is natural), how desperate must the course needs be! The provocation is expressed by *treasuring up wrath.* Those that go on in a course of sin are treasuring up unto themselves wrath. A treasure denotes abundance. It is a treasure that will be spending to eternity, and yet never exhausted; and yet sinners are still adding to it as to a treasure. Every wilful sin adds to the score, and will inflame the reckoning; it brings a *branch to their wrath,* as some read that (Ezek. viii. 17), they *put the branch to their nose.* A treasure denotes secrecy. The treasury or magazine of wrath is the heart of God himself, in which it lies hid, as treasures in some secret place sealed up; see Deut. xxxii. 34; Job xiv. 17. But withal it denotes reservation to some further occasion; as the treasures of the hail are reserved against the day of battle and war, Job xxxviii. 22, 23. These treasures will be broken open like the fountains of the great deep, Gen. vii. 11. They are treasured up *against the day of wrath,* when they will be dispensed by the wholesale, poured out by full vials. Though the present day be a day of patience and forbearance towards sinners, yet there is a day of wrath coming—wrath, and nothing but wrath. Indeed, every day is to sinners a day of wrath, for God is *angry with the wicked every day* (Ps. vii. 11), but there is the *great day of wrath* coming, Rev. vi. 17. And that day of wrath will be *the day of the revelation of the righteous judgment of God.* The wrath of God is not like our wrath, a heat and passion; no, fury is not in him (Isa. xxvii. 4): but it is a righteous judgment, his will to punish sin, because he hates it as contrary to his nature. This righteous judgment of God is now many times concealed in the prosperity and success of sinners, but shortly it will be manifested before all the world, these seeming disorders set to rights, and the heavens shall declare his righteousness, Ps. l. 6. *Therefore judge nothing before the time.*

IV. He describes the measures by which God proceeds in his judgment. Having mentioned the righteous judgment of God in *v.* 5, he here illustrates that judgment, and the righteousness of it, and shows what we may expect from God, and by what rule he will judge the world. The equity of distributive justice is the dispensing of frowns and favours with respect to deserts and without respect to persons: such is the righteous judgment of God.

1. He will *render to every man according to his deeds* (*v.* 6), a truth often mentioned in scripture, to prove that the Judge of all the earth does right.

(1.) In dispensing his favours; and this is mentioned twice here, both in *v.* 7 and *v.* 10. For he delights to show mercy. Observe,

[1.] The objects of his favour: *Those who by patient continuance,* &c. By this we may try our interest in the divine favour, and may hence be directed what course to take, that we may obtain it. Those whom the righteous God will reward are, *First,* Such as fix to themselves the right end, that *seek for glory, and honour, and immortality;* that is, the glory and honour which are immortal—acceptance with God here and for ever. There is a holy ambition which is at the bottom of all practical religion, This is seeking the kingdom of God, looking in our desires and aims as high as heaven, and resolved to take up with nothing short of it. This seeking implies a loss, sense of that loss, desire to retrieve it, and pursuits and endeavours consonant to those desires. *Secondly,* Such as, having fixed the right end, adhere to the right way: *A patient continuance in well-doing.* 1 There must be well-doing, working good, *v.* 10. It is not enough to know well, and speak well, and profess well, and promise well, but we must do well: do that which is good, not only for the matter of it, but for the manner of it. We must do it well. 2. A continuance in well-doing. Not for a fit and a start, like the morning cloud and the early dew; but we must endure to the end: it is perseverance that wins the crown. 3. A patient continuance. This patience respects not only the length of the work, but the difficulties of it and the oppositions and hardships we may meet with in it. Those that will do well and continue in it must put on a great deal of patience.

[2.] The product of his favour. He will render to such eternal life. Heaven is life, eternal life, and it is the reward of those that patiently continue in well-doing; and it is called (*v.* 10) *glory, honour, and peace.* Those that seek for glory and honour (*v.* 7) shall have them. Those that seek for the vain glory and honour of this world often miss of them, and are disappointed; but those that seek for immortal glory and honour shall have them, and not only *glory and honour*, but *peace*. Worldly glory and honour are commonly attended with trouble; but heavenly glory and honour have peace with them, undisturbed everlasting peace.

(2.) In dispensing his frowns (*v.* 8, 9). Observe, [1.] The objects of his frowns. In general those that do evil, more particularly described to be *such as are contentious and do not obey the truth*. Contentious against God. Every wilful sin is a quarrel with God, it is *striving with our Maker* (Isa. xlv. 9), the most desperate contention. The Spirit of God strives with sinners (Gen. vi. 3), and impenitent sinners strive against the Spirit, rebel against the light (Job xxiv. 13), hold fast deceit, strive to retain that sin which the Spirit strives to part them from. *Contentious, and do not obey the truth.* The truths of religion are not only to be known, but to be obeyed; they are directing, ruling, commanding; truths relating to practice. Disobedience to the truth is interpreted a striving against it. *But obey unrighteousness*—do what unrighteousness bids them do. Those that refuse to be the servants of truth will soon be the slaves of unrighteousness. [2.] The products or instances of these frowns: *Indignation and wrath, tribulation and anguish.* These are the wages of sin. *Indignation and wrath* the causes—*tribulation and anguish* the necessary and unavoidable effects. And this *upon the soul;* souls are the vessels of that wrath, the subjects of that tribulation and anguish. Sin qualifies the soul for this wrath. The soul is that in or of man which is alone immediately capable of this indignation, and the impressions or effects of anguish therefrom. Hell is eternal tribulation and anguish, the product of wrath and indignation. This comes of contending with God, of setting briers and thorns before a consuming fire, Isa. xxvii. 4. Those that will not bow to his golden sceptre will certainly be broken by his iron rod. Thus will God render to every man according to his deeds.

2 *There is no respect of persons with God*, *v.* 11. As to the spiritual state, there is a respect of persons; but not as to outward relation or condition. Jews and Gentiles stand upon the same level before God. This was Peter's remark upon the first taking down of the partition-wall (Acts x. 34), that God is no respecter of persons; and it is explained in the next words, that *in every nation he that fears God, and works righteousness, is accepted of him.* God does not save men with respect to their external privileges or their barren knowledge and profession of the truth, but according as their state and disposition really are. In dispensing both his frowns and favours it is both to Jew and Gentile. If to *the Jews first,* who had greater privileges, and made a greater profession, yet *also to the Gentiles,* whose want of such privileges will neither excuse them from the punishment of their ill-doing nor bar them out from the reward of their well-doing (see Col. iii. 11); for shall not the Judge of all the earth do right?

V. He proves the equity of his proceedings with all, when he shall actually come to Judge them (*v.* 12—16), upon this principle, that that which is the rule of man's obedience is the rule of God's judgment. Three degrees of light are revealed to the children of men:—

1. The light of nature. This the Gentiles have, and by this they shall be judged: *As many as have sinned without law shall perish without law;* that is, the unbelieving Gentiles, who had no other guide but natural conscience, no other motive but common mercies, and had not the law of Moses nor any supernatural revelation, shall not be reckoned with for the transgression of the law they never had, nor come under the aggravation of the Jews' sin against and judgment by the written law; but they shall be judged by, as they sin against, the law of nature, not only as it is in their hearts, corrupted, defaced, and imprisoned in unrighteousness, but as in the uncorrupt original the Judge keeps by him. Further to clear this (*v.* 14, 15), in a parenthesis, he evinces that the light of nature was to the Gentiles instead of a written law. He had said (*v.* 12) they had *sinned without law,* which looks like a contradiction; for where there is no law there is no transgression. But, says he, though they had not the written law (Ps. cxlvii. 20), they had that which was equivalent, not to the ceremonial, but to the moral law. They *had the work of the law.* He does not mean that work which the law commands, as if they could produce a perfect obedience; but that work which the law does. The work of the law is to direct us what to do, and to examine us what we have done. Now, (1.) They had that which directed them what to do by the light of nature: by the force and tendency of their natural notions and dictates they apprehended a clear and vast difference between good and evil. They *did by nature the things contained in the law.* They had a sense of justice and equity, honour and purity, love and charity; the light of nature taught obedience to parents, pity to the miserable, conservation of public peace and order, forbade murder, stealing, lying, perjury, &c. Thus they were a *law unto themselves.* (2.) They had that which examined them as to what they had done: *Their conscience also bearing witness.* They had that within them which approved and commended what was well done and which reproached them for what was done amiss. Conscience is a witness, and first or last will bear witness, though for a time it may be bribed or brow-beaten. It is instead of a thousand witnesses, testifying of that which is most secret; and their *thoughts accusing or excusing,* passing a judgment upon the testimony of conscience

by applying the law to the fact. Conscience is that candle of the Lord which was not quite put out, no, not in the Gentile world. The heathen have witnessed to the comfort of a good conscience.

> ———Hic murus aheneus esto,
> Nil conscire sibi———
>
> Be this thy brazen bulwark of defence,
> Still to preserve thy conscious innocence.—Hor.

and to the terror of a bad one:

> ——— Quos diri conscia facti
> Mens habet attonitos, et surdo verbere cædit—
>
> No lash is heard, and yet the guilty heart
> Is tortur'd with a self-inflicted smart—Juv. Sat. 13.

Their *thoughts the meanwhile, μεταξὺ ἀλλήλων—among themselves*, or one with another. The same light and law of nature that witnesses against sin in them, and witnessed against it in others, accused or excused one another. *Vicissim*, so some read it, *by turns;* according as they observed or broke these natural laws and dictates, their consciences did either acquit or condemn them. All this did evince that they had that which was to them instead of a law, which they might have been governed by, and which will condemn them, because they were not so guided and governed by it. So that the guilty Gentiles are left without excuse. God is justified in condemning them. They cannot plead ignorance, and therefore are likely to perish if they have not something else to plead.

2. The light of the law. This the Jews had, and by this they shall be judged (*v.* 12): *As many as have sinned in the law shall be judged by the law.* They sinned, not only having the law, but ἐν νόμῳ—*in the law*, in the midst of so much law, in the face and light of so pure and clear a law, the directions of which were so very full and particular, and the sanctions of it so very cogent and enforcing. These shall be judged *by the law;* their punishment shall be, as their sin is, so much the greater for their having the law. *The Jew first, v.* 9. It shall be more tolerable for Tyre and Sidon. Thus Moses did accuse them (John v. 45), and they fell under the many stripes of him that knew his master's will, and did it not, Luke xii. 47. The Jews prided themselves very much in the law; but, to confirm what he had said, the apostle shows (*v.* 13) that their having, and hearing, and knowing the law, would not justify them, but their doing it. The Jewish doctors bolstered up their followers with an opinion that all that were Jews, how bad soever they lived, should have a place in the world to come. This the apostle here opposes: it was a great privilege that they had the law, but not a saving privilege, unless they lived up to the law they had, which it is certain the Jews did not, and therefore they had need of a righteousness wherein to appear before God. We may apply it to the gospel: it is not hearing, but doing that will save us, John xiii. 17; James i. 22.

3. The light of the gospel: and according to this those that enjoyed the gospel shall be judged (*v.* 16): *According to my gospel;* not meant of any fifth gospel written by Paul, as some conceit; or of the gospel written by *Luke*, as Paul's amanuensis *(Euseb. Hist.* lib iii. cap. 8), but the gospel in general, called Paul's because he was a preacher of it. As many as are under that dispensation shall be judged according to that dispensation, Mark xvi. 16. Some refer those words, *according to my gospel*, to what he says of the day of judgment: "There will come a day of judgment, according as I have in my preaching often told you; and that will be the day of the final judgment both of Jews and Gentiles." It is good for us to get acquainted with what is revealed concerning that day. (1.) There is a day set for a general judgment. The day, the great day, his day that is coming, Ps. xxxvii. 13. (2.) The judgment of that day will be put into the hands of Jesus Christ. God shall judge by Jesus Christ, Acts xvii. 31. It will be part of the reward of his humiliation. Nothing speaks more terror to sinners, or more comfort to saints, than this, that Christ shall be the Judge. (3.) The secrets of men shall then be judged. Secret services shall be then rewarded, secret sins shall be then punished, hidden things shall be brought to light. That will be the great discovering day, when that which is now done in corners shall be proclaimed to all the world.

17 Behold, thou art called a Jew,
and restest in the law, and makest
thy boast of God, 18 And knowest
his will, and approvest the things
that are more excellent, being instructed out of the law; 19 And
art confident that thou thyself art a
guide of the blind, a light of them
which are in darkness, 20 An instructor of the foolish, a teacher of
babes, which hast the form of knowledge and of the truth in the law. 21
Thou therefore which teachest another,
teachest thou not thyself? thou that
preachest a man should not steal, dost
thou steal? 22 Thou that sayest a
man should not commit adultery, dost
thou commit adultery? thou that ab-
horrest idols, dost thou commit sacrilege? 23 Thou that makest thy boast
of the law, through breaking the law
dishonourest thou God? 24 For the
name of God is blasphemed among
the Gentiles through you, as it is
written. 25 For circumcision verily
profiteth, if thou keep the law: but
if thou be a breaker of the law, thy
circumcision is made uncircumcision.

26 Therefore if the uncircumcision
keep the righteousness of the law,
shall not his uncircumcision be counted for circumcision ? 27 And shall not
uncircumcision which is by nature, if it
fulfil the law, judge thee, who by the
letter and circumcision dost trangress
the law? 28 For he is not a Jew, which
is one outwardly ; neither *is that* circumcision, which is outward in the
flesh : 29 But he *is* a Jew, which is
one inwardly ; and circumcision *is*
that of the heart, in the spirit, *and*
not in the letter ; whose praise *is* not
of men, but of God.

In the latter part of the chapter the apostle directs his discourse more closely to the Jews, and shows what sins they were guilty of, notwithstanding their profession and vain pretensions. He had said (*v.* 13) that not the hearers but the doers of the law are justified; and he here applies that great truth to the Jews. Observe,

I. He allows their profession (*v.* 17—20) and specifies their particular pretensions and privileges in which they prided themselves, that they might see he did not condemn them out of ignorance of what they had to say for themselves; no, he knew the best of their cause.

1. They were a peculiar people, separated and distinguished from all others by their having the written law and the special presence of God among them. (1.) *Thou art called a Jew;* not so much in parentage as profession. It was a very honourable title. Salvation was of the Jews; and this they were very proud of, to be a people by themselves; and yet many that were so called were the vilest of men. It is no new thing for the worst practices to be shrouded under the best names, for many of the synagogue of Satan to say they are Jews (Rev. ii. 9), for a generation of vipers to boast they have *Abraham to their father*, Matt. iii. 7—9. (2.) *And restest in the law;* that is, they took a pride in this, that they had the law among them, had it in their books, read it in their synagogues. They were mightily puffed up with this privilege, and thought this enough to bring them to heaven, though they did not live up to the law. To rest in the law, with a rest of complacency and acquiescence, is good; but to rest in it with a rest of pride, and slothfulness, and carnal security, is the ruin of souls. *The temple of the Lord*, Jer. vii. 4. *Bethel their confidence*, Jer. xlviii. 13. *Haughty because of the holy mountain*, Zeph. iii. 11. It is a dangerous thing to rest in external privileges, and not to improve them. (3.) *And makest thy boast of God.* See how the best things may be perverted and abused. A believing, humble, thankful glorying in God, is the root and summary of all religion, Ps. xxxiv. 2; Isa. xlv. 25; 1 Cor. i. 31. But a proud vainglorious boasting in God, and in the outward profession of his name, is the root and summary of all hypocrisy. Spiritual pride is of all kinds of pride the most dangerous.

2. They were a knowing people (*v.* 18): *and knowest his will,* τὸ θέλημα—*the will.* God's will is the will, the sovereign, absolute, irresistible will. The world will then, and not till then, be set to rights, when God's will is the only will, and all other wills are melted into it. They did not only know the truth of God, but the will of God, that which he would have them do. It is possible for a hypocrite to have a great deal of knowledge in the will of God.—*And approvest the things that are more excellent*—δοκιμάζεις τὰ διαφέροντα. Paul prays for it for his friends as a very great attainment, Phil. i. 10. 'Εις το δοκιμάζειν ὑμᾶς τὰ διαφέροντα. Understand it, (1.) Of a good apprehension in *the things of God*, reading it thus, *Thou discernest things that differ*, knowest how to distinguish between good and evil, to separate between the precious and the vile (Jer. xv. 19), to make a difference between the unclean and the clean, Lev. xi. 47. Good and bad lie sometimes so near together that it is not easy to distinguish them; but the Jews, having the touchstone of the law ready at hand, were, or at least thought they were, able to distinguish, to cleave the hair in doubtful cases. A man may be a good casuist and yet a bad Christian—accurate in the notion, but loose and careless in the application. Or, we may, with *De Dieu*, understand *controversies* by the τά διαφέροντα. A man may be well skilled in the controversies of religion, and yet a stranger to the power of godliness. (2.) Of a warm affection to the things of God, as we read it, *Approvest the things that are excellent.* There are excellences in religion which a hypocrite may approve of: there may be a consent of the practical judgment *to the law, that it is good*, and yet that consent overpowered by the lusts of the flesh, and of the mind :—

————Video meliora proboque
Deteriora sequor.

I see the better, but pursue the worse.

and it is common for sinners to make that approbation an excuse which is really a very great aggravation of a sinful course. They got this acquaintance with, and affection to, that which is good, by being *instructed out of the law*, κατηχούμενος—*being catechised.* The word signifies an early instruction in childhood. It is a great privilege and advantage to be well catechised betimes. It was the custom of the Jews to take a great deal of pains in teaching their children when they were young, and all their lessons were *out of the law;* it were well if Christians were but as industrious to teach their children *out of the gospel.* Now this is called (*v.* 20), *The form of knowledge, and of the truth in the law,* that is, the show and appearance of it. Those whose knowledge rests in an empty notion, and does not make an impression on their hearts, have only the form of it, like a picture well drawn and in good colours, but which wants life. A form of knowledge produces but a form of godliness, 2 Tim. iii. 5. A form of knowledge may deceive men, but cannot impose upon the piercing eye of the heart-searching God. A form may be the vehicle of the power; but he that takes up with that only is *like sounding brass and a tinkling cymbal.*

3. They were a teaching people, or at least thought themselves so (*v.* 19, 20): *And art confident that thou thyself art a guide of the blind.* Apply it, (1.) To the Jews in general. They thought themselves guides to the poor blind Gentiles that sat in darkness, were very proud of this, that whoever would have the knowledge of God must be beholden to them for it. All other nations must come to school to them, to learn what is good, and what the Lord requires; for they had the lively oracles. (2.) To their rabbies, and doctors, and leading men among them, who were especially those that judged others, *v.* 1. These prided themselves much in the possession they had got of Moses's chair, and the deference which the vulgar paid to their dictates; and the apostle expresses this in several terms, *a guide of the blind, a light of those who are in darkness, an instructor of the foolish, a teacher of babes,* the better to set forth their proud conceit of themselves, and contempt of others. This was a string they loved to be harping upon, heaping up titles of honour upon themselves. The best work, when it is prided in, is unacceptable to God. It is good to instruct the foolish, and to teach the babes: but considering our own ignorance, and folly, and inability to make these teachings successful without God, there is nothing in it to be proud of.

II. He aggravates their provocations (*v.* 21—24) from two things:—

1. That they sinned against their knowledge and profession, did that themselves which they taught others to avoid: *Thou that teachest another, teachest thou not thyself?* Teaching is a piece of that charity which begins at home, though it must not end there. It was the hypocrisy of the Pharisees *that they did not do as they taught* (Matt. xxiii. 3), but pulled down with their lives what they built up with their preaching; for who will believe those who do not believe themselves? Examples will govern more than rules. The greatest obstructors of the success of the word are those whose bad lives contradict their good doctrine, who in the pulpit preach so well that it is a pity they should ever come out, and out of the pulpit live so ill that it is a pity they should ever come in. He specifies three particular sins that abound among the Jews:—(1.) Stealing. This is charged upon some that declared God's statutes (Ps. l. 16, 18), *When thou sawest a thief, then thou consentedst with him.* The Pharisees are charged with devouring widows' houses (Matt. xxiii. 14), and that is the worst of robberies. (2.) Adultery, *v.* 22. This is likewise charged upon that sinner (Ps. l. 18), *Thou hast been partaker with adulterers.* Many of the Jewish rabbin are said to have been notorious for this sin. (3.) Sacrilege—robbing in holy things, which were then by special laws dedicated and devoted to God; and this is charged upon those that professed to abhor idols. So the Jews did remarkably, after their captivity in Babylon; that furnace separated them for ever from the dross of their idolatry, but they dealt very treacherously in the worship of God. It was in the latter days of the Old-Testament church that they were charged *with robbing God in tithes and offerings* (Mal. iii. 8, 9), converting that to their own use, and to the service of their lusts, which was, in a special manner, set apart for God. And this is almost equivalent to idolatry, though this sacrilege was cloked with the abhorrence of idols. Those will be severely reckoned with another day who, while they condemn sin in others, do the same, or as bad, or worse, themselves.

2. That they dishonoured God by their sin, *v.* 23, 24. While God and his law were an honour to them, which they boasted of and prided themselves in, they were a dishonour to God and his law, by giving occasion to those that were without to reflect upon their religion, as if that did countenance and allow of such things, which, as it is their sin who draw such inferences (for the faults of professors are not to be laid upon professions), so it is their sin who give occasion for those inferences, and will greatly aggravate their miscarriages. This was the condemnation in David's case, *that he had given great occasion to the enemies of the Lord to blaspheme,* 2 Sam. xii. 14. And the apostle here refers to the same charge against their forefathers: *As it is written, v.* 24. He does not mention the place, because he wrote this to those that were instructed in the law (in labouring to convince, it is some advantage to deal with those that have knowledge and are acquainted with the scripture), but he seems to point at Isa. lii. 5; Ezek. xxxvi. 22, 23; and 2 Sam. xii. 14. It is a lamentation that those who were made *to be to God for a name and for a praise* should be to him a shame and dishonour. The great evil of the sins of professors is the dishonour done to God and religion by their profession. "*Blasphemed through you;* that is, you give the occasion for it, it is through your folly and carelessness. The reproaches you bring upon yourselves reflect upon your God, and religion is wounded through your sides." A good caution to professors to walk circumspectly. See 1 Tim. vi. 1.

III. He asserts the utter insufficiency of

their profession to clear them from the guilt of these provocations (*v.* 25—29): *Circumcision verily profiteth, if thou keep the law;* that is, obedient Jews shall not lose the reward of their obedience, but will gain this by their being Jews, that they have a clearer rule of obedience than the Gentiles have. God did not give the law nor appoint circumcision in vain. This must be referred to the state of the Jews before the ceremonial polity was abolished, otherwise circumcision to one that professed faith in Christ was forbidden, Gal. v. 2. But he is here speaking to the Jews, whose Judaism would benefit them, if they would but live up to the rules and laws of it; but if not "*thy circumcision is made uncircumcision;* that is, thy profession will do thee no good; thou wilt be no more justified than the uncircumcised Gentiles, but more condemned for sinning against greater light." The uncircumcised are in scripture branded as *unclean* (Isa. lii. 1), as *out of the covenant,* (Eph. ii. 11, 12) and wicked Jews will be dealt with as such. See Jer. ix. 25, 26. Further to illustrate this,

1. He shows that the uncircumcised Gentiles, if they live up to the light they have, stand upon the same level with the Jews; if *they keep the righteousness of the law* (*v.* 26), *fulfil the law* (*v.* 27); that is, by submitting sincerely to the conduct of natural light, perform the matter of the law. Some understand it as putting the case of a perfect obedience to the law: "If the Gentiles could perfectly keep the law, they would be justified by it as well as the Jews." But it seems rather to be meant of such an obedience as some of the Gentiles did attain to. The case of Cornelius will clear it. Though he was a Gentile, and uncircumcised, yet, *being a devout man, and one that feared God with all his house* (Acts x. 2), he was accepted, *v.* 4. Doubtless, there were many such instances: and *they were the uncircumcision, that kept the righteousness of the law;* and of such he says, (1.) That they were accepted with God, as if they had been circumcised. *Their uncircumcision was counted for circumcision.* Circumcision was indeed *to the Jews* a commanded duty, but it was not to all the world a necessary condition of justification and salvation. (2.) That their obedience was a great aggravation of the disobedience of the Jews, who had the letter of the law, *v.* 27. *Judge thee,* that is, help to add to thy condemnation, who *by the letter and circumcision dost transgress.* Observe, To carnal professors the law is but the letter; they read it as a bare writing, but are not ruled by it as a law. They did transgress, not only notwithstanding the letter and circumcision, but by it, that is, they thereby hardened themselves in sin. External privileges, if they do not do us good, do us hurt. The obedience of those that enjoy less means, and make a less profession, will help to condemn those that enjoy greater means, and make a greater profession, but do not live up to it.

2. He describes the true circumcision, *v.* 28, 29. (1.) It is *not that which is outward in the flesh and in the letter.* This is not to drive us off from the observance of external institutions (they are good in their place), but from trusting to them and resting in them as sufficient to bring us to heaven, taking up with a name to live, without being alive indeed. *He is not a Jew,* that is, shall not be accepted of God as the seed of believing Abraham, nor owned as having answered the intention of the law. To be Abraham's children is to do the works of Abraham, John viii. 39, 40. (2.) It is *that which is inward, of the heart, and in the spirit.* It is the heart that God looks at, the circumcising of the heart that renders us acceptable to him. See Deut. xxx. 6. This is *the circumcision that is not made with hands,* Col. ii. 11, 12. *Casting away the body of sin.* So it is in the spirit, in our spirit as the subject, and wrought by God's Spirit as the author of it. (3.) The praise thereof, though it be *not of men,* who judge according to outward appearance, yet it is *of God,* that is, God himself will own and accept and crown this sincerity; for *he seeth not as man seeth.* Fair pretences and a plausible profession may deceive men: but God cannot be so deceived; he sees through shows to realities. This is alike true of Christianity. He is not a Christian that is one outwardly, nor is that baptism which is outward in the flesh; but he is a Christian that is one inwardly, and baptism is that of the heart, in the spirit, and not in the letter, whose praise is not of men but of God

CHAP. III.

The apostle, in this chapter, carries on his discourse concerning justification. He had already proved the guilt both of Gentiles and Jews. Now in this chapter, I. He answers some objections that might be made against what he had said about the Jews, ver. 1—8. II. He asserts the guilt and corruption of mankind in common, both Jews and Gentiles, ver. 9—18. III. He argues thence that justification must needs be by faith, and not by the law, which he gives several reasons for, ver. 19, to the end. The many digressions in his writings render his discourse sometimes a little difficult, but his scope is evident.

WHAT advantage then hath the Jew? or what profit *is there*
of circumcision? 2 Much every way:
chiefly, because that unto them were
committed the oracles of God. 3
For what if some did not believe;
shall their unbelief make the faith of
God without effect? 4 God forbid;
yea, let God be true, but every man
a liar; as it is written, That thou
mightest be justified in thy sayings,
and mightest overcome when thou
art judged. 5 But if our unrighteousness commend the righteousness of
God, what shall we say? *Is* God
unrighteous who taketh vengeance?
(I speak as a man) 6 God forbid:
for then how shall God judge the
world? 7 For if the truth of God

hath more abounded through my lie
unto his glory; why yet am I also
judged as a sinner? 8 And not
rather, (as we be slanderously reported, and as some affirm that we
say,) Let us do evil, that good may
come? whose damnation is just. 9
What then? are we better *than they?*
No, in no wise: for we have before
proved both Jews and Gentiles, that
they are all under sin; 10 As it is
written, There is none righteous, no,
not one: 11 There is none that
understandeth, there is none that
seeketh after God. 12 They are all
gone out of the way, they are together
become unprofitable; there is none
that doeth good, no, not one. 13
Their throat *is* an open sepulchre;
with their tongues they have used
deceit; the poison of asps *is* under
their lips: 14 Whose mouth *is* full
of cursing and bitterness: 15 Their
feet *are* swift to shed blood: 16
Destruction and misery *are* in their
ways: 17 And the way of peace
have they not known: 18 There is
no fear of God before their eyes.

I. Here the apostle answers several objections, which might be made, to clear his way. No truth so plain and evident but wicked wits and corrupt carnal hearts will have something to say against it; but divine truths must be cleared from cavil.

Object. 1. If Jew and Gentile stand so much upon the same level before God, *what advantage then hath the Jew?* Hath not God often spoken with a great deal of respect for the Jews, as a non-such people (Deut. xxxiii. 29), a holy nation, a peculiar treasure, the seed of Abraham his friend: Did not he institute circumcision as a badge of their church-membership, and a seal of their covenant-relation to God? Now does not this levelling doctrine deny them all such prerogatives, and reflect dishonour upon the ordinance of circumcision, as a fruitless insignificant thing.

Answer. The Jews are, notwithstanding this, a people greatly privileged and honoured, have great means and helps, though these be not infallibly saving (*v.* 2): *Much every way.* The door is open to the Gentiles as well as the Jews, but the Jews have a fairer way up to this door, by reason of their church-privileges, which are not to be undervalued, though many that have them perish eternally for not improving them. He reckons up many of the Jews' privileges Rom. ix. 4, 5; here he mentions but one (which is indeed *instar omnium—equivalent to all), that unto them were committed the oracles of God,* that is, the scriptures of the Old Testament, especially the law of Moses, which is called *the lively oracles* (Acts vii. 38), and those types, promises, and prophecies, which relate to Christ and the gospel. The scriptures are the oracles of God: they are a divine revelation, they come from heaven, are of infallible truth, and of eternal consequence as oracles. The Septuagint call the Urim and Thummim the *λόγια—the oracles.* The scripture is our breast-plate of judgment. We must have recourse to the law and to the testimony, as to an oracle. The gospel is called the oracles of God, Heb. v. 12; 1 Pet. iv. 11. Now these oracles were committed to the Jews; the Old Testament was written in their language; Moses and the prophets were of their nation, lived among them, preached and wrote primarily to and for the Jews. They were committed to them as trustees for succeeding ages and churches. The Old Testament was deposited in their hands, to be carefully preserved pure and uncorrupt, and so transmitted down to posterity. The Jews were the Christians' library-keepers, were entrusted with that sacred treasure for their own use and benefit in the first place, and then for the advantage of the world; and, in preserving the letter of the scripture, they were very faithful to their trust, did not lose one iota or tittle, in which we are to acknowledge God's gracious care and providence. The Jews had the means of salvation, but they had not the monopoly of salvation. Now this he mentions with a *chiefly*, *πρῶτον μὲν γὰρ*—this was their prime and principal privilege. The enjoyment of God's word and ordinances is the chief happiness of a people, is to be put in the *imprimis* of their advantages, Deut. iv. 8; xxxiii. 3; Ps. cxlvii. 20.

Object. 2. Against what he had said of the advantages the Jews had in the lively oracles, some might object the unbelief of many of them. To what purpose were the oracles of God committed to them, when so many of them, notwithstanding these oracles, continued strangers to Christ, and enemies to his gospel? *Some did not believe, v.* 3.

Answer. It is very true that some, nay most of the present Jews, do not believe in Christ; *but shall their unbelief make the faith of God without effect?* The apostle startles at such a thought: *God forbid!* The infidelity and obstinacy of the Jews could not invalidate and overthrow those prophecies of the Messiah which were contained in the oracles committed to them. Christ will be glorious, *though Israel be not gathered,* Isa. xlix. 5. God's words shall be accomplished, his purposes performed, and all his ends answered, though there be a generation that by their unbelief go about to make God a liar. *Let God be true but every man a liar;* let us abide by this principle, that God is true to every word which he has spoken, and will let none of his oracles fall to the ground, though thereby we give the lie to man; better question and overthrow the credit of all the men in the world than doubt of the faithfulness of God. What David said in his haste (Ps. cxvi. 11), that all men are liars, Paul here asserts deliberately. Lying is a limb of that old man which we every one of us come into the world clothed with. All men are fickle, and mutable, and given to change, *vanity and a lie* (Ps. lxii. 9), *altogether vanity*, Ps. xxxix. 5. All men are liars, compared with God. It is very comfortable, when we find every man a liar (no faith in man), that God is faithful. When *they speak vanity every one with his neighbour*, it is very comfortable to think *that the words of the Lord are pure words*, Ps. xii. 2. 6. For the further proof of this he quotes Ps. li. 4, *That thou mightest be justified*, the design of which is to show, 1. That God does and will preserve his own honour in the world, notwithstanding the sins of men. 2. That it is our duty, in all our conclusions concerning ourselves and others, to justify God and to assert and maintain his justice, truth, and goodness, however it goes. David lays a load upon himself in his confession, that he might justify God, and acquit him from any injustice. So here, Let the credit or reputation of man shift for itself, the matter is not great whether it sink or swim; let us hold fast this conclusion, how specious soever the premises may be to the contrary, that *the Lord is righteous in all his ways, and holy in all his works.* Thus is God justified in his sayings, and cleared when he judges (as it is Ps. li. 4), or when *he is judged*, as it is here rendered. When men presume to quarrel with God and his proceedings, we may be sure the sentence will go on God's side

Object. 3. Carnal hearts might hence take occasion to encourage themselves in sin. He had said that the universal guilt and corruption of mankind gave occasion to the manifestation of God's righteousness in Jesus Christ. Now it may be suggested, If all our sin be so far from overthrowing God's honour that it commends it, and his ends are secured, so that there is no harm done, is it not unjust for God to punish our sin and unbelief so severely? If the unrighteousness of the Jews gave occasion to the calling in of the Gentiles, and so to God's greater glory, why are the Jews so much censured? *If our unrighteousness commend the righteousness of God, what shall we say? v.* 5. What inference may be drawn from this? *Is God unrighteous,* μὴ ἄδικος ὁ Θεὸς—*Is not God unrighteous* (so it may be read, more in the form of an objection), *who taketh vengeance?* Unbelieving hearts will gladly take any occasion to quarrel with the equity of God's proceedings, and to condemn him that is most just, Job xxxiv. 17. *I speak as a man*, that is, I object this as the language of carnal hearts; it is suggested like a man, a vain, foolish, proud creature.

Answer. God forbid; far be it from us to imagine such a thing. Suggestions that reflect dishonour upon God and his justice and holiness are rather to be startled at than parleyed with. Get thee behind me, Satan; never entertain such a thought. *For then how shall God judge the world? v.* 6. The argument is much the same with that of Abraham (Gen. xviii. 25): *Shall not the Judge of all the earth do right?* No doubt, he shall. If he were not infinitely just and righteous, he would be unfit to be the judge of all the earth. *Shall even he that hateth right govern?* Job xxxiv. 17. Compare *v.* 18, 19. The sin has never the less of malignity and demerit in it though God bring glory to himself out of it. It is only accidentally that sin commends God's righteousness. No thanks to the sinner for that, who intends no such thing. The consideration of God's judging the world should for ever silence all our doubtings of, and reflections upon, his justice and equity. It is not for us to arraign the proceedings of such an absolute Sovereign. The sentence of the supreme court, whence lies no appeal, is not to be called in question.

Object. 4. The former objection is repeated and prosecuted (*v.* 7, 8), for proud hearts will hardly be beaten out of their refuge of lies, but will hold fast the deceit. But his setting off the objection in its own colours is sufficient to answer it: *If the truth of God has more abounded through my lie.* He supposes the sophisters to follow their objection thus: "If my lie, that is, my sin" (for there is something of a lie in every sin, especially in the sins of professors) "have occasioned the glorifying of God's truth and faithfulness, why *should I be judged* and condemned *as a sinner, and not rather* thence take encouragement to go on in my sin, that grace may abound?" an inference which at first sight appears too black to be argued, and fit to be cast out with abhorrence. Daring sinners take occasion to boast in mischief, because the *goodness of God endures continually*, Ps. lii. 1. *Let us do evil that good may come* is oftener in the heart than in the mouth of sinners, so justifying themselves in their wicked ways. Mentioning this wicked thought, he observes, in a parenthesis, that there were those who charged such doctrines as this upon Paul and his fellow-ministers: Some affirm that we say so. It is no new thing for the best of God's people and ministers to be charged with holding and teaching such things as they do most detest and abhor; and it is not to be thought strange, when our Master himself was said to be in league with Beelzebub. Many have been reproached as if they had said that the contrary of which they maintain: it is an old artifice of Satan thus to cast dirt upon Christ's ministers, *Fortiter calumniari, aliquid adhærebit—Lay slander thickly on, for some will be sure to stick.* The best men and the best truths are subject to slander. Bishop Sanderson makes a further remark upon this, *as we are slanderously reported*—βλασφημούμεθα. Blasphemy in scripture usually signifies the highest degree of slander, speaking ill of God. The slander of a minister and his regular doctrine is a more than ordinary slander, it is a kind of blasphemy, not for his person's sake, but for his calling's sake and his work's sake, 1 Thess. v. 13.

Answer. He says no more by way of confutation but that, whatever they themselves may argue, the damnation of those is just. Some understand it of the slanderers; God will justly condemn those who unjustly condemn his truth. Or, rather, it is to be applied to those who embolden themselves in sin under a pretence of God's getting glory to himself out of it. Those who deliberately do evil that good may come of it will be so far from escaping, under the shelter of that excuse, that it will rather justify their damnation, and render them the more inexcusable; for sinning upon such a surmise, and in such a confidence, argues a great deal both of the wit and of the will in the sin—a wicked will deliberately to choose the evil, and a wicked wit to palliate it with the pretence of good arising from it. Therefore their damnation is just; and, whatever excuses of this kind they may now please themselves with, they will none of them stand good in the great day, but God will be justified in his proceedings, and all flesh, even the proud flesh that now lifts up itself against him, shall be silent before him. Some think Paul herein refers to the approaching ruin of the Jewish church and nation, which their obstinacy and self-justification in their unbelief hastened upon them apace.

II. Paul, having removed these objections, next revives his assertion of the general guilt and corruption of mankind in common, both of Jews and Gentiles, *v.* 9—18. "*Are we better than they,* we Jews, to whom were committed the oracles of God? Does this recommend us to God, or will this justify us? No, by no means." Or, "Are we Christians (Jews and Gentiles) so much better antecedently than the unbelieving part as to have merited God's grace? Alas! no: before free grace made the difference, those of us that had been Jews and those that had been Gentiles were all alike corrupted." They *are all under sin.* Under the guilt of sin: under it as under a sentence;—under it as under a bond, by which they are bound over to eternal ruin and damnation;—under it as under a burden (Ps. xxxviii. 4) that will sink them to the lowest hell: we are guilty before God, *v.* 19. Under the government and dominion of sin: under it as under a tyrant and cruel task-master, enslaved to it;—under it as under a yoke;—under the power of it, sold to work wickedness. And this he had proved, προῃτιασάμεθα. It is a law term: *We have charged them with it,* and have made good our charge; we have proved the indictment, we have convicted them by the notorious evidence of the fact. This charge and conviction he here further illustrates by several scriptures out of the Old Testament, which describe the corrupt depraved state of all men, till grace restrain or change them; so that herein as in a glass we may all of us behold our natural face. The 10th, 11th, and 12th verses are taken from Ps. xiv. 1—3, which are repeated as containing a very weighty truth, Ps. liii. 1—3. The rest that follows here is found in the Septuagint translation of the 14th Psalm, which some think the apostle chooses to follow as better known; but I rather think that Paul took these passages from other places of scripture here referred to, but in later copies of the LXX. they were all added in Ps. xiv. from this discourse of Paul. It is observable that, to prove the general corruption of nature, he quotes some scriptures which speak of the particular corruptions of particular persons, as of Doeg (Ps. cxl. 3), of the Jews (Isa. lix. 7, 8), which shows that the same sins that are committed by one are in the nature of all. The times of David and Isaiah were some of the better times, and yet to their days he refers. What is said Ps. xiv. is expressly spoken of *all the children of men,* and that upon a particular view and inspection made by God himself. The *Lord looked down,* as upon the old world, Gen. vi. 5. And this judgment of God was according to truth. He who, when he himself had made all, looked upon every thing that he had made, and behold all was very good, now that man had marred all, looked, and behold all was very bad. Let us take a view of the particulars. Observe,

1. That which is habitual, which is twofold:—

(1.) An habitual defect of every thing that is good. [1.] *There is none righteous,* none that has an honest good principle of virtue, or is governed by such a principle, none that retains any thing of that image of God, consisting in righteousness, wherein man was created; *no, not one;* implying that, if there had been but one, God would have found him out. When all the world was corrupt, God had his eye upon one righteous Noah. Even those who through grace are justified and sanctified were none of them righteous by nature. No righteousness is born with us. The man after God's own heart owns himself conceived in sin. [2.] *There is none that understandeth, v.* 11. The fault lies in the corruption of the understanding; that is blinded, depraved, perverted. Religion and righteousness have so much reason on their side that if people had but any understanding they would be better and do better. But they do not understand. Sinners are fools. [3.] *None that seeketh after God,* that is, none that has any regard to God, any desire after him. Those may justly be reckoned to have no understanding that do not seek after God.

The carnal mind is so far from seeking after God that really it is enmity against him. [4.] *They are together become unprofitable*, *v.* 12. Those that have forsaken God soon grow good for nothing, useless burdens of the earth. Those that are in a state of sin are the most unprofitable creatures under the sun; for it follows, [5.] *There is none that doeth good;* no, not a just man upon the earth, that doeth good, and sinneth not, Eccl. vii. 23. Even in those actions of sinners that have some goodness in them there is a fundamental error in the principle and end; so that it may be said, There is none that doeth good. *Malum oritur ex quolibet defectu---Every defect is the source of evil.*

(2.) An habitual defection to every thing that is evil: *They are all gone out of the way.* No wonder that those miss the right way who do not seek after God, the highest end. God made man in the way, set him in right, but he hath forsaken it. The corruption of mankind is an apostasy.

2. That which is actual. And what good can be expected from such a degenerate race? He instances,

(1.) In their words (*v.* 13, 14), in three things particularly:—[1.] Cruelty: *Their throat is an open sepulchre,* ready to swallow up the poor and innocent, waiting an opportunity to do mischief, like the old serpent seeking to devour, whose name is Abaddon and Apollyon, the destroyer. And when they do not openly avow this cruelty, and vent it publicly, yet they are underhand intending mischief: the *poison of asps is under their lips* (Jam. iii. 8), the most venomous and incurable poison, with which they blast the good name of their neighbour by reproaches, and aim at his life by false witness. These passages are borrowed from Ps. v. 9 and cxl. 3. [2.] Cheating: *With their tongues they have used deceit.* Herein they show themselves the devil's children, for he is a liar, and the father of lies. They *have used* it: it intimates that they make a trade of lying; it is their constant practice, especially belying the ways and people of God. [3.] Cursing: reflecting upon God, and blaspheming his holy name; wishing evil to their brethren: *Their mouth is full of cursing and bitterness.* This is mentioned as one of the great sins of the tongue, Jam. iii. 9. But those that thus love cursing shall have enough of it, Ps. cix. 17—19. How many, who are called Christians, do by these sins evince that they are still under the reign and dominion of sin, still in the condition that they were born in.

(2.) In their ways (*v.* 15—17): *Their feet are swift to shed blood;* that is, they are very industrious to compass any cruel design, ready to lay hold of all such opportunities. Wherever they go, *destruction and misery* go along with them; these are their companions—destruction and misery to the people of God, to the country and neighbourhood where they live, to the land and nation, and to themselves at last. Besides the destruction and misery that are at the end of their ways (death is the end of these things), destruction and misery are in their ways; their sin is its own punishment: a man needs no more to make him miserable than to be a slave to his sins.—*And the way of peace have they not known*; that is, they know not how to preserve peace with others, nor how to obtain peace for themselves. They may talk of peace, such a peace as is in the devil's palace, while he keeps it, but they are strangers to all true peace; they know not the things that belong to their peace. These are quoted from Prov. i. 16, Isa. lix. 7, 8.

(3.) The root of all this we have: *There is no fear of God before their eyes, v.* 18. The fear of God is here put for all practical religion, which consists in an awful and serious regard to the word and will of God as our rule, to the honour and glory of God as our end. Wicked people have not this before their eyes; that is, they do not steer by it; they are governed by other rules, aim at other ends. This is quoted from Ps. xxxvi. 1. Where no fear of God is, no good is to be expected. The fear of God would lay a restraint upon our spirits, and keep them right, Neh. v. 15. When once fear is cast off, prayer is restrained (Job xv. 4), and then all goes to wreck and ruin quickly. So that we have here a short account of the general depravity and corruption of mankind; and may say, O Adam! what hast thou done? God made man upright, but thus he hath sought out many inventions.

19 Now we know that what things
soever the law saith, it saith to them
who are under the law: that every
mouth may be stopped, and all the
world may become guilty before God.
20 Therefore by the deeds of the law
there shall no flesh be justified in his
sight: for by the law *is* the knowledge of sin. 21 But now the
righteousness of God without the
law is manifested, being witnessed by
the law and the prophets; 22 Even
the righteousness of God *which is* by
faith of Jesus Christ unto all and
upon all them that believe: for there
is no difference: 23 For all have
sinned, and come short of the glory
of God; 24 Being justified freely by
his grace through the redemption
that is in Christ Jesus: 25 Whom
God hath set forth *to be* a propitiation through faith in his blood, to
declare his righteousness for the
remission of sins that are past,

through the forbearance of God; 26
To declare, *I say*, at this time his
righteousness: that he might be just,
and the justifier of him which believeth in Jesus. 27 Where *is*
boasting then? It is excluded. By
what law? of works? Nay: but by
the law of faith. 28 Therefore we
conclude that a man is justified by
faith without the deeds of the law.
29 *Is he* the God of the Jews only?
is he not also of the Gentiles? Yes,
of the Gentiles also: 30 Seeing *it*
is one God, which shall justify the
circumcision by faith, and uncircumcision through faith. 31 Do we then
make void the law through faith?
God forbid: yea, we establish the law.

From all this Paul infers that it is in vain to look for justification by the works of the law, and that it is to be had only by faith, which is the point he has been all along proving, from *ch.* i. 17, and which he lays down (*v.* 28) as the summary of his discourse, with a *quod erat demonstrandum—which was to be demonstrated. We conclude that a man is justified by faith, without the deeds of the law;* not by the deeds of the first law of pure innocence, which left no room for repentance, nor the deeds of the law of nature, how highly soever improved, nor the deeds of the ceremonial law (the blood of bulls and goats could not take away sin), nor the deeds of the moral law, which are certainly included, for he speaks of that law by which is the knowledge of sin and those works which might be matter of boasting. Man, in his depraved state, under the power of such corruption, could never, by any works of his own, gain acceptance with God; but it must be resolved purely into the free grace of God, given through Jesus Christ to all true believers that receive it as a free gift. If we had never sinned, our obedience to the law would have been our righteousness: "Do this, and live." But having sinned, and being corrupted, nothing that we can do will atone for our former guilt. It was by their obedience to the moral law that the Pharisees looked for justification, Luke xviii. 11. Now there are two things from which the apostle here argues: the guiltiness of man, to prove that we cannot be justified by the works of the law, and the glory of God, to prove that we must be justified by faith

I. He argues from man's guiltiness, to show the folly of expecting justification by the works of the law. The argument is very plain: we can never be justified and saved by the law that we have broken. A convicted traitor can never come off by pleading the statute of 25 *Edward* III., for that law discovers his crime and condemns him: indeed, if he had never broken it, he might have been justified by it; but now it is past that he has broken it, and there is no way of coming off but by pleading the act of indemnity, upon which he has surrendered and submitted himself, and humbly and penitently claiming the benefit of it and casting himself upon it. Now concerning the guiltiness of man,

1. He fastens it particularly upon the Jews; for they were the men that made their boast of the law, and set up for justification by it. He had quoted several scriptures out of the Old Testament to show this corruption: Now, says he (*v.* 19), *this that the law says, it says to those who are under the law;* this conviction belongs to the Jews as well as others, for it is written in their law. The Jews boasted of their being under the law, and placed a great deal of confidence in it: "But," says he, "the law convicts and condemns you—you see it does." That *every mouth may be stopped*—that all boasting may be silenced. See the method that God takes both in justifying and condemning: he stops every mouth; those that are justified have their mouths stopped by a humble conviction; those that are condemned have their mouths stopped too, for they shall at last be convinced (Jude 15), and sent speechless to hell, Matt. xxii. 12. *All iniquity shall stop her mouth,* Ps. cvii. 42.

2. He extends it in general to all the world: *That all the world may become guilty before God.* If the world lies in wickedness (1 John v. 19), to be sure it is guilty.—*May become guilty;* that is, may be proved guilty, liable to punishment, all by nature *children of wrath,* Eph. ii. 3. They must all plead guilty; those that stand most upon their own justification will certainly be cast. Guilty before God is a dreadful word, before an all-seeing God, that is not, nor can be, deceived in his judgment—before a just and righteous judge, who will by no means clear the guilty. All are guilty, and therefore all have need of a righteousness wherein to appear before God. *For all have sinned* (*v.* 23); all are sinners by nature, by practice, and *have come short of the glory of God*—have failed of that which is the chief end of man. *Come short,* as the archer comes short of the mark, as the runner comes short of the prize; so come short, as not only not to win, but to be great losers. *Come short of the glory of God.* (1.) Come short of glorifying God. See *ch.* i. 21, *They glorified him not as God.* Man was placed at the head of the visible creation, actively to glorify that great Creator whom the inferior creatures could glorify only objectively; but man by sin comes short of this, and, instead of glorifying God, dishonours him. It is a very melancholy consideration, to look upon the children of men, who were made to glorify God, and to think how few there are that do it. (2.)

Come short of glorying *before God.* There is no boasting of innocency: if we go about to glory before God, to boast of any thing we are, or have, or do, this will be an everlasting estoppel—that we have all sinned, and this will silence us. We may glory before men, who are short-sighted, and cannot search our hearts,—who are corrupt, as we are, and well enough pleased with sin; but there is no glorying before God, who cannot endure to look upon iniquity. (3.) Come short of being glorified by God. Come short of justification, or acceptance with God, which is glory begun—come short of the holiness or sanctification which is the glorious image of God upon man, and have overthrown all hopes and expectations of being glorified with God in heaven by any righteousness of their own. It is impossible now to get to heaven in the way of spotless innocency. That passage is blocked up. There is a cherub and a flaming sword set to keep that way to the tree of life.

3. Further to drive us off from expecting justification by the law, he ascribes this conviction to the law (*v.* 20): *For by the law is the knowledge of sin.* That law which convicts and condemns us can never justify us. The law is the straight rule, that *rectum* which is *index sui et obliqui—that which points out the right and the wrong;* it is the proper use and intendment of the law to open our wound, and therefore not likely to be the remedy. That which is searching is not sanative. Those that would know sin must get the knowledge of the law in its strictness, extent, and spiritual nature. If we compare our own hearts and lives with the rule, we shall discover wherein we have turned aside. Paul makes this use of the law, *ch.* vii. 9, *Therefore by the deeds of the law shall no flesh be justified in his sight.* Observe, (1.) *No flesh shall be justified,* no man, no corrupted man (Gen. vi. 3), *for that he also is flesh,* sinful and depraved; therefore not justified, because we are flesh. The corruption that remains in our nature will for ever obstruct any justification by our own works, which, coming from flesh, must needs taste of the cask, Job xiv. 4. (2.) Not justified in his sight. He does not deny that justification which was by the deeds of the law in the sight of the church: they were, in their church-estate, as embodied in a polity, a holy people, a nation of priests; but as the conscience stands in relation to God, *in his sight,* we cannot be justified by the deeds of the law. The apostle refers to Ps. cxliii. 2.

II. He argues from God's glory to prove that justification must be expected only by faith in Christ's righteousness. There is no justification by the works of the law. Must guilty man then remain eternally under wrath? Is there no hope? Is the wound become incurable because of transgression? No, blessed be God, it is not (*v.* 21, 22); there is another way laid open for us, *the righteousness of God without the law is manifested* now under the gospel. Justification may be obtained without the keeping of Moses's law: and this is called *the righteousness of God,* righteousness of his ordaining, and providing, and accepting,—righteousness which he confers upon us; as the Christian armour is called *the armour of God,* Eph. vi. 11.

1. Now concerning this righteousness of God observe, (1.) That it is manifested. The gospel-way of justification is a high-way, a plain way, it is laid open for us: the brazen serpent is lifted up upon the pole; we are not left to grope our way in the dark, but it is manifested to us. (2.) It is *without the law.* Here he obviates the method of the judaizing Christians, who would needs join Christ and Moses together—owning Christ for the Messiah, and yet too fondly retaining the law, keeping up the ceremonies of it, and imposing it upon the Gentile converts: no, says he, it is without the law. The righteousness that Christ hath brought in is a complete righteousness. (3.) Yet *it is witnessed by the law and the prophets;* that is, there were types, and prophecies, and promises, in the Old Testament, that pointed at this. The law is so far from justifying us that it directs us to another way of justification, points at Christ as our righteousness, to whom bear all the prophets witness. See Acts x. 43. This might recommend it to the Jews, who were so fond of the law and the prophets. (4.) It is by the *faith of Jesus Christ,* that faith which hath Jesus Christ for its object—an *anointed Saviour,* so Jesus Christ signifies. Justifying faith respects Christ as a Saviour in all his three anointed offices, as prophet, priest, and king—trusting in him, accepting of him, and adhering to him, in all these. It is by this that we become interested in that righteousness which God has ordained, and which Christ has brought in. (5.) It is *to all, and upon all, those that believe.* In this expression he inculcates that which he had been often harping upon, that Jews and Gentiles, if they believe, stand upon the same level, and are alike welcome to God through Christ; *for there is no difference.* Or, it is εἰς πάντας—*to all,* offered to all in general; the gospel excludes none that do not exclude themselves; but it is ἐπὶ πάντας τοὺς πιστεύοντας, *upon all that believe,* not only tendered to them, but put upon them as a crown, as a robe; they are, upon their believing, interested in it, and entitled to all the benefits and privileges of it.

2. But now how is this for God's glory?

(1.) It is for the glory of his grace (*v.* 24): *Justified freely by his grace*—δωρεὰν τῇ αὐτοῦ χάριτι. It is *by his grace,* not by the grace wrought in us as the papists say, confounding justification and sanctification, but by the gracious favour of God to us, without any merit in us so much as foreseen. And, to make it the more emphatic, he says it is *freely by his grace,* to show that it must be understood of grace in the most proper and genuine sense. It is said that *Joseph found grace* in the sight of his master (Gen. xxxix. 4), but there was a reason; he saw that what he did prospered. There was something in Joseph to invite that grace; but the grace of God communicated to us comes *freely, freely;* it is free grace, mere mercy; nothing in us to deserve such favours: no, it is all *through the redemption that is in Jesus Christ.* It comes freely to us, but Christ bought it, and paid dearly for it, which yet is so ordered as not to derogate from the honour of free grace. Christ's purchase is no bar to the freeness of God's grace; for grace provided and accepted this vicarious satisfaction.

(2.) It is for the glory of his justice and righteousness (*v.* 25, 26): *Whom God hath set forth to be a propitiation,* &c. Note, [1.] Jesus Christ is the great propitiation, or propitiatory sacrifice, typified by the ἱλαστήριον, or *mercy-seat,* under the law. He is our throne of grace, in and through whom atonement is made for sin, and our persons and performances are accepted of God, 1 John ii. 2. He is all in all in our reconciliation, not only the maker, but the matter of it—our priest, our sacrifice, our altar, our all. God was in Christ as in his mercy-seat, reconciling the world unto himself. [2.] *God hath set him forth* to be so. God, the party offended, makes the first overtures towards a reconciliation, appoints the days-man; προέθετο—*fore-ordained* him to this, in the counsels of his love from eternity, appointed, anointed him to it, qualified him for it, and has exhibited him to a guilty world as their propitiation. See Matt. iii. 17, and xvii. 5. [3.] That *by faith in his blood* we become interested in this propitiation. Christ is the propitiation; there is the healing plaster provided. Faith is the applying of this plaster to the wounded soul. And this faith in the business of justification hath a special regard to *the blood of Christ,* as that which made the atonement; for such was the divine appointment that without blood there should be no remission, and no blood but his would do it effectually. Here may be an allusion to the sprinkling of the blood of the sacrifices under the law, as Exod. xxiv. 8. Faith is the bunch of hyssop, and the blood of Christ is the blood of sprinkling. [4.] That all who by faith are interested in this propitiation have *the remission of their sins that are past.* It was for this that Christ was set forth to be a propitiation, in order to remission, to which the reprieves of his patience and forbearance were a very encouraging preface. *Through the forbearance of God.* Divine patience has kept us out of hell, that we might have space to repent, and get to heaven. Some refer the *sins that are past* to the sins of the Old-Testament saints, which were pardoned for the sake of the atonement which Christ in the fulness of time was to make, which looked backward as well as forward. *Past through the forbearance of God.* It is owing to the divine forbearance that we were not taken in the very act of sin. Several Greek copies make ἐν τῃ ἀνοχῃ τοῦ Θεοῦ—*through the forbearance of God,* to begin *v.* 26, and they denote two precious fruits of Christ's merit and God's grace:—Remission: διὰ τὴν πάρεσιν—*for the remission*; and reprieves: the *forbearance* of God. It is owing to the master's goodness and the dresser's mediation that barren trees are let alone in the vineyard; and in both God's righteousness is declared, in that without a mediator and a propitiation he would not only not pardon, but not so much as forbear, not spare a moment; it is owing to Christ that there is ever a sinner on this side hell. [5.] That God does in all this *declare his righteousness.* This he insists upon with a great deal of emphasis: *To declare, I say, at this time his righteousness.* It is repeated, as that which has in it something surprising. He declares his righteousness, *First,* In the propitiation itself. Never was there such a demonstration of the justice and holiness of God as there was in the death of Christ. It appears that he hates sin, when nothing less than the blood of Christ would satisfy for it. Finding sin, though but imputed, upon his own Son, he did not spare him, because he had made himself sin for us, 2 Cor. v. 21. The iniquities of us all being laid upon him, though he was the Son of his love, yet it pleased the Lord to bruise him, Isa. liii. 10. *Secondly,* In the pardon upon that propitiation; so it follows, by way of explication: *That he might be just, and the justifier of him that believeth.* Mercy and truth are so met together, righteousness and peace have so kissed each other, that it is now become not only an act of grace and mercy, but an act of righteousness, in God, to pardon the sins of penitent believers, having accepted the satisfaction that Christ by dying made to his justice for them. It would not comport with his justice to demand the debt of the principal when the surety has paid it and he has accepted that payment in full satisfaction. See 1 John i. 9. He is just, that is, faithful to his word.

(3.) It is for God's glory; for boasting is thus excluded, *v.* 27. God will have the great work of the justification and salvation of sinners carried on from first to last in such a way as to exclude boasting, that no flesh may glory in his presence, 1 Cor. i. 29—31. Now, if justification were by the works of the law, boasting would not be excluded. How should it? If we were saved by our own works, we might put the crown upon our own heads. But the *law of faith,* that is, the way of justification by faith, doth for ever exclude boasting; for faith is a depending, self-emptying, self-denying grace, and casts every crown before the throne; therefore it is most for God's glory that thus we should be justified. Observe, He speaks of *the law of faith.* Believers are not left lawless: faith is a law, it is a working grace, wherever it is in truth; and yet, because it acts in a strict and close dependence upon Jesus Christ, it excludes boasting.

From all this he draws this conclusion (*v.* 28): *That a man is justified by faith without the deeds of the law.*

III. In the close of the chapter he shows the extent of this privilege of justification by faith, and that it is not the peculiar privilege of the Jews, but pertains to the Gentiles also; for he had said (*v.* 22) that there is no difference: and as to this, 1. He asserts and proves it (*v.* 29, 30): *Is he the God of the Jews only?* He argues from the absurdity of such a supposition. Can it be imagined that a God of infinite love and mercy should limit and confine his favours to that little perverse people of the Jews, leaving all the rest of the children of men in a condition eternally desperate? This would by no means agree with the idea we have of the divine goodness, for his *tender mercies are over all his works;* therefore it is one God of grace that *justifies the circumcision by faith, and the uncircumcision through faith,* that is, both in one and the same way. However the Jews, in favour of themselves, will needs fancy a difference, really there is no more difference than between *by* and *through,* that is, no difference at all. 2. He obviates an objection (*v.* 31), as if this doctrine did nullify the law, which they knew came from God: "No," says he, "though we do say that the law will not justify us, yet we do not therefore say that it was given in vain, or is of no use to us; no, *we establish the right use of the law,* and secure its standing, by fixing it on the right basis. The law is still of use to convince us of what is past, and to direct us for the future; though we cannot be saved by it as a covenant, yet we own it, and submit to it, as a rule in the hand of the Mediator, subordinate to the law of grace; and so are so far from overthrowing that we establish the law." Let those consider this who deny the obligation of the moral law on believers.

CHAP. IV.

The great gospel doctrine of justification by faith without the works of the law was so very contrary to the notions the Jews had learnt from those that sat in Moses's chair, that it would hardly go down with them; and therefore the apostle insists very largely upon it, and labours much in the confirmation and illustration of it. He had before proved it by reason and argument, now in this chapter he proves it by example, which in some places serves for confirmation as well as illustration. The example he pitches upon is that of Abraham, whom he chooses to mention because the Jews gloried much in their relation to Abraham, put it in the first rank of their external privileges that they were Abraham's seed, and truly they had Abraham for their father. Therefore this instance was likely to be more taking and convincing to the Jews than any other. His argument stands thus: "All that are saved are justified in the same way as Abraham was; but Abraham was justified by faith, and not by works; therefore all that are saved are so justified;" for it would easily be acknowledged that Abraham was the father of the faithful. Now this is an argument, not only à pari—from an equal case, as they say, but à fortiori—from a stronger case. If Abraham, a man so famous for works, so eminent in holiness and obedience, was nevertheless justified by faith only, and not by those works, how much less can any other, especially any of those that spring from him, and come so far short of him in works, set up for a justification by their own works? And it proves likewise, ex abundanti—the more abundantly, as some observe, that we are not justified, no not by those good works which flow from faith, as the matter of our righteousness; for such were Abraham's works, and are we better than he? The whole chapter is taken up with his discourse upon this instance, and there is this in it, which hath a particular reference to the close of the foregoing chapter, where he had asserted that, in the business of justification, Jews and Gentiles stand upon the same level. Now in this chapter, with a great deal of cogency of argument, I. He proves that Abraham was justified not by works, but by faith, ver. 1—8. II. He observes when and why he was so justified, ver. 9—17. III. He describes and commends that faith of his, ver. 17—22. IV. He applies all this to us, ver. 22—25. And, if he had now been in the school of Tyrannus, he could not have disputed more argumentatively.

WHAT shall we then say that
Abraham, our father as pertaining to the flesh, hath found? 2
For if Abraham were justified by
works, he hath *whereof* to glory; but
not before God. 3 For what saith
the scripture? Abraham believed
God, and it was counted unto him
for righteousness. 4 Now to him
that worketh is the reward not
reckoned of grace, but of debt. 5
But to him that worketh not, but
believeth on him that justified the
ungodly, his faith is counted for
righteousness. 6 Even as David also
describeth the blessedness of the man,
unto whom God imputeth righteousness without works. 7 *Saying,*
Blessed *are* they whose iniquities are
forgiven, and whose sins are covered.
8 Blessed *is* the man to whom the
Lord will not impute sin.

Here the apostle proves that Abraham was justified not by works, but by faith. Those that of all men contended most vigorously for a share in righteousness by the privileges they enjoyed, and the works they performed, were the Jews, and therefore he appeals to the case of Abraham their father, and puts his own name to the relation, being a Hebrew of the Hebrews: *Abraham our father.* Now surely his prerogative must needs be as great as theirs who claim it as his seed according to the flesh. Now *what has he found?* All the world is seeking; but, while the most are wearying themselves for very vanity, none can be truly reckoned to have found, but those who are justified before God; and thus Abraham, like a wise merchant, seeking goodly pearls, found this one pearl of great price. What has he found, κατὰ σάρκα—*as pertaining to the flesh,* that is, by circumcision and his external privileges and performances? These the apostle calls *flesh,* Phil. iii. 3. Now what did he get by these? Was he justified by them? Was it the merit of his works that recommended him to God's acceptance? No, by no means, which he proves by several arguments.

I. If he had been justified by works, room would have been left for boasting, which must for ever be excluded. If so, *he hath whereof to glory* (*v.* 2), which is not to be allowed. "But," might the Jews say, "was not his name made great (Gen. xii. 2), and then might not he glory?" Yes, but not before God; he might deserve well of men, but he could never merit of God. Paul himself had *whereof to glory before men*, and we have him sometimes glorying in it, yet with humility; but nothing to glory in before God, 1 Cor. iv. 4; Phil. iii. 8, 9. So Abraham. Observe, He takes it for granted that man must not pretend to glory in any thing before God; no, not Abraham, as great and as good a man as he was; and therefore he fetches an argument from it: it would be absurd for him *that glorieth to glory in any but the Lord.*

II. It is expressly said that Abraham's faith was counted to him for righteousness. *What saith the scripture? v.* 3. In all controversies in religion this must be our question, *What saith the scripture?* It is not what this great man, and the other good man, say, but What saith the scripture? Ask counsel at this Abel, and so end the matter, 2 Sam. xx. 18. *To the law, and to the testimony* (Isa. viii. 20), thither is the last appeal. Now the scripture saith that *Abraham believed, and this was counted to him for righteousness* (Gen. xv. 6); therefore he had not whereof to glory before God, it being purely of free grace that it was so imputed, and having not in itself any of the formal nature of a righteousness, further than as God himself was graciously pleased so to count it to him. It is mentioned in Genesis, upon occasion of a very signal and remarkable act of faith concerning the promised seed, and is the more observable in that it followed upon a grievous conflict he had had with unbelief; his faith was now a victorious faith, newly returned from the battle. It is not the perfect faith that is required to justification (there may be acceptable faith where there are remainders of unbelief), but the prevailing faith, the faith that has the upper hand of unbelief.

III. If he had been justified by faith, the reward would have been *of debt, and not of grace,* which is not to be imagined. This is his argument (*v.* 4, 5): Abraham's reward was God himself; so he had told him but just before (Gen. xv. 1), *I am thy exceeding great reward.* Now, if Abraham had merited this by the perfection of his obedience, it had not been an act of grace in God, but Abraham might have demanded it with as much confidence as ever any labourer in the vineyard demanded the penny he had earned. But this cannot be; it is impossible for man, much more guilty man, to make God a debtor to him, Rom. xi. 35. No, God will have free grace to have all the glory, grace for grace's sake, John i. 16. And therefore *to him that worketh not*—that can pretend to no such merit, nor show any worth or value in his work, which may answer such a reward, but disclaiming any such pretension casts himself wholly upon the free grace of God in Christ, by a lively, active, obedient faith—to such a one *faith is counted for righteousness,* is accepted of God as the qualification required in all those that shall be pardoned and saved. *Him that justifieth the ungodly,* that is, him that was before ungodly. His former ungodliness was no bar to his justification upon his believing: τὸν ἀσεβῆ—*that ungodly one,* that is, Abraham, who, before his conversion, it should seem, was carried down the stream of the Chaldean idolatry, Josh. xxiv. 2. No room therefore is left for despair; though God clears not the impenitent guilty, yet through Christ he justifies the ungodly.

IV. He further illustrates this by a passage out of the Psalms, where David speaks of the remission of sins, the prime branch of justification, as constituting the happiness and blessedness of a man, pronouncing blessed, not the man who has no sin, or none which deserved death (for then, while man is so sinful, and God so righteous, where would be the blessed man?) but *the man to whom the Lord imputeth not sin,* who though he cannot plead, Not guilty, pleads the act of indemnity, and his plea is allowed. It is quoted from Ps. xxxii. 1, 2, where observe, 1. The nature of forgiveness. It is the remission of a debt or a crime; it is the covering of sin, as a filthy thing, as the nakedness and shame of the soul, God is said *to cast sin behind his back, to hide his face from it,* which, and the like expressions, imply that the ground of our blessedness is not our innocency, or our not having sinned (a thing is, and is filthy, though covered; justification does not make the sin not to have been, or not to have been sin), but God's not laying it to our charge, as it follows here: it is God's *not imputing sin* (*v.* 8), which makes it wholly a gracious act of God, not dealing with us in strict justice as we have deserved, not entering into judgment, not marking iniquities, all which being purely acts of grace, the acceptance and the reward cannot be expected as debts; and therefore Paul infers (*v.* 6) that it is the imputing of righteousness without works. 2. The blessedness of it: *Blessed are they.* When it is said, *Blessed are the undefiled in the way, blessed is the man that walketh not in the counsel of the wicked,* &c., the design is to show the characters of those that are blessed; but when it is said, *Blessed are those whose iniquities are forgiven,* the design is to show what that blessedness is, and what is the ground and foundation of it. Pardoned people are the only blessed people. The sentiments of the world are, Those are happy that have a clear estate, and are out of debt to man; but the sentence of the word is, Those are happy that have their debts to God discharged. O how much therefore is it our interest to make it sure to ourselves that our sins are pardoned! For this is the foundation of all other benefits. So and so I will do for them; for I will be merciful, Heb. viii. 12.

9 *Cometh* this blessedness then
upon the circumcision *only*, or upon
the uncircumcision also? for we say
that faith was reckoned to Abraham
for righteousness. 10 How was it
then reckoned? when he was in circumcision, or in uncircumcision?
Not in circumcision, but in uncircumcision. 11 And he received the
sign of circumcision, a seal of the
righteousness of the faith which *he*
had yet being uncircumcised: that he
might be the father of all them that
believe, though they be not circumcised; that righteousness might be
imputed unto them also: 12 And
the father of circumcision to them
who are not of the circumcision only,
but who also walk in the steps of that
faith of our father Abraham, which
he had being *yet* uncircumcised. 13
For the promise, that he should be
the heir of the world, *was* not to
Abraham, or to his seed, through the
law, but through the righteousness of
faith. 14 For if they which are of
the law *be* heirs, faith is made void,
and the promise made of none effect:
15 Because the law worketh wrath:
for where no law is, *there is* no
transgression. 16 Therefore *it is* of
faith, that *it might be* by grace; to the
end the promise might be sure to all the
seed; not to that only which is of the
law, but to that also which is of the
faith of Abraham; who is the father
of us all, 17 (As it is written, I have
made thee a father of many nations,)

St. Paul observes in this paragraph when and why Abraham was thus justified; for he has several things to remark upon that. It was before he was circumcised, and before the giving of the law; and there was a reason for both.

I. It was before he was circumcised, *v.* 10. His faith was counted to him for righteousness while he was in uncircumcision. It was imputed, Gen. xv. 6, and he was not circumcised till *ch.* xvii. Abraham is expressly said to be justified by faith *fourteen years,* some say *twenty-five years, before he was circumcised.* Now this the apostle takes notice of in answer to the question (*v.* 9), *Cometh this blessedness then on the circumcision only, or on the uncircumcision also?* Abraham was pardoned and accepted in uncircumcision, a circumstance which, as it might silence the fears of the poor uncircumcised Gentiles, so it might lower the pride and conceitedness of the Jews, who gloried in their circumcision, as if they had the monopoly of all happiness. Here are two reasons why Abraham was justified by faith in circumcision:—

1. That circumcision might be *a seal of the righteousness of faith, v.* 11. The tenour of the covenants must first be settled before the seal can be annexed. Sealing supposes a previous bargain, which is confirmed and ratified by that ceremony. After Abraham's justification by faith had continued several years only a grant by parole, for the confirmation of Abraham's faith God was pleased to appoint a sealing ordinance, and Abraham received it; though it was a bloody ordinance, yet he submitted to it, and even received it as a special favour, *the sign of circumcision,* &c. Now we may hence observe, (1.) The nature of sacraments in general: they are signs and seals—signs to represent and instruct, seals to ratify and confirm. They are signs of absolute grace and favour; they are seals of the conditional promises; nay, they are mutual seals: God does in the sacraments seal to us to be to us a God, and we do therein seal to him to be to him a people. (2.) The nature of circumcision in particular: it was the initiating sacrament of the Old Testament; and it is here said to be, [1.] *A sign*—a sign of that original corruption which we are all born with, and which is cut off by spiritual circumcision,—a commemorating sign of God's covenant with Abraham,—a distinguishing sign between Jews and Gentiles,—a sign of admission into the visible church,—a sign prefiguring baptism, which comes in the room of circumcision, now under the gospel, when (the blood of Christ being shed) all bloody ordinances are abolished; it was *an outward and sensible sign of an inward and spiritual grace signified thereby.* [2.] *A seal of the righteousness of the faith.* In general, it was a seal of the covenant of grace, particularly of justification by faith—the covenant of grace, called *the righteousness which is of faith* (*ch.* x. 6), and it refers to an Old-Testament promise, Deut. xxx. 12. Now if infants were then capable of receiving a seal of the covenant of grace, which proves that they then were within the verge of that covenant, how they come to be now cast out of the covenant and incapable of the seal, and by what severe sentence they were thus rejected and incapacitated, those are concerned to make out that not only reject, but nullify and reproach, the baptism of the seed of believers.

2. *That he might be the father of all those that believe.* Not but that there were those that were justified by faith before Abraham; but of Abraham first it is particularly observed, and in him commenced a much

clearer and fuller dispensation of the covenant of grace than any that had been before extant; and therefore he is called *the father of all that believe,* because he was so eminent a believer, and so eminently justified by faith, as Jabal was the father of shepherds and Jubal of musicians, Gen. iv. 20, 21. *The father of all those that believe;* that is, a standing *pattern of faith,* as parents are examples to their children; and a standing precedent of justification by faith, as the liberties, privileges, honours, and estates, of the fathers descend to their children. Abraham was the father of believers, because to him particularly the *magna charta* was renewed. (1.) The father of believing Gentiles, *though they be not circumcised.* Zaccheus, a publican, if he believe, is reckoned a son of Abraham, Luke xix. 9. Abraham being himself uncircumcised when he was justified by faith, uncircumcision can never be a bar. Thus were the doubts and fears of the poor Gentiles anticipated and no room left to question but that righteousness might be imputed to them also, Col. iii. 11; Gal. v. 6. (2.) The father of believing Jews, not merely as circumcised, and of the seed of Abraham according to the flesh, but because believers, because they *are not of the circumcision only* (that is, are not only circumcised), *but walk in the steps of that faith*—have not only the sign, but the thing signified—not only are of Abraham's family, but follow the example of Abraham's faith. See here who are the genuine children and lawful successors of those that were the church's fathers: not those that sit in their chairs, and bear their names, but those that tread in their steps; this is the line of succession, which holds, notwithstanding interruptions. It seems, then, those were most loud and forward to call Abraham father that had least title to the honours and privileges of his children. Thus those have most reason to call Christ Father, not that bear his name in being Christians in profession, but that tread in his steps.

II. It was before the giving of the law, *v* 13—16. The former observation is levelled against those that confined justification to the circumcision, this against those that expected it by the law; now the promise was made to Abraham long before the law. Compare Gal. iii. 17, 18. Now observe,

1. What that promise was—*that he should be the heir of the world,* that is, of the land of Canaan, the choicest spot of ground in the world,—or the father of many nations of the world, who sprang from him, besides the Israelites,—or the heir of the comforts of the life which now is. The meek are said to *inherit the earth,* and the world is theirs. Though Abraham had so little of the world in possession, yet he was heir of it all. Or, rather, it points at Christ, the seed here mentioned; compare Gal. iii. 16, *To thy seed, which is Christ.* Now Christ is the heir of the world, the ends of the earth are his possession, and it is in him that Abraham was so. And it refers to that promise (Gen. xii. 3), *In thee shall all the families of the earth be blessed.*

2. How it was made to him: *Not through the law, but through the righteousness of faith. Not through the law,* for that was not yet given: but it was upon that believing which was counted to him for righteousness; it was upon his trusting God, in his leaving his own country when God commanded him, Heb. xi. 8. Now, being by faith, it could not be by the law, which he proves by the opposition there is between them (*v.* 14, 15): *If those who are of the law be heirs;* that is, those, and those only, and they by virtue of the law (the Jews did, and still do, boast that they are the rightful heirs of the world, because to them the law was given), then *faith is made void;* for, if it were requisite to an interest in the promise that there should be a perfect performance of the whole law, then the promise can never take its effect, nor is it to any purpose for us to depend upon it, since the way to life by perfect obedience to the law, and spotless sinless innocency, is wholly blocked up, and the law in itself opens no other way. This he proves, *v.* 15. *The law worketh wrath*—wrath in us to God; it irritates and provokes that carnal mind which is enmity to God, as the damming up of a stream makes it swell—wrath in God against us. It works this, that is, it discovers it, or our breach of the law works it. Now it is certain that we can never expect the inheritance by a law that worketh wrath. How the law works wrath he shows very concisely in the latter part of the verse: *Where no law is there is no transgression,* an acknowledged maxim, which implies, Where there is a law there is transgression and that transgression is provoking, and so the law worketh wrath.

3. Why the promise was made to him by faith; for three reasons, *v.* 16. (1.) *That it might be by grace,* that grace might have the honour of it; *by grace, and not by the law; by grace, and not of debt, not of merit;* that *Grace, grace,* might be cried to every stone, especially to the top-stone, in this building. Faith hath particular reference to grace granting, as grace hath reference to faith receiving. *By grace,* and therefore *through faith,* Eph. ii. 8. For God will have every crown thrown at the feet of grace, free grace, and every song in heaven sung to that tune, *Not unto us, O Lord, not unto us, but unto thy name be the praise.* (2.) *That the promise might be sure.* The first covenant, being a covenant of works, was not sure: but, through man's failure, the benefits designed by it were cut off; and therefore, the more effectually to ascertain and ensure the conveyance of the new covenant, there is another way found out, *not by works* (were it so, the promise would not be sure, because of the continual frailty and infirmity of the flesh), *but by faith,* which receives all from Christ, and acts in a continual dependence upon him, as the great trustee of

our salvation, and in whose keeping it is safe. The covenant is therefore sure, because it is so well ordered in all things, 2 Sam. xxiii. 5. (3.) *That it might be sure to all the seed.* If it had been *by the law,* it had been limited to the Jews, *to whom pertained the glory, and the covenants, and the giving of the law* (*ch.* ix. 4); but therefore it was by faith that Gentiles as well as Jews might become interested in it, the spiritual as well as the natural seed of faithful Abraham. God would contrive the promise in such a way as might make it most extensive, to comprehend all true believers, that circumcision and uncircumcision might break no squares; and for this (*v.* 17) he refers us to Gen. xvii. 5, where the reason of the change of his name from *Abram—a high father, to Abraham —the high father of a multitude,* is thus rendered : *For a father of many nations have I made thee;* that is, all believers, both before and since the coming of Christ in the flesh, should take Abraham for their pattern, and call him *father.* The Jews say Abraham was the father of all proselytes to the Jewish religion. *Behold, he is the father of all the world, which are gathered under the wings of the Divine Majesty.*—Maimonides.

17 — Before him whom he believed, *even* God, who quickeneth
the dead, and calleth those things
which be not as though they were.
18 Who against hope believed in
hope, that he might become the
father of many nations, according to
that which was spoken, So shall thy
seed be. 19 And being not weak in
faith, he considered not his own body
now dead, when he was about an
hundred years old, neither yet the
deadness of Sarah's womb : 20 He
staggered not at the promise of God
through unbelief; but was strong in
faith, giving glory to God; 21 And
being fully persuaded that, what he
had promised, he was able also to
perform. 22 And therefore it was
imputed to him for righteousness.

Having observed when Abraham was justified by faith, and why, for the honour of Abraham and for example to us who call him father, the apostle here describes and commends the faith of Abraham, where observe,

I. Whom he believed : *God who quickeneth.* It is God himself that faith fastens upon : *other foundation can no man lay.* Now observe what in God Abraham's faith had an eye to—to that, certainly, which would be most likely to confirm his faith concerning the things promised :—1. *God who quickeneth the dead.* It was promised that he should be *the father of many nations,* when he and his wife were now as good as dead (Heb. xi. 11, 12), and therefore he looks upon God as a God that could breathe life into dry bones. He that quickeneth the dead can do any thing, can give a child to Abraham when he is old, can bring the Gentiles, who are *dead in trespasses and sins,* to a divine and spiritual life, Eph. ii. 1. Compare Eph. i. 19, 20. 2. *Who calleth things which are not as though they were;* that is, creates all things by the word of his power, as in the beginning, Gen. i. 3; 2 Cor. iv. 6. The justification and salvation of sinners, the espousing of the Gentiles that had not been a people, were a gracious calling of things which are not as though they were, giving being to things that were not. This expresses the sovereignty of God and his absolute power and dominion, a mighty stay to faith when all other props sink and totter. It is the holy wisdom and policy of faith to fasten particularly on that in God which is accommodated to the difficulties wherewith it is to wrestle, and will most effectually answer the objections. It is faith indeed to build upon the all-sufficiency of God for the accomplishment of that which is impossible to any thing but that all-sufficiency. Thus Abraham became *the father of many nations before him whom he believed,* that is, in the eye and account of God; or *like him whom he believed;* as God was a common Father, so was Abraham. It is by faith in God that we become accepted of him, and conformable to him.

II. How he believed. He here greatly magnifies the strength of Abraham's faith, in several expressions. 1. *Against hope, he believed in hope, v.* 18. There was a hope against him, a natural hope All the arguments of sense, and reason, and experience, which in such cases usually beget and support hope, were against him; no second causes smiled upon him, nor in the least favoured his hope. But, against all those inducements to the contrary, he believed; for he had a hope for him : *He believed in hope,* which arose, as his faith did, from the consideration of God's all-sufficiency. *That he might become the father of many nations.* Therefore God, by his almighty grace, enabled him thus to believe against hope, that he might pass for a pattern of great and strong faith to all generations. It was fit that he who was to be the father of the faithful should have something more than ordinary in his faith—that in him faith should be set in its highest elevation, and so the endeavours of all succeeding believers be directed, raised, and quickened. Or this is mentioned as the matter of the promise that he believed; and he refers to Gen. xv. 5, *So shall thy seed be,* as the stars of heaven, so innumerable, so illustrious. This was that which he believed, when it was counted to him for righteousness, *v.* 6. And it is observable that this particular instance of his faith was *against hope,* against the surmises and suggestions of his unbelief. He had just before been concluding hardly that he should go childless, that one born in his house was his heir (*v.* 2, 3); and this unbelief was a foil to his faith, and bespeaks it a believing against hope. 2. *Being not weak in faith, he considered not his own body, v.* 19. Observe, His own body was now dead —become utterly unlikely to beget a child, though the new life and vigour that God gave him continued after Sarah was dead, witness his children by Keturah. When God intends some special blessing, some child of promise, for his people, he commonly puts a sentence of death upon the blessing itself, and upon all the ways that lead to it. Joseph must be enslaved and imprisoned before he be advanced. But Abraham did not consider this, *οὐ κατενόησε—he did not dwell in his thoughts upon it.* He said indeed, *Shall a child be born to him that is a hundred years old?* Gen. xvii. 17. But that was the language of his admiration and his desire to be further satisfied, not of his doubting and distrust; his faith passed by that consideration, and thought of nothing but the faithfulness of the promise, with the contemplation whereof he was swallowed up, and this kept up his faith. *Being not weak in faith, he considered not.* It is mere weakness of faith that makes a man lie poring upon the difficulties and seeming impossibilities that lie in the way of a promise. Though it may seem to be the wisdom and policy of carnal reason, yet it is the weakness of faith, to look into the bottom of all the difficulties that arise against the promise. 3. *He staggered not at the promise of God through unbelief* (*v.* 20), and he therefore staggered not because he considered not the frowns and discouragements of second causes; *οὐ διεκρίθη—he disputed not;* he did not hold any self-consultation about it, did not take time to consider whether he should close with it or no, did not hesitate nor stumble at it, but by a resolute and peremptory act of his soul, with a holy boldness, ventured all upon the promise. He took it not for a point that would admit of argument or debate, but presently determined it as a ruled case, did not at all hang in suspense about it: he *staggered not through unbelief.* Unbelief is at the bottom of all our staggerings at God's promises. It is not the promise that fails, but our faith that fails when we stagger. 4. He *was strong in faith, giving glory to God, ἐνεδυναμώθη—he was strengthened* in faith, his faith *got ground by exercise—crescit eundo.* Though weak faith shall not be rejected, the bruised reed not broken, the smoking flax not quenched, yet strong faith shall be commended and honoured. The strength of his faith appeared in the victory it won over his fears. And hereby he gave glory to God; for, as unbelief dishonours God by making him a liar (1 John v. 10), so faith honours God by setting to its seal that he is true, John iii. 33. Abraham's faith gave God the glory of his wisdom, power, holiness, goodness, and especially of his faithfulness, resting upon the word that he had spoken. Among men we say, "He that trusts another, gives him credit, and honours him by taking his word;" thus Abraham gave glory to God by trusting him. We never hear our Lord Jesus commending any thing so much as great faith (Matt. viii. 10 and xv. 28): therefore God gives honour to faith, great faith, because faith, great faith, gives honour to God. 5. He was *fully persuaded that what God had promised he was able to perform, πληροφορηθεὶς—was carried on with the greatest confidence* and assurance; it is a metaphor taken from ships that come into the harbour with full sail. Abraham saw the storms of doubts, and fears, and temptations likely to rise against the promise, upon which many a one would have shrunk back, and lain by for fairer days, and waited a smiling gale of sense and reason. But Abraham, having taken God for his pilot, and the promise for his card and compass, resolves to weather his point, and like a bold adventurer sets up all his sails, breaks through all the difficulties, regards neither winds nor clouds, but trusts to the strength of his bottom and the wisdom and faithfulness of his pilot, and bravely makes to the harbour, and comes home an unspeakable gainer. Such was his full persuasion, and it was built on the omnipotence of God: *He was able.* Our waverings rise mainly from our distrust of the divine power; and therefore to fix us it is requisite we believe not only that he is faithful, but that he is able, that hath promised. *And therefore it was imputed to him for righteousness, v.* 22. Because with such a confidence he ventured his all in the divine promise, God graciously accepted him, and not only answered, but out-did, his expectation. This way of glorifying God by a firm reliance on his bare promise was so very agreeable to God's design, and so very conducive to his honour, that he graciously accepted it as a righteousness, and justified him, though there was not that in the thing itself which could merit such an acceptance. This shows why faith is chosen to be the prime condition of our justification, because it is a grace that of all others gives glory to God.

23 Now it was not written for his
sake alone, that it was imputed to
him; 24 But for us also, to whom
it shall be imputed, if we believe on
him that raised up Jesus our Lord
from the dead; 25 Who was delivered for our offences, and was raised
again for our justification.

In the close of the chapter, he applies all to us; and, having abundantly proved that Abraham was justified by faith, he here concludes that his justification was to be the pattern or sampler of ours: *It was not written for his sake alone.* It was not intended only for an historical commendation of Abraham, or a relation of something peculiar to him (as some antipædobaptists will needs understand that circumcision was a *seal of the righteousness of the faith* (*v.* 11), only to Abraham himself, and no other); no, the scripture did not intend hereby to describe some singular way of justification that belonged to Abraham as his prerogative. The accounts we have of the Old-Testament saints were not intended for histories only, barely to inform and divert us, but for precedents to direct us, for ensamples (1 Cor. x. 11) for *our learning, ch.* xv. 4. And this particularly concerning Abraham was written *for us also,* to assure us what that righteousness is which God requireth and accepteth to our salvation,—for us also, that are mean and vile, that come so far short of Abraham in privileges and performances, us Gentiles as well as the Jews, for the blessing of Abraham comes upon the Gentiles through Christ,—for us on whom the ends of the world are come, as well as for the patriarchs; for the grace of God is the same yesterday, to-day, and for ever. His application of it is but short. Only we may observe,

I. Our common privilege; it shall be imputed to us, that is, righteousness shall. The gospel way of justification is by an imputed righteousness, μέλλει λογίζεσθαι—*it shall be imputed;* he uses a future verb, to signify the continuation of this mercy in the church, that as it is the same now so it will be while God has a church in the world, and there are any of the children of men to be justified; for there is a fountain opened that is inexhaustible.

II. Our common duty, the condition of this privilege, and that is believing. The proper object of this believing is a divine revelation. The revelation to Abraham was concerning a Christ to come; the revelation to us is concerning a Christ already come, which difference in the revelation does not alter the case. Abraham believed the power of God in raising up an Isaac from the dead womb of Sarah; we are to believe the same power exerted in a higher instance, the resurrection of Christ from the dead. The resurrection of Isaac was in a figure (Heb. xi. 19); the resurrection of Christ was real. Now we are to believe on him that raised up Christ; not only believe his power, that he could do it, but depend upon his grace in raising up Christ as our surety; so he explains it, *v.* 25, where we have a brief account of the meaning of Christ's death and resurrection, which are the two main hinges on which the door of salvation turns. 1. He was *delivered for our offences.* God the Father delivered him, he delivered up himself as a sacrifice for sin. He died indeed as a malefactor, because he died for sin; but it was not his own sin, but the sins of the people. He died to make atonement for our sins, to expiate our guilt, to satisfy divine justice. 2. He was *raised again for our justification,* for the perfecting and completing of our justification. By the merit of his death he paid our debt, in his resurrection he took out our acquittance. When he was buried he lay a prisoner in execution for our debt, which as a surety he had undertaken to pay; on the third day an angel was sent to roll away the stone, and so to discharge the prisoner, which was the greatest assurance possible that divine justice was satisfied, the debt paid, or else he would never have released the prisoner: and therefore the apostle puts a special emphasis on Christ's resurrection; it is Christ that died, *yea, rather, that has risen again, ch.* viii. 34. So that upon the whole matter it is very evident that we are not justified by the merit of our own works, but by a fiducial obediential dependence upon Jesus Christ and his righteousness, as the condition on our part of our right to impunity and salvation, which was the truth that Paul in this and the foregoing chapter had been fixing as the great spring and foundation of all our comfort.

CHAP. V.

The apostle, having made good his point, and fully proved justification by faith, in this chapter proceeds in the explication, illustration, and application of that truth. I. He shows the fruits of justification, ver. 1—5. II. He shows the fountain and foundation of justification in the death of Jesus Christ, which he discourses of at large in the rest of the chapter.

THEREFORE being justified by
faith, we have peace with God
through our Lord Jesus Christ: 2
By whom also we have access by
faith into this grace wherein we stand,
and rejoice in hope of the glory of
God. 3 And not only *so*, but we
glory in tribulations also: knowing
that tribulation worketh patience; 4
And patience, experience; and experience, hope: 5 And hope maketh
not ashamed; because the love of God
is shed abroad in our hearts by the
Holy Ghost which is given unto us.

The precious benefits and privileges which flow from justification are such as should quicken us all to give diligence to make it sure to ourselves that we are justified, and then to take the comfort it renders to us, and to do the duty it calls for from us. The fruits of this tree of life are exceedingly precious.

I. *We have peace with God, v.* 1. It is sin that breeds the quarrel between us and God, creates not only a strangeness, but an enmity; the holy righteous God cannot in honour be at peace with a sinner while he continues under the guilt of sin. Justification takes away the guilt, and so makes way for peace. And such are the benignity and good-will of God to man that, immediately upon the removing of that obstacle, the peace is made. By faith we lay hold of God's arm and of his strength, and so are at peace, Isa. xxvii. 4, 5. There is more in this peace than barely a cessation of enmity, there is friendship and loving-kindness, for God is either the worst enemy or th best friend. Abraham, being justified by faith, was called *the friend of God* (Jam. ii. 23), which was his honour, but not his peculiar honour: Christ has called his disciples *friends*, John xv. 13—15. And surely a man needs no more to make him happy than to have God his friend! But this is *through our Lord Jesus Christ*—through him as the great peace-maker, *the Mediator between God and man*, that blessed Day's-man that has laid his hand upon us both. Adam, in innocency, had peace with God immediately; there needed no such mediator. But to guilty sinful man it is a very dreadful thing to think of God out of Christ; *for he is our peace*, Eph. ii. 14, not only the maker, but the matter and maintainer, of our peace, Col. i. 20.

II. *We have access by faith into this grace wherein we stand*, *v.* 2. This is a further privilege, not only peace, but grace, that is, this favour. Observe, 1. The saints' happy state. It is a state of grace, God's loving-kindness to us and our conformity to God; he that hath God's love and God's likeness is in a state of grace. Now into this grace we have access προσαγωγὴν—*an introduction*, which implies that we were not born in this state; we are *by nature children of wrath*, and *the carnal mind is enmity against God;* but we are brought into it. We could not have got into it of ourselves, nor have conquered the difficulties in the way, but we have a manuduction, a leading by the hand,—are led into it as blind, or lame, or weak people are led,—are introduced as pardoned offenders,—are introduced by some favourite at court to kiss the king's hand, as strangers, that are to have audience, are conducted. Προσαγωγὴν ἐσχήκαμεν—*We have had access.* He speaks of those that have been already brought out of a state of nature into a state of grace. Paul, in his conversion, had this access; then he was made nigh. Barnabas introduced him *to the apostles* (Acts ix. 27), and there were others *that led him by the hand to Damascus* (*v.* 8), but it was Christ that introduced and led him by the hand into this grace. *By whom we have access by faith.* By Christ as the author and principal agent, by faith as the means of this access. Not by Christ in consideration of any merit or desert of ours, but in consideration of our believing dependence upon him and resignation of ourselves to him. 2. Their happy standing in this state: *Wherein we stand.* Not only wherein we are, but wherein we stand, a posture that denotes our discharge from guilt; *we stand in the judgment* (Ps. i. 5), not cast, as convicted criminals, but our dignity and honour secured, not thrown to the ground, as abjects. The phrase denotes also our progress; while we stand, we are going. We must not lie down, as if we had already attained, but stand as those that are pressing forward, stand as servants attending on Christ our master. The phrase denotes, further, our perseverance: we stand firmly and safely, upheld by the power of God; stand as soldiers stand, that keep their ground, not borne down by the power of the enemy. It denotes not only our admission to, but our confirmation in, the favour of God. It is not in the court of heaven as in earthly courts, where high places are slippery places: but we stand in a humble confidence of this very thing *that he who has begun the good work will perform it*, Phil. i. 6.

III. *We rejoice in hope of the glory of God.* Besides the happiness in hand, there is a happiness in hope, *the glory of God*, the glory which God will put upon the saints in heaven, glory which will consist in the vision and fruition of God. 1. Those, and those only, that have access by faith into the grace of God now may hope for the glory of God hereafter. There is no good hope of glory but what is founded in grace; grace is glory begun, the earnest and assurance of glory. *He will give grace and glory*, Ps. lxxxiv. 11. 2. Those who hope for the glory of God hereafter have enough to rejoice in now. It is the duty of those that hope for heaven to rejoice in that hope.

IV. *We glory in tribulations also;* not only notwithstanding our tribulations (these do not hinder our rejoicing in hope of the glory of God), but even in our tribulations, as they are working for us the weight of glory, 2 Cor. iv. 17. Observe, What a growing increasing happiness the happiness of the saints is: *Not only so.* One would think such peace, such grace, such glory, and such a joy in hope of it, were more than such poor undeserving creatures as we are could pretend to; and yet it is *not only so:* there are more instances of our happiness—*we glory in tribulations also*, especially tribulations for righteousness' sake, which seemed the greatest objection against the saints' happiness, whereas really their happiness did not only consist with, but take rise from, those tribulations. *They rejoiced that they were counted worthy to suffer*, Acts v. 41. This being the hardest point, he sets himself to show the grounds and reasons of it. How come we to glory in tribulations? Why, because tribulations, by a chain of causes, greatly befriend hope, which he shows in the method of its influence. 1. *Tribulation worketh patience*, not in and of itself, but the powerful grace of God working in and with the tribulation. It proves, and by proving improves, patience, as parts and gifts increase by exercise. It is not the efficient cause, but yields the occasion, as steel is hardened by the fire. See how God brings meat out of the eater, and sweetness out of the strong. That which worketh patience is matter of joy; for patience does us more good than tribulations can do us hurt. Tribulation in itself worketh impatience; but, as it is sanctified to the saints, it worketh patience. 2. *Patience experience,* v. 4. It works an experience of God, and the songs he gives in the night; the patient sufferers have the greatest experience of the divine consolations, which abound as afflictions abound. It works an experience of ourselves. It is by tribulation that we make an experiment of our own sincerity, and therefore such tribulations are called trials. It works, δοκιμὴν—*an approbation,* as he is approved that has passed the test. Thus Job's tribulation wrought patience, and that patience produced an approbation, that still he *holds fast his integrity,* Job ii. 3. 3. *Experience hope.* He who, being thus tried, comes forth as gold, will thereby be encouraged to hope. This experiment, or approbation, is not so much the ground, as the evidence, of our hope, and a special friend to it. Experience of God is a prop to our hope; he that hath delivered doth and will. Experience of ourselves helps to evidence our sincerity. 4. This *hope maketh not ashamed;* that is, it is a hope that will not deceive us. Nothing confounds more than disappointment. Everlasting shame and confusion will be caused by the perishing of the expectation of the wicked, *but the hope of the righteous shall be gladness,* Prov. x. 28. See Ps. xxii. 5; lxxi. 1. Or, It maketh not ashamed of our sufferings. Though *we are counted as the offscouring of all things, and trodden under foot as the mire in the streets,* yet, having hopes of glory, we are not ashamed of these sufferings, It is in a good cause, for a good Master, and in good hope; and therefore we are not ashamed. We will never think ourselves disparaged by sufferings that are likely to end so well. *Because the love of God is shed abroad.* This hope will not disappoint us, because it is sealed with the Holy Spirit as a Spirit of love. It is the gracious work of the blessed Spirit to shed abroad the love of God in the hearts of all the saints. *The love of God,* that is, the sense of God's love to us, drawing out love in us to him again. Or, The great effects of his love: (1.) Special grace; and, (2.) The pleasant gust or sense of it. *It is shed abroad,* as sweet ointment, perfuming the soul, as rain watering it and making it fruitful. The ground of all our comfort and holiness, and perseverance in both, is laid in the *shedding abroad of the love of God in our hearts;* it is this which constrains us, 2 Cor. v. 14. Thus are we drawn and held by the bonds of love. Sense of God's love to us will make us not ashamed, either of our hope in him or our sufferings for him.

6 For when we were yet without
strength, in due time Christ died for
the ungodly. 7 For scarcely for a
righteous man will one die: yet peradventure for a good man some would
even dare to die. 8 But God commendeth his love toward us, in that,
while we were yet sinners, Christ died
for us. 9 Much more then, being
now justified by his blood, we shall
be saved from wrath through him.
10 For if, when we were enemies, we
were reconciled to God by the death
of his Son, much more, being reconciled, we shall be saved by his life.
11 And not only *so,* but we also joy
in God through our Lord Jesus
Christ, by whom we have now received the atonement. 12 Wherefore, as by one man sin entered into
the world, and death by sin; and so
death passed upon all men, for that
all have sinned: 13 (For until the
law sin was in the world: but sin is
not imputed when there is no law.
14 Nevertheless death reigned from
Adam to Moses, even over them that
had not sinned after the similitude of
Adam's transgression, who is the
figure of him that was to come. 15
But not as the offence, so also *is* the
free gift. For if through the offence
of one many be dead, much more the
grace of God, and the gift by grace,
which is by one man, Jesus Christ,
hath abounded unto many. 16 And
not as *it was* by one that sinned, *so*
is the gift: for the judgment *was* by
one to condemnation, but the free
gift *is* of many offences unto justification. 17 For if by one man's
offence death reigned by one; much
more they which receive abundance
of grace and of the gift of righteousness shall reign in life by one, Jesus
Christ.) 18 Therefore as by the
offence of one *judgment came* upon
all men to condemnation; even so by
the righteousness of one *the free gift*
came upon all men unto justification
of life. 19 For as by one man's disobedience many were made sinners,
so by the obedience of one shall many
be made righteous. 20 Moreover
the law entered, that the offence
might abound. But where sin
abounded, grace did much more
abound: 21 That as sin hath
reigned unto death, even so might
grace reign through righteousness

unto eternal life by Jesus Christ our Lord.

The apostle here describes the fountain and foundation of justification, laid in the death of the Lord Jesus. The streams are very sweet, but, if you run them up to the spring-head, you will find it to be Christ's dying for us; it is in the precious stream of Christ's blood that all these privileges come flowing to us: and therefore he enlarges upon this instance of the love of God which is shed abroad. Three things he takes notice of for the explication and illustration of this doctrine: — 1. The persons he died for, *v.* 6—8. 2. The precious fruits of his death, *v.* 9—11. 3. The parallel he runs between the communication of sin and death by the first Adam and of righteousness and life by the second Adam, *v.* 12, to the end.

I. The character we were under when Christ died for us.

1. *We were without strength* (*v.* 6), in a sad condition; and, which is worse, altogether unable to help ourselves out of that condition —lost, and no visible way open for our recovery—our condition deplorable, and in a manner desperate; and therefore our salvation is here said to come *in due time.* God's time to help and save is when those that are to be saved are without strength, that his own power and grace may be the more magnified, Deut. xxxii. 36. It is the manner of God to help at a dead lift,

2. *He died for the ungodly;* not only helpless creatures, and therefore likely to perish, but guilty sinful creatures, and therefore deserving to perish; not only mean and worthless, but vile and obnoxious, unworthy of such favour with the holy God. Being ungodly, they had need of one to die for them, to satisfy for guilt, and to bring in a righteousness. This he illustrates (*v.* 7, 8) as an unparalleled instance of love; herein God's thoughts and ways were above ours. Compare John xv. 13, 14, *Greater love has no man.* (1.) One would hardly *die for a righteous man,* that is, an innocent man, one that is unjustly condemned; every body will pity such a one, but few will put such a value upon his life as either to hazard, or much less to deposit, their own in his stead. (2.) It may be, one might perhaps be persuaded *to die for a good man,* that is, a useful man, who is more than barely a righteous man. Many that are good themselves yet do but little good to others; but those that are useful commonly get themselves well beloved, and meet with some that in a case of necessity would venture to be their ἀντιψυχοὶ —*would engage life for life,* would be their bail, body for body. Paul was, in this sense, a very good man, one that was very useful, and he met with some that for his life laid down their own necks, *ch.* xvi. 4. And yet observe how he qualifies this: it is but some that would do so, and it is a daring act if they do it, it must be some bold venturing soul; and, after all, it is but a *peradventure.* (3.) *But Christ died for sinners* (*v.* 8), neither righteous nor good; not only such as were useless, but such as were guilty and obnoxious; not only such as there would be no loss of should they perish, but such whose destruction would greatly redound to the glory of God's justice, being malefactors and criminals that ought to die. Some think he alludes to a common distinction the Jews had of their people into צדיקים —*righteous,* חסדים—*merciful* (compare Isa. lvii. 1), and רשעים—*wicked.* Now herein *God commended his love,* not only proved or evidenced his love (he might have done that at a cheaper rate), but magnified it and made it illustrious. This circumstance did greatly magnify and advance his love, not only put it past dispute, but rendered it the object of the greatest wonder and admiration: "Now my creatures shall see that I love them, I will give them such an instance of it as shall be without parallel." *Commendeth his love,* as merchants commend their goods when they would put them off. This commending of his love was in order to the shedding abroad of his love in our hearts by the Holy Ghost. He evinces his love in the most winning, affecting, endearing way imaginable. *While we were yet sinners,* implying that we were not to be always sinners, there should be a change wrought; for he died to save us, not in our sins, but from our sins; but we were yet sinners when he died for us. (4.) Nay, which is more, *we were enemies* (*v.* 10), not only malefactors, but traitors and rebels, in arms against the government; the worst kind of malefactors and of all malefactors the most obnoxious. The carnal mind is not only an enemy to God, but enmity itself, *ch.* viii. 7; Col. i. 21. This enmity is a mutual enmity, God loathing the sinner, and the sinner loathing God, Zech. xi. 8. And that for such as these Christ should die is such a mystery, such a paradox, such an unprecedented instance of love, that it may well be our business to eternity to adore and wonder at it. This is a commendation of love indeed. Justly might he who had thus loved us make it one of the laws of his kingdom that we should love our enemies.

II. The precious fruits of his death.

1. Justification and reconciliation are the first and primary fruit of the death of Christ: *We are justified by his blood* (*v.* 9), *reconciled by his death, v.* 10. Sin is pardoned, the sinner accepted as righteous, the quarrel taken up, the enmity slain, an end made of iniquity, and an everlasting righteousness brought in. This is done, that is, Christ has done all that was requisite on his part to be done in order hereunto, and, immediately upon our believing, we are actually put into a state of justification and reconciliation. *Justified by his blood.* Our justification is ascribed to the blood of Christ because *with-*

out blood there is no remission, Heb. ix. 22. *The blood is the life,* and that must go to make atonement. In all the propitiatory sacrifices, the sprinkling of the blood was of the essence of the sacrifice. It was *the blood that made an atonement for the soul,* Lev. xvii. 11.

2. Hence results salvation from wrath: *Saved from wrath* (*v.* 9), *saved by his life, v.* 10. When that which hinders our salvation is taken away, the salvation must needs follow. Nay, the argument holds very strongly; if God justified and reconciled us when we were enemies, and put himself to so much charge to do it, much more will he save us when we are justified and reconciled. He that has done the greater, which is of enemies to make us friends, will certainly do the less, which is when we are friends to use us friendly and to be kind to us. And therefore the apostle, once and again, speaks of it with a *much more.* He that hath digged so deep to lay the foundation will no doubt build upon that foundation.—*We shall be saved from wrath,* from hell and damnation. It is the wrath of God that is the fire of hell; *the wrath to come,* so it is called, 1 Thess. i. 10. The final justification and absolution of believers at the great day, together with the fitting and preparing of them for it, are the salvation from wrath here spoken of; it is the perfecting of the work of grace.—*Reconciled by his death, saved by his life.* His life here spoken of is not to be understood of his life in the flesh, but his life in heaven, that life which ensued after his death. Compare *ch.* xiv. 9. *He was dead, and is alive,* Rev. i. 18. We are reconciled by Christ humbled, we are saved by Christ exalted. The dying Jesus laid the foundation, in satisfying for sin, and slaying the enmity, and so making us salvable; thus is the partition-wall broken down, atonement made, and the attainder reversed; but it is the living Jesus that perfects the work: *he lives to make intercession,* Heb. vii. 25. It is Christ, in his exaltation, that by his word and Spirit effectually calls, and changes, and reconciles us to God, is our Advocate with the Father, and so completes and consummates our salvation. Compare *ch.* iv. 25 and viii. 34. Christ dying was the testator, who bequeathed us the legacy; but Christ living is the executor, who pays it. Now the arguing is very strong. He that puts himself to the charge of purchasing our salvation will not decline the trouble of applying it.

3. All this produces, as a further privilege, our *joy in God, v.* 11. God is now so far from being a terror to us that he is our *joy, and our hope in the day of evil,* Jer. xvii. 17. *We are reconciled and saved from wrath.* Iniquity, blessed be God, *shall not be our ruin. And not only so,* there is more in it yet, a constant stream of favours; we not only go to heaven, but go to heaven triumphantly; not only get into the harbour, but come in with full sail: *We joy in God,* not only saved from his wrath, but solacing ourselves in his love, and this through Jesus Christ, who is the Alpha and the Omega, the foundation-stone and the top-stone of all our comforts and hopes—not only *our salvation, but our strength and our song;* and all this (which he repeats as a string he loved to be harping upon) by virtue of the atonement, for by him we Christians, we believers, have now, now in gospel times, or now in this life, *received the atonement,* which was typified by the sacrifices under the law, and is an earnest of our happiness in heaven. True believers do by Jesus Christ receive the atonement. Receiving the atonement is our actual reconciliation to God in justification, grounded upon Christ's satisfaction. To *receive the atonement* is, (1.) To give our consent to the atonement, approving of, and agreeing to, those methods which Infinite Wisdom has taken of saving a guilty world by the blood of a crucified Jesus, being willing and glad to be saved in a gospel way and upon gospel terms. (2.) To take the comfort of the atonement, which is the fountain and the foundation of our joy in God. Now *we joy in God,* now we do indeed *receive the atonement,* *καυχώμενοι*—*glorying* in it. God hath received the atonement (Matt. iii. 17; xvii. 5; xxviii. 2): if we but receive it, the work is done.

III. The parallel that the apostle runs between the communication of sin and death by the first Adam and of righteousness and life by the second Adam (*v.* 12, to the end), which not only illustrates the truth he is discoursing of, but tends very much to the commending of the love of God and the comforting of the hearts of true believers, in showing a correspondence between our fall and our recovery, and not only a like, but a much greater power in the second Adam to make us happy, than there was in the first to make us miserable. Now, for the opening of this, observe,

1. A general truth laid down as the foundation of his discourse—that Adam was a type of Christ (*v.* 14): *Who is the figure of him that was to come.* Christ is therefore called the *last Adam,* 1 Cor. xv. 45. Compare *v.* 22. In this Adam was a type of Christ, that in the covenant-transactions that were between God and him, and in the consequent events of those transactions, Adam was a public person. God dealt with Adam and Adam acted as such a one, as a common father and factor, root and representative, of and for all his posterity; so that what he did in that station, as agent for us, we may be said to have done in him, and what was done to him may be said to have been done to us in him. Thus Jesus Christ, the Mediator, acted as a public person, the head of all the elect, dealt with God for them, as their father, factor, root, and representative—died for them, rose for them, entered within the veil for them, did all for them. When Adam

failed, we failed with him; when Christ performed, he performed for us. Thus was Adam τύπος τοῦ μέλλοντος—*the figure of him that was to come*, to come to repair that breach which Adam had made.

2. A more particular explication of the parallel, in which observe,

(1.) How Adam, as a public person, communicated sin and death to all his posterity (*v.* 12): *By one man sin entered.* We see the world under a deluge of sin and death, full of iniquities and full of calamities. Now, it is worth while to enquire what is the spring that feeds it, and you will find it to be the general corruption of nature; and at what gap it entered, and you will find it to have been Adam's first sin. It was *by one man*, and he the first man (for if any had been before him they would have been free), that one man from whom, as from the root, we all spring. [1.] By him *sin entered.* When God pronounced all very good (Gen. i. 31) there was no sin in the world; it was when Adam ate forbidden fruit that sin made its entry. Sin had before entered into the world of angels, when many of them revolted from their allegiance and left their first estate; but it never entered into the world of mankind till Adam sinned. Then it entered as an enemy, to kill and destroy, as a thief, to rob and despoil; and a dismal entry it was. Then entered the guilt of Adam's sin imputed to posterity, and a general corruption and depravedness of nature. 'Εφ' ᾧ—*for that* (so we read it), rather *in whom, all have sinned.* Sin entered into the world by Adam, for in him we all sinned. As, 1 Cor. xv. 22, *in Adam all die;* so here, *in him all have sinned;* for it is agreeable to the law of all nations that the acts of a public person be accounted theirs whom they represent; and what a whole body does every member of the same body may be said to do. Now Adam acted thus as a public person, by the sovereign ordination and appointment of God, and yet that founded upon a natural necessity; for God, as the author of nature, had made this the law of nature, that man should beget in his own likeness, and so the other creatures. In Adam therefore, as in a common receptacle, the whole nature of man was reposited, from him to flow down in a channel to his posterity; for all mankind are made *of one blood* (Acts xvii. 26), so that according as this nature proves through his standing or falling, before he puts it out of his hands, accordingly it is propagated from him. Adam therefore sinning and falling, the nature became guilty and corrupt, and is so derived. Thus in him all have sinned. [2.] *Death by sin*, for death is the wages of sin. Sin, when it is finished, brings forth death. When sin came, of course death came with it. Death is here put for all that misery which is the due desert of sin, temporal, spiritual, eternal death. If Adam had not sinned, he had not died; the threatening was, *In the day thou eatest thou shall surely die*, Gen. ii. 17. [3.] *So death passed*, that is, a sentence of death was passed, as upon a criminal, διῆλθεν—*passed through* all men, as an infectious disease passes through a town, so that none escape it. It is the universal fate, without exception: death passes upon all. There are common calamities incident to human life which do abundantly prove this. *Death reigned, v.* 14. He speaks of death as a mighty prince, and his monarchy the most absolute, universal, and lasting monarchy. None are exempted from its sceptre; it is a monarchy that will survive all other earthly rule, authority, and power, for it is the last enemy, 1 Cor. xv. 26. Those sons of Belial that will be subject to no other rule cannot avoid being subject to this. Now all this we may thank Adam for; from him sin and death descend. Well may we say, as that good man, observing the change that a fit of sickness had made in his countenance, *O Adam!* what hast thou done?

Further, to clear this, he shows that sin did not commence with the law of Moses, but was *in the world until*, or *before*, that law; therefore that law of Moses is not the only rule of life, for there was a rule, and that rule was transgressed, before the law was given. It likewise intimates that we cannot be justified by our obedience to the law of Moses, any more than we were condemned by and for our disobedience to it. Sin was in the world before the law; witness Cain's murder, the apostasy of the old world, the wickedness of Sodom. His inference hence is, Therefore there was a law; for *sin is not imputed where there is no law.* Original sin is a want of conformity to, and actual sin is a transgression of, the law of God: therefore all were under some law. His proof of it is, *Death reigned from Adam to Moses, v.* 14. It is certain that death could not have reigned if sin had not set up the throne for him. This proves that sin was in the world before the law, and original sin, for death reigned over those that had not sinned any actual sin, that *had not sinned after the similitude of Adam's transgression*, never sinned in their own persons as Adam did—which is to be understood of infants, that were never guilty of actual sin, and yet died, because Adam's sin was imputed to them. This reign of death seems especially to refer to those violent and extraordinary judgments which were long before Moses, as the deluge and the destruction of Sodom, which involved infants. It is a great proof of original sin that little children, who were never guilty of any actual transgression, are yet liable to very terrible diseases, casualties, and deaths, which could by no means be reconciled with the justice and righteousness of God if they were not chargeable with guilt.

(2.) How, in correspondence to this,

Christ, as a public person, communicates righteousness and life to all true believers, who are his spiritual seed. And in this he shows not only wherein the resemblance holds, but, *ex abundanti,* wherein the communication of grace and love by Christ *goes beyond* the communication of guilt and wrath by Adam. Observe,

[1.] Wherein the resemblance holds. This is laid down most fully, *v.* 18, 19.

First, By the offence and disobedience of one many were made sinners, and judgment came upon all men to condemnation. Here observe, 1. That Adam's sin was disobedience, disobedience to a plain and express command: and it was a command of trial. The thing he did was therefore evil because it was forbidden, and not otherwise; but this opened the door to other sins, though itself seemingly small. 2. That the malignity and poison of sin are very strong and spreading, else the guilt of Adam's sin would not have reached so far, nor have been so deep and long a stream. Who would think there should be so much evil in sin? 3. That by Adam's sin many are made sinners: *many,* that is, all his posterity; said to be many, in opposition to the one that offended. *Made sinners, κατεστάθησαν.* It denotes the making of us such by a judicial act: we were cast as sinners by due course of law. 4. That judgment is come to condemnation upon all those that by Adam's disobedience were made sinners. Being convicted, we are condemned. All the race of mankind lie under a sentence, like an attainder upon a family. There is judgment given and recorded against us in the court of heaven; and, if the judgment be not reversed, we are likely to sink under it to eternity.

Secondly, In like manner, *by the righteousness and obedience of one* (and that one is Jesus Christ, the second Adam), *are many made righteous,* and so the *free gift comes upon all.* It is observable how the apostle inculcates this truth, and repeats it again and again, as a truth of very great consequence. Here observe, 1. The nature of Christ's righteousness, how it is brought in; it is by his obedience. The disobedience of the first Adam ruined us, the obedience of the second Adam saves us,—his obedience to the law of mediation, which was that he should fulfil all righteousness, and then make his soul an offering for sin. By his obedience to this law he wrought out a righteousness for us, satisfied God's justice, and so made way for us into his favour. 2. The fruit of it. (1.) There is a *free gift come upon all men,* that is, it is made and offered promiscuously to all. The salvation wrought is a *common salvation;* the proposals are general, the tender free; whoever will may come, and take of these waters of life. This free gift is to all believers, upon their believing, *unto justification of life.* It is not only a justification that frees from death, but that entitles to life. (2.) *Many shall be made righteous*—many compared with one, or as many as belong to the election of grace, which, though but a few as they are scattered up and down in the world, yet will be a great many when they come all together. *Καταστaθήσονται—they shall be constituted* righteous, as by letters patent. Now the antithesis between these two, our ruin by Adam and our recovery by Christ, is obvious enough.

[2.] Wherein the communication of grace and love by Christ goes beyond the communication of guilt and wrath by Adam; and this he shows, *v.* 15—17. It is designed for the magnifying of the riches of Christ's love, and for the comfort and encouragement of believers, who, considering what a wound Adam's sin has made, might begin to despair of a proportionable remedy. His expressions are a little intricate, but this he seems to intend:—*First,* If guilt and wrath be communicated, much more shall grace and love; for it is agreeable to the idea we have of the divine goodness to suppose that he should be more ready to save upon an imputed righteousness than to condemn upon an imputed guilt: *Much more the grace of God, and the gift by grace.* God's goodness is, of all his attributes, in a special manner his glory, and it is that grace that is the root (his favour to us in Christ), and the gift is by grace. We know that God is rather inclined to show mercy; punishing is his strange work. *Secondly,* If there was so much power and efficacy, as it seems there was, in the sin of a man, who was of the earth, earthy, to condemn us, much more are there power and efficacy in the righteousness and grace of Christ, who is the Lord from heaven, to justify and save us. The *one man* that saves us is Jesus Christ. Surely Adam could not propagate so strong a poison but Jesus Christ could propagate as strong an antidote, and much stronger. 3. It is but the guilt of one single offence of Adam's that is laid to our charge: *The judgment was ἐξ ἑνὸς εἰς κατάκριμα, by one,* that is, by one offence, *v.* 16, 17, *Margin.* But from Jesus Christ we receive and derive an *abundance of grace, and of the gift of righteousness.* The stream of grace and righteousness is deeper and broader than the stream of guilt; for this righteousness does not only take away the guilt of that one offence, but of many other offences, even of all. God in Christ forgives all trespasses, Col. ii. 13. 4. By Adam's sin *death reigned;* but by Christ's righteousness there is not only a period put to the reign of death, but believers are preferred to *reign in life, v.* 17. In and by the righteousness of Christ we have not only a charter of pardon, but a patent of honour, are not only freed from our chains, but, like Joseph, advanced to the second chariot, and made unto our God kings and priests—not only pardoned, but preferred. See this observed, Rev. i. 5, 6; v. 9, 10. We are by Christ and his righteousness entitled to, and instated in, more and greater privileges than we lost by the offence of Adam. The plaster is wider than the wound, and more healing than the wound is killing

IV. In the last two verses the apostle seems to anticipate an objection which is expressed, Gal. iii. 19, *Wherefore then serveth the law?* Answer, 1. *The law entered that the offence might abound.* Not to make sin to abound the more in itself, otherwise than as sin takes occasion by the commandment, but to discover the abounding sinfulness of it. The glass discovers the spots, but does not cause them. When the commandment came into the world sin revived, as the letting of a clearer light into a room discovers the dust and filth which were there before, but were not seen. It was like the searching of a wound, which is necessary to the cure. *The offence, τὸ παράπτωμα—that offence,* the sin of Adam, the extending of the guilt of it to us, and the effect of the corruption in us, are the abounding of that offence which appeared upon the entry of the law. 2. *That grace might much more abound*—that the terrors of the law might make gospel-comforts so much the sweeter. Sin abounded among the Jews; and, to those of them that were converted to the faith of Christ, did not grace much more abound in the remitting of so much guilt and the subduing of so much corruption? The greater the strength of the enemy, the greater the honour of the conqueror. This abounding of grace he illustrates, *v.* 21. As the reign of a tyrant and oppressor is a foil to set off the succeeding reign of a just and gentle prince and to make it the more illustrious, so doth the reign of sin set off the reign of grace. *Sin reigned unto death;* it was a cruel bloody reign. But *grace reigns* to life, *eternal life,* and this *through righteousness,* righteousness imputed to us for justification, implanted in us for sanctification; and both by *Jesus Christ our Lord,* through the power and efficacy of Christ, the great prophet, priest, and king, of his church.

CHAP. VI.

The apostle having at large asserted, opened, and proved, the great doctrine of justification by faith, for fear lest any should suck poison out of that sweet flower, and turn that grace of God into wantonness and licentiousness, he, with a like zeal, copiousness of expression, and cogency of argument, presses the absolute necessity of sanctification and a holy life, as the inseparable fruit and companion of justification; for, wherever Jesus Christ is made of God unto any soul righteousness, he is made of God unto that soul sanctification, 1 Cor. i. 30. The water and the blood came streaming together out of the pierced side of the dying Jesus. And what God hath thus joined together let not us dare to put asunder.

WHAT shall we say then? Shall
we continue in sin, that grace
may abound? 2 God forbid. How
shall we, that are dead to sin, live any
longer therein? 3 Know ye not,
that so many of us as were baptized
into Jesus Christ were baptized into
his death? 4 Therefore we are
buried with him by baptism into
death: that like as Christ was raised
up from the dead by the glory of the
Father, even so we also should walk
in newness of life. 5 For if we have
been planted together in the likeness
of his death, we shall be also *in the*
likeness of *his* resurrection: 6 Knowing this, that our old man is crucified
with *him,* that the body of sin might
be destroyed, that henceforth we
should not serve sin. 7 For he that
is dead is freed from sin. 8 Now if
we be dead with Christ, we believe
that we shall also live with him: 9
Knowing that Christ being raised
from the dead dieth no more; death
hath no more dominion over him.
10 For in that he died, he died unto
sin once: but in that he liveth, he
liveth unto God. 11 Likewise reckon
ye also yourselves to be dead indeed
unto sin, but alive unto God through
Jesus Christ our Lord. 12 Let not
sin therefore reign in your mortal
body, that ye should obey it in the
lusts thereof. 13 Neither yield ye
your members *as* instruments of unrighteousness unto sin: but yield
yourselves unto God, as those that
are alive from the dead, and your
members *as* instruments of righteousness unto God. 14 For sin shall
not have dominion over you: for ye
are not under the law, but under
grace. 15 What then? shall we sin,
because we are not under the law,
but under grace? God forbid. 16
Know ye not, that to whom ye yield
yourselves servants to obey, his servants ye are to whom ye obey; whether of sin unto death, or of obedience
unto righteousness? 17 But God be
thanked, that ye were the servants of
sin, but ye have obeyed from the
heart that form of doctrine which was
delivered you. 18 Being then made
free from sin, ye became the servants
of righteousness. 19 I speak after
the manner of men because of the
infirmity of your flesh: for as ye
have yielded your members servants
to uncleanness and to iniquity unto
iniquity; even so now yield your
members servants to righteousness

unto holiness. 20 For when ye
were the servants of sin, ye were free
from righteousness. 21 What fruit
had ye then in those things whereof
ye are now ashamed? for the end of
those things *is* death. 22 But now
being made free from sin, and become
servants to God, ye have your fruit
unto holiness, and the end everlasting life. 23 For the wages of sin *is*
death; but the gift of God *is* eternal
life through Jesus Christ our Lord.

The apostle's transition, which joins this discourse with the former, is observable: "*What shall we say then? v.* 1. What use shall we make of this sweet and comfortable doctrine? Shall we do evil that good may come, as some say we do? *ch.* iii. 8. *Shall we continue in sin that grace may abound?* Shall we hence take encouragement to sin with so much the more boldness, because the more sin we commit the more will the grace of God be magnified in our pardon? Is this a use to be made of it? No, it is an abuse, and the apostle startles at the thought of it (*v.* 2): "*God forbid;* far be it from us to think such a thought." He entertains the objection as Christ did the devil's blackest temptation (Matt. iv. 10): *Get thee hence, Satan.* Those opinions that give any countenance to sin, or open a door to practical immoralities, how specious and plausible soever they be rendered, by the pretension of advancing free grace, are to be rejected with the greatest abhorrence; for the truth as it is in Jesus is a truth *according to godliness,* Tit. i. 1. The apostle is very full in pressing the necessity of holiness in this chapter, which may be reduced to two heads:—His exhortations to holiness, which show the nature of it; and his motives or arguments to enforce those exhortations, which show the necessity of it.

I. For the first, we may hence observe the nature of sanctification, what it is, and wherein it consists. In general it has two things in it, mortification and vivification—dying to sin and living to righteousness, elsewhere expressed by putting off the old man and putting on the new, ceasing to do evil and learning to do well.

1. Mortification, putting off the old man; several ways this is expressed. (1.) We must *live no longer in sin* (*v.* 2), we must not be as we have been nor do as we have done. The time past of our life must suffice, 1 Peter iv. 3. Though there are none that live without sin, yet, blessed be God, there are those that do not live in sin, do not live in it as their element, do not make a trade of it: this is to be sanctified. (2.) *The body of sin must be destroyed, v.* 6 The corruption that dwelleth in us is the body of sin, consisting of many parts and members, as a body. This is the root to which the axe must be laid. We must not only cease from the acts of sin (this may be done through the influence of outward restraints, or other inducements), but we must get the vicious habits and inclinations weakened and destroyed; not only cast away the idols out of the sanctuary, but the idols of iniquity out of the heart.—*That henceforth we should not serve sin.* The actual transgression is certainly in a great measure prevented by the crucifying and killing of the original corruption. Destroy the body of sin, and then, though there should be Canaanites remaining in the land, yet the Israelites will not be slaves to them. It is the body of sin that sways the sceptre, wields the iron rod; destroy this, and the yoke is broken. The destruction of Eglon the tyrant is the deliverance of oppressed Israel from the Moabites. (3.) *We must be dead indeed unto sin, v.* 11. As the death of the oppressor is a release, so much more is the death of the oppressed, Job iii. 17, 18. Death brings a writ of ease to the weary. Thus must we be dead to sin, obey it, observe it, regard it, fulfil its will no more than he that is dead doth his *quondam* task-masters—be as indifferent to the pleasures and delights of sin as a man that is dying is to his former diversions. He that is dead is separated from his former company, converse, business, enjoyments, employments, is not what he was, does not what he did, has not what he had. Death makes a mighty change; such a change doth sanctification make in the soul, it cuts off all correspondence with sin. (4.) *Sin must not reign in our mortal bodies that we should obey it, v.* 12. Though sin may remain as an outlaw, though it may oppress as a tyrant, yet let it not reign as a king. Let it not make laws, nor preside in councils, nor command the militia; let it not be uppermost in the soul, so that we should obey it. Though we may be sometimes overtaken and overcome by it, yet let us never be obedient to it in the lusts thereof; let not sinful lusts be a law to you, to which you would yield a consenting obedience. *In the lusts thereof—ἐν ταῖς ἐπιθυμίαις αὐτοῦ.* It refers to the body, not to sin. Sin lies very much in the gratifying of the body, and humouring that. And there is a reason implied in the phrase *your mortal body;* because it is a mortal body, and hastening apace to the dust, therefore let not sin reign in it. It was sin that made our bodies mortal, and therefore do not yield obedience to such an enemy. (5.) We must not *yield our members as instruments of unrighteousness, v.* 13. The members of the body are made use of by the corrupt nature as tools, by which the wills of the flesh are fulfilled; but we must not consent to that abuse. The members of the body are fearfully and wonderfully made; it is a pity they should be the devil's tools of *unrighteousness unto sin,* instruments of the sinful actions,

according to the sinful dispositions. Unrighteousness is unto sin; the sinful acts confirm and strengthen the sinful habits; one sin begets another; it is like the letting forth of water, therefore leave it before it be meddled with. The members of the body may perhaps, through the prevalency of temptation, be forced to be instruments of sin; but do not yield them to be so, do not consent to it. This is one branch of sanctification, the mortification of sin.

2. Vivification, or living to righteousness; and what is that? (1.) It is to *walk in newness of life, v.* 4. Newness of life supposes newness of heart, for out of the heart are the issues of life, and there is no way to make the stream sweet but by making the spring so. Walking, in scripture, is put for the course and tenour of the conversation, which must be new. Walk by new rules, towards new ends, from new principles. Make a new choice of the way. Choose new paths to walk in, new leaders to walk after, new companions to walk with. Old things should pass away, and all things become new. The man is what he was not, does what he did not. (2.) It is to be *alive unto God through Jesus Christ our Lord, v.* 11. To converse with God, to have a regard to him, a delight in him, a concern for him, the soul upon all occasions carried out towards him as towards an agreeable object, in which it takes a complacency: this is to be alive to God. The love of God reigning in the heart is the life of the soul towards God. *Anima est ubi amat, non ubi animat—The soul is where it loves, rather than where it lives.* It is to have the affections and desires alive towards God. Or, *living* (our life in the flesh) *unto God,* to his honour and glory as our end, by his word and will as our rule—in all our ways to acknowledge him, and to have our eyes ever towards him; this is to live unto God. —*Through Jesus Christ our Lord.* Christ is our spiritual life; there is no living to God but through him. He is the Mediator; there can be no comfortable receivings from God, nor acceptable regards to God, but in and through Jesus Christ; no intercourse between sinful souls and a holy God, but by the mediation of the Lord Jesus. Through Christ as the author and maintainer of this life; through Christ as the head from whom we receive vital influence; through Christ as the root by which we derive sap and nourishment, and so live. In living to God, Christ is all in all. (3.) It is to *yield ourselves to God, as those that are alive from the dead, v.* 13. The very life and being of holiness lie in the dedication of ourselves to the Lord, giving our own selves to the Lord, 2 Cor. viii. 5. "Yield yourselves to him, not only as the conquered yields to the conqueror, because he can stand it out no longer; but as the wife yields herself to her husband, to whom her desire is, as the scholar yields himself to the teacher, the apprentice to his master, to be taught and ruled by him. Not yield your estates to him, but yield yourselves; nothing less than your whole selves;" *παραστήσατε ἑαυτοὺς, accommodate vos ipsos Deo—accommodate yourselves to God;* so *Tremellius,* from the *Syriac.* "Not only submit to him, but comply with him; not only present yourselves to him once for all, but be always ready to serve him. Yield yourselves to him as wax to the seal, to take any impression, to be, and have, and do, what he pleases." When Paul said, *Lord, what wilt thou have me to do?* (Acts ix. 6) he was then yielded to God. *As those that are alive from the dead.* To yield a dead carcase to a living God is not to please him, but to mock him: "Yield yourselves as those that are alive and good for something, a *living sacrifice, ch.* xii. 1. The surest evidence of our spiritual life is the dedication of ourselves to God. It becomes those that are alive from the dead (it may be understood of a death in law), that are justified and delivered from death, to give themselves to him that hath so redeemed them. (4.) It is to yield *our members as instruments of righteousness to God.* The members of our bodies, when withdrawn from the service of sin, are not to lie idle, but to be made use of in the service of God. When the strong man armed is dispossessed, let him whose right it is divide the spoils. Though the powers and faculties of the soul be the immediate subjects of holiness and righteousness, yet the members of the body are to be instruments; the body must be always ready to serve the soul in the service of God. Thus (*v.* 19), "*Yield your members servants to righteousness unto holiness.* Let them be under the conduct and at the command of the righteous law of God, and that principle of inherent righteousness which the Spirit, as sanctifier, plants in the soul." *Righteousness unto holiness,* which intimates growth, and progress, and ground obtained. As every sinful act confirms the sinful habit, and makes the nature more and more prone to sin (hence the members of a natural man are here said to be servants to *iniquity unto iniquity*—one sin makes the heart more disposed for another), so every gracious act confirms the gracious habit: serving righteousness is unto holiness; one duty fits us for another; and the more we do the more we may do for God. Or serving righteousness, *εἰς ἁγιασμὸν —as an evidence of sanctification.*

II. The motives or arguments here used to show the necessity of sanctification. There is such an antipathy in our hearts by nature to holiness that it is no easy matter to bring them to submit to it: it is the Spirit's work, who persuades by such inducements as these set home upon the soul.

1. He argues from our sacramental conformity to Jesus Christ. Our baptism, with the design and intention of it, carries in it a great reason why we should die to sin, and live to righteousness. Thus we must im-

prove our baptism as a bridle of restraint to keep us in from sin, as a spur of constraint to quicken us to duty. Observe this reasoning.

(1.) In general, we are *dead to sin,* that is, in profession and in obligation. Our baptism signifies our cutting off from the kingdom of sin. We profess to have no more to do with sin. We are dead to sin by a participation of virtue and power for the killing of it, and by our union with Christ and interest in him, in and by whom it is killed. All this is in vain if we persist in sin; we contradict a profession, violate an obligation, return to that to which we were dead, like walking ghosts, than which nothing is more unbecoming and absurd. For (*v.* 7) *he that is dead is freed from sin;* that is, he that is dead to it is freed from the rule and dominion of it, as the servant that is dead is freed from his master, Job iii. 19. Now shall we be such fools as to return to that slavery from which we are discharged? When we are delivered out of Egypt, shall we talk of going back to it again?

(2.) In particular, being *baptized into Jesus Christ, we were baptized into his death, v.* 3. We were baptized εἰς Χριστὸν—*unto Christ,* as 1 Cor. x. 2, εἰς Μωσῆν—*unto Moses.* Baptism binds us to Christ, it binds us apprentice to Christ as our teacher, it is our allegiance to Christ as our sovereign. Baptism is *externa ansa Christi—the external handle of Christ,* by which Christ lays hold on men, and men offer themselves to Christ. Particularly, we were baptized into his death, into a participation of the privileges purchased by his death, and into an obligation both to comply with the design of his death, which was to redeem us from all iniquity, and to conform to the pattern of his death, that, as Christ died for sin, so we should die to sin. This was the profession and promise of our baptism, and we do not do well if we do not answer this profession, and make good this promise.

[1.] Our conformity to the death of Christ obliges us to die unto sin; thereby we know the *fellowship of his sufferings,* Phil. iii. 10. Thus we are here said to be *planted together in the likeness of his death* (*v.* 5), τῷ ὁμοιώματι, not only a conformity, but a conformation, as the engrafted stock is planted together into the likeness of the shoot, of the nature of which it doth participate. Planting is in order to life and fruitfulness: we are planted in the vineyard in a likeness to Christ, which likeness we should evidence in sanctification. Our creed concerning Jesus Christ is, among other things, that he was *crucified, dead, and buried;* now baptism is a sacramental conformity to him in each of these, as the apostle here takes notice. *First, Our old man is crucified with him, v.* 6. The death of the cross was a slow death; the body, after it was nailed to the cross, gave many a throe and many a struggle: but it was a sure death, long in expiring, but expired at last; such is the mortification of sin in believers. It was a cursed death, Gal. iii. 13. Sin dies as a malefactor, devoted to destruction; it is an accursed thing. Though it be a slow death, yet this must needs hasten it that it is an old man that is crucified; not in the prime of its strength, but decaying: that which waxeth old is ready to vanish away, Heb. viii. 13. *Crucified with him*—συνεσταυρώθη, not in respect of time, but in respect of causality. The crucifying of Christ for us has an influence upon the crucifying of sin in us. *Secondly,* We are dead with Christ, *v.* 8. Christ was obedient to death: when he died, we might be said to die with him, as our dying to sin is an act of conformity both to the design and to the example of Christ's dying for sin. Baptism signifies and seals our union with Christ, our engrafting into Christ; so that we are dead with him, and engaged to have no more to do with sin than he had. *Thirdly, We are buried with him by baptism, v.* 4. Our conformity is complete. We are in profession quite cut off from all commerce and communion with sin, as those that are buried are quite cut off from all the world; not only not of the living, but no more among the living, have nothing more to do with them. Thus must we be, as Christ was, separate from sin and sinners. We are buried, namely, in profession and obligation: we profess to be so, and we are bound to be so: it was our convenant and engagement in baptism; we are sealed to be the Lord's, therefore to be cut off from sin. Why this burying in baptism should so much as allude to any custom of dipping under water in baptism, any more than our baptismal crucifixion and death should have any such references, I confess I cannot see. It is plain that it is not the sign, but the thing signified, in baptism, that the apostle here calls being buried with Christ, and the expression of burying alludes to Christ's burial. As Christ was buried, that he might rise again to a new and more heavenly life, so we are in baptism buried, that is, cut off from the life of sin, that we may rise again to a new life of faith and love.

[2.] Our conformity to the resurrection of Christ obliges us to rise again to newness of life. This is *the power of his resurrection* which Paul was so desirous to know, Phil. iii. 10. Christ was raised up *from the dead by the glory of the Father,* that is, by the power of the Father. The power of God is his glory; it is glorious power, Col. i. 11. Now in baptism we are obliged to conform to that pattern, to be planted in the *likeness of his resurrection* (*v.* 5), to *live with him, v.* 8. See Col. ii. 12. Conversion is the first resurrection from the death of sin to the life of righteousness; and this resurrection is conformable to Christ's resurrection. This conformity of the saints to the resurrection of Christ seems to be intimated in the rising of so many of the bodies of the saints, which, though mentioned before by anticipation, is supposed to have been concomitant with Christ's resurrection, Matt. xxvii. 52. We have all risen with Christ. In two things we must conform to the resurrection of Christ:—*First,* He rose to die no more, *v.* 9. We read of many others that were raised from the dead, but they rose to die again. But, when Christ rose, he rose to die no more; therefore he left his grave-clothes behind him, whereas Lazarus, who was to die again, brought them out with him, as one that should have occasion to use them again: but over Christ *death has no more dominion;* he was dead indeed, but he is alive, and so alive that he lives for evermore, Rev. i. 18. Thus we must rise from the grave of sin never again to return to it, nor to have any more fellowship with the works of darkness, having quitted that grave, that land of darkness as darkness itself. *Secondly,* He rose to live unto God (*v.* 10), to live a heavenly life, to receive that glory which was set before him. Others that were raised from the dead returned to the same life in every respect which they had before lived; but so did not Christ: he rose again to leave the world. *Now I am no more in the world,* John xiii. 1; xvii. 11. He rose to *live to God,* that is, to intercede and rule, and all to the glory of the Father. Thus must we rise to live to God: this is what he calls *newness of life* (*v.* 4), to live from other principles, by other rules, with other aims, than we have done. A life devoted to God is a new life; before, self was the chief and highest end, but now God. To live indeed is to live to God, with our eyes ever towards him, making him the centre of all our actions.

2. He argues from the precious promises and privileges of the new covenant, *v.* 14. It might be objected that we cannot conquer and subdue sin, it is unavoidably too hard for us: "No," says he, "you wrestle with an enemy that may be dealt with and subdued, if you will but keep your ground and stand to your arms; it is an enemy that is already foiled and baffled; there is strength laid up in the covenant of grace for your assistance, if you will but use it. *Sin shall not have dominion.*" God's promises to us are more powerful and effectual for the mortifying of sin than our promises to God. Sin may struggle in a believer, and may create him a great deal of trouble, but it shall not have dominion; it may vex him, but shall not rule over him. *For we are not under the law, but under grace,* not under the law of sin and death, but under the law of the spirit of life, which is in Christ Jesus: we are actuated by other principles than we have been: new lords, new laws. Or, not under the covenant of works, which requires brick, and gives no straw, which condemns upon the least failure, which runs thus, "Do this, and live; do it not, and die;" but under the covenant of grace, which accepts sincerity as our gospel perfection, which requires nothing but what it promises strength to perform, which is herein well ordered, that every transgression in the covenant does not put us out of covenant, and especially that it does not leave our salvation in our own keeping, but lays it up in the hands of the Mediator, who undertakes for us that sin shall not have dominion over us, who hath himself condemned it, and will destroy it; so that, if we pursue the victory, we shall come off more than conquerors. Christ rules by the golden sceptre of grace, and he will not let sin have dominion over those that are willing subjects to that rule. This is a very comfortable word to all true believers. If we were under the law, we were undone, for the law curses every one that continues not in every thing; but we are under grace, grace which accepts the willing mind, which is not extreme to mark what we do amiss, which leaves room for repentance, which promises pardon upon repentance; and what can be to an ingenuous mind a stronger motive than this to have nothing to do with sin? Shall we sin against so much goodness, abuse such love? Some perhaps might suck poison out of this flower, and disingenuously use this as an encouragement to sin. See how the apostle starts at such a thought (*v.* 15): *Shall we sin because we are not under the law, but under grace? God forbid.* What can be more black and ill-natured than from a friend's extraordinary expressions of kindness and good-will to take occasion to affront and offend him? To spurn at such bowels, to spit in the face of such love, is that which, between man and man, all the world would cry out shame on.

3. He argues from the evidence that this will be of our state, making for us, or against us (*v.* 16): *To whom you yield yourselves servants to obey, his servants you are.* All the children of men are either the servants of God, or the servants of sin; these are the two families. Now, if we would know to which of these families we belong, we must enquire to which of these masters we yield obedience. Our obeying the laws of sin will be an evidence against us that we belong to that family on which death is entailed. As, on the contrary, our obeying the laws of Christ will evidence our relation to Christ's family.

4. He argues from their former sinfulness, *v.* 17—21, where we may observe,

(1.) What they had been and done formerly. We have need to be often reminded of our former state. Paul frequently remembers it concerning himself, and those to whom he writes. [1.] *You were the servants of sin.* Those that are now the servants of God would do well to remember the time when they were the servants of sin, to keep them humble, penitent, and watchful, and to quicken them in the service of God. It is a reproach to the service of sin that so many thousands have quitted the service, and shaken off the yoke; and never any that sincerely deserted it, and gave up themselves to the service of God, have returned to the former drudgery. "*God be thanked that you were so*, that is, that though you were so, yet you have obeyed. You were so; God be thanked that we can speak of it as a thing past: you were so, but you are not now so. Nay, your having been so formerly tends much to the magnifying of divine mercy and grace in the happy change. God be thanked that the former sinfulness is such a foil and such a spur to your present holiness." [2.] *You have yielded your members servants to uncleanness, and to iniquity unto iniquity*, v. 19. It is the misery of a sinful state that the body is made a drudge to sin, than which there could not be a baser or a harder slavery, like that of the prodigal that was sent into the fields to feed swine. *You have yielded.* Sinners are voluntary in the service of sin. The devil could not force them into the service, if they did not yield themselves to it. This will justify God in the ruin of sinners, that they sold themselves to work wickedness: it was their own act and deed. *To iniquity unto iniquity.* Every sinful act strengthens and confirms the sinful habit: to iniquity as the work unto iniquity as the wages. Sow the wind, and reap the whirlwind; growing worse and worse, more and more hardened. This he speaks *after the manner of men*, that is, he fetches a similitude from that which is common among men, even the change of services and subjections. [3.] *You were free from righteousness* (v. 20); not free by any liberty given, but by a liberty taken, which is licentiousness: "*You were* altogether void of that which is good,—void of any good principles, motions, or inclinations,—void of all subjection to the law and will of God, of all conformity to his image; and this you were highly pleased with, as a freedom and a liberty; but a freedom from righteousness is the worst kind of slavery."

(2.) How the blessed change was made, and wherein it did consist.

[1.] *You have obeyed from the heart that form of doctrine which was delivered to you*, v. 17. This describes conversion, what it is; it is our conformity to, and compliance with, the gospel which was delivered to us by Christ and his ministers.—*Margin. Whereto you were delivered; εἰς ὃν παρεδόθητε—into which you were delivered.* And so observe, *First*, The rule of grace, *that form of doctrine—τύπον διδαχῆς.* The gospel is the great rule both of truth and holiness; it is the stamp, grace is the impression of that stamp; it is the form of healing words, 2 Tim. i. 13. *Secondly*, The nature of grace, as it is our conformity to that rule. 1. It is to *obey from the heart.* The gospel is a doctrine not only to be believed, but to be obeyed, and that from the heart, which denotes the sincerity and reality of that obedience; not in profession only, but in power—from the heart, the innermost part, the commanding part of us. 2. It is to be *delivered into it*, as into a mould, as the wax is cast into the impression of the seal, answering it line for line, stroke for stroke, and wholly representing the shape and figure of it. To be a Christian indeed is to be transformed into the likeness and similitude of the gospel, our souls answering to it, complying with it, conformed to it—understanding, will, affections, aims, principles, actions, all according to that form of doctrine.

[2.] *Being made free from sin, you became servants of righteousness* (v. 18), *servants to God, v.* 22. Conversion is, *First*, A freedom from the service of sin; it is the shaking off of that yoke, resolving to have no more to do with it. *Secondly*, A resignation of ourselves to the service of God and righteousness, to God as our master, to righteousness as our work. When we are made free from sin, it is not that we may live as we list, and be our own masters; no: when we are delivered out of Egypt, we are, as Israel, led to the holy mountain, to receive the law, and are there brought into the bond of the covenant. Observe, We cannot be made the servants of God till we are freed from the power and dominion of sin; we cannot serve two masters so directly opposite one to another as God and sin are. We must, with the prodigal, quit the drudgery of the citizen of the country, before we can come to our Father's house.

(3.) What apprehensions they now had of their former work and way. He appeals to themselves (v. 21), whether they had not found the service of sin, [1.] An unfruitful service: "*What fruit had you then?* Did you ever get any thing by it? Sit down, and cast up the account, reckon your gains, what fruit had you then?" Besides the future losses, which are infinitely great, the very present gains of sin are not worth mentioning. *What fruit?* Nothing that deserves the name of fruit. The present pleasure and profit of sin do not deserve to be called fruit; they are but chaff, ploughing iniquity, sowing vanity, and reaping the same. [2.] It is an unbecoming service; it is that of which we *are now ashamed*—ashamed of the folly, ashamed of the filth, of it. Shame came into the world with sin, and is still the certain product of it—either the shame of repentance, or, if not that, eternal shame and contempt. Who would wilfully do that which sooner or later he is sure to be ashamed of?

5. He argues from the end of all these things. It is the prerogative of rational creatures that they are endued with a power of prospect, are capable of looking forward, considering the latter end of things. To persuade us from sin to holiness here are blessing and cursing, good and evil, life and death, set before us; and we are put to our choice.

(1.) The end of sin is death (*v.* 21): *The end of those things is death.* Though the way may seem pleasant and inviting, yet the end is dismal: at the last it bites; it will be bitterness in the latter end. *The wages of sin is death, v.* 23. Death is as due to a sinner when he hath sinned as wages are to a servant when he hath done his work. This is true of every sin. There is no sin in its own nature venial. Death is the wages of the least sin. Sin is here represented either as the work for which the wages are given, or as the master by whom the wages are given; all that are sin's servants and do sin's work must expect to be thus paid. (2.) If the fruit be unto holiness, if there be an active principle of true and growing grace, the end will be everlasting life—a very happy end!—Though the way be up-hill, though it be narrow, and thorny, and beset, yet everlasting life at the end of it is sure. So, *v.* 23, *The gift of God is eternal life.* Heaven is life, consisting in the vision and fruition of God; and it is eternal life, no infirmities attending it, no death to put a period to it. This is the gift of God. The death is the wages of sin, it comes by desert; but the life is a gift, it comes by favour. Sinners merit hell, but saints do not merit heaven. There is no proportion between the glory of heaven and our obedience; we must thank God, and not ourselves, if ever we get to heaven. And this gift is *through Jesus Christ our Lord.* It is Christ that purchased it, prepared it, prepares us for it, preserves us to it; he is *the Alpha and Omega,* All in all in our salvation.

CHAP. VII.

We may observe in this chapter, I. Our freedom from the law further urged as an argument to press upon us sanctification, ver. 1—6. II. The excellency and usefulness of the law asserted and proved from the apostle's own experience, notwithstanding, ver. 7—14. III. A description of the conflict between grace and corruption in the heart, ver. 14, 15, to the end.

KNOW ye not, brethren, (for I speak to them that know the law,) how that the law hath dominion over a man as long as he liveth? 2
For the woman which hath a husband is bound by the law to *her* husband so long as he liveth; but if the husband be dead, she is loosed from the law of *her* husband. 3 So
then if, while *her* husband liveth, she be married to another man, she shall be called an adulteress: but if her husband be dead, she is free from that law; so that she is no adulteress, though she be married to another
man. 4 Wherefore, my brethren, ye also are become dead to the law by the body of Christ; that ye should be married to another, *even* to him who is raised from the dead, that we should
bring forth fruit unto God. 5 For
when we were in the flesh, the motions of sin, which were by the law, did work in our members to bring
forth fruit unto death. 6 But now
we are delivered from the law, that being dead wherein we were held; that we should serve in newness of spirit, and not *in* the oldness of the letter.

Among other arguments used in the foregoing chapter to persuade us against sin, and to holiness, this was one (*v.* 14), that *we are not under the law;* and this argument is here further insisted upon and explained (*v.* 6): *We are delivered from the law.* What is meant by this? And how is it an argument why sin should not reign over us, and why we should walk in newness of life? 1. We are delivered from that power of the law which curses and condemns us for the sin committed by us. The sentence of the law against us is vacated and reversed, by the death of Christ, to all true believers. The law saith, *The soul that sins shall die;* but we are delivered from the law. *The Lord has taken away thy sin, thou shalt not die.* We are *redeemed from the curse of the law,* Gal. iii. 13. 2. We are delivered from that power of the law which irritates and provokes the sin that dwelleth in us. This the apostle seems especially to refer to (*v.* 5): *The motions of sins which were by the law.* The law, by commanding, forbidding, threatening, corrupt and fallen man, but offering no grace to cure and strengthen, did but stir up the corruption, and, like the sun shining upon a dunghill, excite and draw up the filthy steams. We being lamed by the fall, the law comes and directs us, but provides nothing to heal and help our lameness, and so makes us halt and stumble the more. Understand this of the law not as a rule, but as a covenant of works. Now each of these is an argument why we should be holy; for here is encouragement to endeavours, though in many things we come short. We are under grace, which promises strength to do what it commands, and pardon upon repentance when we do amiss. This is the scope of these verses in general, that, in point of profession and privilege, we are under a covenant of grace, and not under a covenant of works—under the gospel of Christ, and not under the law of Moses. The difference between a law-state and a gospel-state he had before illustrated by the similitude of rising to a new life, and serving a new master; now here he speaks of it under the similitude of being married to a new husband.

I. Our first marriage was to the law, which, according to the law of marriage, was to continue only during the life of the law. The law of marriage is binding till the death of one of the parties, no matter which, and no longer. The death of either discharges both. For this he appeals to themselves, as persons knowing the law (*v.* 1): *I speak to those that know the law.* It is a great advantage to discourse with those that have knowledge, for such can more readily understand and apprehend a truth. Many of the Christians at Rome were such as had been Jews, and so were well acquainted with the law. One has some hold of knowing people. *The law hath power over a man as long as he liveth;* in particular, the law of marriage hath power; or, in general, every law is so limited—the laws of nations, of relations, of families, &c. 1. The obligation of laws extends no further; by death the servant who, while he lived, was under the yoke, is *freed from his master,* Job iii. 19. 2. The condemnation of laws extends no further; death is the finishing of the law. *Actio moritur cum personâ—The action expires with the person.* The severest laws could but kill the body, and after that there is no more that they can do. Thus while we were alive to the law we were under the power of it—while we were in our Old-Testament state, before the gospel came into the world, and before it came with power into our hearts. Such is the law of marriage (*v.* 2), the woman is bound to her husband during life, so bound to him that she cannot marry another; if she do, she shall be reckoned an adulteress, *v.* 3. It will make her an adulteress, not only to be defiled by, but to be married to, another man; for that is so much the worse, upon this account, that it abuses an ordinance of God, by making it to patronise the uncleanness. Thus were we married to the law (*v.* 5): *When we were in the flesh,* that is, in a carnal state, under the reigning power of sin and corruption—in the flesh as in our element—then *the motions of sins which were by the law did work in our members,* we were carried down the stream of sin, and the law was but as an imperfect dam, which made the stream to swell the higher, and rage the more. Our desire was towards sin, as that of the wife towards her husband, and sin ruled over us. We embraced it, loved it, devoted all to it, conversed daily with it, made it our care to please it. We were under a law of sin and death, as the wife under the law of marriage; and the product of this marriage was fruit brought forth unto death, that is, actual transgressions were produced by the original corruptions, such as deserve death. Lust, having conceived by the law (which is the strength of sin, 1 Cor. xv. 56), *bringeth forth sin, and sin, when it is finished, bringeth forth death,* Jam. i. 15. This is the posterity that springs from this marriage to sin and the law. This comes of the motions of sin working in our members. And this continues during life, while the law is alive to us, and we are alive to the law.

II. Our second marriage is to Christ: and how comes this about? Why,

1. We are freed, by death, from our obligation to the law as a covenant, as the wife is from her obligation to her husband, *v.* 3. This resemblance is not very close, nor needed it to be. *You are become dead to the law, v.* 4. He does not say, "The law is dead" (some think because he would avoid giving offence to those who were yet zealous for the law), but, which comes all to one, *You are dead to the law.* As the crucifying of the world to us, and of us to the world, amounts to one and the same thing, so doth the law dying, and our dying to it. We are *delivered from the law* (*v.* 6), κατηργήθημεν—*we are nulled* as to the law; our obligation to it as a husband is cassated and made void. And then he speaks of the law being dead as far as it was a law of bondage to us: *That being dead wherein we were held;* not the law itself, but its obligation to punishment and its provocation to sin. It is dead, it has lost its power; and this (*v.* 4) *by the body of Christ,* that is, by the sufferings of Christ in his body, by his crucified body, which abrogated the law, answered the demands of it, made satisfaction for our violation of it, purchased for us a covenant of grace, in which righteousness and strength are laid up for us, such as were not, nor could be, by the law. We are dead to the law by our union with the mystical body of Christ. By being incorporated into Christ in our baptism professedly, in our believing powerfully and effectually, we are dead to the law, have no more to do with it than the dead servant, that is free from his master, hath to do with his master's yoke.

2. We are married to Christ. The day of our believing is the day of our espousals to the Lord Jesus. We enter upon a life of dependence on him and duty to him: *Married to another, even to him who is raised from the dead,* a periphrasis of Christ very pertinent here; for as our dying to sin and the law is in conformity to the death of Christ, and the crucifying of his body, so our devotedness to Christ in newness of life is in conformity to the resurrection of Christ. We are married to the raised exalted Jesus, a very honourable marriage. Compare 2 Cor. xi. 2; Eph. v. 29. Now we are thus married to Christ, (1.) *That we should bring forth fruit unto God, v.* 4. One end of marriage is fruitfulness: God instituted the ordinance that he might seek a *godly seed,* Mal. ii. 15. The wife is compared to the fruitful vine, and children are called the fruit of the womb. Now the great end of our marriage to Christ is our fruitfulness in love, and grace, and every good work. This is fruit unto God, pleasing to God, according to his will, aiming at his glory. As our old marriage to sin produced fruit unto death, so our second marriage to Christ produces fruit unto God, fruits of righteousness. Good works are the children of the new nature, the products of our union with Christ, as the fruitfulness of the vine is the product of its union with the root. Whatever our professions and pretensions may be, there is no fruit brought forth to God till we are married to Christ; it is in Christ Jesus that we are

created unto good works, Eph. ii. 10. The only fruit which turns to a good account is that which is brought forth in Christ. This distinguishes the good works of believers from the good works of hypocrites and self-justifiers that they are brought forth in marriage, done in union with Christ, in the name of the Lord Jesus, Col. iii. 17. This is, without controversy, one of the great mysteries of godliness. (2.) *That we should serve in newness of spirit, and not in the oldness of the letter, v.* 6. Being married to a new husband, we must change our way. Still we must serve, but it is a service that is perfect freedom, whereas the service of sin was a perfect drudgery: we must now serve in newness of spirit, by new spiritual rules, from new spiritual principles, in spirit and in truth, John iv. 24. There must be a renovation of our spirits wrought by the spirit of God, and in that we must serve. *Not in the oldness of the letter;* that is, we must not rest in mere external services, as the carnal Jews did, who gloried in their adherence to the letter of the law, and minded not the spiritual part of worship. The letter is said to kill with its bondage and terror, but we are delivered from that yoke that we may serve God without fear, in holiness and righteousness, Luke i. 74, 75. We are under the dispensation of the Spirit, and therefore must be spiritual, and serve in the spirit. Compare with this 2 Cor. iii. 3, 6, &c. It becomes us to worship within the veil, and no longer in the outward court.

7 What shall we say then? *Is*
the law sin? God forbid. Nay,
I had not known sin, but by the law:
for I had not known lust, except the
law had said, Thou shalt not covet.
8 But sin, taking occasion by the
commandment, wrought in me all
manner of concupiscence. For without the law sin *was* dead. 9 For I
was alive without the law once: but
when the commandment came, sin
revived, and I died. 10 And the
commandment, which *was ordained*
to life, I found *to be* unto death. 11
For sin, taking occasion by the commandment, deceived me, and by it slew
me. 12 Wherefore the law *is* holy,
and the commandment holy, and just,
and good. 13 Was then that which
is good made death unto me? God
forbid. But sin, that it might appear
sin, working death in me by that
which is good; that sin by the commandment might become exceeding
sinful. 14 For we know that the
law is spiritual:—

To what he had said in the former paragraph, the apostle here raises an objection, which he answers very fully: *What shall we say then? Is the law sin?* When he had been speaking of the dominion of sin, he had said so much of the influence of the law as a covenant upon that dominion that it might easily be misinterpreted as a reflection upon the law, to prevent which he shows from his own experience the great excellency and usefulness of the law, not as a covenant, but as a guide; and further discovers how sin took occasion by the commandment. Observe in particular,

I. The great excellency of the law in itself. Far be it from Paul to reflect upon the law; no, he speaks honourably of it. 1. It is *holy, just, and good, v.* 12. The law in general is so, and every particular commandment is so. Laws are as the law-makers are. God, the great lawgiver, is holy, just, and good, therefore his law must needs be so. The matter of it is holy: it commands holiness, encourages holiness; it is holy, for it is agreeable to the holy will of God, the original of holiness. It is just, for it is consonant to the rules of equity and right reason: the ways of the Lord are right. It is good in the design of it; it was given for the good of mankind, for the conservation of peace and order in the world. It makes the observers of it good; the intention of it was to better and reform mankind. Wherever there is true grace there is an assent to this—that the law is holy, just, and good. 2. *The law is spiritual* (*v.* 14), not only in regard to the effect of it, as it is a means of making us spiritual, but in regard to the extent of it; it reaches our spirits, it lays a restraint upon, and gives a direction to, the motions of the inward man; *it is a discerner of the thoughts and intents of the heart,* Heb. iv. 12. It forbids spiritual wickedness, heart-murder, and heart-adultery. It commands spiritual service, requires the heart, obliges us to worship God in the spirit. It is a spiritual law, for it is given by God, who is a Spirit and the Father of spirits; it is given to man, whose principal part is spiritual; the soul is the best part, and the leading part of the man, and therefore the law to the man must needs be a law to the soul. Herein the law of God is above all other laws, that it is a spiritual law. Other laws may forbid *compassing and imagining,* &c., which are treason in the heart, but cannot take cognizance thereof, unless there be some overt act; but the law of God takes notice of the iniquity regarded in the heart, though it go no further. *Wash thy heart from wickedness,* Jer. iv. 14. *We know this.* Wherever there is true grace there is an experimental knowledge of the spirituality of the law of God.

II. The great advantage that he had found by the law. 1. It was discovering: *I had not known sin but by the law, v.* 7. As that which is straight discovers that which is crooked, as the looking-glass shows us our natural face with all its spots and deformities, so there is no way of coming to that knowledge of sin which is necessary to repentance, and consequently to peace and pardon, but by comparing our hearts and lives with the law. Particularly he came to the knowledge of the sinfulness of lust by the law of the tenth commandment. By lust he means sin dwelling in us, sin in its first motions and workings, the corrupt principle. This he came to know when the law said, *Thou shalt not covet.* The law spoke in other language than the scribes and Pharisees made it to speak in; it spoke in the spiritual sense and meaning of it. By this he knew that lust was sin and a very sinful sin, that those motions and desires of the heart towards sin which never came into act were sinful, exceedingly sinful. Paul had a very quick and piercing judgment, all the advantages and improvements of education, and yet never attained the right knowledge of indwelling sin till the Spirit by the law made it known to him. There is nothing about which the natural man is more blind than about original corruption, concerning which the understanding is altogether in the dark till the Spirit by the law reveal it, and make it known. Thus *the law is a schoolmaster, to bring us to Christ,* opens and searches the wound, and so prepares it for healing. Thus sin by the commandment does appear sin (*v.* 13); it appears in its own colours, appears to be what it is, and you cannot call it by a worse name than its own. Thus by the commandment it becomes *exceedingly sinful;* that is, it appears to be so. We never see the desperate venom or malignity there is in sin, till we come to compare it with the law, and the spiritual nature of the law, and then we see it to be an evil and a bitter thing. 2. It was humbling (*v.* 9): *I was alive.* He thought himself in a very good condition; he was alive in his own opinion and apprehension, very secure and confident of the goodness of his state. Thus he was *once*, πότε—*in times past,* when he was a Pharisee; for it was the common temper of that generation of men that they had a very good conceit of themselves; and Paul was then like the rest of them, and the reason was he was then *without the law.* Though brought up at the feet of Gamaliel, a doctor of the law, though himself a great student in the law, a strict observer of it, and a zealous stickler for it, yet *without the law.* He had the letter of the law, but he had not the spiritual meaning of it—the shell, but not the kernel. He had the law in his hand and in his head, but he had it not in his heart; the notion of it, but not the power of it. There are a great many who are spiritually dead in sin, that yet are alive in their own opinion of themselves, and it is their strangeness to the law that is the cause of the mistake. *But when the commandment came,* came in the power of it (not to his eyes only, but to his heart), *sin revived,* as the dust in a room rises (that is, appears) when the sun-shine is let into it. Paul then saw that in sin which he had never seen before; he then saw sin in its causes, the bitter root, the corrupt bias, the bent to backslide,—sin in its colours, deforming, defiling, breaking a righteous law, affronting an awful Majesty, profaning a sovereign crown by casting it to the ground,—sin in its consequences, sin with death at the heels of it, sin and the curse entailed upon it. "Thus sin revived, and then I died; I lost that good opinion which I had had of myself, and came to be of another mind. *Sin revived, and I died;* that is, the Spirit, by the commandment, convinced me that I was in a state of sin, and in a state of death because of sin." Of this excellent use is the law; it is a lamp and a light; it converts the soul, opens the eyes, prepares the way of the Lord in the desert, rends the rocks, levels the mountains, makes ready a people prepared for the Lord.

III. The ill use that his corrupt nature made of the law notwithstanding. 1. *Sin, taking occasion by the commandment, wrought in me all manner of concupiscence, v.* 8. Observe, Paul had in him all manner of concupiscence, though one of the best unregenerate men that ever was; as touching the righteousness of the law, blameless, and yet sensible of all manner of concupiscence. And it was sin that wrought it, indwelling sin, his corrupt nature (he speaks of a sin that did work sin), and it took occasion by the commandment. The corrupt nature would not have swelled and raged so much if it had not been for the restraints of the law; as the peccant humours in the body are raised, and more inflamed, by a purge that is not strong enough to carry them off. It is incident to corrupt nature, *in vetitum niti—to lean towards what is forbidden.* Ever since Adam ate forbidden fruit, we have all been fond of forbidden paths; the diseased appetite is carried out most strongly towards that which is hurtful and prohibited. *Without the law sin was dead,* as a snake in winter, which the sunbeams of the law quicken and irritate. 2. It *deceived me.* Sin puts a cheat upon the sinner, and it is a fatal cheat, *v.* 11. *By it* (by the commandment) *slew me.* There being in the law no such express threatening against sinful lustings, sin, that is, his own corrupt nature, took occasion thence to promise him impunity, and to say, as the serpent to our first parents, *You shall not surely die.* Thus it deceived and slew him. 3. It *wrought death in me by that which is good, v.* 13. That which works concupiscence works death, for sin bringeth forth death. Nothing so good but a corrupt and vicious nature will pervert it, and make it an occasion of sin; no flower so sweet but sin will suck poison out of it. Now in this sin appears sin. The worst thing that sin does, and most like itself, is the perverting of the law, and taking occasion from it to be so much the more malignant. Thus the commandment, which was ordained to life, was intended as a guide in the way to comfort and happiness, proved unto death, through the corruption of nature, *v.* 10. Many a precious soul splits upon the rock of salvation; and the same word which to some is an occasion of life unto life is to others an occasion of death unto death. The same sun that makes the garden of flowers more fragrant makes the dunghill more noisome; the same heat that softens wax hardens clay; and the same child was set for the fall and rising again of many in Israel. The way to prevent this mischief is to bow our souls to the commanding authority of the word and law of God, not striving against, but submitting to it.

14 — But I am carnal, sold under
sin. 15 For that which I do I allow
not: for what I would, that do I not;
but what I hate, that do I. 16 If
then I do that which I would not, I
consent unto the law that *it is* good.
17 Now then it is no more I that do
it, but sin that dwelleth in me. 18
For I know that in me (that is, in
my flesh,) dwelleth no good thing:
for to will is present with me; but
how to perform that which is good
I find not. 19 For the good that I
would I do not: but the evil which
I would not, that I do. 20 Now if I
do that I would not, it is no more I
that do it, but sin that dwelleth in
me. 21 I find then a law, that, when
I would do good, evil is present with
me. 22 For I delight in the law of
God after the inward man: 23 But
I see another law in my members,
warring against the law of my mind,
and bringing me into captivity to the
law of sin which is in my members.
24 O wretched man that I am! who
shall deliver me from the body of this
death? 25 I thank God through
Jesus Christ our Lord. So then
with the mind I myself serve the law
of God; but with the flesh the law
of sin.

Here is a description of the conflict between grace and corruption in the heart, between the law of God and the law of sin. And it is applicable two ways:—1. To the struggles that are in a convinced soul, but yet unregenerate, in the person of whom it is supposed, by some, that Paul speaks. 2. To the struggles that are in a renewed sanctified soul, but yet in a state of imperfection, as others apprehend. And a great controversy there is of which of these we are to understand the apostle here. So far does the evil prevail here, when he speaks of one sold under sin, doing it, not performing that which is good, that it seems difficult to apply it to the regenerate, who are described to walk not after the flesh, but after the Spirit; and yet so far does the good prevail in hating sin, consenting to the law, delighting in it, serving the law of God with the mind, that it is more difficult to apply it to the unregenerate that are dead in trespasses and sins.

I. Apply it to the struggles that are felt in a convinced soul, that is yet in a state of sin, knows his Lord's will, but does it not, approves the things that are more excellent, being instructed out of the law, and yet lives in the constant breach of it, *ch.* ii. 17—23. Though he has that within him that witnesses against the sin he commits, and it is not without a great deal of reluctancy that he does commit it, the superior faculties striving against it, natural conscience warning against it before it is committed and smiting for it afterwards, yet the man continues a slave to his reigning lusts. It is not thus with every unregenerate man, but with those only that are convinced by the law, but not changed by the gospel. The apostle had said (*ch.* vi. 14), *Sin shall not have dominion, because you are not under the law, but under grace,* for the proof of which he here shows that a man under the law, and not under grace, may be, and is, under the dominion of sin. The law may discover sin, and convince of sin, but it cannot conquer and subdue sin, witness the predominancy of sin in many that are under very strong legal convictions. It discovers the defilement, but will not wash it off. It makes a man weary and heavy laden (Matt. xi. 28), burdens him with his sin; and yet, if rested in, it yields no help towards the shaking off of that burden; this is to be had only in Christ. The law may make a man cry out, *O wretched man that I am! who shall deliver me?* and yet leave him thus fettered and captivated, as being too weak to deliver him (*ch.* viii. 3), give him a spirit of bondage to fear, *ch.* viii. 15. Now a soul advanced thus far by the law is in a fair way towards a state of liberty by Christ, though many rest here and go no further. Felix trembled, but never came to Christ. It is possible for a man to go to hell with his eyes open (Num. xxiv. 3, 4), illuminated with common convictions, and to carry about with him a self-accusing conscience, even in the service of the devil. He may *consent to the law that it is good,* delight to know God's ways (as they, Isa. lviii. 2), may have that within him that witnesses against sin and for holiness; and yet all this overpowered by the reigning love of sin. Drunkards and unclean persons have some faint desires to leave off their sins, and yet persist in them notwithstanding, such is the impotency and such the insufficiency of their convictions. Of such as these there are many that will needs have all this understood, and contend earnestly for it: though it is very hard to imagine why, if the apostle intended this, he should speak all along in his own person; and not only so, but in the present tense. Of his own state under conviction he had spoken at large, as of a thing past (*v.* 7, &c.): *I died; the commandment I found to be unto death;* and if here he speaks of the same state as his present state, and the condition he was now in, surely he did not intend to be so understood: and therefore,

II. It seems rather to be understood of the struggles that are maintained between grace and corruption in sanctified souls. That there are remainders of indwelling corruption, even where there is a living principle of grace, is past dispute; that this corruption is daily breaking forth in sins of infirmity (such as are consistent with a state of grace) is no less certain. If we say that we have no sin, we deceive ourselves, 1 John i. 8, 10. That true grace strives against these sins and corruptions, does not allow of them, hates them, mourns over them, groans under them as a burden, is likewise certain (Gal. v. 17): *The flesh lusteth against the spirit, and the spirit against the flesh; and these are contrary the one to the other, so that you cannot do the things that you would.* These are the truths which, I think, are contained in this discourse of the apostle. And his design is further to open the nature of sanctification, that it does not attain to a sinless perfection in this life; and therefore to quicken us to, and encourage us in, our conflicts with remaining corruptions. Our case is not singular, that which we do sincerely strive against, shall not be laid to our charge, and through grace the victory is sure at last. The struggle here is like that between Jacob and Esau in the womb, between the Canaanites and Israelites in the land, between the house of Saul and the house of David; but great is the truth and will prevail. Understanding it thus, we may observe here,

1. What he complains of—the remainder of indwelling corruptions, which he here speaks of, to show that the law is insufficient to justify even a regenerate man, that the best man in the world hath enough in him to condemn him, if God should deal with him according to the law, which is not the fault of the law, but of our own corrupt nature, which cannot fulfil the law. The repetition of the same things over and over again in this discourse shows how much Paul's heart was affected with what he wrote, and how deep his sentiments were. Observe the particulars of this complaint. (1.) *I am carnal, sold under sin, v.* 14. He speaks of the Corinthians as carnal, 1 Cor. iii. 1. Even where there is spiritual life there are remainders of carnal affections, and so far a man may be *sold under sin;* he does not sell himself to work wickedness, as Ahab did (1 Kings xxi. 25), but he was sold by Adam when he sinned and fell—sold, as a poor slave that does his master's will against his own will—sold under sin, because conceived in iniquity and born in sin. (2.) *What I would, that I do not; but what I hate, that do I, v.* 15. And to the same purport, *v.* 19, 21, *When I would do good, evil is present with me.* Such was the strength of corruptions, that he could not attain that perfection in holiness which he desired and breathed after. Thus, while he was pressing forward towards perfection, yet he acknowledges that he had not already attained, neither was already perfect, Phil. iii. 12. Fain he would be free from all sin, and perfectly do the will of God, such was his settled judgment; but his corrupt nature drew him another way: it was like a clog, that checked and kept him down when he would have soared upward, like the bias in a bowl, which, when it is thrown straight, yet draws it aside. (3.) *In me, that is in my flesh, dwelleth no good, v.* 18. Here he explains himself concerning the corrupt nature, which he calls flesh; and as far as that goes there is no good to be expected, any more than one would expect good corn growing upon a rock, or on the sand which is by the sea-side. As the new nature, as far as that goes, cannot commit sin (1 John iii. 9), so the flesh, the old nature, as far as that goes, cannot perform a good duty. How should it? For the flesh serveth the law of sin (*v.* 25), it is under the conduct and government of that law; and, while it is so, it is not likely to do any good. The corrupt nature is elsewhere called flesh (Gen. vi. 3, John iii. 6); and, though there may be good things dwelling in those that have this flesh, yet, as far as the flesh goes, there is no good, the flesh is not a subject capable of any good. (4.) *I see another law in my members warring against the law of my mind, v.* 23. The corrupt and sinful inclination is here compared to a law, because it controlled and checked him in his good motions. It is said to be seated in his members, because, Christ having set up his throne in his heart, it was only the rebellious members of the body that were the instruments of sin—in the sensitive appetite; or we may take it more generally for all that corrupt nature which is the seat not only of sensual but of more refined lusts. This wars against the law of the mind, the new nature; it draws the contrary way, drives on a contrary interest, which corrupt disposition and inclination are as great a burden and grief to the soul as the worst drudgery and captivity could be. *It brings me into captivity.* To the same purport (*v.* 25), *With the flesh I serve the law of sin;* that is, the corrupt nature, the unregenerate part, is continually working towards sin. (5.) His general complaint we have *v.* 24, *O wretched man that I am! who shall deliver me from the body of this death?* The thing he complains of is a body of death; either the body of flesh, which is a mortal dying body (while we carry this body about

with us, we shall be troubled with corruption; when we are dead, we shall be freed from sin, and not before), or the body of sin, the old man, the corrupt nature, which tends to death, that is, to the ruin of the soul. Or, comparing it to a dead body, the touch of which was by the ceremonial law defiling, if actual transgressions be dead works (Heb. ix. 14), original corruption is a dead body. It was as troublesome to Paul as if he had had a dead body tied to him, which he must have carried about with him. This made him cry out, *O wretched man that I am!* A man that had learned in every state to be content yet complains thus of his corrupt nature. Had I been required to speak of Paul, I should have said, "O blessed man that thou art, an ambassador of Christ, a favourite of heaven, a spiritual father of thousands!" But in his own account he was a wretched man, because of the corruption of nature, because he was not so good as he fain would be, had not yet attained, neither was already perfect. Thus miserably does he complain. *Who shall deliver me?* He speaks like one that was sick of it, that would give any thing to be rid of it, looks to the right hand and to the left for some friend that would part between him and his corruptions. The remainders of indwelling sin are a very grievous burden to a gracious soul.

2. What he comforts himself with. The case was sad, but there were some allays. Three things comforted him:—

(1.) That his conscience witnessed for him that he had a good principle ruling and prevailing in him, notwithstanding. It is well when all does not go one way in the soul. The rule of this good principle which he had was the law of God, to which he here speaks of having a threefold regard, which is certainly to be found in all that are sanctified, and no others. [1.] *I consent unto the law that it is good, v.*16. *σύμφημι—I give my vote* to the law; here is the approbation of the judgment. Wherever there is grace there is not only a dread of the severity of the law, but a consent to the goodness of the law. "It is good in itself, it is good for me." This is a sign that the law is written in the heart, that the soul is delivered into the mould of it. To consent to the law is so far to approve of it as not to wish it otherwise constituted than it is. The sanctified judgment not only concurs to the equity of the law, but to the excellency of it, as convinced that a conformity to the law is the highest perfection of human nature, and the greatest honour and happiness we are capable of. [2.] *I delight in the law of God after the inward man, v.* 22. His conscience bore witness to a complacency in the law. He delighted not only in the promises of the word, but in the precepts and prohibitions of the word; *συνήδομαι* expresses a becoming *delight.* He did herein concur in affection with all the saints. All that are savingly regenerate or born again do truly delight in the law of God, delight to know it, to do it—cheerfully submit to the authority of it, and take a complacency in that submission, never better pleased than when heart and life are in the strictest conformity to the law and will of God. *After the inward man;* that is, *First,* The mind or rational faculties, in opposition to the sensitive appetites and wills of the flesh. The soul is the inward man, and that is the seat of gracious delights, which are therefore sincere and serious, but secret; it is the renewing of the inward man, 2 Cor. iv. 16. *Secondly,* The new nature. The new man is called the *inner man* (Eph. iii. 16), the *hidden man of the heart,* 1 Pet. iii. 4. Paul, as far as he was sanctified, had a delight in the law of God. [3.] *With the mind I myself serve the law of God, v.* 25. It is not enough to consent to the law, and to delight in the law, but we must serve the law; our souls must be entirely delivered up into the obedience of it. Thus it was with Paul's mind; thus it is with every sanctified renewed mind; this is the ordinary course and way; thitherward goes the bent of the soul. *I myself—αὐτὸς ἐγὼ,* plainly intimating that he speaks in his own person, and not in the person of another.

(2.) That the fault lay in that corruption of his nature which he did really bewail and strive against: *It is no more I that do it, but sin that dwelleth in me.* This he mentions twice (*v.* 17, 20), not as an excuse for the guilt of his sin (it is enough to condemn us, if we were under the law, that the sin which does the evil dwelleth in us), but as a salvo for his evidences, that he might not sink in despair, but take comfort from the covenant of grace, which accepts the willingness of the spirit, and has provided pardon for the weakness of the flesh. He likewise herein enters a protestation against all that which this indwelling sin produced. Having professed his consent to the law of God, he here professes his dissent from the law of sin. "It is not I; I disown the fact; it is against my mind that it is done." As when in the senate the major part are bad, and carry every thing the wrong way, it is indeed the act of the senate, but the honest party strive against it, bewail what is done, and enter their protestation against it; so that it is no more they that do it.—*Dwelleth in me,* as the Canaanites among the Israelites, though they were put under tribute: dwelleth in me, and is likely to dwell there, while I live.

(3.) His great comfort lay in Jesus Christ (*v.* 25): *I thank God, through Jesus Christ our Lord.* In the midst of his complaints he breaks out into praises. It is a special remedy against fears and sorrows to be much in praise: many a poor drooping soul hath found it so. And, in all our praises, this should be the burden of the song, "Blessed be God for Jesus Christ." *Who shall deliver me?* says he (*v.* 24), as one at a loss for help. At length he finds an all-sufficient friend, even Jesus Christ. When we are under the sense of the remaining power of sin and and corruption, we shall see reason to bless God through Christ (for, as he is the mediator of all our prayers, so he is of all our praises)—to bless God for Christ; it is he that stands between us and the wrath due to us for this sin. If it were not for Christ, this iniquity that dwells in us would certainly be our ruin. He is our advocate with the Father, and through him God pities, and spares, and pardons, and lays not our iniquities to our charge. It is Christ that has purchased deliverance for us in due time. Through Christ death will put an end to all these complaints, and waft us to an eternity which we shall spend without sin or sigh. *Blessed be God that giveth us this victory through our Lord Jesus Christ!*

CHAP VIII.

The apostle, having fully explained the doctrine of justification, and pressed the necessity of sanctification, in this chapter applies himself to the consolation of the Lord's people. Ministers are helpers of the joy of the saints. "Comfort ye, comfort ye my people," so runs our commission, Isa. xl. 1. It is the will of God that his people should be a comforted people. And we have here such a draught of the gospel charter, such a display of the unspeakable privileges of true believers, as may furnish us with abundant matter for joy and peace in believing, that by all these immutable things, in which it is impossible for God to lie, we might have strong consolation. Many of the people of God have, accordingly, found this chapter a well-spring of comfort to their souls, living and dying, and have sucked and been satisfied from these breasts of consolation, and with joy drawn water out of these wells of salvation. There are three things in this chapter: I. The particular instances of Christians' privileges, ver. 1—28. II. The ground thereof laid in predestination, ver. 29, 30. III. The apostle's triumph herein, in the name of all the saints, ver. 31, to the end.

THERE *is* therefore now no condemnation to them which are
in Christ Jesus, who walk not after
the flesh, but after the Spirit. 2 For
the law of the Spirit of life in Christ
Jesus hath made me free from the
law of sin and death. 3 For what
the law could not do, in that it was
weak through the flesh, God sending
his own Son in the likeness of sinful
flesh, and for sin, condemned sin in
the flesh: 4 That the righteousness
of the law might be fulfilled in us,
who walk not after the flesh, but after
the Spirit. 5 For they that are after
the flesh do mind the things of the
flesh; but they that are after the
Spirit the things of the Spirit. 6
For to be carnally minded *is* death;
but to be spiritually minded *is* life
and peace. 7 Because the carnal
mind *is* enmity against God: for it is
not subject to the law of God, neither indeed can be. 8 So then they
that are in the flesh cannot please
God. 9 But ye are not in the flesh,
but in the Spirit, if so be that the
Spirit of God dwell in you. Now if
any man have not the Spirit of Christ,
he is none of his.

I. The apostle here begins with one signal privilege of true Christians, and describes the character of those to whom it belongs: *There is therefore now no condemnation to those that are in Christ Jesus, v.* 1. This is his triumph after that melancholy complaint and conflict in the foregoing chapter—sin remaining, disturbing, vexing, but, blessed be God, not ruining. The complaint he takes to himself, but humbly transfers the comfort with himself to all true believers, who are all interested in it. 1. It is the unspeakable privilege and comfort of all those that are in Christ Jesus that there is therefore now no condemnation to them. He does not say, "There is no accusation against them," for this there is; but the accusation is thrown out, and the indictment quashed. He does not say, "There is nothing in them that deserves condemnation," for this there is, and they see it, and own it, and mourn over it, and condemn themselves for it; but it shall not be their ruin. He does not say, "There is no cross, no affliction to them or no displeasure in the affliction," for this there may be; but *no condemnation.* They may be chastened of the Lord, but not condemned with the world. Now this arises from their being in Christ Jesus; by virtue of their union with him through faith they are thus secured. They are in Christ Jesus, as in their city of refuge, and so are protected from the avenger of blood. He is their advocate, and brings them off. There is therefore no condemnation, because they are interested in the satisfaction that Christ by dying made to the law. In Christ, God does not only not condemn them, but is well pleased with them, Matt. xvii.5. 2. It is the undoubted character of all those who are so in Christ Jesus as to be freed from condemnation that *they walk not after the flesh but after the Spirit.* Observe, The character is given from their walk, not from any one particular act, but from their course and way. And the great question is, What is the principle of the walk, the flesh or the spirit, the old or the new nature, corruption or grace? Which of these do we mind, for which of these do we make provision, by which of these are we governed, which of these do we take part with?

II. This great truth, thus laid down, he illustrates in the following verses; and shows how we come by this great privilege, and how we may answer this character.

1. How we come by these privileges—the privilege of justification, that *there is no condemnation to us*—the privilege of sanctification, that *we walk after the Spirit, and not after the flesh,* which is no less our privilege than it is our duty. How comes it about?

(1.) The law could not do it, *v.* 3. It could neither justify nor sanctify, neither free us from the guilt nor from the power of sin, having not the promises either of pardon or grace. The law made nothing perfect: *It was weak.* Some attempt the law made towards these blessed ends, but, alas! it was weak, it could not accomplish them: yet that weakness was not through any defect in the law, but *through the flesh,* through the corruption of human nature, by which we became incapable either of being justified or sanctified by the law. We had become unable to keep the law, and, in case of failure, the law, as a covenant of works, made no provision, and so left us as it found us. Or understand it of the ceremonial law; that was a plaster not wide enough for the wound, it could never take away sin, Heb. x. 4.

(2.) *The law of the Spirit of life in Christ Jesus* does it, *v.* 2. The covenant of grace made with us in Christ is a treasury of merit and grace, and thence we receive pardon and a new nature, *are freed from the law of sin and death,* that is, both from the guilt and power of sin—from the course of the law, and the dominion of the flesh. We are under another covenant, another master, another husband, under the *law of the Spirit,* the law that gives the Spirit, spiritual life to qualify us for eternal. The foundation of this freedom is laid in Christ's undertaking for us, of which he speaks *v.* 3, *God sending his own Son.* Observe, When the law failed, God provided another method. Christ comes to do that which the law could not do. Moses brought the children of Israel to the borders of Canaan, and then died, and left them there; but Joshua did that which Moses could not do, and put them in possession of Canaan. Thus what the law could not do Christ did. The best exposition of this verse we have Heb. x. 1—10. To make the sense of the words clear, which in our translation is a little intricate, we may read it thus, with a little transposition:—*God sending his own Son in the likeness of sinful flesh, and a sacrifice for sin, condemned sin in the flesh, which the law could not do, in that it was weak through the flesh,* &c. *v.* 4. Observe, [1.] How Christ appeared: *In the likeness of sinful flesh.* Not sinful, for he was holy, harmless, undefiled; but in the likeness of that flesh which was sinful. He took upon him that nature which was corrupt, though perfectly abstracted from the corruptions of it. His being circumcised, redeemed, baptized with John's baptism, bespeaks the likeness of sinful flesh. The bitings of the fiery serpents were cured by a serpent of brass, which had the shape, though free from the venom, of the serpents that bit them. It was great condescension that he who was God should be made in the likeness of flesh; but much greater that he who was holy should be made in the likeness of sinful flesh. *And for sin,*—here the best Greek copies place the comma. God sent him, ἐν ὁμοιώματι σαρκὸς ἁμαρτίας, καὶ περὶ ἁμαρτίας—*in the likeness of sinful flesh, and as a sacrifice for sin.* The LXX. call a sacrifice for sin no more than περὶ ἁμαρτίας—*for sin;* so Christ was a sacrifice; he was sent to be so, Heb. ix. 26. [2.] What was done by this appearance of his: Sin *was condemned,* that is, God did therein more than ever manifest his hatred of sin; and not only so, but for all that are Christ's both the damning and the domineering power of sin is broken and taken out of the way. He that is condemned can neither accuse nor rule; his testimony is null, and his authority null. Thus by Christ is sin condemned; though it live and remain, its life in the saints is still but like that of a condemned malefactor. It was by the condemning of sin that death was disarmed, and the devil, who had the power of death, destroyed. The condemning of sin saved the sinner from condemnation. Christ was made sin for us (2 Cor. v. 21), and, being so made, when he was condemned sin was condemned in the flesh of Christ, condemned in the human nature: So was satisfaction made to divine justice, and way made for the salvation of the sinner. [3.] The happy effect of this upon us (*v.* 4): *That the righteousness of the law might be fulfilled in us.* Both in our justification and in our sanctification, the righteousness of the law is fulfilled. A righteousness of satisfaction for the breach of the law is fulfilled by the imputation of Christ's complete and perfect righteousness, which answers the utmost demands of the law, as the mercy-seat was as long and as broad as the ark. A righteousness of obedience to the commands of the law is fulfilled in us, when by the Spirit the law of love is written upon the heart, and that love is the fulfilling of the law, *ch.* xiii. 10. Though the righteousness of the law is not fulfilled by us, yet, blessed be God, it is fulfilled in us; there is that to be found upon and in all true believers which answers the intention of the law. *Us who walk not after the flesh, but after the Spirit.* This is the description of all those that are interested in this privilege—they act from spiritual and not from carnal principles; as for others, the righteousness of the law will be fulfilled upon them in their ruin. Now,

2. Observe how we may answer to this character, *v.* 5, &c.

(1.) By looking to our minds. How may we know whether we are after the flesh or after the Spirit? By examining what we mind, the things of the flesh or the things of the spirit. Carnal pleasure, worldly profit and honour, the things of sense and time, are the things of the flesh, which unregenerate people mind. The favour of God, the welfare of the soul, the concerns of eternity, are the things of the Spirit, which those that are after the Spirit do mind. The man is as the mind is. The mind is the forge of thoughts. *As he thinketh in his heart, so is he,* Prov. xxiii. 7. Which way do the thoughts move with most pleasure? On what do they dwell with most satisfaction? The mind is the seat of wisdom. Which way go the projects and contrivances? whether are we more wise for the world or for our souls? φρονοῦσι τα τῆς σαρκὸς—*they savour the things of the flesh*; so the word is rendered, Matt. xvi. 23. It is a great matter what our savour is, what truths, what tidings, what comforts, we do most relish, and are most agreeable to us. Now, to caution us against this carnal-mindedness, he shows the great misery and malignity of it, and compares it with the unspeakable excellency and comfort of spiritual-mindedness. [1.] It is death, *v.* 6. It is spiritual death, the certain way to eternal death. It is the death of the soul; for it is its alienation from God, in union and communion with whom the life of the soul consists. A carnal soul is a dead soul, dead as a soul can die. She that *liveth in pleasure is dead* (1 Tim. v. 6), not only dead in law as guilty, but dead in state as carnal. Death includes all misery; carnal souls are miserable souls. But to be *spiritually minded*, φρόνημα τοῦ πνεύματος—*a spiritual savour* (the wisdom that is from above, a principle of grace) is *life and peace*; it is the felicity and happiness of the soul. The life of the soul consists in its union with spiritual things by the mind. A sanctified soul is a living soul, and that life is peace; it is a very comfortable life. All the paths of spiritual wisdom are paths of peace. It is life and peace in the other world, as well as in this. Spiritual-mindedness is eternal life and peace begun, and an assuring earnest of the perfection of it. [2.] It is enmity to God (*v.* 7), and this is worse than the former. The former speaks the carnal sinner a dead man, which is bad; but this speaks him a devil of a man. It is not only an enemy, but enmity itself. It is not only the alienation of the soul from God, but the opposition of the soul against God; it rebels against his authority, thwarts his design, opposes his interest, spits in his face, spurns at his bowels. Can there be a greater enmity? An enemy may be reconciled, but enmity cannot. How should this humble us for, and warn us against, carnal-mindedness! Shall we harbour and indulge that which is enmity to God our creator, owner, ruler, and benefactor? To prove this, he urges that *it is not subject to the law of God, neither indeed can be.* The holiness of the law of God, and the unholiness of the carnal mind, are as irreconcilable as light and darkness. The carnal man may, by the power of divine grace, be made subject to the law of God, but the *carnal mind* never can; this must be broken and expelled. See how wretchedly the corrupt will of man is enslaved to sin; as far as the carnal mind prevails, there is no inclination to the law of God; therefore wherever there is a change wrought it is by the power of God's grace, not by the freedom of man's will. Hence he infers (*v.* 8), *Those that are in the flesh cannot please God.* Those that are in a carnal unregenerate state, under the reigning power of sin, cannot do the things that please God, wanting grace, the pleasing principle, and an interest in Christ, the pleasing Mediator. The very *sacrifice of the wicked is an abomination*, Prov. xv. 8. Pleasing God is our highest end, of which those that are in the flesh cannot but fall short; they cannot please him, nay, they cannot but displease him. We may know our state and character,

(2.) By enquiring whether we have the Spirit of God and Christ, or not (*v.* 9): *You are not in the flesh, but in the Spirit.* This expresses states and conditions of the soul vastly different. All the saints have flesh and spirit in them; but to be in the flesh and to be in the Spirit are contrary. It denotes our being overcome and subdued by one of these principles. As we say, A man is *in love*, or *in drink*, that is, overcome by it. Now the great question is whether we are in the flesh or in the Spirit; and how may we come to know it? Why, by enquiring whether the Spirit of God dwell in us. The Spirit dwelling in us is the best evidence of our being in the Spirit, for the indwelling is mutual (1 John iv. 16): *Dwelleth in God, and God in him.* The Spirit visits many that are unregenerate with his motions, which they resist and quench; but in all that are sanctified he dwells; there he resides and rules. He is there as a man at his own house, where he is constant and welcome, and has the dominion. Shall we put this question to our own hearts, Who dwells, who rules, who keeps house, here? Which interest has the ascendant? To this he subjoins a general rule of trial: *If any man has not the Spirit of Christ, he is none of his.* To be Christ's (that is, to be a Christian indeed, one of his children, his servants, his friends, in union with him) is a privilege and honour which many pretend to that have no part nor lot in the matter. None are his but those that have his Spirit; that is, [1.] That are spirited as he was spirited—are meek, and lowly, and humble, and peaceable, and patient, and charitable, as he was. We cannot tread in his steps unless we have his spirit; the frame and disposition of our souls must be conformable to Christ's pattern. [2.] That are actuated and guided by the Holy Spirit of God, as a sanctifier, teacher, and comforter Having the Spirit of Christ is the same with having the Spirit of God to dwell in us. But those two come much to one; for all that are actuated by the Spirit of God as their rule are conformable to the spirit of Christ as their pattern. Now this description of the character of those to whom belongs this first privilege of freedom from condemnation is to be applied to all the other privileges that follow.

10 And if Christ *be* in you, the

body *is* dead because of sin ; but the
Spirit *is* life because of righteousness.
11 But if the Spirit of him that raised
up Jesus from the dead dwell in you,
he that raised up Christ from the
dead shall also quicken your mortal
bodies by his Spirit that dwelleth in
you. 12 Therefore, brethren, we are
debtors, not to the flesh, to live after
the flesh. 13 For if ye live after the
flesh, ye shall die : but if ye through
the Spirit do mortify the deeds of the
body, ye shall live. 14 For as many
as are led by the Spirit of God, they
are the sons of God. 15 For ye
have not received the spirit of bondage again to fear ; but ye have received
the Spirit of adoption, whereby we
cry, Abba, Father. 16 The Spirit
itself beareth witness with our spirit,
that we are the children of God :—

In these verses the apostle represents two more excellent benefits, which belong to true believers.

I. Life. The happiness is not barely a negative happiness, not to be condemned; but it is positive, it is an advancement to a life that will be the unspeakable happiness of the man (*v.* 10, 11): *If Christ be in you.* Observe, If the Spirit be in us, Christ is in us. He dwells in the heart by faith, Eph. iii. 17. Now we are here told what becomes of the bodies and souls of those in whom Christ is.

1. We cannot say but that *the body is dead ;* it is a frail, mortal, dying body, and it will be dead shortly; it is a house of clay, whose foundation is in the dust. The life purchased and promised does not immortalize the body in its present state. It is dead, that is, it is appointed to die, it is under a sentence of death: as we say one that is condemned is a dead man. In the midst of life we are in death: be our bodies ever so strong, and healthful, and handsome, they are as good as dead (Heb. xi. 12), and this *because of sin.* It is sin that kills the body. This effect the first threatening has (Gen. iii. 19): *Dust thou art.* Methinks, were there no other argument, love to our bodies should make us hate sin, because it is such an enemy to our bodies. The death even of the bodies of the saints is a remaining token of God's displeasure against sin.

2. But the spirit, the precious soul, that is life; it is now spiritually alive, nay, it is life. Grace in the soul is its new nature; the life of the saint lies in the soul, while the life of the sinner goes no further than the body. When the body dies, and returns to the dust, *the spirit is life ;* not only living and immortal, but swallowed up of life. Death to the saints is but the freeing of the heaven-born spirit from the clog and load of this body, that it may be fit to partake of eternal life. When Abraham was dead, yet God was the God of Abraham, for even then his spirit was life, Matt. xxii. 31, 32. See Ps. xlix. 15. And this *because of righteousness.* The righteousness of Christ imputed to them secures the soul, the better part, from death; the righteousness of Christ inherent in them, the renewed image of God upon the soul, preserves it, and, by God's ordination, at death elevates it, and improves it, and makes it meet to partake of the inheritance of the saints in light. The eternal life of the soul consists in the vision and fruition of God, and both assimilating, for which the soul is qualified by the righteousness of sanctification. I refer to Ps. xvii. 15, *I will behold thy face in righteousness.*

3. There is a life reserved too for the poor body at last: *He shall also quicken your mortal bodies, v.* 11. The Lord is for the body; and though at death it is cast aside as a despised broken vessel, a vessel in which is no pleasure, yet God will have a desire to the work of his hands (Job xiv. 15), will remember his covenant with the dust, and will not lose a grain of it; but the body shall be reunited to the soul, and clothed with a glory agreeable to it. Vile bodies shall be newly fashioned, Phil. iii. 21; 1 Cor. xv. 42. Two great assurances of the resurrection of the body are mentioned:—(1.) The resurrection of Christ: He *that raised up Christ from the dead shall also quicken.* Christ rose as the head, and first-fruits, and forerunner of all the saints, 1 Cor. xv. 20. The body of Christ lay in the grave, under the sin of all the elect imputed, and broke through it. O grave, then, where is thy victory? It is in the virtue of Christ's resurrection that we shall rise. (2.) The indwelling of the Spirit. The same Spirit that raiseth the soul now will raise the body shortly: *By his Spirit that dwelleth in you.* The bodies of the saints are the temples of the Holy Ghost, 1 Cor. iii. 16; vi. 19. Now, though these temples may be suffered for awhile to lie in ruins, yet they shall be rebuilt. The tabernacle of David, which has fallen down, shall be repaired, whatever great mountains may be in the way. The Spirit, breathing upon dead and dry bones, will make them live, and the saints even in their flesh shall see God. Hence the apostle by the way infers how much it is our duty to walk not after the flesh, but after the Spirit, *v.* 12, 13. Let not our life be after the wills and motions of the flesh. Two motives he mentions here: —[1.] We are not debtors to the flesh, neither by relation, gratitude, nor any other bond or obligation. We owe no suit nor service to our carnal desires; we are indeed bound to clothe, and feed, and take care of the body, as a servant to the soul in the service of God, but no further. We are not debtors to it; the flesh never did us so much kindness as to oblige us to serve it. It is implied that we are debtors to Christ and to the Spirit: there

we owe our all, all we have and all we can do, by a thousand bonds and obligations. Being delivered from so great a death by so great a ransom, we are deeply indebted to our deliverer. See 1 Cor. vi. 19, 20. [2.] Consider the consequences, what will be at the end of the way. Here are life and death, blessing and cursing, set before us. *If you live after the flesh, you shall die;* that is, die eternally. It is the pleasing, and serving, and gratifying, of the flesh, that are the ruin of souls; that is, the second death. Dying indeed is the soul's dying: the death of the saints is but a sleep. But, on the other hand, *You shall live,* live and be happy to eternity; that is the true life: *If you through the Spirit mortify the deeds of the body,* subdue and keep under all fleshly lusts and affections, deny yourselves in the pleasing and humouring of the body, and this through the Spirit; we cannot do it without the Spirit working it in us, and the Spirit will not do it without our doing our endeavour. So that in a word we are put upon this dilemma, either to displease the body or destroy the soul.

II. The *Spirit of adoption* is another privilege belonging to those that are in Christ Jesus, *v.* 14—16.

1. All that are Christ's are taken into the relation of children to God, *v.* 14. Observe, (1.) Their property: They are *led by the Spirit of God,* as a scholar in his learning is led by his tutor, as a traveller in his journey is led by his guide, as a soldier in his engagements is led by his captain; not driven as beasts, but led as rational creatures, drawn with the cords of a man and the bands of love. It is the undoubted character of all true believers that they are led by the Spirit of God. Having submitted themselves in believing to his guidance, they do in their obedience follow that guidance, and are sweetly led into all truth and all duty. (2.) Their privilege: *They are the sons of God,* received into the number of God's children by adoption, owned and loved by him as his children.

2. And those that are the sons of God have the Spirit,

(1.) To work in them the disposition of children.

[1.] *You have not received the spirit of bondage again to fear, v.* 15. Understand it, *First,* Of that spirit of bondage which the Old-Testament church was under, by reason of the darkness and terror of that dispensation. The veil signified bondage, 2 Cor. iii. 15. Compare *v.* 17. The Spirit of adoption was not then so plentifully poured out as now; for the law opened the wound, but little of the remedy. Now you are not under that dispensation, you have not received that spirit. *Secondly,* Of that spirit of bondage which many of the saints themselves were under at their conversion, under the convictions of sin and wrath set home by the Spirit; as those in Acts ii. 37, the jailer (Acts xvi. 30), Paul, Acts ix. 6. Then the Spirit himself was to the saints a spirit of bondage: "But," says the apostle, "with you this is over." "God as a Judge," says Dr. Manton, "by the spirit of bondage, sends us to Christ as Mediator, and Christ as Mediator, by the spirit of adoption, sends us back again to God as a Father." Though a child of God may come under fear of bondage again, and may be questioning his sonship, yet the blessed Spirit is not again a spirit of bondage, for then he would witness an untruth.

[2.] But you *have received the Spirit of adoption.* Men may give a charter of adoption; but it is God's prerogative, when he adopts, to give a spirit of adoption—the nature of children. The Spirit of adoption works in the children of God a filial love to God as a Father, a delight in him, and a dependence upon him, as a Father. A sanctified soul bears the image of God, as the child bears the image of the father. *Whereby we cry, Abba, Father.* Praying is here called *crying,* which is not only an earnest, but a natural expression of desire; children that cannot speak vent their desires by crying. Now, the Spirit teaches us in prayer to come to God as a Father, with a holy humble confidence, emboldening the soul in that duty. *Abba, Father. Abba* is a Syriac word signifying *father* or *my father;* πάτηρ, a Greek word; and why both, *Abba, Father?* Because Christ said so in prayer (Mark xiv. 36), *Abba, Father:* and we have received the Spirit of the Son. It denotes an affectionate endearing importunity, and a believing stress laid upon the relation. Little children, begging of their parents, can say little but *Father, Father,* and that is rhetoric enough. It also denotes that the adoption is common both to Jews and Gentiles: the Jews call him *Abba* in their language, the Greeks may call him πάτηρ in their language; for in Christ Jesus there is neither Greek nor Jew.

(2.) To witness to the relation of children, *v.* 16. The former is the work of the Spirit as a Sanctifier; this as a Comforter. *Beareth witness with our spirit.* Many a man has the witness of his own spirit to the goodness of his state who has not the concurring testimony of the Spirit. Many speak peace to themselves to whom the God of heaven does not speak peace. But those that are sanctified have God's Spirit witnessing with their spirits, which is to be understood not of any immediate extraordinary revelation, but an ordinary work of the Spirit, in and by the means of comfort, speaking peace to the soul. This testimony is always agreeable to the written word, and is therefore always grounded upon sanctification; for the Spirit in the heart cannot contradict the Spirit in the word. The Spirit witnesses to none the privileges of children who have not the nature and disposition of children.

17 And if children, then heirs;
heirs of God, and joint-heirs with

Christ; if so be that we suffer with
him, that we may be also glorified
together. 18 For I reckon that the
sufferings of this present time *are*
not worthy *to be compared* with the
glory which shall be revealed in us.
19 For the earnest expectation of the
creature waiteth for the manifestation
of the sons of God. 20 For the
creature was made subject to vanity,
not willingly, but by reason of him
who hath subjected *the same* in hope.
21 Because the creature itself also
shall be delivered from the bondage
of corruption into the glorious liberty
of the children of God. 22 For we
know that the whole creation groan-
eth and travaileth in pain together
until now. 23 And not only *they*,
but ourselves also, which have the
firstfruits of the Spirit, even we ourselves groan within ourselves, waiting
for the adoption, *to wit*, the redemption of our body. 24 For we are
saved by hope: but hope that is seen
is not hope: for what a man seeth,
why doth he yet hope for? 25 But
if we hope for that we see not, *then*
do we with patience wait for *it*.

In these words the apostle describes a fourth illustrious branch of the happiness of believers, namely, a title to the future glory. This is fitly annexed to our sonship; for as the adoption of sons entitles us to that glory, so the disposition of sons fits and prepares us for it. *If children, then heirs*, *v.* 17. In earthly inheritances this rule does not hold, only the first-born are heirs; but the church is a church of first-born, for they are all heirs. Heaven is an inheritance that all the saints are heirs to. They do not come to it as purchasers by any merit or procurement of their own; but as heirs, purely by the act of God; for God makes heirs. The saints are heirs though in this world they are heirs under age; see Gal. iv. 1, 2. Their present state is a state of education and preparation for the inheritance. How comfortable should this be to all the children of God, how little soever they have in possession, that, being heirs, they have enough in reversion! But the honour and happiness of an heir lie in the value and worth of that which he is heir to: we read of those that inherit the wind; and therefore we have here an abstract of the premises. 1. *Heirs of God.* The Lord himself is the portion of the saints' inheritance (Ps. xvi. 5), a goodly heritage, *v.* 6. The saints are spiritual priests, that have the Lord for their inheritance, Num. xviii. 20. The vision of God and the fruition of God make up the inheritance the saints are heirs to. God himself will be with them, and will be their God, Rev. xxi. 3. 2. *Joint-heirs with Christ.* Christ, as Mediator, is said to be the heir of all things (Heb. i. 2), and true believers, by virtue of their union with him, *shall inherit all things*, Rev. xxi. 7. Those that now partake of the Spirit of Christ, as his brethren, shall, as his brethren, partake of his glory (John xvii. 24), shall sit down with him upon his throne, Rev. iii. 21. Lord, what is man, that thou shouldst thus magnify him! Now this future glory is further spoken of as the reward of present sufferings and as the accomplishment of present hopes.

I. As the reward of the saints' present sufferings; and it is a rich reward: *If so be that we suffer with him* (*v.* 17), or *forasmuch as we suffer with him.* The state of the church in this world always is, but was then especially, an afflicted state; to be a Christian was certainly to be a sufferer. Now, to comfort them in reference to those sufferings, he tells them that they suffered with Christ—for his sake, for his honour, and for the testimony of a good conscience, and should be glorified with him. Those that suffered with David in his persecuted state were advanced by him and with him when he came to the crown; see 2 Tim. ii. 12. See the gains of suffering for Christ; though we may be losers for him, we shall not, we cannot, be losers by him in the end. This the gospel is filled with the assurances of. Now, that suffering saints may have strong supports and consolations from their hopes of heaven, he holds the balance (*v.* 18), in a comparison between the two, which is observable. 1. In one scale he puts the *sufferings of this present time.* The sufferings of the saints are but sufferings of this present time, strike no deeper than the things of time, last no longer than the present time (2 Cor. iv. 17), light affliction, and but for a moment. So that on the sufferings he writes *tekel*, weighed in the balance and found light. 2. In the other scale he puts the glory, and finds that a weight, an exceeding and eternal weight: *Glory that shall be revealed.* In our present state we come short, not only in the enjoyment, but in the knowledge of that glory (1 Cor. ii. 9; 1 John iii. 2): it shall be revealed. It surpasses all that we have yet seen and known: present vouchsafements are sweet and precious, very precious, very sweet; but there is something to come, something behind the curtain, that will outshine all. *Shall be revealed in us;* not only revealed to us, to be seen, but revealed in us, to be enjoyed. The kingdom of God is within you, and will be so to eternity. 3. He concludes the sufferings *not worthy to be compared with the glory*—*οὐκ ἄξια πρὸς τὴν δόξαν.* They cannot merit that glory; and, if suffering for Christ will not merit, much less will doing. They should not at all deter and frighten us from the diligent and earnest pursuit of that glory. The sufferings are small and short, and concern the body only; but the glory is rich and great, and concerns the soul, and is eternal. This he reckons. *I reckon*—λογίζομαι. It is not a rash and sudden determination, but the product of a very serious and deliberate consideration. He had reasoned the case within himself, weighed the arguments on both sides, and thus at last resolves the point. O how vastly different is the sentence of the word from the sentiment of the world concerning the sufferings of this present time! *I reckon,* as an arithmetician that is balancing an account. He first sums up what is disbursed for Christ in the sufferings of this present time, and finds they come to very little; he then sums up what is secured to us by Christ in the glory that shall be revealed, and this he finds to be an infinite sum, transcending all conception, the disbursement abundantly made up and the losses infinitely countervailed. And who would be afraid then to suffer for Christ, who as he is beforehand with us in suffering, so he will not be behind-hand with us in recompence? Now Paul was as competent a judge of this point as ever any mere man was. He could reckon not by art only, but by experience; for he knew both. He knew what the sufferings of this present time were; see 2 Cor. xi. 23—28. He knew what the glory of heaven is; see 2 Cor. xii. 3, 4. And, upon the view of both, he gives this judgment here. There is nothing like a believing view of the glory which shall be revealed to support and bear up the spirit under all the sufferings of this present time. The reproach of Christ appears riches to those who have respect to the recompence of reward, Heb. xi. 26.

II. As the accomplishment of the saints' present hopes and expectations, *v.* 19, &c. As the saints are suffering for it, so they are waiting for it. Heaven is therefore sure; for God by his Spirit would not raise and encourage those hopes only to defeat and disappoint them. He will establish that word unto his servants on which he has caused them to hope (Ps. cxix. 49), and heaven is therefore sweet; for, if hope deferred makes the heart sick, surely when the desire comes it will be a tree of life, Prov xiii. 12. Now he observes an expectation of this glory,

1. In the creatures *v.* 19—22. That must needs be a great, a transcendent glory, which all the creatures are so earnestly expecting and longing for. This observation in these verses has some difficulty in it, which puzzles interpreters a little; and the more because it is a remark not made in any other scripture, with which it might be compared. By the *creature* here we understand, not as some do the Gentile world, and their expectation of Christ and the gospel, which is an exposition very foreign and forced, but the whole frame of nature, especially that of this lower world—the whole creation, the compages of inanimate and sensible creatures, which, because of their harmony and mutual dependence, and because they all constitute and make up one world, are spoken of in the singular number as the *creature* The sense of the apostle in these four verses we may take in the following observations:—(1.) That there is a present vanity to which the creature, by reason of the sin of man, is made subject, *v.* 20. When man sinned, the ground was cursed for man's sake, and with it all the creatures (especially of this lower world, where our acquaintance lies) became subject to that curse, became mutable and mortal. *Under the bondage of corruption, v.* 21. There is an impurity, deformity, and infirmity, which the creature has contracted by the fall of man: the creation is sullied and stained, much of the beauty of the world gone. There is an enmity of one creature to another; they are all subject to continual alteration and decay of the individuals, liable to the strokes of God's judgments upon man. When the world was drowned, and almost all the creatures in it, surely then it was subject to vanity indeed. The whole species of creatures is designed for, and is hastening to, a total dissolution by fire. And it is not the least part of their vanity and bondage that they are used, or abused rather, by men as instruments of sin. The creatures are often abused to the dishonour of their Creator, the hurt of his children, or the service of his enemies. When the creatures are made the food and fuel of our lusts, they are subject to vanity, they are captivated by the law of sin. And this *not willingly,* not of their own choice. All the creatures desire their own perfection and consummation; when they are made instruments of sin it is not willingly. Or, They are thus captivated, not for any sin of their own, which they had committed, but for man's sin: *By reason of him who hath subjected the same.* Adam did it meritoriously; the creatures being delivered to him, when he by sin delivered himself he delivered them likewise into the bondage of corruption. God did it judicially; he passed a sentence upon the creatures for the sin of man, by which they became subject. And this yoke (poor creatures) they bear in hope that it will not be so always. Ἐπ' ἐλπίδι ὅτι καὶ, &c.—*in hope that the creature itself;* so many Greek copies join the words. We have reason to pity the poor creatures that for our sin have become subject to vanity. (2.) That the creatures *groan and travail in pain* together under this vanity and corruption, *v.* 22. It is a figurative expression. Sin is a burden to the whole creation; the sin of the Jews, in crucifying Christ, set the earth a quaking under them. The idols were a burden to the weary beast, Isa. xlvi. 1. There is a general outcry of the whole creation against the sin of man: the stone crieth out of the wall (Hab. ii. 11), the land cries, Job xxxi. 38. (3.) That the creature, that is now thus burdened, shall, at the time of the restitution of all things, be *delivered from this bondage into the glorious*

liberty of the children of God (*v.* 21)—they shall no more be subject to vanity and corruption, and the other fruits of the curse; but, on the contrary, this lower world shall be renewed: when there will be new heavens there will be a new earth (2 Pet. iii. 13; Rev. xxi. 1); and there shall be a glory conferred upon all the creatures, which shall be (in the proportion of their natures) as suitable and as great an advancement as the glory of the children of God shall be to them. The fire at the last day shall be a refining, not a destroying annihilating fire. What becomes of the souls of brutes, that go downwards, none can tell. But it should seem by the scripture that there will be some kind of restoration of them. And if it be objected, What use will they be of to glorified saints? we may suppose them of as much use as they were to Adam in innocency; and if it be only to illustrate the wisdom, power, and goodness of their Creator, that is enough. Compare with this Ps. xcvi. 10—13; xcviii. 7—9. *Let the heavens rejoice before the Lord, for he cometh.* (4.) That the creature doth therefore earnestly expect and wait for the *manifestation of the children of God, v.* 19. Observe, At the second coming of Christ there will be a manifestation of the children of God. Now the saints are God's hidden ones, the wheat seems lost in a heap of chaff; but then they shall be manifested. It does not yet appear what we shall be (1 John iii. 2), but then the glory shall be revealed. The children of God shall appear in their own colours. And this redemption of the creature is reserved till then; for, as it was with man and for man that they fell under the curse, so with man and for man they shall be delivered. All the curse and filth that now adhere to the creature shall be done away then when those that have suffered with Christ upon earth shall reign with him upon the earth. This the whole creation looks and longs for; and it may serve as a reason why now a good man should be merciful to his beast.

2. In the saints, who are new creatures, *v.* 23—25. Observe, (1.) The grounds of this expectation in the saints. It is our having received *the first-fruits of the Spirit,* which both quickens our desires and encourages our hopes, and both ways raises our expectations. The first-fruits did both sanctify and ensure the lump. Grace is the first-fruits of glory, it is glory begun. We, having received such clusters in this wilderness, cannot but long for the full vintage in the heavenly Canaan. *Not only they*—not only the creatures which are not capable of such a happiness as the first-fruits of the Spirit, but even we, who have such present rich receivings, cannot but long for something more and greater. In having the first-fruits of the Spirit we have that which is very precious, but we have not all we would have. *We groan within ourselves,* which denotes the strength and secrecy of these desires; not making a loud noise, as the hypocrites howling upon the bed for corn and wine, but with silent groans, which pierce heaven soonest of all. Or, *We groan among ourselves.* It is the unanimous vote, the joint desire, of the whole church, all agree in this: *Come, Lord Jesus, come quickly.* The groaning denotes a very earnest and importunate desire, the soul pained with the delay. Present receivings and comforts are consistent with a great many groans; not as the pangs of one dying, but as the throes of a woman in travail—groans that are symptoms of life, not of death. (2.) The object of this expectation. What is it we are thus desiring and waiting for? What would we have? *The adoption, to wit, the redemption of our body.* Though the soul be the principal part of the man, yet the Lord has declared himself for the body also, and has provided a great deal of honour and happiness for the body. The resurrection is here called *the redemption of the body.* It shall then be rescued from the power of death and the grave, and the bondage of corruption; and, though a vile body, yet it shall be refined and beautified, and made like that glorious body of Christ, Phil. iii. 21; 1 Cor. xv. 42. This is called *the adoption.* [1.] It is the adoption manifested before all the world, angels and men. Now are we the sons of God, but it does not yet appear, the honour is now clouded; but then God will publicly own all his children. The deed of adoption, which is now written, signed, and sealed, will then be recognized, proclaimed, and published. As Christ was, so the saints will be, declared to be the sons of God with power, by the resurrection from the dead, *ch.* i. 4. It will then be put past dispute. [2.] It is the adoption perfected and completed. The children of God have bodies as well as souls; and, till those bodies are brought into the glorious liberty of the children of God, the adoption is not perfect. But then it will be complete, when the Captain of our salvation shall bring the many sons to glory, Heb. ii. 10. This is that which we expect, in hope of which our flesh rests, Ps. xvi. 9, 10. All the days of our appointed time we are waiting, till this change shall come, when he shall call, and we shall answer, and he will have a desire to the work of his hands, Job xiv. 14, 15. (3.) The agreeableness of this to our present state, *v.* 24, 25. Our happiness is not in present possession: *We are saved by hope.* In this, as in other things, God hath made our present state a state of trial and probation—that our reward is out of sight. Those that will deal with God must deal upon trust. It is acknowledged that one of the principal graces of a Christian is hope (1 Cor. xiii. 13), which necessarily implies a good thing to come, which is the object of that hope. Faith respects the promise, hope the thing promised. Faith is the evidence, hope the expectation, of things not seen. Faith is the mother of hope.

We do with patience wait. In hoping for this glory we have need of patience, to bear the sufferings we meet with in the way to it and the delays of it. Our way is rough and long; but he that shall come will come, and will not tarry; and therefore, though he seem to tarry, it becomes us to wait for him.

26 Likewise the Spirit also helpeth our infirmities: for we know not what we should pray for as we ought: but the Spirit itself maketh intercession for us with groanings which cannot be uttered. 27 And he that searcheth the hearts knoweth what *is* the mind of the Spirit, because he maketh intercession for the saints according to *the will of* God. 28 And we know that all things work together for good to them that love God, to them who are the called according to *his* purpose.

The apostle here suggests two privileges more to which true Christians are entitled:—

I. The help of the Spirit in prayer. While we are in this world, hoping and waiting for what we see not, we must be praying. Hope supposes desire, and that desire offered up to God is prayer; we groan. Now observe,

1. Our weakness in prayer: *We know not what we should pray for as we ought.* (1.) As to the matter of our requests, we know not what to ask. We are not competent judges of our own condition. *Who knows what is good for a man in this life?* Eccl. vi. 12. We are short-sighted, and very much biassed in favour of the flesh, and apt to separate the end from the way. *You know not what you ask,* Matt. xx. 22. We are like foolish children, that are ready to cry for fruit before it is ripe and fit for them; see Luke ix. 54, 55. (2.) As to the manner, we know not how to pray as we ought. It is not enough that we do that which is good, but we must do it well, seek in a due order; and here we are often at a loss—graces are weak, affections cold, thoughts wandering, and it is not always easy to *find the heart to pray,* 2 Sam. vii. 27. The apostle speaks of this in the first person: *We know not.* He puts himself among the rest. Folly, and weakness, and distraction in prayer, are what all the saints are complaining of. If so great a saint as Paul knew not what to pray for, what little reason have we to go forth about that duty in our own strength!

2. The assistances which the Spirit gives us in that duty. He *helps our infirmities,* meant especially of our praying infirmities, which most easily beset us in that duty, against which the Spirit helps. The Spirit in the word helps; many rules and promises there are in the word for our help. The Spirit in the heart helps, dwelling in us, working in us, as a Spirit of grace and supplication, especially with respect to the infirmities we are under when we are in a suffering state, when our faith is most apt to fail; for this end the Holy Ghost was poured out. *Helpeth, συναντιλαμβάνεται—heaves with us, over against us,* helps as we help one that would lift up a burden, by lifting over against him at the other end—helps with us, that is, with us doing our endeavour, putting forth the strength we have. We must not sit still, and expect that the Spirit should do all; when the Spirit goes before us we must bestir ourselves. We cannot without God, and he will not without us. What help? Why, the *Spirit itself makes intercession for us,* dictates our requests, indites our petitions, draws up our plea for us. Christ intercedes for us in heaven, the Spirit intercedes for us in our hearts; so graciously has God provided for the encouragement of the praying remnant. The Spirit, as an enlightening Spirit, teaches us what to pray for, as a sanctifying Spirit works and excites praying graces, as a comforting Spirit silences our fears, and helps us over all our discouragements. The Holy Spirit is the spring of all our desires and breathings towards God. Now this intercession which the Spirit makes is, (1.) *With groanings that cannot be uttered.* The strength and fervency of those desires which the Holy Spirit works are hereby intimated. There may be praying in the Spirit where there is not a word spoken; as Moses prayed (Exod. xiv. 15), and Hannah, 1 Sam. i. 13. It is not the rhetoric and eloquence, but the faith and fervency, of our prayers, that the Spirit works, as an intercessor, in us. *Cannot be uttered;* they are so confused, the soul is in such a hurry with temptations and troubles, we know not what to say, nor how to express ourselves. Here is the Spirit interceding with groans that cannot be uttered. When we can but cry, *Abba, Father,* and refer ourselves to him with a holy humble boldness, this is the work of the Spirit. (2.) *According to the will of God, v.* 27. The Spirit in the heart never contradicts the Spirit in the word. Those desires that are contrary to the will of God do not come from the Spirit. The Spirit interceding in us evermore melts our wills into the will of God. *Not as I will, but as thou wilt.*

3. The sure success of these intercessions: *He that searches the heart knoweth what is the mind of the Spirit, v.* 27. To a hypocrite, all whose religion lies in his tongue, nothing is more dreadful than that God searches the heart and sees through all his disguises. To a sincere Christian, who makes heart-work of his duty, nothing is more comfortable than that God searches the heart, for then he will hear and answer those desires which we want words to express. He knows what we have need of before we ask, Matt. vi. 8. He knows what is the mind of his own Spirit in us. And, as he always hears the Son interceding for us, so he always hears the Spirit

interceding in us, because his intercession is according to the will of God. What could have been done more for the comfort of the Lord's people, in all their addresses to God? Christ had said, "Whatever you ask the Father according to his will he will give it you." But how shall we learn to ask according to his will. Why, the Spirit will teach us that. Therefore it is that the seed of Jacob never seek in vain.

II. The concurrence of all providences for the good of those that are Christ's, *v.* 28. It might be objected that, notwithstanding all these privileges, we see believers compassed about with manifold afflictions; though the Spirit makes intercession for them, yet their troubles are continued. It is very true; but in this the Spirit's intercession is always effectual, that, however it goes with them, all this is working together for their good. Observe here.

1. The character of the saints, who are interested in this privilege; they are here described by such properties as are common to all that are truly sanctified. (1.) *They love God.* This includes all the out-goings of the soul's affections towards God as the chief good and highest end. It is our love to God that makes every providence sweet, and therefore profitable. Those that love God make the best of all he does, and take all in good part. (2.) *They are the called according to his purpose,* effectually called according to the eternal purpose. The call is effectual, not according to any merit or desert of ours, but according to God's own gracious purpose.

2. The privilege of the saints, that *all things work together for good to them,* that is, all the providences of God that concern them. All that God performs he performs for them, Ps. lvii. 2. Their sins are not of his performing, therefore not intended here, though his permitting sin is made to work for their good, 2 Chron. xxxii. 31. But all the providences of God are theirs—merciful providences, afflicting providences, personal, public. They are all for good; perhaps for temporal good, as Joseph's troubles; at least, for spiritual and eternal good. That is good for them which does their souls good. Either directly or indirectly, every providence has a tendency to the spiritual good of those that love God, breaking them off from sin, bringing them nearer to God, weaning them from the world, fitting them for heaven. *Work together.* They work, as physic works upon the body, various ways, according to the intention of the physician; but all for the patient's good. *They work together,* as several ingredients in a medicine concur to answer the intention. God hath set the one over against the other (Eccl. vii. 14): *συνεργεῖ*, a verb singular, with a noun plural, denoting the harmony of Providence and its uniform designs, all the wheels as one wheel, Ezek. x. 13. *He worketh all things together for good;* so some read it. It is not from any specific quality in the providences themselves, but from the power and grace of God working in, with, and by, these providences. All this *we know*—know it for a certainty, from the word of God, from our own experience, and from the experience of all the saints.

29 For whom he did foreknow, he also did predestinate *to be* conformed to the image of his Son, that he might be the firstborn among many brethren. 30 Moreover whom he did predestinate, them he also called: and whom he called, them he also justified: and whom he justified, them he also glorified.

The apostle, having reckoned up so many ingredients of the happiness of true believers, comes here to represent the ground of them all, which he lays in predestination. These precious privileges are conveyed to us by the charter of the covenant, but they are founded in the counsel of God, which infallibly secures the event. That Jesus Christ, the purchaser, might not labour in vain, nor spend his strength and life for nought and in vain, there is a remnant given him, a seed that he shall see, so that the good pleasure of the Lord shall prosper in his hands. For the explication of this he here sets before us the order of the causes of our salvation, a golden chain, which cannot be broken. There are four links of it:—

I. *Whom he did foreknow he also did predestinate to be conformed to the image of his Son.* All that God designed for glory and happiness as the end he decreed to grace and holiness as the way. Not, whom he did foreknow to be holy those he predestinated to be so. The counsels and decrees of God do not truckle to the frail and fickle will of men; no, God's foreknowledge of the saints is the same with that everlasting love wherewith he is said to have loved them, Jer. xxxi. 3. God's knowing his people is the same with his owning them, Ps. i. 6; John x. 14; 2 Tim. ii. 19. See *ch.* xi. 2. Words of knowledge often in scripture denote affection; so here: *Elect according to the foreknowledge of God,* 1 Pet. i. 2. And the same word is rendered *fore-ordained,* 1 Pet. i. 20. *Whom he did foreknow,* that is, whom he designed for his friends and favourites. *I know thee by name,* said God to Moses, Exod. xxxiii. 12. Now those whom God thus foreknew he did predestinate to be conformed to Christ. 1. Holiness consists in our conformity to the image of Christ. This takes in the whole of sanctification, of which Christ is the great pattern and sampler. To be spirited as Christ was, to walk and live as Christ did, to bear our sufferings patiently as Christ did. Christ is the express image of his Father, and the saints are conformed to the image of Christ. Thus it is by the mediation and interposal of Christ that we have God's love restored to us and God's likeness renewed upon us, in which two things consists the happiness of man. 2. All that God hath from eternity foreknown with favour he hath predestinated to this conformity. It is not we that can conform ourselves to Christ. Our giving ourselves to Christ takes rise in God's giving us to him; and, in giving us to him, he predestinated us to be conformable to his image. It is a mere cavil therefore to call the doctrine of election a licentious doctrine, and to argue that it gives encouragement to sin, as if the end were separated from the way and happiness from holiness. None can know their election but by their conformity to the image of Christ; for all that are chosen are chosen to sanctification (2 Thess. ii. 13), and surely it cannot be a temptation to any to be conformed to the world to believe that they were predestinated to be conformed to Christ. 3. That which is herein chiefly designed is the honour of Jesus Christ, that he might be the *first-born among many brethren;* that is, that Christ might have the honour of being the great pattern, as well as the great prince, and in this, as in other things, might have pre-eminence. It was in the first-born that all the children were dedicated to God under the law. The first-born was the head of the family, on whom all the rest did depend: now in the family of the saints Christ must have the honour of being the first-born. And blessed be God that there are many brethren; though they seem but a few in one place at one time, yet, when they come all together, they will be a great many. There is, therefore, a certain number predestinated, that the end of Christ's undertaking might be infallibly secured. Had the event been left at uncertainties in the divine counsels, to depend upon the contingent turn of man's will, Christ might have been the first-born among but few or no brethren—a captain without soldiers and a prince without subjects—to prevent which, and to secure to him many brethren, the decree is absolute, the thing ascertained, that he might be sure to see his seed, there is a remnant predestinated to be conformed to his image, which decree will certainly have its accomplishment in the holiness and happiness of that chosen race; and so, in spite of all the opposition of the powers of darkness, Christ will be the first-born among many, very many brethren.

II. *Whom he did predestinate those he also called,* not only with the external call (so many are called that were not chosen, Matt. xx. 16; xxii. 14), but with the internal and effectual call. The former comes to the ear only, but this to the heart. All that God did from eternity predestinate to grace and glory he does, in the fulness of time, effectually call. The call is then effectual when we come at the call; and we then come at the call when the Spirit draws us, convinces the conscience of guilt and wrath, enlightens the understanding, bows the will, persuades and enables us to embrace Christ in the promises, makes us willing in the day of his power. It is an effectual call from self and earth to God, and Christ, and heaven, as our end—from sin and vanity to grace, and holiness, and seriousness as our way. This is the gospel call. *Them he called,* that the purpose of God, according to election, might stand: we are called to that to which we were chosen. So that the only way to make our election sure is to make sure our calling, 2 Pet. i. 10.

III. *Whom he called those he also justified.* All that are effectually called are justified, absolved from guilt, and accepted as righteous through Jesus Christ. They are *recti in curia—right in court;* no sin that ever they have been guilty of shall come against them, to condemn them. The book is crossed, the bond cancelled, the judgment vacated, the attainder reversed; and they are no longer dealt with as criminals, but owned and loved as friends and favourites. Blessed is the man whose iniquity is thus forgiven. None are thus justified but those that are effectually called. Those that stand it out against the gospel call abide under guilt and wrath.

IV. *Whom he justified those he also glorified.* The power of corruption being broken in effectual calling, and the guilt of sin removed in justification, all that which hinders is taken out of the way, and nothing can come between that soul and glory. Observe, It is spoken of as a thing done: *He glorified,* because of the certainty of it; he *hath* saved us, and called us with a holy calling. In the eternal glorification of all the elect, God's design of love has its full accomplishment. This was what he aimed at all along—to bring them to heaven. Nothing less than that glory would make up the fulness of his covenant relation to them as God; and therefore, in all he does for them, and in them, he has this in his eye. Are they chosen? It is to salvation. Called? It is to his kingdom and glory. Begotten again? It is to an inheritance incorruptible. Afflicted? It is to work for them this exceeding and eternal weight of glory. Observe, The author of all these is the same. It is God himself that predestinated, calleth, justifieth, glorifieth; so *the Lord alone did lead him, and there was no strange God with him.* Created wills are so very fickle, and created powers so very feeble, that, if any of these did depend upon the creature, the whole would shake. But God himself hath undertaken the doing of it from first to last, that we might abide in a constant dependence upon him and subjection to him, and ascribe all the praise to him—that every crown may be cast before the throne. This is a mighty encouragement to our faith and hope; for, as for God, his way, his work, is perfect. He that hath laid the foundation will build upon it, and the top-stone will at length be brought forth with shoutings, and it will be our eternal work to cry, Grace, grace to it.

31 What shall we then say to these
things? If God *be* for us, who *can*
be against us? 32 He that spared
not his own Son, but delivered him
up for us all, how shall he not with
him also freely give us all things?
33 Who shall lay any thing to the
charge of God's elect? *It is* God
that justifieth. 34 Who *is* he that
condemneth? *It is* Christ that died,
yea rather, that is risen again, who is
even at the right hand of God, who
also maketh intercession for us. 35
Who shall separate us from the love
of Christ? *shall* tribulation, or distress, or persecution, or famine, or
nakedness, or peril, or sword? 36
As it is written, For thy sake we are
killed all the day long; we are accounted as sheep for the slaughter.
37 Nay, in all these things we are
more than conquerors through him
that loved us. 38 For I am persuaded, that neither death, nor life,
nor angels, nor principalities, nor
powers, nor things present, nor things
to come, 39 Nor height, nor depth,
nor any other creature, shall be able
to separate us from the love of God,
which is in Christ Jesus our Lord.

The apostle closes this excellent discourse upon the privileges of believers with a holy triumph, in the name of all the saints. Having largely set forth the mystery of God's love to us in Christ, and the exceedingly great and precious privileges we enjoy by him, he concludes like an orator: *What shall we then say to these things?* What use shall we make of all that has been said? He speaks as one amazed and swallowed up with the contemplation and admiration of it, wondering at the height and depth, and length and breadth, of the love of Christ, which passeth knowledge. The more we know of other things the less we wonder at them; but the further we are led into an acquaintance with gospel mysteries the more we are affected with the admiration of them. If Paul was at a loss what to say to these things, no marvel if we be. And what does he say? Why, if ever Paul rode in a triumphant chariot on this side heaven, here it was: with such a holy height and bravery of spirit, with such a fluency and copiousness of expression, does he here comfort himself and all the people of God, upon the consideration of these privileges. In general, he here makes a challenge, throws down the gauntlet, as it were, dares all the enemies of the saints to do their worst: *If God be for us, who can be against us?* The ground of the challenge is God's being for us; in this he sums up all our privileges. This includes all, that *God is for us;* not only reconciled to us, and so not against us, but in covenant with us, and so engaged for us—all his attributes for us, his promises for us. All that he is, and has, and does, is for his people. He performs all things for them. He is for them, even when he seems to act against them. And, if so, *who can be against us,* so as to prevail against us, so as to hinder our happiness? Be they ever so great and strong, ever so many, ever so mighty, ever so malicious, what can they do? While God is for us, and we keep in his love, we may with a holy boldness defy all the powers of darkness. Let Satan do his worst, he is chained; let the world do its worst, it is conquered: principalities and powers are spoiled and disarmed, and triumphed over, in the cross of Christ. Who then dares fight against us, while God himself is fighting for us? And this we say to these things, this is the inference we draw from these premises. More particularly.

I. We have supplies ready in all our wants (*v.* 32): *He that spared,* &c. Who can be against us, to strip us, to deprive us of our comforts? Who can cut off our streams, while we have a fountain to go to? 1. Observe what God has done for us, on which our hopes are built: *He spared not his own Son.* When he was to undertake our salvation, the Father was willing to part with him, did not think him too precious a gift to bestow for the salvation of poor souls; now we may know that he loves us, in that he hath not withheld his Son, his own Son, his only Son, from us, as he said of Abraham, Gen. xxii. 12. If nothing less will save man, rather than man shall perish let him go, though it were out of his bosom. Thus did he *deliver him up for us all,* that is, for all the elect; *for us all,* not only for our good, but in our stead, as a sacrifice of atonement to be a propitiation for sin. When he had undertaken it, he did not spare him. Though he was his own Son, yet, being made sin for us, it pleased the Lord to bruise him. 'Ουκ ἐφεισατο—*he did not abate* him a farthing of that great debt, but charged it home. *Awake, O sword.* He did not *spare his own Son that served him,* that he might spare us, though we have done him so much disservice. 2. What we may therefore expect he will do: He will *with him freely give us all things.* (1.) It is implied that he will give us Christ, for other things are bestowed with him: not only with him given for us, but with him given to us. He that put himself to so much charge to make the purchase for us surely will not hesitate at making the application to us. (2.) He will with him freely give us all things, all things that he sees to be needful and necessary for us, all good things, and more we should not desire, Ps. xxxiv. 10. And Infinite Wisdom shall be the judge whether it be good for us and needful for us or no. *Freely give*—freely, without reluctancy; he is ready to give, meets us with his favours;—and freely, without recompence, without money, and without price. *How shall he not?* Can it be imagined that he should do the greater and not do the less? that he should give so great a gift for us when we were enemies, and should deny us any good thing, now that through him we are friends and children? Thus may we by faith argue against our fears of want. He that hath prepared a crown and kingdom for us will be sure to give us enough to bear our charges in the way to it. He that hath designed us for the inheritance of sons when we come to age will not let us want necessaries in the mean time.

II. We have an answer ready to all accusations and a security against all condemnations (*v.* 33, 34): *Who shall lay any thing?* Doth the law accuse them? Do their own consciences accuse them? Is the devil, the accuser of the brethren, accusing them before our God day and night? This is enough to answer all those accusations, *It is God that justifieth.* Men may justify themselves, as the Pharisees did, and yet the accusations may be in full force against them; but, if God justifies, this answers all. He is the judge, the king, the party offended, and his judgment is according to truth, and sooner or later all the world will be brought to be of his mind; so that we may challenge all our accusers to come and put in their charge. This overthrows them all; it is God, the righteous faithful God, that justifieth. *Who is he that condemneth?* Though they cannot make good the charge, yet they will be ready to condemn; but we have a plea ready to move in arrest of judgment, a plea which cannot be overruled. *It is Christ that died,* &c. It is by virtue of our interest in Christ, our relation to him, and our union with him, that we are thus secured. 1. His death: *It is Christ that died.* By the merit of his death he paid our debt; and the surety's payment is a good plea to an action of debt. It is Christ, an able all-sufficient Saviour. 2. His resurrection: *Yea, rather, that has risen again.* This is a much greater encouragement, for it is a convincing evidence that divine justice was satisfied by the merit of his death. His resurrection was his acquittance, it was a legal discharge. Therefore the apostle mentions it with a *yea, rather.* If he had died, and not risen again, we had been where we were. 3. His sitting at the right hand of God: He is *even at the right hand of God*—a further evidence that he has done his work, and a mighty encouragement to us in reference to all accusations, that we have a friend, such a friend, in court. At *the right hand of God,* which denotes that he is ready there—always at hand; and that he is ruling there—all power is given to him. Our friend is himself the judge. 4. The intercession which he makes there. He is there, not unconcerned about us, not forgetful of us, but *making intercession.* He is agent for us there, an advocate for us, to answer all accusations, to put in our plea, and to prosecute it with effect, to appear for us and to present our petitions. And is not this abundant matter for comfort? What shall we say to these things? Is this the manner of men, O Lord God? What room is left for doubting and disquietment? Why art thou cast down, O my soul? Some understand the accusation and condemnation here spoken of of that which the suffering saints met with from men. The primitive Christians had many black crimes laid to their charge—heresy, sedition, rebellion, and what not? For these the ruling powers condemned them: "But no matter for that" (says the apostle); "while we stand right at God's bar it is of no great moment how we stand at men's. To all the hard censures, the malicious calumnies, and the unjust and unrighteous sentences of men, we may with comfort oppose our justification before God through Christ Jesus as that which doth abundantly countervail," 1 Cor. iv. 3, 4.

III. We have good assurance of our preservation and continuance in this blessed state, *v.* 35, to the end. The fears of the saints lest they should lose their hold of Christ are often very discouraging and disquieting, and create them a great deal of disturbance; but here is that which may silence their fears, and still such storms, that nothing can separate them. We have here from the apostle,

1. A daring challenge to all the enemies of the saints to separate them, if they could, from the love of Christ. *Who shall?* None shall, *v.* 35—37. God having manifested his love in giving his own Son for us, and not hesitating at that, can we imagine that any thing else should divert or dissolve that love? Observe here,

(1.) The present calamities of Christ's beloved ones supposed—that they meet with *tribulation* on all hands, are in *distress,* know not which way to look for any succour and relief in this world, are followed with *persecution* from an angry malicious world that always hated those whom Christ loved, pinched with *famine,* and starved with *nakedness,* when stripped of all *creature-comforts,* exposed to the greatest *perils,* the *sword* of the magistrate drawn against them, ready to be sheathed in their bowels, bathed in their blood. Can a case be supposed more black and dismal? It is illustrated (*v.* 36) by a passage quoted from Ps. xliv. 22, *For thy sake we are killed all the day long,* which intimates that we are not to think strange, no not concerning the fiery bloody trial. We see the Old-Testament saints had the same lot; so persecuted they the prophets that were before us. *Killed all the day long,* that is, continually exposed to and expecting the fatal stroke There is still every day, and all the day long, one or other of the people of God bleeding and dying under the rage of persecuting enemies. *Accounted as sheep for the slaughter;* they make no more of killing a Christian than of butchering a sheep. Sheep are killed, not because they are hurtful while they live, but because they are useful when they are dead. They kill the Christians to please themselves, to be food to their malice. *They eat up my people as they eat bread,* Ps. xiv. 4.

(2.) The inability of all these things to separate us from the love of Christ. Shall they, can they, do it? No, by no means. All this will not cut the bond of love and friendship that is between Christ and true believers. [1.] Christ doth not, will not, love us the less for all this. All these troubles are very consistent with the strong and constant love of the Lord Jesus. They are neither a cause nor an evidence of the abatement of his love. When Paul was whipped, and beaten, and imprisoned, and stoned, did Christ love him ever the less? Were his favours intermitted? his smiles any whit suspended? his visits more shy? By no means, but the contrary. These things separate us from the love of other friends. When Paul was brought before Nero all men forsook him, but then the Lord stood by him, 2 Tim. iv. 16, 17. Whatever persecuting enemies may rob us of, they cannot rob us of the love of Christ, they cannot intercept his love-tokens, they cannot interrupt nor exclude his visits: and therefore, let them do their worst, they cannot make a true believer miserable. [2.] We do not, will not, love him the less for this; and that for this reason, because we do not think that he loves us the less. Charity thinks no evil, entertains no misgiving thoughts, makes no hard conclusions, no unkind constructions, takes all in good part that comes from love. A true Christian loves Christ never the less though he suffer for him, thinks never the worse of Christ though he lose all for him.

(3.) The triumph of believers in this (*v.* 37): *Nay, in all these things we are more than conquerors.*

[1.] We are conquerors: though killed all the day long, yet conquerors. A strange way of conquering, but it was Christ's way; thus he triumphed over principalities and powers in his cross. It is a surer and a nobler way of conquest by faith and patience than by fire and sword. The enemies have sometimes confessed themselves baffled and overcome by the invincible courage and constancy of the martyrs, who thus overcame the most victorious princes by not loving their lives to the death, Rev. xii. 11.

[2.] We are more than conquerors. In our patiently bearing these trials we are not only conquerors, but more than conquerors, that is, triumphers. Those are more than conquerors that conquer, *First,* With little loss. Many conquests are dearly bought; but what do the suffering saints lose? Why, they lose that which the gold loses in the furnace, nothing but the dross. It is no great loss to lose things which are not—a body that is of the earth, earthy. *Secondly,* With great gain. The spoils are exceedingly rich; glory, honour, and peace, a crown of righteousness that fades not away. In this the suffering saints have triumphed; not only have not been separated from the love of Christ, but have been taken into the most sensible endearments and embraces of it. As afflictions abound, consolations much more abound, 2 Cor. i. 5. There is one more than a conqueror, when pressed above measure. He that embraced the stake, and said, "Welcome the cross of Christ, welcome everlasting life,"—he that dated his letter from the delectable orchard of the Leonine prison,—he that said, "In these flames I feel no more pain than if I were upon a bed of down,"—she who, a little before her martyrdom, being asked how she did, said, "Well and merry, and going to heaven,"—those that have gone smiling to the stake, and stood singing in the flames—these were more than conquerors.

[3.] It is only *through Christ that loved us,* the merit of his death taking the sting out of all these troubles, the Spirit of his grace strengthening us, and enabling us to bear them with holy courage and constancy, and coming in with special comforts and supports. Thus we are conquerors, not in our own strength, but in the grace that is in Christ Jesus. We are conquerors by virtue of our interest in Christ's victory. He hath overcome the world for us (John xvi. 33), both the good things and the evil things of it; so that we have nothing to do but to pursue the victory, and to divide the spoil, and so are more than conquerors.

2. A direct and positive conclusion of the whole matter: *For I am persuaded, v.* 38, 39. It denotes a full, and strong, and affectionate persuasion, arising from the experience of the strength and sweetness of the divine love. And here he enumerates all those things which might be supposed likely to separate between Christ and believers, and concludes that it could not be done. (1.) *Neither death nor life*—neither the terrors of death on the one hand nor the comforts and pleasures of life on the other, neither the fear of death nor the hope of life. Or, We shall not be separated from that love either in death or in life. (2.) *Nor angels, nor principalities, nor powers.* Both the good angels and the bad are called principalities and powers: the good, Eph. i. 21; Col. i. 16; the bad, Eph. vi. 12; Col. ii. 15. And neither shall do it. The good angels will not, the bad shall not; and neither can. The good angels are engaged friends, the bad are restrained enemies. (3.) *Nor things present, nor things to come*—neither the sense of troubles present nor the fear of troubles to come. Time shall not separate us, eternity

shall not. Things present separate us from things to come, and things to come separate and cut us off from things present; but neither from the love of Christ, whose favour is twisted in with both present things and things to come. (4.) *Nor height, nor depth*—neither the height of prosperity and preferment, nor the depth of adversity and disgrace; nothing from heaven above, no storms, no tempests; nothing on earth below, no rocks, no seas, no dungeons. (5.) *Nor any other creature*—any thing that can be named or thought of. It will not, it cannot, separate us from the love of God, which is in Christ Jesus our Lord. It cannot cut off or impair our love to God, or God's to us; nothing does it, can do it, but sin. Observe, The love that exists between God and true believers is through Christ. He is the Mediator of our love: it is in and through him that God can love us and that we dare love God. This is the ground of the stedfastness of the love; therefore God rests in his love (Zeph. iii. 17), because Jesus Christ, in whom he loves us, is the same yesterday, to-day, and for ever.

Mr. Hugh Kennedy, an eminent Christian of Ayr, in Scotland, when he was dying, called for a Bible; but, finding his sight gone, he said, "Turn me to the eighth of the Romans, and set my finger at these words, *I am persuaded that neither death nor life*," &c. "Now," said he, "is my finger upon them?" And, when they told him it was, without speaking any more, he said, "Now, God be with you, my children; I have breakfasted with you, and shall sup with my Lord Jesus Christ this night;" and so departed.

CHAP. IX.

The apostle, having plainly asserted and largely proved that justification and salvation are to be had by faith only, and not by the works of the law, by Christ and not by Moses, comes in this and the following chapters to anticipate an objection which might be made against this. If this be so, then what becomes of the Jews, of them all as a complex body, especially those of them that do not embrace Christ, nor believe the gospel? By this rule they must needs come short of happiness; and then what becomes of the promise made to the fathers, which entailed salvation upon the Jews? Is not that promise nullified and made of none effect? Which is not a thing to be imagined concerning any word of God. That doctrine therefore, might they say, is not to be embraced, from which flows such a consequence as this. That the consequence of the rejection of the unbelieving Jews follows from Paul's doctrine he grants, but endeavours to soften and mollify, ver. 1—5. But that from this it follows that the word of God takes no effect he denies (ver. 6), and proves the denial in the rest of the chapter, which serves likewise to illustrate the great doctrine of predestination, which he had spoken of (ch. viii. 28) as the first wheel which in the business of salvation sets all the other wheels a-going.

I SAY the truth in Christ, I lie not,
my conscience also bearing me
witness in the Holy Ghost, 2 That
I have great heaviness and continual
sorrow in my heart. 3 For I could wish
that myself were accursed from Christ
for my brethren, my kinsmen according to the flesh: 4 Who are Israelites; to whom *pertaineth* the adoption,
and the glory, and the covenants, and
the giving of the law, and the service
of God, and the promises; 5 Whose
are the fathers, and of whom as concerning the flesh Christ *came*, who is
over all, God blessed for ever. Amen.

We have here the apostle's solemn profession of a great concern for the nation and people of the Jews—that he was heartily troubled that so many of them were enemies to the gospel, and out of the way of salvation. For this he had *great heaviness and continual sorrow.* Such a profession as this was requisite to take off the odium which otherwise he might have contracted by asserting and proving their rejection. It is wisdom as much as may be to mollify those truths which sound harshly and seem unpleasant: dip the nail in oil, it will drive the better. The Jews had a particular pique at Paul above any of the apostles, as appears by the history of the Acts, and therefore were the more apt to take things amiss of him, to prevent which he introduces his discourse with this tender and affectionate profession, that they might not think he triumphed or insulted over the rejected Jews or was pleased with the calamities that were coming upon them. Thus Jeremiah appeals to God concerning the Jews of his day, whose ruin was hastening on (Jer. xvii. 16), *Neither have I desired the woeful day, thou knowest.* Nay, Paul was so far from desiring it that he most pathetically deprecates it. And lest this should be thought only a copy of his countenance, to flatter and please them,

I. He asserts it with a solemn protestation (*v.* 1): *I say the truth in Christ,* "I speak it as a Christian, one of God's people, children that will not lie, as one that knows not how to give flattering titles." Or, "I appeal to Christ, who searches the heart, concerning it." He appeals likewise to his own conscience, which was instead of a thousand witnesses. That which he was going to assert was not only a great and weighty thing (such solemn protestations are not to be thrown away upon trifles), but it was likewise a secret; it was concerning a sorrow in his heart to which none was a capable competent witness but God and his own conscience.—*That I have great heaviness, v.* 2. He does not say for what; the very mention of it was unpleasant and invidious; but it is plain that he means for the rejection of the Jews.

II. He backs it with a very serious imprecation, which he was ready to make, out of love to the Jews. *I could wish;* he does not say, I do wish, for it was no proper means appointed for such an end; but, if it were, *I could wish that myself were accursed from Christ for my brethren*—a very high pang of zeal and affection for his countrymen. He would be willing to undergo the greatest misery to do them good. Love is apt to be thus bold, and venturous, and self-denying. Because the glory of God's grace in the salvation of many is to be preferred before the welfare and happiness of a single person,

Paul, if they were put in competition, would be content to forego all his own happiness to purchase theirs. 1. He would be content to be cut off from the land of the living, in the most shameful and ignominious manner, as an anathema, or a devoted person. They thirsted for his blood, persecuted him as the most obnoxious person in the world, the curse and plague of his generation, 1 Cor. iv. 13; Acts xxii. 22. "Now," says Paul, "I am willing to bear all this, and a great deal more, for your good. Abuse me as much as you will, count and call me at your pleasure; your unbelief and rejection create in my heart a heaviness so much greater than all these troubles can that I could look upon them not only as tolerable, but as desirable, rather than this rejection." 2. He would be content to be excommunicated from the society of the faithful, to be separated from the church, and from the communion of saints, as a heathen man and a publican, if that would do them any good. He could wish himself no more remembered among the saints, his name blotted out of the church-records; though he had been so great a planter of churches, and the spiritual father of so many thousands, yet he would be content to be disowned by the church, cut off from all communion with it, and have his name buried in oblivion or reproach, for the good of the Jews. It may be, some of the Jews had a prejudice against Christianity for Paul's sake; such a spleen they had at him that they hated the religion he was of: "If this stumble you," says Paul, "I could wish I might be cast out, not embraced as a Christian, so you might but be taken in." Thus Moses (Exod. xxxii. 33), in a like holy passion of concern, *Blot me, I pray thee, out of the book which thou hast written.* 3. Nay, some think that the expression goes further, and that he could be content to be cut off from all his share of happiness in Christ, if that might be a means of their salvation. It is a common charity that begins at home; this is something higher, and more noble and generous.

III. He gives us the reason of this affection and concern.

1. Because of their relation to them: *My brethren, my kinsmen, according to the flesh.* Though they were very bitter against him upon all occasions, and gave him the most unnatural and barbarous usage, yet thus respectfully does he speak of them. It shows him to be a man of a forgiving spirit. *Not that I had aught to accuse my nation of*, Acts xxviii. 19. *My kinsmen.* Paul was a Hebrew of the Hebrews. We ought to be in a special manner concerned for the spiritual good of our relations, our brethren and kinsmen. To them we lie under special engagements, and we have more opportunity of doing good to them; and concerning them, and our usefulness to them, we must in a special manner give account.

2. Especially because of their relation to God (*v.* 4, 5): *Who are Israelites*, the seed of Abraham, God's friend, and of Jacob his chosen, taken into the covenant of peculiarity, dignified and distinguished by visible church-privileges, many of which are here mentioned:—(1.) *The adoption;* not that which is saving, and which entitles to eternal happiness, but that which was external and typical, and entitled them to the land of Canaan. *Israel is my son*, Exod. iv. 22. (2.) *And the glory;* the ark with the mercy-seat, over which God dwelt between the cherubim —this was the glory of Israel, 1 Sam. iv. 21. The many symbols and tokens of the divine presence and guidance, the cloud, the Shechinah, the distinguishing favours conferred upon them—these were the glory. (3.) *And the covenants*—the covenant made with Abraham, and often renewed with his seed upon divers occasions. There was a covenant at Sinai (Exod. xxiv.), in the plains of Moab (Deut. xxix.), at Shechem (Josh. xxiv.), and often afterwards; and still these pertained to Israel. Or, the covenant of peculiarity, and in that, as in the type, the covenant of grace. (4.) *And the giving of the law.* It was to them that the ceremonial and judicial law were given, and the moral law in writing pertained to them. It is a great privilege to have the law of God among us, and it is to be accounted so, Ps. cxlvii. 19, 20. This was the grandeur of Israel, Deut. iv. 7, 8. (5.) *And the service of God.* They had the ordinances of God's worship among them—the temple, the altars, the priests, the sacrifices, the feasts, and the institutions relating to them. They were in this respect greatly honoured, that, while other nations were worshipping and serving stocks, and stones, and devils, and they knew not what other idols of their own invention, the Israelites were serving the true God in the way of his own appointment. (6.) *And the promises*—particular promises added to the general covenant, promises relating to the Messiah and the gospel state. Observe, The promises accompany the giving of the law, and the service of God; for the comfort of the promises is to be had in obedience to that law and attendance upon that service. (7.) *Whose are the fathers* (*v.* 5), Abraham, Isaac, and Jacob, those men of renown, that stood so high in the favour of God. The Jews stand in relation to them, are their children, and proud enough they are of it: *We have Abraham to our father.* It was for the fathers' sake that they were taken into covenant, *ch.* xi. 28. (8.) But the greatest honour of all was that *of them as concerning the flesh* (that is, as to his human nature) *Christ came;* for he took on him the seed of Abraham, Heb. ii. 16. As to his divine nature, he is the Lord from heaven; but, as to his human nature, he is of the seed of Abraham. This was the great privilege of the Jews, that Christ was of kin to them. Mentioning Christ, he interposes a very great word concerning him, that he is *over all, God*

blessed for ever. Lest the Jews should think meanly of him, because he was of their alliance, he here speaks thus honourably concerning him: and it is a very full proof of the Godhead of Christ; he is not only over all, as Mediator, but he is God blessed for ever. Therefore, how much sorer punishment were they worthy of that rejected him! It was likewise the honour of the Jews, and one reason why Paul had a kindness for them, that, seeing God blessed for ever would be a man, he would be a Jew; and, considering the posture and character of that people at that time, it may well be looked upon as a part of his humiliation.

6 Not as though the word of God
hath taken none effect. For they *are*
not all Israel, which are of Israel: 7
Neither, because they are the seed of
Abraham, *are they* all children: but,
In Isaac shall thy seed be called. 8
That is, They which are the children
of the flesh, these *are* not the children
of God: but the children of the promise are counted for the seed. 9 For
this *is* the word of promise, At this
time will I come, and Sarah shall
have a son. 10 And not only *this;*
but when Rebecca also had conceived
by one, *even* by our father Isaac;
11 (For *the children* being not yet
born, neither having done any good
or evil, that the purpose of God according to election might stand, not
of works, but of him that calleth;)
12 It was said unto her, The elder
shall serve the younger. 13 As it is
written, Jacob have I loved, but Esau
have I hated.

The apostle, having made his way to that which he had to say, concerning the rejection of the body of his countrymen, with a protestation of his own affection for them and a concession of their undoubted privileges, comes in these verses, and the following part of the chapter, to prove that the rejection of the Jews, by the establishment of the gospel dispensation, did not at all invalidate the word of God's promise to the patriarchs: *Not as though the word of God hath taken no effect* (*v.* 6), which, considering the present state of the Jews, which created to Paul so much *heaviness and continual sorrow* (*v.* 2), might be suspected. We are not to ascribe inefficacy to any word of God: nothing that he has spoken does or can fall to the ground; see Isa. lv. 10, 11. The promises and threatenings shall have their accomplishment; and, one way or other, he will magnify the law and make it honourable. This is to be understood especially of the promise of God, which by subsequent providences may be to a wavering faith very doubtful; but it is not, it cannot be, made of no effect; at the end it will speak and not lie.

Now the difficulty is to reconcile the rejection of the unbelieving Jews with the word of God's promise, and the external tokens of the divine favour, which had been conferred upon them. This he does in four ways:—1. By explaining the true meaning and intention of the promise, *v.* 6—13. 2. By asserting and proving the absolute sovereignty of God, in disposing of the children of men, *v.* 14—24. 3. By showing how this rejection of the Jews, and the taking in of the Gentiles, were foretold in the Old Testament, *v.* 25—29. 4. By fixing the true reason of the Jews' rejection, *v.* 30, to the end.

In this paragraph the apostle explains the true meaning and intention of the promise. When we mistake the word, and misunderstand the promise, no marvel if we are ready to quarrel with God about the accomplishment; and therefore the sense of this must first be duly stated. Now he here makes it out that, when God said he would be *a God to Abraham, and to his seed* (which was the famous promise made unto the fathers), he did not mean it of all his seed according to the flesh, as if it were a necessary concomitant of the blood of Abraham; but that he intended it with a limitation only to such and such. And as from the beginning it was appropriated to Isaac and not to Ishmael, to Jacob and not to Esau, and yet for all this the word of God was not made of no effect; so now the same promise is appropriated to believing Jews that embrace Christ and Christianity, and, though it throws off multitudes that refuse Christ, yet the promise is not therefore defeated and invalidated, any more than it was by the typical rejection of Ishmael and Esau.

I. He lays down this proposition—that *they are not all Israel who are of Israel* (*v.* 6), *neither because they are,* &c. *v.* 7. Many that descended from the loins of Abraham and Jacob, and were of that people who were surnamed by the name of Israel, yet were very far from being Israelites indeed, interested in the saving benefits of the new covenant. They are not all really Israel that are so in name and profession. It does not follow that, because they are the seed of Abraham, therefore they must needs be the children of God, though they themselves fancied so, boasted much of, and built much upon, their relation to Abraham, Matt. iii. 9; John viii. 38, 39. But it does not follow. Grace does not run in the blood; nor are saving benefits inseparably annexed to external church privileges, though it is common for people thus to stretch the meaning of God's promise, to bolster themselves up in a vain hope.

II. He proves this by instances; and therein shows not only that some of Abraham's seed were chosen, and others not, but that God therein wrought according to the counsel of his own will; and not with regard to that law of commandments to which the present unbelieving Jews were so strangely wedded.

1. He specifies the case of Isaac and Ishmael, both of them the seed of Abraham; and yet Isaac only taken into covenant with God, and Ishmael rejected and cast out. For this he quotes Gen. xxi. 12, *In Isaac shall thy seed be called*, which comes in there as a reason why Abraham must be willing to cast out the bond-woman and her son, because the covenant was to be established with Isaac, Gen. xvii. 19. And yet the word which God had spoken, that he would be a God to Abraham and to his seed, did not therefore fall to the ground; for the blessings wrapt up in that great word, being communicated by God as a benefactor, he was free to determine on what head they should rest, and accordingly entailed them upon Isaac, and rejected Ishmael. This he explains further (*v.* 8, 9), and shows what God intended to teach us by this dispensation. (1.) That the children of the flesh, as such, by virtue of their relation to Abraham according to the flesh, are not therefore the children of God, for then Ishmael had put in a good claim. This remark comes home to the unbelieving Jews, who boasted of their relation to Abraham according to the flesh, and looked for justification in a fleshly way, by those carnal ordinances which Christ had abolished. They had confidence in the flesh, Phil. iii. 3. Ishmael was a child of the flesh, conceived by Hagar, who was young and fresh, and likely enough to have children. There was nothing extraordinary or supernatural in his conception, as there was in Isaac's; he was born after the flesh (Gal. iv. 29), representing those that expect justification and salvation by their own strength and righteousness. (2.) That the *children of the promise are counted for the seed.* Those that have the honour and happiness of being counted for the seed have it not for the sake of any merit or desert of their own, but purely by virtue of the promise, in which God hath obliged himself of his own good pleasure to grant the promised favour. Isaac was a child of promise; this he proves, *v.* 9, quoted from Gen. xviii. 10. He was a child promised (so were many others), and he was also conceived and born by force and virtue of the promise, and so a proper type and figure of those who are now counted for the seed, even true believers, who are born, not of the will of the flesh, nor of the will of man, but of God—of the incorruptible seed, even the word of promise, by virtue of the special promise of a new heart: see Gal. iv. 28. It was through faith that Isaac was conceived, Heb. xi. 11. Thus were the great mysteries of salvation taught under the Old Testament, not in express words, but by significant types and dispensations of providence, which to them then were not so clear as they are to us now, when the veil is taken away, and the types are expounded by the antitypes.

2. The case of Jacob and Esau (*v.* 10—13), which is much stronger, to show that the carnal seed of Abraham were not, as such, interested in the promise, but only such of them as God in sovereignty had appointed. There was a previous difference between Ishmael and Isaac, before Ishmael was cast out: Ishmael was the son of the bond-woman, born long before Isaac, was of a fierce and rugged disposition, and had mocked or persecuted Isaac, to all which it might be supposed God had regard when he appointed Abraham to cast him out. But, in the case of Jacob and Esau, it was neither so nor so: they were both the sons of Isaac by one mother; they were conceived ἐξ ἑνὸς—*by one conception;* ἐξ ἑνὸς κοίτου, so some copies read it. The difference was made between them by the divine counsel before they were born, or had done any good or evil. Both lay struggling alike in their mother's womb, when it was said, *The elder shall serve the younger*, without respect to good or bad works done or foreseen, *that the purpose of God according to election might stand*—that this great truth may be established, that God chooses some and refuses others as a free agent, by his own absolute and sovereign will, dispensing his favours or withholding them as he pleases. This difference that was put between Jacob and Esau he further illustrates by a quotation from Mal. i. 2, 3, where it is said, not of Jacob and Esau the persons, but the Edomites and Israelites their posterity, *Jacob have I loved, and Esau have I hated.* The people of Israel were taken into the covenant of peculiarity, had the land of Canaan given them, were blessed with the more signal appearances of God for them in special protections, supplies, and deliverances, while the Edomites were rejected, had no temple, altar, priests, nor prophets—no such particular care taken of them nor kindness shown to them. Such a difference did God put between those two nations, that both descended from the loins of Abraham and Isaac, as at first there was a difference put between Jacob and Esau, the distinguishing heads of those two nations. So that all this choosing and refusing was typical, and intended to shadow forth some other election and rejection. (1.) Some understand it of the election and rejection of conditions or qualifications. As God chose Isaac and Jacob, and rejected Ishmael and Esau, so he might and did choose faith to be the condition of salvation and reject the works of the law. Thus Arminius understands it, *De rejectis et assumptis talibus, certa qualitate notatis—Concerning such as are rejected and such as are chosen, being distinguished by appropriate qualities;* so John Goodwin. But this very much strains the scripture; for the apostle speaks all along of

persons, he has mercy on whom (he does not say on what kind of people) he will have mercy, besides that against this sense those two objections (*v.* 14, 19) do not at all arise, and his answer to them concerning God's absolute sovereignty over the children of men is not at all pertinent if no more be meant than his appointing the conditions of salvation. (2.) Others understand it of the election and rejection of particular persons—some loved, and others hated, from eternity. But the apostle speaks of Jacob and Esau, not in their own persons, but as ancestors—Jacob the people, and Esau the people; nor does God condemn any, or decree so to do, merely because he will do it, without any reason taken from their own deserts. (3.) Others therefore understand it of the election and rejection of people considered complexly. His design is to justify God, and his mercy and truth, in calling the Gentiles, and taking them into the church, and into covenant with himself, while he suffered the obstinate part of the Jews to persist in unbelief, and so to un-church themselves—thus hiding from their eyes the things that belonged to their peace. The apostle's reasoning for the explication and proof of this is, however, very applicable to, and, no doubt (as is usual in scripture) was intended for the clearing of the methods of God's grace towards particular persons, for the communication of saving benefits bears some analogy to the communication of church-privileges. The choosing of Jacob the younger, and preferring him before Esau the elder (so crossing hands), were to intimate that the Jews, though the natural seed of Abraham, and the first-born of the church, should be laid aside; and the Gentiles, who were as the younger brother, should be taken in in their stead, and have the birthright and blessing. The Jews, considered as a body politic, a nation and people, knit together by the bond and cement of the ceremonial law, the temple and priesthood, the centre of their unity, had for many ages been the darlings and favourites of heaven, a kingdom of priests, a holy nation, dignified and distinguished by God's miraculous appearances among them and for them. Now that the gospel was preached, and Christian churches were planted, this national body was thereby abandoned, their church-polity dissolved; and Christian churches (and in process of time Christian nations), embodied in like manner, become their successors in the divine favour, and those special privileges and protections which were the products of that favour. To clear up the justice of God in this great dispensation is the scope of the apostle here.

14 What shall we say then ? *Is*
there unrighteousness with God ?
God forbid. 15 For he saith to
Moses, I will have mercy on whom I
will have mercy, and I will have
compassion on whom I will have
compassion. 16 So then *it is* not of
him that willeth, nor of him that runneth, but of God that showeth mercy.
17 For the scripture saith unto Pharaoh, Even for this same purpose
have I raised thee up, that I might
show my power in thee, and that my
name might be declared throughout
all the earth. 18 Therefore hath he
mercy on whom he will *have mercy*,
and whom he will he hardeneth. 19
Thou wilt say then unto me, Why
doth he yet find fault ? For who
hath resisted his will ? 20 Nay but,
O man, who art thou that repliest
against God ? Shall the thing formed
say to him that formed *it*, Why hast
thou made me thus ? 21 Hath not
the potter power over the clay, of the
same lump to make one vessel unto
honour, and another unto dishonour ?
22 *What* if God, willing to show *his*
wrath, and to make his power known,
endured with much long-suffering the
vessels of wrath fitted to destruction :
23 And that he might make known
the riches of his glory on the vessels
of mercy, which he had afore prepared
unto glory, 24 Even us, whom he
hath called, not of the Jews only, but
also of the Gentiles ?

The apostle, having asserted the true meaning of the promise, comes here to maintain and prove the absolute sovereignty of God, in disposing of the children of men, with reference to their eternal state. And herein God is to be considered, not as a rector and governor, distributing rewards and punishments according to his revealed laws and covenants, but as an owner and benefactor, giving to the children of men such grace and favour as he has determined in and by his secret and eternal will and counsel: both the favour of visible church-membership and privileges, which is given to some people and denied to others, and the favour of effectual grace, which is given to some particular persons and denied to others.

Now this part of his discourse is in answer to two objections.

I. It might be objected, *Is there unrighteousness with God?* If God, in dealing with the children of men, do thus, in an arbitrary manner, choose some and refuse others, may it not be suspected that there is unrighteousness with him? This the apostle startles at the thought of: *God forbid!* Far be it from us to think such a thing; shall not the judge of all the earth do right? Gen. xviii. 25; *ch.*

iii. 5, 6. He denies the consequences, and proves the denial.

1. In respect of those to whom he shows mercy, *v.* 15, 16. He quotes that scripture to show God's sovereignty in dispensing his favours (Exod. xxxiii. 19): *I will be gracious to whom I will be gracious.* All God's reasons of mercy are taken from within himself. All the children of men being plunged alike into a state of sin and misery, equally under guilt and wrath, God, in a way of sovereignty, picks out some from this fallen apostatized race, to be vessels of grace and glory. He dispenses his gifts to whom he will, without giving us any reason: according to his own good pleasure he pitches upon some to be monuments of mercy and grace, preventing grace, effectual grace, while he passes by others. The expression is very emphatic, and the repetition makes it more so: *I will have mercy on whom I will have mercy.* It imports a perfect absoluteness in God's will; he will do what he will, and giveth not account of any of his matters, nor is it fit he should. As these great words, *I am that I am* (Exod. iii. 14) do abundantly express the absolute independency of his being, so these words, *I will have mercy on whom I will have mercy,* do as fully express the absolute prerogative and sovereignty of his will. To vindicate the righteousness of God, in showing mercy to whom he will, the apostle appeals to that which God himself had spoken, wherein he claims this sovereign power and liberty. God is a competent judge, even in his own case. Whatsoever God does, or is resolved to do, is both by the one and the other proved to be just. Ἐλεήσω ὃν ἂν ἐλεῶ—*I will have mercy on whom I will have mercy.* When I begin, I will make an end. Therefore God's mercy endures for ever, because the reason of it is fetched from within himself; therefore his gifts and callings are without repentance. Hence he infers (*v.* 16), *It is not of him that willeth.* Whatever good comes from God to man, the glory of it is not to be ascribed to the most generous desire, nor to the most industrious endeavour, of man, but only and purely to the free grace and mercy of God. In Jacob's case it was *not of him that willeth, nor of him that runneth;* it was not the earnest will and desire of Rebecca that Jacob might have the blessing; it was not Jacob's haste to get it (for he was compelled to run for it) that procured him the blessing, but only the mercy and grace of God. Wherein the holy happy people of God differ from other people, it is God and his grace that make them differ. Applying this general rule to the particular case that Paul has before him, the reason why the unworthy, undeserving, ill-deserving Gentiles are called, and grafted into the church, while the greatest part of the Jews are left to perish in unbelief, is not because those Gentiles were better deserving or better disposed for such a favour, but because of God's free grace that made that difference. The Gentiles did neither will it, nor run for it, for they *sat in darkness,* Matt. iv. 16. In darkness, therefore not willing what they knew not; *sitting* in darkness, a contented posture, therefore not running to meet it, but anticipated with these invaluable blessings of goodness. Such is the method of God's grace towards all that partake of it, for he is found of those that sought him not (Isa. lxv. 1); in this preventing, effectual, distinguishing grace, he acts as a benefactor, whose grace is his own. Our eye therefore must not be evil because his is good; but, of all the grace that we or others have, he must have the glory: *Not unto us,* Ps. cxv. 1.

2. In respect of those who perish, *v.* 17. God's sovereignty, manifested in the ruin of sinners, is here discovered in the instance of Pharaoh; it is quoted from Exod. ix. 16 Observe,

(1.) What God did with Pharaoh. He raised him up, brought him into the world, made him famous, gave him the kingdom and power,—set him up as a beacon upon a hill, as the mark of all his plagues (compare Exod. ix. 14)—hardened his heart, as he had said he would (Exod. iv. 21): *I will harden his heart,* that is, withdraw softening grace, leave him to himself, let Satan loose against him, and lay hardening providences before him. Or, by raising him up may be meant the intermission of the plagues which gave Pharaoh respite, and the reprieve of Pharaoh in those plagues. In the Hebrew, *I have made thee stand,* continued thee yet in the land of the living. Thus doth God raise up sinners, make them for himself, even for the day of evil (Prov. xvi. 4), raise them up in outward prosperity, external privileges (Matt. xi. 23), sparing mercies.

(2.) What he designed in it: *That I might show my power in thee.* God would, by all this, serve the honour of his name, and manifest his power in baffling the pride and insolence of that great and daring tyrant, who bade defiance to Heaven itself, and trampled upon all that was just and sacred. If Pharaoh had not been so high and mighty, so bold and hardy, the power of God had not been so illustrious in the ruining of him; but the taking off of the spirit of such a prince, who hectored at that rate, did indeed proclaim God glorious in holiness, fearful in praises, doing wonders, Exod. xv. 11. This is Pharaoh, and all his multitude.

(3.) His conclusion concerning both these we have, *v.* 18. *He hath mercy on whom he will have mercy, and whom he will he hardeneth.* The various dealings of God, by which he makes some to differ from others, must be resolved into his absolute sovereignty He is debtor to no man, his grace is his own, and he may give it or withhold it as it pleaseth him; we have none of us deserved it, nay, we have all justly forfeited it a thousand times, so that herein the work of our salvation is admirably well ordered that those who are saved must thank God only, and those who perish must thank themselves only, Hos. xiii. 9. We are bound, as God hath bound us, to do our utmost for the salvation of all we have to do with; but God is bound no further than he has been pleased to bind himself by his own covenant and promise, which is his revealed will; and that is that he will receive, and not cast out, those that come to Christ; but the drawing of souls in order to that coming is a preventing distinguishing favour to whom he will. Had he mercy on the Gentiles? It was because he would have mercy on them. Were the Jews hardened? It was because it was his own pleasure to deny them softening grace, and to give them up to their chosen affected unbelief. *Even so, Father, because it seemed good unto thee.* That scripture excellently explains this, Luke x. 21, and, as this, shows the sovereign will of God in giving or withholding both the means of grace and the effectual blessing upon those means.

II. It might be objected, *Why doth he yet find fault? For who hath resisted his will? v.* 19. Had the apostle been arguing only for God's sovereignty in appointing and ordering the terms and conditions of acceptance and salvation, there had not been the least colour for this objection; for he might well find fault if people refused to come up to the terms on which such a salvation is offered; the salvation being so great, the terms could not be hard. But there might be colour for the objection against his arguing for the sovereignty of God in giving and withholding differencing and preventing grace; and the objection is commonly and readily advanced against the doctrine of distinguishing grace. If God, while he gives effectual grace to some, denies it to others, why doth he find fault with those to whom he denies it? If he hath rejected the Jews, and hid from their eyes the things that belong to their peace, why doth he find fault with them for their blindness? If it be his pleasure to discard them as not a people, and not obtaining mercy, their knocking off themselves was no resistance of his will. This objection he answers at large,

1. By reproving the objector (*v.* 20): *Nay but, O man.* This is not an objection fit to be made by the creature against his Creator, by man against God. The truth, as it is in Jesus, is that which abases man as nothing, less than nothing, and advances God as sovereign Lord of all. Observe how contemptibly he speaks of man, when he comes to argue with God his Maker: "*Who art thou,* thou that art so foolish, so feeble, so short-sighted, so incompetent a judge of the divine counsels? art thou able to fathom such a depth, dispute such a case, to trace that way of God which is in the sea, his path in the great waters?" *That repliest against God.* It becomes us to submit to him, not to reply against him; to lie down under his hand, not to fly in his face, nor to charge him with folly. Ὁ ἀνταποκρινόμενος—*That answerest again.* God is our master, and we are his servants; and it does not become servants to answer again, Tit. ii. 9.

2. By resolving all into the divine sovereignty. We are the thing formed, and he is the former; and it does not become us to challenge or arraign his wisdom in ordering and disposing of us into this or that shape of figure. The rude and unformed mass of matter hath no right to this or that form, but is shaped at the pleasure of him that formeth it. God's sovereignty over us is fitly illustrated by the power that the potter hath over the clay; compare Jer. xviii. 6, where, by a like comparison, God asserts his dominion over the nation of the Jews, when he was about to magnify his justice in their destruction by Nebuchadnezzar.

(1.) He gives us the comparison, *v.* 21. The potter, out of the same lump, may make either a fashionable vessel, and a vessel fit for creditable and honourable uses, or a contemptible vessel, and a vessel in which is no pleasure; and herein he acts arbitrarily, as he might have chosen whether he would make any vessel of it at all, or whether he would leave it in the hole of the pit, out of which it was dug.

(2.) The application of the comparison, *v.* 22—24. Two sorts of vessels God forms out of the great lump of fallen mankind:—[1.] *Vessels of wrath*—vessels filled with wrath, as a vessel of wine is a vessel filled with wine; *full of the fury of the Lord,* Isa. li. 20. In these God is willing to show his wrath, that is, his punishing justice, and his enmity to sin. This must be shown to all the world. God will make it appear that he hates sin. He will likewise make his power known, τὸ δύνατον ἀυτοῦ. It is a power of strength and energy, an inflicting power, which works and effects the destruction of those that perish; it is a destruction that proceeds from the *glory of his power,* 2 Thess. i. 9. The eternal damnation of sinners will be an abundant demonstration of the power of God; for he will act in it himself immediately, his wrath preying as it were upon guilty consciences, and his arm stretched out totally to destroy their well-being, and yet at the same instant wonderfully to preserve the being of the creature. In order to this, God *endured them with much long-suffering*—exercised a great deal of patience towards them, let them alone to fill up the measure of sin, to grow till they were ripe for ruin, and so they became *fitted for destruction,* fitted by their own sin and self-hardening. The reigning corruptions and wickedness of the soul are its preparedness and disposedness for hell: a soul is hereby made combustible matter, fit for the flames of hell. When Christ said to the Jews (Matt. xxiii. 32), *Fill you up then the measure of your fathers, that upon you may come all the righteous blood* (*v.* 35), he did, as it were, endure them with much long-suffering, that they might, by their own obstinacy and wilfulness in sin, fit themselves for destruction. [2.] *Vessels of mercy*—filled with mercy. The happiness bestowed upon the saved remnant is the fruit, not of their merit, but of God's mercy. The spring of all the joy and glory of heaven is that mercy of God which endures for ever. Vessels of honour must to eternity own themselves vessels of mercy. Observe, *First,* What he designs in them: *To make known the riches of his glory,* that is, of his goodness; for God's goodness is his greatest glory, especially when it is communicated with the greatest sovereignty. *I beseech thee show me thy glory,* says Moses, Exod. xxxiii. 18. *I will make all my goodness to pass before thee,* says God (*v.* 19), and that given out freely: *I will be gracious to whom I will be gracious.* God makes known his glory, this goodness of his, in the preservation and supply of all the creatures: the earth is full of his goodness, and the year crowned with it; but when he would demonstrate the riches of his goodness, unsearchable riches, he does it in the salvation of the saints, that will be to eternity glorious monuments of divine grace. *Secondly,* What he does for them: he does before *prepare them to glory.* Sanctification is the preparation of the soul for glory, making it meet to partake of the inheritance of the saints in light. This is God's work. We can destroy ourselves fast enough, but we cannot save ourselves. Sinners fit themselves for hell, but it is God that prepares saints for heaven; and all those that God designs for heaven hereafter he prepares and fits for heaven now: he works them to the self-same thing, 2 Cor. v. 5. And would you know who these *vessels of mercy are?* Those whom he hath called (*v.* 24); for whom he did predestinate those he also called with an effectual call: and these not of the Jews only, but of the Gentiles; for, the partition-wall being taken down, the world was laid in common, and not (as it had been) God's favour appropriated to the Jews, and they put a degree nearer his acceptance than the rest of the world. They now stood upon the same level with the Gentiles; and the question is not now whether of the seed of Abraham or no, that is neither here nor there, but whether or no called according to his purpose.

25 As he saith also in Osee, I will
call them my people, which were not
my people; and her beloved, which
was not beloved. 26 And it shall
come to pass, *that* in the place where
it was said unto them, Ye *are* not my
people; there shall they be called the
children of the living God. 27
Esaias also crieth concerning Israel,
Though the number of the children
of Israel be as the sand of the sea, a
remnant shall be saved: 28 For he
will finish the work, and cut *it* short
in righteousness: because a short
work will the Lord make upon the
earth. 29 And as Esaias said before,
Except the Lord of Sabaoth had left
us a seed, we had been as Sodoma,
and been made like unto Gomorrha.

Having explained the promise, and proved the divine sovereignty, the apostle here shows how the rejection of the Jews, and the taking in of the Gentiles, were foretold in the Old Testament, and therefore must needs be very well consistent with the promise made to the fathers under the Old Testament. It tends very much to the clearing of a truth to observe how the scripture is fulfilled in it. The Jews would, no doubt, willingly refer it to the Old Testament, the scriptures of which were committed to them. Now he shows how this, which was so uneasy to them, was there spoken of.

I. By the prophet Hosea, who speaks of the taking in of a great many of the Gentiles, Hos. ii. 23 and Hos. i. 10. The Gentiles had not been the people of God, not owning him, nor being owned by him in that relation: "But," says he, "*I will call them my people,* make them such and own them as such, notwithstanding all their unworthiness." A blessed change! Former badness is no bar to God's present grace and mercy.—*And her beloved which was not beloved.* Those whom God calls his people he calls beloved: he loves those that are his own. And lest it might be supposed that they should become God's people only by being proselyted to the Jewish religion, and made members of that nation, he adds, from Hos. i. 10, *In the place where it was said,* &c., *there shall they be called.* They need not be embodied with the Jews, nor go up to Jerusalem to worship; but, wherever they are scattered over the face of the earth, there will God own them. Observe the great dignity and honour of the saints, that they are called the children of the living God; and his calling them so makes them so. Behold, what manner of love! This honour have all his saints.

II. By the prophet Isaiah, who speaks of the casting off of many of the Jews, in two places:

1. One is Isa. x. 22, 23, which speaks of the saving of a remnant, that is, but a remnant, which, though in the prophecy it seems to refer to the preservation of a remnant from the destruction and desolation that were coming upon them by Sennacherib and his army, yet is to be understood as looking further, and sufficiently proves that it is no strange thing for God to abandon to ruin a great many of the seed of Abraham, and yet

maintain his word of promise to Abraham in full force and virtue. This is intimated in the supposition that the number of children of Israel was as the sand of the sea, which was part of the promise made to Abraham, Gen. xxii. 17. And yet only a remnant shall be saved; for many are called, but few are chosen. In this salvation of the remnant we are told (*v.* 28) from the prophet, (1.) That he will complete the work: *He will finish the work.* When God begins he will make an end, whether in ways of judgment or of mercy. The rejection of the unbelieving Jews God would finish in their utter ruin by the Romans, who soon after this quite took away their place and nation. The assuming of Christian churches into the divine favour, and the spreading of the gospel in other nations, was a work which God would likewise finish, and be known by his name JEHOVAH. As for God, his work is perfect. Margin, *He will finish the account.* God, in his eternal counsels, has taken an account of the children of men, allotted them to such or such a condition, to such a share of privileges; and, as they come into being, his dealings with them are pursuant to these counsels: and he will finish the account, complete the mystical body, call in as many as belong to the election of grace, and then the account will be finished. (2.) That he will contract it; not only finish it, but finish it quickly. Under the Old Testament he seemed to tarry, and to make a longer and more tedious work of it. The wheels moved but slowly towards the extent of the church; but now he will *cut it short,* and make a short work upon the earth. Gentile converts were now flying as a cloud. But he will cut it short *in righteousness,* both in wisdom and in justice. Men, when they cut short, do amiss; they do indeed despatch causes; but, when God cuts short, it is always in righteousness. So the fathers generally apply it. Some understand it of the evangelical law and covenant, which Christ has introduced and established in the world: he has in that finished the work, put an end to the types and ceremonies of the Old Testament. Christ said, *It is finished,* and then the veil was rent, echoing as it were to the word that Christ said upon the cross. And he will cut it short. *The work* (it is λόγος—*the word,* the law) was under the Old Testament very long; a long train of institutions, ceremonies, conditions: but now it is cut short. Our duty is now, under the gospel, summed up in much less room than it was under the law; the covenant was abridged and contracted; religion is brought into a less compass. And it is in righteousness, in favour to us, in justice to his own design and counsel. With us contractions are apt to darken things:—

———Brevis esse laboro,
Obscurus fio ———

I strive to be concise, but prove obscure

but it is not so in this case. Though it be cut short, it is clear and plain; and, because short, the more easy.

2. Another is quoted from Isa. i. 9, where the prophet is showing how in a time of general calamity and destruction God would preserve a seed. This is to the same purport with the former; and the scope of it is to show that it was no strange thing for God to leave the greatest part of the people of the Jews to ruin, and to reserve to himself only a small remnant: so he had done formerly, as appears by their own prophets; and they must not wonder if he did so now. Observe, (1.) What God is. He is *the Lord of sabaoth,* that is, the Lord of hosts—a Hebrew word retained in the Greek, as James v. 4. All the host of heaven and earth are at his beck and disposal. When God secures a seed to himself out of a degenerate apostate world, he acts as Lord of sabaoth. It is an act of almighty power and infinite sovereignty. (2.) What his people are; they are a *seed,* a small number. The corn reserved for next year's seedings is but little, compared with that which is spent and eaten. But they are a useful number—the seed, the substance, of the next generation, Isa. vi. 13. It is so far from being an impeachment of the justice and righteousness of God that so many perish and are destroyed, that it is a wonder of divine power and mercy that all are not destroyed, that there are any saved; for even those that are left to be a seed, if God had dealt with them according to their sins, had perished with the rest. This is the great truth which this scripture teacheth us.

30 What shall we say then? That
the Gentiles, which followed not after
righteousness, have attained to righteousness, even the righteousness
which is of faith. 31 But Israel,
which followed after the law of righteousness, hath not attained to the
law of righteousness. 32 Wherefore? Because *they sought it* not by
faith, but as it were by the works of
the law. For they stumbled at that
stumblingstone; 33 As it is written,
Behold, I lay in Sion a stumbling-
stone and rock of offence: and whosoever believeth on him shall not be
ashamed.

The apostle comes here at last to fix the true reason of the reception of the Gentiles, and the rejection of the Jews. There was a difference in the way of their seeking, and therefore there was that different success, though still it was the free grace of God that made them differ. He concludes like an orator, *What shall we say then?* What is the conclusion of the whole dispute?

I. Concerning the Gentiles observe, 1.

How they had been alienated from righteousness: they followed not after it; they knew not their guilt and misery, and therefore were not at all solicitous to procure a remedy. In their conversion preventing grace was greatly magnified: God was *found of those that sought him not*, Isa. lxv. 1. There was nothing in them to dispose them for such a favour more than what free grace wrought in them. Thus doth God delight to dispense grace in a way of sovereignty and absolute dominion. 2. How they attained to righteousness, notwithstanding: *By faith;* not by being proselyted to the Jewish religion, and submitting to the ceremonial law, but by embracing Christ, and believing in Christ, and submitting to the gospel. They attained to that by the short cut of believing sincerely in Christ for which the Jews had been long in vain beating about the bush.

II. Concerning the Jews observe, 1. How they missed their end: they *followed after the law of righteousness* (*v.* 31)—they talked much of justification and holiness, seemed very ambitious of being the people of God and the favourites of heaven, but they did not attain to it, that is, the greatest part of them did not; as many as stuck to their old Jewish principles and ceremonies, and pursued a happiness in those observances, embracing the shadows now that the substance was come, these fell short of acceptance with God, were not owned as his people, nor went to their house justified. 2. How they mistook their way, which was the cause of their missing the end, *v.* 32, 33. They sought, but not in the right way, not in the humbling way, not in the instituted appointed way. *Not by faith,* not by embracing the Christian religion, and depending upon the merit of Christ, and submitting to the terms of the gospel, which were the very life and end of the law. But they sought by the *works of the law;* as if they were to expect justification by their observance of the precepts and ceremonies of the law of Moses. This was the *stumbling-stone at which they stumbled.* They could not get over this corrupt principle which they had espoused, That the law was given them for no end but that merely by their observance of it, and obedience to it, they might be justified before God: and so they could by no means be reconciled to the doctrine of Christ, which brought them off from that to expect justification through the merit and satisfaction of another. Christ himself is to some a stone of stumbling, for which he quotes Isa. viii. 14; xxviii. 16. It is sad that Christ should be set for the fall of any, and yet it is so (Luke ii. 34), that ever poison should be sucked out of the balm of Gilead, that the foundation-stone should be to any a stone of stumbling, and the rock of salvation a rock of offence; so he is to multitudes; so he was to the unbelieving Jews, who rejected him, because he put an end to the ceremonial law. But still there is a remnant that do believe on him; and they *shall not be ashamed,* that is, their hopes and expectations of justification by him shall not be disappointed, as theirs are who expect it by the law. So that, upon the whole, the unbelieving Jews have no reason to quarrel with God for rejecting them; they had a fair offer of righteousness, and life, and salvation, made to them upon gospel terms, which they did not like, and would not come up to; and therefore, if they perish, they may thank themselves—their blood is upon their own heads.

CHAP. X.

The dissolving of the peculiar church-state of the Jews, and the rejection of that polity by the repealing of their ceremonial law, the vacating of all the institutions of it, the abolishing of their priesthood, the burning of their temple, and the taking away of their place and nation, and in their room the substituting and erecting of a catholic church-state among the Gentile nations, though to us, now that these things have long since been done and completed, they may seem no great matter, yet to those who lived when they were doing, who knew how high the Jews had stood in God's favour, and how deplorable the condition of the Gentile world had been for many ages, it appeared very great and marvellous, and a mystery hard to be understood. The apostle, in this chapter, as in the foregoing and that which follows, is explaining and proving it; but with several very useful digressions, which a little interrupt the thread of his discourse. To two great truths I would reduce this chapter:—I. That there is a great difference between the righteousness of the law, which the unbelieving Jews were wedded to, and the righteousness of faith offered in the gospel, ver. 1—11. II. That there is no difference between Jews and Gentiles; but, in point of justification and acceptance with God, the gospel sets them both upon the same level, ver. 12, to the end.

BRETHREN, my heart's desire
and prayer to God for Israel is,
that they might be saved. 2 For I
bear them record that they have a
zeal of God, but not according to
knowledge. 3 For they being ignorant of God's righteousness, and going
about to establish their own righteousness, have not submitted themselves unto the righteousness of God
4 For Christ *is* the end of the law
for righteousness to every one that
believeth. 5 For Moses describeth
the righteousness which is of the law,
That the man which doeth those
things shall live by them. 6 But
the righteousness which is of faith
speaketh on this wise, Say not in
thine heart, Who shall ascend into
heaven? (that is, to bring Christ
down *from above:*) 7 Or, Who
shall descend into the deep? (that is,
to bring up Christ again from the
dead.) 8 But what saith it? The
word is nigh thee, *even* in thy mouth,
and in thy heart: that is, the word of
faith, which we preach; 9 That if
thou shalt confess with thy mouth
the Lord Jesus, and shalt believe in
thine heart that God hath raised him
from the dead, thou shalt be saved.
10 For with the heart man believeth

unto righteousness; and with the mouth confession is made unto salvation. 11 For the scripture saith, Whosoever believeth on him shall not be ashamed.

The scope of the apostle in this part of the chapter is to show the vast difference between the righteousness of the law and the righteousness of faith, and the great pre-eminence of the righteousness of faith above that of the law; that he might induce and persuade the Jews to believe in Christ, aggravate the folly and sin of those that refused, and justify God in the rejection of such refusers.

I. Paul here professes his good affection to the Jews, with the reason of it (*v.* 1, 2), where he gives them a good wish, and a good witness.

1. A good wish (*v.* 1), a wish that they might be saved—saved from the temporal ruin and destruction that were coming upon them—saved from the wrath to come, eternal wrath, which was hanging over their heads. It is implied in this wish that they might be convinced and converted; he could not pray in faith that they might be saved in their unbelief. Though Paul preached against them, yet he prayed for them. Herein he was merciful, as God is, who is *not willing that any should perish* (2 Pet. iii. 9), desires not the death of sinners. It is our duty truly and earnestly to desire the salvation of the souls of others, next to the salvation of our own. This, he says, was *his heart's desire and prayer*, which intimates, (1.) The strength and sincerity of his desire. It was *his heart's desire;* it was not a formal compliment, as good wishes are with many from the teeth outward, but a real desire. This it was before it was his prayer. The soul of prayer is the heart's desire. Cold desires do but beg denials; we must even breathe out our souls in every prayer. (2.) The offering up of this desire to God. It was not only his heart's desire, but it was his prayer. There may be desires in the heart, and yet no prayer, unless those desires be presented to God. Wishing and woulding, if that be all, are not praying.

2. A good witness, as a reason of his good wish (*v.* 2): *I bear them record that they have a zeal of God.* The unbelieving Jews were the most bitter enemies Paul had in the world, and yet Paul gives them as good a character as the truth would bear. We should say the best we can even of our worst enemies; this is blessing those that curse us. Charity teaches us to have the best opinion of persons, and to put the best construction upon words and actions, that they will bear. We should take notice of that which is commendable even in bad people. *They have a zeal of God.* Their opposition to the gospel is from a principle of respect to the law, which they know to have come from God. There is such a thing as a blind misguided zeal: such was that of the Jews, who, when they hated Christ's people and ministers, and cast them out, said, *Let the Lord be glorified* (Isa. lxvi. 5); nay, they killed them, and thought they did God good service, John xvi. 2.

II. He here shows the fatal mistake that the unbelieving Jews were guilty of, which was their ruin. Their zeal was *not according to knowledge.* It is true God gave them that law for which they were so zealous; but they might have known that, by the appearance of the promised Messiah, an end was put to it. He introduced a new religion and way of worship, to which the former must give place. He proved himself the Son of God, gave the most convincing evidence that could be of his being the Messiah; and yet they did not know and would not own him, but shut their eyes against the clear light, so that their zeal for the law was blind. This he shows further, *v.* 3, where we may observe,

1. The nature of their unbelief. They *have not submitted themselves to the righteousness of God,* that is, they have not yielded to gospel-terms, nor accepted the tender of justification by faith in Christ, which is made in the gospel. Unbelief is a non-submission to the righteousness of God, standing it out against the gospel proclamation of indemnity. *Have not submitted.* In true faith, there is need of a great deal of submission; therefore the first lesson Christ teaches is to deny ourselves. It is a great piece of condescension for a proud heart to be content to be beholden to free grace; we are loth to sue *sub forma pauperis—as paupers.*

2. The causes of their unbelief, and these are two:—(1.) Ignorance of God's righteousness. They did not understand, and believe, and consider, the strict justice of God, in hating and punishing sin, and demanding satisfaction, did not consider what need we have of a righteousness wherein to appear before him; if they had, they would never have stood out against the gospel offer, nor expected justification by their own works, as if they could satisfy God's justice. Or, being ignorant of God's way of justification, which he has now appointed and revealed by Jesus Christ. They did not know it, because they would not; they shut their eyes against the discoveries of it, and loved darkness rather. (2.) A proud conceit of their own righteousness: *Going about to establish their own*—a righteousness of their own devising, and of their own working out, by the merit of their works, and by their observance of the ceremonial law. They thought they needed not to be beholden to the merit of Christ, and therefore depended upon their own performances as sufficient to make up a righteousness wherein to appear before God. They could not with Paul disclaim a dependence upon this (Phil. iii. 9), *Not having my own righteousness.* See an instance of this pride in the Pharisee, Luke xviii. 10, 11. Compare *v.* 14.

III. He here shows the folly of that mistake, and what an unreasonable thing it was for them to be seeking justification by the works of the law, now that Christ had come, and had brought in an everlasting righteousness; considering,

1. The subserviency of the law to the gospel (*v.* 4): *Christ is the end of the law for righteousness.* The design of the law was to lead people to Christ. The moral law was but for the searching of the wound, the ceremonial law for the shadowing forth of the remedy; but Christ is the end of both. See 2 Cor. iii. 7, and compare Gal. iii. 23, 24. The use of the law was to direct people for righteousness to Christ. (1.) Christ is the end of the ceremonial law; he is the period of it, because he is the perfection of it. When the substance comes, the shadow is gone. The sacrifices, and offerings, and purifications appointed under the Old Testament, prefigured Christ, and pointed at him; and their inability to take away sin discovered the necessity of a sacrifice that should, by being once offered, take away sin. (2.) Christ is the end of the moral law in that he did what the law could not do (*ch.* viii. 3), and secured the great end of it. The end of the law was to bring men to perfect obedience, and so to obtain justification. This is now become impossible, by reason of the power of sin and the corruption of nature; but Christ is the end of the law. The law is not destroyed, nor the intention of the lawgiver frustrated, but, full satisfaction being made by the death of Christ for our breach of the law, the end is attained, and we are put in another way of justification. Christ is thus the end of the law for righteousness, that is, for justification; but it is only to *every one that believeth.* Upon our believing, that is, our humble consent to the terms of the gospel, we become interested in Christ's satisfaction, and so are justified through the redemption that is in Jesus.

2. The excellency of the gospel above the law. This he proves by showing the different constitution of these two.

(1.) What is the righteousness which is of the law? This he shows, *v.* 5. The tenour of it is, *Do, and live.* Though it directs us to a better and more effectual righteousness in Christ, yet in itself, considered as a law, abstracted from its respect to Christ and the gospel (for so the unbelieving Jews embraced and retained it), it owneth nothing as a righteousness sufficient to justify a man but that of perfect obedience. For this he quotes that scripture (Lev. xviii. 5), *You shall therefore keep my statutes and my judgments, which if a man do, he shall live in them.* To this he refers likewise, Gal. iii. 12, *The man that doeth them, shall live in them. Live,* that is, be happy, not only in the land of Canaan, but in heaven, of which Canaan was a type and figure. The doing supposed must be perfect and sinless, without the least breach or violation. The law which was given upon mount Sinai, though it was not a pure covenant of works (for who then could be saved under that dispensation?) yet, that it might be the more effectual to drive people to Christ and to make the covenant of grace welcome, it had a very great mixture of the strictness and terror of the covenant of works. Now, was it not extreme folly in the Jews to adhere so closely to this way of justification and salvation, which was in itself so hard, and by the corruption of nature now become impossible, when there was a new and a living way opened?

(2.) What is that righteousness which is of faith, *v.* 6, &c. This he describes in the words of Moses, in Deuteronomy, in the *second law* (so Deuteronomy signifies), where there was a much clearer revelation of Christ and the gospel than there was in the first giving of the law: he quotes it from Deut. xxx. 11—14, and shows,

[1.] That it is not at all hard or difficult. The way of justification and salvation has in it no such depths or knots as may discourage us, no insuperable difficulties attending it; but, as was foretold, it is a high-way, Isa. xxxv. 8. We are not put to climb for it—it is not in heaven; we are not put to dive for it—it is not in the deep. *First,* We need not go to heaven, to search the records there, or to enquire into the secrets of the divine counsel. It is true Christ is in heaven; but we may be justified and saved without going thither, to fetch him thence, or sending a special messenger to him. *Secondly,* We need not go to the deep, to fetch Christ out of the grave, or from the state of the dead: *Into the deep, to bring up Christ from the dead.* This plainly shows that Christ's descent into the *deep,* or into ᾅδης, was no more tha nhis going into the state of the dead, in allusion to Jonah. It is true that Christ was in the grave, and it is as true that he is now in heaven; but we need not perplex and puzzle ourselves with fancied difficulties, nor must we create to ourselves such gross and carnal ideas of these things as if the method of salvation were impracticable, and the design of the revelation were only to amuse us. No, salvation is not put at so vast a distance from us.

[2.] But it is very plain and easy: *The word is nigh thee.* When we speak of looking upon Christ, and receiving Christ, and feeding upon Christ, it is not Christ in heaven, nor Christ in the deep, that we mean; but Christ in the promise, Christ exhibited to us, and offered, in the word. Christ is nigh thee, for the word is nigh thee: nigh thee indeed: it is *in thy mouth, and in thy heart;* there is no difficulty in understanding, believing, and owning it. The work thou hast to do lies within thee: *the kingdom of God is within you,* Luke xvii. 21. Thence thou must fetch thy evidences, not out of the records of heaven. *It is,* that is, it is promised that it shall be, *in thy mouth* (Isa. lix.

21), *and in thy heart*, Jer. xxxi. 33. All that which is to be done for us is already done to our hands. Christ is come down from heaven; we need not go to fetch him. He is come up from the deep; we need not perplex ourselves how to bring him up. There is nothing now to be done, but a work in us; this must be our care, to look to our heart and mouth. Those that were under the law were to do all themselves, *Do this, and live;* but the gospel discovers the greatest part of the work done already, and what remains cut short in righteousness, salvation offered upon very plain and easy terms, brought to our door, as it were, in the word which is nigh us. It is in our mouth—we are reading it daily; it is in our heart—we are, or should be, thinking of it daily. Even *the word of faith:* the gospel and the promise of it, called the word of faith because it is the object of faith about which it is conversant, the word which we believe;—because it is the precept of faith, commanding it, and making it the great condition of justification;—and because it is the ordinary means by which faith is wrought and conveyed. Now what is this word of faith? We have the tenour of it, *v.* 9, 10, the sum of the gospel, which is plain and easy enough. Observe,

First, What is promised to us: *Thou shalt be saved.* It is salvation that the gospel exhibits and tenders—saved from guilt and wrath, with the salvation of the soul, an eternal salvation, which Christ is the author of, a Saviour to the uttermost.

Secondly, Upon what terms.

a. Two things are required as conditions of salvation:—(*a.*) *Confessing the Lord Jesus*—openly professing relation to him and dependence on him, as our prince and Saviour, owning Christianity in the face of all the allurements and affrightments of this world, standing by him in all weathers. Our Lord Jesus lays a great stress upon this confessing of him before men; see Matt. x. 32, 33. It is the product of many graces, evinces a great deal of self-denial, love to Christ, contempt of the world, a mighty courage and resolution. It was a very great thing, especially, when the profession of Christ and Christianity hazarded estate, honour, preferment, liberty, life, and all that is dear in this world, which was the case in the primitive times. (*b.*) *Believing in the heart that God raised him from the dead.* The profession of faith with the mouth, if there be not the power of it in the heart, is but a mockery; the root of it must be laid in an unfeigned assent to the revelation of the gospel concerning Christ, especially concerning his resurrection, which is the fundamental article of the Christian faith, for thereby he was declared to be the Son of God with power, and full evidence was given that God accepted his satisfaction.

b. This is further illustrated (*v.* 10), and the order inverted, because there must first be faith in the heart before there can be an acceptable confession with the mouth. (*a.*) Concerning faith: It is *with the heart that man believeth*, which implies more than an assent of the understanding, and takes in the consent of the will, an inward, hearty, sincere, and strong consent. It is not believing (not to be reckoned so) if it be not with the heart. This is *unto righteousness.* There is the righteousness of justification and the righteousness of sanctification. Faith is to both; it is the condition of our justification (*ch.* v. 1), and it is the root and spring of our sanctification; in it it is begun; by it it is carried on, Acts xv. 9. (*b.*) Concerning profession: It is with *the mouth that confession is made*—confession to God in prayer and praise (*ch.* xv. 6), confession to men by owning the ways of God before others, especially when we are called to it in a day of persecution. It is fit that God should be honoured with the mouth, for he made man's mouth (Exod. iv. 11), and at such a time has promised to give his faithful people a *mouth and wisdom*, Luke xxi. 15. It is part of the honour of Christ that every tongue shall confess, Phil. ii. 11. And this is said to be *unto salvation*, because it is the performance of the condition of that promise, Matt. x. 32. Justification by faith lays the foundation of our title to salvation; but by confession we build upon that foundation, and come at last to the full possession of that to which we were entitled. So that we have here a brief summary of the terms of salvation, and they are very reasonable; in short this, that we must devote, dedicate, and give up, to God, our souls and our bodies—our souls in believing with the heart, and our bodies in confessing with the mouth. This do, and thou shalt live. For this (*v.* 11) he quotes Isa. xxviii. 16, *Whosoever believeth on him shall not be ashamed; οὐ καταισχυνθήσεται.* That is, [*a.*] He will not be ashamed to own that Christ in whom he trusts; he that believes in the heart will not be ashamed to confess with the mouth. It is sinful shame that makes people deny Christ, Mark viii. 38. He that believeth will not make haste (so the prophet has it)—will not make haste to run away from the sufferings he meets with in the way of his duty, will not be ashamed of a despised religion. [*b.*] He shall not be ashamed of his hope in Christ; he shall not be disappointed of his end. It is our duty that we must not, it is our privilege that we shall not, be ashamed of our faith in Christ. He shall never have cause to repent his confidence in reposing such a trust in the Lord Jesus.

12 For there is no difference between the Jew and the Greek: for
the same Lord over all is rich unto
all that call upon him. 13 For whosoever shall call upon the name of

the Lord shall be saved. 14 How
then shall they call on him in whom
they have not believed? and how
shall they believe in him of whom
they have not heard? and how shall
they hear without a preacher? 15
And how shall they preach, except
they be sent? as it is written, How
beautiful are the feet of them that
preach the gospel of peace, and bring
glad tidings of good things! 16 But
they have not all obeyed the gospel.
For Esaias saith, Lord, who hath
believed our report? 17 So then
faith *cometh* by hearing, and hearing
by the word of God. 18 But I say,
Have they not heard? Yes verily,
their sound went into all the earth,
and their words unto the ends of the
world. 19 But I say, Did not Israel
know? First Moses saith, I will
provoke you to jealousy by *them that
are* no people, *and* by a foolish nation
I will anger you. 20 But Esaias is
very bold, and saith, I was found of
them that sought me not; I was
made manifest unto them that asked
not after me. 21 But to Israel he
saith, All day long I have stretched
forth my hands unto a disobedient
and gainsaying people.

The first words express the design of the apostle through these verses, that there is no difference between Jews and Gentiles, but they stand upon the same level in point of acceptance with God. In Jesus Christ there is neither Greek nor Jew, Col. iii. 11. God doth not save any nor reject any because they are Jews, nor because they are Greeks, but doth equally accept both upon gospel terms: *There is no difference.* For the proof of this he urges two arguments:—

I. That God is the same to all: *The same Lord over all is rich unto all.* There is not one God to the Jews who is more kind, and another to the Gentiles who is less kind; but he is the same to all, a common father to all mankind. When he proclaimed his name, *The Lord, the Lord God, gracious and merciful,* he thereby signified not only what he was to the Jews, but what he is and will be to all his creatures that seek unto him: not only good, but rich, plenteous in goodness: he hath wherewith to supply them all, and he is free and ready to give out to them; he is both able and willing: not only rich, but rich unto us, liberal and bountiful in dispensing his favours *to all that call upon him.* Something must be done by us, that we may reap of this bounty; and it is as little as can be, we must call upon him. He will for this be enquired of (Ezek. xxxvi. 37), and surely that which is not worth the asking is not worth the having. We have nothing to do but to draw out by prayer, as there is occasion.

II. That the promise is the same to all (*v.* 13): *Whoever shall call*—one as well as another, without exception. This extent, this undifferencing extent, of the promise both to Jews and Gentiles he thinks should not be surprising, for it was foretold by the prophet, Joel ii. 32. Calling upon the name of the Lord is here put for all practical religion. What is the life of a Christian but a life of prayer? It implies a sense of our dependence on him, an entire dedication of ourselves to him, and a believing expectation of our all from him. He that thus calls upon him shall be saved. It is but ask and have; what would we have more? For the further illustration of this he observes,

1. How necessary it was that the gospel should be preached to the Gentiles, *v.* 14, 15. This was what the Jews were so angry with Paul for, that he was the apostle of the Gentiles, and preached the gospel to them. Now he shows how needful it was to bring them within the reach of the forementioned promise, an interest in which they should not envy to any of their fellow-creatures. (1.) *They cannot call on him in whom they have not believed.* Except they believe that he is God, they will not call upon him by prayer; to what purpose should they? The grace of faith is absolutely necessary to the duty of prayer; we cannot pray aright, nor pray to acceptation, without it. He that comes to God by prayer must believe, Heb. xi. 6. Till they believed the true God, they were calling upon idols, O Baal, hear us. (2.) *They cannot believe in him of whom they have not heard.* Some way or other the divine revelation must be made known to us, before we can receive it and assent to it; it is not born with us. In hearing is included reading, which is tantamount, and by which many are brought to believe (John xx. 31): *These things are written that you may believe.* But hearing only is mentioned, as the more ordinary and natural way of receiving information. (3.) *They cannot hear without a preacher;* how should they? Somebody must tell them what they are to believe. Preachers and hearers are correlates; it is a blessed thing when they mutually rejoice in each other—the hearers in the skill and faithfulness of the preacher, and the preacher in the willingness and obedience of the hearers. (4.) *They cannot preach except they be sent,* except they be both commissioned and in some measure qualified for their preaching work. How shall a man act as an ambassador, unless he have both his credentials and his instructions from the prince that sends him? This proves that to the regular ministry there must be a regular

mission and ordination. It is God's prerogative to send ministers; he is the Lord of the harvest, and therefore to him we must *pray that he would send forth labourers,* Matt. ix. 38. He only can qualify men for, and incline them to, the work of the ministry. But the competency of that qualification, and the sincerity of that inclination, must not be left to the judgment of every man for himself: the nature of the thing will by no means admit this; but, for the preservation of due order in the church, this must needs be referred and submitted to the judgment of a competent number of those who are themselves in that office and of approved wisdom and experience in it, who, as in all other callings, are presumed the most able judges, and who are empowered to set apart such as they find so qualified and inclined to this work of the ministry, that by this preservation of the succession the name of Christ may endure for ever and his throne as the days of heaven. And those that are thus set apart, not only may, but must preach, as those that are sent.

2. How welcome the gospel ought to be to those to whom it was preached, because it showed the way to salvation, *v.* 15. For this he quotes Isa. lii. 7. The like passage we have, Nah. i. 15, which, if it point at the glad tidings of the deliverance of Israel out of Babylon in the type, yet looks further to the gospel, the good news of our salvation by Jesus Christ. Observe, (1.) What the gospel is: It is *the gospel of peace;* it is the word of reconciliation between God and man. *On earth peace,* Luke ii. 14. Or, peace is put in general for all good; so it is explained here; it is *glad tidings of good things.* The things of the gospel are good things indeed, the best things; tidings concerning them are the most joyful tidings, the best news that ever came from heaven to earth. (2.) What the work of ministers is: To preach this gospel, to *bring these glad tidings;* to *evangelize peace* (so the original is), to evangelize good things. Every preacher is in this sense an evangelist: he is not only a messenger to carry the news, but an ambassador to treat; and the first gospel preachers were angels, Luke ii. 13, &c. (3.) How acceptable they should therefore be to the children of men for their work's sake: *How beautiful are the feet,* that is, how welcome are they! Mary Magdalene expressed her love to Christ by kissing his feet, and afterwards by holding him by the feet, Matt. xxviii. 9. And, when Christ was sending forth his disciples, he washed their feet. Those that preach the gospel of peace should see to it that their feet (their life and conversation) be beautiful: the holiness of ministers' lives is the beauty of their feet. *How beautiful!* namely, in the eyes of those that hear them. Those that welcome the message cannot but love the messengers. See 1 Thess. v. 12, 13.

3. He answers an objection against all this, which might be taken from the little success which the gospel had in many places (*v.* 16): *But they have not all obeyed the gospel.* All the Jews have not, all the Gentiles have not; far the greater part of both remain in unbelief and disobedience. Observe, The gospel is given us not only to be known and believed, but to be obeyed. It is not a system of notions, but a rule of practice. This little success of the word was likewise foretold by the prophet (Isa. liii. 1): *Who hath believed our report?* Very few have, few to what one would think should have believed it, considering how faithful a report it is and how well worthy of all acceptation,—very few to the many that persist in unbelief. It is no strange thing, but it is a very sad and uncomfortable thing, for the ministers of Christ to bring the report of the gospel, and not to be believed in it. Under such a melancholy consideration it is good for us to go to God and make our complaint to him. *Lord, who hath believed,* &c. In answer to this,

(1.) He shows that the word preached is the ordinary means of working faith (*v.* 17): *So then, ἄρα—however;* though many that hear do not believe, yet those that believe have first heard. *Faith cometh by hearing.* It is the summary of what he had said before, *v.* 14. The beginning, progress, and strength of faith, are by hearing. The word of God is therefore called *the word of faith:* it begets and nourishes faith. God gives faith, but it is by the word as the instrument. *Hearing* (that hearing which works faith) is *by the word of God.* It is not hearing the enticing words of man's wisdom, but hearing the word of God, that will befriend faith, and hearing it as the word of God. See 1 Thess. ii. 13.

(2.) That those who would not believe the report of the gospel, yet, having heard it, were thereby left inexcusable, and may thank themselves for their own ruin, *v.* 18, *to the end.*

[1.] The Gentiles have heard it (*v.* 18): *Have they not heard?* Yes, more or less, they have either heard the gospel, or at least heard of it. *Their sound went into all the earth;* not only a confused sound, but their *words* (more distinct and intelligible notices of these things) are *gone unto the ends of the world.* The commission which the apostles received runs thus: *Go you into all the world—preach to every creature—disciple all nations;* and they did with indefatigable industry and wonderful success pursue that commission. See the extent of Paul's province, *ch.* xv. 19. To this remote island of Britain, one of the utmost corners of the world, not only the sound, but the words, of the gospel came within a few years after Christ's ascension. It was in order to this that the gift of tongues was at the very first poured so plentifully upon the apostles,

Acts ii. In the expression here he plainly alludes to Ps. xix. 4, which speaks of the notices which the visible works of God in the creation give to all the world of the power and Godhead of the Creator. As under the Old Testament God provided for the publishing of the work of creation by the sun, moon, and stars, so now for the publishing of the work of redemption to all the world by the preaching of gospel ministers, who are therefore called *stars*.

[2.] The Jews have heard it too, *v.* 19—21. For this he appeals to two passages of the Old Testament, to show how inexcusable they are too. *Did not Israel know* that the Gentiles were to be called in? They might have known it from Moses and Isaiah.

First, One is taken from Deut. xxxii. 21, *I will provoke you to jealousy.* The Jews not only had the offer, but saw the Gentiles accepting it and benefitted by that acceptance, witness their vexation at the event. They had the refusal: *To you first,* Acts iii. 26. In all places where the apostles came still the Jews had the first offer, and the Gentiles had but their leavings. If one would not, another would. Now this provoked them to jealousy. They, as the elder brother in the parable (Luke xv.) envied the reception and entertainment of the prodigal Gentiles upon their repentance. The Gentiles are here called *no people,* and *a foolish nation,* that is, not the professing people of God. How much soever there be of the wit and wisdom of the world, those that are not the people of God are, and in the end will be found to be, a foolish people. Such was the state of the Gentile world, who yet were made the people of God, and Christ to them the wisdom of God. What a provocation it was to the Jews to see the Gentiles taken into favour we may see, Acts xiii. 45; xvii. 5, 13, and especially Acts xxii. 22. It was an instance of the great wickedness of the Jews that they were thus enraged; and this in Deuteronomy is the matter of a threatening. God often makes people's sin their punishment. A man needs no greater plague than to be left to the impetuous rage of his own lusts.

Secondly, Another is taken from Isa. lxv. 1, 2, which is very full, and in it Esaias is very bold—bold indeed, to speak so plainly of the rejection of his own countrymen. Those that will be found faithful have need to be very bold. Those that are resolved to please God must not be afraid to displease any man. Now Esaias speaks boldly and plainly,

a. Of the preventing grace and favour of God in the reception and entertainment of the Gentiles (*v.* 20): *I was found of those that sought me not.* The prescribed method is, Seek and find; this is a rule for us, not a rule for God, who is often found of those that do not seek. His grace is his own, distinguishing grace his own, and he dispenses it in a way of sovereignty, gives or withholds it at pleasure—anticipates us with the blessings, the richest choicest blessings, of his goodness. Thus he manifested himself to the Gentiles, by sending the light of the gospel among them, when they were so far from seeking him and asking after him that they were following after lying vanities, and serving dumb idols. Was not this our own particular case? Did not God begin in love, and manifest himself to us when we did not ask after him? And was not that a time of love indeed, to be often remembered with a great deal of thankfulness?

b. Of the obstinacy and perverseness of Israel, notwithstanding the fair offers and affectionate invitations they had, *v.* 21. Observe,

(*a.*) God's great goodness to them: *All day long I have stretched forth my hands.* [*a.*] His offers: *I have stretched forth my hands,* offering them life and salvation with the greatest sincerity and seriousness that can be, with all possible expressions of earnestness and importunity, showing them the happiness tendered, setting it before them with the greatest evidence, reasoning the case with them. Stretching forth the hands is the gesture of those that require audience (Acts xxvi. 1), or desire acceptance, Prov. i. 24. Christ was crucified with his hands stretched out. *Stretched forth my hands* as offering reconciliation—come let us shake hands and be friends; and our duty is to give the hand to him, 2 Chron. xxx. 8. [*b.*] His patience in making these offers: *All day long.* The patience of God towards provoking sinners is admirable. He waits to be gracious. The time of God's patience is here called a day, lightsome as a day and fit for work and business, but limited as a day, and a night at the end of it. He bears long, but he will not bear always.

(*b.*) Their great badness to him. They were a *disobedient gainsaying people.* One word in the Hebrew, in Isaiah, is here well explained by two; not only disobedient to the call, not yielding to it, but gainsaying, and quarrelling with it, which is much worse. Many that will not accept of a good proposal will yet acknowledge that they have nothing to say against it: but the Jews who believed not rested not there, but contradicted and blasphemed. God's patience with them was a very great aggravation of their disobedience, and rendered it the more exceedingly sinful; as their disobedience advanced the honour of God's patience and rendered it the more exceedingly gracious. It is a wonder of mercy in God that his goodness is not overcome by man's badness; and it is a wonder of wickedness in man that his badness is not overcome by God's goodness.

CHAP. XI.

The apostle, having reconciled that great truth of the rejection of the Jews with the promise made unto the fathers, is, in this chapter, further labouring to mollify the harshness of it, and to reconcile it to the divine goodness in general. It might be said, "Hath God then cast away his people?" The apostle therefore sets himself, in this chapter, to make a reply to this objection,

and that two ways:—I. He shows at large what the mercy is that is mixed with this wrath, ver. 1—32. II. He infers thence the infinite wisdom and sovereignty of God, with the adoration of which he concludes this chapter and subject, ver. 33—36.

I SAY then, hath God cast away
his people? God forbid. For
I also am an Israelite, of the seed of
Abraham, *of* the tribe of Benjamin.
2 God hath not cast away his people,
which he foreknew. Wot ye not
what the scripture saith of Elias?
how he maketh intercession to God
against Israel, saying, 3 Lord, they
have killed thy prophets, and digged
down thine altars; and I am left
alone, and they seek my life. 4 But
what saith the answer of God unto
him? I have reserved to myself
seven thousand men, who have not
bowed the knee to *the image of* Baal.
5 Even so then at this present time
also there is a remnant according to
the election of grace. 6 And if by
grace, then *is it* no more of works:
otherwise grace is no more grace.
But if *it be* of works, then it is no
more grace: otherwise work is no
more work. 7 What then? Israel
hath not obtained that which he
seeketh for; but the election hath
obtained it, and the rest were blinded.
8 (According as it is written, God
hath given them the spirit of slumber,
eyes that they should not see, and
ears that they should not hear;) unto
this day. 9 And David saith, Let
their table be made a snare, and a
trap, and a stumblingblock, and a
recompence unto them: 10 Let
their eyes be darkened, that they may
not see, and bow down their back
alway. 11 I say then, Have they
stumbled that they should fall? God
forbid: but *rather* through their fall
salvation *is come* unto the Gentiles,
for to provoke them to jealousy. 12
Now if the fall of them *be* the riches
of the world, and the diminishing of
them the riches of the Gentiles; how
much more their fulness? 13 For I
speak to you Gentiles, inasmuch as
I am the apostle of the Gentiles, I
magnify mine office: 14 If by any
means I may provoke to emulation
them which are my flesh, and might
save some of them. 15 For if the
casting away of them *be* the reconciling of the world, what *shall* the
receiving *of them be*, but life from the
dead? 16 For if the firstfruit *be*
holy, the lump *is* also *holy*: and if
the root *be* holy, so *are* the branches.
17 And if some of the branches be
broken off, and thou, being a wild
olive tree, wert graffed in among
them, and with them partakest of the
root and fatness of the olive tree;
18 Boast not against the branches.
But if thou boast, thou bearest not
the root, but the root thee. 19 Thou
wilt say then, The branches were
broken off, that I might be graffed
in. 20 Well; because of unbelief
they were broken off, and thou standest by faith. Be not high-minded,
but fear: 21 For if God spared not
the natural branches, *take heed* lest
he also spare not thee. 22 Behold
therefore the goodness and severity
of God: on them which fell, severity;
but toward thee, goodness, if thou
continue in *his* goodness: otherwise
thou also shalt be cut off. 23 And
they also, if they abide not in unbelief, shall be graffed in: for God is
able to graff them in again. 24 For
if thou wert cut out of the olive tree
which is wild by nature, and wert
graffed contrary to nature into a good
olive tree: how much more shall
these, which be the natural *branches*,
be graffed into their own olive tree?
25 For I would not, brethren, that ye
should be ignorant of this mystery,
lest ye should be wise in your own
conceits; that blindness in part is
happened to Israel, until the fulness
of the Gentiles be come in. 26 And
so all Israel shall be saved: as it is
written, There shall come out of Sion
the Deliverer, and shall turn away
ungodliness from Jacob: 27 For
this *is* my covenant unto them, when
I shall take away their sins. 28 As
concerning the gospel, *they are* enemies for your sakes: but as touching
the election, *they are* beloved for the
fathers' sakes. 29 For the gifts and
calling of God *are* without repentance. 30 For as ye in times past

have not believed God, yet have now
obtained mercy through their unbelief: 31 Even so have these also
now not believed, that through your
mercy they also may obtain mercy.
32 For God hath concluded them all
in unbelief, that he might have mercy
upon all.

The apostle proposes here a plausible objection, which might be urged against the divine conduct in casting off the Jewish nation (*v.* 1): "*Hath God cast away his people?* Is the rejection total and final? Are they all abandoned to wrath and ruin, and that eternal? Is the extent of the sentence so large as to be without reserve, or the continuance of it so long as to be without repeal? Will he have no more a peculiar people to himself? In opposition to this, he shows that there was a great deal of goodness and mercy expressed along with this seeming severity, particularly he insists upon three things:—1. That, though some of the Jews were cast off, yet they were not all so. 2. That, though the body of the Jews were cast off, yet the Gentiles were taken in. And, 3. That, though the Jews were cast off at present, yet in God's due time they should be taken into his church again.

I. The Jews, it is true, were many of them cast off, but not all. The supposition of this he introduces with a *God forbid.* He will by no means endure such a suggestion. God had made a distinction between some of them and others.

1. There was a chosen remnant of believing Jews, that obtained righteousness and life by faith in Jesus Christ, *v.* 1—7. These are said to be such as he *foreknew* (*v.* 2), that is, had thoughts of love to, before the world was; for whom he thus foreknew he did predestinate. Here lies the ground of the difference. They are called the *election* (*v.* 7), that is, the elect, God's chosen ones, whom he calls the election, because that which first distinguished them from and dignified them above others was God's electing love. Believers are the *election,* all those and those only whom God hath chosen. Now,

(1.) He shows that he himself was one of them: *For I also am an Israelite;* as if he had said, "Should I say that all the Jews are rejected, I should cut off my own claims, and see myself abandoned." Paul was a chosen vessel (Acts ix. 15), and yet he was of the *seed of Abraham,* and particularly of the tribe of Benjamin, the least and youngest of all the tribes of Israel.

(2.) He suggests that as in Elias's time, so now, this chosen remnant was really more and greater than one would think it was, which intimates likewise that it is no new nor unusual thing for God's grace and favour to Israel to be limited and confined to a remnant of that people: for so it was in Elijah's time. The scripture saith it of Elias, ἐν Ἠλίᾳ—*in the story of Elias,* the great reformer of the Old Testament. Observe, [1.] His mistake concerning Israel; as if their apostasy in the days of Ahab was so general that he himself was the only faithful servant God had in the world. He refers to 1 Kings xix. 14, where (it is here said) *he maketh intercession to God against Israel.* A strange kind of intercession: ἐντυγχάνει τῷ Θεῷ κατὰ τοῦ Ἰσραὴλ—*He deals with God against Israel;* so it may be read; so ἐντυγχάνω is translated, Acts xxv. 24. The Jews ἐνέτυχόν μοι—*have dealt with me.* In prayer we deal with God, commune with him, discourse with him: it is said of Elijah (Jam. v. 17) that he *prayed in praying.* We are then likely to pray in praying, to make a business of that duty, when we pray as those that are dealing with God in the duty. Now Elijah in this prayer spoke as if there were none left faithful in Israel but himself. See to what a low ebb the profession of religion may sometimes be brought, and how much the face of it may be eclipsed, that the most wise and observing men may give it up for gone. So it was in Elijah's time. That which makes the show of a nation is the powers and the multitude. The powers of Israel were then persecuting powers: They have *killed thy prophets, and digged down thine altars,* and they *seek my life.* The multitude of Israel were then idolatrous: *I am left alone.* Thus those few that were faithful to God were not only lost in the crowd of idolaters, but crushed and driven into corners by the rage of persecutors. *When the wicked rise, a man is hidden,* Prov. xxviii. 12.—*Digged down thine altars;* not only neglected them, and let them go out of repair, but digged them down. When altars were set up for Baal, it is no wonder if God's altars were pulled down; they could not endure that standing testimony against their idolatry. This was his intercession *against Israel;* as if he had said, "Lord, is not this a people ripe for ruin, worthy to be cast off? What else canst thou do for thy great name?" It is a very sad thing for any person or people to have the prayers of God's people against them, especially of God's prophets, for God espouses, and sooner or later will visibly own, the cause of his praying people. [2.] The rectifying of this mistake by the answer of God (*v.* 4): *I have reserved.* Note, *First,* Things are often much better with the church of God than wise and good men think they are. They are ready to conclude hardly, and to give up all for gone, when it is not so. *Secondly,* In times of general apostasy, there is usually a remnant that keep their integrity—some, though but a few; all do not go one way. *Thirdly,* That when there is a remnant who keep their integrity in times of general apostasy it is God that reserves to himself that remnant. If he had left them to themselves, they had gone down the stream with the rest. It is his free and almighty grace that makes the difference between them and others.—*Seven thousand:* a competent number to bear their testimony against the idolatry of Israel, and yet, compared with the many thousands of Israel, a very small number, one of a city, and two of a tribe, like the grape-gleanings of the vintage. Christ's flock is but a little flock; and yet, when they come all together at last, they will be a great and innumerable multitude, Rev. vii. 9. Now the description of this remnant is that *they had not bowed the knee to the image of Baal,* which was then the reigning sin of Israel. In court, city, and country, Baal had the ascendant; and the generality of people, more or less, paid their respect to Baal. The best evidence of integrity is a freedom from the present prevailing corruptions of the times and places that we live in, to swim against the stream when it is strong. Those God will own for his faithful witnesses that are bold in bearing their testimony to the *present* truth, 2 Pet. i. 12. This is thank-worthy, not to bow to Baal when every body bows. Sober singularity is commonly the badge of true sincerity. [3.] The application of this instance to the case in hand: *Even so at this present time, v.* 5—7. God's methods of dispensation towards his church are as they used to be. As it has been, so it is. In Elijah's time there was a remnant, and so there is now. If then there was a remnant left under the Old Testament, when the displays of grace were less clear and the pourings out of the Spirit less plentiful, much more now under the gospel, when the grace of God, which bringeth salvation, appears more illustrious.—*A remnant,* a few of many, a remnant of believing Jews when the rest were obstinate in their unbelief. This is called *a remnant according to the election of grace;* they are such as were chosen from eternity in the counsels of divine love to be vessels of grace and glory. Whom he did predestinate those he called. If the difference between them and others be made purely by the grace of God, as certainly it is *(I have reserved them,* saith he, *to myself),* then it must needs be according to the election; for we are sure that whatever God does he does it according to the counsel of his own will. Now concerning this remnant we may observe, *First,* Whence it takes its rise, from the free grace of God (*v.* 6), that grace which excludes works. The eternal election, in which the difference between some and others is first founded, is purely of grace, free grace; not for the sake of works done or foreseen; if so, it would not be *grace. Gratia non est ullo modo gratia, si non sit omni modo gratuita—It is not grace, properly so called, if it be not perfectly free.* Election is purely according to the good pleasure of his will, Eph. i. 5. Paul's heart was so full of the freeness of God's grace that in the midst of his discourse he turns aside, as it were, to make this remark, *If of grace, then not of works.* And some observe that faith itself, which in the matter of justification is opposed to works, is here included in them; for faith has a peculiar fitness to receive the free grace of God for our justification, but not to receive that grace for our election. *Secondly,* What it obtains: that which Israel, that is, the body of that people, in vain sought for (*v.* 7): *Israel hath not obtained that which he seeketh for,* that is, justification, and acceptance with God (see *ch.* ix. 31), but the *election have obtained it.* In them the promise of God has its accomplishment, and God's ancient kindness for that people is remembered. He calls the remnant of believers, not the elect, but the *election,* to show that the sole foundation of all their hopes and happiness is laid in election. They were the persons whom God had in his eye in the counsels of his love; they are the election; they are God's choice. Such was the favour of God to the chosen remnant. But,

2. *The rest were blinded, v.* 7. Some are chosen and called, and the call is made effectual. But others are left to perish in their unbelief; nay, they are made worse by that which should have made them better. The gospel, which to those that believed was the savour of life unto life, to the unbelieving was the savour of death unto death. The same sun softens wax and hardens clay. Good old Simeon foresaw that the child Jesus was set for the fall, as well as for the rising again, of many in Israel, Luke ii. 34.—*Were blinded; ἐπωρώθησαν—they were hardened;* so some. They were seared, and made brawny and insensible. They could neither see the light, nor feel the touch, of gospel grace. Blindness and hardness are expressive of the same senselessness and stupidity of spirit. They shut their eyes, and would not see; this was their sin: and then God, in a way of righteous judgment, blinded their eyes, that they could not see; this was their punishment. This seemed harsh doctrine: to qualify it, therefore, he vouches two witnesses out of the Old Testament, who speak of such a thing.

(1.) Isaiah, who spoke of such a judgment in his day, *ch.* xxix. 10; vi. 9. The *spirit of slumber,* that is, an indisposedness to mind either their duty or interest. They are under the power of a prevailing unconcernedness, like people that are slumbering and sleeping; not affected with any thing that is said or done. They were resolved to continue as they were, and would not stir. The following words explain what is meant by the spirit of slumber: *Eyes, that they should not see, and ears, that they should not hear.* They had the faculties, but in the things that belonged to their peace they had not the use of those faculties; they were quite infatuated, they saw Christ, but they did not believe in him; they heard his word, but they did not receive it; and so both their hearing and their seeing were in vain. It was all one as if they had neither seen nor heard. Of all judgments spiritual judgments are the sorest, and most to be dreaded, though they make the least noise.—*Unto this day.* Ever since Esaias prophesied, this hardening work has been in the doing; some among them have been blind and senseless. Or, rather, ever since the first preaching of the gospel: though they have had the most convincing evidences that could be of the truth of it, the most powerful preaching, the fairest offers, the clearest calls from Christ himself, and from his apostles, yet to this day they are blinded. It is still true concerning multitudes of them, even to this day in which we live; they are hardened and blinded, the obstinacy and unbelief go by succession from generation to generation, according to their own fearful imprecation, which entailed the curse: *His blood be upon us and upon our children.*

(2.) David (*v.* 9, 10), quoted from Ps. lxix. 22. 23, where David having in the Spirit foretold the sufferings of Christ from his own people the Jews, particularly that of their giving him *vinegar to drink* (*v.* 21, which was literally fulfilled, Matt. xxvii. 48), an expression of the greatest contempt and malice that could be, in the next words, under the form of an imprecation, he foretels the dreadful judgments of God upon them for it: *Let their table become a snare,* which the apostle here applies to the present blindness of the Jews, and the offence they took at the gospel, which increased their hardness. This teaches us how to understand other prayers of David against his enemies; they are to be looked upon as prophetic of the judgments of God upon the public and obstinate enemies of Christ and his kingdom. His prayer that it might be so was a prophecy that it should be so, and not the private expression of his own angry resentments. It was likewise intended to justify God, and to clear his righteousness in such judgments. He speaks here, [1.] Of the ruin of their comforts: *Let their table be made a snare,* that is, as the psalmist explains it, Let that which should be for their welfare be a trap to them. The curse of God will turn meat into poison. It is a threatening like that in Mal. ii. 2, *I will curse your blessings.* Their table a snare, that is, an occasion of sin and an occasion of misery. Their very food, that should nourish them, shall choke them. [2.] Of the ruin of their powers and faculties (*v.* 10), their eyes darkened, their backs bowed down, that they can neither find the right way, nor, if they could, are they able to walk in it. The Jews, after their national rejection of Christ and his gospel, became infatuated in their politics, so that their very counsels turned against them, and hastened their ruin by the Romans. They looked like a people designed for slavery and contempt, their backs bowed down, to be ridden and trampled upon by all the nations about them. Or, it may be understood spiritually; their backs are bowed down in carnality and worldly-mindedness. *Curvæ in terris animæ—They mind earthly things.* This is an exact description of the state and temper of the present remainder of that people, than whom, if the accounts we have of them be true, there is not a more worldly, wilful, blind, selfish, ill-natured, people in the world. They are manifestly to this day under the power of this curse. Divine curses will work long. It is a sign we have our eyes darkened if we are bowed down in worldly-mindedness.

II. Another thing which qualified this doctrine of the rejection of the Jews was that though they were cast off and unchurched, yet the Gentiles were taken in (*v.* 11—14), which he applies by way of caution to the Gentiles, *v.* 17—22.

1. The rejection of the Jews made room for the reception of the Gentiles. The Jews' leavings were a feast for the poor Gentiles (*v.* 11): "*Have they stumbled that they should fall?* Had God no other end in forsaking and rejecting them than their destruction?" He startles at this, rejecting the thought with abhorrence, as usually he does when any thing is suggested which seems to reflect upon the wisdom, or righteousness, or goodness of God: *God forbid!* no, *through their fall salvation is come to the Gentiles.* Not but that salvation might have come to the Gentiles if they had stood; but by the divine appointment it was so ordered that the gospel should be preached to the Gentiles upon the Jews' refusal of it. Thus in the parable (Matt. xxii. 8, 9), *Those that were* first *bidden were not worthy—Go ye therefore into the highways,* Luke xiv. 21. And so it was in the history (Acts xiii. 46): *It was necessary that the word of God should first have been spoken to you; but, seeing you put it from you, lo, we turn to the Gentiles;* so Acts xviii. 6. God will have a church in the world, will have the wedding furnished with guests; and, if one will not come, another will, or why was the offer made? The Jews had the refusal, and so the tender came to the Gentiles. See how Infinite Wisdom brings light out of darkness, good out of evil, meat out of the eater, and sweetness out of the strong. To the same purport he says (*v.* 12), *The fall of them was the riches of the world,* that is, it hastened the gospel so much the sooner into the Gentile world. The gospel is the greatest riches of the place where it is; it is better than thousands of gold and silver. Or, The riches of the Gentiles was the multitude of converts among them. True believers are God's jewels. To the same purport (*v.* 15): *The casting away of them is the reconciling of the world.* God's displeasure towards them made way for his favour towards the Gentiles. God was in Christ *reconciling the*

world, 2 Cor. v. 19. And therefore he took occasion from the unbelief of the Jews openly to disavow and disown them, though they had been his peculiar favourites, to show that in dispensing his favours he would now no longer act in such a way of peculiarity and restriction, but that in every nation he that feared God and wrought righteousness should be accepted of him, Acts x. 34, 35.

2. The use that the apostle makes of this doctrine concerning the substitution of the Gentiles in the room of the Jews.

(1.) As a kinsman to the Jews, here is a word of excitement and exhortation to them, to stir them up to receive and embrace the gospel-offer. This God intended in his favour to the Gentiles, to provoke the Jews to jealousy (*v.* 11), and Paul endeavours to enforce it accordingly (*v.* 14): *If by any means I might provoke to emulation those who are my flesh.* "Shall the despised Gentiles run away with all the comforts and privileges of the gospel, and shall not we repent of our refusal, and now at last put in for a share? Shall not we believe and obey, and be pardoned and saved, as well as the Gentiles?" See an instance of such an emulation in Esau, Gen. xxviii. 6—9. There is a commendable emulation in the affairs of our souls: why should not we be as holy and happy as any of our neighbours? In this emulation there needs no suspicion, undermining or countermining; for the church has room enough, and the new covenant grace and comfort enough, for us all. The blessings are not lessened by the multitudes of the sharers.—*And might save some of them.* See what was Paul's business, to save souls; and yet the utmost he promises himself is but to save some. Though he was such a powerful preacher, spoke and wrote with such evidence and demonstration of the Spirit, yet of the many he dealt with he could but save some. Ministers must think their pains well bestowed if they can but be instrumental to save some.

(2.) As an apostle to the Gentiles, here is a word of caution for them: "*I speak to you Gentiles.* You believing Romans, you hear what riches of salvation are come to you by the fall of the Jews, but take heed lest you do any thing to forfeit it." Paul takes this, as other occasions, to apply his discourse to the Gentiles, because he was the apostle of the Gentiles, appointed for the service of their faith, to plant and water churches in the Gentile nations. This was the purport of his extraordinary mission, Acts xxii. 21, *I will send thee far hence unto the Gentiles;* compare Acts ix. 15. It was likewise the intention of his ordination, Gal. ii. 9. Compare Acts xiii. 2. It ought to be our great and special care to do good to those that are under our charge: we must particularly mind that which is our own work. It was an instance of God's great love to the poor Gentiles that he appointed Paul, who in gifts and graces excelled all the apostles, to be the apostle of the Gentiles. The Gentile world was a wider province; and the work to be done in it required a very able, skilful, zealous, courageous workman: such a one was Paul. God calls those to special work whom he either sees or makes fit for it.—*I magnify my office.* There were those that vilified it, and him because of it. It was because he was the apostle of the Gentiles that the Jews were so outrageous against him (Acts xxii. 21, 22), and yet he thought never the worse of it, though it set him up as the butt of all the Jewish rage and malice. It is a sign of true love to Jesus Christ to reckon that service and work for him truly honourable which the world looks upon with scorn, as mean and contemptible. The office of the ministry is an office to be *magnified.* Ministers are ambassadors for Christ, and stewards of the mysteries of God, and for their work's sake are to be esteemed highly in love.—*My office; τὴν διακονίαν μου—my ministry,* my service, not my lordship and dominion. It was not the dignity and power, but the duty and work, of an apostle, that Paul was so much in love with. Now two things he exhorts the Gentiles to, with reference to the rejected Jews:—

[1.] To have a respect for the Jews, notwithstanding, and to desire their conversion. This is intimated in the prospect he gives them of the advantage that would accrue to the church by their conversion, *v.* 12, 15. It would be as life from the dead; and therefore they must not insult and triumph over those poor Jews, but rather pity them, and desire their welfare, and long for the receiving of them in again.

[2.] To take heed to themselves, lest they should stumble and fall, as the Jews had done, *v.* 17—22. Here observe,

First, The privilege which the Gentiles had by being taken into the church. They were grafted in (*v.* 17), as a branch of a wild olive into a good olive, which is contrary to the way and custom of the husbandman, who grafts the good olive into the bad; but those that God grafts into the church he finds wild and barren, and good for nothing. Men graft to mend the tree; but God grafts to mend the branch. 1. The church of God is an olive-tree, flourishing and fruitful as an olive (Ps. lii. 8; Hos. xiv. 6), the fruit useful for the honour both of God and man, Judg. ix. 9. 2. Those that are out of the church are as wild olive-trees, not only useless, but what they do produce is sour and unsavoury: *Wild by nature, v.* 24. This was the state of the poor Gentiles, that wanted church privileges, and in respect of real sanctification; and it is the natural state of every one of us, to be wild by nature. 3. Conversion is the grafting in of wild branches into the good olive. We must be cut off from the old stock, and be brought into union with a new root. 4. Those that are grafted into the good olive-tree partake of the root and fatness of the olive. It is applicable to a saving union with Christ; all that are by a lively faith grafted into Christ partake of him as the branches of the root—receive from his fulness. But it is here spoken of a visible church-membership, from which the Jews were as branches broken off; and so the Gentiles were grafted in, *αὐτοῖς—among those* that continued, or in the room of those that were broken off. The Gentiles, being grafted into the church, partake of the same privileges that the Jews did, *the root and fatness.* The olive-tree is the visible church (called so Jer. xi. 16); the root of this tree was Abraham, not the root of communication, so Christ only is the root, but the root of administration, he being the first with whom the covenant was so solemnly made. Now the believing Gentiles partake of this root: *he also is a son of Abraham* (Luke xix. 9), the *blessing of Abraham comes upon the Gentiles* (Gal. iii. 14), the same fatness of the olive-tree, the same for substance, special protection, lively oracles, means of salvation, a standing ministry, instituted ordinances; and, among the rest, the visible church-membership of their infant seed, which was part of the fatness of the olive-tree that the Jews had, and cannot be imagined to be denied to the Gentiles.

Secondly, A caution not to abuse these privileges. 1. "Be not proud (*v.* 18): *Boast not against the branches.* Do not therefore trample upon the Jews as a reprobate people, nor insult over those that are broken off, much less over those that do continue." Grace is given, not to make us proud, but to make us thankful. The law of faith excludes all boasting either of ourselves or against others. "Do not say (*v.* 19): *They were broken off that I might be grafted in;* that is, do not think that thou didst merit more at the hand of God than they, or didst stand higher in his favour." "But remember, *thou bearest not the root, but the root thee.* Though thou art grafted in, thou art still but a branch borne by the root; nay, and an engrafted branch, brought into the good olive *contrary to nature* (*v.* 24), not free-born, but by an act of grace enfranchised and naturalized. Abraham, the root of the Jewish church, is not beholden to thee; but thou art greatly obliged to him, as the trustee of the covenant and the father of many nations. Therefore, *if thou boast,* know (this word must be supplied to clear the sense) *thou bearest not the root but the root thee.*" 2. "Be not secure (*v.* 20): *Be not high-minded, but fear.* Be not too confident of your own strength and standing." A holy fear is an excellent preservative against high-mindedness: happy is the man that thus feareth always. We need not fear but God will be true to his word; all the danger is lest we be false to ours. *Let us therefore fear,* Heb. iv. 1. The church of Rome now boasts of a patent of perpetual preservation; but the apostle here, in his epistle to that church when she was in her infancy and integrity, enters an express caveat against that boast, and all claims of that kind.—*Fear* what? "Why fear lest thou commit a forfeiture as they have done, lest thou lose the privileges thou now enjoyest, as they have lost theirs." The evils that befal others should be warnings to us. *Go* (saith God to Jerusalem Jer. vii. 12), and *see what I did to* Shiloh; so now, let all the churches of God go and see what he did to Jerusalem, and what is become of the day of their visitation, that we may hear and fear, and take heed of Jerusalem's sin. The patent which churches have of their privileges is not for a certain term, nor entailed upon them and their heirs; but it runs as long as they carry themselves well, and no longer. Consider, (1.) "How they were broken off. It was not undeservedly, by an act of absolute sovereignty and prerogative, but *because of unbelief.*" It seems, then, it is possible for churches that have long stood by faith to fall into such a state of infidelity as may be their ruin. Their unbelief did not only provoke God to cut them off, but they did by this cut themselves off: it was not only the meritorious, but the formal cause of their separation. "Now, thou art liable to the same infirmity and corruption that they fell by." Further observe, They were *natural branches* (*v.* 21), not only interested in Abraham's covenant, but descending from Abraham's loins, and so born upon the premises, and thence had a kind of tenant-right: yet, when they sunk into unbelief, God did not spare them. Prescription, long usage, the faithfulness of their ancestors, would not secure them. It was in vain to plead, though they insisted much upon it, that they were Abraham's seed, Matt. iii. 9; John viii. 33. It is true they were the husbandmen to whom the vineyard was first let out; but, when they forfeited it, it was justly taken from them, Matt. xxi. 41, 43. This is called here *severity, v.* 22. God laid righteousness to the line and judgment to the plummet, and dealt with them according to their sins. Severity is a word that sounds harshly; and I do not remember that it is any where else in scripture ascribed to God; and it is here applied to the unchurching of the Jews. God is most severe towards those that have been in profession nearest to him, if they rebel against him, Amos iii. 2. Patience and privileges abused turn to the greatest wrath. Of all judgments, spiritual judgments are the sorest; for of these he is here speaking, *v.* 8. (2.) "How thou standest, thou that art engrafted in." He speaks to the Gentile churches in general, though perhaps tacitly reflecting on some particular person, who might have expressed some such pride and triumph in the Jews rejection. "Consider then," [1.] "By what means thou standest: *By faith,* which is a depending grace, and fetches in strength from heaven. Thou dost not stand in any strength of thy own, of which thou mightest be confident: thou art no more than the free grace of God makes thee, and his grace is his own, which he gives or withholds at pleasure. That which ruined them was unbelief, and by faith thou standest; therefore thou hast no faster hold than they had, thou standest on no firmer foundation than they did." [2.] "On what terms (*v.* 22): *Towards thee goodness, if thou continue in his goodness,* that is, continue in a dependence upon and compliance with the free grace of God, the want of which it was that ruined the Jews—if thou be careful to keep up thine interest in the divine favour, by being continually careful to please God and fearful of offending him." The sum of our duty, the condition of our happiness, is to keep ourselves in the love of God. *Fear the Lord and his goodness.* Hos. iii. 5.

III. Another thing that qualifies this doctrine of the Jews' rejection is that, though for the present they are cast off, yet the rejection is not final; but, when the fulness of time is come, they will be taken in again. They are not cast off for ever, but mercy is remembered in the midst of wrath. Let us observe,

1. How this conversion of the Jews is here described. (1.) It is said to be their fulness (*v.* 12), that is, the addition of them to the church, the filling up again of that place which became vacant by their rejection. This would be the enriching of the world (that is, the church in the world) with a great deal of light and strength and beauty. (2.) It is called the receiving of them. The conversion of a soul is the receiving of that soul, so the conversion of a nation. They shall be received into favour, into the church, into the love of Christ, whose arms are stretched out for the receiving of all those that will come to him. And this will be as *life from the dead*—so strange and surprising, and yet withal so welcome and acceptable. The conversion of the Jews will bring great joy to the church. See Luke xv. 32, *He was dead, and is alive;* and therefore *it was meet we should make merry and be glad.* (3.) It is called the *grafting of them in again* (*v.* 23), into the church, from which they had been broken off. That which is grafted in receives sap and virtue from the root; so does a soul that is truly grafted into the church receive life, and strength, and grace from Christ the quickening root. They shall be *grafted into their own olive-tree* (*v.* 24); that is, into the church of which they had formerly been the most eminent and conspicuous members, to retrieve those privileges of visible church-membership which they had so long enjoyed, but have now sinned away and forfeited by their unbelief. (4.) It is called the *saving of all Israel, v.* 26. True conversion may well be called salvation; it is salvation begun. See Acts ii. 47. The adding of them to the church is the saving of them: τοὺς σωζωμένους, in the present tense, *are saved.* When conversion-work goes on, salvation-work goes on.

2. What it is grounded upon, and what reason we have to look for it.

(1.) Because of the holiness of the first-fruits and the root, *v.* 16. Some by the first-fruits understand those of the Jews that were already converted to the faith of Christ and received into the church, who were as the first-fruits dedicated to God, as earnests of a more plentiful and sanctified harvest. A good beginning promises a good ending. Why may we not suppose that others may be savingly wrought upon as well as those who are already brought in? Others by the first-fruits understand the same with the root, namely, the patriarchs, Abraham, Isaac, and Jacob, from whom the Jews descended, and with whom, as the prime trustees, the covenant was deposited: and so they were the root of the Jews, not only as a people, but as a church. Now, if they were holy, which is not meant so much of inherent as of federal holiness—if they were in the church and in the covenant—then we have reason to conclude that God hath a kindness for the *lump*—the body of that people; and for the *branches*—the particular members of it. The Jews are in a sense a holy nation (Exod. xix. 6), being descended from holy parents. Now it cannot be imagined that such a holy nation should be totally and finally cast off. This proves that the seed of believers, as such, are within the pale of the visible church, and within the verge of the covenant, till they do, by their unbelief, throw themselves out; for, *if the root be holy, so are the branches.* Though real qualifications are not propagated, yet relative privileges are. Though a wise man does not beget a wise man, yet a free man begets a free man. Though grace does not run in the blood, yet external privileges do (till they are forfeited), even to a thousand generations. Look how they will answer it another day that cut off the entail, by turning the seed of the faithful out of the church, and so not allowing the blessing of Abraham to come upon the Gentiles. The Jewish branches are reckoned holy, because the root was so. This is expressed more plainly (*v.* 28): *They are beloved for the fathers' sakes.* In this love to the fathers the first foundation of their church-state was laid (Deut. iv. 37): *Because he loved thy fathers, therefore he chose their seed after them.* And the same love would revive their privileges, for still the ancient loving-kindness is remembered; they are *beloved for the fathers' sakes.* It is God's usual method of grace Kindness to the children for the father's sake is therefore called the *kindness of God,* 2 Sam. ix. 3, 7. Though, as concerning the gospel (namely, in the present dispensation of it), they are enemies to it *for your sakes,* that is, for the sake of the Gentiles, against whom they have such an antipathy; yet, when God's time shall come, this will wear off, and God's love to their fathers will be remembered. See a promise that points at this, Lev. xxvi. 42. The iniquity of the fathers is visited but to the third and fourth generation; but there is mercy kept for thousands. Many fare the better for the sake of their godly ancestors. It is upon this account that the church is called their own *olive-tree*. Long it had been their own peculiar, which is some encouragement to us to hope that there may be room for them in it again, for old acquaintance-sake. That which hath been may be again. Though particular persons and generations wear off in unbelief, yet there having been a national church-membership, though for the present suspended, we may expect that it will be revived.

(2.) Because of the power of God (*v.* 23): *God is able to graft them in again.* The conversion of souls is a work of almighty power; and when they seem most hardened, and blinded, and obstinate, our comfort is that God is able to work a change, able to graft those in that have been long cast out and withered. When the house is kept by the strong man armed, with all his force, yet God is stronger than he, and is able to dispossess him. The condition of their restoration is faith: *If they abide not still in unbelief.* So that nothing is to be done but to remove that unbelief that is the great obstacle; and God is able to take that away, though nothing less than an almighty power will do it, the same power that raised up Christ from the dead, Eph. i. 19, 20. Otherwise, can these dry bones live?

(3.) Because of the grace of God manifested to the Gentiles. Those that have themselves experienced the grace of God, preventing, distinguishing grace, may thence take encouragement to hope well concerning others. This is his argument (*v.* 24): "If thou wast grafted into a good olive, that was wild by nature, much more shall these that were the natural branches, and may therefore be presumed somewhat nearer to the divine acceptance." This is a suggestion very proper to check the insolence of those Gentile Christians that looked with disdain and triumph upon the condition of the rejected Jews, and trampled upon them; as if he had said, "Their condition, bad as it is, is not so bad as yours was before your conversion; and therefore why may it not be made as good as yours is?" This is his argument (*v.* 30, 31): *As you in times past have not,* &c. It is good for those that have found mercy with God to be often thinking what they were in time past, and how they obtained that mercy. This would help to soften our censures of those that still continue in unbelief, and quicken our prayers for them. He argues further from the occasion of the Gentiles' call, that is, the unbelief of the Jews; thence it took rise: "*You have obtained mercy through their unbelief;* much more shall they obtain mercy through your mercy. If the putting out of their candle was the lighting of yours, by that power of God which brings good out of evil, much more shall the continued light of your candle, when God's time shall come, be a means of lighting theirs again." "*That through your mercy they might obtain mercy,* that is, that they may be beholden to you, as you have been to them." He takes it for granted that the believing Gentiles would do their utmost endeavour to work upon the Jews—that, when God had persuaded Japhet, Japhet would be labouring to persuade Shem. True grace hates monopolies. Those that have found mercy themselves should endeavour that through their mercy others also may obtain mercy.

(4.) Because of the promises and prophecies of the Old Testament, which point at this. He quotes a very remarkable one, *v.* 26, from Isa. lix. 20, 21. Where we may observe, [1.] The coming of Christ promised: *There shall come out of Zion the deliverer.* Jesus Christ is the great deliverer, which supposes mankind in a state of misery and danger. In Isaiah it is, *the Redeemer shall come to Zion.* There he is called the Redeemer; here the deliverer; he delivers in a way of redemption, by a price. There he is said to come to Zion, because when the prophet prophesied he was yet to come into the world, and Zion was his first head-quarters. Thither he came, there he took up his residence: but, when the apostle wrote this, he had come, he had been in Zion; and he is speaking of the fruits of his appearing, which shall come *out of Zion;* thence, as from the spring, issued forth those streams of living water which in the everlasting gospel watered the nations. *Out of Zion went forth the law,* Isa. ii. 3. Compare Luke xxiv. 47. [2.] The end and purpose of this coming: *He shall turn away ungodliness from Jacob.* Christ's errand into the world was to turn away ungodliness, to turn away the guilt by the purchase of pardoning mercy, and to turn away the power by the pouring out of renewing grace, to save his people from their sins (Matt. i. 21), to separate between us and our sins, that iniquity might not be our ruin, and that it might not be our ruler. Especially to turn it away from Jacob, which is that for the sake of which he quotes the text, as a proof of the great kindness God intended for the seed of Jacob. What greater kindness could he do them than to turn away ungodliness from them, to take away that which comes between them and all happiness, take away sin, and then make way for all good? This is the blessing that Christ was sent to bestow upon the world, and to tender it to the Jews in the first place (Acts iii. 26), to turn people from their iniquities. In Isaiah it is, *The Redeemer shall come to Zion, and unto those that turn from transgression in Jacob,* which shows who in Zion were to have a share in and to reap benefit by the deliverance promised, those and those only that leave their sins and turn to God; to them Christ comes as a Redeemer, but as an avenger to those that persist in impenitence. See Deut. xxx. 2, 3. Those that turn from sin will be owned as the true citizens of Zion (Eph. ii. 19), the right Jacob, Ps. xxiv. 4, 6. Putting both these readings together, we learn that none have an interest in Christ but those that turn from their sins, nor can any turn from their sins but by the strength of the grace of Christ.—*For this is my covenant with them*—this, that the deliverer shall come to them—this, that my Spirit shall not depart from them, as it follows, Isa. lix. 21. God's gracious intentions concerning Israel were made the matter of a covenant, which the God that cannot lie could not but be true and faithful to. They were the *children of the covenant,* Acts iii. 25. The apostle adds, *When I shall take away their sins,* which some think refers to Isa. xxvii. 9, or only to the foregoing words, to *turn away ungodliness.* Pardon of sin is laid as the foundation of all the blessings of the new covenant (Heb. viii. 12): *For I will be merciful.* Now from all this he infers that certainly God had great mercy in store for that people, something answerable to the extent of these rich promises: and he proves his inference (*v.* 29) by this truth · *For the gifts and callings of God are without repentance.* Repentance is sometimes taken for a change of mind, and so God never repents, for he is in one mind and who can turn him? Sometimes for a change of way, and that is here understood, intimating the constancy and unchangeableness of that love of God which is founded in election. Those gifts and callings are immutable; whom he so loves, he loves to the end. We find God repenting that he had given man a being (Gen. vi. 6, *It repented the Lord that he had made man),* and repenting that he had given a man honour and power (1 Sam. xv. 11, *It repenteth me that I have set up Saul to be king);* but we never find God repenting that he had given a man grace, or effectually called him; those gifts and callings are without repentance.

3. The time and extent of this conversion, when and where it is to be expected. It is called a mystery (*v.* 25), that which was not obvious, and which one would not expect upon the view of the present state of that people, who appeared generally so obstinate against Christ and Christianity that it was a riddle to talk of their unanimous conversion. The conversion of the Gentiles is called a mystery, Eph. iii. 3, 6, 9. The case of the rejected Jews seemed as bad now as that of the Gentiles had been. The work of conversion was carried on in a mystery. Now he would have them know so much of this mystery as to keep them humble: lest *you be wise in your own conceit,* that is, lest you be so much puffed up with your church-membership, and trample upon the Jews. Ignorance is the cause of our self-conceitedness. *I would not have you ignorant, lest you be wise in your own conceits.* Observe, (1.) Their present state: *Blindness, in part, is happened to Israel, v.* 25. Here is something to qualify it, that it is but in part; there is a remnant that see the things which belong to their peace, though part, the far greater part, are in blindness, *v.* 7, 8. To the same purport (*v.* 32): *God has concluded them all in unbelief,* shut them up as in a prison, given them over to their own hearts' lusts. Shutting up is sometimes put for conviction, as Gal. iii. 22. They all stand before God convicted of unbelief. They would not believe. "Why then," saith God, "you shall not." They peremptorily refused to submit to Christ and his government, which refusal of theirs was, as it were, entered upon record in the court of heaven, and was conclusive against them. (2.) When this blessed change should be: when the *fulness of the Gentiles shall come in,* when the gospel has had its intended success, and made its progress in the Gentile world; compare *v.* 12. The Jews shall continue in blindness, till God hath performed his whole work among the Gentiles, and then their turn will come next to be remembered. This was the purpose and ordination of God, for wise and holy ends; things should not be ripe for the Jews' conversion till the church was replenished with the Gentiles, that it might appear that God's taking them again was not because he had need of them, but of his own free grace. (3.) The extent of it: *All Israel shall be saved, v.* 26. He will *have mercy upon all, v.* 32. Not every individual person, but the body of the people. Not that ever they should be restored to their covenant of peculiarity again, to have their priesthood, and temple, and ceremonies again (an end is put to all those things); but they should be brought to believe in Christ the true Messiah whom they crucified, and be incorporated in the Christian church, and become one sheep-fold with the Gentiles under Christ the great Shepherd. But the question is concerning the accomplishment of all this. [1.] Some think it is done already, when before, and in, and after, the destruction of Jerusalem by the Romans, multitudes of the Jews were convinced of their infidelity, and turned Christians; so many that, considering how many millions of them were cut off in the destruction, we may reasonably conclude that of those who survived the greater part were Christians, and embodied in the Christian church, and it was a very inconsiderable number that persisted obstinately. For many ages Judea had, as other Christian provinces, their ministers and churches, and a face of religion. And most of this work, they suppose, was done towards the close of the ministry of the apostles, when the Gentiles had generally come in. [2.] Others think that it is yet to have its accomplishment towards the end of the world—that those Jews which yet wonder-

fully remain distinct from the rest of the nations by their names, customs, and religion, and are very numerous, especially in the Levant parts, shall, by the working of the Spirit with the word, be convinced of their sin, and brought generally to embrace the Christian faith, and to join in with the Christian churches, which will contribute much to their strength and beauty. Alas! who shall live when God doeth this?

33 O the depth of the riches both
of the wisdom and knowledge of God!
how unsearchable *are* his judgments,
and his ways past finding out! 34
For who hath known the mind of the
Lord? or who hath been his counsellor? 35 Or who hath first given to
him, and it shall be recompensed unto
him again? 36 For of him, and
through him, and to him, *are* all
things: to whom *be* glory for ever.
Amen.

The apostle having insisted so largely, through the greatest part of this chapter, upon reconciling the rejection of the Jews with the divine goodness, he concludes here with the acknowledgment and admiration of the divine wisdom and sovereignty in all this. Here the apostle does with great affection and awe adore,

I. The secrecy of the divine counsels: *O the depth!* in these proceedings towards the Jews and Gentiles; or, in general, the whole mystery of the gospel, which we cannot fully comprehend.—*The riches of the wisdom and knowledge of God,* the abundant instances of his wisdom and knowledge in contriving and carrying on the work of our redemption by Christ, a depth which the angels pry into, 1 Pet. i. 12. Much more may it puzzle any human understanding to give an account of the methods, and reasons, and designs, and compass of it. Paul was as well acquainted with the mysteries of the kingdom of God as ever any mere man was; and yet he confesses himself at a loss in the contemplation, and, despairing to find the bottom, he humbly sits down at the brink, and adores the depth. Those that know most in this state of imperfection cannot but be most sensible of their own weakness and short-sightedness, and that after all their researches, and all their attainments in those researches, while they are here they cannot order their speech by reason of darkness. Praise is silent to thee, Ps. lxv. 1.—*The depth of the riches.* Men's riches of all kinds are shallow, you may soon see the bottom; but God's riches are deep (Ps. xxxvi. 6): *Thy judgments are a great deep.* There is not only depth in the divine counsels, but riches too, which denotes an abundance of that which is precious and valuable, so complete are the dimensions of the divine counsels; they have not only depth and height, but *breadth and length* (Eph. iii. 18), and that passing knowledge, *v.* 19.—*Riches of the wisdom and knowledge of God.* His seeing all things by one clear, and certain, and infallible view—all things that are, or ever were, or ever shall be,—that all is naked and open before him: there is his knowledge. His ruling and ordering all things, directing and disposing them to his own glory, and bringing about his own purposes and counsels in all; this is his *wisdom.* And the vast extent of both these is such a depth as is past our fathoming, and we may soon lose ourselves in the contemplation of them. Such *knowledge is too wonderful for me,* Ps. cxxxix. 6. Compare *v.* 17, 18.—*How unsearchable are his judgments!* that is, his counsels and purposes: and his *ways,* that is, the execution of these counsels and purposes. We know not what he designs. When the wheels are set in motion, and Providence has begun to work, yet we know not what he has in view; it is *past finding out.* This does not only overturn all our positive conclusions about the divine counsels, but it also checks all our curious enquiries. Secret things belong not to us, Deut. xxix. 29. God's way is in the sea, Ps. lxxvii. 19. Compare Job xxiii. 8, 9; Ps. xcvii. 2. What he does we know not now, John xiii. 7. We cannot give a reason of God's proceedings, nor by searching find out God. See Job v. 9; ix. 10. The judgments of his mouth, and the way of our duty, blessed be God, are plain and easy, it is a high-way; but the judgments of his hands, and the ways of his providence, are dark and mysterious, which therefore we must not pry into, but silently adore and acquiesce in. The apostle speaks this especially with reference to that strange turn, the casting off of the Jews and the entertainment of the Gentiles, with a purpose to take in the Jews again in due time; these were strange proceedings, the choosing of some, the refusing of others, and neither according to the probabilities of human conjecture. Even so, Father, because it seemed good in thine eyes. These are methods unaccountable, concerning which we must say, *O the depth!—Past finding out, ἀνεξιχνίαστοι—cannot be traced.* God leaves no prints nor footsteps behind him, does not make a path to shine after him; but his paths of providence are new every morning. He does not go the same way so often as to make a track of it. *How little a portion is heard of him!* Job xxvi. 14. It follows (*v.* 34), *For who hath known the mind of the Lord?* Is there any creature made of his cabinet-council, or laid, as Christ was, in the bosom of the Father? Is there any to whom he has imparted his counsels, or that is able, upon the view of his providences, to know the way that he takes? There is so vast a distance and disproportion between God and man, between the Creator and the creature, as for ever excludes the thought of such an intimacy and familiarity. The apostle makes the same challenge (1 Cor. ii. 16): *For who hath known the mind of the Lord?* And yet there he adds, *But we have the mind of Christ*, which intimates that through Christ true believers, who have his Spirit, know so much of the mind of God as is necessary to their happiness. He that knew the mind of the Lord has declared him, John i. 18. And so, though we know not the mind of the Lord, yet, if we have the mind of Christ, we have enough. *The secret of the Lord is with those that fear him*, Ps. xxv. 14. *Shall I hide from Abraham the thing which I do?* See John xv. 15.—*Or who has been his counsellor?* He needs no counsellor, for he is infinitely wise; nor is any creature capable of being his counsellor; this would be like lighting a candle to the sun. This seems to refer to that scripture (Isa. xl. 13, 14), *Who hath directed the Spirit of the Lord, or, being his counsellor, hath taught him? With whom took he counsel?* &c. It is the substance of God's challenge to Job concerning the work of creation (Job xxxviii.), and is applicable to all the methods of his providence. It is nonsense for any man to prescribe to God, or to teach him how to govern the world.

II. The sovereignty of the divine counsels. In all these things God acts as a free agent, does what he will, because he will, and gives not account of any of his matters (Job xxiii. 13; xxxiii. 13), and yet there is no unrighteousness with him. To clear which,

1. He challenges any to prove God a debtor to him (*v.* 35): *Who hath first given to him?* Who is there of all the creatures that can prove God is beholden to him? Whatever we do for him, or devote to him, it must be with that acknowledgment, which is for ever a bar to such demands (1 Chron. xxix. 14): *Of thine own we have given thee.* All the duties we can perform are not requitals, but rather restitutions. If any can prove that God is his debtor, the apostle here stands bound for the payment, and proclaims, in God's name, that payment is ready: *It shall be recompensed to him again.* It is certain God will let nobody lose by him; but never any one yet durst make a demand of this kind, or attempt to prove it. This is here suggested, (1.) To silence the clamours of the Jews. When God took away their visible church-privileges from them, he did but take his own: and may he not do what he will with his own—give or withhold his grace where and when he pleases? (2.) To silence the insultings of the Gentiles. When God sent the gospel among them, and gave so many of them grace and wisdom to accept of it, it was not because he owed them so much favour, or that they could challenge it as a debt, but of his own good pleasure.

2. He resolves all into the sovereignty of God (*v.* 36): *For of him, and through him, and to him, are all things*, that is, God is all in all. All things in heaven and earth (especially those things which relate to our salvation, the things which belong to our peace) are of him by way of creation, through him by way of providential influence, that they may be to him in their final tendency and result. Of God as the spring and fountain of all, through Christ, God-man, as the conveyance, to God as the ultimate end. These three include, in general, all God's causal relations to his creatures: of him as the first efficient cause, through him as the supreme directing cause, to him as the ultimate final cause; for the Lord hath made all for himself, Rev. iv. 11. If all be of him and through him, there is all the reason in the world that all should be to him and for him. It is a necessary circulation; if the rivers receive their waters from the sea, they return them to the sea again, Eccl. i. 7. To do all to the glory of God is to make a virtue of necessity; for all shall in the end be to him, whether we will or no. And so he concludes with a short doxology: *To whom be glory for ever, Amen.* God's universal agency as the first cause, the sovereign ruler, and the last end, ought to be the matter of our adoration. Thus all his works do praise him objectively; but his saints do bless him actively; they hand that praise to him which all the creatures do minister matter for, Ps. cxlv. 10. Paul had been discoursing at large of the counsels of God concerning man, sifting the point with a great deal of accuracy; but, after all, he concludes with the acknowledgment of the divine sovereignty, as that into which all these things must be ultimately resolved, and in which alone the mind can safely and sweetly rest. This is, if not the scholastic way, yet the Christian way, of disputation. Whatever are the premises, let God's glory be the conclusion; especially when we come to talk of the divine counsels and actings, it is best for us to turn our arguments into awful and serious adorations. The glorified saints, that see furthest into these mysteries, never dispute, but praise to eternity.

CHAP. XII.

The apostle, having at large cleared and confirmed the prime fundamental doctrines of Christianity, comes in the next place to press the principal duties. We mistake our religion if we look upon it only as a system of notions and a guide to speculation. No, it is a practical religion, that tends to the right ordering of the conversation. It is designed not only to inform our judgments, but to reform our hearts and lives. From the method of the apostle's writing in this, as in some other of the epistles (as from the management of the principal ministers of state in Christ's kingdom) the stewards of the mysteries of God may take direction how to divide the word of truth: not to press duty abstracted from privilege, nor privilege abstracted from duty; but let both go together, with a complicated design, they will greatly promote and befriend each other. The duties are drawn from the privileges, by way of inference. The foundation of Christian practice must be laid in Christian knowledge and faith. We must first understand how we receive Christ Jesus the Lord, and then we shall know the better how to walk in him. There is a great deal of duty prescribed in this chapter. The exhortations are short and pithy, briefly summing up what is good, and what the Lord our God in Christ requires of us. It is an abridgment of the Christian directory, an excellent collection of rules for the right ordering of the conversation, as becomes the gospel. It is joined to the foregoing discourse by the word "therefore." It is the practical application of doctrinal truths that is the life of preaching. He had been discoursing at large of justification by faith, and of the riches of free grace, and the pledges and assurances we have of the glory that is to be revealed. Hence carnal libertines would be apt to infer, "Therefore we may live as we list, and walk in the way of our hearts and the sight of our eyes." No this does not follow; the faith that justifies is a faith that "works by love." And there is no other way to heaven but the way of holiness and obedience. Therefore what God hath joined together let no man put asunder. The particular exhortations of this chapter are reducible to the three principal heads of Christian duty: our duty to God, to ourselves, and to our brother. The grace of God teaches us, in general, to live "godly, soberly, and righteously;" and to deny all that which is contrary hereunto. Now this chapter will give us to understand what godliness, sobriety, and righteousness, are, though somewhat intermixed.

I BESEECH you therefore, brethren, by the mercies of God,
that ye present your bodies a living
sacrifice, holy, acceptable unto God,
which is your reasonable service. 2
And be not conformed to this world:
but be ye transformed by the renewing of your mind, that ye may
prove what *is* that good, and acceptable, and perfect, will of God. 3
For I say, through the grace given
unto me, to every man that is among
you, not to think *of himself* more
highly than he ought to think; but
to think soberly, according as God
hath dealt to every man the measure
of faith. 4 For as we have many
members in one body, and all members have not the same office: 5
So we, *being* many, are one body
in Christ, and every one members
one of another. 6 Having then
gifts differing according to the grace
that is given to us, whether prophecy, *let us prophesy* according to
the proportion of faith; 7 Or ministry, *let us wait* on *our* ministering: or he that teacheth, on teaching; 8 Or he that exhorteth, on
exhortation: he that giveth, *let him
do it* with simplicity; he that ruleth,
with diligence; he that showeth
mercy, with cheerfulness. 9 *Let*
love be without dissimulation. Abhor that which is evil; cleave to
that which is good. 10 *Be* kindly
affectioned one to another with brotherly love; in honour preferring
one another; 11 Not slothful in
business; fervent in spirit; serving
the Lord; 12 Rejoicing in hope;
patient in tribulation; continuing
instant in prayer; 13 Distributing
to the necessity of saints; given to
hospitality. 14 Bless them which
persecute you: bless, and curse not.
15 Rejoice with them that do rejoice, and weep with them that weep.
16 *Be* of the same mind one toward
another. Mind not high things, but
condescend to men of low estate.
Be not wise in your own conceits.
17 Recompense to no man evil for
evil. Provide things honest in the
sight of all men. 18 If it be possible, as much as lieth in you, live
peaceably with all men. 19 Dearly
beloved, avenge not yourselves, but
rather give place unto wrath: for it is
written, Vengeance *is* mine; I will repay, saith the Lord. 20 Therefore if
thine enemy hunger, feed him; if he
thirst, give him drink: for in so doing
thou shalt heap coals of fire on his
head. 21 Be not overcome of evil,
but overcome evil with good.

We may observe here, according to the scheme mentioned in the contents, the apostle's exhortations,

I. Concerning our duty to God. We see what is godliness.

1. It is to surrender ourselves to God, and so to lay a good foundation. We must first give our own selves unto the Lord, 2 Cor. viii. 5. This is here pressed as the spring of all duty and obedience, *v.* 1, 2. Man consists of body and soul, Gen. ii. 7; Eccl. xii. 7.

(1.) The body must be presented to him, *v.* 1. *The body is for the Lord, and the Lord for the body,* 1 Cor. vi. 13, 14. The exhortation is here introduced very pathetically: *I beseech you, brethren.* Though he was a great apostle, yet he calls the meanest Christians *brethren,* a term of affection and concern. He uses entreaty; this is the gospel way: *As though God did beseech you by us,* 2 Cor. v. 20. Though he might with authority command, yet for love's sake he rather beseeches, Philem. *v.* 8, 9. The *poor useth entreaty,* Prov. xviii. 23. This is to insinuate the exhortation, that it might come with the more pleasing power. Many are sooner wrought upon if they be accosted kindly, are more easily led than driven. Now observe,

[1.] The duty pressed—to present our *bodies a living sacrifice,* alluding to the sacrifices under the law, which were presented or set before God at the altar, ready to be offered to him. *Your bodies*—your whole selves; so expressed because under the law the bodies of beasts were offered in sacrifice, 1 Cor. vi. 20. Our bodies and spirits are intended. The offering was sacrificed by the priest, but presented by the offerer, who transferred to God all his right, title, and interest in it, by laying his hand on the head of it. Sacrifice is here taken for whatsoever is by God's own appointment dedicated to himself; see 1 Pet. ii. 5. We are temple, priest, and sacrifice, as Christ was in his peculiar sacrificing. There were sacrifices of atonement and sacrifices of acknowledgment.

Christ, who was once offered to bear the sins of many, is the only sacrifice of atonement; but our persons and performances, tendered to God through Christ our priest, are as sacrifices of acknowledgment to the honour of God. Presenting them denotes a voluntary act, done by virtue of that absolute despotic power which the will has over the body and all the members of it. It must be a free-will offering. Your bodies; not your beasts. Those legal offerings, as they had their power from Christ, so they had their period in Christ. The presenting of the body to God implies not only the avoiding of the sins that are committed with or against the body, but the using of the body as a servant of the soul in the service of God. It is to *glorify God with our bodies* (1 Cor. vi. 20), to engage our bodies in the duties of immediate worship, and in a diligent attendance to our particular callings, and be willing to suffer for God with our bodies, when we are called to it. It is to yield the members of our bodies as instruments of righteousness, *ch.* vi. 13. Though bodily exercise alone profits little, yet in its place it is a proof and product of the dedication of our souls to God. *First,* Present them a living sacrifice; not killed, as the sacrifices under the law. A Christian makes his body a sacrifice to God, though he does not give it to be burned. A body sincerely devoted to God is a living sacrifice. A living sacrifice, by way of allusion—that which was dead of itself might not be eaten, much less sacrificed, Deut. xiv. 21; and by way of opposition—"The sacrifice was to be slain, but you may be sacrificed, and yet live on"—an unbloody sacrifice. The barbarous heathen sacrificed their children to their idol-gods, not living, but slain sacrifices: but God will have mercy, and not such sacrifice, though life is forfeited to him. A *living* sacrifice, that is, inspired with the spiritual life of the soul. It is Christ living in the soul by faith that makes the body a living sacrifice, Gal. ii. 20. Holy love kindles the sacrifices, puts life into the duties; see *ch.* vi. 13. *Alive,* that is, to God, *v.* 11. *Secondly,* They must be holy. There is a relative holiness in every sacrifice, as dedicated to God. But, besides this, there must be that real holiness which consists in an entire rectitude of heart and life, by which we are conformed in both to the nature and will of God: even our bodies must not be made the instruments of sin and uncleanness, but set apart for God, and put to holy uses, as the vessels of the tabernacle were holy, being devoted to God's service. It is the soul that is the proper subject of holiness; but a sanctified soul communicates a holiness to the body it actuates and animates. That is holy which is according to the will of God; when the bodily actions are so, the body is holy. They are the *temples of the Holy Ghost,* 1 Cor. vi. 19. *Possess the body in sanctification,* 1 Thess. iv. 4, 5.

[2.] The arguments to enforce this, which are three:—*First,* Consider the mercies of God: *I beseech you by the mercies of God.* An affectionate obtestation, and which should melt us into a compliance: διὰ τῶν οἰκτιρμῶν τοῦ Θεοῦ. This is an argument most sweetly cogent. There is the mercy that is in God and the mercy that is from God—mercy in the spring and mercy in the streams: both are included here; but especially gospel-mercies (mentioned *ch.* xi.), the transferring of what the Jews forfeited and lost by their unbelief unto us Gentiles (Eph. iii. 4—6) the sure mercies of David, Isa. lv. 3. God is a merciful God, therefore let us present our bodies to him; he will be sure to use them kindly, and knows how to consider the frames of them, for he is of infinite compassion. We receive from him every day the fruits of his mercy, particularly mercy to our bodies: he made them, he maintains them, he bought them, he has put a great dignity upon them. It is of the Lord's mercies that we are not consumed, that our souls are held in life; and the greatest mercy of all is that Christ hath made not his body only, but his soul, an offering for sin, that he gave himself for us and gives himself to us. Now surely we cannot but be studying what we shall render to the Lord for all this. And what shall we render? Let us render ourselves as an acknowledgment of all these favours—all we are, all we have, all we can do; and, after all, it is but very poor returns for very rich receivings: and yet, because it is what we have, *Secondly,* It is *acceptable to God.* The great end we should all labour after is to be accepted of the Lord (2 Cor. v. 9), to have him well-pleased with our persons and performances. Now these living sacrifices are acceptable to God; while the sacrifices of the wicked, though fat and costly, are an abomination to the Lord. It is God's great condescension that he will vouchsafe to accept of any thing in us; and we can desire no more to make us happy; and, if the presenting of ourselves will but please him, we may easily conclude that we cannot bestow ourselves better. *Thirdly,* It is our *reasonable service.* There is an act of reason in it; for it is the soul that presents the body. Blind devotion, that has ignorance for the mother and nurse of it, is fit to be paid only to those dunghill-gods that have eyes and see not. Our God must be served in the spirit and with the understanding. There is all the reason in the world for it, and no good reason can possibly be produced against it. *Come now, and let us reason together,* Isa. i. 18. God does not impose upon us any thing hard or unreasonable, but that which is altogether agreeable to the principles of right reason. Τὴν λογικὴν λατρείαν ὑμῶν—*your service according to the word;* so it may be read. The word of God does not leave out the body in holy worship. That service only is acceptable to God which is according to the written word. It must be gospel worship, spiritual worship. That is a reasonable service which we are able and ready to give a reason for, in which we understand ourselves. God deals with us as with rational creatures, and will have us so to deal with him. Thus must the body be presented to God.

(2.) The mind must be renewed for him. This is pressed (*v.* 2): "*Be you transformed by the renewing of your mind;* see to it that there be a saving change wrought in you, and that it be carried on." Conversion and sanctification are the renewing of the mind, a change not of the substance, but of the qualities of the soul. It is the same with making a new heart and a new spirit—new dispositions and inclinations, new sympathies and antipathies; the understanding enlightened, the conscience softened, the thoughts rectified; the will bowed to the will of God, and the affections made spiritual and heavenly: so that the man is not what he was—old things are passed away, all things are become new; he acts from new principles, by new rules, with new designs. The mind is the acting ruling part of us; so that the renewing of the mind is the renewing of the whole man, for out of it are the *issues of life*, Prov. iv. 23. The progress of sanctification, dying to sin more and more and living to righteousness more and more, is the carrying on of this renewing work, till it be perfected in glory. This is called the *transforming* of us; it is like putting on a new shape and figure. Μεταμορφοῦσθε—*Be you metamorphosed.* The transfiguration of Christ is expressed by this word (Matt. xvii. 2), when he put on a heavenly glory, which made his face to shine like the sun; and the same word is used 2 Cor. iii. 18, where we are said to be *changed into the same image from glory to glory.* This transformation is here pressed as a duty; not that we can work such a change ourselves: we could as soon make a new world as make a new heart by any power of our own; it is God's work, Ezek. xi. 19; xxxvi. 26, 27. But *be you transformed,* that is, "use the means which God hath appointed and ordained for it." It is God that turns us, and then we are turned; but we must *frame our doings to turn,* Hos. v. 4. "Lay your souls under the changing transforming influences of the blessed Spirit; seek unto God for grace in the use of all the means of grace." Though the new man be created of God, yet we must put it on (Eph. iv. 24), and be pressing forward towards perfection. Now in this verse we may further observe,

[1.] What is the great enemy to this renewing, which we must avoid; and that is, conformity to this world: *Be not conformed to this world.* All the disciples and followers of the Lord Jesus must be nonconformists to this world. Μὴ συσχηματίζεσθε—*Do not fashion yourselves* according to the world. We must not conform to the things of the world; they are mutable, and the fashion of them is passing away. Do not conform either to the lusts of the flesh or the lusts of the eye. We must not conform to the men of the world, of that world which lies in wickedness, not walk according *to the course of this world* (Eph. ii. 2); that is, we must not follow a multitude to do evil, Exod. xxiii. 2. If sinners entice us, we must not consent to them, but in our places witness against them. Nay, even in things indifferent, and which are not in themselves sinful, we must so far not conform to the custom and way of the world as not to act by the world's dictates as our chief rule, nor to aim at the world's favours as our highest end. True Christianity consists much in a sober singularity. Yet we must take heed of the extreme of affected rudeness and moroseness, which some run into. In civil things, the light of nature and the custom of nations are intended for our guidance; and the rule of the gospel in those cases is a rule of direction, not a rule of contrariety.

[2.] What is the great effect of this renewing, which we must labour after: *That you may prove what is that good, and acceptable, and perfect will of God.* By the will of God here we are to understand his revealed will concerning our duty, what the Lord our God requires of us. This is the will of God in general, even our sanctification, that will which we pray may be done by us as it is done by the angels; especially his will as it is revealed in the New Testament, where he hath in these last days spoken to us by his Son. *First,* The will of God is *good, and acceptable, and perfect;* three excellent properties of a law. It is good (Mic. vi. 8); it is exactly consonant to the eternal reason of good and evil. It is good in itself. It is good for us. Some think the evangelical law is here called good, in distinction from the ceremonial law, which consisted of *statutes that were not good,* Ezek. xx. 25. It is acceptable, it is pleasing to God; that and that only is so which is prescribed by him. The only way to attain his favour as the end is to conform to his will as the rule. It is perfect, to which nothing can be added. The revealed will of God is a sufficient rule of faith and practice, containing all things which tend to the perfection of the man of God, to furnish us thoroughly to every good work, 2 Tim. iii. 16, 17. *Secondly,* That it concerns Christians to prove what is that will of God which is good, and acceptable, and perfect; that is, to know it with judgment and approbation, to know it experimentally, to know the excellency of the will of God by the experience of a conformity to it. It is to approve *things that are excellent* (Phil. i. 10); it is δοκιμάζειν (the same word that is used here) *to try* things that differ, in doubtful cases readily to apprehend what the will of God is and to close in with it. It is to be *of quick understanding in the fear of the Lord,* Isa. xi. 3. *Thirdly,* That those are best able to prove what is the good, and acceptable, and perfect will of God, who are transformed by the renewing of their mind. A living principle of grace is in the soul, as far as it prevails, an unbiassed unprejudiced judgment concerning the things of God. It disposes the soul to receive and entertain the revelations of the divine will. The promise is (John vii. 17), *If any man will do his will, he shall know of the doctrine.* A good wit can dispute and distinguish about the will of God; while an honest, humble heart, that has spiritual senses exercised, and is delivered into the mould of the word, loves it, and practises it, and has the relish and savour of it. Thus to be godly is to surrender ourselves to God.

2. When this is done, to serve him in all manner of gospel obedience. Some hints of this we have here (*v.* 11, 12), *Serving the Lord.* Wherefore do we present ourselves to him, but that we may serve him? Acts xxvii. 23, *Whose I am;* and then it follows, *whom I serve.* To be religious is to serve God. How? (1.) We must make a business of it, and not be slothful in that business. *Not slothful in business.* There is the business of the world, that of our particular calling, in which we must not be slothful, 1 Thess. iv. 11. But this seems to be meant of the business of serving the Lord, our Father's business, Luke ii. 49. Those that would approve themselves Christians indeed must make religion their business—must choose it, and learn it, and give themselves to it; they must love it, and employ themselves in it, and abide by it, as their great and main business. And, having made it our business, we must not be slothful in it: not desire our own ease, and consult that, when it comes in competition with our duty. We must not drive on slowly in religion. Slothful servants will be reckoned with as wicked servants. (2.) We must be *fervent in spirit, serving the Lord.* God must be served with the spirit (*ch.* i. 9; John iv. 24), under the influences of the Holy Spirit. Whatever we do in religion it is pleasing to God no further than it is done with our spirits wrought upon by the Spirit of God. And there must be fervency in the spirit—a holy zeal, and warmth, and ardency of affection in all we do, as those that love God not only with the heart and soul, but with all our hearts, and with all our souls. This is the holy fire that kindles the sacrifice, and carries it up to heaven, an offering of a sweet-smelling savour.—*Serving the Lord.* Τῷ καιρῷ δουλεύοντες (so some copies read it), *serving the time,* that is, improving your opportunities and making the best of them, complying with the present seasons of grace. (3.) *Rejoicing in hope.* God is worshipped and honoured by our hope and trust in him, especially when we rejoice in that hope, take a complacency in that confidence, which argues a great assurance of the reality and a great esteem of the excellency of the good hoped for. (4.) *Patient in tribulation.* Thus also God is served, not only by working for him when he calls us to work, but by sitting still quietly when he calls us to suffer. Patience for God's sake, and with an eye to his will and glory, is true piety. Observe, Those that rejoice in hope are likely to be patient in tribulation. It is a believing prospect of the joy set before us that bears up the spirit under all outward pressure. (5.) *Continuing instant in prayer.* Prayer is a friend to hope and patience, and we do in it serve the Lord. Προσκαρτεροῦντες. It signifies both fervency and perseverance in prayer. We should not be cold in the duty, nor soon weary of it, Luke xviii. 1; 1 Thess. v. 17; Eph. vi. 18; Col. iv. 2. This is our duty which immediately respects God.

II. Concerning our duty which respects ourselves; this is sobriety.

1. A sober opinion of ourselves, *v.* 3. It is ushered in with a solemn preface: *I say, through the grace given unto me:* the grace of wisdom, by which he understood the necessity and excellency of this duty; the grace of apostleship, by which he had authority to press and enjoin it. "I say it, who am commissioned to say it, in God's name. I say it, and it is not for you to gainsay it." It is said to every one of us, one as well as another. Pride is a sin that is bred in the bone of all of us, and we have therefore each of us need to be cautioned and armed against it.—*Not to think of himself more highly than he ought to think.* We must take heed of having too great an opinion of ourselves, or putting too high a valuation upon our own judgments, abilities, persons, performances. We must not be self-conceited, nor esteem too much our own wisdom and other attainments, not think ourselves to be something, Gal. vi. 3. There is a high thought of ourselves which we may and must have to think ourselves too good to be the slaves of sin and drudges to this world. But, on the other hand, we should think soberly, that is, we must have a low and modest opinion of ourselves and our own abilities, our gifts and graces, according to what we have received from God, and not otherwise. We must not be confident and hot in matters of doubtful disputation; not stretch ourselves beyond our line; not judge and censure those that differ from us; not desire to make a fair show in the flesh. These and the like are the fruits of a sober opinion of ourselves. The words will bear yet another sense agreeable enough. *Of himself* is not in the original; therefore it may be read, *That no man be wise above what he ought to be wise, but be wise unto sobriety.* We must not exercise ourselves in things too high for us (Ps. cxxxi. 1, 2), not intrude into those things which we have not seen (Col. ii. 18), those secret things which belong not to

us (Deut. xxix. 29), not covet to be wise above what is written. There is a knowledge that puffs up, which reaches after forbidden fruit. We must take heed of this, and labour after that knowledge which tends to sobriety, to the rectifying of the heart and the reforming of the life. Some understand it of the sobriety which keeps us in our own place and station, from intruding into the gifts and offices of others. See an instance of this sober modest care in the exercise of the greatest spiritual gifts, 2 Cor. x. 13—15. To this head refers also that exhortation (*v.* 16), *Be not wise in your own conceits.* It is good to be wise, but it is bad to think ourselves so; for there is more hope of a fool than of him that is wise in his own eyes. It was an excellent thing for Moses to have his face shine and not know it. Now the reasons why we must have such a sober opinion of ourselves, our own abilities and attainments, are these:—

(1.) Because whatever we have that is good, *God hath dealt* it to us; every good and perfect gift *comes from above,* James i. 17. What have we that we have not received? And, if we have received it, why then do we boast? 1 Cor. iv. 7. The best and most useful man in the world is no more, no better, than what the free grace of God makes him every day. When we are thinking of ourselves, we must remember to think not how we have attained, as though our might and the power of our hand had gotten us these gifts; but think how kind God hath been to us, for it is he that gives us power to do any thing that is good, and in him is all our sufficiency.

(2.) Because God deals out his gifts in a certain measure: According to *the measure of faith.* Observe, The measure of spiritual gifts he calls the measure of faith, for this is the radical grace. What we have and do that is good is so far right and acceptable as it is founded in faith, and flows from faith, and no further. Now faith, and other spiritual gifts with it, are dealt by measure, according as Infinite Wisdom sees meet for us. Christ had the Spirit given him without measure, John iii. 34. But the saints have it by measure; see Eph. iv. 7. Christ, who had gifts without measure, was meek and lowly; and shall we, that are stinted, be proud and self-conceited?

(3.) Because God has dealt out gifts to others as well as to us: *Dealt to every man.* Had we the monopoly of the Spirit, or a patent to be sole proprietors of spiritual gifts, there might be some pretence for this conceitedness of ourselves; but others have their share as well as we. God is a common Father, and Christ a common root, to all the saints, who all derive virtue from him; and therefore it ill becomes us to lift up ourselves, and to despise others, as if we only were the people in favour with Heaven, and wisdom should die with us. This reasoning he illustrates by a comparison taken from the members of the natural body (as 1 Cor. xii. 12; Eph. iv. 16): *As we have many members in one body,* &c. *v.* 4, 5. Here observe, [1.] All the saints make up one body in Christ, who is the head of the body, and the common centre of their unity. Believers lie not in the world as a confused disorderly heap, but are organized and knit together, as they are united to one common head, and actuated and animated by one common Spirit. [2.] Particular believers are members of this body, constituent parts, which speak them less than the whole, and in relation to the whole, deriving life and spirits from the head. Some members in the body are bigger and more useful than others, and each receives spirits from the head according to its proportion. If the little finger should receive as much nourishment as the leg, how unseemly and prejudicial would it be! We must remember that we are not the whole; we think above what is meet if we think so; we are but parts and members. [3.] All *the members have not the same office* (*v.* 4), but each hath its respective place and work assigned it. The office of the eye is to see, the office of the hand is to work, &c. So in the mystical body, some are qualified for, and called to, one sort of work; others are, in like manner, fitted for, and called to, another sort of work. Magistrates, ministers, people, in a Christian commonwealth, have their several offices, and must not intrude one upon another, nor clash in the discharge of their several offices. [4.] Each member hath its place and office, for the good and benefit of the whole, and of every other member. We are not only members of Christ, but we are *members one of another, v.* 5. We stand in relation one to another; we are engaged to do all the good we can one to another, and to act in conjunction for the common benefit. See this illustrated at large, 1 Cor. xii. 14, &c. Therefore we must not be puffed up with a conceit of our own attainments, because, whatever we have, as we received it, so we received it not for ourselves, but for the good of others.

2. A sober use of the gifts that God hath given us. As we must not on the one hand be proud of our talents, so on the other hand we must not bury them. Take heed lest, under a pretence of humility and self-denial, we be slothful in laying out ourselves for the good of others. We must not say, "I am nothing, therefore I will sit still, and do nothing;" but, "I am nothing in myself, and therefore I will lay out myself to the utmost in the strength of the grace of Christ." He specifies the ecclesiastical offices appointed in particular churches, in the discharge of which each must study to do his own duty, for the preserving of order and the promoting of edification in the church, each knowing his place and fulfilling it. *Having then gifts.*

The following induction of particulars supplies the sense of this general. *Having gifts,* let us use them. Authority and ability for the ministerial work are the gift of God.—*Gifts differing.* The immediate design is different, though the ultimate tendency of all is the same. *According to the grace, χαρίσματα κατὰ τὴν χάριν.* The free grace of God is the spring and original of all the gifts that are given to men. It is grace that appoints the office, qualifies and inclines the person, works both to will and to do. There were in the primitive church extraordinary gifts of tongues, of discerning, of healing; but he speaks here of those that are ordinary. Compare 1 Cor. xii. 4; 1 Tim. iv. 14; 1 Pet. iv. 10. Seven particular gifts he specifies (*v.* 6—8), which seem to be meant of so many distinct offices, used by the prudential constitution of many of the primitive churches, especially the larger. There are two general ones here expressed by prophesying and ministering, the former the work of the bishops, the latter the work of the deacons, which were the only two standing officers, Phil. i. 1. But the particular work belonging to each of these might be, and it should seem was, divided and allotted by common consent and agreement, that it might be done the more effectually, because that which is every body's work is nobody's work, and he despatches his business best that is *vir unius negotii—a man of one business.* Thus David sorted the Levites (1 Chron. xxiii. 4, 5), and in this wisdom is profitable to direct. The five latter will therefore be reduced to the two former.

(1.) *Prophecy. Whether prophecy, let us prophesy according to the proportion of faith.* It is not meant of the extraordinary gifts of foretelling things to come, but the ordinary office of preaching the word: so *prophesying* is taken, 1 Cor. xiv. 1—3, &c.; xi. 4; 1 Thess. v. 20. The work of the Old-Testament prophets was not only to foretel future things, but to warn the people concerning sin and duty, and to be their remembrancers concerning that which they knew before. And thus gospel preachers are prophets, and do indeed, as far as the revelation of the word goes, foretel things to come. Preaching refers to the eternal condition of the children of men, points directly at a future state. Now those that preach the word must do it *according to the proportion of faith—κατὰ τὴν ἀναλογίαν τῆς πίστεως,* that is, [1.] As to the manner of our prophesying, it must be according to the proportion of the grace of faith. He had spoken (*v.* 3) of the measure of faith dealt to every man. Let him that preaches set all the faith he hath on work, to impress the truths he preaches upon his own heart in the first place. As people cannot hear well, so ministers cannot preach well, without faith. First believe and then speak, Ps. cxvi. 10; 2 Cor. iv. 13. And we must remember the proportion of faith—that, though all men have not faith, yet a great many have besides ourselves; and therefore we must allow others to have a share of knowledge and ability to instruct, as well as we, even those that in less things differ from us. "*Hast thou faith? Have it to thyself;* and do not make it a ruling rule to others, remembering that thou hast but thy proportion." [2.] As to the matter of our prophesying, it must be according to the proportion of the doctrine of faith, as it is revealed in the holy scriptures of the Old and New Testament. By this rule of faith the Bereans tried Paul's preaching, Acts xvii. 11. Compare Acts xxvi. 22; Gal. i. 9. There are some staple-truths, as I may call them, some *prima axiomata—first axioms,* plainly and uniformly taught in the scripture, which are the touchstone of preaching, by which (though we must not despise prophesying) we must *prove all things,* and then *hold fast that which is good,* 1 Thess. v. 20, 21. Truths that are more dark must be examined by those that are more clear; and then entertained when they are found to agree and comport with the analogy of faith; for it is certain one truth can never contradict another. See here what ought to be the great care of preachers—to preach sound doctrine, according to the form of wholesome words, Tit. ii. 8; 2 Tim. i. 13. It is not so necessary that the prophesying be according to the proportion of art, the rules of logic and rhetoric; but it is necessary that it be according to the proportion of faith: for it is the word of faith that we preach. Now there are two particular works which he that prophesieth hath to mind—teaching and exhorting, proper enough to be done by the same person at the same time, and when he does the one let him mind that, when he does the other let him do that too as well as he can. If, by agreement between the ministers of a congregation, this work be divided, either constantly or interchangeably, so that one teaches and the other exhorts (that is, in our modern dialect, one expounds and the other preaches), let each do his work according to the proportion of faith. *First,* Let him that teacheth wait on teaching. Teaching is the bare explaining and proving of gospel truths, without practical application, as in the expounding of the scripture. *Pastors and teachers* are the same office (Eph. iv. 11), but the particular work is somewhat different. Now he that has a faculty of teaching, and has undertaken that province, let him stick to it. It is a good gift, let him use it, and give his mind to it. *He that teacheth, let him be in his teaching;* so some supply it, Ὁ διδάσκων, ἐν τῇ διδασκαλίᾳ. Let him be frequent and constant, and diligent in it; let him abide in that which is his proper work, and be in it as his element. See 1 Tim. iv. 15, 16, where it is explained by two words, ἐν τούτοις ἴσθι, and ἐπίμενε ἀυτοῖς, *be in these things* and *continue in them. Secondly,* Let him that *exhorteth* wait *on exhortation.* Let him give himself to that. This is the work of the pastor, as the former of the teacher; to apply gospel truths and rules more closely to the case and condition of the people, and to press upon them that which is more practical. Many that are very accurate in teaching may yet be very cold and unskilful in exhorting; and on the contrary. The one requires a clearer head, the other a warmer heart. Now where these gifts are evidently separated (that the one excels in the one and the other in the other) it conduces to edification to divide the work accordingly; and, whatsoever the work is that we undertake, let us mind it. To wait on our work is to bestow the best of our time and thoughts upon it, to lay hold of all opportunities for it, and to study not only to do it, but to do it well.

(2.) *Ministry.* If a man hath διακονίαν—*the office of a deacon,* or assistant to the pastor and teacher, let him use that office well—a churchwarden (suppose), an elder, or an overseer of the poor; and perhaps there were more put into these offices, and there was more solemnity in them, and a greater stress of care and business lay upon them in the primitive churches, than we are now well aware of. It includes all those offices which concern the τὰ ἔξω of the church, *the outward business of the house of God.* See Neh. xi. 16. *Serving tables,* Acts vi. 2. Now let him on whom this care of ministering is devolved attend to it with faithfulness and diligence; particularly, [1.] *He that giveth, let him do it with simplicity.* Those church-officers that were the stewards of the church's alms, collected money, and distributed it according as the necessities of the poor were. Let them do it ἐν ἁπλότητι—*liberally* and faithfully; not converting what they receive to their own use, nor distributing it with any sinister design, or with respect of persons: not froward and peevish with the poor, nor seeking pretences to put them by; but with all sincerity and integrity, having no other intention in it than to glorify God and do good. Some understand it in general of all almsgiving: He that hath wherewithal, let him give, and give plentifully and liberally; so the word is translated, 2 Cor. viii. 2; ix. 13. God loves a cheerful bountiful giver. [2.] *He that ruleth with diligence.* It should seem, he means those that were assistants to the pastors in exercising church-discipline, as their eyes, and hands, and mouth, in the government of the church, or those ministers that in the congregation did chiefly undertake and apply themselves to this ruling work; for we find those ruling that laboured in the word and doctrine, 1 Tim. v. 17. Now such must do it with diligence. The word denotes both care and industry to discover what is amiss, to reduce those that go astray, to reprove and admonish those that have fallen, to keep the church pure. Those must take a great deal of pains that will approve themselves faithful in the discharge of this trust, and not let slip any opportunity that may facilitate and advance that work. [3.] *He that showeth mercy with cheerfulness.* Some think it is meant in general of all that in any thing show mercy: Let them be willing to do it, and take a pleasure in it; God loves a cheerful giver. But it seems to be meant of some particular church-officers, whose work it was to take care of the sick and strangers; and those were generally widows that were in this matter servants to the church—deaconesses (1 Tim. v. 9, 10), though others, it is likely, might be employed. Now this must be done with cheerfulness. A pleasing countenance in acts of mercy is a great relief and comfort to the miserable; when they see it is not done grudgingly and unwillingly, but with pleasant looks and gentle words, and all possible indications of readiness and alacrity. Those that have to do with such as are sick and sore, and commonly cross and peevish, have need to put on not only patience, but cheerfulness, to make the work the more easy and pleasant to them, and the more acceptable to God.

III. Concerning that part of our duty which respects our brethren, of which we have many instances, in brief exhortations. Now all our duty towards one another is summed up in one word, and that a sweet word, *love.* In that is laid the foundation of all our mutual duty; and therefore the apostle mentions this first, which is the livery of Christ's disciples, and the great law of our religion: *Let love be without dissimulation;* not in compliment and pretence, but in reality; *not in word and tongue only,* 1 John iii. 18. The right love is love unfeigned; not as the kisses of an enemy, which are deceitful. We should be glad of an opportunity to *prove the sincerity of our love,* 2 Cor. viii. 8. More particularly, there is a love owing to our friends, and to our enemies. He specifies both.

1. To our friends. He that hath friends must show himself friendly. There is a mutual love that Christians owe, and must pay.

(1.) An affectionate love (*v.* 10): *Be kindly affectioned one to another, with brotherly love,* φιλόστοργοι—it signifies not only love, but a readiness and inclination to love, the most genuine and free affection, kindness flowing out as from a spring. It properly denotes the love of parents to their children, which, as it is the most tender, so it is the most natural, of any, unforced, unconstrained; such must our love be to one another, and such it will be where there is a new nature and the law of love is written in the heart. This kind affection puts us on to express ourselves both in word and action with the greatest courtesy and obligingness that may be.—*One to another.* This may recommend the grace of love to us, that, as it is made our duty to love others, so it is as much their duty to love us. And what can be sweeter on this side heaven than to love and be beloved? He that thus watereth shall be watered also himself.

(2.) A respectful love: *In honour preferring one another.* Instead of contending for superiority, let us be forward to give to others the pre-eminence. This is explained, Phil. ii. 3, *Let each esteem other better than themselves.* And there is this good reason for it, because, if we know our own hearts, we know more evil by ourselves than we do by any one else in the world. We should be forward to take notice of the gifts, and graces, and performances of our brethren, and value them accordingly, be more forward to praise another, and more pleased to hear another praised, than ourselves; *τῇ τιμῇ ἀλλήλους προηγοῦμενοι—going before,* or *leading one another in honour;* so some read it: not in taking honour, but in giving honour. "Strive which of you shall be most forward to pay respect to those to whom it is due, and to perform all Christian offices of love (which are all included in the word honour) to your brethren, as there is occasion. Let all your contention be which shall be most humble, and useful, and condescending." So the sense is the same with Tit. iii. 14, *Let them learn, προΐστασθαι—to go before in good works.* For though we must prefer others (as our translation reads it), and put on others, as more capable and deserving than ourselves, yet we must not make that an excuse for our lying by and doing nothing, nor under a pretence of honouring others, and their serviceableness and performances, indulge ourselves in ease and slothfulness. Therefore he immediately adds (*v.* 11), *Not slothful in business.*

(3.) A liberal love (*v.* 13): *Distributing to the necessities of saints.* It is but a mock love which rests in the verbal expressions of kindness and respect, while the wants of our brethren call for real supplies, and it is in the power of our hands to furnish them. [1.] It is no strange thing for saints in this world to want necessaries for the support of their natural life. In those primitive times prevailing persecutions must needs reduce many of the suffering saints to great extremities; and, still the poor, even the poor saints, we have always with us. Surely the things of this world are not the best things; if they were, the saints, who are the favourites of heaven, would not be put off with so little of them. [2.] It is the duty of those who have wherewithal to *distribute,* or (as it might better be read) to *communicate* to those necessities. It is not enough to draw out the soul, but we must draw out the purse, to the hungry. See Jam. ii. 15, 16; 1 John iii. 17. *Communicating—κοινωνοῦντες.* It intimates that our poor brethren have a kind of interest in that which God hath given us; and that our relieving them should come from a sense and fellow-feeling of their wants, as though we suffered with them. The charitable benevolence of the Philippians to Paul is called their communicating with his affliction, Phil. iv. 14. We must be ready, as we have ability and opportunity, to relieve any that are in want; but we are in a special manner bound to communicate to the saints. There is a common love owing to our fellow-creatures, but a special love owing to our fellow-christians (Gal. vi. 10), *Especially to those who are of the household of faith. Communicating, ταῖς μνείαις—to the memories* of the saints; so some of the ancients read it, instead of *ταῖς χρείαις.* There is a debt owing to the memory of those who through faith and patience inherit the promises—to value it, to vindicate it, to embalm it. Let the memory of the just be blessed; so some read Prov. x. 7. He mentions another branch of this bountiful love: *Given to hospitality.* Those who have houses of their own should be ready to entertain those who go about doing good, or who, for fear of persecution, are forced to wander for shelter. They had not then so much of the convenience of common inns as we have; or the wandering Christians durst not frequent them; or they had not wherewithal to bear the charges, and therefore it was a special kindness to bid them welcome on free-cost. Nor is it yet an antiquated superseded duty; as there is occasion, we must welcome strangers, for we know not the heart of a stranger. *I was a stranger, and you took me in,* is mentioned as one instance of the mercifulness of those that shall obtain mercy: *τὴν φιλοξενίαν διώκοντες—following* or *pursuing* hospitality. It intimates, not only that we must take opportunity, but that we must seek opportunity, thus to show mercy. As Abraham, who sat at the tent-door (Gen. xviii. 1), and Lot, who sat in the gate of Sodom (Gen. xix. 1), expecting travellers, whom they might meet and prevent with a kind invitation, and so they entertained angels unawares, Heb. xiii. 2.

(4.) A sympathizing love (*v.* 15): *Rejoice with those that do rejoice, and weep with those that weep.* Where there is a mutual love between the members of the mystical body, there will be such a fellow-feeling. See 1 Cor. xii. 26. True love will interest us in the sorrows and joys of one another, and teach us to make them our own. Observe the common mixture in this world, some rejoicing, and others weeping (as the people, Ezra iii. 12, 13), for the trial, as of other graces, so of brotherly love and Christian sympathy. Not that we must participate in the sinful mirths or mournings of any, but only in just and reasonable joys and sorrows: not envying those that prosper, but rejoicing with them; truly glad that others have the success and comfort which we have not; not despising those that are in trouble, but concerned for them, and ready to help them, as being ourselves in the body. This is to do as God does, who not only has *pleasure in the prosperity of his servants* (Ps. xxxv. 27), but is likewise *afflicted in all their afflictions,* Isa. lxiii. 9.

(5.) A united love: "*Be of the same mind one towards another* (*v.* 16), that is, labour, as much as you can, to agree in apprehension; and, wherein you come short of this, yet agree in affection; endeavour to be all one, not affecting to clash, and contradict, and thwart one another; but keep the unity of the Spirit in the bond of peace, Phil. ii. 2; iii. 15. 16; 1 Cor. i. 10; τὸ αὐτο εἰς ἀλλήλους φρονοῦντες—*wishing the same good* to others that you do to yourselves;" so some understand it. This is to love our brethren as ourselves, desiring their welfare as our own.

(6.) A condescending love: *Mind not high things, but condescend to men of low estate, v.* 16. True love cannot be without lowliness, Eph. iv. 1, 2; Phil. ii. 3. When our Lord Jesus washed his disciples' feet, to teach us brotherly love (John xiii. 5; xiv. 34), it was designed especially to intimate to us that to love one another aright is to be willing to stoop to the meanest offices of kindness for the good of one another. Love is a condescending grace: *Non bene conveniunt—majestas et amor—Majesty and love do but ill assort with each other.* Observe how it is pressed here. [1.] *Mind not high things.* We must not be ambitious of honour and preferment, nor look upon worldly pomp and dignity with any inordinate value or desire, but rather with a holy contempt. When David's advancements were high, his spirit was humble (Ps. cxxxi. 1): *I do not exercise myself in great matters.* The Romans, living in the imperial city, which reigned over the kings of the earth (Rev. xvii. 18), and was at that time in the meridian of its splendour, were perhaps ready to take occasion thence to think the better of themselves. Even the holy seed were tainted with this leaven. Roman Christians would be ready to look scornfully upon other Christians, as some citizens do upon the country; and therefore the apostle so often cautions them against high-mindedness; compare *ch.* xi. 20. They lived near the court, and conversed daily with the gaiety and grandeur of it: "Well," saith he, "do not mind it, be not in love with it." [2.] *Condescend to men of low estate*—Τοῖς ταπεινοῖς συναπαγόμενοι. *First,* It may be meant of *mean things,* to which we must condescend. If our condition in the world be poor and low, our enjoyments coarse and scanty, our employments despicable and contemptible, yet we must bring our minds to it, and acquiesce in it. So the margin: *Be contented with mean things.* Be reconciled to the place which God in his providence hath put us in, whatever it be. We must account nothing below us but sin: stoop to mean habitations, mean fare, mean clothing, mean accommodations when they are our lot, and not grudge. Nay, we must be carried with a kind of impetus, by the force of the new nature (so the word συναπάγομαι properly signifies, and it is very significant), towards mean things, when God appoints us to them; as the old corrupt nature is carried out towards high things. We must accommodate ourselves to mean things. We should make a low condition and mean circumstances more the centre of our desires than a high condition. *Secondly,* It may be meant of *mean persons;* so we read it (I think both are to be included)· *Condescend to men of low estate.* We must associate with, and accommodate ourselves to, those that are poor and mean in the world, if they be such as fear God. David, though a king upon the throne, was a companion for all such, Ps. cxix. 63. We need not be ashamed to converse with the lowly, while the great God overlooks heaven and earth to look at such. True love values grace in rags as well as in scarlet. A jewel is a jewel, though it lie in the dirt. The contrary to this condescension is reproved, Jam. ii. 1—4. *Condescend;* that is, suit yourselves to them, stoop to them for their good; as Paul, 1 Cor. ix. 19, &c. Some think the original word is a metaphor taken from travellers, when those that are stronger and swifter of foot stay for those that are weak and slow, make a halt, and take them with them; thus must Christians be tender towards their fellow travellers. As a means to promote this, he adds, *Be not wise in your own conceits;* to the same purport with *v.* 3. We shall never find in our hearts to condescend to others while we find there so great a conceit of ourselves: and therefore this must needs be mortified. Μὴ γίνεσθε φρόνιμοι παρ' ἑαυτοῖς—"*Be not wise by yourselves,* be not confident of the sufficiency of your own wisdom, so as to despise others, or think you have no need of them (Prov. iii. 7), nor be shy of communicating what you have to others. We are members one of another, depend upon one another, are obliged to one another; and therefore, *Be not wise by yourselves,* remembering it is the merchandise of wisdom that we profess; now merchandise consists in commerce, receiving and returning."

(7.) A love that engages us, as much as lies in us, *to live peaceably with all men, v.* 18. Even those with whom we cannot live intimately and familiarly, by reason of distance in degree or profession, yet we must with such live peaceably; that is, we must be harmless and inoffensive, not giving others occasion to quarrel with us; and we must be gall-less and unrevengeful, not taking occasion to quarrel with them. Thus must we labour to preserve the peace, that it be not broken, and to piece it again when it is broken. The wisdom from above is pure and peaceable. Observe how the exhortation is limited. It is not expressed so as to oblige us to impossibilities: *If it be possible, as much as lies in you.* Thus Heb. xii. 14, *Follow peace.* Eph. iv. 3, *Endeavouring to keep.* Study the things that make for peace.—*If it be possible.* It is not possible to preserve the peace when we cannot do it without offending God and wounding conscience: *Id possumus quod jure possumus—That is possible which is possible without incurring blame.* The wisdom that is from above is first pure and then peaceable, Jam. iii. 17. Peace without purity is the peace of the devil's palace.—*As much as lieth in you.* There must be two words to the bargain of peace. We can but speak for ourselves. We may be unavoidably striven with; as Jeremiah, who was a *man of contention* (Jer. xv. 10), and this we cannot help; our care must be that nothing be wanting on our parts to preserve the peace, Ps. cxx. 7. I am for peace, though, when I speak, they are for war.

2. To our enemies. Since men became enemies to God, they have been found very apt to be enemies one to another. Let but the centre of love be once forsaken, and the lines will either clash and interfere, or be at an uncomfortable distance. And, of all men, those that embrace religion have reason to expect to meet with enemies in a world whose smiles seldom concur with Christ's. Now Christianity teaches us how to behave towards our enemies; and in this instruction it quite differs from all other rules and methods, which generally aim at victory and dominion; but this at inward peace and satisfaction. Whoever are our enemies, that wish us ill and seek to do us ill, our rule is to do them no hurt, but all the good we can.

(1.) To do them no hurt (*v.* 17): *Recompense to no man evil for evil,* for that is a brutish recompence, and befitting only those animals which are not conscious either of any being above them or of any state before them. Or, if mankind were made (as some dream) in a state of war, such recompences as these were agreeable enough; but we have not so learned God, who does so much for his enemies (Matt. v. 45), much less have we so learned Christ, who died for us when we were enemies (*ch.* v. 8, 10), so loved that world which hated him without a cause.—"*To no man;* neither to Jew nor Greek; not to one that has been thy friend, for by recompensing evil for evil thou wilt certainly lose him; not to one that has been thine enemy, for by not recompensing evil for evil thou mayest perhaps gain him." To the same purport, *v.* 19, *Dearly beloved, avenge not yourselves.* And why must this be ushered in with such an affectionate compellation, rather than any other of the exhortations of this chapter? Surely because this is intended for the composing of angry spirits, that are hot in the resentment of a provocation. He addresses himself to such in this endearing language, to mollify and qualify them. Any thing that breathes love sweetens the blood, lays the storm, and cools the intemperate heat. Would you pacify a brother offended? Call him dearly beloved. Such a soft word, fitly spoken, may be effectual to turn away wrath. *Avenge not yourselves;* that is, when any body has done you any ill turn, do not desire nor endeavour to bring the like mischief or inconvenience upon him. It is not forbidden to the magistrate to do justice to those that are wronged, by punishing the wrong-doer; nor to make and execute just and wholesome laws against malefactors; but it forbids private revenge, which flows from anger and ill-will; and this is fitly forbidden, for it is presumed that we are incompetent judges in our own case. Nay, if persons wronged in seeking the defence of the law, and magistrates in granting it, act from any particular personal pique or quarrel, and not from a concern that public peace and order be maintained and right done, even such proceedings, though seemingly regular, will fall under this prohibited self-revenging. See how strict the law of Christ is in this matter, Matt. v. 38—40. It is forbidden not only to take it into our own hands to avenge ourselves, but to desire and thirst after even that judgment in our case which the law affords, for the satisfying of a revengeful humour. This is a hard lesson to corrupt nature; and therefore he subjoins, [1.] A remedy against it: *Rather give place unto wrath.* Not to our own wrath; to give place to this is to give place to the devil, Eph. iv. 26, 27. We must resist, and stifle, and smother, and suppress this; but, *First,* To the wrath of our enemy. "Give place to it, that is, be of a yielding temper; do not answer wrath with wrath, but with love rather. *Yielding pacifies great offences,* Eccl. x. 4. Receive affronts and injuries, as a stone is received into a heap of wool, which gives way to it, and so it does not rebound back, nor go any further." So it explains that of our Saviour (Matt. v. 39), *Whosoever shall smite thee on thy right cheek, turn to him the other also.* Instead of meditating how to revenge one wrong, prepare to receive another. When men's passions are up, and the stream is strong, let it have its course, lest by an unseasonable opposition it be made to rage and swell the more. When others are angry, let us be calm; this is a remedy against revenge, and seems to be the genuine sense. But, *Secondly,* Many apply it to the wrath of God: "Give place to this, make room for him to take the throne of judgment, and let him alone to deal with thine adversary." [2.] A reason against it: *For it is written, Vengeance is mine.* We find it written, Deut. xxxii. 35. God is the sovereign King, the righteous Judge, and to him it belongs to administer justice; for, being a God of infinite knowledge, by him actions are weighed in unerring balances; and, being a God of infinite purity, he hates sin and cannot endure to look upon iniquity. Some of this power he hath trusted in the hands of the civil magistrates (Gen. ix. 6; *ch.* xiii. 4); their legal punishments therefore are to be looked upon as a branch of God's revengings. This is a good reason why we should not avenge ourselves; for, if vengeance be God's, then, *First,* We may not do it. We step into the throne of God if we do and take his work out of his hand. *Secondly,* We need not do it. For God will, if we meekly leave the matter with him; he will avenge us as far as there is reason or justice for it, and further we cannot desire it. See Ps. xxxviii. 14, 15, *I heard not, for thou wilt hear;* and if God hears what need is there for me to hear?

(2.) We must not only not do hurt to our enemies, but our religion goes higher, and teaches us to do them all the good we can. It is a command peculiar to Christianity, and which does highly commend it: *Love your enemies,* Matt. v. 44. We are here taught to show that love to them both in word and deed.

[1.] In word: *Bless those who persecute you, v.* 14. It has been the common lot of God's people to be persecuted, either with a powerful hand or with a spiteful tongue. Now we are here taught to bless those that so persecute us. *Bless* them; that is, *First,* "Speak well of them. If there be any thing in them that is commendable and praiseworthy, take notice of it, and mention it to their honour." *Secondly,* "Speak respectfully to them, according as their place is, not rendering railing for railing, and bitterness for bitterness." And, *Thirdly,* We must wish well to them, and desire their good, so far from seeking any revenge. Nay, *Fourthly,* We must offer up that desire to God, by prayer for them. If it be not in the power of our hand to do any thing else for them, yet we can testify our good-will by praying for them, for which our master hath given us not only a rule, but an example to back that rule, Luke xxiii. 34.—*Bless, and curse not.* It denotes a thorough good-will in all the instances and expressions of it; not, "Bless them when you are at prayer, and curse them at other times;" but, "Bless them always, and curse not at all." Cursing ill becomes the mouths of those whose work it is to bless God, and whose happiness it is to be blessed of him.

[2.] In deed (*v.* 20): "*If thine enemy hunger,* as thou hast ability and opportunity, be ready and forward to show him any kindness, and do him any office of love for his good; and be never the less forward for his having been thine enemy, but rather the more, that thou mayest thereby testify the sincerity of thy forgiveness of him." It is said of archbishop Cranmer that the way for a man to make him his friend was to do him an ill turn. The precept is quoted from Prov. xxv. 21, 22; so that, high as it seems to be, the Old Testament was not a stranger to it. Observe here, *First,* What we must do. We must do good to our enemies. "*If he hunger,* do not insult over him, and say, Now God is avenging me of him, and pleading my cause; do not make such a construction of his wants. But *feed him. Then,* when he has need of thy help, and thou hast an opportunity of starving him and trampling upon him, then *feed him* (*ψώμιζε αὐτόν,* a significant word)—"feed him abundantly, nay, feed him carefully and indulgently:" *frustulatim pasce—feed him with small pieces,* "feed him, as we do children and sick people, with much tenderness. Contrive to do it so as to express thy love. *If he thirst, give him drink: πότιζε αὐτόν—drink to him,* in token of reconciliation and friendship. So confirm your love to him." *Secondly,* Why we must do this. Because in so doing thou shalt heap *coals of fire on his head.* Two senses are given of this, which I think are both to be taken in disjunctively. *Thou shalt heap coals of fire on his head;* that is, "Thou shalt either,' 1. "Melt him into repentance and friendship, and mollify his spirit towards thee" (alluding to those who melt metals; they not only put fire under them, but heap fire upon them; thus Saul was melted and conquered with the kindness of David, 1 Sam. xxiv. 16; xxvi. 21)—"thou wilt win a friend by it, and if thy kindness have not that effect then," 2. "It will aggravate his condemnation, and make his malice against thee the more inexcusable. Thou wilt hereby hasten upon him the tokens of God's wrath and vengeance." Not that this must be our intention in showing him kindness, but, for our encouragement, such will be the effect. To this purpose is the exhortation in the last verse, which suggests a paradox not easily understood by the world, that in all matters of strife and contention those that revenge are the conquered, and those that forgive are the conquerors. (1.) "*Be not overcome of evil.* Let not the evil of any provocation that is given you have such a power over you, or make such an impression upon you, as to dispossess you of yourselves, to disturb your peace, to destroy your love, to ruffle and discompose your spirits, to transport you to any indecencies, or to bring you to study or attempt any revenge." He that cannot quietly bear an injury is perfectly conquered by it. (2.) "*But overcome evil with good,* with the good of patience and forbearance, nay, and of kindness and beneficence to those that wrong you. Learn to defeat their ill designs against you, and either to change them, or at least to preserve your own peace. He that hath this rule over his spirit is better than the mighty.

3. To conclude, there remain two exhortations yet untouched, which are general, and which recommend all the rest as good in themselves, and of good report.

(1.) As good in themselves (*v.* 9): *Abhor that which is evil, cleave to that which is good.* God hath shown us what is good: these Christian duties are enjoined; and that is evil which is opposite to them. Now observe, [1.] We must not only not do evil, but we must *abhor that which is evil.* We must hate sin with an utter and irreconcilable hatred, have an antipathy to it as the worst of evils, contrary to our new nature, and to our true interest—hating all the appearances of sin, even the garment spotted with the flesh. [2.] We must not only do that which is good, but we must cleave to it. It denotes a deliberate choice of, a sincere affection for, and a constant perseverance in, that which is good. "So cleave to it as not to be allured nor affrighted from it, cleave *to him that is good,* even to the Lord (Acts xi. 23), with a dependence and acquiescence." It is subjoined to the precept of brotherly love, as directive of it; we must love our brethren, but not love them so much as for their sakes to commit any sin, or omit any duty; not think the better of any sin for the sake of the person that commits it, but forsake all the friends in the world, to cleave to God and duty.

(2.) As of good report (*v.* 17): "*Provide things honest in the sight of all men;* that is, not only do, but study and forecast and take care to do, that which is amiable and creditable, and recommends religion to all with whom you converse." See Phil. iv. 8. These acts of charity and beneficence are in a special manner of good report among men, and therefore are to be industriously regarded by all that consult the glory of God and the credit of their profession.

CHAP. XIII.

There are three good lessons taught us in this chapter, where the apostle enlarges more upon his precepts than he had done in the foregoing chapter, finding them more needful to be fully pressed. I. A lesson of subjection to lawful authority, ver. 1—6. II. A lesson of justice and love to our brethren, ver. 7—10. III. A lesson of sobriety and godliness in ourselves, ver. 11, to the end.

LET every soul be subject unto
the higher powers. For there
is no power but of God: the powers
that be are ordained of God. 2 Whosoever therefore resisteth the power,
resisteth the ordinance of God: and
they that resist shall receive to
themselves damnation. 3 For rulers
are not a terror to good works,
but to the evil. Wilt thou then
not be afraid of the power? Do that
which is good, and thou shalt have
praise of the same: 4 For he is the
minister of God to thee for good.
But if thou do that which is evil, be
afraid; for he beareth not the sword
in vain: for he is the minister of
God, a revenger to *execute* wrath
upon him that doeth evil. 5 Wherefore *ye* must needs be subject, not
only for wrath, but also for conscience
sake. 6 For this cause pay ye tribute also: for they are God's ministers, attending continually upon this
very thing.

We are here taught how to conduct ourselves towards magistrates, and those that are in authority over us, called here the *higher powers,* intimating their authority (they are powers), and their dignity (they are higher powers), including not only the king as supreme, but all inferior magistrates under him and yet it is expressed, not by the persons that are in that power, but the place of power itself, in which they are. However the persons themselves may be wicked, and of those vile persons whom the citizen of Zion contemneth (Ps. xv. 4), yet the just power which they have must be submitted to and obeyed. The apostle had taught us, in the foregoing chapter, not to avenge ourselves, nor to recompense evil for evil; but, lest it should seem as if this did cancel the ordinance of a civil magistracy among Christians, he takes occasion to assert the necessity of it, and of the due infliction of punishment upon evil doers, however it may look like recompensing evil for evil. Observe,

I. The duty enjoined: *Let every soul be subject.* Every soul—every person, one as well as another, not excluding the clergy, who call themselves spiritual persons, however the church of Rome may not only exempt such from subjection to the civil powers, but place them in authority above them, making the greatest princes subject to the pope, who thus exalteth himself above all that is called God.—*Every soul.* Not that our consciences are to be subjected to the will of any man. It is God's prerogative to make laws immediately to bind conscience, and we must render to God the things that are God's. But it intimates that our subjection must be free and voluntary, sincere and hearty. *Curse not the king, no, not in thy thought,* Eccl. x. 20. To compass and imagine are treason begun. The subjection of soul here required includes inward honour (1 Pet. ii. 17) and outward reverence and respect, both in speaking to them and in speaking of them—obedience to their commands in things lawful and honest, and in other things a patient subjection to the penalty without resistance—a conformity in every thing to the place and duty of subjects, bringing our minds to the relation and condition, and the inferiority and subordination of it. "They are *higher powers;* be content they should be so, and submit to them accordingly." Now there was good reason for the pressing of this duty of subjection to civil magistrates, 1. Because of the reproach which the Christian religion lay under in the world, as an enemy to public peace, order, and government, as a sect that turned the world upside down, and the embracers of it as enemies to Cæsar, and the more because the leaders were Galileans—an old slander. Jerusalem was represented as a *rebellious city, hurtful to kings and provinces,* Ezra iv. 15, 16. Our Lord Jesus was so reproached, though he told them his kingdom was not of this world: no marvel, then, if his followers have been loaded in all ages with the like calumnies, called *factious, seditious,* and *turbulent,* and looked upon as the troublers of the land, their enemies having found such representations needful for the justifying of their barbarous rage against them. The apostle therefore, for the obviating of this reproach and the clearing of Christianity from it, shows that obedience to civil magistrates is one of the laws of Christ, whose religion helps to make people good subjects; and it was very unjust to charge upon Christianity that faction and rebellion to which its principles and rules are so directly contrary. 2. Because of the temptation which the Christians lay under to be otherwise affected to civil magistrates, some of them being originally Jews, and so leavened with a principle that it was unmeet for any of the seed of Abraham to be subject to one of another nation—their king must be of their brethren, Deut. xvii. 15. Besides, Paul had taught them that they were *not under the law,* they were made free by Christ. Lest this liberty should be turned into licentiousness, and misconstrued to countenance faction and rebellion, the apostle enjoins obedience to civil government, which was the more necessary to be pressed now because the magistrates were heathens and unbelievers, which yet did not destroy their civil power and authority. Besides, the civil powers were persecuting powers; the body of the law was against them.

II. The reasons to enforce this duty. Why must we be subject?

1. For *wrath's sake.* Because of the danger we run ourselves into by resistance. Magistrates bear the sword, and to oppose them is to hazard all that is dear to us in this world; for it is to no purpose to contend with him that bears the sword. The Christians were then in those persecuting times obnoxious to the sword of the magistrate for their religion, and they needed not make themselves more obnoxious by their rebellion. The least show of resistance or sedition in a Christian would soon be aggravated and improved, and would be very prejudicial to the whole society; and therefore they had more need than others to be exact in their subjection, that those who had so much occasion against them in the matter of their God might have no other occasion. To this head must that argument be referred (*v.* 2), *Those that resist shall receive to themselves damnation: κρίμα λήψονται,* they shall be called to an account for it. God will reckon with them for it, because the resistance reflects upon him. The magistrates will reckon with them for it. They will come under the lash of the law, and will find the higher powers too high to be trampled upon, all civil governments being justly strict and severe against treason and rebellion; so it follows (*v.* 3), *Rulers are a terror.* This is a good argument, but it is low for a Christian.

2. We must be subject, *not only for wrath, but for conscience' sake;* not so much *formidine pœnæ—from the fear of punishment,* as *virtutis amore—from the love of virtue.* This makes common civil offices acceptable to God, when they are done for *conscience' sake,* with an eye to God, to his providence putting us into such relations, and to his precept making subjection the duty of those relations. Thus the same thing may be done from a very different principle. Now to oblige conscience to this subjection he argues, *v.* 1—4, 6,

(1.) From the institution of magistracy: *There is no power but of God.* God as the ruler and governor of the world hath appointed the ordinance of magistracy, so that all civil power is derived from him as from its original, and he hath by his providence put the administration into those hands, whatever they are that have it. By him kings reign, Prov. viii. 15. The usurpation of power and the abuse of power are not of God, for he is not the author of sin; but the power itself is. As our natural powers, though often abused and made instruments of sin, are from God's creating power, so civil powers are from God's governing power. The most unjust and oppressive princes in the world have no power but what is given them from above (John xix. 11), the divine providence being in a special manner conversant about those changes and revolutions of governments which have such an influence upon states and kingdoms, and such a multitude of particular persons and smaller communities. Or, it may be meant of government in general: it is an instance of God's wisdom, power, and goodness, in the management of mankind, that he has disposed them into such a state as distinguishes between governors and governed, and has not left them like the fishes of the sea, where the greater devour the less. He did herein consult the benefit of his creatures.—*The powers that be:* whatever the particular form and method of government are—whether by monarchy, aristocracy, or democracy—wherever the governing power is lodged, it is an ordinance of God, and it is to be received and submitted to accordingly; though immediately an ordinance of man (1 Pet. ii. 13), yet originally an ordinance of God.—*Ordained of God—τεταγμέναι·* a military word, signifying not only the ordination of magistrates, but the subordination of inferior magistrates to the supreme, as in an army; for among magistrates there is a diversity of gifts, and trusts, and services. Hence it follows (*v.* 2) that whosoever *resisteth the power resisteth the ordinance of God.* There are other things from God that are the greatest calamities; but magistracy is from God as an ordinance, that is, it is a great law, and it is a great blessing: so that the children of Belial, that will not endure the yoke of government, will be found breaking a law and despising a blessing. Magistrates are therefore called gods (Ps. lxxxii. 6), because they bear the image of God's authority. And those who spurn at their power reflect upon God himself. This is not at all applicable to the particular rights of kings and kingdoms, and the branches of their constitution; nor can any certain rule be fetched from this for the modelling of the original contracts between the governors and governed; but it is intended for direction to private persons in their private capacity, to behave themselves quietly and peaceably in the sphere in which God has set them, with a due regard to the civil powers which God in his providence has set over them, 1 Tim. ii. 1, 2. Magistrates are here again and again called God's ministers. He is the *minister of God, v.* 4, 6. Magistrates are in a more peculiar manner God's servants; the dignity they have calls for duty. Though they are lords to us, they are servants to God, have work to do for him, and an account to render to him. In the administration of public justice, the determining of quarrels, the protecting of the innocent, the righting of the wronged, the punishing of offenders, and the preserving of national peace and order, that every man may not do what is right in his own eyes—in these things it is that magistrates act as God's ministers. As the killing of an inferior magistrate, while he is actually doing his duty, is accounted treason against the prince, so the resisting of any magistrates in the discharge of these duties of their place is the resisting of an ordinance of God.

(2.) From the intention of magistracy: *Rulers are not a terror to good works, but to the evil,* &c. Magistracy was designed to be,

[1.] A terror to evil works and evil workers. They bear the sword; not only the sword of war, but the sword of justice. They are *heirs of restraint,* to put offenders to shame; Laish wanted such, Judg. xviii. 7. Such is the power of sin and corruption that many will not be restrained from the greatest enormities, and such as are most pernicious to human society, by any regard to the law of God and nature or the wrath to come; but only by the fear of temporal punishments, which the wilfulness and perverseness of degenerate mankind have made necessary. Hence it appears that laws with penalties for the lawless and disobedient (1 Tim. i. 9) must be constituted in Christian nations, and are agreeable with, and not contradictory to, the gospel. When men are become such beasts, such ravenous beasts, one to another, they must be dealt with accordingly, taken and destroyed *in terrorem—to deter others.* The horse and the mule must thus be held in with bit and bridle. In this work the magistrate is the *minister of God, v.* 4. He acts as God's agent, to whom vengeance belongs; and therefore must take heed of infusing into his judgments any private personal resentments of his own.—*To execute wrath upon him that doeth evil.* In this the judicial processes of the most vigilant faithful magistrates, though some faint resemblance and prelude of the judgments of the great day, yet come far short of the judgment of God: they reach only to the evil act, can execute wrath only on him that *doeth* evil: but God's judgment extends to the evil thought, and is a discerner of the intents of the heart.—*He beareth not the sword in vain.* It is not for nothing that God hath put such a power into the magistrate's hand; but it is intended for the restraining and suppressing of disorders. And therefore, "*If thou do that which is evil,* which falls under the cognizance and censure of the civil magistrate, *be afraid;* for civil powers have quick eyes and long arms." It is a good thing when the punishment of malefactors is managed as an ordinance of God, instituted and appointed by him. *First,* As a holy God, that hates sin, against which, as it appears and puts up its head, a public testimony is thus borne. *Secondly,* As King of nations, and the God of peace and order, which are hereby preserved. *Thirdly,* As the protector of the good, whose persons, families, estates, and names, are by this means hedged about. *Fourthly,* As one that desires not the eternal ruin of sinners, but by the punishment of some would terrify others, and so prevent the like wickedness, that others may hear and fear, and do no more presumptuously. Nay, it is intended for a kindness to those that are punished, that by the destruction of the flesh the spirit may be saved in the day of the Lord Jesus.

[2.] A praise to those that do well. Those that keep in the way of their duty shall have the commendation and protection of the civil powers, to their credit and comfort. "Do that which is good (*v.* 3), and thou needest not be *afraid of the power,* which, though terrible, reaches none but those that by their own sin make themselves obnoxious to it; the fire burns only that which is combustible: nay, thou shalt have praise of it." This is the intention of magistracy, and therefore we must, for conscience' sake, be subject to it, as a constitution designed for the public good, to which all private interests must give way. But pity it is that ever this gracious intention should be perverted, and that those who bear the sword, while they countenance and connive at sin, should be a terror to those who do well. But so it is, when the vilest men are exalted (Ps. xii. 1, 8); and yet even then the blessing and benefit of a common protection, and a face of government and order, are such that it is our duty in that case rather to submit to persecution for well-doing, and to take it patiently, than by any irregular and disorderly practices to attempt a redress. Never did sovereign prince pervert the ends of government as Nero did, and yet to him Paul appealed, and under him had the protection of the law and the inferior magistrates more than once. Better a bad government than none at all.

(3.) From our interest in it: "He is *the minister of God to thee for good.* Thou hast the benefit and advantage of the government, and therefore must do what thou canst to preserve it, and nothing to disturb it." Protection draws allegiance. If we have protection from the government, we owe subjection to it; by upholding the government, we keep up our own hedge. This subjection is likewise consented to by the tribute we pay (*v.* 6): "*For this cause pay you tribute,* as a testimony of your submission, and an acknowledgment that in conscience you think it to be due. You do by paying taxes contribute your share to the support of the power; if therefore you be not subject, you do but pull down with one hand what you support with the other; and is that conscience?" "By your paying tribute you not only own the magistrate's authority, but the blessing of that authority to yourselves, a sense of which you thereby testify, giving him that as a recompence for the great pains he takes in the government; for honour is a burden: and, if he do as he ought, *he is attending continually upon this very thing,* for it is enough to take up all a man's thoughts and time, in consideration of which fatigue, we pay tribute, and must be subject."—*Pay you tribute, φόρους τελεῖτε.* He does not say, "You give it as an alms," but, "You pay it as a just debt, or lend it to be repaid in all the blessings and advantages of public government, of which you reap the benefit." This is the lesson the apostle teaches, and it becomes all Christians to learn and practise it, that the godly in the land may be found (whatever others are) the quiet and the peaceable in the land.

7 Render therefore to all their
dues: tribute to whom tribute *is due;*
custom to whom custom; fear to
whom fear; honour to whom honour.
8 Owe no man any thing, but to love
one another: for he that loveth another hath fulfilled the law. 9 For
this, Thou shalt not commit adultery, Thou shalt not kill, Thou shalt
not steal, Thou shalt not bear false
witness, Thou shalt not covet; and if
there be any other commandment, it
is briefly comprehended in this saying,
namely, Thou shalt love thy neighbour
as thyself. 10 Love worketh no ill to
his neighbour: therefore love *is* the
fulfilling of the law.

We are here taught a lesson of justice and charity.

I. Of justice (*v.* 7): *Render therefore to all their dues,* especially to magistrates, for this refers to what goes before; and likewise to all with whom we have to do. To be just is to give to all their due, to give every body his own. What we have we have as stewards; others have an interest in it, and must have their dues. "Render to God his due in the first place, to yourselves, to your families, your relations, to the commonwealth, to the church, to the poor, to those that you have dealings with in buying, selling, exchanging, &c. Render to all their dues; and that readily and cheerfully, not tarrying till you are by law compelled to it." He specifies, 1. Due taxes: *Tribute to whom tribute is due, custom to whom custom.* Most of the countries where the gospel was first preached were subject at this time to the Roman yoke, and were made provinces of the empire. He wrote this to the Romans, who, as they were rich, so they were drained by taxes and impositions, to the just and honest payment of which they are here pressed by the apostle. Some distinguish between tribute and custom, understanding by the former constant standing taxes, and by the latter those which were occasionally required, both which are to be faithfully and conscientiously paid as they become legally due. Our Lord was born when his mother went to be taxed; and he enjoined the payment of tribute to Cæsar. Many, who in other things seem to be just, yet make no conscience of this, but pass it off with a false ill-favoured maxim, that it is no sin to cheat the king, directly contrary to Paul's rule, *Tribute to whom tribute is due.* 2. Due respect: *Fear to whom fear, honour to whom honour.* This sums up the duty which we owe not only to magistrates, but to all superiors, parents, masters, all that are over us in the Lord, according to the fifth commandment: *Honour thy father and mother.* Compare Lev. xix. 3, *You shall fear every man his mother and his father;* not with a fear of amazement, but a loving, reverent, respectful, obediential fear. Where there is not this respect in the heart to our superiors, no other duty will be paid aright. 3. Due payment of debts (*v.* 8): "*Owe no man any thing;* that is, do not continue in any one's debt, while you are able to pay it, further than by, at least, the tacit consent of the person to whom you are indebted. Give every one his own. Do not spend that upon yourselves, much less heap it up for yourselves, which you owe to others." The *wicked borroweth, and payeth not again,* Ps. xxxvii. 21. Many that are very sensible of the trouble think little of the sin of being in debt.

II. Of charity: *Owe no man any thing; ὀφείλετε—you do owe* no man any thing; so some read it: "Whatever you owe to any relation, or to any with whom you have to do, it is eminently summed up and included in this debt of love. But to *love one another,* this is a debt that must be always in the paying, and yet always owing." Love is a debt. The law of God and the interest of mankind make it so. It is not a thing which we are left at liberty about, but it is enjoined us, as the principle and summary of all duty owing one to another; for love *is the fulfilling of the law;* not perfectly, but it is a good step towards it. It is inclusive of all the duties of the second table, which he specifies, *v.* 9, and these suppose the love of God. See 1 John iv. 20. If the love be sincere, it is accepted as the *fulfilling of the law.* Surely we serve a good master, that has summed up all our duty in one word, and that a short word and a sweet word—*love,* the beauty and harmony of the universe. Loving and being loved is all the pleasure, joy, and happiness, of an intelligent being. *God is love* (1 John iv. 16), and love is his image upon the soul: where it is, the soul is well moulded, and the heart fitted for every good work. Now, to prove that love is the fulfilling of the law, he gives us, 1. An induction of particular precepts, *v.* 9. He specifies the last five of the ten commandments, which he observes to be all summed up in this royal law, *Thou shalt love thy neighbour as thyself*—with an *as* of quality, not of equality—"with the same sincerity that thou lovest thyself, though not in the same measure and degree." He that loves his neighbour as himself will be desirous of the welfare of his neighbour's body, goods, and good name, as of his own. On this is built that golden rule of doing as we would be done by. Were there no restraints of human laws in these things, no punishments incurred (which the malignity of human nature hath made necessary), the law of love would of itself be effectual to prevent all such wrongs and injuries, and to keep peace and good order among us. In the enumeration of these commandments, the apostle puts the seventh before the sixth, and mentions this first, *Thou shalt not commit adultery;* for though this commonly goes under the name of love (pity it is that so good a word should be so abused) yet it is really as great a violation of it as killing and stealing is, which shows that true brotherly love is love to the souls of our brethren in the first place. He that tempts others to sin, and defiles their minds and consciences, though he may pretend the most passionate love (Prov. vii. 15, 18), does really hate them, just as the devil does, who wars against the soul. 2. A general rule concerning the nature of brotherly love: *Love worketh no ill* (*v.* 10)—he that walks in love, that is actuated and governed by a principle of love, *worketh no ill;* he neither practises nor contrives any ill *to his neighbour,* to any one that he has any thing to do with: οὐκ ἐργάζεται. The projecting of evil is in effect the performing of it. Hence devising iniquity is called *working evil* upon the bed, Mic. ii. 1. Love intends and designs no ill to any body, is utterly against the doing of that which may turn to the prejudice, offence, or grief of any. It *worketh no ill;* that is, it prohibits the working of any ill: more is implied than is expressed; it not only worketh no ill, but it worketh all the good that may be, deviseth liberal things. For it is a sin not only to devise evil against thy neighbour, but to withhold good from those to whom it is due; both are forbidden together, Prov. iii. 27—29. This proves that love is the fulfilling of the law, answers all the end of it; for what else is that but to restrain us from evil-doing, and to constrain us to well-doing? Love is a living active principle of obedience to the whole law. The whole law is written in the heart, if the law of love be there.

11 And that, knowing the time,
that now *it is* high time to awake out
of sleep: for now *is* our salvation
nearer than when we believed. 12
The night is far spent, the day is at
hand: let us therefore cast off the
works of darkness, and let us put on
the armour of light. 13 Let us walk
honestly, as in the day; not in rioting and drunkenness, not in chambering and wantonness, not in strife
and envying. 14 But put ye on the
Lord Jesus Christ, and make not
provision for the flesh, to *fulfil* the
lusts *thereof.*

We are here taught a lesson of sobriety and godliness in ourselves. Our main care must be to look to ourselves. Four things we are here taught, as a Christian's directory for his day's work: when to awake, how to dress ourselves, how to walk, and what provision to make.

I. When to awake: *Now it is high time to awake* (*v.* 11), to awake out of the sleep of sin (for a sinful condition is a sleeping condition), out of the sleep of carnal security, sloth and negligence, out of the sleep of spiritual death, and out of the sleep of spiritual deadness; both the wise and foolish virgins slumbered and slept, Matt. xxv. 5. We have need to be often excited and stirred up to awake. The word of command to all Christ's disciples is, *Watch.* "*Awake*—be concerned about your souls and your eternal interest; take heed of sin, be ready to, and serious in, that which is good, and live in a constant expectation of the coming of our Lord. Considering," 1. "The time we are cast into: *Knowing the time.* Consider what time of day it is with us, and you will see it is high time to awake. It is gospel time, it is the accepted time, it is working time; it is a time when more is expected than was in the times of that ignorance which God winked at, when people sat in darkness. It is high time to awake; for the sun has been up a great while, and shines in our faces. Have we this light to sleep in? See 1 Thess. v. 5, 6. It is high time to awake; for others are awake and up about us. Know the time to be a busy time; we have a great deal of work to do, and our Master is calling us to it again and again. Know the time to be a perilous time. We are in the midst of enemies and snares. It is high time to awake, for the Philistines are upon us; our neighbour's house is on fire, and our own in danger. It is time to awake, for we have slept enough (1 Pet. iv. 3), high time indeed, for *behold the bridegroom cometh.*" 2. "The salvation we are upon the brink of: *Now is our salvation nearer than when we believed*—than when we first believed, and so took upon us the profession of Christianity. The eternal happiness we chose for our portion is now nearer to us than it was when we became Christians. Let us mind our way and mend our pace, for we are now nearer our journey's end than we were when we had our first love. The nearer we are to our centre the quicker should our motion be. Is there but a step between us and heaven, and shall we be so very slow and dull in our Christian course, and move so heavily? The more the days are shortened, and the more grace is increased, the nearer is our salvation, and the more quick and vigorous we should be in our spiritual motions."

II. How to dress ourselves. This is the next care, when we are awake and up: "The *night is far spent, the day is at hand;* therefore it is time to dress ourselves. Clearer discoveries will be quickly made of gospel grace than have been yet made, as light gets ground. The night of Jewish rage and cruelty is just at an end; their persecuting power is near a period; the day of our deliverance from them is at hand, that day of redemption which Christ promised, Luke xxi. 28. And the day of our complete salvation, in the heavenly glory, is at hand. Observe then,"

1. "What we must put off; put off our night-clothes, which it is a shame to appear abroad in: *Cast off the works of darkness.*" Sinful works are works of darkness; they come from the darkness of ignorance and mistake, they covet the darkness of privacy and concealment, and they end in the darkness of hell and destruction. Let us therefore, who are of the day, cast them off; not only cease from the practice of them, but detest and abhor them, and have no more to do with them. Because eternity is just at the door, let us take heed lest we be found doing that which will then make against us," 2 Pet. iii. 11, 14.

2. "What we must put on." Our care must be *wherewithal we shall be clothed,* how shall we dress our souls? (1.) *Put on the armour of light.* Christians are soldiers in the midst of enemies, and their life a warfare, therefore their array must be armour, that they may stand upon their defence—the *armour of God,* to which we are directed, Eph. vi. 13, &c. A Christian may reckon himself undressed if he be unarmed. The graces of the Spirit are this armour, to secure the soul from Satan's temptations and the assaults of this present evil world. This is called the armour of light, some think alluding to the bright glittering armour which the Roman soldiers used to wear; or such armour as it becomes us to wear in the day-light. The graces of the Spirit are suitable splendid ornaments, are in the sight of God of great price. (2.) *Put on the Lord Jesus Christ, v.* 14. This stands in opposition to a great many base lusts, mentioned *v.* 13. *Rioting and drunkenness* must be cast off: one would think it should follow, but, "Put on sobriety, temperance, chastity," the opposite virtues: no, "*Put on Christ,* this includes all. Put on the righteousness of Christ for justification; be found in him (Phil. iii. 9) as a man is found in his clothes; put on the priestly garments of the elder brother, that in them you may obtain the blessing. Put on the spirit and grace of Christ for sanctification; put on the *new man* (Eph. iv. 24); get the habit of grace confirmed, the acts of it quickened." Jesus Christ is the best clothing for Christians to adorn themselves with, to arm themselves with; it is decent, distinguishing, dignifying, and defending. Without Christ, we are naked, deformed; all other things are filthy rags, fig-leaves, a sorry shelter. God has provided us coats of skins —large, strong, warm, and durable. By baptism we have in profession put on Christ, Gal. iii. 27. Let us do it in truth and sincerity. *The Lord Jesus Christ.* "Put him on as Lord to rule you, as Jesus to save you, and in both as Christ, anointed and appointed by the Father to this ruling saving work."

III. How to walk. When we are up and dressed, we are not to sit still in an affected closeness and privacy, as monks and hermits. What have we good clothes for, but to appear abroad in them?—*Let us walk.* Christianity teaches us how to walk so as to please God, whose eye is upon us: 1 Thess. iv. 1 *Walk honestly as in the day.* Compare Eph v. 8, *Walk as children of light.* Our conversation must be as becomes the gospel. *Walk honestly; εὐσχημόνως—decently* and becomingly, so as to credit your profession, and to adorn the doctrine of God our Saviour, and recommend religion in its beauty to others. Christians should be in a special manner careful to conduct themselves well in those things wherein men have an eye upon them, and to study that which is lovely and of good report. Particularly, here are three pairs of sins we are cautioned against:—1. We must not walk in *rioting and drunkenness;* we must abstain from all excess in eating and drinking. We must not give the least countenance to revelling, nor indulge our sensual appetite in any private excesses. Christians must not overcharge their hearts with surfeiting and drunkenness, Luke xxi. 34. This is not walking as in the day; for those that are *drunk are drunk in the night*, 1 Thess. v. 7. 2. *Not in chambering and wantonness;* not in any of those lusts of the flesh, those works of darkness, which are forbidden in the seventh commandment. Downright adultery and fornication are the chambering forbidden. Lascivious thoughts and affections, lascivious looks, words, books, songs, gestures, dances, dalliances, which lead to, and are degrees of, that uncleanness, are the wantonness here forbidden—whatsoever trangresseth the pure and sacred law of chastity and modesty. 3. Not in *strife and envying*. These are also works of darkness; for, though the acts and instances of strife and envy are very common, yet none are willing to own the principles, or to acknowledge themselves envious and contentious. It may be the lot of the best saints to be envied and striven with; but to strive and to envy ill becomes the disciples and followers of the peaceable and humble Jesus. Where there are riot and drunkenness, there usually are chambering and wantonness, and strife and envy. Solomon puts them all together, Prov. xxiii. 29, &c. Those that tarry long at the wine (*v.* 30) have contentions and wounds without cause (*v.* 29) and their eyes behold strange women, *v.* 33.

IV. What provision to make (*v.* 14): "*Make not provision for the flesh.* Be not careful about the body." Our great care must be to provide for our souls; but must we take no care about our bodies? Must we not provide for them, when they need it? Yes, but two things are here forbidden:—1. Perplexing ourselves with an inordinate care, intimated in these words, πρόνοιαν μὴ ποιεῖσθε. "Be not solicitous in forecasting for the body; do not stretch your wits, nor set your thoughts upon the tenter-hooks, in making this provision; be not careful and cumbered about it; do not *take thought*," Matt. vi. 31. It forbids an anxious encumbering care. 2. Indulging ourselves in an irregular desire. We are not forbidden barely to provide for the body (it is a lamp that must be supplied with oil), but we are forbidden to fulfil the lusts thereof. The necessities of the body must be considered, but the lusts of it must not be gratified. Natural desires must be answered, but wanton appetites must be checked and denied. To ask meat for our necessities is duty: we are taught to pray for daily bread; but to ask meat for our lusts is provoking, Ps. lxxviii. 18. Those who profess to walk in the spirit must not fulfil the lusts of the flesh, Gal. v. 16.

CHAP. XIV.

The apostle having, in the former chapter, directed our conduct one towards another in civil things, and prescribed the sacred laws of justice, peaceableness, and order, to be observed by us as members of the commonwealth, comes in this and part of the following chapter in like manner to direct our demeanour one towards another in sacred things, which pertain more immediately to conscience and religion, and which we observe as members of the church. Particularly, he gives rules how to manage our different apprehensions about indifferent things, in the management of which, it seems, there was something amiss among the Roman Christians, to whom he wrote, which he here labours to redress. But the rules are general, and of standing use in the church, for the preservation of that Christian love which he had so earnestly pressed in the foregoing chapter as the fulfilling of the law. It is certain that nothing is more threatening, nor more often fatal, to Christian societies, than the contentions and divisions of their members. By these wounds the life and soul of religion expire. Now in this chapter we are furnished with the sovereign balm of Gilead; the blessed apostle prescribes like a wise physician. "Why then is not the hurt of the daughter of my people recovered," but because his directions are not followed? This chapter, rightly understood, made use of, and lived up to, would set things to rights, and heal us all.

HIM that is weak in the faith
receive ye, *but* not to doubtful disputations. 2 For one believeth
that he may eat all things: another,
who is weak, eateth herbs. 3 Let not
him that eateth despise him that eateth not; and let not him which eateth
not judge him that eateth: for God
hath received him. 4 Who art thou
that judgest another man's servant?
to his own master he standeth or
falleth. Yea, he shall be holden up:
for God is able to make him stand.
5 One man esteemeth one day above
another: another esteemeth every day
alike. Let every man be fully persuaded in his own mind. 6 He that
regardeth the day, regardeth *it* unto
the Lord; and he that regardeth not
the day, to the Lord he doth not regard *it*. He that eateth, eateth to
the Lord, for he giveth God thanks;
and he that eateth not, to the Lord
he eateth not, and giveth God thanks.
7 For none of us liveth to himself,
and no man dieth to himself. 8 For
whether we live, we live unto the
Lord; and whether we die, we die
unto the Lord: whether we live
therefore, or die, we are the Lord's.
9 For to this end Christ both died,
and rose, and revived, that he might
be Lord both of the dead and living.
10 But why dost thou judge thy
brother? or why dost thou set at
nought thy brother? for we shall all
stand before the judgment seat of
Christ. 11 For it is written, *As* I
live, saith the Lord, every knee shall
bow to me, and every tongue shall
confess to God. 12 So then every
one of us shall give account of himself to God. 13 Let us not therefore judge one another any more: but
judge this rather, that no man put a
stumblingblock or an occasion to fall
in *his* brother's way. 14 I know,

and am persuaded by the Lord Jesus,
that *there is* nothing unclean of itself:
but to him that esteemeth any thing
to be unclean, to him *it is* unclean.
15 But if thy brother be grieved
with *thy* meat, now walkest thou not
charitably. Destroy not him with
thy meat, for whom Christ died. 16
Let not then your good be evil spoken
of: 17 For the kingdom of God is
not meat and drink; but righteousness, and peace, and joy in the Holy
Ghost. 18 For he that in these
things serveth Christ *is* acceptable to
God, and approved of men. 19 Let
us therefore follow after the things
which make for peace, and things
wherewith one may edify another.
20 For meat destroy not the work of
God. All things indeed *are* pure;
but *it is* evil for that man who eateth
with offence. 21 *It is* good neither
to eat flesh, nor to drink wine, nor
any thing whereby thy brother stumbleth, or is offended, or is made weak.
22 Hast thou faith? have *it* to thyself before God. Happy *is* he that
condemneth not himself in that thing
which he alloweth. 23 And he that
doubteth is damned if he eat, because
he eateth not of faith: for whatsoever
is not of faith is sin.

We have in this chapter,

I. An account of the unhappy contention which had broken out in the Christian church. Our Master had foretold that offences would come; and, it seems, so they did, for want of that wisdom and love which would have prevented discord, and kept up union among them.

1. There was a difference among them about the distinction of meats and days; these are the two things specified. There might be other similar occasions of difference, while these made the most noise, and were most taken notice of. The case was this: The members of the Christian church at Rome were some of them originally Gentiles, and others of them Jews. We find Jews at Rome believing, Acts xxviii. 24. Now those that had been Jews were trained up in the observance of the ceremonial appointments touching meats and days. This, which had been bred in the bone with them, could hardly be got out of the flesh, even after they turned Christians; especially with some of them, who were not easily weaned from what they had long been wedded to. They were not well instructed touching the cancelling of the ceremonial law by the death of Christ, and therefore retained the ceremonial institutions, and practised accordingly; while other Christians that understood themselves better, and knew their Christian liberty, made no such difference. (1.) Concerning meats (*v.* 2): *One believeth that he may eat all things*—he is well satisfied that the ceremonial distinction of meats into clean and unclean is no longer in force, but that every creature of God is good, and nothing to be refused; nothing *unclean of itself*, *v.* 14. This he was assured of, not only from the general tenour and scope of the gospel, but particularly from the revelation which Peter, the apostle of the circumcision (and therefore more immediately concerned in it), had to this purport, Acts x. 15, 28. This the strong Christian is clear in, and practises accordingly, eating what is set before him, and asking no question for conscience' sake, 1 Cor. x. 27. On the other hand, *another, who is weak*, is dissatisfied in this point, is not clear in his Christian liberty, but rather inclines to think that the meats forbidden by the law remain still unclean; and therefore, to keep at a distance from them, he will eat no flesh at all, but *eateth herbs*, contenting himself with only the fruits of the earth. See to what degrees of mortification and self-denial a tender conscience will submit. None know but those that experience it how great both the restraining and the constraining power of conscience is. (2.) Concerning days, *v.* 5. Those who thought themselves still under some kind of obligation by the ceremonial law esteemed *one day above another*—kept up a respect to the times of the passover, pentecost, new moons, and feast of tabernacles; thought those days better than other days, and solemnized them accordingly with particular observances, binding themselves to some religious rest and exercise on those days. Those who knew that all these things were abolished and done away by Christ's coming esteemed every day alike. We must understand it with an exception of the Lord's day, which all Christians unanimously observed; but they made no account, took no notice, of those antiquated festivals of the Jews. Here the apostle speaks of the distinction of meats and days as a thing indifferent, when it went no further than the opinion and practice of some particular persons, who had been trained up all their days to such observances, and therefore were the more excusable if they with difficulty parted with them. But in the epistle to the Galatians, where he deals with those that were originally Gentiles, but were influenced by some judaizing teachers, not only to believe such a distinction and to practise accordingly, but to lay a stress upon it as necessary to salvation, and to make the observance of the Jewish festivals public and congregational, here the case was altered, and it is charged upon them as the frustrating of the design of the gospel, falling from grace, Gal. iv. 9—11. The Romans did it out of weakness, the Galatians did it out of wilfulness and wicked-

ness; and therefore the apostle handles them thus differently. This epistle is supposed to have been written some time before that to the Galatians. The apostle seems willing to let the ceremonial law wither by degrees, and to let it have an honourable burial; now these weak Romans seem to be only following it weeping to its grave, but those Galatians were raking it out of its ashes.

2. It was not so much the difference itself that did the mischief as the mismanagement of the difference, making it a bone of contention. (1.) Those who were strong, and knew their Christian liberty, and made use of it, despised the weak, who did not. Whereas they should have pitied them, and helped them, and afforded them meek and friendly instruction, they trampled upon them as silly, and humoursome, and superstitious, for scrupling those things which they knew to be lawful: so apt are those who have knowledge to be puffed up with it, and to look disdainfully and scornfully upon their brethren. (2.) Those who were weak, and durst not use their Christian liberty, judged and censured the strong, who did, as if they were loose Christians, carnal professors, that cared not what they did, but walked at all adventures, and stuck at nothing. They judged them as breakers of the law, contemners of God's ordinance, and the like. Such censures as these discovered a great deal of rashness and uncharitableness, and would doubtless tend much to the alienating of affection. Well, this was the disease, and we see it remaining in the church to this day; the like differences, in like manner mismanaged, are still the disturbers of the church's peace. But,

II. We have proper directions and suggestions laid down for allaying this contention, and preventing the ill consequences of it. The apostle, as a wise physician, prescribes proper remedies for the disease, which are made up of rules and reasons. Such gentle methods does he take, with such cords of a man does he draw them together; not by excommunicating, suspending, and silencing either side, but by persuading them both to a mutual forbearance: and as a faithful daysman he lays his hand upon them both, reasoning the case with the strong that they should not be so scornful, and with the weak that they should not be so censorious. If the contending parties will but submit to this fair arbitration, each abate of his rigour, and sacrifice their differences to their graces, all will be well quickly. Let us observe the rules he gives, some to the strong and some to the weak, and some to both, for they are interwoven; and reduce the reasons to their proper rules.

1. Those who are weak must be *received, but not to doubtful disputations, v.* 1. Take this for a general rule; spend your zeal in those things wherein you and all the people of God are agreed, and do not dispute about matters that are doubtful. *Receive him, προσλαμβάνεσθε—take him to you,* bid him welcome, receive him with the greatest affection and tenderness; *porrigite manum* (so the Syriac): *lend him your hand,* to help him, to fetch him to you, to encourage him. Receive him into your company, and converse, and communion, entertain him with readiness and condescension, and treat him with all possible endearments. Receive him: not to quarrel with him, and to argue about uncertain points that are in controversy, which will but confound him, and fill his head with empty notions, perplex him, and shake his faith. Let not your Christian friendship and fellowship be disturbed with such vain janglings and strifes of words.—*Not to judge his doubtful thoughts* (so the margin), "not to pump out his weak sentiments concerning those things which he is in doubt about, that you may censure and condemn him. Receive him, not to expose him, but to instruct and strengthen him. See 1 Cor. i. 10; Phil. iii. 15, 16.

2. Those who are strong must by no means despise the weak; nor those who are weak judge the strong, *v.* 3. This is levelled directly against the fault of each party. It is seldom that any such contention exists but there is a fault on both sides, and both must mend. He argues against both these jointly: we must not despise nor judge our brethren. Why so?

(1.) Because God hath received them; and we reflect upon him if we reject those whom he hath received. God never cast off any one that had true grace, though he was but weak in it; never broke the bruised reed. Strong believers and weak believers, those that eat and those that eat not, if they be true believers, are accepted of God. It will be good for us to put this question to ourselves, when we are tempted to behave scornfully towards our brethren, to disdain and censure them: "Has not God owned them; and, if he has, dare I disown them?" "Nay, God doth not only receive him, but *hold him up, v.* 4. You think that he who eateth will fall by his presumption, or that he who eateth not will sink under the weight of his own fears and scruples; but if they have true faith, and an eye to God, the one in the intelligent use of his Christian liberty and the other in the conscientious forbearance of it, they shall be held up—the one in his integrity, and the other in his comfort. This hope is built upon the power of God, for *God is able to make him stand;* and, being able, no doubt he is willing to exert that power for the preservation of those that are his own." In reference to spiritual difficulties and dangers (our own and others), much of our hope and comfort are grounded upon the divine power, 1 Pet. i. 5; Jude 24.

(2.) Because they are servants to their own master (*v.* 4): *Who art thou that judgest another man's servant?* We reckon it a piece of ill manners to meddle with other people's servants, and to find fault with them and censure them. Weak and strong Christians are indeed our brethren, but they are not our servants. This rash judging is reproved, Jam. iii. 1, under the notion of being many masters. We make ourselves our brethren's masters, and do in effect usurp the throne of God, when we take upon us thus to judge them, especially to judge their thoughts and intentions, which are out of our view, to judge their persons and state, concerning which it is hard to conclude by those few indications which fall within our cognizance. God sees not as man sees; and he is their master, and not we. In judging and censuring our brethren, we meddle with that which does not belong to us: we have work enough to do at home; and, if we must needs be judging, let us exercise our faculty upon our own hearts and ways.—*To his own master he stands or falls;* that is, his doom will be according to his master's sentence, and not according to ours. How well for us is it that we are not to stand nor fall by the judgment one of another, but by the righteous and unerring judgment of God, which is according to truth! "While thy brother's cause is before thy judgment, it is *coram non judice—before one who is not the judge;* the court of heaven is the proper court for trial, where, and where only, the sentence is definitive and conclusive; and to this, if his heart be upright, he may comfortably appeal from thy rash censure."

(3.) Because both the one and the other, if they be true believers, and are right in the main, have an eye to God, and do approve themselves to God in what they do, *v.* 6. He *that regards the day*—that makes conscience of the observance of the Jewish fasts and festivals, not imposing it upon others, nor laying a stress upon it, but willing to be as he thinks on the surer side, as thinking there is no harm in resting from worldly labours, and worshipping God on those days—it is well. We have reason to think, because in other things he conducts himself like a good Christian, that in this also his eye is single, and that *he regardeth it unto the Lord;* and God will accept of his honest intention, though he be under a mistake about the observance of days; for the sincerity and uprightness of the heart were never rejected for the weakness and infirmity of the head: so good a master do we serve. On the other hand, he *that regards not the day*—that does not make a difference between one day and another, does not call one day holy and another profane, one day lucky and another unlucky, but esteems every day alike—he does not do it out of a spirit of opposition, contradiction, or contempt of his brother. If he be a good Christian, he does not, he dares not, do it from such a principle; and therefore we charitably conclude that to the *Lord he does not regard it.* He makes no such difference of days only because he knows God hath made none; and therefore intends his honour in endeavouring to dedicate every day to him. So for the other instance: *He that eateth* whatever is set before him, though it be blood, though it be swine's flesh, if it be food convenient for him, he *eateth to the Lord.* He understands the liberty that God has granted him, and uses it to the glory of God, with an eye to his wisdom and goodness in enlarging our allowance now under the gospel, and taking off the yoke of legal restraints; and he *giveth God thanks* for the variety of food he has, and the liberty he has to eat it, and that in those things his conscience is not fettered. On the other hand, *he that eateth not* those meats which were forbidden by the ceremonial law, *to the Lord he eateth not.* It is for God's sake, because he is afraid of offending God by eating that which he is sure was once prohibited; and he *giveth God thanks too* that there is enough besides. If he conscientiously deny himself that which he takes to be forbidden fruit, yet he blesses God that of other trees in the garden he may freely eat. Thus, while both have an eye to God in what they do, and approve themselves to him in their integrity, why should either of them be judged or despised? Observe, Whether we eat flesh, or eat herbs, it is a thankful regard to God, the author and giver of all our mercies, that sanctifies and sweetens it. Bishop Sanderson, in his 34th sermon, upon 1 Tim. iv. 4, justly makes this observation: It appears by this that *saying grace* (as we commonly call it, perhaps from 1 Cor. x. 30) before and after meat was the common known practice of the church, among Christians of all sorts, weak and strong: an ancient, commendable, apostolical, Christian practice, derived down from Christ's example through all the ages of the church, Matt. xiv. 19; xv. 36; Luke ix. 16; John vi. 11; Matt. xxvi. 26, 27; Acts xxvii. 35. Blessing the creatures in the name of God before we use them, and blessing the name of God for them after, are both included; for εὐλογεῖν and εὐχαριστεῖν are used promiscuously. To clear this argument against rash judging and despising, he shows how essential it is to true Christianity to have a regard to God and not to ourselves, which therefore, unless the contrary do manifestly appear, we must presume concerning those that in minor things differ from us. Observe his description of true Christians, taken from their end and aim (*v.* 7, 8), and the ground of it, *v.* 9.

[1.] Our end and aim: not self, but the Lord. As the particular end specifies the action, so the general scope and tendency specify the state. If we would know what way we walk in, we must enquire what end we walk towards. *First,* Not to self. We have learned to deny ourselves; this was our first lesson: *None of us liveth to himself.* This is a thing in which all the people of God are one, however they differ in other things;

though some are weak and others are strong, yet both agree in this, not to live to themselves. Not one that hath given up his name to Christ is allowedly a self-seeker; it is contrary to the foundation of true Christianity. We neither *live to ourselves nor die to ourselves.* We are not our own masters, nor our own proprietors—we are not at our own disposal. The business of our lives is not to please ourselves, but to please God. The business of our deaths, to which we are every day exposed and delivered, is not to make ourselves talked of; we run not such hazards out of vain-glory, while we are dying daily. When we come to die actually, neither is that to ourselves; it is not barely that we would be unclothed, and eased of the burden of the flesh, but it is to the Lord, that we may depart and be with Christ, may be present with the Lord. *Secondly,* But *to the Lord* (*v.* 8), to the Lord Christ, to whom all power and judgment are committed, and in whose name we are taught, as Christians, to do every thing we do (Col. iii. 17), with an eye to the will of Christ as our rule, to the glory of Christ as our end, Phil. i. 21. Christ is the gain we aim at, living and dying. We live to glorify him in all the actions and affairs of life; we die, whether a natural or a violent death, to glorify him, and to go to be glorified with him. Christ is the centre, in which all the lines of life and death do meet. This is true Christianity, which makes Christ all in all. So that, *whether we live or die, we are the Lord's,* devoted to him, depending on him, designed and designing for him. Though some Christians are weak and others strong,—though of different sizes, capacities, apprehensions, and practices, in minor things, yet they are all the Lord's—all eying, and serving, and approving themselves to Christ, and are accordingly owned and accepted of him. Is it for us then to judge or despise them, as if we were their masters, and they were to make it their business to please us, and to stand or fall by our dooms?

[2.] The ground of this, *v.* 9. It is grounded upon Christ's absolute sovereignty and dominion, which were the fruit and end of his death and resurrection. *To this end he both died, and rose, and revived* (he, having risen, entered upon a heavenly life, the glory which he had before) *that he might be Lord both of dead and living*—that he might be universal monarch, Lord of all (Acts x. 36), all the animate and inanimate creatures; for he is head over all things to the church. He is Lord of those that are living to rule them, of those that are dead to receive them and raise them up. This was that *name above every name* which God gave him as the reward of his humiliation, Phil. ii. 8, 9. It was after he had died and risen that he said, *All power is given unto me* (Matt. xxviii. 18), and presently he exerts that power in issuing out commissions, *v.* 19, 20. Now if Christ paid so dearly for his dominion over souls and consciences, and has such a just and undisputed right to exercise that dominion, we must not so much as seem to invade it, nor intrench upon it, by judging the consciences of our brethren, and arraigning them at our bar. When we are ready to reproach and reflect upon the name and memory of those that are dead and gone, and to pass a censure upon them (which some the rather do, because such judgments of the dead are more likely to pass uncontrolled and uncontradicted), we must consider that Christ is Lord of the dead, as well as of the living. If they are dead, they have already given up their account, and let that suffice. And this leads to another reason against judging and despising,

(4.) Because both the one and the other must shortly give an account, *v.* 10—12. A believing regard to the judgment of the great day would silence all these rash judgings: *Why dost thou* that art weak *judge thy brother* that is strong? And *why dost thou* that art strong *set at nought thy brother* that is weak? Why is all this clashing, and contradicting, and censuring, among Christians? *We shall all stand before the judgment-seat of Christ,* 2 Cor. v. 10. Christ will be the Judge, and he has both authority and ability to determine men's eternal state according to their works, and before him we shall stand as persons to be tried, and to give up an account, expecting our final doom from him, which will be eternally conclusive. To illustrate this (*v.* 11), he quotes a passage out of the Old Testament, which speaks of Christ's universal sovereignty and dominion, and that established with an oath: *As I live* (saith the Lord), *every knee shall bow to me.* It is quoted from Isa. xlv. 23. There it is, *I have sworn by myself;* here it is, *As I live.* So that whenever God saith *As I live,* it is to be interpreted as swearing by himself; for it is God's prerogative to have life in himself: there is a further ratification of it there, *The word is gone out of my mouth.* It is a prophecy, in general, of Christ's dominion; and here very fully applied to the judgment of the great day, which will be the highest and most illustrious exercise of that dominion. Here is a proof of Christ's Godhead: he is the Lord and he is God, equal with the Father. Divine honour is due to him, and must be paid. It is paid to God through him as Mediator. God will judge the world by him, Acts xvii. 31. The bowing of the knee to him, and the confession made with the tongue, are but outward expressions of inward adoration and praise. *Every knee* and *every tongue,* either freely or by force.

[1.] All his friends do it freely, are made willing in the day of his power. Grace is the soul's cheerful, entire, and avowed subjection to Jesus Christ. *First,* Bowing to him—the understanding bowed to his truths, the will to his laws, the whole man to his authority; and this expressed by the bowing of the knee, the posture of adoration and prayer. It is proclaimed before our Joseph, *Bow the knee,* Gen. xli. 43. Though bodily exercise alone profits little, yet, as it is guided by inward fear and reverence, it is accepted. *Secondly,* Confessing to him—acknowledging his glory, grace, and greatness—acknowledging our own meanness and vileness, confessing our sins to him; so some understand it.

[2.] All his foes shall be constrained to do it, whether they will or no. When he shall come in the clouds, and every eye shall see him, then, and not till then, will all those promises which speak of his victories over his enemies and their subjection to him have their full and complete accomplishment; then his foes shall be his footstool, and all his enemies shall lick the dust. Hence he concludes (*v.* 12), *Every one of us shall give account of himself to God.* We must not give account for others, nor they for us; but every one for himself. We must give account how we have spent our time, how we have improved our opportunities, what we have done and how we have done it. And therefore, *First,* We have little to do to judge others, for they are not accountable to us, nor are we accountable for them (Gal. ii. 6): *Whatsoever they were, it maketh no matter to me, God accepteth no man's person.* Whatever they are, and whatever they do, they must give account to their own master, and not to us; if we can in any thing be helpers of their joy, it is well; but we have not dominion over their faith. And, *Secondly,* We have the more to do to judge ourselves. We have an account of our own to make up, and that is enough for us; let every *man prove his own work* (Gal. vi. 4), state his own accounts, search his own heart and life; let this take up his thoughts, and he that is strict in judging himself and abasing himself will not be apt to judge and despise his brother. Let all these differences be referred to the arbitration of Christ at the great day.

(5.) Because the stress of Christianity is not to be laid upon these things, nor are they at all essential to religion, either on the one side or on the other. This is his reason (*v.* 17, 18), which is reducible to this branch of exhortation. Why should you spend your zeal either for or against those things which are so minute and inconsiderable in religion? Some make it a reason why, in case of offence likely to be taken, we should refrain the use of our Christian liberty; but it seems directed in general against that heat about those things which he observed on both sides. *The kingdom of God is not meat,* &c. Observe here,

[1.] The nature of true Christianity, what it is: it is here called, *The kingdom of God;* it is a religion intended to rule us, a kingdom: it stands in a true and hearty subjection to God's power and dominion. The gospel dispensation is in a special manner called *the kingdom of God,* in distinction from the legal dispensation, Matt. iii. 2; iv. 17. *First,* It is *not meat and drink:* it does not consist either in using or in abstaining from such and such meats and drinks. Christianity gives no rule in that case, either in one way or another. The Jewish religion consisted much in meats and drinks (Heb. ix 10), abstaining from some meats religiously (Lev. xi. 2), eating other meats religiously, as in several of the sacrifices, part of which were to be eaten before the Lord: but all those appointments are now abolished and are no more, Col. ii. 21, 22. The matter is left at large. Every *creature of God is good,* 1 Tim. iv. 4. So, as to other things, it is neither circumcision nor uncircumcision (Gal. v. 6; vi. 15; 1 Cor. vii. 19), it is not being of this party and persuasion, of this or the other opinion in minor things, that will recommend us to God. It will not be asked at the great day, "Who ate flesh, and who ate herbs?" "Who kept holy days, and who did not?" Nor will it be asked, "Who was conformist and who was nonconformist?" But it will be asked, "Who feared God and worked righteousness, and who did not?" Nothing more destructive to true Christianity than placing it in modes, and forms, and circumstantials, which eat out the essentials. *Secondly, It is righteousness, and peace, and joy in the Holy Ghost.* These are some of the essentials of Christianity, things in which all the people of God are agreed, in the pursuit of which we must spend our zeal, and which we must mind with an excelling care. Righteousness, peace, and joy, are very comprehensive words; and each of them includes much both of the foundation and the superstructure of religion. Might I limit the sense of them, it should be thus:—As to God, our great concern is *righteousness*—to appear before him justified by the merit of Christ's death, sanctified by the Spirit of his grace; for the righteous Lord loveth righteousness. As to our brethren, it is *peace*—to live in peace and love, and charity with them, following peace with all men: Christ came into the world to be the great peace-maker. As to ourselves, it is *joy in the Holy Ghost*—that spiritual joy which is wrought by the blessed Spirit in the hearts of believers, which respects God as their reconciled Father and heaven as their expected home. Next to our compliance with God, the life of religion consists in our complacency in him; to delight ourselves always in the Lord. Surely we serve a good Master, who makes peace and joy so essential to our religion. Then and then only we may expect peace and joy in the Holy Ghost when the foundation is laid in righteousness, Isa. xxxii. 17. *Thirdly,* It is in these things to *serve Christ* (*v.* 18), to do all this out of respect to Christ himself as our Master, to his will as our rule and to his glory as our end. That which puts an acceptableness upon all our good duties is a regard to Christ in the doing of them. We are to serve his interests and designs in the world, which are in the first place to reconcile us to God and then to reconcile us one to another. What is Christianity but the serving of Christ? And we may well afford to serve him who for us and for our salvation took upon him the form of a servant.

[2.] The advantages of it. He that duly observeth these things, *First,* Is acceptable to God. God is well pleased with such a one, though he be not in every thing just of our length. He has the love and favour of God; his person, his performances, are accepted of God, and we need no more to make us happy. If God now accepts thy works, thou mayest eat thy bread with joy. Those are most pleasing to God that are best pleased with him; and they are those that abound most in peace and joy in the Holy Ghost. *Secondly,* He is approved of men—of all wise and good men, and the opinion of others is not to be regarded. The persons and things which are acceptable to God should be approved of us. Should not we be pleased with that which God is pleased with? What is it to be sanctified, but to be of God's mind? Observe, The approbation of men is not to be slighted; for we must provide things honest in the sight of all men, and study those things that are lovely and of good report: but the acceptance of God is to be desired and aimed at in the first place, because, sooner or later, God will bring all the world to be of his mind.

3. Another rule here given is this, that in these doubtful things every one not only may, but must, walk according to the light that God hath given him. This is laid down *v.* 5, *Let every man be fully persuaded in his own mind;* that is, "Practise according to your own judgment in these things, and leave others to do so too. Do not censure the practice of others; let them enjoy their own opinion; if they be persuaded in their own mind that they ought to do so and so, do not condemn them, but, if your sober sentiments be otherwise, do not make their practice a rule to you, any more than you must prescribe yours as a rule to them. Take heed of acting contrary to the dictates of a doubting conscience. First be persuaded that what you do is lawful, before you venture to do it." In doubtful things, it is good keeping on the sure side of the hedge. If a weak Christian doubts whether it be lawful to eat flesh, while he remains under that doubt he had best forbear, till he be fully persuaded in his own mind. We must not pin our faith upon any one's sleeve, nor make the practice of others our rule; but follow the dictates of our own understanding. To this purport he argues, *v.* 14 and 23, which two verses explain this, and give us a rule not to act against the dictates,

(1.) Of a mistaken conscience, *v.* 14. If a thing be indifferent, so that it is not in itself a sin not to do it, if we really think it a sin to do it it is to us a sin, though not to others, because we act against our consciences, though mistaken and misinformed. He specifies the case in hand, concerning the difference of meats. Observe,

[1.] His own clearness in this matter. "*I know and am persuaded*—I am fully persuaded, I am acquainted with my Christian liberty, and am satisfied in it, without any doubt or scruple, that there *is nothing unclean of itself,* that is, no kind of meat that lies under any ceremonial uncleanness, nor is forbidden to be eaten, if it be food proper for human bodies." Several kinds of meat were forbidden to the Jews, that in that, as in other things, they might be a peculiar and separate people, Lev. xi. 44; Deut. xiv. 2, 3. Sin had brought a curse upon the whole creation: *Cursed is the ground for thy sake;* the use of the creatures and dominion over them were forfeited, so that to man they were all unclean (Tit. i. 15), in token of which God in the ceremonial law prohibited the use of some, to show what he might have done concerning all; but now that Christ has removed the curse the matter is set at large again, and that prohibition is taken away. Therefore Paul says that he was persuaded by the Lord Jesus, not only as the author of that persuasion, but as the ground of it; it was built upon the efficacy of Christ's death, which removed the curse, took off the forfeiture, and restored our right to the creature in general, and consequently put a period to that particular distinguishing prohibition. So that now there is nothing unclean of itself, every creature of God is good; nothing *common:* so the margin, *οὐδὲν κοινὸν·* nothing which is common to others to eat, from the use of which the professors of religion are restrained: nothing profane; in this sense the Jews used the word *common.* It is explained by the word *ἀκάθαρτον,* Acts x. 14, nothing *common* or *unclean.* It was not only from the revelation made to Peter in this matter, but from the tenour and tendency of the whole gospel, and from the manifest design of Christ's death in general, that Paul learned to count nothing common or unclean. This was Paul's own clearness, and he practised accordingly.

[2.] But here is a caution he gives to those who had not that clearness in this matter which he had: *To him that esteemeth any thing to be unclean,* though it be his error, yet *to him it is unclean.* This particular case, thus determined, gives a general rule, That he who does a thing which he verily believes to be unlawful, however the thing be in itself, to him it is a sin. This arises from that unchangeable law of our creation, which is, that our wills, in all their choices, motions, and directions, should follow the dictates of our understandings. This is the order of nature, which order is broken if the understanding (though misguided) tell us that such a thing is a sin, and yet we will do it. This is a *will* to do evil; for, if it appears to us to be sin, there is the same pravity and corruption of the will in the doing of it as if really it were a sin; and therefore we ought not to do it. Not that it is in the power of any man's conscience to alter the nature of the action in itself, but only as to himself. It must be understood likewise with this proviso, though men's judgments and opinions may make that which is good in itself to become evil to them, yet they cannot make that which is evil in itself to become good, either in itself or to them. If a man were verily persuaded (it is Dr. Sanderson's instance, sermon on *ch.* xiv. 23) that it were evil to ask his father's blessing, that mispersuasion would make it become evil to him: but, if he should be as verily persuaded that it were good to curse his father, this would not make it become good. The Pharisees taught people to plead conscience, when they made *corban* an excuse for denying relief to their parents, Matt. xv. 5, 6. But this would not serve any more than Paul's erroneous conscience would justify his rage against Christianity (Acts xxvi. 9), or theirs, John xvi. 2.

(2.) Nor must we act against the dictates of a doubting conscience. In those indifferent things which we are sure it is no sin not to do, and yet are not clear that it is lawful to do them, we must not do them while we continue under those doubts; for he *that doubteth is damned if he eat* (*v.* 23), that is, it turns into sin to him; he is *damned, κατακέκριται—he is condemned* of his own conscience, because he *eateth not of faith,* because he does that which he is not fully persuaded he may lawfully do. He is not clear that it is lawful for him to eat swine's flesh (suppose), and yet is drawn, notwithstanding his doubts, to eat it, because he sees others do it, because he would gratify his appetite with it, or because he would not be reproached for his singularity. Here his own heart cannot but condemn him as a transgressor. Our rule is, to walk as far as we have attained, not further, Phil. iii. 15, 16.—*For whatsoever is not of faith is sin.* Taking it in general, it is the same with that of the apostle (Heb. xi. 6), *Without faith it is impossible to please God.* Whatever we do in religion, it will not turn to any good account, except we do it from a principle of faith, with a believing regard to the will of Christ as our rule, to the glory of Christ as our end, and to the righteousness of Christ as our plea. Here it seems to be taken more strictly; whatever is not of faith (that is, whatever is done while we are not clearly persuaded of the lawfulness of it), is a sin against conscience. He that will venture to do that which his own conscience suggests to him to be unlawful, when it is not so in itself, will by a like temptation be brought to do that which his conscience tells him is unlawful when it is really so. The spirit of a man is the candle of the Lord, and it is a dangerous thing to debauch and put a force upon conscience, though it be under a mistake. This seems to be the meaning of that aphorism, which sounds somewhat darkly (*v.* 22), *Happy is he that condemns not himself in that thing which he allows.* Many a one allows himself in practice to do that which yet in his judgment and conscience he condemns himself for—allows it for the sake of the pleasure, profit, or credit of it—allows it in conformity to the custom; and yet whilst he does it, and pleads for it, his own heart gives him the lie, and his conscience condemns him for it. Now, happy is the man who so orders his conversation as not in any action to expose himself to the challenges and reproaches of his own conscience—that does not make his own heart his adversary, as he must needs do who does that which he is not clear he may lawfully do. He is happy that has peace and quietness within, for the testimony of conscience will be a special cordial in troublesome times. Though men condemn us, it is well enough if our own hearts condemn us not, 1 John iii. 21.

4. Another rule here prescribed is to those who are clear in these matters, and know their Christian liberty, yet to take heed of using it so as to give offence to a weak brother. This is laid down *v.* 13, *Let us not judge one another any more.* "Let it suffice that you have hitherto continued in this uncharitable practice, and do so no more." The better to insinuate the exhortation, he puts himself in; Let us not; as if he had said, "It is what I have resolved against, therefore do you leave it: but *judge this rather,* instead of censuring the practice of others, let us look to our own, that no *man put a stumbling-block, or an occasion to fall, in his brother's way,*"—πρόσκομμα, ἢ σκάνδαλον. We must take heed of saying or doing any thing which may occasion our brother to stumble or fall; the one signifies a less, the other a greater degree of mischief and offence—that which may be an occasion,

(1.) Of grief to our brother, "One that is weak, and thinks it unlawful to eat such and such meats, will be greatly troubled to see thee eat them, out of a concern for the honour of the law which he thinks forbids them, and for the good of thy soul which he thinks is wronged by them, especially when thou dost it wilfully and with a seeming presumption, and not with that tenderness and that care to give satisfaction to thy weak brother which would become thee." Christians should take heed of grieving one another, and of saddening the hearts of Christ's little ones. See Matt. xviii. 6, 10.

(2.) Of guilt to our brother. The former is a *stumbling-block,* that gives our brother a great shake, and is a hindrance and discouragement to him; but this is an *occasion to fall.* "If thy weak brother, purely by thy example and influence, without any satisfaction received concerning his Christian liberty, be drawn to act against his conscience and to walk contrary to the light he has, and so to contract guilt upon his soul, though the thing were lawful to thee, yet not being so to him (he having not yet *thereto attained)*, thou art to be blamed for giving the occasion." See this case explained, 1 Cor. viii. 9—11. To the same purport (*v.* 21) he recommends it to our care not to give offence to any one by the use of lawful things : *It is good neither to eat flesh nor to drink wine ;* these are things lawful indeed and comfortable, but not necessary to the support of human life, and therefore we may, and must, deny ourselves in them, rather than give offence. *It is good*—pleasing to God, profitable to our brother, and no harm to ourselves. Daniel and his fellows were in better liking with pulse and water than those were who ate the portion of the king's meat. It is a generous piece of self-denial, for which we have Paul's example (1 Cor. viii. 13), *If meat make my brother to offend ;* he does not say, *I will eat no meat*, that is to destroy himself; but *I will eat no flesh*, that is to deny himself, *while the world stands.* This is to be extended to all such indifferent things whereby thy brother stumbleth, or is offended, is involved either in sin or in trouble: or *is made weak*—his graces weakened, his comforts weakened, his resolutions weakened. *Is made weak*, that is, takes occasion to show his weakness by his censures and scruples. We must not weaken those that are weak; that is to quench the smoking flax and to break the bruised reed. Observe the motives to enforce this caution.

[1.] Consider the royal law of Christian love and charity, which is hereby broken (*v.* 15): *If thy brother be grieved with thy meat*—be troubled to see thee eat those things which the law of Moses did forbid, which yet thou mayest lawfully do; possibly thou art ready to say, "Now he talks foolishly and weakly, and it is no great matter what he says." We are apt, in such a case, to lay all the blame on that side. But the reproof is here given to the stronger and more knowing Christian : *Now walkest thou not charitably.* Thus the apostle takes part with the weakest, and condemns the defect in love on the one side more than the defect in knowledge on the other side; agreeably to his principles elsewhere, that the way of love is the *more excellent way*, 1 Cor. xii. 31. Knowledge puffeth up, but charity edifieth, 1 Cor. viii. 1—3. *Now walkest thou not charitably.* Charity to the souls of our brethren is the best charity. True love would make us tender of their peace and purity, and beget a regard to their consciences as well as to our own. Christ deals gently with those that have true grace, though they are weak in it.

[2.] Consider the design of Christ's death: *Destroy not him with thy meat for whom Christ died, v.* 15. *First*, Drawing a soul to sin threatens the destruction of that soul. By shaking his faith, provoking his passion, and tempting him to act against the light of his own conscience, thou dost, as much as in thee lies, destroy him, giving him an occasion to return to judaism. Μὴ ἀπόλλυε. It denotes an utter destruction. The begining of sin is as the letting forth of water; we are not sure that it will stop any where on this side eternal destruction. *Secondly*, The consideration of the love of Christ in dying for souls should make us very tender of the happiness and salvation of souls, and careful not to do any thing which may obstruct and hinder them. Did Christ quit a life for souls, such a life, and shall not we quit a morsel of meat for them ? Shall we despise those whom Christ valued at so high a rate ? Did he think it worth while to deny himself so much for them as to die for them, and shall not we think it worth while to deny ourselves so little for them as abstaining from flesh comes to ?—*With thy meat.* Thou pleadest that it is thy own meat, and thou mayest do what thou wilt with it; but remember that, though the meat is thine, the brother offended by it is Christ's, and a part of his purchase. While thou destroyest thy brother thou art helping forward the devil's design, for he is the great destroyer; and, as much as in thee lies, thou art crossing the design of Christ, for he is the great Saviour, and dost not only offend thy brother, but offend Christ; for the work of salvation is that which his heart is upon. But are any destroyed for whom Christ died? If we understand it of the sufficiency and general intendment of Christ's death, which was to save all upon gospel terms, no doubt but multitudes are. If of the particular determination of the efficacy of his death to the elect, then, though none that were given to Christ shall perish (John vi. 39), yet thou mayest, as much as is in thy power, destroy such. No thanks to thee if they be not destroyed; by doing that which has a tendency to it, thou dost manifest a great opposition to Christ. Nay, and thou mayest utterly destroy some whose profession may be so justifiable that thou art bound to believe, in a judgment of charity, that Christ died for them. Compare this with 1 Cor. viii. 10, 11.

[3.] Consider the work of God (*v.* 20): "*For meat destroy not the work of God*—the work of grace, particularly the work of faith in thy brother's soul." The works of peace and comfort are destroyed by such an offence given; take heed of it therefore; do not undo that which God hath done. You should work together with God, do not countermine his work. *First*, The work of grace and peace is the work of God; it is wrought by him, it is wrought for him; it is a good work of his beginning, Phil. i. 6. Observe, The same for whom Christ died (*v.* 15) are here called the work of God; besides the work that is wrought for us there is a work to be wrought in us, in order to our salvation. Every saint is God's workmanship, his husbandry, his building, Eph. ii. 10; 1 Cor. iii. 9. *Secondly,* We must be very careful to do nothing which tends to the destruction of this work, either in ourselves or others. We must deny ourselves in our appetites, inclinations, and in the use of Christian liberty, rather than obstruct and prejudice our own or others' grace and peace. Many do for meat and drink destroy the work of God in themselves (nothing more destructive to the soul than pampering and pleasing the flesh, and fulfilling the lusts of it), so likewise in others, by wilful offence given. Think what thou destroyest—*the work of God,* whose work is honourable and glorious; think for what thou destroyest it—*for meat,* which was but for the belly, and the belly for it.

[4.] Consider the evil of giving offence, and what an abuse it is of our Christian liberty. He grants that *all things indeed are pure.* We may lawfully eat flesh, even those meats which were prohibited by the ceremonial law; but, if we abuse this liberty, it turns into sin to us: *It is evil to him that eats with offence.* Lawful things may be done unlawfully.—*Eats with offence,* either carelessly or designedly giving offence to his brethren. It is observable that the apostle directs his reproof most against those who gave the offence; not as if those were not to be blamed who causelessly and weakly took the offence from their ignorance of Christian liberty, and the want of that charity which is not easily provoked and which thinketh no evil (he several times tacitly reflects upon them), but he directs his speech to the strong, because they were better able to bear the reproof, and to begin the reformation. For the further pressing of this rule, we may here observe two directions which have relation to it:—*First, Let not then your good be evil spoken of* (*v.* 16)—take heed of doing any thing which may give occasion to others to speak evil, either of the Christian religion in general, or of your Christian liberty in particular. The gospel is your good; the liberties and franchises, the privileges and immunities, granted by it, are your good; your knowledge and strength of grace to discern and use your liberty in things disputed are your good, a good which the weak brother hath not. Now let not this be evil spoken of. It is true we cannot hinder loose and ungoverned tongues from speaking evil of us, and of the best things we have; but we must not (if we can help it) give them any occasion to do it. Let not the reproach arise from any default of ours; as 1 Tim. iv. 12, *Let no man despise thee,* that is, do not make thyself despicable. So here, Do not use your knowledge and strength in such a manner as to give occasion to people to call it presumption and loose walking, and disobedience to God's law. We must deny ourselves in many cases for the preservation of our credit and reputation, forbearing to do that which we rightly know we may lawfully do, when our doing it may be a prejudice to our good name; as, when it is suspicious and has the appearance of evil, or when it becomes scandalous among good people, or has any way a brand upon it. In such a case we must rather cross ourselves than shame ourselves. Though it be but a little folly, it may be like a dead fly, very prejudicial to one that is in reputation for wisdom and honour, Eccl. x. 1. We may apply it more generally. We should manage all our good duties in such a manner that they may not be evil spoken of. That which for the matter of it is good and unexceptionable may sometimes, by mismanagement, be rendered liable to a great deal of censure and reproach. Good praying, preaching, and discourse, may often, for want of prudence in ordering the time, the expression, and other circumstances to edification, be evil spoken of. It is indeed their sin who do speak evil of that which is good for the sake of any such circumstantial errors, but it is our folly if we give any occasion to do so. As we tender the reputation of the good we profess and practise, let us so order it that it may not be evil spoken of. *Secondly, Hast thou faith? Have it to thyself before God, v.* 22. It is not meant of justifying faith (that must not be hid, but manifested by our works), but of a knowledge and persuasion of our Christian liberty in things disputed. "Hast thou clearness in such a particular? Art thou satisfied that thou mayest eat all meats, and observe all days (except the Lord's day) alike? *Have it to thyself,* that is, enjoy the comfort of it in thy own bosom, and do not trouble others by the imprudent use of it, when it might give offence, and cause thy weak brother to stumble and fall." In these indifferent things, though we must never contradict our persuasion, yet we may sometimes conceal it, when the avowing of it will do more hurt than good. *Have it to thyself*—a rule to thyself (not to be imposed upon others, or made a rule to them), or a rejoicing to thyself. Clearness in doubtful matters contributes very much to our comfortable walking, as it frees us from those scruples, jealousies, and suspicions, which those who have not such clearness are entangled in endlessly. Compare Gal. vi. 4, *Let every man prove his own work,* that is, bring it to the touchstone of the word and try it by that so exactly as to be well satisfied in what he does; and then he *shall have rejoicing in himself alone, and not in another.* Paul had faith in these things: *I am persuaded that there is nothing unclean of itself;* but he had it to himself, so as not to use his liberty to the offence of others. How happy were it for the church if those that have a clearness in disputable things would be satisfied to have it to themselves before God, and not impose those things upon others, and make them terms of communion, than which nothing is more opposite to Christian liberty, nor more destructive both to the peace of churches and the peace of consciences. That healing method is not the less excellent for being common: in things necessary let there be unity, in things unnecessary let there be liberty, and in both let there be charity, then all will be well quickly.—*Have it to thyself before God.* The end of such knowledge is that, being satisfied in our liberty, we may have a conscience void of offence towards God, and let that content us. That is the true comfort which we have before God. Those are right indeed that are so in God's sight.

5. There is one rule more laid down here; and it is general: *Let us therefore follow after the things which make for peace, and things wherewith one may edify another, v.* 19. Here is the sum of our duty towards our brethren. (1.) We must study mutual peace. Many wish for peace, and talk loudly for it, that do not follow the things that make for peace, but the contrary. Liberty in things indifferent, condescension to those that are weak and tender, zeal in the great things of God wherein we are all agreed; these are things that make for peace. Meekness, humility, self-denial, and love, are the springs of peace, the things that make for our peace. We are not always so happy as to obtain peace; there are so many that delight in war: but the God of peace will accept us if we follow after the things that make for peace, that is, if we do our endeavour. (2.) We must study mutual edification. The former makes way for this. We cannot edify one another, while we are quarrelling and contending. There are many ways by which we might edify one another, if we did but seriously mind it; by good counsel, reproof, instruction, example, building up not only ourselves, but one another, in our most holy faith. We are God's building, God's temple, and have need to be edified; and therefore must study to promote the spiritual growth one of another. None so strong but they may be edified; none so weak but may edify; and, while we edify others, we benefit ourselves.

CHAP. XV.

The apostle, in this chapter, continues the discourse of the former, concerning mutual forbearance in indifferent things; and so draws towards a conclusion of the epistle. Where such differences of apprehension, and consequently distances of affection, are among Christians, there is need of precept upon precept, line upon line, to allay the heat, and to beget a better temper. The apostle, being desirous to drive the nail home, as a nail in a sure place, follows his blow, unwilling to leave the subject till he has some hopes of prevailing, to which end he orders the cause before them and fills his mouth with the most pressing arguments. We may observe, in this chapter, I. His precepts to them. II. His prayers for them. III. His apology for writing to them. IV. His account of himself and his own affairs. V. His declaration of his purpose to come and see them. VI. His desire of a share in their prayers.

WE then that are strong ought
to bear the infirmities of the
weak, and not to please ourselves.
2 Let every one of us please *his*
neighbour for *his* good to edification.
3 For even Christ pleased not himself; but, as it is written, The reproaches of them that reproached
thee fell on me. 4 For whatsoever
things were written aforetime were
written for our learning, that we
through patience and comfort of the
scriptures might have hope.

The apostle here lays down two precepts, with reasons to enforce them, showing the duty of the strong Christian to consider and condescend to the weakest.

I. We must *bear the infirmities of the weak. v.* 1. We all have our infirmities; but the weak are more subject to them than others—the weak in knowledge or grace, the bruised reed and the smoking flax. We must consider these; not trample upon them, but encourage them, and bear with their infirmities. If through weakness they judge and censure us, and speak evil of us, we must bear with them, pity them, and not have our affections alienated from them. Alas! it is their weakness, they cannot help it. Thus Christ bore with his weak disciples, and apologised for them. But there is more in it; we must also bear their infirmities by sympathizing with them, concerning ourselves for them, ministering strength to them, as there is occasion. This is bearing one another's burdens.

II. We must not please ourselves, but our neighbour, *v.* 1, 2. We must deny our own humour, in consideration of our brethren's weakness and infirmity.

1. Christians must not please themselves. We must not make it our business to gratify all the little appetites and desires of our own heart; it is good for us to cross ourselves sometimes, and then we shall the better bear others crossing of us. We shall be spoiled (as Adonijah was) if we be always humoured. The first lesson we have to learn is to deny ourselves, Matt. xvi. 24.

2. Christians must please their brethren. The design of Christianity is to soften and meeken the spirit, to teach us the art of obliging and true complaisance; not to be servants to the lust of any, but to the necessities and infirmities of our brethren—to comply with all that we have to do with as far as we can with a good conscience. Christians should study to be pleasing. As we must not please ourselves in the use of our Christian liberty (which was allowed us, not for our own pleasure, but for the glory of God and the profit and edification of others), so we must please our neighbour. How amiable and comfortable a society would the church of Christ be if Christians would study to please one another, as now we see them commonly industrious to cross, and thwart, and contradict one another!—*Please his neighbour*, not in every thing, it is not an unlimited rule; but *for his good*, especially for the good of his soul: not please him by serving his wicked wills, and humouring him in a sinful way, or consenting to his enticements, or suffering sin upon him; this is a

base way of pleasing our neighbour to the ruin of his soul: if we thus please men, we are not the servants of Christ; but please him for his good; not for our own secular good, or to make a prey of him, but for his spiritual good.—*To edification,* that is, not only for his profit, but for the profit of others, to edify the body of Christ, by studying to oblige one another. The closer the stones lie, and the better they are squared to fit one another, the stronger is the building. Now observe the reason why Christians must please one another: *For even Christ pleased not himself.* The self-denial of our Lord Jesus is the best argument against the selfishness of Christians. Observe,

(1.) That Christ pleased not himself. He did not consult his own worldly credit, ease, safety, nor pleasure; he had not where to lay his head, lived upon alms, would not be made a king, detested no proposal with greater abhorrence than that, *Master, spare thyself,* did not *seek his own will* (John v. 30), washed his disciples' feet, endured the contradiction of sinners against himself, troubled himself (John xi. 33), did not consult his own honour, and, in a word, emptied himself, and made himself of no reputation: and all this for our sakes, to bring in a righteousness for us, and to set us an example. His whole life was a self-denying self-displeasing life. He bore the *infirmities of the weak,* Heb. iv. 15.

(2.) That herein the scripture was fulfilled: *As it is written, The reproaches of those that reproached thee fell on me.* This is quoted out of Ps. lxix. 9, the former part of which verse is applied to Christ (John ii. 17), *The zeal of thine house hath eaten me up;* and the latter part here; for David was a type of Christ, and his sufferings of Christ's sufferings. It is quoted to show that Christ was so far from pleasing himself that he did in the highest degree displease himself. Not as if his undertaking, considered on the whole, were a task and grievance to him, for he was very willing to it and very cheerful in it; but in his humiliation the content and satisfaction of natural inclination were altogether crossed and denied. He preferred our benefit before his own ease and pleasure. This the apostle chooses to express in scripture language; for how can the things of the Spirit of God be better spoken of than in the Spirit's own words? And this scripture he alleges, *The reproaches of those that reproached thee fell on me.* [1.] The shame of those reproaches, which Christ underwent. Whatever dishonour was done to God was a trouble to the Lord Jesus. He was grieved for the hardness of people's hearts, beheld a sinful place with sorrow and tears. When the saints were persecuted, Christ so far displeased himself as to take what was done to them as done against himself: *Saul, Saul, why persecutest thou me?* Christ also did himself endure the greatest indignities; there was much of reproach in his sufferings. [2.] The sin of those reproaches, for which Christ undertook to satisfy; so many understand it. Every sin is a kind of reproach to God, especially presumptuous sins; now the guilt of these fell upon Christ, when he was made sin, that is, a sacrifice, a sin-offering for us. When the Lord laid upon him the iniquities of us all, and he bore our sins in his own body upon the tree, they fell upon him as upon our surety. *Upon me be the curse.* This was the greatest piece of self-displacency that could be: considering his infinite spotless purity and holiness, the infinite love of the Father to him, and his eternal concern for his Father's glory, nothing could be more contrary to him, nor more against him, than to be made sin and a curse for us, and to have the reproaches of God fall upon him, especially considering for whom he thus displeased himself, for strangers, enemies, and traitors, the *just for the unjust,* 1 Pet. iii. 18. This seems to come in as a reason why we should bear the infirmities of the weak. We must not please ourselves, for Christ pleased not himself; we must bear the infirmities of the weak, for Christ bore the reproaches of those that reproached God. He bore the guilt of sin and the curse for it; we are only called to bear a little of the trouble of it. He bore the presumptuous sins of the wicked; we are called only to bear the infirmities of the weak.—*Even Christ; καὶ γὰρ ὁ Χριστὸς.* Even he who was infinitely happy in the enjoyment of himself, who needed not us nor our services,—even he who thought it no robbery to be equal with God, who had reason enough to please himself, and no reason to be concerned, much less to be crossed, for us,—even he pleased not himself, even he bore our sins. And should not we be humble, and self-denying, and ready to consider one another, who are members one of another?

(3.) That therefore we must go and do likewise: *For whatsoever things were written aforetime were written for our learning.* [1.] That which is written of Christ, concerning his self-denial and sufferings, is *written for our learning;* he hath left us an example. If Christ denied himself, surely we should deny ourselves, from a principle of ingenuousness and of gratitude, and especially of conformity to his image. The example of Christ, in what he did and said, is recorded for our imitation. [2.] That which is written in the scriptures of the Old Testament in the general is written for our learning. What David had said in his own person Paul had just now applied to Christ. Now lest this should look like a straining of the scripture, he gives us this excellent rule in general, that all the scriptures of the Old Testament (much more those of the New) were written for our learning, and are not to be looked upon as of private interpretation. What happened to the Old-Testament saints happened to them for ensample; and the scriptures of the Old Testament have many fulfillings. The scriptures are left for a standing rule to us: they are *written*, that they might remain for our use and benefit. *First*, For our learning. There are many things to be learned out of the scriptures; and that is the best learning which is drawn from these fountains. Those are the most learned that are most mighty in the scriptures. We must therefore labour, not only to understand the literal meaning of the scripture, but to learn out of it that which will do us good; and we have need of help therefore not only to roll away the stone, but to draw out the water, for in many places the well is deep. Practical observations are more necessary than critical expositions. *Secondly, That we through patience and comfort of the scriptures might have hope.* That hope which hath eternal life for its object is here proposed as the end of scripture-learning. The scripture was written that we might know what to hope for from God, and upon what grounds, and in what way. This should recommend the scripture to us that it is a special friend to Christian hope. Now the way of attaining this hope is *through patience and comfort of the scripture.* Patience and comfort suppose trouble and sorrow; such is the lot of the saints in this world; and, were it not so, we should have no occasion for patience and comfort. But both these befriend that hope which is the life of our souls. Patience works experience, and experience hope, which maketh not ashamed, *ch.* v. 3—5. The more patience we exercise under troubles the more hopefully we may look through our troubles; nothing more destructive to hope than impatience. And the *comfort of the scriptures*, that comfort which springs from the word of God (that is the surest and sweetest comfort) is likewise a great stay to hope, as it is an earnest in hand of the good hoped for. The Spirit, as a comforter, is the earnest of our inheritance.

5 Now the God of patience and consolation grant you to be like-minded one toward another according to Christ Jesus: 6 That ye may with one mind *and* one mouth glorify God, even the Father of our Lord Jesus Christ.

The apostle, having delivered two exhortations, before he proceeds to more, intermixes here a prayer for the success of what he had said. Faithful ministers water their preaching with their prayers, because, whoever sows the seed, it is God that gives the increase. We can but speak to the ear; it is God's prerogative to speak to the heart. Observe,

I. The title he gives to God: *The God of patience and consolation*, who is both the author and the foundation of all the patience and consolation of the saints, from whom it springs and on whom it is built. He gives the grace of patience; he confirms and keeps it up as the God of consolation; for the comforts of the Holy Ghost help to support believers, and to bear them up with courage and cheerfulness under all their afflictions. When he comes to beg the pouring out of the spirit of love and unity he addresses himself to God as the God of patience and consolation; that is, 1. As a God that bears with us and comforts us, is not extreme to mark what we do amiss, but is ready to comfort those that are cast down—to teach us so to testify our love to our brethren, and by these means to preserve and maintain unity, by being patient one with another and comfortable one to another. Or, 2. As a God that gives us patience and comfort. He had spoken (*v.* 4) of patience and comfort of the scriptures; but here he looks up to God as the God of patience and consolation: it comes through the scripture as the conduit-pipe, but from God as the fountain-head. The more patience and comfort we receive from God, the better disposed we are to love one another. Nothing breaks the peace more than an impatient, and peevish, and fretful melancholy temper.

II. The mercy he begs of God: *Grant you to be like-minded one towards another, according to Christ Jesus.* 1. The foundation of Christian love and peace is laid in like-mindedness, a consent in judgment as far as you have attained, or at least a concord and agreement in affection. Τὸ αὐτὸ φρονεῖν—*to mind the same thing*, all occasions of difference removed, and all quarrels laid aside. 2. This like-mindedness must be *according to Christ Jesus*, according to the precept of Christ, the royal law of love, according to the pattern and example of Christ, which he had propounded to them for their imitation, *v.* 3. Or, "Let Christ Jesus be the centre of your unity. Agree in the truth, not in any error." It was a cursed concord and harmony of those who were of one mind to give their power and strength to the beast (Rev. xvii. 13); this was not a like-mindedness according to Christ, but against Christ; like the Babel-builders, who were one in their rebellion, Gen. xi. 6. The method of our prayer must be first for truth, and then for peace; for such is the method of the wisdom that is from above*: it is first pure, then peaceable.* This is to be like-minded according to Christ Jesus. 3. Like-mindedness among Christians, according to Christ Jesus, is the gift of God; and a precious gift it is, for which we must earnestly seek unto him. He is the *Father of spirits*, and fashions the hearts of men alike (Ps. xxxiii. 15), opens the understanding, softens the heart, sweetens the affections, and gives the grace of love, and the Spirit as a Spirit of love, to those that ask him. We are taught to pray that the will of God may be done on earth as it is done in heaven . now there it is done unanimously, among the angels, who are one in their praises and services; and our desire must be that the saints on earth may be so too.

III. The end of his desire: that God may be glorified, *v.* 6. This is his plea with God in prayer, and is likewise an argument with them to seek it. We should have the glory of God in our eye in every prayer; therefore our first petition, as the foundation of all the rest, must be, *Hallowed be thy name.* Like-mindedness among Christians is in order to our glorifying God, 1. *With one mind and one mouth.* It is desirable that Christians should agree in every thing, that so they may agree in this, to praise God together. It tends very much to the glory of God, who is one, and his name one, when it is so. It will not suffice that there be one mouth, but there must be one mind, for God looks at the heart; nay, there will hardly be one mouth where there is not one mind, and God will scarcely be glorified where there is not a sweet conjunction of both. One mouth in confessing the truths of God, in praising the name of God—one mouth in common converse, not jarring, biting, and devouring one another—one mouth in the solemn assembly, one speaking, but all joining. 2. As *the Father of our Lord Jesus Christ.* This is his New-Testament style. God must be glorified as he has now revealed himself in the face of Jesus Christ, according to the rules of the gospel, and with an eye to Christ, in whom he is our Father. The unity of Christians glorifies *God as the Father of our Lord Jesus Christ,* because it is a kind of counter-part or representation of the oneness that is between the Father and the Son. We are warranted so to speak of it, and, with that in our eye, to desire it, and pray for it, from John xvii. 21, *That they all may be one, as thou, Father, art in me, and I in thee:* a high expression of the honour and sweetness of the saints' unity. And it follows, *That the world may believe that thou hast sent me;* and so God may be glorified as the Father of our Lord Jesus Christ.

7 Wherefore receive ye one another,
as Christ also received us to the glory
of God. 8 Now I say that Jesus
Christ was a minister of the circumcision for the truth of God, to confirm
the promises *made* unto the fathers:
9 And that the Gentiles might glorify
God for *his* mercy; as it is written,
For this cause I will confess to thee
among the Gentiles, and sing unto
thy name. 10 And again he saith,
Rejoice, ye Gentiles, with his people.
11 And again, Praise the Lord, all ye
Gentiles; and laud him, all ye people.
12 And again, Esaias saith, There
shall be a root of Jesse, and he that
shall rise to reign over the Gentiles;
in him shall the Gentiles trust.

The apostle here returns to his exhortation to Christians. What he says here (*v.* 7) is to the same purport with the former; but the repetition shows how much the apostle's heart was upon it. "Receive one another into your affection, into your communion, and into your common conversation, as there is occasion." He had exhorted the strong to receive the weak (*ch.* xiv. 1), here, *Receive one another;* for sometimes the prejudices of the weak Christian make him shy of the strong, as much as the pride of the strong Christian makes him shy of the weak, neither of which ought to be. Let there be a mutual embracing among Christians. Those that have received Christ by faith must receive all Christians by brotherly love; though poor in the world, though persecuted and despised, though it may be matter of reproach and danger to you to receive them, though in the less weighty matters of the law they are of different apprehensions, though there may have been occasion for private piques, yet, laying aside these and the like considerations, *receive you one another.* Now the reason why Christians must receive one another is taken, as before, from the condescending love of Christ to us: *As Christ also received us, to the glory of God.* Can there be a more cogent argument? Has Christ been so kind to us, and shall we be so unkind to those that are his? Was he so forward to entertain us, and shall we be backward to entertain our brethren? Christ has received us into the nearest and dearest relations to himself: has received us into his fold, into his family, into the adoption of sons, into a covenant of friendship, yea, into a marriage-covenant with himself; he has received us (though we were strangers and enemies, and had played the prodigal) into fellowship and communion with himself. Those words, *to the glory of God,* may refer both to Christ's receiving us, which is our pattern, and to our receiving one another, which is our practice according to that pattern.

I. Christ hath received us to the glory of God. The end of our reception by Christ is that we might glorify God in this world, and be glorified with him in that to come. It was the glory of God, and our glory in the enjoyment of God, that Christ had in his eye when he condescended to receive us. We are called to an eternal glory by Christ Jesus, John xvii. 24. See to what he received us—to a happiness transcending all comprehension; see for what he received us—for his Father's glory; he had this in his eye in all the instances of his favour to us.

II. We must receive one another to the glory of God. This must be our great end in all our actions, that God may be glorified; and nothing more conduces to this than the mutual love and kindness of those that profess religion; compare *v.* 6, *That you may with one mind and one mouth glorify God.* That which was a bone of contention among them was a different apprehension about meats and drinks, which took rise in distinction between Jews and Gentiles. Now, to prevent and make up this difference, he shows how Jesus Christ has received both Jews and Gentiles; in him they are both one, *one new man,* Eph. ii. 14—16. Now it is a rule, *Quæ conveniunt in aliquo tertio, inter se conveniunt—Things which agree with a third thing agree with each other.* Those that agree in Christ, who is the Alpha and the Omega, the first and the last, and the great centre of unity, may well afford to agree among themselves. This coalescence of the Jews and Gentiles in Christ and Christianity was a thing that filled and affected Paul so much that he could not mention it without some enlargement and illustration.

1. He received the Jews, *v.* 8. Let not any think hardly or scornfully therefore of those that were originally Jews, and still, through weakness, retain some savour of their old Judaism; for, (1.) Jesus Christ was a *minister of the circumcision.* That he was a *minister, διάκονος—a servant,* bespeaks his great and exemplary condescension, and puts an honour upon the ministry: but that he was a minister of the circumcision, was himself circumcised and made under the law, and did in his own person preach the gospel to the Jews, who were of the circumcision—this makes the nation of the Jews more considerable than otherwise they appear to be. Christ conversed with the Jews, blessed them, looked upon himself as primarily sent to the *lost sheep of the house of Israel, laid hold of the seed of Abraham* (Heb. ii. 16, *margin),* and by them, as it were, caught at the whole body of mankind. Christ's personal ministry was appropriated to them, though the apostles had their commission enlarged. (2.) He was so for the truth of God. That which he preached to them was the truth; for he came into the world to bear witness to the truth, John xviii. 37. And he is himself the truth, John xiv. 6. Or, for the truth of God, that is, to make good the promises given to the patriarchs concerning the special mercy God had in store for their seed. It was not for the merit of the Jews, but for the truth of God, that they were thus distinguished—that God might approve himself true to this word which he had spoken.—*To confirm the promises made unto the fathers.* The best confirmation of promises is the performance of them. It was promised that in the seed of Abraham all the nations of the earth should be blessed, that Shiloh should come from between the feet of Judah, that out of Israel should he proceed that should have the dominion, that out of Zion should go forth the law, and many the like. There were many intermediate providences which seemed to weaken those promises, providences which threatened the fatal decay of that people; but when Messiah the Prince appeared in the fulness of time, as a minister of the circumcision, all these promises were confirmed, and the truth of them was made to appear; for in Christ all the promises of God, both those of the Old Testament and those of the New, are Yea, and in him Amen. Understanding by *the promises made to the fathers* the whole covenant of grace, darkly administered under the Old Testament, and brought to a clearer light now under the gospel, it was Christ's great errand to confirm that covenant, Dan. ix. 27. He confirmed it by shedding the blood of the covenant.

2. He received the Gentiles likewise. This he shows, *v.* 9—12.

(1.) Observe Christ's favour to the Gentiles, in taking them in to praise God—the work of the church on earth and the wages of that in heaven. One design of Christ was that the Gentiles likewise might be converted, that they might be one with the Jews in Christ's mystical body. A good reason why they should not think the worse of any Christian for his having been formerly a Gentile; for Christ has received him. He invites the Gentiles, and welcomes them. Now observe how their conversion is here expressed: *That the Gentiles might glorify God for his mercy.* A periphrasis of conversion. [1.] They shall have matter for praise, even the mercy of God. Considering the miserable and deplorable condition that the Gentile world was in, the receiving of them appears more as an act of mercy than the receiving of the Jews. Those that were *Lo-ammi—not a people,* were *Lo-ruhama—not obtaining mercy,* Hos. i. 6, 9; ii. 23. The greatest mercy of God to any people is the receiving of them into covenant with himself: and it is good to take notice of God's mercy in receiving us. [2.] They shall have a heart for praise. They shall glorify God for his mercy. Unconverted sinners do nothing to glorify God; but converting grace works in the soul a disposition to speak and do all to the glory of God; God intended to reap a harvest of glory from the Gentiles, who had been so long turning his glory into shame.

(2.) The fulfilling of the scriptures in this. The favour of God to the Gentiles was not only mercy, but truth. Though there were not promises directly given to them, as to the fathers of the Jews, yet there were many prophesies concerning them, which related to the calling of them, and the embodying of them in the church, some of which he mentions because it was a thing that the Jews were hardly persuaded to believe. Thus, by referring them to the Old Testament, he labours to qualify their dislike of the Gentiles, and so to reconcile the parties at variance. [1.] It was foretold that the Gentiles should have the gospel preached to them: "*I will confess to thee among the Gentiles* (*v.* 9), that is, thy name shall be known and owned in the Gentile world, there shall gospel grace and love be celebrated." This is quoted from Ps. xviii. 49, *I will give thanks unto thee, O Lord, among the heathen.* A thankful explication and commemoration of the name of God are an excellent means of drawing others to know and praise God. Christ, in and by his apostles and ministers, whom he sent to disciple all nations, did confess to God among the Gentiles. The exaltation of Christ, as well as the conversion of sinners, is set forth by the praising of God. Christ's declaring God's name to his brethren is called *his praising God in the midst of the congregation,* Ps. xxii. 22. Taking these words as spoken by David, they were spoken when he was old and dying, and he was not likely to confess to God among the Gentiles; but when David's psalms are read and sung among the Gentiles, to the praise and glory of God, it may be said that David is *confessing to God among the Gentiles, and singing to his name.* He that was the sweet psalmist of Israel is now the sweet psalmist of the Gentiles. Converting grace makes people greatly in love with David's psalms. Taking them as spoken by Christ, the Son of David, it may be understood of his spiritual indwelling by faith in the hearts of all the praising saints. If any confess to God among the Gentiles, and sing to his name, it is not they, but Christ and his grace in them. *I live, yet not I, but Christ liveth in me;* so, I praise, yet not I, but Christ in me. [2.] That the Gentiles should *rejoice with his people, v.* 10. This is quoted from that song of Moses, Deut. xxxii. 43. Observe, Those who were incorporated among his people are said to rejoice with his people. No greater joy can come to any people than the coming of the gospel among them in power. Those Jews that retain a prejudice against the Gentiles will by no means admit them to any of their joyful festivities; for (say they) a stranger intermeddleth not with the joy, Prov. xiv. 10. But, the partition-wall being taken down, the Gentiles are welcome to rejoice with his people. Being brought into the church, they share in its sufferings, are companions in patience and tribulation, to recompense which they share in the joy. [3.] That they should praise God (*v.* 11): *Praise the Lord, all ye Gentiles.* This is quoted out of that short psalm, Ps. cxvii. 1. Converting grace sets people a praising God, furnishes with the richest matter for praise, and gives a heart to it. The Gentiles had been, for many ages, praising their idols of wood and stone, but now they are brought to praise the Lord; and this David in spirit speaks of. In calling upon all the nations to praise the Lord, it is intimated that they shall have the knowledge of him. [4.] That they should believe in Christ (*v.* 12), quoted from Isa. xi. 10, where observe, *First,* The revelation of Christ, as the Gentiles' king. He is here called *the root of Jesse,* that is, such a branch from the family of David as is the very life and strength of the family: compare Isa. xi. 1. Christ was David's Lord, and yet withal he was the Son of David (Matt. xxii. 45), for he was the *root and offspring of David,* Rev. xxii. 16. Christ, as God, was David's root; Christ, as man, was David's offspring.—*And he that shall rise to reign over the Gentiles.* This explains the figurative expression of the prophet, he shall *stand for an ensign of the people.* When Christ rose from the dead, when he ascended on high, it was to reign over the Gentiles. *Secondly,* The recourse of the Gentiles to him: *In him shall the Gentiles trust.* Faith is the soul's confidence in Christ and dependence on him. The prophet has it, *to him shall the Gentiles seek.* The method of faith is first to seek unto Christ, as to one proposed to us for a Saviour; and, finding him able and willing to save, then to trust in him. Those that know him will trust in him. Or, this seeking to him is the effect of a trust in him; seeking him by prayer, and pursuant endeavours. We shall never seek to Christ till we trust in him. Trust is the mother; diligence in the use of means the daughter. Jews and Gentiles being thus united in Christ's love, why should they not be united in one another's love?

13 Now the God of hope fill you with all joy and peace in believing, that ye may abound in hope, through the power of the Holy Ghost.

Here is another prayer directed to God, as the God of hope; and it is, as the former (*v.* 5, 6), for spiritual blessings: these are the best blessings, and to be first and chiefly prayed for.

I. Observe how he addresses himself to God, as the *God of hope.* It is good in prayer to fasten upon those names, titles, and attributes of God, which are most suitable to the errand we come upon, and will best serve to encourage our faith concerning it. Every word in the prayer should be a plea. Thus should the cause be skilfully ordered, and the mouth filled with arguments. God is the God of hope. He is the foundation on which our hope is built, and he is the builder that doth himself raise it: he is both the object of our hope, and the author of it. That hope is but fancy, and will deceive us, which is not fastened upon God (as the goodness hoped for, and the truth hoped in), and which is not of his working in us. We have both together, Ps. cxix. 49. *Thy word*—there is God the object; *on which thou hast caused me to hope*—there is God the author of our hope, 1 Pet. i. 3.

II. What he asks of God, not for himself, but for them.

1. *That they might be filled with all joy and peace in believing.* Joy and peace are two of those things in which the kingdom of God consists, *ch.* xiv. 17. Joy in God, peace of conscience, both arising from a sense of our justification; see *ch.* v. 1, 2. Joy and peace in our own bosoms would promote a cheerful unity and unanimity with our brethren. Observe, (1.) How desirable this joy and peace are · they are filling. Carnal joy puffs up the soul, but cannot fill it; therefore in laughter the heart is sad. True, heavenly, spiritual joy is filling to the soul; it has a satisfaction in it, answerable to the soul's vast and just desires. Thus does God satiate and replenish the weary soul. Nothing more than this joy, only more of it, even the perfection of it in glory, is the desire of the soul that hath it, Ps. iv. 6, 7; xxxvi. 8; lxiii. 5; lxv. 4. (2.) How it is attainable. [1.] By prayer. We must go to God for it; he will for this be enquired of. Prayer fetches in spiritual joy and peace. [2.] By believing; that is the means to be used. It is vain, and flashy, and transient joy, that is the product of fancy; true substantial joy is the fruit of faith. *Believing, you rejoice with joy unspeakable,* 1 Pet. i. 8. It is owing to the weakness of our faith that we are so much wanting in joy and peace. Only believe; believe the goodness of Christ, the love of Christ, the promises of the covenant, and the joys and glories of heaven; let faith be the substance and evidence of these things, and the result must needs be joy and peace. Observe, It is *all* joy and peace—all sorts of true joy and peace. When we come to God by prayer we must enlarge our desires; we are not straitened in him, why should we be straitened in ourselves? Ask for all joy; open thy mouth wide, and he will fill it.

2. That they might *abound in hope through the power of the Holy Ghost.* The joy and peace of believers arise chiefly from their hopes. What is laid out upon them is but little, compared with what is laid up for them; therefore the more hope they have the more joy and peace they have. We do then abound in hope when we hope for great things from God, and are greatly established and confirmed in these hopes. Christians should desire and labour after an abundance of hope, such hope as will not make ashamed. This is through the power of the Holy Ghost. The same almighty power that works grace begets and strengthens this hope. Our own power will never reach it; and therefore where this hope is, and is abounding, the blessed Spirit must have all the glory.

14 And I myself also am persuaded of
you, my brethren, that ye also are full
of goodness, filled with all knowledge,
able also to admonish one another.
15 Nevertheless, brethren, I have
written the more boldly unto you in
some sort, as putting you in mind,
because of the grace that is given to
me of God, 16 That I should be the
minister of Jesus Christ to the Gentiles, ministering the gospel of God,
that the offering up of the Gentiles
might be acceptable, being sanctified
by the Holy Ghost.

Here, I. He commends these Christians with the highest characters that could be. He began his epistle with their praises (*ch.* i. 8), *Your faith is spoken of throughout the world,* thereby to make way for his discourse: and, because sometimes he had reproved them sharply, he now concludes with the like commendation, to qualify them, and to part friends. This he does like an orator. It was not a piece of idle flattery and compliment, but a due acknowledgment of their worth, and of the grace of God in them. We must be forward to observe and commend in others that which is excellent and praiseworthy; it is part of the present recompence of virtue and usefulness, and will be of use to quicken others to a holy emulation. It was a great credit to the Romans to be commended by Paul, a man of such great judgment and integrity, too skilful to be deceived and too honest to flatter. Paul had no personal acquaintance with these Christians, and yet he says he was persuaded of their excellencies, though he knew them only by hearsay. As we must not, on the one hand, be so simple as to believe every word; so, on the other hand, we must not be so sceptical as to believe nothing; but especially we must be forward to believe good concerning others: in this case charity hopeth all things, and believeth all things, and (if the probabilities be any way strong, as here they were) is persuaded. It is safer to err on this side. Now observe what it was that he commended them for. 1. That they *were full of goodness;* therefore the more likely to take in good part what he had written, and to account it a kindness; and not only so, but to comply with it, and to put it in practice, especially that which relates to their union and to the healing of their differences. A good understanding of one another, and a good will to one another, would soon put an end to strife. 2. *Filled with all knowledge.* Goodness and knowledge together! A very rare and an excellent conjunction; the head and the heart of the new man. All knowledge, all necessary knowledge, all the knowledge of those things which belong to their everlasting peace. 3. *Able to admonish one another.* To this there is a further gift requisite, even the gift of utterance. Those that have goodness and knowledge should communicate what they have for the use and benefit of others. "You that excel so much in good gifts may think you have no need of any instructions of mine." It is a comfort to faithful ministers to see their work superseded by the gifts and graces of their people. How gladly would ministers leave off their admonishing work, if people were able and willing to admonish one another! Would to God that all the Lord's people were prophets. But that which is every body's work is nobody's work; and therefore,

II. He clears himself from the suspicion of intermeddling needlessly with that which did not belong to him, *v.* 15. Observe how affectionately he speaks to them: *My brethren* (*v.* 14), and again, *brethren, v.* 15. He had himself, and taught others, the art of obliging. He calls them all his brethren, to teach them brotherly love one to another. Probably he wrote the more courteously to them because, being Roman citizens living near the court, they were more genteel, and made a better figure; and therefore Paul, who became all things to all men, was willing, by the respectfulness of his style, to please them for their good. He acknowledges he had written *boldly in some sort*—*τολμηρότερον ἀπὸ μέρους*, in a manner that looked like boldness and presumption, and for which some might perhaps charge him with taking too much upon him. But then consider,

1. He did it only as their remembrancer: *As putting you in mind.* Such humble thoughts had Paul of himself, though he excelled in knowledge, that he would not pretend to tell them that which they did not know before, but only to remind them of that in which they had formerly been by others instructed. So Peter, 2 Pet. i. 12; iii. 1. People commonly excuse themselves from hearing the word with this, that the minister can tell them nothing but what they knew before. If it be so, yet have they not need to know it better, and to be put in mind of it?

2. He did it as the apostle of the Gentiles. It was in pursuance of his office: *Because of the grace* (that is, the *apostleship, ch.* i. 5) *given to me of God,* to be the minister *of Jesus Christ to the Gentiles, v.* 16. Paul reckoned it a great favour, and an honour that God had put upon him, in putting him into that office, *ch.* i. 13. Now, because of this grace given to him, he thus laid out himself among the Gentiles, that he might not receive that grace of God in vain. Christ received that he might give; so did Paul; so have we talents which must not be buried. Places and offices must be filled up with duty. It is good for ministers to be often remembering the grace that is given unto them of God. *Minister verbi es, hoc age*—*You are a minister of the word; give yourself wholly to it,* was Mr. Perkins's motto. Paul was a minister. Observe here, (1.) Whose minister he was: the *minister of Jesus Christ,* 1 Cor. iv. 1. He is our Master; his we are, and him we serve. (2.) To whom: to the Gentiles. So God had appointed him, Acts xxii. 21. So Peter and he had agreed, Gal. ii. 7—9. These Romans were Gentiles: "Now," says he, "I do not thrust myself upon you, nor seek any lordship over you; I am appointed to it: if you think I am rude and bold, my commission is my warrant, and must bear me out. (3.) What he ministered: the *gospel of God; ἱερουργοῦντα τὸ εὐαγγέλιον*—*ministering as about holy things* (so the word signifies), executing the office of a Christian priest, more spiritual, and therefore more excellent, than the Levitical priesthood. (4.) For what end: *that the offering up* (or sacrificing) *of the Gentiles might be acceptable*—that God might have the glory which would redound to his name by the conversion of the Gentiles. Paul laid out himself thus to bring about something that might be acceptable to God. Observe how the conversion of the Gentiles is expressed: it is the *offering up of the Gentiles;* it is *προσφορὰ τῶν ἐθνῶν*—*the oblation of the Gentiles,* in which the Gentiles are looked upon either, [1.] As the priests, offering the oblation of prayer and praise, and other acts of religion. Long had the Jews been the holy nation, the kingdom of priests, but now the Gentiles are made priests unto God (Rev. v. 10), by their conversion to the Christian faith consecrated to the service of God, that the scripture may be fulfilled, *In every place incense shall be offered, and a pure offering,* Mal. i. 11. The converted Gentiles are said to be *made nigh* (Eph. ii. 13)—the periphrasis of priests. Or, [2.] The Gentiles are themselves the sacrifice offered up to God by Paul, in the name of Christ, a living sacrifice, holy, acceptable to God, *ch.* xii. 1. A sanctified soul is offered up to God in the flames of love, upon Christ the altar. Paul gathered in souls by his preaching, not to keep them to himself, but to offer them up to God: *Behold, I, and the children that God hath given me.* And it is an acceptable offering, *being sanctified by the Holy Ghost.* Paul preached to them, and dealt with them; but that which made them sacrifices to God was their sanctification; and this was not his work, but the work of the Holy Ghost. None are acceptably offered to God but those that are sanctified: unholy things can never be pleasing to the holy God.

17 I have therefore whereof I may
glory through Jesus Christ in those
things which pertain to God. 18
For I will not dare to speak of any of
those things which Christ hath not
wrought by me, to make the Gentiles obedient, by word and deed,
19 Through mighty signs and won-
ders, by the power of the Spirit of
God; so that from Jerusalem, and
round about unto Illyricum, I have
fully preached the gospel of Christ.

20 Yea, so have I striven to preach the gospel, not where Christ was named, lest I should build upon another man's foundation: 21 But as it is written, To whom he was not spoken of, they shall see: and they that have not heard shall understand.

The apostle here gives some account of himself and of his own affairs. Having mentioned his ministry and apostleship, he goes on further to magnify his office in the efficacy of it, and to mention to the glory of God the great success of his ministry and the wonderful things that God had done by him, for encouragement to the Christian church at Rome, that they were not alone in the profession of Christianity, but though, compared with the multitude of their idolatrous neighbours, they were but a little flock, yet, up and down the country, there were many that were their companions in the kingdom and patience of Jesus Christ. It was likewise a great confirmation of the truth of the Christian doctrine that it had such strange success, and was so far propagated by such weak and unlikely means, such multitudes captivated to the obedience of Christ by the foolishness of preaching. Therefore Paul gives them this account, which he makes the matter of his glorying; not vain glory, but holy gracious glorying, which appears by the limitations; it is *through Jesus Christ.* Thus does he centre all his glorying in Christ; he teaches us so to do, 1 Cor. i. 31. *Not unto us,* Ps. cxv. 1. And it is *in those things which pertain to God.* The conversion of souls is one of those things that pertain to God, and therefore is the matter of Paul's glorying; not the things of the flesh. *Whereof I may glory,* ἔχω οὖν καύχησιν ἐν Χριστῷ Ἰησοῦ τὰ πρὸς Θεόν. I would rather read it thus: *Therefore I have a rejoicing in Christ Jesus* (it is the same word that is used, 2 Cor. i. 12, and Phil. iii. 3, where it is the character of the circumcision that they *rejoice*—καυχώμενοι, in Christ Jesus) *concerning the things of God*; or those things that are offered to God—the living sacrifices of the Gentiles, *v.* 16. Paul would have them to rejoice with him in the extent and efficacy of his ministry, of which he speaks not only with the greatest deference possible to the power of Christ, and the effectual working of the Spirit as all in all; but with a protestation of the truth of what he said (*v.* 18): *I will not dare to speak of any of those things which Christ hath not wrought by me.* He would not boast of things without his line, nor take the praise of another man's work, as he might have done when he was writing to distant strangers, who perhaps could not contradict him; but (says he) I dare not do it: a faithful man dares not lie, however he be tempted, dares be true, however he be terrified. Now, in this account of himself, we may observe,

I. His unwearied diligence and industry in his work. He was one that laboured *more abundantly than they all.*

1. He preached in many places: *From Jerusalem,* whence the law went forth as a lamp that shineth, and *round about unto Illyricum,* many hundred miles distant from Jerusalem. We have in the book of the Acts an account of Paul's travels. There we find him, after he was sent forth to preach to the Gentiles (Acts xiii.), labouring in that blessed work in Seleucia, Cyprus, Pamphylia, Pisidia, and Lycaonia (Acts xiii. xiv.), afterwards travelling through Syria and Cilicia, Phrygia, Galatia, Mysia, Troas, and thence called over to Macedonia, and so into Europe, Acts xv. xvi. Then we find him very busy at Thessalonica, Berea, Athens, Corinth, Ephesus, and the parts adjacent. Those that know the extent and distance of these countries will conclude Paul an active man, rejoicing as a strong man to run a race. Illyricum is the country now called Sclavonia, bordering upon Hungary. Some take it for the same with Bulgaria; others for the lower Pannonia: however, it was a great way from Jerusalem. Now it might be suspected that if Paul undertook so much work, surely he did it by the halves. "No," says he, "*I have fully preached the Gospel of Christ*—have given them a full account of the truth and terms of the gospel, have not shunned to declare the whole counsel of God (Acts xx. 27), have kept back nothing that was necessary for them to know." *Filled the gospel,* so the word is; πεπληρωκέναι τὸ εὐαγγέλιον, filled it as the net is filled with fishes in a large draught; or filled the gospel, that is, filled them with the gospel. Such a change does the gospel make that, when it comes in power to any place, it fills the place. Other knowledge is airy, and leaves souls empty, but the knowledge of the gospel is filling.

2. He preached in places that had not heard the gospel before, *v.* 20, 21. He broke up the fallow ground, laid the first stone in many places, and introduced Christianity where nothing had reigned for many ages but idolatry and witchcraft, and all sorts of diabolism. Paul broke the ice, and therefore must needs meet with the more difficulties and discouragements in his work. Those who preached in Judea had upon this account a much easier task than Paul, who was the apostle of the Gentiles; for they entered into the labours of others, John iv. 38. Paul, being a hardy man, was called out to the hardest work; there were many instructors, but Paul was the great father—many that watered, but Paul was the great planter. Well, he was a bold man that made the first attack upon the palace of the strong man armed in the Gentile world, that first assaulted Satan's interest there, and Paul was that man who ventured the first onset in many places, and suffered greatly for it. He mentions this as a proof of his apostle-

ship; for the office of the apostles was especially to bring in those that were without, and to lay the foundations of the new Jerusalem; see Rev. xxi. 14. Not but that Paul preached in many places where others had been at work before him; but he principally and mainly laid himself out for the good of those that sat in darkness. He was in care not to *build upon another man's foundation,* lest he should thereby disprove his apostleship, and give occasion to those who sought occasion to reflect upon him. He quotes a scripture for this out of Isa. lii. 15, *To whom he was not spoken of, they shall see. That which had not been told them, shall they see;* so the prophet has it, much to the same purport. This made the success of Paul's preaching the more remarkable. The transition from darkness to light is more sensible than the after-growth and increase of that light. And commonly the greatest success of the gospel is at its first coming to a place; afterwards people become sermon-proof.

II. The great and wonderful success that he had in his work: It was effectual to *make the Gentiles obedient.* The design of the gospel is to bring people to be *obedient;* it is not only a truth to be believed, but a law to be obeyed. This Paul aimed at in all his travels; not his own wealth and honour (if he had, he had sadly missed his aim), but the conversion and salvation of souls: this his heart was upon, and for this he travailed in birth again. Now how was this great work wrought? 1. Christ was the principal agent. He does not say, "which I worked," but "which Christ wrought by me," *v.* 18. Whatever good we do, it is not we, but Christ by us, that does it; the work is his, the strength his; he is all in all, he works all our works, Phil. ii. 13; Isa. xxvi. 12. Paul takes all occasions to own this, that the whole praise might be transmitted to Christ. 2. Paul was a very active instrument: *By word and deed,* that is, by his preaching, and by the miracles he wrought to confirm his doctrine; or his preaching and his living. Those ministers are likely to win souls that preach both by word and deed, by their conversation showing forth the power of the truths they preach. This is according to Christ's example, who began both to do and teach, Acts i. 1.—*Through mighty signs and wonders: ἐν δυνάμει σημείων—by the power,* or in the strength, of signs and wonders. These made the preaching of the word so effectual, being the appointed means of conviction, and the divine seal affixed to the gospel-charter, Mark xvi. 17, 18. 3. The *power of the Spirit of God* made this effectual, and crowned all with the desired success, *v.* 19. (1.) The power of the Spirit in Paul, as in the other apostles, for the working of those miracles. Miracles were wrought by the power of the Holy Ghost (Acts i. 8), therefore reproaching the miracles is called the blasphemy against the Holy Ghost. Or, (2.) The power of the Spirit in the hearts of those to whom the word was preached, and who saw the miracles, making these means effectual to some and not to others. It is the Spirit's operation that makes the difference. Paul himself, as great a preacher as he was, with all his mighty signs and wonders, could not make one soul obedient further than the power of the Spirit of God accompanied his labours. It was the Spirit of the Lord of hosts that made those great mountains plain before this Zerubbabel. This is an encouragement to faithful ministers, who labour under the sense of great weakness and infirmity, that it is all one to the blessed Spirit to work by many, or by those that have no power. The same almighty Spirit that wrought with Paul often perfects strength in weakness, and ordains praise out of the mouths of babes and sucklings. This success which he had in preaching is that which he here rejoices in; for the converted nations were his joy and crown of rejoicing: and he tells them of it, not only that they might rejoice with him, but that they might be the more ready to receive the truths which he had written to them, and to own him whom Christ had thus signally owned.

22 For which cause also I have
been much hindered from coming to
you. 23 But now having no more
place in these parts, and having a
great desire these many years to
come unto you; 24 Whensoever I
take my journey into Spain, I will
come to you: for I trust to see you
in my journey, and to be brought on
my way thitherward by you, if first I
be somewhat filled by your *company.*
25 But now I go unto Jerusalem to
minister unto the saints. 26 For it
hath pleased them of Macedonia and
Achaia to make a certain contribution
for the poor saints which are at Jerusalem. 27 It hath pleased them
verily; and their debtors they are.
For if the Gentiles have been made
partakers of their spiritual things,
their duty is also to minister unto
them in carnal things. 28 When
therefore I have performed this, and
have sealed to them this fruit, I will
come by you into Spain. 29 And I
am sure that, when I come unto you,
I shall come in the fulness of the
blessing of the gospel of Christ.

St. Paul here declares his purpose to come and see the Christians at Rome. Upon this head his matter is but common and ordinary, appointing a visit to his friends; but the manner of his expression is gracious and savoury, very instructive, and for our imitation. We should learn by it to speak of our common affairs in the language of Canaan. Even our common discourse should have an air of grace; by this it will appear what country we belong to. It should seem that Paul's company was very much desired at Rome. He was a man that had as many friends and as many enemies as most men ever had: he passed through evil report and good report. No doubt they had heard much of him at Rome, and longed to see him. Should the apostle of the Gentiles be a stranger at Rome, the metropolis of the Gentile world? Why as to this he excuses it that he had not come yet, he promises to come shortly, and gives a good reason why he could not come now.

I. He excuses it that he never came yet. Observe how careful Paul was to keep in with his friends, and to prevent or anticipate any exceptions against him; not as one that lorded it over God's heritage. 1. He assures them that he had a great desire to see them; not to see Rome, though it was now in its greatest pomp and splendour, nor to see the emperor's court, nor to converse with the philosophers and learned men that were then at Rome, though such conversation must needs be very desirable to so great a scholar as Paul was, but *to come unto you* (*v.* 3), a company of poor despised saints in Rome, hated of the world, but loving God, and beloved of him. These were the men that Paul was ambitious of an acquaintance with at Rome; they were the excellent ones in whom he delighted, Ps. xvi. 3. And he had a special desire to see them, because of the great character they had in all the churches for faith and holiness; they were men that excelled in virtue, and therefore Paul was so desirous to come to them. This desire Paul had had for many years, and yet could never compass it. The providence of God wisely overrules the purposes and desires of men. God's dearest servants are not always gratified in every thing that they have a mind to. Yet all that delight in God have the desire of their heart fulfilled (Ps. xxxvii. 4), though all the desires in their heart be not humoured. 2. He tells them that the reason why he could not come to them was because he had so much work cut out for him elsewhere. *For which cause*, that is, because of his labours in other countries, he was so much *hindered.* God had opened a wide door for him in other places, and so turned him aside. Observe in this, (1.) The gracious providence of God conversant in a special manner about his ministers, casting their lot, not according to their contrivance, but according to his own purpose. Paul was several times crossed in his intentions; sometimes hindered by Satan (as 1 Thess. ii. 18), sometimes forbidden by the Spirit (Acts xvi. 7), and here diverted by other work. Man purposes but God disposes, Prov. xvi. 9; xix. 21; Jer. x. 23. Ministers purpose, and their friends purpose concerning them, but God overrules both, and orders the journeys, removals, and settlements, of his faithful ministers as he pleases. The stars are in the right hand of Christ, to shine where he sets them. The gospel does not come by chance to any place, but by the will and counsel of God. (2.) The gracious prudence of Paul, in bestowing his time and pains where there was most need. Had Paul consulted his own ease, wealth, and honour, the greatness of the work would never have hindered him from seeing Rome, but would rather have driven him thither, where he might have had more preferment and taken less pains. But Paul sought the things of Christ more than his own things, and therefore would not leave his work of planting churches, no, not for a time, to go and see Rome. The Romans were whole, and needed not the physician as other poor places that were sick and dying. While men and women were every day dropping into eternity, and their precious souls perishing for lack of vision, it was no time for Paul to trifle. There was now a gale of opportunity, the fields were white unto the harvest; such a season slipped might never be retrieved; the necessities of poor souls were pressing, and called aloud, and therefore Paul must be busy. It concerns us all to do that first which is most needful. True grace teaches us to prefer that which is necessary before that which is unnecessary, Luke x. 41, 42. And Christian prudence teaches us to prefer that which is more necessary before that which is less so. This Paul mentions as a sufficient satisfying reason. We must not take it ill of our friends if they prefer necessary work, which is pleasing to God, before unnecessary visits and compliments, which may be pleasing to us. In this, as in other things, we must deny ourselves.

II. He promised to come and see them shortly, *v* 23, 24, 29. *Having no more place in these parts*, namely, in Greece, where he then was. The whole of that country being more or less leavened with the savour of the gospel, churches being planted in the most considerable towns and pastors settled to carry on the work which Paul had begun, he had little more to do there. He had driven the chariot of the gospel to the sea-coast, and having thus conquered Greece he is ready to wish there were another Greece to conquer. Paul was one that went through with his work, and yet then did not think of taking his ease, but set himself to contrive more work, to devise liberal things. Here was a workman that needed not to be ashamed. Observe,

1. How he forecasted his intended visit. His project was to see them in his way to Spain. It appears by this that Paul intended a journey into Spain, to plant Christianity there. The difficulty and peril of the work, the distance of the place, the danger of the

voyage, the other good works (though less needful, he thinks) which Paul might find to do in other places, did not quench the flame of his holy zeal for the propagating of the gospel, which did even eat him up, and make him forget himself. But it is not certain whether ever he fulfilled his purpose, and went to Spain. Many of the best expositors think he did not, but was hindered in this as he was in others of his purposes. He did indeed come to Rome, but he was brought thither a prisoner, and there was detained two years; and whither he went after is uncertain: but several of his epistles which he wrote in prison intimate his purpose to go eastward, and not towards Spain. However, Paul, forasmuch as it was in thine heart to bring the light of the gospel into Spain, thou didst well, in that it was in thine heart; as God said to David, 2 Chron. vi. 8. The grace of God often with favour accepts the sincere intention, when the providence of God in wisdom prohibits the execution. And do not we serve a good Master then? 2 Cor. viii. 12. Now, in his way to Spain he proposed to come to them. Observe his prudence. It is wisdom for every one of us to order our affairs so that we may do the most work in the least time. Observe how doubtfully he speaks: *I trust to see you:* not, "I am resolved I will," but, "I hope I shall." we must purpose all our purposes and make all our promises in like manner with a submission to the divine providence; not boasting ourselves of to-morrow, because we know not what a day may bring forth, Prov. xxvii. 1; James iv. 13—15.

2. What he expected in his intended visit. (1.) What he expected from them. He expected they would bring him on his way towards Spain. It was not a stately attendance, such as princes have, but a loving attendance, such as friends give, that Paul expected. Spain was then a province of the empire, well known to the Romans, who had a great correspondence with it, and therefore they might be helpful to Paul in his voyage thither; and it was not barely their accompanying him part of the way, but their furthering him in his expedition, that he counted upon: not only out of their respect to Paul, but out of respect to the souls of those poor Spaniards that Paul was going to preach to. It is justly expected from all Christians that they should lay out themselves for the promoting and furthering of every good work, especially that blessed work of the conversion of souls, which they should contrive to make as easy as may be to their ministers, and as successful as may be to poor souls. (2.) What he expected in them: to *be somewhat filled with their company.* That which Paul desired was their company and conversation. The good company of the saints is very desirable and delightful. Paul was himself a man of great attainments in knowledge and grace, taller by head and shoulders than other Christians in these things, and yet see how he pleased himself with the thoughts of good company; for as iron sharpens iron so does a man the countenance of his friend. He intimates that he intended to make some stay with them, for he would be filled with their company; not just look at them, and away: and yet he thinks their converse so pleasant that he should never have enough of it; it is but somewhat filled, he thought he should leave them with a desire of more of their company. Christian society, rightly managed and improved, is a heaven upon earth, a comfortable earnest of our gathering together unto Christ at the great day. Yet observe, It is but somewhat filled, *ἀπὸ μέρους—in part.* The satisfaction we have in communion with the saints in this world is but partial; we are but somewhat filled. It is partial compared with our communion with Christ; that, and that only, will completely satisfy, that will fill the soul. It is partial compared with the communion we hope to have with the saints in the other world. When we shall sit down with Abraham, and Isaac, and Jacob, with all the saints, and none but saints, and saints made perfect, we shall have enough of that society, and be quite filled with that company. (3.) What he expected from God with them, *v.* 29. He expected to come *in the fulness of the blessing of the gospel of Christ.* Observe, Concerning what he *expected* from *them* he speaks doubtfully: *I trust to be brought on my way, and to be filled with your company.* Paul had learnt not to be too confident of the best. These very men slipped from him afterwards, when he had occasion to use them (2 Tim. iv. 16), *At my first answer, no man stood by me;* none of the Christians at Rome. The Lord teach us to cease from man. But concerning what he expected from God he speaks confidently. It was uncertain whether he should come or no, but *I am sure when I do come I shall come in the fulness,* &c. We cannot expect too little from man, nor too much from God. Now Paul expected that God would bring him to them, loaded with blessings, so that he should be an instrument of doing a great deal of good among them, and fill them with the blessings of the gospel. Compare *ch.* i. 11, *That I may impart unto you some spiritual gift.* The blessing of the gospel of Christ is the best and most desirable blessing. When Paul would raise their expectation of something great and good in his coming, he directs them to hope for the blessings of the gospel, spiritual blessings, knowledge, and grace, and comfort. There is then a happy meeting between people and ministers, when they are both under the fulness of the blessing. The blessing of the gospel is the treasure which we have in earthen vessels. When ministers are fully prepared to give out, and people fully prepared to receive, this blessing, both are

happy. Many have the gospel who have not the blessing of the gospel, and so they have it in vain. The gospel will not profit, unless God bless it to us; and it is our duty to wait upon him for that blessing, and for the fulness of it.

III. He gives them a good reason why he could not come and see them now, because he had other business upon his hands, which required his attendance, upon which he must first make a journey to Jerusalem, *v.* 25—28. He gives a particular account of it, to show that the excuse was real. He was going to Jerusalem, as the messenger of the church's charity to the poor saints there. Observe what he says,

1. Concerning this charity itself. And he speaks of that upon this occasion probably to excite the Roman Christians to do the like, according to their ability. Examples are moving, and Paul was very ingenious at begging, not for himself, but for others. Observe, (1.) For whom it was intended: *For the poor saints which are at Jerusalem, v.* 26. It is no strange thing for saints to be poor. Those whom God favours the world often frowns upon; therefore riches are not the best things, nor is poverty a curse. It seems, the saints at Jerusalem were poorer than other saints, either because the wealth of that people in general was now declining, as their utter ruin was hastening on (and, to be sure, if any must be kept poor, the saints must), or because the famine that was over all the world in the days of Claudius Cæsar did in a special manner prevail in Judea, a dry country; and, God having called the poor of this world, the Christians smarted most by it. This was the occasion of that contribution mentioned Acts xi. 28—30. Or, because the saints at Jerusalem suffered most by persecution; for of all people the unbelieving Jews were most inveterate in their rage and malice against the Christians, wrath having come upon them to the uttermost, 1 Thess. ii. 16. The Christian Hebrews are particularly noted too as having had their goods spoiled (Heb. x. 34), in consideration of which this contribution was made for them. Though the saints at Jerusalem were at a great distance from them, yet they thus extended their bounty and liberality to them, to teach us as we have ability, and as there is occasion, to stretch out the hand of our charity to all that are of the household of faith, though in places distant from us. Though in personal instances of poverty every church should take care to maintain their own poor (for such poor we have always with us), yet sometimes, when more public instances of poverty are presented as objects of our charity, though a great way off from us, we must extend our bounty, as the sun his beams; and, with the virtuous woman, *stretch out our hands to the poor, and reach forth our hands to the needy,* Prov. xxxi. 20. (2.) By whom it was collected: *By those of Macedonia* (the chief of whom were the Philippians) *and Achaia* (the chief of whom were the Corinthians), two flourishing churches, though yet in their infancy, newly converted to Christianity. And I wish the observation did not hold that people are commonly more liberal at their first acquaintance with the gospel than they are afterwards, that, as well as other instances of the first love and the love of the espousals, being apt to cool and decay after a while. It seems those of Macedonia and Achaia were rich and wealthy, while those at Jerusalem were poor and needy, Infinite Wisdom ordering it so that some should have what others want, and so this mutual dependence of Christians one upon another might be maintained.—*It pleased them.* This intimates how ready they were to it—they were not pressed nor constrained to it, but they did it of their own accord; and how cheerful they were in it—they took a pleasure in doing good; and God loves a cheerful giver.—*To make a certain contribution; κοινωνίαν τινὰ—a communication,* in token of the communion of saints, and their fellow-membership, as in the natural body one member communicates to the relief, and succour, and preservation of another, as there is occasion. Every thing that passes between Christians should be a proof and instance of that common union which they have one with another in Jesus Christ. Time was when the saints at Jerusalem were on the giving hand, and very liberal they were, when they laid their estates at the apostles' feet for charitable uses, and took special care that the Grecian widows should not be neglected in the daily ministration, Act vi. 1, &c. And now that the providence of God had turned the scale, and made them necessitous, they found the Grecians kind to them; for the merciful shall obtain mercy. We should give a portion to seven, and also to eight, because we know not what evil may be on the earth, which may make us glad to be beholden to others. (3.) What reason there was for it (*v.* 27): *And their debtors they are.* Alms are called righteousness, Ps. cxii. 9. Being but stewards of what we have, we owe it where our great Master (by the calls of providence, concurring with the precepts of the word) orders us to dispose of it: but here there was a special debt owing; the Gentiles were greatly beholden to the Jews, and were bound in gratitude to be very kind to them. From the stock of Israel came Christ himself, according to the flesh, who is the light to enlighten the Gentiles; out of the same stock came the prophets, and apostles, and first preachers of the gospel. The Jews, having had the lively oracles committed to them, were the Christians' library-keepers—*out of Zion went forth the law, and the word of the Lord from Jerusalem;* their political church-state was dissolved, and they were cut off, that the Gentiles might be admitted in. Thus did the Gentiles partake of their spiritual things, and receive

the gospel of salvation as it were at second-hand from the Jews; and therefore *their duty is,* they are bound in gratitude to *minister unto them in carnal things:* it is the least they can do: λειτουργῆσαι—*to minister as unto God in holy things;* so the word signifies. A conscientious regard to God in works of charity and almsgiving makes them an acceptable service and sacrifice to God, and fruit abounding to a good account. Paul mentions this, probably, as the argument he had used with them to persuade them to it, and it is an argument of equal cogency to other Gentile churches.

2. Concerning Paul's agency in this business. He could himself contribute nothing; silver and gold he had none, but lived upon the kindness of his friends; yet he *ministered unto the saints* (*v.* 25) by stirring up others, receiving what was gathered, and transmitting it to Jerusalem. Many good works of that kind stand at a stay for want of some one active person to lead in them, and to set the wheels a going. Paul's labour in this work is not to be interpreted as any neglect of his preaching-work, nor did Paul leave the word of God, to serve tables; for, besides this, Paul had other business in this journey, to visit and confirm the churches, and took this by the bye; this was indeed a part of the trust committed to him, in which he was concerned to approve himself faithful (Gal. ii. 10): *They would that we should remember the poor.* Paul was one that laid out himself to do good every way, like his Master, to the bodies as well as to the souls of people. Ministering to the saints is good work, and is not below the greatest apostles. This Paul had undertaken, and therefore he resolves to go through with it, before he fell upon other work (*v.* 28): *When I have sealed to them this fruit.* He calls the alms *fruit,* for it is one of the fruits of righteousness; it sprang from a root of grace in the givers, and redounded to the benefit and comfort of the receivers. And his sealing it intimates his great care about it, that what was given might be kept entire, and not embezzled, but disposed of according to the design of the givers. Paul was very solicitous to approve himself faithful in the management of this matter: an excellent pattern for ministers to write after, that the ministry may in nothing be blamed.

30 Now I beseech you, brethren,
for the Lord Jesus Christ's sake, and
for the love of the Spirit, that ye
strive together with me in *your*
prayers to God for me; 31 That I
may be delivered from them that do
not believe in Judæa; and that my
service which *I have* for Jerusalem
may be accepted of the saints; 32
That I may come unto you with joy
by the will of God, and may with you
be refreshed. 33 Now the God of
peace *be* with you all. Amen.

Here we have, I. St. Paul's desire of a share in the prayers of the Romans for him, expressed very earnestly, *v.* 30—32. Though Paul was a great apostle, yet he begged the prayers of the meanest Christians, not here only, but in several other of the epistles. He had prayed much for them, and this he desires as the return of his kindness. Interchanging prayers is an excellent token of the interchanging of loves. Paul speaks like one that knew himself, and would hereby teach us how to value the effectual fervent prayer of the righteous. How careful should we be lest we do any thing to forfeit our interest in the love and prayers of God's praying people!

1. Observe why they must pray for him. He begs it with the greatest importunity. He might suspect they would forget him in their prayers, because they had no personal acquaintance with him, and therefore he urges it so closely, and begs it with the most affectionate obtestations, by all that is sacred and valuable: *I beseech you,* (1.) "*For the Lord Jesus Christ's sake.* He is my Master, I am going about his work, and his glory is interested in the success of it: if you have any regard to Jesus Christ, and to his cause and kingdom, pray for me. You love Christ, and own Christ; for his sake then do me this kindness." (2.) "*For the love of the Spirit.* As a proof and instance of that love which the Spirit works in the hearts of believers one to another, pray for me; as a fruit of that communion which we have one with another by the Spirit though we never saw one another. If ever you experienced the Spirit's love to you, and would be found returning your love to the Spirit, be not wanting in this office of kindness."

2. How they must pray for him: *That you strive together.* (1.) That *you strive in prayer.* We must put forth all that is within us in that duty; pray with fixedness, faith, and fervency; wrestle with God, as Jacob did; pray in praying, as Elias did (Jam. v. 17), and stir up ourselves to take hold on God (Isa. lxiv. 7); and this not only when we are praying for ourselves, but when we are praying for our friends. True love to our brethren should make us as earnest for them as sense of our own need makes us for ourselves. (2.) That you strive together with me. When he begged their prayers for him, he did not intend thereby to excuse his praying for himself; no, "*Strive together with me,* who am wrestling with God daily, upon my own and my friends' account." He would have them to ply the same oar. Paul and these Romans were distant in place, and likely to be so, and yet they might join together in prayer; those who are put far asunder by the disposal of God's providence may yet meet together at the throne of his grace.

Those who beg the prayers of others must not neglect to pray for themselves

3. What they must beg of God for him. He mentions particulars; for, in praying both for ourselves and for our friends, it is good to be particular. *What wilt thou that I shall do for thee?* So says Christ, when he holds out the golden sceptre. Though he knows our state and wants perfectly, he will know them from us. He recommends himself to their prayers, with reference to three things:—(1.) The dangers which he was exposed to: *That I may be delivered from those that do not believe in Judea.* The unbelieving Jews were the most violent enemies Paul had and most enraged against him, and some prospect he had of trouble from them in this journey; and therefore they must pray that God would deliver him. We may, and must, pray against persecution. This prayer was answered in several remarkable deliverances of Paul, recorded Acts xxi. xxii. xxiii. xxiv. (2.) His services: *Pray that my service which I have for Jerusalem may be accepted of the saints.* Why, was there any danger that it would not be accepted? Can money be otherwise than acceptable to the poor? Yes, there was some ground of suspicion in this case; for Paul was the apostle of the Gentiles, and as the unbelieving Jews looked spitefully at him, which was their wickedness, so those that believed were shy of him upon that account, which was their weakness. He does not say, "Let them choose whether they will accept it or no; if they will not, it shall be better bestowed;" but, "Pray that it may be accepted." As God must be sought unto for the restraining of the ill will of our enemies, so also for the preserving and increasing of the good will of our friends; for God has the hearts both of the one and of the other in his hands. (3.) His journey to them. To engage their prayers for him, he interests them in his concerns (*v.* 32): *That I may come unto you with joy.* If his present journey to Jerusalem proved unsuccessful, his intended journey to Rome would be uncomfortable. If he should not do good, and prosper, in one visit, he thought he should have small joy of the next: may *come with joy, by the will of God.* All our joy depends upon the will of God. The comfort of the creature is in every thing according to the disposal of the Creator.

II. Here is another prayer of the apostle for them (*v.* 33): *Now the God of peace be with you all, Amen.* The Lord of hosts, the God of battle, is the God of peace, the author and lover of peace. He describes God under this title here, because of the divisions among them, to recommend peace to them; if God be the God of peace, let us be men of peace. The Old-Testament blessing was, *Peace be with you;* now, *The God of peace be with you.* Those who have the fountain cannot want any of the streams. *With you all;* both weak and strong. To dispose them to a nearer union, he puts them altogether in this prayer. Those who are united in the blessing of God should be united in affection one to another.

CHAP. XVI.

Paul is now concluding this long and excellent epistle, and he does it with a great deal of affection. As in the main body of the epistle he appears to have been a very knowing man, so in these appurtenances of it he appears to have been a very loving man. So much knowledge and so much love are a very rare, but (where they exist) a very excellent and amiable composition; for what is heaven but knowledge and love made perfect? It is observable how often Paul speaks as if he were concluding, and yet takes fresh hold again. One would have thought that solemn benediction which closed the foregoing chapter should have ended the epistle; and yet here he begins again, and in this chapter he repeats the blessing (ver. 20), "The grace of our Lord Jesus Christ be with you, Amen." And yet he has something more to say; nay, again he repeats the blessing (ver. 24), and yet has not done; an expression of his tender love. These repeated benedictions, which stand for valedictions, speak Paul loth to part. Now, in this closing chapter, we may observe, I. His recommendation of one friend to the Roman Christians, and his particular salutation of several among them, ver. 1—16. II. A caution to take heed of those who caused divisions, ver. 17—20. III. Salutations added from some who were with Paul, ver. 21—24. IV. He concludes with a solemn celebration of the glory of God, ver. 25—27.

I COMMEND unto you Phebe
our sister, which is a servant of
the church which is at Cenchrea: 2
That ye receive her in the Lord, as
becometh saints, and that ye assist
her in whatsoever business she hath
need of you: for she hath been a
succourer of many, and of myself
also. 3 Greet Priscilla and Aquila
my helpers in Christ Jesus: 4 Who
have for my life laid down their own
necks: unto whom not only I give
thanks, but also all the churches of
the Gentiles. 5 Likewise *greet* the
church that is in their house. Salute
my wellbeloved Epenetus, who is the
firstfruits of Achaia unto Christ. 6
Greet Mary, who bestowed much
labour on us. 7 Salute Andronicus
and Junia, my kinsmen, and my
fellowprisoners, who are of note
among the apostles, who also were in
Christ before me. 8 Greet Amplias
my beloved in the Lord. 9 Salute
Urbane, our helper in Christ, and
Stachys my beloved. 10 Salute
Apelles approved in Christ. Salute
them which are of Aristobulus' *house-*
hold. 11 Salute Herodion my kinsman. Greet them that be of the
household of Narcissus, which are in
the Lord. 12 Salute Tryphena and
Tryphosa, who labour in the Lord.
Salute the beloved Persis, which
laboured much in the Lord. 13
Salute Rufus chosen in the Lord, and
his mother and mine. 14 Salute
Asyncritus, Phlegon, Hermas, Patro-

ZELLERS STORE 104
SALE

1 TEA & COFFEE POTS				
1@	1.99	70140264		1.99
2 PRE SCHOOL TOYS				
1@	5.00	50447010		5.00
3 FLANNELSHIRTS				
1@	5.77	21061122	SALE	5.77
4 FLANNELSHIRTS				
1@	5.77	21060546	SALE	5.77

SUBTOTAL	18.53
GST	1.30
PST	1.30
TOTAL	21.13
CASH	22.13
CHANGE	1.00

GST REGISTRATION #121968549

TRAN#	TERM#	OPER#	STOR#	DATE	TIME
4203	2	124	104	10/29/93	03:57PM

RETAIN RECEIPT FOR REFUND WITHIN 14 DAYS

bas, Hermes, and the brethren which are with them. 15 Salute Philologus, and Julia, Nereus, and his sister, and Olympas, and all the saints which are with them. 16 Salute one another with a holy kiss. The churches of Christ salute you.

Such remembrances as these are usual in letters between friends; and yet Paul, by the savouriness of his expressions, sanctifies these common compliments.

I. Here is the recommendation of a friend, by whom (as some think) this epistle was sent—one *Phebe, v.* 1, 2. It should seem that she was a person of quality and estate, who had business which called her to Rome, where she was a stranger; and therefore Paul recommends her to the acquaintance of the Christians there: an expression of his true friendship to her. Paul was as well skilled in the art of obliging as most men. True religion, rightly received, never made any man uncivil. Courtesy and Christianity agree well together. It is not in compliment to her, but in sincerity, that,

1. He gives a very good character of her. (1.) As a sister to Paul: *Phebe our sister;* not in nature, but in grace; not in affinity or consanguinity, but in pure Christianity: his own sister in the faith of Christ, loving Paul, and beloved of him, with a pure and chaste and spiritual love, as a sister; for there is neither male nor female, but all are one in Christ Jesus, Gal. iii. 28. Both Christ and his apostles had some of their best friends among the devout (and upon that account honourable) women. (2.) As a *servant to the church at Cenchrea: διάκονον,* a servant by office, a stated servant, not to preach the word (that was forbidden to women), but in acts of charity and hospitality Some think she was one of the widows that ministered to the sick, and were taken into the church's number, 1 Tim. v. 9. But those were old and poor, whereas Phebe seems to have been a person of some account; and yet it was no disparagement to her to be a servant to the church. Probably they used to meet at her house, and she undertook the care of entertaining the ministers, especially strangers. Every one in his place should strive to serve the church, for therein he serves Christ, and it will turn to a good account another day. Cenchrea was a small sea-port town adjoining to Corinth, about twelve furlongs distant. Some think there was a church there, distinct from that at Corinth, though, being so near, it is very probable that the church of Corinth is called *the church of Cenchrea,* because their place of meeting might be there, on account of the great opposition to them in the city (Acts xviii. 12), as at Philippi they met out of the city by the water-side, Acts xvi. 13. So the reformed church of Paris might be called *the church at Charenton,* where they formerly met, out of the city. (3.) As a *succourer of many,* and particularly of Paul, *v.* 2 She relieved many that were in want and distress—a good copy for women to write after that have ability. She was kind to those that needed kindness, intimated in her succouring them; and her bounty was extensive, she was a succourer of many. Observe the gratitude of Paul in mentioning her particular kindness to him: *And to myself also.* Acknowledgment of favours is the least return we can make. It was much to her honour that Paul left this upon record; for wherever this epistle is read her kindness to Paul is told for a memorial of her.

2. He recommends her to their care and kindness, as one worthy to be taken notice of with peculiar respect. (1.) "*Receive her in the Lord.* Entertain her; bid her welcome." This pass, under Paul's hand, could not but recommend her to any Christian church. "*Receive her in the Lord,*" that is, "for the Lord's sake; receive her as a servant and friend of Christ." *As it becometh saints* to receive, who love Christ, and therefore love all that are his for his sake; or, as *becometh saints* to be received, with love and honour and the tenderest affection. There may be occasion sometimes to improve our interest in our friends, not only for ourselves, but for others also, *interest* being a price in the hand for doing good. (2.) *Assist her in whatsoever business she has need of you.* Whether she had business of trade, or law-business at the court, is not material; however being a woman, a stranger, a Christian, she had need of help: and Paul engaged them to be assistant to her. It becomes Christians to be helpful one to another in their affairs, especially to be helpful to strangers; for we are members one of another and we know not what need of help we may have ourselves. Observe, Paul bespeaks help for one that had been so helpful to many; he that watereth shall be watered also himself.

II. Here are commendations to some particular friends among those to whom he wrote, more than in any other of the epistles. Though the care of all the churches came upon Paul daily, enough to distract an ordinary head, yet he could retain the remembrance of so many; and his heart was so full of love and affection as to send salutations to each of them with particular characters of them, and expressions of love to them and concern for them. *Greet* them, *salute* them; it is the same word, ἀσπάσασθε. "Let them know that I remember them, and love them, and wish them well." There is something observable in several of these salutations.

1. Concerning Aquila and Priscilla, a famous couple, that Paul had a special kindness for. They were originally of Rome, but were banished thence by the edict of Claudius, Acts xviii. 2. At Corinth, Paul became acquainted with them, wrought with them at the trade of tent-making; after some time, when the edge of that edict was rebated, they

returned to Rome, and thither he now sends commendations to them. He calls them his *helpers in Christ Jesus,* by private instructions and converse furthering the success of Paul's public preaching, one instance of which we have in their instructing Apollos, Acts xviii. 26. Those are helpers to faithful ministers that lay out themselves in their families and among their neighbours to do good to souls. Nay, they did not only do much, but they ventured much, for Paul: They have *for my life laid down their own necks.* They exposed themselves to secure Paul, hazarded their own lives for the preservation of his, considering how much better they might be spared than he. Paul was in a great deal of danger at Corinth, while he sojourned with them; but they sheltered him, though they thereby made themselves obnoxious to the enraged multitude, Acts xviii. 12, 17. It was a good while ago that they had done Paul this kindness; and yet he speaks as feelingly of it as if it had been but yesterday. *To whom* (says he) *not only I give thanks, but also all the churches of the Gentiles*; who were all beholden to these good people for helping to save the life of him that was the apostle of the Gentiles. Paul mentions this, to engage the Christians at Rome to be the more kind to Aquila and Priscilla. He sends likewise greeting to the *church in their house, v.* 5. It seems then, a church in a house is no such absurd thing as some make it to be. Perhaps there was a congregation of Christians that used to meet at their house at stated times; and then, no doubt, it was, like the house of Obed-Edom, blessed for the ark's sake. Others think that the church was no more than a religious, pious, well-governed family, that kept up the worship of God. Religion, in the power of it, reigning in a family, will turn a house into a church. And doubtless it had a good influence upon this that Priscilla the good wife of the family was so very eminent and forward in religion, so eminent that she is often named first. A virtuous woman, that looks well to the ways of her household, may do much towards the advancement of religion in a family. When Priscilla and Aquila were at Ephesus, though but sojourners there, yet there also they had a church in their house, 1 Cor. xvi. 19. A truly godly man will be careful to take religion along with him wherever he goes. When Abraham removed his tent, he renewed his altar, Gen. xiii. 18.

2. Concerning Epenetus, *v.* 5. He calls him his *well-beloved.* Where the law of love is in the heart the law of kindness will be in the tongue. Endearing language should pass among Christians to express love, and to engage love. So he calls Amplias, *beloved in the Lord,* with true Christian love for Christ's sake; and Stachys, his *beloved:* a sign that Paul had been in the third heaven, he was so much made up of love. Of Epenetus it is further said that he was the *first-fruit of Achaia unto Christ;* not only one of the most eminent believers in that country, but one of the first that was converted to the faith of Christ: one that was offered up to God by Paul, as the first-fruits of his ministry there; an earnest of a great harvest; for in Corinth, the chief city of Achaia, God had much people, Acts xviii. 10. Special respect is to be paid to those that set out early, and come to work in the vineyard at the first hour, at the first call. The *household of Stephanas* is likewise said to be the *first-fruits of Achaia,* 1 Cor. xvi. 15. Perhaps Epenetus was one of that household; or, at least, he was one of the *first three;* not the first alone, but one of the first fleece of Christians, that the region of Achaia afforded.

3. Concerning Mary, and some others who were laborious in that which is good, industrious Christians: *Mary,* who *bestowed much labour on us.* True love never sticks at labour, but rather takes a pleasure in it; where there is much love there will be much labour. Some think this Mary had been at some of those places where Paul was, though now removed to Rome, and had personally ministered to him; others think Paul speaks of her labour as bestowed upon him because it was bestowed upon his friends and fellow-labourers, and he took what was done to them as done to himself. He says of Tryphena and Tryphosa, two useful women in their places, that they laboured in the Lord (*v.* 12), and of the beloved Persis, another good woman, that she laboured much in the Lord, more than others, abounding more in the work of the Lord.

4. Concerning Andronicus and Junia, *v.* 7. Some take them for a man and his wife, and the original will well enough bear it; and, considering the name of the latter, this is more probable than that they should be two men, as others think, and brethren. Observe, (1.) They were Paul's *cousins,* akin to him; so was Herodion, *v.* 11. Religion does not take away, but rectifies, sanctifies, and improves, our respect to our kindred, engaging us to lay out ourselves most for their good, and to rejoice in them the more, when we find them related to Christ by faith. (2.) They were his fellow-prisoners. Partnership in suffering sometimes does much towards the union of souls and the knitting of affections. We do not find in the story of the Acts any imprisonment of Paul before the writing of this epistle, but that at Philippi, Acts xvi. 23. But Paul was *in prisons more frequent* (2 Cor. xi. 23), in some of which, it seems, he met with his friends Andronicus and Junia, yoke-fellows, as in other things, so in suffering for Christ and bearing his yoke. (3.) They were *of note among the apostles,* not so much perhaps because they were persons of estate and quality in the world as because they were eminent for knowledge, and gifts, and graces, which made them famous among the apostles, who were competent judges of those things, and were endued with a spirit of discerning not

only the sincerity, but the eminency, of Christians. (4.) *Who also were in Christ before me,* that is, were converted to the Christian faith. In time they had the start of Paul, though he was converted the next year after Christ's ascension. How ready was Paul to acknowledge in others any kind of precedency!

5. Concerning Apelles, who is here said to be *approved in Christ* (*v.* 10), a high character! He was one of known integrity and sincerity in his religion, one that had been tried; his friends and enemies had tried him, and he was as gold. He was of approved knowledge and judgment, approved courage and constancy; a man that one might trust and repose a confidence in.

6. Concerning Aristobulus and Narcissus; notice is taken of their household, *v.* 10, 11. Those of their household who *are in the Lord* (as it is limited, *v.* 11), that were Christians. How studious was Paul to leave none out of his salutations that he had any knowledge of or acquaintance with! Aristobulus and Narcissus themselves, some think, were absent, or lately dead; others think they were unbelievers, and such as did not themselves embrace Christianity; so Pareus: and some think this Narcissus was the same with one of that name who is frequently mentioned in the life of Claudius, as a very rich man that had a great family, but was very wicked and mischievous. It seems, then, there were some good servants, or other retainers, even in the family of a wicked man, a common case, 1 Tim. vi. 1. Compare *v.* 2. The poor servant is called, and chosen, and faithful, while the rich master is passed by, and left to perish in unbelief. Even so, Father, because it seemed good unto thee.

7. Concerning Rufus (*v.* 13), *chosen in the Lord.* He was a choice Christian, whose gifts and graces evinced that he was eternally chosen in Christ Jesus. He was one of a thousand for integrity and holiness.—*And his mother and mine,* his mother by nature and mine by Christian love and spiritual affection; as he calls Phebe his sister, and teaches Timothy to treat the elder women as mothers, 1 Tim. v. 2. This good woman, upon some occasion or other, had been as a mother to Paul, in caring for him, and comforting him; and Paul here gratefully owns it, and calls her mother.

8. Concerning the rest this is observable, that he salutes the *brethren who are with them* (*v.* 14), and the *saints who are with them* (*v.* 15), with them in family-relations, with them in the bond of Christian communion. It is the good property of saints to delight in being together; and Paul thus joins them together in his salutations to endear them one to another. Lest any should find themselves aggrieved, as if Paul had forgotten them, he concludes with the remembrance of the rest, as brethren and saints, though not named. In Christian congregations there should be smaller societies linked together in love and converse, and taking opportunities of being often together. Among all those to whom Paul sends greeting here is not a word of Peter, which gives occasion to suspect that he was not bishop of Rome, as the Papists say he was; for, if he was, we cannot but suppose him resident, or at least how could Paul write so long an epistle to the Christians there, and take no notice of him?

Lastly, He concludes with the recommendation of them to the love and embraces one of another: *Salute one another with a holy kiss.* Mutual salutations, as they express love, so they increase and strengthen love, and endear Christians one to another: therefore Paul here encourages the use of them, and only directs that they may be holy—a chaste kiss, in opposition to that which is wanton and lascivious; a sincere kiss, in opposition to that which is treacherous and dissembling, as Judas's, when he betrayed Christ with a kiss. He adds, in the close, a general salutation to them all, in the name of the churches of Christ (*v.* 16): "*The churches of Christ salute you;* that is, the churches which I am with, and which I am accustomed to visit personally, as knit together in the bonds of the common Christianity, desire me to testify their affection to you and good wishes for you." This is one way of maintaining the communion of saints.

17 Now I beseech you, brethren,
mark them which cause divisions and
offences contrary to the doctrine
which ye have learned; and avoid
them. 18 For they that are such
serve not our Lord Jesus Christ, but
their own belly; and by good words
and fair speeches deceive the hearts
of the simple. 19 For your obedience
is come abroad unto all *men.* I am
glad therefore on your behalf: but
yet I would have you wise unto that
which is good, and simple concerning
evil. 20 And the God of peace shall
bruise Satan under your feet shortly.
The grace of our Lord Jesus Christ
be with you. Amen.

The apostle having endeavoured by his endearing salutations to unite them together, it was not improper to subjoin a caution to take heed of those whose principles and practices were destructive to Christian love. And we may observe,

I. The caution itself, which is given in the most obliging manner that could be: *I beseech you, brethren.* He does not will and command, as one that lorded it over God's heritage, but for love's sake beseeches. How earnest, how endearing, are Paul's exhortations! He teaches them, 1. To see their danger: *Mark those who cause divisions and offences.* Our Master had himself foretold that divisions and offences would come, but had entailed a woe on those by whom they come (Matt. xviii. 7), and against such we are here cautioned. Those who burden the church with dividing and offending impositions, who uphold and enforce those impositions, who introduce and propagate dividing and offending notions, which are erroneous or justly suspected, who out of pride, ambition, affectation of novelty, or the like, causelessly separate from their brethren, and by perverse disputes, censures, and evil surmisings, alienate the affections of Christians one from another—these cause divisions and offences, contrary to, or different from (for that also is implied, it is παρὰ τὴν διδαχὴν), the *doctrine which we have learned.* Whatever varies from the form of sound doctrine which we have in the scriptures opens a door to divisions and offences. If truth be once deserted, unity and peace will not last long. Now, *mark* those that thus cause divisions, *σκοπεῖν.* Observe them, the method they take, the end they drive at. There is need of a piercing watchful eye to discern the danger we are in from such people; for commonly the pretences are plausible, when the projects are very pernicious. Do not look only at the divisions and offences, but run up those streams to the fountain, and mark those that cause them, and especially that in them which causes these divisions and offences, those lusts on each side whence come these wars and fightings. A danger discovered is half prevented. 2. To shun it: "*Avoid them.* Shun all unnecessary communion and communication with them, lest you be leavened and infected by them. Do not strike in with any dividing interests, nor embrace any of those principles or practices which are destructive to Christian love and charity, or to the truth which is according to godliness.—*Their word will eat as doth a canker.*" Some think he especially warns them to take heed of the judaizing teachers, who, under the covert of the Christian name, kept up the Mosaical ceremonies, and preached the necessity of them, who were industrious in all places to draw disciples after them, and whom Paul in most of his epistles cautions the churches to take heed of.

II. The reasons to enforce this caution.

1. Because of the pernicious policy of these seducers, *v.* 18. The worse they are, the more need we have to watch against them. Now observe his description of them, in two things:—(1.) The master they serve: not *our Lord Jesus Christ.* Though they call themselves Christians, they do not serve Christ; do not aim at his glory, promote his interest, nor do his will, whatever they pretend. How many are there who call Christ Master and Lord, that are far from serving him! But they *serve their own belly*—their carnal, sensual, secular interests. It is some base lust or other that they are pleasing; pride, ambition, covetousness, luxury, lasciviousness, these are the designs which they are really carrying on. Their *God is their belly*, Phil. iii. 19. What a base master do they serve, and how unworthy to come in competition with Christ, that serve their own bellies, that make gain their godliness, and the gratifying of a sensual appetite the very scope and business of their lives, to which all other purposes and designs must truckle and be made subservient. (2.) The method they take to compass their design: *By good words and fair speeches they deceive the hearts of the simple.* Their words and speeches have a show of holiness and zeal for God (it is an easy thing to be godly from the teeth outward), and a show of kindness and love to those into whom they instil their corrupt doctrines, accosting them courteously when they intend them the greatest mischief. Thus by good words and fair speeches the serpent beguiled Eve. Observe, They corrupt their heads by deceiving their hearts, pervert their judgments by slily insinuating themselves into their affections. We have great need therefore to keep our hearts with all diligence, especially when seducing spirits are abroad.

2. Because of the peril we are in, through our proneness and aptness to be inveigled and ensnared by them: "For *your obedience has come abroad unto all men*—you are noted in all the churches for a willing, tractable, complying people." And, (1.) Therefore, because it was so, these seducing teachers would be the more apt to assault them. The devil and his agents have a particular spite against flourishing churches and flourishing souls. The ship that is known to be richly laden is most exposed to privateers. The adversary and enemy covets such a prey, therefore look to yourselves, 2 John *v.* 8. "The false teachers hear that you are an obedient people, and therefore they will be likely to come among you, to see if you will be obedient to them." It has been the common policy of seducers to set upon those who are softened by convictions, and begin to enquire what they shall do, because such do most easily receive the impressions of their opinions. Sad experience witnesses how many who have begun to ask the way to Zion, with their faces thitherward, have fatally split upon this rock, which proves it to be much the duty of ministers, with a double care, to feed the lambs of the flock, to lay a good foundation, and gently to lead those that are with young. (2.) Though it were so, yet they were in danger from these seducers. This Paul suggests with a great deal of modesty and tenderness; not as one suspicious of them, but as one solicitous for them: "Your *obedience has come abroad unto all men;* we grant this and rejoice in it: *I am glad therefore on your behalf.*" Thus does he insinuate their commendation, the better to make way for the caution. A holy jealousy of our friends may

very well comport with a holy joy in them. "You think yourselves a very happy people, and so do I too: but for all that you must not be secure: *I would have you wise unto that which is good, and simple concerning evil.* You are a willing good-natured people, but you had best take heed of being imposed upon by those seducers." A pliable temper is good when it is under good government; but otherwise it may be very ensnaring; and therefore he gives two general rules:—[1.] To be *wise unto that which is good,* that is, to be skilful and intelligent in the truths and ways of God. "Be wise to try the spirits, to prove all things, and then to hold fast that only which is good." There is need of a great deal of wisdom in our adherence to good truths, and good duties, and good people, lest in any of these we be imposed upon and deluded. *Be ye therefore wise as serpents* (Matt. x. 16), wise to discern that which is really good and that which is counterfeit; wise to distinguish things that differ, to improve opportunities. While we are in the midst of so many deceivers, we have great need of that wisdom of the prudent which is to understand his way, Prov. xiv. 8. [2.] To be *simple concerning evil*—so wise as not to be *deceived,* and yet so simple as not to be deceivers. It is a holy simplicity, not to be able to contrive, nor palliate, nor carry on, any evil design; ἀκεραίους—*harmless,* unmixed, inoffensive. *In malice be you children,* 1 Cor. xiv. 20. The wisdom of the serpent becomes Christians, but not the subtlety of the old serpent. We must withal *be harmless as doves.* That is a wisely simple man that knows not how to do any thing against the truth. Now Paul was the more solicitous for the Roman church, that it might preserve its integrity, because it was so famous; it was a city upon a hill, and many eyes were upon the Christians there, so that an error prevailing there would be a bad precedent, and have an ill influence upon other churches: as indeed it has since proved in fact, the great apostasy of the latter days taking its rise from that capital city. The errors of leading churches are leading errors. When the bishop of Rome fell as a *great star* from heaven (Rev. viii. 10), *his tail drew a third part of the stars* after him, Rev. xii. 4.

3. Because of the promise of God, that we shall have victory at last, which is given to quicken and encourage, not to supersede, our watchful cares and vigorous endeavours. It is a very sweet promise (*v.* 20): *The God of peace shall bruise Satan under your feet.*

(1.) The titles he gives to God: *The God of peace,* the author and giver of all good. When we come to God for spiritual victories, we must not only eye him as the Lord of hosts, whose all power is, but as the God of peace, a God at peace with us, speaking peace to us, working peace in us, creating peace for us. Victory comes from God more as the God of peace than as the God of war; for, in all our conflicts, peace is the thing we must contend for. God, as the God of peace, will restrain and vanquish all those that cause divisions and offences, and so break and disturb the peace of the church.

(2.) The blessing he expects from God—a victory over Satan. If he mean primarily those false doctrines and seducing spirits spoken of before, of which Satan was the prime founder and author, yet, doubtless, it comprehends all the other designs and devices of Satan against souls, to defile, disturb, and destroy them, all his attempts to keep us from the purity of heaven, the peace of heaven here, and the possession of heaven hereafter. Satan tempting and troubling, acting as a deceiver and as a destroyer, the *God of peace* will *bruise under our feet.* He had cautioned them before against simplicity: now they, being conscious of their own great weakness and folly, might think, "How shall we evade and escape these snares that are laid for us? Will not these adversaries of our souls be at length too hard for us?" "No," says he, "fear not; though you cannot overcome in your own strength and wisdom, yet the God of peace will do it for you; and through him that loved us we shall be more than conquerors." [1.] The victory shall be complete: *He shall bruise Satan under your feet,* plainly alluding to the first promise the Messiah made in paradise (Gen. iii. 15), that the seed of the woman should break the serpent's head, which is in the fulfilling every day, while the saints are enabled to resist and overcome the temptations of Satan, and will be perfectly fulfilled when, in spite of all the powers of darkness, all that belong to the election of grace shall be brought triumphantly to glory. When Joshua had conquered the kings of Canaan, he called the captains of Israel to set their feet upon the necks of those kings (Josh. x. 24), so will Christ, our Joshua, enable all his faithful servants and soldiers to set their feet upon Satan's neck, to trample upon, and triumph over, their spiritual enemies. Christ hath overcome for us; disarmed the strong man armed, broken his power, and we have nothing to do but to pursue the victory and divide the spoil. Let this quicken us to our spiritual conflict, to fight the good fight of faith—we have to do with a conquered enemy, and the victory will be perfect shortly. [2.] The victory shall be speedy: He shall do it *shortly.* Yet a little while, and he that shall come will come. He hath said it, *Behold, I come quickly.* When Satan seems to have prevailed, and we are ready to give up all for lost, then will the God of peace cut the work short in righteousness. It will encourage soldiers when they know the war will be at an end quickly, in such a victory. Some refer it to the happy period of their contentions in true love and unity; others to the period of the church's persecutions in the conversion of the powers of the empire to Christianity, when the bloody enemies of the church were subdued and trampled on by Constantine, and the church under his government. It is rather to be applied to the victory which all the saints shall have over Satan when they come to heaven, and shall be for ever out of his reach, together with the present victories which through grace they obtain in earnest of that. Hold out therefore, faith and patience, yet a little while; when we have once got through the Red Sea, we shall see our spiritual enemies dead on the shore, and triumphantly sing the song of Moses and the song of the Lamb. To this therefore he subjoins the benediction, *The grace of our Lord Jesus Christ be with you*—the good-will of Christ towards you, the good work of Christ in you. This will be the best preservative against the snares of heretics, and schismatics, and false teachers. If the grace of Christ be with us, who can be against us so as to prevail? *Be strong therefore in the grace which is in Christ Jesus.* Paul, not only as a friend, but as a minister and an apostle, who had received grace for grace, thus with authority blesses them with this blessing, and repeats it, *v.* 24.

21 Timotheus my workfellow, and
Lucius, and Jason, and Sosipater,
my kinsmen, salute you. 22 I Tertius, who wrote *this* epistle, salute
you in the Lord. 23 Gaius mine
host, and of the whole church, saluteth you. Erastus the chamberlain
of the city saluteth you, and Quartus
a brother. 24 The grace of our Lord
Jesus Christ *be* with you all. Amen.

As the apostle had before sent his own salutations to many of this church, and that of the churches round him to them all, he here adds an affectionate remembrance of them from some particular persons who were now with him, the better to promote acquaintance and fellowship among distant saints, and that the subscribing of these worthy names, known to them, might the more recommend this epistle. He mentions, 1. Some that were his particular friends, and probably known to the Roman Christians: *Timotheus my work-fellow.* Paul sometimes calls Timothy his son, as an inferior; but here he styles him his work-fellow, as one equal with him, such a respect does he put upon him: and *Lucius,* probably Lucius of Cyrene, a noted man in the church of Antioch (Acts xiii. 1), as Jason was at Thessalonica, where he suffered for entertaining Paul (Acts xvii. 5, 6): and *Sosipater,* supposed to be the same with Sopater of Berea, mentioned Acts xx. 4. These Paul calls his kinsmen; not only more largely, as they were Jews, but as they were in blood or affinity nearly allied to him. It seems, Paul was of a good family, that he met with so many of his kindred in several places. It is a very great comfort to see the holiness and usefulness of our kindred. 2. One that was Paul's amanuensis (*v.* 22): *I Tertius, who wrote this epistle.* Paul made use of a scribe, not out of state nor idleness, but because he wrote a bad hand, which was not very legible, which he excuses, when he writes to the Galatians with his own hand (Gal. vi. 11): *πηλίκοις γράμμασι—with what kind of letters.* Perhaps this Tertius was the same with Silas; for Silas (as some think) signifies *the third* in Hebrew, as *Tertius* in Latin. Tertius either wrote as Paul dictated, or transcribed it fairly over out of Paul's foul copy. The least piece of service done to the church, and the ministers of the church, shall not pass without a remembrance and a recompence. It was an honour to Tertius that he had a hand, though but as a scribe, in writing this epistle. 3. Some others that were of note among the Christians (*v.* 23): *Gaius my host.* It is uncertain whether this was Gaius of Derbe (Acts xx. 4), or Gaius of Macedonia (Acts xix. 29), or rather Gaius of Corinth (1 Cor. i. 14), and whether any of these was he to whom John wrote his third epistle. However, Paul commends him for his great hospitality; not only my host, but of the *whole church*—one that entertained them all as there was occasion, opened his doors to their church-meetings, and eased the rest of the church by his readiness to treat all Christian strangers that came to them. *Erastus, the chamberlain of the city* is another; he means the city of Corinth, whence this epistle was dated. It seems he was a person of honour and account, one in public place, steward or treasurer. Not many mighty, not many noble, are called, but some are. His estate, and honour, and employment, did not take him off from attending on Paul and laying out himself for the good of the church, it should seem, in the work of the ministry; for he is joined with Timothy (Acts xix. 22), and is mentioned 2 Tim. iv. 20. It was no disparagement to the chamberlain of the city to be a preacher of the gospel of Christ. *Quartus* is likewise mentioned, and called a brother; for as one is our Father, even Christ, so all we are brethren.

25 Now to him that is of power to
stablish you according to my gospel,
and the preaching of Jesus Christ,
according to the revelation of the
mystery, which was kept secret since
the world began, 26 But now is
made manifest, and by the scriptures
of the prophets, according to the
commandment of the everlasting God,
made known to all nations for the
obedience of faith: 27 To God only
wise, *be* glory through Jesus Christ
for ever. Amen.

Here the apostle solemnly closes his epistle

with a magnificent ascription of glory to the blessed God, as one that terminated all in the praise and glory of God, and studied to return all to him, seeing all is of him and from him. He does, as it were, breathe out his soul to these Romans in the praise of God, choosing to make that the end of his epistle which he made the end of his life. Observe here,

I. A description of the gospel of God, which comes in in a parenthesis; having occasion to speak of it as the means by which the power of God establishes souls, and the rule of that establishment: *To establish you according to my gospel.* Paul calls it his gospel, because he was the preacher of it and because he did so much glory in it. Some think he means especially that declaration, explication, and application, of the doctrine of the gospel, which he had now made in this epistle; but it rather takes in all the preaching and writing of the apostles, among whom Paul was a principal labourer. Through their word (John xvii. 20), the word committed to them. Ministers are the ambassadors, and the gospel is their embassy. Paul had his head and heart so full of the gospel that he could scarcely mention it without a digression to set forth the nature and excellency of it.

1. It is the *preaching of Jesus Christ.* Christ was the preacher of it himself; it began to be spoken by the Lord, Heb. ii. 3. So pleased was Christ with his undertaking for our salvation that he would himself be the publisher of it. Or, Christ is the subject-matter of it; the sum and substance of the whole gospel is Jesus Christ and him crucified. We preach not ourselves, says Paul, but Christ Jesus the Lord. That which establishes souls is the plain preaching of Jesus Christ.

2. *It is the revelation of the mystery which was kept secret since the world began, and by the scriptures of the prophets made known.* The subject-matter of the gospel is a mystery. Our redemption and salvation by Jesus Christ, in the foundation, method, and fruits of it, are, without controversy, a great mystery of godliness, 1 Tim. iii. 16. This bespeaks the honour of the gospel; it is no vulgar common thing, hammered out by any human wit, but it is the admirable product of the eternal wisdom and counsel of God, and has in it such an inconceivable height, such an unfathomable depth, as surpass knowledge. It is a mystery which the angels desire to look into, and cannot find the bottom of. And yet, blessed be God, there is as much of this mystery made plain as will suffice to bring us to heaven, if we do not wilfully neglect so great salvation. Now,

(1.) This mystery was kept secret since the world began: χρόνοις αἰωνίοις σεσιγημένου. It was *wrapped up in silence from eternity*; so some—*à temporibus æternis*; it is no new and upstart notion, no late invention, but took rise from the days of eternity and the purposes of God's everlasting love. Before the foundation of the world was laid, the mystery was hid in God, Eph. iii. 9. Or, *since the world began*, so we translate it. During all the times of the Old-Testament this mystery was comparatively kept secret in the types and shadows of the ceremonial law, and the dark predictions of the prophets, which pointed at it, but so that they could not stedfastly look to the end of those things, 2 Cor. iii. 13. Thus it was hid from ages and generations, even among the Jews, much more among the Gentiles that sat in darkness and had no notices at all of it. Even the disciples of Christ themselves, before his resurrection and ascension, were very much in the dark about the mystery of redemption, and their notion of it was very much clouded and confused; such a secret was it for many ages. But,

(2.) It is now made manifest. The veil is rent, the shadows of the evening are done away, and life and immortality are brought to light by the gospel, and the Sun of righteousness has risen upon the world Paul does not pretend to have the monopoly of this discovery, as if he alone knew it; no, it is made manifest to many others. But how is it made manifest by the scriptures of the prophets? Surely, because now the event has given the best exposition to the prophecies of the Old Testament. Being accomplished, they are explained. The preaching of the prophets, as far as it related to this mystery, was in a great measure dark and unintelligible in the ages wherein they lived; but the scriptures of the prophets, the things which they left in writing, are now not only made plain in themselves, but by them this mystery is made known to all nations. The Old Testament does not only borrow light from, but return light to, the revelation of the New Testament. If the New Testament explains the Old, the Old Testament, by way of requital, very much illustrates the New. Thus the Old-Testament prophets prophesy again, now their prophecies are fulfilled, *before many people, and nations, and tongues.* I refer to Rev. x. 11, which this explains. Now Christ appears to have been the treasure hid in the field of the Old Testament. To him bear *all the prophets witness.* See Luke xxiv. 27.

(3.) It is manifested *according to the commandment of the everlasting God*—the purpose, counsel, and decree of God from eternity, and the commission and appointment given first to Christ and then to the apostles, in the fulness of time. They received commandment from the Father to do what they did in preaching the gospel. Lest any should object, "Why was this mystery kept secret so long, and why made manifest now?"—he resolves it into the will of God, who is an absolute sovereign, and gives not an account of any of his matters. The commandment of the everlasting God was enough to bear out the apostles and ministers of the gospel in their preaching. *The everlasting God.* This attribute of eternity is here given up to God very emphatically. [1.] He is from everlasting, which intimates that though he had kept this mystery secret since the world began, and had but lately revealed it, yet he had framed and contrived it from everlasting, before the worlds were. The oaths and covenants in the written word are but the copy of the oath and covenant which were between the Father and the Son from eternity : those the extracts, these the original And, [2.] He is to everlasting, intimating the eternal continuance of this revelation and its eternal consequence to us. We must never look for any new revelation, but abide by this, for this is according to the commandment of the everlasting God. Christ, in the gospel, is the same yesterday, to-day, and for ever.

(4.) It is *made known to all nations for the obedience of faith.* The extent of this revelation he often takes notice of ; that whereas hitherto in Judah only God was known, now Christ is salvation to the ends of the earth, to all nations. And the design of it is very observable ; it is for the obedience of faith—that they may believe and obey it, receive it and be ruled by it. The gospel is revealed, not to be talked of and disputed about, but to be submitted to. The obedience of faith is that obedience which is paid to the word of faith (see that phrase, Acts vi. 7), and which is produced by the grace of faith. See here what is the right faith—even that which works in obedience ; and what is the right obedience—even that which springs from faith ; and what is the design of the gospel—to bring us to both.

II. A doxology to that God whose gospel it is, ascribing glory to him for ever (*v.* 27), acknowledging that he is a glorious God, and adoring him accordingly, with the most awful affections, desiring and longing to be at this work with the holy angels, where we shall be doing it to eternity. This is praising God, ascribing glory to him for ever. Observe,

1. The matter of this praise. In thanking God, we fasten upon his favours to us ; in praising and adoring God, we fasten upon his perfections in himself. Two of his principal attributes are here taken notice of :—(1.) His power (*v.* 25) : *To him that is of power to establish you.* It is no less than a divine power that establishes the saints. Considering the disposition there is in them to fall, the industry of their spiritual enemies that seek to overthrow them, and the shaking times into which their lot is cast, no less than an almighty power will establish them That power of God which is put forth for the establishment of the saints is and ought to be the matter of our praise, as Jude 24, *To him that is able to keep you from falling.* In giving God the glory of this power we may, and must, take to ourselves the comfort of it—that whatever our doubts, and difficulties, and fears, may be, our God, whom we serve, is of power to establish us. See 1 Pet. i. 5 ; John x. 29. (2.) His wisdom (*v.* 27) : *To God only wise.* Power to effect without wisdom to contrive, and wisdom to contrive without power to effect, are alike vain and fruitless ; but both together, and both infinite, make a perfect being. He is only wise ; not the Father only wise, exclusive of the Son, but Father, Son, and Holy Ghost, three persons and one God, only wise, compared with the creatures. Man, the wisest of all the creatures in the lower world, is born like a wild ass's colt ; nay, the angels themselves are charged with folly, in comparison with God. He only is perfectly and infallibly wise ; he only is originally wise, in and of himself ; for he is the spring and fountain of all the wisdom of the creatures, the Father of all the lights of wisdom that any creature can pretend to (James i. 17) : with him are strength and wisdom, the deceived and deceiver are his.

2. The Mediator of this praise : *Through Jesus Christ. To God only wise through Jesus Christ ;* so some. It is in and through Christ that God is manifested to the world as the only wise God ; for he is the wisdom of God, and the power of God. Or rather, as we read it, *glory through Jesus Christ.* All the glory that passes from fallen man to God, so as to be accepted of him, must go through the hands of the Lord Jesus, in whom alone it is that our persons and performances are, or can be, pleasing to God. Of his righteousness therefore we must make mention, even of his only, who, as he is the Mediator of all our prayers, so he is, and I believe will be to eternity, the Mediator of all our praises.

AN

EXPOSITION,

WITH PRACTICAL OBSERVATIONS,

OF THE FIRST EPISTLE OF ST. PAUL TO THE

CORINTHIANS.

CORINTH was a principal city of Greece, in that particular division of it which was called *Achaia*. It was situated on the isthmus (or neck of land) that joined Peloponnesus to the rest of Greece, on the southern side, and had two ports adjoining, one at the bottom of the Corinthian Gulf, called *Lechæum*, not far from the city, whence they traded to Italy and the west, the other at the bottom of the Sinus Saronicus, called *Cenchrea*, at a more remote distance, whence they traded to Asia. From this situation, it is no wonder that Corinth should be a place of great trade and wealth; and, as affluence is apt to produce luxury of all kinds, neither is it to be wondered at if a place so famous for wealth and arts should be infamous for vice. It was in a particular manner noted for fornication, insomuch that a *Corinthian woman* was a proverbial phrase for a strumpet, and κορινθιάζειν, κορινθιάσεσθαι—*to play the Corinthian*, is to play the whore, or indulge whorish inclinations. Yet in this lewd city did Paul, by the blessing of God on his labours, plant and raise a Christian church, chiefly among the Gentiles, as seems very probable from the history of this matter, Acts xviii. 1—18, compared with some passages in this epistle, particularly *ch.* xii. 2, where the apostle tells them, *You know that you were Gentiles, carried away to those dumb idols even as you were led*, though it is not improbable that many Jewish converts might be also among them, for we are told that *Crispus, the chief ruler of the synagogue, believed on the Lord, with all his house*, Acts xviii. 8. He continued in this city nearly two years, as is plain from Acts xviii. 11 and 18 compared, and laboured with great success, being encouraged by a divine vision assuring him God *had much people in that city*, Acts xviii. 9, 10. Nor did he use to stay long in a place where his ministry met not with acceptance and success.

Some time after he left them he wrote this epistle to them, to water what he had planted and rectify some gross disorders which during his absence had been introduced, partly from the interest some false teacher or teachers had obtained amongst them, and partly from the leaven of their old maxims and manners, that had not been thoroughly purged out by the Christian principles they had entertained. And it is but too visible how much their wealth had helped to corrupt their manners, from the several faults for which the apostle reprehends them. Pride, avarice, luxury, lust (the natural offspring of a carnal and corrupt mind), are all fed and prompted by outward affluence. And with all these either the body of this people or some particular persons among them are here charged by the apostle. Their pride discovered itself in their parties and factions, and the notorious disorders they committed in the exercise of their spiritual gifts. And this vice was not wholly fed by their wealth, but by the insight they had into the Greek learning and philosophy. Some of the ancients tell us that the city abounded with rhetoricians and philosophers. And these were men naturally vain, full of self-conceit, and apt to despise the plain doctrine of the gospel, because it did not feed the curiosity of an inquisitive and disputing temper, nor please the ear with artful speeches and a flow of fine words. Their avarice was manifest in their law-suits and litigations about *meum—mine*, and *tuum—thine*, before heathen judges. Their luxury appeared in more instances than one, in their dress, in their debauching themselves even at the Lord's table, when the rich, who were most faulty on this account, were guilty also of a very proud and criminal contempt of their poor brethren. Their lust broke out in a most flagrant and infamous instance, such as had not been named among the Gentiles, not spoken of without detestation—that a man should have his father's wife, either as his wife, or so as to commit fornication with her. This indeed seems to be the fault of a particular person; but the whole church were to blame that they had his crime in no greater abhorrence, that they could endure one of such very corrupt morals and of so flagitious a behaviour among them. But their participation in his sin was yet greater, if, as some of the ancients tell us, they were puffed up on behalf of the great learning and eloquence of this incestuous person. And it is plain from other passages of the epistle that they were not so entirely free from their former lewd inclinations as not to need very strict cautions and strong arguments against fornication: see *ch.* vi. 9—20. The pride of their learning had also carried many of them so far as to disbelieve or dispute against the doctrine of the resurrection. It is not improbable that they treated this question problematically, as they did many questions in philosophy, and tried their skill by arguing it *pro* and *con*.

It is manifest from this state of things that there was much that deserved reprehension, and needed correction, in this church. And the apostle, under the direction and influence of the Holy Spirit, sets himself to do both with all wisdom and faithfulness, and with a due mixture of tenderness and authority, as became one in so elevated and important a station in the church. After a short introduction at the beginning of the epistle, he first blames them for their discord and factions, enters into the origin and source of them, shows them how much pride and vanity, and the affectation of science, and learning, and eloquence, flattered by false teachers, contributed to the scandalous schism; and prescribes humility, and submission to divine instruction, the teaching of God by his Spirit, both by external revelation and internal illumination, as a remedy for the evils that abounded amongst them. He shows them the vanity of their pretended science and eloquence on many accounts. This he does through the first four chapters. In the fifth he treats of the case of the incestuoùs person, and orders him to be put out from among them. Nor is what the ancients say improbable, that this incestuous person was a man in great esteem, and head of one party at least among them. The apostle seems to tax them with being puffed up on his account, *ch.* v. 2. In the sixth chapter he blames them for their law-suits, carried on before heathen judges, when their disputes about property should have been amicably determined amongst themselves, and in the close of the chapter warns them against the sin of fornication, and urges his caution with a variety of arguments. In the seventh chapter he gives advice upon a case of conscience, which some of that church had proposed to him in an epistle, about marriage, and shows it to be appointed of God as a remedy against fornication, that the ties of it were not dissolved, though a husband or wife continued a heathen, when the other became a Christian; and, in short, that Christianity made no change in men's civil states and relations. He gives also some directions here about virgins, in answer, as is probable, to the Corinthians' enquiries. In the eighth he directs them about meats offered to idols, and cautions them against abusing their Christian liberty. From this he also takes occasion, in the ninth chapter, to expatiate a little on his own conduct upon this head of liberty. For, though he might have insisted on a maintenance from the churches where he ministered, he waived this demand, that *he might make the gospel of Christ without charge*, and did in other things comply with and suit himself to the tempers and circumstances of those among whom he laboured, for their good. In the tenth chapter he dissuades them, from the example of the Jews, against having communion with idolaters, by eating of their sacrifices, inasmuch as they could not be at once partakers of the Lord's table and the table of devils, though they were not bound to enquire concerning meat sold in the shambles, or set before them at a feast made by unbelievers, whether it were a part of the idol-sacrifices or no, but were at liberty to eat without asking questions. In the eleventh chapter he gives direction about their habit in public worship, blames them for their gross irregularities and scandalous disorders in receiving the Lord's supper, and solemnly warns them against the abuse of so sacred an institution. In the twelfth chapter he enters on the consideration of spiritual gifts, which were poured forth in great abundance on this church, upon which they were not a little elated. He tells them, in this chapter, that all came from the same original, and were all directed to the same end. They issued from one Spirit, and were intended for the good of the church, and must be abused when they were not made to minister to this purpose. Towards the close he informs them that they were indeed valuable gifts, but he could recommend to them something far more excellent, upon which he breaks out, in the thirteenth chapter, into the commendation and characteristics of charity. And then, in the fourteenth, he directs them how to keep up decency and order in the churches in the use of their spiritual gifts, in which they seem to have been exceedingly irregular, through pride of their gifts and a vanity of showing them. The fifteenth chapter is taken up in confirming and explaining the great doctrine of the resurrection. The last chapter consists of some particular advices and salutations; and thus the epistle closes.

CHAP. I.

In this chapter we have, I. The preface or introduction to the whole epistle, ver. 1—9. II. One principal occasion of writing it hinted, namely, their divisions and the origin of them, ver. 10—13. III. An account of Paul's ministry among them, which was principally preaching the gospel, ver. 14—17. IV. The manner wherein he preached the gospel, and the different success of it, with an account how admirably it was fitted to bring glory to God and beat down the pride and vanity of men, ver. 17, to the end.

PAUL, called *to be* an apostle of
Jesus Christ through the will of
God, and Sosthenes *our* brother, 2
Unto the church of God which is at
Corinth, to them that are sanctified
in Christ Jesus, called *to be* saints,
with all that in every place call upon
the name of Jesus Christ our Lord,
both their's and our's: 3 Grace *be*
unto you, and peace, from God our
Father, and *from* the Lord Jesus
Christ. 4 I thank my God always
on your behalf, for the grace of God
which is given you by Jesus Christ;
5 That in every thing ye are enriched
by him, in all utterance, and *in* all
knowledge; 6 Even as the testimony
of Christ was confirmed in you: 7
So that ye come behind in no gift;
waiting for the coming of our Lord
Jesus Christ: 8 Who shall also
confirm you unto the end, *that ye may*
be blameless in the day of our Lord

Jesus Christ. 9 God *is* faithful, by whom ye were called unto the fellowship of his Son Jesus Christ our Lord.

We have here the apostle's preface to his whole epistle, in which we may take notice,

I. Of the inscription, in which, according to the custom of writing letters then, the name of the person by whom it was written and the persons to whom it was written are both inserted. 1. It is an epistle from Paul, the apostle of the Gentiles, to the church of Corinth, which he himself had planted, though there were some among them that now questioned his apostleship (*ch.* ix. 1, 2), and vilified his person and ministry, 2 Cor. x. 10. The most faithful and useful ministers are not secure from this contempt. He begins with challenging this character: *Paul, called to be an apostle of Jesus Christ, through the will of God.* He had not taken this honour to himself, but had a divine commission for it. It was proper at any time, but necessary at this time, to assert his character, and magnify his office, when false teachers made a merit of running him down, and their giddy and deluded followers were so apt to set them up in competition with him. It was not pride in Paul, but faithfulness to his trust, in this juncture, to maintain his apostolical character and authority. And, to make this more fully appear, he joins Sosthenes with him in writing, who was a minister of a lower rank. Paul, and Sosthenes his brother, not a fellow-apostle, but a fellow-minister, once a ruler of the Jewish synagogue, afterwards a convert to Christianity, a Corinthian by birth, as is most probable, and dear to this people, for which reason Paul, to ingratiate himself with them, joins him with himself in his first salutations. There is no reason to suppose he was made a partaker of the apostle's inspiration, for which reasons he speaks, through the rest of the epistle, in his own name, and in the singular number. Paul did not in any case lessen his apostolical authority, and yet he was ready upon all occasions to do a kind and condescending thing for their good to whom he ministered. The persons to whom this epistle was directed were *the church of God that was at Corinth, sanctified in Christ Jesus, and called to be saints.* All Christians are thus far sanctified in Christ Jesus, that they are by baptism dedicated and devoted to him, they are under strict obligations to be holy, and they make profession of real sanctity. If they be not truly holy, it is their own fault and reproach. Note, It is the design of Christianity to sanctify us in Christ. *He gave himself for us, to redeem us from all iniquity, and purify us to himself a peculiar people, zealous of good works.* In conjunction with the church at Corinth, he directs the epistle *to all that in every place call on the name of Christ Jesus our Lord, both theirs and ours.* Hereby Christians are distinguished from the profane and atheistical, that they dare not live without prayer; and hereby they are distinguished from Jews and Pagans, that they call on the name of Christ. He is their common head and Lord. Observe, In every place in the Christian world there are some that call on the name of Christ. God hath a remnant in all places; and we should have a common concern for and hold communion with all that call on Christ's name.

II. Of the apostolical benediction. *Grace be to you, and peace, from God our Father, and from the Lord Jesus Christ.* An apostle of the prince of peace must be a messenger and minister of peace. This blessing the gospel brings with it, and this blessing every preacher of the gospel should heartily wish and pray may be the lot of all among whom he ministers. Grace and peace—the favour of God, and reconciliation to him. It is indeed the summary of all blessings. *The Lord lift up his countenance upon thee, and give thee peace,* was the form of benediction under the Old Testament (Num. vi. 26), but this advantage we have by the gospel, 1. That we are directed how to obtain that peace from God: it is in and by Christ. Sinners can have no peace with God, nor any good from him, but through Christ. 2. We are told what must qualify us for this peace; namely, grace: first grace, and then peace. God first reconciles sinners to himself, before he bestows his peace upon them.

III. Of the apostle's thanksgiving to God on their behalf. Paul begins most of his epistles with thanksgiving to God for his friends and prayer for them. Note, The best way of manifesting our affection to our friends is by praying and giving thanks for them. It is one branch of the communion of saints to give thanks to God mutually for our gifts, graces, and comforts. He gives thanks, 1. For their conversion to the faith of Christ: *For the grace which was given you through Jesus Christ, v.* 4. He is the great procurer and disposer of the favours of God. Those who are united to him by faith, and made to partake of his Spirit and merits, are the objects of divine favour. God loves them, bears them hearty good-will, and bestows on them his fatherly smiles and blessings. 2. For the abundance of their spiritual gifts. This the church of Corinth was famous for. They did not come behind any of the churches in any gift, *v.* 7. He specifies *utterance and knowledge, v.* 5. Where God has given these two gifts, he has given great capacity for usefulness. Many have the flower of utterance that have not the root of knowledge, and their converse is barren. Many have the treasure of knowledge, and want utterance to employ it for the good of others, and then it is in a manner wrapped up in a napkin. But, where God gives both, a man is qualified for eminent usefulness. When the church of Corinth was enriched with all utterance and all knowledge, it was fit that a large tribute of praise should be rendered to God, especially when these gifts were a testimony to the truth of the Christian doctrine, a confirmation of the testimony of Christ among them, *v.* 6. They were *signs and wonders and gifts of the Holy Ghost*, by which God did bear witness to the apostles, both to their mission and doctrine (Heb. ii. 4), so that the more plentifully they were poured forth on any church the more full attestation was given to that doctrine which was delivered by the apostles, the more confirming evidence they had of their divine mission. And it is no wonder that when they had such a foundation for their faith they should live in expectation of the coming of their Lord Jesus Christ, *v.* 7. It is the character of Christians that they wait for Christ's second coming; all our religion has regard to this: we believe it, and hope for it, and it is the business of our lives to prepare for it, if we are Christians indeed. And the more confirmed we are in the Christian faith the more firm is our belief of our Lord's second coming, and the more earnest our expectation of it.

IV. Of the encouraging hopes the apostle had of them for the time to come, founded on the power and love of Christ, and the faithfulness of God, *v.* 8, 9. He who had begun a good work in them, and carried it on thus far, would not leave it unfinished. Those that wait for the coming of our Lord Jesus Christ will be kept by him, and confirmed to the end; and those that are so *will be blameless in the day of Christ:* not upon the principle of strict justice, but gracious absolution; not in rigour of law, but from rich and free grace. How desirable is it to be confirmed and kept of Christ for such a purpose as this! How glorious are the hopes of such a privilege, whether for ourselves or others! To be kept by the power of Christ from the power of our own corruption and Satan's temptation, that we may appear without blame in the great day! O glorious expectation, especially when the faithfulness of God comes in to support our hopes! He *who hath called us into the fellowship of his Son is faithful, and will do it,* 1 Thess. v. 24. He who hath brought us into near and dear relation to Christ, into sweet and intimate communion with Christ, is faithful; he may be trusted with our dearest concerns. Those that come at his call shall never be disappointed in their hopes in him. If we approve ourselves faithful to God, we shall never find him unfaithful to us. *He will not suffer his faithfulness to fail,* Ps. lxxxix. 33.

10 Now I beseech you, brethren,
by the name of our Lord Jesus
Christ, that ye all speak the same
thing, and *that* there be no divisions
among you; but *that* ye be perfectly
joined together in the same mind, and
in the same judgment. 11 For it
hath been declared unto me of you,
my brethren, by them *which are of
the house* of Chloe, that there are
contentions among you. 12 Now
this I say, that every one of you saith,
I am of Paul; and I of Apollos; and
I of Cephas; and I of Christ. 13
Is Christ divided? was Paul crucified for you? or were ye baptized in
the name of Paul?

Here the apostle enters on his subject.

I. He exhorts them to unity and brotherly love, and reproves them for their divisions. He had received an account from some that wished them well of some unhappy differences among them. It was neither ill-will to the church, nor to their ministers, that prompted them to give this account; but a kind and prudent concern to have these heats qualified by Paul's interposition. He writes to them in a very engaging way: "*I beseech you, brethren, by the name of our Lord Jesus Christ;* if you have any regard to that dear and worthy name by which you are called, be unanimous. *Speak all the same thing;* avoid *divisions* or *schisms*" (as the original is), "that is, all alienation of affection from each other. *Be perfectly joined together in the same mind,* as far as you can. In the great things of religion be of a mind: but, when there is not a unity of sentiment, let there be a union of affections. The consideration of being agreed in greater things should extinguish all feuds and divisions about minor ones."

II. He hints at the origin of these contentions. Pride lay at the bottom, and this made them factious. *Only of pride cometh contention,* Prov. xiii. 10. They quarrelled about their ministers. Paul and Apollos were both faithful ministers of Jesus Christ, and helpers of their faith and joy: but those who were disposed to be contentious broke into parties, and set their ministers at the head of their several factions: some cried up Paul, perhaps as the most sublime and spiritual teacher; others cried up Apollos, perhaps as the most eloquent speaker; some Cephas, or Peter, perhaps for the authority of his age, or because he was the apostle of the circumcision; and some were for none of them, but Christ only. So liable are the best things in the world to be corrupted, and the gospel and its institutions, which are at perfect harmony with themselves and one another, to be made the engines of variance, discord, and contention. This is no reproach to our religion, but a very melancholy evidence of the corruption and depravity of human nature. Note, How far will pride carry Christians in opposition to one another! Even so far as to set Christ and his own apostles at variance, and make them rivals and competitors.

III. He expostulates with them upon their discord and quarrels: "*Is Christ divided?* No, there is but one Christ, and therefore

Christians should be of one heart. *Was Paul crucified for you?* Was he your sacrifice and atonement? Did I ever pretend to be your saviour, or any more than his minister? Or, *were you baptized in the name of Paul?* Were you devoted to my service, or engaged to be my disciples, by that sacred rite? Did I challenge that right in you, or dependence from you, which is the proper claim of your God and Redeemer?" No; ministers, however instrumental they are of good to us, are not to be put in Christ's stead. They are not to usurp Christ's authority, nor encourage any thing in the people that looks like transferring his authority to them. He is our Saviour and sacrifice, he is our Lord and guide. And happy were it for the churches if there were no name of distinction among them, as Christ is not divided.

14 I thank God that I baptized
none of you, but Crispus and Gaius;
15 Lest any should say that I had
baptized in mine own name. 16
And I baptized also the household of
Stephanas: besides, I know not whether I baptized any other.

Here the apostle gives an account of his ministry among them. He thanks God he had baptized but a few among them, *Crispus*, who had been a ruler of a synagogue at Corinth (Acts xviii. 8), *Gaius, and the household of Stephanas,* besides whom, he says, he did not remember that he had baptized any. But how was this a proper matter for thankfulness? Was it not a part of the apostolical commission to baptize all nations? And could Paul give thanks to God for his own neglect of duty? He is not to be understood in such a sense as if he were thankful for not having baptized at all, but for not having done it in present circumstances, lest it should have had this very bad construction put upon it—that he had baptized in his own name, made disciples for himself, or set himself up as the head of a sect. He left it to other ministers to baptize, while he set himself to more useful work, and filled up his time with preaching the gospel. This, he thought, was more his business, because the more important business of the two. He had assistants that could baptize, when none could discharge the other part of his office so well as himself. In this sense he says, *Christ sent him not to baptize, but to preach the gospel*—not so much to baptize as to preach. Note, Ministers should consider themselves sent and set apart more especially to that service in which Christ will be most honoured and the salvation of souls promoted, and for which they are best fitted, though no part of their duty is to be neglected. The principal business Paul did among them was to preach *the gospel* (*v.* 17), *the cross* (*v.* 18), *Christ crucified, v.* 23. Ministers are the soldiers of Christ, and are to erect and display the banner of the cross. He did not preach his own fancy, but the gospel—the glad tidings of peace, and reconciliation to God, through the mediation of a crucified Redeemer. This is the sum and substance of the gospel. Christ crucified is the foundation of all our hopes and the fountain of all our joys. By his death we live. This is what Paul preached, what all ministers should preach, and what all the saints live upon.

17 For Christ sent me not to baptize, but to preach the gospel: not
with wisdom of words, lest the cross
of Christ should be made of none
effect. 18 For the preaching of the
cross is to them that perish foolishness; but unto us which are saved it
is the power of God. 19 For it is
written, I will destroy the wisdom of
the wise, and will bring to nothing
the understanding of the prudent.
20 Where *is* the wise? where *is* the
scribe? where *is* the disputer of this
world? hath not God made foolish
the wisdom of this world? 21 For
after that in the wisdom of God the
world by wisdom knew not God, it
pleased God by the foolishness of
preaching to save them that believe.
22 For the Jews require a sign, and
the Greeks seek after wisdom: 23
But we preach Christ crucified, unto
the Jews a stumblingblock, and unto
the Greeks foolishness; 24 But
unto them which are called, both
Jews and Greeks, Christ the power
of God, and the wisdom of God. 25
Because the foolishness of God is
wiser than men; and the weakness of
God is stronger than men. 26 For
ye see your calling, brethren, how
that not many wise men after the
flesh, not many mighty, not many
noble, *are called*: 27 But God hath
chosen the foolish things of the world
to confound the wise; and God hath
chosen the weak things of the world
to confound the things which are
mighty; 28 And base things of the
world, and things which are despised,
hath God chosen, *yea*, and things
which are not, to bring to nought
things that are: 29 That no flesh
should glory in his presence. 30
But of him are ye in Christ Jesus,
who of God is made unto us wisdom,

and righteousness, and sanctification, and redemption: 31 That, according as it is written, He that glorieth, let him glory in the Lord.

We have here,

I. The manner in which Paul preached the gospel, and the cross of Christ: *Not with the wisdom of words* (*v.* 17), *the enticing words of man's wisdom* (*ch.* ii. 4), the flourish of oratory, or the accuracies of philosophical language, upon which the Greeks so much prided themselves, and which seem to have been the peculiar recommendations of some of the heads of the faction in this church that most opposed this apostle. He did not preach the gospel in this manner, lest *the cross of Christ should be of no effect*, lest the success should be ascribed to the force of art, and not of truth; not to the plain doctrine of a crucified Jesus, but to the powerful oratory of those who spread it, and hereby the honour of the cross be diminished or eclipsed. Paul had been bred up himself in Jewish learning at the feet of Gamaliel, but in preaching the cross of Christ he laid his learning aside. He preached a crucified Jesus in plain language, and told the people that that Jesus who was crucified at Jerusalem was the Son of God and Saviour of men, and that all who would be saved must repent of their sins, and believe in him, and submit to his government and laws. This truth needed no artificial dress; it shone out with the greatest majesty in its own light, and prevailed in the world by its divine authority, and the demonstration of the Spirit, without any human helps. The plain preaching of a crucified Jesus was more powerful than all the oratory and philosophy of the heathen world.

II. We have the different effects of this preaching: To those who perish it is foolishness, *but to those who are saved it is the power of God*, *v.* 18. *It is to the Jews a stumbling-block, and to the Greeks foolishness; but unto those who are called, both Jews and Greeks, Christ the power of God and the wisdom of God*, *v.* 23, 24. 1. Christ crucified is a stumbling-block to the Jews. They could not get over it. They had a conceit that their expected Messiah was to be a great temporal prince, and therefore would never own one who made so mean an appearance in life, and died so accursed a death, for their deliverer and king. They despised him, and looked upon him as execrable, because he was hanged on a tree, and because he did not gratify them with a sign to their mind, though his divine power shone out in innumerable miracles. The Jews require a sign, *v.* 22. See Matt. xii. 38. 2. He was to the Greeks foolishness. They laughed at the story of a crucified Saviour, and despised the apostles' way of telling it. They sought for wisdom. They were men of wit and reading, men that had cultivated arts and sciences, and had, for some ages, been in a manner the very mint of knowledge and learning. There was nothing in the plain doctrine of the cross to suit their taste, nor humour their vanity, nor gratify a curious and wrangling temper: they entertained it therefore with scorn and contempt. What, hope to be saved by one that could not save himself! And trust in one who was condemned and crucified as a malefactor, a man of mean birth and poor condition in life, and cut off by so vile and opprobrious a death! This was what the pride of human reason and learning could not relish. The Greeks thought it little better than stupidity to receive such a doctrine, and pay this high regard to such a person: and thus were they justly left to perish in their pride and obstinacy. Note, It is just with God to leave those to themselves who pour such proud contempt on divine wisdom and grace. 3. To those who are called and saved *he is the wisdom of God, and the power of God*. Those who are called and sanctified, who receive the gospel, and are enlightened by the Spirit of God, discern more glorious discoveries of God's wisdom and power in the doctrine of Christ crucified than in all his other works. Note, Those who are saved *are reconciled to the doctrine of the cross*, and led into an experimental acquaintance with the mysteries of Christ crucified.

III. We have here the triumphs of the cross over human wisdom, according to the ancient prophecy (Isa. xxix. 14): *I will destroy the wisdom of the wise, and bring to nothing the understanding of the prudent. Where is the wise? Where is the scribe? Where is the disputer of this world? Hath not God made foolish the wisdom of this world? v.* 19, 20. All the valued learning of this world was confounded, baffled, and eclipsed, by the Christian revelation and the glorious triumphs of the cross. The heathen politicians and philosophers, the Jewish rabbies and doctors, the curious searchers into the secrets of nature, were all posed and put to a nonplus. This scheme lay out of the reach of the deepest statesmen and philosophers, and the greatest pretenders to learning both among the Jews and Greeks. When God would save the world, he took a way by himself; and good reason, for *the world by wisdom knew not God, v.* 21. All the boasted science of the heathen world did not, could not, effectually bring home the world to God. In spite of all their wisdom, ignorance still prevailed, iniquity still abounded. Men were puffed up by their imaginary knowledge, and rather further alienated from God; and therefore *it pleased him, by the foolishness of preaching, to save those that believe*. By the *foolishness of preaching*—not such in truth, but in vulgar reckoning.

1. The thing preached was foolishness in the eyes of worldly-wise men. Our living through one who died, our being blessed by

one who was made a curse, our being justified by one who was himself condemned, was all folly and inconsistency to men blinded with self-conceit and wedded to their own prejudices and the boasted discoveries of their reason and philosophy.

2. The manner of preaching the gospel was foolishness to them too. None of the famous men for wisdom or eloquence were employed to plant the church or propagate the gospel. A few fishermen were called out, and sent upon this errand. These were commissioned to disciple the nations: these vessels chosen to convey the treasure of saving knowledge to the world. There was nothing in them that at first view looked grand or august enough to come from God; and the proud pretenders to learning and wisdom despised the doctrine for the sake of those who dispensed it. And yet *the foolishness of God is wiser than men*, *v.* 25. Those methods of divine conduct that vain men are apt to censure as unwise and weak have more true, solid, and successful wisdom in them, than all the learning and wisdom that are among men: "*You see your calling, brethren, how that not many wise men after the flesh, not many mighty, not many noble, are called*, *v.* 26, &c. You see the state of Christianity; not many men of learning, or authority, or honourable extraction, are called." There is a great deal of meanness and weakness in the outward appearance of our religion. For, (1.) Few of distinguished character in any of these respects were chosen for the work of the ministry. God did not choose philosophers, nor orators, nor statesmen, nor men of wealth and power and interest in the world, to publish the gospel of grace and peace. Not the wise men after the flesh, though men would be apt to think that a reputation for wisdom and learning might have contributed much to the success of the gospel. Not the mighty and noble, however men might be apt to imagine that secular pomp and power would make way for its reception in the world. But God seeth not as man seeth. He hath chosen the foolish things of the world, the weak things of the world, the base and despicable things of the world, men of mean birth, of low rank, of no liberal education, to be the preachers of the gospel and planters of the church. *His thoughts are not as our thoughts, nor his ways as our ways.* He is a better judge than we what instruments and measures will best serve the purposes of his glory. (2.) Few of distinguished rank and character were called to be Christians. As the preachers were poor and mean, so generally were the converts. Few of the wise, and mighty, and noble, embraced the doctrine of the cross. The first Christians, both among Jews and Greeks, were weak, and foolish, and base; men of mean furniture as to their mental improvements, and very mean rank and condition as to their outward estate; and yet what glorious discoveries are there of divine wisdom in the whole scheme of the gospel, and in this particular circumstance of its success!

IV. We have an account how admirably all is fitted, 1. To beat down the pride and vanity of men. God hath chosen *the foolish things of the world to confound the wise*—men of no learning to confound the most learned; *the weak things of the world to confound the mighty*—men of mean rank and circumstances to confound and prevail against all the power and authority of earthly kings; *and base things, and things which are despised*—things which men have in the lowest esteem, or in the utmost contempt, to pour contempt and disgrace on all they value and have in veneration; *and things which are not, to bring to nought (to abolish) things that are*—the conversion of the Gentiles (of whom the Jews had the most contemptuous and vilifying thoughts) was to open a way to the abolishing of that constitution of which they were so fond, and upon which they valued themselves so much as for the sake of it to despise the rest of the world. It is common for the Jews to speak of the Gentiles under this character, as *things that are not.* Thus, in the apocryphal book of Esther, she is brought in praying that God would not give his sceptre to those *who are not*, Esth. xiv. 11. Esdras, in one of the apocryphal books under his name, speaks to God *of the heathen as those who are reputed as nothing*, 2 Esdras vi. 56, 57. And the apostle Paul seems to have this common language of the Jews in his view when he calls Abraham the *father of us all before him whom he believed, God, who calleth those things that are not as though they were*, Rom. iv. 17. The gospel is fitted to bring down the pride of both Jews and Greeks, to shame the boasted science and learning of the Greeks, and to take down that constitution on which the Jews valued themselves and despised all the world besides, *that no flesh should glory in his presence* (*v.* 29), that there might be no pretence for boasting. Divine wisdom alone had the contrivance of the method of redemption; divine grace alone revealed it, and made it known. It lay, in both respects, out of human reach. And the doctrine and discovery prevailed, in spite of all the opposition it met with from human art or authority: so effectually did God veil the glory and disgrace the pride of man in all. The gospel dispensation is a contrivance to humble man. But, 2. It is as admirably fitted to glorify God. There is a great deal of power and glory in the substance and life of Christianity. Though the ministers were poor and unlearned, and the converts generally of the meanest rank, yet the hand of the Lord went along with the preachers, and was mighty in the hearts of the hearers; and Jesus Christ was made both to ministers and Christians what was truly great and honourable. All we have we have from God as the fountain, and in and through Christ as the channel of conveyance. He is made of God to us *wisdom, righteousness, sanctification, and redemption* (*v.* 30): all we need, or can desire. We are foolishness, ignorant and blind in the things of God, with all our boasted knowledge; and he is made wisdom to us. We are guilty, obnoxious to justice; and he is made righteousness, our great atonement and sacrifice. We are depraved and corrupt; and he is made sanctification, the spring of our spiritual life; from him, the head, it is communicated to all the members of his mystical body by his Holy Spirit. We are in bonds, and he is made redemption to us, our Saviour and deliverer. Observe, Where Christ is made righteousness to any soul, he is also made sanctification. He never discharges from the guilt of sin, without delivering from the power of it; and he is made righteousness and sanctification, that he may in the end be made complete redemption, may free the soul from the very being of sin, and loose the body from the bonds of the grave: and what is designed in all is *that all flesh may glory in the Lord*, *v.* 31. Observe, It is the will of God that all our glorifying should be in the Lord: and, our salvation being only through Christ, it is thereby effectually provided that it should be so. Man is humbled, and God glorified and exalted, by the whole scheme.

CHAP. II.

The apostle proceeds with his argument in this chapter, and, I. Reminds the Corinthians of the plain manner wherein he delivered the gospel to them, ver. 1–5. But yet, II. Shows them that he had communicated to them a treasure of the truest and highest wisdom, such as exceeded all the attainments of learned men, such as could never have entered into the heart of man if it had not been revealed, nor can be received and improved to salvation but by the light and influence of that Spirit who revealed it, ver. 6, to the end.

AND I, brethren, when I came
to you, came not with excellency of speech or of wisdom, declaring unto you the testimony of God.
2 For I determined not to know any
thing among you, save Jesus Christ,
and him crucified. 3 And I was with
you in weakness, and in fear, and in
much trembling. 4 And my speech
and my preaching *was* not with enticing words of man's wisdom, but in
demonstration of the Spirit and of
power: 5 That your faith should
not stand in the wisdom of men, but
in the power of God.

In this passage the apostle pursues his design, and reminds the Corinthians how he acted when he first preached the gospel among them.

I. As to the matter or subject he tell us (*v.* 2), *He determined to know nothing among them but Jesus Christ and him crucified*—to make a show of no other knowledge than this, to preach nothing, to discover the knowledge of nothing, but Jesus Christ, and him crucified. Note, Christ, in his person and offices, is the sum and substance of the gospel, and ought to be the great subject of a gospel minister's preaching. His business is to display the banner of the cross, and invite people under it. Any one that heard Paul preach found him to harp so continually on this string that he would say he knew nothing but Christ and him crucified. Whatever other knowledge he had, this was the only knowledge he discovered, and showed himself concerned to propagate among his hearers.

II. The manner wherein he preached Christ is here also observable. 1. Negatively. *He came not among them with excellency of speech or wisdom, v.* 1. *His speech and preaching were not with enticing words of man's wisdom, v.* 4. He did not affect to appear a fine orator or a deep philosopher; nor did he insinuate himself into their minds, by a flourish of words, or a pompous show of deep reason and extraordinary science and skill. He did not set himself to captivate the ear by fine turns and eloquent expressions, nor to please and entertain the fancy with lofty flights of sublime notions. Neither his speech, nor the wisdom he taught, savoured of human skill: he learnt both in another school Divine wisdom needed not to be set off with such human ornaments. 2. Positively. He came among them *declaring the testimony of God, v.* 1. He published a divine revelation, and gave in sufficient vouchers for the authority of it, both by its consonancy to ancient predictions and by present miraculous operations; and there he left the matter. Ornaments of speech and philosophical skill and argument could add no weight to what came recommended by such authority. *He was also among them in weakness and fear, and in much trembling;* and yet *his speech and preaching were in demonstration of the Spirit and of power, v.* 3, 4. His enemies in the church of Corinth spoke very contemptuously of him: *His bodily presence, say they, is weak, and his speech contemptible,* 2 Cor. x. 10. Possibly he had a little body, and a low voice; but, though he had not so good an elocution as some, it is plain that he was no mean speaker. The men of Lystra looked on him to be the heathen god Mercury, come down to them in the form of a man, because he was the chief speaker, Acts xiv. 12. Nor did he want courage nor resolution to go through his work; he was *in nothing terrified by his adversaries.* Yet he was no boaster. He did not proudly vaunt himself, like his opposers. He acted in his office with much modesty, concern, and care. He behaved with great humility among them; not as one grown vain with the honour and authority conferred on him, but as one concerned to approve himself faithful, and fearful of himself, lest he should mismanage in his trust. Observe, None know the fear and trembling of faithful ministers, who are jealous over souls with a godly jealousy; and a deep sense of their own weakness is the occasion of this fear and trembling. They know how insufficient they are, and are therefore fearful for themselves. But, though Paul managed with this modesty and concern, yet he spoke with authority: *In the demonstration of the Spirit and of power.* He preached the truths of Christ in their native dress, with plainness of speech. He laid down the doctrine as the Spirit delivered it; and left the Spirit, by his external operation in signs and miracles, and his internal influences on the hearts of men, to demonstrate the truth of it, and procure its reception.

III. Here is the end mentioned for which he preached Christ crucified in this manner: *That your faith should not stand in the wisdom of man, but the power of God* (*v.* 5)—that they might not be drawn by human motives, nor overcome by mere human arguments, lest it should be said that either rhetoric or logic had made them Christians. But, when nothing but Christ crucified was plainly preached, the success must be entirely attributed to a divine power accompanying the word. Their faith must be founded, not on human wisdom, but divine evidence and operation. The gospel was so preached that God might appear and be glorified in all.

6 Howbeit we speak wisdom among
them that are perfect: yet not the
wisdom of this world, nor of the
princes of this world, that come to
nought: 7 But we speak the wisdom of God in a mystery, *even* the
hidden *wisdom*, which God ordained
before the world unto our glory: 8
Which none of the princes of this
world knew: for had they known *it*,
they would not have crucified the
Lord of glory. 9 But as it is written,
Eye hath not seen, nor ear heard,
neither have entered into the heart of
man, the things which God hath prepared for them that love him. 10
But God hath revealed *them* unto us
by his Spirit: for the Spirit searcheth
all things, yea, the deep things of
God. 11 For what man knoweth
the things of a man, save the spirit of
man which is in him? even so the
things of God knoweth no man, but
the Spirit of God. 12 Now we have
received, not the spirit of the world,
but the spirit which is of God, that
we might know the things that are
freely given to us of God. 13 Which
things also we speak, not in the words
which man's wisdom teacheth, but
which the Holy Ghost teacheth;
comparing spiritual things with spiritual. 14 But the natural man receiveth not the things of the Spirit of
God: for they are foolishness unto
him: neither can he know *them*,
because they are spiritually discerned.
15 But he that is spiritual judgeth all
things, yet he himself is judged of no
man. 16 For who hath known the
mind of the Lord, that he may instruct him? But we have the mind
of Christ.

In this part of the chapter the apostle shows them that though he had not come to them with the excellency of human wisdom, with any of the boasted knowledge and literature of the Jews or Greeks, yet he had communicated to them a treasure of the truest and the highest wisdom: *We speak wisdom among those who are perfect* (*v.* 6), among those who are well instructed in Christianity, and come to some maturity in the things of God. Those that receive the doctrine as divine, and, having been illuminated by the Holy Spirit, have looked well into it, discover true wisdom in it. They not only understand the plain history of Christ, and him crucified, but discern the deep and admirable designs of the divine wisdom therein. Though what we preach is foolishness to the world, it is wisdom to them. They are made wise by it, and can discern wisdom in it. Note, Those who are wise themselves are the only proper judges of what is wisdom; *not* indeed *the wisdom of this world, nor of the princes of this world*, but *the wisdom of God in a mystery* (*v.* 6, 7); not worldly wisdom, but divine; not such as the men of this world could have discovered, nor such as worldly men, under the direction of pride, and passion, and appetite, and worldly interest, and destitute of the Spirit of God, can receive. Note, How different is the judgment of God from that of the world! *He seeth not as man seeth.* The wisdom he teaches is of a quite different kind from what passes under that notion in the world. It is not the wisdom of politicians, nor philosophers, nor rabbies (see *v.* 6), not such as they teach nor such as they relish; *but the wisdom of God in a mystery, the hidden wisdom of God*—what he had a long time kept to himself, and concealed from the world, and the depth of which, now it is revealed, none but himself can fathom. *It is the mystery which hath been hid from ages and generations, though now made manifest to the saints* (Col. i. 26), hid in a manner entirely from the heathen world, and made mysterious to the Jews, by being wrapped up in dark types and distant prophecies, but revealed and made known to us by the Spirit of God. Note, See the privilege of those who enjoy the gospel revelation: to them types are unveiled, mysteries made plain, prophecies interpreted, and the secret counsels of God published and laid open. The wisdom of God in a mystery is now made manifest to the saints. Now, concerning this wisdom, observe,

I. The rise and origin of it: *It was ordained of God, before the world, to our glory, v.* 7. It was ordained of God; he had determined long ago to reveal and make it known, from many ages past, from the beginning, nay, from eternity; and that to our glory, *the glory of us,* either us apostles or us Christians. It was a great honour put upon the apostles, to be entrusted with the revelation of this wisdom. It was a great and honourable privilege for Christians to have this glorious wisdom discovered to them. And the wisdom of God discovered in the gospel, the divine wisdom taught by the gospel, prepares for our everlasting glory and happiness in the world to come. The counsels of God concerning our redemption are dated from eternity, and designed for the glory and happiness of the saints. And what deep wisdom was in these counsels! Note, The wisdom of God is both employed and displayed for the honour of his saints—employed from eternity, and displayed in time, to make them glorious both here and hereafter, in time and to eternity. What honour does he put on his saints!

II. The ignorance of the great men of the world about it: *Which none of the princes of this world knew* (*v.* 8), the principal men in authority and power, or in wisdom and learning. The Roman governor, and the guides and rulers of the Jewish church and nation, seem to be the persons here chiefly meant. These were the princes of this world, or this age, who, had they known this true and heavenly wisdom, would not have crucified the Lord of glory. This Pilate and the Jewish rulers literally did when our Redeemer was crucified upon the sentence of the one and the clamorous demands of the other. Observe, Jesus Christ is the Lord of glory, a title much too great for any creature to bear: and the reason why he was hated was because he was not known. Had his crucifiers known him, known who and what he was, they would have withheld their impious hands, and not have taken and slain him. This he pleaded with his Father for their pardon: *Father, forgive them, for they know not what they do,* Luke xxiii. 34. Note, There are many things which people would not do if they knew the wisdom of God in the great work of redemption. They act as they do because they are blind or heedless. They know not the truth, or will not attend to it.

III. It is such wisdom as could not have been discovered without a revelation, according to what the prophet Isaiah says (Isa. lxiv. 4), *Eye hath not seen, nor ear heard, nor have entered into the heart of man the things which God hath prepared for those that love him—for him that waiteth for him,* that waiteth for his mercy, so the LXX. It was a testimony of love to God in the Jewish believers to live in expectation of the accomplishment of evangelical promises. Waiting upon God is an evidence of love to him. *Lo, this is our God, we have waited for him,* Isa. xxv. 9. Observe, There are things which God hath prepared for those that love him, and wait for him. There are such things prepared in a future life for them, things which sense cannot discover, no present information can convey to our ears, nor can yet enter our hearts. *Life and immortality are brought to light through the gospel,* 2 Tim. i. 10. But the apostle speaks here of the subject-matter of the divine revelation under the gospel. These are such as eye hath not seen nor ear heard. Observe, The great truths of the gospel are things lying out of the sphere of human discovery: *Eye hath not seen, nor ear heard them, nor have they entered into the heart of man.* Were they objects of sense, could they be discovered by an eye of reason, and communicated by the ear to the mind, as matters of common human knowledge may, there had been no need of a revelation. But, lying out of the sphere of nature, we cannot discover them but by the light of revelation. And therefore we must take them as they lie in the scriptures, and as God has been pleased to reveal them.

IV. We here see by whom this wisdom is discovered to us: *God hath revealed them to us by his Spirit, v.* 10. The scripture is given by inspiration of God. *Holy men spoke of old as they were moved by the Holy Ghost,* 2 Pet. i. 21. And the apostles spoke by inspiration of the same Spirit, as he taught them, and gave them utterance. Here is a proof of the divine authority of the holy scriptures. Paul wrote what he taught: and what he taught was revealed of God by his Spirit, *that Spirit that searches all things, yea, the deep things of God, and knows the things of God, as the spirit of a man that is in him knows the things of a man, v.* 11. A double argument is drawn from these words in proof of the divinity of the Holy Ghost:—1. Omniscience is attributed to him: *He searches all things, even the deep things of God.* He has exact knowledge of all things, and enters into the very depths of God, penetrates into his most secret counsels. Now who can have such a thorough knowledge of God but God? 2. This allusion seems to imply that the Holy Spirit is as much in God as a man's mind is in himself. Now the mind of the man is plainly essential to him. He cannot be without his mind. Nor can God be without his Spirit. He is as much and as intimately one with God as the man's mind is with the man. The man knows his own mind because his mind is one with himself. The Spirit of God knows the things of God because he is one with God. And as no man can come at the knowledge of what is in another man's mind till he communicates and reveals it, so neither can we know the secret counsels and purposes of God till they are made known to us by his Holy Spirit. We cannot know them at all till he has proposed them objectively (as it is called) in the external revelation; we cannot know or believe them to salvation till he enlightens the faculty, opens the eye of the mind, and gives us such a knowledge and faith of them. And it was by this Spirit that the apostles had received the *wisdom of God in a mystery*, which they spoke. "*Now we have received not the spirit of the world, but the Spirit which is of God, that we might know the things freely given to us of God* (*v.* 12); not the spirit which is in the *wise men of the world* (*v.* 6), nor in the *rulers of the world* (*v.* 8), but the *Spirit which is of God*, or proceedeth from God. We have what we deliver in the name of God by inspiration from him; and it is by his gracious illumination and influence that *we know the things freely given to us of God* unto salvation"—that is, "the great privileges of the gospel, which are the free gift of God, distributions of mere and rich grace." Though these things are given to us, and the revelation of this gift is made to us, we cannot know them to any saving purpose till we have the Spirit. The apostles had the revelation of these things from the Spirit of God, and the saving impression of them from the same Spirit.

V. We see here in what manner this wisdom was taught or communicated: *Which things we speak, not in the words which man's wisdom teaches, but which the Holy Ghost teaches, v.* 13. They had received the wisdom they taught, not from the wise men of the world, not from their own enquiry nor invention, but from the Spirit of God. Nor did they put a human dress on it, but plainly declared the doctrine of Christ, in terms also taught them by the Holy Spirit. He not only gave them the knowledge of these things, but gave them utterance. Observe, The truths of God need no garnishing by human skill or eloquence, but look best in the words which the Holy Ghost teaches. The Spirit of God knows much better how to speak of the things of God than the best critics, orators, or philosophers. *Comparing spiritual things with spiritual*—one part of revelation with another, the revelation of the gospel with that of the Jews, the discoveries of the New Testament with the types and prophecies of the Old. The comparing of matters of revelation with matters of science, things supernatural with things natural and common, is going by a wrong measure. Spiritual things, when brought together, will help to illustrate one another; but, if the principles of human art and science are to be made a test of revelation, we shall certainly judge amiss concerning it, and the things contained in it. Or, *adapting spiritual things to spiritual*—speaking of spiritual matters, matters of revelation, and the spiritual life, in language that is proper and plain. The language of the Spirit of God is the most proper to convey his meaning.

VI. We have an account how this wisdom is received.

1. *The natural man receiveth not the things of God, for they are foolishness to him, neither can he know them, because they are spiritually discerned, v.* 14. The *natural man, the animal man.* Either, (1.) The man under the power of corruption, and never yet illuminated by the Spirit of God, such as Jude calls *sensual, not having the Spirit, v.* 19. Men unsanctified receive not the things of God. The understanding, through the corruption of nature by the fall, and through the confirmation of this disorder by customary sin, is utterly unapt to receive the rays of divine light; it is prejudiced against them. The truths of God are foolishness to such a mind. The man looks on them as trifling and impertinent things, not worth his minding. *The light shineth in darkness, and the darkness comprehendeth it not,* John i. 5. Not that the natural faculty of discerning is lost, but evil inclinations and wicked principles render the man unwilling to enter into the mind of God, in the spiritual matters of his kingdom, and yield to their force and power. It is the quickening beams of the Spirit of truth and holiness that must help the mind to discern their excellency, and to so thorough a conviction of their truth as heartily to receive and embrace them. Thus the natural man, the man destitute of the Spirit of God, cannot know them, because they are spiritually discerned. Or, (2.) The natural man, that is, the wise man of the world (*ch.* i. 19, 20), the wise man after the flesh, or according to the flesh (*v.* 26), one who hath the wisdom of the world, man's wisdom (*ch.* ii. 4—6), a man, as some of the ancients, that would learn all truth by his own ratiocinations, receive nothing by faith, nor own any need of supernatural assistance. This was very much the character of the pretenders to philosophy and the Grecian learning and wisdom in that day. Such a man receives not the things of the Spirit of God. Revelation is not with him a principle of science; he looks upon it as delirium and dotage, the extravagant thought of some deluded dreamer. It is no way to wisdom among the famous masters of the world; and for that reason he can have no knowledge of things revealed, because they are only spiritually discerned, or made known by the revelation of the Spirit, which is a principle of science or knowledge that he will not admit.

2. *But he that is spiritual judgeth all things, yet he himself is judged,* or discerned, *of no man, v.* 15. Either, (1.) He who is sanctified and made spiritually-minded (Rom. viii. 6) judgeth all things, or discerneth all things—he is capable of judging about matters of human wisdom, and has also a relish and savour of divine truths; he sees divine wisdom, and experiences divine power, in gospel revelations and mysteries, which the carnal and unsanctified mind looks upon as

weakness and folly, as things destitute of all power and not worthy any regard. It is the sanctified mind that must discern the real beauties of holiness; but, by the refinement of its faculties, they do not lose their power of discerning and judging about common and natural things. The spiritual man may judge of all things, natural and supernatural, human and divine, the deductions of reason and the discoveries of revelation. But he himself is judged or discerned of NO MAN. God's saints are his hidden ones, Ps. lxxxiii. 3. *Their life is hid with Christ in God*, Col. iii. 3. The carnal man knows no more of a spiritual man than he does of other spiritual things He is a stranger to the principles, and pleasures, and actings, of the divine life. The spiritual man does not lie open to his observation. Or, (2.) *He that is spiritual* (who has had divine revelations made to him, receives them as such, and founds his faith and religion upon them) can judge both of common things and things divine; he can discern what is, and what is not, the doctrine of the gospel and of salvation, and whether a man preaches the truths of God or not. He does not lose the power of reasoning, nor renounce the principles of it, by founding his faith and religion on revelation. But *he himself is judged of no man*—can be judged, so as to be confuted, by no man; nor can any man who is not spiritual, not under a divine *afflatus* himself (see *ch.* xiv. 37), or not founding his faith on a divine revelation, discern or judge whether what he speaks be true or divine, or not. In short, he who founds all his knowledge upon principles of science, and the mere light of reason, can never be a judge of the truth or falsehood of what is received by revelation. *For who hath known the mind of the Lord, that he may instruct him* (*v.* 16), that is, the *spiritual man?* Who can enter so far into the mind of God as to instruct him who has the Spirit of God, and is under his inspiration? He only is the person to whom God immediately communicates the knowledge of his will. And who can inform or instruct him in the mind of God who is so immediately under the conduct of his own Spirit? Very few have known any thing of the mind of God by a natural power. *But*, adds the apostle, *we have the mind of Christ:* and the mind of Christ is the mind of God. He is God, and the principal messenger and prophet of God. And the apostles were empowered by his Spirit to make known his mind to us. And in the holy scriptures the mind of Christ, and the mind of God in Christ, are fully revealed to us. Observe, It is the great privilege of Christians that they have the mind of Christ revealed to them by his Spirit.

CHAP. III.

In this chapter the apostle, I. Blames the Corinthians for their carnality and divisions, ver. 1—4. II. He instructs them how what was amiss among them might be rectified, by remembering, 1. That their ministers were no more than ministers, ver. 5. 2. That they were unanimous, and carried on the same design, ver. 6—10. 3. That they built on one and the same foundation, ver. 11—15. III. He exhorts them to give due honour to their bodies, by keeping them pure (ver. 16, 17), and to humility and self-diffidence, ver. 18—21. IV. And dehorts them from glorying in particular ministers, because of the equal interest they had in all, ver. 22, to the end.

AND I, brethren, could not speak
unto you as unto spiritual, but
as unto carnal, *even* as unto babes in
Christ. 2 I have fed you with milk,
and not with meat: for hitherto ye
were not able *to bear it*, neither yet
now are ye able. 3 For ye are yet
carnal: for whereas *there is* among
you envying, and strife, and divisions,
are ye not carnal, and walk as men?
4 For while one saith, I am of Paul;
and another, I *am* of Apollos; are ye
not carnal?

Here, I. Paul blames the Corinthians for their weakness and nonproficiency. Those who are sanctified are so only in part: there is still room for growth and increase both in grace and knowledge, 2 Pet. iii. 18. Those who through divine grace are renewed to a spiritual life may yet in many things be defective. The apostle tells *them he could not speak to them as unto spiritual* men, *but as unto carnal* men, *as to babes in Christ*, *v.* 1. They were so far from forming their maxims and measures upon the ground of divine revelation, and entering into the spirit of the gospel, that it was but too evident they were much under the command of carnal and corrupt affections. They were still mere babes in Christ. They had received some of the first principles of Christianity, but had not grown up to maturity of understanding in them, or of faith and holiness; and yet it is plain, from several passages in this epistle, that the Corinthians were very proud of their wisdom and knowledge. Note, It is but too common for persons of very moderate knowledge and understanding to have a great measure of self-conceit. The apostle assigns their little proficiency in the knowledge of Christianity as a reason why he had communicated no more of the deep things of it to them. They could not bear such food, they needed to be fed with milk, not with meat, *v.* 2. Note, It is the duty of a faithful minister of Christ to consult the capacities of his hearers and teach them as they can bear. And yet it is natural for babes to grow up to men; and babes in Christ should endeavour to grow in stature, and become men in Christ. It is expected that their advances in knowledge should be in proportion to their means and opportunities, and their time of professing religion, that they may be able to bear discourses on the mysteries of our religion, and not always rest in plain things. It was a reproach to the Corinthians that they had so long sat under the ministry of Paul and had made no more improvement in Christian knowledge. Note, Christians are utterly to blame who do not endeavour to grow in grace and knowledge.

II. He blames them for their carnality, and mentions their contention and discord about their ministers as evidence of it: *For you are yet carnal; for whereas there are among you envyings, and strifes, and divisions, are you not carnal, and walk as men? v.* 3. They had mutual emulations, and quarrels, and factions among them, upon the account of their ministers, *while one said, I am of Paul; and another, I am of Apollos, v.* 4. These were proofs of their being carnal, that fleshly interests and affections too much swayed them. Note, Contentions and quarrels about religion are sad evidences of remaining carnality. True religion makes men peaceable and not contentious. Factious spirits act upon human principles, not upon principles of true religion; they are guided by their own pride and passions, and not by the rules of Christianity: *Do you not walk as men?* Note, It is to be lamented that many who should walk as Christians, that is, above the common rate of men, do indeed walk as men, live and act too much like other men.

5 Who then is Paul, and who *is*
Apollos, but ministers by whom ye
believed, even as the Lord gave to
every man? 6 I have planted, Apollos watered; but God gave the increase. 7 So then neither is he that
planteth any thing, neither he that
watereth; but God that giveth the
increase. 8 Now he that planteth
and he that watereth are one: and
every man shall receive his own reward according to his own labour.
9 For we are labourers together with
God: ye are God's husbandry, *ye are*
God's building. 10 According to
the grace of God which is given unto
me, as a wise master-builder, I have
laid the foundation, and another
buildeth thereon. But let every
man take heed how he buildeth thereupon.

Here the apostle instructs them how to cure this humour, and rectify what was amiss among them upon this head,

I. By reminding them that the ministers about whom they contended were but ministers: *Who then is Paul, and who is Apollos, but ministers by whom you believed? Even as the Lord gave to every man, v.* 5. They are but ministers, mere instruments used by the God of all grace. Some of the factious people in Corinth seem to have made more of them, as if they were lords of their faith, authors of their religion. Note, We should take care not to deify ministers, nor put them into the place of God. Apostles were not the authors of our faith and religion, though they were authorized and qualified to reveal and propagate it. They acted in this office as God gave to every man. Observe, All the gifts and powers that even apostles discovered and exerted in the work of the ministry were from God. They were intended to manifest their mission and doctrine to be divine. It was perfectly wrong, upon their account, to transfer that regard to the apostles which was solely to be paid to the divine authority by which they acted, and to God, from whom they had their authority. *Paul had planted and Apollos had watered, v.* 6. Both were useful, one for one purpose, the other for another. Note, God makes use of variety of instruments, and fits them to their several uses and intentions. Paul was fitted for planting work, and Apollos for watering work, but God gave the increase. Note, The success of the ministry must be derived from the divine blessing: *Neither he that planteth is any thing, nor he that watereth, but God who giveth the increase, v.* 7. Even apostolical ministers are nothing of themselves, can do nothing with efficacy and success unless God give the increase. Note, The best qualified and most faithful ministers have a just sense of their own insufficiency, and are very desirous that God should have all the glory of their success. Paul and Apollos are nothing at all in their own account, but God is all in all.

II. By representing to them the unanimity of Christ's ministers: *He that planteth and he that watereth are one* (*v.* 8), employed by one Master, entrusted with the same revelation, busied in one work, and engaged in one design—in harmony with one another, however they may be set in opposition to each other by factious party-makers. They have their different gifts from one and the same Spirit, for the very same purposes; and they heartily carry on the same design. Planters and waterers are but fellow-labourers in the same work. Note, All the faithful ministers of Christ are one in the great business and intention of their ministry. They may have differences of sentiment in minor things; they may have their debates and contests; but they heartily concur in the great design of honouring God and saving souls, by promoting true Christianity in the world. All such may expect a glorious recompence of their fidelity, and in proportion to it: *Every man shall receive his own reward, according to his own labour.* Their business is one, but some may mind it more than others: their end or design is one, but some may pursue it more closely than others: their Master also is one, and yet this good and gracious Master may make a difference in the rewards he gives, according to the different service they do: *Every one's own work shall have its own reward.* Those that work hardest shall fare best. Those that are most faithful shall have the greatest reward; and glorious work it is in which all faithful ministers are employed. *They are labourers with God,* συνεργοί—*co-workers, fellow-labourers* (*v.* 9), not indeed in the same order and degree, but in subordination to him, as instruments in his hand. They are engaged in his business. They are working together with God, in promoting the purposes of his glory, and the salvation of precious souls; and he who knows their work will take care they do not labour in vain. Men may neglect and vilify one minister while they cry up another, and have no reason for either: they may condemn when they should commend, and applaud what they should neglect and avoid; but the judgment of God is according to truth. He never rewards but upon just reason, and he ever rewards in proportion to the diligence and faithfulness of his servants. Note, Faithful ministers, when they are ill used by men, should encourage themselves in God. And it is to God, the chief agent and director of the great work of the gospel, to whom those that labour with him should endeavour to approve themselves. They are always under his eye, employed in his husbandry and building; and therefore, to be sure, he will carefully look over them: "*You are God's husbandry, you are God's building;* and therefore are neither of Paul nor of Apollos; neither belong to one nor the other, but to God: they only plant and water you, but it is the divine blessing on his own husbandry that alone can make it yield fruit. You are not our husbandry, but God's. We work under him, and with him, and for him. It is all for God that we have been doing among you. You are God's husbandry and building." He had employed the former metaphor before, and now he goes on to the other of a building: *According to the grace of God which is given unto me, as a wise master-builder, I have laid the foundation, and another buildeth thereon.* Paul here calls himself a wise master-builder, a character doubly reflecting honour on him. It was honourable to be a master-builder in the edifice of God; but it added to his character to be a wise one. Persons may be in an office for which they are not qualified, or not so thoroughly qualified as this expression implies Paul was. But, though he gives himself such a character, it is not to gratify his own pride, but to magnify divine grace. He was a wise master-builder, but the grace of God made him such. Note, It is no crime in a Christian, but much to his commendation, to take notice of the good that is in him, to the praise of divine grace. Spiritual pride is abominable: it is making use of the greatest favours of God to feed our own vanity, and make idols of ourselves. But to take notice of the favours of God to promote our gratitude to him, and to speak of them to his honour (be they of what sort they will), is but a proper expression of the duty and regard we owe him. Note, Ministers should not be proud of their gifts or graces; but the better qualified they are for their work, and the more success they have in it, the more thankful should they be to God for his distinguishing goodness: *I have laid the foundation, and another buildeth thereon.* As before he had said, *I have planted, Apollos watered.* It was Paul that laid the foundation of a church among them. He had *begotten them through the gospel, ch.* iv. 15. Whatever instructors they had besides, *they had not many fathers.* He would derogate from none that had done service among them, nor would he be robbed of his own honour and respect. Note, Faithful ministers may and ought to have a concern for their own reputation. Their usefulness depends much upon it. *But let every man take heed how he buildeth thereon.* This is a proper caution; there may be very indifferent building on a good foundation. It is easy to err here; and great care should be used, not only to lay a sure and right foundation, but to erect a regular building upon it. Nothing must be laid upon it but what the foundation will bear, and what is of a piece with it. Gold and dirt must not be mingled together. Note, Ministers of Christ should take great care that they do not build their own fancies or false reasonings on the foundation of divine revelation. What they preach should be the plain doctrine of their Master, or what is perfectly agreeable with it.

11 For other foundation can no
man lay than that is laid, which is
Jesus Christ. 12 Now if any man
build upon this foundation gold, silver, precious stones, wood, hay,
stubble; 13 Every man's work shall
be made manifest: for the day shall
declare it, because it shall be revealed
by fire; and the fire shall try every
man's work of what sort it is. 14
If any man's work abide which he
hath built thereupon, he shall receive
a reward. 15 If any man's work
shall be burned, he shall suffer loss:
but he himself shall be saved; yet so
as by fire.

Here the apostle informs us what foundation he had laid at the bottom of all his labours among them—*even Jesus Christ, the chief corner-stone,* Eph. ii. 20. Upon this foundation all the faithful ministers of Christ build. Upon this rock all Christians found their hopes. Those that build their hopes of heaven on any other foundation build upon the sand. *Other foundation can no man lay besides what is laid—even Jesus Christ.* Note, The doctrine of our Saviour and his mediation is the principal doctrine of Christianity. It lies at the bottom, and is the foundation, of all the rest. Leave out this, and you lay waste all our comforts, and leave no foundation for our hopes as sinners. It is in Christ *only that God is reconciling a sinful world to himself*, 2 Cor. v. 19. But of those that hold the foundation, and embrace the general doctrine of Christ's being the mediator between God and man, there are two sorts:—

I. Some build upon this foundation *gold, silver, and precious stones* (*v.* 12), namely, those who receive and propagate the pure truths of the gospel, who hold nothing but the *truth as it is in Jesus*, and preach nothing else. This is building well upon a good foundation, making all of apiece, when ministers not only depend upon Christ as the great prophet of the church, and take him for their guide and infallible teacher, but receive and spread the doctrines he taught, in their purity, without any corrupt mixtures, without adding or diminishing.

II. Others *build wood, hay, and stubble*, on this foundation; that is, though they adhere to the foundation, they depart from the mind of Christ in many particulars, substitute their own fancies and inventions in the room of his doctrines and institutions, and build upon the good foundation what will not abide the test when the day of trial shall come, and the fire must make it manifest, as wood, hay, and stubble, will not bear the trial by fire, but must be consumed in it. There is a time coming when a discovery will be made of what men have built on this foundation: *Every man's work shall be made manifest*, shall be laid open to view, to his own view and that of others. Some may, in the simplicity of their hearts, build wood and stubble on the good foundation, and know not, all the while, what they have been doing; but in the day of the Lord their own conduct shall appear to them in its proper light. Every man's work shall be made manifest to himself, and made manifest to others, both those that have been misled by him and those that have escaped his errors. Now we may be mistaken in ourselves and others; but there is a day coming that will cure all our mistakes, and show us ourselves, and show us our actions in the true light, without covering or disguise: *For the day shall declare it* (that is, every man's work), *because it shall be revealed by fire; and the fire shall try every man's work, of what sort it is*, *v.* 13. The day shall declare and make it manifest, the last day, the great day of trial; see *ch.* iv. 5. Though some understand it of the time when the Jewish nation was destroyed and their constitution thereby abolished, when the superstructure which judaizing teachers would have raised on the Christian foundation was manifested to be no better than hay and stubble, that would not bear the trial. The expression carries in it a plain allusion to the refiner's art, in which the fire separates and distinguishes the dross from the gold and silver; as it also will silver and gold and precious stones, that will endure the fire, from wood and hay and stubble, that will be consumed in it. Note, There is a day coming that will as nicely distinguish one man from another, and one man's work from another's, as the fire distinguishes gold from dross, or metal that will bear the fire from other materials that will be consumed in it. In that day, 1. Some men's works will *abide the trial*—will be found standard. It will appear that they not only held the foundation, but that they built regularly and well upon it—that they laid on proper materials, and in due form and order. The foundation and the superstructure were all of a piece. The foundation-truths, and those that had a manifest connection with them, were taught together. It may not be so easy to discern this connection now, nor know what works will abide the trial then; but that day will make a full discovery. And such a builder shall not, cannot fail of a reward. He will have praise and honour in that day, and eternal recompence after it. Note, Fidelity in the ministers of Christ will meet with a full and ample reward in a future life. Those who spread true and pure religion in all the branches of it, and whose work will abide in the great day, shall receive a reward. And, Lord, how great! how much exceeding their deserts! 2. There are others *whose works shall be burnt* (*v.* 15), whose corrupt opinions and doctrines, or vain inventions and usages in the worship of God, shall be discovered, disowned, and rejected, in that day—shall be first manifested to be corrupt, and then disapproved of God and rejected. Note, The great day will pluck off all disguises, and make things appear as they are: *He whose work shall be burnt will suffer loss.* If he have built upon the right foundation wood and hay and stubble, he will suffer loss. His weakness and corruption will be the lessening of his glory, though he may in the general have been an honest and an upright Christian. This part of his work will be lost, turning no way to his advantage, though he himself may be saved. Observe, Those who hold the foundation of Christianity, though they build hay, wood, and stubble, upon it, may be saved. This may help to enlarge our charity. We should not reprobate men for their weakness; for nothing will damn men but wickedness. He shall be saved, *yet so as by fire*, saved out of the fire. He himself shall be snatched out of that flame which will consume his work. This intimates that it will be difficult for those that corrupt and deprave Christianity to be saved. God will have no mercy on their works, though he may pluck them as brands out of the burning. On this passage of scripture the papists found their doctrine of purgatory, which is certainly hay and stubble: a doctrine never originally fetched from scripture, but invented in barbarous ages, to feed the avarice and ambition of the clergy, at the cost of those who would rather part with their money than their lusts, for the salvation of their souls. It can have no countenance from this text, (1.) Because this is plainly meant of a figurative fire, not of a real one: for what real fire can consume religious rites or doctrines? (2.) Because this fire is to *try men's works, of what sort they are;* but purgatory-fire is not for trial, not to bring men's actions to the test, but to punish for them. They are supposed to be venial sins, not satisfied for in this life, for which satisfaction must be made by suffering the fire of purgatory. (3.) Because this fire is to *try every man's works,* those of Paul and Apollos, as well as those of others. Now, no papists will have the front to say apostles must have passed through purgatory fires.

16 Know ye not that ye are the temple of God, and *that* the Spirit of God dwelleth in you? 17 If any man defile the temple of God, him shall God destroy; for the temple of God is holy, which *temple* ye are.

Here the apostle resumes his argument and exhortation, founding it on his former allusion, *You are God's building, v.* 9, and here, *Know you not that you are the temple of God, and the Spirit of God dwelleth in you? If any man defile* (corrupt and destroy) *the temple of God, him shall God destroy* (the same word is in the original in both clauses); *for the temple of God is holy, which temple you are.* It looks from other parts of the epistle, where the apostle argues to the very same purport (see *ch.* vi. 13—20), as if the false teachers among the Corinthians were not only loose livers, but taught licentious doctrines, and what was particularly fitted to the taste of this lewd city, on the head of fornication. Such doctrine was not to be reckoned among hay and stubble, which would be consumed while the person who laid them on the foundation escaped the burning; for it tended to corrupt, to pollute, and destroy the church, which was a building erected for God, and consecrated to him, and therefore should be kept pure and holy. Those who spread principles of this sort would provoke God to destroy them. Note, Those who spread loose principles, that have a direct tendency to pollute the church of God, and render it unholy and unclean, are likely to bring destruction on themselves. It may be understood also as an argument against their discord and factious strifes, division being the way to destruction. But what I have been mentioning seems to be the proper meaning of the passage: *Know you not that you are the temple of God, and that the Spirit of God dwelleth in you?* It may be understood of the church of Corinth collectively, or of every single believer among them; Christian churches are temples of God. He dwells among them by his Holy Spirit. *They are built together for a habitation of God through the Spirit,* Eph. ii. 22. Every Christian is a living temple of the living God. God dwelt in the Jewish temple, took possession of it, and resided in it, by that glorious cloud that was the token of his presence with that people. So Christ by his Spirit dwells in all true believers. The temple was devoted and consecrated to God, and set apart from every common to a holy use, to the immediate service of God. So all Christians are separated from common uses, and set apart for God and his service. They are sacred to him—a very good argument this against all fleshly lusts, and all doctrines that give countenance to them. If we are the temples of God, we must do nothing that shall alienate ourselves from him, or corrupt and pollute ourselves, and thereby unfit ourselves for his use; and we must hearken to no doctrine nor doctor that would seduce us to any such practices. Note, Christians are holy by profession, and should be pure and clean both in heart and conversation. We should heartily abhor, and carefully avoid, what will defile God's temple, and prostitute what ought to be sacred to him.

18 Let no man deceive himself. If any man among you seemeth to be wise in this world, let him become a fool, that he may be wise. 19 For the wisdom of this world is foolishness with God. For it is written, He taketh the wise in their own craftiness. 20 And again, The Lord knoweth the thoughts of the wise, that they are vain.

Here he prescribes humility, and a modest opinion of themselves, for the remedy of the irregularities in the church of Corinth, the divisions and contests among them: "*Let no man deceive himself, v.* 18. Do not be led away from the truth and simplicity of the gospel by pretenders to science and eloquence, by a show of deep learning, or a flourish of words, by rabbies, orators, or philosophers." Note, We are in great danger of deceiving ourselves when we have too high an opinion of human wisdom and arts; plain and pure Christianity will be likely to be despised by those who can suit their doctrines to the corrupt taste of their hearers, and set them off with fine language, or support them with a show of deep and strong reasoning. But *he who seems to be wise must become a fool that he may be wise.* He must be sensible of his own ignorance, and lament it; he must distrust his own understanding, and not lean on it. To have a high opinion of our own wisdom is but to flatter ourselves, and self-flattery is the very next step to self-deceit. The way to true wisdom is to sink our opinion of our own to a due level, and be willing to be taught of God. He must become a fool who would be truly and thoroughly wise. The person who resigns his own understanding, that he may follow the instruction of God, is in the way to true and everlasting wisdom. *The meek will he guide in judgment, the meek will he teach his way,* Ps. xxv. 9. He that has a low opinion of his own knowledge and powers will submit to better information; such a person may be informed and improved by revelation: but the proud man, conceited of his own wisdom and understanding, will undertake to correct even divine wisdom itself, and prefer his own shallow reasonings to the revelations of infallible truth and wisdom. Note, We must abase ourselves before God if we would be either truly wise or good: *For the wisdom of this world is foolishness with God,* **v.** 19. The wisdom which worldly men esteem (policy, philosophy, oratory) *is foolishness with God.* It is so in a way of comparison with his wisdom. *He chargeth his angels with folly* (Job iv. 18), and much more the wisest among the children of men. *His understanding is infinite,* Ps. cxlvii. 5. There can be no more comparison between his wisdom and ours than between his power and being and ours. There is no common measure by which to compare finite and infinite. And much more is the wisdom of man foolishness with God when set in competition with his. How justly does he despise, how easily can he baffle and confound it! *He taketh the wise in their own craftiness* (Job v. 13), he catches them in their own nets, and entangles them in their own snares: he turns their most studied, plausible, and promising schemes against themselves, and ruins them by their own contrivance. Nay, *He knows the thoughts of the wise, that they are vain* (*v.* 20), that they are vanity, Ps. xciv. 11. Note, God has a perfect knowledge of the thoughts of men, the deepest thoughts of the wisest men, their most secret counsels and purposes: nothing is hidden from him, but *all things are naked and bare* before him, Heb. iv. 13. And he knows them to be vanity. The thoughts of the wisest men in the world have a great mixture of vanity, of weakness and folly, in them; and before God their wisest and best thoughts are very vanity, compared, I mean, with his thoughts of things. And should not all this teach us modesty, diffidence in ourselves, and a deference to the wisdom of God, make us thankful for his revelations, and willing to be taught of God, and not be led away by specious pretences to human wisdom and skill, from the simplicity of Christ, or a regard to his heavenly doctrine? Note, He who would be wise indeed must learn of God, and not set his own wisdom up in competition with God's.

21 Therefore let no man glory in
men. For all things are your's; 22
Whether Paul, or Apollos, or Cephas,
or the world, or life, or death, or
things present, or things to come; all
are your's; 23 And ye are Christ's;
and Christ *is* God's.

Here the apostle founds an exhortation against over-valuing their teachers on what he had just said, and on the consideration that they had an equal interest in all their ministers: *Therefore let no man glory in men* (*v.* 21)—forget that their ministers are men, or pay that deference to them that is due only to God, set them at the head of parties, have them in immoderate esteem and admiration, and servilely and implicitly follow their directions and submit to their dictates, and especially in contradiction to God and the truths taught by his Holy Spirit. Mankind are very apt to make the mercies of God cross their intentions. The ministry is a very useful and very gracious institution, and faithful ministers are a great blessing to any people; yet the folly and weakness of people may do much mischief by what is in itself a blessing. They may fall into factions, side with particular ministers, and set them at their head, glory in their leaders, and be carried by them they know not whither. The only way to avoid this mischief is to have a modest opinion of ourselves, a due sense of the common weakness of human understanding, and an entire deference to the wisdom of God speaking in his word. Ministers are not to be set up in competition with one another. All faithful ministers are serving one Lord and pursuing one purpose. They were appointed of Christ, for the common benefit of the church: "*Paul, and Apollos, and Cephas, are all yours.* One is not to be set up against another, but all are to be valued and used for your own spiritual benefit." Upon this occasion also he gives in an inventory of the church's possessions, the spiritual riches of a true believer: "*All is yours*—ministers of all ranks, ordinary and extraordinary. Nay, the world itself is yours." Not that saints are proprietors of the world, but it stands for their sake, they have as much of it as Infinite Wisdom sees to be fit for them, and they have all they have with the divine blessing. "*Life is yours,* that you may have season and opportunity to prepare for the life of heaven; and *death is yours,* that you may go to the possession of it. It is the kind messenger that will fetch you to your Father's house. *Things present* are yours, for your support on the road; *things to come* are yours, to enrich and regale you for ever at your journey's end." Note, If we belong to Christ, and are true to him, all good belongs to us, and is sure to us. All is ours, time and eternity, earth and heaven, life and death. *We shall want no good thing,* Ps. lxxxiv. 11. But it must be remembered, at the same time, *that we are Christ's,* the subjects of his kingdom, his property. He is Lord over us, and we must own his dominion, and cheerfully submit to his command and yield themselves to his pleasure, if we would have all things minister to our advantage. All things are ours, upon no other ground than our being Christ's. Out of him we are without just title or claim to any thing that is good. Note Those that would be safe for time, and happy to eternity, must be Christ's. *And Christ is God's.* He is the Christ of God, anointed of God, and commissioned by him, to bear the office of a Mediator, and to act therein for the purposes of his glory. Note, All things are the believer's, that Christ might have honour in his great undertaking, and God in all might have the glory. God in Christ reconciling a sinful world to himself, and shedding abroad the riches of his grace on a reconciled world, is the sum and substance of the gospel.

CHAP IV.

In this chapter the apostle, I. Directs them how to account of him and his fellow-ministers, and therein, tacitly at least, reproves them for their unworthy carriage towards him, ver. 1—6. II. He cautions them against pride and self-elation, and hints at the many temptations they had to conceive too highly of themselves, and despise him and other apostles, because of the great diversity in their circumstances and condition, ver. 7—13. III. He challenges their regard to him as their father in Christ, ver. 14—16. IV. He tells them of his having sent Timothy to them, and of his own purpose to come to them shortly, however some among them had pleased themselves, and grown vain, upon the quite contrary expectation, ver. 17, to the end.

LET a man so account of us, as of
the ministers of Christ, and
stewards of the mysteries of God.
2 Moreover it is required in stewards,
that a man be found faithful. 3 But
with me it is a very small thing that
I should be judged of you, or of
man's judgment: yea, I judge not
mine own self. 4 For I know nothing by myself; yet am I not hereby
justified: but he that judgeth me is
the Lord. 5 Therefore judge nothing
before the time, until the Lord come,
who both will bring to light the hidden things of darkness, and will make
manifest the counsels of the hearts:
and then shall every man have praise
of God. 6 And these things, brethren, I have in a figure transferred to
myself and *to* Apollos for your sakes;
that ye might learn in us not to think
of men above that which is written,
that no one of you be puffed up for
one against another.

Here, I. The apostle challenges the respect due to him on account of his character and office, in which many among them had at least very much failed: *Let a man so account of us as of the ministers of Christ, and stewards of the mysteries of God* (*v.* 1), though possibly others might have valued them too highly, by setting him up as the head of a party, and professing to be his disciples. In our opinion of ministers, as well as all other things, we should be careful to avoid extremes. Apostles themselves were, 1. Not to be over-valued, for they were ministers, not masters; stewards, not lords. They were servants of Christ, and no more, though they were servants of the highest rank, that had the care of his household, that were to provide food for the rest, and appoint and direct their work. Note, It is a very great abuse of their power, and highly criminal in common ministers, to lord it over their fellow-servants, and challenge authority over their faith or practice. For even apostles were but servants of Christ, employed in his work, and sent on his errand, and dispensers of the mysteries of God, or those truths which had been hidden from the world in ages and generations past. They had no authority to propagate their own fancies, but to spread Christian faith. 2. Apostles were not to be undervalued; for, though they were ministers, they were ministers of Christ. The character and dignity of their Master put an honour on them. Though they are but stewards, they are not stewards of the common things of the world, but of divine mysteries. They had a great trust, and for that reason had an honourable office. They were stewards of God's household, high-stewards in his kingdom of grace. They did not set up for masters, but they deserved respect and esteem in this honourable service. Especially,

II. When they did their duty in it, and approved themselves faithful: *It is required in stewards that a man be found faithful* (*v.* 2), trustworthy. The stewards in Christ's family must appoint what he hath appointed. They must not set their fellow-servants to work for themselves. They must not require any thing from them without their Master's warrant. They must not feed them with the chaff of their own inventions, instead of the wholesome food of Christian doctrine and truth. They must teach what he hath commanded, and not the doctrines and commandments of men. They must be true to the interest of their Lord, and consult his honour. Note, The ministers of Christ should make it their hearty and continual endeavour to approve themselves trustworthy; and when they have the testimony of a good conscience, and the approbation of their Master, they must slight the opinions and censures of their fellow-servants: *But with me,* saith the apostle, *it is a small thing that I should be judged of you, or of man's judgment, v.* 3. Indeed, reputation and esteem among men are a good step towards usefulness in the ministry; and Paul's whole argument upon this head shows he had a just concern for his own reputation. But he that would make it his chief endeavour to please men would hardly approve himself a faithful servant of Christ, Gal. i. 10. He that would be faithful to Christ must despise the censures of men for his sake. He must look upon it as a very little thing (if his Lord approves him) what judgment men form of him. They may think very meanly or very hardly of him, while he is doing his duty; but it is not by their judgment that he must stand or fall. And happy is it for faithful ministers that they have a more just and candid judge than their fellow-servants; one who knows and pities their imperfections, though he has none of his own. It is better *to fall into the hands of God than into the hands of men*, 2 Sam. xxiv. 14. The best of men are too apt to iudge rashly, and harshly, and unjustly; but his judgment is always according to truth. It is a comfort that men are not to be our final judges. Nay, we are not thus to judge ourselves: "*Yea, I judge not myself. For though I know nothing by myself*, cannot charge myself with unfaithfulness, *yet am I not thereby justified*, this will not clear me of the charge; *but he that judgeth me is the Lord.* It is his judgment that must determine me. By his sentence I must abide. Such I am as he shall find and judge me to be." Note, It is not judging well of ourselves, justifying ourselves, that will prove us safe and happy. Nothing will do this but the acceptance and approbation of our sovereign Judge. *Not he that commendeth himself is approved, but he whom the Lord commendeth*, 2 Cor. x. 18.

III. The apostle takes occasion hence to caution the Corinthians against censoriousness—the forward and severe judging of others: *Therefore judge nothing before the time, until the Lord come, v.* 5. It is judging out of season, and judging at an adventure. He is not to be understood of judging by persons in authority, within the verge of their office, nor of private judging concerning facts that are notorious; but of judging persons' future state, or the secret springs and principles of their actions, or about facts doubtful in themselves. To judge in these cases, and give decisive sentence, is to assume the seat of God and challenge his prerogative. Note, How bold a sinner is the forward and severe censurer! How ill-timed and arrogant are his censures! But there is one who will judge the censurer, and those he censures, without prejudice, passion, or partiality. And there is a time coming when men cannot fail of judging aright concerning themselves and others, by following his judgment. This should make them now cautious of judging others, and careful in judging themselves. There is a time coming when *the Lord will bring to light the hidden things of darkness, and make manifest the counsels of the hearts*—deeds of darkness that are now done in secret, and all the secret inclinations, purposes, and intentions, of the hidden man of the heart. Note, There is a day coming that will dispel the darkness and lay open the face of the deep, will fetch men's secret sins into open day and discover the secrets of their hearts: *The day shall declare it.* The Judge will bring these things to light. The Lord Jesus Christ will manifest the counsels of the heart, of all hearts. Note, The Lord Jesus Christ must have the knowledge of the counsels of the heart, else he could not make them manifest. This is a divine prerogative (Jer. xvii. 10), and yet it is what our Saviour challenges to himself in a very peculiar manner (Rev. ii. 23): *All the churches shall know that I am HE who searcheth the reins and hearts, and I will give to every one of you according to your works.* Note, We should be very careful how we censure others, when we have to do with a Judge from whom we cannot conceal ourselves. Others do not lie open to our notice, but we lie all open to his: and, when he shall come to judge, *every man shall have praise of God. Every man*, that is, every one qualified for it, every one who has done well. Though none of God's servants can deserve any thing from him, though there be much that is blamable even in their best services, yet shall their fidelity be commended and crowned by him; and should they be condemned, reproached, or vilified, by their fellow-servants, he will roll away all such unjust censures and reproaches, and show them in their own amiable light. Note, Christians may well be patient under unjust censures, when they know such a day as this is coming, especially when they have their consciences testifying to their integrity. But how fearful should they be of loading any with reproaches now whom their common Judge shall hereafter commend.

IV. The apostle here lets us into the reason why he had used his own name and that of Apollos in this discourse of his. He had done *it in a figure*, and *he had done it for their sakes.* He chose rather to mention his own name, and the name of a faithful fellow-labourer, than the names of any heads of factions among them, that hereby he might avoid what would provoke, and so procure for his advice the greater regard. Note, Ministers should use prudence in their advices and admonitions, but especially in their reproofs, lest they lose their end. The advice the apostle would by this means inculcate was *that they might learn not to think of men above what is written* (above what he had been writing), *nor be puffed up for one against another* (*v.* 6). Apostles were not to be esteemed other than planters or waterers in God's husbandry, master-builders in his building, stewards of his mysteries, and servants of Christ. And common ministers cannot bear these characters in the same sense that apostles did. Note, We must be very careful not to transfer the honour and authority of the Master to his servant. *We must call no man Master on earth; one is our Master, even Christ*, Matt. xxiii. 8, 10. We must not think of them above what is written. Note, The word of God is the best rule by which to judge concerning men.

And again, judging rightly concerning men, and not judging more highly of them than is fit, is one way to prevent quarrels and contentions in the churches. Pride commonly lies at the bottom of these quarrels. Self-conceit contributes very much to our immoderate esteem of our teachers, as well as ourselves. Our commendation of our own taste and judgment commonly goes along with our unreasonable applause, and always with a factious adherence to one teacher, in opposition to others that may be equally faithful and well qualified. But to think modestly of ourselves, and not above what is written of our teachers, is the most effectual means to prevent quarrels and contests, sidings and parties, in the church. We shall not be puffed up for one against another if we remember that they are all instruments employed by God in his husbandry and building, and endowed by him with their various talents and qualifications.

7 For who maketh thee to differ
from another? and what hast thou
that thou didst not receive? now if
thou didst receive *it*, why dost thou
glory, as if thou hadst not received
it? 8 Now ye are full, now ye are
rich, ye have reigned as kings without
us: and I would to God ye did reign,
that we also might reign with you.
9 For I think that God hath set forth
us the apostles last, as it were appointed to death: for we are made a
spectacle unto the world, and to
angels, and to men. 10 We *are*
fools for Christ's sake, but ye *are*
wise in Christ; we *are* weak, but ye
are strong; ye *are* honourable, but
we *are* despised. 11 Even unto this
present hour we both hunger, and
thirst, and are naked, and are buffeted, and have no certain dwelling-place;
12 And labour, working with
our own hands: being reviled, we
bless: being persecuted, we suffer it:
13 Being defamed, we intreat: we
are made as the filth of the world, *and*
are the offscouring of all things unto
this day.

Here the apostle improves the foregoing hint to a caution against pride and self-conceit, and sets forth the temptations the Corinthians had to despise him, from the difference of their circumstances.

I. He cautions them against pride and self-conceit by this consideration, that all the distinction made among them was owing to God: *Who maketh thee to differ? And what hast thou that thou didst not receive?* *v.* 7. Here the apostle turns his discourse to the ministers who set themselves at the head of these factions, and did but too much encourage and abet the people in those feuds. What had they to glory in, when all their peculiar gifts were from God? They had received them, and could not glory in them as their own, without wronging God. At the time when they reflected on them to feed their vanity, they should have considered them as so many debts and obligations to divine bounty and grace. But it may be taken as a general maxim: We have no reason to be proud of our attainments, enjoyments, or performances; all that we have, or are, or do, that is good, is owing to the free and rich grace of God. Boasting is for ever excluded. There is nothing we have that we can properly call our own: all is received from God. It is foolish in us therefore, and injurious to him, to boast of it; those who receive all should be proud of nothing, Ps. cxv. 1. Beggars and dependents may glory in their supports; but to glory in themselves is to be proud at once of meanness, impotence, and want. Note, Due attention to our obligations to divine grace would cure us of arrogance and self-conceit.

II. He presses the duty of humility upon them by a very smart irony, or at least reproves them for their pride and self-conceit: "*You are full, you are rich, you have reigned as kings without us.* You have not only a sufficiency, but an affluence, of spiritual gifts; nay, you can make them the matter of your glory *without us*, that is, in my absence, and without having any need of me." There is a very elegant gradation from sufficiency to wealth, and thence to royalty, to intimate how much the Corinthians were elated by the abundance of their wisdom and spiritual gifts, which was a humour that prevailed among them while the apostle was away from them, and made them forget what an interest he had in all. See how apt pride is to overrate benefits and overlook the benefactor, to swell upon its possessions and forget from whom they come; nay, it is apt to behold them in a magnifying-glass: "*You have reigned as kings*," says the apostle, "that is, in your own conceit; and *I would to God you did reign, that we also might reign with you.* I wish you had as much of the true glory of a Christian church upon you as you arrogate to yourselves. I should come in then for a share of the honour: *I should reign with you;* I should not be overlooked by you as now I am, but valued and regarded as a minister of Christ, and a very useful instrument among you." Note, Those do not commonly know themselves best who think best of themselves, who have the highest opinion of themselves. The Corinthians might have reigned, and the apostle with them, if they had not been blown up with an imaginary royalty. Note, Pride is a great prejudice to our improvement. He is stopped from growing wiser or better who thinks himself at the height; not only full, but rich, nay, a king.

III. He comes to set forth his own circumstances and those of the other apostles, and compares them with theirs. 1. To set forth the case of the apostles: *For I think it hath pleased God to set forth us the apostles last, as it were appointed to death. For we are made a spectacle to the world, and to angels, and to men.* Paul and his fellow-apostles were exposed to great hardships. Never were any men in this world so hunted and worried. They carried their lives in their hands: *God hath set forth us the apostles last, as it were appointed to death, v.* 9. An allusion is made to some of the bloody spectacles in the Roman amphitheatres, where men were exposed to fight with wild beasts, or to cut one another to pieces, to make diversion for the populace, where the victor did not escape with his life, though he should destroy his adversary, but was only reserved for another combat, and must be devoured or cut in pieces at last; so that such wretched criminals (for they were ordinarily condemned persons that were thus exposed) might very properly be called ἐπιθανάτιοι—*persons devoted or appointed to death.* They are said to be set forth last, because the meridian gladiators, those who combated one another in the after-part of the day, were most exposed, being obliged to fight naked; so that (as Seneca says, *epist.* 7) this was perfect butchery, and those exposed to beasts in the morning were treated mercifully in comparison with these. The general meaning is that the apostles were exposed to continual danger of death, and that of the worst kinds, in the faithful discharge of their office. God had set them forth, brought them into view, as the Roman emperors brought their combatants into the arena, the place of show, though not for the same purposes. They did it to please the populace, and humour their own vanity, and sometimes a much worse principle. The apostles were shown to manifest the power of divine grace, to confirm the truth of their mission and doctrine, and to propagate religion in the world. These were ends worthy of God—noble views, fit to animate them to the combat. But they had like difficulties to encounter, and were in a manner as much exposed as these miserable Roman criminals. Note, The office of an apostle was, as an honourable, so a hard and hazardous one: "*For we are made a spectacle to the world, and to angels, and to men, v.* 9. A *show.* We are brought into the theatre, brought out to the public view of the world. Angels and men are witnesses to our persecutions, sufferings, patience, and magnanimity. They all see that we suffer for our fidelity to Christ, and how we suffer; how great and imminent are our dangers, and how bravely we encounter them; how sharp our sufferings, and how patiently we endure them, by the power of divine grace and our Christian principles. Ours is hard work, but honourable; it is hazardous, but glorious. God wil have honour from us, religion will be credited by us. The world cannot but see and wonder at our undaunted resolution, our invincible patience and constancy." And how contentedly could they be exposed, both to sufferings and scorn, for the honour of their Master! Note, The faithful ministers and disciples of Christ should contentedly undergo any thing for his sake and honour. 2. He compares his own case with that of the Corinthians: "*We are fools for Christ's sake, but you are wise in Christ; we are weak, but you are strong; you are honourable, but we are despised, v.* 10. *We are fools for Christ's sake;* such in common account, and we are well content to be so accounted. We can pass for fools in the world, and be despised as such, so that the wisdom of God and the honour of the gospel may by this means be secured and displayed." Note, Faithful ministers can bear being despised, so that the wisdom of God and the power of his grace be thereby displayed. "*But you are wise in Christ.* You have the fame of being wise and learned Christians, and you do not a little value yourselves upon it. We are under disgrace for delivering the plain truths of the gospel, and in as plain a manner: you are in reputation for your eloquence and human wisdom, which among many make you pass for wise men in Christ. *We are weak, but you are strong.* We are suffering for Christ's sake" (so being weak plainly signifies, 2 Cor. xii. 10), "when you are in easy and flourishing circumstances." Note, All Christians are not alike exposed. Some suffer greater hardships than others who are yet engaged in the same warfare. The standard-bearers in an army are most struck at. So ministers in a time of persecution are commonly the first and greatest sufferers. Or else, "We pass upon the world for persons of but mean endowments, mere striplings in Christianity; but you look upon yourselves, and are looked upon by others, as men, as those of a much more advanced growth and confirmed strength." Note, Those are not always the greatest proficients in Christianity who think thus of themselves, or pass for such upon others. It is but too easy and common for self-love to commit such a mistake. The Corinthians may think themselves, and be esteemed by others, as wiser and stronger men in Christ than the apostles themselves. But O! how gross is the mistake!

IV. He enters into some particularities of their sufferings: *Even to this present hour;* that is, after all the service we have been doing among you and other churches, *we hunger and thirst, and are naked, and are buffeted, and have no certain dwelling-place, and labour, working with our own hands, v.* 11, 12. Nay, they were *made as the filth of the world, and the off-scouring of all things, v.* 13. They were forced to labour with their own hands to get subsistence, and had so much, and so much greater, business to mind, that they could not attend enough to this, to get a comfortable livelihood, but were exposed to hunger, thirst, and nakedness—many times wanted meat, and drink, and clothes. They were driven about the world, without having any fixed abode, any stated habitation. Poor circumstances indeed, for the prime ministers of our Saviour's kingdom to have no house nor home, and to be destitute of food and raiment! But yet no poorer than his who had not *where to lay his head,* Luke ix. 58. But O glorious charity and devotion, that would carry them through all these hardships! How ardently did they love God, how vehemently did they thirst for the salvation of souls! Theirs was voluntary, it was pleasing poverty. They thought they had a rich amends for all the outward good things they wanted, if they might but serve Christ and save souls. Nay, though they *were made the filth of the world, and the off-scouring of all things.* They were treated as men not fit to live, *περικαθάρματα.* It is reasonably thought by the critics that an allusion is here made to a common custom of many heathen nations, to offer men in sacrifice in a time of pestilence, or other like grievous calamity. These were ordinarily the vilest of men, persons of the lowest rank and worst character. Thus, in the first ages, Christians were counted the source of all public calamities, and were sacrificed to the people's rage, if not to appease their angry deities. And apostles could not meet with better usage. They suffered in their persons and characters as the very worst and vilest men, as the most proper to make such a sacrifice: or else as the very dirt of the world, that was to be swept away: nay, as the *off-scouring of all things,* the dross, the filings of all things. They were the common-sewer into which all the reproaches of the world were to be poured. To be the off-scouring of any thing is bad, but what is it to be the off-scouring of all things! How much did the apostles resemble their Master, *and fill up that which was behind of his afflictions, for his body's sake, which is the church!* Col. i. 24. They suffered for him, and they suffered after his example. Thus poor and despised was he in his life and ministry. And every one who would be faithful in Christ Jesus must prepare for the same poverty and contempt. Note, Those may be very dear to God, and honourable in his esteem, whom men may think unworthy to live, and use and scorn as the very dirt and refuse of the world. *God seeth not as man seeth,* 1 Sam. xvi. 7.

V. We have here the apostles' behaviour under all; and the return they made for this mal-treatment: *Being reviled, we bless; being persecuted, we suffer it; being defamed, we entreat, v.* 12, 13. They returned blessings for reproaches, and entreaties and kind exhortations for the rudest slanders and defamation, and were patient under the sharpest persecutions. Note, The disciples of Christ, and especially his ministers, should hold fast their integrity, and keep a good conscience, whatever opposition or hardships they meet with from the world. Whatever they suffer from men, they must follow the example, and fulfil the will and precepts, of their Lord. They must be content, with him and for him, to be despised and abused.

14 I write not these things to shame you, but as my beloved sons I warn *you.* 15 For though ye have ten thousand instructors in Christ, yet *have ye* not many fathers: for in Christ Jesus I have begotten you through the gospel. 16 Wherefore I beseech you, be ye followers of me.

Here Paul challenges their regard to him as their father. He tells them, 1. That what he had written was not for their reproach, but admonition; not with the gall of an enemy, but the bowels of a father (*v.* 14): *I write not to shame you, but as my beloved children I warn you.* Note, In reproving for sin, we should have a tender regard to the reputation, as well as the reformation, of the sinner. We should aim to distinguish between them and their sins, and take care not to discover any spite against them ourselves, nor expose them to contempt and reproach in the world. Reproofs that expose commonly do but exasperate, when those that kindly and affectionately warn are likely to reform. When the affections of a father mingle with the admonitions of a minister, it is to be hoped that they may at once melt and mend; but to lash like an enemy or executioner will provoke and render obstinate. To expose to open shame is but the way to render shameless. 2. He shows them upon what foundation he claimed paternal relation to them, and called them his sons. They might have other pedagogues or instructors, but he was their father; *for in Christ Jesus he had begotten them by the gospel, v.* 15. They were made Christians by his ministry. He had laid the foundation of a church among them. Others could only build upon it. Whatever other teachers they had, he was their spiritual father. He first brought them off from pagan idolatry to the faith of the gospel and the worship of the true and living God. He was the instrument of their new birth, and therefore claimed the relation of a father to them, and felt the bowels of a father towards them. Note, There commonly is, and always ought to be, an endeared affection between faithful ministers and those they beget in Christ Jesus through the gospel. They should love like parents and children. 3. We have here the special advice he urges on them: *Wherefore I beseech you be you fol-*

lowers of me, v. 16. This he elsewhere explains and limits (*ch.* xi. 1): "*Be you followers of me, as I also am of Christ.* Follow me as far as I follow Christ. Come up as close as you can to my example in those instances wherein I endeavour to copy after his pattern. Be my disciples, as far as I manifest myself to be a faithful minister and disciple of Christ, and no further. I would not have you be my disciples, but his. But I hope I have approved myself a faithful steward of the mysteries of Christ, and a faithful servant of my master Christ; so far follow me, and tread in my steps." Note, Ministers should so live that their people may take pattern from them, and live after their copy. They should guide them by their lives as well as their lips, go before them in the way to heaven, and not content themselves with pointing it out. Note, As ministers are to set a pattern, others must take it. They should follow them as far as they are satisfied that they follow Christ in faith and practice.

17 For this cause have I sent unto
you Timotheus, who is my beloved
son, and faithful in the Lord, who
shall bring you into remembrance of
my ways which be in Christ, as I
teach every where in every church.
18 Now some are puffed up, as though
I would not come to you. 19 But I
will come to you shortly, if the Lord
will, and will know, not the speech of
them which are puffed up, but the
power. 20 For the kingdom of God
is not in word, but in power. 21
What will ye ? shall I come unto you
with a rod, or in love, and *in* the
spirit of meekness ?

Here, I. He tells them of his having sent Timothy to them, *to bring them into remembrance of his ways in Christ, as he taught every where in every church* (*v.* 17)—to remind them of his ways in Christ, to refresh their memory as to his preaching and practice, what he taught, and how he lived among them. Note, Those who have had ever so good teaching are apt to forget, and need to have their memories refreshed. The same truth, taught over again, if it give no new light, may make new and quicker impression. He also lets them know that *his teaching was the same every where, and in every church.* He had not one doctrine for one place and people, and another for another. He kept close to his instructions. What *he received of the Lord, that he delivered, ch.* xi. 23. This was the gospel revelation, which was the equal concern of all men, and did not vary from itself. He therefore taught the same things in every church, and lived after the same manner in all times and places. Note, The truth of Christ is one and invariable. What one apostle taught every one taught. What one apostle taught at one time and in one place, he taught at all times and in all places. Christians may mistake and differ in their apprehensions, but Christ and Christian truth *are the same yesterday, today, and for ever,* Heb. xiii. 8. To render their regard to Timothy the greater, he gives them his character. He was *his beloved son,* a spiritual child of his, as well as themselves. Note, Spiritual brotherhood should engage affection as well as what is common and natural. The children of one father should have one heart. But he adds, "*He is faithful in the Lord*—trustworthy, as one that feared the Lord. He will be faithful in the particular office he has now received of the Lord, the particular errand on which he comes; not only from me, but from Christ. He knows what I have taught, and what my conversation has been in all places, and, you may depend upon it, he will make a faithful report." Note, It is a great commendation of any minister that he is faithful in the Lord, faithful to his soul, to his light, to his trust from God; this must go a great way in procuring regard to his message with those that fear God.

II. He rebukes the vanity of those who imagined he would not come to them, by letting them know this was his purpose, though he had sent Timothy: "*I will come to you shortly,* though some of you are so vain as to think I will not." But he adds, *if the Lord will.* It seems, as to the common events of life, apostles knew no more than other men, nor were they in these points under inspiration. For, had the apostle certainly known the mind of God in this matter, he would not have expressed himself with this certainty. But he sets a good example to us in it. Note, All our purposes must be formed with a dependence on Providence, and a reserve for the overruling purposes of God. *If the Lord will, we shall live, and do this and that,* Jam. iv. 15.

III. He lets them know what would follow upon his coming to them: *I will know, not the speech of those that are puffed up, but the power, v.* 19. He would bring the great pretenders among them to a trial, would know what they were, not by their rhetoric or philosophy, but by the authority and efficacy of what they taught, whether they could confirm it by miraculous operations, and whether it was accompanied with divine influences and saving effects on the minds of men. For, adds he, *the kingdom of God is not in word, but in power.* It is not set up, nor propagated, nor established, in the hearts of men, by plausible reasonings nor florid discourses, but by the external power of the Holy Spirit in miraculous operations at first, and the powerful influence of divine truth on the minds and manners of men. Note, It is a good way in the general to judge of a preacher's doctrine, to see whether the effects of it upon men's hearts be truly divine. That is most likely to come from God which in its own nature is most fit, and in event is found to produce most likeness to God, to spread piety and virtue, to change men's hearts and mend their manners.

IV. He puts it to their choice how he should come among them, *whether with a rod or in love and the spirit of meekness* (*v.* 21); that is, according as they were they would find him. If they continued perverse among themselves and with him, it would be necessary to come with a rod; that is, to exert his apostolical power in chastising them, by making some examples, and inflicting some diseases and corporal punishments, or by other censures for their faults. Note, Stubborn offenders must be used with severity. In families, in Christian communities, paternal pity and tenderness, Christian love and compassion, will sometimes force the use of the rod. But this is far from being desirable, if it may be prevented. And therefore the apostle adds that it was in their own option whether he should come with a rod or in a quite different disposition and manner: *Or in love and the spirit of meekness.* As much as if he had said, "Take warning, cease your unchristian feuds, rectify the abuses among you, and return to your duty, and you shall find me as gentle and benign as you can wish. It will be a force upon my inclination to proceed with severity. I had rather come and display the tenderness of a father among you than assert his authority. Do but your duty, and you have no reason to avoid my presence." Note, It is a happy temper in a minister to have the spirit of love and meekness predominant, and yet to maintain his just authority.

CHAP. V.

In this chapter the apostle, I. Blames them for their indulgence in the case of the incestuous person, and orders him to be excommunicated, and delivered to Satan, ver. 1—6. II. He exhorts them to Christian purity, by purging out the old leaven, ver. 7, 8. And, III. Directs them to shun even the common conversation of Christians who were guilty of any notorious and flagitious wickedness, ver. 9, to the end.

IT is reported commonly *that there*
is fornication among you, and
such fornication as is not so much as
named among the Gentiles, that one
should have his father's wife. 2 And
ye are puffed up, and have not rather
mourned, that he that hath done this
deed might be taken away from
among you. 3 For I verily, as absent in body, but present in spirit,
have judged already, as though I were
present, *concerning* him that hath so
done this deed, 4 In the name of
our Lord Jesus Christ, when ye are
gathered together, and my spirit,
with the power of our Lord Jesus
Christ, 5 To deliver such a one
unto Satan for the destruction of the
flesh, that the spirit may be saved in
the day of the Lord Jesus. 6 Your
glorying *is* not good. Know ye not
that a little leaven leaveneth the whole
lump?

Here the apostle states the case; and,

I. Lets them know what was the common or general report concerning them, that one of their community was guilty of fornication, *v.* 1. It was told in all places, to their dishonour, and the reproach of Christians. And it was the more reproachful because it could not be denied. Note, The heinous sins of professed Christians are quickly noted and noised abroad. We should walk circumspectly, for many eyes are upon us, and many mouths will be opened against us if we fall into any scandalous practice. This was not a common instance of fornication, but *such as was not so much as named among the Gentiles, that a man should have his father's wife*—either marry her while his father was alive, or keep her as his concubine, either when he was dead or while he was alive. In either of these cases, his criminal conversation with her might be called *fornication;* but had his father been dead, and he, after his decease, married to her, it had been incest still, but neither fornication nor adultery in the strictest sense. But to marry her, or keep her as a concubine, while his father was alive, though he had repudiated her, or she had deserted him, whether she were his own mother or not, was incestuous fornication: *Scelus incredibile* (as Cicero calls it), *et præter unum in omni vitâ inauditum* (Orat. pro Cluent.), when a woman had caused her daughter to be put away, and was married to her husband. *Incredible wickedness!* says the orator; *such I never heard of in all my life besides.* Not that there were no such instances of incestuous marriages among the heathens; but, whenever they happened, they gave a shock to every man of virtue and probity among them. They could not think of them without horror, nor mention them without dislike and detestation. Yet such a horrible wickedness was committed by one in the church of Corinth, and, as is probable, a leader of one of the factions among them, a principal man. Note, The best churches are, in this state of imperfection, liable to very great corruptions. Is it any wonder when so horrible a practice was tolerated in an apostolical church, a church planted by the great apostle of the Gentiles?

II. He greatly blames them for their own conduct hereupon: *They were puffed up* (*v.* 2), *they gloried,* 1. Perhaps on account of this very scandalous person. He might be a man of great eloquence, of deep science, and for this reason very greatly esteemed, and followed, and cried up, by many among them. They were proud that they had such a leader

Instead of mourning for his fall, and their own reproach upon his account, and renouncing him and removing him from the society, they continued to applaud him and pride themselves in him. Note, Pride or self-esteem often lies at the bottom of our immoderate esteem of others, and this makes us as blind to their faults as to our own. It is true humility that will bring a man to a sight and acknowledgment of his errors. The proud man either wholly overlooks or artfully disguises his faults, or endeavours to transform his blemishes into beauties. Those of the Corinthians that were admirers of the incestuous person's gifts could overlook or extenuate his horrid practices. Or else, 2. It may intimate to us that some of the opposite party were puffed up. They were proud of their own standing, and trampled upon him that fell. Note, It is a very wicked thing to glory over the miscarriages and sins of others. We should lay them to heart, and mourn for them, not be puffed up with them. Probably this was one effect of the divisions among them. The opposite party made their advantage of this scandalous lapse, and were glad of the opportunity. Note, It is a sad consequence of divisions among Christians that it makes them apt to rejoice in iniquity. The sins of others should be our sorrow. Nay, churches should mourn for the scandalous behaviour of particular members, and, if they be incorrigible, should remove them. He that had done this wicked deed should have been taken away from among them.

III. We have the apostle's direction to them how they should now proceed with this scandalous sinner. He would have him excommunicated and delivered to Satan (*v.* 3—5); *as absent in body, yet present in spirit, he had judged already as if he had been present;* that is, he had, by revelation and the miraculous gift of discerning vouchsafed him by the Spirit, as perfect a knowledge of the case, and had hereupon come to the following determination, not without special authority from the Holy Spirit. He says this to let them know that, though he was at a distance, he did not pass an unrighteous sentence, nor judge without having as full cognizance of the case as if he had been on the spot. Note, Those who would appear righteous judges to the world will take care to inform them that they do not pass sentence without full proof and evidence. The apostle adds, *him who hath so done this deed.* The fact was not only heinously evil in itself, and horrible to the heathens, but there were some particular circumstances that greatly aggravated the offence. He had so committed the evil as to heighten the guilt by the manner of doing it. Perhaps he was a minister, a teacher, or a principal man among them. By this means the church and their profession were more reproached. Note, In dealing with scandalous sinners, not only are they to be charged with the fact, but the aggravating circumstances of it. Paul had judged that *he should be delivered to Satan* (*v.* 5), and this was to be done *in the name of Christ*, with the power of Christ, and in a full assembly, where the apostle would be also present in spirit, or by his spiritual gift of discerning at a distance. Some think that this is to be understood of a mere ordinary excommunication, and that delivering him to Satan for the destruction of the flesh is only meant of disowning him, and casting him out of the church, that by this means he might be brought to repentance, and his flesh might be mortified. Christ and Satan divide the world : and those that live in sin, when they profess relation to Christ, belong to another master, and by excommunication should be delivered up to him ; and this in the name of Christ. Note, Church-censures are Christ's ordinances, and should be dispensed in his name. It was to be done also *when they were gathered together*, in full assembly. The more public the more solemn, and the more solemn the more likely to have a good effect on the offender. Note, Church-censures on notorious and incorrigible sinners should be passed with great solemnity. Those who sin in this manner *are to be rebuked before all, that all may fear*, 1 Tim. v. 20. Others think the apostle is not to be understood of mere excommunication, but of a miraculous power or authority they had of delivering a scandalous sinner into the power of Satan, to have bodily diseases inflicted, and to be tormented by him with bodily pains, which is the meaning of the *destruction of the flesh.* In this sense the destruction of the flesh has been a happy occasion of the salvation of the spirit. It is probable that this was a mixed case. It was an extraordinary instance : and the church was to proceed against him by just censure ; the apostle, when they did so, put forth an act of extraordinary power, and gave him up to Satan, not for his destruction, but for his deliverance, at least for the destruction of the flesh, that the soul might be saved. Note, The great end of church-censures is the good of those who fall under them, their spiritual and eternal good. It is that their spirit may be saved in the day of the Lord Jesus, *v.* 5. Yet it is not merely a regard to their benefit that is to be had in proceeding against them. For,

IV. He hints the danger of contagion from this example : *Your glorying is not good. Know you not that a little leaven leaveneth the whole lump?* The bad example of a man in rank and reputation is very mischievous, spreads the contagion far and wide. It did so, probably, in this very church and case : see 2 Cor. xii. 21. They could not be ignorant of this. The experience of the whole world was for it ; *one scabbed sheep infects a whole flock.* A little leaven will quickly spread the ferment through a great lump. Note, Concern for their purity and preservation should engage Christian churches to remove gross and scandalous sinners.

7 Purge out therefore the old leaven, that ye may be a new lump, as
ye are unleavened. For even Christ
our passover is sacrificed for us: 8
Therefore let us keep the feast, not
with old leaven, neither with the
leaven of malice and wickedness; but
with the unleavened *bread* of sincerity
and truth.

Here the apostle exhorts them to purity, by purging out the old leaven. In this observe,

I. The advice itself, addressed either, 1. To the church in general; and so purging out the old leaven, that they might be a new lump, refers to the *putting away from themselves that wicked person, v.* 13. Note, Christian churches should be pure and holy, and not bear such corrupt and scandalous members. They are to be unleavened, and should endure no such heterogeneous mixture to sour and corrupt them. Or, 2. To each particular member of the church. And so it implies that they should purge themselves from all impurity of heart and life, especially from this kind of wickedness, to which the Corinthians were addicted to a proverb. See the *argument* at the beginning. This old leaven was in a particular manner to be purged out, that they might become a new lump. Note, Christians should be careful to keep themselves clean, as well as purge polluted members out of their society. And they should especially avoid the sins to which they themselves were once most addicted, and the reigning vices of the places and the people where they live. They were also to purge themselves from malice and wickedness—all ill-will and mischievous subtlety. This is leaven that sours the mind to a great degree. It is not improbable that this was intended as a check to some who gloried in the scandalous behaviour of the offender, both out of pride and pique. Note, Christians should be careful to keep free from malice and mischief. Love is the very essence and life of the Christian religion. It is the fairest image of God, *for God is love* (1 John iv. 16), and therefore it is no wonder if it be the greatest beauty and ornament of a Christian. But malice is murder in its principles: He that hates his brother is a murderer (1 John iii. 15), he bears the image and proclaims himthe offspring of him *who was a murderer from the beginning,* John viii. 44. How hateful should every thing be to a Christian that looks like malice and mischief.

II. The reason with which this advice is enforced: *For Christ our passover is sacrificed for us, v.* 7. This is the great doctrine of the gospel. The Jews, after they had killed the passover, kept the feast of unleavened bread. So must we; not for seven days only, but all our days. We should die with our Saviour to sin, be planted into the likeness of his death by mortifying sin, and into the likeness of his resurrection by rising again to newness of life, and that internal and external. We must have new hearts and new lives. Note, The whole life of a Christian must be a feast of unleavened bread. His common conversation and his religious performances must be holy. *He must purge out the old leaven, and keep the feast of unleavened bread of sincerity and truth.* He must be without guilt in his conduct towards God and man. And the more there is of sincerity in our own profession, the less shall we censure that of others. Note, On the whole, The sacrifice of our Redeemer is the strongest argument with a gracious heart for purity and sincerity. How sincere a regard did he show to our welfare, in dying for us! and how terrible a proof was his death of the detestable nature of sin, and God's displeasure against it! Heinous evil, that could not be expiated but with the blood of the Son of God! And shall a Christian love the murderer of his Lord? God forbid.

9 I wrote unto you in an epistle
not to company with fornicators: 10
Yet not altogether with the fornicators of this world, or with the covetous, or extortioners, or with idolaters;
for then must ye needs go out of the
world. 11 But now I have written
unto you not to keep company, if any
man that is called a brother be a fornicator, or covetous, or an idolater,
or a railer, or a drunkard, or an extortioner; with such a one no not
to eat. 12 For what have I to do to
judge them also that are without? do
not ye judge them that are within.
13 But them that are without God
judgeth. Therefore put away from
among yourselves that wicked person.

Here the apostle advises them to shun the company and converse of scandalous professors. Consider,

I. The advice itself: *I wrote to you in a letter not to company with fornicators, v* 9 Some think this was an epistle written to them before, which is lost. Yet we have lost nothing by it, the Christian revelation being entire in those books of scripture which have come down to us, which are all that were intended by God for the general use of Christians, or he could and would in his providence have preserved more of the writings of inspired men. Some think it is to be understood of this very epistle, that he had written this advice before he had full information of their whole case, but thought it needful now to be more particular. And therefore on this occasion he tells them that if any man called a brother, any one professing Christianity, and being a member of a Christian church, were *a fornicator, or covetous, or an idolater, or a railer*, that they should not *keep company with him, nor so much as eat with such a one*. They were to avoid all familiarity with him; they were to have no commerce with him: but, that they might shame him, and bring him to repentance, must disclaim and shun him. Note, Christians are to avoid the familiar conversation of fellow-christians that are notoriously wicked, and under just censure for their flagitious practices. Such disgrace the Christian name. They may call themselves *brethren in Christ*, but they are not Christian brethren. They are only fit companions for their brethren in iniquity; and to such company they should be left, till they *mend their ways and doings*.

II. How he limits this advice. He does not forbid Christians the like commerce with scandalously wicked heathens. He does not forbid their eating nor conversing with the *fornicators of this world*, &c. They know no better. They profess no better. The gods they serve, and the worship they render to many of them, countenance such wickedness. "*You must needs go out of the world* if you will have no conversation with such men. Your Gentile neighbours are generally vicious and profane; and it is impossible, as long as you are in the world, and have any worldly business to do, but you must fall into their company. This cannot be wholly avoided." Note, Christians may and ought to testify more respect to loose worldlings than to loose Christians. This seems a paradox. Why should we shun the company of a profane or loose Christian, rather than that of a profane or loose heathen?

III. The reason of this limitation is here assigned. It is impossible the one should be avoided. Christians must have gone out of the world to avoid the company of loose heathens. But this was impossible, as long as they had business in the world. While they are minding their duty, and doing their proper business, God can and will preserve them from contagion. Besides, they carry an antidote against the infection of their bad example, and are naturally upon their guard. They are apt to have a horror at their wicked practices. But the dread of sin wears off by familiar converse with wicked Christians. Our own safety and preservation are a reason of this difference. But, besides, heathens were such as Christians had nothing to do to judge and censure, and avoid upon a censure passed; for *they are without* (*v.* 12), and must be left to *God's judgment*, *v.* 13. But, as to members of the church, they are within, are professedly bound by the laws and rules of Christianity, and not only liable to the judgment of God, but to the censures of those who are set over them, and the fellow-members of the same body, when they transgress those rules. Every Christian is bound to judge them unfit for communion and familiar converse. They are to be punished, by having this mark of disgrace put upon them, that they may be shamed, and, if possible, reclaimed thereby: and the more because the sins of such much more dishonour God than the sins of the openly wicked and profane can do. The church therefore is obliged to clear herself from all confederacy with them, or connivance at them, and to bear testimony against their wicked practices. Note, Though the church has nothing to do with those without, it must endeavour to keep clear of the guilt and reproach of those within.

IV. How he applies the argument to the case before him: "*Therefore put away from among yourselves that wicked person, v.* 13. Cast him out of your fellowship, and avoid his conversation."

CHAP. VI.

In this chapter the apostle, I. Reproves them for going to law with one another about small matters, and bringing the cause before heathen judges, ver. 1—8. II. He takes occasion hence to warn them against many gross sins, to which they had been formerly addicted, ver. 9—11. III. And, having cautioned them against the abuse of their liberty, he vehemently dehorts them from fornication, by various arguments, ver. 12, to the end.

DARE any of you, having a matter
against another, go to law before the unjust, and not before the
saints? 2 Do ye not know that the
saints shall judge the world? and if
the world shall be judged by you, are
ye unworthy to judge the smallest
matters? 3 Know ye not that we
shall judge angels? how much more
things that pertain to this life? 4 If
then ye have judgments of things
pertaining to this life, set them to
judge who are least esteemed in the
church. 5 I speak to your shame.
Is it so, that there is not a wise man
among you? no, not one that shall be
able to judge between his brethren?
6 But brother goeth to law with brother, and that before the unbelievers.
7 Now therefore there is utterly a
fault among you, because ye go to
law one with another. Why do ye
not rather take wrong? why do ye
not rather *suffer yourselves to* be defrauded? 8 Nay, ye do wrong, and
defraud, and that *your* brethren.

Here the apostle reproves them for going to law with one another before heathen judges for little matters; and therein blames all *vexatious law-suits*. In the previous chapter he had directed them to punish heinous sins among themselves by church-censures. Here he directs them to determine controversies with one another by church-counsel and advice, concerning which observe,

I. The fault he blames them for: it was

going to law. Not but that *the law is good, if a man use it lawfully.* But, 1. *Brother went to law with brother* (*v.* 6), one member of the church with another. The near relation could not preserve peace and good understanding. The bonds of fraternal love were broken through. *And a brother offended,* as Solomon says, *is harder to be won than a strong city;* their contentions are like the bars of a castle, Prov. xviii. 19. Note, Christians should not contend with one another, for they are brethren. This, duly attended to, would prevent law-suits, and put an end to quarrels and litigations. 2. They brought the matter before the heathen magistrates: *they went to law before the unjust, not before the saints* (*v.* 1), brought the controversy before unbelievers (*v.* 6), and did not compose it among themselves, Christians and saints, at least in profession. This tended much to the reproach of Christianity. It published at once their folly and unpeaceableness; whereas they pretended to be the children of wisdom, and the followers of the Lamb, the meek and lowly Jesus, the *prince of peace.* And therefore, says the apostle, "*Dare any of you,* having a controversy with another, go to law, implead him, bring the matter to a hearing before the unjust?" Note, Christians should not dare to do any thing that tends to the reproach of their Christian name and profession. 3. Here is at least an intimation that they went to law for trivial matters, things of little value; for the apostle blames them that they did not suffer wrong rather than go to law (*v.* 7), which must be understood of matters not very important. In matters of great damage to ourselves or families, we may use lawful means to right ourselves. We are not bound to sit down and suffer the injury tamely, without stirring for our own relief; but, in matters of small consequence, it is better to put up with the wrong. Christians should be of a forgiving temper. And it is more for their ease and honour to suffer small injuries and inconveniences than seem to be contentious.

II. He lays before them the aggravations of their fault: *Do you not know that the saints shall judge the world* (*v.* 2), *shall judge angels? v.* 3. And are they unworthy *to judge the smallest matters, the things of this life?* It was a dishonour to their Christian character, a forgetting of their real dignity, as saints, for them to carry little matters, about the things of life, before heathen magistrates. When they were to judge the world, nay, to judge angels, it is unaccountable that they could not determine little controversies among one another. By judging the world and angels, some think, is to be understood, their being assessors to Christ in the great judgment-day; it being said of our Saviour's disciples that they should at that day *sit on twelve thrones, judging the twelve tribes of Israel,* Matt. xix. 28. And elsewhere we read of our *Lord's coming with ten thousand of his saints to execute judgment on all,* &c., Jude 14, 15. *He will come to judgment with all his saints,* 1 Thess. iii. 13. They themselves are indeed to be judged (see Matt. xxv. 31—41), but they may first be acquitted, and then advanced to the bench, to approve and applaud the righteous judgment of Christ both on men and angels. In no other sense can they be judges. They are not partners in their Lord's commission, but they have the honour to sit by, and see his proceeding against the wicked world, and approve it. Others understand this judging of the world to be meant when the empire should become Christian. But it does not appear that the Corinthians had knowledge of the empire's becoming Christian; and, if they had, in what sense could Christian emperors be said to judge angels? Others understand it of their condemning the world by their faith and practice, and casting out evil angels by miraculous power, which was not confined to the first ages, nor to the apostles. The first sense seems to be most natural; and at the same time it gives the utmost force to the argument. "Shall Christians have the honour to sit with the sovereign Judge at the last day, whilst he passes judgment on sinful men and evil angels, and are they not worthy to judge of the trifles about which you contend before heathen magistrates? Cannot they make up your mutual differences? Why must you bring them before heathen judges? When you are to judge them, is it fit to appeal to their judicature? Must you, about *the affairs of this life, set those to judge who are of no esteem in the church?*" (so some read, and perhaps most properly, *v.* 4), *heathen* magistrates, ἐξουθενημένους, the *things that are not, ch.* i. 28. "Must those be called in to judge in your controversies of whom you ought to entertain so low an opinion? Is not this shameful?" *v.* 5. Some who read it as our translators make it an ironical speech: "If you have such controversies depending, set those to judge who are of least esteem among yourselves. The meanest of your own members are able surely to determine these disputes. Refer the matters in variance to any, rather than go to law about them before heathen judges. They are trifles not worth contending about, and may easily be decided, if you have first conquered your own spirits, and brought them into a truly Christian temper. *Bear and forbear,* and the men of meanest skill among you may end your quarrels. *I speak it to your shame,*" *v.* 5. Note, It is a shame that little quarrels should grow to such a head among Christians, that they cannot be determined by arbitration of the brethren.

III. He puts them on a method to remedy this fault. And this twofold:—1. By referring it to some to make it up: "*Is it so that there is no wise man among you, no one able to judge between his brethren?* v. 5. You who value yourselves so much upon your wisdom and knowledge, who are so puffed up upon your extraordinary gifts and endowments, is there none among you fit for this office, none that has wisdom enough to judge in these differences? Must brethren quarrel, and the heathen magistrate judge, in a church so famous as yours for knowledge and wisdom? It is a reproach to you that quarrels should run so high, and none of your wise men interpose to prevent them." Note, Christians should never engage in law-suits till all other remedies have been tried in vain. Prudent Christians should prevent, if possible, their disputes, and not courts of judicature decide them, especially in matters of no great importance. 2. By suffering wrong rather than taking this method to right themselves: *It is utterly a fault among you to go to law in this matter:* it is always a fault of one side to go to law, except in a case where the title is indeed dubious, and there is a friendly agreement of both parties to refer it to the judgment of those learned in the law to decide it. And this is referring it, rather than contending about it, which is the thing the apostle here seems chiefly to condemn: *Should you not rather take wrong, rather suffer yourselves to be defrauded?* Note, A Christian should rather put up with a little injury than tease himself, and provoke others, by a litigious contest. The peace of his own mind, and the calm of his neighbourhood, are more worth than victory in such a contest, or reclaiming his own right, especially when the quarrel must be decided by those who are enemies to religion. But the apostle tells them they were so far from bearing injuries *that they actually did wrong, and defrauded, and that their brethren.* Note, It is utterly a fault to wrong and defraud any; but it is an aggravation of this fault to defraud our Christian brethren. The ties of mutual love ought to be stronger between them than between others. And *love worketh no ill to his neighbour,* Rom. xiii. 10. Those who love the brotherhood can never, under the influence of this principle, hurt or injure them.

9 Know ye not that the unrighteous shall not inherit the kingdom of God? Be not deceived: neither fornicators, nor idolaters, nor adulterers, nor effeminate, nor abusers of themselves with mankind, 10 Nor thieves, nor covetous, nor drunkards, nor revilers, nor extortioners, shall inherit the kingdom of God. 11 And such were some of you: but ye are washed, but ye are sanctified, but ye are justified in the name of the Lord Jesus, and by the Spirit of our God.

Here he takes occasion to warn them against many heinous evils, to which they had been formerly addicted.

I. He puts it to them as a plain truth, of which they could not be ignorant, that such sinners should not inherit the kingdom of God. The meanest among them must know thus much, that *the unrighteous shall not inherit the kingdom of God* (v. 9), shall not be owned as true members of his church on earth, nor admitted as glorious members of the church in heaven. All unrighteousness is sin; and all reigning sin, nay, every actual sin committed deliberately, and not repented of, shuts out of the kingdom of heaven. He specifies several sorts of sins: against the first and second commandments, as *idolaters;* against the seventh, as *adulterers, fornicators, effeminate,* and *Sodomites;* against the eighth, as *thieves* and *extortioners,* that by force or fraud wrong their neighbours; against the ninth, as *revilers;* and against the tenth, as *covetous* and *drunkards,* as those who are in a fair way to break all the rest. Those who knew any thing of religion must know that heaven could never be intended for these. The scum of the earth are no ways fit to fill the heavenly mansions. Those who do the devil's work can never receive God's wages, at least no other than *death, the just wages of sin,* Rom. vi. 23.

II. Yet he warns them against deceiving themselves: *Be not deceived.* Those who cannot but know the fore-mentioned truth are but too apt not to attend to it. Men are very much inclined to flatter themselves that *God is such a one as themselves,* and that they may live in sin and yet die in Christ, may lead the life of the devil's children and yet go to heaven with the children of God. But this is all a gross cheat. Note, It is very much the concern of mankind that they do not cheat themselves in the matters of their souls. We cannot hope to sow to the flesh and yet reap everlasting life.

III. He puts them in mind what a change the gospel and grace of God had made in them: *Such were some of you* (v. 11), such notorious sinners as he had been reckoning up. The Greek word is ταῦτα—*such things* were some of you, very monsters rather than men. Note, Some that are eminently good after their conversion have been as remarkably wicked before. *Quantum mutatus ab illo! How glorious a change does grace make!* It changes the vilest of men into saints and the children of God. Such were some of you, but you are not what you were. *You are washed, you are sanctified, you are justified in the name of Christ, and by the Spirit of our God.* Note, The wickedness of men before conversion is no bar to their regeneration and reconciliation to God. The blood of Christ, and *the washing of regeneration,* can purge away all guilt and defilement. Here is a rhetorical change of the natural order: *You are sanctified, you are justified.* Sanctification is mentioned before justification : and yet the name of Christ, by which we are justified, is placed before the Spirit of God, by whom we are sanctified. Our justification is owing to the merit of Christ ; our sanctification to the operation of the Spirit : but both go together. Note, None are cleansed from the guilt of sin, and reconciled to God through Christ, but those who are also sanctified by his Spirit. All who are made righteous in the sight of God are made holy by the grace of God.

12 All things are lawful unto me,
but all things are not expedient : all
things are lawful for me, but I will
not be brought under the power of
any. 13 Meats for the belly, and
the belly for meats : but God shall
destroy both it and them. Now the
body *is* not for fornication, but for
the Lord ; and the Lord for the body.
14 And God hath both raised up the
Lord, and will also raise up us by his
own power. 15 Know ye not that
your bodies are the members of
Christ ? shall I then take the members of Christ, and make *them* the
members of a harlot ? God forbid.
16 What ? know ye not that he which
is joined to a harlot is one body ?
for two, saith he, shall be one flesh.
17 But he that is joined unto the
Lord is one spirit. 18 Flee fornication. Every sin that a man doeth is
without the body; but he that committeth fornication sinneth against his
own body. 19 What ? know ye not
that your body is the temple of the
Holy Ghost *which is* in you, which ye
have of God, and ye are not your
own ? 20 For ye are bought with a
price : therefore glorify God in your
body, and in your spirit, which are
God's.

The twelfth verse and former part of the thirteenth seem to relate to that early dispute among Christians about the distinction of meats, and yet to be prefatory to the caution that follows against fornication. The connection seems plain enough if we attend to the famous determination of the apostles, Acts xv., where the prohibition of certain foods was joined with that of fornication. Now some among the Corinthians seem to have imagined that they were as much at liberty in the point of fornication as of meats, especially because it was not a sin condemned by the laws of their country. They were ready to say, even in the case of fornication, *All things are lawful for me.* This pernicious conceit Paul here sets himself to oppose: he tells them that many things lawful in themselves were not expedient at certain times, and under particular circumstances ; and Christians should not barely consider what is in itself lawful to be done, but what is fit for them to do, considering their profession, character, relations, and hopes : they should be very careful that by carrying this maxim too far they be not brought into bondage, either to a crafty deceiver or a carnal inclination. *All things are lawful for me,* says he, *but I will not be brought under the power of any, v.* 12. Even in lawful things, he would not be subject to the impositions of a usurped authority : so far was he from apprehending that in the things of God it was lawful for any power on earth to impose its own sentiments. Note, There is a liberty wherewith Christ has made us free, in which we must stand fast. But surely he would never carry this liberty so far as to put himself into the power of any bodily appetite. Though all meats were supposed lawful, he would not become a glutton nor a drunkard. And much less would he abuse the maxim of lawful liberty to countenance the sin of fornication, which, though it might be allowed by the Corinthian laws, was a trespass upon the law of nature, and utterly unbecoming a Christian. He would not abuse this maxim about eating and drinking to encourage any intemperance, nor indulge a carnal appetite : "*Though meats are for the belly and the belly for meats* (*v.* 13), though the belly was made to receive food, and food was originally ordained to fill the belly, yet if it be not convenient for me, and much more if it be inconvenient, and likely to enslave me, if I am in danger of being subjected to my belly and appetite, I will abstain. *But God shall destroy both it and them,* at least as to their mutual relation. There is a time coming when the human body will need no further recruits of food." Some of the ancients suppose that this is to be understood of abolishing the belly as well as the food ; and that though the same body will be raised at the great day, yet not with all the same members, some being utterly unnecessary in a future state, as the belly for instance, when the man is never to hunger, nor thirst, nor eat, nor drink more. But, whether this be true or no, there is a time coming when the need and use of food shall be abolished. Note, The expectation we have of being without bodily appetites in a future life is a very good argument against being under their power in the present life. This seems to me the sense of the apostle's argument ; and that this passage is plainly to be connected with his caution against fornication, though some make it a part of the former argument against litigious law-suits, especially before heathen magistrates and the enemies of true religion. These suppose that the apostle argues that though it may be lawful to claim our rights yet it is not always expedient, and it is utterly unfit for Christians to put themselves into the power of infidel judges, lawyers, and solicitors, on these accounts. But this connection seems not so natural. The transition to his arguments against fornication, as I have laid it, seems very natural: *But the body is not for fornication, but for the Lord, and the Lord for the body, v.* 13. Meats and the belly are for one another; not so fornication and the body.

I. The body is not for fornication, but for the Lord. This is the first argument he uses against this sin, for which the heathen inhabitants of Corinth were infamous, and the converts to Christianity retained too favourable an opinion of it. It is making things to cross their intention and use. The *body is not for fornication;* it was never formed for any such purpose, *but for the Lord,* for the service and honour of God. It is to be an instrument *of righteousness to holiness* (Rom. vi. 19), and therefore is never to be made an instrument of uncleanness. It is to be a member of Christ, and therefore must not be made the member of a harlot, *v.* 15. And *the Lord is for the body,* that is, as some think, Christ is to be Lord of the body, to have property in it and dominion over it, having assumed a body and been made to partake of our nature, that he might be head of his church, and head over all things, Heb. ii. 5, 18. Note, We must take care that we do not use what belongs to Christ as if it were our own, and much less to his dishonour.

II. Some understand this last passage, *The Lord is for the body,* thus: He is for its resurrection and glorification, according to what follows, *v.* 14, which is a second argument against this sin, the honour intended to be put on our bodies: *God hath both raised up our Lord, and will raise us up by his power* (*v.* 14), by the power of him who *shall change our vile body, and make it like to his glorious body by that power whereby he is able to subdue all things to himself,* Phil. iii. 21. It is an honour done to the body that Jesus Christ was raised from the dead: and it will be an honour to our bodies that they will be raised. Let us not abuse those bodies by sin, and make them vile, which, if they be kept pure, shall, notwithstanding their present vileness, be made like to *Christ's glorious body.* Note, The hopes of a resurrection to glory should restrain Christians from dishonouring their bodies by fleshly lusts.

III. A third argument is the honour already put on them: *Know you not that your bodies are the members of Christ? v.* 15. If the soul be united to Christ by faith, the whole man is become a member of his mystical body. The body is in union with Christ as well as the soul. How honourable is this to the Christian! His very flesh is a part of the mystical body of Christ. Note, It is good to know in what honourable relations we stand, that we may endeavour to become them. *But now,* says the apostle, *shall I take the members of Christ, and make them the members of a harlot? God forbid.* Or, *take away* the members of Christ? Would not this be a gross abuse, and the most notorious injury? Would it not be dishonouring Christ, and dishonouring ourselves to the very last degree? What, make Christ's members the members of a harlot, prostitute them to so vile a purpose! The thought is to be abhorred. God forbid. *Know you not that he who is joined to a harlot is one body* with hers? *For two,* says he, *shall be one flesh. But he who is joined to the Lord is one spirit, v.* 16, 17. Nothing can stand in greater opposition to the honourable relations and alliances of a Christian man than this sin. He is joined to the Lord in union with Christ, and made partaker by faith of his Spirit. One spirit lives and breathes and moves in the head and members. Christ and his faithful disciples are one, John xvii. 21, 22. *But he that is joined to a harlot is one body, for two shall be one flesh,* by carnal conjunction, which was ordained of God only to be in a married state. Now shall one in so close a union with Christ as to be one spirit with him yet be so united to a harlot as to become one flesh with her? Were not this a vile attempt to make a union between Christ and harlots? And can a greater indignity he offered to him or ourselves? Can any thing be more inconsistent with our profession or relation? Note, The sin of fornication is a great injury in a Christian to his head and lord, and a great reproach and blot on his profession. It is no wonder therefore that the apostle should say, "*Flee fornication* (*v.* 18), avoid it, keep out of the reach of temptations to it, of provoking objects. Direct the eyes and mind to other things and thoughts." *Alia vitia pugnando, sola libido fugiendo vincitur—Other vices may be conquered in fight, this only by flight;* so speak many of the fathers.

IV. A fourth argument is that it is a sin against our own bodies. *Every sin that a man does is without the body; he that committeth fornication sinneth against his own body* (*v.* 18); every sin, that is, every other sin, every external act of sin besides, is without the body. It is not so much an abuse of the body as of somewhat else, as of wine by the drunkard, food by the glutton, &c. Nor does it give the power of the body to another person. Nor does it so much tend to the reproach of the body and to render it vile. This sin is in a peculiar manner styled uncleanness, pollution, because no sin has so much external turpitude in it, especially in a Christian. He sins against his own body; he defiles it, he degrades it, making it one with the body of that vile creature with whom he sins. He casts vile reproach on what his Redeemer has dignified to the last degree by taking it into union with himself. Note, We should not make our present vile bodies more vile by sinning against them.

V. The fifth argument against this sin is that the bodies of Christians are *the temples of the Holy Ghost which is in them, and which they have of God, v.* 19. He that is joined to Christ is one spirit. He is yielded up to him, is consecrated thereby, and set apart for his use, and is hereupon possessed, and occupied, and inhabited, by his Holy Spirit. This is the proper notion of a temple—a place where God dwells, and sacred to his use, by his own claim and his creature's surrender. Such temples real Christians are of the Holy Ghost. Must he not therefore be God? But the inference is plain that hence we are not our own. We are yielded up to God, and possessed by and for God; nay, and this in virtue of a purchase made of us: *You are bought with a price.* In short, our bodies were made for God, they were purchased for him. If we are Christians indeed they are yielded to him, and he inhabits and occupies them by his Spirit: so that our bodies are not our own, but his. And shall we desecrate his temple, defile it, prostitute it, and offer it up to the use and service of a harlot? Horrid sacrilege! This is robbing God in the worst sense. Note, The temple of the Holy Ghost must be kept holy. Our bodies must be kept as his whose they are, and fit for his use and residence.

VI. The apostle argues from the obligation we are under *to glorify God both with our body and spirit, which are his, v.* 20. He made both, he bought both, and therefore both belong to him and should be used and employed for him, and therefore should not be defiled, alienated from him, and prostituted by us. No, they must be kept as vessels fitted for our Master's use. We must look upon our whole selves as holy to the Lord, and must use our bodies as property which belongs to him and is sacred to his use and service. We are to honour *him with our bodies and spirits, which are his;* and therefore, surely, must abstain from fornication; and not only from the outward act, but from the *adultery of the heart,* as our Lord calls it, Matt. v. 28. Body and spirit are to be kept clean, that God may be honoured by both. But God is dishonoured when either is defiled by so beastly a sin. Therefore flee fornication, nay, and every sin. Use your bodies for the glory and service of their Lord and Maker. Note, We are not proprietors of ourselves, nor have power over ourselves, and therefore should not use ourselves according to our own pleasure, but according to his will, and for his glory, *whose we are, and whom we should serve,* Acts xxvii. 23.

CHAP. VII.

In this chapter the apostle answers some cases proposed to him by the Corinthians about marriage. He, I. Shows them that marriage was appointed as a remedy against fornication, and therefore that persons had better marry than burn, ver. 1–9. II. He gives direction to those who are married to continue together, though they might have an unbelieving relative, unless the unbeliever would part, in which case a Christian would not be in bondage, ver. 10–16. III. He shows them that becoming Christians does not change their external state; and therefore advises every one to continue, in the general, in that state in which he was called, ver. 17–24. IV. He advises them, by reason of the present distress, to keep themselves unmarried; hints the shortness of time, and how they should improve it, so as to grow dead and indifferent to the comforts of the world; and shows them how worldly cares hinder their devotions, and distract them in the service of God, ver. 25—35. V. He directs them in the disposal of their virgins, ver. 36—38. VI. And closes the chapter with advice to widows how to dispose of themselves in that state, ver. 39, 40.

NOW concerning the things wher-
of ye wrote unto me: *It is*
good for a man not to touch a woman.
2 Nevertheless, *to avoid* fornication,
let every man have his own wife, and
let every woman have her own husband. 3 Let the husband render
unto the wife due benevolence: and
likewise also the wife unto the husband. 4 The wife hath not power of
her own body, but the husband: and
likewise also the husband hath not
power of his own body, but the wife.
5 Defraud ye not one the other, except *it be* with consent for a time,
that ye may give yourselves to fasting
and prayer; and come together again,
that Satan tempt you not for your
incontinency. 6 But I speak this by
permission, *and* not of commandment.
7 For I would that all men were even
as I myself. But every man hath his
proper gift of God, one after this
manner, and another after that. 8 I
say therefore to the unmarried and
widows, It is good for them if they
abide even as I. 9 But if they cannot contain, let them marry: for it is
better to marry than to burn.

The apostle comes now, as a faithful and skilful casuist, to answer some cases of conscience which the Corinthians had proposed to him. Those were *things whereof they wrote to him, v.* 1. As the lips of ministers should *keep knowledge,* so the people should *ask the law at their mouths.* The apostle was as ready to resolve as they were to propose their doubts. In the former chapter, he warns them to avoid fornication; here he gives some directions about marriage, the remedy God had appointed for it. He tells them in general,

I. That it was good, in that juncture of time at least, to abstain from marriage altogether: *It is good for a man not to touch a woman* (not to take her to wife), by good here not understanding what is so conformable to the mind and will of God as if to do otherwise were sin, an extreme into which many of the ancients have run in favour of celibacy and virginity. Should the apostle be understood in this sense, he would contradict much of the rest of his discourse. But it is good, that is, either abstracting from circumstances there are many things in which the state of celibacy has the advantage above the marriage state; or else *at this juncture*, by reason of the distresses of the Christian church, it would be a convenience for Christians to keep themselves single, provided they have the gift of continency, and at the same time can keep themselves chaste. The expression also may carry in it an intimation that Christians must avoid all occasions of this sin, and flee all fleshly lusts, and incentives to them; must neither look on nor touch a woman, so as to provoke lustful inclinations. Yet,

II. He informs them that marriage, and the comforts and satisfactions of that state, are by divine wisdom prescribed for preventing fornication (*v.* 2), Πορνείας—*Fornications*, all sorts of lawless lust. To avoid these, *Let every man*, says he, *have his own wife, and every woman her own husband;* that is, marry, and confine themselves to their own mates. And, when they are married, let each render the other *due benevolence* (*v.* 3), consider the disposition and exigency of each other, and render conjugal duty, which is owing to each other. For, as the apostle argues (*v.* 4), in the married state neither person has power over his own body, but has delivered it into the power of the other, the wife hers into the power of the husband, the husband his into the power of the wife. Note, Polygamy, or the marriage of more persons than one, as well as adultery, must be a breach of marriage-covenants, and a violation of the partner's rights. And therefore they should not defraud one another of the use of their bodies, nor any other of the comforts of the conjugal state, appointed of God for keeping *the vessel in sanctification and honour*, and preventing the lusts of uncleanness, except it be *with mutual consent* (*v.* 5) and *for a time* only, while they employ themselves in some extraordinary duties of religion, *or give themselves to fasting and prayer*. Note, Seasons of deep humiliation require abstinence from lawful pleasures. But this separation between husband and wife must not be for a continuance, lest they expose themselves to Satan's temptations, by reason of their incontinence, or inability to contain. Note, Persons expose themselves to great danger by attempting to perform what is above their strength, and at the same time not bound upon them by any law of God. If they abstain from lawful enjoyments, they may be ensnared into unlawful ones. The remedies God hath provided against sinful inclinations are certainly best.

III. The apostle limits what he had said about *every man's having his own wife*, &c. (*v.* 2): *I speak this by permission, not of command.* He did not lay it as an injunction upon every man to marry without exception. Any man might marry. No law of God prohibited the thing. But, on the other hand, no law bound a man to marry so that he sinned if he did not; I mean, unless his circumstances required it for preventing the lust of uncleanness. It was a thing in which men, by the laws of God, were in a great measure left at liberty. And therefore Paul did not bind every man to marry, though every man had an allowance. No, he *could wish all men were as himself* (*v.* 7), that is, single, and capable of living continently in that state. There were several conveniences in it, which at that season, if not at others, made it more eligible in itself. Note, It is a mark of true goodness to wish all men as happy as ourselves. But it did not answer the intentions of divine Providence as well for all men to have as much command of this appetite as Paul had. It was a gift vouchsafed to such persons as Infinite Wisdom thought proper: *Every one hath his proper gift of God, one after this manner and another after that.* Natural constitutions vary; and, where there may not be much difference in the constitution, different degrees of grace are vouchsafed, which may give some a greater victory over natural inclination than others. Note, The gifts of God, both in nature and grace, are variously distributed. Some have them after this manner and some after that. Paul could wish all men were as himself, but *all men cannot receive such a saying, save those to whom it is given,* Matt. xix. 11.

IV. He sums up his sense on this head (*v.* 9, 10): *I say therefore to the unmarried and widows*, to those in a state of virginity or widowhood, *It is good for them if they abide even as I.* There are many conveniences, and especially at this juncture, in a single state, to render it preferable to a married one. It is convenient therefore *that the unmarried abide as I*, which plainly implies that Paul was at that time unmarried. *But, if they cannot contain, let them marry; for it is better to marry than to burn.* This is God's remedy for lust. The fire may be quenched by the means he has appointed. And marriage, with all its inconveniences, is much better than to burn with impure and lustful desires. *Marriage is honourable in all;* but it is a duty in those who cannot contain nor conquer those inclinations.

10 And unto the married I command, *yet* not I, but the Lord, Let
not the wife depart from *her* husband: 11 But and if she depart, let
her remain unmarried, or be reconciled to *her* husband: and let not the
husband put away *his* wife. 12 But
to the rest speak I, not the Lord: If
any brother hath a wife that believeth
not, and she be pleased to dwell with
him, let him not put her away. 13
And the woman which hath a hus-

band that believeth not, and if he be
pleased to dwell with her, let her not
leave him. 14 For the unbelieving
husband is sanctified by the wife, and
the unbelieving wife is sanctified by
the husband: else were your children
unclean; but now are they holy. 15
But if the unbelieving depart, let him
depart. A brother or a sister is not
under bondage in such *cases:* but
God hath called us to peace. 16 For
what knowest thou, O wife, whether
thou shalt save *thy* husband? or how
knowest thou, O man, whether thou
shalt save *thy* wife?

In this paragraph the apostle gives them direction in a case which must be very frequent in that age of the world, especially among the Jewish converts; I mean whether they were to live with heathen relatives in a married state. Moses's law permitted divorce; and there was a famous instance in the Jewish state, when the people were obliged to put away their idolatrous wives, Ezra x. 3. This might move a scruple in many minds, whether converts to Christianity were not bound to put away or desert their mates, continuing infidels. Concerning this matter the apostle here gives direction. And,

I. In general, he tells them that marriage, by Christ's command, is for life; and therefore those who are married must not think of separation. The wife *must not depart from the husband* (*v.* 10), nor the *husband put away his wife, v.* 11. This *I command,* says the apostle; *yet not I, but the Lord.* Not that he commanded any thing of his own head, or upon his own authority. Whatever he commanded was the Lord's command, dictated by his Spirit and enjoined by his authority. But his meaning is that the Lord himself, with his own mouth, had forbidden such separations, Matt. v. 32; xix. 9; Mark x. 11; Luke xvi. 18. Note, Man and wife cannot separate at pleasure, nor dissolve, when they will, their matrimonial bonds and relation. They must not separate for any other cause than what Christ allows. And therefore the apostle advises that if any woman had been separated, either by a voluntary act of her own or by an act of her husband, she should continue unmarried, and seek reconciliation with her husband, that they might cohabit again. Note, Husbands and wives should not quarrel at all, or should be quickly reconciled. They are bound to each other for life. The divine law allows of no separation. They cannot throw off the burden, and therefore should set their shoulders to it, and endeavour to make it as light to each other as they can.

II. He brings the general advice home to the case of such as had an unbelieving mate (*v.* 12): *But to the rest speak I, not the Lord;* that is, the Lord had not so expressly spoken to this case as to the former divorce. It does not mean that the apostle spoke without authority from the Lord, or decided this case by his own wisdom, without the inspiration of the Holy Ghost. He closes this subject with a declaration to the contrary (*v.* 40), I think *also that I have the Spirit of God.* But, having thus prefaced his advice, we may attend,

1. To the advice itself, which is that if an unbelieving husband or wife were pleased to dwell with a Christian relative, the other should not separate. The husband should not put away an unbelieving wife, nor the wife leave an unbelieving husband, *v.* 12, 13. The Christian calling did not dissolve the marriage covenant, but bind it the faster, by bringing it back to the original institution, limiting it to two persons, and binding them together for life. The believer is not by faith in Christ loosed from matrimonial bonds to an unbeliever, but is at once bound and made apt to be a better relative. But, though a believing wife or husband should not separate from an unbelieving mate, yet, if the unbelieving relative desert the believer, and no means can reconcile to a cohabitation, in such *a case a brother or sister is not in bondage* (*v.* 15), not tied up to the unreasonable humour, and bound servilely to follow or cleave to the malicious deserter, or not bound to live unmarried after all proper means for reconciliation have been tried, at least if the deserter contract another marriage or be guilty of adultery, which was a very easy supposition, because a very common instance among the heathen inhabitants of Corinth. In such a case the deserted person must be free to marry again, and it is granted on all hands. And some think that such a malicious desertion is as much a dissolution of the marriage-covenant as death itself. For how is it possible that *the two shall be one flesh* when the one is maliciously bent to part from or put away the other? Indeed, the deserter seems still bound by the matrimonial contract; and therefore the apostle says (*v.* 11), *If the woman depart from her husband* upon account of his infidelity, *let her remain unmarried.* But the deserted party seems to be left more at liberty (I mean supposing all the proper means have been used to reclaim the deserter, and other circumstances make it necessary) to marry another person. It does not seem reasonable that they should be still bound, when it is rendered impossible to perform conjugal duties or enjoy conjugal comforts, through the mere fault of their mate: in such a case marriage would be a state of servitude indeed. But, whatever liberty be indulged Christians in such a case as this, they are not allowed, for the mere infidelity of a husband or wife, to separate; but, if the unbeliever be willing, they should

continue in the relation, and cohabit as those who are thus related. This is the apostle's general direction.

2. We have here the reasons of this advice. (1.) Because the relation or state is sanctified by the holiness of either party: *For the unbelieving husband is sanctified by the wife, and the unbelieving wife by the husband* (*v.* 14), or *hath been sanctified.* The relation itself, and the conjugal use of each other, are sanctified to the believer. *To the pure all things are pure,* Tit. i. 15. Marriage is a divine institution; it is a compact for life, by God's appointment. Had converse and congress with unbelievers in that relation defiled the believer, or rendered him or her offensive to God, the ends of marriage would have been defeated, and the comforts of it in a manner destroyed, in the circumstances in which Christians then were. But the apostle tells them that, though they were yoked with unbelievers, yet, if they themselves were holy, marriage was to them a holy state, and marriage comforts, even with an unbelieving relative, were sanctified enjoyments. It was no more displeasing to God for them to continue to live as they did before, with their unbelieving or heathen relation, than if they had become converts together. If one of the relatives had become holy, nothing of the duties or lawful comforts of the married state could defile them, and render them displeasing to God, though the other were a heathen. He is sanctified for the wife's sake. She is sanctified for the husband's sake. Both are one flesh. He is to be reputed clean who is one flesh with her that is holy, and *vice versâ: Else were your children unclean, but now are they holy* (*v.* 14), that is, they would be heathen, out of the pale of the church and covenant of God. They would not be of the holy seed (as the Jews are called, Isa. vi. 13), but common and unclean, in the same sense as heathens in general were styled in the apostle's vision, Acts x. 28. This way of speaking is according to the dialect of the Jews, among whom a child begotten by parents yet heathens, was said to be begotten *out of holiness;* and a child begotten by parents made proselytes was said to be begotten *intra sanctitatem—within the holy enclosure.* Thus Christians are called commonly *saints;* such they are by profession, separated to be a peculiar people of God, and as such distinguished from the world; and therefore the children born to Christians, though married to unbelievers, are not to be reckoned as part of the world, but of the church, a holy, not a common and unclean seed. "Continue therefore to live even with unbelieving relatives; for, if you are holy, the relation is so, the state is so, you may make a holy use even of an unbelieving relative, in conjugal duties, and your seed will be holy too." What a comfort is this, where both relatives are believers! (2.) Another reason is that *God hath called Christians to peace, v.* 15. The Christian religion obliges us to act peaceably in all relations, natural and civil. We are bound, *as much as in us lies, to live peaceably with all men* (Rom. xii. 18), and therefore surely to promote the peace and comfort of our nearest relatives, those with whom we are one flesh, nay, though they should be infidels. Note, It should be the labour and study of those who are married to make each other as easy and happy as possible. (3.) A third reason is that it is possible for the believing relative to be an instrument of the other's salvation (*v.* 16): *What knowest thou, O wife, whether thou shalt save thy husband?* Note, It is the plain duty of those in so near a relation to seek the salvation of those to whom they are related. "Do not separate. There is other duty now called for. The conjugal relation calls for the most close and endeared affection; it is a contract for life. And should a Christian desert a mate, when an opportunity offers to give the most glorious proof of love? Stay, and labour heartily for the conversion of thy relative. Endeavour to save a soul. Who knows but this may be the event? It is not impossible. And, though there be no great probability, saving a soul is so good and glorious a service that the bare possibility should put one on exerting one's self." Note, Mere possibility of success should be a sufficient motive with us to use our diligent endeavours for saving the souls of our relations. "*What know I but I may save his soul?* should move me to attempt it."

17 But as God hath distributed to
every man, as the Lord hath called
every one, so let him walk. And so
ordain I in all churches. 18 Is any
man called being circumcised? let
him not become uncircumcised. Is
any called in uncircumcision? let him
not be circumcised. 29 Circumcision
is nothing, and uncircumcision is nothing, but the keeping of the commandments of God. 20 Let every
man abide in the same calling wherein
he was called. 21 Art thou called
being a servant? care not for it: but
if thou mayest be made free, use *it*
rather. 22 For he that is called in
the Lord, *being* a servant, is the
Lord's freeman: likewise also he that
is called, *being* free, is Christ's servant. 23 Ye are bought with a price;
be not ye the servants of men. 24
Brethren, let every man, wherein he
is called, therein abide with God.

Here the apostle takes occasion to advise them to continue in the state and condition in which Christianity found them, and in which they became converts to it. And here,

I. He lays down this rule in general—*as God hath distributed to every one.* Note, Our states and circumstances in this world are distributions of divine Providence. *This fixes the bounds of men's habitations,* and orders their steps. God setteth up and pulleth down. And again, *As the Lord hath called every one, so let him walk.* Whatever his circumstances or condition was when he was converted to Christianity, let him abide therein, and suit his conversation to it. The rules of Christianity reach every condition. And in every state a man may live so as to be a credit to it. Note, It is the duty of every Christian to suit his behaviour to his condition and the rules of religion, to be content with his lot, and conduct himself in his rank and place as becomes a Christian. The apostle adds that this was a general rule, to be observed at all times and in all places: *So ordain I in all churches.*

II. He specifies particular cases; as, 1. That of circumcision. *Is any man called being circumcised? Let him not be uncircumcised. Is any man called being uncircumcised? Let him not be circumcised.* It matters not whether a man be a Jew or Gentile, within the covenant of peculiarity made with Abraham or without it. He who is converted, being a Jew, has no need to give himself uneasiness upon that head, and wish himself uncircumcised. Nor is he who is converted from Gentilism under an obligation to be circumcised: nor should he be concerned because he wants that mark of distinction which did heretofore belong to the people of God. For, as the apostle goes on, *circumcision is nothing, and uncircumcision is nothing, but keeping the commandments of God, v.* 19. In point of acceptance with God, it is neither here nor there whether men be circumcised or not. Note, It is practical religion, sincere obedience to the commands of God, on which the gospel lays stress. External observances without internal piety are as nothing. Therefore let every man abide *in the calling* (the state) *wherein he was called, v.* 20. 2. That of servitude and freedom. It was common in that age of the world for many to be in a state of slavery, bought and sold for money, and so the property of those who purchased them. "Now," says the apostle, "*art thou called being a servant? Care not for it.* Be not over-solicitous about it. It is not inconsistent with thy duty, profession, or hopes, as a Christian. *Yet, if thou mayest be made free, use it rather,*" *v.* 21. There are many conveniences in a state of freedom above that of servitude: a man has more power over himself, and more command of his time, and is not under the control of another lord; and therefore liberty is the more eligible state. But men's outward condition does neither hinder nor promote their acceptance with God. For he that is called *being a servant is the Lord's freed-man—ἀπελεύθερος, as he that is called being free is the Lord's servant.* Though he be not discharged from his master's service, he is freed from the dominion and vassalage of sin. Though he be not enslaved to Christ, yet he is bound to yield himself up wholly to his pleasure and service; and yet that service is perfect freedom. Note, Our comfort and happiness depend on what we are to Christ, not what we are in the world. The goodness of our outward condition does not discharge us from the duties of Christianity, nor the badness of it debar us from Christian privileges. He who is a slave may yet be a Christian freeman; he who is a freeman may yet be Christ's servant. He is bought with a price, and should not therefore be the servant of man. Not that he must quit the service of his master, or not take all proper measures to please him (this were to contradict the whole scope of the apostle's discourse); but he must not be so the servant of men but that Christ's will must be obeyed, and regarded, more than his master's. He has paid a much dearer price for him, and has a much fuller property in him. He is to be served and obeyed without limitation or reserve. Note, The servants of Christ should be at the absolute command of no other master besides himself, should serve no man, any further than is consistent with their duty to him. *No man can serve two masters.* Though some understand this passage of persons being bought out of slavery by the bounty and charity of fellow-Christians; and read the passage thus, *Have you been redeemed out of slavery with a price? Do not again become enslaved;* just as before he had advised that, if in slavery they had any prospect of being made free, they should choose it rather. This meaning the words will bear, but the other seems the more natural. See *ch.* vi. 20.

III. He sums up his advice: *Let every man wherein he is called abide therein with God, v.* 24. This is to be understood of the state wherein a man is converted to Christianity. No man should make his faith or religion an argument to break through any natural or civil obligations. He should quietly and comfortably abide in the condition in which he is; and this he may well do, when he may abide therein with God. Note, The special presence and favour of God are not limited to any outward condition or performance. He may enjoy it who is circumcised; and so may he who is uncircumcised. He who is bound may have it as well as he who is free. In this respect *there is neither Greek nor Jew, circumcision nor uncircumcision, barbarian nor Scythian, bond nor free,* Col. iii. 11. The favour of God is not bound.

25 Now concerning virgins I have no commandment of the Lord: yet I give my judgment, as one that hath obtained mercy of the Lord to be faithful. 26 I suppose therefore that

this is good for the present distress,
I say, that *it is* good for a man so to
be. 27 Art thou bound unto a wife?
seek not to be loosed. Art thou
loosed from a wife? seek not a wife.
28 But and if thou marry, thou hast
not sinned; and if a virgin marry, she
hath not sinned. Nevertheless such
shall have trouble in the flesh: but
I spare you. 29 But this I say,
brethren, the time *is* short: it remaineth, that both they that have
wives be as though they had none;
30 And they that weep, as though
they wept not; and they that rejoice,
as though they rejoiced not; and they
that buy, as though they possessed
not; 31 And they that use this
world, as not abusing *it*: for the
fashion of this world passeth away.
32 But I would have you without
carefulness. He that is unmarried
careth for the things that belong to
the Lord, how he may please the
Lord: 33 But he that is married
careth for the things that are of the
world, how he may please *his* wife.
34 There is difference *also* between a
wife and a virgin. The unmarried
woman careth for the things of the
Lord, that she may be holy both in
body and in spirit: but she that is
married careth for the things of the
world, how she may please *her* husband. 35 And this I speak for your
own profit; not that I may cast a
snare upon you, but for that which is
comely, and that ye may attend upon
the Lord without distraction.

The apostle here resumes his discourse, and gives directions to virgins how to act, concerning which we may take notice,

I. Of the manner wherein he introduces them: "*Now concerning virgins I have no commandment of the Lord, v.* 25. I have no express and universal law delivered by the Lord himself concerning celibacy; but *I give my judgment, as one who hath obtained mercy of the Lord to be faithful*," namely, in the apostleship. He acted faithfully, and therefore his direction was to be regarded as a rule of Christ: for he gave judgment as one who was a faithful apostle of Christ. Though Christ had before delivered no universal law about that matter, he now gives direction by an inspired apostle, one who had obtained mercy of the Lord to be faithful. Note, Faithfulness in the ministry is owing to the grace and mercy of Christ. It is what Paul was ready to acknowledge upon all occasions: *I laboured more abundantly than they all; yet not I, but the grace of God which was with me, ch.* xv. 10. And it is a great mercy which those obtain from God who prove faithful in the ministry of his word, either ordinary or extraordinary.

II. The determination he gives, which, considering the present distress, was that a state of celibacy was preferable: *It is good for a man so to be*, that is, *to be single. I suppose*, says the apostle, or it is my opinion. It is worded with modesty, but delivered, notwithstanding, with apostolical authority. It is not the mere opinion of a private man, but the very determination of the Spirit of God in an apostle, though it be thus spoken. And it was thus delivered to give it the more weight. Those that were prejudiced against the apostle might have rejected this advice had it been given with a mere authoritative air. Note, Ministers do not lose their authority by prudent condescensions. They must become all things to all men, that they may do them the more good. *This is good*, says he, *for the present distress*. Christians, at the first planting of their religion, were grievously persecuted. Their enemies were very bitter against them, and treated them very cruelly. They were continually liable to be tossed and hurried by persecution. This being the then state of things, he did not think it so advisable for Christians that were single to change conditions. The married state would bring more care and cumber along with it (*v.* 33, 34), and would therefore make persecution more terrible, and render them less able to bear it. Note, Christians, in regulating their conduct, should not barely consider what is lawful in itself, but what may be expedient for them.

III. Notwithstanding he thus determines, he is very careful to satisfy them that he does not condemn marriage in the gross, nor declare it unlawful. And therefore, though he says, "If thou *art loosed from a wife* (in a single state, whether bachelor or widower, virgin or widow) *do not seek a wife*, do not hastily change conditions;" yet he adds, "*If thou art bound to a wife, do not seek to be loosed.* It is thy duty to continue in the married relation, and do the duties of it." And though such, if they were called to suffer persecution, would find peculiar difficulties in it; yet, to avoid these difficulties, they must not cast off nor break through the bonds of duty. Duty must be done, and God trusted with events. But to neglect duty is the way to put ourselves out of the divine protection. He adds therefore, *If thou marry thou hast not sinned; or if a virgin marry skeh ath not sinned: but such shall have trouble in the flesh.* Marrying is not in itself a sin, but marrying at that time was likely to bring inconvenience upon them, and add to the calamities of the times; and therefore he thought it advisable and expedient that such as could contain should refrain from it; but adds that he would not lay celibacy on them as a yoke, nor, by seeming to urge it too far, draw them into any snare; and therefore says, *But I spare you.* Note, How opposite in this are the papist casuists to the apostle Paul! They forbid many to marry, and entangle them with vows of celibacy, whether they can bear the yoke or no.

IV. He takes this occasion to give general rules to all Christians to carry themselves with a holy indifferency towards the world, and every thing in it. 1. *As to relations:* Those *that had wives must be as though they had none;* that is, they must not set their hearts too much on the comforts of the relation; they must be as though they had none. They know not how soon they shall have none. This advice must be carried into every other relation. Those that have children should be as though they had none. Those that are their comfort now may prove their greatest cross. And soon may the flower of all comforts be cut down. 2. As to afflictions: *Those that weep must be as though they wept not;* that is, we must not be dejected too much with any of our afflictions, nor indulge ourselves in the sorrow of the world, but keep up a holy joy in God in the midst of all our troubles, so that even in sorrow the heart may be joyful, and the end of our grief may be gladness. *Weeping may endure for a night, but joy will come in the morning.* If we can but get to heaven at last, *all tears shall be wiped from our eyes;* and the prospect of it now should make us moderate our sorrows and refrain our tears. 3. As to worldly enjoyments: *Those that rejoice should be as though they rejoiced not;* that is, they should not take too great a complacency in any of their comforts. They must be moderate in their mirth, and sit loose to the enjoyments they most value. Here is not their rest, nor are these things their portion; and therefore their hearts should not be set on them, nor should they place their solace or satisfaction in them. 4. As to worldly traffic and employment: *Those that buy must be as though they possessed not.* Those that prosper in trade, increase in wealth, and purchase estates, should hold these possessions as though they held them not. It is but setting their hearts on that which is not (Prov. xxiii. 5) to do otherwise. Buying and possessing should not too much engage our minds. They hinder many people altogether from minding the better part. Purchasing land and trying oxen kept the guests invited from the wedding-supper, Luke xiv. 18, 19. And, when they do not altogether hinder men from minding their chief business, they do very much divert them from a close pursuit. Those are most likely to run so as to obtain the prize who ease their minds of all foreign cares and cumbrances. 5. As to all worldly concerns: *Those that use this world as not abusing it, v.* 31. The world may be used, but must not be abused. It is abused when it is not used to those purposes for which it is given, to honour God and do good to men—when, instead of being oil to the wheels of our obedience, it is made fuel to lust—when, instead of being a servant, it is made our master, our idol, and has that room in our affections which should be reserved for God. And there is great danger of abusing it in all these respects, if our hearts are too much set upon it. We must keep the world as much as may be out of our hearts, that we may not abuse it when we have it in our hands.

V. He enforces these advices with two reasons:—1. *The time is short, v.* 29. We have but little time to continue in this world; but a short season for possessing and enjoying worldly things; καιρὸς συνεσταλμένος. It is contracted, reduced to a narrow compass. It will soon be gone. It is just ready to be wrapped up in eternity, swallowed up of eternity. Therefore do not set your hearts on worldly enjoyments. Do not be overwhelmed with worldly cares and troubles. Possess what you must shortly leave without suffering yourselves to be possessed by it. Why should your hearts be much set on what you must quickly resign? 2. *The fashion of this world passeth away* (*v.* 31), σχῆμα—*the habit,* figure, appearance, of the world, passeth away. It is daily changing countenance. It is in a continual flux. It is not so much a world as the appearance of one. All is show, nothing solid in it; and it is transient show too, and will quickly be gone. How proper and powerful an argument is this to enforce the former advice! How irrational is it to be affected with the images, the fading and transient images, of a dream! *Surely man walketh in a vain show* (Ps. xxxix. 6), in an image, amidst the faint and vanishing appearances of things. And should he be deeply affected, or grievously afflicted, with such a scene?

VI. He presses his general advice by warning them against the embarrassment of worldly cares: *But I would have you without carefulness, v.* 32. Indeed to be careless is a fault; a wise concern about worldly interests is a duty; but to be careful, full of care, to have an anxious and perplexing care about them, is a sin. All that care which disquiets the mind, and distracts it in the worship of God, is evil; for God must *be attended upon without distraction, v.* 35. The whole mind should be engaged when God is worshipped. The work ceases while it diverts to any thing else, or is hurried and drawn hither and thither by foreign affairs and concerns. Those who are engaged in divine worship should attend to this very thing, should make it their whole business. But how is this possible when the mind is swallowed up of the cares of this life? Note, It is the wisdom of a Christian so to order his outward affairs, and choose such a condition in life, as to be without distracting cares, that he may attend upon the Lord with a mind at leisure and disengaged. This is the general maxim by which the apostle would have Christians govern themselves. In the application of it Christian prudence must direct. That condition of life is best for every man which is best for his soul, and keeps him most clear of the cares and snares of the world. By this maxim the apostle solves the case put to him by the Corinthians, whether it were advisable to marry? To this he says, That, by reason of the present distress, and it may be in general, at that time, when Christians were married to infidels, and perhaps under a necessity of being so, if married at all: I say, in these circumstances, to continue unmarried would be the way to free themselves from any cares and incumbrances, and allow them more vacation for the service of God. Ordinarily, the less care we have about the world the more freedom we have for the service of God. Now the married state at that time (if not at all times) did bring most worldly care along with it. *He that is married careth for the things of the world, that he may please his wife, v.* 33. *And she that is married careth for the things of the world, how she may please her husband.* But the unmarried man and woman mind the things of the Lord, that they may please the Lord, and be holy both in body and spirit, *v.* 32, 34. Not but the married person may be holy both in body and spirit too. Celibacy is not in itself a state of greater purity and sanctity than marriage; but the unmarried would be able to make religion more their business at that juncture, because they would have less distraction from worldly cares. Marriage is that condition of life that brings care along with it, though sometimes it brings more than at others. It is the constant care of those in that relation to please each other; though this is more difficult to do at some reasons, and in some cases, than in others. At that season, therefore, the apostle advises that those who were single should abstain from marriage, if they were under no necessity to change conditions. And, where the same reason is plain at other times, the rule is as fit to be observed. And the very same rule must determine persons for marriage where there is the same reason, that is, if in the unmarried state persons are likely to be more distracted in the service of God than if they were married, which is a case supposable in many respects. This is the general rule, which every one's discretion must apply to his own particular case; and by it should he endeavour to determine, whether it be for marriage or against. That condition of life should be chosen by the Christian in which it is most likely he will have the best helps, and the fewest hindrances, in the service of God and the affairs of his own salvation.

36 But if any man think that he
behaveth himself uncomely toward
his virgin, if she pass the flower of
her age, and need so require, let him
do what he will, he sinneth not: let
them marry. 37 Nevertheless he
that standeth stedfast in his heart,
having no necessity, but hath power
over his own will, and hath so decreed in his heart that he will keep
his virgin, doeth well. 38 So then
he that giveth *her* in marriage doeth
well; but he that giveth *her* not in
marriage doeth better.

In this passage the apostle is commonly supposed to give advice about the disposal of children in marriage, upon the principle of his former determination. In this view the general meaning is plain. It was in that age, and those parts of the world, and especially among the Jews, reckoned a disgrace for a woman to remain unmarried past a certain number of years: it gave a suspicion of somewhat that was not for her reputation. "Now," says the apostle, "if any man thinks he behaves unhandsomely towards his daughter, and that it is not for her credit to remain unmarried, when she is of full age, and that upon this principle it is needful to dispose of her in marriage, he may use his pleasure. It is no sin in him to dispose of her to a suitable mate. But if a man has determined in himself to keep her a virgin, and stands to this determination, and is under no necessity to dispose of her in marriage, but is at liberty, with her consent, to pursue his purpose, he does well in keeping her a virgin. In short, he that gives her in marriage does well; but he that keeps her single, if she can be easy and innocent in such a state, does what is better; that is, more convenient for her in the present state of things, if not at all times and seasons." Note, 1. Children should be at the disposal of their parents, and not dispose of themselves in marriage. Yet, 2. Parents should consult their children's inclinations, both to marriage in general and to the person in particular, and not reckon they have uncontrollable power to do with them, and dictate to them, as they please. 3. It is our duty not only to consider what is lawful, but in many cases, at least, what is fit to be done, before we do it.

But I think the apostle is here continuing his former discourse, and advising unmarried persons, who are at their own disposal, what to do, the man's virgin being meant of his virginity. Τηρεῖν τὴν ἑαυτοῦ παρθένον seems to be rather meant of preserving his own virginity than keeping his daughter a virgin, though it be altogether uncommon to use the word in this sense. Several other reasons may be seen in Locke and Whitby, by those who will consult them. And it was a common matter of reproach among Jews and civilized heathens, for a man to continue single beyond such a term of years, though all did not agree in limiting the single life to the same term. The general meaning of the apostle is the same, that it was no sin to marry, if a man thought there was a necessity upon him, to avoid popular reproach, much less to avoid the hurrying fervours of lust. But he that was in his own power, stood firm in his purpose, and found himself under no necessity to marry, would, at that season, and in the circumstances of Christians at that time, at least, make a choice every way most for his own conveniency, ease, and advantage, as to his spiritual concerns. And it is highly expedient, if not a duty, for Christians to be guided by such a consideration.

39 The wife is bound by the law as long as her husband liveth; but if her husband be dead, she is at liberty to be married to whom she will; only in the Lord. 40 But she is happier if she so abide, after my judgment: and I think also that I have the Spirit of God.

The whole is here closed up with advice to widows: *As long as the husband liveth the wife is bound by the law*, confined to one husband, and bound to continue and cohabit with him. Note, The marriage-contract is for life; death only can annul the bond. *But, the husband being dead, she is at liberty to marry whom she will.* There is no limitation by God's law to be married only for such a number of times. It is certain, from this passage, that second marriages are not unlawful; for then the widow could not be at liberty to marry whom she pleased, nor to marry a second time at all. But the apostle asserts she has such a liberty, when her husband is dead, only with a limitation that *she marry in the Lord.* In our choice of relations, and change of conditions, we should always have an eye to God. Note, Marriages are likely to have God's blessing only when they are made in the Lord, when persons are guided by the fear of God, and the laws of God, and act in dependence on the providence of God, in the change and choice of a mate—when they can look up to God, and sincerely seek his direction, and humbly hope for his blessing upon their conduct. *But she is happier*, says the apostle, *if she so abide* (that is, continue a widow) *in my judgment; and I think I have the Spirit of God, v.* 40. At this juncture, at least, if not ordinarily, it will be much more for the peace and quiet of such, and give them less hindrance in the service of God, to continue unmarried. And this, he tells them, was by inspiration of the Spirit. "Whatever your false apostles may think of me, I think, and have reason to know, that I have the Spirit of God." Note, Change of condition in marriage is so important a matter that it ought not to be made but upon due deliberation, after careful consideration of circumstances, and upon very probable grounds, at least, that it will be a change to advantage in our spiritual concerns.

CHAP. VIII.

The apostle, in this chapter, answers another case proposed to him by some of the Corinthians, about eating those things that had been sacrificed to idols. I. He hints at the occasion of this case, and gives a caution against too high an esteem of their knowledge, ver. 1—3. II. He asserts the vanity of idols, the unity of the Godhead, and the sole mediation of Christ between God and man, ver. 4—6. III. He tells them that upon supposition that it were lawful in itself to eat of things offered to idols (for that they themselves are nothing), yet regard must be had to the weakness of Christian brethren, and nothing done that would lay a stumbling-block before them, and occasion their sin and destruction, ver. 7, to the end.

NOW as touching things offered unto idols, we know that we all have knowledge. Knowledge puffeth up, but charity edifieth. 2 And if any man think that he knoweth any thing, he knoweth nothing yet as he ought to know. 3 But if any man love God, the same is known of him.

The apostle comes here to the case of things that had been offered to idols, concerning which some of them sought satisfaction: a case that frequently occurred in that age of Christianity, when the church of Christ was among the heathen, and the Israel of God must live among the Canaanites. For the better understanding of it, it must be observed that it was a custom among the heathens to make feasts on their sacrifices, and not only to eat themselves, but invite their friends to partake with them. These were usually kept in the temple, where the sacrifice was offered (*v.* 10), and, if any thing was left when the feast ended, it was usual to carry away a portion to their friends; what remained, after all, belonged to the priests, who sometimes sold it in the markets. See *ch.* x. 25. Nay, feasts, as Athenæus informs us, were always accounted, among the heathen, sacred and religious things, so that they were wont to sacrifice before all their feasts; and it was accounted a very profane thing among them, ἄθυτα ἐσθίειν, to eat at their private tables any meat whereof they had not first sacrificed on such occasions. In this circumstance of things, while Christians lived among idolaters, had many relations and friends that were such, with whom they must keep up acquaintance and maintain good neighbourhood, and therefore have occasion to eat at their tables, what should they do if any thing that had been sacrificed should be set before them? What, if they should be invited to feast with them in their temples? It seems as if some of the Corinthians had imbibed an opinion that even this might be done, because they knew an idol was nothing in the world, *v.* 4. The apostle seems to answer more directly to the case (*ch.* x.), and here to argue, upon supposition of their being right in this thought, against their abuse of their liberty to the prejudice of others; but he plainly condemns such liberty in *ch.* x. The apostle introduces his discourse with some remarks about knowledge that seem to carry in them a censure of such pretences to knowledge as I have mentioned: *We know,* says the apostle, *that we all have knowledge* (*v.* 1); as if he had said, "You who take such liberty are not the only knowing persons; we who abstain know as much as you of the vanity of idols, and that they are nothing; but we know too that the liberty you take is very culpable, and that even lawful liberty must be used with charity and not to the prejudice of weaker brethren. *Knowledge puffeth up, but charity edifieth, v.* 1. Note, 1. The preference of charity to conceited knowledge. That is best which is fitted to do the greatest good. Knowledge, or at least a high conceit of it, is very apt to swell the mind, to fill it with wind, and so puff it up. This tends to no good to ourselves, but in many instances is much to the hurt of others. But true love, and tender regard to our brethren, will put us upon consulting their interest, and acting as may be for their edification. Observe, 2. That there is no evidence of ignorance more common than a conceit of knowledge: *If any man think that he knoweth any thing, he knoweth nothing yet as he ought to know.* He that knows most best understands his own ignorance, and the imperfection of human knowledge. He that imagines himself a knowing man, and is vain and conceited on this imagination, has reason to suspect that he knows nothing aright, *nothing as he ought to know it.* Note, It is one thing to know truth, and another to know it as we ought, so as duly to improve our knowledge. Much may be known when nothing is known to any good purpose, when neither ourselves nor others are the better for our knowledge. And those who think they know any thing, and grow vain hereupon, are of all men most likely to make no good use of their knowledge; neither themselves nor others are likely to be benefited by it. *But,* adds the apostle, *if any man love God, the same is known* of God. If any man love God, and is thereby influenced to love his neighbour, the same is known of God; that is, as some understand it, is made by him to know, is taught of God. Note, Those that love God are most likely to be taught of God, and be made by him to know as they ought. Some understand it thus: He shall be approved of God; he will accept him and have pleasure in him. Note, The charitable person is most likely to have God's favour. Those who love God, and for his sake love their brethren and seek their welfare, are likely to be beloved of God; and how much better is it to be approved of God than to have a vain opinion of ourselves!

4 As concerning therefore the eating of those things that are offered
in sacrifice unto idols, we know that
an idol *is* nothing in the world, and
that *there is* none other God but one.
5 For though there be that are called
gods, whether in heaven or in earth,
(as there be gods many, and lords
many), 6 But to us *there is but* one
God, the Father, of whom *are* all
things, and we in him; and one Lord
Jesus Christ, by whom *are* all things,
and we by him.

In this passage he shows the vanity of idols: *As to the eating of things that have been sacrificed to idols, we know that an idol is nothing in the world;* or, there is no idol in the world; or, an idol can do nothing in the world: for the form of expression in the original is elliptical. The meaning in the general is, that heathen idols have no divinity in them; and therefore in the Old Testament they are commonly called *lies* and *vanities,* or *lying vanities.* They are merely imaginary gods, and many of them no better than imaginary beings; they have no power to pollute the creatures of God, and thereby render them unfit to be eaten by a child or servant of God. *Every creature of God is good, if it be received with thanksgiving,* 1 Tim. iv. 4. It is not in the power of the vanities of the heathens to change its nature.—*And there is no other God but one.* Heathen idols are not gods, nor to be owned and respected as gods, for there is no other God but one. Note, The unity of the Godhead is a fundamental principle in Christianity, and in all right religion. The gods of the heathens must be nothing in the world, must have no divinity in them, nothing of real godhead belonging to them; for there is no other God but one. Others may be called gods: *There are that are called gods, in heaven and earth, gods many, and lords many;* but they are falsely thus called. The heathens had many such, some in heaven and some on earth, celestial deities, that were of highest rank and repute among them, and terrestrial ones, men made into gods, that were to mediate for men with the former, and were deputed by them to preside over earthly affairs. These are in scripture commonly called *Baalim.* They had gods of higher and lower degree; nay, many in each order: *gods many, and lords many;* but all titular deities and mediators: so called, but not such in truth. All their divinity and mediation were imaginary. For, 1. *To us there is but one God,* says the apostle, *the Father, of whom are all things, and we in or for him.* We Christians are better informed; we well know there is but one God, the fountain of being, the author of all things, maker, preserver, and governor of the whole world, of whom and for whom are all things. Not one God to govern one part of mankind, or one rank and order of men, and another to govern another. One God made all, and therefore has power over all. All things are of him, and we, and all things else, are for him. Called the *Father* here, not in contradistinction to the other persons of the sacred Trinity, and to exclude them from the Godhead, but in contradistinction to all creatures that were made by God, and whose formation is attributed to each of these three in other places of scripture, and not appropriated to the Father alone. God the Father, as *Fons et fundamentum Trinitatis—as the first person in the Godhead, and the original of the other two*, stands here for the Deity, which yet comprehends all three, the name God being sometimes in scripture ascribed to the Father, κατ' ἐξοχὴν, or *by way of eminency*, because he is *fons et principium Deitatis* (as Calvin observes), *the fountain of the Deity* in the other two, they having it by communication from him: so that there is but one God the Father, and yet the Son is God too, but is not another God, the Father, with his Son and Spirit, being the one God, but not without them, or so as to exclude them from the Godhead. 2. There is to us but one Lord, one Mediator between God and men, even Jesus Christ. Not many mediators, as the heathen imagined, but one only, by whom all things were created and do consist, and to whom all our hope and happiness are owing—the man Christ Jesus; but a man in personal union with the divine Word, or God the Son. This very man hath God made both Lord and Christ, Acts ii. 36. Jesus Christ, in his human nature and mediatorial state, has a delegated power, a name given him, though above every name, that at his name every knee should bow, and every tongue confess that he is Lord. And thus he is the only Lord, and only Mediator, that Christians acknowledge, the only person who comes between God and sinners, administers the world's affairs under God, and mediates for men with God. All the lords of this sort among heathens are merely imaginary ones. Note, It is the great privilege of us Christians that we know the true God, and true Mediator between God and man: *the true God, and Jesus Christ whom he hath sent*, John xvii. 3.

7 Howbeit *there is* not in every
man that knowledge: for some with
conscience of the idol unto this hour
eat *it* as a thing offered unto an idol;
and their conscience being weak is
defiled. 8 But meat commendeth us
not to God: for neither, if we eat, are
we the better; neither, if we eat not,
are we the worse. 9 But take heed
lest by any means this liberty of your's
become a stumblingblock to them
that are weak. 10 For if any man
see thee which hast knowledge sit at
meat in the idol's temple, shall not the
conscience of him which is weak be
emboldened to eat those things which
are offered to idols; 11 And through
thy knowledge shall the weak brother
perish, for whom Christ died? 12
But when ye sin so against the brethren, and wound their weak conscience, ye sin against Christ. 13
Wherefore, if meat make my brother
to offend, I will eat no flesh while the
world standeth, lest I make my brother to offend.

The apostle, having granted, and indeed confirmed, the opinion of some among the Corinthians, that idols were nothing, proceeds now to show them that their inference from this assumption was not just, namely, that therefore they might go into the idol-temple, and eat of the sacrifices, and feast there with their heathen neighbours. He does not indeed here so much insist upon the unlawfulness of the thing in itself as the mischief such freedom might do to weaker Christians, persons that had not the same measure of knowledge with these pretenders. And here,

I. He informs them that every Christian man, at that time, was not so fully convinced and persuaded that an idol was nothing: *Howbeit, there is not in every man this knowledge; for some, with conscience of the idol, unto this hour, eat it as a thing offered unto an idol:* with conscience of the idol; that is, some confused veneration for it. Though they were converts to Christianity, and professed the true religion, they were not perfectly cured of the old leaven, but retained an unaccountable respect for the idols they had worshipped before. Note, Weak Christians may be ignorant, or have but a confused knowledge of the greatest and plainest truths. Such were those of the one God and one Mediator. And yet some of those who were turned from heathenism to Christianity among the Corinthians seem to have retained a veneration for their idols, utterly irreconcilable with those great principles; so that when an opportunity offered to eat things offered to idols they did not abstain, to testify their abhorrence of idolatry, nor eat with a professed contempt of the idol, by declaring they looked upon it to be nothing; and *so their conscience, being weak, was defiled;* that is, they contracted guilt; they ate out of respect to the idol, with an imagination that it had something divine in it, and so committed idolatry: whereas the design of the gospel was to turn men from dumb idols to the living God. They were weak in their understanding, not thoroughly apprized of the vanity of idols; and, while they ate what was sacrificed to them out of veneration for them, contracted the guilt of idolatry, and so greatly polluted themselves. This seems to be the sense of the place; though some understand it of weak Christians defiling themselves by eating what was offered to an idol with an apprehension that thereby it became unclean, and made those so in a moral sense who should eat it, every one not having a knowledge that the idol was nothing, and therefore that it could not render what was offered to it in this sense unclean. Note, We should be careful to do nothing that may occasion weak Christians to defile their consciences.

II. He tells them that mere eating and drinking had nothing in them virtuous nor criminal, nothing that could make them better nor worse, pleasing nor displeasing to God: *Meat commendeth us not to God; for neither if we eat are we the better, nor if we eat not are we the worse*, *v.* 8. It looks as if some of the Corinthians made a merit of their eating what had been offered to idols, and that in their very temples too (*v.* 10), because it plainly showed that they thought the idols nothing. But eating and drinking are in themselves actions indifferent. It matters little what we eat. What goes into the man of this sort neither purifies nor defiles. Flesh offered to idols may in itself be as proper for food as any other; and the bare eating, or forbearing to eat, has no virtue in it. Note, It is a gross mistake to think that distinction of food will make any distinction between men in God's account. Eating this food, and forbearing that, have nothing in them to recommend a person to God.

III. He cautions them against abusing their liberty, the liberty they thought they had in this matter. For that they mistook this matter, and had no allowance to sit at meat in the idol's temple, seems plain from *ch.* x. 20, &c. But the apostle argues here that, even upon the supposition that they had such power, they must be cautious how they use it; it might be a *stumbling-block to the weak* (*v.* 9), it might occasion their falling into idolatrous actions, perhaps their falling off from Christianity and revolting again to heathenism. "If a man see thee, who hast knowledge (hast superior understanding to his, and hereupon conceitest that thou hast a liberty to sit at meat, or feast, in an idol's temple, because an idol, thou sayest, is nothing), shall not one who is less thoroughly informed in this matter, and thinks an idol something, be emboldened to eat what was offered to the idol, not as common food, but sacrifice, and thereby be guilty of idolatry?" Such an occasion of falling they should be careful of laying before their weak brethren, whatever liberty or power they themselves had. The apostle backs this caution with two considerations:—1. The danger that might accrue to weak brethren, even those weak brethren for whom Christ died. We must deny ourselves even what is lawful rather than occasion their stumbling, and endanger their souls (*v.* 11): *Through thy knowledge shall thy weak brother perish, for whom Christ died?* Note, Those whom Christ hath redeemed with his most precious blood should be very precious and dear to us. If he had such compassion as to die for them, that they might not perish, we should have so much compassion for them as to deny ourselves, for their sakes, in various instances, and not use our liberty to their hurt, to occasion their stumbling, or hazard their ruin. That man has very little of the spirit of the Redeemer who had rather his brother should perish than himself be abridged, in any respect, of his liberty. He who hath the Spirit of Christ in him will love those whom Christ loved, so as to die for them, and will study to promote their spiritual and eternal warfare, and shun every thing that would unnecessarily grieve them, and much more every thing that would be likely to occasion their stumbling, or falling into sin. 2. The hurt done to them Christ takes as done to himself: *When you sin so against the weak brethren and wound their consciences, you sin against Christ, v.* 12. Note, Injuries done to Christians are injuries to Christ, especially to babes in Christ, to weak Christians; and most of all, involving them in guilt: wounding their consciences is wounding him. He has a particular care of the lambs of the flock: *He gathers them in his arm and carries them in his bosom,* Isa. xl. 11. Strong Christians should be very careful to avoid what will offend weak ones, or lay a stumbling-block in their way. Shall we be void of compassion for those to whom Christ has shown so much? Shall we sin against Christ who suffered for us? Shall we set ourselves to defeat his gracious designs, and help to ruin those whom he died to save?

IV. He enforces all with his own example (*v.* 13): *Wherefore if meat make my brother to offend I will eat no flesh while the world standeth, lest I make my brother to offend.* He does not say that he will never eat more. This were to destroy himself, and to commit a heinous sin, to prevent the sin and fall of a brother. Such evil must not be done that good may come of it. But, though it was necessary to eat, it was not necessary to eat flesh. And therefore, rather than occasion sin in a brother, he would abstain from it as long as he lived. He had such a value for the soul of his brother that he would willingly deny himself in a matter of liberty, and forbear any particular food, which he might have lawfully eaten and might like to eat, rather than lay a stumbling-block in a weak brother's way, and occasion him to sin, by following his example, without being clear in his mind whether it were lawful or no. Note, We should be very tender of doing any thing that may be an occasion of stumbling to others, though it may be innocent in itself. Liberty is valuable, but the weakness of a brother should induce, and sometimes bind, us to waive it. We must not rigorously claim nor use our own rights, to the hurt and ruin of a brother's soul, and so to the injury of our Redeemer, who died for him. When it is certainly foreseen that my doing what I may forbear will occasion a fellow-christian to do what he ought to forbear, I shall offend, scandalize, or lay a stumbling-block in his way, which to do is a sin, however lawful the thing itself be which is done. And, if we must be so careful not to occasion other men's sins, how careful should we be to avoid sin ourselves! If we must not endanger other men's souls, how much should we be concerned not to destroy our own!

CHAP IX.

In this chapter the apostle seems to answer some cavils against himself. I. He asserts his apostolical mission and authority, and gives in his success among them as a testimony to it, ver. 1, 2. II. He claims a right to subsist by his ministry, and defends it by several arguments from natural reason and the Mosaical law, and asserts it also to be a constitution of Christ, ver. 3—14 III. He shows that he had willingly waived this privilege and power for their benefit, ver. 15—18. IV. He specifies several other things, in which he had denied himself for the sake of other men's spiritual interest and salvation, ver. 19—23. And, V. Concludes his argument by showing what animated him to this course, even the prospect of an incorruptible crown, ver. 24, to the end.

AM I not an apostle? am I not
free? have I not seen Jesus
Christ our Lord? are not ye my work
in the Lord? 2 If I be not an
apostle unto others, yet doubtless I
am to you: for the seal of mine
apostleship are ye in the Lord.

Blessed Paul, in the work of his ministry, not only met with opposition from those without, but discouragement from those within. He was under reproach; false brethren questioned his apostleship, and were very industrious to lessen his character and sink his reputation; particularly here at Corinth, a place to which he had been instrumental in doing much good, and from which he had deserved well; and yet there were those among them who upon these heads created him great uneasiness. Note, It is no strange nor new thing for a minister to meet with very unkind returns for great good-will to a people, and diligent and successful services among them. Some among the Corinthians questioned, if they did not disown, his apostolical character. To their cavils he here answers, and in such a manner as to set forth himself as a remarkable example of that self-denial, for the good of others, which he had been recommending in the former chapter. And, 1. He asserts his apostolical mission and character: *Am I not an apostle? Have I not seen Jesus Christ our Lord?* To be a witness of his resurrection was one great branch of the apostolical charge. "Now," says Paul, "have not I seen the Lord, though not immediately after his resurrection, yet since his ascent?" See *ch.* iv. 8. "*Am I not free?* Have I not the same commission, and charge, and powers, with the other apostles? What respect, or honour, or subsistence, can they challenge, which I am not at liberty to demand as well as they?" It was not because he had no right to live of the gospel that he maintained himself with his own hands, but for other reasons. 2 He offers the success of his ministry among them, and the good he had done to them, as a proof of his apostleship: *Are not you my work in the Lord?* Through the blessing of Christ on my labours, have not I raised a church among you? *The seal of my apostleship are you in the Lord.* Your conversion by my means is a confirmation from God of my mission." Note, The ministers of Christ should not think it strange to be put upon the proof of their ministry by some who have had experimental evidence of the power of it and the presence of God with it. 3. He justly upbraids the Corinthians with their disrespect: "*Doubtless, if I am not an apostle to others, I am so to you, v.* 2. I have laboured so long, and with so much success, among you, that you, above all others, should own and honour my character, and not call it in question." Note, It is no new thing for faithful ministers to meet with the worst treatment where they might expect the best. This church at Corinth had as much reason to believe, and as little reason to question, his apostolical mission, as any; they had as much reason, perhaps more than any church, to pay him respect. He had been instrumental in bringing them to the knowledge and faith of Christ; he laboured long among them, nearly two years, and he laboured to good purpose, *God having much people among them.* See Acts xviii. 10, 11. It was aggravated ingratitude for this people to call in question his authority.

3 Mine answer to them that do
examine me is this, 4 Have we not
power to eat and to drink? 5 Have
we not power to lead about a sister, a
wife, as well as other apostles, and *as*
the brethren of the Lord, and Cephas?
6 Or I only and Barnabas, have not
we power to forbear working? 7 Who
goeth a warfare any time at his own
charges? who planteth a vineyard,
and eateth not of the fruit thereof?
or who feedeth a flock, and eateth not
of the milk of the flock? 8 Say I
these things as a man? or saith not
the law the same also? 9 For it is
written in the law of Moses, Thou
shalt not muzzle the mouth of the ox
that treadeth out the corn. Doth God
take care for oxen? 10 Or saith he *it*
altogether for our sakes? For our
sakes, no doubt, *this* is written: that
he that plougheth should plough in
hope; and that he that thresheth in
hope should be partaker of his hope.

11 If we have sown unto you spiritual things, *is it* a great thing if we
shall reap your carnal things? 12 If
others be partakers of *this* power over
you, *are* not we rather? Nevertheless
we have not used this power; but
suffer all things, lest we should hinder
the gospel of Christ. 13 Do ye not
know that they which minister about
holy things live *of the things* of the
temple? and they which wait at the
altar are partakers with the altar?
14 Even so hath the Lord ordained
that they which preach the gospel
should live of the gospel.

Having asserted his apostolical authority, he proceeds to claim the rights belonging to his office, especially that of being maintained by it.

I. These he states, *v.* 3—6. "*My answer to those that do examine me* (that is, enquire into my authority, or the reasons of my conduct, if I am an apostle) is this: *Have we not power to eat and drink* (*v.* 4), or a right to maintenance? *Have we not power to lead about a sister, a wife, as well as other apostles, and the brethren of the Lord, and Cephas;* and, not only to be maintained ourselves, but have them maintained also? Though Paul was at that time single, he had a right to take a wife when he pleased, and to lead her about with him, and expect a maintenance for her, as well as himself, from the churches. Perhaps Barnabas had a wife, as the other apostles certainly had, and led them about with them. For that a wife is here to be understood by the *sister-woman*—ἀδελφὴν γυναῖκα, is plain from this, that it would have been utterly unfit for the apostles to have carried about women with them unless they were wives. The word implies that they had power over them, and could require their attendance on them, which none could have over any but wives or servants. Now the apostles, who worked for their bread, do not seem to have been in a capacity to buy or have servants to carry with them. Not to observe that it would have raised suspicion to have carried about even women-servants, and much more other women to whom they were not married, for which the apostles would never give any occasion. The apostle therefore plainly asserts he had a right to marry as well as other apostles, and claim a maintenance for his wife, nay, and his children too, if he had any, from the churches, without labouring with his own hands to procure it. *Or I only and Barnabas, have not we power to forbear working? v.* 6. In short, the apostle here claims a maintenance from the churches, both for him and his. This was due from them, and what he might claim.

II. He proceeds, by several arguments, to prove his claim. 1. From the common practice and expectations of mankind. Those who addict and give themselves up to any way of business in the world expect to live out of it. Soldiers expect to be paid for their service. Husbandmen and shepherds expect to get a livelihood out of their labours. If they plant vineyards, and dress and cultivate them, it is with expectation of fruit; if they feed a flock, it is with the expectation of being fed and clothed by it! *Who goeth a warfare at any time at his own charge? Who planteth a vineyard, and eateth not the fruit thereof? Who feedeth a flock, and eateth not the milk thereof? v.* 7—9. Note, It is very natural, and very reasonable, for ministers to expect a livelihood out of their labours. 2. He argues it out of the Jewish law: *Say I these things as a man? Or saith not the law the same also? v.* 8. Is this merely a dictate of common reason and according to common usage only? No, it is also consonant to the old law. God had therein ordered that the ox should not be muzzled while he was treading out the corn, nor hindered from eating while he was preparing the corn for man's use, and treading it out of the ear. But this law was not chiefly given out of God's regard to oxen, or concern for them, but to teach mankind that all due encouragement should be given to those who are employed by us, or labouring for our good—that the labourers should taste of the fruit of their labours. *Those who plough should plough in hope; and those who thresh in hope should be partakers of their hope, v.* 10. The law saith this about oxen for our sakes. Note, Those that lay themselves out to do our souls good should not have their mouths muzzled, but have food provided for them. 3. He argues from common equity: *If we have sown unto you spiritual things, is it a great thing if we shall reap your carnal things?* What they had sown was much better than they expected to reap. They had taught them the way to eternal life, and laboured heartily to put them in possession of it. It was no great matter, surely, while they were giving themselves up to this work, to expect a support of their own temporal life. They had been instruments of conveying to them the greater spiritual blessings; and had they no claim to as great a share in their carnal things as was necessary to subsist them? Note, Those who enjoy spiritual benefits by the ministry of the word should not grudge a maintenance to such as are employed in this work. If they have received a real benefit, one would think they could not grudge them this. What, get so much good by them, and yet grudge to do so little good to them! Is this grateful or equitable? 4. He argues from the maintenance they afforded others: "*If others are partakers of this power over you, are not we rather?* You allow others this maintenance, and confess their claim just; but who has so just a claim as I from the church of Corinth? Who has given greater evidence of the apostolical mission? Who has laboured so much for your good, or done like service among you?" Note, Ministers should be valued and provided for according to their worth. "*Nevertheless*," says the apostle, "*we have not used this power; but suffer all things, lest we should hinder the gospel of Christ.* We have not insisted on our right, but have rather been in straits to serve the interests of the gospel, and promote the salvation of souls." He renounced his right, rather than by claiming it he would hinder his success. He denied himself, for fear of giving offence; but asserted his right lest his self-denial should prove prejudicial to the ministry. Note, He is likely to plead most effectually for the rights of others who shows a generous disregard to his own. It is plain, in this case, that justice, and not self-love, is the principle by which he is actuated. 5. He argues from the old Jewish establishment: "*Do you not know that those who minister about holy things live of the things of the temple, and those who wait at the altar are partakers with the altar? v.* 13. And, if the Jewish priesthood was maintained out of the holy things that were then offered, shall not Christ's ministers have a maintenance out of their ministry? Is there not as much reason that we should be maintained as they? He asserts it to be the institution of Christ: "*Even so hath the Lord ordained that those who preach the gospel should live of the gospel* (*v.* 14), should have a right to a maintenance, though not bound to demand it, and insist upon it." It is the people's duty to maintain their minister, by Christ's appointment, though it be not a duty bound on every minister to call for or accept it. He may waive his right, as Paul did, without being a sinner; but those transgress an appointment of Christ who deny or withhold it. Those who preach the gospel have a right to live by it; and those who attend on their ministry, and yet take no thought about their subsistence, fail very much in their duty to Christ, and the respect owing to them.

15 But I have used none of these
things: neither have I written these
things, that it should be so done unto
me: for *it were* better for me to die,
than that any man should make my
glorying void. 16 For though I
preach the gospel, I have nothing to
glory of: for necessity is laid upon
me; yea, woe is unto me, if I preach
not the gospel! 17 For if I do this
thing willingly, I have a reward: but
if against my will, a dispensation *of*
the gospel is committed unto me. 18
What is my reward then? *Verily*
that, when I preach the gospel, I
may make the gospel of Christ without
charge, that I abuse not my
power in the gospel.

Here he tells them that he had, notwithstanding, waived his privilege, and lays down his reason for doing it.

I. He tells them that he had neglected to claim his right in times past: *I have used none of these things, v.* 15. He neither ate nor drank himself at their cost, nor led about a wife to be maintained by them, nor forbore working to maintain himself. From others he received a maintenance, but not from them, for some special reasons. Nor did he write this to make his claim now. Though he here asserts his right, yet he does not claim his due; but denies himself for their sakes, and the gospel.

II. We have the reason assigned of his exercising this self-denial. He would not have his glorying made void: *It were better for him to die than that any man should make his glorying void, v.* 15. This glorying did imply nothing in it of boasting, or self-conceit, or catching at applause, but a high degree of satisfaction and comfort. It was a singular pleasure to him to preach the gospel without making it burdensome; and he was resolved that among them he would not lose this satisfaction. His advantages for promoting the gospel were his glory, and he valued them above his rights, or his very life: *Better were it for him to die than to have his glorying made void,* than to have it justly said that he preferred his wages to his work. No, he was ready to deny himself for the sake of the gospel. Note, It is the glory of a minister to prefer the success of his ministry to his interest, and deny himself, that he may serve Christ, and save souls. Not that in so doing he does more than he ought; he is still acting within the bounds of the law of charity. But he acts upon truly noble principles, he brings much honour to God in so doing; and those that honour him he will honour. It is what God will approve and commend, what a man may value himself for and take comfort in, though he cannot make a merit of it before God.

III. He shows that this self-denial was more honourable in itself, and yielded him much more content and comfort, than his preaching did: "*Though I preach the gospel, I have nothing whereof to glory; for necessity is laid upon me; yea, woe is unto me, if I preach not the gospel, v.* 16. It is my charge, my business; it is the work for which I am constituted an apostle, *ch.* i. 17. This is a duty expressly bound upon me. It is not in any degree a matter of liberty. *Necessity is upon me.* I am false and unfaithful to my trust, I break a plain and express command, and *woe be to me, if I do not preach the gospel.*" Those who are set apart to the office of the ministry have it in charge to preach the gospel. Woe be to them if they do not. From this none is excepted. But it is not given in charge to all, nor any preacher of the gospel, to do his work gratis, to preach and have no maintenance out of it. It is not said, "Woe be to him if he do not preach the gospel, and yet maintain himself." In this point he is more at liberty. It may be his duty to preach at some seasons, and under some circumstances, without receiving a maintenance for it; but he has, in the general, a right to it, and may expect it from those among whom he labours. When he renounces this right for the sake of the gospel and the souls of men, though he does not supererogate, yet he denies himself, waives his privilege and right; he does more than his charge and office in general, and at all times, obliges him to. Woe be to him if he do not preach the gospel; but it may sometimes be his duty to insist on his maintenance for so doing, and whenever he forbears to claim it he parts with his right, though a man may sometimes be bound to do so by the general duties of love to God and charity to men. Note, It is a high attainment in religion to renounce our own rights for the good of others; this will entitle to a peculiar reward from God. For,

IV. The apostle here informs us that doing our duty with a willing mind will meet with a gracious recompence from God: *If I do this thing,* that is, either preach the gospel or take no maintenance, *willingly, I have a reward.* Indeed, it is willing service only that is capable of reward from God. It is not the bare doing of any duty, but the doing of it heartily (that is, willingly and cheerfully) that God has promised to reward. Leave the heart out of our duties, and God abhors them: they are but the carcasses, without the life and spirit, of religion. Those must preach willingly who would be accepted of God in this duty. They must make their business a pleasure, and not esteem it a drudgery. And those who, out of regard to the honour of God or good of souls, give up their claim to a maintenance, should do this duty willingly, if they would be accepted in it or rewarded for it. But whether the duty of the office be done willingly or with reluctance, whether the heart be in it or averse from it, all in office have a trust and charge from God, for which they must be accountable. Ministers have a dispensation of the gospel, or *stewardship—οἰκονομία* (Luke xvi. 2), committed to them. Note, Christ's willing servants shall not fail of a recompence, and that proportioned to their fidelity, zeal, and diligence; and his slothful and unwilling servants shall all be called to an account. Taking his name, and professing to do his business, will make men accountable at his bar. And how sad an account have slothful servants to give!

V. The apostle sums up the argument, by laying before them the encouraging hope he had of a large recompence for his remarkable self-denial: *What is my reward then?* v. 18. What is it I expect a recompence from God for? *That when I preach the gospel I may make it without charge, that I abuse not my power in the gospel.* Or, "not so to claim my rights as to make them destroy the great intentions and ends of my office, but renounce them for the sake of these." It is an abuse of power to employ it against the very ends for which it is given. And the apostle would never use his power, or privilege of being maintained by his ministry, so as to frustrate the ends of it, but would willingly and cheerfully deny himself for the honour of Christ and the interest of souls. That minister who follows his example may have cheerful expectations of a full recompence.

19 For though I be free from all
men, yet have I made myself servant
unto all, that I might gain the more.
20 And unto the Jews I became as a
Jew, that I might gain the Jews; to
them that are under the law, as under
the law, that I might gain them that
are under the law; 21 To them that
are without law, as without law, (being
not without law to God, but under the
law to Christ,) that I might gain them
that are without law. 22 To the
weak became I as weak, that I might
gain the weak: I am made all things
to all *men*, that I might by all means
save some. 23 And this I do for the
gospel's sake, that I might be partaker thereof with *you*.

The apostle takes occasion from what he had before discoursed to mention some other instances of his self-denial and parting with his liberty for the benefit of others.

I. He asserts his liberty (*v.* 19): *Though I be free from all men.* He was free-born, a citizen of Rome. He was in bondage to none, nor depended upon any for his subsistence; *yet he made himself a servant to all, that he might gain the more.* He behaved as a servant; he laboured for their good as a servant; he was careful to please, as a servant to his master; he acted in many cases as if he had no privileges; and this that he might gain the more, or make the more converts to Christianity. He made himself a servant, that they might be made free.

II. He specifies some particulars wherein he made himself a servant to all. He accommodated himself to all sorts of people. 1. *To the Jews, and those under the law, he became a Jew,* and as under the law, to gain them. Though he looked on the ceremonial law as a yoke taken off by Christ, yet in many instances he submitted to it, that he might work upon the Jews, remove their prejudices, prevail with them to hear the gospel, and win them over to Christ. 2. *To those that are without the law as without law* that is, to the Gentiles, whether converted to the Christian faith or not. In innocent things he could comply with people's usages or humours for their advantage. He would reason with the philosophers in their own way. And, as to converted Gentiles, he behaved among them as one that was not under the bondage of the Jewish laws, as he had asserted and maintained concerning them, though he did not act as a lawless person, but as one who was bound by the laws of Christ. He would transgress no laws of Christ to please or humour any man; but he would accommodate himself to all men, where he might do it lawfully, to gain some. Paul was the apostle of the Gentiles, and so, one would have thought, might have excused himself from complying with the Jews; and yet, to do them good, and win them over to Christ, he did, in innocent things, neglect the power he had to do otherwise, and conformed to some of their usages and laws. And though he might, by virtue of that character, have challenged authority over the Gentiles, yet he accommodated himself, as much as he innocently might, to their prejudices and ways of thinking. Doing good was the study and business of his life; and, so that he might reach this end, he did not stand on privileges and punctilios. 3. *To the weak he became as weak, that he might gain the weak, v.* 22. He was willing to make the best of them. He did not despise nor judge them, but became as one of them, forbore to use his liberty for their sake, and was careful to lay no stumbling-block in their way. Where any, through the weakness of their understanding, or the strength of their prejudices, were likely to fall into sin, or fall off from the gospel into heathen idolatry, through his use of his liberty, he refrained himself. He denied himself for their sakes, that he might insinuate into their affections, and gain their souls. In short, *he became all things to all men, that he might by all means* (all lawful means) *gain some.* He would not sin against God to save the soul of his neighbour, but he would very cheerfully and readily deny himself. The rights of God he could not give up, but he might resign his own, and he very often did so for the good of others.

III. He assigns his reason for acting in this manner (*v.* 23): *This I do for the gospel's sake, and that I may be partaker thereof with you;* that is, for the honour of Christ, whose the gospel is, and for the salvation of souls, for which it was designed, and that he and they might communicate in the privileges of it, or partake together of them. For these ends did he thus condescend, deny himself as to his liberty, and accommodate himself to the capacities and usages of those with whom he had to do, where he lawfully might. Note, A heart warmed with zeal for God, and breathing after the salvation of men, will not plead and insist upon rights and privileges in bar to this design. Those manifestly abuse their power in the gospel who employ it not to edification but destruction, and therefore breathe nothing of its spirit.

24 Know ye not that they which
run in a race run all, but one receiveth
the prize? So run, that ye may obtain.
25 And every man that striveth
for the mastery is temperate in all
things. Now they *do it* to obtain a
corruptible crown; but we an incorruptible.
26 I therefore so run, not
as uncertainly; so fight I, not as one
that beateth the air: 27 But I keep
under my body, and bring *it* into subjection:
lest that by any means, when
I have preached to others, I myself
should be a castaway.

In these verses the apostle hints at the great encouragement he had to act in this manner. He had a glorious prize, an incorruptible crown, in view. Upon this head he compares himself to the racers and combatants in the Isthmian games, an allusion well known to the Corinthians, because they were celebrated in their neighbourhood: "*Know you not that those who run in a race run all, but one obtaineth the prize? v.* 24. All run at your games, but only one gets the race and wins the crown." And here,

I. He excites them to their duty: "*So run that you may obtain.* It is quite otherwise in the Christian race than in your races; only one wins the prize in them. You may all run so as to obtain. You have great encouragement, therefore, to persist constantly, and diligently, and vigorously, in your course. There is room for all to get the prize. You cannot fail if you run well. Yet there should be a noble emulation; you should endeavour to outdo one another. And it is a glorious contest who shall get first to heaven, or have the best rewards in that blessed world. I make it my endeavour to run; so do you, as you see me go before you." Note, It is the duty of Christians to follow their ministers closely in the chace of eternal glory, and the honour and duty of ministers to lead them in the way.

II. He directs them in their course, by setting more fully to view his own example, still carrying on the allusion. 1. Those that ran in their games were kept to a set diet: "*Every man that strives for the mastery is temperate in all things, v.* 23. The fighters and wrestlers in your exercises are kept to strict diet and discipline; nay, they keep themselves to it. They do not indulge themselves, but restrain themselves from the food they eat and so from the liberties they use on other occasions. And should not Christians much more abridge themselves of their liberty, for so glorious an end as winning the race, and obtaining the prize set before them?

They used a very spare diet, and coarse food, and denied themselves much, to prepare for their race and combat; so do I; so should you, after my example. It is hard if, for the heavenly crown, you cannot abstain from heathen sacrifices." 2. They were not only temperate, but inured themselves to hardships. Those who fought with one another in these exercises prepared themselves by beating the air, as the apostle calls it, or by throwing out their arms, and thereby inuring themselves, beforehand, to deal about their blows in close combat, or brandish them by way of flourish. There is no room for any such exercise in the Christian warfare. Christians are ever in close combat. Their enemies make fierce and hearty opposition, and are ever at hand; and for this reason they must lay about them in earnest, and never drop the contest, nor flag and faint in it. They must fight, not as those that beat the air, but must strive against their enemies with all their might. One enemy the apostle here mentions, namely, the body; this must be kept under, beaten black and blue, as the combatants were in these Grecian games, and thereby brought into subjection. By the body we are to understand fleshly appetites and inclinations. These the apostle set himself to curb and conquer, and in this the Corinthians were bound to imitate him. Note, Those who would aright pursue the interests of their souls must beat down their bodies, and keep them under. They must combat hard with fleshly lusts, till they have subdued them; and not indulge a wanton appetite, and long for heathenish sacrifices, nor eat them, to please their flesh, at the hazard of their brethren's souls. The body must be made to serve the mind, not suffered to lord over it.

III. The apostle presses this advice on the Corinthians by proper arguments drawn from the same contenders. 1. They take pains, and undergo all those hardships, *to obtain a corruptible crown* (*v.* 25), *but we an incorruptible.* Those who conquered in these games were crowned only with the withering leaves or boughs of trees, of olive, bays, or laurel. But Christians have an incorruptible crown in view, a crown of glory that never fadeth away, an inheritance incorruptible, reserved in heaven for them. And would they yet suffer themselves to be outdone by these racers or wrestlers? Can they use abstinence in diet, exert themselves in racing, expose their bodies to so much hardship in a combat, who have no more in view than the trifling huzzas of a giddy multitude, or a crown of leaves? And shall not Christians, who hope for the approbation of the sovereign Judge, and a crown of glory from his hands, stretch forward in the heavenly race, and exert themselves in beating down their fleshly inclinations, and the strong-holds of sin? 2. The racers in these games run at uncertainty. All run, but one receives the prize, *v.* 24. Every racer, therefore, is at a great uncertainty whether he shall win it or no. But the Christian racer is at no such uncertainty. Every one may run here so as to obtain; but then he must run within the lines, he must keep to the path of duty prescribed, which, some think, is the meaning of *running not as uncertainly, v.* 26. He who keeps within the limits prescribed, and keeps on in his race, will never miss his crown, though others may get theirs before him. And would the Grecian racers keep within their bounds, and exert themselves to the very last, when one only could win, and all must be uncertain which that one would be? And shall not Christians be much more exact and vigorous when all are sure of a crown when they come to the end of their race? 3. He sets before himself and them the danger of yielding to fleshly inclinations, and pampering the body and its lusts and appetites: *I keep my body under, lest that by any means, when I have preached to others, I myself should be a cast-away* (*v.* 27), *rejected, disapproved,* ἀδόκιμος, one to whom the βραβευτὴς—*the judge* or *umpire* of the race, will not decree the crown. The allusion to the games runs through the whole sentence. Note, A preacher of salvation may yet miss it. He may show others the way to heaven, and never get thither himself. To prevent this, Paul took so much pains in subduing and keeping under bodily inclinations, lest by any means he himself, who had preached to others, should yet miss the crown, be disapproved and rejected by his sovereign Judge. A holy fear of himself was necessary to preserve the fidelity of an apostle; and how much more necessary is it to our preservation? Note, Holy fear of ourselves, and not presumptuous confidence, is the best security against apostasy from God, and final rejection by him.

CHAP. X.

In this chapter the apostle prosecutes the argument at the close of the last, and, I. Warns the Corinthians against security, by the example of the Jews, who, notwithstanding their profession and privileges, were terribly punished of God for their many sins, their history being left upon record for the admonition of Christians, ver. 1—14. II. He resumes his former argument (ch. 8), about eating things offered to idols; and shows that it was utterly inconsistent with true Christianity, that it was downright gross idolatry, to eat them as things offered to idols; it is having fellowship with devils, which cannot consist with having fellowship with God, ver. 15—22. III. He lets them yet know that though they must not eat of things sacrificed to idols as such, and out of any regard to the idol, yet they might buy such flesh in the markets, or eat it at the table of heathen acquaintances, without asking any questions; for that the heathens' abuse of them did not render the creatures of God unfit to be the food of his servants. Yet liberty of this kind must be used with a due regard to weak consciences, and no offence given by it to Jew nor Gentile, nor to the church of God, ver. 23, to the end.

MOREOVER, brethren, I would
not that ye should be ignorant,
how that all our fathers were under
the cloud, and all passed through the
sea; 2 And were all baptized unto
Moses in the cloud and in the sea;
3 And did all eat the same spiritual
meat; 4 And did all drink the same

spiritual drink: for they drank of that
spiritual Rock that followed them:
and that Rock was Christ. 5 But
with many of them God was not well
pleased: for they were overthrown in
the wilderness.

In order to dissuade the Corinthians from communion with idolaters, and security in any sinful course, he sets before them the example of the Jews, the church under the Old Testament. They enjoyed great privileges, but, having been guilty of heinous provocations, they fell under very grievous punishments. In these verses he reckons up their privileges, which, in the main, were the same with ours.

I. He prefaces this discourse with a note of regard: "*Moreover, brethren, I would not that you should be ignorant.* I would not have you without the knowledge of this matter; it is a thing worthy both of your knowledge and attention. It is a history very instructive and monitory." Judaism was Christianity under a veil, wrapt up in types and dark hints. The gospel was preached to them, in their legal rites and sacrifices. And the providence of God towards them, and what happened to them notwithstanding these privileges, may and ought to be warnings to us.

II. He specifies some of their privileges. He begins, 1. With their deliverance from Egypt: "*Our fathers,* that is, the ancestors of us Jews, were *under the cloud, and all passed through the sea.* They were all under the divine covering and conduct." The cloud served for both purposes: it sometimes contracted itself into a cloudy pillar, shining on one side to show them their way, dark on the other to hide them from their pursuing enemies; and sometimes spread itself over them as a mighty sheet, to defend them from the burning sun in the sandy desert, Ps. cv. 39. They were miraculously conducted through the Red Sea, where the pursuing Egyptians were drowned: it was a lane to them, but a grave to these: a proper type of our redemption by Christ, who saves us by conquering and destroying his enemies and ours. They were very dear to God, and much in his favour, when he would work such miracles for their deliverance, and take them so immediately under his guidance and protection. 2. They had sacraments like ours. (1.) *They were all baptized unto Moses in the cloud, and in the sea* (*v.* 2), or into Moses, that is, brought under obligation to Moses's law and covenant, as we are by baptism under the Christian law and covenant. It was to them a typical baptism. (2.) *They did all eat of the same spiritual meat, and drink of the same spiritual drink,* that we do. The manna on which they fed was a type of Christ crucified, the bread which came down from heaven, which whoso eateth shall live for ever. Their drink was a stream fetched from a rock which followed them in all their journeyings in the wilderness; and this rock was Christ, that is, in type and figure. He is the rock on which the Christian church is built; and of the streams that issue from him do all believers drink, and are refreshed. Now all the Jews did eat of this meat, and drink of this rock, called here a spiritual rock, because it typified spiritual things. These were great privileges. One would think that this should have saved them; that all who ate of that spiritual meat, and drank of that spiritual drink, should have been holy and acceptable to God. Yet was it otherwise: *With many of them God was not well pleased; for they were overthrown in the wilderness, v.* 5. Note, Men may enjoy many and great spiritual privileges in this world, and yet come short of eternal life. Many of those *who were baptized unto Moses in the cloud and sea,* that is, had their faith of his divine commission confirmed by these miracles, were yet overthrown in the wilderness, and never saw the promised land. Let none presume upon their great privileges, or profession of the truth; these will not secure heavenly happiness, nor prevent judgments here on earth, except the *root of the matter* be in us.

6 Now these things were our examples, to the intent we should not
lust after evil things, as they also
lusted. 7 Neither be ye idolaters, as
were some of them; as it is written,
The people sat down to eat and drink,
and rose up to play. 8 Neither let
us commit fornication, as some of
them committed, and fell in one day
three and twenty thousand. 9 Neither let us tempt Christ, as some
of them also tempted, and were
destroyed of serpents. 10 Neither
murmur ye, as some of them also murmured, and were destroyed of the destroyer. 11 Now all these things happened unto them for ensamples: and
they are written for our admonition,
upon whom the ends of the world are
come. 12 Wherefore let him that
thinketh he standeth take heed lest
he fall. 13 There hath no temptation
taken you but such as is common to
man: but God *is* faithful, who will
not suffer you to be tempted above
that ye are able; but will with the
temptation also make a way to escape,
that ye may be able to bear *it*. 14
Wherefore, my dearly beloved, flee
from idolatry.

The apostle, having recited their privileges, proceeds here to an account of their faults and punishments, their sins and plagues, which are left upon record for an example to us, a warning against the like sins, if we would escape the like punishments. We must not do as they did, lest we suffer as they suffered.

I. Several of their sins are specified as cautions to us; as, 1. We should shun inordinate desires after carnal objects: *Not lust after evil things, as they lusted, v.* 6. God fed them with manna, but they must have flesh, Num. xi. 4. They had food for their supply, but, not content with this, they asked *meat for their lusts,* Ps. cvi. 14. Carnal desires get head by indulgence, and therefore should be observed and checked in their first rise: if once they prevail, and bear sway in us, we know not whither they will carry us. This caution stands first, because carnal appetites indulged are the root and source of much sin. 2. He warns against idolatry (*v.* 7): *Neither be you idolaters, as were some of them; as it is written, The people sat down to eat and drink, and rose up to play.* The sin of the golden calf is referred to, Exod. xxxii. 6. They first sacrificed to their idol, then feasted on the sacrifices, and then danced before it. Though only eating and drinking are mentioned here, yet the sacrifice is supposed. The apostle is speaking to the case of the Corinthians, who were tempted to feast on the heathen sacrifices, things offered to idols, though they do not seem to have been under any temptation to offer sacrifice themselves. Even eating and drinking of the sacrifices before the idol, and as things sacrificed, was idolatry, which, by the example of the Israelites, they should be warned to avoid. 3. He cautions against fornication, a sin to which the inhabitants of Corinth were in a peculiar manner addicted. They had a temple among them dedicated to Venus (that is, to lust), with above a thousand priestesses belonging to it, all common prostitutes. How needful was a caution against fornication to those who lived in so corrupt a city, and had been used to such dissolute manners, especially when they were under temptations to idolatry too! and spiritual whoredom did in many cases lead to bodily prostitution. Most of the gods whom the heathens served were represented as patterns of lewdness; and much lewdness was committed in the very worship of many of them. Many of the Jewish writers, and many Christians after them, think that such worship was paid to Baal-Peor; and that fornication was committed with the daughters of Moab in the worship of that idol. They were enticed by these women both to spiritual and corporal whoredom; first to feast on the sacrifice, if not to do more beastly acts, in honour of the idol, and then to defile themselves with strange flesh (Num. xxv.), which brought on a plague, that in one day slew twenty-three thousand, besides those who fell by the hand of public justice. Note, Whoremongers and adulterers God will judge, in whatever external relation they may stand to him, and whatever outward privileges he may bestow upon them. Let us fear the sins of Israel, if we would shun their plagues. 4. He warns us against *tempting Christ (as some of them tempted, and were destroyed of serpents, v.* 9), or provoking him to jealousy, *v.* 22. He was with the church in the wilderness; he was the angel of the covenant, who went before them. But he was greatly grieved and provoked by them in many ways: *They spoke against him and Moses, Wherefore have you brought us out of Egypt to die in the wilderness?* for which reason God sent fiery serpents among them (Num. xxi. 5, 6), by which many of them were stung mortally. And it is but just to fear that such as tempt Christ under the present dispensation will be left by him in the power of the old serpent. 5. He warns against murmuring: *Neither murmur you as some of them also murmured, and were destroyed of the destroyer* (*v.* 10), by a destroying angel, an executioner of divine vengeance. They quarrelled with God, and murmured against Moses his minister, when any difficulties pressed them. When they met with discouragements in the way to Canaan, they were very apt to fly in the face of their leaders, were for displacing them, and going back to Egypt under the conduct of others of their own choosing. Something like this seems to have been the case of the Corinthians; they murmured against Paul, and in him against Christ, and seem to have set up other teachers, who would indulge and soothe them in their inclinations, and particularly in a revolt to idolatry. Rather let them feast on idol sacrifices than bear the reproach, or expose themselves to the ill-will, of heathen neighbours. Such conduct was very provoking to God, and was likely to bring upon them swift destruction, as it did on the Israelites, Num. xiv. 37. Note, Murmuring against divine disposals and commands is a sin that greatly provokes, especially when it grows to such a head as to issue in apostasy, and a revolt from him and his good ways.

II. The apostle subjoins to these particular cautions a more general one (*v.* 11): *All these things happened to them for ensamples, and were written for our admonition.* Not only the laws and ordinances of the Jews, but the providences of God towards them, were typical. Their sins against God, and backslidings from him, were typical of the infidelity of many under the gospel. God's judgments on them were types of spiritual judgments now. Their exclusion from the earthly Canaan typified the exclusion of many under the gospel out of the heavenly Canaan, for their unbelief. Their history was written, to be a standing monitor to the church, even under the last and most perfect dispensation: *To us, on whom the end of the world is come,* the concluding period of God's gracious government over men. Note, Nothing in scripture is written in vain. God had wise and gracious purposes towards us in leaving the Jewish history upon record; and it is our wisdom and duty to receive instruction from it. Upon this hint the apostle grounds a caution (*v.* 12): *Let him that thinketh he standeth take heed lest he fall.* Note, The harms sustained by others should be cautions to us. He that thinks he stands should not be confident and secure, but upon his guard. Others have fallen, and so may we. And then we are most likely to fall when we are most confident of our own strength, and thereupon most apt to be secure, and off our guard. Distrust of himself, putting him at once upon vigilance and dependence on God, is the Christian's best security against all sin. Note, He who thinks he stands is not likely to keep his footing, if he fears no fall, nor guards against it. God has not promised to keep us from falling, if we do not look to ourselves: his protection supposes our own care and caution.

III. But to this word of caution he adds a word of comfort, *v.* 13. Though it is displeasing to God for us to presume, it is not pleasing to him for us to despair. If the former be a great sin, the latter is far from being innocent. Though we must fear and take heed lest we fall, yet should we not be terrified and amazed; for either our trials will be proportioned to our strength, or strength will be supplied in proportion to our temptations. We live indeed in a tempting world, where we are compassed about with snares. Every place, condition, relation, employment, and enjoyment, abounds with them; yet what comfort may we fetch from such a passage! For, 1. "*No temptation,*" says the apostle, "*hath yet taken you, but such as is common to man,* what is human; that is, such as you may expect from men of such principles as heathens, and such power; or else such as is common to mankind in the present state; or else such as the spirit and resolution of mere men may bear you through." Note, The trials of common Christians are but common trials: others have the like burdens and the like temptations; what they bear up under, and break through, we may also. 2. *God is faithful.* Though Satan be a deceiver, God is true. Men may be false, and the world may be false; but God is faithful, and our strength and security are in him. He keepeth his covenant, and will never disappoint the filial hope and trust of his children. 3. He is wise as well as faithful, and will proportion our burden to our strength. *He will not suffer us to be tempted above what we are able.* He knows what we can bear, and what we can bear up against; and he will, in his wise providence, either proportion our temptations to our strength or make us able to grapple with them. He will take care that we be not overcome, if we rely upon him, and resolve to approve ourselves faithful to him. We need not perplex ourselves with the difficulties in our way when God will take care that they shall not be too great for us to encounter, especially, 4. When he will make them to issue well. *He will make a way to escape,* either the trial itself, or at least the mischief of it. There is no valley so dark but he can find a way through it, no affliction so grievous but he can prevent, or remove, or enable us to support it, and in the end overrule it to our advantage.

IV. And upon this argument he grounds another caution against idolatry: *Wherefore, my dearly beloved, flee from idolatry.* Observe, 1. How he addresses them: *My dearly beloved.* It is out of tender affection to them that he presses this advice upon them. 2. The matter of his advice: "*Flee idolatry;* shun it, and all approaches towards it." Idolatry is the most heinous injury and affront to the true God; it is transferring his worship and honour to a rival. 3. The ground of this advice: "Seeing you have such encouragement to trust God, and to be faithful, do you approve yourselves men, be not shaken by any discouragements your heathen enemies may lay before you. God will succour and assist, help you in your trials, and help you out of them; and therefore be not guilty of any idolatrous compliances." Note, We have all the encouragement in the world to flee sin and prove faithful to God. We cannot fall by a temptation if we cleave fast to him.

15 I speak as to wise men; judge
ye what I say. 16 The cup of blessing which we bless, is it not the communion of the blood of Christ? The
bread which we break, is it not the
communion of the body of Christ?
17 For we *being* many are one bread,
and one body: for we are all partakers
of that one bread. 18 Behold Israel
after the flesh: are not they which
eat of the sacrifices partakers of the
altar? 19 What say I then? that the
idol is any thing, or that which is
offered in sacrifice to idols is any
thing? 20 But *I say,* that the things
which the Gentiles sacrifice, they sacrifice to devils, and not to God: and
I would not that ye should have fellowship with devils. 21 Ye cannot
drink the cup of the Lord, and the
cup of devils: ye cannot be partakers
of the Lord's table, and of the table of
devils. 22 Do we provoke the Lord
to jealousy? are we stronger than he?

In this passage the apostle urges the general caution against idolatry, in the particular case of eating the heathen sacrifices as such, and out of any religious respect to the idol to whom they were sacrificed.

I. He prefaces his argument with an appeal to their own reason and judgment: "*I speak to wise men, judge you what I say, v.* 15. You are great pretenders to wisdom, to close reasoning and argument; I can leave it with your own reason and conscience whether I do not argue justly." Note, It is no dishonour to an inspired teacher, nor disadvantage to his argument, to appeal for the truth of it to the reason and consciences of his hearers. It comes upon them with the greater force when it comes with this conviction. Paul, an inspired apostle, would yet, in some cases, leave it with the Corinthians to judge whether what he taught was not conformable to their own light and sense.

II. He lays down his argument from the Lord's supper: *The cup which we bless, is it not the communion of the blood of Christ? The bread which we break, is it not the communion of the body of Christ?* Is not this sacred rite an instrument of communion with God? Do we not therein profess to be in friendship, and to have fellowship, with him? Is it not a token whereby we professedly hold communion with Christ, whose body was broken, and blood shed, to procure remission of our sins, and the favour of God? And can we be in alliance with Christ, or friendship with God, without being devoted to him? In short, the Lord's supper is a feast on the sacrificed body and blood of our Lord, *epulum ex oblatis.* And to eat of the feast is to partake of the sacrifice, and so to be his guests to whom the sacrifice was offered, and this in token of friendship with him. Thus to partake of the Lord's table is to profess ourselves his guests and covenant people. This is the very purpose and intention of this symbolical eating and drinking; it is holding communion with God, and partaking of those privileges, and professing ourselves under those obligations, which result from the death and sacrifice of Christ; and this in conjunction with all true Christians, with whom we have communion also in this ordinance. *Because the bread is one, we, being many, are one body, for we are made partakers of one bread,* or loaf (*v.* 17), which I think is thus more truly rendered: "By partaking of one broken loaf, the emblem of our Saviour's broken body, who is the only true bread that came down from heaven, we coalesce into one body, become members of him and one another." Those who truly partake by faith have this communion with Christ, and one another; and those who eat the outward elements make profession of having this communion, of belonging to God and the blessed fraternity of his people and worshippers. This is the true meaning of this holy rite.

III. He confirms this from the Jewish worship and customs: *Behold Israel after the flesh: are not those who eat of the sacrifices partakers of the altar,* that is, of the sacrifice offered upon it? Those who were admitted to eat of the offerings were reckoned to partake of the sacrifice itself, as made for them, and to be sanctified thereby; and therefore surely to worship God, and be in alliance or covenant with him, even the God of Israel, to whom the sacrifice was made: this was a symbol or token of holding communion with him.

IV. He applies this to the argument against feasting with idolaters on their sacrifices, and to prove those that do so idolaters. This he does, 1. By following the principle on which they would argue it to be lawful, namely, that an idol was nothing. Many of them were nothing at all, none of them had any divinity in them. What was sacrificed to idols was nothing, no way changed from what it was before, but was every whit as fit for food, considered in itself. They indeed seem to argue that, because an idol was nothing, what was offered was no sacrifice, but common and ordinary food, of which they might therefore eat with as little scruple. Now the apostle allows that the food was not changed as to its nature, was as fit to be eaten as common food, where it was set before any who knew not of its having been offered to an idol But, 2. He proves that the eating of it as a part of a heathen sacrifice was, (1.) A partaking with them in their idolatry. *It was having fellowship with devils,* because what the Gentiles sacrificed they sacrificed to devils; and to feast with them upon these sacrifices was to partake in the sacrifice, and therefore to worship the god to whom it was made, and have fellowship or communion with him: just as he who eats the Lord's supper is supposed to partake in the Christian sacrifice; or as those who ate the Jewish sacrifices partook of what was offered on their altar. But heathens sacrificed to devils: "Therefore do not feast on their sacrifices. Doing it is a token of your having fellowship with the demons to whom they are offered. I would not have you be in communion with devils." (2.) It was a virtual renouncing of Christianity: *You cannot drink the cup of the Lord, and the cup of devils: you cannot be partakers of the Lord's table, and the table of devils, v.* 21. To partake of this Christian feast was to have communion with Christ: to partake of the feasts made in honour of the heathen idols, and made of things sacrificed to them, was to have communion with devils. Now this was to compound contraries; it was by no means consistent. Communion with Christ, and communion with devils, could never be had at once. One must be renounced, if the other was maintained. He who held communion with Christ must renounce that with devils; he who held communion with devils must by that very deed renounce communion with Christ. And what a manifest self-contradiction must that man's conduct be that would partake of the Lord's table, and yet partake of the table of demons! God and mammon can never be served together, nor fellowship be at once had with Christ and Satan. Those who communicate with devils must virtually renounce Christ. This may also intimate that such as indulge themselves in gluttony or drunkenness, and by so doing make their own table the table of devils, or keep up fellowship with Satan by a course of known and wilful wickedness, cannot partake truly of the cup and table of the Lord. They may use the sign, but do not the thing signified thereby. For a man can never be at once in communication with Christ and his church and yet in fellowship with Satan. Note, How much reason have we to look to it that every sin and idol be renounced by us, when we eat and drink at the Lord's table.

V. He warns them, upon the whole, against such idolatry, by signifying to them that God is a jealous God (*v.* 22): *Do we provoke the Lord to jealousy? Are we stronger than he?* It is very probable that many among the Corinthians made light of being at these heathen feasts, and thought there was no harm in it. But the apostle bids them beware. The reason with which the second commandment is enforced is, *I am a jealous God.* God cannot endure a rival in matter of worship; nor give his glory, nor suffer it to be given, to another. Those who have fellowship with other gods provoke him to jealousy, Deut. xxxii. 16. And, before this be done, persons should consider whether they are stronger than he. It is a dangerous thing to provoke God's anger, unless we could withstand his power. But *who can stand before him when he is angry?* Nah. i. 6. This should be considered by all who continue in the love and liking of sin, and in league with it, while yet they profess to keep up communion with Christ. Is not this the way to provoke his jealousy and indignation? Note, Attention to the greatness of God's power should restrain us from provoking his jealousy, from doing any thing to displease him. Shall we rouse almighty wrath? And how shall we withstand it? Are we a match for God? Can we resist his power, or control it? And, if not, shall we arm it against us, by provoking him to jealousy? No, let us fear his power, and let this restrain us from all provocation.

23 All things are lawful for me,
but all things are not expedient: all
things are lawful for me, but all things
edify not. 24 Let no man seek his
own, but every man another's *wealth.*
25 Whatsoever is sold in the shambles, *that* eat, asking no question for
conscience sake: 26 For the earth
is the Lord's, and the fulness thereof.
27 If any of them that believe not
bid you *to a feast,* and ye be disposed
to go; whatsoever is set before you,
eat, asking no question for conscience
sake. 28 But if any man say unto
you, This is offered in sacrifice unto
idols, eat not for his sake that showed
it, and for conscience sake: for the
earth *is* the Lord's, and the fulness
thereof: 29 Conscience, I say, not
thine own, but of the other: for why
is my liberty judged of another *man's*
conscience? 30 For if I by grace be
a partaker, why am I evil spoken of
for that for which I give thanks? 31
Whether therefore ye eat, or drink,
or whatsoever ye do, do all to the
glory of God. 32 Give none offence,
neither to the Jews, nor to the Gentiles, nor to the church of God: 33
Even as I please all *men* in all *things,*
not seeking mine own profit, but the
profit of many, that they may be
saved.

In this passage the apostle shows in what instances, notwithstanding, Christians might lawfully eat what had been sacrificed to idols. They must not eat it out of religious respect to the idol, nor go into his temple, and hold a feast there, upon what they knew was an idol-sacrifice; nor perhaps out of the temple, if they knew it was a feast held upon a sacrifice, but there were cases wherein they might without sin eat what had been offered. Some such the apostle here enumerates.—But,

I. He gives a caution against abusing our liberty in lawful things. That may be lawful which is not expedient, which will not edify. A Christian must not barely consider what is lawful, but what is expedient, and for the use of edification. A private Christian should do so even in his private conduct. *He must not seek his own only, but his neighbour's wealth.* He must be concerned not to hurt his neighbour, nay, he must be concerned to promote his welfare; and must consider how to act so that he may help others, and not hinder them in their holiness, comfort, or salvation. Those who allow themselves in every thing not plainly sinful in itself will often run into what is evil by accident, and do much mischief to others. Every thing lawful in itself to be done is not therefore lawfully done. Circumstances may make that a sin which in itself is none. These must be weighed, and the expediency of an action, and its tendency to edification, must be considered before it be done. Note, The welfare of others, as well as our own convenience, must be consulted in many things we do, if we would do them well.

II. He tells them that what was *sold in the shambles they might eat without asking questions.* The priest's share of heathen sacrifices was thus frequently offered for sale, after it had been offered in the temple. Now the apostle tells them they need not be so scrupulous as to ask the butcher in the market whether the meat he sold had been offered to an idol? It was there sold as common food, and as such might be bought and used; *for the earth is the Lord's, and the fulness thereof* (*v.* 26), and the fruit and products of the earth were designed by him, the great proprietor, for the use and subsistence of mankind, and more especially of his own children and servants. *Every creature of God is good, and nothing to be refused, if it be received with thanksgiving; for it is sanctified by the word of God and prayer,* 1 Tim. iv. 4, 5. *To the pure all things are pure,* Tit. i. 15. Note, Though it is sinful to use any food in an idolatrous manner, it is no sin, after such abuse, to apply it, in a holy manner, to its common use.

III. He adds that if they were invited by any heathen acquaintances to a feast, *they might go, and eat what was set before them, without asking questions* (*v.* 27), *nay, though* they knew things sacrificed to idols were served up at such entertainments, as well as sold in the shambles. Note, The apostle does not probibit their going to a feast upon the invitation of those that believed not. There is a civility owing even to infidels and heathens. Christianity does by no means bind us up from the common offices of humanity, nor allow us an uncourteous behaviour to any of our own kind, however they may differ from us in religious sentiments or practices. And when Christians were invited to feast with infidels they were not to ask needless questions about the food set before them, but eat without scruple. Needless enquiries might perplex their minds and consciences, for which reason they were to be avoided. Any thing fit to be eaten, that was set before them at a common entertainment, they might lawfully eat. And why then should they scrupulously enquire whether what was set before them had been sacrificed? It is to be understood of civil feasting, not religious; for the latter among the heathens was feasting upon their sacrifices, which he had condemned before as a participation in their idolatrous worship. At a common feast they might expect common food; and they needed not to move scruples in their own minds whether what was set before them was otherwise or no. Note, Though Christians should be very careful to know and understand their duty, yet they should not, by needless enquiries, perplex themselves.

IV. Yet, even at such an entertainment, he adds, if any should say it was a thing that had been offered to idols, they should refrain: *Eat not, for his sake that showed it, and for conscience' sake.* Whether it were the master of the feast or any of the guests, whether it were spoken in the hearing of all or whispered in the ear, they should refrain for his sake who suggested this to them, whether he were an infidel or an infirm Christian; and for conscience' sake, out of regard to conscience, that they might show a regard to it in themselves, and keep up a regard to it in others. This he backs with the same reason as the former: *For the earth is the Lord's.* There is food enough provided by our common Lord, of which we may eat without scruple. The same doctrine may be variously improved, as here: "The earth is the Lord's, therefore you may eat any thing without scruple that is set before you as common food; and yet, because the earth is the Lord's, eat nothing that will give offence, lay a stumbling-block before others, and encourage some in idolatry, or tempt others to eat when they are not clear in their own mind that it is lawful, and so sin, and wound their own consciences." Note, Christians should be very cautious of doing what may thus prejudice the consciences of others, and weaken their authority with them, which is by all means to be kept up.

V. He urges them to refrain where they will give offence, while yet he allows it lawful to eat what was set before them as common food, though it had been offered in sacrifice. "Another man's conscience is no measure to our conduct. What he thinks unlawful is not thereby made unlawful to me, but may be a matter of liberty still; and as long as I own God as the giver of my food, and render him thanks for it, it is very unjust to reproach me for using it. This must be understood abstracted from the scandal given by eating in the circumstance mentioned. Though some understand it to mean, "Why should I, by using the liberty I have, give occasion to those who are scandalized to speak evil of me?" According to that advice of the apostle (Rom. xiv. 16), *Let not your good be evil spoken of.* Note, Christians should take care not to use their liberty to the hurt of others, nor their own reproach.

VI. The apostle takes occasion from this discourse to lay down a general rule for Christians' conduct, and apply it to this particular case (*v.* 31, 32), namely, that in eating and drinking, and in all we do, we should aim at the glory of God, at pleasing and honouring him. This is the fundamental principle of practical godliness. The great end of all practical religion must direct us where particular and express rules are wanting. Nothing must be done against the glory of God, and the good of our neighbours, connected with it. Nay, the tendency of our behaviour to the common good, and the credit of our holy religion, should give direction to it. And therefore nothing should be done by us to offend any, *whether Jew, or Gentile, or the church, v.* 32. The Jews should not be unnecessarily grieved nor prejudiced, who have such an abhorrence of idols that they reckon every thing offered to them thereby defiled, and that it will pollute and render culpable all who partake of it; nor should heathens be countenanced in their idolatry by any behaviour of ours, which they may construe as homage or honour done to their idols; nor young converts from Gentilism take any encouragement from our conduct to retain any veneration for the heathen gods and worship, which they have renounced: nor should we do any thing that may be a means to pervert any members of the church from their Christian profession or practice. Our own humour and appetite must not determine our practice, but the honour of God and the good and edification of the church. We should not so much consult our own pleasure and interest as the advancement of the kingdom of God among men. Note, A Christian should be a man devoted to God, and of a public spirit.

VII. He presses all upon them by his own example: *Even as I please all men* (or study to do it) *in all things* (that I lawfully can), *not seeking my own profit, but that of many, that they may be saved, v.* 33. Note, A preacher may press his advice home with boldness and authority when he can enforce it with his own example. He is most likely to promote a public spirit in others who can give evidence of it in himself. And it is highly commendable in a minister to neglect his own advantage that he may promote the salvation of his hearers. This shows that he has a spirit suitable to his function. It is a station for public usefulness, and can never be faithfully discharged by a man of a narrow spirit and selfish principles.

CHAP. XI.

In this chapter the apostle blames, and endeavours to rectify, some great indecencies and manifest disorders in the church of Corinth; as, I. The misconduct of their women (some of whom seem to have been inspired) in the public assembly, who laid by their veils, the common token of subjection to their husbands in that part of the world. This behaviour he reprehends, requires them to keep veiled, asserts the superiority of the husband, yet so as to remind the husband that both were made for mutual help and comfort, ver. 1--16. II. He blames them for their discord, riot, and neglec and contempt of the poor, at the Lord's supper, ver. 17--22. III. To rectify these scandalous disorders, he sets before them the nature and intentions of this holy institution, directs them how they should attend on it, and warns them of the danger of a conduct so indecent as theirs, and of all unworthy receiving, ver. 23, to the end.

BE ye followers of me, even as I
also *am* of Christ. 2 Now I
praise you, brethren, that ye remember me in all things, and keep the
ordinances, as I delivered *them* to
you. 3 But I would have you know,
that the head of every man is Christ;
and the head of the woman *is* the
man; and the head of Christ *is* God.
4 Every man praying or prophesying, having *his* head covered, dishonoureth his head. 5 But every
woman that prayeth or prophesieth
with *her* head uncovered dishonoureth
her head: for that is even all one as
if she were shaven. 6 For if the
woman be not covered, let her also be
shorn: but if it be a shame for a
woman to be shorn or shaven, let her
be covered. 7 For a man indeed
ought not to cover *his* head, forasmuch as he is the image and glory of
God: but the woman is the glory of
the man. 8 For the man is not of
the woman; but the woman of the
man. 9 Neither was the man created
for the woman; but the woman for
the man. 10 For this cause ought
the woman to have power on *her* head
because of the angels. 11 Nevertheless neither is the man without the
woman, neither the woman without
the man, in the Lord. 12 For as the
woman *is* of the man, even so *is* the
man also by the woman; but all things
of God. 13 Judge in yourselves: is
it comely that a woman pray unto God
uncovered? 14 Doth not even nature itself teach you, that, if a man
have long hair, it is a shame unto him?
15 But if a woman have long hair, it
is a glory to her: for *her* hair is given
her for a covering. 16 But if any
man seem to be contentious, we have
no such custom, neither the churches
of God.

Paul, having answered the cases put to him, proceeds in this chapter to the redress of grievances. The first verse of the chapter is put, by those who divided the epistle into chapters, as a preface to the rest of the epistle, but seems to have been a more proper close to the last, in which he had enforced the cautions he had given against the abuse of liberty, by his own example: *Be ye followers of me, as I also am of Christ* (*v.* 1), fitly closes his argument; and the way of speaking in the next verse looks like a transition to another. But, whether it more properly belong to this or the last chapter, it is plain from it that Paul not only preached such doctrine as they ought to believe, but led such a life as they ought to imitate. "Be ye followers of me," that is, "Be imitators of me; live as you see me live." Note, Ministers are likely to preach most to the purpose when they can press their hearers to follow their example. Yet would not Paul be followed blindly neither. He encourages neither implicit faith nor obedience. He would be followed himself no further than he followed Christ. Christ's pattern is a copy without a blot; so is no man's else. Note, We should follow no leader further than he follows Christ. Apostles should be left by us when they deviate from the example of their Master. He passes next to reprehend and reform an indecency among them, of which the women were more especially guilty, concerning which observe,

I. How he prefaces it. He begins with a commendation of what was praiseworthy in them (*v.* 2): *I praise you, that you remember me in all things, and keep the ordinances as I delivered them to you.* Many of them, it is probable, did this in the strictest sense of the expression: and he takes occasion thence to address the body of the church under this good character; and the body might, in the main, have continued to observe the ordinances and institutions of Christ, though in some things they deviated from, and corrupted, them Note, When we reprove what is amiss in any, it is very prudent and fit to commend what is good in them; it will show that the reproof is not from ill-will, and a humour of censuring and finding fault; and it will therefore procure the more regard to it.

II. How he lays the foundation for his reprehension by asserting the superiority of the man over the woman: *I would have you know that the head of every man is Christ, and the head of the woman is the man, and the head of Christ is God.* Christ, in his mediatorial character and glorified humanity, is at the head of mankind. He is not only first of the kind, but Lord and Sovereign. He has a name above every name: though in this high office and authority he has a superior, God being his head. And as God is the head of Christ, and Christ the head of the whole human kind, so the man is the head of the two sexes: not indeed with such dominion as Christ has over the kind or God has over the man Christ Jesus; but a superiority and headship he has, and the woman should be in subjection and not assume or usurp the man's place. This is the situation in which God has placed her; and for that reason she should have a mind suited to her rank, and not do any thing that looks like an affectation of changing places. Something like this the women of the church of Corinth seem to have been guilty of, who were under inspiration, and prayed and prophesied even in their assemblies, *v.* 5. It is indeed an apostolical canon, that the women *should keep silence in the churches* (*ch.* xiv. 34; 1 Tim. ii 12), which some understand without limitation, as if a woman under inspiration also must keep silence, which seems very well to agree with the connection of the apostle's discourse, *ch.* xiv. Others with a limitation: though a woman might not from her own abilities pretend to teach, or so much as question and debate any thing in the church, yet when under inspiration the case was altered, she had liberty to speak. Or, though she might not preach even by inspiration (because teaching is the business of a superior), yet she might pray or utter hymns by inspiration, even in the public assembly. She did not show any affectation of superiority over the man by such acts of public worship. It is plain the apostle does not in this place prohibit the thing, but reprehend the manner of doing it. And yet he might utterly disallow the thing and lay an unlimited restraint on the woman in another part of the epistle. These things are not contradictory. It is to his present purpose to reprehend the manner wherein the women prayed and prophesied in the church, without determining in this place whether they did well or ill in praying or prophesying. Note, The manner of doing a thing enters into the morality of it. We must not only be concerned to do good, but that the good we do be well done.

III. The thing he reprehends is the woman's praying or prophesying uncovered, or the man's doing either covered *v.* 4, 5. To understand this, it must be observed that it was a signification either of shame or subjection for persons to be veiled, or covered, in the eastern countries, contrary to the custom of ours, where the being bare-headed betokens subjection, and being covered superiority and dominion. And this will help us the better to understand,

IV. The reasons on which he grounds his reprehension. 1. *The man that prays or prophesies with his head covered dishonoureth his head,* namely, Christ, the head of every man (*v.* 3), by appearing in a habit unsuitable to the rank in which God has placed him. Note, We should, even in our dress and habits, avoid every thing that may dishonour Christ. *The woman,* on the other hand, *who prays or prophesies with her head uncovered dishonoureth her head,* namely, the man, *v.* 3. She appears in the dress of her superior, and throws off the token of her subjection. She might, with equal decency, cut her hair short, or cut it close, which was the custom of the man in that age. This would be in a manner to declare that she was desirous of changing sexes, a manifest affectation of that superiority which God had conferred on the other sex. And this was probably the fault of these prophetesses in the church of Corinth. It was doing a thing which, in that age of the world, betokened superiority, and therefore a tacit claim of what did not belong to them but the other sex. Note, The sexes should not affect to change places. The order in which divine wisdom has placed persons and things is best and fittest: to endeavour to amend it is to destroy all order, and introduce confusion. The woman should keep to the rank God has chosen for her, and not dishonour her head; for this, in the result, is to dishonour God. If she was made out of the man, and for the man, and made to be the glory of the man, she should do nothing, especially in public, that looks like a wish of having this order inverted. 2. Another reason against this conduct is that *the man is the image and glory of God,* the representative of that glorious dominion and headship which God has over the world. It is the man who is set at the head of this lower creation, and therein he bears the resemblance of God. The woman, on the other hand, *is the glory of the man* (*v.* 7): she is his representative. Not but she has dominion over the inferior creatures, as she is a partaker of human nature, and so far is God's representative too, but it is at second-hand. She is the image of God, inasmuch as she is the image of the man: *For the man was not made out of the woman, but the woman out of the man, v.* 8. The man was first made, and made head of the creation here below, and therein the image of the divine dominion; and the woman was made out of the man, and shone with a reflection of his glory, being made superior to the other creatures here below, but in subjection to her husband, and deriving that honour from him out of whom she was made. 3. *The woman was made for the man,* to be his help-meet, *and not the man for the woman.* She was naturally, therefore, made subject to him, because made for him, for his use, and help, and comfort. And she who was intended to be always in subjection to the man should do nothing, in Christian assemblies, that looks like an affetaction of equality. 4. *She ought to have power on her head, because of the angels.* Power, that is, a veil, the token, not of her having the power or superiority, but being under the power of her husband, subjected to him, and inferior to the other sex. Rebekah, when she met Isaac, and was delivering herself into his possession, put on her veil, in token of her subjection, Gen. xxiv. 65. Thus would the apostle have the women appear in Christian assemblies, even though they spoke there by inspiration, *because of the angels,* that is, say some, because of the evil angels. The woman *was first in the transgression, being deceived by the devil* (1 Tim. ii. 14), which increased her subjection to man, Gen. iii. 16. Now, because evil angels will be sure to mix in all Christian assemblies, therefore should women wear the token of their shamefacedness and subjection, which in that age and country was a veil. Others say because of the good angels. Jews and Christians have had an opinion that these ministering spirits are many of them present in their assemblies. Their presence should restrain Christians from all indecencies in the worship of God. Note, We should learn from all to behave in the public assemblies of divine worship so as to express a reverence for God, and a content and satisfaction with that rank in which he has placed us.

V. He thinks fit to guard his argument with a caution lest the inference be carried too far (*v.* 11, 12): ***Nevertheless, neither is the man without the woman, nor the woman*** *without the man in the Lord.* They were made for one another. *It is not good for him to be alone* (Gen. ii. 18), and therefore was a woman made, and made for the man; and the man was intended to be a comfort, and help, and defence, to the woman, though not so directly and immediately made for her. They were made to be a mutual comfort and blessing, not one a slave and the other a tyrant. *Both were to be one flesh* (Gen. ii. 24), and this for the propagation of a race of mankind. They are reciprocal instruments of each other's production. As the woman was first formed out of the man, the man is ever since propagated by the woman (*v.* 12), all by the divine wisdom and power of the First Cause so ordaining it. The authority and subjection should be no greater than are suitable to two in such near relation and close union to each other. Note, As it is the will of God that the woman know her place, so it is his will also that the man abuse not his power.

VI. He enforces his argument from the natural covering provided for the woman (*v.* 13—15): "*Judge in yourselves*—consult your own reason, hearken to what nature suggests—*is it comely for a woman to pray to God uncovered?* Should there not be a distinction kept up between the sexes in wearing their hair, since nature has made one? Is it not a distinction which nature has kept up among all civilized nations? The woman's hair is a natural covering; to wear it long is a glory to her; but for a man to have long hair, or cherish it, is a token of softness and effeminacy." Note, It should be our concern, especially in Christian and religious assemblies, to make no breach upon the rules of natural decency.

VII. He sums up all by referring those who were contentious to the usages and customs of the churches, *v.* 16. Custom is in a great measure the rule of decency. And the common practice of the churches is what he would have them govern themselves by. He does not silence the contentious by mere authority, but lets them know that they would appear to the world as very odd and singular in their humour if they would quarrel for a custom to which all the churches of Christ were at that time utter strangers, or against a custom in which they all concurred, and that upon the ground of natural decency. It was the common usage of the churches for women to appear in public assemblies, and join in public worship, veiled; and it was manifestly decent that they should do so. Those must be very contentious indeed who would quarrel with this, or lay it aside.

17 Now in this that I declare *unto*
you I praise *you* not, that ye come
together not for the better, but for the
worse. 18 For first of all, when ye
come together in the church, I hear
that there be divisions among you;
and I partly believe it. 19 For there

must be also heresies among you, that they which are approved may be made manifest among you. 20 When ye come together therefore into one place, *this* is not to eat the Lord's supper. 21 For in eating every one taketh before *other* his own supper: and one is hungry, and another is drunken. 22 What? have ye not houses to eat and to drink in? or despise ye the church of God, and shame them that have not? What shall I say to you? shall I praise you in this? I praise *you* not.

In this passage the apostle sharply rebukes them for much greater disorders than the former, in their partaking of the Lord's supper, which was commonly done in the first ages, as the ancients tell us, with a love-feast annexed, which gave occasion to the scandalous disorders which the apostle here reprehends, concerning which observe,

I. The manner in which he introduces his charge: "*Now in this that I declare to you I praise you not, v.* 17. I cannot commend, but must blame and condemn you. It is plain, from the beginning of the chapter, that he was willing and pleased to commend as far as he could. But such scandalous disorders, in so sacred an institution, as they were guilty of, called for a sharp reprehension. They quite turned the institution against itself. It was intended to make them better, to promote their spiritual interests; but it really made them worse. *They came together, not for the better, but for the worse.* Note, The ordinances of Christ, if they do not make us better, will be very apt to make us worse; if they do not do our souls good, they do us harm; if they do not melt and mend, they will harden. Corruptions will be confirmed in us, if the proper means do not work a cure of them.

II. He enters upon his charge against them in more particulars than one. 1. He tells them that, upon coming together, they fell into *divisions, schisms—σχίσματα*. Instead of concurring unanimously in celebrating the ordinance, they fell a quarrelling with one another. Note, There may be schism where there is no separation of communion. Persons may come together in the same church, and sit down at the same table of the Lord, and yet be schismatics. Uncharitableness, alienation of affection, especially if it grows up to discord, and feuds, and contentions, constitute schism. Christians may separate from each other's communion, and yet be uncharitable one towards another; they may continue in the same communion, and yet be uncharitable. This latter is schism, rather than the former. The apostle had heard a report of the Corinthians' divisions, and he tells them he had too much reason to believe it. For, adds he, there must be heresies also; not only quarrels, but factions, and perhaps such corrupt opinions as strike at the foundation of Christianity, and all sound religion. Note, No marvel there should be breaches of Christian love in the churches, when such offences will come as shall make shipwreck of faith and a good conscience. Such offences must come. Not that men are necessitated to be guilty of them; but the event is certain, and God permits them, that those who are approved (such honest hearts as will bear the trial) may be set to view, and appear faithful by their constant adherence to the truths and ways of God, notwithstanding the temptations of seducers. Note, The wisdom of God can make the wickedness and errors of others a foil to the piety and integrity of the saints 2. He charges them not only with discord and division, but with scandalous disorder: *For in eating every one taketh before the other his own supper; and one is hungry, and another is drunken, v.* 21. Heathens used to drink plentifully at their feasts upon their sacrifices. Many of the wealthier Corinthians seem to have taken the same liberty at the Lord's table, or at least at their Ἀγάπαι, or *love-feasts*, that were annexed to the supper. They would not stay for one another; the rich despised the poor, and ate and drank up the provisions they themselves brought, before the poor were allowed to partake; and thus some wanted, while others had more than enough. This was profaning a sacred institution, and corrupting a divine ordinance, to the last degree. What was appointed to feed the soul was employed to feed their lusts and passions. What should have been a bond of mutual amity and affection was made an instrument of discord and disunion. The poor were deprived of the food prepared for them, and the rich turned a feast of charity into a debauch. This was scandalous irregularity.

III. The apostle lays the blame of this conduct closely on them, 1. By telling them that their conduct perfectly destroyed the purpose and use of such an institution: *This is not to eat the Lord's supper, v.* 20. It was coming to the Lord's table, and not coming. They might as well have staid away. Thus to eat the outward elements was not to eat Christ's body. Note, There is a careless and irregular eating of the Lord's supper which is as none at all; it will turn to no account, but to increase guilt. Such an eating was that of the Corinthians; their practices were a direct contradiction to the purposes of this sacred institution. 2. Their conduct carried in it a contempt of God's house, or of the church, *v.* 22. If they had a mind to feast, they might do it at home in their own houses; but to come to the Lord's table, and cabal and quarrel, and keep the poor from their share of the provision there made for them as well as the rich, was such an abuse of the ordinance, and such a contempt of the poorer members of the church more especially, as merited a very sharp rebuke. Such a behaviour tended much to the shame and discouragement of the poor, whose souls were as dear to Christ, and cost him as much, as those of the rich. Note, Common meals may be managed after a common manner, but religious feasts should be attended religiously. Note also, It is a heinous evil, and severely to be censured, for Christians to treat their fellow-christians with contempt and insolence, but especially at the Lord's table. This is doing what they can to pour contempt on divine ordinances. And we should look carefully to it that nothing in our behaviour at the Lord's table have the appearance of contemning so sacred an institution.

23 For I have received of the
Lord that which also I delivered unto
you, That the Lord Jesus the *same*
night in which he was betrayed took
bread: 24 And when he had given
thanks, he brake *it*, and said, Take,
eat: this is my body, which is broken
for you: this do in remembrance of
me. 25 After the same manner also
he took the cup, when he had supped,
saying, This cup is the new testament
in my blood: this do ye, as oft as ye
drink *it*, in remembrance of me. 26
For as often as ye eat this bread, and
drink this cup, ye do show the Lord's
death till he come. 27 Wherefore
whosoever shall eat this bread, and
drink *this* cup of the Lord, unworthily,
shall be guilty of the body and blood
of the Lord. 28 But let a man examine himself, and so let him eat of
that bread and drink of *that* cup.
29 For he that eateth and drinketh
unworthily, eateth and drinketh damnation to himself, not discerning the
Lord's body. 30 For this cause
many *are* weak and sickly among
you, and many sleep. 31 For if we
would judge ourselves, we should not
be judged. 32 But when we are
judged, we are chastened of the Lord,
that we should not be condemned
with the world. 33 Wherefore, my
brethren, when ye come together to
eat, tarry one for another. 34 And
if any man hunger, let him eat at
home; that ye come not together
unto condemnation. And the rest
will I set in order when I come.

To rectify these gross corruptions and irregularities, the apostle sets the sacred institution here to view. This should be the rule in the reformation of all abuses.

I. He tells us how he came by the knowledge of it. He was not among the apostles at the first institution; but *he had received from the Lord what he delivered to them, v.* 23 He had the knowledge of this matter by revelation from Christ: and what he had received he communicated, without varying from the truth a tittle, without adding or diminishing.

II. He gives us a more particular account of the institution than we meet with elsewhere. We have here an account,

1. Of the author—our Lord Jesus Christ. The king of the church only has power to institute sacraments.

2. The time of the institution: *It was the very night wherein he was betrayed;* just as he was entering on his sufferings which are therein to be commemorated.

3. The institution itself. Our Saviour took bread, and when he had given thanks, or *blessed* (as it is in Matt. xxvi. 26), *he broke, and said, Take, eat; this is my body, broken for you; this do in remembrance of me. And in like manner he took the cup, when he had supped, saying, This cup is the New Testament in my blood; this do, as oft as you drink it, in remembrance of me, v.* 24, 25. Here observe,

(1.) The materials of this sacrament; both, [1.] As to the visible signs: these are bread and the cup, the former of which is called bread many times over in this passage, even after what the papists call consecration. What is eaten is called bread, though it be at the same time said to be *the body of the Lord*, a plain argument that the apostle knew nothing of their monstrous and absurd doctrine of transubstantiation. The latter is as plainly a part of this institution as words can make it. St. Matthew tells us, our Lord bade them all drink of it (*ch.* xxvi. 27), as if he would, by this expression, lay in a caveat against the papists' depriving the laity of the cup. Bread and the cup are both made use of, because it is a holy feast. Nor is it here, or any where, made necessary, that any particular liquor should be in the cup. In one evangelist, indeed, it is plain that wine was the liquor used by our Saviour, though it was, perhaps, mingled with water, according to the Jewish custom; *vide* Lightfoot on Matt. xxvi. But this by no means renders it unlawful to have a sacrament where persons cannot come at wine. In every place of scripture in which we have an account of this part of the institution it is always expressed by a figure. The cup is put for what was in it, without once specifying what the liquor was, in the words of the institution. [2.] The things signified by these outward signs: they are Christ's body and blood, his body broken, his blood shed, together with all the benefits which flow from his death and sacrifice: *it is the New Testament in his blood*

His blood is the seal and sanction of all the privileges of the new covenant; and worthy receivers take it as such, at this holy ordinance. They have the New Testament, and their own title to all the blessings of the new covenant, confirmed to them by his blood.

(2.) We have here the sacramental actions, the manner in which the materials of the sacrament are to be used. [1.] Our Saviour's actions, which are taking the bread and cup, giving thanks, breaking the bread, and giving about both the one and the other. [2.] The actions of the communicants, which were to take the bread and eat, to take the cup and drink, and both in remembrance of Christ. But the external acts are not the whole nor the principal part of what is to be done at this holy ordinance; each of them has a significancy. Our Saviour, having undertaken to make an offering of himself to God, and procure, by his death, the remission of sins, with all other gospel benefits, for true believers, did, at the institution, deliver his body and blood, with all the benefits procured by his death, to his disciples, and continues to do the same every time the ordinance is administered to true believers. This is here exhibited, or set forth, as the food of souls. And as food, though ever so wholesome or rich, will yield no nourishment without being eaten, here the communicants are to take and eat, or to receive Christ and feed upon him, his grace and benefits, and by faith convert them into nourishment to their souls. They are to take him as their Lord and life, yield themselves up to him, and live upon him. *He is our life*, Col. iii. 4.

(3.) We have here an account of the ends of this institution. [1.] It was appointed to be done *in remembrance of Christ*, to keep fresh in our minds an ancient favour, his dying for us, as well as to remember an absent friend, even Christ interceding for us, in virtue of his death, at God's right hand. The best of friends, and the greatest acts of kindness, are here to be remembered, with the exercise of suitable affections and graces. The motto on this ordinance, and the very meaning of it, is, *When this you see, remember me.* [2.] It was *to show forth Christ's death*, to declare and publish it. It is not barely in remembrance of Christ, of what he has done and suffered, that this ordinance was instituted; but to commemorate, to celebrate, his glorious condescension and grace in our redemption. We declare his death to be our life, the spring of all our comforts and hopes. And we glory in such a declaration; we show forth his death, and spread it before God, as our accepted sacrifice and ransom. We set it in view of our own faith, for our own comfort and quickening: and we own before the world, by this very service, that we are the disciples of Christ, who trust in him alone for salvation and acceptance with God.

(4.) It is moreover hinted here, concerning this ordinance, [1.] That it should be frequent: *As often as you eat this bread*, &c. Our bodily meals return often; we cannot maintain life and health without this. And it is fit that this spiritual diet should be taken often too. The ancient churches celebrated this ordinance every Lord's day, if not every day when they assembled for worship. [2.] That it must be perpetual. It is to be celebrated *till the Lord shall come;* till he shall come the second time, without sin, for the salvation of those that believe, and to judge the world. This is our warrant for keeping this feast. It was our Lord's will that we should thus celebrate the memorials of his death and passion, till he come in his own glory, and his Father's glory, with his holy angels, and put an end to the present state of things, and his own mediatorial administration, by passing the final sentence. Note, The Lord's supper is not a temporary, but a standing and perpetual ordinance.

III. He lays before the Corinthians the danger of receiving unworthily, of prostituting this institution as they did, and using it to the purposes of feasting and faction, with intentions opposite to its design, or a temper of mind altogether unsuitable to it; or keeping up the covenant with sin and death, while they are there professedly renewing and confirming their covenant with God. 1. It is great guilt which such contract. They shall *be guilty of the body and blood of the Lord* (*v.* 27), of violating this sacred institution, of despising his body and blood. They act as if they *counted the blood of the covenant, wherewith they are sanctified, an unholy thing*, Heb. x. 29. They profane the institution, and in a manner crucify their Saviour over again. Instead of being cleansed by his blood, they are guilty of his blood. 2. It is a great hazard which they run: *They eat and drink judgment to themselves*, *v.* 29. They provoke God, and are likely to bring down punishment on themselves. No doubt but they incur great guilt, and so render themselves liable to damnation, to spiritual judgments and eternal misery. Every sin is in its own nature damning; and therefore surely so heinous a sin as profaning such a holy ordinance is so. And it is profaned in the grossest sense by such irreverence and rudeness as the Corinthians were guilty of. But fearful believers should not be discouraged from attending at this holy ordinance by the sound of these words, as if they bound upon themselves the sentence of damnation by coming to the table of the Lord unprepared. This sin, as well as all others, leaves room for forgiveness upon repentance; and the Holy Spirit never indited this passage of scripture to deter serious Christians from their duty, though the devil has often made this advantage of it, and robbed good Christians of their choicest comforts. The Corinthians came to the Lord's table as to a common feast, *not discerning the Lord's body*—

not making a difference or distinction between that and common food, but setting both on a level: nay, they used much more indecency at this sacred feast than they would have done at a civil one. This was very sinful in them, and very displeasing to God, and brought down his judgments on them: *For this cause many are weak and sickly among you, and many sleep.* Some were punished with sickness, and some with death. Note, A careless and irreverent receiving of the Lord's supper may bring temporal punishments. Yet the connection seems to imply that even those who were thus punished were in a state of favour with God, at least many of them: *They were chastened of the Lord, that they should not be condemned with the world, v.* 32. Now divine chastening is a sign of divine love: *Whom the Lord loveth he chasteneth* (Heb. xii. 6), especially with so merciful a purpose, to prevent their final condemnation. In the midst of judgment, God remembers mercy: he frequently punishes those whom he tenderly loves. It is kindness to use the rod to prevent the child's ruin. He will visit such iniquity as this under consideration with stripes, and yet make those stripes the evidence of his loving-kindness. Those were in the favour of God who yet so highly offended him in this instance, and brought down judgments on themselves; at least many of them were; for they were punished by him out of fatherly good-will, punished now that they might not perish for ever. Note, It is better to bear trouble in this world than to be miserable to eternity. And God punishes his people now, to prevent their eternal woe.

IV. He points out the duty of those who would come to the Lord's table. 1. In general: *Let a man examine himself* (*v.* 28), try and approve himself. Let him consider the sacred intention of this holy ordinance, its nature, and use, and compare his own views in attending on it and his disposition of mind for it; and, when he has approved himself to his own conscience in the sight of God, then let him attend. Such self-examination is necessary to a right attendance at this holy ordinance. Note, Those who, through weakness of understanding, cannot try themselves, are by no means fit to eat of this bread and drink of this cup; nor those who, upon a fair trial, have just ground to charge themselves with impenitency, unbelief, and alienation from the life of God. Those should have the wedding-garment on who would be welcome at this marriage-feast—grace in habit, and grace in exercise. 2. The duty of those who were yet unpunished for their profanation of this ordinance: *If we would judge ourselves, we should not be judged, v.* 31. If we would thoroughly search and explore ourselves, and condemn and correct what we find amiss, we should prevent divine judgments. Note, To be exact and severe on ourselves and our own conduct is the most proper way in the world not to fall under the just severity of our heavenly Father. We must not judge others, lest we be judged (Matt. vii. 1); but we must judge ourselves, to prevent our being judged and condemned by God. We may be critical as to ourselves, but should be very candid in judging others.

V. He closes all with a caution against the irregularities of which they were guilty (*v.* 33, 34), charging them to avoid all indecency at the Lord's table. They were to eat for hunger and pleasure only at home, and not to change the holy supper to a common feast; and much less eat up the provisions before those who could bring none did partake of them, lest they should come together for condemnation. Note, Our holy duties, through our own abuse, may prove matter of condemnation. Christians may keep Sabbaths, hear sermons, attend at sacraments, and only aggravate guilt, and bring on a heavier doom. A sad but serious truth! O! let all look to it that they do not come together at any time to God's worship, and all the while provoke him, and bring down vengeance on themselves. Holy things are to be used in a holy manner, or else they are profaned. What else was amiss in this matter, he tells them, he would rectify when he came to them.

CHAP. XII.

In this chapter the apostle, I. Considers the case of spiritual gifts, which were very plentifully poured out on the Corinthian church. He considers their original, that they are from God; their variety and use, that they were all intended for one and the same general end, the advancement of Christianity and the church's edification, ver. 1—11. II. He illustrates this by an allusion to a human body, in which all the members have a mutual relation and subserviency, and each has its proper place and use, ver. 12—26. III. He tells us that the church is the body of Christ, and the members are variously gifted for the benefit of the whole body, and each particular member, ver. 27—30. And then, IV. Closes with an exhortation to seek somewhat more beneficial than these gifts, ver. 31.

NOW concerning spiritual *gifts*,
brethren, I would not have you
ignorant. 2 Ye know that ye were
Gentiles, carried away unto these
dumb idols, even as ye were led.
3 Wherefore I give you to understand, that no man speaking by the
Spirit of God calleth Jesus accursed:
and *that* no man can say that Jesus is
the Lord, but by the Holy Ghost.
4 Now there are diversities of gifts,
but the same spirit. 5 And there are
differences of administrations, but the
same Lord. 6 And there are diversities of operations, but it is the same
God which worketh all in all. 7 But
the manifestation of the Spirit is given
to every man to profit withal. 8 For
to one is given by the Spirit the word
of wisdom; to another the word of
knowledge by the same Spirit; 9 To

another faith by the same Spirit; to
another the gifts of healing by the
same Spirit; 10 To another the working of miracles; to another prophecy;
to another discerning of spirits; to
another *divers* kind of tongues; to
another the interpretation of tongues:
11 But all these worketh that one and
the selfsame Spirit, dividing to every
man severally as he will.

The apostle comes now to treat of spiritual gifts, which abounded in the church of Corinth, but were greatly abused. What these gifts were is at large told us in the body of the chapter; namely, extraordinary offices and powers, bestowed on ministers and Christians in the first ages, for conviction of unbelievers, and propagation of the gospel. Gifts and graces, χαρίσματα and χάρις, greatly differ. Both indeed were freely given of God. But where grace is given it is for the salvation of those who have it. Gifts are bestowed for the advantage and salvation of others. And there may be great gifts where there is not a dram of grace, but persons possessed of them are utterly out of the divine favour. They are great instances of divine benignity to men, but do not by themselves prove those who have them to be the objects of divine complacency. This church was rich in gifts, but there were many things scandalously out of order in it. Now concerning these spiritual gifts, that is, the extraordinary powers they had received from the Spirit,

I. The apostle tells them he would not have them ignorant either of their original or use. They came from God, and were to be used for him. It would lead them far astray if they were ignorant of one or the other of these. Note, Right information is of great use as to all religious practice. It is wretched work which gifted men make who either do not know or do not advert to the nature and right use of the gifts with which they are endowed.

II. He puts them in mind of the sad state out of which they had been recovered: *You were Gentiles, carried away to dumb idols, even as you were led*, *v.* 2. While they were so, they could have no pretensions to be spiritual men, nor to have spiritual gifts. While they were under the conduct of the spirit of Gentilism, they could not be influenced by the Spirit of Christ. If they well understood their former condition, they could not but know that all true spiritual gifts were from God. Now concerning this observe, 1. Their former character: they *were Gentiles.* Not God's peculiar people, but of the nations whom he had in a manner abandoned. The Jews were, before, his chosen people, distinguished from the rest of the world by his favour. To them the knowledge and worship of the true God were in a manner confined. The rest of the world were strangers to the covenant of promise, aliens from the commonwealth of Israel, and in a manner without God, Eph. ii. 12. Such Gentiles were the body of the Corinthians, before their conversion to Christianity. What a change was here! Christian Corinthians were once Gentiles. Note, It is of great use to the Christian, and a proper consideration to stir him up both to duty and thankfulness, to think what once he was: *You were Gentiles.* 2. The conduct they were under: *Carried away to these dumb idols, even as you were led.* They were hurried upon the grossest idolatry, the worship even of stocks and stones, through the force of a vain imagination, and the fraud of their priests practising on their ignorance. for, whatever were the sentiments of their philosophers, this was the practice of the herd. The body of the people paid their homage and worship to dumb idols, *that had ears but could not hear, and mouths but could not speak*, Ps. cxv. 5, 6. Miserable abjectness of mind! And those who despised these gross conceptions of the vulgar yet countenanced them by their practice. O dismal state of Gentilism! Could the Spirit of God be among such stupid idolaters, or they be influenced by it? How did the prince of this world triumph in the blindness of mankind! How thick a mist had he cast over their minds!

III. He shows them how they might discern those gifts that were from the Spirit of God, true spiritual gifts: *No man, speaking by the Spirit, calls Jesus accursed.* Thus did both Jews and Gentiles: they blasphemed him as an impostor, and execrated his name, and deemed it abominable. And yet many Jews, who were exorcists and magicians, went about, pretending to work wonders by the Spirit of God (vid. Lightfoot's *Horæ in loc.*), and many among the Gentiles pretended to inspiration. Now the apostle tells them none could act under the influence, nor by the power, of the Spirit of God, who disowned and blasphemed Christ: for the Spirit of God bore uncontrollable witness to Christ by prophecy, miracles, his resurrection from the dead, the success of his doctrine among men, and its effect upon them; and could never so far contradict itself as to declare him accursed. And on the other hand *no man could say Jesus was the Lord* (that is, live by this faith, and work miracles to prove it), *but it must be by the Holy Ghost.* To own this truth before men, and maintain it to the death, and live under the influence of it, could not be done without the sanctification of the Holy Ghost. No man can call Christ *Lord,* with a believing subjection to him and dependence upon him, unless that faith be wrought by the Holy Ghost. No man can confess this truth in the day of trial but by the Holy Ghost animating and encouraging him. Note, We have as necessary a dependence on the Spirit's operation and influence for our sanctification and perseverance as on the mediation of Christ for our reconciliation and acceptance with God: and no man could confirm this truth with a miracle but by the Holy Ghost. No evil spirit would lend assistance, if it were in his power, to spread a doctrine and religion so ruinous to the devil's kingdom. The substance of what the apostle asserts and argues here is that whatever pretences there were to inspiration or miracles, among those who were enemies to Christianity, they could not be from the Spirit of God; but no man could believe this with his heart, nor prove with a miracle that Jesus was Christ, but by the Holy Ghost: so that the extraordinary operations and powers among them did all proceed from the Spirit of God. He adds,

IV. These spiritual gifts, though proceeding from the same Spirit, are yet various. They have one author and original, but are themselves of various kinds. A free cause may produce variety of effects; and the same giver may bestow various gifts, *v.* 4. *There are diversities of gifts*, such as revelations, tongues, prophecy, interpretations of tongues; *but the same Spirit.* There are differences of administrations, or different offices, and officers to discharge them, different ordinances and institutions (see *v.* 28—30), but the same Lord, who appointed all, *v.* 6. *There are diversities of operations*, or miraculous powers, called ἐνεργήματα δυνάμεων (*v.* 10), as here ἐνεργήματα, *but it is the same God that worketh all in all.* There are various gifts, administrations, and operations, but all proceed from one God, one Lord, one Spirit; that is, from Father, Son, and Holy Ghost, the spring and origin of all spiritual blessings and bequests: all issue from the same fountain; all have the same author. However different they may be in themselves, in this they agree; all are from God. And several of the kinds are here specified, *v.* 8—10. Several persons had their several gifts, some one, some another, all from and by the same Spirit. To one was given the *word of wisdom;* that is, say some, a knowledge of the mysteries of the gospel, and ability to explain them, an exact understanding of the design, nature, and doctrines, of the Christian religion. Others say an uttering of grave sentences, like Solomon's proverbs. Some confine this word of wisdom to the revelations made to and by the apostles.—*To another the word of knowledge, by the same Spirit;* that is, say some, the knowledge of mysteries (*ch.* ii. 13): wrapped up in the prophecies, types, and histories of the Old Testament: say others, a skill and readiness to give advice and counsel in perplexed cases.—*To another faith, by the same Spirit;* that is, the faith of miracles, or a faith in the divine power and promise, whereby they were enabled to work miracles; or an extraordinary impulse from above, whereby they were enabled to trust God in any emergency, and go on in the way of their duty, and own and profess the truths of Christ, whatever was the difficulty or danger.—*To another the gift of healing, by th same Spirit;* that is, healing the sick, eith by laying on of hands, or anointing with oi or with a bare word.—*To another the workin of miracles;* the efficacies of powers, ἐνεργήματα δυνάμεων, such as raising the dea restoring the blind to sight, giving speech t the dumb, hearing to the deaf, and the use limbs to the lame.—*To another prophecy*, th is, ability to foretel future events, which i the more usual sense of prophecy; or t explain scripture by a peculiar gift of th Spirit. See *ch.* xiv. 24.—*To another the discerning of Spirits*, power to distinguish between true and false prophets, or to discer the real and internal qualifications of an person for an office, or to discover the inwar workings of the mind by the Holy Ghost, a Peter did those of Ananias, Acts v. 3.—*T another divers kinds of tongues*, or ability t speak languages by inspiration.—*To anothe the interpretation of tongues*, or ability t render foreign languages readily and properly into their own. With such variety o spiritual gifts were the first ministers an churches blessed.

V. The end for which these gifts were bestowed: *The manifestation of the Spirit i given to every man to profit withal*, *v.* 7. Th Spirit was manifested by the exercise of thes gifts; his influence and interest appeared i them. But they were not distributed for th mere honour and advantage of those wh had them, but for the benefit of the churcl to edify the body, and spread and advanc the gospel. Note, Whatever gifts God confers on any man, he confers them that h may do good with them, whether they b common or spiritual. The outward gifts o his bounty are to be improved for his glory and employed in doing good to others. N man has them merely for himself. They ar a trust put into his hands, to profit withal and the more he profits others with them, th more abundantly will they turn to his accoun in the end, Phil. iv. 17. Spiritual gifts ar bestowed, that men may with them profit th church and promote Christianity. They ar not given for show, but for service; not fo pomp and ostentation, but for edification not to magnify those that have them, but t edify others.

VI. The measure and proportion in whicl they are given: *All these worketh one and th same Spirit, dividing to every man as he will* It is according to the sovereign pleasure o the donor. What more free than a gift? An shall not the Spirit of God do what he wil with his own? May he not give to what persons he pleases, and in what proportion h pleases; one gift to one man, and another t another; to one more, and another fewer, a he thinks fit? Is he not the best judge hov his own purposes shall be served, and hi own donatives bestowed? It is not as me will, nor as they may think fit, but as th

Spirit pleases. Note, The Holy Ghost is a divine person. He works divine effects and divides divine gifts as he will, by his own power, and according to his own pleasure, without dependence or control. But though he distributes these gifts freely and uncontrollably, they are intended by him, not for private honour and advantage, but for public benefit, for the edification of the body, the church.

12 For as the body is one, and
hath many members, and all the members of that one body, being many,
are one body: so also *is* Christ. 13
For by one Spirit are we all baptized
into one body, whether *we be* Jews or
Gentiles, whether *we be* bond or free;
and have been all made to drink into
one Spirit. 14 For the body is not
one member, but many. 15 If the
foot shall say, Because I am not the
hand, I am not of the body; is it
therefore not of the body? 16 And
if the ear shall say, Because I am not
the eye, I am not of the body; is it
therefore not of the body? 17 If the
whole body *were* an eye, where *were*
the hearing? If the whole *were* hearing, where *were* the smelling? 18
But now hath God set the members
every one of them in the body, as it
hath pleased him. 19 And if they
were all one member, where *were* the
body? 20 But now *are they* many
members, yet but one body. 21 And
the eye cannot say unto the hand, I
have no need of thee: nor again the
head to the feet, I have no need of
you. 22 Nay, much more those
members of the body, which seem to
be more feeble, are necessary: 23
And those *members* of the body,
which we think to be less honourable, upon these we bestow more
abundant honour; and our uncomely
parts have more abundant comeliness. 24 For our comely *parts*
have no need: but God hath tempered the body together, having given
more abundant honour to that *part*
which lacked: 25 That there should
be no schism in the body; but *that*
the members should have the same
care one for another. 26 And whether
one member suffer, all the members
suffer with it; or one member be
honoured, all the members rejoice
with it.

The apostle here makes out the truth of what was above asserted, and puts the gifted men among the Corinthians in mind of their duty, by comparing the church of Christ to a human body.

I. By telling us that one body may have many members, and that the many members of the same body make but one body (*v.* 12): *As the body is one, and hath many members, and all the members of that one body, being many, are one body, so also is Christ;* that is, Christ mystical, as divines commonly speak. Christ and his church making one body, as head and members, this body is made up of many parts or members, yet but one body; for all the members are *baptized into the same body, and made to drink of the same Spirit, v.* 13. Jews and Gentiles, bond and free, are upon a level in this: all are baptized into the same body, and made partakers of the same Spirit. Christians become members of this body by baptism: they are baptized into one body. The outward rite is of divine institution, significant of the new birth, called therefore *the washing of regeneration,* Tit. iii. 5. But it is by the Spirit, by the renewing of the Holy Ghost, that we are made members of Christ's body. It is the Spirit's operation, signified by the outward administration, that makes us members. And by communion at the other ordinance we are sustained; but then it is not merely by drinking the wine, but by drinking into one Spirit. The outward administration is a means appointed of God for our participation in this great benefit; but it is baptism by the Spirit, it is internal renovation and drinking into one Spirit, partaking of his sanctifying influence from time to time, that makes us true members of Christ's body, and maintains our union with him. Being animated by one Spirit makes Christians one body. Note, All who have the spirit of Christ, without difference, are the members of Christ, whether Jew or Gentile, bond or free; and none but such. And all the members of Christ make up one body; the members many, but the body one. They are one body, because they have one principle of life; all are quickened and animated by the same Spirit.

II. Each member has its particular form, place, and use. 1. The meanest member makes a part of the body. The foot and ear are less useful, perhaps, than the hand and eye; but because one is not a hand, and the other an eye, shall they say, therefore, that they do not belong to the body? *v.* 15, 16. So every member of the body mystical cannot have the same place and office; but what then? Shall it hereupon disown relation to the body? Because it is not fixed in the same station, or favoured with the same gifts as others, shall it say, "I do not belong to Christ?" No, the meanest member of his body is as much a member as the noblest, and as truly regarded by him. All his members are dear to him. 2. There must be a distinction of members in the body: *Were the whole body eye, where were the hearing? Were the whole ear, where were the smelling? v.* 17. *If all were one member, where were the body? v.* 19. *They are many members,* and for that reason must have distinction among them, *and yet are but one body, v.* 20. One member of a body is not a body; this is made up of many; and among these many there must be a distinction, difference of situation, shape, use, &c. So it is in the body of Christ; its members must have different uses, and therefore have different powers, and be in different places, some having one gift, and others a different one. Variety in the members of the body contributes to the beauty of it. What a monster would a body be if it were all ear, or eye, or arm! So it is for the beauty and good appearance of the church that there should be diversity of gifts and offices in it. 3. The disposal of members in a natural body, and their situation, are as God pleases: *But now hath God set the members, every one of them, in the body, as it hath pleased him, v.* 18. We may plainly perceive the divine wisdom in the distribution of the members; but it was made according to the counsel of his will; he distinguished and distributed them as he pleased. So is it also in the members of Christ's body: they are chosen out to such stations, and endued with such gifts, as God pleases. He who is sovereign Lord of all disposes his favours and gifts as he will. And who should gainsay his pleasure? What foundation is here for repining in ourselves, or envying others? We should be doing the duties of our own place, and not murmuring in ourselves, nor quarrelling with others, that we are not in theirs. 4. All the members of the body are, in some respect, useful and necessary to each other: *The eye cannot say to the hand, I have no need of thee; nor the head to the feet, I have no need of you:* nay, those members of the body *which seem to be more feeble* (the bowels, &c.) *are necessary* (*v* 21, 22); God has so fitted and tempered them together that they are all necessary to one another, and to the whole body; there is no part redundant and unnecessary. Every member serves some good purpose or other: it is useful to its fellow-members, and necessary to the good state of the whole body. Nor is there a member of the body of Christ but may and ought to be useful to his fellow-members, and at some times, and in some cases, is needful to them. None should despise and envy another, seeing God has made the distinction between them as he pleased, yet so as to keep them all in some degree of mutual dependence, and make them valuable to each other, and concerned for each other, because of their mutual usefulness. Those who excel in any gift cannot say that they have no need of those who in that gift are their inferiors, while perhaps, in other gifts, they exceed them. Nay, the lowest members of all have their use, and the highest cannot do well without them. The eye has need of the hand, and the head of the feet. 5. Such is the man's concern for his whole body that *on the less honourable members more abundant honour is bestowed, and our uncomely parts have more abundant comeliness.* Those parts which are not fit, like the rest, to be exposed to view, which are either deformed or shameful, we most carefully clothe and cover; whereas the comely parts have no such need. The wisdom of Providence has so contrived and tempered things that the most abundant regard and honour should be paid to that which most wanted it, *v.* 24. So should the members of Christ's body behave towards their fellow-members: instead of despising them, or reproaching them, for their infirmities, they should endeavour to cover and conceal them, and put the best face upon them that they can. 6. Divine wisdom has contrived and ordered things in this manner that the members of the body should not be schismatics, divided from each other and acting upon separate interests, but well affected to each other, tenderly concerned for each other, having a fellow-feeling of each other's griefs and a communion in each other's pleasures and joys, *v.* 25, 26. God has tempered the members of the body natural in the manner mentioned, that *there might be no schism in the body* (*v.* 25), no rupture nor disunion among the members, nor so much as the least mutual disregard. This should be avoided also in the spiritual body of Christ. There should be no schism in this body, but the members should be closely united by the strongest bonds of love. All decays of this affection are the seeds of schism. Where Christians grow cold towards each other, they will be careless and unconcerned for each other. And this mutual disregard is a schism begun. The members of the natural body are made to have a care and concern for each other, to prevent a schism in it. So should it be in Christ's body; the members should sympathize with each other. As in the natural body the pain of the one part afflicts the whole, the ease and pleasure of one part affects the whole, so should Christians reckon themselves honoured in the honours of their fellow-christians, and should suffer in their sufferings. Note, Christian sympathy is a great branch of Christian duty. We should be so far from slighting our brethren's sufferings that we should suffer with them, so far from envying their honours that we should rejoice with them and reckon ourselves honoured in them.

27 Now ye are the body of Christ,
and members in particular. 28 And

God hath set some in the church, first
apostles, secondarily prophets, thirdly
teachers, after that miracles, then gifts
of healings, helps, governments, diversities of tongues. 29 *Are* all apostles?
are all prophets? *are* all teachers? *are*
all workers of miracles? 30 Have all
the gifts of healing? do all speak
with tongues? do all interpret? 31
But covet earnestly the best gifts:
and yet show I unto you a more excellent way.

I. Here the apostle sums up the argument, and applies this similitude to the church of Christ, concerning which observe,

1. The relation wherein Christians stand to Christ and one another. The church, or whole collective body of Christians, in all ages, is his body. Every Christian is a member of his body, and every other Christian stands related to him as a fellow-member (*v.* 27): *Now you are the body of Christ, and members in particular,* or particular members. Each is a member of the body, not the whole body; each stands related to the body as a part of it, and all have a common relation to one another, dependence upon one another, and should have a mutual care and concern. Thus are the members of the natural body, thus should the members of the mystical body be, disposed. Note, Mutual indifference, and much more contempt, and hatred, and envy, and strife, are very unnatural in Christians. It is like the members of the same body being destitute of all concern for one another, or quarrelling with each other. This is the apostle's scope in this argument. He endeavours in it to suppress the proud, vaunting, and contentious spirit, that had prevailed among the Corinthians, by reason of their spiritual gifts.

2. The variety of offices instituted by Christ, and gifts or favours dispensed by him (*v.* 28): *God hath set some in the church; first, apostles,* the chief ministers entrusted with all the powers necessary to found a church, and make an entire revelation of God's will. *Secondarily, prophets,* or persons enabled by inspiration to prophesy, interpret scripture, or write by inspiration, as the evangelists did. *Thirdly, teachers,* those who labour in word and doctrine, whether with pastoral charge or without it. After that, *miracles,* or miracle-workers. *Then gifts of healing,* or those who had power to heal diseases; *helps,* or such as had compassion on the sick and weak, and ministered to them; *governments,* or such as had the disposal of the charitable contributions of the church, and dealt them out to the poor; *diversities of tongues,* or such as could speak divers languages. Concerning all these observe, (1.) The plenteous variety of these gifts and offices. What a multitude are they! A good God was free in his communications to the primitive church; he was no niggard of his benefits and favours. No, he provided richly for them. They had no want, but a store—all that was necessary, and even more; what was convenient for them too. (2.) Observe the order of these offices and gifts. They are here placed in their proper ranks. Those of most value have the first place. Apostles, prophets, and teachers, were all intended to instruct the people, to inform them well in the things of God, and promote their spiritual edification: without them, neither evangelical knowledge nor holiness could have been promoted. But the rest, however fitted to answer the great intentions of Christianity, had no such immediate regard to religion, strictly so called. Note, God does, and we should, value things according to their real worth: and the use of things is the best criterion of their real worth. Those are most valuable that best answer the highest purposes. Such were apostolical powers, compared with theirs who had only the gift of healing and miracles. What holds the last and lowest rank in this enumeration is diversity of tongues. It is by itself the most useless and insignificant of all these gifts. Healing diseases, relieving the poor, helping the sick, have their use: but how vain a thing is it to speak languages, if a man does it merely to amuse or boast himself! This may indeed raise the admiration, but cannot promote the edification, of the hearers, nor do them any good. And yet it is manifest from *ch.* xiv. that the Corinthians valued themselves exceedingly on this gift. Note, How proper a method it is to beat down pride to let persons know the true value of what they pride themselves in! It is but too common a thing for men to value themselves most on what is least worth: and it is of great use to bring them to a sober mind by letting them know how much they are mistaken. (3.) The various distribution of these gifts, not all to one, nor to every one alike. All members and officers had not the same rank in the church, nor the same endowments (*v.* 29, 30): *Are all apostles? Are all prophets?* This were to make the church a monster: all one as if the body were all ear or all eye. Some are fit for one office and employment, and some for another; and the Spirit distributes to every one as he will. We must be content with our own rank and share, if they be lower and less than those of others. We must not be conceited of ourselves, and despise others, if we are in the higher rank and have greater gifts. Every member of the body is to preserve its own rank, and do its own office; and all are to minister to one another, and promote the good of the body in general, without envying, or despising, or neglecting, or ill-using, any one particular member. How blessed a constitution were the Christian church, if all the members did their duty!

II. He closes this chapter with an advice

(as the generality read it) and a hint. 1. An advice to covet the best gifts, χαρίσματα τὰ κρείττονα—*dona potiora, præstantiora*, either the most valuable in themselves or the most serviceable to others; and these are, in truth, most valuable in themselves, though men may be apt to esteem those most that will raise their fame and esteem highest. Those are truly best by which God will be most honoured and his church edified. Such gifts should be most earnestly coveted. Note, We should desire that most which is best, and most worth. Grace is therefore to be preferred before gifts; and, of gifts, those are to be preferred which are of greatest use. But some read this passage, not as an advice, but a charge: ζηλοῦτε, *You are envious* at each other's gifts. In *ch.* xiii. 4, the same word is thus translated. You quarrel and contend about them. This they certainly did. And this behaviour the apostle here reprehends, and labours to rectify. *Only of pride cometh contention.* These contests in the church of Corinth sprang from this original. It was a quarrel about precedency (as most quarrels among Christians are, with whatever pretences they are gilded over); and it is no wonder that a quarrel about precedency should extinguish charity. When all would stand in the first rank, no wonder if they jostle, or throw down, or thrust back, their brethren. Gifts may be valued for their use, but they are mischievous when made the fuel of pride and contention. This therefore the apostle endeavours to prevent. 2. By giving them the hint of a more excellent way, namely, of charity, of mutual love and good-will. This was the only right way to quiet and cement them, and make their gifts turn to the advantage and edification of the church. This would render them kind to each other, and concerned for each other, and therefore calm their spirits, and put an end to their little piques and contests, their disputes about precedency. Those would appear to be in the foremost rank, according to the apostle, who had most of true Christian love. Note, True charity is greatly to be preferred to the most glorious gifts. To have the heart glow with mutual love is vastly better than to glare with the most pompous titles, offices, or powers.

CHAP. XIII.

In this chapter the apostle goes on to show more particularly what that more excellent way was of which he had just before been speaking. He recommends it, I. By showing the necessity and importance of it, ver. 1—3. II. By giving a description of its properties and fruits, ver. 4—7. III. By showing how much it excels the best of gifts and other graces, by its continuance, when they shall be no longer in being, or of any use, ver. 8, to the end.

THOUGH I speak with the
tongues of men and of angels,
and have not charity, I am become
as sounding brass, or a tinkling cymbal. 2 And though I have *the gift
of* prophecy, and understand all mysteries, and all knowledge; and though

I have all faith, so that I could remove
mountains, and have not charity, I
am nothing. 3 And though I bestow
all my goods to feed *the poor*, and
though I give my body to be burned,
and have not charity, it profiteth me
nothing.

Here the apostle shows what more excellent way he meant, or had in view, in the close of the former chapter, namely, *charity*, or, as it is commonly elsewhere rendered, *love*—ἀγάπη: not what is meant by charity in our common use of the word, which most men understand of alms-giving, but love in its fullest and most extensive meaning, true love to God and man, a benevolent disposition of mind towards our fellow-christians, growing out of sincere and fervent devotion to God. This living principle of all duty and obedience is the more excellent way of which the apostle speaks, preferable to all gifts. Nay, without this the most glorious gifts are nothing, of no account to us, of no esteem in the sight of God. He specifies, 1. The gift of tongues: *Though I speak with the tongues of men and of angels, and have not charity, I am become as sounding brass, or a tinkling cymbal, v.* 1. Could a man speak all the languages on earth, and that with the greatest propriety, elegance, and fluency, could he talk like an angel, and yet be without charity, it would be all empty noise, mere unharmonious and useless sound, that would neither profit nor delight. It is not talking freely, nor finely, nor learnedly, of the things of God, that will save ourselves, or profit others, if we are destitute of holy love. It is the charitable heart, not the voluble tongue, that is acceptable with God. The apostle specifies first this gift because hereupon the Corinthians seemed chiefly to value themselves and despise their brethren. 2. Prophecy, and the understanding of mysteries, and all knowledge. This without charity is as nothing, *v.* 2. Had a man ever so clear an understanding of the prophecies and types under the old dispensation, ever so accurate a knowledge of the doctrines of Christianity, nay, and this by inspiration, from the infallible dictates and illumination of the Spirit of God, without charity he would be nothing; all this would stand him in no stead. Note, A clear and deep head is of no signification, without a benevolent and charitable heart. It is not great knowledge that God sets a value upon, but true and hearty devotion and love. 3. Miraculous faith, the faith of miracles, or the faith by which persons were enabled to work miracles: *Had I all faith* (the utmost degree of this kind of faith), *that I could remove mountains* (or say to them, "Go hence into the midst of the sea," and have my command obeyed, Mark xi. 23), *and had no charity, I am nothing.* The most wonder-working faith, to which nothing is in a manner impossible, is itself nothing without charity. Moving mountains is a great achievement in the account of men; but one dram of charity is, in God's account, of much greater worth than all the faith of this sort in the world. Those may do many wondrous works in Christ's name whom yet he will disown, and bid depart from him, as workers of iniquity, Matt. vii. 22, 23. Saving faith is ever in conjunction with charity, but the faith of miracles may be without it. 4. The outward acts of charity: *Bestowing his goods to feed the poor, v.* 3. Should all a man has be laid out in this manner, if he had no charity, it would profit him nothing. There may be an open and lavish hand, where there is no liberal and charitable heart. The external act of giving alms may proceed from a very ill principle. Vain-glorious ostentation, or a proud conceit of merit, may put a man to large expense this way who has no true love to God nor men. Our doing good to others will do none to us, if it be not well done, namely, from a principle of devotion and charity, love to God, and good-will to men. Note, If we leave charity out of religion, the most costly services will be of no avail to us. If we give away all we have, while we withhold the heart from God, it will not profit. 5. Even sufferings, and even those of the most grievous kind: *If we give our bodies to be burnt, without charity, it profiteth nothing, v.* 3. Should we sacrifice our lives for the faith of the gospel, and be burnt to death in maintenance of its truth, this will stand us in no stead without charity, unless we be animated to these sufferings by a principle of true devotion to God, and sincere love to his church and people, and good-will to mankind. The outward carriage may be plausible, when the invisible principle is very bad. Some men have thrown themselves into the fire to procure a name and reputation among men. It is possible that the very same principle may have worked up some to resolution enough to die for their religion who never heartily believed and embraced it. But vindicating religion at the cost of our lives will profit nothing if we feel not the power of it; and true charity is the very heart and spirit of religion. If we feel none of its sacred heat in our hearts, it will profit nothing, though we be burnt to ashes for the truth. Note, The most grievous sufferings, the most costly sacrifices, will not recommend us to God, if we do not love the brethren; should we give our own bodies to be burnt, it would not profit us. How strange a way of recommending themselves to God are those got into who hope to do it by burning others, by murdering, and massacring, and tormenting their fellow-christians, or by any injurious usage of them! *My soul, enter not thou into their secrets.* If I cannot hope to recommend myself to God by giving my own body to be burnt while I have no charity, I will never hope to do it by burning or maltreating others, in open defiance to all charity.

4 Charity suffereth long, *and* is
kind; charity envieth not; charity
vaunteth not itself, is not puffed up,
5 Doth not behave itself unseemly,
seeketh not her own, is not easily
provoked, thinketh no evil; 6 Rejoiceth not in iniquity, but rejoiceth
in the truth; 7 Beareth all things,
believeth all things, hopeth all things,
endureth all things.

The apostle gives us in these verses some of the properties and effects of charity, both to describe and commend it, that we may know whether we have this grace, and that if we have not we may fall in love with what is so exceedingly amiable, and not rest till we have obtained it. It is an excellent grace, and has a world of good properties belonging to it. As,

I. *It is long suffering—μακροθυμεῖ.* It can endure evil, and injury, and provocation, without being filled with resentment, indignation, or revenge. It makes the mind firm, gives it power over the angry passions, and furnishes it with a persevering patience, that shall rather wait and wish for the reformation of a brother than fly out in resentment of his conduct. It will put up with many slights and neglects from the person it loves, and wait long to see the kindly effects of such patience on him.

II. *It is kind—χρηστεύεται.* It is benign, bountiful; it is courteous and obliging. *The law of kindness is in her lips;* her heart is large, and her hand open. She is ready to show favours and to do good. She seeks to be useful; and not only seizes on opportunities of doing good, but searches for them. This is her general character. She is patient under injuries, and apt and inclined to do all the good offices in her power. And under these two generals all the particulars of the character may be reduced.

III. Charity suppresses envy: *It envieth not;* it is not grieved at the good of others; neither at their gifts nor at their good qualities, their honours nor their estates. If we love our neighbour we shall be so far from envying his welfare, or being displeased with it, that we shall share in it and rejoice at it. His bliss and sanctification will be an addition to ours, instead of impairing or lessening it. This is the proper effect of kindness and benevolence: envy is the effect of ill-will. The prosperity of those to whom we wish well can never grieve us; and the mind which is bent on doing good to all can never wish ill to any.

IV. Charity subdues pride and vain-glory: *It vaunteth not itself, is not puffed up,* is not bloated with self-conceit, does not swell upon its acquisitions, nor arrogate to itself that honour, or power, or respect, which does not belong to it. It is not insolent, apt to despise others, or trample on them, or treat them with contempt and scorn. Those who are animated with a principle of true brotherly love will in honour prefer one another, Rom. xii. 10. They will *do nothing out* of a spirit of contention or *vain-glory, but in lowliness of mind will esteem others better than themselves*, Phil. ii. 3. True love will give us an esteem of our brethren, and raise our value for them; and this will limit our esteem of ourselves, and prevent the tumours of self-conceit and arrogance. These ill qualities can never grow out of tender affection for the brethren, nor a diffusive benevolence. The word rendered in our translation *vaunteth itself* bears other significations; nor is the proper meaning, as I can find, settled; but in every sense and meaning true charity stands in opposition to it. The Syriac renders it, *non tumultuatur—does not raise tumults* and disturbances. Charity calms the angry passions, instead of raising them. Others render it, *Non perperàm et perversè agit—It does not act insidiously with any,* seek to ensnare them, nor tease them with needless importunities and addresses. It is not froward, nor stubborn and untractable, nor apt to be cross and contradictory. Some understand it of dissembling and flattery, when a fair face is put on, and fine words are said, without any regard to truth, or intention of good. Charity abhors such falsehood and flattery. Nothing is commonly more pernicious, nor more apt to cross the purposes of true love and good will.

V. Charity is careful not to pass the bounds of decency; οὐκ ἀσχημονεῖ—*it behaveth not unseemly;* it does nothing indecorous, nothing that in the common account of men is base or vile. It does nothing out of place or time; but behaves towards all men as becomes their rank and ours, with reverence and respect to superiors, with kindness and condescension to inferiors, with courtesy and good-will towards all men. It is not for breaking order, confounding ranks, bringing all men on a level; but for keeping up the distinction God has made between men, and acting decently in its own station, and minding its own business, without taking upon it to mend, or censure, or despise, the conduct of others. Charity will do nothing that misbecomes it.

VI. Charity is an utter enemy to selfishness: *Seeketh not its own,* does not inordinately desire nor seek its own praise, or honour, or profit, or pleasure. Indeed self-love, in some degree, is natural to all men, enters into their very constitution. And a reasonable love of self is by our Saviour made the measure of our love to others, that charity which is here described, *Thou shalt love thy neighbour as thyself.* The apostle does not mean that charity destroys all regard to self; he does not mean that the charitable man should never challenge what is his own, but utterly neglect himself and all his interests. Charity must then root up that principle which is wrought into our nature. But charity never seeks its own to the hurt of others, or with the neglect of others. It often neglects its own for the sake of others; prefers their welfare, and satisfaction, and advantage, to its own; and it ever prefers the weal of the public, of the community, whether civil or ecclesiastical, to its private advantage. It would not advance, nor aggrandize, nor enrich, nor gratify itself, at the cost and damage of the public.

VII. It tempers and restrains the passions. Οὐ παροξύνεται—*is not exasperated.* It corrects a sharpness of temper, sweetens and softens the mind, so that it does not suddenly conceive, nor long continue, a vehement passion. Where the fire of love is kept in, the flames of wrath will not easily kindle, nor long keep burning. Charity will never be angry without a cause, and will endeavour to confine the passions within proper limits, that they may not exceed the measure that is just, either in degree or duration. Anger cannot rest in the bosom where love reigns. It is hard to be angry with those we love, but very easy to drop our resentments and be reconciled.

VIII. Charity *thinks no evil.* It cherishes no malice, nor gives way to revenge: so some understand it. It is not soon, nor long, angry; it is never mischievous, nor inclined to revenge; it does not suspect evil of others, οὐ λογίζεται τὸ κακὸν—*it does not reason out* evil, charge guilt upon them by inference and *innuendo,* when nothing of this sort appears open. True love is not apt to be jealous and suspicious; it will hide faults that appear, and draw a veil over them, instead of hunting and raking out those that lie covered and concealed: it will never indulge suspicion without proofs, but will rather incline to darken and disbelieve evidence against the person it affects. It will hardly give into an ill opinion of another, and it will do it with regret and reluctance when the evidence cannot be resisted; hence it will never be forward to suspect ill, and reason itself into a bad opinion upon mere appearances, nor give way to suspicion without any. It will not make the worst construction of things, but put the best face that it can on circumstances that have no good appearance.

IX. The matter of its joy and pleasure is here suggested: 1. Negatively: *It rejoiceth not in iniquity.* It takes no pleasure in doing injury or hurt to any. It thinks not evil of any, without very clear proof. It wishes ill to none, much less will it hurt or wrong any, and least of all make this the matter of its delight, rejoice in doing harm and mischief. Nor will it rejoice at the faults and failings of others, and triumph over them, either out of pride or ill-will, because it will set off its own excellences or gratify its spite. The sins of others are rather the grief of a charitable spirit than its sport or delight; they will touch it to the quick, and stir all its compassion, but can give it no entertainment. It is the very height of malice to take pleasure in the misery of a fellow-creature. And is not falling into sin the greatest calamity that can befal one? How inconsistent is it with Christian charity, to rejoice at such fall! 2. Affirmatively: *It rejoiceth in the truth,* is glad of the success of the gospel, commonly called *the truth,* by way of emphasis, in the New Testament; and rejoices to see men moulded into an evangelical temper by it, and made good. It takes no pleasure in their sins, but is highly delighted to see them do well, to approve themselves men of probity and integrity. It gives it much satisfaction to see truth and justice prevail among men, innocency cleared, and mutual faith and trust established, and to see piety and true religion flourish.

X. *It beareth all things, it endureth all things,* πάντα στέγει, πάντα ὑπομένει. Some read the first, *covers all things.* So the original also signifies. *Charity will cover a multitude of sins,* 1 Pet. iv. 8. It will draw a veil over them, as far as it can consistently with duty. It is not for blazing nor publishing the faults of a brother, till duty manifestly demands it. Necessity only can extort this from the charitable mind. Though such a man be free to tell his brother his faults in private, he is very unwilling to expose him by making them public. Thus we do by our own faults, and thus charity would teach us to do by the faults of others; not publish them to their shame and reproach, but cover them from public notice as long as we can, and be faithful to God and to others. Or, it *beareth all things,*—will pass by and put up with injuries, without indulging anger or cherishing revenge, will be patient upon provocation, and long patient, πάντα ὑπομένει—holds firm, though it be much shocked, and borne hard upon; sustains all manner of injury and ill usage, and bears up under it, such as curses, contumacies, slanders, prison, exile, bonds, torments, and death itself, for the sake of the injurious, and of others; and perseveres in this firmness. Note, What a fortitude and firmness fervent love will give the mind! What cannot a lover endure for the beloved and for his sake! How many slights and injuries will he put up with! How many hazards will he run and how many difficulties encounter!

XI. Charity believes and hopes well of others: *Believeth all things; hopeth all things.* Indeed charity does by no means destroy prudence, and, out of mere simplicity and silliness, believe every word, Prov. xiv. 15. Wisdom may dwell with love, and charity be cautious. But it is apt to believe well of all, to entertain a good opinion of them when there is no appearance to the contrary; nay, to believe well when there may be some dark appearances, if the evidence of ill be not clear. All charity is full of candour, apt to make the best of every thing, and put on it the best face and appearance? it will judge well, and believe well, as far as it can with any reason, and will rather stretch its faith beyond appearances for the support of a kind opinion; but it will go into a bad one with the utmost reluctance, and fence against it as much as it fairly and honestly can. And when, in spite of inclination, it cannot believe well of others, it will yet hope well, and continue to hope as long as there is any ground for it. It will not presently conclude a case desperate, but wishes the amendment of the worst of men, and is very apt to hope for what it wishes. How well-natured and amiable a thing is Christian charity? How lovely a mind is that which is tinctured throughout with such benevolence, and has it diffused over its whole frame! Happy the man who has this heavenly fire glowing in his heart, flowing out of his mouth, and diffusing its warmth over all with whom he has to do! How lovely a thing would Christianity appear to the world, if those who profess it were more actuated and animated by this divine principle, and paid a due regard to a command on which its blessed author laid a chief stress! *A new commandment give I to you, that you love one another, as I have loved you, that you also love one another,* John xiii. 34. *By this shall all men know that you are my disciples, v.* 35. Blessed Jesus! how few of thy professed disciples are to be distinguished and marked out by this characteristic!

8 Charity never faileth: but whether *there be* prophecies, they shall
fail; whether *there be* tongues, they
shall cease; whether *there be* knowledge, it shall vanish away. 9 For
we know in part, and we prophesy in
part. 10 But when that which is
perfect is come, then that which is
in part shall be done away. 11
When I was a child, I spake as a
child, I understood as a child, I
thought as a child: but when I became a man, I put away childish
things. 12 For now we see through
a glass, darkly; but then face to face:
now I know in part; but then shall
I know even as also I am known. 13
And now abideth faith, hope, charity,
these three; but the greatest of these
is charity.

Here the apostle goes on to commend charity, and show how much it is preferable to the gifts on which the Corinthians were so apt to pride themselves, to the utter neglect, and almost extinction, of charity. This he makes out,

I. From its longer continuance and duration: *Charity never faileth.* It is a permanent and perpetual grace, lasting as eternity; whereas the extraordinary gifts on which the Corinthians valued themselves were of short continuance. They were only to edify the church on earth, and that but for a time, not during its whole continuance in this world; but in heaven would be all superseded, which yet is the very seat and element of love. *Prophecy must fail,* that is, either the prediction of things to come (which is its most common sense) or the interpretation of scripture by immediate inspiration. *Tongues will cease,* that is, the miraculous power of speaking languages without learning them. There will be but one language in heaven. There is no confusion of tongues in the region of perfect tranquillity. And *knowledge will vanish away.* Not that, in the perfect state above, holy and happy souls shall be unknowing, ignorant: it is a very poor happiness that can consist with utter ignorance. The apostle is plainly speaking of miraculous gifts, and therefore of knowledge to be had out of the common way (see *ch.* xiv. 6), a knowledge of mysteries supernaturally communicated. Such knowledge was to vanish away. Some indeed understand it of common knowledge acquired by instruction, taught and learnt. This way of knowing is to vanish away, though the knowledge itself, once acquired, will not be lost. But it is plain that the apostle is here setting the grace of charity in opposition to supernatural gifts. And it is more valuable, because more durable; *it* shall last, when *they* shall be no more; *it* shall enter into heaven, where *they* will have no place, because they will be of no use, though, in a sense, even our common knowledge may be said to cease in heaven, by reason of the improvement that will then be made in it. The light of a candle is perfectly obscured by the sun shining in its strength.

II. He hints that these gifts are adapted only to a state of imperfection: *We know in part, and we prophesy in part, v.* 9. Our best knowledge and our greatest abilities are at present like our condition, narrow and temporary. Even the knowledge they had by inspiration was but in part. How little a portion of God, and the unseen world, was heard even by apostles and inspired men! How much short do others come of them! But these gifts were fitted to the present imperfect state of the church, valuable in themselves, but not to be compared with charity, because they were to vanish with the imperfections of the church, nay, and long before, whereas charity was to last for ever.

III. He takes occasion hence to show how much better it will be with the church hereafter than it can be here. A state of perfection is in view (*v.* 10): *When that which is perfect shall come, then that which is in part shall be done away.* When the end is once attained, the means will of course be abolished. There will be no need of tongues, and prophecy, and inspired knowledge, in a future life, because then the church will be in a state of perfection, complete both in knowledge and holiness. God will be known then clearly, and in a manner by intuition, and as perfectly as th capacity of glorified minds will allow; not b such transient glimpses, and little portion as here. The difference between these tw states is here pointed at in two particulars 1. The present state is a state of childhooc the future that of manhood: *When I was a chila I spoke as a child* (that is, as some think spoke with tongues), *I understood as a child* ἐφρόνουν—*sapiebam* (that is, "I prophesied, was taught the mysteries of the kingdom o heaven, in such an extraordinary way as ma nifested I was not out of my childish state"), *thought,* or reasoned, ἐλογιζόμην, *as a child but, when I became a man, I put away childis things.* Such is the difference between eartl and heaven. What narrow views, what con fused and indistinct notions of things, hav children, in comparison of grown men! Anc how naturally do men, when reason is ripenec and matured, despise and relinquish thei infant thoughts, put them away, reject them, esteem them as nothing! Thus shall we think of our most valued gifts and acquisitions in this world, when we come to heaven. We shall despise our childish folly, in priding ourselves in such things when we are grown up to men in Christ. 2. Things are all dark and confused now, in comparison of what they will be hereafter: *Now we see through a glass darkly* (ἐν αἰνίγματι, *in a riddle), then face to face; now we know in part, but then we shall know as we are known.* Now we can only discern things at a great distance, as through a telescope, and that involved in clouds and obscurity; but hereafter the things to be known will be near and obvious, open to our eyes; and our knowledge will be free from all obscurity and error. God is to be seen *face to face;* and we *are to know him* as *we are known by him;* not indeed as perfectly, but in some sense in the same manner. We are known to him by mere inspection; he turns his eye towards us, and sees and searches us throughout. We shall then fix our eye on him, *and see him as he is,* 1 John iii. 2. We shall know how we are known, enter into all the mysteries of divine love and grace. O glorious change! To pass from darkness to light, from clouds to the clear sunshine of our Saviour's face, and in God's own light to see light! Ps. xxxvi. 9. Note, It is the light of heaven only that will remove all clouds and darkness from the face of God. It is at best but twilight while we are in this world; there it will be perfect and eternal day.

IV. To sum up the excellences of charity, he prefers it not only to gifts, but to other graces, to faith and hope (*v.* 13): *And now abide faith, hope, and charity; but the greatest of these is charity.* True grace is much more excellent than any spiritual gifts whatever. And faith, hope, and love, are the three principal graces, of which charity is the chief, being the end to which the other two are but means. This is the divine nature, the soul's felicity, or its complacential rest in God, and holy delight in all his saints. And it is everlasting work, when faith and hope shall be no more. Faith fixes on the divine revelation, and assents to that: hope fastens on future felicity, and waits for that: and in heaven faith will be swallowed up in vision, and hope in fruition. There is no room to believe and hope, when we see and enjoy. But love fastens on the divine perfections themselves, and the divine image on the creatures, and our mutual relation both to God and them. These will all shine forth in the most glorious splendours in another world, and there will love be made perfect; there we shall pefectly love God, because he will appear amiable for ever, and our hearts will kindle at the sight, and glow with perpetual devotion. And there shall we perfectly love one another, when all the saints meet there, when none but saints are there, and saints made perfect. O blessed state! How much surpassing the best below! O amiable and excellent grace of charity! How much does it exceed the most valuable gift, when it outshines every grace, and is the everlasting consummation of them! When faith and hope are at an end, true charity will burn for ever with the brightest flame. Note, Those border most upon the heavenly state and perfection whose hearts are fullest of this divine principle, and burn with the most fervent charity. It is the surest offspring of God, and bears his fairest impression. For God is love, 1 John iv. 8, 16. And where God is to be seen as he is, and face to face, there charity is in its greatest height—there, and there only, will it be perfected.

CHAP. XIV.

In this chapter the apostle directs them about the use of their spiritual gifts, preferring those most that are best and fitted to do the greatest good. I. He begins with advising them of all spiritual gifts to prefer prophesying, and shows that this is much better than speaking with tongues, ver. 1—5. II. He goes on to show them how unprofitable the speaking of foreign languages is, and useless to the church; it is like piping in one tone, like sounding a trumpet without any certain note, like talking gibberish; whereas gifts should be used for the good of the church, ver. 6—14. III. He advises that worship should be celebrated so that the most ignorant might understand, and join in prayer and praise, and presses the advice by his own example, ver. 15—20. IV. He informs them that tongues were a sign for unbelievers rather than those that believe; and represents the advantage of prophecy above speaking with tongues, from the different suggestions they would give to the mind of an unbeliever coming into their assemblies, ver. 21—25. V. He blames them for the disorder and confusion they had brought into the assembly, by their vanity and ostentation of their gifts; and directs them in using the gifts both of tongues and prophecy, ver. 26—33. VI. He forbids women speaking in the church; and closes this subject by requiring them to perform every thing in the public worship with order and decency, ver. 34, to the end.

FOLLOW after charity, and desire
spiritual *gifts*, but rather that ye
may prophesy. 2 For he that speaketh
in an *unknown* tongue speaketh not
unto men, but unto God: for no man
understandeth *him;* howbeit in the
spirit he speaketh mysteries. 3 But
he that prophesieth, speaketh unto
men *to* edification, and exhortation,
and comfort. 4 He that speaketh in
an *unknown* tongue edifieth himself;
but he that prophesieth edifieth the
church. 5 I would that ye all spake
with tongues, but rather that ye prophesied: for greater *is* he that prophesieth than he that speaketh with tongues, except he interpret, that the church may receive edifying.

The apostle, in the foregoing chapter, had himself preferred, and advised the Corinthians to prefer, Christian charity to all spiritual gifts. Here he teaches them, among spiritual gifts, which they should prefer, and by what rules they should make comparison. He begins the chapter,

I. With an exhortation to charity (*v.* 1): *Follow after charity,* pursue it. The original, διώκετε, when spoken of a thing, signifies a singular concern to obtain it; and is commonly taken in a good and laudable sense. It is an exhortation to obtain charity, to get this excellent disposition of mind upon any terms, whatever pains or prayers it may cost: as if he had said, "In whatever you fail, see you do not miss of this; the principal of all graces is worth your getting at any rate."

II. He directs them which spiritual gift to prefer, from a principle of charity: "*Desire spiritual gifts, but rather that you may prophesy,* or chiefly that you may prophesy." While they were in close pursuit of charity, and made this Christian disposition their chief scope, they might be zealous of spiritual gifts, be ambitious of them in some measure, but especially of prophesying, that is, of interpreting scripture. This preference would most plainly discover that they were indeed upon such pursuit, that they had a due value for Christian charity, and were intent upon it. Note, Gifts are fit objects of our desire and pursuit, in subordination to grace and charity. That should be sought first and with the greatest earnestness which is most worth.

III. He assigns the reasons of this preference. And it is remarkable here that he only compares prophesying with speaking with tongues. It seems, this was the gift on which the Corinthians principally valued themselves. This was more ostentatious than the plain interpretation of scripture, more fit to gratify pride, but less fit to pursue the purposes of Christian charity; it would not equally edify nor do good to the souls of men. For, 1. He that spoke with tongues must wholly speak between God and himself; for, whatever mysteries might be communicated in his language, none of his own countrymen could understand them, because they did not understand the language, *v.* 2. Note, What cannot be understood can never edify. No advantage can be reaped from the most excellent discourses, if delivered in unintelligible language, such as the audience can neither speak nor understand: but he that prophesies speaks to the advantage of his hearers; they may profit by his gift. Interpretation of scripture will be for their edification; they may be exhorted and comforted by it, *v.* 3. And indeed these two must go together. Duty is the proper way to comfort; and those that would be comforted must bear being exhorted. 2. He that speaks with tongues may edify himself, *v.* 4. He may understand and be affected with what he speaks; and so every minister should; and he that is most edified himself is in the disposition and fitness to do good to others by what he speaks; but he that speaks with tongues, or language unknown, can only edify himself; others can reap no benefit from his speech. Whereas the end of speaking in the church is to edify the church (*v.* 4), to which prophesying, or interpreting scripture by inspiration or otherwise, is immediately adapted. Note, That is the best and most eligible gift which best answers the purposes of charity and does most good; not that which can edify ourselves only, but that which will edify the church. Such is prophesying, or preaching, and interpreting scripture, compared with speaking in an unknown tongue. 3. Indeed, no gift is to be despised, but the best gifts are to be preferred. *I could wish,* says the apostle, *that you all spoke with tongues, but rather that you prophesied, v.* 5. Every gift of God is a favour from God, and may be improved for his glory, and as such is to be valued and thankfully received; but then those are to be most valued that are most useful. *Greater is he that prophesieth than he that speaketh with tongues, unless he interpret, that the church may receive edifying, v.* 5. Benevolence makes a man truly great. *It is more blessed to give than to receive.* And it is true magnanimity to study and seek to be useful to others, rather than to raise their admiration and draw their esteem. Such a man has a large soul, copious and diffused in proportion to his benevolence and bent of mind for public good. Greater is he who interprets scripture to edify the church than he who speaks tongues to recommend himself. And what other end he who spoke with tongues could have, unless he interpreted what he spoke, is not easy to say. Note, That makes most for the honour of a minister which is most for the church's edification, not that which shows his gifts to most advantage. He acts in a narrow sphere, while he aims at himself; but his spirit and character increase in proportion to his usefulness, I mean his own intention and endeavours to be useful.

6 Now, brethren, if I come unto
you speaking with tongues, what shall
I profit you, except I shall speak to
you either by revelation, or by knowledge, or by prophesying, or by doctrine? 7 And even things without
life giving sound, whether pipe or
harp, except they give a distinction
in the sounds, how shall it be known
what is piped or harped? 8 For if
the trumpet give an uncertain sound,
who shall prepare himself to the
battle? 9 So likewise ye, except ye
utter by the tongue words easy to be
understood, how shall it be known
what is spoken? for ye shall speak
into the air. 10 There are, it may
be, so many kinds of voices in the
world, and none of them *is* without
signification. 11 Therefore if I know
not the meaning of the voice, I shall
be unto him that speaketh a barbarian,
and he that speaketh *shall be* a barbarian unto me. 12 Even so ye, forasmuch as ye are zealous of spiritual
gifts, seek that ye may excel to the
edifying of the church. 13 Wherefore let him that speaketh in an *unknown* tongue pray that he may
interpret. 14 For if I pray in an
unknown tongue, my spirit prayeth,
but my understanding is unfruitful.

In this paragraph he goes on to show how vain a thing the ostentation of speaking unknown and unintelligible language must be. It was altogether unedifying and unprofitable (*v.* 6): *If I come to you speaking with tongues, what will it profit you, unless I speak to you by revelation, or by knowledge, or by prophesying, or by doctrine?* It would signify nothing to utter any of these in an unknown tongue. An apostle, with all his furniture, could not edify, unless he spoke to the capacity of his hearers. New revelations, the most clear explications of old ones, the most instructive discourses in themselves, would be unprofitable in a language not understood. Nay, interpretations of scripture made in an unknown tongue would need to be interpreted over again, before they could be of any use.

I. He illustrates this by several allusions. 1. To a pipe and a harp playing always in one tone. Of what use can this be to those who are dancing? If there be no distinction of sounds, how should they order their steps or motions? Unintelligible language is like piping or harping without distinction of sounds: it gives no more direction how a man should order his conversation than a pipe with but one stop or a harp with but one string can direct a dancer how he should order his steps, *v.* 7. 2. To a trumpet giving an *uncertain sound,* ἄδηλον φωνὴν, a sound not manifest; either not the proper sound for the purpose, or not distinct enough to be discerned from every other sound. If, instead of sounding an onset, it sounded a retreat, or sounded one knew not what, who would prepare for the battle? To talk in an unknown language in a Christian assembly is altogether as vain and to no purpose as for a trumpet to give no certain sound in the field or day of battle. The army in one case, and the congregation in the other, must be all in suspense, and at a perfect nonplus. To speak words that have no significancy to those who hear them is to leave them ignorant of what is spoken; it is speaking to the air, *v.* 9. Words without a meaning can convey no notion nor instruction to the mind; and words not understood have no meaning with those who do not understand them: to talk to them in such language is to waste our breath. 3. He compares the speaking in an unknown tongue to the gibberish of barbarians. There are, as he says (*v.* 10), many kinds of voices in the world, none of which is without its proper signification. This is true of the several languages spoken by different nations. All of them have their proper signification. Without this they would be *φώναι ἄφωνοι—a voice, and no voice.* For that is no language, nor can it answer the end of speaking, which has no meaning. But whatever proper signification the words of any language may have in themselves, and to those who understand them, they are perfect gibberish to men of another language, who understand them not. In this case, speaker and hearers are barbarians to each other (*v.* 11), they talk and hear only sounds without sense; for this is to be a barbarian. For thus says the polite Ovid, when banished into Pontus,

> Barbarus hic ego sum, quia non intelligor ulli.
> I am a barbarian here, none understand me.

To speak in the church in an unknown tongue is to talk gibberish; it is to play the barbarian; it is to confound the audience, instead of instructing them; and for this reason is utterly vain and unprofitable.

II. Having thus established his point, in the two next verses he applies it, 1. By advising them to be chiefly desirous of those gifts that were most for the church's edification, *v.* 12. "Forasmuch as you are zealous of spiritual gifts, this way it will become commendable zeal, be zealous to edify the church, to promote Christian knowledge and practice, and covet those gifts most that will do the best service to men's souls." This is the great rule he gives, which, 2. He applies to the matter in hand, that, if they did speak a foreign language, they should beg of God the gift of interpreting it, *v.* 13. That these were different gifts, see *ch.* xii. 10. Those might speak and understand a foreign language who could not readily translate it into their own: and yet was this necessary to the church's edification; for the church must understand, that it might be edified, which yet it could not do till the foreign language was translated into its own. Let him therefore pray for the gift of interpreting what he speaks in an unknown tongue; or rather covet and ask of God the gift of interpreting than of speaking in a language that needs interpretation, this being most for the church's benefit, and therefore among the gifts that excel; *vide v.* 12. Some understand it, "Let him pray so as to interpret what he utters in prayer in a language unintelligible without it." The sum is that they should perform all religious exercises in their assemblies so that all might join in them and profit by them. 3. He enforces this advice with a proper reason, that, if *he prayed in an unknown tongue, his spirit might pray,* that is, a spiritual gift might be exercised in prayer, or his own mind might be devoutly engaged, *but his understanding would be unfruitful* (*v.* 14), that is, the sense and meaning of his words would be unfruitful, he would not be understood, nor therefore would others join with him in his devotions. Note, It should be the concern of such as pray in public to pray intelligibly, not in a foreign language, nor in a language that, if it be not foreign, is above the level of his audience. Language that is most obvious and easy to be understood is the most proper for public devotion and other religious exercises.

15 What is it then? I will pray
with the spirit, and I will pray with
the understanding also: I will sing
with the spirit, and I will sing with
the understanding also. 16 Else when
thou shalt bless with the spirit, how
shall he that occupieth the room of
the unlearned say Amen at thy giving
of thanks, seeing he understandeth
not what thou sayest? 17 For thou
verily givest thanks well, but the other
is not edified. 18 I thank my God,
I speak with tongues more than ye
all: 19 Yet in the church I had
rather speak five words with my understanding, that *by my voice* I might
teach others also, than ten thousand
words in an *unknown* tongue. 20
Brethren, be not children in understanding: howbeit in malice be ye
children, but in understanding be men.

The apostle here sums up the argument hitherto, and,

I. Directs them how they should sing and pray in public (*v.* 15): *What is it then? I will pray with the spirit, and I will pray with the understanding also. I will sing with the spirit,* &c. He does not forbid their praying or singing under a divine *afflatus,* or when they were inspired for this purpose, or had such a spiritual gift communicated to them; but he would have them perform both so as to be understood by others, that others might join with them. Note, Public worship should be performed so as to be understood.

II. He enforces the argument with several reasons.

1. That otherwise the unlearned could not say Amen to their prayers or thanksgivings, could not join in the worship, for they did not understand it, *v.* 16. He who fills up or occupies the place of the unlearned, that is, as the ancients interpret it, the body of the people, who, in most Christian assemblies, are illiterate; how should they say *Amen* to prayers in an unknown tongue? How should they declare their consent and concurrence? This is saying *Amen,* So be it. *God grant the thing we have requested;* or, We join in the confession that has been made of sin, and in the acknowledgment that has been made of divine mercies and favours. This is the import of saying *Amen.* All should say *Amen* inwardly; and it is not improper to testify this inward concurrence in public prayers and devotions, by an audible *Amen.* The ancient Christians said *Amen* aloud. *Vide* Just. Mart. *apol.* 2. *prope fin.* Now, how should the people say *Amen* to what they did not understand? Note, There can be no concurrence in those prayers that are not understood. The intention of public devotions is therefore entirely destroyed if they are performed in an unknown tongue. He who performs may pray well, and give thanks well, but not in that time and place, because others are not, cannot be, edified (*v.* 17) by what they understand not.

2. He alleges his own example, to make the greater impression, concerning which observe, (1.) That he did not come behind any of them in this spiritual gift: "*I thank my God, I speak with tongues more than you all* (*v.* 18); not only more than any single person among you, but more than all together." It was not envy at their better furniture that made Paul depreciate what they so highly valued and so much vaunted of; he surpassed them all in this very gift of tongues, and did not vilify their gift because he had it not. This spirit of envy is too common in the world. But the apostle took care to guard against this misconstruction of his purpose, by letting them know there was more ground for them to envy him upon this head than for him to envy them. Note, When we beat down men's unreasonable value for themselves, or any of their possessions or attainments, we should let them see, if possible, that this does not proceed from an envious and grudging spirit. We miss our aim if they can fairly give our conduct this invidious turn. Paul could not be justly censured, nor suspected for any such principle in this whole argument. He spoke more languages than they all. Yet, (2.) He had rather *speak five words with understanding,* that is, so as to be understood, and instruct and edify others, *than ten thousand words in an unknown tongue, v.* 19. He was so far from valuing himself upon talking languages, or making ostentation of his talents of this kind, that he had rather speak five intelligible words, to benefit others, than make a thousand, ten thousand fine discourses, that would do no one else any good, because they did not understand them. Note, A truly Christian minister will value himself much more upon doing the least spiritual good to men's souls than upon procuring the greatest applause and commendation to himself. This is true grandeur and nobleness of spirit; it is acting up to his character; it is approving himself the servant of Christ, and not a vassal to his own pride and vanity.

3. He adds a plain intimation that the fondness then discovered for this gift was but too plain an indication of the immaturity of their judgment: *Brethren, be not children in understanding; in malice be you children, but in understanding be men, v.* 20. Children are apt to be struck with novelty and strange appearances. They are taken with an outward show, without enquiring into the true nature and worth of things. Do not you act like them, and prefer noise and show to worth and substance; show a greater ripeness of judgment, and act a more manly part; be like children in nothing but an innocent and inoffensive disposition. A double rebuke is couched in this passage, both of their pride upon account of their gifts, and their arrogance and haughtiness towards each other, and the contests and quarrels proceeding from them. Note, Christians should be harmless and inoffensive as children, void of all guile and malice; but should have wisdom and knowledge that are ripe and mature. They should not be unskilful in the word of righteousness (Heb. v. 13), though they should be unskilful in all the arts of mischief.

21 In the law it is written, With
men of other tongues and other lips
will I speak unto this people; and
yet for all that will they not hear
me, saith the Lord. 22 Wherefore
tongues are for a sign, not to them
that believe, but to them that believe
not: but prophesying *serveth* not for
them that believe not, but for them
which believe. 23 If therefore the
whole church be come together into
one place, and all speak with tongues,
and there come in *those that are* unlearned, or unbelievers, will they not
say that ye are mad? 24 But if all
prophesy, and there come in one that
believeth not, or *one* unlearned, he is
convinced of all, he is judged of all:
25 And thus are the secrets of his
heart made manifest; and so falling
down on *his* face he will worship God,

and report that God is in you of a truth.

In this passage the apostle pursues the argument, and reasons from other topics; as,

I. Tongues, as the Corinthians used them, were rather a token of judgment from God than mercy to any people (*v.* 21): *In the law* (that is, the Old Testament) *it is written, With men of other tongues and other lips will I speak to this people; and yet for all this will they not hear me, saith the Lord,* Isa. xxviii. 11. Compare Deut. xxviii. 46, 49. To both these passages, it is thought, the apostle refers. Both are delivered by way of threatening, and one is supposed to interpret the other. The meaning in this view is that it is an evidence that a people are abandoned of God when he gives them up to this sort of instruction, to the discipline of those who speak in another language. And surely the apostle's discourse implies, "You should not be fond of the tokens of divine displeasure. God can have no gracious regards to those who are left merely to this sort of instruction, and taught in language which they cannot understand. They can never be benefited by such teaching as this; and, when they are left to it, it is a sad sign that God gives them over as past cure." And should Christians covet to be in such a state, or to bring the churches into it? Yet thus did the Corinthian preachers in effect, who would always deliver their inspirations in an unknown tongue.

II. Tongues were rather a sign to unbelievers than to believers, *v.* 22. They were a spiritual gift, intended for the conviction and conversion of infidels, that they might be brought into the Christian church; but converts were to be built up in Christianity by profitable instructions in their own language. The gift of tongues was necessary to spread Christianity, and gather churches; it was proper and intended to convince unbelievers of that doctrine which Christians had already embraced; but prophesying, and interpreting scripture in their own language, were most for the edification of such as did already believe: so that speaking with tongues in Christian assemblies was altogether out of time and place; neither one nor the other was proper for it. Note, That gifts may be rightly used, it is proper to know the ends which they are intended to serve. To go about the conversion of infidels, as the apostles did, had been a vain undertaking without the gift of tongues, and the discovery of this gift; but, in an assembly of Christians already converted to the Christian faith, to make use and ostentation of this gift would be perfectly impertinent, because it would be of no advantage to the assembly; not for conviction of truth, because they had already embraced it; not for their edification, because they did not understand, and could not get benefit without understanding, what they heard.

III. The credit and reputation of their assemblies among unbelievers required them to prefer prophesying before speaking with tongues. For, 1. If, when they were all assembled for Christian worship, their ministers, or all employed in public worship, should talk unintelligible language, and infidels should drop in, they would conclude them to be mad, to be no better than a parcel of wild fanatics. Who in their right senses could carry on religious worship in such a manner? Or what sort of religion is that which leaves out sense and understanding? Would not this make Christianity ridiculous to a heathen, to hear the ministers of it pray, or preach, or perform any other religious exercise, in a language that neither he nor the assembly understood? Note, The Christian religion is a sober and reasonable thing in itself, and should not, by the ministers of it, be made to look wild or senseless. Those disgrace their religion, and vilify their own character, who do any thing that has this aspect. But, on the other hand, 2. If, instead of speaking with tongues, those who minister plainly interpret scripture, or preach, in language intelligible and proper, the great truths and rules of the gospel, a heathen or unlearned person, coming in, will probably be convinced, and become a convert to Christianity (*v.* 24, 25); his conscience will be touched, the secrets of his heart will be revealed to him, he will be condemned by the truth he hears, and so will be brought to confess his guilt, to pay his homage to God, and own that he is indeed among you, present in the assembly. Note, Scripture-truth, plainly and duly taught, has a marvellous aptness to awaken the conscience, and touch the heart. And is not this much more for the honour of our religion than that infidels should conclude the ministers of it a set of madmen, and their religious exercises only fits of phrensy? This last would at once cast contempt on them and their religion too. Instead of procuring applause for them, it would render them ridiculous, and involve their profession in the same censure: whereas prophesying would certainly edify the church, much better keep up their credit, and might probably convince and convert infidels who might occasionally hear them. Note, Religious exercises in Christian assemblies should be such as are fit to edify the faithful, and convince, affect, and convert unbelievers. The ministry was not instituted to make ostentation of gifts and parts, but to save souls.

26 How is it then, brethren? when
ye come together, every one of you
hath a psalm, hath a doctrine, hath a
tongue, hath a revelation, hath an interpretation. Let all things be done
unto edifying. 27 If any man speak
in an *unknown* tongue, *let it be* by

two, or at the most *by* three, and *that*
by course; and let one interpret. 28
But if there be no interpreter, let him
keep silence in the church; and let
him speak to himself, and to God.
29 Let the prophets speak two or
three, and let the other judge. 30 If
any thing be revealed to another that
sitteth by, let the first hold his peace.
31 For ye may all prophesy one by
one, that all may learn, and all may
be comforted. 32 And the spirits of
the prophets are subject to the prophets. 33 For God is not *the author*
of confusion, but of peace, as in all
churches of the saints.

In this passage the apostle reproves them for their disorder, and endeavours to correct and regulate their conduct for the future.

I. He blames them for the confusion they introduced into the assembly, by ostentation of their gifts (*v.* 26): *When you come together every one hath a psalm, hath a doctrine, hath a tongue,* &c.; that is, "You are apt to confound the several parts of worship; and, while one has a psalm to utter by inspiration, another has a doctrine, or revelation;" or else, "You are apt to be confused in the same branch of worship, many of you having psalms or doctrines to propose at the same time, without staying for one another. Is not this perfect uproar? Can this be edifying? And yet all religious exercises in public assemblies should have this view, *Let all things be done to edifying.*"

II. He corrects their faults, and lays down some regulations for their future conduct. 1. As to speaking in an unknown tongue, he orders that no more than two or three should do it at one meeting, and this not altogether, but successively, one after another. And even this was not to be done unless there were some one to interpret (*v.* 27, 28), some other interpreter besides himself, who spoke; for to speak in an unknown tongue what he himself was afterwards to interpret could only be for ostentation. But, if another were present who could interpret, two miraculous gifts might be exercised at once, and thereby the church edified, and the faith of the hearers confirmed at the same time. But, if there were none to interpret, he was to be silent in the church, and only exercise his gift between God and himself (*v.* 28), that is (as I think) in private, at home; for all who are present at public worship should join in it, and not be at their private devotions in public assemblies. Solitary devotions are out of time and place when the church has met for social worship. 2. As to prophesying he orders, (1.) That two or three only should speak at one meeting (*v.* 20), and this successively, not all at once; and that the other should examine and judge what he delivered, that is, discern and determine concerning it, whether it were of divine inspiration or not. There might be false prophets, mere pretenders to divine inspiration; and the true prophets were to judge of these, and discern and discover who was divinely inspired, and by such inspiration interpreted scripture, and taught the church, and who was not—what was of divine inspiration and what was not. This seems to be the meaning of this rule. For where a prophet was known to be such, and under the divine *afflatus,* he could not be judged; for this were to subject even the Holy Spirit to the judgment of men. He who was indeed inspired, and known to be so, was above all human judgment. (2.) He orders that, if any assistant prophet had a revelation, while another was prophesying, the other should hold his peace, be silent (*v.* 30), before the inspired assistant uttered his revelation. Indeed, it is by many understood that the former speaker should immediately hold his peace. But this seems unnatural, and not so well to agree with the context. For why must one that was speaking by inspiration be immediately silent upon another man's being inspired, and suppress what was dictated to him by the same Spirit? Indeed, he who had the new revelation might claim liberty of speech in his turn, upon producing his vouchers; but why must liberty of speech be taken from him who was speaking before, and his mouth stopped, when he was delivering the dictates of the same Spirit, and could produce the same vouchers? Would the Spirit of God move one to speak, and, before he had delivered what he had to say, move another to interrupt him, and put him to silence? This seems to me an unnatural thought. Nor is it more agreeable to the context, and the reason annexed (*v.* 31): *That all might prophesy, one by one,* or one after another, which could not be where any one was interrupted and silenced before he had done prophesying; but might easily be if he who was afterwards inspired forbore to deliver his new revelation till the former prophet had finished what he had to say. And, to confirm this sense, the apostle quickly adds, *The spirits of the prophets are subject to the prophets* (*v.* 33); that is, the spiritual gifts they have leave them still possessed of their reason, and capable of using their own judgment in the exercise of them. Divine inspirations are not, like the diabolical possessions of heathen priests, violent and ungovernable, and prompting them to act as if they were beside themselves; but are sober and calm, and capable of regular conduct. The man inspired by the Spirit of God may still act the man, and observe the rules of natural order and decency in delivering his revelations. His spiritual gift is thus far subject to his pleasure, and to be managed by his discretion.

III. The apostle gives the reasons of these regulations. As, 1. That they would be for the church's benefit, their instruction and consolation. It is that *all may learn, and all may be comforted or exhorted,* that the prophets were to speak in the orderly manner the apostle advises. Note, The instruction, edification, and comfort of the church, is that for which God instituted the ministry. And surely ministers should, as much as possible, fit their ministrations to these purposes. 2. He tells them, *God is not the God of confusion, but of peace and good order,* *v.* 33. Therefore divine inspiration should by no means throw Christian assemblies into confusion, and break through all rules of common decency, which yet would be unavoidable if several inspired men should all at once utter what was suggested to them by the Spirit of God, and not wait to take their turns. Note, The honour of God requires that things should be managed in Christian assemblies so as not to transgress the rules of natural decency. If they are managed in a tumultuous and confused manner, what a notion must this give of the God who is worshipped, to considerate observers! Does it look as if he were the God of peace and order, and an enemy to confusion? Things should be managed so in divine worship that no unlovely nor dishonourable notion of God should be formed in the minds of observers. 3. He adds that things were thus orderly managed in all the other churches: *As in all the churches of the saints* (*v.* 33); they kept to these rules in the exercise of their spiritual gifts, which was a manifest proof that the church of Corinth might observe the same regulations. And it would be perfectly scandalous for them, who exceeded most churches in spiritual gifts, to be more disorderly than any in the exercise of them. Note, Though other churches are not to be our rule, yet the regard they pay to the rules of natural decency and order should restrain us from breaking these rules. Thus far they may be proposed as examples, and it is a shame not to follow them.

34 Let your women keep silence in the churches: for it is not permitted unto them to speak; but *they are commanded* to be under obedience, as also saith the law. 35 And if they will learn any thing, let them ask their husbands at home: for it is a shame for women to speak in the church.

Here the apostle, 1. Enjoins silence on their women in public assemblies, and to such a degree that they must not ask questions for their own information in the church, but ask their husbands at home. *They are to learn in silence with all subjection; but,* says the apostle, *I suffer them not to teach,* 1 Tim. ii. 11, 12. There is indeed an intimation (*ch.* xi. 5) as if the women sometimes did pray and prophecy in their assemblies, which the apostle, in that passage, does not simply condemn, but the manner of performance, that is, praying or prophesying with the head uncovered, which, in that age and country, was throwing off the distinction of sexes, and setting themselves on a level with the men. But here he seems to forbid all public performances of theirs. They are not permitted to speak (*v.* 34) in the church, neither in praying nor prophesying. The connection seems plainly to include the latter, in the limited sense in which it is taken in this chapter, namely, for preaching, or interpreting scripture by inspiration. And, indeed, for a woman to prophesy in this sense were to teach, which does not so well befit her state of subjection. A teacher of others has in that respect a superiority over them, which is not allowed the woman over the man, nor must she therefore be allowed to teach in a congregation: *I suffer them not to teach.* But praying, and uttering hymns inspired, were not teaching. And seeing there were women who had spiritual gifts of this sort in that age of the church (see Acts xxii. 9), and might be under this impulse in the assembly, must they altogether suppress it? Or why should they have this gift, if it must never be publicly exercised? For these reasons, some think that these general prohibitions are only to be understood in common cases; but that upon extraordinary occasions, when women were under a divine *afflatus,* and known to be so, they might have liberty of speech. They were not ordinarily to teach, nor so much as to debate and ask questions in the church, but learn in silence there; and, if difficulties occurred, *ask their own husbands at home.* Note, As it is the woman's duty to learn in subjection, it is the man's duty to keep up his superiority, by being able to instruct her; if it be her duty to ask her husband at home, it is his concern and duty to endeavour at least to be able to answer her enquiries; if it be a shame for her to speak in the church, where she should be silent, it is a shame for him to be silent when he should speak, and not be able to give an answer, when she asks him at home. 2. We have here the reason of this injunction: It is God's law and commandment that they should be under obedience (*v.* 34); they are placed in subordination to the man, and it is a shame for them to do any thing that looks like an affectation of changing ranks, which speaking in public seemed to imply, at least in that age, and among that people, as would public teaching much more: so that the apostle concludes it was a shame for women to speak in the church, in the assembly. Shame is the mind's uneasy reflection on having done an indecent thing. And what more indecent than for a woman to quit her rank, renounce the subordination of her sex, or do what in common account had such aspect and appearance? Note, Our spirit and conduct should be suitable to our rank. The natural distinctions God has made, we should observe. Those he has placed in subjection to others should not set themselves on a level, nor affect or assume superiority. The woman was made subject to the man, and she should keep her station and be content with it. For this reason women must be silent in the churches, not set up for teachers; for this is setting up for superiority over the man.

36 What? came the word of God out
from you? or came it unto you only?
37 If any man think himself to be a
prophet, or spiritual, let him acknowledge that the things that I
write unto you are the commandments
of the Lord. 38 But if any man be
ignorant, let him be ignorant. 39
Wherefore, brethren, covet to prophesy, and forbid not to speak with
tongues. 40 Let all things be done
decently and in order.

In these verses the apostle closes his argument, 1. With a just rebuke of the Corinthians for their extravagant pride and self-conceit: they so managed with their spiritual gifts as no church did like them; they behaved in a manner by themselves, and would not easily endure control nor regulation. Now, says the apostle, to beat down this arrogant humour, "*Came the gospel out from you? Or came it to you only? v.* 36. Did Christianity come out of Corinth? was its original among you? Or, if not, is it now limited and confined to you? are you the only church favoured with divine revelations, that you will depart from the decent usages of all other churches, and, to make ostentation of your spiritual gifts, bring confusion into Christian assemblies? How intolerably assuming is this behaviour! Pray bethink yourselves." When it was needful or proper the apostle could rebuke with all authority; and surely his rebukes, if ever, were proper here. Note, Those must be reproved and humbled whose spiritual pride and self-conceit throw Christian churches and assemblies into confusion, though such men will hardly bear even the rebukes of an apostle. 2. He lets them know that what he said to them was the command of God; nor durst any true prophet, any one really inspired, deny it (*v.* 37): "*If any man think himself a prophet, or spiritual, let him acknowledge,* &c., nay, let him be tried by this very rule. If he will not own what I deliver on this head to be the will of Christ, he himself never had the Spirit of Christ. The Spirit of Christ can never contradict itself; if it speak in me, and in them, it must speak the same things in both. If their revelations contradict mine, they do not come from the same Spirit either I or they must be false prophets. *By this therefore you may know them.* If they say that my directions in this matter are no divine commandments, you may depend upon it they are not divinely inspired. But if any continue after all, through prejudice or obstinacy, uncertain or ignorant whether they or I speak by the Spirit of God, they must be left under the power of this ignorance. If their pretences to inspiration can stand in competition with the apostolical character and powers which I have, I have lost all my authority and influence; and the persons who allow of this competition against me are out of the reach of conviction, and must be left to themselves." Note, It is just with God to leave those to the blindness of their own minds who wilfully shut out the light. Those who would be ignorant in so plain a case were justly left under the power of their mistake. 3. He sums up all in two general advices:—(1.) That though they should not despise the gift of tongues, nor altogether disuse it, under the regulations mentioned, yet they should prefer prophesying. This is indeed the scope of the whole argument. It was to be preferred to the other, because it was the more useful gift. (2.) He charges them to let all things be done decently and in order (*v.* 40), that is, that they should avoid every thing that was manifestly indecent and disorderly. Not that they should hence take occasion to bring into the Christian church and worship any thing that a vain mind might think ornamental to it, or that would help to set it off. Such indecencies and disorders as he had remarked upon were especially to be shunned. They must do nothing that was manifestly childish (*v.* 20), or that would give occasion to say they were mad (*v.* 23), nor must they act so as to breed confusion, *v.* 33. This would be utterly indecent; it would make a tumult and mob of a Christian assembly. But they were to do things in order; they were to speak one after another, and not all at once; take their turns, and not interrupt one another. To do otherwise was to destroy the end of a Christian ministry, and all assemblies for Christian worship. Note, Manifest indecencies and disorders are to be carefully kept out of all Christian churches, and every part of divine worship. They should have nothing in them that is childish, absurd, ridiculous, wild, or tumultuous; but all parts of divine worship should be carried on in a manly, grave, rational, composed, and orderly manner. God is not to be dishonoured, nor his worship disgraced, by our unbecoming and disorderly performance of it and attendance at it.

CHAP. XV.

In this chapter the apostle treats of that great article of Christianity—the resurrection of the dead. I. He establishes the certainty of our Saviour's resurrection, ver. 1—11. II. He, from this truth, sets himself to refute those who said, There is no resurrection of the dead, ver. 12—19. III. From our Saviour's resurrection he establishes the resurrection of the dead and confirms the Corinthians in the belief of it by some other considerations, ver. 20—34. IV. He answers an objection against this truth, and takes occasion thence to show what a vast change will be made in the bodies of believers at the resurrection, ver. 35—50. V. He informs us what a change will be made in those who shall be living at the sound of the last trumpet, and the complete conquest the just shall then obtain over death and the grave, ver. 51—57. And, VI. He sums up the argument with a very serious exhortation to Christians, to be resolved and diligent in their Lord's service, because they know they shall be so gloriously rewarded by him, ver. 58.

MOREOVER, brethren, I declare
unto you the gospel which I
preached unto you, which also ye
have received, and wherein ye stand;
2 By which also ye are saved, if ye
keep in memory what I preached
unto you, unless ye have believed in
vain. 3 For I delivered unto you
first of all that which I also received,
how that Christ died for our sins according to the scriptures; 4 And
that he was buried, and that he rose
again the third day according to the
scriptures: 5 And that he was seen
of Cephas, then of the twelve: 6
After that, he was seen of above five
hundred brethren at once; of whom
the greater part remain unto this
present, but some are fallen asleep.
7 After that, he was seen of James;
then of all the apostles. 8 And last
of all he was seen of me also, as of
one born out of due time. 9 For I
am the least of the apostles, that am
not meet to be called an apostle, because I persecuted the church of God.
10 But by the grace of God I am
what I am: and his grace which *was
bestowed* upon me was not in vain;
but I laboured more abundantly than
they all: yet not I, but the grace of
God which was with me. 11 Therefore whether *it were* I or they, so we
preach, and so ye believed.

It is the apostle's business in this chapter to assert and establish the doctrine of the resurrection of the dead, which some of the Corinthians flatly denied, *v.* 12. Whether they turned this doctrine into allegory, as did Hymeneus and Philetus, by saying it was already past (2 Tim. ii. 17, 18), and several of the ancient heretics, by making it mean no more than a changing of their course of life; or whether they rejected it as absurd, upon principles of reason and science; it seems they denied it in the proper sense. And they disowned a future state of recompences, by denying the resurrection of the dead. Now that heathens and infidels should deny this truth does not seem so strange; but that Christians, who had their religion by revelation, should deny a truth so plainly discovered is surprising, especially when it is a truth of such importance. It was time for the apostle to confirm them in this truth, when the staggering of their faith in this point was likely to shake their Christianity; and they were yet in great danger of having their faith staggered. He begins with an epitome or summary of the gospel, what he had preached among them, namely, the death and resurrection of Christ. Upon this foundation the doctrine of the resurrection of the dead is built. Note, Divine truths appear with greatest evidence when they are looked upon in their mutual connection. The foundation may be strengthened, that the superstructure may be secured. Now concerning the gospel observe,

I. What a stress he lays upon it (*v.* 1, 2): *Moreover, brethren, I declare unto you the gospel which I preached to you.* 1. It was what he constantly preached. His word was not yea and nay: he always preached the same gospel, and taught the same truth. He could appeal to his hearers for this. Truth is in its own nature invariable; and the infallible teachers of divine truth could never be at variance with themselves or one another. The doctrine which Paul had heretofore taught, he still taught. 2. It was what they had received; they had been convinced of the faith, believed it in their hearts, or at least made profession of doing so with their mouths. It was no strange doctrine. It was that very gospel in which, or by which, they had hitherto stood, and must continue to stand. If they gave up this truth, they left themselves no ground to stand upon, no footing in religion. Note, The doctrine of Christ's death and resurrection is at the foundation of Christianity. Remove this foundation, and the whole fabric falls, all our hopes for eternity sink at once. And it is by holding this truth firmly that Christians are made to stand in a day of trial, and kept faithful to God. 3. It was that alone by which they could hope for salvation (*v.* 2), for there is *no salvation in any other name; no name given under heaven by which we may be saved, but by the name of Christ.* And there is no salvation in his name, but upon supposition of his death and resurrection. These are the saving truths of our holy religion. The crucifixion of our Redeemer and his conquest over death are the very source of our spiritual life and hopes. Now concerning these saving truths observe, (1.) They must be retained in mind, they must be held fast (so the word is translated, Heb. x. 23): *Let us hold fast the profession of our faith.* Note, The saving truths of the gospel must be fixed in our mind, revolved much in our thoughts, and maintained and held fast to the end, if we would be saved. They will not save us, if we do not attend to them, and yield to their power, and continue to do so to the end. *He only that endureth to the end shall be saved,* Matt. x. 22. (2.) We believe in vain, unless we continue and persevere in the faith of the gospel. We shall be never the better for a temporary faith; nay, we shall aggravate our guilt by relapsing into infidelity. And in vain is it to profess Christianity, or our faith in Christ, if we deny the resurrection; for this must imply and involve the denial of his resurrection; and, take away this, you make nothing of Christianity, you leave nothing for faith or hope to fix upon.

II. Observe what this gospel is, on which the apostle lays such stress. It was that doctrine which he had received, and delivered to them, ἐν πρώτοις — *among the first, the principal.* It was a doctrine of the first rank, a most necessary truth, That Christ died for our sins, and was buried, and rose again: or, in other words, that *he was delivered for our offences and rose again for our justification* (Rom. iv. 25), that he was offered in sacrifice for our sins, and rose again, to show that he had procured forgiveness for them, and was accepted of God in this offering. Note, Christ's death and resurrection are the very sum and substance of evangelical truth. Hence we derive our spiritual life now, and here we must found our hopes of everlasting life hereafter.

III. Observe how this truth is confirmed,

1. By Old-Testament predictions. He died for our sins, according to the scriptures; he was buried, and rose from the dead, according to the scriptures, according to the scripture-prophecies, and scripture-types. Such prophecies as Ps. xvi. 10; Isa. liii. 4—6; Dan. ix. 26, 27; Hos. vi. 2. Such scripture-types as Jonah (Matt. xii. 4), as Isaac, who is expressly said by the apostle to have been *received from the dead in a figure,* Heb. xi. 19. Note, It is a great confirmation of our faith of the gospel to see how it corresponds with ancient types and prophecies.

2. By the testimony of many eye-witnesses, who saw Christ after he had risen from the dead. He reckons up five several appearances, beside that to himself. He *was seen of Cephas, or Peter, then of the twelve,* called so, though Judas was no longer among them, because this was their usual number; then he was *seen of above five hundred brethren at once,* many of whom were living when the apostle wrote this epistle, though some had fallen asleep. This was in Galilee, Matt. xxviii. 10. After that, he was seen of James singly, and then by all the apostles when he was taken up into heaven. This was on mount Olivet, Luke xxiv. 50. Compare Acts i. 2, 5—7. Note, How uncontrollably evident was Christ's resurrection from the dead, when so many eyes saw him at so many different times alive, and when he indulged the weakness of one disciple so far as to let him handle him, to put his resurrection out of doubt! And what reason have we to believe those who were so steady in maintaining this truth, though they hazarded all that was dear to them in this world, by endeavouring to assert and propagate it! Even Paul himself was last of all favoured with the sight of him. It was one of the peculiar offices of an apostle to be a witness of our Saviour's resurrection (Luke xxiv. 48); and, when Paul was called to the apostolical office, he was made an evidence of this sort; the Lord Jesus appeared to him by the way to Damascus, Acts ix. 17. Having mentioned this favour, Paul takes occasion from it to make a humble digression concerning himself. He was highly favoured of God, but he always endeavoured to keep up a mean opinion of himself, and to express it. So he does here, by observing, (1.) That he was *one born out of due time* (*v.* 8), an abortive, ἔκτρωμα, a child dead born, and out of time. Paul resembled such a birth, in the suddenness of his new birth, in that he was not matured for the apostolic function, as the others were, who had personal converse with our Lord. He was called to the office when such conversation was not to be had, he was out of time for it. He had not known nor followed the Lord, nor been formed in his family, as the others were, for this high and honourable function. This was in Paul's account a very humbling circumstance. (2.) By owning himself inferior to the other apostles: *Not meet to be called an apostle.* The least, because the last of them; called latest to the office, and not worthy to be called an apostle, to have either the office or the title, because he had been *a persecutor of the church of God, v.* 9. Indeed, he tells us elsewhere that he was *not a whit behind the very chief apostles* (2 Cor. xi. 5)—for gifts, graces, service, and sufferings, inferior to none of them. Yet some circumstances in his case made him think more meanly of himself than of any of them. Note, A humble spirit, in the midst of high attainments, is a great ornament to any man; it sets his good qualities off to much greater advantage. What kept Paul low in an especial manner was the remembrance of his former wickedness, his raging and destructive zeal against Christ and his members. Note, How easily God can bring a good out of the greatest evil! When sinners are by divine grace turned into saints, he makes the remembrance of their former sins very serviceable, to make them humble, and diligent, and faithful. (3.) By ascribing all that was valuable in him to divine grace: *But by the grace of God I am what I am, v.* 10. It is God's prerogative to say, *I am that I am;* it is our privilege to be able to say, "By God's grace we are what we are." We are nothing but what God makes us, nothing in religion but what his grace makes us. All that is good in us is a stream from this fountain. Paul was sensible of this, and kept humble and thankful by this conviction; so should we. Nay, though he was conscious of his own diligence, and zeal, and service, so that he could say of himself, *the grace of God was not given him in vain, but he laboured more abundantly than they all:* he thought himself so much more the debtor to divine

grace. *Yet not I, but the grace of God which was with me.* Note, Those who have the grace of God bestowed on them should take care that it be not in vain. They should cherish, and exercise, and exert, this heavenly principle. So did Paul, and therefore laboured with so much heart and so much success. And yet the more he laboured, and the more good he did, the more humble he was in his opinion of himself, and the more disposed to own and magnify the favour of God towards him, his free and unmerited favour. Note, A humble spirit will be very apt to own and magnify the grace of God. A humble spirit is commonly a gracious one. Where pride is subdued there it is reasonable to believe grace reigns.

After this digression, the apostle returns to his argument, and tells them (*v.* 11) that he not only preached the same gospel himself at all times, and in all places, but that all the apostles preached the same: *Whether it were they or I, so we preached, and so you believed.* Whether Peter, or Paul, or any other apostle, had converted them to Christianity, all maintained the same truth, told the same story, preached the same doctrine, and confirmed it by the same evidence. All agreed in this that Jesus Christ, and him crucified and slain, and then rising from the dead, was the very sum and substance of Christianity; and this all true Christians believe. All the apostles agreed in this testimony; all Christians agree in the belief of it. By this faith they live. In this faith they die.

12 Now if Christ be preached that
he rose from the dead, how say some
among you that there is no resurrection of the dead? 13 But if there
be no resurrection of the dead, then
is Christ not risen: 14 And if Christ
be not risen, then *is* our preaching
vain, and your faith *is* also vain. 15
Yea, and we are found false witnesses
of God; because we have testified of
God that he raised up Christ: whom
he raised not up, if so be that the
dead rise not. 16 For if the dead
rise not, then is not Christ raised:
17 And if Christ be not raised, your
faith *is* vain; ye are yet in your sins.
18 Then they also which are fallen
asleep in Christ are perished. 19 If in
this life only we have hope in Christ,
we are of all men most miserable.

Having confirmed the truth of our Saviour's resurrection, the apostle goes on to refute those among the Corinthians who said there would be none: *If Christ be preached that he rose from the dead, how say some among you that there is no resurrection of the dead?* *v.* 12. It seems from this passage, and the course of the argument, there were some among the Corinthians who thought the resurrection an impossibility. This was a common sentiment among the heathens. But against this the apostle produces an incontestable fact, namely, the resurrection of Christ; and he goes on to argue against them from the absurdities that must follow from their principle. As,

I. *If there be* (can be) *no resurrection of the dead, then Christ has not risen* (*v.* 13); and again, "*If the dead rise not,* cannot be raised or recovered to life, *then is Christ not raised, v.* 16. And yet it was foretold in ancient prophecies that he should rise; and it has been proved by multitudes of eye-witnesses that he has risen. And will you say, will any among you dare to say, that is not, cannot be, which God long ago said should be, and which is now undoubted matter of fact?"

II. It would follow hereupon that the preaching and faith of the gospel would be vain: *If Christ be not risen, then is our preaching vain, and your faith vain, v.* 14. This supposition admitted, would destroy the principal evidence of Christianity; and so, 1. Make preaching vain. "*We* apostles should *be found false witnesses of God;* we pretend to be God's witnesses for this truth, and to work miracles by his power in confirmation of it, and are all the while deceivers, liars for God, if in his name, and by power received from him, we go forth, and publish and assert a thing false in fact, and impossible to be true. And does not this make us the vainest men in the world, and our office and ministry the vainest and most useless thing in the world? What end could we propose to ourselves in undertaking this hard and hazardous service, if we knew our religion stood on no better foundation, nay, if we were not well assured of the contrary? What should we preach for? Would not our labour be wholly in vain? We can have no very favourable expectations in this life; and we could have none beyond it. If Christ be not raised, the gospel is a jest; it is chaff and emptiness." 2. This supposition would make the faith of Christians vain, as well as the labours of ministers: *If Christ be not raised, your faith is vain; you are yet in your sins* (*v.* 17), yet under the guilt and condemnation of sin, because it is through his death and sacrifice for sin alone that forgiveness is to be had. *We have redemption through his blood, the forgiveness of sins,* Eph. i. 7. No remission of sins is to be had but through the shedding of his blood. And had his blood been shed, and his life taken away, without ever being restored, what evidence could we have had that through him we should have justification and eternal life? Had he remained under the power of death, how could he have delivered us from its power? And how vain a thing is faith in him, upon this supposition! He must rise for our justification who was delivered for our sins, or in vain we look for any such benefit by him. There had been no justification nor salvation if Christ had not risen. And must not faith in Christ be vain, and of no signification, if he be still among the dead?

III. Another absurdity following from this supposition is that *those who have fallen asleep in Christ have perished.* If there be no resurrection, they cannot rise, and therefore are lost, even those who have died in the Christian faith, and for it. It is plain from this that those among the Corinthians who denied the resurrection meant thereby a state of future retribution, and not merely the revival of the flesh; they took death to be the destruction and extinction of the man, and not merely of the bodily life; for otherwise the apostle could not infer the utter loss of those who slept in Jesus, from the supposition that they would never rise more or that they had no hopes in Christ after life; for they might have hope of happiness for their minds if these survived their bodies, and this would prevent the limiting of their hopes in Christ to this life only. "Upon supposition there is no resurrection in your sense, no after-state and life, then dead Christians are quite lost. How vain a thing were our faith and religion upon this supposition!" And this,

IV. Would infer that Christ's ministers and servants were *of all men most miserable,* as having *hope in him in this life only* (*v.* 19), which is another absurdity that would follow from asserting no resurrection. Their condition who hope in Christ would be worse than that of other men. *Who hope in Christ.* Note, All who believe in Christ have hope in him; all who believe in him as a Redeemer hope for redemption and salvation by him; but if there be no resurrection, or state of future recompence (which was intended by those who denied the resurrection at Corinth), their hope in him must be limited to this life: and, if all their hopes in Christ lie within the compass of this life, they are in a much worse condition than the rest of mankind, especially at that time, and under those circumstances, in which the apostles wrote; for then they had no countenance nor protection from the rulers of the world, but were hated and persecuted by all men. Preachers and private Christians therefore had a hard lot if in this life only they had hope in Christ. Better be any thing than a Christian upon these terms; for in this world they are hated, and hunted, and abused, stripped of all worldly comforts and exposed to all manner of sufferings: they fare much harder than other men in this life, and yet have no further nor better hopes. And is it not absurd for one who believes in Christ to admit a principle that involves so absurd an inference? Can that man have faith in Christ who can believe concerning him that he will leave his faithful servants, whether ministers or others, in a worse state than his enemies? Note, It were a gross absurdity in a Christian to admit the supposition of no resurrection or future state. It would leave no hope beyond this world, and would frequently make his condition the worst in the world. Indeed, the Christian is by his religion crucified to this world, and taught to live upon the hope of another. Carnal pleasures are insipid to him in a great degree; and spiritual and heavenly pleasures are those which he affects and pants after. How sad is his case indeed, if he must be dead to worldly pleasures and yet never hope for any better!

20 But now is Christ risen from
the dead, *and* become the first fruits
of them that slept. 21 For since by
man *came* death, by man *came* also
the resurrection of the dead. 22 For
as in Adam all die, even so in Christ
shall all be made alive. 23 But every
man in his own order: Christ the
firstfruits; afterward they that are
Christ's at his coming. 24 Then
cometh the end, when he shall have
delivered up the kingdom to God,
even the Father; when he shall have
put down all rule and all authority
and power. 25 For he must reign,
till he hath put all enemies under his
feet. 26 The last enemy *that* shall
be destroyed *is* death. 27 For he
hath put all things under his feet.
But when he saith, All things are put
under *him, it is* manifest that he is
excepted, which did put all things
under him. 28 And when all things
shall be subdued unto him, then
shall the Son also himself be subject
unto him that put all things under
him, that God may be all in all. 29
Else what shall they do which are
baptized for the dead, if the dead rise
not at all? why are they then baptized for the dead? 30 And why
stand we in jeopardy every hour? 31
I protest by your rejoicing which I
have in Christ Jesus our Lord, I die
daily. 32 If after the manner of
men I have fought with beasts at
Ephesus, what advantageth it me, if
the dead rise not? let us eat and
drink; for to morrow we die. 33
Be not deceived: evil communications corrupt good manners. 34
Awake to righteousness, and sin
not; for some have not the know-

ledge of God: I speak *this* to your shame.

In this passage the apostle establishes the truth of the resurrection of the dead, the holy dead, the dead in Christ,

I. On the resurrection of Christ. 1. Because he is indeed *the first-fruits of those that slept*, *v.* 20. He has truly risen himself, and he has risen in this very quality and character, as the first-fruits of those who sleep in him. As he has assuredly risen, so in his resurrection there is as much an earnest given that the dead in him shall rise as there was that the Jewish harvest in general should be accepted and blessed by the offering and acceptance of the first-fruits. The whole lump was made holy by the consecration of the first-fruits (Rom. xi. 16), and the whole body of Christ, all that are by faith united to him, are by his resurrection assured of their own. As he has risen, they shall rise; just as the lump is holy because the first-fruits are so. He has not risen merely for himself, but as head of the body, the church; and *those that sleep in him God will bring with him*, 1 Thess. iv. 14. Note, Christ's resurrection is a pledge and earnest of ours, if we are true believers in him; because he has risen, we shall rise. We are a part of the consecrated lump, and shall partake of the acceptance and favour vouchsafed the first-fruits. This is the first argument used by the apostle in confirmation of the truth; and it is, 2. Illustrated by a parallel between the first and second Adam. For, since by man came death, it was every way proper that by man should come deliverance from it, or, which is all one, a resurrection, *v.* 21. And so, *as in Adam all die, in Christ shall all be made alive;* as through the sin of the first Adam all men became mortal, because all derived from him the same sinful nature, so through the merit and resurrection of Christ shall all who are made to partake of the Spirit, and the spiritual nature, revive, and become immortal. All who die die through the sin of Adam; all who are raised, in the sense of the apostle, rise through the merit and power of Christ. But the meaning is not that, as all men died in Adam, so all men, without exception, shall be made alive in Christ; for the scope of the apostle's argument restrains the general meaning. Christ rose as the first-fruits; therefore *those that are Christ's* (*v.* 23) shall rise too. Hence it will not follow that all men without exception shall rise too; but it will fitly follow that all who thus rise, rise in virtue of Christ's resurrection, and so that their revival is owing to the man Christ Jesus, as the mortality of all mankind was owing to the first man; and so, as by man came death, by man came deliverance. Thus it seemed fit to the divine wisdom that, as the first Adam ruined his posterity by sin, the second Adam should raise his seed to a glorious immortality. 3. Before he leaves the argument he states that there will be an order observed in their resurrection. What that precisely will be we are nowhere told, but in the general only here that there will be order observed. Possibly those may rise first who have held the highest rank, and done the most eminent service, or suffered the most grievous evils, or cruel deaths, for Christ's sake. It is only here said that the first-fruits are supposed to rise first, and afterwards all who are Christ's, when he shall come again. Not that Christ's resurrection must in fact go before the resurrection of any of his, but it must be laid as the foundation: as it was not necessary that those who lived remote from Jerusalem must go thither and offer the first-fruits before they could account the lump holy, yet they must be set apart for this purpose, till they could be offered, which might be done at any time from pentecost till the feast of dedication. See Bishop Patrick on Num. xxvi. 2. The offering of the first-fruits was what made the lump holy; and the lump was made holy by this offering, though it was not made before the harvest was gathered in, so it were set apart for that end, and duly offered afterwards. So Christ's resurrection must, in order of nature, precede that of his saints, though some of these might rise in order of time before him. It is because he has risen that they rise. Note, Those that are Christ's must rise, because of their relation to him.

II. He argues from the continuance of the mediatorial kingdom till all Christ's enemies are destroyed, the last of which is death, *v.* 24—26. He has risen, and, upon his resurrection, was invested with sovereign empire, *had all power in heaven and earth put into his hands* (Matt xxviii. 18), *had a name given him above every name, that every knee might bow to him, and every tongue confess him Lord.* Phil. ii. 9—11. And the administration of this kingdom must continue in his hands till all opposing *power, and rule, and authority, be put down* (*v.* 24), *till all enemies are put under his feet* (*v.* 25), and *till the last enemy is destroyed,* which is death, *v.* 26.

1. This argument implies in it all these particulars:—(1.) That our Saviour rose from the dead to have all power put into his hands, and have and administer a kingdom, as Mediator: *For this end he died, and rose, and revived, that he might be Lord both of the dead and living,* Rom. xiv. 9. (2.) That this mediatorial kingdom is to have an end, at least as far as it is concerned in bringing his people safely to glory, and subduing all his and their enemies: *Then cometh the end, v.* 24. (3.) That it is not to have an end till all opposing power be put down, and all enemies brought to his feet, *v.* 24, 25. (4.) That, among other enemies, death must be destroyed (*v.* 26) or abolished; its powers over its members must be disannulled. Thus far the apostle is express; but he leaves us to make the inference that therefore the saints must rise, else death and the grave would have power over them, nor

would our Saviour's kingly power prevail against the last enemy of his people and annul its power. When saints shall live again, and die no more, then, and not till then, will death be abolished, which must be brought about before our Saviour's mediatorial kingdom is delivered up, which yet must be in due time. The saints therefore shall live again and die no more. This is the scope of the argument; but,

2. The apostle drops several hints in the course of it which it will be proper to notice: as, (1.) That our Saviour, as man and mediator between God and man, has a delegated royalty, a kingdom given: *All things are put under him, he excepted that did put all things under him, v.* 27. As man, all his authority must be delegated. And, though his mediation supposes his divine nature, yet as Mediator he does not so explicitly sustain the character of God, but a middle person between God and man, partaking of both natures, human and divine, as he was to reconcile both parties, God and man, and receiving commission and authority from God the Father to act in this office. The Father appears, in this whole dispensation, in the majesty and with the authority of God: the Son, made man, appears as the minister of the Father, though he is God as well as the Father. Nor is this passage to be understood of the eternal dominion over all his creatures which belongs to him as God, but of a kingdom committed to him as Mediator and God-man, and that chiefly after his resurrection, when, having overcome, he sat down with his Father on his throne, Rev. iii. 21. Then was the prediction verified, *I have set my king upon my holy hill of Zion* (Ps. ii. 6), placed him on his throne. This is meant by the phrase so frequent in the writings of the New Testament, of *sitting at the right hand of God* (Mark xvi. 19; Rom. viii. 34; Col. iii. 1, &c.), *on the right hand of power* (Mark xiv. 62; Luke xxii. 69), *on the right hand of the Majesty on high* (Heb. i. 3), *on the right hand of the throne of God* (Heb. xii. 2), *on the right hand of the throne of the Majesty in the heavens,* Heb. viii. 1. Sitting down in this seat is taking upon him the exercise of his mediatorial power and royalty, which was done upon his ascension into heaven, Mark xvi. 19. And it is spoken of in scripture as a recompence made him for his deep humiliation and self-abasement, in becoming man, and dying for man the accursed death of the cross, Phil. ii. 6—12. Upon his ascension, he was made head over all things to the church, had power given him to govern and protect it against all its enemies, and in the end destroy them and complete the salvation of all that believe in him. This is not a power appertaining to Godhead as such; it is not original and unlimited power, but power given and limited to special purposes. And though he who has it is God, yet, inasmuch as he is somewhat else besides God, and in this whole dispensation acts not as God, but as Mediator, not as the offended Majesty, but as one interposing in favour of his offending creatures, and this by virtue of his consent and commission who acts and appears always in that character, he may properly be said to have this power given him; he may reign as God, with power unlimited, and yet may reign as Mediator, with a power delegated, and limited to these particular purposes. (2.) That this delegated royalty must at length *be delivered up to the Father,* from whom it was received (*v.* 24); for it is a power received for particular ends and purposes, a power to govern and protect his church till all the members of it be gathered in, and the enemies of it for ever subdued and destroyed (*v.* 25, 26), and when these ends shall be obtained the power and authority will not need to be continued. The Redeemer must reign till his enemies be destroyed, and the salvation of his church and people accomplished; and, when this end is attained, then will he deliver up the power which he had only for this purpose, though he may continue to reign over his glorified church and body in heaven; and in this sense it may notwithstanding be said that *he shall reign for ever and ever* (Rev. xi. 15), *that he shall reign over the house of Jacob for ever, and of his kingdom there shall be no end* (Luke i. 33), *that his dominion is an everlasting dominion, which shall not pass away,* Dan. vii. 14. See also Mich. iv. 7. (3.) The Redeemer shall certainly reign till the last enemy of his people be destroyed, till death itself be abolished, till his saints revive and recover perfect life, never to be in fear and danger of dying any more. He shall have all power in heaven and earth till then—*he who loved us, and gave himself for us, and washed us from our sins in his own blood*—he who is so nearly related to us, and so much concerned for us. What support should this be to his saints in every hour of distress and temptation! *He is alive who was dead, and liveth for ever,* and doth reign, and will continue to reign, till the redemption of his people be completed, and the utter ruin of their enemies effected. (4.) When this is done, *and all things are put under his feet, then shall the Son become subject to him that put all things under him, that God may be all in all, v.* 28. The meaning of this I take to be that then the man Christ Jesus, who hath appeared in so much majesty during the whole administration of his kingdom, shall appear upon giving it up to be a subject of the Father. Things are in scripture many times said *to be* when they are *manifested* and *made to appear;* and this delivering up of the kingdom will make it manifest that he who appeared in the majesty of the sovereign king was, during this administration, a subject of God. The glorified humanity of our Lord Jesus Christ, with all the dignity and power conferred on it, was no more than a glorious creature. This will appear when the kingdom shall be delivered up; and it will appear to the divine glory, that God may be all

in all, that the accomplishment of our salvation may appear altogether divine, and God alone may have the honour of it. Note, Though the human nature must be employed in the work of our redemption, yet God was all in all in it. *It was the Lord's doing and should be marvellous in our eyes.*

III. He argues for the resurrection, from the case of those who were baptized for the dead (*v.* 29): *What shall those do who are baptized for the dead, if the dead rise not at all? Why are they baptized for the dead?* What shall they do if the dead rise not? What have they done? How vain a thing hath their baptism been! Must they stand by it, or renounce it? why are they baptized for the dead, if the dead rise not? *ὑπὲρ τῶν νεκρῶν.* But what is this baptism for the dead? It is necessary to be known, that the apostle's argument may be understood; whether it be only *argumentum ad hominem,* or *ad rem*; that is, whether it conclude for the thing in dispute universally, or only against the particular persons who were baptized for the dead. But who shall interpret this very obscure passage, which, though it consists of no more than three words, besides the articles, has had more than three times three senses put on it by interpreters? It is not agreed what is meant by baptism, whether it is to be taken in a proper or figurative sense, and, if in a proper sense, whether it is to be understood of Christian baptism properly so called, or some other ablution. And as little is it agreed who are the dead, or in what sense the preposition *ὑπὲρ* is to be taken. Some understand the dead of our Saviour himself; *vide* Whitby *in loc.* Why are persons baptized in the name of a dead Saviour, a Saviour who remains among the dead, if the dead rise not? But it is, I believe, an instance perfectly singular for *οἱ νεκροὶ* to mean no more than one dead person; it is a signification which the words have nowhere else. And the *οἱ βαπτιζόμενοι (the baptized)* seem plainly to mean some particular persons, not Christians in general, which yet must be the signification if the *οἱ νεκροὶ (the dead)* be understood of our Saviour. Some understand the passage of the martyrs: Why do they suffer martyrdom for their religion? This is sometimes called the baptism of blood by the ancients, and, by our Saviour himself, baptism indefinitely, Matt. xx. 22; Luke xii. 50. But in what sense can those who die martyrs for their religion be said to be baptized (that is, die martyrs) for the dead? Some understand it of a custom that was observed, as some of the ancients tell us, among many who professed the Christian name in the first ages, of baptizing some in the name and stead of catechumens dying without baptism. But this savoured of such superstition that, if the custom had prevailed in the church so soon, the apostle would hardly have mentioned it without signifying a dislike of it. Some understand it of baptizing over the dead, which was a custom, they tell us, that early obtained; and this to testify their hope of the resurrection. This sense is pertinent to the apostle's argument, but it appears not that any such practice was in use in the apostle's time. Others understand it of those who have been baptized for the sake, or on occasion, of the martyrs, that is, the constancy with which they died for their religion. Some were doubtless converted to Christianity by observing this: and it would have been a vain thing for persons to have become Christians upon this motive, if the martyrs, by losing their lives for religion, became utterly extinct, and were to live no more. But the church at Corinth had not, in all probability, suffered much persecution at this time, or seen many instances of martyrdom among them, nor had many converts been made by the constancy and firmness which the martyrs discovered. Not to observe that *οἱ νεκροὶ* seems to be too general an expression to mean only the martyred dead. It is as easy an explication of the phrase as any I have met with, and as pertinent to the argument, to suppose the *οἱ νεκροὶ* to mean some among the Corinthians, who had been taken off by the hand of God. We read that *many were sickly among them, and many slept* (*ch.* xi. 30), because of their disorderly behaviour at the Lord's table. These executions might terrify some into Christianity; as the miraculous earthquake did the jailer, Acts xvi. 29, 30, &c. Persons baptized on such an occasion might be properly said to be baptized for the dead, that is, on their account. And the *οἱ βαπτιζόμενοι (the baptized)* and the *οἱ νεκροὶ (the dead)* answer to one another; and upon this supposition the Corinthians could not mistake the apostle's meaning. "Now," says he, "what shall they do, and why were they baptized, if the dead rise not? You have a general persuasion that these men have done right, and acted wisely, and as they ought, on this occasion; but why, if the dead rise not, seeing they may perhaps hasten their death, by provoking a jealous God, and have no hopes beyond it?" But whether this be the meaning, or whatever else be, doubtless the apostle's argument was good and intelligible to the Corinthians. And his next is as plain to us.

IV. He argues from the absurdity of his own conduct and that of other Christians upon this supposition,

1. It would be a foolish thing for them to run so many hazards (*v.* 30): "*Why stand we in jeopardy every hour?* Why do we expose ourselves to continual peril—we Christians, especially we apostles?" Every one knows that it was dangerous being a Christian, and much more a preacher and an apostle, at that time. "Now," says the apostle, "what fools are we to run these hazards, if we have no better hopes beyond death, if when we die we die wholly, and revive no more!" Note, Christianity were a foolish

profession if it proposed no hopes beyond this life, at least in such hazardous times as attended the first profession of it; it required men to risk all the blessings and comforts of this life, and to face and endure all the evils of it, without any future prospects. And is this a character of his religion fit for a Christian to endure? And must he not fix this character on it if he give up his future hopes, and deny the resurrection of the dead? This argument the apostle brings home to himself: "*I protest*," says he, "*by your rejoicing in Jesus Christ*, by all the comforts of Christianity, and all the peculiar succours and supports of our holy faith, that *I die daily*," *v.* 31. He was in continual danger of death, and carried his life, as we say, in his hand. And why should he thus expose himself, if he had no hopes after life? To live in daily view and expectation of death, and yet have no prospect beyond it, must be very heartless and uncomfortable, and his case, upon this account, a very melancholy one. He had need be very well assured of the resurrection of the dead, or he was guilty of extreme weakness, in hazarding all that was dear to him in this world, and his life into the bargain. He had encountered very great difficulties and fierce enemies; he had *fought with beasts at Ephesus* (*v.* 32), and was in danger of being pulled to pieces by an enraged multitude, stirred up by Demetrius and the other craftsmen (Acts xix. 24, &c.), though some understand this literally of Paul's being exposed to fight with wild beasts in the amphitheatre, at a Roman show in that city. And Nicephorus tells a formal story to this purport, and of the miraculous complaisance of the lions to him when they came near him. But so remarkable a trial and circumstance of his life, methinks, would not have been passed over by Luke, and much less by himself, when he gives us so large and particular a detail of his sufferings, 2 Cor. xi. 24, *ad fin.* When he mentioned that he was five times scourged of the Jews, thrice beaten with rods, once stoned, thrice shipwrecked, it is strange that he should not have said that he was once exposed to fight with the beasts. I take it, therefore, that this fighting with beasts is a figurative expression, that the beasts intended were men of a fierce and ferine disposition, and that this refers to the passage above cited. "Now," says he, "what advantage have I from such contests, if the dead rise not? Why should I die daily, expose myself daily to the danger of dying by violent hands, if the dead rise not? And if *post mortem nihil—if I am to perish by death*, and expect nothing after it, could any thing be more weak?" Was Paul so senseless? Had he given the Corinthians any ground to entertain such a thought of him? If he had not been well assured that death would have been to his advantage, would he, in this stupid manner, have thrown away his life? Could any thing but the sure hopes of a better life after death have extinguished the love of life in him to this degree? "*What advantageth it me, if the dead rise not?* What can I propose to myself?" Note, It is very lawful and fit for a Christian to propose advantage to himself by his fidelity to God. Thus did Paul. Thus did our blessed Lord himself, Heb. xii. 2. And thus we are bidden to do after his example, and have our fruit to holiness, that our end may be everlasting life. This is the very end of our faith, even the salvation of our souls (1 Pet. i. 9), not only what it will issue in, but what we should aim at.

2. It would be a much wiser thing to take the comforts of this life: *Let us eat and drink, for to-morrow we die* (*v.* 32); let us turn epicures. Thus this sentence means in the prophet, Isa. xxii. 13. Let us even live like beasts, if we must die like them. This would be a wiser course, if there were no resurrection, no after-life or state, than to abandon all the pleasures of life, and offer and expose ourselves to all the miseries of life, and live in continual peril of perishing by savage rage and cruelty. This passage also plainly implies, as I have hinted above, that those who denied the resurrection among the Corinthians were perfect Sadducees, of whose principles we have this account in the holy writings, that they say, *There is no resurrection, neither angel nor spirit* (Acts xxiii. 8), that is, "Man is all body, there is nothing in him to survive the body, nor will that, when once he is dead, ever revive again." Such Sadducees were the men against whom the apostle argued; otherwise his arguments had no force in them; for, though the body should never revive, yet, as long as the mind survived it, he might have much advantage from all the hazards he ran for Christ's sake. Nay, it is certain that the mind is to be the principal seat and subject of the heavenly glory and happiness. But, if there were no hopes after death, would not every wise man prefer an easy comfortable life before such a wretched one as the apostle led; nay, and endeavour to enjoy the comforts of life as fast as possible, because the continuance of it is short? Note, Nothing but the hopes of better things hereafter can enable a man to forego all the comforts and pleasures here, and embrace poverty, contempt, misery, and death. Thus did the apostles and primitive Christians; but how wretched was their case, and how foolish their conduct, if they deceived themselves, and abused the world with vain and false hopes!

V. The apostle closes his argument with a caution, exhortation, and reproof. 1. A caution against the dangerous conversation of bad men, men of loose lives and principles: *Be not deceived*, says he; *evil communications corrupt good manners*, *v.* 33. Possibly, some of those who said that there was no resurrection of the dead were men of loose lives, and endeavoured to countenance their vicious practices by so corrupt a principle; and had that speech often in their mouths

Let us eat and drink, for to-morrow we die. Now, the apostle grants that their talk was to the purpose if there was no future state. But, having confuted their principle, he now warns the Corinthians how dangerous such men's conversation must prove. He tells them that they would probably be corrupted by them, and fall in with their course of life, if they gave into their evil principles. Note, Bad company and conversation are likely to make bad men. Those who would keep their innocence must keep good company. Error and vice are infectious: and, if we would avoid the contagion, we must keep clear of those who have taken it. *He that walketh with wise men shall be wise; but a companion of fools shall be destroyed,* Prov. xiii. 20. 2. Here is an exhortation to break off their sins, and rouse themselves, and lead a more holy and righteous life (*v.* 34): *Awake to righteousness,* or *awake righteously, ἐκνήψατε δικαίως, and sin not,* or sin no more. "Rouse yourselves, break off your sins by repentance: renounce and forsake every evil way, correct whatever is amiss, and do not, by sloth and stupidity, be led away into such conversation and principles as will sap your Christian hopes, and corrupt your practice." The disbelief of a future state destroys all virtue and piety. But the best improvement to be made of the truth is to cease from sin, and set ourselves to the business of religion, and that in good earnest. If there will be a resurrection and a future life, we should live and act as those who believe it, and should not give into such senseless and sottish notions as will debauch our morals, and render us loose and sensual in our lives. 3. Here is a reproof, and a sharp one, to some at least among them: *Some of you have not the knowledge of God; I speak this to your shame.* Note, It is a shame in Christians not to have the knowledge of God. The Christian religion gives the best information that can be had about God, his nature, and grace, and government. Those who profess this religion reproach themselves, by remaining without the knowledge of God; for it must be owing to their own sloth, and slight of God, that they are ignorant of him. And is it not a horrid shame for a Christian to slight God, and be so wretchedly ignorant in matters that so nearly and highly concern him? Note also, It must be ignorance of God that leads men into the disbelief of a resurrection and future life. Those who know God know that he will not abandon his faithful servants, nor leave them exposed to such hardships and sufferings without any recompence or reward. They know he is not unfaithful nor unkind, to forget their labour and patience, their faithful services and cheerful sufferings, or let their *labour be in vain.* But I am apt to think that the expression has a much stronger meaning; that there were atheistical people among them who hardly owned a God, or one who had any concern with or took cognizance of human affairs. These were indeed a scandal and shame to any Christian church. Note, Real atheism lies at the bottom of men's disbelief of a future state. Those who own a God and a providence, and observe how unequal the distributions of the present life are, and how frequently the best men fare worst, can hardly doubt an after state, where every thing will be set to rights.

35 But some *man* will say, How
are the dead raised up? and with
what body do they come? 36 *Thou*
fool, that which thou sowest is not
quickened, except it die: 37 And
that which thou sowest, thou sowest
not that body that shall be, but bare
grain, it may chance of wheat, or of
some other *grain:* 38 But God
giveth it a body as it hath pleased
him, and to every seed his own body.
39 All flesh *is* not the same flesh:
but *there is* one *kind of* flesh of men,
another flesh of beasts, another of
fishes, *and* another of birds. 40 *There*
are also celestial bodies, and bodies
terrestrial: but the glory of the celestial
is one, and the *glory* of the
terrestrial *is* another. 41 *There is*
one glory of the sun, and another
glory of the moon, and another glory
of the stars: for *one* star differeth
from *another* star in glory. 42 So
also *is* the resurrection of the dead.
It is sown in corruption; it is raised
in incorruption: 43 It is sown in
dishonour; it is raised in glory: it is
sown in weakness; it is raised in
power: 44 It is sown a natural body;
it is raised a spiritual body. There
is a natural body, and there is a spiritual
body. 45 And so it is written,
The first man Adam was made a
living soul; the last Adam *was made*
a quickening spirit. 46 Howbeit that
was not first which is spiritual, but
that which is natural; and afterward
that which is spiritual. 47 The first
man *is* of the earth, earthy: the
second man *is* the Lord from heaven.
48 As *is* the earthy, such *are* they
also that are earthy: and as *is* the
heavenly, such *are* they also that are
heavenly. 49 And as we have borne
the image of the earthy, we shall also
bear the image of the heavenly. 50
Now this I say, brethren, that flesh
and blood cannot inherit the kingdom

of God; neither doth corruption inherit incorruption.

The apostle comes now to answer a plausible and principal objection against the doctrine of the resurrection of the dead, concerning which observe the proposal of the objection: *Some man will say, How are the dead raised up? And with what body do they come? v.* 35. The objection is plainly twofold. *How are they raised up?* that is, "By what means? How can they be raised? What power is equal to this effect? It was an opinion that prevailed much among the heathens, and the Sadducees seem to have been in the same sentiment, that it was not within the compass of divine power, *mortales æternitate donare, aut revocare defunctos—to make mortal men immortal, or revive and restore the dead.* Such sort of men those seem to have been who among the Corinthians denied the resurrection of the dead, and object here, "How are they raised? How should they be raised? Is it not utterly impossible?" The other part of the objection is about the quality of their bodies, who shall rise: "*With what body will they come?* Will it be with the same body, with like shape, and form, and stature, and members, and qualities, or various?" The former objection is that of those who opposed the doctrine, the latter the enquiry of curious doubters.

I. To the former the apostle replies by telling them this was to be brought about by divine power, that very power which they had all observed to do something very like it, year after year, in the death and revival of the corn; and therefore it was an argument of great weakness and stupidity to doubt whether the resurrection of the dead might not be effected by the same power: *Thou fool! that which thou sowest is not quickened unless it die, v.* 36. It must first corrupt, before it will quicken and spring up. It not only sprouts after it is dead, but it must die that it may live. And why should any be so foolish as to imagine that the man once dead cannot be made to live again, by the same power which every year brings the dead grain to life? This is the substance of the apostle's answer to the first question. Note, It is a foolish thing to question the divine power to raise the dead, when we see it every day quickening and reviving things that are dead.

II. But he is longer in replying to the second enquiry.

1. He begins by observing that there is a change made in the grain that is sown: It is *not that body which shall be* that is sown, but *bare grain,* of wheat or barley, &c.; but God gives it such a body as he will, and in such way as he will, only so as to distinguish the kinds from each other. Every seed sown has its *proper body,* is constituted of such materials, and figured in such a manner, as are proper to it, proper to that kind. This is plainly in the divine power, though we no more know how it is done than we know how a dead man is raised to life again. It is certain the grain undergoes a great change, and it is intimated in this passage that so will the dead, when they rise again, and live again, in their bodies, after death.

2. He proceeds hence to observe that there is a great deal of variety among other bodies, as there is among plants: as, (1.) In bodies of flesh: *All flesh is not the same;* that of men is of one kind, that of beasts another, another that of fishes, and that of birds another, *v.* 39. There is a variety in all the kinds, and somewhat peculiar in every kind, to distinguish it from the other. (2.) In bodies celestial and terrestrial there is also a difference; and what is for the glory of one is not for the other; for the true glory of every being consists in its fitness for its rank and state. Earthly bodies are not adapted to the heavenly regions, nor heavenly bodies fitted to the condition of earthly beings. Nay, (3.) There is a variety of glory among heavenly bodies themselves: *There is one glory of the sun, and another glory of the moon, and another glory of the stars; for one star differs from another star in glory, v.* 41. All this is to intimate to us that the bodies of the dead, when they rise, will be so far changed, that they will be fitted for the heavenly regions, and that there will be a variety of glories among the bodies of the dead, when they shall be raised, as there is among the sun, and moon, and stars, nay, among the stars themselves. All this carries an intimation along with it that it must be as easy to divine power to raise the dead, and recover their mouldered bodies, as out of the same materials to form so many different kinds of flesh and plants, and, for aught we know, celestial bodies as well as terrestrial ones. The sun and stars may, for aught we know, be composed of the same materials as the earth we tread on, though as much refined and changed by the divine skill and power. And can he, out of the same materials, form such various beings, and yet not be able to raise the dead? Having thus prepared the way, he comes,

3. To speak directly to the point: *So also,* says he, *is the resurrection of the dead;* so (as the plant growing out of the putrefied grain), so as no longer to be a terrestrial but a celestial body, and varying in glory from the other dead, who are raised, as one star does from another. But he specifies some particulars: as, (1.) *It is sown in corruption, it is raised in incorruption. It is sown.* Burying the dead is like sowing them; it is like committing the seed to the earth, that it may spring out of it again. And our bodies, which are sown, are corruptible, liable to putrefy and moulder, and crumble to dust; but, when we rise, they will be out of the power of the grave, and never more be liable to corruption. (2.) *It is sown in dishonour,*

it is raised in glory. Ours is at present a vile body, Phil. iii. 21. Nothing is more loathsome than a dead body; it is thrown into the grave as a despised and broken vessel, in which there is no pleasure. But at the resurrection a glory will be put upon it; it will be made like the glorious body of our Saviour; it will be purged from all the dregs of earth, and refined into an ethereal substance, and shine out with a splendour resembling his. (3.) *It is sown in weakness, it is raised in power.* It is laid in the earth, a poor helpless thing, wholly in the power of death, deprived of all vital capacities and powers, of life and strength: it is utterly unable to move or stir. But when we arise our bodies will have heavenly life and vigour infused into them; they will be hale, and firm, and durable, and lively, and liable no more to any infirmity, weakness, or decay. (4.) *It is sown a natural,* or *animal* body, *σῶμα ψυχικὸν*, a body fitted to the low condition and sensitive pleasures and enjoyments of this life, which are all gross in comparison of the heavenly state and enjoyments. But when we rise it will be quite otherwise; our body will rise spiritual. Not that body would be changed into spirit: this would be a contradiction in our common conceptions; it would be as much as to say, Body changed into what is not body, matter made immaterial. The expression is to be understood comparatively. We shall at the resurrection have bodies purified and refined to the last degree, made light and agile; and, though they are not changed into spirit, yet made fit to be perpetual associates of spirits made perfect. And why should it not be as much in the power of God to raise incorruptible, glorious, lively, spiritual bodies, out of the ruins of those vile, corruptible, lifeless, and animal ones, as first to make matter out of nothing, and then, out of the same mass of matter, produce such variety of beings, both in earth and heaven? *To God all things are possible;* and this cannot be impossible.

4. He illustrates this by a comparison of the first and second Adam: *There is an animal body,* says he, *and there is a spiritual body;* and then goes into the comparison in several instances. (1.) As we have our natural body, the animal body we have in this world, from the first Adam, we expect our spiritual body from the second. This is implied in the whole comparison. (2.) This is but consonant to the different characters these two persons bear: *The first Adam was made a living soul,* such a being as ourselves, and with a power of propagating such beings as himself, and conveying to them a nature and animal body like his own, but none other, nor better. The *second Adam is a quickening Spirit;* he is the resurrection and the life, John xi. 25. He hath life in himself, and quickeneth whom he will, John v. 20, 21. *The first man was of the earth,* made out of the earth, and was earthy; his body was fitted to the region of his abode: *but the second Adam is the Lord from heaven;* he who came down from heaven, and giveth life to the world (John vi. 33); he who came down from heaven and was in heaven at the same time (John iii. 13); the Lord of heaven and earth. If the first Adam could communicate to us natural and animal bodies, cannot the second Adam make our bodies spiritual ones? If the deputed lord of this lower creation could do the one, cannot the Lord from heaven, the Lord of heaven and earth, do the other? (3.) We must first have natural bodies from the first Adam before we can have spiritual bodies from the second (*v.* 49); we *must bear the image of the earthy before we can bear the image of the heavenly.* Such is the established order of Providence. We must have weak, frail, mortal bodies by descent from the first Adam, before we can have lively, spiritual, and immortal ones by the quickening power of the second. We must die before we can live to die no more. (4.) Yet if we are Christ's, true believers in him (for this whole discourse relates to the resurrection of the saints), it is as certain that we shall have spiritual bodies as it is now that we have natural or animal ones. By these we are as the first Adam, earthy, we bear his image; by those we shall be as the second Adam, have bodies like his own, heavenly, and so bear his image. And we are as certainly intended to bear the one as we have borne the other. As surely therefore as we have had natural bodies, we shall have spiritual ones. The dead in Christ shall not only rise, but shall rise thus gloriously changed.

5. He sums up this argument by assigning the reason of this change (*v.* 50): *Now this I say that flesh and blood cannot inherit the kingdom of God; nor doth corruption inherit incorruption.* The natural body is flesh and blood, consisting of bones, muscles, nerves, veins, arteries, and their several fluids; and, as such, it is of a corruptible frame and form, liable to dissolution, to rot and moulder. But no such thing shall inherit the heavenly regions; for this were for corruption to inherit incorruption, which is little better than a contradiction in terms. The heavenly inheritance is incorruptible, and never fadeth away, 1 Pet. i. 4. How can this be possessed by flesh and blood, which is corruptible and will fade away? It must be changed into ever-during substance, before it can be capable of possessing the heavenly inheritance. The sum is that the bodies of the saints, when they shall rise again, will be greatly changed from what they are now, and much for the better. They are now corruptible, flesh and blood; they will be then incorruptible, glorious, and spiritual bodies, fitted to the celestial world and state, where they are ever afterwards to dwell, and have their eternal inheritance.

51 Behold, I show you a mystery;
We shall not all sleep, but we shall
all be changed, 52 In a moment, in
the twinkling of an eye, at the last
trump: for the trumpet shall sound,
and the dead shall be raised incorruptible, and we shall be changed.
53 For this corruptible must put on
incorruption, and this mortal *must* put
on immortality. 54 So when this
corruptible shall have put on incorruption, and this mortal shall have
put on immortality, then shall be
brought to pass the saying that is
written, Death is swallowed up in
victory. 55 O death, where *is* thy
sting? O grave, where *is* thy victory?
56 The sting of death *is* sin; and the
strength of sin *is* the law. 57 But
thanks *be* to God, which giveth us
the victory through our Lord Jesus
Christ.

To confirm what he had said of this change,

I. He here tells them what had been concealed from or unknown to them till then—that all the saints would not die, but all would be changed. Those that are alive at our Lord's coming will be caught up into the clouds, without dying, 1 Thess. iv. 11. But it is plain from this passage that it will not be without changing from corruption to incorruption. The frame of their living bodies shall be thus altered, as well as those that are dead; and this *in a moment, in the twinkling of an eye, v.* 52. What cannot almighty power effect? That power that calls the dead into life can surely thus soon and suddenly change the living; for changed they must be as well as the dead, because flesh and blood cannot inherit the kingdom of God. This is the mystery which the apostle shows the Corinthians: *Behold, I show you a mystery;* or bring into open light a truth dark and unknown before. Note, There are many mysteries shown to us in the gospel; many truths that before were utterly unknown are there made known; many truths that were but dark and obscure before are there brought into open day, and plainly revealed; and many things are in part revealed that will never be fully known, nor perhaps clearly understood. The apostle here makes known a truth unknown before, which is that the saints living at our Lord's second coming will not die, but be changed, that this change will be made in a moment, in the twinkling of an eye, and *at the sound of the last trump;* for, as he tells us elsewhere, the *Lord himself shall descend with a shout, with the voice of the archangel, and with the trump of God* (1 Thess. iv. 16), so here, *the trumpet must sound.* It is the loud summons of all the living and all the dead to come and appear at the tribunal of Christ. At this summons the graves shall open, the dead saints shall rise incorruptible, and the living saints be changed to the same incorruptible state, *v.* 52.

II. He assigns the reason of this change (*v.* 53): *For this corruptible must put on incorruption, and this mortal must put on immortality.* How otherwise could the man be a fit inhabitant of the incorruptible regions, or be fitted to possess the eternal inheritance? How can that which is corruptible and mortal enjoy what is incorruptible, permanent, and immortal? This corruptible body must be made incorruptible, this mortal body must be changed into immortal, that the man may be capable of enjoying the happiness designed for him. Note, It is this corruptible that must put on incorruption; the demolished fabric that must be reared again. What is sown must be quickened. Saints will come in their own bodies (*v.* 38), not in other bodies.

III. He lets us know what will follow upon this change of the living and dead in Christ: *Then shall be brought to pass that saying, Death is swallowed up in victory;* or, *He will swallow up death in victory,* Isa. xxv. 8. For *mortality shall be then swallowed up of life* (2 Cor. v. 4), and death perfectly subdued and conquered, and saints for ever delivered from its power. Such a conquest shall be obtained over it that it shall for ever disappear in those regions to which our Lord will bear his risen saints. And therefore will the saints hereupon sing their ἐπινίκιον, their *song of triumph.* Then, when this mortal shall have put on immortality, will death be swallowed up, for ever swallowed up, εἰς νῖκος. Christ hinders it from swallowing his saints when they die; but, when they rise again, death shall, as to them, be swallowed for ever. And upon this destruction of death will they break out into a song of triumph.

1. They will glory over death as a vanquished enemy, and insult this great and terrible destroyer: "*O death! where is thy sting?* Where is now thy sting, thy power to hurt? What mischief hast thou done us? We are dead; but behold we live again, and shall die no more. Thou art vanquished and disarmed, and we are out of the reach of thy deadly dart. Where now is thy fatal artillery? Where are thy stores of death? We fear no further mischiefs from thee, nor heed thy weapons, but defy thy power, and despise thy wrath. And, *O grave! where is thy victory?* Where now is thy victory? What has become of it? Where are the spoils and trophies of it? Once we were thy prisoners, but the prison-doors are burst open, the locks and bolts have been forced to give way, our shackles are knocked off, and we are for ever released. Captivity is taken captive. The imaginary victor is conquered, and forced to resign his conquest and release his captives. Thy triumphs, grave, are at

an end. The bonds of death are loosed, and we are at liberty, and are never more to be hurt by death, nor imprisoned in the grave." In a moment, the power of death, and the conquests and spoils of the grave, are gone; and, as to the saints, the very signs of them will not remain. Where are they? Thus will they raise themselves, when they become immortal, to the honour of their Saviour and the praise of divine grace: they shall glory over vanquished death.

2. The foundation for this triumph is here intimated, (1.) In the account given whence death had its power to hurt: *The sting of death is sin.* This gives venom to his dart: this alone puts it into the power of death to hurt and kill. Sin unpardoned, and nothing else, can keep any under his power. And the *strength of sin is the law;* it is the divine threatening against the transgressors of the law, the curse there denounced, that gives power to sin. Note, Sin is the parent of death, and gives it all its hurtful power. *By one man sin entered into the world, and death by sin,* Rom. v. 12. It is its cursed progeny and offspring. (2.) In the account given of the victory saints obtain over it through Jesus Christ, *v.* 56. *The sting of death is sin;* but Christ, by dying, has taken out this sting. He has made atonement for sin; he has obtained remission of it. It may hiss therefore, but it cannot hurt. *The strength of sin is the law;* but the curse of the law is removed by our Redeemer's *becoming a curse for us.* So that sin is deprived of its strength and sting, through Christ, that is, by his incarnation, suffering, and death. Death may seize a believer, but cannot sting him, cannot hold him in his power. There is a day coming when the grave shall open, the bands of death be loosed, the dead saints revive, and become incorruptible and immortal, and put out of the reach of death for ever. And then will it plainly appear that, as to them, death will have lost its strength and sting; and all by the mediation of Christ, by his dying in their room. By dying, he conquered death, and spoiled the grave; and, through faith in him, believers become sharers in his conquests. They often rejoice beforehand, in the hope of this victory; and, when they arise glorious from the grave, they will boldly triumph over death. Note, It is altogether owing to the grace of God in Christ that sin is pardoned and death disarmed. The law puts arms into the hand of death, to destroy the sinner; but pardon of sin takes away this power from the law, and deprives death of its strength and sting. It is *by the grace of God, through the redemption which is in Christ Jesus, that we are freely justified,* Rom. iii. 24. It is no wonder, therefore, (3.) If this triumph of the saints over death should issue in thanksgiving to God: *Thanks be to God, who giveth us the victory through Christ Jesus, our Lord, v.* 57. The way to sanctify all our joy is to make it tributary to the praise of God. Then only do we enjoy our blessings and honours in a holy manner when God has his revenue of glory out of it, and we are free to pay it to him. And this really improves and exalts our satisfaction. We are conscious at once of having done our duty and enjoyed our pleasure. And what can be more joyous in itself than the saints' triumph over death, when they shall rise again? And shall they not then rejoice in the Lord, and be glad in the God of their salvation? Shall not their souls magnify the Lord? When he shows *such wonders to the dead, shall they not arise and praise him?* Ps. lxxxviii. 10. Those who remain under the power of death can have no heart to praise; but such conquests and triumphs will certainly tune the tongues of the saints to thankfulness and praise—praise for the victory (it is great and glorious in itself), and for the means whereby it is obtained (it is given of God through Christ Jesus), a victory obtained not by our power, but the power of God; not given because we are worthy, but because Christ is so, and has by dying obtained this conquest for us. Must not this circumstance endear the victory to us, and heighten our praise to God? Note, How many springs of joy to the saints and thanksgiving to God are opened by the death and resurrection, the sufferings and conquests, of our Redeemer! With what acclamations will saints rising from the dead applaud him! How will the heaven of heavens resound his praises for ever! *Thanks be to God* will be the burden of their song; and angels will join the chorus, and declare their consent with a loud Amen, Hallelujah.

58 Therefore, my beloved brethren, be ye stedfast, unmoveable, always abounding in the work of the Lord, forasmuch as ye know that your labour is not in vain in the Lord.

In this verse we have the improvement of the whole argument, in an exhortation, enforced by a motive resulting plainly from it.

I. An exhortation, and this threefold:—1. That they should be stedfast—ἑδραῖοι, firm, fixed in the faith of the gospel, that gospel which he had preached and they had received, namely, *That Christ died for our sins, and arose again the third day, according to the scriptures* (*v.* 3, 4), and fixed in the faith of the glorious resurrection of the dead, which, as he had shown, had so near and necessary a connection with the former. "Do not let your belief of these truths be shaken or staggered. They are most certain, and of the last importance." Note, Christians should be stedfast believers of this great article of the resurrection of the dead. It is evidently founded on the death of Christ. *Because he lives, his servants shall live also,* John xiv. 19. And it is of the last importance; a disbelief of a future life will open a way to all manner of licentiousness, and corrupt men's morals to the last degree. It will be easy and natural to infer hence that we may live like beasts, and eat and drink, for to-morrow we die. 2. He exhorts them to be *immovable,* namely, in their expectation of this great privilege of being raised incorruptible and immortal. Christians should not be moved away from this hope of the gospel (Col. i. 23), this glorious and blessed hope; they should not renounce nor resign their comfortable expectations. They are not vain, but solid hopes, built upon sure foundations, the purchase and power of their risen Saviour, and the promise of God, to whom it is impossible to lie—hopes that shall be their most powerful supports under all the pressures of life, the most effectual antidotes against the fears of death, and the most quickening motives to diligence and perseverance in Christian duty. Should they part with these hopes? Should they suffer them to be shaken? Note, Christians should live in the most firm expectation of a blessed resurrection. This hope should be an anchor to their souls, firm and sure, Heb. vi. 19. 3. He exhorts them *to abound in the work of the Lord,* and that *always,* in the Lord's service, in obeying the Lord's commands. They should be diligent and persevering herein, and going on towards perfection; they should be continually making advances in true piety, and ready and apt for every good work. The most cheerful duty, the greatest diligence, the most constant perseverance, become those who have such glorious hopes. Can we too much abound in zeal and diligence in the Lord's work, when we are assured of such abundant recompences in a future life? What vigour and resolution, what constancy and patience, should those hopes inspire! Note, Christians should not stint themselves as to their growth in holiness, but be always improving in sound religion, and abounding in the work of the Lord.

II. The motive resulting from the former discourse is that their *labour shall not be in vain in the Lord;* nay, they know it shall not. They have the best grounds in the world to build upon: they have all the assurance that can rationally be expected: as surely as Christ is risen, they shall rise; and Christ is as surely risen as the scriptures are true, and the word of God. The apostles saw him after his death, testified this truth to the world in the face of a thousand deaths and dangers, and confirmed it by miraculous powers received from him. Is there any room to doubt a fact so well attested? Note, True Christians have undoubted evidence that their labour will not be in vain in the Lord; not their most diligent services, nor their most painful sufferings; they will not be in vain, not be vain and unprofitable. Note, The labour of Christians will not be lost labour; they may lose for God, but they will lose nothing by him; nay, there is more implied than is expressed in this phrase: it means that they shall be abundantly rewarded. He will never be found unjust to forget their labour of love, Heb. vi. 10. Nay, he will do exceedingly abundantly above what they can now ask or think. Neither the services they do for him, nor the sufferings they endure for him here, are worthy to be compared with the joy hereafter to be revealed in them, Rom. viii. 18. Note, Those who serve God have good wages; they cannot do too much nor suffer too much for so good a Master. If they serve him now, they shall see him hereafter; if they suffer for him on earth, they shall reign with him in heaven; if they die for his sake, they shall rise again from the dead, be crowned with glory, honour, and immortality, and inherit eternal life.

CHAP XVI.

In this chapter the apostle, I. Gives directions about some charitable collection to be made in this church, for the afflicted and impoverished churches in Judea, ver. 1—4. II. He talks of paying them a visit, ver. 5—9. III. He recommends Timothy to them, and tells them Apollos intended to come to them, ver. 10—12. IV. He presses them to watchfulness, constancy, charity, and to pay a due regard to all who helped him and his fellow-labourers in their work, ver. 13—19. V. After salutations from others, and his own, he closes the epistle with a solemn admonition to them, and his good wishes for them, ver. 20, to the end.

NOW concerning the collection
for the saints, as I have given
order to the churches of Galatia, even
so do ye. 2 Upon the first *day* of
the week let every one of you lay by
him in store, as *God* hath prospered
him, that there be no gatherings when
I come. 3 And when I come, whomsoever ye shall approve by *your* letters, them will I send to bring your
liberality unto Jerusalem. 4 And if
it be meet that I go also, they shall
go with me.

In this chapter Paul closes this long epistle with some particular matters of less moment; but, as all was written by divine inspiration, it is all profitable for our instruction. He begins with directing them about a charitable collection on a particular occasion, the distresses and poverty of Christians in Judea, which at this time were extraordinary, partly through the general calamities of that nation and partly through the particular sufferings to which they were exposed. Now concerning this observe,

I. How he introduces his direction. It was not a peculiar service which he required of them; he had given similar *orders to the churches of Galatia, v.* 1. He desired them only to conform to the same rules which he had given to other churches on a similar occasion. *He did not desire that others should be eased and they burdened,* 2 Cor. viii. 13. He also prudently mentions these orders of his to the churches of Galatia, to excite emulation, and stir them up to be liberal, according to their circumstances, and the occasion. Those who exceeded most churches in spiritual gifts, and, as it is probable, in worldly wealth (see the argument), surely would not suffer themselves to come behind any in their bounty to their afflicted brethren. Note, The good examples of other Christians and churches should excite in us a holy emulation. It is becoming a Christian not to bear to be outdone by a fellow-christian in any thing virtuous and praise-worthy, provided this consideration only makes him exert himself, not envy others; and the more advantages we have above others the more should we endeavour to exceed them. The church of Corinth should not be outdone in this service of love by the churches of Galatia, which do not appear to have been enriched with equal spiritual gifts nor outward ability.

II. The direction itself, concerning which observe,

1. The manner in which the collection was to be made: *Every one was to lay by in store* (*v.* 2), have a treasury, or fund, with himself, for this purpose. The meaning is that he should lay by as he could spare from time to time, and by this means make up a sum for this charitable purpose. Note, It is a good thing to lay up in store for good uses. Those who are rich in this world should be rich in good works, 1 Tim. vi. 17, 18. The best way to be so is to appropriate of their income, and have a treasury for this purpose, a stock for the poor as well as for themselves. By this means they will be ready to every good work as the opportunity offers; and many who labour with their own hands for a livelihood should so work that they may have to give to him that needeth, Eph. iv. 28. Indeed their treasury for good works can never be very large (though, according to circumstances, it may considerably vary); but the best way in the world for them to get a treasury for this purpose is to lay by from time to time, as they can afford. Some of the Greek fathers rightly observe here that this advice was given for the sake of the poorer among them. They were to lay by from week to week, and not bring in to the common treasury, that by this means their contributions might be easy to themselves, and yet grow into a fund for the relief of their brethren. "Every little," as the proverb says, "would make a mickle." Indeed all our charity and benevolence should be free and cheerful, and for that reason should be made as easy to ourselves as may be. And what more likely way to make us easy in this matter than thus to lay by? We may cheerfully give when we know that we can spare, and that we have been laying by in store that we may.

2. Here is the measure in which they are to lay by: *As God hath prospered them; τι ἂν εὐοδῶται*, as he has been prospered, namely, by divine Providence, as God has been pleased to bless and succeed his labours and business. Note, All our business and labour are that to us which God is pleased to make them. It is not the diligent hand that will make rich by itself, without the divine blessing, Prov. x. 4, 22. Our prosperity and success are from God and not from ourselves; and he is to be owned in all and honoured with all. It is his bounty and blessing to which we owe all we have; and whatever we have is to be used, and employed, and improved, for him. His right to ourselves and all that is ours is to be owned and yielded to him. And what argument more proper to excite us to charity to the people and children of God than to consider all we have as his gift, as coming from him? Note, When God blesses and prospers us, we should be ready to relieve and comfort his needy servants; when his bounty flows forth upon us, we should not confine it to ourselves, but let it stream out to others. The good we receive from him should stir us up to do good to others, to resemble him in our beneficence; and therefore the more good we receive from God the more we should do good to others. They were to lay by as God had blessed them, in that proportion. The more they had, through God's blessing, gained by their business or labour, their traffic or work, the more they were to lay by. Note, God expects that our beneficence to others should hold some proportion to his bounty to us. All we have is from God; the more he gives (circumstances being considered), the more he enables us to give, and the more he expects we should give, that we should give more than others who are less able, that we should give more than ourselves when we were less able. And, on the other hand, from him to whom God gives less he expects less. He is no tyrant nor cruel taskmaster, to exact brick without straw, or expect men shall do more good than he gives ability. Note, *Where there is a willing mind he accepts according to what a man hath, and not according to what he hath not* (2 Cor. viii. 12); but as he prospers and blesses us, and puts us in a capacity to do good, he expects we should. The greater ability he gives, the more enlarged should our hearts be, and the more open our hands; but, where the ability is less, the hands cannot be as open, however willing the mind and however large the heart; nor does God expect it.

3. Here is the time when this is to be done: *The first day of the week, κατὰ μίαν σαββάτων* (Luke xxiv. 1), the Lord's day, the Christian holiday, when public assemblies were held and public worship was celebrated, and the Christian institutions and mysteries (as the ancients called them) were attended upon; then let every one lay by him. It is a day of holy rest; and the more vacation the mind has from worldly cares and toils the more disposition has it to show mercy: and the other duties of the day should stir us up to the performance of this; works of charity should always accompany works of piety. True piety towards God will beget kind and friendly dispositions towards men. *This commandment have we from him that he who loveth God love his brother also,* 1 John

iv. 21. Works of mercy are the genuine fruits of true love to God, and therefore are a proper service on his own day. Note, God's day is a proper season on which to lay up for charitable uses, or lay out in them, according as he has prospered us; it is paying tribute for the blessings of the past week, and it is a proper way to procure his blessing on the work of our hands for the next.

4. We have here the disposal of the collections thus made: the apostle would have every thing ready against he came, and therefore gave direction as before: *That there be no gatherings when I come, v.* 2. But, when he came, as to the disposal of it, he would leave it much to themselves. The charity was theirs, and it was fit they should dispose of it in their own way, so it answered its end, and was applied to the right use. Paul no more pretended to lord it over the purses of his hearers than over their faith; he would not meddle with their contributions without their consent. (1.) He tells them that they should give letters of credence, and send messengers of their own with their liberality, *v.* 3. This would be a proper testimony of their respect and brotherly love to their distressed brethren, to send their gift by members of their own body, trusty and tenderhearted, who would have compassion on their suffering brethren, and a Christian concern for them, and not defraud them. It would argue that they were very hearty in this service, when they should send some of their own body on so long and hazardous a journey or voyage, to convey their liberality. Note, We should not only charitably relieve our poor fellow-christians but do it in such a way as will best signify our compassion to them and care of them. (2.) He offers to go with their messengers, if they think proper, *v.* 4. His business, as an apostle, was not to serve tables, but to give himself to the word and prayer; yet he was never wanting to set on foot, or help forward, a work of charity, when an opportunity offered. He would go to Jerusalem, to carry the contributions of the church at Corinth to their suffering brethren, rather than they should go without them, or the charity of the Corinthians fail of a due effect. It was no hindrance to his preaching work, but a great furtherance to the success of it, to show such a tender and benign disposition of mind. Note, Ministers are doing their proper business when they are promoting or helping in works of charity. Paul stirs up the Corinthians to gather for the relief of the churches in Judea, and he is ready to go with their messengers, to convey what is gathered; and he is still in the way of his duty, in the business of his office.

5 Now I will come unto you, when
I shall pass through Macedonia: for
I do pass through Macedonia. 6
And it may be that I will abide, yea,
and winter with you, that ye may
bring me on my journey whithersoever I go. 7 For I will not see you
now by the way; but I trust to tarry
awhile with you, if the Lord permit.
8 But I will tarry at Ephesus until
Pentecost. 9 For a great door and
effectual is opened unto me, and *there
are* many adversaries.

In this passage the apostle notifies and explains his purpose of visiting them, concerning which, observe, 1. His purpose: he intended to pass out of Asia, where he now was (*vide v.* 8, 19) and to go through Macedonia into Achaia, where Corinth was, and to stay some time with them, and perhaps the winter, *v.* 5, 6. He had long laboured in this church, and done much good among them, and had his heart set upon doing much more (if God saw fit), and therefore he had it in his thoughts to see them, and stay with them. Note, The heart of a truly Christian minister must be much towards that people among whom he has long laboured, and with remarkable success. No wonder that Paul was willing to see Corinth and stay with them as long as the other duties of his office would permit. Though some among this people despised him, and made a faction against him, doubtless there were many who loved him tenderly, and paid him all the respect due to an apostle and their spiritual father. And is it any wonder that he should be willing to visit them, and stay with them? And as to the rest, who now manifested great disrespect, he might hope to reduce them to a better temper, and thereby rectify what was out of order in the church, by staying among them for some time. It is plain that he hoped for some good effect, because he says he intended to stay, *that they might bring him on his journey whithersoever he went* (*v.* 6); not that they might accompany him a little way on the road, but expedite and furnish him for his journey, help and encourage him to it, and provide him for it. He is to be understood of being brought forward in his journey after a godly sort (as it is expressed, 3 John 6), so that nothing might be wanting to him, as he himself speaks, Tit. iii. 13. His stay among them, he hoped, would cure their factious humour, and reconcile them to himself and their duty. Note, It was a just reason for an apostle to make his abode in a place that he had a prospect of doing good. 2. His excuse for not seeing them now, because it would be *only by the way* (*v.* 7), *ἐν παρόδῳ—in transitu—en passant: it would only be a transient visit.* He would not see them because he could not stay with them. Such a visit would give neither him nor them any satisfaction or advantage; it would rather raise the appetite than regale it, rather heighten their desires of being together than satisfy them. He loved them so much that he longed for an opportunity to stay with them, take up his abode among them for some length of time. This would be more pleasing to himself, and more serviceable to them, than a cursory visit in his way; and therefore he would not see them now, but another time, when he could tarry longer. 3. We have the limitation of this purpose: *I trust to tarry awhile with you, if the Lord permit*, v. 7. Though the apostles wrote under inspiration, they did not know thereby how God would dispose of them. Paul had a purpose of coming to Corinth, and staying there, and hoped to do good thereby. This was not a purpose proceeding from any extraordinary motion or impulse of the Spirit of God; it was not the effect of inspiration; for had it been such he could not have spoken of it in this manner. A purpose formed thus in him must have been the purpose of God, signified to him by his Spirit; and could he say he would come to Corinth upon this view only, if God permit, that is, that he would execute God's own purpose concerning himself, with God's permission? It is to be understood then of a common purpose, formed in his own spirit. And concerning all our purposes it is fit we should say, "We will execute them if the Lord permit." Note, All our purposes must be made with submission to the divine providence. We should say, *If the Lord will, we shall live, and do this and that*, James iv. 15. It is not in us to effect our own designs, without the divine leave. It is by God's power and permission, and under his direction, that we must do every thing. Heathens have concurred in acknowledging this concern of Providence in all our actions and concerns; surely we should readily own it, and frequently and seriously attend to it. 4. We have his purpose expressed of staying at Ephesus for the present. He says he would stay there till pentecost, *v.* 8. It is very probable that at the time of writing this epistle he was in Ephesus, from this passage, compared with *v.* 19, where he says, *The churches of Asia salute you.* A proper salutation from Ephesus, but hardly so proper had he been at Philippi, as the subscription to this epistle in our common copies has it. "*The churches of Macedonia salute you*" had been much more properly inserted in the close of a letter from Philippi, than the other. But, 5. We have the reason given for his staying at Ephesus for the present: *Because a great door, and effectual, was opened to him, and there were many adversaries*, v. 9. A great door and effectual was opened to him; many were prepared to receive the gospel at Ephesus, and God gave him great success among them; he had brought over many to Christ, and he had great hope of bringing over many more. For this reason he determined to stay awhile at Ephesus. Note, Success, and a fair prospect of more, was a just reason to determine an apostle to stay and labour in a particular place. And there were many adversaries, because a great door, and an effectual, was opened. Note, Great success in the work of the gospel commonly creates many enemies. The devil opposes those most, and makes them most trouble, who most heartily and successfully set themselves to destroy his kingdom. There were many adversaries; and therefore the apostle determined to stay. Some think he alludes in this passage to the custom of the Roman Circus, and the doors of it, at which the charioteers were to enter, as their antagonists did at the opposite doors. True courage is whetted by opposition; and it is no wonder that the Christian courage of the apostle should be animated by the zeal of his adversaries. They were bent to ruin him, and prevent the effect of his ministry at Ephesus; and should he at this time desert his station, and disgrace his character and doctrine? No, the opposition of adversaries only animated his zeal. He was in nothing daunted by his adversaries; but the more they raged and opposed the more he exerted himself. Should such a man as he flee? Note, Adversaries and opposition do not break the spirits of faithful and successful ministers, but only enkindle their zeal, and inspire them with fresh courage. Indeed, to labour in vain is heartless and discouraging. This damps the spirits, and breaks the heart. But success will give life and vigour to a minister, though enemies rage, and blaspheme, and persecute. It is not the opposition of enemies, but the hardness and obstinacy of his hearers, and the backslidings and revolt of professors, that damp a faithful minister, and break his heart.

10 Now if Timotheus come, see
that he may be with you without
fear: for he worketh the work of the
Lord, as I also *do*. 11 Let no man
therefore despise him: but conduct
him forth in peace, that he may come
unto me: for I look for him with the
brethren. 12 As touching *our* brother Apollos, I greatly desired him
to come unto you with the brethren:
but his will was not at all to come at
this time; but he will come when he
shall have convenient time.

In this passage,

I. He recommends Timothy to them, in several particulars. As, 1. He bids them take care that he should *be among them without fear*, v. 10. Timothy was sent by the apostle to correct the abuses which had crept in among them; and not only to direct, but to blame, and censure, and reprove, those who were culpable. They were all in factions, and no doubt the mutual strife and hatred ran very high among them. There were some very rich, as it is probable; and many very proud, upon account both of their outward wealth and spiritual gifts. Proud spirits cannot easily bear reproof. It was reasonable therefore to think young Timothy might be roughly used; hence the apostle warns them against using him ill. Not but that he was prepared for the worst; but, whatever his firmness and prudence might be, it was their duty to behave themselves well towards him, and not discourage and dishearten him in his Lord's work. They should not fly out into resentment at his reproof. Note, Christians should bear faithful reproofs from their ministers, and not terrify and discourage them from doing their duty. 2. He warns them against despising him, *v.* 11. He was but a young man, and alone, as Œcumenius observes. He had no one to back him, and his own youthful face and years commanded but little reverence; and therefore the great pretenders to wisdom among them might be apt to entertain contemptuous thoughts of him. "Now," says the apostle, "guard against this." Not that he distrusted Timothy; he knew that Timothy would do nothing to bring contempt on his character, nothing to make his youth despicable. But pride was a reigning sin among the Corinthians, and such a caution was but too necessary. Note, Christians should be very careful not to pour contempt on any, but especially on ministers, the faithful ministers of Christ. These, whether young or old, are to be had in high esteem for their work's sake. 3. He tells them they should give him all due encouragement, use him well while he was with them; and, as an evidence of this, they should send him away in friendship, and well prepared for his journey back again to Paul. This, as I have before observed, is the meaning of bringing him on his journey in peace, *v.* 11. Note, Faithful ministers are not only to be well received by a people among whom they may for a season minister, but are to be sent away with due respect.

II. He assigns the reasons why they should behave thus towards Timothy. 1. Because he was employed in the same work as Paul, and acted in it by the same authority, *v.* 10. He did not come on Paul's errand among them, nor to do his work, but the work of the Lord. Though he was not an apostle, he was assistant to one, and was sent upon this very business by a divine commission. And therefore to vex his spirit would be to grieve the Holy Spirit; to despise him would be to despise him that sent him, not Paul, but Paul's Lord and theirs. Note, Those who work the work of the Lord should be neither terrified nor despised, but treated with all tenderness and respect. Such are all the faithful ministers of the word, though not all in the same rank and degree. Pastors and teachers, as well as apostles and evangelists, while they are doing their duty, are to be treated with honour and respect. 2. Another reason is implied; as they were to esteem him for his work's sake, so also for Paul's sake, who had sent him to Corinth; not of his own errand indeed, but to work the work of the Lord: *Conduct him forth in peace, that he may come to me, for I look for him with the brethren* (*v.* 11); or *I with the brethren look for him* (the original will bear either), ἐκδέχομαι γὰρ αὐτὸν μετὰ τῶν ἀδελφῶν—"I am expecting his return, and his report concerning you; and shall judge by your conduct towards him what your regard and respect for me will be. Look to it that you send him back with no evil report." Paul might expect from the Corinthians, that a messenger from him, upon such an errand, should be regarded, and well treated. His services and success among them, his authority with them as an apostle, would challenge this at their hands. They would hardly dare to send back Timothy with a report that would grieve or provoke the apostle. "I and the brethren expect his return, wait for the report he is to make; and therefore do not use him ill, but respect him, regard his message, and let him return in peace."

III. He informs them of Apollos's purpose to see them. 1. He himself had greatly desired him to come to them, *v.* 12. Though one party among them had declared for Apollos against Paul (if that passage is to be understood literally, *vide ch.* iv. 6), yet Paul did not hinder Apollos from going to Corinth in his own absence, nay, he pressed him to go thither. He had no suspicions of Apollos, as if he would lessen Paul's interest and respect among them, to the advancement of his own. Note, Faithful ministers are not apt to entertain jealousies of each other, nor suspect of such selfish designs. True charity and brotherly love think no evil. And where should these reign, if not in the breasts of the ministers of Christ? 2. Apollos could not be prevailed on for the present to come, but would at a more convenient season. Perhaps their feuds and factions might render the present season improper. He would not go to be set at the head of a party and countenance the dividing and contentious humour. When this had subsided, through Paul's epistle to them and Timothy's ministry among them, he might conclude a visit would be more proper. Apostles did not vie with each other, but consulted each other's comfort and usefulness. Paul intimates his great regard to the church of Corinth, when they had used him ill, by entreating Apollos to go to them; and Apollos shows his respect to Paul, and his concern to keep up his character and authority, by declining the journey till the Corinthians were in better temper. Note, It is very becoming the ministers of the gospel to have and manifest a concern for each other's reputation and usefulness.

13 Watch ye, stand fast in the
faith, quit you like men, be strong.
14 Let all your things be done with

charity. 15 I beseech you, brethren,
(ye know the house of Stephanas, that
it is the firstfruits of Achaia, and *that*
they have addicted themselves to the
ministry of the saints,) 16 That ye
submit yourselves unto such, and to
every one that helpeth with *us*, and
laboureth. 17 I am glad of the coming of Stephanas and Fortunatus and
Achaicus: for that which was lacking
on your part they have supplied. 18
For they have refreshed my spirit and
your's: therefore acknowledge ye
them that are such.

In this passage the apostle gives,

I. Some general advices; as, 1. That they should watch (*v.* 13), be wakeful and upon their guard. A Christian is always in danger, and therefore should ever be on the watch; but the danger is greater at some times and under some circumstances. The Corinthians were in manifest danger upon many accounts: their feuds ran high, the irregularities among them were very great, there were deceivers got among them, who endeavoured to corrupt their faith in the most important articles, those without which the practice of virtue and piety could never subsist. And surely in such dangerous circumstances it was their concern to watch. Note, If a Christian would be secure, he must be on his guard; and the more his danger the greater vigilance is needful for his security. 2. He advises them to *stand fast in the faith*, to keep their ground, adhere to the revelation of God, and not give it up for the wisdom of the world, nor suffer it to be corrupted by it—stand for the faith of the gospel, and maintain it even to death; and stand in it, so as to abide in the profession of it, and feel and yield to its influence. Note, A Christian should be fixed in the faith of the gospel, and never desert nor renounce it. It is by this faith alone that he will be able to keep his ground in an hour of temptation; it is by faith that we stand (2 Cor. i. 24); it is by this that we must overcome the world (1 John v. 4), both when it fawns and when it frowns, when it tempts and when it terrifies. We must stand therefore in the faith of the gospel, if we would maintain our integrity. 3. He advises them to act like men, and be strong: "Act the manly, firm, and resolved part: behave strenuously, in opposition to the bad men who would divide and corrupt you, those who would split you into factions or seduce you from the faith: be not terrified nor inveigled by them; but show yourselves men in Christ, by your steadiness, by your sound judgment and firm resolution." Note, Christians should be manly and firm in all their contests with their enemies, in defending their faith, and maintaining their integrity. They should, in an especial manner, be so in those points of faith that lie at the foundation of sound and practical religion, such as were attacked among the Corinthians: these must be maintained with solid judgment and strong resolution. 4. He advises them to do every thing in charity, *v.* 14. Our zeal and constancy must be consistent with charity. When the apostle would have us play the man for our faith or religion, he puts in a caution against playing the devil for it. We may defend our faith, but we must, at the same time, maintain our innocence, and not devour and destroy, and think with ourselves that the wrath of man will work the righteousness of God, James i. 24. Note, Christians should be careful that charity not only reign in their hearts, but shine out in their lives, nay, in their most manly defences of the faith of the gospel. There is a great difference between constancy and cruelty, between Christian firmness and feverish wrath and transport. Christianity never appears to so much advantage as when the charity of Christians is most conspicuous, when they can bear with their mistaken brethren, and oppose the open enemies of their holy faith in love, when every thing is done in charity, when they behave towards one another, and towards all men, with a spirit of meekness and good will.

II. Some particular directions how they should behave towards some that had been eminently serviceable to the cause of Christ among them.

1. He gives us their character (1.) The household of Stephanas is mentioned by him, and their character is, that they were the first-fruits of Achaia, the first converts to Christianity in that region of Greece in which Corinth was. Note, It is an honourable character to any man to be early a Christian, betimes in Christ. But they had moreover addicted themselves to the ministry of the saints, to serve the saints. They have *disposed and devoted themselves*—ἔταξαν ἑαυτοὺς, to serve the saints, to do service to the saints. It is not meant of the ministry of the word properly, but of serving them in other respects, supplying their wants, helping and assisting them upon all occasions, both in their temporal and spiritual concerns. The family of Stephanas seems to have been a family of rank and importance in those parts, and yet they willingly offered themselves to this service. Note, It is an honour to persons of the highest rank to devote themselves to the service of the saints. I do not mean to change ranks, and become proper servants to the inferiors, but freely and voluntarily to help them, and do good to them in all their concerns. (2.) He mentions Stephanas, and Fortunatus, and Achaicus, as coming to him from the church of Corinth. The account he gives of them is that they supplied the deficiencies of the church towards him, and by

so doing *refreshed his spirit and theirs, v.* 17, 18. They gave him a more perfect account of the state of the church by word of mouth than he could acquire by their letter, and by that means much quieted his mind, and upon their return from him would quiet the minds of the Corinthians. Report had made their cause much worse than it was in fact, and their letters had not explained it sufficiently to give the apostle satisfaction; but he had been made more easy by converse with them. It was a very good office they did, by truly stating facts, and removing the ill opinion Paul had received by common fame. They came to him with a truly Christian intention, to set the apostle right, and give him as favourable sentiments of the church as they could, as peace-makers. Note, It is a great refreshment to the spirit of a faithful minister to hear better of a people by wise and good men of their own body than by common report, to find himself misinformed concerning them, that matters are not so bad as they had been represented. It is a grief to him to hear ill of those he loves; it gladdens his heart to hear the report thereof is false. And the greater value he has for those who give him this information, and the more he can depend upon their veracity, the greater is his joy.

2. Upon this account of the men, he directs how they should behave towards them; and, (1.) He would have them acknowledged (*v.* 11), that is, owned and respected. They deserve it for their good offices. Those who serve the saints, those who consult the honour and good esteem of the churches, and are concerned to wipe off reproaches from them, and take off from the ill opinion fame had propagated, are to be valued, and esteemed, and loved. Those who discover so good a spirit cannot easily be over-valued. (2.) He advises that they should *submit themselves to such, and to all who helped with the apostles, and laboured, v.* 16. This is not to be understood of subjection to proper superiors, but of a voluntary acknowledgment of their worth. They were persons to whom they owed peculiar respect, and whom they should have in veneration. Note, It is a venerable character which those bear who serve the saints and labour hard to help the success of the gospel, who countenance and encourage the faithful ministers of Christ, and endeavour to promote their usefulness. Such should be had in honourable esteem.

19 The churches of Asia salute
you. Aquila and Priscilla salute you
much in the Lord, with the church
that is in their house. All the brethren greet you. Greet ye one another with a holy kiss. 21 The
salutation of *me* Paul with mine own
hand. 22 If any man love not the
Lord Jesus Christ, let him be Anathema Maran-atha. 23 The grace of
our Lord Jesus Christ *be* with you.
24 My love *be* with you all in Christ
Jesus. Amen.

The apostle closes his epistle,

I. With salutations to the church of Corinth, first from those of Asia, from *Priscilla* and *Aquila* (who seem to have been at this time inhabitants of Ephesus, *vid.* Acts xviii. 26), *with the church in their house* (*v.* 19), and from *all the brethren* (*v.* 20) at Ephesus, where, it is highly probable at least, he then was. All these saluted the church at Corinth, by Paul. Note, Christianity does by no means destroy civility and good manners. Paul could find room in an epistle treating of very important matters to send the salutations of friends. Religion should promote a courteous and obliging temper towards all. Those misrepresent and reproach it who would take any encouragement from it to be sour and morose. Some of these *salute them much in the Lord.* Note, Christian salutations are not empty compliments; they carry in them real expressions of good-will, and are attended with hearty recommendations to the divine grace and blessing. Those who salute in the Lord wish their brethren all good from the Lord, and breathe out their good wishes in fervent prayers. We read also of a church in a private family, *v.* 19. It is very probable that the family itself is called *the church in their house.* Note, Every Christian family should in some respects be a Christian church. In some cases (as, for instance, were they cast away on a foreign shore, where there are no other Christians), they should be a church themselves, if large enough, and live in the use of all ordinances; but in common cases they should live under the direction of Christian rules, and daily offer up Christian worship. Wherever two or three are gathered together, and Christ is among them, there is a church. To these salutations he subjoins, 1. An advice, that *they should greet one another with a holy kiss* (*v.* 20), or with sincere good-will, a tacit reproof of their feuds and factions. When the churches of Asia, and the Christian brethren so remote, did so heartily salute them in the Lord, and own and love them as brethren, and expressed so much good-will to them, it would be a shame for them not to own and love one another as brethren. Note, The love of the brethren should be a powerful incentive to mutual love. When the other churches of Christ love us all, we are very culpable if we do not love one another. 2. He subjoins his own salutation: *The salutation of me Paul with my own hand, v.* 21. His *amanuensis,* it is reasonable to think, wrote the rest of his epistle from his mouth, but at the close it was fit that himself should sign it, that they might know it to be genuine; and therefore it is added (2 Thess. iii. 17), *Which is my token in every epistle,* the mark of its being genuine; so he wrote in every epistle which he did not wholly pen, as he did that to the Galatians, Gal. vi. 11. Note, Those churches to whom apostolical letters were sent were duly certified of their being authentic and divine. Nor would Paul be behind the rest of the brethren in respect to the Corinthians; and therefore, after he has given their salutations, he adds his own.

II. With a very solemn warning to them: *If any man love not the Lord Jesus Christ, let him be Anathema, Maran-atha, v.* 22. We sometimes need words of threatening, that we may fear. *Blessed is he,* says the wise man, *who feareth always.* Holy fear is a very good friend both to holy faith and holy living. And how much reason have all Christians to fear falling under this doom! *If any man love not the Lord Jesus Christ, let him be Anathema, Maran-atha.* Here observe, 1. The person described, who is liable to this doom: *He that loveth not the Lord Jesus Christ.* A μείωσις, as some think; he who blasphemes Christ disowns his doctrine, slights and contemns his institutions, or, through pride of human knowledge and learning, despises his revelations. It stands here as a warning to the Corinthians and a rebuke of their criminal behaviour. It is an admonition to them not to be led away from the simplicity of the gospel, or those principles of it which were the great motives to purity of life, by pretenders to science, by the wisdom of the world, which would call their religion folly, and its most important doctrines absurd and ridiculous. Those men had a spite at Christ; and, if the Corinthians gave ear to their seducing speeches, they were in danger of apostatizing from him. Against this he gives them here a very solemn caution. "Do not give into such conduct, if you would escape the severest vengeance." Note, Professed Christians will, by contempt of Christ, and revolt from him, bring upon themselves the most dreadful destruction. Some understand the words as they lie, in their plain and obvious meaning, for such as are without holy and sincere affection for the Lord Jesus Christ. Many who have his name much in their mouths have no true love to him in their hearts, will not have him to rule over them (Luke xix. 27), no, not though they have very towering hopes of being saved by him. And none love him in truth who do not love his laws and keep his commandments. Note, There are many Christians in name who do not love Christ Jesus the Lord in sincerity. But can any thing be more criminal or provoking? What, not love the most glorious lover in the world! Him who loved us, and gave himself for us, who shed his blood for us, to testify his love to us, and that after heinous wrong and provocation! What had we a power of loving for, if we are unmoved with such love as this, and without affection to such a Saviour? But, 2. We have here the doom of the person described: "*Let him be Anathema, Maran-atha,* lie under the heaviest and most dreadful curse. Let him be separated from the people of God, from the favour of God, and delivered up to his final, irrevocable, and inexorable vengeance" *Maran-atha* is a Syriac phrase, and signifies *The Lord cometh.* That very Lord whom they do not love, to whom they are inwardly and really disaffected whatever outward profession they make, is coming to execute judgment. And to be exposed to his wrath, to be divided to his left hand, to be condemned by him, how dreadful! If he will destroy, who can save? Those who fall under his condemning sentence must perish, and that for ever. Note, Those who love not the Lord Jesus Christ must perish without remedy. *The wrath of God abides on every one who believes not on the Son,* John iii. 36. And true faith in Christ will evermore be productive of sincere love to him. Those who love him not cannot be believers in him.

III. With his good wishes for them and expressions of good-will to them. 1. With his good wishes: *The grace of our Lord Jesus Christ be with you, v.* 23. As much as if he had said, "Though I warn you against falling under his displeasure, I heartily wish you an interest in his dearest love and his eternal favour." The grace of our Lord Jesus Christ comprehends in it all that is good, for time or eternity. To wish our friends may have this grace with them is wishing them the utmost good. And this we should wish all our friends and brethren in Christ. We can wish them nothing more, and we should wish them nothing less. We should heartily pray that they may value, and seek, and obtain, and secure, the grace and good-will of their Lord and Judge. Note, The most solemn warnings are the result of the tenderest affection and the greatest good-will. We may tell our brethren and friends with great plainness and pathos that, if they love not the Lord Jesus Christ, they must perish, while we heartily wish the grace of Christ may be with them. Nay, we may give them this warning that they may prize and lay hold of this grace. Note also, How much true Christianity enlarges our hearts; it makes us wish those whom we love the blessings of both worlds; for this is implied in wishing the grace of Christ to be with them. And therefore it is no wonder that the apostle should close all, 2. With the declaration of his love to them in Christ Jesus: *My love be with you all, in Christ Jesus, Amen, v.* 24. He had dealt very plainly with them in this epistle, and told them of their faults with just severity; but, to show that he was not transported with passion, he parts with them in love, makes solemn profession of his love to them, nay, to them all in Christ Jesus, that is, for Christ's sake. He tells them that his heart was with them, that he truly loved them; but lest this, after all, should be deemed flattery and insinuation, he adds that his affection was the result of his religion, and would be guided by the rules of it. His heart would be with them, and he would bear them dear affection as long as their hearts were with Christ, and they bore true affection to his cause and interest. Note, We should be cordial lovers of all who are in Christ, and who love him in sincerity. Not but we should love all men, and wish them well, and do them what good is in our power; but *those* must have our dearest affection who are dear to Christ, and lovers of him. May our love be with all those who are in Christ Jesus! Amen.

AN

EXPOSITION,

WITH PRACTICAL OBSERVATIONS,

OF THE SECOND EPISTLE OF ST. PAUL TO THE

CORINTHIANS.

In his former epistle the apostle had signified his intentions of *coming to Corinth, as he passed through Macedonia* (*ch.* xvi. 5), but, being providentially hindered for some time, he writes this second epistle to them about a year after the former; and there seem to be these two urgent occasions:—1. The case of the incestuous person, who lay under censure, required that with all speed he should be restored and received again into communion. This therefore he gives directions about (*ch.* ii.), and afterwards (*ch.* vii.) he declares the satisfaction he had upon the intelligence he received of their good behaviour in that affair. 2. There was a contribution now making for the poor saints at Jerusalem, in which he exhorts the Corinthians to join, *ch.* viii. ix.

There are divers other things very observable in this epistle; for example, I. The account the apostle gives of his labours and success in preaching the gospel in several places, *ch.* ii. II. The comparison he makes between the Old and New-Testament dispensation, *ch.* iii. III. The manifold sufferings that he and his fellow-labourers met with, and the motives and encouragements for their diligence and patience, *ch.* iv. v. IV. The caution he gives the Corinthians against mingling with unbelievers, *ch.* vi. V. The way and manner in which he justifies himself and his apostleship from the opprobrious insinuations and accusations of false teachers, who endeavoured to ruin his reputation at Corinth, *ch.* x.—xii., and throughout the whole epistle.

CHAP. I.

After the introduction (ver. 1, 2) the apostle begins with the narrative of his troubles and God's goodness, which he had met with in Asia, by way of thanksgiving to God (ver. 3—6), and for the edification of the Corinthians, ver. 7—11. Then he attests his and his fellow-labourers' integrity (ver. 12—14), and afterwards vindicates himself from the imputation of levity and inconstancy, ver. 15—24.

PAUL, an apostle of Jesus Christ by the will of God, and Timothy *our* brother, unto the church of God which is at Corinth, with all the saints which are in all Achaia:
2 Grace *be* to you and peace from God our Father, and *from* the Lord Jesus Christ.

This is the introduction to this epistle, in which we have,

I. The inscription; and therein, 1. The person from whom it was sent, namely, Paul, who calls himself *an apostle of Jesus Christ by the will of God*. The apostleship itself was ordained by Jesus Christ, according to the will of God; and Paul was called to it by Jesus Christ, according to the will of God. He joins Timotheus with himself in writing this epistle; not because he needed his assistance, but that out of the mouth of two witnesses the word might be established; and his dignifying Timothy with the title of *brother* (either in the common faith, or in the work of the ministry) shows the humility of this great apostle, and his desire to recommend Timothy (though he was then a young man) to the esteem of the Corinthians, and give him a reputation among the churches. 2. The persons to whom this epistle was sent, namely, *the church of God at Corinth:* and not only to them, but also *to all the saints in all Achaia,* that is, to all the Christians who lived in the region round about. Note, In Christ Jesus no distinction is made between the inhabitants of city and country; all Achaia stands upon a level in his account.

II. The salutation or apostolical benediction, which is the same as in his former epistle; and therein the apostle desires the two great and comprehensive blessings, grace and peace, for those Corinthians. These two benefits are fitly joined together, because there is no good and lasting peace without true grace; and both of them come *from God our Father, and from the Lord Jesus Christ,* who is the procurer and dispenser of those benefits to fallen man, and is prayed to as God.

3 Blessed *be* God, even the Father
of our Lord Jesus Christ, the Father
of mercies, and the God of all comfort; 4 Who comforteth us in all
our tribulation, that we may be able
to comfort them which are in any
trouble by the comfort wherewith we
ourselves are comforted of God. 5
For as the sufferings of Christ abound
in us, so our consolation also aboundeth by Christ. 6 And whether we
be afflicted *it is* for your consolation
and salvation, which is effectual in
the enduring of the same sufferings
which we also suffer: or whether we
be comforted, *it is* for your consolation and salvation.

After the foregoing preface, the apostle begins with the narrative of God's goodness to him and his fellow-labourers in their manifold tribulations, which he speaks of by way of thanksgiving to God, and to advance the divine glory (*v.* 3—6); and it is fit that in all things, and in the first place, God be glorified. Observe,

I. The object of the apostle's thanksgiving, to whom he offers up blessing and praise, namely, the blessed God, who only is to be praised, whom he describes by several glorious and amiable titles. 1. *The God and Father of our Lord Jesus Christ:* ὁ Θεὸς καὶ πατὴρ τοῦ Κυρίου ἡμῶν Ἰησοῦ Χριστοῦ. God is the Father of Christ's divine nature by eternal generation, of his human nature by miraculous conception in the womb of the virgin, and of Christ as God-man, and our Redeemer, by covenant-relation, and in and through him as Mediator our God and our Father, John xx. 17. In the Old Testament we often meet with this title, *The God of Abraham, and of Isaac, and of Jacob,* to denote God's covenant-relation to them and their seed; and in the New Testament God is styled *the God and Father of our Lord Jesus Christ,* to denote his covenant-relation to the Mediator and his spiritual seed. Gal. iii. 16. 2. *The Father of mercies.* There is a multitude of tender mercies in God essentially, and all mercies are from God originally: mercy is his genuine offspring and his delight. *He delighteth in mercy,* Mic. vii. 18. 3. *The God of all comfort;* from him proceedeth the COMFORTER, John xv. 26. He giveth the earnest of the Spirit in our hearts, *v.* 22. All our comforts come from God, and our sweetest comforts are in him.

II. The reasons of the apostle's thanksgivings, which are these:—

1. The benefits that he himself and his companions had received from God; for God *had comforted* them *in all their tribulations, v.* 4. In the world they had trouble, but in Christ they had peace. The apostles met with many tribulations, but they found comfort in them all: their sufferings (which are called *the sufferings of Christ* (*v.* 5) because Christ sympathized with his members when suffering for his sake) did abound, but their consolation by Christ did abound also. Note, (1.) Then are we qualified to receive the comfort of God's mercies when we set ourselves to give him the glory of them. (2.) Then we speak best of God and his goodness when we speak from our own experience, and, in telling others, tell God also what he has done for our souls.

2. The advantage which others might receive; for God intended that they *should be able to comfort others* in trouble (*v.* 4), by communicating to them their experiences of the divine goodness and mercy; and the sufferings of good men have a tendency to this good end (*v.* 6) when they are endued with faith and patience. Note, (1.) What favours God bestows on us are intended not only to make us cheerful ourselves, but also that we may be useful to others. (2.) If we do imitate the faith and patience of good men in their afflictions, we may hope to partake of their consolations here and their salvation hereafter.

7 And our hope of you *is* stedfast,
knowing, that as ye are partakers of
the sufferings, so *shall ye be* also of
the consolation. 8 For we would
not, brethren, have you ignorant of
our trouble which came to us in Asia,
that we were pressed out of measure,
above strength, insomuch that we
despaired even of life: 9 But we
had the sentence of death in ourselves, that we should not trust in
ourselves, but in God which raiseth
the dead: 10 Who delivered us from
so great a death, and doth deliver: in
whom we trust that he will yet deliver
us; 11 Ye also helping together by
prayer for us, that for the gift *bestowed*
upon us by the means of many persons thanks may be given by many
on our behalf.

In these verses the apostle speaks for the encouragement and edification of the Corinthians; and tells them (*v.* 7) of his persuasion or stedfast hope that they should receive benefit by the troubles he and his companions in labour and travel had met with, that their faith should not be weakened, but their consolations increased. In order to this he tells them, 1. What their sufferings had been (*v.* 8): *We would not have you ignorant of our trouble.* It was convenient for the churches to know what were the sufferings of their ministers. It is not certain what particular troubles in Asia are here referred to; whether the tumult raised by Demetrius at Ephesus, mentioned Acts xix., or the fight with beasts at Ephesus, mentioned in the former epistle (*ch.* xv.), or some other trouble; for the apostle was in deaths often. This however is evident, that they were great tribulations. They *were pushed out of measure,* to a very extraordinary degree, above the common strength of men, or of ordinary Christians, to bear up under them, insomuch that they *despaired even of life* (*v.* 8), and thought they should have been killed, or have fainted away and expired. 2. What they did in their distress: *They trusted in God.* And they were brought to this extremity in order *that they should not trust in themselves but in God, v.* 9. Note, God often brings his people into great straits, that they may apprehend their own insufficiency to help themselves, and may be induced to place their trust and hope in his all-sufficiency. Our extremity is God's opportunity. *In the mount will the Lord be seen;* and we may safely trust in *God, who raiseth the dead, v.* 9. God's raising the dead is a proof of his almighty power. He that can do this can do any thing, can do all things, and is worthy to be trusted in at all times. Abraham's faith fastened upon this instance of the divine power: *He believed God who quickeneth the dead,* Rom. iv. 17. If we should be brought so low as to despair even of life, yet we may then trust in God, who can bring back not only from the gates, but from the jaws, of death. 3. What the deliverance was that they had obtained; and this was seasonable and continued. Their hope and trust were not in vain, nor shall any who trust in him be ashamed. God had delivered them, and did still deliver them, *v.* 10. *Having obtained help of God, they continued to that day,* Acts xxvi. 22. 4. What use they made of this deliverance: *We trust that he will yet deliver us* (*v.* 10), that God will deliver to the end, and *preserve to his heavenly kingdom.* Note, Past experiences are great encouragements to faith and hope, and they lay great obligations to trust in God for time to come. We reproach our experiences if we distrust God in future straits, who hath delivered as in former troubles. David, even when a young man, and when he had but a small stock of experiences, argued after the manner of the apostle here, 1 Sam. xvii. 37. 5. What was desired of the Corinthians upon this account: *That they would help together by prayer for them* (*v.* 11), by social prayer, agreeing and joining together in prayer on their behalf. Note, Our trusting in God must not supersede the use of any proper and appointed means; and prayer is one of those means. We should pray for ourselves and for one another. The apostle had himself a great interest in the throne of grace, yet he desires the help of others' prayers. If we thus help one another by our prayers, we may hope for an occasion of *giving thanks by many* for answer of prayer. And it is our duty not only to help one another with prayer, but in praise and thanksgiving, and thereby to make suitable returns for benefits received.

12 For our rejoicing is this, the
testimony of our conscience, that in
simplicity and godly sincerity, not
with fleshly wisdom, but by the grace
of God, we have had our conversation
in the world, and more abundantly to
you-ward. 13 For we write none
other things unto you, than what ye
read or acknowledge; and I trust ye
shall acknowledge even to the end;
14 As also ye have acknowledged us
in part, that we are your rejoicing,
even as ye also *are* our's in the day
of the Lord Jesus.

The apostle in these verses attests their integrity by the sincerity of their conversation. This he does not in a way of boasting and vain-glory, but as one good reason for desiring the help of prayer, as well as for the more comfortably trusting in God (Heb. xiii. 18), and for the necessary vindication of himself from the aspersions of some persons at Corinth, who reproached his person and questioned his apostleship. Here,

I. He appeals to the testimony of conscience with rejoicing (*v.* 12), in which observe, 1. The witness appealed to, namely, conscience, which is instead of a thousand witnesses. This is God's deputy in the soul, and the voice of conscience is the voice of God. They rejoiced in the testimony of conscience, when their enemies reproached them, and were enraged against them. Note, The testimony of conscience for us, if that be right and upon good grounds, will be matter of rejoicing at all times and in all conditions. 2. The testimony this witness gave. And here take notice, Conscience witnessed, (1.) Concerning their conversation, their constant course and tenour of life: by that we may judge of ourselves, and not by this or that single act. (2.) Concerning the nature or manner of their conversation; that it was in simplicity and godly sincerity. This blessed apostle was a true Israelite, a man of plain dealing; you might know where to have him. He was not a man who seemed to be one thing and was another, but a man of sincerity. (3.) Concerning the principle they acted from in all their conversation, both in the world and towards these Corinthians; and that was not fleshly wisdom, nor carnal politics and worldly views, but it was the grace of God, a vital gracious principle in their hearts, that cometh from God, and tendeth to God. Then will our conversation be well ordered when we live and act under the influence and command of such a gracious principle in the heart.

II. He appeals to the knowledge of the Corinthians with hope and confidence, *v.* 13, 14. Their conversation did in part fall under the observation of the Corinthians; and these knew how they behaved themselves, *how holily, and justly, and unblamably;* they never found any thing in them unbecoming an honest man. This they had acknowledged in part already, and he doubted not but they would still do so to the end, that is, that they would never have any good reason to think or say otherwise of him, but that he was an honest man. And so there would be mutual rejoicing in one another. *We are your rejoicing, even as you also are ours in the day of the Lord Jesus.* Note, It is happy when ministers and people do rejoice in each other here; and this joy will be complete in that day when the great Shepherd of the sheep shall appear.

15 And in this confidence I was
minded to come unto you before, that
ye might have a second benefit; 16
And to pass by you into Macedonia,
and to come again out of Macedonia
unto you, and of you to be brought
on my way toward Judæa. 17 When
I therefore was thus minded, did I
use lightness? or the things that I
purpose, do I purpose according to
the flesh, that with me there may be
yea yea, and nay nay? 18 But *as*
God *is* true, our word toward you
was not yea and nay. 19 For the
Son of God, Jesus Christ, who was
preached among you by us, *even* by
me and Silvanus and Timotheus, was
not yea and nay, but in him was yea.
20 For all the promises of God in
him *are* yea, and in him Amen, unto
the glory of God by us. 21 Now he
which stablisheth us with you in
Christ, and hath anointed us, *is* God;
22 Who hath also sealed us, and
given the earnest of the Spirit in our
hearts. 23 Moreover I call God for
a record upon my soul, that to spare
you I came not as yet unto Corinth.
24 Not for that we have dominion
over your faith, but are helpers of
your joy: for by faith ye stand.

The apostle here vindicates himself from the imputation of levity and inconstancy, in that he did not hold his purpose of coming to them at Corinth. His adversaries there sought all occasions to blemish his character, and reflect upon his conduct; and, it seemed, they took hold of this handle to reproach his person and discredit his ministry. Now, for his justification,

I. He avers the sincerity of his intention (*v.* 15—17), and he does this in confidence of their good opinion of him, and that they would believe him, when he assured them he *was minded,* or did really intend, *to come* to them, and that with the design, not that he might receive, but that they might receive a *second benefit,* that is, a further advantage by his ministry. He tells them that he had not herein *used lightness* (*v.* 17), that, as he aimed not at any secular advantage to himself (for his purpose was not *according to the flesh,* that is, with carnal views and aims), so it was not a rash and inconsiderate resolution that he had taken up, for he had laid his measures thus of *passing by them to Macedonia, and coming again to them from Macedonia in his way to Judea* (*v.* 16), and therefore they might conclude that it was for some weighty reasons that he had altered his purpose; and that with him there was not yea yea, and nay nay, *v.* 17. He was not to be accused of levity and inconstancy, nor a contradiction between his words and intentions. Note, Good men should be careful to preserve the reputation of sincerity and constancy; they should not resolve but upon mature deliberation, and they will not change their resolves but for weighty reasons.

II. He would not have the Corinthians to infer that his gospel was false or uncertain, nor that it was contradictory in itself, nor unto truth, *v.* 18, 19. For if it had been so, that he had been fickle in his purposes, or even false in the promises he made of coming to them (which he was not justly to be accused of, and so some understand this expression (*v.* 18), *Our word towards you was not yea and nay),* yet it would not follow that the gospel preached not only by him, but also by others in full agreement with him, was either false or doubtful. For *God is true,* and *the Son of God, Jesus Christ,* is true. The true God, and eternal life. Jesus Christ, whom the apostle preached, is not *yea* and *nay,* but in him was *yea* (*v.* 19), nothing but infallible truth. And the promises of God in Christ are not yea and nay, but yea and amen, *v.* 20. There is an inviolable constancy and unquestionable sincerity and certainty in all the parts of the gospel of Christ. If in the promises that the ministers of the gospel make as common men, and about their own affairs, they see cause sometimes to vary from them, yet the promises of the gospel covenant, which they preach, stand firm and inviolable. Bad men are false; good men are fickle; but *God is true,* neither fickle nor false. The apostle, having mentioned the stability of the divine promises, makes a digression to illustrate this great and sweet truth, that all the promises of God are yea and amen. For, 1. They are the promises of the God of truth (*v.* 20), of him *that cannot lie,* whose truth as well as mercy endureth for ever. 2. They are made in Christ Jesus (*v.* 20), the Amen, the true and faithful witness; he hath purchased and ratified the covenant of promises, and is the *surety of the covenant,* Heb. vii. 22. 3. They are confirmed by the Holy Spirit. He does establish Christians in the faith of the gospel; he has anointed them with his sanctifying grace, which in scripture is often compared to oil; he has sealed them, for their security and confirmation; and he is given *as an earnest in their hearts, v.* 21, 22. An earnest secures the promise, and is part of the payment. The illumination of the Spirit is an earnest of everlasting light; the quickening of the Spirit is an earnest of everlasting life; and the comforts of the Spirit are an earnest of everlasting joy. Note, The veracity of God, the mediation of Christ, and the operation of the Spirit, are all engaged that the promises shall be sure to all the seed, and the accomplishment of them shall be to the *glory of God* (*v.* 20), for the glory of his rich and sovereign grace, and never-failing truth and faithfulness.

III. The apostle gives a good reason why he did not come to Corinth, as was expected, *v.* 23. It was that he might spare them. They ought therefore to own his kindness and tenderness. He knew there were things amiss among them, and such as deserved censure, but was desirous to show tenderness. He assures them that this is the true reason, after this very solemn manner: *I call God for a record upon my soul*—a way of speaking not justifiable where used in trivial matters; but this was very justifiable in the apostle, for his necessary vindication, and for the credit and usefulness of his ministry, which was struck at by his opposers. He adds, to prevent mistakes, that he did not pretend to have any dominion over their faith, *v.* 24. Christ only is the Lord of our faith; he is the *author and finisher of our faith,* Heb. xii. 2. He reveals to us what we must believe. Paul, and Apollos, and the rest of the apostles, were *but ministers by whom they believed* (1 Cor. iii. 5), and so the *helpers of their joy,* even the joy of faith. For by faith we stand firmly, and live safely and comfortably. Our strength and ability are owing to faith, and our comfort and joy must flow from faith.

CHAP. II.

In this chapter the apostle proceeds in the account of the reasons why he did not come to Corinth, ver. 1—4. Then he writes concerning the incestuous person who lay under censure; and gives direction for restoring him, together with the reasons for their so doing (ver. 5—11), and afterwards informs them of his labours and success in preaching the gospel in several places, ver. 12—17.

BUT I determined this with myself,
that I would not come again to
you in heaviness. 2 For if I make
you sorry, who is he then that maketh
me glad, but the same which is made
sorry by me? 3 And I wrote this
same unto you, lest, when I came, I
should have sorrow from them of
whom I ought to rejoice; having
confidence in you all, that my joy is
the joy of you all. 4 For out of
much affliction and anguish of heart
I wrote unto you with many tears;
not that ye should be grieved, but
that ye might know the love which I
have more abundantly unto you.

In these verses, 1. The apostle proceeds in giving an account of the reason why he did not come to Corinth, as was expected; namely, because he was unwilling to grieve them, or be grieved by them, *v.* 1, 2. *He had determined not to come to them in heaviness,* which yet he would have done had he come and found scandal among them not duly animadverted upon: this would have been cause of grief both to him and them, for their sorrow or joy at meeting would have been mutual. If he had made them sorry, that would have been a sorrow to himself, for there would have been none to have made him glad. But his desire was to have a cheerful meeting with them, and not to have it embittered by any unhappy occasion of disagreeing. 2. He tells them it was to the same intent that he wrote his former epistle, *v.* 3, 4. (1.) *That he might not have sorrow from those of whom he ought to rejoice;* and that he had written to them in confidence of their doing what was requisite, in order to their benefit and his comfort. The particular thing referred to, as appears by the following verses, was the case of the incestuous person about whom he had written in the first epistle, *ch.* v. Nor was the apostle disappointed in his expectation. (2.) He assures them that he did not design to grieve them, but to testify his love to them, and that he wrote to them with much *anguish and affliction* in his own heart, and with great affection to them. He had *written with tears, that they might know his abundant love to them.* Note, [1.] Even in reproofs, admonitions, and acts of discipline, faithful ministers show their love. [2.] Needful censures, and the exercise of church-discipline towards offenders, are a grief to tender-spirited ministers, and are administered with regret.

5 But if any have caused grief, he
hath not grieved me but in part: that
I may not overcharge you all. 6 Suf-

ficient to such a man *is* this punishment, which *was inflicted* of many. 7
So that contrariwise ye *ought* rather
to forgive *him*, and comfort *him*, lest
perhaps such a one should be swallowed up with overmuch sorrow. 8
Wherefore I beseech you that ye
would confirm *your* love toward him.
9 For to this end also did I write,
that I might know the proof of you,
whether ye be obedient in all things.
10 To whom ye forgive any thing, I
forgive also: for if I forgave any
thing, to whom I forgave *it*, for your
sakes *forgave I it* in the person of
Christ; 11 Lest Satan should get
an advantage of us: for we are not
ignorant of his devices.

In these verses the apostle treats concerning the incestuous person who had been excommunicated, which seems to be one principal cause of his writing this epistle. Here observe, 1. He tells them that the crime of that person had grieved him *in part;* and that he was grieved also with a part of them, who, notwithstanding this scandal had been found among them, were *puffed up and had not mourned*, 1 Cor. v. 2. However, he was unwilling to lay too heavy a charge upon the whole church, especially seeing they had cleared themselves in that matter by observing the directions he had formerly given them. 2. He tells them that the punishment which had been inflicted upon this offender was sufficient, *v.* 6. The desired effect was obtained, for the man was humbled, and they had shown the proof of their obedience to his directions. 3. He therefore directs them, with all speed, to restore the excommunicated person, or to receive him again to their communion, *v.* 7, 8. This is expressed several ways. He beseeches them to forgive him, that is, to release him from church-censures, for they could not remit the guilt or offence against God; and also to comfort him, for in many cases the comfort of penitents depends upon their reconciliation not only with God, but with men also, whom they have scandalized or injured. They must also confirm their love to him; that is, they should show that their reproofs and censures proceeded from love to his person, as well as hatred to his sin, and that their design was to reform, not to ruin him. Or thus: If his fall had weakened their love to him, that they could not take such satisfaction in him as formerly; yet, now that he was recovered by repentance, they must renew and confirm their love to him. 4. He uses several weighty arguments to persuade them to do thus, sa, (1.) The case of the penitent called for this; for he was in danger of being *swallowed up with over-much sorrow, v.* 7. He was so sensible of this fault, and so much afflicted under his punishment, that he was in danger of falling into despair. When sorrow is excessive it does hurt; and even sorrow for sin is too great when it unfits for other duties, and drives men to despair. (2.) They had shown obedience to his directions in passing a censure upon the offender and now he would have them comply with his desire to restore him, *v.* 9. (3.) He mentions his readiness to forgive this penitent, and concur with them in this matter "*To whom you forgive I forgive also, v.* 10. I will readily concur with you in forgiving him." And this he would do for their sakes, for love to them and for their advantage; and for Christ's sake, or in his name, as his apostle, and in conformity to his doctrine and example, which are so full of kindness and tender mercy towards all those who truly repent. (4.) He gives another weighty reason (*v.* 11): *Lest Satan get an advantage against us.* Not only was there danger lest Satan should get an advantage against the penitent, by driving him to despair; but against the churches also, and the apostles or ministers of Christ, by representing them as too rigid and severe, and so frightening people from coming among them. In this, as in other things, *wisdom is profitable to direct,* so to manage according as the case may be that the *ministry may not be blamed,* for indulging sin on the one hand, or for too great severity towards sinners on the other hand. Note, Satan is a subtle enemy, and uses many stratagems to deceive us; and we should not be *ignorant of his devices:* he is also a watchful adversary, ready to take all advantages against us, and we should be very cautious lest we give him any occasion so to do.

12 Furthermore, when I came to
Troas to *preach* Christ's gospel, and
a door was opened unto me of the
Lord, 13 I had no rest in my spirit,
because I found not Titus my brother: but taking my leave of them, I
went from thence into Macedonia.
14 Now thanks *be* unto God, which
always causeth us to triumph in
Christ, and maketh manifest the
savour of his knowledge by us in
every place. 15 For we are unto
God a sweet savour of Christ, in
them that are saved, and in them
that perish: 16 To the one *we are*
the savour of death unto death; and
to the other the savour of life unto
life. And who *is* sufficient for these
things? 17 For we are not as many,
which corrupt the word of God: but
as of sincerity, but as of God, in the
sight of God speak we in Christ.

After these directions concerning the excommunicated person the apostle makes a long digression, to give the Corinthians an account of his travels and labours for the furtherance of the gospel, and what success he had therein, declaring at the same time how much he was concerned for them in their affairs, how he *had no rest in his spirit,* when he found not Titus at Troas (*v.* 13), as he expected, from whom he hoped to have understood more perfectly how it fared with them. And we find afterwards (*ch.* vii. 5—7) that when the apostle had come into Macedonia he was comforted by the coming of Titus, and the information he gave him concerning them. So that we may look upon all that we read from this second chapter, *v.* 12, to *ch.* vii. 5, as a kind of parenthesis. Observe here,

I. Paul's unwearied labour and diligence in his work, *v.* 12, 13. He travelled from place to place, to preach the gospel. He went to Troas from Philippi by sea (Acts xx. 6), and thence he went to Macedonia; so that he was prevented from passing by Corinth, as he had designed, *ch.* i. 16. But, though he was prevented in his design as to the place of working, yet he was unwearied in his work.

II. His success in his work: A *great door was opened to him of the Lord,* v 12. He had a great deal of work to do wherever he came, and had good success in his work; for God *made manifest the savour of his knowledge* by him in every place where he came. He had an opportunity to open the door of his mouth freely, and God opened the hearts of his hearers, as the heart of Lydia (Acts xvi. 14), and the apostle speaks of this as a matter of thankfulness to God and of rejoicing to his soul: *Thanks be to God, who always causeth us to triumph in Christ.* Note, 1. A believer's triumphs are all in Christ. In ourselves we are weak, and have neither joy nor victory; but in Christ we may rejoice and triumph. 2. True believers have constant cause of triumph in Christ, for they are more than conquerors through him who hath loved them, Rom. viii. 37. 3. God causeth them to triumph in Christ. It is God who has given us matter for triumph, and hearts to triumph. To him therefore be the praise and glory of all. 4. The good success of the gospel is a good reason for a Christian's joy and rejoicing.

III. The comfort that the apostle and his companions in labour found, even when the gospel was not successful to the salvation of some who heard it, *v.* 15—17. Here observe,

1. The different success of the gospel, and its different effects upon several sorts of persons to whom it is preached. The success is different; for some are saved by it, while others perish under it. Nor is this to be wondered at, considering the different effects the gospel has. For, (1.) Unto some it is a *savour of death unto death.* Those who are willingly ignorant, and wilfully obstinate, disrelish the gospel, as men dislike an ill savour, and therefore they are blinded and hardened by it: it stirs up their corruptions, and exasperates their spirits. They reject the gospel, to their ruin, even to spiritual and eternal death. (2.) Unto others the gospel is a *savour of life unto life.* To humble and gracious souls the preaching of the word is most delightful and profitable. As it is sweeter than honey to the taste, so it is more grateful than the most precious odours to the senses, and much more profitable; for as it quickened them at first, *when they were dead in trespasses and sins,* so it makes them more lively, and will end in eternal life.

2. The awful impressions this matter made upon the mind of the apostle, and should also make upon our spirits: *Who is sufficient for these things? v.* 16. Τίς ἱκανός—who is *worthy* to be employed in such weighty work, a work of such vast importance, because of so great consequence? Who is able to perform such a difficult work, that requires so much skill and industry? The work is great and our strength is small; yea, of ourselves we have no strength at all; *all our sufficiency is of God.* Note, If men did seriously consider what great things depend upon the preaching of the gospel, and how difficult the work of the ministry is, they would be very cautious how they enter upon it, and very careful to perform it well.

3. The comfort which the apostle had under this serious consideration, (1.) Because faithful ministers shall be accepted of God, whatever their success be: *We are,* if faithful, *unto God a sweet savour of Christ* (*v.* 15), in those who are saved and in those also who perish. God will accept of sincere intentions, and honest endeavours, though with many they are not successful. Ministers shall be accepted, and recompensed, not according to their success, but according to their fidelity. *Though Israel be not gathered, yet shall I be glorious in the eyes of the Lord,* Isa. xlix. 5. (2.) Because his conscience witnessed to his faithfulness, *v.* 17. Though many *did corrupt the word of God,* yet the apostle's conscience witnessed to his fidelity. He did not mix his own notions with the doctrines and institutions of Christ; he durst not add to, nor diminish from, the word of God; he was faithful in dispensing the gospel, as he received it from the Lord, and had no secular turn to serve; his aim was to approve himself to God, remembering that his eye was always upon him; he therefore spoke and acted always as in the sight of God, and therefore in sincerity. Note, What we do in religion is not of God, does not come from God, will not reach to God, unless it be done in sincerity, as in the sight of God.

CHAP. III.

The apostle makes an apology for his seeming to commend himself, and is careful not to assume too much to himself, but to ascribe all praise unto God, ver. 1—5. He then draws a comparison between the Old Testament and the New, and shows the excellency of the latter above the former (ver. 6—11), whence he infers what is the duty of gospel ministers, and the advantage of those who live under the gospel abov those who lived under the law, ver. 12, to the end.

DO we begin again to commend
ourselves? or need we, as some
others, epistles of commendation to
you, or *letters* of commendation from
you? 2 Ye are our epistle written
in our hearts, known and read of all
men: 3 *Forasmuch as ye are* manifestly declared to be the epistle of
Christ ministered by us, written not
with ink, but with the Spirit of the
living God; not in tables of stone,
but in fleshy tables of the heart. 4
And such trust have we through
Christ to God-ward: 5 Not that we
are sufficient of ourselves to think any
thing as of ourselves; but our sufficiency *is* of God;

In these verses,

I. The apostle makes an apology for seeming to commend himself. He thought it convenient to protest his sincerity to them, because there were some at Corinth who endeavoured to blast his reputation; yet he was not desirous of vain-glory. And he tells them, 1. That he neither needed nor desired any verbal commendation to them, nor letters testimonial from them, as some others did, meaning the false apostles or teachers, *v.* 1. His ministry among them had, without controversy, been truly great and honourable, how little soever his person was in reality, or how contemptible soever some would have him thought to be. 2. The Corinthians themselves were his real commendation, and a good testimonial for him, that God was with him of a truth, that he was sent of God: *You are our epistle, v.* 2. This was the testimonial he most delighted in, and what was most dear to him—they were written *in his heart;* and this he could appeal to upon occasion, for it was, or might be, *known and read of all men.* Note, There is nothing more delightful to faithful ministers, nor more to their commendation, than the success of their ministry, evidenced in the hearts and lives of those among whom they labour.

II. The apostle is careful not to assume too much to himself, but to ascribe all the praise to God. Therefore, 1. He says they were the *epistle of Christ, v.* 3. The apostle and others were but instruments, Christ was the author of all the good that was in them. The law of Christ was written in their hearts, and the love of Christ shed abroad in their hearts. This epistle was not written with *ink, but with the Spirit of the living God;* nor was it written in *tables of stone,* as the law of God given to Moses, but on the *heart;* and that heart not a stony one, but a heart of flesh, upon the *fleshy* (not *fleshly,* as fleshliness denotes sensuality) *tables of the heart,* that is, upon hearts that are softened and renewed by divine grace, according to that gracious promise, *I will take away the stony heart, and I will give you a heart of flesh,* Ezek. xxxvi. 26. This was the good hope the apostle had concerning these Corinthians (*v.* 4) that their hearts were like the ark of the covenant, containing the tables of the law and the gospel, written with the finger, that is, by the Spirit, of the living God. 2. He utterly disclaims the taking of any praise to themselves, and ascribes all the glory to God: "*We are not sufficient of ourselves, v.* 5. We could never have made such good impressions on your hearts, nor upon our own. Such are our weakness and inability that we cannot of ourselves think a good thought, much less raise any good thoughts or affections in other men. *All our sufficiency is of God;* to him therefore are owing all the praise and glory of that good which is done, and from him we must receive grace and strength to do more." This is true concerning ministers and all Christians; the best are no more than what the grace of God makes them. Our hands are not sufficient for us, but our sufficiency is of God; and his grace is sufficient for us, to furnish us for every good word and work.

6 Who also hath made us able
ministers of the new testament; not
of the letter, but of the spirit: for the
letter killeth, but the spirit giveth life.
7 But if the ministration of death,
written *and* engraven in stones, was
glorious, so that the children of Israel
could not stedfastly behold the face
of Moses for the glory of his countenance; which *glory* was to be done
away: 8 How shall not the ministration of the spirit be rather glorious?
9 For if the ministration of condemnation *be* glory, much more doth the
ministration of righteousness exceed
in glory. 10 For even that which
was made glorious had no glory in
this respect, by reason of the glory
that excelleth. 11 For if that which
is done away *was* glorious, much more
that which remaineth *is* glorious.

Here the apostle makes a comparison between the Old Testament and the New, the law of Moses and the gospel of Jesus Christ, and values himself and his fellow-labourers by this, that *they were able ministers of the New Testament,* that God had made them so, *v.* 6. This he does in answer to the accusations of false teachers, who magnify greatly the law of Moses.

I. He distinguishes between the letter and the spirit even of the New Testament, *v.* 6. As able ministers of the New Testament, they were ministers not merely of the letter, to read the written word, or to preach the letter of the gospel only, but they were ministers of the Spirit also; the Spirit of God did accompany their ministrations. The *letter killeth;* this the letter of the law does, for that is the ministration of death; and if we rest only in the letter of the gospel we shall be never the better for so doing, for even that will be a *savour of death unto death;* but the Spirit of the gospel, going along with the ministry of the gospel, giveth life spiritual and life eternal.

II. He shows the difference between the Old Testament and the New, and the excellency of the gospel above the law. For, 1. The Old-Testament dispensation was the *ministration of death* (*v.* 7), whereas that of the New Testament is the *ministration of life.* The law discovered sin, and the wrath and curse of God. This showed us a God above us and a God against us; but the gospel discovers grace, and *Emmanuel,* God with us. Upon this account the gospel is more glorious than the law; and yet that had a glory in it, witness the shining of Moses's face (an indication thereof) when he came down from the mount with the tables in his hand, that reflected rays of brightness upon his countenance. 2. The law was the *ministration of condemnation,* for that condemned and cursed every one who *continued not in all things written therein to do them;* but the gospel is the *ministration of righteousness:* therein the righteousness of God by faith is revealed. This shows us that the just shall live by his faith. This reveals the grace and mercy of God through Jesus Christ, for obtaining the remission of sins and eternal life. The gospel therefore so much exceeds in glory that in a manner it eclipses the glory of the legal dispensation, *v.* 10. As the shining of a burning lamp is lost, or not regarded, when the sun arises and goes forth in his strength; so there was no glory in the Old Testament, in comparison with that of the New. 3. The law is done away, but the gospel does and shall *remain, v.* 11. Not only did the glory of Moses's face go away, but the glory of Moses's law is done away also; yea, the law of Moses itself is now abolished. That dispensation was only to continue for a time, and then to vanish away; whereas the gospel shall remain to the end of the world, and is always fresh and flourishing and remains glorious.

12 Seeing then that we have such
hope, we use great plainness of
speech: 13 And not as Moses, *which*
put a veil over his face, that the
children of Israel could not stedfastly
look to the end of that which is
abolished: 14 But their minds were
blinded: for until this day remaineth
the same veil untaken away in the
reading of the old testament; which
veil is done away in Christ. 15 But
even unto this day, when Moses is
read, the veil is upon their heart. 16
Nevertheless when it shall turn to the
Lord, the veil shall be taken away.
17 Now the Lord is that Spirit: and
where the Spirit of the Lord *is,* there
is liberty. 18 But we all, with open
face beholding as in a glass the glory
of the Lord, are changed into the
same image from glory to glory, *even*
as by the Spirit of the Lord.

In these verses the apostle draws two inferences from what he had said about the Old and New Testament:—

I. Concerning the duty of the ministers of the gospel to use great plainness or clearness of speech. They ought not, like Moses, to put a veil upon their faces, or obscure and darken those things which they should make plain. The gospel is a more clear dispensation than the law; the things of God are revealed in the New Testament, not in types and shadows, and ministers are much to blame if they do not set spiritual things, and gospel-truth and grace, in the clearest light that is possible. Though the Israelites could not look *stedfastly to the end* of what was commanded, but is now abolished, yet we may. We may see the meaning of those types and shadows by the accomplishment, seeing the veil is done away in, Christ and he is come, who was the end of the law for righteousness to all those who believe, and whom Moses and all the prophets pointed to, and wrote of.

II. Concerning the privilege and advantage of those who enjoy the gospel, above those who lived under the law. For, 1. Those who lived under the legal dispensation had their minds blinded (*v.* 14), and there was a *veil upon their hearts, v.* 15. Thus it was formerly, and so it was especially as to those who remained in Judaism after the coming of the Messiah and the publication of his gospel. Nevertheless, the apostle tells us, there is a time coming when this *veil also shall be taken away,* and *when it* (the body of that people) *shall turn to the Lord, v.* 16. Or, when any particular person is converted to God, then the veil of ignorance is taken away; the blindness of the mind, and the hardness of the heart, are cured. 2. The condition of those who enjoy and believe the gospel is much more happy. For, (1.) They have liberty: *Where the Spirit of the Lord is,* and where he worketh, as he does under the gospel-dispensation, *there is liberty* (*v.* 17), freedom from the yoke of the ceremonial law, and from the servitude of corruption; liberty of access to God, and freedom of speech in prayer. The heart is set at liberty, and enlarged, to run the ways of God's commandments. (2.) They have *light;* for with *open face we behold the glory of the Lord, v.* 18. The Israelites saw the glory of God in a cloud, which was dark and dreadful; but Christians see the glory of the Lord as in a glass, more clearly and comfortably. It was the peculiar privilege of Moses for God to converse with him face to face, in a friendly manner; but now all true Christians see him more clearly with open face. He showeth them his glory. (3.) This light and liberty *are transforming;* we are changed into the *same image, from glory to glory* (*v.* 18), from one degree of glorious grace unto another, till grace here be consummated in glory for ever. How much therefore should Christians prize and improve these privileges! We should not rest contented without an experimental knowledge of the transforming power of the gospel, by the operation of the Spirit, bringing us into a conformity to the temper and tendency of the glorious gospel of our Lord and Saviour Jesus Christ.

CHAP. IV.

In this chapter we have an account, I. Of the constancy of the apostle and his fellow-labourers in their work. Their constancy is declared (ver. 1), their sincerity is vouched (ver. 2), an objection is obviated (ver. 3, 4), and their integrity proved, ver. 5—7. II. Of their courage and patience under their sufferings. Where see what their sufferings were, together with their allays (ver. 8—12), and what it was that kept them from sinking and fainting under them, ver. 13, to the end.

THEREFORE seeing we have
this ministry, as we have received
mercy, we faint not; 2 But have
renounced the hidden things of dishonesty, not walking in craftiness,
nor handling the word of God deceitfully; but by manifestation of the
truth commending ourselves to every
man's conscience in the sight of God.
3 But if our gospel be hid, it is hid
to them that are lost: 4 In whom
the god of this world hath blinded
the minds of them which believe not,
lest the light of the glorious gospel
of Christ, who is the image of God,
should shine unto them. 5 For we
preach not ourselves, but Christ Jesus the Lord; and ourselves your
servants for Jesus' sake. 6 For God,
who commanded the light to shine
out of darkness, hath shined in our
hearts, to *give* the light of the knowledge of the glory of God in the face
of Jesus Christ. 7 But we have this
treasure in earthen vessels, that the
excellency of the power may be of
God, and not of us.

The apostle had, in the foregoing chapter, been *magnifying his office,* upon the consideration of the excellency or glory of that gospel about which he did officiate; and now in this chapter his design is to vindicate their ministry from the accusation of false teachers, who charged them as deceitful workers, or endeavoured to prejudice the minds of the people against them on account of their sufferings. He tells them, therefore, how they believed, and how they showed their value for their office as ministers of the gospel. They were not puffed up with pride, but spurred on to great diligence: "*Seeing we have this ministry,* are so much distinguished and dignified, we do not take state upon ourselves, nor indulge in idleness, but are excited to the better performance of our duty."

I. Two things in general we have an account of:—Their constancy and sincerity in their work and labour, concerning which observe, 1. Their constancy and perseverance in their work are declared: *We faint not* (*v.* 1) under the difficulty of our work, nor do we desist from our labour." And this their stedfastness was owing to the *mercy of God.* From the same mercy and grace from which they received the apostleship (Rom. i. 5), they received strength to persevere in the work of that office. Note, As it is great mercy and grace to be called to be saints, and especially to be *counted faithful, and be put into the ministry* (1 Tim. i. 12), so it is owing to the mercy and grace of God if we continue faithful and persevere in our work with diligence. The best men in the world would faint in their work, and under their burdens, if they did not receive mercy from God. *By the grace of God I am what I am,* said this great apostle in his former epistle to these Corinthians, *ch.* xv. 10. And that mercy which has helped us out, and helped us on, hitherto, we may rely upon to help us even to the end. 2. Their sincerity in their work is avouched (*v.* 2) in several expressions: *We have renounced the hidden things of dishonesty.* The things of dishonesty are hidden things, that will not bear the light; and those who practise them are, or should be, ashamed of them, especially when they are known. Such things the apostle did not allow of, but did renounce and avoid with indignation: *Not walking in craftiness,* or in disguise, acting with art and cunning, but in great simplicity, and with open freedom. They had no base and wicked designs covered with fair and specious pretences of something that was good. Nor did they in their preaching *handle the word of God deceitfully;* but, as he said before, they used *great plainness of speech,* and did not make their ministry serve a turn, or truckle to base designs. They had not cheated the people with falsehood instead of truth. Some think the apostle alludes to the deceit which treacherous gamesters use, or that of hucksters in the market, who mix bad wares with good. The apostles acted not like such persons, but they *manifested the truth to every man's conscience,* declaring nothing but what in their own conscience they believed to be true, and what might serve for the conviction of their consciences who heard them, who were to judge for themselves, and to give an account for themselves. And all this they did *as in the sight of God,* desirous thus to commend themselves to God, and to the consciences of men, by their undisguised sincerity. Note, A stedfast adherence to the truths of the gospel will commend ministers and people; and sincerity or uprightness will preserve a man's reputation, and the good opinion of wise and good men concerning him.

II. An objection is obviated, which might be thus formed: "If it be thus, how then does it come to pass, that the gospel is hid, and proves ineffectual, as to some who hear it?" To which the apostle answers, by showing that this was not the fault of the gospel, nor of the preachers thereof. But the true reasons of this are, 1. *Those are lost souls* to whom the gospel is hid, or is ineffectual, *v.* 3. Christ came to *save that which was lost* (Matt. xviii. 11), and the gospel of Christ is sent to save such; and, if this do not find and save them, they are lost for ever; they must never expect any thing else to save them, for there is no other method or means of salvation. The hiding of the gospel therefore from souls is both an evidence and cause of their ruin. 2. *The god of this world hath blinded their minds, v.* 4. They are under the influence and power of the devil, who is here called *the god of this world,* and elsewhere *the prince of this world,* because of the great interest he has in this world, the homage that is paid to him by multitudes in this world, and the great sway that, by divine permission, he bears in the world, and in the hearts of his subjects, or rather slaves. And as he is the prince of darkness, and ruler of the darkness of this world, so he darkens the understandings of men, and increases their prejudices, and supports his interest by keeping them in the dark, blinding their minds with ignorance, and error, and prejudices, that they should not *behold the light of the glorious gospel of Christ, who is the image of God.* Observe, (1.) Christ's design by his gospel is to make a glorious discovery of God to the minds of men. Thus, as the image of God, he demonstrates the power and wisdom of God, and the grace and mercy of God for their salvation. But, (2.) The design of the devil is to keep men in ignorance; and, when he cannot keep the light of the gospel out of the world, he makes it his great business to keep it out of the hearts of men.

III. A proof of their integrity is given, *v.* 5. They made it their business to preach Christ, and not themselves: *We preach not ourselves.* Self was not the matter nor the end of the apostles' preaching: they did not give their own notions and private opinions, nor their passions and prejudices, for the word and will of God; nor did they seek themselves, to advance their own secular interest or glory. But they *preached Christ Jesus the Lord;* and thus it did become them and behove them to do, as being Christ's servants. Their business was to make their Master known to the world as the Messiah, or the Christ of God, and as Jesus, the only Saviour of men, and as the rightful Lord, and to advance his honour and glory. Note, All the lines of Christian doctrine centre in Christ; and in preaching Christ we preach all we should preach. "As to *ourselves,*" says the apostle, "*we preach,* or declare, that *we are your servants for Jesus' sake.*" This was no compliment, but a real profession of a readiness to do good to their souls, and to promote their spiritual and eternal interest, and that for *Jesus' sake;* not for their own sake or their own advantage, but for Christ's sake, that they might imitate his great example, and advance his glory. Note, Ministers should not be of proud spirits, *lording it over God's heritage,* who are servants to the souls of men: yet, at the same time, they must avoid the meanness of spirit implied in becoming the servants of the humours or the lusts of men; if they should thus *seek to please men, they would not be the servants of Christ,* Gal. i. 10. And there was good reason, 1. Why they should preach Christ. For by gospel light we have the *knowledge of the glory of God,* which shines in the *face of Jesus Christ, v.* 6. And the light of this *Sun of righteousness* is more glorious than that light which God commanded to shine out of darkness. It is a pleasant thing for the eye to behold the sun in the firmament; but it is more pleasant and profitable when the gospel shines in the heart. Note, As light was the first-born of the first creation, so it is in the new creation: the illumination of the Spirit is his first work upon the soul. The grace of God created such a light in the soul that those who *were sometimes darkness are made light in the Lord,* Eph. v. 8. 2. Why they should not preach themselves: because they were but earthen vessels, things of little or no worth or value. Here seems to be an allusion to the lamps which Gideon's soldiers carried in earthen pitchers, Jud. vii. 16. The treasure of gospel light and grace is put into earthen vessels. The ministers of the gospel are weak and frail creatures, and *subject to like passions* and infirmities as other men; they are mortal, and soon broken in pieces. And God has so ordered it that the weaker the vessels are the stronger his power may appear to be, that the treasure itself should be valued the more. Note, There is an excellency of power in the gospel of Christ, to enlighten the mind, to convince the conscience, to convert the soul, and to rejoice the heart; but all this power is from God the author, and not from men, who are but instruments, so that God in all things must be glorified.

8 *We are* troubled on every side,
yet not distressed; *we are* perplexed,
but not in despair; 9 Persecuted,

but not forsaken; cast down, but not
destroyed; 10 Always bearing about
in the body the dying of the Lord
Jesus, that the life also of Jesus might
be made manifest in our body. 11
For we which live are alway delivered
unto death for Jesus' sake, that the
life also of Jesus might be made
manifest in our mortal flesh. 12 So
then death worketh in us, but life in
you. 13 We having the same spirit of
faith, according as it is written, I believed, and therefore have I spoken;
we also believe, and therefore speak;
14 Knowing that he which raised up
the Lord Jesus shall raise up us also
by Jesus, and shall present *us* with
you. 15 For all things *are* for your
sakes, that the abundant grace might
through the thanksgiving of many
redound to the glory of God. 16
For which cause we faint not; but
though our outward man perish, yet
the inward *man* is renewed day by
day. 17 For our light affliction,
which is but for a moment, worketh
for us a far more exceeding *and* eternal weight of glory; 18 While we
look not at the things which are seen,
but at the things which are not seen:
for the things which are seen *are* temporal; but the things which are not
seen *are* eternal.

In these verses the apostle gives an account of their courage and patience under all their sufferings, where observe,

I. How their sufferings, and patience under them, are declared, *v.* 8—12. The apostles were great sufferers; therein they followed their Master: Christ had told them *that in the world they should have tribulation,* and so they had; yet they met with wonderful support, great relief, and many allays of their sorrows. "*We are,*" says the apostle, "*troubled on every side,* afflicted many ways, and we meet with almost all sorts of troubles; *yet not distressed, v.* 8. We are not hedged in nor cooped up, because we can see help in God, and help from God, and have liberty of access to God." Again, "We are *perplexed,* often uncertain, and in doubt what will become of us, and not always without anxiety in our minds on this account; *yet not in despair* (*v.* 8), even in our greatest perplexities, knowing that God is able to support us, and to deliver us, and in him we always place our trust and hope." Again, "We are *persecuted* by men, pursued with hatred and violence from place to place, as men not worthy to live; yet *not forsaken* of God," *v.* 9. Good men may be sometimes forsaken of their friends, as well as persecuted by their enemies; but God will never leave them nor forsake them. Again, "We are sometimes dejected, or *cast down;* the enemy may in a great measure prevail, and our spirits begin to fail us; there may be fears within, as well as fightings without; yet we are *not destroyed,*" *v.* 9. Still they were preserved, and kept their heads above water. Note, Whatever condition the children of God may be in, in this world, they have a "*but not*" to comfort themselves with; their case sometimes is bad, yea very bad, but not so bad as it might be. The apostle speaks of their sufferings as constant, and as a counterpart of the sufferings of Christ, *v.* 10. The sufferings of Christ were, after a sort, re-acted in the sufferings of Christians; thus did they *bear about the dying of the Lord Jesus* in their body, setting before the world the great example of a suffering Christ, *that the life of Jesus might also be made manifest,* that is, that people might see the power of Christ's resurrection, and the efficacy of grace in and from the living Jesus, manifested in and towards them, who did yet live, though they were always *delivered to death* (*v.* 11), and though *death worked in them* (*v.* 12), they being exposed to death, and ready to be swallowed up by death continually. So great were the sufferings of the apostles that, in comparison with them, other Christians were, even at this time, in prosperous circumstances: *Death worketh in us; but life in you, v.* 12.

II. What it was that kept them from sinking and fainting under their sufferings, *v.* 13—18. Whatever the burdens and troubles of good men may be, they have cause enough not to faint.

1. Faith kept them from fainting: *We have the same spirit of faith* (*v.* 13), that faith which is of the operation of the Spirit; the same faith by which the saints of old did and suffered such great things. Note, The grace of faith is a sovereign cordial, and an effectual antidote against fainting-fits in troublous times. The spirit of faith will go far to bear up the spirit of a man under his infirmities; and as the apostle had David's example to imitate, who said (Ps. cxvi. 10), *I have believed, and therefore have I spoken,* so he leaves us his example to imitate: *We also believe,* says he, *and therefore speak.* Note, As we receive help and encouragement from the good words and examples of others, so we should be careful to give a good example to others.

2. Hope of the resurrection kept them from sinking, *v.* 14. They knew that Christ was raised, and that his resurrection was an earnest and assurance of theirs. This he had treated of largely in his former epistle to these Corinthians, *ch.* xv. And therefore their hope was firm, being well grounded, that he who raised up Christ the head will also raise up all his members. Note, The hope of the resurrection will encourage us in a suffering

day, and set us above the fear of death: for what reason has a good Christian to fear death, that dies in hope of a joyful resurrection?

3. The consideration of the glory of God and the benefit of the church, by means of their sufferings, kept them from fainting, *v.* 15. Their sufferings were for the church's advantage (*ch.* i. 6), and thus did redound to God's glory. For, when the church is edified, then God is glorified; and we may well afford to bear sufferings patiently and cheerfully when we see others are the better for them—if they are instructed and edified, if they are confirmed and comforted. Note, The sufferings of Christ's ministers, as well as their preaching and conversation, are intended for the good of the church and the glory of God.

4. The thoughts of the advantage their souls would reap by the sufferings of their bodies kept them from fainting: *Though our outward man perish, our inward man is renewed day by day, v.* 16. Here note, (1.) We have every one of us an outward and an inward man, a body and a soul. (2.) If the outward man perish, there is no remedy, it must and will be so, it was made to perish. (3.) It is our happiness if the decays of the outward man do contribute to the renewing of the inward man, if afflictions outwardly are gain to us inwardly, if when the body is sick, and weak, and perishing, the soul is vigorous and prosperous. The best of men have need of further renewing of the inward man, even day by day. Where the good work is begun there is more work to be done, for carrying it forward. And as in wicked men things grow every day worse and worse, so in godly men they grow better and better.

5. The prospect of eternal life and happiness kept them from fainting, and was a mighty support and comfort. As to this observe, (1.) The apostle and his fellow-sufferers saw their afflictions working towards heaven, and that they would end at last (*v.* 17), whereupon they weighed things aright in the balance of the sanctuary; they did as it were put the heavenly glory in one scale and their earthly sufferings in the other; and, pondering things in their thoughts, they found afflictions to be light, and the glory of heaven to be *a far more exceeding weight.* That which sense was ready to pronounce heavy and long, grievous and tedious, faith perceived to be light and short, and but for a moment. On the other hand, the worth and weight of the crown of glory, as they are exceedingly great in themselves, so they are esteemed to be by the believing soul—far exceeding all his expressions and thoughts; and it will be a special support in our sufferings when we can perceive them appointed as the way and preparing us for the enjoyment of the future glory. (2.) Their faith enabled them to make this right judgment of things: *We look not at the things which are seen, but at the things which are not seen, v.* 18. It is by faith that we see God, who is invisible (Heb. xi. 27), and by this we look to an unseen heaven and hell, and faith is the *evidence of things not seen.* Note, [1.] There are unseen things, as well as things that are seen. [2.] There is this vast difference between them: unseen things are eternal, seen things but temporal, or temporary only. [3.] By faith we not only discern these things, and the great difference between them, but by this also we take our aim at unseen things, and chiefly regard them, and make it our end and scope, not to escape present evils, and obtain present good, both of which are temporal and transitory, but to escape future evil and obtain future good things, which, though unseen, are real, and certain, and eternal; and faith is *the substance of things hoped for,* as well as the evidence of things not seen, Heb. xi. 1.

CHAP. V.

The apostle proceeds in showing the reasons why they did not faint under their afflictions, namely, their expectation, desire, and assurance of happiness after death (ver. 1—5), and deduces an inference for the comfort of believers in their present state (ver. 6—8), and another to quicken them in their duty, ver. 9—11. Then he makes an apology for seeming to commend himself, and gives a good reason for his zeal and diligence (ver. 12—15), and mentions two things that are necessary in order to our living to Christ, regeneration and reconciliation, ver. 16, to the end.

FOR we know that if our earthly
house of *this* tabernacle were
dissolved, we have a building of God,
an house not made with hands, eternal in the heavens. 2 For in this we
groan, earnestly desiring to be clothed
upon with our house which is from
heaven: 3 If so be that being clothed
we shall not be found naked. 4 For
we that are in *this* tabernacle do groan,
being burdened: not for that we would
be unclothed, but clothed upon, that
mortality might be swallowed up of
life. 5 Now he that hath wrought
us for the selfsame thing *is* God, who
also hath given unto us the earnest
of the Spirit. 6 Therefore *we are*
always confident, knowing that, whilst
we are at home in the body, we are
absent from the Lord: 7 (For we
walk by faith, not by sight:) 8 We
are confident, *I say,* and willing rather
to be absent from the body, and to
be present with the Lord. 9 Wherefore we labour, that, whether present
or absent, we may be accepted of him.
10 For we must all appear before the
judgment seat of Christ; that every
one may receive the things *done* in
his body, according to that he hath
done, whether *it be* good or bad. 11
Knowing therefore the terror of the
Lord, we persuade men; but we are
made manifest unto God; and I trust

also are made manifest in your consciences.

The apostle in these verses pursues the argument of the former chapter, concerning the grounds of their courage and patience under afflictions. And,

I. He mentions their expectation, and desire, and assurance, of eternal happiness after death, *v.* 1—5. Observe particularly,

1. The believer's expectation of eternal happiness after death, *v.* 1. He does not only know, or is well assured by faith of the truth and reality of the thing itself—that there is another and a happy life after this present life is ended, but he has good hope through grace of his interest in that everlasting blessedness of the unseen world: "We know that we have a building of God, we have a firm and well-grounded expectation of the future felicity." Let us take notice, (1.) What heaven is in the eye and hope of a believer. He looks upon it as a house, or habitation, a dwelling-place, a resting-place, a hiding-place, our Father's house, where there are many mansions, and our everlasting home. It is a house in the heavens, in that high and holy place which as far excels all the palaces of this earth as the heavens are high above the earth. It is a building of God, whose builder and maker is God, and therefore is worthy of its author; the happiness of the future state is what God hath prepared for those that love him. It is eternal in the heavens, everlasting habitations, not like the earthly tabernacles, the poor cottages of clay in which our souls now dwell, which are mouldering and decaying, and *whose foundations are in the dust.* (2.) When it is expected this happiness shall be enjoyed—immediately after death, so soon as *our house of this earthly tabernacle is dissolved.* Note, [1.] That the body, this earthly house, is but a tabernacle, that must be dissolved shortly; the nails or pins will be drawn, and the cords be loosed, and then the body will return to dust as it was. [2.] When this comes to pass, then comes the house not made with hands. The spirit returns to God who gave it; and such as have walked with God here shall dwell with God for ever.

2. The believer's earnest desire after this future blessedness, which is expressed by this word, στενάζομεν—*we groan,* which denotes, (1.) A groaning of sorrow under a heavy load; so believers groan under the burden of life: *In this we groan earnestly, v.* 2. *We that are in this tabernacle groan, being burdened, v.* 4. The body of flesh is a heavy burden, the calamities of life are a heavy load. But believers groan because burdened with a body of sin, and the many corruptions that are still remaining and raging in them. This makes them complain, *O wretched man that I am!* Rom. vii. 24. (2.) There is a groaning of desire after the happiness of another life; and thus believers groan: *Earnestly desiring to be clothed upon with our house which is from heaven* (*v.* 2), to obtain a blessed immortality, *that mortality might be swallowed up of life* (*v.* 4), *that being found clothed, we may not be naked* (*v.* 3), that, if it were the will of God, we might not sleep, but be changed; for it is not desirable in itself to be unclothed. Death considered merely as a separation of soul and body is not to be desired, but rather dreaded; but, considered as a passage to glory, the believer is *willing rather* to die than live, *to be absent from the body, that he may be present with the Lord* (*v.* 1), to leave this body that he may go to Christ, and to put off these rags of mortality that he may put on the robes of glory. Note, [1.] Death will strip us of the clothing of flesh, and all the comforts of life, as well as put an end to all our troubles here below. Naked we came into this world, and naked shall we go out of it. But, [2.] Gracious souls are not found naked in the other world; no, they are clothed with garments of praise, with robes of righteousness and glory. They shall be delivered out of all their troubles, and shall have washed their robes and made them white in the blood of the Lamb, Rev. vii. 14.

3. The believer's assurance of his interest in this future blessedness, on a double account:—(1.) From the experience of the grace of God, in preparing and making him meet for this blessedness. He that hath *wrought us for the self-same thing is God, v.* 5. Note, All who are designed for heaven hereafter are wrought or prepared for heaven while they are here; the stones of that spiritual building and temple above are squared and fashioned here below. And he that hath wrought us for this is God, because nothing less than a divine power can make a soul partaker of a divine nature; no hand less than the hand of God can work us for this thing. A great deal is to be done to prepare our souls for heaven, and that preparation of the heart is from the Lord. (2.) The *earnest of the Spirit* gave them this assurance: for an earnest is part of payment, and secures the full payment. The present graces and comforts of the Spirit are earnests of everlasting grace and comfort.

II. The apostle deduces an inference for the comfort of believers in their present state and condition in this world, *v.* 6—8. Here observe, 1. What their present state or condition is: they *are absent from the Lord* (*v.* 6); they are pilgrims and strangers in this world; they do but sojourn here in their earthly home, or in this tabernacle; and though God is with us here, by his Spirit, and in his ordinances, yet we are not with him as we hope to be: we cannot see his face while we live: *For we walk by faith, not by sight, v.* 7. We have not the vision and fruition of God, as of an object that is present with us, and as we hope for hereafter, when we *shall see as we are seen.* Note, Faith is for this world, and sight is reserved for the other world: and it is our duty, and will be our interest, to walk by faith, till we come to live by sight. 2. How comfortable and courageous we ought to be in all the troubles of life, and in the hour of death: *Therefore we are*, or ought to be, *always confident* (*v.* 6), and again (*v.* 8), *We are confident, and willing rather to be absent from the body.* True Christians, if they duly considered the prospect faith gives them of another world, and the good reasons of their hope of blessedness after death, would be comforted under the troubles of life, and supported in the hour of death: they should take courage, when they are encountering the last enemy, and be willing rather to die than live, when it is the will of God that they should *put off this tabernacle.* Note, As those who are born from above long to be there, so it is but being absent from the body, and we shall very soon be present with the Lord—but to die, and be with Christ—but to close our eyes to all things in this world, and we shall open them in a world of glory. Faith will be turned into sight.

III. He proceeds to deduce an inference to excite and quicken himself and others to duty, *v.* 9—11. So it is that well-grounded hopes of heaven will be far from giving the least encouragement to sloth and sinful security; on the contrary, they should stir us up to use the greatest care and diligence in religion: *Wherefore*, or because we hope to be present with the Lord, *we labour* and take pains, *v.* 9. Φιλοτιμούμεθα—*We are ambitious*, and labour as industriously as the most ambitious men do to obtain what they aim at. Here observe, 1. What it was that the apostle was thus ambitious of—*acceptance with God.* We labour that, living and dying, whether present in the body or absent from the body, *we may be accepted of him*, the Lord (*v.* 9), that we *may please him who hath chosen us*, that our great Lord may say to us, *Well done.* This they coveted as the greatest favour and the highest honour: it was the summit of their ambition. 2. What further quickening motives they had to excite their diligence, from the consideration of the judgment to come, *v.* 10, 11. There are many things relating to this great matter that should awe the best of men into the utmost care and diligence in religion; for example, the certainty of this judgment, for we must appear; the universality of it, for we must all appear; the great Judge before whose judgment-seat we must appear, the Lord Jesus Christ, who himself will appear in flaming fire; the recompence to be then received, for things done in the body, which will be very particular (unto every one), and very just, according to what we have done, whether good or bad. The apostle calls this awful judgment *the terror of the Lord* (*v.* 11), and, by the consideration thereof, was excited to persuade men to repent, and live a holy life, that, when Christ shall appear terribly, they may appear before him comfortably. And, concerning his fidelity and diligence, he comfortably appeals unto God, and the consciences of those he wrote to: *We are made manifest unto God, and I trust also are made manifest in your consciences.*

12 For we commend not ourselves
again unto you, but give you occasion
to glory on our behalf, that ye may
have somewhat to *answer* them which
glory in appearance, and not in heart.
13 For whether we be beside ourselves, *it is* to God: or whether we
be sober, *it is* for your cause. 14
For the love of Christ constraineth
us; because we thus judge, that if
one died for all, then were all dead:
15 And *that* he died for all, that they
which live should not henceforth live
unto themselves, but unto him which
died for them, and rose again.

Here observe, I. The apostle makes an apology for seeming to commend himself and his fellow-labourers (*v.* 13), and tells them, 1. It was not to commend themselves, nor for their own sakes, that he had spoken of their fidelity and diligence in the former verses; nor was he willing to suspect their good opinion of him. But, 2. The true reason was this, to put an argument in their mouths wherewith to answer his accusers, who made vain boastings, and gloried in appearances only; that he might give them *an occasion to glory on their behalf*, or to defend them against the reproaches of their adversaries. And if the people can say that the word has been manifested to their consciences, and been effectual to their conversion and edification, this is the best defence they can make for the ministry of the word, when they are vilified and reproached.

II. He gives good reasons for their great zeal and diligence. Some of Paul's adversaries had, it is likely, reproached him for his zeal and fervour, as if he had been a madman, or, in the language of our days, a fanatic; they imputed all to enthusiasm, as the Roman governor told him, *Much learning has made thee mad*, Acts xxvi. 24. But the apostle tells them, 1. It was for the glory of God, and the good of the church, that he was thus zealous and industrious: "*Whether we be beside ourselves, or whether we be sober* (whether you or others do think the one or the other), it is *to God*, and for his glory: and it is *for your cause*, or to promote your good, *v.* 13. If they manifested the greatest ardour and vehemency at some times, and used the greatest calmness in strong reasonings at other times, it was for the best ends; and in both methods they had good reason for what they did. For, 2. *The love of Christ constrained them*, *v.* 14. They were under the sweetest and strongest constraints to do what they did. Love has a constraining virtue to excite ministers and private Christians in their duty. Our love to Christ will have this virtue; and Christ's love to us, which was manifested in this great instance of his dying for us, will have this effect upon us, if it be duly considered and rightly judged of. For observe how the apostle argues for the reasonableness of love's constraints, and declares, (1.) What we were before, and must have continued to be, had not Christ died for us: *We were dead, v.* 14. *If one died for all, then were all dead;* dead in law, under sentence of death; dead in sins and trespasses, spiritually dead. Note, This was the deplorable condition of all those for whom Christ died: they were lost and undone, dead and ruined, and must have remained thus miserable for ever if Christ had not died for them. (2.) What such should do, for whom Christ died; namely, that they should live to him. This is what Christ designed, that *those who live,* who are made alive unto God by means of his death, *should live to him that died for them, and rose again* for their sakes also, and that they should not live *to themselves, v.* 15. Note, We should not make ourselves, but Christ, the end of our living and actions: and it was one end of Christ's death to cure us of this self-love, and to excite us always to act under the commanding influence of his love. A Christian's life should be consecrated to Christ; and then do we live as we ought to live when we live to Christ, who died for us.

16 Wherefore henceforth know we
no man after the flesh: yea, though
we have known Christ after the flesh,
yet now henceforth know we *him* no
more. 17 Therefore if any man *be*
in Christ, *he is* a new creature: old
things are passed away; behold, all
things are become new. 18 And all
things *are* of God, who hath reconciled us to himself by Jesus Christ,
and hath given to us the ministry of
reconciliation; 19 To wit, that God
was in Christ, reconciling the world unto himself, not imputing their trespasses unto them; and hath committed unto us the word of
reconciliation. 20 Now then we are
ambassadors for Christ, as though God did beseech *you* by us: we pray *you* in Christ's stead, be ye reconciled
to God. 21 For he hath made him
to be sin for us, who knew no sin; that we might be made the righteousness of God in him.

In these verses the apostle mentions two things that are necessary in order to our living to Christ, both of which are the consequences of Christ's dying for us; namely, regeneration and reconciliation.

I. Regeneration, which consists of two things; namely, 1. Weanedness from the world: "*Henceforth we know no man after the flesh, v.* 16. We do not own nor affect any person or thing in this world for carnal ends and outward advantage: we are enabled, by divine grace, not to mind nor regard this world, nor the things of this world, but to live above it. The love of Christ is in our hearts, and the world is under our feet." Note, Good Christians must enjoy the comforts of this life, and their relations in this world, with a holy indifference. *Yea, though we have known Christ after the flesh, yet,* says the apostle, *we know him no more.* It is questioned whether Paul had seen Christ in the flesh. However, the rest of the apostles had, and so might some among those he was now writing to. However, he would not have them value themselves upon that account; for even the bodily presence of Christ is not to be desired nor doted upon by his disciples. We must live upon his spiritual presence, and the comfort it affords. Note, Those who make images of Christ, and use them in their worship, do not take the way that God has appointed for strengthening their faith and quickening their affections; for it is the will of God that we should not know Christ any more after the flesh. 2. A thorough change of the heart: *For if any man be in Christ,* if any man be a Christian indeed, and will approve himself such, *he is,* or he must be, *a new creature, v.* 17. Some read it, *Let him be a new creature.* This ought to be the care of all who profess the Christian faith, that they be new creatures; not only that they have a new name, and wear a new livery, but that they have a new heart and new nature. And so great is the change the grace of God makes in the soul, that, as it follows, *old things are passed away*—old thoughts, old principles, and old practices, are passed away; and *all* these *things must become new.* Note, Regenerating grace creates a new world in the soul; all things are new. The renewed man acts from new principles, by new rules, with new ends, and in new company.

II. Reconciliation, which is here spoken of under a double notion:—

1. As an unquestionable privilege, *v.* 18, 19. Reconciliation supposes a quarrel, or breach of friendship; and sin has made a breach, it has broken the friendship between God and man. The heart of the sinner is filled with enmity against God, and God is justly offended with the sinner. Yet, behold, there may be a reconciliation; the offended Majesty of heaven is willing to be reconciled. And observe, 1. He has appointed the Mediator of reconciliation. He has reconciled us to himself by Jesus Christ, *v.* 18. God is to be owned from first to last in the

undertaking and performance of the Mediator. All things relating to our reconciliation by Jesus Christ are of God, who by the mediation of Jesus Christ has reconciled the world to himself, and put himself into a capacity of being actually reconciled to offenders, without any wrong or injury to his justice or holiness, and does not impute to men their trespasses, but recedes from the rigour of the first covenant, which was broken, and does not insist upon the advantage he might justly take against us for the breach of that covenant, but is willing to enter into a new treaty, and into a new covenant of grace, and, according to the tenour thereof, freely to forgive us all our sins, and justify freely by his grace all those who do believe. 2. He has appointed the *ministry of reconciliation, v.* 18. By the inspiration of God the scriptures were written, which contain the word of reconciliation, showing us that peace was made by the blood of the cross, that reconciliation is wrought, and directing us how we may be interested therein. And he has appointed the office of the ministry, which is a *ministry of reconciliation:* ministers are to open and proclaim to sinners the terms of mercy and reconciliation, and persuade them to comply therewith. For,

2. Reconciliation is here spoken of as our indispensable duty, *v.* 20. As God is willing to be reconciled to us, we ought to be reconciled to God. And it is the great end and design of the gospel, that word of reconciliation, to prevail upon sinners to lay aside their enmity against God. Faithful ministers are Christ's ambassadors, sent to treat with sinners on peace and reconciliation: they come in God's name, with his entreaties, and act in Christ's stead, doing the very thing he did when he was upon this earth, and what he wills to be done now that he is in heaven. Wonderful condescension! Though God can be no loser by the quarrel, nor gainer by the peace, yet by his ministers he beseeches sinners to lay aside their enmity, and accept of the terms he offers, that they would be reconciled to him, to all his attributes, to all his laws, and to all his providences, to believe in the Mediator, to accept the atonement, and comply with his gospel, in all the parts of it and in the whole design of it. And for our encouragement so to do the apostle subjoins what should be well known and duly considered by us (*v.* 21), namely, (1.) The purity of the Mediator: *He knew no sin.* (2.) The sacrifice he offered: *He was made sin;* not a sinner, but *sin,* that is, a sin-offering, a sacrifice for sin. (3.) The end and design of all this: that *we might be made the righteousness of God in him,* might be justified freely by the grace of God through the redemption which is in Christ Jesus. Note, [1.] As Christ, who knew no sin of his own, was made sin for us, so we, who have no righteousness of our own, are made the righteousness of God in him. [2.] Our reconciliation to God is only through Jesus Christ, and for the sake of his merit: on him therefore we must rely, and make mention of his righteousness and his only.

CHAP. VI.

In this chapter the apostle gives an account of his general errand to all to whom he preached; with the several arguments and methods he used, ver. 1—10. Then he addresses himself particularly to the Corinthians, giving them good cautions with great affection and strong arguments, ver. 11—18.

WE then, *as* workers together
with him, beseech *you* also
that ye receive not the grace of God
in vain. 2 (For he saith, I have
heard thee in a time accepted, and in
the day of salvation have I succoured
thee: behold, now *is* the accepted
time; behold, now *is* the day of
salvation.) 3 Giving no offence in
any thing, that the ministry be not
blamed: 4 But in all *things* approving ourselves as the ministers of God,
in much patience, in afflictions, in necessities, in distresses, 5 In stripes,
in imprisonments, in tumults, in labours, in watchings, in fastings; 6
By pureness, by knowledge, by long-
suffering, by kindness, by the Holy
Ghost, by love unfeigned, 7 By the
word of truth, by the power of God,
by the armour of righteousness on
the right hand and on the left, 8 By
honour and dishonour, by evil report
and good report: as deceivers, and
yet true; 9 As unknown, and *yet*
well known; as dying, and, behold,
we live; as chastened, and not killed;
10 As sorrowful, yet alway rejoicing;
as poor, yet making many rich; as
having nothing, and *yet* possessing
all things.

In these verses we have an account of the apostle's general errand and exhortation to all to whom he preached in every place where he came, with the several arguments and methods he used. Observe,

I. The errand or exhortation itself, namely, to comply with the gospel offers of reconciliation—that, being favoured with the gospel, they would not receive this *grace of God in vain, v.* 1. The gospel is a word of grace sounding in our ears; but it will be in vain for us to hear it, unless we believe it, and comply with the end and design of it. And as it is the duty of the ministers of the gospel to exhort and persuade their hearers to accept of grace and mercy which are offered to them, so they are honoured with this high title of *co-workers with* God. Note, 1. They must work; and must work for God and his glory, for souls and their good: and they are workers with God, yet under him, as instruments only; however, if they be faithful, they may hope to find God working with them, and their labour will be effectual. 2. Observe the language and way of the spirit of the gospel: it is not with roughness and severity, but with all mildness and gentleness, to beseech and entreat, to use exhortations and arguments, in order to prevail with sinners and overcome their natural unwillingness to be reconciled to God and to be happy for ever.

II. The arguments and method which the apostle used. And here he tells them,

1. The present time is the only proper season to accept of the grace that is offered, and improve that grace which is afforded: Now *is the accepted time,* NOW *is the day of salvation, v.* 2. The gospel day is a day of salvation, the means of grace the means of salvation, the offers of the gospel the offers of salvation, and the present time the only proper time to accept of these offers: *To-day, while it is called to-day.* The morrow is none of ours: we know not what will be on the morrow, nor where we shall be; and we should remember that present seasons of grace are short and uncertain, and cannot be recalled when they are past. It is therefore our duty and interest to improve them while we have them, and no less than our salvation depends upon our so doing.

2. What caution they used not to give offence that might hinder the success of their preaching: *Giving no offence in any thing, v.* 3. The apostle had great difficulty to behave prudently and inoffensively towards the Jews and Gentiles, for many of both sorts watched for his halting, and sought occasion to blame him and his ministry, or his conversation; therefore he was very cautious not to give offence to those who were so apt to take offence, that he might not offend the Jews by unnecessary zeal against the law, nor the Gentiles by unnecessary compliances with such as were zealous for the law. He was careful, in all his words and actions, not to give offence, or occasion of guilt or grief. Note, When others are too apt to take offence, we should be cautious lest we give offence; and ministers especially should be careful lest they do any thing that may bring blame on their ministry or render that unsuccessful.

3. Their constant aim and endeavour in all things to approve themselves faithful, as became the ministers of God, *v.* 4. We see how much stress the apostle upon all occasions lays on fidelity in our work, because much of our success depends upon that. His eye was single, and his heart upright, in all his ministrations; and his great desire was to be the servant of God, and to approve himself so. Note, Ministers of the gospel should look upon themselves as God's servants or ministers, and act in every thing suitably to that character. So did the apostle, (1.) By much patience in afflictions. He was a great sufferer, and met with many afflictions, was often in necessities, and wanted the conveniences, if not the necessaries, of life; in distresses, being straitened on every side, hardly knowing what to do; in stripes often (*ch.* xi. 24); in imprisonments; in tumults raised by the Jews and Gentiles against him; in labours, not only in preaching the gospel, but in travelling from place to place for that end, and working with his hands to supply his necessities; in watchings and in fastings, either voluntary or upon a religious account, or involuntary for the sake of religion: but he exercised much patience in all, *v.* 4, 5. Note, [1.] It is the lot of faithful ministers often to be reduced to great difficulties, and to stand in need of much patience. [2.] Those who would approve themselves to God must approve themselves faithful in trouble as well as in peace, not only in doing the work of God diligently, but also in bearing the will of God patiently. (2.) By acting from good principles. The apostle went by a good principle in all he did, and tells them what his principles were (*v.* 6, 7); namely, pureness; and there is no piety without purity. A care to keep ourselves unspotted from the world is necessary in order to our acceptance with God. Knowledge was another principle; and zeal without this is but madness. He also acted with *long-suffering and kindness,* being not easily provoked, but bearing with the hardness of men's hearts, and hard treatment from their hands, to whom he kindly endeavoured to do good. He acted under the influence of the Holy Ghost, from the noble principle of unfeigned love, according to the rule of the word of truth, under the supports and assistances of the power of God, having on the armour of righteousness (a consciousness of universal righteousness and holiness), which is the best defence against the temptations of prosperity on the right hand, and of adversity on the left. (3.) By a due temper and behaviour under all the variety of conditions in this world, *v.* 8—10. We must expect to meet with many alterations of our circumstances and conditions in this world; and it will be a great evidence of our integrity if we preserve a right temper of mind, and duly behave ourselves, under them all. The apostles met with honour and dishonour, good report and evil report: good men in this world must expect to meet with some dishonour and reproaches, to balance their honour and esteem; and we stand in need of the grace of God to arm us against the temptations of honour on the one hand, so as to bear good report without pride, and of dishonour on the other hand, so as to bear reproaches without impatience or recrimination. It should seem that persons differently represented the apostles in their reports; that some represented them as the best, and others as the worst, of men: by some they were counted deceivers, and run down as

such; by others as true, preaching the gospel of truth, and men who were true to the trust reposed in them. They were slighted by the men of the world as unknown, men of no figure or account, not worth taking notice of; yet in all the churches of Christ they were well known, and of great account: they were looked upon as dying, being killed all the day long, and their interest was thought to be a dying interest; "and yet behold," says the apostle, "we live, and live comfortably, and bear up cheerfully under all our hardships, and go on conquering and to conquer." They were chastened, and often fell under the lash of the law, yet not killed: and though it was thought that they were sorrowful, a company of mopish and melancholy men, always sighing and mourning, yet they were always rejoicing in God, and had the greatest reason to rejoice always. They were despised as poor, upon the account of their poverty in this world; and yet they made many rich, by preaching the unsearchable riches of Christ. They were thought to have nothing, and silver and gold they had none, houses and lands they had none; yet they possessed all things: they had nothing in this world, but they had a treasure in heaven. Their effects lay in another country, in another world. They had nothing in themselves, but possessed all things in Christ. Such a paradox is a Christian's life, and through such a variety of conditions and reports lies our way to heaven; and we should be careful in all these things to approve ourselves to God.

11 O *ye* Corinthians, our mouth is
open unto you, our heart is enlarged.
12 Ye are not straitened in us, but
ye are straitened in your own bowels.
13 Now for a recompence in the same,
(I speak as unto *my* children,) be
ye also enlarged. 14 Be ye not
unequally yoked together with unbelievers:
for what fellowship hath
righteousness with unrighteousness?
and what communion hath light with
darkness? 15 And what concord
hath Christ with Belial? or what part
hath he that believeth with an infidel?
16 And what agreement hath the
temple of God with idols? for ye are
the temple of the living God; as God
hath said, I will dwell in them, and
walk in *them;* and I will be their
God, and they shall be my people.
17 Wherefore come out from among
them, and be ye separate, saith the
Lord, and touch not the unclean
thing; and I will receive you, 18
And will be a father unto you, and ye
shall be my sons and daughters, saith
the Lord Almighty.

The apostle proceeds to address himself more particularly to the Corinthians, and cautions them against mingling with unbelievers. Here observe,

I. How the caution is introduced with a profession, in a very pathetic manner, of the most tender affection to them, *even like that of a father to his children, v.* 11—13. Though the apostle was happy in a great fluency of expressions, yet he seemed to want words to express the warm affections he had for these Corinthians. As if he had said, "O ye Corinthians, to whom I am now writing, I would fain convince you how well I love you: we are desirous to promote the spiritual and eternal welfare of all to whom we preach, yet *our mouth is open unto you, and our heart is enlarged unto* you, in a special manner." And, because his heart was thus enlarged with love to them, therefore he opened his mouth so freely to them in kind admonitions and exhortations: "*You are not,*" says he, "*straitened in us;* we would gladly do you all the service we can, and promote your comfort, as helpers of your faith and your joy; and, if it be otherwise, the fault is in yourselves; it is because you are straitened in yourselves, and fail in suitable returns to us, through some misapprehensions concerning us; and all we desire as a recompence is only that you would be proportionably affected towards us, as children should love their father." Note, It is desirable that there should be a mutual good affection between ministers and their people, and this would greatly tend to their mutual comfort and advantage.

II. The caution or exhortation itself, not to mingle with unbelievers, not to be *unequally yoked* with them, *v.* 14. Either,

1. In stated relations. It is wrong for good people to join in affinity with the wicked and profane; these will draw different ways, and that will be galling and grievous. Those relations that are our choice must be chosen by rule; and it is good for those who are themselves the children of God to join with those who are so likewise; for there is more danger that the bad will damage the good than hope that the good will benefit the bad.

2. In common conversation. We should not yoke ourselves in friendship and acquaintance with wicked men and unbelievers. Though we cannot wholly avoid seeing, and hearing, and being with such, yet we should never choose them for our bosom-friends.

3. Much less should we join in religious communion with them; we must not join with them in their idolatrous services, nor concur with them in their false worship, nor any abominations; we must not confound together the table of the Lord and the table of devils, the house of God and the house of Rimmon. The apostle gives several good

reasons against this corrupt mixture. (1.) It is a very great absurdity, *v.* 14, 15. It is an unequal yoking of things together that will not agree together; as bad as for the Jews to have ploughed with an ox and an ass or to have sown divers sorts of grain intermixed. What an absurdity is it to think of joining righteousness and unrighteousness, or mingling light and darkness, fire and water, together! Believers are, and should be, righteous; but unbelievers are unrighteous. Believers are made light in the Lord, but unbelievers are in darkness; and what comfortable communion can these have together? Christ and Belial are contrary one to the other; they have opposite interests and designs, so that it is impossible there should be any concord or agreement between them. It is absurd, therefore, to think of enlisting under both; and, if the believer has part with an infidel, he does what in him lies to bring Christ and Belial together. (2.) It is a dishonour to the Christian's profession (*v.* 16); for Christians are by profession, and should be in reality, the *temples of the living God*—dedicated to, and employed for, the service of God, who has promised to reside in them, *to dwell and walk in them,* to stand in a special relation to them, and take a special care of them, that he will be their God and they shall be his people. Now there can be no agreement between *the temple of God and idols.* Idols are rivals with God for his honour, and God is a jealous God, and will not give his glory to another. (3.) There is a great deal of danger in communicating with unbelievers and idolaters, danger of being defiled and of being rejected; therefore the exhortation is (*v.* 17) *to come out from among them,* and keep at a due distance, *to be separate,* as one would avoid the society of those who have the leprosy or the plague, for fear of taking infection, and not *to touch the unclean thing,* lest we be defiled. Who can touch pitch, and not be defiled by it? We must take care not to defile ourselves by converse with those who defile themselves with sin; so is the will of God, as we ever hope to be received, and not rejected, by him. (4.) It is base ingratitude to God for all the favours he has bestowed upon believers and promised to them, *v.* 18. God has promised to be a Father to them, and that they shall be his sons and his daughters; and is there a greater honour or happiness than this? How ungrateful a thing then must it be if those who have this dignity and felicity should degrade and debase themselves by mingling with unbelievers! *Do we thus requite the Lord, O foolish and unwise?*

CHAP. VII.

This chapter begins with an exhortation to progressive holiness and a due regard to the ministers of the gospel, ver. 1—4. Then the apostle returns from a long digression to speak further of the affair concerning the incestuous person, and tells them what comfort he received in his distress about that matter, upon his meeting with Titus (ver. 5—7), and how he rejoiced in their repentance, with the evidences thereof, ver. 8—11. And, lastly, he concludes with endeavouring to comfort the Corinthians, upon whom his admonitions had had so good an effect, ver. 12—16.

HAVING therefore these promises, dearly beloved, let us cleanse ourselves from all filthiness of the flesh and spirit, perfecting holiness in the fear of God. 2 Receive us; we have wronged no man, we have corrupted no man, we have defrauded no man. 3 I speak not *this* to condemn *you:* for I have said before, that ye are in our hearts to die and live with *you.* 4 Great *is* my boldness of speech toward you, great *is* my glorying of you: I am filled with comfort, I am exceeding joyful in all our tribulation.

These verses contain a double exhortation:—

I. To make a progress in holiness, or *to perfect holiness in the fear of God, v.* 1. This exhortation is given with most tender affection to those who were dearly beloved, and enforced by strong arguments, even the consideration of those exceedingly great and precious promises which were mentioned in the former chapter, and which the Corinthians had an interest in and a title to. The promises of God are strong inducements to sanctification, in both the branches thereof; namely, 1. The dying unto sin, or mortifying our lusts and corruptions: we must *cleanse ourselves from all filthiness of flesh and spirit.* Sin is filthiness, and there are defilements of body and mind. There are sins of the flesh, that are committed with the body, and sins of the spirit, spiritual wickednesses; and we must cleanse ourselves from the filthiness of both, for God is to be glorified both with body and soul. 2. The living unto righteousness and holiness. If we hope God is our Father, we must endeavour to be *partakers of his holiness,* to be holy as he is holy, and perfect as our Father in heaven is perfect. We must be still perfecting holiness, and not be contented with sincerity (which is our gospel perfection), without aiming at sinless perfection, though we shall always come short of it while we are in this world; and this we must do in the *fear of God,* which is the root and principle of all religion, and there is no holiness without it. Note, Faith and hope in the promises of God must not destroy our fear of God, *who taketh pleasure in those that fear him and hope in his mercy.*

II. To show a due regard to the ministers of the gospel: *Receive us, v.* 2. Those who labour in the word and doctrine should *be had in reputation,* and *be highly esteemed for their work's sake*: and this would be a help to making progress in holiness. If the ministers of the gospel are thought contemptible because of their office, there is danger lest the gospel itself be contemned also. The apostle did not think it any disparagement to court the favour of the Corinthians; and, though we must flatter none, yet we must be gentle towards all. He tells them, 1. He had done nothing to forfeit their esteem and good-will, but was cautious not to do any thing to deserve their ill-will (*v.* 2): "*We have wronged no man:* we have done you no harm, but always designed your good." *I have coveted no man's silver, nor gold, nor apparel,* said he to the elders of Ephesus, Acts xx. 33. "*We have corrupted no man,* by false doctrines or flattering speeches. *We have defrauded no man;* we have not sought ourselves, nor to promote our own secular interests by crafty and greedy measures, to the damage of any persons." This is an appeal like that of Samuel, 1 Sam. xii. Note, Then may ministers the more confidently expect esteem and favour from the people when they can safely appeal to them that they are guilty of nothing that deserves disesteem or displeasure. 2. He did not herein reflect upon them for want of affection to him, *v.* 3, 4. So tenderly and cautiously did the apostle deal with the Corinthians, among whom there were some who would be glad of any occasion to reproach him, and prejudice the minds of others against him. To prevent any insinuations against him on account of what he had said, as if he intended to charge them with wronging him, or unjust accusations of him for having wronged them, he assures them again of his great affection to them, insomuch that he could spend his last breath at Corinth, and *live and die with them,* if his business with other churches, and his work as an apostle (which was not to be confined to one place only), would permit him to do so. And he adds it was his great affection to them that made him use such *boldness* or freedom of *speech towards them,* and caused him to *glory,* or make his boast of them, in all places, and upon all occasions, being *filled with comfort, and exceedingly joyful in all their tribulations.*

5 For, when we were come into
Macedonia, our flesh had no rest, but
we were troubled on every side;
without *were* fightings, within *were*
fears. 6 Nevertheless God, that
comforteth those that are cast down,
comforted us by the coming of Titus;
7 And not by his coming only, but
by the consolation wherewith he was
comforted in you, when he told us
your earnest desire, your mourning,
your fervent mind toward me; so that
I rejoiced the more. 8 For though
I made you sorry with a letter, I do
not repent, though I did repent: for
I perceive that the same epistle hath
made you sorry, though *it were* but
for a season. 9 Now I rejoice, not
that ye were made sorry, but that ye
sorrowed to repentance: for ye were
made sorry after a godly manner, that
ye might receive damage by us in
nothing. 10 For godly sorrow worketh
repentance to salvation not to be
repented of: but the sorrow of the
world worketh death. 11 For behold
this selfsame thing, that ye sorrowed
after a godly sort, what carefulness it
wrought in you, yea, *what* clearing of
yourselves, yea, *what* indignation, yea,
what fear, yea, *what* vehement desire,
yea, *what* zeal, yea, *what* revenge!
In all *things* ye have approved yourselves to be clear in this matter.

There seems to be a connection between *ch.* ii. 13 (where the apostle said he had no rest in his spirit when he found not Titus at Troas) and the fifth verse of this chapter: and so great was his affection to the Corinthians, and his concern about their behaviour in relation to the incestuous person, that, in his further travels, he still had no rest till he heard from them. And now he tells them,

I. How he was distressed, *v.* 5. He was troubled when he did not meet with Titus at Troas, and afterwards when for some time he did not meet with him in Macedonia: this was a grief to him, because he could not hear what reception he met with at Corinth, nor how their affairs went forward. And, besides this, they met with other troubles, with incessant storms of persecutions; there were *fightings without,* or continual contentions with, and opposition from, Jews and Gentiles; and there were *fears within,* and great concern for such as had embraced the Christian faith, lest they should be corrupted or seduced, and give scandal to others, or be scandalized.

II. How he was comforted, *v.* 6, 7. Here observe, 1. The very coming of Titus was some comfort to him. It was matter of joy to see him, whom he long desired and expected to meet with. The very coming of Titus and his company, who was dear to him as his *own son in the common faith* (Tit. i. 4), was a great comfort to the apostle in his travels and troubles. But, 2. The good news which Titus brought concerning the Corinthians was matter of greater consolation. He found Titus to be comforted in them; and this filled the apostle with comfort, especially when he acquainted him with their earnest desire to give good satisfaction in the things about which the apostle had written to them; and of their mourning for the scandal that was found among them and the great grief they had caused to others, and their fervent mind or great affection towards the apostle, who had dealt so faithfully with them in reproving their faults: so true is the observation of Solomon (Prov. xxviii. 23), *He that rebuketh a man afterwards shall find more favour than he that flattereth with his tongue.* 3. He ascribes all his comfort to God as the author. It was God who comforted him by the coming of Titus, even the God of all comfort: *God, who comforteth those that are cast down, v.* 6. Note, We should look above and beyond all means and instruments, unto God, as the author of all the consolation and the good that we enjoy.

III. How greatly he rejoiced at their repentance, and the evidences thereof. The apostle was sorry that he had grieved them, that some pious persons among them laid to heart very greatly what he said in his former epistle, or that it was needful he should make those sorry whom he would rather have made glad, *v.* 8. But now he rejoiced, when he found they had *sorrowed to repentance, v.* 9. Their sorrow in itself was not the cause of his rejoicing; but the nature of it, and the effect of it (*repentance unto salvation, v.* 10), made him rejoice; for now it appeared that they had received damage by him in nothing. Their sorrow was *but for a season;* it was turned into joy, and that joy was durable. Observe here,

1. The antecedent of true repentance is godly sorrow; this worketh repentance. It is not repentance itself, but it is a good preparative to repentance, and in some sense the cause that produces repentance. The offender had great sorrow, he was in danger of being *swallowed up with overmuch sorrow;* and the society was greatly sorrowful which before was puffed up: and this sorrow of theirs was after a godly manner, or according to God (as it is in the original), that is, it was according to the will of God, tended to the glory of God, and was wrought by the Spirit of God. It was a godly sorrow, because a sorrow for sin, as an offence against God, an instance of ingratitude, and a forfeiture of God's favour. There is a great difference between this sorrow of a godly sort and the sorrow of this world. Godly sorrow produces repentance and reformation, and will end in salvation; but worldly sorrow worketh death. The sorrows of worldly men for worldly things will bring down gray hairs the sooner to the grave, and such a sorrow even for sin as Judas had will have fatal consequences, as his had, which wrought death. Note, (1.) Repentance will be attended with salvation. Therefore, (2.) True penitents will never repent that they have repented, nor of any thing that was conducive thereto. (3.) Humiliation and godly sorrow are previously necessary in order to repentance, and both of them are from God, the giver of all grace.

2. The happy fruits and consequences of true repentance are mentioned (*v.* 11); and those *fruits that are meet for repentance* are the best evidences of it. Where the heart is changed, the life and actions will be changed too. The Corinthians made it evident that their sorrow was a godly sorrow, and such as wrought repentance, because it wrought in them great carefulness about their souls, and to avoid sin, and please God; it wrought also a clearing of themselves, not by insisting upon their own justification before God, especially while they persisted in their sin, but by endeavours to put away the accursed thing, and so free themselves from the just imputation of approving the evil that had been done. It wrought indignation at sin, at themselves, at the tempter and his instruments; it wrought fear, a fear of reverence, a fear of watchfulness, and a fear of distrust, not a distrust of God, but of themselves; an awful fear of God, a cautious fear of sin, and a jealous fear of themselves. It wrought vehement desires after a thorough reformation of what had been amiss, and of reconciliation with God whom they had offended. It wrought zeal, a mixture of love and anger, a zeal for duty, and against sin. It wrought, lastly, revenge against sin and their own folly, by endeavours to make all due satisfaction for injuries that might be done thereby. And thus *in all things had they approved themselves to be clear in that matter.* Not that they were innocent, but that they were penitent, and therefore clear of guilt before God, who would pardon and not punish them; and they ought no longer to be reproved, much less to be reproached, by men, for what they had truly repented of.

12 Wherefore, though I wrote unto you, *I did it* not for his cause that had done the wrong, nor for his cause that suffered wrong, but that our care for you in the sight of God might appear unto you. 13 Therefore we were comforted in your comfort: yea, and exceedingly the more joyed we for the joy of Titus, because his spirit was refreshed by you all. 14 For if I have boasted any thing to him of you, I am not ashamed; but as we spake all things to you in truth, even so our boasting, which *I made* before Titus, is found a truth. 15 And his inward affection is more abundant toward you, whilst he remembereth the obedience of you all, how with fear and trembling ye received him. 16 I rejoice therefore that I have confidence in you in all *things.*

In these verses the apostle endeavours to comfort the Corinthians, upon whom his admonitions had had such good effect. And in order thereto, 1. He tells them he had a good design in his former epistle, which might be thought severe, *v.* 12. It was not chiefly *for his cause that did the wrong,* not only for his benefit, much less merely that he should be punished; nor was it merely *for his cause that suffered wrong,* namely, the injured father, and that he might have what satisfaction could be given him; but it was also to manifest his great and sincere concern and *care for them,* for the whole church, lest that should suffer by letting such a crime, and the scandal thereof, remain among them without due remark and resentment. 2. He acquaints them with the joy of Titus as well as of himself upon the account of their repentance and good behaviour. Titus was rejoiced, and his spirit refreshed, with their comfort, and this comforted and rejoiced the apostle also (*v.* 13); and, as Titus was comforted while he was with them, so when he remembered his reception among them, expressing their obedience to the apostolical directions, and their fear and trembling at the reproofs that were given them, the thoughts of these things inflamed and increased his affections to them, *v.* 15. Note, Great comfort and joy follow upon godly sorrow. As sin occasions general grief, so repentance and reformation occasion general joy. Paul was glad, and Titus was glad, and the Corinthians were comforted, and the penitent ought to be comforted; and well may all this joy be on earth, when there is joy in heaven over one sinner that repenteth. 3. He concludes this whole matter with expressing the entire confidence he had in them: He was not ashamed of his boasting concerning them to Titus (*v.* 14); for he was not disappointed in his expectation concerning them, which he signified to Titus, and he could now with great joy declare what confidence he still had in them as to all things, that he did not doubt of their good behaviour for the time to come. Note, It is a great comfort and joy to a faithful minister to have to do with a people whom he can confide in, and who he has reason to hope will comply with every thing he proposes to them that is for the glory of God, the credit of the gospel, and their advantage.

CHAP. VIII.

In this and the following chapter Paul is exhorting and directing the Corinthians about a particular work of charity—to relieve the necessities of the poor saints at Jerusalem and in Judea, according to the good example of the churches in Macedonia, Rom. xv. 26. The Christians at Jerusalem, through war, famine, and persecution, had become poor, many of them had fallen into decay, and perhaps most of them were but poor when they first embraced Christianity; for Christ said, "The poor receive the gospel." Now Paul, though he was the apostle of the Gentiles, had a tender regard, and kind concern, for those among the Jews who were converted to the Christian faith; and, though many of them had not so much affection to the Gentile converts as they ought to have had, yet the apostle would have the Gentiles to be kind to them, and stirred them up to contribute liberally for their relief. Upon this subject he is very copious, and writes very affectingly. In this eighth chapter he acquaints the Corinthians with, and commends, the good example of the Macedonians in this work of charity, and that Titus was sent to Corinth to collect their bounty, ver. 1—6. He then proceeds to urge this duty with several cogent arguments (ver. 7—15), and commends the persons who were employed in this affair, ver. 16—24.

MOREOVER, brethren, we do
you to wit of the grace of God
bestowed on the churches of Macedonia; 2 How that in a great trial
of affliction the abundance of their
joy and their deep poverty abounded
unto the riches of their liberality. 3
For to *their* power, I bear record,
yea, and beyond *their* power *they were*
willing of themselves; 4 Praying us
with much entreaty that we would
receive the gift, and *take upon us* the
fellowship of the ministering to the
saints. 5 And *this they did,* not as
we hoped, but first gave their own
selves to the Lord, and unto us by
the will of God. 6 Insomuch that
we desired Titus, that as he had begun, so he would also finish in you
the same grace also.

Observe here,

I. The apostle takes occasion from the good example of the churches of Macedonia, that is, of Philippi, Thessalonica, Berea, and others in the region of Macedonia, to exhort the Corinthians and the Christians in Achaia to the good work of charity. And,

1. He acquaints them with their great liberality, which he calls *the grace of God bestowed on the churches, v.* 1. Some think the words should be rendered, *the gift of God given in or by the churches.* He certainly means the charitable gifts of these churches, which are called the grace or gifts of God, either because they were very large, or rather because their charity to the poor saints did proceed from God as the author, and was accompanied with true love to God, which also was manifested this way. The grace of God must be owned as the root and fountain of all the good that is in us, or done by us, at any time; and it is great grace and favour from God, and bestowed on us, if we are made useful to others, and are forward to any good work.

2. He commends the charity of the Macedonians, and sets it forth with good advantage. He tells them, (1.) They were but in a low condition, and themselves in distress, yet they contributed to the relief of others. *They were in great tribulation and deep poverty, v.* 2. It was a time of great affliction with them, as may be seen, Acts xviii. 17. The Christians in these parts met with ill treatment, which had reduced them to deep poverty; yet, as they had abundance of joy in the midst of tribulation, they abounded in their liberality; they gave out of a little, trusting in God to provide for them, and make it up to them. (2.) They gave very largely, with *the riches of liberality* (*v.* 2), that is, as liberally as if they had been rich. It was a large contribution they made, all things considered; it was *according to,* yea *beyond, their power* (*v.* 3), as much as could well be expected from them, if not more. Note, Though men may condemn the indiscretion, yet God will accept the pious zeal, of those who in real works of piety and charity do rather beyond their power. (3.) They were very ready and forward to this

good work. *They were willing of themselves* (*v.* 3), and were so far from needing that Paul should urge and press them with many arguments that they *prayed him with much entreaty to receive the gift*, *v.* 4. It seems Paul was backward to undertake this trust, for *he would give himself to the word and prayer;* or, it may be, he was apprehensive how ready his enemies would be to reproach and blacken him upon all occasions, and might take a handle against him upon account of so large a sum deposited in his hands, to suspect or accuse him of indiscretion and partiality in the distribution, if not of some injustice. Note, How cautious ministers should be, especially in money-matters, not to give occasion to those who seek occasion to speak reproachfully! (4.) Their charity was founded in true piety, and this was the great commendation of it. They performed this good work in a right method: *First they gave themselves to the Lord, and then* they gave unto us their contributions, *by the will of God* (*v.* 5), that is, according as it was the will of God they should do, or to be disposed of as the will of God should be, and for his glory. This, it seems, exceeded the expectation of the apostle; it was more than he hoped for, to see such warm and pious affections shining in these Macedonians, and this good work performed with so much devotion and solemnity. They solemnly, jointly, and unanimously, made a fresh surrender of themselves, and all they had, unto the Lord Jesus Christ. They had done this before, and now they do it again upon this occasion; sanctifying their contributions to God's honour, by first giving themselves to the Lord. Note, [1.] We should give ourselves to God; we cannot bestow ourselves better. [2.] When we give ourselves to the Lord, we then give him all we have, to be called for and disposed of according to his will. [3.] Whatever we use or lay out for God, it is only giving to him what is his own. [4.] What we give or bestow for charitable uses will not be accepted of God, nor turn to our advantage, unless we first give ourselves to the Lord.

II. The apostle tells them that Titus was desired to go and make a collection among them (*v.* 6), and Titus, he knew, would be an acceptable person to them. He had met with a kind reception among them formerly. They had shown good affection to him, and he had a great love for them. Besides, Titus had already begun this work among them, therefore he was desired to finish it. So that he was, on all accounts, a proper person to be employed; and, when so good a work had already prospered in so good a hand, it would be a pity if it should not proceed and be finished. Note, It is an instance of wisdom to use proper instruments in a work we desire to do well; and the work of charity will often succeed the best when the most proper persons are employed to solicit contributions and dispose of them.

7 Therefore, as ye abound in every
thing, *in* faith, and utterance, and
knowledge, and *in* all diligence, and
in your love to us, *see* that ye abound
in this grace also. 8 I speak not by
commandment, but by occasion of
the forwardness of others, and to
prove the sincerity of your love. 9
For ye know the grace of our Lord
Jesus Christ, that, though he was
rich, yet for your sakes he became
poor, that ye through his poverty
might be rich. 10 And herein I give
my advice: for this is expedient for
you, who have begun before, not only
to do, but also to be forward a year
ago. 11 Now therefore perform the
doing *of it;* that as *there was* a readiness to will, so *there may be* a performance also out of that which ye
have. 12 For if there be first a
willing mind, *it is* accepted according
to that a man hath, *and* not according
to that he hath not. 13 For *I mean*
not that other men be eased, and ye
burdened: 14 But by an equality,
that now at this time your abundance
may be a supply for their want, that
their abundance also may be *a supply*
for your want: that there may be
equality: 15 As it is written, He
that *had gathered* much had nothing
over; and he that *had gathered* little
had no lack.

In these verses the apostle uses several cogent arguments to stir up the Corinthians to this good work of charity.

I. He urges upon them the consideration of their eminence in other gifts and graces, and would have them excel in this of charity also, *v.* 7. Great address and much holy art are here used by the apostle. When he would persuade the Corinthians to this good thing, he commends them for other good things that were found in them. Most people love to be complimented, especially when we ask a gift of them for ourselves or others; and it is a justice we owe to those in whom God's grace shines to give them their due commendation. Observe here, What it was that the Corinthians abounded in. Faith is mentioned first, for that is the root; and, as *without faith it is impossible to please God* (Heb. xi. 6), so those who abound in faith will abound in other graces and good works also; and this will work and show itself by love. To their faith was added utterance, which is an excellent gift, and redounds much to the glory of God and the good of the church.

Many have faith who want utterance. But these Corinthians excelled most churches in spiritual gifts, and particularly in utterance; and yet this was not in them, as in too many, both the effect and evidence of ignorance; for with their utterance there appeared knowledge, abundance of knowledge. They had a treasury of things new and old, and in their utterance they brought out of this treasury. They abounded also in all diligence. Those who have great knowledge and ready utterance are not always the most diligent Christians. Great talkers are not always the best doers; but these Corinthians were diligent to do, as well as know and talk, well. And further, they had abundant love to their ministers; and were not like too many, who, having gifts of their own, are but too apt to slight their ministers, and neglect them. Now to all these good things the apostle desires them to add this grace also, to abound in charity to the poor; that, where so much good was found, there should be found yet more good. Before the apostle proceeds to another argument he takes care to prevent any misapprehensions of his design to impose on them, or to bind heavy burdens upon them by his authority; and tells them (*v.* 8) he does not speak by commandment, or in a way of authority. I give *my advice, v.* 10. He took occasion from the forwardness of others to propose what would be expedient for them, and would prove the sincerity of their love, or be the genuine effect and evidence thereof. Note, A great difference should be made between plain and positive duty, and the improvement of a present opportunity of doing or getting good. Many a thing which is good for us to do, yet cannot be said to be, by express and indispensable commandment, our duty at this or that time.

II. Another argument is taken from the consideration of the grace of our Lord Jesus Christ. The best arguments for Christian duties are those that are taken from the love of Christ, *that constraineth us.* The example of the churches of Macedonia was such as the Corinthians should imitate; but the example of our Lord Jesus Christ should have much greater influence. And *you know,* saith the apostle, *the grace of our Lord Jesus Christ* (*v.* 9), *that though he was rich,* as being God, equal in power and glory with the Father, rich in all the glory and blessedness of the upper world, *yet for your sakes he became poor;* not only did become man for us, but he became poor also. He was born in poor circumstances, lived a poor life, and died in poverty; and this was for our sakes, that we thereby might be made rich, rich in the love and favour of God, rich in the blessings and promises of the new covenant, rich in the hopes of eternal life, being heirs of the kingdom. This is a good reason why we should be charitable to the poor out of what we have, because we ourselves live upon the charity of the Lord Jesus Christ.

III. Another argument is taken from their good purposes, and their forwardness to begin this good work. As to this he tells them, 1. It was expedient for them to perform what they purposed, and finish what they had begun, *v.* 10, 11. What else did their good purposes and good beginnings signify? Good purposes, indeed, are good things; they are like buds and blossoms, pleasant to behold, and give hopes of good fruit; but they are lost, and signify nothing, without performances. So good beginnings are amiable; but we shall lose the benefit unless there be perseverance, and we bring forth fruit to perfection. Seeing therefore the Corinthians had shown a readiness to will, he would have them be careful also in the performance, according to their ability. For, 2. This would be acceptable to God. *This willing mind is accepted* (*v.* 12), when accompanied with sincere endeavours. When men purpose that which is good, and endeavour, according to their ability, to perform also, God will accept of what they have, or can do, and not reject them for what they have not, and what is not in their power to do: and this is true as to other things besides the work of charity. But let us note here that this scripture will by no means justify those who think good meanings are enough, or that good purposes, and the profession of a willing mind, are sufficient to save them. It is accepted, indeed, where there is a performance as far as we are able, and when Providence hinders the performance, as in David's case concerning building a house for the Lord, 2 Sam. vii.

IV. Another argument is taken from the discrimination which the divine Providence makes in the distribution of the things of this world, and the mutability of human affairs, *v.* 13—15. The force of the arguing seems to be this:—Providence gives to some more of the good things of this world, and to some less, and that with this design, that those who have a greater *abundance may supply those who are in want,* that there may be room for charity. And further, considering the mutability of human affairs, and how soon there may be an alteration, so that those who now have an abundance may stand in need of being supplied themselves in their wants, this should induce them to be charitable while they are able. It is the will of God that, by our mutually supplying one another, there should *be some sort of equality;* not an *absolute* equality indeed, or such a levelling as would destroy property, for in such a case there could be no exercise of charity. But as in works of charity there should be an equitable proportion observed, that the burden should not lie too heavy on some, while others are wholly eased, so all should think themselves concerned to supply those who are in want. This is illustrated by the instance of gathering and distributing manna in the wilderness, concerning which (as we may read, Exod. xvi.) it was the duty of every family, and all in the family, to gather what they could, which, when it was gathered, was put into some common receptacle for each family, whence the master of the family distributed to every one as he had occasion, to some more than they were able, through age and infirmity, to gather up; to others less than they gathered, because they did not need so much: and thus *he that had gathered much* (more than he had occasion for) had nothing over, when a communication was made to him *that had gathered little*, who by this method had no lack. Note, Such is the condition of men in this world that we mutually depend on one another, and should help one another. Those who have ever so much of this world have no more than food and raiment; and those who have but a little of this world seldom want these; nor, indeed, should those who have abundance suffer others to want, but be ready to afford supply.

16 But thanks *be* to God, which
put the same earnest care into the
heart of Titus for you. 17 For indeed he accepted the exhortation;
but being more forward, of his own
accord he went unto you. 18 And
we have sent with him the brother,
whose praise *is* in the gospel throughout all the churches; 19 And not
that only, but who was also chosen
of the churches to travel with us with
this grace, which is administered by
us to the glory of the same Lord, and
declaration of your ready mind: 20
Avoiding this, that no man should
blame us in this abundance which is
administered by us: 21 Providing
for honest things, not only in the
sight of the Lord, but also in the
sight of men. 22 And we have sent
with them our brother, whom we have
oftentimes proved diligent in many
things, but now much more diligent,
upon the great confidence which *I*
have in you. 23 Whether *any do*
enquire of Titus, *he is* my partner
and fellowhelper concerning you: or
our brethren *be enquired of*, *they are*
the messengers of the churches, *and*
the glory of Christ. 24 Wherefore
show ye to them, and before the
churches, the proof of your love, and
of our boasting on your behalf.

In these verses the apostle commends the brethren who were sent to them to collect their charity; and, as it were, gives them letters credential, that, if they *were enquired after* v. 23), if any should be inquisitive or suspicious concerning them, it might be known who they were and how safely they might be trusted.

I. He commends Titus, 1. For his earnest care and great concern of heart for them, and desire in all things to promote their welfare. This is mentioned with thankfulness to God (*v.* 16), and it is cause of thankfulness if God hath put it into the hearts of any to do us or others any good. 2. For his readiness to this present service. He accepted the office, and was forward to go upon this good errand, *v.* 17. Asking charity for the relief of others is by many looked upon as a thankless office; yet it is a good office, and what we should not be shy of when we are called to it.

II. He commends another brother, who was sent with Titus. It is generally thought that this was Luke. He is commended, 1. As a man whose *praise was in the gospel through all the churches*, *v.* 18. His ministerial services of several kinds were well known, and he had approved himself praiseworthy in what he had done. 2. As one chosen of the churches (*v.* 19) and joined with the apostle in his ministration. This was done, it is most likely, at the motion and request of Paul himself; for this reason, *that no man might blame him in that abundance which was administered by him* (*v.* 20), so cautious was the apostle to avoid all occasions that evil-minded men might lay hold on to blacken him. He would not give occasion to any to accuse him of injustice or partiality in this affair, and thought it to be his duty, as it is the duty of all Christians, *to provide for things honest, not only in the sight of the Lord, but also in the sight of men;* that is, to act so prudently as to prevent, as far as we can, all unjust suspicions concerning us, and all occasions of scandalous imputations. Note, We live in a censorious world, and should cut off occasion from those who seek occasion to speak reproachfully. It is the crime of others if they reproach or censure us without occasion; and it is our imprudence at least if we give them any occasion, when there may not be a just cause for them so to do.

III. He commends also another brother who was joined with the two former in this affair. This brother is thought to be Apollos. Whoever he was, he had *approved himself diligent in many things;* and therefore was fit to be employed in this affair. Moreover, he had great desire to this work, because of the confidence or good opinion he had of the Corinthians (*v.* 22), and it is a great comfort to see those employed in good works who have formerly approved themselves diligent.

IV. He concludes this point with a general good character of them all (*v.* 23), as *fellow-labourers with him* for their welfare; as the *messengers of the churches;* as the *glory of Christ,* who were to him for a name and a praise, who brought glory to Christ as instru ments and had obtained honour from Christ to be counted faithful and employed in his service. Wherefore, upon the whole, he exhorts them to show their liberality, answerable to the great expectation others had concerning them at this time, that these messengers of the churches, and the churches themselves, might see a full *proof of their love* to God and to their afflicted brethren, and that it was with good reason the apostle had even *boasted on their behalf, v.* 24. Note, The good opinion others entertain of us should be an argument with us to do well.

CHAP. IX.

In this chapter the apostle seems to excuse his earnestness in pressing the Corinthians to the duty of charity (ver. 1—5), and proceeds to give directions about the acceptable way and manner of performing it, namely, bountifully, deliberately, and freely; and gives good encouragement for so doing, ver. 6, to the end.

FOR as touching the ministering
to the saints, it is superfluous
for me to write to you: 2 For I
know the forwardness of your mind,
for which I boast of you to them of
Macedonia, that Achaia was ready a
year ago; and your zeal hath provoked
very many. 3 Yet have I
sent the brethren, lest our boasting
of you should be in vain in this
behalf; that, as I said, ye may be
ready: 4 Lest haply if they of
Macedonia come with me, and find
you unprepared, we (that we say not,
ye) should be ashamed in this same
confident boasting. 5 Therefore I
thought it necessary to exhort the
brethren, that they would go before
unto you, and make up beforehand
your bounty, whereof ye had notice
before, that the same might be ready,
as *a matter* of bounty, and not as *of*
covetousness.

In these verses the apostle speaks very respectfully to the Corinthians, and with great skill; and, while he seems to excuse his urging them so earnestly to charity, still presses them thereto, and shows how much his heart was set upon this matter.

I. He tells them it was needless to press them with further arguments to afford relief to their poor brethren (*v.* 1), being satisfied he had said enough already to prevail with those of whom he had so good an opinion. For, 1. *He knew their forwardness* to every good work, and how they had begun this good work a year ago, insomuch that, 2. He had boasted of their zeal to the Macedonians, and this had provoked many of them to do as they had done. Wherefore he was persuaded, that, as they had begun well, they would go on well; and so, commending them for what they had done, he lays an obligation on them to proceed and persevere.

II. He seems to apologize for sending Titus and the other brethren to them. He is unwilling they should be offended at him for this, as if he were too earnest, and pressed too hard upon them; and tells the true reasons why he sent them, namely, 1. That, having this timely notice, they might be fully ready (*v.* 3), and not surprised with hasty demands, when he should come to them. When we would have others to do that which is good we must act towards them prudently and tenderly, and give them time. 2. That he might not be ashamed of his boasting concerning them, if they should be found unready, *v.* 3, 4. He intimates that some from Macedonia might *haply come with him:* and, if the collection should not then be made, this would make him, not to say them, ashamed, considering the boasting of the apostle concerning them. Thus careful was he to preserve their reputation and his own. Note, Christians should consult the reputation of their profession, and endeavour to *adorn the doctrine of God our Saviour.*

6 But this *I say,* He which soweth
sparingly shall reap also sparingly;
and he which soweth bountifully
shall reap also bountifully. 7 Every
man according as he purposeth in
his heart, *so let him give;* not
grudgingly, or of necessity: for God
loveth a cheerful giver. 8 And God
is able to make all grace abound
toward you; that ye, always having
all sufficiency in all *things,* may
abound to every good work: 9 (As
it is written, He hath dispersed
abroad; he hath given to the poor:
his righteousness remaineth for ever.
10 Now he that ministereth seed to
the sower both minister bread for
your food, and multiply your seed
sown, and increase the fruits of your
righteousness;) 11 Being enriched
in every thing to all bountifulness,
which causeth through us thanksgiving
to God. 12 For the administration
of this service not only supplieth
the want of the saints, but is
abundant also by many thanksgivings
unto God; 13 Whiles by the experiment
of this ministration they
glorify God for your professed subjection
unto the gospel of Christ,
and for *your* liberal distribution unto
them, and unto all *men;* 14 And by
their prayer for you, which long
after you for the exceeding grace of

God in you. 15 Thanks *be* unto God for his unspeakable gift.

Here we have,

I. Proper directions to be observed about the right and acceptable manner of bestowing charity; and it is of great concernment that we not only do what is required, but do it as is commanded. Now, as to the manner in which the apostle would have the Corinthians give, observe, 1. It should be bountifully; this was intimated, *v.* 5, that a liberal contribution was expected, a matter of bounty, not what savoured of covetousness; and he offers to their consideration that men who expect a good return at harvest are not wont to pinch and spare in sowing their seed, for the return is usually proportionable to what they sow, *v.* 6. 2. It should be deliberately: *Every man, according as he purposes in his heart, v.* 7. Works of charity, like other good works, should be done with thought and design; whereas some do good only by accident. They comply, it may be hastily, with the importunity of others, without any good design, and give more than they intended, and then repent of it afterwards. Or possibly, had they duly considered all things, they would have given more. Due deliberation, as to this matter of our own circumstances, and those of the persons we are about to relieve, will be very helpful to direct us how liberal we should be in our contributions for charitable uses. 3. It should be freely, whatever we give, be it more or less: *Not grudgingly, nor of necessity,* but cheerfully, *v.* 7. Persons sometimes will give merely to satisfy the importunity of those who ask their charity, and what they give is in a manner squeezed or forced from them, and this unwillingness spoils all they do. We ought to give more freely than the modesty of some necessitous persons will allow them to ask: we should not only deal out bread, but draw out our souls to the hungry, Isa. lviii. 10. We should give liberally, with an open hand, and cheerfully, with an open countenance, being glad we have ability and an opportunity to be charitable.

II. Good encouragement to perform this work of charity in the manner directed. Here the apostle tells the Corinthians,

1. They themselves would be no losers by what they gave in charity. This may serve to obviate a secret objection in the minds of many against this good work who are ready to think they may want what they give away; but such should consider that what is given to the poor in a right manner is far from being lost; as the precious seed which is cast into the ground is not lost, though it is buried there for a time, for it will spring up, and bear fruit; the sower shall receive it again with increase, *v.* 6. Such good returns may those expect who give freely and liberally in charity. For, (1.) God loveth a cheerful giver (*v.* 7), and what may not those hope to receive who are the objects of the divine love? Can a man be a loser by doing that with which God is pleased? May not such a one be sure that he shall some way or other be a gainer? Nay, are not the love and favour of God better than all other things, *better than life* itself? (2.) God is able to make our charity redound to our advantage, *v.* 8. We have no reason to distrust the goodness of God, and surely we have no reason to question his power; he is *able to make all grace abound* towards us, and abound in us; to give a large increase of spiritual and temporal good things. He can cause us to have a sufficiency in all things, to be content with what we have, to make up what we give, to be able to give yet more: as it is written (Ps. cxii. 9) concerning the charitable man, *He hath dispersed abroad. He hath given to the poor. His righteousness,* that is, his almsgiving, *endureth for ever.* The honour of it is lasting, the reward of it eternal, and he is still able to live comfortably himself and to give liberally to others. (3.) The apostle puts up a prayer to God in their behalf that they might be gainers, and not losers, *v.* 10, 11. Here observe, [1.] To whom the prayer is made—to God, *who ministereth seed to the sower,* who by his providence giveth such an increase of the fruits of the earth that we have not only bread sufficient to eat for one year, but enough to sow again for a future supply: or thus, It is God who giveth us not only a competency for ourselves, but that also wherewith we may supply the wants of others, and so should be as seed to be sown. [2.] For what he prayeth. There are several things which he desires for them, namely, that they may have *bread for their food,* always a competency for themselves, *food convenient,*—that God will *multiply their seed sown,* that they may still be able to do more good,—and that there may be *an increase of the fruits of righteousness,* that they may reap plentifully, and have the best and most ample returns of their charity, so as to be *enriched in every thing to all bountifulness* (*v.* 11),—that upon the whole they may find it true that they shall be no losers, but great gainers. Note, Works of charity are so far from impoverishing us that they are the proper means truly to enrich us, or make us truly rich.

2. While they would be no losers, the poor distressed saints would be gainers; for this service would *supply their wants, v.* 12. If we have reason to think them to be saints, whom we believe to be of the household of faith, whose wants are great, how ready should we be to do them good! Our goodness cannot extend unto God, but we should freely extend it to these *excellent ones of the earth,* and thus show that we delight in them.

3. This would redound to the praise and glory of God. Many thanksgivings would be given to God on this account, by the apostle, and by those who were employed in

this ministration, *v.* 11. These would bless God, who had made them happy instruments in so good a work, and rendered them successful in it. Besides these, others also would be thankful; the poor, who were supplied in their wants, would not fail to be very thankful to God, and bless God for them; and all who wished well to the gospel would *glorify God for this experiment,* or proof *of subjection to the gospel of Christ,* and true love to all men, *v.* 13. Note, (1.) True Christianity is a subjection to the gospel, a yielding of ourselves to the commanding influence of its truths and laws. (2.) We must evince the sincerity of our subjection to the gospel by works of charity. (3.) This will be for the credit of our profession, and to the praise and glory of God.

4. Those whose wants were supplied would make the best return they were able, by sending up many prayers to God for those who had relieved them, *v.* 14. And thus should we recompense the kindnesses we receive when we are not in a capacity of recompensing them in any other way; and, as this is the only recompence the poor can make, so it is often greatly for the advantage of the rich.

Lastly, The apostle concludes this whole matter with this doxology, *Thanks be to God for his unspeakable gift, v.* 15. Some think that by this unspeakable gift he means the gift of grace bestowed on the churches, in making them able and willing to supply the necessities of the saints, which would be attended with unspeakable benefit both to the givers and receivers. It should seem rather that he means Jesus Christ, who is indeed the unspeakable gift of God unto this world, a gift we have all reason to be very thankful for.

CHAP. X.

There was no place in which the apostle Paul met with more opposition from false apostles than at Corinth; he had many enemies there. Let not any of the ministers of Christ think it strange if they meet with perils, not only from enemies, but from false brethren; for blessed Paul himself did so. Though he was so blameless and inoffensive in all his carriage, so condescending and useful to all, yet there were those who bore him ill-will, who envied him, and did all they could to undermine him, and lesson his interest and reputation. Therefore he vindicates himself from their imputations, and arms the Corinthians against their insinuations. In this chapter the apostle, in a mild and humble manner, asserts the power of his preaching, and to punish offenders, ver. 1—6. He then proceeds to reason the case with the Corinthians, asserting his relation to Christ, and his authority as an apostle of Christ (ver. 7—11), and refuses to justify himself, or to act by such rules as the false teachers did, but according to the better rules he had fixed for himself, ver. 12, to the end.

NOW I Paul myself beseech you by the meekness and gentleness of Christ, who in presence *am* base among you, but being absent am bold toward you:
2 But I beseech *you,* that I may not be bold when I am present with that confidence wherewith I think to be bold against some, which think of us as if we walked according to the flesh.
3 For though we walk in the flesh, we do not war after the flesh:
4 (For the weapons of our warfare *are* not carnal, but mighty through God to the pulling down of strong holds;)
5 Casting down imaginations, and every high thing that exalteth itself against the knowledge of God, and bringeth into captivity every thought to the obedience of Christ;
6 And having in a readiness to revenge all disobedience, when your obedience is fulfilled.

Here we may observe,

I. The mild and humble manner in which the blessed apostle addresses the Corinthians, and how desirous he is that no occasion may be given him to use severity. 1. He addresses them in a very mild and humble manner: *I Paul myself beseech you, v.* 1. We find, in the introduction to this epistle, he joined Timothy with himself; but now he speaks only for himself, against whom the false apostles had particularly levelled their reproaches; yet in the midst of the greatest provocations he shows humility and mildness, from the consideration of the *meekness and gentleness of Christ,* and desires this great example may have the same influence on the Corinthians. Note, When we find ourselves tempted or inclined to be rough and severe towards any body, we should think of the meekness and gentleness of Christ, that appeared in him in the days of his flesh, in the design of his undertaking, and in all the acts of his grace towards poor souls. How humbly also does this great apostle speak of himself, as *one in presence base among them!* So his enemies spoke of him with contempt, and he seems to acknowledge it; while others thought meanly, and spoke scornfully of him, he had low thoughts of himself, and spoke humbly of himself. Note, We should be sensible of our own infirmities, and think humbly of ourselves, even when men reproach us for them.

2. He is desirous that no occasion may be given to use severity, *v.* 2. *He beseeches them* to give no occasion for him to be bold, or to exercise his authority against them in general, as he had resolved to do against some who unjustly charged him as *walking according to the flesh,* that is, regulating his conduct, even in his ministerial actions, according to carnal policy or with worldly views. This was what the apostle had renounced, and this is contrary to the spirit and design of the gospel, and was far from being the aim and design of the apostle. Hereupon,

II. He asserts the power of his preaching and his power to punish offenders.

1. The power of his preaching, *v.* 3, 5. Here observe, (1.) The work of the ministry is a warfare, not *after the flesh* indeed, for it is a spiritual warfare, with spiritual enemies and for spiritual purposes. And though ministers walk in the flesh, or live in the

body, and in the common affairs of life act as other men, yet in their work and warfare they must not go by the maxims of the flesh, nor should they design to please the flesh: this must be crucified with its affections and lusts; it must be mortified and kept under. (2.) The doctrines of the gospel and discipline of the church are the weapons of this warfare; and these are not carnal: outward force, therefore, is not the method of the gospel, but strong persuasions, by the power of truth and the meekness of wisdom. A good argument this is against persecution for conscience' sake: conscience is accountable to God only; and people must be persuaded to God and their duty, not driven by force of arms. And so the weapons of our warfare are mighty, or very powerful; the evidence of truth is convincing and cogent. This indeed is through God, or owing to him, because they are his institutions, and accompanied with his blessing, which makes all opposition to fall before his victorious gospel. We may here observe, [1.] What opposition is made against the gospel by the powers of sin and Satan in the hearts of men. Ignorance, prejudices, beloved lusts, are Satan's strong-holds in the souls of some; vain imaginations, carnal reasonings, and high thoughts, or proud conceits, in others, *exalt themselves against the knowledge of God,* that is, by these ways the devil endeavours to keep men from faith and obedience to the gospel, and secures his possession of the hearts of men, as his own house or property. But then observe, [2.] The conquest which the word of God gains. These strong-holds are pulled down by the gospel as the means, through the grace and power of God accompanying it as the principal efficient cause. Note, The conversion of the soul is the conquest of Satan in that soul.

2. The apostle's power to punish offenders (and that in an extraordinary manner) is asserted in *v.* 6. The apostle was a prime-minister in the kingdom of Christ, and chief officer in his army, and *had in readiness* (that is, he had power and authority at hand) *to revenge all disobedience,* or to punish offenders in a most exemplary and extraordinary manner. The apostle speaks not of personal revenge, but of punishing disobedience to the gospel, and disorderly walking among church-members, by inflicting church-censures. Note, Though the apostle showed meekness and gentleness, yet he would not betray his authority; and therefore intimates that when he would commend those whose obedience was fulfilled or manifested others would fall under severe censures.

7 Do ye look on things after the
outward appearance? If any man
trust to himself that he is Christ's,
let him of himself think this again,
that, as he *is* Christ's, even so *are*
we Christ's. 8 For though I should
boast somewhat more of our authority, which the Lord hath given us
for edification, and not for your destruction, I should not be ashamed:
9 That I may not seem as if I would
terrify you by letters. 10 For *his*
letters, say they, *are* weighty and
powerful; but *his* bodily presence *is*
weak, and *his* speech contemptible.
11 Let such a one think this, that,
such as we are in word by letters
when we are absent, such *will we be*
also in deed when we are present.

In these verses the apostle proceeds to reason the case with the Corinthians, in opposition to those who despised him, judged him, and spoke hardly of him: "*Do you,*" says he, "*look on things after the outward appearance? v.* 7. Is this a fit measure or rule to make an estimate of things or persons by, and to judge between me and my adversaries?" In outward appearance, Paul was mean and despicable with some; he did not make a figure, as perhaps some of his competitors might do: but this was a false rule to make a judgment by. It should seem that some boasted mighty things of themselves, and made a fair show. But there are often false appearances. A man may seem to be learned who has not learned Christ, and appear virtuous when he has not a principle of grace in his heart. However, the apostle asserts two things of himself:—

I. His relation to Christ: *If any man trust to himself that he is Christ's, even so are we Christ's, v.* 7. It should seem by this that Paul's adversaries boasted of their relation to Christ as his ministers and servants. Now the apostle reasons thus with the Corinthians: "Suppose it to be so, allowing what they say to be true (and let us observe that, in fair arguing, we should allow all that may be reasonably granted, and should not think it impossible but those who differ from us very much may yet belong to Christ, as well as we), allowing them," might the apostle say, "what they boast of, yet they ought also to allow this to us, that *we also are Christ's.*" Note, 1. We must not, by the most charitable allowances we make to others who differ from us, cut ourselves off from Christ, nor deny our relation to him. For, 2. There is room in Christ for many; and those who differ much from one another may yet be one in him. It would help to heal the differences that are among us if we would remember that, how confident soever we may be that we belong to Christ, yet, at the same time, we must allow that those who differ from us may belong to Christ too, and therefore should be treated accordingly. We must not think that we are the people, and that none belong to Christ but ourselves. This we may plead for ourselves, against those who judge us and despise us that, how weak soever we are, yet, as they are Christ's, so are we: we profess the same faith, we walk by the same rule, we build upon the same foundation, and hope for the same inheritance.

II. His authority from Christ as an apostle. This he had mentioned before (*v.* 6), and now he tells them that he might speak of it again, and that with some sort of boasting, seeing it was a truth, that the *Lord had given it to him,* and it was more than his adversaries could justly pretend to. It was certainly what he should not be ashamed of, *v.* 8. Concerning this observe, 1. The nature of his authority: it was for *edification, and not for destruction.* This indeed is the end of all authority, civil and ecclesiastical, and was the end of that extraordinary authority which the apostles had, and of all church-discipline. 2. The caution with which he speaks of his authority, professing that his design was not to terrify them with big words, nor by angry letters, *v.* 9. Thus he seems to obviate an objection that might have been formed against him, *v.* 10. But the apostle declares he did not intend to frighten those who were obedient, nor did he write any thing in his letters that he was not able to make good by deeds against the disobedient; and he would have his adversaries *know this* (*v.* 11), that he would, by the exercise of his apostolical power committed to him, make it appear to have a real efficacy.

12 For we dare not make ourselves
of the number, or compare ourselves
with some that commend themselves:
but they measuring themselves by
themselves, and comparing themselves
among themselves, are not wise. 13
But we will not boast of things without *our* measure, but according to the
measure of the rule which God hath
distributed to us, a measure to reach
even unto you. 14 For we stretch
not ourselves beyond *our measure*, as
though we reached not unto you: for
we are come as far as to you also in
preaching the gospel of Christ: 15
Not boasting of things without *our*
measure, *that is,* of other men's labours; but having hope, when your
faith is increased, that we shall be
enlarged by you according to our rule
abundantly, 16 To preach the gospel
in the *regions* beyond you, *and* not to
boast in another man's line of things
made ready to our hand. 17 But he
that glorieth, let him glory in the
Lord. 18 For not he that commendeth himself is approved, but
whom the Lord commendeth.

In these verses observe,

I. The apostle refuses to justify himself, or to act by such rules as the false apostles did, *v.* 12. He plainly intimates that they took a wrong method to commend themselves, in *measuring themselves by themselves, and comparing themselves among themselves,* which was *not wise.* They were pleased, and did pride themselves, in their own attainments, and never considered those who far exceeded them in gifts and graces, in power and authority; and this made them haughty and insolent. Note, If we would compare ourselves with others who excel us, this would be a good method to keep us humble; we should be pleased and thankful for what we have of gifts or graces, but never pride ourselves therein, as if there were none to be compared with us or that did excel us. The apostle would not be of the number of such vain men: let us resolve that we will not make ourselves of that number.

II. He fixes a better rule for his conduct, namely, *not to boast of things without his measure,* which was the measure *God had distributed* to him, *v.* 13. His meaning is, either that he would not boast of more gifts or graces, or power and authority, than God had really bestowed on him; or, rather, that he would not act beyond his commission as to persons or things, nor go beyond the line prescribed to him, which he plainly intimates the false apostles did, while they *boasted of other men's labours.* The apostle's resolution was to keep within his own province, and that compass of ground which God had marked out for him. His commission as an apostle was to preach the gospel every where, especially among the Gentiles, and he was not confined to one place; yet he observed the directions of Providence, and the Holy Spirit, as to the particular places whither he went or where he did abide.

III. He acted according to this rule: *We stretch not ourselves beyond our measure, v.* 14. And, particularly, he acted according to this rule in preaching at Corinth, and in the exercise of his apostolical authority there; for he came thither by divine direction, and there he converted many to Christianity; and, therefore, in boasting of them as his charge, he acted not contrary to his rule, he boasted not of *other men's labours, v.* 15.

IV. He declares his success in observing this rule. His hope was that their faith was increased, and that others beyond them, even in the remoter parts of Achaia, would embrace the gospel also; and in all this he exceeded not his commission, nor acted in another man's line.

V. He seems to check himself in this matter, as if he had spoken too much in his own praise. The unjust accusations and reflections of his enemies had made it needful he should justify himself; and the wrong methods they took gave him good occasion to mention the better rule he had observed:

yet he is afraid of boasting, or taking any praise to himself, and therefore he mentions two things which ought to be regarded:— 1. *He that glorieth should glory in the Lord, v.* 17. If we are able to fix good rules for our conduct, or act by them, or have any good success in so doing, the praise and glory of all are owing unto God. Ministers in particular must be careful not to glory in their performances, but must give God the glory of their work, and the success thereof. 2. *Not he that commendeth himself is approved, but he whom the Lord commendeth, v.* 18. Of all flattery, self-flattery is the worst, and self-applause is seldom any better than self-flattery and self-deceit. At the best, self-commendation is no praise, and it is oftentimes as foolish and vain as it is proud; therefore, instead of praising or commending ourselves, we should strive to approve ourselves to God, and his approbation will be our best commendation.

CHAP XI.

In this chapter the apostle goes on with his discourse, in opposition to the false apostles, who were very industrious to lessen his interest and reputation among the Corinthians, and had prevailed too much by their insinuations. I. He apologizes for going about to commend himself, and gives the reason for what he did, ver. 1—4. II. He mentions, in his own necessary vindication, his equality with the other apostles, and with the false apostles in this particular of preaching the gospel to the Corinthians freely, without wages, ver. 5—15. III. He makes another preface to what he was about further to say in his own justification, ver. 16—21. And, IV. He gives a large account of his qualifications, labours, and sufferings, in which he exceeded the false apostles, ver. 22, to the end.

WOULD to God ye could bear
with me a little in *my* folly,
and indeed bear with me. 2 For I
am jealous over you with godly jealousy: for I have espoused you to one
husband, that I may present *you as* a
chaste virgin to Christ. 3 But I
fear, lest by any means, as the serpent
beguiled Eve through his subtlety, so
your minds should be corrupted from
the simplicity that is in Christ. 4
For if he that cometh preacheth another Jesus, whom we have not
preached, or *if* ye receive another
spirit, which ye have not received,
or another gospel, which ye have not
accepted, ye might well bear with *him*.

Here we may observe, 1. The apology the apostle makes for going about to commend himself. He is loth to enter upon this subject of self-commendation: *Would to God you could bear with me a little in my folly, v.* 1. He calls this folly, because too often it is really no better. In his case it was necessary; yet, seeing others might apprehend it to be folly in him, he desires them to bear with it. Note, As much against the grain as it is with a proud man to acknowledge his infirmities, so much is it against the grain with a humble man to speak in his own praise. It is no pleasure to a good man to speak well of himself, yet in some cases it is lawful, namely, when it is for the advantage of others, or for our own necessary vindication; as thus it was here. For, 2. We have the reasons for what the apostle did. (1.) To preserve the Corinthians from being corrupted by the insinuations of the false apostles, *v.* 2, 3. He tells them *he was jealous over them with godly jealousy;* he was afraid lest their faith should be weakened by hearkening to such suggestions as tended to lessen their regard to his ministry, by which they were brought to the Christian faith. He had *espoused them to one husband*, that is, converted them to Christianity (and the conversion of a soul is its marriage to the Lord Jesus); and he was desirous to *present them as a chaste virgin*—pure, and spotless, and faithful, not having *their minds corrupted* with false doctrines by false teachers, as *Eve was beguiled by the subtlety of the serpent.* This godly jealousy in the apostle was a mixture of love and fear; and faithful ministers cannot but be afraid and concerned for their people, lest they should lose that which they have received, and turn from what they have embraced, especially when *deceivers have gone abroad*, or have *crept in among them.* (2.) To vindicate himself against the false apostles, forasmuch as they could not pretend they had another Jesus, or another Spirit, or another gospel, to preach to them, *v.* 4. If this had been the case, there would have been some colour of reason to bear with them, or to hearken to them. But seeing there is but one Jesus, one Spirit, and one gospel, that is, or at least that ought to be, preached to them and received by them, what reason could there be why the Corinthians should be prejudiced against him, who first converted them to the faith, by the artifices of any adversary? It was a just occasion of jealousy that such persons designed to preach another Jesus, another Spirit, and another gospel.

5 For I suppose I was not a whit
behind the very chiefest apostles. 6
But though *I be* rude in speech, yet
not in knowledge; but we have
been thoroughly made manifest among
you in all things. 7 Have I committed an offence in abasing myself
that ye might be exalted, because I
have preached to you the gospel of
God freely? 8 I robbed other
churches, taking wages *of them*, to do
you service. 9 And when I was
present with you, and wanted, I was
chargeable to no man: for that which
was lacking to me the brethren which
came from Macedonia supplied: and
in all *things* I have kept myself from
being burdensome unto you, and *so*
will I keep *myself*. 10 As the truth

of Christ is in me, no man shall stop
me of this boasting in the regions of
Achaia. 11 Wherefore? because I
love you not? God knoweth. 12
But what I do, that I will do, that I
may cut off occasion from them which
desire occasion; that wherein they
glory, they may be found even as
we. 13 For such *are* false apostles,
deceitful workers, transforming themselves into the apostles of Christ. 14
And no marvel; for Satan himself is
transformed into an angel of light. 15
Therefore *it is* no great thing if his
ministers also be transformed as the
ministers of righteousness; whose end
shall be according to their works.

After the foregoing preface to what he was about to say, the apostle in these verses mentions,

I. His equality with the other apostles—that *he was not a whit behind the very chief of the apostles, v.* 5. This he expresses very modestly: *I suppose so.* He might have spoken very positively. The apostleship, as an office, was equal in all the apostles; but the apostles, like other Christians, differed one from another. These *stars differed one from another in glory,* and Paul was indeed of the first magnitude; yet he speaks modestly of himself, and humbly owns his personal infirmity, that he was *rude in speech,* had not such a graceful delivery as some others might have. Some think that he was a man of very low stature, and that his voice was proportionably small; others think that he may have had some impediment in his speech, perhaps a stammering tongue. However, he was not rude *in knowledge;* he was not unacquainted with the best rules of oratory and the art of persuasion, much less was he ignorant of the mysteries of the kingdom of heaven, as had been *thoroughly manifested among them.*

II. His equality with the false apostles in this particular—the preaching of the gospel unto them freely, without wages. This the apostle largely insists on, and shows that, as they could not but own him to be a minister of Christ, so they ought to acknowledge he had been a good friend to them. For, 1. He had preached the gospel to them freely, *v.* 7—10. He had proved at large, in his former epistle to them, the lawfulness of ministers' receiving maintenance from the people, and the duty of the people to give them an honourable maintenance; and here he says he himself had *taken wages of other churches* (*v.* 8), so that he had a right to have asked and received from them: yet he waived his right, and chose rather to abase himself, by working with his hands in the trade of tent-making to maintain himself, than be burdensome to them, that they might *be exalted,* or encouraged to receive the gospel, which they had so cheaply; yea, he chose rather to be supplied from Macedonia than to be chargeable unto them. 2. He informs them of the reason of this his conduct among them. It was not because *he did not love them* (*v.* 11), or was unwilling to receive tokens of their love (for love and friendship are manifested by mutual giving and receiving), but it was to avoid offence, that *he might cut off occasion from those that desired occasion.* He would not give occasion for any to accuse him of worldly designs in preaching the gospel, or that he intended to make a trade of it, to enrich himself; and that others who opposed him at Corinth might not in this respect gain an advantage against him: that wherein *they gloried,* as to this matter, *they might be found even as he, v.* 12. It is not improbable to suppose that the chief of the false teachers at Corinth, or some among them, were rich, and taught (or deceived) the people freely, and might accuse the apostle or his fellow-labourers as mercenary men, who received hire or wages, and therefore the apostle kept to his resolution not to be chargeable to any of the Corinthians.

III. The false apostles are charged *as deceitful workers* (*v.* 13), and that upon this account, because they would *transform themselves* into the likeness of the apostles of Christ, and, though they were the ministers of Satan, would seem to be the *ministers of righteousness.* They would be as industrious and as generous in promoting error as the apostles were in preaching truth; they would endeavour as much to undermine the kingdom of Christ as the apostles did to establish it. There were counterfeit prophets under the Old Testament, who wore the garb and learned the language of the prophets of the Lord. So there were counterfeit apostles under the New Testament, who seemed in many respects like the true apostles of Christ. And no marvel (says the apostle); hypocrisy is a thing not to be much wondered at in this world, especially when we consider the great influence Satan has upon the minds of many, who *rules in the hearts of the children of disobedience.* As he can turn himself into any shape, and put on almost any form, and look sometimes *like an angel of light,* in order to promote his kingdom of darkness, so he will teach his ministers and instruments to do the same. But it follows, *Their end is according to their works* (*v.* 15); the end will discover them to be deceitful workers, and their work will end in ruin and destruction.

16 I say again, Let no man think
me a fool; if otherwise, yet as a fool
receive me, that I may boast myself
a little. 17 That which I speak, I
speak *it* not after the Lord, but as
it were foolishly, in this confidence

of boasting. 18 Seeing that many
glory after the flesh, I will glory also.
19 For ye suffer fools gladly, seeing
ye *yourselves* are wise. 20 For ye
suffer, if a man bring you into bondage, if a man devour *you*, if a man
take *of you*, if a man exalt himself,
if a man smite you on the face. 21 I
speak as concerning reproach, as
though we had been weak. Howbeit
whereinsoever any is bold, (I speak
foolishly,) I am bold also.

Here we have a further excuse that the apostle makes for what he was about to say in his own vindication. 1. He would not have them think he was guilty of folly, in saying what he said to vindicate himself: *Let no man think me a fool, v.* 16. Ordinarily, indeed, it is unbecoming a wise man to be much and often speaking in his own praise. Boasting of ourselves is usually not only a sign of a proud mind, but a mark of folly also. However, says the apostle, yet *as a fool receive me;* that is, if you count it folly in me to *boast a little,* yet give due regard to what I shall say. 2. He mentions a caution, to prevent the abuse of what he should say, telling them that what he spoke, *he did not speak after the Lord, v.* 17. He would not have them think that boasting of ourselves, or glorying in what we have, is a thing commanded by the Lord in general unto Christians, nor yet that this is always necessary in our own vindication; though it may be lawfully used, because not contrary to the Lord, when, strictly speaking, it is not after the Lord. It is the duty and practice of Christians, in obedience to the command and example of the Lord, rather to humble and abase themselves; yet prudence must direct in what circumstances it is needful to do that which we may do lawfully, even speak of what God has wrought for us, and in us, and by us too. 3. He gives a good reason why they should suffer him to boast a little; namely, because they suffered others to do so who had less reason. *Seeing many glory after the flesh* (of carnal privileges, or outward advantages and attainments), *I will glory also, v.* 18. But he would not glory in those things, though he had as much or more reason than others to do so. But he gloried in his infirmities, as he tells them afterwards. The Corinthians thought themselves wise, and might think it an instance of wisdom to bear with the weakness of others, and therefore suffered others to do what might seem folly; therefore the apostle would have them bear with him. Or these words, *You suffer fools gladly, seeing you yourselves are wise* (*v.* 19), may be ironical, and then the meaning is this: "Notwithstanding all your wisdom, you willingly suffer yourselves to be *brought into bondage* under the Jewish yoke, or suffer others to tyrannize over you; nay, to *devour you,* or make a prey of you, and *take of you* hire for their own advantage, and to *exalt themselves* above you, and lord it over you; nay, even to *smite you on the face,* or impose upon you to your very faces (*v.* 20), upbraiding you while they reproach me, as if you had been very weak in showing regard to me," *v.* 21. Seeing this was the case, that the Corinthians, or some among them, could so easily bear all this from the false apostles, it was reasonable for the apostle to desire, and expect, they should bear with what might seem to them an indiscretion in him, seeing the circumstances of the case were such as made it needful that *whereinsoever any were bold* he should be *bold also, v.* 21.

22 Are they Hebrews? so *am* I.
Are they Israelites? so *am* I. Are
they the seed of Abraham? so *am* I.
23 Are they ministers of Christ? (I
speak as a fool) I *am* more; in labours
more abundant, in stripes above measure, in prisons more frequent, in
deaths oft. 24 Of the Jews five times
received I forty *stripes* save one. 25
Thrice was I beaten with rods, once
was I stoned, thrice I suffered shipwreck, a night and a day I have been
in the deep; 26 *In* journeyings
often, *in* perils of waters, *in* perils
of robbers, *in* perils by *mine own*
countrymen, *in* perils by the heathen, *in* perils in the city, *in*
perils in the wilderness, *in* perils
in the sea, *in* perils among false
brethren; 27 In weariness and
painfulness, in watchings often, in
hunger and thirst, in fastings often,
in cold and nakedness. 28 Beside
those things that are without, that
which cometh upon me daily, the
care of all the churches. 29 Who is
weak, and I am not weak? who is
offended, and I burn not? 30 If I must
needs glory, I will glory of the things
which concern mine infirmities. 31
The God and Father of our Lord Jesus
Christ, which is blessed for evermore,
knoweth that I lie not. 32 In Damascus the governor under Aretas
the king kept the city of the Dama-
scenes with a garrison, desirous to
apprehend me: 33 And through a
window in a basket was I let down
by the wall, and escaped his hands.

Here the apostle gives a large account of

his own qualifications, labours, and sufferings (not out of pride or vain-glory, but to the honour of God, who had enabled him to do and suffer so much for the cause of Christ), and wherein he excelled the false apostles, who would lessen his character and usefulness among the Corinthians. Observe,

I. He mentions the privileges of his birth (*v.* 22), which were equal to any they could pretend to. He was a Hebrew of the Hebrews; of a family among the Jews that never intermarried with the Gentiles. He was also an Israelite, and could boast of his being descended from the beloved Jacob as well as they, and was also of the seed of Abraham, and not of the proselytes. It should seem from this that the false apostles were of the Jewish race, who gave disturbance to the Gentile converts.

II. He makes mention also of his apostleship, that he was more than an ordinary minister of Christ, *v.* 23. God had counted him faithful, and had put him into the ministry. He had been a useful minister of Christ unto them; they had found full proofs of his ministry: *Are they ministers of Christ? I am more so.*

III. He chiefly insists upon this, that he had been an extraordinary sufferer for Christ; and this was what he gloried in, or rather he gloried in the grace of God that had enabled him to be more *abundant in labours,* and to endure very great sufferings, such as *stripes above measure, frequent imprisonments,* and *often* the dangers of *death, v.* 23. Note, When the apostle would prove himself an extraordinary minister, he proves that he had been an extraordinary sufferer. Paul was the apostle of the Gentiles, and for that reason was hated of the Jews. They did all they could against him; and among the Gentiles also he met with hard usage. Bonds and imprisonments were familiar to him; never was the most notorious malefactor more frequently in the hands of public justice than Paul was for righteousness' sake. The jail and the whipping-post, and all other hard usages of those who are accounted the worst of men, were what he was accustomed to. As to the Jews, whenever he fell into their hands, they never spared him. *Five times* he fell under their lash, and received *forty stripes save one, v.* 24. Forty stripes was the utmost their law allowed (Deut. xxv. 3), but it was usual with them, that they might not exceed, to abate one at least of that number. And to have the abatement of one only was all the favour that ever Paul received from them. The Gentiles were not tied up to that moderation, and among them *he was thrice beaten with rods,* of which we may suppose once was at Philippi, Acts xvi. 22. *Once he was stoned* in a popular tumult, and was taken up for dead, Acts xiv. 19. He says that *thrice he suffered shipwreck;* and we may believe him, though the sacred history gives a relation but of one. *A night and a day he had been in the deep* (*v.* 25), in some deep dungeon or other, shut up as a prisoner. Thus he was all his days a constant confessor; perhaps scarcely a year of his life, after his conversion, passed without suffering some hardship or other for his religion; yet this was not all, for, whereever he went, he went in perils; he was exposed to perils of all sorts. If he journeyed by land, or voyaged by sea, he was in perils of robbers, or enemies of some sort; the Jews, his own countrymen, sought to kill him, or do him a mischief; the heathen, to whom he was sent, were not more kind to him, for among them he was in peril. If he was in the city, or in the wilderness, still he was in peril. He was in peril not only among avowed enemies, but among those also who called themselves brethren, but were false brethren, *v.* 26. Besides all this, he had great weariness and painfulness in his ministerial labours, and these are things that will come into account shortly, and people will be reckoned with for all the care and pains of their ministers concerning them. Paul was a stranger to wealth and plenty, power and pleasure, preferment and ease; he was in *watchings often,* and exposed to *hunger and thirst;* in *fastings often,* it may be out of necessity; and endured *cold and nakedness, v.* 27. Thus was he, who was one of the greatest blessings of the age, used as if he had been the burden of the earth, and the plague of his generation. And yet this is not all; for, as an apostle, the *care of all the churches* lay on him, *v.* 28. He mentions this last, as if this lay the heaviest upon him, and as if he could better bear all the persecutions of his enemies than the scandals that were to be found in the churches he had the oversight of. *Who is weak, and I am not weak? Who is offended, and I burn not? v.* 29. There was not a weak Christian with whom he did not sympathize, nor any one scandalized, but he was affected therewith. See what little reason we have to be in love with the pomp and plenty of this world, when this blessed apostle, one of the best of men that ever lived, excepting Jesus Christ, felt so much hardship in it. Nor was he ashamed of all this, but, on the contrary, it was what he accounted his honour; and therefore, much against the grain as it was with him to glory, yet, says he, *if I must needs glory,* if my adversaries will oblige me to it in my own necessary vindication, *I will glory in these my infirmities, v.* 30. Note, Sufferings for righteousness' sake will, the most of any thing, redound to our honour.

In the last two verses, he mentions one particular part of his sufferings out of its place, as if he had forgotten it before, or because the deliverance God wrought for him was most remarkable; namely, the danger he was in at Damascus, soon after he was converted, and not settled in Christianity, at least in the ministry and apostleship. This is recorded,

Acts ix. 24, 25. This was his first great danger and difficulty, and the rest of his life was of a piece with this. And it is observable that, lest it should be thought he spoke more than was true, the apostle confirms this narrative with a solemn oath, or appeal to the omniscience of God, *v.* 31. It is a great comfort to a good man that *the God and Father of our Lord Jesus Christ,* who is an omniscient God, knows the truth of all he says, and knows all he does and all he suffers for his sake.

CHAP. XII.

In this chapter the apostle proceeds in maintaining the honour of his apostleship. He magnified his office when there were those who vilified it. What he says in his own praise was only in his own justification and the necessary defence of the honour of his ministry, the preservation of which was necessary to its success. First, He makes mention of the favour God had shown him, the honour done him, the methods God took to keep him humble, and the use he made of this dispensation, ver. 1—10. Then he addresses himself to the Corinthians, blaming them for what was faulty among them, and giving a large account of his behaviour and kind intentions towards them, ver. 11, to the end.

IT is not expedient for me doubtless
to glory. I will come to visions
and revelations of the Lord. 2 I
knew a man in Christ about fourteen
years ago, (whether in the body, I
cannot tell; or whether out of the
body, I cannot tell: God knoweth;)
such a one caught up to the third
heaven. 3 And I knew such a man,
(whether in the body, or out of the
body, I cannot tell: God knoweth;)
4 How that he was caught up into
paradise, and heard unspeakable
words, which it is not lawful for a
man to utter. 5 Of such a one will
I glory: yet of myself I will not
glory, but in mine infirmities. 6 For
though I would desire to glory, I
shall not be a fool; for I will say the
truth: but *now* I forbear, lest any
man should think of me above that
which he seeth me *to be,* or *that* he
heareth of me. 7 And lest I should
be exalted above measure through
the abundance of the revelations,
there was given to me a thorn in the
flesh, the messenger of Satan to buffet
me, lest I should be exalted above
measure. 8 For this thing I besought
the Lord thrice, that it might depart
from me. 9 And he said unto me,
My grace is sufficient for thee: for
my strength is made perfect in weakness. Most gladly therefore will I
rather glory in my infirmities, that
the power of Christ may rest upon
me. 10 Therefore I take pleasure in
infirmities, in reproaches, in necessities, in persecutions, in distresses for
Christ's sake: for when I am weak,
then am I strong.

Here we may observe,

I. The narrative the apostle gives of the favours God had shown him, and the honour he had done him; for doubtless he himself is the man in Christ of whom he speaks. Concerning this we may take notice, 1. Of the honour itself which was done to the apostle: he was *caught up into the third heaven, v.* 2. When this was we cannot say, whether it was during those three days that he lay without sight at his conversion or at some other time afterwards, much less can we pretend to say *how* this was, whether by a separation of his soul from his body or by an extraordinary transport in the depth of contemplation. It would be presumption for us to determine, if not also to enquire into, this matter, seeing the apostle himself says, *Whether in the body or out of the body, I cannot tell.* It was certainly a very extraordinary honour done him: in some sense he was caught up into the *third heaven,* the heaven of the blessed, above the aërial heaven, in which the fowls fly, above the starry heaven, which is adorned with those glorious orbs: it was into the third heaven, where God most eminently manifests his glory. We are not capable of knowing all, nor is it fit we should know very much, of the particulars of that glorious place and state; it is our duty and interest to give diligence to make sure to ourselves a mansion there; and, if that be cleared up to us, then we should long to be removed thither, to abide there for ever. This third heaven is called paradise (*v.* 4), in allusion to the earthly paradise out of which Adam was driven for his transgression; it is called the paradise of God (Rev. ii. 7), signifying to us that by Christ we are restored to all the joys and honours we lost by sin, yea, to much better. The apostle does not mention what he saw in the third heaven or paradise, but tells us that *he heard unspeakable words,* such as it is not possible for a man to utter—such are the sublimity of the matter and our unacquaintedness with the language of the upper world: nor was it lawful to utter those words, because, while we are here in this world, we have a more sure word of prophecy than such visions and revelations. 2 Pet. i. 19. We read of the tongue of angels as well as of men, and Paul knew as much of that as ever any man upon earth did, and yet preferred charity, that is, the sincere love of God and our neighbour. This account which the apostle gives us of his vision should check our curious desires after forbidden knowledge, and teach us to improve the revelation God has given us in his word. Paul himself, who had been in the third heaven, did not publish to the world what he had heard there, but adhered to the doctrine of Christ: on this foundation the church is built, and on this we must build our faith and hope. 2. The modest and humble manner in which the apostle mentions this matter is observable. One would be apt to think that one who had had such visions and revelations as these would have boasted greatly of them; but, says he, *It is not expedient for me doubtless to glory, v.* 1. He therefore did not mention this immediately, nor till *above fourteen years* after, *v.* 2. And then it is not without some reluctancy, as a thing which in a manner he was forced to by the necessity of the case. Again, he speaks of himself in the third person, and does not say, I am the man who was thus honoured above other men. Again, his humility appears by the check he seems to put upon himself (*v.* 6), which plainly shows that he delighted not to dwell upon this theme. Thus was he, who was not behind the chief of the apostles in dignity, very eminent for his humility. Note, It is an excellent thing to have a lowly spirit in the midst of high advancements; and those who abase themselves shall be exalted.

II. The apostle gives an account of the methods God took to keep him humble, and to prevent his *being lifted up above measure;* and this he speaks of to balance the account that was given before of the visions and revelations he had had. Note, When God's people communicate their experiences, let them always remember to take notice of what God has done to keep them humble, as well as what he has done in favour to them and for their advancement. Here observe,

1. The apostle was pained with a thorn in the flesh, and buffeted with a messenger of Satan, *v.* 7. We are much in the dark what this was, whether some great trouble or some great temptation. Some think it was an acute bodily pain or sickness; others think it was the indignities done him by the false apostles, and the opposition he met with from them, particularly on the account of his speech, which was contemptible. However this was, God often brings this good out of evil, that the reproaches of our enemies help to hide pride from us; and this is certain, that what the apostle calls a thorn in his flesh was for a time very grievous to him: but the thorns Christ wore for us, and with which he was crowned, sanctify and make easy all the thorns in the flesh we may at any time be afflicted with; for *he suffered, being tempted, that he might be able to succour those that are tempted.* Temptations to sin are most grievous thorns; they are messengers of Satan, to buffet us. Indeed it is a great grievance to a good man to be so much as tempted to sin.

2. The design of this was to keep the apostle humble: *Lest he should be exalted above measure, v.* 7. Paul himself knew he *had not yet attained, neither was already perfect;* and yet he was in danger of being lifted up with pride. If God love us, he will hide pride from us, and keep us from being exalted above measure; and spiritual burdens are ordered, to cure spiritual pride. This thorn in the flesh is said to be a messenger of Satan, which he did not send with a good design, but, on the contrary, with ill intentions, to discourage the apostle (who had been so highly favoured of God) and hinder him in his work. But God designed this for good, and he overruled it for good, and made this messenger of Satan to be so far from being a hindrance that it was a help to the apostle.

3. The apostle prayed earnestly to God for the removal of this sore grievance. Note, Prayer is a salve for every sore, a remedy for every malady; and when we are afflicted with thorns in the flesh we should give ourselves to prayer. Therefore we are sometimes tempted that we may learn to pray. The apostle *besought the Lord thrice, that it might depart from him, v.* 8. Note, Though afflictions are sent for our spiritual benefit, yet we may pray to God for the removal of them: we ought indeed to desire also that they may reach the end for which they are designed. The apostle prayed earnestly, and repeated his requests; he besought the Lord *thrice,* that is, often. So that if an answer be not given to the first prayer, nor to the second, we must hold on, and hold out, till we receive an answer. Christ himself prayed to his Father thrice. As troubles are sent to teach us to pray, so they are continued to teach us to continue instant in prayer.

4. We have an account of the answer given to the apostle's prayer, that, although the trouble was not removed, yet an equivalent should be granted: *My grace is sufficient for thee.* Note, (1.) Though God accepts the prayer of faith, yet he does not always answer it in the letter; as he sometimes grants in wrath, so he sometimes denies in love. (2.) When God does not remove our troubles and temptations, yet, if he gives us grace sufficient for us, we have no reason to complain, nor to say that he deals ill by us. It is a great comfort to us, whatever thorns in the flesh we are pained with, that God's grace is sufficient for us. Grace signifies two things:— [1.] The good-will of God towards us, and this is enough to enlighten and enliven us, sufficient to strengthen and comfort us, to support our souls and cheer up our spirits, in all afflictions and distresses. [2.] The good work of God in us, the grace we receive from the fulness that is in Christ our head; and from him there shall be communicated that which is suitable and seasonable, and sufficient for his members. Christ Jesus understands our case, and knows our need, and will proportion the remedy to our malady, and not only strengthen us, but glorify *himself. His strength is made perfect in our weakness.* Thus his grace is manifested and magnified; he ordains his praise out of the mouths of babes and sucklings.

III. Here is the use which the apostle makes of this dispensation: *He gloried in his infirmities* (*v.* 9), and took pleasure in them, *v.* 10. He does not mean his sinful infirmities (those we have reason to be ashamed of and grieved at), but he means his afflictions, his reproaches, necessities, persecutions, and distresses for Christ's sake, *v.* 10. And the reason of his glory and joy on account of these things was this—they were fair opportunities for Christ to manifest the power and sufficiency of his grace resting upon him, by which he had so much experience of the strength of divine grace that he could say, *When I am weak, then am I strong.* This is a Christian paradox: when we are weak in ourselves, then we are strong in the grace of our Lord Jesus Christ; when we see ourselves weak in ourselves, then we go out of ourselves to Christ, and are qualified to receive strength from him, and experience most of the supplies of divine strength and grace.

11 I am become a fool in glorying;
ye have compelled me: for I ought
to have been commended of you:
for in nothing am I behind the very
chiefest apostles, though I be nothing.
12 Truly the signs of an apostle were
wrought among you in all patience, in
signs, and wonders, and mighty deeds.
13 For what is it wherein you were
inferior to other churches, except *it*
be that I myself was not burdensome
to you? forgive me this wrong. 14
Behold, the third time I am ready to
come to you; and I will not be burdensome to you: for I seek not your's,
but you: for the children ought not
to lay up for the parents, but the
parents for the children. 15 And I
will very gladly spend and be spent
for you; though the more abundantly
I love you, the less I be loved. 16
But be it so, I did not burden you:
nevertheless, being crafty, I caught
you with guile. 17 Did I make a
gain of you by any of them whom I
sent unto you? 18 I desired Titus,
and with *him* I sent a brother. Did
Titus make a gain of you? walked
we not in the same spirit? *walked we*
not in the same steps? 19 Again,
think ye that we excuse ourselves
unto you? we speak before God in
Christ: but *we do* all things, dearly
beloved, for your edifying. 20 For
I fear, lest, when I come, I shall not
find you such as I would, and *that* I
shall be found unto you such as ye
would not: lest *there be* debates,
envyings, wraths, strifes, backbitings,
whisperings, swellings, tumults: 21
And lest, when I come again, my God
will humble me among you, and *that*
I shall bewail many which have sinned
already, and have not repented of
the uncleanness and fornication and
lasciviousness which they have committed.

In these verses the apostle addresses himself to the Corinthians two ways:—

I. He blames them for what was faulty in them; namely, that they had not stood up in his defence as they ought to have done, and so made it the more needful for him to insist so much on his own vindication. They in manner compelled him to commend himself, who *ought to have been commended of them* *v.* 11. And had they, or some among them, not failed on their part, it would have been less needful for him to have said so much on his own behalf. He tells them further that they in particular had good reason to speak well of him, as being *in nothing behind the very chief apostles,* because he had given them full proof and evidence of his apostleship; for *the signs of an apostle were wrought among them in all patience, in signs, and wonders, and mighty deeds.* Note, 1. It is a debt we owe to good men to stand up in the defence of their reputation; and we are under special obligations to those we have received benefit by, especially spiritual benefit, to own them as instruments in God's hand of good to us, and to vindicate them when they are calumniated by others. 2. How much soever we are, or ought to be, esteemed by others, we ought always to think humbly of ourselves. See an example of this in this great apostle, who thought himself to be nothing, though in truth he was not behind the greatest apostles—so far was he from seeking praise from men, though he tells them their duty to vindicate his reputation—so far was he from applauding himself, when he was forced to insist upon his own necessary self-defence.

II. He gives a large account of his behaviour and kind intentions towards them, in which we may observe the character of a faithful minister of the gospel. 1. He was not willing to be burdensome to them, nor did he seek theirs, but them. He says (*v.* 13) he had not been burdensome to them, for the time past, and tells them (*v.* 14) he would not be burdensome to them for the time to come, when he should come to them. He spared their purses, and did not covet their money: *I seek not yours but you.* He sought not to enrich himself, but to save their souls: he did not desire to make a property of them to himself, but to gain them over to Christ, whose servant he was. Note, Those who aim at clothing themselves with the fleece of the flock, and take no care of the sheep, are hirelings, and not good shepherds. 2. He would gladly spend and be spent for them (*v.* 15); that is, he was willing to take pains and to suffer loss for their good. He would spend his time, his parts, his strength, his interest, his all, to do them service; nay, so spend as to be spent, and be like a candle, which consumes itself to give light to others. 3. He did not abate in his love to them, notwithstanding their unkindness and ingratitude to him; and therefore was contented and glad to take pains with them, though *the more abundantly he loved them the less he was loved,* *v.* 15. This is applicable to other relations: if others be wanting in their duty to us it does not follow therefore that we may neglect our duty to them. 4. He was careful not only that he himself should not be burdensome, but that none he employed should. This seems to be the meaning of what we read, *v.* 16—18. If it should be objected by any that though he did not himself burden them, *yet, being crafty, he caught them with guile,* that is, he sent those among them who pillaged them, and afterwards he shared with them in the profit: "This was not so," says the apostle; "I did not make a gain of you myself, nor by any of those whom I sent; nor did Titus, nor any others We walked by the same spirit and in the same steps." They all agreed in this matter to do them all the good they could, without being burdensome to them, to promote the gospel among them and make it as easy to them as possible. Or, this may be read with an interrogation, as utterly disclaiming any guile in himself and others towards them. 5. He was a man who did all things for edifying, *v.* 19. This was his great aim and design, to do good, to lay the foundation well, and then with care and diligence to build the superstructure. 6. He would not shrink from his duty for fear of displeasing them, though he was so careful to make himself easy to them. Therefore he was resolved to be faithful in reproving sin, though he was therein *found to be such as they would not, v.* 20. The apostle here mentions several sins that are too commonly found among professors of religion, and are very reprovable: *debates, envyings, wraths, strifes, backbitings, whisperings, swellings, tumults;* and, though those who are guilty of these sins can hardly bear to be reproved for them, yet faithful ministers must not fear offending the guilty by sharp reproofs, as they are needful, in public and in private. 7. He was grieved at the apprehension that he should find scandalous sins among them not duly repented of. This, he tells them, would be the cause of great humiliation and lamentation. Note, (1.) The falls and miscarriages of professors cannot but be a humbling consideration to a good minister; and God sometimes takes this way to humble those who might be under temptation to be lifted up: *I fear lest my God will humble me among you.* (2.) We have reason to bewail those who sin and do not repent, to *bewail many that have sinned, and have not repented, v.* 21. If these have not, as yet, grace to mourn and lament their own case, their case is the more lamentable; and those who love God, and love them, should mourn for them.

CHAP. XIII.

In this chapter the apostle threatens to be severe against obstinate sinners, and assigns the reason thereof (ver. 1—6); then he makes a suitable prayer to God on the behalf of the Corinthians, with the reasons inducing him thereto (ver. 7—10), and concludes his epistle with a valediction and a benediction, ver. 11—14.

THIS *is* the third *time* I am coming
to you. In the mouth of two
or three witnesses shall every word
be established. 2 I told you before,
and foretel you, as if I were present,
the second time; and being absent
now I write to them which heretofore
have sinned, and to all other, that, if
I come again, I will not spare: 3
Since ye seek a proof of Christ speaking in me, which to you-ward is not
weak, but is mighty in you. 4 For
though he was crucified through weakness, yet he liveth by the power of
God. For we also are weak in him,
but we shall live with him by the power
of God toward you. 5 Examine
yourselves, whether ye be in the
faith; prove your own selves. Know
ye not your own selves, how that
Jesus Christ is in you, except ye be
reprobates? 6 But I trust ye shall
know that we are not reprobates.

In these verses observe,

I. The apostle threatens to be severe against obstinate sinners when he should come to Corinth, having now sent to them a first and second epistle, with proper admonitions and exhortations, in order to reform what was amiss among them. Concerning this we may notice, 1. The caution with which he proceeded in his censures: he was not hasty in using severity, but gave a first and second admonition. So some understand his words (*v* 1): *This is the third time I am coming to you,* referring to his first and second epistles, by which he admonished them, as if he were present with them, though in person he was absent, *v.* 2. According to this interpretation, these two epistles are the witnesses he means in the first verse, referring rather to the direction of our Saviour (Matt. xviii. 16) concerning the manner how Christians should deal with offenders before they proceed to extremity than to the law of Moses (Deut. xvii. 6; xix. 15) for the behaviour of judges in criminal matters. We should go, or send, to our brother, once and again, to tell him of his fault. Thus the apostle had told these Corinthians before, in his former epistle, and now he tells them, or *writes to those who heretofore had sinned, and to all others,* giving warning unto all before he came in person *the third time,* to exercise severity against scandalous offenders. Others think that the apostle had designed and prepared for his journey to Corinth twice already, but was providentially hindered, and now informs them of his intentions a third time to come to them. However this be, it is observable that he kept an account how often he endeavoured, and what pains he took with these Corinthians for their good: and we may be sure that an account is kept in heaven, and we must be reckoned with another day for the helps we have had for our souls, and how we have improved them. 2. The threatening itself: *That if* (or when) *he came again* (in person) *he would not spare* obstinate sinners, and such as were impenitent, in their scandalous enormities. He had told them before, he feared *God would humble him among them,* because he should find some who *had sinned and had not repented;* and now he declares he would not spare such, but would inflict church-censures upon them, which are thought to have been accompanied in those early times with visible and extraordinary tokens of divine displeasure. Note, Though it is God's gracious method to bear long with sinners, yet he will not bear always; at length he will come, and will not spare those who remain obstinate and impenitent, notwithstanding all his methods to reclaim and reform them.

II. The apostle assigns a reason why he would be thus severe, namely, for *a proof of Christ's speaking in him,* which they *sought after, v.* 3. The evidence of his apostleship was necessary for the credit, confirmation, and success, of the gospel he preached; and therefore such as denied this were justly and severely to be censured. It was the design of the false teachers to make the Corinthians call this matter into question, of which yet they had not weak, but strong and mighty proofs (*v.* 3), notwithstanding the mean figure he made in the world and the contempt which by some was cast upon him. Even as Christ himself *was crucified through weakness,* or appeared in his crucifixion as a weak and contemptible person, *but liveth by the power of God,* or in his resurrection and life manifests his divine power (*v.* 4), so the apostles, how mean and contemptible soever they appeared to the world, did yet, as instruments, manifest the power of God, and particularly the power of his grace, in converting the world to Christianity. And therefore, as a proof to those who among the *Corinthians sought a proof of* Christ's speaking in the apostle, he puts them upon proving their Christianity (*v.* 5): *Examine yourselves,* &c. Hereby he intimates that, if they could prove their own Christianity, this would be a proof of his apostleship; for if they were in the faith, if Jesus Christ was in them, this was a proof that Christ spoke in him, because it was by his ministry that they did believe. He had been not only an instructor, but a father to them. He had begotten them again by the gospel of Christ. Now it could not be imagined that a divine power should go along with his ministrations if he had not his commission from on high. If therefore they could prove themselves *not to be reprobates,* not to be rejected of Christ, *he trusted they would know that he was not a reprobate* (*v.* 6), not disowned by Christ. What the apostle here says of the duty of the Corinthians to *examine themselves,* &c., with the particular view already mentioned, is applicable to the great duty of all who call themselves Christians, to examine themselves concerning their spiritual state. We should examine whether we be in the faith, because it is a matter in which we may be easily deceived, and wherein a deceit is highly dangerous: we are therefore concerned to *prove our own selves,* to put the question to our own souls, whether Christ be in us, or not; and *Christ is in us, except we be reprobates:* so that either we are true Christians or we are great cheats; and what a reproachful thing is it for a man not to know himself, not to know his own mind!

7 Now I pray to God that ye do
no evil; not that we should appear
approved, but that ye should do that
which is honest, though we be as
reprobates. 8 For we can do nothing against the truth, but for the
truth. 9 For we are glad, when we
are weak, and ye are strong: and this
also we wish, *even* your perfection.
10 Therefore I write these things
being absent, lest being present I
should use sharpness, according to
the power which the Lord hath given
me to edification, and not to destruction.

Here we have,

I. The apostle's prayer to God on the behalf of the Corinthians, that they might *do no evil, v.* 7. This is the most desirable thing we can ask of God, both for ourselves and for our friends, to be kept from sin, that we and they may do no evil; and it is most needful that we often pray to God for his grace to keep us, because without this we cannot keep ourselves. We are more concerned to pray that we may not do evil than that we may not suffer evil.

II. The reasons why the apostle put up this prayer to God on behalf of the Corinthians, which reasons have a special reference to their case, and the subject-matter about which he was writing to them. Observe, he tells them, 1. It was not so much for his own personal reputation as for the honour of religion: "*Not that we should appear approved, but that you should do that which is honest,* or decent, and for the credit of religion, though we should be reproached and vilified, and accounted as reprobates," *v.* 7. Note, (1.) The great desire of faithful ministers of the gospel is that the gospel they preach may be honoured, however their persons may be vilified. (2.) The best way to adorn our holy religion is *to do that which is honest,* and of good report, to walk as becomes the gospel of Christ. 2. Another reason was this: that they might be free from all blame and censure when he should come to them. This is intimated in *v.* 8, *We can do nothing against the truth, but for the truth.* If therefore they did not do evil, nor act contrary to their profession of the gospel, the apostle had no power nor authority to punish them. He had said before (*ch.* x. 8) and says here (*v.* 10) that the power which the Lord had given him was to edification, not to destruction; so that, although the apostle had great powers committed to him for the credit and advancement of the gospel, yet he could not do any thing to the disparagement of the truth, nor the discouragement of those who obeyed it. He could not, that is, he would not, he dared not, he had no commission to act against the truth; and it is remarkable how the apostle did rejoice in this blessed impotency: "*We are glad,*" says he (*v.* 9), "*when we are weak and you are strong;* that is, that we have no power to censure those who are strong in faith and fruitful in good works." Some understand this passage thus: "Though we are weak through persecutions and contempt, we bear it patiently, and also joyfully, while we see that you are strong, that you are prosperous in holiness, and persevering in well-doing." For, 3. He desired their perfection (*v.* 9); that is, that they might be sincere, and aim at perfection (sincerity is our gospel-perfection), or else he wished there might be a thorough reformation among them. He not only desired that they might be kept from sin, but also that they might grow in grace, and increase in holiness, and that all that was amiss among them might be rectified and reformed. This was the great end of his writing this epistle, and that freedom he used with them by *writing these things* (those friendly admonitions and warnings), *being absent, that so, being present, he should not use sharpness* (*v.* 10), that is, not proceed to the utmost extremity in the exercise of the power which the Lord had given him as an apostle, *to revenge all disobedience, ch.* x. 6.

11 Finally, brethren, farewell. Be
perfect, be of good comfort, be of one
mind, live in peace; and the God of
love and peace shall be with you. 12
Greet one another with a holy kiss.
13 All the saints salute you. 14 The
grace of the Lord Jesus Christ, and
the love of God, and the communion
of the Holy Ghost, *be* with you all.
Amen.

Thus the apostle concludes this epistle with,

I. A valediction. He gives them a parting farewell, and takes his leave of them for the present, with hearty good wishes for their spiritual welfare. In order to this,

1. He gives them several good exhortations. (1.) To be perfect, or to be knit together in love, which would tend greatly to their advantage as a church, or Christian society. (2.) To be of good comfort under all the sufferings and persecutions they might endure for the cause of Christ, or any calamities and disappointments they might meet with in the world. (3.) To be of one mind, which would greatly tend to their comfort; for the more easy we are with our brethren the more ease we shall have in our own souls. The apostle would have them, as far as was possible, to be of the same opinion and judgment; however, if this could not be attained, yet, (4.) He exhorts them to live in peace, that difference in opinion should not cause an alienation of affections—that they should be at peace among themselves. He would have all the schisms that were among them healed, that there should be no more contention and wrath found among them, to prevent which they should avoid *debates, envyings, backbitings, whisperings,* and such like enemies to peace.

2. He encourages them with the promise of God's presence among them: *The God of love and peace shall be with you, v.* 11. Note, (1.) God is the God of love and peace. He is the author of peace, and lover of concord. He hath loved us, and is willing to be at peace with us; he commands us to love him, and to be reconciled to him, and also that we love one another, and be at peace among ourselves. (2.) God will be with those who live in love and peace. He will love those who love peace; he will dwell with them here, and they shall dwell with him for ever. Such shall have God's gracious presence here, and be admitted to his glorious presence hereafter.

3. He gives directions to them to salute each other, and sends kind salutations to them from those who were with him, *v.* 12, 13. He would have them testify their affection to one another by the sacred rite of a kiss of charity, which was then used, but has long been disused, to prevent all occasions of wantonness and impurity, in the more declining and degenerate state of the church.

II. The apostolical benediction (*v.* 14): *The grace of the Lord Jesus Christ, and the love of God, and the communion of the Holy Ghost, be with you all.* Thus the apostle concludes his epistle, and thus it is usual and proper to dismiss worshipping assemblies. This plainly proves the doctrine of the gospel, and is an acknowledgment that Father, Son, and Spirit, are three distinct persons, yet but one God; and herein the same, that they are the fountain of all blessings to men. It likewise intimates our duty, which is to have an eye by faith to Father, Son, and Holy

Ghost—to live in a continual regard to the three persons in the Trinity, into whose name we were baptized, and in whose name we are blessed. This is a very solemn benediction, and we should give all diligence to inherit this blessing. The grace of Christ, the love of God, and the communion (or communication) of the Holy Ghost: the grace of Christ as Redeemer, the love of God who sent the Redeemer, and all the communications of this grace and love, which come to us by the Holy Ghost; it is the communications of the Holy Ghost that qualify us for an interest in the grace of Christ, and the love of God: and we can desire no more to make us happy than the grace of Christ, the love of God, and the communion of the Holy Ghost. *Amen.*

AN

EXPOSITION,

WITH PRACTICAL OBSERVATIONS,

OF THE EPISTLE OF ST. PAUL TO

THE GALATIANS.

This epistle of Paul is directed not to the church or churches of a single city, as some others are, but of a country or province, for so Galatia was. It is very probable that these Galatians were first converted to the Christian faith by his ministry; or, if he was not the instrument of planting, yet at least he had been employed in watering these churches, as is evident from this epistle itself, and also from Acts xviii. 23, where we find him going over all the country of Galatia and Phrygia in order, strengthening all the disciples. While he was with them, they had expressed the greatest esteem and affection both for his person and ministry; but he had not been long absent from them before some judaizing teachers got in among them, by whose arts and insinuations they were soon drawn into a meaner opinion both of the one and of the other. That which these false teachers chiefly aimed at was to draw them off from the truth as it is in Jesus, particularly in the great doctrine of justification, which they grossly perverted, by asserting the necessity of joining the observance of the law of Moses with faith in Christ in order to it: and, the better to accomplish this their design, they did all they could to lessen the character and reputation of the apostle, and to raise up their own on the ruins of his, representing him as one who, if he was to be owned as an apostle, yet was much inferior to others, and particularly who deserved not such a regard as Peter, James, and John, whose followers, it is likely, they pretended to be: and in both these attempts they had but too great success. This was the occasion of his writing this epistle, wherein he expresses his great concern that they had suffered themselves to be so soon turned aside from the faith of the gospel, vindicates his own character and authority as an apostle against the aspersions of his enemies, showing that his mission and doctrine were both divine, and that he was not, upon any account, *behind the very chief of the apostles*, 2 Cor. xi. 5. He then sets himself to assert and maintain the great gospel doctrine of justification by faith without the works of the law, and to obviate some difficulties that might be apt to arise in their minds concerning it: and, having established this important doctrine, he exhorts them to stand fast in the liberty wherewith Christ had made them free, cautions them against the abuse of this liberty, gives them several very needful counsels and directions and then concludes the epistle by giving them a just description of those false teachers by whom they had been ensnared, and, on the contrary, of his own temper and behaviour. In all this his great scope and design were to recover those who had been perverted, to settle those who might be wavering, and to confirm such among them as had kept their integrity.

CHAP. I.

In this chapter, after the preface or introduction (v. 1—5), the apostle severely reproves these churches for their defection from the faith (ver. 6—9), and then proves his own apostleship, which his enemies had brought them to question, I. From his end and design in preaching the gospel, ver. 10. II. From his having received it by immediate revelation, ver. 11, 12. For the proof of which he acquaints them, 1. What his former conversation was, ver. 13, 14. 2. How he was converted, and called to the apostleship, ver. 15, 16. 3. How he behaved himself afterwards, ver. 16, to the end.

PAUL, an apostle, (not of men,
neither by man, but by Jesus
Christ, and God the Father, who
raised him from the dead;) 2 And
all the brethren which are with me,
unto the churches of Galatia: 3
Grace *be* to you and peace from God
the Father, and *from* our Lord Jesus
Christ, 4 Who gave himself for our
sins, that he might deliver us from

this present evil world, according to
the will of God and our Father: 5
To whom *be* glory for ever and ever.
Amen.

In these verses we have the preface or introduction to the epistle, where observe,

I. The person or persons from whom this epistle is sent—from Paul *an apostle,* &c., *and all the brethren that were with him.* 1. The epistle is sent from Paul; he only was the penman of it. And, because there were some among the Galatians who endeavoured to lessen his character and authority, in the very front of it he gives a general account both of his office and of the manner in which he was called to it, which afterwards, in this and the following chapter, he enlarges more upon. As to his office, he was an apostle. He is not afraid to style himself so, though his enemies would scarcely allow him this title: and, to let them see that he did not assume this character without just ground, he acquaints them how he was called to this dignity and office, and assures them that his commission to it was wholly divine, for he was an apostle, *not of man, neither by man;* he had not the common call of an ordinary minister, but an extraordinary call from heaven to this office. He neither received his qualification for it, nor his designation to it, by the mediation of men, but had both the one and the other directly from above; for he was an apostle *by Jesus Christ,* he had his instructions and commission immediately from him, and consequently from *God the Father,* who was one with him in respect of his divine nature, and who had appointed him, as Mediator, to be the apostle and high priest of our profession, and as such to authorize others to this office. He adds, *Who raised him from the dead,* both to acquaint us that herein God the Father gave a public testimony to Christ's being his Son and the promised Messiah, and also that, as his call to the apostleship was immediately from Christ, so it was after his resurrection from the dead, and when he had entered upon his exalted state; so that he had reason to look upon himself, not only as standing upon a level with the other apostles, but as in some sort preferred above them; for, whereas they were called by him when on earth, he had his call from him when in heaven. Thus does the apostle, being constrained to it by his adversaries, magnify his office, which shows that though men should by no means be proud of any authority they are possessed of, yet at certain times and upon certain occasions it may become needful to assert it. But, 2. He joins all the brethren that were with him in the inscription of the epistle, and writes in their name as well as his own. By *the brethren that were with him* may be understood either the Christians in common of that place where he now was, or such as were employed as ministers of the gospel. These, notwithstanding his own superior character and attainments, he is ready to own as his brethren; and, though he alone wrote the epistle, yet he joins them with himself in the inscription of it. Herein, as he shows his own great modesty and humility, and how remote he was from an assuming temper, so he might do this to dispose these churches to a greater regard to what he wrote, since hereby it would appear that he had their concurrence with him in the doctrine which he had preached, and was now about to confirm, and that it was no other than what was both published and professed by others as well as himself.

II. To whom this epistle is sent—*to the churches of Galatia.* There were several churches at that time in this country, and it should seem that all of them were more or less corrupted through the arts of those seducers who had crept in among them; and therefore Paul, on whom *came daily the care of all the churches,* being deeply affected with their state, and concerned for their recovery to the faith and establishment in it, writes this epistle to them. He directs it to all of them, as being all more or less concerned in the matter of it; and he gives them the name of *churches,* though they had done enough to forfeit it, for corrupt churches are never allowed to be churches: no doubt there were some among them who still continued in the faith, and he was not without hope that others might be recovered to it.

III. The apostolical benediction, *v.* 3. Herein the apostle, and the brethren who were with him, wish these churches *grace and peace from God the Father, and from the Lord Jesus Christ.* This is the usual blessing wherewith he blesses the churches in the name of the Lord—*grace and peace.* Grace includes God's good-will towards us and his good work upon us; and peace implies in it all that inward comfort, or outward prosperity, which is really needful for us; and they come from God the Father as the fountain, through Jesus Christ as the channel of conveyance. Both these the apostle wishes for these Christians. But we may observe, First grace, and then peace, for there can be no true peace without grace. Having mentioned the Lord Jesus Christ, he cannot pass without enlarging upon his love; and therefore adds (*v.* 4), *Who gave himself for our sins, that he might deliver,* &c. Jesus Christ gave himself for our sins, as a great sacrifice to make atonement for us; this the justice of God required, and to this he freely submitted for our sakes. One great end hereof was *to deliver us from this present evil world;* not only to redeem us from the wrath of God, and the curse of the law, but also to recover us from the corruption that is in the world through lust, and to rescue us from the vicious practices and customs of it, unto which we are naturally enslaved; and possibly also to set us free from the Mosaic constitution, for so αἰῶν οὗτος is used, 1 Cor. ii. 6, 8

From this we may note, 1. This present world is an evil world: it has become so by the sin of man, and it is so on account of the sin and sorrow with which it abounds and the many snares and temptations to which we are exposed as long as we continue in it. But, 2. Jesus Christ has died to deliver us from this present evil world, not presently to remove his people out of it, but to rescue them from the power of it, to keep them from the evil of it, and in due time to possess them of another and better world. This, the apostle informs us, he has done *according to the will of God and our Father.* In offering up himself a sacrifice for this end and purpose, he acted by the appointment of the Father, as well as with his own free consent; and therefore we have the greatest reason to depend upon the efficacy and acceptableness of what he has done and suffered for us; yea, hence we have encouragement to look upon God as our Father, for thus the apostle here represents him: as he is the Father of our Lord Jesus, so in and through him he is also the Father of all true believers, as our blessed Saviour himself acquaints us (John xx. 17), when he tells his disciples that he was ascending to his Father and their Father.

The apostle, having thus taken notice of the great love wherewith Christ hath loved us, concludes this preface with a solemn ascription of praise and glory to him (*v.* 5): *To whom be glory for ever and ever. Amen.* Intimating that on this account he is justly entitled to our highest esteem and regard. Or this doxology may be considered as referring both to God the Father and our Lord Jesus Christ, from whom he had just before been wishing grace and peace. They are both the proper objects of our worship and adoration, and all honour and glory are perpetually due to them, both on account of their own infinite excellences, and also on account of the blessings we receive from them.

6 I marvel that ye are so soon removed from him that called you into
the grace of Christ unto another
gospel: 7 Which is not another;
but there be some that trouble you,
and would pervert the gospel of
Christ. 8 But though we, or an
angel from heaven, preach any other
gospel unto you than that which we
have preached unto you, let him be
accursed. 9 As we said before, so
say I now again, If any *man* preach
any other gospel unto you than that
ye have received, let him be accursed.

Here the apostle comes to the body of the epistle; and he begins it with a more general reproof of these churches for their unsteadiness in the faith, which he afterwards, in some following parts of it, enlarges more upon. Here we may observe,

I. How much he was concerned at their defection: *I marvel,* &c. It filled him at once with the greatest surprise and sorrow. Their sin and folly were that they did not hold fast the doctrine of Christianity as it had been preached to them, but suffered themselves to be removed from the purity and simplicity of it. And there were several things by which their defection was greatly aggravated; as, 1. That they were *removed from him that had called them;* not only from the apostle, who had been the instrument of calling them into the fellowship of the gospel, but from God himself, by whose order and direction the gospel was preached to them, and they were invited to a participation of the privileges of it: so that herein they had been guilty of a great abuse of his kindness and mercy towards them. 2. That they had been *called into the grace of Christ.* As the gospel which had been preached to them was the most glorious discovery of divine grace and mercy in Christ Jesus; so thereby they had been called to partake of the greatest blessings and benefits, such as justification, and reconciliation with God here, and eternal life and happiness hereafter. These our Lord Jesus has purchased for us at the expense of his precious blood, and freely bestows upon all who sincerely accept of him: and therefore, in proportion to the greatness of the privilege they enjoyed, such were their sin and folly in deserting it and suffering themselves to be drawn off from the established way of obtaining these blessings. 3. That they were *so soon removed.* In a very little time they lost that relish and esteem of this grace of Christ which they seemed to have, and too easily fell in with those who taught justification by the works of the law, as many did, who had been bred up in the opinions and notions of the Pharisees, which they mingled with the doctrine of Christ, and so corrupted it; and this, as it was an instance of their weakness, so it was a further aggravation of their guilt. 4. That they were removed to *another gospel, which yet was not another.* Thus the apostle represents the doctrine of these judaizing teachers; he calls it another gospel, because it opened a different way of justification and salvation from that which was revealed in the gospel, namely, by works, and not by faith in Christ. And yet he adds, "*Which is not another*—you will find it to be no gospel at all—not really another gospel, but the perverting of the gospel of Christ, and the overturning of the foundations of that"—whereby he intimates that those who go about to establish any other way to heaven than what the gospel of Christ has revealed are guilty of a gross perversion of it, and in the issue will find themselves wretchedly mistaken. Thus the apostle endeavours to impress upon these Galatians a due sense of their guilt in forsaking the gospel way of justification; and yet at the same time he tempers his reproof with mildness and tenderness towards them, and represents them as rather drawn into it by the arts and industry of some that troubled them than as coming into it of their own accord, which, though it did not excuse them, yet was some extenuation of their fault. And hereby he teaches us that, in reproving others, as we should be faithful, so we should also be gentle, and endeavour *to restore them in the spirit of meekness, ch.* vi. 1.

II. How confident he was that the gospel he had preached to them was the only true gospel. He was so fully persuaded of this that he pronounced an anathema upon those who pretended to preach any other gospel (*v.* 8), and, to let them see that this did not proceed from any rashness or intemperate zeal in him, he repeated it, *v.* 9. This will not justify our thundering out anathemas against those who differ from us in minor things. It is only against those who forge a new gospel, who overturn the foundation of the covenant of grace, by setting up the works of the law in the place of Christ's righteousness, and corrupting Christianity with Judaism, that Paul denounces this. He puts the case: "Suppose we should preach any other gospel; nay, suppose an angel from heaven should:" not as if it were possible for an angel from heaven to be the messenger of a lie; but it is expressed so the more to strengthen what he was about to say. "If you have any other gospel preached to you by any other person, under our name, or under colour of having it from an angel himself, you must conclude that you are imposed upon: and whoever preaches another gospel lays himself under a curse, and is in danger of laying you under it too."

10 For do I now persuade men, or
God? or do I seek to please men?
for if I yet pleased men, I should not
be the servant of Christ. 11 But I
certify you, brethren, that the gospel
which was preached of me is not
after man. 12 For I neither received
it of man, neither was I taught *it*, but
by the revelation of Jesus Christ. 13
For ye have heard of my conversation
in time past in the Jews' religion,
how that beyond measure I persecuted
the church of God, and wasted
it: 14 And profited in the Jews' religion
above many my equals in mine
own nation, being more exceedingly
zealous of the traditions of my fathers.
15 But when it pleased God, who
separated me from my mother's womb,
and called *me* by his grace, 16 To
reveal his Son in me, that I might
preach him among the heathen; immediately
I conferred not with flesh
and blood: 17 Neither went I up
to Jerusalem to them which were
apostles before me; but I went into
Arabia, and returned again unto Damascus.
18 Then after three years
I went up to Jerusalem to see Peter,
and abode with him fifteen days. 19
But other of the apostles saw I none
save James the Lord's brother. 20
Now the things which I write unto
you, behold, before God, I lie not.
21 Afterwards I came into the regions
of Syria and Cicilia; 22 And was
unknown by face unto the churches
of Judæa which were in Christ: 23
But they had heard only, That he
which persecuted us in times past
now preacheth the faith which once
he destroyed. 24 And they glorified
God in me.

What Paul had said more generally, in the preface of this epistle, he now proceeds more particularly to enlarge upon. There he had declared himself to be an apostle of Christ; and here he comes more directly to support his claim to that character and office. There were some in the churches of Galatia who were prevailed with to call this in question; for those who preached up the ceremonial law did all they could to lessen Paul's reputation, who preached the pure gospel of Christ to the Gentiles: and therefore he here sets himself to prove the divinity both of his mission and doctrine, that thereby he might wipe off the aspersions which his enemies had cast upon him, and recover these Christians into a better opinion of the gospel he had preached to them. This he gives sufficient evidence of,

I. From the scope and design of his ministry, which was *not to persuade men, but God,* &c. The meaning of this may be either that in his preaching the gospel he did not act in obedience to men, but God, who had called him to this work and office; or that his aim therein was to bring persons to the obedience, not of men, but of God. As he professed to act by a commission from God; so that which he chiefly aimed at was to promote his glory, by recovering sinners into a state of subjection to him. And as this was the great end he was pursuing, so, agreeably hereunto, *he did not seek to please men.* He did not, in his doctrine, accommodate himself to the humours of persons, either to gain their affection or to avoid their resentment; but his great care was to approve himself to God. The judaizing teachers, by whom these churches were corrupted, had discovered a very different temper; they mixed works with faith, and the law with the gospel, only to please the Jews, whom they were willing to court and keep in with, that they might escape persecution. But Paul was a man of another spirit; he was not so solicitous to please them, nor to mitigate their rage against him, as to alter the doctrine of Christ either to gain their favour or to avoid their fury. And he gives this very good reason for it, that, *if he yet pleased men, he would not be the servant of Christ.* These he knew were utterly inconsistent, and that no man could serve two such masters; and therefore, though he would not needlessly displease any, yet he dared not allow himself to gratify men at the expense of his faithfulness to Christ. Thus, from the sincerity of his aims and intentions in the discharge of his office, he proves that he was truly an apostle of Christ. And from this his temper and behaviour we may note, 1. That the great end which ministers of the gospel should aim at is to bring men to God. 2. That those who are faithful will not seek to please men, but to approve themselves to God. 3. That they must not be solicitous to please men, if they would approve themselves faithful servants to Christ. But, if this argument should not be thought sufficient, he goes on to prove his apostleship,

II. From the manner wherein he received the gospel which he preached to them, concerning which he assures them (*v.* 11, 12) that he had it not by information from others, but by revelation from heaven. One thing peculiar in the character of an apostle was that he had been called to, and instructed for, this office immediately by Christ himself. And in this he here shows that he was by no means defective, whatever his enemies might suggest to the contrary. Ordinary ministers, as they receive their call to preach the gospel by the mediation of others, so it is by means of the instruction and assistance of others that they are brought to the knowledge of it. But Paul acquaints them that he had his knowledge of the gospel, as well as his authority to preach it, directly from the Lord Jesus: the gospel which he preached was not *after man; he neither received it of man, nor was he taught it by man,* but by immediate inspiration, or revelation from Christ himself. This he was concerned to make out, to prove himself an apostle: and to this purpose,

1. He tells them what his education was, and what, accordingly, his conversation in time past had been, *v.* 13, 14. Particularly, he acquaints them that he had been brought up in the Jewish religion, and *that he had profited in it above many his equals of his own nation*—that *he had been exceedingly zealous of the traditions of the elders,* such doctrines and customs as had been invented by their fathers, and conveyed down from one generation to another; yea, to such a degree that, in his zeal for them, *he had beyond measure persecuted the church of God, and wasted it.* He had not only been a rejecter of the Christian religion, notwithstanding the many evident proofs that were given of its divine origin; but he had been a persecutor of it too, and had applied himself with the utmost violence and rage to destroy the professors of it. This Paul often takes notice of, for the magnifying of that free and rich grace which had wrought so wonderful a change in him, whereby of so great a sinner he was made a sincere penitent, and from a persecutor had become an apostle. And it was very fit to mention it here; for it would hence appear that he was not led to Christianity, as many others are, purely by education, since he had been bred up in an enmity and opposition to it; and they might reasonably suppose that it must be something very extraordinary which had made so great a change in him, which had conquered the prejudices of his education, and brought him not only to profess, but to preach, that doctrine, which he had before so vehemently opposed.

2. In how wonderful a manner he was turned from the error of his ways, brought to the knowledge and faith of Christ, and appointed to the office of an apostle, *v.* 15, 16. This was not done in an ordinary way, nor by ordinary means, but in an extraordinary manner; for, (1.) God had *separated him hereunto from his mother's womb:* the change that was wrought in him was in pursuance of a divine purpose concerning him, whereby he was appointed to be a Christian and an apostle, before he came into the world, or had done either good or evil. (2.) He was *called by his grace.* All who are savingly converted are called by the grace of God; their conversion is the effect of his good pleasure concerning them, and is effected by his power and grace in them. But there was something peculiar in the case of Paul, both in the suddenness and in the greatness of the change wrought in him, and also in the manner wherein it was effected, which was not by the mediation of others, as the instruments of it, but by Christ's personal appearance to him, and immediate operation upon him, whereby it was rendered a more special and extraordinary instance of divine power and favour. (3.) He had Christ *revealed in him.* He was not only revealed to him, but in him. It will but little avail us to have Christ revealed to us if he is not also revealed in us; but this was not the case of Paul. It pleased God *to reveal his Son in him,* to bring him to the knowledge of Christ and his gospel by special and immediate revelation. And, (4.) It was with this design, that he should preach him among the heathen; not only that he should embrace him himself, but preach him to others; so that he was both a Christian and an apostle by revelation.

3. He acquaints them how he behaved himself hereupon, from *v.* 16, to the end.

Being thus called to this work and office, *he conferred not with flesh and blood.* This may be taken more generally, and so we may learn from it that, when God calls us by his grace, we must not consult flesh and blood. But the meaning of it here is that he did not consult men; he did not apply to any others for their advice and direction; *neither did he go up to Jerusalem, to those that were apostles before him,* as though he needed to be approved by them, or to receive any further instructions or authority from them: but, instead of that, he steered another course, and *went into Arabia,* either as a place of retirement proper for receiving further divine revelations, or in order to preach the gospel there among the Gentiles, being appointed to be the apostle of the Gentiles; and thence *he returned again to Damascus,* where he had first begun his ministry, and whence he had with difficulty escaped the rage of his enemies, Acts ix. It was not till *three years after* his conversion that *he went up to Jerusalem, to see Peter;* and when he did so he made but a very short stay with him, no more than *fifteen days;* nor, while he was there, did he go much into conversation; for *others of the apostles he saw none, but James, the Lord's brother.* So that it could not well be pretended that he was indebted to any other either for his knowledge of the gospel or his authority to preach it; but it appeared that both his qualifications for, and his call to, the apostolic office were extraordinary and divine. This account being of importance, to establish his claim to this office, to remove the unjust censures of his adversaries, and to recover the Galatians from the impressions they had received to his prejudice, he confirms it by a solemn oath (*v.* 20), declaring, as in the presence of God, that what he had said was strictly true, and that he had not in the least falsified in what he had related, which, though it will not justify us in solemn appeals to God upon every occasion, yet shows that, in matters of weight and moment, this may sometimes not only be lawful, but duty. After this he acquaints them that *he came into the regions of Syria and Cilicia:* having made this short visit to Peter, he returns to his work again. He had no communication at that time with the *churches of Christ in Judea,* they had not so much as *seen his face; but, having heard that he who persecuted them in times past now preached the faith which he once destroyed, they glorified God* because of him; thanksgivings were rendered by many unto God on that behalf; the very report of this mighty change in him, as it filled them with joy, so it excited them to give glory to God on the account of it.

CHAP. II.

The apostle, in this chapter, continues the relation of his past life and conduct, which he had begun in the former; and, by some further instances of what had passed between him and the other apostles, makes it appear that he was not beholden to them either for his knowledge of the gospel or his authority as an apostle, as his adversaries would insinuate; but, on the contrary, that he was owned and approved even by them, as having an equal commission with them to this office. I. He particularly informs them of another journey which he took to Jerusalem many years after the former, and how he behaved himself at that time, ver. 1—10. And, II. Gives them an account of another interview he had with the apostle Peter at Antioch, and how he was obliged to behave himself towards him there. From the subject-matter of that conversation, he proceeds to discourse on the great doctrine of justification by faith in Christ, without the works of the law, which it was the main design of this epistle to establish, and which he enlarges more upon in the two following chapters.

THEN fourteen years after I went
up again to Jerusalem with Barnabas, and took Titus with *me* also.
2 And I went up by revelation, and
communicated unto them that gospel
which I preach among the Gentiles,
but privately to them which were of
reputation, lest by any means I should
run, or had run, in vain. 3 But
neither Titus, who was with me,
being a Greek, was compelled to be
circumcised: 4 And that because
of false brethren unawares brought
in, who came in privily to spy out
our liberty which we have in Christ
Jesus, that they might bring us into
bondage: 5 To whom we gave place
by subjection, no, not for an hour;
that the truth of the gospel might
continue with you. 6 But of those
who seemed to be somewhat, whatsoever they were, it maketh no matter
to me: God accepteth no man's person: for they who seemed *to be somewhat* in conference added nothing to
me: 7 But contrariwise, when they
saw that the gospel of the uncircumcision was committed unto me, as *the
gospel* of the circumcision was unto
Peter; 8 (For he that wrought
effectually in Peter to the apostleship
of the circumcision, the same was
mighty in me toward the Gentiles:)
9 And when James, Cephas, and
John, who seemed to be pillars, perceived the grace that was given unto
me, they gave to me and Barnabas
the right hands of fellowship; that
we *should go* unto the heathen, and
they unto the circumcision. 10 Only
they would that we should remember
the poor; the same which I also was
forward to do.

It should seem, by the account Paul gives of himself in this chapter, that, from the very first preaching and planting of Christianity, there was a difference of apprehension between those Christians who had first been Jews and those who had first been Gentiles. Many of those who had first been Jews retained a regard to the ceremonial law, and strove to keep up the reputation of that; but those who had first been Gentiles had no regard to the law of Moses, but took pure Christianity as perfective of natural religion, and resolved to adhere to that. Peter was the apostle of the circumcision, and preached the gospel to them; and the ceremonial law, though dead with Christ, yet not being as yet buried, he connived at the respect kept up for it. But Paul was the apostle of the Gentiles; and, though he was a Hebrew of the Hebrews, yet he adhered to pure Christianity. Now in this chapter he tells us what passed between him and the other apostles, and particularly between him and Peter hereupon.

In these verses he informs us of another journey which he took to Jerusalem, and of what passed between him and the other apostles there, *v.* 1—10. Here he acquaints us,

I. With some circumstances relating to this his journey thither. As particularly, 1. With the time of it: that it was not till *fourteen years* after the former (mentioned *ch.* i. 18), or, as others choose to understand it, from his conversion, or from the death of Christ. It was an instance of the great goodness of God that so useful a person was for so many years preserved in his work. And it was some evidence that he had no dependence upon the other apostles, but had an equal authority with them, that he had been so long absent from them, and was all the while employed in preaching and propagating pure Christianity, without being called into question by them for it, which it may be thought he would have been, had he been inferior to them, and his doctrine disapproved by them. 2. With his companions in it: *he went up with Barnabas, and took with him Titus also.* If the journey here spoken of was the same with that recorded Acts xv. (as many think), then we have a plain reason why Barnabas went along with him; for he was chosen by the Christians at Antioch to be his companion and associate in the affair he went about. But, as it does not appear that Titus was put into the same commission with him, so the chief reason of his taking him along with him seems to have been to let those at Jerusalem see that he was neither ashamed nor afraid to own the doctrine which he had constantly preached; for though Titus had now become not only a convert to the Christian faith, but a preacher of it too, yet he was by birth a Gentile and uncircumcised, and therefore, by making him his companion, it appeared that their doctrine and practice were of a piece, and that as he had preached the non-necessity of circumcision, and observing the law of Moses, so he was ready to own and converse with those who were uncircumcised. 3. With the reason of it, which was a divine revelation he had concerning it: *he went up by revelation;* not of his own head, much less as being summoned to appear there, but by special order and direction from Heaven. It was a privilege with which this apostle was often favoured to be under a special divine direction in his motions and undertakings; and, though this is what we have no reason to expect, yet it should teach us, in every thing of moment we go about, to endeavour, as far as we are capable, to see our way made plain before us, and to commit ourselves to the guidance of Providence.

II. He gives us an account of his behaviour while he was at Jerusalem, which was such as made it appear that he was not in the least inferior to the other apostles, but that both his authority and qualifications were every way equal to theirs. He particularly acquaints us,

1. That *he there communicated the gospel to them, which he preached among the Gentiles, but privately,* &c. Here we may observe both the faithfulness and prudence of our great apostle. (1.) His faithfulness in giving them a free and fair account of the doctrine which he had all along preached among the Gentiles, and was still resolved to preach—that of pure Christianity, free from all mixtures of Judaism. This he knew was a doctrine that would be ungrateful to many there, and yet he was not afraid to own it, but in a free and friendly manner lays it open before them and leaves them to judge whether or no it was not the true gospel of Christ. And yet, (2.) He uses prudence and caution herein, for fear of giving offence. He chooses rather to do it in a more private than in a public way, and *to those that were of reputation,* that is, to the apostles themselves, or to the chief among the Jewish Christians, rather than more openly and promiscuously to all, because, when he came to Jerusalem, *there were multitudes that believed, and yet continued zealous for the law,* Acts xxi. 20. And the reason of this his caution was *lest he should run, or had run, in vain,* lest he should stir up opposition against himself and thereby either the success of his past labours should be lessened, or his future usefulness be obstructed; for nothing more hinders the progress of the gospel than differences of opinion about the doctrines of it, especially when they occasion quarrels and contentions among the professors of it, as they too usually do. It was enough to his purpose to have his doctrine owned by those who were of greatest authority, whether it was approved by others or not. And therefore, to avoid offence, he judges it safest to communicate it privately to them, and not in public to the whole church. This conduct of the apostle may teach all, and especially ministers, how much need they have of prudence, and how careful they should be to use it upon all occasions, as far as is consistent with their faithfulness.

2. That in his practice he firmly adhered to the doctrine which he had preached. Paul was a man of resolution, and would adhere

to his principles; and therefore, though he had Titus with him, who was a Greek, yet he would not suffer him to be circumcised, because he would not betray the doctrine of Christ, as he had preached it to the Gentiles. It does not appear that the apostles at all insisted upon this; for, though they connived at the use of circumcision among the Jewish converts, yet they were not for imposing it upon the Gentiles. But there were others who did, whom the apostle here calls *false brethren,* and concerning whom he informs us that they were *unawares brought in,* that is, into the church, or into their company, and that they came only to *spy out their liberty which they had in Christ Jesus,* or to see whether Paul would stand up in defence of that freedom from the ceremonial law which he had taught as the doctrine of the gospel, and represented as the privilege of those who embraced the Christian religion. Their design herein was *to bring them into bondage,* which they would have effected could they have gained the point they aimed at; for, had they prevailed with Paul and the other apostles to have circumcised Titus, they would easily have imposed circumcision upon other Gentiles, and so have brought them under the bondage of the law of Moses. But Paul, seeing their design, would by no means yield to them; he would not *give place by subjection, no, not for an hour,* not in this one single instance; and the reason of it was *that the truth of the gospel might continue with them*—that the Gentile Christians, and particularly the Galatians, might have it preserved to them pure and entire, and not corrupted with the mixtures of Judaism, as it would have been had he yielded in this matter. Circumcision was at that time a thing indifferent, and what in some cases might be complied with without sin; and accordingly we find even Paul himself sometimes giving way to it, as in the case of Timothy, Acts xvi. 3. But when it is insisted on as necessary, and his consenting to it, though only in a single instance, is likely to be improved as giving countenance to such an imposition, he has too great a concern for the purity and liberty of the gospel, to submit to it; he would not yield to those who were for the Mosaic rites and ceremonies, but would stand fast in the liberty wherewith Christ hath made us free, which conduct of his may give us occasion to observe that what under some circumstances may lawfully be complied with, yet, when that cannot be done without betraying the truth, or giving up the liberty, of the gospel, it ought to be refused.

3. That, though he conversed with the other apostles, yet he did not receive any addition to his knowledge or authority from them, *v.* 6. By *those who seemed to be somewhat* he means the other apostles, particularly James, Peter, and John, whom he afterwards mentions by name, *v.* 9. And concerning these he grants that they were deservedly had in reputation by all, that they were looked upon (and justly too) as pillars of the church, who were set not only for its ornament, but for its support, and that on some accounts they might seem to have the advantage of him, in that they had seen Christ in the flesh, which he had not, and were apostles before him, yea, even while he continued a persecutor. But yet, *whatever they were, it was no matter to him.* This was no prejudice to his being equally an apostle with them; for God does not accept the persons of men on the account of any such outward advantages. As he had called them to this office, so he was at liberty to qualify others for it, and to employ them in it. And it was evident in this case that he had done so; for *in conference they added nothing to him,* they told him nothing but what he before knew by revelation, nor could they except against the doctrine which he communicated to them, whence it appeared that he was not at all inferior to them, but was as much called and qualified to be an apostle as they themselves were.

4. That the issue of this conversation was that the other apostles were fully convinced of his divine mission and authority, and accordingly acknowledged him as their fellow-apostle, *v.* 7—10. They were not only satisfied with his doctrine, but they saw a divine power attending him, both in preaching it and in working miracles for the confirmation of it: *that he who wrought effectually in Peter to the apostleship of the circumcision, the same was mighty in him towards the Gentiles.* And hence they justly concluded *that the gospel of the uncircumcision was committed to Paul, as the gospel of the circumcision was to Peter.* And therefore, *perceiving the grace that was given to him* (that he was designed to the honour and office of an apostle as well as themselves) *they gave unto him and Barnabas the right hand of fellowship,* a symbol whereby they acknowledged their equality with them, and agreed that *these should go to the heathen, while they continued to preach to the circumcision,* as judging it most agreeable to the mind of Christ, and most conducive to the interest of Christianity, so to divide their work. And thus this meeting ended in an entire harmony and agreement; they approved both Paul's doctrine and conduct, they were fully satisfied in him, heartily embraced him as an apostle of Christ, and had nothing further to add, *only that they would remember the poor,* which of his own accord *he was very forward to do.* The Christians of Judea were at that time labouring under great wants and difficulties; and the apostles, out of their compassion to them and concern for them, recommend their case to Paul, that he should use his interest with the Gentile churches to procure a supply for them. This was a reasonable request; *for, if the Gentiles were made partakers of their spiritual things, it was their duty to minister to them in carnal things,* as Rom. xv.

27. And he very readily falls in with it, whereby he showed his charitable and catholic disposition, how ready he was to own the Jewish converts as brethren, though many of them could scarcely allow the like favour to the converted Gentiles, and that mere difference of opinion was no reason with him why he should not endeavour to relieve and help them. Herein he has given us an excellent pattern of Christian charity, and has taught us that we should by no means confine it to those who are just of the same sentiments with us, but be ready to extend it to all whom we have reason to look upon as the disciples of Christ.

11 But when Peter was come to
Antioch, I withstood him to the face,
because he was to be blamed. 12
For before that certain came from
James, he did eat with the Gentiles:
but when they were come, he withdrew and separated himself, fearing
them which were of the circumcision.
13 And the other Jews dissembled
likewise with him; insomuch that
Barnabas also was carried away with
their dissimulation. 14 But when I
saw that they walked not uprightly
according to the truth of the gospel,
I said unto Peter before *them* all, If
thou, being a Jew, livest after the
manner of the Gentiles, and not as
do the Jews, why compellest thou
the Gentiles to live as do the Jews?
15 We *who are* Jews by nature, and
not sinners of the Gentiles, 16 Knowing that a man is not justified by the
works of the law, but by the faith of
Jesus Christ, even we have believed
in Jesus Christ, that we might be
justified by the faith of Christ, and
not by the works of the law: for by
the works of the law shall no flesh be
justified. 17 But if, while we seek
to be justified by Christ, we ourselves
also are found sinners, *is* therefore
Christ the minister of sin? God
forbid. 18 For if I build again the
things which I destroyed, I make
myself a transgressor. 19 For I
through the law am dead to the law,
that I might live unto God. 20 I
am crucified with Christ: nevertheless I live; yet not I, but Christ
liveth in me: and the life which I
now live in the flesh I live by the
faith of the Son of God, who loved
me, and gave himself for me. 21 I
do not frustrate the grace of God:
for if righteousness *come* by the law,
then Christ is dead in vain.

I. From the account which Paul gives of what passed between him and the other apostles at Jerusalem, the Galatians might easily discern both the falseness of what his enemies had insinuated against him and their own folly and weakness in departing from that gospel which he had preached to them. But to give the greater weight to what he had already said, and more fully to fortify them against the insinuations of the judaizing teachers, he acquaints them with another interview which he had with the apostle Peter at Antioch, and what passed between them there, *v.* 11—14. Antioch was one of the chief churches of the Gentile Christians, as Jerusalem was of those Christians who turned from Judaism to the faith of Christ. There is no colour of reason for the supposition that Peter was bishop of Antioch. If he had, surely Paul would not have withstood him in his own church, as we here find he did; but, on the contrary, it is here spoken of as an occasional visit which he made thither. In their other meeting, there had been good harmony and agreement. Peter and the other apostles had both acknowledged Paul's commission and approved his doctrine, and they parted very good friends. But in this Paul finds himself obliged to oppose Peter, for *he was to be blamed*, a plain evidence that he was not inferior to him, and consequently of the weakness of the pope's pretence to supremacy and infallibility, as the successor of Peter. Here we may observe,

1. Peter's fault. When he came among the Gentile churches, he complied with them, and did eat with them, though they were not circumcised, agreeably to the instructions which were given in particular to him (Acts x.), when he was warned by the heavenly vision *to call nothing common or unclean.* But, when there came some Jewish Christians from Jerusalem, he grew more shy of the Gentiles, only to humour those of the circumcision and for fear of giving them offence, which doubtless was to the great grief and discouragement of the Gentile churches. Then *he withdrew, and separated himself.* His fault herein had a bad influence upon others, for *the other Jews also dissembled with him;* though before they might be better disposed, yet now, from his example, they took on them to scruple eating with the Gentiles, and pretended they could not in conscience do it, because they were not circumcised. And (would you think it?) Barnabas himself, one of the apostles of the Gentiles, and one who had been instrumental in planting and watering the churches of the Gentiles, *was carried away with their dissimulation.* Here note, (1.) The weakness and inconstancy of the best of men, when left to themselves, and

how apt they are to falter in their duty to God, out of an undue regard to the pleasing of men. And, (2.) The great force of bad examples, especially the examples of great men and good men, such as are in reputation for wisdom and honour.

2. The rebuke which Paul gave him for his fault. Notwithstanding Peter's character, yet, when he observes him thus behaving himself to the great prejudice both of the truth of the gospel and the peace of the church, he is not afraid to reprove him for it. Paul adhered resolutely to his principles, when others faltered in theirs; he was as good a Jew as any of them (for he was a Hebrew of the Hebrews), but he would magnify his office as the apostle of the Gentiles, and therefore would not see them discouraged and trampled upon. *When he saw that they walked not uprightly, according to the truth of the gospel*—that they did not live up to that principle which the gospel taught, and which they had professed to own and embrace, namely, that by the death of Christ the partition-wall between Jew and Gentile was taken down, and the observance of the law of Moses was no longer in force—when he observed this, as Peter's offence was public, so he publicly reproved him for it: *He said unto him before them all, If thou, being a Jew, livest after the manner of the Gentiles, and not as do the Jews, why compellest thou the Gentiles to live as do the Jews?* Herein one part of his conduct was a contradiction to the other; for if he, who was a Jew, could himself sometimes dispense with the use of the ceremonial law, and live after the manner of the Gentiles, this showed that he did not look upon the observance of it as still necessary, even for the Jews themselves; and therefore that he could not, consistently with his own practice, impose it upon the Gentile Christians. And yet Paul charges him with this, yea, represents him as compelling the Gentiles to live as did the Jews—not by open force and violence, but this was the tendency of what he did; for it was in effect to signify this, that the Gentiles must comply with the Jews, or else not be admitted into Christian communion.

II. Paul having thus established his character and office, and sufficiently shown that he was not inferior to any of the apostles, no, not to Peter himself, from the account of the reproof he gave him he takes occasion to speak of that great fundamental doctrine of the gospel—That justification is only by faith in Christ, and not by the works of the law (though some think that all he says to the end of the chapter is what he said to Peter at Antioch), which doctrine condemned Peter for his symbolizing with the Jews. For, if it was the principle of his religion that the gospel is the instrument of our justification and not the law, then he did very ill in countenancing those who kept up the law, and were for mixing it with faith in the business of our justification. This was the doctrine which Paul had preached among the Galatians, to which he still adhered, and which it is his great business in this epistle to mention and confirm. Now concerning this Paul acquaints us,

1. With the practice of the Jewish Christians themselves: "*We*," says he, "*who are Jews by nature, and not sinners of the Gentiles* (even we who have been born and bred in the Jewish religion, and not among the impure Gentiles), *knowing that a man is not justified by the works of the law, but by the faith of Jesus Christ, even we ourselves have believed in Jesus Christ, that we might be justified by the faith of Christ, and not by the works of the law.* And, if we have thought it necessary to seek justification by the faith of Christ, why then should we hamper ourselves with the law? What did we believe in Christ for? Was it not that we might be justified by the faith of Christ? And, if so, is it not folly to go back to the law, and to expect to be justified either by the merit of moral works or the influence of any ceremonial sacrifices or purifications? And if it would be wrong in us who are Jews by nature to return to the law, and expect justification by it, would it not be much more so to require this of the Gentiles, who were never subject to it, since *by the works of the law no flesh shall be justified?*" To give the greater weight to this he adds (*v.* 17), "*But if, while we seek to be justified by Christ, we ourselves also are found sinners, is Christ the minister of sin?* If, while we seek justification by Christ alone, and teach others to do so, we ourselves are found giving countenance or indulgence to sin, or rather are accounted sinners of the Gentiles, and such as it is not fit to have communion with, unless we also observe the law of Moses, *is Christ the minister of sin?* Will it not follow that he is so, if he engage us to receive a doctrine that gives liberty to sin, or by which we are so far from being justified that we remain impure sinners, and unfit to be conversed with?" This, he intimates, would be the consequence, but he rejects it with abhorrence: "*God forbid*," says he, "that we should entertain such a thought of Christ, or of his doctrine, that thereby he should direct us into a way of justification that is defective and ineffectual, and leave those who embrace it still unjustified, or that would give the least encouragement to sin and sinners." This would be very dishonourable to Christ, and it would be very injurious to them also. "*For*," says he (*v.* 18), "*if I build again the things which I destroyed*—if I (or any other), who have taught that the observance of the Mosaic law is not necessary to justification, should now, by word or practice, teach or intimate that it is necessary—*I make myself a transgressor;* I own myself to be still an impure sinner, and to remain under the guilt of sin, notwithstanding my faith in Christ; or I shall be liable to be charged with deceit and prevarication, and acting inconsistently with

myself." Thus does the apostle argue for the great doctrine of justification by faith without the works of the law from the principles and practice of the Jewish Christians themselves, and from the consequences that would attend their departure from it, whence it appeared that Peter and the other Jews were much in the wrong in refusing to communicate with the Gentile Christians, and endeavouring to bring them under the bondage of the law.

2. He acquaints us what his own judgment and practice were. (1.) That he was dead to the law. Whatever account others might make of it, yet, for his part, he was dead to it. He knew that the moral law denounced a curse against all that continue not in all things written therein, to do them; and therefore he was dead to it, as to all hope of justification and salvation that way. And as for the ceremonial law, he also knew that it was now antiquated and superseded by the coming of Christ, and therefore, the substance having come, he had no longer any regard to the shadow. He was thus dead to the law, *through the law itself;* it discovered itself to be at an end. By considering the law itself, he saw that justification was not to be expected by the works of it (since none could perform a perfect obedience to it) and that there was now no further need of the sacrifices and purifications of it, since they were done away in Christ, and a period was put to them by his offering up himself a sacrifice for us; and therefore, the more he looked into it the more he saw that there was no occasion for keeping up that regard to it which the Jews pleaded for. But, though he was thus *dead to the law,* yet he did not look upon himself as *without law.* He had renounced all hopes of justification by the works of it, and was unwilling any longer to continue under the bondage of it; but he was far from thinking himself discharged from his duty to God; on the contrary, he was dead to the law, *that he might live unto God.* The doctrine of the gospel, which he had embraced, instead of weakening the bond of duty upon him, did but the more strengthen and confirm it; and therefore, though he was dead to the law, yet it was only in order to his living a new and better life to God (as Rom. vii. 4, 6), such a life as would be more agreeable and acceptable to God than his observance of the Mosaic law could now be, that is, a life of faith in Christ, and, under the influence thereof, of holiness and righteousness towards God. Agreeably hereunto he acquaints us, (2.) That, as he was dead to the law, so he was alive unto God through Jesus Christ (*v.* 20): *I am crucified with Christ,* &c. And here in his own person he gives us an excellent description of the mysterious life of a believer. [1.] He is crucified, and yet he lives; the old man is crucified (Rom. vi. 6), but the new man is living; he is dead to the world, and dead to the law, and yet alive to God and Christ; sin is mortified, and grace quickened. [2.] *He lives, and yet not he.* This is strange: *I live, and yet not I;* he lives in the exercise of grace; he has the comforts and the triumphs of grace; and yet that grace is not from himself, but from another. Believers see themselves living in a state of dependence. [3.] *He is crucified with Christ,* and yet *Christ lives in him;* this results from his mystical union with Christ, by means of which he is interested in the death of Christ, so as by virtue of that to die unto sin; and yet interested in the life of Christ, so as by virtue of that to live unto God. [4.] *He lives in the flesh,* and yet *lives by faith;* to outward appearance he lives as other people do, his natural life is supported as others are; yet he has a higher and nobler principle that supports and actuates him, that of faith in Christ, and especially as eyeing the wonders of his love in giving himself for him. Hence it is that, though he lives in the flesh, yet he does not live after the flesh. Note, Those who have true faith live by that faith; and the great thing which faith fastens upon is Christ's loving us and giving himself for us. The great evidence of Christ's loving us is his giving himself for us; and this is that which we are chiefly concerned to mix faith with, in order to our living to him.

Lastly, The apostle concludes this discourse with acquainting us that by the doctrine of justification by faith in Christ, without the works of the law (which he asserted, and others opposed), he avoided two great difficulties, which the contrary opinion was loaded with:—1. *That he did not frustrate the grace of God,* which the doctrine of justification by the works of the law did; for, as he argues (Rom. xi. 6), *If it be of works, it is no more of grace.* 2. That he did not frustrate the death of Christ; whereas, *if righteousness come by* the law, then it must follow *that Christ has died in vain;* for, if we look for salvation by the law of Moses, then we render the death of Christ needless: for to what purpose should he be appointed to die, if we might have been saved without it?

CHAP. III.

The apostle in this chapter, I. Reproves the Galatians for their folly, in suffering themselves to be drawn away from the faith of the gospel, and endeavours, from several considerations, to impress them with a sense of it. II. He proves the doctrine which he had reproved them for departing from—that of justification by faith without the works of the law, 1. From the example of Abraham's justification. 2. From the nature and tenour of the law. 3. From the express testimony of the Old Testament; and, 4. From the stability of the covenant of God with Abraham. Lest any should hereupon say, "Wherefore then serveth the law?" he answers, (1.) It was added because of transgressions. (2.) It was given to convince the world of the necessity of a Saviour. (3.) It was designed as a schoolmaster, to bring us to Christ. And then he concludes the chapter by acquainting us with the privilege of Christians under the gospel state.

O FOOLISH Galatians, who hath
bewitched you, that ye should
not obey the truth, before whose eyes
Jesus Christ hath been evidently set
forth, crucified among you? 2 This
only would I learn of you, Received
ye the Spirit by the works of the law,

or by the hearing of faith? 3 Are
ye so foolish? having begun in the
Spirit, are ye now made perfect by
the flesh? 4 Have ye suffered so
many things in vain? if *it be* yet in
vain. 5 He therefore that ministereth to you the Spirit, and worketh
miracles among you, *doeth he it* by the
works of the law, or by the hearing
of faith?

The apostle is here dealing with those who, having embraced the faith of Christ, still continued to seek for justification by the works of the law; that is, who depended upon their own obedience to the moral precepts as their righteousness before God, and, wherein that was defective, had recourse to the legal sacrifices and purifications to make it up. These he first sharply reproves, and then endeavours, by the evidence of truth, to convince them. This is the right method, when we reprove any for a fault or an error, to convince them that it is an error, that it is a fault.

He reproves them, and the reproof is very close and warm: he calls them *foolish Galatians, v.* 1. Though as Christians they were Wisdom's children, yet as corrupt Christians they were foolish children. Yea, he asks, *Who hath bewitched you?* whereby he represents them as enchanted by the arts and snares of their seducing teachers, and so far deluded as to act very unlike themselves. That wherein their folly and infatuation appeared was that *they did not obey the truth;* that is, they did not adhere to the gospel way of justification, wherein they had been taught, and which they had professed to embrace. Note, It is not enough to know the truth, and to say we believe it, but we must obey it too; we must heartily submit to it, and stedfastly abide by it. Note, also, Those are spiritually bewitched who, when the truth as it is in Jesus is plainly set before them, will not thus obey it. Several things proved and aggravated the folly of these Christians.

1. *Jesus Christ had been evidently set forth as crucified among them;* that is, they had had the doctrine of the cross preached to them, and the sacrament of the Lord's supper administered among them, in both which Christ crucified had been set before them. Now, it was the greatest madness that could be for those who had acquaintance with such sacred mysteries, and admittance to such great solemnities, not to obey the truth which was thus published to them, and signed and sealed in that ordinance. Note, The consideration of the honours and privileges we have been admitted to as Christians should shame us out of the folly of apostasy and backsliding.

2. He appeals to the experiences they had had of the working of the Spirit upon their souls (*v.* 2); he puts them in mind that, upon their becoming Christians, *they had received the Spirit,* that many of them at least had been made partakers not only of the sanctifying influences, but of the miraculous gifts, of the Holy Spirit, which were eminent proofs of the truth of the Christian religion and the several doctrines of it, and especially of this, that justification is by Christ only, and not by the works of the law, which was one of the peculiar and fundamental principles of it. To convince them of the folly of their departing from this doctrine, he desires to know how they came by these gifts and graces: Was it *by the works of the law,* that is, the preaching of the necessity of these in order to justification? This they could not say, for that doctrine had not then been preached to them, nor had they, as Gentiles, any pretence to justification in that way. Or was it by the *hearing of faith,* that is, the preaching of the doctrine of faith in Christ as the only way of justification? This, if they would say the truth, they were obliged to own, and therefore must be very unreasonable if they should reject a doctrine of the good effects of which they had had such experience. Note, (1.) It is usually by the ministry of the gospel that the Spirit is communicated to persons. And, (2.) Those are very unwise who suffer themselves to be turned away from the ministry and doctrine which have been blessed to their spiritual advantage.

3. He calls upon them to consider their past and present conduct, and thence to judge whether they were not acting very weakly and unreasonably (*v.* 3, 4): he tells them that *they had begun in the Spirit,* but now were seeking *to be made perfect by the flesh;* they had embraced the doctrine of the gospel, by means of which they had received the Spirit, and wherein only the true way of justification is revealed. And thus they had begun well; but now they were turning to the law, and expected to be advanced to higher degrees of perfection by adding the observance of it to faith in Christ, in order to their justification, which could end in nothing but their shame and disappointment: for this, instead of being an improvement upon the gospel, was really a perversion of it; and, while they sought to be justified in this way, they were so far from being more perfect Christians that they were more in danger of becoming no Christians at all; hereby they were pulling down with one hand what they had built with the other, and undoing what they had hitherto done in Christianity. Yea, he further puts them in mind that they had not only embraced the Christian doctrine, but suffered for it too; and therefore their folly would be the more aggravated, if now they should desert it: for in this case all that they had suffered would be in vain—it would appear that they had been foolish in suffering for what they now deserted, and their sufferings would be altogether in vain, and of no advantage to them. Note, (1.) It is the folly of apostates that they lose the benefit of all they have done in religion, or

suffered for it. And, (2.) It is very sad for any to live in an age of services and sufferings, of sabbaths, sermons, and sacraments, in vain; in this case former righteousness shall not be mentioned.

4. He puts them in mind that they had had ministers among them (and particularly himself) who came with a divine seal and commission; for they had *ministered the Spirit to them, and wrought miracles among them:* and he appeals to them whether they did it *by the works of the law or by the hearing of faith,* whether the doctrine that was preached by them, and confirmed by the miraculous gifts and operations of the Spirit, was that of justification by the works of the law or by the faith of Christ; they very well knew that it was not the former, but the latter; and therefore must needs be inexcusable in forsaking a doctrine which had been so signally owned and attested, and exchanging it for one that had received no such attestations.

6 Even as Abraham believed God,
and it was accounted to him for
righteousness. 7 Know ye therefore that they which are of faith, the
same are the children of Abraham.
8 And the scripture, foreseeing that
God would justify the heathen through
faith, preached before the gospel unto
Abraham, *saying,* In thee shall all
nations be blessed. 9 So then they
which be of faith are blessed with
faithful Abraham. 10 For as many
as are of the works of the law are
under the curse: for it is written,
Cursed *is* every one that continueth
not in all things which are written in
the book of the law to do them. 11
But that no man is justified by the
law in the sight of God, *it is* evident:
for, The just shall live by faith. 12
And the law is not of faith: but, The
man that doeth them shall live in them.
13 Christ hath redeemed us from the
curse of the law, being made a curse
for us: for it is written, Cursed *is*
every one that hangeth on a tree: 14
That the blessing of Abraham might
come on the Gentiles through Jesus
Christ; that we might receive the
promise of the Spirit through faith.
15 Brethren, I speak after the manner of men; Though *it be* but a man's
covenant, yet *if it be* confirmed, no
man disannulleth, or addeth thereto.
16 Now to Abraham and his seed
were the promises made. He saith
not, And to seeds, as of many; but
as of one, And to thy seed, which is
Christ. 17 And this I say, *that* the
covenant, that was confirmed before
of God in Christ, the law, which was
four hundred and thirty years after,
cannot disannul, that it should make
the promise of none effect. 18 For
if the inheritance *be* of the law, *it is*
no more of promise: but God gave
it to Abraham by promise.

The apostle having reproved the Galatians for not obeying the truth, and endeavoured to impress them with a sense of their folly herein, in these verses he largely proves the doctrine which he had reproved them for rejecting, namely, that of justification by faith without the works of the law. This he does several ways.

I. From the example of Abraham's justification. This argument the apostle uses, Rom. iv. *Abraham believed God, and that was accounted to him for righteousness* (*v.* 6); that is, his faith fastened upon the word and promise of God, and upon his believing he was owned and accepted of God as a righteous man: as on this account he is represented as the father of the faithful, so the apostle would have us to know *that those who are of faith are the children of Abraham* (*v.* 7), not according to the flesh, but according to the promise; and, consequently, that they are justified in the same way that he was. Abraham was justified by faith, and so are they. To confirm this, the apostle acquaints us that the promise made to Abraham (Gen. xii. 3), *In thee shall all nations be blessed,* had a reference hereunto, *v.* 8. The scripture is said to *foresee,* because he that indited the scripture did foresee, that God would justify the heathen world in the way of faith; and therefore in Abraham, that is, in the seed of Abraham, which is Christ, not the Jews only, but the Gentiles also, should be blessed; not only blessed in the seed of Abraham, but blessed as Abraham was, being justified as he was. This the apostle calls *preaching the gospel to Abraham;* and thence infers (*v.* 9) that *those who are of faith,* that is, true believers, of what nation soever they are, *are blessed with faithful Abraham.* They are blessed with Abraham the father of the faithful, by the promise made to him, and therefore by faith as he was. It was through faith in the promise of God that he was blessed, and it is only in the same way that others obtain this privilege.

II. He shows that we cannot be justified but by faith fastening on the gospel, because the law condemns us. If we put ourselves upon trial in that court, and stand to the sentence of it, we are certainly cast, and lost, and undone; *for as many as are of the works of the law are under the curse,* as many as depend upon the merit of their own works as their righteousness, as plead not guilty, and insist upon their own justification, the cause will certainly go against them; *for it is written, Cursed is every one that continueth not in all things which are written in the book of the law, to do them, v.* 10, and Deut. xxvii. 26. The condition of life, by the law, is perfect, personal, and perpetual, obedience; the language of it is, *Do this and live;* or, as *v.* 12, *The man that doeth them shall live in them:* and for every failure herein the law denounces a curse. Unless our obedience be universal, continuing in all things that are written in the book of the law, and unless it be perpetual too (if in any instance at any time we fail and come short), we fall under the curse of the law. The curse is wrath revealed, and ruin threatened: it is a separation unto all evil, and this is in full force, power, and virtue, against all sinners, and therefore against all men; for all have sinned and become guilty before God: and if, as transgressors of the law, we are under the curse of it, it must be a vain thing to look for justification by it. But, though this is not to be expected from the law, yet the apostle afterwards acquaints us that there is a way open to our escaping this curse, and regaining the favour of God, namely, through faith in Christ, who (as he says, *v.* 13) *hath redeemed us from the curse of the law,* &c. A strange method it was which Christ took to redeem us from the curse of the law; it was *by his being himself made a curse for us.* Being made sin for us, he was made a curse for us; not separated from God, but laid for the present under that infamous token of the divine displeasure upon which the law of Moses had put a particular brand, Deut. xxi. 23. The design of this was *that the blessing of Abraham might come on the Gentiles through Jesus Christ*—that all who believed on Christ, whether Jews or Gentiles, might become heirs of Abraham's blessing, and particularly of that great promise of the Spirit, which was peculiarly reserved for the times of the gospel. Hence it appeared that it was not by putting themselves under the law, but by faith in Christ, that they became the people of God and heirs of the promise. Here note, 1. The misery which as sinners we are sunk into—we are under the curse and condemnation of the law. 2. The love and grace of our Lord Jesus Christ towards us—he has submitted to be made a curse for us, that he might redeem us from the curse of the law. 3. The happy prospect which we now have through him, not only of escaping the curse, but of inheriting the blessing. And, 4. That it is only through faith in him that we can hope to obtain this favour.

III. To prove that justification is by faith, and not by the works of the law, the apostle alleges the express testimony of the Old Testament, *v.* 11. The place referred to is Habak. ii. 4, where it is said, *The just shall live by faith;* it is again quoted, Rom. i. 17, and Heb. x. 38. The design of it is to show that those only are just or righteous who do truly live, who are freed from death and wrath, and restored into a state of life in the favour of God; and that it is only through faith that persons become righteous, and as such obtain this life and happiness—that they are accepted of God, and enabled to live to him now, and are entitled to an eternal life in the enjoyment of him hereafter. Hence the apostle says, *It is evident that no man is justified by the law in the sight of God.* Whatever he may be in the account of others, yet he is not so in the sight of God; for *the law is not of faith*—that says nothing concerning faith in the business of justification, nor does it give life to those who believe; but the language of it is, *The man that doeth them shall live in them,* as Lev. xviii. 5. It requires perfect obedience as the condition of life, and therefore now can by no means be the rule of our justification. This argument of the apostle's may give us occasion to remark that justification by faith is no new doctrine, but what was established and taught in the church of God long before the times of the gospel. Yea, it is the only way wherein any sinners ever were, or can be, justified.

IV. To this purpose the apostle urges the stability of the covenant which God made with Abraham, which was not vacated nor disannulled by the giving of the law to Moses, *v.* 15, &c. Faith had the precedence of the law, for Abraham was justified by faith. It was a promise that he built upon, and promises are the proper objects of faith. God entered into covenant with Abraham (*v.* 8), and this covenant was firm and steady; even men's covenants are so, and therefore much more his. When a deed is executed, or articles of agreement are sealed, both parties are bound, and it is too late then to settle things otherwise; and therefore it is not to be supposed that by the subsequent law the covenant of God should be vacated. The original word διαθήκη signifies both a covenant and a testament. Now the promise made to Abraham was rather a testament than a covenant. When a testament has become of force by the death of the testator, it is not capable of being altered; and therefore, the promise that was given to Abraham being of the nature of a testament, it remains firm and unalterable. But, if it should be said that a grant or testament may be defeated for want of persons to claim the benefit of it (*v.* 16), he shows that there is no danger of that in this case. Abraham is dead, and the prophets are dead, but the covenant is made with Abraham and his seed. And he gives us a very surprising exposition of this. We should have thought it had been meant only of the people of the Jews. "Nay," says the apostle, "it is in the singular number, and points at a single person—*that seed is Christ.*" So that the covenant is still in force; for Christ abideth for ever in his person, and in his spiritual seed, who are his by faith. And if it be objected that the law which was given by Moses did disannul this covenant, because that insisted so much upon works, and there was so little in it of faith or of the promised Messiah, he answers that the subsequent law could not disannul the previous covenant or promise (*v.* 18): *If the inheritance be of the law, it is no more of promise; but,* says he, *God gave it to Abraham by promise,* and therefore it would be inconsistent with his holiness, wisdom, and faithfulness, by any subsequent act to set aside the promise, and so alter the way of justification which he had thus established. If the inheritance was given to Abraham by promise, and thereby entailed upon his spiritual seed, we may be sure that God would not retract that promise; for he is not a man that he should repent.

19 Wherefore then *serveth* the law?
It was added because of transgressions, till the seed should come to
whom the promise was made; *and it*
was ordained by angels in the hand
of a mediator. 20 Now a mediator
is not *a mediator* of one, but God is
one. 20 *Is* the law then against the
promises of God? God forbid: for
if there had been a law given which
could have given life, verily righteousness should have been by the law. 22
But the scripture hath concluded all
under sin, that the promise by faith
of Jesus Christ might be given to
them that believe. 23 But before
faith came, we were kept under the
law, shut up unto the faith which
should afterwards be revealed. 24
Wherefore the law was our schoolmaster *to bring us* unto Christ, that
we might be justified by faith. 25
But after that faith is come, we are
no longer under a schoolmaster. 26
For ye are all the children of God by
faith in Christ Jesus. 27 For as
many of you as have been baptized
into Christ have put on Christ. 28
There is neither Jew nor Greek,
there is neither bond nor free, there
is neither male nor female: for ye
are all one in Christ Jesus. 29 And
if ye *be* Christ's, then are ye Abraham's seed, and heirs according to
the promise.

The apostle having just before been speaking of the promise made to Abraham, and representing that as the rule of our justification, and not the law, lest they should think he did too much derogate from the law, and render it altogether useless, he thence takes occasion to discourse of the design and tendency of it, and to acquaint us for what purposes it was given. It might be asked, "If that promise be sufficient for salvation, wherefore then serveth the law? Or, Why did God give the law by Moses?" To this he answers,

I. The law *was added because of transgressions, v.* 19. It was not designed to disannul the promise, and to establish a different way of justification from that which was settled by the promise; but *it was added* to it, annexed on purpose to be subservient to it, and it was so *because of transgressions.* The Israelites, though they were chosen to be God's peculiar people, were sinners as well as others, and therefore the law was given to convince them of their sin, and of their obnoxiousness to the divine displeasure on the account of it; *for by the law is the knowledge of sin* (Rom. iii. 20), and *the law entered that sin might abound,* Rom. v. 20. And it was also intended to restrain them from the commission of sin, to put an awe upon their minds, and be a curb upon their lusts, that they should not run into that excess of riot to which they were naturally inclined; and yet at the same time it was designed to direct them to the true and only way whereby sin was to be expiated, and wherein they might obtain the pardon of it; namely, through the death and sacrifice of Christ, which was the special use for which the law of sacrifices and purifications was given.

The apostle adds that the law was given for this purpose *till the seed should come to whom the promise was made;* that is, either till Christ should come (the principal seed referred to in the promise, as he had before shown), or till the gospel dispensation should take place, when Jews and Gentiles, without distinction, should, upon believing, become the seed of Abraham. The law was added because of transgressions, till this fulness of time, or this complete dispensation, should come. But when the seed came, and a fuller discovery of divine grace in the promise was made, then the law, as given by Moses, was to cease; that covenant, being found faulty, was to give place to another, and a better, Heb. viii. 7, 8. And though the law, considered as the law of nature, is always in force, and still continues to be of use, to convince men .of sin and to restrain them from it, yet we are now no longer under the bondage and terror of that legal covenant. The law then was not intended to discover another way of justification, different from that revealed by the promise, but only to lead men to see their need of the promise, by showing them the sinfulness of sin, and to point them to Christ, through whom alone they could be pardoned and justified.

As a further proof that the law was not designed to vacate the promise, the apostle adds, *It was ordained by angels in the hand of a mediator.* It was given to different persons, and in a different manner from the promise, and therefore for different purposes. The promise was made to Abraham, and all his spiritual seed, including believers of all nations, even of the Gentiles as well as the Jews; but the law was given to the Israelites as a peculiar people, and separated from the rest of the world. And, whereas the promise was given immediately by God himself, the law was given *by the ministry of angels, and the hand of a mediator.* Hence it appeared that the law could not be designed to set aside the promise; for (*v.* 20), *A mediator is not a mediator of one,* of one party only; *but God is one,* but one party in the promise or covenant made with Abraham: and therefore it is not to be supposed that by a transaction which passed only between him and the nation of the Jews he should make void a promise which he had long before made to Abraham and all his spiritual seed, whether Jews or Gentiles. This would not have been consistent with his wisdom, nor with his truth and faithfulness. Moses was only a mediator between God and the Israelites, not between God and the spiritual seed of Abraham; and therefore the law that was given by him could not affect the promise made to them, much less be subversive of it.

II. The law was given to convince men of the necessity of a Saviour. The apostle asks (*v.* 21), as what some might be willing to object, "*Is the law then against the promises of God?* Do they really clash and interfere with each other? Or do you not set the covenant with Abraham, and the law of Moses, at variance with one another?" To this he answers, *God forbid;* he was far from entertaining such a thought, nor could it be inferred from what he had said. The law is by no means inconsistent with the promise, but subservient to it, as the design of it is to discover men's transgressions, and to show them the need they have of a better righteousness than that of the law. That consequence would much rather follow from their doctrine than from his; *for, if there had been a law given that could have given life, verily righteousness would have been by the law,* and in that case the promise would have been superseded and rendered useless. But that in our present state could not be, *for the scripture hath concluded all under sin* (*v.* 22), or declared that all, both Jew and Gentile, are in a state of guilt, and therefore unable to attain to righteousness and justification by the works of the law. The law discovered their wounds, but could not afford them a remedy: it showed that they were guilty, because it appointed sacrifices and purifications, which were manifestly insufficient to take away sin: and therefore the great design of it was *that the promise by faith of Jesus Christ might be given to those that believe,* that being convinced of their guilt, and the insufficiency of the law to effect a righteousness for them, they might be persuaded to believe on Christ, and so obtain the benefit of the promise.

III. The law was designed for *a schoolmaster, to bring men to Christ, v.* 24. In the foregoing verse, the apostle acquaints us with the state of the Jews under the Mosaic economy, that *before faith came,* or before Christ appeared and the doctrine of justification by faith in him was more fully discovered, *they were kept under the law,* obliged, under severe penalties, to a strict observance of the various precepts of it; and at that time they were shut up, held under the terror and discipline of it, as prisoners in a state of confinement: the design of this was that hereby they might be disposed more readily to embrace *the faith which should afterwards be revealed,* or be persuaded to accept Christ when he came into the world, and to fall in with that better dispensation he was to introduce, whereby they were to be freed from bondage and servitude, and brought into a state of greater light and liberty. Now, in that state, he tells them, *the law was their schoolmaster, to bring them to Christ, that they might be justified by faith.* As it declared the mind and will of God concerning them, and at the same time denounced a curse against them for every failure in their duty, so it was proper to convince them of their lost and undone condition in themselves, and to let them see the weakness and insufficiency of their own righteousness to recommend them to God. And as it obliged them to a variety of sacrifices, &c., which, though they could not of themselves take away sin, were typical of Christ, and of the great sacrifice which he was to offer up for the expiation of it, so it directed them (though in a more dark and obscure manner) to him as their only relief and refuge. And thus it was their schoolmaster, to instruct and govern them in their state of minority, or, as the word παιδαγωγὸς most properly signifies, their *servant,* to lead and conduct them to Christ (as children were wont to be led to school by those servants who had the care of them); that they might be more fully instructed by him as their schoolmaster, in the true way of justification and salvation, which is only by faith in him, and of which he was appointed to give the fullest and clearest discoveries. But lest it should be said, If the law was of this use and service under the Jewish, why may it not continue to be so under the Christian state too, the apostle adds (*v.* 25) that *after faith has come,* and the gospel dispensation has taken place, under which Christ, and the way of pardon and life through faith in him, are set in the clearest light, *we are no longer under a schoolmaster*—we have no such need of the law to direct us to him as there was then. Thus the apostle acquaints us for what uses and purposes the law served; and, from what he says concerning this matter, we may observe,

1. The goodness of God to his people of old, in giving the law to them; for though, in comparison of the gospel state, it was a dispensation of darkness and terror, yet it furnished them with sufficient means and helps both to direct them in their duty to God and to encourage their hopes in him.

2. The great fault and folly of the Jews, in mistaking the design of the law, and abusing it to a very different purpose from that which God intended in the giving of it; for they expected to be justified by the works of it, whereas it was never designed to be the rule of their justification, but only a means of convincing them of their guilt and of their need of a Saviour, and of directing them to Christ, and faith in him, as the only way of obtaining this privilege. See Rom. ix. 31, 32; x. 3, 4.

3. The great advantage of the gospel state above the legal, under which we not only enjoy a clearer discovery of divine grace and mercy than was afforded to the Jews of old, but are also freed from the state of bondage and terror under which they were held. We are not now treated as children in a state of minority, but as sons grown up to a full age, who are admitted to greater freedoms, and instated in larger privileges, than they were. This the apostle enlarges upon in the following verses. For, having shown for what intent the law was given, in the close of the chapter he acquaints us with our privilege by Christ, where he particularly declares,

(1.) That *we are the children of God by faith in Christ Jesus, v.* 26. And here we may observe, [1.] The great and excellent privilege which real Christians enjoy under the gospel: *They are the children of God;* they are no longer accounted servants, but *sons;* they are not now kept at such a distance, and under such restraints, as the Jews were, but are allowed a nearer and freer access to God than was granted to them; yea, they are admitted into the number, and have a right to all the privileges, of his children. [2.] How they come to obtain this privilege, and that is *by faith in Christ Jesus.* Having accepted him as their Lord and Saviour, and relying on him alone for justification and salvation, they are hereupon admitted into this happy relation to God, and are entitled to the privileges of it; for (John i. 12) *as many as received him, to them gave he power to become the sons of God, even to those that believe on his name.* And this faith in Christ, whereby they became the children of God, he reminds us (*v.* 27), was what they professed in baptism; for he adds, *As many of you as have been baptized into Christ have put on Christ.* Having in baptism professed their faith in him, they were thereby devoted to him, and had, as it were, put on his livery, and declared themselves to be his servants and disciples; and, having thus become the members of Christ, they were through him owned and accounted as the children of God. Here note, *First,* Baptism is now the solemn rite of our admission into the Christian church, as circumcision was into that of the Jews. Our Lord Jesus appointed it to be so, in the commission he gave to his apostles (Matt. xxviii. 19), and accordingly it was their practice to baptize those whom they had discipled to the Christian faith; and perhaps the apostle might take notice of their baptism here, and of their becoming the children of God through faith in Christ, professed therein, to obviate a further objection, which the false teachers might be apt to urge in favour of circumcision. They might be ready to say, "Though it should be allowed that the law, as given at mount Sinai, was abrogated by the coming of Christ the promised seed, yet why should circumcision be set aside too, when that was given to Abraham together with the promise, and long before the giving of the law by Moses?" But this difficulty is sufficiently removed when the apostle says, *Those who are baptized into Christ have put on Christ;* for thence it appears that under the gospel baptism comes in the room of circumcision, and that those who by baptism are devoted to Christ, and do sincerely believe in him, are to all intents and purposes as much admitted into the privileges of the Christian state as the Jews were by circumcision into those of the legal (Phil. iii. 3), and therefore there was no reason why the use of that should still be continued. Note, *Secondly,* In our baptism we put on Christ; therein we profess our discipleship to him, and are obliged to behave ourselves as his faithful servants. Being baptized into Christ, we are baptized into his death, that as he died and rose again, so, in conformity thereunto, we should die unto sin, and walk in newness of life (Rom. vi. 3, 4); it would be of great advantage to us did we oftener remember this.

(2.) That this privilege of being the children of God, and of being by baptism devoted to Christ, is now enjoyed in common by all real Christians. The law indeed made a difference between Jew and Greek, giving the Jews on many accounts the pre-eminence: that also made a difference between *bond and free,* master and servant, and between *male and female,* the males being circumcised. But it is not so now; they all stand on the same level, *and are all one in Christ Jesus:* as the one is not accepted on the account of any national or personal advantages he may enjoy above the other, so neither is the other rejected for the want of them; but all who sincerely believe on Christ, of what nation, or sex, or condition, soever they be, are accepted of him, and become the children of God through faith in him.

(3.) That, *being Christ's, we are Abraham's seed, and heirs according to the promise.* Their judaizing teachers would have them believe that they must be circumcised and keep the law of Moses, or they could not be saved: "No," says the apostle, "there is no need of that; for *if you be Christ's*, if you sincerely believe on him, who is the promised seed, in whom all the nations of the earth were to be blessed, you therefore become the true *seed of Abraham*, the father of the faithful, and as such *are heirs according to the promise*, and consequently are entitled to the great blessings and privileges of it." And therefore upon the whole, since it appeared that justification was not to be attained by the works of the law, but only by faith in Christ, and that the law of Moses was a temporary institution and was given for such purposes as were only subservient to and not subversive of the promise, and that now, under the gospel, Christians enjoy much greater and better privileges than the Jews did under that dispensation, it must needs follow that they were very unreasonable and unwise, in hearkening to those who at once endeavoured to deprive them of the truth and liberty of the gospel.

CHAP. IV.

The apostle, in this chapter, is still carrying on the same general design as in the former—to recover these Christians from the impressions made upon them by the judaizing teachers, and to represent their weakness and folly in suffering themselves to be drawn away from the gospel doctrine of justification, and to be deprived of their freedom from the bondage of the law of Moses. For this purpose he makes use of various considerations; such as, I. The great excellence of the gospel state above the legal, ver. 1—7. II The happy change that was made in them at their conversion, ver. 8—11. III. The affection they had had for him and his ministry, ver. 12—16. IV. The character of the false teachers by whom they had been perverted, ver. 17, 18. V. The very tender affection he had for them, ver. 19, 20. VI. The history of Isaac and Ishmael, by a comparison taken from which he illustrates the difference between such as rested in Christ and such as trusted in the law. And in all these, as he uses great plainness and faithfulness with them, so he expresses the tenderest concern for them.

NOW I say, *That* the heir, as
long as he is a child, differeth
nothing from a servant, though he be
lord of all; 2 But is under tutors
and governors until the time appointed of the father. 3 Even so we,
when we were children, were in bondage under the elements of the world:
4 But when the fulness of the time
was come, God sent forth his Son,
made of a woman, made under the
law, 5 To redeem them that were
under the law, that we might receive
the adoption of sons. 6 And because
ye are sons, God hath sent forth the
Spirit of his Son into your hearts,
crying, Abba, Father. 7 Wherefore
thou art no more a servant, but a son;
and if a son, then an heir of God
through Christ.

In this chapter the apostle deals plainly with those who hearkened to the judaizing teachers, who cried up the law of Moses in competition with the gospel of Christ, and endeavoured to bring them under the bondage of it. To convince them of their folly, and to rectify their mistake herein, in these verses he prosecutes the comparison of a child under age, which he had touched upon in the foregoing chapter, and thence shows what great advantages we have now, under the gospel, above what they had under the law. And here.

I. He acquaints us with the state of the Old-Testament church: it was like a child under age, and it was used accordingly, being kept in a state of darkness and bondage, in comparison of the greater light and liberty which we enjoy under the gospel. That was indeed a dispensation of grace, and yet it was comparatively a dispensation of darkness; for as the heir, in his minority, is *under tutors and governors till the time appointed of his father*, by whom he is educated and instructed in those things which at present he knows little of the meaning of, though afterwards they are likely to be of great use to him; so it was with the Old-Testament church—the Mosaic economy, which they were under, was what they could not fully understand the meaning of; for, as the apostle says (2 Cor. iii. 13), *They could not stedfastly look to the end of that which is abolished.* But to the church, when grown up to maturity, in gospel days, it becomes of great use. And as that was a dispensation of darkness, so of bondage too; for *they were in bondage under the elements of the world*, being tied to a great number of burdensome rites and observances, by which, as by a kind of first rudiments, they were taught and instructed, and whereby they were kept in a state of subjection, like a child under tutors and governors. The church then lay more under the character of *a servant*, being obliged to do every thing according to the command of God, without being fully acquainted with the reason of it; but the service under the gospel appears to be more reasonable than that was. The time appointed of the Father having come, when the church was to arrive at its full age, the darkness and bondage under which it before lay are removed, and we are under a dispensation of greater light and liberty.

II. He acquaints us with the much happier state of Christians under the gospel-dispensation, *v.* 4—7. *When the fulness of time had come*, the time appointed of the Father, when he would put an end to the legal dispensation, and set up another and a better in the room of it, *he sent forth his Son*, &c. The person who was employed to introduce this new dispensation was no other than the Son of God himself, the only-begotten of the Father, who, as he had been prophesied of and promised from the foundation of the world, so in due time he was manifested for this purpose. He, in pursuance of the great design he had undertaken, submitted to be *made of a woman*—there is his incarnation; and to be *made under the law*—there is his subjection. He who was truly God for our sakes became man; and he who was Lord of all consented to come into a state of subjection and to take upon him the form of a servant; and one great end of all this was *to redeem those that were under the law*—to save us from that intolerable yoke and to appoint gospel ordinances more rational and easy. He had indeed something more and greater in his view, in coming into the world, than merely to deliver us from the bondage of the ceremonial law; for he came in our nature, and consented to suffer and die for us, that hereby he might redeem us from the wrath of God, and from the curse of the moral law, which, as sinners, we all lay under. But that was one end of it, and a mercy reserved to be bestowed at the time of his manifestation; then the more servile state of the church was to come to a period, and a better to succeed in the place of it; for he was sent to redeem us, *that we might receive the adoption of sons*—that we might no longer be accounted and treated as servants, but as sons grown up to maturity, who are allowed greater freedoms, and admitted to larger privileges, than while they were under tutors and governors. This the course of the apostle's argument leads us to take notice of, as one thing intended by this expression, though no doubt it may also be understood as signifying that gracious adoption which the gospel so often speaks of as the privilege of those who believe in Christ. Israel was God's son, his first-born, Rom. ix. 4. But now, under the gospel, particular believers receive the adoption; and, as an earnest and evidence of it, they have together therewith the Spirit of adoption, putting them upon the duty of prayer, and enabling them in prayer to eye God as a Father (*v.* 6): *Because you are sons, God hath sent forth the Spirit of his Son into your hearts, crying Abba, Father.* And hereupon (*v.* 7) the apostle concludes this argument by adding, *Wherefore thou art no more a servant, but a son; and, if a son, then an heir of God through Christ;* that is, Now, under the gospel state, we are no longer under the servitude of the law, but, upon our believing in Christ, become the sons of God; we are thereupon accepted of him, and adopted by him; and, being the sons, we are also heirs of God, and are entitled to the heavenly inheritance (as he also reasons Rom. viii. 17), and therefore it must needs be the greatest weakness and folly to turn back to the law, and to seek justification by the works of it. From what the apostle says in these verses, we may observe,

1. The wonders of divine love and mercy towards us, particularly of God the Father, in sending his Son into the world to redeem and save us,—of the Son of God, in submitting so low, and suffering so much, for us, in pursuance of that design,—and of the Holy Spirit, in condescending to dwell in the hearts of believers for such gracious purposes.

2. The great and invaluable advantages which Christians enjoy under the gospel; for, (1.) We receive *the adoption of sons.* Whence note, It is the great privilege which believers have through Christ that they are adopted children of the God of heaven. We who by nature are children of wrath and disobedience have become by grace children of love. (2.) We receive *the Spirit of adoption.* Note, [1.] All who have the privilege of adoption have the Spirit of adoption—all who are received into the number partake of the nature of the children of God; for he will have all his children to resemble him. [2.] The Spirit of adoption is always the Spirit of prayer, and it is our duty in prayer to eye God as a Father. Christ has taught us in prayer to eye God as our Father in heaven. [3.] If we are his sons, then his heirs. It is not so among men, with whom the eldest son is heir; but all God's children are heirs. Those who have the nature of sons shall have the inheritance of sons.

8 Howbeit then, when ye knew not God, ye did service unto them which by nature are no gods. 9 But now, after that ye have known God, or rather are known of God, how turn ye again to the weak and beggarly elements, whereunto ye desire again to be in bondage? 10 Ye observe days, and months, and times, and years. 11 I am afraid of you, lest I have bestowed upon you labour in vain.

In these verses the apostle puts them in mind of what they were before their conversion to the faith of Christ, and what a blessed change their conversion had made upon them; and thence endeavours to convince them of their great weakness in hearkening to those who would bring them under the bondage of the law of Moses.

I. He reminds them of their past state and behaviour, and what they were before the gospel was preached to them. Then *they knew not God;* they were grossly ignorant of the true God, and the way wherein he is to be worshipped: and at that time they were under the worst of slaveries, for *they did service to those which by nature were no gods,* they were employed in a great number of superstitious and idolatrous services to those who, though they were accounted gods, were yet really no gods, but mere creatures, and perhaps of their own making, and therefore were utterly unable to hear and help them. Note, 1. Those who are ignorant of the true God cannot but be inclined to false gods. Those who forsook the God who made the world, rather than be without gods, worshipped such as they themselves made. 2. Religious worship is due to none but to him who is by nature God; for, when the apostle blames the doing service to such as by nature were no gods, he plainly shows that he only who is by nature God is the proper object of our religious worship.

II. He calls upon them to consider the happy change that was made in them by the preaching of the gospel among them. Now *they had known God* (they were brought to the knowledge of the true God and of his Son Jesus Christ, whereby they were recovered out of the ignorance and bondage under which they before lay) *or rather were known of God;* this happy change in their state, whereby they were turned from idols to the living God, and through Christ had received the adoption of sons, was not owing to themselves, but to him; it was the effect of his free and rich grace towards them, and as such they ought to account it; and therefore hereby they were laid under the greater obligation to adhere to the liberty wherewith he had made them free. Note, All our acquaintance with God begins with him; we know him, because we are known of him.

III. Hence he infers the unreasonableness and madness of their suffering themselves to be brought again into a state of bondage. He speaks of it with surprise and deep concern of mind that such as they should do so: *How turn you again,* &c., says he, *v.* 9. "How is it that you, who have been taught to worship God in the gospel way, should now be persuaded to comply with the ceremonial way of worship? that you, who have been acquainted with a dispensation of light, liberty, and love, as that of the gospel is, should now submit to a dispensation of darkness, and bondage, and terror, as that of the law is?" This they had the less reason for, since they had never been under the law of Moses, as the Jews had been; and therefore on this account they were more inexcusable than the Jews themselves, who might be supposed to have some fondness for that which had been of such long standing among them. Besides, what they suffered themselves to be brought into bondage to were but *weak and beggarly elements,* such things as had no power in them to cleanse the soul, nor to afford any solid satisfaction to the mind, and which were only designed for that state of pupillage under which the church had been, but which had now come to a period; and therefore their weakness and folly were the more aggravated, in submitting to them, and in symbolizing with the Jews in observing their various festivals, here signified by *days, and months, and times, and years.* Here note, 1. It is possible for those who have made great professions of religion to be afterwards drawn into very great defections from the purity and simplicity of it, for this was the case of these Christians. And, 2. The more mercy God has shown to any, in bringing them into an acquaintance with the gospel, and the liberties and privileges of it, the greater are their sin and folly in suffering themselves to be deprived of them; for this the apostle lays a special stress upon, that after they had known God, or rather were known of him, they desired to be in bondage under the weak and beggarly elements of the law.

IV. Hereupon he expresses his fears concerning them, *lest he had bestowed on them labour in vain.* He had been at a great deal of pains about them, in preaching the gospel to them, and endeavouring to confirm them in the faith and liberty of it; but now they were giving up these, and thereby rendering his labour among them fruitless and ineffectual, and with the thoughts of this he could not but be deeply affected. Note, 1. A great deal of the labour of faithful ministers is labour in vain; and, when it is so, it cannot but be a great grief to those who desire the salvation of souls. Note, 2. The labour of ministers is in vain upon those who begin in the Spirit and end in the flesh, who, though they seem to set out well, yet afterwards turn aside from the way of the gospel. Note, 3. Those will have a great deal to answer for upon whom the faithful ministers of Jesus Christ bestow labour in vain.

12 Brethren, I beseech you, be as
I *am;* for I *am* as ye *are:* ye have
not injured me at all. 13 Ye know
how through infirmity of the flesh I
preached the gospel unto you at the
first. 14 And my temptation which
was in my flesh ye despised not, nor
rejected; but received me as an angel
of God, *even* as Christ Jesus. 15
Where is then the blessedness ye
spake of? for I bear you record,
that, if *it had been* possible, ye would
have plucked out your own eyes, and
have given them to me. 16 Am I
therefore become your enemy, because
I tell you the truth?

That these Christians might be the more ashamed of their defection from the truth of the gospel which Paul had preached to them, he here reminds them of the great affection they formerly had for him and his ministry, and puts them upon considering how very unsuitable their present behaviour was to what they then professed. And here we may observe,

I. How affectionately he addresses himself to them. He styles them brethren, though he knew their hearts were in a great measure alienated from him. He desires that all resentments might be laid aside, and that they would bear the same temper of mind towards him which he did to them; he would have them *to be as he was, for he was as they were,* and moreover tells them that *they had not injured him at all.* He had no quarrel with them upon his own account. Though, in blaming their conduct, he had expressed himself with some warmth and concern of mind-he assured them that it was not owing to any sense of personal injury or affront (as they might be ready to think), but proceeded wholly from a zeal for the truth and purity of the gospel, and their welfare and happiness. Thus he endeavours to mollify their spirits towards him, that so they might be the better disposed to receive the admonitions he was giving them. Hereby he teaches us that in reproving others we should take care to convince them that our reproofs do not proceed from any private pique or resentment, but from a sincere regard to the honour of God and religion and their truest welfare; for they are then likely to be most successful when they appear to be most disinterested.

II. How he magnifies their former affection to him, that hereby they might be the more ashamed of their present behaviour towards him. To this purpose, 1. He puts them in mind of the difficulty under which he laboured when he came first among them: *I knew*, says he, *how, through infirmity of the flesh, I preached the gospel unto you at the first.* What this *infirmity of the flesh* was, which in the following words he expresses by *his temptation that was in his flesh* (though, no doubt, it was well known to those Christians to whom he wrote), we can now have no certain knowledge of: some take it to have been the persecutions which he suffered for the gospel's sake; others, to have been something in his person, or manner of speaking, which might render his ministry less grateful and acceptable, referring to 2 Cor. x. 10, and to *ch.* xii. 7—10. But, whatever it was, it seems it made no impression on them to his disadvantage. For, 2. He takes notice that, notwithstanding this his infirmity (which might possibly lessen him in the esteem of some others), they did not despise nor reject him on the account of it, but, on the contrary, *received him as an angel of God, even as Christ Jesus.* They showed a great deal of respect to him, he was a welcome messenger to them, even as though an angel of God or Jesus Christ himself had preached to them; yea, so great was their esteem of him, that, if it would have been any advantage to him, *they could have plucked out their own eyes, and have given them to him.* Note, How uncertain the respects of people are, how apt they are to change their minds, and how easily they are drawn into contempt of those for whom they once had the greatest esteem and affection, so that they are ready to pluck out the eyes of those for whom they would before have plucked out their own! We should therefore labour to be accepted of God, *for it is a small thing to be judged of man's judgment,* 1 Cor. iv. 3.

III. How earnestly he expostulates with them hereupon: *Where is then,* says he, *the blessedness you spoke of?* As if he had said, "Time was when you expressed the greatest joy and satisfaction in the glad tidings of the gospel, and were very forward in pouring out your blessings upon me as the publisher of them; whence is it that you are now so much altered, that you have so little relish of them or respect for me? You once thought yourselves happy in receiving the gospel; have you now any reason to think otherwise?" Note, Those who have left their first love would do well to consider, Where is now the blessedness they once spoke of? What has become of that pleasure they used to take in communion with God, and in the company of his servants? The more to impress upon them a just shame of their present conduct, he again asks (*v.* 16), "*Am I become your enemy, because I tell you the truth?* How is it that I, who was heretofore your favourite, am now accounted your enemy? Can you pretend any other reason for it than that I have told you the truth, endeavoured to acquaint you with, and to confirm you in, the truth of the gospel? And, if not, how unreasonable must your disaffection be!" Note, 1. It is no uncommon thing for men to account those their enemies who are really their best friends; for so, undoubtedly, those are, whether ministers or others, who tell them the truth, and deal freely and faithfully with them in matters relating to their eternal salvation, as the apostle now did with these Christians. 2. Ministers may sometimes create enemies to themselves by the faithful discharge of their duty; for this was the case of Paul, he was accounted their enemy for telling them the truth. 3. Yet ministers must not forbear speaking the truth, for fear of offending others and drawing their displeasure upon them. 4. They may be easy in their own minds, when they are conscious to themselves that, if others have become their enemies, it is only for telling them the truth.

17 They zealously affect you, *but* not well; yea, they would exclude you, that ye might affect them. 18 But *it is* good to be zealously affected always in *a* good *thing,* and not only when I am present with you.

The apostle is still carrying on the same design as in the foregoing verses, which was, to convince the Galatians of their sin and folly in departing from the truth of the gospel: having just before been expostulating with them about the change of their behaviour towards him who endeavoured to establish them in it, he here gives them the character of those false teachers who made it their business to draw them away from it, which if they would attend to, they might soon see how little reason they had to hearken to them: whatever opinion they might have of them, he tells them they were designing men, who were aiming to set up themselves, and who, under their specious pretences, were more consulting their own interest than theirs: "*They zealously affect you,*" says he;

"they show a mighty respect for you, and pretend a great deal of affection to you, *but not well;* they do it not with any good design, they are not sincere and upright in it, for *they would exclude you, that you might affect them.* That which they are chiefly aiming at is to engage your affections to them; and, in order to this, they are doing all they can to draw off your affections from me and from the truth, that so they may engross you to themselves." This, he assures them, was their design, and therefore they must needs be very unwise in hearkening to them. Note, 1. There may appear to be a great deal of zeal where yet there is but little truth and sincerity. 2. It is the usual way of seducers to insinuate themselves into people's affections, and by that means to draw them into their opinions. 3. Whatever pretences such may make, they have usually more regard to their own interest than that of others, and will not stick at ruining the reputation of others, if by that means they can raise their own. On this occasion the apostle gives us that excellent rule which we have, *v.* 18, *It is good to be zealously affected always in a good thing.* What our translation renders *in a good thing* some choose to render *to a good man,* and so consider the apostle as pointing to himself; this sense, they think, is favoured both by the preceding context and also by the words immediately following, *and not only when I am present with you,* which may be as if he had said, "Time was when you were zealously affected towards me; you once took me for a good man, and have now no reason to think otherwise of me; surely then it would become you to show the same regard to me, now that I am absent from you, which you did when I was present with you." But, if we adhere to our own translation, the apostle here furnishes us with a very good rule to direct and regulate us in the exercise of our zeal: there are two things which to this purpose he more especially recommends to us:—(1.) That it be exercised only upon that which is good; for zeal is then only good when it is in a good thing: those who are zealously affected to that which is evil will thereby only do so much the more hurt. And, (2.) That herein it be constant and steady: it is good to be zealous always in a good thing; not for a time only, or now and then, like the heat of an ague-fit, but, like the natural heat of the body, constant. Happy would it be for the church of Christ if this rule were better observed among Christians!

19 My little children, of whom I travail in birth again until Christ be formed in you. 20 I desire to be present with you now, and to change my voice for I stand in doubt of you.

That the apostle might the better dispose these Christians to bear with him in the reproofs which he was obliged to give them, he here expresses his great affection to them, and the very tender concern he had for their welfare: he was not like them—one thing when among them and another when absent from them. Their disaffection to him had not removed his affection from them; but he still bore the same respect to them which he had formerly done, nor was he like their false teachers, who pretended a great deal of affection to them, when at the same time they were only consulting their own interest; but he had a sincere concern for their truest advantage; he sought not theirs, but them. They were too ready to account him their enemy, but he assures them that he was their friend; nay, not only so, but that he had the bowels of a parent towards them. He calls them *his children,* as he justly might, since he had been the instrument of their conversion to the Christian faith; yea, he styles them his *little children,* which, as it denotes a greater degree of tenderness and affection to them, so it may possibly have a respect to their present behaviour, whereby they showed themselves too much like little children, who are easily wrought upon by the arts and insinuations of others. He expresses his concern for them, and earnest desire of their welfare and soul-prosperity, by the pangs of a travailing woman: *He travailed in birth for them:* and the great thing which he was in so much pain about, and which he was so earnestly desirous of, was not so much that they might affect him as *that Christ might be formed in them,* that they might become Christians indeed, and be more confirmed and established in the faith of the gospel. From this we may note, 1. The very tender affection which faithful ministers bear towards those among whom they are employed; it is like that of the most affectionate parents to their little children. 2. That the chief thing they are longing and even travailing in birth for, on their account, is that Christ may be formed in them; not so much that they may gain their affections, much less that they may make a prey of them, but that they may be renewed in the spirit of their minds, wrought into the image of Christ, and more fully settled and confirmed in the Christian faith and life: and how unreasonably must those people act who suffer themselves to be prevailed upon to desert or dislike such ministers! 3. That Christ is not fully formed in men till they are brought off from trusting in their own righteousness, and made to rely only upon him and his righteousness.

As a further evidence of the affection and concern which the apostle had for these Christians, he adds (*v.* 20) that *he desired to be then present with them*—that he would be glad of an opportunity of being among them, and conversing with them, and that thereupon he might find occasion *to change his voice* towards them; for at present *he stood in doubt of them.* He knew not well what to think of them. He was not so fully acquainted with their state as to know how to accommodate himself to them. He was full of fears and jealousies concerning them, which was the reason of his writing to them in such a manner as he had done; but he would be glad to find that matters were better with them than he feared, and that he might have occasion to commend them, instead of thus reproving and chiding them. Note, Though ministers too often find it necessary to reprove those they have to do with, yet this is no grateful work to them; they had much rather there were no occasion for it, and are always glad when they can see reason to change their voice towards them.

21 Tell me, ye that desire to be
under the law, do ye not hear the
law? 22 For it is written, that
Abraham had two sons, the one by a
bondmaid, the other by a freewoman.
23 But he *who was* of the bondwoman
was born after the flesh; but he of
the freewoman *was* by promise. 24
Which things are an allegory: for
these are the two covenants; the one
from the mount Sinai, which gendereth to bondage, which is Agar. 25
For this Agar is mount Sinai in
Arabia, and answereth to Jerusalem
which now is, and is in bondage with
her children. 26 But Jerusalem
which is above is free, which is the
mother of us all. 27 For it is written, Rejoice, *thou* barren that bearest
not; break forth and cry, thou that
travailest not: for the desolate hath
many more children than she which
hath a husband. 28 Now we, brethren, as Isaac was, are the children
of promise. 29 But as then he that
was born after the flesh persecuted
him *that was born* after the Spirit,
even so *it is* now. 30 Nevertheless
what saith the scripture? Cast out
the bondwoman and her son; for the
son of the bondwoman shall not be
heir with the son of the freewoman.
31 So then, brethren, we are not
children of the bondwoman, but of
the free.

In these verses the apostle illustrates the difference between believers who rested in Christ only and those judaizers who trusted in the law, by a comparison taken from the story of Isaac and Ishmael. This he introduces in such a manner as was proper to strike and impress their minds, and to convince them of their great weakness in departing from the truth, and suffering themselves to be deprived of the liberty of the gospel: *Tell me,* says he, *you that desire to be under the law, do you not hear the law?* He takes it for granted that they did hear the law, for among the Jews it was wont to be read in their public assemblies every sabbath day; and, since they were so very fond of being under it, he would have them duly to consider what is written therein (referring to what is recorded Gen. xvi. and xxi.), for, if they would do this, they might soon see how little reason they had to trust in it. And here, 1. He sets before them the history itself (*v.* 22, 23): *For it is written, Abraham had two sons,* &c. Here he represents the different state and condition of these two sons of Abraham—that the one, Ishmael, *was by a bond-maid,* and the other, Isaac, *by a free-woman;* and that whereas the former *was born after the flesh,* or by the ordinary course of nature, the other *was by promise,* when in the course of nature there was no reason to expect that Sarah should have a son. 2. He acquaints them with the meaning and design of this history, or the use which he intended to make of it (*v.* 24—27): *These things,* says he, *are an allegory,* wherein, besides the literal and historical sense of the words, the Spirit of God might design to signify something further to us, and that was, That these two, Agar and Sarah, *are the two covenants,* or were intended to typify and prefigure the two different dispensations of the covenant. The former, Agar, represented that which was given from mount Sinai, and *which gendereth to bondage,* which, though it was a dispensation of grace, yet, in comparison of the gospel state, was a dispensation of bondage, and became more so to the Jews, through their mistake of the design of it, and expecting to be justified by the works of it. *For this Agar is mount Sinai in Arabia* (mount Sinai was then called Agar by the Arabians), *and it answereth to Jerusalem which now is, and is in bondage with her children;* that is, it justly represents the present state of the Jews, who, continuing in their infidelity and adhering to that covenant, are still in bondage with their children. But the other, Sarah, was intended to prefigure Jerusalem which is above, or the state of Christians under the new and better dispensation of the covenant, which is free both from the curse of the moral and the bondage of the ceremonial law, and *is the mother of us all*—a state into which all, both Jews and Gentiles, are admitted, upon their believing in Christ. And to this greater freedom and enlargement of the church under the gospel dispensation, which was typified by Sarah the mother of the promised seed, the apostle refers that of the prophet, Isa. liv. 1, where it is written, *Rejoice, thou barren that bearest not; break forth and cry, thou that travailest not: for the desolate hath many more children than she who hath a husband.* 3. He applies the history thus explained to the present case (*v.* 28): *Now we, brethren,* says he, *as Isaac was, are the children of the promise.* We Christians, who have accepted Christ, and rely upon him, and look for justification and salvation by him alone, as hereby we become the spiritual, though we are not the natural, seed of Abraham, so we are entitled to the promised inheritance and interested in the blessings of it. But lest these Christians should be stumbled at the opposition they might meet with from the Jews, who were so tenacious of their law as to be ready to persecute those who would not submit to it, he tells them that this was no more than what was pointed to in the type; for *as then he that was born after the flesh persecuted him that was born after the Spirit,* they must expect it would be *so now.* But, for their comfort in this case, he desires them to consider what the scripture saith (Gen. xxi. 10), *Cast out the bond-woman and her son, for the son of the bond-woman shall not be heir with the son of the free-woman.* Though the judaizers should persecute and hate them, yet the issue would be that Judaism would sink, and wither, and perish; but true Christianity should flourish and last for ever. And then, as a general inference from the whole of the sum of what he had said, he concludes (*v.* 31), *So then, brethren, we are not children of the bond-woman, but of the free.*

CHAP. V.

In this chapter the apostle comes to make application of his foregoing discourse. He begins it with a general caution, or exhortation (ver 1), which he afterwards enforces by several considerations, ver 2—12 He then presses them to serious practical godliness, which would be the best antidote against the snares of their false teachers; particularly, I. That they should not strive with one another, ver. 13—15. II. That they would strive against sin, where he shows, 1. That there is in every one a struggle between flesh and spirit, ver. 17. 2. That it is our duty and interest, in this struggle, to side with the better part, ver. 16, 18. 3. He specifies the works of the flesh, which must be watched against and mortified, and the fruits of the Spirit, which must be brought forth and cherished, and shows of what importance it is that they be so, ver. 19—24. And then concludes the chapter with a caution against pride and envy.

STAND fast therefore in the liberty
wherewith Christ hath made us
free, and be not entangled again with
the yoke of bondage. 2 Behold, I Paul
say unto you, that if ye be circumcised, Christ shall profit you nothing.
3 For I testify again to every man
that is circumcised, that he is a
debtor to do the whole law. 4 Christ
is become of no effect unto you, whosoever of you are justified by the law;
ye are fallen from grace. 5 For we
through the Spirit wait for the hope
of righteousness by faith. 6 For in
Jesus Christ neither circumcision
availeth any thing, nor uncircumcision; but faith which worketh by
love. 7 Ye did run well; who did
hinder you that ye should not obey
the truth? 8 This persuasion *cometh*
not of him that calleth you. 9 A little
leaven leaveneth the whole lump. 10
I have confidence in you through the
Lord, that ye will be none otherwise
minded: but he that troubleth you
shall bear his judgment, whosoever
he be. 11 And I, brethren, if I yet
preach circumcision, why do I yet
suffer persecution? then is the offence
of the cross ceased. 12 I would they
were even cut off which trouble you.

In the former part of this chapter the apostle cautions the Galatians to take heed of the judaizing teachers, who endeavoured to bring them back under the bondage of the law. He had been arguing against them before, and had largely shown how contrary the principles and spirit of those teachers were to the spirit of the gospel; and now this is as it were the general inference or application of all that discourse. Since it appeared by what had been said that we can be justified only by faith in Jesus Christ, and not by the righteousness of the law, and that the law of Moses was no longer in force, nor Christians under any obligation to submit to it, therefore he would have them to *stand fast in the liberty wherewith Christ hath made us free, and not to be again entangled with the yoke of bondage.* Here observe, 1. Under the gospel we are enfranchised, we are brought into a state of liberty, wherein we are freed from the yoke of the ceremonial law and from the curse of the moral law; so that we are no longer tied to the observance of the one, nor tied up to the rigour of the other, which curses every one that continues not in all things written therein to do them, *ch.* iii. 10. 2. We owe this liberty to Jesus Christ. It is he who *has made us free;* by his merits he has satisfied the demands of the broken law, and by his authority as a king he has discharged us from the obligation of those carnal ordinances which were imposed on the Jews. And, 3. It is therefore our duty to *stand fast in this liberty,* constantly and faithfully to adhere to the gospel and to the liberty of it, and not to suffer ourselves, upon any consideration, *to be again entangled in the yoke of bondage,* nor persuaded to return back to the law of Moses. This is the general caution or exhortation, which in the following verses the apostle enforces by several reasons or arguments. As,

I. That their submitting to circumcision, and depending on the works of the law for righteousness, were an implicit contradiction of their faith as Christians and a forfeiture of all their advantages by Jesus Christ, *v.* 2—4. And here we may observe, 1. With what solemnity the apostle asserts and declares this: *Behold, I Paul say unto you* (*v.* 2), and he repeats it (*v.* 3), *I testify unto you;* as if he had said, "I, who have proved myself an apostle of Christ, and to have received my authority and instructions from him, do declare, and am ready to pawn my credit and reputation upon it, *that if you be circumcised Christ shall profit you nothing*, &c.," wherein he shows that what he was now saying was not only a matter of great importance, but what might be most assuredly depended on. He was so far from being a preacher of circumcision (as some might report him to be) that he looked upon it as a matter of the greatest consequence that they did not submit to it. 2. What it is which he so solemnly, and with so much assurance, declares: it is that, *if they were circumcised, Christ would profit them nothing*, &c. We are not to suppose that it is mere circumcision which the apostle is here speaking of, or that it was his design to say that none who are circumcised could have any benefit by Christ; for all the Old-Testament saints had been circumcised, and he himself had consented to the circumcising of Timothy. But he is to be understood as speaking of circumcision in the sense in which the judaizing teachers imposed it, who taught *that except they were circumcised, and kept the law of Moses, they could not be saved*, Acts xv. 1. That this is his meaning appears from *v.* 4, where he expresses the same thing by their being *justified by the law*, or seeking justification by the works of it. Now in this case, if they submitted to circumcision in this sense, he declares that *Christ would profit them nothing, that they were debtors to do the whole law*, that *Christ had become of no effect to them*, and that *they were fallen from grace*. From all these expressions it appears that thereby they renounced that way of justification which God had established; yea, that they laid themselves under an impossibility of being justified in his sight, for they became debtors to do the whole law, which required such an obedience as they were not capable of performing, and denounced a curse against those who failed in it, and therefore condemned, but could not justify them; and, consequently, that having thus revolted from Christ, and built their hopes upon the law, Christ would profit them nothing, nor be of any effect to them. Thus, as by being circumcised they renounced their Christianity, so they cut themselves off from all advantage by Christ; and therefore there was the greatest reason why they should stedfastly adhere to that doctrine which they had embraced, and not suffer themselves to be brought under this yoke of bondage. Note, (1.) Though Jesus Christ is able to save to the uttermost, yet there are multitudes whom he will profit nothing. (2.) All those who seek to be justified by the law do thereby render Christ of no effect to them. By building their hopes on the works of the law, they forfeit all their hopes from him; for he will not be the Saviour of any who will not own and rely upon him as their only Saviour.

II. To persuade them to stedfastness in the doctrine and liberty of the gospel, he sets before them his own example, and that of other Jews who had embraced the Christian religion, and acquaints them what their hopes were, namely, That *through the Spirit they were waiting for the hope of righteousness by faith*. Though they were Jews by nature, and had been bred up under the law, yet being, through the Spirit, brought to the knowledge of Christ, they had renounced all dependence on the works of the law, and looked for justification and salvation only by faith in him; and therefore it must needs be the greatest folly in those who had never been under the law to suffer themselves to be brought into subjection to it, and to found their hopes upon the works of it. Here we may observe, 1. What it is that Christians are waiting for: it is *the hope of righteousness*, by which we are chiefly to understand the happiness of the other world. This is called the hope of Christians, as it is the great object of their hope, which they are above every thing else desiring and pursuing; and the hope of righteousness, as their hopes of it are founded on righteousness, not their own, but that of our Lord Jesus: for, though a life of righteousness is the way that leads to this happiness, yet it is the righteousness of Christ alone which has procured it for us, and on account of which we can expect to be brought to the possession of it. 2. How they hope to obtain this happiness, namely, by faith, that is, in our Lord Jesus Christ, not by the works of the law, or any thing they can do to deserve it, but only by faith, receiving and relying upon him as the Lord our righteousness. It is in this way only that they expect either to be entitled to it here or possessed of it hereafter. And, 3. Whence it is that they are thus waiting for the hope of righteousness: it is *through the Spirit*. Herein they act under the direction and influence of the Holy Spirit; it is under his conduct, and by his assistance, that they are both persuaded and enabled to believe on Christ, and to look for the hope of righteousness through him. When the apostle thus represents the case of Christians, it is implied that if they expected to be justified and saved in any other way they were likely to meet with a disappointment, and therefore that they were greatly concerned to adhere to the doctrine of the gospel which they had embraced.

III. He argues from the nature and design of the Christian institution, which was to abolish the difference between Jew and Gentile, and to establish faith in Christ as the way of our acceptance with God. He tells them (*v.* 6) that *in Christ Jesus*, or under the gospel dispensation, *neither circumcision availeth any thing nor uncircumcision*. Though, while the legal state lasted, there was a difference put between Jew and Greek, between those who were and those who were not circumcised, the former being admitted to those privileges of the church of God from which the other were excluded, yet it was otherwise in the gospel state: Christ, who is *the end of the law,* having come, now it was neither here nor there whether a man were circumcised or uncircumcised; he was neither the better for the one nor the worse for the other, nor would either the one or the other recommend him to God; and therefore as their judaizing teachers were very unreasonable in imposing circumcision upon them, and obliging them to observe the law of Moses, so they must needs be very unwise in submitting to them herein. But, though he assures them that neither circumcision nor uncircumcision would avail to their acceptance with God, yet he informs them what would do so, and that is *faith, which worketh by love:* such a faith in Christ as discovers itself to be true and genuine by a sincere love to God and our neighbour. If they had this, it mattered not whether they were circumcised or uncircumcised, but without it nothing else would stand them in any stead. Note, 1. No external privileges nor profession will avail to our acceptance with God, without a sincere faith in our Lord Jesus. 2. Faith, where it is true, is a working grace: it works by love, love to God and love to our brethren; and faith, thus working by love, is all in all in our Christianity.

IV. To recover them from their backslidings, and engage them to greater stedfastness for the future, he puts them in mind of their good beginnings, and calls upon them to consider whence it was that they were so much altered from what they had been, *v.* 7.

1. He tells them that *they did run well;* at their first setting out in Christianity they had behaved themselves very commendably, they had readily embraced the Christian religion, and discovered a becoming zeal in the ways and work of it; as in their baptism they were devoted to God, and had declared themselves the disciples of Christ, so their behaviour was agreeable to their character and profession. Note, (1.) The life of a Christian is a race, wherein he must run, and hold on, if he would obtain the prize. (2.) It is not enough that we run in this race, by a profession of Christianity, but we must run well, by living up to that profession. Thus these Christians had done for awhile, but they had been obstructed in their progress, and were either turned out of the way or at least made to flag and falter in it. Therefore,

2. He asks them, and calls upon them to ask themselves, *Who did hinder you?* How came it to pass that they did not hold on in the way wherein they had begun to run so well? He very well knew who they were, and what it was that hindered them; but he would have them to put the question to themselves, and seriously consider whether they had any good reason to hearken to those who gave them this disturbance, and whether what they offered was sufficient to justify them in their present conduct. Note, (1.) Many who set out fair in religion, and run well for awhile—run within the bounds appointed for the race, and run with zeal and alacrity too—are yet by some means or other hindered in their progress, or turned out of the way. (2.) It concerns those who have run well, but now begin either to turn out of the way or to tire in it, to enquire what it is that hinders them. Young converts must expect that Satan will be laying stumbling-blocks in their way, and doing all he can to divert them from the course they are in; but, whenever they find themselves in danger of being turned out of it, they would do well to consider who it is that hinders them. Whoever they were that hindered these Christians, the apostle tells them that by hearkening to them they were kept from *obeying the truth,* and were thereby in danger of losing the benefit of what they had done in religion. The gospel which he had preached to them, and which they had embraced and professed, he assures them was the truth; it was therein only that the true way of justification and salvation was fully discovered, and, in order to their enjoying the advantage of it, it was necessary that they should obey it, that they should firmly adhere to it, and continue to govern their lives and hopes according to the directions of it. If therefore they should suffer themselves to be drawn away from it they must needs be guilty of the greatest weakness and folly. Note, [1.] The truth is not only to be believed, but to be obeyed, to be received not only in the light of it, but in the love and power of it. [2.] Those do not rightly obey the truth, who do not stedfastly adhere to it. [3.] There is the same reason for our obeying the truth that there was for our embracing it: and therefore those act very unreasonably who, when they have begun to run well in the Christian race, suffer themselves to be hindered, so as not to persevere in it.

V. He argues for their stedfastness in the faith and liberty of the gospel from the ill rise of that persuasion whereby they were drawn away from it (*v.* 8): *This persuasion,* says he, *cometh not of him that calleth you.* The opinion or persuasion of which the apostle here speaks was no doubt that of the necessity of their being circumcised, and keeping the law of Moses, or of their mixing the works of the law with faith in Christ in the business of justification. This was what the judaizing teachers endeavoured to impose upon them, and what they had too easily fallen into. To convince them of their folly herein, he tells them that this persuasion did not come of him that called them, that is, either of God, by whose authority the gospel had been preached to them and they had been called into the fellowship of it, or of the apostle himself, who had been employed as the instrument of calling them hereunto. It could not come from God, for it was contrary to that way of justification and salvation which he had established; nor could they have received it from Paul himself; for, whatever some might pretend, he had all along been an opposer and not a preacher of circumcision, and, if in any instance he had submitted to it for the sake of peace, yet he had never pressed the use of it upon Christians, much less imposed it upon them as necessary to salvation. Since then this persuasion did not come of him that had called them, he leaves them to judge whence it must arise, and sufficiently intimates that it could be owing to none but Satan and his instruments, who by this means were endeavouring to overthrow their faith and obstruct the progress of the gospel, and therefore that the Galatians had every reason to reject it, and to continue stedfast in the truth which they had before embraced. Note, 1. In order to our judging aright of the different persuasions in religion which there are among Christians, it concerns us to enquire whether they come of him that calleth us, whether or no they are founded upon the authority of Christ and his apostles. 2. If, upon enquiry, they appear to have no such foundation, how forward soever others may be to impose them upon us, we should by no means submit to them, but reject them.

VI. The danger there was of the spreading of this infection, and the ill influence it might have upon others, are a further argument which the apostle urges against their complying with their false teachers in what they would impose on them. It is possible that, to extenuate their fault, they might be ready to say that there were but few of those teachers among them who endeavoured to draw them into this persuasion and practice, or that they were only some smaller matters wherein they complied with them—that though they submitted to be circumcised, and to observe some few rites of the Jewish laws, yet they had by no means renounced their Christianity and gone over to Judaism. Or, suppose their complying thus far was as faulty as he could represent it, yet perhaps they might further say that there were but few among them who had done so, and therefore he needed not be so much concerned about it. Now, to obviate such pretences as these, and to convince them that there was more danger in it than they were aware of, he tells them (*v.* 9) that *a little leaven leaveneth the whole lump*—that the whole lump of Christianity may be tainted and corrupted by one such erroneous principle, or that the whole lump of the Christian society may be infected by one member of it, and therefore that they were greatly concerned not to yield in this single instance, or, if any had done so, to endeavour by all proper methods to purge out the infection from among them. Note, It is dangerous for Christian churches to encourage those among them who entertain, especially who set themselves to propagate, destructive errors. This was the case here. The doctrine which the false teachers were industrious to spread, and which some in these churches had been drawn into, was subversive of Christianity itself, as the apostle had before shown; and therefore, though the number either of the one or the other of these might be but small, yet, considering the fatal tendency of it and the corruption of human nature, whereby others were too much disposed to be infected with it, he would not have them on that account to be easy and unconcerned, but remember that *a little leaven leaveneth the whole lump.* If these were indulged the contagion might soon spread further and wider; and, if they suffered themselves to be imposed upon in this instance, it might soon issue in the utter ruin of the truth and liberty of the gospel.

VII. That he might conciliate the greater regard to what he had said, he expresses the hopes he had concerning them (*v.* 10): *I have confidence in you,* says he, *through the Lord, that you will be none otherwise minded.* Though he had many fears and doubts about them (which was the occasion of his using so much plainness and freedom with them), yet he hoped that through the blessing of God upon what he had written they might be brought to be of the same mind with him, and to own and abide by that truth and that liberty of the gospel which he had preached to them, and was now endeavouring to confirm them in. Herein he teaches us that we ought to hope the best even of those concerning whom we have cause to fear the worst. That they might be the less offended at the reproofs he had given them for their unstedfastness in the faith, he lays the blame of it more upon others than themselves; for he adds, *But he that troubleth you shall bear his judgment, whosoever he be.* He was sensible that there were *some that troubled them, and would pervert the gospel of Christ* (as *ch.* i. 7), and possibly he may point to some one particular man who was more busy and forward than others, and might be the chief instrument of the disorder that was among them; and to this he imputes their defection or inconstancy more than to any thing in themselves. This may give us occasion to observe that, in reproving sin and error, we should always distinguish between the leaders and the led, such as set themselves to draw others thereinto and such as are drawn aside by them. Thus the apostle softens and alleviates the fault of these Christians, even while he is reproving them, that he might the better persuade them to return to, and stand fast in, the liberty wherewith Christ had made them free: but as for him or those that troubled them, whoever he or they were, he declares they *should bear their judgment,* he did not doubt but God would deal with them according to their deserts, and out of his just indignation against them, as enemies of Christ and his church, he wishes that *they were even cut off*—not cut off from Christ and all hopes of salvation by him, but cut off by the censures of the church, which ought to witness against those teachers who thus corrupted the purity of the gospel. Those, whether ministers or others, who set themselves to overthrow the faith of the gospel, and disturb the peace of Christians, do thereby forfeit the privileges of Christian communion and deserve to be cut off from them.

VIII. To dissuade these Christians from hearkening to their judaizing teachers, and to recover them from the ill impressions they had made upon them, he represents them as men who had used very base and disingenuous methods to compass their designs; for they had misrepresented him, that they might the more easily gain their ends upon them. That which they were endeavouring was to bring them to submit to circumcision, and to mix Judaism with their Christianity; and, the better to accomplish this design, they had given out among them that Paul himself was a preacher of circumcision: for when he says (*v.* 11), *And I brethren, if I yet preach circumcision*, it plainly appears that they had reported him to have done so, and that they had made use of this as an argument to prevail with the Galatians to submit to it. It is probable that they grounded this report upon his having circumcised Timothy, Acts xvi. 3. But, though for good reasons he had yielded to circumcision in that instance, yet that he was a preacher of it, and especially in that sense wherein they imposed it, he utterly denies. To prove the injustice of that charge upon him, he offers such arguments as, if they would allow themselves to consider, could not fail to convince them of it. 1. If he would have preached circumcision, he might have avoided persecution. If I yet preach circumcision, says he, *why do I yet suffer persecution?* It was evident, and they could not but be sensible of it, that he was hated and persecuted by the Jews; but what account could be given of this their behaviour towards him, if he had so far symbolized with them as to preach up circumcision, and the observance of the law of Moses, as necessary to salvation? This was the great point they were contending for; and, if he had fallen in with them herein, instead of being exposed to their rage he might have been received into their favour. When therefore he was suffering persecution from them, this was a plain evidence that he had not complied with them; yea, that he was so far from preaching the doctrine he was charged with, that, rather than do so, he was willing to expose himself to the greatest hazards. 2. If he had yielded to the Jews herein, *then would the offence of the cross have ceased.* They would not have taken so much offence against the doctrine of Christianity as they did, nor would he and others have been exposed to so much suffering on the account of it as they were. He informs us (1 Cor. i. 23) that the preaching of the cross of Christ (or the doctrine of justification and salvation only by faith in Christ crucified) *was to the Jews a stumbling-block.* That which they were most offended at in Christianity was, that thereby circumcision, and the whole frame of the legal administration, were set aside, as no longer in force. This raised their greatest outcries against it, and stirred them up to oppose and persecute the professors of it. Now if Paul and others could have given into this opinion, that circumcision was still to be retained, and the observance of the law of Moses joined with faith in Christ as necessary to salvation, then their offence against it would have been in a great measure removed, and they might have avoided the sufferings they underwent for the sake of it. But though others, and particularly those who were so forward to asperse him as a preacher of this doctrine, could easily come into it, yet so could not he. He rather chose to hazard his ease and credit, yea his very life itself, than thus to corrupt the truth and give up the liberty of the gospel. Hence it was that the Jews continued to be so much offended against Christianity, and against him as the preacher of it. Thus the apostle clears himself from the unjust reproach which his enemies had cast upon him, and at the same time shows how little regard was due to those men who could treat him in such an injurious manner, and how much reason he had to wish that they were even cut off.

13 For, brethren, ye have been
called unto liberty; only *use* not
liberty for an occasion to the flesh,
but by love serve one another. 14
For all the law is fulfilled in one
word, *even* in this; Thou shalt love
thy neighbour as thyself. 15 But if
ye bite and devour one another, take
heed that ye be not consumed one of
another. 16 *This* I say then, Walk
in the Spirit, and ye shall not fulfil
the lust of the flesh. 17 For the
flesh lusteth against the Spirit, and
the Spirit against the flesh: and these
are contrary the one to the other: so that
ye cannot do the things that ye would.
18 But if ye be led of the Spirit, ye
are not under the law. 19 Now the
works of the flesh are manifest, which
are *these;* Adultery, fornication,
uncleanness, lasciviousness, 20 Idolatry, witchcraft, hatred, variance,
emulations, wrath, strife, seditions,
heresies, 21 Envyings, murders,
drunkenness, revellings, and such like:
of the which I tell you before, as I have
also told *you* in time past, that they

which do such things shall not inherit
the kingdom of God. 22 But the
fruit of the Spirit is love, joy, peace,
longsuffering, gentleness, goodness,
faith, 23 Meekness, temperance:
against such there is no law. 24
And they that are Christ's have crucified the flesh with the affections
and lusts. 25 If we live in the
Spirit, let us also walk in the Spirit.
26 Let us not be desirous of vain
glory, provoking one another, envying
one another.

In the latter part of this chapter the apostle comes to exhort these Christians to serious practical godliness, as the best antidote against the snares of the false teachers. Two things especially he presses upon them:—

I. That they should not strive with one another, but love one another. He tells them (*v.* 13) that *they had been called unto liberty*, and he would have them to stand fast in the liberty wherewith Christ had made them free; but yet he would have them be very careful that they did not *use this liberty as an occasion to the flesh*—that they did not thence take occasion to indulge themselves in any corrupt affections and practices, and particularly such as might create distance and disaffection, and be the ground of quarrels and contentions among them: but, on the contrary, he would have them *by love to serve one another*, to maintain that mutual love and affection which, notwithstanding any minor differences there might be among them, would dispose them to all those offices of respect and kindness to each other which the Christian religion obliged them to. Note, 1. The liberty we enjoy as Christians is not a licentious liberty: though Christ has redeemed us from the curse of the law, yet he has not freed us from the obligation of it; the gospel is a *doctrine according to godliness* (1 Tim. vi. 3), and is so far from giving the least countenance to sin that it lays us under the strongest obligations to avoid and subdue it. 2. Though we ought to stand fast in our Christian liberty, yet we should not insist upon it to the breach of Christian charity; we should not use it as an occasion of strife and contention with our fellow Christians, who may be differently minded from us, but should always maintain such a temper towards each other as may dispose us by love to serve one another. To this the apostle endeavours to persuade these Christians, and there are two considerations which he sets before them for this purpose:—(1.) *That all the law is fulfilled in one word, even in this, Thou shalt love thy neighbour as thyself, v.* 14. Love is the sum of the whole law; as love to God comprises the duties of the first table, so love to our neighbour those of the second. The apostle takes notice of the latter here, because he is speaking of their behaviour towards one another; and, when he makes use of this as an argument to persuade them to mutual love, he intimates both that this would be a good evidence of their sincerity in religion and also the most likely means of rooting out those dissensions and divisions that were among them. It will appear that we are the disciples of Christ indeed when we have love one to another (John xiii. 35); and, where this temper is kept up, if it do not wholly extinguish those unhappy discords that are among Christians, yet at least it will so far accommodate them that the fatal consequences of them will be prevented. (2.) The sad and dangerous tendency of a contrary behaviour (*v.* 15): *But*, says he, if instead of serving one another in love, and therein fulfilling the law of God, *you bite and devour one another, take heed that you be not consumed one of another.* If, instead of acting like men and Christians, they would behave themselves more like brute beasts, in tearing and rending one another, they could expect nothing as the consequence of it, but that they would be consumed one of another; and therefore they had the greatest reason not to indulge themselves in such quarrels and animosities. Note, Mutual strifes among brethren, if persisted in, are likely to prove a common ruin; those that devour one another are in a fair way to be consumed one of another. Christian churches cannot be ruined but by their own hands; but if Christians, who should be helps to one another and a joy one to another, be as brute beasts, biting and devouring each other, what can be expected but that the God of love should deny his grace to them, and the Spirit of love should depart from them, and that the evil spirit, who seeks the destruction of them all, should prevail?

II. That they should all strive against sin; and happy would it be for the church if Christians would let all their quarrels be swallowed up of this, even a quarrel against sin—if, instead of biting and devouring one another on account of their different opinions, they would all set themselves against sin in themselves and the places where they live. This is what we are chiefly concerned to fight against, and that which above every thing else we should make it our business to oppose and suppress. To excite Christians hereunto, and to assist them herein, the apostle shows,

1. That there is in every one a struggle between the flesh and the spirit (*v.* 17): *The flesh* (the corrupt and carnal part of us) *lusts* (strives and struggles with strength and vigour) *against the spirit:* it opposes all the motions of the Spirit, and resists every thing that is spiritual. On the other hand, *the spirit* (the renewed part of us) strives *against the flesh,* and opposes the will and desire of it: and hence it comes to pass *that we cannot do the things that we would.* As the princi-

ple of grace in us will not suffer us to do all the evil which our corrupt nature would prompt us to, so neither can we do all the good that we would, by reason of the oppositions we meet with from that corrupt and carnal principle. Even as in a natural man there is something of this struggle (the convictions of his conscience and the corruption of his own heart strive with one another; his convictions would suppress his corruptions, and his corruptions silence his convictions), so in a renewed man, where there is something of a good principle, there is a struggle between the old nature and the new nature, the remainders of sin and the beginnings of grace; and this Christians must expect will be their exercise as long as they continue in this world.

2. That it is our duty and interest in this struggle to side with the better part, to side with our convictions against our corruptions and with our graces against our lusts. This the apostle represents as our duty, and directs us to the most effectual means of success in it. If it should be asked, What course must we take that the better interest may get the better? he gives us this one general rule, which, if duly observed, would be the most sovereign remedy against the prevalence of corruption; and that is to walk in the Spirit (*v.* 16): *This I say, then, Walk in the Spirit, and you shall not fulfil the lust of the flesh.* By the *Spirit* here may be meant either the Holy Spirit himself, who condescends to dwell in the hearts of those whom he has renewed and sanctified, to guide and assist them in the way of their duty, or that gracious principle which he implants in the souls of his people and which lusts against the flesh, as that corrupt principle which still remains in them does against it. Accordingly the duty here recommended to us is that we set ourselves to act under the guidance and influence of the blessed Spirit, and agreeably to the motions and tendency of the new nature in us; and, if this be our care in the ordinary course and tenour of our lives, we may depend upon it that, though we may not be freed from the stirrings and oppositions of our corrupt nature, we shall be kept from fulfilling it in the lusts thereof; so that though it remain in us, yet it shall not obtain a dominion over us. Note, The best antidote against the poison of sin is to walk in the Spirit, to be much in conversing with spiritual things, to mind the things of the soul, which is the spiritual part of man, more than those of the body, which is his carnal part, to commit ourselves to the guidance of the word, wherein the Holy Spirit makes known the will of God concerning us, and in the way of our duty to act in a dependence on his aids and influences. And, as this would be the best means of preserving them from fulfilling the lusts of the flesh, so it would be a good evidence that they were Christians indeed; for, says the apostle (*v.* 18), *If you be led by the Spirit, you are not under the law.* As if he had said, "You must expect a struggle between flesh and spirit as long as you are in the world, that the flesh will be lusting against the spirit as well as the spirit against the flesh; but if, in the prevailing bent and tenour of your lives, you be *led by the Spirit,*—if you act under the guidance and government of the Holy Spirit and of that spiritual nature and disposition he has wrought in you,—if you make the word of God your rule and the grace of God your principle,—it will hence appear that you are not under the law, not under the condemning, though you are still under the commanding, power of it; for *there is now no condemnation to those that are in Christ Jesus, who walk not after the flesh, but after the Spirit;* and *as many as are led by the Spirit of God, they are the sons of God,*" Rom. viii. 1—14.

3. The apostle specifies the works of the flesh, which must be watched against and mortified, and the fruits of the Spirit, which must be cherished and brought forth (*v.* 19, &c.); and by specifying particulars he further illustrates what he is here upon. (1.) He begins with *the works of the flesh,* which, as they are many, so they are manifest. It is past dispute that the things he here speaks of are the works of the flesh, or the product of corrupt and depraved nature; most of them are condemned by the light of nature itself, and all of them by the light of scripture. The particulars he specifies are of various sorts; some are sins against the seventh commandment, such as *adultery, fornication, uncleanness, lasciviousness,* by which are meant not only the gross acts of these sins, but all such thoughts, and words, and actions, as have a tendency towards the great transgression. Some are sins against the first and second commandments, as *idolatry* and *witchcraft.* Others are sins against our neighbour, and contrary to the royal law of brotherly love, such as *hatred, variance, emulations, wrath, strife,* which too often occasion *seditions, heresies, envyings,* and sometimes break out into *murders,* not only of the names and reputation, but even of the very lives, of our fellow-creatures. Others are sins against ourselves, such as *drunkenness and revellings;* and he concludes the catalogue with an *et cætera,* and gives fair warning to all to take care of them, as they hope to see the face of God with comfort. Of these and *such like,* says he, *I tell you before, as I have also told you in times past,* that *those who do such things,* how much soever they may flatter themselves with vain hopes, *shall not inherit the kingdom of God.* These are sins which will undoubtedly shut men out of heaven. The world of spirits can never be comfortable to those who plunge themselves in the filth of the flesh; nor will the righteous and holy God ever admit such into his favour and presence, unless they be first *washed and sanctified, and justified in the name of our*

Lord Jesus, and by the Spirit of our God, 1 Cor. vi. 11. (2.) He specifies the fruits of the Spirit, or the renewed nature, which as Christians we are concerned to bring forth, *v.* 22, 23. And here we may observe that as sin is called *the work of the flesh,* because the flesh, or corrupt nature, is the principle that moves and excites men to it, so grace is said to be *the fruit of the Spirit,* because it wholly proceeds from the Spirit, as the fruit does from the root: and whereas before the apostle had chiefly specified those works of the flesh which were not only hurtful to men themselves but tended to make them so to one another, so here he chiefly takes notice of those fruits of the Spirit which had a tendency to make Christians agreeable one to another, as well as easy to themselves; and this was very suitable to the caution or exhortation he had before given (*v.* 13), that they should *not use their liberty as an occasion to the flesh, but by love serve one another.* He particularly recommends to us, *love,* to God especially, and to one another for his sake,—*joy,* by which may be understood cheerfulness in conversation with our friends, or rather a constant delight in God,—*peace,* with God and conscience, or a peaceableness of temper and behaviour towards others,—*long-suffering,* patience to defer anger, and a contentedness to bear injuries,—*gentleness,* such a sweetness of temper, and especially towards our inferiors, as disposes us to be affable and courteous, and easy to be entreated when any have wronged us,—*goodness* (kindness, beneficence), which shows itself in a readiness to do good to all as we have opportunity,—*faith,* fidelity, justice, and honesty, in what we profess and promise to others,—*meekness,* wherewith to govern our passions and resentments, so as not to be easily provoked, and, when we are so, to be soon pacified,—and *temperance,* in meat and drink, and other enjoyments of life, so as not to be excessive and immoderate in the use of them. Concerning these things, or those in whom these fruits of the Spirit are found, the apostle says, *There is no law against them,* to condemn and punish them. Yea, hence it appears that they are not under the law, but under grace; for these fruits of the Spirit, in whomsoever they are found, plainly show that such are *led by the Spirit,* and consequently that they are not *under the law,* as *v.* 18. And as, by specifying these works of the flesh and fruits of the Spirit, the apostle directs us both what we are to avoid and oppose and what we are to cherish and cultivate, so (*v.* 24) he informs us that this is the sincere care and endeavour of all real Christians: *And those that are Christ's,* says he (those who are Christians indeed, not only in show and profession, but in sincerity and truth), *have crucified the flesh with the affections and lusts.* As in their baptism they were obliged hereunto (for, being baptized into Christ, they were baptized into his death, Rom. vi. 3), so they are now sincerely employing themselves herein, and, in conformity to their Lord and head, are endeavouring to die unto sin, as he had died for it. They have not yet obtained a complete victory over it; they have still flesh as well as Spirit in them, and that has its affections and lusts, which continue to give them no little disturbance, but as it does not now *reign in their mortal bodies, so as that they obey it in the lusts thereof* (Rom. vi. 12), so they are seeking the utter ruin and destruction of it, and to put it to the same shameful and ignominious, though lingering death, which our Lord Jesus underwent for our sakes. Note, If we would approve ourselves to be Christ's, such as are united to him and interested in him, we must make it our constant care and business to crucify the flesh with its corrupt affections and lusts. Christ will never own those as his who yield themselves the servants of sin. But though the apostle here only mentions the crucifying of the flesh with the affections and lusts, as the care and character of real Christians, yet, no doubt, it is also implied that, on the other hand, we should show forth those fruits of the Spirit which he had just before been specifying; this is no less our duty than that, nor is it less necessary to evidence our sincerity in religion. It is not enough that we cease to do evil, but we must learn to do well. Our Christianity obliges us not only to die unto sin, but to live unto righteousness; not only to oppose the works of the flesh, but to bring forth the fruits of the Spirit too. If therefore we would make it appear that we do indeed belong to Christ, this must be our sincere care and endeavour as well as the other; and that it was the design of the apostle to represent both the one and the other of these as our duty, and as necessary to support our character as Christians, may be gathered from what follows (*v.* 25), where he adds, *If we live in the Spirit, let us also walk in the Spirit;* that is, "If we profess to have received the Spirit of Christ, or that we are renewed in the spirit of our minds, and endued with a principle of spiritual life, let us make it appear by the proper fruits of the Spirit in our lives." He had before told us that the Spirit of Christ is a privilege bestowed on all the children of God, *ch.* iv. 6. "Now," says he, "if we profess to be of this number, and as such to have obtained this privilege, let us show it by a temper and behaviour agreeable hereunto; let us evidence our good principles by good practices." Our conversation will always be answerable to the principle which we are under the guidance and government of: as *those that are after the flesh do mind the things of the flesh,* so *those that are after the Spirit do mind the things of the Spirit,* Rom. viii. 5. If therefore we would have it appear that we are Christ's, and that we are partakers of his Spirit, it must be by our *walking not after the flesh, but after the spirit.* We must set ourselves in good earnest both to mortify the deeds of the body, and to walk in newness of life.

4. The apostle concludes this chapter with a caution against pride and envy, *v.* 26. He had before been exhorting these Christians *by love to serve one another* (*v.* 13), and had put them in mind of what would be the consequence if, instead of that, they did *bite and devour one another*, *v.* 15. Now, as a means of engaging them to the one and preserving them from the other of these, he here cautions them against being desirous of vain-glory, or giving way to an undue affectation of the esteem and applause of men, because this, if it were indulged, would certainly lead them to provoke one another and to envy one another. As far as this temper prevails among Christians, they will be ready to slight and despise those whom they look upon as inferior to them, and to be put out of humour if they are denied that respect which they think is their due from them, and they will also be apt to envy those by whom their reputation is in any danger of being lessened: and thus a foundation is laid for those quarrels and contentions which, as they are inconsistent with that love which Christians ought to maintain towards each other, so they are greatly prejudicial to the honour and interest of religion itself. This therefore the apostle would have us by all means to watch against. Note, (1.) The glory which comes from men is vain-glory, which, instead of being desirous of, we should be dead to. (2.) An undue regard to the approbation and applause of men is one great ground of the unhappy strifes and contentions that exist among Christians.

CHAP VI.

This chapter chiefly consists of two parts. In the former the apostle gives us several plain and practical directions, which more especially tend to instruct Christians in their duty to one another, and to promote the communion of saints in love, ver. 1—10. In the latter he revives the main design of the epistle, which was to fortify the Galatians against the arts of their judaizing teachers, and confirm them in the truth and liberty of the gospel, for which purpose he, I. Gives them the true character of these teachers, and shows them from what motives, and with what views, they acted, ver. 11—14. And, II. On the other hand he acquaints them with his own temper and behaviour. From both these they might easily see how little reason they had to slight him, and to fall in with them. And then he concludes the epistle with a solemn benediction.

BRETHREN, if a man be overtaken in a fault, ye which are
spiritual, restore such a one in the
spirit of meekness; considering thyself, lest thou also be tempted. 2
Bear ye one another's burdens, and
so fulfil the law of Christ. 3 For if
a man think himself to be something,
when he is nothing, he deceiveth
himself. 4 But let every man prove
his own work, and then shall he have
rejoicing in himself alone, and not in
another. 5 For every man shall bear
his own burden. 6 Let him that is
taught in the word communicate unto
him that teacheth in all good things.
7 Be not deceived; God is not mocked:
for whatsoever a man soweth, that
shall he also reap. 8 For he that
soweth to his flesh shall of the flesh
reap corruption; but he that soweth
to the Spirit shall of the Spirit reap
life everlasting. 9 And let us not
be weary in well doing: for in due
season we shall reap, if we faint not.
10 As we have therefore opportunity,
let us do good unto all *men*, especially
unto them who are of the household
of faith.

The apostle having, in the foregoing chapter, exhorted Christians *by love to serve one another* (*v.* 13), and also cautioned us (*v.* 26) against a temper which, if indulged, would hinder us from showing the mutual love and serviceableness which he had recommended, in the beginning of this chapter he proceeds to give some further directions, which, if duly observed, would both promote the one and prevent the other of these, and render our behaviour both more agreeable to our Christian profession and more useful and comfortable to one another: particularly,

I. We are here taught to deal tenderly with those who are overtaken in a fault, *v.* 1. He puts a common case: *If a man be overtaken in a fault*, that is, be brought to sin by the surprise of temptation. It is one thing to overtake a fault by contrivance and deliberation, and a full resolution in sin, and another thing to be overtaken in a fault. The latter is the case here supposed, and herein the apostle shows that great tenderness should be used. *Those who are spiritual*, by whom is meant, not only the ministers (as if none but they were to be called spiritual persons), but other Christians too, especially those of the higher form in Christianity; these must *restore such a one with the spirit of meekness.* Here observe, 1. The duty we are directed to—to restore such; we should labour, by faithful reproofs, and pertinent and seasonable councils, to bring them to repentance. The original word, καταρτίζετε, signifies *to set in joint*, as a dislocated bone; accordingly we should endeavour to set them in joint again, to bring them to themselves, by convincing them of their sin and error, persuading them to return to their duty, comforting them in a sense of pardoning mercy thereupon, and, having thus recovered them, confirming our love to them. 2. The manner wherein this is to be done: *With the spirit of meekness;* not in wrath and passion, as those who triumph in a brother's falls, but with meekness, as those who rather mourn for them. Many needful reproofs lose their efficacy by being given in wrath; but when they are managed with calmness and tenderness, and appear to proceed from sincere affection and concern for the welfare of those to whom they are given, they are likely to make a due impression. 3. A very good reason why this should be done with meekness: *Considering thyself, lest thou also be tempted.* We ought to deal very tenderly with those who are overtaken in sin, because we none of us know but it may some time or other be our own case. We also may be tempted, yea, and overcome by the temptation; and therefore, if we rightly consider ourselves, this will dispose us to do by others as we desire to be done by in such a case.

II. We are here directed *to bear one another's burdens, v.* 2. This may be considered either as referring to what goes before, and so may teach us to exercise forbearance and compassion towards one another, in the case of those weaknesses, and follies, and infirmities, which too often attend us—that, though we should not wholly connive at them, yet we should not be severe against one another on account of them; or as a more general precept, and so it directs us to sympathize with one another under the various trials and troubles that we may meet with, and to be ready to afford each other the comfort and counsel, the help and assistance, which our circumstances may require. To excite us hereunto, the apostle adds, by way of motive, that so we shall *fulfil the law of Christ.* This is to act agreeably to the law of his precept, which is the law of love, and obliges us to a mutual forbearance and forgiveness, to sympathy with and compassion towards each other; and it would also be agreeable to his pattern and example, which have the force of a law to us. He bears with us under our weaknesses and follies, he is *touched with a fellow-feeling of our infirmities;* and therefore there is good reason why we should maintain the same temper towards one another. Note, Though as Christians we are freed from the law of Moses, yet we are under the law of Christ; and therefore, instead of laying unnecessary burdens upon others (as those who urged the observance of Moses's law did), it much more becomes us to fulfil the law of Christ by bearing one another's burdens. The apostle being aware how great a hindrance pride would be to the mutual condescension and sympathy which he had been recommending, and that a conceit of ourselves would dispose us to censure and contemn our brethren, instead of bearing with their infirmities and endeavouring to restore them when overtaken with a fault, he therefore (*v.* 3) takes care to caution us against this; he supposes it as a very possible thing (and it would be well if it were not too common) for a man to think himself to be something—to entertain a fond opinion of his own sufficiency, to look upon himself as wiser and better than other men, and as fit to dictate and prescribe to them—when in truth he is nothing, has nothing of substance or solidity in him, or that can be a ground of the confidence and superiority which he assumes. To dissuade us from giving way to this temper he tells us that such a one does but deceive himself; while he imposes upon others, by pretending to what he has not, he puts the greatest cheat upon himself, and sooner or later will find the sad effects of it. This will never gain him that esteem, either with God or good men, which he is ready to expect; he is neither the freer from mistakes nor will he be the more secure against temptations for the good opinion he has of his own sufficiency, but rather the more liable to fall into them, and to be overcome by them; for *he that thinks he stands has need to take heed lest he fall.* Instead therefore of indulging such a vain-glorious humour, which is both destructive of the love and kindness we owe to our fellow-christians and also injurious to ourselves, it would much better become us to accept the apostle's exhortation (Phil. ii. 3), *Do nothing through strife nor vain-glory; but in lowliness of mind let each esteem others better than himself.* Note, Self-conceit is but self-deceit: as it is inconsistent with that charity we owe to others (for *charity vaunteth not itself, is not puffed up,* 1 Cor. xiii. 4), so it is a cheat upon ourselves; and there is not a more dangerous cheat in the world than self-deceit. As a means of preventing this evil,

III. We are advised every one to prove his own work, *v.* 4. By our own work is chiefly meant our own actions or behaviour. These the apostle directs us to prove, that is, seriously and impartially to examine them by the rule of God's word, to see whether or no they are agreeable to it, and therefore such as God and conscience do approve. This he represents as the duty of every man; instead of being forward to judge and censure others, it would much more become us to search and try our own ways; our business lies more at home than abroad, with ourselves than with other men, *for what have we to do to judge another man's servant?* From the connection of this exhortation with what goes before it appears that if Christians did duly employ themselves in this work they might easily discover those defects and failings in themselves which would soon convince them how little reason they have either to be conceited of themselves or severe in their censures of others; and so it gives us occasion to observe that the best way to keep us from being proud of ourselves is to prove our own-selves: the better we are acquainted with our own hearts and ways, the less liable shall we be to despise and the more disposed to compassionate and help others under their infirmities and afflictions. That we may be persuaded to this necessary and profitable duty of proving our own work, the apostle urges two considerations very proper for this purpose:—

1. This is the way to *have rejoicing in ourselves alone.* If we set ourselves in good earnest to *prove our own work,* and, upon the

trial, can approve ourselves to God, as to our sincerity and uprightness towards him, then may we expect to have comfort and peace in our own souls, having the testimony of our own consciences for us (as 2 Cor. i. 12), and this, he intimates, would be a much better ground of joy and satisfaction than to be able to rejoice *in another,* either in the good opinion which others may have of us or in having gained over others to our opinion, which the false teachers were wont to glory in (as we see *v.* 13), or by comparing ourselves with others, as, it should seem, some did, who were ready to think well of themselves, because they were not so bad as some others. Too many are apt to value themselves upon such accounts as these; but the joy that results thence is nothing to that which arises from an impartial trial of ourselves by the rule of God's word, and our being able thereupon to approve ourselves to him. Note, (1.) Though we have nothing in ourselves to boast of, yet we may have the matter of rejoicing in ourselves: our works can merit nothing at the hand of God; but, if our consciences can witness for us that they are such as he for Christ's sake approves and accepts, we may upon good ground rejoice therein. (2.) The true way to have *rejoicing in ourselves* is to be much in *proving our own works,* in examining ourselves by the unerring rule of God's word, and not by the false measures of what others are, or may think of us. (3.) It is much more desirable to have matter of glorying in ourselves than in another. If we have the testimony of our consciences that we are accepted of God, we need not much concern ourselves about what others think or say of us; and without this the good opinion of others will stand us in little stead.

2. The other argument which the apostle uses to press upon us this duty of proving our own work is that every man shall bear his own burden (*v.* 5), the meaning of which is that at the great day every one shall be reckoned with according as his behaviour here has been. He supposes that there is a day coming when we must all give an account of ourselves to God; and he declares that then the judgment will proceed, and the sentence pass, not according to the sentiments of the world concerning us, or any ungrounded opinion we may have had of ourselves, or upon our having been better or worse than others, but according as our state and behaviour have really been in the sight of God. And, if there be such an awful time to be expected, when he will *render to every one according to his works,* surely there is the greatest reason why we should prove our own works now: if we must certainly be called to an account hereafter, surely we ought to be often calling ourselves to an account here, to see whether or no we are such as God will own and approve then: and, as this is our duty, so if it were more our practice we should entertain more becoming thoughts both of ourselves and our fellow-christians, and instead of bearing hard upon one another, on account of any mistakes or failings we may be guilty of, we should be more ready to fulfil that law of Christ by which we must be judged in bearing one another's burdens.

IV. Christians are here exhorted to be free and liberal in maintaining their ministers (*v.* 6): *Let him that is taught in the word communicate to him that teacheth, in all good things.* Here we may observe, 1. The apostle speaks of it as a thing known and acknowledged, that, as there are some to be taught, so there are others who are appointed to teach them. The office of the ministry is a divine institution, which does not lie open in common to all, but is confined to those only whom God has qualified for it and called to it: even reason itself directs us to put a difference between the teachers and the taught (for, if all were teachers, there would be none to be taught), and the scriptures sufficiently declare that it is the will of God we should do so. 2. It is the word of God wherein ministers are to teach and instruct others; that which they are to preach is *the word,* 2 Tim. iv. 2. That which they are to declare is *the counsel of God,* Acts xx. 27. They are not *lords of our faith, but helpers of our joy,* 2 Cor. i. 24. It is the word of God which is the only rule of faith and life; this they are concerned to study, and to open, and improve, for the edification of others, but they are no further to be regarded than as they speak according to this rule. 3. It is the duty of those who are taught in the word to support those who are appointed to teach them; for they are *to communicate to them in all good things,* freely and cheerfully to contribute, of the good things with which God has blessed them, what is needful for their comfortable subsistence. Ministers are *to give attendance to reading, to exhortation, to doctrine* (1 Tim. iv. 13); they are not to *entangle themselves with the affairs of this life* (2 Tim. ii. 4), and therefore it is but fit and equitable that, while they are *sowing to others spiritual things, they should reap their carnal things.* And this is the appointment of God himself; for as, under the law, *those who ministered about holy things lived of the things of the temple, so hath the Lord ordained that those who preach the gospel should live of the gospel,* 1 Cor. ix. 11, 13, 14.

V. Here is a caution to take heed of mocking God, or of deceiving ourselves, by imagining that he can be imposed upon by mere pretensions or professions (*v.* 7): *Be not deceived, God is not mocked.* This may be considered as referring to the foregoing exhortation, and so the design of it is to convince those of their sin and folly who endeavoured by any plausible pretences to excuse themselves from doing their duty in supporting their ministers: or it may be taken in a more general view, as respecting the whole business of religion, and so as designed to take men off from entertaining any vain hopes of enjoying its rewards while they live in the neglect of its duties. The apostle here supposes that many are apt to excuse themselves from the work of religion, and especially the more self-denying and chargeable parts of it, though at the same time they may make a show and profession of it; but he assures them that *this their way is their folly*, for, though hereby they may possibly impose upon others, yet they do but deceive themselves if they think to impose upon God, who is perfectly acquainted with their hearts as well as actions, and, as he cannot be deceived, so he will not be mocked; and therefore, to prevent this, he directs us to lay down as a rule to ourselves, *That whatsoever a man soweth that shall he also reap;* or that according as we behave ourselves now, so will our account be in the great day. Our present time is seed-time: in the other world there will be a great harvest; and, as the husbandman reaps in the harvest according as he sows in the seedness, so we shall reap then as we sow now. And he further informs us (*v.* 8) that, as there are two sorts of seedness, sowing to the flesh and sowing to the Spirit, so accordingly will the reckoning be hereafter: *If we sow to the flesh, we shall of the flesh reap corruption.* If we sow the wind, we shall reap the whirlwind. Those who live a carnal sensual life, who, instead of employing themselves to the honour of God and the good of others, spend all their thoughts, and care, and time, about the flesh, must expect no other fruit of such a course than corruption—a mean and short-lived satisfaction at present, and ruin and misery at the end of it. But, on the other hand, *those who sow to the Spirit,* who under the guidance and influence of the Spirit do live a holy and spiritual life, a life of devotedness to God and of usefulness and serviceableness to others, may depend upon it that *of the Spirit they shall reap life everlasting*—they shall have the truest comfort in their present course, and an eternal life and happiness at the end of it. Note, Those who go about to mock God do but deceive themselves. Hypocrisy in religion is the greatest folly as well as wickedness, since the God we have to do with can easily see through all our disguises, and will certainly deal with us hereafter, not according to our professions, but our practices.

VI. Here is a further caution given us, *not to be weary in well doing, v.* 9. As we should not excuse ourselves from any part of our duty, so neither should we grow weary in it. There is in all of us too great a proneness to this; we are very apt to flag and tire in duty, yea to fall off from it, particularly that part of it to which the apostle has here a special regard, that of doing good to others. This therefore he would have us carefully to watch and guard against; and he gives this very good reason for it, because *in due season we shall reap, if we faint not,* where he assures us that there is a recompence of reward in reserve for all who sincerely employ themselves in well doing; that this reward will certainly be bestowed on us in the proper season—if not in this world, yet undoubtedly in the next; but then that it is upon supposition that we faint not in the way of our duty; if we grow weary of it, and withdraw from it, we shall not only miss of this reward, but lose the comfort and advantage of what we have already done; but, if we hold on and hold out in well-doing, though our reward may be delayed, yet it will surely come, and will be so great as to make us an abundant recompence for all our pains and constancy. Note, Perseverance in well-doing is our wisdom and interest, as well as our duty, for to this only is the reward promised

VII. Here is an exhortation to all Christians to do good in their places (*v.* 10): *As we have therefore an opportunity,* &c. It is not enough that we be good ourselves, but we must do good to others, if we would approve ourselves to be Christians indeed. The duty here recommended to us is the same that is spoken of in the foregoing verses; and, as there the apostle exhorts us to sincerity and perseverance in it, so here he directs us both as to the objects and rule of it. 1. The objects of this duty are more generally all men. We are not to confine our charity and beneficence within too narrow bounds, as the Jews and judaizing Christians were apt to do, but should be ready to extend it to all who partake of the same common nature with us, as far as we are capable and they stand in need of us. But yet, in the exercise of it, we are to have a special regard to the household of faith, or to those who profess the same common faith, and are members of the same body of Christ, with us: though others are not to be excluded, yet these are to be preferred. The charity of Christians should be extensive charity; but yet therein a particular respect is to be had to good people. God does good to all, but in an especial manner he is good to his own servants; and we must in doing good be *followers of God as dear children.* 2. The rule which we are to observe in doing good to others is *as we have opportunity,* which implies, (1.) That we should be sure to do it while we have opportunity, or while our life lasts, which is the only season wherein we are capable of doing good to others. If therefore we would behave ourselves aright in this matter, we must not, as too many do, neglect it in our life-time, and defer it till we come to die, under a pretence of doing something of this nature then: for, as we cannot be sure that we shall then have an opportunity for it, so neither, if we should, have we any ground to expect that what we do will be so acceptable to God, much less that we can atone for our past neglects by leaving something behind us for the good of others, when we can no longer keep it ourselves. But we should take care to do good in our life-time, yea, to make this the business of our lives. And, (2.) That we be ready to improve every opportunity for it: we should not content ourselves in having done some good already; but, whenever fresh occasions offer themselves, as far as our capacity reaches we should be ready to embrace them too, for we are directed to *give a portion to seven and also to eight*, Eccl. xi. 2. Note, [1.] As God has made it our duty to do good to others, so he takes care in his providence to furnish us with opportunities for it. *The poor we have always with us*, Matt. xxvi. 11. [2.] Whenever God gives us an opportunity of being useful to others, he expects we should improve it, according to our capacity and ability. [3.] We have need of godly wisdom and discretion to direct us in the exercise of our charity or beneficence, and particularly in the choice of the proper objects of it; for, though none who stand in need of us are to be wholly overlooked, yet there is a difference to be made between some and others.

11 Ye see how large a letter I have
written unto you with mine own hand.
12 As many as desire to make a fair
show in the flesh, they constrain you
to be circumcised; only lest they
should suffer persecution for the cross
of Christ. 13 For neither they themselves who are circumcised keep the
law; but desire to have you circumcised, that they may glory in your
flesh. 14 But God forbid that I
should glory, save in the cross of our
Lord Jesus Christ, by whom the
world is crucified unto me, and I
unto the world. 15 For in Christ
Jesus neither circumcision availeth
any thing, nor uncircumcision, but a
new creature. 16 And as many as
walk according to this rule, peace *be*
on them, and mercy, and upon the
Israel of God. 17 From henceforth
let no man trouble me: for I bear in
my body the marks of the Lord Jesus.
18 Brethren, the grace of our Lord
Jesus Christ *be* with your spirit.
Amen.

The apostle, having at large established the doctrine of the gospel, and endeavoured to persuade these Christians to a behaviour agreeable to it, seems as if he intended here to have put an end to the epistle, especially when he had acquainted them that, as a particular mark of his respect for them, he had written this large letter with his own hand, and had not made use of another as his amanuensis, and only subscribed his name to it, as he was wont to do in his other epistles: but such is his affection to them such his concern to recover them from the bad impressions made upon them by their false teachers, that he cannot break off till he has once again given them the true character of those teachers, and an account of his own contrary temper and behaviour, that by comparing these together they might the more easily see how little reason they had to depart from the doctrine he had taught them and to comply with theirs.

I. He gives them the true character of those teachers who were industrious to seduce them, in several particulars. As, 1. They were men who *desired to make a fair show in the flesh, v.* 12. They were very zealous for the externals of religion, forward to observe, and to oblige others to observe, the rites of the ceremonial law, though at the same time they had little or no regard to real piety; for, as the apostle says of them in the following verse, *neither do they themselves keep the law.* Proud, vain, and carnal hearts desire nothing more than to make a fair show in the flesh, and they can easily be content with so much religion as will help them to keep up such a fair show; but frequently those have least of the substance of religion who are most solicitous to make a show of it. 2. They were men who were afraid of suffering, for they constrained the Gentile Christians to be circumcised, *only lest they should suffer persecution for the cross of Christ.* It was not so much out of a regard to the law as to themselves; they were willing to sleep in a whole skin, and to save their worldly cargo, and cared not though they made shipwreck of faith and a good conscience. That which they chiefly aimed at was to please the Jews, and to keep up their reputation among them, and so to prevent the trouble that Paul, and other faithful professors of the doctrine of Christ, lay open to. And, 3. Another part of their character was that they were men of a party spirit, and who had no further zeal for the law than as it subserved their carnal and selfish designs; for they desired to have these Christians circumcised, *that they might glory in their flesh* (*v.* 13), that they might say they had gained them over to their side, and made proselytes of them, of which they carried the mark in their flesh. And thus, while they pretended to promote religion, they were the greatest enemies of it; for nothing has been more destructive to the interest of religion than men-siding and party-making.

II. He acquaints us, on the other hand, with his own temper and behaviour, or makes profession of his own faith, hope, and joy; particularly,

1. That his principal glory was in the cross of Christ: *God forbid*, says he, *that I should glory, save in the cross of our Lord Jesus Christ, v.* 14. By the cross of Christ is here meant his sufferings and death on the cross, or the doctrine of salvation by a cruci-

fied Redeemer. This was what the Jews stumbled at and the Greeks accounted foolishness; and the judaizing teachers themselves, though they had embraced Christianity, yet were so far ashamed of it that in compliance with the Jews, and to avoid persecution from them, they were for mixing the observance of the law of Moses with faith in Christ, as necessary to salvation. But Paul had a very different opinion of it; he was so far from being offended at the cross of Christ, or ashamed of it, or afraid to own it, that he gloried in it; yea, he desired to glory in nothing else, and rejected the thought of setting up any thing in competition with it, as the object of his esteem, with the utmost abhorrence: *God forbid*, &c. This was the ground of all his hope as a Christian: this was the doctrine which, as an apostle, he was resolved to preach; and, whatever trials his firm adherence to it might bring upon him, he was ready, not only to submit to them, but to rejoice in them. Note, The cross of Christ is a good Christian's chief glory, and there is the greatest reason why we should glory in it, for to it we owe all our joys and hopes.

2. That he was dead to the world. By Christ, or by the cross of Christ, *the world was crucified to him, and he to the world;* he had experienced the power and virtue of it in weaning him from the world, and this was one great reason of his glorying in it. The false teachers were men of a worldly temper, their chief concern was about their secular interests, and therefore they accommodated their religion thereunto. But Paul was a man of another spirit; as the world had no kindness for him, so neither had he any great regard to it; he had got above both the smiles and the frowns of it, and had become as indifferent to it as one who is dying out of it. This is a temper of mind that all Christians should be labouring after; and the best way to attain it is to converse much with the cross of Christ. The higher esteem we have of him the meaner opinion shall we have of the world, and the more we contemplate the sufferings our dear Redeemer met with from the world the less likely shall we be to be in love with it.

3. That he did not lay the stress of his religion on one side or the other of the contesting interests, but on sound Christianity, *v.* 15. There was at that time an unhappy division among Christians; circumcision and uncircumcision had become names by which they were distinguished from each other; for (*ch.* ii. 9, 12) the Jewish Christians are called *the circumcision,* and *those of the circumcision.* The false teachers were very zealous for circumcision; yea, to such a degree as to represent it as necessary to salvation, and therefore they did all they could to constrain the Gentile Christians to submit to it. In this they had carried the matter much further than others did; for, though the apostles connived at the use of it among the Jewish converts, yet they were by no means for imposing it upon the Gentiles. But what they laid so great a stress upon Paul made very little account of. It was indeed of great importance to the interest of Christianity that circumcision should not be imposed on the Gentile converts, and therefore this he had set himself with the utmost vigour to oppose; but as for mere circumcision or uncircumcision, whether those who embraced the Christian religion had been Jews or Gentiles, and whether they were for or against continuing the use of circumcision, so that they did not place their religion in it—this was comparatively a matter of little moment with him; for he very well knew that *in Jesus Christ*, that is, in his account, or under the Christian dispensation, *neither circumcision availed any thing nor uncircumcision,* as to men's acceptance with God, *but a new creature.* Here he instructs us both wherein real religion does not and wherein it does consist. It does not consist in circumcision or uncircumcision, in our being in this or the other denomination of Christians; but it consists in our being new creatures; not in having a new name, or putting on a new face, but in our being renewed in the spirit of our minds and having Christ formed in us: this is of the greatest account with God, and so it was with the apostle. If we compare this text with some others, we may more fully see what it is that renders us most acceptable to God, and about which we should therefore be chiefly concerned. Here we are told that it is *a new creature,* and in *ch.* v. 6 that it is *faith which worketh by love,* and in 1 Cor. vii. 19 that it is *the keeping of the commandments of God,* from all which it appears that it is a change of mind and heart, whereby we are disposed and enabled to believe in the Lord Jesus and to live a life of devotedness to God; and that where this inward, vital, practical religion is wanting, no outward professions, nor particular names, will ever stand us in any stead, or be sufficient to recommend us to him. Were Christians duly concerned to experience this in themselves, and to promote it in others, if it did not make them lay aside their distinguishing names, yet it would at least take them off from laying so great a stress upon them as they too often do. Note, Christians should take care to lay the stress of their religion where God has laid it, namely, on those things which are available to our acceptance with him; so we see the apostle did, and it is our wisdom and interest herein to follow his example. The apostle having shown what was of chief consideration in religion, and what he laid the greatest stress upon, namely, not a mere empty name or profession, but a sound and saving change, in *v.* 16 he pronounces a blessing upon all those who walk according to this rule: *And as many as walk according to this rule peace be upon them, and mercy upon the*

Israel of God. The rule which he here speaks of may signify more generally the whole word of God, which is the complete and perfect rule of faith and life, or that doctrine of the gospel, or way of justification and salvation, which he had laid down in this epistle, namely, by faith in Christ without the works of the law; or it may be considered as more immediately referring to the new creature, of which he had just before been speaking. The blessings which he desires for those who walk according to this rule, or which he gives them the hope and prospect of (for the words may be taken either as a prayer or a promise), are *peace and mercy*—peace with God and conscience, and all the comforts of this life as far as they are needful for them, and mercy, or an interest in the free love and favour of God in Christ, which are the spring and fountain of all other blessings. A foundation is laid for these in that gracious change which is wrought in them; and while they behave themselves as new creatures, and govern their lives and hopes by the rule of the gospel, they may most assuredly depend upon them. These, he declares, shall be the portion of *all the Israel of God*, by whom he means all sincere Christians, whether Jews or Gentiles, all who are Israelites indeed, who, though theymay notbe the natural, yet are become the spiritual seed of Abraham; these, being heirs of his faith, are also heirs together with him of the same promise, and consequently entitled to the peace and mercy here spoken of. The Jews and judaizing teachers were for confining these blessings to such as were circumcised and kept the law of Moses; but, on the contrary, the apostle declares that they belong to all who walk according to the rule of the gospel, or of the new creature, even to all the Israel of God, intimating that those only are the true Israel of God who walk according to this rule, and not that of circumcision, which they insisted so much upon, and therefore that this was the true way to obtain peace and mercy. Note, (1.) Real Christians are such as walk by rule; not a rule of their own devising, but that which God himself has prescribed to them. (2.) Even those who walk according to this rule do yet stand in need of the mercy of God. But, (3.) All who sincerely endeavour to walk according to this rule may be assured that peace and mercy will be upon them: this is the best way to have peace with God, ourselves, and others; and hereupon, as we may be sure of the favour of God now, so we may be sure that we shall find mercy with him hereafter.

4. That he had cheerfully suffered persecution for the sake of Christ and Christianity, *v.* 17. As the cross of Christ, or the doctrine of salvation by a crucified Redeemer, was what he chiefly gloried in, so he had been willing to run all hazards rather than he would betray this truth, or suffer it to be corrupted. The false teachers were afraid of persecution, and this was the great reason why they were zealous for circumcision, as we see, *v.* 12. But this was the least of Paul's concern; he was not moved at any of the afflictions he met with, *nor did he count his life dear to him, so that he might finish his course with joy, and the ministry which he had received of the Lord Jesus, to testify the gospel of the grace of God,* Acts. xx. 24. He had already suffered much in the cause of Christ, for *he bore in his body the marks of the Lord Jesus,* the scars of those wounds which he had sustained from persecuting enemies, for his steady adherence to him, and that doctrine of the gospel which he had received from him. As from this it appeared that he was firmly persuaded of the truth and importance of it, and that he was far from being a favourer of circumcision, as they had falsely reported him to be, so hereupon, with a becoming warmth and vehemence, suitable to his authority as an apostle and to the deep concern of mind he was under, he insists upon it that no man should henceforth trouble him, namely by opposing his doctrine or authority, or by any such calumnies and reproaches as had been cast upon him; for as, both from what he had said and what he had suffered, they appeared to be highly unjust and injurious, so also those were very unreasonable who either raised or received them. Note, (1.) It may justly be presumed that men are fully persuaded of those truths in the defence of which they are willing to suffer. And, (2.) It is very unjust to charge those things upon others which are contrary not only to their profession, but their sufferings too.

III. The apostle, having now finished what he intended to write for the conviction and recovery of the churches of Galatia, concludes the epistle with his apostolical benediction, *v.* 18. He calls them his brethren, wherein he shows his great humility, and the tender affection he had for them, notwithstanding the ill treatment he had met with from them; and takes his leave of them with this very serious and affectionate prayer, that *the grace of our Lord Jesus Christ may be with their spirit.* This was a usual farewell wish of the apostle's, as we see, Rom. xvi. 20, 24, and 1 Cor. xvi. 23. And herein he prays that they might enjoy the favour of Christ, both in its special effects and its sensible evidences, that they might receive from him all that grace which was needful to guide them in their way, to strengthen them in their work, to establish them in their Christian course, and to encourage and comfort them under all the trials of life and the prospect of death itself. This is fitly called *the grace of our Lord Jesus Christ,* as he is both the sole purchaser and the appointed dispenser of it; and though these churches had done enough to forfeit it, by suffering themselves to be drawn into an opinion and practice highly dishonourable to Christ, as well as dangerous to them, yet, out of his great concern for them, and knowing of what importance it was to them, he earnestly desires it on their behalf; yea, that it might *be with their spirit,* that they might continually experience the influences of it upon their souls, disposing and enabling them to act with sincerity and uprightness in religion. We need desire no more to make us happy than the grace of our Lord Jesus Christ. This the apostle begs for these Christians, and therein shows us what we are chiefly concerned to obtain; and, both for their and our encouragement to hope for it, he adds his *Amen.*

AN

EXPOSITION,

WITH PRACTICAL OBSERVATIONS,

OF THE EPISTLE OF ST. PAUL TO

THE EPHESIANS.

Some think that this epistle to the Ephesians was a circular letter sent to several churches, and that the copy directed to the Ephesians happened to be taken into the canon, and so it came to bear that particular inscription. And they have been induced the rather to think this because it is the only one of all Paul's epistles that has nothing in it peculiarly adapted to the state or case of that particular church; but it has much of common concernment to all Christians, and especially to all who, having been Gentiles in times past, were converted to Christianity. But then it may be observed, on the other hand, that the epistle is expressly inscribed (*ch.* i. 1) *to the saints which are at Ephesus;* and in the close of it he tells them that he had sent Tychicus unto them, whom, in 2 Tim. iv. 12, he says he had sent to Ephesus. It is an epistle that bears date out of a prison: and some have observed that what this apostle wrote when he was a prisoner had the greatest relish and savour in it of the things of God. When his tribulations did abound, his consolations and experiences did much more abound, whence we may observe that the afflictive exercises of God's people, and particularly of his ministers, often tend to the advantage of others as well as to their own. The apostle's design is to settle and establish the Ephesians in the truth, and further to acquaint them with the mystery of the gospel, in order to it. In the former part he represents the great privilege of the Ephesians, who, having been in time past idolatrous heathens, were now converted to Christianity and received into covenant with God, which he illustrates from a view of their deplorable state before their conversion, *ch.* i—iii. In the latter part (which we have in the 4th, 5th, and 6th chapters) he instructs them in the principal duties of religion, both personal and relative, and exhorts and quickens them to the faithful discharge of them. Zanchy observes that we have here an epitome of the whole Christian doctrine, and of almost all the chief heads of divinity.

CHAP. I.

In this chapter we have, I. The introduction to the whole epistle, which is much the same as in others, ver. 1, 2. II. The apostle's thanksgivings and praises to God for his inestimable blessings bestowed on the believing Ephesians, ver. 3—14. III. His earnest prayers to God in their behalf, ver. 15—23. This great apostle was wont to abound in prayers and in thanksgivings to almighty God, which he generally so disposes and orders that at the same time they carry with them and convey the great and important doctrines of the Christian religion, and the most weighty instructions to all those who seriously peruse them.

PAUL, an apostle of Jesus Christ by the will of God, to the saints which are at Ephesus, and to the faithful in Christ Jesus: 2 Grace *be* to you, and peace, from God our Father, and *from* the Lord Jesus Christ.

Here is, 1. The title St. Paul takes to himself, as belonging to him—*Paul, an apostle of Jesus Christ,* &c. He reckoned it a great honour to be employed by Christ, as one of his messengers to the sons of men. The apostles were prime officers in the Christian church, being extraordinary ministers appointed for a time only. They were furnished by their great Lord with extraordinary gifts and the immediate assistance of the Spirit, that they might be fitted for publishing and spreading the gospel and for governing the church in its infant state. Such a one Paul was, and that not *by the will* of man conferring that office upon him, nor by his own intrusion into it; but *by the will of God,* very expressly and plainly intimated to him, he being immediately called (as the other apostles were) by Christ himself to the work. Every faithful minister of Christ (though his call and office are not of so extraordinary a nature) may, with our apostle, reflect on it as an honour and comfort to himself that he is what he is *by the will of God.* 2. The persons to whom this epistle is sent: *To the saints who are at Ephesus,* that is, to the Christians who were members of the church at Ephesus, the metropolis of Asia. He calls them saints, for such they were in profession, such they were bound to be in truth and reality, and many of them were such. All Christians must be saints; and, if they come not under that character on earth, they will never be saints in glory. He calls them *the faithful in Christ Jesus,* believers in him, and firm and constant in their adherence to him and to his truths and ways. Those are not saints who are not faithful, believing in Christ, firmly adhering to him, and true to the profession they make of relation to their Lord. Note, It is the honour not only of ministers, but of private Christians too, to have obtained mercy of the Lord to be faithful.—*In Christ Jesus,* from whom they derive all their grace and spiritual strength, and in whom their persons, and all that they perform, are made accepted. 3. The apostolical benediction: *Grace be to you,* &c. This is the token in every epistle; and it expresses the apostle's good-will to his friends, and a real desire of their welfare. By *grace* we are to understand the free and undeserved love and favour of God, and those graces of the Spirit which proceed from it; by *peace* all other blessings, spiritual and temporal, the fruits and product of the former. No peace without grace. No peace, nor grace, but *from God the Father, and from the Lord Jesus Christ.* These peculiar blessings proceed from God, not as a Creator, but as a Father by special relation: and they come from our Lord Jesus Christ, who, having purchased them for his people, has a right to bestow them upon them. Indeed the saints, and the faithful in Christ Jesus, had already received grace and peace; but the increase of these is very desirable, and the best saints stand in need of fresh supplies of the graces of the Spirit, and cannot but desire to improve and grow: and therefore they should pray, each one for himself and all for one another, that such blessings may still abound unto them.

After this short introduction he comes to the matter and body of the epistle; and, though it may seem somewhat peculiar in a letter, yet the Spirit of God saw fit that his discourse of divine things in this chapter should be cast into prayers and praises, which, as they are solemn addresses to God, so they convey weighty instructions to others. Prayer may preach; and praise may do so too.

3 Blessed *be* the God and Father
of our Lord Jesus Christ, who hath
blessed us with all spiritual blessings
in heavenly *places* in Christ: 4 According as he hath chosen us in him
before the foundation of the world,
that we should be holy and without
blame before him in love: 5 Having
predestinated us unto the adoption of
children by Jesus Christ to himself,
according to the good pleasure of his
will, 6 To the praise of the glory of
his grace, wherein he hath made us
accepted in the beloved. 7 In whom
we have redemption through his
blood, the forgiveness of sins, according to the riches of his grace; 8
Wherein he hath abounded toward
us in all wisdom and prudence: 9
Having made known unto us the
mystery of his will, according to his
good pleasure which he hath purposed in himself: 10 That in the
dispensation of the fulness of times
he might gather together in one all
things in Christ, both which are in
heaven, and which are on earth; *even*
in him: 11 In whom also we have
obtained an inheritance, being predestinated according to the purpose
of him who worketh all things after
the counsel of his own will: 12 That
we should be to the praise of his
glory, who first trusted in Christ.
13 In whom ye also *trusted,* after
that ye heard the word of truth, the
gospel of your salvation: in whom
also after that ye believed, ye were
sealed with that holy Spirit of promise, 14 Which is the earnest of
our inheritance until the redemption
of the purchased possession, unto the
praise of his glory.

He begins with thanksgivings and praise, and enlarges with a great deal of fluency and copiousness of affection upon the exceedingly great and precious benefits which we enjoy by Jesus Christ. For the great privileges of our religion are very aptly recounted and enlarged upon in our praises to God.

I. In general he blesses God for *spiritual blessings, v.* 3, where he styles him *the God and Father of our Lord Jesus Christ;* for, as Mediator, the Father was his God; as God, and the second person in the blessed Trinity, God was his Father. It bespeaks the mystical union between Christ and believers, that the God and Father of our Lord Jesus Christ is their God and Father, and that in and through him. All blessings come from God as the Father of our Lord Jesus Christ. No good can be expected from a righteous and holy God to sinful creatures, but by his mediation. *He hath blessed us with all spiritual blessings.* Note, Spiritual blessings are the best blessings with which God blesses us, and for which we are to bless him. He blesses us by bestowing such things upon us as make us really blessed. We cannot thus bless God again; but must do it by praising, and magnifying, and speaking well of him on that account. Those whom God blesses with some he blesses with all spiritual blessings; to whom he gives Christ, he freely gives all these things. It is not so with temporal blessings; some are favoured with health, and not with riches; some with riches, and not with health, &c. But, where God blesses with spiritual blessings, he blesses with all. They are *spiritual blessings in heavenly places;* that is, say some, in the church, distinguished from the world, and called out of it. Or it may be read, *in heavenly things,* such as come from heaven, and are designed to prepare men for it, and to secure their reception into it. We should hence learn to mind spiritual and heavenly things as the principal things, spiritual and heavenly blessings as the best blessings, with which we cannot be miserable and without which we cannot but be so. *Set not your affections on things on the earth, but on those things which are above.* These we are blessed with in Christ; for, as all our services ascend to God through Christ, so all our blessings are conveyed to us in the same way, he being the Mediator between God and us.

II. The particular spiritual blessings with which we are blessed in Christ, and for which we ought to bless God, are (many of them) here enumerated and enlarged upon. 1. Election and predestination, which are the secret springs whence the others flow, *v.* 4, 5, 11. *Election,* or choice, respects that lump or mass of mankind out of which some are chosen, from which they are separated and distinguished. Predestination has respect to the blessings they are designed for; particularly *the adoption of children,* it being the purpose of God that in due time we should become his adopted children, and so have a right to all the privileges and to the inheritance of children. We have here the date of this act of love: it was *before the foundation of the world;* not only before God's people had a being, but before the world had a beginning; for they were chosen in the counsel of God from all eternity. It magnifies these blessings to a high degree that they are the products of eternal counsel. The alms which you give to beggars at your doors proceed from a sudden resolve; but the provision which a parent makes for his children is the result of many thoughts, and is put into his last will and testament with a great deal of solemnity. And, as this magnifies divine love, so it secures the blessings to God's elect; for *the purpose of God according to election shall stand.* He acts in pursuance of his eternal purpose in bestowing spiritual blessings upon his people. *He hath blessed us——according as he hath chosen us in him,* in Christ the great head of the election, who is emphatically called *God's elect, his chosen;* and in the chosen Redeemer an eye of favour was cast upon them. Observe here one great end and design of this choice: *chosen——that we should be holy;* not because he foresaw they would be holy, but because he determined to make them so. All who are chosen to happiness as the end are chosen to holiness as the means. Their sanctification, as well as their salvation, is the result of the counsels of divine love.—*And without blame before him*—that their holiness might not be merely external and in outward appearance, so as to prevent blame from men, but internal and real, and what God himself, who *looketh at the heart,* will account such, such holiness as proceeds from love to God and to our fellow-creatures, this charity being the principle of all true holiness. The original word signifies such an innocence as no man can carp at; and therefore some understand it of that perfect holiness which the saints shall attain in the life to come, which will be eminently before God, they being in his immediate presence for ever. Here is also the rule and the fontal cause of God's election: it is *according to the good pleasure of his will* (*v.* 5), not for the sake of any thing in them foreseen, but because it was his sovereign will, and a thing highly pleasing to him. It is *according to the purpose,* the fixed and unalterable will, *of him who worketh all things after the counsel of his own will* (*v.* 11), who powerfully accomplishes whatever concerns his elect, as he has wisely and freely foreordained and decreed, the last and great end and design of all which is his own glory: *To the praise of the glory of his grace* (*v.* 6), *that we should be to the praise of his glory* (*v.* 12), that is, that we should live and behave ourselves in such a manner that his rich grace might be magnified, and appear glorious, and worthy of the highest praise. *All is of God, and from him, and through him,* and therefore all must be to him, and centre in his praise. Note, The glory of God is his own end, and it should be ours in all that we do. This passage has been understood by some in a very different sense, and with a special reference to the conversion of these Ephesians to Christianity. Those who have a mind to see what is said to this purpose may consult Mr. Locke, and other well-known writers, on the place. 2. The next spiritual blessing the apostle takes notice of is acceptance with God through Jesus Christ: *Wherein,* or by which grace, *he hath made us accepted in the beloved, v.* 6. Jesus Christ is the beloved of his Father (Matt. iii. 17), as well as of angels and saints. It is our great privilege to be accepted of God, which implies his love to us and his taking us under his care and into his family. We cannot be thus accepted of God, but in and through Jesus Christ. He loves his people for the sake of the beloved. 3. Remission of sins, and redemption through the blood of Jesus, *v.* 7. No remission without redemption. It was by reason of sin that we were captivated, and we cannot be released from our captivity but by the remission of our sins. This redemption we have in Christ, and this remission through his blood. The guilt and the stain of sin could be no otherwise removed than by the blood of Jesus. All our spiritual blessings flow down to us in that stream. This great benefit, which comes freely to us, was dearly bought and paid for by our blessed Lord; and yet it is according to the riches of God's grace. Christ's satisfaction and God's rich grace are very consistent in the great affair of man's redemption. God was satisfied by Christ as our substitute and surety; but it was rich grace that would accept of a surety, when he might have executed the severity of the law upon the transgressor, and it was rich grace to provide such a surety as his own Son, and freely to deliver him up, when nothing of that nature could have entered into our thoughts, nor have been any otherwise found out for us. In this instance he has not only manifested riches of grace, but *has abounded towards us in all wisdom and prudence* (*v.* 8), wisdom in contriving the dispensation, and prudence in executing the counsel of his will, as he has done. How illustrious have the divine wisdom and prudence rendered themselves, in so happily adjusting the matter between justice and mercy in this grand affair, in securing the honour of God and his law, at the same time that the recovery of sinners and their salvation are ascertained and made sure! 4. Another privilege which the apostle here blesses God for is divine revelation—that God hath *made known to us the mystery of his will* (*v.* 9), that is, so much of his good-will to men, which had been concealed for a long time, and is still concealed from so great a part of the world: this we owe to Christ, who, having lain in the bosom of the Father from eternity, came to declare his will to the children of men. *According to his good pleasure,* his secret counsels concerning man's redemption, *which he had purposed,* or resolved upon, merely in and from himself, and not for any thing in them. In this revelation, and in his *making known unto us the mystery of his will,* the wisdom and the prudence of God do abundantly shine forth. It is described (*v.* 13) *as the word of truth, and the gospel of our salvation.* Every word of it is true. It contains and instructs us in the most weighty and important truths, and it is confirmed and sealed by the very oath of God, whence we should learn to *betake ourselves to it in all our searches after divine truth.* It is the gospel of our salvation: it publishes the glad tidings of salvation, and contains the offer of it: it points out the way that leads to it; and the blessed Spirit renders the reading and the ministration of it effectual to the salvation of souls. O, how ought we to prize this glorious gospel and to bless God for it! This is the light shining in a dark place, for which we have reason to be thankful, and to which we should take heed. 5. Union in and with Christ is a great privilege, a spiritual blessing, and the foundation of many others. *He gathers together in one all things in Christ, v.* 10. All the lines of divine revelation meet in Christ; all religion centres in him. Jews and Gentiles were united to each other by being both united to Christ. *Things in heaven and things on earth* are gathered together in him; peace made, correspondence settled, between heaven and earth, through him. The innumerable company of angels become one with the church through Christ: this God *purposed in himself,* and it was his design in that dispensation which was to be accomplished by his sending Christ in the fulness of time, at the exact time that God had prefixed and settled. 6. The eternal inheritance is the great blessing with which we are blessed in Christ: *In whom also we have obtained an inheritance, v.* 11. Heaven is the inheritance, the happiness of which is a sufficient portion for a soul: it is conveyed in the way of an inheritance, being the gift of a Father to his children. *If children, then heirs.* All the blessings that we have in hand are but small if compared with the inheritance. What is laid out upon an heir in his minority is nothing to what is reserved for him when he comes to age. Christians are said to have obtained this inheritance, as they have a present right to it, and even actual possession of it, in Christ their head and representative. 7. The seal and earnest of the Spirit are of the number of these blessings. We are said to be *sealed with that Holy Spirit of promise, v.* 13. The blessed Spirit is holy himself, and he makes us holy. He is called *the Spirit of promise,* as he is the promised Spirit. By him believers are sealed; that is, separated and set apart for God, and distinguished and marked as belonging to him. The Spirit *is the earnest of our inheritance, v.* 14. The earnest is part of payment, and it secures the full sum: so is the gift of the Holy Ghost; all his influences and operations, both as a sanctifier and a comforter, are heaven begun, glory in the seed and bud. The Spirit's illumination is an earnest of everlasting light; sanctification is an earnest of perfect holiness; and his comforts are earnests of everlasting joys. He is said to be the earnest, *until the redemption of the purchased possession.* It may be called here the possession, because this earnest makes it as sure to the heirs as though they were already possessed of it; and it is purchased for them by the blood of Christ. The redemption of it is mentioned because it was mortgaged and forfeited by sin; and Christ restores it to us, and so is said to redeem it, in allusion to the law of redemption. Observe, from all this, what a gracious promise that is which secures the gift of the Holy Ghost to those who ask him.

The apostle mentions the great end and design of God in bestowing all these spiritual privileges, *that we should be to the praise of his glory who first trusted in Christ*—we to whom the gospel was first preached, and who were first converted to the faith of Christ, and to the placing of our hope and trust in him. Note, Seniority in grace is a preferment: *Who were in Christ before me*, says the apostle (Rom. xvi. 7); those who have for a longer time experienced the grace of Christ are under more special obligations to glorify God. They should be strong in faith, and more eminently glorify him; but this should be the common end of all. For this we were made, and for this we were redeemed; this is the great design of our Christianity, and of God in all that he has done for us: *unto the praise of his glory*, *v.* 14. He intends that his grace and power and other perfections should by this means become conspicuous and illustrious, and that the sons of men should magnify him.

15 Wherefore I also, after I heard
of your faith in the Lord Jesus, and
love unto all the saints, 16 Cease
not to give thanks for you, making
mention of you in my prayers; 17
That the God of our Lord Jesus
Christ, the Father of glory, may give
unto you the spirit of wisdom and
revelation in the knowledge of him:
18 The eyes of your understanding
being enlightened; that ye may know
what is the hope of his calling, and
what the riches of the glory of his
inheritance in the saints, 19 And
what *is* the exceeding greatness of
his power to us-ward who believe,
according to the working of his
mighty power, 20 Which he wrought
in Christ, when he raised him from
the dead, and set *him* at his own
right hand in the heavenly *places*,
21 Far above all principality, and
power, and might, and dominion,
and every name that is named, not
only in this world, but also in that
which is to come: 22 And hath put
all *things* under his feet, and gave
him *to be* the head over all *things* to
the church, 23 Which is his body,
the fulness of him that filleth all in all.

We have come to the last part of this chapter, which consists of Paul's earnest prayer to God in behalf of these Ephesians. We should pray for the persons for whom we give thanks. Our apostle blesses God for what he had done for them, and then he prays that he would do more for them. He gives thanks for spiritual blessings, and prays for further supplies of them; for God *will for this be enquired of by the house of Israel, to do it for them.* He has laid up these spiritual blessings for us in the hands of his Son, the Lord Jesus; but then he has appointed us to draw them out, and fetch them in, by prayer. We have no part nor lot in the matter, any further than we claim it by faith and prayer. One inducement to pray for them was the good account he had of them, *of their faith in the Lord Jesus and love to all the saints, v.* 15. Faith in Christ, and love to the saints, will be attended with all other graces. Love to the saints, as such, and because they are such, must include love to God. Those who love saints, as such, love all saints, how weak in grace, how mean in the world, how fretful and peevish soever, some of them may be. Another inducement to pray for them was because they had received the earnest of the inheritance: this we may observe from the words being connected with the preceding ones by the particle *wherefore.* "Perhaps you will think that, having received the earnest, it should follow, therefore you are happy enough, and need take no further care: you need not pray for yourselves, nor I for you. No, quite the contrary. *Wherefore——I cease not to give thanks for you, making mention of you in my prayers, v.* 16. While he blesses God for giving them the Spirit, he ceases not to pray that he would give unto them the Spirit (*v.* 17), that he would give greater measures of the Spirit. Observe, Even the best of Christians need to be prayed for: and, while we hear well of our Christian friends, we should think ourselves obliged to intercede with God for them, that they may abound and increase yet more and more. Now what is it that Paul prays for in behalf of the Ephesians? Not that they might be freed from persecution; nor that they might possess the riches, honours, or pleasures of the world; but the great thing he prays for is the illumination of their understandings, and that their knowledge might increase and abound: he means it of a practical and experimental knowledge. The graces and comforts of the Spirit are communicated to the soul by the enlightening of the understanding. In this way he gains and keeps possession. Satan takes a contrary way: he gets possession by the senses and passions, Christ by the understanding. Observe,

I. Whence this knowledge must come from *the God of our Lord Jesus Christ, v.* 17. The Lord *is a God of knowledge,* and there is no sound saving knowledge but what comes from him; and therefore to him we must look for it, who is *the God of our Lord Jesus Christ* (see *v.* 3) *and the Father of glory.* It is a Hebraism. God is infinitely glorious in himself all glory is due to him from his creatures, and he is the author of all that glory with which his saints are or shall be invested. Now he gives knowledge by giving the Spirit of knowledge; for the Spirit of God is the teacher of the saints, *the Spirit of wisdom and revelation.* We have the revelation of the Spirit in the word: but will that avail us, if we have not the wisdom of the Spirit in the heart? If the same Spirit who indited the sacred scriptures do not take the veil from off our hearts, and enable us to understand and improve them, we shall be never the better.—*In the knowledge of him*, or for the acknowledgment of him; not only a speculative knowledge of Christ, and of what relates to him, but an acknowledgment of Christ's authority by an obedient conformity to him, which must be by the help of *the Spirit of wisdom and revelation.* This knowledge is first in the understanding. He prays that *the eyes of their understanding may be enlightened, v.* 18. Observe, Those who have their eyes opened, and have some understanding in the things of God, have need to be more and more enlightened, and to have their knowledge more clear, and distinct, and experimental. Christians should not think it enough to have warm affections, but they should labour to have clear understandings; they should be ambitious of being knowing Christians, and judicious Christians.

II. What it is that he more particularly desires they should grow in the knowledge of. 1. *The hope of his calling, v.* 18. Christianity is our calling. God has called us to it, and on that account it is said to be his calling. There is a hope in this calling; for those who deal with God deal upon trust. And it is a desirable thing to know what this hope of our calling is, to have such an acquaintance with the immense privileges of God's people, and the expectations they have from God, and with respect to the heavenly world, as to be quickened thereby to the utmost diligence and patience in the Christian course. We ought to labour after, and pray earnestly for, a clearer insight into, and a fuller acquaintance with, the great objects of a Christian's hopes. 2. *The riches of the glory of his inheritance in the saints.* Besides the heavenly inheritance prepared for the saints, there is a present inheritance in the saints; for grace is glory begun, and holiness is happiness in the bud. There is a glory in this inheritance, riches of glory, rendering the Christian more excellent and more truly honourable than all about him: and it is desirable to know this experimentally, to be acquainted with the principles, pleasures, and powers, of the spiritual and divine life. It may be understood of the glorious inheritance in or among the saints in heaven, where God does, as it were, lay forth all his riches, to make them happy and glorious, and where all that the saints are in possession of is transcendently glorious, as the knowledge that can be attained of this upon earth is very desirable, and must be exceedingly entertaining and delightful. Let us endeavour then, by reading, contemplation, and prayer, to know as much of heaven as we can, that we may be desiring and longing to be there. 3. *The exceeding greatness of God's power towards those who believe, v.* 19. The practical belief of the all-sufficiency of God, and of the omnipotence of divine grace, is absolutely necessary to a close and steady walking with him. It is a desirable thing to know experimentally the mighty power of that grace beginning and carrying on the work of faith in our souls. It is a difficult thing to bring a soul to believe in Christ, and to venture its all upon his righteousness, and upon the hope of eternal life. It is nothing less than an almighty power that will work this in us. The apostle speaks here with a mighty fluency and copiousness of expression, and yet, at the same time, as if he wanted words to express the *exceeding greatness of God's almighty power*, that power which God exerts towards his people, and by which *he raised Christ from the dead, v.* 20. That indeed was the great proof of the truth of the gospel to the world: but the transcript of that in ourselves (our sanctification, and rising from the death of sin, in conformity to Christ's resurrection) is the great proof to us. Though this cannot prove the truth of the gospel to another who knows nothing of the matter (there the resurrection of Christ is the proof), yet to be able to speak experimentally, as the Samaritans, "*We have heard him ourselves,* we have felt a mighty change in our hearts," will make us able to say, with the fullest satisfaction, *Now we believe, and are sure, that this is the Christ, the Son of God.* Many understand the apostle here as speaking of that *exceeding greatness of power* which God will exert for raising the bodies of believers to eternal life, even the same *mighty power which he wrought in Christ when he raised him,* &c. And how desirable a thing must it be to become at length acquainted with that power, by being raised out of the grave thereby unto eternal life!

Having said something of Christ and his resurrection, the apostle digresses a little from the subject he is upon to make some further honourable mention of the Lord Jesus and his exaltation. He sits at the Father's *right hand in the heavenly places,* &c. *v.* 20, 21. Jesus Christ is advanced above all, and he is set in authority over all, they being made subject to him. All the glory of the upper world, and all the powers of both worlds, are entirely devoted to him. The Father *hath put all things under his feet* (*v.* 22), according to the promise, Ps. cx. 1. All creatures whatsoever are in subjection to him; they must either yield him sincere obedience or fall under the weight of his sceptre, and receive their doom from him. God GAVE *him to be head over all things.* It was a gift to Christ, considered as a Mediator, to be advanced to such dominion and headship, and to have such a mystical body prepared for him: and it was a gift to the church, to be provided with a head endued with so much power and authority. God *gave him to be the head over all things.* He gave him all power both in heaven and in earth. *The Father loves the Son, and hath given* ALL *things into his hands.* But that which completes the comfort of this is that he is the head over all things to the church; he is entrusted with all power, that is, that he may dispose of all the affairs of the providential kingdom in subserviency to the designs of his grace concerning his church. With this therefore we may answer the messengers of the nations, that the Lord hath founded Zion. The same power that supports the world supports the church; and we are sure he loves his church, for it *is his body* (*v.* 23), his mystical body, and he will care for it. It is *the fulness of him that filleth all in all.* Jesus Christ filleth all in all; he supplies all defects in all his members, filling them with his Spirit, and even with *the fulness of God, ch.* iii. 19. And yet the church is said to be his fulness, because Christ as Mediator would not be complete if he had not a church. How could he be a king if he had not a kingdom? This therefore comes in to the honour of Christ, *as Mediator, that the church is his fulness.*

CHAP. II.

This chapter contains an account, I. Of the miserable condition of these Ephesians by nature (ver. 1—3) and again, ver. 11, 12. II. Of the glorious change that was wrought in them by converting grace (ver. 4—10) and again, ver. 13. III. Of the great and mighty privileges that both converted Jews and Gentiles receive from Christ, ver. 14—22. The apostle endeavours to affect them with a due sense of the wonderful change which divine grace had wrought in them; and this is very applicable to that great change which the same grace works in all those who are brought into a state of grace. So that we have here a lively picture both of the misery of unregenerate men and of the happy condition of converted souls, enough to awaken and alarm those who are yet in their sins and to put them upon hastening out of that state, and to comfort and delight those whom God hath quickened, with a consideration of the mighty privileges with which they are invested.

AND you *hath he quickened,* who were dead in trespasses and sins; 2 Wherein in time past ye walked according to the course of this world, according to the prince of the power of the air, the spirit that now worketh in the children of disobedience: 3 Among whom also we all had our conversation in times past in the lusts of our flesh, fulfilling the desires of the flesh and of the mind; and were by nature the children of wrath, even as others.

The miserable condition of the Ephesians by nature is here in part described. Observe, 1. Unregenerate souls are dead in trespasses and sins. All those who are in their sins, are dead in sins; yea, in trespasses and sins, which may signify all sorts of sins, habitual and actual, sins of heart and of life. Sin is the death of the soul. Wherever that prevails there is a privation of all spiritual life. Sinners are dead in state, being destitute of the principles, and powers of spiritual life; and cut off from God, the fountain of life: and they are dead in law, as a condemned malefactor is said to be a dead man. 2. A state of sin is a state of conformity to this world, *v.* 2. In the first verse he speaks of their internal state, in this of their outward conversation: *Wherein,* in which trespasses and sins, *in time past you walked,* you lived and behaved yourselves in such a manner as the men of the world are used to do. 3. We are by nature bond-slaves to sin and Satan. Those who walk in trespasses and sins, and according to the course of this world, walk *according to the prince of the power of the air.* The devil, or the prince of devils, is thus described. See Matt. xii. 24, 26. The legions of apostate angels are as one power united under one chief; and therefore what is called *the powers of darkness* elsewhere is here spoken of in the singular number. The air is represented as the seat of his kingdom: and it was the opinion of both Jews and heathens that the air is full of spirits, and that there they exercise and exert themselves. The devil seems to have some power (by God's permission) in the lower region of the air; there he is at hand to tempt men, and to do as much mischief to the world as he can: but it is the comfort and joy of God's people that he who is *head over all things to the church* has conquered the devil and has him in his chain. But wicked men are slaves to Satan, for they walk according to him; they conform their lives and actions to the will and pleasure of this great usurper. The course and tenour of their lives are according to his suggestions, and in compliance with his temptations; they are subject to him, and are led captive by him at his will, whereupon he is called the god of this world, and *the spirit that now worketh in the children of disobedience. The children of disobedience* are such as choose to disobey God, and to serve the devil; in these he works very powerfully and effectually. As the good Spirit works that which is good in obedient souls, so this evil spirit works that which is evil in wicked men; and he now works, not only heretofore, but even since the world has been blessed with the light of the glorious gospel The apostle adds, *Among whom also we all had our conversation in times past,* which words refer to the Jews, whom he signifies here to have been in the like sad and miserable condition by nature, and to have been as vile and wicked as the unregenerate Gentiles themselves, and whose natural state he further describes in the next words. 4. We are by nature drudges to the flesh, and to our corrupt affections, *v.* 3. By *fulfilling the desires of the flesh and of the mind,* men contract that filthiness of flesh and spirit from which the apostle exhorts Christians to cleanse themselves, 2 Cor. vii. 1. The fulfilling of the desires of the flesh and of the mind includes all the sin and wickedness that are acted in and by both the inferior and the higher or nobler powers of the soul. We lived in the actual commission of all those sins to which corrupt nature inclined us. The carnal mind makes a man a perfect slave to his vicious appetite.—*The fulfilling of the wills of the flesh,* so the words may be rendered, denoting the efficacy of these lusts, and what power they have over those who yield themselves up unto them. 5. We are *by nature the children of wrath, even as others.* The Jews were so, as well as the Gentiles; and one man is as much so as another by nature, not only by custom and imitation, but from the time when we began to exist, and by reason of our natural inclinations and appetites. All men, being naturally children of disobedience, are also by nature children of wrath: God is angry with the wicked every day. Our state and course are such as deserve wrath, and would end in eternal wrath, if divine grace did not interpose. What reason have sinners then to be looking out for that grace that will make them, of children of wrath, children of God and heirs of glory! Thus far the apostle has described the misery of a natural state in these verses, which we shall find him pursuing again in some following ones.

4 But God, who is rich in mercy,
for his great love wherewith he loved
us, 5 Even when we were dead in
sins, hath quickened us together with
Christ, (by grace ye are saved;) 6
And hath raised *us* up together, and
made *us* sit together in heavenly
places in Christ Jesus: 7 That in
the ages to come he might show the
exceeding riches of his grace in *his*
kindness toward us through Christ
Jesus. 8 For by grace are ye saved
through faith; and that not of yourselves: *it is* the gift of God: 9 Not
of works, lest any man should boast.
10 For we are his workmanship,
created in Christ Jesus unto good
works, which God hath before ordained that we should walk in them.

Here the apostle begins his account of the glorious change that was wrought in them by converting grace, where observe,

I. By whom, and in what manner, it was brought about and effected. 1. Negatively: *Not of yourselves, v.* 8. Our faith, our conversion, and our eternal salvation, are not the mere product of any natural abilities, nor of any merit of our own: *Not of works, lest any man should boast, v.* 9. These things are not brought to pass by any thing done by us, and therefore all boasting is excluded; he who glories must not glory in himself, but in the Lord. There is no room for any man's boasting of his own abilities and power; or as though he had done any thing that might deserve such immense favours from God. 2. Positively: *But God, who is rich in mercy,* &c. *v.* 4. God himself is the author of this great and happy change, and his great love is the spring and fontal cause of it; hence he resolved to show mercy. Love is his inclination to do us good considered simply as creatures; mercy respects us as apostate and as miserable creatures. Observe, God's eternal love or good-will towards his creatures is the fountain whence all his mercies vouchsafed to us proceed; and that love of God is great love, and that mercy of his is rich mercy, inexpressibly great and inexhaustibly rich. And then *by grace you are saved* (*v.* 5), and *by grace are you saved through faith—it is the gift of* God, *v.* 8. Note, Every converted sinner is a saved sinner. Such are delivered from sin and wrath; they are brought into a state of salvation, and have a right given them by grace to eternal happiness. The grace that saves them is the free undeserved goodness and favour of God; and he saves them, not *by the works of the law,* but through faith in Christ Jesus, by means of which they come to partake of the great blessings of the gospel; and both that faith and that salvation on which it has so great an influence are the gift of God. The great objects of faith are made known by divine revelation, and made credible by the testimony and evidence which God hath given us; and that we believe to salvation and obtain salvation through faith is entirely owing to divine assistance and grace; God has ordered all so that the whole shall appear to be of grace. Observe,

II. Wherein this change consists, in several particulars, answering to the misery of our natural state, some of which are enumerated in this section, and others are mentioned below. 1. We who were dead are quickened (*v.* 5), we are saved from the death of sin and have a principle of spiritual life implanted in us. Grace in the soul is a new life in the soul. As death locks up the senses, seals up all the powers and faculties, so does a state of sin, as to any thing that is good. Grace unlocks and opens all, and enlarges the soul. Observe, A regenerate sinner becomes a living soul: he lives a life of sanctification, being born of God; and he lives in the sense of the law, being delivered from the guilt of sin by pardoning and justifying grace. *He hath quickened us together with Christ.* Our spiritual life results from our union with Christ; it is in him that we live: *Because I live, you shall live also.* 2. We who were buried are raised up, *v.* 6. What remains yet to be done is here spoken of as though it were already past, though indeed we are raised up in virtue of our union with him whom God hath raised from the dead. When he raised Christ from the dead, he did in effect raise up all believers together with him, he being their common head; and when he placed him at his right hand in heavenly places, he advanced and glorified them in and with him, their raised and exalted head and forerunner.—*And made us sit together in heavenly places in Christ Jesus.* This may be understood in another sense. Sinners roll themselves in the dust; sanctified souls sit in heavenly places, are raised above the world; the world is as nothing to them, compared with what it has been, and compared with what the other world is. Saints are not only Christ's freemen, but they are assessors with him; by the assistance of his grace they have ascended with him above this world to converse with another, and they live in the constant expectation of it. They are not only servants to the best of masters in the best work, but they are exalted to reign with him; they sit upon the throne with Christ, *as he has sat down with his Father on his throne.*

III. Observe what is the great design and aim of God in producing and effecting this change: And this, 1. With respect to others: *That in the ages to come he might show,* &c. (*v.* 7), that he might give a specimen and proof of his great goodness and mercy, for the encouragement of sinners in future time. Observe, The goodness of God in converting and saving sinners heretofore is a proper encouragement to others in after-time to hope in his grace and mercy, and to apply themselves to these. God having this in his design, poor sinners should take great encouragement from it. And what may we not hope for from such grace and kindness, from riches of grace, and from exceeding riches of grace, to which this change is owing? *Through Christ Jesus,* by and through whom God conveys all his favour and blessings to us. 2. With respect to the regenerated sinners themselves: *For we are his workmanship, created in Christ Jesus unto good works,* &c. *v.* 10. It appears that all is of grace, because all our spiritual advantages are from God. *We are his workmanship;* he means in respect of the new creation; not only as men, but as saints. The new man is a new creature; and God is its Creator. It is a new birth, and we are born or begotten of his will. *In Christ Jesus,* that is, on the account of what he has done and suffered, and by the influence and operation of his blessed Spirit. *Unto good works,* &c. The apostle having before ascribed this change to divine grace in exclusion of works, lest he should seem thereby to discourage good works, he here observes that though the change is to be ascribed to nothing of that nature (*for we are the workmanship of God*), yet God, in his new creation, has designed and prepared us for good works: *Created unto good works,* with a design that we should be fruitful in them. Wherever God by his grace implants good principles, they are intended to be for good works. *Which God hath before ordained,* that is, decreed and appointed. Or, the words may be read, *To which God hath before prepared us,* that is, by blessing us with the knowledge of his will, and with the assistance of his Holy Spirit; and by producing such a change in us. *That we should walk in them,* or glorify God by an exemplary conversation and by our perseverance in holiness.

11 Wherefore remember, that ye *being* in time past Gentiles in the flesh, who are called Uncircumcision by that which is called the Circumcision in the flesh made by hands;
12 That at that time ye were without Christ, being aliens from the commonwealth of Israel, and strangers from the covenants of promise, having no hope, and without God in the world:
13 But now in Christ Jesus ye who sometimes were far off are made nigh by the blood of Christ.

In these verses the apostle proceeds in his account of the miserable condition of these Ephesians by nature. *Wherefore remember,* &c. *v.* 11. As if he had said, "You should remember what you have been, and compare it with what you now are, in order to humble yourselves and to excite your love and thankfulness to God." Note, Converted sinners ought frequently to reflect upon the sinfulness and misery of the state they were in by nature. *Gentiles in the flesh,* that is, living in the corruption of their natures, and being destitute of circumcision, the outward sign of an interest in the covenant of grace. *Who are called uncircumcision by that,* &c., that is, "You were reproached and upbraided for it by the formal Jews, who made an external profession, and who looked no further than the outward ordinance." Note, Hypocritical professors are wont to value themselves chiefly on their external privileges, and to reproach and despise others who are destitute of them. The apostle describes the misery of their case in several particulars, *v.* 12. "*At that time,* while you were Gentiles, and in an unconverted state, you were," 1. "In a Christless condition, without the knowledge of the Messiah, and without any saving interest in him or relation to him." It is true of all unconverted sinners, all those who are destitute of faith, that they have no saving interest in Christ; and it must be a sad and deplorable thing for a soul to be without a Christ. Being without Christ, they were, 2. *Aliens from the commonwealth of Israel;* they did not belong to Christ's church, and had no communion with it, that being confined to the Israelitish nation. It is no small privilege to be placed in the church of Christ, and to share with the members of it in the advantages peculiar to it. 3. *They are strangers from the covenants of promise.* The covenant of grace has ever been the same for substance, though, having undergone various additions and improvements in the several ages of the church, it is called covenants; and the covenants of promise, because it is made up of promises, and particularly contains the great promise of the Messiah, and of eternal life through him. Now the Ephesians, in their gentilism, were strangers to this covenant, having never had any information nor overture of it; and all unregenerate sinners are strangers to it, as they have no interest in it. Those who are without Christ, and so have no interest in the Mediator of the covenant, have none in the promises of the covenant. 4. They had no hope, that is, beyond this life—no well-grounded hope in God, no hope of spiritual and eternal blessings. Those who are without Christ, and strangers from the covenant, can have no good hope; for Christ and the covenant are the ground and foundation of all the Christian's hopes. They were in a state of distance and estrangement from God: *Without God in the world;* not without some general knowledge of a deity, for they worshipped idols, but living without any due regard to him, any acknowledged dependence on him, and any special interest in him. The words are, *atheists in the world;* for, though they worshipped many gods, yet they were without the true God.

The apostle proceeds (*v.* 13) further to illustrate the happy change that was made in their state: *But now, in Christ Jesus, you who sometimes were far off,* &c. They were far off from Christ, from his church, from the promises, from the Christian hope, and from God himself; and therefore from all good, like the prodigal son in the far country: this had been represented in the preceding verses. Unconverted sinners remove themselves at a distance from God, and God puts them at a distance: *He beholds the proud afar off.* "*But now in Christ Jesus,* &c., upon your conversion, by virtue of union with Christ, and interest in him by faith, you are made nigh." They were brought home to God, received into the church, taken into the covenant, and possessed of all other privileges consequent upon these. Note, *The saints are a people near to God. Salvation is far from the wicked;* but God is a help at hand to his people; and this is *by the blood of Christ,* by the merit of his sufferings and death. Every believing sinner owes his nearness to God, and his interest in his favour, to the death and sacrifice of Christ.

14 For he is our peace, who hath
made both one, and hath broken
down the middle wall of partition
between us; 15 Having abolished in
his flesh the enmity, *even* the law of
commandments *contained* in ordinances; for to make in himself of
twain one new man, *so* making peace;
16 And that he might reconcile both
unto God in one body by the cross,
having slain the enmity thereby: 17
And came and preached peace to you
which were afar off, and to them that
were nigh. 18 For through him we
both have access by one Spirit unto
the Father. Now therefore ye are
no more strangers and foreigners, but
fellowcitizens with the saints, and of
the household of God; 20 And are
built upon the foundation of the
apostles and prophets, Jesus Christ
himself being the chief corner *stone;*
21 In whom all the building fitly
framed together groweth unto a holy
temple in the Lord: 22 In whom ye
also are builded together for an habitation of God through the Spirit.

We have now come to the last part of the chapter, which contains an account of the great and mighty privileges that converted Jews and Gentiles both receive from Christ. The apostle here shows that those who were in a state of enmity are reconciled. Between the Jews and the Gentiles there had been a great enmity; so there is between God and every unregenerate man. Now Jesus Christ is our peace, *v.* 14. He made peace by the sacrifice of himself; and came to reconcile, 1. Jews and Gentiles to each other. He *made both one,* by reconciling these two divisions of men, who were wont to malign, to hate, and to reproach each other before. He *broke down the middle wall of partition,* the ceremonial law, that made the great feud, and was the badge of the Jews' peculiarity, called *the partition-wall* by way of allusion to the partition in the temple, which separated the court of the Gentiles from that into which the Jews only had liberty to enter. Thus *he abolished in his flesh the enmity, v.* 15. By his sufferings in the flesh, he took away the binding power of the ceremonial law (so removing that cause of enmity and distance between them), which is here called *the law of commandments contained in ordinances,* because it enjoined a multitude of external rites and ceremonies, and consisted of many institutions and appointments about the outward parts of divine worship. *The legal ceremonies were abrogated by Christ, having their accomplishment in him.* By taking these out of the way, he formed one church of believers, whether they had been Jews or Gentiles. Thus he made *in himself of twain one new man.* He framed both these parties into one new society, or body of God's people, uniting them to himself as their common head, they being renewed by the Holy Ghost, and now concurring in a new way of gospel worship, *so making peace* between these two parties, who were so much at variance before. 2. There is an enmity between God and sinners, whether Jews or Gentiles; and Christ came to slay that enmity, and to reconcile them both to God, *v.* 16. Sin breeds a quarrel between God and men. Christ came to take up the quarrel, and to bring it to an end, by reconciling both Jew and Gentile, now collected and gathered into one body, to a provoked and an offended God: and this *by the cross,* or by the sacrifice of himself upon the cross, *having slain the enmity thereby.* He, being slain or sacrificed, slew the enmity that there was between God and poor sinners. The apostle proceeds to illustrate the great advantages which both parties gain by the mediation of our Lord Jesus Christ, *v.* 17. Christ, who purchased peace on the cross, came, partly in his own person, as to the Jews, who are here said to have been nigh, and partly in his apostles, whom he commissioned to preach the gospel to the Gentiles, who are said to have been afar off, in the sense that has been given before. *And preached peace,* or published the terms of reconciliation with God and of eternal life. Note here, When the messengers of Christ deliver his truths, it is in effect the same as if he did it immediately himself. He is said to preach by them, insomuch that he who receiveth them receiveth him, and he who despiseth them (acting by virtue of his commission, and delivering his message) despiseth and rejecteth Christ himself. Now the effect of this peace is the free access which both Jews and Gentiles have unto God (*v.* 18): *For through him,* in his name and by virtue of his mediation, *we both have access* or admission into the presence of God, who has become the common reconciled Father of both: the throne of grace is erected for us to come to, and liberty of approach to that throne is allowed us. Our access is by the Holy Spirit. Christ purchased for us leave to come to God, and the Spirit gives us a heart to come and strength to come, even grace to serve God acceptably. Observe, We draw nigh to God, through Jesus Christ, by the help of the Spirit. The Ephesians, upon their conversion, having such an access to God, as well as the Jews, and by the same Spirit, the apostle tells them, *Now therefore you are no more strangers and foreigners, v.* 19. This he mentions by way of opposition to what he had observed of them in their heathenism: they were now no longer *aliens from the commonwealth of Israel,* and no longer what the Jews were wont to account all the nations of the earth besides themselves (namely, strangers to God), *but fellow-citizens with the saints, and of the household of God,* that is, members of the church of Christ, and having a right to all the privileges of it. Observe here, The church is compared to a city, and every converted sinner is free of it. It is also compared to a house, and every converted sinner is one of the domestics, one of the family, a servant and a child in God's house. In *v.* 20 the church is compared to a building. The apostles and prophets are *the foundation* of that building. They may be so called in a secondary sense, Christ himself being the primary foundation; but we are rather to understand it of the doctrine delivered by the prophets of the Old Testament and the apostles of the New. It follows, *Jesus Christ himself being the chief corner-stone.* In him both Jews and Gentiles meet, and constitute one church; and Christ supports the building by his strength: *In whom all the building, fitly framed together,* &c. *v.* 21. All believers, of whom it consists, being united to Christ by faith, and among themselves by Christian charity, *grow unto a holy temple,* become a sacred society, in which there is much communion between God and his people, as in the temple, they worshipping and serving him, he manifesting himself unto them, they offering up spiritual sacrifices to God and he dispensing his blessings and favours to them Thus the building, for the nature of it, is a temple, a holy temple; for the church is the place which God hath chosen to put his name there, and it becomes such a temple by grace and strength derived from himself—*in the Lord.* The universal church being built upon Christ as the foundation-stone, and united in Christ as the corner-stone, comes at length to be glorified in him as the top-stone: *In whom you also are built together,* &c., *v.* 22. Observe, Not only the universal church is called the temple of God, but particular churches; and even every true believer is a living temple, is *a habitation of God through the Spirit.* God dwells in all believers now, they having become the temple of God through the operations of the blessed Spirit, and his dwelling with them now is an earnest of their dwelling together with him to eternity.

CHAP. III.

This chapter consists of two parts. I. Of the account which Paul gives the Ephesians concerning himself, as he was appointed by God to be the apostle of the Gentiles, ver. 1—13. II. Of his devout and affectionate prayer to God for the Ephesians, ver. 14—21. We may observe it to have been very much the practice of this apostle to intermix, with his instructions and counsels, intercessions and prayers to God for those to whom he wrote, as knowing that all his instructions and teachings would be useless and vain, except God did co-operate with them, and render them effectual. This is an example that all the ministers of Christ should copy after, praying earnestly that the efficacious operations of the divine Spirit may attend their ministrations, and crown them with success.

FOR this cause I Paul, the prisoner
of Jesus Christ for you Gentiles,
2 (If ye have heard of the dispensation of the grace of God which is
given me to you-ward: 3 How that
by revelation he made known unto
me the mystery; (as I wrote afore in
few words, 4 Whereby, when ye
read, ye may understand my knowledge in the mystery of Christ) 5
Which in other ages was not made
known unto the sons of men, as it is
now revealed unto his holy apostles
and prophets by the Spirit; 6 That
the Gentiles should be fellowheirs,

and of the same body, and partakers
of his promise in Christ by the gospel: 7 Whereof I was made a minister, according to the gift of the
grace of God given unto me by the
effectual working of his power. 8
Unto me, who am less than the least
of all saints, is this grace given, that
I should preach among the Gentiles
the unsearchable riches of Christ; 9
And to make all *men* see what *is* the
fellowship of the mystery, which from
the beginning of the world hath been
hid in God, who created all things by
Jesus Christ: 10 To the intent
that now unto the principalities and
powers in heavenly *places* might be
known by the church the manifold
wisdom of God, 11 According to
the eternal purpose which he purposed in Christ Jesus our Lord: 12
In whom we have boldness and access
with confidence by the faith of him.
13 Wherefore I desire that ye faint
not at my tribulations for you, which
is your glory.

Here we have the account which Paul gives the Ephesians concerning himself, as he was appointed by God the apostle of the Gentiles.

I. We may observe that he acquaints them with the tribulations and sufferings which he endured in the discharge of that office, *v.* 1. The first clause refers to the preceding chapter, and may be understood either of these two ways:—1. "*For this cause,*—for having preached the doctrine contained in the foregoing chapter, and for asserting that the great privileges of the gospel belong not only to the Jews, but to believing Gentiles also, though they are not circumcised,—for this I am now a prisoner, but a *prisoner of Jesus Christ,* as I suffer in his cause and for his sake, and continue his faithful servant and the object of his special protection and care, while I am thus suffering for him." Observe, Christ's servants, if they come to be prisoners, are his prisoners; and he despises not his prisoners. He thinks never the worse of them for the bad character which the world gives them, or the evil treatment that they met with in it. Paul adhered to Christ, and Christ owned him, when he was in prison.—*For you, Gentiles;* the Jews persecuted and imprisoned him because he was the apostle of the Gentiles, and preached the gospel to them. We may learn hence that the faithful ministers of Christ are to dispense his sacred truths, however disagreeable they may be to some, and whatever they themselves may suffer for doing so. Or, 2. The words may be thus understood:—"*For this cause,*—since *you are no more strangers and foreigners* (as *ch.* ii. 19), but are united to Christ, and admitted into communion with his church,—*I Paul,* who am *the prisoner of Jesus Christ,* pray that you may be enabled to act as becomes persons thus favoured by God, and made partakers of such privileges." To this purport you find him expressing himself in *v.* 14, where, after the digression contained in the several verses intervening, he proceeds with what he began in the first verse. Observe, Those who have received grace and signal favours from God stand in need of prayer, that they may improve and advance, and continue to act as becomes them. And, seeing Paul while he was a prisoner employed himself in such prayers to God in behalf of the Ephesians, we should learn that no particular sufferings of our own should make us so solicitous about ourselves as to neglect the cases of others in our supplications and addresses to God. He speaks again of his sufferings: *Wherefore I desire that you faint not at my tribulation for you, which is your glory, v.* 13. While he was in prison, he suffered much there; and, though it was upon their account that he suffered, yet he would not have them discouraged nor dismayed at this, seeing God had done such great things for them by his ministry. What a tender concern was here for these Ephesians! The apostle seems to have been more solicitous lest they should be discouraged and faint upon his tribulations than about what he himself endured; and, to prevent this, he tells them that his sufferings were their glory, and would be so far from being a real discouragement, if they duly considered the matter, that they ministered cause to them for glorying and for rejoicing, as this discovered the great esteem and regard which God bore to them, in that he not only sent his apostles to preach the gospel to them, but even to suffer for them, and to confirm the truths they delivered by the persecutions they underwent. Observe, Not only the faithful ministers of Christ themselves, but their people too, have some special cause for joy and glorying, when they suffer for the sake of dispensing the gospel.

II. The apostle informs them of God's appointing him to the office, and eminently fitting and qualifying him for it, by a special revelation that he made unto him. 1. God appointed him to the office: *If you have heard of the dispensation of the grace of God, which is given me to you-ward, v.* 2. They could not have heard of this, and therefore he does not design to speak doubtfully of this matter. Εἴγε is sometimes an affirmative particle, and we may read it, *Since you have heard,* &c. He styles the gospel *the grace of God* here (as in other places) because it is the gift of divine grace to sinful men; and all the gracious overtures that it makes, and the joyful tidings that it contains, proceed from the rich grace of God; and it is also the great instrument in the hands of the Spirit by which God works grace in the souls of men. He speaks of the dispensation of this grace given to him; he means as he was authorized and commissioned by God to dispense the doctrine of the gospel, which commission and authority were given to him chiefly for the service of the Gentiles: *to you-ward.* And again, speaking of the gospel, he says, *Whereof I was made a minister,* &c. *v.* 7. Here he again asserts his authority. He *was* MADE *a minister*—he did not make himself such; he took not to himself that honour—and he was made such *according to the gift of the grace of God unto* him. God supplied and furnished him for his work; and in the performance of it suitably assisted him with all needful gifts and graces, both ordinary and extraordinary, and that *by the effectual working of his power,* in himself more especially, and also in great numbers of those to whom he preached, by which means his labours among them were successful. Observe, What God calls men to he fits them for, and does it with an almighty power. An effectual working of divine power attends the gifts of divine grace. 2. As God appointed him to the office, so he eminently qualified him for it, by a special revelation that he made unto him. He makes mention both of the mystery that was revealed and of the revelation of it. (1.) The mystery revealed is *that the Gentiles should be fellow-heirs, and of the same body, and partakers of his promise in Christ, by the gospel* (*v.* 6); that is, that they should be joint-heirs with the believing Jews of the heavenly inheritance; and that they should be members of the same mystical body, be received into the church of Christ, and be interested in the gospel-promises, as well as the Jews, and particularly in that great promise of the Spirit. And this *in Christ,* being united to Christ, *in whom all the promises are yea and amen; and by the gospel,* that is, in the times of the gospel, as some understand it; or, *by the gospel* preached to them, which is the great instrument and means by which God works faith in Christ, as others. This was the great truth revealed to the apostles, namely, that God would call the Gentiles to salvation by faith in Christ, and that without the works of the law. (2.) Of the revelation of this truth he speaks, *v.* 3—5. Here we may observe that the coalition of Jews and Gentiles in the gospel church was a mystery, a great mystery, what was designed in the counsel of God before all worlds, but what could not be fully understood for many ages, till the accomplishment expounded the prophecies of it. It is called a mystery because the several circumstances and peculiarities of it (such as the time and manner and means by which it should be effected) were concealed and kept secret in God's own breast, till by an immediate *revelation he made them known to* his servant. See Acts xxvi. 16—18. And it is called the mystery of Christ because it was revealed by him (Gal. i. 12), and because it relates so very much to him. Of this the apostle has given some hints *afore,* or a little before; that is, in the preceding chapters. *Whereby, when you read;* or, as those words may be read, *unto which attending* (and it is not enough for us barely to read the scriptures, unless we attend to them, and seriously consider and lay to heart what we read), *you may understand my knowledge in the mystery of Christ;* so as to perceive how God had fitted and qualified him to be an apostle to the Gentiles, which might be to them an evident token of his divine authority. *This mystery,* he says, *in other ages was not made known unto the sons of men, as it is now revealed unto his holy apostles and prophets by the Spirit* (*v.* 5); that is, "It was not so fully and clearly discovered in the ages before Christ as it is now revealed unto the prophets of this age, the prophets of the New Testament, who are immediately inspired and taught by the Spirit." Let us observe, that the conversion of the Gentile world to the faith of Christ was an adorable mystery, and we ought to bless God for it. Who would have imagined that those who had been so long in the dark, and at so great a distance, would be enlightened with the marvellous light, and be made nigh? Let us learn hence not to despair of the worst, of the worst of persons, and the worst of nations. Nothing is too hard for divine grace to do: none so unworthy but God may please to confer great grace upon them. And how much are we ourselves interested in this affair; not only as we live in a time in which the mystery is revealed, but particularly as we are a part of the nations which in times past were foreigners and strangers, and lived in gross idolatry; but are now enlightened with the everlasting gospel, and partake of its promises!

III. The apostle informs them how he was employed in this office, and that with respect to the Gentiles, and to all men.

1. With respect to the Gentiles, he *preached* to them *the unsearchable riches of Christ, v.* 8. Observe, in this verse, how humbly he speaks of himself, and how highly he speaks of Jesus Christ. (1.) How humbly he speaks of himself: *I am less than the least of all saints.* St. Paul, who was the chief of the apostles, calls himself *less than the least of all saints:* he means on account of his having been formerly a persecutor of the followers of Christ. He was, in his own esteem, as little as could be. What can be less than the least? To speak himself as little as could be, he speaks himself less than could be. Observe, Those whom God advances to honourable employments he humbles and makes low in their own eyes; and, where God gives grace to be humble, there he gives all other grace. You may also observe in what a different

manner the apostle speaks of himself and of his office. While he magnifies his office, he debases himself. Observe, A faithful minister of Christ may be very humble, and think very meanly of himself, even when he thinks and speaks very highly and honourably of his sacred function. (2.) How highly he speaks of Jesus Christ: *The unsearchable riches of Christ*. There is a mighty treasury of mercy, grace, and love, laid up in Christ Jesus, and that both for Jews and Gentiles. Or, the riches of the gospel are here spoken of as the riches of Christ: the riches which Christ purchased for, and bestows upon, all believers. And they are unsearchable riches, which we cannot find the bottom of, which human sagacity could never have discovered, and men could no otherwise attain to the knowledge of them but by revelation. Now it was the apostle's business and employment to *preach* these *unsearchable riches of Christ among the Gentiles:* and it was a favour he greatly valued, and looked upon it as an unspeakable honour to him: "*Unto me is this grace given;* this special favour God has granted to such an unworthy creature as I am." And it is an unspeakable favour to the Gentile world that to them *the unsearchable riches of Christ* are preached. Though many remain poor, and are not enriched with these riches, yet it is a favour to have them preached among us, to have an offer of them made to us; and, if we are not enriched with them, it is our own fault.

2. With respect to all men, *v.* 9. His business and employment were *to make all men see* (to publish and make known to the whole world) *what is the fellowship of the mystery* (that the Gentiles who have hitherto been strangers to the church, shall be admitted into communion with it) *which from the beginning of the world hath been hid in God* (kept secret in his purpose), *who created all things by Jesus Christ:* as John i. 3, *All things were made by him, and without him was not any thing made that was made;* and therefore no wonder that he saves the Gentiles as well as the Jews; for he is the common Creator of them both: and we may conclude that he is able to perform the work of their redemption, seeing he was able to accomplish the great work of creation. It is true that both the first creation, when God made all things out of nothing, and the new creation, whereby sinners are made new creatures by converting grace, are of God by Jesus Christ. The apostle adds, *To the intent that now unto the principalities and powers in heavenly places might be known, by the church, the manifold wisdom of God, v.* 10. This was one thing, among others, which God had in his eye in revealing this mystery, that the good angels, who have a pre-eminence in governing the kingdoms and principalities of the world, and who are endued with great power to execute the will of God on this earth (though their ordinary residence is in heaven) may be informed, from what passes in the church and is done in and by it, *of the manifold wisdom of God;* that is, of the great variety with which God wisely dispenses things, or of his wisdom manifested in the many ways and methods he takes in ordering his church in the several ages of it, and especially in receiving the Gentiles into it. The holy angels, who look into the mystery of our redemption by Christ, could not but take notice of this branch of that mystery, that among the Gentiles is preached the unsearchable riches of Christ. And this is *according to the eternal purpose which he purposed in Christ Jesus our Lord, v.* 11. Some translate the words κατὰ πρόθεσιν τῶν αἰώνων thus, *According to the fore-disposing of the ages which he made,* &c. So Dr. Whitby, &c. "In the first of the ages," says this author, "his wisdom seeing fit to give the promise of a Saviour to a fallen Adam: in the second age to typify and represent him to the Jews in sacred persons, rites, and sacrifices: and in the age of the Messiah, or the last age, to reveal him to the Jews, and preach him to the Gentiles." Others understand it, according to our translation, of the eternal purpose which God purposed to execute in and through Jesus Christ, the whole of what he has done in the great affair of man's redemption being in pursuance of his eternal decree about that matter. The apostle, having mentioned our Lord Jesus Christ, subjoins concerning him, *In whom we have boldness and access with confidence by the faith of him* (*v.* 12); that is, "By (or through) whom we have liberty to open our minds freely to God, as to a Father, and a well-grounded persuasion of audience and of acceptance with him; and this by means of the faith we have in him, as our great Mediator and Advocate." We may come with humble boldness to hear from God, knowing that the terror of the curse is done away; and we may expect to hear from him good words and comfortable. We may have access with confidence to speak to God, knowing that we have such a Mediator between God and us, and such an Advocate with the Father.

14 For this cause I bow my knees
unto the Father of our Lord Jesus
Christ, 15 Of whom the whole
family in heaven and earth is named,
16 That he would grant you, according to the riches of his glory, to be
strengthened with might by his Spirit
in the inner man; 17 That Christ
may dwell in your hearts by faith;
that ye, being rooted and grounded
in love, 18 May be able to comprehend with all saints what *is* the
breadth, and length, and depth, and
height; 19 And to know the love of
Christ, which passeth knowledge, that

ye might be filled with all the fulness
of God. 20 Now unto him that is
able to do exceeding abundantly above
all that we ask or think, according to
the power that worketh in us, 21
Unto him *be* glory in the church by
Christ Jesus throughout all ages,
world without end. Amen.

We now come to the second part of this chapter, which contains Paul's devout and affectionate prayer to God for his beloved Ephesians.—*For this cause.* This may be referred either to the immediately foregoing verse, *That you faint not,* &c., or, rather, the apostle is here resuming what he began at the first verse, from which he digressed in those which are interposed. Observe,

I. To whom he prays—to God, as *the Father of our Lord Jesus Christ,* of which see *ch.* i. 3.

II. His outward posture in prayer, which was humble and reverent: *I bow my knees.* Note, When we draw nigh to God, we should reverence him in our hearts, and express our reverence in the most suitable and becoming behaviour and gesture. Here, having mentioned Christ, he cannot pass without an honourable encomium of his love, *v.* 15. The universal church has a dependence upon the Lord Jesus Christ: *Of whom the whole family in heaven and earth is named.* The Jews were wont to boast of Abraham as their father, but now Jews and Gentiles are both denominated from Christ (so some); while others understand it of the saints in heaven, who wear the crown of glory, and of saints on earth who are going on in the work of grace here. Both the one and the other make but one family, one household; and from him they are *named* CHRISTIANS, as they really are such, acknowledging their dependence upon, and their relation to, Christ.

III. What the apostle asks of God for these his friends—spiritual blessings, which are the best blessings, and the most earnestly to be sought and prayed for by every one of us, both for ourselves and for our friends. 1. Spiritual strength for the work and duty to which they were called, and in which they were employed: *That he would grant you, according to the riches of his grace, to be strengthened,* &c. *The inner man* is the heart or soul. To be *strengthened with might* is to be mightily strengthened, much more than they were at present; to be endued with a high degree of grace, and spiritual abilities for discharging duty, resisting temptations, enduring persecutions, &c. And the apostle prays that this may be *according to the riches of his glory,* or according to his glorious riches—answerable to that great abundance of grace, mercy, and power, which resides in God, and is his glory: and this by his Spirit, who is the immediate worker of grace in the souls of God's people. Observe from these things, That strength from the Spirit of God in the inner man is the best and most desirable strength, strength in the soul, the strength of faith and other graces, strength to serve God and to do our duty, and to persevere in our Christian course with vigour and with cheerfulness. And let us further observe that *as the work of grace is first begun so it is continued and carried on, by the blessed Spirit of God.* 2. The indwelling of Christ in their hearts, *v.* 17. Christ is said to dwell in his people, as he is always present with them by his gracious influences and operations. Observe, It is a desirable thing to have Christ dwell in our hearts; and if the law of Christ be written there, and the love of Christ be shed abroad there, then Christ dwells there. Christ is an inhabitant in the soul of every good Christian. Where his Spirit dwells, there he dwells; and he dwells in the heart by faith, by means of the continual exercise of faith upon him. Faith opens the door of the soul, to receive Christ; faith admits him, and submits to him. By faith we are united to Christ, and have an interest in him. 3. The fixing of pious and devout affections in the soul: *That you being rooted and grounded in love,* stedfastly fixed in your love to God, the Father of our Lord Jesus Christ, and to all the saints, the beloved of our Lord Jesus Christ. Many have some love to God and to his servants, but it is a flash, like the crackling of thorns under a pot, it makes a great noise, but is gone presently. We should earnestly desire that good affections may be fixed in us, that we may be *rooted and grounded in love.* Some understand it of their being settled and established in the sense of God's love to them, which would inspire them with greater ardours of holy love to him, and to one another. And how very desirable is it to have a settled fixed sense of the love of God and Christ to our souls, so as to be able to say with the apostle at all times, *He has loved me!* Now the best way to attain this is to be careful that we maintain a constant love to God in our souls; this will be the evidence of the love of God to us. *We love him, because he first loved us.* In order to this he prays, 4. For their experimental acquaintance with the love of Jesus Christ. The more intimate acquaintance we have with Christ's love to us, the more our love will be drawn out to him, and to those who are his, for his sake: *That you may be able to comprehend with all saints,* &c. (*v.* 18, 19); that is, more clearly to understand, and firmly to believe, the wonderful love of Christ to his, which the saints do understand and believe in some measure, and shall understand more hereafter. Christians should not aim to comprehend above all saints; but be content that God deals with them as he uses to do with those who love and fear his name: we should desire to comprehend *with all saints,* to have so much knowledge as the saints are allowed to have in this world. We should be ambitious of coming up with *the first three;* but not of going beyond what is the measure of the stature of other saints. It is observable how magnificently the apostle speaks of the love of Christ. The dimensions of redeeming love are admirable: *The breadth, and length, and depth, and height.* By enumerating these dimensions, the apostle designs to signify the exceeding greatness of the love of Christ, the unsearchable riches of his love, which is *higher than heaven, deeper than hell, longer than the earth, and broader than the sea,* Job xi. 8, 9. Some describe the particulars thus: By the breadth of it we may understand the extent of it to all ages, nations, and ranks of men; by the length of it, its continuance from everlasting to everlasting; by the depth of it, its stooping to the lowest condition, with a design to relieve and save those who have sunk into the depths of sin and misery; by its height, its entitling and raising us up to the heavenly happiness and glory. We should desire to comprehend this love: it is the character of all the saints that they do so; for they all have a complacency and a confidence in the love of Christ: *And to know the love of Christ which passeth knowledge, v.* 19. If it passeth knowledge, how can we know it? We must pray and endeavour to know something, and should still covet and strive to know more and more of it, though, after the best endeavours, none can fully comprehend it: in its full extent it surpasses knowledge. Though the love of Christ may be better perceived and known by Christians than it generally is, yet it cannot be fully understood on this side heaven. 5. He prays that they may *be filled with all the fulness of God.* It is a high expression: we should not dare to use it if we did not find it in the scriptures. It is like those other expressions, of being *partakers of a divine nature,* and of being *perfect as our Father in heaven is perfect.* We are not to understand it of his fulness as God in himself, but of his fulness as a God in covenant with us, as a God to his people: such a fulness as God is ready to bestow, who is willing to fill them all to the utmost of their capacity, and that with all those gifts and graces which he sees they need. Those who receive grace for grace from Christ's fulness may be said to be *filled with the fulness of God,* according to their capacity, all which is in order to their arriving at the highest degree of the knowledge and enjoyment of God, and an entire conformity to him.

The apostle closes the chapter with a doxology, *v.* 20, 21. It is proper to conclude our prayers with praises. Our blessed Saviour has taught us to do so. Take notice how he describes God, and how he ascribes glory to him. He describes him as a God that *is able to do exceedingly abundantly above all that we ask or think.* There is an inexhaustible fulness of grace and mercy in God, which the prayers of all the saints can never draw dry. Whatever we may ask, or think to ask, still God is still able to do more, abundantly more, exceedingly abundantly more. Open thy mouth ever so wide, still he hath wherewithal to fill it. Note, In our applications to God we should encourage our faith by a consideration of his all-sufficiency and almighty power. *According to the power which worketh in us.* As if he had said, We have already had a proof of this power of God, in what he hath wrought in us and done for us, having quickened us by his grace, and converted us to himself. The power that still worketh for the saints is according to that power that hath wrought in them. Wherever God gives of his fulness he gives to experience his power. Having thus described God, he ascribes glory to him. When we come to ask for grace from God, we ought to give glory to God. Unto him be glory in the church by Christ Jesus. In ascribing glory to God, we ascribe all excellences and perfections to him, glory being the effulgency and result of them all. Observe, The seat of God's praises is in the church. That little rent of praise which God receives from this world is from the church, a sacred society constituted for the glory of God, every particular member of which, both Jew and Gentile, concurs in this work of praising God. The Mediator of these praises is Jesus Christ. All God's gifts come from him to us through the hand of Christ; and all our praises pass from us to him through the same hand. And God should and will be praised thus *throughout all ages, world without end;* for he will ever have a church to praise him, and he will ever have his tribute of praise from his church. *Amen.* So be it; and so it will certainly be.

CHAP. IV.

We have gone through the former part of this epistle, which consists of several important doctrinal truths, contained in the three preceding chapters. We enter now on the latter part of it, in which we have the most weighty and serious exhortations that can be given. We may observe that in this, as in most others of Paul's epistles, the former part is doctrinal, and fitted to inform the minds of men in the great truths and doctrines of the gospel, the latter is practical, and designed for the direction of their lives and manners, all Christians being bound to endeavour after soundness in the faith, and regularity in life and practice. In what has gone before we have heard of Christian privileges, which are the matter of our comfort. In what follows we shall hear of Christian duties, and what the Lord our God requires of us in consideration of such privileges vouchsafed to us. The best way to understand the mysteries and partake of the privileges of which we have read before is conscientiously to practise the duties prescribed to us in what follows: as, on the other hand, a serious consideration and belief of the doctrines that have been taught us in the foregoing chapters will be a good foundation on which to build the practice of the duties prescribed in those which are yet before us. Christian faith and Christian practice mutually befriend each other. In this chapter we have divers exhortations to important duties. I. One that is more general, ver. 1. II. An exhortation to mutual love, unity, and concord, with the proper means and motives to promote them, ver. 2—16. III. An exhortation to Christian purity and holiness of life; and that both more general (ver. 17—24) and in several particular instances, ver. 25, to the end.

I THEREFORE, (the prisoner of the Lord,) beseech you that ye walk worthy of the vocation wherewith ye are called,

This is a general exhortation to walk as becomes our Christian profession. Paul was now a prisoner at Rome; and he was the *prisoner of the Lord,* or in the Lord, which signifies as much as for the Lord See of this, *ch.* iii. 1. He mentions this once and again, to show that he was not ashamed of his bonds, well knowing that he suffered not as an evil doer: and likewise to recommend what he wrote to them with the greater tenderness and with some special advantage. It was a doctrine he thought worth suffering for, and therefore surely they should think it worthy their serious regards and their dutiful observance. We have here the petition of a poor prisoner, one of Christ's prisoners: "*I therefore, the prisoner of the Lord, beseech you,* &c. Considering what God has done for you, and to what a state and condition he has called you, as has been discoursed before, I now come with an earnest request to you (not to send me relief, nor to use your interest for the obtaining of my liberty, the first thing which poor prisoners are wont to solicit from their friends, but) that you would approve yourselves good Christians, and live up to your profession and calling: *That you walk worthily,* agreeably, suitably, and congruously to those happy circumstances into which the grace of God has brought you, whom he has converted from heathenism to Christianity. Observe, Christians ought to accommodate themselves to the gospel by which they are called, and to the glory to which they are called; both are their vocation. We are called Christians; we must answer that name, and live like Christians. We are called to God's kingdom and glory; that kingdom and glory therefore we must mind, and walk as becomes the heirs of them.

2 With all lowliness and meekness,
with longsuffering, forbearing one
another in love; 3 Endeavouring
to keep the unity of the Spirit in the
bond of peace. 4 *There is* one body,
and one Spirit, even as ye are called
in one hope of your calling; 5 One
Lord, one faith, one baptism, 6 One
God and Father of all, who *is* above
all, and through all, and in you all.
7 But unto every one of us is given
grace according to the measure of the
gift of Christ. 8 Wherefore he saith,
When he ascended up on high, he led
captivity captive, and gave gifts unto
men. 9 (Now that he ascended, what
is it but that he also descended first
into the lower parts of the earth? 10
He that descended is the same also
that ascended up far above all heavens, that he might fill all things.)
11 And he gave some, apostles; and
some, prophets; and some, evangelists; and some, pastors and teachers;
12 For the perfecting of the saints,
for the work of the ministry, for the
edifying of the body of Christ: 13
Till we all come in the unity of the
faith, and of the knowledge of the
Son of God, unto a perfect man, unto
the measure of the stature of the fulness of Christ: 14 That we *henceforth* be no more children, tossed to
and fro, and carried about with every
wind of doctrine, by the sleight of
men, *and* cunning craftiness, whereby
they lie in wait to deceive; 15 But
speaking the truth in love, may grow
up into him in all things, which is the
head, *even* Christ: 16 From whom
the whole body fitly joined together
and compacted by that which every
joint supplieth, according to the effectual working in the measure of every
part, maketh increase of the body
unto the edifying of itself in love.

Here the apostle proceeds to more particular exhortations. Two he enlarges upon in this chapter:—To unity and love, purity and holiness, which Christians should very much study. We do not *walk worthy of the vocation wherewith we are called* if we be not faithful friends to all Christians, and sworn enemies to all sin.

This section contains the exhortation to mutual love, unity, and concord, with the proper means and motives to promote them. Nothing is pressed upon us more earnestly in the scriptures than this. Love is the law of Christ's kingdom, the lesson of his school, the livery of his family. Observe,

I. The means of unity: *Lowliness and meekness, long-suffering, and forbearing one another in love, v.* 2. By lowliness we are to understand humility, entertaining mean thoughts of ourselves, which is opposed to pride. By *meekness,* that excellent disposition of soul which makes men unwilling to provoke others, and not easily to be provoked or offended with their infirmities; and it is opposed to angry resentments and peevishness. *Long-suffering* implies a patient bearing of injuries, without seeking revenge. *Forbearing one another in love* signifies bearing their infirmities out of a principle of love, and so as not to cease to love them on the account of these. The best Christians have need to bear one with another, and to make the best one of another, to provoke one another's graces and not their passions. We find much in ourselves which it is hard to forgive ourselves; and therefore we must not think it much if we find that in others which we think hard to forgive them, and yet we must forgive them as we forgive ourselves. Now without these things unity cannot be preserved. The first step towards unity is humility; without this there will be no meekness, no patience, or forbearance; and without these no unity. Pride and passion break the peace, and make all the mischief. Humility and meekness restore the peace, and keep it. *Only by pride comes contention;* only by humility comes love. The more lowly-mindedness the more like-mindedness. We do not walk worthy of the vocation wherewith we are called if we be not meek and lowly of heart: for he by whom we are called, he to whom we are called, was eminent for meekness and lowliness of heart, and has commanded us therein to learn of him.

II. The nature of that unity which the apostle prescribes: it is *the unity of the Spirit, v.* 3. The seat of Christian unity is in the heart or spirit: it does not lie in one set of thoughts, nor in one form and mode of worship, but in one heart and one soul. This unity of heart and affection may be said to be of the Spirit of God; it is wrought by him, and is one of the fruits of the Spirit. This we should endeavour to keep. *Endeavouring* is a gospel word. We must do our utmost. If others will quarrel with us, we must take all possible care not to quarrel with them. If others will despise and hate us, we must not despise and hate them. *In the bond of peace.* Peace is a bond, as it unites persons, and makes them live friendly one with another. A peaceable disposition and conduct bind Christians together, whereas discord and quarrelling disband and disunite their hearts and affections. Many slender twigs, bound together, become strong. The bond of peace is the strength of society. Not that it can be imagined that all good people, and all the members of societies, should be in every thing just of the same length, and the same sentiments, and the same judgment: but the bond of peace unites them all together, with a *non obstante* to these. As in a bundle of rods, they may be of different lengths and different strength; but, when they are tied together by one bond, they are stronger than any, even than the thickest and strongest was of itself.

III. The motives proper to promote this Christian unity and concord. The apostle urges several, to persuade us thereto.

1. Consider how many unities there are that are the joy and glory of our Christian profession. There should be one heart; for *there is one body, and one Spirit, v.* 4. Two hearts in one body would be monstrous. If there be but one body, all that belong to that body should have one heart. The Catholic church is one mystical body of Christ, and all good Christians make up but one body, incorporated by one charter, that of the gospel, animated by one Spirit, the same Holy Spirit who by his gifts and graces quickens, enlivens, and governs that body. If we belong to Christ, we are all actuated by one and the same Spirit, and therefore should be one. *Even as you are called in one hope of your calling.* Hope is here put for its object, the thing hoped for, the heavenly inheritance, to the hope of which we are called. All Christians are called to the same hope of eternal life. There is one Christ that they all hope in, and one heaven that they are all hoping for; and therefore they should be of one heart. *One Lord* (*v.* 5), that is, Christ, the head of the church, to whom, by God's appointment, all Christians are immediately subject. *One faith,* that is, the gospel, containing the doctrine of the Christian faith: or, it is the same grace of faith (faith in Christ) whereby all Christians are saved. *One baptism,* by which we profess our faith, being baptized in the name of the Father, Son, and Holy Ghost; and so the same sacramental covenant, whereby we engage ourselves to the Lord Christ. *One God and Father of all, v.* 6. One God, who owns all the true members of the church for his children; for he is the Father of all such by special relation, as he is the Father of all men by creation: and he *is above all,* by his essence, and with respect to the glorious perfections of his nature, and as he has dominion over all creatures and especially over his church, *and through all,* by his providence upholding and governing them: *and in you all,* in all believers, in whom he dwells as in his holy temple, by his Spirit and special grace. If then there be so many *ones,* it is a pity but there should be one more—one heart, or one soul.

2. Consider the variety of gifts that Christ has bestowed among Christians: *But unto every one of us is given grace according to the measure of the gift of Christ.* Though the members of Christ's church agree in so many things, yet there are some things wherein they differ: but this should breed no difference of affection among them, since they are all derived from the same bountiful author and designed for the same great ends. Unto every one of us Christians is given grace, some gift of grace, in some kind or degree or other, for the mutual help of one another. Unto every one of us ministers is given grace; to some a greater measure of gifts, to others a less measure. The different gifts of Christ's ministers proved a great occasion of contention among the first Christians: one was for Paul, and another for Apollos. The apostle shows that they had no reason to quarrel about them, but all the reason in the world to agree in the joint use of them, for common edification; because all was given *according to the measure of the gift of Christ,* in such a measure as seemed best to Christ to bestow upon every one. Observe, All the ministers, and all the members of Christ, owe all the gifts and graces that they are possessed of to him; and this is a good reason why we should love one another, *because to every one of us is given grace.* All to whom Christ has given grace, and on whom he has bestowed his gifts (though they are of different sizes, different names, and different

sentiments, yet) *ought to love one another.* The apostle takes this occasion to specify some of the gifts which Christ bestowed. And that they were bestowed by Christ he makes appear by those words of David wherein he foretold this concerning him (Ps. lxviii. 18), *Wherefore he saith* (*v.* 8), that is, the Psalmist saith, *When he ascended up on high, he led captivity captive, and gave gifts unto men.* David prophesied of the ascension of Christ; and the apostle descants upon it here, and in the three following verses. *When he ascended up on high.* We may understand the apostle both of the place into which he ascended in his human nature, that is, the highest heavens, and particularly of the state to which he was advanced, he being then highly exalted, and eminently glorified, by his Father. Let us set ourselves to think of the ascension of Jesus Christ: that our blessed Redeemer, having risen from the dead, is gone to heaven, where he sits at the right hand of the Majesty on high, which completed the proof of his being the Son of God. As great conquerors, when they rode in their triumphal chariots, used to be attended with the most illustrious of their captives led in chains, and were wont to scatter their largesses and bounty among the soldiers and other spectators of their triumphs, so Christ, when he ascended into heaven, as a triumphant conqueror, *led captivity captive.* It is a phrase used in the Old Testament to signify a conquest over enemies, especially over such as formerly had led others captive; see Judges v. 12. Captivity is here put for captives, and signifies all our spiritual enemies, who brought us into captivity before. He conquered those who had conquered us; such as sin, the devil, and death. Indeed, he triumphed over these *on the cross;* but the triumph was completed at his ascension, when he became Lord over all, and had the keys of death and hades put into his hands. *And he gave gifts unto men*: in the psalm it is, *He received gifts for men.* He received for them, that he might give to them, a large measure of gifts and graces; particularly, he enriched his disciples with the gift of the Holy Ghost. The apostle, thus speaking of the ascension of Christ, takes notice that he *descended first, v.* 9. As much as if he had said, "When David speaks of Christ's ascension, he intimates the knowledge he had of Christ's humiliation on earth; for, when it is said that he ascended, this implies that he first descended: for what is it but a proof or demonstration of his having done so? *Into the lower parts of the earth;* this may refer either to his incarnation, according to that of David, Ps. cxxxix. 15, *My substance was not hidden from thee, when I was made in secret, and curiously wrought in the lowest parts of the earth;* or, to his burial, according to that of Ps. lxiii. 9, *Those that seek my soul to destroy it shall go into the lower parts of the earth.* He calls his death (say some of the fathers) *his descent into the lower parts of the earth.* He descended to the earth in his incarnation. He descended into the earth in his burial. *As Jonas was three days and three nights in the whale's belly, so was the Son of man in the heart of the earth. He that descended is the same also that ascended up far above all heavens* (*v.* 10), far above the airy and starry (which are the visible) heavens, into the heaven of heavens; *that he might fill all things,* all the members of his church, with gifts and graces suitable to their several conditions and stations. Observe, Our Lord humbled himself first, and then he was exalted. He descended first, and then ascended. The apostle next tells us what were Christ's gifts at his ascension: *He gave some apostles,* &c. *v.* 11. Indeed he sent forth some of these before his ascension, Matt. x. 1—5. But one was then added, Acts i. 26. And all of them were more solemnly installed, and publicly confirmed, in their office, by his visibly pouring forth the Holy Ghost in an extraordinary manner and measure upon them. Note, The great gift that Christ gave to the church at his ascension was that of the ministry of peace and reconciliation. The gift of the ministry is the fruit of Christ's ascension. And ministers have their various gifts, which are all given them by the Lord Jesus. The officers which Christ gave to his church were of two sorts—*extraordinary* ones advanced to a higher office in the church: such were *apostles, prophets,* and *evangelists.* The apostles were chief. These Christ immediately called, furnished them with extraordinary gifts and the power of working miracles, and with infallibility in delivering his truth; and, they having been the witnesses of his miracles and doctrine, he sent them forth to spread the gospel and to plant and govern churches. The prophets seem to have been such as expounded the writings of the Old Testament, and foretold things to come. The evangelists were ordained persons (2 Tim. i. 6) whom the apostles took for their companions in travel (Gal. ii. 1), and sent them out to settle and establish such churches as the apostles themselves had planted (Acts xix. 22), and, not being fixed to any particular place, they were to continue till recalled, 2 Tim. iv. 9. And then there are *ordinary* ministers, employed in a lower and narrower sphere; as *pastors* and *teachers.* Some take these two names to signify one office, implying the duties of ruling and teaching belonging to it. Others think they design two distinct offices, both ordinary, and of standing use in the church; and then pastors are such as are fixed at the head of particular churches, with design to guide, instruct, and feed them in the manner appointed by Christ; and they are frequently called bishops and elders: and the teachers were those whose work it was also to preach the gospel and to instruct the people by way of exhortation. We see here that it is Christ's prerogative to appoint what officers and offices he pleases in his church. And how rich is the church, that had at first such a variety of officers and has still such a variety of gifts! How kind is Christ to his church! How careful of it and of its edification! When he ascended, he procured the gift of the Holy Ghost; and the gifts of the Holy Ghost are various: some have greater, others have less measures; but all for the good of the body, which brings us to the third argument,

3. Which is taken from Christ's great end and design in giving gifts unto men. The gifts of Christ were intended for the good of his church, and in order to advance his kingdom and interest among men. All these being designed for one common end is a good reason why all Christians should agree in brotherly love, and not envy one another's gifts. All are *for the perfecting of the saints* (*v.* 12); that is, according to the import of the original, to bring into an orderly spiritual state and frame those who had been as it were dislocated and disjointed by sin, and then to strengthen, confirm, and advance them therein, that so each, in his proper place and function, might contribute to the good of the whole.—*For the work of the ministry,* or *for the work of dispensation;* that is, that they might dispense the doctrines of the gospel, and successfully discharge the several parts of their ministerial function.—*For the edifying of the body of Christ;* that is, to build up the church, which is Christ's mystical body, by an increase of their graces, and an addition of new members. All are designed to prepare us for heaven: *Till we all come,* &c., *v.* 13. The gifts and offices (some of them) which have been spoken of are to continue in the church till the saints be perfected, which will not be *till they all come in the unity of the faith* (till all true believers meet together, by means of the same precious faith) *and of the knowledge of the Son of God,* by which we are to understand, not a bare speculative knowledge, or the acknowledging of Christ to be the Son of God and the great Mediator, but such as is attended with appropriation and affection, with all due honour, trust, and obedience.—*Unto a perfect man,* to our full growth of gifts and graces, free from those childish infirmities that we are subject to in the present world.—*Unto the measure of the stature of the fulness of Christ,* so as to be Christians of a full maturity and ripeness in all the graces derived from Christ's fulness: or, according to the measure of that stature which is to make up the fulness of Christ, which is to complete his mystical body. Now we shall never come to the perfect man, till we come to the perfect world. There is a fulness in Christ, and a fulness to be derived from him; and a certain stature of that fulness, and a measure of that stature, are assigned in the counsel of God to every believer, and we never come to that measure till we come to heaven. God's children, as long as they are in this world, are growing. Dr. Lightfoot understands the apostle as speaking here of Jews and Gentiles knit in the unity of the faith and of the knowledge of the Son of God, so making a perfect man, and the measure of the stature of the fulness of Christ. The apostle further shows, in the following verses, what was God's design in his sacred institutions, and what effect they ought to have upon us. As, (1.) *That we henceforth be no more children,* &c. (*v.* 14); that is, that we may be no longer children in knowledge, weak in the faith, and inconstant in our judgments, easily yielding to every temptation, readily complying with every one's humour, and being at every one's beck. Children are easily imposed upon. We must take care of this, and of being *tossed to and fro,* like ships without ballast, *and carried about,* like clouds in the air, with such doctrines as have no truth nor solidity in them, but nevertheless spread themselves far and wide, and are therefore compared to wind. *By the sleight of men;* this is a metaphor taken from gamesters, and signifies the mischievous subtlety of seducers: *and cunning craftiness,* by which is meant their skilfulness in finding ways to seduce and deceive; for it follows, *whereby they lie in wait to deceive,* as in an ambush, in order to circumvent the weak, and draw them from the truth. Note, Those must be very wicked and ungodly men who set themselves to seduce and deceive others into false doctrines and errors. The apostle describes them here as base men, using a great deal of devilish art and cunning, in order thereunto. The best method we can take to fortify ourselves against such is to study the sacred oracles, and to pray for the illumination and grace of the Spirit of Christ, that we may know the truth as it is in Jesus, and be established in it. (2.) That we should *speak the truth in love* (*v.* 15), or follow the truth in love, or be sincere in love to our fellow-christians. While we adhere to the doctrine of Christ, which is the truth, we should live in love one with another. Love is an excellent thing; but we must be careful to preserve truth together with it. Truth is an excellent thing; yet it is requisite that we speak it in love, and not in contention. These two should go together—truth and peace. (3.) That we should *grow up into Christ in all things.* Into Christ, so as to be more deeply rooted in him. In all things; in knowledge, love, faith, and all the parts of the new man. We should grow up towards maturity, which is opposed to being children. Those are improving Christians who grow up into Christ. The more we grow into an acquaintance with Christ, faith in him, love to him, dependence upon him, the more we shall flourish in every grace. He is the head; and we should thus grow, that we may thereby honour our head. The Christian's growth tends to the glory of Christ. (4.) We should be assisting and

helpful one to another, as members of the same body, *v.* 16. Here the apostle makes a comparison between the natural body and Christ's mystical body, that body of which Christ is the head: and he observes that as there must be communion and mutual communications of the members of the body among themselves, in order to their growth and improvement, so there must be mutual love and unity, together with the proper fruits of these, among Christians, in order to their spiritual improvement and growth in grace. *From whom,* says he (that is, from Christ their head, who conveys influence and nourishment to every particular member), *the whole body of Christians, fitly joined together and compacted* (being orderly and firmly united among themselves, every one in his proper place and station), *by that which every joint supplies* (by the assistance which every one of the parts, thus united, gives to the whole, or by the Spirit, faith, love, sacraments, &c., which, like the veins and arteries in the body, serve to unite Christians to Christ their head, and to one another as fellow-members), *according to the effectual working in the measure of every part* (that is, say some, according to the power which the Holy Ghost exerts to make God's appointed means effectual for this great end, in such a measure as Christ judges to be sufficient and proper for every member, according to its respective place and office in the body; or, as others, according to the power of Christ, who, as head, influences and enlivens every member; or, according to the effectual working of every member, in communicating to others of what it has received, nourishment is conveyed to all in their proportions, and according to the state and exigence of every part) *makes increase of the body,* such an increase as is convenient for the body. Observe, Particular Christians receive their gifts and graces from Christ for the sake and benefit of the whole body. *Unto the edifying of itself in love.* We may understand this two ways:—Either that all the members of the church may attain to a greater measure of love to Christ and to one another; or that they are moved to act in the manner mentioned from love to Christ and to one another. Observe, Mutual love among Christians is a great friend to spiritual growth: it is in love that the body edifies itself; whereas *a kingdom divided against itself cannot stand.*

17 This I say therefore, and testify
in the Lord, that ye henceforth walk
not as other Gentiles walk, in the
vanity of their mind, 18 Having the
understanding darkened, being alienated from the life of God through the
ignorance that is in them, because of
the blindness of their heart: 19 Who
being past feeling have given themselves over unto lasciviousness, to
work all uncleanness with greediness.
20 But ye have not so learned Christ;
21 If so be that ye have heard him,
and have been taught by him, as the
truth is in Jesus: 22 That ye put
off concerning the former conversation the old man, which is corrupt according to the deceitful lusts; 23 And
be renewed in the spirit of your mind;
24 And that ye put on the new man,
which after God is created in righteousness and true holiness. 25 Wherefore putting away lying, speak every
man truth with his neighbour: for
we are members one of another. 26
Be ye angry, and sin not: let not the
sun go down upon your wrath: 27
Neither give place to the devil. 28
Let him that stole steal no more:
but rather let him labour, working
with *his* hands the thing which is
good, that he may have to give to
him that needeth. 29 Let no corrupt communication proceed out of
your mouth, but that which is good
to the use of edifying, that it may
minister grace unto the hearers. 30
And grieve not the holy Spirit of
God, whereby ye are sealed unto the
day of redemption. 31 Let all bitterness, and wrath, and anger, and
clamour, and evil speaking, be put
away from you, with all malice: 32
And be ye kind one to another, tender-
hearted, forgiving one another, even as
God for Christ's sake hath forgiven you.

The apostle having gone through his exhortation to mutual love, unity, and concord, in the foregoing verses, there follows in these an exhortation to Christian purity and holiness of heart and life, and that both more general (*v.* 17—24) and in several particular instances, *v.* 25—32. This is solemnly introduced: "*This I say therefore, and testify in the Lord;* that is, seeing the matter is as above described, seeing you are members of Christ's body and partakers of such gifts, this I urge upon your consciences, and bear witness to as your duty in the Lord's name, and by virtue of the authority I have derived from him." Consider,

I. The more general exhortation to purity and holiness of heart and life.

1. It begins thus, "*That you henceforth walk not as other Gentiles walk*—that for the time to come you do not live, and behave yourselves, as ignorant and unconverted heathens do, who are wholly guided by an understanding employed about vain things, their idols and

their worldly possessions, things which are no way profitable to their souls, and which will deceive their expectations." Converted Gentiles must not live as unconverted Gentiles do. Though they live among them, they must not live like them. Here,

(1.) The apostle takes occasion to describe the wickedness of the Gentile world, out of which regenerate Christians were snatched as brands out of the burning. [1.] Their *understandings were darkened, v.* 18. They were void of all saving knowledge; yea, ignorant of many things concerning God which the light of nature might have taught them. They sat in darkness, and they loved it rather than light: and by their ignorance they were *alienated from the life of God.* They were estranged from, and had a dislike and aversion to, a life of holiness, which is not only that way of life which God requires and approves, and by which we live to him, but which resembles God himself, in his purity, righteousness, truth, and goodness. Their wilful ignorance was the cause of their estrangement from this life of God, which begins in light and knowledge. Gross and affected ignorance is destructive to religion and godliness. And what was the cause of their being thus ignorant? It was *because of the blindness* or the hardness *of their heart.* It was not because God did not make himself known to them by his works, but because they would not admit the instructive rays of the divine light. They were ignorant because they would be so. Their ignorance proceeded from their obstinacy and the hardness of their hearts, their resisting the light and rejecting all the means of illumination and knowledge. [2.] Their consciences were debauched and seared: *Who being past feeling, v.* 19. They had no sense of their sin, nor of the misery and danger of their case by means of it; whereupon they *gave themselves over unto lasciviousness.* They indulged themselves in their filthy lusts; and, yielding themselves up to the dominion of these, they became the slaves and drudges of sin and the devil, *working all uncleanness with greediness.* They made it their common practice to commit all sorts of uncleanness, and even the most unnatural and monstrous sins, and that with insatiable desires. Observe, When men's consciences are once seared, there are no bounds to their sins. When they set their hearts upon the gratification of their lusts, what can be expected but the most abominable sensuality and lewdness, and that their horrid enormities will abound? This was the character of the Gentiles; but,

(2.) These Christians must distinguish themselves from such Gentiles: *You have not so learned Christ, v.* 20. It may be read, *But you not so; you have learned Christ.* Those who have learned Christ are saved from the darkness and defilement which others lie under; and, as they know more, they are obliged to live in a better manner than others. It is a good argument against sin that we have not so learned Christ. Learn Christ! Is Christ a book, a lesson, a way, a trade? The meaning is, "You have not so learned Christianity—the doctrines of Christ and the rules of life prescribed by him. Not so as to do as others do. *If so be,* or since, *that you have heard him* (*v.* 21), have heard his doctrine preached by us, *and have been taught by him,* inwardly and effectually, by his Spirit." Christ is the lesson; we must learn Christ: and Christ is the teacher; we are taught by him. *As the truth is in Jesus.* This may be understood two ways: either, "You have been taught the real truth, as held forth by Christ himself, both in his doctrine and in his life." Or thus, "The truth has made such an impression on your hearts, in your measure, as it did upon the heart of Jesus." The truth of Christ then appears in its beauty and power, when it appears as in Jesus.

2. Another branch of the general exhortation follows in those words, *That you put off, concerning the former conversation, the old man,* &c., *v.* 22—24. "This is a great part of the doctrine which has been taught you, and which you have learned." Here the apostle expresses himself in metaphors taken from garments. The principles, habits, and dispositions of the soul must be changed, before there can be a saving change of the life. There must be sanctification, which consists of these two things:—(1.) The old man must be put off. The corrupt nature is called a man, because, like the human body, it consists of divers parts, mutually supporting and strengthening one another. It is the old man, as old Adam, from whom we derive it. It is bred in the bone, and we brought it into the world with us. It is subtle as an old man; but in all God's saints decaying and withering as an old man, and ready to pass away. It is said to be corrupt; for sin in the soul is the corruption of its faculties: and, where it is not mortified, it grows daily worse and worse, and so tends to destruction. *According to the deceitful lusts.* Sinful inclinations and desires are deceitful lusts: they promise men happiness, but render them more miserable, and if not subdued and mortified betray them into destruction. These therefore must be put off as an old garment that we should be ashamed to be seen in: they must be subdued and mortified. These lusts prevailed against them in their *former conversation,* that is, during their state of unregeneracy and heathenism. (2.) The new man must be put on. It is not enough to shake off corrupt principles, but we must be actuated by gracious ones. We must embrace them, espouse them, and get them written on our hearts: it is not enough to cease to do evil, but we must learn to do well. "*Be renewed in the spirit of your mind* (*v.* 23); that is, use the proper and prescribed means in order to have the mind, which is a spirit, renewed more and more." *And that you put on the new man, v.* 24. By

the new man is meant the new nature, the new creature, which is actuated by a new principle, even regenerating grace, enabling a man to lead a new life, that life of righteousness and holiness which Christianity requires. This new man *is created,* or produced out of confusion and emptiness, by God's almighty power, whose workmanship it is, truly excellent and beautiful. *After God,* in imitation of him, and in conformity to that grand exemplar and pattern. The loss of God's image upon the soul was both the sinfulness and misery of man's fallen state; and that resemblance which it bears to God is the beauty, the glory, and the happiness, of the new creature. *In righteousness* towards men, including all the duties of the second table; *and in holiness* towards God, signifying a sincere obedience to the commands of the first table; *true holiness* in opposition to the outward and ceremonial holiness of the Jews. We are said to put on this new man when, in the use of all God's appointed means, we are endeavouring after this divine nature, this new creature. This is the more general exhortation to purity and holiness of heart and life.

II. The apostle proceeds to some things more particular. Because generals are not so apt to affect, we are told what are those particular limbs of the old man that must be mortified, those filthy rags of the old nature that must be put off, and what are the peculiar ornaments of the new man wherewith we should adorn our Christian profession. 1. Take heed of lying, and be ever careful to speak the truth (*v.* 25): "*Wherefore,* since you have been so well instructed in your duty, and are under such obligations to discharge it, let it appear, in your future behaviour and conduct, that there is a great and real change wrought in you, particularly by *putting away lying.*" Of this sin the heathen were very guilty, affirming that a profitable lie was better than a hurtful truth; and therefore the apostle exhorts them to cease from lying, from every thing that is contrary to truth. This is a part of the old man that must be put off; and that branch of the new man that must be put on in opposition to it is *speaking the truth* in all our converse with others. It is the character of God's people that they are *children who will not lie,* who dare not lie, who hate and abhor lying. All who have grace make conscience of speaking the truth, and would not tell a deliberate lie for the greatest gain and benefit to themselves. The reason here given for veracity is, *We are members one of another.* Truth is a debt we owe to one another; and, if we love one another, we shall not deceive nor lie one to another. We belong to the same society or body, which falsehood or lying tends to dissolve; and therefore we should avoid it, and speak truth. Observe, Lying is a very great sin, a peculiar violation of the obligations which Christians are under, and very injurious and hurtful to Christian society. 2. "Take heed of anger and ungoverned passions. *Be you angry, and sin not,*" *v.* 26. This is borrowed from the LXX. translation of Ps. iv. 4, where we render it, *Stand in awe, and sin not.* Here is an easy concession; for as such we should consider it, rather than as a command. *Be you angry.* This we are apt enough to be, God knows: but we find it difficult enough to observe the restriction, *and sin not.* "If you have a just occasion to be angry at any time, see that it be without sin; and therefore take heed of excess in your anger." If we would be angry and not sin (says one), we must be angry at nothing but sin; and we should be more jealous for the glory of God than for any interest or reputation of our own. One great and common sin in anger is to suffer it to burn into wrath, and then to let it rest; and therefore we are here cautioned against that. "If you have been provoked and have had your spirits greatly discomposed, and if you have bitterly resented any affront that has been offered, before night calm and quiet your spirits, be reconciled to the offender, and let all be well again: *Let not the sun go down upon your wrath.* If it burn into wrath and bitterness of spirit, O see to it that you suppress it speedily." Observe, Though anger in itself is not sinful, yet there is the utmost danger of its becoming so if it be not carefully watched and speedily suppressed. And therefore, though anger may come into the bosom of a wise man, *it rests* only *in the bosom of fools. Neither give place to the devil, v.* 27. Those who persevere in sinful anger and in wrath let the devil into their hearts, and suffer him to gain upon them, till he bring them to malice, mischievous machinations, &c. "*Neither give place to the* calumniator, or the false accuser" (so some read the words); that is, "let your ears be deaf to whisperers, talebearers, and slanderers." 3. We are here warned against the sin of stealing, the breach of the eighth commandment, and advised to honest industry and to beneficence: *Let him that stole steal no more, v.* 28. It is a caution against all manner of wrong-doing, by force or fraud. "Let those of you who, in the time of your gentilism, have been guilty of this enormity, be no longer guilty of it." But we must not only take heed of the sin, but conscientiously abound in the opposite duty: not only not steal, *but rather let him labour, working with his hands the thing that is good.* Idleness makes thieves. So Chrysostom, Τὸ γὰρ κλέπτειν ἀργίας ἐστὶν—*Stealing is the effect of idleness.* Those who will not work, and who are ashamed to beg, expose themselves greatly to temptations to thievery. Men should therefore be diligent and industrious, not in any unlawful way, but in some honest calling: *Working the thing which is good.* Industry, in some honest way, will keep people out of temptation of doing wrong. But there is another reason why men ought to be industrious, namely, that they may be capable of doing some good, as well as that they may be preserved from temptation: *That he may have to give to him that needeth.* They must labour not only that they may live themselves, and live honestly, but they may distribute for supplying the wants of others. Observe, Even those who get their living by their labour should be charitable out of their little to those who are disabled for labour. So necessary and incumbent a duty is it to be charitable to thepoor that even labourers and servants, and those who have but little for themselves, must cast their mite into the treasury. God must have his dues and the poor are his receivers. Observe further, Those alms that are likely to be acceptable to God must not be the produce of unrighteousness and robbery but of honesty and industry. *God hates robbery for burnt-offerings.* 4. We are here warned against corrupt communication; and directed to that which is useful and edifying, *v.* 29. Filthy and unclean words and discourse are poisonous and infectious, as putrid rotten meat: they proceed from and prove a great deal of corruption in the heart of the speaker, and tend to corrupt the minds and manners of others who hear them; and therefore Christians should beware of all such discourse. It may be taken in general for all that which provokes the lusts and passions of others. We must not only put off corrupt communication, but *put on that which is good to the use of edifying.* The great use of speech is to edify those with whom we converse. Christians should endeavour to promote a useful conversation: *that it may minister grace unto the hearers;* that it may be good for, and acceptable to, the hearers, in the way of information, counsel, pertinent reproof, or the like. Observe, It is the great duty of Christians to take care that they offend not with their lips, and that they improve discourse and converse, as much as may be, for the good of others. 5. Here is another caution against wrath and anger, with further advice to mutual love and kindly dispositions towards each other, *v.* 31, 32. By *bitterness, wrath,* and *anger,* are meant violent inward resentment and displeasure against others: and, by *clamour,* big words, loud threatenings, and other intemperate speeches, by which bitterness, wrath, and anger, vent themselves. Christians should not entertain these vile passions in their hearts nor be clamorous with their tongues. *Evil speaking* signifies all railing, reviling, and reproachful speeches, against such as we are angry with. And by *malice* we are to understand that rooted anger which prompts men to design and to do mischief to others. The contrary to all this follows: *Be you kind one to another.* This implies the principle of love in the heart, and the outward expression of it, in an affable, humble, courteous behaviour. It becomes the disciples of Jesus to be kind one to another, as those who have learned, and would teach, the art of obliging. *Tender-hearted;* that is, merciful, and having a tender sense of the distresses and sufferings of others, so as to be quickly moved to compassion and pity. *Forgiving one another.* Occasions of difference will happen among Christ's disciples; and therefore they must be placable, and ready to forgive, therein resembling God himself, who *for Christ's sake hath forgiven them,* and that more than they can forgive one another. Note, With God there is forgiveness; and he forgives sin for the sake of Jesus Christ, and on account of that atonement which he has made to divine justice. Note again, Those who are forgiven of God should be of a forgiving spirit, and should forgive even as God forgives, sincerely and heartily, readily and cheerfully, universally and for ever, upon the sinner's sincere repentance, as remembering that they pray, *Forgive us our trespasses, as we forgive those who trespass against us.* Now we may observe concerning all these particulars that the apostle has insisted on that they belong to the second table, whence Christians should learn the strict obligations they are under to the duties of the second table, and that he who does not conscientiously discharge them can never fear nor love God in truth and in sincerity, whatever he may pretend to.

In the midst of these exhortations and cautions the apostle interposes that general one, *And grieve not the Holy Spirit of God, v.* 30. By looking to what precedes, and to what follows, we may see what it is that grieves the Spirit of God. In the previous verses it is intimated that all lewdness and filthiness, lying, and corrupt communications that stir up filthy appetites and lusts, grieve the Spirit of God. In what follows it is intimated that those corrupt passions of bitterness, and wrath, and anger, and clamour, and evil speaking, and malice, grieve this good Spirit. By this we are not to understand that this blessed Being could properly be grieved or vexed as we are; but the design of the exhortation is that we act not towards him in such a manner as is wont to be grievous and disquieting to our fellow-creatures: we must not do that which is contrary to his holy nature and his will; we must not refuse to hearken to his counsels, nor rebel against his government, which things would provoke him to act towards us as men are wont to do towards those with whom they are displeased and grieved, withdrawing themselves and their wonted kindness from such, and abandoning them to their enemies. O provoke not the blessed Spirit of God to withdraw his presence and his gracious influences from you! It is a good reason why we should not grieve him that *by him we are sealed unto the day of redemption.* There is to be a day of redemption; the body is to be redeemed from the power of the grave at the resurrection-day, and then God's people will be delivered from all the effects of sin, as well as from all sin and misery, which they are not till rescued out of the grave: and then their full and complete happiness commences. All true believers are sealed to that day. God has distinguished them from others, having set his mark upon them; and he gives them the earnest and assurance of a joyful and a glorious resurrection; and the Spirit of God is the seal. Wherever that blessed Spirit is as a sanctifier, he is the earnest of all the joys and glories of the redemption-day; and we should be undone should God take away his Holy Spirit from us.

CHAP. V.

We had several important exhortations in the close of the foregoing chapter, and they are continued in this: particularly, I. We have here an exhortation to mutual love and charity, ver. 1, 2. II. Against all manner of uncleanness, with proper arguments and remedies proposed against such sins: and some further cautions are added, and other duties recommended, ver. 3—20. III. The apostle directs to the conscientious discharge of relative duties, from ver. 21, throughout this, and in the beginning of the next chapter.

BE ye therefore followers of God,
as dear children; 2 And walk
in love, as Christ also hath loved us,
and hath given himself for us an offering and a sacrifice to God for a
sweetsmelling savour.

Here we have the exhortation to mutual love, or to Christian charity. The apostle had been insisting on this in the former chapter, and particularly in the last verses of it, to which the particle *therefore* refers, and connects what he had said there with what is contained in these verses, thus: "Because God, for Christ's sake, has forgiven you, therefore be you followers of God, or *imitators* of him;" for so the word signifies. Pious persons should imitate the God whom they worship, as far as he has revealed himself as imitable by them. They must conform themselves to his example, and have his image renewed upon them. This puts a great honour upon practical religion, that it is the imitating of God. We must be holy as God is holy, merciful as he is merciful, perfect as he is perfect. But there is no one attribute of God more recommended to our imitation than that of his goodness. Be you imitators of God, or resemble him, in every grace, and especially in his love, and in his pardoning goodness. God *is love; and those that dwell in love dwell in God and God in them.* Thus he has proclaimed his name, *Gracious and merciful, and abundant in goodness. As dear children,* as children (who are wont to be greatly beloved by their parents) usually resemble them in the lineaments and features of their faces, and in the dispositions and qualities of their minds; or as becomes the children of God, who are beloved and cherished by their heavenly Father. Children are obliged to imitate their parents in what is good, especially when dearly beloved by them. The character that we bear of God's children obliges us to resemble him, especially in his love and goodness, in his mercy and readiness to forgive. And those only are God's dear children who imitate him in these. It follows, *And walk in love, v.* 2. This godlike grace should conduct and influence our whole conversation, which is meant by walking in it. It should be the principle from which we act; it should direct the ends at which we aim. We should be more careful to give proof of the sincerity of our love one to another. *As Christ also hath loved us.* Here the apostle directs us to the example of Christ, whom Christians are obliged to imitate, and in whom we have an instance of the most free and generous love that ever was, that great love wherewith he hath loved us. We are all joint sharers in that love, and partakers of the comfort of it, and therefore should love one another, Christ having loved us all and given such proof of his love to us; for *he hath given himself for us.* The apostle designedly enlarges on the subject; for what can yield us more delightful matter for contemplation than this? Christ gave himself to die for us; and the death of Christ was the great sacrifice of atonement: *An offering and a sacrifice to God;* or an offering, even a sacrifice—a propitiatory sacrifice, to expiate our guilt, which had been prefigured in the legal oblations and sacrifices; and this *for a sweet-smelling savour* Some observe that the sin-offerings were never said to be of a sweet-smelling savour; but this is said of *the Lamb of God, which taketh away the sin of the world.* As he offered himself with a design to be accepted of God, so God did accept, was pleased with, and appeased by, that sacrifice. Note, As the sacrifice of Christ was efficacious with God, so his example should be prevailing with us, and we should carefully copy after it.

3 But fornication, and all uncleanness, or covetousness, let it not be
once named among you, as becometh
saints; 4 Neither filthiness, nor
foolish talking, nor jesting, which are
not convenient: but rather giving of
thanks. 5 For this ye know, that no
whoremonger, nor unclean person,
nor covetous man, who is an idolater
hath any inheritance in the kingdom
of Christ and of God. 6 Let no
man deceive you with vain words:
for because of these things cometh
the wrath of God upon the children
of disobedience. 7 Be not ye therefore partakers with them. 8 For ye
were sometimes darkness, but now
are ye light in the Lord: walk as
children of light: 9 (For the fruit of
the Spirit *is* in all goodness and
righteousness and truth;) 10 Proving what is acceptable unto the Lord.
11 And have no fellowship with the
unfruitful works of darkness, but

rather reprove *them.* 12 For it is a
shame even to speak of those things
which are done of them in secret.
13 But all things that are reproved
are made manifest by the light: for
whatsoever doth make manifest is
light. 14 Wherefore he saith, Awake
thou that sleepest, and arise from the
dead, and Christ shall give thee light.
15 See then that ye walk circumspectly, not as fools, but as wise,
16 Redeeming the time, because the
days are evil. 17 Wherefore be ye
not unwise, but understanding what
the will of the Lord *is.* 18 And be
not drunk with wine, wherein is
excess; but be filled with the Spirit;
19 Speaking to yourselves in psalms
and hymns and spiritual songs, singing and making melody in your heart
to the Lord; 20 Giving thanks
always for all things unto God and
the Father in the name of our Lord
Jesus Christ—

These verses contain a caution against all manner of uncleanness, with proper remedies and arguments proposed: some further cautions are added, and other duties recommended. Filthy lusts must be suppressed, in order to the supporting of holy love. *Walk in love,* and *shun fornication and all uncleanness. Fornication* is folly committed between unmarried persons. *All uncleanness* includes all other sorts of filthy lusts, which were too common among the Gentiles. Or *covetousness,* which being thus connected, and mentioned as a thing which should not be *once named,* some understand it, in the chaste style of the scripture, of unnatural lust; while others take it in the more common sense, for an immoderate desire of gain or an insatiable love of riches, which is spiritual adultery; for by this the soul, which was espoused to God, goes astray from him, and embraces the bosom of a stranger, and therefore carnal worldlings are called adulterers: *You adulterers and adulteresses, know you not that the friendship of the world is enmity with God?* Now these sins must be dreaded and detested in the highest degree: *Let it not be once named among you,* never in a way of approbation nor without abhorrence, *as becometh saints,* holy persons, who are separated from the world, and dedicated unto God. The apostle not only cautions against the gross acts of sin, but against what some may be apt to make light of, and think to be excusable. *Neither filthiness* (*v.* 4), by which may be understood all wanton and unseemly gestures and behaviour; *nor foolish talking,* obscene and lewd discourse, or, more generally, such vain discourse as betrays much folly and indiscretion, and is far from edifying the hearers; *nor jesting.* The Greek word εὐτραπελία is the same which Aristotle, in his Ethics, makes a virtue: pleasantness of conversation. And there is no doubt an innocent and inoffensive jesting, which we cannot suppose the apostle here forbids. Some understand him of such scurrilous and abusive reflections as tend to expose others and to make them appear ridiculous. This is bad enough: but the context seems to restrain it to such pleasantry of discourse as is filthy and obscene, which he may also design by that *corrupt,* or putrid and rotten, communication that he speaks of, *ch.* iv. 29. Of these things he says, *They are not convenient.* Indeed there is more than inconvenience, even a great deal of mischief, in them. They are so far from being profitable that they pollute and poison the hearers. But the meaning is, Those things do not become Christians, and are very unsuitable to their profession and character. Christians are allowed to be cheerful and pleasant; but they must be merry and wise. The apostle adds, *But rather giving of thanks:* so far let the Christian's way of mirth be from that of obscene and profane wit, that he may delight his mind, and make himself cheerful, by a grateful remembrance of God's goodness and mercy to him, and by blessing and praising him on account of these. Note, 1. We should take all occasions to render thanksgivings and praises to God for his kindness and favours to us. 2. A reflection on the grace and goodness of God to us, with a design to excite our thankfulness to him, is proper to refresh and delight the Christian's mind, and to make him cheerful. Dr. Hammond thinks that εὐχαριστία may signify gracious, pious, religious discourse in general, by way of opposition to what the apostle condemns. Our cheerfulness, instead of breaking out into what is vain and sinful, and a profanation of God's name, should express itself as becomes Christians, and in what may tend to his glory. If men abounded more in good and pious expressions, they would not be so apt to utter ill and unbecoming words; for shall *blessing* and *cursing,* lewdness and thanksgivings, *proceed out of the same mouth?*

I. To fortify us against the sins of uncleanness, &c., the apostle urges several arguments, and prescribes several remedies, in what follows,

1. He urges several arguments, As, (1.) Consider that these are sins which shut persons out of heaven: *For this you know,* &c., *v.* 5. They knew it, being informed of it by the Christian religion. By *a covetous man* some understand a lewd lascivious libertine, who indulges himself in those vile lusts which were accounted the certain marks of a heathen and an idolater. Others understand it in the common acceptation of the word; and such a man is an idolater because

there is spiritual idolatry in the love of this world. As the epicure makes a god of his belly, so the covetous man makes a god of his money, sets those affections upon it, and places that hope, confidence, and delight, in worldly good, which should be reserved for God only. He serves mammon instead of God. Of these persons it is said that they *have no inheritance in the kingdom of Christ and of God;* that is, the kingdom of Christ, who is God, or the kingdom which is God's by nature, and Christ's as he is Mediator, the kingdom which Christ has purchased and which God bestows. Heaven is here described as a kingdom (as frequently elsewhere) with respect to its eminency and glory, its fulness and sufficiency, &c. In this kingdom the saints and servants of God have an inheritance; for it is the *inheritance of the saints in light.* But those who are impenitent, and allow themselves either in the lusts of the flesh or the love of the world, are not Christians indeed, and so belong not to the kingdom of grace, nor shall they ever come to the kingdom of glory. Let us then be excited to be on our guard against those sins which would exclude and shut us out of heaven. (2.) These sins bring the wrath of God upon those who are guilty of them: "*Let no man deceive you with vain words,* &c., *v.* 6. Let none flatter you, as though such things were tolerable and to be allowed of in Christians, or as though they were not very provoking and offensive unto God, or as though you might indulge yourselves in them and yet escape with impunity. These are *vain words.*" Observe, Those who flatter themselves and others with hopes of impunity in sin do but put a cheat upon themselves and others. Thus Satan deceived our first parents with vain words when he said to them, *You shall not surely die.* They are *vain words* indeed; for those who trust to them will find themselves wretchedly imposed upon, *for because of these things cometh the wrath of God upon the children of disobedience.* By *children of disobedience* may be meant the Gentiles, who disbelieved, and refused to comply with, and to submit themselves to, the gospel: or, more generally, all obstinate sinners, who will not be reclaimed, but are given over to disobedience. Disobedience is the very malignity of sin. And it is by a usual Hebraism that such sinners are called children of disobedience; and such indeed they are from their childhood, going astray as soon as they are born. *The wrath of God comes upon* such, because of their sins; sometimes in this world, but more especially in the next. And dare we make light of that which will lay us under the wrath of God? O no. *Be not you therefore partakers with them, v.* 7. Do not partake with them in their sins, that you may not share in their punishment." We partake with other men in their sins, not only when we live in the same sinful manner that they do, and consent and comply with their temptations and solicitations to sin, but when we encourage them in their sins, prompt them to sin, and do not prevent and hinder them, as far as it may be in our power to do so. (3.) Consider what obligations Christians are under to live at another rate than such sinners do: *For you were sometimes darkness, but now,* &c., *v.* 8. The meaning is, "Such courses are very unsuitable to your present condition; for, whereas in your Gentile and your unregenerate state you were darkness, you have now undergone a great change." The apostle calls their former condition *darkness* in the abstract, to express the great darkness they were in. They lived wicked and profane lives, being destitute of the light of instruction without and of the illumination and grace of the blessed Spirit within. Note, A state of sin is a state of darkness. Sinners, like men in the dark, are going they know not whither, and doing they know not what. But the grace of God had produced a mighty change in their souls: *Now are you light in the Lord,* savingly enlightened by the word and the Spirit of God. *Now,* upon your believing in Christ, and your receiving the gospel. *Walk as children of light.* Children of light, according to the Hebrew dialect, are those who are in a state of light, endued with knowledge and holiness. "Now, being such, let your conversation be suitable to your condition and privileges, and accordingly live up to the obligation you are under by that knowledge and those advantages you enjoy.—*Proving what is acceptable unto the Lord* (*v.* 10), examining and searching diligently what God has revealed to be his will, and making it appear that you approve it by conforming yourselves to it. Observe, We must not only dread and avoid that which is displeasing to God, but enquire and consider what will be acceptable to him, searching the scriptures with this view, thus keeping at the greatest distance from these sins.

2. The apostle prescribes some remedies against them. As, (1.) If we would not be entangled by the lusts of the flesh, we must bring forth *the fruits of the Spirit, v.* 9. This is expected from the children of light, that, being illuminated, they be also sanctified by the Spirit, and thereupon bring forth his fruit, which *is in all goodness,* an inclination to do good and to show mercy, *and righteousness,* which signifies justice in our dealings. Thus they are taken more strictly; but, more generally, all religion is goodness and righteousness. And in and with these must be *truth,* or sincerity and uprightness of heart. (2.) We must have no fellowship with sin nor sinners, *v.* 11. Sinful works are works of darkness: they come from the darkness of ignorance, they seek the darkness of concealment, and they lead to the darkness of hell. These works of darkness are *unfruitful works;* there is nothing got by them in the long run, whatever profit is pretended by sin, it will by no means balance the loss; for it issues in

the utter ruin and destruction of the impenitent sinner. We must therefore *have no fellowship with* these unfruitful works; as we must not practise them ourselves, so we must not countenance others in the practice of them. There are many ways of our being accessary to the sins of others, by commendation, counsel, consent, or concealment. And, if we share with others in their sin, we must expect to share with them in their plagues. Nay, if we thus have fellowship with them, we shall be in the utmost danger of acting as they do ere long. But, rather than have fellowship with them, we must *reprove them,* implying that if we do not reprove the sins of others we have fellowship with them. We must prudently and in our places witness against the sins of others, and endeavour to convince them of their sinfulness, when we can do it seasonably and pertinently, in our words; but especially by the holiness of our lives, and a religious conversation. Reprove their sins by abounding in the contrary duties. One reason given is, *For it is a shame even to speak of those things,* &c., *v.* 12. They are so filthy and abominable that it is a shame to mention them, except in a way of reproof, much more must it be a shame to have any fellowship with them. *The things which are done of them in secret.* The apostle seems to speak here of the Gentile idolaters, and of their horrid mysteries, which abounded with detestable wickedness, and which none were permitted to divulge upon pain of death. Observe, A good man is ashamed to speak that which many wicked people are not ashamed to act; but, as far as their wickedness appears, it should be reproved by good men. There follows another reason for such reproof: *But all things that are reproved are made manifest by the light, v.* 13. The meaning of this passage may be this: "All those unfruitful works of darkness which you are called upon to reprove are laid open, and made to appear in their proper colours to the sinners themselves, by the light of doctrine or of God's word in your mouths, as faithful reprovers, or by that instructive light which is diffused by the holiness of your lives and by your exemplary walk." Observe, The light of God's word, and the exemplification of it in a Christian conversation, are proper means to convince sinners of their sin and wickedness. It follows, *For whatsoever doth make manifest is light;* that is, it is the light that discovers what was concealed before in darkness; and accordingly it becomes those who are *children of light,* who are *light in the Lord,* to discover to others their sins, and to endeavour to convince them of the evil and danger of them, thus shining as lights in the world. The apostle further urges this duty from the example of God or Christ: *Wherefore he saith,* &c. (*v.* 14); as if he had said, "In doing this, you will copy after the great God, who has set himself to awaken sinners from their sleep, and to raise them from the death of sin, that they might receive light from Christ." *He saith.* The Lord is constantly saying in his word what is more particularly expressed in Isa. lx. 1. Or, Christ, by his ministers, who preach the everlasting gospel, is continually calling upon sinners to this effect: *Awake, thou that sleepest, and arise from the dead.* The same thing in the main is designed by these different expressions; and they serve to remind us of the great stupidity and the wretched security of sinners, how insensible they are of their danger, and how unapt they naturally are to spiritual motions, sensations, and actions. When God calls upon them to awake, and to arise, his meaning is that they would break off their sins by repentance, and enter on a course of holy obedience, and he encourages them to essay and do their utmost that way, by that gracious promise, *And Christ shall give thee light;* or *Christ shall enlighten thee,* or *shall shine upon thee.* "He shall bring thee into a state of knowledge, holiness, and comfort, assisting thee with his grace, and refreshing thy mind with joy and peace here and rewarding thee with eternal glory at length." Observe, When we are endeavouring to convince sinners, and to reform them from their sins, we are imitating God and Christ in that which is their great design throughout the gospel. Some indeed understand this as a call to sinners and to saints: to sinners to repent and turn; to saints to stir up themselves to their duty. The former must arise from their spiritual death; and the latter must awake from their spiritual deadness. (3.) Another remedy against sin is circumspection, care, or caution (*v.* 15): *See then,* &c. This may be understood either with respect to what immediately precedes, "If you are to reprove others for their sins, and would be faithful to your duty in this particular, you must look well to yourselves, and to your own behaviour and conduct" (and, indeed, those only are fit to reprove others who walk with due circumspection and care themselves): or else we have here another remedy or rather preservative from the before-mentioned sins; and this I take to be the design of the apostle, being impossible to maintain purity and holiness of heart and life without great circumspection and care. *Walk circumspectly,* or, as the word signifies, accurately, exactly, in the right way, in order to which we must be frequently consulting our rule, and the directions we have in the sacred oracles. *Not as fools,* who walk at all adventures, and who have no understanding of their duty, nor of the worth of their souls, and through neglect, supineness, and want of care, fall into sin, and destroy themselves; *but as wise,* as persons taught of God and endued with wisdom from above. Circumspect walking is the effect of true wisdom, but the contrary is the effect of folly. It follows, *redeeming the time* (*v* 16), literally, *buying the opportunity.* It is a metaphor taken from merchants and traders who diligently observe and improve the seasons for merchandise and trade. It is a great part of Christian wisdom to redeem the time. Good Christians must be good husbands of their time, and take care to improve it to the best of purposes, by watching against temptations, by doing good while it is in the power of their hands, and by filling it up with proper employment—one special preservative from sin. They should make the best use they can of the present seasons of grace. Our time is a talent given us by God for some good end, and it is misspent and lost when it is not employed according to his design. If we have lost our time heretofore, we must endeavour to redeem it by doubling our diligence in doing our duty for the future. The reason given is *because the days are evil,* either by reason of the wickedness of those who dwell in them, or rather " as they are troublesome and dangerous times to you who live in them." Those were times of persecution wherein the apostle wrote this: the Christians were in jeopardy every hour. When the days are evil we have one superadded argument to redeem time, especially because we know not how soon they may be worse. People are very apt to complain of bad times; it were well if that would stir them up to redeem time. " *Wherefore,*" says the apostle (*v.* 17), " because of the badness of the times, *be you not unwise,* ignorant of your duty and negligent about your souls, *but understanding what the will of the Lord is.* Study, consider, and further acquaint yourselves with the will of God, as determining your duty." Observe, Ignorance of our duty, and neglect of our souls, are evidences of the greatest folly; while an acquaintance with the will of God, and a care to comply with it, bespeak the best and truest wisdom.

II. In the three following verses the apostle warns against some other particular sins, and urges some other duties. 1. He warns against the sin of drunkenness: *And be not drunk with wine, v.* 18. This was a sin very frequent among the heathens; and particularly on occasion of the festivals of their gods, and more especially in their Bacchanalia: then they were wont to inflame themselves with wine, and all manner of inordinate lusts were consequent upon it: and therefore the apostle adds, *wherein,* or in which drunkenness, *is excess.* The word ἀσωτία may signify *luxury* or *dissoluteness;* and it is certain that drunkenness is no friend to chastity and purity of life, but it virtually contains all manner of extravagance, and transports men into gross sensuality and vile enormities. Note, Drunkenness is a sin that seldom goes alone, but often involves men in other instances of guilt: it is a sin very provoking to God, and a great hindrance to the spiritual life. The apostle may mean all such intemperance and disorder as are opposite to the sober and prudent demeanour he intends in his advice, to redeem the time. 2. Instead of being filled with wine, he exhorts them to *be filled with the Spirit.* Those who are full of drink are not likely to be full of the Spirit; and therefore this duty is opposed to the former sin. The meaning of the exhortation is that men should labour for a plentiful measure of the graces of the Spirit, that would fill their souls with great joy, strength, and courage, which things sensual men expect their wine should inspire them with. We cannot be guilty of any excess in our endeavours after these: nay, we ought not to be satisfied with a little of the Spirit, but to be aspiring after greater measures, so as to be filled with the Spirit. Now by this means we shall come to *understand what the will of the Lord is;* for the Spirit of God is given as a Spirit of wisdom and of understanding. And because those who are filled with the Spirit will be carried out in acts of devotion, and all the proper expressions of it, therefore the apostle exhorts, 3. To sing unto the Lord, *v.* 19. Drunkards are wont to sing obscene and profane songs. The heathens, in their Bacchanalia, used to sing hymns to Bacchus, whom they called the god of wine. Thus they expressed their joy; but the joy of Christians should express itself in songs of praise to their God. In these they should *speak to themselves* in their assemblies and meetings together, for mutual edification. By *psalms* may be meant David's psalms, or such composures as were fitly sung with musical instruments. By *hymns* may be meant such others as were confined to matter of praise, as those of Zacharias, Simeon, &c. *Spiritual songs* may contain a greater variety of matter, doctrinal, prophetical, historical, &c. Observe here, (1.) The singing of psalms and hymns is a gospel ordinance: it is an ordinance of God, and appointed for his glory. (2.) Though Christianity is an enemy to profane mirth, yet it encourages joy and gladness, and the proper expressions of these in the professors of it. God's people have reason to rejoice, and to sing for joy. They are to *sing and to make melody in their hearts;* not only with their voices, but with inward affection, and then their doing this will be as delightful and acceptable to God as music is to us: and it must be with a design to please him, and to promote his glory, that we do this; and then it will be done to the Lord. 4. Thanksgiving is another duty that the apostle exhorts to, *v.* 20. We are appointed to sing psalms, &c., for the expression of our thankfulness to God; but, though we are not always singing, we should be *always giving thanks;* that is, we should never want a disposition for this duty, as we never want matter for it. We must continue it throughout the whole course of our lives; and we should give thanks *for all things;* not only for spiritual blessings enjoyed, and eternal ones expected (for what of the former we have in hand, and for what of the other we have in hope), but for temporal mercies too; not only for our comforts, but also for our sanctified afflictions; not only for what immediately concerns ourselves, but for the instances of God's kindness and favour to others also. It is our duty in *every thing to give thanks unto God and the Father,* to God as the Father of our Lord Jesus Christ and our Father in him, in whose name we are to offer up all our prayers, and praises, and spiritual services, that they may be acceptable to God.

21 Submitting yourselves one to
another in the fear of God. 22 Wives,
submit yourselves unto your own husbands, as unto the Lord. 23 For the
husband is the head of the wife, even
as Christ is the head of the church:
and he is the saviour of the body.
24 Therefore as the church is subject
unto Christ, so *let* the wives *be* to
their own husbands in every thing.
25 Husbands, love your wives, even
as Christ also loved the church,
and gave himself for it; 26 That
he might sanctify and cleanse it
with the washing of water by the
word, 27 That he might present it
to himself a glorious church, not
having spot, or wrinkle, or any such
thing; but that it should be holy
and without blemish. 28 So ought
men to love their wives as their own
bodies. He that loveth his wife
loveth himself. 29 For no man ever
yet hated his own flesh; but nou-
risheth and cherisheth it, even as the
Lord the church: 30 For we are
members of his body, of his flesh,
and of his bones. 31 For this cause
shall a man leave his father and
mother, and shall be joined unto his
wife, and they two shall be one flesh.
32 This is a great mystery: but I
speak concerning Christ and the
church. 33 Nevertheless let every
one of you in particular so love his
wife even as himself; and the wife
see that she reverence *her* husband.

Here the apostle begins his exhortation to the discharge of relative duties. As a general foundation for these duties, he lays down that rule *v.* 21. There is a mutual submission that Christians owe one to another, condescending to bear one another's burdens: not advancing themselves above others, nor domineering over one another and giving laws to one another. Paul was an example of this truly Christian temper, for he *became all things to all men.* We must be of a yielding and of a submissive spirit, and ready to all the duties of the respective places and stations that God has allotted to us in the world. *In the fear of God,* that is, so far as is consistent with the fear of God, for his sake, and out of conscience towards him, and that hereby we may give proof that we truly fear him. Where there is this mutual condescension and submission, the duties of all relations will be the better performed. From *v.* 22 to the end he speaks of the duties of husbands and wives; and he speaks of these in a Christian manner, setting the church as an example of the wife's subjection, and Christ as an example of love in husbands.

I. The duty prescribed to wives is submission to their husbands in the Lord (*v.* 22), which submission includes the honouring and obeying of them, and that from a principle of love to them. They must do this in compliance with God's authority, who has commanded it, which is doing it *as unto the Lord;* or it may be understood by way of similitude and likeness, so that the sense may be, "as, being devoted to God, you submit yourselves unto him." From the former sense we may learn that by a conscientious discharge of the duties we owe to our fellow-creatures we obey and please God himself; and, from the latter, that God not only requires and insists on those duties which immediately respect himself, but such as respect our neighbours too. The apostle assigns the reason of this submission from wives: *For the husband is the head of the wife, v.* 23. The metaphor is taken from the head in the natural body, which, being the seat of reason, of wisdom, and of knowledge, and the fountain of sense and motion, is more excellent than the rest of the body. God has given the man the pre-eminence and a right to direct and govern by creation, and in that original law of the relation, *Thy desire shall be to thy husband, and he shall rule over thee.* Whatever there is of uneasiness in this, it is an effect of sin coming into the world. Generally, too, the man has (what he ought to have) a superiority in wisdom and knowledge. He is therefore the head, *even as Christ is the head of the church.* There is a resemblance of Christ's authority over the church in that superiority and headship which God has appointed to the husband. The apostle adds, *and he is the Saviour of the body.* Christ's authority is exercised over the church for the saving of her from evil, and the supplying of her with every thing good for her. In like manner should the husband be employed for the protection and comfort of his spouse; and therefore she should the more cheerfully submit herself unto him. So it follows, *Therefore as the church is subject unto Christ* (*v.* 24), with cheerfulness, with fidelity, with humility, *so let the wives be to their own husbands in every thing*—in every thing to which their authority justly extends itself, in every thing lawful and consistent with duty to God.

II. The duty of husbands on the other

hand), is to love their wives (*v.* 25); for without this they would abuse their superiority and headship, and, wherever this prevails as it ought to do, it will infer the other duties of the relation, it being a special and peculiar affection that is required in her behalf. The love of Christ to the church is proposed as an example of this, which love of his is a sincere, a pure, an ardent, and a constant affection, and that notwithstanding the imperfections and failures that she is guilty of. The greatness of his love to the church appeared in his giving himself unto the death for it. Observe, As the church's subjection to Christ is proposed as an exemplar to wives, so the love of Christ to his church is proposed as a pattern to husbands; and while such exemplars are offered to both, and so much is required of each, neither has reason to complain of the divine injunctions. The love which God requires from the husband in behalf of his wife will make amends for the subjection which he demands from her to her husband; and the prescribed subjection of the wife will be an abundant return for that love of the husband which God has made her due. The apostle, having mentioned Christ's love to the church, enlarges upon it, assigning the reason why he gave himself for it, namely, that he might sanctify it in this world, and glorify it in the next: *That he might sanctify and cleanse it, with the washing of water by the word* (*v.* 26)—that he might endue all his members with a principle of holiness, and deliver them from the guilt, the pollution, and the dominion of sin. The instrumental means whereby this is effected are the instituted sacraments, particularly the washing of baptism and the preaching and reception of the gospel. *And that he might present it to himself,* &c. *v.* 27. Dr. Lightfoot thinks the apostle alludes here to the Jews' extraordinary carefulness in their washings for purification. They were careful that there should be no wrinkle to keep the flesh from the water, and no spot nor dirt which was not thoroughly washed. Others understand him as alluding to a garment come newly out of the fuller's hand, purged from spots, stretched from wrinkles, the former newly contracted, the latter by long time and custom. *That he might present it to himself*—that he might perfectly unite it to himself in the great day, *a glorious church,* perfect in knowledge and in holiness, *not having spot, nor wrinkle, nor any such thing,* nothing of deformity or defilement remaining, but being entirely amiable and pleasing in his eye, *holy and without blemish,* free from the least remains of sin. The church in general, and particular believers, will not be without spot or wrinkle till they come to glory. From this and the former verse together we may take notice that the glorifying of the church is intended in the sanctifying of it: and that those, and those only, who are sanctified now, will be glorified hereafter.—*So ought men to love their wives as their own bodies,* &c. *v.* 28. The wife being made one with her husband (not in a natural, but in a civil and in a relative sense), this is an argument why he should love her with as cordial and as ardent an affection as that with which he loves himself. *For no man ever yet hated his own flesh, v.* 29—(no man in his right senses ever hated himself, however deformed, or whatever his imperfections might be); so far from it that *he nourishes and cherishes it:* he uses himself with a great deal of care and tenderness, and is industrious to supply himself with every thing convenient or good for him, with food and clothing, &c. *Even as the Lord the church:* that is, as the Lord nourishes and cherishes the church, which he furnishes with all things that he sees needful or good for her, with whatever conduces to her everlasting happiness and welfare. The apostle adds, *For we are members of his body, of his flesh and of his bones, v.* 30. He assigns this as a reason why Christ nourishes and cherishes his church—because all who belong to it *are members of his body,* that is, of his mystical body. Or, we are members *out of his body:* all the grace and glory which the church has are from Christ, as Eve was taken out of the man. But, as one observes, it being the manner of the sacred writings to express a complex body by the enumeration of its several parts, as the heaven and earth for the world, evening and morning for the natural day, sc here, by body, flesh, and bones, we are tc understand himself, the meaning of the verse being that we are members of Christ.—*For this cause* (because they are one, as Christ and his church are one) *shall a man leave his father and mother;* the apostle refers to the words of Adam, when Eve was given to him for a meet help, Gen. ii. 24. We are not to understand by this that a man's obligation to other relations is cancelled upon his marriage, but only that this relation is to be preferred to all others, there being a nearer union between these two than between any others, that the man must rather leave any of those than his wife.—*And they two shall be one flesh,* that is, by virtue of the matrimonial bond. *This is a great mystery, v.* 32. Those words of Adam, just mentioned by the apostle, are spoken literally of marriage; but they have also a hidden mystical sense in them, relating to the union between Christ and his church, of which the conjugal union between Adam and the mother of us all was a type: though not instituted or appointed by God to signify this, yet it was a kind of natural type, as having a resemblance to it: *I speak concerning Christ and the church.*

After this, the apostle concludes this part of his discourse with a brief summary of the duty of husbands and wives, *v.* 33. "*Nevertheless* (though there be such a secret mystical sense, yet the plain literal sense concerns you) *let every one of you in particular so love his wife even as himself,* with such a sincere, peculiar, singular, and prevailing affection as that is which he bears to himself. *And the wife see that she reverence her husband.*" Reverence consists of love and esteem, which produce a care to please, and of fear, which awakens a caution lest just offence be given. That the wife thus reverence her husband is the will of God and the law of the relation.

CHAP. VI.

In this chapter, I. The apostle proceeds in the exhortation to relative duties which he began in the former, particularly he insists on the duties of children and parents, and of servants and masters, ver. 1—9. II. He exhorts and directs Christians how to behave themselves in the spiritual warfare with the enemies of their souls; and to the exercise of several Christian graces, which he proposes to them as so many pieces of spiritual armour, to preserve and defend them in the conflict, ver. 10—18. III. We have here the conclusion of the epistle, in which he takes his leave of them, recommending himself to the prayers of the believing Ephesians, and praying for them, ver. 19—24.

CHILDREN, obey your parents
in the Lord: for this is right.
2 Honour thy father and mother;
which is the first commandment with
promise; 3 That it may be well
with thee, and thou mayest live long
on the earth. 4 And, ye fathers,
provoke not your children to wrath:
but bring them up in the nurture and
admonition of the Lord. 5 Servants,
be obedient to them that are *your*
masters according to the flesh, with
fear and trembling, in singleness of
your heart, as unto Christ; 6 Not
with eyeservice, as menpleasers; but
as the servants of Christ, doing the
will of God from the heart; 7 With
good will doing service, as to the
Lord, and not to men: 8 Knowing
that whatsoever good thing any man
doeth, the same shall he receive of
the Lord, whether *he be* bond or free.
9 And, ye masters, do the same
things unto them, forbearing threatening: knowing that your Master
also is in heaven; neither is there
respect of persons with him.

Here we have further directions concerning relative duties, in which the apostle is very particular.

I. The duty of children to their parents. *Come, you children, hearken to me, I will teach you the fear of the Lord.* The great duty of children is to obey their parents (*v.* 1), parents being the instruments of their being, God and nature having given them an authority to command, in subserviency to God; and, if children will be obedient to their pious parents, they will be in a fair way to be pious as they are. That obedience which God demands from their children, in their behalf, includes an inward reverence, as well as the outward expressions and acts. Obey in the Lord. Some take this as a limitation, and understand it thus: "as far as is consistent with your duty to God." We must not disobey our heavenly Father in obedience to earthly parents; for our obligation to God is prior and superior to all others. I take it rather as a reason: "Children, obey your parents; for the Lord has commanded it: obey them therefore for the Lord's sake, and with an eye to him." Or it may be a particular specification of the general duty: "Obey your parents, especially in those things which relate to the Lord. Your parents teach you good manners, and therein you must obey them. They teach you what is for your health, and in this you must obey them: but the chief things in which you are to do it are the things pertaining to the Lord." Religious parents charge their children to keep the ways of the Lord, Gen. xviii. 19. They command them to be found in the way of their duty towards God, and to take heed of those sins most incident to their age; in these things especially they must see that they be obedient. There is a general reason given: *For this is right*, there is a natural equity in it, God has enjoined it, and it highly becomes Christians. It is the order of nature that parents command and children obey. Though this may seem a hard saying, yet it is duty, and it must be done by such as would please God and approve themselves to him. For the proof of this the apostle quotes the law of the fifth commandment, which Christ was so far from designing to abrogate and repeal that he came to confirm it, as appears by his vindicating it, Matt. xv. 4, &c. *Honour thy father and mother* (*v.* 2), which honour implies reverence, obedience, and relief and maintenance, if these be needed. The apostle adds, *which is the first commandment with promise.* Some little difficulty arises from this, which we should not overlook, because some who plead for the lawfulness of images bring this as a proof that we are not bound by *the second commandment.* But there is no manner of force in the argument. The second commandment has not a particular promise; but only a general declaration or assertion, which relates to the whole law of God's keeping mercy for thousands. And then by this is not meant the first commandment of the decalogue that has a promise, for there is no other after it that has, and therefore it would be improper to say it is the first; but the meaning may be this: "This is a prime or chief commandment, and it has a promise; it is the first commandment in the second table, and it has a promise. The promise is, *That it may be well with thee*, &c., *v.* 3. Observe, Whereas the promise in the commandment has reference to the land of Canaan, the apostle hereby shows that this and other promises which we have in the Old Testament relating to the land of Canaan are to be understood more generally. That you may not think that the Jews only, to whom God gave the land of Canaan, were bound by the fifth commandment, he here gives it a further sense, *That it may be well with thee,* &c. Outward prosperity and long life are blessings promised to those who keep this commandment. This is the way to have it well with us, and obedient children are often rewarded with outward prosperity. Not indeed that it is always so; there are instances of such children who meet with much affliction in this life: but *ordinarily* obedience is thus rewarded, and, where it is not, it is made up with something better. Observe, 1. The gospel has its temporal promises, as well as spiritual ones. 2. Although the authority of God be sufficient to engage us in our duty, yet we are allowed to have respect to the promised reward: and, 3. Though it contains some temporal advantage, even this may be considered as a motive and encouragement to our obedience.

II. The duty of parents: *And you fathers, v.* 4. Or, you parents, 1. "*Do not provoke your children to wrath.* Though God has given you power, you must not abuse that power, remembering that your children are, in a particular manner, pieces of yourselves, and therefore ought to be governed with great tenderness and love. Be not impatient with them; use no unreasonable severities and lay no rigid injunctions upon them. When you caution them, when you counsel them, when you reprove them, do it in such a manner as not to *provoke them to wrath.* In all such cases deal prudently and wisely with them, endeavouring to convince their judgments and to work upon their reason." 2. "*Bring them up* well, *in the nurture and admonition of the Lord,* in the discipline of proper and of compassionate correction, and in the knowledge of that duty which God requires of them and by which they may become better acquainted with him. Give them a good education." It is the great duty of parents to be careful in the education of their children: "Not only bring them up, as the brutes do, taking care to provide for them; but bring them up in nurture and admonition, in such a manner as is suitable to their reasonable natures. Nay, not only bring them up as men, in nurture and admonition, but as Christians, in the admonition of the Lord. Let them have a religious education. Instruct them to fear sinning; and inform them of, and excite them to, the whole of their duty towards God."

III. The duty of servants. This also is summed up in one word, which is, *obedience.* He is largest on this article, as knowing there was the greatest need of it. These servants were generally slaves. Civil servitude is not inconsistent with Christian liberty. Those may be the Lord's freemen who are slaves to men. "*Your masters according to the flesh* (*v.* 5), that is, who have the command of your bodies, but not of your souls and consciences: God alone has dominion over these." Now, with respect to servants, he exhorts, 1. That they obey *with fear and trembling.* They are to reverence those who are over them, fearing to displease them, and trembling lest they should justly incur their anger and indignation. 2. That they be sincere in their obedience: *In singleness of heart;* not pretending obedience when they design disobedience, but serving them with faithfulness. 3. They should have an eye to Jesus Christ in all the service that they perform to their masters (*v.* 5—7), *doing service as to the Lord, and not to men;* that is, not to men only or principally. When servants, in the discharge of the duty of their places, have an eye to Christ, this puts an honour upon their obedience, and an acceptableness into it. Service done to their earthly masters, with an eye to him, becomes acceptable service to him also. To have an eye to Christ is to remember that he sees them and is ever present with them, and that his authority obliges them to a faithful and conscientious discharge of the duties of their station. 4. They must not serve their masters *with eye-service* (*v.* 6)—that is, only when their master's eye is upon them; but they must be as conscientious in the discharge of their duty, when they are absent and out of the way, because then their Master in heaven beholds them: and therefore they must not act as *men-pleasers*—as though they had no regard to the pleasing of God, and approving themselves to him, if they can impose upon their masters. Observe, A steady regard to the Lord Jesus Christ will make men faithful and sincere in every station of life. 5. What they do they must do cheerfully: *Doing the will of God from the heart,* serving their masters as God wills they should, not grudgingly, nor by constraint, but from a principle of love to them and their concerns. This is *doing it with good-will* (*v.* 7), which will make their service easy to themselves, pleasing to their masters, and acceptable to the Lord Christ. There should be *good-will* to their masters, good-will to the families they are in; and especially a readiness to do their duty to God. Observe, Service, performed with conscience, and from a regard to God, though it be to unrighteous masters, will be accounted by Christ as service done to himself. 6. Let faithful servants trust God for their wages, while they do their duty in his fear: *Knowing that whatsoever good thing* (*v.* 8), how poor and mean soever it may be, considered in itself,——*the same shall he receive of the Lord,* that is, by a metonymy, the reward of the same. Though his master on earth should neglect or abuse him, instead of rewarding him, he shall certainly be rewarded by the Lord Christ, *whether he be bond or free,* whether he be a poor bond-servant or a freeman or master. Christ regards not these differences of men at present; nor will he in the great and final judgment. You think, "A prince, or a magistrate, or a minister, that does his duty here, will be sure to receive his reward in heaven: but what capacity am I, a poor servant, in, of recommending myself to the favour of God." Why,

God will as certainly reward thee for the meanest drudgery that is done from a sense of duty and with an eye to himself. And what can be said more proper either to engage or to encourage servants to their duty?

IV The duty of masters: "*And you masters, do the same things unto them* (*v.* 9); that is, act after the same manner. Be just to them, as you expect they should be to you: show the like good-will and concern for them, and be careful herein to approve yourselves to God." Observe, Masters are under as strict obligations to discharge their duty to their servants as servants are to be obedient and dutiful to them. "*Forbearing threatening; ἀνιέντες—moderating* threatening, and remitting the evils with which you threaten them. Remember that your servants are made of the same mould with yourselves, and therefore be not tyrannical and imperious over them, *knowing that your Master also is in heaven:*" some copies read, both *your* and *their* Master. "You have a Master to obey who makes this your duty; and you and they are but fellow-servants in respect of Christ. You will be as punishable by him, for the neglect of your duty, or for acting contrary to it, as any others of meaner condition in the world. You are therefore to show favour to others, as ever you expect to find favour with him; and you will never be a match for him, though you may be too hard for your servants." *Neither is there respect of persons with him;* a rich, a wealthy, and a dignified master, if he be unjust, imperious, and abusive, is not a jot the nearer being accepted of God for his riches, wealth, and honour. He will call masters and servants to an impartial account for their conduct one to another, and will neither spare the former because they are more advanced nor be severe towards the latter because they are inferior and mean in the world. If both masters and servants would consider their relation and obligation to God and the account they must shortly give to him, they would be more careful of their duty to each other. Thus the apostle concludes his exhortation to relative duties.

10 Finally, my brethren, be strong
in the Lord, and in the power of his
might. 11 Put on the whole armour
of God, that ye may be able to stand
against the wiles of the devil. 12
For we wrestle not against flesh
and blood, but against principalities,
against powers, against the rulers of
the darkness of this world, against
spiritual wickedness in high *places*.
13 Wherefore take unto you the
whole armour of God, that ye may
be able to withstand in the evil day,
and having done all, to stand. 14
Stand therefore, having your loins
girt about with truth, and having on
the breastplate of righteousness; 15
And your feet shod with the preparation of the gospel of peace; 16 Above
all, taking the shield of faith, wherewith ye shall be able to quench all
the fiery darts of the wicked. 17
And take the helmet of salvation,
and the sword of the Spirit, which is
the word of God: 18 Praying always
with all prayer and supplication in the
Spirit, and watching thereunto with
all perseverance and supplication for
all saints.

Here is a general exhortation to constancy in our Christian course, and to courage in our Christian warfare. Is not our life a warfare? It is so; for we struggle with the common calamities of human life. Is not our religion much more a warfare? It is so; for we struggle with the opposition of the powers of darkness, and with many enemies who would keep us from God and heaven. We have enemies to fight against, a captain to fight for, a banner to fight under, and certain rules of war by which we are to govern ourselves. "*Finally, my brethren* (*v.* 10), it yet remains that you apply yourselves to your work and duty as Christian soldiers." Now it is requisite that a soldier be both stout-hearted and well armed. If Christians be soldiers of Jesus Christ,

I. They must see that they be stout-hearted. This is prescribed here: *Be strong in the Lord,* &c. Those who have so many battles to fight, and who, in their way to heaven, must dispute every pass, with dint of sword, have need of a great deal of courage. *Be strong therefore,* strong for service, strong for suffering, strong for fighting. Let a soldier be ever so well armed without, if he have not within a good heart, his armour will stand him in little stead. Note, Spiritual strength and courage are very necessary for our spiritual warfare. Be strong in the Lord, either in his cause and for his sake or rather in his strength. We have no sufficient strength of our own. Our natural courage is as perfect cowardice, and our natural strength as perfect weakness; but all our sufficiency is of God. In his strength we must go forth and go on. By the actings of faith, we must fetch in grace and help from heaven to enable us to do that which of ourselves we cannot do, in our Christian work and warfare. We should stir up ourselves to resist temptations in a reliance upon God's all-sufficiency and the omnipotence of his might.

II. They must be well armed: "*Put on the whole armour of God* (*v.* 11), make use of all the proper defensives and weapons for repelling the temptations and stratagems of Satan—get and exercise all the Christian graces, the whole armour, that no part be naked and exposed to the enemy." Observe, Those who would approve themselves to have true grace must aim at all grace, the whole armour. It is called the armour of God, because he both prepares and bestows it. We have no armour of our own that will be armour of proof in a trying time. Nothing will stand us in stead but the armour of God. This armour is prepared for us, but we must put it on; that is, we must pray for grace, we must use the grace given us, and draw it out into act and exercise as there is occasion. The reason assigned why the Christian should be completely armed is *that he may be able to stand against the wiles of the devil*—that he may be able to hold out, and to overcome, notwithstanding all the devil's assaults, both of force and fraud, all the deceits he puts upon us, all the snares he lays for us, and all his machinations against us. This the apostle enlarges upon here, and shows,

1. What our danger is, and what need we have to put on this whole armour, considering what sort of enemies we have to deal with—the devil and all the powers of darkness: *For we wrestle not against flesh and blood*, &c., *v.* 12. The combat for which we are to be prepared is not against ordinary human enemies, not barely against men compounded of *flesh and blood,* nor against our own corrupt natures singly considered, but against the several ranks of devils, who have a government which they exercise in this world. (1.) We have to do with a subtle enemy, an enemy who uses wiles and stratagems, as *v.* 11. He has a thousand ways of beguiling unstable souls: hence he is called a serpent for subtlety, an old serpent, experienced in the art and trade of tempting. (2.) He is a powerful enemy: *Principalities,* and *powers,* and *rulers.* They are numerous, they are vigorous; and rule in those heathen nations which are yet in darkness. The dark parts of the world are the seat of Satan's empire. Yea, they are usurping princes over all men who are yet in a state of sin and ignorance. Satan's is a kingdom of darkness; whereas Christ's is a kingdom of light. (3.) They are spiritual enemies: *Spiritual wickedness in high places,* or wicked spirits, as some translate it. The devil is a spirit, a wicked spirit; and our danger is the greater from our enemies because they are unseen, and assault us ere we are aware of them. The devils are wicked spirits, and they chiefly annoy the saints with, and provoke them to, spiritual wickednesses, pride, envy, malice, &c. These enemies are said to be *in high places,* or in heavenly places, so the word is, taking heaven (as one says) for the whole *expansum,* or spreading out of the air between the earth and the stars, the air being the place from which the devils assault us. Or the meaning may be, "*We wrestle* about heavenly places or heavenly things;" so some of the ancients interpret it. Our enemies strive to prevent our ascent to heaven, to deprive us of heavenly blessings and to obstruct our communion with heaven. They assault us in the things that belong to our souls, and labour to deface the heavenly image in our hearts; and therefore we have need to be upon our guard against them. We have need of faith in our Christian warfare, because we have spiritual enemies to grapple with, as well as of faith in our Christian work, because we have spiritual strength to fetch in. Thus you see your danger.

2. What our duty is: to take and put on the whole armour of God, and then to stand our ground, and withstand our enemies.

(1.) We must *withstand, v.* 13. We must not yield to the devil's allurements and assaults, but oppose them. Satan is said *to stand up against us,* 1 Chron. xxi. 1. If he stand up against us, we must stand against him; set up, and keep up, an interest in opposition to the devil. Satan is the wicked one, and his kingdom is the kingdom of sin: to stand against Satan is to strive against sin. *That you may be able to withstand in the evil day,* in the day of temptation, or of any sore affliction.

(2.) We must stand our ground: *And, having done all, to stand.* We must resolve, by God's grace, not to yield to Satan. Resist him, and he will flee. If we give back, he will get ground. If we distrust our cause, or our leader, or our armour, we give him advantage. Our present business is to withstand the assaults of the devil, and to stand it out; and then, having done all that is incumbent on the good soldiers of Jesus Christ, our warfare will be accomplished, and we shall be finally victorious.

(3.) We must stand armed; and this is here most enlarged upon. Here is a Christian in complete armour: and the armour is divine: *Armour of God, armour of light,* Rom. xiii. 12. *Armour of righteousness,* 2 Cor. vi. 7. The apostle specifies the particulars of this armour, both offensive and defensive. The military girdle or belt, the breast-plate, the greaves (or soldier's shoes), the shield, the helmet, and the sword. It is observable that, among them all, there is none for the back; if we turn our back upon the enemy, we lie exposed. [1.] Truth or sincerity is our girdle, *v.* 14. It was prophesied of Christ (Isa. xi. 5) that *righteousness should be the girdle of his loins and faithfulness the girdle of his reins.* That which Christ was girded with all Christians must be girded with. God desires truth, that is, sincerity, in the inward parts. This is the strength of our loins; and it girds on all other pieces of our armour, and therefore is first mentioned. I know no religion without sincerity. Some understand it of the doctrine of the truths of the gospel: they should cleave to us as the girdle does to the loins, Jer. xiii. 11. This will restrain from libertinism and licentiousness, as a girdle retrains and keeps in the body. This is the Christian soldier's belt: ungirded with this, he is unblessed. [2.] Righteousness must be our breast-plate. The breast-plate secures the vitals, shelters the heart. The righteousness of Christ imputed to us is our breast-plate against the arrows of divine wrath. The righteousness of Christ implanted in us is our breast-plate to fortify the heart against the attacks which Satan makes against us. The apostle explains this in 1 Thess. v. 8, *Putting on the breast-plate of faith and love.* Faith and love include all Christian graces; for by faith we are united to Christ and by love to our brethren. These will infer a diligent observance of our duty to God, and a righteous deportment towards men, in all the offices of justice, truth, and charity. [3.] Resolution must be as the greaves to our legs: *And their feet shod with the preparation of the gospel of peace, v.* 15. Shoes, or greaves of brass, or the like, were formerly part of the military armour (1 Sam. xvii. 6): the use of them was to defend the feet against the gall-traps, and sharp sticks, which were wont to be laid privily in the way, to obstruct the marching of the enemy, those who fell upon them being unfit to march. *The preparation of the gospel of peace* signifies a prepared and resolved frame of heart, to adhere to the gospel and abide by it, which will enable us to walk with a steady pace in the way of religion, notwithstanding the difficulties and dangers that may be in it. It is styled *the gospel of peace* because it brings all sorts of peace, peace with God, with ourselves, and with one another. It may also be meant of that which prepares for the entertainment of the gospel, namely, repentance. With this our feet must be shod: for by living a life of repentance we are armed against temptations to sin, and the designs of our great enemy. Dr. Whitby thinks this may be the sense of the words: "That you may be ready for the combat, be shod with the gospel of peace, endeavour after that peaceable and quiet mind which the gospel calls for. Be not easily provoked, nor prone to quarrel: but show all gentleness and all long-suffering to all men, and this will certainly preserve you from many great temptations and persecutions, as did those shoes of brass the soldiers from those gall-traps," &c. [4.] Faith must be our shield: *Above all,* or chiefly, *taking the shield of faith, v.* 16. This is more necessary than any of them. Faith is all in all to us in an hour of temptation. The breast-plate secures the vitals; but with the shield we turn every way. *This is the victory over the world, even our faith.* We are to be fully persuaded of the truth of all God's promises and threatenings, such a faith being of great use against temptations. Consider faith as it *is the evidence of things not seen and the substance of things hoped for,* and it will appear to be of admirable use for this purpose. Faith, as receiving Christ and the benefits of redemption, so deriving grace from him, is like a shield, a sort of universal defence. Our enemy the devil is here called *the wicked one.* He is wicked himself, and he endeavours to make us wicked. His temptations are called *darts,* because of their swift and undiscerned flight, and the deep wounds that they give to the soul; *fiery darts,* by way of allusion to the poisonous darts which were wont to inflame the parts which were wounded with them, and therefore were so called, as the serpents with poisonous stings are called fiery serpents. Violent temptations, by which the soul is set on fire of hell, are the darts which Satan shoots at us. Faith is the shield with which we must quench these fiery darts, wherein we should receive them, and so render them ineffectual, that they may not hit us, or at least that they may not hurt us. Observe, Faith, acted upon the word of God and applying that, acted upon the grace of Christ and improving that, quenches the darts of temptation. [5.] Salvation must be our helmet (*v.* 17); that is, *hope,* which has salvation for its object; so 1 Thess. v. 8. The helmet secures the head. A good hope of salvation, well founded and well built, will both purify the soul and keep it from being defiled by Satan, and it will comfort the soul and keep it from being troubled and tormented by Satan. He would tempt us to despair; but good hope keeps us trusting in God, and rejoicing in him. [6.] The word of God is the sword of the Spirit. The sword is a very necessary and useful part of a soldier's furniture. The word of God is very necessary, and of great use to the Christian, in order to his maintaining the spiritual warfare and succeeding in it. It is called *the sword of the Spirit,* because it is of the Spirit's inditing and he renders it efficacious and powerful, and *sharper than a two-edged sword.* Like Goliath's sword, none like that; with this we assault the assailants. Scripture-arguments are the most powerful arguments to repel temptation with. Christ himself resisted Satan's temptations with, *It is written,* Matt. iv. 4, 6, 7, 10. This, being hid in the heart, will preserve from sin (Ps. cxix. 11), and will mortify and kill those lusts and corruptions that are latent there. [7.] Prayer must buckle on all the other parts of our Christian armour, *v.* 18. We must join prayer with all these graces, for our defence against these spiritual enemies, imploring help and assistance of God, as the case requires: and we must pray always. Not as though we were to do nothing else but pray, for there are other duties of religion and of our respective stations in the world that are to be done in their place and season; but we should keep up constant times of prayer, and be constant to them. We must pray upon all occasions, and as often as our own and others' necessities call us to it. We must always keep up a disposition to prayer, and should intermix ejaculatory prayers with other duties, and with common business. Though set and solemn prayer may sometimes be unseasonable (as when other duties are to be done), yet pious ejaculations *can* never be so. We must pray *with all prayer and supplication*, with all kinds of prayer: public, private, and secret, social and solitary, solemn and sudden; with all the parts of prayer: confession of sin, petition for mercy, and thanksgivings for favours received. We must pray *in the Spirit;* our spirits must be employed in the duty and we must do it by the grace of God's good Spirit. We must *watch thereunto*, endeavouring to keep our hearts in a praying frame, and taking all occasions, and improving all opportunities, for the duty: we must watch to all the motions of our own hearts towards the duty. When God says, *Seek my face*, our hearts must comply, Ps. xxvii. 8. This we must do *with all perseverance.* We must abide by the duty of prayer, whatever change there may be in our outward circumstances; and we must continue in it as long as we live in the world. We must persevere in a particular prayer; not cutting it short, when our hearts are disposed to enlarge, and there is time for it, and our occasions call for it. We must likewise persevere in particular requests, notwithstanding some present discouragements and repulses. And we must pray *with supplication*, not for ourselves only, but *for all saints;* for we are members one of another. Observe, None are so much saints, and in so good a condition in this world, but they need our prayers, and they ought to have them. The apostle passes hence to the conclusion of the epistle.

19 And for me, that utterance may
be given unto me, that I may open
my mouth boldly, to make known
the mystery of the gospel, 20 For
which I am an ambassador in bonds:
that therein I may speak boldly, as I
ought to speak. 21 But that ye also
may know my affairs, *and* how I do,
Tychicus, a beloved brother and faithful minister in the Lord, shall make
known to you all things: 22 Whom
I have sent unto you for the same
purpose, that ye might know our
affairs, and *that* he might comfort
your hearts. 23 Peace *be* to the
brethren, and love with faith, from
God the Father and the Lord Jesus
Christ. 24 Grace *be* with all them
that love our Lord Jesus Christ in
sincerity. Amen.

Here, I. He desires their prayers for him, *v.* 19. Having mentioned *supplication for all saints*, he puts himself into the number. We must pray for all saints, and particularly for God's faithful ministers. *Brethren, pray for us, that the word of the Lord may run and be glorified.* Observe what it is he would have them pray for in his behalf: "*That utterance may be given unto me;* that I may be enlarged from my present restraints, and so have liberty to propagate the faith of Christ; that I may have ability to express myself in a suitable and becoming manner; *and that I may open my mouth boldly*, that is, that I may deliver the whole counsel of God, without any base fear, shame, or partiality." *To make known the mystery of the gospel;* some understand it of that part of the gospel which concerns the calling of the Gentiles, which had hitherto, as a mystery, been concealed. But the whole gospel was a mystery, till made known by divine revelation; and it is the work of Christ's ministers to publish it. Observe, Paul had a great command of language; they called him Mercury, because he was the chief speaker (Acts xiv. 12), and yet he would have his friends ask of God the gift of utterance for him. He was a man of great courage, and often signalized himself for it; yet he would have them pray that God would give him boldness. He knew as well what to say as any man; yet he desires them to pray for him, that he may *speak as he ought to speak.* The argument with which he enforces his request is that for the sake of the gospel he was *an ambassador in bonds*, *v.* 20. He was persecuted and imprisoned for preaching the gospel; though, notwithstanding, he continued in the embassy committed to him by Christ, and persisted in preaching it. Observe, 1. It is no new thing for Christ's ministers to be in bonds. 2. It is a hard thing for them to speak boldly when that is their case. 3. The best and most eminent ministers have need of, and may receive advantage by, the prayers of good Christians; and therefore should earnestly desire them. Having thus desired their prayers,

II. He recommends Tychicus unto them, *v.* 21, 22. He sent him with this epistle, that he might acquaint them with what other churches were informed of, namely, how he did, and what he did; how he was used by the Romans in his bonds, and how he behaved himself in his present circumstances. It is desirable to good ministers both that their Christian friends should know their state and that they should be acquainted with the condition of their friends; for by this means they may the better help each other in their prayers.—*And that he might comfort their hearts*, by giving such an account of his sufferings, of the cause of them, and of the temper of his mind and his behaviour under them, as might prevent their fainting at his tribulations and even minister matter of joy and thanksgiving unto them. He tells them that Tychicus was *a beloved brother and faithful minister in the Lord.* He was a sincere Christian, and so a brother in Christ: he was a faithful minister in the work of Christ, and he was very dear to Paul, which makes Paul's love to these Christian Ephesians the more observable, in that he should now part with so good and dear a friend for their sakes, when his company and conversation must have been peculiarly delightful and serviceable to himself. But the faithful servants of Jesus Christ are wont to prefer the public good to their own private or personal interests.

III. He concludes with his good wishes and prayers for them, and not for them only, but for all the brethren, *v.* 23, 24. His usual benediction was, *Grace and peace;* here it is, *Peace be to the brethren, and love with faith.* By peace we are to understand all manner of peace—peace with God, peace with conscience, peace among themselves: and all outward prosperity is included in the word; as if he had said, "I wish the continuance and increase of all happiness to you." *And love with faith.* This in part explains what he means in the following verse by grace; not only grace in the fountain, or the love and favour of God, but grace in the streams, the grace of the Spirit flowing from that divine principle, faith and love including all the rest. It is the continuance and increase of these that he desires for them, in whom they were already begun. It follows, *from God the Father,* &c. All grace and blessings are derived to the saints from God, through the merit and intercession of Jesus Christ our Lord. The closing benediction is more extensive than the former; for in this he prays for all true believers at Ephesus, and every where else. It is the undoubted character of all the saints that they love our Lord Jesus Christ. Our love to Christ is not acceptable, unless it be in sincerity: indeed there is no such thing as love to Christ, whatever men may pretend, where there is not sincerity. The words may be read, *Grace be with all those who love our Lord Jesus Christ in incorruption,* who continue constant in their love to him, so as not to be corrupted out of it by any baits or seductions whatsoever, and whose love to him is uncorrupted by any opposite lust, or the love of any thing displeasing to him. Grace, that is, the favour of God, and all good (spiritual and temporal), that is, the product of it, are and shall be with all those who thus love our Lord Jesus Christ. And it is, or ought to be, the desire and prayer of every lover of Christ that it may be so with all his fellow-christians. *Amen,* so be it.

AN

EXPOSITION,

WITH PRACTICAL OBSERVATIONS,

OF THE EPISTLE OF ST. PAUL TO

THE PHILIPPIANS.

PHILIPPI was a chief city of the western part of Macedonia, πρώτη τῆς μερίδος τῆς Μακεδονίας πόλις, Acts xvi. 12. It took its name from Philip, the famous king of Macedon, who repaired and beautified it, and it was afterwards made a Roman colony. Near this place were the *Campi Philippici,* remarkable for the famous battles between Julius Cæsar and Pompey the Great, and that between Augustus and Antony on one side and Cassius and Brutus on the other. But it is most remarkable among Christians for this epistle, which was written when Paul was a prisoner at Rome, A.D. 62. Paul seems to have had a very particular kindness for the church at Philippi, which he himself had been instrumental in planting; and, though he had *the care of all the churches,* he had, upon that account, a particular fatherly tender care of this. To those to whom God has employed us to do any good we should look upon ourselves both as encouraged and engaged to study to do more good. He looked upon them as his children, and, having *begotten them by the gospel,* he was desirous by the same gospel to nourish and nurse them up. I. He was called in an extraordinary manner to preach the gospel at Philippi, Acts xvi. 9. A vision appeared to Paul in the night: *There stood a man of Macedonia, and prayed him, saying, Come over into Macedonia, and help us.* He saw God going before him, and was encouraged to use all means for carrying on the good work which was begun among them, and building upon the foundation which was laid. II. At Philippi he suffered hard things; he was scourged, and put into the stocks (Acts xvi. 23, 24); yet he had not the less kindness for the place for the hard usage he met with there. We must never love our friends the less for the ill treatment which our enemies give us. III. The beginnings of that church were very small; Lydia was converted there, and the jailer, and a few more: yet that did not discourage him. If good be not done at first, it may be done afterwards, and the last works may be more abundant. We must not be discouraged by small beginnings. IV. It seems, by many passages in this epistle, that this church at Philippi grew into a flourishing church, and particularly that the brethren were very kind to Paul. He had reaped of their temporal things, and he made a return in spiritual things. He acknowledges the receipt of a present they had sent him (*ch.* iv. 18), and this when no other church communicated with him as concerning giving and receiving (*v.* 15); and he gives them a prophet's, an apostle's reward, in this epistle, which is of more value than thousands of gold and silver.

CHAP. I.

He begins with the inscription and benediction, ver. 1, 2. He gives thanks for the saints at Philippi, ver. 3—6. He speaks of his great affection and concern for their spiritual welfare (ver. 7, 8), his prayers for them (ver. 9—11), his care to prevent their offence at his sufferings (ver. 12—20), his readiness to glorify Christ by life or death (ver. 21—26), and then concludes with a double exhortation to strictness and constancy, ver. 27—30.

PAUL and Timotheus, the servants of Jesus Christ, to all the saints in Christ Jesus which are at Philippi, with the bishops and deacons: 2 Grace *be* unto you, and peace, from God our Father, and *from* the Lord Jesus Christ.

We have here the inscription and benediction. Observe,

I. The persons writing the epistle—*Paul and Timotheus.* Though Paul was alone divinely inspired, he joins Timothy with himself, to express his own humility, and put honour upon Timothy. Those who are aged, and strong, and eminent, should pay respect to, and support the reputation of, those who are younger, and weaker, and of less note. *The servants of Jesus Christ;* not only in the common relation of his disciples, but in the peculiar work of the ministry, the high office of an apostle and an evangelist. Observe, The highest honour of the greatest apostle, and most eminent ministers, is to be the servants of Jesus Christ; not the masters of the churches, but the servants of Christ. Observe,

II. The persons to whom it is directed. 1. To *all the saints in Christ who are at Philippi.* He mentions the church before the ministers, because the ministers are for the church, for their edification and benefit, not the churches for the ministers, for their dignity, dominion, and wealth. *Not for that we have dominion over your faith, but are helpers of your joy,* 2 Cor. i. 24. They are not only the servants of Christ, but the servants of the church for his sake. *Ourselves your servants for Jesus' sake,* 2 Cor. iv 5. Observe, The Christians here are called saints; set apart for God, or sanctified by his Spirit, either by visible profession or real holiness. And those who are not really saints on earth will never be saints in heaven. Observe, It is directed to *all the saints,* one as well as another, even the meanest, the poorest, and those of the least gifts. Christ makes no difference; the rich and the poor meet together in him: and the ministers must not make a difference in their care and tenderness upon these accounts. We must not *have the faith of our Lord Jesus Christ with respect of persons,* James ii. 1. *Saints in Christ Jesus;* saints are accepted only by virtue of their being in Christ Jesus, or as they are Christians. Out of Christ the best saints will appear sinners, and unable to stand before God. 2. It is directed to the ministers, or church-officers—*with the bishops and deacons,* the bishops or elders, in the first place, whose office it was to teach and rule, and the deacons, or overseers of the poor, who took care of the outward business of the house of God: the place, the furniture, the maintenance of the ministers, and provision for the poor. These were all the offices which were then known in the church, and which were of divine appointment. The apostle, in the direction of his epistle to a Christian church, acknowledges but two orders, which he calls bishops and deacons. And whosoever shall consider that the same characters and titles, the same qualifications, the same acts of office, and the same honour and respect, are every where ascribed throughout the New Testament to those who are called bishops and presbyters (as Dr. Hammond and other learned men allow), will find it difficult to make them a different office or distinct order of ministry in the scripture times.

III. Here is the apostolical benediction: *Grace be unto you, and peace, from God our Father, and from the Lord Jesus Christ, v.* 2. This is the same, almost word for word, in all the epistles, to teach us that we must not be shy of forms, though we are not to be tied down to them, especially such as are not scriptural. The only form in the Old Testament is that of a benediction (Num. vi. 23—26), *On this wise you shall bless the children of Israel, saying unto them, The Lord bless thee and keep thee: the Lord make his face shine upon thee, and be gracious unto thee: the Lord lift up the light of his countenance upon thee, and give thee peace.* So in the New Testament, the good which is wished is spiritual good, *grace and peace*—the free favour and good-will of God, and all the blessed fruits and effects of it, and that *from God our Father, and from the Lord Jesus Christ,* jointly from them both, though in a different way. Observe, 1. No peace without grace. Inward peace springs from a sense of divine favour. 2. No grace and peace but from God our Father, the fountain and original of all blessings, the *Father of lights, from whom cometh down every good and perfect gift,* James i. 17. 3. No grace and peace from

God our Father, but in and through our Lord Jesus Christ. Christ, as Mediator, is the channel of conveyance of all spiritual blessings to the church, and directs the disposal of them to all his members.

3 I thank my God upon every remembrance of you, 4 Always in every prayer of mine for you all making request with joy, 5 For your fellowship in the gospel from the first day until now; 6 Being confident of this very thing, that he which hath begun a good work in you will perform *it* until the day of Jesus Christ:

The apostle proceeds after the inscription and benediction to thanksgiving for the saints at Philippi. He tells them what it was he thanked God for, upon their account. Observe here,

I. Paul remembered them: he bore them much in his thoughts; and though they were out of sight, and he was at a distance from them, yet they were not out of his mind: or, *Upon every mention of you—ἐπὶ πάσῃ τῇ μνείᾳ ὑμῶν.* As he often thought of them, so he often spoke of them, and delighted to hear them spoken of. The very mention of them was grateful to him: it is a pleasure to hear of the welfare of an absent friend.

II. He remembered them with joy. At Philippi he was maltreated; there he was scourged and put into the stocks, and for the present saw little of the fruit of his labour; and yet he remembers Philippi with joy. He looked upon his sufferings for Christ as his credit, his comfort, his crown, and was pleased at every mention of the place where he suffered. So far was he from being ashamed of them, or loth to hear of the scene of his sufferings, that he remembered it with joy.

III. He remembered them in prayer: *Always in every prayer of mine for you all, v.* 4. The best remembrance of our friends is to remember them at the throne of grace. Paul was much in prayer for his friends, for all his friends, for these particularly. It should seem, by this manner of expression, that he mentioned at the throne of grace the several churches he was interested in and concerned for particularly and by name. He had seasons of prayer for the church at Philippi. God gives us leave to be thus free with him, though, for our comfort, he knows whom we mean when we do not name them.

IV. He thanked God upon every joyful remembrance of them. Observe, Thanksgiving must have a part in every prayer; and whatsoever is the matter of our rejoicing ought to be the matter of our thanksgiving. What we have the comfort of, God must have the glory of. He thanked God, as well as made requests with joy. As holy joy is the heart and soul of thankful praise, so thankful praise is the lip and language of holy joy.

V. As in our prayers, so in our thanksgiving, we must eye God as our God: *I thank my God.* It encourages us in prayer, and enlarges the heart in praise, to see every mercy coming from the hand of God as our God.—*I thank my God upon every remembrance of you.* We must thank our God for others' graces and comforts, and gifts and usefulness, as we receive the benefit of them, and God receives glory by them. But what is the matter of this thanksgiving? 1. He gives thanks to God for the comfort he had in them: for *your fellowship in the gospel, from the first day until now, v.* 5. Observe, Gospel fellowship is a good fellowship; and the meanest Christians have fellowship in the gospel with the greatest apostles, for the gospel salvation is a *common salvation* (Jude 3), and they *obtain like precious faith* with them, 2 Pet. i. 1. Those who sincerely receive and embrace the gospel have fellowship in it *from the very first day:* a new-born Christian, if he is trueborn, is interested in all the promises and privileges of the gospel from the first day of his becoming such.—*Until now.* Observe, It is a great comfort to ministers when those who begin well hold on and persevere. Some, by their *fellowship in the gospel,* understand their liberality towards propagating the gospel, and translate *κοίνωνια,* not *communion,* but *communication.* But, comparing it with Paul's thanksgiving on the account of other churches, it rather seems to be taken more generally for the fellowship which they had, in faith, and hope, and holy love, with all good Christians—a fellowship in gospel promises, ordinances, privileges, and hopes; and this from the *first day until now.* 2. For the confidence he had concerning them (*v.* 6): *Being confident of this very thing,* &c. Observe, The confidence of Christians is the great comfort of Christians, and we may fetch matter of praise from our hopes as well as from our joys; we must give thanks not only for what we have the present possession and evidence of, but for what we have the future prospect of. Paul speaks with much confidence concerning the good estate of others, hoping well concerning them in the judgment of charity, and being confident in the judgment of faith that if they were sincere they would be happy: *That he who has begun a good work in you will perform it unto the day of Jesus Christ.* A good work *among you—ἐν ὑμῖν,* so it may be read: understand it, in the general, of the planting of the church among them. He who hath planted Christianity in the world will preserve it as long as the world stands. Christ will have a church till the mystery of God shall be finished and the mystical body completed. The church is built upon a rock, and the *gates of hell shall not prevail against it.* But it is rather to be applied to particular persons, and then it speaks of the certain accomplishment of the work of grace wherever it is begun. Observe here, (1.) The work of grace is a good work, a blessed work; for it makes us good, and is an earnest of good to us. It makes us like God, and fits us for the enjoyment of God. That may well be called a good work which does us the greatest good. (2.) Wherever this good work is begun it is of God's beginning: *He has begun a good work in you.* We could not begin it ourselves, for we are by nature *dead in trespasses and sins:* and what can dead men do towards raising themselves to life; or how can they begin to act till they are enlivened in the same respect in which they are said to be dead? It is God who quickens those who are thus dead, Eph. ii. 1; Col. ii. 13. (3.) The work of grace is but begun in this life; it is not finished here; as long as we are in this imperfect state there is something more to be done. (4.) If the same God who begins the good work did not undertake the carrying on and finishing of it, it would lie for ever unfinished. He must perform it who began it. (5.) We may be confident, or well persuaded, that God not only will not forsake, but that he will finish and crown the work of his own hands. For, *as for God, his work is perfect.* (6.) The work of grace will never be perfected *till the day of Jesus Christ,* the day of his appearance. When he shall come to judge the world, and finish his mediation, then this work will be complete, and the top-stone will be brought forth with shouting. We have the same expression, *v.* 10.

7 Even as it is meet for me to think
this of you all, because I have you in
my heart; inasmuch as both in my
bonds, and in the defence and confirmation of the gospel, ye all are
partakers of my grace. 8 For God
is my record, how greatly I long after
you all in the bowels of Jesus Christ.

The apostle expresses the ardent affection he had for them, and his concern for their spiritual welfare: *I have you in my heart, v.* 7. He loved them as his own soul, and they lay near his heart. He thought much of them, and was in care about them. Observe, 1. Why he had them in his heart: *Inasmuch as both in my bonds, and in the defence and confirmation of the gospel, you all are partakers of my grace;* that is, they had received benefit by him and by his ministry; they were partakers of that grace of God which by him, and through his hands, was communicated to them. This makes people dear to their ministers—their receiving benefit by their ministry. Or, "*You are partakers of my grace,* you have joined with me in doing and suffering." They were partakers of his affliction by sympathy and concern, and readiness to assist him. This he calls being partakers of his grace; for those who suffer with the saints are and shall be comforted with them; and those shall share in the reward, who bear their part of the burden. He loved them because they adhered to him in his bonds, and in the *defence and confirmation of the gospel:* they were as ready to appear in their places, and according to their capacity, for the defence of the gospel, as the apostle was in his; and therefore he had them in his heart. Fellow sufferers should be dear one to another; those who have ventured and suffered in the same good cause of God and religion should for that reason love one another dearly: or, because *you have me at heart*—διὰ τὸ ἔχειν με ἐν τῇ καρδίᾳ ὑμᾶς. They manifested their respect for him by adhering firmly to the doctrine he preached, and readily suffering for it along with him. The truest mark of respect towards our ministers is receiving and abiding by the doctrine they preach. 2. The evidence of it: *It is meet for me to think this of you all, because I have you in my heart.* By this it appeared that he had them in his heart, because he had a good opinion of them and good hopes concerning them. Observe, It is very proper to think the best of other people, and as well as we can of them—to suppose as well of them as the matter will admit in all cases. 3. An appeal to God concerning the truth of this (*v.* 8): *For God is my record how greatly I long after you all in the bowels of Jesus Christ.* Having them in his heart, he longed after them; either he longed to see them, longed to hear from them, or he longed for their spiritual welfare and their increase and improvement in knowledge and grace. He had *joy in them* (*v.* 4), because of the good he saw and heard of among them; yet still he longed after them, to hear of more of it among them; and he *longed after them all,* not only those among them who were witty and wealthy, but even the meanest and poorest; and he *longed greatly* after them, or with strong affection and great good-will; and this *in the bowels of Jesus Christ,* with that tender concern which Christ himself has and has shown to precious souls. Paul was herein a follower of Christ, and all good ministers should aim to be so. O the bowels of compassion which are in Jesus Christ to poor souls! It was in compassion to them that he undertook their salvation, and put himself to so vast an expense to compass it. Now, in conformity to the example of Christ, Paul had a compassion for them, and longed after them all *in the bowels of Jesus Christ.* Shall not we pity and love those souls whom Christ had such a love and pity for? For this he appeals to God: *God is my record.* It was an inward disposition of mind that he expressed towards them, to the sincerity of which God only was witness, and therefore to him he appeals. "Whether you know it or not, or are sensible of it, God, who knows the heart, knows it."

9 And this I pray, that your love
may abound yet more and more in
knowledge and *in* all judgment; 10

That ye may approve things that are
excellent; that ye may be sincere and
without offence till the day of Christ;
11 Being filled with the fruits of righteousness, which are by Jesus Christ,
unto the glory and praise of God.

These verses contain the prayers he put up for them. Paul often let his friends know what it was he begged of God for them, that they might know what to beg for themselves and be directed in their own prayers, and that they might be encouraged to hope they should receive from God the quickening, strengthening, everlasting, comforting grace, which so powerful an intercessor as Paul asked of God for them. It is an encouragement to us to know that we are prayed for by our friends, who, we have reason to think, have an interest at the throne of grace. It was intended likewise for their direction in their walk, and that they might labour to answer his prayers for them; for by this it would appear that God had answered them. Paul, in praying thus for them, expected good concerning them. It is an inducement to us to do our duty, that we may not disappoint the expectations of praying friends and ministers. He prayed, 1. That they might be a loving people, and that good affections might abound among them: *That your love might abound yet more and more.* He means it of their love to God, and one another, and all men. Love is the fulfilling both of the law and of the gospel. Observe, Those who abound much in any grace have still need to abound more and more, because there is still something wanting in it and we are imperfect in our best attainments. 2. That they might be a knowing and judicious people: that love might abound *in knowledge and in all judgment.* It is not a blind love that will recommend us to God, but a love grounded upon knowledge and judgment. We must love God because of his infinite excellence and loveliness, and love our brethren because of what we see of the image of God upon them. Strong passions, without knowledge and a settled judgment, will not make us complete in the will of God, and sometimes do more hurt than good. The Jews had a zeal of God, but not according to knowledge, and were transported by it to violence and rage, Rom. x. 2; John xvi. 2. 3. That they might be a discerning people. This would be the effect of their knowledge and judgment: *That you may approve the things which are excellent* (*v.* 10); or, as it is in the margin, *Try the things which differ; εἰς τὸ δοκιμάζειν ὑμᾶς τὰ διαφέροντα,* that we may approve the things which are excellent upon the trial of them, and discern their difference from other things. Observe, The truths and laws of Christ are excellent things; and it is necessary that we every one approve them, and esteem them such. We only need to try them, to approve of them; and they will easily recommend themselves to any searching and discerning mind. 4. That they might be an honest upright-hearted people: *That you may be sincere.* Sincerity is our gospel perfection, that in which we should have our conversation in the world, and which is the glory of all our graces. When the eye is single, when we are inward with God in what we do, are really what we appear to be, and mean honestly, then we are sincere. 5. That they might be an inoffensive people: that you may be *without offence until the day of Christ;* not apt to take offence; and very careful not to give offence to God or their brethren, to *live in all good conscience before God* (Acts xxiii. 1), and to *exercise ourselves to have always a conscience void of offence towards God and towards men,* Acts xxiv. 16. And we must continue to the end *blameless,* that we may be presented so at the *day of Christ.* He will present the church *without spot or wrinkle* (Eph. v. 27), and *present* believers *faultless before the presence of his glory with exceeding joy,* Jude 24. 6. That they might be a fruitful useful people (*v.* 11): *Being filled with the fruits of righteousness,* &c. From God is our fruit found, and therefore from him it must be asked. The *fruits of righteousness* are the evidences and effects of our sanctification, the duties of holiness springing from a renewed heart, the *root of the matter in us. Being filled* with them. Observe, Those who do much good should still endeavour to do more. The fruits of righteousness, brought forth for the glory of God and edification of his church, should really fill us, and wholly take us up. Fear not being emptied by bringing forth the fruits of righteousness, for you will be filled with them. These fruits are *by Jesus Christ,* by his strength and grace, for *without him we can do nothing.* He is the root of the good olive, from which it derives its fatness. We are *strong in the grace which is in Christ Jesus* (2 Tim. ii. 1) and *strengthened with might by his Spirit* (Eph. iii. 16), and they are *unto the glory and praise of God.* We must not aim at our own glory in our fruitfulness, but at the *praise and glory of God,* that *God may be glorified in all things* (1 Peter iv. 11), and *whatsoever we do we must do all to the glory of God,* 1 Cor. x. 31. It is much for the honour of God, when Christians not only are good, but do good, and *abound in good works.*

12 But I would ye should understand, brethren, that the things *which
happened* unto me have fallen out
rather unto the furtherance of the
gospel; 13 So that my bonds in
Christ are manifest in all the palace,
and in all other *places;* 14 And
many of the brethren in the Lord,
waxing confident by my bonds, are
much more bold to speak the word

without fear. 15 Some indeed preach
Christ even of envy and strife; and
some also of good will: 16 The one
preach Christ of contention, not sincerely, supposing to add affliction to
my bonds: 17 But the other of
love, knowing that I am set for the
defence of the gospel. 18 What
then? notwithstanding, every way,
whether in pretence, or in truth,
Christ is preached; and I therein do
rejoice, yea, and will rejoice. 19 For
I know that this shall turn to my
salvation through your prayer, and
the supply of the Spirit of Jesus
Christ, 20 According to my earnest
expectation and *my* hope, that in
nothing I shall be ashamed, but *that*
with all boldness, as always, *so* now
also Christ shall be magnified in my
body, whether *it be* by life, or by death.

We see here the care the apostle takes to prevent their being offended at his sufferings. He was now a prisoner at Rome; this might be a stumbling-block to those who had received the gospel by his ministry. They might be tempted to think, If this doctrine were indeed of God, God would not suffer one who was so active and instrumental in preaching and propagating it to be thrown by as a despised broken vessel. They might be shy of owning this doctrine, lest they should be involved in the same trouble themselves. Now to take off the offence of the cross, he expounds this dark and hard chapter of his sufferings, and makes it very easy and intelligible, and reconcilable to the wisdom and goodness of God who employed him.

I. He suffered by the sworn enemies of the gospel, who laid him in prison, and aimed at taking away his life; but they should not be stumbled at this, for good was brought out of it, and it tended to the furtherance of the gospel (*v.* 12): *The things which happened unto me have fallen out rather unto the furtherance of the gospel.* A strange chemistry of Providence this, to extract so great a good as the enlargement of the gospel out of so great an evil as the confinement of the apostle. "*I suffer trouble as an evil-doer, even unto bonds; but the word of God is not bound,* 2 Tim. ii. 9. They cannot imprison the word of God; that has its free course, though I am confined." But how was this?

1. It alarmed those who were without (*v.* 13): "*My bonds in Christ,* or for Christ, *are manifest in all the palace and in all other places.* The emperor, the courtiers, the magistrates, are convinced that I do not suffer as an evil-doer, but as an honest man, with a good conscience. They know that I suffer for Christ, and not for any wickedness." Observe, (1.) Paul's sufferings made him known at court, where perhaps he would never have otherwise been known; and this might lead some of them to enquire after the gospel for which he suffered, which they might otherwise have never heard of. (2.) When his bonds were manifest in the palace, they were manifest in all other places. *The sentiments of the court have a great influence on the sentiments of all people—Regis ad exemplum totus componitur orbis.*

2. It emboldened those who were within. As his enemies were startled at his sufferings, so his friends were encouraged by them. *Upright men shall be astonished at this, and the innocent shall stir up himself against the hypocrite. The righteous also shall hold on his way, and he who has clean hands shall be stronger and stronger,* Job xvii. 8, 9. So it was here: *Many of the brethren in the Lord waxing confident by my bonds, v.* 14. The expectation of trouble for their religion, in general, perhaps disheartened and discouraged them; but, when they saw Paul imprisoned for Christ, they were so far from being deterred from preaching Christ and praising his name, that it made them the more bold; for they could gladly suffer in Paul's company. If they should be hurried from the pulpit to the prison, they could be reconciled to it, because they would be there in such good company. Besides, the comfort which Paul had in his sufferings, his extraordinary consolations received from Christ in a suffering state, greatly encouraged them. They saw that those who served Christ served a good Master, who could both bear them up and bear them out, in their sufferings for him. *Waxing confident by my bonds.* Πεποιθότας. They were more fully satisfied and persuaded by what they saw. Observe the power of divine grace; that which was intended by the enemy to discourage the preachers of the gospel was overruled for their encouragement. And *are much more bold to speak the word without fear:* they see the worst of it, and therefore are not afraid to venture. Their confidence gave them courage, and their courage preserved them from the power of fear.

II. He suffered from false friends as well as from enemies (*v.* 15, 16): *Some preach Christ even of envy and strife. The one preach Christ of contention, not sincerely.* Now this would be a stumbling-block and discouragement to some, that there were those who envied Paul's reputation in the churches, and the interest he had among the Christians, and endeavoured to supplant and undermine him. They were secretly pleased when he was laid up in prison, that they might have the better opportunity to steal away the people's affections; and they laid themselves out the more in preaching, that they might gain to themselves the reputation they envied him: *Supposing to add affliction to my bonds.* They thought hereby to grieve his spirit, and make him afraid of losing his interest, uneasy under his confinement, and impatient for release. It is sad that there should be men who profess the gospel, especially who preach it, who are governed by such principles as these, who should preach Christ in spite to Paul, and to increase the affliction of his bonds. Let us not think it strange if in these later and more degenerate ages of the church there should be any such. However, there were others who were animated by Paul's sufferings to preach Christ the more vigorously: *Some also of good will, and love:* from sincere affection to the gospel, that the work might not stand while the workman was laid up.—*Knowing that I am set for the defence of the gospel.* They knew that he was appointed to support and propagate the gospel in the world, against all the violence and opposition of its enemies, and were afraid lest the gospel should suffer by his confinement. This made them the more bold to preach the word and *supply his lack of service* to the church.

III. It is very affecting to see how easy he was in the midst of all: *Notwithstanding every way, whether in pretence or in truth, Christ is preached; and I therein do rejoice, yea, and I will rejoice, v.* 18. Note, The preaching of Christ is the joy of all who wish well to his kingdom among men. Since it may tend to the good of many, we ought to rejoice in it, though it be done in pretence, and not in reality. It is God's prerogative to judge of the principles men act upon; this is out of our line. Paul was so far from envying those who had liberty to preach the gospel while he was under confinement that he rejoiced in the preaching of it even by those who do it in pretence, and not in truth. How much more then should we rejoice in the preaching of the gospel by those who do it in truth, yea, though it should be with much weakness and some mistake! Two things made the apostle rejoice in the preaching of the gospel:—

1. Because it tended to the salvation of the souls of men: *I know that this shall turn to my salvation, v.* 19. Observe, God can bring good out of evil; and what does not turn to the salvation of the ministers may yet, by the grace of God, be made to turn to the salvation of the people. What reward can those expect who preach Christ out *of strife, and envy, and contention,* and to add affliction to a faithful minister's bonds? who preach in pretence, and not in truth? And yet even this may turn to the salvation of others; and Paul's rejoicing in it turned to his salvation too. This is one of the things which *accompany salvation*—to be able to rejoice that Christ is preached, though it be to the diminution of us and our reputation. This noble spirit appeared in John the Baptist, at the first public preaching of Christ: "*This my joy therefore is fulfilled. He must increase, but I must decrease,* John iii. 29, 30. Let him shine, though I be obscured; and his glory be exalted, though upon my ruins." Others understand this expression of the malice of his enemies being defeated, and contributing towards his deliverance from his confinement. *Through your prayers, and the supply of the Spirit of Christ.* Note, Whatever turns to our salvation is by the supply or the aids and assistance of the Spirit of Christ; and prayer is the appointed means of fetching in that supply. The prayers of the people may bring a supply of the Spirit to their ministers, to support them in suffering, as well as in preaching the gospel.

2. Because it would turn to the glory of Christ, *v.* 20, where he takes occasion to mention his own entire devotedness to the service and honour of Christ: *According to my earnest expectation and hope, that in nothing I shall be ashamed,* &c. Here observe, (1.) The great desire of every true Christian is that Christ may be magnified and glorified, that his name may be great, and his kingdom come. (2.) Those who truly desire that Christ may be magnified desire that he may be *magnified in their body.* They present their *bodies a living sacrifice* (Rom. xii. 1), and *yield their members as instruments of righteousness unto God,* Rom. vi. 13. They are willing to serve his designs, and be instrumental to his glory, with every member of their body, as well as faculty of their soul. (3.) It is much for the glory of Christ that we should serve him boldly and not be ashamed of him, with freedom and liberty of mind, and without discouragement: *That in nothing I shall be ashamed, but that with all boldness Christ may be magnified.* The boldness of Christians is the honour of Christ. (4.) Those who make Christ's glory their desire and design may make it their expectation and hope. If it be truly aimed at, it shall certainly be attained. If in sincerity we pray, *Father, glorify thy name,* we may be sure of the same answer to that prayer which Christ had: *I have glorified it, and I will glorify it again,* John xii. 28. (5.) Those who desire that Christ may be magnified in their bodies have a holy indifference *whether it be by life or by death.* They refer it to him which way he will make them serviceable to his glory, whether by their labours or sufferings, by their diligence or patience, by their living to his honour in working for him or dying to his honour in suffering for him.

21 For to me to live *is* Christ, and
to die *is* gain. 22 But if I live in
the flesh, this *is* the fruit of my
labour: yet what I shall choose I
wot not. 23 For I am in a strait
betwixt two, having a desire to depart, and to be with Christ; which
is far better: 24 Nevertheless to
abide in the flesh *is* more needful

for you. 25 And having this confidence, I know that I shall abide and continue with you all for your furtherance and joy of faith; 26 That your rejoicing may be more abundant in Jesus Christ for me by my coming to you again.

We have here an account of the life and death of blessed Paul: his life was Christ, and his death was gain. Observe, 1. It is the undoubted character of every good Christian that to him to live is Christ. The glory of Christ ought to be the end of our life, the grace of Christ the principle of our life, and the word of Christ the rule of it. The Christian life is derived from Christ, and directed to him. He is the principle, rule, and end of it. 2. All those to whom to live is Christ to them to die *will be gain:* it is great gain, a present gain, everlasting gain. Death is a great loss to a carnal worldly man; for he loses all his comforts and all his hopes: but to a good Christian it is gain, for it is the end of all his weakness and misery and the perfection of his comforts and accomplishment of his hopes; it delivers him from all the evils of life, and brings him to the possession of the chief good. Or, *To me to die is gain;* that is, "to the gospel as well as to myself, which will receive a further confirmation by the seal of my blood, as it had before by the labours of my life." So Christ would be *magnified by his death, v.* 20. Some read the whole expression thus: *To me, living and dying, Christ is gain;* that is, "I desire no more, neither while I live nor when I die, but to win Christ and be found in him." It might be thought, if death were gain to him, he would be weary of life, and impatient for death. No, says he,

I. *If I live in the flesh, this is the fruit of my labour* (*v.* 22), that is, Christ is. He reckoned his labour well bestowed, if he could be instrumental to advance the honour and interest of the kingdom of Christ in the world. It is *the fruit of my labour—καρπὸς ἔργου—operæ pretium.* It is worth while for a good Christian and a good minister to live in the world as long as he can glorify God and do good to his church. *Yet what I shall choose I wot not; for I am in a strait betwixt two.* It was a blessed strait which Paul was in, not between two evil things, but between two good things. David was in a strait by three judgments—sword, famine, and pestilence: Paul was in a strait between two blessings—living to Christ, and being with him. Here we have him reasoning with himself upon the matter.

1. His inclination was for death. See the power of faith and of divine grace; it can reconcile the mind to death, and make us willing to die, though death is the destruction of our present nature and the greatest natural evil. We have naturally an aversion to death, but he had an inclination to it (*v.* 23); *Having a desire to depart, and to be with Christ,* Observe, (1.) It is being with Christ which makes a departure desirable to a good man. It is not simply dying, or putting off the body, it is not of itself and for its own sake a desirable thing; but it may be necessarily connected with something else which may make it truly so. If I cannot be with Christ without departing, I shall reckon it desirable on that account to depart. (2.) As soon as ever the soul departs, it is immediately with Christ. *This day shalt thou be with me in paradise,* Luke xxiii. 43. *Absent from the body and present with the Lord* (2 Cor. v. 8), without any interval between. *Which is far better, πολλῷ γὰρ μᾶλλον κρεῖσσον—very much exceeding,* or *vastly preferable.* Those who know the value of Christ and heaven will readily acknowledge it far better to be in heaven than to be in this world, to be with Christ than to be with any creature; for in this world we are compassed about with sin, born to trouble, born again to it; but, if we come to be with Christ, farewell sin and temptation, farewell sorrow and death, for ever.

2. His judgment was rather to live awhile longer in this world, for the service of the church (*v.* 24): *Nevertheless to abide in the flesh is more needful for you.* It is needful for the church to have ministers; and faithful ministers can ill be spared when the *harvest is plenteous and the labourers are few.* Observe, Those who have most reason to desire to depart should be willing to continue in the world as long as God has any work for them to do. Paul's strait was not between living in this world and living in heaven; between these two there is no comparison: but his strait was between serving Christ in this world and enjoying him in another. Still it was Christ that his heart was upon: though, to advance the interest of Christ and his church, he chose rather to tarry here, where he met with oppositions and difficulties, and to deny himself for awhile the satisfaction of his reward.

II. *And, having this confidence, I know that I shall abide and continue with you all for your furtherance and joy of faith, v.* 25. Observe here, 1. What a great confidence Paul had in the divine Providence, that it would order all for the best to him. "Having this confidence that it will be needful for you that I should abide in the flesh, I know that I shall abide." 2. Whatsoever is best for the church, we may be sure God will do. If we know what is needful for building up the body of Christ, we may certainly know what will be; for he will take care of its interests, and do what is best, all things considered, in every condition it is in. 3. Observe what ministers are continued for: *For our furtherance and joy of faith,* our further advancement in holiness and comfort. 4. What promotes our *faith and joy of faith* is very much for our furtherance in the way to heaven. The more faith the more joy, and the more faith and joy the more we are furthered in our Christian course. 5. There is need of a settled ministry, not only for the conviction and conversion of sinners, but for the edification of saints, and their furtherance in spiritual attainments.

III. *That your rejoicing may be more abundant in Jesus Christ for me, by my coming to you again, v.* 26. They rejoiced in the hope of seeing him, and enjoying his further labours among them. Observe, 1. The continuance of ministers with the church ought to be the rejoicing of all who wish well to the church, and to its interests. 2. All our joys should terminate in Christ. Our joy in good ministers should be our joy *in Christ Jesus for them;* for they are but the *friends of the bridegroom,* and are to be received in his name, and for his sake.

27 Only let your conversation be
as it becometh the gospel of Christ:
that whether I come and see you, or
else be absent, I may hear of your
affairs, that ye stand fast in one spirit,
with one mind striving together for
the faith of the gospel; 28 And in
nothing terrified by your adversaries:
which is to them an evident token of
perdition, but to you of salvation,
and that of God. 29 For unto you
it is given in the behalf of Christ,
not only to believe on him, but also
to suffer for his sake; 30 Having
the same conflict which ye saw in me,
and now hear *to be* in me.

The apostle concludes the chapter with two exhortations:—

I. He exhorts them to strictness of conversation (*v.* 27): *Only let your conversation be as becometh the gospel of Christ.* Observe, Those who profess the gospel of Christ should have their conversation as becomes the gospel, or in a suitableness and agreeableness to it. Let it be as becomes those who believe gospel truths, submit to gospel laws, and depend upon gospel promises; and with an answerable faith, holiness, and comfort. Let it be in all respects as those who belong to the kingdom of God among men, and are members and subjects of it. It is an ornament to our profession when our conversation is of a piece with it.—*That whether I come and see you, or else be absent, I may hear of your affairs.* He had spoken in *v.* 26 of his coming to them again, and had spoken it with some assurance, though he was now a prisoner; but he would not have them build upon that. Our religion must not be bound up in the hands of our ministers: "Whether I come or no, let me hear well of you, and do you stand fast." Whether ministers come or no, Christ is always at hand. He is nigh to us, never far from us; and hastens his second coming. *The coming of the Lord draws nigh,* James v. 8. Let me hear of you *that you stand fast in one spirit, with one mind striving together for the faith of the gospel.* Three things he desired to hear of them; and they are all such as become the gospel:—1. It becomes those who profess the gospel to strive for it, to use a holy violence in taking the kingdom of heaven. The *faith of the gospel* is the doctrine of faith, or the religion of the gospel. There is that in the faith of the gospel which is worth striving for. If religion is worth any thing, it is worth every thing. There is much opposition, and there is need of striving. A man may sleep and go to hell; but he who will go to heaven must look about him and be diligent. 2. The unity and unanimity of Christians become the gospel: *Strive together,* not strive one with another; all of you must strive against the common adversary. One spirit and one mind become the gospel; for *there is one Lord, one faith, one baptism.* There may be a oneness of heart and affection among Christians, where there is diversity of judgment and apprehensions about many things. 3. Stedfastness becomes the gospel: *Stand fast in one spirit, with one mind.* Be *stedfast and immovable* by any opposition. It is a shame to religion when the professors of it are off and on, unfixed in their minds, and unstable as water; for they will never excel. Those who would strive for the faith of the gospel must stand firm to it.

II. He exhorts them to courage and constancy in suffering: *And in nothing terrified by your adversaries, v.* 28. The professors of the gospel have all along met with adversaries, especially at the first planting of Christianity. Our great care must be to keep close to our profession, and be constant to it: whatever oppositions we meet with, we must not be frightened at them, considering that the condition of the persecuted is much better and more desirable than the condition of the persecutors; for persecuting is an *evident token of perdition.* Those who oppose the gospel of Christ, and injure the professors of it, are marked out for ruin. But being persecuted is a token of salvation. Not that it is a certain mark; many hypocrites have suffered for their religion; but it is a good sign that we are in good earnest in religion, and designed for salvation, when we are enabled in a right manner to suffer for the cause of Christ.—*For to you it is given on the behalf of Christ not only to believe, but also to suffer for his name, v.* 29. Here are two precious gifts given, and both on the behalf of Christ:—1. To believe in him. Faith is God's gift on the behalf of Christ, who purchased for us not only the blessedness which is the object of faith, but the grace of faith itself: the ability or disposition to believe is from God. 2. To suffer for the sake of Christ is a valuable gift too: it is a great honour and a great advantage; for we may be very serviceable to the glory of God, which is the end of our creation, and encourage and confirm the faith of others. And there is a great reward attending it too: *Blessed are you when men shall persecute you, for great is your reward in heaven,* Matt. v. 11, 12. And, if *we suffer with him, we shall also reign with him,* 2 Tim. ii. 12. If we suffer reproach and loss for Christ, we are to reckon it a great gift, and prize it accordingly, always provided we behave under our sufferings with the genuine temper of martyrs and confessors (*v.* 30): "*Having the same conflict which you saw in me, and now hear to be in me;* that is, suffering in the same manner as you saw and now hear of me that I suffer." It is not simply the suffering, but the cause, and not only the cause, but the spirit, which makes the martyr. A man may suffer in a bad cause, and then he suffers justly; or in a good cause, but with a wrong mind, and then his sufferings lose their value.

CHAP. II.

The apostle proceeds to further exhortations to several duties, to be like-minded, and lowly-minded, which he presses from the example of Christ (ver. 1—11), to be diligent and serious in the Christian course (ver. 12, 13), and to adorn their Christian profession by several suitable graces, ver. 14—18. He then concludes with particular notice and commendation of two good ministers, Timothy and Epaphroditus, whom he designed to send to them, ver 19—30.

IF *there be* therefore any consolation
in Christ, if any comfort of love,
if any fellowship of the Spirit, if any
bowels and mercies, 2 Fulfil ye my
joy, that ye be likeminded, having
the same love, *being* of one accord,
of one mind. 3 *Let* nothing *be done*
through strife or vainglory; but in
lowliness of mind let each esteem
other better than themselves. 4
Look not every man on his own
things, but every man also on the
things of others. 5 Let this mind
be in you, which was also in Christ
Jesus: 6 Who, being in the form
of God, thought it not robbery to be
equal with God: 7 But made himself of no reputation, and took upon
him the form of a servant, and was
made in the likeness of men: 8 And
being found in fashion as a man, he
humbled himself, and became obedient unto death, even the death of
the cross. 9 Wherefore God also
hath highly exalted him, and given
him a name which is above every
name: 10 That at the name of
Jesus every knee should bow, of
things in heaven, and *things* in earth,
and *things* under the earth; 11 And
that every tongue should confess that
Jesus Christ *is* Lord, to the glory of
God the Father.

The apostle proceeds in this chapter where he left off in the last, with further exhortations to Christian duties. He presses them largely to like-mindedness and lowly-mindedness, in conformity to the example of the Lord Jesus, the great pattern of humility and love. Here we may observe,

I. The great gospel precept pressed upon us; that is, to love one another. This is the law of Christ's kingdom, the lesson of his school, the livery of his family. This he represents (*v.* 2) by being *like-minded, having the same love, being of one accord, of one mind.* We are of a like mind when we have the same love. Christians should be one in affection, whether they can be one in apprehension or no. This is always in their power, and always their duty, and is the likeliest way to bring them nearer in judgment. *Having the same love.* Observe, The same love that we are required to express to others, others are bound to express to us. Christian love ought to be mutual love. Love, and you shall be loved. *Being of one accord, and of one mind;* not crossing and thwarting, or driving on separate interests, but unanimously agreeing in the great things of God and keeping the *unity of the Spirit* in other differences. Here observe,

1. The pathetic pressing of the duty. He is very importunate with them, knowing what an evidence it is of our sincerity, and what a means of the preservation and edification of the body of Christ. The inducements to brotherly love are these:—(1.) "If there is any *consolation in Christ.* Have you experienced consolation in Christ? Evidence that experience by loving one another." The sweetness we have found in the doctrine of Christ should sweeten our spirits. Do we expect consolation in Christ? If we would not be disappointed, we must love one another. If we have not consolation in Christ, where else can we expect it? Those who have an interest in Christ have consolation in him, strong and everlasting consolation (Heb. vi. 18; 2 Thess. ii. 16), and therefore ought to love one another. (2.) "*Comfort of love.* If there is any comfort in Christian love, in God's love to you, in your love to God, or in your brethren's love to us, in consideration of all this, be you like-minded. If you have ever found that comfort, if you would find it, if you indeed believe that the grace of love is a comfortable grace, abound in it." (3.) "*Fellowship of the Spirit.* If there is such a thing as communion with God and Christ by the Spirit, such a thing as the communion of saints, by virtue of their being animated and actuated by *one and the same Spirit,* be you like-minded; for Christian love and like-mindedness will preserve to us our communion with God and with one another." (4.) "*Any bowels and mercies,* in God and

Christ, towards you. If you expect the benefit of God's compassions to yourselves, be you compassionate one to another. If there is such a thing as mercy to be found among the followers of Christ, if all who are sanctified have a disposition to holy pity, make it appear this way." How cogent are these arguments! One would think them enough to tame the most fierce, and mollify the hardest, heart. (5.) Another argument he insinuates is the comfort it would be to him: *Fulfil you my joy.* It is the joy of ministers to see people like-minded and living in love. He had been instrumental in bringing them to the grace of Christ and the love of God. "Now," says he, "if you have found any benefit by your participation of the gospel of Christ, if you have any comfort in it, or advantage by it, *fulfil the joy* of your poor minister, who preached the gospel to you."

2. He proposes some means to promote it. (1.) *Do nothing through strife and vain glory, v.* 3. There is no greater enemy to Christian love than pride and passion. If we do things in contradiction to our brethren, this is doing them through strife; if we do them through ostentation of ourselves, this is doing them through vain-glory: both are destructive of Christian love and kindle unchristian heats. Christ came to slay all enmities; therefore let there not be among Christians a spirit of opposition. Christ came to humble us, and therefore let there not be among us a spirit of pride. (2.) We must *esteem others in lowliness of mind better than ourselves,* be severe upon our own faults and charitable in our judgment of others, be quick in observing our own defects and infirmities, but ready to overlook and make favourable allowances for the defects of others. We must esteem the good which is in others above that which is in ourselves; for we best know our own unworthiness and imperfections. (3.) We must interest ourselves in the concerns of others, not in a way of curiosity and censoriousness, or as *busy-bodies in other men's matters,* but in Christian love and sympathy: *Look not every man on his own things, but every man also on the things of others, v.* 4. A selfish spirit is destructive of Christian love. We must be concerned not only for our own credit, and ease, and safety, but for those of others also; and rejoice in the prosperity of others as truly as in our own. We must love our neighbour as ourselves, and make his case our own.

II. Here is a gospel pattern proposed to our imitation, and that is the example of our Lord Jesus Christ: *Let this mind be in you which was also in Christ Jesus, v.* 5. Observe, Christians must be of Christ's mind. We must bear a resemblance to his life, if we would have the benefit of his death. *If we have not the Spirit of Christ, we are none of his,* Rom. viii. 9. Now what was the mind of Christ? He was eminently humble, and this is what we are peculiarly to learn of him. *Learn of me, for I am meek and lowly in heart,* Matt. xi. 29. If we were lowly-minded, we should be like-minded; and, if we were like Christ, we should be lowly-minded. We must walk in the same spirit and in the same steps with the Lord Jesus, who humbled himself to sufferings and death for us; not only to satisfy God's justice, and pay the price of our redemption, but to set us an example, and that we might *follow his steps.* Now here we have the two natures and the two states of our Lord Jesus. It is observable that the apostle, having occasion to mention the Lord Jesus, and the mind which was in him, takes the hint to enlarge upon his person, and to give a particular description of him. It is a pleasing subject, and a gospel minister needs not think himself out of the way when he is upon it; any fit occasion should be readily taken.

1. Here are the two natures of Christ: his divine nature and his human nature. (1.) Here is his divine nature: *Who being in the form of God* (*v.* 6), partaking of the divine nature, as the eternal and only begotten Son of God. This agrees with John i. 1, *In the beginning was the Word, and the Word was with God:* it is of the same import with being the *image of the invisible* God (Col. i. 15), and the *brightness of his glory, and express image of his person,* Heb. i. 3. *He thought it no robbery to be equal with God;* did not think himself guilty of any invasion of what did not belong to him, or assuming another's right. He said, *I and my Father are one,* John x. 30. It is the highest degree of robbery for any mere man or mere creature to pretend to be equal with God, or profess himself *one with the Father.* This is for a man to rob God, not in tithes and offerings, but of the rights of his Godhead, Mal. iii. 8. Some understand *being in the form of God*—ἐν μορφῇ Θεοῦ ὑπάρχων, of his appearance in a divine majestic glory to the patriarchs, and the Jews, under the Old Testament, which was often called the *glory,* and the *Shechinah.* The word is used in such a sense by the LXX. and in the New Testament. *He appeared to the two disciples,* ἐν ἑτέρᾳ μορφῇ—*in another form,* Mark xvi. 12. Μετεμορφώθη—*he was transfigured* before them, Matt. xvii. 2. And *he thought it no robbery to be equal with God;* he did not greedily *catch at,* nor covet and affect to appear in that glory; he laid aside the majesty of his former appearance while he was here on earth, which is supposed to be the sense of the peculiar expression, οὐκ ἁρπαγμὸν ἡγήσατο. Vid. *Bishop Bull's Def.* cap. ii. sect. 4. et alibi, and *Whitby* in loc. (2.) His human nature: He was *made in the likeness of men,* and *found in fashion as a man.* He was really and truly man, *took part of our flesh and blood,* appeared in the nature and habit of man. And he voluntarily assumed human nature; it was his own act, and by his own consent. We cannot say that our participation of the human nature is so. Herein he *emptied himself,* divested himself of the

honours and glories of the upper world, and of his former appearance, to clothe himself with the rags of human nature. *He was in all things like to us*, Heb. ii. 17.

2. Here are his two estates, of humiliation and exaltation. (1.) His estate of humiliation. He not only took upon him the likeness and fashion of a man, but the *form of a servant*, that is, a man of mean estate. He was not only God's servant whom he had chosen, but he came to minister to men, and was among them as one who serveth in a mean and servile state. One would think that the Lord Jesus, if he would be a man, should have been a prince, and appeared in splendour. But quite the contrary: *He took upon him the form of a servant.* He was brought up meanly, probably working with his supposed father at his trade. His whole life was a life of humiliation, meanness, poverty, and disgrace; he had nowhere to lay his head, lived upon alms, was a *man of sorrows and acquainted with grief*, did not appear with external pomp, or any marks of distinction from other men. This was the humiliation of his life. But the lowest step of his humiliation was his dying the death of the cross. *He became obedient to death, even the death of the cross.* He not only suffered, but was actually and voluntarily obedient; he obeyed the law which he brought himself under as Mediator, and by which he was obliged to die. *I have power to lay down my life, and I have power to take it again: this commandment have I received of my Father*, John x. 18. And he was *made under the law*, Gal. iv. 4. There is an emphasis laid upon the manner of his dying, which had in it all the circumstances possible which are humbling: *Even the death of the cross*, a cursed, painful, and shameful death,—a death accursed by the law *(Cursed is he that hangeth on a tree)*—full of pain, the body nailed through the nervous parts (the hands and feet) and hanging with all its weight upon the cross,—and the death of a malefactor and a slave, not of a free-man,—exposed as a public spectacle. Such was the condescension of the blessed Jesus. (2.) His exaltation: *Wherefore God also hath highly exalted him.* His exaltation was the reward of his humiliation. Because he humbled himself, God exalted him; and he *highly exalted him*, ὑπερύψωσε, raised him to an exceeding height. He exalted his whole person, the human nature as well as the divine; for he is spoken of as being in the form of God as well as in the fashion of man. As it respects the divine nature, it could only be the recognizing of his rights, or the display and appearance of the *glory he had with the Father before the world was* (John xvii. 5), not any new acquisition of glory; and so the Father himself is said to be exalted. But the proper exaltation was of his human nature, which alone seems to be capable of it, though in conjunction with the divine. His exaltation here is made to consist in honour and power. In honour; so *he had a name above every name*, a title of dignity above all the creatures, men and angels. And in power: *Every knee must bow to him.* The whole creation must be in subjection to him: *things in heaven, and things in earth, and things under the earth*, the inhabitants of heaven and earth, the living and the dead. *At the name of Jesus;* not at the sound of the word, but the authority of Jesus; all should pay a solemn homage. And that *every tongue should confess that Jesus Christ is Lord*—every nation and language should publicly own the universal empire of the exalted Redeemer, and that *all power in heaven and earth is given to him*, Matt. xxviii. 18. Observe the vast extent of the kingdom of Christ; it reaches to heaven and earth, and to all the creatures in each, to angels as well as men, and to the dead as well as the living.—*To the glory of God the Father.* Observe, It is to the glory of God the Father to confess that Jesus Christ is Lord; for it is his will that *all men should honour the Son as they honour the Father*, John v. 23. Whatever respect is paid to Christ redounds to the honour of the Father. *He who receiveth me receiveth him who sent me*, Matt. x. 40.

12 Wherefore, my beloved, as ye
have always obeyed, not as in my
presence only, but now much more
in my absence, work out your own
salvation with fear and trembling.
13 For it is God which worketh in
you both to will and to do of *his*
good pleasure.

I. He exhorts them to diligence and seriousness in the Christian course: *Work out your own salvation.* It is the salvation of our souls (1 Pet. i. 9), and our eternal salvation (Heb. v. 9), and contains deliverance from all the evils sin had brought upon us and exposed us to, and the possession of all good and whatsoever is necessary to our complete and final happiness. Observe, It concerns us above all things to secure the welfare of our souls: whatever becomes of other things, let us take care of our best interests. It is our own salvation, the salvation of our own souls. It is not for us to judge other people; we have enough to do to look to ourselves; and, though we must promote the common salvation (Jude 3) as much as we can, yet we must upon no account neglect our own. We are required to *work out our salvation*, κατεργάζεσθε. The word signifies *working thoroughly* at a thing, and taking *true pains*. Observe, We must be diligent in the use of all the means which conduce to our salvation. We must not only work at our salvation, by doing something now and then about it; but we must work out our salvation, by doing all that is to be done, and persevering therein to the end. Salvation is the great thing we should mind, and set our hearts upon; and we cannot attain salvation without the utmost care and diligence. He adds, *With fear and trembling,* that is, with great care and circumspection: "Trembling for fear lest you miscarry and come short. Be careful to do every thing in religion in the best manner, and fear lest under all your advantages you should so much as *seem to come short,*" Heb. iv. 1. Fear is a great guard and preservative from evil.

II. He urges this from the consideration of their readiness always to obey the gospel: "*As you have always obeyed, not as in my presence only, but now much more in my absence, v.* 12. You have been always willing to comply with every discovery of the will of God; and that in my absence as well as presence. You make it to appear that regard to Christ, and care of your souls, sway more with you than any mode of showing respect whatsoever." They were not merely awed by the apostle's presence, but did it even *much more in his absence.* "And because *it is God who worketh in you,* do you work out your salvation. Work, for he worketh." It should encourage us to do our utmost, because our *labour shall not be in vain.* God is ready to concur with his grace, and assist our faithful endeavours. Observe, Though we must use our utmost endeavours in working out our salvation, yet still we must go forth, and go on, in a dependence upon the grace of God. His grace works in us in a way suitable to our natures, and in concurrence with our endeavours; and the operations of God's grace in us are so far from excusing, that they are intended to quicken and engage our endeavours. "And work out our salvation *with fear and trembling,* for *he worketh in you.*" All our working depends upon his working in us. "Do not trifle with God by neglects and delays, lest you provoke him to withdraw his help, and all your endeavours prove in vain. Work with *fear,* for he works of his *good pleasure.*" —*To will and to do:* he gives the whole ability. It is the grace of God which inclines the will to that which is good: and then enables us to perform it, and to act according to our principles. *Thou hast wrought all our works in us,* Isa. xxvi. 12. *Of his good pleasure.* As there is no strength in us, so there is no merit in us. As we cannot act without God's grace, so we cannot claim it, nor pretend to deserve it. God's good will to us is the cause of his good work in us; and he is under no engagements to his creatures, but those of his gracious promise.

14 Do all things without murmurings and disputings:
15 That ye may be blameless and harmless, the sons of God, without rebuke, in the midst of a crooked and perverse nation, among whom ye shine as lights in the world;
16 Holding forth the word of life; that I may rejoice in the day of Christ, that I have not run in vain, neither laboured in vain.
17 Yea, and if I be offered upon the sacrifice and service of your faith, I joy, and rejoice with you all.
18 For the same cause also do ye joy, and rejoice with me.

The apostle exhorts them in these verses to adorn their Christian profession by a suitable temper and behaviour, in several instances. 1. By a cheerful obedience to the commands of God (*v.* 14): "*Do all things,* do your duty in every branch of it, *without murmurings.* Do it, and do not find fault with it. Mind your work, and do not quarrel with it." God's commands were given to be obeyed, not to be disputed. This greatly adorns our profession, and shows we serve a good Master, whose service is freedom and whose work is its own reward. 2. By peaceableness and love one to another. "Do all things *without disputing,* wrangling, and debating one with another; because the light of truth and the life of religion are often lost in the heats and mists of disputation." 3. By a blameless conversation towards all men (*v.* 15): "*That you may be blameless and harmless, the sons of God, without rebuke;* that you be not injurious to any in word or deed, and give no just occasion of offence." We should endeavour not only to be harmless, but to be blameless; not only not to do hurt, but not to come under the just suspicion of it. *Blameless and sincere;* so some read it. Blameless before men, sincere towards God. The *sons of God.* It becomes those to be blameless and harmless who stand in such a relation, and are favoured with such a privilege. The children of God should differ from the sons of men. *Without rebuke—ἀμώμητα.* Momus was a carping deity among the Greeks, mentioned by Hesiod and Lucian, who did nothing himself, and found fault with every body and every thing. From him all carpers at other men, and rigid censurers of their works, were called *Momi.* The sense of the expression is, "Walk so circumspectly that Momus himself may have no occasion to cavil at you, that the severest censurer may find no fault with you." We should aim and endeavour, not only to get to heaven, but to get thither without a blot; and, like Demetrius, to *have a good report of all men, and of the truth,* 3 John 12. *In the midst of a crooked and perverse generation;* that is, among the heathens, and those who are without. Observe, Where there is no true religion, little is to be expected but crookedness and perverseness; and the more crooked and perverse others are among whom we live, and the more apt to cavil, the more careful we should be to keep ourselves blameless and harmless. Abraham and Lot must not *strive, because the Canaanite and Perizzite dwelt in the land,* Gen. xiii. 7. *Among whom you shine as lights in the world.* Christ is the light of the world, and good Christians are lights in the world. When God raises up a good man in any place, he sets up a light in that place. Or it may be read imperatively: *Among whom shine you as lights:* compare Matt. v. 16, *Let your light so shine before men.* Christians should endeavour not only to approve themselves to God, but to recommend themselves to others, that they may also glorify God. They must shine as well as be sincere.—*Holding forth the word of life, v.* 16. The gospel is called the word of life because it reveals and proposes to us eternal life through Jesus Christ. *Life and immortality are brought to light by the gospel,* 2 Tim. i. 10. It is our duty not only to hold fast, but to hold forth the word of life; not only to hold it fast for our own benefit, but to hold it forth for the benefit of others, to hold it forth as the candlestick holds forth the candle, which makes it appear to advantage all around, or as the luminaries of the heavens, which shed their influence far and wide. This Paul tells them would be his joy: "*That I may rejoice in the day of Christ;* not only rejoice in your stedfastness, but in your usefulness." He would have them think his pains well bestowed, and that *he had not run in vain, nor laboured in vain.* Observe, (1.) The work of the ministry requires the putting forth of the whole man: all that is within us is little enough to be employed in it; as in running and labouring. Running denotes vehemence and vigour, and continual pressing forward; labour denotes constancy and close application. (2.) It is a great joy to ministers when they perceive that they have not *run in vain, nor laboured in vain;* and it will be their rejoicing in the day of Christ, when their converts will be their crown. *What is our hope, or joy, or crown of rejoicing? Are not even you in the presence of our Lord Jesus Christ at his coming? For you are our glory and joy,* 1 Thess. ii. 19, 20. The apostle not only ran and laboured for them with satisfaction, but shows that he was ready to suffer for their good (*v.* 17): *Yea, and if I be offered upon the sacrifice and service of your faith, I joy and rejoice with you all.* He could reckon himself happy if he could promote the honour of Christ, the edification of the church, and the welfare of the souls of men; though it were not only by hazarding, but by laying down, his life: he could willingly be a sacrifice at their altars, to serve the faith of God's elect. Could Paul think it worth while to shed his blood for the service of the church, and shall we think it much to take a little pains? Is not that worth our labour which he thought worth his life? *If I be offered,* or *poured* out as the wine of the *drink-offerings,* σπένδομαι. 2 Tim. iv. 6, *I am now ready to be offered.* He could rejoice to seal his doctrine with his blood (*v.* 18): *For the same cause also do you joy and rejoice with me.* It is the will of God that good Christians should be much in rejoicing; and those who are happy in good ministers have a great deal of reason to joy and rejoice with them. If the minister loves the people, and is willing to spend and be spent for their welfare, the people have reason to love the minister and to *joy and rejoice with him.*

19 But I trust in the Lord Jesus
to send Timotheus shortly unto you,
that I also may be of good comfort,
when I know your state. 20 For I
have no man likeminded, who will naturally care for your state. 21 For all
seek their own, not the things which
are Jesus Christ's. 22 But ye know
the proof of him, that, as a son with
the father, he hath served with me
in the gospel. 23 Him therefore I
hope to send presently, so soon as I
shall see how it will go with me.
24 But I trust in the Lord that I
also myself shall come shortly. 25
Yet I supposed it necessary to send
to you Epaphroditus, my brother,
and companion in labour, and fellow-soldier, but your messenger, and he
that ministered to my wants. 26
For he longed after you all, and was
full of heaviness, because that ye had
heard that he had been sick. 27 For
indeed he was sick nigh unto death:
but God had mercy on him; and not
on him only, but on me also, lest I
should have sorrow upon sorrow. 28
I sent him therefore the more carefully, that, when ye see him again,
ye may rejoice, and that I may be
the less sorrowful. 29 Receive him
therefore in the Lord with all gladness; and hold such in reputation:
30 Because for the work of Christ he
was nigh unto death, not regarding
his life, to supply your lack of service toward me.

Paul takes particular notice of two good ministers; for though he was himself a great apostle, and *laboured more abundantly than they all,* yet he took all occasions to speak with respect of those who were far his inferiors.

I. He speaks of Timothy, whom he intended to send to the Philippians, that he might have an account of their state. See Paul's care of the churches, and the comfort he had in their well-doing. He was in pain when he had not heard of them for a good while, and therefore would send Timothy to enquire, and bring him an account: *For I have no man like-minded, who will naturally care for your state.* Timothy was a non-such. There were, no doubt, many good ministers, who were in care for the souls of those for whom they preached; but none comparable to Timothy, a man of an excellent spirit and tender heart. *Who will naturally care for your state.* Observe, It is best with us when our duty becomes in a manner natural to us. Timothy was a genuine son of blessed Paul, and walked in the same spirit and the same steps. *Naturally*, that is, sincerely, and not in pretence only: with a willing heart and upright view, so agreeably to the make of his mind. Note, 1. It is the duty of ministers to care for the state of their people and be concerned for their welfare: *I seek not yours, but you*, 2 Cor. xii. 14. 2. It is a rare thing to find one who does it naturally: such a one is remarkable and distinguished among his brethren. *All seek their own, not the things which are Jesus Christ's, v.* 21. Did Paul say this in haste, as David said, *All men are liars?* Ps. cxvi. 11 Was there so general a corruption among ministers so early that there was not one among them who cared for the state of their people? We must not understand it so: he means the generality; *all*, that is, either the most, or all in comparison of Timothy. Note, Seeking our own interest to the neglect of Jesus Christ is a very great sin, and very common among Christians and ministers. Many prefer their own credit, ease, and safety, before truth, holiness, and duty, the things of their own pleasure and reputation before the things of Christ's kingdom and his honour and interest in the world: but Timothy was none of these.—*You know the proof of him, v.* 22. Timothy was a man who had been tried, and had made *full proof of his ministry* (2 Tim. iv. 5), and was faithful in all that befel him. All the churches with whom he had acquaintance knew the proof of him. He was a man as good as he seemed to be; and *served Christ so as to be acceptable to God*, and *approved of men*, Rom. xiv. 18. "You not only know the name of him, and the face of him, but the proof of him, and have experienced his affection and fidelity in your service, *that, as a son with a father, he hath served with me in the gospel.* He was Paul's assistant in many places where he preached, and served with him in the gospel with all the dutiful respect which a child pays to a father, and with all the love and cheerfulness with which a child is serviceable to his father. Their ministrations together were with great respect on the one side and great tenderness and kindness on the other—an admirable example to elder and younger ministers united in the same service. Paul designed to send him shortly: *Him therefore I hope to send presently, as soon as I shall see how it will go with me, v.* 23. He was now a prisoner, and did not know what would be the issue; but, according as it turned, he would dispose of Timothy. Nay, he hoped to come himself (*v.* 24): *But I trust in the Lord that I also myself shall come shortly.* He hoped he should soon be set at liberty, and be able to pay them a visit. Paul desired his liberty, not that he might take his pleasure, but that he might do good.—*I trust in the Lord.* He expresses his hope and confidence of seeing them, with a humble dependence and submission to the divine will. See Acts xviii. 21; 1 Cor. iv. 19; James iv. 15; and Heb. vi. 3.

II. Concerning Epaphroditus, whom he calls *his brother, and companion in labour, and fellow-soldier*, his Christian brother, to whom he bore a tender affection,—his companion in the work and sufferings of the gospel, who submitted to the same labours and hardships with himself,—and their messenger, one who was sent by them to him, probably to consult him about some affairs relating to their church, or to bring a present from them for his relief for he adds, and *who ministered to my wants* He seems to be the same who is called *Epaphras*, Col. iv. 12. He had an earnest desire to come to them, and Paul was willing he should. It seems, 1 Epaphroditus had been sick: *They had heard that he had been sick, v.* 26. And *indeed he was sick, nigh unto death, v.* 27. Sickness is a calamity common to men, to good men and ministers. But why did not the apostle heal him, who was endued with a power of curing diseases, as well as raising the dead? Acts xx. 10. Probably because that was intended as a sign to others, and to confirm the truth of the gospel, and therefore needed not be exercised one towards another. *These signs shall follow those who believe, they shall lay hands on the sick, and they shall recover*, Mark xvi. 17. 18. And perhaps they had not that power at all times, and at their own discretion, but only when some great end was to be served by it, and when God saw fit. It was proper to Christ, who had *the Spirit above measure.* 2. The Philippians were exceedingly sorry to hear of his sickness. They were full of heaviness, as well as he, upon the tidings of it: for he was one, it seems, for whom they had a particular respect and affection, and thought fit to choose out to send to the apostle. 3. It pleased God to recover and spare him: *But God had mercy on him, v.* 27. The apostle owns it is a great mercy to himself, as well as to Epaphroditus and others. Though the church was blessed at that time with extraordinary gifts, they could even then ill spare a good minister. He was sensibly touched with the thoughts of so great a loss: *Lest I should have sorrow upon sorrow;* that is, "Lest, besides the sorrow of my own imprisonment, I should have the sorrow of his death." Or perhaps some other good ministers had died lately, which had been a great affliction to him: and, if this had died now, it would have been a fresh grief to him, and *sorrow added to sorrow.* 4. Epaphroditus was willing to pay a visit to the Philippians, that he might be comforted with those who had sorrowed for him when he was sick: "*That when you see him again you may rejoice* (*v.* 28), that you may yourselves see how well he has recovered, and what reason you have for thankfulness and joy upon his account." He gave himself the pleasure of comforting them by the sight of so dear a friend. 5. Paul recommends him to their esteem and affection: "*Receive him therefore in the Lord with all gladness, and hold such in reputation:* account such men valuable, who are zealous and faithful, and let them be highly loved and regarded. Show your joy and respect by all the expressions of hearty affection and good opinion." It seems he had caught his illness in the work of God: *It was for the work of Christ that he was nigh to death, and to supply their lack of service to him.* The apostle does not blame him for his indiscretion in hazarding his life, but reckons they ought to love him the more upon that account. Observe, (1.) Those who truly love Christ, and are hearty in the interests of his kingdom, will think it very well worth their while to hazard their health and life to do him service, and promote the edification of his church. (2.) They were to receive him with joy, as newly recovered from sickness. It is an endearing consideration to have our mercies restored to us after danger of removal, and should make them the more valued and improved. What is given us in answer to prayer should be received with great thankfulness and joy.

CHAP. III.

He cautions them against judaizing seducers (ver. 1—3) and proposes his own example: and here he enumerates the privileges of his Jewish state which he rejected (ver. 4—8), describes the matter of his own choice (ver. 9—16), and closes with an exhortation to beware of wicked men, and to follow his example, ver. 17—21.

FINALLY, my brethren, rejoice in the Lord. To write the same things to you, to me indeed *is* not grievous, but for you *it is* safe. 2
Beware of dogs, beware of evil workers, beware of the concision. 3 For
we are the circumcision, which worship God in the spirit, and rejoice in Christ Jesus, and have no confidence in the flesh.

It seems the church of the Philippians, though a faithful and flourishing church, was disturbed by the judaizing teachers, who endeavoured to keep up the law of Moses, and mix the observances of it with the doctrine of Christ and his institutions. He begins the chapter with warnings against these seducers.

I. He exhorts them to *rejoice in the Lord* (*v.* 1), to rest satisfied in the interest they had in him and the benefit they hoped for by him. It is the character and temper of sincere Christians to rejoice in Christ Jesus. The more we take of the comfort of our religion the more closely we shall cleave to it: the more we rejoice in Christ the more willing we shall be to do and suffer for him, and the less danger we shalt be in of being drawn away from him. The *joy of the Lord is our strength,* Neh. viii. 10.

II. He cautions them to take heed of those false teachers: *To write the same thing to you to me indeed is not grievous, but for you it is safe;* that is, the same things which I have already preached to you; as if he had said, "What has been presented to your ears shall be presented to your eyes: what I have spoken formerly shall now be written; to show that I am still of the same mind." *To me indeed is not grievous.* Observe, 1. Ministers must not think any thing grievous to themselves which they have reason to believe is safe and edifying to the people. 2. It is good for us often to hear the same truths, to revive the remembrance and strengthen the impression of things of importance. It is a wanton curiosity to desire always to hear some new thing. It is a needful caution he here gives: *Beware of dogs, v.* 2. The prophet calls the false prophets dumb dogs (Isa. lvi. 10), to which the apostle here seems to refer. *Dogs,* for their malice against the faithful professors of the gospel of Christ, barking at them and biting them. They cried up good works in opposition to the faith of Christ; but Paul calls them evil workers: they boasted themselves to be of the circumcision; but he calls them the concision: they rent and tore the church of Christ, and cut it to pieces; or contended for an abolished rite, a mere insignificant cutting of the flesh.

III. He describes true Christians, who are indeed the circumcision, the spiritual circumcision, the peculiar people of God, who are in covenant with him, as the Old-Testament Israelites were: *We are the circumcision, who worship God in the spirit, and rejoice in Christ Jesus, and have no confidence in the flesh.* Here are three characters:—1. They worshipped in the spirit, in opposition to the carnal ordinances of the Old Testament, which consist in meats, and drinks, and divers washings, &c. Christianity takes us off from these things, and teaches us to be inward with God in all the duties of religious worship. We must *worship God in spirit,* John iv. 24. The work of religion is to no purpose any further than the heart is employed in it. *Whatsoever we do, we must do it heartily as unto the Lord;* and we must worship God in the strength and grace of the Divine Spirit, which is so peculiar to the gospel state, which is the *ministration of the spirit,* 2 Cor. iii. 8. 2. They *rejoice in Christ Jesus,* and not in the peculiar privileges of the Jewish church, or what answers to them in the Christian church—mere outward enjoyments and performances. They rejoice in their relation to

Christ and interest in him. God made it the duty of the Israelites to rejoice before him in the courts of his house; but now that the substance has come the shadows are done away, and we are to rejoice in Christ Jesus only. 3. They have no *confidence in the flesh,* in those carnal ordinances and outward performances. We must be taken off from trusting in our own bottom, that we may build only on Jesus Christ, the everlasting foundation. Our confidence, as well as our joy, is proper to him.

4 Though I might also have confidence in the flesh. If any other man
thinketh that he hath whereof he
might trust in the flesh, I more: 5
Circumcised the eighth day, of the
stock of Israel, *of* the tribe of Benjamin, a Hebrew of the Hebrews; as
touching the law, a Pharisee; 6 Concerning zeal, persecuting the church;
touching the righteousness which is
in the law, blameless. 7 But what
things were gain to me, those I
counted loss for Christ. 8 Yea
doubtless, and I count all things *but*
loss for the excellency of the knowledge of Christ Jesus my Lord: for
whom I have suffered the loss of all
things, and do count them *but* dung,
that I may win Christ,—

The apostle here proposes himself for an example of trusting in Christ only, and not in his privileges as an Israelite.

I. He shows what he had to boast of as a Jew and a Pharisee. Let none think that the apostle despised these things (as men commonly do) because he had them not himself to glory in. No, if he would have gloried and trusted in the flesh, he had as much cause to do so as any man: *If any other man thinketh that he hath whereof to trust in the flesh, I more, v.* 4. He had as much to boast of as any Jew of them all. 1. His birth-right privileges. He was not a proselyte, but a native Israelite: *of the stock of Israel.* And he was *of the tribe of Benjamin,* in which tribe the temple stood, and which adhered to Judah when all the other tribes revolted. Benjamin was the father's darling, and this was a favourite tribe. *A Hebrew of the Hebrews,* an Israelite on both sides, by father and mother, and from one generation to another; none of his ancestors had matched with Gentiles. 2. He could boast of his relations to the church and the covenant, for he was *circumcised the eighth day;* he had the token of God's covenant in his flesh, and was circumcised the very day which God had appointed. 3. For learning, he was a Pharisee, brought up at the feet of Gamaliel, an eminent doctor of the law: and was a scholar learned in all the learning of the Jews, taught according to the perfect manner of the laws of the fathers, Acts xxii. 3. He was a *Pharisee, the son of a Pharisee* (Acts xxiii. 6), and *after the most strict sect of his religion lived a Pharisee,* Acts xxvi. 5. 4. He had a blameless conversation: *Touching the righteousness which is of the law, blameless:* as far as the Pharisees' exposition of the law went, and as to the mere letter of the law and outward observance of it, he could acquit himself from the breach of it and could not be accused by any. 5. He had been an active man for his religion. As he made a strict profession of it, under the title and character of a Pharisee, so he persecuted those whom he looked upon as enemies to it. *Concerning zeal, persecuting the church.* 6. He showed that he was in good earnest, though he had a zeal without knowledge to direct and govern the exercise of it: *I was zealous towards God, as you all are this day, and I persecuted this way unto the death,* Acts xxii. 3, 4. All this was enough to have made a proud Jew confident, and was stock sufficient to set up with for his justification. But,

II. The apostle tells us here how little account he made of these, in comparison of his interest in Christ and his expectations from him: *But what things were gain to me those have I counted loss for Christ* (*v.* 7); that is, those things which he had counted gain while he was a Pharisee, and which he had before reckoned up, *these he counted loss for Christ.* "I should have reckoned myself an unspeakable loser if, to adhere to them, I had lost my interest in Jesus Christ." He counted them loss; not only insufficient to enrich him, but what would certainly impoverish and ruin him, if he trusted to them, in opposition to Christ. Observe, The apostle did not persuade them to do any thing but what he himself did, to quit any thing but what he had himself quitted, nor venture on any bottom but what he himself had ventured his immortal soul upon.—*Yea doubtless, and I count all things but loss for the excellency of the knowledge of Christ Jesus my Lord, v.* 8. Here the apostle explains himself. 1. He tells us what it was that he was ambitious of and reached after: it was the knowledge of Christ Jesus his Lord, a believing experimental acquaintance with Christ as Lord; not a merely notional and speculative, but a practical and efficacious knowledge of him. So knowledge is sometimes put for faith: *By his knowledge,* or the knowledge of him, *shall my righteous servant justify many,* Isa. liii. 11. And it is the excellency of knowledge. There is an abundant and transcendent excellency in the doctrine of Christ, or the Christian religion above all the knowledge of nature, and improvements of human wisdom; for it is suited to the case of fallen sinners, and furnishes them with all they need and all they can desire and hope for, with all saving wisdom and saving grace. 2. He shows how he had quitted his privileges as a Jew and a Pharisee: *Yea doubtless;* his expression rises with a holy triumph and elevation, ἀλλὰ μὲν οὖν γε καί. There a five particles in the original: *But indeed even also do I count all things but loss.* He had spoken before of *those things,* his Jewish privileges: here he speaks of *all things,* all worldly enjoyments and mere outward privileges whatsoever, things of a like kind or any other kind which could stand in competition with Christ for the throne in his heart, or pretend to merit and desert. There he had said that he did count them but loss; but it might be asked, "Did he continue still in the same mind, did he not repent his renouncing them?" No, now he speaks in the present tense: *Yea doubtless, I do count them but loss.* But it may be said, "It is easy to say so; but what would he do when he came to the trial?" Why he tells us that he had himself practised according to this estimate of the case: *For whom I have suffered the loss of all things.* He had quitted all his honours and advantages, as a Jew and a Pharisee, and submitted to all the disgrace and suffering which attended the profession and preaching of the gospel. When he embarked in the bottom of the Christian religion, he ventured all in it, and suffered the loss of all for the privileges of a Christian. Nay, he not only counted them loss, but dung, σκύβαλα—*offals* thrown to dogs; they are not only less valuable than Christ, but in the highest degree contemptible, when they come in competition with him. Note, The New Testament never speaks of saving grace in any terms of diminution, but on the contrary represents it as the fruits of the divine Spirit and the image of God in the soul of man; as a divine nature, and the seed of God: and faith is called precious faith; and meekness is in the *sight of God of great price,* 1 Pet. iii. 4; 2 Pet. i. 1, &c.

9 And be found in him, not having
mine own righteousness, which is of
the law, but that which is through
the faith of Christ, the righteousness
which is of God by faith: 10 That
I may know him, and the power of
his resurrection, and the fellowship of
his sufferings, being made conformable unto his death; 11 If by any
means I might attain unto the resurrection of the dead. 12 Not as
though I had already attained, either
were already perfect: but I follow
after, if that I may apprehend that
for which also I am apprehended of
Christ Jesus. 13 Brethren, I count
not myself to have apprehended: but
this one thing I do, forgetting those
things which are behind, and reaching
forth unto those things which are
before, 14 I press toward the mark
for the prize of the high calling of
God in Christ Jesus.

We have heard what the apostle renounced; let us now see what he laid hold on, and resolved to cleave to, namely, Christ and heaven. He had his heart on these two great peculiarities of the Christian religion.

I. The apostle had his heart upon Christ as his righteousness. This is illustrated in several instances. 1. He desired to win Christ; and an unspeakable gainer he would reckon himself if he had but an interest in Christ and his righteousness, and if Christ became his Lord and his Saviour: *That I may win him;* as the runner wins the prize, as the sailor makes the port he is bound for. The expression intimates that we have need to strive for him and after him, and that all is little enough to win him. 2. That he *might be found in him* (*v.* 9), as the manslayer was found in the city of refuge, where he was safe from the avenger of blood, Num. xxxv. 25. Or it alludes to a judicial appearance; so we are to be found of our Judge in peace, 2 Pet. iii. 14. We are undone without a righteousness wherein to appear before God, for we are guilty. There is a righteousness provided for us in Jesus Christ, and it is a complete and perfect righteousness. None can have interest or benefit by it but those who come off from confidence in themselves, and are brought heartily to believe in him. "*Not having my own righteousness, which is of the law;* not thinking that my outward observances and good deeds are able to atone for my bad ones, or that by setting the one over against the other I can come to balance accounts with God. No, the righteousness which I depend upon is that *which is through the faith of Christ,* not a legal, but evangelical righteousness: *The righteousness which is of God by faith,* ordained and appointed of God." The Lord Jesus Christ is the Lord our righteousness, Isa. xlv. 24; Jer. xxiii. 6. Had he not been God, he could not have been our righteousness; the transcendent excellence of the divine nature put such a value upon, and such a virtue into, his sufferings, that they became sufficient to satisfy for the sins of the world, and to bring in a righteousness which will be effectual to all that believe. Faith is the ordained means of actual interest and saving benefit in all the purchase of his blood. It is *by faith in his blood,* Rom. iii. 25. 3. That he might know Christ (*v.* 10): *That I may know him, and the power of his resurrection, and the fellowship of his sufferings.* Faith is called knowledge, Isa. liii. 11. Knowing him here is believing in him: it is an experimental knowledge of the *power of his resurrection, and the fellowship of his sufferings,* or feeling the transforming efficacy and virtue of them. Observe, The apostle was as ambitious of being sanctified as he was of being justified. He was as desirous to know the power of Christ's death and resurrection killing sin in him, and raising him up to newness of life, as he was to receive the benefit of Christ's death and resurrection in his justification. 4. That he might be conformable unto him, and this also is meant of his sanctification. We are then made conformable to his death when we die to sin, as Christ died for sin, when we are crucified with Christ, the flesh and affections of it mortified, and the *world is crucified to us,* and *we to the world, by virtue of the cross of Christ.* This is our conformity to his death.

II. The apostle had his hear tupon heaven as his happiness: *If by any means I might attain to the resurrection of the dead, v.* 11.

1. The happiness of heaven is here called the resurrection of the dead, because, though the souls of the faithful, when they depart, are immediately with Christ, yet their happiness will not be complete till the general resurrection of the dead at the last day, when soul and body shall be glorified together. Ἀνάστασις sometimes signifies the future state. This the apostle had his eye upon; this he would attain. There will be a resurrection of the unjust, who shall arise to *shame and everlasting contempt;* and our care must be to escape that: but the joyful and glorious resurrection of saints is called *the resurrection, κατ' ἐξοχὴν—by eminence,* because it is in virtue of Christ's resurrection, as their head and first-fruits; whereas the wicked shall rise only by the power of Christ, as their judge. To the saints it will be indeed a resurrection, a return to bliss, and life, and glory; while the resurrection of the wicked is a rising from the grave, but a return to a second death. It is called the *resurrection of the just,* and the *resurrection of life* (John v. 29), and they are *counted worthy to obtain that world and the resurrection from the dead,* Luke xx. 35.

2. This joyful resurrection the apostle pressed towards. He was willing to do any thing, or suffer any thing, that he might attain that resurrection. The hope and prospect of it carried him with so much courage and constancy through all the difficulties he met with in his work. He speaks as if they were in danger of missing it, and coming short of it. A holy fear of coming short is an excellent means of perseverance. Observe, His care to be found in Christ was in order to his attaining the resurrection of the dead. Paul himself did not hope to attain it through his own merit and righteousness, but through the merit and righteousness of Jesus Christ. "Let me be found in Christ, that I may attain the resurrection of the dead, be found a believer in him, and interested in him by faith," Observe,

(1.) He looks upon himself to be in a state of imperfection and trial: *Not as though I had already attained, or were already perfect, v.* 12. Observe, The best men in the world will readily own their imperfection in the present state. We have not yet attained, are not already perfect; there is still much wanting in all our duties, and graces, and comforts. If Paul had not attained to perfection (who had reached to so high a pitch of holiness), much less have we. Again, *Brethren, I count not myself to have apprehended* (*v.* 13), *οὐ λογίζομαι.* "I make this judgment of the case; I thus reason with myself." Observe, Those who think they have grace enough give proof that they have little enough, or rather that they have none at all; because, wherever there is true grace, there is a desire of more grace, and a pressing towards the perfection of grace.

(2.) What the apostle's actings were under this conviction. Considering that he had not already attained, and had not apprehended, he pressed forward: "*I follow after* (*v.* 12), *διώκω—I pursue* with vigour, as one following after the game. I endeavour to get more grace and do more good, and never think I have done enough: *If that I may apprehend that for which also I am apprehended of Christ Jesus.*" Observe, [1.] Whence our grace comes—from our being apprehended of Christ Jesus. It is not our laying hold of Christ first, but his laying hold of us, which is our happiness and salvation. *We love him because he first loved us,* 1 John iv. 19. Not our keeping hold of Christ, but his keeping hold of us, is our safety. We are *kept by his mighty power through faith unto salvation,* 1 Pet. i. 5. Observe, [2.] What the happiness of heaven is: it is *to apprehend that for which we are apprehended of Christ.* When Christ laid hold of us, it was to bring us to heaven; and to apprehend that for which he apprehended us is to attain the perfection of our bliss. He adds further (*v.* 13): *This one thing I do* (this was his great care and concern), *forgetting those things which are behind, and reaching forth to those things which are before.* There is a sinful forgetting of past sins and past mercies, which ought to be remembered for the exercise of constant repentance and thankfulness to God. But Paul forgot the things which were behind so as not to be content with present measures of grace: he was still for having more and more. So he *reached forth, ἐπεκτεινόμενος—stretched* himself forward, bearing towards his point: it is expressive of a vehement concern.

(3.) The apostle's aim in these actings: *I press towards the mark, for the prize of the high calling of God in Christ Jesus, v.* 14. He pressed towards the mark. As he who runs a race never takes up short of the end, but is still making forwards as fast as he can, so those who have heaven in their eye must still be pressing forward to it in holy desires and hopes, and constant endeavours and preparations. The fitter we grow for heaven the faster we must press towards it Heaven is called here the mark, because it is that which every good Christian has in his eye; as the archer has his eye fixed upon the mark he designs to hit. *For the prize of the high calling.* Observe, A Christian's calling is a high calling: it is from heaven, as its original; and it is to heaven in its tendency. Heaven is the *prize of the high calling; τὸ βραβεῖον—the prize* we fight for, and run for, and wrestle for, what we aim at in all we do, and what will reward all our pains. It is of great use in the Christian course to keep our eye upon heaven. This is proper to give us measures in all our service, and to quicken us every step we take; and it is of God, from whom we are to expect it. *Eternal life is the gift of God* (Rom. vi. 23), but it is in Christ Jesus; through his hand it must come to us, as it is procured for us by him. There is no getting to heaven as our home but by Christ as our way.

15 Let us therefore, as many as be
perfect, be thus minded: and if in
any thing ye be otherwise minded,
God shall reveal even this unto you.
16 Nevertheless, whereto we have
already attained, let us walk by the
same rule, let us mind the same thing.

The apostle, having proposed himself as an example, urges the Philippians to follow it. Let the same mind be in us which was in blessed Paul. We see here how he was minded; let us be like-minded, and set our hearts upon Christ and heaven, as he did. 1. He shows that this was the thing wherein all good Christians were agreed, to make Christ all in all, and set their hearts upon another world. This is that whereto we have all attained. However good Christians may differ in their sentiments about other things, this is what they are agreed in, that Christ is a Christian's all, that to win Christ and to be found in him involve our happiness both here and hereafter. And therefore let us walk by the same rule, and mind the same thing. Having made Christ our all, *to us to live must be Christ.* Let us agree to press towards the mark, and make heaven our end. 2. That this is a good reason why Christians who differ in smaller matters should yet bear with one another, because they are agreed in the main matter: "*If in any thing you be otherwise minded*—if you differ from one another, and are not of the same judgment as to meats and days, and other matters of the Jewish law—yet you must not judge one another, while you all meet now in Christ as your centre, and hope to meet shortly in heaven as your home. As for other matters of difference, lay no great stress upon them, *God shall reveal even this unto you.* Whatever it is wherein you differ, you must wait till God give you a better understanding, which he will do in his due time. In the mean time, *as far as you have attained,* you must go together in the ways of God, join together in all the great things in which you are agreed, and wait for further light in the minor things wherein you differ."

17 Brethren, be followers together
of me, and mark them which walk so
as ye have us for an ensample. 18
(For many walk, of whom I have told
you often, and now tell you even
weeping, *that they are* the enemies of
the cross of Christ: 19 Whose end
is destruction, whose God *is their*
belly, and *whose* glory *is* in their
shame, who mind earthly things.) 20
For our conversation is in heaven;
from whence also we look for the Saviour,
the Lord Jesus Christ: 21
Who shall change our vile body, that
it may be fashioned like unto his
glorious body, according to the working
whereby he is able even to subdue
all things unto himself.

He closes the chapter with warnings and exhortations.

I. He warns them against following the examples of seducers and evil teachers (*v.* 18, 19): *Many walk, of whom I have told you often, and now tell you weeping, that they are the enemies of the cross of Christ.* Observe,

1. There are many called by Christ's name who are enemies to Christ's cross, and the design and intention of it. Their walk is a surer evidence what they are than their profession. By *their fruits you shall know them,* Matt. vii. 20. The apostle warns people against such, (1.) Very frequently: *I have told you often.* We so little heed the warnings given us that we have need to have them repeated. *To write the same things is safe, v.* 1. (2.) Feelingly and affectionately: *I now tell you weeping.* Paul was upon proper occasions a weeping preacher, as Jeremiah was a weeping prophet. Observe, An old sermon may be preached with new affections; what we say often we may say again, if we say it affectionately, and are ourselves under the power of it.

2. He gives us the characters of those who were the enemies of the cross of Christ. (1.) Whose God is their belly. They minded nothing but their sensual appetites. A wretched idol it is, and a scandal for any, but especially for Christians, to sacrifice the favour of God, the peace of their conscience, and their eternal happiness to it. Gluttons and drunkards make a god of their belly, and all their care is to please it and make provision for it. The same observance which good people give to God epicures give to their appetites. Of such he says, *They serve not the Lord Jesus Christ, but their own bellies,* Rom. xvi. 18. (2.) They glory in their shame. They not only sinned, but boasted of it and gloried in

that of which they ought to have been ashamed. Sin is the sinner's shame, especially when it is gloried in. "They value themselves for what is their blemish and reproach." (3.) They mind earthly things. Christ came by his cross to *crucify the world to us and us to the world;* and those who mind earthly things act directly contrary to the cross of Christ, and this great design of it. They relish earthly things, and have no relish of the things which are spiritual and heavenly. They set their hearts and affections on earthly things; they love them, and even dote upon them, and have a confidence and complacency in them. He gives them this character, to show how absurd it would be for Christians to follow the example of such or be led away by them; and, to deter us all from so doing, he reads their doom. (4.) Whose end is destruction. Their way seems pleasant, but death and hell are at the end of it. *What fruit had you then in those things whereof you are now ashamed? For the end of those things is death,* Rom. vi. 21. It is dangerous following them, though it is going down the stream; for, if we choose their way, we have reason to fear their end. Perhaps he alludes to the total destruction of the Jewish nation.

II. He proposes himself and his brethren for an example, in opposition to these evil examples: *Brethren, be followers together of me, and mark those who walk as you have us for an example, v.* 17. Mark them out for your pattern. He explains himself (*v.* 20) by their regard to Christ and heaven: *For our conversation is in heaven.* Observe, Good Christians, even while they are here on earth, have their conversation in heaven. Their *citizenship* is there, *πολίτευμα.* As if he had said, We stand related to that world, and are citizens of the New Jerusalem. This world is not our home, but that is. There our greatest privileges and concerns lie. And, because our citizenship is there, our conversation is there; being related to that world, we keep up a correspondence with it. The life of a Christian is in heaven, where his head is, and his home is, and where he hopes to be shortly; he *sets his affections upon things above;* and where his heart is there will his conversation be. The apostle had pressed them to follow him and other ministers of Christ: "Why," might they say, "you are a company of poor, despised, persecuted people, who make no figure, and pretend to no advantages in the world; who will follow you?" "Nay," says he, "but our conversation is in heaven. We have a near relation and a great pretension to the other world, and are not so mean and despicable as we are represented." It is good having fellowship with those who have fellowship with Christ, and conversation with those whose conversation is in heaven.

1. Because we look for the Saviour from heaven (*v.* 20): *Whence also we look for the Saviour, the Lord Jesus Christ.* He is not here, he has ascended, he has entered within the veil for us; and we expect his second coming thence, to gather in all the citizens of that New Jerusalem to himself.

2. Because at the second coming of Christ we expect to be happy and glorified there. There is good reason to have our conversation in heaven, not only because Christ is now there, but because we hope to be there shortly: *Who shall change our vile bodies, that they may be fashioned like unto his glorious body, v.* 21. There is a glory reserved for the bodies of the saints, which they will be instated in at the resurrection. The body is now at the best a *vile body, τὸ σῶμα τῆς ταπεινώσεως ἡμῶν—the body of our humiliation:* it has its rise and origin from the earth, it is supported out of the earth, and is subject to many diseases and to death at last. Besides, it is often the occasion and instrument of much sin, which is called the *body of this death,* Rom. vii. 24. Or it may be understood of its vileness when it lies in the grave; at the resurrection it will be found a vile body, resolved into rottenness and dust; the *dust will return to the earth as it was,* Eccl. xii. 7. But it will be made a glorious body; and not only raised again to life, but raised to great advantage. Observe, (1.) The sample of this change, and that is, the glorious body of Christ; when he was transfigured upon the mount, *his face did shine as the sun, and his raiment was white as the light,* Matt. xvii. 2. He went to heaven clothed with a body, that he might take possession of the inheritance in our nature, and be not only the *first-born from the dead,* but the *first-born* of the *children of the resurrection.* We shall be *conformed to the image of his Son, that he may be the first-born among many brethren,* Rom. viii. 29. (2.) The power by which this change will be wrought: *According to the working whereby he is able even to subdue all things unto himself.* There is an efficacy of power, an *exceeding greatness of power,* and the *working of mighty power,* Eph. i. 19. It is matter of comfort to us that he can subdue all things to himself, and sooner or later will bring over all into his interest And the resurrection will be wrought by this power. *I will raise him up at the last day,* John vi. 44. Let this confirm our faith of the resurrection, that we not only have the scriptures, which assure us it shall be, but we *know the power of God,* which can effect it, Matt. xxii. 29. As Christ's resurrection was a glorious instance of the divine power, and therefore *he is declared to be the Son of God with power, by the resurrection from the dead* (Rom. i. 4), so will our resurrection be: and his resurrection is a standing evidence, as well as pattern, of ours. And then all the enemies of the Redeemer's kingdom will be completely conquered. Not only he *who had the power of death,* that is, *the devil* (Heb. ii. 14), but the *last enemy, shall be destroyed,* that is, *death,* 1 Cor. xv. 26, *shall be swallowed up in victory, v.* 54

CHAP IV.

Exhortations to several Christian duties, as stedfastness, unanimity, joy, &c. ver. 1—9. The apostle's grateful acknowledgments of the Philippians' kindness to him, with expressions of his own content, and desire of their good, ver. 10—19. He concludes the epistle with praise, salutations, and blessing, ver. 20—23.

THEREFORE, my brethren,
dearly beloved and longed for,
my joy and crown, so stand fast in
the Lord, *my* dearly beloved. 2 I
beseech Euodias, and beseech Syntyche, that they be of the same mind
in the Lord. 3 And I entreat thee
also, true yokefellow, help those women which laboured with me in the
gospel, with Clement also, and *with*
other my fellowlabourers, whose names
are in the book of life. 4 Rejoice in
the Lord alway: *and* again I say, Rejoice. 5 Let your moderation be
known unto all men. The Lord *is* at
hand. 6 Be careful for nothing; but
in every thing by prayer and supplication with thanksgiving let your requests be made known unto God. 7
And the peace of God, which passeth
all understanding, shall keep your
hearts and minds through Christ
Jesus. 8 Finally, brethren, whatsoever things are true, whatsoever
things *are* honest, whatsoever things
are just, whatsoever things *are* pure,
whatsoever things *are* lovely, whatsoever things *are* of good report; if
there be any virtue, and if *there be*
any praise, think on these things. 9
Those things, which ye have both
learned, and received, and heard, and
seen in me, do: and the God of peace
shall be with you.

The apostle begins the chapter with exhortations to divers Christian duties.

I. To stedfastness in our Christian profession, *v.* 1. It is inferred from the close of the foregoing chapter: *Therefore stand fast,* &c. Seeing our *conversation is in heaven,* and we look for the Saviour to come thence and fetch us thither, *therefore let us stand fast.* Note, The believing hope and prospect of eternal life should engage us to be steady, even, and constant, in our Christian course. Observe here,

1. The compellations are very endearing: *My brethren, dearly beloved and longed for, my joy and crown;* and again, *My dearly beloved.* Thus he expresses the pleasure he took in them, the kindness he had for them, to convey his exhortations to them with so much the greater advantage. He looked upon them as his brethren, though he was a great apostle. *All we are brethren.* There is difference of gifts, graces, and attainments, yet, being renewed by the same Spirit, after the same image, we are brethren; as the children of the same parents, though of different ages, statures, and complexions. Being brethren, (1.) He loved them, and loved them dearly: *Dearly beloved;* and again, *My dearly beloved.* Warm affections become ministers and Christians towards one another. Brotherly love must always go along with the brotherly relation. (2.) He loved them and longed for them, longed to see them and hear from them, longed for their welfare and was earnestly desirous of it. *I long after you all in the bowels of Jesus Christ, ch.* i. 8. (3.) He loved them and rejoiced in them. They were his joy; he had no greater joy than to hear of their spiritual health and prosperity. *I rejoiced greatly that I found of thy children walking in the truth,* 2 John 4; 3 John 4. (4.) He loved them and gloried in them. They were his crown as well as his joy. Never was proud ambitious man more pleased with the ensigns of honour than Paul was with the evidences of the sincerity of their faith and obedience. All this is to prepare his way to greater regard.

2. The exhortation itself: *So stand fast in the Lord.* Being in Christ, they must stand fast in him, be even and steady in their walk with him, and close and constant unto the end. Or, To *stand fast in the Lord* is to stand fast in his strength and by his grace; not trusting in ourselves, and disclaiming any sufficiency of our own. We must be *strong in the Lord, and in the power of his might,* Eph. vi. 10. "So stand fast, so as you have done hitherto, stand fast unto the end, so as you are my beloved, and my joy and crown; so stand fast as those in whose welfare and perseverance I am so nearly interested and concerned."

II. He exhorts them to unanimity and mutual assistance (*v.* 2, 3): *I beseech Euodias and Syntyche that they be of the same mind in the Lord.* This is directed to some particular persons. Sometimes there is need of applying the general precepts of the gospel to particular persons and cases. Euodias and Syntyche, it seems, were at variance, either one with the other or with the church; either upon a civil account (it may be they were engaged in a law-suit) or upon a religious account—it may be they were of different opinions and sentiments. "Pray," says he, "desire them from me to be of the same mind in the Lord, to keep the peace and live in love, to be of the same mind one with another, not thwarting and contradicting, and to be of the same mind with the rest of the church, not acting in opposition to them." Then he exhorts to mutual assistance (*v.* 3), and this exhortation he directs to particular persons: *I entreat thee also, true yoke-fellow.* Who this person was whom he calls true yoke-fellow is uncertain. Some think Epaphroditus, who is supposed to have been one of the pastors of the church of the Philippians. Others think it was some eminently good woman, perhaps Paul's wife, because he exhorts his yoke-fellow to *help the women who laboured with him.* Whoever was the yoke-fellow with the apostle must be a yoke-fellow too with his friends. It seems, there were women who laboured with Paul in the gospel; not in the public ministry (for the apostle expressly forbids that, 1 Tim. ii. 12, *I suffer not a woman to teach),* but by entertaining the ministers, visiting the sick, instructing the ignorant, convincing the erroneous. Thus women may be helpful to ministers in the work of the gospel. Now, says the apostle, *do thou help them.* Those who help others should be helped themselves when there is occasion. "*Help them,* that is, join with them, strengthen their hands, encourage them in their difficulties."—*With Clement also, and other my fellow-labourers.* Paul had a kindness for all his fellow-labourers; and, as he had found the benefit of their assistance, he concluded how comfortable it would be to them to have the assistance of others. Of his fellow-labourers he says, *Whose names are in the book of life;* either they were chosen of God from all eternity, or registered and enrolled in the corporation and society to which the privilege of eternal life belongs, alluding to the custom among the Jews and Gentiles of registering the inhabitants or the freemen of the city. So we read of their *names being written in heaven* (Luke x. 20), *not blotting his name out of the book of life* (Rev. iii. 5), and of *those who are written in the Lamb's book of life,* Rev. xxi. 27. Observe, There is a book of life; there are names in that book and not characters and conditions only. We cannot search into that book, or know whose names are written there; but we may, in a judgment of charity, conclude that those who labour in the gospel, and are faithful to the interest of Christ and souls, have their names in the book of life.

III. He exhorts to holy joy and delight in God: *Rejoice in the Lord always, and again I say, Rejoice, v.* 4. All our joy must terminate in God; and our thoughts of God must be delightful thoughts. *Delight thyself in the Lord* (Ps. xxxvii 4), *in the multitude of our thoughts within us* (grievous and afflicting thoughts) *his comforts delight our souls* (Ps. xciv. 19), and our *meditation of him is sweet,* Ps. civ. 34. Observe, It is our duty and privilege to rejoice in God, and to rejoice in him always; at all times, in all conditions; even when we suffer for him, or are afflicted by him. We must not think the worse of him or of his ways for the hardships we meet with in his service. There is enough in God to furnish us with matter of joy in the worst circumstance on earth. He had said it before (*ch.* iii. 1): *Finally, my brethren, rejoice in the Lord.* Here he says it again, *Rejoice in the Lord always; and again I say, Rejoice.* Joy in God is a duty of great consequence in the Christian life; and Christians need to be again and again called to it. If good men have not a continual feast, it is their own fault.

IV. We are here exhorted to candour and gentleness, and good temper towards our brethren: "*Let your moderation be known to all men, v.* 5. In things indifferent do not run into extremes; avoid bigotry and animosity; judge charitably concerning one another." The word τὸ ἐπιεικὲς signifies a good disposition towards other men; and this moderation is explained, Rom. xiv. Some understand it of the patient bearing of afflictions, or the sober enjoyment of worldly good; and so it well agrees with the following verse. The reason is, *the Lord is at hand.* The consideration of our Master's approach, and our final account, should keep us from smiting our fellow-servants, support us under present sufferings, and moderate our affections to outward good. "He will take vengeance on your enemies, and reward your patience."

V. Here is a caution against disquieting perplexing care (*v.* 6): *Be careful for nothing*—μηδὲν μεριμνᾶτε: the same expression with that Matt vi. 25, *Take no thought for your life;* that is, avoid anxious care and distracting thought in the wants and difficulties of life. Observe, It is the duty and interest of Christians to live without care. There is a care of diligence which is our duty, and consists in a wise forecast and due concern; but there is a care of diffidence and distrust which is our sin and folly, and which only perplexes and distracts the mind. "*Be careful for nothing,* so as by your care to distrust God, and unfit yourselves for his service."

VI. As a sovereign antidote against perplexing care he recommends to us constant prayer: *In every thing by prayer and supplication, with thanksgiving, let your requests be made known to God.* Observe, 1. We must not only keep up stated times for prayer, but we must pray upon every particular emergency: *In every thing by prayer.* When any thing burdens our spirits, we must ease our minds by prayer; when our affairs are perplexed or distressed, we must seek direction and support. 2. We must join thanksgiving with our prayers and supplications. We must not only seek supplies of good, but own receipts of mercy. Grateful acknowledgments of what we have argue a right disposition of mind, and are prevailing motives for further blessings. 3. Prayer is the offering up of our desires to God, or making them known to him: *Let your requests be made known to God* Not that God needs to be told either our wants or desires; for he knows them better than we can tell him: but he will know them from us, and have us show our regards and concern, express our value of the mercy and sense of our dependence on him. 4. The effect of this will be the *peace of God keeping our hearts, v.* 7. The *peace of God,* that is, the comfortable sense of our reconciliation to God and interest in his favour, and the hope of the heavenly blessedness, and enjoyment of God hereafter, *which passeth all understanding,* is a greater good than can be sufficiently valued or duly expressed. *It has not entered into the heart of man,* 1 Cor. ii. 9. This peace will *keep our hearts and minds through Christ Jesus;* it will keep us from sinning under our troubles, and from sinking under them; keep us calm and sedate, without discomposure of passion, and with inward satisfaction. *Thou wilt keep him in perfect peace whose mind is stayed on thee,* Isa. xxvi. 3.

VII. We are exhorted to get and keep a good name, a name for good things with God and good men: *Whatsoever things are true and honest* (*v.* 8), a regard to truth in our words and engagements, and to decency and becomingness in our behaviour, suitable to our circumstances and condition of life. Whatsoever things are *just and pure,*—agreeable to the rules of justice and righteousness in all our dealings with men, and without the impurity or mixture of sin. Whatsoever things are *lovely and of good report,* that is, amiable; that will render us beloved, and make us well spoken of, as well as well thought of, by others. *If there is any virtue, if there is any praise*—any thing really virtuous of any kind and worthy of commendation. Observe, 1. The apostle would have the Christians learn any thing which was good of their heathen neighbours: "*If there be any virtue, think of these things*—imitate them in what is truly excellent among them, and let not them outdo you in any instance of goodness." We should not be ashamed to learn any good thing of bad men, or those who have not our advantages. 2. Virtue has its praise, and will have. We should walk in all the ways of virtue, and abide therein; and then, whether our praise be of men or no, it will be of God, Rom. ii. 29.

In these things he proposes himself to them for an example (*v.* 9): *Those things which you have learned, and received, and heard and seen in me, do.* Observe, Paul's doctrine and life were of a piece. What they saw in him was the same thing with what they heard from him. He could propose himself as well as his doctrine to their imitation. It gives a great force to what we say to others when we can appeal to what they have seen in us. And this is the way to have the *God of peace with us*—to keep close to our duty to him. The *Lord is with us while we are with him.*

10 But I rejoiced in the Lord greatly, that now at the last your care of me hath flourished again; wherein ye were also careful, but ye lacked opportunity. 11 Not that I speak in respect of want: for I have learned, in whatsoever state I am, *therewith* to be content. 12 I know both how to be abased, and I know how to abound: every where and in all things I am instructed both to be full and to be hungry, both to abound and to suffer need. 13 I can do all things through Christ which strengtheneth me. 14 Notwithstanding ye have well done, that ye did communicate with my affliction. 15 Now ye Philippians know also, that in the beginning of the gospel, when I departed from Macedonia, no church communicated with me as concerning giving and receiving, but ye only. 16 For even in Thessalonica ye sent once and again unto my necessity. 17 Not because I desire a gift: but I desire fruit that may abound to your account. 18 But I have all, and abound: I am full, having received of Epaphroditus the things *which were sent* from you, an odour of a sweet smell, a sacrifice acceptable, wellpleasing to God. 19 But my God shall supply all your need according to his riches in glory by Christ Jesus.

In these verses we have the thankful grateful acknowledgment which the apostle makes of the kindness of the Philippians in sending him a present for his support, now that he was a prisoner at Rome. And here,

I. He takes occasion to acknowledge their former kindnesses to him, and to make mention of them, *v.* 15, 16. Paul had a grateful spirit; for, though what his friends did for him was nothing in comparison of what he deserved from them and the obligations he had laid upon them, yet he speaks of their kindness as if it had been a piece of generous charity, when it was really far short of a just debt. If they had each of them contributed half their estates to him, they had not given him too much, since they *owed to him even their own souls;* and yet, when they send a small present to him, how kindly does he take it, how thankfully does he mention it, even in this epistle which was to be left upon record, and read in the churches, through all ages; so that wherever this epistle shall be read there shall this which they did to Paul be told for a memorial of them. Surely never was present so well repaid. He reminds them that *in the beginning of the gospel no church communicated with him as to giving and receiving but they only, v.* 15. They not only maintained him comfortably while he was with them, but when *he departed from Macedonia* they sent tokens of their kindness after him; and this when no other church did so. None besides sent after him of their carnal things, in consideration of what they had reaped of his spiritual things. In works of charity, we are ready to ask what other people do. But the church of the Philippians never considered that. It redounded so much the more to their honour that they were the only church who were thus just and generous. *Even in Thessalonica* (after he had departed from Macedonia) *you sent once and again to my necessity, v.* 16. Observe, 1. It was but little which they sent; they sent only to his necessity, just such things as he had need of; perhaps it was according to their ability, and he did not desire superfluities nor dainties. 2. It is an excellent thing to see those to whom God has abounded in the gifts of his grace abounding in grateful returns to his people and ministers, according to their own ability and their necessity: *You sent once and again.* Many people make it an excuse for their charity that they have given once; why should the charge come upon them again? But the Philippians sent once and again; they often relieved and refreshed him in his necessities. He makes this mention of their former kindness, not only out of gratitude, but for their encouragement.

II. He excuses their neglect of late. It seems, for some time they had not sent to enquire after him, or sent him any present; but *now at the last their care of him flourished again* (*v.* 10), like a tree in the spring, which seemed all the winter to be quite dead. Now, in conformity to the example of his great Master, instead of upbraiding them for their neglect, he makes an excuse for them: *Wherein you were also careful, but you lacked opportunity.* How could they lack opportunity, if they had been resolved upon it? They might have sent a messenger on purpose. But the apostle is willing to suppose, in favour of them, that they would have done it if a fair opportunity had offered. How contrary is this to the behaviour of many to their friends, by whom neglects which really are excusable are resented very heinously, when Paul excused that which he had reason enough to resent.

III. He commends their present liberality: *Notwithstanding, you have well done that you did communicate with my affliction, v.* 14. It is a good work to succour and help a good minister in trouble. Here see what is the nature of true Christian sympathy; not only to be concerned for our friends in their troubles, but to do what we can to help them. They *communicated with his affliction,* in relieving him under it. He who says, *Be you warmed, be you filled, and giveth not those things they have need of, what doth it profit?* Jam. ii. 16. He rejoiced greatly in it (*v.* 10), because it was an evidence of their affection to him and the success of his ministry among them. When the fruit of their charity abounded towards the apostle, it appeared that the fruit of his ministry abounded among them.

IV. He takes care to obviate the bad use some might make of his taking so much notice of what was sent him. It did not proceed either from discontent and distrust (*v.* 11) or from covetousness and love of the world, *v.* 12. 1. It did not come from discontent, or distrust of Providence: *Not that I speak in respect of want* (*v.* 11); not in respect of any want he felt, nor of any want he feared. As to the former, he was content with the little he had, and that satisfied him; as to the latter, he depended upon the providence of God to provide for him from day to day, and that satisfied him: so that he did not speak in respect of want any way. *For I have learned, in whatsoever state I am, therewith to be content.* We have here an account of Paul's learning, not that which he got at the feet of Gamaliel, but that which he got at the feet of Christ. He had learnt to be content; and that was the lesson he had as much need to learn as most men, considering the hardships and sufferings with which he was exercised. He was in bonds, and imprisonments, and necessities, often; but in all he had learnt to be content, that is, to bring his mind to his condition, and make the best of it.—*I know both how to be abased and I know how to abound, v.* 12. This is a special act of grace, to accommodate ourselves to every condition of life, and carry an equal temper of mind through all the varieties of our state. (1.) To accommodate ourselves to an afflicted condition—to know how to be abased, how to be hungry, how to suffer want, so as not to be overcome by the temptations of it, either to lose our comfort in God or distrust his providence, or to take any indirect course for our own supply. (2.) To a prosperous condition—to know how to abound, how to be full, so as not to be proud, or secure, or luxurious. And this is as hard a lesson as the other; for the temptations of fulness and prosperity are not less than those of affliction and want. But how must we learn it? *I can do all things through Christ who strengthens me, v.* 13. We have need of strength from Christ, to enable us to perform not only those duties which are purely Christian, but even those which are the fruit of moral virtue. We need his strength to teach us to be content in every condition. The apostle had seemed to boast of himself, and of his own strength: *I know how to be abased* (*v.* 12); but here he transfers all the praise to Christ. "What do I talk of *knowing how to be abased, and how to abound?* It is only *through Christ who strengthens me* that I can do it, not in my own strength." So we are required to be *strong in the Lord, and in the power of his might* (Eph. vi. 10), and to be *strong in the grace which is in Christ Jesus* (2 Tim. ii. 1); and we are *strengthened with might by his Spirit in the inner man,* Eph. iii. 16. The word in the original is a participle of the present tense, ἐν τῷ ἐνδυναμοῦντί με Χριστῷ, and denotes a present and continued act; as if he had said, "Through Christ, who is strengthening me, and does continually strengthen me; it is by his constant and renewed strength I am enabled to act in every thing; I wholly depend upon him for all my spiritual power." 2. It did not come from covetousness, or an affection to worldly wealth: "*Not because I desired a gift* (*v.* 17); that is, I welcome your kindness, not because it adds to my enjoyments, but because it adds to your account." He desired not so much for his own sake, but theirs: "*I desire fruit that may abound to your account*, that is, that you may be enabled to make such a good use of your worldly possessions that you may give an account of them with joy. It is not with any design to draw more from you, but to encourage you to such an exercise of beneficence as will meet with a glorious reward hereafter. "For my part," says he, "*I have all, and abound*, *v.* 18. What can a man desire more than enough? I do not desire a gift for the gift's sake, for *I have all, and abound.*" They sent him a small token, and he desired no more; he was not solicitous for a present superfluity, or a future supply: *I am full, having received from Epaphroditus the things which were sent by you.* Note, A good man will soon have enough of this world; not only of living in it, but of receiving from it. A covetous worldling, if he has ever so much, would still have more; but a heavenly Christian, though he has little, has enough.

V. The apostle assures them that God did accept, and would recompense, their kindness to him. 1. He did accept it: *It is an odour of a sweet smell, a sacrifice acceptable, well-pleasing to God.* Not a sacrifice of atonement, for none makes atonement for sin but Christ; but a sacrifice of acknowledgment, and *well-pleasing to God.* It was more acceptable to God as it was the fruit of their grace than it was to Paul as it was the supply of his want. *With such sacrifices God is well pleased*, Heb. xiii. 16. 2. He would recompense it: *But my God shall supply all your wants according to his riches in glory by Christ Jesus, v.* 19. He does as it were draw a bill upon the exchequer in heaven, and leaves it to God to make them amends for the kindness they had shown him. "He shall do it, not only as your God, but as my God, who takes what is done to me as done to himself. You supplied my needs, according to your poverty; and he shall supply yours, according to his riches." But still it is by Christ Jesus; through him we have grace to do that which is good, and through him we must expect the reward of it. Not of debt, but of grace; for the more we do for God the more we are indebted to him, because we receive the more from him.

20 Now unto God and our Father
be glory for ever and ever. Amen.
21 Salute every saint in Christ Jesus.
The brethren which are with me greet
you. 22 All the saints salute you,
chiefly they that are of Cæsar's
household. 23 The grace of our
Lord Jesus Christ *be* with you all.
Amen.

The apostle concludes the epistle in these verses,

1 With praises to God: *Now unto God and our Father be glory for ever and ever, Amen, v.* 20. Observe, (1.) God is to be considered by us as our Father: *Now unto God and our Father.* It is a great condescension and favour in God to own the relation of Father to sinners, and allow us to say to him, *Our Father;* and it is a title peculiar to the gospel dispensation. It is also a great privilege and encouragement to us to consider him as our Father, as one so nearly related and who bears so tender an affection towards us. We should look upon God, under all our weaknesses and fears, not as a tyrant or an enemy, but as a Father, who is disposed to pity us and help us. (2.) We must ascribe glory to God as a Father, the glory of his own excellence and of all his mercy unto us. We must thankfully own the receipt of all from him, and give the praise of all to him. And our praise must be constant and perpetual; it must be *glory for ever and ever.*

2. With salutations to his friends at Philippi: "*Salute every saint in Christ Jesus* (*v.* 21); give my hearty love to all the Christians in your parts." He desires remembrances not only to the bishops and deacons, and the church in general, but to every particular saint. Paul had a kind affection to all good Christians.

3. He sends salutations from those who were at Rome: *The brethren who are with me salute you;* the *ministers*, and all the saints here, send their affectionate remembrances to you. *Chiefly those who are of Cæsar's household;* the Christian converts who belonged to the emperor's court." Observe, (1.) There were saints in Cæsar's household. Though Paul was imprisoned at Rome, for preaching the gospel, by the emperor's command, yet there were some Christians in his own family. The gospel early obtained among some of the rich and great. Perhaps the apostle fared the better, and received some favour, by means of his friends at court. (2.) *Chiefly those*, &c. Observe, They, being bred at court, were more complaisant than the rest. See what an ornament to religion sanctified civility is.

4. The apostolical benediction, as usual: "*The grace of our Lord Jesus Christ be with you all, Amen.* The free favour and good will of Christ be your portion and happiness."

AN

EXPOSITION,

WITH PRACTICAL OBSERVATIONS,

OF THE EPISTLE OF ST. PAUL TO

THE COLOSSIANS.

Colosse was a considerable city of Phrygia, and probably not far from Laodicea and Hierapolis; we find these mentioned together, *ch.* iv. 13. It is now buried in ruins, and the memory of it chiefly preserved in this epistle. The design of the epistle is to warn them of the danger of the Jewish zealots, who pressed the necessity of observing the ceremonial law; and to fortify them against the mixture of the Gentile philosophy with their Christian principles. He professes a great satisfaction in their stedfastness and constancy, and encourages them to perseverance. It was written about the same time with the epistles to the Ephesians and Philippians, A. D. 62, and in the same place, while he was now a prisoner at Rome. He was not idle in his confinement, and the word of God was not bound.

This epistle, like that to the Romans, was written to those he had never seen, nor had any personal acquaintance with. The church planted at Colosse was not by Paul's ministry, but by the ministry of Epaphras or Epaphroditus, an evangelist, one whom he delegated to preach the gospel among the Gentiles; and yet, I. There was a flourishing church at Colosse, and one which was eminent and famous among the churches. One would have thought none would have come to be flourishing churches but those which Paul himself had planted; but here was a flourishing church planted by Epaphras. God is sometimes pleased to make use of the ministry of those who are of less note, and lower gifts, for doing great service to his church. God uses what hands he pleases, and is not tied to those of note, that the *excellence of the power may appear to be of God and not of men*, 2 Cor. iv. 7. II. Though Paul had not the planting of this church, yet he did not therefore neglect it; nor, in writing his epistles, does he make any difference between that and other churches. The Colossians, who were converted by the ministry of Epaphras, were as dear to him, and he was as much concerned for their welfare, as the Philippians, or any others who were converted by his ministry. Thus he put an honour upon an inferior minister, and teaches us not to be selfish, nor think all that honour lost which goes beside ourselves. We learn, in his example, not to think it a disparagement to us to water what others have planted, or build upon the foundation which others have laid: as he himself, as a *wise master-builder, laid the foundation, and another built thereon*, 1 Cor. iii. 10.

CHAP. I.

We have here, I. The inscription, as usual, ver. 1, 2. II. His thanksgiving to God for what he had heard concerning them—their faith, love, and hope, ver. 3—8. III. His prayer for their knowledge, fruitfulness, and strength, ver. 9—11. IV. An admirable summary of the Christian doctrine concerning the operation of the Spirit, the person of the Redeemer, the work of redemption, and the preaching of it in the gospel, ver. 12—29.

PAUL, an apostle of Jesus Christ by the will of God, and Timotheus *our* brother, 2 To the saints and faithful brethren in Christ which are at Colosse: Grace *be* unto you, and peace, from God our Father and the Lord Jesus Christ.

I. The inscription of this epistle is much the same with the rest; only it is observable that, 1. He calls himself an *apostle of Jesus Christ by the will of God.* An apostle is a prime-minister in the kingdom of Christ, immediately called by Christ, and extraordinarily qualified; his work was peculiarly to plant the Christian church, and confirm the Christian doctrine. He attributes this not to his own merit, strength, or sufficiency; but to the free grace and good-will of God. He thought himself engaged to do his utmost, as an apostle, because he was made so by the will of God. 2. He joins Timothy in commission with himself, which is another instance of his humility; and, though he elsewhere calls him his son (2 Tim. ii. 1), yet here he calls him his brother, which is an example to the elder and more eminent ministers to look upon the younger and more obscure as their brethren, and to treat them accordingly with kindness and respect. 3. He calls the Christians at Colosse *saints, and faithful brethren in Christ.* As all good ministers, so all good Christians, are brethren one to another, who stand in a near relation and owe a mutual love. Towards God they must be saints, consecrated to his honour and sanctified by his grace, bearing his image and aiming at his glory. And in both these, as saints to God and as brethren to one another, they must be faithful. Faithfulness runs through every character and relation of the Christian life, and is the crown and glory of them all.

II. The apostolical benediction is the same as usual: *Grace be unto you, and peace, from God our Father, and the Lord Jesus Christ.* He wishes them *grace and peace,* the free favour of God and all the blessed fruits of it; every kind of spiritual blessings, and that *from God our Father, and the Lord Jesus Christ;* jointly from both, and distinctly from each; as in the former epistle.

3 We give thanks to God and
the Father of our Lord Jesus Christ,
praying always for you, 4 Since we
heard of your faith in Christ Jesus,
and of the love *which ye have* to all
the saints, 5 For the hope which is
laid up for you in heaven, whereof ye
heard before in the word of the truth
of the gospel; 6 Which is come
unto you, as *it is* in all the world;
and bringeth forth fruit, as *it doth*
also in you, since the day ye heard
of it, and knew the grace of God in
truth: 7 As ye also learned of Epaphras our dear fellowservant, who is
for you a faithful minister of Christ;
8 Who also declared unto us your
love in the Spirit.

Here he proceeds to the body of the epistle, and begins with thanksgiving to God for what he had heard concerning them, though he had no personal acquaintance with them, and knew their state and character only by the reports of others.

I. He gave thanks to God for them, that they had embraced the gospel of Christ, and given proofs of their fidelity to him. Observe, In his prayers for them he gave thanks for them. Thanksgiving ought to be a part of every prayer; and whatever is the matter of our rejoicing ought to be the matter of our thanksgiving. Observe, 1. Whom he gives thanks to: *To God, even the Father of our Lord Jesus Christ.* In our thanksgiving we must have an eye to God as God (he is the object of thanksgiving as well as prayer), and as the Father of our Lord Jesus Christ, in and through whom all good comes to us. He is the Father of our Lord Jesus Christ as well as our Father; and it is matter of encouragement, in all our addresses to God, that we can look to him as Christ's Father and our Father, as his God and our God, John xx. 17. Observe, 2. What he gives thanks to God for—for the graces of God in them, which were evidences of the grace of God towards them: *Since we heard of your faith in Christ Jesus, and of the love you have to all the saints; for the hope which is laid up for you in heaven, v.* 4, 5. Faith, hope, and love, are the three principal graces in the Christian life, and proper matter of our prayer and thanksgiving. (1.) He gives thanks for their faith in Christ Jesus, that they were brought to believe in him, and take upon them the profession of his religion, and venture their souls upon his undertaking. (2.) For their love. Besides the general love which is due to all men, there is a particular love owing to the saints, or those who are of the Christian *brotherhood,* 1 Pet. ii. 17. We must love all the saints, bear an extensive kindness and good-will to good men, notwithstanding smaller points of difference, and many real weaknesses. Some understand it of their charity to the saints in necessity, which is one branch and evidence of Christian love. (3.) For their hope: *The hope which is laid up for you in heaven, v.* 5. The happiness of heaven is called their hope, because it is the *thing hoped for, looking for the blessed hope,* Tit. ii. 13. What is laid out upon believers in this world is much; but what is laid up for them in heaven is much more. And we have reason to give thanks to God for the hope of heaven which good Christians have, or their well-grounded expectation of the future glory. Their faith in Christ, and love to the saints, had an eye to the *hope laid up for them in heaven.* The more we fix our hopes on the recompence of reward in the other world, the more free and liberal shall we be of our earthly treasure upon all occasions of doing good.

II. Having blessed God for these graces, he blesses God for the means of grace which they enjoyed: *Wherein you heard before in the word of the truth of the gospel.* They had heard in the word of the truth of the gospel concerning this *hope laid up for them in heaven.* Observe, 1. The gospel is the word of truth, and what we may safely venture our immortal souls upon: it proceeds from the God of truth and the Spirit of truth, and is a faithful saying. He calls it *the grace of God in truth, v.* 6. 2. It is a great mercy to hear this word of truth; for the great thing we learn from it is the happiness of heaven. Eternal life is brought to light by the gospel, 2 Tim. i. 10. They heard of the hope laid up in heaven in the word of the truth of the gospel. "*Which has come unto you, as it hath to all the world, and bringeth forth fruit, as it doth also in you, v.* 6. This gospel is preached and brings forth fruit in other nations; it has come to you, *as it hath to all the world,* according to the commission, *Go preach the gospel in all the nations,* and to *every creature.*" Observe, (1.) All who hear the word of the gospel ought to bring forth the fruit of the gospel, that is, be obedient to it, and have their principles and lives formed according to it. This was the doctrine first preached: *Bring forth therefore fruits meet for repentance,* Matt. iii. 8. And our Lord says, *If you know these things, happy are you if you do them,* John xiii. 17. Observe, (2.) Wherever the gospel comes, it will bring forth fruit to the honour and glory of God: *It bringeth forth fruit, as it doth also in you.* We mistake, if we think to monopolise the comforts and benefits of the gospel to ourselves. Does the gospel bring forth fruit in us? So it does in others.

III. He takes this occasion to mention the minister by whom they believed (*v.* 7, 8): *As you also learned of Epaphras, our dear fellow-servant, who is for you a faithful minister of Christ.* He mentions him with great respect, to engage their love to him. 1. He calls him his fellow-servant, to signify not only that they served the same Master, but that they were engaged in the same work. They were fellow-labourers in the work of the Lord, though one was an apostle and the other an ordinary minister. 2. He calls him his dear fellow-servant: all the servants of Christ ought to love one another, and it is an endearing consideration that they are engaged in the same service. 3. He represents him as one who was a faithful minister of Christ to them, who discharged his trust and fulfilled his ministry among them. Observe, Christ is our proper Master, and we are his ministers. He does not say who is your minister; but *who is the minister of Christ for you.* It is by his authority and appointment, though for the people's service. 4. He represents him as one who gave them a good word: *Who also declared unto us your love in the Spirit, v.* 8. He recommends him to their affection, from the good report he made of their sincere love to Christ and all his members, which was wrought in them by the Spirit, and is agreeable to the spirit of the gospel. Faithful ministers are glad to be able to speak well of their people.

9 For this cause we also, since the
day we heard *it*, do not cease to pray
for you, and to desire that ye might
be filled with the knowledge of his
will in all wisdom and spiritual understanding; 10 That ye might walk
worthy of the Lord unto all pleasing,
being fruitful in every good work, and
increasing in the knowledge of God;
11 Strengthened with all might according to his glorious power, unto
all patience and longsuffering with
joyfulness;

The apostle proceeds in these verses to pray for them. He heard that they were good, and he prayed that they might be better. He was constant in this prayer: *We do not cease to pray for you.* It may be he could hear of them but seldom, but he constantly prayed for them.—*And desire that you may be filled with the knowledge,* &c. Observe what it is that he begs of God for them,

I. That they might be knowing intelligent Christians: *filled with the knowledge of his will, in all wisdom and spiritual understanding.* Observe, 1. The knowledge of our duty is the best knowledge. A mere empty notion of the greatest truths is insignificant. Our knowledge of the will of God must be always practical: we must know it, in order to do it. 2. Our knowledge is then a blessing indeed when it is in wisdom, when we know how to apply our general knowledge to our particular occasions, and to suit it to all emergencies. 3. Christians should endeavour to be filled with knowledge; not only to know the will of God, but to know more of it, and to *increase in the knowledge of God* (as it is *v.* 10), and to *grow in grace, and in the knowledge of our Lord and Saviour,* 2 Pet. iii. 18.

II. That their conversation might be good. Good knowledge without a good life will not profit. Our understanding is then a spiritual understanding when we exemplify it in our way of living: *That you may walk worthy of the Lord unto all pleasing* (*v.* 10), that is, as becomes the relation we stand in to him and the profession we make of him. The agreeableness of our conversation to our religion is pleasing to God as well as to good men. We walk unto all well-pleasing when we walk in all things according to the will of God. *Being fruitful in every good work.* This is what we should aim at. Good words will not do without good works. We must abound in good works, and in every good work: not in some only, which are more easy, and suitable, and safe, but in all, and every instance of them. There must be a regular uniform regard to all the will of God. And the more fruitful we are in good works the more we shall *increase in the knowledge of God. He who doeth his will shall know of the doctrine whether it be of God,* John vii. 17.

III. That they might be strengthened: *Strengthened with all might, according to his glorious power* (*v.* 11), fortified against the temptations of Satan and furnished for all their duty. It is a great comfort to us that he who undertakes to give strength to his people is a God of power and of glorious power. Where there is spiritual life there is still need of spiritual strength, strength for all the actions of the spiritual life. To be strengthened is to be furnished by the grace of God for every good work, and fortified by that grace against every evil one: it is to be enabled to do our duty, and still to hold fast our integrity. The blessed Spirit is the author of this strength; for we are *strength-*

ened with might by his Spirit in the inward man, Eph. iii. 16. The word of God is the means of it, by which he conveys it; and it must be fetched in by prayer. It was in answer to earnest prayer that the apostle obtained sufficient grace. In praying for spiritual strength we are not straitened in the promises, and therefore should not be straitened in our own hopes and desires. Observe, 1. He prayed that they might be strengthened with might: this seems a tautology; but he means, that they might be mightily strengthened, or strengthened with might derived from another. 2. It is with all might. It seems unreasonable that a creature should be strengthened with all might, for that is to make him *almighty;* but he means, with all that might which we have occasion for, to enable us to discharge our duty or preserve our innocence, that grace which is sufficient for us in all the trials of life and able to help us in time of need. 3. It is *according to his glorious power*. He means, according to the grace of God: but the grace of God in the hearts of believers is the power of God; and there is a glory in this power; it is an excellent and sufficient power. And the communications of strength are not according to our weakness, to whom the strength is communicated, but according to his power, from whom it is received. When God gives he gives like himself, and when he strengthens he strengthens like himself. 4. The special use of this strength was for suffering work: *That you may be strengthened unto all patience and long-suffering with joyfulness.* He prays not only that they may be *supported* under their troubles, but *strengthened* for them. the reason is there is work to be done even when we are suffering. And those who are strengthened *according to his glorious power* are strengthened, (1.) To all patience. When patience *hath its perfect work* (Jam. i. 4) then we are strengthened to all patience—when we not only bear our troubles patiently, but receive them as gifts from God, and are thankful for them. To you *it is given to suffer*, Phil. i. 29. When we bear our troubles well, though ever so many, and the circumstances of them ever so aggravating, then we bear them with all patience. And the same reason for bearing one trouble will hold for bearing another, if it be a good reason. All patience includes all the kinds of it; not only bearing patience, but waiting patience. (2.) This is even unto long-suffering, that is, drawn out to a great length: not only to bear trouble awhile, but to bear it as long as God pleases to continue it. (3.) It is with joyfulness, to rejoice in tribulation, to take joyfully the spoiling of our goods, and rejoice that we are counted worthy to suffer for his name, to have joy as well as patience in the troubles of life. This we could never do by any strength of our own, but as we are strengthened by the grace of God.

12 Giving thanks unto the Father,
which hath made us meet to be partakers of the inheritance of the saints
in light: 13 Who hath delivered us
from the power of darkness, and hath
translated *us* into the kingdom of his
dear Son: 14 In whom we have
redemption through his blood, *even*
the forgiveness of sins: 15 Who is
the image of the invisible God, the
firstborn of every creature: 16 For
by him were all things created, that
are in heaven, and that are in earth,
visible and invisible, whether *they
be* thrones, or dominions, or principalities, or powers: all things were
created by him, and for him: 17
And he is before all things, and by
him all things consist. 18 And he
is the head of the body, the church:
who is the beginning, the firstborn
from the dead; that in all *things* he
might have the pre-eminence. 19
For it pleased *the Father* that in him
should all fulness dwell; 20 And,
having made peace through the blood
of his cross, by him to reconcile all
things unto himself; by him, *I say*,
whether *they be* things in earth, or
things in heaven. 21 And you, that
were sometime alienated and enemies
in *your* mind by wicked works, yet
now hath he reconciled 22 In the
body of his flesh through death, to
present you holy and unblameable
and unreproveable in his sight: 23
If ye continue in the faith grounded
and settled, and *be* not moved away
from the hope of the gospel, which ye
have heard, *and* which was preached
to every creature which is under
heaven; whereof I Paul am made a
minister; 24 Who now rejoice in
my sufferings for you, and fill up
that which is behind of the afflictions
of Christ in my flesh for his body's
sake, which is the church: 25
Whereof I am made a minister, according to the dispensation of God
which is given to me for you, to
fulfil the word of God; 26 *Even*
the mystery which hath been hid
from ages and from generations, but
now is made manifest to his saints
27 To whom God would make known

what *is* the riches of the glory of this mystery among the Gentiles; which is Christ in you, the hope of glory:
28 Whom we preach, warning every man, and teaching every man in all wisdom; that we may present every man perfect in Christ Jesus: 29
Whereunto I also labour, striving according to his working, which worketh in me mightily.

Here is a summary of the doctrine of the gospel concerning the great work of our redemption by Christ. It comes in here not as the matter of a sermon, but as the matter of a thanksgiving; for our salvation by Christ furnishes us with abundant matter of thanksgiving in every view of it: *Giving thanks unto the Father, v.* 12. He does not discourse of the work of redemption in the natural order of it; for then he would speak of the purchase of it first, and afterwards of the application of it. But here he inverts the order, because, in our sense and feeling of it, the application goes before the purchase. We first find the benefits of redemption in our hearts, and then are led by those streams to the original and fountain-head. The order and connection of the apostle's discourse may be considered in the following manner:—

I. He speaks concerning the operations of the Spirit of grace upon us. We must give thanks for them, because by these we are qualified for an interest in the mediation of the Son: *Giving thanks to the Father,* &c. *v.* 12, 13. It is spoken of as the work of the Father, because the Spirit of grace is the Spirit of the Father, and the Father works in us by his Spirit. Those in whom the work of grace is wrought must give thanks unto the Father. If we have the comfort of it, he must have the glory of it. Now what is it which is wrought for us in the application of redemption? 1. "He hath *delivered us from the power of darkness, v.* 13. He has rescued us from the state of heathenish darkness and wickedness. He hath saved us from the dominion of sin, which is darkness (1 John i. 6), from the dominion of Satan, who is the *prince of darkness* (Eph. vi. 12), and from the damnation of hell, which is *utter darkness,*" Matt. xxv. 30. They are *called out of darkness,* 1 Pet. ii. 9. 2. "He hath *translated us into the kingdom of his dear Son,* brought us into the gospel-state, and made us members of the church of Christ, which is a state of light and purity." *You were once darkness, but now are you light in the Lord,* Eph. v. 8. *Who hath called you out of darkness into his marvellous light,* 1 Pet. ii. 9. Those were made willing subjects of Christ who were the slaves of Satan. The conversion of a sinner is the translation of a soul into the kingdom of Christ out of the kingdom of the devil. The power of sin is shaken off, and the power of Christ submitted to. The law of the Spirit of life in Christ Jesus makes them free from the law of sin and death; and it is the kingdom of his dear Son, or the Son of his peculiar love, his beloved Son (Matt. iii. 17), and eminently the beloved, Eph. i. 6. 3. "He hath not only done this, but hath *made us meet to partake of the inheritance of the saints in light, v.* 12. He hath prepared us for the eternal happiness of heaven, as the Israelites divided the promised land by lot; and has given us the earnest and assurance of it." This he mentions first because it is the first indication of the future blessedness, that by the grace of God we find ourselves in some measure prepared for it. God gives *grace and glory,* and we are here told what they both are. (1.) What that glory is. It is the *inheritance of the saints in light.* It is an inheritance, and belongs to them as children, which is the best security and the sweetest tenure: *If children, then heirs,* Rom. viii. 17. And it is an inheritance of the saints—proper to sanctified souls. Those who are not saints on earth will never be saints in heaven. And it is an inheritance in light; the perfection of knowledge, holiness, and joy, by communion with God, who is light, and the Father of lights, Jam. i. 17; 1 John i. 5. (2.) What this grace is. It is a meetness for the inheritance: *"He hath made us meet to be partakers,* that is, suited and fitted us for the heavenly state by a proper temper and habit of soul; and he makes us meet by the powerful influence of his Spirit." It is the effect of the divine power to change the heart, and make it heavenly. Observe, All who are designed for heaven hereafter are prepared for heaven now. As those who live and die unsanctified go out of the world with their hell about them, so those who are sanctified and renewed go out of the world with their heaven about them. Those who have the inheritance of sons have the education of sons and the disposition of sons: they *have the Spirit of adoption, whereby they cry, Abba, Father.* Rom. viii. 15. *And, because you are sons, God hath sent forth the Spirit of his Son into your hearts, crying, Abba, Father,* Gal. iv. 6. This meetness for heaven is the earnest of the Spirit in our heart, which is part of payment, and assures the full payment. Those who are sanctified shall be glorified (Rom. viii. 30), and will be for ever indebted to the grace of God, which hath sanctified them.

II. Concerning the person of the Redeemer Glorious things are here said of him; for blessed Paul was full of Christ, and took all occasions to speak honourably of him. He speaks of him distinctly as God, and as Mediator. 1. As God he speaks of him, *v.* 15—17. (1.) He is the *image of the invisible God.* Not as man was made *in the image of God* (Gen. i. 27), in his natural faculties and dominion over the creatures: no, he is the *express image of his person*, Heb. i. 3. He is so the image of God as the son is the image of his father, who has a natural likeness to him; so that he who has seen him has *seen the Father*, and his *glory was the glory of the only-begotten of the Father*, John i. 14; xiv. 9. (2.) He is the *first-born of every creature.* Not that he is himself a creature; for it is πρωτότοκος πάσης κτίσεως—*born* or *begotten before all the creation*, or before any creature was made, which is the scripture-way of representing eternity, and by which the eternity of God is represented to us: *I was set up from everlasting, from the beginning, or ever the earth was; when there was no depth, before the mountains were settled, while as yet he had not made the earth*, Prov. viii. 23—26. It signifies his dominion over all things, as the first-born in a family is heir and lord of all, so he is the *heir of all things*, Heb. i. 2. The word, with only the change of the accent, πρωτοτόκος, signifies actively the first begetter or producer of all things, and so it well agrees with the following clause. *Vid. Isidor. Peleus. epist.* xxx. *lib.* 3. (3.) He is so far from being himself a creature that he is the Creator: *For by him were all things created, which are in heaven and earth, visible and invisible, v.* 16. He made all things out of nothing, the highest angel in heaven, as well as men upon earth. He made the world, the upper and lower world, with all the inhabitants of both. *All things were made by him, and without him was not any thing made which was made*, John i. 3. He speaks here as if there were several orders of angels: *Whether thrones, or dominions, or principalities, or powers*, which must signify either different degrees of excellence or different offices and employments. *Angels, authorities, and powers*, 1 Pet. iii. 22. Christ is the eternal wisdom of the Father, and the world was made in wisdom. He is the eternal Word, and the world was made by the word of God. He is the *arm of the Lord*, and the world was made by that arm. *All things are created by him and for him;* δἰ αὐτοῦ καὶ εἰς αὐτὸν. Being created by him, they were created for him; being made by his power, they were made according to his pleasure and for his praise. He is the end, as well as the cause of all things. *To him are all things*, Rom. xi. 36; εἰς αὐτὸν τὰ πάντα. (4.) He *was before all things.* He had a being before the world was made, before the beginning of time, and therefore from all eternity. Wisdom was with the Father, and possessed by him in the beginning of his ways, before his works of old, Prov. viii. 22. And in the beginning the Word was with God and was God, John i. 1. He not only had a being before he was born of the virgin, but he had a being before all time. (5.) *By him all things consist.* They not only subsist in their beings, but consist in their order and dependences. He not only created them all at first, but it is by the word of his power that they are still upheld, Heb. i. 3. The whole creation is kept together by the power of the Son of God, and made to consist in its proper frame. It is preserved from disbanding and running into confusion.

2. The apostle next shows what he is as Mediator, *v.* 18, 19. (1.) He is the *head of the body the church:* not only a head of government and direction, as the king is the head of the state and has right to prescribe laws, but a head of vital influence, as the head in the natural body: for all grace and strength are derived from him; and the church is his body, *the fulness of him who filleth all in all*, Eph. i. 22, 23. (2.) He is the *beginning, the first-born from the dead*, ἀρχὴ, πρωτότοκος—the principle, the first-born from the dead; the principle of our resurrection, as well as the first-born himself. All our hopes and joys take their rise from him who is the author of our salvation. Not that he was the first who ever rose from the dead, but the first and only one who rose by his own power, and was *declared to be the Son of God, and Lord of all things.* And he is the head of the resurrection, and has given us an example and evidence of our resurrection from the dead. He rose as the first-fruits, 1 Cor. xv. 20. (3.) He hath in *all things the pre-eminence.* It was the will of the Father that he should have *all power in heaven and earth*, that he might be preferred above angels and all the powers in heaven (he has *obtained a more excellent name than they*, Heb. i. 4), and that in all the affairs of the kingdom of God among men he should have the pre-eminence. He has the pre-eminence in the hearts of his people above the world and the flesh; and by giving him the pre-eminence we comply with the Father's will, That *all men should honour the Son even as they honour the Father*, John v. 23. (4.) All fulness dwells in him, and it pleased the Father it should do so (*v.* 19), not only a fulness of abundance for himself, but redundance for us, a fulness of merit and righteousness, of strength and grace. As the head is the seat and source of the animal spirits, so is Christ of all graces to his people. *It pleased the Father* that all fulness should dwell in him; and we may have free resort to him for all that grace for which we have occasion. He not only intercedes for it, but is the trustee in whose hands it is lodged to dispense to us: *Of his fulness we receive, and grace for grace*, grace in us answering to that grace which is in him (John i. 16), and *he fills all in all*, Eph. i. 23.

III. Concerning the work of redemption. He speaks of the nature of it, or wherein it consists; and of the means of it, by which it was procured.

1. Wherein it consists. It is made to lie in two things:—(1.) In the remission of sin: *In whom we have redemption, even the forgive-*

ness of sins, v. 14. It was sin which sold us, sin which enslaved us: if we are redeemed, we must be redeemed from sin; and this is by forgiveness, or remitting the obligation to punishment. So Eph. i. 7, *In whom we have redemption, the forgiveness of sins, according to the riches of his grace.* (2.) In reconciliation to God. God by him *reconciled all things to himself, v.* 20. He is the Mediator of reconciliation, who procures peace as well as pardon for sinners, who brings them into a state of friendship and favour at present, and will bring all holy creatures, angels as well as men, into one glorious and blessed society at last: *things in earth, or things in heaven.* So Eph. i. 10, *He will gather together in one all things in Christ, both which are in heaven and which are on earth.* The word is ἀνακεφαλαιώσασθαι—*he will bring them all under one head.* The Gentiles, who were alienated, and *enemies in their minds by wicked works, yet now hath he reconciled, v.* 21. Here see what was their condition by nature, and in their Gentile state—estranged from God, and at enmity with God: and yet this *enmity is slain,* and, notwithstanding this distance, we are now reconciled. Christ has laid the foundation for our reconciliation; for he has paid the price of it, has purchased the proffer and promise of it, proclaims it as a prophet, applies it as a king. Observe, The greatest enemies to God, who have stood at the greatest distance and bidden him defiance, may be reconciled, if it be not their own fault.

2. How the redemption is procured: *it is through his blood* (*v.* 14); he has *made peace through the blood of his cross* (*v.* 20), and it is *in the body of his flesh through death, v.* 22. It was the *blood which made an atonement, for the blood is the life; and without the shedding of blood there is no remission,* Heb. ix. 22. There was such a value in the blood of Christ that, on account of Christ's shedding it, God was willing to deal with men upon new terms to bring them under a covenant of grace, and *for his sake,* and in consideration of his death upon the cross, to pardon and accept to favour all who comply with them.

IV. Concerning the preaching of this redemption. Here observe,

1. To whom it was preached: *To every creature under heaven* (*v.* 23), that is, it was ordered to be preached to every creature, Mark xvi. 15. It may be preached to every creature; for the gospel excludes none who do not exclude themselves. More or less it has been or will be preached to every nation, though many have sinned away the light of it and perhaps some have never yet enjoyed it.

2. By whom it was preached: *Whereof I Paul am made a minister.* Paul was a great apostle; but he looks upon it as the highest of his titles of honour to be a minister of the gospel of Jesus Christ. Paul takes all occasions to speak of his office; for he *magnified his office,* Rom. xi. 13. And again in *v.* 25, *Whereof I am made a minister.* Observe here,

(1.) Whence Paul had his ministry: it was *according to the dispensation of God which was given to him* (*v.* 25), the economy or wise disposition of things in the house of God. He was steward and master-builder, and this was given to him: he did not usurp it, nor take it to himself; and he could not challenge it as a debt. He received it from God as a gift, and took it as a favour.

(2.) For whose sake he had his ministry: "*It is for you,* for your benefit: *ourselves your servants for Jesus' sake,* 2 Cor. iv. 5. We are Christ's ministers for the good of his people, to *fulfil the word of God* (that is, fully to preach it), of which you will have the greater advantage. The more we fulfil our ministry, or fill up all the parts of it, the greater will be the benefit of the people; they will be the more filled with knowledge, and furnished for service."

(3.) What kind of preacher Paul was. This is particularly represented.

[1.] He was a suffering preacher: *Who now rejoice in my sufferings for you, v.* 24. He suffered in the cause of Christ, and for the good of the church. He suffered for preaching the gospel to them. And, while he suffered in so good a cause, he could rejoice in his sufferings, *rejoice that he was counted worthy to suffer,* and esteem it an honour to him. *And fill up that which is behind of the afflictions of Christ in my flesh.* Not that the afflictions of Paul, or any other, were expiations for sin, as the sufferings of Christ were. There was nothing wanting in them, nothing which needed to *be filled up.* They were perfectly sufficient to answer the intention of them, the satisfaction of God's justice, in order to the salvation of his people. But the sufferings of Paul and other good ministers made them conformable to Christ; and they followed him in his suffering state: so they are said to fill up what was behind of the sufferings of Christ, as the wax fills up the vacuities of the seal, when it receives the impression of it. Or it may be meant not of Christ's sufferings, but of his suffering for Christ. He *filled that which was behind.* He had a certain rate and measure of suffering for Christ assigned him; and, as his sufferings were agreeable to that appointment, so he was still filling up more and more what was behind, or remained of them to his share.

[2.] He was a close preacher: he preached not only in public, but *from house to house,* from person to person. *Whom we preach, warning every man, and teaching every man in all wisdom, v.* 28. Every man has need to be warned and taught, and therefore let every man have his share. Observe, *First,* When we warn people of what they do amiss, we must teach them to do better: warning and teaching must go together. *Secondly,* Men must be warned and taught in all wisdom. We must choose the fittest seasons, and use the likeliest means, and accommodate ourselves to the different circumstances and capacities of those we have to do with, and teach them as they are able to bear. That which he aimed at was *to present every man perfect in Christ Jesus*, τέλειος, either perfect in the knowledge of the Christian doctrine (*Let us therefore, as many as are perfect, be thus minded*, Phil. iii. 15; 2 Tim. iii. 17), or else crowned with a glorious reward hereafter, when he will *present to himself a glorious church* (Eph. v. 27), and bring them to the *spirits of just men made perfect*, Heb. xii. 23. Observe, Ministers ought to aim at the improvement and salvation of every particular person who hears them. *Thirdly*, He was a laborious preacher, and one who took pains: he was no loiterer, and did not do his work negligently (*v.* 29): *Whereunto I also labour, striving according to his working, which worketh in me mightily*. He laboured and strove, used great diligence and contended with many difficulties, according to the measure of grace afforded to him and the extraordinary presence of Christ which was with him. Observe, As Paul laid out himself to do much good, so he had this favour, that the power of God wrought in him the more effectually. The more we labour in the work of the Lord the greater measure of help we may expect from him in it (Eph. iii. 7): *According to the gift of the grace of God given unto me, by the effectual working of his power*.

3. The gospel which was preached. We have an account of this: *Even the mystery which hath been hid from ages, and from generations, but is now made manifest to his saints, v.* 26, 27. Observe, (1.) The mystery of the gospel was long hidden: it was concealed from ages and generations, the several ages of the church under the Old-Testament dispensation. They were in a state of minority, and training up for a more perfect state of things, and could not look to the end of those things which were ordained, 2. Cor. iii. 13. (2.) This mystery now, in the fulness of time, is made manifest to the saints, or clearly revealed and made apparent. The veil which was over Moses's face is done away in Christ, 2 Cor. iii. 14. The meanest saint under the gospel understands more than the greatest prophets under the law. He who is least in the kingdom of heaven is greater than they. The *mystery of Christ, which in other ages was not made known unto the sons of men, is now revealed unto his holy apostles and prophets by the Spirit*, Eph. iii. 4, 5. And what is this mystery? It is the riches of God's glory among the Gentiles. The peculiar doctrine of the gospel was a mystery which was before hidden, and is now made manifest and made known. But the great mystery here referred to is the breaking down of the partition-wall between the Jew and Gentile, and preaching the gospel to the Gentile world, and making those partakers of the privileges of the gospel state who before lay in ignorance and idolatry: *That the Gentiles should be fellow-heirs, and of the same body, and partakers together of his promise in Christ by the gospel*, Eph. iii. 6. This mystery, thus made known, *is Christ in you* (or among you) *the hope of glory*. Observe, Christ is the hope of glory. The ground of our hope is Christ in the word, or the gospel revelation, declaring the nature and methods of obtaining it. The evidence of our hope is Christ in the heart, or the sanctification of the soul, and its preparation for the heavenly glory.

4. The duty of those who are interested in this redemption: *If you continue in the faith, grounded and settled, and be not moved away from the hope of the gospel which you have heard, v.* 23. We must continue in the faith grounded and settled, and not be moved away from the hope of the gospel; that is, we must be so well fixed in our minds as not to be moved from it by any temptations. We must be stedfast and immovable (1 Cor. xv. 58) and *hold fast the profession of our faith without wavering*, Heb. x. 23. Observe, We can expect the happy end of our faith only when we continue in the faith, and are so far grounded and settled in it as not to be moved from it. We must not *draw back unto perdition*, but *believe unto the saving of the soul*, Heb. x. 39. We must be faithful to death, through all trials, that we may receive the *crown of life, and receive the end of our faith, the salvation of our souls*, 1 Pet. i. 9.

CHAP. II.

I. The apostle expresses concern for the Colossians, ver. 1—3. II. He repeats it again, ver. 5. III. He cautions them against false teachers among the Jews (ver. 4, 6, 7), and against the Gentile philosophy, ver. 8—12. IV. He represents the privileges of Christians, ver. 13—15. And, V. Concludes with a caution against the judaizing teachers, and those who would introduce the worship of angels, ver. 16—23.

FOR I would that ye knew what great conflict I have for you, and *for* them at Laodicea, and *for* as many as have not seen my face in the flesh; 2 That their hearts might be comforted, being knit together in love, and unto all riches of the full assurance of understanding, to the acknowledgment of the mystery of God, and of the Father, and of Christ; 3 In whom are hid all the treasures of wisdom and knowledge.

We may observe here the great concern which Paul had for these Colossians and the other churches which he had not any personal knowledge of. The apostle had never been at Colosse, and the church planted there was not of his planting; and yet he had as tender a care of it as if it had been the only people of his charge (*v.* 1): *For I would that you knew what great conflict I have for you, and for those at Laodicea, and for as many as have not seen my face in the flesh*. Observe, 1. Paul's care of the church was such as amounted to a conflict. He was in a sort of agony, and had a constant fear respecting what would become of them. Herein he was a follower of his Master, who was in an agony for us, and was *heard in that he feared.* (2.) We may keep up a communion by faith, hope, and holy love, even with those churches and fellow-christians of whom we have no personal knowledge, and with whom we have no conversation. We can think, and pray, and be concerned for one another, at the greatest distance; and those we never saw in the flesh we may hope to meet in heaven. But,

I. What was it that the apostle desired for them? *That their hearts may be comforted, being knit together in love,* &c., *v.* 2. It was their spiritual welfare about which he was solicitous. He does not say that they may be healthy, and merry, and rich, and great, and prosperous; but that their *hearts may be comforted.* Note, The prosperity of the soul is the best prosperity, and what we should be most solicitous about for ourselves and others. We have here a description of soul-prosperity.

1. When our knowledge grows to an understanding of the mystery of God, and of the Father, and of Christ,—when we come to have a more clear, distinct, methodical knowledge of the truth as it is in Jesus, then the soul prospers: *To understand the mystery,* either what was before concealed, but is now made known concerning the Father and Christ, or the mystery before mentioned, of calling the Gentiles into the Christian church, as the Father and Christ have revealed it in the gospel; and not barely to speak of it by rote, or as we have been taught it by our catechisms, but to be led into it, and enter into the meaning and design of it. This is what we should labour after, and then the soul prospers.

2 When our faith grows to a full assurance and bold acknowledgment of this mystery. (1.) To a full assurance, or a well-settled judgment, upon their proper evidence, of the great truths of the gospel, without doubting, or calling them in question, but embracing them with the highest satisfaction, as faithful sayings and worthy of all acceptation. (2.) When it comes to a free acknowledgment, and we not only believe with the heart, but are ready, when called to it, to make confession with our mouth, and are not ashamed of our Master and our holy religion, under the frowns and violence of their enemies. This is called the *riches of the full assurance of understanding.* Great knowledge and strong faith make a soul rich. This is being rich towards God, and rich in faith, and having the true riches, Luke xii. 21; xvi. 11; Jam. ii. 5.

3. It consists in the abundance of comfort in our souls: *That their hearts might be comforted.* The soul prospers when it is filled with joy and peace (Rom. xv. 13), and has a satisfaction within which all the troubles without cannot disturb, and is able to joy in the Lord when all other comforts fail, Hab. iii 17, 18.

4. The more intimate communion we have with our fellow-christians the more the soul prospers: *Being knit together in love.* Holy love knits the hearts of Christians one to another; and faith and love both contribute to our comfort. The stronger our faith is, and the warmer our love, the greater will our comfort be. Having occasion to mention Christ (*v.* 2), according to his usual way, he makes this remark to his honour (*v.* 3): *In whom are hidden all the treasures of wisdom and knowledge.* He had said (*ch.* i. 19) *that all fulness dwells in him:* here he mentions particularly the *treasures of wisdom and knowledge.* There is a fulness of wisdom in him, as he has perfectly revealed the will of God to mankind. Observe, The treasures of wisdom are hidden not from us, but for us, in Christ. Those who would be wise and knowing must make application to Christ. We must spend upon the stock which is laid up for us in him, and draw from the treasures which are hidden in him. He is the wisdom of God, and is *of God made unto us wisdom,* &c., 1 Cor. i. 24, 30.

II. His concern for them is repeated (*v.* 5): *Though I am absent in the flesh, yet am I with you in the spirit, joying, and beholding your order, and the stedfastness of your faith in Christ.* Observe, 1. We may be present in spirit with those churches and Christians from whom we are absent in body; for the communion of saints is a spiritual thing. Paul had heard concerning the Colossians that they were orderly and regular; and though he had never seen them, nor was present with them, he tells them he could easily think himself among them, and look with pleasure upon their good behaviour. 2. The order and stedfastness of Christians are matter of joy to ministers; they joy when they behold their order, their regular behaviour and stedfast adherence to the Christian doctrine. 3. The more stedfast our faith in Christ is, the better order there will be in our whole conversation; for we live and walk by faith, 2 Cor. v. 7; Heb. x. 38.

4 And this I say, lest any man
should beguile you with enticing
words. 5 For though I be absent
in the flesh, yet am I with you in
the spirit, joying and beholding your
order, and the stedfastness of your
faith in Christ. 6 As ye have therefore received Christ Jesus the Lord,
so walk ye in him: 7 Rooted and
built up in him, and stablished in
the faith, as ye have been taught,
abounding therein with thanksgiving.
8 Beware lest any man spoil you
through philosophy and vain deceit,
after the tradition of men, after the
rudiments of the world, and not after
Christ. 9 For in him dwelleth all
the fulness of the Godhead bodily.
10 And ye are complete in him,

which is the head of all principality
and power: 11 In whom also ye
are circumcised with the circumcision
made without hands, in putting off
the body of the sins of the flesh by
the circumcision of Christ: 12 Buried with him in baptism, wherein
also ye are risen with *him* through
the faith of the operation of God,
who hath raised him from the dead.

The apostle cautions the Colossians against deceivers (*v.* 4): *And this I say lest any man beguile you with enticing words;* and *v.* 8, *Lest any man spoil you.* He insists so much upon the perfection of Christ and the gospel revelation, to preserve them from the ensnaring insinuations of those who would corrupt their principles. Note, 1. The way in which Satan spoils souls is by beguiling them. He deceives them, and by this means slays them. He is the *old serpent who beguiled Eve through his subtlety,* 2 Cor. xi. 3. He could not ruin us if he did not cheat us; and he could not cheat us but by our own fault and folly. 2. Satan's agents, who aim to spoil them, beguile them with enticing words. See the danger of enticing words; how many are ruined by the flattery of those who lie in wait to deceive, and by the false disguises and fair appearances of evil principles and wicked practices. *By good words, and fair speeches, they deceive the hearts of the simple,* Rom. xvi. 18. "You ought to stand upon your guard against enticing words, and be aware and afraid of those who would entice you to any evil; for that which they aim at is to spoil you." *If sinners entice thee, consent thou not,* Prov. i. 10. Observe,

I. A sovereign antidote against seducers (*v* 6, 7): *As you have therefore received Christ Jesus the Lord, so walk you in him, rooted and built up,* &c. Here note, 1. All Christians have, in profession at least, *received Jesus Christ the Lord,* received him as Christ, the great prophet of the church, anointed by God to reveal his will; as Jesus the great high priest, and Saviour from sin and wrath, by the expiatory sacrifice of himself; and as Lord, or sovereign and king, whom we are to obey and be subject to.—*Received him,* consented to him, taken him for ours in every relation and every capacity, and for all the purposes and uses of them. 2. The great concern of those who have received Christ is *to walk in him*—to make their practices conformable to their principles and their conversation agreeable to their engagements. As we have received Christ, or consented to be his, so we must walk with him in our daily course and keep up our communion with him. 3. The more closely we walk with Christ the more we are *rooted and established in the faith.* A good conversation is the best establishment of a good faith. If we walk in him, we shall be rooted in him; and the more firmly we are rooted in him the more closely we shall walk in him: *Rooted and built up.* Observe, We cannot be built up in Christ, unless we be first rooted in him. We must be united to him by a lively faith, and heartily consent to his covenant, and then we shall *grow up in him in all things.—As you have been taught*—"according to the rule of the Christian doctrine, in which you have been instructed." Observe, A good education has a good influence upon our establishment. We must be *established in the faith, as we have been taught, abounding therein.* Observe, Being established in the faith, we must abound therein, and improve in it more and more; and this with thanksgiving. The way to have the benefit and comfort of God's grace is to be much in giving thanks for it. We must join thanksgiving to all our improvements, and be sensible of the mercy of all our privileges and attainments. Observe,

II. The fair warning given us of our danger: *Beware lest any man spoil you through philosophy and vain deceit, after the tradition of men, after the rudiments of the world, and not after Christ, v.* 8. There is a philosophy which is a noble exercise of our reasonable faculties, and highly serviceable to religion, such a study of the works of God as leads us to the knowledge of God and confirms our faith in him. But there is a philosophy which is vain and deceitful, which is prejudicial to religion, and sets up the wisdom of man in competition with the wisdom of God, and while it pleases men's fancies ruins their faith; as nice and curious speculations about things above us, or of no use and concern to us; or a care of words and terms of art, which have only an empty and often a cheating appearance of knowledge. *After the tradition of men, after the rudiments of the world:* this plainly reflects upon the Jewish pedagogy or economy, as well as the Pagan learning. The Jews governed themselves by the traditions of their elders and the rudiments or elements of the world, the rites and observances which were only preparatory and introductory to the gospel state; the Gentiles mixed their maxims of philosophy with their Christian principles; and both alienated their minds from Christ. Those who pin their faith on other men's sleeves, and walk in the way of the world, have turned away from following after Christ. The deceivers were especially the Jewish teachers, who endeavoured to keep up the law of Moses in conjunction with the gospel of Christ, but really in competition with it and contradiction to it. Now here the apostle shows,

1. That we have in Christ the substance of all the shadows of the ceremonial law; for example, (1.) Had they then the Shechinah, or special presence of God, called the glory, from the visible token of it? So have we now in Jesus Christ (*v.* 9): *For in him dwelleth all the fulness of the Godhead bodily.* Under

the law, the presence of God dwelt between the cherubim, in a cloud which covered the mercy-seat; but now it dwells in the person of our Redeemer, who partakes of our nature, and is bone of our bone and flesh of our flesh, and has more clearly declared the Father to us. It dwells in him bodily; not as the body is opposed to the spirit, but as the body is opposed to the shadow. The fulness of the Godhead dwells in Christ really, and not figuratively; for he is both God and man. (2.) Had they circumcision, which was the seal of the covenant? In Christ we are *circumcised with the circumcision made without hands* (*v.* 11), by the work of regeneration in us, which is the spiritual or Christian circumcision. *He is a Jew who is one inwardly, and circumcision is that of the heart,* Rom. ii. 29. This is owing to Christ, and belongs to the Christian dispensation. *It is made without hands;* not by the power of any creature, but by the power of the blessed Spirit of God. We are *born of the Spirit,* John iii. 5. And it is *the washing of regeneration, and renewing of the Holy Spirit,* Tit. iii. 5. It consists *in putting off the body of the sins of the flesh,* in renouncing sin and reforming our lives, not in mere external rites. It is not the *putting away of the filth of the flesh, but the answer of a good conscience towards God,* 1 Pet. iii. 21. And it is not enough to put away some one particular sin, but we must put off the whole body of sin. The *old man must be crucified, and the body of sin destroyed,* Rom. vi. 6. Christ was circumcised, and, by virtue of our union to him, we partake of that effectual grace which puts off the *body of the sins of the flesh.* Again, The Jews thought themselves complete in the ceremonial law; but we are *complete in Christ, v.* 10. That was imperfect and defective; *if the first covenant had been faultless, there would no place have been sought for the second* (Heb. viii. 7), and the *law was but a shadow of good things, and could never, by those sacrifices, make the comers thereunto perfect,* Heb. x. 1. But all the defects of it are made up in the gospel of Christ, by the complete sacrifice for sin and revelation of the will of God. *Which is the head of all principality and power.* As the Old-Testament priesthood had its perfection in Christ, so likewise had the kingdom of David, which was the eminent principality and power under the Old Testament, and which the Jews valued themselves so much upon. And he is the Lord and head of all the powers in heaven and earth, of angels and men. *Angels, and authorities, and powers are subject to him,* 1 Pet. iii. 22.

2. We have communion with Christ in his whole undertaking (*v.* 12): *Buried with him in baptism, wherein also you have risen with him.* We are both buried and rise with him, and both are signified by our baptism; not that there is any thing in the sign or ceremony of baptism which represents this burying and rising, any more than the crucifixion of Christ is represented by any visible resemblance in the Lord's supper: and he is speaking of the *circumcision made without hands;* and says it is *through the faith of the operation of God.* But the thing signified by our baptism is that we are buried with Christ, as baptism is the seal of the covenant and an obligation to our dying to sin; and that we are raised with Christ, as it is a seal and obligation to our living to righteousness, or newness of life. God in baptism engages to be to us a God, and we become engaged to be his people, and by his grace to die to sin and to live to righteousness, or put off the old man and put on the new.

13 And you, being dead in your
sins and the uncircumcision of your
flesh, hath he quickened together
with him, having forgiven you all
trespasses; 14 Blotting out the
handwriting of ordinances that was
against us, which was contrary to us,
and took it out of the way, nailing it
to his cross; 15 *And* having spoiled
principalities and powers, he made
a show of them openly, triumphing
over them in it.

The apostle here represents the privileges we Christians have above the Jews, which are very great.

I. Christ's death is our life: *And you, being dead in your sins and the uncircumcision of your flesh, hath he quickened together with him, v.* 13. A state of sin is a state of spiritual death. Those who are in sin are dead in sin. As the death of the body consists in its separation from the soul, so the death of the soul consists in its separation from God and the divine favour. As the death of the body is the corruption and putrefaction of it, so sin is the corruption or depravation of the soul. As a man who is dead is unable to help himself by any power of his own, so an habitual sinner is morally impotent: though he has a natural power, or the power of a reasonable creature, he has not a spiritual power, till he has the divine life or a renewed nature. It is principally to be understood of the Gentile world, who *lay in wickedness.* They were *dead in the uncircumcision of their flesh,* being *aliens to the covenant of promise, and without God in the world,* Eph. ii. 11, 12. By reason of their uncircumcision they were dead in their sins. It may be understood of the spiritual uncircumcision or corruption of nature; and so it shows that we are dead in law, and dead in state. Dead in law, as a condemned malefactor is called a dead man because he is under a sentence of death; so sinners by the guilt of sin are under the sentence of the law and *condemned already,* John iii. 18. And dead in state, by reason of the *uncircumcision of our flesh.* An unsanctified heart is called an *uncircumcised heart:* this is our state. Now through Christ we, who were dead in sins, are quickened; that is, effectual provision is made for taking away the guilt of sin, and breaking the power and dominion of it. *Quickened together with him*—by virtue of our union to him, and in conformity to him. Christ's death was the death of our sins; Christ's resurrection is the quickening of our souls.

II. Through him we have the remission of sin: *Having forgiven you all trespasses.* This is our quickening. The pardon of the crime is the life of the criminal: and this is owing to the resurrection of Christ, as well as his death; for, as he *died for our sins,* so he *rose again for our justification,* Rom. iv. 25.

III. Whatever was in force against us is taken out of the way He has obtained for us a legal discharge from the *hand-writing of ordinances, which was against us* (*v.* 14), which may be understood, 1. Of that obligation to punishment in which consists the guilt of sin. The curse of the law is the hand-writing against us, like the hand-writing on Belshazzar's wall. *Cursed is every one who continues not in every thing.* This was a hand-writing which was *against us, and contrary to us;* for it threatened our eternal ruin. This was removed when he *redeemed us from the curse of the law, being made a curse for us,* Gal. iii. 13. He cancelled the obligation for all who repent and believe. "Upon me be the curse, my father." He vacated and disannulled the judgment which was against us. When he was nailed to the cross, the curse was as it were nailed to the cross. And our indwelling corruption is crucified with Christ, and by virtue of his cross. When we remember the dying of the Lord Jesus, and see him nailed to the cross, we should see the hand-writing against us taken out of the way. Or rather, 2. It must be understood of the ceremonial law, the *hand-writing of ordinances,* the ceremonial institutions or *the law of commandments contained in ordinances* (Eph. ii. 15), which was a yoke to the Jews and a partition-wall to the Gentiles. The Lord Jesus *took it out of the way, nailed it to his cross*; that is, disannulled the obligation of it, that all might see and be satisfied that it was no more binding. When the substance came, the shadows fled away. It is abolished (2 Cor. iii. 13), and *that which decayeth and waxeth old is ready to vanish away,* Heb. viii. 13. The expressions are in allusion to the ancient methods of cancelling a bond, either by crossing the writing or striking it through with a nail.

IV. He has obtained a glorious victory for us over the powers of darkness: *And, having spoiled principalities and powers, he made a show of them openly, triumphing over them in it, v.* 15. As the curse of the law was against us, so the power of Satan was against us. He treated with God as the Judge, and redeemed us out of the hands of his justice by a price; but out of the hands of Satan the executioner he redeemed us by power and with a high hand. *He led captivity captive.* The devil and all the powers of hell were conquered and disarmed by the dying Redeemer. The first promise pointed at this; the bruising of the heel of Christ in his sufferings was the breaking of the serpent's head, Gen. iii. 15. The expressions are lofty and magnificent: let us turn aside and see this great sight. The Redeemer conquered by dying. See his crown of thorns turned into a crown of laurels. He *spoiled them,* broke the devil's power, and conquered and disabled him, and *made a show of them openly*—exposed them to public shame, and made a show of them to angels and men. Never had the devil's kingdom such a mortal blow given to it as was given by the Lord Jesus. He tied them to his chariot-wheels, and rode forth conquering and to conquer—alluding to the custom of a general's triumph, who returned victorious.—*Triumphing over them in it;* that is, either in his cross and by his death; or, as some read it, in himself, by his own power; for he *trod the wine-press alone, and of the people there was none with him.*

16 Let no man therefore judge you
in meat, or in drink, or in respect of
an holyday, or of the new moon, or
of the sabbath *days:* 17 Which are
a shadow of things to come; but the
body *is* of Christ. 18 Let no man
beguile you of your reward in a
voluntary humility and worshipping
of angels, intruding into those things
which he hath not seen, vainly puffed
up by his fleshly mind, 19 And not
holding the Head, from which all the
body by joints and bands having
nourishment ministered, and knit
together, increaseth with the increase
of God. 20 Wherefore if ye be dead
with Christ from the rudiments of
the world, why, as though living in
the world, are ye subject to ordinances, 21 (Touch not; taste not;
handle not; 22 Which all are to
perish with the using;) after the commandments and doctrines of men? 23
Which things have indeed a show of
wisdom in will worship, and humility,
and neglecting of the body; not in any
honour to the satisfying of the flesh.

The apostle concludes the chapter with exhortations to proper duty, which he infers from the foregoing discourse.

I. Here is a caution to take heed of judaizing teachers, or those who would impose upon Christians the yoke of the ceremonial law: *Let no man therefore judge you in meat nor in drink,* &c., *v.* 16. Much of the ceremonies of the law of Moses consisted in the distinction of meats and days. It appears by Rom. xiv. that there were those who were for keeping up those distinctions: but here the apostle shows that since Christ has come, and has cancelled the ceremonial law, we ought not to keep it up. "Let no man impose those things upon you, for God has not imposed them: if God has made you free, be not you again *entangled in that yoke of bondage.*" And this the rather because these things *were shadows of things to come* (*v.* 17), intimating that they had no intrinsic worth in them and that they are now done away. *But the body is of Christ:* the body, of which they were shadows, has come; and to continue the ceremonial observances, which were only types and shadows of Christ and the gospel, carries an intimation that Christ has not yet come and the gospel state has not yet commenced. Observe the advantages we have under the gospel, above what they had under the law: they had the shadows, we have the substance.

II. He cautions them to take heed of those who would introduce the worship of angels as mediators between God and them, as the Gentile philosophers did: *Let no man beguile you of your reward, in a voluntary humility and worshipping of angels, v.* 18. It looked like a piece of modesty to make use of the mediation of angels, as conscious to ourselves of our unworthiness to speak immediately to God; but, though it has a show of humility, it is a voluntary, not a commanded humility; and therefore it is not acceptable, yea, it is not warrantable: it is taking that honour which is due to Christ only and giving it to a creature. Besides, the notions upon which this practice was grounded were merely the inventions of men and not by divine revelation,—the proud conceits of human reason, which make a man presume to dive into things, and determine them, without sufficient knowledge and warrant: *Intruding into those things which he hath not seen, vainly puffed up by his fleshly mind*—pretending to describe the order of angels, and their respective ministries, which God has hidden from us; and therefore, though there was a show of humility in the practice, there was a real pride in the principle. They advanced those notions to gratify their own carnal fancy, and were fond of being thought wiser than other people. Pride is at the bottom of a great many errors and corruptions, and even of many evil practices, which have a great show and appearance of humility. Those who do so do *not hold the head, v.* 19. They do in effect disclaim Christ, who is the only Mediator between God and man. It is the highest disparagement to Christ, who is the head of the church, for any of the members of it to make use of any intercessors with God but him. When men let go their hold of Christ, they catch at that which is next them and will stand them in no stead.—*From which all the body, by joints and bands, having nourishment ministered, and knit together, increaseth with the increase of God.* Observe, 1. Jesus Christ is not only a head of government over the church, but a head of vital influence to it. They are knit to him by joints and bands, as the several members of the body are united to the head, and receive life and nourishment from him. 2. The body of Christ is a growing body: *it increaseth with the increase of God.* The new man is increasing, and the nature of grace is to grow, where there is not an accidental hindrance.—*With the increase of God,* with an increase of grace which is from God as its author; or, in a usual Hebraism, with a large and abundant increase.—*That you may be filled with all the fulness of God,* Eph. iii. 19. See a parallel expression, *Which is the head, even Christ, from whom the whole body, fitly joined together, maketh increase of the body,* Eph. iv. 15, 16.

III. He takes occasion hence to warn them again: "*Wherefore, if you be dead with Christ from the rudiments of the world, why, as though living in the world, are you subject to ordinances? v.* 20. If as Christians you are dead to the observances of the ceremonial law, why are you subject to them? Such observances as, *Touch not, taste not, handle not," v.* 21, 22. Under the law there was a ceremonial pollution contracted by touching a dead body, or any thing offered to an idol; or by tasting any forbiden meats, &c., *which all are to perish with the using,* having no intrinsic worth in themselves to support them, and those who used them saw them perishing and passing away; or, which tend to corrupt the Christian faith, having no other authority than the traditions and injunctions of men.—*Which things have indeed a show of wisdom in will-worship and humility.* They thought themselves wiser than their neighbours, in observing the law of Moses together with the gospel of Christ, that they might be sure in the one, at least, to be in the right; but, alas! it was but a show of wisdom, a mere invention and pretence. So they seem to neglect the body, by abstaining from such and such meats, and mortifying their bodily pleasures and appetites; but there is nothing of true devotion in these things, for the gospel teaches us to worship God in spirit and truth and not by ritual observances, and through the mediation of Christ alone and not of any angels. Observe, 1. Christians are freed by Christ from the ritual observances of Moses's law, and delivered from that yoke of bondage which God himself had laid upon them. 2. Subjection to ordinances, or human appointments in the worship of God, is highly blamable, and contrary to the freedom and liberty of the gospel. The apostle requires Christians *to stand fast in the liberty with which Christ hath made them free, and not to be entangled again with the yoke of bondage,* Gal. v. 1. And the imposition of them is invading the authority of Christ, the head of the church, and *introducing another law of commandments contained in ordinances,* when Christ has abolished the old one, Eph. ii. 15. 3. Such things have only a show of wisdom, but are really folly. It is true wisdom to keep close to the appointments of the gospel, and an entire subjection to Christ, the only head of the church.

CHAP. III.

I. The apostle exhorts us to set our hearts upon heaven and take them off from this world, ver. 1—4. II. He exhorts to the mortification of sin, in the various instances of it, ver. 5—11. III. He earnestly presses to mutual love and compassion, ver. 12—17. And concludes with exhortations to relative duties, of wives and husbands, parents and children, masters and servants, ver. 18—25.

IF ye then be risen with Christ, seek those things which are above, where Christ sitteth on the right hand of God. 2 Set your affection on things above, not on things on the earth. 3 For ye are dead, and your life is hid with Christ in God. 4 When Christ, *who is* our life, shall appear, then shall ye also appear with him in glory.

The apostle, having described our privileges by Christ in the former part of the epistle, and our discharge from the yoke of the ceremonial law, comes here to press upon us our duty as inferred thence. Though we are made free from the obligation of the ceremonial law, it does not therefore follow that we may live as we list. We must walk the more closely with God in all the instances of evangelical obedience. He begins with exhorting them to set their hearts on heaven, and take them off from this world: *If you then have risen with Christ.* It is our privilege that we have risen with Christ; that is, have benefit by the resurrection of Christ, and by virtue of our union and communion with him are justified and sanctified, and shall be glorified. Hence he infers that we must *seek those things which are above.* We must mind the concerns of another world more than the concerns of this. We must make heaven our scope and aim, seek the favour of God above, keep up our communion with the upper world by faith, and hope, and holy love, and make it our constant care and business to secure our title to and qualifications for the heavenly bliss. And the reason is because *Christ sits at the right hand of God.* He who is our best friend and our head is advanced to the highest dignity and honour in heaven, and has gone before to secure to us the heavenly happiness; and therefore we should seek and secure what he has purchased at so vast an expense, and is taking so much care about. We must live such a life as Christ lived here on earth and lives now in heaven, according to our capacities.

I. He explains this duty (*v.* 2): *Set your affections on things above, not on things on the earth.* Observe, To seek heavenly things is to set our affections upon them, to love them and let our desires be towards them. Upon the wings of affection the heart soars upwards, and is carried forth towards spiritual and divine objects. We must acquaint ourselves with them, esteem them above all other things, and lay out ourselves in preparation for the enjoyment of them. David gave this proof of his *loving the house of God,* that he diligently sought after it, and prepared for it, Ps. xxvii. 4. This is to be spiritually minded (Rom. viii. 6), and to *seek and desire a better country, that is, a heavenly,* Heb. xi. 14, 16. *Things on earth* are here set in opposition to *things above.* We must not dote upon them, nor expect too much from them, that we may set our affections on heaven; for heaven and earth are contrary one to the other, and a supreme regard to both is inconsistent; and the prevalence of our affection to one will proportionably weaken and abate our affection to the other.

II. He assigns three reasons for this, *v.* 3, 4.

1. That we are dead; that is, to present things, and as our portion. We are so in profession and obligation; for we are *buried with Christ, and planted into the likeness of his death.* Every Christian is *crucified unto the world,* and *the world is crucified unto him,* Gal. vi. 14. And if we are dead to the earth, and have renounced it as our happiness, it is absurd for us to *set our affections* upon it, and *seek* it. We should be like a dead thing to it, unmoved and unaffected towards it.

2. Our true life lies in the other world: *You are dead, and your life is hid with Christ in God, v.* 3. The new man has its livelihood thence. It is born and nourished from above; and the perfection of its life is reserved for that state. It is *hid with Christ:* not hid from us only, in point of secrecy, but hid for us, denoting security. The life of a Christian *is hid with Christ. Because I live you shall live also,* John xiv. 19. Christ is at present a hidden Christ, or one *whom we have not seen;* but this is our comfort, that our *life is hid with him,* and laid up safely with him. As we have reason to *love him whom we have not seen* (1 Pet. i. 8), so we may take the comfort of a happiness out of sight, and *reserved in heaven for us.*

3. Because at the second coming of Christ we hope for the perfection of our happiness. If we live a life of Christian purity and devotion now, *when Christ, who is our life, shall appear, we shall also appear with him in glory, v.* 4. Observe, (1.) Christ is a believer's life. *I live, yet not I, but Christ lives in me,* Gal. ii. 20. He is the principle and end of the Christian's life. He lives *in* us by his Spirit, and we live to him in all we do. *To me to live is Christ,* Phil. i. 21. (2.) Christ will appear again. He is now *hid;* and the *heavens must contain* him; but he will appear in all the pomp of the upper world, with his *holy angels,* and in *his own glory and his*

Father's glory, Mark viii. 38; Luke ix. 26. (3.) We shall then appear with him in glory. It will be his glory to have his redeemed with him; he will come to be glorified in his saints (2 Thess. i. 10); and it will be their glory to come with him, and be with him for ever. At the second coming of Christ there will be a general meeting of all the saints; and those whose life is now *hid with Christ* shall then appear with Christ in that glory which he himself enjoys, John xvii. 24. Do we look for such a happiness, and should we not set our affections upon that world, and live above this? What is there here to make us fond of it? What is there not there to draw our hearts to it? Our head is there, our home is there, our treasure is there, and we hope to be there for ever.

5 Mortify therefore your members which are upon the earth; fornication, uncleanness, inordinate affection, evil concupiscence, and covetousness, which is idolatry:
6 For which things' sake the wrath of God cometh on the children of disobedience:
7 In the which ye also walked some time, when ye lived in them.

The apostle exhorts the Colossians to the mortification of sin, the great hindrance to seeking the things which are above. Since it is our duty to set our affections upon heavenly things, it is our duty to mortify our *members which are upon the earth,* and which naturally incline us to the things of the world: "Mortify them, that is, subdue the vicious habits of mind which prevailed in your Gentile state. Kill them, suppress them, as you do weeds or vermin which spread and destroy all about them, or as you kill an enemy who fights against you and wounds you."—*Your members which are upon the earth;* either the members of the body, which are the earthly part of us, and were *curiously wrought in the lower parts of the earth* (Ps. cxxxix. 15), or the corrupt affections of the mind, which lead us to earthly things, the members of the body of death, Rom. vii. 24. He specifies,

I. The lusts of the flesh, for which they were before so very remarkable: *Fornication, uncleanness, inordinate affection, evil concupiscence*—the various workings of the carnal appetites and fleshly impurities, which they indulged in their former course of life, and which were so contrary to the Christian state and the heavenly hope.

II. The love of the world: *And covetousness, which is idolatry;* that is, an inordinate love of present good and outward enjoyments, which proceeds from too high a value in the mind, puts upon too eager a pursuit, hinders the proper use and enjoyment of them, and creates anxious fear and immoderate sorrow for the loss of them. Observe, Covetousness is spiritual idolatry: it is the giving of that love and regard to worldly wealth which are due to God only, and carries a greater degree of malignity in it, and is more highly provoking to God, than is commonly thought. And it is very observable that among all the instances of sin which good men are recorded in the scripture to have fallen into (and there is scarcely any but some or other, in one or other part of their life, have fallen into) there is no instance in all the scripture of any good man charged with covetousness. He proceeds to show how necessary it is to mortify sins, *v.* 6, 7. 1. Because, if we do not kill them, they will kill us: *For which things' sake the wrath of God cometh on the children of disobedience, v.* 6. See what we are all by nature more or less: we are *children of disobedience:* not only disobedient children, but under the power of sin and naturally prone to disobey. The *wicked are estranged from the womb; they go astray as soon as they are born, speaking lies,* Ps. lviii. 3. And, being children of disobedience, we are *children of wrath,* Eph. ii. 3. The wrath of God comes upon all the children of disobedience. Those who do not obey the precepts of the law incur the penalties of it. The sins he mentions were their sins in their heathen and idolatrous state, and they were then especially the children of disobedience; and yet these sins brought judgments upon them, and exposed them to the wrath of God. 2. We should mortify these sins because they have lived in us: *In which you also walked some time, when you lived in them, v.* 7. Observe, The consideration that we have formerly lived in sin is a good argument why we should now forsake it. We have walked in by-paths, therefore let us walk in them no more. *If I have done iniquity, I will do no more,* Job xxxiv. 32. The time past of our lives may suffice us to have wrought the will of the Gentiles, when we walked in lasciviousness, 1 Pet. iv. 3.—*When you lived among those who did such things* (so some understand it), then you walked in those evil practices. It is a hard thing to live among those who do the works of darkness and not have fellowship with them, as it is to walk in the mire and contract no soil. Let us keep out of the way of evil-doers.

8 But now ye also put off all these; anger, wrath, malice, blasphemy, filthy communication out of your mouth.
9 Lie not one to another, seeing that ye have put off the old man with his deeds;
10 And have put on the new *man,* which is renewed in knowledge after the image of him that created him:
11 Where there is neither Greek nor Jew, circumcision nor uncircumcision, Barbarian, Scythian, bond *nor* free: but Christ *is* all, and in all.

As we are to mortify inordinate appetites,

so we are to mortify inordinate passions (*v.* 8): *But now you also put off all these, anger, wrath, malice;* for these are contrary to the design of the gospel, as well as grosser impurities; and, though they are more spiritual wickedness, have not less malignity in them. The gospel religion introduces a change of the higher as well as the lower powers of the soul, and supports the dominion of right reason and conscience over appetite and passion. Anger and wrath are bad, but malice is worse, because it is more rooted and deliberate; it is anger heightened and settled. And, as the corrupt principles in the heart must be cut off, so the product of them in the tongue; as *blasphemy,* which seems there to mean, not so much speaking ill of God as speaking ill of men, giving ill language to them, or raising ill reports of them, and injuring their good name by any evil arts,—*filthy communication,* that is, all lewd and wanton discourse, which comes from a polluted mind in the speaker and propagates the same defilements in the hearers,—and lying: *Lie not one to another* (*v.* 9), for it is contrary both to the law of truth and the law of love, it is both unjust and unkind, and naturally tends to destroy all faith and friendship among mankind. Lying makes us like the devil (who is the *father of lies*), and is a prime part of the devil's image upon our souls; and therefore we are cautioned against this sin by this general reason: Seeing *you have put off the old man with his deeds, and have put on the new man, v.* 10. The consideration that we have by profession put away sin and espoused the cause and interest of Christ, that we have renounced all sin and stand engaged to Christ, should fortify us against this sin of lying. Those who have put off the old man have put it off with its deeds; and those who have put on the new man must put on all its deeds—not only espouse good principles but act them in a good conversation. The new man is said to be *renewed in knowledge,* because an ignorant soul cannot be a good soul. Without knowledge the heart cannot be good, Prov. xix. 2. The grace of God works upon the will and affections by renewing the understanding. Light is the first thing in the new creation, as it was in the first: *after the image of him who created him.* It was the honour of man in innocence that he was made after the image of God; but that image was defaced and lost by sin, and is renewed by sanctifying grace: so that a renewed soul is something like what Adam was in the day he was created. In the privilege and duty of sanctification *there is neither Greek nor Jew, circumcision nor uncircumcision, Barbarian, Scythian, bond nor free, v.* 11. There is now no difference arising from different country or different condition and circumstance of life: it is as much the duty of the one as of the other to be holy, and as much the privilege of the one as of the other to receive from God the grace to be so. Christ came to take down all partition-walls, that all might stand on the same level before God, both in duty and privilege. And for this reason, because *Christ is all in all.* Christ is a Christian's all, his only Lord and Saviour, and all his hope and happiness. And to those who are sanctified, one as well as another and whatever they are in other respects, he is *all in all,* the *Alpha* and *Omega,* the *beginning and the end:* he is all in all things to them.

12 Put on therefore, as the elect
of God, holy and beloved, bowels
of mercies, kindness, humbleness of
mind, meekness, longsuffering; 13
Forbearing one another, and forgiving one another, if any man have a
quarrel against any: even as Christ
forgave you, so also *do* ye. 14 And
above all these things *put on* charity,
which is the bond of perfectness. 15
And let the peace of God rule in your
hearts, to the which also ye are called
in one body; and be ye thankful. 16
Let the word of Christ dwell in you
richly in all wisdom; teaching and
admonishing one another in psalms
and hymns and spiritual songs, singing with grace in your hearts to the
Lord. 17 And whatsoever ye do in
word or deed, *do* all in the name of
the Lord Jesus, giving thanks to
God and the Father by him.

The apostle proceeds to exhort to mutual love and compassion: *Put on therefore bowels of mercy, v.* 12. We must not only put off anger and wrath (as *v.* 8), but we must put on compassion and kindness; not only cease to do evil, but learn to do well; not only not do hurt to any, but do what good we can to all.

I. The argument here used to enforce the exhortation is very affecting: *Put on, as the elect of God, holy and beloved.* Observe, 1. Those who are holy are the elect of God; and those who are the elect of God, and holy, are beloved—beloved of God, and ought to be so of all men. 2. Those who are the elect of God, holy and beloved, ought to conduct themselves in every thing as becomes them, and so as not to lose the credit of their holiness, nor the comfort of their being chosen and beloved. It becomes those who are holy towards God to be lowly and loving towards all men. Observe, What we must put on in particular. (1.) Compassion towards the miserable: *Bowels of mercy,* the tenderest mercies. Those who owe so much to mercy ought to be merciful to all who are proper objects of mercy. *Be you merciful, as your Father is merciful,* Luke vi. 36. (2.) *Kindness* towards our friends, and those who love us. A courteous disposition becomes the elect of God; for the design of the gospel is not only to soften the minds of men, but to sweeten them, and to promote friendship among men as well as reconciliation with God. (3.) *Humbleness of mind,* in submission to those above us, and condescension to those below us. There must not only be a humble demeanour, but a humble mind. *Learn of me, for I am meek and lowly in heart,* Matt. xi. 29. (4.) *Meekness* towards those who have provoked us, or been any way injurious to us. We must not be transported into any indecency by our resentment of indignities and neglects; but must prudently bridle our own anger, and patiently bear the anger of others. (5.) *Long-suffering* towards those who continue to provoke us. *Charity suffereth long,* as well *as is kind,* 1 Cor. xiii. 4. Many can bear a short provocation who are weary of bearing when it grows long. But we must suffer long both the injuries of men and the rebukes of divine Providence. If God is long-suffering to us, under all our provocations of him, we should exercise long-suffering to others in like cases. (6.) Mutual forbearance, in consideration of the infirmities and deficiencies under which we all labour: *Forbearing one another.* We have all of us something which needs to be borne with, and this is a good reason why we should bear with others in what is disagreeable to us. We need the same good turn from others which we are bound to show them. (7.) A readiness to forgive injuries: *Forgiving one another, if any man have a quarrel against any.* While we are in this world, where there is so much corruption in our hearts, and so much occasion of difference and contention, quarrels will sometimes happen, even among the elect of God, who are holy and beloved, as Paul and Barnabas had a *sharp contention, which parted them asunder one from the other* (Acts xv. 39), and Paul and Peter, Gal. ii. 14. But it is our duty to forgive one another in such cases; not to bear any grudge, but put up with the affront and pass it by. And the reason is: *Even as Christ forgave you, so also do you.* The consideration that we are forgiven by Christ so many offences is a good reason why we should forgive others. It is an argument of the divinity of Christ that he had *power on earth to forgive sins;* and it is a branch of his example which we are obliged to follow, if we ourselves would be forgiven. *Forgive us our trespasses, as we forgive those who trespass against us,* Matt. vi. 12.

II. In order to all this, we are exhorted here to several things:—1. To clothe ourselves with love (*v.* 14): *Above all things put on charity:* ἐπὶ πᾶσι δὲ τούτοις—*over all things.* Let this be the upper garment, the robe, the livery, the mark of our dignity and distinction. Or, Let this be principal and chief, as the whole sum and abstract of the second table. *Add to faith virtue, and to brotherly-kindness charity,* 2 Pet. i. 5—7. He lays the foundation in faith, and the top-stone in charity, *which is the bond of perfectness,* the cement and centre of all happy society. Christian unity consists of unanimity and mutual love. 2. To submit ourselves to the government of the *peace of God* (*v.* 15): *Let the peace of God rule in your hearts,* that is, God's being at peace with you, and the comfortable sense of his acceptance and favour: or, a disposition to peace among yourselves, a peaceable spirit, that keeps the peace, and makes peace. This is called the *peace of God,* because it is of his working in all who are his. The *kingdom of God is righteousness and peace,* Rom. xiv. 17. "Let this peace *rule in your heart*—prevail and govern there, or as an umpire decide all matters of difference among you."—*To which you are called in one body.* We are called to this peace, to peace with God as our privilege and peace with our brethren as our duty. Being united in one body, we are called to be at peace one with another, as the members of the natural body; for *we are the body of Christ, and members in particular,* 1 Cor. xii. 27. To preserve in us this peaceable disposition, we must be thankful. The work of thanksgiving to God is such a sweet and pleasant work that it will help to make us sweet and pleasant towards all men. "Instead of envying one another upon account of any particular favours and excellence, be thankful for his mercies, which are common to all of you." 3. To let the *word of Christ dwell in us richly, v.* 16. The gospel is the word of Christ, which has come to us; but that is not enough, it must dwell in us, or *keep house*—ἐνοικείτω, not as a servant in a family, who is under another's control, but as a master, who has a right to prescribe to and direct all under his roof. We must take our instructions and directions from it, and our portion of meat and strength, of grace and comfort, in due season, as from the *master of the household.* It must dwell in us; that is, be always ready and at hand to us in every thing, and have its due influence and use. We must be familiarly acquainted with it, and *know it for our good,* Job v. 27. It must dwell in us richly: not only keep house in our hearts, but keep a good house. Many have the word of Christ dwelling in them, but it dwells in them but poorly; it has no mighty force and influence upon them. Then the soul prospers when the word of God *dwells in us richly,* when we have abundance of it in us, and are full of the scriptures and of the grace of Christ. And this in all wisdom. The proper office of wisdom is to apply what we know to ourselves, for our own direction. The word of Christ must dwell in us, not in all notion and speculation, to make us doctors, but in all wisdom, to make us good Christians, and enable us to conduct ourselves in every thing as becomes Wisdom's children. 4. To teach and admonish one another. This would contribute very much to our furtherance in all grace; for we sharpen ourselves by quickening others, and improve our knowledge by communicating it for their edification. We must *admonish one another in psalms and hymns.* Observe, Singing of psalms is a gospel ordinance; ψαλμοῖς καὶ ὕμνοις καὶ ᾠδαῖς—the Psalms of David, and spiritual hymns and odes, collected out of the scripture, and suited to special occasions, instead of their lewd and profane songs in their idolatrous worship. Religious poesy seems countenanced by these expressions and is capable of great edification. But, when we sing psalms, we make no melody unless we sing with grace in our hearts, unless we are suitably affected with what we sing and go along in it with true devotion and understanding. Singing of psalms is a teaching ordinance as well as a praising ordinance; and we are not only to quicken and encourage ourselves, but to *teach and admonish one another,* mutually excite our affections, and convey instructions. 5. All must be done in the name of Christ (*v.* 17): *And whatsoever you do in word or deed, do all in the name of the Lord Jesus,* according to his command and in compliance with his authority, by strength derived from him, with an eye to his glory, and depending upon his merit for the acceptance of what is good and the pardon of what is amiss, *Giving thanks to God and the Father by him.* Observe, (1.) We must give thanks in all things; whatsoever we do, we must still give thanks, Eph. v. 20, *Giving thanks always for all things.* (2.) The Lord Jesus must be the Mediator of our praises as well as of our prayers. *We give thanks to God and the Father in the name of the Lord Jesus Christ,* Eph. v. 20. Those who do all things in Christ's name will never want matter of thanksgiving to God, even the Father.

18 Wives, submit yourselves unto your own husbands, as it is fit in the Lord. 19 Husbands, love *your* wives, and be not bitter against them. 20 Children, obey *your* parents in all things: for this is wellpleasing unto the Lord. 21 Fathers, provoke not your children *to anger,* lest they be discouraged. 22 Servants, obey in all things *your* masters according to the flesh; not with eyeservice, as menpleasers; but in singleness of heart, fearing God: 23 And whatsoever ye do, do *it* heartily, as to the Lord, and not unto men; 24 Knowing that of the Lord ye shall receive the reward of the inheritance: for ye serve the Lord Christ. 25 But he that doeth wrong shall receive for the wrong which he hath done: and there is no respect of persons.

The apostle concludes the chapter with exhortations to relative duties, as before in the epistle to the Ephesians. The epistles which are most taken up in displaying the glory of divine grace, and magnifying the Lord Jesus, are the most particular and distinct in pressing the duties of the several relations. We must never separate the privileges and duties of the gospel religion.

I. He begins with the duties of wives and husbands (*v.* 18): *Wives, submit yourselves unto your own husbands, as it is fit in the Lord.* Submission is the duty of wives, ὑποτάσσεσθε. It is the same word which is used to express our duty to magistrates (Rom. xiii. 1, *Let every soul be* subject *to the higher powers),* and is expressed by subjection and reverence, Eph. v. 24, 33. The reason is that *Adam was first formed, then Eve: and Adam was not deceived, but the woman, being deceived, was in the transgression,* 1 Tim. ii. 13, 14. He was first in the creation and last in the transgression. The *head of the woman is the man;* and the *man is not of the woman, but the woman of the man; neither was the man created for the woman, but the woman for the man,* 1 Cor. xi. 3, 8, 9. It is agreeable to the order of nature and the reason of things, as well as the appointment and will of God. But then it is submission, not to a rigorous lord or absolute tyrant, who may do his will and is without restraints, but to a husband, and to her own husband, who stands in the nearest relation, and is under strict engagements to proper duty too. And *this is fit in the Lord,* it is becoming the relation, and what they are bound in duty to do, as an instance of obedience to the authority and law of Christ. On the other hand, *husbands must love their wives, and not be bitter against them, v.* 19. They must love them with tender and faithful affection, as Christ loved the church, and as their own bodies, and even as themselves (Eph. v. 25, 28, 33), with a love peculiar to the nearest relation and the greatest comfort and blessing of life. And they must not be bitter against them, not use them unkindly, with harsh language or severe treatment, but be kind and obliging to them in all things; for the *woman was made for the man, neither is the man without the woman,* and the *man also is by the woman,* 1 Cor. xi. 9, 11, 12.

II. The duties of children and parents: *Children, obey your parents in all things, for this is well-pleasing unto the Lord, v.* 20. They must be willing to do all their lawful commands, and be at their direction and disposal; as those who have a natural right and are fitter to direct them than themselves. The apostle (Eph. vi. 2) requires them to honour as well as obey their parents; they must esteem them and think honourably of them, as the obedience of their lives must proceed from the esteem and opinion of their minds. And this is *well-pleasing to God,* or acceptable to him; for it is the *first commandment with promise* (Eph. vi. 2), with an explicit promise annexed to it, namely, *That it shall be well with them, and they shall live long on the earth.* Dutiful children are the most likely to prosper in the world and enjoy long life. And parents must be tender, as well as children obedient (*v.* 21): "*Fathers, provoke not your children to anger, lest they be discouraged.* Let not your authority over them be exercised with rigour and severity, but with kindness and gentleness, lest you raise their passions and discourage them in their duty, and by holding the reins too tight make them fly out with the greater fierceness." The bad temper and example of imprudent parents often prove a great hindrance to their children and a stumbling-block in their way; see Eph. vi. 4. And it is by the tenderness of parents, and dutifulness of children, that God ordinarily furnishes his church with a seed to serve him, and propagates religion from age to age.

III. Servants and masters: *Servants, obey your masters in all things according to the flesh, v.* 22. Servants must do the duty of the relation in which they stand, and obey their master's commands in *all things* which are consistent with their duty to God their heavenly Master. *Not with eye-service, as men-pleasers*—not only when their master's eye is upon them, but when they are from under their master's eye. They must be both just and diligent. *In singleness of heart, fearing God*—without selfish designs, or hypocrisy and disguise, as those who fear God and stand in awe of him. Observe, The fear of God ruling in the heart will make people good in every relation. Servants who fear God will be just and faithful when they are from under their master's eye, because they know they are under the eye of God. See Gen. xx. 11, *Because I thought, Surely the fear of God is not in this place.* Neh. v. 15, *But so did not I, because of the fear of God.* "And *whatsoever you do, do it heartily* (*v.* 23), with diligence, not idly and slothfully:" or, "Do it cheerfully, not discontented at the providence of God which put you in that relation."—*As to the Lord, and not as to men.* It sanctifies a servant's work when it is done as unto God—with an eye to his glory and in obedience to his command, and not merely as unto men, or with regard to them only. Observe, We are really doing our duty to God when we are faithful in our duty to men. And, for servants' encouragement, let them know that a good and faithful servant is never the further from heaven for his being a servant: "*Knowing that of the Lord you shall receive the reward of the inheritance, for you serve the Lord Christ, v.* 24. Serving your masters according to the command of Christ, you serve Christ, and he will be your paymaster: you will have a glorious reward at last. Though you are now servants, you will receive the inheritance of sons. But, on the other hand, *He who does wrong will receive for the wrong which he has done," v.* 25. There is a righteous God, who, if servants wrong their masters, will reckon with them for it, though they may conceal it from their master's notice. And he will be sure to punish the unjust as well as reward the faithful servant: and so if masters wrong their servants.—*And there is no respect of persons with him.* The righteous Judge of the earth will be impartial, and carry it with an equal hand towards master and servant; not swayed by any regard to men's outward circumstances and condition of life. The one and the other will stand upon a level at his tribunal.

It is probable that the apostle has a particular respect, in all these instances of duty, to the case mentioned 1 Cor. vii. of relations of a different religion, as a Christian and heathen, a Jewish convert and an uncircumcised Gentile, where there was room to doubt whether they were bound to fulfil the proper duties of their several relations to such persons. And, if it hold in such cases, it is much stronger upon Christians one towards another, and where both are of the same religion. And how happy would the gospel religion make the world, if it every where prevailed; and how much would it influence every state of things and every relation of life!

CHAP. IV.

I. He continues his account of the duty of masters, from the close of the former chapter, ver. 1. II. He exhorts to the duty of prayer (ver. 2—4), and to a prudent and decent conduct towards those with whom we converse, ver. 5, 6. III. He closes the epistle with the mention of several of his friends, of whom he gives an honourable testimony, ver. 7—18.

MASTERS, give unto *your* servants that which is just and equal; knowing that ye also have a Master in heaven.

The apostle proceeds with the duty of masters to their servants, which might have been joined to the foregoing chapter, and is a part of that discourse. Here observe, 1. Justice is required of them: *Give unto your servants that which is just and equal* (*v.* 1), not only strict justice, but equity and kindness. Be faithful to your promises to them, and perform your agreements; not defrauding them of their dues, nor *keeping back by fraud the hire of the labourers,* Jam. v. 4. Require no more of them than they are able to perform; and do not lay unreasonable burdens upon them, and beyond their strength. Provide for them what is fit, supply proper food and physic, and allow them such liberties as may fit them the better for cheerful service and make it the easier to them, and this though they be employed in the meanest and lowest offices, and of another country and a different religion from yourselves. 2. A good reason for this regard: "*Knowing that you also have a Master in heaven.* You who are masters of others have a Master yourself, and are servants of another Lord. You are not lords of yourselves, and are accountable to one above you. Deal with your servants as you expect God should deal with you, and as those who believe they must give an account.

You are both servants of the same Lord in the different relations in which you stand, and are equally accountable to him at last. *Knowing that your Master also is in heaven, neither is there respect of persons with him,"* Eph. vi. 9.

2 Continue in prayer, and watch
in the same with thanksgiving; 3
Withal praying also for us, that God
would open unto us a door of utterance, to speak the mystery of Christ,
for which I am also in bonds: 4
That I may make it manifest, as I
ought to speak.

If this be considered as connected with the foregoing verse, then we may observe that it is part of the duty which masters owe their servants to pray with them, and to pray daily with them, or *continue in prayer.* They must not only do justly and kindly by them, but act a Christian and religious part, and be concerned for their souls as well as their bodies: "As parts of your charge, and under your influence, be concerned for the blessing of God upon them, as well as the success of your affairs in their hands." And this is the duty of every one—to *continue in prayer.* "Keep up your constant times of prayer, without being diverted from it by other business; keep your hearts close to the duty, without wandering or deadness, and even to the end of it: *Watching in the same.*" Christians should lay hold of all opportunities for prayer, and choose the fittest seasons, which are least liable to disturbance from other things, and keep their minds lively in the duty, and in suitable frames.—*With thanksgiving,* or solemn acknowledgment of the mercies received. Thanksgiving must have a part in every prayer.—*Withal praying also for us, v.* 3. The people must pray particularly for their ministers, and bear them upon their hearts at all times at the throne of grace. As if he had said, "Do not forget us, whenever you pray for yourselves," Eph. vi. 19; 1 Thess. v. 25; Heb. xiii. 18. *That God would open to us a door of utterance,* that is, either afford opportunity to preach the gospel (so he says, *a great door and effectual is opened to me,* 1 Cor. xvi. 9), or else give me ability and courage, and enable me with freedom and faithfulness; so Eph. vi. 19, *And for me, that utterance may be given to me, that I may open my mouth boldly, to speak the mystery of Christ, for which I am also in bonds;* that is, either the deepest doctrines of the gospel with plainness, of which Christ is the principal subject (he calls it the *mystery of the gospel,* Eph. vi. 19), or else he means the preaching of the gospel to the Gentile world, which he calls the *mystery hidden from ages* (*ch.* i. 26) and the *mystery of Christ,* Eph. iii. 4. For this he was now in bonds. He was a prisoner at Rome, by the violent opposition of the malicious Jews. He would have them pray for him, that he might not be discouraged in his work, nor driven from it by his sufferings: *That I may make it manifest, as I ought to speak, v.* 4. That I may make this mystery known to those who have not heard of it, and make it plain to their understanding, in such a manner as I ought to do." He had been particular in telling them what he prayed for on their behalf, *ch.* i. Here he tells them particularly what he would have them pray for on his behalf. Paul knew as well as any man how to speak; and yet he begged their prayers for him, that he might be taught to speak. The best and most eminent Christians need the prayers of meaner Christians, and are not above asking them. The chief speakers need prayer, that God would give them a door of utterance, and that they may speak as they ought to speak.

5 Walk in wisdom toward them
that are without, redeeming the time.
6 Let your speech *be* alway with
grace, seasoned with salt, that ye
may know how ye ought to answer
every man.

The apostle exhorts them further to a prudent and decent conduct towards all those with whom they conversed, towards the heathen world, or those out of the Christian church among whom they lived (*v.* 5): *Walk in wisdom towards those who are without.* Be careful, in all your converse with them, to get no hurt by them, or contract any of their customs; for *evil communications corrupt good manners;* and to do no hurt to them, or increase their prejudices against religion, and give them an occasion of dislike. Yea, do them all the good you can, and by all the fittest means and in the proper seasons recommend religion to them.—*Redeeming the time;* that is, either "improving every opportunity of doing them good, and making the best use of your time in proper duty" (diligence in redeeming time very much recommends religion to the good opinion of others), or else "walking cautiously and with circumspection, to give them no advantage against you, nor expose yourselves to their malice and ill-will," Eph. v. 15, 16. *Walk circumspectly, redeeming the time, because the days are evil,* that is, dangerous, or times of trouble and suffering. And towards others, or those who are within as well as those who are without, "Let *your speech be always with grace, v.* 6. Let all your discourse be as becomes Christians, suitable to your profession—savoury, discreet, seasonable." Though it be not always of grace, it must be always with grace; and, though the matter of our discourse be that which is common, yet there must be an air of piety upon it and it must be in a Christian manner · *seasoned with salt.* Grace is the salt which seasons our discourse, makes it savoury, and keeps it from corrupting. *That you may know how to answer every man.* One answer is proper for one man, and another for another man Prov. xxvi. 4, 5. We have need of a great deal of wisdom and grace to give proper answers to every man, particularly in answering the questions and objections of adversaries against our religion, giving the reasons of our faith, and showing the unreasonableness of their exceptions and cavils to the best advantage for our cause and least prejudice to ourselves. *Be ready always to give an answer to every man who asketh you a reason of the hope that is in you, with meekness and fear,* 1 Pet. iii. 15.

7 All my state shall Tychicus
declare unto you, *who* is a beloved
brother, and a faithful minister and
fellowservant in the Lord: 8 Whom
I have sent unto you for the same
purpose, that he might know your
estate, and comfort your hearts; 9
With Onesimus, a faithful and beloved brother, who is *one* of you.
They shall make known unto you
all things which *are done* here. 10
Aristarchus my fellowprisoner saluteth you, and Marcus, sister's son to
Barnabas, (touching whom ye received
commandments: if he come unto you,
receive him;) 11 And Jesus, which
is called Justus, who are of the circumcision. These only *are my* fellow-
workers unto the kingdom of God,
which have been a comfort unto me.
12 Epaphras, who is *one* of you, a
servant of Christ, saluteth you, always
labouring fervently for you in prayers,
that ye may stand perfect and complete in all the will of God. 13 For
I bear him record, that he hath a great
zeal for you, and them *that are* at
Laodicea, and them in Hierapolis.
14 Luke, the beloved physician, and
Demas, greet you. 15 Salute the
brethren which are in Laodicea, and
Nymphas, and the church which is
in his house. 16 And when this
epistle is read among you, cause that
it be read also in the church of the
Laodiceans; and that ye likewise
read the *epistle* from Laodicea. 17
And say to Archippus, Take heed to
the ministry which thou hast received
in the Lord, that thou fulfil it. 18
The salutation by the hand of me
Paul. Remember my bonds. Grace
be with you. Amen.

In the close of this epistle the apostle does several of his friends the honour to leave their names upon record, with some testimony of his respect, which will be spoken of wherever the gospel comes, and last to the end of the world.

I. Concerning Tychicus, *v.* 7. By him this epistle was sent; and he does not give them an account in writing of his present state, because Tychicus would do it by word of mouth more fully and particularly. He knew they would be glad to hear how it fared with him. The churches cannot but be concerned for good ministers and desirous to know their state. He gives him this character, *A beloved brother and faithful minister.* Paul, though a great apostle, owns a faithful minister for a brother and a beloved brother. Faithfulness in any one is truly lovely, and renders him worthy our affection and esteem. *And a fellow-servant in the Lord.* Ministers are servants to Christ, and fellow-servants to one another. They have one Lord, though they have different stations and capacities of service. Observe, It adds much to the beauty and strength of the gospel ministry when ministers are thus loving and condescending one to another, and by all just means support and advance one another's reputation. Paul sent him not only to tell them of his affairs, but to bring him an account of theirs: *Whom I have sent unto you for the same purpose, that he might know your estate, and comfort your hearts, v.* 8. He was as willing to hear from them as they could be to hear from him, and thought himself as much obliged to sympathize with them as he thought them obliged to sympathize with him. It is a great comfort, under the troubles and difficulties of life, to have the mutual concern of fellow-christians.

II. Concerning Onesimus (*v.* 9): *With Onesimus, a faithful and beloved brother, who is one of you.* He was sent back from Rome along with Tychicus. This was he whom Paul had begotten in his bonds, Philem. 10. He had been servant to Philemon, and was a member, if not a minister, of their church. He was converted at Rome, whither he had fled from his master's service; and was now sent back, it is probable, with the epistle to Philemon, to introduce him again into his master's family. Observe, Though he was a poor servant, and had been a bad man, yet, being now a convert, Paul calls him a *faithful and beloved brother.* The meanest circumstance of life, and greatest wickedness of former life, make no difference in the spiritual relation among sincere Christians: they partake of the same privileges, and are entitled to the same regards. The *righteousness of God by faith of Jesus Christ is unto all and upon all those that believe; for there is no difference* (Rom. iii. 22): and *there is neither Jew nor Greek, neither bond nor free, for you are all one in Christ Jesus,* Gal. iii. 28. Perhaps this was some time after he was converted and sent back to Philemon, and by this time he had entered into the ministry, because Paul calls him a brother.

III. *Aristarchus, a fellow-prisoner.* Those who join in services and sufferings should be thereby engaged to one another in holy love. Paul had a particular affection for his fellow-servants and his fellow-prisoners.

IV. *Marcus, sister's son to Barnabas.* This is supposed to be the same who wrote the gospel which bears his name. *If he come unto you receive him.* Paul had a quarrel with Barnabas upon the account of this Mark, who was his nephew, and *thought not good to take him with them, because he departed from them from Pamphylia, and went not with them to the work,* Acts xv. 38. He would not take Mark with him, but took Silas, because Mark had deserted them; and yet Paul is not only reconciled to him himself, but recommends him to the respect of the churches, and gives a great example of a truly Christian and forgiving spirit. If men have been guilty of a fault, it must not be always remembered against them. We must forget as well as forgive. *If a man be overtaken in a fault, you who are spiritual restore such a one in the spirit of meekness,* Gal. vi. 1.

V. Here is one who is called *Jesus,* which is the Greek name for the Hebrew *Joshua. If Jesus had given them rest, then would he not afterwards have spoken of another day,* Heb. iv. 8. *Who is called Justus.* It is probable that he changed his name for that of Justus, in honour to the name of the Redeemer. Or else Jesus was his Jewish name, for he was of the circumcision; and Justus his Roman or Latin name. *These are my fellow-labourers unto the kingdom of God, who have been a comfort unto me.* Observe, What comfort the apostle had in the communion of saints and ministers! One is his fellow-servant, another his fellow-prisoner, and all his fellow-workers, who were working out their own salvation and endeavouring to promote the salvation of others. Good ministers take great comfort in those who are their fellow-workers unto the kingdom of God. Their friendship and converse together are a great refreshment under the sufferings and difficulties in their way.

VI. *Epaphras* (*v.* 12), the same with *Epaphroditus.* He is *one of you,* one of your church; *he salutes you,* or sends his service to you, and his best affections and wishes. *Always labouring fervently for you in prayers.* Epaphras had learned of Paul to be much in prayer for his friends. Observe, 1. In what manner he prayed for them. He laboured in prayer, laboured fervently, and always laboured fervently for them. Those who would succeed in prayer must take pains in prayer; and we must be earnest in prayer, not only for ourselves, but for others also. It is the effectual fervent prayer which is the prevailing prayer, and availeth much (Jam. v. 16), and *Elias prayed earnestly that it might not rain, v.* 17. 2. What is the matter of this prayer: *That you may stand perfect and complete in all the will of God.* Observe, To stand perfect and complete in the will of God is what we should earnestly desire both for ourselves and others. We must stand complete in all the will of God; in the will of his precepts by a universal obedience, and in the will of his providence by a cheerful submission to it: and we stand perfect and complete in both by constancy and perseverance unto the end. The apostle was witness for Epaphras that he had a great zeal for them: "*I bear him record;* I can testify for him that he has a great concern for you, and that all he does for you proceeds from a warm desire for your good." And his zeal extended to all about them: to *those who are in Laodicea and Hierapolis.* He had a great concern for the Christian interest in the neighbouring places, as well as among them.

VII. *Luke* is another here mentioned, whom he calls the *beloved physician.* This is he who wrote the Gospel and Acts, and was Paul's companion. Observe, He was both a physician and an evangelist. Christ himself both taught and healed, and was the great physician as well as prophet of the church. He was the beloved physician; one who recommended himself more than ordinary to the affections of his friends. Skill in physic is a useful accomplishment in a minister and may be improved to more extensive usefulness and greater esteem among Christians.

VIII. *Demas.* Whether this was written before the second epistle to Timothy or after is not certain. There we read (2 Tim. iv. 10), *Demas hath forsaken me, having loved this present world.* Some have thought that this epistle was written after; and then it is an evidence that, though Demas forsook Paul, yet he did not forsake Christ; or he forsook him but for a time, and recovered himself again, and Paul forgave him and owned him as a brother. But others think more probably that this epistle was written before the other; this in *anno* 62, that in 66, and then it is an evidence how considerable a man Demas was, who yet afterwards revolted. Many who have made a great figure in profession, and gained a great name among Christians, have yet shamefully apostatized: *They went forth from us, because they were not of us,* 1 John ii. 19.

IX. The *brethren in Laodicea* are here mentioned, as living in the neighbourhood of Colosse: and Paul sends salutations to them, and orders that this epistle should be read in the church of the Laodiceans (*v.* 16), that a copy of it should be sent thither, to be read publicly in their congregation. And some think Paul sent another epistle at this time to Laodicea, and ordered them to send for that from Laodicea, and read it in their church: *And that you likewise read the epistle from Laodicea.* If so, that epistle is now lost, and did not belong to the canon; for all the epistles which the apostles ever wrote were not preserved, any more than the words and actions of our blessed Lord. *There are many other things which Jesus did, which if they should be written every one, I suppose the world itself could not contain the books which would be written,* John xxi. 25. But some think it was the epistle to the Ephesians, which is still extant.

X. *Nymphas* is mentioned (*v.* 15) as one who lived at Colosse, and had a church in his house; that is, either a religious family, where the several parts of worship were daily performed; or some part of the congregation met there, when they had no public places of worship allowed, and they were forced to assemble in private houses for fear of their enemies. *The disciples were assembled for fear of the Jews* (John xx. 19), and the apostle preached in his *own lodging and hired house,* Acts xxviii. 23, 30. In the former sense it showed his exemplary piety; in the latter his zeal and public spirit.

XI. Concerning *Archippus,* who was one of their ministers at Colosse. They are bidden to admonish him to mind his work as a minister, to *take heed to it, and to fulfil it*—to be diligent and careful of all the parts of it, and to persevere in it unto the end. They must attend to the main design of their ministry, without troubling themselves or the people with things foreign to it, or of less moment. Observe, (1.) The ministry we have received is a great honour; for it is *received in the Lord,* and is by his appointment and command. (2.) Those who have received it must fulfil it, or do the full duty of it. Those betray their trust, and will have a sad account at last, who *do this work of the Lord negligently.* (3.) The people may put their ministers in mind of their duty, and excite them to it: *Say to Archippus, Take heed to the ministry,* though no doubt with decency and respect, not from pride and conceit.

XII. Concerning himself (*v.* 18): *The salutation of me Paul. Remember my bonds.* He had a scribe to write all the rest of the epistle, but these words he wrote with his own hand: *Remember my bonds.* He does not say, "Remember I am a prisoner, and send me supply;" but, "Remember I am in bonds as the apostle of the Gentiles, and let this confirm your faith in the gospel of Christ:" it adds weight to this exhortation: *I therefore, the prisoner of the Lord, beseech you to walk worthy,* Eph. iv. 1. "*Grace be with you.* The favour of God, and all good, the blessed fruits and effects of it, be with you, and be your portion."

AN

EXPOSITION,

WITH PRACTICAL OBSERVATIONS,

OF THE FIRST EPISTLE OF ST. PAUL TO THE

THESSALONIANS.

Thessalonica was formerly the metropolis of Macedonia; it is now called *Salonichi,* and is the best peopled, and one of the best towns for commerce, in the Levant. The apostle Paul, being diverted from his design of going into the provinces of Asia, properly so called, and directed after an extraordinary manner to preach the gospel in Macedonia (Acts xvi. 9, 10), in obedience to the call of God went from Troas to Samothracia, thence to Neapolis, and thence to Philippi, where he had good success in his ministry, but met with hard usage, being cast into prison with Silas his companion in travel and labour, from which being wonderfully delivered, they comforted the brethren there, and departed. Passing through Amphipolis and Apollonia, they came to Thessalonica, where the apostle planted a church that consisted of some believing Jews and many converted Gentiles, Acts xvii. 1—4. But a tumult being raised in the city by the unbelieving Jews, and the lewd and baser sort of the inhabitants, Paul and Silas, for their safety, were sent away by night unto Berea, and afterwards Paul was conducted to Athens, leaving Silas and Timotheus behind him, but sent directions that they should come to him with all speed. When they came, Timotheus was sent to Thessalonica, to enquire after their welfare and to establish them in the faith (1 Thess. iii. 2), and, returning to Paul while he tarried at Athens, was sent again, together with Silas, to visit the churches in Macedonia. So that Paul, being left at Athens alone (1 Thess. iii. 1), departed thence to Corinth, where he continued a year and a half, in which time Silas and Timotheus returned to him from Macedonia (Acts

xviii. 5), and then he wrote this epistle to the church of Christ at Thessalonica, which, though it is placed after the other epistles of this apostle, is supposed to be first in time of all Paul's epistles, and to be written about A. D. 51. The main scope of it is to express the thankfulness of this apostle for the good success his preaching had among them, to establish them in the faith, and persuade them to a holy conversation.

CHAP. I.

After the introduction (ver. 1) the apostle begins with a thanksgiving to God for the saving benefits bestowed on them, ver. 2—5. And then mentions the sure evidences of the good success of the gospel among them, which was notorious and famous in several other places, ver. 6—10.

PAUL, and Silvanus, and Timotheus, unto the church of the Thessalonians *which is* in God the Father and *in* the Lord Jesus Christ: Grace *be* unto you, and peace, from God our Father, and the Lord Jesus Christ.

In this introduction we have,

I. The inscription, where we have, 1. The persons from whom this epistle came, or by whom it was written. Paul was the inspired apostle and writer of this epistle, though he makes no mention of his apostleship, which was not doubted of by the Thessalonians, nor opposed by any false apostle among them. He joins Silvanus (or Silas) and Timotheus with himself (who had now come to him with an account of the prosperity of the churches in Macedonia), which shows this great apostle's humility, and how desirous he was to put honour upon the ministers of Christ who were of an inferior rank and standing. A good example this is to such ministers as are of greater abilities and reputation in the church than some others. 2. The persons to whom this epistle is written, namely, the church of the Thessalonians, the converted Jews and Gentiles in Thessalonica; and it is observable that this church is said to *be in God the Father and in the Lord Jesus Christ:* they had fellowship with the Father, and his Son Jesus Christ, 1 John i. 3. They were a Christian church, because they believed in God the Father and in the Lord Jesus Christ. They believed the principles both of natural and revealed religion. The Gentiles among them were turned to God from idols, and the Jews among them believed Jesus to be the promised Messias. All of them were devoted and dedicated to God the Father and the Lord Jesus Christ: to God as their chief good and highest end, to Jesus Christ as their Lord and Mediator between God and man. God the Father is the original and centre of all natural religion; and Jesus Christ is the author and centre of all revealed religion. *You believe in God,* says our Saviour, *believe also in me,* John xiv. 1.

II. The salutation or apostolical benediction: *Grace be with you, and peace from God our Father and the Lord Jesus Christ.* This is the same for substance as in the other epistles. Grace and peace are well joined together; for the free grace or favour of God is the spring or fountain of all the peace and prosperity we do or can enjoy; and where there are gracious dispositions in us we may hope for peaceful thoughts in our own breasts; both grace and peace, and all spiritual blessings, come to us from God the Father and the Lord Jesus Christ; from God the original of all good, and from the Lord Jesus the purchaser of all good for us; from God in Christ, and so our Father in covenant, because he is the God and Father of our Lord Jesus Christ. Note, As all good comes from God, so no good can be hoped for by sinners but from God in Christ. And the best good may be expected from God as our Father for the sake of Christ.

2 We give thanks to God always for you all, making mention of you in our prayers; 3 Remembering without ceasing your work of faith, and labour of love, and patience of hope in our Lord Jesus Christ, in the sight of God and our Father; 4 Knowing, brethren beloved, your election of God. 5 For our gospel came not unto you in word only, but also in power, and in the Holy Ghost, and in much assurance; as ye know what manner of men we were among you for your sake.

I. The apostle begins with thanksgiving to God. Being about to mention the things that were matter of joy to him, and highly praiseworthy in them, and greatly for their advantage, he chooses to do this by way of thanksgiving to God, who is the author of all that good that comes to us, or is done by us, at any time. God is the object of all religious worship, of prayer and praise. And thanksgiving to God is a great duty, to be performed always or constantly; even when we do not actually give thanks to God by our words, we should have a grateful sense of God's goodness upon our minds. Thanksgiving should be often repeated; and not only should we be thankful for the favours we ourselves receive, but for the benefits bestowed on others also, upon our fellow-creatures and fellow-christians. The apostle gave thanks not only for those who were his most intimate friends, or most eminently favoured of God, but for them all.

II. He joined prayer with his praise or thanksgiving. When we in every thing by prayer and supplication make our requests known to God, we should join thanksgiving therewith, Phil. iv. 6. So when we give thanks for any benefit we receive we should join prayer. We should pray always and without ceasing, and should pray not only for ourselves, but for others also, for our friends, and should make mention of them in our prayers. We may sometimes mention their names, and should make mention of their case and condition; at least, we should have their persons and circumstances in our minds, remembering them without ceasing. Note, As there is much that we ought to be thankful for on the behalf of ourselves and our friends, so there is much occasion of constant prayer for further supplies of good.

III. He mentions the particulars for which he was so thankful to God; namely,

1. The saving benefits bestowed on them. These were the grounds and reasons of his thanksgiving. (1.) Their faith and their work of faith. Their faith he tells them (*v.* 8) was very famous, and spread abroad. This is the radical grace; and their faith was a true and living faith, because a working faith. Note, Wherever there is a true faith,it will work: it will have an influence upon heart and life; it will put us upon working for God and for our own salvation. We have comfort in our own faith and the faith of others when we perceive the work of faith. *Show me thy faith by thy works,* Jam. ii. 18. (2.) Their love and the labour of love. Love is one of the cardinal graces; it is of great use to us in this life and will remain and be perfected in the life to come. *Faith works by love;* it shows itself in the exercise of love to God and love to our neighbour; as love will show itself by labour, it will put us upon taking pains in religion. (3.) Their hope and the patience of hope. *We are saved by hope.* This grace is compared to the soldier's helmet and sailor's anchor, and is of great use in times of danger. Wherever there is a well-grounded hope of eternal life, it will appear by the exercise of patience; in a patient bearing of the calamities of the present time and a patient waiting for the glory to be revealed. *For, if we hope for that we see not, then do we with patience wait for it,* Rom. viii. 25.

2. The apostle not only mentions these three cradinal graces, faith, hope, and love, but also takes notice, (1.) Of the object and efficient cause of these graces, namely, our Lord Jesus Christ. (2.) Of the sincerity of them: being in the *sight of God even our Father.* The great motive to sincerity is the apprehension of God's eye as always upon us; and it is a sign of sincerity when in all we do we endeavour to approve ourselves to God, and that is right which is so in the sight of God. Then is the work of faith, or labour of love, or patience of hope, sincere, when it is done as under the eye of God. (3.) He mentions the fountain whence these graces flow, namely, God's electing love: *Knowing, brethren beloved, your election of God, v.* 4. Thus he runs up these streams to the fountain, and that was God's eternal election. Some by their election of God would understand only the temporary separation of the Thessalonians from the unbelieving Jews and Gentiles in their conversion; but this was according to the *eternal purpose of him who worketh all things according to the counsel of his own will,* Eph. i. 11. Speaking of their election, he calls them, *brethren beloved;* for the original of the brotherhood that is between Christians and the relation wherein they stand one to another is election. And it is a good reason why we should *love one another,* because we are all beloved of God, and were beloved of him in his counsels when there was not any thing in us to merit his love. The election of these Thessalonians was known to the apostles, and therefore might be known to themselves, and that by the fruits and effects thereof—their sincere faith, and hope, and love, by the successful preaching of the gospel among them. Observe, [1.] All those who in the fulness of time are effectually called and sanctified were from eternity elected and chosen to salvation. [2.] The election of God is of his own good pleasure and mere grace, not for the sake of any merit in those who are chosen. [3.] The election of God may be known by the fruits thereof. [4.] Whenever we are giving thanks to God for his grace either to ourselves or others, we should run up the streams to the fountain, and give thanks to God for his electing love, by which we are made to differ.

3. Another ground or reason of the apostle's thanksgiving is the success of his ministry among them. He was thankful on his own account as well as theirs, that he had not laboured in vain. He had the seal and evidence of his apostleship hereby, and great encouragement in his labours and sufferings. Their ready acceptance and entertainment of the gospel he preached to them were an evidence of their being elected and beloved of God. It was in this way that he knew their election. It is true he had been in the third heavens; but he had not searched the records of eternity, and found their election there, but knew this by the success of the gospel among them (*v.* 5), and he takes notice with thankfulness, (1.) That the gospel came to them also not in word only, but in power; they not only heard the sound of it, but submitted to the power of it. It did not merely tickle the ear and please the fancy, not merely fill their heads with notions and amuse their minds for awhile, but it affected their hearts: a divine power went along with it for convincing their consciences and amending their lives. Note, By this we may know our election, if we not only speak of the things of God by rote as parrots, but feel the influence of these things in our hearts, mortifying our lusts, weaning us from the world, and raising us up to heavenly things. (2.)

It came in the Holy Ghost, that is, with the powerful energy of the divine Spirit. Note, Wherever the gospel comes in power, it is to be attributed to the operation of the Holy Ghost; and unless the Spirit of God accompany the word of God, to render it effectual by his power, it will be to us but as a dead letter; and the letter killeth, it is the Spirit that giveth life. (3.) The gospel came to them in much assurance. Thus did they entertain it by the power of the Holy Ghost. They were fully convinced of the truth of it, so as not to be easily shaken in mind by objections and doubts; they were willing to leave all for Christ, and to venture their souls and everlasting condition upon the verity of the gospel revelation. The word was not to them, like the sentiments of some philosophers about matters of opinion and doubtful speculation, but the object of their faith and assurance. Their *faith was the evidence of things not seen;* and the Thessalonians thus knew what manner of men the apostle and his fellow-labourers were among them, and what they did for their sake, and with what good success.

6 And ye became followers of us,
and of the Lord, having received the
word in much affliction, with joy of
the Holy Ghost: 7 So that ye were
ensamples to all that believe in Macedonia and Achaia. 8 For from you
sounded out the word of the Lord
not only in Macedonia and Achaia,
but also in every place your faith to
God-ward is spread abroad; so that
we need not to speak any thing. 9
For they themselves show of us what
manner of entering in we had unto
you, and how ye turned to God from
idols to serve the living and true
God; 10 And to wait for his Son
from heaven, whom he raised from
the dead, *even* Jesus, which delivered
us from the wrath to come.

In these words we have the evidence of the apostle's success among the Thessalonians, which was notorious and famous in several places. For,

I. They were careful in their holy conversation to imitate the good examples of the apostles and ministers of Christ, *v.* 6. As the apostle took care to demean himself well, not only for his own credit's sake, but for the benefit of others, by a conversation suitable to his doctrine, that he might not pull down with one hand what he built up with the other, so the Thessalonians, who observed what manner of men they were among them, how their preaching and living were all of a piece, showed a conscientious care to be followers of them, or to imitate their good example. Herein they became also followers of the Lord, who is the perfect example we must strive to imitate; and we should be followers of others no further than they are followers of Christ, 1 Cor. xi. 1. The Thessalonians acted thus, notwithstanding their affliction, that much affliction which the apostles and themselves also were exposed to. They were willing to share in the sufferings that attended the embracing and professing of Christianity. They entertained the gospel, notwithstanding the troubles and hardships which attended the preachers and professors of it too. Perhaps this made the word more precious, being dear-bought; and the examples of the apostles shone very bright under their afflictions; so that the Thessalonians embraced the word cheerfully, and followed the example of the suffering apostles joyfully, *with joy in the Holy Ghost*—such solid and spiritual and lasting joy as the Holy Ghost is the author of, who, when our afflictions abound, makes our consolations much more to abound.

II. Their zeal prevailed to such a degree that they were themselves examples to all about them, *v.* 7, 8. Observe here,

1. Their example was very effectual to make good impressions upon many others. They were τυποὶ—*stamps,* or instruments to make impression with. They had themselves received good impressions from the preaching and conversation of the apostles, and they made good impressions, and their conversation had an influence upon others. Note, Christians should be so good as by their example to influence others.

2. It was very extensive, and reached beyond the confines of Thessalonica, even to the believers of all Macedonia, and further, in Achaia; the Philippians, and others who received the gospel before the Thessalonians, were edified by their example. Note, Some who were last hired into the vineyard may sometimes outstrip those who come in before them, and become examples to them.

3. It was very famous. The word of the Lord, or its wonderful effects upon the Thessalonians, sounded, or was famous and well known, in the regions round about that city, and *in every place;* not strictly every where, but here and there, up and down in the world: so that, from the good success of the gospel among them, many others were encouraged to entertain it, and to be willing, when called, to suffer for it. Their faith was spread abroad. (1.) The readiness of their faith was famed abroad. These Thessalonians embraced the gospel as soon as it was preached to them; so that every body took notice what manner of entering in among them the apostles had, that there were no such delays as at Philippi, where it was a great while before much good was done. (2.) The effects of their faith were famous. [1.] They quitted their idolatry; they turned from their idols, and abandoned all the false wor-

ship they had been educated in. [2.] They gave themselves up to God, to the living and true God, and devoted themselves to his service. [3.] They set themselves to wait for the Son of God from heaven, *v.* 10. And this is one of the peculiarities of our holy religion, to wait for Christ's second coming, as those who believe he will come and hope he will come to our joy. The believers under the Old Testament waited for the coming of the Messiah, and believers now wait for his second coming; he is yet to come. And there is good reason to believe he will come, because God has raised him from the dead, which is a full assurance unto all men that he will come to judgment, Acts xvii. 31. And there is good reason to hope and wait for his coming, because he has delivered us from the wrath to come. He came to purchase salvation, and will, when he comes again, bring salvation with him, full and final deliverance from sin, and death, and hell, from that wrath which is yet to come upon unbelievers, and which, when it has once come, will be yet to come, because it is *everlasting fire* prepared for the devil and his angels, Matt. xxv. 41.

CHAP. II.

In this chapter the apostle puts the Thessalonians in mind of the manner of his preaching among them, ver. 1—6. Then of the manner of his conversation among them, ver. 7—12. Afterwards of the success of his ministry, with the effects both on himself and on them (ver. 13—16), and then apologizes for his absence, ver. 17—20.

FOR yourselves, brethren, know
our entrance in unto you, that
it was not in vain: 2 But even after
that we had suffered before, and were
shamefully entreated, as ye know, at
Philippi, we were bold in our God to
speak unto you the gospel of God
with much contention. 3 For our
exhortation *was* not of deceit, nor of
uncleanness, nor in guile: 4 But as
we were allowed of God to be put in
trust with the gospel, even so we
speak; not as pleasing men, but
God, which trieth our hearts. 5 For
neither at any time used we flattering
words, as ye know, nor a cloak of
covetousness; God *is* witness: 6
Nor of men sought we glory, neither
of you, nor *yet* of others, when we
might have been burdensome, as the
apostles of Christ.

Here we have an account of Paul's manner of preaching, and his comfortable reflection upon his entrance in among the Thessalonians. As he had the testimony of his own conscience witnessing to his integrity, so he could appeal to the Thessalonians how faithfully he, and Silas, and Timotheus, his helpers in the work of the Lord, had discharged their office: *You yourselves, brethren, know our entrance in unto you.* Note, It is a great comfort to a minister to have his own conscience and the consciences of others witnessing for him that he set out well, with good designs and from good principles; and that *his preaching was not in vain,* or, as some read it, *was not vain.* The apostle here comforts himself either in the success of his ministry, that it was not fruitless or in vain (according to our translation), or, as others think, reflecting upon the sincerity of his preaching, that it was not vain and empty, or deceitful and treacherous. The subject-matter of the apostle's preaching was not vain and idle speculations about useless niceties and foolish questions, but sound and solid truth, such as was most likely to profit his hearers. A good example this is, to be imitated by all the ministers of the gospel. Much less was the apostle's preaching vain or deceitful. He could say to these Thessalonians what he told the Corinthians (2 Cor. iv. 2): *We have renounced the hidden things of dishonesty, not walking in craftiness, nor handling the word of God deceitfully.* He had no sinister or worldly design in his preaching, which he puts them in mind to have been,

I. With courage and resolution: *We were bold in our God to speak unto you the gospel of God, v.* 2. The apostle was inspired with a holy boldness, nor was he discouraged at the afflictions he met with, or the opposition that was made against him. He had met with ill usage at Philippi, as these Thessalonians well knew. There it was that he and Silas were shamefully treated, being put in the stocks; yet no sooner were they set at liberty than they went to Thessalonica, and preached the gospel with as much boldness as ever. Note, Suffering in a good cause should rather sharpen than blunt the edge of holy resolution. The gospel of Christ, at its first setting out in the world, met with much opposition; and those who preached it preached it *with contention,* with great agony, which denoted either the apostles' striving in their preaching or their striving against the opposition they met with. This was Paul's comfort; he was neither daunted in his work, nor driven from it.

II. With great simplicity and godly sincerity: *Our exhortation was not of deceit, nor of uncleanness, nor in guile, v.* 3. This, no doubt, was matter of the greatest comfort to the apostle—the consciousness of his own sincerity; and was one reason of his success. It was the sincere and uncorrupted gospel that he preached and exhorted them to believe and obey. His design was not to set up a faction, to draw men over to a party, but to promote *pure religion and undefiled before God and the Father.* The gospel he preached was without deceit, it was true and faithful; it was not fallacious, nor a cunningly-devised fable. Nor was it of uncleanness. His gospel was pure and holy, worthy of its holy author, tending to discountenance all manner of impurity. *The word of God is pure.* There should be no corrupt mixtures therewith; and, as the matter of the apostle's exhortation was thus true and pure, the manner of his speaking was without guile. He did not pretend one thing and intend another. *He believed, and therefore he spoke.* He had no sinister and secular aims and views, but was in reality what he seemed to be. The apostle not only asserts his sincerity, but subjoins the reasons and evidences thereof. The reasons are contained, *v.* 4.

1. They were stewards, *put in trust* with the gospel: and it is required of a steward that he be faithful. The gospel which Paul preached was not his own, but the gospel of God. Note, Ministers have a great favour shown them, and honour put upon them, and trust committed to them. They must not dare to corrupt the word of God: they must diligently make use of what is entrusted with them, so as God hath allowed and commanded, knowing they shall be called to an account, when they must be no longer stewards.

2. Their design was to please God and not men. God is a God of truth, and requires truth in the inward parts; and, if sincerity be wanting, all that we do cannot please God. The gospel of Christ is not accommodated to the vain fancies and lusts of men, to gratify their appetites and passions; but, on the contrary, it was designed for the mortifying of their corrupt affections, and delivering them from the power of fancy, that they might be brought under the power of faith. *If I yet pleased men, I should not be the servant of Christ*, Gal. i. 10.

3. They acted under the consideration of God's omniscience, as in the sight of him who *tries our hearts.* This is indeed the great motive to sincerity, to consider that God not only seeth all that we do, but knoweth our thoughts afar off, and searcheth the heart. He is well acquainted with all our aims and designs, as well as our actions. And it is from this God who trieth our hearts that we must receive our reward. The evidences of the apostle's sincerity follow; and they are these:—(1.) He avoided flattery: *Neither at any time used we flattering words, as you know, v.* 5. He and his fellow-labourers preached Christ and him crucified, and did not aim to gain an interest in men's affections for themselves, by glorying, and fawning and wheedling them. No, he was far from this; nor did he flatter men in their sins; nor tell them, if they would be of his party, they might live as they listed. He did not flatter them with vain hopes, nor indulge them in any evil work or way, promising them life, and so *daubing with untempered mortar.* (2.) He avoided covetousness. He did not make the ministry *a cloak*, or a covering, for *covetousness, as God was witness, v.* 5. His design was not to enrich himself by preaching the gospel, so far from this, he did not stipulate with them for bread. He was not like the false apostles, who, *through covetousness, with feigned words made merchandise* of the people, 2 Pet. ii. 3. (3.) He avoided ambition and vain-glory: *Nor of men sought we glory, neither of you nor yet of others, v.* 6. They expected neither people's purses nor their caps, neither to be enriched by them nor caressed, and adored, and called Rabbi by them. This apostle exhorts the Galatians (*ch.* v. 26) *not to be desirous of vain-glory;* his ambition was to obtain *that honour which comes from God*, John v. 44. He tells them that they might have used greater authority as apostles, and expected greater esteem, and demanded maintenance, which is meant by the phrase of *being burdensome*, because perhaps some would have thought this too great a burden for them to bear.

7 But we were gentle among you,
even as a nurse cherisheth her children: 8 So being affectionately desirous of you, we were willing to have imparted unto you, not the gospel of God only, but also our own souls, because ye were dear unto us. 9
For ye remember, brethren, our labour and travail: for labouring night and day, because we would not be chargeable unto any of you, we preached unto you the gospel of God. 10 Ye *are* witnesses, and God *also*, how holily and justly and unblameably we behaved ourselves among you that believe: 11 As ye know how we exhorted and comforted and charged every one of you, as a father *doth* his children, 12 That
ye would walk worthy of God, who hath called you unto his kingdom and glory.

In these words the apostle reminds the Thessalonians of the manner of his conversation among them. And,

I. He mentions the gentleness of their behaviour: *We were gentle among you, v.* 7. He showed great mildness and tenderness who might have acted with the authority of an apostle of Christ. Such a behaviour greatly recommends religion, and is most agreeable to God's gracious dealing with sinners, in and by the gospel. This great apostle, though he abhorred and avoided flattery, was most condescending to all men. He accommodated himself to all men's capacities, *and became all things to all men.* He showed the kindness and care of a nurse that cherishes her children. This is the way to win people, rather than to rule with rigour. The word of God is indeed powerful; and as it comes often with awful authority upon the minds of men, as it always has enough in it to convince every impartial judgment, so it comes with the more pleasing power, when the ministers of the gospel recommend themselves to the affections of the people. And as a nursing mother bears with frowardness in a child, and condescends to mean offices for its good, and draws out her breast, cherishing it in her bosom, so in like manner should the ministers of Christ behave towards their people. The *servant of the Lord must not strive, but be gentle unto all men, and patient,* 2 Tim. ii. 24. This gentleness and goodness the apostle expressed several ways. 1. By the most affectionate desire of their welfare: *Being affectionately desirous of you, v.* 8. The apostle had a most affectionate love to their persons, and sought them, not theirs; themselves, not their goods; and to gain them, not to be a gainer by them, or to make a merchandise of them: it was their spiritual and eternal welfare and salvation that he was earnestly desirous of. 2. By great readiness to do them good, willingly imparting to them, *not the gospel of God only, but also our own souls, v* 8. See here the manner of Paul's preaching. He spared no pains therein. He was willing to run hazards, and venture his soul, or life, in preaching the gospel. He was willing to spend and be spent in the service of men's souls; and, as those who give bread to the hungry from a charitable principle are said to impart their souls in what they give (Isa. lviii. 10), so did the apostles in giving forth the bread of life; so dear were these Thessalonians in particular to this apostle, and so great was his love to them. 3. By bodily labour to prevent their charge, or that his ministry might not be expensive and burdensome to them: *You remember our labour and travail; for, labouring night and day,* &c., *v.* 9. He denied himself the liberty he had of taking wages from the churches. To the labour of the ministry he added that of his calling, as a tent-maker, that he might get his own bread. We are not to suppose that the apostle spent the whole night and day in bodily labour, or work, to supply the necessities of his body; for then he would have had no time for the work of the ministry. But he spent part of the night, as well as the day, in this work; and was willing to forego his rest in the night, that he might have an opportunity to do good to the souls of men in the day time. A good example is here set before the ministers of the gospel, to be industrious for the salvation of men's souls, though it will not follow that they are always obliged to preach freely. There is no general rule to be drawn from this instance, either that ministers may at no time work with their hands, for the supply of their outward necessities, or that they ought always to do so. 4. By the holiness of their conversation, concerning which he appeals not only to them, but to God also (*v.* 10): *You are witnesses, and God also.* They were observers of their outward conversation in public before men, and God was witness not only of their behaviour in secret, but of the inward principles from which they acted. Their behaviour was holy towards God, just towards all men, and unblamable, without giving cause of scandal or offence; and they were careful to give no offence either to those who were without, or to those who believed, that they might give no ill example; that their preaching and living might be all of a piece. Herein, said this apostle, *do I exercise myself, to have always a conscience void of offence towards God, and towards men,* Acts xxiv. 16.

II. He mentions their faithful discharge of the work and office of the ministry, *v.* 11, 12. Concerning this also he could appeal to them as witnesses. Paul and his fellow-labourers were not only good Christians, but faithful ministers. And we should not only be good as to our general calling as Christians, but in our particular callings and relations. Paul exhorted the Thessalonians, not only informing them in their duty, but exciting and quickening them to the performance of it, by proper motives and arguments. And he comforted them also, endeavouring to cheer and support their spirits under the difficulties and discouragements they might meet with. And this he did not only publicly, but privately also, and from house to house (Acts xx. 20), *and charged every one* of them by personal addresses: this, some think, is intended by the similitude of a father's charging his children. This expression also denotes the affectionate and compassionate counsels and consolations which this apostle used. He was their spiritual father; and, as he cherished them like a nursing mother, so he charged them as a father, with a father's affection rather than a father's authority. As *my beloved sons, I warn you,* 1 Cor. iv. 14. The manner of this apostle's exhortation ought to be regarded by ministers in particular for their imitation, and the matter of it is greatly to be regarded by them and all others; namely, that *they would walk worthy of God, who hath called them to his kingdom and glory, v.* 12. Observe, 1. What is our great gospel privilege—that God has called us to his kingdom and glory. The gospel calls us into the kingdom and state of grace here and unto the kingdom and state of glory hereafter, to heaven and happiness as our end and to holiness as the way to that end. 2. What is our great gospel duty—that we walk worthy of God, that the temper of our minds and tenour of our lives be answerable to this call and suitable to this privilege. We should accommodate ourselves to the intention and design of the gospel, and live suitably to our profession and privileges, our hopes and expectations, as becomes those who are called with such a high and holy calling.

13 For this cause also thank we God without ceasing, because, when

ye received the word of God which
ye heard of us, ye received *it* not *as*
the word of men, but as it is in
truth, the word of God, which effectually worketh also in you that believe.
14 For ye, brethren, became followers
of the churches of God which in
Judæa are in Christ Jesus: for ye
also have suffered like things of your
own countrymen, even as they *have*
of the Jews: 15 Who both killed
the Lord Jesus, and their own prophets, and have persecuted us; and
they please not God, and are contrary
to all men: 16 Forbidding us to
speak to the Gentiles that they might
be saved, to fill up their sins alway:
for the wrath is come upon them to
the uttermost.

Here observe, I. The apostle makes mention of the success of his ministry among these Thessalonians (*v.* 13), which is expressed,

1. By the manner of their receiving the word of God: *When you received the word of God, which you heard of us, you received it, not as the word of men, but (as it is in truth) the word of God.* Where note, (1.) The word of the gospel is preached by men like ourselves, men of like passions and infirmities with others: *We have this treasure in earthen vessels.* The word of God, which these Thessalonians received, they heard from the apostles. (2.) However, it is in truth the word of God. Such was the word the apostles preached by divine inspiration, and such is that which is left upon record, written in the scriptures by divine inspiration; and such is that word which in our days is preached, being either contained, or evidently founded on, or deduced from, these sacred oracles. (3.) Those are greatly to blame who give out their own fancies or injunctions for the word of God. This is the vilest way of imposing upon a people, and to deal unfaithfully. (4.) Those are also to blame who, in hearing the word, look no further than to the ministry of men, or the words of men, who are only, or chiefly, pleased with the elegance of the style, or the beauty of the composition, or the voice and manner in which the word is preached, and expect to receive their advantage herein. (5.) We should receive the word of God as the word of God, with affections suitable to the holiness, wisdom, verity, and goodness, thereof. The words of men are frail and perishing, like themselves, and sometimes false, foolish, and fickle: but God's word is holy, wise, just, and faithful; and, like its author, lives and abides for ever. Let us accordingly receive and regard it.

2. By the wonderful operation of this word they received: *It effectually worketh in those that believe, v.* 13. Those who by faith receive the word find it profitable. *It does good to those that walk uprightly,* and by its wonderful effects evidences itself to be the word of God. This converts their souls, and enlightens their minds, and rejoices their hearts (Ps. xix.); and such as have this inward testimony of the truth of the scriptures, the word of God, by the effectual operations thereof on their hearts, have the best evidence of their divine original to themselves, though this is not sufficient to convince others who are strangers thereto.

II. He mentions the good effects which his successful preaching had,

1. Upon himself and fellow-labourers. It was a constant cause of thankfulness: *For this cause thank we God without ceasing, v.* 13. The apostle expressed his thankfulness to God so often upon this account that he seemed to think he never could be sufficiently thankful that God had counted him faithful, and put him into the ministry, and made his ministrations successful.

2. Upon them. The word wrought effectually in them, not only to be examples unto others in faith and good works (which he had mentioned before), but also in constancy and patience under sufferings and trials for the sake of the gospel: *You became followers of the churches of God, and have suffered like things as they have done* (*v.* 14), and with like courage and constancy, with like patience and hope. Note, The cross is the Christian's mark: if we are called to suffer we are called only to be followers of the churches of God; *so persecuted they the prophets that were before you,* Matt. v. 12. It is a good effect of the gospel when we are enabled to suffer for its sake. The apostle mentions the sufferings of the churches of God, which *in Judea were in Christ Jesus.* Those in Judea first heard the gospel, and they first suffered for it: for the Jews were the most bitter enemies Christianity had, and were especially enraged against their countrymen who embraced Christianity. Note, Bitter zeal and fiery persecution will set countrymen at variance, and break through all the bonds of nature, as well as contradict all the rules of religion. In every city where the apostles went to preach the gospel the Jews stirred up the inhabitants against them. They were the ringleaders of persecution in all places; so in particular it was at Thessalonica: Acts xvii. 5, *The Jews that believed not, moved with envy, took unto them certain lewd fellows of the baser sort, and gathered a company, and set all the city in an uproar.* Upon this occasion, the apostle gives a character of the unbelieving Jews (*v.* 15), enough to justify their final rejection and the ruin of their place, and church, and nation, which was now approaching. (1.) They *killed the Lord Jesus,* and impudently and presumptuously wished that his blood might be on

them and their children. (2.) They killed *their own prophets:* so they had done all along; their fathers had done so: they had been a persecuting generation. (3) They hated the apostles, and did them all the mischief they could. They persecuted them, and drove and chased them from place to place: and no marvel, if they killed the Lord Jesus, that they persecuted his followers. (4.) They *pleased not God.* They had quite lost all sense of religion, and due care to do their duty to God. It was a most fatal mistake to think that they did God service by killing God's servants. Murder and persecution are most hateful to God and cannot be justified on any pretence; they are so contrary to natural religion that no zeal for any true or only pretended institution of religion can ever excuse them. (5.) They were *contrary to all men.* Their persecuting spirit was a perverse spirit; contrary to the light of nature, and contrary to humanity, contrary to the welfare of all men, and contrary to the sentiments of all men not under the power of bigotry. (6.) They had *an implacable enmity to the Gentiles,* and envied them the offers of the gospel: *Forbidding the apostles to speak to the Gentiles, that they might be saved.* The means of salvation had long been confined to the Jews. *Salvation is of the Jews,* says our Saviour. And they were envious against the Gentiles, and angry that they should be admitted to share in the means of salvation. Nothing provoked them more than our Saviour's speaking to them at any time concerning this matter; this enraged the Jews at Jerusalem, when, in his defence, Paul told them, *he was sent unto the Gentiles,* Acts xxii. 21. They heard him patiently till he uttered these words, but then could endure no longer, but *lifted up their voices, and said, Away with such a fellow from the earth, for it is not fit that he should live.* Thus did the Jews fill up their sins; and nothing tends more to any person or people's filling up the measure of their sins than opposing the gospel, obstructing the progress of it, and hindering the salvation of precious souls. For the sake of these things *wrath has come upon them to the uttermost;* that is, wrath was determined against them, and would soon overtake them. It was not many years after this that Jerusalem was destroyed, and the Jewish nation cut off by the Romans. Note, When the measure of any man's iniquity is full, and he has sinned to the uttermost, then comes wrath, and that to the uttermost.

17 But we, brethren, being taken
from you a short time in presence,
not in heart, endeavoured the more
abundantly to see your face with great
desire. 18 Wherefore we would have
come unto you, even I Paul, once
and again; but Satan hindered us.
19 For what *is* our hope, or joy, or
crown of rejoicing? *Are* not even ye
in the presence of our Lord Jesus
Christ at his coming? 20 For ye are
our glory and joy.

In these words the apostle apologizes for his absence. Here observe, 1. He tells them they were involuntarily forced from them: *We, brethren, were taken from you, v.*17. Such was the rage of his persecutors. He was unwillingly sent away by night to Berea, Acts xvii. 10. 2. Though he was absent in body, yet he was present in heart. He had still a remembrance of them, and great care for them. 3. Even his bodily absence was but for a short time, the time of an hour. Time is short, all our time on earth is short and uncertain, whether we are present with our friends or absent from them. This world is not a place where we are always, or long, to be together. It is in heaven that holy souls shall meet, and never part more. 4. He earnestly desired and endeavoured to see them again: *We endeavoured more abundantly to see your face with great desire, v.* 17. So that the apostle at least intended his absence should be but for a short time. His desire and endeavour were to return again very soon to Thessalonica. But men of business are not masters of their own time. Paul did his endeavour, and he could do no more, *v.* 18. 5. He tells them that Satan hindered his return (*v.* 18), that is, either some enemy or enemies, or the great enemy of mankind, who stirred up opposition to Paul, either in his return to Thessalonica, when he intended to return thither, or stirred up such contentions or dissensions in those places whether he went as made his presence necessary. Note, Satan is a constant enemy to the work of God, and does all he can to obstruct it. 6. He assures them of his affection and high esteem for them, though he was not able, as yet, to be present with them according to his desire. They were his *hope, and joy, and crown of rejoicing; his glory and joy.* These are expressions of great and endeared affection, and high estimation. And it is happy when ministers and people have such mutual affection and esteem of each other, and especially if they shall thus rejoice, if those that sow and those that reap shall rejoice together, *in the presence of our Lord Jesus Christ at his coming.*

The apostle here puts the Thessalonians in mind that though he could not come to them as yet, and though he should never be able to come to them, yet our Lord Jesus Christ will come, nothing shall hinder this. And further, when he shall come, all must appear in his presence, or before him. Ministers and people must all appear before him, and faithful people will be the glory and joy of faithful ministers in that great and glorious day.

CHAP. III.

In this chapter the apostle gives further evidence of his love to the Thessalonians, reminding them of his sending Timothy to them, with the mention of his design therein and his inducements so to do, ver. 1—5. He acquaints them also with his great satisfaction at the return of Timothy, with good tidings concerning them, ver. 6—10. And concludes with fervent prayer for them, ver. 11, to the end.

WHEREFORE when we could
no longer forbear, we thought
it good to be left at Athens alone; 2
And sent Timotheus, our brother, and
minister of God, and our fellowlabourer
in the gospel of Christ, to establish
you, and to comfort you concerning
your faith: 3 That no man should
be moved by these afflictions: for
yourselves know that we are appointed thereunto. 4 For verily,
when we were with you, we told you
before that we should suffer tribulation; even as it came to pass, and
ye know. 5 For this cause, when I
could no longer forbear, I sent to
know your faith, lest by some means
the tempter have tempted you, and
our labour be in vain.

In these words the apostle gives an account of his sending Timothy to the Thessalonians. Though he was hindered from going to them himself, yet his love was such that he could not forbear sending Timothy to them. Though Timothy was very useful to him, and he could not well spare him, yet Paul was content, for their good, *to be left alone at Athens.* Note, Those ministers do not duly value the establishment and welfare of their people who cannot deny themselves in many things for that end. Observe,

I. The character he gives of Timothy (*v.* 2): *We sent Timotheus, our brother.* Elsewhere he calls him his son; here he calls him brother. Timothy was Paul's junior in age, his inferior in gifts and graces, and of a lower rank in the ministry: for Paul was an apostle, and Timothy but an evangelist; yet Paul calls him brother. This was an instance of the apostle's humility, and showed his desire to put honour upon Timothy and to recommend him to the esteem of the churches. He calls him also a minister of God Note, Ministers of the gospel of Christ are ministers of God, to promote the kingdom of God among men. He calls him also his fellow-labourer in the gospel of Christ. Note, Ministers of the gospel must look upon themselves as labourers in the Lord's vineyard; they have an honourable office and hard work, yet a good work. *This is a true saying, If any man desire the office of a bishop, he desires a good work,* 1 Tim. iii. 1. And ministers should look upon one another, and strengthen one another's hands, not strive and contend one with another (which will hinder their work), but strive together to carry on the great work they are engaged in, namely, to preach and publish the gospel of Christ, and to persuade people to embrace and entertain it and live suitably thereto.

II. The end and design why Paul sent Timothy: *To establish you and to comfort you concerning your faith, v.* 2. Paul had converted them to the Christian faith, and now he was desirous that they might be confirmed and comforted, that they might be confirmed in the choice they had made of the Christian religion, and be comforted in the profession and practice of it. Note, The more we are comforted, the more we shall be confirmed, because, when we find pleasure in the ways of God, we shall thereby be engaged to continue and persevere therein. The apostle's design was to establish and comfort the Thessalonians concerning their faith,—concerning the object of their faith, namely, the truths of the gospel, and particularly that Jesus Christ was the Saviour of the world, and so wise and good, so powerful and faithful, that they might rely upon him,—concerning the recompence of faith, which was more than sufficient to balance all their losses and reward all their labours.

III. The motive inducing Paul to send Timothy for this end, namely, a godly fear or jealousy, lest they should be moved from the faith of Christ, *v.* 3. He was desirous that no man, no one among them, should be moved or shaken in mind, that they should not apostatize or waver in the faith. And yet,

1. He apprehended there was danger, and feared the consequence.

(1.) There was danger, [1.] By reason of *affliction* and persecution for the sake of the gospel, *v.* 3. These Thessalonians could not but perceive what afflictions the apostles and preachers of the gospel met with, and this might possibly stumble them; and also those who made profession of the gospel were persecuted, and without doubt these Thessalonians themselves were afflicted. [2.] By reason of the tempter's subtlety and malice. The apostle was afraid lest by any means the tempter had tempted them, *v.* 5. The devil is a subtle and unwearied tempter, who seeks an opportunity to beguile and destroy us, and takes all advantages against us, both in a time of prosperity and adversity; and he has often been successful in his attacks upon persons under afflictions. He has often prejudiced the minds of men against religion on account of the sufferings its professors are exposed to. We have reason therefore to be jealous over ourselves and others, lest we be ensnared by him.

(2.) The consequence the apostle feared was lest his labour should be in vain. And thus it would have been, if the tempter had tempted them, and prevailed against them, to move them from the faith. They would have lost what they had wrought, and the apostle would have lost what he laboured for. Note, It is the devil's design to hinder the good fruit and effect of the preaching of the gospel. If he cannot hinder ministers from labouring in the word and doctrine, he will, if he be able, hinder them of the success of their labours. Note also, Faithful ministers are much concerned about the success of their labours. No one would willingly labour in vain; and ministers are loth to spend their strength, and pains, and time, for nought.

2. To prevent this danger, with its bad consequence, the apostle tells them what care he took in sending Timothy, (1.) To put them in mind of what he had told them before concerning suffering tribulation (*v.* 4), he says (*v.* 3), *We are appointed thereunto,* that is, unto afflictions. So is the will and purpose of God that *through many afflictions we must enter into his kingdom.* Their troubles and persecutions did not come by chance, not merely from the wrath and malice of the enemies of religion, but by the *appointment of God.* The event only came to pass according as God had determined, and they knew he had told them before it would be; so that they should not think it strange, and, being fore-warned, they should be fore-armed. Note, The apostles were so far from flattering people with an expectation of worldly prosperity in religion that, on the contrary, they told them plainly they must count upon trouble in the flesh. And herein they followed the example of their great Master, the author of our faith. Besides, it might prove a confirmation of their faith, when they perceived that it only happened to them as was predicted before. (2.) To know their faith, that so he might inform the apostles whether they remained stedfast under all their sufferings, whether their faith failed or not, because, if their faith did not fail, they would be able to stand their ground against the tempter and all his temptations: their faith would be a *shield, to defend them against all the fiery darts of the wicked,* Eph. vi. 16.

6 But now when Timotheus came
from you unto us, and brought us good
tidings of your faith and charity, and
that ye have good remembrance of us
always, desiring greatly to see us, as
we also *to see* you: 7 Therefore,
brethren, we were comforted over
you in all your affliction and distress
by your faith: 8 For now we live,
if ye stand fast in the Lord. 9 For
what thanks can we render to God
again for you, for all the joy wherewith we joy for your sakes before our
God; 10 Night and day praying
exceedingly that we might see your
face, and might perfect that which is
lacking in your faith?

Here we have Paul's great satisfaction upon the return of Timothy with good tidings from the Thessalonians, in which we may observe,

I. The good report Timothy made concerning them, *v.* 6. Without question, he was a willing messenger of these good tidings. *Concerning their faith,* that is, concerning their stedfastness in the faith, that they were not shaken in mind, nor turned aside from the profession of the gospel. *Their love* also continued; their love to the gospel, and the ministers of the gospel. For they had a good and a kind remembrance of the apostles, and that constantly, or always. The names of the apostles were very dear to them, and the thoughts of them, and what they themselves had received from them, were very precious, insomuch that they *desired greatly to see them again,* and receive some spiritual gift from them; and there was no love lost, for the apostle was as desirous to see them. It is happy where there is such mutual love between minister and people. This tends to promote religion, and the success of the gospel. The world hates them, and therefore they should love one another.

II. The great comfort and satisfaction the apostle had in this good report concerning them (*v.* 7, 8): *Therefore, brethren, we were comforted in all our affliction and distress.* The apostle thought this good news of them was sufficient to balance all the troubles he met with. It was easy to him to bear affliction, or persecution, or fightings from without, when he found the good success of his ministry and the constancy of the converts he had made to Christianity; and his distress of mind on account of his fears within, lest he had laboured in vain, was now in a good measure over, when he understood their faith and the perseverance of it. This put new life and spirit into the apostle and made him vigorous and active in the work of the Lord. Thus he was not only comforted, but greatly rejoiced also: *Now we live, if you stand fast in the Lord, v.* 8. It would have been a killing thing to the apostles if the professors of religion had been unsteady, or proved apostates; whereas nothing was more encouraging than their constancy.

III. The effects of this were thankfulness and prayer to God on their behalf. Observe, 1. How thankful the apostle was, *v.* 9. He was full of joy, and full of praise and thanksgiving. When we are most cheerful we should be most thankful. What we rejoice in we should give thanks for. This is to rejoice before our God, to spiritualize our joy. Paul speaks as if he could not tell how to express his thankfulness to God, or his joy and rejoicing for their sakes. But he was careful God should not lose the glory of the comfort he received in the welfare of his friends. His heart was enlarged with love to them and with thanksgiving to God. He was willing to express the one and the other as well as he could. As to thankfulness to God, this especially is very imperfect in the present state; but, when we come to heaven, we shall do this work better than now we can. 2. He prayed for them night and day (*v.* 10), evening and morning, or very frequently, in the midst of the business of the day or slumber of the night lifting up his heart to God in prayer. Thus we should pray always. And Paul's prayer was fervent prayer. He prayed exceedingly, and was earnest in his supplication. Note, When we are most thankful we should always give ourselves to prayer; and those we give thanks for have yet need to be prayed for. Those whom we most rejoice in, and who are our greatest comforts, must be our constant care, while in this world of temptation and imperfection. There was something still lacking in their faith; Paul desired that this might be perfected, and to see their face in order thereunto. Note, (1.) The best of men have something wanting in their faith, if not as to the matter of it, there being some mysteries or doctrines not sufficiently known or believed by them, yet as to the clearness and certainty of their faith, there being some remaining darkness and doubtings, or at least as to the effects and operations of it, these being not so conspicuous and perfect as they should be. And, (2.) The ministry of the word and ordinances is helpful, and to be desired and used for the perfecting of that which is lacking in our faith.

11 Now God himself and our
Father, and our Lord Jesus Christ,
direct our way unto you. 12 And
the Lord make you to increase and
abound in love one toward another,
and toward all *men*, even as we *do*
toward you: 13 To the end he may
stablish your hearts unblameable in
holiness before God, even our Father,
at the coming of our Lord Jesus Christ
with all his saints.

In these words we have the earnest prayer of the apostle. He desired to be instrumental in the further benefit of the Thessalonians; and the only way to be so while at a distance was by prayer for them, together with his writing or sending to them. He desired that their faith might be perfected, which he could not be the proper cause or author of; for he pretended not to dominion over their faith, nor to have the donation of it, and he therefore concludes with prayer for them. Observe,

I. Whom he prays to, namely, God and Christ. Prayer is a part of religious worship, and all religious worship is due unto God only. Prayer is here made to God, even the Father and our Father; and also to Christ, even our Lord Jesus Christ. Therefore Jesus Christ our Lord is God, even as God our Father is God. Prayer is to be offered to God as our Father. So Christ taught his disciples to pray; and so the Spirit of adoption prompts them to pray, to cry, *Abba, Father.* Prayer is not only to be offered in the name of Christ, but offered up to Christ himself, as our Lord and our Saviour.

II. What he prays for, with respect to himself and his fellow-labourers, and on behalf of the Thessalonians

1. He prays that himself and fellow-labourers might have a prosperous journey to them by the will of God, that their way might be directed to them, *v.* 11. The taking of a journey to this or that place, one would think, is a thing depending so much on a man's own will, and lies so much in his own power, that Paul needed not by prayer to go to God about it. But the apostle knew that *in God we live, and move, and have our being,* that we depend upon God in all our motions and actions, as well as for the continuance of life and being, that divine Providence orders all our affairs and that it is owing thereto if we prosper therein, that God our Father directs and orders his children whither they shall go and what they shall do, that our Lord Jesus Christ in a particular manner directs the motions of his faithful ministers, those stars which he holds in his right hand. Let us acknowledge God in all our ways, and he will direct our paths.

2. He prays for the prosperity of the Thessalonians. Whether he should have an opportunity of coming to them or not, yet he earnestly prayed for the prosperity of their souls. And there are two things he desired for them, which we should desire for ourselves and friends:—(1.) That they might increase and abound in love (*v.* 12), in love to one another and in love to all men. Note, Mutual love is required of all Christians, and not only that they love one another, but that they also have a charitable disposition of mind and due concern for the welfare of all men. Love is of God, and is the fulfilling of the gospel as well as of the law. Timothy brought good tidings of their faith, yet something was lacking therein; and of their charity, yet the apostle prays that this might increase and abound. Note, We have reason to desire to grow in every grace, and have need of the Spirit's influence in order to growth in grace; and the way to obtain this is by prayer. We are beholden to God not only for the stock put into our hands at first, but for the improvement of it also. And to our prayer we must add endeavour. To excite this in the Thessalonians the apostle again mentions his love, his abounding love, towards them. The more we are beloved, the more affectionate we should be. (2.) That they might be established unblamable in holiness, *v.* 13. This spiritual benefit is mentioned as an effect of increasing and abounding love: *To the end that he* (the Lord) *may establish your hearts.* Note, The more we grow and abound in grace, and particularly in the grace of love, the more we are established and confirmed in it. Note also, Holiness is required of all those who would go to heaven, and therein we must be unblamable; that is, we must act in every thing so that we may not in the least contradict the profession we make of holiness. Our desire

should be to have our hearts established in holiness before God, and be preserved safe, to the coming of the Lord Jesus Christ; and that we may be unblamable before God, even the Father, now, and be presented blameless before the throne of his glory, when the Lord Jesus shall come with all his saints. Note, [1.] The Lord Jesus will certainly come, and come in his glory. [2.] When he comes, his saints will come with him: *They shall appear with him in glory.* [3.] Then the excellency as well as the necessity of holiness will appear, because without this no hearts shall be established at that day, nor shall any one be unblamable, or avoid everlasting condemnation.

CHAP. IV.

In this chapter the apostle gives earnest exhortations to abound in holiness, with a caution against uncleanness, enforced with several arguments, ver. 1—8. He then mentions the great duties of brotherly love, and quietness with industry in our callings, ver. 9—12. And concludes with comforting those who mourned for their relations and friends that died in the Lord, ver. 13—18.

FURTHERMORE then we be-
seech you, brethren, and exhort
you by the Lord Jesus, that as ye
have received of us how ye ought to
walk and to please God, *so* ye would
abound more and more. 2 For ye
know what commandments we gave
you by the Lord Jesus. 3 For this
is the will of God, *even* your sanctification, that ye should abstain from
fornication: 4 That every one of
you should know how to possess his
vessel in sanctification and honour;
5 Not in the lust of concupiscence,
even as the Gentiles which know not
God: 6 That no *man* go beyond and
defraud his brother in *any* matter:
because that the Lord *is* the avenger
of all such, as we also have forewarned
you and testified. 7 For God hath
not called us unto uncleanness, but
unto holiness. 8 He therefore that
despiseth, despiseth not man, but
God, who hath also given unto us
his holy Spirit.

Here we have,

I. An exhortation to abound in holiness, to *abound more and more* in that which is good, *v.* 1, 2. We may observe,

1. The manner in which the exhortation is given—very affectionately. The apostle entreats them as brethren; he calls them so, and loved them as such. Because his love to them was very great, he exhorts them very earnestly: *We beseech and exhort you.* The apostle was unwilling to take any denial, and therefore repeats his exhortation again and again.

2. The matter of his exhortation—that they would abound more and more in holy walking, or excel in those things that are good, in good works. Their faith was justly famed abroad, and they were already examples to other churches: yet the apostle would have them yet further to excel others, and to make further progress in holiness. Note (1.) Those who most excel others fall short of perfection. The very best of us should *forget those things which are behind, and reach forth unto those things which are before.* (2.) It is not enough that we abide in the faith of the gospel, but we must abound in the work of faith. We must not only persevere to the end, but we should grow better, and walk more evenly and closely with God.

3. The arguments with which the apostle enforces his exhortation. (1.) They had been informed of their duty. They knew their Master's will, and could not plead ignorance as an excuse. Now as faith, so knowledge, is dead without practice. They had received of those who had converted them to Christianity, or been taught of them, *how they ought to walk.* Observe, The design of the gospel is to teach men not only what they should believe, but also how they ought to live; not so much to fill men's minds with notions as to regulate their temper and behaviour. The apostle taught them how to walk, not how to talk. To talk well without living well will never bring us to heaven: for the character of those who are in Christ Jesus is this: *They walk not after the flesh, but after the Spirit.* (2.) Another argument is that the apostle taught and exhorted them in the name, or by the authority, of the Lord Jesus Christ. He was Christ's minister and ambassador, declaring to them what was the will and command of the Lord Jesus. (3.) Another argument is this. Herein they would please God. Holy walking is most pleasing to the holy God, *who is glorious in holiness.* This ought to be the aim and ambition of every Christian, to please God and to be accepted of him. We should not be men-pleasers, nor flesh-pleasers, but should walk so as to please God. (4.) The rule according to which they ought to walk and act—*the commandments they had given them by the Lord Jesus Christ,* which were the commandments of the Lord Jesus Christ himself, because given by authority and direction from him and such as were agreeable to his will. The apostles of our Lord Jesus Christ were only commissioned by him to teach men to observe all things *whatsoever he had commanded them,* Matt. xxviii. 20. Though they had great authority from Christ, yet that was to teach men what Christ had commanded, not to give forth commandments of their own. They did not act as lords over God's heritage (1 Pet. v. 3), nor should any do so that pretend to be their successors. The apostle could appeal to the Thessalonians, who knew what commandments he gave them, that they were no other than what he had received from the Lord Jesus.

II. A caution against uncleanness, this

being a sin directly contrary to sanctification, or that holy walking to which he so earnestly exhorts them. This caution is expressed, and also enforced by many arguments.

1. It is expressed in these words: *That you should abstain from fornication* (*v.* 3), by which we are to understand all uncleanness whatsoever, either in a married or unmarried state. Adultery is of course included, though fornication is particularly mentioned. And other sorts of uncleanness are also forbidden, of which it is a shame even to speak, though they are done by too many in secret. All that is contrary to chastity in heart, speech, and behaviour, is contrary to the command of God in the decalogue, and contrary to that holiness which the gospel requires.

2. There are several arguments to enforce this caution. As, (1.) This branch of sanctification in particular is the will of God, *v.* 3. It is the will of God in general that we should be holy, because *he that called us is holy*, and because we are *chosen unto salvation through the sanctification of the Spirit;* and not only does God require holiness in the heart, but also purity in our bodies, and that we should cleanse ourselves from all *filthiness both of flesh and spirit,* 2 Cor. vii. 1. Wherever the body is, as it ought to be, devoted to God, and dedicated and set apart for him, it should be kept clean and pure for his service; and, as chastity is one branch of our sanctification, so this is one thing which God commands in his law, and what his grace effects in all true believers. (2.) This will be greatly for our honour: so much is plainly implied, *v.* 4. Whereas the contrary will be a great dishonour. *And his reproach shall not be wiped away,* Prov. vi. 33. The body is here called the vessel of the soul, which dwells therein (so 1 Sam. xxi. 5), and it must be kept pure from defiling lusts. Every one should be careful in this matter, as he values his own honour and will not be contemptible on this account, that his inferior appetites and passions gain not the ascendant, tyrannizing over his reason and conscience, and enslaving the superior faculties of his soul. What can be more dishonourable than for a rational soul to be enslaved by bodily affections and brutal appetites? (3.) To indulge the lust of concupiscence is to live and act like heathens? *Even as the Gentiles who know not God, v.* 5. The Gentiles, and especially the Grecians, were commonly guilty of some sins of uncleanness which were not so evidently forbidden by the light of nature. But they did not know God, nor his mind and will, so well as Christians know, and should know, this his will, namely *our sanctification* in this branch of it. It is not so much to be wondered at, therefore, if the Gentiles indulge their fleshly appetites and lusts; but Christians should not walk as unconverted Gentiles, *in lasciviousness, lusts, excess of wine, revellings, banquetings,* &c. (1 Pet. iv. 3), because those who are in Christ *have crucified the flesh with its affections and lusts.* (4.) The sin of uncleanness, especially adultery, is a great piece of injustice that God will be the avenger of; so we may understand those words, *That no man go beyond or defraud his brother* (*v.* 6) *in any matter*—ἐν τῷ πράγματι, in *this* matter of which the apostle is speaking in the preceding and following verses, namely, the sin of uncleanness. Some understand these words as a further warning and caution against injustice and oppression, all fraud and deceit in our dealings with men, which are certainly criminal, and contrary to the gospel. And Christians should not impose upon the ignorance and necessity of those they deal with, and so go beyond them, nor should they by equivocations or lying arts defraud them; and although this may be practised by some and lie long undiscovered, and so go unpunished among men, yet the righteous God will render a recompence. But the meaning may rather be to show the injustice and wrong that in many cases are done by the sin of uncleanness. Not only are fornication and other acts of uncleanness sins against his own body who commits them (1 Cor. vi. 18), not only are they very injurious to the sinner himself both in soul and body, but sometimes they are very injurious, and no less than defrauding, acts of injustice to others, particularly to those who are joined together in the marriage covenant and to their posterity. And, as this sin is of such a heinous nature, so it follows that God will be the avenger of it. *Whoremongers and adulterers God will judge,* Heb. xiii. 4. This the apostle had forewarned and testified by his gospel, which, as it contained exceedingly great and precious promises, so also it *revealed from heaven the wrath of God against all ungodliness and unrighteousness among men,* Rom. i. 18. (5.) The sin of uncleanness is contrary to the nature and design of our Christian calling: *For God hath called us not unto uncleanness, but unto holiness, v.* 7. The law of God forbids all impurity, and the gospel requires the greatest purity; it calls us from uncleanness unto holiness. (6.) The contempt therefore of God's law and gospel is the contempt of God himself: *He that despises despises God, not man* only. Some might possibly make light of the precepts of purity and holiness, because they heard them from men like themselves; but the apostle lets them know that they were God's commands, and to violate them was no less than to despise God. He adds, *God hath given Christians his Spirit,* intimating that all sorts of uncleanness do in an especial manner grieve the Holy Spirit, and will provoke him to withdraw from us; and also the Holy Spirit is given unto us to arm us against these sins, and to help us to mortify these deeds of the body, that we may live, Rom. viii. 13.

9 But as touching brotherly love

ye need not that I write unto you:
for ye yourselves are taught of God
to love another. 10 And indeed ye
do it toward all the brethren which
are in all Macedonia: but we beseech
you, brethren, that ye increase more
and more; 11 And that ye study
to be quiet, and to do your own
business, and to work with your own
hands, as we commanded you; 12
That ye may walk honestly toward
them that are without, and *that* ye
may have lack of nothing.

In these words the apostle mentions the great duties,

I. Of brotherly love. This he exhorts them to increase in yet more and more. The exhortation is introduced, not with a compliment, but with a commendation, because they were remarkable in the exercise of it, which made it less needful that he should write to them about it, *v.* 9. Thus by his good opinion of them he insinuated himself into their affections, and so made way for his exhortation to them. Note, We should take notice of that in others which is good, to their praise, that by so doing we may lay engagements upon them to abound therein more and more. Observe,

1. What it is that the apostle commends in them. It was not so much their own virtue as God's grace; yet he takes notice of the evidence they gave of the grace of God in them. (1.) It was God's grace that he took special notice of: that God had taught them this good lesson: *You yourselves are taught of God to love one another*, *v.* 9. Whoever does that which is good is taught of God to do it, and God must have the glory. All who are savingly taught of God are taught this lesson, to love one another. This is the livery of Christ's family. Note also, The teaching of the Spirit exceeds the teaching of men; and, as no man should teach contrary to what God teaches, so none can teach so effectually as he teaches; and men's teaching is vain and useless unless God teach also. (2.) The Thessalonians gave good evidence of their being taught of God by *their love to the brethren in all Macedonia*, *v.* 10. They not only loved those of their own city and society, or such as were near them and just of their own sentiments, but their love was extensive. And a true Christian's is so to all the saints, though distant from him in place, and differing from him in some opinions or practices of less moment.

2. The exhortation itself is to increase more and more in this great grace and duty of brotherly love, *v.* 10. Though these Thessalonians had in some sense no need of an exhortation to brotherly love, as if it were wholly wanting, yet they must be exhorted to pray for more, and labour for more. There are none on this side heaven who love in perfection. Those who are eminent in this or any other grace have need of increase therein as well as of perseverance unto the end.

II. Of quietness and industry in their callings. Observe, 1. The apostle exhorts to these duties: that they should *study to be quiet, v.* 11. It is the most desirable thing to have a calm and quiet temper, and to be of a peaceable and quiet behaviour. This tends much to our own and others' happiness; and Christians should study how to be quiet. We should be ambitious and industrious how to be calm and quiet in our minds, in patience to possess our own souls, and to be quiet towards others; or of a meek and mild, a gentle and peaceable disposition, not given to strife, contention, or division. Satan is very busy to disquiet us; and we have that in our own hearts that disposes us to be disquiet; therefore let us study to be quiet. It follows, *Do your own business.* When we go beyond this, we expose ourselves to a great deal of inquietude. Those who are busy-bodies, meddling in other men's matters, generally have but little quiet in their own minds and cause great disturbances among their neighbours; at least they seldom mind the other exhortation, to be diligent in their own calling, *to work with their own hands*; and yet this was what the apostle commanded them, and what is required of us also. Christianity does not discharge us from the work and duty of our particular callings, but teaches us to be diligent therein. 2. The exhortation is enforced with a double argument; namely, (1.) So we shall live creditably. Thus we shall walk honestly, or decently and creditably, towards those that are without, *v.* 12. This will be to act as becomes the gospel, and will gain a good report from those that are strangers, yea, enemies to it. Note, It is a great ornament to religion when the professors of it are of meek and quiet spirits, diligent to do their own business, and not busy-bodies in other men's matters. (2.) We shall live comfortably, and have lack of nothing, *v.* 12. People often by their slothfulness bring themselves into narrow circumstances, and reduce themselves to great straits, and are liable to many wants, when such as are diligent in their own business live comfortably and have lack of nothing. They are not burdensome to their friends, nor scandalous to strangers. They earn their own bread, and have the greatest pleasure in so doing.

13 But I would not have you to be
ignorant, brethren, concerning them
which are asleep, that ye sorrow not,
even as others which have no hope.
14 For if we believe that Jesus died
and rose again, even so them also

which sleep in Jesus will God bring
with him. 15 For this we say unto
you by the word of the Lord, that
we which are alive *and* remain unto
the coming of the Lord shall not
prevent them which are asleep. 16
For the Lord himself shall descend
from heaven with a shout, with the
voice of the archangel, and with the
trump of God: and the dead in
Christ shall rise first: 17 Then we
which are alive *and* remain shall be
caught up together with them in the
clouds, to meet the Lord in the air:
and so shall we ever be with the
Lord. 18 Wherefore comfort one
another with these words.

In these words the apostle comforts the Thessalonians who mourned for the death of their relations and friends that died in the Lord. His design is to dissuade them from excessive grief, or inordinate sorrow, on that account. *All* grief for the death of friends is far from being unlawful; we may weep at least for ourselves if we do not weep for them, weep for own loss, though it may be their gain. Yet we must not be immoderate in our sorrows, because,

I. This looks as if we had no hope, *v.* 13. It is to act too much like the Gentiles, who had no hope of a better life after this; whereas we Christians, who have a most sure hope, the hope of eternal life after this, *which God who cannot lie hath promised us,* should moderate all our joys and our sorrows on account of any worldly thing. This hope is more than enough to balance all our griefs upon account of any of the crosses of the present time.

II. This is an effect of ignorance concerning those who are dead, *v.* 13. There are some things which we cannot but be ignorant of concerning those that are asleep; for the land they are removed to is a land of darkness, which we know but little of and have no correspondence with. To go among the dead is to go among we know not whom, and to live we know not how. Death is an unknown thing, and the state of the dead, or the state after death, we are much in the dark about; yet there are some things concerning those especially who die in the Lord that we need not, and ought not, to be ignorant of; and, if these things be really understood and duly considered, they will be sufficient to allay our sorrow concerning them.

1. They sleep in Jesus. They are asleep, *v.* 13. They have *fallen asleep in Christ,* 1 Cor. xv. 18. Death does not annihilate them. It is but a sleep to them. It is their rest, and undisturbed rest. They have retired out of this troublesome world, to rest from all their labours and sorrows, and they sleep in Jesus, *v.* 14. Being still in union with him, they sleep in his arms and are under his special care and protection. Their souls are in his presence, and their dust is under his care and power; so that they are not lost, nor are they losers, but great gainers by death, and their removal out of this world is into a better.

2. They shall be raised up from the dead, and awakened out of their sleep, for *God will bring them with him, v.* 14. They then are with God, and are better where they are than when they were here; and when God comes he will bring them with him. The doctrine of the resurrection and the second coming of Christ is a great antidote against the fear of death and inordinate sorrow for the death of our Christian friends; and this doctrine we have a full assurance of, because we *believe that Jesus died and rose again, v.* 14. It is taken for granted that as Christians they knew and believed this. The death and resurrection of Christ are fundamental articles of the Christian religion, and give us hope of a joyful resurrection; for *Christ, having risen from the dead, has become the first fruits of those that slept;* and therefore *those who have fallen asleep in him have not perished nor are lost,* 1 Cor. xv. 18, 20. His resurrection is a full confirmation of all that is said in the gospel, or by the word of the Lord, which has *brought life and immortality to light.*

3. Their state and condition shall be glorious and happy at the second coming of Christ. This the apostle informs the Thessalonians of *by the word of the Lord* (*v.* 15), by divine revelation from the Lord Jesus; for though the resurrection of the dead, and a future state of blessedness, were part of the creed of the Old-Testament saints, yet they are much more clearly revealed in and by the gospel. By this word of the Lord we know, (1.) That the Lord Jesus will come down from heaven in all the pomp and power of the upper world (*v.* 16): *The Lord himself shall descend from heaven with a shout.* He ascended into heaven after his resurrection, and passed through these material heavens into the third heaven, which must retain him till the restitution of all things; and then he will come again, and appear in his glory. He will descend from heaven into this our air, *v.* 17. The appearance will be with pomp and power, *with a shout*—the shout of a king, and the power and authority of a mighty king and conqueror, with *the voice of the archangel;* an innumerable company of angels will attend him. Perhaps *one,* as general of those hosts of the Lord, will give notice of his approach, and the glorious appearance of this great Redeemer and Judge will be proclaimed and ushered in by the *trump of God. For the trumpet shall sound,* and this will awaken those that sleep in the dust of the earth, and will summon all the world to appear. For, (2.) The dead shall be raised: *The dead in Christ shall rise first* (*v*

16), before those who are *found alive at Christ's coming shall be changed;* and so it appears that those who shall then *be found alive shall not prevent those that are asleep, v.* 15. The first care of the Redeemer in that day will be about his dead saints; he will raise them before the great change passes on those that shall be found alive: so that those who did not sleep in death will have no greater privilege or joy at that day than those who fell asleep in Jesus. (3.) Those that shall be found alive will then be changed. They shall *be caught up together with them in the clouds, to meet the Lord in the air, v.* 17. At, or immediately before, this rapture into the clouds, those who are alive will undergo a mighty change, which will be equivalent to dying. This change is so mysterious that we cannot comprehend it: we know little or nothing of it, 1 Cor. xv. 51. Only, in the general, *this mortal must put on immortality,* and these bodies will be made fit to inherit the kingdom of God, which flesh and blood in its present state are not capable of. This change will be *in a moment, in the twinkling of an eye* (1 Cor. xv. 52), in the very instant, or not long after the raising up of those that sleep in Jesus. And those who are raised, and thus changed, shall meet together in the clouds, and there meet with their Lord, to congratulate him on his coming, to receive the crown of glory he will then bestow upon them, and to be assessors with him in judgment, approving and applauding the sentence he will then pass upon the prince of the power of the air, and all the wicked, who shall be doomed to destruction with the devil and his angels. (4.) Here is the bliss of the saints at that day: they shall *be ever with the Lord, v.* 17. It will be some part of their felicity that all the saints shall meet together, and remain together for ever; but the principal happiness of heaven is this, *to be with the Lord,* to see him, live with him, and enjoy him, for ever. This should comfort the saints upon the death of their friends, that, although death has made a separation, yet their souls and bodies will meet again; we and they shall meet together again: we and they with all the saints shall meet our Lord, and be with him for ever, no more to be separated either from him or from one another for ever. And the apostle would have us *comfort one another with these words, v.* 18. We should endeavour to support one another in times of sorrow, not deaden one another's spirits, nor weaken one another's hands, but should comfort one another; and this may be done by serious consideration and discourse on the many good lessons to be learned from the doctrine of the resurrection of the dead, the second coming of Christ, and the glory of the saints in that day.

CHAP. V.

The apostle, having spoken in the end of the foregoing chapter concerning the resurrection, and the second coming of Christ, proceeds to speak concerning the uselessness of enquiring after the particular time of Christ's coming, which would be sudden and terrible to the wicked, but comfortable to the saints, ver. 1—5. He then exhorts them to the duties of watchfulness, sobriety, and the exercise of faith, love, and hope, as being suitable to their state, ver. 6—10. In the next words he exhorts them to several duties they owed to others, or to one another (ver. 11—15), afterwards to several other Christian duties of great importance (ver. 16—22), and then concludes this epistle, ver. 23—28.

BUT of the times and the seasons,
brethren, ye have no need that
I write unto you. 2 For yourselves
know perfectly that the day of the
Lord so cometh as a thief in the
night. 3 For when they shall say,
Peace and safety; then sudden destruction cometh upon them, as
travail upon a woman with child;
and they shall not escape. 4 But
ye, brethren, are not in darkness,
that that day should overtake you as
a thief. 5 Ye are all the children of
light, and the children of the day: we
are not of the night, nor of darkness.

In these words observe,

I. The apostle tells the Thessalonians it was needless or useless to enquire about the particular time of Christ's coming: *Of the times and seasons you need not that I write unto you, v.* 1. The thing is certain that Christ will come, and there is a certain time appointed for his coming; but there was no need that the apostle should write about this, and therefore he had no revelation given him; nor should they or we enquire into this secret, *which the Father has reserved in his own power. Of that day and hour knoweth no man.* Christ himself did not reveal this while upon earth; it was not in his commission as the great prophet of the church: nor did he reveal this to his apostles; there was *no need* of this. There are times and seasons for us to do our work in: these it is our duty and interest to know and observe; but the time and season when we must give up our account we know not, nor is it needful that we should know them. Note, There are many things which our vain curiosity desires to know which there is no necessity at all of our knowing, nor would our knowledge of them do us good.

II. He tells them that the coming of Christ would be sudden, and a great surprise to most men, *v.* 2. And this is what they knew perfectly, or might know, because our Lord himself had so said: *In such an hour as you think not, the Son of man cometh,* Matt. xxiv. 44. So Mark xiii. 35, 36, *Watch you therefore, for you know not when the master of the house cometh; lest, coming suddenly, he find you sleeping.* And no doubt the apostle had told them, as of the coming of Christ, so also of his coming suddenly, which is the meaning of his coming *as a thief in the night,* Rev. xvi. 15. As the thief usually cometh in the dead time of the night, when he is least expected, such a *surprise* will the day of the Lord be; so sudden and surprising will be his appearance.

The knowledge of this will be more useful than to know the exact time, because this should awaken us to stand upon our watch, that we may be ready whenever he cometh.

III. He tells them how terrible Christ's coming would be to the ungodly, *v.* 3. It will be to their destruction in that day of the Lord. The righteous God will bring ruin upon his and his people's enemies; and this their destruction, as it will be total and final, so, 1. It will be sudden. It will overtake them, and fall upon them, in the midst of their carnal security and jollity, when they say in their hearts, *Peace and safety,* when they dream of felicity and please themselves with vain amusements of their fancies or their senses, and think not of it,—*as travail cometh upon a woman with child,* at the set time indeed, but not perhaps just then expected, nor greatly feared. 2. It will be unavoidable destruction too: *They shall not escape;* they shall in no wise escape. There will be no means possible for them to avoid the terror nor the punishment of that day. There will be *no place where the workers of iniquity shall be able to hide themselves,* no shelter from the storm, nor shadow from the burning heat that shall consume the wicked.

IV. He tells them how comfortable this day will be to the righteous, *v.* 4, 5. Here observe, 1. Their character and privilege. They are not in darkness; they are the children of the light, &c. This was the happy condition of the Thessalonians as it is of all true Christians. They were not in a state of sin and ignorance as the heathen world. They were *some time darkness, but were made light in the Lord.* They were favoured with the divine revelation of things that are unseen and eternal, particularly concerning the coming of Christ, and the consequences thereof. They were the *children of the day,* for the day-star had risen upon them; yea, the Sun of righteousness had arisen on them with healing under his wings. They were no longer under the darkness of heathenism, nor under the shadows of the law, but under the gospel, which brings life and immortality to light. 2 Tim. i. 10. 2. Their great advantage on this account: that *that day should not overtake them as a thief, v.* 4. It was at least their own fault if they were surprised by that day. They had fair warning, and sufficient helps to provide against that day, and might hope to stand with comfort and confidence before the Son of man. This would be a time of *refreshing to them from the presence of the Lord,* who to *those that look for him will appear without sin unto their salvation,* and will come to them as a friend in the day, not as a thief in the night.

6 Therefore, let us not sleep, as
do others; but let us watch and be
sober. 7 For they that sleep sleep in
the night; and they that be drunken
are drunken in the night. 8 But let
us, who are of the day, be sober,
putting on the breastplate of faith
and love; and, for an helmet, the
hope of salvation. 9 For God hath
not appointed us to wrath, but to
obtain salvation by our Lord Jesus
Christ, 10 Who died for us, that,
whether we wake or sleep, we should
live together with him.

On what had been said, the apostle grounds seasonable exhortations to several needful duties.

I. To watchfulness and sobriety, *v.* 6. These duties are distinct, yet they mutually befriend one another. For, while we are compassed about with so many temptations to intemperance and excess, we shall not keep sober, unless we be upon our guard, and, unless we keep sober, we shall not long watch. 1. Then *let us not sleep as do others, but let us watch;* we must not be secure and careless, nor indulge spiritual sloth and idleness. We must not be off our watch, but continually upon our guard against sin, and temptation to it. The generality of men are too careless of their duty and regardless of their spiritual enemies. They say, *Peace and safety,* when they are in the greatest danger, doze away their precious moments on which eternity depends, indulging idle dreams, and have no more thoughts nor cares about another world than men that are asleep have about this. Either they do not consider the things of another world at all, because they are asleep; or they do not consider them aright, because they dream. But let us watch, and act like men that are awake, and that stand upon their guard. 2. Let us also *be sober,* or temperate and moderate. Let us keep our natural desires and appetites after the things of this world within due bounds. Sobriety is usually opposed to excess in meats and drinks, and here particularly it is opposed to drunkenness; but it also extends to all other temporal things. Thus our Saviour warned his disciples to *take heed lest their hearts should be overcharged with surfeiting and drunkenness, and cares of this life, and so that day come on them unawares,* Luke xxi. 34. *Our moderation* then, as to all temporal things, *should be known to all men, because the Lord is at hand.* Besides this, watchfulness and sobriety are most suitable to the Christian's character and privilege, as being *children of the day;* because *those that sleep sleep in the night, and those that are drunken are drunken in the night, v.* 7. It is a most reproachful thing for men to sleep away the day-time, which is for work and not for sleep, to be drunken in the day, when so many eyes are upon them, to behold their shame. It was not so strange if those who had not the benefit of divine revelation suffered themselves to be lulled asleep by the devil in carnal security, and if they laid the reins upon the neck of their appetites, and indulged themselves in all manner of riot and excess; for it was night-time with them. They were not sensible of their danger, therefore they *slept;* they were not sensible of their duty, therefore they were drunk: but it ill becomes Christians to do thus. What! shall Christians, who have the light of the blessed gospel shining in their faces, be careless about their souls, and unmindful of another world? Those who have so many eyes upon them should conduct themselves with peculiar propriety.

II. To be well armed as well as watchful: to put on the whole armour of God. This is necessary in order to such sobriety as becomes us and will be a preparation for the day of the Lord, because our spiritual enemies are many, and mighty, and malicious. They draw many to their interest, and keep them in it, by making them careless, secure, and presumptuous, by making them drunk—drunk with pride, drunk with passion, drunk and giddy with self-conceit, drunk with the gratifications of sense: so that we have need to arm ourselves against their attempts, by putting on the spiritual breast-plate to keep the heart, and the spiritual helmet to secure the head; and this spiritual armour consists of the three great graces of Christians, faith, love, and hope, *v.* 8. 1. We must live by faith, and this will keep us watchful and sober. If we believe that the eye of God (who is a spirit) is always upon us, that we have spiritual enemies to grapple with, that there is a world of spirits to prepare for, we shall see reason to watch and be sober. Faith will be our best defence against the assaults of our enemies. 2. We must get a heart inflamed with love; and this also will be our defence. True and fervent love to God, and the things of God, will keep us watchful and sober, and hinder our apostasy in times of trouble and temptation. 3. We must make salvation our hope, and should have a lively hope of it. This good hope, through grace, of eternal life, will be as a helmet to defend the head, and hinder our being intoxicated with the pleasures of sin, which are but for a season. If we have hope of salvation, let us take heed of doing any thing that shall shake our hopes, or render us unworthy of or unfit for the great salvation we hope for. Having mentioned salvation and the hope of it, the apostle shows what grounds and reasons Christians have to hope for this salvation, as to which observe, He says nothing of their meriting it. No, the doctrine of our merits is altogether unscriptural and antiscriptural; there is no foundation of any good hope upon that account. But our hopes are to be grounded, (1.) Upon God's appointment: because *God hath not appointed us to wrath, but to obtain salvation, v.* 9. If we would trace our salvation to the first cause, that is God's appointment. Those who live and die in darkness and ignorance, who sleep and are drunken as in the night, are, it is but too plain, *appointed to wrath;* but as for those who are of the day, if they watch and be sober, it is evident that they are *appointed to obtain salvation.* And the sureness and firmness of the divine appointment are the great support and encouragement of our hope. Were we to obtain salvation by our own merit or power, we could have but little or no hope of it; but seeing we are to obtain it by virtue of God's appointment, which we are sure cannot be shaken *(for his purpose, according to election, shall stand)*, on this we build unshaken hope, especially when we consider, (2.) Christ's merit and grace, and that salvation is by our Lord Jesus Christ, who died for us. Our salvation therefore is owing to, and our hopes of it are grounded on, Christ's atonement as well as God's appointment: and, as we should think on God's gracious design and purpose, so also on Christ's death and sufferings, for this end, *that whether we wake or sleep* (whether we live or die, for death is but a sleep to believers, as the apostle had before intimated) *we should live together with Christ* live in union and in glory with him for ever. And, as it is the salvation that Christians hope for to *be for ever with the Lord,* so one foundation of their hope is their union with him. And if they are united with Christ, and live in him, and live to him, here, the sleep of death will be no prejudice to the spiritual life, much less to the life of glory hereafter. On the contrary, Christ died for us, that, living and dying, we might be his; that we might live to him while we are here, and live with him when we go hence.

11 Wherefore comfort yourselves
together, and edify one another, even
as also ye do. 12 And we beseech
you, brethren, to know them which
labour among you, and are over you
in the Lord, and admonish you; 13
And to esteem them very highly in
love for their work's sake. *And* be
at peace among yourselves. 14 Now
we exhort you, brethren, warn them
that are unruly, comfort the feeble-
minded, support the weak, be patient
toward all *men.* 15 See that none
render evil for evil unto any *man;* but
ever follow that which is good, both
among yourselves, and to all *men.*

In these words the apostle exhorts the Thessalonians to several duties.

I. Towards those who were nearly related one to another. Such should comfort themselves, or exhort one another, and edify one another, *v.* 11. 1. They must comfort or exhort themselves and one another; for the original word may be rendered both these ways. And we may observe, As those are most able and likely to comfort others who can comfort themselves, so the way to have comfort ourselves, or to administer comfort to others, is by compliance with the exhortation of the word. Note, We should not only be careful about our own comfort and welfare, but to promote the comfort and welfare of others also. He was a Cain that said, *Am I my brother's keeper?* We *must bear one another's burdens, and so fulfil the law of Christ.* 2. They must edify one another, by *following after those things whereby one may edify another,* Rom. xiv. 19. As Christians are lively stones built up together a spiritual house, they should endeavour to promote the good of the whole church by promoting the work of grace in one another. And it is the duty of every one of us to study that which is for the edification of those with whom we converse, *to please all men for their* real *profit.* We should communicate our knowledge and experiences one to another. We should join in prayer and praise one with another. We should set a good example one before another. And it is the duty of those especially who live in the same vicinity and family thus to comfort and edify one another; and this is the best neighbourhood, the best means to answer the end of society. Such as are nearly related together and have affection for one another, as they have the greatest opportunity, so they are under the greatest obligation, to do this kindness one to another. This the Thessalonians did *(which also you do),* and this is what they are exhorted to continue and increase in doing. Note, Those who do that which is good have need of further exhortations to excite them to do good, to do more good, as well as continue in doing what they do.

II. He shows them their duty towards their ministers, *v.* 12, 13. Though the apostle himself was driven from them, yet they had others who laboured among them, and to whom they owed these duties. The apostle here exhorts them to observe,

1. How the ministers of the gospel are described by the work of their office; and they should rather mind the work and duty they are called to than affect venerable and honourable names that they may be called by. Their work is very weighty, and very honourable and useful. (1.) Ministers must labour among their people, labour with diligence, and unto weariness (so the word in the original imports); *they must labour in the word and doctrine,* 1 Tim. v. 17. They are called labourers, and should not be loiterers. They must labour with their people, to instruct, comfort, and edify them. And, (2.) Ministers are to rule their people also, so the word is rendered, 1 Tim. v. 17. They must rule, not with rigour, but with love. They must not exercise dominion as temporal lords; but rule as spiritual guides, by setting a good example to the flock. They are over the people in the Lord, to distinguish them from civil magistrates, and to denote also that they are but ministers under Christ, appointed by him, and must rule the people by Christ's laws, and not by laws of their own. This may also intimate the end of their office and all their labour; namely, the service and honour of the Lord. (3.) They must also admonish the people, and that not only publicly, but privately, as there may be occasion. They must instruct them to do well, and should reprove when they do ill. It is their duty not only to give good counsel, but also to give admonition, to give warning to the flock of the dangers they are liable to, and reprove for negligence or what else may be amiss.

2. What the duty of the people is towards their ministers. There is a mutual duty between ministers and people. If ministers should labour among the people, then, (1.) The people must know them. As the shepherd should know his flock, so the sheep must know their shepherd. They must know his person, hear his voice, acknowledge him for their pastor, and pay due regard to his teaching, ruling, and admonitions. (2.) They must esteem their ministers highly in love; they should greatly value the office of the ministry, honour and love the persons of their ministers, and show their esteem and affection in all proper ways, and this for their work's sake, because their business is to promote the honour of Christ and the welfare of men's souls. Note, Faithful ministers ought to be so far from being lightly esteemed because of their work that they should be highly esteemed on account of it. The work of the ministry is so far from being a disgrace to those who upon other accounts deserve esteem, that it puts an honour upon those who are faithful and diligent, to which otherwise they could lay no claim, and will procure them that esteem and love among good people which otherwise they could not expect.

III. He gives divers other exhortations touching the duty Christians owe to one another. 1. *To be at peace among themselves,* *v.* 13. Some understand this exhortation (according to the reading in some copies) as referring to the people's duty to their ministers, to live peaceably with them, and not raise nor promote dissensions at any time between minister and people, which will certainly prove a hindrance to the success of a minister's work and the edification of the people. This is certain, that ministers and people should avoid every thing that tends to alienate their affections one from another And the people should be at peace among themselves, doing all they can to hinder any differences from rising or continuing among them, and using all proper means to preserve peace and harmony. 2. *To warn the unruly,* *v.* 14. There will be in all societies some who walk disorderly, who go out of their rank and station; and it is not only the duty of ministers, but of private Christians also, to warn and admonish them. Such should be reproved for their sin, warned of their danger, and told plainly of the injury they do their own souls, and the hurt they may do to others. Such should be put in mind of what they should do, and be reproved for doing otherwise. 3. *To comfort the feeble-minded,* v. 14. By these are intended the timorous and faint-hearted, or such as are dejected and of a sorrowful spirit. Some are cowardly, afraid of difficulties, and disheartened at the thoughts of hazards, and losses, and afflictions; now such should be encouraged; we should not despise them, but comfort them; and who knows what good a kind and comfortable word may do them? 4. *To support the weak,* v. 14. Some are not well able to perform their work, nor bear up under their burdens; we should therefore support them, help their infirmities, and lift at one end of the burden, and so help to bear it. It is the grace of God, indeed, that must strengthen and support such; but we should tell them of that grace, and endeavour to minister of that grace to them. 5. *To be patient towards all men,* v. 14. We must bear and forbear. We must be long-suffering, and suppress our anger, if it begin to rise upon the apprehension of affronts or injuries; at least we must not fail to moderate our anger: and this duty must be exercised towards all men, good and bad, high and low. We must not be high in our expectations and demands, nor harsh in our resentments, nor hard in our impositions, but endeavour to make the best we can of every thing, and think the best we can of every body. 6. *Not to render evil for evil to any man,* v. 15. This we must look to, and be very careful about, that is, we must by all means forbear to avenge ourselves. If others do us an injury, this will not justify us in returning it, in doing the same, or the like, or any other injury to them. It becomes us to forgive, as those that are, and that hope to be, forgiven of God. 7. *Ever to follow that which is good,* v. 15. In general, we must study to do what is our duty, and pleasing to God, in all circumstances, whether men do us good turns or ill turns; whatever men do to us, we must do good to others. We must always endeavour to be beneficent and instrumental to promote the welfare of others, both among ourselves (in the first place to those that *are of the household of faith),* and then, *as we have opportunity, unto all men,* Gal. vi. 10.

16 Rejoice evermore. 17 Pray
without ceasing. 18 In every thing
give thanks: for this is the will of
God in Christ Jesus concerning you.
19 Quench not the Spirit. 20 Despise not prophesyings. 21 Prove
all things; hold fast that which is
good. 22 Abstain from all appearance of evil.

Here we have divers short exhortations, that will not burden our memories, but will be of great use to direct the motions of our hearts and lives; for the duties are of great importance, and we may observe how they are connected together, and have a dependence upon one another. 1. *Rejoice evermore,* v. 16. This must be understood of spiritual joy; for we must rejoice in our creature-comforts as if we rejoiced not, and must not expect to live many years, and rejoice in them all; but, if we do rejoice in God, we may do that evermore. In him our joy will be full; and it is our fault if we have not a continual feast. If we are sorrowful upon any worldly account, yet still we may always rejoice, 2 Cor. vi. 10. Note, A religious life is a pleasant life, it is a life of constant joy. 2. *Pray without ceasing,* v. 17. Note, The way to rejoice evermore is to pray without ceasing. We should rejoice more if we prayed more. We should keep up stated times for prayer, and continue instant in prayer. We should pray always, and not faint: pray without weariness, and continue in prayer, till we come to that world where prayer shall be swallowed up in praise. The meaning is not that men should do nothing but pray, but that nothing else we do should hinder prayer in its proper season. Prayer will help forward and not hinder all other lawful business, and every good work. 3. *In every thing give thanks,* v. 18. If we pray without ceasing, we shall not want matter for thanksgiving *in every thing.* As we must in every thing make our requests known to God by supplications, so we must not omit thanksgiving, Phil. iv. 6. We should be thankful in every condition, even in adversity as well as prosperity. It is never so bad with us but it might be worse. If we have ever so much occasion to make our humble complaints to God, we never can have any reason to complain of God, and have always much reason to praise and give thanks: the apostle says, This is the *will of God in Christ Jesus concerning us, that we give thanks,* seeing God is reconciled to us in Christ Jesus; in him, through him, and for his sake, he allows us to rejoice evermore, and appoints us in every thing to give thanks. It is pleasing to God. 4. *Quench not the Spirit* (v. 19), for it is this Spirit of grace and supplication that helpeth our infirmities, that assisteth us in our prayers and thanksgivings. Christians are said to *be baptized with the Holy Ghost and with fire.* He worketh as fire, by enlightening, enlivening, and purifying the souls of men. We must be careful not to quench this holy fire. As fire is put out by withdrawing fuel, so we quench the Spirit if we do not stir up our spirits, and all that is within us, to comply with the motions of the good Spirit; and as fire is quenched by pouring water, or putting a great quantity of dirt upon it, so we must be careful not to quench the Holy Spirit by indulging carnal lusts and affections, or minding only earthly things. 5. *Despise not prophesyings* (v. 20); for, if we neglect the means of grace, we forfeit the Spirit of grace. By *prophesyings* here we are to understand the preaching of the word, the interpreting and applying of the scriptures; and this we must not despise, but should prize and value, because it is the ordinance of God, appointed of him for our furtherance and increase in knowledge and grace, in holiness and comfort. We must not despise preaching, though it be plain, and not with enticing words of men's wisdom, and though we be told no more than what we knew before. It is useful, and many times needful, to have our minds stirred up, our affections and resolutions excited, to those things that we knew before to be our interest and our duty. 6. *Prove all things, but hold fast that which is good, v.* 21. This is a needful caution, to prove all things; for, though we must put a value on preaching, we must not take things upon trust from the preacher, but try them by the law and the testimony. We must search the scriptures, whether what they say be true or not. We must not believe every spirit, but must try the spirits. But we must not be always trying, always unsettled; no, at length we must be settled, and hold fast that which is good. When we are satisfied that any thing is right, and true, and good, we must hold it fast, and not let it go, whatever opposition or whatever persecution we meet with for the sake thereof. Note, The doctrines of human infallibility, implicit faith, and blind obedience, are not the doctrines of the Bible. Every Christian has, and ought to have, the judgment of discretion, and should have *his senses exercised in discerning between good and evil,* truth and falsehood, Heb. v 13, 14. And proving all things must be in order to holding fast that which is good. We must not always be seekers, or fluctuating in our minds, *like children tossed to and fro with every wind of doctrine.* 7. *Abstain from all appearance of evil, v.* 22. This is a good means to prevent our being deceived with false doctrines, or unsettled in our faith; for our Saviour has told us (John vii. 17), *If a man will do his will, he shall know of the doctrine whether it be of God.* Corrupt affections indulged in the heart, and evil practices allowed of in the life, will greatly tend to promote fatal errors in the mind; whereas purity of heart, and integrity of life, will dispose men to receive the truth in the love of it. We should therefore abstain from evil, and all appearances of evil, from sin, and that which looks like sin, leads to it, and borders upon it. He who is not shy of the appearances of sin, who shuns not the occasions of sin, and who avoids not the temptations and approaches to sin, will not long abstain from the actual commission of sin.

23 And the very God of peace
sanctify you wholly; and I *pray
God* your whole spirit and soul and
body be preserved blameless unto the
coming of our Lord Jesus Christ. 24
Faithful *is* he that calleth you, who
also will do *it.* 25 Brethren, pray
for us. 26 Greet all the brethren
with a holy kiss. 27 I charge you
by the Lord that this epistle be read
unto all the holy brethren. 28 The
grace of our Lord Jesus Christ *be*
with you. Amen.

In these words, which conclude this epistle, observe,

I. Paul's prayer for them, *v.* 23. He had told them, in the beginning of this epistle, that he always made mention of them in his prayers; and, now that he is writing to them, he lifts up his heart to God in prayer for them. Take notice, 1. To whom the apostle prays, namely, *The very God of peace.* He is the God of grace, and the God of peace and love. He is the author of peace and lover of concord; and by their peaceableness and unity, from God as the author, those things would best be obtained which he prays for. 2. The things he prays for on behalf of the Thessalonians are their sanctification, that *God would sanctify them wholly;* and their preservation, that they might be *preserved blameless.* He prays that they may be wholly sanctified, that the whole man may be sanctified, and then that the whole man, spirit, soul, and body, may be preserved: or, he prays that they may be wholly sanctified, that is, more perfectly, for the best are sanctified but in part while in this world; and therefore we should pray for and press towards complete sanctification. Where the good work of grace is begun, it shall be carried on, be protected and preserved; and all those who are sanctified in Christ Jesus shall be preserved to the coming of our Lord Jesus Christ. And because, if God did not carry on his good work in the soul, it would miscarry, we should pray to God to perfect his work, and *preserve us blameless,* free from sin and impurity, till at length we are *presented faultless before the throne of his glory with exceeding joy.*

II. His comfortable assurance that God would hear his prayer: *Faithful is he who calleth you, who will also do it, v.* 24. The kindness and love of God had appeared to them in calling them to the knowledge of his truth, and the faithfulness of God was their security that they should persevere to the end; and therefore, the apostle assures them, God would do what he desired; he would effect what he had promised; he would accomplish all the good pleasure of his goodness towards them. Note, Our fidelity to God depends upon his faithfulness to us.

III. His request of their prayers: *Brethren, pray for us, v.* 25. We should pray for one another; and brethren should thus express brotherly love. This great apostle did not think it beneath him to call the Thessalonians brethren, nor to request their prayers

Ministers stand in need of their people's prayers; and the more people pray for their ministers the more good ministers may have from God, and the more benefit people may receive by their ministry.

IV. His salutation: *Greet all the brethren with a holy kiss, v.* 26. Thus the apostle sends a friendly salutation from himself, and Silvanus, and Timotheus, and would have them salute each other in their names; and thus he would have them signify their mutual love and affection to one another by the kiss of charity (1 Pet. v. 14), which is here called a holy kiss, to intimate how cautious they should be of all impurity in the use of this ceremony, then commonly practised; as it should not be a treacherous kiss like that of Judas, so not a lascivious kiss like that of the harlot, Prov. vii. 13.

V. His solemn charge for the reading of this epistle, *v.* 27. This is not only an exhortation, but an adjuration by the Lord. And this epistle was to be read to all the holy brethren. It is not only allowed to the common people to read the scriptures, and what none should prohibit, but it is their indispensable duty, and what they should be persuaded to do. In order to this, these holy oracles should not be kept concealed in an unknown tongue, but translated into the vulgar languages, that all men, being concerned to know the scriptures, may be able to read them, and be acquainted with them. The public reading of the law was one part of the worship of the sabbath among the Jews in their synagogues, and the scriptures should be read in the public assemblies of Christians also.

VI. The apostolical benediction that is usual in other epistles: *The grace of our Lord Jesus Christ be with you. Amen, v.* 28. We need no more to make us happy than to know that grace which our Lord Jesus Christ has manifested, be interested in that grace which he has purchased, and partake of that grace which dwells in him as the head of the church. This is an ever-flowing and overflowing fountain of grace to supply all our wants.

AN

EXPOSITION,

WITH PRACTICAL OBSERVATIONS,

OF THE SECOND EPISTLE OF ST. PAUL TO THE

THESSALONIANS.

THIS Second Epistle was written soon after the former, and seems to have been designed to prevent a mistake, which might arise from some passages in the former epistle, concerning the second coming of Christ, as if it were near at hand. The apostle in this epistle is careful to prevent any wrong use which some among them might make of those expressions of his that were agreeable to the dialect of the prophets of the Old Testament, and informs them that there were many intermediate counsels yet to be fulfilled before that day of the Lord should come, though, because it is sure, he had spoken of it as near. There are other things that he writes about for their consolation under sufferings, and exhortation and direction in duty.

CHAP. I.

After the introduction (ver. 1, 2) the apostle begins this epistle with an account of his high esteem for these Thessalonians, ver. 3, 4. He then comforts them under their afflictions and persecutions, ver. 5—10, and tells them what his prayers were to God for them, ver. 11, 12.

PAUL, and Silvanus, and Timotheus, unto the church of the
Thessalonians in God our Father and
the Lord Jesus Christ: 2 Grace unto
you, and peace, from God our Father
and the Lord Jesus Christ. 3 We
are bound to thank God always for
you, brethren, as it is meet, because
that your faith groweth exceedingly,
and the charity of every one of you
all toward each other aboundeth; 4
So that we ourselves glory in you in
the churches of God for your patience
and faith in all your persecutions and
tribulations that ye endure—

Here we have,

I. The introduction (*v.* 1, 2), in the same words as in the former epistle, from which we may observe that as this apostle did not count it grievous to him to write the same things (Phil. iii. 1) in his epistles that he had delivered in preaching, so he willingly wrote the same things to one church that he did to another. The occurrence of the same words in this epistle as in the former shows us that ministers ought not so much to regard the variety of expression and elegance of style as the truth and usefulness of the doctrines they preach. And great care should be taken lest, from an affectation of novelty in method and phrases, we advance new notions or doctrines, contrary to the principles of natural or revealed religion, upon which this church of the Thessalonians was built, as all true churches are; namely, *in God our Father and the Lord Jesus Christ.*

II. The apostle's expression of the high esteem he had for them. He not only had a great affection for them (as he had expressed in his former epistle, and now again in his pious wish of grace and peace for them), but he also expresses his great esteem for them, concerning which observe,

1. How his esteem of them is expressed. (1.) He glorified God on their behalf: *We are bound to thank God always for you, brethren, as it is meet*, v. 3. He chose rather to speak of what was praiseworthy in them in a way of thanksgiving to God than by commendation of them; and, as what he mentions was matter of his rejoicing, he accounted it matter of thanksgiving, and it was meet or fit it should be so, for we are bound, and it is our duty, to be thankful to God for all the good that is found in us or others: and it not only is an act of kindness to our fellow-christians, but our duty, to thank God on their behalf. (2.) He also *glories in them before the churches of God, v.* 4. The apostle never flattered his friends, but he took pleasure in commending them, and speaking well of them, to the glory of God and for the excitement and encouragement of others. Paul did not glory in his own gifts, nor in his labour among them, but he gloried in the grace of God which was bestowed upon them, and so his glorying was good, because all the commendation he gave to them, and the pleasure he took himself, centred in the praise and glory of God.

2. For what he esteemed them and thanked God; namely, the increase of their faith, and love, and patience. In his former epistle (*ch.* i. 3) he gave thanks for their faith, love, and patience; here he gives thanks for the increase of all those graces, that they were not only true Christians, but growing Christians. Note, Where there is the truth of grace there will be increase of it. *The path of the just is as the shining light, which shines more and more unto the perfect day.* And where there is the increase of grace God must have all the glory of it. We are as much indebted to him for the improvement of grace, and the progress of that good work, as we are for the first work of grace and the very beginning of it. We may be tempted to think that though when we were bad we could not make ourselves good, yet when we are good we can easily make ourselves better; but we have as much dependence on the grace of God for increasing the grace we have as for planting grace when we had it not. The matter of the apostle's thanksgiving and glorying on behalf of the Thessalonians was, (1.) That their faith grew exceedingly, *v.* 3. They were more confirmed in the truth of gospel-revelations, confided in gospel-promises, and had lively expectations of another world. The growth of their faith appeared by the works of faith; and, where faith grows, all other graces grow proportionably. (2.) Their charity abounded (*v.* 3), their love to God and man. Note, Where faith grows love will abound, for faith works by love; and not only the charity of some few of them, but of every one to each other, did abound. There were no such divisions among them as in some other churches. (3.) Their patience as well as faith increased in all their persecutions and tribulations. And patience has then its perfect work when it extends itself to all trials. There were many persecutions which the Thessalonians endured for the sake of righteousness, as well as other troubles which they met with in this calamitous life; yet they endured all these, by faith *seeing him that is invisible*, and looking to the *recompence of reward;* and endured them with. patience, not with an insensibility under them, but with patience arising from Christian principles, which kept them quiet and submissive, and afforded them inward strength and support.

5 *Which is* a manifest token of the
righteous judgment of God, that ye
may be counted worthy of the kingdom of God, for which ye also suffer:
6 Seeing *it is* a righteous thing with
God to recompense tribulation to them
that trouble you; 7 And to you who
are troubled rest with us, when the
Lord Jesus shall be revealed from
heaven with his mighty angels, 8 In
flaming fire, taking vengeance on them
that know not God, and that obey not
the gospel of our Lord Jesus Christ:
9 Who shall be punished with everlasting destruction from the presence
of the Lord, and from the glory of
his power; 10 When he shall come
to be glorified in his saints, and to be
admired in all them that believe (because our testimony among you was
believed) in that day.

Having mentioned their persecutions and tribulations, which they endured principally for the cause of Christ, the apostle proceeds to offer several things for their comfort under them; as,

I. He tells them of the present happiness and advantage of their sufferings, *v.* 5. Their faith being thus tried, and patience exercised, they were improved by their sufferings, insomuch that they were *counted worthy of the kingdom of God.* Their sufferings were a manifest token of this, that they were worthy or meet to be accounted Christians indeed, seeing they could suffer for Christianity. And the truth is, Religion, if it is worth any thing, is worth every thing; and those either have no religion at all, or none that is worth having, or know not how to value it, that cannot find in their hearts to suffer for it. Besides, from their patient suffering, it appeared that, according to the righteous judgment of God, they should be counted worthy of the heavenly glory: not by worthiness of condignity, but of congruity only; not that they could merit heaven, but they were made meet for heaven. We cannot by all our sufferings, any more than by our services, merit heaven as a debt; but by our patience under our sufferings we are qualified for the joy that is promised to patient sufferers in the cause of God.

II. He tells them next of the future recompence that shall be given to persecutore and persecuted.

1. In this future recompence there will be, (1.) A punishment inflicted on persecutors: God will *recompense tribulation to those that trouble you, v.* 6. And there is nothing that more infallibly marks a man for eternal ruin than a spirit of persecution, and enmity to the name and people of God: as the faith, patience, and constancy of the saints are to them an earnest of everlasting rest and joy, so the pride, malice, and wickedness of their persecutors are to them an earnest of everlasting misery; for every man carries about with him, and carries out of the world with him, either his heaven or his hell. God will render a recompence, and will trouble those that trouble his people. This he has done sometimes in this world, witness the dreadful end of many persecutors; but especially this he will do in the other world, where the portion of the wicked must be *weeping, and wailing, and gnashing of teeth.* (2.) A reward for those that are persecuted: God will recompense their trouble with rest, *v.* 7. There is a rest that remains for the people of God, a rest from sin and sorrow. Though many may be the troubles of the righteous now, yet God will deliver them out of them all. The future rest will abundantly recompense all their present troubles. The sufferings of this present time are not worthy to be compared with the glory that shall be revealed. There is enough in heaven to countervail all that we may lose or suffer for the name of Christ in this world. The apostle says, *To you who are troubled rest with us.* In heaven, ministers and people shall rest together, and rejoice together, who suffer together here; and the meanest Christian shall rest with the greatest apostle: nay, what is far more, if we suffer for Christ, we shall also reign with him, 2 Tim. ii. 12.

2. Concerning this future recompence we are further to observe,

(1.) The certainty of it, proved by the righteousness and justice of God: *It is a righteous thing with God* (*v.* 6) to render to every man according to his works. The thoughts of this should be terrible to wicked men and persecutors, and the great support of the righteous and such as are persecuted; fo·, seeing there is a righteous God, there will be a righteous recompence. God's suffering people will lose nothing by their sufferings, and their enemies will gain nothing by their advantages against them.

(2.) The time when this righteous recompence shall be made: *When the Lord Jesus shall be revealed from heaven, v.* 7. That will be the day of the *revelation of the righteous judgment of God;* for then will God judge the world in righteousness by that man whom he hath appointed, even Jesus Christ the righteous Judge. The righteousness of God does not so visibly appear to all men in the procedure of his providence as it will in the process of the great judgment-day. The scripture has made known to us the judgment to come, and we are bound to receive the revelation here given concerning Christ. As,

[1.] That the Lord Jesus will in that day appear from heaven. Now the heavens retain him, they conceal him; but then he will be revealed and made manifest. He will come in all the pomp and power of the upper world, *whence we look for the Saviour.*

[2.] He will be revealed with his mighty angels (*v.* 7), or the angels of his power: these will attend upon him, to grace the solemnity of that great day of his appearance; they will be the ministers of his justice and mercy in that day; they will summon the criminals to his tribunal, and gather in the elect, and be employed in executing his sentence.

[3.] He will come in flaming fire, *v.* 8. A fire goeth before him, which shall consume his enemies. The earth, and all the works that are therein, shall be burnt up, and the elements shall melt with fervent heat. This will be a trying fire, to try every man's work, —a refining fire, to purify the saints, who shall share in the purity, and partake of the felicity, of the new heaven and the new earth, —a consuming fire to the wicked. His light will be piercing, and his power consuming, to all those who in that day shall be found as chaff.

[4.] The effects of this appearance will be terrible to some and joyful to others.

First, They will be terrible to some; for he will then take vengeance on the wicked. 1. On those that sinned against the principles of natural religion, and rebelled against the light of nature, *that knew not God* (*v.* 8), though the invisible things of him are manifested in the things that are seen. 2. On those that rebel against the light of revelation, that *obey not the gospel of our Lord Jesus Christ.* And this is the condemnation, that light is come into the world, and men love darkness rather than light. This is the great crime of multitudes—the gospel is revealed to them, and they will not believe it; or, if they pretend to believe it, they will not obey it. Note, Believing the truths of the gospel is in order to our obeying the precepts of the gospel: there must be the obedience of faith. To such persons as are here mentioned the revelation of our Lord Jesus Christ will be terrible, because of their doom, which is mentioned, *v.* 9. Here observe, (1.) They will then be punished. Though sinners may be long reprieved, yet they will be punished at last. Their misery will be a proper punishment for their crimes, and only what they have deserved. They did sin's work, and must receive sin's wages. (2.) Their punishment will be no less than destruction, not of their being, but of their bliss; not that of the body alone, but both as to body and soul. (3.) This destruction will be everlasting. They shall be always dying, and yet never die. Their misery will run parallel with the line of eternity. The chains of darkness are everlasting chains, and the fire is everlasting fire. It must needs be so, since the punishment is inflicted by an eternal God, fastening upon an immortal soul, set out of the reach of divine mercy and grace. (4.) This destruction shall come from the *presence of the Lord*, that is, immediately from God himself. Here God punishes sinners by creatures, by instruments; but then he will take the work into his own hands. It will be destruction from the Almighty, more terrible than the consuming fire which consumed Nadab and Abihu, which came from before the Lord. (5.) It shall come from the *glory of his power*, or from his glorious power. Not only the justice of God, but his almighty power, will be glorified in the destruction of sinners; and who knows the power of his anger? He is able to cast into hell.

Secondly, It will be a joyful day to some, even to the saints, unto those that believe and obey the gospel. And then the apostle's testimony concerning this day will be confirmed and *believed* (*v.* 10); in that bright and blessed day, 1. Christ Jesus will be glorified and admired by his saints. They will behold his glory, and admire it with pleasure; they will glorify his grace, and admire the wonders of his power and goodness towards them, and sing hallelujahs to him in that day of his triumph, for their complete victory and happiness. 2. Christ will be glorified and admired in them. His grace and power will then be manifested and magnified, when it shall appear what he has purchased for, and wrought in, and bestowed upon, all those who believe in him. As his wrath and power will be made known in and by the destruction of his enemies, so his grace and power will be magnified in the salvation of his saints. Note, Christ's dealings with those who believe will be what the world one day shall wonder at. Now, they are a wonder to many; but how will they be wondered at in this great and glorious day; or, rather, how will Christ, whose name is Wonderful, be admired, when the mystery of God shall be finished! Christ will not be so much admired in the glorious esteem of angels that he will bring from heaven with him as in the many saints, *the many sons*, that he will bring to glory.

11 Wherefore also we pray always for you, that our God would count you worthy of *this* calling, and fulfil all the good pleasure of *his* goodness, and the work of faith with power:
12 That the name of our Lord Jesus Christ may be glorified in you, and ye in him, according to the grace of our God and the Lord Jesus Christ.

In these verses the apostle again tells the Thessalonians of his earnest and constant prayer for them. He could not be present with them, yet he had a constant remembrance of them; they were much upon his thoughts; he wished them well, and could not express his good-will and good wishes to them better than in earnest constant prayer to God for them: *Wherefore also we pray*, &c. Note, The believing thoughts and expectation of the second coming of Christ should put us upon prayer to God for ourselves and others. We should watch and pray, so our Saviour directs his disciples (Luke xxi. 36), *Watch therefore, and pray always, that you may be counted worthy to stand before the Son of man.* Observe,

I. What the apostle prayed for, *v.* 11. It is a great concern to be well instructed what to pray for; and without divine instruction we know not what to pray for, as without divine assistance we shall not pray in such a manner as we ought. Our prayers should be suitable to our expectations. Thus the apostle prays for them, 1. That God would begin his good work of grace in them; so we may understand this expression: *That our God would count you* (or, as it might be read, *make you) worthy of this calling.* We are called with a high and holy calling; we are called to God's kingdom and glory; and no less than the inheritance of the saints is the hope of our calling, nothing less than the enjoyment of that glory and felicity which shall be revealed when Christ Jesus shall be revealed from heaven. Now, if this be our calling, our great concern should be to be worthy of it, or meet and prepared for this glory: and because we have no worthiness of our own, but what is owing purely to the grace of God, we should pray that he would make us worthy, and then count us worthy, of this calling, or that he would make us meet to partake of the inheritance of the saints in light, Col. i. 12. 2. That God would carry on the good work that is begun, and *fulfil all the good pleasure of his goodness.* The good pleasure of God denotes his gracious purposes towards his people, which flow from his goodness, and are full of goodness towards them; and it is thence that all good comes to us. If there be any good in us, it is the fruit of God's good-will to us, it is owing to the good pleasure of his goodness, and therefore is called grace. Now, there are various and manifold purposes of grace and good-will in God towards his people; and the apostle prays that all of them may be fulfilled or accomplished towards these Thessalonians. There are several good works of grace begun in the hearts of God's people, which proceed from this good pleasure of God's goodness, and we should desire that they may be completed and perfected. In particular, the apostle prays that God would fulfil in them the *work of faith with power.* Note, (1.) The fulfilling of the work of faith is in order to the fulfilling of every other good work. And, (2.) It is the power of God that not only begins, but that carries on and perfects the work of faith.

II. Why the apostle prayed for these things (*v.* 12): *That the name of the Lord Jesus may be glorified;* this is the end we should aim at in every thing we do and desire, that God and Christ in all things may be glorified. Our own happiness and that of others should be subordinate to this ultimate end. Our good works should so shine before men that others may glorify God, that Christ may be glorified in and by us, and then we shall be glorified in and with him. And this is the great end and design of the grace of our God and the Lord Jesus Christ, which is manifested to us and wrought in us. Or thus: it is according to the grace of God and Christ, that is, it is an agreeable thing, considering the grace that is manifested to us and bestowed on us, by God and Christ, that we direct all we do to the glory of our Creator and Redeemer.

CHAP. II.

The apostle is very careful to hinder the spreading of an error into which some among them had fallen concerning the coming of Christ, as being very near, ver. 1—3. Then he proceeds to confute the error he cautioned them against, by telling them of two great events that were antecedent to the coming of Christ—a general apostasy, and the revelation of antichrist, concerning whom the apostle tells them many remarkable things, about his name, his character, his rise, his fall, his reign, and the sin and ruin of his subjects, ver. 4—12, He then comforts them against the terror of this apostasy, and exhorts them to stedfastness, ver. 13—15. And concludes with a prayer for them, ver. 16, 17.

NOW we beseech you, brethren,
by the coming of our Lord
Jesus Christ, and *by* our gathering
together unto him, 2 That ye be
not soon shaken in mind, or be
troubled, neither by spirit, nor by
word, nor by letter as from us, as
that the day of Christ is at hand.
3 Let no man deceive you by any
means—

From these words it appears that some among the Thessalonians had mistaken the apostle's meaning, in what he had written in his former epistle about the coming of Christ, by thinking that it was near at hand,—that Christ was just ready to appear and come to judgment. Or, it may be, some among them pretended that they had the knowledge of this by particular revelation from the Spirit, or from some words they had heard from the apostle, when he was with them, or some letter he had written or they pretended he had written to them or some other person: and hereupon the apostle is careful to rectify this mistake, and to prevent the spreading of this error. Observe, If errors and mistakes arise among Christians, we should take the first opportunity to rectify them, and hinder the spreading thereof; and good men will be especially careful to suppress errors that may arise from a mistake of their words and actions, though that which was spoken or done was ever so innocent or well. We have a subtle adversary, who watches all opportunities to do mischief, and will sometimes promote errors even by means of the words of scripture. Observe,

I. How very earnest and solicitous this apostle was to prevent mistakes: *We beseech you, brethren,* &c., *v.* 1. He entreats them as brethren who might have charged them as a father charges his children: he shows great kindness and condescension, and insinuates himself into their affections. And this is the best way to deal with men when we would preserve or recover them from errors, to deal gently and affectionately with them: rough and rigorous treatment will but exasperate their spirits, and prejudice them against the reasons we may offer. He obtests and even conjures them in the most solemn manner: *By the coming of Christ,* &c. The words are in the form of an oath; and his meaning is that if they believed Christ would come, and if they desired he would come, and rejoiced in the hope of his coming, they should be careful to avoid the error, and the evil consequences of it, against which he was now cautioning them. From this form of obtestation used by the apostle, we may observe,

1. It is most certain that the Lord Jesus Christ will come to judge the world, that he will come in all the pomp and power of the upper world in the last day, to execute judgment upon all. Whatever uncertainty we are at, or whatever mistakes may arise about the time of his coming, his coming itself is certain. This has been the faith and hope of all Christians in all ages of the church; nay, it was the faith and hope of the Old-Testament saints, ever since Enoch the seventh from Adam, who said, *Behold, the Lord cometh,* &c., Jude 14.

2. At the second coming of Christ all the saints will be gathered together to him; and this mention of the gathering of the saints together unto Christ at his coming shows that the apostle speaks of Christ's coming to judgment at the last day, and not of his coming to destroy Jerusalem. He speaks of a proper, and not a metaphorical advent: and, as it will be part of Christ's honour in that day, so it will be the completing of the happiness of his saints. (1.) That they all shall be gathered together. There will then be a general meeting of all the saints, and none but saints; all the Old-Testament saints, who got acquaintance with Christ by the dark shadows of the law, and saw this day at a distance; and all the New-Testament saints, to whom life and immortality were brought to light by the gospel; they will all be gathered together. There will then come from the four winds of heaven all that are, or ever were, or ever shall be, from the beginning to the end of time. All shall be gathered together. (2.) That they shall be gathered *together to Christ.* He will be the great centre of their unity. They shall be gathered together to him, to be attendants on him, to be assessors with him, to be presented by him to the Father, to be with him for ever, and altogether happy in his presence to all eternity. (3.) The doctrine of Christ's coming and our gathering together to him is of great moment and importance to Christians; otherwise it would not be the proper matter of the apostle's obtestation. We ought therefore not only to believe these things, but highly to account of them also, and look upon them as things we are greatly concerned in and should be much affected with.

II. The thing itself against which the apostle cautions the Thessalonians is that they should not be deceived about the time of Christ's coming, and so *be shaken in mind, or be troubled.* Note, Errors in the mind tend greatly to weaken our faith, and cause us trouble; and such as are weak in faith and of troubled minds are oftentimes apt to be deceived, and fall a prey to seducers. 1. The apostle would not have them be deceived: *Let no man deceive you by any means,* v. 3. There are many who lie in wait to deceive, and they have many ways of deceiving; we have reason therefore to be cautious and stand upon our guard. Some deceivers will pretend new revelations, others misinterpret scripture, and others will be guilty of gross forgeries; divers means and artifices of deceit men will use; but we must be careful that no man deceive us by any means. The particular matter in which the apostle cautions them not to be deceived is about the near approach of Christ's coming, as if it was to have been in the apostle's days; and harmless as this error might seem to many, yet, because it was indeed an error, it would have proved of bad consequence to many persons. Therefore, 2. He gives them warning, and would not have them be soon shaken in mind, nor be troubled. (1.) He would not have their faith weakened. We should firmly believe the second coming of Christ, and be settled and established in the faith of this; but there was danger lest the Thessalonians, if they apprehended the coming of Christ was just at hand, upon finding that they, or others whom they too much regarded, were mistaken as to the time, should thereupon question the truth or certainty of the thing itself; whereas they ought not to waver in their minds as to this great thing, which is the faith and hope of all the saints. False doctrines are like the winds, that toss the water to and fro, and they are apt to unsettle the minds of men, who are sometimes as unstable as water. Then, (2.) He would not have their comforts lessened, that they should not be troubled nor affrighted with false alarms. It is probable that the coming of Christ was represented in so much terror as to trouble many serious Christians among them, though in itself it should be matter of the believer's hope and joy; or else many might be troubled with the thought how surprising this day would be, or with the fear of their unpreparedness, or upon the reflection on their mistake about the time of Christ's coming: we should always watch and pray, but must not be discouraged nor uncomfortable at the thought of Christ's coming.

3—For *that day shall not come,*
except there come a falling away first,
and that man of sin be revealed, the
son of perdition; 4 Who opposeth
and exalteth himself above all that is
called God, or that is worshipped; so
that he as God sitteth in the temple
of God, showing himself that he is
God. 5 Remember ye not, that,
when I was yet with you, I told you
these things? 6 And now ye know
what withholdeth that he might be
revealed in his time. 7 For the
mystery of iniquity doth already
work: only he who now letteth *will
let,* until he be taken out of the way.
8 And then shall that Wicked be
revealed, whom the Lord shall consume with the spirit of his mouth,
and shall destroy with the brightness
of his coming: 9 *Even him,* whose
coming is after the working of Satan
with all power and signs and lying
wonders, 10 And with all deceivableness of unrighteousness in them
that perish; because they received
not the love of the truth, that they
might be saved. 11 And for this

cause God shall send them strong delusion, that they should believe a lie: 12 That they all might be damned who believed not the truth, but had pleasure in unrighteousness.

In these words the apostle confutes the error against which he had cautioned them, and gives the reasons why they should not expect the coming of Christ as just at hand. There were several events previous to the second coming of Christ; in particular, he tells them there would be

I. A general apostasy, *there would come a falling away first*, *v.* 3. By this apostasy we are not to understand a defection in the state, or from civil government, but in spiritual or religious matters, from sound doctrine, instituted worship and church government, and a holy life. The apostle speaks of some very great apostasy, not only of some converted Jews or Gentiles, but such as should be very general, though gradual, and should give occasion to the revelation or rise of *antichrist*, that *man of sin*. This, he says (*v.* 5), he had told them of when he was with them, with design, no doubt, that they should not take offence nor be stumbled at it. And let us observe that no sooner was Christianity planted and rooted in the world than there began to be a defection in the Christian church. It was so in the Old-Testament church; presently after any considerable advance made in religion there followed a defection: soon after the promise there was revolting; for example, soon after men began to call upon the name of the Lord all flesh corrupted their way,—soon after the covenant with Noah the Babel-builders bade defiance to heaven,—soon after the covenant with Abraham his seed degenerated in Egypt,—soon after the Israelites were planted in Canaan, when the first generation was worn off, they forsook God and served Baal,—soon after God's covenant with David his seed revolted, and served other gods,—soon after the return out of captivity there was a general decay of piety, as appears by the story of Ezra and Nehemiah; and therefore it was no strange thing that after the planting of Christianity there should come a falling away.

II. A revelation of that man of sin, that is (*v.* 3), antichrist would take his rise from this general apostasy. The apostle afterwards speaks of the revelation of that wicked one (*v.* 8), intimating the discovery which should be made of his wickedness, in order to his ruin: here he seems to speak of his rise, which should be occasioned by the general apostasy he had mentioned, and to intimate that all sorts of false doctrines and corruptions should centre in him. Great disputes have been as to who or what is intended by this man of sin and son of perdition: and, if it be not certain that the papal power and tyranny are principally or only intended, yet this is plain, What is here said does very exactly agree thereto. For observe,

1. The names of this person, or rather the state and power here spoken of. He is called the man of sin, to denote his egregious wickedness; not only is he addicted to, and practises, wickedness himself, but he also promotes, countenances, and commands sin and wickedness in others; and he is the son of perdition, because he himself is devoted to certain destruction, and is the instrument of destroying many others both in soul and body. These names may properly be applied, for these reasons, to the papal state; and thereto agree also,

2. The characters here given, *v.* 4. (1.) That he *opposes and exalts himself above all that is called God, or is worshipped;* and thus have the bishops of Rome not only opposed God's authority, and that of the civil magistrates, who are called gods, but have exalted themselves above God and earthly governors, in demanding greater regard to their commands than to the commands of God or the magistrate. (2.) *As God, he sits in the temple of God, showing himself that he is God.* As God was in the temple of old, and worshipped there, and is in and with his church now, so the antichrist here mentioned is some usurper of God's authority in the Christian church, who claims divine honours; and to whom can this better apply than to the bishops of Rome, to whom the most blasphemous titles have been given, as *Dominus Deus noster papa—Our Lord God the pope; Deus alter in terrâ—Another God on earth; Idem est dominium Dei et papæ—The dominion of God and the pope is the same?*

3. His rise is mentioned, *v.* 6, 7. Concerning this we are to observe two things:—(1.) There was something that hindered or withheld, or *let, until it was taken away.* This is supposed to be the power of the Roman empire, which the apostle did not think fit to mention more plainly at that time; and it is notorious that, while this power continued, it prevented the advances of the bishops of Rome to that height of tyranny to which soon afterwards they arrived. (2.) This mystery of iniquity was gradually to arrive at its height; and so it was in effect that the universal corruption of doctrine and worship in the Romish church came in by degrees, and the usurpation of the bishops of Rome was gradual, not all at once; and thus the mystery of iniquity did the more easily, and almost insensibly, prevail. The apostle justly calls it a *mystery of iniquity*, because wicked designs and actions were concealed under false shows and pretences, at least they were concealed from the common view and observation. By pretended devotion, superstition and idolatry were advanced; and, by a pretended zeal for God and his glory, bigotry and persecution were promoted. And he tells us that this

mystery of iniquity did even then begin, or did *already work*. While the apostles were yet living, *the enemy came, and sowed tares;* there were then the *deeds of the Nicolaitans*, persons who pretended zeal for Christ, but really opposed him. Pride, ambition, and worldly interest of church-pastors and church-rulers, as in Diotrephes and others, were the early working of the mystery of iniquity, which, by degrees, came to that prodigious height which has been visible in the church of Rome.

4. The fall or ruin of the antichristian state is declared, *v.* 8. The head of this antichristian kingdom is called *that wicked one*, or that lawless person who sets up a human power in competition with, and contradiction to, the divine dominion and power of the Lord Jesus Christ; but, as he would thus manifest himself to be the man of sin, so the revelation or discovery of this to the world would be the sure presage and the means of his ruin. The apostle assures the Thessalonians that the Lord would consume and destroy him; the consuming of him precedes his final destruction, and that is by the *Spirit of his mouth*, by his word of command; the pure word of God, accompanied with the Spirit of God, will discover this mystery of iniquity, and make the power of antichrist to consume and waste away; and in due time it will be totally and finally destroyed, and this will be by the brightness of Christ's coming. Note, The coming of Christ to destroy the wicked will be with peculiar glory and eminent lustre and brightness.

5 The apostle further describes the reign and rule of this man of sin. Here we are to observe, (1.) The manner of his coming, or ruling, and working: in general, that it is after the example of Satan, the grand enemy of souls, the great adversary of God and man. He is the great patron of error and lies, the sworn enemy of the truth as it is in Jesus and all the faithful followers of Jesus. More particularly, it is with Satanical power and deceit. A divine power is pretended for the support of this kingdom, but it is only after the working of Satan. Signs and wonders, visions and miracles, are pretended; by these the papal kingdom was first set up, and has all along been kept up, but they have false signs to support false doctrines; and lying wonders, or only pretended miracles that have served their cause, things false in fact, or fraudulently managed, to impose upon the people: and the diabolical deceits with which the antichristian state has been supported are notorious. The apostle calls it *all deceivableness of unrighteousness*, *v.* 10. Others may call them pious frauds, but the apostle called them unrighteous and wicked frauds; and, indeed, all fraud (which is contrary to truth) is an impious thing. Many are the subtle artifices the man of sin has used, and various are the plausible pretences by which he has beguiled unwary and unstable souls to embrace false doctrines, and submit to his usurped dominion. (2.) The persons are described who are his willing subjects, or most likely to become such, *v.* 10. They are such as *love not the truth that they may be saved.* They heard the truth (it may be), but they did not love it; they could not bear sound doctrine, and therefore easily imbibed false doctrines; they had some notional knowledge of what was true, but they indulged some powerful prejudices, and so became a prey to seducers. Had they loved the truth, they would have persevered in it, and been preserved by it; but no wonder if they easily parted with what they never had any love to. And of these persons it is said that they perish or are lost; they are in a lost condition, and in danger to be lost for ever. For,

6. We have the *sin and ruin of the subjects* of antichrist's kingdom declared, *v.* 11, 12. (1.) Their sin is this: *They believed not the truth, but had pleasure in unrighteousness:* they did not love the truth, and therefore they did not believe it; and, because they did not believe the truth, therefore they had pleasure in unrighteousness, or in wicked actions, and were pleased with false notions. Note, An erroneous mind and vicious life often go together and help forward one another. (2.) Their ruin is thus expressed: *God shall send them strong delusions, to believe a lie.* Thus he will punish men for their unbelief, and for their dislike of the truth and love to sin and wickedness; not that God is the author of sin, but in righteousness he sometimes withdraws his grace from such sinners as are here mentioned; he gives them over to Satan, or leaves them to be deluded by his instruments; he gives them up to their own hearts' lusts, and leaves them to themselves, and then sin will follow of course, yea, the worst of wickedness, that shall end at last in eternal damnation. God is just when he inflicts spiritual judgments here, and eternal punishments hereafter, upon those who have no love to the truths of the gospel, who will not believe them, nor live suitably to them, but indulge false doctrines in their minds, and wicked practices in their lives and conversations.

13 But we are bound to give thanks
alway to God for you, brethren beloved
of the Lord, because God hath from
the beginning chosen you to salvation
through sanctification of the Spirit and
belief of the truth: 14 Whereunto
he called you by our gospel to the
obtaining of the glory of our Lord
Jesus Christ. 15 Therefore, brethren,
stand fast, and hold the traditions
which ye have been taught, whether
by word, or our epistle.

Here observe, I. The consolation the

Thessalonians might take against the terrors of this apostasy, *v.* 13, 14. For they were chosen to salvation, and called to the obtaining of glory. Note, When we hear of the apostasy of many, it is matter of great comfort and joy that there is a remnant according to the election of grace which does and shall persevere; and especially we should rejoice if we have reason to hope that we are of that number. The apostle reckoned himself bound in duty to be thankful to God on this account: *We are bound to give thanks to God always for you.* He had often given thanks on their behalf, and he is still abounding in thanksgiving for them; and there was good reason, because they were beloved by the Lord, as appeared in this matter—their security from apostatizing. This preservation of the saints is owing,

1. To the stability of the election of grace, *v.* 13. Therefore were they beloved of the Lord, because God had chosen them from the beginning. He had loved them with an everlasting love. Concerning this election of God we may observe, (1.) The eternal date of it—it is from the beginning; not the beginning of the gospel, but the beginning of the world, before the foundation of the world, Eph. i. 4. Then, (2.) The end to which they were chosen—salvation, complete and eternal salvation from sin and misery, and the full fruition of all good. (3.) The means in order to obtaining this end—*sanctification of the spirit and belief of the truth.* The decree of election therefore connects the end and the means, and these must not be separated. We are not elected of God because we were holy, but that we might be holy. Being chosen of God, we must not live as we list; but, if we are chosen to salvation as the end, we must be prepared for it by sanctification as the necessary means to obtain that end, which sanctification is by the operation of the Holy Spirit as the author and by faith on our part. There must be the belief of the truth, without which there can be no true sanctification, nor perseverance in grace, nor obtaining of salvation. Faith and holiness must be joined together, as well as holiness and happiness; therefore our Saviour prayed for Peter that his faith might not fail (Luke xxii. 32), and for his disciples (John xvii. 17), *Sanctify them by thy truth; thy word is truth.*

2. To the efficacy of the gospel call, *v.* 14. As they were chosen to salvation, so they were called thereunto by the gospel. Whom he did predestinate those he also called, Rom. viii. 30. The outward call of God is by the gospel; and this is rendered effectual by the inward operation of the Spirit. Note, Wherever the gospel comes it calls and invites men to the obtaining of glory; it is a call to honour and happiness, even the *glory of our Lord Jesus Christ,* the glory he has purchased, and the glory he is possessed of, to be communicated unto those who believe in him and obey his gospel; such shall be with Christ, to behold his glory, and they shall be glorified with Christ and partake of his glory. Hereupon there follows,

II. An exhortation to stedfastness and perseverance: *Therefore, brethren, stand fast, v.* 15. Observe, He does not say, "You are chosen to salvation, and therefore you may be careless and secure;" but *therefore stand fast.* God's grace in our election and vocation is so far from superseding our diligent care and endeavour that it should quicken and engage us to the greatest resolution and diligence. So the apostle John having told those to whom he wrote that they had received the anointing which should abide in them, and that they should abide in him (in Christ), subjoins this exhortation, *Now abide in him,* 1 John ii. 27, 28. The Thessalonians are exhorted to stedfastness in their Christian profession, to *hold fast the traditions which they had been taught,* or the doctrine of the gospel, which had been delivered by the apostle, by word or epistle. As yet the canon of scripture was not complete, and therefore some things were delivered by the apostles in their preaching, under the guidance of the infallible Spirit, which Christians were bound to observe as coming from God; other things were afterwards by them committed to writing, as the apostle had written a former epistle to these Thessalonians; and these epistles were written as the writers were moved by the Holy Ghost. Note, There is no argument hence for regarding oral traditions in our days, now that the canon of scripture is complete, as of equal authority with the sacred writings. Such doctrines and duties as were taught by the inspired apostles we must stedfastly adhere to; but we have no certain evidence of any thing delivered by them more than what we find contained in the holy scriptures.

16 Now our Lord Jesus Christ himself, and God, even our Father, which hath loved us, and hath given *us* everlasting consolation and good hope through grace,
17 Comfort your hearts, and stablish you in every good word and work.

In these words we have the apostle's earnest prayer for them, in which observe,

I. To whom he prays: *Our Lord Jesus Christ himself, and God, even our Father.* We may and should direct our prayers, not only to God the Father, through the mediation of our Lord Jesus Christ, but also *to our Lord Jesus Christ himself;* and should pray in his name unto God, not only as his Father but as our Father in and through him.

II. From what he takes encouragement in his prayer—from the consideration of what God had already done for him and them: *Who hath loved us, and given us everlasting consolation and good hope through grace, v.* 16.

Here observe, 1. The love of God is the spring and fountain of all the good we have or hope for; our election, vocation, justification, and salvation, are all owing to the love of God in Christ Jesus. 2. From this fountain in particular all our consolation flows. And the consolation of the saints is an everlasting consolation. The comforts of the saints are not dying things; they shall not die with them. The spiritual consolations God gives none shall deprive them of; and God will not take them away: because he loves them with an everlasting love, therefore they shall have everlasting consolations. 3. Their consolation is founded on the hope of eternal life. They rejoice in hope of the glory of God, and are not only patient, but joyful, in tribulations; and there is good reason for these strong consolations, because the saints have good hope: their hope is grounded on the love of God, the promise of God, and the experience they have had of the power, the goodness, and the faithfulness of God, and it is good hope through grace; the free grace and mercy of God are what they hope for, and what their hopes are founded on, and not on any worth or merit of their own.

III. What it is that he asks of God for them—that *he would comfort their hearts, and establish them in every good word and work, v.* 17. God had given them consolations, and he prayed that they might have more abundant consolation. There was good hope, through grace, that they would be preserved, and he prayed that they might be established: it is observable how comfort and establishment are here joined together. Note therefore, 1. Comfort is a means of establishment; for the more pleasure we take in the word, and work, and ways of God, the more likely we shall be to persevere therein. And, 2. Our establishment in the ways of God is a likely means in order to comfort; whereas, if we are wavering in faith, and of a doubtful mind, or if we are halting and faltering in our duty, no wonder if we are strangers to the pleasures and joys of religion. What is it that lies at the bottom of all our uneasiness, but our unsteadiness in religion? We must be established in every good word and work, in the word of truth and the work of righteousness: Christ must be honoured by our good works and good words; and those who are sincere will endeavour to do both, and in so doing they may hope for comfort and establishment, till at length their holiness and happiness be completed.

CHAP. III.

In the close of the foregoing chapter, the apostle had prayed earnestly for the Thessalonians, and now he desires their prayers, encouraging them to trust in God, to which he subjoins another petition for them, ver. 1—5. He then proceeds to give them commands and directions for correcting some things he was informed were amiss among them, ver. 6—15, and concludes with benedictions and prayers, ver. 16—18.

FINALLY, brethren, pray for us,
that the word of the Lord may
have *free* course, and be glorified,
even as *it is* with you: 2 And that
we may be delivered from unreasonable and wicked men: for all *men*
have not faith. 3 But the Lord is
faithful, who shall stablish you, and
keep *you* from evil. 4 And we have
confidence in the Lord touching you,
that ye both do and will do the things
which we command you. 5 And the
Lord direct your hearts into the love
of God, and into the patient waiting
for Christ.

In these words observe,

I. The apostle desires the prayers of his friends: *Finally, brethren, pray for us, v.* 1. He always remembered them in his prayers, and would not have them forget him and his fellow-labourers, but bear them on their hearts at the throne of grace. Note, 1. This is one way by which the communion of saints is kept up, not only by their praying together, or with one another, but by their praying for one another when they are absent one from another. And thus those who are at a great distance may meet together at the throne of grace; and thus those who are not capable of doing or receiving any other kindness may yet this way do and receive real and very great kindness. 2. It is the duty of people to pray for their ministers; and not only for their own pastors, but also for all good and faithful ministers. And, 3. Ministers need, and therefore should desire, the prayers of their people. How remarkable is the humility, and how engaging the example, of this great apostle, who was so mighty in prayer himself, and yet despised not the prayers of the meanest Christian, but desired an interest in them. Observe, further, what they are desired and directed to pray for; namely, (1.) For the success of the gospel ministry: *That the word of the Lord may have free course, and be glorified, v.* 1. This was the great thing that Paul was most solicitous about. He was more solicitous that God's name might be sanctified, his kingdom advanced, and his will done, than he was about his own daily bread. He desired that the word of the Lord might run (so it is in the original), that it might get ground, that the interest of religion in the world might go forward and not backward, and not only go forward, but go apace. All the forces of hell were then, and still are, more or less, raised and mustered to oppose the word of the Lord, to hinder its publication and success. We should pray, therefore, that oppositions may be removed, that so the gospel may have free course to the ears, the hearts, and the consciences of men, that it may be glorified in the conviction and conversion of sinners, the confutation, of gainsayers, and the holy conversation of the saints. God, who magnified the law, and made it honourable, will glorify the gospel, and make that honourable, and so will glorify his own name; and good ministers and good Christians may very well be contented to be little, to be any thing, to be nothing, if Christ be magnified and his gospel be glorified. Paul was now at Athens, or, as some think, at Corinth, and would have the Thessalonians pray that he might have as good success there as he had at Thessalonica, that it might be as well with others even as it was with them. Note, If ministers have been successful in one place, they should desire to be successful in every place where they may preach the gospel. (2.) For the safety of gospel ministers. He asks their prayers, not for preferment, but for preservation: *That we may be delivered from unreasonable and wicked men, v.* 2. Note, Those who are enemies to the preaching of the gospel, and persecutors of the faithful preachers of it, are unreasonable and wicked men. They act against all the rules and laws of reason and religion, and are guilty of the greatest absurdity and impiety. Not only in the principles of atheism and infidelity, but also in the practice of vice and immorality, and especially in persecution, there is the greatest absurdity in the world, as well as impiety. There is need of the spiritual protection, as well as the assistance, of godly and faithful ministers, for these are as the standard-bearers, who are most struck at; and therefore all who wish well to the interest of Christ in the world should pray for them. *For all men have not faith;* that is, many do not believe the gospel; they will not embrace it themselves, and no wonder if such are restless and malicious in their endeavours to oppose the gospel, decry the ministry, and disgrace the ministers of the word; and too many have not common faith or honesty; there is no confidence that we can safely put in them, and we should pray to be delivered from those who have no conscience nor honour, who never regard what they say or do. We may sometimes be in as much or more danger from false and pretended friends as from open and avowed enemies.

II. He encourages them to trust in God. We should not only pray to God for his grace, but also place our trust and confidence in his grace, and humbly expect what we pray for. Observe,

1. What the good is which we may expect from the grace of God—establishment, and preservation from evil; and the best Christians stand in need of these benefits. (1.) That God would establish them. This the apostle had prayed for on their behalf (*ch.* ii. 17), and now he encourages them to expect this favour. We stand no longer than God holds us up; unless he *hold up our goings in his paths, our feet will slide,* and we shall fall. (2.) That God will keep them from evil. We have as much need of the grace of God for our perseverance to the end as for the beginning of the good work. The evil of sin is the greatest evil, but there are other evils which God will also preserve his saints from—the evil that is in the world, yea, from all evil, to his heavenly kingdom.

2. What encouragement we have to depend upon the grace of God: *The Lord is faithful.* He is faithful to his promises, and is the Lord who cannot lie, who will not alter the thing that has gone out of his mouth. When once the promise therefore is made, performance is sure and certain. He is faithful to his relation, a faithful God and a faithful friend; we may depend upon his filling up all the relations he stands in to his people. Let it be our care to be true and faithful in our promises, and to the relations we stand in to this faithful God. He adds,

3. A further ground of hope that God would do this for them, seeing they did and would do the things they were commanded, *v.* 4. The apostle had this confidence in them, and this was founded upon his confidence in God; for there is otherwise no confidence in man. Their obedience is described by doing what he and his fellow-labourers had commanded them, which was no other thing than the commandments of the Lord; for the apostles themselves had no further commission than to teach men *to observe and to do what the Lord had commanded,* Matt. xxviii. 20. And as the experience the apostle had of their obedience for the time past was one ground of his confidence that they would do the things commanded them for the time to come, so this is one ground to hope that *whatsoever we ask of God we shall receive of him, because we keep his commandments, and do those things that are pleasing in his sight,* 1 John iii. 22.

III. He makes a short prayer for them, *v.* 5. It is a prayer for spiritual blessings. Two things of the greatest importance the apostle prays for:—1. That their hearts may be brought into the love of God, to be in love with God as the most excellent and amiable Being, the best of all beings; and this is not only most reasonable and necessary in order to our happiness, but is our happiness itself; it is a great part of the happiness of heaven itself, where this love shall be made perfect. We can never attain to this unless God by his grace direct our hearts aright, for our love is apt to go astray after other things. Note, We sustain a great deal of damage by misplacing our affections; it is our sin and our misery that we place our affections upon wrong objects. If God direct our love aright upon himself, the rest of the affections will thereby be rectified. 2. That a *patient waiting for Christ* may be joined with this love of God. There is no true love of God without faith in Jesus Christ. We must wait for Christ, which supposes our faith in him, that we believe he came once in flesh and will come again in glory: and we must expect this second coming of Christ, and be careful to get ready for it; there must be a patient waiting, enduring with courage and constancy all that we may meet with in the mean time: and we *have need of patience*, and need of divine grace to exercise Christian patience, the *patience of Christ* (as some read the word), patience for Christ's sake and after Christ's example.

6 Now we command you, brethren,
in the name of our Lord Jesus Christ,
that ye withdraw yourselves from every
brother that walketh disorderly, and
not after the tradition which he received of us. 7 For yourselves know
how ye ought to follow us: for we
behaved not ourselves disorderly
among you; 8 Neither did we eat
any man's bread for nought; but
wrought with labour and travail
night and day, that we might not
be chargeable to any of you: 9
Not because we have not power, but
to make ourselves an ensample unto
you to follow us. 10 For even when
we were with you, this we commanded
you, that if any would not work, neither
should he eat. 11 For we hear that
there are some which walk among you
disorderly, not working at all, but are
busybodies. 12 Now them that are
such we command and exhort by our
Lord Jesus Christ, that with quietness
they work, and eat their own bread.
13 But ye, brethren, be not weary in
well doing. 14 And if any man obey
not our word by this epistle, note
that man, and have no company with
him, that he may be ashamed. 15
Yet count *him* not as an enemy, but
admonish *him* as a brother.

The apostle having commended their obedience for the time past, and mentioned his confidence in their obedience for the time to come, proceeds to give them commands and directions to some who were faulty, correcting some things that were amiss among them. Observe, The best society of Christians may have some faulty persons among them, and some things that ought to be reformed. Perfection is not to be found on this side heaven: but evil manners beget good laws; the disorders that Paul heard of as existing among the Thessalonians occasioned the good laws we find in these verses, which are of constant use to us, and all others whom they may concern. Observe,

I. That which was amiss among the Thessalonians, which is expressed,

1. More generally. There were some who *walked disorderly, not after the tradition they received* from the apostle, *v.* 6. Some of the brethren were guilty of this disorderly walking; they did not live regularly, nor govern themselves according to the rules of Christianity, nor agreeably to their profession of religion; not according to the precepts delivered by the apostle, which they had received, and pretended to pay a regard to. Note, It is required of those who have received the gospel, and who profess a subjection to it, that they live according to the gospel. If they do not, they are to be counted disorderly persons.

2. In particular, there were among them some *idle persons and busy-bodies, v.* 11. This the apostle was so credibly informed of that he had sufficient reason to give commands and directions with relation to such persons, how they ought to behave, and how the church should act towards them. (1.) There were some among them who were idle, *not working at all*, or doing nothing. It does not appear that they were gluttons or drunkards, but idle, and therefore disorderly people. It is not enough for any to say they do no hurt; for it is required of all persons that they do good in the places and relations in which Providence has placed them It is probable that these persons had a notion (by misunderstanding some passages in the former epistle) concerning the near approach of the coming of Christ, which served them for a pretence to leave off the work of their callings, and live in idleness. Note, It is a great error, or abuse of religion, to make it a cloak for idleness or any other sin. If we were sure that the day of judgment were ever so near, we must, notwithstanding, do the work of the day in its day, that when our Lord comes he may find us so doing. The servant who waits for the coming of his Lord aright must be working as his Lord has commanded, that all may be ready when he comes. Or, it may be, these disorderly persons pretended that the liberty wherewith Christ had made them free discharged them from the services and business of their particular callings and employments in the world: whereas they were *to abide in the same calling wherein they were called of God, and therein abide with God,* 1 Cor. vii. 20, 24. Industry in our particular callings as men is a duty required of us by our general calling as Christians. Or perhaps the general charity there was then among Christians to their poor brethren encouraged some to live in idleness, as knowing the church would maintain them: whatever was the cause, they were much to blame. (2.) There were busy-bodies among them: and it should seem, by the connection, that the same persons who were idle were busy-bodies also. This may seem to be a contradiction; but so it is, that most commonly those persons who have no business of their own to do, or who neglect it, busy themselves in other men's matters. If we are idle, the devil and a corrupt heart will

soon find us something to do. The mind of man is a busy thing; if it be not employed in doing good, it will be doing evil. Note, Busy-bodies are disorderly walkers, such as are guilty of vain curiosity, and impertinent meddling with things that do not concern them, and troubling themselves and others with other men's matters. The apostle warns Timothy (1 Tim. v. 13) to beware of such *as learn to be idle, wandering about from house to house, and are not only idle, but tatlers also, and busy-bodies, speaking things which they ought not.*

II. The good laws which were occasioned by these evil manners, concerning which we may take notice,

1. Whose laws they are: they are commands of the apostles of our Lord, given in the name of their Lord and ours, that is, the commands of our Lord himself. *We command you, brethren, in the name of the Lord Jesus Christ, v.* 6. Again, *We command and exhort you by our Lord Jesus Christ, v.* 12. The apostle uses words of authority and entreaty: and, where disorders are to be rectified or prevented, there is need of both. The authority of Christ should awe our minds to obedience, and his grace and goodness should allure us.

2. What the good laws and rules are. The apostle gives directions to the whole church, commands to those disorderly persons, and an exhortation to those in particular who did well among them.

(1.) His commands and directions to the whole church regard, [1.] Their behaviour towards the disorderly persons who were among them, which is thus expressed (*v.* 6), to *withdraw themselves from such,* and afterwards to *mark that man, and have no company with him, that he may be ashamed; yet not to count him as an enemy, but to admonish him as a brother.* The directions of the apostle are carefully to be observed in our conduct towards disorderly persons. We must be very cautious in church-censures and church-discipline. We must, *First,* Note that man who is suspected or charged with not obeying the word of God, or walking contrary thereto, that is, we must have sufficient proof of his fault before we proceed further. We must, *Secondly,* Admonish him in a friendly manner; we must put him in mind of his sin, and of his duty; and this should be done privately (Matt. xviii. 15); then, if he will not hear, we must, *Thirdly,* Withdraw from him, and not keep company with him, that is, we must avoid familiar converse and society with such, for two reasons, namely, that we may not learn his evil ways; for he who follows vain and idle persons, and keeps company with such, is in danger of becoming like them. Another reason is for the shaming, and so the reforming, of those that offend, that when idle and disorderly persons see how their loose practices are disliked by all wise and good people they may be ashamed of them, and walk more orderly. Love therefore to the persons of our offending brethren, even when we hate their vices, should be the motive of our withdrawing from them; and even those who are under the censures of the church must not be accounted as enemies (*v.* 15); for, if they be reclaimed and reformed by these censures, they will recover their credit and comfort, and right to church-privileges as brethren. [2.] Their general conduct and behaviour ought to be according to the good example the apostle and those who were with him had given them: *Yourselves know how you ought to follow us, v.* 7. Those who planted religion among them had set a good example before them; and the ministers of the gospel should be ensamples to the flock. It is the duty of Christians not only to walk according to the traditions of the apostles, and the doctrines they preached, but also according to the good example they set before them, *to be followers of them so far as they were followers of Christ.* The particular good example the apostle mentions was their diligence, which was so different from what was found in the disorderly walkers he takes notice of: "*We behaved not ourselves disorderly among you* (*v.* 7), we did not spend our time idly, in idle visits, idle talk, idle sports." They took pains in their ministry, in preaching the gospel, and in getting their own living. *Neither did we eat any man's bread for nought, v.* 8. Though he might justly have demanded a maintenance, because those who preach the gospel may of right expect to live by the gospel. This is a just debt that people owe to their ministers, and the apostle had power or authority to have demanded this (*v.* 9); but he waived his right from affection to them, and for the sake of the gospel, and that he might be an example for them to follow (*v.* 9), that they might learn how to fill up time, and always be employed in something that would turn to good account.

(2.) He commands and directs those that lived idle lives to reform, and set themselves to their business. He had given commandments to this purport, as well as a good example of this, when he was among them: *Even when we were with you, this we commanded you, that if any man would not work neither should he eat, v.* 10. It was a proverbial speech among the Jews, *He who does not labour does not deserve to eat.* The labourer is worthy of his meat; but what is the loiterer worthy of? It is the will of God that every man should have a calling, and mind his calling, and make a business of it, and that none should live like useless drones in the world. Such persons do what in them lies to defeat the sentence, *In the sweat of thy face shalt thou eat thy bread.* It was not the mere humour of the apostle, who was an active stirring man himself and therefore would have every body else to be so too, but it was the command of our Lord Jesus Christ, that *with quietness we work, and eat our own bread*, v. 12. Men ought some way or other to earn their own living, otherwise they do not eat their own bread. Observe, There must be work or labour, in opposition to idleness; and there must be quietness, in opposition to being busy-bodies in other men's matters. We must study to be quiet, and do our own business. This is an excellent but rare composition, to be of an active yet quiet spirit, active in our own business and yet quiet as to other people's.

(3.) He exhorts *those that did well not* to be *weary in well-doing* (v. 13); as if he had said, "Go on and prosper. The Lord is with you while you are with him. See that whatever you do, that is good, you persevere therein. Hold on your way, and hold out to the end. You must never give over, nor tire in your work. It will be time enough to rest when you come to heaven, that *everlasting rest which remains for the people of God.*"

16 Now the Lord of peace himself give you peace always by all means. The Lord *be* with you all. 17 The salutation of Paul with mine own hand, which is the token in every epistle: so I write. 18 The grace of our Lord Jesus Christ *be* with you all. Amen.

In this conclusion of the epistle we have the apostle's benediction and prayers for these Thessalonians. Let us desire them for ourselves and our friends. There are three blessings pronounced upon them, or desired for them:—

I. That God would give them peace. Note, 1. Peace is the blessing pronounced or desired. By peace we may understand all manner of prosperity; here it may signify, in particular, peace with God, peace in their own minds and consciences, peace among themselves, and peace with all men. 2. This peace is desired for them always, or in every thing; and he desired they might have all good things at all times. 3. Peace by all means: that, as they enjoyed the means of grace, they might with success use all the means and methods of peace too; for peace is often difficult, as it is always desirable. 4. That God would give them peace, who is the Lord of peace. If we have any peace that is desirable, God must give it, who is the *author of peace and lover of concord.* We shall neither have peaceable dispositions ourselves nor find men disposed to be at peace with us, unless the God of peace give us both.

II. That the presence of God might be with them: *The Lord be with you all.* We need nothing more to make us safe and happy, nor can we desire any thing better for ourselves and our friends, than to have God's gracious presence with us and them. This will be a guide and guard in every way that we may go, and our comfort in every condition we may be in. It is the presence of God that makes heaven to be heaven, and this will make this earth to be like heaven. No matter where we are if God be with us, nor who is absent if God be present with us.

III. That the *grace of our Lord Jesus Christ might be with them.* So this apostle concluded his first epistle to these Thessalonians; and it is through the grace of our Lord Jesus Christ that we may comfortably hope to have peace with God and enjoy the presence of God, for he has made those nigh that were afar off. It is this grace that is all in all to make us happy. This is what the apostle admired and magnified on all occasions, what he delighted and trusted in; and by this salutation or benediction, written with his own hand, as the token of every epistle (when the rest was written by an amanuensis), he took care lest the churches he wrote to should be imposed on by counterfeit epistles, which he knew would be of dangerous consequence.

Let us be thankful that we have the canon of scripture complete, and by the wonderful and special care of divine Providence preserved pure and uncorrupt through so many successive ages, and not dare to add to it, nor diminish from it. Let us believe the divine original of the sacred scriptures, and conform our faith and practice to this our sufficient and only rule, *which is able to make us wise unto salvation, through faith which is in Christ Jesus.* Amen.

AN

EXPOSITION,

WITH PRACTICAL OBSERVATIONS,

OF THE FIRST EPISTLE OF ST. PAUL

TO TIMOTHY.

HITHERTO Paul's epistles were directed to churches; now follow some to particular persons: two to Timothy, one to Titus, and another to Philemon—all three ministers. Timothy and Titus were evangelists, an inferior order to the apostles, as appears by Eph. iv. 11, *Some prophets, some apostles, some evangelists.* Their commission and work was much the same with that of the apostles, to plant churches, and water the churches that were planted; and accordingly they were itinerants, as we find Timothy was. Timothy was first converted by Paul, and therefore he calls him his *own son in the faith:* we read of his conversion, Acts xvi. 3.

The scope of these two epistles is to direct Timothy how to discharge his duty as an evangelist at Ephesus, where he now was, and where Paul ordered him for some time to reside, to perfect the good work which he had begun there. As for the ordinary pastoral charge of that church, he had very solemnly committed it to the presbytery, as appears from Acts xx. 28, where he charges the presbyters *to feed the flock of God, which he had purchased with his own blood.*

CHAP. I.

After the inscription (ver. 1, 2) we have, I. The charge given to Timothy, ver 3, 4. II. The true end of the law (ver. 5—11), where he shows that it is entirely agreeable to the gospel. III. He mentions his own call to be an apostle, for which he expresses his thankfulness, ver. 12—16. IV. His doxology, ver. 17. V. A renewal of the charge to Timothy, ver. 18. And of Hymeneus and Alexander, ver. 19, 20.

PAUL, an apostle of Jesus Christ
by the commandment of God
our Saviour, and Lord Jesus Christ,
which is our hope; 2 Unto Timothy,
my own son in the faith: Grace,
mercy, *and* peace, from God our
Father and Jesus Christ our Lord.
3 As I besought thee to abide still at
Ephesus, when I went into Macedonia, that thou mightest charge some
that they teach no other doctrine, 4
Neither give heed to fables and endless
genealogies, which minister questions,
rather than godly edifying which is in
faith: *so do.*

Here is, I. The inscription of the epistle, from whom it is sent: *Paul an apostle of Jesus Christ,* constituted an apostle *by the commandment of God our Saviour, and Lord Jesus Christ.* His credentials were unquestionable. He had not only a commission, but a commandment, not only from God our Saviour, but from Jesus Christ: he was a preacher of the gospel of Christ, and a minister of the kingdom of Christ. Observe, God is our Saviour.—*Jesus Christ, who is our hope.* Observe, Jesus Christ is a Christian's hope; our hope is in him, all our hope of eternal life is built upon him; Christ is in us the hope of glory, Col. i. 27. He calls Timothy his own son, because he had been an instrument of his conversion, and because he had been a son that served him, served with him in the gospel, Phil. ii. 22. Timothy had not been wanting in the duty of a son to Paul, and Paul was not wanting in the care and tenderness of a father to him.

II. The benediction is, *grace, mercy, and peace, from God our Father.* Some have observed that whereas in all the epistles to the churches the apostolical benediction is *grace and peace,* in these two epistles to Timothy and that to Titus it is *grace, mercy, and peace:* as if ministers had more need of God's mercy than other men. Ministers need more grace than others, to discharge their duty faithfully; and they need more mercy than others, to pardon what is amiss in them: and if Timothy, so eminent a minister, must be indebted to the mercy of God, and needed the increase and continuance of it, how much more do we ministers, in these times, who have so little of his excellent spirit!

III. Paul tells Timothy what was the end of his appointing him to this office: *I besought thee to abide at Ephesus.* Timothy had a mind to go with Paul, was loth to go from under his wing, but Paul would have it so; it was necessary for the public service:

I besought thee, says he. Though he might assume an authority to command him, yet for love's sake he chose rather to beseech him. Now his business was to take care to fix both the ministers and the people of that church: *Charge them that they teach no other doctrine* than what they have received, that they do not add to the Christian doctrine, under pretence of improving it or making up the defects of it, that they do not alter it, but cleave to it as it was delivered to them. Observe, 1. Ministers must not only be charged to preach the true doctrine of the gospel, but charged to preach no other doctrine. *If an angel from heaven preach any other doctrine, let him be anathema,* Gal. i. viii. 2. In the times of the apostles there were attempts made to corrupt Christianity *(we are not as many, who corrupt the word,* 2 Cor. ii. 17), otherwise this charge to Timothy might have been spared. 3. He must not only see to it that he did not preach any other doctrine, but he must charge others that they might not add any thing of their own to the gospel, or take any thing from it, but that they preach it pure and uncorrupt. He must also take care to prevent their regarding *fables, and endless genealogies,* and strifes of words. This is often repeated in these two epistles (as *ch.* iv. 7; vi. 4; 2 Tim. ii. 23), as well as in the epistle to Titus. As among the Jews there were some who brought Judaism into Christianity; so among the Gentiles there were some who brought paganism into Christianity. "Take heed of these," says he, "watch against them, or they will be the corrupting and ruining of religion among you, for *they minister questions rather than edifying.*" That which ministers questions is not for edifying; that which gives occasion for doubtful disputes pulls down the church rather than builds it up. And I think, by a parity of reason, every thing else that ministers questions rather than godly edifying should be disclaimed and disregarded by us, such as an uninterrupted succession in the ministry from the apostles down to these times, the absolute necessity of episcopal ordination, and of the intention of the minister to the efficacy and validity of the sacraments he ministers. These are as bad as Jewish fables and endless genealogies, for they involve us in inextricable difficulties, and tend only to shake the foundations of a Christian's hope and to fill his mind with perplexing doubts and fears. Godly edifying is the end ministers should aim at in all their discourses, that Christians may be improving in godliness and growing up to a greater likeness to the blessed God. Observe, further, Godly edifying must be in faith: the gospel is the foundation on which we build; it is by faith that we come to God at first (Heb. xi. 6), and it must be in the same way, and by the same principle of faith, that we must be edified. Again, Ministers should avoid, as much as may be, what will occasion disputes; and would do well to insist on the great and practical points of religion, about which there can be no disputes; for even disputes about great and necessary truths draw off the mind from the main design of Christianity, and eat out the vitals of religion, which consist in practice and obedience as well as in faith, that we may not hold the truth in unrighteousness, but may keep the mystery of the faith in a pure conscience.

5 Now the end of the commandment is charity out of a pure heart,
and *of* a good conscience, and *of* faith
unfeigned: 6 From which some
having swerved have turned aside
unto vain jangling; 7 Desiring to
be teachers of the law; understanding
neither what they say, nor whereof
they affirm. 8 But we know that
the law *is* good, if a man use it lawfully; 9 Knowing this, that the law
is not made for a righteous man, but
for the lawless and disobedient, for
the ungodly and for sinners, for unholy and profane, for murderers of
fathers and murderers of mothers, for
manslayers, 10 For whoremongers,
for them that defile themselves with
mankind, for menstealers, for liars,
for perjured persons, and if there be
any other thing that is contrary to
sound doctrine; 11 According to
the glorious gospel of the blessed God,
which was committed to my trust.

Here the apostle instructs Timothy how to guard against the judaizing teachers, or others who mingled fables and endless genealogies with the gospel. He shows the use of the law, and the glory of the gospel.

I. He shows the end and uses of the law: it is intended to promote love, *for love is the fulfilling of the law,* Rom. xiii. 10.

1. *The end of the commandment is charity,* or love, Rom. xiii. 8. The main scope and drift of the divine law are to engage us to the love of God and one another; and whatever tends to weaken either our love to God or love to the brethren tends to defeat the end of the commandment: and surely the gospel, which obliges us to love our enemies, to do good to those who hate us (Matt. v. 44) does not design to lay aside or supersede a commandment the end whereof is love; so far from it that, on the other hand, we are told that though we had all advantages and wanted charity, we are but as sounding brass and a tinkling cymbal, 1 Cor. xiii. 1. *By this shall all men know that you are my disciples, if you love one another,* John xiii. 35. Those therefore who boasted of their know-

ledge of the law, but used it only as a colour for the disturbance that they gave to the preaching of the gospel (under pretence of zeal for the law, dividing the church and distracting it), defeated that which was the very end of the commandment, and that is love, love *out of a pure heart,* a heart purified by faith, purified from corrupt affections. In order to the keeping up of holy love our hearts must be cleansed from all sinful love; our love must arise *out of a good conscience,* kept without offence. Those answer the end of the commandment who are careful to keep a good conscience, from a real belief of the truth of the word of God which enjoins it, here called a *faith unfeigned.* Here we have the concomitants of that excellent grace charity; they are three:—(1.) A pure heart; there it must be seated, and thence it must take its rise. (2.) A good conscience, in which we must exercise ourselves daily, that we may not only get it, but that we may keep it, Acts xxiv. 16. (3.) Faith unfeigned must also accompany it, for it is love without dissimulation: the faith that works by it must be of the like nature, genuine and sincere. Now some who set up for teachers of the law swerved from the very end of the commandment: they set up for disputers, but their disputes proved vain jangling; they set up for teachers, but they pretended to teach others what they themselves did not understand. If the church be corrupted by such teachers, we must not think it strange, for we see from the beginning it was so. Observe, [1.] When persons, especially ministers, swerve from the great law of charity—the end of the commandment, they will turn aside to vain jangling; when a man misses his end and scope, it is no wonder that every step he takes is out of the way. [2.] Jangling, especially in religion, is vain; it is unprofitable and useless as to all that is good, and it is very pernicious and hurtful: and yet many people's religion consists of little else but vain jangling. [3.] Those who deal much in vain jangling are fond and ambitious to be teachers of others; they desire (that is, they affect) the office of teaching. [4.] It is too common for men to intrude into the office of the ministry when they are very ignorant of those things about which they are to speak: they understand neither what they say nor whereof they affirm; and by such learned ignorance, no doubt, they edify their hearers very much !.

2. The use of the law (*v.* 8): *The law is good, if a man use it lawfully.* The Jews used it unlawfully, as an engine to divide the church, a cover to the malicious opposition they made to the gospel of Christ; they set it up for justification, and so used it unlawfully. We must not therefore think to set it aside, but use it lawfully, for the restraint of sin. The abuse which some have made of the law does not take away the use of it; but, when a divine appointment has been abused, call it back to its right use and take away the abuses, for the law is still very useful as a rule of life; though we are not under it as under a covenant of works, yet it is good to teach us what is sin and what is duty. It is not made for a righteous man, that is, it is not made for those who observe it; for, if we could keep the law, righteousness would be by the law (Gal. iii. 21): but it is made for wicked persons, to restrain them, to check them, and to put a stop to vice and profaneness. It is the grace of God that changes men's hearts; but the terrors of the law may be of use to tie their hands and restrain their tongues. A righteous man does not want those restraints which are necessary for the wicked; or at least the law is not made primarily and principally for the righteous, but for sinners of all sorts, whether in a greater or less measure, *v.* 9, 10. In this black roll of sinners, he particularly mentions breaches of the second table, duties which we owe to our neighbour; against the fifth and sixth commandments, *murderers of fathers and mothers, and manslayers;* against the seventh, *whoremongers, and those that defile themselves with mankind;* against the eighth, *men-stealers;* against the ninth, *liars and perjured persons;* and then he closes his account with this, *and if there be any other thing that is contrary to sound doctrine.* Some understand this as an institution of a power in the civil magistrate to make laws against such notorious sinners as are specified, and to see those laws put in execution.

II. He shows the glory and grace of the gospel. Paul's epithets are expressive and significant; and frequently every one is a sentence: as here (*v.* 11), *According to the glorious gospel of the blessed God.* Let us learn hence, 1. To call God the blessed God, infinitely happy in the enjoyment of himself and his own perfections. 2. To call the gospel the glorious gospel, for so it is: much of the glory of God appears in the works of creation and providence, but much more in the gospel, where it shines in the face of Jesus Christ. Paul reckoned it a great honour put upon him, and a great favour done him, that this glorious gospel was committed to his trust; that is, the preaching of it, for the framing of it is not committed to any man or company of men in the world. The settling of the terms of salvation in the gospel of Christ is God's own work; but the publishing of it to the world is committed to the apostles and ministers. Note here, (1.) The ministry is a trust, for the gospel was committed unto this apostle; it is an office of trust as well as of power, and the former more than the latter; for this reason ministers are called stewards, 1 Cor. iv. 1. (2.) It is a glorious trust, because the gospel committed to them is a glorious gospel; it is a trust of very great importance. God's glory is very much concerned in it. Lord, what a trust is committed to us! How much grace do we want, to be found faithful in this great trust!

12 And I thank Christ Jesus our
Lord, who hath enabled me, for that
he counted me faithful, putting me
into the ministry; 13 Who was
before a blasphemer, and a persecutor, and injurious: but I obtained
mercy, because I did *it* ignorantly, in
unbelief. 14 And the grace of our
Lord was exceeding abundant with
faith and love which is in Christ
Jesus. 15 This *is* a faithful saying,
and worthy of all acceptation, that
Christ Jesus came into the world to
save sinners; of whom I am chief.
16 Howbeit for this cause I obtained
mercy, that in me first Jesus Christ
might show forth all longsuffering,
for a pattern to them which should
hereafter believe on him to life everlasting. 17 Now unto the King
eternal, immortal, invisible, the only
wise God, *be* honour and glory for
ever and ever. Amen.

Here the apostle, I. Returns thanks to Jesus Christ for putting him into the ministry. Observe, 1. It is Christ's work to put men into the ministry, Acts xxvi. 16, 17. God condemned the false prophets among the Jews in these words, *I have not sent these prophets, yet they ran: I have not spoken to them, yet they prophesied*, Jer. xxiii. 21. Ministers, properly speaking, cannot make ministers, much less can persons make themselves ministers; for it is Christ's work, as king and head, prophet and teacher, of his church. 2. Those whom he puts into the ministry he fits for it; whom he calls he qualifies. Those ministers who are no way fit for their work, nor have ability for it, are not of Christ's putting into the ministry, though there are different qualifications as to gifts and graces. 3. Christ gives not only ability, but fidelity, to those whom he puts into the ministry: He *counted me faithful;* and none are counted faithful but those whom he makes so. Christ's ministers are trusty servants, and they ought to be so, having so great a trust committed to them. 4. A call to the ministry is a great favour, for which those who are so called ought to give thanks to Jesus Christ: *I thank Christ Jesus our Lord, who hath put me into the ministry.*

II. The more to magnify the grace of Christ in putting him into the ministry, he gives an account of his conversion.

1. What he was before his conversion: *A blasphemer, a persecutor, and injurious.* Saul breathed out threatenings and slaughter against the disciples of the Lord, Acts ix. 1 He made havoc of the church, Acts viii. 3. He was a blasphemer of God, a persecutor of the saints, and injurious to both. Frequently those who are designed for great and eminent services are left to themselves before their conversion, to fall into great wickedness, that the mercy of God may be the more glorified in their remission, and the grace of God in their regeneration. The greatness of sin is no bar to our acceptance with God, no, nor to our being employed for him, if it be truly repented of. Observe here, (1.) Blasphemy, persecution, and injuriousness, are very great and heinous sins, and those who are guilty of them are sinners before God exceedingly. To blaspheme God is immediately and directly to strike at God; to persecute his people is to endeavour to wound him through their sides; and to be injurious is to be like Ishmael, whose hand was against every one, and every one was against him; for such invade God's prerogative, and encroach upon the liberties of their fellow-creatures. (2.) True penitents, to serve a good purpose, will not be backward to own their former condition before they were brought home to God: this good apostle often confessed what his former life had been, as Acts xxii. 4; xxvi. 10, 11.

2 The great favour of God to him: *But I obtained mercy.* This was a blessed *but* indeed, a great favour, that so notorious a rebel should find mercy with his prince.

(1.) If Paul had persecuted the Christians wilfully, knowing them to be the people of God, for aught I know he had been guilty of the unpardonable sin; but, because he did it ignorantly and in unbelief, he obtained mercy. Note, [1.] What we do ignorantly is a less crime than what we do knowingly; yet a sin of ignorance is a sin, for he that knew not his Master's will, but did commit things worthy of stripes, shall be beaten with few stripes, Luke xii. 48. Ignorance in some cases will extenuate a crime, though it do not take it away. [2.] Unbelief is at the bottom of what sinners do ignorantly; they do not believe God's threatenings, otherwise they could not do as they do. [3.] For these reasons Paul obtained mercy: *But I obtained mercy, because I did it ignorantly, in unbelief.* [4.] Here was mercy for a blasphemer, a persecutor, and an injurious person: "*But I obtained mercy*, I a blasphemer," &c

(2.) Here he takes notice of the abundant grace of Jesus Christ, *v.* 14. The conversion and salvation of great sinners are owing to the grace of Christ, his exceedingly abundant grace, even that grace of Christ which appears in his glorious gospel (*v.* 15): *This is a faithful saying*, &c. Here we have the sum of the whole gospel, *that Jesus Christ came into the world.* The Son of God took upon him our nature, was made flesh, and dwelt among us, John i. 14. He came into the world, *not to call the righteous but sinners to repentance,*

Matt. ix. 13. His errand into the world was to seek and find, and so save, *those that were lost,* Luke xix. 10. The ratification of this is *that it is a faithful saying, and worthy of all acceptation.* It is good news, worthy of all acceptation; and yet not too good to be true, for it is a faithful saying. It is a faithful saying, and therefore worthy to be embraced in the arms of faith: it is worthy of all acceptation, and therefore to be received with holy love, which refers to the foregoing verse, where the grace of Christ is said to abound in faith and love. In the close of the verse Paul applies it to himself: *Of whom I am chief.* Paul was a sinner of the first rank; so he acknowledges himself to have been, for he breathed out threatenings and slaughter against the disciples of the Lord, &c., Acts ix. 1, 2. Persecutors are some of the worst of sinners: such a one Paul had been. Or, *of whom I am chief,* that is, of pardoned sinners I am chief. It is an expression of his great humility; he that elsewhere calls himself the *least of all saints* (Eph. iii. 8) here calls himself the chief of sinners. Observe, [1.] Christ Jesus has come into the world; the prophecies concerning his coming are now fulfilled. [2.] He came to save sinners; he came to save those who could not save and help themselves. [3.] Blasphemers and persecutors are the chief of sinners, so Paul reckoned them. [4.] The chief of sinners may become the chief of saints; so this apostle was, for he was not a whit behind the very chief apostles (2 Cor. xi. 5), for Christ came to save the chief of sinners. [5.] This is a very great truth, it is a faithful saying; these are true and faithful words, which may be depended on. [6.] It deserves to be received, to be believed by us all, for our comfort and encouragement.

(3.) The mercy which Paul found with God, notwithstanding his great wickedness before his conversion, he speaks of,

[1.] For the encouragement of others to repent and believe (*v.* 16): *For this cause I obtained mercy, that in me first Jesus Christ might show forth all long-suffering, for a pattern to those who should hereafter believe.* It was an instance of the long-suffering of Christ that he would bear so much with one who had been so very provoking; and it was designed for a pattern to all others, that the greatest sinners might not despair of mercy with God. Note here, *First,* Our apostle was one of the first great sinners converted to Christianity. *Secondly,* He was converted, and obtained mercy, for the sake of others as well as of himself; he was a pattern to others. *Thirdly,* The Lord Jesus Christ shows great long-suffering in the conversion of great sinners. *Fourthly,* Those who obtain mercy believe on the Lord Jesus Christ; for without faith it is impossible to please God, Heb. xi. 6. *Fifthly,* Those who believe on Christ believe on him to life everlasting; they believe to the saving of the soul, Heb. x. 39.

[2.] He mentions it to the glory of God having spoken of the mercy he had found with God, he could not go on with his letter without inserting a thankful acknowledgment of God's goodness to him: *Now unto the King eternal, immortal, invisible, the only wise God, be honour and glory for ever and ever. Amen.* Observe, *First,* That grace which we have the comfort of God must have the glory of. Those who are sensible of their obligations to the mercy and grace of God will have their hearts enlarged in his praise. Here is praise ascribed to him, as *the King eternal, immortal, invisible. Secondly,* When we have found God good we must not forget to pronounce him great; and his kind thoughts of us must not at all abate our high thoughts of him, but rather increase them. God had taken particular cognizance of Paul, and shown him mercy, and taken him into communion with himself, and yet he calls him the King eternal, &c. God's gracious dealings with us should fill us with admiration of his glorious attributes. He is eternal, without beginning of days, or end of life, or change of time. He is the Ancient of days, Dan. vii. 9. He is immortal, and the original of immortality; he only has immortality (1 Tim. vi. 16), for he cannot die. He is invisible, for he cannot be seen with mortal eyes, dwelling in the light to which no man can approach, whom no man hath seen nor can see, 1 Tim. vi. 16. He is *the only wise God* (Jude 25); he only is infinitely wise, and the fountain of all wisdom. "*To him be glory for ever and ever,*" or, "Let me be for ever employed in giving honour and glory to him, as the thousands of thousands do," Rev. v. 12, 13.

18 This charge I commit unto thee, son Timothy, according to the prophecies which went before on thee, that thou by them mightest war a good warfare; 19 Holding faith, and a good conscience; which some having put away concerning faith have made shipwreck: 20 Of whom is Hymenæus and Alexander; whom I have delivered unto Satan, that they may learn not to blaspheme.

Here is the charge he gives to Timothy to proceed in his work with resolution, *v.* 18. Observe here, The gospel is a charge committed to the ministers of it; it is committed to their trust, to see that it be duly applied according to the intent and meaning of it, and the design of its great Author. It seems, there had been prophecies before concerning Timothy, that he should be taken into the ministry, and should prove eminent in the work of the ministry; this encouraged Paul to commit this charge to him. Observe, 1. The ministry is a warfare, it is a good warfare against sin and Satan: and under the banner of the Lord Jesus, who is the Captain of our salvation (Heb. ii. 10), and in his cause, and against his enemies, ministers are in a particular manner engaged. 2. Ministers must war this good warfare, must execute their office diligently and courageously, notwithstanding oppositions and discouragements. 3. The prophecies which went before concerning Timothy are here mentioned as a motive to stir him up to a vigorous and conscientious discharge of his duty; so the good hopes that others have entertained concerning us should excite us to our duty: *That thou by them mightest war a good warfare.* 4. We must hold both faith and a good conscience: *Holding faith and a good conscience, v.* 19. Those that put away a good conscience will soon make shipwreck of faith. Let us live up to the directions of a renewed enlightened conscience, and keep conscience void of offence (Acts xxiv. 16), a conscience not debauched by any vice or sin, and this will be a means of preserving us sound in the faith; we must look to the one as well as the other, for the mystery of the faith must be held in a pure conscience, *ch.* iii. 9. As for those who had made shipwreck of the faith, he specifies two, *Hymeneus and Alexander,* who had made a profession of the Christian religion, but had quitted that profession; and Paul had delivered them to Satan, had declared them to belong to the kingdom of Satan, and, as some think, had, by an extraordinary power, delivered them to be terrified or tormented by Satan, *that they might learn not to blaspheme* not to contradict or revile the doctrine of Christ and the good ways of the Lord. Observe, The primary design of the highest censure in the primitive church was to prevent further sin and to reclaim the sinner. In this case it was for the destruction of the flesh, that the spirit might be saved in the day of the Lord Jesus, 1 Cor. v. 5. Observe, (1.) Those who love the service and work of Satan are justly delivered over to the power of Satan: *Whom I have delivered over to Satan.* (2.) God can, if he please, work by contraries: Hymeneus and Alexander are delivered to Satan, that they may learn not to blaspheme, when one would rather think they would learn of Satan to blaspheme the more. (3.) Those who have put away a good conscience, and made shipwreck of faith, will not stick at any thing, blasphemy not excepted. (4.) Therefore let us hold faith and a good conscience, if we would keep clear of blasphemy; for, if we once let go our hold of these, we do not know where we shall stop.

CHAP. II.

In this chapter Paul treats, I. Of prayer, with many reasons for it, ver. 1—8. II. Of women's apparel, ver. 9, 10. III. Of their subjection, with the reasons of it, ver. 11—14. IV. A promise given for their encouragement in child-bearing, ver. 15.

I EXHORT therefore, that, first of
all, supplications, prayers, intercessions, *and* giving of thanks, be
made for all men; 2 For kings,
and *for* all that are in authority; that
we may lead a quiet and peaceable
life in all godliness and honesty 3
For this *is* good and acceptable in
the sight of God our Saviour; 4
Who will have all men to be saved,
and to come unto the knowledge of
the truth. 5 For *there is* one God,
and one mediator between God and
men, the man Christ Jesus; 6 Who
gave himself a ransom for all, to be
testified in due time. 7 Whereunto
I am ordained a preacher, and an
apostle, (I speak the truth in Christ,
and lie not;) a teacher of the Gentiles in faith and verity. 8 I will
therefore that men pray every where,
lifting up holy hands, without wrath
and doubting.

Here is, I. A charge given to Christians to pray for all men in general, and particularly for all in authority. Timothy must take care that this be done. Paul does not send him any prescribed form of prayer, as we have reason to think he would if he had intended that ministers should be tied to that way of praying; but, in general, that they should make *supplications, prayers, intercessions, and giving of thanks:* supplications for the averting of evil, prayers for the obtaining of good, intercessions for others, and thanksgivings for mercies already received. Paul thought it enough to give them general heads; they, having the scripture to direct them in prayer and the Spirit of prayer poured out upon them, needed not any further directions. Observe, The design of the Christian religion is to promote prayer; and the disciples of Christ must be praying people. Pray *always with all prayer,* Eph. vi. 18. There must be prayers for ourselves in the first place; this is implied here. We must also pray *for all men,* for the world of mankind in general, for particular persons who need or desire our prayers. See how far the Christian religion was from being a sect, when it taught men this diffusive charity, to pray, not only for those of their own way, but for all men. Pray for kings (*v.* 2); though the kings at this time were heathens, enemies to Christianity, and persecutors of Christians, yet they must pray for them, because it is for the public good that there should be civil government, and proper persons entrusted with the administration of it, for whom therefore we ought to pray, yea, though we ourselves suffer under them. *For kings, and all that are in authority,* that is, inferior magistrates: we must pray for them, and we must give thanks for them, pray for their welfare and for the welfare of their kingdoms, and therefore must not plot against them, that in the peace thereof we may have peace, and give thanks for them and for the benefit we have under their government, that *we may lead a quiet and peaceable life in all godliness and honesty.* Here see what we must desire for kings, that God will so turn their hearts, and direct them and make use of them, that we under them may lead a quiet and peaceable life. He does not say, "that we may get preferments under them, grow rich, and be in honour and power under them;" no, the summit of the ambition of a good Christian is to lead a quiet and peaceable life, to get through the world unmolested in a low private station. We should desire that we and others may lead a peaceable life *in all godliness and honesty,* implying that we cannot expect to be kept quiet and peaceable unless we keep in all godliness and honesty. Let us mind our duty, and then we may expect to be taken under the protection both of God and the government. *In all godliness and honesty.* Here we have our duty as Christians summed up in two words: godliness, that is, the right worshipping of God; and honesty, that is, a good conduct towards all men. These two must go together; we are not truly honest if we are not godly, and do not render to God his due; and we are not truly godly if we are not honest, for God hates robbery for burnt-offering. Here we may observe, 1. Christians are to be men much given to prayer: they ought to abound herein, and should use themselves to prayers, supplications, &c. 2. In our prayers we are to have a generous concern for others as well as for ourselves; we are to pray for all men, and to give thanks for all men; and must not confine our prayers nor thanksgivings to our own persons or families. 3. Prayer consists of various parts, of supplications, intercessions, and thanksgivings; for we must pray for the mercies we want, as well as be thankful for mercies already received; and we are to deprecate the judgments which our own sins or the sins of others have deserved. 4. All men, yea, kings themselves, and those who are in authority, are to be prayed for. They want our prayers, for they have many difficulties to encounter, many snares to which their exalted stations expose them. 5. In praying for our governors, we take the most likely course to lead a peaceable and quiet life. The Jews at Babylon were commanded to seek the peace of the city whither the Lord had caused them to be carried captives, and to pray to the Lord for it; for in the peace thereof they should have peace, Jer. xxix. 7. 6. If we would lead a peaceable and quiet life, we must live in all godliness and honesty; we must do our duty to God and man. *He that will love life, and see good days, let him refrain his tongue from evil, and his lips that they speak no guile; let him eschew evil, and do good; let him seek peace, and pursue it,* 1 Pet. iii. 10, 11. Now the reason he gives for this is *because this is good in the sight of God our Saviour;* that is, the gospel of Christ requires this. That which is acceptable in the sight of God our Saviour we should do, and should abound in.

II. As a reason why we should in our prayers concern ourselves for all men, he shows God's love to mankind in general, *v.* 4.

1. One reason why all men are to be prayed for is because there is one God, and that God bears a good will to all mankind. There is one God (*v.* 5), and one only, there is no other, there can be no other, for there can be but one infinite. This one God *will have all men to be saved;* he desires not the death and destruction of any (Ezek. xxxiii. 11), but the welfare and salvation of all. Not that he has decreed the salvation of all. for then all men would be saved; but he has a good will to the salvation of all, and none perish but by their own fault, Matt. xxiii. 37. He will have all to be saved, *and to come to the knowledge of the truth,* to be saved in the way that he has appointed and not otherwise. It concerns us to get the knowledge of the truth, because that is the way to be saved; *Christ is the way and the truth, and so he is the life.*

2. There is one Mediator, and that Mediator gave himself a ransom for all. As the mercy of God extends itself to all his works, so the mediation of Christ extends itself thus far to all the children of men that he paid a price sufficient for the salvation of all mankind; he brought mankind to stand upon new terms with God, so that they are not now under the law as a covenant of works, but as a rule of life. They are under grace; not under the covenant of innocence, but under a new covenant: *He gave himself a ransom.* Observe, The death of Christ was a ransom, a counter-price. We deserved to have died. Christ died for us, to save us from death and hell; he gave himself a ransom voluntarily, a ransom for all; so that all mankind are put in a better condition than that of devils. He died to work out a common salvation: in order hereunto, he put himself into the office of Mediator between God and man. A mediator supposes a controversy. Sin had made a quarrel between us and God; Jesus Christ is a Mediator who undertakes to make peace, to bring God and man together, in the nature of an umpire or arbitrator, a days-man who lays his hand upon us both, Job ix. 33. He is a ransom that *was to be testified in due time;* that is, in the Old-Testament times, his sufferings and the glory that should follow were spoken of as things to be revealed in the last times, 1 Pet. i. 10, 11. And they are accordingly revealed, Paul himself having been ordained a preacher and an apostle, to publish to the Gentiles the glad tidings of redemption and salvation by Jesus Christ. This doctrine of Christ's mediation Paul was entrusted to

preach to every creature, Mark xvi. 15. He was appointed to be a teacher of the Gentiles; besides his general call to the apostleship, he was commissioned particularly to preach to the Gentiles, *in faith and truth*, or faithfully and truly. Note, (1.) It is good and acceptable in the sight of God our Saviour that we pray for kings and for all men, and also that we lead a peaceable and quiet life; and this is a very good reason why we should do the one as well as the other. (2.) God has a good will to the salvation of all; so that it is not so much the want of a will in God to save them as it is a want of will in themselves to be saved in God's way. Here our blessed Lord charges the fault: *You will not come unto me that you may have life*, John v. 40. *I would have gathered you, and you would not.* (3.) Those who are saved must come to the knowledge of the truth, for this is God's appointed way to save sinners. Without knowledge the heart cannot be good; if we do not know the truth, we cannot be ruled by it. (4.) It is observable that the unity of God is asserted, and joined with the unity of the Mediator; and the church of Rome might as well maintain a plurality of gods as a plurality of mediators. (5.) He that is a Mediator in the New-Testament sense, gave himself a ransom. Vain then is the pretence of the Romanists that there is but one Mediator of satisfaction, but many of intercession; for, according to Paul, Christ's giving himself a ransom was a necessary part of the Mediator's office; and indeed this lays the foundation for his intercession. (6.) Paul was ordained a minister, to declare this to the Gentiles, that Christ is the one Mediator between God and men, who gave himself a ransom for all. This is the substance of which all ministers are to preach, to the end of the world; and Paul magnified his office, as he was the apostle of the Gentiles, Rom. xi. 13. (7.) Ministers must preach the truth, what they apprehend to be so, and they must believe it themselves; they are, like our apostle, to preach in faith and verity, and they must also be faithful and trusty.

III. A direction how to pray, *v.* 8. 1. Now, under the gospel, prayer is not to be confined to any one particular house of prayer, but men must pray every where: no place is amiss for prayer, no place more acceptable to God than another, John iv. 21. *Pray every where.* We must pray in our closets, pray in our families, pray at our meals, pray when we are on journeys, and pray in the solemn assemblies, whether more public or private. 2. It is the will of God that in prayer we should lift up holy hands: *Lifting up holy hands*, or pure hands, pure from the pollution of sin, washed in the fountain opened for sin and uncleanness. *I will wash my hands*, &c., Ps. xxvi. 6. 3. We must pray in charity: *Without wrath*, or malice, or anger at any person. 4. We must pray in faith *without doubting* (Jam. i. 6), or, as some read it, *without disputing*, and then it falls under the head of charity.

9 In like manner also, that women adorn themselves in modest apparel, with shamefacedness and sobriety; not with broidered hair, or gold, or pearls, or costly array; 10 But (which becometh women professing godliness) with good works. 11 Let the woman learn in silence with all subjection. 12 But I suffer not a woman to teach, nor to usurp authority over the man, but to be in silence. 13 For Adam was first formed, then Eve. 14 And Adam was not deceived, but the woman being deceived was in the transgression. 15 Notwithstanding she shall be saved in childbearing, if they continue in faith and charity and holiness with sobriety.

I. Here is a charge, that women who profess the Christian religion should be modest, sober, silent, and submissive, as becomes their place. 1. They must be very modest in their apparel, not affecting gaudiness, gaiety, or costliness (you may read the vanity of a person's mind in the gaiety and gaudiness of his habit), because they have better ornaments with which they should *adorn themselves, as becometh women professing godliness, with good works.* Note, Good works are the best ornament; these are, in the sight of God, of great price. Those that profess godliness should, in their dress, as well as other things, act as becomes their profession; instead of laying out their money on fine clothes, they must lay it out in works of piety and charity, which are properly called good works. 2. Women must learn the principles of their religion, learn Christ, learn the scriptures; they must not think that their sex excuses them from that learning which is necessary to salvation. 3. They must be silent, submissive, and subject, and not usurp authority. The reason given is because *Adam was first formed, then Eve* out of him, to denote her subordination to him and dependence upon him; and that she was made for him, to be a help-meet for him. And as she was last in the creation, which is one reason for her subjection, so she was first in the transgression, and that is another reason. *Adam was not deceived*, that is, not first; the serpent did not immediately set upon him, but the woman was first in the transgression (2 Cor. xi. 3), and it was part of the sentence, *Thy desire shall be to thy husband, and he shall rule over thee*, Gen. iii. 16. But it is a word of comfort (*v.* 15) that those who continue in sobriety shall be *saved in child-bearing*, or *with* child-bearing—the Messiah, who was born of a woman, should break the serpent's head (Gen. iii. 15); or the sentence which they are under for sin shall be no bar to their acceptance with Christ, *if they continue in faith, and charity, and holiness, with sobriety.*

II. Here observe, 1. The extensiveness of the rules of Christianity; they reach not only to men, but to women, not only to their persons, but also to their dress, which must be modest, like their sex; and to their outward deportment and behaviour, it must be in silence, with all subjection. 2. Women are to profess godliness as well as men; for they are baptized, and thereby stand engaged to exercise themselves to godliness; and, to their honour be it spoken, many of them were eminent professors of Christianity in the days of the apostles, as the book of Acts will inform us. 3. Women being more in danger of exceeding in their apparel, it was more necessary to caution them in this respect. 4. The best ornaments for professors of godliness are good works. 5. According to Paul, women must be learners, and are not allowed to be public teachers in the church; for teaching is an office of authority, and the woman must not usurp authority over the man, but is to be in silence. But, notwithstanding this prohibition, good women may and ought to teach their children at home the principles of religion. Timothy from a child had known the holy scriptures; and who should teach him but his mother and grandmother? 2 Tim. iii. 15. Aquila and his wife Priscilla expounded unto Apollos the way of God more perfectly; but then they did it privately, for *they took him unto them,* Acts xviii. 26. 6. Here are two very good reasons given for the man's authority over the woman, and her subjection to the man, *v.* 13, 14. Adam was first formed, then Eve; she was created for the man, and not the man for the woman (1 Cor. xi. 9); then she was deceived, and brought the man into the transgression. 7. Though the difficulties and dangers of child-bearing are many and great, as they are part of the punishment inflicted on the sex for Eve's transgression, yet here is much for her support and encouragement: *Notwithstanding she shall be saved,* &c. Though in sorrow, yet she shall bring forth, and be a living mother of living children; with this proviso, that they continue in faith, and charity, and holiness, with sobriety: and women, under the circumstance of child-bearing should by faith lay hold of this promise for their support in the needful time.

CHAP. III.

In this chapter our apostle treats of church-officers. He specifies, I. The qualifications of a person to be admitted to the office of a bishop, ver. 1—7. II. The qualifications of deacons (ver. 8—10), and of their wives (ver. 11), again of the deacons, ver. 12, 13. III. The reasons of his writing to Timothy, whereupon he speaks of the church and the foundation-truth professed therein, ver. 14, to the end.

THIS *is* a true saying, If a man
desire the office of a bishop, he
desireth a good work. 2 A bishop
then must be blameless, the husband
of one wife, vigilant, sober, of good
behaviour, given to hospitality, apt
to teach; 3 Not given to wine, no
striker, not greedy of filthy lucre;
but patient, not a brawler, not covetous; 4 One that ruleth well his
own house, having his children in
subjection with all gravity; 5 (For
if a man know not how to rule his
own house, how shall he take care of
the church of God?) 6 Not a novice,
lest being lifted up with pride he fall
into the condemnation of the devil.
7 Moreover he must have a good
report of them which are without;
lest he fall into reproach and the
snare of the devil.

The two epistles to Timothy, and that to Titus, contain a scripture-plan of church-government, or a direction to ministers. Timothy, we suppose, was an evangelist who was left at Ephesus, to take care of those whom the Holy Ghost had made bishops there, that is, the presbyters, as appears by Acts xx. 28, where the care of the church was committed to the presbyters, and they were called bishops. It seems they were very loth to part with Paul, especially because he told them they should *see his face no more* (Acts xx. 38); for their church was but newly planted, they were afraid of undertaking the care of it, and therefore Paul left Timothy with them to set them in order. And here we have the character of a gospel minister, whose office it is, as a bishop, to preside in a particular congregation of Christians: *If a man desires the office of a bishop, he desires a good work, v.* 1. Observe,

I. The ministry is a work. However the office of a bishop may be now thought a good preferment, then it was thought a good work. 1. The office of a scripture-bishop is an office of divine appointment, and not of human invention. The ministry is not a creature of the state, and it is a pity that the minister should be at any time the tool of the state. The office of the ministry was in the church before the magistrate countenanced Christianity, for this office is one of the great gifts Christ has bestowed on the church, Eph. iv. 8—11. 2. This office of a Christian bishop is a work, which requires diligence and application: the apostle represents it under the notion and character of a work; not of great honour and advantage, for ministers should always look more to their work than to the honour and advantage of their office. 3. It is a good work, a work of the greatest importance, and designed for the greatest good: the ministry is conversant about no lower concerns than the life and happiness of immortal souls; it is a good work, because designed to illustrate the divine perfections in bringing many sons to glory; the ministry is appointed to open men's eyes, and to turn them from darkness to light, and from the power of Satan unto God, &c., Acts xxvi. 18. 4. There ought to be an earnest desire of the office in those who would be put into it; if a man desire, he should earnestly desire it for the prospect he has of bringing greater glory to God, and of doing the greatest good to the souls of men by this means. This is the question proposed to those who offer themselves to the ministry of the church of England: "Do you think you are moved by the Holy Ghost to take upon you this office?"

II. In order to the discharge of this office, the doing of this work, the workman must be duly qualified. 1. A minister must be blameless, he must not lie under any scandal; he must give as little occasion for blame as can be, because this would be a prejudice to his ministry and would reflect reproach upon his office. 2. He must be the husband of one wife; not having given a bill of divorce to one, and then taken another, or not having many wives at once, as at that time was too common both among Jews and Gentiles, especially among the Gentiles. 3. He must be vigilant and watchful against Satan, that subtle enemy; he must watch over himself, and the souls of those who are committed to his charge, of whom having taken the *oversight*, he must improve all opportunities of doing them good. A minister ought to be vigilant, because our adversary the devil goes about like a roaring lion, seeking whom he may devour, 1 Pet. v. 8. 4. He must be sober, temperate, moderate in all his actions, and in the use of all creature-comforts. Sobriety and watchfulness are often in scripture put together, because they mutually befriend one another: *Be sober, be vigilant.* 5. He must be of good behaviour, composed and solid, and not light, vain, and frothy. 6. He must be given to hospitality, open-handed to strangers, and ready to entertain them according to his ability, as one who does not set his heart upon the wealth of the world and who is a true lover of his brethren. 7. Apt to teach. Therefore this is a preaching bishop whom Paul describes, one who is both able and willing to communicate to others the knowledge which God has given him, one who is fit to teach and ready to take all opportunities of giving instruction, who is himself *well instructed in the things of the kingdom of heaven*, and is communicative of what he knows to others. 8. No drunkard: *Not given to wine.* The priests were not to drink wine when they went in to minister (Lev. x. 8, 9), lest they should drink and pervert the law. 9. No striker; one who is not quarrelsome, nor apt to use violence to any, but does every thing with mildness, love, and gentleness. The servant of the Lord must not strive, but be gentle towards all, &c., 2 Tim. ii. 24. 10. One who is not greedy of filthy lucre, who does not make his ministry to truckle to any secular design or interest, who uses no mean, base, sordid ways of getting money, who is dead to the wealth of this world, lives above it, and makes it appear he is so. 11. He must be patient, and not a brawler, of a mild disposition. Christ, the great Shepherd and Bishop of souls, is so. Not apt to be angry or quarrelsome; as not a striker with his hands, so not a brawler with his tongue; for how shall men teach others to govern their tongues who do not make conscience of keeping them under good government themselves? 12. Not covetous. Covetousness is bad in any, but it is worst in a minister, whose calling leads him to converse so much with another world. 13. He must be one who keeps his family in good order: *That rules well his own house*, that he may set a good example to other masters of families to do so too, and that he may thereby give a proof of his ability to take care of the church of God: *For, if a man know not how to rule his own house, how shall he take care of the church of God.* Observe, The families of ministers ought to be examples of good to all other families. Ministers must have their children in subjection; then it is the duty of ministers' children to submit to the instructions that are given them.—*With all gravity.* The best way to keep inferiors in subjection, is to be grave with them. Not having his children in subjection with all austerity, but with all gravity. 14. He must not be a novice, not one newly brought to the Christian religion, or not one who is but meanly instructed in it, who knows no more of religion than the surface of it, for such a one is apt to be lifted up with pride: the more ignorant men are the more proud they are: *Lest, being lifted up with pride, he fall into the condemnation of the devil.* The devils fell through pride, which is a good reason why we should take heed of pride, because it is a sin that turned angels into devils. 15. He must be of good reputation among his neighbours, and under no reproach from former conversation; for the devil will make use of that to ensnare others, and work in them an aversion to the doctrine of Christ preached by those who have not had a good report

III. Upon the whole, having briefly gone through the qualifications of a gospel-bishop, we may infer, 1. What great reason we have to cry out, as Paul does, *Who is sufficient for these things?* 2 Cor. ii. 16. *Hic labor, hoc opus—This is a work indeed.* What piety, what prudence, what zeal, what courage, what faithfulness, what watchfulness over ourselves, our lusts, appetites, and passions, and over those under our charge; I say, what holy watchfulness is necessary in this work! 2. Have not the best qualified and the most faithful and conscientious ministers just reason to complain against themselves, that so much is requisite by way of qualification, and so much work is necessary to be done? And, alas! how far short do the best come of what they should be and what they should do! 3. Yet let those bless God, and be thankful, whom the Lord has enabled, and counted faithful, putting them into the ministry: if God is pleased to make any in some degree able and faithful, let him have the praise and glory of it. 4. For the encouragement of all faithful ministers, we have Christ's gracious word of promise, *Lo, I am with you always, even unto the end of the world,* Matt. xxviii. 20. And, if he be with us, he will fit us for our work in some measure, will carry us through the difficulties of it with comfort, graciously pardon our imperfections, and reward our faithfulness with a crown of glory that fadeth not away, 1 Pet. v. 4.

8 Likewise *must* the deacons *be* grave, not doubletongued, not given to much wine, not greedy of filthy lucre; 9 Holding the mystery of the faith in a pure conscience. 10 And let these also first be proved; then let them use the office of a deacon, being *found* blameless. 11 Even so *must their* wives *be* grave, not slanderers, sober, faithful in all things. 12 Let the deacons be the husbands of one wife, ruling their children and their own houses well. 13 For they that have used the office of a deacon well purchase to themselves a good degree, and great boldness in the faith which is in Christ Jesus.

We have here the character of deacons: these had the care of the temporal concerns of the church, that is, the maintenance of the ministers and provision for the poor: they served tables, while the ministers or bishops gave themselves only to the ministry of the word and prayer, Acts vi. 2, 4. Of the institution of this office, with that which gave occasion to it, you have an account in Acts vi. 1—7. Now it was requisite that deacons should have a good character, because they were assistants to the ministers, appeared and acted publicly, and had a great trust reposed in them. They must be *grave.* Gravity becomes all Christians, but especially those who are in office in the church. *Not doubled-tongued;* that will say one thing to one and another thing to another, according as their interest leads them: a double tongue comes from a double heart; flatterers and slanderers are doubled-tongued. *Not given to much wine;* for this is a great disparagement to any man, especially to a Christian, and one in office, unfits men for business, opens the door to many temptations. *Not greedy of filthy lucre;* this would especially be bad in the deacons, who were entrusted with the church's money, and, if they were covetous and greedy of filthy lucre, would be tempted to embezzle it, and convert that to their own use which was intended for the public service. *Holding the mystery of faith in a pure conscience, v.* 9. Note, The mystery of faith is best held in a pure conscience. The practical love of truth is the most powerful preservative from error and delusion. If we keep a pure conscience (take heed of every thing that debauches conscience, and draws us away from God), this will preserve in our souls the mystery of faith. *Let these also first be proved, v.* 10. It is not fit that the public trusts should be lodged in the hands of any, till they have been first proved, and found fit for the business they are to be entrusted with; the soundness of their judgments, their zeal for Christ, and the blamelessness of their conversation, must be proved. Their wives likewise must have a good character (*v.* 11); they must be of a grave behaviour, not slanderers, tale-bearers, carrying stories to make mischief and sow discord; they must be *sober and faithful in all things,* not given to any excess, but trusty in all that is committed to them. All who are related to ministers must double their care to walk as becomes the gospel of Christ, lest, if they in any thing walk disorderly, the ministry be blamed. As he said before of the bishops or ministers, so here of the deacons, they must be *the husband of one wife,* such as had not put away their wives, upon dislike, and married others; they must *rule their children and their own houses well:* the families of deacons should be examples to other families. And the reason why the deacons must be thus qualified is (*v.* 13) because, though the office of a deacon be of an inferior degree, yet it is a step towards the higher degree; and those who had served tables well the church might see cause afterwards to discharge from that service, and prefer to serve in preaching the word and in prayer. Or it may be meant of the good reputation that a man would gain by his fidelity in this office: *they will purchase to themselves great boldness in the faith that is in Christ Jesus.* Observe, 1. In the primitive church there were but two orders of ministers or officers, *bishops* and *deacons,* Phil. i. 1. After-ages have invented the rest. The office of the bishop, presbyter, pastor, or minister, was confined to prayer and to the ministry of the word; and the office of the deacon was confined to, or at least principally conversant about, serving tables. Clemens Romanus, in his epistle to the Christians (*cap.* 42, 44), speaks very fully and plainly to this effect, that the apostles, foreknowing, by our Lord Jesus Christ, that there would arise in the Christian church a controversy about the name *episcopacy,* appointed the forementioned orders, bishops and deacons. 2. The scripture-deacon's main employment was to serve tables, and not to preach or baptize. It is true, indeed, that Philip did preach and baptize in Samaria (Acts viii.), but you read that he was an evangelist (Acts xxi. 8), and he might preach and baptize, and perform any other part of the ministerial office, under that character; but still the design of the deacon's office was to mind the temporal concerns of the church, such as the salaries of the ministers and providing for the poor. 3. Several qualifications were very necessary, even for these inferior officers: *The deacons must be grave,* &c. 4. Some trial should be made of persons qualifications before they are admitted into office in the church, or have any trust committed to them: *Let these also first be proved.* 5. Integrity and uprightness in an inferior office are the way to be preferred to a higher station in the church: *They purchase to themselves a good degree.* 6. This will also give a man great boldness in the faith, whereas a want of integrity and uprightness will make a man timorous, and ready to tremble at his own shadow. *The wicked fleeth when no man pursueth, but the righteous are bold as a lion,* Prov. xxviii. 1.

14 These things write I unto thee, hoping to come unto thee shortly:
15 But if I tarry long, that thou mayest know how thou oughtest to behave thyself in the house of God, which is the church of the living God, the pillar and ground of the truth. 16
And without controversy great is the mystery of godliness: God was manifest in the flesh, justified in the Spirit, seen of angels, preached unto the Gentiles, believed on in the world, received up into glory.

He concludes the chapter with a particular direction to Timothy. He hoped shortly to come to him, to give him further directions and assistance in his work, and to see that Christianity was well planted, and took root well, at Ephesus; he therefore wrote the more briefly to him. But he wrote *lest he should tarry long, that* Timothy *might know how to behave himself in the house of God,* how to conduct himself as became an evangelist, and the apostle's substitute. Observe,

I. Those who are employed in the house of God must see to it that they behave themselves well, lest they bring reproach upon the house of God, and that worthy name by which they are called. Ministers ought to behave themselves well, and to look not only to their praying and preaching, but to their behaviour: their office binds them to their good behaviour, for any behaviour will not do in this case. Timothy must know how to behave himself, not only in the particular church where he was now appointed to reside for some time, but being an evangelist, and the apostle's substitute, he must learn how to behave himself in other churches, where he should in like manner be appointed to reside for some time; and therefore it is not the church of Ephesus, but the catholic church, which is here called *the house of God, which is the church of the living God.* Observe here, 1. God is the living God; he is the fountain of life, he is life in himself, and he gives life, breath, and all things to his creatures; in him we live, and move, and have our being, Acts xvii. 25, 28. 2. The church is the house of God, he dwells there; the Lord has chosen Zion, to dwell there. "This is my rest, here will I dwell, for I have chosen it;" there may we see God's power and glory, Ps. lxiii. 2.

II. It is the great support of the church that it is the church of the living *God,* the true God in opposition to false gods, dumb and dead idols.

1. As the church of God, it is *the pillar and ground of truth;* that is, either, (1.) The church itself is the pillar and ground of truth. Not that the authority of the scriptures depends upon that of the church, as the papists pretend, for truth is the pillar and ground of the church; but the church holds forth the scripture and the doctrine of Christ, as the pillar to which a proclamation is affixed holds forth the proclamation. *Even to the principalities and powers in heavenly places is made known by the church the manifold wisdom of God,* Eph. iii. 10. (2.) Others understand it of Timothy. He, not he himself only, but he as an evangelist, he and other faithful ministers, are the pillars and ground of truth; it is their business to maintain, hold up, and publish, the truths of Christ in the church. It is said of the apostles that *they seemed to be pillars,* Gal. ii. 9. [1.] Let us be diligent and impartial in our own enquiries after truth; let us buy the truth at any rate, and not think much of any pains to discover it. [2.] Let us be careful to keep and preserve it. "*Buy the truth, and sell it not* (Prov. xxiii. 23), do not part with it on any consideration." [3.] Let us take care to publish it, and to transmit it safe and uncorrupted unto posterity. [4.] When the church ceases to be the pillar and ground of truth, we may and ought to forsake her; for our regard to truth should be greater than our regard to the church; we are no longer obliged to continue in the church than she continues to be the pillar and ground of truth.

2. But what is the truth which the churches and ministers are the pillars and grounds of? He tells us (*v.* 16) that *without controversy great is the mystery of godliness.* The learned Camero joins this with what goes before, and then it runs thus: "The pillar and ground of the truth, and *without controversy great is the mystery of godliness.*" He supposes this mystery to be the pillar, &c. Observe,

(1.) Christianity is a mystery, a mystery that could not have been found out by reason or the light of nature, and which cannot be comprehended by reason, because it is above reason, though not contrary thereto. It is a mystery, not of philosophy or speculation; but of godliness, designed to promote godliness; and herein it exceeds all the mysteries of the Gentiles. It is also a revealed mystery, not shut up and sealed; and it does not cease to be a mystery because now in part revealed. But,

(2.) What is the mystery of godliness? It is Christ; and here are six things concerning Christ, which make up the mystery of godliness. [1.] That he is God manifest in the flesh: *God was manifest in the flesh.* This proves that he is God, the eternal Word, that was made flesh and was manifest in the flesh. When God was to be manifested to man he was pleased to manifest himself in the incarnation of his own Son: *The Word was made flesh,* John i. 14. [2.] He is *justified in the Spirit.* Whereas he was reproached as a sinner, and put to death as a malefactor, he was raised again by the Spirit, and so was justified from all the calumnies with which he was loaded. *He was made sin for us, and was delivered for our offences;* but, being raised again, he was justified in the Spirit; that is, it was made to appear that his sacrifice was accepted, and so he rose again for our justification, as he was delivered for our offences, Rom. iv. 25. He was put to death in the flesh, but quickened by the Spirit, 1 Pet. iii. 18. [3.] He was *seen of angels.* They worshipped him (Heb. i. 6); they attended his incarnation, his temptation, his agony, his death, his resurrection, his ascension; this is much to his honour, and shows what a mighty interest he had in the upper world, that angels ministered to him, for he is the Lord of angels. [4.] He is *preached unto the Gentiles.* This is a great part of the mystery of godliness, that Christ was offered to the Gentiles a Redeemer and Saviour; that whereas, before, salvation was of the Jews, the partition-wall was now taken down, and the Gentiles were taken in. *I have set thee to be a light of the Gentiles,* Acts. xiii. 47. [5.] That he was *believed on in the world,* so that he was not preached in vain. Many of the Gentiles welcomed the gospel which the Jews rejected. Who would have thought that the world, which lay in wickedness, would believe in the Son of God, would take him to be their Saviour who was himself crucified at Jerusalem? But, notwithstanding all the prejudices they laboured under, he was believed on, &c. [6.] He was *received up into glory,* in his ascension. This indeed was before he was believed on in the world; but it is put last, because it was the crown of his exaltation, and because it is not only his ascension that is meant, but his sitting at the right hand of God, where he ever lives, making intercession, and has all power, both in heaven and earth, and because, in the apostasy of which he treats in the following chapter, his remaining in heaven would be denied by those who pretend to bring him down on their altars in the consecrated wafers. Observe, *First,* He who was manifest in flesh was God, really and truly God, God by nature, and not only so by office, for this makes it to be a mystery. *Secondly,* God was manifest in flesh, real flesh. *Forasmuch as the children are partakers of flesh and blood, he also himself likewise took part of the same,* Heb. ii. 14. And, what is more amazing, he was manifest in the flesh after all flesh had corrupted his way, though he himself was holy from the womb. *Thirdly,* Godliness is a mystery in all its parts and branches, from the beginning to the end, from Christ's incarnation to his ascension. *Fourthly,* It being a great mystery, we should rather humbly adore it, and piously believe it, than curiously pry into it, or be too positive in our explications of it and determinations about it, further than the holy scriptures have revealed it to us.

CHAP. IV.

Paul here foretels, I. A dreadful apostasy, ver. 1—3. II. He treats of Christian liberty, ver. 4, 5. III. He gives Timothy divers directions with respect to himself, his doctrine, and the people under his care, ver. 6, to the end.

NOW the Spirit speaketh expressly,
that in the latter times some shall
depart from the faith, giving heed to
seducing spirits, and doctrines of devils;
2 Speaking lies in hypocrisy; having
their conscience seared with a hot
iron; 3 Forbidding to marry, *and
commanding* to abstain from meats,
which God hath created to be received
with thanksgiving of them which believe and know the truth. 4 For
every creature of God *is* good, and
nothing to be refused, if it be received
with thanksgiving: 5 For it is sanctified by the word of God and prayer.

We have here a prophecy of the apostasy of the latter times, which he had spoken of as a thing expected and taken for granted among Christians, 2 Thess. ii.

I. In the close of the foregoing chapter, we had the mystery of godliness summed up; and therefore very fitly, in the beginning of this chapter, we have the mystery of iniquity summed up: *The Spirit speaks expressly that in the latter times some shall depart from the faith;* whether he means the Spirit in the Old Testament, or the Spirit in the prophets of the New Testament, or both. The prophecies concerning antichrist, as well as the prophecies concerning Christ, came from the Spirit. The Spirit in both spoke expressly of a general apostasy from the faith of Christ and the pure worship of God. This should come in the *latter times,* during the Christian dispensation, for these are called the latter days; in the following ages of the church, for the mystery of iniquity now began to work. *Some shall depart from the faith,* or there shall be an apostasy from the faith. Some, not all; for in the worst of times God will have a remnant, according to the election of grace. *They shall depart from the faith,* the faith delivered to the saints (Jude 3), which was delivered at once, the sound doctrine of the gospel. *Giving heed to seducing spirits,* men who pretended to the Spirit, but were not really guided by the Spirit, 1 John iv. 1, *Beloved, believe not every spirit,* every one who pretends to the Spirit. Now here observe,

1. One of the great instances of the apostasy, namely, giving heed to doctrines of demons, or concerning demons; that is, those doctrines which teach the worship of saints and angels, as a middle sort of deities, between the immortal God and mortal men, such as the heathen called demons, and worshipped under that notion. Now this plainly agrees to the church of Rome, and it was one of the first steps towards that great apostasy, the enshrining of the relics of martyrs, paying divine honours to them, erecting altars, burning incense, consecrating images and temples, and making prayers and praises to the honour of saints departed. This demon-worship is paganism revived, the image of the first beast.

2. The instruments of promoting and propagating this apostasy and delusion. (1.) It will be done by hypocrisy of those that speak lies, the agents and emissaries of Satan, who promote these delusions by lies and forgeries and pretended miracles, *v.* 2. It is done by their hypocrisy, professing honour to Christ, and yet at the same time fighting against all his anointed offices, and corrupting or profaning all his ordinances. This respects also the hypocrisy of those who have *their consciences seared with a red-hot iron,* who are perfectly lost to the very first principles of virtue and moral honesty. If men had not their consciences seared as with a hot iron, they could never maintain a power to dispense with oaths for the good of the catholic cause, could never maintain that no faith is to be kept with heretics, could never divest themselves of all remains of humanity and compassion, and clothe themselves with the most barbarous cruelty, under pretence of promoting the interest of the church. (2.) Another part of their character is that they forbid to marry, forbid their clergy to marry, and speak very reproachfully of marriage, though an ordinance of God; and that they command *to abstain from meats,* and place religion in such abstinence at certain times and seasons, only to exercise a tyranny over the consciences of men.

3. On the whole observe, (1.) The apostasy of the latter times should not surprise us, because it was expressly foretold by the Spirit. (2.) The Spirit is God, otherwise he could not certainly foresee such distant events, which as to us are uncertain and contingent, depending on the tempers, humours, and lusts of men. (3.) The difference between the predictions of the Spirit and the oracles of the heathen is remarkable; the Spirit speaks expressly, but the oracles of the heathen were always doubtful and uncertain. (4.) It is comfortable to think that in such general apostasies all are not carried away, but only some. (5.) It is common for seducers and deceivers to pretend to the Spirit, which is a strong presumption that all are convinced that this is the most likely to work in us an approbation of what pretends to come from the Spirit. (6.) Men must be hardened, and their consciences seared, before they can depart from the faith, and draw in others to side with them. (7.) It is a sign that men have departed from the faith when they will command what God has forbidden, such as saint and angel or demon-worship; and forbid what God has allowed or commanded, such as marriage and meats.

II. Having mentioned their hypocritical fastings, the apostle takes occasion to lay down the doctrine of the Christian liberty, which we enjoy under the gospel, of using God's good creatures,—that, whereas under the law there was a distinction of meats between clean and unclean (such sorts of flesh they might eat, and such they might not eat), all this is now taken away; and we are to call nothing common or unclean, Acts x. 15. Here observe, 1. We are to look upon our food as that which God has created; we have it from him, and therefore must use it for him. 2. God, in making those things, had a special regard to *those who believe and know the truth,* to good Christians, who have a covenant right to the creatures, whereas others have only a common right. 3. What God has created is to be *received with thanksgiving.* We must not refuse the gifts of God's bounty, nor be scrupulous in making differences where God has made none; but receive them, and be thankful, acknowledging the power of God the Maker of them, and the bounty of God the giver of them: *Every creature of God is good, and nothing to be refused, v.* 4. This plainly sets us at liberty from all the distinctions of meats appointed by the ceremonial law, as particularly that of swine's flesh, which the Jews were forbidden to eat, but which is allowed to us Christians, by this rule, *Every creature of God is good,* &c. Observe, God's good creatures are then good, and doubly sweet to us, when they are received with thanksgiving.—*For it is sanctified by the word of God and prayer, v.* 5. It is a desirable thing to have a sanctified use of our creature-comforts. Now they are sanctified to us, (1.) By the word of God; not only his permission, allowing us the liberty of the use of these things, but his promise to feed us with food convenient for us. This gives us a sanctified use of our creature-comforts. (2.) By prayer, which blesses our meat to us. The word of God and prayer must be brought to our common actions and affairs, and then we do all in faith. Here observe,

[1.] Every creature is God's, for he made all. *Every beast in the forest is mine* (says God), *and the cattle upon a thousand hills. I know all the fowls of the mountains, and the wild beasts of the field are mine,* Ps. l. 10, 11. [2.] Every creature of God is good: when the blessed God took a survey of all his works, God saw all that was made, and, behold, it was very good, Gen. i. 31. [3.] The blessing of God makes every creature nourishing to us; man lives not by bread alone, but by every word that proceeds out of the mouth of God (Matt. iv. 4), and therefore nothing ought to be refused. [4.] We ought therefore to ask his blessing by prayer, and so to sanctify the creatures we receive by prayer.

6 If thou put the brethren in
remembrance of these things, thou
shalt be a good minister of Jesus
Christ, nourished up in the words of
faith and of good doctrine, whereunto
thou hast attained. 7 But refuse
profane and old wives' fables, and
exercise thyself *rather* unto godliness.
8 For bodily exercise profiteth little:
but godliness is profitable unto all
things, having promise of the life
that now is, and of that which is to
come. 9 This *is* a faithful saying
and worthy of all acceptation. 10
For therefore we both labour and
suffer reproach, because we trust in
the living God, who is the saviour of
all men, specially of those that believe.
11 These things command and teach.
12 Let no man despise thy youth;
but be thou an example of the believers, in word, in conversation, in
charity, in spirit, in faith, in purity.
13 Till I come, give attendance to
reading, to exhortation, to doctrine.
14 Neglect not the gift that is in
thee, which was given thee by prophecy, with the laying on of the
hands of the presbytery. 15 Meditate upon these things; give thyself
wholly to them; that thy profiting
may appear to all. 16 Take heed
unto thyself, and unto the doctrine;
continue in them: for in doing this
thou shalt both save thyself, and them
that hear thee.

The apostle would have Timothy to instil into the minds of Christians such sentiments as might prevent their being seduced by the judaizing teachers. Observe, Those are good ministers of Jesus Christ who are diligent in their work; not that study to advance new notions, but that *put the brethren in remembrance of those things which they have received and heard. Wherefore I will not be negligent to put you always in remembrance of these things, though you knew them,* 2 Pet. i. 12. And elsewhere, *I stir up your pure minds by way of remembrance,* 2 Pet. iii. 1. And, says the apostle Jude, *I will therefore put you in remembrance,* Jude 5. You see that the apostles and apostolical men reckoned it a main part of their work to put their hearers in remembrance; for we are apt to forget, and slow to learn and remember, the things of God. —*Nourished up in the words of faith and good doctrine, whereunto thou hast attained.* Observe, 1. Even ministers themselves have need to be growing and increasing in the knowledge of Christ and his doctrine: they must be nourished up in the words of faith. 2. The best way for ministers to grow in knowledge and faith is to put the brethren in remembrance; while we teach others, we teach ourselves. 3. Those whom ministers teach are brethren, and are to be treated like brethren; for ministers are not lords of God's heritage.

I. Godliness is here pressed upon him and others: *Refuse profane and old wives' sayings, v.* 7, 8, The Jewish traditions, which some people fill their heads with, have nothing to do with them. *But exercise thyself rather unto godliness;* that is, mind practical religion. Those who would be godly must exercise themselves unto godliness; it requires a constant exercise. The reason is taken from the gain of godliness; *bodily exercise profits little,* or for a little time. Abstinence from meats and marriage, and the like, though they pass for acts of mortification and self-denial, yet profit little, they turn to little account. What will it avail us to mortify the body if we do not mortify sin? Observe, 1. There is a great deal to be got by godliness; it will be of use to us in the whole of our life, for it has *the promise of the life that now is, and of that which is to come.* 2. The gain of godliness lies much in the promise: and the promises made to godly people relate to the life that now is, but especially they relate to the life that is to come. Under the Old Testament the promises were mostly of temporal blessings, but under the New Testament of spiritual and eternal blessings. If godly people have but little of the good things of the life that now is, yet it shall be made up to them in the good things of the life that is to come. 3. There were profane and old wives' fables in the days of the apostles; and Timothy, though an excellent man, was not above such a word of advice, *Refuse profane,* &c. 4. It is not enough that we refuse profane and old wives fables, but we must exercise ourselves to godliness; we must not only cease to do evil, but we must learn to do well (Isa. i. 16, 17), and we must make a practice of exercising ourselves to godliness. And, 5. Those who are truly godly shall not be losers at last, whatever becomes of those who content themselves with bodily exercise, for godliness has the promise, &c.

II. The encouragement which we have to proceed in the ways of godliness, and to exercise ourselves to it, notwithstanding the difficulties and discouragements that we meet with in it. He had said (*v.* 8) that it *is profitable for all things, having the promise of the life which now is.* But the question is, Will the profit balance the loss? For, if it will not, it is not profit. Yes, we are sure it will. Here is another of Paul's faithful sayings, worthy of all acceptation—that all our labours and losses in the service of God and the work of religion will be abundantly recompensed, so that though we lose for Christ we shall not lose by him. *Therefore we labour and suffer reproach, because we trust in the living God, v.* 10. Observe,

1. Godly people must labour and expect reproach; they must do well, and yet expect at the same time to suffer ill: toil and trouble are to be expected by us in this world, not only as men, but as saints.

2. Those who labour and suffer reproach in the service of God and the work of religion may depend upon the living God that they shall not lose by it. Let this encourage them, *We trust in the living God.* The consideration of this, that the God who has undertaken to be our pay-master is the living God, who does himself live for ever and is the fountain of life to all who serve him, should encourage us in all our services and in all our sufferings for him, especially considering that he is *the Saviour of all men.* (1.) By his providences he protects the persons, and prolongs the lives, of the children of men. (2.) He has a general good-will to the eternal salvation of all men thus far that he is not willing that any should perish, but that all should come to repentance. He desires not the death of sinners; he is thus far the Saviour of all men that none are left in the same desperate condition that fallen angels are in. Now, if he be thus the Saviour of all men, we may hence infer that much more he will be the rewarder of those who seek and serve him; if he has such a good-will for all his creatures, much more will he provide well for those who are new creatures, who are born again. He is the Saviour of all men, but *especially of those that believe;* and the salvation he has in store for those that believe is sufficient to recompense them for all their services and sufferings. Here we see, [1.] The life of a Christian is a life of labour and suffering: *We labour and suffer.* [2.] The best we can expect to suffer in the present life is reproach for our well-doing, for our work of faith and labour of love. [3.] True Christians trust in the living God; for cursed is the man that trusts in man, or in any but the living God; and those that trust in him shall never be ashamed. *Trust in him at all times.* [4.] God is the general Saviour of all men, as he has put them into a salvable state; but he is in a particular manner the Saviour of true believers; there is then a general and a special redemption.

III. He concludes the chapter with an exhortation to Timothy,

1. To *command and teach these things* that he had now been teaching him. "Command them to exercise themselves unto godliness, teach them the profit of it, and that if they serve God they serve one who will be sure to bear them out."

2. To conduct himself with that gravity and prudence which might gain him respect, notwithstanding his youth: "*Let no man despise thy youth;* that is, give no man an occasion to despise thy youth." Men's youth will not be despised if they do not by youthful vanities and follies make themselves despicable; and this men may do who are old, who may therefore thank themselves if they be despised.

3. To confirm his doctrine by a good example: *Be thou an example of the believers,* &c. Observe, Those who teach by their doctrine must teach by their life, else they pull down with one hand what they build up with the other: they must be examples both *in word and conversation.* Their discourse must be edifying, and this will be a good example: their conversation must be strict, and this will be a good example: they must be examples *in charity,* or love to God and all good men, examples *in spirit,* that is, in spiritual-mindedness, in spiritual worship,—*in faith,* that is, in the profession of Christian faith,—and *in purity* or chastity.

4. He charges him to study hard: *Till I come, give attendance to reading, to exhortation, to doctrine, to meditation upon these things, v.* 13. Though Timothy had extraordinary gifts, yet he must use ordinary means. Or it may be meant of the public reading of the scriptures; he must *read and exhort,* that is, read and expound, read and press what he read upon them; he must expound it both by way of exhortation and by way of doctrine; he must teach them both what to do and what to believe. Observe, (1.) Ministers must teach and command the things that they are themselves taught and commanded to do; they must teach people to observe all things whatsoever Christ has commanded, Matt. xxviii. 20. (2.) The best way for ministers to avoid being despised is to teach and practise the things that are given them in charge. No wonder if ministers are despised who do not teach these things, or who, instead of being examples of good to believers, act directly contrary to the doctrines they preach; for ministers are to be ensamples of their flock. (3.) Those ministers that are the best accomplished for their work must yet mind their studies, that they may be improving in knowledge; and they must mind also their work; they are to give

attendance to reading, to exhortation, to doctrine.

5. He charges him to beware of negligence: *Neglect not the gift that is in thee, v.* 14. The gifts of God will wither if they be neglected. It may be understood either of the office to which he was advanced, or of his qualifications for that office; if of the former, it was ordination in an ordinary way; if of the latter, it was extraordinary. It seems to be the former, for it was by *laying on of hands,* &c. Here see the scripture-way of ordination: it was by the laying on of hands, and the laying on of the hands of the presbytery. Observe, Timothy was ordained by men in office. It was an extraordinary gift that we read of elsewhere as being conferred on him by the laying on of Paul's hands, but he was invested in the office of the ministry by the laying on of the hands of the presbytery. (1.) We may note, The office of the ministry is a gift, it is the gift of Christ; when he ascended on high, he received gifts for men, and he gave some apostles, and some pastors and teachers (Eph. iv. 8, 11), and this was a very kind gift to his church. (2.) Ministers ought not to neglect the gift bestowed upon them, whether by gift we are here to understand the office of the ministry or the qualifications for that office; neither the one nor the other must be neglected. (3.) Though there was prophecy in the case of Timothy (the gift was given by prophecy), yet this was accompanied by the laying on of the hands of the presbytery, that is, a number of presbyters; the office was conveyed to him this way; and I should think here is a sufficient warrant for ordination by presbyters, since it does not appear that Paul was concerned in Timothy's ordination. It is true, extraordinary gifts were conferred on him by the laying on of the apostle's hands (2 Tim. i. 6), but, if he was concerned in his ordination, the presbytery was not excluded, for that is particularly mentioned, whence it seems pretty evident that the presbytery have the inherent power of ordination.

6. Having this work committed to him, he must *give himself wholly* to it: "Be wholly in those things, *that thy profiting may appear.*" He was a wise knowing man, and yet must still be profiting, and make it appear that he improved in knowledge. Observe, (1.) Ministers are to be much in meditation. They are to consider beforehand how and what they must speak. They are to meditate on the great trust committed to them, on the worth and value of immortal souls, and on the account they must give at the last. (2.) Ministers must be wholly in these things, they must mind these things as their principal work and business: *Give thyself wholly to them.* (3.) By this means their profiting will appear in all things, as well as to all persons; this is the way for them to profit in knowledge and grace, and also to profit others.

7. He presses it upon him to be very cautious: "*Take heed to thyself and to the doctrine,* consider what thou preachest; *continue in them,* in the truths that thou hast received; and this will be the way to *save thyself, and those that hear thee.*" Observe, (1.) Ministers are engaged in saving work, which makes it a good work. (2.) The care of ministers should be in the first place to save themselves: "Save thyself in the first place, so shalt thou be instrumental to save those that hear thee." (3.) Ministers in preaching should aim at the salvation of those that hear them, next to the salvation of their own souls. (4.) The best way to answer both these ends is to take heed to ourselves, &c.

CHAP. V.

Here the apostle, I. Directs Timothy how to reprove, ver. 1, 2. II. Adverts to widows, both elder and younger, ver. 3—16. III. To elders, ver. 17—19. IV. Treats of public reproof, ver. 20. V. Gives a solemn charge concerning ordination, ver. 21, 22. VI. Refers to his health (ver. 23), and states men's sins to be very different in their effects, ver. 24, 25.

REBUKE not an elder, but intreat
him as a father; *and* the younger
men as brethren; 2 The elder women
as mothers; the younger as sisters,
with all purity.

Here the apostle gives rules to Timothy, and in him to other ministers, in reproving. Ministers are reprovers by office; it is a part, though the least pleasing part, of their office; they are to preach the word, to reprove and rebuke, 2 Tim. iv. 2. A great difference is to be made in our reproofs, according to the age, quality, and other circumstances, of the persons rebuked; thus, an elder in age or office must be entreated as a father; *on some have compassion, making a difference,* Jude 22 Now the rule is, 1. To be very tender in rebuking elders—elders in age, elders by office. Respect must be had to the dignity of their years and place, and therefore they must not be rebuked sharply nor magisterially; but Timothy himself, though an evangelist, must entreat them as fathers, for this would be the likeliest way to work upon them, and to win upon them. 2. The younger must be rebuked as brethren, with love and tenderness; not as desirous to spy faults or pick quarrels, but as being willing to make the best of them. There is need of a great deal of meekness in reproving those who deserve reproof. 3. The elder women must be reproved, when there is occasion, as mothers. Hos. ii. 2, *Plead with your mother, plead.* 4. The younger women must be reproved, but reproved as *sisters, with all purity.* If Timothy, so mortified a man to this world and to the flesh and the lusts of it, had need of such a caution as this, much more have we.

3 Honour widows that are widows
indeed. 4 But if any widow have
children or nephews, let them learn
first to show piety at home, and to
requite their parents: for that is good

and acceptable before God. 5 Now
she that is a widow indeed, and
desolate, trusteth in God, and continueth in supplications and prayers
night and day. 6 But she that liveth
in pleasure is dead while she liveth.
7 And these things give in charge,
that they may be blameless. 8 But
if any provide not for his own, and
specially for those of his own house,
he hath denied the faith, and is worse
than an infidel. 9 Let not a widow
be taken into the number under
threescore years old, having been the
wife of one man, 10 Well reported
of for good works; if she have brought
up children, if she have lodged strangers, if she have washed the saints'
feet, if she have relieved the afflicted,
if she have diligently followed every
good work. 11 But the younger
widows refuse: for when they have
begun to wax wanton against Christ,
they will marry; 12 Having damnation, because they have cast off
their first faith. 13 And withal they
learn *to be* idle, wandering about from
house to house; and not only idle,
but tattlers also and busybodies,
speaking things which they ought
not. 14 I will therefore that the
younger women marry, bear children,
guide the house, give none occasion
to the adversary to speak reproachfully. 15 For some are already
turned aside after Satan. 16 If any
man or woman that believeth have
widows, let them relieve them, and
let not the church be charged; that
it may relieve them that are widows
indeed.

Directions are here given concerning the taking of widows into the number of those who were employed by the church and had maintenance from the church: *Honour widows that are widows indeed.* Honour them, that is, maintain them, admit them into office. There was in those times an office in the church in which widows were employed, and that was to tend the sick and the aged, to look to them by the direction of the deacons. We read of the care taken of widows immediately upon the first forming of the Christian church (Acts vi. 1), where the Grecians thought their widows were neglected in the daily ministration and provision made for poor widows. The general rule is to *honour widows that are widows indeed,* to maintain them, to relieve them with respect and tenderness.

I. It is appointed that those widows only should be relieved by the charity of the church who were pious and devout, and not wanton widows that *lived in pleasure, v.* 5, 6. She is to be reckoned a widow indeed, and fit to be maintained at the church's charge, who, being *desolate, trusteth in God.* Observe, It is the duty and comfort of those who are desolate to trust in God. *Therefore* God sometimes brings his people into such straits that they have nothing else to trust to, that they may with more confidence trust in him. Widowhood is a desolate estate; but *let the widows trust in me* (Jer. xlix. 11), and rejoice that they have a God to trust to. Again, Those who trust in God must *continue in prayer.* If by faith we confide in God, by prayer we must give glory to God and commit ourselves to his guidance. Anna was a widow indeed, who *departed not from the temple* (Luke ii. 37), *but served God with fasting and prayer night and day.* But she is not a widow indeed *that lives in pleasure* (*v.* 6), or who lives licentiously. A jovial widow is not a widow indeed, not fit to be taken under the care of the church. *She that lives in pleasure is dead while she lives,* is no living member of the church, but as a carcase in it, or a mortified member. We may apply it more generally; those who live in pleasure are dead while they live, spiritually dead, *dead in trespasses and sins;* they are in the world to no purpose, buried alive as to the great ends of living.

II. Another rule he gives is that the church should not be charged with the maintenance of those widows who had relations of their own that were able to maintain them. This is mentioned several times (*v.* 4): *If any widow have children or nephews,* that is grandchildren or near relations, let them maintain them, and let not the church be burdened. So *v.* 16. This is called showing *piety at home* (*v.* 4), or showing piety towards their own families. Observe, The respect of children to their parents, with their care of them, is fitly called piety. This is requiting their parents. Children can never sufficiently requite their parents for the care they have taken of them, and the pains they have taken with them; but they must endeavour to do it. It is the indispensable duty of children, if their parents be in necessity, and they in ability to relieve them, to do it to the utmost of their power, *for this is good and acceptable before God.* The Pharisees taught that a gift to the altar was more acceptable to God than relieving a poor parent, Matt. xv. 5. But here we are told that this *is better than all burnt-offerings and sacrifices; this is good and acceptable,* &c. He speaks of this again (*v.* 8), *If any provide not for his own,* &c. If any men or women do not maintain their own poor relations who belong to them, they do in effect *deny the faith;* for the design of

Christ was to confirm the law of Moses, and particularly the law of the fifth commandment, which is, *Honour thy father and mother;* so that those deny the faith who disobey that law, much more if they provide not for their wives and children, who are parts of themselves; if they spend that upon their lusts which should maintain their families, they have denied the faith *and are worse than infidels.* One reason why this care must be taken that those who are rich should maintain their poor relations, and not burden the church with them is (*v.* 16) *that it may relieve those who are widows indeed.* Observe, Charity misplaced is a great hindrance to true charity; there should be prudence in the choice of the objects of charity, that it may not be thrown away upon those who are not properly so, that there may be the more for those who are real objects of charity.

III. He gives directions concerning the characters of the widows that were to be taken into the number to receive the church's charity: not under sixty years old, nor any who have divorced their husbands or been divorced from them and have married again; she must have been *the wife of one man,* such as had been a housekeeper, had a good name for hospitality and charity, *well reported of for good works.* Observe, Particular care ought to be taken to relieve those, when they fall into decay, who, when they had wherewithal, were ready to every good work. Here are instances of such good works as are proper to be done by good wives: *If she have brought up children:* he does not say, If she have borne children (*children are a heritage of the Lord*), that depends on the will of God; but, if she had not children of her own, yet if she had brought up children. *If she have lodged strangers,* and *washed the saints' feet;* if she have been ready to give entertainment to good Christians and good ministers, when they were in their travels for the spreading of the gospel. Washing of the feet of their friends was a part of their entertainments. *If she have relieved the afflicted* when she had ability, let her be relieved now. Observe, Those who would find mercy when they are in distress must show mercy when they are in prosperity.

IV. He cautions them to take heed of admitting into the number those who are likely to be no credit to them (*v.* 11): *The younger widows refuse;* they will be weary of their employments in the church, and of living by rule, as they must do; so they *will marry, and cast off their first faith.* You read of a first love (Rev. ii. 4), and here of a first faith, that is, the engagements they gave to the church to behave well, and as became the trust reposed in them: it does not appear that by their first faith is meant their vow not to marry, for the scripture is very silent on that head; besides the apostle here advises the younger widows to marry (*v.* 14), which he would not if hereby they must have broken their vows. Dr. Whitby well observes, "If this faith referred to a promise made to the church not to marry, it could not be called their first faith." *Withal they learn to be idle, and not only idle, but tattlers,* &c., *v.* 13. Observe, It is seldom that those who are idle are idle only, they learn *to be tattlers and busy-bodies,* and to make mischief among neighbours, and sow discord among brethren. Those who had not attained to such a gravity of mind as was fit for the deaconesses (or the widows who were taken among the church's poor), let them *marry, bear children,* &c., *v.* 14. Observe, If housekeepers do not mind their business, but are tattlers, they give occasion to the adversaries of Christianity to reproach the Christian name, which, it seems, there were some instances of, *v.* 15. We learn hence, 1. In the primitive church there was care taken of poor widows, and provision made for them; and the churches of Christ in these days should follow so good an example, as far as they are able. 2. In the distribution of the church's charity, or alms, great care is to be taken that those share in the public bounty who most want it and best deserve it. A widow was not to be taken into the primitive church that had relations who were able to maintain her, or who was not well reported of for good works, but lived in pleasure: *But the younger widows refuse, for, when they have begun to wax wanton against Christ, they will marry.* 3. The credit of religion, and the reputation of Christian churches, are very much concerned in the character and behaviour of those that are taken into any employment in the church, though of a lower nature (such as the business of deaconesses), or that receive alms of the church; if they do not behave well, but are tatlers and busy-bodies, they will give occasion to the adversary to speak reproachfully. 4. Christianity obliges its professors to relieve their indigent friends, particularly poor widows, that the church may not be charged with them, that it may relieve those that are widows indeed: rich people should be ashamed to burden the church with their poor relations, when it is with difficulty that those are supplied who have no children or nephews, that is, grand-children, who are in a capacity to relieve them.

17 Let the elders that rule well
be counted worthy of double honour,
especially they who labour in the word
and doctrine. 18 For the scripture
saith, Thou shalt not muzzle the ox
that treadeth out the corn. And,
The labourer *is* worthy of his reward.
19 Against an elder receive not an
accusation, but before two or three
witnesses. 20 Them that sin rebuke
before all, that others also may fear.
21 I charge *thee* before God, and

the Lord Jesus Christ, and the elect
angels, that thou observe these things
without preferring one before another,
doing nothing by partiality. 22 Lay
hands suddenly on no man, neither
be partaker of other men's sins: keep
thyself pure. 23 Drink no longer
water, but use a little wine for thy
stomach's sake and thine often infirmities. 24 Some men's sins are open
beforehand, going before to judgment;
and some *men* they follow after. 25
Likewise also the good works *of some*
are manifest beforehand; and they
that are otherwise cannot be hid.

Here are directions,

I. Concerning the supporting of ministers. Care must be taken that they be honourably maintained (*v.* 17): *Let the elders that rule well be counted worthy of double honour* (that is, of double maintenance, double to what they have had, or to what others have), *especially those who labour in the word and doctrine,* those who are more laborious than others. Observe, The presbytery ruled, and the same that ruled were those *who laboured in the word and doctrine*: they had not one to preach to them and another to rule them, but the work was done by one and the same person. Some have imagined that by the *elders that rule well* the apostle means lay-elders, who were employed in ruling but not in teaching, who were concerned in church-government, but did not meddle with the administration of the word and sacraments; and I confess this is the plainest text of scripture that can be found to countenance such an opinion. But it seems a little strange that mere ruling elders should be accounted worthy of double honour, when the apostle preferred preaching to baptizing, and much more would he prefer it to ruling the church; and it is more strange that the apostle should take no notice of them when he treats of church-officers; but, as it is hinted before, they had not, in the primitive church, one to preach to them and another to rule them, but ruling and teaching were performed by the same persons, only some might labour more in the word and doctrine than others. Here we have, 1. The work of ministers; it consists principally in two things: ruling well and labouring in the word and doctrine. This was the main business of elders or presbyters in the days of the apostles. 2. The honour due to those who were not idle, but laborious in this work; they were worthy of double honour, esteem, and maintenance. He quotes a scripture to confirm this command concerning the maintenance of ministers that we might think foreign; but it intimates what a significancy there was in many of the laws of Moses, and particularly in this, *Thou shalt not muzzle the ox that treads out the corn,* Deut. xxv. 4. The beasts that were employed in treading out the corn (for that way they took instead of threshing it) were allowed to feed while they did the work, so that the more work they did the more food they had; therefore let the elders that labour in the word and doctrine be well provided for; *for the labourer is worthy of his reward* (Matt. x. 10), and there is all the reason in the world that he should have it. We hence learn, (1.) God, both under the law, and now under the gospel, has taken care that his ministers be well provided for. Does God take care for oxen, and will he not take care of his own servants? The ox only treads out the corn of which they make the bread that perishes; but ministers break the bread of life which endures for ever. (2.) The comfortable subsistence of ministers, as it is God's appointment that those who preach the gospel should live of the gospel (1 Cor. ix. 14), so it is their just due, as much as the reward of the labourer; and those who would have ministers starved, or not comfortably provided for, God will require it of them another day.

II. Concerning the accusation of ministers (*v.* 19): *Against an elder receive not an accusation, but before two or three witnesses.* Here is the scripture-method of proceeding against an elder, when accused of any crime. Observe, 1. There must be an accusation; it must not be a flying uncertain report, but an accusation, containing a certain charge, must be drawn up. Further, He is not to be proceeded against by way of enquiry; this is according to the modern practice of the inquisition, which draws up articles for men to purge themselves of such crimes, or else to accuse themselves; but, according to the advice of Paul, there must be an accusation brought against an elder. 2. This accusation is not to be received unless supported by two or three credible witnesses; and the accusation must be received before them, that is, the accused must have the accusers face to face, because the reputation of a minister is, in a particular manner, a tender thing; and therefore, before any thing be done in the least to blemish that reputation, great care should be taken that the thing alleged against him be well proved, that he be not reproached upon an uncertain surmise; "but (*v.* 20) *those that sin rebuke before all;* that is, thou needest not be so tender of other people, but rebuke them publicly." Or "those that sin before all rebuke before all, that the plaster may be as wide as the wound, and that those who are in danger of sinning by the example of their fall may take warning by the rebuke given them for it, *that others also may fear.*" Observe, (1.) Public scandalous sinners must be rebuked publicly: as their sin has been public, and committed before many, or at least come to the hearing of all, so their reproof must be public, and before all. (2.)

Public rebuke is designed for the good of others, that they may fear, as well as for the good of the party rebuked; hence it was ordered under the law that public offenders should receive public punishment, that *all Israel* might *hear, and fear, and do no more wickedly.*

III. Concerning the ordination of ministers (*v.* 22): *Lay hands suddenly on no man;* it seems to be meant of the ordaining of men to the office of the ministry, which ought not to be done rashly and inconsiderately, and before due trial made of their gifts and graces, their abilities and qualifications for it. Some understand it of absolution: "Be not too hasty in laying hands on any; remit not the censure of the church to any, till time be first taken for the proof of their sincerity in their repentance, *neither be partakers of other men's sins,* implying that those who are too easy in remitting the censures of the church encourage others in the sins which are thus connived at, and make themselves thereby guilty. Observe, We have great need to watch over ourselves at all times, that we do not make ourselves partakers of other men's sins. "Keep thyself pure, not only from doing the like thyself, but from countenancing it, or being any way accessary to it, in others." Here is, 1. A caution against the rash ordination of ministers, or absolution of those who have been under church-censures: *Lay hands suddenly on no man.* 2. Those who are rash, either in the one case or the other, will make themselves partakers in other men's sins. 3. We must keep ourselves pure, if we will be pure; the grace of God makes and keeps us pure, but it is by our own endeavours.

IV. Concerning absolution, to which *v.* 24, 25, seem to refer: *Some men's sins are open beforehand, going before to judgment, and some follow after,* &c. Observe, Ministers have need of a great deal of wisdom, to know how to accommodate themselves to the variety of offences and offenders that they have occasion to deal with. Some men's sins are so plain and obvious, and not found by secret search, that there is no dispute concerning the bringing of them under the censures of the church; they *go before to judgment,* to lead them to censure.—*Others they follow after;* that is, their wickedness does not presently appear, nor till after a due search has been made concerning it. Or, as some understand it, some men's sins continue after they are censured; they are not reformed by the censure, and in that case there must be no absolution. So, also, as to the evidences of repentance: *The good works of some are manifest beforehand. And those that are otherwise,* whose good works do not appear, their wickedness *cannot be hid,* and so it will be easy to discern who are to be absolved, and who are not. Observe, 1. There are secret, and there are open sins; some men's sins are open beforehand, and going before unto judgment, and some they follow after. 2. Sinners must be differently dealt with by the church. 3. The effects of church-censures are very different; some are thereby humbled and brought to repentance, so that their good works are manifest beforehand, while it is quite otherwise with others. 4. The incorrigible cannot be hid; for God will bring to light the hidden things of darkness, and make manifest the counsels of all hearts.

V. Concerning Timothy himself. 1. Here is a charge to him to be careful of his office; and a solemn charge it is: *I charge thee before God, as thou wilt answer it to God before the holy and elect angels, observe these things without partiality, v.* 21. Observe, It ill becomes ministers to be partial, and to have respect of persons, and to prefer one before another upon any secular account. He charges him, by all that is dear, *before God, and the Lord Jesus Christ, and the elect angels,* to guard against partiality. Ministers must give an account to God and the Lord Jesus Christ, whether, and how, they have observed all things given them in charge: and woe to them if they have been partial in their ministrations, out of any worldly politic view. 2. He charges him to take care of his health: *Drink no longer water,* &c. It seems, Timothy was a mortified man to the pleasures of sense; he drank water, and he was a man of no strong constitution of body, and for this reason Paul advises him to use wine for the helping of his stomach and the recruiting of his nature. Observe, It is a little wine, for ministers must not be given to much wine; so much as may be for the health of the body, not so as to distemper it, for God has made wine to rejoice man's heart. Note, (1.) It is the will of God that people should take all due care of their bodies. As we are not to make them our masters, so neither our slaves; but to use them so that they may be most fit and helpful to us in the service of God. (2.) Wine is most proper for sickly and weak people, whose stomachs are often out of order, and who labour under infirmities. *Give strong drink to him that is ready to perish, and wine to those that are of heavy hearts,* Prov. xxxi. 6. (3.) Wine should be used as a help, and not a hindrance, to our work and usefulness.

CHAP. VI.

I. He treats of the duty of servants, ver. 1, 2. II. Of false teachers, ver. 3—5. III. Of godliness and covetousness, ver. 6—10. IV. What Timothy was to flee, and what to follow, ver. 11, 12. V. A solemn charge, ver. 13—16. VI. A charge for the rich, ver. 17—19. And lastly, A charge to Timothy, ver. 20, 21.

LET as many servants as are under the yoke count their own masters worthy of all honour, that the name of God and *his* doctrine be not blasphemed. 2 And they that have believing masters, let them not despise *them,* because they are bre-

thren; but rather do *them* service,
because they are faithful and beloved,
partakers of the benefit. These things
teach and exhort. 3 If any man
teach otherwise, and consent not to
wholesome words, *even* the words
of our Lord Jesus Christ, and to
the doctrine which is according to
godliness; 4 He is proud, knowing
nothing, but doting about questions
and strifes of words, whereof cometh
envy, strife, railings, evil surmisings,
5 Perverse disputings of men of corrupt minds, and destitute of the truth,
supposing that gain is godliness: from
such withdraw thyself.

I. Here is the duty of servants. The apostle had spoken before of church-relations, here of our family-relations. Servants are here said to be *under the yoke,* which denotes both subjection and labour; they are yoked to work, not to be idle. If Christianity finds servants under the yoke, it continues them under it; for the gospel does not cancel the obligations any lie under either by the law of nature or by mutual consent. They must respect their masters, *count them worthy of all honour* (because they are their masters), of all the respect, observance, compliance, and obedience, that are justly expected from servants to their masters. Not that they were to think that of them which they were not; but as heir masters they must count them worthy of all that honour which was fit for them to receive, *that the name of God be not blasphemed.* If servants that embraced the Christian religion should grow insolent and disobedient to their masters, the doctrine of Christ would be reflected on for their sakes, as if it had made men worse livers than they had been before they received the gospel. Observe, If the professors of religion misbehave themselves, *the name of God and his doctrine* are in danger of being blasphemed by those who seek occasion *to speak evil of that worthy name by which we are called.* And this is a good reason why we should all conduct ourselves well, that we may prevent the occasion which many seek, and will be very apt to lay hold of, to speak ill of religion for our sakes. Or suppose the master were a Christian, and a believer, and the servant a believer too, would not this excuse him, because *in Christ there is neither bond nor free?* No, by no means, for Jesus Christ did not come to dissolve the bond of civil relation, but to strengthen it: *Those that have believing masters, let them not despise them because they are brethren;* for this brotherhood relates only to spiritual privileges, not to any outward dignity or advantage (those misunderstand and abuse their religion who make it a pretence for denying the duties that they owe to their relations); nay, *rather do them service, because they are faithful and beloved.* They must think themselves the more obliged to serve them because the faith and love that bespeak men Christians oblige them to do good; and that is all wherein their service consists. Observe, It is a great encouragement to us in doing our duty to our relations if we have reason to think they are faithful and beloved, *and partakers of the benefit,* that is, of the benefit of Christianity. Again, Believing masters and servants are brethren, and partakers of the benefit; for in Christ Jesus there is neither bond nor free, for you are all one in Christ Jesus, Gal. iii. 28. Timothy is appointed to *teach and exhort these things.* Ministers must preach not only the general duties of all, but the duties of particular relations.

II. Paul here warns Timothy to withdraw from those who corrupted the doctrine of Christ, and made it the subject of strife, debate, and controversy: *If any man teach otherwise* (*v.* 3—5, do not preach practically, do not teach and exhort that which is for the promoting of serious godliness—if he will not consent to wholesome words, words that have a direct tendency to heal the soul—if he will *not consent* to these, even the *words of our Lord Jesus Christ.* Observe, We are not required to consent to any words as wholesome words except the words of our Lord Jesus Christ; but to those we must give our unfeigned assent and consent, and *to the doctrine which is according to godliness.* Observe, The doctrine of our Lord Jesus is a doctrine according to godliness; it has a direct tendency to make people godly. But he that does not consent to the words of Christ *is proud* (*v.* 4) and contentious, ignorant, and does a great deal of mischief to the church, knowing nothing. Observe, Commonly those are most proud who know least; for with all their knowledge they do not know themselves.—*But doting about questions.* Those who fall off from the plain practical doctrines of Christianity fall in with controversies, which eat out the life and power of religion; they dote about questions *and strifes of words,* which do a great deal of mischief in the church, are the occasion of *envy, strife, railings, evil surmisings.* When men are not content with the words of the Lord Jesus Christ, and the doctrine which is according to godliness, but will frame notions of their own and impose them, and that too in their own words, which man's wisdom teaches, and not in the words which the Holy Ghost teaches (1 Cor. ii. 13), they sow the seeds of all mischief in the church. Hence come *perverse disputings of men of corrupt minds* (*v.* 5), disputes that are all subtlety, and no solidity. Observe, Men of corrupt minds are *destitute of the truth.* The reason why men's minds are corrupt is because they do not stick to *the truth as it is in Jesus:*

supposing that gain is godliness, making religion truckle to their secular interest. From such as these Timothy is warned to withdraw himself. We observe, 1. The words of our Lord Jesus Christ are wholesome words, they are the fittest to prevent or heal the church's wounds, as well as to heal a wounded conscience; for Christ has the tongue of the learned, to speak a word in season to him that is weary, Isa. l. 4. The words of Christ are the best to prevent ruptures in the church; for none who profess faith in him will dispute the aptness or authority of his words who is their Lord and teacher, and it has never gone well with the church since the words of men have claimed a regard equal to his words, and in some cases a much greater. 2. Whoever teaches otherwise, and does not consent to these wholesome words, he is proud, knowing nothing; for pride and ignorance commonly go together. 3. Paul sets a brand only on those who consent not to the words of our Lord Jesus Christ, and the doctrine which is according to godliness; they are proud, knowing nothing: other words more wholesome he knew not. 4. We learn the sad effects of doting about questions and strifes of words; of such doting about questions comes envy, strife, evil surmisings, and perverse disputings; when men leave the wholesome words of our Lord Jesus Christ, they will never agree in other words, either of their own or other men's invention, but will perpetually wrangle and quarrel about them; and this will produce envy, when they see the words of others preferred to those they have adopted for their own; and this will be attended with jealousies and suspicions of one another, called here *evil surmisings;* then they will proceed to perverse disputings. 5. Such persons as are given to perverse disputings appear to be men of corrupt minds, and destitute of the truth; especially such as act in this manner for the sake of gain, which is all their godliness, supposing gain to be godliness, contrary to the apostle's judgment, who reckoned godliness great gain. 6. Good ministers and Christians will withdraw themselves from such. "Come out from among them, my people, and be ye separate," says the Lord: *frôm such withdraw thyself.*

6 But godliness with contentment
is great gain. 7 For we brought
nothing into *this* world, *and it is*
certain we can carry nothing out. 8
And having food and raiment let us
be therewith content. 9 But they
that will be rich fall into temptation
and a snare, and *into* many foolish
and hurtful lusts, which drown men
in destruction and perdition. 10 For
the love of money is the root of all
evil: which while some coveted after,
they have erred from the faith, and
pierced themselves through with many
sorrows. 11 But thou, O man of
God, flee these things; and follow
after righteousness, godliness, faith,
love, patience, meekness. 12 Fight
the good fight of faith, lay hold on
eternal life, whereunto thou art also
called, and hast professed a good
profession before many witnesses.

From the mention of the abuse which some put upon religion, making it to serve their secular advantages, the apostle,

I. Takes occasion to show the excellency of contentment and the evil of covetousness.

1. The excellency of contentment, *v.* 6—8. Some account Christianity an advantageous profession for this world. In the sense they mean this is false; yet it is undoubtedly true that, though Christianity is the worst trade, it is the best calling in the world. Those that make a trade of it, merely to serve their turn for this world, will be disappointed, and find it a sorry trade; but those that mind it as their calling, and make a business of it, will find it a gainful calling, for it has the promise of the life that now is, as well as of that which is to come.

(1.) The truth he lays down is that *godliness with contentment is great gain.* Some read it, *godliness with a competency;* that is, if a man have but a little in this world, yet, if he have but enough to carry him through it, he needs desire no more, his godliness with that will be his great gain. *For a little which a righteous man has is better than the riches of many wicked,* Ps. xxxvii. 16. We read it, *godliness with contentment;* godliness is itself great gain, it is profitable to all things; and, wherever there is true godliness, there will be contentment; but those that have arrived at the highest pitch of contentment with their godliness are certainly the easiest happiest people in this world. *Godliness with contentment,* that is, Christian contentment (content must come from principles of godliness) is great gain; it is all the wealth in the world. He that is godly is sure to be happy in another world; and if withal he do by contentment accommodate himself to his condition in this world he has enough. Here we have, [1.] A Christian's gain; it is godliness with contentment, this is the true way to gain, yea, it is gain itself. [2.] A Christian's gain is great: it is not like the little gain of worldlings, who are so fond of a little worldly advantage. [3.] Godliness is ever accompanied with contentment in a greater or less degree; all truly godly people have learned with Paul, in whatever state they are, to be therewith content, Phil. iv. 11. They are content with what God allots for them, well knowing that this is best for them. Let us all then endeavour after godliness with contentment.

(2.) The reason he gives for it is, *For we brought nothing with us into this world, and it is certain we can carry nothing out, v.* 7. This is a reason why we should be content with a little. [1.] Because we can challenge nothing as a debt that is due to us, for we came naked into the world. Whatever we have had since, we are obliged to the providence of God for it; but he that gave may take what and when he pleases. We had our beings, our bodies, our lives (which are more than meat, and which are more than raiment), when we came into the world, though we came naked, and brought nothing with us; may we not then be content while our beings and lives are continued to us, though we have not every thing we would have? We brought nothing with us into this world, and yet God provided for us, care was taken of us, we have been fed all our lives long unto this day; and therefore, when we are reduced to the greatest straits, we cannot be poorer than when we came into this world, and yet then we were provided for; therefore let us trust in God for the remaining part of our pilgrimage. [2.] We shall carry nothing with us out of this world. A shroud, a coffin, and a grave, are all that the richest man in the world can have from his thousands. Therefore why should we covet much? Why should we not be content with a little, because, how much soever we have, we must leave it behind us? Eccl. v. 15, 16.

(3.) Hence he infers, *having food and raiment, let us be therewith content, v.* 8. Food and a *covering*, including habitation as well as raiment. Observe, If God give us the necessary supports of life, we ought to be content therewith, though we have not the ornaments and delights of it. If nature should be content with a little, grace should be content with less; though we have not dainty food, though we have not costly raiment, if we have but food and raiment convenient for us we ought to be content. This was Agur's prayer: *Give me neither poverty nor riches; feed me with food convenient for me*, Prov. xxx. 8. Here we see, [1.] The folly of placing our happiness in these things, when we did not bring any thing into this world with us, and we can carry nothing out. What will worldlings do when death shall strip them of their happiness and portion, and they must take an everlasting farewell of all these things, on which they have so much doted? They may say with poor Micah, *You have taken away my gods; and what have I more?* Jud. xviii. 24. [2.] The necessaries of life are the bounds of a true Christian's desire, and with these he will endeavour to be content; his desires are not insatiable; no, a little, a few comforts of this life, will serve him, and these he may hope to enjoy: *Having food and raiment.*

2. The evil of covetousness. *Those that will be rich* (that set their hearts upon the wealth of this world, and are resolved, right or wrong, they will have it) *fall into temptation and a snare, v* 9. It is not said, those that are rich, but those that will be rich, that is, that place their happiness in worldly wealth, that covet it inordinately, and are eager and violent in the pursuit of it. Those that are such *fall into temptation and a snare*, unavoidably; for, when the devil sees which way their lusts carry them, he will soon bait his hook accordingly. He knew how fond Achan would be of a wedge of gold, and therefore laid that before him. They fall into *many foolish and hurtful lusts.* Observe,

(1.) The apostle supposes that, [1.] Some will be rich; that is, they are resolved upon it, nothing short of a great abundance will satisfy. [2.] Such will not be safe nor innocent, for they will be in danger of ruining themselves for ever; they fall into temptation, and a snare, &c. [3.] Worldly lusts are foolish and hurtful, for they drown men in destruction and perdition. [4.] It is good for us to consider the mischievousness of worldly fleshly lusts. They are foolish, and therefore we should be ashamed of them, hurtful, and therefore we should be afraid of them, especialy considering to what degree they are hurtful, for they *drown men in destruction and perdition.*

(2.) The apostle affirms that *the love of money is the root of all evil, v.* 10. What sins will not men be drawn to by the love of money? Particularly this was at the bottom of the apostasy of many from the faith of Christ; while they coveted money, they *erred from the faith*, they quitted their Christianity, and *pierced themselves through with many sorrows.* Observe, [1.] What is the root of all evil; the love of money: people may have money, and yet not love it; but, if they love it inordinately, it will push them on to all evil. [2.] Covetous persons will quit the faith, if that be the way to get money: *Which while some coveted after, they have erred from the faith. Demas hath forsaken me, having loved this present world*, 2 Tim. iv. 10. For the world was dearer to him than Christianity. Observe, Those that err from the faith pierce themselves with many sorrows; those that depart from God do but treasure up sorrows for themselves.

II. Hence he takes occasion to caution Timothy, and to counsel him to keep in the way of God and his duty, and particularly to fulfil the trust reposed in him as a minister. He addresses himself to him as *a man of God.* Ministers are men of God, and ought to conduct themselves accordingly in every thing; they are men employed for God, devoted to his honour more immediately. The prophets under the Old Testament were called men of God. 1. He charges Timothy to take heed of the love of money, which had been so pernicious to many: *Flee these things.* It ill becomes any men, but especially men of God, to set their hearts upon the things of this world; men of God should be taken up with the things of God. 2. To arm him against the love of the world, he directs him to follow that which is good *Follow after righteousness, godliness, faith, love, patience, meekness*: righteousness in his conversation towards men, godliness towards God, faith and love as living principles, to support him and carry him on in the practice both of righteousness and godliness. Those that follow after righteousness and godliness, from a principle of faith and love, have need to put on patience and meekness—patience to bear both the rebukes of Providence and the reproaches of men, and meekness wherewith to instruct gainsayers and pass by the affronts and injuries that are done us. Observe, It is not enough that men of God flee these things, but they must follow after what is directly contrary thereto. Further, What excellent persons men of God are, who follow after righteousness! They are the excellent of the earth, and, being acceptable to God, they should be approved of men. 3. He exhorts him to do the part of a soldier: *Fight the good fight of faith.* Note, Those who will get to heaven must fight their way thither. There must be a conflict with corruption and temptations, and the opposition of the powers of darkness. Observe, It is a good fight, it is a good cause, and it will have a good issue. It is the fight of faith; we do not war after the flesh, for the weapons of our warfare are not carnal, 2 Cor. x. 3, 4. 4. He exhorts him to *lay hold on eternal life.* Observe, (1.) Eternal life is the crown proposed to us, for our encouragement to war, and to fight the good fight of faith, the good warfare. (2.) This we must lay hold on, as those that are afraid of coming short of it and losing it. Lay hold, and take heed of losing your hold. *Hold fast that which thou hast, that no man take thy crown,* Rev. iii. 11. (3.) We are called to the fight, and to lay hold on eternal life. (4.) The profession Timothy and all faithful ministers make before many witnesses is a good profession; for they profess and engage to fight the good fight of faith, and to lay hold on eternal life; their calling and their own profession oblige them to this.

13 I give thee charge in the sight
of God, who quickeneth all things,
and *before* Christ Jesus, who before
Pontius Pilate witnessed a good confession; 14 That thou keep *this*
commandment without spot, unre-
bukeable, until the appearing of our
Lord Jesus Christ: 15 Which in
his times he shall show, *who is* the
blessed and only Potentate, the King
of kings, and Lord of lords; 16 Who
only hath immortality, dwelling in
the light which no man can approach
unto; whom no man hath seen, nor
can see: to whom *be* honour and
power everlasting. Amen. 17 Charge
them that are rich in this world, that
they be not highminded, nor trust in
uncertain riches, but in the living
God, who giveth us richly all things
to enjoy; 18 That they do good,
that they be rich in good works, ready
to distribute, willing to communicate;
19 Laying up in store for themselves
a good foundation against the time
to come, that they may lay hold on
eternal life. 20 O Timothy, keep
that which is committed to thy trust,
avoiding profane *and* vain babblings,
and oppositions of science falsely so
called: 21 Which some professing
have erred concerning the faith. Grace
be with thee. Amen.

The apostle here charges Timothy *to keep this commandment* (that is, the whole work of his ministry, all the trust reposed in him, all the service expected from him) *without spot, unrebukable;* he must conduct himself so in his ministry that he might not lay himself open to any blame nor incur any blemish. What are the motives to move him to this?

I. He gives him a solemn charge: *I give thee charge in the sight of God that thou do this.* He charges him as he will answer it at the great day to that God whose eyes are upon us all, who sees what we are and what we do: *God, who quickens all things,* who has life in himself and is the fountain of life. This should quicken us to the service of God that we serve a God who quickens all things. He charges him before Christ Jesus, to whom in a peculiar manner he stood related as a minister of his gospel: *Who before Pontius Pilate witnessed a good confession.* Observe, Christ died not only as a sacrifice, but as a martyr; and he witnessed a good confession when he was arraigned before Pilate, saying (John xviii. 36, 37), *My kingdom is not of this world: I am come to bear witness unto the truth.* That good confession of his before Pilate, *My kingdom is not of this world,* should be effectual to draw off all his followers, both ministers and people, from the love of this world.

II. He reminds him of the confession that he himself had made: *Thou hast professed a good profession before many witnesses* (*v.* 12), namely, when he was ordained by the laying on of the hands of the presbytery. The obligation of that was still upon him, and he must live up to that, and be quickened by that, to do the work of his ministry.

III. He reminds him of Christ's second coming: "*Keep this commandment——until the appearing of our Lord Jesus Christ;* keep it as long as thou live, till Christ come at death to give thee a discharge. Keep it with an eye to his second coming, when we must all give an account of the talents we have been entrusted with," Luke xvi. 2. Observe, The Lord Jesus Christ will appear, and it will be a glorious appearing, not like his first appearing in the days of his humiliation. Ministers should have an eye to this appearing of the Lord Jesus Christ in all their ministrations, and, till his appearing, they are to keep this commandment without spot, unrebukable. Mentioning the appearing of Christ, as one that loved it, Paul loves to speak of it, and loves to speak of him who shall then appear. The appearing of Christ is certain *(he shall show it)*, but it is not for us to know the time and season of it, which the Father has kept in his own power: let this suffice us, that in time he will show it, in the time that he thinks fit for it. Observe,

1. Concerning Christ and God the Father the apostle here speaks great things. (1.) That God is the only Potentate; the powers of earthly princes are all derived from him, and depend upon him. The powers that exist are ordained of God, Rom. xiii. 1. He is the only Potentate that is absolute and sovereign, and perfectly independent. (2.) He is the blessed and the only Potentate, infinitely happy, and nothing can in the least impair his happiness. (3.) He is King of kings, and Lord of lords. All the kings of the earth derive their power from him; he gave them their crowns, they hold them under him, and he has a sovereign dominion over them. This is Christ's title (Rev. xix. 16), *upon his vesture and his thigh;* for he has a name higher than the kings of the earth. (4.) He only has immortality. He only is immortal in himself, and has immortality as he is the fountain of it, for the immortality of angels and spirits is derived from him. (5.) He dwells in inaccessible light, *light which no man can approach unto:* no man can get to heaven but those whom he is pleased to bring thither, and admit into his kingdom. (6.) He is invisible: *Whom no man hath seen, nor can see.* It is impossible that mortal eyes should bear the brightness of the divine glory. No man can see God and live.

2. Having mentioned these glorious attributes, he concludes with a doxology: *To him be honour and power everlasting. Amen.* God having all power and honour to himself, it is our duty to ascribe all power and honour to him. (1.) What an evil is sin, when committed against such a God, the blessed and only Potentate! The evil of it rises in proportion to the dignity of him against whom it is committed. (2.) Great is his condescension, to take notice of such mean and vile creatures as we are. What are we then, that the blessed God, the King of kings and Lord of lords, should seek after us? (3.) Blessed are those who are admitted to dwell with this great and blessed Potentate. *Happy are thy men* (says the queen of Sheba to king Solomon), *happy are these thy servants, who stand continually before thee,* 1 Kings x. 8. Much more happy are those who are allowed to stand before the King of kings. (4.) Let us love, adore, and praise, the great God; for *who shall not fear thee, O Lord, and glorify thy name? For thou only art holy,* Rev. xv. 4.

IV. The apostle adds, by way of postscript, a lesson for rich people, *v.* 17—19.

1. Timothy must charge those that are rich to beware of the temptations, and improve the opportunities, of their prosperous estate. (1.) He must caution them to take heed of pride. This is a sin that easily besets rich people, upon whom the world smiles. Charge them *that they be not high-minded,* or think of themselves above what is meet, or be puffed up with their wealth. (2.) He must caution them against vain confidence in their wealth. Charge them that they *trust not in uncertain riches.* Nothing is more uncertain than the wealth of this world; many have had much of it one day and been stripped of all the next. Riches make themselves wings, and fly away as an eagle, &c., Prov. xxiii. 5. (3.) He must charge them to *trust in God, the living God,* to make him their hope, *who giveth us richly all things to enjoy.* Those who are rich must see God giving them their riches, and giving them to enjoy them richly; for many have riches, but enjoy them poorly, not having a heart to use them. (4.) He must charge them to do good with what they have (for what is the best estate worth, any more than as it gives a man an opportunity of doing so much the more good?): *That they be rich in good works.* Those are truly rich who are rich in good works. That they be *ready to distribute, willing to communicate:* not only to do it, but to do it willingly, for *God loves a cheerful giver.* (5.) He must charge them to think of another world, and prepare for that which is to come by works of charity: *Laying up in store a good foundation against the time to come,* that they may take hold on eternal life.

2. Hence we may observe, (1.) Ministers must not be afraid of the rich; be they ever so rich, they must speak to them, and charge them. (2.) They must caution them against pride, and vain confidence in their riches: *That they be not high-minded, nor trust in uncertain riches.* Stir them up to works of piety and charity: *That they do good,* &c. (3.) This is the way for the rich to lay up in store for themselves for the time to come, that they may lay hold on eternal life; in the way of well-doing we are to seek for glory, honour, and immortality, *and eternal life will be the end of all,* Rom. ii. 7. (4.) Here is a lesson for ministers in the charge given to Timothy: *Keep that which is committed to thy trust.* Every minister is a trustee, and it is a treasure committed to his trust, which he has to keep. The truths of God, the ordinances of God, keep these, *avoiding profane and vain babblings;* not affecting human eloquence, which

the apostle calls vain babbling, or human learning, which often opposes the truths of God, but keep close to the written word, for that is committed to our trust. Some who have been very proud of their learning, their *science, which is falsely so called*, have by that been debauched in their principles and been drawn away from the faith of Christ, which is a good reason why we should keep to the plain word of the gospel, and resolve to live and die by that. Observe, [1.] Ministers cannot be too earnestly exhorted to keep what is committed to their trust, because it is a great trust lodged with them: *O Timothy, keep that which is committed to thy trust!* as if he had said, "I cannot conclude without charging thee again; whatever thou doest, be sure to keep this trust, for it is too great a trust to be betrayed." [2.] Ministers are to avoid babblings, if they would keep what is committed to them, because they are vain and profane. [3.] That science which opposes the truth of the gospel is falsely so called; it is not true science, for if it were it would approve of the gospel and consent to it. [4.] Those who are so fond of such science are in great danger of erring concerning the faith; those who are for advancing reason above faith are in danger of leaving faith.

V. Our apostle concludes with a solemn prayer and benediction: *Grace be with thee. Amen.* Observe, this is a short, yet comprehensive prayer for our friends, for grace comprehends in it all that is good, and grace is an earnest, yea, a beginning, of glory; for, wherever God gives grace, he will give glory, and will not withhold any good thing from him who walketh uprightly. Grace be with you all. Amen.

AN

EXPOSITION,

WITH PRACTICAL OBSERVATIONS,

OF THE SECOND EPISTLE OF ST. PAUL

TO TIMOTHY.

This second epistle Paul wrote to Timothy from Rome, when he was a prisoner there and in danger of his life; this is evident from these words, *I am now ready to be offered, and the time of my departure is at hand, ch.* iv. 6. It appears that his removal out of this world, in his own apprehension, was not far off, especially considering the rage and malice of his persecutors; and that he had been brought before the emperor Nero, which he calls *his first answer, when no man stood with him, but all men forsook him, ch.* iv. 16. And interpreters agree that this was the last epistle he wrote. Where Timothy now was is not certain. The scope of this epistle somewhat differs from that of the former, not so much relating to his office as an evangelist as to his personal conduct and behaviour.

CHAP. I.

After the introduction (ver. 1, 2) we have, I. Paul's sincere love to Timothy, ver. 3—5. II. Divers exhortations given to him, ver. 6—14. III. He speaks of Phygellus and Hermogenes, with others, and closes with Onesiphorus, ver. 15, to the end.

PAUL, an apostle of Jesus Christ
by the will of God, according to
the promise of life which is in Christ
Jesus. 2 To Timothy, *my* dearly
beloved son: Grace, mercy, *and*
peace, from God the Father and
Christ Jesus our Lord. 3 I thank
God, whom I serve from *my* forefathers with pure conscience, that
without ceasing I have remembrance
of thee in my prayers night and day;
4 Greatly desiring to see thee, being
mindful of thy tears, that I may be
filled with joy; 5 When I call to
remembrance the unfeigned faith that
is in thee, which dwelt first in thy
grandmother Lois, and thy mother
Eunice; and I am persuaded that in
thee also.

Here is, I. The inscription of the epistle. Paul calls himself *an apostle by the will of*

God, merely by the good pleasure of God, and by his grace, which he professes himself unworthy of. *According to the promise of life which is in Christ Jesus*, or according to the gospel. The gospel is the promise of life in Christ Jesus; life is the end, and Christ the way, John. xiv. 6. The life is put into the promise, and both are sure in Christ Jesus the faithful witness; *for all the promises of God in Christ Jesus are yea, and all amen*, 2 Cor. i. 20. He calls Timothy his *beloved son.* Paul felt the warmest affection for him both because he had been an instrument of his conversion and because as a son with his father he had served with him in the gospel. Observe, 1. Paul was an apostle of Jesus Christ by the will of God; as he did not receive the gospel of man, nor was taught it, but had it by the revelation of Jesus Christ (Gal. i. 12), so his commission to be an apostle was not by the will of man, but of God: in the former epistle he says it was *by the commandment of God our Saviour*, and here *by the will of God.* God called him to be an apostle. 2. We have the promise of life, blessed be God for it: *In hope of eternal life, which God, who cannot lie, promised before the world began*, Tit. i. 2. It is a promise to discover the freeness and certainty of it. 3. This, as well as all other promises, is in and through Jesus Christ; they all take their rise from the mercy of God in Christ, and they are sure, so that we may safely depend on them. 4. The grace, mercy, and peace, which even Paul's dearly beloved son Timothy wanted, comes from God the Father and Christ Jesus our Lord; and therefore the one as well as the other is the giver of these blessings, and ought to be applied to for them. 5. The best want these blessings, and they are the best we can ask for our dearly-beloved friends, that they may have grace to help them in the time of need, and mercy to pardon what is amiss, and so may have peace with God the Father and Christ Jesus our Lord.

II. Paul's thanksgiving to God for Timothy's faith and holiness: he thanks God that he remembered Timothy in his prayers. Observe, Whatever good we do, and whatever good office we perform for our friends, God must have the glory of it, and we must give him thanks. It is he who puts it into our hearts to remember such and such in our prayers. Paul was much in prayer, he prayed night and day; in all his prayers he was mindful of his friends, he particularly prayed for good ministers, he prayed for Timothy, and *had remembrance of him in his prayers night and day;* he did this without ceasing; prayer was his constant business, and he never forgot his friends in his prayers, as we often do. Paul served God from his forefathers with a pure conscience. It was a comfort to him that he was born in God's house, and was of the seed of those that served God; as likewise that he had served him with a pure conscience, according to the best of his light; he had kept a conscience void of offence, and made it his daily exercise to do so, Acts xxiv. 16. *He greatly desired to see Timothy*, out of the affection he had for him, that he might have some conversation with him, *being mindful of his tears* at their last parting. Timothy was sorry to part with Paul, he wept at parting, and therefore Paul desired to see him again, because he had perceived by that what a true affection he had for him. He thanks God that Timothy kept up the religion of his ancestors, *v.* 5. Observe, The entail of religion descended upon Timothy by the mother's side; he had a good mother, and a good grandmother: they believed, though his father did not, Acts xvi. 1. It is a comfortable thing when children imitate the faith and holiness of their godly parents, and tread in their steps, 3 John 4.—*Dwelt in thy grandmother and thy mother, and I am persuaded that in thee also.* Paul had a very charitable opinion of his friends; was very willing to hope the best concerning them; indeed he had a great deal of reason to believe well of Timothy, for he had *no man like-minded*, Phil. ii. 20. Observe, 1. We are, according to St. Paul, to serve God with a pure conscience, so did his and our pious forefathers; this is to draw *near with a true heart, in full assurance of faith, having our heart sprinkled from an evil conscience*, Heb. x. 22. 2. In our prayers we are to remember without ceasing our friends, especially the faithful ministers of Christ. Paul had remembrance of his dearly beloved son Timothy in his prayers night and day. 3. The faith that dwells in real believers is unfeigned; it is without hypocrisy, it is a faith that will stand the trial, and it dwells in them as a living principle. It was the matter of Paul's thanksgiving that Timothy inherited the faith of his mother Eunice and his grandmother Lois, and ought to be ours whenever we see the like; we should rejoice wherever we see the grace of God; so did Barnabas, Acts xi. 23, 24. *I rejoiced greatly that I found of thy children walking in the truth*, 2 John 4.

6 Wherefore I put thee in remembrance that thou stir up the gift of
God, which is in thee by the putting
on of my hands. 7 For God hath
not given us the spirit of fear; but
of power, and of love, and of a sound
mind. 8 Be not thou therefore
ashamed of the testimony of our
Lord, nor of me his prisoner: but
be thou partaker of the afflictions of
the gospel according to the power of
God; 9 Who hath saved us, and
called *us* with a holy calling, not
according to our works, but according
to his own purpose and grace, which
was given us in Christ Jesus before

the world began; 10 But is now
made manifest by the appearing of
our Saviour Jesus Christ, who hath
abolished death, and hath brought
life and immortality to light through
the gospel: 11 Whereunto I am
appointed a preacher, and an apostle,
and a teacher of the Gentiles. 12
For the which cause I also suffer
these things: nevertheless I am not
ashamed: for I know whom I have
believed, and am persuaded that he
is able to keep that which I have
committed unto him against that
day. 13 Hold fast the form of sound
words, which thou hast heard of me,
in faith and love which is in Christ
Jesus. 14 That good thing which
was committed unto thee keep by the
Holy Ghost which dwelleth in us.

Here is an exhortation and excitation of Timothy to his duty (*v.* 6): *I put thee in remembrance.* The best men need remembrancers; what we know we should be reminded of. 2 Pet. iii. 1, I write this, *to stir up your pure minds by way of remembrance.*

I. He exhorts him to stir *up the gift of God* that was *in him.* Stir it up as fire under the embers. It is meant of all the gifts and graces that God had given him, to qualify him for the work of an evangelist, the gifts of the Holy Ghost, the extraordinary gifts that were conferred by the imposition of the apostle's hands. These he must stir up; he must exercise them, and so increase them: use gifts, and have gifts. *To him that hath shall be given,* Matt. xxv. 29. He must take all opportunities to use these gifts, and so stir them up, for that is the best way of increasing them. Whether the gift of God in Timothy was ordinary or extraordinary (though I incline to the latter), he must stir it up, otherwise it would decay. Further, you see that this gift was in him by the putting on of the apostle's hands, which I take to be distinct from his ordination, for that was performed by the hands of the presbytery, 1 Tim. iv. 14. It is probable that Timothy had the Holy Ghost, in his extraordinary gifts and graces, conferred on him by the laying on of the apostle's hands (for I reckon that none but the apostles had the power of giving the Holy Ghost), and afterwards, being thus richly furnished for the work of the ministry, was ordained by the presbytery. Observe, 1. The great hindrance of usefulness in the increase of our gifts is slavish fear. Paul therefore warns Timothy against this: *God hath not given us the spirit of fear, v.* 7. It was through base fear that the evil servant buried his talent, and did not trade with it, Matt. xxv. 25. Now God hath therefore armed us against the spirit of fear, by often bidding us fear not. "Fear not the face of man; fear not the dangers you may meet with in the way of your duty." God hath delivered us from the spirit of fear, and hath given us the spirit *of power, and of love, and of a sound mind.* The spirit of power, or of courage and resolution to encounter difficulties and dangers;—the spirit of love to God, which will carry us through the opposition we may meet with, as Jacob made nothing of the hard service he was to endure for Rachel: the spirit of love to God will set us above the fear of man, and all the hurt that man can do us;—and the spirit of a sound mind, or quietness of mind, a peaceable enjoyment of ourselves, for we are oftentimes discouraged in our way and work by the creatures of our own fancy and imagination, which a sober, solid, thinking mind would obviate, and would easily answer. 2. The spirit God gives to his ministers is not a fearful, but a courageous spirit; it is a spirit of power, for they speak in his name who has all power, both in heaven and earth; and it is a spirit of love, for love to God and the souls of men must inflame ministers in all their service; and it is a spirit of a sound mind, for they speak the words of truth and soberness.

II. He exhorts him to count upon afflictions, and get ready for them: "*Be not thou therefore ashamed of the testimony of our Lord, nor of me his prisoner.* Be not thou ashamed of the gospel, of the testimony thou hast borne to it." Observe,

1. The gospel of Christ is what we have none of us reason to be ashamed of. We must not be ashamed of those who are suffering for the gospel of Christ. Timothy must not be ashamed of good old Paul, though he was now in bonds. As he must not himself be afraid of suffering, so he must not be afraid of owning those who were sufferers for the cause of Christ. (1.) The gospel is the testimony of our Lord; in and by this he bears testimony of himself to us, and by professing our adherence to it we bear testimony of him and for him. (2.) Paul was the Lord's prisoner, his prisoner, Eph. iv. 1. For his sake he was bound with a chain. (3.) We have no reason to be ashamed either of the testimony of our Lord or of his prisoners; if we are ashamed of either now, Christ will be ashamed of us hereafter. "*But be thou partaker of the afflictions of the gospel, according to the power of God,* that is, expect afflictions for the gospel's sake, prepare for them, count upon them, be willing to take thy lot with the suffering saints in this world. *Be partaker of the afflictions of the gospel;*" or, as it may be read, *Do thou suffer with the gospel;* "not only sympathize with those who suffer for it, but be ready to suffer with them and suffer like them." If at any time the gospel be in distress, he who hopes for life and salvation by it will be content to suffer with it. Observe, [1.] Then we are likely to bear

afflictions well, when we fetch strength and power from God to enable us to bear them: *Be thou partaker of the afflictions of the gospel, according to the power of God.* [2.] All Christians, but especially ministers, must expect afflictions and persecutions for the sake of the gospel. [3.] These shall be proportioned, according to the power of God (1 Cor. x. 13) resting upon us.

2. Mentioning God and the gospel, he takes notice what great things God has done for us by the gospel, *v.* 9, 10. To encourage him to suffer, he urges two considerations:—

(1.) The nature of that gospel which he was called to suffer for, and the glorious and gracious designs and purposes of it. It is usual with Paul, when he mentions Christ, and the gospel of Christ, to digress from his subject, and enlarge upon them; so full was he of that which is all our salvation, and ought to be all our desire. Observe, [1.] The gospel aims at our salvation: *He has saved us,* and we must not think much to suffer for that which we hope to be saved by. He has begun to save us, and will complete it in due time; for God calls those things that are not (that are not yet completed) as though they were (Rom. iv. 17); therefore he says, who *has* saved us. [2.] It is designed for our sanctification: *And called us with a holy calling,* called us to holiness. Christianity is a calling, a holy calling; it is the calling wherewith we are called, the calling to which we are called, to labour in it. Observe, All who shall be saved hereafter are sanctified now. Wherever the call of the gospel is an effectual call, it is found to be a holy call, making those holy who are effectually called. [3.] The origin of it is the free grace and eternal purpose of God in Christ Jesus. If we had merited it, it had been hard to suffer for it; but our salvation by it is of free grace, and not according to our works, and therefore we must not think much to suffer for it This grace is said to be given us *before the world began,* that is, in the purpose and designs of God from all eternity; *in Christ Jesus,* for all the gifts that come from God to sinful man come in and through Christ Jesus. [4.] The gospel is the manifestation of this purpose and grace: *By the appearing of our Saviour Jesus Christ,* who had lain in the bosom of the Father from eternity. and was perfectly apprised of all his gracious purposes. By his appearing this gracious purpose was made manifest to us. Did Jesus Christ suffer for it, and shall we think much to suffer for it? [5.] By the gospel of Christ death is abolished: *He has abolished death,* not only weakened it, but taken it out of the way, has broken the power of death over us; by taking away sin he has abolished death (for the sting of death is sin, 1 Cor. xv. 56), in altering the property of it, and breaking the power of it. Death now of an enemy has become a friend; it is the gate by which we pass out of a troublesome, vexatious, sinful world, into a world of perfect peace and purity; and the power thereof is broken, for death does not triumph over those who believe the gospel, but they triumph over it. *O death! where is thy sting? O grave! where is thy victory?* 1 Cor. xv. 55. [6.] He has *brought life and immortality to light by the gospel;* he has shown us another world more clearly than it was before discovered under any former dispensation, and the happiness of that world, the certain recompence of our obedience by faith: we all with open face, as in a glass, behold the glory of God. He has brought it to light, not only set it before us, but offered it to us, by the gospel. Let us value the gospel more than ever, as it is that whereby life and immortality are brought to light, for herein it has the pre-eminence above all former discoveries; so that it is the gospel of life and immortality, as it discovers them to us, and directs us in the ready way that leads thereto, as well as proposes the most weighty motives to excite our endeavours in seeking after glory, honour, and immortality.

(2.) Consider the example of blessed Paul, *v.* 11, 12. He was appointed to preach the gospel, and particularly appointed to teach the Gentiles. He thought it a cause worth suffering for, and why should not Timothy think so too? No man needs to be afraid nor ashamed to suffer for the cause of the gospel: *I am not ashamed,* says Paul, *for I know whom I have believed, and am persuaded that he is able to keep that which I have committed unto him against that day.* Observe, [1.] Good men often suffer many things for the best cause in the world: *For which cause I suffer these things;* that is, "for my preaching, and adhering to the gospel." [2.] They need not be ashamed, the cause will bear them out; but those who oppose it shall be clothed with shame. [3.] Those who trust in Christ know whom they have trusted. The apostle speaks with a holy triumph and exultation, as much as to say, "I stand on firm ground. I know I have lodged the great trust in the hands of the best trustee." *And am persuaded,* &c. What must we commit to Christ? The salvation of our souls, and their preservation to the heavenly kingdom; and what we so commit to him he will keep. There is a day coming when our souls will be enquired after: "Man! Woman! thou hadst a soul committed to thee, what hast thou done with it? To whom was it offered, to God or Satan? How was it employed, in the service of sin or in the service of Christ?" There is a day coming, and it will be a very solemn and awful day, when we must give an account of our stewardship (Luke xvi. 2), give an account of our souls: now, if by an active obedient faith we commit it to Jesus Christ, we may be sure he is able to keep it, and it shall be forthcoming to our comfort in that day.

III. He exhorts him to *hold fast the form of sound words, v.* 13. 1. "*Have* a form of sound words" (so it may be read), "a short form, a catechism, an abstract of the first principles of religion, according to the scriptures, a scheme of sound words, a brief summary of the Christian faith, in a proper method, drawn out by thyself from the holy scriptures for thy own use;" or, rather, by the form of sound words I understand the holy scriptures themselves. 2. "Having it, *hold it fast,* remember it, retain it, adhere to it. Adhere to it in opposition to all heresies and false doctrine, which corrupt the Christian faith. Hold that fast *which thou hast heard of me.*" Paul was divinely inspired. It is good to adhere to those forms of sound words which we have in the scriptures; for these, we are sure, were divinely inspired. That is sound speech, which cannot be condemned, Tit. ii. 8. But how must it be held fast? *In faith and love;* that is, we must assent to it as *a faithful saying,* and bid it welcome as *worthy of all acceptation.* Hold it fast in a good heart, this is the ark of the covenant, in which the tables both of law and gospel are most safely and profitably deposited, Ps. cxix. 11. Faith and love must go together; it is not enough to believe the sound words, and to give an assent to them, but we must love them, believe their truth and love their goodness, and we must propagate the form of sound words in love; speaking the truth in love, Eph. iv. 15. *Faith and love which are in Christ Jesus;* it must be Christian faith and love, faith and love fastening upon Jesus Christ, in and by whom God speaks to us and we to him. Timothy, as a minister, must *hold fast the form of sound words,* for the benefit of others. *Of healing words,* so it may read; there is a healing virtue in the word of God; *he sent his word, and healed them.* To the same purport is that (*v.* 14), *That good thing which was committed unto thee keep by the Holy Ghost, which dwelleth in us.* That good thing was the form of sound words, the Christian doctrine, which was committed to Timothy in his baptism and education as he was a Christian, and in his ordination as he was a minister. Observe, (1.) The Christian doctrine is a trust committed to us. It is committed to Christians in general, but to ministers in particular. It is a good thing, of unspeakable value in itself, and which will be of unspeakable advantage to us; it is a good thing indeed, it is an inestimable jewel, for it discovers to us the unsearchable riches of Christ, Eph. iii. 8. It is committed to us to be preserved pure and entire, and to be transmitted to those who shall come after us, and we must keep it, and not contribute any thing to the corrupting of its purity, the weakening of its power, or the diminishing of its perfection: *Keep it by the Holy Ghost that dwelleth in us.* Observe, Even those who are ever so well taught cannot keep what they have learned, any more than they could at first learn it, without the assistance of the Holy Spirit. We must not think to keep it by our own strength, but keep it by the Holy Ghost. (2.) The Holy Ghost dwells in all good ministers and Christians; they are his temples, and he enables them to keep the gospel pure and uncorrupt; and yet they must use their best endeavours to keep this good thing, for the assistance and indwelling of the Holy Ghost do not exclude men's endeavours, but they very well consist together.

15 This thou knowest, that all
they which are in Asia be turned
away from me; of whom are Phygellus and Hermogenes. 16 The
Lord give mercy unto the house of
Onesiphorus: for he oft refreshed
me, and was not ashamed of my
chain: 17 But, when he was in
Rome, he sought me out very diligently, and found *me.* 18 The Lord
grant unto him that he may find
mercy of the Lord in that day: and
in how many things he ministered
unto me at Ephesus, thou knowest
very well.

Having (*v.* 13, 14) exhorted Timothy to hold fast,

I. He mentions the apostasy of many from the doctrine of Christ, *v.* 15. It seems, in the best and purest ages of the church, there were those that had embraced the Christian faith, and yet afterwards revolted from it, nay, there were many such. He does not say that they had turned away from the doctrine of Christ (though it should seem they had) but they had turned away from him, they had turned their backs upon him, and disowned him in the time of his distress. And should we wonder at it, when many turned their backs on a much better than Paul? I mean the Lord Jesus Christ, John vi. 66.

II. He mentions the constancy of one that adhered to him, namely, Onesiphorus: *For he often refreshed me, and was not ashamed of my chain, v.* 16. Observe, 1. What kindness Onesiphorus had shown to Paul: he refreshed him, he often refreshed him with his letters, and counsels, and comforts, and he was not ashamed of his chains. He was not ashamed of him, notwithstanding the disgrace he was now under. He was kind to him not once or twice, but often; not only when he was at Ephesus among his own friends, but when Onesiphorus was at Rome; he took care to seek Paul *out very diligently, and found him, v.* 17. Observe, A good man will seek opportunities of doing good, and will not shun any that offer. At Ephesus he had ministered to him, and been very kind to him: Timothy knew it. 2. How Paul returns his kindness, *v.* 16—18. He that receives a prophet shall have a prophet's reward. He repays him with his prayers: *The Lord give mercy to Onesiphorus.* It is probable that Onesiphorus was now absent from home, and in company with Paul; Paul therefore prays that his house might be kept during his absence. Though the papists will have it that he was now dead; and, from Paul's praying for him that he might find mercy, they conclude the warrantableness of praying for the dead; but who told them that Onesiphorus was dead? And can it be safe to ground a doctrine and practice of such importance on a mere supposition and very great uncertainty?

III. He prays for Onesiphorus himself, as well as for his house: *That he may find mercy in that day,* in the day of death and of judgment, when Christ will account all the good offices done to his poor members as done to himself. Observe, 1. The day of death and judgment is an awful day, and may be emphatically called *that day.* 2. We need desire no more to make us happy than to find mercy of the Lord in that day, when those that have shown no mercy will have judgment without mercy. 3. The best Christians will want mercy in that day; *looking for the mercy of our Lord Jesus Christ,* Jude 21. 4. If you would have mercy then, you must seek for it now of the Lord. 5. It is of and from the Lord that we must have mercy; for, unless the Lord has mercy on us, in vain will be the pity and compassion of men or angels. 6. We are to seek and ask for mercy of the Lord, who is the giver and bestower of it; for the Lord Jesus Christ has satisfied justice, that mercy might be displayed. We are to come to a throne of grace, that we may obtain mercy, and find grace to help in the time of need. 7. The best thing we can ask, either for ourselves or our friends, is that the Lord will grant to them that they may find mercy of the Lord in that day, when they must pass out of time into eternity, and exchange this world for the other, and appear before the judgment-seat of Christ: the Lord then grant unto all of us that we may find mercy of the Lord in that day.

CHAP. II.

In this chapter our apostle gives Timothy many exhortations and directions, which may be of great use to others, both ministers and Christians, for whom they were designed as well as for him. I. He encourages him in his work, showing him whence he must fetch help, ver. 1. II. He must take care of a succession in the ministry, that the office might not die with him, ver. 2. III. He exhorts him to constancy and perseverance in this work, as a soldier and as a husbandman, considering what would be the end of all his sufferings, &c. ver. 3—15. IV. He must shun profane and vain babblings (ver. 16—18), for they will be pernicious and mischievous. V. He speaks of the foundation of God, which standeth sure, ver. 19—21. VI. What he is to avoid—youthful lusts, and foolish and unlearned questions; and what to do, ver. 22, to the end.

THOU therefore, my son, be strong
in the grace that is in Christ Jesus.
2 And the things that thou hast heard
of me among many witnesses, the same
commit thou to faithful men, who shall
be able to teach others also. 3 Thou
therefore endure hardness, as a good
soldier of Jesus Christ. 4 No man
that warreth entangleth himself with
the affairs of *this* life; that he may
please him who hath chosen him to
be a soldier. 5 And if a man also
strive for masteries, *yet* is he not
crowned, except he strive lawfully.
6 The husbandman that laboureth
must be first partaker of the fruits.
7 Consider what I say; and the Lord
give thee understanding in all things.

Here Paul encourages Timothy to constancy and perseverance in his work: *Be strong in the grace that is in Christ Jesus, v.* 1. Observe, Those who have work to do for God must stir up themselves to do it, and strengthen themselves for it. Being strong in the grace that is in Christ Jesus may be understood in opposition to the weakness of grace. Where there is the truth of grace there must be a labouring after the strength of grace. As our trials increase, we have need to grow stronger and stronger in that which is good; our faith stronger, our resolution stronger, our love to God and Christ stronger. Or it may be understood in opposition to our being strong in our own strength: "Be strong, not confiding in thy own sufficiency, but in the grace that is in Jesus Christ." Compare Eph. vi. 10, *Be strong in the Lord, and in the power of his might.* When Peter promised rather to die for Christ than to deny him he was strong in his own strength; had he been strong in the grace that is in Christ Jesus, he would have kept his standing better. Observe, 1. There is grace in Christ Jesus; for the law was given by Moses, but grace and truth came by Jesus Christ, John i. 17. There is grace enough in him for all of us. 2. We must be strong in this grace; not in ourselves, in our own strength, or in the grace we have already received, but in the grace that is in him, and that is the way to be strong in grace. 3. As a father exhorts his son, so does Paul exhort Timothy, with great tenderness and affection: *Thou, therefore, my son, be strong,* &c. Observe,

I. Timothy must count upon sufferings, even unto blood, and therefore he must train up others to succeed him in the ministry of the gospel, *v.* 2. He must instruct others, and train them up for the ministry, and so commit to them the things which he had heard; and he must also ordain them to the ministry, lodge the gospel as a trust in their hands, and so commit to them the things which he had heard. Two things he must have an eye to in ordaining ministers:—Their fidelity or integrity ("Commit them to *faithful men,* who will sincerely aim at the glory of God, the honour of Christ, the welfare of souls, and the advancement of the kingdom of the Redeemer among men"), and also their ministerial ability. They must not only be knowing themselves, but be able to teach others also, and be apt to teach. Here we have, 1. The things Timothy was to commit to others—what he had heard of the apostle among many witnesses; he must not deliver any thing besides, and what Paul delivered to him and others he had received of the Lord Jesus Christ. 2. He was to commit them as a trust, as a sacred deposit, which they were to keep, and to transmit pure and uncorrupt unto others. 3. Those to whom he was to commit these things must be faithful, that is, trusty men, and who were skilful to teach others. 4. Though men were both faithful and able to teach others, yet these things must be committed to them by Timothy, a minister, a man in office; for none must intrude themselves into the ministry, but must have these things committed to them by those already in that office.

II. He must *endure hardness* (*v.* 3): *Thou therefore,* &c. 1. All Christians, but especially ministers, *are soldiers of Jesus Christ;* they fight under his banner, in his cause, and against his enemies, for he is the captain of our salvation, Heb. ii. 10. 2. The soldiers of Jesus Christ must approve themselves good soldiers, faithful to their captain, resolute in his cause, and must not give over fighting till *they are made more than conquerors, through him that loved them,* Rom. viii. 37. 3. Those who would approve themselves good soldiers of Jesus Christ must endure hardness; that is, we must expect it and count upon it in this world, must endure and accustom ourselves to it, and bear it patiently when it comes, and not be moved by it from our integrity.

III. He must not entangle himself in the affairs of this world, *v.* 4. A soldier, when he has enlisted, leaves his calling, and all the business of it, that he may attend his captain's orders. If we have given up ourselves to be Christ's soldiers, we must sit loose to this world; and though there is no remedy, but we must employ ourselves in the affairs of this life while we are here (we have something to do here), we must not entangle ourselves with those affairs, so as by them to be diverted and drawn aside from our duty to God and the great concerns of our Christianity. Those who will war the good warfare must sit loose to this world. *That we may please him who hath chosen us to be soldiers.* Observe, 1. The great care of a soldier should be to please his general; so the great care of a Christian should be to please Christ, to approve ourselves to him. The way to please him who hath chosen us to be soldiers is not to entangle ourselves with the affairs of this life, but to be free from such entanglements as would hinder us in our holy warfare.

IV. He must see to it that in carrying on the spiritual warfare he went by rule, that he observed the laws of war (*v.* 5): *If a man strive for masteries, yet is he not crowned, except he strive lawfully.* We are striving for mastery, to get the mastery of our lusts and corruptions, to excel in that which is good, but we cannot expect the prize unless we observe the laws. In doing that which is good we must take care that we do it in a right manner, that our good may not be evil spoken of. Observe here, 1. A Christian is to strive for masteries; he must aim at mastering his own lusts and corruptions. 2. Yet he must strive according to the laws given to him; he must strive lawfully. 3. Those who do so shall be crowned at last, after a complete victory is obtained.

V. He must be willing to wait for a recompence (*v.* 6): *The husbandman that laboureth must be first partaker of the fruits.* Or, as it should be read, *The husbandman labouring first must partake of the fruits,* as appears by comparing it with Jam. v. 7. If we would be partakers of the fruits, we must labour; if we would gain the prize, we must run the race. And, further, we must first labour as the husbandman does, with diligence and patience, before we are partakers of the fruit; we must do the will of God, before we receive the promises, for which reason we have need of patience, Heb. x. 36.

The apostle further commends what he had said to the attention of Timothy, and expresses his desire and hope respecting him: *Consider what I say, and the Lord give thee understanding in all things, v.* 7. Here, 1. Paul exhorts Timothy to consider those things about which he admonished him. Timothy must be reminded to use his considering faculties about the things of God. Consideration is as necessary to a good conversation as to a sound conversion. 2. He prays for him: *The Lord give thee understanding in all things.* Observe, It is God who gives understanding. The most intelligent man needs more and more of this gift. If he who gave the revelation in the word does not give the understanding in the heart, we are nothing. Together with our prayers for others, that the Lord would give them understanding in all things, we must exhort and stir them up to consider what we say, for consideration is the way to understand, remember, and practise, what we hear or read.

8 Remember that Jesus Christ of
the seed of David was raised from
the dead according to my gospel: 9
Wherein I suffer trouble, as an evil
doer, *even* unto bonds; but the word
of God is not bound. 10 Therefore
I endure all things for the elect's
sakes, that they may also obtain the
salvation which is in Christ Jesus
with eternal glory. 11 *It is* a faithful
saying: For if we be dead with *him,*

we shall also live with *him:* 12 If
we suffer, we shall also reign with *him:*
if we deny *him,* he also will deny us:
13 If we believe not, *yet* he abideth
faithful: he cannot deny himself.

I. To encourage Timothy in suffering, the apostle puts him in mind of the resurrection of Christ (*v.* 8): *Remember that Jesus Christ, of the seed of David, was raised from the dead, according to my gospel.* This is the great proof of his divine mission, and therefore a great confirmation of the truth of the Christian religion; and the consideration of it should make us faithful to our Christian profession, and should particularly encourage us in suffering for it. Let suffering saints remember this. Observe, 1. We are to look to Jesus, the author and finisher of our faith, who, for the joy that was set before him, endured the cross, despised the shame, and has now sat down at the right hand of the throne of God, Heb. xii. 2. 2. The incarnation and resurrection of Jesus Christ, heartily believed and rightly considered, will support a Christian under all sufferings in the present life.

II. Another thing to encourage him in suffering was that he had Paul for an example. Observe,

1. How the apostle suffered (*v.* 9): *Wherein I suffer as an evil-doer;* and let not Timothy the son expect any better treatment than Paul the father. Paul was a man who did good, and yet suffered as an evil-doer: we must not think it strange if those who do well fare ill in this world, and if the best of men meet with the worst of treatment; but this was his comfort *that the word of God was not bound.* Persecuting powers may silence ministers and restrain them, but they cannot hinder the operation of the word of God upon men's hearts and consciences; that cannot be bound by any human force. This might encourage Timothy not to be afraid of bonds for the testimony of Jesus; for the word of Christ, which ought to be dearer to him than liberty, or life itself, should in the issue suffer nothing by those bonds. Here we see, (1.) The good apostle's treatment in the world: *I suffer trouble;* to this he was called and appointed. (2.) The pretence and colour under which he suffered: *I suffer as an evil-doer;* so the Jews said to Pilate concerning Christ, *If he were not a malefactor, we would not have delivered him up to thee,* John xviii. 30. (3.) The real and true cause of his suffering trouble as an evil-doer: *Wherein;* that is, in or for the sake of the gospel. The apostle suffered trouble unto bonds, and afterwards he resisted unto blood, striving against sin, Heb. xii. 4. Though the preachers of the word are often bound, yet the word is never bound.

2. Why he suffered cheerfully: *I endure all things for the elects' sake, v.* 10. Observe, (1.) Good ministers may and should encourage themselves in the hardest services and the hardest sufferings, with this, that God will certainly bring good to his church, and benefit to his elect, out of them.—*That they may obtain the salvation which is in Christ Jesus.* Next to the salvation of our own souls we should be willing to do and suffer any thing to promote the salvation of the souls of others. (2.) The elect are designed to obtain salvation: *God hath not appointed us to wrath, but to obtain salvation,* 1 Thess. v. 9. (3.) This salvation is in Christ Jesus, in him as the fountain, the purchaser, and the giver of it; and it is accompanied with eternal glory: there is no salvation in Christ Jesus without it. (4.) The sufferings of our apostle were for the elects' sake, for their confirmation and encouragement.

III. Another thing with which he encourages Timothy is the prospect of a future state.

1. Those who faithfully adhere to Christ and to his truths and ways, whatever it cost them, will certainly have the advantage of it in another world: *If we be dead with him, we shall live with him, v.* 11. If, in conformity to Christ, we be dead to this world, its pleasures, profits, and honours, we shall go to live with him in a better world, to be for ever with him. Nay, though we be called out to suffer for him, we shall not lose by that. *Those who suffer for Christ* on earth shall reign with Christ in heaven, *v.* 12. Those who suffered with David in his humiliation were preferred with him in his exaltation: so it will be with those who suffer with the Son of David.

2. It is at our peril if we prove unfaithful to him: *If we deny him, he also will deny us.* If we deny him before man, he will deny us before his Father, Matt. x. 33. And that man must needs be for ever miserable whom Christ disowns at last. This will certainly be the issue, whether we believe it or no (*v.* 13): *If we believe not, yet he abideth faithful; he cannot deny himself.* He is faithful to his threatenings, faithful to his promises; neither one nor the other shall fall to the ground, no, not the least jot nor tittle of them. If we be faithful to Christ, he will certainly be faithful to us. If we be false to him, he will be faithful to his threatenings: *he cannot deny himself,* cannot recede from any word that he hath spoken, for he is yea, and amen, the faithful witness. Observe, (1.) Our being dead with Christ precedes our living with him, and is connected with it: the one is in order to the other; so our suffering for him is the way to reign with him. *You that have followed me in the regeneration, when the Son of man shall sit on the throne of his glory, you also shall sit upon twelve thrones, judging the twelve tribes of Israel* Matt. xix. 28. (2.) This is a faithful saying, and may be depended on and ought

to be believed. But, (3.) If we deny him, out of fear, or shame, or for the sake of some temporal advantage, he will deny and disown us, and will not deny himself, but will continue faithful to his word when he threatens as well as when he promises.

14 Of these things put *them* in
remembrance, charging *them* before
the Lord that they strive not about
words to no profit, *but* to the subverting of the hearers. 15 Study to
show thyself approved unto God,
a workman that needeth not to be
ashamed, rightly dividing the word
of truth. 16 But shun profane *and*
vain babblings: for they will increase
unto more ungodliness. 17 And
their word will eat as doth a canker:
of whom is Hymenæus and Philetus;
18 Who concerning the truth have
erred, saying that the resurrection is
past already; and overthrow the faith
of some.

Having thus encouraged Timothy to suffer, he comes in the next place to direct him in his work.

I. He must make it his business to edify those who were under his charge, *to put them in remembrance* of those things which they did already know; for this is the work of ministers; not to tell people that which they never knew before, but to put them in mind of that which they do know, *charging them that they strive not about words.* Observe, Those that are disposed to strive commonly strive about matters of very small moment. Strifes of words are very destructive to the things of God. That they strive not about words *to no profit.* If people did but consider of what little use most of the controversies in religion are, they would not be so zealous in their strifes of words, *to the subverting of the hearers,* to the drawing of them away from the great things of God, and occasioning unchristian heats and animosities, by which truth is often in danger of being lost. Observe, People are very prone to strive about words, and such strifes never answer any other ends than to shake some and subvert others; they are not only useless, but they are very hurtful, and therefore ministers are to charge the people that they do not strive about words, and they are most likely to be regarded when they charge them before the Lord, that is, in his name and from his word; when they produce their warrant for what they say.—*Study to show thyself approved unto God, v.* 15. Observe, The care of ministers must be to approve themselves unto God, to be accepted of him, and to show that they are so approved unto God. In order thereunto, there must be constant care and industry: *Study to show thyself* such a one, *a workman that needs not be ashamed.* Ministers must be workmen; they have work to do, and they must take pains in it. Workmen that are unskilful, or unfaithful, or lazy, have need to be ashamed; but those who mind their business, and keep to their work, are workmen that need not be ashamed. And what is their work? It is *rightly to divide the word of truth.* Not to invent a new gospel, but rightly to divide the gospel that is committed to their trust. To speak terror to those to whom terror belongs, comfort to whom comfort; to give every one *his portion in due season,* Matt. xxiv. 45. Observe here, 1. The word which ministers preach is the word of truth, for the author of it is the God of truth. 2. It requires great wisdom, study, and care, to divide this word of truth rightly; Timothy must study in order to do this well.

II. He must take heed of that which would be a hindrance to him in his work, *v.* 16. He must take heed of error: *Shun profane and vain babblings.* The heretics, who boasted of their notions and their arguments, thought their performances such as might recommend them; but the apostle calls them *profane and vain babblings:* when once men become fond of those *they will increase unto more ungodliness.* The way of error is down-hill; one absurdity being granted or contended for, a thousand follow: *Their word will eat as doth a canker, or gangrene;* when errors or heresies come into the church, the infecting of one often proves the infecting of many, or the infecting of the same person with one error often proves the infecting of him with many errors. Upon this occasion the apostle mentions some who had lately advanced erroneous doctrines: *Hymeneus and Philetus.* He names these corrupt teachers, by which he sets a brand upon them, to their perpetual infamy, and warns all people against hearkening to them. They have *erred concerning the truth,* or concerning one of the fundamental articles of the Christian religion, which is truth. The resurrection of the dead is one of the great doctrines of Christ. Now see the subtlety of the serpent and the serpent's seed. They did not deny the resurrection (for that had been boldly and avowedly to confront the word of Christ), but they put a corrupt interpretation upon that true doctrine, saying that the resurrection was past already, that what Christ spoke concerning the resurrection was *to be understood mystically* and by way of allegory, that it must be meant of a spiritual resurrection only. It is true, there is a spiritual resurrection, but to infer thence that there will not be a true and real resurrection of the body at the last day is to dash one truth of Christ in pieces against another. By this they *overthrew the faith of some,* took them off from the belief of the resurrection of the dead; and if there be no resurrection of the dead, no future state, no recompence of our services and sufferings in another world, we are of all men the most miserable, 1 Cor. xv. 19. Whatever takes away the doctrine of a future state overthrows the faith of Christians. The apostle had largely disproved this error (1 Cor. xv.), and therefore does not here enter into the arguments against it. Observe, 1. The babblings Timothy was to shun were profane and vain; they were empty shadows, and led to profaneness: *For they will increase unto more ungodliness.* 2. Error is very productive, and on that account the more dangerous: it *will eat like a gangrene.* 3. When men err concerning the truth, they always endeavour to have some plausible pretence for it. Hymeneus and Philetus did not deny a resurrection, but pretended it was already past. 4. Error, especially that which affects the foundation, will overthrow the faith of some.

19 Nevertheless the foundation of God standeth sure, having this seal, The Lord knoweth them that are his. And, Let every one that nameth the name of Christ depart from iniquity. 20 But in a great house there are not only vessels of gold and silver, but also of wood and earth; and some to honour, and some to dishonour. 21 If a man therefore purge himself from these, he shall be a vessel unto honour, sanctified, and meet for the master's use, *and* prepared unto every good work.

Here we see what we may comfort ourselves with, in reference to this, and the little errors and heresies that both infect and infest the church, and do mischief.

I. It may be a great comfort to us that the unbelief of men cannot make the promise of God of no effect. Though the faith of some particular persons be overthrown, yet *the foundation of God standeth sure* (*v.* 19); it is not possible that they should deceive the elect. Or it may be meant of the truth itself, which they impugn. All the attacks which the powers of darkness have made upon the doctrine of Christ cannot shake it; it stands firm, and weathers all the storms which have been raised against it. The prophets and apostles, that is, the doctrines of the Old and New Testament, are still firm; and they have a seal with two mottoes upon it, one on the one side, and the other on the other, as is usual in a broad seal. 1. One expresses our comfort—that *the Lord knows those that are his,* and those that are not; knows them, that is, he owns them, so knows them that he will never lose them. Though the faith of some be overthrown, yet the Lord is said to know the ways of the righteous, Ps. i. 6. None can overthrow the faith of any whom God hath chosen. 2. Another declares our duty—that every one who names the name of Christ must depart from iniquity. Those who would have the comfort of the privilege must make conscience of the duty. If the name of Christ be called upon us, we must depart from iniquity, else he will not own us; he will say in the great day (Matt. vii. 23), *Depart from me, I never knew you, you workers of iniquity.* Observe, (1.) Whatever errors are introduced into the church, the foundation of God standeth sure, his purpose can never be defeated. (2.) God hath some in the church who are his and whom he knows to be his. (3.) Professing Christians name the name of Christ, are called by his name, and therefore are bound to depart from iniquity; for Christ *gave himself for us, that he might redeem us from all iniquity,* Tit. ii. 14.

II. Another thing that may comfort us is that though there are some whose faith is overthrown, yet there are others who keep their integrity, and hold it fast (*v.* 20): *In a great house there are not only vessels of gold,* &c. The church of Christ is a great house, a well-furnished house: now some of the furniture of this house is of great value, as the plate in a house; some of small value, and put to mean uses, as the vessels of wood and earth; so it is in the church of God. There are some professors of religion that are like the vessels of wood and earth, they are vessels of dishononr. But at the same time all are not vessels of dishonour; there are *vessels of gold and silver,* vessels of honour, *that are sanctified and meet for the Master's use.* When we are discouraged by the badness of some, we must encourage ourselves by the consideration of the goodness of others. Now we should see to it that we be vessels of honour: we must *purge ourselves from these corrupt opinions,* that we may be sanctified for our Master's use. Observe, 1. In the church there are some vessels of honour and some of dishonour; there are some vessels of mercy and other vessels of wrath, Rom. ix. 22, 23. Some dishonour the church by their corrupt opinions and wicked lives; and others honour and credit it by their exemplary conversation. 2. A man must purge himself from these before he can be a vessel of honour, or meet for his Master's use. 3. Every vessel must be fit for its Master's use; every one in the church whom God approves must be devoted to his Master's service and meet for his use. 4. Sanctification in the heart is our preparation for every good work. The tree must be made good, and then the fruit will be good.

22 Flee also youthful lusts: but follow righteousness, faith, charity, peace, with them that call on the Lord out of a pure heart. 23 But foolish and unlearned questions avoid, knowing that they do gender strifes. 24 And the servant of the Lord must

not strive; but be gentle unto all *men*, apt to teach, patient, 25 In meekness instructing those that oppose themselves; if God peradventure will give them repentance to the acknowledging of the truth; 26 And *that* they may recover themselves out of the snare of the devil, who are taken captive by him at his will.

I. Paul here exhorts Timothy to beware of *youthful lusts, v.* 22. Though he was a holy good man, very much mortified to the world, yet Paul thought it necessary to caution him against youthful lusts: "*Flee* them, take all possible care and pains to keep thyself pure from them." The lusts of the flesh are youthful lusts, which young people must carefully watch against, and the best must not be secure. He prescribes an excellent remedy against youthful lusts: *Follow righteousness, faith, charity, peace,* &c. Observe, 1. Youthful lusts are very dangerous, for which reason even hopeful young people should be warned of them, for they war against the soul, 1 Pet. ii. 11. 2. The exciting of our graces will be the extinguishing of our corruptions; the more we follow that which is good the faster and the further we shall flee from that which is evil. Righteousness, and faith, and love, will be excellent antidotes against youthful lusts. Holy love will cure impure lust.—*Follow peace with those that call on the Lord.* The keeping up of the communion of saints will take us off from all fellowship with unfruitful works of darkness. See the character of Christians: they are such as *call on the Lord Jesus Christ, out of a pure heart.* Observe, Christ is to be prayed to. It is the character of all Christians that they call upon him; but our prayers to God and Christ are not acceptable nor successful except they come out of a pure heart.

II. He cautions him against contention, and, to prevent this (*v.* 23), cautions him against *foolish and unlearned questions,* that tend to no benefit, strifes of words. Those who advanced them, and doted upon them, thought themselves wise and learned; but Paul calls them foolish and unlearned. The mischief of these is that they *gender strifes,* that they breed debates and quarrels among Christians and ministers. It is very remarkable how often, and with what seriousness, the apostle cautions Timothy against disputes in religion, which surely was not without some such design as this, to show us that religion consists more in believing and practising what God requires than in subtle disputes.—*The servant of the Lord must not strive, v.* 24. Nothing worse becomes the servant of the Lord Jesus, who himself did not strive nor cry (Matt. xii. 19), but was a pattern of meekness, and mildness, and gentleness to all, than strife and contention. The servant of the Lord must be *gentle to all men,* and thereby show that he is himself subject to the commanding power of that holy religion which he is employed in preaching and propagating.—*Apt to teach.* Those are unapt to teach who are apt to strive, and are fierce and froward. Ministers must be patient, bearing with evil, and *in meekness instructing* (*v.* 25) not only those who subject themselves, but those who oppose themselves. Observe, 1. Those who oppose themselves to the truth are to be instructed; for instruction is the scripture-method of dealing with the erroneous, which is more likely to convince them of their errors than fire and faggot: he does not bid us kill their bodies, under pretence of saving their souls. 2. Such as oppose themselves are to be instructed in meekness, for our Lord is meek and lowly (Matt. xi. 29), and this agrees well with the character of the servant of the Lord (*v.* 24): *He must not strive, but be gentle to all men, apt to teach, patient.* This is the way to convey truth in its light and power, and to overcome evil with good, Rom. xii. 21. 3. That which ministers must have in their eyes, in instructing those who oppose themselves, must be their recovery: *If God, peradventure, will give them repentance to the acknowledging of the truth.* Observe, (1.) Repentance is God's gift. (2.) It is a gift with a *peradventure* in the case of those who oppose themselves; and therefore, though we are not to despair of the grace of God, yet we must take heed of presuming upon it. *To the acknowledging of the truth.* (3.) The same God who gives us the discovery of the truth does by his grace bring us to the acknowledging of it, otherwise our hearts would continue in rebellion against it, for we are to confess with our mouths as well as to believe with our hearts, Rom. x. 9, 10. And thus sinners recover themselves out of the snare of the devil; see here, [1.] The misery of sinners: they are in the *snare of the devil, and are led captive by him at his will, v.* 26 They are slaves to the worst of task-masters; he is the spirit that now worketh in the children of disobedience, Eph. ii. 2. They are taken in a snare, and in the worst snare, because it is the devil's; they are as fishes that are taken in an evil net, and as the birds that are caught in the snare. Further, They are under Ham's curse (*a servant of servants shall he be,* Gen. ix. 25), they are slaves to him who is but a slave and vassal. [2.] The happiness of those who repent: they recover themselves out of this snare, as a bird out of the snare of the fowler; the snare is broken, and they have escaped; and the greater the danger the greater the deliverance. When sinners repent, those who before were led captive by the devil at his will come to be led into the glorious liberty of the children of God, and have their wills melted into the will of the Lord Jesus. The good Lord recover us all out of the snare.

CHAP. III.

I. The apostle forewarns Timothy what the last days would be, with the reasons thereof, ver. 1—9. II. Prescribes various remedies against them (ver. 10, to the end), particularly his own example ("But thou hast fully known my doctrine," &c.) and the knowledge of the holy scriptures, which are able to make us wise unto salvation, and will be the best antidote against the corruptions of the times we live in. In this chapter Paul tells Timothy how bad others would be, and therefore how good he should be; and this use we should make of the badness of others, thereby to engage us to hold our own integrity so much the firmer.

THIS know also, that in the last
days perilous times shall come.
2 For men shall be lovers of their
own selves, covetous, boasters, proud,
blasphemers, disobedient to parents,
unthankful, unholy, 3 Without natural affection, trucebreakers, false
accusers, incontinent, fierce, despisers
of those that are good, 4 Traitors,
heady, highminded, lovers of pleasures more than lovers of God; 5
Having a form of godliness, but
denying the power thereof: from
such turn away. 6 For of this sort
are they which creep into houses,
and lead captive silly women laden
with sins, led away with divers lusts,
7 Ever learning, and never able to
come to the knowledge of the truth.
8 Now as Jannes and Jambres withstood Moses, so do these also resist
the truth: men of corrupt minds,
reprobate concerning the faith. 9
But they shall proceed no further:
for their folly shall be manifest unto
all *men*, as their's also was.

Timothy must not think it strange if there were in the church bad men; for the net of the gospel was to enclose both good fish and bad, Matt. xiii. 47, 48. Jesus Christ had foretold (Matt. xxiv.) that there would come seducers, and therefore we must not be offended at it, nor think the worse of religion or the church for it. Even in gold ore there will be dross, and a great deal of chaff among the wheat when it lies on the floor.

I. Timothy must know that in the *last days* (*v.* 1), in gospel times, there would *come perilous times*. Though gospel times were times of reformation in many respects, let him know that even in gospel times there would be perilous times; not so much on account of persecution from without as on account of corruptions within. These would be difficult times, wherein it would be difficult for a man to keep a good conscience. He does not say, "Perilous times shall come, for both Jews and Gentiles shall be combined to root out Christianity;" but "perilous times shall come, for such as have *the form of godliness* (*v.* 5) shall be corrupt and wicked, and do a great deal of damage to the church." Two traitors within the garrison may do more hurt to it than two thousand besiegers without. Perilous times shall come, for men shall be wicked. Note, 1. Sin makes the times perilous. When there is a general corruption of manners, and of the tempers of men, this makes the times dangerous to live in; for it is hard to keep our integrity in the midst of general corruption. 2. The coming of perilous times is an evidence of the truth of scripture-predictions; if the event in this respect did not answer to the prophecy, we might be tempted to question the divinity of the Bible. 3. We are all concerned to know this, to believe and consider it, that we may not be surprised when we see the times perilous: *This know also.*

II. Paul tells Timothy what would be the occasion of making these times perilous, or what shall be the marks and signs whereby these times may be known, *v.* 2, &c. 1. Self-love will make the times perilous. Who is there who does not love himself? But this is meant of an irregular sinful self-love. Men love their carnal selves better than their spiritual selves. Men love to gratify their own lusts, and make provision for them, more than to please God and do their duty. Instead of Christian charity, which takes care for the good of others, they will mind themselves only, and prefer their own gratification before the church's edification. 2. Covetousness. Observe, Self-love brings in a long train of sins and mischiefs. When men are lovers of themselves, no good can be expected from them, as all good may be expected from those who love God with all their hearts. When covetousness generally prevails, when every man is for what he can get and for keeping what he has, this makes men dangerous to one another, and obliges every man to stand on his guard against his neighbour. 3. Pride and vain-glory. The times are perilous when men, being proud of themselves, are *boasters and blasphemers*, boasters before men whom they despise and look upon with scorn, and blasphemers of God and of his name. When men do not fear God they will not regard man, and so *vice versâ*. 4. When children are disobedient to their parents, and break through the obligations which they lie under to them both in duty and gratitude, and frequently in interest, having their dependence upon them and their expectation from them, they make the times perilous; for what wickedness will those stick at who will be abusive to their own parents and rebel against them? 5. Unthankfulness and unholiness make the times perilous, and these two commonly go together. What is the reason that men are unholy and without the fear of God, but that they are unthankful for the mercies of God? Ingratitude and impiety go together; for call a man ungrateful, and you can call him by no worse name. Unthankful, and impure, defiled with fleshly lusts, which is an instance of great ingratitude to that God who has provided so well for the support of the body; we abuse his gifts, if we make them the food and fuel of our lusts. 6. The times are perilous when men will not be held by the bonds either of nature or common honesty, when they are *without natural affection,* and *truce-breakers, v.* 3. There is a natural affection due to all. Wherever there is the human nature, there should be humanity towards those of the same nature, but especially between relations. Times are perilous when children are disobedient to their parents (*v.* 2) and when parents are without natural affection to their children, *v.* 3. See what a corruption of nature sin is, how it deprives men even of that which nature has implanted in them for the support of their own kind; for the natural affection of parents to their children is that which contributes very much to the keeping up of mankind upon the earth. And those who will not be bound by natural affection, no marvel that they will not be bound by the most solemn leagues and covenants. *They are truce-breakers,* that make no conscience of the engagements they have laid themselves under. 7. The times are perilous when men are *false accusers* one of another, *διάβολοι—devils* one to another, having no regard to the good name of others, or to the religious obligations of an oath, but thinking themselves at liberty to say and do what they please, Ps. xii. 4. 8. When men have no government of themselves and their own appetites: not of their own appetites, for they are *incontinent;* not of their own passions, for they are *fierce;* when they have no rule over their own spirits, and therefore are like a city that is broken down, and has no walls; they are soon fired, upon the least provocation. 9. When that which is good and ought to be honoured is generally despised and looked upon with contempt. It is the pride of persecutors that they look with contempt upon good people, though they are more excellent than their neighbours. 10. When men are generally treacherous, wilful, and haughty, the times are perilous (*v.* 4)—when men are *traitors, heady, high-minded.* Our Saviour has foretold that the brother shall betray the brother to death and the father the child (Matt. x. 21), and those are the worst sort of traitors: those who delivered up their Bibles to persecutors were called *traditores,* for they betrayed the trust committed to them. When men are petulant and puffed up, behaving scornfully to all about them, and when this temper generally prevails, then the times are perilous. 11. When men are generally *lovers of pleasure more than lovers of God.* When there are more epicures than true Christians, then the times are bad indeed. God is to be loved above all. That is a carnal mind, and is full of enmity against him, which prefers any thing before him, especially such a sordid thing as carnal pleasure is. 12. When, notwithstanding all this, they *have the form of godliness* (*v.* 5), are called by the Christian name, baptized into the Christian faith, and make a show of religion; but, how plausible soever their form of godliness is, they deny the power of it. When they take upon them the form which should and would bring along with it the power thereof, they will put asunder what God hath joined together: they will assume the form of godliness, to take away their reproach; but they will not submit to the power of it, to take away their sin. Observe here, (1.) Men may be very bad and wicked under a profession of religion; they may be lovers of themselves, &c., yet have a form of godliness. (2.) A form of godliness is a very different thing from the power of it; men may have the one and be wholly destitute of the other; yea, they deny it, at least practically in their lives. (3.) From such good Christians must withdraw themselves.

III. Here Paul warns Timothy to take heed of certain seducers, not only that he might not be drawn away by them himself, but that he might arm those who were under his charge against their seduction. 1. He shows how industrious they were to make proselytes (*v.* 6): they applied themselves to particular persons, visited them in their houses, not daring to appear openly; for those that do evil hate the light, John iii. 20. They were not forced into houses, as good Christians often were by persecution; but they of choice crept into houses, to insinuate themselves into the affections and good opinion of people, and so to draw them over to their party. And see what sort of people those were that they gained, and made proselytes of; they were such as were weak, *silly women;* and such as were wicked, *laden with sins, and led away with divers lusts.* A foolish head and a filthy heart make persons, especially women, an easy prey to seducers. 2. He shows how far they were from coming to the knowledge of the truth, though they pretended to be *ever learning, v.* 7. In one sense we must all be ever learning, that is, growing in knowledge, following on to know the Lord, pressing forward; but these were sceptics, giddy and unstable, who were forward to imbibe every new notion, under pretence of advancement in knowledge, but never came to a right understanding of the truth as it is in Jesus. 3. He foretels the certain stop that should be put to their progress (*v.* 8, 9), comparing them to the Egyptian magicians who withstood Moses, and who are here named, *Jannes* and *Jambres;* though the names are not to be met with in the story of the Old Testament, yet they are found in some old Jewish writers. When Moses came with a divine command to fetch Israel out of Egypt, these magicians opposed him. Thus those heretics *resisted the truth* and like them were men *of corrupt minds,* men who had their understandings perverted, biassed and prejudiced against the truth, and *reprobate concerning the faith,* or very far from being true Christians; *but they shall proceed no further,* or not much further, as some read it. Observe, (1.) Seducers seek for corners, and love obscurity; for they are afraid to appear in public, and therefore creep into houses. Further, They attack those who are the least able to defend themselves, silly and wicked women. (2.) Seducers in all ages are much alike. Their characters are the same—namely, *Men of corrupt minds,* &c.; their conduct is much the same—they resist the truth, as Jannes and Jambres withstood Moses; and they will be alike in their disappointment. (3.) Those who resist the truth are guilty of folly, yea, of egregious folly; for *magna est veritas, et prævalebit—Great is the truth, and shall prevail.* (4.) Though the spirit of error may be let loose for a time, God has it in a chain. Satan can deceive the nations and the churches no further and no longer than God will permit him: *Their folly shall be manifest,* it shall appear that they are impostors, and every man shall abandon them.

10 But thou hast fully known my
doctrine, manner of life, purpose, faith,
longsuffering, charity, patience, 11
Persecutions, afflictions, which came
unto me at Antioch, at Iconium, at
Lystra; what persecutions I endured:
but out of *them* all the Lord delivered
me. 12 Yea, and all that will live
godly in Christ Jesus shall suffer
persecution. 13 But evil men and
seducers shall wax worse and worse,
deceiving, and being deceived. 14
But continue thou in the things
which thou hast learned and hast
been assured of, knowing of whom
thou hast learned *them;* 15 And
that from a child thou hast known
the holy scriptures, which are able to
make thee wise unto salvation through
faith which is in Christ Jesus. 16
All scripture *is* given by inspiration
of God, and *is* profitable for doctrine,
for reproof, for correction, for instruction in righteousness: 17 That the
man of God may be perfect, thoroughly
furnished unto all good works.

Here the apostle, to confirm Timothy in that way wherein he walked,

I. Sets before him his own example, which Timothy had been an eye-witness of, having long attended Paul (*v.* 10): *Thou hast fully known my doctrine.* The more fully we know the doctrine of Christ and the apostles, the more closely we shall cleave to it; the reason why many sit loose to it is because they do not fully know it. Christ's apostles had no enemies but those who did not know them, or not know them fully; those who knew them best loved and honoured them the most. Now what is it that Timothy had so fully known in Paul? 1. The doctrine that he preached. Paul kept back nothing from his hearers, but declared to them the whole counsel of God (Acts xx. 27), so that if it were not their own fault they might fully know it. Timothy had a great advantage in being trained up under such a tutor, and being apprised of the doctrine he preached. 2. He had fully known his conversation: *Thou hast fully known my doctrine, and manner of life;* his manner of life was of a piece with his doctrine, and did not contradict it. He did not pull down by his living what he built up by his preaching. Those ministers are likely to do good, and leave lasting fruits of their labours, whose manner of life agrees with their doctrine; as, on the contrary, those cannot expect to profit the people at all that preach well and live ill. 3. Timothy fully knew what was the great thing that Paul had in view, both in his preaching and in his conversation: "Thou hast known *my purpose,* what I drive at, how far it is from any worldly, carnal, secular design, and how sincerely I aim at the glory of God and the good of the souls of men." 4. Timothy fully knew Paul's good character, which he might gather from his doctrine, manner of life, and purpose; for he gave proofs of his *faith* (that is, of his integrity and fidelity, or his faith in Christ, his faith concerning another world, by which Paul lived), his *long-suffering* towards the churches to which he preached and over which he presided, his *charity* towards all men, and his *patience.* These were graces that Paul was eminent for, and Timothy knew it. 5. He knew that he had suffered ill for doing well (*v.* 11): "Thou hast fully known the *persecutions and afflictions that came unto me*" (he mentions those only which happened to him while Timothy was with him, *at Antioch, at Iconium, at Lystra);* "and therefore let it be no surprise to thee if thou suffer hard things, it is no more than I have endured before." 6. He knew what care God had taken of him: *Notwithstanding out of them all the Lord delivered me;* as he never failed his cause, so his God never failed him. Thou hast fully known my *afflictions.* When we know the afflictions of good people but in part, they are a temptation to us to decline that cause which they suffer for; when we know only the hardships they undergo for Christ, we may be ready to say, "We will renounce that cause that is likely to cost us so dear in the owning of it;" but when we *fully* know the afflictions, not only how they suffer, but how they are supported and comforted under their sufferings, then, instead of being discouraged, we shall be animated by them, especially considering that we are told before that we must count upon such things (*v.* 12): *All that will live godly in Christ Jesus shall suffer persecution:*

not always alike; at that time those who professed the faith of Christ were more exposed to persecution than at other times; but at all times, more or less, those who will live godly in Christ Jesus shall suffer persecution. They must expect to be despised, and that their religion will stand in the way of their preferment; those who will live godly must expect it, especially those who will live godly *in Christ Jesus,* that is, according to the strict rules of the Christian religion, those who will wear the livery and bear the name of the crucified Redeemer. All who will show their religion in their conversation, who will not only be godly, but live godly, let them expect persecution, especially when they are resolute in it. Observe, (1.) The apostle's life was very exemplary for three things. for his *doctrine,* which was according to the will of God; for his *life,* which was agreeable to his doctrine; and for his *persecutions and sufferings.* (2.) Though his life was a life of great usefulness, yet it was a life of great sufferings; and none, I believe, came nearer to their great Master for eminent services and great sufferings than Paul: he suffered almost in every place; the Holy Ghost witnessed that bonds and afflictions did abide him, Acts xx. 23. Here he mentions his persecutions and afflictions at *Antioch,* at *Iconium,* at *Lystra,* besides what he suffered elsewhere. (3.) The apostle mentions the Lord's delivering him out of them all, for Timothy's and our encouragement under sufferings. (4.) We have the practice and treatment of true Christians: they live godly in Jesus Christ—this is their practice; and they shall suffer persecution—this is the usage they must expect in this world.

II. He warns Timothy of the fatal end of seducers, as a reason why he should stick closely to the truth as it is in Jesus: *But evil men and seducers shall wax worse and worse,* &c., *v.* 13. Observe, As good men, by the grace of God, grow better and better, so bad men, through the subtlety of Satan and the power of their own corruptions, grow worse and worse. The way of sin is down-hill; for such proceed from bad to worse, *deceiving and being deceived.* Those who deceive others do but deceive themselves; those who draw others into error run themselves into more and more mistakes, and they will find it so at last, to their cost.

III. He directs him to keep close to a good education, and particularly to what he had learned out of the holy scriptures (*v.* 14, 15): *Continue thou in the things which thou hast learned.* Note, It is not enough to learn that which is good, but we must continue in it, and persevere in it unto the end. Then are we Christ's disciples indeed, John viii. 31. We should not be any more *children, tossed to and fro, and carried about with every wind of doctrine, by the sleight of men and cunning craftiness, whereby they lie in wait to deceive,* Eph. iv. 14. *Be not carried about with divers and strange doctrines; for it is a good thing that the heart be established with grace,* Heb. xiii. 9. And for this reason we should continue in the things we have learned from the holy scriptures; not that we ought to continue in any errors and mistakes which we may have been led into, in the time of our childhood and youth (for these, upon an impartial enquiry and full conviction, we should forsake); but this makes nothing against our continuing in those things which the holy scriptures plainly assert, and which he that runs may read. If Timothy would adhere to the truth as he had been taught it, this would arm him against the snares and insinuations of seducers. Observe, Timothy must *continue in the things which he had learned and had been assured of.*

1. It is a great happiness to know the certainty of the things wherein we have been instructed (Luke i. 4); not only to know what the truths are, but to know that they are of undoubted certainty. What we have learned we must labour to be more and more assured of, that, being grounded in the truth, we may be guarded against error, for certainty in religion is of great importance and advantage: *Knowing,* (1.) "That thou hast had good teachers. Consider of *whom thou hast learned them;* not of evil men and seducers, but good men, who had themselves experienced the power of the truths they taught thee, and been ready to suffer for them, and thereby would give the fullest evidence of their belief of these truths." (2.) "Knowing especially the firm foundation upon which thou hast built, namely, that of the scripture (*v.* 15): *That from a child thou hast known the holy scriptures.*

2. Those who would acquaint themselves with the things of God, and be assured of them, must know the holy scriptures, for these are the summary of divine revelation.

3. It is a great happiness to know the holy scriptures from our childhood; and children should betimes get the knowledge of the scriptures. The age of children is the learning age; and those who would get true learning must get it out of the scriptures.

4. The scriptures we are to know are the holy scriptures; they come from the holy God, were delivered by holy men, contain holy precepts, treat of holy things, and were designed to make us holy and to lead us in the way of holiness to happiness; being called the *holy scriptures,* they are by this distinguished from profane writings of all sorts, and from those that only treat of morality, and common justice and honesty, but do not meddle with holiness. If we would know the holy scriptures, we must read and search them daily, as the noble Bereans did, Acts xvii. 11. They must not lie by us neglected, and seldom or never looked into. Now here observe,

(1.) What is the excellency of the scripture. It is *given by inspiration of God* (*v.* 16), and therefore is his word. It is a divine revelation, which we may depend upon as infallibly true. The same Spirit that breathed reason into us breathes revelation among us: *For the prophecy came not in old time by the will of man, but holy men spoke as they were moved or carried forth by the Holy Ghost,* 2 Pet. i. 21 The prophets and apostles did not speak from themselves, but what they received of the Lord that they delivered unto us. That the scripture was given by inspiration of God appears from the majesty of its style,—from the truth, purity, and sublimity, of the doctrines contained in it,—from the harmony of its several parts,—from its power and efficacy on the minds of multitudes that converse with it,—from the accomplishment of many prophecies relating to things beyond all human foresight,—and from the uncontrollable miracles that were wrought in proof of its divine original: *God also bearing them witness, both with signs and wonders, and with divers miracles and gifts of the Holy Ghost, according to his own will,* Heb. ii. 4.

(2.) What use it will be of to us. [1.] *It is able to make us wise to salvation;* that is, it is a sure guide in our way to eternal life. Note, Those are wise indeed who are wise to salvation. The scriptures are able to make us truly wise, wise for our souls and another world. "To make thee wise to salvation *through faith.*" Observe, The scriptures will make us wise to salvation, if they be mixed with faith, and not otherwise, Heb. iv. 2. For, if we do not believe their truth and goodness, they will do us no good. [2.] It is *profitable* to us for all the purposes of the Christian life, *for doctrine, for reproof, for correction, for instruction in righteousness.* It answers all the ends of divine revelation. It instructs us in that which is true, reproves us for that which is amiss, directs us in that which is good. It is of use to all, for we all need to be instructed, corrected, and reproved: it is of special use to ministers, who are to give instruction, correction, and reproof; and whence can they fetch it better than from the scripture? [3.] *That the man of God may be perfect, v.* 17. The Christian, the minister, is the man of God. That which finishes a man of God in this world is the scripture. By it we are *thoroughly furnished for every good work.* There is that in the scripture which suits every case. Whatever duty we have to do, whatever service is required from us, we may find enough in the scriptures to furnish us for it.

(3.) On the whole we here see, [1.] That the scripture has various uses, and answers divers ends and purposes: *It is profitable for doctrine, for reproof, for correction* of all errors in judgment and practice, and *for instruction in righteousness.* [2.] The scripture is a perfect rule of faith and practice, and was designed for the man of God, the minister as well as the Christian who is devoted to God, for it is *profitable for doctrine,* &c. [3.] If we consult the scripture, which was given by inspiration of God, and follow its directions, we shall be made men of God, *perfect, and thoroughly furnished to every good work.* [4.] There is no occasion for the writings of the philosopher, nor for rabbinical fables, nor popish legends, nor unwritten traditions, to make us perfect men of God, since the scripture answers all these ends and purposes. O that we may love our Bibles more, and keep closer to them than ever! and then shall we find the benefit and advantage designed thereby, and shall at last attain the happiness therein promised and assured to us.

CHAP. IV.

In this chapter, I. Paul with great solemnity and earnestness presses Timothy to the diligent and conscientious discharge of his work and office as an evangelist; and the charge given to him all gospel ministers are to take to themselves, ver. 1—5. II. The reason of his concern in this case, Why must Timothy now be instant in season, &c., in a particular manner? Because the church was likely to be deprived of the apostle's labours, for his departure was at hand, ver. 6—8. III. Divers particular matters, with a hint and caution, about Alexander the coppersmith, ver. 9—15. IV. He informs him of what befel him at his first answer; though men forsook him, the Lord stood by him, and this encouraged him to hope for future deliverance, ver. 16—18. And then he concludes with salutations and a benediction, ver. 19, to the end.

I CHARGE *thee* therefore before
God, and the Lord Jesus Christ,
who shall judge the quick and the
dead at his appearing and his kingdom; 2 Preach the word; be instant
in season, out of season; reprove, rebuke, exhort with all longsuffering and
doctrine. 3 For the time will come
when they will not endure sound
doctrine; but after their own lusts
shall they heap to themselves teachers, having itching ears; 4 And they
shall turn away *their* ears from the
truth, and shall be turned unto fables.
5 But watch thou in all things, endure
afflictions, do the work of an evangelist, make full proof of thy ministry.
6 For I am now ready to be offered,
and the time of my departure is at
hand. 7 I have fought a good fight,
I have finished *my* course, I have kept
the faith: 8 Henceforth there is
laid up for me a crown of righteousness, which the Lord, the righteous
judge, shall give me at that day: and
not to me only, but unto all them
also that love his appearing.

Observe, I. How awfully this charge is introduced (*v.* 1): *I charge thee before God, and the Lord Jesus Christ, who shall judge the quick and the dead at his appearing and his kingdom.* Observe, The best of men have need to be awed into the discharge of their duty. The work of a minister is not an indifferent thing, but absolutely necessary. Woe be to him if he preach not the gospel, 1 Cor. ix. 16. To induce him to faithfulness, he must consider, 1. That the eye of God and Jesus Christ was upon him: *I charge thee before God and the Lord Jesus Christ;* that is, "as thou tenderest the favour of God and Jesus Christ; as thou wilt approve thyself to God and Jesus Christ, by the obligations both of natural and revealed religion; as thou wilt make due returns to the God who made thee and the Lord Jesus Christ who redeemed thee." 2. He charges him as he will answer it at the great day, reminding him of the judgment to come, which is committed to the Lord Jesus. He shall judge the quick and the dead *at his appearing and his kingdom,* that is, when he appears in his kingdom. It concerns all, both ministers and people, seriously to consider the account that they must shortly give to Jesus Christ of all the trusts reposed in them. Christ shall *judge the quick and the dead,* that is, those that at the last day shall be found alive, and those who shall be raised to life out of the grave. Note, (1.) The Lord Jesus Christ shall judge the quick and dead. *God hath committed all judgment unto the Son,* and hath appointed him the Judge of quick and dead, Acts x. 42. (2.) He will appear; he will come the second time, and it will be a glorious appearance, as the word ἐπιφανεία signifies. (3.) Then his kingdom shall appear in its glory: *At his appearing and kingdom;* for he will then appear in his kingdom, sitting on a throne, to judge the world.

II. What is the matter of the charge, *v.* 2—5. He is charged,

1. To *preach the word.* This is ministers' business; a dispensation is committed to them. It is not their own notions and fancies that they are to preach, but the pure plain word of God; and they must not corrupt it, but as of sincerity, but as of God, in the sight of God, they speak in Christ, 2 Cor. ii. 17.

2. To urge what he preached, and to press it with all earnestness upon his hearers: "*Be instant in season and out of season, reprove, rebuke, exhort;* do this work with all fervency of spirit. Call upon those under thy charge to take heed of sin, to do their duty: call upon them to repent, and believe, and live a holy life, and this both in season and out of season. *In season,* when they are at leisure to hear thee, when some special opportunity offers itself of speaking to them with advantage. Nay, do it *out of season,* even when there is not that apparent probability of fastening something upon them, because thou dost not know but the Spirit of God may fasten upon them; for the wind bloweth where it listeth; and *in the morning we must sow our seed, and in the evening not withhold our hand,*" Eccl. xi. 6. We must do it in season, that is, let slip no opportunity; and do it out of season, that is, not shift off the duty, under pretence that it is out of season.

3. He must tell people of their faults: "*Reprove them, rebuke them.* Convince wicked people of the evil and danger of their wicked courses. Endeavour, by dealing plainly with them, to bring them to repentance. Rebuke them with gravity and authority, in Christ's name, that they may take thy displeasure against them as an indication of God's displeasure.

4. He must direct, encourage, and quicken those who began well. "*Exhort them* (persuade them to hold on, and endure to the end) and this *with all long-suffering and doctrine.*" (1.) He must do it very patiently: *With all long-suffering.* "If thou do not see the effect of thy labours presently, yet do not therefore give up the cause; be not weary of speaking to them." While God shows to them all long-suffering, let ministers exhort with all long-suffering. (2.) He must do it rationally, not with passion, but *with doctrine,* that is, "In order to the reducing of them to good practices, instil into them good principles. Teach them the truth as it is in Jesus, reduce them to a firm belief of it, and this will be a means both to reclaim them from evil and to bring them to good." Observe, [1.] A minister's work has various parts: he is to *preach the word,* to *reprove, rebuke,* and *exhort.* [2.] He is to be very diligent and careful; he must be *instant in season and out of season;* he must spare no pains nor labour, but must be urgent with them to take care of their souls and their eternal concerns.

5. He must *watch in all things.* "Seek an opportunity of doing them a kindness; let no fair occasion slip, through thy negligence. Watch to thy work; watch against the temptations of Satan, by which thou mayest be diverted from it; watch over the souls of those who are committed to thy charge."

6. He must count upon afflictions, and endure them, make the best of them. Κακοπάθησον, endure *patiently.* "Be not discouraged by the difficulties thou meetest with, but bear them with an evenness of spirit. Inure thyself to hardships."

7. He must remember his office, and discharge its duties: *Do the work of an evangelist.* The office of the evangelist was, as the apostles' deputies, to water the churches that they planted. They were not settled pastors, but for some time resided in, and presided over, the churches that the apostles had planted, till they were settled under a standing ministry. This was Timothy's work.

8. He must fulfil his ministry: *Make full proof of it.* It was a great trust that was reposed in him, and therefore he must answer it, and perform all the parts of his office with diligence and care. Observe, (1.) A minister must expect afflictions in the faithful discharge of his duty. (2.) He must endure them patiently, like a Christian hero. (3.) These must not discourage him in

his work, for he must do his work, and fulfil his ministry. (4.) The best way to make full proof of our ministry is to fulfil it, to fill it up in all its parts with proper work.

III. The reasons to enforce the charge.

1. Because errors and heresies were likely to creep into the church, by which the minds of many professing Christians would be corrupted (*v.* 3, 4): "*For the time will come when they will not endure sound doctrine.* Therefore improve the present time, when they will endure it. Be busy now, for it is seed-time; when the fields are white unto the harvest, put in the sickle, for the present gale of opportunity will be soon over. *They will not endure sound doctrine.* There will be those who will *heap to themselves corrupt teachers, and will turn away their ears from the truth;* and therefore secure as many as thou canst, that, when these storms and tempests do arise, they may be well fixed, and their apostasy may be prevented." People must hear, and ministers must preach, for the time to come, and guard against the mischiefs that are likely to arise hereafter, though they do not yet arise. They will *turn away their ears from the truth;* they will grow weary of the old plain gospel of Christ, and then they will be greedy of fables, and take pleasure in them, and God will give them up to those strong delusions, because they received not the truth in the love of it, 2 Thess. ii. 11, 12. Observe, (1.) These teachers were of their own heaping up, and not of God's sending; but they chose them, to gratify their lusts, and to please their itching ears. (2.) People do so when they will not endure sound doctrine, that preaching which is searching, plain, and to the purpose; then they will have teachers of their own. (3.) There is a wide difference between the word of God and the word of such teachers; the one is sound doctrine, the word of truth, the other is only fables. (4.) Those that are turned unto fables first turn away their ears from the truth, for they cannot hear and mind both, any more than they can serve two masters. Nay, further, it is said, *They shall be turned unto fables.* God justly suffers those to turn to fables who grow weary of the truth, and gives them up to be led aside from the truth by fables.

2. Because Paul for his part had almost done his work: *Do thou make full proof of thy ministry, for I am now ready to be offered, v.* 6. And,

(1.) "Therefore there will be the more occasion for thee." When labourers are removed out of the vineyard, it is no time for those to loiter that are left behind, but to double their diligence. The fewer hands there are to work the more industrious those hands must be that are at work.

(2.) "I have done the work of my day and generation; do thou in like manner do the work of thy day and generation."

(3.) The comfort and cheerfulness of Paul, in the prospect of his approaching departure, might encourage Timothy to the utmost industry, and diligence, and seriousness in his work. Paul was an old soldier of Jesus Christ, Timothy was but newly enlisted. "Come," says Paul, "I have found our Master kind and the cause good; I can look back upon my warfare with a great deal of pleasure and satisfaction; and therefore be not afraid of the difficulties thou must meet with. The crown of life is as sure to thee as if it were already upon thy head; and therefore endure afflictions, and make full proof of thy ministry." The courage and comfort of dying saints and ministers, and especially dying martyrs, are a great confirmation of the truth of the Christian religion, and a great encouragement to living saints and ministers in their work. Here the apostle looks forward, upon his death approaching: *I am now ready to be offered.* The Holy Ghost witnessed in every city that bonds and afflictions did abide him, Acts xx. 23. He was now at Rome, and it is probable that he had particular intimations from the Spirit that there he should seal the truth with his blood; and he looks upon it now as near at hand: I am *already poured out;* so it is in the original, ἤδη σπένδομαι· that is, I am already a martyr in affection. It alludes to the pouring out of the drink-offerings; for the blood of the martyrs, though it was not a sacrifice of atonement, was a sacrifice of acknowledgment to the honour of the grace of God and his truths. Observe,

[1.] With what pleasure he speaks of dying. He calls it his departure; though it is probable that he foresaw he must die a violent bloody death, yet he calls it his departure, or his release. Death to a good man is his release from the imprisonment of this world and his departure to the enjoyments of another world; he does not cease to be, but is only removed from one world to another.

[2.] With what pleasure he looks back upon the life he had lived (*v.* 7): *I have fought a good fight, I have finished my course,* &c. He did not fear death, because he had the testimony of his conscience that by the grace of God he had in some measure answered the ends of living. As a Christian, as a minister, he had fought a good fight. He had done the service, gone through the difficulties of his warfare, and had been instrumental in carrying on the glorious victories of the exalted Redeemer over the powers of darkness. His life was a course, and he had now finished it; as his warfare was accomplished, so his race was run. "*I have kept the faith.* I have kept the doctrines of the gospel, and never betrayed any of them." Note, *First,* The life of a Christian, but especially of a minister, is a warfare and a race, sometimes compared to the one in the scripture, and sometimes to the other. *Secondly,* It is a good fight, a good warfare; the cause is good, and the victory is sure, if we continue faithful and courageous. *Thirdly,* We must fight this good fight; we must fight it out, and finish our course; we must not give over till we are made more than conquerors through him who hath loved us, Rom. viii. 37. *Fourthly,* It is a great comfort to a dying saint, when he can look back upon his past life and say with our apostle, "*I have fought,* &c. I have kept the faith, the doctrine of faith and the grace of faith." Towards the end of our days to be able to speak in this manner, what comfort, unspeakable comfort, will it afford! Let it then be our constant endeavour, by the grace of God, that we may finish our course with joy, Acts xx. 24.

[3.] With what pleasure he looks forward to the life he was to live hereafter (*v.* 8): *Henceforth there is laid up for me a crown of righteousness,* &c. He had lost for Christ, but he was sure he should not lose by him, Phil. iii. 8. Let this encourage Timothy to endure hardness as a good soldier of Jesus Christ that there is a crown of life before us, the glory and joy of which will abundantly recompense all the hardships and toils of our present warfare. Observe, It is called *a crown of righteousness,* because it will be the recompence of our services, which *God is not unrighteous to forget;* and because our holiness and righteousness will there be perfected, and will be our crown. God will give it as *a righteous Judge,* who will let none lose by him. And yet this crown of righteousness was not peculiar to Paul, as if it belonged only to apostles and eminent ministers and martyrs, but *to all those also that love his appearing.* Observe, It is the character of all the saints that they love the appearing of Jesus Christ: they loved his first appearing, when he appeared to take away sin by the sacrifice of himself (Heb. ix. 26); they love to think of it; they love his second appearing at the great day; love it, and long for it: and, with respect to those who love the appearing of Jesus Christ, he shall appear to their joy; there is a crown of righteousness reserved for them, which shall then be given them, Heb. ix. 28. We learn hence, *First,* The Lord is the righteous Judge, for his judgment is according to truth. *Secondly,* The crown of believers is a crown of righteousness, purchased by the righteousness of Christ, and bestowed as the reward of the saints' righteousness. *Thirdly,* This crown, which believers shall wear, is laid up for them; they have it not at present, for here they are but heirs; they have it not in possession, and yet it is sure, for it is laid up for them. *Fourthly,* The righteous Judge will give it to all who love, prepare, and long for his appearing. *Surely I come quickly. Amen, even so come, Lord Jesus.*

9 Do thy diligence to come shortly
unto me: 10 For Demas hath forsaken me, having loved this present
world, and is departed unto Thessalonica; Crescens to Galatia, Titus
unto Dalmatia. 11 Only Luke is
with me. Take Mark, and bring
him with thee: for he is profitable
to me for the ministry. 12 And
Tychicus have I sent to Ephesus.
13 The cloak that I left at Troas
with Carpus, when thou comest,
bring *with thee,* and the books, *but*
especially the parchments. 14 Alexander the coppersmith did me much
evil: the Lord reward him according
to his works: 15 Of whom be thou
ware also; for he hath greatly withstood our words.

Here are divers particular matters which Paul mentions to Timothy, now at the closing of the epistle. 1. He bids him hasten to him, if possible (*v.* 9): *Do thy diligence to come shortly to me.* For Timothy was an evangelist, one who was not a fixed pastor of any one place, but attended the motions of the apostles, to build upon their foundation. Paul wanted Timothy's company and help; and the reason he gives is because several had left him (*v.* 10); one from an ill principle, namely, *Demas,* who abides under an ill name for it: *Demas hath forsaken me, having loved this present world.* He quitted Paul and his interest, either for fear of suffering (because Paul was now a prisoner, and he was afraid of coming into trouble upon his account) or being called off from his ministry by secular affairs, in which he entangled himself; his first love to Christ and his gospel was forsaken and forgotten, and he fell in love with the world. Note, Love to this present world is often the cause of apostasy from the truths and ways of Jesus Christ. He has gone off, has *departed to Thessalonica,* called thither perhaps by trade, or by some other worldly business. *Crescens* had gone one way and *Titus* another way. *Luke* however remained with Paul (*v.* 11, 12), and was not this enough? Paul did not think it so; he loved the company of his friends. 2. He speaks respectfully concerning *Mark: He is profitable to me for the ministry.* It is supposed that this Mark was he about whom Paul and Barnabas had contended, Acts xv. 39. Paul would not take him with him to the work, because he had once flinched and drawn back: but now, says he, *Take Mark, and bring him with thee.* By this it appears that Paul was now reconciled to Mark, and had a better opinion of him than he had had formerly. This teaches us to be of a forgiving spirit; we must not therefore disclaim for ever making use of those that are profitable and useful, though they may have done amiss. 3. Paul orders Timothy to come to him, bids him as he came through Troas to bring with him thence those things which he had left behind him there (*v.* 13), the cloak he had left there, which, it may be, Paul had the more occasion for in a cold prison. It is probable that it was the habit Paul usually wore, a plain dress. Some read it, the *roll of parchment I left at Troas;* others, the *desk* that I left. Paul was guided by divine inspiration, and yet he would have his books with him. Whereas he had exhorted Timothy to give attendance to reading, so he did himself, though he was now ready to be offered. As long as we live, we must be still learning. *But especially the parchments,* which some think were the originals of his epistles; others think they were the skins of which he made his tents, whereby he obtained a livelihood, working with his own hands. 4. He mentions *Alexander*, and the mischief that he had done him, *v.* 14, 15. This is he who is spoken of Acts xix. 33. It should seem, he had been a professor of the Christian religion, a forward professor, for he was there particularly maligned by the worshippers of Diana, and yet he did Paul much evil. Paul was in as much danger from false brethren (2 Cor. xi. 26) as from open enemies. Paul foretels that God would reckon with him. It is a prophetical denunciation of the just judgment of God that would befal him: The Lord *will reward him according to his works.* He cautions Timothy to take heed of him: "*Of whom be thou aware also*, that he do not, under pretence of friendship, betray thee to mischief." It is dangerous having any thing to do with those who would be enemies to such a man as Paul. Observe, (1.) Some who were once Paul's hearers and admirers did not give him reason to remember them with much pleasure; for one forsook him, and another did him much evil, and greatly withstood his words. Yet, (2.) At the same time he mentions some with pleasure; the badness of some did not make him forget the goodness of others; such as *Timothy, Titus, Mark,* and *Luke.* (3.) The apostle has left a brand on the names and memory of two persons; the one is *Demas,* who forsook him, having loved the present world, and the other is *Alexander,* who greatly withstood his words. (4.) God will reward evil-doers, particularly apostates, according to their works. (5.) Of such as are of Alexander's spirit and temper we should beware; for they will do us no good, but all the mischief that is in their power.

16 At my first answer no man
stood with me, but all *men* forsook
me: *I pray God* that it may not be
laid to their charge. 17 Notwithstanding the Lord stood with me,
and strengthened me; that by me
the preaching might be fully known,
and *that* all the Gentiles might hear:
and I was delivered out of the mouth
of the lion. 18 And the Lord shall
deliver me from every evil work, and
will preserve *me* unto his heavenly
kingdom: to whom *be* glory for ever
and ever. Amen. 19 Salute Prisca
and Aquila, and the household of
Onesiphorus. 20 Erastus abode at
Corinth: but Trophimus have I left
at Miletum sick. 21 Do thy diligence to come before winter. Eubulus greeteth thee, and Pudens, and
Linus, and Claudia, and all the brethren. 22 The Lord Jesus Christ *be* with
thy spirit. Grace *be* with you. Amen.

Here, I. He gives Timothy an account of his own present circumstances.

1. He had lately been called to appear before the emperor, upon his appeal to Cæsar; and then *no man stood with him* (*v.* 16), to plead his cause, to bear testimony for him, or so much as to keep him in countenance, but *all men forsook him.* This was strange, that so good a man as Paul should have nobody to own him, even at Rome, where there were many Christians, whose faith was spoken of throughout the world, Rom. i. 8. But men are but men. The Christians at Rome were forward to go and meet him (Acts xxviii.); but when it came to the pinch, and they would be in danger of suffering with him, then they all forsook him. He prays that God would not lay it to their charge, intimating that it was a great fault, and God might justly be angry with them, but he prays God to forgive them. See what a distinction is put between sins of presumption and sins of infirmity. Alexander the coppersmith, who maliciously withstood Paul, he prays against: *The Lord reward him according to his works;* but respecting these Christians, who through weakness shrunk from Paul in time of trial, he says, *The Lord lay it not to their charge.* Observe, (1.) Paul had his trials in his friends' forsaking him in a time of danger as well as in the opposition made by enemies: all forsook him. (2.) It was their sin not to appear for the good apostle, especially at his first answer; but it was a sin of weakness, and therefore the more excusable. Yet, (3.) God might lay it to their charge, but Paul endeavours to prevent it by his earnest prayers: *Let it not be laid to their charge.*

2. *Notwithstanding this God stood by him* (*v.* 17), gave him extraordinary wisdom and courage, to enable him to speak so much the better himself. When he had nobody to keep him in countenance, God made his face to shine.—*That by me the preaching might be fully known,* that is, "God brought me out from that difficulty that I might preach the gospel, which is my business." Nay, it should seem, that he might preach the gospel at that time; for Paul knew how to preach at the bar as well as in the pulpit. *And that all the*

Gentiles might hear; the emperor himself and the great men who would never have heard Paul preach if he had not been brought before them. *And I was delivered out of the mouth of the lion,* that is, of Nero (as some think) or some other judge. Some understand it only as a proverbial form of speech, to signify that he was in imminent danger. *And the Lord shall deliver me from every evil work.* See how Paul improved his experiences: "*He that hath delivered doth deliver, and we trust he will yet deliver,* will deliver me *from every evil work,* from any ill done to me by others. *And shall preserve me to his heavenly kingdom.*" And for this he gives glory to God, rejoicing in hope of the glory of God. Observe, (1.) If the Lord stand by us, he will strengthen us, in a time of difficulty and danger, and his presence will more than supply every one's absence. (2.) When the Lord preserves his servants from great and imminent danger, it is for eminent work and service. Paul was preserved that by him the preaching might be fully known, &c. (3.) Former deliverances should encourage future hopes. (4.) There is a heavenly kingdom, to which the Lord will preserve his faithful witnessing or suffering servants. (5.) We ought to give God the glory of all past, present, and future deliverances: *To whom be glory for ever and ever. Amen.*

II. He sends salutations to *Aquila, and Priscilla, and the household of Onesiphorus, v.* 19. He mentions his leaving *Trophimus sick at Miletum* (*v.* 20), by which it appears that though the apostles healed all manner of diseases miraculously, for the confirmation of their doctrine, yet they did not exert that power upon their own friends, lest it should have looked like a collusion.

III. He hastens Timothy to *come to him before winter* (*v.* 21), because he longed to see him, and because in the winter the journey or voyage would be more dangerous.

IV. He sends commendations to him from *Eubulus, Pudens, Linus, Claudia,* and all the *brethren.* One of the heathen writers at this time mentions one Pudens and his wife Claudia, and says that Claudia was a Briton, whence some have gathered that it was this Pudens, and that Claudia here was his wife, and that they were eminent Christians at Rome.

V. He concludes with a prayer, that the *Lord Jesus would be with his spirit.* We need no more to make us happy than to have the Lord Jesus Christ with our spirits; for in him all spiritual blessings are summed up. And it is the best prayer we can put up for our friends, that the Lord Jesus Christ may be with their spirits, to sanctify and save them, and at last to receive them to himself; as Stephen the proto-martyr prayed, *Lord Jesus, receive my spirit,* Acts vii. 59. "Lord Jesus, receive that spirit which thou hast been with while it was united to the body; do not now leave it in its separate state." *Grace be with you. Amen.* This was our apostle's token in every epistle; so he wrote. *The grace of our Lord Jesus Christ be with you all. Amen,* 2 Thess. iii. 17, 18. And if grace be with us here to convert and change us, to make us holy, to keep us humble, and to enable us to persevere to the end, glory will crown us hereafter: *for the Lord is a sun, and a shield; the Lord will give grace and glory, and no good thing will he withhold from those that walk uprightly. O Lord of hosts, blessed is the man that trusteth in thee,* Ps. lxxxiv. 11, 12. *Now unto the King eternal, immortal, invisible, the only wise God our Saviour, be honour and glory for ever and ever.* Amen.

AN

EXPOSITION,

WITH PRACTICAL OBSERVATIONS,

OF THE EPISTLE OF ST. PAUL TO

TITUS.

THIS Epistle of Paul to Titus is much of the same nature with those to Timothy; both were converts of Paul, and his companions in labours and sufferings; both were in the office of evangelists, whose work was to water the churches planted by the apostles, and to set in order the things that were wanting in them: they were vice-apostles, as it were, *working the work of the Lord, as they did,* and mostly under their direction, though not despotic and arbitrary, but with the concurring exercise of their own prudence and judgment, 1 Cor. xvi. 10, 12. We read much of this Titus, his titles, character, and active usefulness, in many places: he was a Greek,

Gal. ii. 3. Paul called him *his son* (Tit. i. 4), *his brother* (2 Cor. ii. 13), *his partner and fellow-helper* (2 Cor. viii. 23), *one that walked in the same spirit and in the same steps with himself.* He went up with the apostles to the church at Jerusalem (Gal. ii. 1), was much conversant at Corinth, for which church he had *an earnest care,* 2 Cor. viii. 16. Paul's second epistle to them, and probably his first also, was sent by his hand, 2 Cor. viii. 16—18, 23; ix. 2—4; xii. 18. He was with the apostle at Rome, and thence went into Dalmatia (2 Tim. iv. 10), after which no more occurs of him in the scriptures. So that by them he appears not to have been a fixed bishop; if such he were, and in those times, the church of Corinth, where he most laboured, had the best title to him. In Crete (now called *Candia,* formerly *Hecatompolis,* from the hundred cities that were in it), a large island at the mouth of the Ægean Sea, the gospel had got some footing; and here were Paul and Titus in one of their travels, cultivating this plantation; but the apostle of the Gentiles, having on him the care of all the churches, could not himself tarry long at this place. He therefore left Titus some time there, to carry on the work which had been begun, wherein, probably, meeting with more difficulty than ordinary, Paul wrote this epistle to him; and yet perhaps not so much for his own sake as for the people's, that the endeavours of Titus, strengthened with apostolic advice and authority, might be more significant and effectual among them. He was to see all the cities furnished with good pastors, to reject and keep out the unmeet and unworthy, to teach sound doctrine, and instruct all sorts in their duties, to set forth the free grace of God in man's salvation by Christ, and withal to show the necessity of maintaining good works by those who have believed in God and hope for eternal life from him.

CHAP. I.

In this chapter we have, I. The preface or introduction to the epistle, showing from and to whom it was written, with the apostle's salutation and prayer for Titus, wishing all blessings to him, ver. 1—4. II. Entrance into the matter, by signifying the end of Titus's being left at Crete, ver. 5. III. And how the same should be pursued in reference both to good and bad ministers, ver. 6, to the end.

PAUL, a servant of God, and an apostle of Jesus Christ, according to the faith of God's elect, and the acknowledging of the truth which is after godliness;
2 In hope of eternal life, which God, that cannot lie, promised before the world began;
3 But hath in due times manifested his word through preaching, which is committed unto me according to the commandment of God our Saviour;
4 To Titus, *mine* own son after the common faith: Grace, mercy, *and* peace, from God the Father and the Lord Jesus Christ our Saviour.

Here is the preface to the epistle, showing,

I. The writer. *Paul,* a Gentile name taken by the apostle of the Gentiles, Acts xiii. 9, 46, 47. Ministers will accommodate even smaller matters, so that they may be any furthering of acceptance in their work. When the Jews rejected the gospel, and the Gentiles received it, we read no more of this apostle by his Jewish name *Saul,* but by his Roman one, *Paul. A servant of God, and an apostle of Jesus Christ.* Here he is described by his relation and office: *A servant of God,* not in the general sense only, as a man and a Christian, but especially as a minister, *serving God in the gospel of his Son,* Rom. i. 9. This is a high honour; it is the glory of angels that they are *ministering spirits, and sent forth to minister for those who shall be heirs of salvation,* Heb. i. 14. Paul is described more especially as a chief minister, *an apostle of Jesus Christ:* one who had seen the Lord, and was immediately called and commissioned by him, and had his doctrine from him. Observe, The highest officers in the church are but servants. (Much divinity and devotion are comprehended in the inscriptions of the epistles.) The apostles of Jesus Christ, who were employed to spread and propagate his religion, were therein also the servants of God; they did not set up any thing inconsistent with the truths and duties of natural religion. Christianity, which they preached, was in order to clear and enforce those natural principles, as well as to advance them, and to superadd what was fit and necessary in man's degenerate and revolted state: therefore the apostles of Jesus Christ were the servants of God, *according to the faith of God's elect.* Their doctrine agreed with the faith of all the elect from the beginning of the world, and was for propagating and promoting the same. Observe, There are elect of God (1 Pet. i. 2), and in these the Holy Spirit works precious divine faith, proper to those who are chosen to eternal life (2 Thess. ii. 13, 14): *God hath from the beginning chosen you to salvation, through sanctification of the Spirit and belief of the truth, whereunto he called you by our gospel.* Faith is the first principle of sanctification. *And the acknowledging of the truth which is after godliness.* The gospel is truth; the great, sure, and saving truth (Col. i. 5), *the word of the truth of the gospel.* Divine faith rests not on fallible reasonings and probable opinions, but on the infallible word, the truth itself, *which is after godliness,* of a godly nature and tendency, pure, and purifying the heart of the believer. By this mark judge of doctrines and of spirits—whether they be of God or not; what is impure, and prejudicial to true piety and practical religion, cannot be of divine original. All gospel truth is after godliness, teaching and nourishing reverence and fear of God, and obedience to him; it is truth not only to be known, but acknowledged; it must be held forth in word and practice, Phil. ii. 15, 16. *With the heart man believes to righteousness, and with the mouth confession is made unto salvation*, Rom. x. 10. Such as retain the truth in unrighteousness neither know nor believe as they ought. To bring to this knowledge and faith, and to the acknowledging and professing of the truth which is after godliness, is the great end of the gospel ministry, even of the highest degree and order in it; their teachings should have this chief aim, to beget faith and confirm in it. *In* (or *for) hope of eternal life, v.* 2. This is the further intent of the gospel, to beget hope as well as faith; to take off the mind and heart from the world, and to raise them to heaven and the things above. The faith and godliness of Christians lead to eternal life, and give hope and well-grounded expectation of it; for *God, that cannot lie, hath promised it.* It is the honour of God that he cannot lie or deceive: and this is the comfort of believers, whose treasure is laid up in his faithful promises. But how is he said to promise before the world began? *Answer*, By promise some understand his decree: he purposed it in his eternal counsels, which were as it were his promise in *embryo:* or rather, say some, πρὸ χρόνων αἰωνίων is *before ancient times*, or many years ago, referring to the promise darkly delivered, Gen. iii. 15. Here is the stability and antiquity of the promise of eternal life to the saints. God, who cannot lie, hath promised before the world began, that is, many ages since. How excellent then is the gospel, which was the matter of divine promise so early! how much to be esteemed by us, and what thanks due for our privilege beyond those before us! *Blessed are your eyes, for they see*, &c. No wonder if the contempt of it be punished severely, since he has not only promised it of old, *but* (*v.* 3) *has in due times manifested his word through preaching;* that is, made that his promise, so darkly delivered of old, *in due time* (the proper season before appointed) more plain *by preaching;* that which some called *foolishness of preaching* has been thus honoured. *Faith comes by hearing, and hearing by the word of God*, by the word preached. *Which is committed unto me.* The ministry is a trust; none taketh this honour, but he who is thereunto appointed; and whoso is appointed and called must preach the word. 1 Cor. ix. 16, *Woe is unto me if I preach not the gospel.* Nonpreaching ministers are none of the apostle's successors. *According to the commandment of God our Saviour.* Preaching is a work appointed by God as a Saviour. See a proof here of Christ's deity, for by him was the gospel committed to Paul when he was converted (Acts ix. 15, 17, and *ch.* xxii. 10, 14, 15), and again when Christ appeared to him, *v.* 17—21 He therefore is this Saviour; not but that the whole Trinity concur therein: the Father saves by the Son through the Spirit, and all concur in sending ministers. Let none rest therefore in men's calling, without God's; he furnishes, inclines, authorises, and gives opportunity for the work.

II. The person written to, who is described, 1. By his name, *Titus*, a Gentile Greek, yet called both to the faith and ministry Observe, the grace of God is free and powerful. What worthiness or preparation was there in one of heathen stock and education? 2. By his spiritual relation to the apostle: *My own* (or *my genuine) son*, not by natural generation, but by supernatural regeneration. *I have begotten you through the gospel*, said he to the Corinthians, 1 Cor. iv. 15. Ministers are spiritual fathers to those whom they are the means of converting, and will tenderly affect and care for them, and must be answerably regarded by them. "*My own son after the common faith*, that faith which is common to all the regenerate, and which thou hast in truth, and expressest to the life." This might be said to distinguish Titus from hypocrites and false teachers, and to recommend him to the regard of the Cretans, as being among them a lively image of the apostle himself, in faith, and life, and heavenly doctrine. To this Titus, deservedly so dear to the apostle, is,

III. The salutation and prayer, wishing all blessings to him: *Grace, mercy, and peace, from God the Father, and the Lord Jesus Christ our Saviour.* Here are, 1. The blessings wished: *Grace, mercy, and peace. Grace*, the free favour of God, and acceptance with him. *Mercy*, the fruits of that favour, in pardon of sins, and freedom from all miseries by it, both here and hereafter. And *peace*, the positive effect and fruit of mercy. Peace with God through Christ who is our peace, and with the creatures and ourselves; outward and inward peace, comprehending all good whatsoever, that makes for our happiness in time and to eternity. Observe, Grace is the fountain of all blessings. Mercy, and peace, and all good, spring out of this. Get into God's favour, and all must be well; for, 2. These are the persons from whom blessings are wished: *From God the Father*, the fountain of all good. Every blessing, every comfort, comes to us from God as a Father; he is the Father of all by creation, but of the good by adoption and regeneration. *And the Lord Jesus Christ our Saviour*, as the way and means of procurement and conveyance. All is from the Father by the Son, who is Lord by nature, heir of all things, and our Lord, Redeemer, and head, ordering and ruling his members. All are put under him; we hold of him, as *in capite*, and owe subjection and obedience to him, who is also Jesus and Christ, the anointed Saviour, and especially our Saviour, who believe in him, delivering us from sin and hell, and bringing us to heaven and happiness.

Thus far is the preface to the epistle; then

follows the entrance into the matter, by signifying the end of Titus's being left in Crete.

5 For this cause left I thee in Crete, that thou shouldest set in order the things that are wanting, and ordain elders in every city, as I had appointed thee.

Here is the end expressed,

I. More generally: *For this cause left I thee in Crete, that thou shouldst set in order the things that are wanting.* This was the business of evangelists (in which office Titus was), to water where the apostles had planted (1 Cor. iii. 6), furthering and finishing what they had begun; so much ἐπιδιορθουν imports, *to order after another.* Titus was to go on in settling what the apostle himself had not time for, in his short stay there. Observe, 1. The apostle's great diligence in the gospel; when he had set things on foot in one place, he hastened away to another. He was debtor to the Greeks and to the barbarians, and laboured to spread the gospel as far as he could among them all. And, 2. His faithfulness and prudence. He neglected not the places that he went from; but left some to cultivate the young plantation, and carry on what was begun. 3. His humility; he disdained not to be helped in his work, and that by such as were not of so high a rank in the ministry, nor of so great gifts and furniture, as himself; so that the gospel might be furthered and the good of souls promoted, he willingly used the hands of others in it: a fit example for exciting zeal and industry, and engaging to faithfulness and care of the flock, and present or absent, living and dying, for ministers, as much as in them lies, to provide for the spiritual edification and comfort of their people. We may here also observe, 4. That Titus, though inferior to an apostle, was yet above the ordinary fixed pastors or bishops, who were to tend particular churches as their peculiar stated charge; but Titus was in a higher sphere, to ordain such ordinary pastors where wanting, and settle things in their first state and form, and then to pass to other places for like service as there might be need. Titus was not only a minister of the catholic church (as all others also are), but a catholic minister. Others had power habitual, and in *actu primo,* to minister any where, upon call and opportunity; but evangelists, such as Titus was, had power in *actu secundo et exercito,* and could exercise their ministry wherever they came, and claim maintenance of the churches. They were every where actually in their diocese or province, and had a right to direct and preside among the ordinary pastors and ministers. Where an apostle could act as an apostle an evangelist could act as an evangelist; for *they worked the work of the Lord as they did* (1 Cor. xvi. 10), in a like unfixed and itinerant manner. Here at Crete Titus was but occasionally, and for a short time; Paul willed him to despatch the business he was left for, and come to him at Nicopolis, where he purposed to winter; after this he was sent to Corinth, was with the apostle at Rome, and was sent thence into Dalmatia, which is the last we read of him in scripture, so that from scripture no fixed episcopacy in him does appear; he left Crete, and we find not that he returned thither any more. But what power had either Paul or Titus here? Was not what they did an encroachment on the rights of civil rulers? In no sort; they came not to meddle with the civil rights of any. Luke xii. 14, *Who made me a judge or a divider over you?* Their work was spiritual, to be carried on by conviction and persuasion, no way interfering with, or prejudicing, or weakening, the power of magistrates, but rather securing and strengthening it; the *things wanting* were not such as civil magistrates are the fountains or authors of, but divine and spiritual ordinances, and appointments for spiritual ends, derived from Christ the king and head of the church: for settling these was Titus left. And observe, No easy thing is it to raise churches, and bring them to perfection. Paul had himself been here labouring, and yet were there things wanting; materials are out of square, need much hewing and fitting, to bring them into right form, and, when they are set therein, to hold and keep them so. The best are apt to decay and to go out of order. Ministers are to help against this, to get what is amiss rectified, and what is wanting supplied. This in general was Titus's work in Crete: and,

II. In special: *To ordain elders in every city,* that is, ministers, who were mostly out of the elder and most understanding and experienced Christians; or, if younger in years, yet such as were grave and solid in their deportment and manners. These were to be set where there was any fit number of Christians, as in larger towns and cities was usually the case; though villages, too, might have them where there were Christians enough for it. These presbyters or elders were to have the ordinary and stated care and charge of the churches; to feed and govern them, and perform all pastoral work and duty in and towards them. The word is used sometimes more largely for any who bear ecclesiastical function in the church, and so the apostles were *presbyters* or *elders* (1 Pet. v. 1); but here it is meant of ordinary fixed pastors, who *laboured in the word and doctrine,* and were *over the churches in the Lord;* such as are described here throughout the chapter. This word *presbyter* some use in the same sense as *sacerdos,* and translate it *priest,* a term not given to gospel ministers, unless in a figurative or allusive way, as all God's people are said to be made *kings and priests unto God* (ἱερεῖς, not πρεσβυτέρους), to offer up spiritual sacrifices of prayers, praises, and alms. But properly we have no priest under the gospel, except Christ alone, *the high priest of our profession* (Heb. iii. 1), who offered up himself a sacrifice to God for us, and ever lives, in virtue thereof, to make intercession in our behalf. Presbyters here therefore are not proper priests, to offer sacrifices, either typical or real; but only gospel ministers, to dispense Christ's ordinances, and to *feed the church of God, over which the Holy Ghost has made them overseers.* Observe, 1. A church without a fixed and standing ministry in it is imperfect and wanting. 2. Where a fit number of believers is, presbyters or elders must be set; their continuance in churches is as necessary as their first appointment, *for perfecting the saints, and edifying the body of Christ, till all come to a perfect man in Christ,* till the whole number of God's chosen be called and united to Christ in one body, and brought to their full stature and strength, and that measure of grace that is proper and designed for them, Eph. iv. 12, 13. This is work that must and will be doing to the world's end, to which therefore the necessary and appointed means for it must last. What praise is due to God for such an institution! What thankfulness from those that enjoy the benefits of it! What pity and prayer for such as want it! *Pray the Lord of the harvest that he will send forth labourers into his harvest. Faith comes by hearing,* and is preserved, maintained, and made fruitful, through it also. Ignorance and corruption, decays of good and increase of all evil, come by want of a teaching and quickening ministry. On such accounts therefore was *Titus left in Crete, to set in order the things that were wanting, and to ordain elders in every city;* but this he was to do, not *ad libitum,* or according to his own will or fancy, but according to apostolic direction.

III. The rule of his proceeding: *As I had appointed thee,* probably when he was going from him, and in the presence and hearing of others, to which he may now refer, not so much for Titus's own sake as for the people's, that they might the more readily yield obedience to Titus, knowing and observing that in what he did he was warranted and supported by apostolic injunction and authority. As under the law all things were to be made according to the pattern shown to Moses in the mount; so under the gospel all must be ordered and managed according to the direction of Christ, and of his chief ministers, who were infallibly guided by him. Human traditions and inventions may not be brought into the church of God. Prudent disposals for carrying on the ends of Christ's appointments, according to the general rules of the word, there may, yea, must be; but none may alter any thing in the substance of the faith or worship, or order and discipline, of the churches. If an evangelist might not do any thing but by appointment, much less may others. The church is the house of God, and to him it belongs to appoint the officers and orders of it, as he pleases: the *as,* here refers to the qualifications and character of the elders that he was to ordain: "*Ordain elders in every city, as I appointed thee,* such as I then described and shall now again more particularly point out to thee," which he does from the sixth verse to the ninth inclusive.

6 If any be blameless, the husband
of one wife, having faithful children,
not accused of riot, or unruly. 7
For a bishop must be blameless, as
the steward of God; not selfwilled,
not soon angry, not given to wine,
no striker, not given to filthy lucre;
8 But a lover of hospitality, a lover
of good men, sober, just, holy, temperate; 9 Holding fast the faithful
word as he hath been taught, that he
may be able by sound doctrine both
to exhort and to convince the gainsayers. 10 For there are many
unruly and vain talkers and deceivers,
specially they of the circumcision: 11
Whose mouths must be stopped, who
subvert whole houses, teaching things
which they ought not, for filthy lucre's
sake. 12 One of themselves, *even*
a prophet of their own, said, The
Cretians *are* always liars, evil beasts,
slow bellies. 13 This witness is true.
Wherefore rebuke them sharply, that
they may be sound in the faith; 14
Not giving heed to Jewish fables, and
commandments of men, that turn from
the truth. 15 Unto the pure all
things *are* pure: but unto them that
are defiled and unbelieving *is* nothing
pure; but even their mind and conscience is defiled. 16 They profess
that they know God; but in works
they deny *him*, being abominable, and
disobedient, and unto every good work
reprobate.

The apostle here gives Titus directions about ordination, showing whom he should ordain, and whom not.

I. Of those whom he should ordain. He points out their qualifications and virtues; such as respect their life and manners, and such as relate to their doctrine: the former in the sixth, seventh, and eighth verses, and the latter in the ninth.

1. Their qualifications respecting their life and manners are,

(1.) More general: *If any be blameless;* not absolutely without fault, so none are, for *there is none that liveth and sinneth not;* nor altogether unblamed, this is rare and difficult. Christ himself and his apostles were blamed, though not worthy of it. In Christ there was certainly nothing blamable; and his apostles were not such as their enemies charged them to be. But the meaning is, He must be one who lies not under an ill character; but rather must have a good report, even *from those that are without;* not grossly or scandalously guilty, so as would bring reproach upon the holy function; he must not be such a one.

(2.) More particularly.

[1.] There is his relative character. In his own person, he must be of conjugal chastity: *The husband of one wife.* The church of Rome says the husband of *no* wife, but from the beginning it was not so; marriage is an ordinance from which no profession nor calling is a bar. 1 Cor. ix. 5, *Have I not power,* says Paul, *to lead about a sister, a wife, as well as other apostles? Forbidding to marry* is one of the erroneous doctrines of the antichristian church, 1 Tim. iv. 3. Not that ministers *must* be married; this is not meant; but *the husband of one wife* may be either not having divorced his wife and married another (as was too common among those of the circumcision, even for slight causes), or *the husband of one wife,* that is, at one and the same time, no bigamist; not that he might not be married to more than one wife successively, but, being married, he must have but one wife at once, not two or more, according to the too common sinful practice of those times, by a perverse imitation of the patriarchs, from which evil custom our Lord taught a reformation. Polygamy is scandalous in any, as also having a harlot or concubine with his lawful wife; such sin, or any wanton libidinous demeanour, must be very remote from such as would enter into so sacred a function. And, as to his children, *having faithful children,* obedient and good, brought up in the true Christian faith, and living according to it, at least as far as the endeavours of the parents can avail. It is for the honour of ministers that their children be faithful and pious, and such as become their religion. *Not accused of riot, nor unruly,* not justly so accused, as having given ground and occasion for it, for otherwise the most innocent may be falsely so charged; they must look to it therefore that there be no colour for such censure. Children so faithful, and obedient, and temperate, will be a good sign of faithfulness and diligence in the parent who has so educated and instructed them; and, from his faithfulness in the less, there may be encouragement to commit to him the greater, the rule and government of the church of God. The ground of this qualification is shown from the nature of his office (*v.* 7): *For a bishop must be blameless, as the steward of God.* Those before termed presbyters, or elders, are in this verse styled bishops; and such they were, having no ordinary fixed and standing officers above them. Titus's business here, it is plain, was but occasional, and his stay short, as was before noted. Having ordained elders, and settled things in their due form, he went and left all (for aught that appears in scripture) in the hands of those elders whom the apostle here calls bishops and stewards of God. We read not in the sacred writings of any successor he had in Crete; but to those elders or bishops was committed the full charge of feeding, ruling, and watching over their flock; they wanted not any powers necessary for carrying on religion and the ministry of it among them, and committing it down to succeeding ages. Now, being such bishops and overseers of the flock, who were to be examples to them, and God's stewards to take care of the affairs of his house, to provide for and dispense to them things needful, there is great reason that their character should be clear and good, that they should be blameless. How else could it be but that religion must suffer, their work be hindered, and souls prejudiced and endangered, whom they were set to save? These are the relative qualifications with the ground of them.

[2.] The more absolute ones are expressed, *First,* Negatively, showing what an elder or bishop must not be: *Not self-willed.* The prohibition is of large extent, excluding self-opinion, or overweening conceit of parts and abilities, and abounding in one's own sense,—self-love, and self-seeking, making self the centre of all,—also self-confidence and trust, and self-pleasing, little regarding or setting by others,—being proud, stubborn, froward, inflexible, set on one's own will and way, or churlish as Nabal: such is the sense expositors have affixed to the term. A great honour it is to a minister not to be thus affected, to be ready to ask and to take advice, to be ready to defer as much as reasonably may be to the mind and will of others, becoming all things to all men, that they may gain some. *Not soon angry,* μὴ ὀργίλον, *not one of a hasty angry temper,* soon and easily provoked and inflamed. How unfit are those to govern a church who cannot govern themselves, or their own turbulent and unruly passions! The minister must be meek and gentle, and patient towards all men. *Not given to wine;* there is no greater reproach on a minister than to be a wine-bibber, one who loves it, and gives himself undue liberty this way who *continues at the wine or strong drink till it inflames him.* Seasonable and moderate use of this, as of the other good creatures of God, is not unlawful. *Use a little wine for thy stomach's sake, and thine often infirmities,* said Paul to Timothy, 1 Tim. v. 23. But excess therein is shameful in all, especially in a minister. *Wine takes away the heart,* turns the man into a brute: here most proper is that exhortation of the apostle (Eph. v. 18), *Be not drunk with wine, wherein is excess; but be filled with the Spirit.* Here is no exceeding, but in the former too easily there may: take heed therefore of going too near the brink. *No striker,* in any quarrelsome or contentious manner, not injuriously nor out of revenge, with cruelty or unnecessary roughness. *Not given to filthy lucre;* not greedy of it (as 1 Tim. iii. 3), whereby is not meant refusing a just return for their labours, in order to their necessary support and comfort; but not making gain their first or chief end, not entering into the ministry nor managing it with base worldly views. Nothing is more unbecoming a minister, who is to direct his own and others' eyes to another world, than to be too intent upon this. It is called *filthy lucre,* from its defiling the soul that inordinately affects or greedily looks after it, as if it were any otherwise desirable than for the good and lawful uses of it. Thus of the negative part of the bishop's character. But, *Secondly,* Positively: he must be (*v.* 8) *a lover of hospitality,* as an evidence that he is not given to filthy lucre, but is willing to use what he has to the best purposes, not laying up for himself, so as to hinder charitable laying out for the good of others; *receiving and entertaining strangers* (as the word imports), a great and necessary office of love, especially in those times of affliction and distress, when Christians were made to fly and wander for safety from persecution and enemies, or in travelling to and fro where there were not such public houses for reception as in our days, nor, it may be, had many poor saints sufficiency of their own for such uses—then to receive and entertain them was good and pleasing to God. And such a spirit and practice, according to ability and occasion, are very becoming such as should be examples of good works. *A lover of good men,* or of *good things;* ministers should be exemplary in both; this will evince their open piety, and likeness to God and their Master Jesus Christ: *Do good to all, but especially to those of the household of faith,* those who are the excellent of the earth, in whom should be all our delight. *Sober,* or *prudent,* as the word signifies; a needful grace in a minister both for his ministerial and personal carriage and management. He should be a wise steward, and one who is not rash, or foolish, or heady; but who can govern well his passions and affections. *Just* in things belonging to civil life, and moral righteousness, and equity in dealings, giving to all their due. *Holy* in what concerns religion; one who reverences and worships God, and is of a spiritual and heavenly conversation. *Temperate;* it comes from a word that signifies *strength,* and denotes one who has power over his appetite and affections, or, in things lawful, can, for good ends, restrain and hold them in. Nothing is more becoming a minister than such things as these, *sobriety, temperance, justice,* and *holiness*—sober in respect of himself, just and righteous towards all men, and holy towards God. And thus of the qualifications respecting the minister's life and manners, relative and absolute, negative and positive, what he must not, and what he must, be and do.

2. As to doctrine,

(1.) Here is his duty: *Holding fast the faithful word, as he has been taught,* keeping close to the doctrine of Christ, *the word of his grace,* adhering thereto according to the instructions he has received—holding it fast in his own belief and profession, and in teaching others. Observe, [1.] The word of God, revealed in the scripture, is a true and infallible word; the word of him that *is the amen, the true and faithful witness,* and whose Spirit guided the penmen of it. *Holy men of God spoke as they were moved by the Holy Ghost.* [2.] Ministers must hold fast, and hold forth, the faithful word in their teaching and life. *I have kept the faith,* was Paul's comfort (2 Tim. iv. 7), and *not shunned to declare the whole counsel of God;* there was his faithfulness, Acts xx. 27.

(2.) Here is the end: *That he may be able, by sound doctrine, both to exhort, and to convince the gainsayers,* to persuade and draw others to the true faith, and to convince the contrary-minded. How should he do this if he himself were uncertain or unsteady, not holding fast that *faithful word and sound doctrine* which should be the matter of this teaching, and the means and ground of convincing those that oppose the truth? We see here summarily the great work of the ministry—to exhort those who are willing to know and do their duty, and to convince those that contradict, both which are to be done by *sound doctrine,* that is, in a rational instructive way, by scripture-arguments and testimonies, which are the infallible words of truth, what all may and should rest and be satisfied in and determined by. And thus of the qualifications of the elders whom Titus was to ordain.

II. The apostle's directory shows whom he should reject or avoid—men of another character, the mention of whom is brought in as a reason of the care he had recommended about the qualifications of ministers, why they should be such, and only such, as he had described. The reasons he takes both from bad teachers and hearers among them, *v.* 10, to the end.

1. From bad teachers. (1.) Those false teachers are described. They were *unruly,* headstrong and ambitious of power, refractory and untractable (as some render it), and such as would not bear nor submit themselves to the discipline and necessary order in the church, impatient of good government and of sound doctrine. *And vain talkers and deceivers,* conceiting themselves to be wise, but really foolish, and thence great talkers, falling into errors and mistakes, and fond of them, and studious and industrious to draw others into the same. Many such there were, *especially those of the circumcision,* converts as

they pretended, at least, from the Jews, who yet were for mingling Judaism and Christianity together, and so making a corrupt medley. These were the false teachers. (2.) Here is the apostle's direction how to deal with them (*v.* 11): *Their mouths must be stopped;* not by outward force (Titus had no such power, nor was this the gospel method), but by confutation and conviction, showing them their error, *not giving place to them even for an hour.* In case of obstinacy indeed, breaking the peace of the church, and corrupting other churches, censures are to have place, the last means for recovering the faulty and preventing the hurt of many. Observe, Faithful ministers must oppose seducers in good time, *that, their folly being made manifest, they may proceed no further.* (3.) The reasons are given for this. [1.] From the pernicious effects of their errors: *They subvert whole houses, teaching things which they ought not* (namely, the necessity of circumcision, and of keeping the law of Moses, &c.), so subverting the gospel and the souls of men; not some few only, but whole families. It was unjustly charged on the apostles *that they turned the world upside down*; but justly on these false teachers that they drew many from the true faith to their ruin: the mouths of such should be stopped, especially considering, [2.] Their base end in what they do: *For filthy lucre's sake,* serving a worldly interest under pretence of religion. *Love of money is the root of all evil.* Most fit it is that such should be resisted, confuted, and put to shame, by sound doctrine, and reasons from the scriptures. Thus of the grounds respecting the bad teachers.

II. In reference to their people or hearers, who are described from ancient testimony given of them.

1. Here is the witness (*v.* 12): *One of themselves, even a prophet of their own,* that is, one of the Cretans, not of the Jews, Epimenides a Greek poet, likely to know and unlikely to slander them. *A prophet of their own;* so their poets were accounted, writers of divine oracles; these often witnessed against the vices of the people: Aratus, Epimenides, and others among the Greeks; Horace, Juvenal, and Persius, among the Latins: much smartness did they use against divers vices.

2. Here is the matter of his testimony: *Κρῆτες ἀεὶ ψεῦσται, κακὰ θηρία, γαστέρες ἀργαί—The Cretans are always liars, evil beasts, slow bellies.* Even to a proverb, they were infamous for falsehood and lying; *κρετίζειν,* to play the *Cretan,* or to lie, is the same; and they were compared to evil beasts for their sly hurtfulness and savage nature, and called slow bellies for their laziness and sensuality, more inclined to eat than to work and live by some honest employment. Observe, Such scandalous vices as were the reproach of heathens should be far from Christians: falsehood and lying, invidious craft and cruelty, all beastly and sensual practices, with idleness and sloth, are sins condemned by the light of nature. For these were the Cretans taxed by their own poets.

3. Here is the verification of this by the apostle himself: *v.* 13. This witness is true, The apostle saw too much ground for that character. The temper of some nations is more inclined to some vices than others. The Cretans were too generally such as here described, slothful and ill-natured, false and perfidious, as the apostle himself vouches. And thence,

4. He instructs Titus how to deal with them: *Wherefore rebuke them sharply.* When Paul wrote to Timothy he bade him instruct with meekness; but now, when he writes to Titus, he bids him rebuke them sharply. The reason of the difference may be taken from the different temper of Timothy and Titus; the former might have more keenness in his disposition, and be apt to be warm in reproving, whom therefore he bids to rebuke with meekness; and the latter might be one of more mildness, therefore he quickens him, and bids him rebuke sharply. Or rather it was from the difference of the case and people: Timothy had a more polite people to deal with, and therefore he must rebuke them with meekness; and Titus had to do with those who were more rough and uncultivated, and therefore he must rebuke them sharply; their corruptions were many and gross, and committed without shame or modesty, and therefore should be dealt with accordingly. There must in reproving be a distinguishing between sins and sins; some are more gross and heinous in their nature, or in the manner of their commission, with openness and boldness, to the greater dishonour of God and danger and hurt to men: and between sinners and sinners; some are of a more tender and tractable temper, apter to be wrought on by gentleness, and to be sunk and discouraged by too much roughness and severity; others are more hardy and stubborn, and need more cutting language to beget in them remorse and shame. Wisdom therefore is requisite to temper and manage reproofs aright, as may be most likely to do good. Jude 22, 23, *Of some have compassion, making a difference; and others save with fear, pulling them out of the fire.* The Cretans' sins and corruptions were many, great, and habitual; therefore they must be rebuked sharply. But that such direction might not be misconstrued,

5. Here is the end of it noted: *That they may be sound in the faith* (*v.* 14), *not giving heed to Jewish fables, and commandments of men, that turn from the truth;* that is, that they may be and show themselves truly and effectually changed from such evil tempers and manners as those Cretans in their natural state lived in, and may not adhere to nor regard (as some who were converted might be too ready to do) the Jewish traditions and he superstitions of the Pharisees, which

would be apt to make them disrelish the gospel, and the sound and wholesome truths of it. Observe, (1.) The sharpest reproofs must aim at the good of the reproved; they must not be of malice, nor hatred, nor ill-will, but of love; not to gratify pride, passion, nor any evil affection in the reprover, but to reclaim and reform the erroneous and the guilty. (2.) Soundness in the faith is most desirable and necessary. This is the soul's health and vigour, pleasing to God, comfortable to the Christian, and what makes ready to be cheerful and constant in duty. (3.) A special means to soundness in the faith is to turn away the ear from fables and the fancies of men (1 Tim. i. 4): *Neither give heed to fables and endless genealogies, that minister questions rather than godly edifying, which is in faith.* So *ch.* iv. 7, *Refuse profane and old wives' fables, and exercise thyself rather to godliness.* Fancies and devices of men in the worship of God are contrary to truth and piety. Jewish ceremonies and rites, that were at first divine appointments, the substance having come and their season and use being over, are now but unwarranted commands of men, which not only stand not with, but turn from, the truth, the pure gospel truth and spiritual worship, set up by Christ instead of that bodily service under the law. (4.) A fearful judgment it is to be turned away from the truth, to leave Christ for Moses, the spiritual worship of the gospel for the carnal ordinances of the law, or the true divine institutions and precepts for human inventions and appointments. *Who hath bewitched you* (said Paul to the Galatians, *ch.* iii. 1, 3) *that you should not obey the truth? Having begun in the Spirit, are you made perfect by the flesh?* Thus having shown the end of sharply reproving the corrupt and vicious Cretans, that they might be sound in the faith, and not heed Jewish fables and commands of men,

6. He gives the reasons of this, from the liberty we have by the gospel from legal observances, and the evil and mischief of a Jewish spirit under the Christian dispensation in the last two verses. To good Christians that are sound in the faith and thereby purified *all things are pure.* Meats and drinks, and such things as were forbidden under the law (the observances of which some still maintain), in these there is now no such distinction, *all are pure* (lawful and free in their use), *but to those that are defiled and unbelieving nothing is pure;* things lawful and good they abuse and turn to sin; they suck poison out of that from which others draw sweetness; their mind and conscience, those leading faculties, being defiled, a taint is communicated to all they do. *The sacrifice of the wicked is an abomination to the Lord,* Prov. xv. 8. And *ch.* xxi. 4, *The ploughing of the wicked is sin,* not in itself, but as done by him; the carnality of the mind and heart mars all the labour of the hand.

Objection. But are not these judaizers (as you call them) men who profess religion, and speak well of God, and Christ, and righteousness of life, and should they be so severely taxed? *Answer, They profess that they know God; but in works they deny him, being abominable, and disobedient, and to every good work reprobate, v.* 16. There are many who in word and tongue profess to know God, and yet in their lives and conversations deny and reject him; their practice is a contradiction to their profession. *They come unto thee as the people cometh, and they sit before thee as my people, and they hear thy words, but they will not do them: with their mouth they show much love, but their heart goeth after their covetousness,* Ezek. xxxiii. 31. *Being abominable, and disobedient, and to every good work reprobate.* The apostle, instructing Titus to rebuke sharply, does himself rebuke sharply; he gives them very hard words, yet doubtless no harder than their case warranted and their need required. *Being abominable*—βδελυκτοὶ, deserving that God and good men should turn away their eyes from them as nauseous and offensive. *And disobedient*—ἀπειθεῖς, *unpersuadable* and *unbelieving.* They might do divers things; but it was not the obedience of faith, nor what was commanded, or short of the command. *To every good work reprobate,* without skill or judgment to do any thing aright. See the miserable condition of hypocrites, such as have a form of godliness, but without the power; yet let us not be so ready to fix this charge on others as careful that it agree not to ourselves, that there be not in us *an evil heart of unbelief, in departing from the living God;* but that we be *sincere and without offence till the day of Christ, being filled with the fruits of righteousness, which are by Jesus Christ unto the glory and praise of God,* Phil. i. 10, 11

CHAP. II.

The apostle here directs Titus about the faithful discharge of his own office generally (ver. 1), and particularly as to several sorts of persons (ver. 2—10) and gives the grounds of these and of other following directions (ver. 11—14), with a summary direction in the close, ver. 15.

BUT speak thou the things which
become sound doctrine: 2 That
the aged men be sober, grave, temperate, sound in faith, in charity, in
patience. 3 The aged women likewise, that *they be* in behaviour as
becometh holiness, not false accusers,
not given to much wine, teachers of
good things; 4 That they may teach
the young women to be sober, to love
their husbands, to love their children,
5 *To be* discreet, chaste, keepers at
home, good, obedient to their own
husbands, that the word of God be
not blasphemed. 6 Young men
likewise exhort to be sober minded.

7 In all things showing thyself a pattern of good works: in doctrine *showing* uncorruptness, gravity, sincerity, 8 Sound speech, that cannot be condemned; that he that is of the contrary part may be ashamed, having no evil thing to say of you. 9 *Exhort* servants to be obedient unto their own masters, *and* to please *them* well in all *things;* not answering again; 10 Not purloining, but showing all good fidelity; that they may adorn the doctrine of God our Saviour in all things.

Here is the third thing in the matter of the epistle. In the chapter foregoing, the apostle had directed Titus about matters of government, and to set in order the things that were wanting in the churches. Now here he exhorts him,

I. Generally, to a faithful discharge of his own office. His ordaining others to preach would not excuse himself from preaching, nor might he take care of ministers and elders only, but he must instruct private Christians also in their duty. The adversative particle (*but*) here points back to the corrupt teachers, who vented *fables*, things vain and unprofitable: in opposition to them, says he, "*But speak thou the things that become sound doctrine,* what is agreeable to the word, which is pure and uncorrupt, healthful and nourishing to eternal life." Observe, (1.) The true doctrines of the gospel are *sound doctrines*, formally and effectively; they are in themselves good and holy, and make the believers so; they make them fit for, and vigorous in, the service of God. (2.) Ministers must be careful to teach only such truths. If the common talk of Christians must *be uncorrupt, to the use of edifying, such as may minister grace to the hearers* (Eph. iv. 29), much more must ministers' preaching be such. Thus the apostle exhorts Titus generally: and then,

II. Specially and particularly, he instructs him to apply this sound doctrine to several sorts of persons, from *v.* 2—10. Ministers must not stay in generals, but must divide to every one his portion, what belongs to his age, or place, or condition of life; they must be particular as well as practical in their preaching; they must teach men their duty, and must teach all and each his duty. Here is an excellent Christian directory, accommodated to the old and to the young; to men and women; to the preacher himself and to servants.

1. To the aged men. By aged men some understand elders by office, including deacons, &c. But it is rather to be taken of the aged in point of years. Old disciples of Christ must conduct themselves in every thing agreeably to the Christian doctrine. *That the aged men be sober,* not thinking that the decays of nature, which they feel in old age, will justify them in any inordinacy or intemperance, whereby they conceit to repair them; they must keep measure in things, both for health and for fitness, for counsel and example to the younger. *Grave:* levity is unbecoming in any, but especially in the aged; they should be composed and stayed, grave in habit, speech, and behaviour; gaudiness in dress, levity and vanity in the behaviour, how unbeseeming in their years! *Temperate,* moderate and prudent, one who governs well his passions and affections, so as not to be hurried away by them to any thing that is evil or indecent. *Sound in the faith,* sincere and stedfast, constantly adhering to the truth of the gospel, not fond of novelties, nor ready to run into corrupt opinions or parties, nor to be taken with Jewish fables or traditions, or the dotages of their rabbin. Those who are full of years should be full of grace and goodness, the inner man renewing more and more as the outer decays. *In charity,* or love; this is fitly joined with *faith,* which works by, and must be seen in, love, love to God and men, and soundness therein. It must be sincere love, without dissimulation: love of God for himself, and of men for God's sake. The duties of the second table must be done in virtue of those of the first; love to men as men, and to the saints as the excellent of the earth, in whom must be special delight; and love at all times, in adversity as well as prosperity. Thus must there be soundness in charity or love. And *in patience.* Aged persons are apt to be peevish, fretful, and passionate; and therefore need to be on their guard against such infirmities and temptations. Faith, love, and patience, are three main Christian graces, and soundness in these is much of gospel perfection. There is *enduring patience* and *waiting patience,* both of which must be looked after; to *bear evils* becomingly, and contentedly to *want the good* till we are fit for it and it for us, being *followers of those who through faith and patience inherit the promises.* Thus as to the aged men.

2. To the aged women. These also must be instructed and warned. Some by these aged women understand the deaconesses, who were mostly employed in looking after the poor and attending the sick; but it is rather to be taken (as we render it) of all aged women professing religion. They must *be in behaviour as becometh holiness:* both men and women must accommodate their behaviour to their profession. Those virtues before mentioned (*sobriety, gravity, temperance, soundness in the faith, charity, and patience*), recommended to aged men, are not proper to them only, but applicable to both sexes, and to be looked to by aged women as well as men. Women are to hear and learn their duty from the word, as well as the men: there is not one way of salvation for one sex or sort, and another for another; but both must learn and practise the same things,

both as aged and as Christians; the virtues and duties are common. *That the aged women likewise* (as well as the men) *be in behaviour as becometh holiness;* or as beseems and is proper for holy persons, such as they profess to be and should be, keeping a pious decency and decorum in clothing and gesture, in looks and speech, and all their deportment, and this from an inward principle and habit of holiness, influencing and ordering the outward conduct at all times. Observe, Though express scripture do not occur, or be not brought, for every word, or look, or fashion in particular, yet general rules there are according to which all must be ordered; as 1 Cor. x. 31, *Whatever you do, do all to the glory of God.* And Phil. iv. 8, *Whatsoever things are true, whatsoever things are honest, whatsoever things are just, whatsoever things are pure, whatsoever things are lovely, whatsoever things are of good report, if there be any virtue, and if there be any praise, think on these things.* And here, whatsoever things are beseeming or unbeseeming holiness form a measure and rule of conduct to be looked to. *Not false accusers*—*μὴ διαβόλους*, no calumniators or sowers of discord, slandering and backbiting their neighbours, a great and too common fault; not only loving to speak, but to speak ill, of people, and to separate very friends. A slanderer is one *whose tongue is set on fire of hell;* so much, and so directly, do these do the devil's work, that for it the devil's name is given to such. This is a sin contrary to the great duties of love, justice, and equity between one another; it springs often from malice and hatred, or envy, and such like evil causes, to be shunned as well as the effect. *Not given to much wine;* the word denotes such addictedness thereto as to be under the power and mastery of it. This is unseemly and evil in any, but especially in this sex and age, and was too much to be found among the Greeks of that time and place. How immodest and shameful, corrupting and destroying purity both of body and mind! Of what evil example and tendency, unfitting for the next thing, which is a positive duty of aged matrons, namely, to be *teachers of good things!* Not public preachers, that is forbidden (1 Cor. xiv. 34, *I permit not a woman to speak in the church),* but otherwise teach they may and should, that is, by example and good life. Hence observe, Those whose actions and behaviour become holiness are thereby teachers of good things; and, besides this, they may and should also teach by doctrinal instruction at home, and in a private way. *The words of king Lemuel, the prophecy his mother taught him.* Such a woman is praised, *She openeth her mouth with wisdom, and in her tongue is the law of kindness,* Prov. xxxi. 1, 26. *Teachers of good things* are opposed to teachers of things corrupt, or to what is trifling and vain, of no good use or tendency, old wives' fables or superstitious sayings and observances; in opposition to these, their business is, and they may be called on to it, to be teachers of good things.

3. There are lessons for young women also, whom the aged women must teach, instructing and advising them in the duties of religion according to their years. For teaching such things aged women have often better access than the men, even than ministers have, which therefore they must improve in instructing the young women, especially the young wives; for he speaks of their duty to their husbands and children. These young women the more aged must teach, (1.) To bear a good personal character: *To be sober and discreet,* contrary to the vanity and rashness which younger years are subject to: discreet in their judgments and sober in their affections and behaviour. *Discreet* and *chaste* stand well together; many expose themselves to fatal temptations by that which at first might be but indiscretion. Prov. ii. 11, *Discretion shall preserve thee, understanding shall keep thee from the evil way. Chaste,* and *keepers at home,* are well joined too. Dinah, when she went to see the daughters of the land, lost her chastity. Those whose home is their prison, it is to be feared, feel that their chastity is their fetters. Not but there are occasions, and will be, of going abroad; but a gadding temper for merriment and company sake, to the neglect of domestic affairs, or from uneasiness at being in her place, is the opposite evil intended, which is commonly accompanied with, or draws after it, other evils. 1 Tim. v. 13, 14, *They learn to be idle, wandering from house to house; and not only idle, but tattlers also and busybodies, speaking things which they ought not.* Their business is *to guide the house,* and they should give no occasion to the enemy to speak reproachfully. *Good,* generally, in opposition to all vice; and specially, in her place, kind, helpful, and charitable; as Dorcas, *full of good works and almsdeeds.* It may also have, as some think, a more particular sense; one of a meek and yet cheerful spirit and temper, not sullen nor bitter; not taunting nor fretting and galling any; not of a troublesome or jarring disposition, uneasy in herself and to those about her; but of a good nature and pleasing conversation, and likewise helpful by her advice and pains: thus *building her house, and doing her husband good, and not evil, all her days.* Thus in their personal character *sober, discreet, chaste, keepers at home,* and *good:* and, (2.) In their relative capacities: *To love their husbands, and to be obedient to them:* and where there is true love this will be no difficult command. God, in nature, and by his will, hath made this subordination: *I suffer not a woman to usurp authority over the man* (1 Tim. ii. 12); and the reason is added: *For Adam was first formed, then Eve. Adam was not deceived, but the woman, being deceived, was in the transgression, v.* 13, 14. She fell first, and was the means

of seducing the husband. She was given to be a helper, but proved a most grievous hinderer, even the instrument of his fall and ruin, on which the bond of subjection was confirmed, and tied faster on her (Gen. iii. 16): *Thy desire shall be to thy husband, and he shall rule over thee*, with less easiness, it may be, than before. It is therefore doubly enjoined: *first in innocency*, when was settled a subordination of nature, Adam being first formed and then Eve, and the woman being taken out of the man; *and then upon the fall*, the woman being first in the transgression, and seducing the man; here now began to be a subjection not so easy and comfortable, being a part of the penalty in her case; yet through Christ is this nevertheless a sanctified state. Eph. v. 22, 23, *Wives submit yourselves unto your own husbands, as unto the Lord*, as owning Christ's authority in them, whose image they bear; *for the husband is the head of the wife, even as Christ is the head of the church: and he is the saviour of the body.* God would have a resemblance of Christ's authority over the church held forth in the husband's over the wife. Christ is the head of the church, to protect and save it, to supply it with all good, and secure or deliver it from evil; and so is the husband over the wife, to keep her from injuries, and to provide comfortably for her, according to his ability. Therefore, as the church is subject unto Christ, so let the *wives be unto their own husbands, as is fit in the Lord* (Col. iii. 18), as comports with the law of Christ, and is for his and the Father's glory. It is not then an absolute, or unlimited, nor a slavish subjection that is required; but a loving subordination, to prevent disorder or confusion, and to further all the ends of the relation. Thus, in reference to the husbands, wives must be instructed in their duties of love and subjection to them. *And to love their children*, not with a natural affection only, but a spiritual, a love springing from a holy sanctified heart and regulated by the word; not a fond foolish love, indulging them in evil, neglecting due reproof and correction where necessary, but a regular Christian love, showing itself in their pious education, forming their life and manners aright, taking care of their souls as well as of their bodies, of their spiritual welfare as well as of their temporal, of the former chiefly and in the first place. The reason is added: *That the word of God may not be blasphemed.* Failures in such relative duties would be greatly to the reproach of Christianity. "What are these the better for this their new religion?" would the infidels be ready to say. The word of God and the gospel of Christ are pure, excellent, and glorious, in themselves; and their excellency should be expressed and shown in the lives and conduct of their professors, especially in relative duties; failures here being disgrace. Rom. ii. 24, *The name of God is blasphemed among the Gentiles through you.* "Judge what a God he is," would they be ready to say, "by these his servants; and what his word, and doctrine, and religion, are by these his followers." Thus would Christ *be wounded in the house of his friends.* Thus of the duties of the younger women.

4. Here is the duty of young men. They are apt to be eager and hot, thoughtless and precipitant; therefore they must be earnestly called upon and exhorted to be considerate, not rash; advisable and submissive, not wilful and head-strong; humble and mild, not haughty and proud; for there are more young people ruined by pride than by any other sin. The young should be grave and solid in their deportment and manners, joining the seriousness of age with the liveliness and vigour of youth. This will make even those younger years to pass to good purpose, and yield matter of comfortable reflection when the evil days come; it will be preventive of much sin and sorrow, and lay the foundation for doing and enjoying much good. Such shall not *mourn at the last*, but have peace and comfort in death, and after it a glorious crown of life.

5. With these instructions to Titus, respecting what he should teach others—the aged men and women, and the younger of both sexes (Titus himself probably at this time being a young man also), the apostle inserts some directions to himself. He could not expect so successfully to teach others, if he did not conduct himself well both in his conversation and preaching. (1.) Here is direction for his conversation: *In all things showing thyself a pattern of good works, v.* 7. Without this, he would pull down with one hand what he built with the other. Observe, Preachers of good works must be patterns of them also; good doctrine and good life must go together. *Thou that teachest another, teachest thou not thyself?* A defect here is a great blemish and a great hindrance. *In all things;* some read, *above all things*, or *above all men.* Instructing others in the particulars of their duty is necessary, and, above all things, example, especially that of the teacher himself, is needful; hereby both light and influence are more likely to go together. "Let them see a lively image of those virtues and graces in thy life which must be in theirs. Example may both teach and impress the things taught; when they see purity and gravity, sobriety and all good life, in thee, they may be more easily won and brought thereto themselves; they may become pious and holy, sober and righteous, as thou art." Ministers must be examples to the flock, and the people followers of them, as they are of Christ. And here is direction, (2.) For his teaching and doctrine, as well as for his life: *In doctrine showing uncorruptness, gravity, sincerity, sound speech, that cannot be condemned, v.* 7, 8. They must make it appear that the design of their preaching is purely to advance the honour of God, the interest of

Christ and his kingdom, and the welfare and happiness of souls; that this office was not entered into nor used with secular views, not from ambition nor covetousness, but a pure aim at the spiritual ends of its institution. In their preaching, therefore, the display of wit or parts, or of human learning or oratory, is not to be affected; but sound speech must be used, which cannot be *condemned;* scripture-language, as far as well may be, in expressing scripture-truths. This is sound speech, that cannot be condemned. We have more than once these duties of a minister set together. 1 Tim. iv. 16, *Take heed to thyself, and to thy doctrine:* and, *v.* 12 of the same chapter, "*Let no man despise thy youth, but be thou an example of believers in word*—in thy speech, as a Christian, being grave, serious, and to the use of edifying; and in thy preaching, that it be the pure word of God, or what is agreeable to it and founded on it. Thus be an example *in word:* and *in conversation,* the life corresponding with the doctrine. In doing this *thou shalt both save thyself and those that hear thee.*" In 2 Tim. iii. 10, *Thou hast fully known my doctrine and manner of life* (says the same apostle), how agreeable these have been. And so must it be with others; their teaching must be agreeable to the word, and their life with their teaching. This is the true and good minister. 1 Thess. ii. 9, 10, *Labouring night and day, we preached to you the gospel of God; and you are witnesses, and God also, how holily, and justly, and unblamably, we behaved ourselves among you.* This must be looked to, as the next words show, which are, (3.) The reason both for the strictness of the minister's life and the gravity and soundness of his preaching: *That he who is of the contrary part may be ashamed, having no evil thing to say of you.* Adversaries would be seeking occasion to reflect, and would do so could they find any thing amiss in doctrine or life; but, if both were right and good, such ministers might set calumny itself at defiance; they would have no evil thing to say justly, and so must be ashamed of their opposition. Observe, Faithful ministers will have enemies watching for their halting, such as will endeavour to find or pick holes in their teaching or behaviour; the more need therefore for them to look to themselves, that no just occasion be found against them. Opposition and calumny perhaps may not be escaped; men of corrupt minds will resist the truth, and often reproach the preachers and professors of it; but let them see that *with well-doing they put to silence the ignorance of foolish men; that, when they speak evil of them as evil-doers, those may be ashamed who falsely accuse their good conversation in Christ.* This is the direction to Titus himself, and so of the duties of free persons, male and female, old and young. Then follow,

6. The directions respecting servants. Servants must not think that their mean and low state puts them beneath God's notice or the obligations of his laws—that, because they are servants of men, they are thereby discharged from serving God. No; servants must know and do their duty to their earthly masters, but with an eye to their heavenly one: and Titus must not only instruct and warn earthly masters of their duties, but servants also of theirs, both in his public preaching and private admonitions. Servants must attend the ordinances of God for their instruction and comfort, as well as the masters themselves. In this direction to Titus there are the duties themselves, to which he must exhort servants, and a weighty consideration wherewith he was to enforce them.

(1.) The duties themselves are these:—

[1.] *To be obedient to their own masters v.* 9. This is the prime duty, that by which they are characterized. Rom. vi. 16, *His servants you are whom you obey.* There must be inward subjection and dutiful respect and reverence in the mind and thoughts. "*If I be a master, where is my fear,* the dutiful affection you show to me, together with the suitable outward significations and expressions of it, in doing what I command you?" This must be in servants; their will must be subject to their master's will, and their time and labour at their master's disposal and command. 1 Pet. ii. 18, *Servants, be subject to your masters with all fear, not only to the good and gentle, but also to the froward.* The duty results from the will of God, and the relation in which, by his providence, he has put such; not from the quality of the person. If he be a master, the duties of a servant are to be paid to him as such. Servants therefore are to be exhorted to be obedient to their own masters. And,

[2.] *To please them well in all things,* in all lawful things, and such as belong to them to command, or at least as are not contrary to the will of their great and superior Lord. We are not to understand it either of obeying or pleasing them absolutely, without any limitation; but always with a reserve of God's right, which may in no case be entrenched upon. If his command and the earthly master's come in competition, we are instructed to obey God rather than man; but then servants must be upon good grounds in this, that there is an inconsistency, else are they not held to be excused. And not only must the will of God be the measure of the servant's obedience, but the reason of it also. All must be done with a respect to him, in virtue of his authority, and for pleasing him primarily and chiefly, Col. iii. 22—24. In serving the earthly master according to Christ's will, he is served; and such shall be rewarded by him accordingly. But how are servants to please their masters in all things, and yet not be men-pleasers? *Answer,* Men-pleasers, in the faulty sense, are such as eye men alone, or chiefly, in what they do, leaving God out, or subordinating him to man; when the will of man shall carry it, though against God's will, or man's pleasure is more regarded than his,—when this can content them, that the earthly master is pleased, though God be displeased,—or when more care, or more satisfaction, is taken in man's being pleased than in God's, this is sinful man-pleasing, of which all must take heed. Eph. vi. 5—7, "*Servants, be obedient to those that are your masters according to the flesh, with fear and trembling, with singleness of your heart, as unto Christ. Not with eye-service, as men-pleasers* (who look at nothing but the favour or displeasure of men, or at nothing so much as this), *but as the servants of Christ, doing the will of God from the heart; with good will doing service, as to the Lord, and not to men;*" not to them chiefly, but to Christ, who requires, and who will reward, any good done, whether by bond or free. Observe therefore, Christian liberty comports well with civil servitude and subjection. Persons may serve men, and yet be the servants of Christ; these are not contrary, but subordinate, so far as serving men is according to Christ's will and for his sake. Christ came not to destroy or prejudice civil order and differences. "*Art thou called, being a servant? Care not for it,* 1 Cor. vii. 21. Let not this trouble thee, as if it were a condition unworthy of a Christian, or wherein the person so called is less pleasing unto God; *for he that is called in the Lord, being a servant, is the Lord's freeman,* not free from that service, but free in it; free spiritually, though not in a civil sense. *Likewise also he that is called, being free, is Christ's servant;* he is bound to him, though he be not under civil subjection to any; so that, *bond or free, all are one in Christ.*" Servants therefore should not regret nor be troubled at their condition, but be faithful and cheerful in the station wherein God hath set them, striving to please their masters in all things. Hard it may be under some churlish Nabals, but it must be aimed at as much as possible.

[3.] *Not answering again;* not contradicting them, nor disputing it with them; not giving them any disrespectful or provoking language. Job complained of his servants, that he *called them, and they gave him no answer;* that was faulty another way: *Non respondere pro convitio est—Such silence is contempt:* but here it is respect, rather to take a check or reproof with humble silence, not making any confident nor bold replies. When conscious of a fault, to palliate or stand in justification of it doubles it. Yet this not answering again excludes not turning away wrath with a soft answer, when season and circumstances admit. Good and wise masters will be ready to hear and do right; but answering unseasonably, or in an unseemly manner, or, where the case admits not excuse, to be pert or confident, shows a want of the humility and meekness which such relation requires.

[4.] *Not purloining, but showing all good fidelity.* This is another great essential of good servants, to be *honest,* never converting that to their own use which is their master's, nor wasting the goods they are entrusted with; that is, *purloining.* They must be just and true, and do for their masters as they would or should for themselves. Prov. xxviii. 24, *Whoso robbeth his father or his mother, and saith, It is no transgression, the same is the companion of a destroyer;* he will be ready to join with him. Thus having such light thoughts of taking beyond what is right, though it be from a parent or master, is likely to harden conscience to go further; it is both wicked in itself, and it tends to more. Be it so that the master is hard and strait, scarcely making sufficient provision for servants; yet they must not be their own carvers, nor go about by theft to right themselves; they must bear their lot, committing their cause to God for righting and providing for them. I speak not of cases of extremity, for preserving life, the necessaries for which the servant has a right to. *Not purloining, but showing all good fidelity;* he must not only not steal nor waste, but must improve his master's goods, and promote his prosperity and thriving, to his utmost. He that increased not his master's talent is accused of unfaithfulness, though he had not embezzled nor lost it. Faithfulness in a servant lies in the ready, punctual, and thorough execution of his master's orders; keeping his secrets and counsels, despatching his affairs, and managing with frugality, and to as much just advantage for his master as he is able; looking well to his trusts, and preventing, as far as he can, all spoil, or loss, or damage. This is a way to bring a blessing upon himself, as the contrary often brings utter ruin. *If you have not been faithful in that which is another man's, who shall give you that which is your own?* Luke xvi. 12. Thus of the duties themselves, to which servants are to be exhorted. Then,

(2.) Here is the consideration with which Titus was to enforce them: *That they may adorn the doctrine of God our Saviour in all things;* that is, that they may recommend the gospel and Christ's holy religion to the good opinion of those that are without, by their meek, humble, obedient, and faithful conduct in all things. Even servants, though they may think that such as they, in so low and inferior a condition, can do little to bring repute to Christianity, or adorn the doctrine of Christ, and set forth the excellences of his truth and ways, yet, if they be careful to do their duty, it will redound to the glory of God and the credit of religion. The unbelieving masters would think the better of that despised way, which was every where spoken against, when they found that those of their servants who were Christians were better than their other servants—more obedient and submissive, more just and faithful, and more diligent in their places. True religion is an honour to the professors of it; and they should see that they do not any dishonour to it, but adorn it rather in all that they are able. Our light must shine among men, so that they, seeing our good works, may glorify our Father who is in heaven. And thus of the apostle's directions to Titus, about the discharge of his office, in reference to several sorts of persons.

11 For the grace of God that bringeth salvation hath appeared to all men, 12 Teaching us that, denying ungodliness and worldly lusts, we should live soberly, righteously, and godly, in this present world; 13 Looking for that blessed hope, and the glorious appearing of the great God and our Saviour Jesus Christ; 14 Who gave himself for us, that he might redeem us from all iniquity, and purify unto himself a peculiar people, zealous of good works.

Here we have the grounds or considerations upon which all the foregoing directions are urged, taken from the nature and design of the gospel, and the end of Christ's death.

I. From the nature and design of the gospel. Let young and old, men and women, masters and servants, and Titus himself, let all sorts do their respective duties, for this is the very aim and business of Christianity, to instruct, and help, and form persons, under all distinctions and relations, to a right frame and conduct. For this,

1. They are put under the dispensation of *the grace of God*, so the gospel is called, Eph. iii. 2. It is grace in respect of the spring of it—the free favour and good-will of God, not any merit or desert in the creature; as manifesting and declaring this good-will in an eminent and signal manner; and as it is the means of conveying and working grace in the hearts of believers. Now grace is obliging and constraining to goodness: *Let not sin reign, but yield yourselves unto God; for you are not under the law, but under grace,* Rom. vi. 12—14. *The love of Christ constrains us* not to live to self, but to him (2 Cor. v. 14, 15); without this effect, grace is received in vain.

2. This gospel grace *brings salvation* (reveals and offers it to sinners and ensures it to believers)—salvation from sin and wrath, from death and hell. Hence it is called *the word of life;* it brings to faith, and so to life, the life of holiness now and of happiness hereafter. The law is the ministration of death, but the gospel the ministration of life and peace. This therefore must be received as salvation (its rules minded, its commands obeyed), that the end of it may be obtained, *the salvation of the soul.* And more inexcusable will the neglecters of this grace of God bringing salvation now be, since,

3. *It hath appeared,* or shone out more clearly and illustriously than ever before. The old dispensation was comparatively dark and shadowy; this is a clear and shining light; and, as it is now more bright, so more diffused and extensive also. For,

4. It hath appeared *to all men;* not to the Jews only, as the glory of God appeared at mount Sinai to that particular people, and out of the view of all others; but gospel grace is open to all, and all are invited to come and partake of the benefit of it, Gentiles as well as Jews. The publication of it is free and general: *Disciple all nations: Preach the gospel to every creature.* The pale is broken down; there is no such enclosure now as formerly. *The preaching of Jesus Christ, which was kept secret since the world began, now is made manifest, and by the scriptures of the prophets, according to the commandment of the everlasting God, made known to all nations for the obedience of faith,* Rom. xvi. 25, 26. The doctrine of grace and salvation by the gospel is for all ranks and conditions of men (slaves and servants, as well as masters), therefore engaging and encouraging all to receive and believe it, and walk suitably to it, adorning it in all things.

5. This gospel revelation is to *teach,* and not by way of information and instruction only, as a schoolmaster does his scholars, but by way of precept and command, as a sovereign who gives laws to his subjects. It directs what to shun and what to follow, what to avoid and what to do. The gospel is not for speculation only or chiefly, but for practice and right ordering of life; for it teaches us,

(1.) To abandon sin: *Denying ungodliness and wordly lusts;* to renounce and have no more to do with these, as we have had: *Put off, concerning the former conversation, the old man which is corrupt;* that is, the whole body of sins, here distributed into *ungodliness* and *worldly lusts.* "Put away ungodliness and irreligion, all unbelief, neglect or disesteem of the divine Being, not loving, nor fearing, nor trusting in him, nor obeying him as we should, neglecting his ordinances, slighting his worship, profaning his name or day. Thus deny ungodliness (hate and put it away); *and worldly lusts,* all corrupt and vicious desires and affections that prevail in worldly men, and carry out to worldly things· *the lusts of the flesh also, and of the eye, and the pride of life,* all sensuality and filthiness, covetous desires and ambition, seeking and valuing more the praise of men than of God; put away all these." An earthly sensual conversation suits not a heavenly calling. *Those that are Christ's have crucified the flesh with the affections and lusts.* They have done it by covenant-engagement and promise, and have initially and prevailingly done it in act; they are going on in the work, cleansing themselves more and more from all filthiness of flesh and spirit. Thus the gospel first unteaches that which is evil, to abandon sin; and then,

(2.) To make conscience of that which is good: *To live soberly, righteously, and godly,* &c. Religion is not made up of negatives only; there must be doing good as well as eschewing evil; in these conjunctly is sincerity proved and the gospel adorned. We should live soberly with respect to ourselves, in the due government of our appetites and passions, keeping the limits of moderation and temperance, avoiding all inordinate excesses; and righteously towards all men, rendering to all their due, and injuring none, but rather doing good to others, according to our ability and their need: this seems a part of justice and righteousness, for we are not born for ourselves alone, and therefore may not live to ourselves only. *We are members one of another,* and *must seek every man another's wealth,* 1 Cor. x. 24; xii. 25. The public, especially, which includes the interests of all, must have the regards of all. Selfishness is a sort of unrighteousness; it robs others of that share in us which is their due. How amiable then will a just and righteous conduct be! It secures and promotes all interests, not particular only, but general and public, and so contributes to the peace and happiness of the world. Live righteously therefore as well as soberly. And godly towards God, in the duties of his worship and service. Regards to him indeed should run through all. *Whether you eat, or drink, or whatsoever you do, do all to the glory of God,* 1 Cor. x. 31. Personal and relative duties must be done in obedience to his commands, with due aim at pleasing and honouring him, from principles of holy love and fear of him. But there is an express and direct duty also that we owe to God, namely, belief and acknowledgment of his being and perfections, paying him internal and external worship and homage,—loving, fearing, and trusting in him,—depending on him, and devoting ourselves to him,—observing all those religious duties and ordinances that he has appointed,—praying to him, praising him, and meditating on his word and works. This is godliness, looking and coming to God, as our state now is, not immediately, but as he has manifested himself in Christ; so does the gospel direct and require. To go to God in any other way, namely, by saints or angels, is unsuitable, yea, contrary to the gospel rule and warrant. All communications from God to us are through his Son, and our returns must also be by him. God in Christ we must look at as the object of our hope and worship. Thus must we exercise ourselves to godliness, without which there can be no adorning of that gospel which is according to it, which teaches and requires such a deportment. A gospel conversation must needs be a godly conversation, expressing our love and fear and reverence of God, our hope and trust and confidence in him, as manifested in his Son. *We are the circumcision* (who have in truth what was signified by that sacrament) *who worship God in the Spirit, and rejoice in Christ Jesus, and have no confidence in the flesh.* See in how small a compass our duty is comprised; it is put into few words, *denying ungodliness and worldly lusts, and living soberly, righteously, and godly, in this present world.* The gospel teaches us not only how to believe and hope well, but also to live well, as becomes that faith and hope in this present world, and as expectants of another and better. There is the world that now is, and that which is to come; the present is the time and place of our trial, and the gospel teaches us to live well here, not, however, as our final state, but with an eye chiefly to a future: for it teaches us in all,

(3.) To look for the glories of another world, to which a sober, righteous, and godly life in this is preparative: *Looking for that blessed hope, and the glorious appearing of the great God and our Saviour Jesus Christ.* Hope, by a metonymy, is put for the thing hoped for, namely, heaven and the felicities thereof, called emphatically *that hope,* because it is the great thing we look and long and wait for; and a *blessed hope,* because, when attained, we shall be completely happy for ever. *And the glorious appearing of the great God and our Saviour Jesus Christ.* This denotes both the time of the accomplishing of our hope and the sureness and greatness of it: it will be at the second appearing of Christ, when he shall come *in his own glory, and in his Father's, and of the holy angels,* Luke ix. 26. His own glory which he had before the world was; and his Father's, being *the express image of his person,* and as God-man, his delegated ruler and Judge; and of the holy angels, as his ministers and glorious attendants. His first coming was in meanness, to satisfy justice and purchase happiness; his second will be in majesty, to bestow and instate his people in it. *Christ was once offered to bear the sins of many; and unto those that look for him will he appear the second time, without sin, unto salvation,* Heb. ix. 28. *The great God and our Saviour* (or *even our Saviour) Jesus Christ;* for they are not two subjects, but one only, as appears by the single article, *τοῦ μεγάλου Θεοῦ καὶ Σωτῆρος,* not *καὶ τοῦ Σωτῆρος,* and so is *καὶ* rendered 1 Cor. xv. 24, *When he shall have delivered up the kingdom to God, even the Father; τῷ Θεῷ καὶ Πατρὶ.* Christ then is the *great God,* not figuratively, as magistrates and others are sometimes called gods, or as appearing and acting in the name of God, but properly and absolutely, *the true God* (1 John v. 20), *the mighty God* (Isa. ix. 6), *who, being in the form of God, thought it not robbery to be equal with God,* Phil. ii. 6. In his second coming he will reward his servants, and bring them to glory with him. Observe, [1.] There is a common and blessed hope for all true Christians in the other world. If in this life only they had hope in Christ, they were of all men the most miserable, 1 Cor. xv. 19. By hope is meant the thing hoped for, namely, Christ himself, who is called *our hope* (1 Tim. i. 1), and blessedness in and through him, even riches of glory (Eph. i. 18), hence fitly termed here *that blessed hope.* [2.] The design of the gospel is to stir up all to a good life by this blessed hope. *Gird up the loins of your mind, be sober, and hope to the end for the grace that is to be brought unto you at the revelation of Jesus Christ,* 1 Pet. i. 13. To the same purport here, *Denying ungodliness and worldly lusts, live soberly, righteously, and godly, in this present world, looking for the blessed hope;* not as mercenaries, but as dutiful and thankful Christians. *What manner of persons ought you to be in all holy conversation and godliness, looking for and hastening to the coming of the day of God!* 2 Pet. iii. 11, 12. Looking and hastening, that is, expecting and diligently preparing for it. [3.] At, and in, the glorious appearing of Christ will the blessed hope of Christians be attained; for their felicity will be this, *To be where he is, and to behold his glory,* John xvii. 24. The glory of the great God and our Saviour will then break out as the sun. Though in the exercise of his judiciary power he will appear as the Son of man, yet will he be mightily declared to be the Son of God too. The divinity, which on earth was much veiled, will shine out then as the sun in its strength. Hence the work and design of the gospel are to raise the heart to wait for this second appearing of Christ. *We are begotten again to a lively hope of it* (1 Pet. i. 3), turned to *serve the living God, and wait for his Son from heaven,* 1 Thess. i. 9, 10. Christians are marked by this, expecting their Master's coming (Luke xii. 36), *loving his appearance,* 2 Tim. iv. 8. Let us then look to this hope; let our loins be girt, and our lights burning, and ourselves like those who wait for their Lord; the day or hour we know not, but *he that shall come will come, and will not tarry,* Heb. x. 37 [4.] The comfort and joy of Christians are that their Saviour is the great God, and will gloriously manifest himself at his second coming. Power and love, majesty and mercy, will then appear together in the highest lustre, to the terror and confusion of the wicked, but to the everlasting triumph and rejoicing of the godly. Were he not thus the great God, and not a mere creature, he could not be their Saviour, nor their hope. Thus of the considerations to enforce the directions of all sorts to their respective duties from the nature and design of the gospel. And herewith is connected another ground, namely,

II. From the end of Christ's death: *Who gave himself for us, that he might redeem us from all iniquity, and purify unto himself a peculiar people, zealous of good works, v.* 14. To bring us to holiness and happiness was the end of Christ's death, as well as the scope of his doctrine. Here we have,

1. The purchaser of salvation—Jesus Christ, *that great God and our Saviour,* who saves not simply as God, much less as man alone; but as God-man, two natures in one person: man, that he might obey, and suffer, and die, for man, and be meet to deal with him and for him; and God, that he might support the manhood, and give worth and efficacy to his undertakings, and have due regard to the rights and honour of the deity, as well as the good of his creature, and bring about the latter to the glory of the former. Such a one became us; and this was,

2. The price of our redemption: *He gave himself.* The Father gave him, but he gave himself too; and, in the freeness and voluntariness, as well as the greatness of the offering, lay the acceptableness and merit of it. *Therefore doth my Father love me, because I lay down my life, that I might take it again. No man taketh it from me, but I lay it down of myself,* John x. 17, 18. So John xvii. 19, "*For their sakes I sanctify myself,* or separate and devote myself to this work, to be both a priest and a sacrifice to God for the sins of men." The human nature was the offering, and the divine the altar, sanctifying the gift, and the whole the act of the person. *He gave himself a ransom for all,* 1 Tim. ii. 6. *Once in the end of the world hath he appeared, to put away sin by the sacrifice of himself.* He was the priest and sacrifice too. *We are redeemed, not with silver and gold, but the precious blood of Christ* (1 Pet. i. 18, 19), called *the blood of God* (Acts xx. 28), that is, of him who is God.

3. The persons for whom: *For us,* us poor perishing sinners, gone off from God, and turned rebels against him. He gave himself *for us,* not only for our good, but in our stead. Messiah was cut off, not for himself, but for us. *He suffered, the just for the unjust, that he might bring us to God,* 1 Pet. iii. 18. *He was made sin for us* (an offering and sacrifice for sin), *that we might be made the righteousness of God in him,* 2 Cor. v. 21. Wonderful condescension and grace! *He loved us, and gave himself for us;* what can we do less than love and give up ourselves to him? Especially considering,

4. The ends of his giving himself for us, (1.) *That he might redeem us from all iniquity.* This is fitted to the first lesson, *denying ungodliness and worldly lusts.* Christ gave himself to redeem us from these, therefore put them away. To love and live in sin is to trample under foot redeeming blood, to despise and reject one of the greatest benefits of it, and to act counter to its design. But how could the short sufferings of Christ redeem us from all iniquity? *Answer,* Through the infinite dignity of his person. He who was God suffered, though not as God. The acts and properties of either nature are attributed to the person. God purchased his

church *with his own blood,* Acts xx. 28. Could payment be made at once, no need of suffering for ever. A mere creature could not do this, from the finiteness of his nature; but God-man could. *The great God and our Saviour gave himself for us:* this accounts for it. *By one offering he hath for ever perfected those that are sanctified,* Heb. ix. 25, 26; x. 14. He needed not to offer himself often, nor could he be holden of death, when he had once undergone it. Happy end and fruit of Christ's death, redemption from all iniquity! Christ died for this: and, (2.) *To purify to himself a peculiar people.* This enforces the second lesson: *To live soberly, righteously, and godly, in this present world.* Christ died to purify as well as to pardon—to obtain grace, to heal the nature, as well as to free from guilt and condemnation. He gave himself for his church, *to cleanse it.* Thus does he make *to himself a peculiar people,* by purifying them. Thus are they distinguished from the world that lies in wickedness; they are born of God, and assimilated to him, bear his image, are holy as their heavenly Father is holy. Observe, Redemption from sin and sanctification of the nature go together, and both make a peculiar people unto God: freedom from guilt and condemnation, freedom from the power of lusts, and purification of soul by the Spirit. These are *a chosen generation, a royal priesthood, a holy nation,* and so *a peculiar people.* And, (3.) *Zealous of good works.* This peculiar people, as they are made so by grace purifying them, so must they be seen to be so by doing good, and a zeal therein. Observe, The gospel is not a doctrine of licentiousness, but of holiness and good life. We are redeemed from our vain conversation, to serve God *in holiness and righteousness all the days of our life.* Let us see then that we do good, and have zeal in it; only looking that zeal be guided by knowledge and spirited with love, directed to the glory of God, and always in some good thing. And thus of the motive to the duties directed, from the end of Christ's death.

15 These things speak, and exhort, and rebuke with all authority. Let no man despise thee.

The apostle closes the chapter (as he began it) with a summary direction to Titus upon the whole, in which we have the matter and manner of ministers' teaching, and a special instruction to Titus in reference to himself.

I. The matter of ministers' teaching: *These things,* namely, those before mentioned: not Jewish fables and traditions, but the truths and duties of the gospel, of avoiding sin, and living soberly, righteously, and godly, in this present world. Observe, Ministers in their preaching must keep close to the word of God. *If any man speak, let him speak as the oracles of God,* 1 Pet. iv. 11, and not the figments and inventions of his own brain.

II. The manner; by doctrine, and exhortation, and reproof with all authority. 2 Tim. iii. 16, *All scripture is given by inspiration of God, and is profitable for doctrine, for reproof, for correction, and for instruction in righteousness;* that is, to teach sound doctrine, to convince of sin and refute error, to reform the life, and to carry forward in what is just and good; *that the man of God* (the Christian or minister) *may be perfect, thoroughly furnished to all good works* that are to be practised by himself or to be taught to others. Here is what will furnish for all parts of his duty, and the right discharge of them. "*These things speak,* or teach; shun not to declare the whole counsel of God." The great and necessary truths and duties of the gospel, especially, these *speak and exhort,* *παρακάλει, press with much earnestness.* Ministers must not be cold and lifeless in delivering heavenly doctrine and precepts, as if they were indifferent things or of little concern; but they must urge them with earnestness suitable to their nature and importance; they must call upon persons to mind and heed, and not be *hearers only, deceiving themselves; but doers of the word, that they may be blessed therein. And rebuke;* convince and reprove such as contradict or gainsay, or neglect and do not receive the truth as they should, or retain it in unrighteousness—those who hear it not with such a believing and obedient mind and heart as they ought, but, instead of this (it may be) live in contrary practices, showing themselves stubborn and disobedient, and to every good work reprobate. *Rebuke with all authority,* as coming in the name of God, and armed with his threatenings and discipline, whoever make light of which will do it at their peril. Ministers are reprovers in the gate.

III. Here is a special instruction to Titus in reference to himself: "*Let no man despise thee;* that is, give no occasion to do so, nor suffer it without reproof, considering that *he who despiseth despiseth not man, but God.*" Or thus, "*Speak and exhort these things,* press them upon all, as they may respectively be concerned; with boldness and faithfulness reprove sin, and carefully look to thyself and thy own conduct, and then none will despise thee." The most effectual way for ministers to secure themselves from contempt is to keep close to the doctrine of Christ, and imitate his example—to preach and live well, and do their duty with prudence and courage; this will best preserve both their reputation and their comfort.

Perhaps too an admonition might be here intended to the people—that Titus, though young, and but a substitute of the apostle, yet should not be contemned by them, but considered and respected as a faithful minister of Christ, and encouraged and supported in his work and office. "*Know those that labour among you, and are over you in the Lord, and admonish you; and esteem them*

very highly in love for their work's sake, 1 Thess. v. 12, 13. Mind their teaching, respect their persons, support them in their function, and, what in you lies, further their endeavours for the honour of God and the salvation of souls."

CHAP. III.

Of duties which concern Christians more in common, and the reasons of them, ver. 1—8. What Titus in teaching should avoid, and how he should deal with a heretic, with some other directions (ver. 9—14), and salutations in the close, ver. 15.

PUT them in mind to be subject
to principalities and powers, to
obey magistrates, to be ready to
every good work, 2 To speak evil
of no man, to be no brawlers, *but*
gentle, showing all meekness unto
all men. 3 For we ourselves also
were sometimes foolish, disobedient,
deceived, serving divers lusts and
pleasures, living in malice and envy,
hateful, *and* hating one another. 4
But after that the kindness and love
of God our Saviour toward man
appeared, 5 Not by works of righteousness which we have done, but
according to his mercy he saved us,
by the washing of regeneration, and
renewing of the Holy Ghost; 6
Which he shed on us abundantly
through Jesus Christ our Saviour;
7 That being justified by his grace,
we should be made heirs according
to the hope of eternal life. 8 *This*
is a faithful saying, and these things
I will that thou affirm constantly,
that they which have believed in
God might be careful to maintain
good works. These things are good
and profitable unto men.

Here is the fourth thing in the matter of the epistle. The apostle had directed Titus in reference to the particular and special duties of several sorts of persons; now he bids him exhort to what concerned them more in common, namely, to quietness and submission to rulers, and readiness to do good, and to equitable and gentle behaviour towards all men—things comely and ornamental of religion; he must therefore put them in mind of such things. Ministers are people's remembrancers of their duty. As they are remembrancers for the people to God in prayers (Isa. lxii. 6), so are they from God to them in preaching: *I will not be negligent to put you always in remembrance,* 2 Pet. i. 12. Forgetfulness of duty is a common frailty; there is need therefore of reminding and quickening them thereto. Here are the duties themselves, and the reasons of them.

I. The duties themselves, which they were to be reminded of. 1. *Put them in mind to be subject to principalities and powers, to obey magistrates.* Magistracy is God's ordinance for the good of all, and therefore must be regarded and submitted to by all; not for wrath and by force only, but willingly and for conscience' sake. *Principalities,* and *powers,* and *magistrates,* that is, all civil rulers, whether supreme and chief or subordinate, in the government under which they live, of whatever form it be; that they be subject to them and obey them in things lawful and honest, and which it belongs to their office to require. The Christian religion was misrepresented by its adversaries as prejudicial to the rights of princes and civil powers, and tending to faction and sedition, and to rebellion against lawful authority; therefore *to put to silence the ignorance of foolish men,* and stop the mouths of malicious enemies, Christians must be reminded to show themselves examples rather of all due subjection and obedience to the government that is over them. Natural desire of liberty must be guided and bounded by reason and scripture. Spiritual privileges do not make void or weaken, but confirm and strengthen, their obligations to civil duties: "Remind them therefore *to be subject to principalities and powers and to obey magistrates.*" And, 2. *To be ready to every good work.* Some refer this to such good works as are required by magistrates and within their sphere: "Whatever tends to good order, and to promote and secure public tranquillity and peace, be not backward, but ready, to promote such things." But, though this be included, if not first intended, yet is it not to be hereto restrained. The precept regards doing good in all kinds, and on every occasion that may offer, whether respecting God, ourselves, or our neighbour—what may bring credit to religion in the world. *Whatsoever things are true, honest, just, pure, lovely, of good report; if there be any virtue, if there be any praise, think on these things* (Phil. iv. 8), to do and follow and further them. Mere harmlessness, or good words and good meanings only, are not enough without good works. *Pure religion and undefiled before God and the Father is this, to visit the fatherless and the widow in their affliction, and keep unspotted from the world.* "Not only take, but seek, occasion for doing good, keep fitness and readiness that way, put it not off to others, but embrace and lay hold on it thyself, delight and rejoice therein, put all in mind of this." And, 3. *To speak evil of no man: μηδένα βλασφημεῖν, to revile,* or *curse,* or *blaspheme none:* or (as our translation more generally) *to speak evil of none,* unjustly and falsely, or unnecessarily, without call, and when it may do hurt but no good to the person himself or any other. If no good can be spoken, rather than speak evil unnecessarily, say nothing. We must never take pleasure in speaking ill of others, nor make the worst of any thing, but the best that we can. We must not go up and down as tale-bearers, carrying ill-natured stories, to the prejudice of our neighbour's good name and the destruction of brotherly love. Misrepresentations, or insinuations of bad intentions, or of hypocrisy in what is done, things out of our reach or cognizance, these come within the reach of this prohibition. As this evil is too common, so it is of great malignity. *If any man seemeth to be religious and bridleth not his tongue, that man's religion is vain,* Jam. i. 26. Such loose uncharitable talk is displeasing to God, and hurtful among men. Prov. xvii. 9, *He that covereth a transgression seeketh love* (that is, to himself by this tenderness and charity, or rather to the transgressor); *but he that repeateth a matter* (that blazes and tells the faults of another abroad) *separateth very friends;* he raises dissensions and alienates his friend from himself, and perhaps from others. This is among the sins to be put off (Eph. iv. 31); for, if indulged, it unfits for Christian communion here and the society of the blessed in heaven, 1 Cor. vi. 10. Remind them therefore to avoid this. And, 4. *To be no brawlers; ἀμάχους εἶναι—no fighters,* either with hand or tongue, no quarrelsome contentious persons, apt to give or return ill and provoking language. A holy contending there is for matters good and important, and in a manner suitable and becoming, not with wrath nor injurious violence. Christians must follow the things that are conducive to peace, and that in a peaceful, not a rough and boisterous and hurtful way, but as becomes the servants of the God of peace and love (Rom. xii. 19), *Dearly beloved, avenge not yourselves, but rather give place unto wrath;* this is the Christian's wisdom and duty. *The glory of a man is to pass over a transgression;* it is the duty of a reasonable, and therefore certainly of a Christian man, whose reason is improved and advanced by religion; such may not, and will not, presently fall foul on one who has offended him, but, like God, will be *slow to anger, and ready to forgive.* Contention and strife arise from men's lusts, and exorbitant unruly passions, which must be curbed and moderated, not indulged; and Christians need to be reminded of these things, that they do not by a wrathful contentious spirit and behaviour displease and dishonour God and discredit religion, promoting feuds in the places where they live. *He that is slow to anger is better than the mighty,* and he *that ruleth his spirit than he that taketh a city.* Wherefore it follows, 5. *But gentle;* ἐπιεικεῖς, *equitable and just,* or candid and fair in constructions of things, not taking words or actions in the worst sense; and for peace sometimes yielding somewhat of strict right. And, 6. *Showing all meekness to all men.* We must be of a mild disposition, and not only have meekness in our hearts, but show it in our speech and conduct. *All meekness*—meekness in all instances and occasions, not towards friends only, but *to all men,* though still with wisdom, as James admonishes, Jam. iii. 13. "Distinguish the person and the sin; pity the one and hate the other. Distinguish between sin and sin; look not on all alike, there are *motes and beams.* Distinguish also between sinner and sinner: *of some have compassion, others save with fear, pulling them out of the fire, thus making a difference,* Jude 22, 23. Mind these things; *the wisdom that is from above is pure and peaceable, gentle and easy to be entreated.*" Meekness of spirit and demeanour renders religion amiable; it is a commanded imitation of Christ the grand exemplar, and what brings its own reward with it, in the ease and comfort of the disposition itself and the blessings accompanying it. These shall be glad and rejoice, shall be taught and guided in their way, and satisfied with bread, and beautified with salvation. Thus of the duties themselves, which Titus was to put people in mind of: for which,

II. He adds the reasons, which are derived

1. From their own past condition. Consideration of men's natural condition is a great means and ground of equity and gentleness, and all meekness, towards those who are yet in such a state. This has a tendency to abate pride and work pity and hope in reference to those who are yet unconverted: "We ourselves also were so and so, corrupt and sinful, therefore we should not be impatient and bitter, hard and severe, towards those who are but as ourselves once were. Should we then have been willing to be contemned, and proudly and rigorously dealt with? No, but treated with gentleness and humanity; and therefore we should now so treat those who are unconverted, according to that rule of equity: *Quod tibi non vis fieri, alteri ne feceris—What you would not have done to you that do not you to another.*" Their past natural condition is set forth in divers particulars. *We ourselves also were sometimes,* (1.) *Foolish;* without true spiritual understanding and knowledge, ignorant of heavenly things. Observe, Those should be most disposed to bear with others' follies who may remember many of their own; those should be meek and gentle, and patient towards others, who once needed and doubtless then expected the same. *We ourselves also were sometimes foolish.* And, (2.) *Disobedient;* heady and unpersuadable, resisting the word, and rebellious even against the natural laws of God, and those which human society requires. Well are these set together, *foolish* and *disobedient.* For what folly like this, to disobey God and his laws, natural or revealed? This is contrary to right reason, and men's true and greatest interests; and what so foolish as to violate and go counter to these? (3.) *Deceived,* or wandering; namely, out of the ways of truth and holiness. Man in this his degenerate state is of a straying nature, thence compared to a lost sheep; this

must be sought and brought back, and guided in the right way, Ps. cxix. 176. He is weak, and ready to be imposed upon by the wiles and subtleties of Satan, and of men lying in wait to seduce and mislead. (4.) *Serving divers lusts and pleasures;* namely, as vassals and slaves under them. Observe, Men deceived are easily entangled and ensnared; they would not serve divers lusts and pleasures as they do, were they not blinded and beguiled into them. See here too what a different notion the word gives of a sensual and fleshly life from what the world generally has of it. Carnal people think they enjoy their pleasures; the word calls it servitude and vassalage: they are very drudges and bond slaves under them; so far are they from freedom and felicity in them that they are captivated by them, and serve them as task-masters and tyrants. Observe further, It is the misery of the servants of sin that they have many masters, one lust hurrying them one way, and another another; pride commands one thing, covetousness another, and often a contrary. What vile slaves are sinners, while they conceit themselves free! the lusts that tempt them promise them liberty, but in yielding they become the servants of corruption; for *of whom a man is overcome of the same is he brought into bondage.* (5.) *Living in malice,* one of those lusts that bear rule in them. Malice desires hurt to another and rejoices in it. (6.) *And envy,* which grudges and repines at another's good, frets at his prosperity and success in any thing: both are roots of bitterness, whence many evils spring: evil thoughts and speeches, tongues *set on fire of hell,* detracting from and impairing the just and due praises of others. *Their words are swords,* wherewith they slay the good name and honour of their neighbour. This was the sin of Satan, and of Cain who was of that evil one, and slew his brother; for wherefore slew he him, but of this envy and malice, *because his own works were evil, and his brother's righteous?* These were some of the sins in which we lived in our natural state. And, (7.) *Hateful,* or odious—deserving to be hated. (8.) *And hating one another.* Observe, Those that are sinful, living and allowing themselves in sin, are hateful to God and all good men. Their temper and ways are so, though not simply their persons. It is the misery of sinners that they hate one another, as it is the duty and happiness of saints to love one another. What contentions and quarrels flow from men's corruptions, such as were in the nature of those who by conversion are now good, but in their unconverted state made them ready to run like furious wild beasts one upon another! The consideration of its having been thus with us should moderate our spirits, and dispose us to be more equal and gentle, meek and tender-hearted, towards those who are such. This is the argument from their own past condition here described. And he reasons,

2. From their present state. "We are delivered out of that our miserable condition by no merit nor strength of our own; but only by the mercy and free grace of God, and merit of Christ, and operation of his Spirit. Therefore we have no ground, in respect of ourselves, to contemn those who are yet unconverted, but rather to pity them, and cherish hope concerning them, that they, though in themselves as unworthy and unmeet as we were, yet may obtain mercy, as we have: and so upon this occasion the apostle again opens the causes of our salvation, *v.* 4—7.

(1.) We have here the prime author of our salvation—God the Father, therefore termed here *God our Saviour. All things are of God, who hath reconciled us to himself by Jesus Christ,* 2 Cor. v. 18. All things belonging to the new creation, and recovery of fallen man to life and happiness, of which the apostle is there speaking, all these things are of God the Father, as contriver and beginner of this work. There is an order in acting, as in subsisting. The Father begins, the Son manages, and the Holy Spirit works and perfects all. God (namely, *the Father)* is a Saviour by Christ, through the Spirit. John iii. 16, *God so loved the world as to give his only begotten Son, that whoever believes in him might not perish, but have everlasting life.* He is the Father of Christ, and through him the Father of mercies; all spiritual blessings are by Christ from him, Eph. i. 3. *We joy in God through Jesus Christ,* Rom. v. 11. *And with one mind, and one mouth, glorify God, even the Father of our Lord Jesus Christ,* Rom. xv. 5.

(2.) The spring and rise of it—the divine *philanthropy,* or *kindness and love of God to man.* By grace we are saved from first to last. This is the ground and motive. God's pity and mercy to man in misery were the first wheel, or rather the Spirit in the wheels, that sets and keeps them all in motion. God is not, cannot be, moved by any thing out of himself. The occasion is in man, namely, his misery and wretchedness. Sin bringing that misery, wrath might have issued out rather than compassion; but God, knowing how to adjust all with his own honour and perfections, would pity and save rather than destroy. He delights in mercy. *Where sin abounded, grace did much more abound.* We read of *riches of goodness and mercy,* Rom. ii. 4; Eph. ii. 7. Let us acknowledge this, and give him the glory of it, not turning it to wantonness, but to thankfulness and obedience.

(3.) Here is the means, or instrumental cause—the shining out of this love and grace of God in the gospel, *after it appeared,* that is, in the word. The appearing of love and grace has, through the Spirit, great virtue to soften and change and turn to God, and so is *the power of God to salvation to every one that believeth.* Thus having asserted God to be the author, his free grace the spring, and the manifestation of this in the gospel the means of salvation, that the honour of all still may be the better secured to him,

(4) False grounds and motives are here removed: *Not by works of righteousness which we have done, but according to his mercy, he saved us;* not for foreseen works of ours, but his own free grace and mercy alone. Works must be in the saved (where there is room for it), but not among the causes of his salvation; they are the way to the kingdom, not the meriting price of it; all is upon the principle of undeserved favour and mercy from first to last. Election is of grace: we are chosen *to be* holy, not because it was antecedently seen that we should be so, Eph. i. 4. It is the fruit, not the cause, of election: *God hath from the beginning chosen you to salvation through sanctification of the Spirit and belief of the truth,* 2 Thess. ii. 13. So effectual calling, in which election breaks out, and is first seen: *He hath saved us, and called us with a holy calling; not according to our works, but according to his own purpose and grace, which was given us in Christ Jesus before the world began,* 2 Tim. i. 9. We *are justified freely by grace* (Rom. iii. 24), and sanctified and saved by grace: *By grace you are saved, through faith; and that not of yourselves, it is the gift of God,* Eph. ii. 8. Faith and all saving graces are God's free gift and his work; the beginning, increase, and perfection of them in glory, all are from him. In building men up to be a holy temple unto God, from the foundation to the top-stone, we must cry nothing but *Grace, grace* unto it. It is *not of works, lest any man should boast; but of grace, that he who glorieth should glory only in the Lord.* Thus the true cause is shown, and the false removed.

(5.) Here is the formal cause of salvation, or that wherein it lies, the beginnings of it at least—in regeneration or spiritual renewing, as it is here called. *Old things pass away, and all things become new,* in a moral and spiritual, not in a physical and natural, sense. It is the same man, but with other dispositions and habits; evil ones are done away, as to the prevalency of them at present; and all remains of them in due time will be so, when the work shall be perfected in heaven. A new prevailing principle of grace and holiness is wrought, which inclines, and sways, and governs, and makes the man a new man, a new creature, having new thoughts, desires, and affections, a new and holy turn of life and actions; the life of God in man, not only from God in a special manner, but conformed and tending to him. Here is salvation begun, and which will be growing and increasing to perfection; therefore it is said, *He saved us.* What is so begun, as sure to be perfected in time, is expressed as if it already were so. Let us look to this therefore without delay; we must be initially saved now, by regeneration, if on good ground we would expect complete salvation in heaven. The change then will be but in degree, not in kind. Grace is glory begun, as glory is but grace in its perfection. How few mind this! Most act as if they were afraid to be happy before the time; they would have heaven, they pretend, at last, yet care not for holiness now; that is, they would have the end without the beginning; so absurd are sinners. But without regeneration, that is, the first resurrection, there is no attaining the second glorious one, the resurrection of the just. Here then is formal salvation, in the new divine life wrought by the gospel.

(6.) Here is the outward sign and seal thereof in baptism, called therefore *the washing of regeneration.* The work itself is inward and spiritual; but it is outwardly signified and sealed in this ordinance. Water is of a cleansing and purifying nature, does away the filth of the flesh, and so was apt to signify the doing away of the guilt and defilement of sin by the blood and Spirit of Christ, though that aptness alone, without Christ's institution, would not have been sufficient. This it is that makes it of this signification on God's part, a seal of righteousness by faith, as circumcision was, in the place of which it succeeds; and on ours an engagement to be the Lord's. Thus baptism saves figuratively and sacramentally, where it is rightly used. *Arise, and be baptized, and wash away thy sins, calling upon the name of the Lord,* Acts xxii. 16. So Eph. v. 26, *That he might sanctify and cleanse us by the washing of water by the word.* Slight not this outward sign and seal, where it may be had according to Christ's appointment; yet rest not in the outward washing, but look to the *answer of a good conscience,* without which the external washing will avail nothing. The covenant sealed in baptism binds to duties, as well as exhibits and conveys benefits and privileges; if the former be not minded, in vain are the latter expected. Sever not what God has joined; in both the outer and inner part is baptism complete; as he that was circumcised became debtor to the whole law (Gal. v. 3), so is he that is baptized to the gospel, to observe all the commands and ordinances thereof, as Christ appointed. *Disciple all nations, baptizing them in the name of the Father, and of the Son, and of the Holy Ghost; teaching them to observe all things whatsoever I have commanded you,* Matt. xxviii. 19, 20. This is the outward sign and seal of salvation, baptism, called here *the washing of regeneration.*

(7.) Here is the principal efficient, namely, the Spirit of God; it is the *renewing of the Holy Ghost;* not excluding the Father and the Son, who in all works without themselves are concurring; nor the use of means, the word and sacraments, by which the Spirit works; through his operation it is that they have their saving effect. In the economy of our salvation, the applying and effecting part is especially attributed to the Holy Spirit. We are said to be born of the Spirit, to be quickened and sanctified by the Spirit, to be led and guided, strengthened and helped, by the Spirit. Through him we mortify sin, perform duty, walk in God's ways; all the acts and operations of the divine life in us, the works and fruits of righteousness without us, all are through this blessed and Holy Spirit, who is therefore called the Spirit of life, and of grace and holiness; all grace is from him. Earnestly therefore is he to be sought, and greatly to be heeded by us, that we quench not his holy motions, nor resist and oppose him in his workings. *Res delicatula est Spiritus—The Spirit is a tender thing.* As we act towards him, so may we expect he will to us; if we slight, and resist, and oppose his workings, he will slacken them; if we continue to vex him, he will retire. *Grieve not therefore the Holy Spirit of God, whereby you are sealed to the day of redemption,* Eph. iv. 30. The Spirit seals by his renewing and sanctifying, his witnessing and assuring work; he distinguishes and marks out for salvation, and fits for it; it is his work: we could not turn to God by any strength of our own, any more than we can be justified by any righteousness of our own.

(8.) Here is the manner of God's communicating this Spirit in the gifts and graces of it; not with a scanty and niggardly hand, but most freely and plentifully: *Which he shed on us abundantly.* More of the Spirit in its gifts and graces is poured out under the gospel than was under the law, whence it is eminently styled *the ministration of the Spirit,* 2 Cor. iii. 8. A measure of the Spirit the church has had in all ages, but more in gospel times, since the coming of Christ, than before. *The law came by Moses, but grace and truth by Jesus Christ;* that is, a more plentiful effusion of grace, fulfilling the promises and prophecies of old. Isa. xliv. 3, *I will pour water upon him that is thirsty, and floods upon the dry ground. I will pour my Spirit upon thy seed, and my blessing upon thy offspring:* this greatest and best of blessings, an effusion of grace, and of the sanctifying gifts of the Spirit. Joel. ii. 28, *I will pour out my Spirit upon all flesh;* not on Jews only, but Gentiles also. This was to be in gospel times; and accordingly (Acts ii. 17, 18, 33), speaking of Christ risen and ascended, *having received of the Father the promise of the Holy Ghost, he hath shed forth* (says Peter) *this that you now see and hear:* and *ch.* x. 44, 45, *The Holy Ghost fell on all those that heard the word,* Gentiles as well as Jews. This indeed was, in a great measure, in the miraculous gifts of the Holy Ghost, but not without his sanctifying graces also accompanying many if not all of them. There was then great abundance of common gifts of illumination, outward calling and profession, and general faith, and of more special gifts of sanctification too, such as faith, and hope, and love, and other graces of the Spirit. Let us get a share in these. What will it signify if much be shed forth and we remain dry? Our condemnation will but be aggravated the more if under such a dispensation of grace we remain void of grace. *Be filled with the Spirit,* says the apostle; it is duty as well as privilege, because of the means which God in the gospel is ready to bless and make effectual; this is the manner of God's communicating grace and all spiritual blessings under the gospel —*plentifully;* he is not straitened towards us, but we towards him and in ourselves.

(9.) Here is the procuring cause of all, namely, Christ: *Through Jesus Christ our Saviour.* He it is who purchased the Spirit and his saving gifts and graces. All come through him, and through him as a Saviour, whose undertaking and work it is to bring to grace and glory; he is our righteousness and peace, and our head, from whom we have all spiritual life and influences. *He is made of God to us wisdom, righteousness, sanctification, and redemption.* Let us praise God for him above all; let us go to the Father by him, and improve him to all sanctifying and saving purposes. Have we grace? Let us thank him with the Father and Spirit for it: *account all things but loss and dung for the excellency of the knowledge of him,* and grow and increase therein more and more.

(10.) Here are the ends why we are brought into this new spiritual condition, namely, justification, and heirship, and hope of eternal life: *That, being justified by his grace, we should be made heirs according to the hope of eternal life.* Justification in the gospel sense is the free remission of a sinner, and accepting him as righteous through the righteousness of Christ received by faith. In it there is the removing of guilt that bound to punishment, and the accepting and dealing with the person as one that now is righteous in God's sight. This God does freely as to us, yet through the intervention of Christ's sacrifice and righteousness, laid hold on by faith (Rom. iii. 20, &c.): *By the deeds of the law shall no flesh be justified;* but through *the righteousness of God, which is by faith of Jesus Christ unto all and upon all those that believe,* whence (*v.* 24) we are said to be *justified freely by his grace, through the redemption that is in Jesus Christ, whom God hath set forth to be a propitiation through faith in his blood, to declare his righteousness for the remission of sins, that he might be just, and the justifier of him that believeth in Jesus.* God, in justifying a sinner in the way of the gospel, is gracious to him, and yet just to himself and his law, forgiveness being through a perfect righteousness, and satisfaction made to justice by Christ, who is the propitiation for sin, and not merited by the sinner himself. So it is here: *Not by works of righteousness which we have done, but ac-*

cording to his mercy he saved us, that, being justified by his grace, we should be made heirs according to the hope of eternal life. It is by grace, as the spring and rise (as was said), though *through the redemption that is in Christ* as making the way, God's law and justice being thereby satisfied, and by faith applying that redemption. *By him* (by Christ) *all that believe are justified from all things from which they could not be justified by the law of Moses,* Acts xiii. 39. Hence the apostle desires *to be found in him, not having his own righteousness, which was of the law, but that which is through the faith of Christ, the righteousness which is of God by faith.* Let us not trust therefore in our own righteousness or merit of good works, but in Christ's righteousness alone, received by faith for justification and acceptance with God. Inherent righteousness we must have, and the fruits of it in works of obedience; not however as our justifying righteousness before God, but as fruits of our justification, and evidences of our interest in Christ and qualification for life and happiness, and the very beginning and part of it; but the procuring of all this is by Christ, that, *being justified by his grace, we should be made heirs.* Observe, Our justification is *by the grace of God,* and our justification by that grace is necessary in order to our being made *heirs of eternal life;* without such justification there can be no adoption and sonship, and so no right of inheritance. John i. 12, *Whoever received him* (namely, Christ), *to them gave he power to become the sons of God, even to those that believed on his name.* Eternal life is set before us in the promise, the Spirit works faith in us and hope of that life, and so are we made heirs of it and have a kind of possession of it even now; faith and hope bring it near, and fill with joy in the well-grounded expectation of it. The meanest believer is a great heir. Though he has not his portion in hand, he has good hope through grace, and may bear up under all difficulties. There is a better state in view. He is waiting for *an inheritance incorruptible, undefiled, and that fadeth not away, reserved in heaven for him.* How well may such comfort themselves with these words! And now all this gives good reason why we should *show all meekness to all men,* because we have experienced so much benefit by the kindness and love of God to us, and may hope that they, in God's time, may be partakers of the like grace as we are. And thus of the reasons of equal and gentle, meek and tender behaviour towards others, from their own bad condition in time past, and the present more happy state into which they are brought, without any merit or deservings of their own, and whereinto by the same grace others may be brought also.

III. The apostle, having opened the duties of Christians in common, with the reasons respecting themselves, adds another from their goodness and usefulness to men. Observe, When he has opened the grace of God towards us, he immediately presses the necessity of good works; for we must not expect the benefit of God's mercy, unless we make conscience of our duty (*v.* 8): *This is a faithful saying, and these things I will that thou affirm constantly* (this is a true Christian doctrine of highest importance, and which ministers must most earnestly and constantly press and inculcate), *that those who have believed in God* do not think that a bare naked faith will save them; but it must be an operative working faith, bringing forth the fruit of righteousness; they must make it their care *to maintain good works,* not to do them occasionally only, and when opportunities come in their way, but to seek opportunities for doing them. *These things are good and profitable unto men:* these *good works,* say some, or *the teaching of these things,* rather than idle questions, as follows. These things are good in themselves, and the teaching of them useful to mankind, making persons a common good in their places. Note, Ministers, in teaching, must see that they deliver what is sound and good in itself, and profitable to those that hear: all must be to the use of edifying both of persons and societies.

9 But avoid foolish questions, and
genealogies, and contentions, and
strivings about the law; for they
are unprofitable and vain. 10 A man
that is a heretic after the first and
second admonition reject; 11 Knowing
that he that is such is subverted, and
sinneth, being condemned of himself.
12 When I shall send Artemas unto
thee, or Tychicus, be diligent to
come unto me to Nicopolis: for I
have determined there to winter. 13
Bring Zenas the lawyer and Apollos
on their journey diligently, that nothing be wanting unto them. 14
And let our's also learn to maintain
good works for necessary uses, that
they be not unfruitful. 15 All that
are with me salute thee. Greet them
that love us in the faith. Grace be
with you all. Amen.

Here is the fifth and last thing in the matter of the epistle: what Titus should avoid in teaching; how he should deal with a heretic; with some other directions. Observe,

I. That the apostle's meaning might be more clear and full, and especially fitted to the time and state of things in Crete, and the many judaizers among them, he tells Titus what, in teaching, he should shun, *v.* 9. There are needful questions to be discussed and cleared, such as make for improvement in useful knowledge; but idle and foolish enquiries, tending neither to God's glory nor the edification of men, must be shunned. Some may have a show of wisdom, but are vain, as many among the Jewish doctors, as well as of later schoolmen, who abound with questions of no moment or use to faith or practice; avoid these.—*And genealogies* (of the gods, say some, that the heathen poets made such noise about; or rather those that the Jews were so curious in): some lawful and useful enquiries might be made into these things, to see the fulfilling of the scriptures in some cases, and especially in the descent of Christ the Messiah; but all that served to pomp only, and to feed vanity, in boasting of a long pedigree, and much more such as the Jewish teachers were ready to busy themselves in and trouble their hearers with, even since Christ had come, and that distinction of families and tribes had been taken away, as if they would build again that policy which now is abolished, these Titus must withstand as foolish and vain.—*And contentions, and strivings about the law.* There were those who were for the Mosaic rites and ceremonies, and would have them continued in the church, though by the gospel and the coming of Christ they were superseded and done away. Titus must give no countenance to these, but avoid and oppose them; *for they are unprofitable and vain:* this is to be referred to all those *foolish questions and genealogies,* as well as those *strivings about the law.* They are so far from instructing and building up in godliness, that they are hindrances of it rather: the Christian religion, and good works, which are to be maintained, will hereby be weakened and prejudiced, the peace of the church disturbed, and the progress of the gospel hindered. Observe, Ministers must not only teach things good and useful, but shun and oppose the contrary, what would corrupt the faith, and hinder godliness and good works; nor should people have itching ears, but love and embrace sound doctrine, which tends most to the use of edifying.

II. But because, after all, there will be *heresies* and *heretics* in the church, the apostle next directs Titus what to do in such a case, and how to deal with such, *v.* 10. He who forsakes the truth as it is in Christ Jesus, who broaches false doctrines and propagates them to the corrupting of the faith in weighty and momentous points, and breaks the peace of the church about them, after due means used to reclaim him, must be rejected. "Admonish him once and again, that, if possible, he may be brought back, and thou mayest gain thy brother; but, if this will not reduce him, that others be not hurt, cast him out of the communion, and warn all Christians to avoid him.—*Knowing that he that is such is subverted* (turned off from the foundation) *and sinneth* grievously, being *self-condemned.* Those who will not be reclaimed by admonitions, but are obstinate in their sins and errors, *are subverted and self-condemned;* they inflict that punishment upon themselves which the governors of the church should inflict upon them: they throw themselves out of the church, and throw off its communion, and so are self-condemned. Observe, 1. How great an evil real heresy is, not lightly therefore to be charged upon any, though greatly to be taken heed of by all. Such a one is *subverted* or perverted—a metaphor from a building so ruined as to render it difficult if not impossible to repair and raise it up again. Real heretics have seldom been recovered to the true faith: not so much defect of judgment, as perverseness of the will, being in the case, through pride, or ambition, or self-willedness, or covetousness, or such like corruption, which therefore must be taken heed of: "Be humble, love the truth and practise it, and damning heresy will be escaped." 2. Pains and patience must be used about those that err most grievously. They are not easily and soon to be given up and cast off, but competent time and means must be tried for their recovery. 3. The church's means even with heretics are persuasive and rational. They must be admonished, instructed, and warned; so much νουθεσία imports. 4. Upon continued obstinacy and irreclaimableness, the church has power, and is obliged, to preserve its own purity, by severing such a corrupt member which discipline may by God's blessing become effectual to reform the offender, or if not it will leave him the more inexcusable in his condemnation.

III. The apostle subjoins some further directions, *v.* 12, 13. Here are two personal things enjoined:—

1. That Titus should hold himself ready to come to Paul at *Nicopolis* (a city of Thrace, as is reckoned, on the borders of Macedonia), as soon as *Artemas or Tychicus* should be sent to Crete, to supply his place, and take care of the churches there when he should leave them. The apostle would not have them in their young and weak state be without one or other of chief sufficiency, to guide and help them. Titus, it seems, was not their ordinary fixed bishop or pastor, but an evangelist, otherwise Paul would not have called him so much from his charge. Of Artemas we read little, but Tychicus is mentioned on many occasions with respect. Paul calls him *a beloved brother, and faithful minister, and fellow-servant in the Lord:* one fit therefore for the service intimated. When Paul says to Titus, *Be diligent to come to me to Nicopolis, for I have determined there to winter,* it is plain that the epistle was not written from Nicopolis, as the postcript would have it, for then he would have said, I determined *here,* not *there,* to winter.

2. The other personal charge to Titus is that he would bring two of his friends **on**

their journey diligently, and see them furnished, so that nothing should be wanting to them. This was to be done, not as a piece of common civility only, but of Christian piety, out of respect both to them and the work they were sent about, which probably was to preach the gospel, or to be in some way serviceable to the churches. *Zenas* is styled *the lawyer,* whether in reference to the Roman or the Mosaic law, as having some time been his profession, is doubtful. *Apollos* was an eminent and faithful minister. Accompanying such persons part of their way, and accommodating them for their work and journeys, was a pious and needful service; and to further this, and lay in for it, what the apostle had before exhorted Titus to teach (*v.* 8) he repeats here: *Let ours also learn to maintain good works for necessary uses, that they be not unfruitful, v.* 14. Let Christians, those who have believed in God, learn to *maintain good works,* especially such as these, supporting ministers in their work of preaching and spreading the gospel, hereby becoming *fellow-helpers to the truth,* 3 John, 5—8. *That they be not unfruitful.* Christianity is not a fruitless profession; the professors of it must be *filled with the fruits of righteousness, which are by Jesus Christ, to the glory and praise of God.* It is not enough that they be harmless, but they must be profitable, doing good, as well as eschewing evil.—“ *Let ours* set up and maintain some honest labour and employment, to provide for themselves and their families, that they be not unprofitable burdens on the earth;” so some understand it. Let them not think that Christianity gives them a writ of ease; no, it lays an obligation upon them to seek some honest work and calling, and therein *to abide with God.* This is of good report, will credit religion and be good to mankind; they will not be unprofitable members of the body, not burdensome and chargeable to others, but enabled to be helpful to those in want. *To maintain good works for necessary uses;* not living like drones on the labours of others, but themselves fruitful to the common benefit.

IV. The apostle concludes with salutations and benedictions, *v.* 5. Though perhaps not personally known (some of them at least), yet all by Paul testify their love and good wishes to Titus, owning him thereby in his work, and stimulating him to go on therein. Great comfort and encouragement it is to have the heart and prayers of other Christians with and for us. *Greet those that love us in the faith,* or *for the faith,* who are our loving fellow-christians. Holiness, or the image of God in any, is the great endearing thing that gives strength to all other bonds, and is itself the best. *Grace be with you all. Amen.* This is the closing benediction, not to Titus alone, but to all the faithful with him, which shows that though the epistle bears the single name of Titus in the inscription, yet it was for the use of the churches there, and they were in the eye, and upon the heart, of the apostle, in the writing of it. “ *Grace be with you all,* the love and favour of God, with the fruits and effects thereof, according to need, spiritual ones especially, and the increase and feeling of them more and more in your souls.” This is the apostle's wish and prayer, showing his affection to them, his desire of their good, and a means of obtaining for them, and bringing down upon them, the thing requested. Observe, Grace is the chief thing to be wished and begged for, with respect to ourselves or others; it is, summarily, all good. *Amen* shuts up the prayer, expressing desire and hope, that so it may, and so it shall be.

AN

EXPOSITION,

WITH PRACTICAL OBSERVATIONS,

OF THE EPISTLE OF ST. PAUL

TO PHILEMON.

THIS epistle to Philemon is placed the last of those with the name of Paul to them, perhaps because the shortest, and of an argument peculiar and different from all the others; yet such as the Spirit of God, who indited it, saw would, in its kind, be very instructive and useful in the churches. The occasion of it was this:—Philemon, one of note and probably a minister in the church of Colosse, a city of Phrygia, had a servant named *Onesimus,* who, having purloined his goods, ran away from him, and in his rambles came to Rome, where Paul was then a prisoner for the gospel, and, providentially coming under his preaching there, was, by the blessing of God, converted by him, after which he ministered awhile to the apostle in bonds, and might have been further useful to him, but, understanding him to be another man's servant, Paul would not, without his consent, detain him, but sends him back with this letter-commendatory, wherein he earnestly sues for his pardon and kind reception.

Before we enter on the exposition, such general things as follow may be taken notice of from the epistle and what relates to it; namely, I. The goodness and mercy of God to a poor wandering sinner, bringing him by his gracious providence under the means, and making them effectual to his conversion. Thus came he to be *sought of him that asked not for him, and to be found of him that sought him not*, Isa. lxv. 1. II. The great and endeared affection between a true convert and him whom God used to be the instrument of his conversion. Paul regards this poor fugitive now as his son in the faith, and terms him his *own bowels;* and Onesimus readily serves Paul in prison, and would gladly have continued to do so, would duty have permitted; but, being another's servant, he must return and submit himself to his master, and be at his disposal. III. The tender and good spirit of this blessed apostle Paul. With what earnestness does he concern himself for the poor slave! Being now, through his preaching, reconciled to God, he labours for reconciliation between him and his master. How pathetic a letter does he here write in his behalf! Scarcely any argument is forgotten that could possibly be used in the case; and all are pressed with such force that, had it been the greatest favour to himself that he was asking, he could not have used more. IV. The remarkable providence of God in preserving such a short writing as this, that might be thought of little concern to the church, being not only a letter to a particular person (as those to Timothy, and Titus, and Gaius, and the elect lady, likewise were), but of a private personal matter, namely, the receiving of a poor fugitive servant into the favour and family of his injured master. What in this is there that concerns the common salvation? And yet over this has there been a special divine care, it being given (as the other scriptures were) by *inspiration of God*, and in some sort, as they are, *profitable for doctrine, for reproof, for correction, and for instruction in righteousness.* God would have extant a proof and instance of his rich and free grace for the encouragement and comfort of the meanest and vilest of sinners, looking to him for mercy and forgiveness; and for instruction to ministers and others not to despise any, much less to judge them as to their final state, as if they were utter cast-aways, but rather to attempt their conversion, hoping they may be saved; likewise how to behave towards them. Joy must be on earth, as well as there is in heaven, over one sinner who repenteth. Such must now be loved, and helped, and confirmed in good, and furthered in it; and, in their outward concerns, their comfort and welfare must be consulted and promoted as much as possible. And, on their part, they must be humble and grateful, acknowledging God and his instruments in what good they have received, ready to all suitable returns, making what reparation they can in case of injuries, and living a life of thankfulness and obedience. To such purposes may this epistle have been written and preserved. And perhaps, V. There may be something further in all this; at least, by way of allusion, it is applicable to the mediation and intercession of Christ for poor sinners. We, like Onesimus, were revolters from God's service, and had injured him in his rights. Jesus Christ finds us, and by his grace works a change in us, and then intercedes for us with the Father, that we may be received into his favour and family again, and past offences may be forgiven; and we are sure that the *Father heareth him always.* There is no reason to doubt but Paul prevailed with Philemon to forgive and receive Onesimus: and more reason have we to be confident that the intercession of Christ with the Father is prevalent for the acceptance of all whose case he takes in hand and recommends to him. From these general observations we come to the epistle itself.

CHAP. I.

In this epistle we have, I. The preface, ver. 1—7. II. The substance and body of it, ver. 8—21. And then the conclusion, ver. 22, to the end.

PAUL, a prisoner of Jesus Christ,
and Timothy *our* brother, unto
Philemon our dearly beloved, and fellowlabourer, 2 And to *our* beloved
Apphia, and Archippus our fellow-
soldier, and to the church in thy
house: 3 Grace to you, and peace,
from God our Father and the Lord
Jesus Christ. 4 I thank my God,
making mention of thee always in
my prayers, 5 Hearing of thy love
and faith, which thou hast toward
the Lord Jesus, and toward all saints;
6 That the communication of thy
faith may become effectual by the
acknowledging of every good thing
which is in you in Christ Jesus. 7
For we have great joy and consolation
in thy love, because the bowels of the
saints are refreshed by thee, brother.

I. In the first two verses of the preface we have the persons from and to whom it is written, with some annexed note or title, implying somewhat of argument to the purpose of the letter.

1. The persons writing: Paul, the principal, who calls himself *a prisoner of Jesus Christ,* that is, for Jesus Christ. To be a prisoner simply is no comfort nor honour; but such as Paul was, *for the faith and preaching of the gospel,* this was true glory,

and proper to move Philemon upon the request made to him by such a one. A petition from one suffering for Christ and his gospel would surely be tenderly regarded by a believer and minister of Christ, especially when strengthened too with the concurrence of Timothy, one eminent in the church, sometimes called by Paul *his son in the faith*, but now, it is likely, grown more in years, he styles him *his brother*. What could be denied to two such petitioners? Paul is not slight in serving a poor convert; he gets all the additional help he can in it.

2. The persons written to are *Philemon and Apphia*, and with them Archippus, and the church in Philemon's house. Philemon, the master of Onesimus, was the principal, to whom the letter is inscribed, the head of the family, in whom were the authority and power of taking in or shutting out, and whose property Onesimus was: with him therefore chiefly lay the business. *To Philemon our dearly beloved, and fellow-labourer;* a good man he was, and probably a minister, and on both accounts dearly beloved by Paul. *A lover of good men* is one property of a good minister (Tit. i. 8), and especially must such love those who labour with them in the work of the gospel, and who are faithful therein. The general calling as Christians knits those together who are Christians; but, when conjunction in the special calling as ministers is added, this will be further endearing. Paul, in the highest degree of ministry, not only calls Timothy, an evangelist, his brother, but Philemon, an ordinary pastor, his dearly beloved fellow-labourer—an example of humility and condescension, and of all affectionate regards, even in those that are highest in the church, towards others that are labourers in the same special heavenly calling. With Philemon Apphia is joined, probably his yoke-fellow; and, having a concern in the domestic affairs, the apostle directs to her likewise. She was a party offended and injured by Onesimus, and therefore proper to be taken notice of in a letter for reconciliation and forgiveness. Justice and prudence would direct Paul to this express notice of her, who might be helpful in furthering the good ends of his writing. She is set before Archippus, as more concerned and having more interest. A kind conjunction there is in domestic matters between husband and wife, whose interests are one, and whose affections and actings must correspond. These are the principal parties written to. The less principal are, *Archippus, and the church in Philemon's house*. Archippus was a minister in the church of Colosse, Philemon's friend, and probably co-pastor with him; Paul might think him one whom Philemon would advise with, and who might be capable of furthering the good work of peace-making and forgiveness, and therefore might judge fit to put him in the inscription of the letter, with the adjunct of *fellow-soldier*. He had called Philemon his *fellow-labourer*. Ministers must look on themselves as labourers and soldiers, who must therefore take pains, and endure hardship; they must stand on their guard, and make good their post; must look on one another as fellow-labourers, and fellow-soldiers, who must stand together, and strengthen one another's hands and hearts in any work of their holy function and calling: they need see to it that they be provided with spiritual weapons, and skill to use them; as labourers they must minister the word, and sacraments, and discipline, and watch over souls, *as those that must give an account of them;* and, as soldiers, they must fight the Lord's battles, and not entangle themselves in the things of this life, but attend to the pleasing of him who hath chosen them to be soldiers, 2 Tim. ii. 4. To these it is added, *And to the church in thy house*, his whole family, in which the worship of God was kept up, so that he had, as it were, a church in his house. Observe, (1.) Families which generally may be most pious and orderly may yet have one or other in them impious and wicked. This was the aggravation of Onesimus's sin, that it was where he might and should have learned better; it is likely that he was secret in his misconduct, till his flight discovered him. Hearts are unknown but to God, till overt acts discover them. (2.) This one evil servant did not hinder Philemon's house from being called and counted a church, for the religious worship and order that were kept up in it; and such should all families be—nurseries of religion, societies where God is called on, his word is read, his sabbaths are observed, and the members are instructed in the knowledge of him and of their duty to him, neglect of which is followed with ignorance and all corruption. Wicked families are nurseries for hell, as good ones are for heaven. (3.) Masters and others of the family may not think it enough to be good, singly and severally in their personal capacities, but they must be socially so; as here Philemon's house was a church; and Paul, for some concern that all might have in this matter of Onesimus, directs to them all, that their affection as well as Philemon's might return to him, and that in their way and place they might further, and not hinder, the reconciliation wished and sought. Desirable it is that all in a family be well affected towards one another, for furthering their particular welfare and for the common good and benefit of all. On such accounts might it be that Paul inscribed his letter here so generally, that all might be the more ready to own and receive this poor convert, and to behave affectionately towards him. Next to this inscription is,

II. The apostle's salutation of those named by him (*v.* 3): *Grace to you and peace from God our Father and the Lord Jesus Christ.* This is the token in every epistle; so the apostle writes. He is a hearty well-wisher to all his friends, and wishes for them the best things; not gold, nor silver, nor any earthly good, in the first or chief place, but *grace and peace from God in Christ;* he cannot give them himself, but he prays for them from him who can bestow them. *Grace,* the free favour and good-will of God, the spring and fountain of all blessings; *and peace,* all good, as the fruit and effect of that grace. *To you,* that is, be bestowed on you, and continued to you, with the comfortable feeling and sense of it in yourselves. *From God our Father and the Lord Jesus Christ.* The Holy Spirit also is understood, though not named; for all acts towards the creatures are of the whole Trinity: from the Father, who is our Father in Christ, the first in order of acting as of subsisting; and from Christ, his favour and good-will as God, and the fruits of it through him as Mediator, God-man. It is in the beloved that we are accepted, and through him we have peace and all good things, who is, with the Father and Spirit, to be looked to and blessed and praised for all, and to be owned, not only as Jesus and Christ, but as Lord also. In 2 Cor. xiii. 14 the apostle's benediction is full: *The grace of the Lord Jesus Christ, and the love of God, and the communion of the Holy Ghost, be with you all, Amen.* Observe, Spiritual blessings are first and especially to be sought for ourselves and others. The favour of God and peace with him, as in itself it is the best and most desirable good, so is it the cause of all other, and what puts sweetness into every mercy and can make happy even in the want of all earthly things. *Though there be no herd in the stall, and the labour of the olive fail,* yet may such *rejoice in the Lord, and joy in the God of their salvation,* Hab. iii. 17, 18. *There are many that say, Who will show us any good?* But, if God *lift up the light of his countenance,* this will put more joy and gladness into the heart than all worldly increase, Ps. iv. 6, 7. And Num. vi. 26, *The Lord lift up the light of his countenance upon thee, and give thee peace.* In this is summarily all good, and from this one fountain, God the *Father, Son,* and *Spirit,* all comes. After this salutation of the apostle to Philemon, and his friends and family, for better making way still for his suit to him,

III. He expresses the singular affection he had for him, by thanksgiving and prayer to God in his behalf, and the great joy for the many good things he knew and heard to be in him, *v.* 4—7. The apostle's thanksgiving and prayer for Philemon are here set forth by the object, circumstance, and matter of them, with the way whereby much of the knowledge of Philemon's goodness came to him.

1. Here is the object of Paul's praises and prayers for Philemon: *I thank my God, making mention of thee in my prayers, v.* 4. Observe, (1.) God is the author of all the good that is in any, or that is done by them. *From me is thy fruit found,* Hos. xiv. 8. To him therefore is all the praise due. 1 Chron. xxix. 13, 14, *But* [or *for*] *who am I, and what is my people, that we should be able to offer so willingly after this sort? For all things come of thee,* both wherewith to offer, and the will and heart to do it. On this account (says he) *we thank thee our God, and praise thy glorious name.* (2.) It is the privilege of good men that in their praises and prayers they come to God as their God: *Our God, we thank thee,* said David; and *I thank my God,* said Paul. (3.) Our prayers and praises should be offered up to God, not for ourselves only, but for others also. Private addresses should not be altogether with a private spirit, minding our own things only, but others must be remembered by us. We must be affected with joy and thankfulness for any good in them, or done by them, or bestowed on them, as far as is known to us, and seek for them what they need. In this lies no little part of the communion of saints. Paul, in his private thanksgivings and prayers, was often particular in remembering his friends: *I thank my God, making mention of thee in my prayers;* sometimes it may be by name, or at least having them particularly in his thoughts; and God knows who is meant, though not named. This is a means of exercising love, and obtaining good for others. *Strive with me, by your prayers to God for me,* said the apostle: and what he desired for himself he surely practised on behalf of others; so should all. *Pray one for another,* says James, v. 16.

2. Here is the circumstance: *Always making mention of thee. Always*—usually, not once or twice only, but frequently. So must we remember Christian friends much and often, as their case may need, bearing them in our thoughts and upon our hearts before our God.

3. Here is the matter both of his praises and prayers, in reference to Philemon.

(1.) Of his praises. [1.] He thanks God for the love which he heard Philemon had towards the Lord Jesus. He is to be loved as God superlatively, as his divine perfections require; and as related to us, the Lord, and our Lord, our Maker, Redeemer, and Saviour, who loved us, and gave himself for us. Paul thanks God for what he heard of this, the signal marks and expressions of it in Philemon. [2.] For his faith in Christ also. Love to Christ, and faith in him, are prime Christian graces, for which there is great ground of praise to God, where he has blessed any with them, as Rom. i. 8, *I thank my God* because *your faith is published throughout the world;* and, in reference to the Colossians (*ch.* i. 3, 4), *We give thanks to God since we heard of your faith in Christ Jesus.* This is a saving grace, and the very principle of Christian life and of all good works. [3.] He praises God likewise for Philemon's love to all the saints. These two must go together; for he who *loveth him that begat must and* will *love those also that are begotten of him.* The apostle joins them in that

(Col. i. 3, 4), *We give thanks to God since we heard of your faith in Christ Jesus, and of the love which you have to all the saints.* These bear the image of Christ, which will be loved by every Christian. Different sentiments and ways in what is not essential will not make a difference of affection as to the truth, though difference in the degrees of love will be according as more or less of that image is discerned. Mere external differences are nothing here. Paul calls a poor converted slave *his bowels.* We must love, as God does, all saints. Paul thanked God for the good that was not only in the churches, but in the particular persons he wrote to, and though this too was known to him merely by report: *Hearing of thy love and faith, which thou hast towards the Lord Jesus, and towards all saints.* This was what he enquired after concerning his friends, the truth, and growth, and fruitfulness of their graces, their faith in Christ, and love to him and to all the saints. Love to saints, if it be sincere, will be catholic and universal love towards all saints; but faith and love, though in the heart they are hidden things, are known by the effects of them. Therefore,

(2.) The apostle joins prayer with his praises, that the fruits of Philemon's faith and love might be more and more conspicuous, so as that the communication of them might constrain others to the acknowledgment of all the good things that were in him and in his house towards Christ Jesus; that their *light might so shine before men that they, seeing their good works, might* be stirred up to imitate them, and to *glorify their Father who is in heaven.* Good works must be done, not of vain-glory to be seen, yet such as may be seen to God's glory and the good of men.

4. He adds a reason, both of his prayer and his praises (*v.* 7): *For "we have great joy and consolation in thy love, because the bowels of the saints are refreshed by thee, brother.* The good thou hast done and still doest is abundant matter of joy and comfort to me and others, who therefore desire you may continue and abound in such good fruits more and more, to God's honour and the credit of religion. *The administration of this service not only supplieth the want of the saints, but is abundant also by many thanksgivings unto God,"* 2 Cor. ix. 12.

8 Wherefore, though I might be
much bold in Christ to enjoin thee
that which is convenient, 9 Yet for
love's sake I rather beseech *thee,* being
such a one as Paul the aged, and now
also a prisoner of Jesus Christ. 10
I beseech thee for my son Onesimus,
whom I have begotten in my bonds:
11 Which in time past was to thee
unprofitable, but now profitable to
thee and to me: 12 Whom I have
sent again: thou therefore receive
him, that is, mine own bowels: 13
Whom I would have retained with
me, that in thy stead he might have
ministered unto me in the bonds of
the gospel: 14 But without thy
mind would I do nothing; that thy
benefit should not be as it were of
necessity, but willingly. 15 For
perhaps he therefore departed for a
season, that thou shouldst receive
him for ever; 16 Not now as a
servant, but above a servant, a brother beloved, specially to me, but
how much more unto thee, both in
the flesh, and in the Lord? 17 If
thou count me therefore a partner,
receive him as myself. 18 If he
hath wronged thee, or oweth *thee*
ought, put that on mine account;
19 I Paul have written *it* with mine
own hand, I will repay *it:* albeit I
do not say to thee how thou owest
unto me even thine own self besides.
20 Yea, brother, let me have joy of
thee in the Lord: refresh my bowels in
the Lord. 21 Having confidence in thy
obedience I wrote unto thee, knowing
that thou wilt also do more than I say.
22 But withal prepare me also a
lodging: for I trust that through
your prayers I shall be given unto
you. 23 There salute thee Epaphras,
my fellowprisoner in Christ Jesus;
24 Marcus, Aristarchus, Demas, Lucas, my fellowlabourers. 25 The grace
of our Lord Jesus Christ *be* with your
spirit. Amen.

We have here,

I. The main business of the epistle, which was to plead with Philemon on behalf of Onesimus, that he would receive him and be reconciled to him. Many arguments Paul urges for this purpose, *v.* 8—21. The

1*st Argument* is taken from what was before noted, and is carried in the illative *wherefore:* "Seeing so much good is reported of thee and found in thee, especially thy love to all saints, now let me see it on a fresh and further occasion; *refresh the bowels of Onesimus and mine also,* in forgiving and receiving him, who is now a convert, and so a saint indeed, and meet for thy favour and love." Observe, A disposition to do good, together with past instances and expressions of it, is a good handle to take hold of for pressing to more. "*Be not weary of* *well-doing*, go on as thou art able, and as new objects and occasions occur, to do the same still." The

2*d Argument* is from the authority of him that was now making this request to him: *I might be very bold in Christ to enjoin thee that which is convenient*, *v.* 8. The apostles had under Christ great power in the church over the ordinary ministers, as well as the members of it, for edification; they might require of them what was fit, and were therein to be obeyed, which Philemon should consider. This was a matter within the compass of the apostle's power to require, though he would not in this instance act up to it. Observe, Ministers, whatever their power be in the church, are to use prudence in the exercise of it; they may not unseasonably, nor further than is requisite, put it forth; in all they must use godly wisdom and discretion. Wherefore this may be a

3*d Argument*, Waiving the authority which yet he had to require, he chooses to entreat it of him (*v.* 9): *Yet for love's sake I rather beseech thee.* Observe, It is no disparagement for those who have power to be condescending, and sometimes even to beseech, where, in strictness of right, they might command; so does Paul here, though an apostle: he entreats where he might enjoin, he argues from love rather than authority, which doubtless must carry engaging influence with it. And especially, which may be a

4*th Argument*, When any circumstance of the person pleading gives additional force to his petition, as here: *Being such a one as Paul the aged, and now also a prisoner of Jesus Christ.* Years bespeak respect; and the motions of such, in things lawful and fit, should be received with regard. The request of an aged apostle, and now suffering for Christ and his gospel, should be tenderly considered. "If thou wilt do any thing for a poor aged prisoner, to comfort me in my bonds, and make my chain lighter, grant me this which I desire: hereby in a manner you will do honour to Christ in the person of an aged suffering servant of his, which doubtless he will take as done to himself." He makes also a

5*th Argument*, From the spiritual relation now between Onesimus and himself: *I beseech thee for my son Onesimus, whom I have begotten in my bonds*, *v.* 10. "Though of right and in a civil respect he be thy servant, yet in a spiritual sense he is now a son to me, God having made me the instrument of his conversion, even here, where I am a prisoner for Christ's sake." Thus does God sometimes honour and comfort his suffering servants, not only working good in themselves by their sufferings, exercising and improving thereby their own graces, but making them a means of much spiritual good to others, either of their conversion, as of Onesimus here, or of their confirmation and strengthening, as Phil. i. 14, *Many brethren, waxing confident by my bonds, are much more bold to speak the word of the Lord without fear.* When God's servants are bound, yet his word and Spirit are not bound; spiritual children may then be born to them. The apostle lays an emphasis here: *My son, whom I have begotten in my bonds;* he was dear to him, and he hoped would be so to Philemon, under this consideration. Prison-mercies are sweet and much set by. Paul makes an argument to Philemon from this dear relation that now was between Onesimus and him, his son begotten in his bonds. And a

6*th Argument* is from Philemon's own interest: *Who in time past was to thee unprofitable, but now profitable to thee and to me*, *v.* 11. Observe, (1.) Unsanctified persons are unprofitable persons; they answer not the great end of their being and relations. Grace makes good for somewhat: "*In time past unprofitable, but now profitable*, inclined and fitted to be so, and will be so to thee, his master, if thou receive him, as he has since his conversion been here to me, ministering to me in my confinement." There seems an allusion to the name Onesimus, which signifies *profitable*. Now he will answer to his name. It may be noted also how the apostle speaks in this matter, not as Onesimus's former case and conduct might warrant; he had wronged his master, and ran away from him, and lived as if he were his own and not his; yet as God covers the sins of penitents, forgives and does not upbraid, so should men. How tenderly does Paul here speak! Not that Onesimus's sin was small, nor that he would have any, much less himself, to take it so; but having been humbled for it, and doubtless taken shame to himself on account thereof, the apostle now would not sink his spirit by continuing to load and burden him therewith, but speaks thus tenderly when he is pleading with Philemon not to make severe reflections on his servant's misconduct, but to forgive. (2.) What happy changes conversion makes—of evil good! of unprofitable useful! Religious servants are a treasure in a family. Such will make conscience of their time and trusts, promoting the interests of those whom they serve, and managing all they can for the best. This then is the argument here urged: "It will now be for thy advantage to receive him: thus changed, as he is, thou mayest expect him to be a dutiful and faithful servant, though in time past he was not so." Whereupon,

7*th Argument*, He urges Philemon from the strong affection that he had to Onesimus. He had mentioned the spiritual relation before, *My son begotten in my bonds;* and now he signifies how dear he was to him: *Thou therefore receive him, that is my own bowels*, *v.* 12. "I love him as I do myself, and have sent him back to thee for this end, that thou shouldst receive him; do it therefore for my sake, receive him as one thus dear to me." Observe, Even good men may sometimes need great earnestness and entreaty to lay their passions, let go their resentments, and forgive those who have injured and offended them. Some have thought it to look this way, when Paul is so pathetic and earnest, mustering up so many pleas and arguments to gain what he requests. Philemon, a Phrygian, might perhaps be naturally of a rough and difficult temper, and thence need no little pains in touching all the springs that might move him to forgiveness and reconciliation; but rather should we strive to be like God, who is *slow to anger, ready to forgive, and abundant in pardons.* And again, an

8*th Argument* is from the apostle's denying himself in sending back Onesimus: though he might have presumed upon Philemon's leave to detain him longer, yet he would not, *v.* 13, 14. Paul was now in prison, and wanted a friend or servant to act for him, and assist him, for which he found Onesimus fit and ready, and therefore would have detained him to minister to him, instead of Philemon himself, whom if he had requested to have come to him in person for such purpose, he might have presumed he would not have refused; much less might he have reckoned that he would be unwilling his servant should do this in his stead; yet he would not take this liberty, though his circumstances needed it: *I have sent him back* to thee, that any good office of thine to me might not be *of necessity, but willingly.* Observe, Good deeds are most acceptable to God and man when done with most freedom. And Paul herein, notwithstanding his apostolical power, would show what regard he had to civil rights, which Christianity does by no means supersede or weaken, but rather confirm and strengthen. Onesimus, he knew, was Philemon's servant, and therefore without his consent not to be detained from him. In his unconverted state he had violated that right, and withdrawn himself, to his master's injury; but, now that he had seen his sin and repented, he was willing and desirous to return to his duty, and Paul would not hinder this, but rather further it. He might indeed have presumed on Philemon's willingness; but, notwithstanding his need, he would deny himself rather than take that way. And he further urges,

9*th Argument,* That such a change was now wrought in Onesimus that Philemon needed not fear his ever running from him, or injuring him any more: *For perhaps he therefore departed for a season, that thou shouldst receive him for ever, v.* 15. There are those of whom Solomon says, *If thou deliver them, thou must do it again* (Prov. xix. 19); but the change wrought in Onesimus was such that he would never again need one thus to intercede for him. Charity would so hope and judge, yea, so it would be; yet the apostle speaks cautiously, that none might be bold to make another such experiment in expectation of a like gracious issue. Observe, (1.) In matters that may be wrested to ill, ministers must speak warily, that kind providences of God towards sinners be not abused to encouragements to sin, or abatements of just abhorrence of it: *Perhaps he therefore departed from thee for a season,* &c. (2.) How tenderly still the sins of penitents are spoken of; he calls it a *departure for a season,* instead of giving it the term that it deserved. As overruled and ordered by God, it was *a departure;* but in itself, and in respect of the disposition and manner of the act, it was a *criminal going away.* When we speak of the nature of any sin or offence against God, the evil of it is not to be lessened; but in the person of a penitent sinner, as God covers it, so must we: "*He departed for a season, that thou shouldst receive him for ever,* that upon conversion he may return, and be a faithful and useful servant to thee as long as he lives." *Bray a fool in a mortar, yet will not his folly depart from him.* But it is not so with true penitents: they will not return to folly. (3.) Observe the wisdom, and goodness, and power of God, in causing that to end so happily which was begun and carried on for some time so wickedly, thus regarding a poor vassal, one of such low rank and condition and so little regarded by men, working so good and great a change in him who was so far gone in evil ways, who had wronged a master so good, had run from a family so pious, from the means of grace, the church in his house, that he should be led into the way of salvation who had fled from it, and find means made effectual at Rome who had been hardened under them at Colosse. What riches are here of divine grace! None so low, nor mean, nor vile, as utterly to be despaired of. God can meet with them when running from him; can make means effectual at one time and place, which have not been so at another. So was it in this instance of Onesimus; having returned to God, he now returns to his master, who will have more service and better hold of him than ever—by conscience of his duty and faithfulness in it to his life's end; his interest therefore it will be now to receive him. So God often brings gain to his people out of their losses. And, besides interest, a

10*th Argument* is taken from the capacity under which Onesimus now would return, and must be received by Philemon (*v.* 16): "*Not now as a servant* (that is, not merely or so much), *but above a servant* (in a spiritual respect), *a brother beloved,* one to be owned as a brother in Christ, and to be beloved as such, upon account of this holy change that is wrought in him, and one therefore who will be useful unto thee upon better principles and in a better manner than before, who will love and promote the best things in thy family, be a blessing in it, and help to keep up the church that is in thy house." Observe (1.) There is a spiritual brotherhood between all true believers, however distinguished in civil and outward respects; they are all children of the same heavenly Father, have a right to the same spiritual privileges and benefits, must love and do all good offices to and for one another as brethren, though still in the same rank, and degree, and station, wherein they were called. Christianity does not annul nor confound the respective civil duties, but strengthens the obligation to them, and directs to a right discharge of them. (2.) Religious servants are more than mere ordinary servants; they have grace in their hearts, and have found grace in God's sight, and so will in the sight of religious masters. Ps. ci. 6, *Mine eyes are upon the faithful of the land, that they may dwell with me. He that walketh in a perfect way, he shall serve me.* "Onesimus having now become such, receive and regard him as one that is partaker of the same common faith, and so *a brother beloved, specially to me* who have been the instrument of his conversion." Good ministers love not so much according to the outward good which they receive as the spiritual good which they do. Paul called Onesimus his *own bowels,* and other converts his *joy and crown.* "*A brother beloved, specially to me, but how much more to thee, both in the flesh and in the Lord;* by a double tie therefore (both civil and religious) thy servant: thy property, one of thy house and family, and now, in a spiritual respect, thy brother in Christ, which heightens the engagement. He is God's servant and thine too; here are more ties than he is under to me. How readily therefore should he be received and loved by thee, as one of thy family and one of the true faith, one of thy house and one of the church in thy house!" This argument is strengthened by another, the

11*th Argument,* From the communion of saints: *If thou count me therefore a partner, receive him as myself, v.* 17. There is a fellowship among saints; they have interest one in another, and must love and act accordingly. "Now show thy love to me, and the interest I have in thee, by loving and receiving one so near and dear to me, even as myself; own and treat him as thou wouldst me, with a like ready and true, though perhaps not equal, affection." But why such concern and earnestness for a servant, a slave, and such a one as had misbehaved? *Answer,* Onesimus being now penitent, it was doubtless to encourage him, and to support him against the fears he might have in returning to a master whom he had so much abused and wronged, to keep him from sinking into despondency and dejection, and encourage him to his duty. Wise and good ministers will have great and tender care of young converts, to encourage and hearten them what they can to and in their duty. *Objection,* But Onesimus had wronged as well as offended his master. The answer to this makes a

12*th Argument,* A promise of satisfaction to Philemon: *If he hath wronged thee, or oweth thee aught,* &c., *v.* 18, 19. Here are three things:

(1.) A confession of Onesimus's debt to Philemon: *If he hath wronged thee, or oweth thee aught.* It is not an *if* of doubting, but of illation and concession; *seeing he hath wronged thee,* and thereby has become indebted to thee; such an *if* as Col. iii. 1 and 2 Pet. ii. 4, &c. Observe, True penitents will be ingenuous in owning their faults, as doubtless Onesimus had been to Paul, upon his being awakened and being brought to repentance; and especially is this to be done in cases of injury to others. Onesimus by Paul owns the wrong. And,

(2.) Paul here engages for satisfaction: *Put that on my account; I Paul have written it with my own hand, I will repay it.* Observe, [1.] The communion of saints does not destroy distinction of property: Onesimus, now converted, and become a brother beloved, is yet Philemon's servant still, and indebted to him for wrongs that he had done, and not to be discharged but by free and voluntary remission, or on reparation made by himself, or some other in his behalf, which part, rather than fail, the apostle undertakes for him. [2.] Suretiship is not in all cases unlawful, but in some is a good and merciful undertaking. Only know the person and case, be not *surety for a stranger* (Prov. xi. 15), and go not beyond ability; help thy friend thou mayest, as far as will comport with justice and prudence. And how happy for us that Christ would be made the surety of a better covenant (Heb. vii. 22), that he would be made *sin for us who knew no sin, that we might be made the righteousness of God in him!* And, [3.] Formal securities by writing, as well as by word and promise, may be required and given. Persons die, and words may be forgotten or mistaken; writing better preserves right and peace, and has been in use with good persons, as well as others, in all ages, Jer. xxxii. 9, &c.; Luke xvi. 5—7. It was much that Paul, who lived on contributions himself, would undertake to make good all loss by an evil servant to his master; but hereby he expresses his real and great affection for Onesimus, and his full belief of the sincerity of his conversion: and he might have hope that, notwithstanding this generous offer, Philemon would not insist on it, but freely remit all, considering,

(3.) The reason of things between him and Philemon: "*Albeit, I do not say to thee how thou owest unto me even thy own self besides;* thou wilt remember, without my reminding thee, that thou art on other accounts more in debt to me than this comes to." Modesty in self-praises is true praise. The apostle glances at the benefits he had conferred on Philemon: "That thou art any thing in grace and acceptation with God, or enjoyest any thing in a right and comfortable manner, it is, under God, owing to my ministry. I have been the instrument in his hand of all that spiritual good to thee; and what thy obligation to me on this account is I leave to thee to consider. Thy forgiving a pecuniary debt to a poor penitent for my sake and at my request, and which, however, I now take upon myself to answer, thy remitting it to him, or to me, now his surety, thou wilt confess, is not so great a thing; here is more *per contra: Thou owest to me even thy ownself besides.*" Observe, How great the endearments are between ministers and those towards whom their endeavours have been blessed to their conversion or spiritual edification! *If it had been possible* (said Paul to the Galatians), *you would have plucked out your own eyes, and have given them to me,* Gal. iv. 15. On the other hand he calls them his *children, of whom he travailed again, till Christ was formed in them,* that is, the likeness of Christ more fully. So 1 Thess. ii. 8, *We were willing to have imparted to you not the gospel of God only, but also our own souls, because you were dear unto us.* By way of allusion, this may illustrate Christ's undertaking for us. We had revolted from God, and by sin had wronged him, but Christ undertakes to make satisfaction, *the just for the unjust, that he might bring us unto God.* "If the sinner owes thee aught, put it upon my account, I will pay the debt; let his iniquity be laid on me, I will bear the penalty." Further, a

13*th Argument* is from the joy and comfort the apostle hereby would have on Philemon's own account, as well as on Onesimus's in such a seasonable and acceptable fruit of Philemon's faith and obedience: *Yea, brother, let me have joy of thee in the Lord: refresh my bowels in the Lord, v.* 20. Philemon was Paul's son in the faith, yet he entreats him as a brother; Onesimus a poor slave, yet he solicits for him as if he were seeking some great thing for himself. How pathetic is he! "*Yea, brother,* or *O my brother* (it is an adverb of wishing or desiring), *let me have joy of thee in the Lord.* Thou knowest that I am now a prisoner of the Lord, for his sake and cause, and need all the comfort and support that my friends in Christ can give me: now this will be a joy to me, I shall *have joy of thee in the Lord,* as seeing such an evidence and fruit of thy own Christian faith and love, and on Onesimus's account, who hereby will be relieved and encouraged." Observe, (1.) Christians should do the things that may rejoice the hearts of one another, both people and minister reciprocally, and ministers of their brethren. From the world they expect trouble; and where may they look for comfort and joy but in one another? (2.) Fruits of faith and obedience in people are the minister's greatest joy, especially the more of love appears in them to Christ and his members, forgiving injuries, showing compassion, being merciful as their heavenly Father is merciful. "*Refresh my bowels in the Lord.* It is not any carnal selfish respect I am actuated by, but what is pleasing to Christ, and that he may have honour therein. Observe, [1.] The Lord's honour and service are a Christian's chief aim in all things. And, [2.] It is meat and drink to a good minister to see people ready and zealous in what is good, especially in acts of charity and beneficence, as occasions occur, forgiving injuries, remitting somewhat of their right, and the like. And, once more, his last, which is the

14*th Argument,* Lies in the good hope and opinion which he expresses of Philemon: *Having confidence in thy obedience, I wrote unto thee, knowing that thou wilt also do more than I say, v.* 21. Good thoughts and expectations of us more strongly move and engage us to do the things expected from us. The apostle knew Philemon to be a good man, and was thence persuaded of his readiness to do good, and that not in a scanty and niggardly manner, but with a free and liberal hand. Observe, Good persons will be ready for good works, and not narrow and pinching, but abundant in them. Isa. xxxii. 8, *The liberal deviseth liberal things.* The Macedonians first gave themselves to the Lord, and then to his apostles by the will of God, to do what good they could with what they had, according as occasions offered.

Thus far is the substance and body of the epistle. We have,

II. The conclusion, where,

1. He signifies his good hope of deliverance, through their prayers, and that shortly he might see them, desiring Philemon to make provision for him: *But withal prepare me also a lodging; for I trust that through your prayers I shall be given unto you, v.* 22. *But withal,* or *moreover.* He comes to another thing, yet, as may seem, not without some eye to the matter which he had been upon, that might be furthered by this intimation that he hoped he should himself soon follow, and know the effect of his epistle, which Philemon would therefore be the more stirred up to see might be to his satisfaction. Now here is,

(1.) The thing requested: *Prepare me also a lodging;* under this all necessaries for a stranger are included. He wills Philemon to do it, intending to be his guest, as most to his purpose. Observe, Hospitality is a great Christian duty, especially in ministers, and towards ministers, such as the apostle was, coming out of such dangers and sufferings for Christ and his gospel. Who would not show the utmost of affectionate regards to such a one? It is an honourable title that he gives Gaius (Rom. xvi. 23), *My host, and of the whole church.* Onesiphorus is also affectionately remembered by the apostle on this account (2 Tim. i. 16, 18), *The Lord give mercy to the house of Onesiphorus; for he oft refreshed me, and was not ashamed of my chain; and in how many things he ministered to me at Ephesus, thou knowest.*

(2.) Here is the ground of the apostle's request: *For I trust that through your prayers I shall be given unto you.* He did not know how God might deal with him, but the benefit of prayer he had often found, and hoped he should again, for deliverance, and liberty to come to them. Observe, [1.] Our dependence is on God for life and liberty and opportunity of service; all is by divine pleasure. [2.] When abridged of these or any other mercies, our trust and hope must be in God, without fainting or succumbing, while our case is depending. But yet, [3.] Trust must be with the use of means, prayer especially, though no other should be at hand; this hath unlocked heaven and opened prison-doors. *The fervent effectual prayer of the righteous availeth much.* [4.] Prayer of people for ministers, especially when they are in distress and danger, is their great duty; ministers need and request it. Paul, though an apostle, did so with much earnestness, Rom. xv. 30; 2 Cor. i. 11; Eph. vi. 18, 19; 1 Thess. v. 25. The least may in this way be helpful to the greatest. Yet, [5.] Though prayer obtains, yet it does not merit the things obtained: they are God's gift, and Christ's purchase. *I trust that through your prayers,* χαρισθήσομαι ὑμῖν—*I shall be freely bestowed on you.* What God gives, he will yet be sought to for, that mercies may be valued the more, and known whence they come, and God may have the praise. Ministers' lives and labours are for the people's good; the office was set up for them; *he gave gifts for men, apostles,* &c. Eph. iv. 8, 11, 12. Their gifts, and labours, and lives, all are for their benefit. 1 Cor. iii. 21, 22, *All things are yours, Apollos, Cephas,* &c. [6.] In praying for faithful ministers, people in effect pray for themselves: "*I trust I shall be given unto you,* for your service, and comfort, and edification in Christ." See 2 Cor. iv. 15. [7.] Observe the humility of the apostle; his liberty, should he have it, he would own to be through their prayers, as well as, or more than, his own; he mentions them only through the high thoughts he had of the prayers of many, and the regard God would show to his praying people. Thus of the first thing in the apostle's conclusion.

2. He sends salutations from one who was his fellow-prisoner, and four more who were his fellow-labourers, *v.* 23, 24. Saluting is wishing health and peace. Christianity is no enemy to courtesy, but enjoins it, 1 Pet. iii. 8. It is a mere expression of love and respect, and a means of preserving and nourishing them. *There salute thee Epaphras, my fellow-prisoner in Christ Jesus.* He was of Colosse, and so countryman and fellow-citizen with Philemon; by office he seems to have been an evangelist, who laboured among the Colossians (if he was not the first converter of them), for whom he had special affection. *Our dear fellow-servant* (said St. Paul), *and for you a faithful minister of Christ* (Col. i. 7), and (*ch.* iv. 12, 13), *A servant of Christ, always labouring for you in prayers. I bear him record that he hath a great zeal for you,* &c. A very eminent person therefore this was, who, being at Rome, perhaps accompanying Paul, and labouring in the same work of preaching and propagating the gospel, was confined in the same prison, and for the same cause; both termed *prisoners in Christ Jesus,* intimating the ground of their imprisonment, not any crime or wickedness, but for the faith of Christ and their service to him. An honour it is to suffer shame for Christ's name. *My fellow-prisoner in Christ Jesus* is mentioned as his glory and the apostle's comfort; not that he was a prisoner and so hindered from his work (this was matter of affliction), but that, seeing God thus permitted and called him to suffer, his providence so ordered it that they suffered together, and so had the benefit and comfort of one another's prayers, and help, it may be, in some things; this was a mercy. So God sometimes lightens the sufferings of his servants by the communion of saints, the sweet fellowship they have one with another in their bonds. Never more enjoyment of God have they found than when suffering together for God. So Paul and Silas, when their feet were fast in the stocks, had their tongues set at liberty, and their hearts tuned for the praises of God.—*Marcus, Aristarchus, Demas, Lucas, my fellow-labourers.* The mention of these seems in a manner to interest them in the business of the latter. How ill would it look by denial of the request of it to slight so many worthy names as most of these, at least, were! *Marcus,* cousin of Barnabas, and son of Mary, who was so hospitable to the saints at Jerusalem (Col. iv. 10, Acts xii. 12), and whose house was the place of meeting for prayer and the worship of God. Though some failing seems to have been in him when Paul and he parted, yet in conjunction with Barnabas he went on with his work, and here Paul and he, we perceive, were reconciled, and differences forgotten, 2 Tim. iv. 11. He bids Mark to be brought to him, *for he is profitable to me for the ministry,* that is, of an evangelist. *Aristarchus* is mentioned with Marcus (Col. iv. 10), and called there by Paul his fellow-prisoner; and speaking there of Marcus, sister's son to Barnabas, he adds, *Touching whom you received commandments; if he come unto you, receive him:* an evidence that he himself had received him, and was reconciled to him. Next is *Demas,* who hitherto, it seems, appeared not faulty, though he is censured (2 Tim. iv. 10) as having forsaken Paul, from *love of this present world.* But how far his forsaking was, whether total from his work and profession, or partial only, and whether he repented and returned to his duty, scripture is silent, and so must we be: no mark of disgrace lay on

him here, but he is joined with others who were faithful, as he is also in Col. iv. 14. *Lucas* is the last, that *beloved physician* and evangelist, who came to Rome, companion with Paul, Col. iv. 14; 2 Tim. iv. 11. He was Paul's associate in his greatest dangers, and his fellow-labourer. The ministry is not a matter of carnal ease nor pleasure, but of pains; if any are idle in it, they answer not their calling. Christ bids his disciples *pray the Lord of the harvest to send forth labourers,* not loiterers, *into his harvest,* Matt. ix. 38. And the people are exhorted to *know those that labour among them, and are over them in the Lord, and to esteem them very highly in love for their work's sake,* 1 Thess. v. 12, 13. *My fellow-labourers,* says the apostle: ministers must be helpers together of the truth; they serve the same Lord, in the same holy work and function, and are expectants of the same glorious reward; therefore they must be assistants to each other in furthering the interest of their great and common Master. Thus of the salutations, and then,

3. Here is the apostle's closing prayer and benediction, *v.* 25. Observe, (1.) What is wished and prayed for: *Grace,* the free favour and love of God, together with the fruits and effects of it in all good things, for soul and body, for time and eternity. Observe, Grace is the best wish for ourselves and others; with this the apostle begins and ends. (2.) From whom: *Our Lord Jesus Christ,* the Son of God, second Person in the Trinity, *Lord* by natural right, *by whom, and for whom, all things were created* (Col. i. 16, John i. 1—3), *and who is heir of all things,* and, as God-man and Mediator, who purchased us, and to whom we are given by the Father. *Jesus,* the Saviour, Matt. i. 21. We were lost and undone; he recovers us, and repairs the ruin. He saves by merit, procuring pardon and life for us; and by power, rescuing us from sin, and Satan, and hell, and renewing us to the likeness, and bringing us to the enjoyment, of God: thus is he Jesus; and Christ, the Messiah or anointed, consecrated and fitted to be king, priest, and prophet, to his church. To all those offices were there anointings under the law with oil, and to them was the Saviour spiritually anointed with the Holy Ghost, Acts x. 38. In none but him were all these together and in such eminence. *He was anointed with the oil of gladness above his fellows,* Ps. xlv. 7. This Lord Jesus Christ is ours by original title to us, and by gospel offers and gift, his purchase of us, and our own acceptance of him, resignation to him, and mystical union with him: *Our Lord Jesus Christ.* Observe, All grace to us is from Christ; he purchased, and he bestows it. *Of his fulness we all receive, and grace for grace,* John i. 16. *He filleth all in all,* Eph. i. 23. (3.) To whom: *Your spirit,* *μετὰ τοῦ πνεύματος ὑμῶν,* not of Philemon only, but of all who were named in the inscription. *With your spirit,* that is, with you, the soul or spirit being the immediate seat of grace, whence it influences the whole man, and flows out in gracious and holy actings. All the house saluted are here joined in the closing benediction, the more to remind and quicken all to further the end of the epistle.

Amen is added, not only for strong and affectionate summing up the prayer and wish, *so let it be;* but as an expression of faith that it will be heard, *so shall it be.* And what need we more to make us happy than to have *the grace of our Lord Jesus Christ with our spirit?* This is the usual benediction, but it may be taken here to have some special respect also to the occasion; the grace of Christ with their spirits, Philemon's especially, would sweeten and mollify them, take off too deep and keen resentments of injuries, and dispose to forgive others as God for Christ's sake hath forgiven us.

AN

EXPOSITION,

WITH PRACTICAL OBSERVATIONS,

OF THE EPISTLE TO

THE HEBREWS.

CONCERNING this epistle we must enquire, I. Into the divine authority of it; for this has been questioned by some, whose distempered eyes could not bear the light of it, or whose errors have been confuted by it; such as the Arians, who deny the Godhead and self-existence of Christ; and the Socinians, who deny his satisfaction; but, after all the attempts of such men to disparage this epistle, the divine original of it shines forth with such strong and unclouded rays that he who runs may read it is an eminent part of the canon of scripture. The divinity of the matter, the sublimity of the style, the excellency of the design, the harmony of this with other parts of scripture, and its general reception in the church of God in all ages—these are the evidences of its divine authority. II. As to the divine amanuensis or penman of this epistle, we are not so certain; it does not bear the name of any in the front of it, as the rest of the epistles do, and there has been some dispute among the learned to whom they should ascribe it. Some have assigned it to Clemens of Rome; others to Luke; and many to Barnabas, thinking that the style and manner of expression is very agreeable to the zealous, authoritative, affectionate temper that Barnabas appears to be of, in the account we have of him in the Acts of the Apostles; and one ancient father quotes an expression out of this epistle as the words of Barnabas. But it is generally assigned to the apostle Paul; and some later copies and translations have put Paul's name in the title. In the primitive times it was generally ascribed to him, and the style and scope of it very well agree with his spirit, who was a person of a clear head and a warm heart, whose main end and endeavour it was to exalt Christ. Some think that the apostle Peter refers to this epistle, and proves Paul to be the penman of it, by telling the Hebrews, to whom he wrote, of Paul's having written to them, 2 Pet. iii. 15. We read of no other epistle that he ever wrote to them but this. And though it has been objected that, since Paul put his name to all his other epistles, he would not have omitted it here; yet others have well answered that he, being the apostle of the Gentiles, who were odious to the Jews, might think fit to conceal his name, lest their prejudices against him might hinder them from reading and weighing it as they ought to do. III. As to the scope and design of this epistle, it is very evident that it was clearly to inform the minds, and strongly to confirm the judgment, of the Hebrews in the transcendent excellency of the gospel above the law, and so to take them off from the ceremonies of the law, to which they were so wedded, of which they were so fond, that they even doted on them, and those of them who were Christians retained too much of the old leaven, and needed to be purged from it. The design of this epistle was to persuade and press the believing Hebrews to a constant adherence to the Christian faith, and perseverance in it, notwithstanding all the sufferings they might meet with in so doing. In order to this, the apostle speaks much of the excellency of the author of the gospel, the glorious Jesus, whose honour he advances, and whom he justly prefers before all others, showing him to be all in all, and this in lofty strains of holy rhetoric. It must be acknowledged that there are many things in this epistle hard to be understood, but the sweetness we shall find therein will make us abundant amends for all the pains we take to understand it. And indeed, if we compare all the epistles of the New Testament, we shall not find any of them more replenished with divine, heavenly matter than this to the Hebrews.

CHAP. I.

In this chapter we have a twofold comparison stated: I. Between the evangelical and legal dispensation; and the excellency of the gospel above that of the law is asserted and proved, ver. 1—3. II. Between the glory of Christ and that of the highest creatures, the angels; where the pre-eminence is justly given to the Lord Jesus Christ, and clearly demonstrated to belong to him, ver. 4, to the end.

GOD, who at sundry times and in divers manners spake in time past unto the fathers by the prophets,
2 Hath in these last days spoken unto us by *his* Son, whom he hath appointed heir of all things, by whom also he made the worlds;
3 Who being the brightness of *his* glory, and the express image of his person, and upholding all things by the word of his power, when he had by himself purged our sins, sat down on the right hand of the Majesty on high;

Here the apostle begins with a general declaration of the excellency of the gospel dispensation above that of the law, which he demonstrates from the different way and manner of God's communicating himself and his mind and will to men in the one and in the other: both these dispensations were of God, and both of them very good, but there is a great difference in the way of their coming from God. Observe,

I. The way wherein God communicated himself and his will to men under the Old Testament. We have here an account, 1. Of the persons by whom God delivered his mind under the Old Testament; they were *the prophets*, that is, persons chosen of God, and qualified by him, for that office of revealing the will of God to men. No man takes this honour to himself, unless called; and whoever are called of God are qualified by him. 2. The persons to whom God spoke by the prophets: *To the fathers*, to all the Old-Testament saints who were under that dispensation. God favoured and honoured them with much clearer light than that of nature, under which the rest of the world were left. 3. The order in which God spoke to men in those times that went before the gospel, those past times: he spoke to his ancient people *at sundry times and in divers manners.* (1.) *At sundry times, or by several parts,* as the word signifies, which may refer either to the several ages of the Old-Testament dispensation—the patriarchal, the Mosaic, and the prophetic; or to the several gradual openings of his mind concerning the Redeemer: to Adam, that the Messiah should come of the seed of the woman,—to Abraham, that he should spring from his loins,—to Jacob, that he should be of the tribe of Judah,—to David, that he should be of his house,—to Micah, that he should be born at Bethlehem,—to Isaiah, that he should be born of a virgin. (2.) *In divers manners,* according to the different ways in which God thought fit to communicate his mind to his prophets; sometimes by the *illapses* of his Spirit, sometimes by *dreams,* sometimes by visions, sometimes by an audible voice, sometimes by legible characters under his own hand, as when he wrote the ten commandments on tables of stone. Of some of these different ways God himself gave an account in Num. xii. 6—8, *If there be a prophet among you, I the Lord will make myself known to him in a vision, and will speak to him in a dream. Not so with my servant Moses: with him I will speak mouth to mouth, even apparently, and not in dark speeches.*

II. God's method of communicating his mind and will under the New-Testament dispensation, these last days as they are called, that is, either towards the end of the world, or the end of the Jewish state. The times of the gospel are the last times, the gospel revelation is the last we are to expect from God. There was first the natural revelation; then the patriarchal, by dreams, visions, and voices; then the Mosaic, in the law given forth and written down; then the prophetic, in explaining the law, and giving clearer discoveries of Christ: but now we must expect no new revelation, but only more of the Spirit of Christ to help us better to understand what is already revealed. Now the excellency of the gospel revelation above the former consists in two things:—

1. It is the final, the finishing revelation, given forth in the last days of divine revelation, to which nothing is to be added, but the canon of scripture is to be settled and sealed: so that now the minds of men are no longer kept in suspense by the expectation of new discoveries, but they rejoice in a complete revelation of the will of God, both preceptive and providential, so far as is necessary for them to know in order to their direction and comfort. For the gospel includes a discovery of the great events that shall befal the church of God to the end of the world.

2. It is a revelation which God has made by his Son, the most excellent messenger that was ever sent into the world, far superior to all the ancient patriarchs and prophets, by whom God communicated his will to his people in former times. And here we have an excellent account of the glory of our Lord Jesus Christ.

(1.) The glory of his office, and that in three respects:—[1.] God hath appointed him to be heir of all things. As God, he was equal to the Father; but, as God-man and Mediator, he was appointed by the Father to be the heir of all things, the sovereign Lord of all, the absolute disposer, director, and governor of all persons and of all things, Ps. ii. 6, 7. *All power in heaven and earth is given to him; all judgment is committed to him,* Matt. xxviii. 18; John v. 22. [2.] By him God made the worlds, both visible and invisible, the heavens and the earth; not as an instrumental cause, but as his essential word and wisdom. By him he made the old creation, by him he makes the new creature, and by him he rules and governs both. [3.] He upholds all things by the word of his power: he keeps the world from dissolving. *By him all things consist.* The weight of the whole creation is laid upon Christ: he supports the whole and all the parts. When, upon the apostasy, the world was breaking to pieces under the wrath and curse of God, the Son of God, undertaking the work of redemption, bound it up again, and established it by his almighty power and goodness. None of the ancient prophets sustained such an office as this, none was sufficient for it.

(2.) Hence the apostle passes to the glory of the person of Christ, who was able to execute such an office: *He was the brightness of his Father's glory, and the express image of his person, v.* 3. This is a high and lofty description of the glorious Redeemer, this is an account of his personal excellency. [1.] He is, in person, the Son of God, the only-begotten Son of God, and as such he must have the same nature. This personal distinction always supposes one and the same nature. Every son of man is man; were not the nature the same, the generation would be monstrous. [2.] The person of the Son is the glory of the Father, shining forth with a truly divine splendour. As the beams are effulgent emanations of the sun, the father and fountain of light, Jesus Christ in his person is God manifest in the flesh, he is light of light, the true Shechinah. [3.] The person of the Son is the true image and character of the person of the Father; being of the same nature, he must bear the same image and likeness. In beholding the power, wisdom, and goodness, of the Lord Jesus Christ, we behold the power, wisdom, and goodness, of the Father; for he hath the nature and perfections of God in him. *He that hath seen the Son hath seen the Father;* that is, he hath seen the same Being. He that hath known the Son hath known the Father, John xiv. 7—9. For the Son is in the Father, and the Father in the Son; the personal distinction is no other than will consist with essential union. This is the glory of the person of Christ; the fulness of the Godhead dwells, not typically, but really, in him.

(3.) From the glory of the person of Christ he proceeds to mention the glory of his grace; his condescension itself was truly glorious. The sufferings of Christ had this great honour in them, to be a full satisfaction for the sins of his people: *By himself he purged away our sins,* that is, by the proper innate merit of his death and bloodshed, by their infinite intrinsic value; as they were the sufferings of himself, he has made atonement for sin. Himself, the glory of his person and nature, gave to his sufferings such merit as was a sufficient reparation of honour to God, who had suffered an infinite injury and affront by the sins of men.

(4.) From the glory of his sufferings we are at length led to consider the glory of his exaltation: *When by himself he had purged away our sins, he sat down at the right hand of the Majesty on high,* at his Father's right hand. As Mediator and Redeemer, he is invested with the highest honour, authority, and activity, for the good of his people; the Father now does all things by him, and receives all the services of his people from him. Having assumed our nature, and suffered in it on earth, he has taken it up with him to heaven, and there it has the high honour to be next to God, and this was the reward of his humiliation.

Now it was by no less a person than this that God in these last days spoke to men; and, since the dignity of the messenger gives authority and excellency to the message, the dispensations of the gospel must therefore exceed, very far exceed, the dispensation of the law.

4 Being made so much better than
the angels, as he hath by inheritance
obtained a more excellent name than
they. 5 For unto which of the angels
said he at any time, Thou art my Son,
this day have I begotten thee? And
again, I will be to him a Father, and
he shall be to me a Son? 6 And
again, when he bringeth in the first-
begotten into the world, he saith,
And let all the angels of God worship
him. 7 And of the angels he saith,
Who maketh his angels spirits, and
his ministers a flame of fire. 8 But
unto the Son *he saith,* Thy throne, O
God, *is* for ever and ever: a sceptre
of righteousness *is* the sceptre of thy
kingdom. 9 Thou hast loved righteousness, and hated iniquity; therefore God, *even* thy God, hath anointed
thee with the oil of gladness above
thy fellows. 10 And, Thou, Lord,
in the beginning hast laid the foundation of the earth; and the heavens
are the works of thine hands: 11
They shall perish; but thou remainest; and they all shall wax old as doth
a garment; 12 And as a vesture shalt
thou fold them up, and they shall be
changed: but thou art the same, and
thy years shall not fail. 13 But to
which of the angels said he at any
time, Sit on my right hand, until I
make thine enemies thy footstool?
14 Are they not all ministering spirits,
sent forth to minister for them who
shall be heirs of salvation?

The apostle, having proved the pre-eminence of the gospel above the law from the pre-eminence of the Lord Jesus Christ above the prophets, now proceeds to show that he is much superior not only to the prophets, but to the angels themselves. In this he obviates an objection that the Jewish zealots would be ready to make, that the law was not only delivered by men, *but ordained by angels* (Gal. iii. 19), who attended at the giving forth of the law, the hosts of heaven being drawn forth to attend the Lord Jehovah on that awful occasion. Now the angels are very glorious beings, far more glorious and excellent than men; the scripture always represents them as the most excellent of all creatures, and we know of no being but God himself that is higher than the angels; and therefore that law that was ordained by angels ought to be held in great esteem. To take off the force of this argument, the penman of this epistle proceeds to state the comparison between Jesus Christ and the holy angels, both in nature and office, and to prove that Christ is vastly superior to the angels themselves: *Being made so much better than the angels, as he hath by inheritance obtained a more excellent name than they.* Here observe,

I. The superior nature of Christ is proved from his superior name. The scripture does not give high and glorious titles without a real foundation and reason in nature; nor would such great things have been said of our Lord Jesus Christ if he had not been as great and excellent as those words import. When it is said that Christ was made so much better than the angels, we are not to imagine that he was a mere creature, as the angels are; the word γενόμενος, when joined with an adjective, is nowhere to be rendered *created,* and here may very well be read, *being more excellent,* as the *Syriac version* hath it. We read γινέσθη ὁ Θεὸς ἀληθὴς—*let God be true,* not made so, but acknowledged to be so.

II. The superiority of the name and nature of Christ above the angels is declared in the holy scriptures, and to be deduced thence. We should have known little or nothing either of Christ or of the angels, without the scriptures; and we must therefore be determined by them in our conceptions of the one and the other. Now here are several passages of scripture cited, in which those things are said of Christ that were never said of the angels.

1. It was said of Christ, *Thou art my Son, this day have I begotten thee* (Ps. ii. 7), which may refer to his eternal generation, or to his resurrection, or to his solemn inauguration into his glorious kingdom at his ascension and session at the right hand of the Father. Now this was never said concerning the angels, and therefore by inheritance he has a more excellent nature and name than they.

2. It is said concerning Christ, but never

concerning the angels, *I will be to him a Father, and he shall be to me a Son;* taken from 2 Sam. vii. 14. Not only, "I am his Father, and he is my Son, by nature and eternal promanation;" but, "I will be his Father, and he shall be my Son, by wonderful conception, and this his son-ship shall be the fountain and foundation of every gracious relation between me and fallen man."

3. It is said of Christ, *When God bringeth his First-begotten into the world, let all the angels of God worship him;* that is, when he is brought into this lower world, at his nativity, let the angels attend and honour him; or when he is brought into the world above, at his ascension, to enter upon his mediatorial kingdom, or when he shall bring him again into the world, to judge the world, then let the highest creatures worship him. God will not suffer an angel to continue in heaven who will not be in subjection to Christ, and pay adoration to him; and he will at last make the fallen angels and wicked men to confess his divine power and authority and to fall before him. Those who would not have him to reign must then be brought forth and slain before him. The proof of this is taken out of Ps. xcvii. 7, *Worship him, all you gods,* that is, "All you that are superior to men, own yourselves to be inferior to Christ in nature and power."

4. God has said concerning Christ, *Thy throne, O God, is for ever and ever,* &c., *v.* 8—12. But of the angels he has only said that *he hath made them spirits, and his ministers a flame of fire, v.* 7. Now, upon comparing what he here says of the angels with what he says to Christ, the vast inferiority of the angels to Christ will plainly appear.

(1.) What does God say here of the angels? *He maketh his angels spirits, and his ministers a flame of fire.* This we have in Ps. civ. 4, where it seems to be more immediately spoken of the winds and lightning, but is here applied to the angels, whose agency the divine Providence makes use of in the winds, and in thunder and lightnings. Observe, [1.] The office of the angels: they are God's ministers, or *servants, to do his pleasure.* It is the glory of God that he has such servants; it is yet more so that he does not need them. [2.] How the angels are qualified for this service; he makes them spirits and a flame of fire, that is, he endows them with light and zeal, with activity and ability, readiness and resolution to do his pleasure: they are no more than what God has made them to be, and they are servants to the Son as well as to the Father. But observe,

(2.) How much greater things are said of Christ by the Father. Here two passages of scripture are quoted.

[1.] One of these is out of Ps. xlv. 6, 7, where God declares of Christ, *First,* His true and real divinity, and that with much pleasure and affection, not grudging him that glory: *Thy throne, O God.* Here one person calls another person God, *O God.* And, if God the Father declares him to be so, he must be really and truly so; for God calls persons and things as they are. And now let who will deny him to be essentially God at their peril, but let us own and honour him as God; for, if he had not been God, he had never been fit to have done the Mediator's work nor to have worn the Mediator's crown. *Secoudly,* God delares his dignity and dominion, as having a throne, a kingdom, and a sceptre of that kingdom. He has all right, rule, authority, and power, both as the God of nature, grace, and glory, and as Mediator; and so he is fully adequate to all the intents and purposes of his mediatorial kingdom. *Thirdly,* God declares the eternal duration of the dominion and dignity of Christ, founded upon the divinity of his person: *Thy throne, O God, is for ever and ever,* from everlasting to everlasting, through all the ages of time, maugre all the attempts of earth and hell to undermine and overthrow it, and through all the endless ages of eternity, when time shall be no more. This distinguishes Christ's throne from all earthly thrones, which are tottering, and will at length tumble down; but the throne of Christ shall be as the days of heaven. *Fourthly,* God declares of Christ the perfect equity of his administration, and of the execution of his power, through all the parts of his government: *A sceptre of righteousness is the sceptre of thy kingdom, v.* 8. He came righteously to the sceptre, and he uses it in perfect righteousness; the righteousness of his government proceeds from the righteousness of his person, from an essential eternal love of righteousness and hatred of iniquity, not merely from considerations of prudence or interest, but from an inward and immovable principle: *Thou lovest righteousness and hatest iniquity, v.* 9. Christ came to fulfil all righteousness, to bring in an everlasting righteousness; and he was righteous in all his ways and holy in all his works. He has recommended righteousness to men, and restored it among them, as a most excellent and amiable thing. He came to finish transgression, and to make an end of sin as a hateful as well as hurtful thing. *Fifthly,* God declares of Christ how he was qualified for the office of Mediator, and how he was installed and confirmed in it (*v.* 9): *Therefore God, even thy God, hath anointed thee with the oil of gladness above thy fellows.* 1. Christ has the name Messiah from his being anointed. God's anointing of Christ signifies both his qualifying him for the office of the Mediator with the Holy Spirit and all his graces, and likewise his inauguration of him into the office, as prophets, priests, and kings, were by anointing. *God, even thy God,* imports the confirmation of Christ in the office of Mediator by the covenant of redemption and peace, that was between the Father and the Son. God is the God of

Christ, as Christ is man and Mediator. 2. This anointing of Christ was *with the oil of gladness,* which signifies both the gladness and cheerfulness with which Christ undertook and went through the office of Mediator (finding himself so absolutely sufficient for it), and also that joy which was set before him as the reward of his service and sufferings, that crown of glory and gladness which he should wear for ever after the suffering of death. 3. This anointing of Christ was above the anointing of his fellows: *God, even thy God, hath anointed thee with the oil of gladness above thy fellows.* Who are Christ's fellows? Has he any equals? Not as God, except the Father and Spirit, but these are not here meant. As man, however, he has his fellows, and as an anointed person; but his unction is beyond all theirs. (1.) Above the angels, who may be said to be his fellows, as they are the sons of God by creation, and God's messengers, whom he employs in his service. (2.) Above all prophets, priests, and kings, that ever were anointed with oil, to be employed in the service of God on earth. (3.) Above all the saints, who are his brethren, children of the same father, as he was a partaker with them of flesh and blood. (4.) Above all those who were related to him as man, above all the house of David, all the tribe of Judah, all his brethren and kinsmen in the flesh. All God's other anointed ones had only the Spirit in a certain measure; Christ had the Spirit above measure, without any limitation. None therefore goes through his work as Christ did, none takes so much pleasure in it as Christ does; for he was anointed with the oil of gladness above his fellows.

[2.] The other passage of scripture in which is the superior excellence of Christ to the angels is taken out of Ps. cii. 25—27, and is recited in *v.* 10—12, where the omnipotence of the Lord Jesus Christ is declared as it appears both in creating the world and in changing it.

First, In creating the world (*v.* 10): *And thou, Lord, in the beginning hast laid the foundation of the earth, and the heavens are the work of thy hands.* The Lord Christ had the original right to govern the world, because he made the world in the beginning. His right, as Mediator, was by commission from the Father. His right, as God with the Father, was absolute, resulting from his creating power. This power he had before the beginning of the world, and he exerted it in giving a beginning and being to the world. He must therefore be no part of the world himself, for then he must give himself a beginning. He was πρὸ πάντων—*before all things,* and *by him all things consist,* Col. i. 17. He was not only above all things in condition, but before all things in existence; and therefore must be God, and self-existent. He laid the foundations of the earth, did not only introduce new forms into pre-existent matter, but made out of nothing the foundations of the earth, the *primordia rerum—the first principles of things;* he not only founded the earth, but the heavens too are the work of his hands, both the habitation and the inhabitants, the hosts of heaven, the angels themselves; and therefore he must needs be infinitely superior to them.

Secondly, In changing the world that he has made; and here the mutability of this world is brought in to illustrate the immutability of Christ. Observe, 1. This world is mutable, all created nature is so; this world has passed through many changes, and shall pass through more; all these changes are by the permission and under the direction of Christ, who made the world (*v.* 11, 12): *They shall perish, they shall all wax old as doth a garment; as a vesture shalt thou fold them up, and they shall be changed.* This our visible world (both the earth and visible heavens) is growing old. Not only men and beasts and trees grow old, but this world itself grows old, and is hastening to its dissolution; it changes like a garment, has lost much of its beauty and strength; it grew old betimes on the first apostasy, and it has been waxing older and growing weaker ever since; it bears the symptoms of a dying world. But then its dissolution will not be its utter destruction, but its change. Christ will fold up this world as a garment not to be abused any longer, not to be any longer so used as it has been. Let us not then set our hearts upon that which is not what we take it to be, and will not be what it now is. Sin has made a great change in the world for the worse, and Christ will make a great change in it for the better. *We look for new heavens and a new earth, wherein dwelleth righteousness.* Let the consideration of this wean us from the present world, and make us watchful, diligent, and desirous of that better world, and let us wait on Christ to change us into a meetness for that new world that is approaching; we cannot enter into it till we be new creatures. 2. Christ is immutable. Thus the Father testifies of him, *Thou remainest, thy years shall not fail.* Christ is the same in himself, the same yesterday, and to-day, and for ever, and the same to his people in all the changes of time. This may well support all who have an interest in Christ under all the changes they meet with in the world, and under all they feel in themselves. Christ is immutable and immortal: his years shall not fail. This may comfort us under all decays of nature that we may observe in ourselves or in our friends, though our flesh and heart fail and our days are hastening to an end. Christ lives to take care of us while we live, and of ours when we are gone, and this should quicken us all to make our interest in him clear and sure, that our spiritual and eternal life may be hid with Christ in God.

III. The superiority of Christ to the angels

appears in this that God never said to the angels what he has said to Christ, *v.* 13, 14.

1. What has God said to Christ? He has said, "*Sit thou at my right hand, till I make thy enemies thy footstool,* Ps. cx. 1. Receive thou glory, dominion, and rest; and remain in the administration of thy mediatorial kingdom until all thy enemies shall either be made thy friends by conversion or thy footstool." Note, (1.) Christ Jesus has his enemies (would one think it?), enemies even among men—enemies to his sovereignty, to his cause, to his people; such as will not have him to reign over them. Let us not think it strange then if we have our enemies. Christ never did any thing to make men his enemies; he has done a great deal to make them all his friends and his Father's friends, and yet he has his enemies. (2.) All the enemies of Christ shall be made his footstool, either by humble submission and entire subjection to his will casting themselves down at his feet, or by utter destruction; he shall trample upon those who continue obstinate, and shall triumph over them. (3.) God the Father has undertaken for this, and he will see it done, yea, he will himself do it; and, though it be not done presently, it shall certainly be done, and Christ waits for it; and so must Christians wait till God has wrought all their works in them, for them, and by them. (4.) Christ shall go on to rule and reign till this be done; he shall not leave any of his great designs unfinished, he shall go on conquering and to conquer. And it becomes his people to go on in their duty, being what he would have them to be, doing what he would have them to do, avoiding what he would have them to avoid, bearing what he would have them to bear, till he make them conquerors and more than conquerors over all their spiritual enemies.

2. What has God said to the angels? He never said to them, as he said to Christ, *Sit you at my right hand;* but he has said of them here that *they are ministering spirits, sent forth to minister for those who shall be the heirs of salvation.* Note, (1.) What the angels are as to their nature: they are spirits, without bodies or inclination to bodies, and yet they can assume bodies, and appear in them, when God pleases. They are spirits, incorporeal, intelligent, active, substances; they excel in wisdom and strength. (2.) What the angels are as to their office: they are ministering spirits. Christ, as Mediator, is the great minister of God in the great work of redemption. The Holy Spirit is the great minister of God and Christ in the application of this redemption. Angels are ministering spirits under the blessed Trinity, to execute the divine will and pleasure; they are the ministers of divine Providence. (3.) The angels are sent forth for this end—to minister to those who shall be the heirs of salvation. Here observe, [1.] The description given of the saints—they are *heirs of salvation;* at present they are under age, heirs, not inheritors. They are heirs because they are children of God; *if children, then heirs.* Let us make sure that we are children by adoption and regeneration, having made a covenant-resignation of ourselves to God, and walking before him in a gospel-conversation, and then we are heirs of God, and joint-heirs with Christ. [2.] The dignity and privilege of the saints—the angels are sent forth to minister for them. Thus they have done in attending and acting at the giving forth of the law, in fighting the battles of the saints, in destroying their enemies. They still minister for them in opposing the malice and power of evil spirits, in protecting and keeping their bodies, pitching their tents about theirs, instructing, quickening, and comforting their souls under Christ and the Holy Ghost; and thus they shall do in gathering all the saints together at the last day. Bless God for the ministration of angels, keep in God's way, and take the comfort of this promise, that he will *give his angels charge over you, to keep you in all your ways. They shall bear you up in their hands, lest you dash your feet against a stone,* Ps. xci. 11, 12.

CHAP. II.

In this chapter the apostle, I. Makes some application of the doctrine laid down in the chapter foregoing concerning the excellency of the person of Christ, both by way of exhortation and argument, ver. 1—4. II. Enlarges further upon the pre-eminence of Christ above the angels, ver. 5—9. III. Proceeds to remove the scandal of the cross, ver. 10—15. IV. Asserts the incarnation of Christ, taking upon him not the nature of angels, but the seed of Abraham, and assigns the reason of his so doing, ver. 16, to the end.

THEREFORE we ought to give
the more earnest heed to the
things which we have heard, lest at
any time we should let *them* slip. 2
For if the word spoken by angels was
stedfast, and every transgression and
disobedience received a just recompence of reward; 3 How shall we
escape, if we neglect so great salvation; which at the first began to be
spoken by the Lord, and was confirmed unto us by them that heard
him; 4 God also bearing *them* witness, both with signs and wonders,
and with divers miracles, and gifts of
the Holy Ghost, according to his own
will?

The apostle proceeds in the plain profitable method of doctrine, reason, and use, through this epistle. Here we have the application of the truths before asserted and proved; this is brought in by the illative particle *therefore,* with which this chapter begins, and which shows its connection with the former, where the apostle having proved Christ to be superior to the angels by whose ministry the law was given, and therefore that the gospel dispensation must be more excellent than the legal, he now comes to apply this doctrine both by way of exhortation and argument.

I. By way of exhortation: *Therefore we ought to give the more diligent heed to the things which we have heard, v.* 1. This is the first way by which we are to show our esteem of Christ and of the gospel. It is the great concern of every one under the gospel to give the most earnest heed to all gospel discoveries and directions, to prize them highly in his judgment as matters of the greatest importance, to hearken to them diligently in all the opportunities he has for that purpose, to read them frequently, to meditate on them closely, and to mix faith with them. We must embrace them in our hearts and affections, retain them in our memories, and finally regulate our words and actions according to them.

II. By way of argument, he adds strong motives to enforce the exhortation.

1. From the great loss we shall sustain if we do not take this earnest heed to the things which we have heard: *We shall let them slip.* They will leak, and run out of our heads, lips, and lives, and we shall be great losers by our neglect. Learn, (1.) When we have received gospel truths into our minds, we are in danger of letting them slip. Our minds and memories are like a leaky vessel, they do not without much care retain what is poured into them; this proceeds from the corruption of our natures, the enmity and subtlety of Satan (he steals away the word), from the entanglements and snares of the world, the thorns that choke the good seed. (2.) Those meet with an inconceivable loss who let gospel truths, which they had received, slip out of their minds; they have lost a treasure far better than thousands of gold and silver; the seed is lost, their time and pains in hearing lost, and their hopes of a good harvest lost; all is lost, if the gospel be lost. (3.) This consideration should be a strong motive both to our attention to the gospel and our retention of it; and indeed, if we do not well attend, we shall not long retain the word of God; inattentive hearers will soon be forgetful hearers.

2. Another argument is taken from the dreadful punishment we shall incur if we do not do this duty, a more dreadful punishment than those fell under who neglected and disobeyed the law, *v.* 2, 3. Here observe, (1.) How the law is described: it was the *word spoken by angels, and declared to be stedfast.* It was the word spoken by angels, because given by the ministration of angels, they sounding the trumpet, and perhaps forming the words according to God's direction; and God, as judge, will make use of the angels to sound the trumpet a second time, and gather all to his tribunal, to receive their sentence, as they have conformed or not conformed to the law. *And this law is declared to be stedfast;* it is like the promise, *yea and amen;* it is truth and faithfulness, and it will abide and have its force whether men obey it or no; *for every transgression and disobedience will receive a just recompence of reward.* If men trifle with the law of God, the law will not trifle with them; it has taken hold of the sinners of former ages, and will take hold of sinners in all ages. God, as a righteous governor and judge, when he had given forth the law, would not let the contempt and breach of it go unpunished; but he has from time to time reckoned with the transgressors of it, and recompensed them according to the nature and aggravation of their disobedience. Observe, The severest punishment God ever inflicted upon sinners is no more than what sin deserves: it is *a just recompence of reward;* punishments are as just, and as much due to sin as rewards are to obedience, yea, more due than rewards are to imperfect obedience. (2.) How the gospel is described. It is salvation, a great salvation; so great salvation that no other salvation can compare with it; so great that none can fully express, no, nor yet conceive, how great it is. It is a great salvation that the gospel discovers, for it discovers a great Saviour, one who has manifested God to be reconciled to our nature, and reconcilable to our persons; it shows how we may be saved from so great sin and so great misery, and be restored to so great holiness and so great happiness. The gospel discovers to us a great sanctifier, to qualify us for salvation and to bring us to the Saviour. The gospel unfolds a great and excellent dispensation of grace, a new covenant; the great charter-deed and instrument is settled and secured to all those who come into the bond of the covenant. (3.) How sinning against the gospel is described: it is declared to be a *neglect of this great salvation;* it is a contempt put upon the saving grace of God in Christ, making light of it, not caring for it, not thinking it worth their while to acquaint themselves with it, not regarding either the worth of gospel grace or their own want of it and undone state without it; not using their endeavours to discern the truth of it, and assent to it, nor to discern the goodness of it, so as to approve of it, or apply it to themselves. In these things they discover a plain neglect of this great salvation. Let us all take heed that we be not found among those wicked wretched sinners who neglect the grace of the gospel. (4.) How the misery of such sinners is described: it is declared to be unavoidable (*v.* 3): *How shall we escape?* This intimates, [1.] That the despisers of this salvation are condemned already, under arrest and in the hands of justice already. So they were by the sin of Adam; and they have strengthened their bonds by their personal transgression. *He that believeth not is condemned already,* John iii. 18. [2.] There is no escaping out of this condemned state, but by accepting the great salvation discovered in the gospel; as for those who neglect

it, the wrath of God is upon them, and it abides upon them; they cannot disengage themselves, they cannot emerge, they cannot get from under the curse. [3.] That there is a yet more aggravated curse and condemnation waiting for all those who despise the grace of God in Christ, and that this most heavy curse they cannot escape; they cannot conceal their persons at the great day, nor deny the fact, nor bribe the judge, nor break the prison. There is no door of mercy left open for them; there will be no more sacrifice for sin: they are irrecoverably lost. The unavoidableness of the misery of such is here expressed by way of question: *How shall we escape?* It is an appeal to universal reason, to the consciences of sinners themselves; it is a challenge to all their power and policy, to all their interest and alliances, whether they, or any for them, can find out, or can force out, a way of escape from the vindictive justice and wrath of God. It intimates that the neglecters of this great salvation will be left not only without power, but without plea and excuse, at the judgment-day; if they be asked what they have to say that the sentence should not be executed upon them, they will be speechless, and self-condemned by their own consciences, even to a greater degree of misery than those fell under who neglected the authority of the law, or sinned without the law.

3. Another argument to enforce the exhortation is taken from the dignity and excellency of the person by whom the gospel began to be spoken (*v.* 3): *It began at first to be spoken by the Lord,* that is, the Lord Jesus Christ, who is Jehovah, the Lord of life and glory, Lord of all, and as such possessed of unerring and infallible wisdom, infinite and inexhaustible goodness, unquestionable and unchangeable veracity and faithfulness, absolute sovereignty and authority, and irresistible power. This great Lord of all was the first who began to speak it plainly and clearly, without types and shadows as it was before he came. Now surely it may be expected that all will reverence this Lord, and take heed to a gospel that began to be spoken by one who spoke so as never *man spoke.*

4. Another argument is taken from the character of those who were witnesses to Christ and the gospel (*v.* 3, 4): *It was confirmed to us by those that heard him, God also bearing them witness.* Observe, (1.) The promulgation of the gospel was continued and confirmed by those who heard Christ, by the evangelists and apostles, who were eye and ear-witnesses of what Jesus Christ began both to do and to teach, Acts i. 1. These witnesses could have no worldly end or interest of their own to serve hereby. Nothing could induce them to give in their evidence but the Redeemer's glory, and their own and others' salvation; they exposed themselves by their testimony to the loss of all that was dear to them in this life, and many of them sealed it with their blood. (2.) *God himself bore witness* to those who were witnesses for Christ; he testified that they were authorized and sent by him to preach Christ and salvation by him to the world. And how did he bear them witness? Not only by giving them great peace in their own minds, great patience under all their sufferings, and unspeakable courage and joy (though these were witnesses to themselves), but he bore them witness *by signs, and wonders, and divers miracles, and gifts of the Holy Ghost, according to his will.* [1.] With *signs,* signs of his gracious presence with them, and of his power working by them. [2.] *Wonders,* works quite beyond the power of nature, and out of the course of nature, filling the spectators with wonder and admiration, stirring them up to attend to the doctrine preached, and to enquire into it. [3.] *Divers miracles,* or mighty works, in which an almighty agency appeared beyond all reasonable controversy. [4.] *Gifts of the Holy Ghost,* qualifying, enabling, and exciting them to do the work to which they were called—*divisions or distributions of the Holy Ghost, diversities of gifts,* 1 Cor. xii. 4, &c. And all this *according to God's own will.* It was the will of God that we should have sure footing for our faith, and a strong foundation for our hope in receiving the gospel. As at the giving forth of the law there were signs and wonders, by which God testified the authority and excellency of it, so he witnessed to the gospel by more and greater miracles, as to a more excellent and abiding dispensation.

5 For unto the angels hath he not put in subjection the world to come, whereof we speak. 6 But one in a certain place testified, saying, What is man, that thou art mindful of him? or the son of man, that thou visitest him? 7 Thou madest him a little lower than the angels; thou crownedst him with glory and honour, and didst set him over the works of thy hands: 8 Thou hast put all things in subjection under his feet. For in that he put all in subjection under him, he left nothing *that is* not put under him. But now we see not yet all things put under him. 9 But we see Jesus, who was made a little lower than the angels for the suffering of death, crowned with glory and honour; that he by the grace of God should taste death for every man.

The apostle, having made this serious application of the doctrine of the personal excellency of Christ above the angels, now returns to that pleasant subject again, and pursues it further (*v.* 5): *For to the angels hath he not put in subjection the world to come, whereof we speak.*

I. Here the apostle lays down a negative proposition, including a positive one—That the state of the gospel-church, which is here called *the world to come*, is *not subjected to the angels*, but under the special care and direction of the Redeemer himself. Neither the state in which the church is at present, nor that more completely restored state at which it shall arrive when the prince of this world is cast out and the kingdoms of the earth shall become the kingdom of Christ, is left to the government of the angels; but Jesus Christ will take to him his great power, and will reign. He does not make that use of the ministration of angels to give the gospel as he did to give the law, which was the state of the old or antiquated world. This new world is committed to Christ, and put in absolute subjection to him only, in all spiritual and eternal concerns. Christ has the administration of the gospel church, which at once bespeaks Christ's honour and the church's happiness and safety. It is certain that neither the first creation of the gospel church, nor its after-edification or administration, nor its final judgment and perfection, is committed to the angels, but to Christ. God would not put so great a trust in his holy ones; his angels were too weak for such a charge.

II. We have a scripture-account of that blessed Jesus to whom the gospel world is put into subjection. It is taken from Ps. viii. 4—6, *But one in a certain place testified, saying, What is man, that thou art mindful of him? or the Son of man, that thou visitest him?* &c. These words are to be considered both as applicable to mankind in general, and as applied here to the Lord Jesus Christ.

1. As applicable to mankind in general, in which sense we have an affectionate thankful expostulation with the great God concerning his wonderful condescension and kindness to the sons of men. (1.) In remembering them, or being mindful of them, when yet they had no being but in the counsels of divine love. The favours of God to men all spring up out of his eternal thoughts and purposes of mercy for them; as all our dutiful regards to God spring forth from our remembrance of him. God is always mindful of us, let us never be forgetful of him. (2.)In visiting them. God's purpose of favours for men is productive of gracious visits to them; he comes to see us, how it is with us, what we ail, what we want, what dangers we are exposed to, what difficulties we have to encounter; and by his visitation our spirit is preserved. Let us so remember God as daily to approach him in a way of duty. (3.) In making man the head of all the creatures in this lower world, the top-stone of this building, the chief of the ways of God on earth, and only a little lower than the angels in place, and respect to the body, while here, and to be made like the angels, and equal to the angels, at the resurrection of the just, Luke xx. 36. (4.) In crowning him with glory and honour, the honour of having noble powers and faculties of soul, excellent organs and parts of body, whereby he is allied to both worlds, capable of serving the interests of both worlds, and of enjoying the happiness of both. (5.) In giving him right to and dominion over the inferior creatures, which did continue so long as he continued in his allegiance and duty to God.

2. As applied to the Lord Jesus Christ, and the whole that is here said can be applied only to him, *v.* 8, 9. And here you may observe, (1.) What is the moving cause of all the kindness God shows to men in giving Christ for them and to them; and that is the grace of God. For *what is man?* (2.) What are the fruits of this free grace of God with respect to the gift of Christ for us and to us, as related in this scripture-testimony. [1.] That God was mindful of Christ for us in the covenant of redemption. [2.] That God visited Christ on our account; and it was concluded between them that in the fulness of time Christ should come into the world, as the great archetypal sacrifice. [3.] That God had made him a little lower than the angels, in his being made man, that he might suffer and humble himself to death. [4.] That God crowned the human nature of Christ with glory and honour, in his being perfectly holy, and having the Spirit without measure, and by an ineffable union with the divine nature in the second person of the Trinity, the fulness of the Godhead dwelling in him bodily; that by his sufferings he might make satisfaction, tasting death for every man, sensibly feeling and undergoing the bitter agonies of that shameful, painful, and cursed death of the cross, hereby putting all mankind into a new state of trial. [5.] That, as a reward of his humiliation in suffering death, he was crowned with glory and honour, advanced to the highest dignity in heaven, and having absolute dominion over all things, thus accomplishing that ancient scripture in Christ, which never was so accomplished or fulfilled in any mere man that ever was upon earth.

10 For it became him, for whom
are all things, and by whom *are* all
things, in bringing many sons unto
glory, to make the captain of their
salvation perfect through sufferings.
11 For both he that sanctifieth and
they who are sanctified *are* all of one:
for which cause he is not ashamed to
call them brethren, 12 Saying, I will
declare thy name unto my brethren,
in the midst of the church will I sing
praise unto thee. 13 And again, I
will put my trust in him. And again,
Behold I and the children which God
hath given me.

Having mentioned the death of Christ, the apostle here proceeds to prevent and remove the scandal of the cross; and this he does by showing both how it became God that Christ should suffer and how much man should be benefited by those sufferings.

I. How it became God that Christ should suffer: *For it became him for whom are all things, and by whom are all things, in bringing many sons to glory, to make the captain of their salvation perfect through sufferings, v.* 10. Here,

1. God is described as the final end and first cause of all things, and as such it became him to secure his own glory in all that he did, not only to act so that he might in nothing dishonour himself, but so that he might from every thing have a revenue of glory.

2. He is declared to have acted up to this glorious character in the work of redemption, as to the choice both of the end and of the means.

(1.) In the choice of the end; and that was to bring many sons to glory, to present glory in enjoying the glorious privileges of the gospel, and to future glory in heaven, which will be glory indeed, an exceeding eternal weight of glory. Here observe, [1.] We must be the sons of God both by adoption and regeneration, before we can be brought to the glory of heaven. Heaven is the inheritance; and only those that are the children are heirs of that inheritance. [2.] All true believers are the children of God: to *those that receive Christ he has granted the power and privilege of being the children of God, even to as many as believe on his name,* John i. 12. [3.] Though the sons of God are but a few in one place and at one time, yet when they shall be all brought together it will appear that they are many. Christ is the first-born among many brethren. [4.] All the sons of God, how many soever they are, or however dispersed and divided, shall at length be brought together to glory.

(2.) In the choice of the means. [1.] In finding out such a person as should be the captain of our salvation; those that are saved must come to that salvation under the guidance of a captain and leader sufficient for that purpose; and they must be all enlisted under the banner of this captain; they must endure hardship as good soldiers of Christ; they must follow their captain, and those that do so shall be brought safely off, and shall inherit great glory and honour. [2.] In making this captain of our salvation perfect through sufferings. God the Father made the Lord Jesus Christ the captain of our salvation (that is, he consecrated, he appointed him to that office, he gave him a commission for it), and he made him a perfect captain: he had perfection of wisdom, and courage, and strength, by the Spirit of the Lord, which he had without measure; he was made perfect through sufferings; that is, he perfected the work of our redemption by shedding his blood, and was thereby perfectly qualified to be a Mediator between God and man. He found his way to the crown by the cross, and so must his people too. The excellent Dr. Owen observes that the Lord Jesus Christ, being consecrated and perfected through suffering, has consecrated the way of suffering for all his followers to pass through unto glory; and hereby their sufferings are made necessary and unavoidable, they are hereby made honourable, useful, and profitable.

II. He shows how much they would be benefited by the cross and sufferings of Christ; as there was nothing unbecoming God and Christ, so there was that which would be very beneficial to men, in these sufferings. Hereby they are brought into a near union with Christ, and into a very endearing relation.

1. Into a near union (*v.* 11): *Both he that sanctifieth and those that are sanctified are all of one.* Observe, Christ is he that sanctifieth; he has purchased and sent the sanctifying Spirit; he is the head of all sanctifying influences. The Spirit sanctifieth as the Spirit of Christ. True believers are those who are sanctified, endowed with holy principles and powers, separated and set apart from mean and vile uses to high and holy uses and purposes; for so they must be before they can be brought to glory. Now Christ, who is the agent in this work of sanctification, and Christians, who are the recipient subjects, are all of one. How? Why, (1.) They are all of one heavenly Father, and that is God. God is the Father of Christ by eternal generation and by miraculous conception, of Christians by adoption and regeneration. (2.) They are of one earthly father, Adam. Christ and believers have the same human nature. (3.) Of one spirit, one holy and heavenly disposition; the same mind is in them that was in Christ, though not in the same measure; the same Spirit informs and actuates the head and all the members.

2. Into an endearing relation. This results from the union. And here first he declares what this relation is, and then he quotes three texts out of the Old Testament to illustrate and prove it.

(1.) He declares what this relation is: he and believers being all of one, he therefore is not ashamed to call them *brethren.* Observe, [1.] Christ and believers are brethren; not only bone of his bone and flesh of his flesh, but spirit of his spirit—brethren by the whole blood, in what is heavenly as well as in what is earthly. [2.] Christ is not ashamed to own this relation; he is not ashamed to call them brethren, which is wonderful goodness and condescension in him, considering their meanness by nature and vileness by sin; but he will never be ashamed of any who are not ashamed of him, and who take care not to be a shame and reproach to him and to themselves.

(2.) He illustrates this from three texts of scripture.

[1.] The first is out of Ps. xxii. 22, *I will declare thy name unto my brethren; in the midst of the church will I sing praise unto thee.* This psalm was an eminent prophecy of Christ; it begins with his words on the cross, *My God, my God, why hast thou forsaken me?* Now here it is foretold, *First,* That Christ should have a church or *congregation* in the world, a company of volunteers, freely willing to follow him. *Secondly,* That these should not only be brethren to one another, but to Christ himself. *Thirdly,* That he would declare his Father's name to them, that is, his nature and attributes, his mind and will: this he did in his own person, while he dwelt among us, and by his Spirit poured out upon his disciples, enabling them to spread the knowledge of God in the world from one generation to another, to the end of the world. *Fourthly,* That Christ would sing praise to his Father in the church. The glory of the Father was what Christ had in his eye; his heart was set upon it, he laid out himself for it, and he would have his people to join with him in it.

[2.] The second scripture is quoted from Ps. xviii. 2, *And again, I will put my trust in him.* That psalm sets forth the troubles that David, as a type of Christ, met with, and how he in all his troubles put his trust in God. Now this shows that besides his divine nature, which needed no supports, he was to take another nature upon him, that would want those supports which none but God could give. He suffered and trusted as our head and president. *Owen in locum.* His brethren must suffer and trust too.

[3.] The third scripture is taken from Isa. viii. 18, *Behold, I and the children which God hath given me.* This proves Christ really and truly man, for parents and children are of the same nature. Christ's children were given him of the Father, in the counsel of his eternal love, and that covenant of peace which was between them. And they are given to Christ at their conversion. When they take hold of his covenant, then Christ receives them, rules over them, rejoices in them, perfects all their affairs, takes them up to heaven, and there presents them to his Father, *Behold, I and the children which thou hast given me.*

14 Forasmuch then as the children
are partakers of flesh and blood, he
also himself likewise took part of the
same; that through death he might
destroy him that had the power of
death, that is, the devil; 15 And
deliver them who through fear of
death were all their lifetime subject
to bondage. 16 For verily he took
not on *him the nature of* angels; but
he took on *him* the seed of Abraham.
17 Wherefore in all things it behoved
him to be made like unto *his* brethren,
that he might be a merciful and faithful high priest in things *pertaining* to
God, to make reconciliation for the
sins of the people. 18 For in that he
himself hath suffered being tempted,
he is able to succour them that are
tempted.

Here the apostle proceeds to assert the incarnation of Christ, as taking upon him not the nature of angels, but the seed of Abraham; and he shows the reason and design of his so doing.

I. The incarnation of Christ is asserted (*v.* 16): *Verily he took not upon him the nature of angels, but he took upon him the seed of Abraham.* He took part of flesh and blood. Though as God he pre-existed from all eternity, yet in the fulness of time he took our nature into union with his divine nature, and became really and truly man. He did not lay hold of angels, but he laid hold of the seed of Abraham. The angels fell, and he let them go, and lie under the desert, defilement, and dominion of their sin, without hope or help. Christ never designed to be the Saviour of the fallen angels; as their tree fell, so it lies, and must lie to eternity, and therefore he did not assume their nature. The nature of angels could not be an atoning sacrifice for the sin of man. Now Christ resolving to recover the seed of Abraham and raise them up from their fallen state, he took upon him the human nature from one descended from the loins of Abraham, that the same nature that had sinned might suffer, to restore human nature to a state of hope and trial, and all that accepted of mercy to a state of special favour and salvation. Now there is hope and help for the chief of sinners in and through Christ. Here is a price paid sufficient for all, and suitable to all, for it was in our nature. Let us all then know the day of our gracious visitation, and improve that distinguishing mercy which has been shown to fallen men, not to the fallen angels.

II. The reasons and designs of the incarnation of Christ are declared.

1. *Because the children were partakers of flesh and blood, he must take part of the same, and be made like his brethren, v.* 14, 15. For no higher nor lower nature than man's that had sinned could so suffer for the sin of man as to satisfy the justice of God, and raise man up to a state of hope, and make believers the children of God, and so brethren to Christ.

2. He became man that he might die; as God he could not die, and therefore he assumed another nature and state. Here the wonderful love of God appeared, that, when Christ knew what he must suffer in our nature, and how he must die in it, yet he so readily took it upon him. The legal sacrifices and offerings God could not accept as

a propitiation. A body was prepared for Christ, and he said, *Lo! I come, I delight to do thy will.*

3. That *through death he might destroy him that had the power of death, that is, the devil, v.* 14. The devil was the first sinner, and the first tempter to sin, and sin was the procuring cause of death; and he may be said to have the power of death, as he draws men into sin, the ways whereof are death, as he is often permitted to terrify the consciences of men with the fear of death, and as he is the executioner of divine justice, haling their souls from their bodies to the tribunal of God, there to receive their doom, and then being their tormentor, as he was before their tempter. In these respects he may be said to have had the power of death. But now Christ has so far destroyed him who had the power of death that he can keep none under the power of spiritual death; nor can he draw any into sin (the procuring cause of death), nor require the soul of any from the body, nor execute the sentence upon any but those who choose and continue to be his willing slaves, and persist in their enmity to God.

4. That he might deliver his own people from the slavish fear of death to which they are often subject. This may refer to the Old-Testament saints, who were more under a spirit of bondage, because life and immortality were not so fully brought to light as now they are by the gospel. Or it may refer to all the people of God, whether under the Old Testament or the New, whose minds are often in perplexing fears about death and eternity. Christ became man, and died, to deliver them from those perplexities of soul, by letting them know that death is not only a conquered enemy, but a reconciled friend, not sent to hurt the soul, or separate it from the love of God, but to put an end to all their grievances and complaints, and to give them a passage to eternal life and blessedness; so that to them death is not now in the hand of Satan, but in the hand of Christ—not Satan's servant, but Christ's servant—has not hell following it, but heaven to all who are in Christ.

5. Christ must be made like unto his brethren, that he might be a merciful and faithful high priest in things pertaining to the justice and honour of God and to the support and comfort of his people. He must be faithful to God and merciful to men. (1.) In things pertaining to God, to his justice, and to his honour—to make reconciliation for the sins of the people, to make all the attributes of the divine nature, and all the persons subsisting therein, harmonize in man's recovery, and fully to reconcile God and man. Observe, There was a great breach and quarrel between God and man, by reason of sin; but Christ, by becoming man and dying, has taken up the quarrel, and made reconciliation so far that God is ready to receive all into favour and friendship who come to him through Christ. (2.) In things pertaining to his people, to their support and comfort: *In that he suffered, being tempted, he is able to succour those that are tempted, v.* 18. Here observe, [1.] Christ's passion: *He suffered being tempted;* and his temptations were not the least part of his sufferings. *He was in all things tempted as we are, yet without sin, ch.* iv. 15. [2.] Christ's compassion: *He is able to succour those that are tempted.* He is touched with a feeling of our infirmities, a sympathizing physician, tender and skilful; he knows how to deal with tempted sorrowful souls, because he has been himself sick of the same disease, not of sin, but of temptation and trouble of soul. The remembrance of his own sorrows and temptations makes him mindful of the trials of his people, and ready to help them. Here observe, *First,* The best of Christians are subject to temptations, to many temptations, while in this world; let us never count upon an absolute freedom from temptations in this world. *Secondly,* Temptations bring our souls into such distress and danger that they need support and succour. *Thirdly,* Christ is ready and willing to succour those who under their temptations apply to him; and he became man, and was tempted, that he might be every way qualified to succour his people.

CHAP. III.

In this chapter the apostle applies what he had said in the chapter foregoing concerning the priesthood of Christ, I. In a serious pathetic exhortation that this great high priest, who was discovered to them, might be seriously considered by them, ver. 1—6. II. He then adds many weighty counsels and cautions, from ver. 7, to the end.

WHEREFORE, holy brethren,
partakers of the heavenly
calling, consider the Apostle and High
Priest of our profession, Christ Jesus;
2 Who was faithful to him that appointed him, as also Moses *was faith-*
ful in all his house. 3 For this *man*
was counted worthy of more glory
than Moses, inasmuch as he who hath
builded the house hath more honour
than the house. 4 For every house
is builded by some *man;* but he that
built all things *is* God. 5. And
Moses verily *was* faithful in all his
house, as a servant, for the testimony
of those things which were to be
spoken after; 6 But Christ as a son
over his own house; whose house are
we, if we hold fast the confidence and
the rejoicing of the hope firm unto
the end.

In these verses we have the application of the doctrine laid down in the close of the last chapter concerning the priesthood of our Lord Jesus Christ. And observe,

I. In how fervent and affectionate a manner the apostle exhorts Christians to have this high priest much in their thoughts, and to make him the object of their close and serious consideration; and surely no one in earth or heaven deserves our consideration more than he. That this exhortation might be made the more effectual, observe,

1. The honourable compellation used towards those to whom he wrote: *Holy brethren, partakers of the heavenly calling.* (1.) Brethren, not only my brethren, but the brethren of Christ, and in him brethren to all the saints. All the people of God are brethren, and should love and live like brethren. (2.) Holy brethren; holy not only in profession and title, but in principle and practice, in heart and life. This has been turned by some into scorn: "These," say they, "are the holy brethren;" but it is dangerous jesting with such edge-tools; *be not mockers, lest your bands be made strong.* Let those that are thus despised and scorned labour to be holy brethren indeed, and approve themselves so to God; and they need not be ashamed of the title nor dread the scoffs of the profane. The day is coming when those that make this a term of reproach would count it their greatest honour and happiness to be taken into this sacred brotherhood. (3.) *Partakers of the heavenly calling*—partakers of the means of grace, and of the Spirit of grace, that came from heaven, and by which Christians are effectually called out of darkness into marvellous light, that calling which brings down heaven into the souls of men, raises them up to a heavenly temper and conversation, and prepares them to live for ever with God in heaven.

2. The titles he gives to Christ, whom he would have them consider, (1.) As the apostle of our profession, the prime-minister of the gospel church, a messenger and a principal messenger sent of God to men, upon the most important errand, the great revealer of that faith which we profess to hold and of that hope which we profess to have. (2.) Not only the apostle, but the high priest too, of our profession, the chief officer of the Old Testament as well as the New, the head of the church in every state, and under each dispensation, upon whose satisfaction and intercession we profess to depend for pardon of sin, and acceptance with God. (3.) As Christ, the Messiah, anointed and every way qualified for the office both of apostle and high priest. (4.) As Jesus, our Saviour, our healer, the great physician of souls, typified by the brazen serpent that Moses lifted up in the wilderness, that those who were stung by the fiery serpents might look to him, and be saved.

II. We have the duty we owe to him who bears all these high and honourable titles, and that is to consider him as thus characterized. Consider what he is in himself, what he is to us, and what he will be to us hereafter and for ever; consider him, fix your thoughts upon him with the greatest attention, and act towards him accordingly; look unto Jesus, the author and finisher of your faith. Here observe, 1. Many that profess faith in Christ have not a due consideration for him; he is not so much thought of as he deserves to be, and desires to be, by those that expect salvation from him. 2. Close and serious consideration of Christ would be of great advantage to us to increase our acquaintance with him, and to engage our love and our obedience to him, and reliance on him. 3. Even those that are holy brethren, and partakers of the heavenly calling, have need to stir up one another to think more of Christ than they do, to have him more in their minds; the best of his people think too seldom and too slightly of him. 4. We must consider Christ as he is described to us in the scriptures, and form our apprehensions of him thence, not from any vain conceptions and fancies of our own.

III. We have several arguments drawn up to enforce this duty of considering Christ the apostle and high priest of our profession.

1. The first is taken from his fidelity, *v.* 2. He was faithful to him that appointed him, as Moses was in all his house. (1.) Christ is an appointed Mediator; God the Father has sent and sealed him to that office, and therefore his mediation is acceptable to the Father. (2.) He is faithful to that appointment, punctually observing all the rules and orders of his mediation, and fully executing the trust reposed in him by his Father and by his people. (3.) That he is as faithful to him that appointed him as Moses was in all his house. Moses was faithful in the discharge of his office to the Jewish church in the Old Testament, and so is Christ under the New; this was a proper argument to urge upon the Jews, who had so high an opinion of the faithfulness of Moses, and yet his faithfulness was but typical of Christ's.

2. Another argument is taken from the superior glory and excellence of Christ above Moses (*v.* 3—6); therefore they were more obliged to consider Christ. (1.) Christ was a maker of the house, Moses but a member in it. By the house we are to understand the church of God, the people of God incorporated together under Christ their maker and head, and under subordinate officers, according to his law, observing his institutions. Christ is the maker of this house of the church in all ages: Moses was a minister in the house, he was instrumental under Christ in governing and edifying the house, but Christ is the maker of all things; for he is God, and no one less than God could build the church, either lay the foundation or carry on the superstructure. No less power was requisite to make the church than to make the world; the world was made out of nothing, the church made out of materials altogether unfit for such a building. Christ, who is God, drew the ground-plan of the church, provided the materials, and by almighty power disposed them to receive the form; he has compacted and united this his house, has

settled the orders of it, and crowned all with his own presence, which is the true glory of this house of God. (2.) Christ was the master of this house, as well as the maker, *v.* 5, 6. This house is styled his house, as the Son of God. Moses was only a faithful servant, for a testimony of those things that were afterwards to be revealed. Christ, as the eternal Son of God, is the rightful owner and sovereign ruler of the church. Moses was only a typical governor, for a testimony of all those things relating to the church which would be more clearly, completely, and comfortably revealed in the gospel by the Spirit of Christ; and therefore Christ is worthy of more glory than Moses, and of greater regard and consideration. This argument the apostle concludes, [1.] With a comfortable accommodation of it to himself and all true believers (*v.* 6)· *Whose house we are:* each of us personally, as we are the temples of the Holy Ghost, and Christ dwells in us by faith; all of us jointly, as we are united by the bonds of graces, truths, ordinances, gospel discipline, and devotions. [2.] With a characteristic description of those persons who constitute this house: "*If we hold fast the confidence, and the rejoicing of the hope, firmly to the end;* that is, if we maintain a bold and open profession of the truths of the gospel, upon which our hopes of grace and glory are built, and live upon and up to those hopes, so as to have a holy rejoicing in them, which shall abide firm to the end, notwithstanding all that we may meet with in so doing." So that you see there must not only be a setting out well in the ways of Christ, but a stedfastness and perseverance therein unto the end. We have here a direction what those must do who would partake of the dignity and privileges of the household of Christ. *First,* They must take the truths of the gospel into their heads and hearts. *Secondly,* They must build their hopes of happiness upon those truths. *Thirdly,* They must make an open profession of those truths. *Fourthly,* They must live so up to them as to keep their evidences clear, that they may rejoice in hope, and then they must in all persevere to the end. In a word, they must walk closely, consistently, courageously, and constantly, in the faith and practice of the gospel, that their Master, when he comes, may own and approve them.

7 Wherefore (as the Holy Ghost
saith, To day if ye will hear his voice.
8 Harden not your hearts, as in the
provocation, in the day of temptation
in the wilderness: 9 When your fathers tempted me, proved me, and
saw my works forty years. 10 Wherefore I was grieved with that generation, and said, They do alway err in
their heart; and they have not known
my ways. 11 So I sware in my
wrath, They shall not enter into my
rest.) 12 Take heed, brethren, lest
there be in any of you an evil heart
of unbelief, in departing from the
living God. 13 But exhort one another daily, while it is called To day;
lest any of you be hardened through
the deceitfulness of sin. 14 For we
are made partakers of Christ, if we
hold the beginning of our confidence
stedfast unto the end; 15 While it
is said, To day if ye will hear his voice,
harden not your hearts, as in the provocation. 16 For some, when they
had heard, did provoke: howbeit not
all that came out of Egypt by Moses.
17 But with whom was he grieved
forty years? *was it* not with them
that had sinned, whose carcases fell
in the wilderness? 18 And to whom
sware he that they should not enter
into his rest, but to them that believed not? 19 So we see they could
not enter in because of unbelief.

Here the apostle proceeds in pressing upon them serious counsels and cautions to the close of the chapter; and he recites a passage out of Ps. xcv. 7, &c., where observe,

I. What he counsels them to do—to give a speedy and present attention to the call of Christ. "Hear his voice, assent to, approve of, and consider, what God in Christ speaks unto you; apply it to yourselves with suitable affections and endeavours, and set about it this very day, for to-morrow it may be too late."

II. What he cautions them against—hardening their hearts, turning the deaf ear to the calls and counsels of Christ: "When he tells you of the evil of sin, the excellency of holiness, the necessity of receiving him by faith as your Saviour, do not shut your ear and heart against such a voice as this." Observe, The hardening of our hearts is the spring of all our other sins.

III. Whose example he warns them by—that of the Israelites their fathers in the wilderness: *As in the provocation and day of temptation;* this refers to that remarkable passage at Massah Meribah, Exod. xvii. 2—7. Observe,

1. Days of temptation are often days of provocation.

2. To provoke God, when he is trying us, and letting us see that we entirely depend and live immediately upon him, is a provocation with a witness.

3. The sins of others, especially our relations, should be a warning to us. Our fathers' sins and punishments should be remembered by us, to deter us from following their evil

examples. Now as to the sin of the fathers of the Jews, here reflected upon, observe,

(1.) The state in which these fathers were, when they thus sinned: they were in the wilderness, brought out of Egypt, but not got into Canaan, the thoughts whereof should have restrained them from sin.

(2.) The sin they were guilty of: they tempted and provoked God; they distrusted God, murmured against Moses, and would not attend to the voice of God.

(3.) The aggravations of their sin: they sinned in the wilderness, where they had a more immediate dependence upon God: they sinned when God was trying them; they sinned when they saw his works—works of wonder wrought for their deliverance out of Egypt, and their support and supply in the wilderness from day to day. They continued thus to sin against God for forty years. These were heinous aggravations.

(4.) The source and spring of such aggravated sins, which were, [1.] They erred in their hearts; and these heart-errors produced many other errors in their lips and lives. [2.] They did not know God's ways, though he had walked before them. They did not know his ways; neither those ways of his providence in which he had walked towards them, nor those ways of his precept in which they ought to have walked towards God; they did not observe either his providences or his ordinances in a right manner.

(5.) The just and great resentment God had at their sins, and yet the great patience he exercised towards them (*v.* 10): *Wherefore I was grieved with that generation.* Note, [1.] All sin, especially sin committed by God's professing privileged people, does not only anger and affront God, but it grieves him. [2.] God is loth to destroy his people in or for their sin, he waits long to be gracious to them. [3.] God keeps an exact account of the time that people go on in sinning against him, and in grieving him by their sins; but at length, if they by their sins continue to grieve the Spirit of God, their sins shall be made grievous to their own spirits, either in a way of judgment or mercy.

(6.) The irreversible doom passed upon them at last for their sins. God swore in his wrath that they should not enter into his rest, the rest either of an earthly or of a heavenly Canaan. Observe, [1.] Sin, long continued in, will kindle the divine wrath, and make it flame out against sinners. [2.] God's wrath will discover itself in its righteous resolution to destroy the impenitent; he will swear in his wrath, not rashly, but righteously, and his wrath will make their condition a restless condition; there is no resting under the wrath of God.

IV. What use the apostle makes of their awful example, *v.* 12, 13, &c. He gives the Hebrews a proper caution, and enforces it with an affectionate compellation.

1. He gives the Hebrews a proper caution; the word is, *Take heed, βλέπετε—look to it.* "Look about you; be upon your guard against enemies both within and without; be circumspect. You see what kept many of your forefathers out of Canaan, and made their carcases fall in the wilderness; take heed lest you fall into the same sin and snare and dreadful sentence. For you see Christ is head of the church, a much greater person than Moses, and your contempt of him must be a greater sin than their contempt of Moses; and so you are in danger of falling under a severer sentence than they." Observe, The ruin of others should be a warning to us to take heed of the rock they split upon. Israel's fall should for ever be a warning to all who come after them; for *all these things happened to them for ensamples* (1 Cor. x. 11), and should be remembered by us. Take heed; all who would get safely to heaven must look about them.

2. He enforces the admonition with an affectionate compellation: "*Brethren,* not only in the flesh, but in the Lord; brethren whom I love, and for whose welfare I labour and long." And here he enlarges upon the matter of the admonition: *Take heed, brethren, lest there be in any of you an evil heart of unbelief in departing from the living God.* Here observe, (1.) A heart of unbelief is an evil heart. Unbelief is a great sin, it vitiates the heart of man. (2.) An evil heart of unbelief is at the bottom of all our sinful departures from God; it is a leading step to apostasy; if once we allow ourselves to distrust God, we may soon desert him. (3.) Christian brethren have need to be cautioned against apostasy. *Let those that think they stand take heed lest they fall.*

3. He subjoins good counsel to the caution, and advises them to that which would be a remedy against this evil heart of unbelief—that they should *exhort one another daily, while it is called to-day, v.* 13. Observe, (1.) We should be doing all the good we can to one another while we are together, which will be but a short and uncertain time. (2.) Since to-morrow is none of ours, we must make the best improvement of to-day. (3.) If Christians do not exhort one another daily, they will be in danger of being hardened through the deceitfulness of sin. Note, [1.] There is a great deal of deceitfulness in sin; it appears fair, but is filthy; it appears pleasant, but is pernicious; it promises much, but performs nothing. [2.] The deceitfulness of sin is of a hardening nature to the soul; one sin allowed prepares for another; every act of sin confirms the habit; sinning against conscience is the way to sear the conscience; and therefore it should be the great concern of every one to exhort himself and others to beware of sin.

4. He comforts those who not only set out well, but hold on well, and hold out to the end (*v.* 14): *We are made partakers of Christ, if we hold the beginning of our confidence*

stedfast to the end. Here observe, (1.) The saints' privilege: they are made partakers of Christ, that is, of the Spirit, nature, graces, righteousness, and life of Christ; they are interested in all that is Christ's, in all that he is, in all that he has done, or can do. (2.) The condition on which they hold that privilege, namely, their perseverance in the bold and open profession and practice of Christ and Christianity unto the end. Not but they shall persevere, being kept by the mighty power of God through faith to salvation, but to be pressed thus to it is one means by which Christ helps his people to persevere. This tends to make them watchful and diligent, and so keeps them from apostasy. Here observe, [1.] The same spirit with which Christians set out in the ways of God they should maintain and evidence to the end. Those who begin seriously, and with lively affections and holy resolutions and humble reliance, should go on in the same spirit. But, [2.] There are a great many who in the beginning of their profession show a great deal of courage and confidence, but do not hold them fast to the end. [3.] Perseverance in faith is the best evidence of the sincerity of our faith.

5. The apostle resumes what he had quoted before from Ps. xcv. 7, &c., and he applies it closely to those of that generation, *v.* 15, 16, &c. While it is said, *To-day if you will hear,* &c.; as if he should say, "What was recited before from that scripture belonged not only to former ages, but to you now, and to all who shall come after you; that you take heed you fall not into the same sins, lest you fall under the same condemnation." The apostle tells them that though some who had heard the voice of God did provoke him, yet all did not so. Observe, (1.) Though the majority of hearers provoked God by unbelief, yet some there were who believed the report. (2.) Though the hearing of the word be the ordinary means of salvation, yet, if it be not hearkened to, it will expose men more to the anger of God. (3.) God will have a remnant that shall be obedient to his voice, and he will take care of such and make mention of them with honour. (4.) If these should fall in a common calamity, yet they shall partake of eternal salvation, while disobedient hearers perish for ever.

6. The apostle puts some queries upon what had been before mentioned, and gives proper answers to them (*v.* 17—19): *But with whom was he grieved forty years? With those that sinned. And to whom did he swear?* &c. Whence observe, (1.) God is grieved only with those of his people who sin against him, and continue in sin. (2.) God is grieved and provoked most by sins publicly committed by the generality of a nation; when sin becomes epidemic, it is most provoking. (3.) Though God grieves long, and bears long, when pressed with the weight of general and prevailing wickedness, yet he will at length ease himself of public offenders by public judgments. (4.) Unbelief (with rebellion which is the consequent of it) is the great damning sin of the world, especially of those who have a revelation of the mind and will of God. This sin shuts up the heart of God, and shuts up the gate of heaven, against them; it lays them under the wrath and curse of God, and leaves them there; so that in truth and justice to himself he is obliged to cast them off for ever.

CHAP. IV.

The apostle, having in the foregoing chapter set forth the sin and punishment of the ancient Jews, proceeds in this, I. To declare that our privileges by Christ under the gospel exceed the privileges of the Jewish church under Moses, as a reason why we should make a right improvement of them, ver. 1—4. II. He assigns the cause why the ancient Hebrews did not profit by their religious privileges, ver. 2. Then, III. Confirms the privileges of those who believe, and the misery of those who continue in unbelief, 3—10. IV. Concludes with proper and powerful arguments and motives to faith and obedience.

LET us therefore fear, lest, a promise being left *us* of entering
into his rest, any of you should seem
to come short of it. 2 For unto us
was the gospel preached, as well as
unto them: but the word preached
did not profit them, not being mixed
with faith in them that heard *it.* 3
For we which have believed do enter
into rest, as he said, As I have sworn
in my wrath, if they shall enter into
my rest: although the works were
finished from the foundation of the
world. 4 For he spake in a certain
place of the seventh *day* on this
wise, And God did rest the seventh
day from all his works. 5 And in
this *place* again, If they shall enter
into my rest. 6 Seeing therefore it
remaineth that some must enter therein, and they to whom it was first
preached entered not in because of
unbelief: 7 (Again, he limiteth a
certain day, saying in David, To day,
after so long a time; as it is said,
To day if ye will hear his voice, harden
not your hearts. 8 For if Jesus had
given them rest, then would he not
afterward have spoken of another day.
9 There remaineth therefore a rest to
the people of God. 10 For he that
is entered into his rest, he also hath
ceased from his own works, as God
did from his.)

Here, I. The apostle declares that our privileges by Christ under the gospel are not only as great, but greater than those enjoyed under the Mosaic law. He specifies this, that we have a promise left us of entering into his rest; that is, of entering into a covenant-relation to Christ, and a state of communion with God through Christ, and of growing up therein, till we are made perfect in glory. We have discoveries of this rest, and proposals, and the best directions how we may attain unto it. This promise of spiritual rest is a promise left us by the Lord Jesus Christ in his last will and testament, as a precious legacy. Our business is to see to it that we be the legatees, that we lay our claim to that rest and freedom from the dominion of sin, Satan, and the flesh, by which the souls of men are kept in servitude and deprived of the true rest of the soul, and may be also set free from the yoke of the law and all the toilsome ceremonies and services of it, and may enjoy peace with God in his ordinances and providences, and in our own consciences, and so have the prospect and earnest of perfect and everlasting rest in heaven.

II. He demonstrates the truth of his assertion, that we have as great advantages as they. For says he (*v.* 2), *To us was the gospel preached as well as unto them;* the same gospel for substance was preached under both Testaments, though not so clearly; not in so comfortable a manner under the Old as under the New. The best privileges the ancient Jews had were their gospel privileges; the sacrifices and ceremonies of the Old Testament were the gospel of that dispensation; and, whatever was excellent in it, was the respect it had to Christ. Now, if this was their highest privilege, we are not inferior to them; for we have the gospel as well as they, and in greater purity and perspicuity than they had.

III. He again assigns the reason why so few of the ancient Jews profited by that dispensation of the gospel which they enjoyed, and that was their want of faith: *The word preached did not profit them because it was not mixed with faith in those that heard him, v.* 2. Observe, 1. The word is preached to us that we may profit by it, that we may gain spiritual riches by it; it is a price put into our hands to get wisdom, the rich endowment of the soul. 2. There have been in all ages a great many unprofitable hearers; many who seem to deal much in sermons, in hearing the word of God, but gain nothing to their souls thereby; and those who are not gainers by hearing are great losers. 3. That which is at the bottom of all our unprofitableness under the word is our unbelief. We do not mix faith with what we hear; it is faith in the hearer that is the life of the word. Though the preacher believes the gospel, and endeavours to mix faith with his preaching, and to speak as one who has believed and so spoken, yet, if the hearers have not faith in their souls to mix with the word, they will be never the better for it. This faith must mingle with every word, and be in act and exercise while we are hearing; and, when we have heard the word, assenting to the truth of it, approving of it, accepting the mercy offered, applying the word to ourselves with suitable affections, then we shall find great profit and gain by the word preached.

IV. On these considerations the apostle grounds his repeated and earnest caution and counsel that those who enjoy the gospel should maintain a holy fear and jealousy over themselves, lest latent unbelief should rob them of the benefit of the word, and of that spiritual rest which is discovered and tendered in the gospel: *Let us fear lest, a promise being left us of entering into his rest, any of you should seem to come short of it, v.* 1. Observe, 1. Grace and glory are attainable by all under the gospel: there is an offer, and a promise to those who shall accept the offer. 2. Those who may attain them may also fall short. Those who might have attained salvation by faith may fall short by unbelief. 3. It is a dreadful thing so much as to seem to fall short of the gospel salvation, to seem so to themselves, to lose their comfortable hope; and to seem so to others, so losing the honour of their holy profession. But, if it be so dreadful to seem to fall short of this rest, it is much more dreadful really to fall short. Such a disappointment must be fatal. 4. One good means to prevent either our real falling short or seeming to fall short is to maintain a holy and religious fear lest we should fall short. This will make us vigilant and diligent, sincere and serious; this fear will put us upon examining our faith and exercising it; whereas presumption is the high road to ruin.

V. The apostle confirms the happiness of all those who truly believe the gospel; and this he does,

1. By asserting so positively the truth of it, from the experience of himself and others: "*We, who have believed, do enter into rest, v.*3. We enter into a blessed union with Christ, and into a communion with God through Christ; in this state we actually enjoy many sweet communications of pardon of sin, peace of conscience, joy in the Holy Ghost, increase of grace and earnests of glory, resting from the servitude of sin, and reposing ourselves in God till we are prepared to rest with him in heaven."

2. He illustrates and confirms it that those who believe are thus happy, and do enter into rest. (1.) From God's finishing his work of creation, and so entering into his rest (*v.* 3, 4), appointing our first parents to rest the seventh day, to rest in God. Now as God finished his work, and then rested from it, and acquiesced in it, so he will cause those who believe to finish their work, and then to enjoy their rest. (2.) From God's continuing the observance of the sabbath, after the fall, and the revelation of a Redeemer. They were to keep the seventh day a holy sabbath to the Lord, therein praising him who had raised them up out of nothing by creating power, and praying to him that he would create them anew by his Spirit of grace, and direct their faith to the promised

Redeemer and restorer of all things, by which faith they find rest in their souls. (3.) From God's proposing Canaan as a typical rest for the Jews who believed: and as those who did believe, Caleb and Joshua, did actually enter into Canaan; so those who now believe shall enter into rest. (4.) From the certainty of another rest besides that seventh day of rest instituted and observed both before and after the fall, and besides that typical Canaan-rest which most of the Jews fell short of by unbelief; for the Psalmist has spoken of another day and another rest, whence it is evident that there is a more spiritual and excellent sabbath remaining for the people of God than that into which Joshua led the Jews (*v.* 6—9), and this rest remaining is, [1.] A rest of grace, and comfort, and holiness, in the gospel state. This is the rest wherewith the Lord Jesus, our Joshua, causes weary souls and awakened consciences to rest, and this is the refreshing. [2.] A rest in glory, the everlasting sabbatism of heaven, which is the repose and perfection of nature and grace too, where the people of God shall enjoy the end of their faith and the object of all their desires. (5.) This is further proved from the glorious forerunners who have actually taken possession of this rest—God and Christ. It is certain that God, after the creating of the world in six days, entered into his rest; and it is certain that Christ, when he had finished the work of our redemption, entered into his rest; and these were not only examples, but earnests, that believers shall enter into their rest: *He that hath entered into rest hath also ceased from his own works as God did from his, v.* 10. Every true believer hath ceased from his own works of sin, from relying on his own works of righteousness, and from the burdensome works of the law, as God and Christ have ceased from their works of creation and redemption.

VI. The apostle confirms the misery of those who do not believe; they shall never enter into this spiritual rest, either of grace here or glory hereafter. This is as certain as the word and oath of God can make it. As sure as God has entered into his rest, so sure it is that obstinate unbelievers shall be excluded. As sure as the unbelieving Jews fell in the wilderness, and never reached the promised land, so sure it is that unbelievers shall fall into destruction, and never reach heaven. As sure as Joshua, the great captain of the Jews, could not give them possession of Canaan because of their unbelief, notwithstanding his eminent valour and conduct, so sure it is that even Jesus himself, the captain of our salvation, notwithstanding all that fulness of grace and strength that dwells in him, will not, cannot, give to final unbelievers either spiritual or eternal rest: it remains only for the people of God; others by their sin abandon themselves to eternal restlessness.

11 Let us labour therefore to enter
into that rest, lest any man fall after
the same example of unbelief. 12
For the word of God *is* quick, and
powerful, and sharper than any two-
edged sword, piercing even to the
dividing asunder of soul and spirit,
and of the joints and marrow, and *is*
a discerner of the thoughts and intents of the heart. 13 Neither is
there any creature that is not manifest in his sight: but all things *are*
naked and opened unto the eyes of him
with whom we have to do. 14 Seeing then that we have a great high
priest, that is passed into the heavens,
Jesus the Son of God, let us hold fast
our profession. 15 For we have not
a high priest which cannot be touched
with the feeling of our infirmities;
but was in all points tempted like as
we are, yet without sin. 16 Let us
therefore come boldly unto the throne
of grace, that we may obtain mercy,
and find grace to help in time of need.

In this latter part of the chapter the apostle concludes, first, with a serious repeated exhortation, and then with proper and powerful motives.

I. Here we have a serious exhortation: *Let us labour therefore to enter into that rest, v.* 11. Observe, 1. The end proposed—rest spiritual and eternal, the rest of grace here and glory hereafter—in Christ on earth, with Christ in heaven. 2. The way to this end prescribed—labour, diligent labour; this is the only way to rest; those who will not work now shall not rest hereafter. After due and diligent labour, sweet and satisfying rest shall follow; and labour now will make that rest more pleasant when it comes. *The sleep of the labouring man is sweet,* Eccl. v. 12. Let us therefore labour, let us all agree and be unanimous in this, and let us quicken one another, and call upon one another to this diligence. It is the truest act of friendship, when we see our fellow-christians loiter, to call upon them to mind their business and labour at it in earnest. "Come, Sirs, let us all go to work; why do we sit still? Why do we loiter? Come, let us labour; now is our working time, our rest remains." Thus should Christians call upon themselves and one another to be diligent in duty; and so much the more as we see the day approaching.

II. Here we have proper and powerful motives to make the advice effectual, which are drawn,

1. From the dreadful example of those who have already perished by unbelief: *Lest any man fall after the same example of unbelief.* To have seen so many fall before us will be a great aggravation of our sin, if we will not take warning by them: their ruin

calls loudly upon us; their lost and restless souls cry to us from their torments, that we do not, by sinning as they did, make ourselves miserable as they are.

2. From the great help and advantage we may have from the word of God to strengthen our faith, and excite our diligence, that we may obtain this rest: *The word of God is quick and powerful, v.* 12. By the word of God we may understand either the essential or the written word: the essential *Word,* that in *the beginning was with God, and was God* (John i. 1), the Lord Jesus Christ, and indeed what is said in this verse is true concerning him; but most understand it of the written word, the holy scriptures, which are the word of God. Now of this word it is said, (1.) That it is *quick;* it is very lively and active, in all its efforts, in seizing the conscience of the sinner, in cutting him to the heart, and in comforting him and binding up the wounds of the soul. Those know not the word of God who call it a dead letter; it is quick, compared to the light, and nothing quicker than the light; it is not only quick, but quickening; it is a vital light; it is a living word, ζῶν. Saints die, and sinners die; but the word of God lives. *All flesh is grass, and all the glory thereof as the flower of grass. The grass withereth, and the flower thereof falleth away, but the word of the Lord endureth for ever,* 1 Pet. i. 24, 25. *Your fathers, where are they? And the prophets, do they live for ever? But my words, which I commanded the prophets, did they not take hold of your fathers?* Zech. i. 5, 6. (2.) It is *powerful.* When God sets it home by his Spirit, it convinces powerfully, converts powerfully, and comforts powerfully. It is so powerful as to pull down strong holds (2 Cor. x. 4, 5), to raise the dead, to make the deaf to hear, the blind to see, the dumb to speak, and the lame to walk. It is powerful to batter down Satan's kingdom, and to set up the kingdom of Christ upon the ruins thereof. (3.) It is *sharper than any two-edged sword;* it cuts both ways; it is *the sword of the Spirit,* Eph. vi. 17. It is the two-edged sword that cometh out of the mouth of Christ, Rev. i. 16. It is sharper than any two-edged sword, for it will enter where no other sword can, and make a more critical dissection: it *pierces to the dividing asunder of the soul and the spirit,* the soul and its habitual prevailing temper; it makes a soul that has been a long time of a proud spirit to be humble, of a perverse spirit to be meek and obedient. Those sinful habits that have become as it were natural to the soul, and rooted deeply in it, and become in a manner one with it, are separated and cut off by this sword, It cuts off ignorance from the understanding, rebellion from the will, and enmity from the mind, which, when carnal, is enmity itself against God. This sword divides between *the joints and the marrow,* the most secret, close, and intimate parts of the body; this sword can cut off the lusts of the flesh as well as the lusts of the mind, and make men willing to undergo the sharpest operation for the mortifying of sin. (4.) It is *a discerner of the thoughts and intents of the heart,* even the most secret and remote thoughts and designs. It will discover to men the variety of their thoughts and purposes, the vileness of them, the bad principles they are actuated by, the sinister and sinful ends they act to. The word will turn the inside of a sinner out, and let him see all that is in his heart. Now such a word as this must needs be a great help to our faith and obedience.

3. From the perfections of the Lord Jesus Christ, both of his person and office.

(1.) His person, particularly his omniscience: *Neither is there any creature that is not manifest in his sight, v.* 13. This is agreeable to what Christ speaks of himself: *All the churches shall know that I am he that searches the reins and hearts,* Rev. ii. 23. None of the creatures can be concealed from Christ; none of the creatures of God, for Christ is the Creator of them all; and there are none of the motions and workings of our heads and hearts (which may be called creatures of our own) but what are open and manifest to him with whom we have to do as the object of our worship, and the high priest of our profession. He, by his omniscience, cuts up the sacrifice we bring to him, that it may be presented to the Father. Now as the high priest inspected the sacrificed beasts, cut them up to the back-bone to see whether they were sound at heart, so all things are thus dissected, and lie open to the piercing eye of our great high priest. And he who now tries our sacrifices will at length, as Judge, try our state. We shall have to do with him as one who will determine our everlasting state. Some read the words, *to whom with us there is an account or reckoning.* Christ has an exact account of us all. He has accounted for all who believe on him; and he will account with all: our accounts are before him. This omniscience of Christ, and the account we owe of ourselves to him, should engage us to persevere in faith and obedience till he has perfected all our affairs.

(2.) We have an account of the excellency and perfection of Christ, as to his office, and this particular office of our high priest. The apostle first instructs Christians in the knowledge of their high priest, what kind of high priest he is, and then puts them in mind of the duty they owe on this account.

[1.] What kind of high priest Christ is (*v.* 14): *Seeing we have such a high priest;* that is, *First,* A great high priest, much greater than Aaron, or any of the priests of his order. The high priests under the law were accounted great and venerable persons; but they were but faint types and shadows of Christ. The greatness of our high priest is set forth, 1. By his having passed into the heavens. The high priest under the law, once a year, went out of the people's sight within the veil, into the holiest of all, where were the sacred signals of the presence of God; but Christ once for all has passed into the heavens, to take the government of all upon him, to send the Spirit to prepare a place for his people, and to make intercession for them. Christ executed one part of his priesthood on earth, in dying for us; the other he executes in heaven, by pleading the cause, and presenting the offerings, of his people. 2. The greatness of Christ is set forth by his name, *Jesus*—a physician and a Saviour, and one of a divine nature, the Son of God by eternal generation; and therefore having divine perfection, able to save to the uttermost all who come to God by him. *Secondly*, He is not only a great, but a gracious high priest, merciful, compassionate, and sympathizing with his people: *We have not a high priest who cannot be touched with the feeling of our infirmities*, *v.* 15. Though he is so great, and so far above us, yet he is very kind, and tenderly concerned for us. He is touched with the feeling of our infirmities in such a manner as none else can be; for he was himself tried with all the afflictions and troubles that are incident to our nature in its fallen state: and this not only that he might be able to satisfy for us, but to sympathize with us. But then, *Thirdly*, He is a sinless high priest: *He was in all things tempted as we are, yet without sin.* He was tempted by Satan, but he came off without sin. We seldom meet with temptations but they give us some shock. We are apt to give back, though we do not yield; but our great high priest came off clear in his encounter with the devil, who could neither find any sin in him nor fix any stain upon him. He was tried severely by the Father. It pleased the Lord to bruise him; and yet he sinned not, either in thought, word, or deed. He had done no violence, neither was there any deceit in his mouth. He was holy, harmless, and undefiled; and such a high priest became us. Having thus told us what a one our high priest is, the apostle proceeds to show us,

[2.] How we should demean ourselves towards him. *First*, Let us hold fast our profession of faith in him, *v.* 14. Let us never deny him, never be ashamed of him before men. Let us hold fast the enlightening doctrines of Christianity in our heads, the enlivening principles of it in our hearts, the open profession of it in our lips, and our practical and universal subjection to it in our lives. Observe here, 1. We ought to be possessed of the doctrines, principles, and practice, of the Christian life. 2. When we are so, we may be in danger of losing our hold, from the corruption of our hearts, the temptations of Satan, and the allurements of this evil world. 3. The excellency of the high priest of our profession would make our apostasy from him most heinous and inexcusable; it would be the greatest folly and the basest ingratitude. 4. Christians must not only set out well, but they must hold out: those who endure to the end will be saved, and none but they. *Secondly*, We should encourage ourselves, by the excellency of our high priest, to come boldly to the throne of grace, *v.* 16. Here observe, 1. There is a throne of grace set up, a way of worship instituted, in which God may with honour meet poor sinners, and treat with them, and they may with hope draw nigh to him, repenting and believing. God might have set up a tribunal of strict and inexorable justice, dispensing death, the wages of sin, to all who were convened before it; but he has chosen to set up a throne of grace. A throne speaks authority, and bespeaks awe and reverence. A throne of grace speaks great encouragement even to the chief of sinners. There grace reigns, and acts with sovereign freedom, power, and bounty. 2. It is our duty and interest to be often found before this throne of grace, waiting on the Lord in all the duties of his worship, private and public. It is good for us to be there. 3. Our business and errand at the throne of grace should be that we *may obtain mercy and find grace to help in time of need.* Mercy and grace are the things we want, mercy to pardon all our sins and grace to purify our souls. 4. Besides the daily dependence we have upon God for present supplies, there are some seasons in which we shall most sensibly need the mercy and grace of God, and we should lay up prayers against such seasons—times of temptation, either by adversity or prosperity, and especially a dying time: we should every day put up a petition for mercy in our last day. The Lord grant unto us that we may find mercy of the Lord at that day, 2 Tim. i. 18. 5. In all our approaches to this throne of grace for mercy, we should come with a humble freedom and boldness, with a liberty of spirit and a liberty of speech; we should ask in faith, nothing doubting; we should come with a Spirit of adoption, as children to a reconciled God and Father. We are indeed to come with reverence and godly fear, but not with terror and amazement; not as if we were dragged before the tribunal of justice, but kindly invited to the mercy-seat, where grace reigns, and loves to exert and exalt itself towards us. 6. The office of Christ, as being our high priest, and such a high priest, should be the ground of our confidence in all our approaches to the throne of grace. Had we not a Mediator, we could have no boldness in coming to God; for we are guilty and polluted creatures. All we do is polluted; we cannot go into the presence of God alone; we must either go in the hand of a Mediator or our hearts and our hopes will fail us. We have boldness to enter into the holiest by the blood of Jesus. He is our Advocate, and, while he pleads for his people, he pleads with the price in his hand, by which he purchased all that our souls want or can desire.

CHAP. V.

In this chapter the apostle continues his discourse upon the priesthood of Christ, a sweet subject, which he would not too soon dismiss. And here, I. He explains the nature of the priestly office in general, ver. 1—3. II. The proper and regular call there must be to this office, ver. 4—6. III. The requisite qualifications for the work, ver. 7—9. IV. The peculiar order of the priesthood of Christ; it was not after the order of Aaron, but of Melchisedec, ver. 6, 7, 10. V. He reproves the Hebrews, that they had not made those improvements in knowledge which might have made them capable of looking into the more abstruse and mysterious parts of scripture, ver. 11—14.

FOR every high priest taken from
among men is ordained for men
in things *pertaining* to God, that he
may offer both gifts and sacrifices for
sins: 2 Who can have compassion
on the ignorant, and on them that are
out of the way: for that he himself
also is compassed with infirmity. 3
And by reason hereof he ought, as for
the people, so also for himself, to
offer for sins. 4 And no man taketh
this honour unto himself, but he that
is called of God, as *was* Aaron. 5 So
also Christ glorified not himself to be
made a high priest; but he that said
unto him, Thou art my Son, to day
have I begotten thee. 6 As he saith
also in another *place*, Thou *art* a priest
for ever after the order of Melchisedec.
7 Who in the days of his flesh, when
he had offered up prayers and supplications with strong crying and tears
unto him that was able to save him
from death, and was heard in that he
feared; 8 Though he were a Son,
yet learned he obedience by the things
which he suffered; 9 And being
made perfect, he became the author
of eternal salvation unto all them
that obey him.

We have here an account of the nature of the priestly office in general, though with an accommodation to the Lord Jesus Christ. We are told,

I. Of what kind of beings the high priest must be. He must be taken from among men; he must be a man, one of ourselves, bone of our bone, flesh of our flesh, and spirit of our spirits, a partaker of our nature, and a standard-bearer among ten thousand. This implies, 1. That man had sinned. 2. That God would not admit sinful man to come to him immediately and alone, without a high priest, who must be taken from among men. 3. That God was pleased to take one from among men, by whom they might approach God in hope, and he might receive them with honour. 4. That every one shall now be welcome to God that comes to him by this his priest.

II. For whom every high priest is ordained: *For men in things pertaining to God,* for the glory of God and the good of men, that he might come between God and man. So Christ did; and therefore let us never attempt to go to God but through Christ, nor expect any favour from God but through Christ.

III. For what purpose every high priest was ordained: *That he might offer both gifts and sacrifices for sin.*

1. That he might offer gifts or free-will offerings, brought to the high priest, so offered for the glory of God, and as an acknowledgment that our all is of him and from him; we have nothing but what he is pleased to give us, and of his own we offer to him an oblation of acknowledgment. This intimates, (1.) That all we bring to God must be free and not forced; it must be a gift; it must be given and not taken away again. (2.) That all we bring to God must go through the high priest's hands, as the great agent between God and man.

2. That he might offer sacrifices for sin; that is, the offerings that were appointed to make atonement, that sin might be pardoned and sinners accepted. Thus Christ is constituted a high priest for both these ends. Our good deeds must be presented by Christ, to render ourselves and them acceptable; and our evil deeds must be expiated by the sacrifice of himself, that they may not condemn and destroy us. And now, as we value acceptance with God and pardon, we must apply ourselves by faith to this our great high priest.

IV. How this high priest must be qualified, *v.* 2.

1. He must be one that can have compassion on two sorts of persons:—(1.) *On the ignorant,* or those that are guilty of sins of ignorance. He must be one who can find in his heart to pity them, and intercede with God for them, one that is willing to instruct those that are dull of understanding. (2.) *On those that are out of the way,* out of the way of truth, duty, and happiness; and he must be one who has tenderness enough to lead them back from the by-paths of error, sin, and misery, into the right way: this will require great patience and compassion, even the compassion of a God.

2. He must also be compassed with infirmity; and so be able from himself feelingly to consider our frame, and to sympathize with us. Thus Christ was qualified. He took upon him our sinless infirmities; and this gives us great encouragement to apply ourselves to him under every affliction; for in all the afflictions of his people he is afflicted.

V. How the high priest was to be called of God. He must have both an internal and external call to his office: *For no man taketh this honour to himself* (*v.* 4), that is, no man ought to do it, no man can do it legally; if any does it, he must be reckoned a usurper, and treated accordingly. Here observe, 1. The office of the priesthood was a very great honour. To be employed to stand between God and man, one while representing God and his will to men, at another time representing man and his case to God, and dealing between them about matters of the highest importance—entrusted on both sides with the honour of God and the happiness of man—must render the office very honourable. 2. The priesthood is an office and honour that no man ought to take to himself; if he does, he can expect no success in it, nor any reward for it, only from himself. He is an intruder who is not called of God, as was Aaron. Observe, (1.) God is the fountain of all honour, especially true spiritual honour. He is the fountain of true authority, whether he calls any to the priesthood in an extraordinary way, as he did Aaron, or in an ordinary way, as he called his successors. (2.) Those only can expect assistance from God, and acceptance with him, and his presence and blessing on them and their administrations, that are called of God; others may expect a blast instead of a blessing.

VI. How this is brought home and applied to Christ: *So Christ glorified not himself, v.* 5. Observe here, Though Christ reckoned it his glory to be made a high priest, yet he would not assume that glory to himself. He could truly say, *I seek not my own glory,* John viii. 50. Considered as God, he was not capable of any additional glory, but as man and Mediator he did not run without being sent; and, if he did not, surely others should be afraid to do it.

VII. The apostle prefers Christ before Aaron, both in the manner of his call and in the holiness of his person. 1. In the manner of his call, in which God said unto him, *Thou art my Son, this day have I begotten thee* (quoted from Ps. ii. 7), referring to his eternal generation as God, his wonderful conception as man, and his perfect qualification as Mediator. Thus God solemnly declared his dear affection to Christ, his authoritative appointment of him to the office of a Mediator, his instalment and approbation of him in that office, his acceptance of him, and of all he had done or should do in the discharge of it. Now God never said thus to Aaron. Another expression that God used in the call of Christ we have in Ps. cx. 4, *Thou art a priest for ever, after the order of Melchisedec, v.* 6. God the Father appointed him a priest of a higher order than that of Aaron. The priesthood of Aaron was to be but temporary; the priesthood of Christ was to be perpetual: the priesthood of Aaron was to be successive, descending from the fathers to the children; the priesthood of Christ, after the order of Melchisedec, was to be personal, and the high priest immortal as to his office, without descent, having neither beginning of days nor end of life, as it is more largely described in the seventh chapter, and will be opened there. 2. Christ is here preferred to Aaron in the holiness of his person. Other priests were to offer up sacrifices, as for the *sins of others, so for themselves, v.* 3. But Christ needed not to offer for sins for himself, *for he had done no violence,* neither was there *any deceit in his mouth,* Isa. liii. 9. And such a high priest became us.

VIII. We have an account of Christ's discharge of this his office, and of the consequences of that discharge, *v.* 7—9.

1. The discharge of his office of the priesthood (*v.* 7): *Who in the days of his flesh, when he had offered up prayers and supplications,* &c. Here observe, (1.) He took to him flesh, and for some days tabernacled therein; he became a mortal man, and reckoned his life by days, herein setting us an example how we should reckon ours. Were we to reckon our lives by days, it would be a means to quicken us to do the work of every day in its day. (2.) Christ, in the days of his flesh, subjected himself to death; he hungered, he was a tempted, bleeding, dying Jesus! His body is now in heaven, but it is a spiritual glorious body. (3.) God the Father was able to save him from death. He could have prevented his dying, but he would not; for then the great design of his wisdom and grace must have been defeated. What would have become of us if God had saved Christ from dying? The Jews reproachfully said, *Let him deliver him now, if he will have him,* Matt. xxvii. 43. But it was in kindness to us that the Father would not suffer that bitter cup to pass away from him; for then we must have drunk the dregs of it, and been miserable for ever. (4.) Christ, in the days of his flesh, offered up prayers and supplications to his Father, as an earnest of his intercession in heaven. A great many instances we have of Christ's praying. This refers to his prayer in his agony (Matt. xxvi. 39, and *ch.* xxvii. 46), and to that before his agony (John xvii.) which he put up for his disciples, and all who should believe on his name. (5.) The prayers and supplications that Christ offered up were joined with strong cries and tears, herein setting us an example not only to pray, but to be fervent and importunate in prayer. How many dry prayers, how few wet ones, do we offer up to God! (6.) Christ was heard in that he feared. How? Why he was answered by present supports in and under his agonies, and in being carried well through death, and delivered from it by a glorious resurrection: *He was heard in that he feared.* He had an awful sense of the wrath of God, of the weight of sin. His human nature was ready to sink under the heavy load, and would have sunk,

had he been quite forsaken in point of help and comfort from God; but he was heard in this, he was supported under the agonies of death. He was carried through death; and there is no real deliverance from death but to be carried well through it. We may have many recoveries from sickness, but we are never saved from death till we are carried well through it. And those that are thus saved from death will be fully delivered at last by a glorious resurrection, of which the resurrection of Christ was the earnest and first-fruits.

2. The consequences of this discharge of his office, *v.* 8, 9, &c.

(1.) By these his sufferings *he learned obedience, though he was a Son, v.* 8. Here observe, [1.] The privilege of Christ: *He was a Son;* the only-begotten of the Father. One would have thought this might have exempted him from suffering, but it did not. Let none then who are the children of God by adoption expect an absolute freedom from suffering. *What Son is he whom the Father chasteneth not?* [2.] Christ made improvement by his sufferings. By his passive obedience, he learned active obedience; that is, he practised that great lesson, and made it appear that he was well and perfectly learned in it; though he never was disobedient, yet he never performed such an act of obedience as when he became obedient to death, even to the death of the cross. Here he has left us an example, that we should learn by all our afflictions a humble obedience to the will of God. We need affliction, to teach us submission.

(2.) By these his sufferings he was made perfect, and became the author of eternal salvation to all who obey him, *v.* 9. [1.] Christ by his sufferings was consecrated to his office, consecrated by his own blood. [2.] By his sufferings he consummated that part of his office which was to be performed on earth, making reconciliation for iniquity; and in this sense he is said to be *made perfect,* a perfect propitiation. [3.] Hereby he has become the author of eternal salvation to men; he has by his sufferings purchased a full deliverance from sin and misery, and a full fruition of holiness and happiness for his people. Of this salvation he has given notice in the gospel; he has made a tender of it in the new covenant, and has sent the Spirit to enable men to accept this salvation. [4.] This salvation is actually bestowed on none but those who obey Christ. It is not sufficient that we have some doctrinal knowledge of Christ, or that we make a profession of faith in him, but we must hearken to his word, and obey him. He is exalted to be a prince to rule us, as well as a Saviour to deliver us; and he will be a Saviour to none but to those to whom he is a prince, and who are willing that he should reign over them; the rest he will account his enemies, and treat them accordingly. But to those who obey him, devoting themselves to him, denying themselves, and taking up their cross, and following him, he will be the author, αἴτιος — the grand cause of their salvation, and they shall own him as such for ever.

10 Called of God a high priest
after the order of Melchisedec. 11
Of whom we have many things to say,
and hard to be uttered, seeing ye are
dull of hearing. 12 For when for the
time ye ought to be teachers, ye have
need that one teach you again which
be the first principles of the oracles of
God; and are become such as have
need of milk, and not of strong meat.
13 For every one that useth milk *is*
unskilful in the word of righteousness: for he is a babe. 14 But strong
meat belongeth to them that are of
full age, *even* those who by reason of
use have their senses exercised to discern both good and evil.

Here the apostle returns to what he had in *v.* 6 cited out of Ps. cx., concerning the peculiar order of the priesthood of Christ, that is, the order of Melchisedec. And here,

I. He declares he had many things which he could say to them concerning this mysterious person called Melchisedec, whose priesthood was eternal, and therefore the salvation procured thereby should be eternal also. We have a more particular account of this Melchisedec in *ch.* vii. Some think the things which the apostle means, that were hard to be uttered, were not so much concerning Melchisedec himself as concerning Christ, of whom Melchisedec was the type. And doubtless this apostle had many things to say concerning Christ that were very mysterious, hard to be uttered; there are great mysteries in the person and offices of the Redeemer; Christianity is the great mystery of godliness.

II. He assigns the reason why he did not say all those things concerning Christ, our Melchisedec, that he had to say, and what it was that made it so difficult for him to utter them, namely, the dulness of the Hebrews to whom he wrote: *You are dull of hearing.* There is a difficulty in the things themselves, and there may be a weakness in the ministers of the gospel to speak clearly about these things; but generally the fault is in the hearers. Dull hearers make the preaching of the gospel a difficult thing, and even many who have some faith are but dull hearers, dull of understanding and slow to believe; the understanding is weak, and does not apprehend these spiritual things; the memory is weak, and does not retain them.

III. He insists upon the faultiness of this infirmity of theirs. It was not a mere natural infirmity, but it was a sinful infirmity, and more in them than others, by reason of the singular advantages they had enjoyed for improving in the knowledge of Christ: *For when, for the time, you ought to be teachers, you have need that one teach you again which are the first principles of the oracles of God*, *v.* 12. Here observe,

1. What proficiency might have been reasonably expected from these Hebrews—that they might have been so well instructed in the doctrine of the gospel as to have been teachers of others. Hence learn, (1.) God takes notice of the time and helps we have for gaining scripture-knowledge. (2.) From those to whom much is given much is expected. (3.) Those who have a good understanding in the gospel should be teachers of others, if not in a public, yet in a private station. (4.) None should take upon them to be teachers of others, but those who have made a good improvement in spiritual knowledge themselves.

2. Observe the sad disappointment of those just expectations: *You have need that one should teach you again*, &c. Here note, (1.) In the oracles of God there are some first principles, plain to be understood and necessary to be learned. (2.) There are also deep and sublime mysteries, which those should search into who have learned the first principles, that so they may stand complete in the whole will of God. (3.) Some persons, instead of going forward in Christian knowledge, forget the very first principles that they had learned long ago; and indeed those that are not improving under the means of grace will be losing. (4.) It is a sin and shame for persons that are men for their age and standing in the church to be children and babes in understanding.

IV. The apostle shows how the various doctrines of the gospel must be dispensed to different persons. There are in the church babes and persons of full age (*v.* 12—14), and there are in the gospel milk and strong meat. Observe, 1. Those that are babes, unskilful in the word of righteousness, must be fed with milk; they must be entertained with the plainest truths, and these delivered in the plainest manner; *there must be line upon line, precept upon precept, here a little, and there a little*, Isa. xxviii. 10. Christ despises not his babes; he has provided suitable food for them. It is good to be babes in Christ, but not always to continue in that childish state; we should endeavour to pass the infant state; we should always remain in malice children, but in understanding we should grow up to a manly maturity. 2. There is strong meat for those that are of full age, *v.* 14. The deeper mysteries of religion belong to those that are of a higher class in the school of Christ, who have learned the first principles and well improved them; so that by reason of use they have their senses exercised to discern both good and evil, duty and sin, truth and error. Observe, (1.) There have been always in the Christian state children, young men, and fathers. (2.) Every true Christian, having received a principle of spiritual life from God, stands in need of nourishment to preserve that life. (3.) The word of God is food and nourishment to the life of grace: *As new-born babes desire the sincere milk of the word that you may grow thereby.* (4.) It is the wisdom of ministers rightly to divide the word of truth, and to give to every one his portion—milk to babes, and strong meat to those of full age. (5.) There are spiritual senses as well as those that are natural. There is a spiritual eye, a spiritual appetite, a spiritual taste; the soul has its sensations as well as the body; these are much depraved and lost by sin, but they are recovered by grace. (6.) It is by use and exercise that these senses are improved, made more quick and strong to taste the sweetness of what is good and true, and the bitterness of what is false and evil. Not only reason and faith, but spiritual sense, will teach men to distinguish between what is pleasing and what is provoking to God, between what is helpful and what is hurtful to our own souls.

CHAP. VI.

In this chapter the apostle proceeds to persuade the Hebrews to make a better proficiency in religion than they had done, as the best way to prevent apostasy, the dreadful nature and consequences of which sin he sets forth in a serious manner (ver. 1—8), and then expresses his good hopes concerning them, that they would persevere in faith and holiness, to which he exhorts them, and sets before them the great encouragement they had from God, both with respect to their duty and happiness, from ver. 9, to the end.

THEREFORE leaving the principles of the doctrine of Christ,
let us go on unto perfection; not laying again the foundation of repentance
from dead works, and of faith toward
God, 2 Of the doctrine of baptisms,
and of laying on of hands, and of resurrection of the dead, and of eternal
judgment. 3 And this will we do, if
God permit. 4 For *it is* impossible
for those who were once enlightened,
and have tasted of the heavenly gift,
and were made partakers of the Holy
Ghost, 5 And have tasted the good
word of God, and the powers of the
world to come, 6 If they shall fall
away, to renew them again unto repentance; seeing they crucify to themselves the Son of God afresh, and
put *him* to an open shame. 7 For
the earth which drinketh in the rain
that cometh oft upon it, and bringeth
forth herbs meet for them by whom it
is dressed, receiveth blessing from
God: 8 But that which beareth thorns

and briers *is* rejected, and *is* nigh unto cursing; whose end *is* to be burned.

We have here the apostle's advice to the Hebrews—that they would grow up from a state of childhood to the fulness of the stature of the new man in Christ. He declares his readiness to assist them all he could in their spiritual progress; and, for their greater encouragement, he puts himself with them: *Let us go on.* Here observe, In order to their growth, Christians must leave the principles of the doctrine of Christ. How must they leave them? They must not lose them, they must not despise them, they must not forget them. They must lay them up in their hearts, and lay them as the foundation of all their profession and expectation; but they must not rest and stay in them, they must not be always laying the foundation, they must go on, and build upon it. There must be a superstructure; for the foundation is laid on purpose to support the building. Here it may be enquired, Why did the apostle resolve to set strong meat before the Hebrews, when he knew they were but babes? *Answer.* 1. Though some of them were but weak, yet others of them had gained more strength; and they must be provided for suitably. And, as those who are grown Christians must be willing to hear the plainest truths preached for the sake of the weak, so the weak must be willing to hear the more difficult and mysterious truths preached for the sake of those who are strong. 2. He hoped they would be growing in their spiritual strength and stature, and so be able to digest stronger meat.

I. The apostle mentions several foundation-principles, which must be well laid at first, and then built upon; neither his time nor theirs must be spent in laying these foundations over and over again. These foundations are six:—

1. Repentance from dead works, that is, conversion and regeneration, repentance from a spiritually dead state and course; as if he had said, "Beware of destroying the life of grace in your souls; your minds were changed by conversion, and so were your lives. Take care that you return not to sin again, for then you must have the foundation to lay again; there must be a second conversion a repenting not only of, but from, dead works." Observe here, (1.) The sins of persons unconverted are dead works; they proceed from persons spiritually dead, and they tend to death eternal. (2.) Repentance for dead works, if it be right, is repentance from dead works, a universal change of heart and life. (3.) Repentance for and from dead works is a foundation-principle, which must not be laid again, though we must renew our repentance daily.

2. Faith towards God, a firm belief of the existence of God, of his nature, attributes, and perfections, the trinity of persons in the unity of essence, the whole mind and will of God as revealed in his word, particularly what relates to the Lord Jesus Christ. We must by faith acquaint ourselves with these things; we must assent to them, we must approve of them, and apply all to ourselves with suitable affections and actions. Observe, (1.) Repentance from dead works, and faith towards God, are connected, and always go together; they are inseparable twins, the one cannot live without the other. (2.) Both of these are foundation-principles, which should be once well laid, but never pulled up, so as to need to be laid over again; we must not relapse into infidelity.

3. The doctrine of baptisms, that is, of being baptized by a minister of Christ with water, in the name of the Father, and of the Son, and of the Holy Ghost, as the initiating sign or seal of the covenant of grace, strongly engaging the person so baptized to get acquainted with the new covenant, to adhere to it, and prepare to renew it at the table of the Lord and sincerely to regulate himself according to it, relying upon the truth and faithfulness of God for the blessings contained in it. And the doctrine of an inward baptism, that of the Spirit sprinkling the blood of Christ upon the soul, for justification, and the graces of the Spirit for sanctification. This ordinance of baptism is a foundation to be rightly laid, and daily remembered, but not repeated.

4. Laying on of hands, on persons passing solemnly from their initiated state by baptism to the confirmed state, by returning the answer of a good conscience towards God, and sitting down at the Lord's table. This passing from incomplete to complete church-membership was performed by laying on of hands, which the extraordinary conveyance of the gift of the Holy Ghost continued. This, once done, all are obliged to abide by, and not to need another solemn admission, as at first, but to go on, and grow up, in Christ. Or by this may be meant ordination of persons to the ministerial office, who are duly qualified for it and inclined to it; and this by fasting and prayer, with laying on of the hands of the presbytery: and this is to be done but once.

5. The resurrection of the dead, that is, of dead bodies; and their re-union with their souls, to be eternal companions together in weal or woe, according as their state was towards God when they died, and the course of life they led in this world.

6. Eternal judgment, determining the soul of every one, when it leaves the body at death, and both soul and body at the last day, to their eternal state, every one to his proper society and employment to which they were entitled and fitted here on earth; the wicked to everlasting punishment, the righteous to life eternal.

These are the great foundation-principles which ministers should clearly and convincingly unfold, and closely apply. In these the people should be well instructed and established, and from these they must never depart; without these, the other parts of religion have no foundation to support them.

II. The apostle declares his readiness and resolution to assist the Hebrews in building themselves up on these foundations till they arrive at perfection: *And this we will do, if God permit, v.* 3. And thereby he teaches them, 1. That right resolution is very necessary in order to progress and proficiency in religion. 2. That that resolution is right which is not only made in the sincerity of our hearts, but in a humble dependence upon God for strength, for assistance and righteousness, for acceptance, and for time and opportunity. 3. That ministers should not only teach people what to do, but go before them, and along with them, in the way of duty.

III. He shows that this spiritual growth is the surest way to prevent that dreadful sin of apostasy from the faith. And here,

1. He shows how far persons may go in religion, and, after all, fall away, and perish for ever, *v.* 4, 5. (1.) They may be *enlightened.* Some of the ancients understand this of their being baptized; but it is rather to be understood of notional knowledge and common illumination, of which persons may have a great deal, and yet come short of heaven. *Balaam was the man whose eyes were opened* (Num. xxiv. 3), and yet with his eyes opened he went down to utter darkness. (2.) They may *taste of the heavenly gift,* feel something of the efficacy of the Holy Spirit in his operations upon their souls, causing them to taste something of religion, and yet be like persons in the market, who taste of what they will not come up to the price of, and so but take a taste, and leave it. Persons may taste religion, and seem to like it, if they could have it upon easier terms than denying themselves, and taking up their cross,. and following Christ. (3.) They may be *made partakers of the Holy Ghost,* that is, of his extraordinary and miraculous gifts; they may have cast out devils in the name of Christ, and done many other mighty works. Such gifts in the apostolic age were sometimes bestowed upon those who had no true saving grace. (4.) They may *taste of the good word of God;* they may have some relish of gospel doctrines, may hear the word with pleasure, may remember much of it, and talk well of it, and yet never be cast into the form and mould of it, nor have it dwelling richly in them. (5.) They may have *tasted of the powers of the world to come;* they may have been under strong impressions concerning heaven and hell, may have felt some desires of heaven, and dread of going to hell. These lengths hypocrites may go, and, after all, turn apostates. Now hence observe, [1.] These great things are spoken here of those who may fall way; yet it is not here said of them that they were truly converted, or that they were justified; there is more in true saving grace than in all that is here said of apostates. [2.] This therefore is no proof of the final apostasy of true saints. These indeed may fall frequently and foully, but yet they will not totally nor finally from God; the purpose and the power of God, the purchase and the prayer of Christ, the promise of the gospel, the everlasting covenant that God has made with them, ordered in all things and sure, the indwelling of the Spirit, and the immortal seed of the word, these are their security. But the tree that has not these roots will not stand.

2. The apostle describes the dreadful case of such as fall away after having gone so far in the profession of religion. (1.) The greatness of the sin of apostasy. It is *crucifying the Son of God afresh, and putting him to open shame.* They declare that they approve of what the Jews did in crucifying Christ, and that they would be glad to do the same thing again if it were in their power. They pour the greatest contempt upon the Son of God, and therefore upon God himself, who expects all should reverence his Son, and honour him as they honour the Father. They do what in them lies to represent Christ and Christianity as a shameful thing, and would have him to be a public shame and reproach. This is the nature of apostasy. (2.) The great misery of apostates. [1.] It is impossible to renew them again unto repentance. It is extremely hazardous. Very few instances can be given of those who have gone so far and fallen away, and yet ever have been brought to true repentance, such a repentance as is indeed a renovation of the soul. Some have thought this is the sin against the Holy Ghost, but without ground. The sin here mentioned is plainly apostasy both from the truth and the ways of Christ. God can renew them to repentance, but he seldom does it; and with men themselves it is impossible. [2.] Their misery is exemplified by a proper similitude, taken from the ground that after much cultivation brings forth nothing but briers and thorns; *and therefore is nigh unto cursing, and its end is to be burned, v.* 8. To give this the greater force here is observed the difference that there is between the good ground and the bad, that these contraries, being set one over against the other, may illustrate each other. *First.* Here is a description of the good ground: It *drinketh in the rain that cometh often upon it.* Believers do not only taste of the word of God, but they drink it in; and this good ground bringeth forth fruit answerable to the cost laid out, for the honour of Christ and the comfort of his faithful ministers, who are, under Christ, dressers of the ground. And this fruit-field or garden receives the blessing. God declares fruitful Christians blessed, and all wise and good men account them blessed: they are blessed

with increase of grace, and with further establishment and glory at last. *Secondly,* Here is the different case of the bad ground: It *bears briers and thorns;* it is not only barren of good fruit, but fruitful in that which is bad, briers and thorns, fruitful in sin and wickedness, which are troublesome and hurtful to all about them, and will be most so to sinners themselves at last; and then such ground is rejected. God will concern himself no more about such wicked apostates; he will let them alone, and cast them out of his care; he will command the clouds that they rain no more upon them. Divine influences shall be restrained; and that is not all, but such ground *is nigh unto cursing;* so far is it from receiving the blessing, that a dreadful curse hangs over it, though as yet, through the patience of God, the curse is not fully executed. *Lastly,* Its end is to be burned. Apostasy will be punished with everlasting burnings, the fire that shall never be quenched. This is the sad end to which apostasy leads, and therefore Christians should go on and grow in grace, lest, if they do not go forward, they should go backward, 'till they bring matters to this woeful extremity of sin and misery.

9 But, beloved, we are persuaded
better things of you, and things that
accompany salvation, though we thus
speak. 10 For God *is* not unrighteous to forget your work and labour
of love, which ye have showed toward
his name, in that ye have ministered
to the saints, and do minister. 11
And we desire that every one of you
do show the same diligence to the full
assurance of hope unto the end: 12
That ye be not slothful, but followers
of them who through faith and patience inherit the promises. 13 For
when God made promise to Abraham,
because he could swear by no greater,
he sware by himself, 14 Saying,
Surely blessing I will bless thee, and
multiplying I will multiply thee. 15
And so, after he had patiently endured, he obtained the promise. 16
For men verily swear by the greater:
and an oath for confirmation *is* to
them an end of all strife. 17 Wherein
God, willing more abundantly to show
unto the heirs of promise the immutability of his counsel, confirmed *it* by
an oath: 18 That by two immutable
things, in which *it was* impossible for
God to lie, we might have a strong
consolation, who have fled for refuge
to lay hold upon the hope set before
us: 19 Which *hope* we have as an
anchor of the soul, both sure and
stedfast, and which entereth into that
within the veil; 20 Whither the
forerunner is for us entered, *even*
Jesus, made a high priest for ever
after the order of Melchisedec.

The apostle, having applied himself to the fears of the Hebrews, in order to excite their diligence and prevent their apostasy, now proceeds to apply himself to their hopes, and candidly declares the good hope he had concerning them, that they would persevere; and proposes to them the great encouragements they had in the way of their duty.

I. He freely and openly declares the good hope he had concerning them, that they would endure to the end: *But beloved, we are persuaded better things of you, v.* 9. Observe, 1. There are things that accompany salvation, things that are never separated from salvation, things that show the person to be in a state of salvation, and will issue in eternal salvation. 2. The things that accompany salvation are better things than ever any hypocrite or apostate enjoyed. They are better in their nature and in their issue. 3. It is our duty to hope well of those in whom nothing appears to the contrary. 4. Ministers must sometimes speak by way of caution to those of whose salvation they have good hopes. And those who have in themselves good hopes, as to their eternal salvation, should yet consider seriously how fatal a disappointment it would be if they should fall short. Thus they are to work out their salvation with fear and trembling.

II. He proposes arguments and encouragements to them to go on in the way of their duty. 1. That God had wrought a principle of holy love and charity in them, which had discovered itself in suitable works that would not be forgotten of God: *God is not unrighteous to forget your labour of love, v.* 10. Good works and labour proceeding from love to God are commendable; and what is done to any in the name of God shall not go unrewarded. What is done to the saints, as such, God takes as done to himself. 2. Those who expect a gracious reward for the labour of love must continue in it as long as they have ability and opportunity: *You have ministered to the saints, and you do minister; and we desire that every one of you do show the same diligence.* 3. Those who persevere in a diligent discharge of their duty shall attain to the full assurance of hope in the end. Observe, (1.) Full assurance is a higher degree of hope, is full assurance of hope; they differ not in nature, but only in degree. (2.) Full assurance is attainable by great diligence and perseverance to the end.

III. He proceeds to set before them caution and counsel how to attain this full assurance of hope to the end. 1. That they should not be slothful. Slothfulness will clothe a man with rags: they must not love their ease, nor lose their opportunities. 2. That they would follow the good examples of those who had gone before, *v.* 12. Here learn, (1.) There are some who from assurance have gone to inherit the promises. They believed them before, now they inherit them; they have got safely to heaven. (2.) The way by which they came to the inheritance was that of faith and patience. These graces were implanted in their souls, and drawn forth into act and exercise in their lives. If we ever expect to inherit as they do, we must follow them in the way of faith and patience; and those who do thus follow them in the way shall overtake them at the end, and be partakers of the same blessedness.

IV. The apostle closes the chapter with a clear and full account of the assured truth of the promises of God, *v.* 13, *to the end.* They are all confirmed by the oath of God, and they are all founded in the eternal counsel of God, and therefore may be depended upon.

1. They are all confirmed by the oath of God. He has not only given his people his word, and his hand and seal, but his oath. And here, you will observe, he specifies the oath of God to Abraham, which, being sworn to him as the father of the faithful, remains in full force and virtue to all true believers: *When God made a promise unto Abraham, because he could swear by no greater, he swore by himself.* Observe, (1.) What was the promise: *Surely, blessing I will bless thee, and multiplying I will multiply thee.* The blessing of God is the blessedness of his people; and those whom he has blessed indeed he will go on to bless, and will multiply blessings, till he has brought them to perfect blessedness. (2.) What was the oath by which this promise was ratified: *He swore by himself.* He staked down his own being and his own blessedness upon it; no greater security can be given or desired. (3.) How was that oath accomplished. Abraham, in due time, obtained the promise. It was made good to him after he had patiently endured. [1.] There is always an interval, and sometimes a long one, between the promise and the performance. [2.] That interval is a trying time to believers, whether they have patience to endure to the end. [3.] Those who patiently endure shall assuredly obtain the blessedness promised, as sure as Abraham did. [4.] The end and design of an oath is to make the promise sure, and to encourage those to whom it is made to wait with patience till the time for performance comes, *v.* 16. An oath with men is for confirmation, and is an end of all strife. This is the nature and design of an oath, in which men swear by the greater, not by creatures, but by the Lord himself; and it is to put an end to all dispute about the matter, both to disputes within our own breasts (doubts and distrusts), and disputes with others, especially with the promiser. Now, if God would condescend to take an oath to his people, he will surely remember the nature and design of it.

2. The promises of God are all founded in his eternal counsel; and this counsel of his is an immutable counsel. (1.) The promise of blessedness which God has made to believers is not a rash and hasty thing, but the result of God's eternal purpose. (2.) This purpose of God was agreed upon in counsel, and settled there between the eternal Father, Son, and Spirit. (3.) These counsels of God can never be altered; they are immutable. God never needs to change his counsels; for nothing new can arise to him who sees the end from the beginning.

3. The promises of God, which are founded upon these immutable counsels of God, and confirmed by the oath of God, may safely be depended upon; for here we have two immutable things, the counsel and the oath of God, in which it is impossible for God to lie, contrary to his nature as well as to his will. Here observe,

(1.) Who they are to whom God has given such full security of happiness. [1.] They are the heirs of the promise: such as have a title to the promises by inheritance, by virtue of their new birth, and union with Christ. We are all by nature children of wrath. The curse is the inheritance we are born to: it is by a new and heavenly birth that any are born heirs to the promise. [2.] They are such as have fled for refuge to the hope set before them. Under the law there were cities of refuge provided for those who were pursued by the avenger of blood. Here is a much better refuge prepared by the gospel, a refuge for all sinners who shall have the heart to flee to it; yea, though they have been the chief of sinners.

(2.) What God's design towards them is, in giving them such securities—that they might have strong consolation. Observe, [1.] God is concerned for the consolation of believers, as well as for their sanctification; he would have his children walk in the fear of the Lord, and in the comforts of the Holy Ghost. [2.] The consolations of God are strong enough to support his people under their strongest trials. The comforts of this world are too weak to bear up the soul under temptation, persecution, and death; but the consolations of the Lord are neither few nor small.

(3.) What use the people of God should make of their hope and comfort, that most refreshing and comfortable hope of eternal blessedness that God has given them. This is, and must be, unto them, for *an anchor to the soul, sure and stedfast,* &c., *v.* 19. Here, [1.] We are in this world as a ship at sea, liable to be tossed up and down, and in danger of being cast away. Our souls are the vessels. The comforts, expectations, graces, and happiness of our souls are the precious cargo with which these vessels are loaded. Heaven is the harbour to which we sail. The temptations, persecutions, and afflictions that we encounter, are the winds and waves that threaten our shipwreck. [2.] We have need of an anchor to keep us sure and steady, or we are in continual danger. [3.] Gospel hope is our anchor; as in our day of battle it is our helmet, so in our stormy passage through this world it is our anchor. [4.] It is sure and stedfast, or else it could not keep us so. *First,* It is sure in its own nature; for it is the special work of God in the soul. It is a good hope through grace; it is not a flattering hope made out of the spider's web, but it is a true work of God, it is a strong and substantial thing. *Secondly,* It is stedfast as to its object; it is an anchor that has taken good hold, it enters that which is within the veil; it is an anchor that is cast upon the rock, the Rock of ages. It does not seek to fasten in the sands, but enters within the veil, and fixes there upon Christ; he is the object, he is the anchor-hold of the believer's hope. As an unseeen glory within the veil is what the believer is hoping for, so an unseen Jesus within the veil is the foundation of his hope; the free grace of God, the merits and mediation of Christ, and the powerful influences of his Spirit, are the grounds of his hope, and so it is a stedfast hope. Jesus Christ is the object and ground of the believer's hope in several respects. 1. As he has entered within the veil, to intercede with God, in virtue of that sacrifice which he offered up without the veil: hope fastens upon his sacrifice and intercession. 2. As he is the forerunner of his people, gone within the veil, to prepare a place for them, and to assure them that they shall follow him; he is the earnest and first-fruits of believers, both in his resurrection and in his ascension. 3. And he abides there, a high priest after the order of Melchisedec, a priest for ever, whose priesthood shall never cease, never fail, till he has accomplished its whole work and design, which is the full and final happiness of all who have believed on Christ. Now this should engage us to clear up our interest in Christ, that we may fix our hopes in him as our forerunner, that has entered thither for us, for our sakes, for our safety, to watch over our highest interest and concerns. Let us then love heaven the more on his account, and long to be there with him, where we shall be for ever safe, and for ever satisfied.

CHAP. VII.

The doctrine of the priestly office of Christ is so excellent in itself, and so essential a part of the Christian faith, that the apostle loves to dwell upon it. Nothing made the Jews so fond of the Levitical dispensation as the high esteem they had of their priesthood, and it was doubtless a sacred and most excellent institution; it was a very severe threatening denounced against the Jews (Hos. iii. 4), that the children of Israel should abide many days without a prince or priest, and without a sacrifice, and without an ephod, and without teraphim. Now the apostle assures them that by receiving the Lord Jesus they would have a much better high priest, a priesthood of a higher order, and consequently a better dispensation or covenant, a better law and testament; this he shows in this chapter, where, I. We have a more particular account of Melchisedec, ver. 1–3. II. The superiority of his priesthood to that of Aaron, ver. 4–10. III. An accommodation of all to Christ, to show the superior excellency of his person, office, and covenant, ver. 11, to the end.

FOR this Melchisedec, king of Salem, priest of the most high
God, who met Abraham returning
from the slaughter of the kings, and
blessed him; 2 To whom also Abraham gave a tenth part of all; first
being by interpretation King of righteousness, and after that also King
of Salem, which is, King of peace;
3 Without father, without mother,
without descent, having neither beginning of days, nor end of life; but
made like unto the Son of God;
abideth a priest continually. 4 Now
consider how great this man *was,*
unto whom even the patriarch Abraham gave the tenth of the spoils. 5
And verily they that are of the sons
of Levi, who receive the office of the
priesthood, have a commandment to
take tithes of the people according to
the law, that is, of their brethren,
though they come out of the loins of
Abraham: 6 But he whose descent
is not counted from them received
tithes of Abraham, and blessed him
that had the promises. 7 And without all contradiction the less is blessed
of the better. 8 And here men that
die receive tithes; but there he *receiveth them,* of whom it is witnessed
that he liveth. 9 And as I may so
say, Levi also, who receiveth tithes,
paid tithes in Abraham. 10 For he
was yet in the loins of his father, when
Melchisedec met him.

The foregoing chapter ended with a repetition of what had been cited once and again before out of Ps. cx. 4, *Jesus, a high priest for ever, after the order of Melchisedec.* Now this chapter is as a sermon upon that text; here the apostle sets before them some of the strong meat he had spoken of before, hoping they would by greater diligence be better prepared to digest it.

I. The great question that first offers itself is, Who was this Melchisedec? All the account we have of him in the Old Testament is in Gen. xiv. 18, &c., and in Ps. cx. 4. Indeed we are much in the dark about him; God has thought fit to leave us so, that this Melchisedec might be a more lively type of him whose generation none can declare. If men will not be satisfied with what is revealed, they must rove about in the dark in endless conjectures, some fancying him to have been an angel, others the Holy Ghost; but,

1. The opinions concerning him that are best worthy our consideration are these three:—(1.) The rabbin, and most of the Jewish writers, think he was Shem the son of Noah,

who was king and priest to their ancestors, after the manner of the other patriarchs; but it is not probable that he should thus change his name. Besides, we have no account of his settling in the land of Canaan. (2.) Many Christian writers have thought him to be Jesus Christ himself, appearing by a special dispensation and privilege to Abraham in the flesh, and who was known to Abraham by the name *Melchisedec,* which agrees very well to Christ, and to what is said, John viii. 56, *Abraham saw* his *day and rejoiced.* Much may be said for this opinion, and what is said in *v.* 3 does not seem to agree with any mere man; but then it seems strange to make Christ a type of himself. (3.) The most general opinion is that he was a Canaanite king, who reigned in Salem, and kept up religion and the worship of the true God; that he was raised to be a type of Christ, and was honoured by Abraham as such.

2. But we shall leave these conjectures, and labour to understand, as far as we can, what is here said of him by the apostle, and how Christ is represented thereby, *v.* 1—3. (1.) Melchisedec was a king, and so is the Lord Jesus—a king of God's anointing; the government is laid upon his shoulders, and he rules over all for the good of his people. (2.) That he was *king of righteousness:* his name signifies *the righteous king.* Jesus Christ is a rightful and a righteous king—rightful in his title, righteous in his government. He is the Lord our righteousness; he has fulfilled all righteousness, and brought in an everlasting righteousness, and he loves righteousness and righteous persons, and hates iniquity. (3.) He was king of Salem, that is, king of peace; first king of righteousness, and after that king of peace. So is our Lord Jesus; he by his righteousness made peace, the fruit of righteousness is peace. Christ speaks peace, creates peace, is our peace-maker. (4.) He was *priest of the most high God,* qualified and anointed in an extraordinary manner to be his priest among the Gentiles. So is the Lord Jesus; he is the priest of the most high God, and the Gentiles must come to God by him; it is only through his priesthood that we can obtain reconciliation and remission of sin. (5.) He was *without father, without mother, without descent, having neither beginning of days nor end of life, v.* 3. This must not be understood according to the letter; but the scripture has chosen to set him forth as an extraordinary person, without giving us his genealogy, that he might be a fitter type of Christ, who as man was without father, as God without mother; whose priesthood is without descent, did not descend to him from another, nor from him to another, but is personal and perpetual. (6.) That he *met Abraham returning from the slaughter of the kings, and blessed him.* The incident is recorded Gen. xiv. 18, &c. He brought forth bread and wine to refresh Abraham and his servants when they were weary; he gave as a king, and blessed as a priest. Thus our Lord Jesus meets his people in their spiritual conflicts, refreshes them, renews their strength, and blesses them. (7.) That *Abraham gave him a tenth part of all* (*v.* 2), that is, as the apostle explains it, of all *the spoils;* and this Abraham did as an expression of his gratitude for what Melchisedec had done for him, or as a testimony of his homage and subjection to him as a king, or as an offering vowed and dedicated to God, to be presented by his priest. And thus are we obliged to make all possible returns of love and gratitude to the Lord Jesus for all the rich and royal favours we receive from him, to pay our homage and subjection to him as our King, and to put all our offerings into his hands, to be presented by him to the Father in the incense of his own sacrifice. (8.) That this Melchisedec was *made like unto the Son of God, and abideth a priest continually.* He bore the image of God in his piety and authority, and stands upon record as an immortal high priest; the ancient type of him who is the eternal and only-begotten of the Father, who abideth a priest for ever.

II. Let us now consider (as the apostle advises) how great this Melchisedec was, and how far his priesthood was above that of the order of Aaron (*v.* 4, 5, &c.): *Now consider how great this man was,* &c. The greatness of this man and his priesthood appears, 1. From Abraham's paying the tenth of the spoils unto him; and it is well observed that Levi paid tithes to Melchisedec in Abraham, *v.* 9. Now Levi received the office of the priesthood from God, and was to take tithes of the people, yet even Levi paid tithes to Melchisedec, as to a greater and higher priest than himself; therefore that high priest who should afterwards appear, of whom Melchisedec was a type, must be much superior to any of the Levitical priests, who paid tithes, in Abraham, to Melchisedec. And now by this argument of persons doing things that are matters of right or injury in the loins of their predecessors we have an illustration how we may be said to have sinned in Adam, and fallen with him in his first transgression. We were in Adam's loins when he sinned, and the guilt and depravity contracted by the human nature when it was in our first parents are equitably imputed and derived to the same nature as it is in all other persons naturally descended from them. They justly adhere to the nature, and it must be by an act of grace if ever they be taken away. 2. From Melchisedec's blessing of Abraham, *who had the promises; and, without contradiction, the less is blessed of the greater, v.* 6, 7. Here observe, (1.) Abraham's great dignity and felicity—that he had the promises. He was one in covenant with God, to whom God had given exceedingly great and precious promises. That man is rich and happy indeed who has an estate in bills and bonds under

God's own hand and seal. These promises are both of the life that now is and of that which is to come; this honour have all those who receive the Lord Jesus, in whom all the promises are yea and amen. (2.) Melchisedec's greater honour—in that it was his place and privilege to bless Abraham; and it is an incontested maxim *that the less is blessed of the greater*, *v.* 7. He who gives the blessing is greater than he who receives it; and therefore Christ, the antitype of Melchisedec, the meriter and Mediator of all blessings to the children of men, must be greater than all the priests of the order of Aaron.

11 If therefore perfection were by
the Levitical priesthood, (for under it
the people received the law,) what
further need *was there* that another
priest should rise after the order of
Melchisedec, and not be called after
the order of Aaron? 12 For the
priesthood being changed, there is
made of necessity a change also of the
law. 13 For he of whom these things
are spoken pertaineth to another tribe,
of which no man gave attendance at
the altar. 14 For *it is* evident that
our Lord sprang out of Juda; of
which tribe Moses spake nothing concerning priesthood. 15 And it is yet
far more evident: for that after the
similitude of Melchisedec there ariseth
another priest, 16 Who is made,
not after the law of a carnal commandment, but after the power of an
endless life. 17 For he testifieth,
Thou *art* a priest for ever after the
order of Melchisedec. 18 For there
is verily a disannulling of the commandment going before for the weakness and unprofitableness thereof. 19
For the law made nothing perfect,
but the bringing in of a better hope
did; by the which we draw nigh unto
God. 20 And inasmuch as not without an oath *he was made priest*: 21
(For those priests were made without
an oath; but this with an oath by
him that said unto him, The Lord
sware and will not repent, Thou *art*
a priest for ever after the order of
Melchisedec:) 22 By so much was
Jesus made a surety of a better testament. 23 And they truly were
many priests, because they were not
suffered to continue by reason of
death: 24 But this *man*, because he
continueth ever, hath an unchangeable priesthood. 25 Wherefore he is
able also to save them to the uttermost that come unto God by him,
seeing he ever liveth to make intercession for them. 26 For such an
high priest became us, *who is* holy,
harmless, undefiled, separate from
sinners, and made higher than the
heavens; 27 Who needeth not daily,
as those high priests, to offer up sacrifice, first for his own sins, and then
for the people's: for this he did once,
when he offered up himself. 28 For
the law maketh men high priests
which have infirmity; but the word
of the oath, which was since the law,
maketh the Son, who is consecrated
for evermore.

Observe the necessity there was of raising up another priest, after the order of Melchisedec and not after the order of Aaron, by whom that perfection should come which could not come by the Levitical priesthood, which therefore must be changed, and the whole economy with it, *v.* 11, 12, &c. Here,

I. It is asserted that perfection could not come by the Levitical priesthood and the law. They could not put those who came to them into the perfect enjoyment of the good things they pointed out to them; they could only show them the way.

II. That therefore another priest must be raised up, after the order of Melchisedec, by whom, and his law of faith, perfection might come to all who obey him; and, blessed be God, that we may have perfect holiness and perfect happiness by Christ in the covenant of grace, according to the gospel, for we are complete in him.

III. It is asserted that the priesthood being changed there must of necessity be a change of the law; there being so near a relation between the priesthood and the law, the dispensation could not be the same under another priesthood; a new priesthood must be under a new regulation, managed in another way, and by rules proper to its nature and order.

IV. It is not only asserted, but proved, that the priesthood and law are changed, *v.* 13, 14. The priesthood and law by which perfection could not come are abolished, and a priest has arisen, and a dispensation is now set up, by which true believers may be made perfect. Now that there is such a change is obvious.

1. There is a change in the tribe of which the priesthood comes. Before, it was the tribe of Levi; but our great high priest sprang out of Judah, of which tribe Moses spoke nothing concerning the priesthood, *v.* 14.

This change of the family shows a real change of the law of priesthood.

2. There is a change in the form and order of making the priests. Before, in the Levitical priesthood, they were made after the law of a carnal commandment; but our great high priest was made after the power of an endless life. The former law appointed that the office should descend, upon the death of the father, to his eldest son, according to the order of carnal or natural generation; for none of the high priests under that law were without father or mother, or without descent: they had not life and immortality in themselves. They had both beginning of days and end of life; and so the carnal commandment, or law of primogeniture, directed their succession, as it did in matters of civil right and inheritance. But the law by which Christ was constituted a priest, after the order of Melchisedec, was the power of an endless life. The life and immortality which he had in himself were his right and title to the priesthood, not his descent from former priests. This makes a great difference in the priesthood, and in the economy too, and gives the preference infinitely to Christ and the gospel. The very law which constituted the Levitical priesthood supposed the priests to be weak, frail, dying, creatures, not able to preserve their own natural lives, but who must be content and glad to survive in their posterity after the flesh; much less could they, by any power or authority they had, convey spiritual life and blessedness to those who came to them. But the high priest of our profession holds his office by that innate power of endless life which he has in himself, not only to preserve himself alive, but to communicate spiritual and eternal life to all those who duly rely upon his sacrifice and intercession. Some think *the law of the carnal commandment* refers to the external rites of consecration, and the carnal offerings that were made; but *the power of an endless life* to the spiritual living sacrifices proper to the gospel, and the spiritual and eternal privileges purchased by Christ, who was consecrated by the eternal Spirit of life that he received without measure.

3. There is a change in the efficacy of the priesthood. The former was weak and unprofitable, made nothing perfect; the latter brought in a better hope, by which we draw near to God, *v.* 18, 19. The Levitical priesthood brought nothing to perfection: it could not justify men's persons from guilt; it could not sanctify them from inward pollution; it could not cleanse the consciences of the worshippers from dead works; all it could do was to lead them to the antitype. But the priesthood of Christ carries in it, and brings along with it, a better hope; it shows us the true foundation of all the hope we have towards God for pardon and salvation; it more clearly discovers the great objects of our hope; and so it tends to work in us a more strong and lively hope of acceptance with God. By this hope we are encouraged to draw nigh unto God, to enter into a covenant-union with him, to live a life of converse and communion with him. We may now draw near with a true heart, and with the full assurance of faith, having our minds sprinkled from an evil conscience. The former priesthood rather kept men at a distance, and under a spirit of bondage.

4. There is a change in God's way of acting in this priesthood. He has taken an oath to Christ, which he never did to any of the order of Aaron. God never gave them any such assurance of their continuance, never engaged himself by oath or promise that theirs should be an everlasting priesthood, and therefore gave them no reason to expect the perpetuity of it, but rather to look upon it as a temporary law. But Christ was made a priest with the oath of God: *The Lord hath sworn, and will not repent, Thou art a priest for ever after the order of Melchisedec, v.* 21. Here God has upon oath declared the immutability, excellency, efficacy, and eternity, of the priesthood of Christ.

5. There is a change in that covenant of which the priesthood was a security and the priest a surety; that is, a change in the dispensation of that covenant. The gospel dispensation is more full, free, perspicuous, spiritual, and efficacious, than that of the law. Christ is in this gospel covenant a surety for us to God and for God to us, to see that the articles be performed on both parts He, as surety, has united the divine and human nature together in his own person, and therein given assurance of reconciliation; and he has, as surety, united God and man together in the bond of the everlasting covenant. He pleads with men to keep their covenant with God, and he pleads with God that he will fulfil his promises to men, which he is always ready to do in a way suitable to his majesty and glory, that is, through a Mediator.

6. There is a remarkable change in the number of the priests under these different orders. In that of Aaron there was a multitude of priests, of high priests, not at once, but successively; but in this of Christ there is but one and the same. The reason is plain, The Levitical priests were many, because *they were not suffered to continue by reason of death.* Their office, how high and honourable soever, could not secure them from dying; and, as one died, another must succeed, and after a while must give place to a third, till the number had become very great. But this our high priest continues for ever, and his priesthood is ἀπαράβατον—*an unchangeable one,* that does not pass from one to another, as the former did; it is always in the same hand. There can be no vacancy in this priesthood, no hour nor moment in which the people are without a priest to negociate their spiritual concerns in heaven.

Such a vacancy might be very dangerous and prejudicial to them; but this is their safety and happiness, that this ever-living high priest is able to save to the utmost—in all times, in al lcases, in every juncture—all who come to God by him, *v.* 25. So that here is a manifest alteration much for the better.

7. There is a remarkable difference in the moral qualifications of the priests. Those who were of the order of Aaron were not only mortal men, but sinful men, who had their sinful as well as natural infirmities; they needed to offer up sacrifices first for their own sins and then for the people. But our high priest, who was consecrated by the word of the oath, needed only to offer up once for the people, never at all for himself; for he has not only an immutable consecration to his office, but an immutable sanctity in his person. He is *such a high priest as became us, holy, harmless, and undefiled,* &c., *v.* 26—28. Here observe, (1.) Our case, as sinners, needed a high priest to make satisfaction and intercession for us. (2.) No priest could be suitable or sufficient for our reconciliation to God but one who was perfectly righteous in his own person; he must be righteous in himself, or he could not be a propitiation for our sin, or our advocate with the Father. (3.) The Lord Jesus was exactly such a high priest as we wanted, for he has a personal holiness, absolutely perfect. Observe the description we have of the personal holiness of Christ expressed in various terms, all of which some learned divines consider as relating to his perfect purity. [1.] He is holy, perfectly free from all the habits or principles of sin, not having the least disposition to it in his nature; no sin dwells in him, though it does in the best of Christians, not the least sinful inclination. [2.] He is harmless, perfectly free from all actual transgression, has done no violence, nor is there any deceit in his mouth, never did the least wrong to God or man. [3.] He is undefiled, he was never accessory to other men's sins. The best of Christians have need to pray that God would forgive them their other men's sins. It is a difficult thing to keep ourselves pure, so as not to partake in the guilt of other men's sins, by contributing in some way towards them, or not doing what we ought to prevent them. Christ was undefiled; though he took upon him the guilt of our sins, yet he never involved himself in the fact and fault of them. [4.] He is separate from sinners, not only in his present state (having entered as our high priest into the holiest of all, into which nothing defiled can enter), but in his personal purity: he has no such union with sinners, either natural or federal, as can devolve upon him original sin. This comes upon us by virtue of our natural and federal union with the first Adam, we descending from him in the ordinary way. But Christ was, by his ineffable conception in the virgin, separate from sinners; though he took a true human nature, yet the miraculous way in which it was conceived set him upon a separate footing from all the rest of mankind. [5.] He is made higher than the heavens. Most expositors understand this concerning his state of exaltation in heaven, at the right hand of God, to perfect the design of his priesthood. But Dr. Goodwin thinks this may be very justly referred to the personal holiness of Christ, which is greater and more perfect than the holiness of the hosts of heaven, that is, the holy angels themselves, who, though they are free from sin, yet are not in themselves free from all possibility of sinning. And therefore we read, *God putteth no trust in his holy ones, and he chargeth his angels with folly* (Job iv. 18), that is, with weakness and peccability. They may be angels one hour and devils another, as many of them were; and that the holy angels shall not now fall does not proceed from an indefectibility of nature, but from the election of God; they are elect angels. It is very probable that this explanation of the words, *made higher than the heavens,* may be thought too much strained, and that it ought to be understood of the dignity of Christ's state, and not the perfect holiness of his person; and the rather because it is said he was *made* higher γενόμενος; but it is well known that this word is used in a neutral sense, as where it is said, γενέσθη ὁ Θεὸς ἀληθὴς—*Let God be true.* The other characters in the verse plainly belong to the personal perfection of Christ in holiness, as opposed to the sinful infirmities of the Levitical priests; and it seems congruous to think this must do so too, if it may be fairly taken in such a sense; and it appears yet more probable, since the validity and prevalency of Christ's priesthood in *v.* 27 are placed in the impartiality and disinterestedness of it. He needed not to offer up for himself: it was a disinterested mediation; he mediated for that mercy for others which he did not need for himself; had he needed it himself, he had been a party, and could not have been a Mediator—a criminal, and could not have been an advocate for sinners. Now, to render his mediation the more impartial and disinterested, it seems requisite not only that he had no present need of that favour for himself which he mediated for in behalf of others, but that he never could stand in need of it. Though he needed it not to-day, yet if he knew he might be in such circumstances as to need it to-morrow, or at any future time, he must have been thought to have had some eye upon his own interest, and therefore could not act with impartial regard and pure zeal for the honour of God on one hand, and tender pure compassion for poor sinners on the other. I pretend not here to follow the notes of our late excellent expositor, into whose labours we have entered, but have taken the liberty to vindicate this notion of the learned Dr. Goodwin from the exceptions that I know have been made

to it; and I have the rather done it because, if it will hold good, it gives us further evidence how necessary it was that the Mediator should be God, since no mere creature is of himself possessed of that impeccability which will set him above all possible need of favour and mercy for himself.

CHAP. VIII.

In this chapter the apostle pursues his former subject, the priesthood of Christ. And, I. He sums up what he had already said, ver. 1, 2. II. He sets before them the necessary parts of the priestly office, ver. 3—5. And, III. Largely illustrates the excellency of the priesthood of Christ, by considering the excellency of that new dispensation or covenant for which Christ is the Mediator, ver. 6, to the end.

NOW of the things which we have
spoken *this is* the sum: We
have such a high priest, who is set
on the right hand of the throne of the
Majesty in the heavens; 2 A minister of the sanctuary, and of the true
tabernacle, which the Lord pitched,
and not man. 3 For every high priest
is ordained to offer gifts and sacrifices: wherefore *it is* of necessity that
this man have somewhat also to offer.
4 For if he were on earth, he should
not be a priest, seeing that there are
priests that offer gifts according to
the law: 5 Who serve unto the example and shadow of heavenly things,
as Moses was admonished of God
when he was about to make the tabernacle: for, See, saith he, *that* thou
make all things according to the
pattern showed to thee in the mount.

Here is, I. A summary recital of what had been said before concerning the excellency of Christ's priesthood, showing what we have in Christ, where he now resides, and what sanctuary he is the minister of, *v.* 1, 2. Observe, 1. What we have in Christ; we have a high priest, and such a high priest as no other people ever had, no age of the world, or of the church, ever produced; all others were but types and shadows of this high priest. He is adequately fitted and absolutely sufficient to all the intents and purposes of a high priest, both with respect to the honour of God and the happiness of men and himself; the great honour of all those who have an interest in him. 2. Where he now resides: *He sits on the right hand of the throne of the Majesty on high*, that is, of the glorious God of heaven. There the Mediator is placed, and he is possessed of all authority and power both in heaven and upon earth. This is the reward of his humiliation. This authority he exercises for the glory of his Father, for his own honour, and for the happiness of all who belong to him; and he will by his almighty power bring every one of them in their own order to the right hand of God in heaven, as members of his mystical body, that where he is they may be also. 3. What is that sanctuary of which he is a minister: *Of the true tabernacle, which the Lord hath pitched, and not man, v.* 2. The tabernacle which was pitched by man, according to the appointment of God. There was an outer part, in which was the altar where they were to offer their sacrifices, which typified Christ dying; and there was an interior part within the veil, which typified Christ interceding for the people in heaven. Now this tabernacle Christ never entered into; but, having finished the work of satisfaction in the true tabernacle of his own body, he is now a minister of the sanctuary, the holy of holies, the true tabernacle in heaven, there taking care of his people's affairs, interceding with God for them, that their sins may be pardoned and their persons and services accepted, through the merit of his sacrifice. He is not only in heaven enjoying great dominion and dignity, but, as the high priest of his church, executing this office for them all in general, and every member of the church in particular.

II. The apostle sets before the Hebrews the necessary parts of Christ's priesthood, or what it was that belonged to that office, in conformity to what every high priest is ordained to, *v.* 3, 4. 1. *Every high priest is ordained to offer gifts and sacrifices.* Whatever was brought by the people to be presented to God, whether expiatory sacrifices, or peace-offerings, or thank-offerings, must be offered by the priest, who was to expiate their guilt by the blood of the sacrifice, and perfume their gifts and services by his holy incense, to render their persons and performances typically acceptable; so then it necessarily belongs to the priesthood of Christ that he should have somewhat to offer; and he, as the antitype, had himself to offer, his human nature upon the altar of his divine nature, as the great atoning sacrifice that finished transgression, and made an end of sin once for all; and he has the incense of his own righteousness and merits too to offer with all that his people offer up to God by him, to render them acceptable. We must not dare to approach to God, or to present any thing to him, but in and through Christ, depending upon his merits and mediation; for if we are accepted, it is in the Beloved. 2. Christ must now execute his priesthood in heaven, in the holy of holies, the true tabernacle which the Lord hath fixed. Thus the type must be fully answered; having finished the work of sacrificing here, he must go into heaven, to present his righteousness and to make intercession there. For, (1.) *If Christ were on earth, he would not be a priest* (*v.* 4), that is, not according to the Levitical law, as not being of the line of that priesthood; and so long as that priesthood continued there must be a strict regard paid to the divine institution in every thing. (2.) All the services of the priest, under the law, as well as every thing in that tabernacle which was framed according to the pattern in the mount, were only exemplars and shadows of heavenly things, *v.* 5. Christ is the substance and end of the law for righteousness. Something therefore there must be in Christ's priesthood that answers to the high priest's entering within the veil to make intercession, without which he could not have been a perfect priest; and what is this but the ascension of Christ into heaven, and his appearance there in the sight of God for his people, to present their prayers, and plead their cause? So that, if he had still continued on earth, he could not have been a perfect priest; and an imperfect one he could not be.

6 But now hath he obtained a more
excellent ministry, by how much also
he is the mediator of a better covenant,
which was established upon better
promises. 7 For if that first *covenant*
had been faultless, then should no
place have been sought for the second.
8 For finding fault with them, he
saith, Behold, the days come, saith
the Lord, when I will make a new
covenant with the house of Israel
and with the house of Judah: 9 Not
according to the covenant that I made
with their fathers in the day when I
took them by the hand to lead them
out of the land of Egypt; because they
continued not in my covenant, and
I regarded them not, saith the Lord.
10 For this *is* the covenant that I
will make with the house of Israel
after those days, saith the Lord; I
will put my laws into their mind, and
write them in their hearts: and I
will be to them a God, and they shall
be to me a people: 11 And they
shall not teach every man his neighbour, and every man his brother,
saying, Know the Lord: for all shall
know me, from the least to the greatest. 12 For I will be merciful to
their unrighteousness, and their sins
and their iniquities will I remember
no more. 13 In that he saith, A new
covenant, he hath made the first old.
Now that which decayeth and waxeth
old *is* ready to vanish away.

In this part of the chapter, the apostle illustrates and confirms the superior excellency of the priesthood of Christ above that of Aaron, from the excellency of that covenant, or that dispensation of the covenant of grace, of which Christ was the Mediator (*v.* 6): his ministry is more excellent, by how much he is the Mediator of a better covenant. The body and soul too of all divinity (as some observe) consist very much in rightly distinguishing between the two covenants—the covenant of works and the covenant of grace; and between the two dispensations of the covenant of grace—that under the Old Testament and that under the New. Now observe,

I. What is here said of the old covenant, or rather of the old dispensation of the covenant of grace: of this it is said, 1. That it was made with the fathers of the Jewish nation at mount Sinai (*v.* 9), and Moses was the Mediator of that covenant, when God took them by the hand, to lead them out of the land of Egypt, which intimates the great affection, condescension, and tender care of God towards them. 2. That this covenant was not found faultless (*v.* 7, 8); it was a dispensation of darkness and dread, tending to bondage, and only a schoolmaster to bring us to Christ; it was perfect in its kind, and fitted to answer its end, but very imperfect in comparison of the gospel. 3. That it was not sure or stedfast; *for the Jews continued not in that covenant, and the Lord regarded them not, v.* 9. They dealt ungratefully with their God, and cruelly with themselves, and fell under God's displeasure. God will regard those who remain in his covenant, but will reject those who cast away his yoke from them. 4. That it is decayed, grown old, and vanisheth away, *v.* 13. It is antiquated, cancelled, out of date, of no more use in gospel times than candles are when the sun has risen. Some think the covenant of peculiarity did not quite decay till the destruction of Jerusalem, though it was forfeited at the death of Christ, and was made old, and was now to vanish and perish, and the Levitical priesthood vanished with it.

II. What is here said of the New-Testament dispensation, to prove the superior excellency of Christ's ministry. It is said,

1. That it is a better covenant (*v.* 6), a more clear and comfortable dispensation and discovery of the grace of God to sinners, bringing in holy light and liberty to the soul. It is without fault, well ordered in all things. It requires nothing but what it promises grace to perform. It accepts of godly sincerity, accounting it gospel perfection. Every transgression does not turn us out of covenant; all is put into a good and safe hand.

2. That it is established upon better promises, more clear and express, more spiritual, more absolute. The promises of spiritual and eternal blessings are in this covenant positive and absolute; the promises of temporal blessings are with a wise and kind proviso, as far as shall be for God's glory and his people's good. This covenant contains in it promises of assistance and acceptance in duty, promises of progress and perseverance in grace and holiness, of bliss and glory in heaven, which were more

obscurely shadowed forth by the promises of the land of Canaan, a type of heaven.

3. It is a new covenant, even that new covenant that God long ago declared he would make with the house of Israel, that is, all the Israel of God; this was promised in Jer. xxxi. 31, 32, and accomplished in Christ. This will always be a new covenant, in which all who truly take hold of it shall be always found preserved by the power of God. It is God's covenant; his mercy, love, and grace moved for it; his wisdom devised it; his Son purchased it; his Spirit brings souls into it, and builds them up in it.

4. The articles of this covenant are very extraordinary, which are sealed between God and his people by baptism and the Lord's supper; whereby they bind themselves to their part, and God assures them he will do his part; and his is the main and principal part, on which his people depend for grace and strength to do theirs. Here,

(1.) God articles with his people *that he will put his laws into their minds and write them in their hearts*, *v.* 10. He once wrote his laws to them, now he will write his laws in them; that is, he will give them understanding to know and to believe his law; he will give them memories to retain them; he will give them hearts to love them and consciences to recognise them; he will give them courage to profess them and power to put them in practice; the whole habit and frame of their souls shall be a table and transcript of the law of God. This is the foundation of the covenant; and, when this is laid, duty will be done wisely, sincerely, readily, easily, resolutely, constantly, and comfortably.

(2.) He articles with them to take them into a near and very honourable relation to himself. [1.] He will be to them a God; that is, he will be all that to them, and do all that for them, that God can be and do. Nothing more can be said in a thousand volumes than is comprehended in these few words: *I will be a God to them.* [2.] They shall be to him a people, to love, honour, observe, and obey him in all things; complying with his cautions, conforming to his commands, comporting with his providences, copying out his example, taking complacency in his favour. This those must do and will do who have God for their God; this they are bound to do as their part of the contract; this they shall do, for God will enable them to do it, as an evidence that he is their God and that they are his people; for it is God himself who first founds the relation, and then fills it up with grace suitable and sufficient, and helps them in their measure to fill it up with love and duty; so that God engages both for himself and them.

(3.) He articles with them that they shall grow more and more acquainted with their God (*v.* 11): *They shall all know me from the least to the greatest,* insomuch that there shall not be so much need of one neighbour teaching another the knowledge of God. Here observe, [1.] In the want of better instruction, one neighbour should be teaching another to know the Lord, as they have ability and opportunity for it. [2.] This private instruction shall not be so necessary under the New Testament as it was under the Old. The old dispensation was shadowy, dark, ritual, and less understood; their priests preached but seldom, and but a few at a time, and the Spirit of God was more sparingly given out. But under the new dispensation there shall be such abundance of public qualified preachers of the gospel, and dispensers of ordinances statedly in the solemn assemblies, and so great a flocking to them, as doves to their windows, and such a plentiful effusion of the Spirit of God to make the ministration of the gospel effectual, that there shall be a mighty increase and spreading of Christian knowledge in persons of all sorts, of each sex, and of all ages. O that this promise might be fulfilled in our days, that the hand of God may be with his ministers, that a great number may believe and be turned to the Lord!

(4.) God articles with them about the pardon of their sins, as what always accompanies the true knowledge of God (*v.* 12): *For I will be merciful to their unrighteousness,* &c. Observe, [1.] The freeness of this pardon. It does not result from merit in man, but from mercy in God; he pardons for his own name's sake. [2.] The fulness of this pardon; it extends to their unrighteousness, sins, and iniquities; to all kinds of sin, to sins highly aggravated. [3.] The fixedness of this pardon. It is so final and so fixed that God will remember their sins no more; he will not recal his pardon; he will not only forgive their sins, but forget them, treat them as if he had forgotten them. This pardoning mercy is connected with all other spiritual mercies. Unpardoned sin prevents mercy, and pulls down judgments; but the pardon of sin prevents judgment, and opens a wide door to all spiritual blessings; it is the effect of that mercy that is from everlasting, and the earnest of that mercy that shall be to everlasting. This is the excellency of the new dispensation, and these are the articles of it; and therefore we have no reason to repine, but great reason to rejoice that the former dispensation is antiquated and has vanished away.

CHAP. IX.

The apostle, having declared the Old-Testament dispensation antiquated and vanishing away, proceeds to let the Hebrews see the correspondence there was between the Old Testament and the New; and that whatever was excellent in the Old was typical and representative of the New, which therefore must as far excel the Old as the substance does the shadow. The Old Testament was never intended to be rested in, but to prepare for the institutions of the gospel. And here he treats, I. Of the tabernacle, the place of worship, ver. 1—5. II. Of the worship and services performed in the tabernacle, ver. 6, 7. III. He delivers the spiritual sense and the main design of all, ver. 8, to the end.

THEN verily the first *covenant* had also ordinances of divine service,

and a worldly sanctuary. 2 For
there was a tabernacle made; the first,
wherein *was* the candlestick, and the
table, and the showbread; which is
called the sanctuary. 3 And after
the second veil, the tabernacle which
is called the Holiest of all; 4 Which
had the golden censer, and the ark of
the covenant overlaid round about
with gold, wherein *was* the golden
pot that had manna, and Aaron's rod
that budded, and the tables of the
covenant; 5 And over it the cheru-
bims of glory shadowing the mercy-
seat; of which we cannot now speak
particularly. 6 Now when these
things were thus ordained, the priests
went always into the first tabernacle,
accomplishing the service *of God*. 7
But into the second *went* the high
priest alone once every year, not
without blood which he offered for himself, and *for* the errors of the people.

Here, I. The apostle gives an account of the tabernacle, that place of worship which God appointed to be pitched on earth; it is called *a worldly* sanctuary, wholly of this world, as to the materials of which it was built, and a building that must be taken down; it is called a worldly *sanctuary*, because it was the court and palace of the King of Israel. God was their King, and, as other kings, had his court or place of residence, and attendants, furniture, and provision, suitable thereto. This tabernacle (of which we have the model, Exod. xxv.—xxvii.) was a moving temple, shadowing forth the unsettled state of the church militant, and the human nature of the Lord Jesus Christ, in whom the fulness of the Godhead dwelt bodily. Now of this tabernacle it is said that it was divided into two parts, called a first and a second tabernacle, an inner and an outer part, representing the two states of the church militant and triumphant, and the two natures of Christ, human and divine. We are also told what was placed in each part of the tabernacle.

1. In the outer part: and there were several things, of which you have here a sort of schedule. (1.) The candlestick; doubtless not an empty and unlighted one, but where the lamps were always burning. And there was need of it, for there were no windows in the sanctuary; and this was to convince the Jews of the darkness and the mysterious nature of that dispensation. Their light was only candle-light, in comparison of the fulness of light which Christ, the Sun of righteousness, would bring along with him, and communicate to his people; for all our light is derived from him the fountain of light. (2.) The table and the show-bread set upon it. This table was set directly opposite to the candlestick, which shows that by light from Christ we must have communion with him and with one another. We must not come in the dark to his table, but by light from Christ must discern the Lord's body. On this table were placed twelve loaves for the twelve tribes of Israel, a loaf for a tribe, which stood from sabbath to sabbath, and on that day were renewed. This show-bread may be considered either as the provision of the palace (though the King of Israel needed it not, yet, in resemblance of the palaces of earthly kings, there must be this provision laid in weekly), or the provision made in Christ for the souls of his people, suitable to the wants and to the relief of their souls. He is the bread of life; in our Father's house there is bread enough and to spare; we may have fresh supplies from Christ, especially every Lord's day. This outer part is called *the sanctuary* or *holy*, because erected to the worship of a holy God, to represent a holy Jesus, and to entertain a holy people, for their further improvement in holiness.

2. We have an account of what was in the inner part of the sanctuary, which was within the second veil, and is called *the holiest of all.* This second veil, which divided between the holy and the most holy place, was a type of the body of Christ, by the rending whereof not only a view, but a way, was opened for us into the holiest of all, the type of heaven itself. Now in this part were, (1.) The golden censer, which was to hold the incense, or the golden altar set up to burn the incense upon; both the one and the other were typical of Christ, of his pleasing and prevailing intercession which he makes in heaven, grounded upon the merits and satisfaction of his sacrifice, upon which we are to depend for acceptance and the blessing from God. (2.) The ark of the covenant overlaid round about with pure gold, *v.* 4. This typified Christ, his perfect obedience to the law and his fulfilling of all righteousness for us. Now here we are told both what was in this ark and what was over it. [1.] What was in it. *First, The golden pot that had manna,* which, when preserved by the Israelites in their own houses, contrary to the command of God, presently putrefied; but now, being by God's appointment deposited here in his house, was kept from putrefaction, always pure and sweet; and this to teach us that it is only in Christ that our persons, our graces, our performances are kept pure. It was also a type of the bread of life we have in Christ, the true ambrosia that gives immortality. This was also a memorial of God's miraculously feeding his people in the wilderness, that they might never forget such signal favour, nor distrust God for the time to come. *Secondly, Aaron's rod that budded,* and thereby showed that God had chosen him of the tribe of Levi to minister before him of all the tribes of

Israel, and so an end was put to the murmuring of the people, and to their attempt to invade the priest's office, Num. xvii. This was that rod of God with which Moses and Aaron wrought such wonders; and this was a type of Christ, who is styled *the man, the branch* (Zech. vi. 12), by whom God has wrought wonders for the spiritual deliverance, defence, and supply of his people, and for the destruction of their enemies. It was a type of divine justice, by which Christ the Rock was smitten, and from whom the cool refreshing waters of life flow into our souls. *Thirdly, The tables of the covenant*, in which the moral law was written, signifying the regard God has to the preservation of his holy law, and the care we all ought to have that we keep the law of God—that this we can only do in and through Christ, by strength from him, nor can our obedience be accepted but through him. [2.] What was over the ark (*v.* 5): *Over it the cherubim of glory shadowing the mercy-seat. First*, The mercy-seat, which was the covering of the ark; it was called *the propitiatory*, and it was of pure gold, as long and as broad as the ark in which the tables of the law were laid. It was an eminent type of Christ, and of his perfect righteousness, ever adequate to the dimensions of the law of God, and covering all our transgressions, interposing between the Shechinah, or symbol of God's presence, and our sinful failures, and covering them. *Secondly, The cherubim of glory* shadowing the mercy-seat, representing the holy angels of God, who take pleasure in looking into the great work of our redemption by Christ, and are ready to perform every good office, under the Redeemer, for those who are the heirs of salvation. The angels attended Christ at his birth, in his temptation, under his agonies, at his resurrection, and in his ascension, and will attend his second coming. God manifest in the flesh was seen, observed, visited, by the angels.

II. From the description of the place of worship in the Old-Testament dispensation, the apostle proceeds to speak of the duties and services performed in those places, *v.* 6. When the several parts and furniture of the tabernacle were thus settled, then what was to be done there?

1. The ordinary priests went always into the first tabernacle, to accomplish the service of God. Observe, (1.) None but priests were to enter into the first part of the tabernacle, and this to teach us all that persons not qualified, not called of God, must not intrude into the office and work of the ministry. (2.) The ordinary priests were only to enter into the first part of the tabernacle, it would have been fatal presumption in them to have gone into the holiest of all; and this teaches us that even ministers themselves must know and keep in their proper stations, and not presume to usurp the prerogative of Christ, by offering up incense of their own, or adding their own inventions to the ordinances of Christ, or lording it over men's consciences. (3.) These ordinary priests were to enter into the first tabernacle always; that is, they were to devote themselves and all their time to the work of their office, and not alienate themselves at any time from it; they were to be in an habitual readiness for the discharge of their office, and at all stated appointed times were actually to attend to their work. (4.) The ordinary priests must enter into the first tabernacle, that they might there accomplish the service of God. They must not do the work of God partially or by halves, but stand complete in the whole of his will and counsel; not only beginning well, but proceeding well, and persevering to the end, fulfilling the ministry they had received.

2. Into the second, the interior part, went the high priest alone, *v.* 7. This part was an emblem of heaven, and Christ's ascension thither. Here observe, (1.) None but the high priest must go into the holiest; so none but Christ could enter into heaven in his own name, by his own right, and by his own merits. (2.) In entering into the holiest, the high priest must first go through the outer sanctuary, and through the veil, signifying that Christ went to heaven through a holy life and a violent death; the veil of his flesh was rent asunder. (3.) The high priest entered but once a year into the holiest, and in this the antitype excels the type (as in every thing else), for he has entered once for all, during the whole dispensation of the gospel. (4.) The high priest must not enter without blood, signifying that Christ, having undertaken to be our high priest, could not have been admitted into heaven without shedding his blood for us, and that none of us can enter either into God's gracious presence here or his glorious presence hereafter, but by the blood of Jesus. (5.) The high priest, under the law, entering into the holiest, offered up that blood for himself and his own errors first, and then for the errors of the people, *v.* 7. This teaches us that Christ is a more excellent person and high priest than any under the law, for he has no errors of his own to offer for. And it teaches us that ministers, when in the name of Christ they intercede for others, must first apply the blood of Christ to themselves for their pardon. (6.) When the legal high priest had offered for himself, he must not stop there, but must also offer for the errors of the people. Our high priest, though he needs not to offer for himself, yet forgets not to offer for his people; he pleads the merit of his sufferings for the benefit of his people on earth. Observe, [1.] Sins are errors, and great errors, both in judgment and practice. We greatly err when we sin against God; and who can understand all his errors? [2.] They are such errors as leave guilt upon the conscience, not to be washed away but by the blood of Christ; and the sinful errors of priests and people must

be all done away by the same means. the application of the blood of Christ; we must plead this blood on earth, while he is pleading it in heaven for us.

8 The Holy Ghost this signifying,
that the way into the holiest of all
was not yet made manifest, while as
the first tabernacle was yet standing:
9 Which *was* a figure for the time
then present, in which were offered
both gifts and sacrifices, that could
not make him that did the service
perfect, as pertaining to the conscience; 10 *Which stood* only in
meats and drinks, and divers washings, and cardinal ordinances, imposed
on them until the time of reformation.
11 But Christ being come a high
priest of good things to come, by a
greater and more perfect tabernacle,
not made with hands, that is to say,
not of this building; 12 Neither by
the blood of goats and calves, but by
his own blood he entered in once into
the holy place, having obtained eternal
redemption *for us*. 13 For if the
blood of bulls and of goats, and the
ashes of a heifer sprinkling the unclean, sanctifieth to the purifying of the
flesh: 14 How much more shall the
blood of Christ, who through the eternal Spirit offered himself without spot
to God, purge your conscience from
dead works to serve the living God?

In these verses the apostle undertakes to deliver to us the mind and meaning of the Holy Ghost in all the ordinances of the tabernacle and legal economy, comprehending both place and worship. The scriptures of the Old Testament were given by inspiration of God; holy men of old spoke and wrote as the Holy Ghost directed them. And these Old-Testament records are of great use and significancy, not only to those who first received them, but even to Christians, who ought not to satisfy themselves with reading the institutes of the Levitical law, but should learn what the Holy Ghost signifies and suggests to them thereby. Now here are several things mentioned as the things that the Holy Ghost signified and certified to his people hereby.

I. That the way into the holiest of all was not yet made manifest, while the first tabernacle was standing, *v.* 8. This was one lesson the Holy Ghost would teach us by these types; the way to heaven was not so clear and plain, nor so much frequented, under the Old Testament as under the New. It is the honour of Christ and the gospel, and the happiness of those who live under it, that now life and immortality are brought to light. There was not that free access to God then that there is now; God has now opened a wider door; and there is room for more, yea, even for as many as are truly willing to return unto him by Christ.

II. That the first tabernacle was only a figure for the time then present, *v.* 9. It was a dark dispensation, and but of short continuance, only designed for awhile to typify the great things of Christ and the gospel, that were in due time to shine forth in their own brightness, and thereby cause all the shadows to flee away and disappear, as the stars before the rising sun.

III. That none of the gifts and sacrifices there offered could make the offerers perfect as pertaining to conscience (*v.* 9); that is, they could not take away the desert, or defilement, or dominion, of sin; they could not deliver conscience from a dread of the wrath of God; they could neither discharge the debts, nor resolve the doubts, of him who did the service. A man might run through them all in their several orders and frequent returns, and continue to do so all his days, and yet not find his conscience either pacified or purified by them; he might thereby be saved from corporal and temporal punishments that were threatened against the non-observers, but he could not be saved by them from sin or hell, as all those are who believe in Christ.

IV. The Holy Ghost hereby signifies that the Old-Testament institutions were but external carnal ordinances imposed upon them until the time of reformation, *v.* 10. Their imperfection lay in three things:—1. Their nature. They were but external and carnal meats and drinks, and divers washings. All these were bodily exercises, which profit little; they could only satisfy the flesh, or at best sanctify to the purifying of the flesh. 2. They were not such as were left indifferent to them to use or disuse, but they were imposed upon them by grievous corporal punishments, and this was ordered on purpose to make them look more to the promised Seed, and long more for him. 3. These were never designed for a perpetuity, but only to continue till the time of reformation, till the better things provided for them were actually bestowed upon them. Gospel times are and should be times of reformation,—of clearer light as to all things necessary to be known,—of greater love, inducing us to bear ill-will to none, but good-will to all, and to have complacency in all that are like God,—of greater liberty and freedom both of spirit and speech—and of a more holy living according to the rule of the gospel. We have far greater advantages under the gospel than they had under the law; and either we must be better or we shall be worse. A conversation becoming the gospel is an excellent way of living; nothing mean, foolish, vain, or servile becomes the gospel.

V. The Holy Ghost signifies to us hereby that we never make the right use of types but when we apply them to the antitype; and, whenever we do so, it will be very evident that the antitype (as in reason it should) greatly excels the type, which is the main drift and design of all that is said. And, as he writes to those who believed that Christ had come and that Jesus was the Christ, so he very justly infers that he is infinitely above all legal high priests (*v.* 11, 12), and he illustrates it very fully. For,

1. *Christ is a high priest of good things to come,* by which may be understood, (1.) All the good things that were to come during the Old Testament, and now have come under the New. All the spiritual and eternal blessings the Old-Testament saints had in their day and under their dispensation were owing to the Messiah to come, on whom they believed. The Old Testament set forth in shadows what was to come; the New Testament is the accomplishment of the Old. (2.) All the good things yet to come and to be enjoyed in a gospel state, when the promises and prophecies made to the gospel church in the latter days shall be accomplished; all these depend upon Christ and his priesthood, and shall be fulfilled. (3.) Of all the good things to come in the heavenly state, which will perfect both the Testaments; as the state of glory will perfect the state of grace, this state will be in a much higher sense the perfection of the New Testament than the New Testament was the perfection of the Old. Observe, All things past, present, and to come, were, and are, founded upon, and flowing from, the priestly office of Christ.

2. Christ is a high priest *by a greater and more perfect tabernacle* (*v.* 11), *a tabernacle not made with hands, that is to say, not of this building,* but his own body, or rather human nature, conceived by the Holy Ghost overshadowing the blessed virgin. This was a new fabric, a new order of building, infinitely superior to all earthly structures, not excepting the tabernacle of the temple itself.

3. Christ, our high priest, has entered into heaven, not as their high priest entered into the holiest, with the blood of bulls and of goats, but by his own blood, typified by theirs, and infinitely more precious. And this,

4. Not for one year only, which showed the imperfection of that priesthood, that it did but typically obtain a year's reprieve or pardon. But our high priest entered into heaven *once for all,* and has obtained not a yearly respite, but eternal redemption, and so needs not to make an annual entrance. In each of the types there was something that showed it was a type, and resembled the antitype, and something that showed it was but a type, and fell short of the antitype, and therefore ought by no means to be set up in competition with the antitype.

5. The Holy Ghost further signified and showed what was the efficacy of the blood of the Old-Testament sacrifices, and thence is inferred the much greater efficacy of the blood of Christ (1.) The efficacy of the blood of the legal sacrifices extended to the purifying of the flesh (*v.* 13): it freed the outward man from ceremonial uncleanness and from temporal punishment, and entitled him to, and fitted him for, some external privileges. (2.) He infers very justly hence the far greater efficacy of the blood of Christ (*v.* 14): *How much more shall the blood of Christ,* &c. Here observe, [1.] What it was that gave such efficacy to the blood of Christ. *First,* It was his offering himself to God, the human nature upon the altar of his divine nature, he being priest, altar, and sacrifice, his divine nature serving for the two former, and his human nature for the last; now such a priest, altar, and sacrifice, could not but be propitiatory. *Secondly,* It was Christ's offering up himself to God through the eternal Spirit, not only as the divine nature supported the human, but the Holy Ghost, which he had without measure, helping him in all, and in this great act of obedience offering himself. *Thirdly,* It was Christ's offering himself to God without spot, without any sinful stain either in his nature or life; this was conformable to the law of sacrifices, which required them to be without blemish. Now further observe, [2.] What the efficacy of Christ's blood is; it is very great. For, *First,* It is sufficient to purge the conscience from dead works, it reaches to the very soul and conscience, the defiled soul, defiled with sin, which is a dead work, proceeds from spiritual death, and tends to death eternal. As the touching of a dead body gave a legal uncleanness, so meddling with sin gives a moral and real defilement, fixes it in the very soul; but the blood of Christ has efficacy to purge it out. *Secondly,* It is sufficient to enable us to serve the living God, not only by purging away that guilt which separates between God and sinners, but by sanctifying and renewing the soul through the gracious influences of the Holy Spirit, purchased by Christ for this purpose, that we might be enabled to serve the living God in a lively manner.

15 And for this cause he is the
mediator of the new testament, that
by means of death, for the redemption of the trangressions *that were*
under the first testament, they which
are called might receive the promise
of eternal inheritance. 16 For where
a testament *is,* there must also of necessity be the death of the testator.
17 For a testament *is* of force after
men are dead: otherwise it is of no
strength at all while the testator liveth.
18 Whereupon neither the first *tes-*

tament was dedicated without blood.
19 For when Moses had spoken every
precept to all the people according to
the law, he took the blood of calves
and of goats, with water, and scarlet
wool, and hyssop, and sprinkled both
the book, and all the people, 20
Saying, This *is* the blood of the testament which God hath enjoined unto
you. 21 Moreover he sprinkled with
blood both the tabernacle, and all
the vessels of the ministry. 22 And
almost all things are by the law
purged with blood; and without
shedding of blood is no remission.

In these verses the apostle considers the gospel under the notion of a will or testament, the new or last will and testament of Christ, and shows the necessity and efficacy of the blood of Christ to make this testament valid and effectual.

I. The gospel is here considered as a testament, the new and last will and testament of our Lord and Saviour Jesus Christ. It is observable that the solemn transactions that pass between God and man are sometimes called a covenant, here a testament. A covenant is an agreement between two or more parties about things that are in their own power, or may be so, and this either with or without a mediator; this agreement takes effect at such time and in such manner as therein declared. A testament is a voluntary act and deed of a single person, duly executed and witnessed, bestowing legacies on such legatees as are described and characterized by the testator, and which can only take effect upon his death. Now observe, Christ is the Mediator of a New Testament (*v.* 15); and he is so for several ends and purposes here mentioned. 1. To redeem persons from their transgressions committed against the law or first testament, which makes every transgression a forfeiture of liberty, and makes men debtors, and slaves or prisoners, who need to be redeemed. 2. To qualify all those that are effectually called to receive the promise of an eternal inheritance. These are the great legacies that Christ by his last will and testament has bequeathed to the truly characterized legatees.

II. To make this New Testament effectual, it was necessary that Christ should die; the legacies accrue by means of death. This he proves by two arguments:—1. From the general nature of every will or testamentary disposition, *v.* 16. Where a testament is, where it acts and operates, there must of necessity be the death of the testator; till then the property is still in the testator's hand, and he has power to revoke, cancel, or alter, his will as he pleases; so that no estate, no right, is conveyed by will, till the testator's death has made it unalterable and effectual. 2. From the particular method that was taken by Moses in the ratification of the first testament, which was not done without blood, *v.* 18, 19, &c. All men by sin had become guilty before God, had forfeited their inheritance, their liberties, and their very lives, into the hands of divine justice; but God, being willing to show the greatness of his mercy, proclaimed a covenant of grace, and ordered it to be typically administered under the Old Testament, but not without the blood and life of the creature; and God accepted the blood of bulls and goats, as typifying the blood of Christ; and by these means the covenant of grace was ratified under the former dispensation. The method taken by Moses, according to the direction he had received from God, is here particularly related. (1.) Moses spoke every precept to all the people, according to the law, *v.* 19. He published to them the tenour of the covenant, the duties required, the rewards promised to those who did their duty, and the punishment threatened against the transgressors, and he called for their consent to the terms of the covenant; and this in an express manner. (2.) Then he took the blood of calves and of goats, with water, and scarlet wool, and hyssop, and applied this blood by sprinkling it. This blood and water signified the blood and water that came out of our Saviour's pierced side, for justification and sanctification, and also shadowed forth the two sacraments of the New Testament, baptism and the Lord's supper, with scarlet wool, signifying the righteousness of Christ with which we must be clothed, the hyssop signifying that faith by which we must apply all. Now with these Moses sprinkled, [1.] The book of the law and covenant, to show that the covenant of grace is confirmed by the blood of Christ and made effectual to our good. [2.] The people, intimating that the shedding of the blood of Christ will be no advantage to us if it be not applied to us. And the sprinkling of both the book and the people signified the mutual consent of both parties, God and man, and their mutual engagements to each other in this covenant through Christ, Moses at the same time using these words, *This is the blood of the testament which God hath enjoined unto you.* This blood, typifying the blood of Christ, is the ratification of the covenant of grace to all true believers. [3.] He sprinkled the tabernacle and all the utensils of it, intimating that all the sacrifices offered up and services performed there were accepted only through the blood of Christ, which procures the remission of that iniquity that cleaves to our holy things, which could not have been remitted but by that atoning blood.

23 *It was* therefore necessary that
the patterns of things in the heavens
should be purified with these; but

the heavenly things themselves with
better sacrifices than these. 24 For
Christ is not entered into the holy
places made with hands, *which are*
the figures of the true; but into heaven itself, now to appear in the presence of God for us: 25 Nor yet
that he should offer himself often, as
the high priest entereth into the holy
place every year with blood of others;
26 For then must he often have suffered since the foundation of the
world: but now once in the end of
the world hath he appeared to put
away sin by the sacrifice of himself.
27 And as it is appointed unto men
once to die, but after this the judgment: 28 So Christ was once offered to
bear the sins of many; and unto them
that look for him shall he appear the
second time without sin unto salvation.

In this last part of the chapter, the apostle goes on to tell us what the Holy Ghost has signified to us by the legal purifications of the patterns of the things in heaven, inferring thence the necessity of better sacrifices to consecrate the heavenly things themselves.

I. The necessity of purifying the patterns of the things in heaven, *v.* 23. This necessity arises both from the divine appointment, which must always be obeyed, and from the reason of that appointment, which was to preserve a proper resemblance between the things typifying and the things typified. It is observable here that the sanctuary of God on earth is a pattern of heaven, and communion with God in his sanctuary is to his people a heaven upon earth.

II. The necessity that the heavenly things themselves should be purified with better sacrifices than of bulls and goats; the things themselves are better than the patterns, and must therefore be consecrated with better sacrifices. These heavenly things are the privileges of the gospel state, begun in grace, perfected in glory. These must be ratified by a suitable sanction or consecration; and this was the blood of Christ. Now it is very evident that the sacrifice of Christ is infinitely better than those of the law, 1. From the places in which the sacrifices under the law, and that under the gospel, were offered. Those under the law were the holy places made with hands, which are but figures of the true sanctuary, *v.* 24. Christ's sacrifice, though offered upon earth, was by himself carried up into heaven, and is there presented in a way of daily intercession; for he appears in the presence of God for us. He has gone to heaven, not only to enjoy the rest and receive the honour due to him, but to appear in the presence of God for us, to present our persons and our performances, to answer and rebuke our adversary and accuser, to secure our interest, to perfect all our affairs, and to prepare a place for us. 2. From the sacrifices themselves, *v.* 26. Those under the law were the lives and blood of other creatures of a different nature from the offerers—the blood of beasts, a thing of small value, and which would have been of none at all in this matter had it not had a typical respect to the blood of Christ; but the sacrifice of Christ was the oblation of himself; he offered his own blood, truly called, by virtue of the hypostatical union, *the blood of God;* and therefore of infinite value. 3. From the frequent repetition of the legal sacrifices. This showed the imperfection of that law; but it is the honour and perfection of Christ's sacrifice that, being once offered, it was sufficient to all the ends of it; and indeed the contrary would have been absurd, for then he must have been still dying and rising again, and ascending and then again descending and dying; and the great work had been always *in fieri—always doing*, and always to do, but never finished, which would be as contrary to reason as it is to revelation, and to the dignity of his person: *But now once in the end of the world hath he appeared, to put away sin by the sacrifice of himself.* The gospel is the last dispensation of the grace of God to men. 4. From the inefficacy of the legal sacrifices, and the efficacy of Christ's sacrifice. The legal sacrifices could not of themselves put away sin, neither procure pardon for it nor power against it. Sin would still have lain upon us, and had dominion over us; but Jesus Christ by one sacrifice has made an end of sin, he has destroyed the works of the devil.

III. The apostle illustrates the argument from the appointment of God concerning men (*v.* 27, 28), and observes something like it in the appointment of God concerning Christ.

1. The appointment of God concerning men contains in it two things:—(1.) That they must once die, or, at least, undergo a change equivalent to death. It is an awful thing to die, to have the vital knot loosed or cut asunder, all relations here dropped at once, an end put to our probation and preparation state, and to enter into another world. It is a great work, and it is a work that can be but once done, and therefore had need to be well done. This is matter of comfort to the godly, that they shall die well and die but once; but it is matter of terror to the wicked, who die in their sins, that they cannot return again to do that great work better. (2.) It is appointed to men that after death they shall come to judgment, to a particular judgment immediately after death; for the soul returns to God as to its judge, to be determined to its eternal state; and men shall be brought to the general judgment, at the end of the world. This is the unalterable decree of God concerning men—they must die, and they must be judged. It is ap-

pointed for them, and it is to be believed and seriously considered by them.

2. The appointment of God concerning Christ, bearing some resemblance to the other. (1.) He must be once offered, to bear the sins of many, of all the Father had given to him, of all who should believe in his name. He was not offered for any sin of his own; he was wounded for our transgressions. God laid on him the iniquity of all his people; and these are many, though not so many as the rest of mankind; yet, when they are all gathered to him, he will be the first-born among many brethren. (2.) It is appointed that Christ shall appear the second time without sin, to the salvation of those who look for him. [1.] He will then appear without sin; at his first appearance, though he had no sin of his own, yet he stood charged with the sins of many; he was the Lamb of God that bore upon him the sins of the world, and then he appeared in the form of sinful flesh; but his second appearance will be without any such charge upon him, he having fully discharged it before, and then his visage shall not be marred, but shall be exceedingly glorious. [2.] This will be to the salvation of all who look for him; he will then perfect their holiness, their happiness; their number shall then be accomplished, and their salvation completed. Observe, It is the distinguishing character of true believers that they are looking for Christ; they look to him by faith; they look for him by hope and holy desires. They look for him in every duty, in every ordinance, in every providence now; and they expect his second coming, and are preparing for it; and though it will be sudden destruction to the rest of the world, who scoff at the report of it, it will be eternal salvation to those who look for it.

CHAP. X.

The apostle knew very well that the Hebrews, to whom he wrote, were strangely fond of the Levitical dispensation, and therefore he fills his mouth with arguments to wean them from it; and in order thereto proceeds in this chapter, I. To lay low the whole of that priesthood and sacrifice, ver. 1—6. II. He raises and exalts the priesthood of Christ very high, that he might effectually recommend him and his gospel to them, ver. 7—18. III. He shows to believers the honours and dignities of their state, and calls them to suitable duties, ver. 19, to the end.

FOR the law having a shadow of
good things to come, *and* not
the very image of the things, can
never with those sacrifices which they
offered year by year continually make
the comers thereunto perfect. 2 For
then would they not have ceased to
be offered? because that the worshippers
once purged should have had
no more conscience of sins. 3 But in
those *sacrifices there is* a remembrance
again *made* of sins every year.
4 For *it is* not possible that the
blood of bulls and of goats should
take away sins. 5 Wherefore when
he cometh into the world, he saith,
Sacrifice and offering thou wouldest
not, but a body hast thou prepared
me: 6 In burnt offerings and *sacrifices*
for sin thou hast had no pleasure.

Here the apostle, by the direction of the Spirit of God, sets himself to lay low the Levitical dispensation; for though it was of divine appointment, and very excellent and useful in its time and place, yet, when it was set up in competition with Christ, to whom it was only designed to lead the people, it was very proper and necessary to show the weakness and imperfection of it, which the apostle does effectually, from several arguments. As,

I. That the law had a shadow, and but a shadow, of good things to come; and who would dote upon a shadow, though of good things, especially when the substance has come? Observe, 1. The things of Christ and the gospel are good things; they are the best things; they are best in themselves, and the best for us: they are realities of an excellent nature. 2. These good things were, under the Old Testament, good things to come, not clearly discovered, nor fully enjoyed. 3. That the Jews then had but the shadow of the good things of Christ, some adumbrations of them; we under the gospel have the substance.

II. That the law was not the very image of the good things to come. An image is an exact draught of the thing represented thereby. The law did not go so far, but was only a shadow, as the image of a person in a looking-glass is a much more perfect representation than his shadow upon the wall The law was a very rough draught of the great design of divine grace, and therefore not to be so much doted on.

III. The legal sacrifices, being offered year by year, could never make the comers thereunto perfect; for then there would have been an end of offering them, *v.* 1, 2. Could they have satisfied the demands of justice, and made reconciliation for iniquity,—could they have purified and pacified conscience,—then they had ceased, as being no further necessary, since the offerers would have had no more sin lying upon their consciences. But this was not the case; after one day of atonement was over, the sinner would fall again into one fault or another, and so there would be need of another day of atonement, and of one every year, besides the daily ministrations. Whereas now, under the gospel, the atonement is perfect, and not to be repeated; and the sinner, once pardoned, is ever pardoned as to his state, and only needs to renew his repentance and faith, that he may have a comfortable sense of a continued pardon.

IV. As the legal sacrifices did not of themselves take away sin, so it was impossible they should, *v.* 4. There was an essential defect in them. 1. They were not of the same nature with us who sinned. 2. They were not of sufficient value to make satisfaction for the affronts offered to the justice and government of God. They were not of the same nature that offended, and so could not be suitable. Much less were they of the same nature that was offended; and nothing less than the nature that was offended could make the sacrifice a full satisfaction for the offence. 3. The beasts offered up under the law could not consent to put themselves in the sinner's room and place. The atoning sacrifice must be one capable of consenting, and must voluntarily substitute himself in the sinner's stead: Christ did so.

V. There was a time fixed and foretold by the great God, and that time had now come, when these legal sacrifices would be no longer accepted by him nor useful to men. God never did desire them for themselves, and now he abrogated them; and therefore to adhere to them now would be resisting God and rejecting him. This time of the repeal of the Levitical laws was foretold by David (Ps. xl. 6, 7), and is recited here as now come. Thus industriously does the apostle lay low the Mosaical dispensation.

7 Then said I, Lo, I come (in the
volume of the book it is written of
me,) to do thy will, O God. 8 Above
when he said, Sacrifice and offering
and burnt offerings and *offering* for
sin thou wouldest not, neither hadst
pleasure *therein;* which are offered
by the law; 9 Then said he, Lo,
I come to do thy will, O God. He
taketh away the first, that he may establish the second. 10 By the which
will we are sanctified through the
offering of the body of Jesus Christ
once *for all.* 11 And every priest
standeth daily ministering and offering
oftentimes the same sacrifices, which
can never take away sins: 12 But
this man, after he had offered one sacrifice for sins, for ever sat down on
the right hand of God; 13 From
henceforth expecting till his enemies
be made his footstool. 14 For by
one offering he hath perfected for ever
them that are sanctified. 15 *Whereof*
the Holy Ghost also is a witness to
us: for after that he had said before,
16 This *is* the covenant that I will
make with them after those days,
saith the Lord, I will put my laws
into their hearts, and in their minds
will I write them; 17 And their
sins and iniquities will I remember
no more. 18 Now where remission
of these *is, there is* no more offering
for sin.

Here the apostle raises up and exalts the Lord Jesus Christ, as high as he had laid the Levitical priethood low. He recommends Christ to them as the true high priest, the true atoning sacrifice, the antitype of all the rest: and this he illustrates,

I. From the purpose and promise of God concerning Christ, which are frequently recorded in the volume of the book of God, *v.* 7. God had not only decreed, but declared by Moses and the prophets, that Christ should come and be the great high priest of the church, and should offer up a perfect and a perfecting sacrifice. It was written of Christ, in the beginning of the book of God, that *the seed of the woman should break the serpent's head;* and the Old Testament abounds with prophecies concerning Christ. Now since he is the person so often promised, so much spoken of, so long expected by the people of God, he ought to be received with great honour and gratitude.

II. From what God had done in preparing a body for Christ (that is, a human nature), that he might be qualified to be our Redeemer and Advocate; uniting the two natures in his own person, he was a fit Mediator to go between God and man; a days-man to lay his hand upon both, a peace-maker, to reconcile them, and an everlasting band of union between God and the creature—"*My ears hast thou opened;* thou hast fully instructed me, furnished and fitted me for the work, and engaged me in it," Ps. xl. 6. Now a Saviour thus provided, and prepared by God himself in so extraordinary a manner, ought to be received with great affection and gladness.

III. From the readiness and willingness that Christ discovered to engage in this work, when no other sacrifice would be accepted, *v.* 7—9. When no less sacrifice would be a proper satisfaction to the justice of God than that of Christ himself, then Christ voluntarily came into it: "*Lo, I come! I delight to do thy will, O God!* Let thy curse fall upon me, but let these go their way. Father, I delight to fulfil thy counsels, and my covenant with thee for them; I delight to perform all thy promises, to fulfil all the prophecies." This should endear Christ and our Bibles to us, that in Christ we have the fulfilling of the scriptures.

IV. From the errand and design upon which Christ came; and this was to do the will of God, not only as a prophet to reveal the will of God, not only as a king to give forth divine laws, but as a priest to satisfy the demands of justice, and to fulfil all righteousness. Christ came to do the will of God in two instances. 1. In taking away the first priesthood, which God had no pleasure in; not only taking away the curse of the covenant of works, and cancelling the sentence denounced against us as sinners, but taking away the insufficient typical priesthood, and blotting out the hand-writing of ceremonial ordinances and nailing it to his cross. 2. In establishing the second, that is, his own priesthood and the everlasting gospel, the most pure and perfect dispensation of the covenant of grace; this is the great design upon which the heart of God was set from all eternity. The will of God centres and terminates in it; and it is not more agreeable to the will of God than it is advantageous to the souls of men; for it is by this will that *we are sanctified, through the offering of the body of Jesus Christ once for all, v.* 10. Observe, (1.) What is the fountain of all that Christ has done for his people—the sovereign will and grace of God. (2.) How we come to partake of what Christ has done for us—by being sanctified, converted, effectually called, wherein we are united to Christ, and so partake of the benefits of his redemption; and this sanctification is owing to the oblation he made of himself to God.

V. From the perfect efficacy of the priesthood of Christ (*v.* 14): *By one offering he hath for ever perfected those that are sanctified;* he has delivered and will perfectly deliver those that are brought over to him, from all the guilt, power, and punishment of sin, and will put them into the sure possession of perfect holiness and felicity. This is what the Levitical priesthood could never do; and, if we indeed are aiming at a perfect state, we must receive the Lord Jesus as the only high priest that can bring us to that state.

VI. From the place to which our Lord Jesus is now exalted, the honour he has there, and the further honour he shall have: *This man, after he had offered one sacrifice for sins, for ever sat down at the right hand of God, henceforth expecting till his enemies be made his footstool, v.* 12, 13. Here observe, 1. To what honour Christ, as man and Mediator, is exalted—to the right hand of God, the seat of power, interest, and activity: the giving hand; all the favours that God bestows on his people are handed to them by Christ: the receiving hand; all the duties that God accepts from men are presented by Christ: the working hand; all that pertains to the kingdoms of providence and grace is administered by Christ; and therefore this is the highest post of honour. 2. How Christ came to this honour—not merely by the purpose or donation of the Father, but by his own merit and purchase, as a reward due to his sufferings; and, as he can never be deprived of an honour so much his due, so he will never quit it, nor cease to employ it for his people's good. 3. How he enjoys this honour—with the greatest satisfaction and rest; he is for ever sitting down there. The Father acquiesces and is satisfied in him; he is satisfied in his Father's will and presence; this is his rest for ever; here he will dwell, for he has both desired and deserved it. 4. He has further expectations, which shall not be disappointed; for they are grounded upon the promise of the Father, who hath said unto him, *Sit thou at my right hand, until I make thine enemies thy footstool,* Ps. cx. 1. One would think such a person as Christ could have no enemies except in hell; but it is certain that he has enemies on earth, very many, and very inveterate ones. Let not Christians then wonder that they have enemies, though they desire to live peaceably with all men. But Christ's enemies shall be made his footstool; some by conversion, others by confusion; and, which way soever it be, Christ will be honoured. Of this Christ is assured, this he is expecting, and his people should rejoice in the expectation of it; for, when his enemies shall be subdued, their enemies, that are so for his sake, shall be subdued also.

VII. The apostle recommends Christ from the witness the Holy Ghost has given in the scriptures concerning him; this relates chiefly to what should be the happy fruit and consequence of his humiliation and sufferings, which in general is that new and gracious covenant that is founded upon his satisfaction, and sealed by his blood (*v.* 15): *Whereof the Holy Ghost is a witness.* The passage is cited from Jer. xxxi. 31, in which covenant God promises, 1. That he will pour out his Spirit upon his people, so as to give them wisdom, will, and power, to obey his word; he will put his laws in their hearts, and write them in their minds, *v.* 16. This will make their duty plain, easy, and pleasant. 2. Their sins and iniquities he will remember no more (*v.* 17), which will alone show the riches of divine grace, and the sufficiency of Christ's satisfaction, that it needs not be repeated, *v.* 18. For there shall be no more remembrance of sin against true believers, either to shame them now or to condemn them hereafter. This was much more than the Levitical priesthood and sacrifices could effect.

And now we have gone through the doctrinal part of the epistle, in which we have met with many things dark and difficult to be understood, which we must impute to the weakness and dulness of our own minds. The apostle now proceeds to apply this great doctrine, so as to influence their affections, and direct their practice, setting before them the dignities and duties of the gospel state.

19 Having therefore, brethren, boldness to enter into the holiest by the
blood of Jesus, 20 By a new and
living way, which he hath consecrated
for us, through the veil, that is to say,
his flesh; 21 And *having* a high
priest over the house of God; 22
Let us draw near with a true heart
in full assurance of faith, having our

hearts sprinkled from an evil conscience, and our bodies washed with
pure water. 23 Let us hold fast the
profession of *our* faith without wavering; (for he *is* faithful that promised;) 24 And let us consider one
another to provoke unto love and to
good works: 25 Not forsaking the
assembling of ourselves together, as
the manner of some *is;* but exhorting *one another:* and so much the
more, as ye see the day approaching.
26 For if we sin wilfully after that
we have received the knowledge of
the truth, there remaineth no more
sacrifice for sins, 27 But a certain
fearful looking for of judgment and
fiery indignation, which shall devour
the adversaries. 28 He that despised
Moses' law died without mercy under
two or three witnesses: 29 Of how
much sorer punishment, suppose ye,
shall he be thought worthy, who hath
trodden under foot the Son of God,
and hath counted the blood of the
covenant, wherewith he was sanctified, an unholy thing, and hath done
despite unto the Spirit of grace? 30
For we know him that hath said, Vengeance *belongeth* unto me, I will recompense, saith the Lord. And again,
The Lord shall judge his people.
31 *It is* a fearful thing to fall into the
hands of the living God. 32 But
call to remembrance the former days,
in which, after ye were illuminated,
ye endured a great fight of afflictions;
33 Partly, whilst ye were made a
gazingstock both by reproaches and
afflictions; and partly, whilst ye became companions of them that were
so used. 34 For ye had compassion
of me in my bonds, and took joyfully
the spoiling of your goods, knowing
in yourselves that ye have in heaven
a better and an enduring substance.
35 Cast not away therefore your confidence, which hath great recompence
of reward. 36 For ye have need of
patience, that, after ye have done the
will of God, ye might receive the promise. 37 For yet a little while, and
he that shall come will come, and
will not tarry. 38 Now the just shall
live by faith: but if *any man* draw
back, my soul shall have no pleasure
in him. 39 But we are not of them
who draw back unto perdition; but
of them that believe to the saving of
the soul.

I. Here the apostle sets forth the dignities of the gospel state. It is fit that believers should know the honours and privileges that Christ has procured for them, that, while they take the comfort, they may give him the glory of all. The privileges are, 1. Boldness to enter into the holiest. They have access to God, light to direct them, liberty of spirit and of speech to conform to the direction; they have a right to the privilege and a readiness for it, assistance to use and improve it and assurance of acceptance and advantage. They may enter into the gracious presence of God in his holy oracles, ordinances, providences, and covenant, and so into communion with God, where they receive communications from him, till they are prepared to enter into his glorious presence in heaven. 2. A high priest over the house of God, even this blessed Jesus, who presides over the church militant, and every member thereof on earth, and over the church triumphant in heaven. God is willing to dwell with men on earth, and to have them dwell with him in heaven; but fallen man cannot dwell with God without a high priest, who is the Mediator of reconciliation here and of fruition hereafter.

II. The apostle tells us the way and means by which Christians enjoy such privileges, and, in general, declares it to be *by the blood of Jesus,* by the merit of that blood which he offered up to God as an atoning sacrifice: he has purchased for all who believe in him free access to God in the ordinances of his grace here and in the kingdom of his glory. This blood, being sprinkled on the conscience, chases away slavish fear, and gives the believer assurance both of his safety and his welcome into the divine presence. Now the apostle, having given this general account of the way by which we have access to God, enters further into the particulars of it, *v.* 20. As, 1. It is the only way; there is no way left but this. The first way to the tree of life is, and has been, long shut up. 2. It is a new way, both in opposition to the covenant of works and to the antiquated dispensation of the Old Testament; it is *via novissima—the last way* that will ever be opened to men. Those who will not enter in this way exclude themselves for ever. It is a way that will always be effectual. 3. It is a living way. It would be death to attempt to come to God in the way of the covenant of works; but this way we may come to God, and live. It is by a living Saviour, who, though he was dead, is alive; and it is a way that gives life and lively hope to those who enter into it. 4. It is a way that Christ has consecrated for us through the veil, that is, his flesh. The veil in the tabernacle and temple signified the body of Christ; when he died, the veil of the temple was rent in sunder, and this was at the time of the evening sacrifice, and gave the people a surprising view into the holy of holies, which they never had before. Our way to heaven is by a crucified Saviour; his death is to us the way of life. To those who believe this he will be precious.

III. He proceeds to show the Hebrews the duties binding upon them on account of these privileges, which were conferred in such an extraordinary way, *v.* 22, 23, &c.

1. They must draw near to God, and that in a right manner. They must draw near to God. Since such a way of access and return to God is opened, it would be the greatest ingratitude and contempt of God and Christ still to keep at a distance from him. They must draw near by conversion, and by taking hold of his covenant. They must draw near in all holy conversation, like Enoch walking with God. They must draw near in humble adorations, worshipping at his footstool. They must draw near in holy dependence, and in a strict observance of the divine conduct towards them. They must draw near in conformity to God, and communion with him, living under his blessed influence, still endeavouring to get nearer and nearer, till they come to dwell in his presence; but they must see to it that they make their approach to God after a right manner. (1.) With a true heart, without any allowed guile or hypocrisy. God is the searcher of hearts, and he requires truth in the inward parts. Sincerity is our gospel perfection, though not our justifying righteousness. (2.) In full assurance of faith, with a faith grown up to a full persuasion that when we come to God by Christ we shall have audience and acceptance. We should lay aside all sinful distrust. Without faith it is impossible to please God; and the stronger our faith is the more glory we give to God. And, (3.) Having our hearts sprinkled from an evil conscience, by a believing application of the blood of Christ to our souls. They may be cleansed from guilt, from filth, from sinful fear and torment, from all aversion to God and duty, from ignorance, and error, and superstition, and whatever evils the consciences of men are subject to by reason of sin. (4.) Our bodies washed with pure water, that is, with the water of baptism (by which we are recorded among the disciples of Christ, members of his mystical body), or with the sanctifying virtue of the Holy Spirit, reforming and regulating our outward conversation as well as our inward frame, cleansing from the filthiness of the flesh as well as of the spirit. The priests under the law were to wash, before they went into the presence of the Lord to offer before him. There must be a due preparation for making our approaches to God.

2. The apostle exhorts believers to hold fast the profession of their faith, Here observe, (1.) The duty itself—to hold fast the profession of our faith, to embrace all the truths and ways of the gospel, to get fast hold of them, and to keep that hold against all temptation and opposition. Our spiritual enemies will do what they can to wrest our faith, and hope, and holiness, and comfort, out of our hands, but we must hold fast our religion as our best treasure. (2.) The manner in which we must do this—without wavering, without doubting, without disputing, without dallying with temptation to apostasy. Having once settled these great things between God and our souls, we must be stedfast and immovable. Those who begin to waver in matters of Christian faith and practice are in danger of falling away. (3.) The motive or reason enforcing this duty: *He is faithful that hath promised.* God has made great and precious promises to believers, and he is a faithful God, true to his word; there is no falseness nor fickleness with him, and there should be none with us. His faithfulness should excite and encourage us to be faithful, and we must depend more upon his promises to us than upon our promises to him, and we must plead with him the promise of grace sufficient.

IV. We have the means prescribed for preventing our apostasy, and promoting our fidelity and perseverance, *v.* 24, 25, &c. He mentions several; as, 1. That we should *consider one another, to provoke to love and to good works.* Christians ought to have a tender consideration and concern for one another; they should affectionately consider what their several wants, weaknesses, and temptations are; and they should do this, not to reproach one another, to provoke one another not to anger, but to love and good works, calling upon themselves and one another to love God and Christ more, to love duty and holiness more, to love their brethren in Christ more, and to do all the good offices of Christian affection both to the bodies and the souls of each other. A good example given to others is the best and most effectual provocation to love and good works. 2. *Not to forsake the assembling of ourselves together, v.* 25. It is the will of Christ that his disciples should assemble together, sometimes more privately for conference and prayer, and in public for hearing and joining in all the ordinances of gospel worship. There were in the apostles' times, and should be in every age, Christian assemblies for the worship of God, and for mutual edification. And it seems even in those times there were some who forsook these assemblies, and so began to apostatize from religion itself. The communion of saints is a great help and privilege, and a good means of steadiness and perseverance; hereby their hearts and hands are mutually strengthened. 3. To exhort one another, to exhort ourselves and each other, to warn ourselves and one another of the sin and danger of backsliding, to put ourselves and our fellow-christians in mind of our duty, of our failures and corruptions, to watch over one another, and be jealous of ourselves and one another with a godly jealousy. This, managed with a true gospel spirit, would be the best and most cordial friendship. 4. That we should observe the approaching of times of trial, and be thereby quickened to greater diligence: *So much the more, as you see the day approaching.* Christians ought to observe the signs of the times, such as God has foretold. There was a day approaching, a terrible day to the Jewish nation, when their city should be destroyed, and the body of the people rejected of God for rejecting Christ. This would be a day of dispersion and temptation to the chosen remnant. Now the apostle puts them upon observing what signs there were of the approach of such a terrible day, and upon being the more constant in meeting together and exhorting one another, that they might be the better prepared for such a day. There is a trying day coming on us all, the day of our death, and we should observe all the signs of its approaching, and improve them to greater watchfulness and diligence in duty.

V. Having mentioned these means of establishment, the apostle proceeds, in the close of the chapter, to enforce his exhortations to perseverance, and against apostasy, by many very weighty considerations, *v.* 26, 27, &c.

1. From the description he gives of the sin of apostasy. It is *sinning wilfully after we have received the knowledge of the truth,* sinning wilfully against that truth of which we have had convincing evidence. This text has been the occasion of great distress to some gracious souls; they have been ready to conclude that every wilful sin, after conviction and against knowledge, is the unpardonable sin: but this has been their infirmity and error. The sin here mentioned is a total and final apostasy, when men with a full and fixed will and resolution despise and reject Christ, the only Saviour,—despise and resist the Spirit, the only sanctifier,—and despise and renounce the gospel, the only way of salvation, and the words of eternal life; and all this after they have known, owned, and professed, the Christian religion, and continue to do so obstinately and maliciously. This is the great transgression: the apostle seems to refer to the law concerning presumptuous sinners, Num. xv. 30, 31. They were to be cut off.

2. From the dreadful doom of such apostates. (1.) There remains no more sacrifice for such sins, no other Christ to come to save such sinners; they sin against the last resort and remedy. There were some sins under the law for which no sacrifices were provided; but yet if those who committed them did truly repent, though they might not escape temporal death, they might escape eternal destruction; for Christ would come, and make atonement. But now those under the gospel who will not accept of Christ, that they may be saved by him, have no other refuge left them. (2.) There remains for them only a certain fearful looking for of judgment, *v.* 27. Some think this refers to the dreadful destruction of the Jewish church and state; but certainly it refers also to the utter destruction that awaits all obstinate apostates at death and judgment, when the Judge will discover a fiery indignation against them, which will devour the adversaries; they will be consigned to the devouring fire and to everlasting burnings. Of this destruction God gives some notorious sinners, while on earth, a fearful foreboding in their own consciences, a dreadful looking for it, with a despair of ever being able either to endure or escape it.

3. From the methods of divine justice with those who despised Moses's law, that is, sinned presumptuously, despising his authority, his threatenings and his power. These, when convicted by two or three witnesses, were put to death; they died without mercy, a temporal death. Observe, Wise governors should be careful to keep up the credit of their government and the authority of the laws, by punishing presumptuous offenders; but then in such cases there should be good evidence of the fact. Thus God ordained in Moses's law; and hence the apostle infers the heavy doom that will fall upon those that apostatize from Christ. Here he refers to their own consciences, to judge how much sorer punishment the despisers of Christ (after they have professed to know him) are likely to undergo; and they may judge of the greatness of the punishment by the greatness of the sin. (1.) They have *trodden under foot the Son of God.* To trample upon an ordinary person shows intolerable insolence; to treat a person of honour in that vile manner is insufferable; but to deal thus with the Son of God, who himself is God, must be the highest provocation—to trample upon his person, denying him to be the Messiah—to trample upon his authority, and undermine his kingdom—to trample upon his members as the offscouring of all things, and not fit to live in the world; what punishment can be too great for such men? (2.) They have *counted the blood of the covenant, wherewith he was sanctified, an unholy thing;* that is, the blood of Christ, with which the covenant was purchased and sealed, and wherewith Christ himself was consecrated, or wherewith the apostate was sanctified, that is, baptized, visibly initiated into the new covenant by baptism, and admitted to the Lord's supper. Observe, There is a kind of sanctification which persons may partake of and yet fall away: they may be distinguished by common gifts and graces, by an outward profession, by a form of godliness, a course of duties, and a set of privileges, and yet fall away finally. Men who have seemed before to have the blood of Christ in high esteem may come to account

it an unholy thing, no better than the blood of a malefactor, though it was the world's ransom, and every drop of it of infinite value. (3) *Those have done despite unto the Spirit of grace,* the Spirit that is graciously given to men, and that works grace wherever it is,—the Spirit of grace, that should be regarded and attended to with the greatest care,—this Spirit they have grieved, resisted, quenched, yea, done despite to him, which is the highest act of wickedness, and makes the case of the sinner desperate, refusing to have the gospel salvation applied to him. Now he leaves it to the consciences of all, appeals to universal reason and equity, whether such aggravated crimes ought not to receive a suitable punishment, a sorer punishment than those who had died without mercy? But what punishment can be sorer than to die without mercy? I answer, To die by mercy, by the mercy and grace which they have despised. How dreadful is the case when not only the justice of God, but his abused grace and mercy call for vengeance!

4. From the description we have in the scripture of the nature of God's vindictive justice, *v.* 30. We know that he has said, *Vengeance is mine.* This is taken out of Ps. xciv. 1, *Vengeance belongs unto me.* The terrors of the Lord are known both by revelation and reason. Vindictive justice is a glorious, though terrible attribute of God; it belongs to him, and he will use and execute it upon the heads of such sinners as despise his grace; he will avenge himself, and his Son, and Spirit, and covenant, upon apostates. And how dreadful then will their case be! The other quotation is from Deut. xxxii. 36, *The Lord will judge his people;* he will search and try his visible church, and will discover and detect those who say they are Jews, and are not, but are of the synagogue of Satan; and he will separate the precious from the vile, and will punish the sinners in Zion with the greatest severity. Now those who know him who hath said, *Vengeance belongeth to me, I will recompense,* must needs conclude, as the apostle does (*v.* 31): *It is a fearful thing to fall into the hands of the living God.* Those who know the joy that results from the favour of God can thereby judge of the power and dread of his vindictive wrath. Observe here, What will be the eternal misery of impenitent sinners and apostates: they shall fall into the hands of the living God; their punishment shall come from God's own hand. He takes them into the hand of his justice; he will deal with them himself; their greatest misery will be the immediate impressions of divine wrath on the soul. When he punishes them by creatures, the instrument abates something of the force of the blow; but, when he does it by his own hand, it is infinite misery. This they shall have at God's hand, they shall lie down in sorrow; their destruction shall come from his glorious powerful presence; when they make their woeful bed in hell, they will find that God is there, and his presence will be their greatest terror and torment. And he is a living God; he lives for ever, and will punish for ever.

5. He presses them to perseverance by putting them in mind of their former sufferings for Christ: *But call to mind the former days, in which, after you were illuminated, you endured a great fight of afflictions, v.* 32. In the early days of the gospel there was a very hot persecution raised up against the professors of the Christian religion, and the believing Hebrews had their share of it: he would have them to remember,

(1.) When they had suffered: *In former days, after* they were *illuminated;* that is, as soon as God had breathed life into their souls, and caused divine light to spring up in their minds, and taken them into his favour and covenant; then earth and hell combined all their force against them. Here observe, A natural state is a dark state, and those who continue in that state meet with no disturbance from Satan and the world; but a state of grace is a state of light, and therefore the powers of darkness will violently oppose it. Those who will live godly in Christ Jesus must suffer persecution.

(2.) What they suffered: they *endured a great fight of afflictions,* many and various afflictions united together against them, and they had a great conflict with them. Many are the troubles of the righteous. [1.] They were afflicted in themselves. In their own persons; they were made gazing-stocks, spectacles to the world, angels, and men, 1 Cor. iv. 9. In their names and reputations (*v.* 33), by many reproaches. Christians ought to value their reputation; and they do so especially because the reputation of religion is concerned: this makes reproach a great affliction. They were afflicted in their estates, by the spoiling of their goods, by fines and forfeitures. [2.] They were afflicted in the afflictions of their brethren: *Partly while you became companions of those that were so used.* The Christian spirit is a sympathizing spirit, not a selfish spirit, but a compassionate spirit; it makes every Christian's suffering our own, puts us upon pitying others, visiting them, helping them, and pleading for them. Christians are one body, are animated by one spirit, have embarkd in one common cause and interest, and are the children of that God who is afflicted in all the afflictions of his people. If one member of the body suffers, all the rest suffer with it. The apostle takes particular notice how they had sympathized with him (*v.* 34): *You had compassion on me in my bonds.* We must thankfully acknowledge the compassions our Christian friends have shown for us under our afflictions.

(3.) How they had suffered. They had been mightily supported under their former sufferings; they took their sufferings patiently, and not only so, but joyfully received it from

God as a favour and honour conferred upon them that they should be thought worthy to suffer reproach for the name of Christ. God can strengthen his suffering people with all might in the inner man, to all patience and long-suffering, and that with joyfulness, Col. i. 11.

(4.) What it was that enabled them thus to bear up under their sufferings. They knew in themselves that they had in heaven a better and a more enduring substance. Observe, [1.] The happiness of the saints in heaven is substance, something of real weight and worth. All things here are but shadows. [2.] It is a better substance than any thing they can have or lose here. [3.] It is an enduring substance, it will out-live time and run parallel with eternity; they can never spend it; their enemies can never take it from them, as they did their earthly goods. [4.] This will make a rich amends for all they can lose and suffer here. In heaven they shall have a better life, a better estate, better liberty, better society, better hearts, better work, every thing better. [5.] Christians should know this in themselves, they should get the assurance of it in themselves (the Spirit of God witnessing with their spirits), for the assured knowledge of this will help them to endure any fight of afflictions they may be encountered with in this world.

6. He presses them to persevere, from that recompence of reward that waited for all faithful Christians (*v.* 35): *Cast not away therefore your confidence, which hath great recompence of reward.* Here, (1.) He exhorts them not to cast away their confidence, that is, their holy courage and boldness, but to hold fast that profession for which they had suffered so much before, and borne those sufferings so well. (2.) He encourages them to this by assuring them that the reward of their holy confidence would be very great. It carries a present reward in it, in holy peace and joy, and much of God's presence and his power resting upon them; and it shall have a great recompence of reward hereafter. (3.) He shows them how necessary a grace the grace of patience is in our present state (*v.* 36): *You have need of patience, that after you have done the will of God you might receive the promise;* that is, this promised reward. Observe, The greatest part of the saints' happiness is in promise. They must first do the will of God before they receive the promise; and, after they have done the will of God, they have need of patience to wait for the time when the promise shall be fulfilled; they have need of patience to live till God calls them away. It is a trial of the patience of Christians, to be content to live after their work is done, and to stay for the reward till God's time to give it them is come. We must be God's waiting servants when we can be no longer his working servants. Those who have had and exercised much patience already must have and exercise more till they die. (4.) To help their patience, he assures them of the near approach of Christ's coming to deliver and to reward them (*v.* 37): *For yet a little while, and he that shall come will come, and will not tarry.* He will soon come to them at death, and put an end to all their sufferings, and give them a crown of life. He will soon come to judgment, and put an end to the sufferings of the whole church (all his mystical body), and give them an ample and glorious reward in the most public manner. There is an appointed time for both, and beyond that time he will not tarry, Hab. ii. 3. The Christian's present conflict may be sharp, but it will be soon over.

7. He presses them to perseverance, by telling them that this is their distinguishing character and will be their happiness; whereas apostasy is the reproach, and will be the ruin, of all who are guilty of it (*v.* 38, 39): *Now the just shall live by faith,* &c. (1.) It is the honourable character of just men that in times of the greatest affliction they can live by faith; they can live upon the assured persuasion they have of the truth of God's promises. Faith puts life and vigour into them. They can trust God, and live upon him, and wait his time: and, as their faith maintains their spiritual life now, it shall be crowned with eternal life hereafter. (2.) Apostasy is the mark and the brand of those in whom God takes no pleasure; and it is a cause of God's severe displeasure and anger. God never was pleased with the formal profession and external duties and services of such as do not persevere. He saw the hypocrisy of their hearts then; and he is greatly provoked when their formality in religion ends in an open apostasy from religion. He beholds them with great displeasure; they are an offence to him. (3.) The apostle concludes with declaring his good hope concerning himself and these Hebrews, that they should not forfeit the character and happiness of the just, and fall under the brand and misery of the wicked (*v.* 39): *But we are not,* &c.; as if he had said, "I hope we are not of those who draw back. I hope that you and I, who have met with great trials already, and have been supported under them by the grace of God strengthening our faith, shall not be at any time left to ourselves to draw back to perdition; but that God will still keep us by his mighty power through faith unto salvation." Observe, [1.] Professors may go a great way, and after all draw back; and this drawing back from God is drawing on to perdition: the further we depart from God the nearer we approach to ruin. [2.] Those who have been kept faithful in great trials for the time past have reason to hope that the same grace will be sufficient to help them still to live by faith, till they receive the end of their faith and patience, even the salvation of their souls. If we live by faith, and die in faith, our souls will be safe for ever

CHAP. XI.

The apostle having, in the close of the foregoing chapter, recommended the grace of faith and a life of faith as the best preservative against apostasy, he now enlarges upon the nature and fruits of this excellent grace. I. The nature of it, and the honour it reflects upon all who live in the exercise of it, ver. 1—3. II. The great examples we have in the Old Testament of those who lived by faith, and did and suffered extraordinary things by the strength of this grace, ver. 4—38. And, III. The advantages that we have in the gospel for the exercise of this grace above what those had who lived in the times of the Old Testament, ver. 39, 40.

NOW faith is the substance of things hoped for, the evidence of things not seen.
2 For by it the elders obtained a good report.
3 Through faith we understand that the worlds were framed by the word of God, so that things which are seen were not made of things which do appear.

Here we have, I. A definition or description of the grace of faith in two parts. 1. It *is the substance of things hoped for.* Faith and hope go together; and the same things that are the object of our hope are the object of our faith. It is a firm persuasion and expectation that God will perform all that he has promised to us in Christ; and this persuasion is so strong that it gives the soul a kind of possession and present fruition of those things, gives them a subsistence in the soul, by the first-fruits and foretastes of them: so that believers in the exercise of faith *are filled with joy unspeakable and full of glory.* Christ dwells in the soul by faith, and the soul is filled with the fulness of God, as far as his present measure will admit; he experiences a substantial reality in the objects of faith. 2. It is *the evidence of things not seen.* Faith demonstrates to the eye of the mind the reality of those things that cannot be discerned by the eye of the body. Faith is the firm assent of the soul to the divine revelation and every part of it, and sets to its seal that God is true. It is a full approbation of all that God has revealed as holy, iust, and good; it helps the soul to make application of all to itself with suitable affections and endeavours; and so it is designed to serve the believer instead of sight, and to be to the soul all that the senses are to the body. That faith is but opinion or fancy which does not realize invisible things to the soul, and excite the soul to act agreeably to the nature and importance of them.

II. An account of the honour it reflects upon all those who have lived in the exercise of it (*v.* 2): *By it the elders obtained a good report*—the ancient believers, who lived in the first ages of the world. Observe, 1. True faith is an old grace, and has the best plea to antiquity: it is not a new invention, a modern fancy; it is a grace that has been planted in the soul of man ever since the covenant of grace was published in the world; and it has been practised from the beginning of the revelation; the eldest and best men that ever were in the world were believers. 2 Their faith was their honour; it reflected honour upon them. They were an honour to their faith, and their faith was an honour to them. It put them upon doing *the things that were of good report,* and God has taken care that a record shall be kept and report made of the excellent things they did in the strength of this grace. The genuine actings of faith will bear to be reported, deserve to be reported, and will, when reported, redound to the honour of true believers.

III. We have here one of the first acts and articles of faith, which has a great influence on all the rest, and which is common to all believers in every age and part of the world, namely, the creation of the *worlds by the word of God,* not out of pre-existent matter, but out of nothing, *v.* 3. The grace of faith has a retrospect as well as prospect; it looks not only forward to the end of the world, but back to the beginning of the world. By faith we understand much more of the formation of the world than ever could be understood by the naked eye of natural reason. Faith is not a force upon the understanding, but a friend and a help to it. Now what does faith give us to understand concerning *the worlds,* that is, the upper, middle, and lower regions of the universe? 1. *That these worlds were* not eternal, nor did they produce themselves, but they were made by another. 2. That the maker of the worlds is God; he is the maker of all things; and whoever is so must be God. 3. That he made the world with great exactness; it was a *framed* work, in every thing duly adapted and disposed to answer its end, and to express the perfections of the Creator. 4. That God made the world by his word, that is, by his essential wisdom and eternal Son, and by his active will, saying, *Let it be done, and it was done,* Ps. xxxiii. 9. 5. That the world was thus framed out of nothing, out of no pre-existent matter, contrary to the received maxim, that "out of nothing nothing can be made," which, though true of created power, can have no place with God, who can call *things that are not as if they were,* and command them into being. These things we understand by faith. The Bible gives us the truest and most exact account of the origin of all things, and we are to believe it, and not to wrest or run down the scripture-account of the creation, because it does not suit with some fantastic hypotheses of our own, which has been in some learned but conceited men the first remarkable step towards infidelity, and has led them into many more.

4 By faith Abel offered unto God a more excellent sacrifice than Cain, by which he obtained witness that he was righteous, God testifying of his gifts: and by it he being dead yet speaketh.
5 By faith Enoch was

translated that he should not see
death; and was not found, because
God had translated him: for before
his translation he had this testimony,
that he pleased God. 6 But without
faith *it is* impossible to please *him:*
for he that cometh to God must believe that he is, and *that* he is a rewarder of them that diligently seek
him. 7 By faith Noah, being warned
of God of things not seen as yet,
moved with fear, prepared an ark to
the saving of his house; by the which
he condemned the world, and became
heir of the righteousness which is by
faith. 8 By faith Abraham, when
he was called to go out into a place
which he should after receive for an
inheritance, obeyed; and he went out,
not knowing whither he went. 9
By faith he sojourned in the land of
promise, as *in* a strange country,
dwelling in tabernacles with Isaac and
Jacob, the heirs with him of the same
promise: 10 For he looked for a
city which hath foundations, whose
builder and maker *is* God. 11 Through
faith also Sara herself received strength
to conceive seed, and was delivered of
a child when she was past age, because
she judged him faithful who had promised. 12 Therefore sprang there
even of one, and him as good as dead,
so many as the stars of the sky in
multitude, and as the sand which is
by the sea shore innumerable. 13
These all died in faith, not having
received the promises, but having
seen them afar off, and were persuaded
of *them*, and embraced *them*, and confessed that they were strangers and
pilgrims on the earth. 14 For they
that say such things declare plainly
that they seek a country. 15 And
truly, if they had been mindful of
that *country* from whence they came
out, they might have had opportunity
to have returned. 16 But now they
desire a better *country*, that is, a
heavenly: wherefore God is not
ashamed to be called their God: for
he hath prepared for them a city.
17 By faith Abraham, when he was
tried, offered up Isaac: and he that
had received the promises offered up
his only begotten *son*, 18 Of whom
it was said, That in Isaac, shall thy
seed be called: 19 Accounting that
God *was* able to raise *him* up, even
from the dead; from whence also he
received him in a figure. 20 By faith
Isaac blessed Jacob and Esau concerning things to come. 21 By faith
Jacob, when he was a dying, blessed
both the sons of Joseph; and worshipped, *leaning* upon the tŏp of his
staff. 22 By faith Joseph, when he
died, made mention of the departing
of the children of Israel; and gave
commandment concerning his bones.
23 By faith Moses, when he was
born, was hid three months of his
parents, because they saw *he was* a
proper child; and they were not
afraid of the king's commandment.
24 By faith Moses, when he was
come to years, refused to be called
the son of Pharaoh's daughter; 25
Choosing rather to suffer affliction
with the people of God, than to enjoy the pleasures of sin for a season;
26 Esteeming the reproach of Christ
greater riches than the treasures in
Egypt: for he had respect unto the
recompence of the reward. 27 By
faith he forsook Egypt, not fearing
the wrath of the king: for he endured, as seeing him who is invisible.
28 Through faith he kept the passover, and the sprinkling of blood,
lest he that destroyed the firstborn
should touch them. 29 By faith they
passed through the Red sea as by
dry *land:* which the Egyptians as-
saying to do were drowned. 30 By
faith the walls of Jericho fell down,
after they were compassed about seven
days. 31 By faith the harlot Rahab
perished not with them that believed
not, when she had received the spies
with peace.

The apostle, having given us a more general account of the grace of faith, now proceeds to set before us some illustrious examples of it in the Old-Testament times, and these may be divided into two classes:— 1. Those whose names are mentioned, and the particular exercise and actings of whose faith are specified. 2. Those whose names are barely mentioned, and an account given in general of the exploits of their faith, which it is left to the reader to accommodate, and apply to the particular persons from what he gathers up in the sacred story. We have here those whose names are not only mentioned, but the particular trials and actings of their faith are subjoined.

I. The leading instance and example of faith here recorded is that of Abel. It is observable that the Spirit of God has not thought fit to say any thing here of the faith of our first parents; and yet the church of God has generally, by a pious charity, taken it for granted that God gave them repentance and faith in the promised seed, that he instructed them in the mystery of sacrificing, that they instructed their children in it, and that they found mercy with God, after they had ruined themselves and all their posterity. But God has left the matter still under some doubt, as a warning to all who have great talents given to them, and a great trust reposed in them, that they do not prove unfaithful, since God would not enrol our first parents among the number of believers in this blessed calendar. It begins with Abel, one of the first saints, and the first martyr for religion, of all the sons of Adam, one who lived by faith, and died for it, and therefore a fit pattern for the Hebrews to imitate. Observe,

1. What Abel did by faith: *He offered up a more acceptable sacrifice than Cain,* a more full and perfect sacrifice, *πλείονα θυσίαν.* Hence learn, (1.) That, after the fall, God opened a new way for the children of men to return to him in religious worship. This is one of the first instances that is upon record of fallen men going in to worship God; and it was a wonder of mercy that all intercourse between God and man was not cut off by the fall. (2.) After the fall, God must be worshipped by sacrifices, a way of worship which carries in it a confession of sin, and of the desert of sin, and a profession of faith in a Redeemer, who was to be a ransom for the souls of men. (3.) That, from the beginning, there has been a remarkable difference between the worshippers. Here were two persons, brethren, both of whom went in to worship God, and yet there was a vast difference. Cain was the elder brother, but Abel has the preference. It is not seniority of birth, but grace, that makes men truly honourable. The difference is observable in their persons: Abel was an upright person, a righteous man, a true believer; Cain was a formalist, had not a principle of special grace. It is observable in their principles: Abel acted under the power of faith; Cain only from the force of education, or natural conscience. There was also a very observable difference in their offerings: Abel brought a sacrifice of atonement, *brought of the firstlings of the flock,* acknowledging himself to be a sinner who deserved to die, and only hoping for mercy through *the great sacrifice;* Cain brought only a sacrifice of acknowledgment, a mere thank-offering, *the fruit of the ground,* which might, and perhaps must, have been offered in innocency; here was no confession of sin, no regard to the ransom; this was an essential defect in Cain's offering. There will always be a difference between those who worship the true God; some will compass him about with lies, others will be faithful with the saints; some, like the Pharisee, will lean to their own righteousness; others, like the publican, will confess their sin, and cast themselves upon the mercy of God in Christ.

2. What Abel gained by his faith: the original record is in Gen. iv. 4, *God had respect to Abel, and to his offering;* first to his person as gracious, then to his offering as proceeding from grace, especially from the grace of faith. In this place we are told that he obtained by his faith some special advantages; as, (1.) *Witness that he was righteous,* a justified, sanctified, and accepted person; this, very probably, was attested by fire from heaven, kindling and consuming his sacrifice. (2.) God gave witness to the righteousness of his person, by testifying his acceptance of his gifts. When the fire, an emblem of God's justice, consumed the offering, it was a sign that the mercy of God accepted the offerer for the sake of the great sacrifice. (3.) *By it he, being dead, yet speaketh.* He had the honour to leave behind him an instructive speaking case; and what does it speak to us? What should we learn from it? [1.] That fallen man has leave to go in to worship God, with hope of acceptance. [2.] That, if our persons and offerings be accepted, it must be through faith in the Messiah. [3.] That acceptance with God is a peculiar and distinguishing favour. [4.] That those who obtain this favour from God must expect the envy and malice of the world. [5.] That God will not suffer the injuries done to his people to remain unpunished, nor their sufferings unrewarded. These are very good and useful instructions, and yet *the blood of sprinkling speaketh better things than that of Abel.* [6.] That God would not suffer Abel's faith to die with him, but would raise up others, who should obtain like precious faith; and so he did in a little time; for in the next verse we read,

II. Of the faith of Enoch, *v.* 5. He is the second of those elders that through faith have a good report. Observe,

1. What is here reported of him. In this place (and in Gen. v. 22, &c.) we read, (1.) *That he walked with God,* that is, that he was really, eminently, actively, progressively, and perseveringly religious in his conformity to God, communion with God, and complacency in God. (2.) *That he was translated, that he should not see death,* nor any part of him be found upon earth; for God took him, soul and body, into heaven, as he will do those of the saints who shall be found alive at his second coming. (3.) *That before his translation he had this testimony, that he pleased God.* He had the evidence of it in

his own conscience, and the Spirit of God witnessed with his spirit. Those who by faith walk with God in a sinful world are pleasing to him, and he will give them marks of his favour, and put honour upon them.

2. What is here said of his faith, *v.* 6. It is said that *without* this *faith it is impossible to please God,* without such a faith as helps us to walk with God, an active faith, and that we cannot come to God unless we *believe that he is, and that he is a rewarder of those that diligently seek him.* (1.) He must believe that God is, and that he is what he is, what he has revealed himself to be in the scripture, a Being of infinite perfections, subsisting in three persons, Father, Son, and Holy Ghost. Observe, The practical belief of the existence of God, as revealed in the word, would be a powerful awe-band upon our souls, a bridle of restraint to keep us from sin, and a spur of constraint to put us upon all manner of gospel obedience. (2.) *That he is a rewarder of those that diligently seek him.* Here observe, [1.] By the fall we have lost God; we have lost the divine light, life, love, likeness, and communion. [2.] God is again to be found of us through Christ, the second Adam. [3.] God has prescribed means and ways wherein he may be found; to wit, a strict attention to his oracles, attendance on his ordinances, and ministers duly discharging their office and associating with his people, observing his providential guidance, and in all things humbly waiting his gracious presence. [4.] Those who would find God in these ways of his must *seek him diligently;* they must seek early, earnestly, and perseveringly. *Then shall they seek him, and find him, if they seek him with all their heart;* and when once they have found him, as their reconciled God, they will never repent the pains they have spent in seeking after him.

III. The faith of Noah, *v.* 7. Observe,

1. The ground of Noah's faith—a warning he had received from God of things as yet not seen. He had a divine revelation, whether by voice or vision does not appear; but it was such as carried in it its own evidence; he was *forewarned of things not seen as yet,* that is, of a great and severe judgment, such as the world had never yet seen, and of which, in the course of second causes, there was not yet the least sign. This secret warning he was to communicate to the world, who would be sure to despise both him and his message. God usually warns sinners before he strikes; and, where his warnings are slighted, the blow will fall the heavier.

2. The actings of Noah's faith, and the influence it had both upon his mind and practice. (1.) Upon his mind; it impressed his soul with a fear of God's judgment: he was *moved with fear.* Faith first influences our affections, then our actions; and faith works upon those affections that are suitable to the matter revealed. If it be some good thing, faith stirs up love and desire; if some evil thing, faith stirs up fear. (2.) His faith influenced his practice. His fear, thus excited by believing God's threatening, moved him to prepare an ark, in which, no doubt, he met with the scorns and reproaches of a wicked generation. He did not dispute with God why he should make an ark, nor how it could be capable of containing what was to be lodged in it, nor how such a vessel could possibly weather out so great a storm. His faith silenced all objections, and set him to work in earnest.

3. The blessed fruits and rewards of Noah's faith. (1.) Hereby himself and his house were saved, when a whole world of sinners were perishing about them. God saved his family for his sake; it was well for them that they were Noah's sons and daughters; it was well for those women that they married into Noah's family; perhaps they might have married to great estates in other families, but then they would have been drowned. We often say, "It is good to be akin to an estate;" but surely it is good to be akin to the covenant. (2.) Hereby he judged and condemned the world; his holy fear condemned their security and vain confidence; his faith condemned their unbelief; his obedience condemned their contempt and rebellion. Good examples will either convert sinners or condemn them. There is something very convincing in a life of strict holiness and regard to God; it commends itself to every man's conscience in the sight of God, and they are judged by it. This is the best way the people of God can take to condemn the wicked; not by harsh and censorious language, but by a holy exemplary conversation. (3.) Hereby *he became an heir of the righteousness which is by faith.* [1.] He was possessed of a true justifying righteousness; he was *heir to it:* and, [2.] This his right of inheritance was through faith in Christ, as *a member of Christ, a child of God,* and, if a child, then an heir. His righteousness was relative, resulting from his adoption, through faith in the promised seed. As ever we expect to be justified and saved *in the great and terrible day of the Lord,* let us now prepare an ark, secure an interest in Christ, and in the ark of the covenant, and do it speedily, before the door be shut, for there is not salvation in any other.

IV. The faith of Abraham, the friend of God, and father of the faithful, in whom the Hebrews boasted, and from whom they derived their pedigree and privileges; and therefore the apostle, that he might both please and profit them, enlarges more upon the heroic achievements of Abraham's faith than of that of any other of the patriarchs; and in the midst of his account of the faith of Abraham he inserts the story of Sarah's faith, whose daughters those women are that continue to do well. Observe,

1. The ground of Abraham's faith, the call and promise of God, *v.* 8. (1.) This call, though it was a very trying call, was the call of God, and therefore a sufficient ground for faith and rule of obedience. The manner in which he was called Stephen relates in Acts vii. 2, 3, *The God of glory appeared to our father Abraham, when he was in Mesopotamia——And said unto him, Get thee out of thy country, and from thy kindred, and come into the land which I will show thee.* This was an effectual call, by which he was converted from the idolatry of his father's house, Gen. xii. 1. This call was renewed after his father's death in Charran. Observe, [1.] The grace of God is absolutely free, in taking some of the worst of men, and making them the best. [2.] God must come to us before we come to him. [3.] In calling and converting sinners, God appears as a God of glory, and works a glorious work in the soul. [4.] This calls us not only to leave sin, but sinful company, and whatever is inconsistent with our devotedness to him. [5.] We need to be called, not only to set out well, but to go on well. [6.] He will not have his people take up that rest any where short of the heavenly Canaan. (2.) The promise of God. God promised Abraham that the place he was called to he should afterwards receive for an inheritance, after awhile he should have the heavenly Canaan for his inheritance, and in process of time his posterity should inherit the earthly Canaan. Observe here, [1.] God calls his people to an inheritance: by his effectual call he makes them children, and so heirs. [2.] This inheritance is not immediately possessed by them; they must wait some time for it: but the promise is sure, and shall have its seasonable accomplishment. [3.] The faith of parents often procures blessings for their posterity.

2. The exercise of Abraham's faith: he yielded an implicit regard to the call of God. (1.) *He went out, not knowing whither he went.* He put himself into the hand of God, to send him whithersoever he pleased. He subscribed to God's wisdom, as fittest to direct; and submitted to his will, as fittest to determine every thing that concerned him. Implicit faith and obedience are due to God, and to him only. All that are effectually called resign up their own will and wisdom to the will and wisdom of God, and it is their wisdom to do so; though they know not always their way, yet they know their guide, and this satisfies them. (2.) *He sojourned in the land of promise as in a strange country.* This was an exercise of his faith. Observe, [1.] How Canaan is called the land of promise, because yet only promised, not possessed. [2.] How Abraham lived in Canaan, not as heir and proprietor, but as a sojourner only. He did not serve an ejectment, or raise a war against the old inhabitants, to dispossess them, but contented himself to live as a stranger, to bear their unkindnesses patiently, to receive any favours from them thankfully, and to keep his heart fixed upon his home, the heavenly Canaan. [3.] He dwelt in tabernacles with Isaac and Jacob, heirs with him of the same promise. He lived there in an ambulatory moving condition, living in a daily readiness for his removal: and thus should we all live in this world. He had good company with him, and they were a great comfort to him in his sojourning state. Abraham lived till Isaac was seventy-five years old, and Jacob fifteen. Isaac and Jacob were heirs of the same promise; for the promise was renewed to Isaac (Gen. xxvi. 3), and to Jacob, Gen. xxviii. 13. All the saints are heirs of the same promise. The promise is made to believers and their children, and to as many as the Lord our God shall call. And it is pleasant to see parents and children sojourning together in this world as heirs of the heavenly inheritance.

3. The supports of Abraham's faith (*v.* 10): *He looked for a city that hath foundations, whose builder and maker is God.* Observe here, (1.) The description given of heaven: it is a city, a regular society, well established, well defended, and well supplied: it is a city that hath foundations, even the immutable purposes and almighty power of God, the infinite merits and mediation of the Lord Jesus Christ, the promises of an everlasting covenant, its own purity, and the perfection of its inhabitants: and it is a city whose builder and maker is God. He contrived the model; he accordingly made it, and he has laid open a new and living way into it, and prepared it for his people; he puts them into possession of it, prefers them in it, and is himself the substance and felicity of it. (2.) Observe the due regard that Abraham had to this heavenly city: he looked for it; he believed there was such a state; he waited for it, and in the mean time he conversed in it by faith; he had exalted and rejoicing hopes, that in God's time and way he should be brought safely to it. (3.) The influence this had upon his present conversation: it was a support to him under all the trials of his sojourning state, helped him patiently to bear all the inconveniences of it, and actively to discharge all the duties of it, persevering therein unto the end.

V. In the midst of the story of Abraham, the apostle inserts an account of the faith of Sarah. Here observe,

1. The difficulties of Sarah's faith, which were very great. As, (1.) The prevalency of unbelief for a time: she laughed at the promise, as impossible to be made good. (2.) She had gone out of the way of her duty through unbelief, in putting Abraham upon taking Hagar to his bed, that he might have a posterity. Now this sin of hers would make it more difficult for her to act by faith afterwards. (3.) The great improbability of the thing promised, that she should be the

mother of a child, when she was of sterile constitution naturally, and now past the prolific age.

2. The actings of her faith. Her unbelief is pardoned and forgotten, but her faith prevailed and is recorded: *She judged him faithful, who had promised, v.* 11. She received the promise as the promise of God; and, being convinced of that, she truly judged he both could and would perform it, how impossible soever it might seem to reason; for the faithfulness of God will not suffer him to deceive his people.

3. The fruits and rewards of her faith. (1.) *She received strength to conceive seed.* The strength of nature, as well as grace, is from God: he can make the barren soul fruitful, as well as the barren womb. (2.) *She was delivered of a child,* a man-child, a child of the promise, the comfort of his parents' advanced years, and the hope of future ages. (3.) From them, by this son, sprang a numerous progeny of illustrious persons, *as the stars of the sky* (*v.* 12)—a great, powerful, and renowned nation, above all the rest in the world; and a nation of saints, the peculiar church and people of God; and, which was the highest honour and reward of all, *of these, according to the flesh, the Messiah came, who is over all, God blessed for evermore.*

VI. The apostle proceeds to make mention of the faith of the other patriachs, Isaac and Jacob, and the rest of this happy family, *v.* 13. Here observe,

1. The trial of their faith in the imperfection of their present state. They had not received the promises,that is, they had not received the things promised, they had not yet been put into possession of Canaan, they had not yet seen their numerous issue, they had not seen Christ in the flesh. Observe, (1.) Many that are interested in the promises do not presently receive the things promised. (2.) One imperfection of the present state of the saints on earth is that their happiness lies more in promise and reversion than in actual enjoyment and possession. The gospel state is more perfect than the patriarchal, because more of the promises are now fulfilled. The heavenly state will be most perfect of all; for there all the promises will have their full accomplishment.

2. The actings of their faith during this imperfect state of things. Though they had not received the promises, yet,

(1.) They saw them afar off. Faith has a clear and a strong eye, and can see promised mercies at a great distance. Abraham saw Christ's day, when it was afar off, and rejoiced, John viii. 56.

(2.) They were persuaded of them, that they were true and should be fulfilled. Faith sets to its seal that God is true, and thereby settles and satisfies the soul.

(3.) They embraced them. Their faith was a faith of consent. Faith has a long arm, and can lay hold of blessings at a great distance, can make them present, can love them, and rejoice in them; and thus antedate the enjoyment of them.

(4.) They *confessed that they were strangers and pilgrims on earth.* Observe, [1.] Their condition: *Strangers and pilgrims.* They are strangers as saints, whose home is heaven; they are pilgrims as they are travelling towards their home, though often meanly and slowly. [2.] Their acknowledgment of this their condition: they were not ashamed to own it; both their lips and their lives confessed their present condition. They expected little from the world. They cared not to engage much in it. They endeavoured to lay aside every weight, to gird up the loins of their minds to mind their way, to keep company and pace with their fellow-travellers, looking for difficulties, and bearing them, and longing to get home.

(5.) Hereby they declared plainly that they sought another country (*v.* 14), heaven, their own country. For their spiritual birth is thence, there are their best relations, and there is their inheritance. This country they seek: their designs are for it; their desires are after it; their discourse is about it; they diligently endeavour to clear up their title to it, to have their temper suited to it, to have their conversation in it, and to come to the enjoyment of it.

(6.) They gave full proof of their sincerity in making such a confession. For, [1.] They were not mindful of that country whence they came, *v.* 15. They did not hanker after the plenty and pleasures of it, nor regret and repent that they had left it; they had no desire to return to it. Note, Those that are once effectually and savingly called out of a sinful state have no mind to return into it again; they now know better things. [2.] They did not take the opportunity that offered itself for their return. They might have had such an opportunity. They had time enough to return. They had natural strength to return. They knew the way. Those with whom they sojourned would have been willing enough to part with them. Their old friends would have been glad to receive them. They had sufficient to bear the charges of their journey; and flesh and blood, a corrupt counsellor, would be sometimes suggesting to them a return. But they stedfastly adhered to God and duty under all discouragements and against all temptations to revolt from him. So should we all do. We shall not want opportunities to revolt from God; but we must show the truth of our faith and profession by a steady adherence to him to the end of our days. Their sincerity appeared not only in not returning to their former country, but in desiring a better country, that is, a heavenly. Observe, *First,* The heavenly country is better than any upon earth; it is better situated, better stored with every thing that is good, better secured from every thing that is evil; the employments, the enjoyments, the society, and every thing in it, are better than the best in this world. *Secondly,* All true believers desire this better country. True faith draws forth sincere and fervent desires; and the stronger faith is the more fervent those desires will be.

(7.) They died in the faith of those promises; not only lived by the faith of them, but died in the full persuasion that all the promises would be fulfilled to them and theirs, *v.* 13. That faith held out to the last. By faith, when they were dying, they received the atonement; they acquiesced in the will of God; they quenched all the fiery darts of the devil; they overcame the terrors of death, disarmed it of its sting, and bade a cheerful farewell to this world and to all the comforts and crosses of it. These were the actings of their faith. Now observe,

3. The gracious and great reward of their faith: *God is not ashamed to be their God, for he hath prepared for them a city, v.* 16. Note, (1.) God is the God of all true believers; faith gives them an interest in God, and in all his fulness. (2.) He is called their God. He calls himself so: *I am the God of Abraham, and the God of Isaac, and the God of Jacob;* he gives them leave to call him so; and he gives them the spirit of adoption, to enable them to cry, *Abba, Father.* (3.) Notwithstanding their meanness by nature, their vileness by sin, and the poverty of their outward condition, God is not ashamed to be called *their God:* such is his condescension, such is his love to them; therefore let them never be ashamed of being called his people, nor of any of those that are truly so, how much soever despised in the world. Above all, let them take care that they be not a shame and reproach to their God, and so provoke him to be ashamed of them; but let them act so as to be to him for a name, and for a praise, and for a glory. (4.) As the proof of this, God has prepared for them a city, a happiness suitable to the relation into which he has taken them. For there is nothing in this world commensurate to the love of God in being the God of his people; and, if God neither could nor would give his people anything better than this world affords, he would be ashamed to be called their God. If he takes them into such a relation to himself, he will provide for them accordingly. If he takes to himself the title of their God, he will fully answer it, and act up to it; and he has prepared that for them in heaven which will fully answer this chatacter and relation, so that it shall never be said, to the reproach and dishonour of God, that he has adopted a people to be his own children and then taken no care to make a suitable provision for them. The consideration of this should inflame the affections, enlarge the desires, and excite the diligent endeavours, of the people of God after this city that he has prepared for them.

VII. Now after the apostle has given this account of the faith of others, with Abraham, he returns to him again, and gives us an instance of the greatest trial and act of faith that stands upon record, either in the story of the father of the faithful or of any of his spiritual seed; and this was his offering up Isaac: *By faith Abraham, when he was tried, offered up Isaac; and he that had received the promises offered up his only-begotten son, v.* 17. In this great example observe,

1. The trial and exercise of Abraham's faith; he was tried indeed. It is said (Gen. xxii. 1), *God in this tempted Abraham;* not to sin, for so God tempteth no man, but only tried his faith and obedience to purpose. God had before this tempted or tried the faith of Abraham, when he called him away from his country and father's house,—when by a famine he was forced out of Canaan into Egypt,—when he was obliged to fight with five kings to rescue Lot,—when Sarah was taken from him by Abimelech, and in many other instances. But this trial was greater than all; he was commanded to offer up his son Isaac. Read the account of it, Gen. xxii. 2. There you will find every word was a trial: "*Take now thy son, thine only son Isaac, whom thou lovest, and get thee into the land of Moriah, and offer him there for a burnt-offering upon one of the mountains which I will tell thee of.* Take thy son, not one of thy beasts or slaves, thy only son by Sarah, Isaac thy laughter, the child of thy joy and delight, whom thou lovest as thine own soul; take him away to a distant place, three days' journey, the land of Moriah; do not only leave him there, but offer him for a burnt-offering." A greater trial was never put upon any creature. The apostle here mentions some things that very much added to the greatness of this trial. (1.) He was put upon it after he had received the promises, that this Isaac should build up his family, that in him his seed should be called (*v.* 18), and that he should be one of the progenitors of the Messiah, and all nations blessed in him; so that, in being called to offer up his Isaac, he seemed to be called to destroy and cut off his own family, to cancel the promises of God, to prevent the coming of Christ, to destroy the whole world, to sacrifice his own soul and his hopes of salvation, and to cut off the church of God at one blow: a most terrible trial! (2.) That this Isaac was his only-begotten son by his wife Sarah, the only one he was to have by her, and the only one that was to be the child and heir of the promise. Ishmael was to be put off with earthly greatness. The promises of a posterity, and of the Messiah, must either be fulfilled by means of this son or not at all; so that, besides his most tender affection to this his son, all his expectations were bound up in him, and, if he perished, must perish with him. If Abraham had ever so many sons, this was the only son who could convey to

all nations the promised blessing. A son for whom he waited so long, whom he received in so extraordinary a manner, upon whom his heart was set—to have this son offered up as a sacrifice, and that by his own hand; it was a trial that would have overset the firmest and the strongest mind that ever informed a human body.

2. The actings of Abraham's faith in so great a trial: he obeyed; he offered up Isaac; he intentionally gave him up by his submissive soul to God, and was ready to have done it actually, according to the command of God; he went as far in it as to the very critical moment, and would have gone through with it if God had not prevented him. Nothing could be more tender and moving than those words of Isaac: *My father, here is the wood, here is the fire; but where is the lamb for the burnt-offering?* little thinking that he was to be the lamb; but Abraham knew it, and yet he went on with the great design.

3. The supports of his faith. They must be very great, suitable to the greatness of the trial: *He accounted that God was able to raise him from the dead, v.* 19. His faith was supported by the sense he had of the mighty power of God, who was able to raise the dead; he reasoned thus with himself, and so he resolved all his doubts. It does not appear that he had any expectation of being countermanded, and prevented from offering up his son; such an expectation would have spoiled the trial, and consequently the triumph, of his faith; but he knew that God was able to raise him from the dead, and he believed that God would do so, since such great things depended upon his son, which must have failed if Isaac had not a further life. Observe, (1.) God is able to raise the dead, to raise dead bodies, and to raise dead souls. (2.) The belief of this will carry us through the greatest difficulties and trials that we can meet with. (3.) It is our duty to be reasoning down our doubts and fears, by the consideration of the almighty power of God.

4. The reward of his faith in this great trial (*v.* 19): he received his son from the dead in a figure, in a parable. (1.) He received his son. He had parted with him to God, and God gave him back again. The best way to enjoy our comforts with comfort is to resign them up to God; he will then return them, if not in kind, yet in kindness. (2.) He received him from the dead, for he gave him up for dead; he was as a dead child to him, and the return was to him no less than a resurrection. (3.) This was a figure or parable of something further. It was a figure of the sacrifice and resurrection of Christ, of whom Isaac was a type. It was a figure and earnest of the glorious resurrection of all true believers, whose life is not lost, but hid with Christ in God. We come now to the faith of other Old-Testament saints, mentioned by name, and by the particular trials and actings of their faith.

VIII. Of the faith of Isaac, *v.* 20. Something of him we had before interwoven with the story of Abraham; here we have something of a distinct nature—that by faith he blessed his two sons, Jacob and Esau, *concerning things to come.* Here observe,

1. The actings of his faith: He *blessed Jacob and Esau concerning things to come.* He blessed them; that is, he resigned them up to God in covenant; he recommended God and religion to them; he prayed for them, and prophesied concerning them, what would be the condition, and the condition of their descendants: we have the account of this in Gen. xxvii. Observe, (1.) Both Jacob and Esau were blessed as Isaac's children, at least as to temporal good things. It is a great privilege to be the offspring of good parents, and often the wicked children of good parents fare the better in this world for their parents' sake, for things present are in the covenant; but they are not the best things, and no man knoweth love or hatred by having or wanting such things. (2.) Jacob had the precedency and the principal blessing, which shows that it is grace and the new birth that exalt persons above their fellows and qualify them for the best blessings, and that it is owing to the sovereign free grace of God that in the same family one is taken and another left, one loved and the other hated, since all the race of Adam are by nature hateful to God—that if one has his portion in this world, and the other in the better world, it is God who makes the difference; for even the comforts of this life are more and better than any of the children of men deserve.

2. The difficulties Isaac's faith struggled with. (1.) He seemed to have forgotten how God had determined the matter at the birth of these his sons, Gen. xxv. 23. This should have been a rule to him all along, but he was rather swayed by natural affection, and by general custom, which gives the double portion of honour, affection, and advantage, to the first-born. (2.) He acted in this matter with some reluctance. When he came to pronounce the blessing, *he trembled very exceedingly* (Gen. xxvii. 33); and he charged Jacob that he had subtly taken away Esau's blessing, *v.* 33, 35. But, notwithstanding all this, Isaac's faith recovered itself, and he ratified the blessing: *I have blessed him, yea, and he shall be blessed.* Rebecca and Jacob are not to be justified in the indirect means they used to obtain this blessing, but God will be justified in overruling even the sins of men to serve the purposes of his glory. Now, the faith of Isaac thus prevailing over his unbelief, it has pleased the God of Isaac to pass by the weakness of his faith, to commend the sincerity of it, and record him among the elders, *who through faith have obtained a good report.* We now go on to,

IX. The faith of Jacob (*v.* 21), who, *when he was dying, blessed both the sons of Joseph, and worshipped, leaning upon the top of his staff.* There were a great many instances of the faith of Jacob; his life was a life of faith, and his faith met with great exercise. But it has pleased God to single two instances out of many of the faith of this patriarch, besides what has been already mentioned in the account of Abraham. Here observe,

1. The actings of his faith here mentioned, and they are two:—

(1.) *He blessed both the sons of Joseph,* Ephraim and Manasseh; he adopted them into the number of his own sons, and so into the congregation of Israel, though they were born in Egypt. It is doubtless a great blessing to be joined to the visible church of God in profession and privilege, but more to be so in spirit and truth. [1.] He made them both heads of different tribes, as if they had been his own immediate sons. [2.] He prayed for them, that they might both be blessed of God. [3.] He prophesied that they should be blessed; but, as Isaac did before, so now Jacob prefers the younger, Ephraim; and though Joseph had placed them so, that the right hand of his father should be laid on Manasseh, the elder, Jacob wittingly laid it on Ephraim, and this by divine direction, for he could not see, to show that the Gentile church, the younger, should have a more abundant blessing than the Jewish church, the elder.

(2.) *He worshipped, leaning on his staff;* that is, he praised God for what he had done for him, and for the prospect he had of approaching blessedness; and he prayed for those he was leaving behind him, that religion might live in his family when he was gone. He did this *leaning on the top of his staff;* not as the papists dream, that he worshipped some image of God engraven on the head of his staff, but intimating to us his great natural weakness, that he was not able to support himself so far as to sit up in his bed without a staff, and yet that he would not make this an excuse for neglecting the worshipping of God; he would do it as well as he could with his body, as well as with his spirit, though he could not do it as well as he would. He showed thereby his dependence upon God, and testified his condition here as a pilgrim with his staff, and his weariness of the world, and willingness to be at rest.

2. The time and season when Jacob thus acted his faith: when he was dying. He lived by faith, and he died by faith and in faith. Observe, Though the grace of faith is of universal use throughout our whole lives, yet it is especially so when we come to die. Faith has its greatest work to do at last, to help believers to finish well, to die to the Lord, so as to honour him, by patience, hope, and joy—so as to leave a witness behind them of the truth of God's word and the excellency of his ways, for the conviction and establishment of all who attend them in their dying moments. The best way in which parents can finish their course is blessing their families and worshipping their God. We have now come to,

X. The faith of Joseph, *v.* 22. And here also we consider,

1. What he did by his faith: *He made mention of the departing of the children of Israel, and gave commandment concerning his bones.* The passage is out of Gen. l. 24, 25 Joseph was eminent for his faith, though he had not enjoyed the helps for it which the rest of his brethren had. He was sold into Egypt. He was tried by temptations, by sin, by persecution, for retaining his integrity. He was tried by preferment and power in the court of Pharaoh, and yet his faith held out and carried him through to the last. (1.) He made mention by faith of the departing of the children of Israel, that the time should come when they should be delivered out of Egypt; and he did this both that he might caution them against the thoughts of settling in Egypt, which was now a place of plenty and ease to them; and also that he might keep them from sinking under the calamities and distresses which he foresaw were coming upon them there; and he does it to comfort himself, that though he should not live to see their deliverance, yet he could die in the faith of it. (2.) He gave commandment concerning his bones, that they should preserve them unburied in Egypt, till God should deliver them out of that house of bondage, and that then they should carry his bones along with them into Canaan and deposit them there. Though believers are chiefly concerned for their souls, yet they cannot wholly neglect their bodies, as being members of Christ and parts of themselves, which shall at length be raised up, and be the happy companions of their glorified souls to all eternity. Now Joseph gave this order, not that he thought his being buried in Egypt would either prejudice his soul or prevent the resurrection of his body (as some of the rabbies fancied that all the Jews who were buried out of Canaan must be conveyed underground to Canaan before they could rise again), but to testify, [1.] That though he had lived and died in Egypt, yet he did not live and die an Egyptian, but an Israelite. [2.] That he preferred a significant burial in Canaan before a magnificent one in Egypt. [3.] That he would go as far with his people as he could, though he could not go as far as he would. [4.] That he believed the resurrection of the body, and the communion that his soul should presently have with departed saints, as his body had with their dead bodies. [5.] To assure them that God would be with them in Egypt, and deliver them out of it in his own time and way.

2. When it was that the faith of Joseph acted after this manner; namely, as in the case of Jacob, when he was dying. God often gives his people living comforts in dying

moments; and when he does it is their duty, as they can, to communicate them to those about them, for the glory of God, for the honour of religion, and for the good of their brethren and friends. We go on now to,

XI. The faith of the parents of Moses, which is cited from Exod. ii. 3, &c. Here observe, 1. The acting of their faith: they hid this their son three months. Though only the mother of Moses is mentioned in the history, yet, by what is here said, it seems his father not only consented to it, but consulted about it. It is a happy thing where yoke-fellows draw together in the yoke of faith, as heirs of the grace of God; and when they do this in a religious concern for the good of their children, to preserve them not only from those who would destroy their lives, but from those who would corrupt their minds. Observe, Moses was persecuted betimes, and forced to be concealed; in this he was a type of Christ, who was persecuted almost as soon as he was born, and his parents were obliged to flee with him into Egypt for his preservation. It is a great mercy to be free from wicked laws and edicts; but, when we are not, we must use all lawful means for our security. In this faith of Moses's parents there was a mixture of unbelief, but God was pleased to overlook it. 2. The reasons of their thus acting. No doubt, natural affection could not but move them; but there was something further. They *saw he was a proper child, a goodly child* (Exod. ii. 2), *exceedingly fair*, as in Acts vii. 20, ἀστεῖος τῷ Θεῷ—*venustus Deo—fair to God.* There appeared in him something uncommon; the beauty of the Lord sat upon him, as a presage that he was born to great things, and that by conversing with God his face should shine (Exod. xxxiv. 29), what bright and illustrious actions he should do for the deliverance of Israel, and how his name should shine in the sacred records. Sometimes, not always, the countenance is the index of the mind. 3. The prevalency of their faith over their fear. They were not afraid of the king's commandment, Exod. i. 22. That was a wicked and a cruel edict, that all the males of the Israelites should be destroyed in their infancy, and so the name of Israel must be destroyed out of the earth. But they did not so fear as presently to give up their child; they considered that, if none of the males were preserved, there would be an end and utter ruin of the church of God and the true religion, and that though in their present state of servitude and oppression one would praise the dead rather than the living, yet they believed that God would preserve his people, and that the time was coming when it would be worth while for an Israelite to live. Some must hazard their own lives to preserve their children, and they were resolved to do it; they knew the king's commandment was evil in itself, contrary to the laws of God and nature, and therefore of no authority nor obligation. Faith is a great preservative against the sinful slavish fear of men, as it sets God before the soul, and shows the vanity of the creature and its subordination to the will and power of God The apostle next proceeds to,

XII. The faith of Moses himself (*v.* 24, 25, &c.), here observe,

1. An instance of his faith in conquering the world.

(1.) He *refused to be called the son of Pharaoh's daughter*, whose foundling he was, and her fondling too; she had adopted him for her son, and he refused it. Observe, [1.] How great a temptation Moses was under. Pharaoh's daughter is said to have been his only child, and was herself childless; and having found Moses, and saved him as she did, she resolved to take him and bring him up as her son; and so he stood fair to be in time king of Egypt, and he might thereby have been serviceable to Israel. He owed his life to this princess; and to refuse such kindness from her would look not only like ingratitude to her, but a neglect of Providence, that seemed to intend his advancement and his brethren's advantage. [2.] How glorious was the triumph of his faith in so great a trial. He *refused to be called the son of Pharaoh's daughter* lest he should undervalue the truer honour of being a son of Abraham, the father of the faithful; *he refused to be called the son of Pharaoh's daughter* lest it should look like renouncing his religion as well as his relation to Israel; and no doubt both these he must have done if he had accepted this honour; he therefore nobly refused it.

(2.) He chose *rather to suffer affliction with the people of God than to enjoy the pleasures of sin for a season, v.* 25. He was willing to take his lot with the people of God here, though it was a suffering lot, that he might have his portion with them hereafter, rather than to enjoy all the sensual sinful pleasures of Pharaoh's court, which would be but for a season, and would then be punished with everlasting misery. Herein he acted rationally as well as religiously, and conquered the temptation to worldly pleasure as he had done before to worldly preferment. Here observe, [1.] The pleasures of sin are and will be but short; they must end in speedy repentance or in speedy ruin. [2.] The pleasures of this world, and especially those of a court, are too often the pleasures of sin; and they are always so when we cannot enjoy them without deserting God and his people. A true believer will despise them when they are offered upon such terms. [3.] Suffering is to be chosen rather than sin, there being more evil in the least sin than there can be in the greatest suffering. [4.] It greatly alleviates the evil of suffering when we suffer with the people of God, embarked in the same interest and animated by the same Spirit.

(3.) He accounted *the reproaches of Christ greater riches than the treasures of Egypt*, *v.* 26. See how Moses weighed matters: in one scale he put the worst of religion—*the reproaches of Christ,* in the other scale the best of the world—*the treasures of Egypt;* and in his judgment, directed by faith, the worst of religion weighed down the best of the world. The reproaches of the church of God are *the reproaches of Christ,* who is, and has ever been, the head of the church. Now here Moses conquered the riches of the world, as before he had conquered its honours and pleasures. God's people are, and always have been, a reproached people. Christ accounts himself reproached in their reproaches; and, while he thus interests himself in their reproaches, they become riches, and greater riches than the treasures of the richest empire in the world; for Christ will reward them with a crown of glory that fades not away. Faith discerns this, and determines and acts accordingly.

2. The circumstance of time is taken notice of, when Moses by his faith gained this victory over the world, in all its honours, pleasures, and treasures: *When he had come to years* (*v.* 24); not only to years of discretion, but of experience, to the age of forty years – when he was great, or had come to maturity. Some would take this as detracting from his victory, that he gained it so late, that he did not make this choice sooner; but it is rather an enhancement of the honour of his self-denial and victory over the world that he made this choice when he had grown ripe for judgment and enjoyment, able to know what he did and why he did it. It was not the act of a child, that prefers counters to gold, but it proceeded from mature deliberation. It is an excellent thing for persons to be seriously religious when in the midst of worldly business and enjoyments, to despise the world when they are most capable of relishing and enjoying it.

3. What it was that supported and strengthened the faith of Moses to such a degree as to enable him to gain such a victory over the world: *He had respect unto the recompence of reward,* that is, say some, the deliverance out of Egypt; but doubtless it means much more—the glorious reward of faith and fidelity in the other world. Observe here, (1.) Heaven is a great reward, surpassing not only all our deservings, but all our conceptions. It is a reward suitable to the price paid for it—the blood of Christ; suitable to the perfections of God, and fully answering to all his promises. It is a recompence of reward, because given by a righteous Judge for the righteousness of Christ to righteous persons, according to the righteous rule of the covenant of grace. (2.) Believers may and ought to have respect to this recompence of reward; they should acquaint themselves with it, approve of it, and live in the daily and delightful expectation of it. Thus it will prove a land-mark to direct their course, a load-stone to draw their hearts, a sword to conquer their enemies, a spur to quicken them to duty, and a cordial to refresh them under all the difficulties of doing and suffering work.

4. We have another instance of the faith of Moses, namely, in forsaking Egypt: *By faith he forsook Egypt, not fearing the wrath of the king, v.* 27. Observe here, (1.) The product of his faith: *He forsook Egypt,* and all its power and pleasures, and undertook the conduct of Israel out of it. Twice Moses forsook Egypt: [1.] As a supposed criminal, when the king's wrath was incensed against him for killing the Egyptian (Exod. ii. 14, 15), where it is said he feared, not with a fear of despondency, but of discretion, to save his life. [2.] As a commander and ruler in Jeshurun, after God had employed him to humble Pharaoh and make him willing to let Israel go. (2.) The prevalency of his faith. It raised him above the fear of the king's wrath. Though he knew that it was great, and levelled at him in particular, and that it marched at the head of a numerous host to pursue him, yet he was not dismayed, and he said to Israel, *Fear not,* Exod. xiv. 13. Those who forsook Egypt must expect the wrath of men; but they need not fear it, for they are under the conduct of that God who is able to make the wrath of man to praise him, and restrain the remainder of it. (3.) The principle upon which his faith acted in these his motions: *He endured, as seeing him that was invisible.* He bore up with invincible courage under all danger, and endured all the fatigue of his employment, which was very great; and this by seeing the invisible God. Observe, [1.] The God with whom we have to do is an invisible God: he is so to our senses, to the eye of the body; and this shows the folly of those who pretend to make images of God, whom no man hath seen, nor can see. [2.] By faith we may see this invisible God. We may be fully assured of his existence, of his providence, and of his gracious and powerful presence with us. [3.] Such a sight of God will enable believers to endure to the end whatever they may meet with in the way.

5. We have yet another instance of the faith of Moses, in keeping *the passover and sprinkling of blood, v.* 28. The account of this we have in Exod. xii. 13—23. Though all Israel kept this passover, yet it was by Moses that God delivered the institution of it; and, though it was a great mystery, Moses by faith both delivered it to the people and kept it that night in the house where he lodged. The passover was one of the most solemn institutions of the Old Testament, and a very significant type of Christ. The occasion of its first observance was extraordinary: it was in the same night that God slew the first-born of the Egyptians; but, though the Israelites lived among them, the destroying angel passed over their houses, and spared them and theirs. Now, to entitle

them to this distinguishing favour, and to mark them out for it, a lamb must be slain; the blood of it must be sprinkled with a bunch of hyssop upon the lintel of the door, and on the two side-posts; the flesh of the lamb must be roasted with fire; and it must be all of it eaten that very night with bitter herbs, in a travelling posture, their loins girt, their shoes on their feet, and their staff in their hand. This was accordingly done, and the destroying angel passed over them, and slew the first-born of the Egyptians. This opened a way for the return of Abraham's posterity into the land of promise. The accommodation of this type is not difficult. (1.) Christ is that Lamb, he is our Passover, he was sacrificed for us. (2.) His blood must be sprinkled; it must be applied to those who have the saving benefit of it. (3.) It is applied effectually only to the Israelites, the chosen people of God. (4.) It is not owing to our inherent righteousness or best performances that we are saved from the wrath of God, but to the blood of Christ and his imputed righteousness. If any of the families of Israel had neglected the sprinkling of this blood upon their doors, though they should have spent all the night in prayer, the destroying angel would have broken in upon them, and slain their first-born. (5.) Wherever this blood is applied, the soul receives a whole Christ by faith, and lives upon him. (6.) This true faith makes sin bitter to the soul, even while it receives the pardon and atonement. (7.) All our spiritual privileges on earth should quicken us to set out early, and get forward, in our way to heaven. (8.) Those who have been marked out must ever remember and acknowledge free and distinguishing grace.

XIII. The next instance of faith is that of the Israelites passing through the Red Sea under the conduct of Moses their leader, *v.* 29. The story we have in Exodus, *ch.* xiv. Observe,

1. The preservation and safe passage of the Israelites through the Red Sea, when there was no other way to escape from Pharaoh and his host, who were closely pursuing them. Here we may observe, (1.) Israel's danger was very great; an enraged enemy with chariots and horsemen behind them; steep rocks and mountains on either hand, and the Red Sea before them. (2.) Their deliverance was very glorious. By faith they passed through the Red Sea as on dry land; the grace of faith will help us through all the dangers we meet with in our way to heaven.

2. The destruction of the Egyptians. They, presumptuously attempting to follow Israel through the Red Sea, being thus blinded and hardened to their ruin, were all drowned. Their rashness was great, and their ruin was grievous. When God judges, he will overcome; and it is plain that the destruction of sinners is of themselves.

XIV. The next instance of faith is that of the Israelites, under Joshua their leader, before the walls of Jericho. The story we have Josh. vi. 5, &c. Here observe, 1. The means prescribed of God to bring down the walls of Jericho. It was ordered that they should compass the walls about once a day for seven days together and seven times the last day, that the priests should carry the ark when they compassed the walls about, and should blow with trumpets made of rams' horns, and sound a longer blast than before, and then all the people should shout, and the walls of Jericho should fall before them. Here was a great trial of their faith. The method prescribed seemed very improbable to answer such an end, and would doubtless expose them to the daily contempt of their enemies; the ark of God would seem to be in danger. But this was the way God commanded them to take, and he loves to do great things by small and contemptible means, that his own arm may be made bare. 2. The powerful success of the prescribed means. The walls of Jericho fell before them. This was a frontier town in the land of Canaan, the first that stood out against the Israelites. God was pleased in this extraordinary manner to slight and dismantle it, in order to magnify himself, to terrify the Canaanites, to strengthen the faith of the Israelites, and to exclude all boasting. God can and will in his own time and way cause all the powerful opposition that is made to his interest and glory to fall down, and the grace of faith is mighty through God for the pulling down of strong-holds; he will make Babylon fall before the faith of his people, and, when he has some great thing to do for them, he raises up great and strong faith in them.

XV. The next instance is the faith of Rahab, *v.* 31. Among the noble army of believing worthies, bravely marshalled by the apostle, Rahab comes in the rear, to show *that God is no respecter of persons.* Here consider,

1. Who this Rahab was. (1.) She was a Canaanite, a *stranger to the commonwealth of Israel,* and had but little help for faith, and yet she was a believer; the power of divine grace greatly appears when it works without the usual means of grace. (2.) She was a harlot, and lived in a way of sin; she was not only a keeper of a public house, but a common woman of the town, and yet she believed that the greatness of sin, if truly repented of, shall be no bar to the pardoning mercy of God. Christ has saved the chief of sinners. *Where sin has abounded, grace has superabounded.*

2. What she did by her faith: *She received the spies in peace,* the men that Joshua had sent to spy out Jericho, Josh. ii. 6, 7. She not only bade them welcome, but she concealed them from their enemies who sought to cut them off, and she made a noble confession of her faith, *v.* 9—11. She engaged them to covenant with her to show fa-

vour to her and hers, when God should show kindness to them, and that they would give her a sign, which they did, a line of scarlet, which she was to hang forth out of the window; she sent them away with prudent and friendly advice. Learn here, (1.) True faith will show itself in good works, especially towards the people of God. (2.) Faith will venture all hazards in the cause of God and his people; a true believer will sooner expose his own person than God's interest and people. (3.) A true believer is desirous, not only to be in covenant with God, but in communion with the people of God, and is willing to cast in his lot with them, and to fare as they fare.

3. What she gained by her faith. She escaped perishing with those that believed not. Observe, (1.) The generality of her neighbours, friends, and fellow-citizens, perished; it was an utter destruction that befel that city: man and beast were cut off. (2.) The cause of the people of Jericho's destruction—unbelief. They believed not that Israel's God was the true God, and that Israel was the peculiar people of God, though they had evidence sufficient of it. (3.) The signal preservation of Rahab. Joshua gave a strict charge that she should be spared, and none but she and hers; and she taking care that the sign, the scarlet thread, should be hung out, her family were marked out for mercy, and perished not. Singular faith, when the generality are not only unbelievers, but against believers, will be rewarded with singular favours in times of common calamity.

32 And what shall I more say?
for the time would fail me to tell of
Gedeon, and *of* Barak, and *of* Samson, and *of* Jephthae; *of* David also,
and Samuel, and *of* the prophets:
33 Who through faith subdued kingdoms, wrought righteousness, obtained promises, stopped the mouths
of lions, 34 Quenched the violence
of fire, escaped the edge of the sword,
out of weakness were made strong,
waxed valiant in fight, turned to flight
the armies of the aliens. 35 Women
received their dead raised to life again:
and others were tortured, not accepting deliverance; that they might obtain a better resurrection: 36 And
others had trial of *cruel* mockings and
scourgings, yea, moreover of bonds
and imprisonment: 37 They were
stoned, they were sawn asunder, were
tempted, were slain with the sword:
they wandered about in sheepskins
and goatskins; being destitute, afflicted, tormented; 38 (Of whom
the world was not worthy:) they
wandered in deserts, and *in* mountains, and *in* dens, and caves of
the earth. 39 And these all, having
obtained a good report through faith,
received not the promise: 40 God
having provided some better thing for
us, that they without us should not
be made perfect.

The apostle having given us a classis of many eminent believers, whose names are mentioned and the particular trials and actings of their faith recorded, now concludes his narrative with a more summary account ot another set of believers, where the particular acts are not ascribed to particular persons by name, but left to be applied by those who are well acquainted with the sacred story; and, like a divine orator, he prefaces this part of the narrative with an elegant expostulation: *What shall I say more? Time would fail me;* as if he had said, "It is in vain to attempt to exhaust this subject; should I not restrain my pen, it would soon run beyond the bounds of an epistle; and therefore I shall but just mention a few more, and leave you to enlarge upon them." Observe, 1. After all our researches into the scripture, there is still more to be learned from them. 2. We must well consider in divine matters what we should say, and suit it as well as we can to the time. 3. We should be pleased to think how great the number of believers was under the Old Testament, and how strong their faith, though the objects thereof were not then so fully revealed. And, 4. We should lament it, that now, in gospel times, when the rule of faith is more clear and perfect, the number of believers should be so small and their faith so weak.

I. In this summary account the apostle mentions,

1. Gideon, whose story we have in Judges vi. 11, &c. He was an eminent instrument raised up of God to deliver his people from the oppression of the Midianites; he was a person of mean tribe and family, called from a mean employment (threshing wheat), and saluted by an angel of God in this surprising manner, *The Lord is with thee, thou mighty man of war.* Gideon could not at first receive such honours, but humbly expostulates with the angel about their low and distressed state. The angel of the Lord delivers him his commission, and assures him of success, confirming the assurance by fire out of the rock. Gideon is directed to offer sacrifice, and, instructed in his duty, goes forth against the Midianites, when his army is reduced from thirty-two thousand to three hundred; yet by these, with their lamps and pitchers, God put the whole army of the Midianites to confusion and ruin: and the same faith that gave Gideon so much courage and honour enabled him to act with great meekness and modesty towards his brethren afterwards. It is the

excellency of the grace of faith that, while it helps men to do great things, it keeps them from having high and great thoughts of themselves.

2. Barak, another instrument raised up to deliver Israel out of the hand of Jabin, king of Canaan, Jud. iv., where we read, (1.) Though he was a soldier, yet he received his commission and instructions from Deborah, a *prophetess of the Lord;* and he insisted upon having this divine oracle with him in his expedition. (2.) He obtained a great victory by his faith over all the host of Sisera. (3.) His faith taught him to return all the praise and glory to God: this is the nature of faith; it has recourse unto God in all dangers and difficulties, and then makes grateful returns to God for all mercies and deliverances.

3. Samson, another instrument that God raised up to deliver Israel from the Philistines: his story we have in Judges xiii., xiv., xv., and xvi., and from it we learn that the grace of faith is the strength of the soul for great service. If Samson had not had a strong faith as well as a strong arm, he had never performed such exploits. Observe, (1.) By faith the servants of God shall overcome even the roaring lion. (2.) True faith is acknowledged and accepted, even when mingled with many failings. (3.) The believer's faith endures to the end, and, in dying, gives him victory over death and all his deadly enemies; his greatest conquest he gains by dying.

4. Jephthah, whose story we have, Jud. xi., before that of Samson. He was raised up to deliver Israel from the Ammonites. As various and new enemies rise up against the people of God, various and new deliverers are raised up for them. In the story of Jephthah observe, (1.) The grace of God often finds out, and fastens upon, the most undeserving and ill-deserving persons, to do great things for them and by them. Jephthah was the son of a harlot. (2.) The grace of faith, wherever it is, will put men upon acknowledging God in all their ways (*ch.* xi. 11): *Jephthah rehearsed all his words before the Lord in Mizpeh.* (3.) The grace of faith will make men bold and venturous in a good cause. (4.) Faith will not only put men upon making their vows to God, but paying their vows after the mercy received; yea, though they have vowed to their own great grief, hurt, and loss, as in the case of Jephthah and his daughter.

5. David, that great man after God's own heart. Few ever met with greater trials, and few ever discovered a more lively faith. His first appearance on the stage of the world was a great evidence of his faith. Having, when young, slain *the lion and the bear,* his faith in God encouraged him to encounter the great Goliath, and helped him to triumph over him. The same faith enabled him to bear patiently the ungrateful malice of Saul and his favourites, and to wait till God should put him into possession of the promised power and dignity. The same faith made him a very successful and victorious prince, and, after a long life of virtue and honour (though not without some foul stains of sin), he died in faith, relying upon the everlasting covenant that God had made with him and his, ordered in all things and sure; and he has left behind him such excellent memoirs of the trials and acts of faith in the book of Psalms as will ever be of great esteem and use, among the people of God.

6. Samuel, raised up to be a most eminent prophet of the Lord to Israel, as well as a ruler over them. God revealed himself to Samuel when he was but a child, and continued to do so till his death. In his story observe, (1.) Those are likely to grow up to some eminency in faith who begin betimes in the exercise of it. (2.) Those whose business it is to reveal the mind and will of God to others had need to be well established in the belief of it themselves.

7. To Samuel he adds, *and of the prophets,* who were extraordinary ministers of the Old-Testament church, employed of God sometimes to denounce judgment, sometimes to promise mercy, always to reprove sin; sometimes to foretel remarkable events, known only to God; and chiefly to give notice of the Messiah, his coming, person, and offices; for in him the prophets as well as the law centre. Now a true and strong faith was very requisite for the right discharge of such an office as this.

II. Having done naming particular persons, he proceeds to tell us what things were done by their faith. He mentions some things that easily apply themselves to one or other of the persons named; but he mentions other things that are not so easy to be accomodated to any here named, but must be left to general conjecture or accommodation.

1. *By faith they subdued kingdoms, v.* 33. Thus did David, Joshua, and many of the judges. Learn hence, (1.) The interests and powers of kings and kingdoms are often set up in opposition to God and his people. (2.) God can easily subdue all those kings and kingdoms that set themselves to oppose him. (3.) Faith is a suitable and excellent qualification of those who fight in the wars of the Lord; it makes them just, bold, and wise.

2. They *wrought righteousness,* both in their public and personal capacities; they turned many from idolatry to the ways of righteousness; they believed God, and it was imputed to them for righteousness; they walked and acted righteously towards God and man. It is a greater honour and happiness to work righteousness than to work miracles; faith is an active principle of universal righteousness.

3. They *obtained promises,* both general and special. It is faith that gives us an interest in the promises; it is by faith that we have the comfort of the promises; and it is

by faith that we are prepared to wait for the promises, and in due time to receive them.

4. They *stopped the mouths of lions;* so did Samson, Judg. xiv. 5, 6., and David, 1 Sam. xvii. 34, 35, and Daniel, vi. 22. Here learn, (1.) The power of God is above the power of the creature. (2.) Faith engages the power of God for his people, whenever it shall be for his glory, to overcome brute beasts and brutish men.

5. They *quenched the violence of the fire, v.* 34. So Moses, by the prayer of faith, quenched the fire of God's wrath that was kindled against the people of Israel, Num. xi. 1, 2. So did the three children, or rather mighty champions, Dan. iii. 17—27. Their faith in God, refusing to worship the golden image, exposed them to the fiery furnace which Nebuchadnezzar had prepared for them, and their faith engaged for them that power and presence of God in the furnace which quenched the violence of the fire, so that not so much as the smell thereof passed on them. Never was the grace of faith more severely tried, never more nobly exerted, nor ever more gloriously rewarded, than theirs was.

6. They *escaped the edge of the sword.* Thus David escaped the sword of Goliath and of Saul; and Mordecai and the Jews escaped the sword of Haman. The swords of men are held in the hand of God, and he can blunt the edge of the sword, and turn it away from his people against their enemies when he pleases. Faith takes hold of that hand of God which has hold of the swords of men; and God has often suffered himself to be prevailed upon by the faith of his people.

7. *Out of weakness they were made strong.* From national weakness, into which the Jews often fell by their unbelief; upon the revival of their faith, all their interest and affairs revived and flourished. From bodily weakness; thus Hezekiah, believing the word of God, recovered out of a mortal distemper, and he ascribed his recovery to the promise and power of God (Isa. xxxviii. 15, 16), *What shall I say? He hath spoken it, and he hath also done it. Lord by these things men live, and in these is the life of my spirit.* And it is the same grace of faith that from spiritual weakness helps men to recover and renew their strength.

8. They *grew valiant in fight.* So did Joshua, the judges, and David. True faith gives truest courage and patience, as it discerns the strength of God, and thereby the weakness of all his enemies. And they were not only valiant, but successful. God, as a reward and encouragement of their faith, *put to flight the armies of the aliens,* of those who were aliens to their commonwealth, and enemies to their religion; God made them flee and fall before his faithful servants. Believing and praying commanders, at the head of believing and praying armies, have been so owned and honoured of God that nothing could stand before them.

9. *Women received their dead raised to life again, v.* 35. So did the widow of Zarepath (1 Kings xvii. 23), and the Shunamite, 2 Kings iv. 36. (1.) *In Christ there is neither male nor female;* many of the weaker sex have been strong in faith. (2.) Though the covenant of grace takes in the children of believers, yet it leaves them subject to natural death. (3.) Poor mothers are loth to resign up their interest in their children, though death has taken them away. (4.) God has sometimes yielded so far to the tender affections of sorrowful women as to restore their dead children to life again. Thus Christ had compassion on the widow of Nain, Luke vii. 12, &c. (5.) This should confirm our faith in the general resurrection.

III. The apostle tells us what these believers endured by faith. 1. They *were tortured, not accepting deliverance, v.* 35. They were put upon the rack, to make them renounce their God, their Saviour, and their religion. They bore the torture, and would not accept of deliverance upon such vile terms; and that which animated them thus to suffer was the hope they had of *obtaining a better resurrection,* and deliverance upon more honourable terms. This is thought to refer to that memorable story, 2 Macc. *ch.* vii. &c. 2. They endured *trials of cruel mockings and scourgings, and bonds and imprisonment, v.* 36. They were persecuted in their reputation by *mockings,* which are cruel to an ingenuous mind; in their persons by *scourging,* the punishment of slaves; in their liberty by *bonds and imprisonment.* Observe how inveterate is the malice that wicked men have towards the righteous, how far it will go, and what a variety of cruelties it will invent and exercise upon those against whom they have no cause of quarrel, except in the matters of their God. 3. They were put to death in the most cruel manner; some *were stoned,* as Zechariah (2 Chron. xxiv. 21), *sawn asunder,* as Isaiah by Manasseh. *They were tempted;* some read it, *burnt,* 2 Macc. vii. 5. *They were slain with the sword.* All sorts of deaths were prepared for them; their enemies clothed death in all the array of cruelty and terror, and yet they boldly met it and endured it. 4. Those who escaped death were used so ill that death might seem more eligible than such a life. Their enemies spared them, only to prolong their misery, and wear out all their patience; for they were forced to *wander about in sheep-skins and goat-skins, being destitute, afflicted,* and *tormented; they wandered about in deserts, and on mountains, and in dens and caves of the earth, v.* 37, 38. They were stripped of the conveniences of life, and turned out of house and harbour. They had not raiment to put on, but were forced to cover themselves with the skins of slain beasts. They were driven out of all human society, and forced to converse with the beasts of the field, to hide themselves in dens and caves, and make their complaint to rocks and rivers, not more obdurate than their enemies. Such sufferings as these they endured then for their faith; and such they endured through the power of the grace of faith: and which shall we most admire, the wickedness of human nature, that is capable of perpetrating such cruelties on fellow-creatures, or the excellency of divine grace, that is able to bear up the faithful under such cruelties, and to carry them safely through all?

IV. What they obtained by their faith. 1. A most honourable character and commendation from God, the true Judge and fountain of honour—that *the world was not worthy* of such men; the world did not deserve such blessings; they did not know how to value them, nor how to use them. Wicked men! The righteous are not worthy to live in the world, and God declares the world is not worthy of them; and, though they widely differ in their judgment, they agree in this, that it is not fit that good men should have their rest in this world; and therefore God receives them out of it, to that world that is suitable to them, and yet far beyond the merit of all their services and sufferings. 2. They *obtained a good report* (*v.* 39) of all good men, and of the truth itself, and have the honour to be enrolled in this sacred calendar of the Old-Testament worthies, God's witnesses; yea, they had a witness for them in the consciences of their enemies, who, while they thus abused them, were condemned by their own consciences, as persecuting those who were more righteous than themselves. 3. They obtained an interest in the promises, though not the full possession of them. They had a title to the promises, though they received not the great things promised. This is not meant of the felicity of the heavenly state, for this they did receive, when they died, in the measure of a part, in one constituent part of their persons, and the much better part; but it is meant of the felicity of the gospel-state: they had types, but not the antitype; they had shadows, but had not seen the substance; and yet, under this imperfect dispensation, they discovered this precious faith. This the apostle insists upon to render their faith more illustrious, and to provoke Christians to a holy jealousy and emulation; that they should not suffer themselves to be outdone in the exercise of faith by those who came so short of them in all the helps and advantages for believing. He tells the Hebrews that God had *provided some better things for* them (*v.* 40), and therefore they might be assured that he expected at least as good things from them; and that since the gospel is the end and perfection of the Old Testament, which had no excellency but in its reference to Christ and the gospel, it was expected that their faith should be as much more perfect than the faith of the Old-Testament saints; for their state and dispensation were more perfect than the former, and were indeed the perfection and completion of the former, for without the gospel-church the Jewish church must have remained in an incomplete and imperfect state. This reasoning is strong, and should be effectually prevalent with us all.

CHAP. XII.

The apostle, in this chapter, applies what he has collected in the chapter foregoing, and makes use of it as a great motive to patience and perseverance in the Christian faith and state, pressing home the argument, I. From a greater example than he had yet mentioned, and that is Christ himself. ver. 1—3. II. From the gentle and gracious nature of the afflictions they endured in their Christian course, ver. 4—17. III. From the communion and conformity between the state of the gospel-church on earth and the triumphant church in heaven, ver. 18, to the end.

WHEREFORE seeing we also are compassed about with so great a cloud of witnesses, let us lay aside every weight, and the sin which doth so easily beset *us*, and let us run with patience the race that is set before us, 2 Looking unto Jesus the author and finisher of *our* faith; who for the joy that was set before him endured the cross, despising the shame, and is set down at the right hand of the throne of God. 3 For consider him that endured such contradiction of sinners against himself, lest ye be wearied and faint in your minds.

Here observe what is the great duty which the apostle urges upon the Hebrews, and which he so much desires they would comply with, and that is, to *lay aside every weight, and the sin that did so easily beset them, and run with patience the race set before them.* The duty consists of two parts, the one preparatory, the other perfective.

I. Preparatory: *Lay aside every weight, and the sin,* &c. 1. *Every weight,* that is, all inordinate affection and concern for the body, and the present life and world. Inordinate care for the present life, or fondness for it, is a dead weight upon the soul, that pulls it down when it should ascend upwards, and pulls it back when it should press forward; it makes duty and difficulties harder and heavier than they would be. 2. *The sin that doth so easily beset us;* the sin that has the greatest advantage against us, by the circumstances we are in, our constitution, our company. This may mean either the damning sin of unbelief or rather the darling sin of the Jews, an over-fondness for their own dispensation. *Let us lay aside* all external and internal hindrances.

II. Perfective: *Run with patience the race that is set before us.* The apostle speaks in the gymnastic style, taken from the Olympic and other exercises.

1. Christians have a race to run, a race of service and a race of sufferings, a course of active and passive obedience.

2. This race is set before them; it is marked out unto them, both by the word of God and the examples of the faithful servants of God, that cloud of witnesses with which they are compassed about. It is set out by proper limits and directions; the mark they run to, and the prize they run for, are set before them.

3. This race must be run with patience and perseverance. There will be need of patience to encounter the difficulties that lie in our way, of perseverance to resist all temptations to desist or turn aside. Faith and patience are the conquering graces, and therefore must be always cultivated and kept in lively exercise.

4. Christians have a greater example to animate and encourage them in their Christian course than any or all who have been mentioned before, and that is the Lord Jesus Christ: *Looking unto Jesus, the author and finisher of our faith, v.* 2. Here observe,

(1.) What our Lord Jesus is to his people: he is *the author and finisher of* their *faith*—the beginning, perfecter, and rewarder of it. [1.] He is the author of their faith; not only the object, but the author. He is the great leader and precedent of our faith, *he trusted in God;* he is the purchaser of the Spirit of faith, the publisher of the rule of faith, the efficient cause of the grace of faith, and in all respects the author of our faith. [2.] He is *the finisher of our faith;* he is the fulfiller and the fulfilling of all scripture-promises and prophecies; he is the perfecter of the canon of scripture; he is the finisher of grace, and of the work of faith with power in the souls of his people; and he is the judge and the rewarder of their faith; he determines who they are that reach the mark, and from him, and in him, they have the prize.

(2.) What trials Christ met with in his race and course. [1.] He *endured the contradiction of sinners against himself* (*v.* 3); he bore the opposition that they made to him, both in their words and behaviour. They were continually contradicting him, and crossing in upon his great designs; and though he could easily have both confuted and confounded them, and sometimes gave them a specimen of his power, yet he endured their evil manners with great patience. Their contradictions were levelled against Christ himself, against his person as God-man, against his authority, against his preaching, and yet he endured all. [2.] He *endured the cross*—all those sufferings that he met with in the world; for he took up his cross betimes, and was at length nailed to it, and endured a painful, ignominious, and accursed death, in which he was numbered with the transgressors, the vilest malefactors; yet all this he endured with invincible patience and resolution. [3.] He *despised the shame.* All the reproaches that were cast upon him, both in his life and at his death, he despised; he was infinitely above them; he knew his own innocency and excellency, and despised the ignorance and malice of his despisers.

(3.) What it was that supported the human soul of Christ under these unparalleled sufferings; and that was *the joy that was set before him.* He had something in view under all his sufferings, which was pleasant to him; he rejoiced to see that by his sufferings he should make satisfaction to the injured justice of God and give security to his honour and government, that he should make peace between God and man, that he should seal the covenant of grace and be the Mediator of it, that he should open a way of salvation to the chief of sinners, and that he should effectually save all those whom the Father had given him, and himself be the first-born among many brethren. This was the joy that was set before him

(4.) The reward of his suffering: he *has sat down at the right hand of the throne of God.* Christ, as Mediator, is exalted to a station of the highest honour, of the greatest power and influence; he is at the right hand of the Father. Nothing passes between heaven and earth but by him; he does all that is done; *he ever lives to make intercession for* his people.

(5.) What is our duty with respect to this Jesus. We must, [1.] Look unto him; that is, we must set him continually before us as our example, and our great encouragement; we must look to him for direction, for assistance, and for acceptance, in all our sufferings. [2.] We must consider him, meditate much upon him, and reason with ourselves from his case to our own. We must *analogize,* as the word is; compare Christ's sufferings and ours; and we shall find that as his sufferings far exceeded ours, in the nature and measure of them, so his patience far excels ours, and is a perfect pattern for us to imitate.

(6.) The advantage we shall reap by thus doing: it will be a means to prevent our weariness and fainting (*v.* 3): *Lest you be weary and faint in your minds.* Observe, [1.] There is a proneness in the best to grow weary and to faint under their trials and afflictions, especially when they prove heavy and of long continuance: this proceeds from the imperfections of grace and the remains of corruption. [2.] The best way to prevent this is to look unto Jesus, and to consider him. Faith and meditation will fetch in fresh supplies of strength, comfort, and courage; for he has assured them, if *they suffer with him, they shall also reign with him:* and this hope will be their helmet.

4 Ye have not yet resisted unto
blood, striving against sin. 5 And
ye have forgotten the exhortation
which speaketh unto you as unto
children, My son, despise not thou
the chastening of the Lord, nor faint

when thou art rebuked of him: 6 For
whom the Lord loveth he chasteneth,
and scourgeth every son whom he receiveth. 7 If ye endure chastening,
God dealeth with you as with sons;
for what son is he whom the father
chasteneth not? 8 But if ye be
without chastisement, whereof all are
partakers, then are ye bastards, and
not sons. 9 Furthermore we have
had fathers of our flesh which corrected *us*, and we gave *them* reverence:
shall we not much rather be in subjection unto the Father of spirits, and
live? 10 For they verily for a few
days chastened *us* after their own
pleasure; but he for *our* profit, that
we might be partakers of his holiness.
11 Now no chastening for the present
seemeth to be joyous, but grievous:
nevertheless afterward it yieldeth the
peaceable fruit of righteousness unto
them which are exercised thereby.
12 Wherefore lift up the hands which
hang down, and the feeble knees;
13 And make straight paths for your
feet, lest that which is lame be turned
out of the way; but let it rather be
healed. 14 Follow peace with all
men, and holiness, without which no
man shall see the Lord: 15 Looking diligently lest any man fail of the
grace of God; lest any root of bitterness springing up trouble *you*, and
thereby many be defiled; 16 Lest
there *be* any fornicator, or profane
person, as Esau, who for one morsel of
meat sold his birthright. 17 For ye
know how that afterward, when he
would have inherited the blessing, he
was rejected: for he found no place
of repentance, though he sought it
carefully with tears.

Here the apostle presses the exhortation to patience and perseverance by an argument taken from the gentle measure and gracious nature of those sufferings which the believing Hebrews endured in their Christian course.

I. From the gentle and moderate degree and measure of their sufferings: *You have not yet resisted unto blood, striving against sin, v.* 4. Observe,

1. He owns that they had suffered much, they had been striving to an agony against sin. Here, (1.) The cause of the conflict was sin, and to be engaged against sin is to fight in a good cause, for sin is the worst enemy both to God and man. Our spiritual warfare is both honourable and necessary; for we are only defending ourselves against that which would destroy us, if it should get the victory over us; we fight for ourselves, for our lives, and therefore ought to be patient and resolute. (2.) Every Christian is enlisted under Christ's banner, to strive against sin, against sinful doctrines, sinful practices, and sinful habits and customs, both in himself and in others.

2. He puts them in mind that they might have suffered more, that they had not suffered as much as others; for they had *not yet resisted unto blood,* they had not been called to martyrdom as yet, though they knew not how soon they might be. Learn here, (1.) Our Lord Jesus, *the captain of our salvation,* does not call his people out to the hardest trials at first, but wisely trains them up by less sufferings to be prepared for greater. He will not put new wine into weak vessels, he is *the gentle shepherd,* who will not overdrive *the young ones of the flock.* (2.) It becomes Christians to take notice of the gentleness of Christ in accommodating their trial to their strength. They should not magnify their afflictions, but should take notice of the mercy that is mixed with them, and should pity those who are called to the fiery trial to *resist to blood;* not to shed the blood of their enemies, but to seal their testimony with their own blood. (3.) Christians should be ashamed to faint under less trials, when they see others bear up under greater, and do not know how soon they may meet with greater themselves. If we have run with the footmen and they have wearied us, how shall we contend with horses? If we be wearied in a land of peace, what shall we do in the swellings of Jordan? Jer. xii. 5.

II. He argues from the peculiar and gracious nature of those sufferings that befal the people of God. Though their enemies and persecutors may be the instruments of inflicting such sufferings on them, yet they are divine chastisements; their heavenly Father has his hand in all, and his wise end to serve by all; of this he has given them due notice, and they should not forget it, *v.* 5. Observe,

1. Those afflictions which may be truly persecution as far as men are concerned in them are fatherly rebukes and chastisements as far as God is concerned in them. Persecution for religion is sometimes a correction and rebuke for the sins of professors of religion. Men persecute them because they are religious; God chastises them because they are not more so: men persecute them because they will not give up their profession; God chastises them because they have not lived up to their profession.

2. God has directed his people how they ought to behave themselves under all their afflictions; they must avoid the extremes that many run into. (1.) They must not

despise the chastening of the Lord; they must not make light of afflictions, and be stupid and insensible under them, for they are the hand and rod of God, and his rebukes for sin. Those who make light of affliction make light of God and make light of sin. (2.) They must not faint when they are rebuked; they must not despond and sink under their trial, nor fret and repine, but bear up with faith and patience. (3.) If they run into either of these extremes, it is a sign they have forgotten their heavenly Father's advice and exhortation, which he has given them in true and tender affection.

3. Afflictions, rightly endured, though they may be the fruits of God's displeasure, are yet proofs of his paternal love to his people and care for them (*v.* 6, 7): *Whom the Lord loveth he chasteneth, and scourgeth every son whom he receiveth.* Observe, (1.) The best of God's children need chastisement. They have their faults and follies, which need to be corrected. (2.) Though God may let others alone in their sins, he will correct sin in his own children; they are of his family, and shall not escape his rebukes when they want them. (3.) In this he acts as becomes a father, and treats them like children; no wise and good father will wink at faults in his own children as he would in others; his relation and his affections oblige him to take more notice of the faults of his own children than those of others. (4.) To be suffered to go on in sin without a rebuke is a sad sign of alienation from God; such are bastards, not sons. They may call him Father, because born in the pale of the church; but they are the spurious offspring of another father, not of God, *v.* 7, 8.

4. Those that are impatient under the discipline of their heavenly Father behave worse towards him than they would do towards earthly parents, *v.* 9, 10. Here, (1.) The apostle commends a dutiful and submissive behaviour in children towards their earthly parents *We gave them reverence,* even when they corrected us. It is the duty of children to give the reverence of obedience to the just commands of their parents, and the reverence of submission to their correction when they have been disobedient. Parents have not only authority, but a charge from God, to give their children correction when it is due, and he has commanded children to take such correction well: to be stubborn and discontented under due correction is a double fault; for the correction supposes there has been a fault already committed against the parent's commanding power, and superadds a further fault against his chastening power. Hence, (2.) He recommends humble and submissive behaviour towards our heavenly Father, when under his correction; and this he does by an argument from the less to the greater. [1.] Our earthly fathers are but *the fathers of our flesh,* but God is *the Father of our spirits.* Our fathers on earth were instrumental in the production of our bodies, which are but flesh, a mean, mortal, vile thing, formed out of the dust of the earth, as the bodies of the beasts are; and yet as they are curiously wrought, and made parts of our persons, a proper tabernacle for the soul to dwell in and an organ for it to act by, we owe reverence and affection to those who were instrumental in their procreation; but then we must owe much more to him who is the Father of our spirits. Our souls are not of a material substance, not of the most refined sort; they are not *ex traduce—by traduction;* to affirm it is bad philosophy, and worse divinity: they are the immediate offspring of God, who, after he had formed the body of man out of the earth, breathed into him a vital spirit, and so he became a living soul. [2.] Our earthly parents *chastened us for their own pleasure.* Sometimes they did it to gratify their passion rather than to reform our manners. This is a weakness the fathers of our flesh are subject to, and this they should carefully watch against; for hereby they dishonour that parental authority which God has put upon them and very much hinder the efficacy of their chastisements. But the Father of our spirits never grieves willingly, nor afflicts the children of men, much less his own children. It is always *for our profit;* and the advantage he intends us thereby is no less than our being partakers of his holiness; it is to correct and cure those sinful disorders which make us unlike to God, and to improve and to increase those graces which are the image of God in us, that we may be and act more like our heavenly Father. God loves his children so that he would have them to be as like himself as can be, and for this end he chastises them when they need it. [3.] The fathers of our flesh corrected us for *a few days,* in our state of childhood, when minors; and, though we were in that weak and peevish state, we owed them reverence, and when we came to maturity we loved and honoured them the more for it. Our whole life here is a state of childhood, minority, and imperfection, and therefore we must submit to the discipline of such a state; when we come to a state of perfection we shall be fully reconciled to all the measures of God's discipline over us now. [4.] God's correction is no condemnation. His children may at first fear lest affliction should come upon that dreadful errand, and we cry, *Do not condemn me,* but *show me wherefore thou contendest with me,* Job. x. 2. But this is so far from being the design of God to his own people that he therefore chastens them now *that they may not be condemned with the world,* 1 Cor. xi. 32. He does it to prevent the death and destruction of their souls, that they may live to God, and be like God, and for ever with him.

5. The children of God, under their afflictions, ought not to judge of his dealings

with them by present sense, but by reason, and faith, and experience: *No chastening for the present seemeth to be joyous, but grievous; nevertheless afterwards it yieldeth the peaceable fruits of righteousness, v.* 11. Here observe,

(1.) The judgment of sense in this case—Afflictions are not grateful to the sense, but grievous; the flesh will feel them, and be grieved by them, and groan under them.

(2.) The judgment of faith, which corrects that of sense, and declares that a sanctified affliction produces the fruits of righteousness; these fruits are peaceable, and tend to the quieting and comforting of the soul. Affliction produces peace, by producing more righteousness; for the fruit of righteousness is peace. And if the pain of the body contribute thus to the peace of the mind, and short present affliction produce blessed fruits of a long continuance, they have no reason to fret or faint under it; but their great concern is that the chastening they are under may be endured by them with patience, and improved to a greater degree of holiness. [1.] That their affliction may be endured with patience, which is the main drift of the apostle's discourse on this subject; and he again returns to exhort them that for the reason before mentioned they should *lift up the hands that hang down and the feeble knees, v.* 12. A burden of affliction is apt to make the Christian's hands hang down, and his knees grow feeble, to dispirit him and discourage him; but this he must strive against, and that for two reasons:—*First,* That he may the better run his spiritual race and course. Faith, and patience, and holy courage and resolution, will make him walk more steadily, keep a straighter path, prevent wavering and wandering. *Secondly,* That he may encourage and not dispirit others that are in the same way with him. There are many that are in the way to heaven who yet walk but weakly and lamely in it. Such are apt to discourage one another, and hinder one another; but it is their duty to take courage, and act by faith, and so help one another forward in the way to heaven. [2.] That their affliction may be improved to a greater degree of holiness. Since this is God's design, it ought to be the design and concern of his children, that with renewed strength and patience they may *follow peace with all men, and holiness, v.* 14. If the children of God grow impatient under affliction, they will neither walk so quietly and peaceably towards men, nor so piously towards God, as they should do; but faith and patience will enable them to follow peace and holiness too, as a man follows his calling, constantly, diligently, and with pleasure. Observe, *First,* It is the duty of Christians, even when in a suffering state, *to follow peace with all men,* yea, even with those who may be instrumental in their sufferings. This is a hard lesson, and a high attainment, but it is what Christ has called his people to. Sufferings are apt to sour the spirit and sharpen the passions; but the children of God must follow peace with all men. *Secondly,* Peace and holiness are connected together; there can be no true peace without holiness. There may be prudence and discreet forbearance, and a show of friendship and good-will to all; but this true Christian peaceableness is never found separate from holiness. We must not, under pretence of living peaceably with all men, leave the ways of holiness, but cultivate peace in a way of holiness. *Thirdly, Without holiness no man shall see the Lord.* The vision of God our Saviour in heaven is reserved as the reward of holiness, and the stress of our salvation is laid upon our holiness, though a placid peaceable disposition contributes much to our meetness for heaven.

6. Where afflictions and sufferings for the sake of Christ are not considered by men as the chastisement of their heavenly Father, and improved as such, they will be a dangerous snare and temptation to apostasy, which every Christian should most carefully watch against (*v.* 15, 16): *Looking diligently lest any man fail of the grace of God,* &c.

(1.) Here the apostle enters a serious caveat against apostasy, and backs it with an awful example.

[1.] He enters a serious caveat against apostasy, *v.* 15. Here you may observe, *First,* The nature of apostasy: it is *failing of the grace of God;* it is to become bankrupts in religion, for want of a good foundation, and suitable care and diligence; it is *failing of the grace of God,* coming short of a principle of true grace in the soul, notwithstanding the means of grace and a profession of religion, and so coming short of the love and favour of God here and hereafter. *Secondly,* The consequences of apostasy: where persons fail of having the true grace of God, a root of bitterness will spring up, corruption will prevail and break forth. A *root of bitterness,* a bitter root, producing bitter fruits to themselves and others. It produces to themselves corrupt principles, which lead to apostasy and are greatly strengthened and radicated by apostasy—damnable errors (to the corrupting of the doctrine and worship of the Christian church) and corrupt practices. Apostates generally grow worse and worse, and fall into the grossest wickedness, which usually ends either in downright atheism or in despair. It also produces bitter fruits to others, to the churches to which these men belonged; by their corrupt principles and practices many are troubled, the peace of the church is broken, the peace of men's minds is disturbed, and *many are defiled,* tainted with those bad principles, and drawn into defiling practices; so that the churches suffer both in their purity and peace. But the apostates themselves will be the greatest sufferers at last.

[2.] The apostle backs the caution with an

awful example, and that is, that of Esau, who though born within the pale of the church, and having the birthright as the eldest son, and so entitled to the privilege of being prophet, priest, and king, in his family, was so profane as to despise these sacred privileges, and to sell his birthright for a morsel of meat. Where observe, *First*, Esau's sin. He profanely despised and sold the birthright, and all the advantages attending it. So do apostates, who to avoid persecution, and enjoy sensual ease and pleasure, though they bore the character of the children of God, and had a visible right to the blessing and inheritance, give up all pretensions thereto. *Secondly*, Esau's punishment, which was suitable to his sin. His conscience was convinced of his sin and folly, when it was too late: *He would afterwards have inherited the blessing*, &c. His punishment lay in two things: 1. He was condemned by his own conscience; he now saw that the blessing he had made so light of was worth the having, worth the seeking, though with much carefulness and many tears. 2. He was rejected of God: *He found no place of repentance* in God nor in his father; the blessing was given to another, even to him to whom he sold it for a mess of pottage. Esau, in his great wickedness, had made the bargain, and God, in his righteous judgment, ratified and confirmed it, and would not suffer Isaac to reverse it.

(2.) We may hence learn, [1.] That apostasy from Christ is the fruit of preferring the gratification of the flesh to the blessing of God and the heavenly inheritance. [2.] Sinners will not always have such mean thoughts of the divine blessing and inheritance as now they have. The time is coming when they will think no pains too great, no cares no tears too much, to obtain the lost blessing. [3.] When the day of grace is over (as sometimes it may be in this life), they will find no place for repentance: they cannot repent aright of their sin; and God will not repent of the sentence he has passed upon them for their sin. And therefore, as the design of all, Christians should never give up their title, and hope of their Father's blessing and inheritance, and expose themselves to his irrevocable wrath and curse, by deserting their holy religion, to avoid suffering, which, though this may be persecution as far as wicked men are concerned in it, is only a rod of correction and chastisement in the hand of their heavenly Father, to bring them near to himself in conformity and communion. This is the force of the apostle's arguing from the nature of the sufferings of the people of God even when they suffer for righteousness' sake; and the reasoning is very strong.

18 For ye are not come unto the
mount that might be touched, and
that burned with fire, nor unto blackness, and darkness, and tempest, 19
And the sound of a trumpet, and the
voice of words; which *voice* they that
heard entreated that the word should
not be spoken to them any more: 20
(For they could not endure that which
was commanded, And if so much as a
beast touch the mountain, it shall be
stoned, or thrust through with a dart:
21 And so terrible was the sight, *that*
Moses said, I exceedingly fear and
quake:) 22 But ye are come unto
mount Sion, and unto the city of the
living God, the heavenly Jerusalem,
and to an innumerable company of
angels, 23 To the general assembly
and church of the firstborn, which
are written in heaven, and to God
the Judge of all, and to the spirits of
just men made perfect, 24 And to
Jesus the mediator of the new covenant, and to the blood of sprinkling,
that speaketh better things than *that*
of Abel. 25 See that ye refuse not
him that speaketh. For if they escaped not who refused him that spake
on earth, much more *shall not* we
escape, if we turn away from him that
speaketh from heaven: 26 Whose
voice then shook the earth: but now
he hath promised, saying, Yet once
more I shake not the earth only, but
also heaven. 27 And this *word*, Yet
once more, signifieth the removing of
those things that are shaken, as of
things that are made, that those things
which cannot be shaken may remain.
28 Wherefore we receiving a kingdom which cannot be moved, let us
have grace, whereby we may serve
God acceptably with reverence and
godly fear: 29 For our God *is* a
consuming fire.

Here the apostle goes on to engage the professing Hebrews to perseverance in their Christian course and conflict, and not to relapse again into Judaism. This he does by showing them how much the state of the gospel church differs from that of the Jewish church, and how much it resembles the state of the church in heaven, and on both accounts demands and deserves our diligence, patience, and perseverance in Christianity.

I. He shows how much the gospel church differs from the Jewish church, and how much it excels. And here we have a very particular description of the state of the church under the Mosaic dispensation, *v.* 18—21. 1. It was a gross sensible state. Mount

Sinai, on which that church-state was constituted, was a *mount that might be touched* (*v.* 18), a gross palpable place; so was the dispensation. It was very much external and earthly, and so more heavy. The state of the gospel church on mount Zion is more spiritual, rational, and easy. 2. It was a dark dispensation. Upon that mount there were blackness and darkness, and that church-state was covered with dark shadows and types: the gospel state is much more clear and bright. 3. It was a dreadful and terrible dispensation; the Jews could not bear the terror of it. The thunder and the lightning, the trumpet sounding, the voice of God himself speaking to them, struck them with such dread that they *entreated that the word might not be so spoken to them any more, v.* 19. Yea, Moses himself said, *I exceedingly fear and quake.* The best of men on earth are not able to converse immediately with God and his holy angels. The gospel state is mild, and kind, and condescending, suited to our weak frame. 4. It was a limited dispensation; all might not approach to that mount, but only Moses and Aaron. Under the gospel we have all access with boldness to God. 5. It was a very dangerous dispensation. The mount burned with fire, and whatever man or beast touched the mount must *be stoned, or thrust through with a dart, v.* 20. It is true, it will be always dangerous for presumptuous and brutish sinners to draw nigh to God; but it is not immediate and certain death, as here it was. This was the state of the Jewish church, fitted to awe a stubborn and hard-hearted people, to set forth the strict and tremendous justice of God, to wean the people of God from that dispensation, and induce them more readily to embrace the sweet and gentle economy of the gospel church, and adhere to it.

II. He shows how much the gospel church represents the church triumphant in heaven, what communication there is between the one and the other. The gospel church is called *mount Zion, the heavenly Jerusalem, which is free,* in opposition to mount Sinai, which tendeth to bondage, Gal. iv. 24. This was the hill on which God set his king the Messiah. Now, in coming to mount Zion, believers come into heavenly places, and into a heavenly society.

1. Into heavenly places. (1.) *Unto the city of the living God.* God has taken up his gracious residence in the gospel church, which on that account is an emblem of heaven. There his people may find him ruling, guiding, sanctifying, and comforting them; there he speaks to them by the gospel ministry; there they speak to him by prayer, and he hears them; there he trains them up for heaven, and gives them the earnest of their inheritance. (2.) To *the heavenly Jerusalem* as born and bred there, as free denizens there. Here believers have clearer views of heaven, plainer evidences for heaven, and a greater meetness and more heavenly temper of soul.

2. To a heavenly society. (1.) *To an innumerable company of angels,* who are of the same family with the saints, under the same head, and in a great measure employed in the same work, ministering to believers for their good, keeping them in all their ways, and pitching their tents about them. These for number are innumerable, and for order and union are a company, and a glorious one. And those who by faith are joined to the gospel church are joined to the angels, and shall at length be like them, and equal with them. (2.) *To the general assembly and church of the first-born, that are written in heaven,* that is, to the universal church, however dispersed. By faith we come to them, have communion with them in the same head, by the same Spirit, and in the same blessed hope, and walk in the same way of holiness, grappling with the same spiritual enemies, and hasting to the same rest, victory, and glorious triumph. Here will be the general assembly of the first-born, the saints of former and earlier times, who saw the promises of the gospel state, but received them not, as well as those who first received them under the gospel, and were regenerated thereby, and so were the first-born, and the first-fruits of the gospel church; and thereby, as the first-born, advanced to greater honours and privileges than the rest of the world. Indeed all the children of God are heirs, and every one has the privileges of the first-born. The names of these are written in heaven, in the records of the church here: they have a name in God's house, are written among the living in Jerusalem; they have a good repute for their faith and fidelity, and are enrolled in the Lamb's book of life, as citizens are enrolled in the livery-books. (3.) *To God the Judge of all,* that great God who will judge both Jew and Gentile according to the law they are under: believers come to him now by faith, make supplication to their Judge, and receive a sentence of absolution in the gospel, and in the court of their consciences now, by which they know they shall be justified hereafter. (4.) *To the spirits of just men made perfect;* to the best sort of men, the righteous, who are more excellent than their neighbours; to the best part of just men, their spirits, and to these in their best state, made perfect. Believers have union with departed saints in one and the same head and Spirit, and a title to the same inheritance, of which those on earth are heirs, those in heaven possessors. (5.) *To Jesus the Mediator of the new covenant, and to the blood of sprinkling, that speaketh better things than that of Abel.* This is none of the least of the many encouragements there are to perseverance in the gospel state, since it is a state of communion with Christ the Mediator of the new covenant, and of communication of his blood, that speaketh better things than the blood of

Abel. [1.] The gospel covenant is a new covenant, distinct from the covenant of works; and it is now under a new dispensation, distinct from that of the Old Testament. [2.] Christ is the Mediator of this new covenant; he is the middle person that goes between both parties, God and man, to bring them together in this covenant, to keep them together notwithstanding the sins of the people and God's displeasure against them for sin, to offer up our prayers to God, and to bring down the favours of God to us, to plead with God for us and to plead with us for God, and at length to bring God and his people together in heaven, and to be a Mediator of fruition between them for ever, they beholding and enjoying God in Christ and God beholding and blessing them in Christ. [3.] This covenant is ratified by the blood of Christ sprinkled upon our consciences, as the blood of the sacrifice was sprinkled upon the altar and the sacrifice. This blood of Christ pacifies God and purifies the consciences of men. [4.] This is speaking blood, and it speaks better things than that of Abel. *First,* It speaks to God in behalf of sinners; it pleads not for vengeance, as the blood of Abel did on him who shed it, but for mercy. *Secondly,* To sinners, in the name of God. It speaks pardon to their sins, peace to their souls; and bespeaks their strictest obedience and highest love and thankfulness.

III. The apostle, having thus enlarged upon the argument to perseverance taken from the heavenly nature of the gospel church state, closes the chapter by improving the argument in a manner suitable to the weight of it (*v.* 25, &c.): *See then that you refuse not him that speaketh*—that speaketh by his blood; and not only speaketh after another manner than the blood of Abel spoke from the ground, but than God spoke by the angels, and by Moses spoke on mount Sinai; then he spoke on earth, now he speaks from heaven. Here observe,

1. When God speaks to men in the most excellent manner he justly expects from them the most strict attention and regard. Now it is in the gospel that God speaks to men in the most excellent manner. For, (1.) He now speaks from a higher and more glorious seat and throne, not from mount Sinai, which was on this earth, but from heaven. (2.) He speaks now more immediately by his inspired word and by his Spirit, which are his witnesses. He speaks not now any new thing to men, but by his Spirit speaks the same word home to the conscience. (3.) He speaks now more powerfully and effectually. Then indeed his voice shook the earth, but now, by introducing the gospel state, he hath shaken not only the earth, but the heavens,—not only shaken the hills and mountains, or the spirits of men, or the civil state of the land of Canaan, to make room for his people,—not only shaken the world, as he then did, but he hath shaken the church, that is, the Jewish nation, and shaken them in their church-state, which was in Old-Testament times a heaven upon earth; this their heavenly spiritual state he hath now shaken. It is by the gospel from heaven that God shook to pieces the civil and ecclesiastical state of the Jewish nation, and introduced a new state of the church, that cannot be removed, shall never be changed for any other on earth, but shall remain till it be made perfect in heaven.

2. When God speaks to men in the most excellent manner, the guilt of those who refuse him is the greater, and their punishment will be more unavoidable and intolerable; there is no escaping, no bearing it, *v.* 25. The different manner of God's dealing with men under the gospel, in a way of grace, assures us that he will deal with the despisers of the gospel after a different manner than he does with other men, in a way of judgment. The glory of the gospel, which should greatly recommend it to our regard, appears in these three things:—(1.) It was by the sound of the gospel trumpet that the former dispensation and state of the church of God were shaken and removed; and shall we despise that voice of God that pulled down a church and state of so long standing and of God's own building? (2.) It was by the sound of the gospel trumpet that a new kingdom was erected for God in the world, which can never be so shaken as to be removed. This was a change made once for all; no other change shall take place *till time shall be no more.* We have now *received a kingdom that cannot be moved,* shall never be removed, never give way to any new dispensation. The canon of scripture is now perfected, *the Spirit of prophecy has ceased,* the mystery of God is finished, he has put his last hand to it. The gospel church may be made more large, more prosperous, more purified from contracted pollution, but it shall never be altered for another dispensation; those who perish under the gospel perish without remedy. And hence the apostle justly concludes, [1.] How necessary it is for us to obtain *grace from God, to serve him acceptably:* if we be not accepted of God under this dispensation, we shall never be accepted at all; and we lose all our labour in religion if we be not accepted of God. [2.] We cannot worship God acceptably, unless we worship him with *godly reverence and fear.* As faith, so holy fear, is necessary to acceptable worship. [3.] It is only the grace of God that enables us to worship God in a right manner: nature cannot come up to it; it can produce neither that precious faith nor that holy fear that is necessary to acceptable worship. [4.] God is the same just and righteous God under the gospel that he appeared to be under the law. Though he be our God in Christ, and now deals with us in a more kind and gracious way, yet he is in himself a consuming fire; that is, a God of strict justice, who will avenge himself on all the despisers of his

grace, and upon all apostates. Under the gospel, the justice of God is displayed in a more awful manner, though not in so sensible a manner as under the law; for here we behold divine justice seizing upon the Lord Jesus Christ, and making him a propitiatory sacrifice, his soul and body an offering for sin, which is a display of justice far beyond what was seen and heard on mount Sinai when the law was given.

CHAP. XIII.

The apostle, having treated largely of Christ, and faith, and free grace, and gospel privileges, and warned the Hebrews against apostasy, now, in the close of all, recommends several excellent duties to them, as the proper fruits of faith (ver. 1—17); he then bespeaks their prayers for him, and offers up his prayers to God for them, gives them some hope of seeing himself and Timothy, and ends with the general salutation and benediction, ver. 18, to the end.

LET brotherly love continue. 2
Be not forgetful to entertain
strangers: for thereby some have entertained angels unawares. 3 Remember them that are in bonds, as
bound with them; *and* them which
suffer adversity, as being yourselves
also in the body. 4 Marriage *is*
honourable in all, and the bed undefiled: but whoremongers and adulterers God will judge. 5 *Let your*
conversation *be* without covetousness;
and be content with such things as ye
have: for he hath said, I will never
leave thee, nor forsake thee. 6 So
that we may boldly say, The Lord *is*
my helper, and I will not fear what
man shall do unto me. 7 Remember
them which have the rule over you,
who have spoken unto you the word
of God: whose faith follow, considering the end of *their* conversation: 8
Jesus Christ the same yesterday, and
to day, and for ever. 9 Be not
carried about with divers and strange
doctrines. For *it is* a good thing
that the heart be established with
grace; not with meats, which have
not profited them that have been occupied therein. 10 We have an
altar, whereof they have no right to
eat which serve the tabernacle. 11 For
the bodies of those beasts, whose
blood is brought into the sanctuary
by the high priest for sin, are burned
without the camp. 12 Wherefore
Jesus also, that he might sanctify the
people with his own blood, suffered
without the gate. 13 Let us go
forth therefore unto him without the
camp, bearing his reproach. 14 For
here have we no continuing city, but
we seek one to come. 15 By him
therefore let us offer the sacrifice of
praise to God continually, that is, the
fruit of *our* lips giving thanks to his
name. 16 But to do good and to
communicate forget not: for with
such sacrifices God is well pleased.
17 Obey them that have the rule over
you, and submit yourselves: for they
watch for your souls, as they that
must give account, that they may do
it with joy, and not with grief: for
that *is* unprofitable for you.

The design of Christ in giving himself for us is that he may purchase *to himself a peculiar people, zealous of good works.* Now the apostle calls the believing Hebrews to the performance of many excellent duties, in which it becomes Christians to excel.

I. To brotherly love (*v.* 1), by which he does not only mean a general affection to all men, as our brethren by nature, all made of the same blood, nor that more limited affection which is due to those who are of the same immediate parents, but that special and spiritual affection which ought to exist among the children of God. 1. It is here supposed that the Hebrews had this love one for another. Though, at this time, that nation was miserably divided and distracted among themselves, both about matters of religion and the civil state, yet there was true brotherly love left among those of them who believed on Christ; and this appeared in a very eminent manner presently after the shedding forth of the Holy Ghost, when they had all things common, and sold their possessions to make a general fund of subsistence to their brethren. The spirit of Christianity is a spirit of love. Faith works by love. The true religion is the strongest bond of friendship; if it be not so, it has its name for nothing. 2. This brotherly love was in danger of being lost, and that in a time of persecution, when it would be most necessary; it was in danger of being lost by those disputes that were among them concerning the respect they ought still to have to the ceremonies of the Mosaic law. Disputes about religion too often produce a decay of Christian affection; but this must be guarded against, and all proper means used to preserve brotherly love. Christians should always love and live as brethren, and the more they grow in devout affection to God their heavenly Father the more they will grow in love to one another for his sake.

II. To hospitality: *Be not forgetful to entertain strangers for his sake, v.* 2. We must add to brotherly kindness charity. Here observe, 1. The duty required—*to entertain strangers,* both those that are strangers to the commonwealth of Israel, and strangers to our persons, especially those who know themselves to be strangers here and are seeking another country, which is the case of the people of God, and was so at this time: the believing Jews were in a desperate and distressed condition. But he seems to speak of strangers as such; though we know not who they are, nor whence they come, yet, seeing they are without any certain dwelling place, we should allow them room in our hearts and in our houses, as we have opportunity and ability. 2. The motive: *Thereby some have entertained angels unawares;* so Abraham did (Gen. xviii.), and Lot (Gen. xix.), and one of those that Abraham entertained was the Son of God; and, though we cannot suppose this will ever be our case, yet what we do to strangers, in obedience to him, he will reckon and reward as done to himself. Matt. xxv. 35, *I was a stranger, and you took me in.* God has often bestowed honours and favours upon his hospitable servants, beyond all their thoughts, *unawares.*

III. To Christian sympathy: *Remember those that are in bonds, v.* 3. Here observe,

1. The duty—to *remember those that are in bonds* and in *adversity.* (1.) God often orders it so that while some Christians and churches are in adversity others enjoy peace and liberty. All are not called at the same time to resist unto blood. (2.) Those that are themselves at liberty must sympathise with those that are in bonds and adversity, as if they were bound with them in the same chain: they must feel the sufferings of their brethren.

2. The reason of the duty: *As being yourselves in the body;* not only in the body natural, and so liable to the like sufferings, and you should sympathise with them now that others may sympathise with you when your time of trial comes; but in the same mystical body, under the same head, *and if one member suffer all the rest suffer with it,* 1 Cor. xii. 26. It would be unnatural in Christians not to bear each other's burdens.

IV. To purity and chastity, *v.* 4. Here you have, 1. A recommendation of God's ordinance of marriage, that it *is honourable in all,* and ought to be so esteemed by all, and not denied to those to whom God has not denied it. It is honourable, for God instituted it for man in paradise, knowing it was not good for him to be alone. He married and blessed the first couple, the first parents of mankind, to direct all to look unto God in that great concern, and to marry in the Lord. Christ honoured marriage with his presence and first miracle. It is honourable as a means to prevent impurity and a defiled bed. It is *honourable* and happy, when persons come together pure and chaste, and preserve the marriage bed undefiled, not only from unlawful but inordinate affections. 2. A dreadful but just censure of impurity and lewdness: *Whoremongers and adulterers God will judge.* (1.) God knows who are guilty of such sins, no darkness can hide them from him. (2.) He will call such sins by their proper names, not by the names of love and gallantry, but of whoredom and adultery, whoredom in the single state and adultery in the married state. (3.) He will bring them into judgment, he will judge them, either by their own consciences here, and *set their sins in order before them* for their deep humiliation (and conscience, when awakened, will be very severe upon such sinners), or he will set them at his tribunal at death, and in the last day; he will convict them, condemn them, and cast them out for ever, if they die under the guilt of this sin.

V. To Christian contentment, *v.* 5, 6. Here observe, 1. The sin that is contrary to this grace and duty—*covetousness,* an over eager desire of the wealth of this world, envying those who have more than we. This sin we must allow no place in our conversation; for, though it be a secret lust lurking in the heart, if it be not subdued it will enter into our conversation, and discover itself in our manner of speaking and acting. We must take care not only to keep this sin down, but to root it out of our souls. 2. The duty and grace that is contrary to covetousness—being satisfied and pleased *with such things as we have;* present things, for past things cannot be recalled, and future things are only in the hand of God. What God gives us from day to day we must be content with, though it fall short of what we have enjoyed heretofore, and though it do not come up to our expectations for the future. We must be content with our present lot. We must bring our minds to our present condition, and this is the sure way to contentment; and those who cannot do it would not be contented though God should raise their condition to their minds, for the mind would rise with the condition. Haman was the great court-favourite, and yet not contented—Ahab on the throne, and yet not contented—Adam in paradise, and yet not contented; yea, the angels in heaven, and yet not contented; but Paul, though abased and empty, had *learned in* every *state, in* any *state, therewith to be content.* 3. What reason Christians have to be contented with their lot. (1.) *God hath said, I will never leave thee, nor forsake thee, v.* 5, 6. This was said to Joshua (*ch.* i. 5), but belongs to all the faithful servants of God. Old-Testament promises may be applied to New-Testament saints. This promise contains the sum and substance of all the promises. *I will never,* no, *never leave thee, nor* ever *forsake thee.* Here are no fewer than five negatives heaped together, to confirm the promise; the true believer shall have the gracious presence of God with him in life, at death, and for ever. (2.) From this comprehensive promise they may assure themselves of help from God: *So that we may boldly say, The Lord is my helper; I will not fear what man shall do unto me, v.* 6. Men can do nothing against God, and God can make all that men do against his people to turn to their good.

VI. To the duty Christians owe to their ministers, and that both to those that are dead and to those that are yet alive.

1. To those that are dead: *Remember those that have had the rule over you, v. 7.* Here observe,

(1.) The description given of them. They were such as had the rule over them, and had spoken to them the word of God; their guides and governors, who had spoken to them the word of God. Here is the dignity to which they were advanced—to be rulers and leaders of the people, not according to their own will, but the will and word of God; and this character they filled up with suitable duty: they did not rule at a distance, and rule by others, but they ruled by personal presence and instruction, according to the word of God.

(2.) The duties owing to them, even when they were dead.

[1.] "*Remember them*—their preaching, their praying, their private counsel, their example."

[2.] "*Follow* their *faith;* be stedfast in the profession of the faith they preached to you, and labour after the grace of faith by which they lived and died so well. *Consider the end of their conversation,* how quickly, how comfortably, how joyfully, they finished their course!" Now this duty of following the same true faith in which they had been instructed the apostle enlarges much upon, and presses them earnestly to it, not only from the remembrance of their faithful deceased guides, but from several other motives.

First, From the immutability and eternity of the Lord Jesus Christ. Though their ministers were some dead, others dying, yet the great head and high priest of the church, *the bishop of their souls,* ever lives, and is ever the same; and they should be stedfast and immovable, in imitation of Christ, and should remember that Christ ever lives to observe and reward their faithful adherence to his truths, and to observe and punish their sinful departure from him. Christ is the same in the Old-Testament day, in the gospel day, and will be so to his people for ever.

Secondly, From the nature and tendency of those erroneous doctrines that they were in danger of falling in with.

a. They were divers and various (*v.* 9), different from what they had received from their former faithful teachers, and inconsistent with themselves.

b. They were strange doctrines: such as the gospel church was unacquainted with foreign to the gospel.

c. They were of an unsettling, distracting nature, like the wind by which the ship is tossed, and in danger of being driven from its anchor, carried away, and split upon the rocks. They were quite contrary to that grace of God which fixes and establishes the heart, which is an excellent thing. These strange doctrines keep the heart always fluctuating and unsettled.

d. They were mean and low as to their subject. They were about external, little, perishing things, such as *meats and drinks,* &c.

e. They were unprofitable. Those who were most taken with them, and employed about them, got no real good by them to their own souls. They did not make them more holy, nor more humble, nor more thankful, nor more heavenly.

f. They would exclude those who embraced them from the privileges of the Christian altar (*v.* 10): *We have an altar.* This is an argument of great weight, and therefore the apostle insists the longer upon it. Observe,

(*a.*) The Christian church has its altar. It was objected against the primitive Christians that their assemblies were destitute of an altar; but this was not true. *We have an altar,* not a material altar, but a personal one, and that is Christ; he is both our altar, and our sacrifice; he sanctifies the gift. The altars under the law were types of Christ; the brazen altar of the sacrifice, the golden altar of his intercession.

(*b.*) This altar furnishes out a feast for true believers, a feast upon the sacrifice, a *feast of fat things,* spiritual strength and growth, and holy delight and pleasure. The Lord's table is not our altar, but it is furnished with provision from the altar. *Christ our passover is sacrificed for us* (1 Cor. v. 7), and it follows, *therefore let us keep the feast.* The Lord's supper is the feast of the gospel passover.

(*c.*) Those who adhere to the tabernacle or the Levitical dispensation, or return to it again, exclude themselves from the privileges of this altar, from the benefits purchased by Christ. If they serve the tabernacle, they are resolved to subject themselves to antiquated rites and ceremonies, to renounce their right to the Christian altar; and this part of the argument he first proves and then improves.

[*a.*] He proves that this servile adherence to the Jewish state is a bar to the privileges of the gospel altar; and he argues thus:—Under the Jewish law, no part of the sin-offering was to be eaten, but all must be burnt without the camp while they dwelt in tabernacles, and without the gates when they dwelt in cities: now, if they will still be subject to that law, they cannot eat at the gospel-altar; for that which is eaten there is furnished from Christ, who is the great sin-offering. Not that it is the very sin-offering itself, as the papists affirm; for then it was not to be eaten, but burnt; but the gospel feast is the fruit and procurement of the sacrifice, which those have no right to who do not acknowledge the sacrifice itself. And that it might appear that Christ was really the antitype of the sin-offering, and, as such, might sanctify or cleanse his people with his own blood, he conformed himself to the type, in suffering without the gate. This was a striking specimen of his humiliation, as if he had not been fit either for sacred or civil society! And this shows how sin, which was the meritorious cause of the sufferings of Christ, is a forfeiture of all sacred and civil rights, and the sinner a common plague and nuisance to all society, if God should be strict to mark iniquity. Having thus shown that adherence to the Levitical law would, even according to its own rules, debar men from the Christian altar, he proceeds,

[*b.*] To improve this argument (*v.* 13—15) in suitable advices. *First, Let us go forth therefore unto him without the camp;* go forth from the ceremonial law, from sin, from the world, from ourselves, our very bodies, when he calls us. *Secondly,* Let us be willing to *bear his reproach,* be willing to be accounted the offscouring of all things, not worthy to live, not worthy to die a common death. This was his reproach, and we must submit to it; and we have the more reason because, whether we go forth from this world to Christ or no, we must necessarily go forth in a little time by death; for *here we have no continuing city.* Sin, sinners, death, will not suffer us to continue long here; and therefore we should go forth now by faith, and seek in Christ the rest and settlement which this world cannot afford us, *v.* 14. *Thirdly,* Let us make a right use of this altar; not only partake of the privileges of it, but discharge the duties of the altar, as those whom Christ has made priests to attend on this altar. Let us bring our sacrifices to this altar, and to this our high priest, and offer them up by him, *v.* 15, 16. Now what are the sacrifices which we must bring and offer on this altar, even Christ? Not any expiatory sacrifices; there is no need of them. Christ has offered the great *sacrifice of atonement,* ours are only the sacrifices of acknowledgment; and they are, 1. The sacrifice of praise to God, which we should offer up to God continually. In this are included all adoration and prayer, as well as thanksgiving; this is *the fruit of our lips;* we must speak forth the praises of God from unfeigned lips; and this must be offered only to God, not to angels, nor saints, nor any creature, but to the name of God alone; and it must be by Christ, in a dependence upon his meritorious satisfaction and intercession. 2. The sacrifice of alms-deeds, and Christian charity: *To do good, and to communicate, forget not; for with such sacrifices God is well pleased, v.* 16. We must, according to our power, *communicate* to the necessities of the souls and bodies of men; not contenting ourselves to offer the sacrifice of our lips, mere words, but the sacrifice of good deeds; and these we must lay down upon this altar, not depending upon the merit of our good deeds, but of our great high priest; and with such sacrifices as these, adoration and alms thus offered up, God is well pleased; he will accept the offering with pleasure, and will accept and bless the offerers through Christ.

2. Having thus told us the duty Christians owe to their deceased ministers, which principally consists in following their faith and not departing from it, the apostle tells us what is the duty that people owe to their living ministers (*v.* 17) and the reasons of that duty: (1.) The duty—to obey them, and submit themselves to them. It is not an implicit obedience, or absolute submission, that is here required, but only so far as is agreeable to the mind and will of God revealed in his word; and yet it is truly obedience and submission, and that not only to God, but to the authority of the ministerial office, which is of God as certainly, in all things belonging to that office, as the authority of parents or of civil magistrates in the things within their sphere. Christians must submit to be instructed by their ministers, and not think themselves too wise, too good, or too great, to learn from them; and, when they find that ministerial instructions are agreeable to the written word, they must obey them. (2.) The motives to this duty. [1.] They have the rule over the people; their office, though not magisterial, yet is truly authoritative. They have no authority to lord it over the people, but to lead them in the ways of God, by informing and instructing them, explaining the word of God to them, and applying it to their several cases. They are not to make laws of their own, but to interpret the laws of God; nor is their interpretation to be immediately received without examination, but the people must search the scriptures, and so far as the instructions of their minister are according to that rule they ought to receive them, *not as the word of men, but, as they are indeed, the word of God, that works effectually in those that believe.* [2.] They watch for the souls of the people, not to ensnare them, but to save them; to gain them, not to themselves, but to Christ; to build them up in knowledge, faith, and holiness. They are to watch against every thing that may be hurtful to the souls of men, and to give them warning of dangerous errors, of the devices of Satan, of approaching judgments; they are to watch for all opportunities of helping the souls of men forward in the way to heaven. [3.] They must give an account how they have discharged their duty, and what has become of the souls committed to their trust, whether any have been lost through their neglect, and whether any of them have been brought in and built up under their ministry. [4.] They would be glad to give a good account of themselves and their hearers. If they can then give in an account of their own fidelity and success, it will be a joyful day to them; those souls that have been converted and confirmed under their ministry *will be their joy, and their crown, in the day of the Lord Jesus.* [5.] If they give up their account

with grief, it will be the people's loss as well as theirs. It is the interest of hearers that the account their ministers give of them may be with joy, and not with grief. If faithful ministers be not successful, the grief will be theirs, but the loss will be the people's. Faithful ministers have delivered their own souls, but a fruitless and faithless people's blood and ruin will be upon their own heads.

18 Pray for us: for we trust we
have a good conscience, in all things
willing to live honestly. 19 But I
beseech *you* the rather to do this, that
I may be restored to you the sooner.
20 Now the God of peace, that
brought again from the dead our Lord
Jesus, that great Shepherd of the
sheep, through the blood of the everlasting covenant, 21 Make you perfect in every good work to do his will,
working in you that which is well-
pleasing in his sight, through Jesus
Christ; to whom *be* glory for ever
and ever. Amen. 22 And I beseech
you, brethren, suffer the word of
exhortation: for I have written a
letter unto you in few words. 23
Know ye that *our* brother Timothy
is set at liberty; with whom, if he
come shortly, I will see you. 24
Salute all them that have the rule
over you, and all the saints. They
of Italy salute you. 25 Grace *be*
with you all. Amen.

Here, I. The apostle recommends himself, and his fellow-sufferers, to the prayers of the Hebrew believers (*v.* 18): "*Pray for us;* for me and Timothy" (mentioned *v.* 23), "and for all those of us who labour in the ministry of the gospel."

1. This is one part of the duty which people owe to their ministers. Ministers need the prayers of the people; and the more earnestly the people pray for their ministers the more benefit they may expect to reap from their ministry. They should pray that God would teach those who are to teach them, that he would make them vigilant, and wise, and zealous, and successful—that he would assist them in all their labours, support them under all their burdens, and strengthen them under all their temptations.

2. There are good reasons why people should pray for their ministers; he mentions two:—

(1.) *We trust we have a good conscience,* &c., *v.* 18. Many of the Jews had a bad opinion of Paul, because he, being a Hebrew of the Hebrews, had cast off the Levitical law and preached up Christ: now he here modestly asserts his own integrity: *We trust we have a good conscience, in all things willing to live honestly. We trust!* he might have said, *We know;* but he chose to speak in a humble style, to teach us all not to be too confident of ourselves, but to maintain a godly jealousy over our own hearts. "We trust we have a *good conscience,* an enlightened and well-informed conscience, a clean and pure conscience, a tender and faithful conscience, a conscience testifying for us, not against us: a good conscience *in all things,* in the duties both of the first and second table, towards God and towards men, and especially in all things pertaining to our ministry; we would act honestly and sincerely in all things." Observe, [1.] A good conscience has a respect to all God's commands and all our duty. [2.] Those who have this good conscience, yet need the prayers of others. [3.] Conscientious ministers are public blessings, and deserve the prayers of the people.

(2.) Another reason why he desires their prayers is that he hoped thereby to be the sooner restored to them (*v.* 19), intimating that he had been formerly among them,—that, now he was absent from them, he had a great desire and real intention to come again to them,—and that the best way to facilitate his return to them, and to make it a mercy to him and them, was to make it a matter of their prayer. When ministers come to a people as a return of prayer, they come with greater satisfaction to themselves and success to the people. We should fetch in all our mercies by prayer.

II. He offers up his prayers to God for them, being willing to do for them as he desired they should do for him: *Now the God of peace,* &c., *v.* 20. In this excellent prayer observe, 1. The title given to God—*the God of peace,* who has found out a way for peace and reconciliation between himself and sinners, and who loves peace on earth and especially in his churches. 2. The great work ascribed to him: *He hath brought again from the dead our Lord Jesus,* &c. Jesus raised himself by his own power; and yet the Father was concerned in it, attesting thereby that justice was satisfied and the law fulfilled. He rose again for our justification; and that divine power by which he was raised is able to do every thing for us that we stand in need of. 3. The titles given to Christ—our Lord Jesus, our sovereign, our Saviour, and the great shepherd of the sheep, promised in Isa. xl. 11, declared by himself to be so, John x. 14, 15. Ministers are under-shepherds, Christ is the great shepherd. This denotes his interest in his people. They are the flock of his pasture, and his care and concern are for them. He feeds them, and leads them, and watches over them. 4. The way and method in which God is reconciled, and Christ raised from the dead: *Through the blood of the everlasting covenant.* The blood of Christ satisfied divine justice, and so procured Christ's release from the prison of the grave, as having paid our debt, according to an eternal covenant or agreement between the Father and the Son; and this blood is the sanction and seal of an everlasting covenant between God and his people. 5. The mercy prayed for: *Make you perfect in every good work*, &c., *v.* 21. Observe, (1.) The perfection of the saints in every good work is the great thing desired by them and for them, that they may here have a perfection of integrity, a clear mind, a clean heart, lively affections, regular and resolved wills, and suitable strength for every good work to which they are called now, and at length a perfection of degrees to fit them for the employment and felicity of heaven. (2.) The way in which God makes his people perfect; it is by working in them always what is pleasing in his sight, and that *through Jesus Christ, to whom be glory for ever*. Observe, [1.] There is no good thing wrought in us but it is the work of God; he works in us, before we are fit for any good work. [2.] No good thing is wrought in us by God, but through Jesus Christ, for his sake and by his Spirit. And therefore, [3.] Eternal glory is due to him, who is the cause of all the good principles wrought in us and all the good works done by us. To this every one should say, *Amen*.

III. He gives the Hebrews an account of Timothy's liberty and his hopes of seeing them with him in a little time, *v.* 23. It seems, Timothy had been a prisoner, doubtless for the gospel, but now he was set at liberty. The imprisonment of faithful ministers is an honour to them, and their enlargement is matter of joy to the people. He was pleased with the hopes of not only seeing Timothy, but seeing the Hebrews with him. Opportunities of writing to the churches of Christ are desired by the faithful ministers of Christ, and pleasant to them.

IV. Having given a brief account of this his letter, and begged their attention to it (*v.* 22), he closes with salutations, and a solemn, though short benediction.

1. The salutation. (1.) From himself to them, directed to all their ministers who had rule over them, and to all the saints; to them all, ministers and people. (2.) From the Christians in Italy to them. It is a good thing to have the law of holy love and kindness written in the hearts of Christians one towards another. Religion teaches men the truest civility and good-breeding. It is not a sour nor morose thing.

2. The solemn, though short benediction (*v.* 25): *Grace be with you all. Amen.* Let the favour of God be towards you, and his grace continually working in you, and with you, bringing forth the fruits of holiness, as the first-fruits of glory. When the people of God have been conversing together by word or writing, it is good to part with prayer, desiring for each other the continuance of the gracious presence of God, that they may meet together again in the world of praise.

AN EXPOSITION, WITH PRACTICAL OBSERVATIONS, OF THE GENERAL EPISTLE OF JAMES.

THE writer of this epistle was not James the son of Zebedee; for he was put to death by Herod (Acts xii.) before Christianity had gained so much ground among the Jews of the dispersion as is here implied. But it was the other James, the son of Alpheus, who was cousin-german to Christ, and one of the twelve apostles, Matt. x. 3. He is called *a pillar* (Gal. ii. 9), and this epistle of his cannot be disputed, without loosening a foundation-stone. It is called a general epistle, because (as some think) not directed to any particular person or church, but such a one as we call a circular letter. Others think it is called general, or catholic, to distinguish it from the epistles of Ignatius, Barnabas, Polycarp, and others who were noted in the primitive times, but not generally received in the church, and on that account not canonical, as this is. Eusebius tells us that this epistle was "generally read in the churches with the other catholic epistles." Hist. Eccles. page 53. Ed. Val. Anno 1678. James, our author, was called the just, for his great piety. He was an eminent example of those graces which he presses upon others. He was so exceedingly revered for his justice, temperance, and devotion, that Josephus the Jewish historian records it as one of the causes of the destruction of Jerusalem, "That St. James was martyred in it." This is mentioned in hopes of procuring the greater regard to what is penned by so holy and excellent a man. The time when this epistle was written is uncertain. The design of it is to reprove Christians for their great degeneracy both in faith and manners, and to prevent the spreading of those libertine doctrines which threatened the destruction of all practical godliness. It was also a special intention of the author of this epistle to awaken the Jewish nation to a sense of the greatness and nearness of those judgments which were coming upon them; and to support all true Christians in the way of their duty, under the calamities and persecutions they might meet with. The truths laid down are very momentous, and necessary to be maintained; and the rules for practice, as here stated, are such as ought to be observed in our times as well as in preceding ages.

CHAP. I.

After the inscription and salutation (ver. 1) Christians are taught how to conduct themselves when under the cross. Several graces and duties are recommended; and those who endure their trials and afflictions as the apostle here directs are pronounced blessed and are assured of a glorious reward, ver. 2—12. But those sins which bring sufferings, or the weaknesses and faults men are chargeable with under them, are by no means to be imputed to God, who cannot be the author of sin, but is the author of all good, ver. 13—18. All passion, and rush anger, and vile affections, ought to be suppressed. The word of God should be made our chief study: and what we hear and know of it we must take care to practise, otherwise our religion will prove but a vain thing. To this is added an account wherein pure religion consists, ver. 19—27.

JAMES, a servant of God and of the Lord Jesus Christ, to the twelve tribes which are scattered abroad, greeting.

We have here the inscription of this epistle, which consists of three principal parts.

I. The character by which our author desires to be known: *James, a servant of God, and of the Lord Jesus Christ.* Though he was a prime-minister in Christ's kingdom, yet he styles himself only a servant. Note hence, Those who are highest in office or attainments in the church of Christ are but servants. They should not therefore act as masters, but as ministers. Further, Though James is called by the evangelist *the brother of our Lord,* yet it was his glory to serve Christ in the spirit, rather than to boast of his being akin according to the flesh. Hence let us learn to prize this title above all others in the world—*the servants of God and of Christ.* Again, it is to be observed that James professes himself *a servant of God and of the Lord Jesus Christ,* to teach us that in all services we should have an eye to the Son as well as the Father. We cannot acceptably serve the Father, unless we are also servants of the Son. God will have *all men to honour the Son as they honour the Father* (John v. 23), looking for acceptance in Christ and assistance from him, and yielding all obedience to him, thus confessing *that Jesus Christ is Lord, to the glory of God the Father.*

II. The apostle here mentions the condition of those to whom he writes: *The twelve tribes which are scattered abroad.* Some understand this of the dispersion upon the persecution of Stephen, Acts viii. But that only reached to Judea and Samaria. Others by the Jews of the dispersion understand those who were in Assyria, Babylon, Egypt, and other kingdoms into which their wars had driven them. The greatest part indeed of ten of the twelve tribes were lost in captivity; but yet some of every tribe were preserved and they are still honoured with the ancient style of *twelve tribes.* These however were scattered and dispersed. 1. They were dispersed in mercy. Having the scriptures of the Old Testament, the providence of God so ordered it that they were scattered in several countries for the diffusing of the light of divine revelation. 2. They began now to be scattered in wrath. The Jewish nation was crumbling into parties and factions, and many were forced to leave their own country, as having now grown too hot for them. Even good people among them shared in the common calamity. 3. These Jews of the dispersion were those who had embraced the Christian faith. They were persecuted and forced to seek for shelter in other countries, the Gentiles being kinder to Christians than the Jews were. Note here, It is often the lot even of God's own tribes to be scattered abroad. The gathering day is reserved for the end of time; when all the dispersed children of God shall be gathered together to Christ their head. In the mean time, while God's tribes are scattered abroad, he will send to look after them. Here is an apostle writing to the scattered; an epistle from God to them, when driven away from his temple, and seemingly neglected by him. Apply here that of the prophet Ezekiel, *Thus saith the Lord God, Although I have cast them far off among the heathen, and although I have scattered them among the countries, yet will I be to them as a little sanctuary in the countries where they shall come,* Ezek. xi. 16. God has a particular care of his outcasts. *Let my outcasts dwell with thee, Moab,* Isa. xvi. 3, 4. God's tribes may be scattered; therefore we should not value ourselves too much on outward privileges. And, on the other hand, we should not despond and think ourselves rejected, under outward calamities, because God remembers and sends comfort to his scattered people.

III. James here shows the respect he had even for the dispersed: *greeting,* saluting them, wishing peace and salvation to them. True Christians should not be the less valued for their hardships. It was the desire of this apostle's heart that those who were scattered might be comforted—that they might do well and fare well, and be enabled to rejoice even in their distresses. God's people have reason to rejoice in all places, and at all times; as will abundantly appear from what follows.

2 My brethren, count it all joy
when ye fall into divers temptations;
3 Knowing *this*, that the trying of your
faith worketh patience. 4 But let patience have *her* perfect work, that ye
may be perfect and entire, wanting
nothing. 5 If any of you lack wisdom,
let him ask of God, that giveth to all
men liberally, and upbraideth not; and
it shall be given him. 6 But let him
ask in faith, nothing wavering. For
he that wavereth is like a wave of the
sea driven with the wind and tossed.
7 For let not that man think that he
shall receive any thing of the Lord.
8 A double minded man *is* unstable
in all his ways. 9 Let the brother of
low degree rejoice in that he is exalted: 10 But the rich, in that he is
made low: because as the flower of
the grass he shall pass away. 11 For
the sun is no sooner risen with a
burning heat, but it withereth the
grass, and the flower thereof falleth,
and the grace of the fashion of it
perisheth: so also shall the rich man
fade away in his ways. 12 Blessed
is the man that endureth temptation:
for when he is tried, he shall receive
the crown of life, which the Lord hath
promised to them that love him.

We now come to consider the matter of this epistle. In this paragraph we have the following things to be observed:—

I. The suffering state of Christians in this world is represented, and that in a very instructive manner, if we attend to what is plainly and necessarily implied, together with what is fully expressed. 1. It is implied that troubles and afflictions may be the lot of the best Christians, even of those who have the most reason to think and hope well of themselves. Such as have a title to the greatest joy may yet endure very grievous afflictions. As good people are liable to be scattered, they must not think it strange if they meet with troubles. 2. These outward afflictions and troubles are temptations to them. The devil endeavours by sufferings and crosses to draw men to sin and to deter them from duty, or unfit them for it; but, as our afflictions are in God's hand, they are intended for the trial and improvement of our graces. The gold is put into the furnace, that it may be purified. 3. These temptations may be numerous and various: *Divers temptations*, as the apostle speaks. Our trials may be of many and different kinds, and therefore we have need to put on the whole armour of God. We must be armed on every side, because temptations lie on all sides. 4. The trials of a good man are such as he does not create to himself, nor sinfully pull upon himself; but they are such as he is said to fall into. And for this reason they are the better borne by him.

II. The graces and duties of a state of trial and affliction are here pointed out to us. Could we attend to these things, and grow in them as we should do, how good would it be for us to be afflicted!

1. One Christian grace to be exercised is joy: *Count it all joy, v.* 2. We must not sink into a sad and disconsolate frame of mind, which would make us faint under our trials; but must endeavour to keep our spirits dilated and enlarged, the better to take in a true sense of our case, and with greater advantage to set ourselves to make the best of it. Philosophy may instruct men to be calm under their troubles; but Christianity teaches them to be joyful, because such exercises proceed from love and not fury in God. In them we are conformable to Christ our head, and they become marks of our adoption. By suffering in the ways of righteousness, we are serving the interests of our Lord's kingdom among men, and edifying the body of Christ; and our trials will brighten our graces now and our crown at last. Therefore there is reason to count it all joy when trials and difficulties become our lot in the way of our duty. And this is not purely a New-Testament paradox, but even in Job's time it was said, *Behold, happy is the man whom God correcteth.* There is the more reason for joy in afflictions if we consider the other graces that are promoted by them.

2. Faith is a grace that one expression supposes and another expressly requires: *Knowing this, that the trial of your faith, v.* 3; and then in *v.* 6, *Let him ask in faith.* There must be a sound believing of the great truths of Christianity, and a resolute cleaving to them, in times of trial. That faith which is spoken of here as tried by afflictions consists in a belief of the power, and word, and promise of God, and in fidelity and constancy to the Lord Jesus.

3. There must be patience: *The trial of faith worketh patience.* The trying of one grace produces another; and the more the suffering graces of a Christian are exercised the stronger they grow. *Tribulation worketh patience,* Rom. v. 3. Now, to exercise Christian patience aright, we must, (1.) Let it work. It is not a stupid, but an active thing. Stoical apathy and Christian patience are very different: by the one men become, in some measure, insensible of their afflic-

tions; but by the other they become triumphant in and over them. Let us take care, in times of trial, that patience and not passion, be set at work in us; whatever is said or done, let patience have the saying and doing of it: let us not allow the indulging of our passions to hinder the operation and noble effects of patience; let us give it leave to work, and it will work wonders in a time of trouble. (2.) We must let it have its perfect work. Do nothing to limit it nor to weaken it; but let it have its full scope: if one affliction come upon the heels of another, and a train of them are drawn upon us, yet let patience go on till its work is perfected. When we bear all that God appoints, and as long as he appoints, and with a humble obedient eye to him, and when we not only bear troubles, but rejoice in them, then patience hath its perfect work. (3.) When the work of patience is complete, then the Christian is entire, and nothing will be wanting: it will furnish us with all that is necessary for our Christian race and warfare, and will enable us to persevere to the end, and then its work will be ended, and crowned with glory. After we have abounded in other graces, we *have need of patience*, Heb. x. 36. But *let patience have its perfect work, and we shall be perfect and entire, wanting nothing.*

4. Prayer is a duty recommended also to suffering Christians; and here the apostle shows, (1.) What we ought more especially to pray for—wisdom: *If any lack wisdom, let him ask of God.* We should not pray so much for the removal of an affliction as for wisdom to make a right use of it. And who is there that does not want wisdom under any great trials or exercises to guide him in his judging of things, in the government of his own spirit and temper, and in the management of his affairs? To be wise in trying times is a special gift of God, and to him we must seek for it. (2.) In what way this is to be obtained—upon our petitioning or asking for it. Let the foolish become beggars at the throne of grace, and they are in a fair way to be wise. It is not said, "Let such ask of man," no, not of any man, but, "Let him ask of God," who made him, and gave him his understanding and reasonable powers at first, of him in whom are all the treasures of wisdom and knowledge. Let us confess our want of wisdom to God and daily ask it of him. (3.) We have the greatest encouragement to do this: *he giveth to all men liberally, and upbraideth not.* Yea, it is expressly promised that *it shall be given, v.* 5. Here is something in answer to every discouraging turn of the mind, when we go to God, under a sense of our own weakness and folly, to ask for wisdom. He to whom we are sent, we are sure, has it to give: and he is of a giving disposition, inclined to bestow this upon those who ask. Nor is there any fear of his favours being limited to some in this case, so as to exclude others, or any humble petitioning soul; for *he gives to all men.* If you should say you want a great deal of wisdom, a small portion will not serve your turn, the apostle affirms, he *gives liberally;* and lest you should be afraid of going to him unseasonably, or being put to shame for your folly, it is added, he *upbraideth not.* Ask when you will, and as often as you will, you will meet with no upbraidings. And if, after all, any should say, "This may be the case with some, but I fear I shall not succeed so well in my seeking for wisdom as some others may," let such consider how particular and express the promise is: *It shall be given him.* Justly then must fools perish in their foolishness, if wisdom may be had for asking, and they will not pray to God for it. But, (4.) There is one thing necessary to be observed in our asking, namely, that we do it with a believing, steady mind: *Let him ask in faith, nothing wavering, v.* 6. The promise above is very sure, taking this proviso along with us; wisdom shall be given to those who ask it of God, provided they believe that God is able to make the simple wise, and is faithful to make good his word to those who apply to him. This was the condition Christ insisted on, in treating with those who came to him for healing: *Believest thou that I am able to do this?* There must be *no wavering,* no staggering at the promise of God through unbelief, or through a sense of any disadvantages that lie on our own part. Here therefore we see,

5. That oneness, and sincerity of intention, and a steadiness of mind, constitute another duty required under affliction: *He that wavereth is like a wave of the sea, driven with the wind, and tossed.* To be sometimes lifted up by faith, and then thrown down again by distrust—to mount sometimes towards the heavens, with an intention to secure glory, and honour, and immortality, and then to sink again in seeking the ease of the body, or the enjoyments of this world—this is very fitly and elegantly compared to a wave of the sea, that rises and falls, swells and sinks, just as the wind tosses it higher or lower, that way or this. A mind that has but one single and prevailing regard to its spiritual and eternal interest, and that keeps steady in its purposes for God, will grow wise by afflictions, will continue fervent in its devotions, and will be superior to all trials and oppositions. Now, for the cure of a wavering spirit and a weak faith, the apostle shows the ill effects of these, (1.) In that the success of prayer is spoiled hereby: *Let not that man think that he shall receive any thing of the Lord, v.* 7. Such a distrustful, shifting, unsettled person is not likely to value a favour from God as he should do, and therefore cannot expect to receive it. In asking for divine and heavenly wisdom we are never likely to prevail if we have not a heart to prize it above rubies, and the greatest things in

this world. (2.) A wavering faith and spirit has a bad influence upon our conversations. *A double-minded man is unstable in all his ways, v.* 8. When our faith and spirits rise and fall with second causes, there will be great unsteadiness in all our conversation and actions. This may sometimes expose men to contempt in the world; but it is certain that such ways cannot please God nor procure any good for us in the end. While we have but one God to trust to, we have but one God to be governed by, and this should keep us even and steady. He that is unstable as water shall not excel. Hereupon,

III. The holy humble temper of a Christian, both in advancement and debasement, is described: and both poor and rich are directed on what grounds to build their joy and comfort, *v.* 9—11. Here we may observe, 1. Those of low degree are to be looked upon as brethren: *Let the brother of low degree,* &c. Poverty does not destroy the relation among Christians. 2. Good Christians may be rich in the world, *v.* 10. Grace and wealth are not wholly inconsistent. Abraham, the father of the faithful, was rich in silver and gold. 3. Both these are allowed to rejoice. No condition of life puts us out of a capacity of rejoicing in God. If we do not rejoice in him always, it is our own fault. Those of low degree may rejoice, if they are exalted to be rich in faith and heirs of the kingdom of God (as Dr. Whitby explains this place); and the rich may rejoice in humbling providences, as they produce a lowly and humble disposition of mind, which is highly valuable in the sight of God. Where any are made poor for righteousness' sake, their very poverty is their exaltation. It is an honour to be dishonoured for the sake of Christ. *To you it is given to suffer,* Phil. i. 29. All who are brought low, and made lowly by grace, may rejoice in the prospect of their exaltation at the last in heaven. 4. Observe what reason rich people have, notwithstanding their riches, to be humble and low in their own eyes, because both they and their riches are passing away: *As the flower of the grass he shall pass away.* He, and his wealth with him, *v.* 11. *For the sun has no sooner risen with a burning heat than it withereth the grass.* Note hence, Worldly wealth is a withering thing. Riches are too uncertain (says Mr. Baxter on this place), too inconsiderable things to make any great or just alteration in our minds. As a flower fades before the heat of the scorching sun, *so shall the rich man fade away in his ways.* His projects, counsels, and managements for this world, are called his *ways;* in these he shall *fade away.* For this reason let him that is rich rejoice, not so much in the providence of God, that makes him rich, as in the grace of God, that makes and keeps him humble; and in those trials and exercises that teach him to seek his felicity in and from God, and not from these perishing enjoyments.

IV. A blessing is pronounced on those who endure their exercises and trials, as here directed: *Blessed is the man that endureth temptation, v.* 12. Observe, 1. It is not the man who suffers only that is blessed, but he who endures, who with patience and constancy goes through all difficulties in the way of his duty. 2. Afflictions cannot make us miserable, if it be not our own fault. A blessing may arise from them, and we may be blessed in them. They are so far from taking away a good man's felicity that they really increase it. 3. Sufferings and temptations are the way to eternal blessedness: *When he is tried, he shall receive the crown of life,* δόκιμος γενόμενος—*when he is approved,* when his graces are found to be true and of the highest worth (so metals are tried as to their excellency by the fire), and when his integrity is manifested, and all is approved of the great Judge. Note hence, To be approved of God is the great aim of a Christian in all his trials; and it will be his blessedness at last, when he shall receive the crown of life. The tried Christian shall be a crowned one: and the crown he shall wear will be a crown of life. It will be life and bliss to him, and will last for ever. We only bear the cross for a while, but we shall wear the crown to eternity. 4. This blessedness, involved in a crown of life, is a promised thing to the righteous sufferer. It is therefore what we may most surely depend upon: for, when heaven and earth shall pass away, this word of God shall not fail of being fulfilled. But withal let us take notice that our future reward comes, not as a debt, but by a gracious promise. 5. Our enduring temptations must be from a principle of love to God and to our Lord Jesus Christ, otherwise we are not interested in this promise: *The Lord hath promised to those that love him.* Paul supposes that a man may for some point of religion even give *his body to be burnt,* and yet not be pleasing to God, nor regarded by him, because of his want of charity, or a prevailing sincere love to God and man, 1 Cor. xiii. 3. 6. The crown of life is promised not only to great and eminent saints, but to all those who have the love of God reigning in their hearts. Every soul that truly loves God shall have its trials in this world fully recompensed in that world above *where love is made perfect.*

13 Let no man say when he is
tempted, I am tempted of God: for
God cannot be tempted with evil,
neither tempteth he any man: 14 But
every man is tempted, when he is
drawn away of his own lust, and enticed. 15 Then when lust hath conceived, it bringeth forth sin: and sin,
when it is finished, bringeth forth
death. 16 Do not err, my beloved
brethren. 17 Every good gift and

every perfect gift is from above, and cometh down from the Father of lights, with whom is no variableness, neither shadow of turning. 18 Of his own will begat he us with the word of truth, that we should be a kind of first-fruits of his creatures.

I. We are here taught that God is not the author of any man's sin. Whoever they are who raise persecutions against men, and whatever injustice and sin they may be guilty of in proceeding against them, God is not to be charged with it. And, whatever sins good men may themselves be provoked to by their exercises and afflictions, God is not the cause of them. It seems to be here supposed that some professors might fall in the hour of temptation, that the rod resting upon them might carry some into ill courses, and make them put forth their hands unto iniquity. But though this should be the case, and though such delinquents should attempt to lay their fault on God, yet the blame of their misconduct must lie entirely upon themselves. For, 1. There is nothing in the nature of God that they can lay the blame upon: *Let no man say, when he is tempted* to take any evil course, or do any evil thing, *I am tempted of God; for God cannot be tempted with evil.* All moral evil is owing to some disorder in the being that is chargeable with it, to a want of wisdom, or of power, or of decorum and purity in the will. But who can impeach the holy God with the want of these, which are his very essence? No exigence of affairs can ever tempt him to dishonour or deny himself, and therefore he cannot be tempted with evil. 2. There is nothing in the providential dispensations of God that the blame of any man's sin can be laid upon (*v.* 13): *Neither tempteth he any man.* As God cannot be tempted with evil himself, so neither can he be a tempter of others. He cannot be a promoter of what is repugnant to his nature. The carnal mind is willing to charge its own sins on God. There is something hereditary in this. Our first father Adam tells God, *The woman thou gavest me* tempted me, thereby, in effect, throwing the blame upon God, for giving him the tempter. Let no man speak thus. It is very bad to sin; but it is much worse, when we have done amiss, to charge it upon God, and say it was owing to him. Those who lay the blame of their sins either upon their constitution or upon their condition in the world, or who pretend they are under a fatal necessity of sinning, wrong God, as if he were the author of sin. Afflictions, as sent by God, are designed to draw out our graces, but not our corruptions.

II. We are taught where the true cause of evil lies, and where the blame ought to be laid (*v.* 14): *Every man is tempted* (in an ill sense) *when he is drawn away of his own lust, and enticed.* In other scriptures the devil is called *the tempter*, and other things may sometimes concur to tempt us; but neither the devil nor any other person or thing is to be blamed so as to excuse ourselves; for the true original of evil and temptation is in our own hearts. The combustible matter is in us, though the flame may be blown up by some outward causes. And therefore, *if thou scornest, thou alone shalt bear it*, Prov. ix. 12. Observe here, 1. The method of sin in its proceeding. First it draws away, then entices. As holiness consists of two parts—forsaking that which is evil and cleaving to that which is good, so these two things, reversed, are the two parts of sin. The heart is carried from that which is good, and enticed to cleave to that which is evil. It is first by corrupt inclinations, or by lusting after and coveting some sensual or worldly thing, estranged from the life of God, and then by degrees fixed in a course of sin. 2. We may observe hence the power and policy of sin. The word here rendered *drawn away* signifies a being forcibly haled or compelled. The word translated *enticed* signifies being wheedled and beguiled by allurements and deceitful representations of things, *ἐξελκόμενος καὶ δελεαζόμενος.* There is a great deal of violence done to conscience and to the mind by the power of corruption: and there is a great deal of cunning and deceit and flattery in sin to gain us to its interests. The force and power of sin could never prevail, were it not for its cunning and guile. Sinners who perish are wheedled and flattered to their own destruction. And this will justify God for ever in their damnation, that they destroyed themselves. Their sin lies at their own door, and therefore their blood will lie upon their own heads. 3. The success of corruption in the heart (*v.* 15): *Then, when lust hath conceived, it bringeth forth sin;* that is, sin being allowed to excite desires in us, it will soon ripen those desires into consent, and then it is said to have *conceived.* The sin truly exists, though it be but in embryo. And, when it has grown to its full size in the mind, it is then brought forth in actual execution. Stop the beginnings of sin therefore, or else all the evils it produces must be wholly charged upon us. 4. The final issue of sin, and how it ends: *Sin, when it is finished, bringeth forth death.* After sin is brought forth in actual commissions, the *finishing of it* (as Dr. Manton observes) is its being strengthened by frequent acts and settled into a habit. And, when the iniquities of men are thus filled up, death is brought forth. There is a death upon the soul, and death comes upon the body. And, besides death spiritual and temporal, the wages of sin is eternal death too. Let sin therefore be repented of and forsaken, before it be finished. *Why will you die, O house of Israel!* Ezek. xxxiii. 11. God has no pleasure in your death, as he has no hand in your sin; but both sin and misery are owing to yourselves.

Your own hearts' lusts and corruptions are your tempters; and when by degrees they have carried you off from God, and finished the power and dominion of sin in you, then they will prove your destroyers.

III. We are taught yet further that, while we are the authors and procurers of all sin and misery to ourselves, *God is the Father and fountain of all good, v.* 16, 17. We should take particular care not to err in our conceptions of God: "*Do not err, my beloved brethren,* μὴ λανᾶσθε—*do not wander,* that is, from the word of God, and the accounts of him you have there. Do not stray into erroneous opinions, and go off from the standard of truth, the things which you have received from the Lord Jesus and by the direction of his Spirit." The loose opinions of Simon, and the Nicolaitans (from whom the Gnostics, a most sensual corrupt set of people, arose afterwards), may perhaps, by the apostle here, be more especially cautioned against. Those who are disposed to look into these may consult the first book of Irenæus against heresies. Let corrupt men run into what notions they will, the truth, as it is in Jesus, stands thus: that God is not, cannot be, the author and patronizer of any thing that is evil; but must be acknowledged as the cause and spring of every thing that is good: *Every good and every perfect gift is from above, and cometh down from the Father of lights, v.* 17. Here observe, 1. God is the Father of lights. The visible light of the sun and the heavenly bodies is from him. He said, *Let there be light, and there was light.* Thus God is at once represented as the Creator of the sun and in some respects compared to it. "As the sun is the same in its nature and influences, though the earth and clouds, oft interposing, make it seem to us as varying, by its rising and setting, and by its different appearances, or entire withdrawment, when the change is not in it; so God is unchangeable, and our changes and shadows are not from any mutability or shadowy alterations in him, but from ourselves."—*Baxter.* The Father of lights, *with whom there is no variableness, neither shadow of turning.* What the sun is in nature, God is in grace, providence, and glory; aye, and infinitely more. For, 2. Every good gift is from him. As the Father of lights, he gives the light of reason. *The inspiration of the Almighty giveth understanding,* Job xxxii. 8. He gives also the light of learning: Solomon's wisdom in the knowledge of nature, in the arts of government, and in all his improvements, is ascribed to God. The light of divine revelation is more immediately from above. The light of faith, purity, and all manner of consolation is from him. So that we have nothing good but what we receive from God, as there is no evil or sin in us, or done by us, but what is owing to ourselves. We must own God as the author of all the powers and perfections that are in the creature, and the giver of all the benefits which we have in and by those powers and perfections: but none of their darknesses, their imperfections, or their ill actions are to be charged on the Father of lights; from him proceeds every good and perfect gift, both pertaining to this life and that which is to come. 3. As every good gift is from God, so particularly the renovation of our natures, our regeneration, and all the holy happy consequences of it, must be ascribed to him (*v.* 18): *Of his own will begat he us with the word of truth.* Here let us take notice, (1.) A true Christian is a creature begotten anew. He becomes as different a person from what he was before the renewing influences of divine grace as if he were formed over again, and born afresh. (2.) The original of this good work is here declared: it is of God's own will; not by our skill or power; not from any good foreseen in us, or done by us, but purely from the good-will and grace of God. (3.) The means whereby this is effected are pointed out: *the word of truth,* that is, the gospel, as Paul expresses it more plainly, 1 Cor iv. 15, *I have begotten you in Jesus Christ through the gospel.* This gospel is indeed a word of truth, or else it could never produce such real, such lasting, such great and noble effects. We may rely upon it, and venture our immortal souls upon it. And we shall find it a means of our sanctification as it is a word of truth, John xvii. 17. (4.) The end and design of God's giving renewing grace is here laid down: *That we should be a kind of first-fruits of his creatures*—that we should be God's portion and treasure, and a more peculiar property to him, as the first-fruits were; and that we should become holy to the Lord, as the first-fruits were consecrated to him. Christ is the first-fruits of Christians, Christians are the first-fruits of creatures.

19 Wherefore, my beloved brethren, let every man be swift to hear,
slow to speak, slow to wrath: 20 For
the wrath of man worketh not the
righteousness of God. 21 Wherefore lay apart all filthiness and superfluity of naughtiness, and receive
with meekness the engrafted word,
which is able to save your souls. 22
But be ye doers of the word, and not
hearers only, deceiving your own
selves. 23 For if any be a hearer of
the word, and not a doer, he is like
unto a man beholding his natural
face in a glass: 24 For he beholdeth
himself, and goeth his way, and
straightway forgetteth what manner
of man he was. 25 But whoso looketh
into the perfect law of liberty, and

continueth *therein*, he being not a
forgetful hearer, but a doer of the
work, this man shall be blessed in his
deed. 26 If any man among you
seem to be religious, and bridleth not
his tongue, but deceiveth his own
heart, this man's religion *is* vain.
27 Pure religion and undefiled before
God and the Father is this, To visit
the fatherless and widows in their
affliction, *and* to keep himself unspotted from the world.

In this part of the chapter we are required,

I. To restrain the workings of passion. This lesson we should learn under afflictions; and this we shall learn if we are indeed begotten again by the word of truth. For thus the connection stands—An angry and hasty spirit is soon provoked to ill things by afflictions, and errors and ill opinions become prevalent through the workings of our own vile and vain affections; but the renewing grace of God and the word of the gospel teach us to subdue these: *Wherefore, my beloved brethren, let every man be swift to hear, slow to speak, slow to wrath, v.* 19. This may refer, 1. To the word of truth spoken of in the verse foregoing. And so we may observe, It is our duty rather to hear God's word, and apply our minds to understand it, than to speak according to our own fancies or the opinions of men, and to run into heat and passion thereupon. Let not such errors as that of God's being the occasion of men's sin ever be hastily, much less angrily, mentioned by you (and so as to other errors); but be ready to hear and consider what God's word teaches in all such cases. 2. This may be applied to the afflictions and temptations spoken of in the beginning of the chapter. And then we may observe, It is our duty rather to hear how God explains his providences, and what he designs by them, than to say as David did in his haste, *I am cut off;* or as Jonah did in his passion, *I do well to be angry.* Instead of censuring God under our trials, let us open our ears and hearts to hear what he will say to us. 3. This may be understood as referring to the disputes and differences that Christians, in those times of trial, were running into among themselves: and so this part of the chapter may be considered without any connection with what goes before. Here we may observe that, whenever matters of difference arise among Christians, each side should be willing to hear the other. People are often stiff in their own opinions because they are not willing to hear what others have to offer against them: whereas we should be swift to hear reason and truth on all sides, and be slow to speak any thing that should prevent this: and, when we do speak, there should be nothing of wrath; for a soft answer turneth away wrath. As this epistle is designed to correct a variety of disorders that existed among Christians, these words, *swift to hear, slow to speak, slow to wrath,* may be very well interpreted according to this last explication. And we may further observe from them that, if men would govern their tongues, they must govern their passions. When Moses's spirit was provoked, *he spoke unadvisedly with his lips.* If we would be slow to speak, we must be slow to wrath.

II. A very good reason is given for suppressing anger: *For the wrath of man worketh not the righteousness of God, v.* 20. It is as if the apostle had said, "Whereas men often pretend zeal for God and his glory, in their heat and passion, let them know that God needs not the passions of any man; his cause is better served by mildness and meekness than by wrath and fury." Solomon says, *The words of the wise are heard in quiet, more than the cry of him that ruleth among fools,* Eccl. ix. 17. Dr. Manton here says of some assemblies, "That if we were as swift to hear as we are ready to speak there would be less of wrath, and more of profit, in our meetings. I remember when a Manichee contested with Augustine, and with importunate clamour cried, *Hear me! hear me!* the father modestly replied, *Nec ego te, nec tu me, sed ambo audiamus apostolum—Neither let me hear thee, nor do thou hear me, but let us both hear the apostle.*" The worst thing we can bring to a religious controversy is anger. This, however it may pretend to be raised by a concern for what is just and right, is not to be trusted. *Wrath* is a human thing, and the wrath of man stands opposed to the righteousness of God. Those who pretend to serve the cause of God hereby show that they are acquainted neither with God nor his cause. This passion must especially be watched against when we are hearing the word of God. See 1 Pet. ii. 1, 2.

III. We are called upon to suppress other corrupt affections, as well as rash anger: *Lay aside all filthiness and superfluity of naughtiness, v.* 21. The word here translated *filthiness* signifies those lusts which have the greatest turpitude and sensuality in them; and the words rendered *superfluity of naughtiness* may be understood of the overflowings of malice or any other spiritual wickednesses. Hereby we are taught, as Christians, to watch against, and lay aside, not only those more gross and fleshly dispositions and affections which denominate a person filthy, but all the disorders of a corrupt heart, which would prejudice it against the word and ways of God. Observe, 1. Sin is a defiling thing; it is called filthiness itself. 2. There is abundance of that which is evil in us, to be watched against; there is *superfluity of naughtiness.* 3. It is not enough to restrain evil affections, but *they must be cast from us, or laid apart.* Isa. xxx. 22, *Thou shalt cast them away as a menstruous cloth; thou shalt say, Get you hence.* 4. This must extend not only to outward sins, and greater abominations, but to all sin of thought and affection as well as speech and practice; πᾶσαν ῥυπαρίαν—*all filthiness*, every thing that is corrupt and sinful. 5. Observe, from the foregoing parts of this chapter, the laying aside of all filthiness is what a time of temptation and affliction calls for, and is necessary to the avoiding of error, and the right receiving and improving of the word of truth: for,

IV. We are here fully, though briefly, instructed concerning hearing the word of God.

1. We are required to prepare ourselves for it (*v.* 21), to get rid of every corrupt affection and of every prejudice and prepossession, and to lay aside those sins which pervert the judgment and blind the mind. *All the filthiness and superfluity of naughtiness*, before explained, must, in an especial manner, be subdued and cast off, by all such as attend on the word of the gospel.

2. We are directed how to hear it: *Receive with meekness the engrafted word, which is able to save your souls.* (1.) In hearing the word of God, we are to receive it—assent to the truths of it—consent to the laws of it; receive it as the stock does the graft; so as that the fruit which is produced may be, not according to the nature of the sour stock, but according to the nature of that word of the gospel which is engrafted into our souls. (2.) We must therefore yield ourselves to the word of God, with most submissive, humble, and tractable tempers: this is to *receive it with meekness.* Being willing to hear of our faults, and taking it not only patiently, but thankfully, desiring also to be moulded and formed by the doctrines and precepts of the gospel. (3.) In all our hearing we should aim at the salvation of our souls. It is the design of the word of God to make us wise to salvation; and those who propose any meaner or lower ends to themselves in attending upon it dishonour the gospel and disappoint their souls. We should come to the word of God (both to read it and hear it), as those who know it is *the power of God unto salvation to every one that believeth*, Rom. i. 16.

3. We are taught what is to be done after hearing (*v.* 22): *But be you doers of the word, and not hearers only, deceiving your own selves.* Observe here, (1.) Hearing is in order to doing; the most attentive and the most frequent hearing of the word of God will not avail us, unless we be also doers of it. If we were to hear a sermon every day of the week, and an angel from heaven were the preacher, yet, if we rested in bare hearing, it would never bring us to heaven. Therefore the apostle insists much upon it (and, without doubt, it is indispensably necessary) that we practise what we hear. "There must be inward practice by meditation, and outward practice in true obedience." *Baxter.* It is not enough to remember what we hear, and to be able to repeat it, and to give testimony to it, and commend it, and write it, and preserve what we have written; that which all this is in order to, and which crowns the rest, is that we be doers of the word. Observe, (2.) Bare hearers are self-deceivers; the original word, παραλογιζόμενοι, signifies men's arguing sophistically to themselves; their reasoning is manifestly deceitful and false when they would make one part of their work discharge them from the obligation they lie under to another, or persuade themselves that filling their heads with notions is sufficient, though their hearts be empty of good affections and resolutions, and their lives fruitless of good works. Self-deceit will be found the worst deceit at last.

4. The apostle shows what is the proper use of the word of God, who they are that do not use it as they ought, and who they are that do make a right use of it, *v.* 23—25. Let us consider each of these distinctly. (1.) The use we are to make of God's word may be learnt from its being compared to a glass, in which a man may *behold his natural face.* As a looking-glass shows us the spots and defilements upon our faces, that they may be remedied and washed off, so the word of God shows us our sins, that we may repent of them and get them pardoned; it shows us what is amiss, that it may be amended. There are glasses that will flatter people; but that which is truly the word of God is no flattering glass. If you flatter yourselves, it is your own fault; *the truth, as it is in Jesus*, flatters no man. Let the word of truth be carefully attended to, and it will set before you the corruption of your nature, the disorders of your hearts and lives; it will tell you plainly what you are. Paul describes himself as insensible of the corruption of his nature till he saw himself in the glass of the law (Rom. vii. 9): "*I was alive without the law;* that is, I took all to be right with me, and thought myself not only clean, but, compared with the generality of the world, beautiful too; *but when the commandment came*, when the glass of the law was set before me, *then sin revived, and I died*—then I saw my spots and deformities, and discovered that amiss in myself which before I was not aware of; and such was the power of the law, and of sin, that I then perceived myself in a state of death and condemnation." Thus, when we attend to *the word of God*, so as to see ourselves, our true state and condition, to rectify what is amiss, and to form and dress ourselves anew by the glass of God's word, this is to make a proper use of it. (2.) We have here an account of those who do not use this glass of the word as they ought: *He that beholds himself, and goes his way, and straightway forgets what manner of man he was*, *v.* 24. This is the true description of one who hears the word of God and does it

not. How many are there who, when they sit under the word, are affected with their own sinfulness, misery, and danger, acknowledge the evil of sin, and their need of Christ; but, when their hearing is over, all is forgotten, convictions are lost, good affections vanish, and pass away like the waters of a land-flood: he *straightway forgets.* "The word of God (as Dr. Manton speaks) discovers how we may do away our sins, and deck and attire our souls with the righteousness of Jesus Christ. *Maculæ sunt peccata, quæ ostendit lex; aqua est sanguis Christi, quem ostendit evangelium—Our sins are the spots which the law discovers; Christ's blood is the laver which the gospel shows.*" But in vain do we hear God's word, and look into the gospel glass, if we go away, and forget our spots, instead of washing them off, and forget our remedy, instead of applying to it. This is the case of those who do not hear the word as they ought. (3.) Those also are described, and pronounced blessed, who hear aright, and who use the glass of God's word as they should do (*v.* 25): *Whoso looketh into the perfect law of liberty, and continueth therein,* &c. Observe here, [1.] The gospel is a law of liberty, or, as Mr. Baxter expresses it, *of liberation,* giving us deliverance from the Jewish law, and from sin and guilt, and wrath and death. The ceremonial law was a yoke of bondage; the gospel of Christ is a law of liberty. [2.] It is a perfect law; nothing can be added to it. [3.] In hearing the word, we look into this perfect law; we consult it for counsel and direction; we look into it, that we may thence take our measures. [4.] Then only do we look into the law of liberty as we should when we *continue therein*—"when we dwell in the study of it, till it turn to a spiritual life, engrafted and digested in us" *(Baxter)*—when we are not forgetful of it, but practise it as our work and business, set it always before our eyes, and make it the constant rule of our conversation and behaviour, and model the temper of our minds by it. [5.] Those who thus do, and *continue in the law and word of God,* are, and *shall be, blessed in their deed; blessed in all their ways,* according to the first psalm, to which, some think, James here alludes. *He that meditates in the law of God, and walks according to it,* the psalmist says, *shall prosper in whatsoever he does.* And *he that is not a forgetful hearer, but a doer of the work* which God's word sets him about, James says, *shall be blessed.* The papists pretend that here we have a clear text to prove we are blessed for our good deeds; but Dr. Manton, in answer to that pretence, puts the reader upon marking the distinctness of scripture-phrase. The apostle does not say, *for* his deeds, that any man is blessed, but *in* his deed. This is a way in which we shall certainly find blessedness, but not the cause of it. This blessedness does not lie in knowing, but in doing the will of God. John xiii. 17, *If you know these things, happy are you if you do them.* It is not talking, but walking, that will bring us to heaven.

V. The apostle next informs us how we may distinguish between a vain religion and that which is pure and approved of God. Great and hot disputes there are in the world about this matter: what religion is false and vain, and what is true and pure. I wish men would agree to let the holy scripture in this place determine the question: and here it is plainly and peremptorily declared,

1. What is a vain religion: *If any man among you seemeth to be religious, and bridleth not his tongue, but deceives his own heart, this man's religion is vain.* Here are three things to be observed:—(1.) In a vain religion there is much of show, and affecting to seem religious in the eyes of others. This, I think, is mentioned in a manner that should fix our thoughts on the word *seemeth.* When men are more concerned to seem religious than really to be so, it is a sign that their religion is but vain. Not that *religion* itself is a vain thing (those do it a great deal of injustice who say, *It is in vain to serve the Lord),* but it is possible for people to make it a vain thing, if they have only a form of godliness, and not the power. (2.) In a vain religion there is much censuring, reviling, and detracting of others. The not bridling the tongue here is chiefly meant of not abstaining from these evils of the tongue. When we hear people ready to speak of the faults of others, or to censure them as holding scandalous errors, or to lessen the wisdom and piety of those about them, that they themselves may seem the wiser and better, this is a sign that they have but a vain religion. The man who has a detracting tongue cannot have a truly humble gracious heart. He who delights to injure his neighbour in vain pretends to love God; therefore a reviling tongue will prove a man a hypocrite. Censuring is a pleasing sin, extremely compliant with nature, and therefore evinces a man's being in a natural state. These sins of the tongue were the great sins of that age in which James wrote (as other parts of this epistle fully show); and it is a strong sign of a vain religion (says Dr. Manton) to be carried away with the evil of the times. This has ever been a leading sin with hypocrites, that the more ambitious they have been to seem well themselves the more free they have been in censuring and running down others; and there is such quick intercourse between the tongue and the heart that the one may be known by the other. On these accounts it is that the apostle has made an ungoverned tongue an undoubted certain proof of a vain religion. There is no strength nor power in that religion which will not enable a man to bridle his tongue. (3.) In a vain religion a man deceives his own heart; he goes on in such a course of detracting from others, and making himself seem somebody, that at last the vanity of his religion is consummated by the deceiving of his own

soul. When once religion comes to be a vain thing, how great is the vanity!

2. It is here plainly and peremptorily declared wherein true religion consists: *Pure religion and undefiled before God and the Father is this, v.* 27. Observe, (1.) It is the glory of religion to be pure and undefiled; not mixed with the inventions of men nor with the corruptions of the world. False religions may be known by their impurity and uncharitableness; according to that of John, *He that doeth not righteousness* is not of God, neither he that *loveth not his brother*, 1 John iii. 10. But, on the other hand, a holy life and a charitable heart show a true religion. Our religion is not (says Dr. Manton) adorned with ceremonies, but purity and charity. And it is a good observation of his that a religion which is pure should be kept undefiled. (2.) That religion is pure and undefiled which is so before God and the Father. That is right which is so in God's eye, and which chiefly aims at his approbation. True religion teaches us to do every thing as in the presence of God; and to seek his favour, and study to please him in all our actions. (3.) Compassion and charity to the poor and distressed from a very great and necessary part of true religion: *Visiting the fatherless and widow in their affliction.* Visiting is here put for all manner of relief which we are capable of giving to others; and fatherless and widows are here particularly mentioned, because they are generally most apt to be neglected or oppressed: but by them we are to understand all who are proper objects of charity, all who are in affliction. It is very remarkable that if the sum of religion be drawn up in two articles this is one—to be charitable and relieve the afflicted. Observe, (4.) An unspotted life must accompany an unfeigned love and charity: *To keep himself unspotted from the world.* The world is apt to spot and blemish the soul, and it is hard to live in it, and have to do with it, and not be defiled; but this must be our constant endeavour. Herein consists pure and undefiled religion. The very things of the world too much taint our spirits, if we are much conversant with them; but the sins and lusts of the world deface and defile them very woefully indeed. John comprises *all that is in the world,* which we are not to love, under three heads: *the lust of the flesh, the lust of the eyes, and the pride of life;* and to keep ourselves unspotted from all these is to keep ourselves unspotted from the world. May God by his grace keep both our hearts and lives clean from the love of the world, and from the temptations of wicked worldly men.

CHAP. II.

In this chapter the apostle condemns a sinful regarding of the rich, and despising the poor, which he imputes to partiality and injustice, and shows it to be an acting contrary to God, who has chosen the poor, and whose interest is often persecuted, and his name blasphemed, by the rich, ver. 1—7. He shows that the whole law is to be fulfilled, and that mercy should be followed, as well as justice, ver. 8—13. He exposes the error and folly of those who boast of faith without works, telling us that this is but a dead faith, and such a faith as devils have, not the faith of Abraham, or of Rahab, ver. 14, to the end.

MY brethren, have not the faith
of our Lord Jesus Christ, *the*
Lord of glory, with respect of persons. 2 For if there come unto your
assembly a man with a gold ring, in
goodly apparel, and there come in
also a poor man in vile raiment; 3
And ye have respect to him that
weareth the gay clothing, and say
unto him, Sit thou here in a good
place; and say to the poor, Stand
thou there, or sit here under my footstool: 4 Are ye not then partial in
yourselves, and are become judges of
evil thoughts? 5 Hearken, my beloved brethren, Hath not God chosen
the poor of this world rich in faith,
and heirs of the kingdom which he
hath promised to them that love him.
6 But ye have despised the poor.
Do not rich men oppress you, and
draw you before the judgment seats?
7 Do not they blaspheme that worthy
name by the which ye are called?

The apostle is here reproving a very corrupt practice. He shows how much mischief there is in the sin of προσωποληψία—*respect of persons,* which seemed to be a very growing evil in the churches of Christ even in those early ages, and which, in these after-times, has sadly corrupted and divided Christian nations and societies. Here we have,

I. A caution against this sin laid down in general: *My brethren, have not the faith of our Lord Jesus Christ, the Lord of glory, with respect of persons, v.* 1. Observe here, 1. The character of Christians fully implied: they are such as have the faith of our Lord Jesus Christ; they embrace it; they receive it; they govern themselves by it; they entertain the doctrine, and submit to the law and government, of Christ; they have it as a trust; they have it as a treasure. 2. How honourably James speaks of Jesus Christ; he calls him *the Lord of glory;* for he is *the brightness of his Father's glory, and the express image of his person.* 3. Christ's being the Lord of glory should teach us not to respect Christians for any thing so much as their relation and conformity to Christ. You who profess to believe the glory of our Lord Jesus Christ, which the poorest Christian shall partake of equally with the rich, and to which all worldly glory is but vanity, you should not make men's outward and worldly advantages the measure of your respect. In professing the faith of our Lord Jesus Christ, we should not show respect to men, so as to cloud or lessen the glory of our glorious Lord: however any may think of it, this is certainly a very heinous sin.

II. We have this sin described and cautioned against, by an instance or example of it (*v.* 2, 3): *For if there come into your assembly a man with a gold ring,* &c. *Assembly* here is meant of those meetings which were appointed for deciding matters of difference among the members of the church, or for determining when censures should be passed upon any, and what those censures should be; therefore the Greek word here used, συναγωγὴ, signifies such an assembly as that in the Jewish synagogues, when they met to do justice. Maimonides says (as I find the passage quoted by Dr. Manton) "That it was expressly provided by the Jews' constitutions that, when a poor man and a rich plead together, the rich shall not be bidden to sit down and the poor stand, or sit in a worse place, but both sit or both stand alike." To this the phrases used by the apostle have a most plain reference, and therefore the assembly here spoken of must be some such as the synagogue-assemblies of the Jews were, when they met to hear causes and to execute justice: to these the arbitrations and censures of their Christian assemblies are compared. But we must be careful not to apply what is here said to the common assemblies for worship; for in these certainly there may be appointed different places for persons according to their rank and circumstances, without sin. Those do not understand the apostle who fix his severity here upon this practice; they do not consider the word judges (used in *v.* 4), nor what is said of their being convicted as transgressors of the law, if they had such a respect of persons as is here spoken of, according to *v.* 9. Thus, now put the case: "*There comes into your assembly* (when of the same nature with some of those at the synagogue) *a man* that is distinguished by his dress, and who makes a figure, *and there comes in also a poor man in vile raiment,* and you act partially, and determine wrong, merely because the one makes a better appearance, or is in better circumstances, than the other." Observe hence, 1. God has his remnant among all sorts of people, among those that wear soft and gay clothing, and among those that wear poor and vile raiment. 2. In matters of religion, rich and poor stand upon a level; no man's riches set him in the least nearer to God, nor does any man's poverty set him at a distance from God. *With the Most High there is no respect of persons,* and therefore in matters of conscience there should be none with us. 3. All undue honouring of worldly greatness and riches should especially be watched against in Christian societies. James does not here encourage rudeness or disorder. Civil respect must be paid, and some difference may be allowed in our carriage towards persons of different ranks; but this respect must never be such as to influence the proceedings of Christian societies in disposing of the offices of the church, or in passing the censures of the church, or in any thing that is purely a matter of religion; here we are to know no man after the flesh. It is the character of a citizen of Zion that *in his eyes a vile person is contemned, but he honoureth those that fear the Lord.* If a poor man be a good man, we must not value him a whit the less for his poverty; and, if a rich man be a bad man (though he may have both gay clothing and a gay profession), we must not value him any whit the more for his riches. 4. Of what importance it is to take care what rule we go by in judging of men; if we allow ourselves commonly to judge by outward appearance, this will too much influence our spirits and our conduct in religious assemblies. There is many a man, whose wickedness renders him vile and despicable, who yet makes a figure in the world; and, on the other hand, there is many a humble, heavenly, good Christian, who is clothed meanly; but neither should he nor his Christianity be thought the worse of on this account.

III. We have the greatness of this sin set forth, *v.* 4, 5. It is great partiality, it is injustice, and it is to set ourselves against God, who has chosen the poor, and will honour and advance them (if good), let who will despise them. 1. In this sin there is shameful partiality: *Are you not then partial in yourselves?* The question is here put, as what could not fail of being answered by every man's conscience that would put it seriously to himself. According to the strict rendering of the original, the question is, "*Have you not made a difference?* And, in that difference, do you not judge by a false rule, and go upon false measures? And does not the charge of a partiality condemned by the law lie fully against you? Does not your own conscience tell you that you are guilty?" Appeals to conscience are of great advantage, when we have to do with such as make a profession, even though they may have fallen into a very corrupt state. 2. This respect of persons is owing to the evil and injustice of the thoughts. As the temper, conduct, and proceedings, are partial, so the heart and thoughts, from which all flows, are evil: "*You have become judges of evil thoughts;* that is, you are judges according to those unjust estimations and corrupt opinions which you have formed to yourselves. Trace your partiality till you come to those hidden thoughts which accompany and support it, and you will find those to be *exceedingly evil.* You secretly prefer outward pomp before inward grace, and the things that are seen before those which are not seen." The deformity of sin is never truly and fully discerned till the evil of our thoughts be disclosed: and it is this which highly aggravates the faults of our tempers and lives—that *the imagination of the thoughts of the heart is evil,* Gen. vi. 5. 3. This respect of persons is a heinous sin, because it is to show ourselves most directly contrary to God (*v.* 5): "*Hath not God chosen the poor of this world, rich in faith?* &c. *But you have despised them*, *v.* 6. God has made those heirs of a kingdom whom you make of no reputation, and has given very great and glorious promises to those to whom you can hardly give a good word or a respectful look. And is not this a monstrous iniquity in you who pretend to be the children of God and conformed to him? *Hearken, my beloved brethren;* by all the love I have for you, and all the regards you have to me, I beg you would consider these things. Take notice that many of the poor of this world are the chosen of God. Their being God's chosen does not prevent their being poor; their being poor does not at all prejudice the evidences of their being chosen. Matt. xi. 5, *The poor are evangelized.*" God designed to recommend his holy religion to men's esteem and affection, not by the external advantages of gaiety and pomp, but by its intrinsic worth and excellency; and therefore chose the poor of this world. Again, take notice that many poor of the world are rich in faith; thus the poorest may become rich; and this is what they ought to be especially ambitious of. It is expected from those who have wealth and estates that they be rich in good works, because the more they have the more they have to do good with; but it is expected from the poor in the world that they be rich in faith, for the less they have here the more they may, and should, live in the believing expectation of better things in a better world. Take notice further, Believing Christians are rich in title, and in being heirs of a kingdom, though they may be very poor as to present possessions. What is laid out upon them is but little; what is laid up for them is unspeakably rich and great. Note again, Where any are rich in faith, there will be also divine love; faith working by love will be in all the heirs of glory. Note once more, under this head, Heaven is a kingdom, and a kingdom promised to those that love God. We read of the crown promised to those that love God, in the former chapter (*v.* 12); we here find there is a kingdom too. And, as the crown is a crown of life, so the kingdom will be an everlasting kingdom. All these things, laid together, show how highly the poor in this world, if rich in faith, are now honoured, and shall hereafter be advanced by God; and consequently how very sinful a thing it was for them to despise the poor. After such considerations as these, the charge is cutting indeed: *But you have despised the poor*, *v.* 6. 4. Respecting persons, in the sense of this place, on account of their riches or outward figure, is shown to be a very great sin, because of the mischiefs which are owing to worldly wealth and greatness, and the folly which there is in Christians' paying undue regards to those who had so little regard either to their God or them: "*Do not rich men oppress you, and draw you before the judgment-seat? Do not they blaspheme that worthy name by which you are called?* *v.* 7. Consider how commonly riches are the incentives of vice and mischief, of blasphemy and persecution: consider how many calamities you yourselves sustain, and how great reproaches are thrown upon your religion and your God by men of wealth, and power, and worldly greatness; and this will make your sin appear exceedingly sinful and foolish, in setting up that which tends to pull you down, and to destroy all that you are building up, and to dishonour that worthy name by which you are called." The name of Christ is a worthy name; it reflects honour, and gives worth to those who wear it.

8 If ye fulfil the royal law according to the scripture, Thou shalt love
thy neighbour as thyself, ye do well:
9 But if ye have respect to persons,
ye commit sin, and are convinced of
the law as transgressors. 10 For
whosoever shall keep the whole law,
and yet offend in one *point*, he is
guilty of all. 11 For he that said,
Do not commit adultery, said also,
Do not kill. Now if thou commit
no adultery, yet if thou kill, thou art
become a transgressor of the law. 12
So speak ye, and so do, as they that
shall be judged by the law of liberty.
13 For he shall have judgment without mercy, that hath showed no mercy;
and mercy rejoiceth against judgment.

The apostle, having condemned the sin of those who had an undue respect of persons, and having urged what was sufficient to convict them of the greatness of this evil, now proceeds to show how the matter may be mended; it is the work of a gospel ministry, not only to reprove and warn, but to teach and direct. Col. i. 28, *Warning every man, and teaching every man.* And here,

I. We have the law that is to guide us in all our regards to men set down in general. *If you fulfil the royal law, according to the scripture, Thou shalt love thy neighbour as thyself, you do well*, *v.* 8. Lest any should think James had been pleading for the poor so as to throw contempt on the rich, he now lets them know that he did not design to encourage improper conduct towards any; they must not hate nor be rude to the rich, any more than despise the poor; but as the scripture teaches us to love all our neighbours, be they rich or poor, as ourselves, so, in our having a steady regard to this rule, *we shall do well.* Observe hence, 1. The rule for Christians to walk by is settled in the scriptures: *If according to the scriptures*, &c. It is not great men, nor worldly wealth, nor corrupt practices among professors themselves, that must guide us, but the scriptures of truth. 2. The scripture gives us this as a law, to love our neighbour as ourselves; it is what still remains in full force, and is rather carried higher and further by Christ than made less important to us. 3. This law is a royal law, it comes from the King of kings. Its own worth and dignity deserve it should be thus honoured; and the state in which all Christians now are, as it is a state of liberty, and not of bondage or oppression, makes this law, by which they are to regulate all their actions to one another, a royal law. 4. A pretence of observing this royal law, when it is interpreted with partiality, will not excuse men in any unjust proceedings. It is implied here that some were ready to flatter rich men, and be partial to them, because, if they were in the like circumstances, they should expect such regards to themselves; or they might plead that to show a distinguished respect to those whom God in his providence had distinguished by their rank and degree in the world was but doing right; therefore the apostle allows that, so far as they were concerned to observe the duties of the second table, they *did well in giving honour to whom honour was due;* but this fair pretence would not cover their sin in that undue *respect of persons* which they stood chargeable with; for,

II. This general law is to be considered together with a particular law: "*If you have respect to persons, you commit sin, and are convinced of the law as transgressors, v.* 9. Notwithstanding the law of laws, *to love your neighbour as yourselves,* and to show that respect to them which you would be apt to look for yourselves if in their circumstances, yet this will not excuse your distributing either the favours or the censures of the church according to men's outward condition; but here you must look to a particular law, which God, who gave the other, has given you together with it, and by this you will stand fully convicted of the sin I have charged you with. This law is in Lev. xix. 15, *Thou shalt do no unrighteousness in judgment; thou shalt not respect the person of the poor nor the person of the mighty; but in righteousness shalt thou judge thy neighbour.* Yea, the very royal law itself, rightly explained, would serve to convict them, because it teaches them to put themselves as much in the places of the poor as in those of the rich, and so to act equitably towards one as well as the other. Hence he proceeds,

III. To show the extent of the law, and how far obedience must be paid to it. They must fulfil the royal law, have a regard to one part as well as another, otherwise it would not stand them in stead, when they pretended to urge it as a reason for any particular actions: *For whosoever shall keep the whole law, and yet offend in one point, is guilty of all, v.* 10. This may be considered, 1. With reference to the case James has been upon: Do you plead for your respect to the rich, because you are to love your neighbour as yourselves? Why then show also an equitable and due regard to the poor, because you are to love your neighbour as yourself: or else your offending in one point will spoil your pretence of observing that law at all. *Whosoever shall keep the whole law, if he offend in one point,* wilfully, avowedly, and with continuance, and so as to think he shall be excused in some matters because of his obedience in others, *he is guilty of all;* that is, he incurs the same penalty, and is liable to the same punishment, by the sentence of the law, as if he had broken it in other points as well as that he stands chargeable with. Not that all sins are equal, but that all carry the same contempt of the authority of the Lawgiver, and so bind over to such punishment as is threatened on the breach of that law. This shows us what a vanity it is to think that our good deeds will atone for our bad deeds, and plainly puts us upon looking for some other atonement. 2. This is further illustrated by putting a case different from that before mentioned (*v.* 11): *For he that said, Do not commit adultery, said also, Do not kill. Now, if thou commit no adultery, yet, if thou kill, thou art become a transgressor of the law.* One, perhaps, is very severe in the case of adultery, or what tends to such pollutions of the flesh; but less ready to condemn murder, or what tends to ruin the health, break the hearts, and destroy the lives, of others: another has a prodigious dread of murder, but has more easy thoughts of adultery; whereas one who looks at the authority of the Lawgiver more than the matter of the command will see the same reason for condemning the one as the other. Obedience is then acceptable when all is done with an eye to the will of God; and disobedience is to be condemned, in whatever instance it be, as it is a contempt of the authority of God; and, for that reason, if we offend in one point, we contemn the authority of him who gave the whole law, and so far are guilty of all. Thus, if you look to the law of old, you stand condemned; for *cursed is every that continueth not in all things that are written in the book of the law to do them,* Gal. iii. 10.

IV. James directs Christians to govern and conduct themselves more especially by the law of Christ. *So speak and so do as those that shall be judged by the law of liberty, v.* 12. This will teach us, not only to be just and impartial, but very compassionate and merciful to the poor; and it will set us perfectly free from all sordid and undue regards to the rich. Observe here, 1. The gospel is called a law. It has all the requisites of a law: precepts with rewards and punishments annexed; it prescribes duty, as well as administers comfort; and Christ is a king to rule us as well as a prophet to teach us, and a priest to sacrifice and intercede for us. *We are under the law to Christ.* 2. It is a *law of liberty*, and one that we have no reason to complain of as a yoke or burden; for the service of God, according to the gospel, is perfect freedom; it sets us at liberty from all slavish regards, either to the persons or the things of this world. 3. We must all be judged by this law of liberty. Men's eternal condition will be determined according to the gospel; this is the book that will be opened, when we shall stand before the judgment-seat; there will be no relief to those whom the gospel condemns, nor will any accusation lie against those whom the gospel justifies. 4. It concerns us therefore so to speak and act now as becomes those who must shortly be judged by this law of liberty; that is, that we come up to gospel terms, that we make conscience of gospel duties, that we be of a gospel temper, and that our conversation be a gospel conversation, because by this rule we must be judged. 5. The consideration of our being judged by the gospel should engage us more especially to be merciful in our regards to the poor (*v.* 13): *For he shall have judgment without mercy that hath shown no mercy; and mercy rejoiceth against judgment.* Take notice here, (1.) The doom which will be passed upon impenitent sinners at last will be judgment without mercy; there will be no mixtures or allays in the cup of wrath and of trembling, the dregs of which they must drink. (2.) Such as show no mercy now shall find no mercy in the great day. But we may note, on the other hand, (3.) That there will be such as shall become instances of the triumph of mercy, in whom mercy rejoices against judgment: all the children of men, in the last day, will be either vessels of wrath or vessels of mercy. It concerns all to consider among which they shall be found; and let us remember that *blessed are the merciful, for they shall obtain mercy.*

14 What *doth it* profit, my brethren,
though a man say he hath faith, and
have not works? can faith save him?
15 If a brother or sister be naked,
and destitute of daily food, 16 And
one of you say unto them, Depart in
peace, be *ye* warmed and filled; notwithstanding ye give them not those
things which are needful to the body;
what *doth it* profit? 17 Even so
faith, if it hath not works, is dead,
being alone. 18 Yea, a man may
say, Thou hast faith, and I have
works: show me thy faith without
thy works, and I will show thee my
faith by my works. 19 Thou believest
that there is one God; thou doest
well: the devils also believe and
tremble. 20 But wilt thou know, O
vain man, that faith without works is
dead? 21 Was not Abraham our
father justified by works, when he
had offered Isaac his son upon the
altar? 22 Seest thou how faith
wrought with his works, and by works
was faith made perfect? 23 And the
scripture was fulfilled which saith,
Abraham believed God, and it was
imputed unto him for righteousness:
and he was called the Friend of God.
24 Ye see then how that by works a
man is justified, and not by faith only.
25 Likewise also was not Rahab the
harlot justified by works, when she
had received the messengers, and had
sent *them* out another way? 26 For
as the body without the spirit is dead,
so faith without works is dead also.

In this latter part of the chapter, the apostle shows the error of those who rested in a bare profession of the Christian faith, as if that would save them, while the temper of their minds and the tenour of their lives were altogether disagreeable to that holy religion which they professed. To let them see, therefore, what a wretched foundation they built their hopes upon, it is here proved at large that a man is justified, not by faith only, but by works. Now,

I. Upon this arises a very great question, namely, how to reconcile Paul and James. Paul, in his epistles to the Romans and Galatians, seems to assert the directly contrary thing to what James here lays down, saying it often, and with a great deal of emphasis, *that we are justified by faith only, and not by the works of the law. Amicæ scripturarum lites, utinam et nostræ—There is a very happy agreement between one part of scripture and another, notwithstanding seeming differences: it were well if the differences among Christians were as easily reconciled.* "Nothing," says Mr. Baxter, "but men's misunderstanding the plain drift and sense of Paul's epistles, could make so many take it for a matter of great difficulty to reconcile Paul and James." A general view of those things which are insisted on by the Antinomians may be seen in Mr. Baxter's Paraphrase: and many ways might be mentioned which have been invented among learned men to make the apostles agree; but it may be sufficient only to observe these few things following:—1. When Paul says that *a man is justified by faith, without the deeds of the law* (Rom. iii. 28), he plainly speaks of another sort of work than James does, but not of another sort of faith. Paul speaks of works wrought in obedience to the law of Moses, and before men's embracing the faith of the gospel; and he had to deal with those who valued themselves so highly upon those works that they rejected the gospel (as Rom. x., at the beginning, most expressly declares); but James speaks of works done in obedience to the gospel, and as the proper and necessary effects and fruits of sound believing in Christ Jesus. Both are concerned to magnify the faith of the gospel, as that which alone could save us and justify us; but Paul magnifies it by showing the insufficiency of any works of the law before faith, or in opposition to the doctrine of justification by Jesus Christ; James magnifies the same faith, by showing what are the genuine and necessary products and operations of it. 2. Paul not only speaks of different works from those insisted on by James, but he speaks of a quite different use that was made of good works from what is here urged and intended. Paul had to do with those who depended on the merit of their works in the sight of God, and thus he might well make them of no manner of account. James had to do with those who cried up faith, but would not allow works to be used even as evidences; they depended upon a bare profession, as sufficient to justify them; and with these he might well urge the necessity and vast importance of good works. As we must not break one table of the law, by dashing it against the other, so neither must we break in pieces the law and the gospel, by making them clash with one another: those who cry up the gospel so as to set aside the law, and those who cry up the law so as to set aside the gospel, are both in the wrong; for we must take our work before us; there must be both faith in Jesus Christ and good works the fruit of faith. 3. The justification of which Paul speaks is different from that spoken of by James; the one speaks of our persons being justified before God, the other speaks of our faith being justified before men: "*Show me thy faith by thy works*," says James, "let thy faith be justified in the eyes of those that behold thee by thy works;" but Paul speaks of justification in the sight of God, who justifies those only that believe in Jesus, and purely on account of the redemption that is in him. Thus we see that our persons are justified before God by faith, but our faith is justified before men by works. This is so plainly the scope and design of the apostle James that he is but confirming what Paul, in other places, says of his faith, that it is a laborious faith, and a faith working by love, Gal. v. 6; 1 Thess. i. 3; Titus iii. 8; and many other places. 4. Paul may be understood as speaking of that justification which is inchoate, James of that which is complete; it is by *faith* only that we are put into a justified state, but then good works come in for the completing of our justification at the last great day; then, *Come you children of my Father——for I was hungry, and you gave me meat*, &c.

II. Having thus cleared this part of scripture from every thing of a contradiction to other parts of it, let us see what is more particularly to be learnt from this excellent passage of James; we are taught,

1. That faith without works will not profit, and cannot save us. *What doth it profit, my brethren, if a man say he hath faith, and have not works? Can faith save him?* Observe here, (1.) That faith which does not save will not really profit us; a bare profession may sometimes seem to be profitable, to gain the good opinion of those who are truly good, and it may procure in some cases worldly good things; but what profit will this be, for any to gain the world and to lose their souls? *What doth it profit?—Can faith save him?* All things should be accounted profitable or unprofitable to us as they tend to forward or hinder the salvation of our souls. And, above all other things, we should take care thus to make account of faith, as that which does not profit, if it do not save, but will aggravate our condemnation and destruction at last. (2.) For a man to have faith, and to say he has faith, are two different things; the apostle does not say, *If a man have faith without works*, for that is not a supposable case; the drift of this place of scripture is plainly to show that an opinion, or speculation, or assent, without works, is not faith; but the case is put thus, *If a man say he hath faith*, &c. Men may boast of that to others, and be conceited of that in themselves, of which they are really destitute.

2. We are taught that, as love or charity is an operative principle, so is faith, and that neither of them would otherwise be good for any thing; and, by trying how it looks for a person to pretend he is very charitable who yet never does any works of charity, you may judge what sense there is in pretending to have faith without the proper and necessary fruits of it: "*If a brother or a sister be naked, and destitute of daily food, and one of you say unto them, Depart in peace, be you warmed and filled, notwithstanding you give them not those things which are needful to the body, what doth it profit? v.* 15—17. What will such a charity as this, that consists in bare words, avail either you or the poor? Will you come before God with such empty shows of charity as these? You might as well pretend that your love and charity will stand the test without acts of mercy as think that a profession of faith will bear you out before God without works of piety and obedience. *Even so faith, if it hath not works, is dead, being alone*," *v.* 17. We are too apt to rest in a bare profession of faith, and to think that this will save us; it is a cheap and easy religion to say, "We believe the articles of the Christian faith;" but it is a great delusion to imagine that this is enough to bring us to heaven. Those who argue thus wrong God, and put a cheat upon their own souls; a mock-faith is as hateful as mock-charity, and both show a heart dead to all real godliness. You may as soon take pleasure in a dead

body, void of soul, or sense, or action, as God take pleasure in a dead faith, where there are no works.

3. We are taught to compare a faith boasting of itself without works and a faith evidenced by works, by looking on both together, to try how this comparison will work upon our minds. *Yea, a man may say, Thou hast faith, and I have works. Show me thy faith without thy works, and I will show thee my faith by my works, v.* 18. Suppose a true believer thus pleading with a boasting hypocrite, "Thou makest a profession, and sayest thou hast faith; I make no such boasts, but leave my works to speak for me. Now give any evidence of having the faith thou professest without works if thou canst, and I will soon let thee see how my works flow from faith and are the undoubted evidences of its existence." This is the evidence by which the scriptures all along teach men to judge both of themselves and others. And this is the evidence according to which Christ will proceed at the day of judgment. *The dead were judged according to their works,* Rev. xx. 12. How will those be exposed then who boast of that which they cannot evidence, or who go about to evidence their faith by any thing but works of piety and mercy!

4. We are taught to look upon a faith of bare speculation and knowledge as the faith of devils: *Thou believest that there is one God; thou doest well; the devils also believe, and tremble, v.* 19. That instance of faith which the apostle here chooses to mention is the first principle of all religion. "*Thou believest that there is a God,* against the atheists; and that there is but one God, against the idolaters; *thou doest well:* so far all is right. But to rest here, and take up a good opinion of thyself, or of thy state towards God, merely on account of thy believing in him, this will render thee miserable: *The devils also believe, and tremble.* If thou contentest thyself with a bare assent to articles of faith, and some speculations upon them, thus far the devils go. And as their faith and knowledge only serve to excite horror, so in a little time will thine." The word tremble is commonly looked upon as denoting a good effect of faith; but here it may rather be taken as a bad effect, when applied to the faith of devils. They tremble, not out of reverence, but hatred and opposition to that one God on whom they believe. To rehearse that article of our creed, therefore, *I believe in God the Father Almighty,* will not distinguish us from devils at last, unless we now give up ourselves to God as the gospel directs, and love him, and delight ourselves in him, and serve him, which the devils do not, cannot do.

5. We are taught that he who boasts of faith without works is to be looked upon at present as a foolish condemned person. *But wilt thou know, O vain man, that faith without works is dead? v.* 20. The words translated *vain man—ἄνθρωπε κενὲ,* are observed to have the same signification with the word *Raca,* which must never be used to private persons, or as an effect of anger (Matt. v. 22), but may be used as here, to denote a just detestation of such a sort of men as are empty of good works, and yet boasters of their faith. And it plainly declares them fools and abjects in the sight of God. Faith without works is said to be *dead,* not only as void of all those operations which are the proofs of spiritual life, but as unavailable to eternal life: such believers as rest in a bare profession of faith *are dead while they live.*

6. We are taught that a justifying faith cannot be without works, from two examples, Abraham and Rahab.

(1.) The first instance is that of Abraham, the father of the faithful, and the prime example of justification, to whom the Jews had a special regard (*v.* 21): *Was not Abraham our father justified by works, when he had offered Isaac his son upon the altar?* Paul, on the other hand, says (in *ch.* iv. of the epistle to the Romans) that Abraham *believed, and it was counted to him for righteousness.* But these are well reconciled, by observing what is said in Heb. xi., which shows that the faith both of Abraham and Rahab was such as to produce those good works of which James speaks, and which are not to be separated from faith as justifying and saving. By what Abraham did, it appeared that he truly believed. Upon this footing, the words of God himself plainly put this matter. Gen. xxii. 16, 17, *Because thou hast done this thing, and hast not withheld thy son, thine only son; therefore in blessing I will bless thee.* Thus the faith of Abraham was a working faith (*v.* 22), *it wrought with his works, and by works was made perfect.* And by this means you come to the true sense of that scripture which saith, Abraham believed God, *and it was imputed unto him for righteousness, v.* 23. And thus he became the *friend of God.* Faith, producing such works, endeared him to the divine Being, and advanced him to very peculiar favours and intimacies with God. It is a great honour done to Abraham that he is called and counted the friend of God. You see then (*v.* 24) how that *by works a man is justified* (comes into such a state of favour and friendship with God), *and not by faith only:* not by a bare opinion, or profession, or believing without obeying, but by having such a faith as is productive of good works. Now besides the explication of this passage and example, as thus illustrating and supporting the argument James is upon, many other useful lessons may be learned by us from what is here said concerning Abraham. [1.] Those who would have Abraham's blessings must be careful to copy after his faith: to boast of being Abraham's seed will not avail any, if they do not believe as he did. [2.] Those works which evidence true faith must be works of self-denial, and such as

God himself commands (as Abraham's offering up his son, his only son, was), and not such works as are pleasing to flesh and blood and may serve our interest, or are the mere fruits of our own imagination and devising. [3.] What we piously purpose and sincerely resolve to do for God is accepted as if actually performed. Thus Abraham is regarded as offering up his son, though he did not actually proceed to make a sacrifice of him. It was a done thing in the mind, and spirit, and resolution of Abraham, and God accepts it as if fully performed and accomplished. [4.] The actings of faith make it grow perfect, as the truth of faith makes it act. [5.] Such an acting faith will make others, as well as Abraham, friends of God. Thus Christ says to his disciples, *I have called you friends*, John xv. 15. All transactions between God and the truly believing soul are easy, pleasant, and delightful. There is one will and one heart, and there is a mutual complacency. *God rejoiceth over those* who truly believe, to do them good; and they delight themselves in him.

(2.) The second example of faith's justifying itself and us with and by works is Rahab: *Likewise also was not Rahab the harlot justified by works, when she had received the messengers, and had sent them out another way? v.* 25. The former instance was of one renowned for his faith all his life long. This is of one noted for sin, whose faith was meaner and of a much lower degree; so that the strongest faith will not do, nor the meanest be allowed to go without works. Some say that the word here rendered *harlot* was the proper name of Rahab. Others tell us that it signifies no more than a *hostess*, or one who keeps a public house, with whom therefore the spies lodged. But it is very probable that her character was infamous; and such an instance is mentioned to show that faith will save the worst, when evidenced by proper works; and it will not save the best without such works as God requires. This Rahab believed the report she had heard of God's powerful presence with Israel; but that which proved her faith sincere was, that, to the hazard of her life, she *received the messengers, and sent them out another way*. Observe here, [1.] The wonderful power of faith in transforming and changing sinners. [2.] The regard which an operative faith meets with from God, to obtain his mercy and favour. [3.] Where great sins are pardoned, there must be great acts of self-denial. Rahab must prefer the honour of God and the good of his people before the preservation of her own country. Her former acquaintance must be discarded, her former course of life entirely abandoned, and she must give signal proof and evidence of this before she can be in a justified state; and even after she is justified, yet her former character must be remembered; not so much to her dishonour as to glorify the rich grace and mercy of God. Though justified, she is called *Rahab the harlot.*

7. And now, upon the whole matter, the apostle draws this conclusion, *As the body without the spirit is dead, so faith without works is dead also, v.* 26. These words are read differently; some reading them, *As the body without the breath is dead, so is faith without works:* and then they show that works are the companions of faith, as breathing is of life. Others read them, *As the body without the soul is dead, so faith without works is dead also:* and then they show that as the body has no action, nor beauty, but becomes a loathsome carcase, when the soul is gone, so a bare profession without works is useless, yea, loathsome and offensive. Let us then take heed of running into extremes in this case. For, (1.) The best works, without faith, are dead; they want their root and principle. It is by faith that any thing we do is really good, as done with an eye to God, in obedience to him, and so as to aim principally at his acceptance. (2.) The most plausible profession of faith, without works, is dead: as the root is dead when it produces nothing green, nothing of fruit. Faith is the root, good works are the fruits, and we must see to it that we have both. We must not think that either, without the other, will justify and save us. This is the grace of God wherein we stand, and we should stand to it.

CHAP. III.

The apostle here reproves ambition, and an arrogant magisterial tongue; and shows the duty and advantage of bridling it because of its power to do mischief. Those who profess religion ought especially to govern their tongues, ver. 1—12. True wisdom makes men meek, and avoiders of strife and envy: and hereby it may easily be distinguished from a wisdom that is earthly and hypocritical, ver. 13, to the end.

MY brethren, be not many masters, knowing that we shall
receive the greater condemnation. 2
For in many things we offend all. If
any man offend not in word, the same
is a perfect man, *and* able also to
bridle the whole body. 3 Behold,
we put bits in the horses' mouths,
that they may obey us; and we turn
about their whole body. 4 Behold
also the ships, which though *they be*
so great, and *are* driven of fierce
winds, yet are they turned about with
a very small helm, whithersoever the
governor listeth. 5 Even so the
tongue is a little member, and boasteth great things. Behold, how great
a matter a little fire kindleth! 6 And
the tongue *is* a fire, a world of
iniquity: so is the tongue among our
members, that it defileth the whole
body, and setteth on fire the course
of nature; and it is set on fire of hell.
7 For every kind of beasts, and of

birds, and of serpents, and of things
in the sea, is tamed, and hath been
tamed of mankind: 8 But the tongue
can no man tame; *it is* an unruly
evil, full of deadly poison. 9 Therewith bless we God, even the Father;
and therewith curse we men, which
are made after the similitude of God.
10 Out of the same mouth proceedeth
blessing and cursing. My brethren,
these things ought not so to be. 11
Doth a fountain send forth at the
same place sweet *water* and bitter?
12 Can the fig tree, my brethren, bear
olive berries? either a vine, figs? so
can no fountain both yield salt water
and fresh.

The foregoing chapter shows how unprofitable and dead faith is without works. It is plainly intimated by what this chapter first goes upon that such a faith is, however, apt to make men conceited and magisterial in their tempers and their talk. Those who set up faith in the manner the former chapter condemns are most apt to run into those sins of the tongue which this chapter condemns. And indeed the best need to be cautioned against a dictating, censorious, mischievous use of their tongues. We are therefore taught,

I. Not to use our tongues so as to lord it over others: *My brethren, be not many masters,* &c., *v.* 1. These words do not forbid doing what we can to direct and instruct others in the way of their duty or to reprove them in a Christian way for what is amiss; but we must not affect to speak and act as those who are continually assuming the chair, we must not prescribe to one another, so as to make our own sentiments a standard by which to try all others, because God gives various gifts to men, and expects from each according to that measure of light which he gives. "Therefore be not many *masters*" (or *teachers,* as some read it); "do not give yourselves the air of teachers, imposers, and judges, but rather speak with the humility and spirit of learners; do not censure one another, as if all must be brought to your standard." This is enforced by two reasons. 1. Those who thus set up for judges and censurers *shall receive the greater condemnation.* Our judging others will but make our own judgment the more strict and severe, Matt. vii. 1, 2. Those who are curious to spy out the faults of others, and arrogant in passing censures upon them, may expect that God will be as extreme in marking what they say and do amiss. 2. Another reason given against such acting the master is because we are all sinners: *In many things we offend all, v.* 2. Were we to think more of our own mistakes and offences, we should be less apt to judge other people. While we are severe against what we count offensive in others, we do not consider how much there is in us which is justly offensive to them. Self-justifiers are commonly self-deceivers. We are all guilty before God; and those who vaunt it over the frailties and infirmities of others little think how many things they offend in themselves. Nay, perhaps their magisterial deportment, and censorious tongues, may prove worse than any faults they condemn in others. Let us learn to be severe in judging ourselves, but charitable in our judgments of other people.

II. We are taught to govern our tongue so as to prove ourselves perfect and upright men, and such as have an entire government over ourselves: *If any man offend not in word, the same is a perfect man, and able also to bridle the whole body.* It is here implied that he whose conscience is affected by tongue-sins, and who takes care to avoid them, is an upright man, and has an undoubted sign of true grace. But, on the other hand, *if a man seemeth to be religious* (as was declared in the first chapter) *and bridleth not his tongue,* whatever profession he makes, *that man's religion is vain.* Further, he that offends not in word will not only prove himself a sincere Christian, but a very much advanced and improved Christian. For the wisdom and grace which enable him to rule his tongue will enable him also to rule all his actions. This we have illustrated by two comparisons:—1. The governing and guiding of all the motions of a horse, by the bit which is put into his mouth: *Behold, we put bits into the horses' mouths, that they may obey us, and we turn about their whole body, v.* 3. There is a great deal of brutish fierceness and wantonness in us. This shows itself very much by the tongue: so that this must be bridled; according to Ps. xxxix. 1, *I will keep my mouth with a bridle* (or, *I will bridle my mouth*) *while the wicked is before me.* The more quick and lively the tongue is, the more should we thus take care to govern it. Otherwise, as an unruly and ungovernable horse runs away with his rider, or throws him, so an unruly tongue will serve those in like manner who have no command over it. Whereas, let resolution and watchfulness, under the influence of the grace of God, bridle the tongue, and then all the motions and actions of the whole body will be easily guided and overruled. 2. The governing of a ship by the right management of the helm: *Behold also the ships, which though they are so great, and are driven of fierce winds, yet are they turned about with a very small helm whithersoever the governor listeth. Even so the tongue is a little member, and boasteth great things, v.* 4, 5. As the helm is a very small part of the ship, so is the tongue a very small part of the body: but the right governing of the helm or rudder will steer and turn the ship as the governor pleases; and a right management of the tongue is, in a great measure, the government of the whole man. There is a wonderful beauty in these comparisons, to show how things of small bulk may yet be of vast use. And hence we should learn to make the due management of our tongues more our study, because, though they are little members, they are capable of doing a great deal of good or a great deal of hurt. Therefore,

III. We are taught to dread an unruly tongue as one of the greatest and most pernicious evils. It is compared to a little fire placed among a great deal of combustible matter, which soon raises a flame and consumes all before it: *Behold, how great a matter a little fire kindleth! And the tongue is a fire, a world of iniquity,* &c., *v.* 5, 6. There is such an abundance of sin in the tongue that it may be called *a world of iniquity.* How many defilements does it occasion! How many and dreadful flames does it kindle! *So is the tongue among the members that it defileth the whole body.* Observe hence, There is a great pollution and defilement in sins of the tongue. Defiling passions are kindled, vented, and cherished by this unruly member. And the whole body is often drawn into sin and guilt by the tongue. Therefore Solomon says, *Suffer not thy mouth to cause thy flesh to sin,* Eccles. v. 6. The snares into which men are sometimes led by the tongue are insufferable to themselves and destructive of others. *It setteth on fire the course of nature.* The affairs of mankind and of societies are often thrown into confusion, and all is on a flame, by the tongues of men. Some read it, *all our generations are set on fire by the tongue.* There is no age of the world, nor any condition of life, private or public, but will afford examples of this. *And it is set on fire of hell.* Observe hence, Hell has more to do in promoting the fire of the tongue than men are generally aware of. It is from some diabolical temptations, and to serve some diabolical designs, that men's tongues are inflamed. The devil is expressly called a liar, a murderer, an accuser of the brethren; and, whenever men's tongues are employed in any of these ways, they are set on fire of hell. The Holy Ghost indeed once descended in *cloven tongues as of fire,* Acts ii. And, where the tongue is thus guided and wrought upon by a fire from heaven, there it kindleth good thoughts, holy affections, and ardent devotions. But when it is set on fire of hell, as in all undue heats it is, there it is mischievous, producing rage and hatred, and those things which serve the purposes of the devil. As therefore you would dread fires and flames, you should dread contentions, revilings, slanders, lies, and every thing that would kindle the fire of wrath in your own spirit or in the spirits of others. But,

IV. We are next taught how very difficult a thing it is to govern the tongue: *For every kind of beasts, and of birds, and of serpents, and of things in the sea, is tamed, and hath been tamed, of mankind. But the tongue can no man tame, v.* 7, 8. As if the apostle had said, "Lions, and the most savage beasts, as well as horses and camels, and creatures of the greatest strength, have been tamed and governed by men: so have birds, notwithstanding their wildness and timorousness, and their wings to bear them up continually out of our reach: even serpents, notwithstanding all their venom and all their cunning, have been made familiar and harmless: and things in the sea have been taken by men, and made serviceable to them. And these creatures have not been subdued nor tamed by miracle only (as the lions crouched to Daniel, instead of devouring him, and ravens fed Elijah, and a whale carried Jonah through the depths of the sea to dry land), but what is here spoken of is something commonly done; not only hath been tamed, but is tamed of mankind. Yet the tongue is worse than these, and cannot be tamed by the power and art which serves to tame these things. No man can tame the tongue without supernatural grace and assistance." The apostle does not intend to represent it as a thing impossible, but as a thing extremely difficult, which therefore will require great watchfulness, and pains, and prayer, to keep it in due order. And sometimes all is too little; *for it is an unruly evil, full of deadly poison.* Brute creatures may be kept within certain bounds, they may be managed by certain rules, and even serpents may be so used as to do no hurt with all their poison; but the tongue is apt to break through all bounds and rules, and to spit out its poison on one occasion or other, notwithstanding the utmost care. So that not only does it need to be watched, and guarded, and governed, as much as an unruly beast, or a hurtful and poisonous creature, but much more care and pains will be needful to prevent the mischievous outbreakings and effects of the tongue. However,

V. We are taught to think of the use we make of our tongues in religion and in the service of God, and by such a consideration to keep it from cursing, censuring, and every thing that is evil on other occasions: *Therewith bless we God, even the Father; and therewith curse we men, who are made after the similitude of God. Out of the same mouth proceed blessing and cursing. My brethren, these things ought not so to be, v.* 9, 10. How absurd is it that those who use their tongues in prayer and praise should ever use them in cursing, slandering, and the like! If we bless God as our Father, it should teach us to speak well of, and kindly to, all who bear his image. That tongue which addresses with reverence the divine Being cannot, without the greatest inconsistency, turn upon fellow-creatures with reviling brawling language. It is said of the seraphim that praise God, they *dare not bring a railing accusation.* And for men to reproach those who have not only the image of God in their natural faculties, but are renewed after the image of God by the grace of the gospel: this is a most shameful contradiction to all their pretensions of honouring the great Original. *These things ought not so to be;* and, if such considerations were always at hand, surely they would not be. Piety is disgraced in all the shows of it, if there be not charity. That tongue confutes itself which one while pretends to adore the perfections of God, and to refer all things to him, and another while will condemn even good men if they do not just come up to the same words or expressions used by it. Further, to fix this thought, the apostle shows that contrary effects from the same causes are monstrous, and not to be found in nature, and therefore cannot be consistent with grace: *Doth a fountain send forth at the same place sweet water and bitter? Can the fig-tree bear olive-berries, or a vine, figs? Or doth the same spring yield both salt water and fresh? v.* 11, 12. True religion will not admit of contradictions; and a truly religious man can never allow of them either in his words or his actions. How many sins would this prevent, and recover men from, to put them upon being always consistent with themselves!

13 Who *is* a wise man and endued
with knowledge among you? let him
show out of a good conversation his
works with meekness of wisdom. 14
But if ye have bitter envying and
strife in your hearts, glory not, and
lie not against the truth. 15 This
wisdom descendeth not from above,
but *is* earthly, sensual, devilish. 16
For where envying and strife *is*, there
is confusion and every evil work.
17 But the wisdom that is from above
is first pure, then peaceable, gentle,
and easy to be entreated, full of mercy
and good fruits, without hypocrisy.
18 And the fruit of righteousness is
sown in peace of them that make peace.

As the sins before condemned arise from an affectation of being thought more wise than others, and being endued with more knowledge than they, so the apostle in these verses shows the difference between men's pretending to be wise and their being really so, and between the wisdom which is from beneath (from earth or hell) and that which is from above.

I. We have some account of true wisdom, with the distinguishing marks and fruits of it: *Who is a wise man, and endued with knowledge among you? Let him show out of a good conversation his works with meekness of wisdom, v.* 13. A truly wise man is a very knowing man: he will not set up for the reputation of being wise without laying in a good stock of knowledge; and he will not value himself merely upon knowing things, if he has not wisdom to make a right application and use of that knowledge. These two things must be put together to make up the account of true wisdom: who is wise, and endued with knowledge? Now where this is the happy case of any there will be these following things:—1. A good conversation. If we are wiser than others, this should be evidenced by the goodness of our conversation, not by the roughness or vanity of it. Words that inform, and heal, and do good, are the marks of wisdom; not those that look great, and do mischief, and are the occasions of evil, either in ourselves or others. 2. True wisdom may be known by its works. The conversation here does not refer only to words, but to the whole of men's practice; therefore it is said, Let him show out of a good conversation his works. True wisdom does not lie in good notions or speculations so much as in good and useful actions. Not he who thinks well, or he who talks well, is in the sense of the scripture allowed to be wise, if he do not live and act well. 3. True wisdom may be known by the meekness of the spirit and temper: *Let him show with meekness,* &c. It is a great instance of wisdom prudently to bridle our own anger, and patiently to bear the anger of others. And as wisdom will evidence itself in meekness, so meekness will be a great friend to wisdom; for nothing hinders the regular apprehension, the solid judgment, and impartiality of thought, necessary to our acting wisely, so much as passion. When we are mild and calm, we are best able to hear reason, and best able to speak it. Wisdom produces meekness, and meekness increases wisdom.

II. We have the glorying of those taken away who are of a contrary character to that now mentioned, and their wisdom exposed in all its boasts and productions: "*If you have bitter envying and strife in your hearts, glory not,* &c., *v.* 14—16. Pretend what you will, and think yourselves ever so wise, yet you have abundance of reason to cease your glorying, if you run down love and peace, and give way to bitter envying and strife. Your zeal for truth or orthodoxy, and your boasts of knowing more than others, if you employ these only to make others hateful, and to show your own spite and heart-burnings against them, are a shame to your profession of Christianity, and a downright contradiction to it. Lie not thus against the truth." Observe, 1. Envying and strife are opposed to the meekness of wisdom. The heart is the seat of both; but envy and wisdom cannot dwell together in the same heart. Holy zeal and bitter envying are as different as the flames of seraphim and the fire of hell. 2. The order of things here laid down. Envying is first and excites strife; strife endeavours to excuse itself by vain-glorying and lying; and then (*v.* 16) hereupon ensue confusion and every evil work. Those who live in malice, envy, and contention, live in confusion, and are liable to be provoked and hurried to any evil work. Such disorders raise many temptations, strengthen temptations, and involve men in a great deal of guilt. One sin begets another, and it cannot be imagined how much mischief is produced: *there* is every evil work. And is such wisdom as produces these effects to be gloried in? This cannot be without giving the lie to Christianity, and pretending that this wisdom is what it is not. For observe, 3. Whence such wisdom cometh: *It descendeth not from above,* but ariseth from beneath; and, to speak plainly, it is *earthly, sensual, devilish, v.* 15. It springs from earthly principles, acts upon earthly motives, and is intent upon serving earthly purposes. It is sensual, indulging the flesh, and making provision to fulfil the lusts and desires of it. Or, according to the original word, ψυχικὴ, it is animal or human—the mere working of natural reason, without any supernatural light. And it is devilish, such wisdom being the wisdom of devils (to create uneasiness and to do hurt), and being inspired by devils, whose condemnation is pride (1 Tim. iii. 6), and who are noted in other places of scripture for their wrath, and their accusing the brethren. And therefore those who are lifted up with such wisdom as this must fall into the condemnation of the devil.

III. We have the lovely picture of that wisdom which is from above more fully drawn, and set in opposition to this which is from beneath: *But the wisdom that is from above is first pure, then peaceable,* &c., *v.* 17, 18. Observe here, True wisdom is God's gift. It is not gained by conversing with men, nor by the knowledge of the world (as some think and speak), but it comes from above. It consists of these several things:—1. It is pure, without mixture of maxims or aims that would debase it: and it is free from iniquity and defilements, not allowing of any known sin, but studious of holiness both in heart and life. 2. The wisdom that is from above is peaceable. Peace follows purity, and depends upon it. Those who are truly wise do what they can to preserve peace, that it may not be broken; and to make peace, that where it is lost it may be restored. In kingdoms, in families, in churches, in all societies, and in all interviews and transactions, heavenly wisdom makes men peaceable. 3. It is gentle, not standing upon extreme right in matters of property; not saying nor doing any thing rigorous in points of censure; not being furious about opinions, urging our own beyond their weight nor theirs who oppose us beyond their intention; not being rude and overbearing in conversation, nor harsh and cruel in temper. Gentleness may thus be opposed to all these. 4. Heavenly wisdom is *easy to be entreated,* εὐπειθὴς· it is very *persuadable,* either to what is good or from what is evil. There is an easiness that is weak and faulty; but it is not a blamable easiness to yield ourselves to the persuasions of God's word, and to all just and reasonable counsels or requests of our fellow-creatures; no, nor to give up a dispute, where there appears a good reason for it and where a good end may be answered by it. 5. Heavenly wisdom is full of mercy and good fruits, inwardly disposed to every thing that is kind and good, both to relieve those who want and to forgive those who offend, and actually to do this whenever proper occasions offer. 6. Heavenly wisdom is without partiality. The original word, ἀδιάκριτος, signifies to be without suspicion, or free from judging, making no undue surmises nor differences in our conduct towards one person more than another. The margin reads it, *without wrangling,* not acting the part of sectaries, and disputing merely for the sake of a party; nor censuring others purely on account of their differing from us. The wisest men are least apt to be censurers. 7. That wisdom which is from above is without hypocrisy. It has no disguises nor deceits. It cannot fall in with those managements which the world counts wise, which are crafty and guileful; but it is sincere and open, steady and uniform, and consistent with itself. O that you and I may always be guided by such wisdom as this! that with Paul we may be able to say, *Not with fleshly wisdom, but in simplicity and godly sincerity, by the grace of God, we have our conversation.* And then, *lastly,* true wisdom will go on to sow the fruits of righteousness in peace, and thus, if it may be, to make peace in the world, *v.* 18. And that which is sown in peace will produce a harvest of joys. Let others reap the fruits of contentions, and all the advantages they can propose to themselves by them; but let us go on peaceably to sow the seeds of righteousness, and we may depend upon it our labour will not be lost. *For light is sown for the righteous, and gladness for the upright in heart; and the work of righteousness shall be peace, and the effect of righteousness quietness and assurance for ever.*

CHAP. IV.

In this chapter we are directed to consider, I. Some causes of contention, besides those mentioned in the foregoing chapter, and to watch against them, ver. 1—5. II. We are taught to abandon the friendship of this world, so as to submit and subject ourselves entirely to God, ver. 4—10. III. All detraction and rash judgment of others are to be carefully avoided, ver. 11, 12. IV. We must preserve a constant regard, and pay the utmost deference to the disposals of divine Providence, ver. 13, to the end.

FROM whence *come* wars and
fightings among you? *come they*
not hence, *even* of your lusts that war
in your members? 2 Ye lust, and
have not: ye kill, and desire to have,
and cannot obtain: ye fight and war,
yet ye have not, because ye ask not.
3 Ye ask, and receive not, because
ye ask amiss, that ye may consume *it*

upon your lusts. 4 Ye adulterers
and adulteresses, know ye not that
the friendship of the world is enmity
with God? whosoever therefore will
be a friend of the world is the enemy
of God. 5 Do ye think that the
scripture saith in vain, The spirit that
dwelleth in us lusteth to envy? 6
But he giveth more grace. Wherefore
he saith, God resisteth the proud, but
giveth grace unto the humble. 7
Submit yourselves therefore to God.
Resist the devil, and he will flee from
you. 8 Draw nigh to God, and he
will draw nigh to you. Cleanse *your*
hands, *ye* sinners; and purify *your*
hearts, *ye* double minded. 9 Be
afflicted, and mourn, and weep: let
your laughter be turned to mourning,
and *your* joy to heaviness. 10 Humble yourselves in the sight of the
Lord, and he shall lift you up.

The former chapter speaks of envying one another, as the great spring of strifes and contentions; this chapter speaks of a lust after worldly things, and a setting too great a value upon worldly pleasures and friendships, as that which carried their divisions to a shameful height.

I. The apostle here reproves the Jewish Christians for their wars, and for their lusts as the cause of them: *Whence come wars and fightings among you? Come they not hence, even of your lusts that war in your members, v.* 1. The Jews were a very seditious people, and had therefore frequent wars with the Romans; and they were a very quarrelsome divided people, often fighting among themselves; and many of those corrupt Christians against whose errors and vices this epistle was written seem to have fallen in with the common quarrels. Hereupon, our apostle informs them that the origin of their wars and fightings was not (as they pretended) a true zeal for their country, and for the honour of God, but that their prevailing lusts were the cause of all. Observe hence, What is sheltered and shrouded under a specious pretence of zeal for God and religion often comes from men's pride, malice, covetousness, ambition, and revenge. The Jews had many struggles with the Roman power before they were entirely destroyed. They often unnecessarily embroiled themselves, and then fell into parties and factions about the different methods of managing their wars with their common enemies; and hence it came to pass that, when their cause might be supposed good, yet their engaging in it and their management of it came from a bad principle. Their worldly and fleshly lusts raised and managed their wars and fightings; but one would think here is enough said to subdue those lusts; for, 1. They make a war within as well as fightings without. Impetuous passions and desires first war in their members, and then raise feuds in their nation. There is war between conscience and corruption, and there is war also between one corruption and another, and from these contentions in themselves arose their quarrels with each other. Apply this to private cases, and may we not then say of fightings and strifes among relations and neighbours that they come from those lusts which war in the members? From lust of power and dominion, lust of pleasure, or lust of riches, from some one or more of these lusts arise all the broils and contentions that are in the world; and, since all wars and fightings come from the corruptions of our own hearts, it is therefore the right method for the cure of contention to lay the axe to the root, and mortify those lusts that war in the members. 2. It should kill these lusts to think of their disappointment: "*You lust, and have not; you kill, and desire to have, and cannot obtain, v.* 2. You covet great things for yourselves, and you think to obtain them by your victories over the Romans or by suppressing this and the other party among yourselves. You think you shall secure great pleasures and happiness to yourselves, by overthrowing every thing which thwarts your eager wishes; but, alas! you are losing your labour and your blood, while you kill one another with such views as these." Inordinate desires are either totally disappointed, or they are not to be appeased and satisfied by obtaining the things desired. The words here rendered *cannot obtain* signify cannot gain the happiness sought after. Note hence, Worldly and fleshly lusts are the distemper which will not allow of contentment or satisfaction in the mind. 3. Sinful desires and affections generally exclude prayer, and the working of our desires towards God: "*You fight and war, yet you have not, because you ask not.* You fight, and do not succeed, because you do not pray· you do not consult God in your undertakings, whether he will allow of them or not; and you do not commit your way to him, and make known your requests to him, but follow your own corrupt views and inclinations: therefore you meet with continual disappointments;" or else, 4. "Your lusts spoil your prayers, and make them an abomination to God, whenever you put them up to him, *v.* 3. *You ask, and receive not, because you ask amiss, that you may consume it upon your lusts.*" As if it had been said, "Though perhaps you may sometimes pray for success against your enemies, yet it is not your aim to improve the advantages you gain, so as to promote true piety and religion either in yourselves or others; but pride, vanity, luxury, and sensuality, are what you would serve by your successes, and by your very prayers. You want to live in great power and plenty, in voluptuousness and a sensual prosperity; and thus you disgrace devotion and dishonour God by such gross and base ends; and therefore your prayers are rejected." Let us learn hence, in the management of all our worldly affairs, and in our prayers to God for success in them, to see that our ends be right. When men follow their worldly business (suppose them tradesmen or husbandmen), and ask of God prosperity, but do not receive what they ask for, it is because they ask with wrong aims and intentions. They ask God to give them success in their callings or undertakings; not that they may glorify their heavenly Father and do good with what they have, but that they may *consume it upon their lusts*—that they may be enabled to eat better meat, and drink better drink, and wear better clothes, and so gratify their pride, vanity, and voluptuousness. But, if we thus seek the things of this world, it is just in God to deny them; whereas, if we seek any thing that we may serve God with it, we may expect he will either give us what we seek or give us hearts to be content without it, and give opportunities of serving and glorifying him some other way. Let us remember this, that when we speed not in our prayers it is *because we ask amiss;* either we do not ask for right ends or not in a right manner, not with faith or not with fervency: unbelieving and cold desires beg denials; and this we may be sure of, that, when our prayers are rather the language of our lusts than of our graces, they will return empty.

II. We have fair warning to avoid all criminal friendships with this world: *You adulterers and adulteresses, know you not that the friendship of the world is enmity with God? v.* 4. Worldly people are here called adulterers and adulteresses, because of their perfidiousness to God, while they give their best affections to the world. Covetousness is elsewhere called idolatry, and it is here called adultery; it is a forsaking of him to whom we are devoted and espoused, to cleave to other things; there is this brand put upon worldly-mindedness—that it is enmity to God. A man may have a competent portion of the good things of this life, and yet may keep himself in the love of God; but he who sets his heart upon the world, who places his happiness in it, and will conform himself to it, and do any thing rather than lose its friendship, he is an enemy to God; it is constructive treason and rebellion against God to set the world upon his throne in our hearts. *Whosoever therefore is the friend of the world is the enemy of God.* He who will act upon this principle, to keep the smiles of the world, and to have its continual friendship, cannot but show himself, in spirit, and in his actions too, an enemy to God. *You cannot serve God and mammon,* Matt. vi. 24. Hence arise wars and fightings, even from this adulterous idolatrous love of the world, and serving of it; for what peace can there be among men, so long as there is enmity towards God? or who can fight against God, and prosper? "Think seriously with yourselves what the spirit of the world is, and you will find that you cannot suit yourselves to it as friends, but it must occasion your being envious, and full of evil inclinations, as the generality of the world are. *Do you think that the scripture saith in vain, The spirit that dwelleth in us lusteth to envy?*" *v.* 5. The account given in the holy scriptures of the hearts of men by nature is *that their imagination is evil, only evil, and that continually,* Gen. vi. 5. Natural corruption principally shows itself by envying, and there is a continual propensity to this. The spirit which naturally dwells in man is always producing one evil imagination or another, always emulating such as we see and converse with and seeking those things which are possessed and enjoyed by them. Now this way of the world, affecting pomp and pleasure, and falling into strifes and quarrels for the sake of these things, is the certain consequence of being friends to the world; for there is no friendship without a oneness of spirit, and therefore Christians, to avoid contentions, must avoid the friendship of the world, and must show that they are actuated by nobler principles and that a nobler spirit dwells in them; for, if we belong to God, he gives more grace than to live and act as the generality of the world do. The spirit of the world teaches men to be churls; God teaches them to be bountiful. The spirit of the world teaches us to lay up, or lay out, for ourselves, and according to our own fancies; God teaches us to be willing to communicate to the necessities and to the comfort of others, and so as to do good to all about us, according to our ability. The grace of God is contrary to the spirit of the world, and therefore the friendship of the world is to be avoided, if we pretend to be friends of God: yea, the grace of God will correct and cure the spirit that naturally dwells in us; where he giveth grace, he giveth another spirit than that of the world.

III. We are taught to observe the difference God makes between pride and humility. *God resisteth the proud, but giveth grace unto the humble, v.* 6. This is represented as the language of scripture in the Old Testament; for so it is declared in the book of *Psalms that God will save the afflicted people* (if their spirits be suited to their condition), *but will bring down high looks* (Ps. xviii. 27); and in the book of Proverbs it is said, *He scorneth the scorners, and giveth grace unto the lowly,* Prov. iii. 34. Two things are here to be observed:—1. The disgrace cast upon the proud: God resists them; the original word, ἀντιτάσσεται, signifies, God's setting himself as in battle array against them; and can there be a greater disgrace than for God to proclaim a man a rebel, an enemy, a traitor to his crown and dignity, and to proceed against him as such? The proud resists God; in his understanding he resists the truths of God; in his will he resists the laws of God; in his passions he resists the providence of God; and therefore no wonder that God sets himself against the proud. Let proud spirits hear this and tremble—*God resists them.* Who can describe the wretched state of those who make God their enemy? He will certainly fill with shame (sooner or later) the faces of such as have filled their hearts with pride. We should therefore resist pride in our hearts, if we would not have God to resist us. 2. The honour and help God gives to the humble. Grace, as opposed to disgrace, is honour; this God gives to the humble; and, where God gives grace to be humble, there he will give all other graces, and, as in the beginning of this sixth verse, he will *give more grace.* Wherever God gives true grace, he will give more; for to him that hath, and useth what he hath aright, more shall be given. He will especially give more grace to the humble, because they see their need of it, will pray for it and be thankful for it; and such shall have it. For this reason,

IV. We are taught to submit ourselves entirely to God: *Submit yourselves therefore to God. Resist the devil, and he will flee from you, v.* 7. Christians should forsake the friendship of the world, and watch against that envy and pride which they see prevailing in natural men, and should by grace learn to glory in their submissions to God. "Submit yourselves to him as subjects to their prince, in duty, and as one friend to another, in love and interest. Submit your understandings to the truths of God; submit your wills to the will of God, the will of his precept, the will of his providence." We are subjects, and as such must be submissive; not only through fear, but through love; *not only for wrath, but also for conscience' sake.* "Submit yourselves to God, as considering how many ways you are bound to this, and as considering what advantage you will gain by it; for God will not hurt you by his dominion over you, but will do you good." Now, as this subjection and submission to God are what the devil most industriously strives to hinder, so we ought with great care and steadiness to resist his suggestions. If he would represent a tame yielding to the will and providence of God as what will bring calamities, and expose to contempt and misery, we must resist these suggestions of fear. If he would represent submission to God as a hindrance to our outward ease, or worldly preferments, we must resist these suggestions of pride and sloth. If he would tempt us to lay any of our miseries, and crosses, and afflictions, to the charge of Providence, so that we might avoid them by following his directions instead of God's, we must resist these provocations to anger, *not fretting ourselves in any wise to do evil.* "Let not the devil, in these or the like attempts, prevail upon you; but *resist him and he will flee from you.*" If we basely yield to temptations, the devil will continually follow us; but if we *put on the whole armour of God,* and stand it out against him, he will be gone from us. Resolution shuts and bolts the door against temptation.

V. We are directed how to act towards God, in our becoming submissive to him, *v.* 8—10. 1. *Draw nigh to God.* The heart that has rebelled must be brought to the foot of God; the spirit that was distant and estranged from a life of communion and converse with God must become acquainted with him: "*Draw nigh to God,* in his worship and institutions, and in every duty he requires of you." 2. *Cleanse your hands.* He who comes unto God must have clean hands. Paul therefore directs to *lift up holy hands without wrath and doubting* (1 Tim. ii. 8), hands free from blood, and bribes, and every thing that is unjust or cruel, and free from every defilement of sin: he is not subject to God who is a servant of sin. The hands must be cleansed by faith, repentance, and reformation, or it will be in vain for us to draw nigh to God in prayer, or in any of the exercises of devotion. 3. The hearts of the double-minded must be purified. Those who halt between God and the world are here meant by *the double-minded.* To *purify the heart* is to be sincere, and to act upon this single aim and principle, rather to please God than to seek after any thing in this world: hypocrisy is heart-impurity; but those who submit themselves to God aright will purify their hearts as well as cleanse their hands. 4. *Be aifflcted, and mourn, and weep.* "What afflictions God sends take them as he would have you, and be duly sensible of them. Be afflicted when afflictions are sent upon you, and do not despise them; or be afflicted in your sympathies with those who are so, and in laying to heart the calamities of the church of God. Mourn and weep for your own sins and the sins of others; times of contention and division are times to mourn in, and the sins that occasion wars and fightings should be mourned for. *Let your laughter be turned to mourning and your joy to heaviness.*" This may be taken either as a prediction of sorrow or a prescription of seriousness. Let men think to set grief at defiance, yet God can bring it upon them; none laugh so heartily but he can turn their laughter into mourning; and this the unconcerned Christians James wrote to are threatened should be their case. They are therefore directed, before things come to the worst, to lay aside their vain mirth and their sensual pleasures, that they might indulge godly sorrow and penitential tears. 5. "*Humble yourselves in the sight of the Lord.* Let the inward acts of the soul be suitable to all those outward expressions of grief, affliction, and sorrow, before mentioned." Humility of spirit is here required, as in the sight of him who looks principally at the spirits of men. "Let there be a thorough humiliation in bewailing every thing that is evil; let there be great humility in doing that which is good: *Humble yourselves.*"

VI. We have great encouragement to act thus towards God: *He will draw nigh to those that draw nigh to him* (*v.* 8), *and he will lift up* those who humble themselves in his sight, *v.* 10. Those that draw nigh to God in a way of duty shall find God drawing nigh to them in a way of mercy. Draw nigh to him in faith, and trust, and obedience, and he will draw nigh to you for your deliverance. If there be not a close communion between God and us, it is our fault, and not his. *He shall lift up the humble.* Thus much our Lord himself declared, *He that shall humble himself shall be exalted,* Matt. xxiii. 12. If we be truly penitent and humble under the marks of God's displeasure, we shall in a little time know the advantages of his favour; he will lift us up out of trouble, or he will lift us up in our spirits and comforts under trouble; he will lift us up to honour and safety in the world, or he will lift us up in our way to heaven, so as to raise our hearts and affections above the world. *God will revive the spirit of the humble* (Isa. lvii. 15), *He will hear the desire of the humble* (Ps. x. 17), and he will at last lift them up to glory. *Before honour is humility.* The highest honour in heaven will be the reward of the greatest humility on earth.

11 Speak not evil one of another,
brethren. He that speaketh evil of
his brother, and judgeth his brother,
speaketh evil of the law, and judgeth
the law: but if thou judge the law,
thou art not a doer of the law, but a
judge. 12 There is one lawgiver, who
is able to save and to destroy: who
art thou that judgest another? 13
Go to now, ye that say, To day or to
morrow we will go into such a city,
and continue there a year, and buy
and sell, and get gain: 14 Whereas ye
know not what *shall be* on the
morrow. For what *is* your life? It is
even a vapour, that appeareth for a
little time, and then vanisheth away.
5 For that ye *ought* to say, If the
Lord will, we shall live, and do this,
or that. 16 But now ye rejoice in
your boastings: all such rejoicing is
evil. 17 Therefore to him that
knoweth to do good, and doeth *it*
not, to him it is sin.

In this part of the chapter,

I. We are cautioned against the sin of evil-speaking: *Speak not evil one of another, brethren, v.* 11. The Greek word, καταλαλεῖτε, signifies speaking any thing that may hurt or injure another; we must not speak evil things of others, though they be true, unless we be called to it, and there be some necessary occasion for it; much less must we report evil things when they are false, or, for aught we know, may be so. Our lips must be guided by the law of kindness, as well as truth and justice. This, which Solomon makes a necessary part of the character of his virtuous woman, *that she openeth her mouth with wisdom, and in her tongue is the law of kindness* (Prov. xxxi. 26), must needs be a part of the character of every true Christian. *Speak not evil one of another,* 1. Because you are brethren. The compellation, as used by the apostle here, carries an argument along with it. Since Christians are brethren, they should not defile nor defame one another. It is required of us that we be tender of the good name of our brethren; where we cannot speak well, we had better say nothing than speak evil; we must not take pleasure in making known the faults of others, divulging things that are secret, merely to expose them, nor in making more of their known faults than really they deserve, and, least of all, in making false stories, and spreading things concerning them of which they are altogether innocent. What is this but to raise the hatred and encourage the persecutions of the world, against those who are engaged in the same interests with ourselves, and therefore with whom we ourselves must stand or fall? "Consider, you are brethren." 2. Because this is to judge the law: *He that speaketh evil of his brother, and judgeth his brother, speaketh evil of the law, and judgeth the law.* The law of Moses says, *Thou shalt not go up and down as a tale-bearer among thy people,* Lev. xix. 16. The law of Christ is, *Judge not, that you be not judged,* Matt. vii. 1. The sum and substance of both is that men should love one another. A detracting tongue therefore condemns the law of God, and the commandment of Christ, when it is defaming its neighbour. To break God's commandments is in effect to speak evil of them, and to judge them, as if they were too strict, and laid too great a restraint upon us. The Christians to whom James wrote were apt to speak very hard things of one another, because of their differences about indifferent things (such as *the observance of meats and days,* as appears from Rom. xiv.): "Now," says the apostle, "he who censures and condemns his brother for not agreeing with him in those things which the law of God has left indifferent thereby censures and condemns the law, as if it had done ill in leaving them indifferent. He who quarrels with his brother, and condemns him for the sake of any thing not determined in the word of God, does thereby reflect on that word of God, as if it were not a perfect rule. Let us take heed of judging the law, for the law of the Lord is perfect; if men break the law, leave that to judge them; if they do not break it, let us not judge them." This is a heinous evil, because it is to forget our place, that we ought to be doers of the law, and it is to set up ourselves above it, as if we were to be judges of it. He who is guilty of the sin here cautioned against is not a doer of the law, but a judge; he assumes an office and a place that do not belong to him, and he will be sure to suffer for his presumption in the end. Those who are most ready to set up for judges of the law generally fail most in their obedience to it. 3. Because God, the Lawgiver, has reserved the power of passing the final sentence on men wholly to himself: *There is one Lawgiver, who is able to save, and to destroy: who art thou that judgest another?* v. 12. Princes and states are not excluded, by what is here said, from making laws; nor are subjects at all encouraged to disobey human laws; but God is still to be acknowledged as the supreme Lawgiver, who only can give law to the conscience, and who alone is to be absolutely obeyed. His right to enact laws is incontestable, because he has such a power to enforce them. He *is able to save, and to destroy*, so as no other can. He has power fully to reward the observance of his laws, and to punish all disobedience; he can save the soul, and make it happy for ever, or he can, after he has killed, cast into hell; and therefore should be feared and obeyed as the great Lawgiver, and all judgment should be committed to him. Since there is one Lawgiver, we may infer that it is not for any man or company of men in the world to pretend to give laws immediately to bind conscience; for that is God's prerogative, which must not be invaded. As the apostle had before warned against being many masters, so here he cautions against being many judges. Let us not prescribe to our brethren, let us not censure and condemn them; it is sufficient that we have the law of God, which is a rule to us all; and therefore we should not set up other rules. Let us not presume to set up our own particular notions and opinions as a rule to all about us; for *there is one Lawgiver*.

II. We are cautioned against a presumptuous confidence of the continuance of our lives, and against forming projects thereupon with assurance of success, *v.* 13, 14. The apostle, having reproved those who were judges and condemners of the law, now reproves such as were disregardful of Providence: *Go to now,* an old way of speaking, designed to engage attention; the Greek word may be rendered, *Behold now*, or "*See, and consider, you that say, To-day or to-morrow we will go into such a city, and continue there a year, and buy and sell, and get gain.* Reflect a little on this way of thinking and talking; call yourselves to account for it." Serious reflection on our words and ways would show us many evils that we are apt, through inadvertency, to run into and continue in. There were some who said of old, as too many say still, *We will go to such a city, and do this or that,* for such a term of time, while all serious regards to the disposals of Providence were neglected. Observe here, 1. How apt worldly and projecting men are to leave God out of their schemes. Where any are set upon earthly things, these have a strange power of engrossing the thoughts of the heart. We should therefore have a care of growing intent or eager in our pursuits after any thing here below. 2. How much of worldly happiness lies in the promises men make to themselves beforehand. Their heads are full of fine visions, as to what they shall do, and be, and enjoy, in some future time, when they can neither be sure of time nor of any of the advantages they promise themselves; therefore observe, 3. How vain a thing it is to look for any thing good in futurity, without the concurrence of Providence. *We will go to such a city* (say they), perhaps to Antioch, or Damascus, or Alexandria, which were then the great places for traffic; but how could they be sure, when they set out, that they should reach any of these cities? Something might possibly stop their way, or call them elsewhere, or cut the thread of life. Many who have set out on a journey have gone to their long home, and never reached their journey's end. But, suppose they should reach the city they designed, how did they know they should continue there? Something might happen to send them back, or to call them thence, and to shorten their stay. Or suppose they should stay the full time they proposed, yet they could not be certain that they should buy and sell there; perhaps they might lie sick there, or they might not meet with those to trade with them that they expected. Yea, suppose they should go to that city, and continue there a year, and should buy and sell, yet they might not get gain; getting of gain in this world is at best but an uncertain thing, and they might probably make more losing bargains than gainful ones. And then, as to all these particulars, the frailty, shortness, and uncertainty of life, ought to check the vanity and presumptuous confidence of such projectors for futurity: *What is your life? It is even a vapour that appeareth for a little time, and then vanisheth away*, *v.* 14. God hath wisely left us in the dark concerning future events, and even concerning the duration of life itself. We *know not what shall be on the morrow;* we may know what we intend to do and to be, but a thousand things may happen to prevent us. We are not sure of life itself, since it is but as a *vapour*, something in appearance, but nothing solid nor certain, easily scattered and gone.

We can fix the hour and minute of the sun's rising and setting to-morrow, but we cannot fix the certain time of a vapour's being scattered; such is our life: *it appears but for a little time, and then vanisheth away;* it vanisheth as to this world, but there is a life that will continue in the other world; and, since this life is so uncertain, it concerns us all to prepare and lay up in store for that to come.

III. We are taught to keep up a constant sense of our dependence on the will of God for life, and all the actions and enjoyments of it: *You ought to say, If the Lord will, we shall live, and do this, or that, v.* 15. The apostle, having reproved them for what was amiss, now directs them how to be and do better: "You ought to say it in your hearts at all times, and with your tongues upon proper occasions, especially in your constant prayers and devotions, that if the Lord will give leave, and if he will own and bless you, you have such and such designs to accomplish." This must be said, not in a slight, formal, and customary way, but so as to think what we say, and so as to be reverent and serious in what we say. It is good to express ourselves thus when we have to do with others, but it is indispensably requisite that we should say this to ourselves in all that we go about. Σὺν Θεῷ—*with the leave and blessing of God,* was used by the Greeks in the beginning of every undertaking. 1. *If the Lord will, we shall live.* We must remember that our times are not in our own hands, but at the disposal of God; we live as long as God appoints, and in the circumstances God appoints, and therefore must be submissive to him, even as to life itself; and then, 2. *If the Lord will, we shall do this or that.* All our actions and designs are under the control of Heaven. Our heads may be filled with cares and contrivances. This and the other thing we may propose to do for ourselves, or our families, or our friends; but Providence sometimes breaks all our measures, and throws our schemes into confusion. Therefore both our counsels for action and our conduct in action should be entirely referred to God; all we design and all we do should be with a submissive dependence on God.

IV. We are directed to avoid vain boasting, and to look upon it not only as a weak, but a very evil thing. *You rejoice in your boastings; all such rejoicing is evil, v.* 16. They promised themselves life and prosperity, and great things in the world, without any just regard to God; and then they boasted of these things. Such is the joy of worldly people, to boast of all their successes, yea, often to boast of their very projects before they know what success they shall have. How common is it for men to boast of things which they have no other title to than what arises from their own vanity and presumption! *Such rejoicing* (says the apostle) *is evil;* it is foolish and it is hurtful. For men to boast of worldly things, and of their aspiring projects, when they should be attending to the humbling duties before laid down (in *v.* 8—10), is a very evil thing. It is a great sin in God's account, it will bring great disappointment upon themselves, and it will prove their destruction in the end. If we rejoice in God that our times are in his hand, that all events are at his disposal, and that he is our God in covenant, this rejoicing is good; the wisdom, power, and providence of God, are then concerned to make all things work together for our good: but, if we rejoice in our own vain confidences and presumptuous boasts, this is evil; it is an evil carefully to be avoided by all wise and good men.

V. We are taught, in the whole of our conduct, to act up to our own convictions, and, whether we have to do with God or men, to see that we never go contrary to our own knowledge (*v.* 17): *To him that knoweth to do good, and doeth it not, to him it is sin;* it is aggravated sin; it is sinning with a witness; and it is to have the worst witness against a man that can be, when he sins against his own conscience. Observe, 1. This stands immediately connected with the plain lesson of saying, *If the Lord will, we shall do this or that;* they might be ready to say, "This is a very obvious thing; who knows not that we all depend upon almighty God *for life, and breath, and all things?*" Remember then, if you do know this, whenever you act unsuitably to such a dependence, that *to him that knows to do good, and does it not, to him it is sin,* the greater sin. 2. Omissions are sins which will come into judgment, as well as commissions. He that does not the good he knows should be done, as well as he who does the evil he knows should not be done, will be condemned. Let us therefore take care that conscience be rightly informed, and then that it be faithfully and constantly obeyed; for, if *our own hearts condemn us not, then have we confidence towards God;* but if we say, *We see,* and do not act suitably to our sight, then *our sin remaineth,* John ix. 41.

CHAP. V.

In this chapter the apostle denounces the judgments of God upon those rich men who oppress the poor, showing them how great their sin and folly are in the sight of God, and how grievous the punishments would be which should fall upon themselves, ver. 1—6. Hereupon, all the faithful are exhorted to patience under their trials and sufferings, ver. 7—11. The sin of swearing is cautioned against, ver. 12. We are directed how to act, both under affliction and in prosperity, ver. 13. Prayer for the sick, and anointing with oil, are prescribed, ver. 14, 15. Christians are directed to acknowledge their faults one to another, and to pray one for another, and the efficacy of prayer is proved, ver. 16—18. And, lastly, it is recommended to us to do what we can for bringing back those that stray from the ways of truth.

GO to now, *ye* rich men, weep and
howl for your miseries that shall
come upon *you.* 2 Your riches are
corrupted, and your garments are
motheaten. 3 Your gold and silver
is cankered; and the rust of them
shall be a witness against you, and
shall eat your flesh as it were fire.

Ye have heaped treasure together for
the last days. 4 Behold, the hire of
the labourers who have reaped down
your fields, which is of you kept back
by fraud, crieth: and the cries of them
which have reaped are entered into
the ears of the Lord of sabaoth. 5
Ye have lived in pleasure on the
earth, and been wanton; ye have
nourished your hearts, as in a day of
slaughter. 6 Ye have condemned *and*
killed the just; *and* he doth not resist you. 7 Be patient therefore,
brethren, unto the coming of the Lord.
Behold, the husbandman waiteth for
the precious fruit of the earth, and
hath long patience for it, until he receive the early and latter rain. 8 Be
ye also patient; stablish your hearts:
for the coming of the Lord draweth
nigh. 9 Grudge not one against
another, brethren, lest ye be condemned: behold, the judge standeth
before the door. 10 Take, my brethren, the prophets, who have spoken
in the name of the Lord, for an
example of suffering affliction, and of
patience. 11 Behold, we count them
happy which endure. Ye have heard
of the patience of Job, and have seen
the end of the Lord; that the Lord
is very pitiful, and of tender mercy.

The apostle is here addressing first sinners and then saints.

I. Let us consider the address to sinners; and here we find James seconding what his great Master had said: *Woe unto you that are rich; for you have received your consolation,* Luke vi. 24. The rich people to whom this word of warning was sent were not such as professed the Christian religion, but the worldly and unbelieving Jews, such as are here said *to condemn and kill the just,* which the Christians had no power to do; and though this epistle was written for the sake of the faithful, and was sent principally to them, yet, by an apostrophe, the infidel Jews may be well supposed here spoken to. They would not hear the word, and therefore it is *written,* that they might read it. It is observable, in the first inscription of this epistle, that it is not directed, as Paul's epistles were, *to the brethren in Christ,* but, in general, *to the twelve tribes;* and the salutation is not, *grace and peace from Christ,* but, in general, *greeting, ch.* i. 1. The poor among the Jews received the gospel, and many of them believed; but the generality of the rich rejected Christianity, and were hardened in their unbelief, and hated and persecuted those who believed on Christ. To these oppressing, unbelieving, persecuting, rich people, the apostle addresses himself in the first six verses.

1. He foretels the judgments of God that should come upon them, *v.* 1—3. They should have miseries come upon them, and such dreadful miseries that the very apprehension of them was enough to make them weep and howl—misery that should arise from the very things in which they placed their happiness, and misery that should be completed by these things witnessing against them at the last, to their utter destruction; and they are now called to reason upon and thoroughly to weigh the matter, and to think how they will stand before God in judgment: *Go to now, you rich men.* (1.) "You may be assured of this that very dreadful calamities are coming upon you, calamities that shall carry nothing of support nor comfort in them, but all misery, misery in time, misery to eternity, misery in your outward afflictions, misery in your inward frame and temper of mind, misery in this world, misery in hell. You have not a single instance of misery only coming upon you, but miseries. The ruin of your church and nation is at hand; and there will come a day of wrath, when riches shall not profit men, but *all the wicked shall be destroyed.*" (2.) The very apprehension of such miseries as were coming upon them is enough to make them weep and howl. Rich men are apt to say to themselves (and others are ready to say to them), *Eat, drink, and be merry;* but God says, *Weep and howl.* It is not said, Weep and repent, for this the apostle does not expect from them (he speaks in a way of denouncing rather than admonishing); but, "*Weep and howl,* for when your doom comes there will be nothing but *weeping, and wailing, and gnashing of teeth.*" Those who live like beasts are called to howl like such. Public calamities are most grievous to rich people, who live in pleasure, and are secure and sensual; and therefore they shall weep and howl more than other people for the miseries that shall come upon them. (3.) Their misery shall arise from the very things in which they placed their happiness. "Corruption, decay, rust, and ruin, will come upon all your goodly things: *Your riches are corrupted and your garments are moth-eaten, v.* 2. Those things which you now inordinately affect will hereafter insupportably wound you: they will be of no worth, of no use to you, but, on the contrary, will *pierce you through with many sorrows;* for," (4.) "*They will witness against you, and they will eat your flesh as it were fire,*" *v.* 3. Things inanimate are frequently represented in scripture as witnessing against wicked men. Heaven, earth, the stones of the field, the production of the ground, and here the very rust and canker of ill-gotten and ill-kept treasures, are said to witness against impious rich men. They think to heap up treasure

for their latter days, to live plentifully upon when they come to be old; but, alas! they are only heaping up treasures to become a prey to others (as the Jews had all taken from them by the Romans), and treasures that will prove at last to be only treasures of wrath, *in the day of the revelation of the righteous judgment of God.* Then shall their iniquities, in the punishment of them, *eat their flesh as it were with fire.* In the ruin of Jerusalem, many thousands perished by fire; in the last judgment the wicked shall be condemned to *everlasting burnings, prepared for the devil and his angels.* The Lord deliver us from the portion of wicked rich men! and, in order to this, let us take care that we do not fall into their sins, which we are next to consider.

2. The apostle shows what those sins are which should bring such miseries. To be in so deplorable a condition must doubtless be owing to some very heinous crimes. (1.) Covetousness is laid to the charge of this people; they laid by their garments till they bred moths and were eaten; they hoarded up their gold and silver till they were rusty and cankered. It is a very great disgrace to these things that they carry in them the principles of their own corruption and consumption—the garment breeds the moth that frets it, the gold and silver breeds the canker that eats it; but the disgrace falls most heavily upon those who hoard and lay up these things till they come to be thus corrupted, and cankered, and eaten. God gives us our worldly possessions that we may honour him and do good with them; but if, instead of this, we sinfully hoard them up, through an undue affection towards them, or a distrust of the providence of God for the future, this is a very heinous crime, and will be witnessed against by the very rust and corruption of the treasure thus heaped together. (2.) Another sin charged upon those against whom James writes is oppression: *Behold, the hire of the labourers, who have reaped down your fields, which is of you kept back by fraud, crieth,* &c., *v.* 4. Those who have wealth in their hands get power into their hands, and then they are tempted to abuse that power to oppress such as are under them. The rich we here find employing the poor in their labours, and the rich have as much need of the labours of the poor as the poor have of wages from the rich, and could as ill be without them; but yet, not considering this, they kept back the hire of the labourers; having power in their hands, it is probable that they made as hard bargains with the poor as they could, and even after that would not make good their bargains as they should have done. This is a crying sin, an iniquity that cries so as to reach the ears of God; and, in this case, God is to be considered as *the Lord of sabaoth,* or *the Lord of hosts,* Κυριον σαβαωθ, a phrase often used in the Old-Testament, when the people of God were defenceless and wanted protection, and when their enemies were numerous and powerful. The Lord of hosts, who has all ranks of beings and creatures at his disposal, and who sets all in their several places, hears the oppressed when they cry by reason of the cruelty or injustice of the oppressor, and he will give orders to some of those hosts that are under him (angels, devils, storms, distempers, or the like) to avenge the wrongs done to those who are dealt with unrighteously and unmercifully. Take heed of this sin of defrauding and oppressing, and avoid the very appearances of it. (3.) Another sin here mentioned is sensuality and voluptuousness. *You have lived in pleasure on the earth, and been wanton, v.* 5. God does not forbid us to use pleasure; but to live in them as if we lived for nothing else is a very provoking sin; and to do this on the earth, where we are but strangers and pilgrims, where we are but to continue for a while, and where we ought to be preparing for eternity—this, this is a grievous aggravation of the sin of voluptuousness. Luxury makes people wanton, as in Hos. xiii. 6, *According to their pasture, so were they filled; they were filled, and their heart was exalted; therefore have they forgotten me.* Wantonness and luxury are commonly the effects of great plenty and abundance; it is hard for people to have great estates, and not too much indulge themselves in carnal, sensual pleasures: "*You have nourished your hearts as in a day of slaughter:* you live as if it were every day a day of sacrifices, a festival; and hereby your hearts are fattened and nourished to stupidity, dulness, pride, and an insensibility to the wants and afflictions of others." Some may say, "What harm is there in good cheer, provided people do not spend above what they have?" What! Is it no harm for people to make gods of their bellies, and to give all to these, instead of abounding in acts of charity and piety? Is it no harm for people to unfit themselves for minding the concerns of their souls, by indulging the appetites of their bodies? Surely that which brought flames upon Sodom, and would bring these miseries for which rich men are here called to weep and howl, must be a heinous evil! Pride, and idleness, and fulness of bread, mean the same thing with living in pleasure, and being wanton, and nourishing the heart as in a day of slaughter. (4.) Another sin here charged on the rich is persecution: *You have condemned and killed the just, and he doth not resist you, v.* 6. This fills up the measure of their iniquity. They oppressed and acted very unjustly, to get estates; when they had them, they gave way to luxury and sensuality, till they had lost all sense and feeling of the wants or afflictions of others; and then they persecute and kill without remorse. They pretend to act legally indeed, they condemn before they kill; but unjust prosecutions, whatever colour of law they may carry in them, will come into the

reckoning when God shall make inquisition for blood, as well as massacres and downright murders. Observe here, The just may be condemned and killed: but then again observe, When such do suffer, and yield without resistance to the unjust sentence of oppressors, this is marked by God, to the honour of the sufferers and the infamy of their persecutors; this commonly shows that judgments are at the door, and we may certainly conclude that a reckoning-day will come, to reward the patience of the oppressed and to break to pieces the oppressor. Thus far the address to sinners goes.

II. We have next subjoined an address to saints. Some have been ready to despise or to condemn this way of preaching, when ministers, in their application, have brought a word to sinners, and a word to saints; but, from the apostle's here taking this method, we may conclude that this is the best way rightly to divide the word of truth. From what has been said concerning wicked and oppressing rich men, occasion is given to administer comfort to God's afflicted people: "Be patient therefore; since God will send such miseries on the wicked, you may see what is your duty, and where your greatest encouragement lies."

1. Attend to your duty: *Be patient* (*v.* 7), *establish your hearts* (*v.* 8), *grudge not one against another, brethren, v.* 9. Consider well the meaning of these three expressions:—(1.) "*Be patient*—bear your afflictions without murmuring, your injuries without revenge; and, though God should not in any signal manner appear for you immediately, wait for him. *The vision is for an appointed time; at the end it will speak, and will not lie; therefore wait for it. It is but a little while, and he that shall come will come, and will not tarry.* Let your patience be lengthened out to long-suffering;" so the word here used, *μακροθυμήσατε*, signifies. When we have done our work, we have need of patience to stay for our reward. This Christian patience is not a mere yielding to necessity, as the moral patience taught by some philosophers was, but it is a humble acquiescence in the wisdom and will of God, with an eye to a future glorious recompence: *Be patient to the coming of the Lord.* And because this is a lesson Christians must learn, though ever so hard or difficult to them, it is repeated in *v.* 8, *Be you also patient.* (2.) "*Establish your hearts*—let your faith be firm, without wavering, your practice of what is good constant and continued, without tiring, and your resolutions for God and heaven fixed, in spite of all sufferings or temptations." The prosperity of the wicked and the affliction of the righteous have in all ages been a very great trial to the faith of the people of God. David tells us *that his feet were almost gone, when he saw the prosperity of the wicked,* Ps. lxxiii. 2, 3. Some of those Christians to whom St. James wrote might probably be in the same tottering condition; and therefore they are called upon to establish their hearts; faith and patience will establish the heart. (3.) *Grudge not one against another;* the words *μὴ στενάζετε* signify, *Groan* not one against another, that is, "Do not make one another uneasy by your murmuring groans at what befals you, nor by your distrustful groans as to what may further come upon you, nor by your revengeful groans against the instruments of your sufferings, nor by your envious groans at those who may be free from your calamities: do not make yourselves uneasy and make one another uneasy by thus groaning to and grieving one another." "The apostle seemeth to me" (says Dr. Manton) "to be here taxing those mutual injuries and animosities wherewith the Christians of those times, having banded under the names of *circumcision* and *uncircumcision,* did grieve one another, and give each other cause to groan; so that they did not only sigh under the oppressions of the rich persecutors, but under the injuries which they sustained from many of the brethren who, together with them, did profess the holy faith." Those who are in the midst of common enemies, and in any suffering circumstances, should be more especially careful not to grieve nor to groan against one another, otherwise judgments will come upon them as well as others; and the more such grudgings prevail the nearer do they show judgment to be.

2. Consider what encouragement here is for Christians to be patient, to establish their hearts, and not to grudge one against another. And, (1.) "Look to the example of the husbandman: *He waits for the precious fruit of the earth, and hath long patience for it, until he receive the early and latter rain.* When you sow your corn in the ground, you wait many months for the former and latter rain, and are willing to stay till harvest for the fruit of your labour; and shall not this teach you to bear a few storms, and to be patient for a season, when you are looking for a kingdom and everlasting felicity? Consider him that waits for a crop of corn; and will not you wait for a crown of glory? If you should be called to wait a little longer than the husbandman does, is it not something proportionably greater and infinitely more worth your waiting for? But," (2.) "Think how short your waiting time may possibly be: *The coming of the Lord draweth nigh, v.* 8; *behold, the Judge standeth before the door, v.* 9. Do not be impatient, do not quarrel with one another; the great Judge, who will set all to rights, who will punish the wicked and reward the good, is at hand: he should be conceived by you to stand as near as one who is just knocking at the door." *The coming of the Lord* to punish the wicked Jews was then very nigh, when James wrote this epistle; and, whenever the patience and other graces of his people are tried in an extraordinary manner, the certainty of Christ's

coming as Judge, and the nearness of it, should establish their hearts. The Judge is now a great deal nearer, in his coming to judge the world, than when this epistle was written, nearer by above seventeen hundred years; and therefore this should have the greater effect upon us. (3.) The danger of our being condemned when the Judge appears should excite us to mind our duty as before laid down: *Grudge not, lest you be condemned.* Fretfulness and discontent expose us to the just judgment of God, and we bring more calamities upon ourselves by our murmuring, distrustful, envious groans and grudgings against one another, than we are aware of. If we avoid these evils, and be patient under our trials, God will not condemn us. Let us encourage ourselves with this. (4.) We are encouraged to be patient by the example of the prophets (*v.* 10): *Take the prophets, who have spoken in the name of the Lord, for an example of suffering affliction, and of patience.* Observe here, The prophets, on whom God put the greatest honour, and for whom he had the greatest favour, were most afflicted: and, when we think that the best men have had the hardest usage in this world, we should hereby be reconciled to affliction. Observe further, Those who were the greatest examples of suffering affliction were also the best and greatest examples of patience: *tribulation worketh patience.* Hereupon James gives it to us as the common sense of the faithful (*v.* 11): *We count those happy who endure:* we look upon righteous and patient sufferers as the happiest people. See *ch.* i. 2—12. (5.) Job also is proposed as an example for the encouragement of the afflicted. *You have heard of the patience of Job, and have seen the end of the Lord,* &c., *v.* 11. In the case of Job you have an instance of a variety of miseries, and of such as were very grievous; but under all he could bless God, and, as to the general bent of his spirit, he was patient and humble: and what came to him in the end? Why, truly, God accomplished and brought about those things for him which plainly prove that *the Lord is very pitiful, and of tender mercy.* The best way to bear afflictions is to look to the end of them; and the pity of God is such that he will not delay the bringing of them to an end when his purposes are once answered; and the tender mercy of God is such that he will make his people an abundant amends for all their sufferings and afflictions. His bowels are moved for them while suffering, his bounty is manifested afterwards. Let us serve our God, and endure our trials, as those who believe the end will crown all.

12 But above all things, my brethren, swear not, neither by heaven,
neither by the earth, neither by any
other oath: but let your yea be yea;
and *your* nay, nay; lest ye fall into
condemnation. 13 Is any among you
afflicted? let him pray. Is any
merry? let him sing psalms. 14 Is
any sick among you? let him call for
the elders of the church; and let
them pray over him, anointing him
with oil in the name of the Lord: 15
And the prayer of faith shall save the
sick, and the Lord shall raise him up;
and if he have committed sins, they
shall be forgiven him. 16 Confess
your faults one to another, and pray
one for another, that ye may be healed.
The effectual fervent prayer of a righteous man availeth much. 17 Elias
was a man subject to like passions as
we are, and he prayed earnestly that
it might not rain: and it rained not
on the earth by the space of three
years and six months. 18 And he
prayed again, and the heaven gave
rain, and the earth brought forth her
fruit. 19 Brethren, if any of you do
err from the truth, and one convert
him; 20 Let him know, that he
which converteth the sinner from the
error of his way shall save a soul from
death, and shall hide a multitude of sins.

This epistle now drawing to a close, the penman goes off very quickly from one thing to another: hence it is that matters so very different are insisted on in these few verses.

I. The sin of swearing is cautioned against: *But above all things, my brethren, swear not,* &c., *v.* 12. Some understand this too restrictedly, as if the meaning were, "Swear not at your persecutors, at *those that reproach you and say all manner of evil of you;* be not put into a passion by the injuries they do you, so as in your passion to be provoked to swear." This swearing is no doubt forbidden here: and it will not excuse those that are guilty of this sin to say they swear only when they are provoked to it, and before they are aware. But the apostle's warning extends to other occasions of swearing as well as this. Some have translated the words, πρὸ πάντων—*before all things;* and so have made the sense of this place to be that they should not, in common conversation, *before every thing they say,* put an oath. All customary needless swearing is undoubtedly forbidden, and all along in scripture condemned, as a very grievous sin. Profane swearing was very customary among the Jews, and, since this epistle is directed in general *to the twelve tribes scattered abroad* (as before has been observed), we may conceive this exhortation sent to those who believed not. It is hard to suppose that swearing should be one of the spots of God's children, since Peter, when he was charged with being a disciple of Christ and would disprove the charge, cursed and swore, thereby thinking most effectually to convince them that he was no disciple of Jesus, it being well known of such that they durst not allow themselves in swearing; but possibly some of the looser sort of those who were called Christians might, among other sins here charged upon them, be guilty also of this. It is a sin that in later years has most scandalously prevailed, even among those who would be thought above all others entitled to the Christian name and privileges. It is very rare indeed to hear of a dissenter from the church of England who is guilty of swearing, but among those who glory in their being of the established church nothing is more common; and indeed the most execrable oaths and curses now daily wound the ears and hearts of all serious Christians. James here says,

1. *Above all things, swear not;* but how many are there who mind this the least of all things, and who make light of nothing so much as common profane swearing! But why *above all things* is swearing here forbidden? (1.) Because it strikes most directly at the honour of God and most expressly throws contempt upon his name and authority. (2.) Because this sin has, of all sins, the least temptation to it: it is not gain, nor pleasure, nor reputation, that can move men to it, but a wantonness in sinning, and a needless showing an enmity to God. *Thy enemies take thy name in vain*, Ps. cxxxix. 20. This is a proof of men's being enemies to God, however they may pretend to call themselves by his name, or sometimes to compliment him in acts of worship. (3.) Because it is with most difficulty left off when once men are accustomed to it, therefore it should above all things be watched against. And, (4.) "*Above all things swear not,* for how can you expect the name of God should be a strong tower to you in your distress if you profane it and play with it at other times?" But (as Mr. Baxter observes) "all this is so far from forbidding necessary oaths that it is but to confirm them, by preserving the due reverence of them." And then he further notes that "The true nature of an oath is, by our speech, *to pawn the reputation of some certain or great thing,* for the *averring of a doubted less thing;* and not (as is commonly held) an appeal to God or other judge." Hence it was that swearing by the heavens, and by the earth, and by the other oaths the apostle refers to, came to be in use. The Jews thought if they did but omit the great oath of *Chi-Eloah,* they were safe. But they grew so profane as to swear by the creature, as if it were God; and so advanced it into the place of God; while, on the other hand, those who swear commonly and profanely by the name of God do hereby put him upon the level with every common thing.

2. *But let your yea be yea, and your nay nay; lest you fall into condemnation;* that is, "let it suffice you to affirm or deny a thing as there is occasion, and be sure to stand to your word, and be true to it, so as to give no occasion for your being suspected of falsehood; and then you will be kept from the condemnation of backing what you say or promise by rash oaths, and from profaning the name of God to justify yourselves. It is being suspected of falsehood that leads men to swearing. Let it be known that you keep to truth, and are firm to your word, and by this means you will find there is no need to swear to what you say. Thus shall you escape the condemnation which is expressly annexed to the third commandment: *The Lord will not hold him guiltless that taketh his name in vain.*"

II. As Christians we are taught to suit ourselves to the dispensations of Providence (*v.* 13): *Is any among you afflicted? Let him pray. Is any merry? Let him sing psalms.* Our condition in this world is various; and our wisdom is to submit to its being so, and to behave as becomes us both in prosperity and under affliction. Sometimes we are in sadness, sometimes in mirth; God has set these one over against the other that we may the better observe the several duties he enjoins, and that the impressions made on our passions and affections may be rendered serviceable to our devotions. Afflictions should put us upon prayer, and prosperity should make us abound in praise. Not that prayer is to be confined to a time of trouble, nor singing to a time of mirth; but these several duties may be performed with special advantage, and to the happiest purposes, at such seasons. 1. In a day of affliction nothing is more seasonable than prayer. The person afflicted must pray himself, as well as engage the prayers of others for him. Times of affliction should be praying times. To this end God sends afflictions, that we may be engaged to seek him early; and that those who at other times have neglected him may be brought to enquire after him. The spirit is then most humble, the heart is broken and tender; and prayer is most acceptable to God when it comes from a contrite humble spirit. Afflictions naturally draw out complaints; and to whom should we complain but to God in prayer? It is necessary to exercise faith and hope under afflictions; and prayer is the appointed means both for obtaining and increasing these graces in us. *Is any afflicted? Let him pray.* 2. In a day of mirth and prosperity singing psalms is very proper and seasonable. In the original it is only said *sing,* ψαλλέτω, without the addition of psalms or any other word: and we learn from the writings of several in the first ages of Christianity (particularly from a letter of Pliny's, and from some passages in Justin Martyr and Tertullian) that the Christians were accustomed to sing hymns, either taken out of scripture, or of more private composure, in their worship of God. Though some have thought that Paul's advising both the Colossians and Ephesians to *speak to one another* ψαλμοῖς καὶ ὕμνοις καὶ ᾠδαῖς πνευματικαῖς—*in psalms, and hymns, and spiritual songs,* refers only to the compositions of scripture, the psalms of David being distinguished in Hebrew by *Shurim, Tehillim,* and *Mizmorim,* words that exactly answer these of the apostle. Let that be as it will, this however we are sure of, that the singing of psalms is a gospel ordinance, and that our joy should be holy joy, consecrated to God. Singing is so directed to here as to show that, if any be in circumstances of mirth and prosperity, he should turn his mirth, though alone, and by himself, into this channel. Holy mirth becomes families and retirements, as well as public assemblies. Let our singing be such as to make *melody with our hearts unto the Lord,* and God will assuredly be well pleased with this kind of devotion.

III. We have particular directions given as to sick persons, and *healing pardoning mercy promised* upon the observance of those directions. *If any be sick,* they are required, 1. To *send for the elders,* πρεσβυτέρους τῆς ἐκκλησίας—*the presbyters,* pastors or ministers *of the church, v.* 14, 15. It lies upon sick people as a duty to send for ministers, and to desire their assistance and their prayers. 2. It is the duty of ministers to pray over the sick, when thus desired and called for. *Let them pray over him;* let their prayers be suited to his case, and their intercessions be as becomes those who are affected with his calamities. 3. In the times of miraculous healing, the *sick were to be anointed with oil in the name of the Lord.* Expositors generally confine this anointing with oil to such as had the power of working miracles; and, when miracles ceased, this institution ceased also. In Mark's gospel we read of the apostle's anointing with oil many that were sick, and healing them, Mark vi. 13. And we have accounts of this being practised in the church two hundred years after Christ; but then the gift of healing also accompanied it, and, when the miraculous gift ceased, this rite was laid aside. The papists indeed have made a sacrament of this, which they call *the extreme unction.* They use it, not to heal the sick, as it was used by the apostles; but as they generally run counter to scripture, in the appointments of their church, so here they ordain that this should be administered only to such as are at the very point of death. The apostle's anointing was in order to heal the disease; the popish anointing is for the expulsion of the relics of sin, and to enable the soul (as they pretend) the better to combat with the powers of the air. When they cannot prove, by any visible effects, that Christ owns them in the continuance of this rite, they would however have people to believe that the invisible effects are very wonderful. But it is surely much better to omit this anointing with oil than to turn it quite contrary to the purposes spoken of in scripture. Some protestants have thought that this anointing was only permitted or approved by Christ, not instituted. But it should seem, by the words of James here, that it was a thing enjoined in cases where there was faith for healing. And some protestants have argued for it with this view. It was not to be commonly used, not even in the apostolical age; and some have thought that it should not be wholly laid aside in any age, but that where there are extraordinary measures of faith in the person anointing, and in those who are anointed, an extraordinary blessing may attend the observance of this direction for the sick. However that be, there is one thing carefully to be observed here, that the saving of the sick is not ascribed to the *anointing with oil,* but to prayer: *The prayer of faith shall save the sick,* &c., *v.* 15. So that, 4. Prayer over the sick must proceed from, and be accompanied with, a lively faith. There must be faith both in the person praying and in the person prayed for. In a time of sickness, it is not the cold and formal prayer that is effectual, but the prayer of faith. 5. We should observe the success of prayer. The Lord shall raise up; that is, if he be a person capable and fit for deliverance, and if God have any thing further for such a person to do in the world. *And, if he have committed sins, they shall be forgiven him;* that is, where sickness is sent as a punishment for some particular sin, that sin shall be pardoned, and in token thereof the sickness shall be removed. As when Christ said to the impotent man, *Go and sin no more, lest a worse thing come unto thee,* it is intimated that some particular sin was the cause of his sickness. The great thing therefore we should beg of God for ourselves and others in the time of sickness is the pardon of sin. Sin is both the root of sickness and the sting of it. If sin be pardoned, either affliction shall be removed in mercy or we shall see there is mercy in the continuance of it. When healing is founded upon pardon, we may say as Hezekiah did: Thou hast, in love to my soul, *delivered it from the pit of corruption,* Isa. xxxviii. 17. When you are sick and in pain, it is most common to pray and cry, *O give me ease! O restore me to health!* But your prayer should rather and chiefly be, *O that God would pardon my sins!*

IV. Christians are directed to *confess their faults one to another, and so to join in their prayers with and for one another, v.* 16 Some expositors connect this with *v.* 14. As if when sick people send for ministers to pray over them they should then confess their faults to them. Indeed, where any are conscious that their sickness is a vindictive punishment of some particular sin, and they cannot look for the removal of their sickness without particular applications to God for the pardon of such a sin, there it may be proper to acknowledge and tell his case, that those who pray over him may know how to plead rightly for him. But the confession here required is that of Christians to one another, and not, as the papists would have it, to a priest. Where persons have injured one another, acts of injustice must be confessed to those against whom they have been committed. Where persons have tempted one another to sin, or have consented in the same evil actions, there they ought mutually to blame themselves and excite each other to repentance. Where crimes are of a public nature, and have done any public mischief, there they ought to be more publicly confessed, so as may best reach to all who are concerned. And sometimes it may be well to confess our faults to some prudent minister or praying friend, that he may help us to plead with God for mercy and pardon. But then we are not to think that James puts us upon telling every thing that we are conscious is amiss in ourselves or in one another; but so far as confession is necessary to our reconciliation with such as are at variance with us, or for reparation of wrongs done to any, or for gaining information in any point of conscience and making our own spirits quiet and easy, so far we should be ready to confess our faults. And sometimes also it may be of good use to Christians to disclose their peculiar weaknesses and infirmities to one another, where there are great intimacies and friendships, and where they may help each other by their prayers to obtain pardon of their sins and power against them. Those who make confession of their faults one to another should thereupon pray with and for one another. The 13th verse directs persons to pray for themselves: *Is any afflicted let him pray;* the 14th directs to seek for the prayers of ministers; and the 16th directs private Christians to pray one for another; so that here we have all sorts of prayer (ministerial, social, and secret) recommended.

V. The great advantage and efficacy of prayer are declared and proved: *The effectual fervent prayer of a righteous man availeth much,* whether he pray for himself or for others: witness the example of Elias, *v.* 17, 18. He who prays must be a righteous man; not righteous in an absolute sense (for this Elias was not, who is here made a pattern to us), but righteous in a gospel sense; not loving nor approving of any known iniquity. *If I regard iniquity in my heart, the Lord will not hear my prayer,* Ps. lxvi. 18. Further, the prayer itself must be a fervent, in-wrought, well-wrought prayer. It must be a pouring out of the heart to God; and it must proceed from a faith unfeigned. Such prayer avails much. It is of great advantage to ourselves, it may be very beneficial to our friends, and we are assured of its being acceptable to God. It is good having those for friends whose prayers are available in the sight of God. The power of prayer is here proved from the success of Elijah. This may be encouraging to us even in common cases, if we consider that Elijah was *a man of like passions with us.* He was a zealous good man and a very great man, but he had his infirmities, and was subject to disorder in his passions as well as others. In prayer we must not look to the merit of man, but to the grace of God. Only in this we should copy after Elijah, that he prayed earnestly, or, as it is in the original, *in prayer he prayed.* It is not enough to say a prayer, but we must pray in prayer. Our thoughts must be fixed, our desires firm and ardent, and our graces in exercise; and, when we thus pray in prayer, we shall speed in prayer. Elijah *prayed that it might not rain;* and God heard him in his pleading against an idolatrous persecuting country, so that *it rained not on the earth for the space of three years and six months. Again he prayed, and the heaven gave rain,* &c. Thus you see prayer is the key which opens and shuts heaven. To this there is an allusion, Rev. xi. 6, where the two witnesses are said to have power *to shut heaven, that it rain not.* This instance of the extraordinary efficacy of prayer is recorded for encouragement even to ordinary Christians to be instant and earnest in prayer. God never says to any of the seed of Jacob, *Seek my face in vain.* If Elijah by prayer could do such great and wonderful things, surely the prayers of no righteous man shall return void. Where there may not be so much of miracle in God's answering our prayers, yet there may be as much of grace.

VI. This epistle concludes with an exhortation to do all we can in our places to promote the conversion and salvation of others, *v.* 19, 20. Some interpret these verses as an apology which the apostle is making for himself that he should so plainly and sharply reprove the Jewish Christians for their many faults and errors. And certainly James gives a very good reason why he was so much concerned to reclaim them from their errors, because in thus doing he should save souls, and hide a multitude of sins. But we are not to restrain this place to the apostle's converting such as erred from the truth; no, nor to other ministerial endeavours of the like nature, since it is said, "If any err, and one convert him, let him be who he will that does so good an office for another, he is therein an instrument of saving a soul from death." Those whom the apostle here calls brethren, he yet supposes liable to err. It is no mark of a wise or a holy man to boast of his being free from error, or to refuse to acknowledge when he is in an error. But if any do err, be they ever so great, you must not be afraid to show them their error; and, be they ever so weak and little, you must not disdain to make them wiser and better. If they err from the truth, that is, from the gospel (the great rule and standard of truth), whether it be in opinion or practice, you must endeavour to bring them again to the rule. Errors in judgment and in life generally go together. There is some doctrinal mistake at the bottom of every practical miscarriage. There is no one habitually bad, but upon some bad principle. Now to convert such is to reduce them from their error, and to reclaim them from the evils they have been led into. We are not presently to accuse and exclaim against an erring brother, and seek to bring reproaches and calamities upon him, but to convert him: and, if by all our endeavours we cannot do this, yet we are nowhere empowered to persecute and destroy him. If we are instrumental in the conversion of any, *we* are said to convert them, though this be principally and efficiently the work of God. And, if we can do no more towards the conversion of sinners, yet we may do this—pray for the grace and Spirit of God to convert and change them. And let those that are in any way serviceable to convert others know what will be the happy consequence of their doing this: they may take great comfort in it at present, and they will meet with a crown at last. He that is said to *err from the truth* in *v.* 19 is described as *erring in his way* in *v.* 20, and we cannot be said to convert any merely by altering their opinions, unless we can bring them to correct and amend their ways. This is conversion—to turn a sinner from the error of his ways, and not to turn him from one party to another, or merely from one notion and way of thinking to another. He who thus converteth a sinner from the error of his ways *shall save a soul from death.* There is a soul in the case; and what is done towards the salvation of the soul shall certainly turn to good account. The soul being the principal part of the man, the saving of that only is mentioned, but it includes the salvation of the whole man: the spirit shall be saved from hell, the body raised from the grave, and both saved from eternal death. And then, by such conversion of heart and life, a *multitude of sins shall be hid.* A most comfortable passage of scripture is this. We learn hence that though our sins are many, even a multitude, yet they may be hid or pardoned; and that when sin is turned from or forsaken it shall be hid, never to appear in judgment against us. Let people contrive to cover or excuse their sin as they will, there is no way effectually and finally to hide it but by forsaking it. Some make the sense of this text to be, that conversion shall *prevent* a multitude of sins; and it is a truth beyond dispute that many sins are prevented in the party converted, many also may be prevented in others that he may have an influence upon, or may converse with. Upon the whole, how should we lay out ourselves with all possible concern for the conversion of sinners! It will be for the happiness and salvation of the converted; it will prevent much mischief, and the spreading and multiplying of sin in the world; it will be for the glory and honour of God; and it will mightily redound to our comfort and renown in the great day. *Those that turn many to righteousness,* and those who help to do so, *shall shine as the stars for ever and ever.*

AN

EXPOSITION,

WITH PRACTICAL OBSERVATIONS,

OF THE FIRST EPISTLE GENERAL

OF PETER.

Two epistles we have enrolled in the sacred canon of the scripture written by Peter, who was a most eminent apostle of Jesus Christ, and whose character shines brightly as it is described in the four Gospels and in the Acts of the Apostles, but, as it is painted by the papists and legendary writers, it represents a person of extravagant pride and ambition. It is certain from scripture that Simon Peter was one of the first of those whom our Lord called to be his disciples and followers, that he was a person of excellent endowments, both natural and gracious, of great parts and ready elocution, quick to apprehend and bold to execute whatever he knew to be his duty. When our Saviour called his apostles, and gave them their commission, he nominated him first in the list; and by his behaviour towards him he seems to have distinguished him as a special favourite among the twelve. Many instances of our Lord's affection to him, both during his life and after his resurrection, are upon record. But there are many things confidently affirmed of this holy man that are directly false: as, That he had a primacy and superior power over the rest of the apostles—that he was more than their equal—that he was their prince, monarch, and sovereign—and that he exercised a jurisdiction over the whole college of the apostles: moreover, That he was the sole and universal pastor over all the Christian world, the only vicar of Christ upon earth—that he was for above twenty years bishop of Rome—that the popes of Rome succeed to St. Peter, and derive from him a universal supremacy and jurisdiction over all churches and Christians upon earth—and that all this was by our Lord's ordering and appointment; whereas Christ never gave him any pre-eminence of this kind, but positively forbade it, and gave precepts to the contrary. The other apostles never consented to any such claim. Paul declares himself *not a whit behind the very chief apostles,* 2 Cor. xi. 5 and xii. 11. Here is no exception of Peter's superior dignity, whom Paul took the freedom to blame, and *withstood him to the face,* Gal. ii. 11. And Peter himself never assumed any thing like it, but modestly styles himself an *apostle of Jesus Christ;* and, when he writes to the presbyters of the church, he humbly places himself in the same rank with them: *The elders who are among you I exhort, who am also an elder, ch.* v. 1. See Dr. Barrow on the pope's supremacy.

The design of this first epistle is, I. To explain more fully the doctrines of Christianity to these newly-converted Jews. II. To direct and persuade them to a holy conversation, in the faithful discharge of all personal and relative duties, whereby they would secure their own peace and effectually confute the slanders and reproaches of their enemies. III. To prepare them for sufferings. This seems to be his principal intention; for he has something to this purport in every chapter, and does, by a great variety of arguments, encourage them to patience and perseverance in the faith, lest the persecutions and sad calamities that were coming upon them should prevail with them to apostatize from Christ and the gospel. It is remarkable that you find not so much as one word savouring of the spirit and pride of a pope in either of these epistles.

CHAP. I.

The apostle describes the persons to whom he writes, and salutes them (ver. 1, 2), blesses God for their regeneration to a lively hope of eternal salvation (ver. 3—5), in the hope of this salvation he shows they had great cause of rejoicing, though for a little while they were in heaviness and affliction, for the trial of their faith, which would produce joy unspeakable and full of glory, ver. 6—9. This is that salvation which the ancient prophets foretold and the angels desire to look into, ver. 10—12. He exhorts them to sobriety and holiness, which he presses from the consideration of the blood of Jesus, the invaluable price of man's redemption (ver. 13—21), and to brotherly love, from the consideration of their regeneration, and the excellency of their spiritual state, ver. 22—25.

PETER, an apostle of Jesus Christ, to the strangers scattered throughout Pontus, Galatia, Cappadocia, Asia, and Bithynia, 2 Elect according to the foreknowledge of God the Father, through sanctification of the Spirit, unto obedience and sprinkling of the blood of Jesus Christ: Grace unto you, and peace, be multiplied.

In this inscription we have three parts:—

I. The author of it, described, 1. By his name—*Peter.* His first name was *Simon,* and Jesus Christ gave him the surname of *Peter,* which signifies *a rock,* as a commendation of his faith, and to denote that he should be an eminent pillar in the church of God, Gal. ii. 9. 2. By his office—*an apostle of Jesus Christ.* The word signifies *one sent, a legate, a messenger,* any one sent in Christ's name and about his work; but more strictly it signifies the highest office in the Christian church. 1 Cor. xii. 28, *God hath set some in the church, first apostles.* Their dignity and pre-eminence lay in these things:—They were immediately chosen by Christ himself,—they were first witnesses, then preachers, of the resurrection of Christ, and so of the entire gospel-dispensation,—their gifts were excellent and extraordinary,—they had a power of working miracles, not at all times, but when Christ pleased,—they were led into all truth, were endowed with the spirit of prophecy, and they had an extent of power and jurisdiction beyond all others; every apostle was a universal bishop in all churches, and over all ministers. In this humble manner Peter, (1.) Asserts his own character as an apostle. Hence learn, A man may lawfully acknowledge, and sometimes is bound to assert, the gifts and graces of God to him. To pretend to what we have not is hypocrisy; and to deny what we have is ingratitude. (2.) He mentions his apostolical function as his warrant and call to write this epistle to these people. Note, It concerns all, but especially ministers, to consider well their warrant and call from God to their work. This will justify them to others, and give them inward support and comfort under all dangers and discouragements.

II. The persons to whom this epistle was addressed, and they are described,

1. By their external condition—*Strangers dispersed throughout Pontus, Galatia,* &c. They were chiefly Jews, descended (as Dr. Prideaux thinks) from those Jews who were translated from Babylon, by order of Antiochus king of Syria, about two hundred years before the coming of Christ, and placed in the cities of Asia Minor. It is very likely that our apostle had been among them, and converted them, being the apostle of the circumcision, and that he afterwards wrote this epistle to them from Babylon, where multitudes of the Jewish nation then resided. At present, their circumstances were poor and afflicted. (1.) The best of God's servants may, through the hardships of times and providences, be dispersed about, and forced to leave their native countries. Those of whom the world was not worthy have been forced to wander in mountains, in dens and caves of the earth. (2.) We ought to

have a special regard to the dispersed persecuted servants of God. These were the objects of this apostle's particular care and compassion. We should proportion our regard to the excellency and to the necessity of the saints. (3.) The value of good people ought not to be estimated by their present external condition. Here was a set of excellent people, beloved of God, and yet strangers, dispersed and poor in the world; the eye of God was upon them in all their dispersions, and the apostle was tenderly careful to write to them for their direction and consolation.

2. They are described by their spiritual condition: *Elect according to the foreknowledge of God the Father*, &c. These poor strangers, who were oppressed and despised in the world, were nevertheless in high esteem with the great God, and in the most honourable state that any person can be in during this life; for they were,

(1.) *Elect according to the foreknowledge of God the Father.* Election is either to an office: so Saul was the man whom the Lord chose to be king (1 Sam. x. 24), and our Lord says to his apostles, *Have not I chosen you twelve?* (John vi. 70); or it is to a church-state, for the enjoyment of special privileges: thus Israel was God's elect (Deut. vii. 6), *For thou art a holy people unto the Lord thy God; the Lord thy God hath chosen thee to be a special people unto himself above all people that are upon the face of the earth;* or it is to eternal salvation: *God hath from the beginning chosen you to salvation, through sanctification of the Spirit and belief of the truth.* This is the election here spoken of, importing God's gracious decree or resolution to save some, and bring them, through Christ, by proper means, to eternal life. [1.] This election is said to be *according to the foreknowledge of God.* Foreknowledge may be taken in two ways:—*First*, for mere prescience, foresight, or understanding, that such a thing will be, before it comes to pass. Thus a mathematician certainly foreknows that at such a time there will be an eclipse. This sort of foreknowledge is in God, who at one commanding view sees all things that ever were, or are, or ever will be. But such a prescience is not the cause why any thing is so or so, though in the event it certainly will be so, as the mathematician who foresees an eclipse does not thereby cause that eclipse to be. *Secondly*, Foreknowledge sometimes signifies counsel, appointment, and approbation. Acts ii. 23, *Him being delivered by the determinate counsel and foreknowledge of God.* The death of Christ was not only foreseen, but fore-ordained, as *v.* 20. Take it thus here; so the sense is, *elect according to the counsel, ordination, and free grace of God.* [2.] It is added, according to the foreknowledge of *God the Father.* By the Father we are here to understand the first person of the blessed Trinity. There is an order among the three persons. though no superiority; they are equal in power and glory, and there is an agreed economy in their works. Thus, in the affair of man's redemption, election is by way of eminency ascribed to the Father, as reconciliation is to the Son and sanctification to the Holy Ghost, though in each of these one person is not so entirely interested as to exclude the other two. Hereby the persons of the Trinity are more clearly discovered to us, and we are taught what obligations we are under to each of them distinctly.

(2.) They were elect *through sanctification of the Spirit, unto obedience, and sprinkling of the blood of Jesus Christ.* The end and last result of election is eternal life and salvation; but, before this can be accomplished, every elect person must be sanctified by the Spirit, and justified by the blood of Jesus. God's decree for man's salvation always operates through sanctification of the Spirit and sprinkling of the blood of Jesus. By sanctification here understand, not a federal sanctification only, but a real one, begun in regeneration, whereby we are renewed after the image of God and made new creatures, and carried on in the daily exercise of holiness, mortifying our sins more and more, and living to God in all the duties of a Christian life, which is here summed up in one word, *obedience*, comprehending all the duties of Christianity. By *the Spirit* some would have the apostle to mean the spirit of man, the subject sanctified. The legal or typical sanctification operated no further than the purifying of the flesh, but the Christian dispensation takes effect upon the spirit of man, and purifies that. Others, with better reason, think that by Spirit is meant the Holy Ghost, the author of sanctification. He renews the mind, mortifies our sins (Rom. viii. 13), and produces his excellent fruits in the hearts of Christians, Gal. v. 22, 23. This sanctification of the Spirit implies the use of means. *Sanctify them through thy truth; thy word is truth*, John xvii. 17. *Unto obedience.* This word, as it is pointed in our translation, is referred to what goes before it, and denotes the end of sanctification, which is, to bring rebellious sinners to obedience again, to universal obedience, to obey the truth and gospel of Christ: *You have purified your souls in obeying the truth through the Spirit*, *v.* 22.

(3.) They were elected also to the *sprinkling of the blood of Jesus.* They were designed by God's decree to be sanctified by the Spirit, and to be purified by the merit and blood of Christ. Here is a manifest allusion to the typical sprinklings of blood under the law, which language these Jewish converts understood very well. The blood of the sacrifices must not only be shed but sprinkled, to denote that the benefits designed thereby are applied and imputed to the offerers. Thus the blood of Christ, the grand and all-sufficient sacrifice, typified by the legal sacrifices, was not only shed, but must be sprinkled and communicated to every one of these elect Christians, *that through faith in his blood they may obtain remission of sins,* Rom. iii. 25. This blood of sprinkling justifies before God (Rom. v. 9), seals the covenant between God and us, of which the Lord's supper is a sign (Luke xxii. 20), cleanses from all sin (1 John i. 7), and admits us into heaven, Heb. x. 19. Note, [1.] God hath elected some to eternal life, some, not all; persons, not qualifications. [2.] All that are chosen to eternal life as the end are chosen to obedience as the way. [3.] Unless a person be sanctified by the Spirit, and sprinkled with the blood of Jesus, there will be no true obedience in the life. [4.] There is a consent and co-operation of all the persons of the Trinity in the affair of man's salvation, and their acts are commensurate one to another: whoever the Father elects the Spirit sanctifies unto obedience, and the Son redeems and sprinkles with his blood. [5.] The doctrine of the Trinity lies at the foundation of all revealed religion. If you deny the proper deity of the Son and Holy Spirit, you invalidate the redemption of the one and the gracious operations of the other, and by this means destroy the foundation of your own safety and comfort.

III. The salutation follows: *Grace unto you, and peace be multiplied.* The blessings desired for them are *grace and peace.* 1. *Grace*—the free favour of God, with all its proper effects, pardoning, healing, assisting, and saving. 2. *Peace.* All sorts of peace may be here intended, domestic, civil, ecclesiastical peace in the church, and spiritual peace with God, with the feeling of it in our own consciences. 3. Here is the request or prayer, in relation to these blessings—that they may be multiplied, which implies that they were already possessed in some degree of these blessings, and he wishes them the continuation, the increase, and the perfection of them. Learn, (1.) Those who possess spiritual blessings in their own souls earnestly desire the communication of the same to others. The grace of God is a generous, not a selfish principle. (2.) The best blessings we can desire for ourselves, or one for another, are grace and peace, with the multiplication of them; therefore the apostles so often make this their prayer in the beginning and end of their epistles. (3.) Solid peace cannot be enjoyed where there is no true grace; first grace, then peace. Peace without grace is mere stupidity; but grace may be true where there is for a time no actual peace; as Heman was distracted with terror, and Christ was once in an agony. (4.) The increase of grace and peace, as well as the first gift of them, is from God. Where he gives true grace he will give more grace; and every good man earnestly desires the improvement and multiplication of these blessings in himself and others.

3 Blessed *be* the God and Father of
our Lord Jesus Christ, which according to his abundant mercy hath begotten us again unto a lively hope by
the resurrection of Jesus Christ from
the dead, 4 To an inheritance incorruptible, and undefiled, and that fadeth
not away, reserved in heaven for you,
5 Who are kept by the power of God
through faith unto salvation ready to
be revealed in the last time.

We come now to the body of the epistle, which begins with,

I. A congratulation of the dignity and happiness of the state of these believers, brought in under the form of a thanksgiving to God. Other epistles begin in like manner, 2 Cor. i. 3; Eph. i. 3. Here we have,

1. The duty performed, which is blessing God. A man blesses God by a just acknowledgment of his excellency and blessedness.

2. The object of this blessing described by his relation to Jesus Christ: *The God and Father of our Lord Jesus Christ.* Here are three names of one person, denoting his threefold office. (1.) He is *Lord,* a universal king or sovereign. (2.) *Jesus,* a priest or Saviour. (3.) *Christ,* a prophet, anointed with the Spirit and furnished with all gifts necessary for the instruction, guidance, and salvation of his church. This God, so blessed, is the God of Christ according to his human nature, and his Father according to his divine nature.

3. The reasons that oblige us to this duty of blessing God, which are comprised in *his abundant mercy.* All our blessings are owing to God's mercy, not to man's merit, particularly regeneration. He *hath begotten us again,* and this deserves our thanksgiving to God, especially if we consider the fruit it produces in us, which is that excellent grace of hope, and that not such a vain, dead, perishing hope as that of worldlings and hypocrites, but a lively hope, a living, strong, quickening, and durable hope, as that hope must needs be that has such a solid foundation as *the resurrection of Jesus Christ from the dead.* Learn, (1.) A good Christian's condition is never so bad but he has great reason still to bless God. As a sinner has always reason to mourn, notwithstanding his present prosperity, so good people, in the midst of their manifold difficulties, have reason still to rejoice and bless God. (2.) In our prayers and praises we should address God as *the Father of our Lord Jesus Christ;* it is only through him that we and our services are accepted. (3.) The best of men owe their best blessings to the abundant mercy of God. All the evil in the world is from man's sin, but all the good in it is from *God's mercy.* Regeneration is expressly ascribed to the abundant mercy of God, and so are all the rest; we subsist entirely upon divine mercy.

Of the nature of regeneration, see on John iii. 3. (4.) Regeneration produces a lively hope of eternal life. Every unconverted person is a hopeless creature; whatever he pretends to of that kind is all confidence and presumption. The right Christian hope is what a man is begotten again unto by the Spirit of God; it is not from nature, but free grace. Those who are begotten to a new and spiritual life are begotten to a new and spiritual hope. (5.) The hope of a Christian has this excellency, it is a living hope. The hope of eternal life in a true Christian is a hope that keeps him alive, quickens him, supports him, and conducts him to heaven. Hope invigorates and spirits up the soul to action, to patience, to fortitude, and perseverance to the end. The delusive hopes of the unregenerate are vain and perishing; the hypocrite and his hope expire and die both together, Job xxvii. 8. (6.) *The resurrection of Jesus Christ from the dead* is the ground or foundation of a Christian's hope. The resurrection of Christ is the act of the Father as a Judge, of the Son as a conqueror. His resurrection demonstrates that the Father accepts his death in full discharge for our ransom, that he is victorious over death, the grave, and all our spiritual enemies; and it is also an assurance of our own resurrection. There being an inseparable union between Christ and his flock, they rise by virtue of his resurrection as a head, rather than by virtue of his power as a Judge. *We have risen with Christ,* Col. iii. 1. From all this taken together, Christians have two firm and solid foundations whereon to build their hope of eternal life.

II. Having congratulated these people on their new birth, and the hope of everlasting life, the apostle goes on to describe that life under the notion of *an inheritance,* a most proper way of speaking to these people; for they were poor and persecuted, perhaps turned out of their inheritances to which they were born; to allay this grievance, he tells them they were new-born to a new inheritance, infinitely better than what they had lost. Besides, they were most of them Jews, and so had a great affection to the land of Canaan, as the land of their inheritance, settled upon them by God himself; and to be driven out from abiding in the inheritance of the Lord was looked upon as a sore judgment, 1 Sam. xxvi. 19. To comfort them under this they are put in mind of a noble inheritance reserved in heaven for them, such a one that the land of Canaan was but a mere shadow in comparison with it. Here note,

1. Heaven is the undoubted inheritance of all the children of God; all that are born again are born to an inheritance, as a man makes his child his heir; the apostle argues, *If children, then heirs,* Rom. viii. 17. God giveth his gifts unto all, but the inheritance to none but his children; those that are his sons and daughters by regeneration and adoption receive the promise of eternal inheritance, Heb. ix. 15. This inheritance is not our purchase, but our Father's gift; not wages that we merit, but the effect of grace, which first makes us children and then settles this inheritance upon us by a firm unalterable covenant.

2. The incomparable excellencies of this inheritance, which are four:—(1.) It is incorruptible, in which respect it is like its Maker, who is called the *incorruptible God,* Rom. i. 23. All corruption is a change from better to worse, but heaven is without change and without end; the house is eternal in the heavens, and the possessors must subsist for ever, *for their corruptible must put on incorruption,* 1 Cor. xv. 53. (2.) This inheritance is undefiled, like the great high priest that is now in possession of it, who is *holy, harmless, and undefiled,* Heb. vii. 26. Sin and misery, the two grand defilements that spoil this world, and mar its beauty, have no place there. (3.) It fadeth not away, but always retains its vigour and beauty, and remains immarcescible, ever entertaining and pleasing the saints who possess it, without the least weariness or distaste. (4.) "*Reserved in heaven for you,*" which expression teaches us, [1.] That it is a glorious inheritance, for it is in heaven, and all that is there is glorious, Eph. i. 18. [2.] It is certain, a reversion in another world, safely kept and preserved till we come to the possession of it. [3.] The persons for whom it is reserved are described, not by their names, but by their character: *for you,* or us, or every one that is *begotten again to a lively hope.* This inheritance is preserved for them, and none but them; all the rest will be shut out for ever.

III. This inheritance being described as future, and distant both in time and place, the apostle supposes some doubt or uneasiness yet to remain upon the minds of these people, whether they might not possibly fall short by the way. "Though the happiness be safe in heaven, yet we are still upon earth, liable to abundance of temptations, miseries, and infirmities. Are we in such a safe state that we shall certainly come thither?" To this he answers that they should be safely guarded and conducted thither; they should be kept and preserved from all such destructive temptations and injuries as would prevent their safe arrival at eternal life. The heir to an earthly estate has no assurance that he shall live to enjoy it, but the heirs of heaven shall certainly be conducted safely to the possession of it. The blessing here promised is preservation: You *are kept;* the author of it is *God;* the means in us made use of for that end are our own *faith* and care; the end to which we are preserved is *salvation;* and the time when we shall see the safe end and issue of all is *the last time.* Note, 1. Such is the tender care of God over his people that he not only gives them grace, but preserves them unto glory. Their being kept implies both danger and deliverance; they may be attacked, but shall not be overcome. 2. The preservation of the regenerate to eternal life is the effect of God's power. The greatness of the work, the number of enemies, and our own infirmities, are such that no power but what is almighty can preserve the soul through all unto salvation; therefore the scripture often represents man's salvation as the effect of divine power, 2 Cor. xii. 9; Rom. xiv. 4. 3. Preservation by God's power does not supersede man's endeavour and care for his own salvation; here are God's power and man's faith, which implies an earnest desire of salvation, a reliance upon Christ according to his invitations and promises, a vigilant care to do every thing pleasing to God and avoid whatever is offensive, an abhorrence of temptations, a *respect to the recompence of reward,* and persevering diligence in prayer. By such a patient, operating, conquering faith, we are kept, under the assistance of divine grace, unto salvation; faith is a sovereign preservative of the soul through a state of grace unto a state of glory. 4. This salvation is *ready to be revealed in the last time.* Here are three things asserted about the salvation of the saints:—(1.) That it is now prepared, and made ready, and reserved in heaven for them. (2.) Though it be made ready now, yet it is in a great measure hidden and unrevealed at present, not only to the ignorant, blind world, that never enquire after it, but even to the heirs of salvation themselves. *It does not yet appear what we shall be,* 1 John iii. 2. (3.) That it shall be fully and completely *revealed in the last time,* or at the last day of judgment. *Life and immortality are now brought to light by the gospel,* but this life will be revealed more gloriously at death, when the soul shall be admitted into the presence of Christ, and behold his glory; and even beyond this there will be a further and a final revelation of the amplitude and transcendency of the saints' felicity at the last day, when their bodies shall be raised and re-united to their souls, and judgment shall pass upon angels and men, and Christ shall publicly honour and applaud his servants in the face of all the world.

6 Wherein ye greatly rejoice, though
now for a season, if need be, ye are in
heaviness through manifold temptations:
7 That the trial of your faith,
being much more precious than of
gold that perisheth, though it be tried
with fire, might be found unto praise
and honour and glory at the appearing
of Jesus Christ: 8 Whom having
not seen ye love; in whom, though
now ye see *him* not, yet believing, ye
rejoice with joy unspeakable and full
of glory: 9 Receiving the end of your
faith, *even* the salvation of *your* souls.

The first word, *wherein,* refers to the apostle's foregoing discourse about the excellency of their present state, and their grand expectations for the future. "In this condition *you greatly rejoice, though now for a season,* or a little while, *if need be, you are made sorrowful through manifold temptations,*" *v.* 6.

I. The apostle grants they were in great affliction, and propounds several things in mitigation of their sorrows. 1. Every sound Christian has always something wherein he may greatly rejoice. Great rejoicing contains more than an inward placid serenity of mind or sensation of comfort; it will show itself in the countenance and conduct, but especially in praise and gratitude. 2. The chief joy of a good Christian arises from things spiritual and heavenly, from his relation to God and to heaven. In these every sound Christian greatly rejoices; his joy arises from his treasure, which consists of matters of great value, and the title to them is sure. 3. The best Christians, those who have reason greatly to rejoice, may yet be in great heaviness through manifold temptations. All sorts of adversities are temptations, or trials of faith, patience, and constancy. These seldom go singly, but are manifold, and come from different quarters, the effect of all which is great heaviness. As men, we are subject to sorrows, personal and domestic. As Christians, our duty to God obliges us to frequent sorrow: and our compassion towards the miserable, the dishonour done to God, the calamities of his church, and the destruction of mankind, from their own folly and from divine vengeance, raise, in a generous and pious mind, almost continual sorrow. *I have great heaviness and continual sorrow in my heart,* Rom. ix. 2. 4. The afflictions and sorrows of good people are but for a little while, they are but for a season; though they may be smart, they are but short. Life itself is but for a little while, and the sorrows of it cannot survive it; the shortness of any affliction does much abate the heaviness of it. 5. Great heaviness is often necessary to a Christian's good: *If need be, you are in heaviness.* God does not afflict his people willingly, but acts with judgment, in proportion to our needs. There is a conveniency and fitness, nay, an absolute necessity in the case, for so the expression signifies: *it must be;* therefore no man should be *moved by these afflictions. For yourselves know that we are appointed thereunto,* 1 Thess. iii. 3. These troubles, that lie heavy, never come upon us but when we have need, and never stay any longer than needs must.

II. He expresses the end of their afflictions and the ground of their joy under them, *v.* 7. The end of good people's afflictions is *the trial of their faith.* As to the nature of this trial, it is *much more precious than of gold that perisheth, though it be tried with fire.* The effect of the trial is this, it will *be found unto praise, honour, and glory at the appearing of Jesus Christ.* Note, 1. The afflictions of serious Christians are designed for the trial of their faith. God's design in afflicting his people is their probation, not their destruction; their advantage, not their ruin: a *trial,* as the word signifies, is an experiment or search made upon a man, by some affliction, to prove the value and strength of his faith. This trial is made upon faith principally, rather than any other grace, because the trial of this is, in effect, the trial of all that is good in us. Our Christianity depends upon our faith; if this be wanting, there is nothing else that is spiritually good in us. Christ prays for this apostle, *that his faith might not fail;* if that be supported, all the rest will stand firm; the faith of good people is tried, that they themselves may have the comfort of it, God the glory of it, and others the benefit of it. 2. A tried faith is much more precious than tried gold. Here is a double comparison of faith and gold, and the trial of the one with the trial of the other. Gold is the most valuable, pure, useful, and durable, of all the metals; so is faith among the Christian virtues; it lasts till it brings the soul to heaven, and then it issues in the glorious fruition of God for ever. The trial of faith is much more precious than the trial of gold; in both there is a purification, a separation of the dross, and a discovery of the soundness and goodness of the things. Gold does not increase and multiply by trial in the fire, it rather grows less; but *faith* is established, improved, and multiplied, by the oppositions and afflictions that it meets with. *Gold* must perish at last—*gold that perisheth;* but *faith* never will. *I have prayed for thee, that thy faith fail not,* Luke xxii. 32. 3. The trial of faith will be found to praise, and honour, and glory. Honour is properly that esteem and value which one has with another, and so God and man will honour the saints. Praise is the expression or declaration of that esteem; so Christ will commend his people in the great day, *Come, you blessed of my Father,* &c. Glory is that lustre wherewith a person, so honoured and praised, shines in heaven. *Glory, honour, and peace, to every man that worketh good,* Rom. ii. 10. If a tried faith be found to praise, honour, and glory, let this recommend faith to you, as much more precious than gold, though it be assaulted and tried by afflictions. If you make your estimate either from present use or the final event of both, this will be found true, however the world may take it for an incredible paradox. 4. Jesus Christ will appear again in glory, and, when he does so, the saints will appear with him, and their graces will appear illustrious; and the more they have been tried the more bright they will then appear. The trial will soon be over, but the glory, honour, and praise will last to eternity. This should reconcile you to your present afflictions: *they work for you a far more exceeding and eternal weight of glory.*

III. He particularly commends the faith of these primitive Christians upon two accounts:—

1. The excellency of its object, the unseen Jesus. The apostle had seen our Lord in the flesh, but these dispersed Jews never did, and yet they believed in him, *v.* 8. It is one thing to believe God, or Christ (so the devils believe), and another thing to believe in him, which denotes subjection, reliance, and expectation of all promised good from him.

2. On account of two notable productions or effects of their faith, *love* and *joy,* and this joy so great as to be above description: *You rejoice with joy unspeakable, and full of glory.* Learn,

(1.) The faith of a Christian is properly conversant about things revealed, but not seen. Sense converses with things sensible and present; reason is a higher guide, which by sure deductions can infer the operation of causes, and the certainty of events; but faith ascends further still, and assures us of abundance of particulars that sense and reason could never have found out, upon the credit of revelation; it is *the evidence of things not seen.*

(2.) True faith is never alone, but produces a strong love to Jesus Christ. True Christians have a sincere love to Jesus, because they believe in him. This love discovers itself in the highest esteem for him, affectionate desires after him, willingness to be dissolved to be with him, delightful thoughts, cheerful services and sufferings, &c.

(3.) Where there are true faith and love to Christ there is, or may be, *joy unspeakable and full of glory.* This joy is inexpressible, it cannot be described by words; the best discovery is by an experimental taste of it; it is *full of glory,* full of heaven. There is much of heaven and the future glory in the present joys of improved Christians; their faith removes the causes of sorrow, and affords the best reasons for joy. Though good people sometimes walk in darkness, it is often owing to their own mistakes and ignorance, or to a fearful or melancholy disposition, or to some late sinful conduct, or perhaps to some sad occurrence of providence, that sinks their comfort for the present, yet they have reason to rejoice in the Lord, and joy in the God of their salvation, Hab. iii. 18. Well might these primitive Christians rejoice with joy unspeakable, since they were every day *receiving the end of their faith, the salvation of their souls v.* 4. Note, [1.] The blessing they were receiving: *The salvation of their souls* (the more noble part being put for the whole man), which salvation is here called *the end of their faith,* the end wherein faith terminates: faith helps to save the soul, then it has done its work, and ceases for ever. [2.] He speaks of the present time: You are now actually *receiving the end of your faith,* &c. [3.] The word used alludes to the games at which the conqueror received or bore away from the judge of the contest a crown or reward, which he carried about in triumph; so the salvation of the soul was the prize these Christians sought for, the crown they laboured for, the end they aimed at, which came nearer and more within their reach every day. Learn, *First,* Every faithful Christian is daily receiving the salvation of his soul; salvation is one permanent thing, begun in this life, not interrupted by death, and continued to all eternity. These believers had the beginnings of heaven in the possession of holiness and a heavenly mind, in their duties and communion with God, in the earnest of the inheritance, and the witness of the divine Spirit. This was properly urged to these distressed people; they were on the losing side in the world, but the apostle puts them in mind of what they were receiving; if they lost an inferior good, they were all the while receiving the salvation of their souls. *Secondly,* It is lawful for a Christian to make the salvation of his soul his end; the glory of God and our own felicity are so connected that if we regularly seek the one we must attain the other.

10 Of which salvation the prophets
have enquired and searched diligently,
who prophesied of the grace *that*
should come unto you: 11 Searching
what, or what manner of time the
Spirit of Christ which was in them did
signify, when it testified beforehand
the sufferings of Christ, and the glory
that should follow. 12 Unto whom
it was revealed, that not unto themselves, but unto us they did minister the things which are now reported unto you by them that have preached the gospel unto you with the Holy Ghost sent down from heaven; which things the angels desire to look into.

The apostle having described the persons to whom he wrote, and declared to them the excellent advantages they were under, goes on to show them what warrant he had for what he had delivered; and because they were Jews, and had a profound veneration for the Old Testament, he produces the authority of the prophets to convince them that the doctrine of salvation by faith in Jesus Christ was no new doctrine, but the same which the old prophets did enquire and search diligently into. Note,

I. Who made this diligent search—*the prophets,* who were persons inspired by God either to do or to say things extraordinary, above the reach of their own studies and abilities, as foretelling things to come, and revealing the will of God, by the direction of the Holy Spirit.

II. The object of their search, which was *salvation,* and *the grace of God which should come unto you;* the general salvation of men of all nations by Jesus Christ, and more especially the salvation afforded to the Jews, *the grace that should come to them* from him who was *not sent but to the lost sheep of the house of Israel.* They foresaw glorious times of light, grace, and comfort, coming upon the church, which made the prophets and righteous men desire to see and hear the things which came to pass in the days of the gospel.

III. The manner of their enquiry: they *enquired and searched diligently.* The words are strong and emphatic, alluding to miners, who dig to the bottom, and break through not only the earth, but the rock, to come to the ore; so these holy prophets had an earnest desire to know, and were proportionably diligent in their enquiries after the grace of God, which was to be revealed in the days of the Messiah: their being inspired did not make their industrious search needless; for, notwithstanding their extraordinary assistance from God, they were obliged to make use of all the ordinary methods of improvement in wisdom and knowledge. Daniel was a man greatly beloved and inspired, yet he understood by books and study the computations of time, *ch.* ix. 2. Even their own revelation required their study, meditation, and prayer; for many prophecies had a double meaning: in their first intention they aimed at some person or event near at hand, but their ultimate design was to describe the person, sufferings, or kingdom of Christ. Observe, 1. The doctrine of man's salvation by Jesus Christ has been the study and admiration of the greatest and wisest of men; the nobleness of the subject, and their own concern in it, have engaged them, with most accurate attention and seriousness to search into it. 2. A good man is much affected and pleased with the grace and mercy of God to others, as well as to himself. *The prophets* were highly delighted with the prospects of mercy to be shown both to Jews and Gentiles at the coming of Christ. 3. Those who would be acquainted with this great salvation, and the grace that shines therein, must enquire and search diligently into it: if it was necessary for an inspired prophet to do so, much more for persons so weak and injudicious as we are. 4. The grace that came by the gospel excels all that was before it; the gospel dispensation is more glorious, evident, intelligible, extensive, and effectual, than any dispensation that ever did precede it.

IV. The particular matters which the ancient prophets chiefly searched into, which are expressed in *v.* 11. Jesus Christ was the main subject of their studies; and, in relation to him, they were most inquisitive into,

1. His humiliation and death, and the glorious consequences of it: *The sufferings of Christ, and the glories that should follow.* This enquiry would lead them into a view of the whole gospel, the sum whereof is this, *that Christ Jesus was delivered for our offences and raised again for our justification.*

2. The time, and the manner of the times, wherein the Messiah was to appear. Undoubtedly these holy prophets earnestly desired to see the days of the Son of man; and therefore, next to the thing itself, their minds were set upon the time of its accomplishment, so far as the Spirit of Christ, which was in them, had signified any thing towards that purpose. The nature of the times was also under their strict consideration, whether they would be quiet or troublesome times, times of peace or times of war. Learn, (1.) Jesus Christ had a being before his incarnation; for his Spirit did then exist in the prophets, and therefore he whose that Spirit then was must be in being also. (2.) The doctrine of the Trinity was not wholly unknown to the faithful in the Old Testament. The prophets knew that they were inspired by a Spirit that was in them; this Spirit they knew to be the Spirit of Christ, and consequently distinct from Christ himself: here is a plurality of persons, and from other parts of the Old Testament a Trinity may be collected. (3.) The works here ascribed to the Holy Ghost prove him to be God. He *did signify*, discover, and manifest to the prophets, many hundred years *beforehand, the sufferings of Christ*, with a multitude of particular circumstances attending them; and he did also *testify*, or give proof and evidence beforehand, of the certainty of that event, by inspiring the prophets to reveal it, to work miracles in confirmation of it, and by enabling the faithful to believe it. These works prove the Spirit of Christ to be God, since he is possessed of almighty power and infinite knowledge. (4.) From the example of Christ Jesus learn to expect a time of services and sufferings before you are received to glory. It was so with him, and *the disciple is not above his Lord.* The suffering time is but short, but the glory is everlasting; let the suffering season be ever so sharp and severe, it shall not hinder, but *work for us a far more exceeding and eternal weight of glory.*

V. The success with which their enquiries were crowned. Their holy endeavours to inform themselves were not slighted, for God gave them a satisfactory revelation to quiet and comfort their minds. They were informed that these things should not come to pass in their time, but yet all was firm and certain, and should come to pass in the times of the apostles: *Not unto themselves, but to us;* and we must report them, under the infallible direction of the Holy Ghost, to all the world. *Which things the angels*, &c.

You have here three sorts of students, or enquirers into the great affair of man's salvation by Jesus Christ:—1. *The prophets*, who *searched diligently* into it. 2. The apostles, who consulted all the prophecies, and were witnesses of the accomplishment of them, and so reported what they knew to others in the preaching of the gospel. 3. The angels, who most attentively pry into these matters. Learn, (1.) A diligent endeavour after the knowledge of Christ and our duty will certainly be answered with good success. The prophets are answered with a revelation. Daniel studies, and receives information: the Bereans search the scriptures, and are confirmed. (2.) The holiest and best of men sometimes have their lawful and pious requests denied. It was both lawful and pious for these prophets to desire to know more than they were permitted to know about the time of the appearance of Christ in the world, but they were denied. It is lawful and pious for good parents to pray for their wicked children, for the poor to pray against poverty, for a good man to pray against death; yet, in these honest requests, they often are denied. God is pleased to answer our necessities rather than our requests. (3.) It is the honour and the practice of a Christian to be useful to others, in many cases, rather than to himself. The prophets ministered to others, not unto themselves. *None of us liveth to himself*, Rom. xiv. 7. Nothing is more contrary to man's nature nor to Christian principles than for a man to make himself his own end, and live to himself. (4.) The revelations of God to his church, though gradual, and given by parcels, are all perfectly consistent; the doctrine of the prophets and that of the apostles exactly agree, as coming from the same Spirit of God. (5.) The efficacy of the evangelical ministry depends upon the Holy Ghost sent down from heaven. The gospel is the ministration of the Spirit; the success of it depends upon his operation and blessing. (6.) The mysteries of the gospel, and the methods of man's salvation, are so glorious that the blessed angels earnestly desire to look into them; they are curious, accurate, and industrious in prying into them; they consider the whole scheme of man's redemption with deep attention and admiration, particularly the points the apostle had been discoursing of: *Which things the angels desire to* stoop down and *look into*, as *the cherubim* did continually *towards the mercy-seat.*

13 Wherefore gird up the loins of
your mind, be sober, and hope to the
end for the grace that is to be brought
unto you at the revelation of Jesus
Christ; 14 As obedient children,
not fashioning yourselves according
to the former lusts in your ignorance:
15 But as he which hath called you

is holy, so be ye holy in all manner
of conversation; 16 Because it is
written, Be ye holy; for I am holy.
17 And if ye call on the Father, who
without respect of persons judgeth
according to every man's work, pass
the time of your sojourning *here* in
fear: 18 Forasmuch as ye know that
ye were not redeemed with corruptible
things, *as* silver and gold, from your
vain conversation *received* by tradition
from your fathers; 19 But with the
precious blood of Christ, as of a lamb
without blemish and without spot:
20 Who verily was foreordained before the foundation of the world, but
was manifest in these last times for
you, 21 Who by him do believe in
God, that raised him up from the
dead, and gave him glory; that your
faith and hope might be in God. 22
Seeing ye have purified your souls in
obeying the truth through the Spirit
unto unfeigned love of the brethren,
see that ye love one another with a
pure heart fervently: 23 Being born
again, not of corruptible seed, but
of incorruptible, by the word of God,
which liveth and abideth for ever.

Here the apostle begins his exhortations to those whose glorious state he had before described, thereby instructing us that Christianity is a doctrine according to godliness, designed to make us not only wiser, but better.

I. He exhorts them to sobriety and holiness.

1. *Wherefore gird up the loins of your mind*, &c., *v.* 13. As if he had said, "*Wherefore,* since you are so honoured and distinguished, as above, *Gird up the loins of your mind.* You have a journey to go, a race to run, a warfare to accomplish, and a great work to do; as the traveller, the racer, the warrior, and the labourer, gather in, and gird up, their long and loose garments, that they may be more ready, prompt, and expeditious in their business, so do you by your minds, your inner man, and affections seated there: *gird them,* gather them in, let them not hang loose and neglected about you; restrain their extravagances, and let the loins or strength and vigour of your minds be exerted in your duty; disengage yourselves from all that would hinder you, and go on resolutely in your obedience. *Be sober,* be vigilant against all your spiritual dangers and enemies, and be temperate and modest in eating, drinking, apparel, recreation, business, and in the whole of your behaviour. Be sober-minded also in opinion, as well as in practice, and humble in your judgment of yourselves." *And hope to the end, for the grace that is to be brought to you at the revelation of Jesus Christ.* Some refer this to the last judgment, as if the apostle directed their hope to the final revelation of Jesus Christ; but it seems more natural to take it, as it might be rendered, "*Hope perfectly,* or *thoroughly, for the grace that is brought to you* in or by *the revelation of Jesus Christ;* that is, by the gospel, *which brings life and immortality to light.* Hope perfectly, trust without doubting to that grace which is now offered to you by the gospel." Learn, (1.) The main work of a Christian lies in the right management of his heart and mind; the apostle's first direction is to gird up the loins of the mind. (2.) The best Christians have need to be exhorted to sobriety. These excellent Christians are put in mind of it; it is required of a bishop (1 Tim. iii. 2), of aged men (Tit. ii. 2), the young women are to be taught it, and the young men are directed to be sober-minded, Tit. ii. 4, 6. (3.) A Christian's work is not over as soon as he has got into a state of grace; he must still hope and strive for more grace. When he has entered the strait gate, he must still walk in the narrow way, and gird up the loins of his mind for that purpose. (4.) A strong and perfect trust in God's grace is very consistent with our best endeavours in our duty; we must hope perfectly, and yet gird up our loins, and address ourselves vigorously to the work we have to do, encouraging ourselves from the grace of Jesus Christ.

2. *As obedient children,* &c., *v.* 14. These words may be taken as a rule of holy living, which is both positive—"You ought to live *as obedient children,* as those whom God hath adopted into his family, and regenerated by his grace;" and negative—"You must *not fashion yourselves according to the former lusts, in your ignorance.*" Or the words may be taken as an argument to press them to holiness from the consideration of what they now are, children of obedience, and what they were when they lived in lust and ignorance. Learn, (1.) The children of God ought to prove themselves to be such by their obedience to God, by their present, constant, universal obedience. (2.) The best of God's children have had their times of lust and ignorance; the time has been when the whole scheme of their lives, their way and fashion, was to accommodate and gratify their unlawful desires and vicious appetites, being grossly ignorant of God and themselves, of Christ and the gospel. (3.) Persons, when converted, differ exceedingly from what they were formerly. They are people of another fashion and manner from what they were before; their inward frame, behaviour, speech, and conversation, are much altered from what they were in times past. (4.) The

lusts and extravagances of sinners are both the fruits and the signs of their ignorance.

3. *But as he who hath called you,* &c., *v.* 15, 16. Here is a noble rule enforced by strong arguments: *Be you holy in all manner of conversation.* Who is sufficient for this? And yet it is required in strong terms, and enforced by three reasons, taken from the grace of God in calling us,—from his command, *it is written,*—and from his example. *Be you holy, for I am holy.* Learn, (1.) The grace of God in calling a sinner is a powerful engagement to holiness. It is a great favour to be called effectually by divine grace out of a state of sin and misery into the possession of all the blessings of the new covenant; and great favours are strong obligations; they enable as well as oblige to be holy. (2.) Complete holiness is the desire and duty of every Christian. Here is a twofold rule of holiness: [1.] It must, for the extent of it, be universal. We must *be holy,* and be so *in all manner of conversation;* in all civil and religious affairs, in every condition, prosperous or reverse; towards all people, friends and enemies; in all our intercourse and business still we must be holy. [2.] For the pattern of it. We must *be holy, as God is holy:* we must imitate him, though we can never equal him. He is perfectly, unchangeably, and eternally holy; and we should aspire after such a state. The consideration of the holiness of God should oblige us to the highest degree of holiness we can attain unto. (3.) The written word of God is the surest rule of a Christian's life, and by this rule we are commanded to be holy every way. (4.) The Old-Testament commands are to be studied and obeyed in the times of the New Testament; the apostle, by virtue of a command delivered several times by Moses, requires holiness in all Christians.

4. *If you call on the Father,* &c., v. 17. The apostle does not there express any doubt at all whether these Christians would call upon their heavenly Father, but supposes they would certainly do it, and from this argues with them to *pass the time of their sojourning here in fear:* "If you own the great God as a Father and a Judge, you ought to live the time of your sojourning here in his fear." Learn, (1.) All good Christians look upon themselves in this world as pilgrims and strangers, as strangers in a distant country, passing to another, to which they properly belong, Ps. xxxix. 12; Heb. xi. 13. (2.) The whole time of our sojourning here is to be passed in the fear of God. (3.) The consideration of God as a Judge is not improper for those who can truly clal him Father. Holy confidence in God as a Father, and an awful fear of him as a Judge, are very consistent; to regard God as a Judge is a singular means to endear him to us as a Father. (4.) The judgment of God will be without respect of persons: *According to every man's work.* No external relation to him will protect any; the Jew may call God Father and Abraham father, but God will not respect persons, nor favour their cause, from personal considerations, but judge them according to their work. The works of men will in the great day discover their persons; God will make all the world to know who are his by their works. We are obliged to faith, holiness, and obedience, and our works will be an evidence whether we have complied with our obligations or not.

5. The apostle having exhorted them to *pass the time of their sojourning in the fear of God* from this consideration, that they *called on the Father,* he adds (*v.* 18) a second argument: *Because* or *forasmuch as you were not redeemed with corruptible things,* &c. Herein he puts them in mind, (1.) That they were redeemed, or bought back again, by a ransom paid to the Father. (2.) What the price paid for their redemption was: *Not with corruptible things, as silver and gold, but with the precious blood of Christ.* (3.) From what they were redeemed: *From a vain conversation received by tradition.* (4.) They knew this: *Forasmuch as you know,* and cannot pretend ignorance of this great affair. Learn, [1.] The consideration of our redemption ought to be a constant and powerful inducement to holiness, and the fear of God. [2.] God expects that a Christian should live answerably to what he knows, and therefore we have great need to be put in mind of what we already know, Ps. xxxix. 4. [3.] Neither silver nor gold, nor any of the corruptible things of this world, can redeem so much as one soul. They are often snares, temptations, and hindrances to man's salvation, but they can by no means purchase or procure it; they are corruptible, and therefore cannot redeem an incorruptible and immortal soul. [4.] The blood of Jesus Christ is the only price of man's redemption. The redemption of man is real, not metaphorical. We are bought with a price, and the price is equal to the purchase, for it is the precious blood of Christ; it is the blood of an innocent person, a lamb without blemish and without spot, whom the paschal lamb represented, and of an infinite person, being the Son of God, and therefore it is called the blood of God, Acts xx. 28. [5.] The design of Christ in shedding his most precious blood was to redeem us, not only from eternal misery hereafter, but from a vain conversation in this world. That conversation is vain which is empty, frivolous, trifling, and unserviceable to the honour of God, the credit of religion, the conviction of unbelievers, and the comfort and satisfaction of a man's own conscience. Not only the open wickedness, but the vanity and unprofitableness of our conversation are highly dangerous. [6.] A man's conversation may carry an appearance of devotion, and may plead antiquity, custom, and tradition, in its defence, and

yet after all be a most vain conversation. The Jews had a deal to say from these heads, for all their formalities; and yet their conversation was so vain that only the blood of Christ could redeem them from it. Antiquity is no certain rule of verity, nor is it a wise resolution, "I will live and die in such a way, because my forefathers did so."

6. Having mentioned the price of redemption, the apostle goes on to speak of some things relating both to the Redeemer and the redeemed, *v.* 20 21.

(1.) The Redeemer is further described, not only as a Lamb without spot, but as one, [1.] That was *fore-ordained before the foundation of the world,* fore-ordained or foreknown. When prescience is ascribed to God, it implies more than bare prospect or speculation. It imports an act of the will, a resolution that the thing shall be, Acts ii. 23. God did not only foreknow, but determine and decree, that his Son should die for man, and this decree was before the foundation of the world. Time and the world began together; before the commencement of time there was nothing but eternity. [2.] That was *manifested in these last days for them.* He was manifested or demonstrated to be that Redeemer whom God had fore-ordained. He was manifested by his birth, by his Father's testimony, and by his own works, especially by his resurrection from the dead, Rom. i. 4. "This was done in these last times of the New Testament and of the gospel, for you, you Jews, you sinners, you afflicted ones; you have the comfort of the manifestation and appearance of Christ, if you believe on him." [3.] That was raised from the dead by the Father, who gave him glory. The resurrection of Christ, considered as an act of power, is common to all the three persons, but as an act of judgment it is peculiar to the Father, who as a Judge released Christ, raised him from the grave, and gave him glory, proclaimed him to all the world to be his Son by his resurrection from the dead, advanced him to heaven, crowned him with glory and honour, invested him with all power in heaven and earth, and glorified him with that glory which he had with God before the world was.

(2.) The redeemed are also described here by their faith and hope, the cause of which is Jesus Christ: "*You do by him believe in God*—by him as the author, encourager, support, and finisher of your faith; your faith and hope now may be in God, as reconciled to you by Christ the Mediator."

(3.) From all this we learn, [1.] The decree of God to send Christ to be a Mediator was from everlasting, and was a just and merciful decree, which yet does not at all excuse man's sin in crucifying him, Acts ii. 23. God had purposes of special favour towards his people long before he made any manifestations of such grace to them. [2.] Great is the happiness of the last times in comparison with what the former ages of the world enjoyed. The clearness of light, the supports of faith, the efficacy of ordinances, and the proportion of comforts—these are all much greater since the manifestation of Christ than they were before. Our gratitude and services should be suitable to such favours. [3.] The redemption of Christ belongs to none but true believers. A general impetration is asserted by some and denied by others, but none pretend to a general application of Christ's death for the salvation of all. Hypocrites and unbelievers will be ruined for ever, notwithstanding the death of Christ. [4.] God in Christ is the ultimate object of a Christian's faith, which is strongly supported by the resurrection of Christ, and the glory that did follow.

II. He exhorts them to brotherly love.

1. He supposes that the gospel had already had such an effect upon them as to purify their souls while they obeyed it through the Spirit, and that it had produced at least an *unfeigned love of the brethren;* and thence he argues with them to proceed to a higher degree of affection, to love one another with a pure heart fervently, *v.* 22. Learn, (1.) It is not to be doubted but that every sincere Christian purifies his soul. The apostle takes this for granted: *Seeing you have,* &c. To purify the soul supposes some great uncleanness and defilement which had polluted it, and that this defilement is removed. Neither the Levitical purifications under the law, nor the hypocritical purifications of the outward man, can effect this. (2.) The word of God is the great instrument of a sinner's purification: *Seeing you have purified your souls in obeying the truth.* The gospel is called truth, in opposition to types and shadows, to error and falsehood. This truth is effectual to purify the soul, if it be obeyed, John xvii. 17. Many hear the truth, but are never purified by it, because they will not submit to it nor obey it. (3.) The Spirit of God is the great agent in the purification of man's soul. The Spirit convinces the soul of its impurities, furnishes those virtues and graces that both adorn and purify, such as faith (Acts xv. 9), hope (1 John iii. 3), the fear of God (Ps. xxxiv. 9), and the love of Jesus Christ. The Spirit excites our endeavours, and makes them successful. The aid of the Spirit does not supersede our own industry; these people purified their own souls, but it was through the Spirit. (4.) The souls of Christians must be purified before they can so much as love one another unfeignedly. There are such lusts and partialities in man's nature that without divine grace we can neither love God nor one another as we ought to do; there is no charity but out of a pure heart. (5.) It is the duty of all Christians sincerely and fervently to love one another. Our affection to one another must be sincere and real, and it must be fervent, constant, and extensive.

2. He further presses upon Christians the duty of loving one another with a pure heart fervently from the consideration of their spiritual relation; they are all *born again, not of corruptible seed, but incorruptible,* &c. Hence we may learn, (1.) That all Christians are born again. The apostle speaks of it as what is common to all serious Christians, and by this they are brought into a new and a near relation to one another, they become brethren by their new birth. (2.) The word of God is the great means of regeneration, Jam. i. 18. The grace of regeneration is conveyed by the gospel. (3.) This new and second birth is much more desirable and excellent than the first. This the apostle teaches by preferring the incorruptible to the corruptible seed. By the one we become the children of men, by the other the sons and daughters of the Most High. The word of God being compared to seed teaches us that though it is little in appearance, yet it is wonderful in operation, though it lies hid awhile, yet it grows up and produces excellent fruit at last. (4.) Those that are regenerate should love one another with a pure heart fervently. Brethren by nature are bound to love one another; but the obligation is double where there is a spiritual relation: they are under the same government, partake of the same privileges, and have embarked in the same interest. (5.) The word of God lives and abides for ever. This word is a living word, or a lively word, Heb. iv. 12. It is a means of spiritual life, to begin it and preserve in it, animating and exciting us in our duty, till it brings us to eternal life: and it is abiding; it remains eternally true, and abides in the hearts of the regenerate for ever.

24 For all flesh *is* as grass, and all the glory of man as the flower of grass. The grass withereth, and the flower thereof falleth away: 25 But the word of the Lord endureth for ever. And this is the word which by the gospel is preached unto you.

The apostle having given an account of the excellency of the renewed spiritual man as born again, not of corruptible but incorruptible seed, he now sets before us the vanity of the natural man, taking him with all his ornaments and advantages about him: *For all flesh is as grass, and all the glory of man as the flower of grass;* and nothing can make him a solid substantial being, but the being born again of the incorruptible seed, the word of God, which will transform him into a most excellent creature, whose glory will not fade like a flower, but shine like an angel; and this word is daily set before you in the preaching of the gospel. Learn, 1. Man, in his utmost flourish and glory, is still a withering, fading, dying creature. Take him singly, all flesh is grass. In his entrance into the world, in his life and in his fall, he is similar to grass, Job xiv. 2; Isa. xl. 6, 7. Take him in all his glory, even this is as the flower of grass; his wit, beauty, strength, vigour, wealth, honour—these are but as the flower of grass, which soon withers and dies away. 2. The only way to render this perishing creature solid and incorruptible is for him to entertain and receive the word of God; for this remains everlasting truth, and, if received, will preserve him to everlasting life, and abide with him for ever. 3. The prophets and apostles preached the same doctrine. This word which Isaiah and others delivered in the Old Testament is the same which the apostles preached in the New.

CHAP. II.

The general exhortation to holiness is continued, and enforced by several reasons taken from the foundation on which Christians are built, Jesus Christ, and from their spiritual blessings and privileges in him. The means of obtaining it, the word of God, is recommended, and all contrary qualities are condemned, ver. 1—12. Particular directions are given how subjects ought to obey the magistrates, and servants their masters, patiently suffering in well doing, in imitation of Christ, ver. 13, to the end.

WHEREFORE laying aside all malice, and all guile, and hypocrisies, and envies, and all evil speakings, 2 As newborn babes, desire the sincere milk of the word, that ye may grow thereby: 3 If so be ye have tasted that the Lord *is* gracious.

The holy apostle has been recommending mutual charity, and setting forth the excellences of the word of God, calling it an *incorruptible seed,* and saying that it *liveth and abideth for ever.* He pursues his discourse, and very properly comes in with this necessary advice, *Wherefore laying aside all malice,* &c. These are such sins as both destroy charity and hinder the efficacy of the word, and consequently they prevent our regeneration.

I. His advice is to lay aside or put off what is evil, as one would do an old rotten garment: "Cast it away with indignation, never put it on more."

1. The sins to be put off, or thrown aside, are, (1.) *Malice,* which may be taken more generally for all sorts of wickedness, as Jam. i. 21; 1 Cor. v. 8. But, in a more confined sense, malice is anger resting in the bosom of fools, settled overgrown anger, retained till it inflames a man to design mischief, to do mischief, or delight in any mischief that befals another. (2.) *Guile,* or deceit in words. So it comprehends flattery, falsehood, and delusion, which is a crafty imposing upon another's ignorance or weakness, to his damage. (3.) *Hypocrisies.* The word being plural comprehends all sorts of hypocrisies. In matters of religion hypocrisy is counterfeit piety. In civil conversation hypocrisy is counterfeit friendship, which is much practised by those who give high compliments, which they do not believe, or make promises which they never intend to perform, or pretend friendship when mischief

lies in their hearts. (4.) *All envies;* every thing that may be called *envy,* which is a grieving at the good and welfare of another, at their abilities, prosperity, fame, or successful labours. (5.) *Evil speaking,* which is detraction, speaking against another, or defaming him; it is rendered *backbiting,* 2 Cor. xii. 20; Rom. i. 30.

2. Hence learn, (1.) The best Christians have need to be cautioned and warned against the worst sins, such as malice, hypocrisy, envy. They are but sanctified in part, and are still liable to temptations. (2.) Our best services towards God will neither please him nor profit us if we be not conscientious in our duties to men. The sins here mentioned are offences against the second table. These must be laid aside, or else we cannot receive the word of God as we ought to do. (3.) Whereas it is said *all malice, all guile,* learn, That one sin, not laid aside, will hinder our spiritual profit and everlasting welfare. (4.) Malice, envy, hatred, hypocrisy, and evil-speaking, generally go together. Evil-speaking is a sign that malice and guile lie in the heart; and all of them combine to hinder our profiting by the word of God.

II. The apostle, like a wise physician, having prescribed the purging out of vicious humours, goes on to direct to wholesome and regular food, that they may grow thereby. The duty exhorted to is a strong and constant desire for the *word of God,* which word is here called *reasonable milk,* only, this phrase not being proper English, our translators rendered it *the milk of the word,* by which we are to understand food proper for the soul, or a reasonable creature, whereby the mind, not the body, is nourished and strengthened. This milk of the word must be *sincere,* not adulterated by the mixtures of men, who often corrupt the word of God, 2 Cor. ii. 17. The manner in which they are to desire this sincere milk of the word is stated thus: *As new-born babes.* He puts them in mind of their regeneration. A new life requires suitable food. They, being newly born, must desire the milk of the word. Infants desire common milk, and their desires towards it are fervent and frequent, arising from an impatient sense of hunger, and accompanied with the best endeavours of which the infant is capable. Such must Christians' desires be for the word of God: and that for this end, that they may grow thereby, that we may improve in grace and the knowledge of our Lord and Saviour, 2 Pet. iii. 18. Learn, 1. Strong desires and affections to the word of God are a sure evidence of a person's being born again. If they be such desires as the babe has for the milk, they prove that the person is new-born. They are the lowest evidence, but yet they are certain. 2. Growth and improvement in wisdom and grace are the design and desire of every Christian; all spiritual means are for edification and improvement. The word of God, rightly used, does not leave a man as it finds him, but improves and makes him better.

III. He adds an argument from their own experience: *If so be,* or *since that,* or *forasmuch as, you have tasted that the Lord is gracious, v.* 3. The apostle does not express a doubt, but affirms that these good Christians had tasted the goodness of God, and hence argues with them. "You ought to lay aside these vile sins (*v.* 1); you ought to desire the word of God; you ought to grow thereby, since you cannot deny but that you have tasted that the Lord is gracious." The next verse assures us that the Lord here spoken of is the Lord Jesus Christ. Hence learn, 1. Our Lord Jesus Christ is very gracious to his people. He is in himself infinitely good; he is very kind, free, and merciful to miserable sinners; he is pitiful and good to the undeserving; he has in him a fulness of grace. 2. The graciousness of our Redeemer is best discovered by an experimental taste of it. There must be an immediate application of the object to the organ of taste; we cannot taste at a distance, as we may see, and hear, and smell. To taste the graciousness of Christ experimentally supposes our being united to him by faith, and then we may taste his goodness in all his providences, in all our spiritual concerns, in all our fears and temptations, in his word and worship every day. 3. The best of God's servants have in this life but a taste of the grace of Christ. A taste is but a little; it is not a draught, nor does it satisfy. It is so with the consolations of God in this life. 4. The word of God is the great instrument whereby he discovers and communicates his grace to men. Those who feed upon the sincere milk of the word taste and experience most of his grace. In our converses with his word we should endeavour always to understand and experience more and more of his grace.

4 To whom coming, *as unto* a
living stone, disallowed indeed of men,
but chosen of God, *and* precious,
5 Ye also, as lively stones, are built
up a spiritual house, a holy priesthood, to offer up spiritual sacrifices,
acceptable to God by Jesus Christ.
6 Wherefore also it is contained in
the scripture, Behold, I lay in Sion a
chief corner stone, elect, precious:
and he that believeth on him shall
not be confounded. 7 Unto you
therefore which believe *he is* precious:
but unto them which be disobedient,
the stone which the builders disallowed, the same is made the head of
the corner, 8 And a stone of stum-

bling, and a rock of offence, *even to*
them which stumble at the word,
being disobedient: whereunto also
they were appointed. 9 But ye *are*
a chosen generation, a royal priesthood, a holy nation, a peculiar people;
that ye should show forth the praises
of him who hath called you out of
darkness into his marvellous light:
10 Which in time past *were* not a
people, but *are* now the people of
God: which had not obtained mercy,
but now have obtained mercy. 11
Dearly beloved, I beseech *you* as
strangers and pilgrims, abstain from
fleshly lusts, which war against the
soul; 12 Having your conversation
honest among the Gentiles: that,
whereas they speak against you as
evildoers, they may by *your* good
works, which they shall behold, glorify
God in the day of visitation.

I. The apostle here gives us a description of Jesus Christ as a living stone; and though to a capricious wit, or an infidel, this description may seem rough and harsh, yet to the Jews, who placed much of their religion in their magnificent temple, and who understood the prophetical style, which calls the Messiah *a stone* (Isa. viii. 14; xxviii. 16), it would appear very elegant and proper.

1. In this metaphorical description of Jesus Christ, he is called a stone, to denote his invincible strength and everlasting duration, and to teach his servants that he is their protection and security, the foundation on which they are built, and a rock of offence to all their enemies. He is the living stone, having eternal life in himself, and being the prince of life to all his people. The reputation and respect he has with God and man are very different. He is disallowed of men, reprobated or rejected by his own countrymen the Jews, and by the generality of mankind; but chosen of God, separated and fore-ordained to be the foundation of the church (as *ch.* i. 20), and precious, a most honourable, choice, worthy person in himself, in the esteem of God, and in the judgment of all who believe on him. To this person so described we are obliged to come: *To whom coming*, not by a local motion, for that is impossible since his exaltation, but by faith, whereby we are united to him at first, and draw nigh to him afterwards. Learn, (1.) Jesus Christ is the very foundation-stone of all our hopes and happiness. He communicates the true knowledge of God (Matt. xi. 27); by him we have access to the Father (John xiv. 6), and through him are made partakers of all spiritual blessings, Eph. i. 3. (2.) Men in general disallow and reject Jesus Christ; they slight him, dislike him, oppose and refuse him, as scripture and experience declare, Isa. liii. 3. (3.) However Christ may be disallowed by an ungrateful world, yet he is chosen of God, and precious in his account. He is chosen and fixed upon to be the Lord of the universe, the head of the church, the Saviour of his people, and the Judge of the world. He is precious in the excellency of his nature, the dignity of his office, and the gloriousness of his services. (4.) Those who expect mercy from this gracious Redeemer must come to him, which is our act, though done by God's grace—an act of the soul, not of the body—a real endeavour, not a fruitless wish.

2. Having described Christ as the foundation, the apostle goes on to speak of the superstructure, the materials built upon him: *You also, as living stones, are built up, v.* 6. The apostle is recommending the Christian church and constitution to these dispersed Jews. It was natural for them to object that the Christian church had no such glorious temple, nor such a numerous priesthood; but its dispensation was mean, the services and sacrifices of it having nothing of the pomp and grandeur which the Jewish dispensation had. To this the apostle answers that the Christian church is a much nobler fabric than the Jewish temple; it is a living temple, consisting not of dead materials, but of living parts. Christ, the foundation, is a living stone. Christians are lively stones, and these make a spiritual house, and they are a holy priesthood; and, though they have no bloody sacrifices of beasts to offer, yet they have much better and more acceptable, and they have an altar too on which to present their offerings; for they offer spiritual sacrifices, acceptable to God by Jesus Christ. Learn, (1.) All sincere Christians have in them a principle of spiritual life communicated to them from Christ their head: therefore, as he is called a living stone, so they are called lively, or living stones; not dead in trespasses and sins, but alive to God by regeneration and the working of the divine Spirit. (2.) The church of God is a spiritual house. The foundation is Christ, Eph. ii. 20. The builders are ministers, 1 Cor. iii. 10. The inhabitant is God, Eph. ii. 22. It is a house for its strength, beauty, variety of parts, and usefulness of the whole. It is spiritual in its foundation, Christ Jesus,—in the materials of it, spiritual persons,—in its furniture, the graces of the Spirit,—in its connection, being held together by the Spirit of God and by one common faith,—and in its use, which is spiritual work, to offer up spiritual sacrifices. This house is daily built up, every part of it improving, and the whole supplied in every age by the addition of new particular members. (3.) All good Christians are a holy priesthood. The apostle speaks here of the generality of Christians, and tells them they are a holy priesthood; they are

all select persons, sacred to God, serviceable to others, well endowed with heavenly gifts and graces, and well employed. (4.) This holy priesthood must and will offer up spiritual sacrifices to God. The spiritual sacrifices which Christians are to offer are their bodies, souls, affections, prayers, praises, alms, and other duties. (5.) The most spiritual sacrifices of the best men are not acceptable to God, but through Jesus Christ; he is the only great high priest, through whom we and our services can be accepted; therefore bring all your oblations to him, and by him present them to God.

II. He confirms what he had asserted of Christ being a *living stone*, &c., from Isa. xxviii. 16. Observe the manner of the apostle's quoting scripture, not by book, chapter, and verse; for these distinctions were not then made, so no more was said than a reference to Moses, David, or the prophets, except once a particular psalm was named, Acts xiii. 33. In their quotations they kept rather to the sense than the words of scripture, as appears from what is recited from the prophet in this place. He does not quote the scripture, neither the Hebrew nor LXX., word for word, yet makes a just and true quotation. The true sense of scripture may be justly and fully expressed in other than in scripture-words. *It is contained.* The verb is active, but our translators render it passively, to avoid the difficulty of finding a nominative case for it, which had puzzled so many interpreters before them. The matter of the quotation is this, *Behold, I lay in Zion.* Learn, 1. In the weighty matters of religion we must depend entirely upon scripture-proof; Christ and his apostles appealed to Moses, David, and the ancient prophets. The word of God is the only rule God hath given us. It is a perfect and sufficient rule; and it is an intelligible and a certain rule. 2. The accounts that God hath given us in scripture concerning his Son Jesus Christ are what require our strictest attention. *Behold, I lay*, &c. John calls for the like attention, John i. 29. These demands of attention to Christ show us the excellency of the matter, the importance of it, and our stupidity and dulness. 3. The constituting of Christ Jesus head of the church is an eminent work of God: *I lay in Zion.* The setting up of the pope for head of the church is a human contrivance and an arrogant presumption; Christ only is the foundation and head of the church of God. 4. Jesus Christ is the chief corner-stone that God hath laid in his spiritual building. The corner-stone stays inseparably with the building, supports it, unites it, and adorns it. So does Christ by his holy church, his spiritual house. 5. Jesus Christ is the corner-stone for the support and salvation of none but such as are his sincere people: none but Zion, and such as are of Zion; not for Babylon, not for his enemies. 6. True faith in Jesus Christ is the only way to prevent a man's utter confusion. Three things put a man into great confusion, and faith prevents them all—disappointment, sin, and judgment. Faith has a remedy for each.

III. He deduces an important inference, *v.* 7. Jesus Christ is said to be the chief corner-stone. Hence the apostle infers with respect to good men, "To you therefore who believe he is precious, or he is an honour. Christ is the crown and honour of a Christian; you who believe will be so far from being ashamed of him that you will boast of him and glory in him for ever." As to wicked men, the disobedient will go on to disallow and reject Jesus Christ; but God is resolved that he shall be, in despite of all opposition, the head of the corner. Learn, 1. Whatever is by just and necessary consequence deduced from scripture may be depended upon with as much certainty as if it were contained in express words of scripture. The apostle draws an inference from the prophet's testimony. The prophet did not expressly say so, but yet he said that from which the consequence was unavoidable. Our Saviour bids them search the scriptures, because they testified of him; and yet no place in those scriptures to which he there refers them said that Jesus of Nazareth was the Messiah. Yet those scriptures do say that he who should be born of a virgin, before the sceptre departed from Judah, during the second temple, and after Daniel's seventy weeks, was the Messiah; but such was Jesus Christ: to collect this conclusion one must make use of reason, history, eye-sight, experience, and yet it is an infallible scripture-conclusion notwithstanding. 2. The business of a faithful minister is to apply general truths to the particular condition and state of his hearers. The apostle quotes a passage (*v.* 6) out of the prophet, and applies it severally to good and bad. This requires wisdom, courage, and fidelity; but it is very profitable to the hearers. 3. Jesus Christ is exceedingly precious to all the faithful. The majesty and grandeur of his person, the dignity of his office, his near relation, his wonderful works, his immense love—every thing engages the faithful to the highest esteem and respect for Jesus Christ. 4. Disobedient people have no true faith. By disobedient people understand those that are unpersuadable, incredulous, and impenitent. These may have some right notions, but no solid faith. 5. Those that ought to be builders of the church of Christ are often the worst enemies that Christ has in the world. In the Old Testament the false prophets did the most mischief; and in the New Testament the greatest opposition and cruelty that Christ met with were from the scribes, pharisees, chief priests, and those who pretended to build and take care of the church still the hierarchy of Rome is the worst enemy in the world to Jesus Christ and his interest. 6.

God will carry on his own work, and support the interest of Jesus Christ in the world, notwithstanding the falseness of pretended friends and the opposition of his worst enemies.

IV. The apostle adds a further description, still preserving the metaphor of a stone, *v.* 8. The words are taken from Isa. viii. 13, 14, *Sanctify the Lord of hosts himself——and he shall be for a stone of stumbling, and for a rock of offence,* whence it is plain that Jesus Christ is the Lord of hosts, and consequently the most high God. Observe,

1. The builders, the chief-priests, refused him, and the people followed their leaders; and so Christ became to them *a stone of stumbling, and a rock of offence,* at which they stumbled and hurt themselves; and in return he fell upon them as a mighty stone or rock, and punished them with destruction. Matt. xxi. 44, *Whosoever shall fall on this stone shall be broken; but on whomsoever it shall fall it will grind him to powder.* Learn, (1.) All those that are disobedient take offence at the word of God: *They stumble at the word, being disobedient.* They are offended with Christ himself, with his doctrine and the purity of his precepts; but the Jewish doctors more especially stumbled at the meanness of his appearance and the proposal of trusting only to him for their justification before God. They could not be brought to seek justification by faith, but as it were by the works of the law; *for they stumbled at that stumbling-stone,* Rom. ix. 32. (2.) The same blessed Jesus who is the author of salvation to some is to others the occasion of their sin and destruction. *He is set for the rising and fall of many in Israel.* He is not the author of their sin, but only the occasion of it; their own disobedience makes them stumble at him and reject him, which he punishes, as a judge, with destruction. Those who reject him as a Saviour will split upon him as a Rock. (3.) God himself hath appointed everlasting destruction to all those who *stumble at the word, being disobedient.* All those who go on resolutely in their infidelity and contempt of the gospel are appointed to eternal destruction; and God from eternity knows who they are. (4.) To see the Jews generally rejecting Christ, and multitudes in all ages slighting him, ought not to discourage us in our love and duty to him; for this had been foretold by the prophets long ago, and is a confirmation of our faith both in the scriptures and in the Messiah.

2. Those who received him were highly privileged, *v.* 9. The Jews were exceedingly tender of their ancient privileges, of being the only people of God, taken into a special covenant with him, and separated from the rest of the world. "Now," say they, "if we submit to the gospel-constitution, we shall lose all this, and stand upon the same level with the Gentiles."

(1.) To this objection the apostle answers, that if they did not submit they were ruined (*v.* 7, 8), but that if they did submit they should lose no real advantage, but continue still what they desired to be, *a chosen generation, a royal priesthood,* &c. Learn, [1.] All true Christians *are a chosen generation;* they all make one family, a sort and species of people distinct from the common world, of another spirit, principle, and practice, which they could never be if they were not chosen in Christ to be such, and sanctified by his Spirit. [2.] All the true servants of Christ are a royal priesthood. They are royal in their relation to God and Christ, in their power with God, and over themselves and all their spiritual enemies; they are princely in the improvements and the excellency of their own spirits, and in their hopes and expectations; they are a royal priesthood, separated from sin and sinners, consecrated to God, and offering to God spiritual services and oblations, acceptable to God through Jesus Christ. [3.] All Christians, wheresoever they be, compose one holy nation. They are one nation, collected under one head, agreeing in the same manners and customs, and governed by the same laws; and they are a holy nation, because consecrated and devoted to God, renewed and sanctified by his Holy Spirit. [4.] It is the honour of the servants of Christ that they are God's peculiar people. They are the people of his acquisition, choice, care, and delight. These four dignities of all genuine Christians are not natural to them; for their first state is a state of horrid darkness, but they are effectually called out of darkness into a state of marvellous light, joy, pleasure, and prosperity, with this intent and view, that they should show forth, by words and actions, the virtues and praises of him who hath called them.

(2.) To make this people content, and thankful for the great mercies and dignities brought unto them by the gospel, the apostle advises them to compare their former and their present state. Time was when they were not a people, nor had they obtained mercy, but they were solemnly disclaimed and divorced (Jer. iii. 8; Hos. i. 6, 9); but now they are taken in again to be the people of God, and have obtained mercy. Learn, [1.] The best people ought frequently to look back upon what they were in time past. [2.] The people of God are the most valuable people in the world; all the rest are not a people, good for little. [3.] To be brought into the number of the people of God is a very great mercy, and it may be obtained.

V He warns them to beware of fleshly lusts, *v.* 11. Even the best of men, *the chosen generation, the people of God,* need an exhortation to abstain from the worst sins, which the apostle here proceeds most earnestly and affectionately to warn them against. Knowing the difficulty, and yet the importance of the duty, he uses his utmost interest in them: *Dearly beloved, I beseech you.* The duty is to abstain from, and to suppress, the first inclination or rise of fleshly lusts. Many of them proceed from the corruption of nature, and in their exercise depend upon the body, gratifying some sensual appetite or inordinate inclination of the flesh. These Christians ought to avoid, considering, 1. The respect they have with God and good men: They are *dearly beloved.* 2. Their condition in the world: *They are strangers and pilgrims,* and should not impede their passage by giving into the wickedness and lusts of the country through which they pass. 3. The mischief and danger these sins do: "*They war against the soul;* and therefore your souls ought to war against them." Learn, (1.) The grand mischief that sin does to man is this, it *wars against the soul;* it destroys the moral liberty of the soul; it weakens and debilitates the soul by impairing its faculties; it robs the soul of its comfort and peace; it debases and destroys the dignity of the soul, hinders its present prosperity, and plunges it into everlasting misery. (2.) Of all sorts of sin, none are more injurious to the soul than *fleshly lusts.* Carnal appetites, lewdness, and sensuality, are most odious to God, and destructive to man's soul. It is a sore judgment to be given up to them.

VI. He exhorts them further to adorn their profession by an honest conversation. Their conversation in every turn, every instance, and every action of their lives, ought to be honest; that is, good, lovely, decent, amiable, and without blame: and that because they lived among the Gentiles, people of another religion, and who were inveterate enemies to them, who did already slander them and constantly spoke evil of them *as of evil-doers.* "A clean, just, good conversation may not only stop their mouths, but may possibly be a means to bring them to glorify God, and turn to you, when they shall see you excel all others in good works. They now call you evil-doers; vindicate yourselves by good works, this is the way to convince them. There is a day of visitation coming, wherein God may call them by his word and his grace to repentance; and then they will glorify God, and applaud you, for your excellent conversation, Luke i. 68. When the gospel shall come among them, and take effect, a good conversation will encourage them in their conversion, but an evil one will obstruct it." Note, 1. A Christian profession should be attended with an honest conversation, Phil. iv. 8. 2. It is the common lot of the best Christians to be evil spoken of by wicked men. 3. Those that are under God's gracious visitation immediately change their opinion of good people, glorifying God and commending those whom before they railed at as evil-doers.

13 Submit yourselves to every ordinance of man for the Lord's sake:
whether it be to the king, as supreme;
14 Or unto governors, as unto them
that are sent by him for the punishment of evildoers, and for the praise
of them that do well. 15 For so is
the will of God, that with well doing
ye may put to silence the ignorance of
foolish men: 16 As free, and not
using *your* liberty for a cloak of
maliciousness, but as the servants of
God. 17 Honour all *men.* Love the
brotherhood. Fear God. Honour
the king. 18 Servants, *be* subject to
your masters with all fear; not only
to the good and gentle, but also to
the froward. 19 For this *is* thank-
worthy, if a man for conscience toward
God endure grief, suffering wrongfully.
20 For what glory *is it,* if, when ye
be buffeted for your faults, ye shall
take it patiently? but if, when ye do
well, and suffer *for it,* ye take it
patiently, this *is* acceptable with God.
21 For even hereunto were ye called:
because Christ also suffered for us,
leaving us an example, that ye should
follow his steps: 22 Who did no
sin, neither was guile found in his
mouth: 23 Who, when he was reviled, reviled not again; when he
suffered, he threatened not; but committed *himself* to him that judgeth
righteously: 24 Who his own self bare
our sins in his own body on the tree,
that we, being dead to sins, should
live unto righteousness: by whose
stripes ye were healed. 25 For ye
were as sheep going astray; but are
now returned unto the Shepherd and
Bishop of your souls.

The general rule of a Christian conversation is this, it must be honest, which it cannot be if there be not a conscientious discharge of all relative duties. The apostle here particularly treats of these distinctly.

I. The case of subjects. Christians were not only reputed innovators in religion, but disturbers of the state; it was highly necessary, therefore, that the apostle should settle the rules and measures of obedience to the civil magistrate, which he does here, where,

1. The duty required is submission, which comprises loyalty and reverence to their persons, obedience to their just laws and commands, and subjection to legal penalties.

2. The persons or objects to whom this submission is due are described, (1.) More generally: *Every ordinance of man.* Magistracy is certainly of divine right; but the

particular form of government, the power of the magistrate, and the persons who are to execute this power, are of human institution, and are governed by the laws and constitutions of each particular country; and this is a general rule, binding in all nations, let the established form of government be what it will. (2.) Particularly: *To the king, as supreme,* first in dignity and most eminent in degree; the king is a legal person, not a tyrant: *or unto governors,* deputies, proconsuls, rulers of provinces, who *are sent by him,* that is, commissioned by him to govern.

3 The reasons to enforce this duty are, (1.) *For the Lord's sake,* who has ordained magistracy for the good of mankind, who has required obedience and submission (Rom. xiii.), and whose honour is concerned in the dutiful behaviour of subjects to their sovereigns.

(2.) From the end and use of the magistrate's office, which are, to punish evil-doers, and to praise and encourage all those that do well. They were appointed for the good of societies; and, where this end is not pursued, the fault is not in their institution but their practice. [1.] True religion is the best support of civil government; it requires submission for the Lord's sake, and for conscience' sake. [2.] All the punishments, and all the magistrates in the world, cannot hinder but there will be evil-doers in it. [3.] The best way the magistrate can take to discharge his own duty, and to amend the world, is to punish well and reward well.

(3.) Another reason why Christians should submit to the civil magistrate is because it *is the will of God,* and consequently their duty; and because it is the way to put to silence the malicious slanders of ignorant and foolish men, *v.* 15. Learn, [1.] *The will of God is,* to a good man, the strongest reason for any duty. [2.] Obedience to magistrates is a considerable branch of a Christian's duty: *So is the will of God.* [3.] A Christian must endeavour, in all relations, to behave himself so as to put to silence the unreasonable reproaches of the most ignorant and foolish men. [4.] Those who speak against religion and religious people are ignorant and foolish.

(4.) He reminds them of the spiritual nature of Christian liberty. The Jews, from Deut. xvii. 15, concluded that they were bound to obey no sovereign but one *taken from among their own brethren;* and the converted Jews thought they were free from subjection, by their relation to Christ. To prevent these mistakes, the apostle tells the Christians that they were free, but from what? Not from duty or obedience to God's law, which requires subjection to the civil magistrate. They were free spiritually from the bondage of sin and Satan, and the ceremonial law; but they must not make their Christian liberty a cloak or covering for any wickedness, or for the neglect of any duty towards God or towards their superiors, but must still remember they were *the servants of God.* Learn, [1.] All the servants of Christ are free men (John viii. 36); they are *free* from Satan's dominion, the law's condemnation, the wrath of God, the uneasiness of duty, and the terrors of death. [2.] The servants of Jesus Christ ought to be very careful not to abuse their Christian liberty; they must not make it a cover or cloak for any wickedness against God or disobedience to superiors.

4. The apostle concludes his discourse concerning the duty of subjects with four admirable precepts:—(1.) *Honour all men.* A due respect is to be given to all men; the poor are not to be despised (Prov. xvii. 5); the wicked must be honoured, not for their wickedness, but for any other qualities, such as wit, prudence, courage, eminency of employment, or the hoary head. Abraham, Jacob, Samuel, the prophets, and the apostles, never scrupled to give due honour to bad men. (2.) *Love the brotherhood.* All Christians are a fraternity, united to Christ the head, alike disposed and qualified, nearly related in the same interest, having communion one with another, and going to the same home; they should therefore love one another with an especial affection. (3.) *Fear God* with the highest reverence, duty, and submission; if this be wanting, none of the other three duties can be performed as they ought. (4.) *Honour the king* with that highest honour that is peculiarly due to him above other men.

II. The case of servants wanted an apostolical determination as well as that of subjects, for they imagined that their Christian liberty set them free from their unbelieving and cruel masters; to this the apostle answers, *Servants, be subject, v.* 18. By *servants* he means those who were strictly such, whether hired, or bought with money, or taken in the wars, or born in the house, or those who served by contract for a limited time, as apprentices. Observe,

1. He orders them to *be subject,* to do their business faithfully and honestly, to conduct themselves, as inferiors ought, with reverence and affection, and to submit patiently to hardships and inconveniences. This subjection they owe to their masters, who have a right to their service; and that *not only to the good and gentle,* such as use them well and abate somewhat of their right, but even to the crooked and perverse, who are scarcely to be pleased at all. Learn, (1.) Servants ought to behave themselves to their masters with submission, and fear of displeasing them. (2.) The sinful misconduct of one relation does not justify the sinful behaviour of the other; the servant is bound to do his duty, though the master be sinfully froward and perverse. (3.) Good people are meek and gentle to their servants and inferiors. Our holy

apostle shows his love and concern for the souls of poor servants, as well as for higher people. Herein he ought to be imitated by all inferior ministers, who should distinctly apply their counsels to the lower, the meaner, the younger, and the poorer sort of their hearers, as well as others.

2. Having charged them to be subject, he condescends to reason with them about it.

(1.) If they were patient under their hardships, while they suffered unjustly, and continued doing their duty to their unbelieving and untoward masters, this would be acceptable to God, and he would reward all that they suffered for conscience towards him; but to be patient when they were justly chastised would deserve no commendation at all; it is only *doing well, and suffering patiently for that, which is acceptable with God, v.* 19, 20. Learn, [1.] There is no condition so mean but a man may live conscientiously in it, and glorify God in it; the meanest servant may do so. [2.] The most conscientious persons are very often the greatest sufferers. *For conscience towards God, they suffer wrongfully; they do well, and suffer for it;* but sufferers of this sort are praiseworthy, they do honour to God and to religion, and they are accepted of him; and this is their highest support and satisfaction. [3.] Deserved sufferings must be endured with patience: *If you* are *buffeted for your faults, you* must *take it patiently.* Sufferings in this world are not always pledges of our future happiness; if children or servants be rude and undutiful, and suffer for it, this will neither be acceptable with God nor procure the praise of men.

(2.) More reasons are given to encourage Christian servants to patience under unjust sufferings, *v.* 21. [1.] From their Christian calling and profession: *Hereunto were you called.* [2.] From the example of Christ, who *suffered for us,* and so became our *example, that we should follow his steps,* whence learn, *First,* Good Christians are a sort of people called to be sufferers, and therefore they must expect it; by the terms of Christianity they are bound to deny themselves, and take up the cross; they are called by the commands of Christ, by the dispensations of Providence, and by the preparations of divine grace; and, by the practice of Jesus Christ, they are bound to suffer when thus called to it. *Secondly,* Jesus Christ *suffered for* you, or *for us;* it was not the Father that suffered, but he whom the Father sanctified, and sent into the world, for that end; it was both the body and soul of Christ that suffered, and he suffered for us, in our stead and for our good, *v.* 24. *Thirdly,* The sufferings of Christ should quiet us under the most unjust and cruel sufferings we meet with in the world. He suffered voluntarily, not for himself, but for us, with the utmost readiness, with perfect patience, from all quarters, and all this though he was God-man; shall not we sinners, who deserve the worst, submit to the light afflictions of this life, which work for us unspeakable advantages afterwards?

3. The example of Christ's subjection and patience is here explained and amplified: *Christ suffered,* (1.) Wrongfully, and without cause; for he *did no sin, v.* 22. *He had done no violence,* no injustice or wrong to any one—he wrought no iniquity of any sort whatever; *neither was guile found in his mouth* (Isa. liii. 9), his words, as well as his actions, were all sincere, just, and right. (2.) Patiently: *When he was reviled, he reviled not again* (*v.* 23); when they blasphemed him, mocked him, called him foul names, he was *dumb, and opened not his mouth;* when they went further, to real injuries, beating, buffeting, and crowning him with thorns, *he threatened not; but committed* both *himself* and his cause *to God that judgeth righteously,* who would in time clear his innocency, and avenge him on his enemies. Learn, [1.] Our blessed Redeemer was perfectly holy, and so free from sin that no temptation, no provocation whatsoever, could extort from him so much as the least sinful or indecent word. [2.] Provocations to sin can never justify the commission of it. The rudeness, cruelty, and injustice of enemies, will not justify Christians in reviling and revenge; the reasons for sin can never be so great, but we have always stronger reasons to avoid it. [3.] The judgment of God will determine justly upon every man and every cause; and thither we ought, with patience and resignation, to refer ourselves.

4. Lest any should think, from what is said, *v.* 21—23, that Christ's death was designed merely for an example of patience under sufferings, the apostle here adds a more glorious design and effect of it: *Who his own self,* &c., where note, (1.) The person suffering — Jesus Christ: *His own self——in his own body.* The expression *his own self* is emphatic, and necessary to show that he verified all the ancient prophecies, to distinguish him from the Levitical priests (who offered the blood of others, but he by *himself purged our sins,* Heb. i. 3), and to exclude all others from participation with him in the work of man's redemption: it is added, *in his body;* not but that he suffered in his soul (Matt. xxvi. 38), but the sufferings of the soul were inward and concealed, when those of the body were visible and more obvious to the consideration of these suffering servants, for whose sake this example is produced. (2.) The sufferings he underwent were *stripes,* wounds, and death, *the death of the cross*—servile and ignominious punishments! (3.) The reason of his sufferings: He *bore our sins,* which teaches, [1.] That Christ, in his sufferings, stood charged with our sins, as one who had undertaken to put them away by *the sacri-*

fice of himself, Isa. liii. 6. [2.] That he bore the punishment of them, and thereby satisfied divine justice. [3.] That hereby he takes away our sins, and removes them away from us; as the scape-goat did typically bear the sins of the people on his head, and then carried them quite away, (Lev. xvi. 21, 22), so the Lamb of God does first bear our sins in his own body, and thereby take away the sins of the world, John i. 29. (4.) The fruits of Christ's sufferings are, [1.] Our sanctification, consisting of the death, the mortification of sin, and a new holy life of righteousness, for both which we have an example, and powerful motives and abilities also, from the death and resurrection of Christ. [2.] Our justification. Christ was bruised and crucified as an expiatory sacrifice, and *by his stripes we are healed.* Learn, *First,* Jesus Christ bore the sins of all his people, and expiated them by his *death upon the cross. Secondly,* No man can depend safely upon Christ, as having borne his sin and expiated his guilt, till he dies unto sin and lives unto righteousness.

5. The apostle concludes his advice to Christian servants, by putting them in mind of the difference between their former and present condition, *v.* 25. They *were as sheep going astray,* which represents, (1.) Man's sin: he goes astray; it is his own act, he is not driven, but does voluntarily go astray. (2.) His misery: he goes astray from the pasture, from the shepherd, and from the flock, and so exposes himself to innumerable dangers. (3.) Here is the recovery of these by conversion: *But are now returned.* The word is passive, and shows that the return of a sinner is the effect of divine grace. This return is from all their errors and wanderings , to Christ, who is the true careful shepherd, that loves his sheep, and laid down his life for them, who is the most vigilant pastor, and bishop, or overseer of souls. Learn, [1.] Sinners, before their conversion, are always going astray; their life is a continued error. [2.] Jesus Christ is the supreme shepherd and bishop of souls, who is always resident with his flock, and watchful over them. [3.] Those that expect the love and care of this universal pastor must return to him, must die unto sin, and live unto righteousness.

CHAP. III.

Wherein the apostle describes the duties of husbands and wives one to another, beginning with the duty of the wife, ver. 1—7 He exhorts Christians to unity, love, compassion, peace, and patience under sufferings; to oppose the slanders of their enemies, not by returning evil for evil, or railing for railing, but by blessing; by a ready account of their faith and hope, and by keeping a good conscience, ver. 8—17. To encourage them to this, he proposes the example of Christ, who suffered, the just for the unjust, but yet punished the old world for their disobedience, and saved the few who were faithful in the days of Noah ver. 18, to the end.

LIKEWISE, ye wives, *be* in subjection to your own husbands;
that, if any obey not the word, they
also may without the word be won
by the conversation of the wives;
2 While they behold your chaste
conversation *coupled* with fear. 3
Whose adorning let it not be that
outward *adorning* of plaiting the hair,
and of wearing of gold, or of putting
on of apparel; 4 But *let it be* the
hidden man of the heart, in that
which is not corruptible, *even the*
ornament of a meek and quiet spirit,
which is in the sight of God of great
price. 5 For after this manner in
the old time the holy women also,
who trusted in God, adorned themselves, being in subjection unto their
own husbands: 6 Even as Sara
obeyed Abraham, calling him lord:
whose daughters ye are, as long as
ye do well, and are not afraid with
any amazement. 7 Likewise, y
husbands, dwell with *them* according
to knowledge, giving honour unto the
wife, as unto the weaker vessel, and
as being heirs together of the grace of
life; that your prayers be not hindered.

The apostle having treated of the duties of subjects to their sovereigns, and of servants to their masters, proceeds to explain the duty of husbands and wives.

I. Lest the Christian matrons should imagine that their conversion to Christ, and their interest in all Christian privileges, exempted them from subjection to their pagan or Jewish husbands, the apostle here tells them,

1. In what the duty of wives consists.

(1.) In *subjection,* or an affectionate submission to the will, and obedience to the just authority, of *their own husbands,* which obliging conduct would be the most likely way to win those disobedient and unbelieving husbands who had rejected the word, or who attended to no other evidence of the truth of it than what they saw in the prudent, peaceable, and exemplary *conversation of their wives.* Learn, [1.] Every distinct relation has its particular duties, which ministers ought to preach, and the people ought to understand. [2.] A cheerful *subjection,* and a loving, reverential respect, are duties which Christian women owe their husbands, whether they be good or bad; these were due from Eve to Adam before the fall, and are still required, though much more difficult now than they were before, Gen. iii. 16; 1 Tim. ii. 11. [3.] Though the design of the word of the gospel is to win and gain souls to Christ Jesus, yet there are many so obstinate that they will not be *won by the word.* [4.] There is nothing more powerful, next to the word of God, to win people, than a good conversation, and the careful discharge of relative duties. [5.]

Irreligion and infidelity do not dissolve the bonds, nor dispense with the duties, of civil relations; *the wife* must discharge her duty *to her own husband,* though he *obey not the word.*

(2.) In *fear,* or reverence to their husbands, Eph. v. 33.

(3.) In a *chaste conversation,* which their unbelieving husbands would accurately observe and attend to. [1.] Evil men are strict observers of the conversation of the professors of religion; their curiosity, envy, and jealousy, make them watch narrowly the ways and lives of good people. [2.] *A chaste conversation,* attended with due and proper respect to every one, is an excellent means to win them to the faith of the gospel and obedience to the word.

(4.) In preferring the ornaments of the mind to those of the body. [1.] He lays down a rule in regard to the dress of religious women, *v.* 3. Here are three sorts of ornaments forbidden: *plaiting of hair,* which was commonly used in those times by lewd women; *wearing of gold,* or ornaments made of *gold,* was practised by Rebecca, and Esther, and other religious women, but afterwards became the attire chiefly of harlots and wicked people; *putting on of apparel,* which is not absolutely forbidden, but only too much nicety and costliness in it. Learn, *First,* Religious people should take care that all their external behaviour be answerable to their profession of Christianity: *They must be holy in all manner of conversation. Secondly,* The outward adorning of the body is very often sensual and excessive; for instance, when it is immoderate, and above your degree and station in the world, when you are proud of it and puffed up with it, when you dress with design to allure and tempt others, when your apparel is too rich, curious, or superfluous, when your fashions are fantastical, imitating the levity and vanity of the worst people, and when they are immodest and wanton. The attire of a harlot can never become a chaste Christian matron. [2.] Instead of the outward adorning of the body, he directs Christian wives to put on much more excellent and beautiful ornaments, *v.* 4. Here note, *First,* The part to be adorned: *The hidden man of the heart;* that is, the soul; the hidden, the inner man. Take care to adorn and beautify your souls rather than your bodies. *Secondly,* The ornament prescribed. It must, in general, be something *not corruptible,* that beautifies the soul, that is, the graces and virtues of God's Holy Spirit. The ornaments of the body are destroyed by the moth, and perish in the using; but the grace of God, the longer we wear it, the brighter and better it is. More especially, the finest ornament of Christian women is *a meek and quiet spirit,* a tractable easy temper of mind, void of passion, pride, and immoderate anger, discovering itself in a quiet obliging behaviour towards their husbands and families. If the husband be harsh, and averse to religion (which was the case of these good wives to whom the apostle gives this direction), there is no way so likely to win him as a prudent meek behaviour. At least, a quiet spirit will make a good woman easy to herself, which, being visible to others, becomes an amiable ornament to a person in the eyes of the world. *Thirdly,* The excellency of it. Meekness and calmness of spirit are, in the sight of God, of great price—amiable in the sight of men, and precious in the sight of God. Learn, 1. A true Christian's chief care lies in the right ordering and commanding of his own spirit. Where the hypocrite's work ends, there the true Christian's work begins. 2. The endowments of the inner man are the chief ornaments of a Christian; but especially a composed, calm, and quiet spirit, renders either man or woman beautiful and lovely.

2. The duties of Christian wives being in their nature difficult, the apostle enforces them by the example, (1.) Of the holy women of old, who trusted in God, *v.* 5. "You can pretend nothing of excuse from the weakness of your sex, but what they might. They lived *in old time,* and had less knowledge to inform them and fewer examples to encourage them; yet in all ages they practised this duty; they were *holy women,* and therefore their example is obligatory; they *trusted in God,* and yet did not neglect their duty to man: the duties imposed upon you, of a quiet spirit and of subjection to your own husbands, are not new, but what have ever been practised by the greatest and best women in the world." (2.) Of Sara, who obeyed her husband, and followed him when he went from Ur of the Chaldeans, *not knowing whither he went,* and *called him lord,* thereby showing him reverence and acknowledging his superiority over her; and all this though she was declared a princess by God from heaven, by the change of her name, "*Whose daughters you are* if you imitate her in faith and good works, and do not, through fear of your husbands, either quit the truth you profess or neglect your duty to them, but readily perform it, without either fear or force, out of conscience towards God and sense of duty to them." Learn, [1.] God takes exact notice, and keeps an exact record, of the actions of all men and women in the world. [2.] The subjection of wives to their husbands is a duty which has been practised universally by holy women in all ages. [3.] The greatest honour of any man or woman lies in a humble and faithful deportment of themselves in the relation or condition in which Providence has placed them. [4.] God takes notice of the good that is in his servants, to their honour and benefit, but covers a multitude of failings; Sara's infidelity and derision are overlooked, when her virtues are celebrated. [5.] Christians ought to do their duty to one another, not out of

fear, nor from force, but from a willing mind, and in obedience to the command of God. Wives should be in subjection to their churlish husbands, not from dread and amazement, but from a desire to do well and to please God.

II. The husband's duty to the wife comes next to be considered.

1. The particulars are, (1.) *Cohabitation,* which forbids unnecessary separation, and implies a mutual communication of goods and persons one to another, with delight and concord. (2.) *Dwelling with the wife according to knowledge;* not according to lust, as brutes; nor according to passion, as devils; but according to knowledge, as wise and sober men, who know the word of God and their own duty. (3.) *Giving honour to the wife*—giving due respect to her, and maintaining her authority, protecting her person, supporting her credit, delighting in her conversation, affording her a handsome maintenance, and placing a due trust and confidence in her.

2. The reasons are, Because she is *the weaker vessel* by nature and constitution, and so ought to be defended: but then the wife is, in other and higher respects, equal to her husband; they are *heirs together of the grace of life,* of all the blessings of this life and another, and therefore should live peaceably and quietly one with another, and, if they do not, their prayers one with another and one for another will be hindered, so that often "you will not pray at all, or, if you do, you will pray with a discomposed ruffled mind, and so without success." Learn, (1.) The weakness of the female sex is no just reason either for separation or contempt, but on the contrary it is a reason for honour and respect: *Giving honour to the wife as unto the weaker vessel.* (2.) There is an honour due to all who are heirs of the grace of life. (3.) All married people should take care to behave themselves so lovingly and peaceably one to another that they may not by their broils hinder the success of their prayers.

8 Finally, *be ye* all of one mind,
having compassion one of another,
love as brethren, *be* pitiful, *be* courteous: 9 Not rendering evil for evil,
or railing for railing: but contrariwise
blessing; knowing that ye are thereunto called, that ye should inherit a
blessing. 10 For he that will love
life, and see good days, let him refrain
his tongue from evil, and his lips that
they speak no guile: 11 Let him
eschew evil, and do good; let him
seek peace, and ensue it. 12 For the
eyes of the Lord *are* over the righteous, and his ears *are open* unto their
prayers: but the face of the Lord *is*
against them that do evil. 13 And
who *is* he that will harm you, if ye be
followers of that which is good? 14
But and if ye suffer for righteousness'
sake, happy *are ye:* and be not afraid
of their terror, neither be troubled;
15 But sanctify the Lord God in
your hearts: and *be* ready always to
give an answer to every man that
asketh you a reason of the hope that
is in you with meekness and fear.

The apostle here passes from special to more general exhortations.

I. He teaches us how Christians and friends should treat one another. He advises Christians to *be all of one mind,* to be unanimous in the belief of the same faith, and the practice of the same duties of religion; and, whereas the Christians at that time were many of them in a suffering condition, he charges them to *have compassion one of another,* to *love as brethren,* to *pity* those who were in distress, and to *be courteous* to all. Hence learn, 1. Christians should endeavour to be all of one mind in the great points of faith, in real affection, and in Christian practice; they should be *like-minded one to another, according to Christ Jesus* (Rom. xv. 5), not according to man's pleasure, but God's word. 2. Though Christians cannot be exactly of the same mind, yet they should have compassion one for another, and love as brethren; they ought not to persecute or hate one another, but love one another with more than common affection; they should love as brethren. 3. Christianity requires pity to the distressed, and civility to all. He must be a flagrant sinner, or a vile apostate, who is not a proper object of civil courtesy, 1 Cor. v. 11; 2 John x. 11.

II. He instructs us how to behave towards enemies. The apostle knew that Christians would *be hated* and evil-entreated *of all men for Christ's sake;* therefore,

1. He warns them not to return *evil for evil, nor railing for railing;* but, on the contrary, "when they rail at you, do you bless them; when they give you evil words, do you give them good ones; for Christ has both by his word and example called you to bless those that curse you, and has settled a blessing on you as your everlasting inheritance, though you were unworthy." To bear evils patiently, and to bless your enemies, is the way to obtain this blessing of God. Learn, (1.) To *render evil for evil, or railing for railing,* is a sinful unchristian practice; the magistrate may punish *evil-doers,* and private men may seek a legal remedy when they are wronged; but private revenge by duelling, scolding, or secret mischief, is forbidden, Prov. xx. 22; Luke vi. 27; Rom. xii. 17; 1 Thess. v. 15. To rail is to revile another in bitter, fierce, and reproachful terms; but for ministers to rebuke sharply, and to preach earnestly against the sins of the times,

is not railing; all the prophets and apostles practised it, Isa. lvi. 10; Zeph. iii. 3; Acts xx. 29. (2.) The laws of Christ oblige us to return blessing for railing. Matt. v. 44, "*Love your enemies, bless those that curse you, do good to those that hate you, and pray for those that persecute you.* You must not justify them in their sin, but you must do for your enemies all that justice requires or charity commands." We must pity, pray for, and love those who rail at us. (3.) A Christian's calling, as it invests him with glorious privileges, so it obliges him to difficult duties. (4.) All the true servants of God shall infallibly inherit a blessing; they have it already in a great degree, but the full possession of it is reserved to another state and world.

2. He gives an excellent prescription for a comfortable happy life in this quarrelsome ill-natured world (*v.* 10): it is quoted from Ps. xxxiv. 12—14. "If you earnestly desire that your life should be long, and your days peaceable and prosperous, keep your tongue from reviling, evil-speaking, and slandering, and your lips from lying, deceit, and dissimulation. Avoid doing any real damage or hurt to your neighbour, but be ever ready to do good, and to overcome evil with good; seek peace with all men, and pursue it, though it retire from you. This will be the best way to dispose people to speak well of you, and live peaceably with you." Learn, (1.) Good people under the Old and New Testament were obliged to the same moral duties; to *refrain the tongue from evil, and the lips from guile,* was a duty in David's time as well as now. (2.) It is lawful to consider temporal advantages as motives and encouragements to religion. (3.) The practice of religion, particularly the right government of the tongue, is the best way to make this life comfortable and prosperous; a sincere, inoffensive, discreet tongue, is a singular means to pass us peaceably and comfortably through the world. (4.) The avoiding of evil, and doing of good, is the way to contentment and happiness both here and hereafter. (5.) It is the duty of Christians not only to embrace peace when it is offered, but to seek and pursue it when it is denied: peace with societies, as well as peace with particular persons, in opposition to division and contention, is what is here intended.

3. He shows that Christians need not fear that such patient inoffensive behaviour as is prescribed will invite and encourage the cruelty of their enemies, for God will thereby be engaged on their side: *For the eyes of the Lord are over the righteous* (*v.* 12); he takes special notice of them, exercises a providential constant government over them, and bears a special respect and affection to them. *His ears are open to their prayers;* so that if any injuries be offered to them they have this remedy, they may complain of it to their heavenly Father, whose ears are always attentive to the prayers of his servants in their distresses, and who will certainly aid them against their unrighteous enemies. *But the face of the Lord is against those that do evil;* his anger, and displeasure, and revenge, will pursue them; for he is more an enemy to wicked persecutors than men are. Observe, (1.) We must not in all cases adhere to the express words of scripture, but study the sense and meaning of them, otherwise we shall be led into blasphemous errors and absurdities: we must not imagine that God hath eyes, and ears, and face, though these are the express words of the scripture. (2.) God hath a special care and paternal affection towards all his righteous people. (3.) God doth always hear the prayers of the faithful, John iv. 31; 1 John v. 14; Heb. iv. 16. (4.) Though God is infinitely good, yet he abhors impenitent sinners, and will pour out his wrath upon those that do evil. He will do himself right, and do all the world justice; and his goodness is no obstruction to his doing so.

4. This patient humble behaviour of Christians is further recommended and urged from two considerations:—(1.) This will be the best and surest way to prevent suffering; for *who is he that will harm you? v.* 13. This, I suppose, is spoken of Christians in an ordinary condition, not in the heat of persecution. "Ordinarily, there will be but few so diabolical and impious as to harm those who live so innocently and usefully as you do." (2.) This is the way to improve sufferings. "*If you be followers of that which is good,* and yet *suffer,* this is suffering for righteousness' sake (*v.* 14), and will be your glory and your happiness, as it entitles you to the blessing promised by Christ (Matt. v. 10); therefore, [1.] "You need not be afraid of any thing they can do to strike you with terror, neither be much troubled nor concerned about the rage or force of your enemies." Learn, *First,* to follow always that which is good is the best course we can take to keep out of harm's way. *Secondly,* To suffer for righteousness sake is the honour and happiness of a Chris tian; to suffer for the cause of truth, a good conscience, or any part of a Christian's duty, is a great honour; the delight of it is greater than the torment, the honour more than the disgrace, and the gain much greater than the loss. *Thirdly,* Christians have no reason to be afraid of the threats or rage of any of their enemies. "Your enemies are God's enemies, *his face is against them,* his power is above them, they are the objects of his curse, and can do nothing to you but by his permission; therefore trouble not yourselves about them." [2.] Instead of terrifying yourselves with the fear of men, be sure to *sanctify the Lord God in your hearts* (*v.* 15); *let him be your fear, and let him be your dread,* Isa. viii. 12, 13. *Fear not those that can only kill the body, but fear him that can destroy body and soul,* Luke xii. 4, 5. We sanctify the Lord God in our

hearts when we with sincerity and fervency adore him, when our thoughts of him are awful and reverend, when we rely upon his power, trust to his faithfulness, submit to his wisdom, imitate his holiness, and give him the glory due to his most illustrious perfections. We sanctify God before others when our deportment is such as invites and encourages others to glorify and honour him; both are required, Lev. x. 3. "When this principle is laid deeply into your hearts, the next thing, as to men, is to be always ready, that is, able and willing, *to give an answer,* or make an apology or defence, of the faith you profess, and that *to every man that asketh a reason of your hope,* what sort of hope you have, for which you suffer such hardships in the world." Learn, *First,* An awful sense of the divine perfections is the best antidote against the fear of sufferings; did we fear God more, we should certainly fear men less. *Secondly,* The hope and faith of a Christian are defensible against all the world. There may be a good reason given for religion; it is not a fancy but a rational scheme revealed from heaven, suited to all the necessities of miserable sinners, and centering entirely in the glory of God through Jesus Christ. *Thirdly,* Every Christian is bound to answer and apologize for the hope that is in him. Christians should have a reason ready for their Christianity, that it may appear they are not actuated either by folly or fancy. This defence may be necessary more than once or twice, so that Christians should be always prepared to make it, either to the magistrate, if he demand it, or to any inquisitive serious Christian, who desires to know it for his information or improvement. *Fourthly,* These confessions of our faith ought to be made *with meekness and fear;* apologies for our religion ought to be made with modesty and meekness, in the fear of God, with jealousy over ourselves, and reverence to our superiors.

16 Having a good conscience; that, whereas they speak evil of you, as of evildoers, they may be ashamed that falsely accuse your good conversation in Christ. 17 For *it is* better, if the will of God be so, that ye suffer for well doing, than for evil doing.

The confession of a Christian's faith cannot credibly be supported but by the two means here specified—*a good conscience* and a *good conversation.* Conscience is good when it does its office well, when it is kept pure and uncorrupt, and clear from guilt; then it will justify you, though men accuse you. *A good conversation in Christ* is a holy life, according to the doctrine and example of Christ. "Look well to your conscience, and to your conversation; and then, though men speak evil of you, and falsely accuse you as evil-doers, you will clear yourselves, and bring them to shame. Perhaps you may think it hard to suffer for well-doing, for keeping a good conscience and a good conversation; but be not discouraged, for it is better for you, though worse for your enemies, that you suffer for well-doing than for evil-doing." Learn, 1. The most conscientious persons cannot escape the censures and slanders of evil men; they will speak evil of them, as of evil-doers, and charge them with crimes which their very souls abhor: Christ and his apostles were so used. 2. A good conscience and a good conversation are the best means to secure a good name; these give a solid reputation and a lasting one. 3. False accusation generally turns to the accuser's shame, by discovering at last the accuser's indiscretion, injustice, falsehood, and uncharitableness. 4. It is sometimes the will of God that good people should suffer for well-doing, for their honesty and for their faith. 5. As well-doing sometimes exposes a good man to suffering, so evil-doing will not exempt an evil man from it. The apostle supposes here that a man may suffer for both. If the sufferings of good people for well-doing be so severe, what will the sufferings of wicked people be for evil-doing? It is a sad condition which that person is in upon whom sin and suffering meet together at the same time; sin makes sufferings to be extreme, unprofitable, comfortless, and destructive.

18 For Christ also hath once suffered for sins, the just for the unjust, that he might bring us to God, being put to death in the flesh, but quickened by the Spirit:
19 By which also he went and preached unto the spirits in prison;
20 Which sometime were disobedient, when once the long-suffering of God waited in the days of Noah, while the ark was a preparing, wherein few, that is, eight souls were saved by water.

Here, I. The example of Christ is proposed as an argument for patience under sufferings, the strength of which will be discerned if we consider the several points contained in the words; observe therefore, 1. Jesus Christ himself was not exempted from sufferings in this life, though he had no guilt of his own and could have declined all suffering if he had pleased. 2. The reason or meritorious cause of Christ's suffering was the sins of men: *Christ suffered for sins.* The sufferings of Christ were a true and proper punishment; this punishment was suffered to expiate and to make an atonement for sin; and it extends to all sin. 3. In the case of our Lord's suffering, it was the just that suffered for the unjust; he substituted himself in our room and stead, and bore our iniquities. He that knew no sin suffered instead of those that knew no righteousness. 4. The merit and perfection of Christ's sacrifice were such that for him to suffer once was enough. The legal sacrifices were repeated from day to day, and from year to year; but the sacrifice of Christ, once offered, purgeth away sin, Heb. vii. 27; ix. 26, 28; x. 10, 12, 14. 5. The blessed end or design of our Lord's sufferings was to bring us to God, to reconcile us to God, to give us access to the Father, to render us and our services acceptable, and to bring us to eternal glory, Eph. ii. 13, 18; iii. 12; Heb. x. 21, 22. 6. The issue and event of Christ's suffering, as to himself, were these, he was put to death in his human nature, but he was quickened and raised again by the Spirit. Now, if Christ was not exempted from sufferings, why should Christians expect it? If he suffered, to expiate sins, why should not we be content when our sufferings are only for trial and correction, but not for expiation? If he, though perfectly just, why should not we, who are all criminals? If he once suffered, and then entered into glory, shall not we be patient under trouble, since it will be but a little time and we shall follow him to glory? If he *suffered, to bring us to God,* shall not we submit to difficulties, since they are of so much use to quicken us in our return to God, and in the performance of our duty to him?

II. The apostle passes from the example of Christ to that of the old world, and sets before the Jews, to whom he wrote, the different event of those who believed and obeyed Christ preaching by Noah, from those that continued disobedient and unbelieving, intimating to the Jews that they were under a like sentence. God would not wait much longer upon them. They had now an offer of mercy; those that accepted of it should be saved, but those who rejected Christ and the gospel should be as certainly destroyed as ever the disobedient in the times of Noah were.

1. For the explication of this we may notice, (1.) The preacher—Christ Jesus, who has interested himself in the affairs of the church and of the world ever since he was first promised to Adam, Gen. iii. 15. *He went,* not by a local motion, but by special operation, as God is frequently said to move, Gen. xi. 5; Hos. v. 15; Mic. i. 3. *He went and preached,* by his Spirit striving with them, and inspiring and enabling Enoch and Noah to plead with them, and *preach righteousness to them,* as 2 Pet. ii. 5. (2.) The hearers. Because they were dead and disembodied when the apostle speaks of them, therefore he properly calls them spirits now *in prison;* not that they were *in prison when Christ preached to them,* as the vulgar Latin translation and the popish expositors pretend. (3.) The sin of these people: They were *disobedient,* that is, *rebellious, unpersuadable,* and *unbelieving,* as the word signifies; this their sin is aggravated from the patience and *long-suffering of God* (which *once waited* upon them for 120 years together, *while Noah was preparing the ark,* and by that, as well as by his preaching, giving them fair warning of what was coming upon them. (4.) The event of all: Their bodies were drowned, and their spirits cast into hell, which is called a prison (Matt. v. 25; 2 Pet. ii. 4, 5); but Noah and his family, who believed and were obedient, *were saved in the ark.*

2. From the whole we learn that, (1.) God takes exact notice of all the means and advantages that people in all ages have had for the salvation of their souls; it is put to the account of the old world that Christ offered them his help, sent his Spirit, gave them fair warning by Noah, and waited a long time for their amendment. (2.) Though the patience of God wait long upon sinners, yet it will expire at last; it is beneath the majesty of the great God always to wait upon man in vain. (3.) The spirits of disobedient sinners, as soon as they are out of their bodies, are committed to the prison of hell, whence there is no redemption. (4.) The way of the most is neither the best, the wisest, nor the safest way to follow: better to follow the eight in the ark than the eight millions drowned by the flood and damned to hell.

21 The like figure whereunto *even* baptism doth also now save us (not the putting away of the filth of the flesh, but the answer of a good conscience toward God,) by the resurrection of Jesus Christ: 22 Who is gone into heaven, and is on the right hand of God; angels and authorities and powers being made subject unto him.

Noah's salvation in the ark upon the water prefigured the salvation of all good Christians in the church by baptism; that temporal salvation by the ark was a type, the antitype whereunto is the eternal salvation of believers by baptism, to prevent mistakes about which the apostle,

I. Declares what he means by saving baptism; not the outward ceremony of washing with water, which, in itself, does no more than put away the filth of the flesh, but it is that baptism wherein there is a faithful answer or restipulation of a resolved good conscience, engaging to believe in, and be entirely devoted to, God, the Father, Son, and Holy Ghost, renouncing at the same time the flesh, the world, and the devil. The baptismal covenant, made and kept, will certainly save us. Washing is the visible sign; this is the thing signified.

II. The apostle shows that the efficacy of baptism to salvation depends not upon the work done, but upon the resurrection of Christ, which supposes his death, and is the foundation of our faith and hope, to which we are rendered conformable by dying to sin, and rising again to holiness and newness of life. Learn, 1. The sacrament of baptism, rightly received, is a means and a pledge of salvation. *Baptism now saveth us.* God is pleased to convey his blessings to us in and by his ordinances, Acts ii. 38; xxii. 16. 2. The external participation of baptism will save no man without an answerable good conscience and conversation. There must be the answer of a good conscience towards God.—*Obj.* Infants cannot make such an answer, and therefore ought not to be baptized.—*Answer,* The true circumcision was that of the heart and of the spirit (Rom. ii. 29), which children were no more capable of then than our infants are capable of making this answer now; yet they were allowed circumcision at eight days old. The infants of the Christian church therefore may be admitted to the ordinance with as much reason as the infants of the Jewish, unless they are barred from it by some express prohibition of Christ.

III. The apostle, having mentioned the death and resurrection of Christ, proceeds to speak of his ascension, and sitting at the right hand of the Father, as a subject fit to be considered by these believers for their comfort in their suffering condition, *v.* 22. If the advancement of Christ was so glorious after his deep humiliation, let not his followers despair, but expect that after these short distresses they shall be advanced to transcendent joy and glory. Learn, 1. Jesus Christ, after he had finished his labours and his sufferings upon earth, ascended triumphantly into heaven, of which see Acts i. 9—11; Mark xvi. 19. He went to heaven to receive his own acquired crown and glory (John xvii. 5), to finish that part of his mediatorial work which could not be done on earth, and make intercession for his people, to demonstrate the fulness of his satisfaction, to take possession of heaven for his people, to prepare mansions for them, and to send down the Comforter, which was to be the first-fruits of his intercession, John xvi. 7. 2. Upon his ascension into heaven, Christ is enthroned at the right hand of the Father. His being said to *sit* there imports absolute rest and cessation from all further troubles and sufferings, and an advancement to the highest personal dignity and sovereign power. 3. Angels, authorities, and powers, are all made subject to Christ Jesus: *all power in heaven and earth,* to command, to give law, issue orders, and pronounce a final sentence, is committed to Jesus, God-man, which his enemies will find to their everlasting sorrow and confusion, but his servants to their eternal joy and satisfaction.

CHAP. IV.

The work of a Christian is twofold—doing the will of God and suffering his pleasure. This chapter directs us in both. The duties we are here exhorted to employ ourselves in are the mortification of sin, living to God, sobriety, prayer, charity, hospitality, and the best improvement of our talents, which the apostle presses upon Christians from the consideration of the time they have lost in their sins, and the approaching end of all things, ver. 1—11. The directions for sufferings are that we should not be surprised at them, but rejoice in them, only take care not to suffer as evil-doers. He intimates that their trials were near at hand, that their souls were in danger as well as their bodies, and that the best way to preserve their souls is to commit them to God in well-doing.

FORASMUCH then as Christ hath
suffered for us in the flesh, arm
yourselves likewise with the same
mind: for he that hath suffered in
the flesh hath ceased from sin; 2
That he no longer should live the rest
of *his* time in the flesh to the lusts of
men, but to the will of God. 3 For
the time past of *our* life may suffice
us to have wrought the will of the
Gentiles, when we walked in lasciviousness, lusts, excess of wine, revellings, banquetings, and abominable idolatries.

The apostle here draws a new inference from the consideration of Christ's sufferings. As he had before made use of it to persuade to patience in suffering, so here to mortification of sin. Observe,

I. How the exhortation is expressed. The antecedent or supposition is *that Christ had suffered* for us in the flesh, or in his human nature. The consequent or inference is, "*Arm* and fortify *yourselves likewise with the same mind,* courage, and resolution." The word flesh in the former part of the verse signifies Christ's human nature, but in the latter part it signifies man's corrupt nature. So the sense is, "As Christ suffered in his human nature, do you, according to your baptismal vow and profession, make your corrupt nature suffer, by putting to death the body of sin by self-denial and mortification; for, if you do thus suffer, you will be conformable to Christ in his death and resurrection, and will *cease from sin.*" Learn, 1. Some of the strongest and best arguments against all sorts of sin are taken from the sufferings of Christ. All sympathy and tenderness for Christ as a sufferer are lost if you do not put away sin. He died to destroy it; and, though he could cheerfully submit to the worst sufferings, yet he could never submit to the least sin. 2. The beginning of all true mortification lies in the mind, not in penances and hardships upon the body. The mind of man is carnal, full of enmity; the understanding is darkened, being alienated from the life of God, Eph. iv. 18. Man is not a sincere creature, but partial, blind, and wicked, till he be renewed and sanctified by the regenerating grace of God.

II. How it is further explained, *v.* 2. The apostle explains what he means by being dead to sin, and ceasing from sin, both negatively and positively. Negatively, a Christian ought *no longer to live the rest of his time in the flesh,* to the sinful lusts and corrupt desires of carnal wicked men; but, positively, he ought to conform himself to the revealed will of the holy God. Learn, 1. The lusts of men are the springs of all their wickedness, Jam. i. 13, 14. Let occasional temptations be what they will, they could not prevail, were it not for men's own corruptions. 2. All good Christians make the will of God, not their own lusts or desires, the rule of their lives and actions. 3. True conversion makes a marvellous change in the heart and life of every one who partakes of it. It brings a man off from all his old, fashionable, and delightful lusts, and from the common ways and vices of the world, to the will of God. It alters the mind, judgment, affections, way, and conversation of every one who has experienced it.

III. How it is enforced (*v.* 3): *For the time past of our life may suffice us to have wrought the will of the Gentiles,* &c. Here the apostle argues from equity. "It is but just, equal, and reasonable, that as you have hitherto all the former part of your life served sin and Satan, so you should now serve the living God." Though those were Jews to whom the apostle wrote, yet living among the Gentiles they had learned their way. Observe, 1. When a man is truly converted, it is very grievous to him to think how the time past of his life has been spent; the hazard he has run so many years, the mischief he has done to others, the dishonour done to God, and the loss he has sustained, are very afflicting to him. 2. While the will of man is unsanctified and corrupt, he walks continually in wicked ways; he makes them his choice and delight, his work and business, and he makes a bad condition daily worse and worse. 3. One sin, allowed, draws on another. Here are six named, and they have a connection and dependence one upon another. (1.) *Lasciviousness* or wantonness, expressed in looks, gesture, or behaviour, Rom. xiii. 13. (2.) *Lusts,* acts of lewdness, such as whoredom and adultery. (3.) *Excess of wine,* though short of drunkenness, an immoderate use of it, to the prejudice of health or business, is here condemned. (4.) *Revellings,* or luxurious feastings, too frequent, too full, or too expensive. (5.) *Banquetings,* by which is meant gluttony or excess in eating. (6.) *Abominable* idolatry; the idol-worship of the Gentiles was attended with lewdness, drunkenness, gluttony, and all sorts of brutality and cruelty; and these Jews living long among them were, some of them at least, debauched and corrupted by such practices. 4. It is a Christian's duty not only to abstain from what is grossly wicked, but also from those things that are generally the occasions of sin, or carry the appearance of evil. *Excess of wine* and immoderate feasting are forbidden as well as lust and idolatry.

4 Wherein they think it strange
that ye run not with *them* to the same
excess of riot, speaking evil of *you*:
5 Who shall give account to him that
is ready to judge the quick and the
dead. 6 For for this cause was the
gospel preached also to them that are
dead, that they might be judged according to men in the flesh, but live
according to God in the spirit.

I. Here you have the visible change wrought in those who in the foregoing verse were represented as having been in the former part of their life very wicked. They no longer run on in the same courses, or with the same companions, as they used to do. Hereupon observe the conduct of their wicked acquaintance towards them. 1. *They think it strange,* they are surprised and wonder at it, as at something new and unusual, that their old friends should be so much altered, and not run with as much violence as they used to do *to the same excess of riot,* to the same sottish excesses and luxury which before they had greedily and madly followed. 2. *They speak evil of them.* Their surprise carries them to blasphemy. They speak evil of their persons, of their way, their religion, and their God. Learn, (1.) Those that are once really converted will not return to their former course of life, though ever so much tempted by the frowns or flatteries of others to do so. Neither persuasion nor reproach will prevail with them to be or to do as they were wont to do. (2.) The temper and behaviour of true Christians seem very strange to ungodly men. That they should despise that which every one else is fond of, that they should believe many things which to others seem incredible, that they should delight in what is irksome and tedious, be zealous where they have no visible interest to serve, and depend so much upon hope, is what the ungodly cannot comprehend. (3.) The best actions of religious people cannot escape the censures and slanders of those who are irreligious. Those actions which cost a good man the most pains, hazard, and self-denial, shall be most censured by the uncharitable and ill-natured world; they will speak evil of good people, though they themselves reap the fruits of their charity, piety, and goodness.

II. For the comfort of the servants of God, it is here added,

1. That all wicked people, especially those who speak evil of such as are not as bad as themselves, shall *give an account,* and be put to give a reason of their behaviour, to him who is ready to judge, who is both able and duly authorized, and who will ere long judge and pass sentence upon all who shall then be found alive, and all such as being dead shall then be raised again, Jam. v. 8, 9; 2 Pet. iii. 7. Observe, The malignant world shall in a little time give an account to the great God of all their evil speeches against his people, Jude 14, 15. They will soon be called to a sad account for all their curses, their

foolish jests, their slanders and falsehoods, uttered against the faithful people of God.

2. That *for this cause was the gospel preached also to those that are dead, that they might be judged according to men in the flesh, but live according to God in the Spirit, v.* 6. Some understand this difficult place thus: *For this cause was the gospel preached* to all the faithful of old, who are now dead in Christ, that thereby they might be taught and encouraged to bear the unrighteous judgments and persecutions which the rage of men put upon them *in the flesh, but might live in the Spirit unto God.* Others take the expression, *that they might be judged according to men in the flesh,* in a spiritual sense, thus: The gospel was preached to them, to judge them, condemn them, and reprove them, for the corruption of their natures, and the viciousness of their lives, while they lived after the manner of the heathen or the mere natural man; and that, having thus mortified their sins, they might live according to God, a new and spiritual life. Take it thus; and thence learn, 1. The mortifying of our sins and living to God are the expected effects of the gospel preached to us. 2. God will certainly reckon with all those who have had the gospel preached to them, but without these good effects produced by it. God is ready to judge all those who have received his gospel in vain. 3. It is no matter how we are judged according to men in the flesh, if we do but live according to God in the Spirit.

7 But the end of all things is at
hand: be ye therefore sober, and
watch unto prayer. 8 And above all
things have fervent charity among
yourselves: for charity shall cover
the multitude of sins. 9 Use hospitality one to another without grudging. 10 As every man hath received
the gift, *even so* minister the same
one to another, as good stewards of
the manifold grace of God. 11 If
any man speak, *let him speak* as the
oracles of God; if any man minister,
let him do it as of the ability which
God giveth: that God in all things
may be glorified through Jesus Christ,
to whom be praise and dominion for
ever and ever. Amen.

We have here an awful position or doctrine, and an inference drawn from it. The position is that the *end of all things is at hand.* The miserable destruction of the Jewish church and nation foretold by our Saviour is now very near; consequently, the time of their persecution and your sufferings is but very short. Your own life and that of your enemies will soon come to their utmost period. Nay, the world itself will not continue very long. The conflagration will put an end to it; and all things must be swallowed up in an endless eternity. The inference from this comprises a series of exhortations.

1. To sobriety and watchfulness: *Be you therefore sober, v.* 7. Let the frame and temper of your minds be grave, stayed, and solid; and observe strict temperance and sobriety in the use of all wordly enjoyments. Do not suffer yourselves to be caught with your former sins and temptations, *v.* 3. *And watch unto prayer.* Take care that you be continually in a calm sober disposition, fit for prayer; and that you be frequent in prayers, lest this end come upon you unawares," Luke xxi. 34; Matt. xxvi. 40, 41. Learn, (1.) The consideration of our approaching end is a powerful argument to make us sober in all worldly matters, and earnest in religious affairs. (2.) Those who would pray to purpose must *watch unto prayer.* They must watch over their own spirits, watch all fit opportunities, and do their duty in the best manner they can. (3.) The right ordering of the body is of great use to promote the good of the soul. When the appetites and inclinations of the body are restrained and governed by God's word and true reason, and the interests of the body are submitted to the interests and necessities of the soul, then it is not the soul's enemy, but its friend and helper.

2. To charity: *And above all things have fervent charity among yourselves, v.* 8. Here is a noble rule in Christianity. Christians ought to love one another, which implies an affection to their persons, a desire of their welfare, and a hearty endeavour to promote it. This mutual affection must not be cold, but fervent, that is, sincere, strong, and lasting. This sort of earnest affection is recommended *above all things,* which shows the importance of it, Col. iii. 14. It is greater than faith or hope, 1 Cor. xiii. 13. One excellent effect of it is that it will *cover a multitude of sins.* Learn, (1.) There ought to be in all Christians a more fervent charity towards one another than towards other men: *Have charity among yourselves.* He does not say for pagans, for idolaters, or for apostates, but among yourselves. *Let brotherly love continue,* Heb. xiii. 1. There is a special relation between all sincere Christians, and a particular amiableness and good in them, which require special affection. (2.) It is not enough for Christians not to bear malice, nor to have common respect for one another, they must intensely and fervently love each other. (3.) It is the property of true charity *to cover a multitude of sins.* It inclines people to forgive and forget offences against themselves, to cover and conceal the sins of others, rather than aggravate them and spread them abroad. It teaches us to love those who are but weak, and who have been guilty of many evil things before their conversion; and it pre-

pares for mercy at the hand of God, who hath promised to forgive those that forgive others, Matt. vi. 14.

3. To hospitality, *v.* 9. The hospitality here required is a free and kind entertainment of strangers and travellers. The proper objects of Christian hospitality are one another. The nearness of their relation, and the necessity of their condition in those times of persecution and distress, obliged Christians to be hospitable one to another. Sometimes Christians were spoiled of all they had, and were driven away to distant countries for safety. In this case they must starve if their fellow-christians would not receive them. Therefore it was a wise and necessary rule which the apostle here laid down. It is elsewhere commanded, Heb. xiii. 1, 2; Rom. xii. 13. The manner of performing this duty is this: it must be done in an easy, kind, handsome manner, *without grudging* or grumbling at the expense or trouble. Learn, (1.) Christians ought not only to be charitable, but hospitable, one to another. (2.) Whatever a Christian does by way of charity or of hospitality, he ought to do it cheerfully, and without grudging. *Freely you have received, freely give.*

4. To the improvement of talents, *v.* 11.

(1.) The rule is that whatever gift, ordinary or extraordinary, whatever power, ability, or capacity of doing good is given to us, we should minister, or do service, with the same *one to another*, accounting ourselves not masters, but only *stewards of the manifold grace*, or the various gifts, of God. Learn, [1.] Whatever ability we have of doing good we must own it to be the gift of God and ascribe it to his grace. [2.] Whatever gifts we have received, we ought to look upon them as received for the use one of another. We must not assume them to ourselves, nor hide them in a napkin, but do service with them *one to another* in the best manner we are able. [3.] In receiving and using the manifold gifts of God we must look upon ourselves as stewards only, and act accordingly. The talents we are entrusted with are our Lord's goods, and must be employed as he directs. And it is required in a steward that he be found faithful.

(2.) The apostle exemplifies his direction about gifts in two particulars—speaking and ministering, concerning which he gives these rules:—[1.] *If any man*, whether a minister in public or a Christian in private conference, *speak* or teach, he must do it *as the oracles of God*, which direct us as to the matter of our speech. What Christians in private, or ministers in public, teach and speak must be the pure word and oracles of God. As to the manner of speaking, it must be with the seriousness, reverence, and solemnity, that become those holy and divine oracles. [2.] *If any man minister*, either as a deacon, distributing the alms of the church and taking care of the poor, or as a private person, by charitable gifts and contributions, *let him do it as of the ability which God giveth.* He who has received plenty and ability from God ought to minister plentifully, and according to his ability. These rules ought to be followed and practised for this end, *that God in all things*, in all your gifts, ministrations, and services, may be glorified, *that others may see your good works, and glorify your Father who is in heaven* (Matt. v. 16), *through Jesus Christ*, who has procured and given these gifts to men (Eph. iv. 8), and through whom alone we and our services are accepted of God (Heb. xiii. 15), to whom, Jesus Christ, *be praise and dominion for ever and ever. Amen.* Learn, *First*, It is the duty of Christians in private, as well as ministers in public, to speak to one another of the things of God, Mal. iii. 16; Eph. iv. 29; Ps. cxlv. 10—12. *Secondly*, It highly concerns all preachers of the gospel to keep close to the word of God, and to treat that word as becomes the oracles of God. *Thirdly*, Christians must not only do the duty of their place, but they must do it with vigour, and according to the best of their abilities. The nature of a Christian's work, which is high work and hard work, the goodness and kindness of the Master, and the excellency of the reward, all require that our endeavours should be serious and vigorous, and that whatever we are called to do for the honour of God and the good of others we should do it with all our might. *Fourthly*, In all the duties and services of life we should aim at the glory of God as our chief end; all other views must be subservient to this, which would sanctify our common actions and affairs, 1 Cor. x. 31. *Fifthly*, God is not glorified by any thing we do if we do not offer it to him through the mediation and merits of Jesus Christ. *God in all things must be glorified through Jesus Christ*, who is the only way to the Father. *Sixthly*, The apostle's adoration of Jesus Christ, and ascribing unlimited and everlasting praise and dominion to him, prove that Jesus Christ is the most high God, over all blessed for evermore. Amen.

12 Beloved, think it not strange
concerning the fiery trial which is to
try you, as though some strange
thing happened unto you: 13 But
rejoice, inasmuch as ye are partakers
of Christ's sufferings; that, when his
glory shall be revealed, ye may be
glad also with exceeding joy. 14 If
ye be reproached for the name of
Christ, happy *are ye*; for the spirit
of glory and of God resteth upon you:
on their part he is evil spoken of, but
on your part he is glorified. 15 But
let none of you suffer as a murderer,

or *as* a thief, or *as* an evildoer, or as
a busybody in other men's matters.
16 Yet if *any man suffer* as a Christian, let him not be ashamed; but let
him glorify God on this behalf. 17
For the time *is come* that judgment
must begin at the house of God: and
if *it* first *begin* at us, what shall the
end *be* of them that obey not the
gospel of God? 18 And if the righteous scarcely be saved, where shall
the ungodly and the sinner appear?
19 Wherefore let them that suffer
according to the will of God commit
the keeping of their souls *to him* in
well doing, as unto a faithful Creator.

The frequent repetition of counsel and comfort to Christians, considered as sufferers, in every chapter of this epistle, shows that the greatest danger these new converts were in arose from the persecutions to which their embracing Christianity exposed them. The good behaviour of Christians under sufferings is the most difficult part of their duty, but yet necessary both for the honour of Christ and their own comfort; and therefore the apostle, having exhorted them in the former part of this chapter to the great duty of mortification, comes here to direct them in the necessary duty of patience under sufferings. An unmortified spirit is very unfit to bear trials. Observe,

I. The apostle's kind manner of address to these poor despised Christians: they were his *beloved*, *v.* 9.

II. His advice to them, relating to their sufferings, which is,

1. That they should not think them strange, nor be surprised at them, as if some unexpected event befel them; for,

(1.) Though they be sharp and fiery, yet they are designed only to try, not to ruin them, to try their sincerity, strength, patience, and trust in God. On the contrary, they ought rather to rejoice under their sufferings, because theirs may properly be called Christ's sufferings. They are of the same kind, and for the same cause, that Christ suffered; they make us conformable to him; he suffers in them, and feels in our infirmities; and, if we be partakers of his sufferings, we shall also be made *partakers of his glory*, and shall meet him with exceeding joy at his great appearing to judge his enemies, and crown his faithful servants, 2 Thess. i. 7, &c. Learn, [1.] True Christians love and own the children of God in their lowest and most distressing circumstances. The apostle owns these poor afflicted Christians, and calls them his beloved. True Christians never look more amiable one to another than in their adversities. [2.] There is no reason for Christians to think strange, or to wonder, at the unkindnesses and persecutions of the world, because they are forewarned of them. Christ himself endured them; and forsaking all, denying ourselves, are the terms upon which Christ accepts of us to be his disciples. [3.] Christians ought not only to be patient, but to rejoice, in their sharpest sorest sufferings for Christ, because they are tokens of divine favour; they promote the gospel and prepare for glory. Those who rejoice in their sufferings for Christ shall eternally triumph and rejoice with him in glory.

(2.) From the fiery trial the apostle descends to a lower degree of persecution—that of the tongue by slander and reproach, *v.* 14. He supposes that this sort of suffering would fall to their lot: they would be reviled, evil-spoken of, and slandered for the name or sake of Christ. In such case he asserts, *Happy are you,* the reason of which is, "Because you have the Spirit of God with you, to fortify and comfort you; and the Spirit of God is also the Spirit of glory, that will carry you through all, bring you off gloriously, and prepare and seal you up for eternal glory. This glorious Spirit *resteth upon you*, resideth with you, dwelleth in you, supporteth you, and is pleased with you; and is not this an unspeakable privilege? By your patience and fortitude in suffering, by your dependence upon the promises of God, and adhering to the word which the Holy Spirit hath revealed, *he is on your part glorified;* but by the contempt and reproaches cast upon you *the Spirit itself* is evil-spoken of and blasphemed." Learn, [1.] The best men and the best things usually meet with reproaches in the world. Jesus Christ and his followers, the Spirit of God and the gospel, are all evil-spoken of. [2.] The happiness of good people not only consists with, but even flows from their afflictions: *Happy are you.* [3.] That man who hath the Spirit of God resting upon him cannot be miserable, let his afflictions be ever so great: *Happy are you; for the Spirit of God*, &c. [4.] The blasphemies and reproaches which evil men cast upon good people are taken by the Spirit of God as cast upon himself: *On their part he is evil-spoken of.* [5.] When good people are vilified *for the name of Christ* his Holy Spirit is glorified in them.

2. That they should take care they did not suffer justly, as evil-doers, *v.* 15. One would think such a caution as this needless to such an excellent set of Christians as these were. But their enemies charged them with these and other foul crimes: therefore the apostle, when he was settling the rules of the Christian religion, thought these cautions necessary, forbidding every one of them to hurt the life or the estate and property of any one, or to do any sort of evil, or, without call and necessity, to play the *bishop in another man's charge*, or busy himself *in other men's mat-*

ters. To this caution he adds a direction, *that if any man suffer* for the cause of Christianity, and with a patient Christian spirit, he ought not to account it a shame, but an honour to him; and ought to glorify God who hath thus dignified him, *v.* 16. Learn, (1.) The best of men need to be warned against the worst of sins. (2.) There is very little comfort in sufferings when we bring them upon ourselves by our own sin and folly. It is not the suffering, but the cause, that makes the martyr. (3.) We have reason to thank God for the honour if he calls us out to suffer for his truth and gospel, for our adherence to any of the doctrines or duties of Christianity.

3. That their trials were now at hand, and they should stand prepared accordingly, *v.* 17, 18.

(1.) He tells them that the time had come when *judgment must begin at the house of God.* The usual method of Providence has been this: When God brings great calamities and sore judgments upon whole nations, he generally begins with his own people, Isa. x. 12; Jer. xxv. 29; Ezek. ix. 6. "Such a time of universal calamity is now at hand, which was foretold by our Saviour, Matt. xxiv. 9, 10. This renders all the foregoing exhortations to patience necessary for you. And you have two considerations to support you." [1.] "That these judgments will but *begin* with you that are God's house and family, and will soon be over: your trials and corrections will not last long." [2.] "Your troubles will be but light and short, in comparison of what shall befal the wicked world, your own countrymen the Jews, and the infidels and idolatrous people among whom you live: *What shall the end be of those who obey not the gospel of God?*" Learn, *First,* The best of God's servants, his own household, have so much amiss in them as renders it fit and necessary that God should sometimes correct and punish them with his judgments: *Judgment begins at the house of God. Secondly,* Those who are the family of God have their worst things in this life. Their worst condition is tolerable, and will soon be over. *Thirdly,* Such persons or societies of men as *disobey the gospel of God* are not of his church and household, though possibly they may make the loudest pretensions. The apostle distinguishes the disobedient from the house of God. *Fourthly,* The sufferings of good people in this life are demonstrations of the unspeakable torments that are coming upon the disobedient and unbelieving: *What shall the end be of those that obey not the gospel?* Who can express or say how dreadful their end will be?

(2.) He intimates the irremediable doom of the wicked: *If the righteous scarcely be saved, where shall the ungodly and sinner appear, v.* 18. This whole verse is taken from Prov. xi. 31, *Behold the righteous shall be recompensed in the earth; how much more the wicked and the sinner?* This the LXX. translate exactly as the apostle here quotes it. Hence we may learn, [1.] The grievous sufferings of good people in this world are sad presages of much heavier judgments coming upon impenitent sinners. But, if we take the salvation here in the highest sense, then we may learn, [2.] It is as much as the best can do to secure the salvation of their souls; there are so many sufferings, temptations, and difficulties to be overcome, so many sins to be mortified, the gate is so strait and the way so narrow, that it is as much as the righteous can do to be saved. Let the absolute necessity of salvation balance the difficulty of it. Consider, Your difficulties are greatest at first; God offers his grace and help; the contest will not last long; be but faithful to the death, *and God will give you the crown of life,* Rev. ii. 10. [3.] The ungodly and the sinner are unquestionably in a state of damnation. *Where shall they appear?* How will they stand before their Judge? Where can they show their heads? *If the righteous scarcely be saved,* the wicked must certainly perish.

4. That when called to suffer, *according to the will of God,* they should look chiefly to the safety of their souls, which are put into hazard by affliction, and cannot be kept secure otherwise than by *committing them to God,* who will undertake the charge, if we commit them to him in well-doing; for he is their Creator, and has out of mere grace made many kind promises to them of eternal salvation, in which he will show himself faithful and true, *v.* 19. Learn, (1.) All the sufferings that befal good people come upon them *according to the will of God.* (2.) It is the duty of Christians, in all their distresses, to look more to the keeping of their souls than to the preserving of their bodies. The soul is of greatest value, and yet in most danger. If suffering from without raise uneasiness, vexation, and other sinful and tormenting passions within, the soul is then the greatest sufferer. If the soul be not well kept, persecution will drive people to apostasy, Ps. cxxv. 3. (3.) The only way to keep the soul well is to commit it to God, in well-doing. Commit your souls to God by solemn dedication, prayer, and patient perseverance in well-doing, Rom. ii. 7. (4.) Good people, when they are in affliction, have great encouragement to commit their souls to God, because he is their Creator, and faithful in all his promises.

CHAP. V.

In which the apostle gives particular directions, first to the elders, how to behave themselves towards their flock, ver. 1—4; then to the younger, to be obedient and humble, and to cast their care upon God, ver. 5—7. He then exhorts all to sobriety, watchfulness against temptations, and stedfastness in the faith, praying earnestly for them; and so concludes his epistle with a solemn doxology, mutual salutations, and his apostolical benediction.

THE elders which are among you I exhort, who am also an elder, and a witness of the sufferings of

Christ, and also a partaker of the
glory that shall be revealed: 2 Feed
the flock of God which is among you,
taking the oversight *thereof*, not by
constraint, but willingly; not for filthy
lucre, but of a ready mind. 3 Neither
as being lords over *God's* heritage,
but being ensamples to the flock. 4
And when the chief Shepherd shall
appear, ye shall receive a crown of
glory, that fadeth not away.

Here we may observe,

I. The persons to whom this exhortation is given—to the presbyters, pastors, and spiritual guides of the church, elders by office, rather than by age, ministers of those churches to whom he wrote this epistle.

II. The person who gives this exhortation—the apostle Peter: *I exhort;* and, to give force to this exhortation, he tells them he was their brother-presbyter or fellow-elder, and so puts nothing upon them but what he was ready to perform himself. He was also *a witness of the sufferings of Christ*, being with him in the garden, attending him to the palace of the high-priest, and very likely being a spectator of his suffering upon the cross, at a distance among the crowd, Acts iii. 15. He adds that he was also *a partaker of the glory* that was in some degree revealed at the transfiguration (Matt. xvii. 1—3), and shall be completely enjoyed at the second coming of Jesus Christ. Learn, 1. Those whose office it is to teach others ought carefully to study their own duty, as well as teach the people theirs. 2. How different the spirit and behaviour of Peter were from that of his pretended successors! He does not command and domineer, but exhort. He does not claim sovereignty over all pastors and churches, nor style himself *prince of the apostles, vicar of Christ*, or *head of the church*, but values himself upon being an *elder*. All the apostles were elders, though every elder was not an apostle. 3. It was the peculiar honour of Peter, and a few more, to be the witnesses of Christ's sufferings; but it is the privilege of all true Christians to be partakers of the glory that shall be revealed.

III. The pastor's duty described, and the manner in which that duty ought to be performed. The pastoral duty is three-fold:—1. *To feed the flock*, by preaching to them the sincere word of God, and ruling them according to such directions and discipline as the word of God prescribes, both which are implied in this expression, *Feed the flock*. 2. The pastors of the church must *take the oversight thereof*. The elders are exhorted to do the office of bishops (as the word signifies), by personal care and vigilance over all the flock committed to their charge. 3. They must be *examples to the flock*, and practise the holiness, self-denial, mortification, and all other Christian duties, which they preach and recommend to their people. These duties must be performed, *not by constraint*, not because you must do them, not from compulsion of the civil power, or the constraint of fear or shame, but from a willing mind that takes pleasure in the work: *not for filthy lucre*, or any emoluments and profits attending the place where you reside, or any perquisite belonging to the office, *but of a ready mind*, regarding the flock more than the fleece, sincerely and cheerfully endeavouring to serve the church of God; *neither as being lords over God's heritage*, tyrannizing over them by compulsion and coercive force, or imposing unscriptural and human inventions upon them instead of necessary duty, Matt. xx. 25, 26; 2 Cor. i. 24. Learn, (1.) The eminent dignity of the church of God, and all the true members of it. These poor, dispersed, suffering Christians were the flock of God. The rest of the world is a brutal herd. These are an orderly flock, redeemed to God by the great Shepherd, living in holy love and communion one with another, *according to the will of God*. They are also dignified with the title of God's *heritage* or *clergy*, his peculiar lot, chosen out of the common multitude for his own people, to enjoy his special favour and to do him special service. The word is never restricted in the New Testament to the ministers of religion. (2.) The pastors of the church ought to consider their people as *the flock of God, as God's heritage*, and treat them accordingly. They are not theirs, to be lorded over at pleasure; but they are God's people, and should be treated with love, meekness, and tenderness, for the sake of him to whom they belong. (3.) Those ministers who are either driven to the work by necessity or drawn to it by filthy lucre can never perform their duty as they ought, because they do not do it willingly, and with a ready mind. (4.) The best way a minister can take to engage the respect of a people is to discharge his own duty among them in the best manner that he can, and to be a constant example to them of all that is good.

IV. In opposition to that filthy lucre which many propose to themselves as their principal motive in undertaking and discharging the pastoral office, the apostle sets before them the crown of glory designed by the great shepherd, Jesus Christ, for all his faithful ministers. Learn, 1. Jesus Christ is *the chief shepherd* of the whole flock and heritage of God. He bought them, and rules them; he defends and saves them for ever. He is also the chief shepherd over all inferior shepherds; they derive their authority from him, act in his name, and are accountable to him at last. 2. This chief shepherd will appear, to judge all ministers and under-shepherds, to call them to account, whether they have faithfully discharged their duty both publicly and privately according to the foregoing directions. 3. Those that are found to have done their duty shall have what is infinitely better than temporal gain; they shall receive from the grand shepherd a high degree of everlasting glory, *a crown of glory that fadeth not away.*

5 Likewise, ye younger, submit yourselves unto the elder. Yea, all *of you* be subject one to another, and be clothed with humility: for God resisteth the proud, and giveth grace to the humble.
6 Humble yourselves therefore under the mighty hand of God, that he may exalt you in due time:
7 Casting all your care upon him; for he careth for you.

Having settled and explained the duty of the pastors or spiritual guides of the church, the apostle comes now to instruct the flock,

I. How to behave themselves to their ministers and to one another. He calls them *the younger*, as being generally younger than their grave pastors, and to put them in mind of their inferiority, the term younger being used by our Saviour to signify an inferior, Luke xxii. 26. He exhorts those that are younger and inferior to *submit themselves to the elder*, to give due respect and reverence to their persons, and to yield to their admonitions, reproof, and authority, enjoining and commanding what the word of God requires, Heb. xiii. 17. As to one another, the rule is that they should all *be subject one to another*, so far as to receive the reproofs and counsels one of another, and be ready to *bear one another's burdens*, and perform all the offices of friendship and charity one to another; and particular persons should submit to the directions of the whole society, Eph. v. 21; Jam. v. 16. These duties of submission to superiors in age or office, and subjection to one another, being contrary to the proud nature and selfish interests of men, he advises them to *be clothed with humility*. "Let your minds, behaviour, garb, and whole frame, be adorned with humility, as the most beautiful habit you can wear; this will render obedience and duty easy and pleasant; but, if you be disobedient and proud, God will set himself to oppose and crush you; for *he resisteth the proud*, when he *giveth grace to the humble.*" Observe, 1. Humility is the great preserver of peace and order in all Christian churches and societies, consequently pride is the great disturber of them, and the cause of most dissensions and breaches in the church. 2. There is a mutual opposition between God and the proud, so the word signifies; they war against him, and he scorns them; *he resisteth the proud*, because they are like the devil, enemies to himself and to his kingdom among men, Prov. iii. 34. 3. Where God giveth grace to be humble, he will give more grace, more wisdom, faith, holiness, and humility. Hence the apostle adds: *Humble yourselves therefore under the mighty hand of God, that he may exalt you in due time, v.* 6. "Since God resisteth the proud, but giveth grace to the humble, therefore humble yourselves, not only one to another, but to the great God, whose judgments are coming upon the world, and must begin at the house of God (*ch.* iv. 17); his hand is almighty, and can easily pull you down if you be proud, or exalt you if you be humble; and it will certainly do it, either in this life, if he see it best for you, or at the day of general retribution. Learn, (1.) The consideration of the omnipotent hand of God should make us humble and submissive to him in all that he brings upon us. (2.) Humbling ourselves to God under his hand is the next way to deliverance and exaltation; patience under his chastisements, submission to his pleasure, repentance, prayer, and hope in his mercy, will engage his help and release in due time, Jam. iv. 7, 10.

II. The apostle, knowing that these Christians were already under very hard circumstances, rightly supposes that what he had foretold of greater hardships yet a coming might excite in them abundance of care and fear about the event of these difficulties, what the issue of them would be to themselves, their families, and the church of God; foreseeing this anxious care would be a heavy burden, and a sore temptation, he gives them the best advice, and supports it with a strong argument. His advice is to *cast all their care*, or *all care of themselves, upon God.* "Throw your cares, which are so cutting and distracting, which wound your souls and pierce your hearts, upon the wise and gracious providence of God; trust in him with a firm composed mind, *for he careth for you.* He is willing to release you of your care, and take the care of you upon himself. He will either avert what you fear, or support you under it. He will order all events to you so as shall convince you of his paternal love and tenderness towards you; and all shall be so ordered that no hurt, but good, shall come unto you," Matt. vi. 25; Ps. lxxxiv. 11; Rom. viii. 28. Learn, 1. The best of Christians are apt to labour under the burden of anxious and excessive care; the apostle calls it, *all your care*, intimating that the cares of Christians are various and of more sorts than one: personal cares, family cares, cares for the present, cares for the future, cares for themselves, for others, and for the church. 2. The cares even of good people are very burdensome, and too often very sinful; when they arise from unbelief and diffidence, when they torture and distract the mind, unfit us for the duties of our place and hinder our delightful service of God, they are very criminal. 3. The best remedy against immoderate care is to *cast our care upon God*, and resign every event to his wise and gracious determination. A firm belief of the rectitude of the divine will and counsels calms the spirit of man. *We ceased, saying, The will of the Lord be done,* Acts xxi 14.

8 Be sober, be vigilant; because your adversary the devil, as a roaring lion, walketh about, seeking whom he may devour: 9 Whom resist stedfast in the faith, knowing that the same afflictions are accomplished in your brethren that are in the world.

Here the apostle does three things:—

I. He shows them their danger from an enemy more cruel and restless than even the worst of men, whom he describes,

1. By his characters and names. (1.) He is an adversary: "*That adversary of yours;* not a common adversary, but an enemy that impleads you, and litigates against you in your grand depending cause, and aims at your very souls." (2.) *The devil, the grand accuser of all the brethren;* this title is derived from a word which signifies to strike through, or to stab. He would strike malignity into our natures, and poison into our souls. If he could have struck these people with passion and murmuring in their sufferings, perhaps he might have drawn them to apostasy and ruin. (3.) He is *a roaring lion,* hungry, fierce, strong, and cruel, the fierce and greedy pursuer of souls.

2. By his business: *He walks about, seeking whom he may devour;* his whole design is to devour and destroy souls. To this end he is unwearied and restless in his malicious endeavours; for he always, night and day, goes about studying and contriving whom he may ensnare to their eternal ruin.

II. Hence he infers that it is their duty, 1. To *be sober,* and to govern both the outward and the inward man by the rules of temperance, modesty, and mortification. 2. To *be vigilant;* not secure or careless, but rather suspicious of constant danger from this spiritual enemy, and, under that apprehension, to be watchful and diligent to prevent his designs and save our souls. 3. To resist him *stedfast in the faith.* It was the faith of these people that Satan aimed at; if he could overturn their faith, and draw them into apostasy, then he knew he should gain his point, and ruin their souls; therefore, to destroy their faith, he raises bitter persecutions, and sets the grand potentates of the world against them. This strong trial and temptation they must resist, by being well-grounded, resolute, and stedfast in the faith: to encourage them to this,

III. He tells them that their care was not singular, for they knew that the like afflictions befel their brethren in all parts of the world, and that all the people of God were their fellow-soldiers in this warfare. Learn, 1. All the great persecutions that ever were in the world were raised, spirited up, and conducted, by the devil; he is the grand persecutor, as well as *the deceiver and accuser, of the brethren;* men are his willing spiteful instruments, but he is the chief adversary that wars against Christ and his people, Gen. iii. 15; Rev. xii. 12. 2. The design of Satan in raising persecutions against the faithful servants of God is to bring them to apostasy, by reason of their sufferings, and so to destroy their souls. 3. Sobriety and watchfulness are necessary virtues at all times, but especially in times of suffering and persecution. "You must moderate your affection to worldly things, or else Satan will soon overcome you." 4. "If you would overcome Satan, as a tempter, an accuser, or a persecutor, you must resist him stedfast in the faith; if your faith give way, you are gone; therefore, *above all, take the shield of faith,*" Eph. vi. 16. 5. The consideration of what others suffer is proper to encourage us to bear our own share in any affliction: *The same afflictions are accomplished in your brethren.*

10 But the God of all grace, who hath called us unto his eternal glory by Christ Jesus, after that ye have suffered a while, make you perfect, stablish, strengthen, settle *you.* 11 To him *be* glory and dominion for ever and ever. Amen. 12 By Silvanus, a faithful brother unto you, as I suppose, I have written briefly, exhorting, and testifying that this is the true grace of God wherein ye stand. 13 The *church that is* at Babylon, elected together with *you,* saluteth you; and *so doth* Marcus my son. 14 Greet ye one another with a kiss of charity. Peace *be* with you all that are in Christ Jesus. Amen.

We come now to the conclusion of this epistle, which,

I. The apostle begins with a most weighty prayer, which he addresses to God as *the God of all grace,* the author and finisher of every heavenly gift and quality, acknowledging, on their behalf, that God had already called them to be partakers of that eternal glory, which, being his own, he had promised and settled upon them, through the merit and intercession of Jesus Christ. Observe,

1. What he prays for on their account; not that they might be excused from sufferings, but that their sufferings might be moderate and short, and, *after they had suffered awhile,* that God would restore them to a settled and peaceable condition, and perfect his work in them—that he would establish them against wavering, either in faith or duty, that he would strengthen those who were weak, and settle them upon Christ the foundation, so firmly that their union with him might be indissoluble and everlasting. Learn, (1.) All grace is from God; it is he

who restrains, converts, comforts, and saves men by his grace. (2.) All who are called into a state of grace are called to partake of eternal glory and happiness. (3.) Those who are called to be heirs of eternal life through Jesus Christ must, nevertheless, suffer in this world, but their sufferings will be but for a little while. (4.) The perfecting, establishing, strengthening, and settling, of good people in grace, and their perseverance therein, is so difficult a work, that only the God of all grace can accomplish it; and therefore he is earnestly to be sought unto by continual prayer, and dependence upon his promises.

2. His doxology, *v.* 11. From this doxology we may learn that those who have obtained grace from the God of all grace should and will ascribe glory, dominion, and power, to him for ever and ever.

II. He recapitulates the design of his writing this epistle to them (*v.* 12), which was, 1. To testify, and in the strongest terms to assure them, that the doctrine of salvation, which he had explained and they had embraced, was the true account of the grace of God, foretold by the prophets and published by Jesus Christ. 2. To exhort them earnestly that, as they had embraced the gospel, they would continue stedfast in it, notwithstanding the arts of seducers, or the persecutions of enemies. (1.) The main thing that ministers ought to aim at in their labours is to convince their people of the certainty and excellency of the Christian religion; this the apostles did *exhort and testify* with all their might. (2.) A firm persuasion that we are in the true way to heaven will be the best motive to stand fast, and persevere therein.

III. He recommends *Silvanus*, the person by whom he sent them this brief epistle, as a brother whom he esteemed faithful and friendly to them, and hoped they would account him so, though he was a minister of the uncircumcision. Observe, An honourable esteem of the ministers of religion tends much to the success of their labours. When we are convinced they are faithful, we shall profit more by their ministerial services. The prejudices that some of these Jews might have against Silvanus, as a minister of the Gentiles, would soon wear off when they were once convinced that he was a faithful brother.

IV. He closes with salutations and a solemn benediction. Observe, 1. Peter, being at Babylon in Assyria, when he wrote this epistle (whither he travelled, as the apostle of the circumcision, to visit that church, which was the chief of the dispersion), sends the salutation of that church to the other churches to whom he wrote (*v.* 13), telling them that God had *elected* or chosen the Christians at Babylon out of the world, to be his church, and to partake of eternal salvation through Christ Jesus, together with them and all other faithful Christians, *ch.* i. 2. In this salutation he particularly joins Mark the evangelist, who was then with him, and who was his son in a spiritual sense, being begotten by him to Christianity. Observe, All the churches of Jesus Christ ought to have a most affectionate concern one for another; they should love and pray for one another, and be as helpful one to another as they possibly can. 2. He exhorts them to fervent love and charity one towards another, and to express this by giving *the kiss of peace* (*v.* 14), according to the common custom of those times and countries, and so concludes with a benediction, which he confines to those *that are in Christ Jesus,* united to him by faith and sound members of his mystical body. The blessing he pronounces upon them is *peace,* by which he means all necessary good, all manner of prosperity; to this he adds his *amen,* in token of his earnest desire and undoubted expectation that the blessing of peace would be the portion of all the faithful.

AN

EXPOSITION,

WITH PRACTICAL OBSERVATIONS,

OF THE SECOND EPISTLE GENERAL OF

PETER.

The penman of this epistle appears plainly to be the same who wrote the foregoing; and, whatever difference some learned men apprehend they discern in the style of this epistle from that of the former, this cannot be a sufficient argument to assert that it was written by Simon who succeeded the apostle James in the church at Jerusalem, inasmuch as he who wrote this epistle calls himself *Simon Peter, and an apostle* (*v.* 1), and says that he was *one of the three apostles that were present at Christ's transfiguration* (*v.* 18), and says expressly *that he had written a former epistle to them,* ch. iii. 1. The design of this second epistle is the same with that of the former, as is evident from the first verse of the third chapter, whence observe that, in the things of God, we have need of *precept upon precept, and line upon line,* and all little enough to keep them in remembrance; and yet these are the things which should be most faithfully recorded and frequently remembered by us.

CHAP. I.

In this chapter we have, I. An introduction, or preface, making way for, and leading to, what is principally designed by the apostle, ver. 1—4. II. An exhortation to advance and improve in all Christian graces, ver. 5—7. III. To enforce this exhortation, and engage them seriously and heartily to comply with it, he adds, 1. A representation of the very great advantage which will thereby accrue to them, ver. 8—11. 2. A promise of the best assistance the apostle was able to give to facilitate and forward this good work, ver. 12—15. 3. A declaration of the certain truth and divine origin of the gospel of Christ, in the grace whereof they were exhorted to increase and persevere.

SIMON Peter, a servant and an apostle of Jesus Christ, to them that have obtained like precious faith with us through the righteousness of God and our Saviour Jesus Christ:
2 Grace and peace be multiplied unto you through the knowledge of God, and of Jesus our Lord, 3 According as his divine power hath given unto us all things that *pertain* unto life and godliness, through the knowledge of him that hath called us to glory and virtue: 4 Whereby are given unto us exceeding great and precious promises: that by these ye might be partakers of the divine nature, having escaped the corruption that is in the world through lust.

The apostle Peter, being moved by the Holy Ghost to write once more to those who from among the Jews were turned to faith in Christ, begins this second epistle with an introduction, wherein the same persons are described and the same blessings are desired that are in the preface to his former letter; but there are some additions or alterations which ought to be taken notice of, in all the three parts of the introduction.

I. We have here a description of the person who wrote the epistle, by the name of *Simon*, as well as *Peter*, and by the title of *servant*, as well as that of *apostle*. *Peter*, being in both epistles, seems to be the name most frequently used, and with which he may be thought to be best pleased, it being given him by our Lord, upon his confessing *Jesus to be Christ the Son of the living God*, and the very name signifying and sealing that truth to be the fundamental article, the rock on which all must build; but the name *Simon*, though omitted in the former epistle, is mentioned in this, lest the total omission of that name, which was given him when he was circumcised, should make the Jewish believers, who were all zealous of the law, to become jealous of the apostle, as if he disclaimed and despised circumcision. He here styles himself *a servant* (as well as an apostle) *of Jesus Christ;* in this he may be allowed to glory, as David does, Ps. cxvi. 16. The service of Christ is the way to the highest honour, John xii. 26. Christ himself is *King of kings, and Lord of lords;* and he makes all his servants *kings and priests unto God*, Rev. i. 6. How great an honour is it to be the servants of this Master! This is what we cannot, without sin, be ashamed of. To triumph in being *Christ's servant* is very proper for those who are engaging others to enter into or abide in the service of Christ.

II. We have an account of the people to whom the epistle is written. They are described in the former epistle as *elect according to the foreknowledge of God the Father*, and here as *having obtained precious faith in our Lord Jesus Christ;* for the faith here mentioned is vastly different from the false faith of the heretic, and the feigned faith of the hypocrite, and the fruitless faith of the formal professor, how orthodox soever he is. It is *the faith of God's elect* (Tit. i. 1), wrought by the Spirit of God in effectual calling. Observe, 1. True saving faith is a precious grace, and that not only as it is very uncommon, very scarce, even in the visible church, a very small number of true believers among a great multitude of visible professors (Matt. xxii. 14), but true faith is very excellent and of very great use and advantage to those who have it. *The just lives by faith*, a truly divine spiritual life; faith procures all the necessary supports and comforts of this excellent life; faith goes to Christ, and buys the wine and milk (Isa. lv. 1) which are the proper nourishment of the new creature; faith buys and brings home the tried gold, the heavenly treasure that enriches; faith takes and puts on the white raiment, the royal robes that clothe and adorn, Rev. iii. 18. Observe, 2. Faith is alike precious in the private Christian and in the apostle; it produces the same precious effects in the one and in the other. Faith unites the weak believer to Christ as really as it does the strong one, and purifies the heart of one as truly as of another; and every sincere believer is by his faith justified in the sight of God, and that from all sins, Acts xiii. 39. Faith, in whomsoever it exists, takes hold of the same *precious* Saviour, and applies the same precious promises. 3. This precious faith is obtained of God. Faith is the gift of God, wrought by the Spirit, who raised up Jesus Christ from the dead. 4. The preciousness of faith, as well as our obtaining it, is through the righteousness of Christ. The satisfactory meritorious righteousness and obedience of Christ gives faith all its value and preciousness: and the righteousness of such a person cannot but be of infinite value to those who by faith receive it. For, (1.) This Jesus Christ is God, yea, *our* God, as it is in the original. He is truly God, an infinite Being, who has wrought out this righteousness, and therefore it must be of infinite value. (2.) *He is the Saviour of those that believe*, and as such he yielded this meritorious obedience; and therefore it is of such great benefit and advantage to them, because, as surety and Saviour, he wrought out this righteousness in their stead.

III. We have the apostolical benediction,

wherein he wishes for the multiplication and increase of the divine favour to them, and the advancement and growth of the work of grace in them, and that peace with God and in their own consciences (which cannot be without *grace)* may abound in them. This is the very same benediction that is in the former epistle; but here he adds,

1. An account of the way and means whereby *grace and peace are multiplied*—it is *through the knowledge of God and Jesus Christ;* this acknowledging or believing in *the only living and true God, and Jesus Christ whom he has sent,* is the great improvement of spiritual life, or it could not be the way to life eternal, John xvii. 3.

2. The ground of the apostle's faith in asking, and of the Christian's hope in expecting, the increase of grace. What we have already received should encourage us to ask for more; he who has begun the work of grace will perfect it. Observe, (1.) The fountain of all spiritual blessings is the divine power of Jesus Christ, who could not discharge all the office of Mediator, unless he was God as well as man. (2.) All things that have any relation to, and influence upon, the true spiritual life, the life and power of godliness, are from Jesus Christ; *in him all fulness dwells,* and it is from him that we receive, *and grace for grace* (John i. 16), even all that is necessary for the preserving, improving, and perfecting of grace and peace, which, according to some expositors, are called here in this verse *godliness and life.* (3.) Knowledge of God, and faith in him, are the channel whereby all spiritual supports and comforts are conveyed to us; but then we must own and acknowledge God as the author of our effectual calling, for so he is here described: *Him that hath called us to glory and virtue.* Observe here, The design of God in calling or converting men is to bring them to *glory and virtue,* that is, *peace and grace,* as some understand it; but many prefer the marginal rendering, *by glory and virtue;* and so we have effectual calling set forth as the work of the glory and virtue, or *the glorious power, of God,* which is described Eph. i. 19. It is the glory of God's power to convert sinners; this is the power and glory of God which are seen and experienced in his sanctuary (Ps. lxiii. 2); this power or virtue is to be extolled by all *that are called out of darkness into marvellous light,* 1 Pet. ii. 9. (4.) In the fourth verse the apostle goes on to encourage their faith and hope in looking for an increase of grace and peace, because the same glory and virtue are employed and evidenced in giving the promises of the gospel that are exercised in our effectual calling. Observe, [1.] The good things which the promises make over are exceedingly great. Pardon of sin is one of the blessings here intended; how great this is all who know any thing of the power of God's anger will readily confess, and this is one of those promised favours in bestowing whereof *the power of the Lord is great,* Num. xiv. 17. To pardon sins that are numerous and heinous (every one of which deserves God's wrath and curse, and that for ever) is a wonderful thing, and is so called, Ps. cxix. 18. [2.] The promised blessings of the gospel are very precious; as the great promise of the Old Testament was *the Seed of the woman,* the Messiah (Heb. xi. 39), so the great promise of the New Testament is the *Holy Ghost* (Luke xxiv. 49), and how precious must the enlivening, enlightening, sanctifying Spirit be! [3.] Those who receive the promises of the gospel *partake of the divine nature.* They are *renewed in the spirit of their mind, after the image of God, in knowledge, righteousness, and holiness;* their hearts are set for God and his service; they have a divine temper and disposition of soul; though the law is *the ministration of death,* and *the letter killeth,* yet the gospel is *the ministration of life,* and *the Spirit quickeneth* those *who* are naturally *dead in trespasses and sins.* [4.] Those in whom the Spirit works the divine nature are freed from the bondage of corruption. Those who are, by the Spirit of grace, *renewed in the spirit of their mind,* are translated into *the liberty of the children of God;* for it is the world in which *corruption reigns.* Those who are *not of the Father, but of the world,* are under the power of sin; the world lies in wickedness, 1 John v. 19. And the dominion that sin has in the men of the world is through lust; their desires are to it, and therefore it rules over them. The dominion that sin has over us is according to the delight we have in it.

5 And beside this, giving all diligence, add to your faith virtue; and
to virtue knowledge; 6 And to
knowledge temperance; and to temperance patience; and to patience
godliness; 7 And to godliness brotherly kindness; and to brotherly
kindness charity. 8 For if these
things be in you, and abound, they
make *you that ye shall* neither *be*
barren nor unfruitful in the knowledge
of our Lord Jesus Christ. 9 But he
that lacketh these things is blind, and
cannot see afar off, and hath forgotten
that he was purged from his old sins.
10 Wherefore the rather, brethren,
give diligence to make your calling
and election sure: for if ye do these
things, ye shall never fall: 11 For
so an entrance shall be ministered
unto you abundantly into the everlasting kingdom of our Lord and Saviour Jesus Christ.

In these words the apostle comes to the

chief thing intended in this epistle—to excite and engage them to advance in grace and holiness, they having already obtained precious faith, and been made partakers of the divine nature. This is a very good beginning, but it is not to be rested in, as if we were already perfect. The apostle had prayed that grace and peace might be multiplied to them, and now he exhorts them to press forward for the obtaining of more grace. We should, as we have opportunity, exhort those we pray for, and excite them to the use of all proper means to obtain what we desire God to bestow upon them; and those who will make any progress in religion must be very diligent and industrious in their endeavours. Without *giving all diligence,* there is no gaining any ground in the work of holiness; those who are slothful in the business of religion will make nothing of it; we must strive if we will *enter in at the strait gate,* Luke xiii. 24.

I. Here we cannot but observe how the believer's way is marked out step by step. 1. He must get *virtue,* by which some understand *justice;* and then the *knowledge, temperance, and patience* that follow, being joined with it, the apostle may be supposed to put them upon pressing after the four cardinal virtues, or the four elements that go to the making up of every virtue or virtuous action. But seeing it is a *faithful saying, and constantly to be asserted, that those who have faith be careful to maintain good works* (Tit. iii. 8), by *virtue* here we may understand *strength* and *courage,* without which the believer cannot stand up for good works, by abounding and excelling in them. The righteous must be bold as a lion (Prov. xxviii. 1); a cowardly Christian, who is afraid to profess the doctrines or practise the duties of the gospel, must expect that Christ will be ashamed of him another day. "Let not your hearts fail you in the evil day, but show yourselves valiant in standing against all opposition, and resisting every enemy, world, flesh, devil, yea, and death too." We have need of virtue while we live, and it will be of excellent use when we come to die. 2. The believer must add *knowledge* to his virtue, prudence to his courage; there is a knowledge of God's name which must go before our faith (Ps. ix. 10), and we cannot approve of the good, and acceptable, and perfect will of God, till we know it; but there are proper circumstances for duty, which must be known and observed; we must use the appointed means, and observe the accepted time. Christian prudence regards the persons we have to do with and the place and company we are in. Every believer must labour after the knowledge and wisdom that are profitable to direct, both as to the proper method and order wherein all Christian duties are to be performed and as to the way and manner of performing them. 3. We must add *temperance* to our knowledge. We must be sober and moderate in our love to, and use of, the good things of this life; and, if we have a right understanding and knowledge of outward comforts, we shall see that their worth and usefulness are vastly inferior to those of spiritual mercies. Bodily exercises and bodily privileges profit but little, and therefore are to be esteemed and used accordingly; the gospel teaches sobriety as well as honesty, Tit. ii. 12. We must be moderate in desiring and using the good things of natural life, such as meat, drink, clothes, sleep, recreations, and credit; an inordinate desire after these is inconsistent with an earnest desire after God and Christ; and those who take more of these than is due can render to neither God nor man what is due to them. 4. Add to temperance *patience,* which must *have its perfect work,* or we cannot *be perfect and entire, wanting nothing* (Jam. i. 4), for we are born to trouble, and must through many tribulations enter into the kingdom of heaven; and it is this tribulation (Rom. v. 3) which worketh patience, that is, requires the exercise and occasions the increase of this grace, whereby we bear all calamities and crosses with silence and submission, without murmuring against God or complaining of him, but justifying him who lays all affliction upon us, owning that our sufferings are less than our sins deserve, and believing they are no more than we ourselves need. 5. To patience we must add *godliness,* and this is the very thing which is produced by patience, for that works experience, Rom. v. 4. When Christians bear afflictions patiently, they get an experimental *knowledge of the loving-kindness of their heavenly Father, which he will not take from his children, even when he visits their iniquity with the rod and their transgression with stripes* (Ps. lxxxix. 32, 33), and hereby they are brought to the child-like fear and reverential love wherein true godliness consists: to this, 6. We must add *brotherly-kindness,* a tender affection to all our fellow-christians, who are children of the same Father, servants of the same Master, members of the same family, travellers to the same country, and heirs of the same inheritance, and therefore are to be loved with a pure heart fervently, with a love of complacency, as those who are peculiarly near and dear to us, in whom we take particular delight, Ps. xvi. 3. 7. *Charity,* or a love of good-will to all mankind, must be added to the love of delight which we have for those who are the children of God. God has made of one blood all nations, and all the children of men are partakers of the same human nature, are all capable of the same mercies, and liable to the same afflictions, and therefore, though upon a spiritual account Christians are distinguished and dignified above those who are without Christ, yet are they to sympathize with others in their calamities, and relieve their necessities, and promote their welfare both in body and soul, as they have opportunity: thus must all believers in

Christ evidence that they are the children of God, who is good to all, but is especially good to Israel.

II. All the forementioned graces must be had, or we shall not be *thoroughly furnished for all good works*—for the duties of the first and second table, for active and passive obedience, and for those services wherein we are to imitate God as well as for those wherein we only obey him—and therefore to engage us to an industrious and unwearied pursuit of them, the apostle sets forth the advantages that redound to all who successfully labour so as to get these things to *be and abound in them, v.* 8—11. These are proposed,

1. More generally, *v.* 8. The having *these things make not barren* (or slothful) *nor unfruitful,* where, according to the style of the Holy Ghost, we must understand a great deal more than is expressed; for when it is said concerning Ahaz, the vilest and most provoking of all the kings of Judah, *that he did not right in the sight of the Lord* (2 Kings xvi. 2), we are to understand as much as if it had been said, He did what was most offensive and abominable, as the following account of his life shows; so, when it is here said that the being and abounding of all Christian graces in us will make us neither inactive nor unfruitful, we are thereby to understand that it will make us very zealous and lively, vigorous and active, in all practical Christianity, and eminently fruitful in the works of righteousness. These will bring much glory to God, by bringing forth much fruit among men, being *fruitful in knowledge, or the acknowledging of our Lord Jesus Christ,* owning him to be their *Lord,* and evidencing themselves to be his servants by their abounding in the work that he has given them to do. This is the necessary consequence of adding one grace to another; for, where all Christian graces are in the heart, they improve and strengthen, encourage and cherish, one another; so they all thrive and grow (as the apostle intimates in the beginning of *v.* 8), and wherever grace abounds there will be an abounding in good works. How desirable it is to be in such a case the apostle evidences, *v.* 9. There he sets forth how miserable it is to be without those quickening fructifying graces; for he who has not the forementioned graces, or, though he pretends or seems to have them, does not exercise and improve them, *is blind,* that is, as to spiritual and heavenly things, as the next words explain it: *He cannot see far off.* This present evil world he can see, and dotes upon, but has no discerning at all of the world to come, so as to be affected with the spiritual privileges and heavenly blessings thereof. He who sees the excellences of Christianity must needs be diligent in endeavours after all those graces that are absolutely necessary for *obtaining glory, honour, and immortality;* but, where these graces are not obtained nor endeavoured after, men are not able to look forward to the things that are but a very little way off in reality, though in appearance, or in their apprehension, they are at a great distance, because they put them far away from them; and how wretched is their condition who are thus blind as to the awfully great things of the other world, who cannot see any thing of the reality and certainty, the greatness and nearness, of the glorious rewards God will bestow on the righteous, and the dreadful punishment he will inflict on the ungodly! But this is not all the misery of those who do not *add to their faith virtue, knowledge,* &c. They are as unable to look backward as forward, their memories are slippery and unable to retain what is past, as their sight is short and unable to discern what is future; they forget that they have been baptized, and had the means, and been laid under the obligations to holiness of heart and life. By baptism we are engaged in a holy war against sin, and are solemnly bound to fight against the flesh, the world, and the devil. Often call to mind, and seriously meditate on, your solemn engagement to be the Lord's, and your peculiar advantages and encouragements to lay aside *all filthiness of flesh and spirit.*

2. The apostle proposes two particular advantages that will attend or follow upon diligence in the work of a Christian: stability in grace, and a triumphant entrance into glory. These he brings in by resuming his former exhortation, and laying it down in other words; for what in *v.* 5 is expressed by *giving diligence to add to faith virtue,* &c., is expressed in *v.* 10 by *giving diligence to make our calling and election sure.* Here we may observe, (1.) It is the duty of believers *to make their election sure,* to clear it up to themselves that they are the chosen of God. (2.) The way to make sure their eternal election is to make out their effectual calling: none can look into the book of God's eternal counsels and decrees; but, inasmuch as *whom God did predestinate those he also called,* if we can find we are effectually called, we may conclude we are chosen to salvation. (3.) It requires a great deal of diligence and labour to make sure our calling and election; there must be a very close examination of ourselves, a very narrow search and strict enquiry, whether we are thoroughly converted, our minds enlightened, our wills renewed, and our whole souls changed as to the bent and inclination thereof; and to come to a fixed certainty in this requires the utmost diligence, and cannot be attained and kept without divine assistance, as we may learn from Ps. cxxxix. 23; Rom. viii. 16. "But, how great soever the labour is, do not think much of it, for great is the advantage you gain by it; for," [1.] "By this you will be kept from falling, and that at all times and seasons, even in those hours of temptation that shall be on the earth." When others shall fall into heinous and scandalous sin,

those who are thus diligent shall be enabled to walk circumspectly and keep on in the way of their duty; and, when many fall into errors, they shall be preserved sound in the faith, and stand perfect and complete in all the will of God. [2.] Those who are diligent in the work of religion shall have a triumphant entrance into glory; while of those few who get to heaven some are scarcely saved (1 Pet. iv. 18), with a great deal of difficulty, *even as by fire* (1 Cor. iii. 15), those who are *growing in grace*, and *abounding in the work of the Lord*, shall have an *abundant entrance into the joy of their Lord*, even that everlasting kingdom where Christ reigns, and they shall *reign with him for ever and ever*.

12 Wherefore I will not be negligent to put you always in remembrance of these things, though ye know *them*, and be established in the present truth. 13 Yea, I think it meet, as long as I am in this tabernacle, to stir you up by putting *you* in remembrance; 14 Knowing that shortly I must put off *this* my tabernacle, even as our Lord Jesus Christ hath showed me. 15 Moreover I will endeavour that ye may be able after my decease to have these things always in remembrance.

I. The importance and advantage of progress and perseverance in grace and holiness made the apostle to be very diligent in doing the work of a minister of Christ, that he might thereby excite and assist them to be diligent in the duty of Christians. If ministers be negligent in their work, it can hardly be expected that the people will be diligent in theirs; therefore Peter *will not be negligent* (that is, at no time or place, in no part of his work, to no part of his charge), but will be exemplarily and universally diligent, and that in the work of a remembrancer. This is the office of the best ministers, even the apostles themselves; they are *the Lord's remembrancers* (Isa. lxii. 6.); they are especially bound to make mention of the promises, and put God in mind of his engagements to do good to his people; and they are the people's remembrancers, making mention of God's precepts, and putting them in mind of the doctrines and duties of Christianity, that they may remember God's commandments, to do them. And this the apostle does, though some persons might think it needless, inasmuch as they already knew those things that he writes about, and were established in the very truth that he insists upon. Observe, 1. We need to be put in mind of what we already know to prevent our forgetting it, and to improve our knowledge, and reduce all to practice. 2. We must be established in the belief of the truth, that we may not be shaken by every wind of doctrine, and especially in that which is the present truth, the truth more peculiarly necessary for us to know in our day, that which belongs to our peace, and which is more especially opposed in our time. The great doctrines of the gospel, *that Jesus is the Christ, that Jesus Christ came into the world to save sinners, that those who believe in the Lord Jesus Christ shall be saved, and all that believe in God must be careful to maintain good works*—these are truths the apostles insisted on in their day; *these are faithful sayings, and worthy of all acceptation* in every age of the Christian church. And, as these must be constantly affirmed by ministers (Tit. iii. 8), so the people are to be well instructed and established therein, and yet must, after all their attainments in knowledge, be put in mind of such things as cannot be too clearly known nor too firmly believed. The most advanced Christians cannot, while in this world, be above ordinances, nor beyond the need of those means which God has appointed and does afford. And, if the people need teaching and exhortation while they are in the body, it is very meet and just that ministers should, as long as they are in this tabernacle, instruct and exhort them, and bring those truths to their remembrance that they have formerly heard, this being a proper means to stir them up to be diligent and lively in a course of gospel-obedience.

II. The apostle, being set upon the work, tell us (*v.* 14) what makes him earnest in this matter, even the knowledge he had, not only that he must certainly, but also that he must shortly, *put off this tabernacle.* Observe, 1. The body is but the tabernacle of the soul. It is a mean and movable structure, whose stakes can be easily removed, and its cords presently broken. 2. This tabernacle must be put of. We are not to continue long in this earthly house. As at night we put off our clothes, and lay them by, so at death we must put off our bodies, and they must be laid up in the grave till the morning of the resurrection. 3. The nearness of death makes the apostle diligent in the business of life. Our Lord Jesus had shown him that the time of his departure was at hand, and therefore he bestirs himself with greater zeal and diligence, because the time is short. He must soon be removed from those to whom he wrote; and his ambition being that they should remember the doctrine he had delivered to them, after he himself was taken away from them, he commits his exhortation to writing. The apostle had not any great opinion of oral tradition. This was not so proper a means to reach the end he was in pursuit of. He would have them always to remember these things, and not only to keep them in mind, but also to make mention of them, as the original words import. *Those who fear the Lord make mention of his name*, and talk of his loving-kindness. This is the way to spread the knowledge of the Lord and this the apostle had at heart: and those who have the written word of God are thereby put into a capacity to do this.

16 For we have not followed cunningly devised fables, when we made known unto you the power and coming of our Lord Jesus Christ, but were eyewitnesses of his majesty.
17 For he received from God the Father honour and glory, when there came such a voice to him from the excellent glory, This is my beloved Son, in whom I am well pleased.
18 And this voice which came from heaven we heard, when we were with him in the holy mount.

Here we have the reason of giving the foregoing exhortation, and that with so much diligence and seriousness. These things are not idle tales, or a vain thing, but of undoubted truth and vast concern. The gospel is not a *cunningly devised fable.* These are not the words of one who hath a devil, nor the contrivance of any number of men who by cunning craftiness endeavour to deceive. The way of salvation by Jesus Christ is eminently the counsel of God, the most excellent contrivance of the infinitely wise Jehovah; it was he that invented this way of saving sinners by Jesus Christ, whose power and coming are set forth in the gospel, and the apostle's preaching was a making of these things known. 1. The preaching of the gospel is a making known the power of Christ, that he is able to save to the uttermost all who come to God by him. He is the mighty God, and therefore can save from both the guilt and the filth of sin. 2. The coming of Christ also is made known by the preaching of the gospel. He who was promised immediately after the fall of man, as in the fulness of time to be born of a woman, has now come in the flesh; and whosoever denies this is an antichrist (1 John iv. 3), he is actuated and influenced by the spirit of antichrist; but those who are the true apostles and ministers of Christ, and are directed and guided by the Spirit of Christ, evidence that Christ has come according to the promise which all the Old-Testament believers died in the faith of, Heb. xi. 39. Christ has come in the flesh. Inasmuch as those whom he undertakes to save *are partakers of flesh and blood, he himself also took part of the same,* that he might suffer in their nature and stead, and thereby make an atonement. This coming of Christ the gospel is very plain and circumstantial in setting forth; but there is a second coming, which it likewise mentions, which the ministers of the gospel ought also to make known, when he shall come in the glory of his Father with all his holy angels, for he is appointed to be Judge both of quick and dead. He will come to judge the world in righteousness by the everlasting gospel, and call us all to give account of all things done in the body, whether good or evil. 3. And though this gospel of Christ has been blasphemously called a *fable* by one of those wretches who call themselves *the successors of St. Peter,* yet our apostle proves that it is of the greatest certainty and reality, inasmuch as during our blessed Saviour's abode here on earth, when he took on him the form of a servant and was found in fashion as a man, he sometimes manifested himself to be God, and particularly to our apostle and the two sons of Zebedee, who *were eye-witnesses of his divine majesty, when he was transfigured before them, and his face did shine as the sun, and his raiment was white as the light, exceedingly white, as snow, so as no fuller on earth can whiten them.* This Peter, James, and John, were eye-witnesses of, and therefore might and ought to attest; and surely their testimony is true, when they witness what they have seen with their eyes, yea, and heard with their ears: for, besides the visible glory that Christ was invested with here on earth, there was an audible voice from heaven. Here observe, (1.) What a gracious declaration was made: *This is my beloved Son, in whom I am well pleased*—the best voice that ever came from heaven to earth; God is well pleased with Christ, and with us in him. This is the Messiah who was promised, through whom all who believe in him shall be accepted and saved. (2.) This declaration is made by God the Father, who thus publicly owns his Son (even in his state of humiliation, when he was in the form of a servant), yea, proclaims him to be his beloved Son, when he is in that low condition; yea, so far are Christ's mean and low circumstances from abating the love of the Father to him that his laying down his life is said to be one special reason of the Father's love, John x. 17. (3.) The design of this voice was to do our Saviour a singular honour while he was here below: *He received honour and glory from God the Father.* This is the person whom God delights to honour. As he requires us to give honour and glory to his Son by confessing him to be our Saviour, so does he give glory and honour to our Saviour by declaring him to be his Son. (4.) This voice is from heaven, called here *the excellent glory,* which still reflects a greater glory upon our blessed Saviour. This declaration is from God the fountain of honour, and from heaven the seat of glory, where God is most gloriously present. (5.) This voice was heard, and that so as to be understood, by Peter, James, and John. They not only heard a sound (as the people did, John xii. 28, 29), but they understood the sense. God opens the ears and understandings of his people to receive what they are concerned to know, when others are like Paul's companions, who only heard a sound of words (Acts ix. 7), but understood not the meaning thereof, and therefore are said not to hear the voice of him that spoke, Acts xxii. 9. Blessed are those who not only hear, but understand, who believe the truth, and feel the power of the voice from heaven, as he did who testifieth these things: and we have all the reason in the world to receive his testimony; for who would refuse to give credit to what is so circumstantially laid down as this account of the voice from heaven, of which the apostle tells us, (6.) It was heard by them *in the holy mount*, when they were with Jesus? The place wherein God affords any peculiarly gracious manifestation of himself is thereby made holy, not with an inherent holiness, but as the ground was holy where God appeared to Moses (Exod. iii. 5), and the mountain holy on which the temple was built, Ps. lxxxvii. 1. Such places are relatively holy, and to be regarded as such during the time that men in themselves experience, or may, by warrant from the word, believingly expect, the special presence and gracious influence of the holy and glorious God.

19 We have also a more sure word of prophecy; whereunto ye do well that ye take heed, as unto a light that shineth in a dark place, until the day dawn, and the day star arise in your hearts: 20 Knowing this first, that no prophecy of the scripture is of any private interpretation. 21 For the prophecy came not in old time by the will of man: but holy men of God spake *as they were* moved by the Holy Ghost.

In these words the apostle lays down another argument to prove the truth and reality of the gospel, and intimates that this second proof is more strong and convincing than the former, and more unanswerably makes out that the doctrine of the power and coming of our Lord Jesus Christ is not a mere fable or cunning contrivance of men, but the wise and wonderful counsel of the holy and gracious God. For this is foretold by the prophets and penmen of the Old Testament, who spoke and wrote under the influence and according to the direction of the Spirit of God. Here note,

I. The description that is given of the scriptures of the Old Testament: they are called *a more sure word of prophecy*. 1. It is a prophetical declaration of the power and coming, the Godhead and incarnation, of our Saviour, which we have in the Old Testament. It is there foretold *that the seed of the woman shall bruise the serpent's head.* His power to destroy the devil and his works, and his being made of a woman, are there foretold; and the great and awful Old-Testament name of God, *Jehovah* (as read by some), signifies only *He will be;* and that name of God (Exod. iii. 14) is rendered by many, *I will be that I will be;* and, thus understood, they point at God's being incarnate in order to the redemption and salvation of his people as what was *to come.* But the New Testament is a history of that whereof the Old Testament is a prophecy. *All the prophets and the law prophesied until John,* Matt. xi. 13. And the evangelists and the apostles have written the history of what was before delivered as prophecy. Now the accomplishment of the Old Testament by the New, and the agreeableness of the New Testament to the Old, are a full demonstration of the truth of both. Read the Old Testament as a prophecy of Christ, and with diligence and thankfulness use the New as the best exposition of the Old. 2. *The Old Testament is a more sure word of prophecy.* It is so to the Jews who received it as the oracles of God. Following prophets confirmed what had been delivered by those who went before, and these prophecies had been written by the express command, and preserved by the special care, and many of them fulfilled by the wonderful providence of God, and therefore were more certain to those who had all along received and read the scriptures than the apostle's account of this voice from heaven. *Moses and the prophets* more powerfully persuade than even miracles themselves, Luke xvi. 31. How firm and sure should our faith be, who have such a firm and sure word to rest upon! All the prophecies of the Old Testament are more sure and certain to us who have the history of the most exact and minute accomplishment of them.

II. The encouragement the apostle gives us to search the scriptures. He tells us, *We do well if we take heed to them;* that is, apply our minds to understand the sense, and our hearts to believe the truth, of this sure word, yea, bend ourselves to it, that we may be moulded and fashioned by it. The word is that form of doctrine into which we must be cast (Rom. vi. 17), *that formulary of knowledge* (Rom. ii. 20) by which we are to regulate our thoughts and sentiments, our words and confessions, our whole life and conversation. If we thus apply ourselves to the word of God, we certainly do well in all respects, what is pleasing to God and profitable to ourselves; and this indeed is but paying that regard which is due to the oracles of God. But, in order to this giving heed to the word, the apostle suggests some things that are of singular use to those who would attend to the scriptures to any good purpose. 1. They must account and use the scripture as a light which God hath sent into and set up in the world, to dispel that darkness which is upon the face of the whole earth. The word is a lamp to the feet of those who use it aright; this discovers the way wherein men ought to walk; this is the means whereby we come to know the way of life. 2. They must acknowledge their own darkness. This world is a place of error and ignorance, and every man in the world is naturally without that knowledge which is necessary in order to attain eternal life. 3. If ever men are made wise to salvation, it is by the shining of the word of God into their hearts. Natural notions of God are not sufficient for fallen man, who does at best actually know a great deal less, and yet does absolutely need to know a great deal more, of God than Adam did while he continued innocent. 4. When the light of the scripture is darted into the blind mind and dark understanding by the Holy Spirit of God, then the *spiritual day dawns and the day-star arises in that soul.* This enlightening of a dark benighted mind is like the day-break that improves and advances, spreads and diffuses itself through the whole soul, till it makes perfect day, Prov. iv. 18. It is a growing knowledge; those who are this way enlightened never think they know enough, till they come to know as they are known. To give heed to this light must needs be the interest and duty of all; and all who do truth come to this light, while evil-doers keep at a distance from it.

III. The apostle lays down one thing as previously necessary in order to our giving heed to, and getting good by, the scriptures, and that is the knowing that all prophecy is of divine origin. Now this important truth he not only asserts, but proves. 1. Observe, No scripture prophecy is of private interpretation (or a man's own proper opinion, an explication of his own mind), but the revelation of the mind of God. This was the difference between the prophets of the Lord and the false prophets who have been in the world. The prophets of the Lord did not speak nor do any thing of their own mind, as Moses, the chief of them, says expressly (Num. xvi. 28), *I have not done any of the works* (nor delivered any of the statutes and ordinances) *of my own mind.* But false prophets *speak a vision of their own heart, not out of the mouth of the Lord,* Jer. xxiii. 16. The prophets and penmen of the scripture spoke and wrote what was the mind of God; and though, when under the influence and guidance of the Spirit, it may well be supposed that they were willing to reveal and record such things, yet it is because God would have them spoken and written. But though the scripture be not the effusion of man's own private opinion or inclination, but the revelation of the mind and will of God, yet every private man ought to search it, and come to understand the sense and meaning thereof. 2. This important truth of the divine origin of the scriptures (that what is contained in them is the mind of God and not of man) is to be known and owned by all who will give heed to the sure word of prophecy. That the scriptures are the word of God is not only an article of the true Christian's faith, but also a matter of science or knowledge. As a man not barely believes, but knows assuredly that that very person is his particular friend in whom he sees all the proper, peculiar, distinguishing marks and characters of his friend, so the Christian knows that book to be the word of God in and upon which he sees all the proper marks and characters of a divinely inspired book. He tastes a sweetness, and feels a power, and sees a glory, in it truly divine. 3. The divinity of the scriptures must be known and acknowledged in the first place, before men can profitably use them, before they can give good heed to them. To call off our minds from all other writings, and apply them in a peculiar manner to these as the only certain and infallible rule, necessarily requires our being fully persuaded that these are divinely inspired, and contain what is truly the mind and will of God.

IV. Seeing it is so absolutely necessary that persons be fully persuaded of the scripture's divine origin, the apostle (*v.* 21) tells us how the Old Testament came to be compiled, and that, 1. Negatively: *It came not by the will of man.* Neither the things themselves that are recorded, and make up the several parts of the Old Testament, are the opinions of men, nor was the will of any of the prophets or penmen of the scriptures the rule or reason why any of those things were written which make up the canon of the scripture. 2. Affirmatively: *Holy men of God spoke as they were moved by the Holy Ghost.* Observe, (1.) They were holy men of God who were employed about that book which we receive as the word of God. If Balaam and Caiaphas, and others who were destitute of holiness, had any thing of the spirit of prophecy, upon occasion, yet such persons were not employed to write any part of the scriptures for the use of the church of God. All the penmen of the scriptures were holy men of God. (2.) *These holy men were moved by the Holy Ghost* in what they delivered as the mind and will of God. The Holy Ghost is the supreme agent, the holy men are but instruments. [1.] The Holy Ghost inspired and dictated to them what they were to deliver of the mind of God. [2.] He powerfully excited and effectually engaged them to speak (and write) what he had put into their mouths. [3.] He so wisely and carefully assisted and directed them in the delivery of what they had received from him that they were effectually secured from any the least mistake in expressing what they revealed; so that the very words of scripture are to be accounted the words of the Holy Ghost, and all the plainness and simplicity, all the power and virtue, all the elegance and propriety, of the very words and expressions are to be regarded by us as proceeding from God. Mix faith therefore with what you find in the scriptures; esteem and reverence your Bible as a book written by holy men, inspired, influenced, and assisted by the Holy Ghost.

CHAP. II.

The apostle, having in the foregoing chapter exhorted them to proceed and advance in the Christian race, now comes to remove, as much as in him lay, what he could not but apprehend would hinder their complying with his exhortation. He therefore gives them fair warning of false teachers, by whom they might be in danger of being seduced. To prevent this, I. He describes these seducers as impious in themselves, and very pernicious to others, ver. 1—3. II. He assures them of the punishment that shall be inflicted on them, ver. 3—6. III. He tells us how contrary the method is which God takes with those who fear him, ver. 7—9. IV. He fills up the rest of the chapter with a further description of those seducers of whom he would have them beware.

BUT there were false prophets also among the people, even as there shall be false teachers among you, who privily shall bring in damnable heresies, even denying the Lord that bought them, and bring upon themselves swift destruction.
2 And many shall follow their pernicious ways; by reason of whom the way of truth shall be evil spoken of.
3 And through covetousness shall they with feigned words make merchandise of you—

I. In the end of the former chapter there is mention made of holy men of God, who lived in the times of the Old Testament, and were used as the amanuenses of the Holy Ghost, in writing the sacred oracles; but in the beginning of this he tells us they had, even at that time, false prophets in the church as well as true. In all ages of the church, and under all dispensations, when God sends true prophets, the devil sends some to seduce and deceive, false prophets in the Old Testament, and false Christs, false apostles, and seducing teachers, in the New. Concerning these observe, 1. Their business is to bring in destructive errors, *even damnable heresies*, as the business of teachers sent of God is to show the way of truth, even the true way to everlasting life. There are damnable heresies as well as damnable practices; and false teachers are industrious to spread pernicious errors. 2. Damnable heresies are commonly brought in privily, under the cloak and colour of truth. 3. Those who introduce destructive heresies *deny the Lord that bought them.* They reject and refuse to hear and learn of the great teacher sent from God, though he is the only Saviour and Redeemer of men, who paid a price sufficient to redeem as many worlds of sinners as there are sinners in the world. 4. Those who bring in errors destructive to others bring swift (and therefore sure) *destruction upon themselves.* Self-destroyers are soon destroyed; and those who are so hardened as to propagate errors destructive to others shall surely and suddenly be destroyed, and that without remedy.

II. He proceeds, in the second verse, to tell us the consequence with respect to others; and here we may learn, 1. Corrupt leaders seldom fail of many to follow them; though the way of error is a pernicious way, yet many are ready to walk therein. Men drink in iniquity like water, and are pleased to live in error. *The prophets prophesy falsely, and the people love to have it so.* 2. The spreading of error will bring up an evil report on the way of truth; that is, the way of salvation by Jesus Christ, who is *the way, the truth, and the life.* The Christian religion is from the God of truth as the author, leads to true happiness in the enjoyment of the true God as the end, and works truth in the inward part as the means of acceptably serving God. And yet this way of truth is traduced and blasphemed by those who embrace and advance destructive errors. This the apostle has foretold as what should certainly come to pass. Let us not be offended at any thing of this in our day, but take care that we give no occasion to the enemy to blaspheme the holy name whereby we are called, or speak evil of that way whereby we hope to be saved.

III. Observe, in the next place, the method seducers take to draw disciples after them: they use *feigned words;* they flatter, and by good words and fair speeches deceive the hearts of the simple, inducing them to yield entirely to the opinions which these seducers endeavour to propagate, and sell and deliver themselves over to the instruction and government of these false teachers, who make a gain of those whom they make their proselytes, serving themselves and making some advantage of them; for all this is through covetousness, with a desire and design to get more wealth, or credit, or commendation, by increasing the number of their followers. The faithful ministers of Christ, who show men the way of truth, desire the profit and advantage of their followers, that they may be saved; but these seducing teachers desire and design only their own temporal advantage and worldly grandeur.

—3 Whose judgment now of a long time lingereth not, and their damnation slumbereth not.
4 For if God spared not the angels that sinned, but cast *them* down to hell, and delivered *them* into chains of darkness, to be reserved unto judgment;
5 And spared not the old world, but saved Noah the eighth *person*, a preacher of righteousness, bringing in the flood upon the world of the ungodly;
6 And turning the cities of Sodom and Gomorrha into ashes condemned *them* with an overthrow, making *them* an ensample unto those that after should live ungodly.

Men are apt to think that a reprieve is the forerunner of a pardon, and that if judgment be not speedily executed it is, or will be, certainly reversed. But the apostle tells us that how successful and prosperous soever false teachers may be, and that for a time, yet their *judgment lingereth not.* God has determined long ago how he will deal with them. Such unbelievers, who endeavour to turn others from the faith, are condemned already, and the wrath of God abideth on them. The righteous Judge will speedily take vengeance; the day of their calamity is at hand, and the things that shall come upon them make haste. To prove this assertion, here are several examples of the righteous judgment of God, in taking vengeance on sinners, proposed to our serious consideration.

I. See how God dealt with the angels who sinned. Observe, 1. No excellency will exempt a sinner from punishment. If the angels, who excel us vastly in strength and knowledge, violate the law of God, the sentence which that law awards shall be executed upon them, and that without mercy or mitigation, for God did not spare them. Hence observe, 2. By how much the more excellent the offender, by so much the more severe the punishment. These angels, who had the advantage of men as to the dignity of their nature, are immediately punished. There is no sparing them for a few days, no favour at all shown them. 3. Sin debases and degrades the persons who commit it. The angels of heaven are cast down from the height of their excellency, and divested of all their glory and dignity, upon their disobedience. Whoever sins against God does a manifest hurt to himself. 4. Those who rebel against the God of heaven shall all be sent down to hell. There is no place nor state between the height of glory and the depth of misery in which they shall be allowed to rest. If creatures sin in heaven, they must suffer in hell. 5. Sin is the work of darkness, and darkness is the wages of sin. The darkness of misery and torment follows the darkness of sin. Those who will not walk according to the light and direction of God's law shall be deprived of the light of God's countenance and the comforts of his presence. 6. As sin binds men over to punishment, so misery and torment hold men under punishment. The darkness which is their misery keeps them so that they cannot get away from their torment. 7. The last degree of torment is not till the day of judgment. The sinning angels, though in hell already, are yet reserved to the judgment of the great day.

II. See how God dealt with the old world, even in much the same way that he dealt with the angels. He spared not the old world. Here observe, 1. The number of offenders signifies no more to procure any favour than the quality. If the sin be universal, the punishment shall likewise extend to all. But, 2. If there be but a few righteous, they shall be preserved. God does not destroy the good with the bad. In wrath he remembers mercy. 3. Those who are *preachers of righteousness* in an age of universal corruption and degeneracy, *holding forth the word of life* in an unblamable and exemplary conversation, shall be preserved in a time of general destruction. 4. God can make use of those creatures as the instruments of his vengeance in punishing sinners which he at first made and appointed for their service and benefit. He destroyed the whole world by water; but observe, 5. What was the procuring cause of this: *it was a world of ungodly men.* Ungodliness puts men out of the divine protection, and exposes them to utter destruction.

III. See how God dealt with Sodom and Gomorrah; though they were situated in a country like the garden of the Lord, yet, if in such a fruitful soil they abound in sin, God can soon turn a fruitful land into barrenness and a well-watered country into dust and ashes. Observe, 1. No political union or confederacy can keep off judgments from a sinful people. Sodom and the neighbouring cities were no more secured by their regular government than the angels by the dignity of their nature or the old world by their vast number. 2. God can make use of contrary creatures to punish incorrigible sinners. He destroys the *old world by water,* and Sodom by fire. He who keeps fire and water from hurting his people (Isa. xliii. 2) can make either to destroy his enemies; therefore they are never safe. 3. Most heinous sins bring most grievous judgments. Those who were abominable in their vices were remarkable for their plagues. Those who are sinners exceedingly before the Lord must expect the most dreadful vengeance. 4. The punishment of sinners in former ages is designed for the example of those who come after. "Follow them, not only in the time of living, but in their *course and way of living.*" Men who live ungodly must see what they are to expect if they go on still in a course of impiety. Let us take warning by all the instances of God's taking vengeance, which are recorded for our admonition, and to prevent our promising ourselves impunity, though we go on in a course of sin.

7 And delivered just Lot, vexed with the filthy conversation of the wicked: 8 (For that righteous man dwelling among them, in seeing and hearing, vexed *his* righteous soul from day to day with *their* unlawful deeds;) 9 The Lord knoweth how to deliver the godly out of temptations, and to reserve the unjust unto the day of judgment to be punished.

When God sends destruction on the ungodly, he commands deliverance for the righteous; and, if he rain fire and brimstone on the wicked, he will cover the head of the just, and they shall be hid in the day of his anger. This we have an instance of in his preserving Lot. Here observe, 1. The character given of Lot; he is called *a just man:* this he was as to the generally prevailing bent of his heart and through the main of his conversation. God does not account men just or unjust from one single act, but from their general course of life. And here is a just man in the midst of a most corrupt and profligate generation universally gone off from all good. He does not follow the multitude to do evil, but in a city of injustice he walks uprightly. 2. The impression the sins of others made upon this righteous man. Though the sinner takes pleasure in his wickedness, it is a grief and vexation to the soul of the righteous. In bad company we cannot escape either guilt or grief. Let the sins of others be a trouble to us, otherwise it will not be possible for us to keep ourselves pure. 3. Here is particular mention of the duration and continuance of this good man's grief and vexation: it was *from day to day.* Being accustomed to hear and see their wickedness did not reconcile him to it, nor abate of the horror that was occasioned by it. This is the righteous man whom God preserved from the desolating judgment that destroyed all round about him. From this instance we are taught to argue that God knows how to deliver his people and punish his enemies. It is here presupposed that the righteous must have their temptations and trials. The devil and his instruments will thrust sore at them, that they may fall; and, if we will get to heaven, it must be through many tribulations. It is therefore our duty to reckon upon and prepare for them. Observe here, (1.) *The Lord knows those that are his.* He has set apart him who is godly for himself; and, if there is but one in five cities, he knows him; and where there is a greater number he cannot be ignorant of nor overlook any one of them. (2.) The wisdom of God is never at a loss about ways and means to deliver his people. They are often utterly at a loss, and can see no way; he can discover a great many. (3.) The deliverance of the godly is the work of God, that which he concerns himself in, both his wisdom to contrive the way and his power to work out the deliverance *out of temptation,* to prevent their falling into sin and their being ruined by their troubles. And surely, if he can deliver out of temptation, he could keep from falling into it if he did not see such trials to be necessary. (4.) God makes a very great difference in his dealings with the godly and the wicked. When he saves his people from destruction, he delivers over his enemies to deserved ruin. The unjust has no share in the salvation God works out for the righteous. The wicked are *reserved to the day of judgment.* Here we see, [1.] There is a day of judgment. *God has appointed a day wherein he will judge the world.* [2.] The preservation of impenitent sinners is only a reserving of them to the day of the revelation of the righteous judgment of God.

10 But chiefly them that walk after
the flesh in the lust of uncleanness,
and despise government. Presumptuous *are they,* selfwilled, they are
not afraid to speak evil of dignities.
11 Whereas angels, which are greater
in power and might, bring not railing
accusation against them before the
Lord. 12 But these, as natural brute
beasts, made to be taken and destroyed, speak evil of the things that
they understand not; and shall utterly perish in their own corruption;
13 And shall receive the reward of
unrighteousness, *as* they that count
it pleasure to riot in the day time.
Spots *they are* and blemishes, sport-
ing themselves with their own de-
ceivings while they feast with you;
14 Having eyes full of adultery, and
that cannot cease from sin; beguiling
unstable souls: a heart they have
exercised with covetous practices;
cursed children: 15 Which have
forsaken the right way, and are gone
astray, following the way of Balaam
the son of Bosor, who loved the wages
of unrighteousness; 16 But was rebuked for his iniquity: the dumb ass
speaking with man's voice forbad the
madness of the prophet. 17 These
are wells without water, clouds that
are carried with a tempest; to whom
the mist of darkness is reserved for
ever. 18 For when they speak great
swelling *words* of vanity, they allure
through the lusts of the flesh, *through*
much wantonness, those that were
clean escaped from them who live in
error. 19 While they promise them
liberty, they themselves are the servants of corruption: for of whom a
man is overcome, of the same is he
brought in bondage. 20 For if after
they have escaped the pollutions of
the world through the knowledge of
the Lord and Saviour Jesus Christ,
they are again entangled therein, and
overcome, the latter end is worse
with them than the beginning. 21
For it had been better for them not
to have known the way of righteousness, than, after they have known *it,*
to turn from the holy commandment
delivered unto them. 22 But it is

happened unto them according to the true proverb, The dog *is* turned to his own vomit again; and the sow that was washed to her wallowing in the mire.

The apostle's design being to warn us of, and arm us against, seducers, he now returns to discourse more particularly of them, and give us an account of their character and conduct, which abundantly justifies the righteous Judge of the world in reserving them in an especial manner for the most severe and heavy doom, as Cain is taken under special protection that he might be kept for uncommon vengeance. But why will God thus deal with these false teachers? This he shows in what follows.

I. *These walk after the flesh;* they follow the devices and desires of their own hearts, they give up themselves to the conduct of their own fleshly mind, refusing to make their reason stoop to divine revelation, and to *bring every thought to the obedience of Christ;* they, in their lives, act directly contrary to God's righteous precepts, and comply with the demands of corrupt nature. Evil opinions are often accompanied with evil practices; and those who are for propagating error are for improving in wickedness. They will not sit down contented in the measure of iniquity to which they have attained, nor is it enough for them to stand up, and maintain, and defend, what wickedness they have already committed, but they *walk after the flesh,* they go on in their sinful course, and increase unto more ungodliness and greater degrees of impurity and uncleanness too; they also pour contempt on those whom God has set in authority over them and requires them to honour. These therefore despise *the ordinance of God,* and we need not wonder at it, for they are bold and daring, obstinate and refractory, and will not only cherish contempt in their hearts, but with their tongues will utter slanderous and reproachful words of those who are set over them.

II. This he aggravates, by setting forth the very different conduct of more excellent creatures, even the *angels,* of whom observe, 1. They *are greater in power and might,* and that even than those who are clothed with authority and power among the sons of men, and much more than those false teachers who are slanderous revilers of magistrates and governors; the good angels vastly exceed us in all natural and moral excellences, in strength, understanding, and holiness too. 2. Good angels are accusers of sinful creatures, either of their own kind, or ours, or both. Those who are allowed to behold the face of God, and stand before his throne, cannot but have a zeal for his honour, and accuse and blame those who dishonour him. 3. *Angels bring* their *accusations* of sinful creatures *before the Lord;* they do not publish their faults, and tell their crimes to their fellow-creatures, in a way of calumny and slander; but it is before the Lord, who is the Judge, and will be the avenger, of all impiety and injustice. 4. Good angels mingle no bitter revilings nor base reproaches with any of the accusations or charges they bring against the wickedest and worst of criminals. Let us, who pray that God's *will may be done on earth as it is in heaven,* imitate the angels in this particular; if we complain of wicked men, let it be to God, and that not with rage and reviling, but with compassion and composedness of mind, that may evidence that we belong to him who is meek and merciful.

III. The apostle, having shown (*v.* 11) how unlike seducing teachers are to the most excellent creatures, proceeds (*v.* 12) to show how like they are to the most inferior: they are *like the horse and mule, which have no understanding;* they are *as natural brute beasts, made to be taken and destroyed.* Men, under the power of sin, are so far from observing divine revelation that they do not exercise reason, nor act according to the direction thereof. They *walk by sight, and not by faith,* and judge of things according to their senses; as these represent things pleasant and agreeable, so they must be approved and esteemed. Brute-creatures follow the instinct of their sensitive appetite, and sinful man follows the inclination of his carnal mind; these refuse to employ the understanding and reason God has given them, and so are ignorant of what they might and ought to know; and therefore observe, 1. Ignorance is the cause of evil-speaking; and, 2. Destruction will be the effect of it. These persons shall be utterly destroyed in their own corruption. Their vices not only expose them to the wrath of God in another world, but often bring them to misery and ruin in this life; and surely such impudent offenders, who *glory in their shame,* and to whom openness in sin is an improvement of the pleasure of sinning, most justly deserve all the plagues of this life and the pains of the next in the greatest extremity. Therefore whatever they meet with is the just *reward of their unrighteousness.* Such sinners as sport themselves in mischief deceive themselves and disgrace all they belong to, for by one sort of sins they prepare themselves for another; their extravagant feastings, their intemperance in eating and drinking, bring them to commit all manner of lewdness, so that their *eyes are full of adultery,* their wanton looks show their own impure lusts and are designed and directed to kindle the like in others; and this is what they *cannot cease* from—the heart is insatiate in lusting and the eye incessant in looking after what may gratify their unclean desires, and those who are themselves impudent and incessant in sin are very diligent and often successful in deceiving others and drawing others into the same excess of riot. But here observe who those are who are in the greatest danger of being led away into error and impiety, even the *unstable*. Those whose hearts are not established with grace are easily turned into the way of sin, or else such sensual wretches would not be able to prevail upon them, for these are not only riotous and lascivious, but *covetous* also, and these practices their hearts are exercised with; they pant after riches, and the desire of their souls is to the wealth of this world: it is a considerable part of their work to contrive to get wealth; in this their hearts are exercised, and then they execute their projects; and, if men abandon themselves to all sorts of lusts, we cannot wonder that the apostle should call them *cursed children*, for they are liable to the curse of God denounced against such *ungodly and unrighteous men*, and they bring a curse upon all who hearken and adhere to them.

IV. The apostle (*v.* 15, 16) proves that they are *cursed children*, even such covetous persons as *the Lord abhors*, by showing, 1. They *have forsaken the right way;* and it cannot be but such self-seekers must be out of the right way, which is a self-denying way. 2. They have gone into a wrong way: they have erred and strayed from the way of life, and gone over into the path which leads to death, and takes hold of hell; and this he makes out by showing it to be *the way of Balaam, the son of Bosor*. (1.) That is a way of unrighteousness into which men are led by the wages of unrighteousness. (2.) Outward temporal good things are the wages sinners expect and promise themselves, though they are often disappointed. (3.) The inordinate love of the good things of this world turns men out of the way which leads to the unspeakably better things of another life; the love of riches and honour turned Balaam out of the way of his duty, although he knew that the way he took displeased the Lord. (4.) Those who from the same principle are guilty of the same practices with notorious sinners are, in the judgment of God, the followers of such vile offenders, and therefore must reckon upon being at last where they are: *they shall have their portion* with those in another world whom they imitated in this. (5.) Heinous and hardened sinners sometimes meet with rebukes for their iniquity. God stops them in their way, and opens the mouth of conscience, or by some startling providence startles and affrights them. (6.) Though some more uncommon and extraordinary rebuke may for a little while cool men's courage, and hinder their violent progress in the way of sin, it will not make them forsake the way of iniquity and go over into the way of holiness. If rebuking a sinner for his iniquity would have made a man return to his duty, surely the rebuke of Balaam must have produced this effect; for here is a surprising miracle wrought: *the dumb ass*, in whose mouth no man can expect to meet with reproof, is enabled to speak, and that with a human voice, and to her owner and master (who is here called a *prophet*, for the Lord appeared and spoke sometimes to him (Num. xxii. 23, 24), but indeed he was among the prophets of the Lord as Judas among the apostles of Jesus Christ), and she exposes *the madness* of his conduct and opposes his going on in this evil way, and yet all in vain. Those who will not yield to usual methods of reproof will be but little influenced by miraculous appearances to turn them from their sinful courses. Balaam was indeed restrained from actually *cursing the people*, but he had so strong a desire after the honours and riches that were promised him that he went as far as he could, and did his utmost to get from under the restraint that was upon him.

V. The apostle proceeds (*v.* 17) to a further description of seducing teachers, whom he sets forth,

1. As *wells*, or fountains, *without water*. Observe, (1.) Ministers should be as wells or fountains, where the people may find instruction, direction, and comfort; but (2.) False teachers have nothing of this to impart to those who consult them: the word of truth is the water of life, which refreshes the souls that receive it; but these deceivers are set upon spreading and promoting error, and therefore are set forth as empty, because there is no truth in them. In vain then are all our expectations of being fed and filled with knowledge and understanding by those who are themselves ignorant and empty.

2. As *clouds carried with a tempest*. When we see a cloud we expect a refreshing shower from it; but these are clouds which yield no rain, for they are driven with the wind, but not of the Spirit, but the stormy wind or tempest of their own ambition and covetousness. They espouse and spread those opinions that will procure most applause and advantage to themselves; and as clouds obstruct the light of the sun, and darken the air, so do these *darken counsel by words without knowledge* and wherein there is no truth; and, seeing these men are for promoting darkness in this world, it is very just that the mist of darkness should be their portion in the next. Utter darkness was prepared for the devil, the great deceiver, and his angels, those instruments that he uses to turn men from the truth, and therefore for them it is reserved, and that for ever; the fire of hell is everlasting, and the smoke of the bottomless pit rises up for ever and ever. And it is just with God to deal thus with them, because (1.) They allure those they deal with, and draw them into a net, or catch them as men do fish; and, (2.) It is *with great swelling words of vanity*, lofty expressions, which have a great sound, but little sense. (3.) They work upon *the corrupt affections* and *carnal fleshly lusts of men*, proposing what is grateful to them. And, (4.) They seduce persons who

in reality avoided and kept at a distance from those who spread and those who embraced hurtful and destructive errors. Observe, [1.] By application and industry men attain a skilfulness and dexterity in promoting error. They are as artful and as successful as the fisher, who makes angling his daily employment. The business of these men is to draw disciples after them, and in their methods and management there are some things worth observing, how they suit their bait to those they desire to catch. [2.] Erroneous teachers have a peculiar advantage to win men over to them, because they have sensual pleasure to take them with; whereas the ministers of Christ put men upon self-denial, and the mortifying of those lusts that others gratify and please: wonder not therefore that truth prevails no more, or that errors spread so much. [3.] Persons who have for a while adhered to the truth, and kept clear of errors, may by the subtlety and industry of seducers be so far deceived as to fall into those errors they had for a while *clean escaped.* "Be therefore always upon your guard, maintain a godly jealousy of yourselves, search the scriptures, pray for the Spirit to instruct and establish you in the truth, walk humbly with God, and watch against every thing that may provoke him to give you up to a reprobate mind, that you may not be taken with the fair and specious pretences of these false teachers, who promise liberty to all who will hearken to them, not true Christian liberty for the service of God, but a licentiousness in sin, to follow the devices and desires of their own hearts." To prevent these men's gaining proselytes, he tells us that, in the midst of all their talk of liberty, they themselves are the vilest slaves, for they are the servants of corruption; their own lusts have gotten a complete victory over them, and they are actually in bondage to them, making *provision for the flesh,* to satisfy its cravings, comply with its directions, and obey its commands. Their minds and hearts are so far corrupted and depraved that they have neither power nor will to refuse the task that is imposed on them. They are conquered and captivated by their spiritual enemies, and yield their members servants of unrighteousness: and what a shame it is to be overcome and commanded by those who are themselves *the servants of corruption, and slaves to their own lusts!* This consideration should prevent our being led away by these seducers; and to this he adds another (*v.* 20): it is not only a shame and disgrace to be seduced by those who are themselves the slaves of sin, and led captive by the devil at his pleasure, but it is a real detriment to those who have clean escaped from those who live in error, for hereby their latter end is made worse than their beginning. Here we see, *First,* It is an advantage to escape the pollutions of the world, to be kept from gross and scandalous sins, though men are not thoroughly converted and savingly changed; for hereby we are kept from grieving those who are truly serious and emboldening those who are openly profane; whereas, if we run with others to the same excess of riot and abandon ourselves to the sins of the age, we afflict and dishearten those who endeavour to walk as becomes the gospel, and strengthen the hands of those who are already engaged in open rebellion against the Most High, as well as alienate ourselves more from God, and harden our hearts against him. *Secondly,* Some men are, for a time, *kept from the pollutions of the world, by the knowledge of Christ,* who are not savingly renewed in the spirit of their mind. A religious education has restrained many whom the grace of God has not renewed: if we receive the light of the truth, and have a notional knowledge of Christ in our heads, it may be of some present service to us; but we must receive the love of the truth, and hide God's word in our heart, or it will not sanctify and save us. *Thirdly,* Those who have, for a time, escaped the pollutions of the world, are at first ensnared and entangled by false teachers, who first perplex men with some plausible and specious objections against the truths of the gospel; and the more ignorant and unstable are hereby made to stagger, and brought to question the truth of doctrines they have received, because they cannot solve all the difficulties, nor answer all the objections, that are urged by these seducers. *Fourthly,* When men are once entangled, they are easily overcome; therefore should Christians keep close to the word of God, and watch against those who seek to perplex and bewilder them, and that because, if men who have once *escaped are again entangled, the latter end is worse with them than the beginning.*

VI. The apostle, in the last two verses of the chapter, sets himself to prove that a state of apostasy is worse than a state of ignorance; for it is a *condemning of the way of righteousness,* after they have had some knowledge of it, and expressed some liking to it; it carries in it a declaring that they have found some iniquity in the way of righteousness and some falsehood in the word of truth. Now to bring up such an evil report upon the good way of God, and such a false charge against the way of truth, must necessarily expose to the heaviest condemnation; the misery of such deserters of Christ and his gospel is more unavoidable and more intolerable than that of other offenders; for, 1. God is more highly provoked by those who by their conduct despise the gospel, as well as disobey the law, and who reproach and pour contempt upon God and his grace. 2. The devil more narrowly watches and more closely confines those whom he has recovered, after they had once gone off from him and professed to be the followers of the Lord Jesus Christ (Matt. xii. 45); they are kept under a stronger guard, and no wonder it should be so when they have licked up their own vomit again, returning to the same errors and impieties that they had once cast off and seemed to detest and loathe, and wallowing in that filthiness from which they appeared once to be really cleansed. Well, if the scripture gives such an account of Christianity on the one hand, and of sin on the other, as we have here in these two verses, we certainly ought highly to approve of the former and persevere therein, because it is a way of righteousness, and a holy commandment, and to loathe and keep at the greatest distance from the latter because it is set forth as most offensive and abominable.

CHAP. III.

The apostle, drawing towards the conclusion of his second epistle, begins this last chapter with repeating the account of his design and scope in writing a second time to them, ver. 1—2. II. He proceeds to mention one thing that induced him to write this second epistle, namely, the coming of scoffers, whom he describes, ver. 3—7. III. He instructs and establishes them in the coming of our Lord Jesus Christ to judgment, ver. 8—10. IV. He sets forth the use and improvement which Christians ought to make of Christ's second coming, and that dissolution and renovation of things which will accompany that solemn coming of our Lord, ver. 11—18.

THIS second epistle, beloved, I
now write unto you; in *both*
which I stir up your pure minds by
way of remembrance: 2 That ye
may be mindful of the words which
were spoken before by the holy prophets, and of the commandment of us the apostles of the Lord and Saviour.

That the apostle might the better reach his end in writing this epistle, which is to make them steady and constant in a fiducial and practical remembrance of the doctrine of the gospel, he, 1. Expresses his special affection and tenderness for them, by calling them *beloved,* hereby evidencing that he *added to godliness brotherly-kindness,* as he had (*ch.* i. 7) exhorted them to do. Ministers must be examples of love and affection, as well as life and conversation. 2. He evinces a sincere love to them, and hearty concern for them, by writing the same thing to them, though in other words. It being safe for them, it shall not be grievous to him to write upon the same subject, and pursue the same design, by those methods which are most likely to succeed. 3. The better to recommend the matter, he tells them that what he would have them to remember are, (1.) *The words spoken by the holy prophets,* who were divinely inspired, both enlightened and sanctified by the Holy Ghost; and, seeing these persons' minds were purified by the sanctifying operation of the same Spirit, they were the better disposed to receive and retain what came from God by the holy prophets. (2.) *The commandments of the apostles of the Lord and Saviour;* and therefore the disciples and servants of Christ ought to regard what those who are sent by him have declared unto them to be the will of their Lord. What God has spoken by the prophets of the Old Testament, and Christ has commanded by the apostles of the New, cannot but demand and deserve to be frequently remembered; and those who meditate on these things will feel the quickening virtues thereof. It is by these things the pure minds of Christians are to be stirred up, that they may be active and lively in the work of holiness, and zealous and unwearied in the way to heaven.

3 Knowing this first, that there shall
come in the last days scoffers, walking
after their own lusts, 4 And saying,
Where is the promise of his coming?
for since the fathers fell asleep all
things continue as *they were* from the
beginning of the creation. 5 For this
they willingly are ignorant of, that by
the word of God the heavens were of
old, and the earth standing out of the
water and in the water: 6 Whereby
the world that then was, being overflowed with water, perished: 7 But
the heavens and the earth, which are
now, by the same word are kept in
store, reserved unto fire against the
day of judgment and perdition of
ungodly men.

To quicken and excite us to a serious minding and firm adhering to what God has revealed to us by the prophets and apostles, we are told that there will be *scoffers,* men who will *make a mock of sin,* and of salvation from it. God's way of saving sinners by Jesus Christ is what men will scoff at, and that *in the last days,* under the gospel. This indeed may seem very strange, that the New-Testament dispensation of the covenant of grace, which is spiritual and therefore more agreeable to the nature of God than the Old, should be ridiculed and reproached; but the spirituality and simplicity of New-Testament worship are directly contrary to the carnal mind of man, and this accounts for what the apostle seems here to hint at, namely, that scoffers shall be more numerous and more bold in the last days than ever before. Though in all ages those who were born and walked after the flesh persecuted, reviled, and reproached those who were born and did walk after the Spirit, yet in the last days there will be a great improvement in the art and impudence of bantering serious godliness, and those who firmly adhere to the circumspection and self-denial which the gospel prescribes. This is what is mentioned as a thing well known to all Christians, and therefore they ought to reckon upon it, that they may not be surprised and shaken, as if some strange thing happened unto them. Now to prevent the true Christian's being overcome, when attacked by these scoffers, we are told,

I. What sort of persons they are: they *walk after their own lusts,* they follow the devices and desires of their own hearts, and carnal corrupt affections, not the dictates and directions of right reason and an enlightened well-informed judgment. This they do in the course of their conversation, they live as they list, and they speak as they list; it is not only their inward minds that are evil and opposite to God, as the mind of every unrenewed sinner is (Rom. viii. 7), alienated from God, ignorant of him, and averse to him; but they have grown to such a height of wickedness that they proclaim openly what is in the hearts of others who are yet carnal; they say, "Our tongues are our own, and our strength, and time, and *who is lord over us?* Who shall contradict or control us, or ever call us to an account for what we say or do?" And, as they scorn to be confined by any laws of God in their conversation, so neither will they bear that the revelation of God should dictate and prescribe to them what they are to believe; as they will walk in their own way, and talk their own language, so will they also think their own thoughts, and form principles which are altogether their own: here also *their own lusts* alone shall be consulted by them. None but such accomplished libertines as are here described can take a seat, at least they cannot sit in the seat of the scornful. "By this you shall know them, that you may the better be upon your guard against them."

II. We also are forewarned how far they will proceed: they will attempt to shake and unsettle us, even as to our belief of Christ's second coming; they will scoffingly say, *Where is the promise of his coming? v.* 4. Without this, all the other articles of the Christian faith will signify very little; this is that which fills up and gives the finishing stroke to all the rest. The promised Messiah has come, he *was made flesh, and dwelt among us;* he is altogether such a one as is stated before, and has done all that for us which has been before taken notice of. These principles the enemies of Christianity have all along endeavoured to overturn; but as these all rest upon facts which are already past, and of which this and the other apostles have given us the most sure and satisfying evidence, it is probable that they will at last grow weary of their opposition to them; and yet, while one very principal article of our faith refers to what is still behind, and only has a promise to rest upon, here they will still attack us, even to the end of time. Till our Lord shall have come, they will not themselves believe that he will come; nay, they will laugh at the very mention of his second coming, and do what in them lies to put all out of countenance who seriously believe and wait for it. Now therefore let us see how this point stands, both on the believer's part and on the part of these seducers: the believer not only desires that he may come, but, having a promise that he will come, a promise that he himself has made and often repeated, a promise received and reported by faithful witnesses, and left upon sure record, he is also firmly and fully persuaded that he will come: on the other hand, these seducers, because they wish he never may, therefore do all that in them lies to cheat themselves and others into a persuasion that he never will come. If they cannot deny that there is a promise, yet they will laugh at that very promise, which argues much higher degrees of infidelity and contempt: *Where is the promise,* say they, *of his coming?*

III. We are also forewarned of the method of their reasoning, for while they laugh they will pretend to argue too. To this purpose they add that *since the fathers fell asleep all things continue as they were from the beginning of the creation, v.* 4. This is a subtle, though not a solid way of reasoning; it is apt to make impressions upon weak minds, and especially upon wicked hearts. *Because sentence against them is not speedily executed,* therefore they flatter themselves that it never will, whereupon *their hearts are fully set in them to do evil* (Eccl. viii. 11); thus they act themselves, and thus they would persuade others to act; so here, say they, "*The fathers have fallen asleep,* those are all dead to whom *the promise was made,* and it was never made good in their time, and there is no likelihood that it ever will be in any time; why should we trouble ourselves about it? If there had been any truth or certainty in the promise you speak of, we should surely have seen somewhat of it before this time, some signs of his coming, some preparatory steps in order to it; whereas we find to this very day *all things continue as they were,* without any change, even *from the beginning of the creation.* Since the world has undergone no changes in the course of so many thousand years, why should we affright ourselves as if it were to have an end?" Thus do these scoffers argue. *Because they see no changes, therefore they fear not God,* Ps. lv. 19. They neither fear him nor his judgments; what he never has done they would conclude he never can do or never will.

IV. Here is the falsehood of their argument detected. Whereas they confidently had said there had not been any change *from the beginning of the creation,* the apostle puts us in remembrance of a change already past, which, in a manner, equals that which we are called to expect and look for, which was the drowning of the world in the days of Noah. This these scoffers had overlooked; they took no notice of it. Though they might have known it, and ought to have known it, yet *this they willingly are ignorant of* (*v.* 5), they choose to pass it over in silence, as if they had never heard or known any thing of it; if they knew it, they did not like to retain it in their knowledge; they did not receive this truth in the love of it, neither did they care to own it. Note, It is hard to persuade men to believe what they are not willing to find true; they are ignorant, in many cases, because they are willing to be ignorant, and they do not know because they do not care to know. But let not sinners think that such ignorance as this will be admitted as an excuse for whatever sin it may betray them into. Those who crucified Christ did not know who he was; for *had they known they would not have crucified the Lord of glory* (1 Cor. ii. 8); but, though ignorant, they were not therefore innocent; their ignorance itself was a sin, willing and wilful ignorance, and one sin can be no excuse for another. So it is here; had these known of the dreadful vengeance with which God swept away a whole world of ungodly wretches at once, they would not surely have scoffed at his threatenings of any after equally terrible judgment; but here *they were willingly ignorant,* they did not know what God had done because they had no mind to know it. Now therefore we shall proceed to consider the representation which the apostle here lays down both of the destruction of the old world by water and that which awaits this present world at the final conflagration. He mentions the one as what God has done, to convince and persuade us the rather to believe that the other both may be and will be.

1. We begin with the apostle's account of the destruction which has once already come upon the world (*v.* 5, 6): *By the word of God the heavens were of old, and the earth standing out of the water and in the water, whereby the world that then was, being overflowed with water, perished.* Originally the world was otherwise situated, the waters were most wisely divided at the creation and most beneficially for us; some of the waters had proper repositories above the firmament, here called the heavens (as it is also Gen. i. 8), and others under the firmament, gathered together unto one place; there were then both sea and dry land, commodious habitation for the children of men. But now, at the time of the universal deluge, the case is strangely altered; the waters which God had divided before, assigning to each part its convenient receptacle, now does he, in anger, throw together again in a heap. *He breaks up the fountain of the great deep, and throws open the windows (that is, the clouds) of heaven* (Gen. vii. 11), till the whole earth is overflowed with water, and not a spot can be found upon the highest mountains but what is *fifteen cubits under water,* Gen. vii. 20. Thus he made known at once his terrible power and his fierce anger, and made an end of a whole world at once: *The world that then was, being overflowed with water, perished, v.* 6. Is not here a change and a most awful change! And then it is to be observed that all this was done by the word of God; it was by his powerful word that the world was made at first, and made in so commodious and beautiful a frame and order, Heb. xi. 3, Κατηρτίσθαι. *He said, Let there be a firmament,* &c., Gen. i. 6, 7. *And let the waters under the heaven be gathered together unto one place,* &c., *v.* 9, 10. Thus he spoke, and it was done, Ps. xxxiii. 9. Thus, says our apostle, *by the word of the Lord the heavens were,* as they were *of old* (that is, at the first creation) *and the earth* (as it was at first a terraqueous globe) *standing out of the water and in the water.* Nor is it only the first frame and order of the world that is here said to be *by the word of God,* but the after-confusion and ruin of the world, as well as the utter destruction of its inhabitants, were also by the same word; none but that God who *stretched out the heavens and laid the foundation of the earth* could destroy and overthrow such a vast fabric at once. This was done by the word of his power, and it was also done according to the word of his promise; God had said that he would destroy man, even all flesh, and that he would do it by bringing a flood of waters upon the earth, Gen. vi. 7, 13, 17. This was the change which God had before brought upon the world, and which these scoffers had overlooked; and now we are to consider,

2. What the apostle says of the destructive change which is yet to come upon it: *The heavens and the earth, which now are, by the same word are kept in store, reserved unto fire against the day of judgment and perdition of ungodly men, v.* 7. Here we have an awful account of the final dissolution of the world, and which we are yet more nearly concerned in. The ruin that came upon the world and its inhabitants by the flood, we read, and hear, and think of, with concern, though those who were swept away by it were such as we never knew; but the judgment here spoken of is yet to come, and will surely come, though we know not when, nor upon what particular age or generation of men; and therefore we are not, we cannot be, sure that it may not happen in our own times: and this makes a very great difference, though it should be admitted that they were equal in every other respect, which yet must not be allowed, for there were some, though very few, who escaped that deluge, but not one can escape in this conflagration. Besides, we were not in reach of the one, but are not sure that we shall not be included in the other calamity. Now therefore to see the world to which we belong destroyed at once—not a single person only, not a particular family only, nor yet a nation (even that which we are most nearly interested in and concerned for), but the whole world, I say, sinking at once, and no ark provided, no possible way left of escaping for any one from the common ruin, this makes a difference between the desolation that has been and what we yet are to expect. The one is already past, and never to return upon us any more (for God has said expressly *that there shall never any more be a flood to destroy the earth,* Gen. ix. 11—17); the other is still behind, and is as certain to come as the truth and the power of God can make it: the one came gradually

upon the world, and was growing upon its inhabitants forty days, before it made an utter end of them (Gen. vii. 12, 17); this other will come upon them swiftly and all at once (2 Pet. ii. 1): besides, there were in that overthrow (as we have said) a few who escaped, but the ruin which yet awaits this world, whenever it comes, will be absolutely a universal one; there will not be any part but what the devouring flames will seize upon, not a sanctuary left any where for the inhabitants to flee to, not a single spot in all this world where any one of them can be safe. Thus, whatever differences may be assigned between that destruction of the world and this here spoken of, they do indeed represent the approaching as the most terrible judgment; yet that the world has once been destroyed by a universal deluge renders it the more credible that it may be again ruined by a universal conflagration. Let therefore the scoffers, who laugh at the coming of our Lord to judgment, at least consider that it *may be.* There is nothing said of it in the word of God but what is within reach of the power of God, and, though they still should laugh, they shall not put us out of countenance; we are well assured that it will be, because he has said it, and we can depend upon his *promise.* They *err, not knowing* (at least not believing) *the scriptures, nor the power of God;* but we know, and we do or ought to depend upon, both. Now that which he has said, and which he will certainly make good, is that *the heavens and the earth which now are* (which we are now related to, which still subsist in all the beauty and order in which we see them, and which are so agreeable and useful to us, as we find they are) *are kept in store,* not to be, what earthly minds would wish to have them, treasures for us, but to be what God will have them, in his treasury, securely lodged and kept safely for his purposes. It follows, they are *reserved unto fire.* Observe, God's following judgments are more terrible than those which went before; the old world was destroyed by water, but this is reserved unto fire, which shall burn up the wicked at the last day; and, though this seems to be delayed, yet, as this wicked world is upheld by the word of God, so it is only reserved for the vengeance of him to whom vengeance belongs, who will at the day of judgment deal with an ungodly world according to their deserts, for the day of judgment is the day of *the perdition of ungodly men.* Those who now scoff at a future judgment shall find it a day of vengeance and utter destruction. "Beware therefore of being among these scoffers; never question but the day of the Lord will come; give diligence therefore to be found in Christ, that that may be a time of refreshment and day of redemption to you which will be a day of indignation and wrath to the ungodly world."

8 But, beloved, be not ignorant of this one thing, that one day *is* with the Lord as a thousand years, and a thousand years as one day.

The apostle comes in these words to instruct and establish Christians in the truth of the coming of the Lord, where we may clearly discern the tenderness and affection wherewith he speaks to them, calling them *beloved;* he had a compassionate concern and a love of good-will for the ungodly wretches who refused to believe divine revelation, but he has a peculiar respect for the true believers, and the remaining ignorance and weakness that he apprehends to be in them make him jealous, and put him on giving them a caution. Here we may observe,

I. The truth which the apostle asserts—*that with the Lord one day is as a thousand years, and a thousand years are as one day.* Though, in the account of men, there is a great deal of difference between a day and a year, and a vast deal more between one day and a thousand years, yet in the account of God, who inhabits eternity, in which there is no succession, there is no difference; for all things past, present, and future, are ever before him, and the delay of a thousand years cannot be so much to him as the deferring of any thing for a day or an hour is to us.

II. The importance of this truth: This is the *one thing* the apostle would not have us ignorant of; a holy awe and reverential fear of God are necessary in order to our worshipping and glorifying him, and a belief of the inconceivable distance between him and us is very proper to beget and maintain that religious fear of the Lord which is the beginning of wisdom. This is a truth that belongs to our peace, and therefore he endeavours that it may not be hidden from our eyes; as it is in the original, *Let not this one thing be hidden from you.* If men have no knowledge or belief of the eternal God, they will be very apt to think him such a one as themselves. Yet how hard is it to conceive of eternity! It is therefore not very easy to attain such a knowledge of God as is absolutely necessary.

9 The Lord is not slack concerning his promise, as some men count slackness; but is longsuffering to us-ward, not willing that any should perish, but that all should come to
repentance. 10 But the day of the
Lord will come as a thief in the night; in the which the heavens shall pass away with a great noise, and the elements shall melt with fervent heat, the earth also and the works that are therein shall be burned up.

We are here told that *the Lord is not slack*—he does not delay beyond the appointed time; as God kept the time that he had appointed for the delivering of Israel out of Egypt, to a day (Exod. xii. 41), so he will keep to the time appointed in coming to judge the world. What a difference is there between the account which God makes and that which men make! Good men are apt to think God stays beyond the appointed time, that is, the time which they have set for their own and the church's deliverance; but they set one time and God sets another, and he will not fail to keep the day which he has appointed. Ungodly men dare charge a culpable slackness upon God, as if he had slipped the time, and laid aside the thoughts of coming. But the apostle assures us,

I. That what men count slackness is truly *long-suffering*, and that *to us-ward;* it is giving more time to his own people, *whom he has chosen before the foundation of the world*, many of whom are not as yet converted; and those who are in a state of grace and favour with God are to advance in knowledge and holiness, and in the exercise of faith and patience, to abound in good works, doing and suffering what they are called to, that they may bring glory to God, and improve in a meetness for heaven; for God is not willing that any of these should perish, but that all of them should come to repentance. Here observe, 1. Repentance is absolutely necessary in order to salvation. *Except we repent, we shall perish*, Luke xiii. 3, 5. 2. God has no delight in the death of sinners: as the punishment of sinners is a torment to his creatures, a merciful God does not take pleasure in it; and though the principal design of God in his long-suffering is the blessedness of those *whom he has chosen to salvation, through sanctification of the spirit, and belief of the truth*, yet his goodness and forbearance do in their own nature invite and call to repentance all those to whom they are exercised; and, if men continue impenitent when God gives them space to repent, he will deal more severely with them, though the great reason why he did not hasten his coming was because he had not accomplished *the number of his elect*. "Abuse not therefore the patience and long-suffering of God, by abandoning yourselves to a course of ungodliness; presume not to go on boldly in the way of sinners, nor to sit down securely in an unconverted impenitent state, as he who said (Matt. xxiv. 48), *My Lord delayeth his coming*, lest he come and surprise you; for,

II. *The day of the Lord will come as a thief in the night, v.* 10. Here we may observe, 1. The certainty of the day of the Lord: though it is now above sixteen hundred years since this epistle was written, and the day has not yet come, it assuredly will come. God has *appointed a day wherein he will judge the world in righteousness*, and he will keep his appointment. *It is appointed to men once to die, and after this the judgment*, Heb. ix. 27. "Settle it therefore in your hearts that the day of the Lord will certainly come, and you shall certainly be called to give an account of all things done in the body, whether good or evil; and let your exact walking before God, and your frequent judging yourselves, evidence your firm belief of a future judgment, when many live as if they were never to give any account at all." 2. The suddenness of this day: It *will come as a thief in the night*, at a time when men are sleeping and secure, and have no manner of apprehension or expectation of the day of the Lord, any more than men have of a thief when they are in a deep sleep, in the dark and silent night. *At midnight there was a cry, Behold, the bridegroom comes* (Matt. xxv. 6), and at that time not only the foolish, but also the wise virgins slumbered and slept. *The Lord will come in a day when we look not for him, and an hour when men are not aware.* The time which men think to be the most improper and unlikely, and when therefore they are most secure, will be the time of the Lord's coming. Let us then beware how we in our thoughts and imaginations put that day far away from us; but rather suppose it to be so much nearer in reality, by how much further off it is in the opinion of the ungodly world. 3. The solemnity of this coming. (1.) *The heavens shall pass away with a great noise.* The visible heavens, as unable to abide when the Lord shall come in his glory, shall pass away; they shall undergo a mighty alteration, and this shall be very sudden, and with such a noise as the breaking and tumbling down of so great a fabric must necessarily occasion. (2.) *The elements shall melt with fervent heat.* At this coming of the Lord it shall not only be very *tempestuous round about him*, so that the very heavens shall pass away as in a mighty violent storm, but *a fire shall go before him, that shall melt the elements* of which the creatures are composed. (3.) *The earth also, and all the works that are therein, shall be burnt up.* The earth, and its inhabitants, and all the works, whether of nature or art, shall be destroyed. The stately palaces and gardens, and all the desirable things wherein worldly-minded men seek and place their happiness, all of them shall be burnt up; all sorts of creatures which God has made, and all the works of men, must submit, all must pass through the fire, which shall be a consuming fire to all that sin has brought into the world, though it may be but a refining fire to the works of God's hand, that the glass of the creation being made much brighter the saints may much better discern the glory of the Lord therein.

And now who can but observe what a difference there will be between the first coming of Christ and the second! Yet that is called *the great and dreadful day of the Lord*, Mal. iv. 5. How much more dreadful must this coming to judgment be! May we be so wise as to prepare for it, that it may not be a day of vengeance and destruction unto us. O! what will become of us, if we set our affections on this earth, and make it our portion, seeing all these things shall be burnt up? Look out therefore, and make sure of a happiness beyond this visible world, which must all be melted down.

11 *Seeing* then *that* all these things
shall be dissolved, what manner *of*
persons ought ye to be in *all* holy
conversation and godliness, 12 Looking for and hasting unto the coming
of the day of God, wherein the heavens being on fire shall be dissolved,
and the elements shall melt with fervent heat? 13 Nevertheless we, according to his promise, look for new
heavens and a new earth, wherein
dwelleth righteousness. 14 Wherefore, beloved, seeing that ye look for
such things, be diligent that ye may
be found of him in peace, without
spot, and blameless. 15 And account *that* the long-suffering of our
Lord *is* salvation; even as our beloved brother Paul also according to
the wisdom given unto him hath
written unto you; 16 As also in all
his epistles, speaking in them of these
things; in which are some things
hard to be understood, which they
that are unlearned and unstable wrest,
as *they do* also the other scriptures,
unto their own destruction. 17 Ye
therefore, beloved, seeing ye know
these things before, beware lest ye
also, being led away with the error of
the wicked, fall from your own stedfastness. 18 But grow in grace, and
in the knowledge of our Lord and
Saviour Jesus Christ. To him *be*
glory both now and for ever. Amen.

The apostle, having instructed them in the doctrine of Christ's second coming,

I. Takes occasion thence to exhort them to purity and godliness in their whole conversation: all the truths which are revealed in scripture should be improved for our advancement in practical godliness: this is the effect that knowledge must produce, or we are never the better for it. *If you know these things, happy are you if you do them.* *Seeing all these things must be dissolved, how holy should we be,* that are assured of it, departing from and dying to sin, that has so corrupted and defiled all the visible creation that there is an absolute need of its dissolution! All that was made for man's use is subject to vanity by man's sin; and if the sin of man has brought the visible heavens, and the elements and earth, under a curse, from which they cannot be freed without being dissolved, what an abominable evil is sin, and how much to be hated by us! And, inasmuch as this dissolution is in order to their being restored to their primitive beauty and excellency, how pure and holy should we be, in order to our being fit for the *new heaven and new earth, wherein dwelleth righteousness!* It is a very exact and universal holiness that he exhorts to, not resting in any lower measure or degree, but labouring to be eminent beyond what is commonly attained—holy in God's house and in our own, holy in our worshipping of God and in our conversing with men. All our conversation, whether with high or low, rich or poor, good or bad, friends or enemies, must be holy. We must *keep ourselves unspotted from the world* in all our converses with it. We must be *perfecting holiness in the fear of God,* and in the love of God too. We must *exercise ourselves unto godliness* of all sorts, in all its parts, trusting in God and delighting in God only, who continues the same when the whole visible creation shall be dissolved, devoting ourselves to the service of God, and designing the glorifying and enjoyment of God, who endures for ever; whereas what worldly men delight in and follow after must all be dissolved. Those things which we now see must in a little while pass away, and be no more as they now are: let us look therefore at what shall abide and continue, which, though it be not present, is certain and not far off. This *looking for the day of God* is one of the directions the apostle gives us, in order to our being eminently *holy and godly in all manner of conversation.* "Look for the day of God as what you firmly believe shall come, and what you earnestly long for." *The coming of the day of God* is what every Christian must hope for and earnestly expect; for it is a day when Christ shall *appear in the glory of the Father,* and evidence his divinity and Godhead even to those who counted him a mere man. The first coming of our Lord Jesus Christ, when he *appeared in the form of a servant,* was what the people of God earnestly waited and looked for: that coming was for *the consolation of Israel,* Luke ii. 25. How much more should they wait with expectation and earnestness for his second coming, which will be the day of their complete redemption, and of his most glorious manifestation! Then he shall *come to be admired in his saints, and glorified in all those that believe.* For though it cannot but terrify and affright the ungodly to see the visible heavens all in a flame, and the elements melting, yet the believer, whose *faith is the evidence of things not seen,* can rejoice in hope of more glorious heavens after these have been melted and refined by that dreadful fire which shall burn up all the dross of this visible creation. Here we must take notice, 1. What true Christians look for: *new heavens and a new earth,* in which a great deal more of the wisdom, power and goodness of our great God and Saviour Jesus Christ will be clearly discerned than we are able to discover in what we now see; for in these new heavens and earth, freed from the vanity the former were subject to, and the sin they were polluted with, only righteousness shall dwell; this is to be the habitation of such righteous persons as do righteousness, and are free from the power and pollution of sin; *all the wicked shall be turned into hell;* those only who are clothed with the righteousness of Christ, and sanctified by the Holy Ghost, shall be admitted to dwell in this holy place. 2. What is the ground and foundation of this expectation and hope—*the promise of God.* To look for any thing which God has not promised is presumption; but if our expectations are according to the promise, both as to the things we look for and the time and way of their being brought about, we cannot meet with a disappointment; *for he is faithful who has promised.* "See therefore that you raise and regulate your expectations of all the great things that are to come according to the word of God; and, as to *the new heaven and new earth,* look for them as God has allowed and directed by the passages we have in this portion of scripture now before you, and in Isa. lxv. 17; lxvi. 22, to which the apostle may be thought to allude."

II. As in *v.* 11 he exhorts to holiness from the consideration that *the heavens and the earth shall be dissolved,* so in *v.* 14 he resumes his exhortation from the consideration that they shall be again renewed. "Seeing you expect the day of God, when our Lord Jesus Christ will appear in his glorious majesty, and these heavens and earth shall be dissolved and melted down, and, being purified and refined, shall be erected and rebuilt, prepare to meet him. It nearly concerns you to see in what state you will be when the Judge of all the world shall come to pass sentence upon men, and to determine how it shall be with them to all eternity. This is the court of judicature whence there lies no appeal; whatever sentence is here passed by this great Judge is irreversible; therefore get ready to *appear before the judgment-seat of Christ:* and see to it,"

1. "That you be *found of him in peace,* in a state of peace and reconciliation with God through Christ, in whom alone God is *reconciling the world to himself.* All that are out of Christ are in a state of enmity, and reject and oppose the Lord and his anointed, and shall therefore *be punished with everlasting destruction from the presence of the Lord, and the glory of his power.* Those whose sins are pardoned and their peace made with God are the only safe and happy people; therefore follow after peace, and that with all." (1.) Peace with God through our Lord Jesus Christ. (2.) Peace in our own consciences, through the Spirit of grace witnessing with our spirits that we are the children of God. (3.) Peace with men, by having a calm and peaceable disposition wrought in us, resembling that of our blessed Lord.

2. That you be *found of Christ without spot, and blameless. Follow after holiness* as well as peace: and even spotless and perfect; we must not only take heed of all spots which are not the spots of God's children (this only prevents our being found of men without spot), but we must be found of Christ without spot, we must be pressing towards spotless purity, absolute perfection. Christians must be *perfecting holiness,* that they may be not only blameless before men, but also in the sight of God; and all this deserves and needs the greatest diligence; he who does this work negligently can never do it successfully. "Never expect to be found at that day of God in peace, if you are lazy and idle in this your day, in which we must finish the work that is given us to do. It is only the diligent Christian who will be the happy Christian in the day of the Lord. Our Lord will suddenly come to us, or shortly call us to him; and would you have him find you idle?" Remember there is a curse denounced against him *who does the work of the Lord negligently,* Marg. Jer. xlviii. 10. Heaven will be a sufficient recompence for all our diligence and industry; therefore let us labour and take pains in the work of the Lord; he will certainly reward us if we be diligent in the work he has allotted us; now, that you may be diligent, *account the long-suffering of our Lord to be salvation.* "Does your Lord delay his coming? Do not think this is to give more time to make provision for your lusts, to gratify them; it is so much space to repen-t and work out your salvation. It proceeds not from a want of concern or compassion for his suffering servants, nor is it designed to give countenance and encouragement to the world of the ungodly, but that men may have time to prepare for eternity. Learn then to make a right use of the patience of our Lord, who does as yet delay his coming. Follow after peace and holiness, or else his coming will be dreadful to you." And inasmuch as it is difficult to prevent men's abuse of God's patience, and engage them in the right improvement thereof, our apostle quotes St. Paul as directing men to make the same good use of the divine forbearance, that in the mouth, or from the pen, of two apostles the truth might be confirmed. And we may here observe with what esteem and affection he speaks of him who had formerly publicly withstood and sharply reproved Peter. If a righteous man smite one who is truly religious, it shall be received as a kindness; and let him reprove, it shall be as an excellent oil, which shall soften and sweeten the good man that is reproved when he does amiss. What an honourable mention does this apostle of the circumcision make of that very man who had openly, *before all, reproved him,* as not

walking uprightly according to the truth of the gospel! (1.) He calls him *brother*, whereby he means not only that he is a fellow-christian (in which sense the word brethren is used 1 Thess. v. 27), or a fellow-preacher (in which sense Paul calls Timothy the evangelist a *brother*, Col. i. 1), but a fellow-apostle, one who had the same extraordinary commission, immediately from Christ himself, to preach the gospel in every place, and to disciple all nations. Though many seducing teachers denied Paul's apostleship, yet Peter owns him to be an apostle. (2.) He calls him *beloved;* and they being both alike commissioned, and both united in the same service of the same Lord, it would have been very unseemly if they had not been united in affection to one another, for the strengthening of one another's hands, mutually desirous of, and rejoicing in, one another's success. (3.) He mentions Paul as one who had an uncommon measure of wisdom given unto him. He was a person of eminent knowledge in the mysteries of the gospel, and did neither in that nor any other qualification come behind any of all the other apostles. How desirable is it that those who preach the same gospel should treat one another according to the pattern Peter here sets them! It is surely their duty to endeavour, by proper methods, to prevent or remove all prejudices that hinder ministers' usefulness, and to beget and improve the esteem and respect in the minds of people towards their ministers that may promote the success of their labours. And let us also here observe, [1.] The excellent wisdom that was in Paul is said to be *given* him. The understanding and knowledge that qualify men to preach the gospel are the gift of God. We must seek for knowledge, and labour to get understanding, in hopes that it shall be given us from above, while we are diligent in using proper means to attain it. [2.] The apostle imparts to men according as he had received from God. He endeavours to lead others as far as he himself was led into the knowledge of the mysteries of the gospel. He is not an intruder into the things he had not seen or been fully assured of, and yet he does not fail to declare the whole counsel of God, Acts xx. 27. [3.] The epistles which were written by the apostle of the Gentiles, and directed to those Gentiles who believed in Christ, are designed for the instruction and edification of those who from among the Jews were brought to believe in Christ; for it is generally thought that what is here alluded to is contained in the epistle to the Romans (*ch.* ii. 4), though in all his epistles there are some things that refer to one or other of the subjects treated of in this and the foregoing chapter; and it cannot seem strange that those who were pursuing the same general design should in their epistles insist upon the same things. But the apostle Peter proceeds to tell us that in those things which are to be met with in Paul's epistles there are some things hard to be understood Among the variety of subjects treated of in scripture, some are not easy to be understood because of their own obscurity, such are prophecies; others cannot be so easily understood because of their excellency and sublimity, as the mysterious doctrines; and others are with difficulty taken in because of the weakness of men's minds, such are the things of the Spirit of God, mentioned 1 Cor. ii. 14. And here the unlearned and unstable make wretched work; for they wrest and torture the scriptures, to make them speak what the Holy Ghost did not intend. Those who are not well instructed and well established in the truth are in great danger of perverting the word of God. Those who have heard and learned of the Father are best secured from misunderstanding and misapplying any part of the word of God; and, where there is a divine power to establish as well as to instruct men in divine truth, persons are effectually secured from falling into errors. How great a blessing this is we learn by observing what is the pernicious consequence of the errors that ignorant and unstable men fall into—even their own destruction. Errors in particular concerning the holiness and justice of God are the utter ruin of multitudes of men. Let us therefore earnestly pray for the Spirit of God to instruct us in the truth, that we may know it as it is in Jesus, and have our hearts established with grace, that we may stand firm and unshaken, even in the most stormy times, when others are tossed to and fro with every wind of doctrine.

III. The apostle gives them a word of caution, *v.* 17, 18, where,

1. He intimates that the knowledge we have of these things should make us very wary and watchful, inasmuch as there is a twofold danger, *v.* 17. (1.) We are in great danger *of* being seduced, and turned away from the truth. The unlearned and unstable, and they are very numerous, do generally wrest the scripture. Many who have the scriptures and read them do not understand what they read; and too many of those who have a right understanding of the sense and meaning of the word are not established in the belief of the truth, and all these are liable to fall into error. Few attain to the knowledge and acknowledgment of doctrinal Christianity; and fewer find, so as to keep in the way of practical godliness, which is the narrow way, which only leadeth unto life. There must be a great deal of self-denial and suspicion of ourselves, and submitting to the authority of Christ Jesus our great prophet, before we can heartily receive all the truths of the gospel, and therefore we are in great danger of rejecting the truth. (2.) We are in great danger *by* being seduced; for, [1.] So far as we are turned from the truth *so far are we turned out of the way to true blessedness,* into the path which leads to destruction. If men corrupt the word of God, it tends to their

own utter ruin. [2.] When men wrest the word of God, *they fall into the error of the wicked,* men without law, who keep to no rules, set no bounds to themselves, a sort of free-thinkers, which the psalmist detests. Ps. cxix. 113, *I hate vain thoughts, but thy law do I love.* Whatever opinions and thoughts of men are not conformable to the law of God, and warranted by it, the good man disclaims and abhors; they are the conceits and counsels of the ungodly, who have forsaken God's law, and, if we imbibe their opinions, we shall too soon imitate their practices. [3.] Those who are led away by error *fall from their own stedfastness.* They are wholly unhinged and unsettled, and know not where to rest, but are at the greatest uncertainty, like a wave of the sea, driven with the wind and tossed. It nearly concerns us therefore to be upon our guard, seeing the danger is so great.

2. That we may the better avoid being led away, the apostle directs us what to do, *v.* 18. And, (1.) We must *grow in grace.* He had in the beginning of the epistle exhorted us to add one grace to another, and here he advises us to grow in all grace, in faith, and virtue, and knowledge. By how much the stronger grace is in us, by so much the more stedfast shall we be in the truth. (2.) We must grow *in the knowledge of our Lord Jesus Christ.* "Follow on to know the Lord. Labour to know him more clearly and more fully, to know more of Christ and to know him to better purpose, so as to be more like him and to love him better." This is the knowledge of Christ the apostle Paul reached after and desired to attain, Phil. iii. 10. Such a knowledge of Christ as conforms us more to him, and endears him more to us, must needs be of great use to us, to preserve us from falling off in times of general apostasy; and those who experience this effect of the knowledge of the Lord and Saviour Jesus Christ will, upon receiving such grace from him, give thanks and praise to him, and join with our apostle in saying, *To him be glory both now and for ever. Amen.*

AN

EXPOSITION,

WITH PRACTICAL OBSERVATIONS,

OF THE FIRST EPISTLE GENERAL OF

JOHN.

Though the continued tradition of the church attests that this epistle came from John the apostle, yet we may observe some other evidence that will confirm (or with some perhaps even outweigh) the certainty of that tradition. It should seem that the penman was one of the apostolical college by the sensible palpable assurance he had of the truth of the Mediator's person in his human nature: *That which we have heard, which we have seen with our eyes, which we have looked upon, and our hands have handled, of the Word of life, v.* 1. He here takes notice of the evidence the Lord gave to Thomas of his resurrection, by calling him to feel the prints of the nails and of the spear, which is recorded by John. And he must have been one of the disciples present when the Lord came on the same day in which he arose from the dead, and showed them his hands and his side, John xx. 20. But, that we may be assured which apostle this was, there is scarcely a critic or competent judge of diction, or style of argument and spirit, but will adjudge this epistle to the writer of that gospel that bears the name of the apostle John. They wonderfully agree in the titles and characters of the Redeemer: *The Word, the Life, the Light; his name was the Word of God.* Compare *ch.* i. 1 and *ch.* v. 7 with John i. 1 and Rev. xix. 13. They agree in the commendation of God's love to us (*ch.* iii. 1 and *ch.* iv. 9; John iii. 16), and in speaking of our regeneration, or being born of God, *ch.* iii. 9; iv. 7; and v. 1; John iii. 5, 6. Lastly (to add no more instances, which may be easily seen in comparing this epistle with that gospel), they agree in the allusion to, or application of, that passage in that gospel which relates (and which alone relates) the issuing of water and blood out of the Redeemer's opened side: *This is he that came by water and blood, ch.* v. 6. Thus the epistle plainly appears to flow from the same pen as that gospel did. Now I know not that the text, or the intrinsic history of any of the gospels, gives us such assurance of its writer or penman as that ascribed to John plainly does. There (viz. *ch.* xxi. 24) the sacred historian thus notifies himself: *This is the disciple that testifieth of these things and wrote these things; and we know that his testimony is true.* Now who is this disciple, but he concerning whom Peter asked, *What shall this man do?* And concerning whom the Lord answered, *If I will that he tarry till I come, what is that to thee? v.* 22. And who (in *v.* 20) is described by these three characters:—1. *That he is the disciple whom Jesus loved,* the Lord's peculiar friend. 2. *That he also leaned on his breast at supper.* 3. That he said unto him, *Lord, who is he that betrayeth thee?* As sure then as it is that that disciple was John, so sure may the church be that that gospel and this epistle came from the beloved John.

The epistle is styled *general,* as being not inscribed to any particular church; it is, as a circular letter (or visitation charge), sent to divers churches (some say of Parthia), in order to confirm them in their stedfast adherence to the Lord Christ, and the sacred doctrines concerning his person and office, against seducers; and to instigate them to adorn that doctrine by love to God and man, and particularly to each other, as being descended from God, united by the same head, and travelling towards the same eternal life.

CHAP. I.

Evidence given concerning Christ's person and excellency, ver. 1, 2. The knowledge thereof gives us communion with God and Christ (ver. 3), and joy, ver. 4. A description of God, ver. 5. How we are thereupon to walk, ver. 6. The benefit of such walking, ver. 7. The way to forgiveness, ver. 9. The evil of denying our sin, ver. 8—10.

THAT which was from the beginning, which we have heard, which we have seen with our eyes, which we have looked upon, and our hands have handled, of the Word of life;
2 (For the life was manifested, and we have seen *it,* and bear witness, and show unto you that eternal life, which was with the Father, and was manifested unto us;)
3 That which we have seen and heard declare we unto you, that ye also may have fellowship with us: and truly our fellowship *is* with the Father, and with his Son Jesus Christ.
4 And these things write we unto you, that your joy may be full.

The apostle omits his name and character (as also the author to the Hebrews does) either out of humility, or as being willing that the Christian reader should be swayed by the light and weight of the things written rather than by the name that might recommend them. And so he begins,

I. With an account or character of the Mediator's person. He is the great subject of the gospel, the foundation and object of our faith and hope, the bond and cement that unite us unto God. He should be well known; and he is represented here, 1. *As the Word of life, v.* 1. In the gospel these two are disjoined, and he is called first *the Word,* John i. 1, and afterwards *Life,* intimating, withal, that he is *intellectual life. In him was life, and that life was* (efficiently and objectively) *the light of men,* John i. 4. Here both are conjoined: *The Word of life,* the vital Word. In that he is the Word, it is intimated that he is the Word of some person or other; and that is God, even the Father. *He is the Word of God,* and so he is intimated to issue from the Father, as truly (though not in the same manner) as a word (or speech, which is a train of words) from a speaker. But he is not a mere vocal word, a bare λόγος προφορικὸς, but a vital one: *the Word of life,* the living word; and thereupon, 2. *As eternal life.* His duration shows his excellency. He was from eternity; and so is, in scripture-account, necessary, essential, uncreated life. That the apostle speaks of his eternity, *à parte ante* (as they say) and as *from everlasting,* seems evident in that he speaks of him as he was in and from the beginning; when he was then with the Father, before his manifestation to us, yea, before the making of all things that were made; as John i. 2. 3. So that he is the eternal, vital, intellectual Word of the eternal living Father. 3. *As life manifested* (*v.* 2), manifested in the flesh, manifested to us. The eternal life would assume mortality, would put on flesh and blood (in the entire human nature), and so dwell among us and converse with us, John i. 14. Here were condescension and kindness indeed, that eternal life (a person of eternal essential life) should come to visit mortals, and to procure eternal life for them, and then confer it on them!

II. With the evidences and convictive assurances that the apostle and his brethren had of the Mediator's presence and converse in this world. There were sufficient demonstrations of the reality of his abode here, and of the excellency and dignity of his person in the way of his manifestation. *The life, the word of life, the eternal life,* as such, could not be seen and felt; but the life manifested might be, and was so. The life was clothed with flesh, put on the state and habit of abased human nature, and as such gave sensible proof of its existence and transactions here. The divine life, or Word incarnate, presented and evinced itself to the very senses of the apostles. As, 1. To their ears: *That which we have heard, v.* 1, 3. The life assumed a mouth and tongue, that he might utter words of life. The apostles not only heard of him, but they heard him himself. Above three years might they attend his ministry, be auditors of his public sermons and private expositions (for he expounded them in the house), and be charmed with the words of him who spoke as never man spoke before or since. The divine word would employ the ear, and the ear should be devoted to the word of life. And it was meet that those who were to be his representatives and imitators to the world should be personally acquainted with his ministrations. 2. To their eyes: *That which we have seen with our eyes, v.* 1—3. The Word would become visible, would not only be heard, but seen, seen publicly, privately, at distance and at nearest approach, which may be intimated in the expression, *with our eyes*—with all the use and exercise that we could make of our eyes. We saw him in his life and ministry, saw him in his transfiguration on the mount, hanging, bleeding, dying, and dead, upon the cross, and we saw him after his return from the grave and resurrection from the dead. His apostles must be eye-witnesses as well as ear-witnesses of him. *Wherefore, of these men that have accompanied with us all the time that the Lord Jesus went in and out among us, beginning from the baptism of John, must one be ordained to be a witness with us of his resurrection,* Acts i. 21, 22. *And we were eye-witnesses of his majesty,* 2 Pet. i. 16. 3. To their internal sense, to the eyes of their mind; for so (possibly) may the next clause be interpreted: *Which we have looked upon.* This may be distinguished from the foregoing perception, *seeing with the eyes;* and may be the same with what the apostle says in his gospel (*ch.* i. 14), *And we beheld—ἐθεασάμεθα, his glory, the glory as of the only-begotten of the Father.* The word is not applied to the immediate object of the eye, but to that which was rationally collected from what they saw. "What we have well discerned, contemplated, and viewed, what we have well known of this Word of life, we report to you." The senses are to be the informers of the mind. 4. To their hands and sense of feeling: *And our hands have handled* (touched and felt) *of the Word of life.* This surely refers to the full conviction our Lord afforded his apostles of the truth, reality, solidity, and organization of his body, after his resurrection from the dead. When he showed them his hands and his side, it is probable that he gave them leave to touch him; at least, he knew of Thomas's unbelief, and his professed resolution too not to believe, till he had found and felt the places and signatures of the wounds by which he died. Accordingly at the next congress he called Thomas, in the presence of the rest, to satisfy the very curiosity of his unbelief. And probably others of them did so too. *Our hands have handled of the Word of life.* The invisible life and Word was no despiser of the testimony of sense. Sense, in its place and sphere, is a means that God has appointed, and the Lord Christ has employed, for our information. Our Lord took care to satisfy (as far as might be) all the senses of his apostles, that they might be the more authentic witnesses of him to the world. Those that apply all this to the hearing of the gospel lose the variety of sensations here mentioned, and the propriety of the expressions, as well as the reason of their inculcation and repetition here: *That which we have seen and heard declare we unto you, v.* 3. The apostles could not be deceived in such long and various exercise of their sense Sense must minister to reason and judgment; and reason and judgment must minister to the reception of the Lord Jesus Christ and his gospel. The rejection of the Christian revelation is at last resolved into the rejection of sense itself. *He upbraided them with their unbelief and hardness of heart, because they believed not those who had seen him after he had risen,* Mark xvi. 14.

III. With a solemn assertion and attestation of these grounds and evidences of the Christian truth and doctrine. The apostles publish these assurances for our satisfaction: *We bear witness, and show unto you, v.* 2. *That which we have seen and heard declare we unto you, v.* 3. It became the apostles to open to the disciples the evidence by which they were led, the reasons by which they were constrained to proclaim and propagate the Christian doctrine in the world. Wisdom and integrity obliged them to demonstrate that it was not either private fancy or a cunningly-devised fable that they presented to the world. Evident truth would open their mouths, and force a public profession. *We cannot but speak the things which we have seen and heard,* Acts iv. 20. It concerned the disciples to be well assured of the truth of the institution they had embraced. They should see the evidences of their holy religion. It fears not the light, nor the most judicious examination. It is able to afford rational conviction and solid persuasion of mind and conscience. *I would that you knew what great conflict* (or concern of mind) *I have for you, and for those at Laodicea, and for as many as have not seen my face in the flesh, that their hearts might be knit together in love, and unto all riches of full assurance of understanding, to the acknowledgment of the mystery of God, even of the Father, and of Christ,* Col. ii. 1, 2.

IV. With the reason of the apostle's exhibiting and asserting this summary of sacred faith, and this breviate of evidence attending it. This reason is twofold:—

1. That the believers of it may be advanced to the same happiness with them (with the apostles themselves): *That which we have seen and heard declare we unto you, that you may have fellowship with us, v.* 3. The apostle means not personal fellowship nor consociation in the same church-administrations, but such as is consistent with personal distance from each other. It is communion with heaven, and in blessings that come thence and tend thither. "This we declare and testify, that you may share with us in our privileges and happiness." Gospel spirits (or those that are made happy by gospel grace) would fain have others happy too. We see, also, there is a fellowship or communion that runs through the whole church of God. There may be some personal distinctions and peculiarities, but there

is a communion (or common participation of privilege and dignity) belonging to all saints, from the highest apostle to the lowest believer. As there is the same precious faith, there are the same precious promises dignifying and crowning that faith and the same precious blessings and glories enriching and filling those promises. Now that believers may be ambitious of this communion, that they may be instigated to retain and hold fast the faith that is the means of such communion, that the apostles also may manifest their love to the disciples in assisting them to the same communion with themselves, they indicate what it is and where it is: *And truly our fellowship* (or communion) *is with the Father and his Son Jesus Christ.* We have communion with the Father, and with the Son of the Father (as 2 John 3, he is most emphatically styled) in our happy relation to them, in our receiving heavenly blessings from them, and in our spiritual converse with them. We have now such supernatural conversation with God and the Lord Christ as is an earnest and foretaste of our everlasting abode with them, and enjoyment of them, in the heavenly glory. See to what the gospel revelation tends—to advance us far above sin and earth and to carry us to blessed communion with the Father and the Son. See for what end the eternal life was made flesh—that he might advance us to eternal life in communion with the Father and himself. See how far those live beneath the dignity, use, and end of the Christian faith and institution, who have not spiritual blessed communion with the Father and his Son Jesus Christ.

2. That believers may be enlarged and advanced in holy joy: *And these things write we unto you that your joy may be full, v.* 4. The gospel dispensation is not properly a dispensation of fear, sorrow, and dread, but of peace and joy. Terror and astonishment may well attend mount Sinai, but exultation and joy mount Zion, where appears *the eternal Word, the eternal life,* manifested in our flesh. The mystery of the Christian religion is directly calculated for the joy of mortals. It should be joy to us that the eternal Son should come to seek and save us, that he has made a full atonement for our sins, that he has conquered sin and death and hell, that he lives as our Intercessor and Advocate with the Father, and that he will come again to perfect and glorify his persevering believers. And therefore those live beneath the use and end of the Christian revelation who are not filled with spiritual joy. Believers should rejoice in their happy relation to God, as his sons and heirs, his beloved and adopted,—in their happy relation to the Son of the Father, as being members of his beloved body, and coheirs with himself,—in the pardon of their sins, the sanctification of their natures, the adoption of their persons, and the prospect of grace and glory that will be revealed at the return of their Lord and head from heaven. Were they confirmed in their holy faith, how would they rejoice! *The disciples were filled with joy, and with the Holy Ghost,* Acts xiii. 52.

5 This then is the message which
we have heard of him, and declare
unto you, that God is light, and
in him is no darkness at all. 6 If we
say that we have fellowship with him,
and walk in darkness, we lie, and do
not the truth: 7 But if we walk in
the light, as he is in the light, we have
fellowship one with another, and the
blood of Jesus Christ his Son cleanseth
us from sin.

The apostle, having declared the truth and dignity of the author of the gospel, brings a message or report from him, from which a just conclusion is to be drawn for the consideration and conviction of the professors of religion, or professed entertainers of this glorious gospel.

I. Here is the message or report that the apostle avers to come from the Lord Jesus: *This then is the message which we have heard of him* (*v.* 5), of his Son Jesus Christ. As he was the immediate sender of the apostles, so he is the principal person spoken of in the preceding context, and the next antecedent also to whom the pronoun *him* can relate. The apostles and apostolical ministers are the messengers of the Lord Jesus; it is their honour, the chief they pretend to, to bring his mind and messages to the world and to the churches. This is the wisdom and present dispensation of the Lord Jesus, to send his messages to us by persons like ourselves. He that put on human nature will honour earthen vessels. It was the ambition of the apostles to be found faithful, and faithfully to deliver the errands and messages they had received. What was communicated to them they were solicitous to impart: *This then is the message which we have heard of him, and declare unto you.* A message from the Word of life, from the eternal Word, we should gladly receive: and the present one is this (relating to the nature of God whom we are to serve, and with whom we should covet all indulged communion)—*That God is light, and in him is no darkness at all, v.* 5. This report asserts the excellency of the divine nature. He is all that beauty and perfection that can be represented to us by light. He is a self-active uncompounded spirituality, purity, wisdom, holiness, and glory. And then the absoluteness and fulness of that excellency and perfection. There is no defect or imperfection, no mixture of any thing alien or contrary to absolute excellency, no mutability nor capacity of any decay in him: *In him is no darkness at all, v.* 5. Or this report may more immediately relate to what is usually called the moral perfection of the divine nature, what we are to imitate, or what is more directly to influence us in our gospel work. And so it will comprehend the holiness of God, the absolute purity of his nature and will, his penetrative knowledge (particularly of hearts), his jealousy and justice, which burn as a most bright and vehement flame. It is meet that to this dark world the great God should be represented as pure and perfect light. It is the Lord Jesus that best of all opens to us the name and nature of the unsearchable God: *The only-begotten, who is in the bosom of the Father, the same hath declared him.* It is the prerogative of the Christian revelation to bring us the most noble, the most august and agreeable account of the blessed God, such as is most suitable to the light of reason and what is demonstrable thereby, most suitable to the magnificence of his works round about us, and to the nature and office of him that is the supreme administrator, governor, and judge of the world. What more (relating to and comprehensive of all such perfection) could be included in one word than in this, *God is light, and in him is no darkness at all?* Then,

II. There is a just conclusion to be drawn from this message and report, and that for the consideration and conviction of professors of religion, or professed entertainers of this gospel. This conclusion issues into two branches:—1. For the conviction of such professors as have no true fellowship with God: *If we say we have fellowship with him, and walk in darkness, we lie, and do not the truth.* It is known that to walk, in scripture account, is to order and frame the course and actions of the moral life, that is, of the life so far as it is capable of subjection to the divine law. *To walk in darkness* is to live and act according to such ignorance, error, and erroneous practice, as are contrary to the fundamental dictates of our holy religion. Now there may be those who may pretend to great attainments and enjoyments in religion; they may profess to have communion with God; and yet their lives may be irreligious, immoral, and impure. To such the apostle would not fear to give the lie: *They lie, and do not the truth.* They belie God; for he holds no heavenly fellowship or intercourse with unholy souls. What communion hath light with darkness? They belie themselves, or lie concerning themselves; for they have no such communications from God nor accesses to him. There is no truth in their profession nor in their practice, or their practice gives their profession and pretences the lie, and demonstrates the folly and falsehood of them. 2. For the conviction and consequent satisfaction of those that are near to God: *But, if we walk in the light, we have fellowship one with another, and the blood of Jesus Christ his Son cleanseth us from all sin.* As the blessed God is the eternal boundless light, and the Mediator is, from him, the light of the world, so the Christian institution is the great luminary that appears in our sphere, and shines here below. A conformity to this in spirit and practice demonstrates fellowship or communion with God. Those that so walk show that they know God, that they have received of the Spirit of God, and that the divine impress or image is stamped upon their souls. *Then we have fellowship one with another,* they with us and we with them, and both with God, in his blessed or beatific communications to us. And this is one of those beatific communications to us—that his Son's blood or death is applied or imputed to us: *The blood of Jesus Christ his Son cleanseth us from all sin.* The eternal life, the eternal Son, hath put on flesh and blood, and so became Jesus Christ. Jesus Christ hath shed his blood for us, or died to wash us from our sins in his own blood. His blood applied to us discharges us from the guilt of all sin, both original and actual, inherent and committed: and so far we stand righteous in his sight; and not only so, but his blood procures for us those sacred influences by which sin is to be subdued more and more, till it is quite abolished, Gal. iii. 13, 14.

8 If we say that we have no sin we
deceive ourselves, and the truth is not
in us. 9 If we confess our sins, he
is faithful and just to forgive us *our*
sins, and to cleanse us from all unrighteousness. 10 If we say that we
have not sinned, we make him a liar,
and his word is not in us.

Here, I. The apostle, having supposed that even those of this heavenly communion have yet their sin, proceeds here to justify that supposition, and this he does by showing the dreadful consequences of denying it, and that in two particulars:—1. *If we say, We have no sin, we deceive ourselves, and the truth is not in us, v.* 8. We must beware of deceiving ourselves in denying or excusing our sins. The more we see them the more we shall esteem and value the remedy. *If we deny them, the truth is not in us,* either the truth that is contrary to such denial (we lie in denying our sin), or the truth of religion, is not in us. The Christian religion is the religion of sinners, of such as have sinned, and in whom sin in some measure still dwells. The Christian life is a life of continued repentance, humiliation for and mortification of sin, of continual faith in, thankfulness for, and love to the Redeemer, and hopeful joyful expectation of a day of glorious redemption, in which the believer shall be fully and finally acquitted, and sin abolished for ever. 2. *If we say, We have not sinned, we make him a liar, and his word is not in us, v.* 10. The denial of our sin not only deceives ourselves, but reflects dishonour upon God. It challenges his veracity. He has abundantly testified of, and testified against, the sin of the world. *And the Lord said in his heart* (determined thus with himself), *I will not again curse the ground* (as he had then lately done) *for man's sake; for* (or, with the learned bishop Patrick, *though) the imagination of man's heart is evil from his youth,* Gen. viii. 21. But God has given his testimony to the continued sin and sinfulness of the world, by providing a sufficient effectual sacrifice for sin, that will be needed in all ages, and to the continued sinfulness of believers themselves by requiring them continually to confess their sins, and apply themselves by faith to the blood of that sacrifice. And therefore, if we say either that we have not sinned or do not yet sin, *the word of God is not in us,* neither in our minds, as to the acquaintance we should have with it, nor in our hearts, as to the practical influence it should have upon us.

II. The apostle then instructs the believer in the way to the continued pardon of his sin. Here we have, 1. His duty in order thereto: *If we confess our sins, v.* 9. Penitent confession and acknowledgment of sin are the believer's business, and the means of his deliverance from his guilt. And, 2. His encouragement thereto, and assurance of the happy issue. This is the veracity, righteousness, and clemency of God, to whom he makes such confession: *He is faithful and just to forgive us our sins, and to cleanse us from all unrighteousness, v.* 9. God is faithful to his covenant and word, wherein he has promised forgiveness to penitent believing confessors. He is just to himself and his glory who has provided such a sacrifice, by which his righteousness is declared in the justification of sinners. He is just to his Son who has not only sent him for such service, but promised to him that those who come through him shall be forgiven on his account. *By his knowledge* (by the believing apprehension of him) *shall my righteous servant justify many,* Isa. liii. 11. He is clement and gracious also, and so will forgive, to the contrite confessor, all his sins, cleanse him from the guilt of all unrighteousness, and in due time deliver him from the power and practice of it.

CHAP. II.

Here the apostle encourages against sins of infirmity (ver. 1, 2), shows the true knowledge and love of God (ver. 3—6), renews the precept of fraternal love (ver. 7—11), addresses the several ages of Christians (ver. 12—14), warns against worldly love (ver. 15—17), against seducers (ver. 18, 19), shows the security of true Christians (ver. 20—27), and advises to abide in Christ, ver. 28, 29.

MY little children, these things write I unto you, that ye sin not. And if any man sin, we have an advocate with the Father, Jesus Christ the righteous: 2 And he is the propitiation for our sins: and not for our's only, but also for *the sins of* the whole world.

These verses relate to the concluding subject of the foregoing chapter, in which the apostle proceeds upon the supposition of the real Christian's sin. And here he gives them both dissuasion and support.

1. Dissuasion. He would leave no room for sin: "*My little children, these things write I unto you, that you sin not, v.* 1. The design or purport of this letter, the design of what I have just said concerning communion with God and the overthrow of it by an irreligious course, is to dissuade and drive you from sin." See the familiar affectionate compellation with which he introduces his admonition: *My little children,* children as having perhaps been begotten by his gospel, *little children* as being much beneath him in age and experience, *my little children* as being dear to him in the bonds of the gospel. Certainly the gospel most prevailed where and when such ministerial love most abounded. Or perhaps the judicious reader will find reason to think that the apostle's meaning in this dissuasion or caution is this, or amounts to this reading: *These things write I unto you, not that you sin.* And so the words will look back to what he had said before concerning the assured pardon of sin: *God is faithful and just to forgive us our sins,* &c., *ch.* i. 9. And so the words are a preclusion of all abuse of such favour and indulgence. "Though sins will be forgiven to penitent confessors, yet this I write, not to encourage you in sin, but upon another account." Or this clause will look forward to what the apostle is going to say about the Advocate for sinners: and so it is a prolepsis, a prevention of like mistake or abuse: *These things write I unto you, not that you sin,* but that you may see your remedy for sin." And so the following particle (as the learned know) may be rendered adversatively: *But, if a man sin,* he may know his help and cure. And so we see,

II. The believer's support and relief in case of sin: *And* (or *but) if any man sin* (any of us, or of our foresaid communion), *we have we an Advocate with the Father,* &c., *v.* 1. Believers themselves, those that are advanced to a happy gospel-state, have yet their sins. There is a great distinction therefore between the sinners that are in the world. There are Christianized (such as are instated in the sacred saving privileges of Christ's mystical or spiritual body) and unchristianized, converted and unconverted sinners. There are some who, though they really sin, yet, in comparison with others, are said *not to sin,* as *ch.* iii. 9. Believers, as they have an atonement applied unto them at their entrance into a state of pardon and justification, so they have an Advocate in heaven still to continue to them that state, and procure their continued forgiveness. And this must be the support, satisfaction, and refuge of believers (or real Christians) in or upon their sins: *We have an Advocate.* The original name is sometimes given to the Holy Ghost, and then it is rendered, *the Comforter.* He acts within us; he puts pleas and arguments into our hearts and mouths; and so is our advocate, by teaching us to intercede for ourselves. But here is an advocate without us, in heaven and with the Father. The proper office and business of an advocate is with the judge; with him he pleads the client's cause. The Judge with whom our advocate pleads is the Father, his Father and ours. He who was our Judge in the legal court (the court of the violated law) is our Father in the gospel court, the court of heaven and of grace. His throne or tribunal is the mercy-seat. And he that is our Father is also our Judge, the supreme arbitrator of our state and circumstances, either for life or death, for time or eternity. *You have come——to God, the Judge of all*, Heb. xii. 23. That believers may be encouraged to hope that their cause will go well, as their Judge is represented to them in the relation of a Father, so their advocate is recommended to them upon these considerations:—1. By his person and personal names. *It is Jesus Christ the Son of the Father*, one anointed by the Father for the whole office of mediation, the whole work of salvation, and consequently for that of the intercessor or advocate. 2. By his qualification for the office. *It is Jesus Christ the righteous*, the righteous one in the court and sight of the Judge. This is not so necessary in another advocate. Another advocate (or an advocate in another court) may be an unjust person himself, and yet may have a just cause (and the cause of a just person in that case) to plead, and may accordingly carry his cause. But here the clients are guilty; their innocence and legal righteousness cannot be pleaded; their sin must be confessed or supposed. It is the advocate's own righteousness that he must plead for the criminals. He has been righteous to the death, righteous for them; he has brought in everlasting righteousness. This the Judge will not deny. Upon this score he pleads, that the clients' sins may not be imputed to them. 3. By the plea he has to make, the ground and basis of his advocacy: *And he is the propitiation for our sins, v.* 2. He is the expiatory victim, the propitiatory sacrifice that has been offered to the Judge for all our offences against his majesty, and law, and government. In vain do the professors of Rome distinguish between an advocate of redemption and an advocate of intercession, or a mediator of such different service. The Mediator of intercession, the Advocate for us, is the Mediator of redemption, the propitiation for our sins. It is his propitiation that he pleads. And we might be apt to suppose that his blood had lost its value and efficacy if no mention had been made of it in heaven since the time it was shed. But now we see it is of esteem there, since it is continually represented in the intercession of the great advocate (the attorney-general) for the church of God. *He ever lives to make intercession for those that come to God through him.* 4. By the extent of his plea, the latitude of his propitiation. It is not confined to one nation; and not particularly to the ancient Israel of God: *He is the propitiation for our sins; and not for ours only* (not only for the sins of us Jews, us that are Abraham's seed according to the flesh), *but also for those of the whole world* (*v.* 2); not only for the past, or us present believers, but for the sins of all who shall hereafter believe on him or come to God through him. The extent and intent of the Mediator's death reach to all tribes, nations, and countries. As he is the only, so he is the universal atonement and propitiation for all that are saved and brought home to God, and to his favour and forgiveness.

3 And hereby we do know that we
know him, if we keep his commandments.
4 He that saith, I know
him, and keepeth not his commandments, is a liar, and the truth is not
in him.
5 But whoso keepeth his
word, in him verily is the love of God
perfected: hereby know we that we
are in him.
6 He that saith he
abideth in him ought himself also so
to walk, even as he walked.

These verses may seem to relate to the seventh verse of the former chapter, between which and these verses there occurred an incidental discourse concerning the believer's duty and relief in case of sin, occasioned by the mention of one of the believer's privileges—his being cleansed from sin by the Mediator's blood. In that verse the apostle asserts the beneficial consequence of *walking in the light*: "*We have then fellowship with one another*, such divine fellowship and communion as are the prerogative of the church of Christ." Here now succeeds the trial or test of our light and of our love.

I. The trial of our light: *And hereby we do know that we know him, if we keep his commandments, v.* 3. Divine light and knowledge are the beauty and improvement of the mind; it becomes the disciples of the Mediator to be persons of wisdom and understanding. Young Christians are apt to magnify their new light and applaud their own knowledge, especially if they have been suddenly or in a short time communicated; and old ones are apt to suspect the sufficiency and fulness of their knowledge; they lament that they know God, and Christ, and the rich contents of his gospel, no more: but here is the evidence of the soundness of our knowledge, if it constrain us to *keep God's commandments*. Each perfection of his nature enforces his authority; the wisdom of his counsels, the riches of his grace, the grandeur of his works, recommend his law and government. A careful conscientious obedience to his commands shows that the apprehension and knowledge of these things are graciously impressed upon the soul; and therefore it must follow in the reverse that *he that saith, I know him, and keepeth not his commandments, is a liar, and the truth is not in him, v.* 4. Professors of the truth are often ashamed of their ignorance, or ashamed to own it; they frequently pretend to great attainments in the knowledge of divine mysteries: *Thou makest thy boast of God, and knowest his will, and approvest* (in thy rational judgment) *the things that are more excellent, being instructed out of the law, and art confident that thou thyself art* (or art fit to be) *a guide to the blind,* &c., Rom. ii. 17, &c. But what knowledge of God can that be which sees not that he is most worthy of the most entire and intense obedience? And, if that be seen and known, how vain and superficial is even this knowledge when it sways not the heart unto obedience! A disobedient life is the confutation and shame of pretended religious knowledge; it gives the lie to such boasts and pretences, and shows that there is neither religion nor honesty in them.

II. The trial of our love: *But whoso keepeth his word in him verily is the love of God perfected; hereby know we that we are in him, v.* 5. To keep the word of God, or of Christ, is sacredly to attend thereto in all the conduct and motion of life; in him that does so is the love of God perfected. Possibly, some may here understand God's love to us; and doubtless his love to us cannot be perfected (or obtain its perfect design and fruit) without our practical observance of his word. We are chosen, to be holy and blameless before him in love; we are *redeemed, to be a peculiar people, zealous of good works;* we are pardoned and justified, that we may be partakers of larger measures of the divine Spirit for sanctification; we are sanctified, that we may walk in ways of holiness and obedience: no act of divine love that here terminates upon us obtains its proper tendency, issue, and effect, without our holy attendance to God's word. But the phrase rather denotes here our love to God; so *v.* 15, *The love of (to) the Father is not in him;* so *ch.* iii. 17, *How dwelleth the love of (to) God in him?* Now light is to kindle love; and love must and will keep the word of God; it enquires wherein the beloved may be pleased and served, and, finding he will be so by observance of his declared will, there it employs and exerts itself; there love is demonstrated; there it has its perfect (or complete) exercise, operation, and delight; and hereby (by this dutiful attendance to the will of God, or Christ) *we know that we are in him* (*v.* 5), we know that we belong to him, and that we are united to him by that Spirit which elevates and assists us to this obedience; and if we acknowledge our relation to him, and our union with him, it must have this continued enforcement upon us: *He that saith he abideth in him ought himself to walk even as he walked, v.* 6. The Lord Christ was an inhabitant of this world, and walked here below; here he gave a shining example of absolute obedience to God. Those who profess to be on his side, and to abide with him, must walk with him, walk after his pattern and example. The partisans of the several sects of philosophers of old paid great regard to the dictates and practice of their respective teachers and sect-masters; much more should the Christian, he who professes to abide in and with Christ, aim to resemble his infallible Master and head, and conform to his course and prescriptions: *Then are you my friends if you do whatsoever I command you,* John xv. 14.

7 Brethren, I write no new commandment unto you, but an old commandment which ye had from the
beginning. The old commandment
is the word which ye have heard from
the beginning. 8 Again, a new commandment I write unto you, which
thing is true in him and in you: because the darkness is past, and the
true light now shineth. 9 He that
saith he is in the light, and hateth his
brother, is in darkness even until
now. 10 He that loveth his brother
abideth in the light, and there is none
occasion of stumbling in him. 11
But he that hateth his brother is in
darkness, and walketh in darkness, and
knoweth not whither he goeth, because
that darkness hath blinded his eyes.

The seventh verse may be supposed either to look backward to what immediately preceded (and then it is *walking as Christ walked* that is here represented as *no new, but an old commandment;* it is that which the apostles would certainly inculcate where-ever they brought Christ's gospel), or to look forward to what the apostle is now going to recommend, and that is the law of fraternal love; this is the message *heard from the beginning* (*ch.* iii. 11), and *the old commandment,* 2 John 5. Now, while the apostle addresses himself to the recommendation of such a practice, he is ready to give an instance thereof in his affectionate appellation: "*Brethren,* you who are dear to me in the bond of that love to which I would solicit you;" and so the precept of fraternal love is recommended,

I. As an old one: *I write no new commandment unto you, but an old commandment, which you had from the beginning, v.* 7. The precept of love must be as old as human nature; but it might admit divers enactions, enforcements, and motives. In the state of innocence, had human nature then been propagated, men must have loved one another as being of one blood, made to dwell on the earth, as being God's offspring, and bearing his image. In the state of sin and promised recovery, they must love one another as related to God their Maker, as related to each other by blood, and as partners in the same hope. When the Hebrews were peculiarly incorporated, they must accordingly love each other, as being the privileged people, whose were the covenants and the adoption, and of whose race the Messiah and head of the church must spring; and the law of love must be conveyed with new obligations to the new Israel of God, to the gospel church, and so it is the *old commandment*, or the word which the children of the gospel Israel have heard from the beginning, *v.* 7.

II. As a new one: "*Again*, to constrain you to this duty the more, *a new commandment I write unto you*, the law of the new society, the Christian corporation, *which thing is true in him*, the matter of which was first true in and concerning the head of it; the truth of it was first and was abundantly in him; *he loved the church, and gave himself for it:* and it is true *in you;* this law is in some measure written upon your hearts; you are taught of God to love one another, and that *because*" (or since, or forasmuch as) "*the darkness is past*, the darkness of your prejudiced unconverted (whether Jewish or Gentile) minds, your deplorable ignorance of God and of Christ is now past, *and the true light now shineth* (*v.* 8); *the light* of evangelical revelation hath shone with life and efficacy into your hearts; hence you have seen the excellency of Christian love, and the fundamental obligation thereto." Hence we see that the fundamentals (and particularly the fundamental precepts) of the Christian religion may be represented either as new or old; the reformed doctrine, or doctrine of religion in the reformed churches, is new and old—new, as taught after long darkness, by the lights of the reformation, new as purged from the adulterations of Rome; but old as having been taught and *heard from the beginning*. We should see that that grace or virtue which was true in Christ be true also in us; we should be conformable to our head. The more our darkness is past, and gospel light shines unto us, the deeper should our subjection be to the commandments of our Lord, whether considered as old or new. Light should produce a suitable heat. Accordingly, here is another trial of our Christian light; before, it was to be approved by obedience to God; here by Christian love. 1. He who wants such love in vain pretends his light: *He that saith he is in the light, and hateth his brother, is in darkness even until now*, *v.* 9. It is proper for sincere Christians to acknowledge what God has done for their souls; but in the visible church there are often those who assume to themselves more than is true, there are those who say they are in the light, the divine revelation has made its impression upon their minds and spirits, and yet they walk in hatred and enmity towards their Christian brethren; these cannot be swayed by the sense of the love of Christ to their brethren, and therefore remain in their dark state, notwithstanding their pretended conversion to the Christian religion. 2. He who is governed by such love approves his light to be good and genuine: *He that loveth his brother* (as his brother in Christ) *abideth in the light*, *v.* 10. He sees the foundation and reason of Christian love; he discerns the weight and value of the Christian redemption; he sees how meet it is that we should love those whom Christ hath loved; and then the consequence will be that *there is no occasion of stumbling in him* (*v.* 10); he will be no scandal, *no stumbling-block, to his brother;* he will conscientiously beware that he neither induce his brother to sin nor turn him out of the way of religion, Christian love teaches us highly to value our brother's soul, and to dread every thing that will be injurious to his innocence and peace. 3. Hatred is a sign of spiritual darkness: *But he that hateth his brother is in darkness*, *v.* 11. Spiritual light is instilled by the Spirit of grace, and one of *the first-fruits of that Spirit is love;* he then who is possessed with malignity towards a Christian brother must needs be destitute of spiritual light; consequently *he walks in darkness* (*v.* 11); his life is agreeable to a dark mind and conscience, *and he knows not whither he goes;* he sees not whither this dark spirit carries him, and particularly that it will carry him to the world of utter darkness, *because darkness hath blinded his eyes*, *v.* 11 The darkness of unregeneracy, evidenced by a malignant spirit, is contrary to the light of life; where that darkness dwells, the mind, the judgment, and the conscience will be darkened, and so will mistake the way to heavenly endless life. Here we may observe how effectually our apostle is now cured of his once hot and flaming spirit. Time was when he was for *calling for fire from heaven* upon poor ignorant Samaritans who received them not, Luke ix. 54. But his Lord had shown him that he knew not his own spirit, nor whither it led him. Having now imbibed more of the Spirit of Christ, he breathes out good-will to man, and love to all the brethren. It is the Lord Jesus that is the great Master of love: it is his school (his own church) that is the school of love. His disciples are the disciples of love, and his family must be the family of love.

12 I write unto you, little children,
because your sins are forgiven you
for his name's sake. 13 I write unto
you, fathers, because ye have known
him *that is* from the beginning I

write unto you, young men, because
ye have overcome the wicked one. I
write unto you, little children, because
ye have known the Father. 14 I have
written unto you, fathers, because
ye have known him *that is* from the
beginning. I have written unto you,
young men, because ye are strong,
and the word of God abideth in you,
and ye have overcome the wicked one.
15 Love not the world, neither the
things *that are* in the world. If any
man love the world, the love of the
Father is not in him. 16 For all
that *is* in the world, the lust of the
flesh, and the lust of the eyes, and the
pride of life, is not of the Father, but
is of the world. 17 And the world
passeth away, and the lust thereof:
but he that doeth the will of God
abideth for ever.

This new command of holy love, with the incentives thereto, may possibly be directed to the several ranks of disciples that are here accosted. The several graduates in the Christian university, the catholic church, must be sure to preserve the bond of sacred love. Or, there being an important dehortation and dissuasion to follow, without the observance of which vital religion in the love of God and love of the brethren cannot subsist, the apostle may justly seem to preface it with a solemn address to the several forms or orders in the school of Christ: let the infants or minors, the adults, the seniors (or the *adepti*, the *τέλειοι*, the most *perfect)*, in the Christian institution, know that they must *not love this world;* and so,

I. We have the address itself made to the various forms and ranks in the church of Christ. All Christians are not of the same standing and stature; there are babes in Christ, there are grown men, and old disciples. As these have their peculiar states, so they have their peculiar duties; but there are precepts and a correspondent obedience common to them all, as particularly mutual love and contempt of the world. We see also that wise pastors will judiciously distribute the word of life, and give to the several members of Christ's family their several suitable portions: *I write unto you children, fathers, and young men.* In this distribution the apostle addresses,

1. The lowest in the Christian school: *I write unto you, little children, v.* 12. There are novices in religion, babes in Christ, those who are learning the rudiments of Christian godliness. The apostle may seem to encourage them by applying to them first; and it may be useful to the greater proficients to hear what is said to their juniors; elements are to be repeated; first principles are the foundation of all. He addresses *the children* in Christianity upon two accounts:—(1.) *Because their sins were forgiven them for his name's sake, v.* 12. The youngest sincere disciple is pardoned; *the communion of saints* is attended with *the forgiveness of sins.* Sins are forgiven either for God's name's sake, for the praise of his glory (his glorious perfections displayed in forgiveness), or *for Christ's name's sake,* upon his score, and upon the account of the redemption that is in him; and those that are forgiven of God are strongly obliged to relinquish this world, which so interferes with *the love of God.* (2.) Because of their knowledge of God: *I write unto you, little children, because you have known the Father, v.* 13. Children are wont to know none so soon as their father. Children in Christianity must and do know God. *They shall all know me, from the least to the greatest,* Heb. viii. 11. Children in Christ should know that God is their Father; it is their wisdom. We say, It is a wise child that knows his father. These children cannot but know theirs; they can well be assured by whose power they are regenerated and by whose grace they are adopted. Those that know the Father may well be withdrawn from the love of this world. Then the apostle, proceeds,

2. To those of the highest station and stature, to the seniors in Christianity, to whom he gives an honourable appellation: *I write unto you, fathers (v.* 13, 14), *unto you, Mnasons, you old disciples,* Acts xxi. 16. The apostle immediately passes from the bottom to the top of the school, from the lowest form to the highest, that those in the middle may hear both lessons, may remember what they have learned and perceive what they must come to: *I write unto you, fathers.* Those that are of longest standing in Christ's school have need of further advice and instruction; the oldest disciple must go to heaven (the university above) with his book, his Bible, in his hand; fathers must be written to, and preached to; none are too old to learn. He writes to them upon the account of their knowledge: *I write unto you, fathers, because you have known him that is from the beginning, v.* 13, 14. Old men have knowledge and experience, and expect deference. The apostle is ready to own the knowledge of old Christians, and to congratulate them thereupon. They know the Lord Christ, particularly *him that was from the beginning;* as *ch.* i. 1. As Christ is *Alpha* and *Omega,* so he must be the beginning and end of our Christian knowledge. *I count all things but loss for the excellency of the knowledge of Christ Jesus my Lord,* Phil. iii. 8. Those who know him that was from the beginning, before this world was made, may well be induced thereby to relinquish this world. Then,

3. To the middle age of Christians, to

those who are in their bloom and flower: *I write unto you, young men, v.* 13, 14. There are the adult in Christ Jesus, those that have arrived at the strength of spirit and sound sense and can discern between good and evil. The apostle applies to them upon these accounts:—(1.) Upon the account of their martial exploits. Dexterous soldiers they are in the camp of Christ: *Because you have overcome the wicked one, v.* 13. There is a wicked one that is continually warring against souls, and particularly against the disciples: but those that are well taught in Christ's school can handle their arms and vanquish the evil one; and those that can vanquish him may be called to vanquish the world too, which is so great an instrument for the devil. (2.) Upon the account of their strength, discovered in this their achievement: *Because you are strong, and you have overcome the wicked one, v.* 14. Young men are wont to glory in their strength; it will be the glory of youthful persons to be strong in Christ and in his grace; it will be their glory, and it will try their strength, to overcome the devil; if they be not too hard for the devil, he will be too hard for them. Let vigorous Christians show their streugth in conquering the world; and the same strength must be exerted in overcoming the world as is employed in overcoming the devil. (3.) Because of their acquaintance with the word of God: *And the word of God abideth in you, v.* 14. The word of God must abide in the adult disciples; it is the nutriment and supply of strength to them; it is the weapon by which they overcome the wicked one; the sword of the Spirit, whereby they quench his fiery darts: and those in whom the word of God dwells are well furnished for the conquest of the world.

II. We have the dehortation or dissuasion thus prefaced and introduced, a caution fundamental to vital practical religion: "*Love not the world, neither the things that are in the world, v.* 15. Be crucified to the world, be mortified to the things, to the affairs and enticements, of it." The several degrees of Christians should unite in this, in being dead to the world. Were they thus united, they would soon unite upon other accounts: their love should be reserved for God; throw it not away upon the world. Now here we see the reasons of this dissuasion and caution. They are several, and had need to be so; it is hard to dispute or dissuade disciples themselves from the love of the world. These reasons are taken,

1. From the inconsistency of this love with the love of God: *If any man love the world, the love of the Father is not in him, v.* 15. The heart of man is narrow, and cannot contain both loves. The world draws down the heart from God; and so the more the love of the world prevails the more the love of God dwindles and decays.

2. From the prohibition of worldly love or lust; it is not ordained of God: *It is not of the Father, but is of the world, v.* 16. This love or lust is not appointed of God) he calls us from it), but it intrudes itself from the world; the world is a usurper of our affection. Now here we have the due consideration and notion of the world, according to which it is to be crucified and renounced. *The world*, physically considered, is good, and is to be admired as the work of God and a glass in which his perfections shine; but it is to be considered in its relation to us now in our corrupted state, and as it works upon our weakness and instigates and inflames our vile affections. There is great affinity and alliance between this world and the flesh, and this world intrudes and encroaches upon the flesh, and thereby makes a party against God. The things of the world therefore are distinguished into three classes, according to the three predominant inclinations of depraved nature; as, (1.) There is *the lust of the flesh. The flesh* here, being distinguished from *the eyes* and *the life*, imports the body. The lust of the flesh is, subjectively, the humour and appetite of indulging fleshly pleasures; and, objectively, all those things that excite and inflame the pleasures of the flesh. This lust is usually called *luxury*. (2.) There is *the lust of the eyes*. The eyes are delighted with treasures; riches and rich possessions are craved by an extravagant eye; this is the lust of covetousness. 3. There is *the pride of life*. A vain mind craves all the grandeur, equipage, and pomp of a vain-glorious life; this is ambition, and thirst after honour and applause. This is, in part, the disease of the ear; it must be flattered with admiration and praise. The objects of these appetites must be abandoned and renounced; as they engage and engross the affection and desire, *they are not of the Father, but of the world, v.* 16. The Father disallows them, and the world should keep them to itself. The lust or appetite to these things must be mortified and subdued; and so the indulging of it is not appointed by the Father, but is insinuated by the ensnaring world.

3. From the vain and vanishing state of earthly things and the enjoyment of them. *And the world passeth away, and the lust thereof, v.* 17. The things of the world are fading and dying apace. The lust itself and the pleasure of it wither and decay; desire itself will ere long fail and cease, Eccl. xii. 5. And what has become of all the pomp and pleasure of all those who now lie mouldering in the grave?

4. From the immortality of the divine lover, the lover of God: *But he that doeth the will of God*, which must be the character of the lover of God, in opposition to this lover or the world, *abideth for ever, v.* 17. The object of his love in opposition to *the world* that *passeth away*, abideth for ever; his sacred passion or affection, in opposition to the lust that passeth away, abideth for ever; love shall never fail; and he himself is an heir of

immortality and endless life, and shall in time be translated thither.

From the whole of these verses we should observe the purity and spirituality of the apostolical doctrine. The animal life must be subjected to the divine; the body with its affections should be subjugated to the soul; the soul should be swayed by religion, or the victorious love of God.

18 Little children, it is the last
time: and as ye have heard that
antichrist shall come, even now are
there many antichrists; whereby we
know that it is the last time. 19
They went out from us, but they were
not of us; for if they had been of us,
they would *no doubt* have continued
with us: but *they went out*, that they
might be made manifest that they
were not all of us.

Here is, I. A moral prognostication of the time; the end is coming: *Little children, it is the last time, v.* 18. Some may suppose that the apostle here addresses the first rank of Christians again; the juniors are most apt to be seduced, and therefore, "*Little children,* you that are young in religion, take heed to yourselves that you be not corrupted." But it may be, as elsewhere, a universal appellation, introductive of an alarm to all Christians: "*Little children, it is the last time;* our Jewish polity in church and state is hastening to an end; the Mosaic institution and discipline are just upon vanishing away; Daniel's weeks are now expiring; the destruction of the Hebrew city and sanctuary is approaching, *the end whereof must be with a flood, and to the end of the war desolations are determined,*" Dan. ix. 26. It is meet that the disciples should be warned of the haste and end of time, and apprised as much as may be of the prophetic periods of time.

II. The sign of this last time: *Even now there are many antichrists* (*v.* 18), many that oppose the person, doctrine, and kingdom of Christ. It is a mysterious portion of providence that antichrists should be permitted; but, when they have come, it is good and safe that the disciples should be informed of them; ministers should be *watchmen to the house of Israel.* Now it should be no great offence nor prejudice to the disciples that there are such antichrists: 1. One great one has been foretold: *As you have heard that antichrist shall come, v.* 18. The generality of the church have been informed by divine revelation that there must be a long and fatal adversary to Christ and his church, 2 Thess. ii. 8—10. No wonder then that there are many harbingers and forerunners of the great one: *Even now there are many antichrists,* the mystery of iniquity already worketh. 2. They were foretold also as the sign of this last time. *For there shall arise false Christs and false prophets, and shall show great signs and wonders, insomuch that, if it were possible, they shall deceive the very elect,* Matt. xxiv. 24. And these were the forerunners of the dissolution of the Jewish state, nation, and religion: *Whereby we know it is the last time, v.* 18. Let the prediction that we see there has been of seducers arising in the Christian world fortify us against their seduction.

III. Some account of these seducers or antichrists. 1. More positively. They were once entertainers or professors of apostolical doctrine: "*They went out from us* (*v.* 19), from our company and communion;" possibly from the church of Jerusalem, or some of the churches of Judea, as Acts xv. 1, *Certain men came down from Judea, and taught the brethren,* &c. The purest churches may have their apostates and revolters; the apostolic doctrine did not convert all whom it convinced of its truth. 2. More privatively. "They were not inwardly such as we are: *But they were not of us;* they had not *from the heart obeyed the form of sound doctrine delivered to them;* they were not of our union with Christ the head." Then here is, (1.) The reason upon which it is concluded that they were not of us, were not what they pretended, or what we are, and that is their actual defection: "*For, if they had been of us, they would* no doubt *have continued with us* (*v.* 19); had the sacred truth been rooted in their hearts it would have held them with us; had they had the anointing from above, by which they had been made true and real Christians, they would not have turned antichrists." Those that apostatize from religion sufficiently indicate that, before, they were hypocrites in religion: those who have imbibed the spirit of gospel truth have a good preservative againt destructive error. (2.) The reason why they are permitted thus to depart from apostolical doctrine and communion—that their insincerity may be detected: *But* this was done (or *they went out) that they might be made manifest that they were not all of us, v.* 19. The church knows not well who are its vital members and who are not; and therefore the church, considered as internally sanctified, may well be styled *invisible.* Some of the hypocritical must be manifested here, and that for their own shame and benefit too, in their reduction to the truth, if they have not sinned unto death, and for the terror and caution of others. *You therefore, beloved, seeing you know these things before, beware lest you also, being led away with the error of the wicked, fall from your own stedfastness. But grow in grace,* &c., 2 Pet. iii. 17, 18.

20 But ye have an unction from
the Holy One, and ye know all things.
21 I have not written unto you because ye know not the truth, but be-

cause ye know it, and that no lie is
of the truth. 22 Who is a liar but he
that denieth that Jesus is the Christ?
He is antichrist, that denieth the Father and the Son. 23 Whosoever
denieth the Son, the same hath not
the Father: [*but*] *he that acknow-*
ledgeth the Son hath the Father also.
24 Let that therefore abide in you,
which ye have heard from the beginning. If that which ye have heard
from the beginning shall remain in
you, ye also shall continue in the Son,
and in the Father. 25 And this is
the promise that he hath promised us,
even eternal life. 26 These *things*
have I written unto you concerning
them that seduce you. 27 But the
anointing which ye have received of
him abideth in you, and ye need not
that any man teach you: but as the
same anointing teacheth you of all
things, and is truth, and is no lie, and
even as it hath taught you, ye shall
abide in him.

Here, I. The apostle encourages the disciples (to whom he writes) in these dangerous times, in this hour of seducers; he encourages them in the assurance of their stability in this day of apostasy: *But you have an unction from the Holy One, and you know all things.* We see, 1. The blessing wherewith they were enriched—an unguent from heaven: *You have an unction.* True Christians are anointed ones, their name intimates as much. They are anointed with the oil of grace, with gifts and spiritual endowments, by the Spirit of grace. They are anointed into a similitude of their Lord's offices, as subordinate prophets, priests, and kings, unto God. The Holy Spirit is compared to oil, as well as to fire and water; and the communication of his salvific grace is our anointing. 2. From whom this blessing comes—*from the Holy One,* either from the Holy Ghost or from the Lord Christ, as Rev. iii. 7, *These things saith he that is holy —the Holy One.* The Lord Christ is glorious in his holiness. The Lord Christ disposes of the graces of the divine Spirit, and he anoints the disciples to make them like himself, and to secure them in his interest. 3. The effect of this unction—it is a spiritual eye-salve; it enlightens and strengthens the eyes of the understanding: "*And* thereby *you know all things* (*v.* 20), all these things concerning Christ and his religion; it was promised and given you for that end," John xiv. 26. The Lord Christ does not deal alike by all his professed disciples; some are more anointed than others There is great danger lest those that are not thus anointed should be so far from being true to Christ that they should, on the contrary, turn antichrists, and prove adversaries to Christ's person, and kingdom, and glory.

II. The apostle indicates to them the mind and meaning with which he wrote to them. 1. By way of negation; not as suspecting their knowledge, or supposing their ignorance in the grand truths of the gospel: "*I have not written unto you because you know not the truth, v.* 21. I could not then be so well assured of your stability therein, nor congratulate you on your unction from above." It is good to surmise well concerning our Christian brethren; we ought to do so till evidence overthrows our surmise: a just confidence in religious persons may both encourage and contribute to their fidelity. 2. By way of assertion and acknowledgment, as relying upon their judgment in these things: *But because you know it* (you know *the truth in Jesus), and that no lie is of the truth.* Those who know the truth in any respect are thereby prepared to discern what is contrary thereto and inconsistent therewith. *Rectum est index sui et obliqui—The line which shows itself to be straight shows also what line is crooked.* Truth and falsehood do not well mix and suit together. Those that are well acquainted with Christian truth are thereby well fortified against antichristian error and delusion. No lie belongs to religion, either natural or revealed. The apostles most of all condemned lies, and showed the inconsistency of lies with their doctrine: they would have been the most self-condemned persons had they propagated the truth by lies. It is a commendation of the Christian religion that it so well accords with natural religion, which is the foundation of it, that it so well accords with the Jewish religion, which contained the elements or rudiments of it. *No lie is of the truth;* frauds and impostures then are very unfit means to support and propagate the truth. I suppose it had been better with the state of religion if they had never been used. The result of them appears in the infidelity of our age; the detection of ancient pious frauds and wiles has almost run our age into atheism and irreligion; but the greatest actors and sufferers for the Christian revelation would assure us that *no lie is of the truth.*

III. The apostle further impleads and arraigns these seducers who had newly arisen. 1. They are *liars,* egregious opposers of sacred truth: *Who is a liar,* or the liar, the notorious liar of the time and age in which we live, *but he that denieth that Jesus is the Christ?* The great and pernicious lies that the father of lies, or of liars, spreads in the world, were of old, and usually are, falsehoods and errors relating to the person of Christ. There is no truth so sacred and fully attested but some or other will contradict or deny it. That Jesus of Nazareth was the Son and the Christ of God had been attested by heaven, and earth, and hell. It should seem that some, in the tremendous judgment of God, are given up to strong delusions. 2. They are direct enemies to God as well as to the Lord Christ: *He is antichrist who denieth the Father and the Son, v.* 22. He that opposes Christ denies the witness and testimony of the Father, and the seal that he hath given to his Son; *for him hath God the Father sealed,* John vi. 27. And he that denies the witness and testimony of the Father, concerning Jesus Christ denies that God is the Father of the Lord Jesus Christ, and consequently abandons the knowledge of God in Christ, and thereupon the whole revelation of God in Christ, and particularly of God in Christ *reconciling the world unto himself:* and therefore the apostle may well infer, *Whosoever denies the Son the same has not the Father* (*v.* 23); he has not the true knowledge of the Father, for the Son has most and best revealed him; he has no interest in the Father, in his favour, and grace, and salvation, *for none cometh to the Father but by the Son. But,* as some copies add, *he that acknowledgeth the Son has the Father also, v.* 23. As there is an intimate relation between the Father and the Son, so there is an inviolable union in the doctrine, knowledge, and interests of both; so that he who has the knowledge of, and right to, the Son, has the knowledge of, and right to, the Father also. Those that adhere to the Christian revelation hold the light and benefit of natural religion withal.

IV. Hereupon the apostle advises and persuades the disciples to continue in the old doctrine at first communicated to them: *Let that therefore abide in you which you have heard from the beginning, v.* 24. Truth is older than error. The truth concerning Christ, that was at first delivered to the saints, is not to be exchanged for novelties. So sure were the apostles of the truth of what they had delivered concerning Christ, and from him, that after all their toils and sufferings they were not willing to relinquish it. The Christian truth may plead antiquity, and be recommended thereby. This exhortation is enforced by these considerations:—

1. From the sacred advantage they will receive by adhering to the primitive truth and faith. (1.) They will continue thereby in holy union with God and Christ: *If that which you have heard from the beginning shall remain in you, you also shall continue in the Son and in the Father, v.* 24. It is the truth of Christ abiding in us that is the means of severing us from sin and uniting us to the Son of God, John xv. 3, 4. The Son is the medium or Mediator by whom we are united to the Father. What value then should we put upon gospel truth! (2.) They will thereby secure the promise of eternal life: *And this is the promise that he* (even God the Father, *ch.* v. 11) *hath promised us, even eternal life, v.* 25. Great is the promise that God makes to his faithful adherents. It is suitable to his own greatness, power, and goodness. It is *eternal life,* which none but God can give. The blessed God puts great value upon his Son, and the truth relating to him, when he is pleased to promise to those who continue in that truth (under the light, and power, and influence of it) *eternal life.* Then the exhortation aforesaid is enforced,

2. From the design of the apostle's writing to them. This letter is to fortify them against the deceivers of the age: "*These things have I written to you concerning those that seduce you* (*v.* 26), and therefore, if you continue not in what *you have heard from the beginning,* my writing and service will be in vain." We should beware lest the apostolical letters, yea, lest the whole scripture of God, should be to us insignificant and fruitless. *I have written to him the great things of my law* (and my gospel too), *but they were counted as a strange thing,* Hos. viii. 12.

3. From the instructive blessing they had received from heaven: *But the anointing which you have received from him abideth in you, v.* 27. True Christians have an inward confirmation of the divine truth they have imbibed: the Holy Spirit has imprinted it on their minds and hearts. It is meet that the Lord Jesus should have a constant witness in the hearts of his disciples. The unction, the pouring out of the gifts of grace upon sincere disciples, is a seal to the truth and doctrine of Christ, since none giveth that seal but God. *Now he who establisheth us with you* (and you with us) *in Christ, and hath anointed us, is God,* 2 Cor. i. 21. This sacred chrism, or divine unction, is commended on these accounts:—(1.) It is durable and lasting; oil or unguent is not so soon dried up as water: it *abideth in you, v.* 27. Divine illumination, in order to confirmation, must be something continued or constant. Temptations, snares, and seductions, arise. The anointing must abide. (2.) It is better than human instruction: "*And you need not that any man teach you, v.* 27. Not that this anointing will teach you without the appointed ministry. It could, if God so pleased; but it will not, though it will teach you better than we can: *And you need not that any man teach you, v.* 27. You were instructed by us before you were anointed; but now our teaching is nothing in comparison to that. *Who teacheth like him?*" Job xxxvi. 22. The divine unction does not supersede ministerial teaching, but surmount it. (3.) It is a sure evidence of truth, and all that it teaches is infallible truth: *But as the same anointing teacheth you of all things, and is truth, and is no lie, v.* 27. The Holy Spirit must needs be *the Spirit of truth,* as he is called, John xiv. 17. The instruction and illumination that he affords must needs be in and of the truth. The Spirit of truth will not lie; and he teacheth all things, that is, all things in the present

dispensation, all things necessary to our knowledge of God in Christ, and their glory in the gospel. And, (4.) It is of a conservative influence; it will preserve those in whom it abides against seducers and their seduction: "*And even as it hath taught you you shall abide in him, v.* 27. It teaches you to abide in Christ; and, as it teaches you, it secures you; it lays a restraint upon your minds and hearts, that you may not revolt from him. *And he that hath anointed us is God, who also hath sealed us* for himself, *and given the earnest of the Spirit in our hearts.*" 2 Cor. i. 21, 22.

28 And now, little children, abide in him; that, when he shall appear, we may have confidence, and not be ashamed before him at his coming.
29 If ye know that he is righteous, ye know that every one that doeth righteousness is born of him.

From the blessing of the sacred unction the apostle proceeds in his advice and exhortation to constancy in and with Christ: *And now, little children, abide in him, v.* 28. The apostle repeats his kind appellation, *little children,* which I suppose does not so much denote their diminutiveness as his affection, and therefore, I judge, may be rendered *dear children.* He would persuade by love, and prevail by endearment as well as by reason. "Not only the love of Christ, but the love of you, constrains us to inculcate your perseverance, and that *you would abide in him,* in the truth relating to his person, and in your union with him and allegiance to him." Evangelical privileges are obligatory to evangelical duties; and those that are anointed by the Lord Jesus are highly obliged to abide with him in opposition to all adversaries whatever. This duty of perseverance and constancy in trying times is strongly urged by the two following considerations:—1. From the consideration of his return at the great day of account: *That when he shall appear we may have confidence, and not be ashamed before him at his coming, v.* 28. It is here taken for granted that the Lord Jesus will come again. This was part of that truth they had heard from the beginning. And, when he shall come again, he will publicly appear, be manifested to all. When he was here before, he came privately, in comparison. He proceeded from a womb, and was introduced into a stable: but, when he shall come again, he will come from the opened heavens, and every eye shall see him; and then those who have continued with him throughout all their temptations shall have confidence, assurance, and joy, in the sight of him. They shall lift up their heads with unspeakable triumph, as knowing that their complete redemption comes along with him. On the contrary, those that have deserted him *shall be ashamed before him;* they shall be ashamed of themselves, ashamed of their unbelief, their cowardice, ingratitude, temerity, and folly, in forsaking so glorious a Redeemer. They shall be ashamed of their hopes, expectations, and pretences, and ashamed of all the wages of unrighteousness, by which they were induced to desert him: *That we may have confidence, and may not be ashamed.* The apostle includes himself in the number. "Let not us be ashamed of you," as well as, "you will not be ashamed of yourselves." Or *μὴ αἰσχυνθῶμεν ἀπ' αὐτοῦ—that we be not ashamed* (made ashamed, or put to shame) *by him at his coming.* At his public appearance he will shame all those who have abandoned him, he will disclaim all acquaintance with them, will cover them with shame and confusion, will abandon them to darkness, devils, and endless despair, by professing before men and angels that he is ashamed of them, Mark viii. 38. To the same advice and exhortation he proceeds, 2. From the consideration of the dignity of those who still adhere to Christ and his religion: *If you know that he is righteous, you know that every one that doeth righteousness is born of him, v.* 29. The particle here rendered *if* seems not to be *vox dubitantis,* but *concedentis;* not so much a conditional particle, as a suppositional one, if I may call it so, a note of allowance or concession, and so seems to be of the same import with our English *inasmuch,* or *whereas,* or *since.* So the sense runs more clearly: *Since you know that he is righteous, you know that every one that doeth righteousness is born of him.* He that doeth righteousness may here be justly enough assumed as another name for him that abideth in Christ. For he that abideth in Christ abideth in the law and love of Christ, and consequently in his allegiance and obedience to him; and so must do, or work, or practise, righteousness, or the parts of gospel holiness. Now such a one must needs *be born of him.* He is renewed by the Spirit of Christ, after the image of Christ, *created in Christ Jesus unto good works, which God hath fore-ordained that he should walk in them,* Eph. ii. 10. "*Since then you know that the Lord Christ is righteous* (righteous in his quality and capacity, the Lord our righteousness, and the Lord our sanctifier or our sanctification, as 1 Cor. i. 30), you cannot but know thereupon" (or know you, it is for your consideration and regard) "that he who by the continued practice of Christianity abideth in him is born of him." The new spiritual nature is derived from the Lord Christ. He that is constant to the practice of religion in trying times gives good evidence that he is born from above, from the Lord Christ. The Lord Christ is an everlasting Father. It is a great privilege and dignity to be born of him. Those that are so are the children of God. *To as many as received him to them gave he power to become the sons of God,* John i. 12. And this introduces the context of the following chapter.

CHAP. III.

The apostle here magnifies the love of God in our adoption, ver. 1, 2. He thereupon argues for holiness (ver. 3), and against sin, ver. 4—19. He presses brotherly love, ver. 11—18. How to assure our hearts before God, ver. 19—22. The precept of faith, ver. 23. And the good of obedience, ver. 24.

BEHOLD, what manner of love
the Father hath bestowed upon
us, that we should be called the sons
of God: therefore the world knoweth
us not, because it knew him not. 2
Beloved, now are we the sons of God,
and it doth not yet appear what we
shall be: but we know that, when he
shall appear, we shall be like him; for
we shall see him as he is. 3 And
every man that hath this hope in him
purifieth himself, even as he is pure.

The apostle, having shown the dignity of Christ's faithful followers, that they are born of him and thereby nearly allied to God, now here,

I. Breaks forth into the admiration of that grace that is the spring of such a wonderful vouchsafement: *Behold* (see you, observe) *what manner of love*, or how great love, *the Father hath bestowed upon us, that we should be called*, effectually called (he who calls things that are not makes them to be what they were not) *the sons of God!* The Father adopts all the children of the Son. The Son indeed calls them, and makes them his brethren; and thereby he confers upon them the power and dignity of the sons of God. It is wonderful condescending love of the eternal Father, that such as we should be made and called his sons—we who by nature are heirs of sin, and guilt, and the curse of God—we who by practice are children of corruption, disobedience, and ingratitude! Strange, that the holy God is not ashamed to be called our Father, and to call us his sons! Thence the apostle,

II. Infers the honour of believers above the cognizance of the world. Unbelievers know little of them. *Therefore* (or wherefore, upon this score) *the world knoweth us not, v.* 1. Little does the world perceive the advancement and happiness of the genuine followers of Christ. They are here exposed to the common calamities of earth and time; all things fall alike to them as to others, or rather they are subject to the greater sorrow, for they have often reason to say, *If in this life only we have hope in Christ, we are of all men most miserable*, 1 Cor. xv. 19. The unchristian world, therefore, that walks by sight, knows not their dignity, their privileges, the enjoyments they have in hand, nor what they are entitled to. Little does the world think that these poor, humble, contemned ones are the favourites of heaven, and will be inhabitants there ere long. And they may bear their case the better since their Lord was here unknown as well as they: *Because it knew him not, v.* 1. Little did the world think how great a person was once sojourning here, that the Maker of it was once an inhabitant of it. Little did the Jewish world think that the God of Abraham, Isaac, and Jacob, was one of their blood, and dwelt in their land; he came to his own, and his own received him not. He came to his own, and his own crucified him; but surely, *had they known him, they would not have crucified the Lord of glory*, 1 Cor. ii. 8. Let the followers of Christ be content with hard fare here, since they are in a land of strangers, among those who little know them, and their Lord was so treated before them. Then the apostle,

III. Exalts these persevering disciples in the prospect of the certain revelation of their state and dignity. Here, 1. Their present honourable relation is asserted: *Beloved* (you may well be our beloved, for you are beloved of God), *now are we the sons of God, v.* 2. We have the nature of sons by regeneration: we have the title, and spirit, and right to the inheritance of sons by adoption. *This honour have all the saints.* 2. The discovery of the bliss belonging and suitable to this relation is denied: *And it doth not yet appear what we shall be, v.* 2. The glory pertaining to the sonship and adoption is adjourned and reserved for another world. The discovery of it here would put a stop to the current of affairs that must now proceed. The sons of God must walk by faith, and live by hope. 3. The time of the revelation of the sons of God in their proper state and glory is determined; and that is when their elder brother comes to call and collect them all together: *But we know that when he shall appear we shall be like him.* The particle ἐὰν, usually translated *if*, is here well rendered *when;* for the Hebrew particle אם (to which this is thought to correspond) is observed so to signify, as Dr. Whitby has here noted; and not only is ἐὰν sometimes used for ὅταν, but some copies even here read ὅταν, *when.* And accordingly it seems proper so to render it in John xiv. 3, where we read it, *And if I go, and prepare a place;* but more naturally and properly, *When I shall have gone, and shall have prepared the place, I will come again, and receive you unto myself*, or παραλήψομαι—*I will take you along with myself, that where I am there you may be also.* When the head of the church, the only-begotten of the Father, shall appear, his members, the adopted of God, shall appear and be manifested together with him. They may then well wait in faith, hope, and earnest desire, for the revelation of the Lord Jesus; as even the creation itself waiteth for their perfection, *and the public manifestation of the sons of God*, Rom. viii. 19. The sons of God will be known and be made manifest by their likeness to their head: *They shall be like him*—like him in honour, and power, and glory. Their vile bodies shall be made like his glorious body; they shall be filled with life, light, and bliss from him. *When he, who is their life, shall appear, they also shall appear with him in glory,* Col. iii. 4. Then, 4. Their likeness to him is argued from the sight they shall have of him: *We shall be like him, for we shall see him as he is.* Their likeness will be the cause of that sight which they shall have of him. Indeed, all shall see him, but not as they do; not as *he is,* namely, to those in heaven. The wicked shall see him in his frowns, in the terror of his majesty, and the splendour of his avenging perfections; but these shall see him in the smiles and beauty of his face, in the correspondence and amiableness of his glory, in the harmony and agreeableness of his beatific perfections. Their likeness shall enable them to see him as the blessed do in heaven. Or the sight of him shall be the cause of their likeness; it shall be a transformative sight: they shall be transformed into the same image by the beatific view that they shall have of him. Then the apostle,

IV. Urges the engagement of these sons of God to the prosecution of holiness: *And every man that hath this hope in him purifies himself even as he is pure, v.* 3. The sons of God know that their Lord is holy and pure; he is of purer heart and eyes than to admit any pollution or impurity to dwell with him. Those then who hope to live with him must study the utmost purity from the world, and flesh, and sin; they must grow in grace and holiness. Not only does their Lord command them to do so, but their new nature inclines them so to do; yea, their hope of heaven will dictate and constrain them so to do. They know that their high priest is holy, harmless, and undefiled. They know that their God and Father is the high and holy one, that all the society is pure and holy, that their inheritance is an inheritance of saints in light. It is a contradiction to such hope to indulge sin and impurity. And therefore, as we are sanctified by faith, we must be sanctified by hope. That we may be saved by hope we must be purified by hope. It is the hope of hypocrites, and not of the sons of God, that makes an allowance for the gratification of impure desires and lusts.

4 Whosoever committeth sin transgresseth also the law: for sin is the
transgression of the law. 5 And ye
know that he was manifested to take
away our sins; and in him is no sin.
6 Whosoever abideth in him sinneth
not: whosoever sinneth hath not seen
him, neither known him. 7 Little
children, let no man deceive you: he
that doeth righteousness is righteous,
even as he is righteous. 8 He that
committeth sin is of the devil; for
the devil sinneth from the beginning.
For this purpose the Son of God was
manifested, that he might destroy the
works of the devil. 9 Whosoever is
born of God doth not commit sin; for
his seed remaineth in him: and he
cannot sin, because he is born of God.
10 In this the children of God are
manifest, and the children of the
devil: whosoever doeth not righteousness is not of God, neither he that
loveth not his brother.

The apostle, having alleged the believer's obligation to purity from his hope of heaven, and of communion with Christ in glory at the day of his appearance, now proceeds to fill his own mouth and the believer's mind with multiplied arguments against sin, and all communion with the impure unfruitful works of darkness. And so he reasons and argues,

I. From the nature of sin and the intrinsic evil of it. It is a contrariety to the divine law: *Whosoever committeth sin transgresseth also* (or *even) the law* (or, whosoever committeth sin even committeth enormity, or aberration from law, or from the law); *for sin is the transgression of the law,* or is lawlessness, *v.* 4. Sin is the destitution or privation of correspondence and agreement with the divine law, that law which is the transcript of the divine nature and purity, which contains his will for the government of the world, which is suitable to the rational nature, and enacted for the good of the world, which shows man the way of felicity and peace, and conducts him to the author of his nature and of the law. The current commission of sin now is the rejection of the divine law, and this is the rejection of the divine authority, and consequently of God himself

II. From the design and errand of the Lord Jesus in and to this world, which was to remove sin: *And you know that he was manifested to take away our sins, and in him is no sin, v.* 5. The Son of God appeared, and was known, in our nature; and he came to vindicate and exalt the divine law, and that by obedience to the precept, and by subjection and suffering under the penal sanction, under the curse of it. *He came therefore to take away our sins,* to take away the guilt of them by the sacrifice of himself, to take away the commission of them by implanting a new nature in us (for we are sanctified by virtue of his death), and to dissuade and save from it by his own example, *and* (or *for) in him was no sin;* or, he takes sin away, that he may conform us to himself, *and in him is no sin.* Those that expect communion with Christ above should study communion with him here in the utmost purity. And the Christian world should know and consider the great end of the Son of God's coming hither: it was to take away our sin: *And you know* (and this knowledge should be deep and effectual) *that he was manifested to take away our sins.*

III. From the opposition between sin and

a real union with or adhesion to the Lord Christ: *Whosoever abideth in him sinneth not, v.* 6. To sin here is the same as to commit sin (*v.* 8, 9), and to commit sin is to practise sin. He that abideth in Christ continues not in the practice of sin. As vital union with the Lord Jesus broke the power of sin in the heart and nature, so continuance therein prevents the regency and prevalence thereof in the life and conduct. Or the negative expression here is put for the positive: *He sinneth not,* that is, he is obedient, *he keeps the commandments* (in sincerity, and in the ordinary course of life) *and does those things that are pleasing in his sight,* as is said *v.* 22. Those that abide in Christ abide in their covenant with him, and consequently watch against the sin that is contrary thereto. They abide in the potent light and knowledge of him; and therefore it may be concluded *that he that sinneth* (abideth in the predominant practice of sin) *hath not seen him* (hath not his mind impressed with a sound evangelical discerning of him), *neither known him,* hath no experimental acquaintance with him. Practical renunciation of sin is the great evidence of spiritual union with, continuance in, and saving knowledge of, the Lord Christ.

IV. From the connection between the practice of righteousness and a state of righteousness, intimating withal that the practice of sin and a justified state are inconsistent; and this is introduced with a supposition that a surmise to the contrary is a gross deceit: "*Little children,* dear children, and as much children as you are, herein *let no man deceive you.* There will be those who will magnify your new light and entertainment of Christianity, who will make you believe that your knowledge, profession, and baptism, will excuse you from the care and accuracy of the Christian life. But beware of such self-deceit. *He that doeth righteousness is righteous.*" It may appear that righteousness may in several places of scripture be justly rendered *religion,* as Matt. v. 10, *Blessed are those that are persecuted for righteousness' sake,* that is, for religion's sake; 1 Pet. iii. 14, *But if you suffer for righteousness' sake* (religion's sake) *happy are you;* and 2 Tim. iii. 16, *All scripture,* or the whole scripture, *is given by inspiration of God, and is profitable for doctrine——and for instruction in righteousness,* that is, in the nature and branches of religion. To do righteousness then, especially being set in opposition to the doing, committing, or practising, of sin, is to practise religion. Now he who practiseth religion is righteous; he is the righteous person on all accounts; he is sincere and upright before God. The practice of religion cannot subsist without a principle of integrity and conscience. He has that righteousness which consists in pardon of sin and right to life, founded upon the imputation of the Mediator's righteousness. He has a title *to the crown of righteousness, which the righteous Judge will give,* according to his covenant and promise, *to those that love his appearing,* 2 Tim. iv. 8. He has communion with Christ, in conformity to the divine law, being in some measure practically righteous as he; and he has communion with him in the justified state, being now relatively righteous together with him.

V. From the relation between the sinner and the devil, and thereupon from the design and office of the Lord Christ against the devil. 1. From the relation between the sinner and the devil. As elsewhere sinners and saints are distinguished (though even saints are sinners largely so called), *so to commit sin* is here so to practise it as sinners do, that are distinguished from saints, to live under the power and dominion of it; and he who does so *is of the devil;* his sinful nature is inspired by, and agreeable and pleasing to, the devil; and he belongs to the party, and interest, and kingdom of the devil. It is he that is the author and patron of sin, and has been a practitioner of it, a tempter and instigator to it, even from the beginning of the world. And thereupon we must see how he argues. 2. From the design and office of the Lord Christ against the devil: *For this purpose the Son of God was manifested, that he might destroy the works of the devil, v.* 8. The devil has designed and endeavoured to ruin the work of God in this world. The Son of God has undertaken the holy war against him. He came into our world, and was manifested in our flesh, that he might conquer him and dissolve his works. Sin will he loosen and dissolve more and more, till he has quite destroyed it. Let not us serve or indulge what the Son of God came to destroy.

VI. From the connection between regeneration and the relinquishment of sin: *Whosoever is born of God doth not commit sin.* To be born of God is to be inwardly renewed, and restored to a holy integrity or rectitude of nature by the power of the Spirit of God. *Such a one committeth not sin,* does not work iniquity nor practise disobedience, which is contrary to his new nature and the regenerate complexion of his spirit; for, as the apostle adds, *his seed remaineth in him,* either the word of God in its light and power *remaineth in him* (as 1 Pet. i. 23, *Being born again, not of corruptible seed, but of incorruptible, by the word of God, which liveth and abideth for ever),* or, *that which is born of the Spirit is spirit;* the spiritual seminal principle of holiness remaineth in him. Renewing grace is an abiding principle. Religion, in the spring of it, is not an art, an acquired dexterity and skill, but a new nature. And thereupon the consequence is the regenerate person *cannot sin.* That he cannot commit an act of sin, I suppose no judicious interpreter understands. This would be contrary to *ch.* i. 9, where it is made our duty to confess our sins, and supposed that our privilege thereupon is to have our sins forgiven.

He therefore cannot sin, in the sense in which the apostle says, *he cannot commit sin.* He cannot continue in the course and practice of sin. He cannot so sin as to denominate him a sinner in opposition to a saint or servant of God. Again, he cannot sin comparatively, as he did before he was born of God, and as others do that are not so. And the reason is *because he is born of God,* which will amount to all this inhibition and impediment. 1. There is that light in his mind which shows him the evil and malignity of sin. 2. There is that bias upon his heart which disposes him to loathe and hate sin. 3. There is the spiritual seminal principle or disposition, that breaks the force and fulness of the sinful acts. They proceed not from such plenary power of corruption as they do in others, nor obtain that plenitude of heart, spirit, and consent, which they do in others. *The spirit lusteth against the flesh.* And therefore in respect to such sin it may be said, *It is no more I that do it, but sin that dwelleth in me.* It is not reckoned the person's sin, in the gospel account, where the bent and frame of the mind and spirit are against it. Then, 4. There is a disposition for humiliation and repentance for sin, when it has been committed. *He that is born of God cannot sin.* Here we may call to mind the usual distinction of natural and moral impotency. The unregenerate person is morally unable for what is religiously good. The regenerate person is happily disabled for sin. There is a restraint, an embargo (as we may say), laid upon his sinning powers. It goes against him sedately and deliberately to sin. We usually say of a person of known integrity, "He cannot lie, he cannot cheat, and commit other enormities." *How can I commit this great wickedness, and sin against God!* Gen. xxxix. 9. And so those who persist in a sinful life sufficiently demonstrate that they are not born of God.

VII. From the discrimination between the children of God and the children of the devil. They have their distinct characters. *In this the children of God are manifest and the children of the devil, v.* 10. In the world (according to the old distinction) there are the seed of God and the seed of the serpent. Now the seed of the serpent is known by these two signatures:—1. By neglect of religion: *Whosoever doeth not righteously* (omits and disregards the rights and dues of God; for religion is but our righteousness towards God, or giving him his due, and whosoever does not conscientiously do this) *is not of God,* but, on the contrary, of the devil. The devil is the father of unrighteous or irreligious souls. And, 2. By hatred of fellow-christians: *Neither he that loveth not his brother, v.* 10. True Christians are to be loved for God's and Christ's sake. Those who so love them not, but despise, and hate, and persecute them, have the serpentine nature still abiding in them.

11 For this is the message that ye
heard from the beginning, that we
should love one another. 12 Not as
Cain, *who* was of that wicked one, and
slew his brother. And wherefore
slew he him? Because his own works
were evil, and his brother's righteous.
13 Marvel not, my brethren, if the
world hate you.

The apostle, having intimated that one mark of the devil's children is hatred of the brethren, takes occasion thence,

I. To recommend fraternal Christian love, and that from the excellence, or antiquity, or primariness of the injunction relating thereto: *And this is the message* (the errand or charge) *which you heard from the beginning* (this came among the principal parts of practical Christianity), *that we should love one another, v.* 11. We should love the Lord Jesus, and value his love, and consequently love all the objects of it, and thereupon all our brethren in Christ.

II. To dissuade from what is contrary thereto, all ill-will towards the brethren, and that by the example of Cain. His envy and malignity should deter us from harbouring the like passion, and that upon these accounts:—1. It showed that he was as the first-born of the serpent's seed; even he, the eldest son of the first man, was of *the wicked one.* He imitated and resembled the first wicked one, the devil. 2. His ill-will had no restraint; it proceeded so far as to contrive and accomplish murder, and that of a near relation, and that in the beginning of the world, when there were but few to replenish it. *He slew his brother, v.* 12. Sin, indulged, knows no bound. And, 3. It proceeded so far, and had in it so much of the devil, that he murdered his brother for religion's sake. He was vexed with the superiority of Abel's service, and envied him the favour and acceptance he had with God. And for these he martyred his brother. *And wherefore slew he him? Because his own works were evil, and his brother's righteous, v.* 12. Ill-will will teach us to hate and revenge what we should admire and imitate. And then,

III. To infer that it is no wonder that good men are so served now: *Marvel not, my brethren, if the world hate you, v.* 13. The serpentine nature still continues in the world. The great serpent himself reigns as the God of this world. Wonder not then that the serpentine world hates and hisses at you who belong to that seed of the woman that is to bruise the serpent's head.

14 We know that we have passed
from death unto life, because we
love the brethren. He that loveth
not *his* brother abideth in death. 15
Whosoever hateth his brother is a

murderer: and ye know that no murderer hath eternal life abiding in him.
16 Hereby perceive we the love *of*
God, because he laid down his life for
us: and we ought to lay down *our*
lives for the brethren. 17 But whoso
hath this world's good, and seeth his
brother have need, and shutteth up
his bowels *of compassion* from him,
how dwelleth the love of God in
him? 18 My little children, let us
not love in word, neither in tongue;
but in deed and in truth. 19 And
hereby we know that we are of the
truth, and shall assure our hearts before him.

The beloved apostle can scarcely touch upon the mention of sacred love, but he must enlarge upon the enforcement of it, as here he does by divers arguments and incentives thereto; as,

I. That it is a mark of our evangelical justification, of our transition into a state of life: *We know that we have passed from death to life, because we love the brethren, v.* 14. We are by nature children of wrath and heirs of death. By the gospel (the gospel-covenant or promise) our state towards another world is altered and changed. We pass from death to life, from the guilt of death to the right of life; and this transition is made upon our believing in the Lord Jesus: *He that believeth on the Son hath everlasting life*, and he that believeth not *hath the wrath of God abiding on him*, John iii. 36. Now this happy change of state we may come to be assured of: *We know that we have passed from death to life;* we may know it by the evidences of our faith in Christ, of which this love to our brethren is one, which leads us to characterize this love that is such a mark of our justified state. It is not a zeal for a party in the common religion, or an affection for, or an affectation of, those who are of the same denomination and subordinate sentiments with ourselves. But this love,

1. Supposes a general love to mankind: the law of Christian love, in the Christian community, is founded on the catholic law, in the society of mankind, *Thou shalt love thy neighbour as thyself.* Mankind are to be loved principally on these two accounts:—(1.) As the excellent work of God, made by him, and made in wonderful resemblance of him. The reason that God assigns for the certain punishment of a murderer is a reason against our hatred of any of the brethren of mankind, and consequently a reason for our love to them: *for in the image of God made he man*, Gen. ix. 6. (2.) As being, in some measure, beloved in Christ. The whole *race of mankind—the gens humana*, should be considered as being, in distinction from fallen angels, a redeemed nation, as having a divine Redeemer designed, prepared, and given for them. *So God loved the world*, even this world, *that he gave his only-begotten Son, that whosoever believeth on him should not perish, but have everlasting life*, John iii. 16. A world so beloved of God should accordingly be loved by us. And this love will exert itself in earnest desires, and prayers, and attempts, for the conversion and salvation of the yet uncalled blinded world. *My heart's desire and prayer for Israel are that they may be saved.* And then this love will include all due love to enemies themselves.

2. It includes a peculiar love to the Christian society, to the catholic church, and that for the sake of her head, as being his body, as being redeemed, justified, and sanctified in and by him; and this love particularly acts and operates towards those of the catholic church that we have opportunity of being personally acquainted with or credibly informed of. They are not so much loved for their own sakes as for the sake of God and Christ, who have loved them. And it is God and Christ, or, if you will, the love of God and grace of Christ, that are beloved and valued in them and towards them. And so this is the issue of faith in Christ, and is thereupon a note of our passage from death to life.

II. The hatred of our brethren is, on the contrary, a sign of our deadly state, of our continuance under the legal sentence of death: *He that loveth not his brother* (his brother in Christ) *abideth in death, v.* 14. He yet stands under the curse and condemnation of the law. This the apostle argues by a clear syllogism: "You know that no murderer hath eternal life abiding in him; but he who hates his brother is a murderer; and therefore you cannot but know that he who hates his brother hath not eternal life abiding in him," *v.* 15. Or, *he abideth in death*, as it is expressed, *v.* 14, *Whosoever hateth his brother is a murderer;* for hatred of the person is, so far as it prevails, a hatred of life and welfare, and naturally tends to desire the extinction of it. Cain hated, and then slew, his brother Hatred will shut up the bowels of compassion from the poor brethren, and will thereby expose them to the sorrows of death. And it has appeared that hatred of the brethren has in all ages dressed them up in ill names, odious characters, and calumnies, and exposed them to persecution and the sword. No wonder, then, that he who has a considerable acquaintance with the heart of man, or is taught by him who fully knows it, who knows the natural tendency and issue of vile and violent passions, and knows withal the fulness of the divine law, declares him who hates his brother to be *a murderer*. Now he who by the frame and disposition of his heart is a murderer *cannot have eternal life abiding in him;* for he who is such must needs be carnally-minded, *and to be carnally-minded is death,* Rom. viii. 6. The apostle, by the expression of *having eternal life abiding in us,* may seem to mean the possession of an internal principle of endless life, according to that of the Saviour, *Whosoever drinketh of the water that I shall give him shall never thirst,* shall never be totally destitute thereof; *but the water that I shall give him shall be in him a well of water springing up into everlasting life,* John iv. 14. And thereupon some may be apt to surmise that the passing from death to life (*v.* 14) does not signify the relative change made in our justification of life, but the real change made in the regeneration to life; and accordingly that the abiding in death mentioned *v.* 14 is continuance in spiritual death, as it is usually called, or abiding in the corrupt deadly temper of nature. But as these passages more naturally denote the state of the person, whether adjudged to life or death, so the relative transition from death to life may well be proved or disproved by the possession or non-possession of the inward principle of eternal life, since washing from the guilt of sin is inseparably united with washing from the filth and power of sin. *But you are washed, but you are sanctified, but you are justified, in the name of the Lord Jesus, and by the Spirit of our God,* 1 Cor. vi. 11.

III. The example of God and Christ should inflame our hearts with this holy love: *Hereby perceive we the love of God, because he laid down his life for us; and we ought to lay down our lives for the brethren, v.* 16. The great God has given his Son to the death for us. But since this apostle has declared that the *Word was God,* and that *he became flesh for us,* I see not why we may not interpret this of God the Word. Here is the love of God himself, of him who in his own person is God, though not the Father, that he assumed a life, that he might lay it down for us! Here is the condescension, the miracle, the mystery of divine love, that God would redeem the church with his own blood! Surely we should love those whom God hath loved, and so loved; and we shall certainly do so if we have any love for God.

IV. The apostle, having proposed this flaming constraining example of love, and motive to it, proceeds to show us what should be the temper and effect of this our Christian love. And, 1. It must be, in the highest degree, so fervent as to make us willing to suffer even to death for the good of the church, for the safety and salvation of the dear brethren: *And we ought to lay down our lives for the brethren* (*v.* 16), either in our ministrations and services to them *(yea, and if I be offered upon the service and sacrifice of your faith, I joy and rejoice with you all*—I shall congratulate your felicity, Phil. ii. 17), or in exposing ourselves to hazards, when called thereto, for the safety and preservation of those that are more serviceable to the glory of God and the edification of the church than we can be. *Who have for my life laid down their own necks; unto whom not only I give thanks, but also all the churches of the Gentiles,* Rom. xvi. 4. How mortified should the Christian be to this life! How prepared to part with it! And how well assured of a better! 2. It must be, in the next degree, compassionate, liberal, and communicative to the necessities of the brethren: For *whoso hath this world's good, and seeth his brother have need, and shutteth up his bowels of compassion from him, how dwelleth the love of God in him? v.* 17. It pleases God that some of the Christian brethren should be poor, for the exercise of the charity and love of those that are rich. And it pleases the same God to give to some of the Christian brethren this world's good, that they may exercise their grace in communicating to the poor saints. And those who have this world's good must love a good God more, and their good brethren more, and be ready to distribute it for their sakes. It appears here that this love to the brethren is founded upon love to God, in that it is here called so by the apostle: *How dwelleth the love of God in him?* This love to the brethren is love to God in them; and where there is none of this love to them there is no true love to God at all. 3. I was going to intimate the third and lowest degree in the next verse; but the apostle has prevented me, by intimating that this last charitable communicative love, in persons of ability, is the lowest that can consist with the love of God. But there may be other fruits of this love; and therefore the apostle desires that in all it should be unfeigned and operative, as circumstances will allow: *My little children* (my dear children in Christ), *let us not love in word, neither in tongue, but in deed and in truth, v.* 18. Compliments and flatteries become not Christians; but the sincere expressions of sacred affection, and the services or labours of love, do. Then,

V. This love will evince our sincerity in religion, and give us hope towards God: *And hereby we know that we are of the truth, and shall assure our hearts before him, v.* 19. It is a great happiness to be assured of our integrity in religion. Those that are so assured may have holy boldness or confidence towards God; they may appeal to him from the censures and condemnation of the world. The way to arrive at the knowledge of our own truth and uprightness in Christianity, and to secure our inward peace, is to abound in love and in the works of love towards the Christian brethren.

20 For if our heart condemn us,
God is greater than our heart, and
knoweth all things. 21 Beloved, if
our heart condemn us not, *then* have
we confidence toward God. 22 And
whatsoever we ask, we receive of him,
because we keep his commandments,

and do those things that are pleasing in his sight.

The apostle, having intimated that there may be, even among us, such a privilege as an assurance or sound persuasion of heart towards God, proceeds here,

I. To establish the court of conscience, and to assert the authority of it: *For, if our heart condemn us, God is greater than our heart, and knoweth all things, v.* 20. Our heart here is our self-reflecting judicial power, that noble excellent ability whereby we can take cognizance of ourselves, of our spirits, our dispositions, and actions, and accordingly pass a judgment upon our state towards God; and so it is the same with conscience, or the power of moral self-consciousness. This power can act as witness, judge, and executioner of judgment; it either accuses or excuses, condemns or justifies; it is set and placed in this office by God himself: *the spirit of man,* thus capacitated and empowered, *is the candle of the Lord,* a luminary lighted and set up by the Lord, *searching all the inward parts of the belly,* taking into scrutiny and viewing the *penetralia—the private recesses* and secret transactions of the inner man, Prov. xx. 27. Conscience is God's vicegerent, calls the court in his name, and acts for him. *The answer of a good conscience towards God,* 1 Pet. iii. 21. God is chief Judge of the court: *If our heart condemn us God is greater than our heart,* superior to our heart and conscience in power and judgment; hence the act and judgment of the court are the act and judgment of God; as, 1. If conscience condemn us, God does so too: *For, if our heart condemn us, God is greater than our heart, and knoweth all things, v.* 20. God is a greater witness than our conscience, and knoweth more against us than it does: *he knoweth all things;* he is a greater Judge than conscience; for, as he is supreme, so his judgment shall stand, and shall be fully and finally executed. This seems to be the design of another apostle when he says, *For I know nothing by myself,* that is, in the case wherein I am censured by some. "I am not conscious of any guile, or allowed unfaithfulness, in my stewardship and ministry. *Yet am I not hereby justified;* it is not by my own conscience that I must ultimately stand or fall; the justification or justifying sentence of my conscience, or self-consciousness, will not determine the controversy between you and me; as you do not appeal to its sentence, so neither will you be determined by its decision; *but he that judgeth me* (supremely and finally judgeth me), and by whose judgment you and I must be determined, *is the Lord,*" 1 Cor. iv. 4. Or, 2. If conscience acquit us, God does so too: *Beloved, if our heart condemn us not, then have we confidence towards God* (*v.* 21), then have we assurance that he accepts us now, and will acquit us in the great day of account. But, possibly, some presumptuous soul may here say, "I am glad of this; my heart does not condemn me, and therefore I may conclude God does not." As, on the contrary, upon the foregoing verse, some pious trembling soul will be ready to cry out, "God forbid! My heart or conscience condemns me, and must I then infallibly expect the condemnation of God?" But let such know that the errors of the witness are not here reckoned as the acts of the court; ignorance, error, prejudice, partiality, and presumption, may be said to be faults of the officers of the court, or of the attendants of the judge (as the mind, the will, appetite, passion, sensual disposition, or disordered brain), or of the jury, who give a false verdict, not of the judge itself; *conscience—συνείδησις,* is properly *self-consciousness.* Acts of ignorance and error are not acts of self-consciousness, but of some mistaken power; and the court of conscience is here described in its process, according to the original constitution of it by God himself, according to which process what is bound in conscience is bound in heaven; let conscience therefore be heard, be well-informed, and diligently attended to.

II. To indicate the privilege of those who have a good conscience towards God. They have interest in heaven and in the court above; their suits are heard there: *And whatsoever we ask we receive of him, v.* 22. It is supposed that the petitioners do not desire, or do not intend to desire, any thing that is contrary to the honour and glory of the court or to their own intended spiritual good, and then they may depend upon receiving the good things they ask for; and this supposition may well be made concerning the petitioners, or they may well be supposed to receive the good things they ask for, considering their qualification and practice: *Because we keep his commandments, and do those things that are pleasing in his sight, v.* 22. Obedient souls are prepared for blessings, and they have promise of audience; those who commit things displeasing to God cannot expect that he should please them in hearing and answering their prayers, Ps. lxvi. 18; Prov. xxviii. 9.

23 And this is his commandment,
That we should believe on the name
of his Son Jesus Christ, and love one
another, as he gave us commandment. 24 And he that keepeth his
commandments dwelleth in him, and
he in him. And hereby we know
that he abideth in us, by the Spirit
which he hath given us.

The apostle, having mentioned keeping the commandments, and pleasing God, as the qualification of effectual petitioners in and with Heaven, here suitably proceeds,

I. To represent to us what those commandments primarily and summarily are;

they are comprehended in this double one: *And this is his commandment, That we should believe on the name of his Son Jesus Christ, and love one another, as he gave us commandment, v.* 23. To believe on the name of his Son Jesus Christ is, 1. To discern what he is, according to his name, to have an intellectual view of his person and office, as the Son of God, and the anointed Saviour of the world. *That every one that seeth the Son, and believeth on him, may have everlasting life,* John vi. 40. 2. To approve him in judgment and conscience, in conviction and consciousness of our case, as one wisely and wonderfully prepared and adapted for the whole work of eternal salvation. 3. To consent to him, and acquiesce in him, as our Redeemer and recoverer unto God. 4. To trust to him, and rely upon him, for the full and final discharge of his saving office. *Those that know thy name will put their trust in thee,* Ps. ix. 10. *I know whom I have believed, and I am persuaded that he is able to keep that which I have committed unto him against that day,* 2 Tim. i. 12. This faith is a needful requisite to those who would be prevalent petitioners with God, because it is by the Son that we must come to the Father; through his grace and righteousness our persons must be accepted or ingratiated with the Father (Eph. i. 6), through his purchase all our desired blessings must come, and through his intercession our prayers must be heard and answered. This is the first part of the commandment that must be observed by acceptable worshippers; the second is that we *love one another, as he gave us commandment, v.* 23. The command of Christ should be continually before our eyes. Christian love must possess our soul when we go to God in prayer. To this end we must remember that our Lord obliges us, (1.) To forgive those who offend us (Matt. vi. 14), and, (2.) To reconcile ourselves to those whom we have offended, Matt. v. 23, 24. As good-will to men was proclaimed from heaven, so good-will to men, and particularly to the brethren, must be carried in the hearts of those who go to God and heaven.

II. To represent to us the blessedness of obedience to these commands. The obedient enjoy communion with God: *And he that keepeth his commandments,* and particularly those of faith and love, *dwelleth in him, and he in him, v.* 24. We dwell in God by a happy relation to him, and spiritual union with him, through his Son, and by a holy converse with him; and God dwells in us by his word, and our faith fixed on him, and by the operations of his Spirit. Then there occurs the trial of his divine inhabitation: *And hereby we know that he abideth in us, by the Spirit which he hath given us* (*v.* 24), by the sacred disposition and frame of soul that he hath conferred upon us, which being a spirit of faith in God and Christ, and of love to God and man, appears to be of God.

CHAP. IV.

In this chapter the apostle exhorts to try spirits (ver. 1), gives a note to try by (ver. 2, 3), shows who are of the world and who of God (ver. 4—6), urges Christian love by divers considerations (ver. 7—16), describes our love to God, and the effect of it, ver. 17—21.

BELOVED, believe not every
spirit, but try the spirits whether
they are of God: because many false
prophets are gone out into the world.
2 Hereby know ye the Spirit of God:
Every spirit that confesseth that
Jesus Christ is come in the flesh is
of God. 3 And every spirit that confesseth not that Jesus Christ is come
in the flesh is not of God: and this
is that *spirit* of antichrist, whereof
ye have heard that it should come;
and even now already is it in the world.

The apostle, having said that God's dwelling in and with us may be known by *the Spirit that he hath given us,* intimates that that Spirit may be discerned and distinguished from other spirits that appear in the world; and so here,

I. He calls the disciples, to whom he writes, to caution and scrutiny about the spirits and spiritual professors that had now risen. 1. To caution: "*Beloved, believe not every spirit;* regard not, trust not, follow not, every pretender to the Spirit of God, or every professor of vision, or inspiration, or revelation from God." Truth is the foundation of simulation and counterfeits; there had been real communications from the divine Spirit, and therefore others pretended thereto. God will take the way of his own wisdom and goodness, though it may be liable to abuse; he has sent inspired teachers to the world, and given us a supernatural revelation, though others may be so evil and so impudent as to pretend the same; every pretender to the divine Spirit, or to inspiration, and extraordinary illumination thereby, is not to be believed. Time was when the spiritual man (the man of the Spirit, who made a great noise about, and boast of, the Spirit) was mad, Hos. ix. 7. 2. To scrutiny, to examination of the claims that are laid to the Spirit: *But try the spirits, whether they be of God, v.* 1. God has given of his Spirit in these latter ages of the world, but not to all who profess to come furnished therewith; to the disciples is allowed a judgment of discretion, in reference to the spirits that would be believed and trusted in the affairs of religion. A reason is given for this trial: *Because many false prophets have gone out into the world, v.* 1. There being much about the time of our Saviour's appearance in the world a general expectation among the Jews of a Redeemer to Israel, and the humiliation, spiritual reformation, and sufferings of the Saviour being taken as a prejudice against him, others were induced to set up as prophets and messiahs to Israel, according to the Saviour's prediction, Matt. xxiv. 23, 24. It should not seem strange to us that false teachers set themselves up in the church: it was so in the apostles' times; fatal is the spirit of delusion, sad that men should vaunt themselves for prophets and inspired preachers that are by no means so!

II. He gives a test whereby the disciples may try these pretending spirits. These spirits set up for prophets, doctors, or dictators in religion, and so they were to be tried by their doctrine; and the test whereby in that day, or in that part of the world where the apostle now resided (for in various seasons, and in various churches, tests were different), must be this: *Hereby know you the Spirit of God, Every spirit that confesseth that Jesus Christ has come in the flesh* (or *that confesseth Jesus Christ that came in the flesh) is of God, v.* 2. Jesus Christ is to be confessed as the Son of God, the eternal life and Word, that was with the Father from the beginning; as the Son of God that came into, and came in, our human mortal nature, and therein suffered and died at Jerusalem. He who confesses and preaches this, by a mind supernaturally instructed and enlightened therein, does it by the Spirit of God, or God is the author of that illumination. On the contrary, "*Every spirit that confesseth not that Jesus Christ has come in the flesh* (or *Jesus Christ that came in the flesh) is not of God, v.* 3. God has given so much testimony to Jesus Christ, who was lately here in the world, and in *the flesh* (or in a fleshly body like ours), though now in heaven, that you may be assured that any impulse or pretended inspiration that contradicts this is far from being from heaven and of God." The sum of revealed religion is comprehended in the doctrine concerning Christ, his person and office. We see then the aggravation of a systematic opposition to him and it. *And this is that spirit of antichrist whereof you have heard that it should come, and even now already is it in the world, v.* 3. It was foreknown by God that antichrists would arise, and antichristian spirits oppose his Spirit and his truth; it was foreknown also that one eminent antichrist would arise, and make a long and fatal war against the Christ of God, and his institution, and honour, and kingdom in the world. This great antichrist would have his way prepared, and his rise facilitated, by other less antichrists, and the spirit of error working and disposing men's minds for him: the antichristian spirit began betimes, even in the apostles' days. Dreadful and unsearchable is the judgment of God, that persons should be given over to an antichristian spirit, and to such darkness and delusion as to set themselves against the Son of God and all the testimony that the Father hath given to the Son! But we have been forewarned that such opposition would arise; we should therefore cease to be offended, and the more we see the word of Christ fulfilled the more confirmed we should be in the truth of it.

4 Ye are of God, little children,
and have overcome them: because
greater is he that is in you, than he
that is in the world. 5 They are of
the world: therefore speak they of
the world, and the world heareth
them. 6 We are of God: he that
knoweth God heareth us; he that is
not of God heareth not us. Hereby
know we the spirit of truth, and the
spirit of error.

In these verses the apostle encourages the disciples against the fear and danger of this seducing antichristian spirit, and that by such methods as these:—1. He assures them of a more divine principle in them: "*You are of God, little children, v.* 4. *You are God's little children. We are of God, v.* 6. *We are born of God,* taught of God, anointed of God, and so secured against infectious fatal delusions. God has his chosen, who shall not be mortally seduced." 2. He gives them hope of victory: "*And have overcome them, v.* 4. You have hitherto overcome these deceivers and their temptations, and there is good ground of hope that you will do so still, and that upon these two accounts:"—(1.) "There is a strong preserver within you: *Because greater is he that is in you than he that is in the world, v.* 4. The Spirit of God dwells in you, and that Spirit is more mighty than men or devils." It is a great happiness to be under the influence of the Holy Ghost. (2.) "You are not of the same temper with these deceivers. The Spirit of God hath framed your mind for God and heaven; *but they are of the world.* The spirit that prevails in them leads them to this world; their heart is addicted thereto; they study the pomp, the pleasure, and interest of the world: *and therefore speak they of the world;* they profess a worldly messiah and saviour; they project a worldly kingdom and dominion; the possessions and treasures of the world would they engross to themselves, forgetting that the true Redeemer's *kingdom is not of this world.* This worldly design procures them proselytes: *The world heareth them, v.* 5. They are followed by such as themselves: the world will love its own, and its own will love it. But those are in a fair way to conquer pernicious seductions who have conquered the love of this seducing world." Then, 3. He represents to them that though their company might be the smaller, yet it was the better; they had more divine and holy knowledge: "*He that knoweth God heareth us.* He who knows the purity and holiness of God, the love and grace of God, the truth and faithfulness of God, the ancient word and prophecies of God, the signals and testimonials of God, must know that he is with us; and he who knows this will attend to us, and abide with us." He that is well furnished with natural religion will the more faithfully cleave to Christianity. *He that knoweth God* (in his natural and moral excellences, revelations, and works) *heareth us, v.* 6. As, on the contrary, "*He that is not of God heareth not us.* He who knows not God regards not us. He that is not *born of God* (walking according to his natural disposition) walks not with us. The further any are from God (as appears in all ages) the further they are from Christ and his faithful servants; and the more addicted persons are to this world the more remote they are from the spirit of Christianity. Thus you have a distinction between us and others: *Hereby know we the Spirit of truth and the spirit of error, v.* 6. This doctrine concerning the Saviour's person leading you from the world to God is a signature of *the Spirit of truth,* in opposition to *the spirit of error.* The more pure and holy any doctrine is the more likely is it to be of God."

7 Beloved, let us love one another:
for love is of God; and every one
that loveth is born of God, and
knoweth God. 8 He that loveth not
knoweth not God; for God is love.
9 In this was manifested the love of
God toward us, because that God
sent his only begotten Son into the
world, that we might live through
him. 10 Herein is love, not that we
loved God, but that he loved us, and
sent his Son *to be* the propitiation for
our sins. 11 Beloved, if God so
loved us, we ought also to love one
another. 12 No man hath seen God
at any time. If we love one another,
God dwelleth in us, and his love is
perfected in us. 13 Hereby know
we that we dwell in him, and he in us,
because he hath given us of his Spirit.

As *the Spirit of truth* is known by doctrine (thus spirits are to be tried), it is known by love likewise; and so here follows a strong fervent exhortation to holy Christian love: *Beloved, let us love one another, v.* 7. The apostle would unite them in his love, that he might unite them in love to each other: "*Beloved,* I beseech you, by the love I bear to you, that you put on unfeigned mutual love." This exhortation is pressed and urged with variety of argument: as,

I. From the high and heavenly descent of love: *For love is of God.* He is the fountain, author, parent, and commander of love; it is the sum of his law and gospel: *And every one that loveth* (whose spirit is framed to judicious holy love) *is born of God, v.* 7. The Spirit of God is the Spirit of love. The new nature in the children of God is the offspring of his love: and the temper and complexion of it is love. *The fruit of the Spirit is love,* Gal. v. 22. Love comes down from heaven.

II. Love argues a true and just apprehension of the divine nature: *He that loveth knoweth God, v.* 7. *He that loveth not knoweth not God, v.* 8. What attribute of the divine Majesty so clearly shines in all the world as his communicative goodness, which is love. The wisdom, the greatness, the harmony, and usefulness of the vast creation, which so fully demonstrate his being, do at the same time show and prove his love; and natural reason, inferring and collecting the nature and excellence of the most absolute perfect being, must collect and find that he is most highly good: and *he that loveth not* (is not quickened by the knowledge he hath of God to the affection and practice of love) *knoweth not God;* it is a convictive evidence that the sound and due knowledge of God dwells not in such a soul; his love must needs shine among his primary brightest perfections; *for God is love* (*v.* 8), his nature and essence are love, his will and works are primarily love. Not that this is the only conception we ought to have of him; we have found that he *is light as well as love* (*ch.* i. 5), and God is principally love to himself, and he has such perfections as arise from the necessary love he must bear to his necessary existence, excellence, and glory; but love is natural and essential to the divine Majesty: *God is love.* This is argued from the display and demonstration that he hath given of it; as, 1. That he hath loved us, such as we are: *In this was manifest the love of God towards us* (*v.* 9), towards us mortals, us ungrateful rebels. *God commendeth his love towards us, in that, while we were yet sinners, Christ died for us,* Rom. v. 8. Strange that God should love impure, vain, vile, dust and ashes! 2. That he has loved us at such a rate, at such an incomparable value as he has given for us; he has given his own, only-beloved, blessed Son for us: *Because that God sent his only-begotten Son into the world, that we might live through him, v.* 9. This person is in some peculiar distinguishing way the Son of God; he is the only-begotten. Should we suppose him begotten as a creature or created being, he is not the only-begotten. Should we suppose him a natural necessary eradiation from the Father's glory or glorious essence or substance, he must be the only-begotten: and then it will be a mystery and miracle of divine love that such a Son should be sent into our world for us! It may be well said, *So* (wonderfully, so amazingly, so incredibly) *God loved the world.* 3. That God loved us first, and in the circumstances in which we lay: *Herein is love* (unusual unprecedented love), *not that we loved God, but that he loved us, v.* 10. He loved us, when we had no love for him, when we lay in our guilt, misery, and blood, when we were undeserving, ill-deserving, polluted, and unclean, and wanted to be washed from our sins in sacred blood. 4. That he gave us his Son for such service and such an end. (1.) For such service, *to be the propitiation for our sins;* consequently to die for us, to die under the law and curse of God, to *bear our sins in his own body,* to be crucified, to be wounded in his soul, and pierced in his side, to be dead and buried for us (*v.* 10); and then, (2.) For such an end, for such a good and beneficial end to us—*that we might live through him* (*v.* 9), might live for ever through him, might live in heaven, live with God, and live in eternal glory and blessedness with him and through him: O what love is here! Then,

III. Divine love to the brethren should constrain ours: *Beloved* (I would adjure you by your interest in my love to remember), *if God so loved us, we ought also to love one another, v.* 11. This should be an invincible argument. The example of God should press us. *We should be followers* (or imitators) *of him, as his dear children.* The objects of the divine love should be the objects of ours. Shall we refuse to love those whom the eternal God hath loved? We should be admirers of his love, and lovers of his love (of the benevolence and complacency that are in him), and consequently lovers of those whom he loves. The general love of God to the world should induce a universal love among mankind. *That you may be the children of your Father who is in heaven; for he maketh his sun to rise on the evil and on the good, and sendeth his rain on the just and on the unjust,* Matt. v. 45. The peculiar love of God to the church and to the saints should be productive of a peculiar love there: *If God so loved us, we ought* surely (in some measure suitably thereto) *to love one another.*

IV. The Christian love is an assurance of the divine inhabitation: *If we love one another, God dwelleth in us, v.* 12. Now God dwelleth in us, not by any visible presence, or immediate appearance to the eye *(no man hath seen God at any time, v.* 12), but by his Spirit (*v.* 13); or, "*No man hath seen God at any time;* he does not here present himself to our eye or to our immediate intuition, and so he does not in this way demand and exact our love; but he demands and expects it in that way in which he has thought meet to deserve and claim it, and that is in the illustration that he has given of himself and of his love (and thereupon of his loveliness too) in the catholic church, and particularly in the brethren, the members of that church. In them, and in his appearance for them and with them, is God to be loved; and thus, *if we love one another, God dwelleth in us.* The sacred lovers of the brethren are the temples of God; the divine Majesty has a peculiar residence there."

V. Herein the divine love attains a considerable end and accomplishment in us: "*And his love is perfected in us, v.* 12. It has obtained its completion in and upon us. God's love is not perfected in him, but in and with us. His love could not be designed to be ineffectual and fruitless upon us; when its proper genuine end and issue are attained and produced thereby, it may be said to be perfected; so faith is perfected by its works, and love perfected by its operations. When the divine love has wrought us to the same image, to the love of God, and thereupon to the love of the brethren, the children of God, for his sake, it is therein and so far perfected and completed, though this love of ours is not at present perfect, nor the ultimate end of the divine love to us." How ambitious should we be of this fraternal Christian love, when God reckons his own love to us perfected thereby! To this the apostle, having mentioned the high favour of God's dwelling in us, subjoins the note and character thereof: *Hereby know we that we dwell in him, and he in us, because he hath given us of his Spirit, v.* 13. Certainly this mutual inhabitation is something more noble and great than we are well acquainted with or can declare. One would think that to speak of God dwelling in us, and we in him, were to use words too high for mortals, had not God gone before us therein. What this indwelling imports has been briefly explained on *ch.* iii. 24. What it fully is must be left to the revelation of the blessed world. But this mutual inhabitation we know, says the apostle, *because he hath given us of his Spirit;* he has lodged the image and fruit of his Spirit in our hearts (*v.* 13), and *the Spirit that he hath given us* appears to be his, or of him, since it is *the Spirit of power,* of zeal and magnanimity for God, *of love* to God and man, *and of a sound mind,* of an understanding well instructed in the affairs of God and religion, and his kingdom among men, 2 Tim. i. 7.

14 And we have seen and do testify
that the Father sent the Son *to be*
the Saviour of the world. 14 Whosoever shall confess that Jesus is the
Son of God, God dwelleth in him,
and he in God. 16 And we have
known and believed the love that God
hath to us. God is love; and he
that dwelleth in love dwelleth in God,
and God in him.

Since faith in Christ works love to God, and love to God must kindle love to the brethren, the apostle here confirms the prime article of the Christian faith as the foundation of such love. Here,

I. He proclaims the fundamental article of the Christian religion, which is so representative of the love of God: *And we have seen, and do testify, that the Father sent the Son to be the Saviour of the world, v.* 14. We here see, 1. The Lord Jesus's relation to God; he is Son to the Father, such a Son as no one else is, and so as to be God with the Father. 2. His relation and office towards us—*the Saviour of the world;* he saves us by his death, example, intercession, Spirit, and power against the enemies of our salvation. 3. The ground on which he became so—by the mission of him: *The Father sent the Son,* he decreed and willed his coming hither, in and with the consent of the Son. 4. The apostle's assurance of this—he and his brethren had seen it; they had seen the Son of God in his human nature, in his holy converse and works, in his transfiguration on the mount, and in his death, resurrection from the dead, and royal ascent to heaven; they had so seen him as to be satisfied that he was the *only-begotten of the Father, full of grace and truth.* 5. The apostle's attestation of this, in pursuance of such evidence: "*We have seen and do testify.* The weight of this truth obliges us to testify it; the salvation of the world lies upon it. The evidence of the truth warrants us to testify it; our eyes, and ears, and hands, have been witnesses of it." Thereupon,

II. The apostle states the excellency, or the excellent privilege attending the due acknowledgment of this truth: *Whosoever shall confess that Jesus is the Son of God, God dwelleth in him, and he in God, v.* 15. This confession seems to include faith in the heart as the foundation of it, acknowledgment with the mouth to the glory of God and Christ, and profession in the life and conduct, in opposition to the flatteries or frowns of the world. Thus *no man says that Jesus is the Lord but by the Holy Ghost,* by the external attestation and internal operation of the Holy Ghost, 1 Cor. xii. 3. And so he who thus confesses Christ, and God in him, is enriched with or possessed by the Spirit of God, and has a complacential knowledge of God and much holy enjoyment of him. Then,

III. The apostle applies this in order to the excitation of holy love. God's love is thus seen and exerted in Christ Jesus; *and* thus *have we known and believed the love that God hath to us, v.* 16. The Christian revelation is, what should endear it to us, the revelation of the divine love; the articles of our revealed faith are but so many articles relating to the divine love. The history of the Lord Christ is the history of God's love to us; all his transactions in and with his Son were but testifications of his love to us, and means to advance us to the love of God: *God was in Christ reconciling the world unto himself,* 2 Cor. v. 19. Hence we may learn,

1. That *God is love* (*v.* 16); he is essential boundless love; he has incomparable incomprehensible love for us of this world, which he has demonstrated in the mission and mediation of his beloved Son. It is the great objection and prejudice against the Christian revelation that the love of God should be so strange and unaccountable as to give his own eternal Son for us; it is the prejudice of many against the eternity and the deity of the Son that so great a person should be given for us. It is, I confess, mysterious and unsearchable; but there are *unsearchable riches in Christ.* It is a pity that the vastness of the divine love should be made a prejudice against the revelation and the belief of it. But what will not God do when he designs to demonstrate the height of any perfection of his? When he would show somewhat of his power and wisdom, he makes such a world as this; when he would show more of his grandeur and glory, he makes heaven for the ministering spirits that are before the throne. What will he not do then when he designs to demonstrate his love, and to demonstrate his highest love, or that he himself is love, or that love is one of the most bright, dear, transcendent, operative excellences of his unbounded nature; and to demonstrate this not only to us, but to the angelic world, and to the principalities and powers above, and this not for our surprise for a while, but for the admiration, and praise, and adoration, and felicity, of our most exalted powers to all eternity? What will not God then do? Surely then it will look more agreeable to the design, and grandeur, and pregnancy of his love (if I may so call it) to give an eternal Son for us, than to make a Son on purpose for our relief. In such a dispensation as that of giving a natural, essential, eternal Son for us and to us, he will commend his love to us indeed; and what will not the God of love do when he designs to commend his love, and to commend it in the view of heaven, and earth, and hell, and when he will commend himself and recommend himself to us, and to our highest conviction, and also affection, as love itself? And what if it should appear at last (which I shall only offer to the consideration of the judicious) that the divine love, and particularly God's love in Christ, should be the foundation of the glories of heaven, in the present enjoyment of those ministering spirits that comported with it, and of the salvation of this world, and of the torments of hell? This last will seem most strange. But what if therein it should appear not only that God is love to himself, in vindicating his own law, and government, and love, and glory, but that the damned ones are made so, or are so punished, (1.) Because they despised the love of God already manifested and exhibited. (2.) Because they refused to be beloved in what was further proposed and promised. (3.) Because they made themselves unmeet to be the objects of divine complacency and delight? If the conscience of the damned should accuse them of these things, and especially of rejecting the highest instance of divine love, and if the far greatest part of the intelligent creation should be everlastingly blessed through the highest instance of the divine love, then may it well be inscribed upon the whole creation of God, *God is love.*

2. That hereupon *he that dwelleth in love dwelleth in God, and God in him, v.* 16. There is great communion between the God of love and the loving soul; that is, him who loves the creation of God, according to its different relation to God, and reception from him and interest in him. He that dwells in sacred love has *the love of God shed abroad upon his heart,* has the impress of God upon his spirit, the Spirit of God sanctifying and sealing him, lives in the meditation, views, and tastes of the divine love, and will ere long go to dwell with God for ever.

17 Herein is our love made perfect,
that we may have boldness in the
day of judgment: because as he is,
so are we in this world. 18 There
is no fear in love; but perfect love
casteth out fear: because fear hath
torment. He that feareth is not
made perfect in love. 19 We love
him, because he first loved us. 20
If a man say, I love God, and hateth
his brother, he is a liar: for he that
loveth not his brother whom he hath
seen, how can he love God whom he
hath not seen? 21 And this commandment have we from him, That he
who loveth God love his brother also.

The apostle, having thus excited and enforced sacred love from the great pattern and motive of it, the love that is and dwells in God himself, proceeds to recommend it further by other considerations; and he recommends it in both the branches of it, both as love to God, and love to our brother or Christian neighbour.

I. As love to God, to the *primum amabile—the first and chief of all amiable beings and objects,* who has the confluence of all beauty, excellence, and loveliness, in himself, and confers on all other beings whatever renders them good and amiable. Love to God seems here to be recommended on these accounts:—1. It will give us peace and satisfaction of spirit in the day when it will be most needed, or when it will be the greatest pleasure and blessing imaginable: *Herein is our love made perfect, that we may have boldness in the day of judgment, v.* 17. There must be a day of universal judgment. Happy they who shall have holy fiducial boldness before the Judge at that day, who shall be able to lift up their heads, and to look him in the face, as knowing he is their friend and advocate! Happy they who have holy boldness and assurance in the prospect of that day, who look and wait for it, and for the Judge's appearance! So do, and so may do, the lovers of God. Their love to God assures them of God's love to them, and consequently of the friendship of the Son of God; the more we love our friend, especially when we are sure that he knows it, the more we can trust his love. As God is good and loving, and faithful to his promise, so we can easily be persuaded of his love, and the happy fruits of his love, when we can say, *Thou that knowest all things knowest that we love thee. And hope maketh not ashamed;* our hope, conceived by the consideration of God's love, will not disappoint us, *because the love of God is shed abroad in our hearts by the Holy Ghost that is given to us,* Rom. v. 5. Possibly here by the love of God may be meant our *love to God,* which is *shed abroad upon our hearts by the Holy Ghost;* this is the foundation of our hope, or of our assurance that our hope will hold good at last. Or, if by the love of God be meant the sense and apprehension of his love to us, yet this must suppose or include us as lovers of him in this case; and indeed the sense and evidence of his love to us do shed abroad upon our hearts love to him; and thereupon we have confidence towards him and peace and joy in him. He will give the crown of righteousness to all that love his appearing. And we have this boldness towards Christ because of our conformity to him: *Because as he is so are we in this world, v.* 17. Love hath conformed us to him; as he was the great lover of God and man, he has taught us in our measure to be so too, and he will not deny his own image. Love teaches us to conform in sufferings too; we suffer for him and with him, and therefore cannot but hope and trust that we shall also be glorified together with him, 2 Tim. ii. 12. 2. It prevents or removes the uncomfortable result and fruit of servile fear: *There is no fear in love* (*v.* 18); so far as love prevails, fear ceases. We must here distinguish, I judge, between fear and being afraid; or, in this case, between the fear of God and being afraid of him. The fear of God is often mentioned and commanded as the substance of religion (1 Pet. ii. 17; Rev. xiv. 7); and so it imports the high regard and veneration we have for God and his authority and government. Such fear is consistent with love, yea, with perfect love, as being in the angels themselves. But then there is a being afraid of God, which arises from a sense of guilt, and a view of his vindictive perfections; in the view of them, God is represented as a consuming fire; and so fear here may be rendered *dread: There is no dread in love.* Love considers its object as good and excellent, and therefore amiable, and worthy to be beloved. Love considers God as most eminently good, and most eminently loving us in Christ, and so puts off dread, and puts on joy in him; and, as love grows, joy grows too; so that *perfect love casteth out fear* or dread. Those who perfectly love God are, from his nature, and counsel, and covenant, perfectly assured of his love, and consequently are perfectly free from any dismal dreadful suspicions of his punitive power and justice, as armed against them; they well know that

God loves them, and they thereupon triumph in his love. That *perfect love casteth out fear* the apostle thus sensibly argues: that which casteth out torment casteth out fear or dread: *Because fear hath torment* (*v.* 18)—fear is known to be a disquieting torturing passion, especially such a fear as is the dread of an almighty avenging God; but perfect love casteth out torment, for it teaches the mind a perfect acquiescence and complacency in the beloved, and therefore *perfect love casteth out fear.* Or, which is here equivalent, *he that feareth is not made perfect in love* (*v.* 18); it is a sign that our love is far from being perfect, since our doubts, and fears, and dismal apprehensions of God, are so many. Let us long for, and hasten to, the world of perfect love, where our serenity and joy in God will be as perfect as our love! 3. From the source and rise of it, which is the antecedent love of God: *We love him, because he first loved us, v.* 19. His love is the incentive, the motive, and moral cause of ours. We cannot but love so good a God, who was first in the act and work of love, who loved us when we were both unloving and unlovely, who loved us at so great a rate, who has been seeking and soliciting our love at the expense of his Son's blood; and has condescended to beseech us to be reconciled unto him. Let heaven and earth stand amazed at such love! His love is the productive cause of ours: *Of his own will* (of his own free loving will) *begat he us. To those that love him all things work together for good, to those who are the called according to his purpose.* Those *that love God are the called* thereto *according to his purpose* (Rom. viii. 28); according to whose purpose they are called is sufficiently intimated in the following clauses: *whom he did predestinate* (or antecedently purpose, to the image of his Son) *those he also called,* effectually recovered thereto. The divine love stamped love upon our souls; may the Lord still and further direct our hearts into the love of God! 2 Thess. iii. 5.

II. As love to our brother and neighbour in Christ; such love is argued and urged on these accounts:—1. As suitable and consonant to our Christian profession. In the profession of Christianity we profess to love God as the root of religion: "*If then a man say,* or profess as much as thereby to say, *I love God,* I am a lover of his name, and house, and worship, *and* yet *hate his brother,* whom he should love for God's sake, *he is a liar* (*v.* 20), he therein gives his profession the lie." That such a one loves not God the apostle proves by the usual facility of loving what is seen rather than what is unseen: *For he that loveth not his brother, whom he hath seen, how can he love God, whom he hath not seen? v.* 20. The eye is wont to affect the heart; things unseen less catch the mind, and thereby the heart. The incomprehensibleness of God very much arises from his invisibility; the member of Christ has much of God visible in him. How then shall the hater of a visible image of God pretend to love the unseen original, the invisible God himself? 2. As suitable to the express law of God, and the just reason of it: *And this commandment have we from him, that he who loveth God love his brother also, v.* 21. As God has communicated his image in nature and in grace, so he would have our love to be suitably diffused. We must love God originally and supremely, and others in him, on the account of their derivation and reception from him, and of his interest in them. Now, our Christian brethren having a new nature and excellent privileges derived from God, and God having his interest in them as well as in us, it cannot but be a natural suitable obligation *that he who loves God should love his brother also.*

CHAP. V.

In this chapter the apostle asserts, I. The dignity of believers, ver. 1. II. Their obligation to love, and the trial of it, ver. 1—3. III. Their victory, ver. 4, 5. IV. The credibility and confirmation of their faith, ver. 6—10. V. The advantage of their faith in eternal life, ver. 11—13. VI. The audience of their prayers, unless for those who have sinned unto death, ver. 14—17. VII. Their preservation from sin and Satan, ver. 18. VIII. Their happy distinction from the world, ver. 19. IX. Their true knowledge of God (ver. 20), upon which they must depart from idols, ver. 21.

WHOSOEVER believeth that Jesus is the Christ is born of God: and every one that loveth him that begat loveth him also that is begotten of him. 2 By this we know that we love the children of God, when we love God, and keep his commandments. 3 For this is the love of God, that we keep his commandments: and his commandments are not grievous. 4 For whatsoever is born of God overcometh the world: and this is the victory that overcometh the world, *even* our faith. 5 Who is he that overcometh the world, but he that believeth that Jesus is the Son of God?

I. The apostle having, in the conclusion of the last chapter, as was there observed, urged Christian love upon those two accounts, as suitable to Christian profession and as suitable to the divine command, here adds a third: Such love is suitable, and indeed demanded, by their eminent relation; our Christian brethren or fellow-believers are nearly related to God; they are his children: *Whosoever believeth that Jesus is the Christ is born of God, v.* 1. Here the Christian brother is, 1. Described by his faith; he that *believeth that Jesus is the Christ*—that he is Messiah the prince, that he is the Son of God by nature and office, that he is the chief of all the anointed world, chief of all the priests, prophets, or kings, who were ever anointed by God or for him, that he is perfectly prepared and furnished for the whole work of the eternal salvation—accordingly yields himself up to his care and direction; and then he is, 2. Dignified by his descent: *He is born of God, v.* 1. This principle of faith, and the new nature that attends it or from which it springs, are ingenerated by the Spirit of God; and so sonship and adoption are not now appropriated *to the seed of Abraham according to the flesh,* nor to the ancient Israel of God; all believers, though by nature sinners of the Gentiles, are spiritually descended from God, and accordingly are to be beloved; as it is added: *Every one that loveth him that begat loveth him also that is begotten of him, v.* 1. It seems but natural that he who loves the Father should love the children also, and that in some proportion to their resemblance to their Father and to the Father's love to them; and so we must first and principally love *the Son of the Father,* as he is most emphatically styled, 2 John 3, *the only* (necessarily) *begotten,* and *the Son of his love,* and then those that are voluntarily begotten, and *renewed by the Spirit of grace.*

II. The apostle shows, 1. How we may discern the truth, or the true evangelical nature of our love to the regenerate. The ground of it must be our love to God, whose they are: *By this we know that we love the children of God, when we love God, v.* 2. Our love to them appears to be sound and genuine when we love them not merely upon any secular account, as because they are rich, or learned, or kind to us, or of our denomination among religious parties; but because they are God's children, his regenerating grace appears in them, his image and superscription are upon them, and so in them God himself is loved. Thus we see what that love to the brethren is that is so pressed in this epistle: it is love to them as the children of God and the adopted brethren of the Lord Jesus. 2. How we may learn the truth of our love to God—it appears in our holy obedience: *When we love God, and keep his commandments, v.* 2. Then we truly, and in gospel account, love God, when we keep his commandments: *For this is the love of God, that we keep his commandments;* and the keeping of his commandments requires a spirit inclined thereto and delighting therein; *and so his commandments are not grievous, v.* 3. Or, *This is the love of God, that,* as thereby we are determined to obedience, and to keep the commandments of God, so his commandments are thereby made easy and pleasant to us. The lover of God says, "*O how I love thy law! I will run the way of thy commandments, when thou shalt enlarge my heart* (Ps. cxix. 32), when thou shalt enlarge it either with love or with thy Spirit, the spring of love." 3. What is and ought to be the result and effect of regeneration—an intellectual spiritual conquest of this world: *For* whatsoever *is born of God,* or, as in some copies, whosoever *is born of God, overcometh the world, v.* 4. He that is born of God is born *for* God, and consequently for another world. He has a temper and disposition that tend to a higher and better world; and he is furnished with such arms, or such a weapon, whereby he can repel and conquer this; as it is added, *And this is the victory that overcometh the world, even our faith, v.* 4. Faith is the cause of victory, the means, the instrument, the spiritual armour and artillery by which we overcome; for, (1.) In and by faith we cleave to Christ, in contempt of, and opposition to, the world. (2.) Faith works in and by love to God and Christ, and so withdraws us from the love of the world. (3.) Faith sanctifies the heart, and purifies it from those sensual lusts by which the world obtains such sway and dominion over souls. (4.) It receives and derives strength from the object of it, the Son of God, for conquering the frowns and flatteries of the world. (5.) It obtains by gospel promise a right to the indwelling Spirit of grace, that is greater than he who dwells in the world. (6.) It sees an invisible world at hand, with which this world is not worthy to be compared, and into which it tells the soul in which it resides it must be continually prepared to enter; and thereupon,

III. The apostle concludes that it is the real Christian that is the true conqueror of the world: *Who is he* then *that overcometh the world, but he that believeth that Jesus is the Son of God? v.* 5. It is the world that lies in our way to heaven, and is the great impediment to our entrance there. But he who believes that Jesus is the Son of God believes therein that Jesus came from God to be the Saviour of the world, and powerfully to conduct us from the world to heaven, and to God, who is fully to be enjoyed there. And he who so believes must needs by this faith overcome the world. For, 1. He must be well satisfied that this world is a vehement enemy to his soul, to his holiness, his salvation, and his blessedness. *For all that is in the world, the lust of the flesh, the lust of the eyes, and the pride of life, is not of the Father, but is of the world, ch.* ii. 16. 2. He sees it must be a great part of the Saviour's work, and of his own salvation, to be redeemed and rescued from this malignant world. *Who gave himself for our sins, that he might deliver us from this present evil world,* Gal. i. 4. 3. He sees in and by the life and conduct of the Lord Jesus on earth that this world is to be renounced and overcome. 4. He perceives that the Lord Jesus conquered the world, not for himself only, but for his followers; and they must study to be partakers of his victory. *Be of good cheer, I have overcome the world.* 5. He is taught and influenced by the Lord Jesus's death to be mortified and crucified to the world. *God forbid that I should glory, save in the cross of our Lord Jesus Christ, by whom the world is crucified to me, and I unto the world,* Gal. vi. 14.

6. He is begotten by the resurrection of Jesus Christ from the dead to the lively hope of a blessed world above, 1 Pet. i. 3. 7. He knows that the Saviour has gone to heaven, and is there preparing a place for his serious believers, John xiv. 2. 8. He knows that his Saviour will come again thence, and will put an end to this world, and judge the inhabitants of it, and receive his believers to his presence and glory, John xiv. 3. 9. He is possessed with a spirit and disposition that cannot be satisfied with this world, that look beyond it, and are still tending, striving, and pressing, towards the world in heaven. *In this we groan, earnestly desiring to be clothed upon with our house which is from heaven,* 2 Cor. v. 2. So that it is the Christian religion that affords its proselytes a universal empire. It is the Christian revelation that is the great means of conquering the world, and gaining another that is most pure and peaceful, blessed and eternal. It is there, in that revelation, that we see what are the occasion and ground of the quarrel and contest between the holy God and this rebellious world. It is there that we meet with sacred doctrine (both speculative and practical), quite contrary to the tenour, temper, and tendency of this world. It is by that doctrine that a spirit is communicated and diffused which is superior and adverse to the spirit of the world. It is there we see that the Saviour himself was not of this world that his kingdom was not and is not so, that it must be separated from the world and gathered out of it for heaven and for God. There we see that the Saviour designs not this world for the inheritance and portion of his saved company. As he has gone to heaven himself, so he assures them he goes to prepare for their residence there, as designing they should always dwell with him, and allowing them to believe that if in this life, and this world only, they had hope in him, they should at last be but miserable. It is there that the eternal blessed world is most clearly revealed and proposed to our affection and pursuit. It is there that we are furnished with the best arms and artillery against the assaults and attempts of the world. It is there that we are taught how the world may be out-shot in its own bow, or its artillery turned against itself; and its oppositions, encounters, and persecutions, be made serviceable to our conquest of the world, and to our motion and ascent to the higher heavenly world: and there we are encouraged by a whole army and cloud of holy soldiers, who have in their several ages, posts, and stations, overcome the world, and won the crown. It is the real Christian that is the proper hero, who vanquishes the world and rejoices in a universal victory. Nor does he (for he is far superior to the Grecian monarch) mourn that there is not another world to be subdued, but lays hold on the eternal world of life, and in a sacred sense takes the kingdom of heaven by violence too. Who in all the world but the believer on Jesus Christ can thus overcome the world?

6 This is he that came by water
and blood, *even* Jesus Christ; not by
water only, but by water and blood.
And it is the Spirit that beareth witness, because the Spirit is truth. 7
For there are three that bear record
in heaven, the Father, the Word, and
the Holy Ghost: and these three are
one. 8 And there are three that bear
witness in earth, the spirit, and the
water, and the blood: and these
three agree in one. 9 If we receive the
witness of men, the witness of God is
greater: for this is the witness of God
which he hath testified of his Son.

The faith of the Christian believer (or the believer in Christ) being thus mighty and victorious, it had need to be well founded, to be furnished with unquestionable celestial evidence concerning the divine mission, authority, and office of the Lord Jesus; and it is so; he brings his credentials along with him, and he brings them in the way by which he came and in the witness that attends him.

I. In the way and manner by which he came; not barely by which he came into the world, but by and with which he came, and appeared, and acted, as a Saviour in the world: *This is he that came by water and blood.* He came to save us from our sins, to give us eternal life, and bring us to God; and, that he might the more assuredly do this, *he came by,* or with, *water and blood. Even Jesus Christ;* Jesus Christ, I say, did so; and none but he. And I say it again, not by or with *water only, but by* and with *water and blood, v.* 6. *Jesus Christ came with water and blood,* as the notes and signatures of the true effectual Saviour of the world; and he came by water and blood as the means by which he would heal and save us. That he must and did thus come in his saving office may appear by our remembering these things:—

1. We are inwardly and outwardly defiled. (1.) Inwardly, by the power and pollution of sin in our nature. For our cleansing from this we need spiritual water; such as can reach the soul and the powers of it. Accordingly, there is in and by Christ Jesus *the washing of regeneration and the renewing of the Holy Ghost.* And this was intimated to the apostles by our Lord, when he washed their feet, and said to Peter, who refused to be washed, *Except I wash thee, thou hast no part in me.* (2.) We are defiled outwardly, by the guilt and condemning power of sin upon our persons. By this we are separated from God, and banished from his favourable, gracious, beatific presence for

ever. From this we must be purged by atoning blood. It is the law or determination in the court of heaven *that without shedding of blood there shall be no remission,* Heb. ix. 22. The Saviour from sin therefore must come with blood.

2 Both these ways of cleansing were represented in the old ceremonial institutions of God. Persons and things must be purified by water and blood. *There were divers washings and carnal ordinances imposed till the time of reformation,* Heb. ix. 10. *The ashes of a heifer,* mixed with water, *sprinkling the unclean, sanctifieth to the purifying of the flesh,* Heb. ix. 13; Num. xix. 9. *And likewise almost all things are, by the law, purged with blood,* Heb. ix. 22. As these show us our double defilement, so they indicate the Saviour's two-fold purgation.

3. At and upon the death of Jesus Christ, his side being pierced with a soldier's spear, out of the wound there immediately issued water and blood. This the beloved apostle saw, and he seems to have been affected with the sight; he alone records it, and seems to reckon himself obliged to record it, as containing something mysterious in it: *And he that saw it bore record, and his record is true. And he knoweth,* being an eye-witness, *that he saith true, that you might believe,* and that you might believe this particularly, that out of his pierced side *forthwith there came water and blood,* John xix. 34, 35. Now this water and blood are comprehensive of all that is necessary and effectual to our salvation. By the water our souls are washed and purified for heaven and the region of saints in light. By the blood God is glorified, his law is honoured, and his vindictive excellences are illustrated and displayed. *Whom God hath set forth,* or purposed, or proposed, *a propitiation through faith in his blood,* or a propitiation in or by his blood through faith, *to declare his righteousness, that he may be just, and the justifier of him that believeth in Jesus,* Rom. iii. 25, 26. By the blood we are justified, reconciled, and presented righteous to God. By the blood, the curse of the law being satisfied, the purifying Spirit is obtained for the internal ablution of our natures. *Christ hath redeemed us from the curse of the law, that the blessing of Abraham might come on the Gentiles, that we might receive the promise of the Spirit,* the promised Spirit, *through faith,* Gal. iii. 13, &c. The water, as well as the blood, issued out of the side of the sacrificed Redeemer. The water and the blood then comprehend all things that can be requisite to our salvation. They will consecrate and sanctify to that purpose all that God shall appoint or make use of in order to that great end. *He loved the church, and gave himself for it, that he might sanctify and cleanse it with the washing of water by the word, that he might present it to himself a glorious church,* Eph. v. 25—27. He who comes by water and blood is an accurate perfect Saviour. And this is he who comes by water and blood, even Jesus Christ! Thus we see in what way and manner, or, if you please, with what utensils, he comes. But we see his credentials also,

II. In the witness that attends him, and that is, the divine Spirit, that Spirit to whom the perfecting of the works of God is usually attributed: *And it is the Spirit that beareth witness, v.* 6. It was meet that the commissioned Saviour of the world should have a constant agent to support his work, and testify of him to the world. It was meet that a divine power should attend him, his gospel, and servants; and notify to the world upon what errand and office they came, and by what authority they were sent: this was done in and by the Spirit of God, according to the Saviour's own prediction, "*He shall glorify me,* even when I shall be rejected and crucified by men, *for he shall receive* or take *of mine.* He shall not receive my immediate office; he shall not die and rise again for you; *but he shall receive of mine,* shall proceed on the foundation I have laid, shall take up my institution, and truth, and cause, *and shall* further *show it unto you,* and by you to the world," John xvi. 14. And then the apostle adds the commendation or the acceptableness of this witness: *Because the Spirit is truth, v.* 6. He is the Spirit of God, and cannot lie. There is a copy that would afford us a very suitable reading thus: *because,* or that, *Christ is the truth.* And so it indicates the matter of the Spirit's testimony, the thing which he attests, and that is, the truth of Christ: *And it is the Spirit that beareth witness that Christ is the truth;* and consequently that Christianity, or the Christian religion, is the truth of the day, the truth of God. But it is not meet that one or two copies should alter the text; and our present reading is very agreeable, and so we retain it. *The Spirit is truth.* He is indeed the Spirit of truth, John xiv. 17. And that the Spirit is truth, and a witness worthy of all acceptation, appears in that he is a heavenly witness, or one of the witnesses that in and from heaven bore testimony concerning the truth and authority of Christ. *Because* (or for) *there are three that bear record in heaven, the Father, the Word, and the Holy Ghost, and these three are one.* And so *v.* 7 most appositely occurs, as a proof of the authenticity of the Spirit's testimony; he must needs be true, or even truth itself, if he be not only a witness in heaven, but *even one* (not in testimony only, for so an angel may be, but in being and essence) *with the Father and the Word.* But here,

1. We are stopped in our course by the contest there is about the genuineness of *v.* 7. It is alleged that many old Greek manuscripts have it not. We shall not here enter into the controversy. It should seem that the critics are not agreed what manuscripts have it and what not; nor do they sufficiently inform us of the integrity and

value of the manuscripts they peruse. Some may be so faulty, as I have an old printed Greek Testament so full of *errata,* that one would think no critic would establish a various lection thereupon. But let the judicious collators of copies manage that business. There are some rational surmises that seem to support the present text and reading. As,

(1.) If we admit *v.* 8, in the room of *v.* 7, it looks too like a tautology and repetition of what was included in *v.* 6, *This is he that came by water and blood, not by water only, but by water and blood; and it is the Spirit that beareth witness. For there are three that bear witness, the Spirit, the water, and the blood.* This does not assign near so noble an introduction of these three witnesses as our present reading does.

(2.) It is observed that many copies read that distinctive clause, *upon the earth: There are three that bear record upon the earth.* Now this bears a visible opposition to some witness or witnesses elsewhere, and therefore we are told, by the adversaries of the text, that this clause must be supposed to be omitted in most books that want *v.* 7. But it should for the same reason be so in all. Take we *v.* 6, *This is he that came by water and blood. And it is the Spirit that beareth witness, because the Spirit is truth.* It would not now naturally and properly be added, *For there are three that bear record on earth,* unless we should suppose that the apostle would tell us that all the witnesses are such as are on earth, when yet he would assure us that one is infallibly true, or even truth itself.

(3.) It is observed that there is a variety of reading even in the Greek text, as in *v.* 7. Some copies read ἕν εἰσι—*are one;* others (at least the *Complutensian*) εἰς τὸ ἕν εἰσιν—*are to one,* or *agree in one;* and in *v.* 8 (in that part that it is supposed should be admitted), instead of the common ἐν τῇ γῇ—*in earth, the Complutensian* reads ἐπὶ τῆς γῆς—*upon earth,* which seems to show that that edition depended upon some Greek authority, and not merely, as some would have us believe, upon the authority either of the vulgar Latin or of *Thomas Aquinas,* though his testimony may be added thereto.

(4.) The seventh verse is very agreeable to the style and the theology of our apostle; as, [1.] He delights in the title *the Father,* whether he indicates thereby God only, or a divine person distinguished from the Son. I *and* the Father *are one. And yet I am not alone; because* the Father *is with me. I will pray* the Father, *and he shall give you another comforter. If any man love the world, the love of* the Father *is not in him. Grace be with you, and peace from God* the Father, *and from the Lord Jesus Christ, the Son of* the Father, 2 John 3. Then, [2.] The name *the Word* is known to be almost (if not quite) peculiar to this apostle. Had the text been devised by another, it had been more easy and obvious, from the form of baptism, and the common language of the church, to have used the name *Son* instead of that of the *Word.* As it is observed that Tertullian and Cyprian use that name, even when they refer to this verse; or it is made an objection against their referring to this verse, because they speak of the Son, not the Word; and yet Cyprian's expression seems to be very clear by the citation of Facundus himself. *Quod Johannis apostoli testimonium beatus Cyprianus, Carthaginensis antistes et martyr, in epistolâ sive libro, quem de Trinitate scripsit, de Patre, Filio, et Spiritu sancto dictum intelligit; ait enim, Dicit Dominus, Ego et Pater unum sumus; et iterum de Patre, Filio, et Spiritu sancto scriptum est, Et hi tres unum sunt.—Blessed Cyprian, the Carthaginian bishop and martyr, in the epistle or book he wrote concerning the Trinity, considered the testimony of the apostle John as relating to the Father, the Son, and the Holy Spirit; for he says, the Lord says, I and the Father are one; and again, of the Father, the Son, and the Holy Spirit it is written, And these three are one.* Now it is nowhere written that these are one, but in *v.* 7. It is probable then that St. Cyprian, either depending on his memory, or rather intending things more than words, persons more than names, or calling persons by their names more usual in the church (both in popular and polemic discourses), called the second by the name of the *Son* rather than of the *Word.* If any man can admit Facundus's fancy, that Cyprian meant that the Spirit, the water, and the blood, were indeed the Father, Word, and Spirit, that John said were one, he may enjoy his opinion to himself. For, *First,* He must suppose that Cyprian not only changed all the names, but the apostle's order too. For the blood (the Son), which Cyprian puts second, the apostle puts last. And, *Secondly,* He must suppose that Cyprian thought that by the blood which issued out of the side of the Son the apostle intended the Son himself, who might as well have been denoted by the water,—that by the water, which also issued from the side of the Son, the apostle intended the person of the Holy Ghost,—that by the Spirit, which in *v.* 6 is said to be truth, and in the gospel is called the Spirit of truth, the apostle meant the person of the Father, though he is nowhere else so called when joined with the Son and the Holy Ghost. We require good proof that the *Carthaginian* father could so understand the apostle. He who so understands him must believe too that the Father, Son, and Holy Spirit, are said to be three witnesses on earth. *Thirdly, Facundus* acknowledges that Cyprian says that of his three it is written, *Et hi tres unum sunt—and these three are one.* Now these are the words, not of *v.* 8, but of *v.* 7. They are not used concerning the three on earth, the Spirit, the water, and the blood; but the three in heaven, the Father, and the Word, and the Holy Ghost. So we are told that the author of the book *De baptismo hæreticorum,* allowed to be contemporary with Cyprian, cites John's words, agreeably to the Greek manuscripts and the ancient versions, thus: *Ait enim Johannes de Domino nostro in epistolâ nos docens, Hic es qui venit per aquam et sanguinem, Jesus Christus, non in aquâ tantùm, sed in aquâ et sanguine; et Spiritus est qui testimonium perhibet, quia Spiritus est veritas; quia tres testimonium perhibent, Spiritus et aqua et sanguis, et isti tres in unum sunt—For John, in his epistle, says concerning our Lord, This is he, Jesus Christ, who came by water and blood, not in water only, but in water and blood; and it is the Spirit that bears witness, because the Spirit is truth; for there are three that bear witness, the Spirit, the water, and the blood, and these three agree in one.* If all the Greek manuscripts and ancient versions say concerning the Spirit, the water, and the blood, that *in unum sunt—they agree in one,* then it was not of them that Cyprian spoke, whatever variety there might be in the copies in his time, when he said it is written, *unum sunt—they are one.* And therefore Cyprian's words seem still to be a firm testimony to *v.* 7, and an intimation likewise that a forger of the text would have scarcely so exactly hit upon the apostolical name for the second witness in heaven, *the Word.* Then, [3.] As only this apostle records the history of the water and blood flowing out of the Saviour's side, so it is he only, or he principally, who registers to us the Saviour's promise and prediction of the Holy Spirit's coming to glorify him, and to testify of him, and to convince the world of its own unbelief and of his righteousness, as in his gospel, *ch.* xiv. 16, 17, 26; xv. 26; xvi. 7—15. It is most suitable then to the diction and to the gospel of this apostle thus to mention the Holy Ghost as a witness for Jesus Christ. Then,

(5.) It was far more easy for a transcriber, by turning away his eye, or by the obscurity of the copy, it being obliterated or defaced on the top or bottom of a page, or worn away in such materials as the ancients had to write upon, to lose and omit the passage, than for an interpolator to devise and insert it. He must be very bold and impudent who could hope to escape detection and shame; and profane too, who durst venture to make an addition to a supposed sacred book. And,

(6.) It can scarcely be supposed that, when the apostle is representing the Christian's faith in overcoming the world, and the foundation it relies upon in adhering to Jesus Christ, and the various testimony that was given to Jesus Christ in the world, he should omit the supreme testimony that attended him, especially when we consider that he meant to infer, as he does (*v.* 9), *If we receive the witness of men, the witness of God is greater; for this* (which he had rehearsed before) *is the witness of God which he hath testified of his Son.* Now in the three witnesses on earth there is neither all the witness of God, nor indeed any witness who is truly and immediately God. The antitrinitarian opposers of the text will deny that either the Spirit, or the water, or the blood, is God himself; but, upon our present reading, here is a noble enumeration of the several witnesses and testimonies supporting the truth of the Lord Jesus and the divinity of his institution. Here is the most excellent abridgment or breviate of the motives to faith in Christ, of the credentials the Saviour brings with him, and of the evidences of our Christianity, that is to be found, I think, in the book of God, upon which single account, even waiving the doctrine of the divine Trinity, the text is worthy of all acceptation.

2. Having these rational grounds on our side, we proceed. The apostle, having told us that the Spirit that bears witness to Christ is truth, shows us that he is so, by assuring us that he is in heaven, and that there are others also who cannot but be true, or truth itself, concurring in testimony with him: *For there are three that bear record in heaven, the Father, the Word, and the Holy Ghost, and these three are one, v.* 7.

(1.) Here is a trinity of heavenly witnesses, such as have testified and vouched to the world the veracity and authority of the Lord Jesus in his office and claims, where, [1.] The first that occurs in order is *the Father;* he set his seal to the commission of the Lord Christ all the while he was here; more especially, *First,* In proclaiming him at his baptism, Matt. iii. 17. *Secondly,* In confirming his character at the transfiguration, Matt. xvii. 5. *Thirdly,* In accompanying him with miraculous power and works: *If I do not the works of my Father, believe me not; but if I do, though you believe not me, believe the works, that you may know and believe that the Father is in me, and I in him,* John x. 37, 38. *Fourthly,* In avouching at his death, Matt. xxvii. 54. *Fifthly,* In raising him from the dead, and receiving him up to his glory: *He shall convince the world——of righteousness, because I go to my Father, and you see me no more,* John xvi. 10, and Rom. i. 4. [2.] The second witness is the Word, a mysterious name, importing the highest nature that belongs to the Saviour Jesus Christ, wherein he existed before the world was, whereby he made the world, and whereby he was truly God with the Father. He must bear witness to the human nature, or to the man Christ Jesus, in and by whom he redeemed and saved us; and he bore witness, *First,* By the mighty works that he wrought. John v. 17, *My Father worketh hitherto, and I work. Secondly,* In conferring a glory upon him at his transfiguration. *And we beheld his glory, the glory as of the only-begotten of the Father,* John i. 14. *Thirdly,* In raising him from the dead. John ii. 19, *Destroy this temple, and in three days will I raise it up.* [3.] The third witness is the Holy Ghost, or the Holy Spirit, an august, venerable name, the possessor, proprietor, and author of holiness. True and faithful must he be to whom the Spirit of holiness sets his seal and solemn testimony. So he did to the Lord Jesus, the head of the Christian world; and that in such instances as these:—*First,* In the miraculous production of his immaculate human nature in the virgin's womb. *The Holy Ghost shall come upon thee,* Luke i. 35, &c. *Secondly,* In the visible descent upon him at his baptism. *The Holy Ghost descended in a bodily shape,* Luke iii. 22, &c. *Thirdly,* In an effectual conquest of the spirits of hell and darkness. *If I cast out devils by the Spirit of God, then the kingdom of God has come unto you,* Matt. xii. 28. *Fourthly,* In the visible potent descent upon the apostles, to furnish them with gifts and powers to preach him and his gospel to the world after he himself had gone to heaven, Acts i. 4, 5; ii. 2—4, &c. *Fifthly,* In supporting the name, gospel, and interest of Christ, by miraculous gifts and operations by and upon the disciples, and in the churches, for two hundred years (1 Cor. xii. 7), concerning which see Dr. Whitby's excellent discourse in the preface to the second volume of his *Commentary on the New Testament.* These are witnesses in heaven; and they bear record from heaven; and they are one, it should seem, not only in testimony (for that is implied in their being three witnesses to one and the same thing), but upon a higher account, as they are in heaven; they are one in their heavenly being and essence; and, if one with the Father, they must be one God.

(2.) To these there is opposed, though with them joined, a trinity of witnesses on earth, such as continue here below: *And there are three that bear witness on earth, the spirit, the water, and the blood; and these three agree in one, v.* 8. [1.] Of these witnesses the first is the *spirit.* This must be distinguished from the person of the Holy Ghost, who is in heaven. We must say then, with the Saviour (according to what is reported by this apostle), *that which is born of the Spirit is spirit,* John iii. 6. The disciples of the Saviour are, as well as others, born after the flesh. They come into the world endued with a corrupt carnal disposition, which is enmity to God. This disposition must be mortified and abolished. A new nature must be communicated. Old lusts and corruptions must be eradicated, and the true disciple become a new creature. The regeneration or renovation of souls is a testimony to the Saviour. It is his actual though initial salvation. It is a testimony on earth, because it continues with the church here, and is not performed in that conspicuous astonishing manner in which signs from heaven are accomplished. To this Spirit belong not only the regeneration and conversion of the church, but its progressive sanctification, victory over the world, her peace, and love, and joy, and all that grace by which she is made meet for the inheritance of the saints in light. [2.] The second is the *water.* This was before considered as a means of salvation, now as a testimony to the Saviour himself, and intimates his purity and purifying power. And so it seems to comprehend, *First,* The purity of his own nature and conduct in the world. *He was holy, harmless, and undefiled. Secondly,* The testimony of John's baptism, who bore witness of him, prepared a people for him, and referred them to him, Mark i. 4, 7, 8. *Thirdly,* The purity of his own doctrine, by which souls are purified and washed. *Now you are clean through the word that I have spoken unto you,* John xv. 3. *Fourthly,* The actual and active purity and holiness of his disciples. His body is the holy catholic church. *Seeing you have purified your souls in obeying the truth through the Spirit,* 1 Pet. i. 22. And this signed and sealed by, *Fifthly,* The baptism that he has appointed for the initiation or introduction of his disciples, in which he signally (or by that sign) says, *Except I wash thee, thou hast no part in me. Not the putting away of the filth of the flesh, but the answer of a good conscience towards God,* 1 Pet. iii. 21. [3.] The third witness is the blood; this he shed, and this was our ransom. This testifies for Jesus Christ, *First,* In that it sealed up and finished the sacrifices of the Old Testament, *Christ, our Passover, was sacrificed for us. Secondly,* In that it confirmed his own predictions, and the truth of all his ministry and doctrine, John xviii. 37. *Thirdly,* In that it showed unparalleled love to God, in that he would die a sacrifice to his honour and glory, in making atonement for the sins of the world, John xiv. 30, 31. *Fourthly,* In that it demonstrated unspeakable love to us; and none will deceive those whom they entirely love, John xiv. 13—15. *Fifthly,* In that it demonstrated the disinterestedness of the Lord Jesus as to any secular interest and advantage. No impostor and deceiver ever proposes to himself contempt and a violent cruel death, John xviii. 36. *Sixthly,* In that it lays obligation on his disciples to suffer and die for him. No deceiver would invite proselytes to his side and interest at the rate that the Lord Jesus did. *You shall be hated of all men for my sake. They shall put you out of their synagogues; and the time comes that whosoever kills you will think that he doeth God service,* John xvi. 2. He frequently calls his servants to a conformity with him in sufferings: *Let us go forth therefore unto him without the camp, bearing his reproach,* Heb. xiii. 13. This shows that neither he nor his kingdom is of this world. *Seventhly,* The benefits accruing and procured by his blood (well understood) must immediately demonstrate that he is indeed the Saviour of the world. And then, *Eighthly,* These are signified and sealed in the institution of his own supper: *This is my blood of the New Testament* (which ratifies the New Testament), *which is shed for many, for the remission of sins,* Matt. xxvi. 28. Such are the witnesses on earth. Such is the various testimony given to the author of our religion. No wonder if the rejecter of all this evidence be judged as a blasphemer of the Spirit of God, and be left to perish without remedy in his sins. These three witnesses (being more different than the three former) are not so properly said to be *one* as to be *for one,* to be for one and the same purpose and cause, *or to agree in one,* in one and the same thing among themselves, and in the same testimony with those who bear record from heaven.

III. The apostle justly concludes, *If we receive the witness of men, the witness of God is greater; for this is the witness of God, that he hath testified of his Son, v.* 9. Here we have, 1. A supposition well founded upon the premises. *Here is the witness of God,* the witness whereby God hath testified of his Son, which surely must intimate some immediate irrefragable testimony, and that of the Father concerning his Son; he has by himself proclaimed and avouched him to the world. 2. The authority and acceptableness of his testimony; and that argued from the less to the greater: *If we receive the witness of men* (and such testimony is and must be admitted in all judicatories and in all nations), *the witness of God is greater.* It is truth itself, of highest authority and most unquestionable infallibility. And then there is, 3. The application of the rule to the present case: *For this is the witness,* and here is the witness, *of God* even of the Father, as well as of the Word and Spirit, *which he hath testified of,* and wherein he hath attested, *his Son. God, that cannot lie,* hath given sufficient assurance to the world that Jesus Christ is his Son, the Son of his love, and Son by office, to reconcile and recover the world unto himself; he testified therefore the truth and divine origin of the Christian religion, and that it is the sure appointed way and means of bringing us to God.

10 He that believeth on the Son
of God hath the witness in himself:
he that believeth not God hath made
him a liar; because he believeth not
the record that God gave of his Son.
11 And this is the record, that God
hath given to us eternal life, and this
life is in his Son. 12 He that hath
the Son hath life; *and* he that hath
not the Son of God hath not life.
13 These things have I written unto
you that believe on the name of the
Son of God; that ye may know that
ye have eternal life, and that ye
may believe on the name of the Son
of God.

In these words we may observe,

I. The privilege and stability of the real Christian: *He that believeth on the Son of God,* hath been prevailed with unfeignedly to cleave to him for salvation, *hath the witness in himself, v.* 10. He hath not only the outward evidence that others have, but he hath in his own heart a testimony for Jesus Christ. He can allege what Christ and the truth of Christ have done for his soul and what he has seen and found in him. As, 1. He has deeply seen his sin, and guilt, and misery, and his abundant need of such a Saviour. 2. He has seen the excellency, beauty, and office of the Son of God, and the incomparable suitableness of such a Saviour to all his spiritual wants and sorrowful circumstances. 3 He sees and admires the wisdom and love of God in preparing and sending such a Saviour to deliver him from sin and hell, and to raise him to pardon, peace, and communion with God. 4. He has found and felt the power of the word and doctrine of Christ, wounding, humbling, healing, quickening, and comforting his soul. 5 He finds that the revelation of Christ, as it is the greatest discovery and demonstration of the love of God, so it is the most apt and powerful means of kindling, fomenting, and inflaming love to the holy blessed God. 6. He is born of God by the truth of Christ, as *v.* 1. He has a new heart and nature, a new love, disposition, and delight, and is not the man that formerly he was. 7. He finds yet such a conflict with himself, with sin, with the flesh, the world, and invisible wicked powers, as is described and provided for in the doctrine of Christ. 8. He finds such prospects and such strength afforded him by the faith of Christ, that he can despise and overcome the world, and travel on towards a better. 9. He finds what interest the Mediator has in heaven, by the audiency and prevalency of those prayers that are sent thither in his name, according to his will, and through his intercession. 10. He is begotten again to a lively hope, to a holy confidence in God, in his good-will and love, to a pleasant victory over terrors of conscience, dread of death and hell, to a comfortable prospect of life and immortality, being enriched with the earnest of the Spirit and sealed to the day of redemption. Such assurance has the gospel believer; he has a witness in himself. Christ is formed in him, and he is growing up to the fulness and perfection, or perfect image of Christ, in heaven.

II. The aggravation of the unbeliever's sin, the sin of unbelief: *He that believeth not God hath made him a liar.* He does, in effect, give God the lie, *because he believeth not the record that God gave of his Son, v.* 10. He must believe that God did not send his Son into the world, when he has given us such manifold evidence that he did, or that Jesus Christ was not the Son of God, when all that evidence relates to and terminates upon him, or that he sent his Son to deceive the world and to lead it into error and misery, or that he permits men to devise a religion which, in all the parts of it, is a pure, holy, heavenly, undefiled institution, and so worthy to be embraced by the reason of mankind, and yet is but a delusion and a lie, and then lends them his Spirit and power to recommend and obtrude it upon the world, which is to make God the Father, the author and abettor, of the lie.

III. The matter, the substance, or contents of all this divine testimony concerning Jesus Christ: *And this is the record, that God hath given to us eternal life, and this life is in his Son, v.* 11. This is the sum of the gospel. This is the sum and epitome of the whole record given us by all the aforesaid six witnesses. 1. That *God hath given to us eternal life.* He has designed it for us in his eternal purpose. He has prepared all the means that are necessary to bring us to it. He has made it over to us by his covenant and promise. And he actually confers a right and title thereto on all who believe on and actually embrace the Son of God. Then, 2. *This life is in the Son.* The Son is life; eternal life in his own essence and person, John i. 4; 1 John i. 2. He is eternal life to us, the spring of our spiritual and glorious life, Col. iii. 4. From him life is communicated to us, both here and in heaven. And thereupon it must follow, (1.) *He that hath the Son hath life, v.* 12. He that is united to the Son is united to life. He who hath a title to the Son hath a title to life, to eternal life. Such honour hath the Father put upon the Son: such honour must we put upon him too. We must come and kiss the Son, and we shall have life. (2.) *He that hath not the Son of God hath not life, v.* 12. He continues under the condemnation of the law (John iii. 36); he refuses the Son, who is life itself, who is the procurer of life, and the way to it; he provokes God to deliver him over to endless death for making him a liar, since he believes not this record that God hath given concerning his Son.

IV. The end and reason of the apostle's preaching this to believers. 1. For their satisfaction and comfort: *These things have I written unto you that believe on the name of the Son of God, that you may know that you have eternal life, v.* 13. Upon all this evidence, and these witnesses, it is but just and meet that there should be those who believe on the name of the Son of God. God increase their number! How much testimony from heaven has the world to answer for! And to three witnesses in heaven must the world be accountable. These believers have eternal life. They have it in the covenant of the gospel, in the beginning and first-fruits of it within them, and in their Lord and head in heaven. These believers may come to know that they have eternal life, and should be quickened, encouraged, and comforted, in the prospect of it: and they should value the scriptures, which are so much written for their consolation and salvation. 2. For their confirmation and progress in their holy faith: *And that you may believe on the name of the Son of God* (*v.* 13), may go on believing. Believers must persevere, or they do nothing. To withdraw from believing on the name of the Son of God is to renounce eternal life, and to draw back unto perdition. Therefore the evidences of religion and the advantage of faith are to be presented to believers, in order to hearten and encourage them to persevere to the end.

14 And this is the confidence that
we have in him, that, if we ask any
thing according to his will, he heareth
us: 15 And if we know that he
hear us, whatsoever we ask, we know
that we have the petitions that we
desired of him. 16 If any man see
his brother sin a sin *which is* not unto
death, he shall ask, and he shall give
him life for them that sin not unto
death. There is a sin unto death: I
do not say that he shall pray for it.
17 All unrighteousness is sin: and
there is a sin not unto death.

Here we have,

I. A privilege belonging to faith in Christ, namely, audience in prayer: *This is the confidence that we have in him, that, if we ask any thing according to his will, he heareth us, v.* 14. The Lord Christ emboldens us to come to God in all circumstances, with all our supplications and requests. Through him our petitions are admitted and accepted of God. The matter of our prayer must be agreeable to the declared will of God. It is not fit that we should ask what is contrary either to his majesty and glory or to our own good, who are his and dependent on him. And then we may have confidence that the prayer of faith shall be heard in heaven.

II. The advantage accruing to us by such privilege: *If we know that he heareth us, whatsoever we ask, we know that we have the petitions that we desired of him, v.* 15. Great are the deliverances, mercies, and blessings, which the holy petitioner needs. To know that his petitions are heard or accepted is as good as to know that they are answered; and therefore that he is so pitied, pardoned, counselled, sanctified, assisted, and saved (or shall be so) as he is allowed to ask of God.

III. Direction in prayer in reference to the sins of others: *If any man see his brother sin a sin which is not unto death, he shall ask, and he shall give him life for those that sin not unto death. There is a sin unto death: I do not say that he shall pray for it, v.* 16. Here we may observe, 1. We ought to pray for others as well as for ourselves; for our brethren of mankind, that they may be enlightened, converted, and saved; for our brethren in the Christian profession, that they may be sincere, that their sins may be pardoned, and that they may be delivered from evils and the chastisements of God, and preserved in Christ Jesus. 2. There is a great distinction in the heinousness and guilt of sin: *There is a sin unto death* (*v.* 16), *and there is a sin not unto death, v.* 17. (1.) *There is a sin unto death.* All sin, as to the merit and legal sentence of it, is unto death. *The wages of sin is death;* and *cursed is every one that continueth not in all things that are written in the book of the law, to do them,* Gal. iii. 10. But there is a sin unto death in opposition to such sin as is here said *not to be unto death.* There is therefore, (2.) *A sin not unto death.* This surely must include all such sin as by divine or human constitution may consist with life; in the human constitution with temporal or corporal life, in the divine constitution with corporal or with spiritual evangelical life. [1.] There are sins which, by human righteous constitution, are not unto death; as divers pieces of injustice, which may be compensated without the death of the delinquent. In opposition to this there are sins which, by righteous constitution, are to death, or to a legal forfeiture of life; such as we call *capital crimes.* [2.] Then there are sins which, by divine constitution, are unto death; and that either death corporal or spiritual and evangelical. *First,* Such as are, or may be, to death corporal. Such may the sins be either of gross hypocrites, as Ananias and Sapphira, or, for aught we know, of sincere Christian brethren, as when the apostle says of the offending members of the church of Corinth, *For this cause many are weak and sickly among you, and many sleep,* 1 Cor. xi. 30. There may be sin unto corporal death among those who may not be condemned with the world. Such sin, I said, is, or may be, to corporal death. The divine penal constitution in the gospel does not positively and peremptorily threaten death to the more visible sins of the members of Christ, but only some gospel-chastisement; *for whom the Lord loveth he chasteneth, and scourgeth every son whom he receiveth,* Heb. xii. 6. There is room left for divine wisdom or goodness, or even gospel severity, to determine how far the chastisement or the scourge shall proceed. And we cannot say but that sometimes it may *(in terrorem—for warning to others)* proceed even to death. Then, *Secondly,* There are sins which, by divine constitution, are unto death spiritual and evangelical, that is, are inconsistent with spiritual and evangelical life, with spiritual life in the soul and with an evangelical right to life above. Such are total impenitence and unbelief for the present. Final impenitence and unbelief are infallibly to death eternal, as also a blaspheming of the Spirit of God in the testimony that he has given to Christ and his gospel, and a total apostasy from the light and convictive evidence of the truth of the Christian religion. These are sins involving the guilt of everlasting death. Then comes,

IV. The application of the direction for prayer according to the different sorts of sin thus distinguished. The prayer is supposed to be for life: *He shall ask, and he* (God) *shall give them life.* Life is to be asked of God. He is the God of life; he gives it when and to whom he pleases, and takes it away either by his constitution or providence, or both, as he thinks meet. In the case of a brother's sin, which is not (in the manner already mentioned) unto death, we may in faith and hope pray for him; and particularly for the life of soul and body. But, in case of the sin unto death in the forementioned ways, we have no allowance to pray. Perhaps the apostle's expression, *I do not say, He shall pray for it,* may intend no more than, "I have no promise for you in that case; no foundation for the prayer of faith." 1. The laws of punitive justice must be executed, for the common safety and benefit of mankind: and even an offending brother in such a case must be resigned to public justice (which in the foundation of it is divine), and at the same time also to the mercy of God. 2. The removal of evangelical penalties (as they may be called), or the prevention of death (which may seem to be so consequential upon, or inflicted for, some particular sin), can be prayed for only conditionally or provisionally, that is, with proviso that it consist with the wisdom, will, and glory of God that they should be removed, and particularly such death prevented. 3. We cannot pray that the sins of the impenitent and unbelieving should, while they are such, be forgiven them, or that any mercy of life or soul, that supposes the forgiveness of sin, should be granted to them, while they continue such. But we may pray for their repentance (supposing them but in the common case of the impenitent world), for their being enriched with faith in Christ, and thereupon for all other saving mercies. 4. In case it should appear that any have committed the irremissible blasphemy against the Holy Ghost, and the total apostasy from the illuminating convictive powers of the Christian religion, it should seem that they are not to be prayed for at all. For *what remains but a certain fearful expectation of judgment, to consume such adversaries?* Heb. x. 27. And these last seem to be the sins chiefly intended by the apostle by the name of *sins unto death.* Then, 5. The apostle seems to argue that there is sin that is not unto death; thus, *All unrighteousness is sin* (*v.* 17); but, were all unrighteousness unto death (since we have all some unrighteousness towards God or man, or both, in omitting and neglecting something that is their due), then we were all peremptorily bound over to death, and, since it is not so (the Christian brethren, generally speaking, having right to life), there must be sin that is not to death. Though there is no venial sin (in the common acceptation), there is pardoned sin, sin that does not involve a plenary obligation to eternal death. If it were not so, there could be no justification nor continuance of the justified state. The gospel constitution or covenant abbreviates, abridges, or rescinds the guilt of sin.

18 We know that whosoever is born of God sinneth not; but he that is begotten of God keepeth himself, and that wicked one toucheth him not. 19 *And* we know that we are of God, and the whole world lieth in wickedness. 20 And we know that the Son of God is come, and hath given us an understanding, that we may know him that is true, and we are in him that is true, *even* in his Son Jesus Christ. This is the true God, and eternal life. 21 Little children, keep yourselves from idols. Amen.

Here we have,

I. A recapitulation of the privileges and advantages of sound Christian believers. 1. They are secured against sin, against the fulness of its dominion or the fulness of its guilt: *We know that whosoever is born of God* (and the believer in Christ is born of God, *v.* 1) *sinneth not* (*v.* 18), *sinneth not* with that fulness of heart and spirit that the unregenerate do (as was said *ch.* iii. 6, 9), and consequently not with that fulness of guilt that attends the sins of others; and so he is secured against that sin which is unavoidably unto death, or which infallibly binds the sinner over unto the wages of eternal death; the new nature, and the inhabitation of the divine Spirit thereby, prevent the admission of such unpardonable sin. 2. They are fortified against the devil's destructive attempts: *He that is begotten of God keepeth himself*, that is, is enabled to guard himself, *and the wicked one toucheth him not* (*v.* 18), that is, that the wicked one may not touch him, namely, to death. It seems not to be barely a narration of the duty or the practice of the regenerate; but an indication of their power by virtue of their regeneration. They are thereby prepared and principled against the fatal touches, the sting, of the wicked one; he touches not their souls, to infuse his venom there as he does in others, or to expel that regenerative principle which is an antidote to his poison, or to induce them to that sin which by the gospel constitution conveys an indissoluble obligation to eternal death. He may prevail too far with them, to draw them to some acts of sin; but it seems to be the design of the apostle to assert that their regeneration secures them from such assaults of the devil as will bring them into the same case and actual condemnation with the devil. 3. They are on God's side and interest, in opposition to the state of the world: *And we know that we are of God, and the whole world lieth in wickedness, v.* 19. Mankind are divided into two great parties or dominions, that which belongs to God and that which belongs to wickedness or to the wicked one. The Christian believers belong to God. They are of God, and from him, and to him, and for him. They succeed into the right and room of the ancient Israel of God, of whom it is said, *The Lord's people is his portion*, his estate in this world; *Jacob is the lot of his inheritance*, the dividend that has fallen to him by the lot of his own determination (Deut. xxxii. 9); while, on the contrary, *the whole world*, the rest, being by far the major part, *lieth in wickedness*, in the jaws in the bowels, of the wicked one. There are, indeed, were we to consider the individuals, many wicked ones, many wicked spirits, in the heavenly or the ethereal places; but they are united in wicked nature, policy, and principle, and they are united also in one head. There is the prince of the devils and of the diabolical kingdom. There is a head of the malignity and of the malignant world; and he has such sway here that he is called *the god of this world*. Strange that such a knowing spirit should be so implacably incensed against the Almighty and all his interests, when he cannot but know that it must end in his own overthrow and everlasting damnation! How tremendous is the judgment of God upon that wicked one! May the God of the Christian world continually demolish his dominion in this world, and translate souls into *the kingdom of his dear Son!* 4. They are enlightened in the knowledge of the true eternal God: "*And we know that the Son of God has come, and has given us an understanding, that we may know him that is true, v.* 20. The Son of God has come into our world, and we have seen him, and know him by all the evidence that has already been asserted; he has revealed unto us the true God (as John i. 18), and he has opened our minds too to understand that revelation, given us an internal light in our understandings, whereby we may discern the glories of the true God; and we are assured that it is the true God that he hath discovered to us. He is infinitely superior in purity, power, and perfection, to all the gods of the Gentiles. He has all the excellences, beauties, and riches, of the living and true God. It is the same God that, according to Moses's account, made the heavens and the earth, the same who took our fathers the patriarchs into peculiar covenant with himself, the same who brought our ancestors out of Egypt, who gave us the fiery law upon mount Sinai, who gave us his holy oracles, and promised the call and conversion of the Gentiles. By his counsels and works, by his love and grace, by his terrors and judgments, we know that he, and he alone, in the fulness of his being, is the living and true God." It is a great happiness to know the true God, to know him in Christ; it is eternal life, John xvii. 3. It is the glory of the Christian revelation that it gives the best account of the true God, and administers the best eye-salve for our discerning the living and true God. 5. They have a happy union with God and his Son: "*And we are in him that is true, even* (or and) *in his Son Jesus Christ, v.* 20. The Son leads us to the Father, and we are in both, in the love and favour of both, in covenant and federal alliance with both, in spiritual conjunction with both by the inhabitation and operation of their Spirit: and, that you may know how great a dignity and felicity this is, you must remember that this true one is *the true God and eternal life*" or rather (as it should seem a more natural construction), "This same Son of God is himself also *the true God and eternal life*" (John i. 1, and here, *ch.* i. 2), "so that in union with either, much more with both, we are united to *the true God and eternal life.*" Then we have,

II. The apostle's concluding monition: "*Little children*" (dear children, as it has been interpreted), "*keep yourselves from idols, v.* 21. Since you know the true God, and are in him, let your light and love guard you against all that is advanced in opposition to him, or competition with him. Flee from the false gods of the heathen world. They are not comparable to the God whose you are and whom you serve. Adore not your God by statues and images, which share in his worship. Your God is an incomprehensible Spirit, and is disgraced by such sordid representations. Hold no communion with your heathen neighbours in their idolatrous worship. Your God is jealous, and would have you come out, and be separated from among them; mortify the flesh, and be crucified to the world, that they may not usurp the throne of dominion in the heart, which is due only to God. The God whom you have known is he who made you, who redeemed you by his Son, who has sent his gospel to you, who has pardoned your sins, begotten you unto himself by his Spirit, and given you eternal life. Cleave to him in faith, and love, and constant obedience, in opposition to all things that would alienate your mind and heart from God. To this living and true God be glory and dominion for ever and ever. *Amen.*"

AN

EXPOSITION,

WITH PRACTICAL OBSERVATIONS,

OF THE SECOND EPISTLE OF

JOHN.

HERE we find a canonical epistle inscribed, principally, not only to a single person, but to one also of the softer sex. And why not to one of that sex? In gospel redemption, privilege, and dignity, *there is neither male nor female;* they are both one *in Christ Jesus.* Our Lord himself neglected his own repast, to commune with the woman of Samaria, in order to show her the fountain of life; and, when almost expiring upon the cross, he would with his dying lips bequeath his blessed mother to the care of his beloved disciple, and thereby instruct him to respect female disciples for the future. It was to one of the same sex that our Lord chose to appear first after his return from the grave, and to send by her the news of his resurrection to this as well as to the other apostles; and we find afterwards a zealous Priscilla so well acquitting herself in her Christian race, and particularly in some hazardous service towards the apostle Paul, that she is not only often mentioned before her husband, but to her as well as to him, not only the apostle himself, but also all the Gentile churches, were ready to return their thankful acknowledgments. No wonder then that a heroine in the Christian religion, honoured by divine providence, and distinguished by divine grace, should be dignified also by an apostolical epistle.

The apostle here salutes an honourable matron and her children, ver. 1—3. Recommends to them faith and love, ver. 5, 6. Warns them of deceivers (ver. 7), and to take heed to themselves, ver. 8. Teaches how to treat those who bring not the doctrine of Christ, ver. 10, 11. And, referring other things to personal discourse, concludes the epistle, ver. 12, 13.

THE elder unto the elect lady and
her children, whom I love in the
truth; and not I only, but also all
they that have known the truth; 2
For the truth's sake, which dwelleth
in us, and shall be with us for ever.
3 Grace be with you, mercy, *and*
peace, from God the Father, and
from the Lord Jesus Christ, the Son
of the Father, in truth and love. 4 I
rejoiced greatly that I found of thy
children walking in truth, as we have
received a commandment from the
Father.

Ancient epistles began, as here, with salutation and good wishes: religion consecrates, as far as may be, old forms, and turns compliments into real expressions of life and love. Here we have, as usually,

I. The saluter, not expressed by name, but by a chosen character: *The elder.* The expression, and style, and love, intimate that the penman was the same with that of the foregoing epistle; he is now *the elder,* emphatically and eminently so, possibly the oldest apostle now living, the chief elder in the church of God. An elder in the ancient house of Israel was reverend, or to be reverenced, much more he who is so in the gospel Israel of God. An old disciple is honourable; an old apostle and leader of disciples is more so. He was now old in holy service and experience, had seen and tasted much of heaven, and was much nearer than when at first he believed.

II. The saluted—a noble Christian matron, and her children: *To the elect lady and her children.* A lady, a person of eminent quality for birth, education, and estate. It is well that the gospel has got among such. It is a pity but lords and ladies should be acquainted with the Lord Christ and his religion. They owe more to him than others do; though usually *not many noble are called.* Here is a pattern for persons of quality of the same sex. *The elect lady;* not only a choice one, but one chosen of God. It is lovely and beautiful to see ladies, by holy walking, demonstrate their election of God. *And her children;* probably the lady was a widow; she *and her children* then are the principal part of the family, and so this may be styled an economical epistle. Families may well be written to and encouraged, and further directed in their domestic love, and order, and duties. We see that children may well be taken notice of in Christian letters, and they should know it too; it may avail to their encouragement and caution. Those who love and commend them will be apt to enquire after them. This *lady and her children* are further notified by the respect paid them, and that, 1. By the apostle himself: *Whom I love in the truth,* or in truth, whom I sincerely and heartily love. He who was the beloved disciple had learnt the art or exercise of love; and he especially loved those who loved him, that Lord who loved him. 2. By all her Christian acquaintance, all the religious who knew her: *And not I only, but also all those that have known the truth.* Virtue and goodness in an elevated sphere shine brightly. Truth demands acknowledgment, and those who see the evidences of pure religion should confess and attest them; it is a good sign and great duty to love and value religion in others. The ground of this love and respect thus paid to this lady and her children was their regard to the truth: *For the truth's sake* (or true religion's sake) *which dwelleth in us, and shall be with us for ever.* Christian love is founded upon the appearance of vital religion. Likeness should beget affection. Those who love truth and piety in themselves should love it in others too, or love others upon the account of it. The apostle and the other Christians loved this lady, not so much for her honour as her holiness; not so much for her bounty as her serious Christianity. We should not be religious merely by fits and starts, in certain moods and moons; but religion should still dwell within us, in our minds and hearts, in our faith and love. It is to be hoped that where religion once truly dwells it will abide for ever. The Spirit of Christianity, we may suppose, will not be totally extinguished: *Which shall be with us for ever.*

III. The salutation, which is indeed an apostolical benediction: *Grace be with you, mercy, and peace, from God the Father and from the Lord Jesus Christ, the Son of the Father, in truth and love, v.* 3. Sacred love pours out blessings upon this honourable Christian family; to those who have shall more be given. Observe,

1. From whom these blessings are craved, (1.) *From God the Father,* the God of all grace. He is the fountain of blessedness, and of all the blessings that must bring us thither. (2.) *From the Lord Jesus Christ.* He is also author and communicator of these heavenly blessings, and he is distinguished by this emphatic character—*the Son of the Father;* such a Son as none else can be; such a Son as is *the brightness of the Father's glory, and the express image of his person,* who, with the Father, is also *eternal life,* 1 John i. 2.

2. What the apostle craves from these divine persons. (1.) *Grace*—divine favour and good-will, the spring of all good things: it is grace indeed that any spiritual blessing should be conferred on sinful mortals. (2.) *Mercy*—free pardon and forgiveness; those who are already rich in grace have need of continual forgiveness. (3.) *Peace*—tranquillity of spirit and serenity of conscience,

in an assured reconciliation with God, together with all safe and sanctified outward prosperity. And these are desired *in truth and love,* either by sincere and ardent affection in the saluter (in faith and love he prays them *from God the Father, and the Lord Jesus Christ),* or as productive of continued truth and love in the saluted; these blessings will continually preserve true faith and love *in the elect lady and her children;* and may they do so!

IV. The congratulation upon the prospect of the exemplary behaviour of other children of this excellent lady. Happy parent, who was blessed with such a numerous religious offspring! *I rejoiced greatly that I found of thy children walking in the truth, as we have received commandment from the Father, v.* 4. Possibly the lady's sons travelled abroad, either for accomplishment and acquaintance with the world, or on the account of their own business or the common affairs of the family, and in their travels might come to Ephesus, where the apostle is supposed to have now resided, and might there happily converse with him. See how good it is to be trained up to early religion! Though religion is not to be founded upon education, yet education may be and often is blessed, and is the way to fortify youth against irreligious infection. Hence too let young travellers learn to carry their religion along with them, and not either leave it at home or learn the ill customs of the countries where they come. It may be observed, also, that sometimes election runs in a direct line; here we have an *elect lady, and her elect children;* children may be beloved for their parents' sake, but both by virtue of free grace. From the apostle's joy herein we may observe that it is pleasant to see children treading in good parent's steps; and those who see this may well congratulate their parents thereupon, and that both to excite their thankfulness to God for, and to enlarge their comfort in, so great a blessing. How happy a lady was this, who had brought forth so many children for heaven and for God! And how great a joy must it be to her ladyship to hear so good an account of them from so good a judge! And we may further see that it is joyful to good old ministers, and accordingly to other good old disciples, to see a hopeful rising generation, who may serve God and support religion in the world when they are dead and gone. We see here also the rule of true walking: *the commandment of the Father.* Then is our walk true, our converse right, when it is managed by the word of God.

5 And now I beseech thee, lady, not
as though I wrote a new commandment unto thee, but that which we
had from the beginning, that we love
one another. 6 And this is love,
that we walk after his commandments. This is the commandment,
That, as ye have heard from the beginning, ye should walk in it.

We come now more into the design and substance of the epistle; and here we have,

I. The apostle's request: *Now, I beseech thee, lady.* Considering what it is that he entreats, the way of address is very remarkable; it is not any particular boon or bounty to himself, but common duty and observance of divine command. Here he might command or charge; but harsher measures are worse than needless where milder will prevail; and the apostolical spirit is, of all other, the most tender and endearing. Whether out of deference to her ladyship, or apostolical meekness, or both, he condescends to beseech: *And now I beseech thee, lady.* He may be supposed speaking as another apostle does to a certain master to whom he writes: *Wherefore, though I might be very bold in Christ* (and according to the power with which Christ hath entrusted me) *to enjoin thee that which is convenient, yet, for love's sake, I rather beseech thee, being such a one as the aged, the elder.* Love will avail where authority will not; and we may often see that the more authority is urged the more it is slighted. The apostolical minister will love and beseech his friends into their duty.

II. The thing requested of *the lady and her children*—Christian sacred love: *That we love one another, v.* 5. Those that are eminent in any Christian virtue have yet room to grow therein. *But, as touching brotherly love, you need not that I write unto you; for you yourselves are taught of God to love one another. But we beseech you, brethren* (and sisters), *that you increase more and more,* 1 Thess. iv. 9, 10.

1. This love is recommended, (1.) From the obligation thereto—*the commandment.* Divine command should sway our mind and heart. (2.) From the antiquity of the obligation: *Not as though I wrote a new commandment unto thee, but that which we had from the beginning, v.* 5. This commandment of mutual Christian love may be said to be a *new* one in respect of its new enaction and sanction by the Lord Christ; but yet, as to the matter of it (mutual holy love), it is as old as natural, Jewish, or Christian religion. This commandment must every where attend Christianity, that the disciples of it must love one another.

2. Then this love is illustrated from the fruitful nature of it: *And this is love, that we walk after his commandments, v.* 5. This is the test of our love to God, our obedience to him. This is love to ourselves, to our own souls, that we walk in obedience to divine commands. *In keeping them there is great reward.* This is love to one another, to engage one another to walk in holiness; and this is the evidence of our sincere, mutual,

Christian love—that we (in other things) walk after God's commands. There may be mutual love that is not religious and Christian; but we know ours to be so, by our attendance to all other commands besides that of mutual love. Universal obedience is the proof of the goodness and sincerity of Christian virtues; and those that aim at all Christian obedience will be sure to attend to Christian love. This is a fundamental duty in the gospel-charter: *This is the commandment, that, as you have heard from the beginning, you should walk in it* (*v.* 6), that is, walk in this love. The foresight of the decay of this love, as well as of other apostasy, might engage the apostle to inculcate this duty, and this primordial command, the more frequently, the more earnestly.

7 For many deceivers are entered
into the world, who confess not that
Jesus Christ is come in the flesh.
This is a deceiver and an antichrist.
8 Look to yourselves, that we lose not
those things which we have wrought,
but that we receive a full reward. 9
Whosoever transgresseth, and abideth
not in the doctrine of Christ, hath
not God. He that abideth in the
doctrine of Christ, he hath both the
Father and the Son.

In this principal part of the epistle we find,

I. The ill news communicated to the lady—seducers are abroad: *For many deceivers have entered into the world.* This report is introduced by a particle that bespeaks a reason of the report. "You have need to maintain your love, *for* there are destroyers of it in the world. Those who subvert the faith destroy the love; the common faith is one ground of the common love;" or, "You must secure your walk according to the commands of God; this will secure you. Your stability is likely to be tried, *for many deceivers have entered into the world.*" Sad and saddening news may be communicated to our Christian friends; not that we should love to make them sorry, but to fore-warn is the way to fore-arm them against their trials. Now here is, 1. The description of the deceiver and his deceit—he *confesses not that Jesus Christ has come in the flesh* (*v.* 7); he brings some error or other concerning the person of the Lord Jesus; he either confesses not that Jesus Christ is the same person, or that Jesus of Nazareth was the Christ, the anointed of God, the Messiah promised of old for the redemption of Israel, or that the promised Messiah and Redeemer has come in the flesh, or into the flesh, into our world and into our nature; such a one pretends that he is yet to be expected. Strange that after such evidence any should deny that the Lord Jesus is the Son of God and Saviour of the world! 2. The aggravation of the case—such a one is *a deceiver and an antichrist* (*v.* 7); he deludes souls and undermines the glory and kingdom of the Lord Christ. He must be an impostor, a wilful deceiver, after all the light that has been afforded, and all the evidence that Christ has given concerning himself, and the attestation God has given concerning his Son; and he is a wilful opposer of the person, and honour, and interest of the Lord Christ, and as such shall be reckoned with when the Lord Christ comes again. Let us not think it strange that there are deceivers and opposers of the Lord Christ's name and dignity now, for there were such of old, even in the apostle's times.

II. The counsel given to this elect household hereupon. Now care and caution are needful: *Look to yourselves, v.* 8. The more deceivers and deceits abound, the more watchful the disciples must be. Delusions may so prevail that even the elect may be endangered thereby. Two things they must beware of:—1. *That they lose not what they have wrought* (*v* 8), what they have done or what they have gained. It is a pity that any religious labour should be in vain; some begin well, but at last lose all their pains. The hopeful gentleman, who had kept the commands of the second table from his youth up, lost all for want of less love to the world and more love to Christ. Professors should take care not to lose what they have gained. Many have not only gained a fair reputation for religion, but much light therein, much conviction of the evil of sin, the vanity of the world, the excellency of religion, and the power of God's word. They have even *tasted of the powers of the world to come,* and the gifts of the Holy Spirit; and yet at last lose all. *You did run well, who hindered you, that you should not obey* (or not go on to obey) *the truth?* Sad it is that fair and splendid attainments in the school of Christ should all be lost at last. 2. That they lose not their reward, none of it, no portion of that honour, or praise, or glory that they once stood fair for. *That we* (or you, as in some copies) *receive a full reward.* "Secure you as full a reward as will be given to any in the church of God; if there are degrees of glory, lose none of that grace (that light, or love, or peace) which is to prepare you for the higher elevation in glory. *Hold fast that which thou hast* (in faith, and hope, and a good conscience), *that no man take thy crown,* that thou neither lose it nor any jewel out of it," Rev. iii. 11. The way to attain the full reward is to abide true to Christ, and constant in religion to the end.

III. The reason of the apostle's counsel, and of their care and caution about themselves, which is twofold:—1. The danger and evil of departure from gospel light and revelation; it is in effect and reality a departure from God himself: *Whosoever transgresseth* (transgresseth at this dismal rate), *and abideth not in the doctrine of Christ, hath not God.* It is the doctrine of Christ that is appointed to guide us to God; it is that whereby God draws souls to salvation and to himself. Those who revolt thence, in so doing revolt from God. 2. The advantage and happiness of firm adherence to Christian truth; it unites us to Christ (the object or subject-matter of that truth), and thereby to the Father also; for they are one. *He that abideth* (rooted and grounded) *in the doctrine of Christ, he hath both the Father and the Son.* By the doctrine of Christ we are enlightened in the knowledge of the Father and the Son; by it we are sanctified for the Father and the Son; thereupon we are enriched with holy love to the Father and the Son; and thereby prepared for the endless enjoyment of the Father and the Son. *Now you are clean through the word which I have spoken to you,* John. xv. 3. This purity makes meet for heaven. The great God, as he has set his seal to the doctrine of Christ, so he puts a value upon it. We must retain that holy doctrine in faith and love, as we hope or desire to arrive at blessed communion with the Father and the Son.

10 If there come any unto you, and bring not this doctrine, receive him not into *your* house, neither bid him God speed: 11 For he that biddeth him God speed is partaker of his evil deeds.

Here, I. Upon due warning given concerning seducers, the apostle gives direction concerning the treatment of such. They are not to be entertained as the ministers of Christ. The Lord Christ will distinguish them from such, and so would he have his disciples. The direction is negative. 1. "Support them not: *If there come any unto you, and bring not this doctrine* (concerning Christ as the Son of God, the Messiah and anointed of God for our redemption and salvation), *receive him not into your house.*" Possibly this lady was like Gaius, of whom we read in the next epistle, a generous housekeeper, and hospitable entertainer of travelling ministers and Christians. These deceivers might possibly expect the same reception with others, or with the best who came there (as the blind are often bold enough), but the apostle allows it not: "Do not welcome them into your family." Doubtless such may be relieved in their pressing necessities, but not encouraged for ill service. Deniers of the faith are destroyers of souls; and it is supposed that even ladies themselves should have good understanding in the affairs of religion. 2. "Bless not their enterprises: *Neither bid him God speed.* Attend not their service with your prayers and good wishes." Bad work should not be consecrated or recommended to the divine benediction. God will be no patron of falsehood, seduction, and sin. We ought to bid God speed to evangelical ministration; but the propagation of fatal error, if we cannot prevent, we must not dare to countenance. Then,

II. Here is the reason of such direction, forbidding the support and patronage of the deceiver: *For he that biddeth him God speed is partaker of his evil deeds.* Favour and affection partake of the sin. We may be sharers in the iniquities of others. How judicious and how cautious should the Christian be! There are many ways of sharing the guilt of other people's transgressions; it may be done by culpable silence, indolence, unconcernedness, private contribution, public countenance and assistance, inward approbation, open apology and defence. The Lord pardon our guilt of other persons' sins!

12 Having many things to write unto you, I would not *write* with paper and ink: but I trust to come unto you, and speak face to face, that our joy may be full. 13 The children of thy elect sister greet thee. Amen.

The apostle concludes this letter, 1. With an adjournment of many things to personal conference: *Having many things to write unto you I would not write with paper and ink; but I trust to come unto you, and speak face to face, that our joy may be full.* Here it is supposed that some things are better spoken than written. The use of pen and ink may be a mercy and a pleasure; but a personal interview may be more so. The apostle was not yet too old for travel, nor consequently for travelling service. The communion of saints should be by all methods maintained; and their communion should tend to their mutual joy. Excellent ministers may have their joy advanced by their Christian friends. *That I may be comforted together with you by the mutual faith both of you and me,* Rom. i. 12. 2. With the presentation of service and salutation from some near relations to the lady: *The children of thy elect sister greet thee.* Grace was abundant towards this family; here are two elect sisters, and probably their elect children. How will they admire this grace in heaven! The apostle condescends to insert the nieces' duty (as we should call it), or dutiful salutation, to their aunt. The duty of inferior relations is to be cherished. Doubtless the apostle was easy of access, and would admit all friendly and pious communication, and was ready to enhance the good lady's joy in her nieces as well as in her children. May there be many such gracious ladies rejoicing in their gracious descendants and other relations! *Amen.*

AN

EXPOSITION,

WITH PRACTICAL OBSERVATIONS,

OF THE THIRD EPISTLE OF

JOHN.

Christian communion is exerted and cherished by letter. Christians are to be commended in the practical proof of their professed subjection to the gospel of Christ. The animating and countenancing of generous and public-spirited persons is doing good to many—to this end the apostle sends this encouraging epistle to his friend Gaius, in which also he complains of the quite opposite spirit and practice of a certain minister, and confirms the good report concerning another more worthy to be imitated.

In this epistle the apostle congratulates Gaius upon the prosperity of his soul (ver. 1, 2), upon the fame he had among good Christians (ver. 3, 4), and upon his charity and hospitality to the servants of Christ, ver. 5, 6. He complains of contemptuous treatment by an ambitious Diotrephes (ver. 9, 10), recommends Demetrius (ver. 12), and expresses his hope of visiting Gaius shortly, ver. 13, 14.

THE elder unto the well-beloved Gaius, whom I love in the truth.
2 Beloved, I wish above all things that thou mayest prosper and be in health, even as thy soul prospereth.

Here we see, I. The sacred penman who writes and sends the letter; not here indeed notified by his name, but a more general character: *The elder,* he that is so by years and by office; honour and deference are due to both. Some have questioned whether this were John the apostle or no; but his style and spirit seem to shine in the epistle. Those that are beloved of Christ will love the brethren for his sake. Gaius could not question from whom the letter came. The apostle might have assumed many more illustrious characters, but it becomes not Christ's ministers to affect swelling pompous titles. He almost levels himself with the more ordinary pastors of the church, while he styles himself the elder. Or, possibly, most of the extraordinary ministers, the apostles, were now dead, and this holy survivor would countenance the continued standing ministry, by assuming the more common title—the elder. *The elders I exhort, who am also an elder,* 1 Pet. v. i.

II. The person saluted and honoured by the letter. The former is directed to an elect lady, this to a choice gentleman; such are worthy of esteem and value. He is notified, 1. By his name,—*Gaius.* We read of several of that name, particularly of one whom the apostle Paul baptized at Corinth, who possibly might be also the apostle's host and kind entertainer there (Rom. xvi. 23); if this be not he, it is his brother in name, estate, and disposition. Then, 2. By the kind expressions of the apostle to him: *The well-beloved,* and *whom I love in the truth.* Love expressed is wont to kindle love. Here seems to be either the sincerity of the apostle's love or the religion of it. The sincerity of it: *Whom I love in truth,* whom I truly cordially love. The religion of it: *Whom I love in the truth,* for the truth's sake, as abiding and walking in the truth as it is in Jesus. To love our friends for the truth's sake is true love, religious gospel love.

III. The salutation or greeting, containing a prayer, introduced by an affectionate compellation—*Beloved,* thou beloved one in Christ. The minister who would gain love must show it himself. Here is, 1. The apostle's good opinion of his friend, that his *soul prospered.* There is such a thing as soul-prosperity—the greatest blessing on this side heaven. This supposes regeneration, and an inward fund of spiritual life; this stock is increasing, and, while spiritual treasures are advancing, the soul is in a fair way to the kingdom of glory. 2. His good wish for his friend that his body may *prosper and be in health* as well as his soul. Grace and health are two rich companions; grace will improve health, health will employ grace. It frequently falls out that a rich soul is lodged in a crazy body; grace must be exercised in submission to such a dispensation; but we may well wish and pray that those who have prosperous souls may have healthful bodies too; their grace will shine in a larger sphere of activity.

3 For I rejoiced greatly, when the
brethren came and testified of the
truth that is in thee, even as thou
walkest in the truth. 4 I have no
greater joy than to hear that my
children walk in truth. 5 Beloved,
thou doest faithfully whatsoever thou
doest to the brethren, and to strangers;
6 Which have borne witness of thy
charity before the church: whom if
thou bring forward on their journey
after a godly sort, thou shalt do well:
7 Because that for his name's sake
they went forth, taking nothing of the
Gentiles. 8 We therefore ought to
receive such, that we might be fellow-
helpers to the truth.

In these verses we have,

I. The good report that the apostle had received concerning this friend of his: *The brethren came and testified of the truth that is in thee* (*v.* 3), *who have borne witness of thy charity before the church, v.* 6. Here we may see, 1. The testimony or thing testified concerning Gaius—the truth that was in him, the reality of his faith, the sincerity of his religion, and his devotedness to God; and this evinced by his charity, which includes his love to the brethren, kindness to the poor, hospitality to Christian strangers, and readiness to accommodate them for the service of the gospel. Faith should work by love; it gives a lustre in and by the offices of love, and induces others to commend its integrity. 2. The witnesses—brethren that came from Gaius testified and bore witness. A good report is due from those who have received good; though a good name is but a small reward for costly service, yet it is *better than precious ointment,* and will not be refused by the ingenuous and religious. 3. The auditory or judicatory before which the report and testimony were given—*before the church.* This seems to be the church at which the apostle now resided. What church this was we are not sure; what occasion they had thus to testify his faith and love before the church we cannot tell; possibly out of the fulness of the heart the mouth spoke; they could not but testify what they found and felt; possibly they would engage the church's prayer for the continued life and usefulness of such a patron, that he might *prosper and be in health as his soul prospered.*

II. The report the apostle himself gives of him, introduced by an endearing appellation again: *Beloved, thou doest faithfully whatsoever thou doest to the brethren, and to strangers, v.* 5. 1. He was hospitable, good to the brethren, even to strangers; it was enough to recommend them to Gaius's house that they belonged to Christ. Or he was good to *the brethren* of the same church with himself, and to those who came from far; all who were of the household of faith were welcome to him. 2. He seems to have been of a catholic spirit; he could overlook the petty differences among serious Christians, and be communicative to all who bore the image and did the work of Christ. And, 3. He was conscientious in what he did: "*Thou doest faithfully* (thou makest faithful work of) *whatsoever thou doest;* thou doest it as a faithful servant, and from the Lord Christ mayest thou expect the reward of the inheritance." Such faithful souls can hear their own praises without being puffed up; the commendation of what is good in us is designed, not for our pride, but for our encouragement to continue therein, and should be accordingly improved.

III. The apostle's joy therein, in the good report itself, and the good ground of it: *I rejoiced greatly when the brethren came and testified,* &c., *v.* 3. *I have no greater joy than to hear that my children walk in the truth,* in the prescripts of the Christian religion. The best evidence of our having the truth is our *walking in the truth.* Good men will greatly rejoice in the soul-prosperity of others; and they are glad to hear of the grace and goodness of others. *They glorified God in me.* Love envieth not, but rejoiceth in the good name of other folks. As it is joy to good parents, it will be joy to good ministers, to see their children evidence their sincerity in religion, and adorn their profession.

IV. The direction the apostle gives his friend concerning further treatment of the brethren that were with him: *Whom if thou bring forward on their journey, after a godly sort, thou shalt do well.* It seems to have been customary in those days of love to attend travelling ministers and Christians, at least some part of their road, 1 Cor. xvi. 6. It is a kindness to a stranger to be guided in his way, and a pleasure to travellers to meet with suitable company: this is a work that may be done *after a godly sort,* in a manner worthy of God, or suitable to the deference and relation we bear to God. Christians should consider not only what they must do, but what they may do, what they may most honourably and laudably do: *the liberal mind deviseth liberal* generous *things.* Christians should do even the common actions of life and of good-will after a godly sort, as serving God therein, and designing his glory.

V. The reasons of this directed conduct; these are two:—1. *Because that for his name's sake these brethren went forth, taking nothing of the Gentiles.* It appears thus that these were ministerial brethren, that they went forth to preach the gospel and propagate Christianity; possibly they might be sent out by this apostle himself: they went forth to convert the Gentiles; this was excellent service: they went forth for God and his name's sake; this is the minister's highest end, and should be his principal spring, and motive, to gather and to build up a people for his name: they went forth also to carry a free gospel about with them, to publish it without charge wherever they came: *Taking nothing of the Gentiles.* These were worthy of double honour. There are those who are not called to preach the gospel themselves who may yet contribute to the progress of it. The gospel should be made without charge to those to whom it is first preached. Those who know it not cannot be expected to value it; churches and Christian patriots ought to concur to support the propagation of holy religion in the pagan countries; public spirits should concur according to their several capacities; those who are freely communicative of Christ's gospel should be assisted by those who are communicative of their purses. 2. *We ought therefore to receive such, that we may be fellow-helpers to the truth,* to true religion. The institution of Christ is the true religion; it has been attested by God. Those that are true in it and true to it will earnestly desire, and pray for, and contribute to, its propagation in the world. In many ways may the truth be befriended and assisted; those who cannot themselves proclaim it may yet receive, accompany, help, and countenance those who do.

9 I wrote unto the church: but
Diotrephes, who loveth to have the
preeminence among them, receiveth
us not. 10 Wherefore, if I come, I
will remember his deeds which he
doeth, prating against us with malicious words: and not content therewith, neither doth he himself receive
the brethren, and forbiddeth them
that would, and casteth *them* out of
the church. 11 Beloved, follow not
that which is evil, but that which is
good. He that doeth good is of God:
but he that doeth evil hath not seen
God.

I. Here is a very different example and character, an officer, a minister in the church, less generous, catholic, and communicative than the private Christians. Ministers may sometimes be out-shone, out-done. In reference to this minister, we see,

1. His name—a Gentile name: *Diotrephes,* attended with an unchristian spirit.

2. His temper and spirit—full of pride and ambition: *He loves to have the pre-eminence* This ferment sprang and wrought betimes. It is an ill unbeseeming character of Christ's ministers to love pre-eminence, to affect presidency and precedency in the church of God.

3. His contempt of the apostle's authority, and letter, and friends. (1.) Of his authority: *The deeds which he doeth* contrary to our appointment, *prating against us with malicious words.* Strange that the contempt should run so high! But ambition will breed malice against those who oppose it. Malice and ill-will in the heart will be apt to vent themselves by the lips. The heart and mouth are both to be watched. (2.) Of his letter: "*I wrote to the church* (*v.* 9), namely, in recommendation of such and such brethren. *But Diotrephes receiveth us not,* admits not our letter and testimony therein." This seems to be the church of which Gaius was a member. A gospel church seems to be such a society as to which a letter may be written and communicated. Gospel churches may well expect and be allowed credentials with the strangers who desire to be admitted among them. The apostle seems to write by and with these brethren. To an ambitious aspiring spirit apostolical authority or epistle signifies but little. (3.) Of his friends, the brethren he recommended: *Neither doth he himself receive the brethren, and forbiddeth those that would, and casteth them out of the church, v.* 10. There might be some differences or different customs between the Jewish and Gentile Christians. Pastors should seriously consider what differences are tolerable. The pastor is not at absolute liberty, nor lord over God's heritage. It is bad to do no good ourselves; but it is worse to hinder those who would. Church-power and church-censures are often abused. Many are cast out of the church who should be received there with satisfaction and welcome. But woe to those who cast out the brethren whom the Lord Christ will take into his own communion and kingdom!

4. The apostle's menace of this proud domineerer: *Wherefore, if I come, I will remember his deeds which he doeth* (*v.* 10), will remember to censure them. This seems to intimate apostolical authority. But the apostle seems not to hold an episcopal court, to which Diotrephes must be summoned; but he will come to take cognizance of this affair in the church to which it belongs. Acts of ecclesiastical domination and tyranny ought to be animadverted upon. May it be better agreed to whom that power belongs!

II. Here is counsel upon that different character, dissuasion from copying such a pattern, and indeed any evil at all: *Beloved, follow not that which is evil, but that which is good, v.* 11. Imitate not such unchristian pernicious evil; but pursue the contrary good, in wisdom, purity, peace, and love. Caution and counsel are not needless to those who are good already. Those cautions and counsels are most likely to be accepted that are seasoned with love. *Beloved, follow not that which is evil.* To this caution and counsel a reason is respectively subjoined. 1. To the counsel: *Follow that which is good;* for *he that doeth good* (naturally and genuinely doeth good, as delighting therein) *is of God,* is born of God. The practice of goodness is the evidence of our filial happy relation to God. 2. To the caution: *Follow not that which is evil,* for *he that doeth evil* (with bent of mind pursues it) *hath not seen God,* is not duly sensible of his holy nature and will. Evil-workers vainly pretend or boast an acquaintance with God.

12 Demetrius hath good report of all *men,* and of the truth itself: yea, and we *also* bear record; and ye know that our record is true.
13 I had many things to write, but I will not with ink and pen write unto thee:
14 But I trust I shall shortly see thee, and we shall speak face to face. Peace *be* to thee. *Our* friends salute thee. Greet the friends by name.

Here we have, I. The character of another person, one *Demetrius,* not much known otherwise. But here his name will live. A name in the gospel, a fame in the churches, is better than that of sons and daughters. His character was his commendation. His commendation was, 1. General: *Demetrius has a good report of all men.* Few are well spoken of by all; and sometimes it is ill to be so. But universal integrity and goodness are the way to (and sometimes obtain) universal applause. 2. Deserved and well founded: *And of the truth itself, v.* 12. Some have a good report, but not of the truth itself. Happy are those whose spirit and conduct commend them before God and men. 3. Confirmed by the apostle's and his friends' testimony: *Yea, and we also bear record;* and that with an appeal to Gaius's own knowledge: *And you* (you and your friends) *know that our record is true.* Probably this Demetrius was known to the church where the apostle now resided, and to that where Gaius was. It is good to be well known, or known for good. We must be ready to bear our testimony to those who are good: it is a debt to virtue and goodness. It is well for those who are commended when those who commend them can appeal to the consciences of those who know them most.

II. The conclusion of the epistle, in which we may observe, 1. The referring of some things to personal interview: *I have many things to write, but I will not with ink and pen, but I trust I shall shortly see thee, v.* 13, 14. Many things may be more proper for immediate communication than for letter. A little personal conference may spare the time, trouble, and charge, of many letters; and good Christians may well be glad to see one another. 2. The benediction: *Peace be to you;* all felicity attend you. Those that are good and happy themselves wish others so too. 3. The public salutation sent to Gaius: *Our friends salute thee.* A friend to the propagation of religion deserves a common remembrance. And these pious persons show their friendship to religion as well as to Gaius. 4. The apostle's particular salutation of the Christians in Gaius's church or vicinity: *Greet the friends by name.* I doubt they were not very many who must be so personally saluted. But we must learn humility as well as love. The lowest in the church of Christ should be greeted. And those may well salute and greet one another on earth who hope to live together in heaven. And the apostle who had lain in Christ's bosom lays Christ's friends in his heart.

AN

EXPOSITION,

WITH PRACTICAL OBSERVATIONS,

OF THE GENERAL EPISTLE OF

JUDE.

THIS epistle is styled (as are some few others) *general* or *Catholic,* because it is not immediately directed to any particular person, family, or church, but to the whole society of Christians of that time, lately converted to the faith of Christ, whether from Judaism or paganism: and it is, and will be, of standing, lasting, and special use in and to the church as long as Christianity, that is, as time, shall last. The general scope of it is much the same with that of the second chapter of the second epistle of Peter, which having been already explained, the less will need to be said on this. It is designed to warn us against seducers and their seduction, to inspire us with a warm love to, and a hearty concern for, truth (evident and important truth), and that in the closest conjunction with holiness, of which charity, or sincere unbiassed brotherly-love, is a most essential character and inseparable branch. The truth we are to hold fast, and endeavour that others may be acquainted with and not depart from, has two special characters :—It is *the truth as it is in Jesus* (Eph. iv. 21 ; and it is *truth after* (or *which is according to) godliness*, Tit. i. 1. The gospel is the gospel of Christ. He has revealed it to us, and he is the main subject of it ; and therefore we are indispensably bound to learn thence all we can of his person, natures, and offices : indifference as to this is inexcusable in any who call themselves *Christians ;* and we know from what fountain we are wholly and solely to draw all necessary saving knowledge. Further, it is also a doctrine of godliness. Whatever doctrines favour the corrupt lusts of men cannot be of God, let the pleas and pretensions for them be what they will. Errors dangerous to the souls of men soon sprang up in the church. *The servants slept and tares were sown.* But such were the wisdom and kindness of Providence that they began sensibly to appear and show themselves, while some, at least, of the apostles were yet alive to confute them, and warn others against them. We are apt to think, If we had lived in their times, we should have been abundantly fenced against the attempts and artifices of seducers ; but we have their testimony and their cautions, which is sufficient ; and, if we will not believe their writings, neither should we have believed or regarded their sayings, if we had lived among them and conversed personally with them.

We have here, I. An account of the penman of this epistle, a character of the church, the blessings and privileges of that happy society, ver. 1, 2. II. The occasion of writing this epistle, ver. 3. III. A character of evil and perverse men, who had already sprung up in that infant state of the church, and would be succeeded by others of the like evil spirit and temper in after-times, ver. 4. IV. A caution against hearkening to and following after such, from the severity of God towards the unbelieving murmuring Israelites at their coming out of Egypt, the angels that fell, the sin and punishment of Sodom and Gomorrah, ver. 5—7. V. To these the apostle likens the seducers against whom he was warning them, and describes them at large, from ver. 8 to 13, inclusive. VI. Then (as specially suitable to his argument) he cites an ancient prophecy of Enoch foretelling and describing the future judgment, ver. 14, 15. VII. He enlarges on the seducers' character, and guards against the offence which honest minds might be apt to take at the so early permission of such things, by showing that it was foretold long before that so it must be, ver. 16—19. VIII. Exhorts them to perseverance in the faith, fervency in prayer, watchfulness against falling from the love of God, and a lively hope of eternal life, ver. 20, 21. IX. Directs them how to act towards the erroneous and scandalous, ver. 22, 23. And, X. Closes with an admirable doxology in the last two verses.

JUDE, the servant of Jesus Christ, and brother of James, to them that are sanctified by God the Father, and preserved in Jesus Christ, *and* called :
2 Mercy unto you, and peace, and love, be multiplied.

Here we have the preface or introduction, in which,

I. We have an account of the penman of this epistle, *Jude*, or *Judas*, or Judah. He was name-sake to one of his ancestors, the patriarch-son of Jacob, the most eminent though not the first-born of his sons, out of whose loins (lineally, in a most direct succession) the Messiah came. This was a name of worth, eminency, and honour ; yet, 1. He had a wicked name-sake. There was one Judas (one of the twelve, surnamed *Iscariot*, from the place of his birth) who was a vile traitor, the betrayer of his and our Lord. The same names may be common to the best and worst persons. It may be instructive to be called after the names of eminently good men, but there can be no inference drawn thence as to what we shall prove, though we may even thence conclude what sort of persons our good parents or progenitors desired and hoped we should be. But, 2. Our Judas was quite another man. He was an apostle, so was Iscariot ; but he was a sincere disciple and follower of Christ, so was not the other. He was a faithful servant of Jesus Christ, the other was his betrayer and murderer ; therefore here the one is very carefully distinguished from the other. Dr. Manton's note upon this is, that God takes great care of the good name of his sincere and useful servants. Why then should we be prodigal of our own or one another's reputation and usefulness ? Our apostle here calls himself a servant of Jesus Christ, esteeming that a most honourable title. It is more honourable to be a sincere and useful servant of Christ than to be an earthly king, how potent and prosperous soever. He might have claimed kindred to Christ according to the flesh, but he waives this, and rather glories in being his servant. Observe, (1.) It is really a greater honour to be a faithful servant of Jesus Christ than to be akin to him according to the flesh. Many of Christ's natural kindred, as well as of his progenitors, perished ; not from want of natural affection in him as man, but from infidelity and obstinacy in themselves, which should make the descendants and near relatives of persons most eminent for sincere and exemplary piety *jealous over themselves with a godly jealousy.* A son of Noah may be saved in the ark from a flood of temporal destruction, and yet be overwhelmed at last in a deluge of divine wrath, and suffer *the vengeance of eternal fire.* Christ himself tells us *that he that heareth his word and doeth it* (that is, he only) *is as his brother, and sister, and mother*, that is, more honourably and advantageously related to him than the nearest and dearest of his natural relatives, considered merely as such. See Matt. xii. 48—50. (2.) In that the apostle Jude styles himself a servant, though an apostle, a dignified officer in Christ's kingdom, it is a great honour to the meanest sincere minister (and it holds proportionably as to every upright Christian) that he is *the servant of Christ Jesus.* The apostles were servants before they were apostles, and they were but servants still. Away then with all pretensions in the ministers of Christ to lordly dominion either over one another or over the flocks committed to their charge. Let us ever have that of our dear Redeemer in actual view, *It shall not be so among you,* Matt. xx. 25, 26.—*And brother of James,* to wit, of him whom the ancients style *the first bishop of Jerusalem,* of whose character and martyrdom Josephus makes mention, ascribing the horrible destruction of that city and nation to this wicked cruelty, as one of its principal causes. Of this James our Jude was brother, whether in the strictest or a larger (though very usual) acceptation I determine not. He however reckons it an honour to him that he was the brother of such a one. We ought to honour those who are above us in age, gifts, graces, station; not to envy them, yet neither to flatter them, nor be led merely by their example, when we have reason to think they act wrong. Thus the apostle Paul withstood his fellow-apostle Peter to the face, notwithstanding the high esteem he had for him and the affectionate love he bore to him, when he saw that he was to be blamed, that is, really blameworthy, Gal. ii. 11, and following verses.

II. We are here informed to whom this epistle is directed; namely, to all those *who are sanctified by God the Father, and preserved in Jesus Christ, and called.* I begin with the last—*called,* that is, called *Christians,* in the judgment of charity, further than which we cannot, nor in justice ought to go, in the judgments or opinions we form or receive of one another; for what appears not is not, nor ought to come into account in all our dealings with and censures of one another, whatever abatements the divine goodness may see fit to make for an honest though misguided zeal. The church pretends not (I am sure it ought not) to judge of *secret or hidden things* (things drawn into the light before the time), lest our rash and preposterous zeal do more harm than ever it has done good, or I am afraid ever will do. *The tares and wheat* (if Christ may be Judge) *must grow together till the harvest* (Matt. xiii. 28—30); and then he himself will, by proper instruments, take timely care to separate them. We ought to think the best we can of every man till the contrary appear; not being forward to receive or propagate, much less invent, disadvantageous characters of our brethren. This is the least we can make of the apostle's large and excellent description of charity (1 Cor. xiii.), and this we ought to make conscience of acting up to, which till we do, the Christian churches will be (as, alas! they are at this day) filled with *envying and strife, confusion and every evil work,* Jam. iii. 16. Or, the apostle may speak of their being *called to be Christians,* by the preaching of the word, which they gladly received, and professed cordially to believe, and so were received into the society and fellowship of the church—Christ the head, and believers the members; real believers really, professed believers visibly. Note, Christians are the called, called out of the world, the evil spirit and temper of it,—above the world, to higher and better things, heaven, things unseen and eternal,—called from sin to Christ, from vanity to seriousness, from uncleanness to holiness; and this in pursuance of divine purpose and grace; *for whom he did predestinate those he also called,* Rom. viii. 30. Now those who are thus called, are, 1. Sanctified: *Sanctified by God the Father.* Sanctification is usually spoken of in scripture as the work of the Holy Spirit, yet here it is ascribed to God the Father, because the Spirit works it as the Spirit of the Father and the Son. Note, All who are effectually called are sanctified, *made partakers of a divine nature* (2 Pet. i. 4); *for without holiness no man shall see the Lord,* Heb. xii. 14. Observe, Our sanctification is not our own work. If any are sanctified, they are so by God the Father, not excluding Son or Spirit, for they are one, one God. Our corruption and pollution are of ourselves; but our sanctification and renovation are of God and his grace; and therefore if we perish in our iniquity we must bear the blame, but if we be sanctified and glorified all the honour and glory must be ascribed to God, and to him alone. I own it is hard to give a clear and distinct account of this, but we must not deny nor disregard necessary truth because we cannot fully reconcile the several parts of it to each other; for, on that supposition, we might deny that any one of us could stir an inch from the place we are at present in, though we see the contrary every day and hour. 2. The called and sanctified are *preserved in Christ Jesus.* As it is God who begins the work of grace in the souls of men, so it is he who carries it on, and perfects it. Where he begins he will perfect; though we are fickle, he is constant. *He will not forsake the work of his own hands,* Ps. cxxxviii. 8. Let us not therefore trust in ourselves, nor in our stock of grace already received, but in him, and in him alone, still endeavouring, by all proper and appointed means, to keep ourselves, as ever we would hope he should keep us. Note, (1.) Believers are *preserved* from the gates of hell, and to the glory of heaven. (2.) All who are preserved are preserved in Jesus Christ, in him as their *citadel and stronghold,* no longer than they abide in him, and solely by virtue of their union with him.

III. We have the apostolical benediction: *Mercy to you,* &c. From the mercy, peace, and love of God all our comfort flows, all our real enjoyment in this life, all our hope of a better. 1. The *mercy* of God is the spring and fountain of all the good we have or hope for; mercy not only to the miserable, but to the guilty. 2. Next to mercy is *peace,* which we have from the sense of having obtained mercy. We can have no true and lasting peace but what flows from our reconciliation with God by Jesus Christ. 3. As from mercy springs peace, so from peace springs *love*, his love to us, our love to him, and our brotherly love (forgotten, wretchedly neglected, grace!) to one another. These the apostle prays may be multiplied, that Christians may not be content with scraps and narrow scantlings of them; but that souls and societies may be full of them. Note, God is ready to supply us with all grace, and a fulness in each grace. If we are straitened, we are not straitened in him, but in ourselves.

3 Beloved, when I gave all diligence to write unto you of the common salvation, it was needful for me
to write unto you, and exhort *you*
that ye should earnestly contend for
the faith which was once delivered
unto the saints. 4 For there are
certain men crept in unawares, who
were before of old ordained to this
condemnation, ungodly men, turning
the grace of our God into lasciviousness, and denying the only Lord God,
and our Lord Jesus Christ. 5 I will
therefore put you in remembrance,
though ye once knew this, how that
the Lord, having saved the people out
of the land of Egypt, afterward destroyed them that believed not. 6
And the angels which kept not their
first estate, but left their own habitation, he hath reserved in everlasting
chains under darkness unto the judgment of the great day. 7 Even as
Sodom and Gomorrha, and the cities
about them in like manner, giving
themselves over to fornication, and
going after strange flesh, are set forth
for an example, suffering the vengeance of eternal fire.

We have here, I. The design of the apostle in writing this epistle to the lately converted Jews and Gentiles; namely, to establish them in the Christian faith, and a practice and conversation truly consonant and conformable thereunto, and in an open and bold profession thereof, especially in times of notorious opposition, whether by artful seduction or violent and inhuman persecution. But then we must see to it very carefully that it be really the Christian faith that we believe, profess, propagate, and contend for; not the discriminating badges of this or the other party, not any thing of later date than the inspired writings of the holy evangelists and apostles. Here observe, 1. The gospel salvation is a common salvation, that is, in a most sincere offer and tender of it to all mankind to whom the notice of it reaches: for so the commission runs (Mark xvi. 15, 16), *Go you into all the world, and preach the gospel to every creature*, &c. Surely God means as he speaks; he does not delude us with vain words, whatever men do; and therefore none are excluded from the benefit of these gracious offers and invitations, but those who obstinately, impenitently, finally exclude themselves. *Whoever will may come and drink of the water of life freely*, Rev. xxii. 17. The application of it is made to all believers, and only to such; it is made to the weak as well as to the strong. Let none discourage themselves on the account of hidden decrees which they can know little of, and with which they have nothing to do. God's decrees are dark, his covenants are plain. "All good Christians meet in Christ the common head, are actuated by one and the same Spirit, are guided by one rule, meet here at one throne of grace, and hope shortly to meet in one common inheritance," a glorious one to be sure, but what or how glorious we cannot, nor at present need to know; but such it will be as vastly to exceed all our present hopes and expectations. 2. This common salvation is the subject-matter of the faith of all the saints. The doctrine of it is what they all most heartily consent to; they esteem it as a *faithful saying, and worthy of all acceptation*, 1 Tim. i. 15. It is the faith once, *or at once, once for all, delivered to the saints*, to which nothing can be added, from which nothing may be detracted, in which nothing more nor less should be altered. Here let us abide; here we are safe; if we stir a step further, we are in danger of being either entangled or seduced. 3. The apostles and evangelists all wrote to us of this common salvation. This cannot be doubted by those who have carefully read their writings. It is strange that any should think they wrote chiefly to maintain particular schemes and opinions, especially such as they never did nor could think of. It is enough that they have fully declared to us, by inspiration of the Holy Ghost, all that is necessary *for every one to believe and do*, in order to obtain a personal interest in the common salvation. 4. Those who preach or write of the common salvation should give all diligence to do it well: they should not allow themselves to offer to God or his people that which costs them nothing, or next to nothing, little or no pains or thought, 2 Sam. xxiv. 24. This were to treat God irreverently, and man unjustly. The apostle (though inspired) gave all diligence to write of the common salvation. What then will become of those who (though uninspired) give no diligence, or next to none, but say to the people (even in the name of God) *quicquid in buccam venerit—whatever comes next*, who, so that they use scripture-words, care not how they interpret or apply them? Those who speak of sacred things ought always to speak of them with the greatest reverence, care, and diligence. 5. Those who have received the doctrine of this common salvation must contend earnestly for it. *Earnestly*, not *furiously*. Those who strive for the Christian faith, or in the Christian course, must strive lawfully, or they lose their labour, and run great hazard of losing their crown, 2 Tim. ii. 5. *The wrath of man worketh not the righteousness of God*, Jam. i. 20. Lying for the truth is bad, and scolding for it is not much better. Observe, Those who have received the truth must contend for it. But how? As the apostles did; by suffering patiently and courageously for it, not by making others suffer if they will not presently embrace every notion that we are pleased (proved or unproved) to call faith, or fundamental. We must not suffer ourselves to be robbed of any essential article of Christian faith, by the cunning craftiness or specious plausible pretences of any who *lie in wait to deceive*, Eph. iv. 14. The apostle Paul tells us he preached the gospel (mind it was the gospel) *with much contention* (1 Thess. ii. 2), that is (as I understand it), with great earnestness, with a hearty zeal, and a great concern for the success of what he preached. But, if we will understand *contention* in the common acceptation of the word, we must impartially consider with whom the apostle contended, and how, the enlarging on which would not be proper for this place.

II. The occasion the apostle had to write to this purport. As evil manners give rise to good laws, so dangerous errors often give just occasion to the proper defence of important truths. Here observe, 1. Ungodly men are the great enemies of the faith of Christ and the peace of the church. Those who deny or corrupt the one, and disturb the other, are here expressly styled *ungodly men*. We might have truth with peace (a most desirable thing) were there none (ministers or private Christians) in our particular churches and congregations but truly godly men—a blessing scarcely to be looked or hoped for on this side heaven. Ungodly men raise scruples, start questions, cause divisions, widen breaches, merely to advance and promote their own selfish, ambitious, and covetous ends. This has been the plague of the church in all past ages, and I am afraid no age is, or will be, wholly free from such men and such practices as long as time shall last. Observe, Nothing cuts us off from the church but that which cuts us off from Christ; namely, reigning infidelity and ungodliness. We must abhor the thought of branding particular parties or persons with this character, especially of doing it without the least proof, or, as it too often happens, the least shadow of it. Those are ungodly men who live *without God in the world*, who have no regard to God and conscience. Those are to be dreaded and consequently to be avoided, not only who are wicked by sins of commission, but also who are ungodly by sins of omission, who, for example, restrain prayer before God, who dare not reprove a rich man, when it is the duty of their place so to do, for fear of losing his favour and the advantage they promise themselves therefrom, who *do the work of the Lord negligently*, &c. 2. Those are *the worst of ungodly men who turn the grace of God into lasciviousness*, who take encouragement to sin more boldly because the grace of God has abounded, and still abounds, so wonderfully, who are hardened in their impieties by the extent and fulness of gospel grace, the design of which is to reduce men from sin, and bring them unto God. Thus therefore to wax wanton under so great grace, and turn it into an occasion of working all uncleanness with greediness, and hardening ourselves in such a course by that very grace which is the last and most forcible means to reclaim us from it, is to render ourselves the vilest, the worst, and most hopeless of sinners. 3. Those who turn the grace of God into lasciviousness do in effect *deny the Lord God, and our Lord Jesus Christ;* that is, they deny both natural and revealed religion. They strike at the foundation of natural religion, for they *deny the only Lord God;* and they overturn all the frame of revealed religion, for they deny *the Lord Jesus Christ*. Now his great design in establishing revealed religion in the world was to bring us unto God. Note, Those who deny our Lord Jesus Christ do in effect deny the only Lord God. To deny revealed religion is virtually to overturn natural religion, for they stand or fall together, and they mutually yield light and force to each other. Would to God our modern deists, who live in the midst of gospel light, would seriously consider this, and cautiously, diligently, and impartially examine what it is that hinders their receiving the gospel, while they profess themselves fully persuaded of all the principles and duties of natural religion! Never two tallies answered more exactly to each other than these do, so that it seems absurd to receive the one and reject the other. One would think it were the fairer way to receive both or reject both; though perhaps the more plausible method, especially in this age, is to act the part they do. 4. Those who turn the grace of God into lasciviousness are ordained unto condemnation. They sin against the last, the greatest, and most perfect remedy; and so are without excuse. Those who thus sin must needs die of their wounds, of their disease, are of old ordained to this condemnation, whatever that expression means. But what if our translators had thought fit to have rendered the words πάλαι προγεγραμμένοι—*of old fore-written of*, as persons who would through their own sin and folly become the proper subjects of this condemnation, where had the harm been? Plain Christians had not been troubled with dark, doubtful, and perplexing thoughts about reprobation, which the strongest heads cannot enter far into, can indeed bear but little of, without much loss and damage. Is it not enough that early notice was given by inspired writers that such seducers and wicked men should arise in later times, and that every one, being forewarned of, should be fore-armed against them? 5. We ought to contend earnestly for the faith, in opposition to those who would corrupt or deprave it, such as have *crept in unawares:* a wretched character, to be sure, but often very ill applied by weak and ignorant people, and even by those who themselves creep in unawares, who think their *ipse dixit* should stand for a law to all their followers and admirers. Surely faithful humble ministers are helpers of their people's joy, peace, and comfort; *not lords of their faith!* Whoever may attempt to corrupt the faith, we ought to contend earnestly against them. The more busy and crafty the instruments and agents of Satan are, to rob us of the truth, the more solicitous should we be to hold it fast, always provided we be very sure that we fasten no wrong or injurious characters on persons, parties, or sentiments.

III. The fair warning which the apostle, in Christ's name, gives to those who, having professed his holy religion, do afterwards desert and prove false to it, *v.* 5—7. We have here a recital of the former judgments of God upon sinners, with design to awaken and terrify those to whom warning is given in this epistle. Observe, The judgments of God are often denounced and executed *in terrorem—for warning to others,* rather than from immediate or particular displeasure against the offenders themselves; not that God is not displeased with them, but perhaps not more with them than with others who, at least for the present, escape. *I will put you in remembrance.* What we already know we still need to be put in remembrance of. Therefore there will always be need and use of a standing stated ministry in the Christian church, though all the doctrines of faith, the essentials, are so plainly revealed in express words, or by the most near, plain, and immediate consequence, that he who runs may read and understand them. There wants no infallible interpreter, really or conceitedly such, for any such end or purpose. Some people (weakly enough) suggest, "If the scriptures do so plainly contain all that is necessary to salvation, what need or use can there be of a standing ministry? Why may we not content ourselves with staying at home, and reading our Bibles?" The inspired apostle has here fully, though not wholly, answered this objection. Preaching is not designed to teach us something new in every sermon, somewhat that we knew nothing of before; but *to put us in remembrance,* to call to mind things forgotten, to affect our passions, and engage and fix our resolutions, that our lives may be answerable to our faith. *Though you know these things,* yet you still need to *know them better.* There are many things which we have known which yet we have unhappily forgotten. Is it of no use or service to be put afresh in remembrance of them?

Now what are these things which we Christians need to be put in remembrance of?

1. The destruction of the unbelieving Israelites in the wilderness, *v.* 5. Paul puts the Corinthians in mind of this, 1 Cor. x. The first ten verses of that chapter (as the scripture is always the best commentary upon itself) are the best explication of the fifth verse of this epistle of Jude. None therefore ought to presume upon their privileges, since many who were brought out of Egypt by a series of amazing miracles, yet perished in the wilderness by reason of their unbelief. *Let us not therefore be high-minded, but fear,* Rom. xi. 20. *Let us fear lest, a promise being left us of entering into his rest, any of you should seem to come short of it,* Heb. iv. 1. They had miracles in abundance: they were their daily bread; yet even they perished in unbelief. We have greater (much greater) advantages than they had; let their error (their so fatal error) be our awful warning.

2. We are here put in remembrance of the fall of the angels, *v.* 6. There were a great number of the angels who *left their own habitation;* that is, who were not pleased with the posts and stations the supreme Monarch of the universe had assigned and allotted to them, but thought (like discontented ministers in our age, I might say in every age) they deserved better; they would, with the title of *ministers,* be *sovereigns,* and in effect their Sovereign should be their minister—do all, and only, what they would have him; thus was pride the main and immediate cause or occasion of their fall. Thus they quitted their post, and rebelled against God, their Creator and sovereign Lord. But God did not spare them (high and great as they were); he would not truckle to them; he threw them off, as a wise and good prince will a selfish and deceitful minister; and the great, the all-wise God, could not be ignorant, as the wisest and best of earthly princes often are, what designs they were hatching. After all, what became of them? They thought to have dared and outfaced Omnipotence itself; but God was too hard for them, he cast them down to hell. Those who would not be servants to their Maker and his will in their first state were made captives to his justice, and are *reserved in everlasting chains under darkness.* Here see what the condition of fallen angels is: they are *in chains,* bound under the divine power and justice, bound over *to the judgment of the great day;* they are *under darkness,* though once *angels of light;* so horribly in the dark are they that they continue to fight against God, as if there were yet some small hope at least left them of prevailing and overcoming in the conflict. Dire infatuation! Light and liberty concur, chains and darkness how well do they agree and suit each other! The devils, once angels in the best sense, are *reserved,* &c. Observe,

There is, undoubtedly there is, a judgment to come; the fallen angels are *reserved to the judgment of the great day;* and shall fallen men escape it? Surely not. Let every reader consider this in due time. Their chains are called everlasting, because it is impossible they should ever break loose from them, or make an escape; they are held fast and sure under them. The decree, the justice, the wrath of God, are the very chains under which fallen angels are held so fast. Hear and fear, O sinful mortals of mankind!

3. The apostle here calls to our remembrance the destruction of Sodom and Gomorrah, *v.* 7. *Even as,* &c. It is in allusion to the destruction of *Pentapolis,* or the five cities, that the miseries of the damned are set forth by a lake that burneth with fire and brimstone; they were guilty of abominable wickedness, not to be named or thought of but with the utmost abhorrence and detestation; their ruin is a particular warning to all people to take heed of, and fly *from, fleshly lusts that war against the soul,* 1 Pet. ii. 11. "These lusts consumed the Sodomites with fire from heaven, and they are now *suffering the vengeance of eternal fire;* therefore take heed, imitate not their sins, lest the same plagues overtake you as did them. God is the same holy, just, pure Being now as then; and can the beastly pleasures of a moment make amends for your suffering the vengeance of eternal fire? *Stand in awe, therefore, and sin not,* Ps. iv. 4.

8 Likewise also these *filthy* dreamers
defile the flesh, despise dominion, and
speak evil of dignities. 9 Yet Michael
the archangel, when contending with
the devil he disputed about the body
of Moses, durst not bring against him
a railing accusation, but said, The
Lord rebuke thee. 10 But these
speak evil of those things which they
know not: but what they know naturally, as brute beasts, in those
things they corrupt themselves. 11
Woe unto them! for they have gone
in the way of Cain, and ran greedily
after the error of Balaam for reward,
and perished in the gainsaying of
Core. 12 These are spots in your
feasts of charity, when they feast with
you, feeding themselves without fear:
clouds *they are* without water, carried
about of winds; trees whose fruit
withereth, without fruit, twice dead,
plucked up by the roots; 13 Raging
waves of the sea, foaming out their
own shame; wandering stars, to whom
is reserved the blackness of darkness
for ever. 14 And Enoch also, the
seventh from Adam, prophesied of
these, saying, Behold, the Lord
cometh with ten thousands of his
saints, 15 To execute judgment upon
all, and to convince all that are ungodly among them of all their ungodly deeds which they have ungodly
committed, and of all their hard
speeches which ungodly sinners have
spoken against him.

The apostle here exhibits a charge against deceivers who were now seducing the disciples of Christ from the profession and practice of his holy religion. He calls them *filthy dreamers,* forasmuch as delusion is a dream, and the beginning of, and inlet to, all manner of filthiness. Note, Sin is filthiness; it renders men odious and vile in the sight of the most holy God, and makes them (sooner or later, as penitent or as punished to extremity and without resource) vile in their own eyes, and in a while they become vile in the eyes of all about them. *These filthy dreamers* dream themselves into a fool's paradise on earth, and into a real hell at last: let their character, course, and end, be our seasonable and sufficient warning; like sins will produce like punishments and miseries. Here,

I. The character of these deceivers is described.

1. They *defile the flesh.* The flesh or body is the immediate seat, and often the irritating occasion, of many horrid pollutions; yet these, though done in and against the body, do greatly defile and grievously maim and wound the soul. *Fleshly lusts do war against the soul,* 1 Pet. ii. 11; and in 2 Cor. vii. 1 we read of *filthiness of flesh and spirit,* each of which, though of different kinds, defiles the whole man.

2. They *despise dominion, and speak evil of dignities,* are of a disturbed mind and a seditious spirit, forgetting that *the powers that be are ordained of God,* Rom. xiii. 1. God requires us to *speak evil of no man* (Tit. iii. 2); but it is a great aggravation of the sin of evil-speaking when what we say is pointed at magistrates, men whom God has set in authority over us, by blaspheming or speaking evil of whom we blaspheme God himself. Or if we understand it, as some do, with respect to religion, which ought to have the dominion in this lower world, such evil-speakers despise the dominion of conscience, make a jest of it, and would banish it out of the world; and as for the word of God, the rule of conscience, they despise it. The revelations of the divine will go for little with them; they are a rule of faith and manners. but not till they have explained them, and imposed their sense of them upon all about them. Or, as others account for the sense of this passage, the people of God, truly and specially so, are the dignities here spoken of or referred to, according to that of the

psalmist, *Touch not mine anointed, and do my prophets no harm*, Ps. cv. 15. They *speak evil*, &c. Religion and its serious professors have been always and every where evil spoken of. Though there is nothing in religion but what is very good, and deserves our highest regards, both as it is perfective of our natures and as it is subservient to our truest and highest interests; yet *this sect*, as its enemies are pleased to call it, *is every where spoken against*, Acts xxviii. 22.

On this occasion the apostle brings in *Michael the archangel*, &c., *v.* 9. Interpreters are at a loss what is here meant by *the body of Moses*. Some think that the devil contended that Moses might have a public and honourable funeral, that the place where he was interred might be generally known, hoping thereby to draw the Jews, so naturally prone thereto, to a new and fresh instance of idolatry. Dr. Scott thinks that by the body of Moses we are to understand the Jewish church, whose destruction the devil strove and contended for, as the Christian church is called the body of Christ in the New-Testament style. Others bring other interpretations, which I will not here trouble the reader with. Though this contest was mightily eager and earnest, and Michael was victorious in the issue, yet he would not *bring a railing accusation against the devil himself;* he knew a good cause needed no such weapons to be employed in its defence. It is said, *He durst not bring*, &c. Why durst he not? Not that he was afraid of the devil, but he believed God would be offended if, in such a dispute, he went that way to work; he thought it below him to engage in a trial of skill with the great enemy of God and man which of them should out-scold or out-rail the other: a memorandum to all disputants, never to bring railing accusations into their disputes. Truth needs no supports from falsehood or scurrility. Some say, Michael would not bring a railing accusation against the devil as knowing beforehand that he would be too hard for him at that weapon. Some think the apostle refers here to the remarkable passage we have, Num. xx. 7—14. Satan would have represented Moses under disadvantageous colours, which he, good man, had at that time, and upon that occasion, given but too much handle for. Now Michael, according to this account, stands up in defence of Moses, and, in the zeal of an upright and bold spirit, says to Satan, *The Lord rebuke thee*. He would not stand disputing with the devil, nor enter into a particular debate about the merits of that special cause. He knew Moses was his fellow-servant, a favourite of God, and he would not patiently suffer him to be insulted, no, not by the prince of devils; but in a just indignation cries out, *The Lord rebuke thee:* like that of our Lord himself (Matt. iv. 10), *Get thee hence, Satan.* Moses was a dignity, a magistrate, one beloved and preferred by the great God; and the archangel thought it insufferable that such a one should be so treated by a vile apostate spirit, of how high an order soever. So the lesson hence is that we ought to stand up in defence of those whom God owns, how severe soever Satan and his instruments may be in their censures of them and their conduct. Those who censure (in particular) upright magistrates, upon every slip in their behaviour, may expect to hear, *The Lord rebuke thee;* and divine rebukes are harder to be borne than careless sinners now think for.

3. *They speak evil of the things which they know not*, &c., *v.* 10. Observe, Those who speak evil of religion and godliness *speak evil of the things which they know not;* for, if they had known them, they would have spoken well of them, for nothing but good and excellent can be truly said of religion, and it is sad that any thing different or opposite should ever be justly said of any of its professors. A religious life is the most safe, happy, comfortable, and honourable life that is. Observe, further, Men are most apt to speak evil of those persons and things that they know least of. How many had never suffered by slanderous tongues if they had been better known! On the other hand, retirement screens some even from just censure. *But what they know naturally*, &c. It is hard, if not impossible, to find any obstinate enemies to the Christian religion, who do not in their stated course live in open or secret contradiction to the very principles of natural religion: this many think hard and uncharitable; but I am afraid it will appear too true in *the day of the revelation of the righteous judgment of God.* The apostle likens such to *brute beasts*, though they often think and boast themselves, if not as the wisest, yet at least as the wittiest part of mankind. *In those things they corrupt themselves;* that is, in the plainest and most natural and necessary things, things that lie most open and obvious to natural reason and conscience; even in those things they corrupt, debase, and defile themselves: the fault, whatever it is, lies not in their understandings or apprehensions, but in their depraved wills and disordered appetites and affections; they could and might have acted better, but then they must have offered violence to those vile affections which they obstinately chose rather to gratify than to mortify.

4. In *v.* 11 the apostle represents them as followers *of Cain*, and in *v.* 12, 13, as atheistical and profane people, who thought little, and perhaps believed not much, of God or a future world—as greedy and covetous, who, so they could but gain present worldly advantages, cared not what came next—rebels against God and man, who, like Core, ran into attempts in which they must assuredly perish, as he did. Of such the apostle further says, (1.) *These are spots in your feasts of charity*—the ἀγάπαι or *love-feasts*, so much

spoken of by the ancients. They happened, by whatever means or mischance, to be admitted among them, but were spots in them, defiled and defiling. Observe, It is a great reproach, though unjust and accidental, to religion, when those who profess it, and join in the most solemn institution of it, are in heart and life unsuitable and even contrary to it: *These are spots.* Yet how common in all Christian societies here on earth, the very best not excepted, are such blemishes! The more is the pity. The Lord remedy it in his due time and way, not in men's blind and rigorous way of plucking up the wheat with the tares. But in the heaven we are waiting, hoping, and preparing for, there is none of this mad work, there are none of these disorderly doings. (2.) *When they feast with you, they feed themselves without fear.* Arrant gluttons, no doubt, they were; such as minded only the gratifying of their appetites with the daintiness and abundance of their fare; they had no regard to Solomon's caution, Prov. xxiii. 2. Note, In common eating and drinking a holy fear is necessary, much more in feasting, though we may sometimes be more easily and insensibly overcome at a common meal than at a feast; for, in the case supposed, we are less upon our guard, and sometimes, at least to some persons, the plenty of a feast is its own antidote, as to others it may prove a dangerous snare. (3.) *Clouds they are without water,* which promise rain in time of drought, but perform nothing of what they promise. Such is the case of formal professors, who at first setting out promise much, like early-blossoming trees in a forward spring, but in conclusion bring forth little or no fruit.—*Carried about of winds,* light and empty, easily driven about this way or that, as the wind happens to set; such are empty, ungrounded professors, an easy prey to every seducer. It is amazing to hear many talk so confidently of so many things of which they know little or nothing, and yet have not the wisdom and humility to discern and be sensible how little they know. How happy would our world be if men either knew more or practically knew how little they know! (4.) *Trees whose fruit withereth,* &c. Trees they are, for they are planted in the Lord's vineyard, yet fruitless ones. Observe, Those whose fruit withereth may be justly said to be without fruit. As good never a whit as never the better. It is a sad thing when men seem to *begin in the Spirit and end in the flesh,* which is almost as common a case as it is an awful one. The text speaks of such as were *twice dead.* One would think to be once dead were enough; we none of us, till grace renew us to a higher degree than ordinary, love to think of dying once, though this is appointed for us all. What then is the meaning of this being twice dead? They had been once dead in their natural, fallen, lapsed state; but they seemed to recover, and, as a man in a swoon, to be brought to life again, when they took upon them the profession of the Christian religion. But now they are dead again by the evident proofs they have given of their hypocrisy: whatever they seemed, they had nothing truly vital in them.—*Plucked up by the roots,* as we commonly serve dead trees, from which we expect no more fruit. They are *dead, dead, dead; why cumber they the ground?* Away with them to the fire. (5.) *Raging waves of the sea,* boisterous, noisy, and clamorous; full of talk and turbulency, but with little (if any) sense or meaning: *Foaming out their own shame,* creating much uneasiness to men of better sense and calmer tempers, which yet will in the end turn to their own greater shame and just reproach. The psalmist's prayer ought always to be that of every honest and good man, "*Let integrity and uprightness preserve me* (Ps. xxv. 21), and, if it will not, let me be unpreserved." If honesty signify little now, knavery will signify much less, and that in a very little while. Raging waves are a terror to sailing passengers; but, when they have got to port, the waves are forgotten as if no longer in being: their noise and terror are for ever ended. (6.) *Wandering stars,* planets that are erratic in their motions, keep not that steady regular course which the fixed ones do, but shift their stations, that one has sometimes much ado to know where to find them. This allusion carries in it a very lively emblem of false teachers, who are sometimes here and sometimes there, so that one knows not where nor how to fix them. In the main things, at least, one would think something should be fixed and steady; and this might be without infallibility, or any pretensions to it in us poor mortals. In religion and politics, the great subjects of present debate, surely there are certain *stamina* in which wise and good, honest and disinterested, men might agree, without throwing the populace into the utmost anguish and distress of mind, or blowing up their passions into rage and fury, without letting them know what they say or whereof they affirm.

II. The doom of this wicked people is declared: *To whom is reserved the blackness of darkness for ever.* False teachers are to expect the worst of punishments in this and a future world: not every one who teaches by mistake any thing that is not exactly true (for who then, in any public assembly, durst open a Bible to teach others, unless he thought himself equal or superior to the angels of God in heaven?) but every one who prevaricates, dissembles, would lead others into by-paths and side-ways, that he may have opportunity to make a gain or prey of them, or (in the apostle's phrase) to make merchandize of them, 2 Pet. ii. 3. But enough of this. As for the blackness of darkness for ever, I shall only say that this terrible expression, with all the horror it imports, belongs to false teachers, truly, not slanderously so called, who *corrupt the word of God, and betray the souls of men.* If this will not make both ministers and people cautious, I know not what will.

Of the prophecy of Enoch (*v.* 14, 15) we have no mention made in any other part or place of scripture; yet now it is scripture that there was such prophecy. One plain text of scripture is proof enough of any one point that we are required to believe, especially when relating to a matter of fact; but in matters of faith, necessary saving faith, God has not seen fit (blessed be his holy name he has not) to try us so far. There is no fundamental article of the Christian religion, truly so called, which is not inculcated over and over in the New Testament, by which we may know on what the Holy Ghost does, and consequently on what we ought, to lay the greatest stress. Some say that this prophecy of Enoch was preserved by tradition in the Jewish church; others that the apostle Jude was immediately inspired with the notice of it: be this as it may, it is certain that there was such a prophecy of ancient date, of long standing, and universally received in the Old-Testament church; and it is a main point of our New-Testament creed. Observe, 1. Christ's coming to judgment was prophesied of as early as the middle of the patriarchal age, and was therefore even then a received and acknowledged truth.—*The Lord cometh with* his holy myriads, including both angels and the spirits of just men made perfect. What a glorious time will that be, when Christ shall *come with ten thousand of these!* And we are told for what great and awful ends and purposes he will come so accompanied and attended, namely, *to execute judgment upon all.* 2. It was spoken of then, so long ago, as a thing just at hand: "*Behold, the Lord cometh;* he is just a coming, he will be upon you before you are aware, and, unless you be very cautious and diligent, before you are provided to meet him comfortably. He *cometh,* (1.) *To execute judgment upon* the wicked. (2.) *To convince* them. Observe, Christ will condemn none without precedent, trial, and conviction, such conviction as shall at least silence themselves. They shall have no excuse or apology to make that they either can or dare then stand by. Then *every mouth shall be stopped,* the Judge and his sentence shall be (by all the impartial) approved and applauded, and even the guilty condemned criminals shall be speechless, though at present they want not bold and specious pleas, which they vent with all assurance and confidence; and yet it is certain that the mock-trials of prisoners in the jail among themselves and the real trial at the bar before the proper judge soon appear to be very different things.

I cannot pass *v.* 15 without taking notice how often, and how emphatically, the word *ungodly* is repeated in it, no fewer than four times: ungodly men, ungodly sinners, ungodly deeds, and, as to the manner, ungodly committed. Godly or ungodly signifies little with men now-a-days, unless it be to scoff at and deride even the very expressions; but it is not so in the language of the Holy Ghost. Note, Omissions, as well as commissions, must be accounted for in the day of judgment. Note, further, Hard speeches of one another, especially if ill-grounded, will most certainly come into account at *the judgment of the great day.* Let us all take care in time. "If thou," says one of our good old puritans, "smite (a miscalled heretic, or) a schismatic, and God find a real saint bleeding, look thou to it, how thou wilt answer it." It may be too late to say before the angel that it was an error, Eccl. v. 6. I only here allude to that expression of the divinely inspired writer.

16 These are murmurers, complainers, walking after their own lusts; and their mouth speaketh great swelling *words,* having men's persons in admiration because of advantage.
17 But, beloved, remember ye the words which were spoken before of the apostles of our Lord Jesus Christ;
18 How that they told you there should be mockers in the last time, who should walk after their own ungodly lusts. 19 These be they who separate themselves, sensual, having not the Spirit. 20 But ye, beloved, building up yourselves on your most holy faith, praying in the Holy Ghost, 21 Keep yourselves in the love of God, looking for the mercy of our Lord Jesus Christ unto eternal life. 22 And of some have compassion, making a difference: 23 And others save with fear, pulling *them* out of the fire; hating even the garment spotted by the flesh. 24 Now unto him that is able to keep you from falling, and to present *you* faultless before the presence of his glory with exceeding joy. 25 To the only wise God our Saviour, *be* glory and majesty, dominion and power, both now and ever. Amen.

Here, I. The apostle enlarges further on the character of these evil men and seducers: they *are murmurers, complainers,* &c., *v.* 16. Observe, A murmuring complaining temper, indulged and expressed, lays men under a very bad character; such are very weak at least, and for the most part very wicked. They murmur against God and his providence, against men and their conduct; they are angry at every thing that happens, and never pleased with their own state and condition in the world, as not thinking it good enough for them. Such *walk after their own lusts;* their will, their appetite, their fancy, are their only rule and law. Note, Those who please their sinful appetites are most prone to yield to their ungovernable passions.

II. He proceeds to caution and exhort those to whom he is writing, *v.* 17—23. Here,

1. He calls them to remember how they had been forewarned: *But, beloved, remember,* &c., *v.* 17. "*Remember,* take heed that you think it not strange (so as to stumble and be offended, and have your faith staggered by it) that such people as the seducers before described and warned against should arise (and that early) in the Christian church, seeing all this was foretold by *the apostles of our Lord Jesus Christ,* and consequently the accomplishment of it in the event is a confirmation of your faith, instead of being in the least an occasion of shaking and unsettling you therein." Note, (1.) Those who would persuade must make it evident that they sincerely love those whom they would persuade. Bitter words and hard usage never did nor ever will convince, much less persuade any body. (2.) The words which inspired persons have spoken (or written), duly remembered and reflected on, are the best preservative against dangerous errors; this will always be so, till men have learnt to speak better than God himself. (3.) We ought not to be offended if errors and persecutions arise and prevail in the Christian church; this was foretold, and therefore we should not think worse of Christ's person, doctrine, or cross, when we see it fulfilled. See 1 Tim. iv. 1, and 2 Tim. iii. 1, and 2 Pet. iii. 3. We must not think it strange, but comfort ourselves with this, that in the midst of all this confusion Christ will maintain his church, and make good his promise, that *the gates of hell shall not prevail against it,* Matt. xvi. 18. (4.) The more religion is ridiculed and persecuted the faster hold we should take and keep of it; being forewarned, we should show that we are fore-armed; under such trials we should stand firm, and *not be soon shaken in mind,* 2 Thess. ii. 2.

2. He guards them against seducers by a further description of their odious character: *These are those who separate,* &c., *v.* 19. Observe, (1.) Sensualists are the worst separatists. They separate themselves from God, and Christ, and his church, to the devil, the world, and the flesh, by their ungodly courses and vicious practices; and this is a great deal worse than separation from any particular branch of the visible church on account of opinions or modes and circumstances of external government or worship, though many can patiently bear with the former, while they are plentifully and almost perpetually railing at the latter, as if no sin were damnable but what they are pleased to call *schism.* (2.) Sensual men have not the Spirit, that is, of God and Christ, the Spirit of holiness, which whoever *has not, is none of Christ's,* does not belong to him, Rom. viii. 9. (3.) The worse others are the better should we endeavour and approve ourselves to be; the more busy Satan and his instruments are to pervert others, in judgment or practice, the more tenacious should we be of sound doctrine and a good conversation, *holding fast the faithful word, as we have been* (divinely) *taught, holding the mystery of the faith in a pure conscience,* Tit. i. 9; 1 Tim. iii. 9.

3. He exhorts them to persevering constancy in truth and holiness.

(1.) *Building up yourselves in your most holy faith, v.* 20. Observe, The way to hold fast our profession is to hold on in it. Having laid our foundation well in a sound faith, and a sincere upright heart, we must build upon it, make further progress continually; and we should take care with what materials we carry on our building, namely, *gold, silver, precious stones,* not *wood, hay, stubble,* 1 Cor. iii. 12. Right principles and a regular conversation will stand the test even of the fiery trial; but, whatever we mix of baser alloy, though we be in the main sincere, we shall suffer loss by it, and though our persons be saved all that part of our work shall be consumed; and, if we ourselves escape, it will be with great danger and difficulty, as from a house on fire on every side.

(2.) *Praying in the Holy Ghost.* Observe, [1.] Prayer is the nurse of faith; the way to *build up ourselves in our most holy faith* is to *continue instant in prayer,* Rom. xii. 12. [2.] Our prayers are then most likely to prevail when we *pray in the Holy Ghost,* that is, under his guidance and influence, according to the rule of his word, with faith, fervency, and constant persevering importunity; this is praying in the Holy Ghost, whether it be done by or without a set prescribed form.

(3.) *Keep yourselves in the love of God, v.* 21. [1.] "Keep up the grace of love to God in its lively vigorous actings and exercises in your souls." [2.] "Take heed of throwing yourselves out of the love of God to you, or its delightful, cheering, strengthening manifestations; keep yourselves in the way of God, if you would continue in his love."

(4.) *Looking for the mercy,* &c. [1.] Eternal life is to be looked for only through *mercy;* mercy is our only plea, not merit; or if merit, not our own, but another's, who has merited for us what otherwise we could have laid no claim to, nor have entertained any well-grounded hope of. [2.] It is said, not only through the mercy of God as our Creator, but through the mercy *of our Lord Jesus Christ* as Redeemer; all who come to heaven must come thither through our Lord Jesus Christ; for *there is no other name under heaven given among men by which we must be saved,* but that of the Lord Jesus only, Acts. iv. 12, compared with *v.* 10. [3.] A believing expectation of eternal life will arm us against the snares of sin (2 Pet. iii. 14); a lively faith of the blessed hope will help us to mortify our cursed lusts.

4. He directs them how to behave towards erring brethren: *And of some have compassion*, &c., *v.* 22, 23. Observe, (1.) We ought to do all we can to rescue others out of the snare of the devil, that they may be saved from (or recovered, when entangled therein, out of) dangerous errors, or pernicious practices. We are not only (under God) our own keepers, but every man ought to be, as much as in him lies, his *brother's keeper;* none but a wicked Cain will contradict this, Gen. iv. 9. We must watch over one another, must faithfully, yet prudently, reprove each other, and set a good example to all about us. (2.) This must be done with *compassion, making a difference.* How is that? We must distinguish between the weak and the wilful. [1.] *Of some* we must *have compassion,* treat them with all tenderness, *restore them in the spirit of meekness,* not be needlessly harsh and severe in our censures of them and their actions, nor proud and haughty in our conduct towards them; not implacable, nor averse to reconciliation with them, or admitting them to the friendship they formerly had with us, when they give evident or even strongly hopeful tokens of a sincere repentance: if God has forgiven them, why should not we? We infinitely more need his forgiveness than they do, or can do, ours, though perhaps neither they nor we are justly or sufficiently sensible of this. [2.] *Others save with fear,* urging upon them *the terrors of the Lord:* "Endeavour to frighten them out of their sins; preach hell and damnation to them." But what if prudence and caution in administering even the most just and severe reproofs be what are primarily and chiefly here intimated—(I do but offer it for consideration); as if he had said, "Fear lest you frustrate your own good intentions and honest designs by rash and imprudent management, that you do not harden, instead of reclaiming, even where greater degrees of severity are requisite than in the immediately foregoing instance." We are often apt to over-do, when we are sure we mean honestly, and think we are right in the main; yet the very worst are not needlessly, nor rashly, nor to extremity, to be provoked, lest they be thereby further hardened through our default.—"*Hating even the garment spotted with the flesh,* that is, keeping yourselves at the utmost distance from what is or appears evil, and designing and endeavouring that others may do so too. Avoid all that leads to sin or that looks like sin," 1 Thess. v. 22.

III. The apostle concludes this epistle with a solemn ascription of glory to the great God, *v.* 24, 25. Note, 1. Whatever is the subject or argument we have been treating of, ascribing glory to God is fittest for us to conclude with. 2. God is able, and he is as willing as able, *to keep us from falling, and to present us faultless before the presence of his glory;* not as those who never have been faulty (for what has once been done can never be rendered undone, even by Omnipotence itself, for that implies a contradiction), but as those whose faults shall not be imputed, to their ruin, which, but for God's mercy and a Saviour's merits, they might most justly have been.—*Before the presence of his glory.* Observe, (1.) The glory of the Lord will shortly be present. We now look upon it as distant, and too many look upon it as uncertain, but it will come, and it will be manifest and apparent. *Every eye shall see him,* Rev. i. 7. This is now the object of our faith, but hereafter (and surely it cannot *now* be long) it will be the object of our sense; whom we now believe in, him we shall shortly see, to our unspeakable joy and comfort or inexpressible terror and consternation. See 1 Pet. i. 8. (2.) All real sincere believers shall be presented, at the Lord Redeemer's appearance and coming, by him their glorious head, to the Father, in order to his approbation, acceptance, and reward. They were given to him of the Father, and *of all that were so given to him he has lost none,* nor will lose any one, not an individual, a single soul, but will present them all perfectly holy and happy, when he shall surrender his mediatorial kingdom to *his God and our God, his Father and our Father,* John vi. 39, with *ch.* xvii. 12, 1 Cor. xv. 24. (3.) When believers shall be presented faultless it will be with exceeding joy. Alas! now our faults fill us with fears, doubts, and sorrows. But *be of good cheer;* if we be sincere, we shall be, our dear Redeemer has undertaken for it, we shall be *presented faultless;* where there is no sin there will be no sorrow; where there is the perfection of holiness, there will be the perfection of joy. Surely, the God who can and will do all this is worthy to have *glory, majesty, dominion, and power,* ascribed to him, *both now and for ever!* And to this we may well, with the apostle, affix our hearty *Amen.*

AN

EXPOSITION,

WITH PRACTICAL OBSERVATIONS,

OF THE

REVELATION OF ST. JOHN

THE DIVINE.

It ought to be no prejudice to the credit and authority of this book that it has been rejected by men of corrupt minds, such as Cerdon and Marcion, and doubted of by men of a better character; for this has been the lot of other parts of holy writ, and of the divine Author of the scripture himself. The image and superscription of this book are truly sacred and divine, and the matter of it agreeable with other prophetical books, particularly Ezekiel and Daniel; the church of God has generally received it, and found good counsel and great comfort in it. From the beginning, the church of God has been blessed with prophecy. That glorious prediction of breaking the serpent's head was the stay and support of the patriarchal age; and the many prophecies there were concerning the Messiah to come were the gospel of the Old Testament. Christ himself prophesied of the destruction of Jerusalem; and, about the time in which that was accomplished, he entrusted the apostle John with this book of revelation, to deliver it to the church as a prediction of the most important events that should happen to it to the end of time, for the support of the faith of his people and the direction of their hope. It is called the *Revelation*, because God therein discovers those things which could never have been sifted out by the reasonings of human understanding, those deep things of God which no man knows, but the Spirit of God, and those to whom he reveals them.

CHAP. I.

This chapter is a general preface to the whole book, and contains, I. An inscription, declaring the original and the design of it, ver. 1, 2. II. The apostolic benediction pronounced on all those who shall pay a due regard to the contents of this book, ver. 3—8. III. A glorious vision or appearance of the Lord Jesus Christ to the apostle John, when he delivered to him this revelation, ver. 9, to the end.

THE Revelation of Jesus Christ, which God gave unto him, to show unto his servants things which must shortly come to pass; and he sent and signified *it* by his angel unto his servant John: 2 Who bare record of the word of God, and of the testimony of Jesus Christ, and of all things that he saw.

Here we have,

I. What we may call the pedigree of this book. 1. It is *the revelation of Jesus Christ*. The whole Bible is so; for all revelation comes through Christ and all centres in him; and especially *in these last days God has spoken to us by his Son*, and concerning his Son. Christ, as the king of his church, has been pleased thus far to let his church know by what rules and methods he will proceed in his government; and, as the prophet of the church, he has made known to us the things that shall be hereafter. 2. It is a revelation *which God gave unto Christ*. Though Christ is himself God, and as such has light and life in himself, yet, as he sustains the office of *Mediator between God and man*, he receives his instructions from the Father. The human nature of Christ, though endowed with the greatest sagacity, judgment, and penetration, could not, in a way of reason, discover these great events, which not being produced by natural causes, but wholly depending upon the will of God, could be the object only of divine prescience, and must come to a created mind only by revelation. Our Lord Jesus is the great trustee of divine revelation; it is to him that we owe the knowledge we have of what we are to expect from God and what he expects from us. 3. This revelation Christ *sent and signified by his angel*. Observe here the admirable order of divine revelation. God gave it to Christ, and Christ employed an angel to communicate it to the churches. The angels are God's messengers; they are ministering spirits to the heirs of salvation. They are Christ's servants: principalities and powers are subject to him; all the angels of God are obliged to worship him. 4. The angels *signified it to the apostle John.* As the angels are the messengers of Christ, the ministers are the messengers of the churches; what they receive from heaven, they are to communicate to the churches. John was the apostle chosen for this service. Some think he was the only one surviving, the rest having sealed their testimony with their blood. This was to be the last book of divine revelation; and therefore notified to the church by the last of the apostles. John was the beloved disciple. He was, under the New Testament, as the prophet Daniel under the Old, *a man greatly beloved.* He was the servant of Christ; he was an apostle, an evangelist, and a prophet; he served Christ in all the three extraordinary offices of the church. James was an apostle, but not a prophet, nor an evangelist; Matthew was an apostle and evangelist, but not a prophet; Luke was an evangelist, but neither a prophet nor an apostle; but John was all three; and so Christ calls him in an eminent sense his *servant John.* 5. John was to deliver this revelation to the church, to all his servants. For the revelation was not designed for the use of Christ's extraordinary servants the ministers only, but for all his servants, the members of the church; they have all a right to the oracles of God, and all have their concern in them.

II. Here we have the subject-matter of this revelation, namely, the things that must shortly come to pass. The evangelists give us an account of the things that are past; prophecy gives us an account of things to come. These future events are shown, not in the clearest light in which God could have set them, but in such a light as he saw most proper, and which would best answer his wise and holy purposes. Had they been as clearly foretold in all their circumstances as God could have revealed them, the prediction might have prevented the accomplishment; but they are foretold more darkly, to beget in us a veneration for the scripture, and to engage our attention and excite our enquiry. We have in this revelation a general idea of the methods of divine providence and government in and about the church, and many good lessons may be learned hereby. These events (it is said) were such as should come to pass not only *surely*, but *shortly;* that is, they would begin to come to pass very shortly, and the whole would be accomplished in a short time. For now the last ages of the world had come.

III. Here is an attestation of the prophecy, *v.* 2. It was signified to John, who bore record of the word of God, and of the testimony of Jesus Christ, and of all things that he saw. It is observable that the historical books of the Old Testament have not always the name of the historian prefixed to them, as in the books of *Judges, Kings, Chronicles;* but in the prophetical books the name is always prefixed, as *Isaiah, Jeremiah,* &c. So in the New Testament, though John did not prefix his name to his first epistle, yet he does to this prophecy, as ready to vouch and answer for the truth of it; and he gives us not only his name, but his office. He was one who bore record of the word of God in general, and of the testimony of Jesus in particular, and of all things that he saw; he was an eye-witness, and he concealed nothing that he saw. Nothing recorded in this revelation was his own invention or imagination; but all was the record of God and the testimony of Jesus; and, as he added nothing to it, so he kept back no part of the counsels of God.

3 Blessed *is* he that readeth, and
they that hear the words of this
prophecy, and keep those things
which are written therein: for the
time *is* at hand. 4 John to the seven
churches which are in Asia: Grace
be unto you, and peace, from him
which is, and which was, and which
is to come; and from the seven
Spirits which are before his throne;
5 And from Jesus Christ, *who is* the
faithful witness, *and* the first begotten
of the dead, and the prince of the
kings of the earth. Unto him that
loved us, and washed us from our
sins in his own blood, 6 And hath
made us kings and priests unto God
and his Father; to him be glory and
dominion for ever and ever. Amen.
7 Behold, he cometh with clouds;
and every eye shall see him, and they
also which pierced him: and all
kindreds of the earth shall wail because of him. Even so, Amen. 8
I am Alpha and Omega, the beginning and the ending, saith the Lord,
which is, and which was, and which
is to come, the Almighty.

We have here an apostolic benediction on those who should give a due regard to this divine revelation; and this benediction is given more generally and more especially.

I. More generally, to all who either read or hear the words of the prophecy. This blessing seems to be pronounced with a design to encourage us to study this book, and not be weary of looking into it upon account of the obscurity of many things in it; it will repay the labour of the careful and attentive reader. Observe, 1. It is a blessed privilege to enjoy the oracles of God. This was one of the principal advantages the Jews had above the Gentiles. 2. It is a blessed thing to study the scriptures; those are well employed who search the scriptures. 3. It is a privilege not only to read the scriptures ourselves, but to hear them read by others, who are qualified to give us the sense of what they read and to lead us into an understanding of them. 4. It is not sufficient to our blessedness that we read and hear the scriptures, but we must keep the things that are written; we must keep them in our memories, in our minds, in our affections, and in practice, and we shall be blessed in the deed. 5. The nearer we come to the accomplishment of the scriptures, the greater regard we shall give to them. The time is at hand, and we should be so much the more attentive as we see the day approaching.

II. The apostolic benediction is pronounced more especially and particularly to the seven Asian churches, *v.* 4. These seven churches are named in *v.* 11, and distinct messages sent to each of them respectively in the chapters following. The apostolic blessing is more expressly directed to these, because they were nearest to him, who was now in the isle of Patmos, and perhaps he had the peculiar care of them and superintendency over them, not excluding any of the rest of the apostles, if any of them were now living. Here observe,

1. What the blessing is which he pronounces on all the faithful in these churches: *Grace and peace,* holiness and comfort. *Grace,* that is, the good-will of God towards us and his good work in us; and *peace,* that is, the sweet evidence and assurance of this grace. There can be no true peace where there is not true grace; and, where grace goes before, peace will follow.

2. Whence this blessing is to come. In whose name does the apostle bless the churches? In the name of God, of the whole Trinity; for this is an act of adoration, and God only is the proper object of it; his ministers must bless the people in no name but his alone. And here, (1.) The Father is first named: God the Father, which may be taken either essentially, for God as God, or personally, for the first person in the ever-blessed Trinity, the God and Father of our Lord Jesus Christ; and he is described as the Jehovah *who is, and who was, and who is to come,* eternal, unchangeable, the same to the Old-Testament church which was, and to the New-Testament church which is, and who will be the same to the church triumphant which is to come. (2.) The Holy Spirit, called *the seven spirits,* not seven in number, nor in nature, but the infinite perfect Spirit of God, in whom there is a diversity of gifts and operations. He is before the throne; for, as God made, so he governs, all things by his Spirit. (3.) The Lord Jesus Christ. He mentions him after the Spirit, because he intended to enlarge more upon the person of Christ, as God manifested in the flesh, whom he had seen dwelling on earth before, and now saw again in a glorious form. Observe the particular account we have here of Christ, *v.* 5. [1.] He *is the faithful witness;* he was from eternity a witness to all the counsels of God (John i. 18), and he was in time a faithful witness to the revealed will of God, who has now spoken to us by his Son; upon his testimony we may safely depend, for he is a faithful witness, cannot be deceived and cannot deceive us. [2.] He is the first-begotten or first-born from the dead, or the first parent and head of the resurrection, the only one who raised himself by his own power, and who will by the same power raise up his people from their graves to everlasting honour; for he has begotten them again to a lively hope by his resurrection from the dead. [3.] He is the prince of the kings of the earth; from him they have their authority; by him their power is limited and their wrath restrained; by him their counsels are over-ruled, and to him they are accountable. This is good news to the church, and it is good evidence of the Godhead of Christ, who is King of kings and Lord of lords. [4.] He is the great friend of his church and people, one who has done great things for them, and this out of pure disinterested affection. He has loved them, and, in pursuance of that everlasting love, he has, *First, Washed them from their sins in his own blood.* Sins leave a stain upon the soul, a stain of guilt and of pollution. Nothing can fetch out this stain but the blood of Christ; and, rather than it should not be washed out, Christ was willing to shed his own blood, to purchase pardon and purity for them. *Secondly,* He has *made them kings and priests to God and his Father.* Having justified and sanctified them, he makes them kings to his Father; that is, in his Father's account, with his approbation, and for his glory. As kings, they overcome the world, mortify sin, govern their own spirits, conquer Satan, have power and prevalency with God in prayer, and shall judge the world. He hath made them priests, given them access to God, enabled them to enter into the holiest and to offer spiritual and acceptable sacrifices, and has given them an unction suitable to this character; and for these high honours and favours they are bound to ascribe to him dominion and glory for ever. [5.] He will be the Judge of the world: *Behold, he cometh, and every eye shall see him, v.* 7. This book, the Revelation, begins and ends with a prediction of the second coming of the Lord Jesus Christ. We should set ourselves to meditate frequently upon the second coming of Christ, and keep it in the eye of our faith and expectation. John speaks as if he saw that day: "*Behold, he cometh,* as sure as if you beheld him with your eyes. *He cometh with clouds,* which are his

chariot and pavilion. He will come publicly: *Every eye shall see him,* the eye of his people, the eye of his enemies, every eye, yours and mine." He shall come, to the terror of those who have pierced him and have not repented and of all who have wounded and crucified him afresh by their apostasy from him, and to the astonishment of the pagan world. For he comes to take vengeance on those who know not God, as well as on those that obey not the gospel of Christ. [6.] This account of Christ is ratified and confirmed by himself, *v.* 8. Here our Lord Jesus justly challenges the same honour and power that is ascribed to the Father, *v.* 4. He is the beginning and the end; all things are from him and for him; he is the Almighty; he is the same eternal and unchangeable one. And surely whoever presumes to blot out one character of this name of Christ deserves to have his name blotted out of the book of life. Those that honour him he will honour; but those who despise him shall be lightly esteemed.

9 I John, who also am your brother, and companion in tribulation,
and in the kingdom and patience of
Jesus Christ, was in the isle that is
called Patmos, for the word of God,
and for the testimony of Jesus Christ.
10 I was in the Spirit on the Lord's
day, and heard behind me a great
voice, as of a trumpet, 11 Saying,
I am Alpha and Omega, the first and
the last: and, What thou seest, write
in a book, and send *it* unto the seven
churches which are in Asia; unto
Ephesus, and unto Smyrna, and unto
Pergamos, and unto Thyatira, and
unto Sardis, and unto Philadelphia,
and unto Laodicea. 12 And I turned
to see the voice that spake with me.
And being turned, I saw seven golden
candlesticks; 13 And in the midst
of the seven candlesticks *one* like
unto the Son of man, clothed with a
garment down to the foot, and girt
about the paps with a golden girdle.
14 His head and *his* hairs *were* white
like wool, as white as snow; and his
eyes *were* as a flame of fire; 15 And
his feet like unto fine brass, as if they
burned in a furnace; and his voice as
the sound of many waters. 16 And
he had in his right hand seven stars:
and out of his mouth went a sharp
twoedged sword: and his countenance *was* as the sun shineth in his
strength. 17 And when I saw him.
I fell at his feet as dead. And he
laid his right hand upon me, saying
unto me, Fear not; I am the first
and the last: 18 *I am* he that liveth,
and was dead; and, behold, I am
alive for evermore, Amen; and have
the keys of hell and of death. 19
Write the things which thou hast
seen, and the things which are, and
the things which shall be hereafter;
20 The mystery of the seven stars
which thou sawest in my right hand,
and the seven golden candlesticks.
The seven stars are the angels of the
seven churches: and the seven candlesticks which thou sawest are the
seven churches.

We have now come to that glorious vision which the apostle had of the Lord Jesus Christ, when he came to deliver this revelation to him, where observe,

I. The account given of the person who was favoured with this vision. He describes himself, 1. By his present state and condition. He was *the brother and companion of these churches in tribulation, and in the kingdom and patience of Christ.* He was, at their time, as the rest of true Christians were, a persecuted man, banished, and perhaps imprisoned, for his adherence to Christ. He was their *brother,* though an apostle; he seems to value himself upon his relation to the church, rather than his authority in it: Judas Iscariot may be an apostle, but not a brother in the family of God. He was their companion: the children of God should choose communion and society with each other. He was their companion in tribulation: the persecuted servants of God did not suffer alone, the same trials are accomplished in others. He was their companion in patience, not only a sharer with them in suffering circumstances, but in suffering graces: if we have the patience of the saints, we should not grudge to meet with their trials. He was their *brother and companion in the patience of the kingdom of Christ,* a sufferer for Christ's cause, for asserting his kingly power over the church and the world, and for adhering to it against all who would usurp upon it. By this account he gives of his present state, he acknowledges his engagements to sympathize with them, and to endeavour to give them counsel and comfort, and bespeaks their more careful attention to what he had to say to them from Christ their common Lord. 2. By the place where he was when he was favoured with this vision: he was in *the isle Patmos.* He does not say who banished him thither. It becomes Christians to speak sparingly and modestly of their own sufferings. Patmos is said to be an island in the Ægean Sea, one of those called Cyclades, and was about thirty-five miles in compass; but under this confinement it was the apostle's comfort that he did not suffer as an evil-doer, but that it was for the testimony of Jesus, for bearing witness to Christ as the Immanuel, the Saviour. This was a cause worth suffering for; and the Spirit of glory and of God rested upon this persecuted apostle. 3. The day and time in which he had this vision: it was *the Lord's day,* the day which Christ had separated and set apart for himself, as the eucharist is called *the Lord's supper.* Surely this can be no other than the Christian sabbath, the first day of the week, to be observed in remembrance of the resurrection of Christ. Let us who call him *our Lord* honour him on his own day, the day which the Lord hath made and in which we ought to rejoice. 4. The frame that his soul was in at this time: *He was in the Spirit.* He was not only in a rapture when he received the vision, but before he received it; he was in a serious, heavenly, spiritual frame, under the blessed gracious influences of the Spirit of God. God usually prepares the souls of his people for uncommon manifestations of himself, by the quickening sanctifying influences of his good Spirit. Those who would enjoy communion with God on the Lord's day must endeavour to abstract their thoughts and affections from flesh and fleshly things, and be wholly taken up with things of a spiritual nature.

II. The apostle gives an account of what he heard when thus in the Spirit. An alarm was given as with the sound of a trumpet, and then *he heard a voice,* the voice of Christ applying to himself the character before given, *the first and the last,* and commanding the apostle to commit to writing the things that were now to be revealed to him, and to send it immediately *to the seven Asian churches,* whose names are mentioned. Thus our Lord Jesus, the captain of our salvation, gave the apostle notice of his glorious appearance, as with the sound of a trumpet.

III We have also an account of what he saw. *He turned to see the voice,* whose it was and whence it came; and then a wonderful scene of vision opened itself to him.

1. He saw a representation of the church under the emblem of *seven golden candlesticks,* as it is explained in the last verse of the chapter. The churches are compared to candlesticks, because they hold forth the light of the gospel to advantage. The churches are not candles: Christ only is our light, and his gospel our lamp; but they receive their light from Christ and the gospel, and hold it forth to others. They are golden candlesticks, for they should be precious and pure, comparable to fine gold; not only the ministers, but the members of the churches ought to be such; their light should so shine before men as to engage others to give glory to God.

2. He saw a representation of the Lord Jesus Christ in the midst of the golden candlesticks; for he has promised to be with his churches always to the end of the world, filling them with light, and life, and love, for he is the very animating informing soul of the church. And here we observe,

(1.) The glorious form in which Christ appeared in several particulars. [1.] He was *clothed with a garment down to the foot,* a princely and priestly robe, denoting righteousness and honour. [2.] *He was girt about with a golden girdle,* the breast-plate of the high priest, on which the names of his people are engraven; he was ready girt to do all the work of a Redeemer. [3.] *His head and hairs were white like wool or snow.* He was the Ancient of days; his hoary head was no sign of decay, but was indeed a crown of glory. [4.] *His eyes were as a flame of fire,* piercing and penetrating into the very hearts and reins of men, scattering terrors among his adversaries. [5.] *His feet were like unto fine burning brass,* strong and stedfast, supporting his own interest, subduing his enemies, and treading them to powder. [6.] *His voice was as the sound of many waters,* of many rivers falling in together. He can and will make himself heard to those who are afar off as well as to those who are near. His gospel is a profluent and mighty stream, fed by the upper springs of infinite wisdom and knowledge. [7.] *He had in his right hand seven stars,* that is, the ministers of the seven churches, who are under his direction, have all their light and influence from him, and are secured and preserved by him. [8.] *Out of his mouth went a two-edged sword,* his word, which both wounds and heals, strikes at sins on the right hand and on the left, [9.] *His countenance was as the sun shining,* its strength too bright and dazzling for mortal eyes to behold.

(2.) The impression this appearance of Christ made upon the apostle John (*v.* 17): *He fell at the feet of Christ as dead;* he was overpowered with the greatness of the lustre and glory in which Christ appeared, though he had been so familiar with him before. How well is it for us that God speaks to us by men like ourselves, whose terrors shall not make us afraid, for none can see the face of God and live!

(3.) The condescending goodness of the Lord Jesus to his disciple: *He laid his hand upon him, v.* 17. He raised him up; he did not plead against him with his great power, but he put strength into him, he spoke kind words to him. [1.] Words of comfort and encouragement: *Fear not.* He commanded away the slavish fears of his disciple. [2.] Words of instruction, telling him particularly who he was that thus appeared to him. And here he acquaints him, *First,* With his divine nature: *The first and the last. Secondly,* With his former sufferings: *I was dead;* the very same that his disciples saw upon the cross dying for the sins of men. *Thirdly,* With his resurrection and life: "*I live, and am alive for evermore,* have conquered death and opened the grave, and am partaker of an endless life." *Fourthly,* With his office and authority: *I have the keys of hell and of death,* a sovereign dominion in and over the invisible world, opening and none can shut, shutting so that none can open, opening the gates of death when he pleases and the gates of the eternal world, of happiness or misery, as the Judge of all, from whose sentence there lies no appeal. *Fifthly,* With his will and pleasure: *Write the things which thou hast seen, and the things which are, and which shall be hereafter.* *Sixthly,* With the meaning of the seven stars, that *they are the ministers of the churches;* and of the seven candlesticks, that *they are the seven churches,* to whom Christ would now send by him particular and proper messages.

CHAP. II.

The apostle John, having in the foregoing chapter written the things which he had seen, now proceeds to write the things that are, according to the command of God (ch. i. 19), that is, the present state of the seven churches of Asia, with which he had a particular acquaintance, and for which he had a tender concern. He was directed to write to every one of them according to their present state and circumstances, and to inscribe every letter to the angel of that church, to the minister or rather ministry of that church, called angels because they are the messengers of God to mankind. In this chapter we have, I. The message sent to Ephesus, ver. 1—7. II. To Smyrna, ver. 8—11. III. To Pergamos, ver. 12—17. IV. To Thyatira, ver. 18, &c.

UNTO the angel of the church of
Ephesus write; These things
saith he that holdeth the seven stars
in his right hand, who walketh in the
midst of the seven golden candlesticks; 2 I know thy works, and
thy labour, and thy patience, and
how thou canst not bear them which
are evil: and thou hast tried them
which say they are apostles, and are
not, and hast found them liars: 3
And hast borne, and hast patience,
and for my name's sake hast laboured,
and hast not fainted. 4 Nevertheless I have *somewhat* against thee,
because thou hast left thy first love.
5 Remember therefore from whence
thou art fallen, and repent, and do
the first works; or else I will come
unto thee quickly, and will remove
thy candlestick out of his place, except thou repent. 6 But this thou
hast, that thou hatest the deeds of
the Nicolaitanes, which I also hate.
7 He that hath an ear, let him
hear what the Spirit saith unto the
churches; To him that overcometh will
I give to eat of the tree of life, which
is in the midst of the paradise of God.

We have here,

I. The inscription, where observe, 1. To whom the first of these epistles is directed: *To the church of Ephesus,* a famous church planted by the apostle Paul (Acts xix.), and afterwards watered and governed by John, who had his residence very much there. We can hardly think that Timothy was the angel, or sole pastor and bishop, of this church at this time,—that he who was of a very excellent spirit, and naturally cared for the good state of the souls of the people, should become so remiss as to deserve the rebukes given to the ministry of this church. Observe, 2. From whom this epistle to Ephesus was sent; and here we have one of those titles that were given to Christ in his appearance to John in the chapter foregoing: *He that holds the seven stars in his right hand, and walks in the midst of the seven golden candlesticks, ch.* i. 13, 16. This title consists of two parts:—(1.) *He that holds the stars in his right hand.* The ministers of Christ are under his special care and protection. It is the honour of God that he knows the number of the stars, calls them by their names, *binds the sweet influences of Pleiades and looses the bands of Orion;* and it is the honour of the Lord Jesus Christ that the ministers of the gospel, who are greater blessings to the church than the stars are to the world, are in his hand. He directs all their motions; he disposes of them into their several orbs; he fills them with light and influence; he supports them, or else they would soon be falling stars; they are instruments in his hand, and all the good they do is done by his hand with them. (2.) *He walks in the midst of the golden candlesticks.* This intimates his relation to his churches, as the other his relation to his ministers. Christ is in an intimate manner present and conversant with his churches; he knows and observes their state; he takes pleasure in them, as a man does to walk in his garden. Though Christ is in heaven, he walks in the midst of his churches on earth, observing what is amiss in them and what it is that they want. This is a great encouragement to those who have the care of the churches, that the Lord Jesus has graven them upon the palms of his hands.

II. The contents of the epistle, in which, as in most of those that follow, we have,

1. The commendation Christ gave this church, ministers and members, which he always brings in by declaring that he knows their works, and therefore both his commendation and reprehension are to be strictly regarded; for he does not in either speak at a venture: he knows what he says. Now the church of Ephesus is commended, (1.) For their diligence in duty: *I know thy works, and thy labour, v.* 2. This may more immediately relate to the ministry of this church, which had been laborious and diligent. Dignity calls for duty. Those that are stars in Christ's hand had need to be always in motion, dispensing light to all about them. *For my name's sake thou hast laboured, and*

hast not fainted, v. 3. Christ keeps an account of every day's work, and every hour's work, his servants do for him, *and their labour shall not be in vain in the Lord.* (2.) For their patience in suffering: *Thy labour and thy patience, v.* 2. It is not enough that we be diligent, but we must be patient, and endure hardness as good soldiers of Christ. Ministers must have and exercise great patience, and no Christian can be without it. There must be bearing patience, to endure the injuries of men and the rebukes of Providence; and there must be waiting patience, that, when they have done the will of God, they may receive the promise: *Thou hast borne, and hast patience, v.* 3. We shall meet with such difficulties in our way and work as require patience to go on and finish well. (3.) For their zeal against what was evil: *Thou canst not bear those that are evil, v.* 2. It consists very well with Christian patience not to dispense with sin, much less allow it; though we must show all meekness to men, yet we must show a just zeal against their sins. This their zeal was the more to be commended because it was according to knowledge, a discreet zeal upon a previous trial made of the pretences, practices, and tenets of evil men: *Thou hast tried those that say they are apostles and are not, and hast found them liars.* True zeal proceeds with discretion; none should be cast off till they be tried. Some had risen up in this church that pretended to be not ordinary ministers, but apostles; and their pretensions had been examined but found to be vain and false. Those that impartially search after truth may come to the knowledge of it.

2. The rebuke given to this church: *Nevertheless, I have somewhat against thee, v.* 4. Those that have much good in them may have something much amiss in them, and our Lord Jesus, as an impartial Master and Judge, takes notice of both; though he first observes what is good, and is most ready to mention this, yet he also observes what is amiss, and will faithfully reprove them for it. The sin that Christ charged this church with was their decay and declension in holy love and zeal: *Thou hast left thy first love;* not left and forsaken the object of it, but lost the fervent degree of it that at first appeared. Observe, (1.) The first affections of men towards Christ, and holiness, and heaven, are usually lively and warm. God remembered the love of Israel's espousals, when she would follow him whithersoever he went. (2.) These lively affections will abate and cool if great care be not taken, and diligence used, to preserve them in constant exercise. (3.) Christ is grieved and displeased with his people when he sees them grow remiss and cold towards him, and he will one way or other make them sensible that he does not take it well from them.

3. The advice and counsel given them from Christ: *Remember therefore whence thou hast fallen, and repent,* &c. (1.) Those that have lost their first love *must remember whence they have fallen;* they must compare their present with their former state, and consider how much better it was with them then than now, how much peace, strength, purity, and pleasure they have lost, by leaving their first love,—how much more comfortably they could lie down and sleep at night,—how much more cheerfully they could awake in the morning,—how much better they could bear afflictions, and how much more becomingly they could enjoy the favours of Providence,—how much easier the thoughts of death were to them, and how much stronger their desires and hopes of heaven. (2.) They must repent. They must be inwardly grieved and ashamed for their sinful declension; they must blame themselves, and shame themselves, for it, and humbly confess it in the sight of God, and judge and condemn themselves for it. (3.) They must return and do their first works. They must as it were begin again, go back step by step, till they come to the place where they took the first false step; they must endeavour to revive and recover their first zeal, tenderness, and seriousness, and must pray as earnestly, and watch as diligently, as they did when they first set out in the ways of God.

4. This good advice is enforced and urged, (1.) By a severe threatening, if it should be neglected: *I will come unto thee quickly, and remove thy candlestick out of its place.* If the presence of Christ's grace and Spirit be slighted, we may expect the presence of his displeasure. He will come in a way of judgment, and that suddenly and surprisingly, upon impenitent churches and sinners; he will unchurch them, take away his gospel, his ministers, and his ordinances from them, and what will the churches or the angels of the churches do when the gospel is removed? (2.) By an encouraging mention that is made of what was yet good among them: *This thou hast, that thou hatest the deeds of the Nicolaitans, which I also hate, v.* 6. "Though thou hast declined in thy love to what is good, yet thou retainest thy hatred to what is evil, especially to what is grossly so." The Nicolaitans were a loose sect who sheltered themselves under the name of Christianity. They held hateful doctrines, and they were guilty of hateful deeds, hateful to Christ and to all true Christians; and it is mentioned to the praise of the church of Ephesus that they had a just zeal and abhorrence of those wicked doctrines and practices. An indifference of spirit between truth and error, good and evil, may be called *charity* and *meekness,* but it is not pleasing to Christ. Our Saviour subjoins this kind commendation to his severe threatening, to make the advice more effectual.

III. We have the conclusion of this epistle, in which, as in those that follow, we have,

1. A call to attention: *He that hath an*

ear, let him hear what the Spirit saith unto the churches. Observe, (1.) What is written in the scriptures is spoken by the Spirit of God. (2.) What is said to one church concerns all the churches, in every place and age. (3.) We can never employ our faculty of hearing better than in hearkening to the word of God: and we deserve to lose it if we do not employ it to this purpose. Those who will not hear the call of God now will wish at length they had never had a capacity of hearing any thing at all.

2. A promise of great mercy to those who overcome. The Christian life is a warfare against sin, Satan, the world, and the flesh. It is not enough that we engage in this warfare, but we must pursue it to the end, we must never yield to our spiritual enemies, but fight the good fight, till we gain the victory, as all persevering Christians shall do; and the warfare and victory shall have a glorious triumph and reward. That which is here promised to the victors is that they shall *eat of the tree of life which is in the midst of the paradise of God.* They shall have that perfection of holiness, and that confirmation therein, which Adam would have had if he had gone well through the course of his trial: he would then have eaten of the tree of life which was in the midst of paradise, and this would have been the sacrament of confirmation to him in his holy and happy state; so all who persevere in their Christian trial and warfare shall derive from Christ, as the tree of life, perfection and confirmation in holiness and happiness in the paradise of God; not in the earthly paradise, but the heavenly, *ch.* xxii. 1, 2.

8 And unto the angel of the church
in Smyrna write; These things saith
the first and the last, which was dead
and is alive; 9 I know thy works,
and tribulation, and poverty, (but
thou art rich) and *I know* the blasphemy of them which say they are
Jews, and are not, but *are* the synagogue of Satan. 10 Fear none of
those things which thou shalt suffer:
behold, the devil shall cast *some* of
you into prison, that ye may be tried;
and ye shall have tribulation ten days:
be thou faithful unto death, and I will
give thee a crown of life. 11 He
that hath an ear, let him hear what
the Spirit saith unto the churches;
He that overcometh shall not be hurt
of the second death.

We now proceed to the second epistle sent to another of the Asian churches, where, as before, observe,

I. The preface or inscription in both parts. 1. The superscription, telling us to whom it was more expressly and immediately directed: *To the angel of the church in Smyrna,* a place well known at this day by our merchants, a city of great trade and wealth, perhaps the only city of all the seven that is still known by the same name, now however no longer distinguished for its Christian church being overrun with Mahomedism. 2. The subscription, containing another of the glorious titles of our Lord Jesus, *the first and the last, he that was dead and is alive,* taken out of *ch.* i. 17, 18. (1.) Jesus Christ is the *first and the last.* It is but a little scantling of time that is allowed to us in this world, but our Redeemer is the first and the last. He is the first, for by him all things were made, and he was before all things with God and was God himself. He is the last, for all things are made for him, and he will be the Judge of all. This surely is the title of God, from everlasting and to everlasting, and it is the title of one that is an unchangeable Mediator between God and man, *Jesus, the same yesterday, to-day, and for ever.* He was the first, for by him the foundation of the church was laid in the patriarchal state; and he is the last, for by him the top-stone will be brought forth and laid in the end of time. (2.) *He was dead and is alive.* He was dead, and died for our sins; he is alive, for he rose again for our justification, and he ever lives to make intercession for us. He was dead, and by dying purchased salvation for us; he is alive, and by his life applies this salvation to us. And *if, when we were enemies, we were reconciled by his death, much more, being reconciled, we shall be saved by his life.* His death we commemorate every sacrament day; his resurrection and life every sabbath day.

II. The subject-matter of this epistle to Smyrna, where, after the common declaration of Christ's omniscience, and the perfect cognizance he has of all the works of men and especially of his churches, he takes notice,

1. Of the improvement they had made in their spiritual state. This comes in in a short parenthesis; yet it is very emphatic: *But thou art rich* (*v.* 9), poor in temporals, but rich in spirituals—poor in spirit, and yet rich in grace. Their spiritual riches are set off by their outward poverty. Many who are rich in temporals are poor in spirituals. Thus it was with the church of Laodicea. Some who are poor outwardly are inwardly rich, rich in faith and in good works, rich in privileges, rich in bonds and deeds of gift, rich in hope, rich in reversion. Spiritual riches are usually the reward of great diligence; *the diligent hand makes rich.* Where there is spiritual plenty, outward poverty may be better borne; and when God's people are impoverished in temporals, for the sake of Christ and a good conscience, he makes all up to them in spiritual riches, which are much more satisfying and enduring.

2. Of their sufferings: *I know thy tribulation and thy poverty*—the persecution they underwent, even to the spoiling of their goods. Those who will be faithful to Christ must expect to go through many tribulations; but Jesus Christ takes particular notice of all their troubles. In all their afflictions, he is afflicted, and he will recompense tribulation to those who trouble them, but to those that are troubled rest with himself.

3. He knows the wickedness and the falsehood of their enemies: *I know the blasphemy of those that say they are Jews, but are not;* that is, of those who pretend to be the only peculiar covenant-people of God, as the Jews boasted themselves to be, even after God had rejected them; or of those who would be setting up the Jewish rites and ceremonies, which were now not only antiquated, but abrogated; these may say that they only are the church of God in the world, when indeed *they are the synagogue of Satan.* Observe, (1.) As Christ has a church in the world, the spiritual Israel of God, so the devil has his synagogue. Those assemblies which are set up in opposition to the truths of the gospel, and which promote and propagate damnable errors,—those which are set up in opposition to the purity and spirituality of gospel worship, and which promote and propagate the vain inventions of men and rites and ceremonies which never entered into the thoughts of God,—and those which are set up to revile and persecute the true worship and worshippers of God,—these are all synagogues of Satan: he presides over them, he works in them, his interests are served by them, and he receives a horrid homage and honour from them. (2.) For the synagogues of Satan to give themselves out to be the church or Israel of God is no less than blasphemy. God is greatly dishonoured when his name is made use of to promote and patronize the interests of Satan; and he has a high resentment of this blasphemy, and will take a just revenge on those who persist in it.

4. He foreknows the future trials of his people, and forewarns them of them, and forearms them against them. (1.) He forewarns them of future trials: *The devil shall cast some of you into prison, and you shall have tribulation, v.* 10. The people of God must look for a series and succession of troubles in this world, and their troubles usually rise higher. They had been impoverished by their tribulations before; now tney must be imprisoned. Observe, It is the devil that stirs up his instruments, wicked men, to persecute the people of God; tyrants and persecutors are the devil's tools, though they gratify their own sinful malignity, and know not that they are actuated by a diabolical malice. (2.) Christ fore-arms them against these approaching troubles, [1.] By his counsel: *Fear none of these things.* This is not only a word of command, but of efficacy, no, only forbidding slavish fear, but subduing its and furnishing the soul with strength and courage. [2.] By showing them how their sufferings would be alleviated and limited. *First,* They should not be universal. It would be some of them, not all, who should be cast into prison, those who were best able to bear it and might expect to be visited and comforted by the rest. *Secondly,* They were not to be perpetual, but for a set time, and a short time: *Ten days.* It should not be everlasting tribulation, *the time should be shortened for the elect's sake. Thirdly,* It should be to try them, not to destroy them, that their faith, and patience, and courage, might be proved and improved, and be found to honour and glory. [3.] By proposing and promising a glorious reward to their fidelity: *Be thou faithful to death, and I will give thee a crown of life.* Observe, *First,* The sureness of the reward: *I will give thee.* He has said it that is able to do it; and he has undertaken that he will do it. They shall have the reward from his own hand, and none of their enemies shall be able to wrest it out of his hand, or to pull it from their heads. *Secondly,* The suitableness of it. 1. *A crown,* to reward their poverty, their fidelity, and their conflict. 2. *A crown of life,* to reward those who are faithful even unto death, who are faithful till they die, and who part with life itself in fidelity to Christ. The life so worn out in his service, or laid down in his cause, shall be rewarded with another and a much better life that shall be eternal.

III. The conclusion of this message, and that, as before, 1. With a call to universal attention, that all men, all the world, should hear what passes between Christ and his churches—how he commends them, how he comforts them, how he reproves their failures, how he rewards their fidelity. It concerns all the inhabitants of the world to observe God's dealings with his own people; all the world may learn instruction and wisdom thereby. 2. With a gracious promise to the conquering Christian: *He that overcometh shall not be hurt of the second death, v.* 11. Observe, (1.) There is not only a first, but a second death, a death after the body is dead. (2.) This second death is unspeakably worse than the first death, both in the dying pangs and agonies of it (which are the agonies of the soul, without any mixture of support) and in the duration; it is *eternal death,* dying the death, to die and to be always dying This is hurtful indeed, fatally hurtful, to all who fall under it. (3.) From this hurtful, this destructive death, Christ will save all his faithful servants; the second death shall have no power over those who are *partakers of the first resurrection:* the first death shall not hurt them, and the second death shall have no power over them.

12 And to the angel of the church in Pergamos write; These things saith he which hath the sharp sword

with two edges; 13 I know thy
works, and where thou dwellest, *even*
where Satan's seat *is:* and thou
holdest fast my name, and hast not
denied my faith, even in those days
wherein Antipas *was* my faithful
martyr, who was slain among you,
where Satan dwelleth. 14 But I have
a few things against thee, because
thou hast there them that hold the
doctrine of Balaam, who taught Balac
to cast a stumblingblock before the
children of Israel, to eat things sacrificed unto idols, and to commit
fornication. 15 So hast thou also
them that hold the doctrine of the
Nicolaitanes, which thing I hate.
16 Repent; or else I will come unto
thee quickly, and will fight against
them with the sword of my mouth.
17 He that hath an ear, let him
hear what the Spirit saith unto the
churches; To him that overcometh
will I give to eat of the hidden manna,
and will give him a white stone, and
in the stone a new name written,
which no man knoweth saving he
that receiveth *it.*

Here also we are to consider,

I. The inscription of this message. 1. To whom it was sent: *To the angel of the church of Pergamos.* Whether this was a city raised up out of the ruins of old Troy, a Troy *nouveau* (as our London was once called), or some other city of the same name, is neither certain nor material; it was a place where Christ had called and constituted a gospel church, by the preaching of the gospel and the grace of his Spirit making the word effectual. 2. Who it was that sent this message to Pergamos: the same Jesus who here describes himself as one that *hath the sharp sword with two edges* (*ch.* i. 16), *out of whose mouth went a sharp two-edged sword.* Some have observed that, in the several titles of Christ which are prefixed to the several epistles, there is something suited to the state of those churches; as in that to Ephesus, what could be more proper to awaken and recover a drowsy and declining church than to hear Christ speaking as one that *held the stars in his hand, and walked in the midst of the golden candlesticks?* &c. The church of Pergamos was infested with men of corrupt minds, who did what they could to corrupt both the faith and manners of the church; and Christ, being resolved to fight against them by the sword of his word, takes the title of him that *hath the sharp sword with two edges.* (1.) The word of God is a sword; it is a weapon both offensive and defensive, it is, in the hand of God, able to slay both sin and sinners. (2.) It is a *sharp sword.* No heart is so hard but it is able to wound it, no knot so closely tied but it is able to cut it; it can divide asunder between the soul and the spirit, that is, between the soul and those sinful habits that by custom have become another soul, or seem to be essential to it. (3.) It is a *sword with two edges;* it turns and cuts every way. There is the *edge* of the law against the transgressors of that dispensation, and the *edge* of the gospel against the despisers of that dispensation; there is an edge to make a wound, and an edge to open a festered wound in order to its healing. There is no escaping the edge of this sword: if you turn aside to the right hand, it has an edge on that side; if on the left hand, you fall upon the edge of the sword on that side; it turns every way.

II. From the inscription we proceed to the contents of the epistle, in which the method is much the same as is observed in the rest. Here,

1. Christ takes notice of the trials and difficulties this church encountered with: *I know thy works, and where thou dwellest,* &c. *v.* 13. The works of God's servants are best known when the circumstances under which they did those works are duly considered. Now that which added very much lustre to the good works of this church was the circumstance of the place where this church was planted, a place where *Satan's seat* was. As our great Lord takes notice of all the advantages and opportunities we have for duty in the places where we dwell, so he takes notice of all the temptations and discouragements we meet with from the places where we dwell, and makes gracious allowances for them. This people dwelt where Satan's seat was, where he kept his court. His *circuit* is throughout the world, his *seat* is in some places that are infamous for wickedness, error, and cruelty. Some think that the Roman governor in this city was a most violent enemy to the Christians; and the seat of persecution is Satan's seat.

2. He commends their stedfastness: *Thou holdest fast my name, and hast not denied my faith.* These two expressions are much the same in sense; the former may, however, signify the effect and the latter the cause or means. (1.) "*Thou holdest fast my name;* thou art not ashamed of thy relation to me, but accountest it thine honour that my name is named on thee, that, as the wife bears the name of the husband, so thou art called by my name; this thou holdest fast, as thine honour and privilege." (2.) "That which has made thee thus faithful is the grace of faith: *thou hast not denied* the great doctrines of the gospel, nor departed from the Christian faith, and by that means thou hast been kept faithful." Our faith will have a great influence upon our faithfulness. Men who deny the faith

of Christ may boast very much of their sincerity, and faithfulness to God and conscience; but it has been seldom known that those who let go the true faith retained their fidelity; usually on that rock on which men make shipwreck of their faith they make shipwreck of a good conscience too. And here our blessed Lord aggrandizes the fidelity of this church from the circumstance of the times, as well as of the place where they lived: they had been stedfast *even in those days wherein Antipas his faithful martyr was slain among them.* Who this person was, and whether there be any thing mysterious in his name, we have no certain account. He was a faithful disciple of Christ, he suffered martyrdom for it, and sealed his faith and fidelity with his blood in the place where Satan dwelt; and though the rest of the believers there knew this, and saw it, yet they were not discouraged nor drawn away from their stedfastness: this is mentioned as an addition to their honour.

3. He reproves them for their sinful failures (*v.* 14): *But I have a few things against thee, because thou hast there those that hold the doctrine of Balaam,* &c., and *those that hold the doctrine of the Nicolaitans, which thing I hate.* There were some who taught that it was lawful to eat things sacrificed to idols, and that simple fornication was no sin; they, by an impure worship, drew men into impure practices, as Balaam did the Israelites. Observe, (1.) The filthiness of the spirit and the filthiness of the flesh often go together. Corrupt doctrines and a corrupt worship often lead to a corrupt conversation. (2.) It is very lawful to fix the name of the leaders of any heresy upon those who follow them. It is the shortest way of telling whom we mean. (3.) To continue in communion with persons of corrupt principles and practices is displeasing to God, draws a guilt and blemish upon the whole society: they become *partakers of other men's sins.* Though the church, as such, has no power to punish the persons of men, either for heresy or immorality, with corporal penalties, yet it has power to exclude them from its communion; and, if it do not so, Christ, the head and lawgiver of the church, will be displeased with it.

4. He calls them to repentance: *Repent, or else I will come unto thee quickly,* &c., *v.* 16. Observe here, (1.) Repentance is the duty of saints as well as sinners; it is a gospel duty. (2.) It is the duty of churches and communities as well as particular persons; those who sin together should repent together. (3.) It is the duty of Christian societies to repent of other men's sins, as far as they have been accessory to them, though but so much as by connivance. (4.) When God comes to punish the corrupt members of a church, he rebukes that church itself for allowing such to continue in its communion, and some drops of the storm fall upon the whole society. (5.) No sword cuts so deep, nor inflicts so mortal a wound, as the sword of Christ's mouth. Let but the threatenings of the word be set home upon the conscience of a sinner, and he will soon be a terror to himself; let these threatenings be executed, and the sinner is utterly cut off. The word of God will take hold of sinners, sooner or later, either for their conviction or their confusion.

III. We have the conclusion of this epistle, where, after the usual demand of universal attention, there is the promise of great favour to those that overcome. They shall *eat of the hidden manna, and have the new name, and the white stone, which no man knoweth, saving he that receiveth it, v.* 17. 1. The hidden manna, the influences and comforts of the Spirit of Christ in communion with him, coming down from heaven into the soul, from time to time, for its support, to let it taste something how saints and angels live in heaven. This is hidden from the rest of the world—*a stranger intermeddles not with* this joy; and it is laid up in Christ, the ark of the covenant, in the holy of holies. 2. The white stone, with a new name engraven upon it. This white stone is absolution from the guilt of sin, alluding to the ancient custom of giving a white stone to those acquitted on trial and a black stone to those condemned. The new name is the name of adoption: adopted persons took the name of the family into which they were adopted. None can read the evidence of a man's adoption but himself; he cannot always read it, but if he persevere he shall have both the evidence of sonship and the inheritance.

18 And unto the angel of the church
in Thyatira write; These things saith
the Son of God, who hath his eyes
like unto a flame of fire, and his feet
are like fine brass; 19 I know thy
works, and charity, and service, and
faith, and thy patience, and thy works;
and the last *to be* more than the first.
20 Notwithstanding I have a few
things against thee, because thou sufferest that woman Jezebel, which
calleth herself a prophetess, to teach
and to seduce my servants to commit
fornication, and to eat things sacrificed
unto idols. 21 And I gave her space
to repent of her fornication; and she
repented not. 22 Behold, I will cast
her into a bed, and them that commit
adultery with her into great tribulation, except they repent of their
deeds. 23 And I will kill her children with death; and all the churches
shall know that I am he which searcheth the reins and hearts: and I will
give unto every one of you according

to your works. 24 But unto you I
say, and unto the rest in Thyatira, as
many as have not this doctrine, and
which have not known the depths of
Satan, as they speak; I will put upon
you none other burden. 25 But that
which ye have *already* hold fast till I
come. 26 And he that overcometh,
and keepeth my works unto the end,
to him will I give power over the nations: 27 And he shall rule them
with a rod of iron; as the vessels of
a potter shall they be broken to
shivers: even as I received of my
Father. 28 And I will give him the
morning star. 29 He that hath an
ear, let him hear what the Spirit saith
unto the churches.

The form of each epistle is very much the same; and in this, as the rest, we have to consider the inscription, contents, and conclusion.

I. The inscription, telling us, 1. To whom it is directed: *To the angel of the church of Thyatira*, a city of the proconsular Asia, bordering upon Mysia on the north and Lydia on the south, a town of trade, whence came the woman named *Lydia, a seller of purple*, who, being at Philippi in Macedonia, probably about the business of her calling, *heard Paul preach there*, and *God opened her heart, that she attended to the things that were spoken, and believed, and was baptized*, and entertained Paul and Silas there. Whether it was by her means that the gospel was brought into her own city, Thyatira, is not certain; but that it was there, and successful to the forming of a gospel church, this epistle assures us. 2. By whom it was sent: by *the Son of God*, who is here described as having *eyes like a flame of fire, and feet like as fine brass*. His general title is here, *the Son of God*, that is, the eternal and only-begotten Son of God, which denotes that he has the same nature with the Father, but with a distinct and subordinate manner of subsistence. The description we have here of him is in two characters:—(1.) That his eyes are like a flame of fire, signifying his piercing, penetrating, perfect knowledge, a thorough insight into all persons and all things, one *who searches the hearts and tries the reins of the children of men* (*v.* 23), and will make all the churches to know he does so. (2.) That his feet are like fine brass, that the outgoings of his providence are steady, awful, and all pure and holy. As he judges with perfect wisdom, so he acts with perfect strength and steadiness.

II. The contents or subject-matter of this epistle, which, as the rest, includes,

1. The honourable character and commendation Christ gives of this church, ministry, and people; and this given by one who was no stranger to them, but well acquainted with them and with the principles from which they acted. Now in this church Christ makes honourable mention, (1.) Of their *charity*, either more general, a disposition to do good to all men, or more special, to the household of faith: there is no religion where there is no charity. (2.) Their *service*, their ministration; this respects chiefly the officers of the church, who had laboured in the word and doctrine. (3.) Their *faith*, which was the grace that actuated all the rest, both their charity and their service. (4.) Their *patience;* for those that are most charitable to others, most diligent in their places, and most faithful, must yet expect to meet with that which will exercise their patience. (5.) Their growing fruitfulness: their last works were better than the first This is an excellent character; when others had *left their first love*, and *lost their first zeal*, these were growing wiser and better. It should be the ambition and earnest desire of all Christians that their last works may be their best works, that they may be better and better every day, and best at last.

2. A faithful reproof for what was amiss. This is not so directly charged upon the church itself as upon some wicked seducers who were among them; the church's fault was that she connived too much at them.

(1.) These wicked seducers are compared to Jezebel, and called by her name. Jezebel was a persecutor of the prophets of the Lord, and a great patroness of idolaters and false prophets. The sin of these seducers was that they attempted to draw the servants of God into fornication, and to offer sacrifices to idols; they called themselves prophets, and so would claim a superior authority and regard to the ministers of the church. Two things aggravated the sin of these seducers, who, being one in their spirit and design, are spoken of as one person:—[1.] They made use of the name of God to oppose the truth of his doctrine and worship; this very much aggravated their sin. [2.] They abused the patience of God to harden themselves in their wickedness. God gave them space for repentance, but they repented not. Observe, *First*, Repentance is necessary to prevent the sinner's ruin. *Secondly*, Repentance requires time, a course of time, and time convenient; it is a great work, and a work of time. *Thirdly*, Where God gives space for repentance, he expects fruits meet for repentance. *Fourthly*, Where the space for repentance is lost, the sinner perishes with a double destruction.

(2.) Now why should the wickedness of this Jezebel be charged upon the church of Thyatira? Because that church suffered her to seduce the people of that city. But how could the church help it? They had not, as a church, civil power to banish or imprison her; but they had ministerial power to censure and to excommunicate her: and it is probable that neglecting to use the power they had made them sharers in her sin.

3. The punishment of this seducer, this Jezebel, *v.* 22, 23, in which is couched a prediction of the fall of Babylon. (1.) *I will cast her into a bed,* into a bed of pain, not of pleasure, into a bed of flames; and those who have sinned with her shall suffer with her; but this may yet be prevented by their repentance. (2.) *I will kill her children with death;* that is, the second death, which does the work effectually, and leaves no hope of future life, no resurrection for those that are killed by the second death, but only to shame and everlasting contempt.

4. The design of Christ in the destruction of these wicked seducers, and this was the instruction of others, especially of his churches: *All the churches shall know that I am he that searcheth the reins and the hearts; and I will give to every one of you according to your works.* God is known by *the judgments that he executes;* and, by this revenge taken upon seducers, he would make known, (1.) His infallible knowledge of the hearts of men, of their principles, designs, frame, and temper, their formality, their indifference, their secret inclinations to symbolize with idolaters. (2.) His impartial justice, in *giving every one according to his work,* that the name of Christians should be no protection, their churches should be no sanctuaries for sin and sinners.

5. The encouragement given to those who keep themselves pure and undefiled: *But to you I say, and unto the rest,* &c., *v.* 24. Observe, (1.) What these seducers called their doctrines—*depths,* profound mysteries, amusing the people, and endeavouring to persuade them that they had a deeper insight into religion than their own ministers had attained to. (2.) What Christ called them—*depths of Satan,* Satanical delusions and devices, diabolical mysteries; for there is a *mystery of iniquity,* as well as *the great mystery of godliness.* It is a dangerous thing to despise the mystery of God, and it is as dangerous to receive the mysteries of Satan. (3.) How tender Christ is of his faithful servants: "*I will lay upon you no other burden; but that which you have already hold fast till I come, v.* 24, 25. I will not overburden your faith with any new mysteries, nor your consciences with any new laws. I only require your attention to what you have received. *Hold that fast till I come,* and I desire no more." Christ is coming to put an end to all the temptations of his people; and, if they hold fast faith and a good conscience till he come, all the difficulty and danger will be over.

III. We now come to the conclusion of this message, *v.* 26—29. Here we have, 1. The promise of an ample reward to the persevering victorious believer, in two parts:—(1.) Very great power and dominion over the rest of the world: *Power over the nations,* which may refer either to the time when the empire should turn Christian, and the world be under the government of the Christian emperor, as in Constantine's time; or to the other world, when believers shall sit down with Christ on his throne of judgment, and join with him in trying, and condemning, and consigning over to punishment the enemies of Christ and the church. *The upright shall have dominion in the morning.* (2.) Knowledge and wisdom, suitable to such power and dominion: *I will give him the morning-star.* Christ is the morning-star. He brings day with him into the soul, the light of grace and of glory; and he will give his people that perfection of light and wisdom which is requisite to the state of dignity and dominion that they shall have in the morning of the resurrection. 2. This epistle ends with the usual demand of attention: *He that hath an ear let him hear what the Spirit saith unto the churches.* In the foregoing epistles, this demand of attention comes before the concluding promise; but in this, and all that follow, it comes after, and tells us that we should all attend to the promises as well as to the precepts that Christ delivers to the churches.

CHAP. III.

Here we have three more of the epistles of Christ to the churches: I. To Sardis, ver. 1—6. II. To Philadelphia, ver. 7—13. III. To Laodicea, ver. 14, to the end.

AND unto the angel of the church
in Sardis write; These things
saith he that hath the seven Spirits of
God, and the seven stars; I know thy
works, that thou hast a name that thou
livest, and art dead. 2 Be watchful,
and strengthen the things which remain,
that are ready to die: for I
have not found thy works perfect before
God. 3 Remember therefore
how thou hast received and heard,
and hold fast, and repent. If therefore
thou shalt not watch, I will come
on thee as a thief, and thou shalt not
know what hour I will come upon
thee. 4 Thou hast a few names even
in Sardis which have not defiled their
garments; and they shall walk with
me in white: for they are worthy.
5 He that overcometh, the same shall
be clothed in white raiment; and I
will not blot out his name out of the
book of life, but I will confess his
name before my Father, and before
his angels. 6 He that hath an ear,
let him hear what the Spirit saith
unto the churches.

Here is, I. The preface, showing, 1. To whom this letter is directed: *To the angel of the church of Sardis,* an ancient city of Lydia, on the banks of the mountain Tmolus, said to have been the chief city of Asia the Less, and the first city in that part of the world that was converted by the preaching of John; and, some say, the first that revolted from Christianity, and one of the first that was laid in its ruins, in which it still lies, without any church or ministry. 2. By whom this message was sent—the Lord Jesus, who here assumes the character of him *that hath the seven spirits of God, and the seven stars,* taken out of *ch.* i. 4, where *the seven spirits are said to be before the throne.* (1.) He hath the seven spirits, that is, the Holy Spirit with his various powers, graces, and operations; for he is personally one, though efficaciously various, and may be said here to be seven, which is the number of the churches, and of the angels of the churches, to show that to every minister, and to every church, there is a dispensation and measure of the Spirit given for them to profit withal—a stock of spiritual influence for that minister and church to improve, both for enlargement and continuance, which measure of the Spirit is not ordinarily withdrawn from them, till they forfeit it by misimprovement. Churches have their spiritual stock and fund, as well as particular believers; and, this epistle being sent to a languishing ministry and church, they are very fitly put in mind that Christ has the seven spirits, the Spirit without measure and in perfection, to whom they may apply themselves for the reviving of his work among them. (2.) He hath the seven stars, the angels of the churches; they are disposed of by him, and accountable to him, which should make them faithful and zealous. He has ministers to employ, and spiritual influences to communicate to his ministers for the good of his church. The Holy Spirit usually works by the ministry, and the ministry will be of no efficacy without the Spirit; the same divine hand holds them both.

II. The body of this epistle. There is this observable in it, that whereas in the other epistles Christ begins with commending what is good in the churches, and then proceeds to tell them what is amiss, in this (and in the epistle to Laodicea) he begins,

1. With a reproof, and a very severe one: *I know thy works, that thou hast a name that thou livest, and art dead.* Hypocrisy, and a lamentable decay in religion, are the sins charged upon this church, by one who knew her well, and all her works. (1.) This church had gained a great reputation; it had a name, and a very honourable one, for a flourishing church, a name for vital lively religion, for purity of doctrine, unity among themselves, uniformity in worship, decency, and order. We read not of any unhappy divisions among themselves. Every thing appeared well, as to what falls under the observation of men. (2.) This church was not really what it was reputed to be. They had a name to live, but they were dead; there was a form of godliness, but not the power, *a name to live,* but not a principle of life. If there was not a total privation of life, yet there was a great deadness in their souls and in their services, a great deadness in the spirits of their ministers, and a great deadness in their ministrations, in their praying, in their preaching, in their converse, and a great deadness in the people in hearing, in prayer, and in conversation; what little life was yet left among them was, in a manner, expiring, ready to die.

2. Our Lord proceeds to give this degenerate church the best advice: *Be watchful, and strengthen the things,* &c., *v.* 2. (1.) He advises them to be upon their watch. The cause of their sinful deadness and declension was that they had let down their watch. Whenever we are off our watch, we lose ground, and therefore must return to our watchfulness against sin, and Satan, and whatever is destructive to the life and power of godliness. (2.) To strengthen the things that remain, and that are ready to die. Some understand this of persons; there were some few who had retained their integrity, but they were in danger of declining with the rest. It is a difficult thing to keep up to the life and *power of godliness* ourselves, when we see a universal deadness and declension prevailing round about us. Or it may be understood of practices, as it follows: *I have not found thy works perfect before God,* not filled up; there is something wanting in them; there is the shell, but not the kernel; there is the carcase, but not the soul—the shadow, but not the substance. The inward thing is wanting, thy works are hollow and empty; prayers are not filled up with holy desires, alms-deeds not filled up with true charity, sabbaths not filled up with suitable devotion of soul to God; there are not inward affections suitable to outward acts and expressions. Now when the spirit is wanting the form cannot long subsist. (3.) To recollect themselves, and *remember how they have received and heard* (*v.* 3); not only to remember what they had received and heard, what messages they had received from God, what tokens of his mercy and favour towards them, what sermons they had heard, but how they had received and heard, what impressions the mercies of God had made upon their souls at first, what affections they felt working under the word and ordinances, the love of their espousals, the kindness of their youth, how welcome the gospel and the grace of God were to them when they first received them. *Where is the blessedness they then spoke of?* (4.) To hold fast what they had received, that they might not lose all, *and repent* sincerely that they had lost so much of the life of religion, and had run the risk of losing all.

3. Christ enforces his counsel with a dreadful threatening in case it should be despised: *I will come unto thee as a thief, and thou shalt not know the hour, v.* 3. Observe, (1.) When Christ leaves a people as to his gracious presence, he comes to them in judgment; and his judicial presence will be very dreadful to those who have sinned away his gracious

presence. (2.) His judicial approach to a dead declining people will be surprising; their deadness will keep them in security, and, as it procures an angry visit from Christ to them, it will prevent their discerning it and preparing for it. (3.) Such a visit from Christ will be to their loss; he will come as a thief, to strip them of their remaining enjoyments and mercies, not by fraud, but in justice and righteousness, taking the forfeiture they have made of all to him.

4. Our blessed Lord does not leave this sinful people without some comfort and encouragement: *In the midst of judgment he remembers mercy* (*v.* 4), and here, (1.) He makes honourable mention of the faithful remnant in Sardis, though but small: *Thou hast a few names in Sardis which have not defiled their garments;* they had not given into the prevailing corruptions and pollution of the day and place in which they lived. God takes notice of the smallest number of those who abide with him; and the fewer they are the more precious in his sight. (2.) He makes a very gracious promise to them: *They shall walk with me in white, for they are worthy*—in the *stola,* the white robes of justification, and adoption, and comfort, or in the white robes of honour and glory in the other world. They shall walk with Christ in the pleasant walks of the heavenly paradise; and what delightful converse will there be between Christ and them when they thus walk together! This is an honour proper and suitable to their integrity, which their fidelity has prepared them for, and which it is no way unbecoming Christ to confer upon them, though it is not a legal but a gospel worthiness that is ascribed to them, not merit but meetness. Those who walk with Christ in the clean garments of real practical holiness here, and keep themselves unspotted from the world, shall walk with Christ in the white robes of honour and glory in the other world: this is a suitable reward.

III. We now come to the conclusion of this epistle, in which, as before, we have,

1. A great reward promised to the conquering Christian (*v.* 5), and it is very much the same with what has been already mentioned: *He that overcometh shall be clothed in white raiment.* The purity of grace shall be rewarded with the perfect purity of glory. Holiness, when perfected, shall be its own reward; glory is the perfection of grace, differing not in kind, but in degree. Now to this is added another promise very suitable to the case: *I will not blot his name out of the book of life, but will confess his name before my Father, and before his angels.* Observe, (1.) Christ has his book of life, a register and roll of all who shall inherit eternal life. [1.] The book of eternal election. [2.] The book of remembrance of all those who have lived to God, and have kept up the life and power of godliness in evil times. (2.) Christ will not blot the names of his chosen and faithful ones out of this book of life; men may be enrolled in the registers of the church, as baptized, as making a profession, as having a name to live, and that name may come to be blotted out of the roll, when it appears that it was but a name, a name to live, without spiritual life; such often lose the very name before they die, they are left of God to blot out their own names by their gross and open wickedness. But the names of those that overcome shall never be blotted out. (3.) Christ will produce this book of life, and confess the names of the faithful who stand there, before God, and all the angels; he will do this as their Judge, when the books shall be opened; he will do this as their captain and head, leading them with him triumphantly to heaven, presenting them to the Father: *Behold me, and the children that thou hast given me.* How great will this honour and reward be!

2. The demand of universal attention finishes the message. Every word from God deserves attention from men; that which may seem more particularly directed to one body of men has something in it instructive to all.

7 And to the angel of the church
in Philadelphia write; These things
saith he that is holy, he that is true,
he that hath the key of David, he that
openeth, and no man shutteth; and
shutteth, and no man openeth; 8 I
know thy works: behold, I have set
before thee an open door, and no
man can shut it: for thou hast a little
strength, and hast kept my word, and
hast not denied my name. 9 Behold,
I will make them of the synagogue of
Satan, which say they are Jews, and
are not, but do lie; behold, I will
make them to come and worship before thy feet, and to know that I have
loved thee. 10 Because thou hast
kept the word of my patience, I also
will keep thee from the hour of
temptation, which shall come upon
all the world, to try them that dwell
upon the earth. 11 Behold, I come
quickly: hold that fast which thou
hast, that no man take thy crown.
12 Him that overcometh will I make
a pillar in the temple of my God, and
he shall go no more out: and I will
write upon him the name of my God,
and the name of the city of my God,
which is new Jerusalem, which cometh
down out of heaven from my God:
and I *will write upon him* my new
name. 13 He that hath an ear let

him hear what the Spirit saith unto the churches.

We have now come to the sixth letter, sent to one of the Asian churches, where observe,

I. The inscription, showing,

1. For whom it was more immediately designed: *The angel of the church of Philadelphia;* this also was a city in Asia Minor, seated upon the borders of Mysia and Lydia, and had its name from that brotherly love for which it was eminent. We can hardly suppose that this name was given to it after it received the Christian religion, and that it was so called from that Christian affection that all believers have, and should have, one for another, as the children of one Father and the brethren of Christ; but rather that it was its ancient name, on account of the love and kindness which the citizens had and showed to each other as a civil fraternity. This was an excellent spirit, and, when sanctified by the grace of the gospel, would render them an excellent church, as indeed they were, for here is no one fault found with this church, and yet, doubtless, there were faults in it of common infirmity; but love covers such faults.

2. By whom this letter was signed; even by the same Jesus who is alone the universal head of all the churches; and here observe by what title he chooses to represent himself to this church: *He that is holy, he that is true, he that hath the key of David,* &c. You have his personal character: *He that is holy* and *he that is true,* holy in his nature, and therefore he cannot but be true to his word, for he hath spoken in his holiness; and you have also his political character: *He hath the key of David, he openeth, and no man shutteth; he hath the key of the house of David,* the key of government and authority in and over the church. Observe, (1.) The acts of his government. [1.] He opens. He opens a door of opportunity to his churches; he opens a door of utterance to his ministers; he opens a door of entrance, opens the heart; he opens a door of admission into the visible church, laying down the terms of communion; and he opens the door of admission into the church triumphant, according to the terms of salvation fixed by him. [2.] He shuts the door. When he pleases, he shuts the door of opportunity and the door of utterance, and leaves obstinate sinners shut up in the hardness of their hearts; he shuts the door of church-fellowship against unbelievers and profane persons; and he shuts the door of heaven against the foolish virgins who have slept away their day of grace, and against the workers of iniquity, how vain and confident soever they may be. (2.) The way and manner in which he performs these acts, and that is absolute sovereignty, independent upon the will of men, and irresistible by the power of men: *He openeth, and no man shutteth; he shutteth, and no man openeth;* he works to will and to do, and, when he works, none can hinder. These were proper characters for him, when speaking to a church that had endeavoured to be conformed to Christ in holiness and truth, and that had enjoyed a wide door of liberty and opportunity under his care and government.

II. The subject-matter of this epistle, where,

1. Christ puts them in mind of what he had done for them: *I have set before thee an open door, and no man can shut it, v.* 8. I have set it open, and kept it open, though there be many adversaries. Learn here, (1.) Christ is to be acknowledged as the author of all the liberty and opportunity his churches enjoy. (2.) He takes notice and keeps account, how long he has preserved their spiritual liberties and privileges for them. (3.) Wicked men envy the people of God their door of liberty, and would be glad to shut it against them. (4.) If we do not provoke Christ to shut this door against us, men cannot do it.

2. This church is commended: *Thou hast a little strength, and hast kept my word, and hast not denied my name, v.* 8. In this there seems to be couched a gentle reproof: "*Thou hast a little strength,* a little grace, which, though it be not proportionate to the wide door of opportunity which I have opened to thee, yet is true grace, and has kept thee faithful." True grace, though weak, has the divine approbation; but, though Christ accepts a little strength, yet believers should not rest satisfied in a little, but should strive to grow in grace, to be *strong in faith, giving glory to God.* True grace, though weak, will do more than the greatest gifts or highest degrees of common grace, for it will enable the Christian to keep the word of Christ, and not to deny his name. Obedience, fidelity, and a free confession of the name of Christ, are the fruits of true grace, and are pleasing to Christ as such.

3. Here is a promise of the great favour God would bestow on this church, *v.* 9, 10. This favour consists in two things:—

(1.) Christ would make this church's enemies subject to her. [1.] Those enemies are described to be such as *said they were Jews,* but lied in saying so—pretended to be the only and peculiar people of God, but were really *the synagogue of Satan.* Assemblies that *worship God in spirit and in truth* are the Israel of God; assemblies that either worship false gods, or the true God in a false manner, are the synagogues of Satan: though they may profess to be the only people o God, their profession is a lie. [2.] Their subjection to the church is described: *They shall worship at thy feet;* not pay a religious and divine honour to the church itself, nor to the ministry of it, but shall be convinced that they have been in the wrong, that this church is in the right and is beloved of Christ, and they shall desire to be taken into communion with her and that they may worship the same God after the same manner.

How shall this great change be wrought? By the power of God upon the hearts of his enemies, and by signal discoveries of his peculiar favour to his church: *They shall know that I have loved thee.* Observe, *First,* The greatest honour and happiness any church can enjoy consist in the peculiar love and favour of Christ. *Secondly,* Christ can discover this his favour to his people in such a manner that their very enemies shall see it, and be forced to acknowledge it. *Thirdly,* This will, by the grace of Christ, soften the hearts of their enemies, and make them desirous to be admitted into communion with them.

(2.) Another instance of favour that Christ promises to this church is persevering grace in the most trying times (*v.* 10), and this as the reward of their past fidelity. *To him that hath shall be given.* Here observe, [1.] The gospel of Christ is the word of his patience. It is the fruit of the patience of God to a sinful world; it sets before men the exemplary patience of Christ in all his sufferings for men; it calls those who receive it to the exercise of patience in conformity to Christ. [2.] This gospel should be carefully kept by all that enjoy it; they must keep up to the faith, and practice, and worship prescribed in the gospel. [3.] After a day of patience we must expect an hour of temptation; a day of gospel peace and liberty is a day of God's patience, and it is seldom so well improved as it should be and therefore it is often followed by an hour of trial and temptation. [4.] Sometimes the trial is more general and universal; it comes upon all the world, and, when it is so general, it is usually the shorter. [5.] Those who keep the gospel in a time of peace shall be kept by Christ in an hour of temptation. By keeping the gospel they are prepared for the trial; and the same divine grace that has made them fruitful in times of peace will make them faithful in times of persecution.

4. Christ calls the church to that duty which he before promised he would enable her to do, and that is, to persevere, *to hold fast that which she had.* (1.) The duty itself: "*Hold fast that which thou hast,* that faith, that truth, that strength of grace, that zeal, that love to the brethren; thou hast been possessed of this excellent treasure, hold it fast." (2.) The motives, taken from the speedy appearance of Christ: "*Behold, I come quickly.* See, I am just a coming to relieve them under the trial, to reward their fidelity, and to punish those who fall away; they shall lose that crown which they once seemed to have a right to, which they hoped for, and pleased themselves with the thoughts of. The persevering Christian shall win the prize from backsliding professors, who once stood fair for it."

III. The conclusion of this epistle, *v.* 12, 13. Here,

1. After his usual manner, our Saviour promises a glorious reward to the victorious believer, in two things:—(1.) He shall be a monumental *pillar in the temple of God;* not a pillar to support the temple (heaven needs no such props), but a monument of the free and powerful grace of God, a monument that shall never be defaced nor removed, as many stately pillars erected in honour to the Roman emperors and generals have been. (2.) On this monumental pillar there shall be an honourable inscription, as in those cases is usual. [1.] *The name of God,* in whose cause he engaged, whom he served, and for whom he suffered in this warfare; *and the name of the city of God,* the church of God, *the new Jerusalem, which came down from heaven.* On this pillar shall be recorded all the services the believer did to the church of God, how he asserted her rights, enlarged her borders, maintained her purity and honour; this will be a greater name than *Asiaticus,* or *Africanus;* a soldier under God in the wars of the church. And then another part of the inscription is, [2.] The *new name* of Christ, the Mediator, the Redeemer, the captain of our salvation; by this it will appear under whose banner this conquering believer had enlisted, under whose conduct he acted, by whose example he was encouraged, and under whose influence he fought the good fight, and came off victorious.

2. The epistle is closed up with the demand of attention: *He that hath an ear, let him hear what the Spirit saith unto the churches,* how Christ loves and values his faithful people, how he commends, and how he will crown their fidelity.

14 And unto the angel of the church
of the Laodiceans write; These things
saith the Amen, the faithful and true
witness, the beginning of the creation
of God; 15 I know thy works, that
thou art neither cold nor hot: I would
thou wert cold or hot. 16 So then
because thou art lukewarm, and neither cold nor hot, I will spue thee
out of my mouth. 17 Because thou
sayest, I am rich, and increased with
goods, and have need of nothing;
and knowest not that thou art
wretched, and miserable, and poor,
and blind, and naked: 18 I counse
thee to buy of me gold tried in the
fire, that thou mayest be rich; and
white raiment, that thou mayest be
clothed, and *that* the shame of thy
nakedness do not appear; and anoint
thine eyes with eye-salve, that thou
mayest see. 19 As many as I love,
I rebuke and chasten: be zealous
therefore, and repent. 20 Behold, I
stand at the door, and knock: if any
man hear my voice, and open the

door, I will come in to him, and will
sup with him, and he with me. 21
To him that overcometh will I grant
to sit with me in my throne, even as
I also overcame, and am set down
with my Father in his throne. 22
He that hath an ear, let him hear what
the Spirit saith unto the churches.

We now come to the last and worst of all the seven Asian churches, the reverse of the church of Philadelphia; for, as there was nothing reproved in that, here is nothing commended in this, and yet this was one of *the seven golden candlesticks,* for a corrupt church may still be a church. Here we have, as before,

I. The inscription, to whom, and from whom. 1. To whom: *To the angel of the church of Laodicea.* This was a once famous city near the river Lycus, had a wall of vast compass, and three marble theatres, and, like Rome, was built on seven hills. It seems, the apostle Paul was very instrumental in planting the gospel in this city, from which he wrote a letter, as he mentions in *the epistle to the Colossians,* the last chapter, in which he sends salutations to them, Laodicea not being above twenty miles distant from Colosse. In this city was held a council in the fourth century, but it has been long since demolished, and lies in its ruins to this day, an awful monument of *the wrath of the Lamb.* 2. From whom this message was sent. Here our Lord Jesus styles himself *the Amen, the faithful and true witness, the beginning of the creation of God.* (1.) *The Amen,* one that is steady and unchangeable in all his purposes and promises, which are all yea, and all amen. (2.) *The faithful and true witness,* whose testimony of God to men ought to be received and fully believed, and whose testimony of men to God will be fully believed and regarded, and will be a swift but true witness against all indifferent lukewarm professors. (3.) *The beginning of the creation of God,* either of the first creation, and so he is the beginning, that is, the first cause, the Creator, and the Governor of it; or of the second creation, the church; and so he is the head of that body, the first-born from the dead, as it is in *ch.* i. 5, whence these titles are taken. Christ, having raised up himself by his own divine power, as the head of a new world, raises up dead souls to be a living temple and church to himself.

II. The subject-matter, in which observe,

1. The heavy charge drawn up against this church, ministers and people, by one who knew them better than they knew themselves: *Thou art neither cold nor hot,* but worse than either; *I would thou wert cold or hot, v.* 15. Lukewarmness or indifference in religion is the worst temper in the world. If religion is a real thing, it is the most excellent thing, and therefore we should be in good earnest in it; if it is not a real thing, it is the vilest imposture, and we should be earnest against it. If religion is worth any thing, it is worth every thing; an indifference here is inexcusable: *Why halt you between two opinions? If God be God, follow him; if Baal* (be God), *follow him.* Here is no room for neutrality. An open enemy shall have fairer quarter than a perfidious neuter; and there is more hope of a heathen than of such. Christ expects that men should declare themselves in earnest either for him or against him.

2. A severe punishment threatened: *I will spue thee out of my mouth.* As lukewarm water turns the stomach, and provokes to a vomit, lukewarm professors turn the heart of Christ against them. He is sick of them, and cannot long bear them. They may call their lukewarmness *charity, meekness, moderation,* and *a largeness of soul;* it is nauseous to Christ, and makes those so that allow themselves in it. They shall be rejected, and finally rejected; for far be it from the holy Jesus to return to that which has been thus rejected.

3. We have one cause of this indifference and inconsistency in religion assigned, and that is self-conceitedness or self-delusion. They thought they were very well already, and therefore they were very indifferent whether they grew better or no: *Because thou sayest, I am rich, and increased with goods,* &c., *v.* 17. Here observe, What a difference there was between the thoughts they had of themselves and the thoughts that Christ had of them. (1.) The high thoughts they had of themselves: *Thou sayest, I am rich, and increased with goods, and have need of nothing,* rich, and growing richer, and increased to such a degree as to be above all want or possibilty of wanting. Perhaps they were well provided for as to their bodies, and this made them overlook the necessities of their souls. Or they thought themselves well furnished in their souls: they had learning, and they took it for religion; they had gifts, and they took them for grace; they had wit, and they took it for true wisdom; they had ordinances, and they took up with them instead of the God of ordinances. How careful should we be not to put the cheat upon our own souls! Doubtless there are many in hell that once thought themselves to be in the way to heaven. Let us daily beg of God that we may not be left to flatter and deceive ourselves in the concerns of our souls. (2.) The mean thoughts that Christ had of them; and he was not mistaken. He knew, though they knew not, that they were *wretched, and miserable, and poor, and blind, and naked.* Their state was wretched in itself, and such as called for pity and compassion from others: though they were proud of themselves, they were pitied by all who knew their case. For, [1.] They were poor, really poor, when they said and thought they were rich; they had no

provision for their souls to live upon; their souls were starving in the midst of their abundance; they were vastly in debt to the justice of God, and had nothing to pay off the least part of the debt. [2.] They were *blind;* they could not see their state, nor their way, nor their danger; they could not see into themselves; they could not look before them; they were blind, and yet they thought they saw; the very light that was in them was darkness, and then how great must that darkness be! They could not see Christ, though evidently set forth, and crucified, before their eyes. They could not see God by faith, though always present in them. They could not see death, though it was just before them. They could not look into eternity, though they stood upon the very brink of it continually. [3.] They were naked, without clothing and without house and harbour for their souls. They were without clothing, had neither the garment of justification nor that of sanctification. Their nakedness both of guilt and pollution had no covering. They lay always exposed to sin and shame. Their righteousnesses were but filthy rags; they were rags, and would not cover them, filthy rags, and would defile them. And they were naked, without house or harbour, for they were without God, and he has been the dwelling-place of his people in all ages; in him alone the soul of man can find rest, and safety, and all suitable accommodations. The riches of the body will not enrich the soul; the sight of the body will not enlighten the soul; the most convenient house for the body will not afford rest nor safety to the soul. The soul is a different thing from the body, and must have accommodation suitable to its nature, or else in the midst of bodily prosperity it will be wretched and miserable.

4. We have good counsel given by Christ to this sinful people, and that is that they drop their vain and false opinion they had of themselves, and endeavour to be that really which they would seem to be: *I counsel thee to buy of me,* &c., *v.* 18. Observe, (1.) Our Lord Jesus Christ continues to give good counsel to those who have cast his counsels behind their backs. (2.) The condition of sinners is never desperate, while they enjoy the gracious calls and counsels of Christ. (3.) Our blessed Lord, the counsellor, always gives the best advice, and that which is most suitable to the sinner's case; as here, [1.] These people were poor; Christ counsels them to buy of him gold tried in the fire, that they might be rich. He lets them know where they might have true riches and how they might have them. *First,* Where they might have them—from himself; he sends them not to the streams of Pactolus, nor to the mines of Potosi, but invites them to himself, the pearl of price. *Secondly,* And how must they have this true gold from him? They must buy it. This seems to be unsaying all again. How can those that are poor buy gold? Just as they may buy of Christ wine and milk, that is, *without money and without price,* Isa. lv. 1 Something indeed must be parted with, but it is nothing of a valuable consideration, it is only to make room for receiving true riches. "Part with sin and self-sufficiency, and come to Christ with a sense of your poverty and emptiness, that you may be filled with his hidden treasure." [2.] These people were naked; Christ tells them where they might have clothing, and such as would cover the shame of their nakedness. This they must receive from Christ; and they must only put off their filthy rags that they might put on the white raiment which he had purchased and provided for them—his own imputed righteousness for justification and the garments of holiness and sanctification. [3.] They were blind; and he *counsels them to buy of him eye-salve, that they might see,* to give up their own wisdom and reason, which are but blindness in the things of God, and resign themselves to his word and Spirit, and their eyes shall be opened to see their way and their end, their duty and their true interest; a new and glorious scene would then open itself to their souls; a new world furnished with the most beautiful and excellent objects, and this light would be marvellous to those who were but just now delivered from the powers of darkness. This is the wise and good counsel Christ gives to careless souls; and, if they follow it, he will judge himself bound in honour to make it effectual.

5. Here is added great and gracious encouragement to this sinful people to take the admonition and advice well that Christ had given them, *v.* 19, 20. He tells them, (1.) It was given them in true and tender affection: "*Whom I love, I rebuke and chasten.* You may think I have given you hard words and severe reproofs; it is all out of love to your souls. I would not have thus openly rebuked and corrected your sinful lukewarmness and vain confidence, if I had not been a lover of your souls; had I hated you, I would have let you alone, to go on in sin till it had been your ruin." Sinners ought to take the rebukes of God's word and rod as tokens of his good-will to their souls, and should accordingly repent in good earnest, and turn to him that smites them; better are the frowns and wounds of a friend than the flattering smiles of an enemy. (2.) If they would comply with his admonitions, he was ready to make them good to their souls: *Behold, I stand at the door and knock,* &c., *v.* 20. Here observe, [1.] Christ is graciously pleased by his word and Spirit to come to the door of the heart of sinners; he draws near to them in a way of mercy, ready to make them a kind visit. [2.] He finds this door shut against him; the heart of man is by nature shut up against Christ by ignorance, unbelief, sinful prejudices. [3.] When he finds the heart

shut, he does not immediately withdraw, but he waits to be gracious, even till his head be filled with the dew. [4.] He uses all proper means to awaken sinners, and to cause them to open to him: he calls by his word, he knocks by the impulses of his Spirit upon their conscience. [5.] Those who open to him shall enjoy his presence, to their great comfort and advantage. He will sup with them; he will accept of what is good in them; he will eat his pleasant fruit; and he will bring the best part of the entertainment with him. If what he finds would make but a poor feast, what he brings will make up the deficiency: he will give fresh supplies of graces and comforts, and thereby stir up fresh actings of faith, and love, and delight; and in all this Christ and his repenting people will enjoy pleasant communion with each other. Alas! what do careless obstinate sinners lose by refusing to open the door of the heart to Christ!

III. We now come to the conclusion of this epistle; and here we have as before,

1. The promise made to the overcoming believer. It is here implied, (1.) That though this church seemed to be wholly overrun and overcome with lukewarmness and self-confidence, yet it was possible that by the reproofs and counsels of Christ they might be inspired with fresh zeal and vigour, and might come off conquerors in their spiritual warfare. (2.) That, if they did so, all former faults should be forgiven, and they should have a great reward. And what is that reward? *They shall sit down with me on my throne, as I also overcame, and have sat down with my Father on his throne, v.* 21. Here it is intimated, [1.] That Christ himself had met with his temptations and conflicts. [2.] That he overcame them all, and was more than a conqueror. [3.] That, as the reward of his conflict and victory, he has sat down with God the Father on his throne, possessed of that glory which he had with the Father from eternity, but which he was pleased very much to conceal on earth, leaving it as it were in the hands of the Father, as a pledge that he would fulfil the work of a Saviour before he reassumed that manifestative glory; and, having done so, then *pignus reposcere—he demands the pledge,* to appear in his divine glory equal to the Father. [4.] That those who are conformed to Christ in his trials and victories shall be conformed to him in his glory; they shall sit down with him on his throne, on his throne of judgment at the end of the world, on his throne of glory to all eternity, shining in his beams by virtue of their union with him and relation to him, as the mystical body of which he is the head.

2. All is closed up with the general demand of attention (*v.* 22), putting all to whom these epistles shall come in mind that what is contained in them is not of private interpretation, not intended for the instruction, reproof, and correction of those particular churches only, but of all the churches of Christ in all ages and parts of the world: and as there will be a resemblance in all succeeding churches to these, both in their graces and sins, so they may expect that God will deal with them as he dealt with these, which are patterns to all ages what faithful and fruitful churches may expect to receive from God, and what those who are unfaithful may expect to suffer from his hand; yea, that God's dealings with his churches may afford useful instruction to the rest of the world, to put them upon considering, *If judgment begin at the house of God, what shall the end of those be that do not obey the gospel of Christ?* 1 Pet. iv. 17. Thus end the messages of Christ to the Asian churches, the epistolary part of this book. We now come to the prophetical part.

CHAP. IV.

In this chapter the prophetical scene opens; and, as the epistolary part opened with a vision of Christ (ch. i.), so this part is introduced with a glorious appearance of the great God, whose throne is in heaven, compassed about with the heavenly host. This discovery was made to John, and in this chapter he, I. Records the heavenly sight he saw, ver. 1—7. And then, II. The heavenly songs he heard, ver. 8, to the end.

AFTER this I looked, and, behold, a door *was* opened in heaven: and the first voice which I heard *was* as it were of a trumpet talking with me; which said, Come up hither, and I will show thee things
which must be hereafter. 2 And
immediately I was in the spirit: and, behold, a throne was set in heaven,
and *one* sat on the throne. 3 And
he that sat was to look upon like a jasper and a sardine stone: and *there was* a rainbow round about the throne,
in sight like unto an emerald. 4 And
round about the throne *were* four and twenty seats: and upon the seats I saw four and twenty elders sitting, clothed in white raiment; and they had on their heads crowns of gold.
5 And out of the throne proceeded lightnings and thunderings and voices: and *there were* seven lamps of fire burning before the throne, which are
the seven Spirits of God. 6 And
before the throne *there was* a sea of glass like unto crystal: and in the midst of the throne, and round about the throne, *were* four beasts full of
eyes before and behind. 7 And the
first beast *was* like a lion, and the second beast like a calf, and the third beast had a face as a man, and the fourth beast *was* like a flying eagle.
8 And the four beasts had each of them six wings about *him;* and *they were* full of eyes within—

We have here an account of a second vision with which the apostle John was favoured: *After this,* that is, not only "after I had seen the vision of Christ walking in the midst of the golden candlesticks," but "after I had taken his messages from his mouth, and written and sent them to the several churches, according to his command, after this I had another vision." Those who well improve the discoveries they have had of God already are prepared thereby for more, and may expect them. Observe,

I. The preparation made for the apostle's having this vision.

1. *A door was opened in heaven.* Hence we learn, (1.) Whatever is transacted on earth is first designed and settled in heaven; there is the model of all the works of God; all of them are therefore before his eye, and he lets the inhabitants of heaven see as much of them as is fit for them. (2.) We can know nothing of future events but what God is pleased to discover to us; they are within the veil, till God opens the door. But, (3.) So far as God reveals his designs to us we may and ought to receive them, and not pretend to be wise above what is revealed.

2. To prepare John for the vision, a trumpet was sounded, and he was called up into heaven, to have a sight there of the things which were to be hereafter. He was called into the third heavens. (1.) There is a way opened into the holiest of all, into which the sons of God may enter by faith and holy affections now, in their spirits when they die, and in their whole persons at the last day. (2.) We must not intrude into the secret of God's presence, but stay till we are called up to it.

3. To prepare for this vision, *the apostle was in the Spirit.* He was in a rapture, as before (*ch.* i. 10), whether in the body or out of the body we cannot tell; perhaps he himself could not; however all bodily actions and sensations were for a time suspended, and his spirit was possessed with the spirit of prophecy, and wholly under a divine influence. The more we abstract ourselves from all corporeal things the more fit we are for communion with God; the body is a veil, a cloud, and clog to the mind in its transactions with God. We should as it were forget it when we go in before the Lord in duty, and be willing to drop it, that we may go up to him in heaven. This was the *apparatus* to the vision. Now observe,

II. The vision itself. It begins with the strange sights that the apostle saw, and they were such as these:—1. He saw *a throne set in heaven,* the seat of honour, and authority, and judgment. Heaven is the throne of God; there he resides in glory, and thence he gives laws to the church and to the whole world, and all earthly thrones are under the jurisdiction of this throne that is set in heaven. 2. He saw a glorious one upon the throne. This throne was not empty; there was one in it who filled it, and that was God, who is here described by those things that are most pleasant and precious in our world: *His countenance was like a jasper and a sardine-stone;* he is not described by any human features, so as to be represented by an image, but only by his transcendant brightness. The jasper is a transparent stone, which yet offers to the eye a variety of the most vivid colours, signifying the glorious perfections of God; the sardine-stone is red, signifying the justice of God, that essential attribute of which he never divests himself in favour of any, but gloriously exerts it in the government of the world, and especially of the church, through our Lord Jesus Christ. This attribute is displayed in pardoning as well as in punishing, in saving as well as in destroying sinners. 3. He saw *a rainbow about the throne, like unto an emerald, v.* 3. The rainbow was the seal and token of the covenant of providence that God made with Noah and his posterity with him, and is a fit emblem of that covenant of promise that God has made with Christ as the head of the church, and all his people in him, which covenant is as the waters of Noah unto God, an everlasting covenant, ordered in all things and sure. This rainbow looked like *the emerald;* the most prevailing colour was a pleasant green, to show the reviving and refreshing nature of the new covenant. 4. He saw *four-and-twenty seats* round about the throne, not empty, but filled with *four-and-twenty elders,* presbyters, representing, very probably, the whole church of God, both in the Old-Testament and in the New-Testament state; not the ministers of the church, but rather the representatives of the people. Their sitting denotes their honour, rest, and satisfaction; their sitting about the throne signifies their relation to God, their nearness to him, the sight and enjoyment they have of him, and their continual regard to him. *They are clothed in white raiment,* the righteousness of the saints, both imputed and inherent; *they had on their heads crowns of gold,* signifying the honour and authority given them of God, and the glory they have with him. All these may in a lower sense be applied to the gospel church on earth, in its worshipping assemblies; and, in the higher sense, to the church triumphant in heaven. 5. He perceived lightnings and voices proceeding out of the throne; that is, the awful declarations that God makes to his church of his sovereign will and pleasure. Thus he gave forth the law on mount Sinai; and the gospel has not less glory and authority than the law, though it be of a more spiritual nature. 6. He saw *seven lamps of fire burning before the throne,* which are explained to be *the seven Spirits of God* (*v.* 5), the various gifts, graces, and operations of the Spirit of God in the churches of Christ; these are all dispensed according to the will and pleasure of him who sits upon the throne. 7. He saw *before the throne a sea of glass, like unto crystal.* As in the temple there was a great vessel of brass filled with water, in which the priests were to wash when they went to minister before the Lord (and this was called a *sea),* so in the gospel church the sea or laver for purification is the blood of the Lord Jesus Christ, who cleanses from all sin, even from sanctuary-sins. In this all those must be washed that are admitted into the gracious presence of God on earth or his glorious presence in heaven. 8. He saw *four animals,* living creatures, between the throne and the circle of the elders (as seems most probable), standing between God and the people; these seem to signify the ministers of the gospel, not only because of this their situation nearer to God, and between him and the elders or representatives of the Christian people, and because fewer in number than the people, but as they are here described, (1.) By their many eyes, denoting sagacity, vigilance, and circumspection. (2.) By their lion-like courage, their great labour and diligence (in which they resemble the ox), their prudence and discretion becoming men, and their sublime affections and speculations, by which they mount up *with wings like eagles towards heaven* (*v.* 7), and these wings full of eyes within, to show that in all their meditations and ministrations they are to act with knowledge, and especially should be well acquainted with themselves and the state of their own souls, and see their own concern in the great doctrines and duties of religion, watching over their own souls as well as the souls of the people. (3.) By their continual employment, and that is, praising God, and not ceasing to do so night and day. The elders sit and are ministered unto; these stand and minister: they rest not night nor day. This now leads to the other part of the representation.

—8 And they rest not day and
night, saying, Holy, holy, holy, Lord
God Almighty, which was, and is, and
is to come. 9 And when those beasts
give glory and honour and thanks to
him that sat on the throne, who liveth
for ever and ever, 10 The four and
twenty elders fall down before him that
sat on the throne, and worship him
that liveth for ever and ever, and cast
their crowns before the throne, saying,
11 Thou art worthy, O Lord, to receive glory and honour and power:
for thou hast created all things, and for
thy pleasure they are and were created.

We have considered the sights that the apostle saw in heaven: now let us observe the songs that he heard, for there is in heaven not only that to be seen which will highly please a sanctified eye, but there is that to be heard which will greatly delight a sanctified ear. This is true concerning the church of Christ here, which is a heaven upon earth, and it will be eminently so in the church made perfect in the heaven of heavens.

I. He heard the song of the four living creatures, of the ministers of the church, which refers to the prophet Isaiah's vision, *ch.* vi. And here, 1. They adore one God, and one only, *the Lord God Almighty,* unchangeable and everlasting. 2. They adore three holies in this one God, the Holy Father, the Holy Son, and the Holy Spirit; and these are one infinitely holy and eternal Being, who sits upon the throne, *and lives for ever and ever.* In this glory the prophet saw Christ, and spoke of him.

II. He heard the adorations of the *four-and-twenty elders,* that is, of the Christian people represented by them; the ministers led, and the people followed, in the praises of God, *v.* 10, 11. Here observe,

1. The object of their worship, the same with that which the ministers adored: *Him that sat on the throne,* the eternal everliving God. The true church of God has one and the same object of worship. Two different objects of worship, either co-ordinate or subordinate, would confound the worship and divide the worshippers. It is unlawful to join in divine worship with those who either mistake or multiply the object. There is but one God, and he alone, as God, is worshipped by the church on earth and in heaven.

2. The acts of adoration. (1.) They *fell down before him that sat on the throne;* they discovered the most profound humility, reverence, and godly fear. (2.) They *cast their crowns before the throne;* they gave God the glory of the holiness wherewith he had crowned their souls on earth and the honour and happiness with which he crowns them in heaven. They owe all their graces and all their glories to him, and acknowledge that his crown is infinitely more glorious than theirs, and that it is their glory to be glorifying God.

3. The words of adoration: they said, *Thou art worthy, O Lord, to receive glory, and honour, and power, v.* 11. Observe, (1.) They do not say, *We give thee glory, and honour, and power;* for what can any creature pretend to give unto God? But they say, *Thou art worthy to receive glory.* (2.) In this they tacitly acknowledge that God is exalted far above all blessing and praise. He was worthy to receive glory, but they were not worthy to praise, nor able to do it according to his infinite excellences.

4. We have the ground and reason of their adoration, which is threefold:—(1.) He is the Creator of all things, the first cause; and none but the Creator of all things should be adored; no made thing can be the object of religious worship. (2.) He is the preserver of all things, and his preservation is a continual creation; they are created still by the sustaining power of God. All beings but God are dependent upon the will and power

of God, and no dependent being must be set up as an object of religious worship. It is the part of the best dependent beings to be worshippers, not to be worshipped. (3.) He is the final cause of all things: *For thy pleasure they are and were created.* It was his will and pleasure to create all things; he was not put upon it by the will of another; there is no such thing as a subordinate creator, that acts under and by the will and power of another; and, if there were, he ought not to be worshipped. As God made all things at his pleasure, so he made them for his pleasure, to deal with them as he pleases and to glorify himself by them one way or other. Though he delights not in the death of sinners, but rather that they should turn and live, *yet he hath made all things for himself,* Prov. xvi. 4. Now if these be true and sufficient grounds for religious worship, as they are proper to God alone, Christ must needs be God, one with the Father and Spirit, and be worshipped as such; for we find the same causality ascribed to him. Col. i. 16, 17, *All things were created by him and for him, and he is before all things, and by him all things consist.*

CHAP. V.

In the foregoing chapter the prophetical scene was opened, in the sight and hearing of the apostle, and he had a sight of God the Creator and ruler of the world, and the great King of the church. He saw God on the throne of glory and government, surrounded with his holy ones, and receiving their adorations. Now the counsels and decrees of God are set before the apostle, as in a book, which God held in his right hand; and this book is represented, I. As sealed in the hand of God, ver. 1—9. II. As taken into the hand of Christ the Redeemer, to be unsealed and opened, ver. 6, to the end.

AND I saw in the right hand of
him that sat on the throne a
book written within and on the back-
side, sealed with seven seals. 2 And
I saw a strong angel proclaiming with
a loud voice, Who is worthy to open
the book, and to loose the seals
thereof? 3 And no man in heaven,
nor in earth, neither under the earth,
was able to open the book, neither to
look thereon. 4 And I wept much,
because no man was found worthy
to open and to read the book, neither
to look thereon. 5 And one of the
elders saith unto me, Weep not: behold, the Lion of the tribe of Juda,
the Root of David, hath prevailed
to open the book, and to loose the
seven seals thereof.

Hitherto the apostle had seen only the great God, the governor of all things, now,

I. He is favoured with a sight of the model and methods of his government, as they are all written down in a book which he holds in his hand; and this we are now to consider as shut up and sealed in the hand of God. Observe, 1. The designs and methods of divine Providence towards the church and the world are stated and fixed; they are resolved upon and agreed to, as that which is written in a book. The great design is laid, every part adjusted, all determined, and every thing passed into decree and made a matter of record. The original and first draught of this book is the book of God's decrees, laid up in his own cabinet, in his eternal mind: but there is a transcript of so much as was necessary to be known in the book of the scripture in general, in the prophetical part of scripture especially, and in this prophecy in particular. 2. God holds this book in his right hand, to declare the authority of the book, and his readiness and resolution to execute all the contents thereof, all the counsels and purposes therein recorded. 3. This book in the hand of God is shut up and sealed; it is known to none but himself, till he allows it to be opened. *Known unto God,* and to him alone, *are all his works, from the beginning of the world;* but it is his glory to conceal the matter as he pleases. The times and seasons, and their great events, he hath kept in his own hand and power. 4. It is *sealed with seven seals.* This tells us with what inscrutable secrecy the counsels of God are laid, how impenetrable by the eye and intellect of the creature; and also points us to seven several parts of this book of God's counsels. Each part seems to have its particular seal, and, when opened, discovers its proper events; these seven parts are not unsealed and opened at once, but successively, one scene of Providence introducing another, and explaining it, till the whole mystery of God's counsel and conduct be finished in the world.

II. He heard a proclamation made concerning this sealed book. 1. The crier was *a strong angel;* not that there are any weak ones among the angels in heaven, though there are many among the angels of the churches. This angel seems to come out, not only as a crier, but as a champion, with a challenge to any or all the creatures to try the strength of their wisdom in opening the counsels of God; and, as a champion, he cried with a loud voice, that every creature might hear. 2. The cry or challenge proclaimed was, "*Who is worthy to open the book, and to loose the seals thereof? v.* 2. If there be any creature who thinks himself sufficient either to explain or execute the counsels of God, let him stand forth, and make the attempt." 3. None in heaven or earth could accept the challenge and undertake the task: none *in heaven,* none of the glorious holy angels, though before the throne of God, and the ministers of his providence; they with all their wisdom cannot dive into the decrees of God: none *on earth,* no man, the wisest or the best of men, none of the magicians and soothsayers, none of the prophets of God, any further than he reveals his mind to them: *none under the earth,* none of the fallen angels, none of the spirits of men departed, though they should return to our world, can open this book. Satan himself, with all his subtlety, cannot do it; the creatures cannot open it, nor look on it; they cannot read it. God only can do it.

III. He felt a great concern in himself about this matter: the apostle *wept much;* it was a great disappointment to him. By what he had seen in him who sat upon the throne, he was very desirous to see and know more of his mind and will: this desire, when not presently gratified, filled him with sorrow, and fetched many tears from his eyes. Here observe, 1. Those who have seen most of God in this world are most desirous to see more; and those who have seen his glory desire to know his will. 2. Good men may be too eager and too hasty to look into the mysteries of divine conduct. 3. Such desires, not presently answered, turn to grief and sorrow. *Hope deferred makes the heart sick.*

IV. The apostle was comforted and encouraged to hope this sealed book would yet be opened. Here observe, 1. Who it was that gave John the hint: *One of the elders.* God had revealed it to his church. If angels do not refuse to learn from the church, ministers should not disdain to do it. God can make his people to instruct and inform their teachers when he pleases. 2. Who it was that would do the thing—the Lord Jesus Christ, called *the lion of the tribe of Judah,* according to his human nature, alluding to Jacob's prophecy (Gen. xlix. 10), and *the root of David* according to his divine nature, though a branch of David according to the flesh. He who is a middle person, God and man, and bears the office of Mediator between God and man, is fit and worthy to open and execute all the counsels of God towards men. And this he does in his mediatorial state and capacity, *as the root of David and the offspring of Judah,* and as the King and head of the Israel of God; and he will do it, to the consolation and joy of all his people.

6 And I beheld, and, lo, in the
midst of the throne and of the four
beasts, and in the midst of the elders,
stood a Lamb as it had been slain,
having seven horns and seven eyes,
which are the seven Spirits of God
sent forth into all the earth. 7 And
he came and took the book out of
the right hand of him that sat upon
the throne. 8 And when he had
taken the book, the four beasts and
four *and* twenty elders fell down before the Lamb, having every one of
them harps, and golden vials full of
odours, which are the prayers of
saints. 9 And they sung a new
song, saying, Thou art worthy to
take the book, and to open the seals
thereof: for thou wast slain, and
hast redeemed us to God by thy
blood out of every kindred, and
tongue, and people, and nation; 10
And hast made us unto our God
kings and priests: and we shall
reign on the earth. 11 And I beheld, and I heard the voice of many
angels round about the throne and
the beasts and the elders: and the
number of them was ten thousand
times ten thousand, and thousands
of thousands; 12 Saying with a
loud voice, Worthy is the Lamb that
was slain to receive power, and riches,
and wisdom, and strength, and honour, and glory, and blessing. 13 And
every creature which is in heaven,
and on the earth, and under the
earth, and such as are in the sea,
and all that are in them, heard I
saying, Blessing, and honour, and
glory, and power, *be* unto him that
sitteth upon the throne, and unto
the Lamb for ever and ever. 14 And
the four beasts said, Amen. And the
four *and* twenty elders fell down and
worshipped him that liveth for ever
and ever.

Here, I. The apostle beholds this book taken into the hands of the Lord Jesus Christ, in order to its being unsealed and opened by him. Here Christ is described, 1. By his place and station: *In the midst of the throne, and of the four beasts, and of the elders.* He was on the same throne with the Father; he was nearer to him than either the elders or ministers of the churches. Christ, as man and Mediator, is subordinate to God the Father, but is nearer to him than all the creatures; *for in him all the fulness of the Godhead dwells bodily.* The ministers stand between God and the people. Christ stands as Mediator between God and both ministers and people. 2. The form in which he appeared. Before he is called *a lion;* here he appears *as a lamb slain.* He is a lion to conquer Satan, a lamb to satisfy the justice of God. He appears with the marks of his sufferings upon him, to show that he intercedes in heaven in the virtue of his satisfaction. He appears as a *lamb, having seven horns and seven eyes,* perfect power to execute all the will of God and perfect wisdom to understand it all and to do it in the most effectual manner; *for he hath the seven Spirits of God,* he has received the Holy Spirit without measure, in all perfection of light, and life, and power, by which he is able to teach and rule all parts of the earth. 3. He is described by his act and deed: *He came, and took the book out of the right hand of him that sat on the throne* (*v.* 7), not by violence, nor by fraud, but he prevailed to do it (as *v.* 5), he prevailed by his merit and worthiness, he did it by authority and by the Father's appointment. God very willingly and justly put the book of his eternal counsels into the hand of Christ, and Christ as readily and gladly took it into his hand; for he delights to reveal and to do the will of his Father.

II. The apostle observes the universal joy and thanksgiving that filled heaven and earth upon this transaction. No sooner had Christ received this book out of the Father's hand than he received the applauses and adorations of angels and men, yea, of *every creature.* And, indeed, it is just matter of joy to all the world to see that God does not deal with men in a way of absolute power and strict justice, but in a way of grace and mercy through the Redeemer. He governs the world, not merely as a Creator and Lawgiver, but as our God and Saviour. All the world has reason to rejoice in this. The song of praise that was offered up to the Lamb on this occasion consists of three parts, one part sung by the church, another by the church and the angels, the third by every creature.

1. The church begins the doxology, as being more immediately concerned in it (*v.* 8), the four living creatures, and *the four-and-twenty elders,* the Christian people, under their minister, lead up the chorus. Here observe, (1.) The object of their worship—*the Lamb,* the Lord Jesus Christ; it is the declared will of God that all men *should honour the Son as they honour the Father;* for he has the same nature. (2.) Their posture: They *fell down before him,* gave him not an inferior sort of worship, but the most profound adoration. (3.) The instruments used in their adorations—*harps and vials;* the harps were the instruments of praise, the vials were full of odours or incense, which signify *the prayers of the saints:* prayer and praise should always go together. (4.) The matter of their song: it was suited to the new state of the church, the gospel-state introduced by the Son of God. In this new song, [1.] They acknowledge the infinite fitness and worthiness of the Lord Jesus for this great work of opening and executing the counsel and purposes of God (*v.* 9): *Thou art worthy to take the book, and to open the seals thereof,* every way sufficient for the work and deserving of the honour. [2.] They mention the grounds and reasons of this worthiness; and though they do not exclude the dignity of his person as God, without which he had not been sufficient for it, yet they chiefly insist upon the merit of his sufferings, which he had endured for them; these more sensibly struck their souls with thankfulness and joy. Here, *First,* They mention his suffering: "*Thou wast slain,* slain as a sacrifice, thy blood was shed." *Secondly,* The fruits of his sufferings. 1. Redemption to God; Christ has redeemed his people from the bondage of sin, guilt, and Satan, redeemed them to God, set them at liberty to serve him and to enjoy him. 2. High exaltation: Thou *hast made us to our God kings and priests, and we shall reign on the earth, v.* 10. Every ransomed slave is not immediately preferred to honour; he thinks it a great favour to be restored to liberty. But when the elect of God were made slaves by sin and Satan, in every nation of the world, Christ not only purchased their liberty for them, but the highest honour and preferment, *made them kings and priests*—kings, to rule over their own spirits, and to overcome the world, and the evil one; and he has made them priests, given them access to himself, and liberty to offer up spiritual sacrifices, and *they shall reign on the earth;* they shall with him judge the world at the great day.

2. The doxology, thus begun by the church, is carried on by the angels; they take the second part, in conjunction with the church, *v.* 11. They are said to be *innumerable,* and to be the attendants on the throne of God and guardians to the church; though they did not need a Saviour themselves, yet they rejoice in the redemption and salvation of sinners, and they agree with the church in acknowledging the infinite merits of the Lord Jesus as dying for sinners, that he is *worthy to receive power, and riches, and wisdom, and strength, and honour, and glory, and blessing.* (1.) He is worthy of that office and that authority which require the greatest power and wisdom, the greatest fund, all excellency, to discharge them aright; and, (2.) He is worthy of all honour, and glory, and blessing, because he is sufficient for the office and faithful in it.

3. This doxology, thus begun by the church, and carried on by the angels, is resounded and echoed by the whole creation, *v.* 13. Heaven and earth ring with the high praises of the Redeemer. The whole creation fares the better for Christ. *By him all things consist;* and all the creatures, had they sense and language, would adore that great Redeemer who delivers the creature from that bondage under which it groans, through the corruption of men, and the just curse denounced by the great God upon the fall; that part which (by a prosopopœia) is made for the whole creation is a song of *blessing, and honour, and glory, and power,* (1.) *To him that sits on the throne,* to God as God, or to God the Father, as the first person in the Trinity and the first in the economy of our salvation; and, (2.) *To the Lamb,* as the second person in the Godhead and the Mediator of the new covenant. Not that the worship paid to the Lamb is of another nature, an inferior worship, for the very same honour and glory are in the same words ascribed *to the Lamb and to him that sits on the throne,* their essence being the same; but,

their parts in the work of our salvation being distinct, they are distinctly adored. We worship and glorify one and the same God for our creation and for our redemption.

We see how the church that began the heavenly anthem, finding heaven and earth join in the concert, closes all with their *Amen*, and end as they began, with a low prostration before the eternal and everlasting God. Thus we have seen this sealed book passing with great solemnity from the hand of the Creator into the hand of the Redeemer.

CHAP. VI.

The book of the divine counsels being thus lodged in the hand of Christ, he loses no time, but immediately enters upon the work of opening the seals and publishing the contents; but this is done in such a manner as still leaves the predictions very abstruse and difficult to be understood. Hitherto the waters of the sanctuary have been as those in Ezekiel's vision, only to the ancles, or to the knees, or to the loins at least; but here they begin to be a river that cannot be passed over. The visions which John saw, the epistles to the churches, the songs of praise, in the two foregoing chapters, had some things dark and hard to be understood; and yet they were rather milk for babes than meat for strong men; but now we are to launch into the deep, and our business is not so much to fathom it as to let down our net to take a draught. We shall only hint at what seems most obvious. The prophecies of this book are divided into seven seals opened, seven trumpets sounding, and seven vials poured out. It is supposed that the opening of the seven seals discloses those providences that concerned the church in the first three centuries, from the ascension of our Lord and Saviour to the reign of Constantine; this was represented in a book rolled up, and sealed in several places, so that, when one seal was opened, you might read so far of it, and so on, till the whole was unfolded. Yet we are not here told what was written in the book, but what John saw in figures enigmatical and hieroglyphic; and it is not for us to pretend to know "the times and the seasons which the Father has put in his own power." In this chapter six of the seven seals are opened, and the visions attending them are related; the first seal in ver. 1, 2, the second seal in ver. 3, 4, the third seal in ver. 5, 6, the fourth seal in ver. 7, 8, the fifth seal in ver. 9—11, the sixth seal in ver. 12, 13, &c.

AND I saw when the Lamb opened one of the seals, and I heard, as it were the noise of thunder, one of the four beasts saying, Come and see.
2 And I saw, and behold a white horse: and he that sat on him had a bow; and a crown was given unto him: and he went forth conquering and to conquer.

Here, 1. Christ, the Lamb, opens the first seal; he now enters upon the great work of opening and accomplishing the purposes of God towards the church and the world. 2. One of the ministers of the church calls upon the apostle, with a voice like thunder, to come near, and observe what then appeared. 3. We have the vision itself, *v.* 2. (1.) The Lord Jesus appears riding on *a white horse.* White horses are generally refused in war, because they make the rider a mark for the enemy; but our Lord Redeemer was sure of the victory and a glorious triumph, and he rides on the white horse of a pure but despised gospel, with great swiftness through the world. (2.) *He had a bow* in his hand. The convictions impressed by the word of God are sharp arrows, they reach at a distance; and, though the ministers of the word draw the bow at a venture, God can and will direct it to the joints of the harness. This bow, in the hand of Christ, abides in strength, and, like that of Jonathan, *never returns empty*. (3.) *A crown was given him*, importing that all who receive the gospel must receive Christ as a king, and must be his loyal and obedient subjects; he will be glorified in the success of the gospel. When Christ was going to war, one would think a helmet had been more proper than a crown; but a crown is given him as the earnest and emblem of victory. (4.) *He went forth conquering, and to conquer.* As long as the church continues militant Christ will be conquering; when he has conquered his enemies in one age he meets with new ones in another age; men go on opposing, and Christ goes on conquering, and his former victories are pledges of future victories. He conquers his enemies in his people; their sins are their enemies and his enemies; when Christ comes with power into their soul he begins to conquer these enemies, and he goes on conquering, in the progressive work of sanctification, till he has gained us a complete victory. And he conquers his enemies in the world, wicked men, some by bringing them to his foot, others by making them his footstool. Observe, From this seal opened, [1.] The successful progress of the gospel of Christ in the world is a glorious sight, worth beholding, the most pleasant and welcome sight that a good man can see in this world. [2.] Whatever convulsions and revolutions happen in the states and kingdoms of the world, the kingdom of Christ shall be established and enlarged in spite of all opposition. [3.] A morning of opportunity usually goes before a night of calamity; the gospel is preached before the plagues are poured forth. [4.] Christ's work is not all done at once. We are ready to think, when the gospel goes forth, it should carry all the world before it, but it often meets with opposition, and moves slowly; however, Christ will do his own work effectually, in his own time and way.

3 And when he had opened the second seal, I heard the second beast say, Come and see.
4 And there went out another horse *that was* red: and *power* was given to him that sat thereon to take peace from the earth, and that they should kill one another: and there was given unto him a great sword.
5 And when he had opened the third seal, I heard the third beast say, Come and see. And I beheld, and lo a black horse; and he that sat on him had a pair of balances in his hand.
6 And I heard a voice in the midst of the four beasts say, A measure of wheat for a penny, and three measures of barley for a penny; and *see* thou hurt not the oil and the wine.
7 And

when he had opened the fourth seal,
I heard the voice of the fourth beast
say, Come and see. 8 And I looked,
and behold a pale horse: and his
name that sat on him was Death, and
Hell followed with him. And power
was given unto them over the fourth
part of the earth, to kill with sword,
and with hunger, and with death, and
with the beasts of the earth.

The next three seals give us a sad prospect of great and desolating judgments with which God punishes those who either refuse or abuse the everlasting gospel. Though some understand them of the persecutions that befel the church of Christ, and others of the destruction of the Jews, they rather seem more generally to represent God's terrible judgments, by which he avenges the quarrel of his covenant upon those who make light of it.

I. Upon opening the second seal, to which John was called to attend, *another horse* appears, of a different colour from the former, *a red horse, v.* 4. This signifies the desolating judgment of war; he that sat upon this red horse had *power to take peace from the earth, and that* the inhabitants of *the earth should kill one another*. Who this was that sat upon the red horse, whether Christ himself, as Lord of hosts, or the instruments that he raised up to conduct the war, is not clear; but this is certain, 1. That those who will not submit to the bow of the gospel must expect to be cut in sunder by the sword of divine justice. 2. That Jesus Christ rules and commands, not only in the kingdom of grace, but of providence. And, 3. That the sword of war is a dreadful judgment; it takes away peace from the earth, one of the greatest blessings, and it puts men upon killing one another. Men, who should love one another and help one another, are, in a state of war, set upon killing one another.

II. Upon opening the third seal, which John was directed to observe, another horse appears, different from the former, *a black horse*, signifying famine, that terrible judgment; *and he that sat on the horse had a pair of balances in his hand* (*v.* 5), signifying that men must now eat their bread by weight, as was threatened (Lev. xxvi. 26), *They shall deliver your bread to you by weight*. That which follows in *v.* 6, of the voice that cried, *A measure of wheat for a penny, and three measures of barley for a penny, and see thou hurt not the oil and the wine*, has made some expositors think this was not a vision of famine, but of plenty; but if we consider the quantity of their measure, and the value of their penny, at the time of this prophecy, the objection will be removed; their measure was but a single quart, and their penny was our sevenpence-halfpenny, and that is a large sum to give for a quart of wheat. However, it seems this famine, as all others, fell most severely upon the poor; whereas the oil and the wine, which were dainties of the rich, were not hurt; but if bread, the staff of life, be broken, dainties will not supply the place of it. Here observe, 1. When a people loathe their spiritual food, God may justly deprive them of their daily bread. 2. One judgment seldom comes alone; the judgment of war naturally draws after it that of famine; and those who will not humble themselves under one judgment must expect another and yet greater, for when God contends he will prevail. The famine of bread is a terrible judgment; but the famine of the word is more so, though careless sinners are not sensible of it.

III. Upon opening the fourth seal, which John is commanded to observe, there appears another horse, of a pale colour. Here observe, 1. The name of the rider—*Death*, the king of terrors; the pestilence, which is death in its empire, death reigning over a place or nation, death on horseback, marching about, and making fresh conquests every hour. 2. The attendants or followers of this king of terrors—*hell*, a state of eternal misery to all those who die in their sins; and, in times of such a general destruction, multitudes go down unprepared into the valley of destruction. It is an awful thought, and enough to make the whole world to tremble, that eternal damnation immediately follows upon the death of an impenitent sinner. Observe, (1.) There is a natural as well as judicial connection between one judgment and another: war is a wasting calamity, and draws scarcity and famine after it; and famine, not allowing men proper sustenance, and forcing them to take that which is unwholesome, often draws the pestilence after it. (2.) God's quiver is full of arrows; he is never at a loss for ways and means to punish a wicked people. (3.) In the book of God's counsels he has prepared judgments for scorners as well as mercy for returning sinners. (4.) In the book of the scriptures God has published threatenings against the wicked as well as promises to the righteous; and it is our duty to observe and believe the threatenings as well as the promises.

IV. After the opening of these seals of approaching judgments, and the distinct account of them, we have this general observation, that God *gave power to them over the fourth part of the earth, to kill with the sword, and with hunger, and with death, and with the beasts of the earth, v.* 8. He gave them power, that is, those instruments of his anger, or those judgments themselves; he who holds the winds in his hand has all public calamities at his command, and they can only go when he sends them and no further than he permits. To the three great judgments of war, famine, and pestilence, is here added *the beasts of the earth*, another of God's sore judgments, mentioned Ezek. xiv. 21, and mentioned here the last, because, when a nation is depopulated by the sword, famine, and pestilence, the small remnant that continue in a waste and howling wilderness encourage the wild beasts to make head against them, and they become an easy prey. Others, by *the beasts of the field,* understand brutish, cruel, savage men, who, having divested themselves of all humanity, delight to be the instruments of the destruction of others.

9 And when he had opened the
fifth seal, I saw under the altar the
souls of them that were slain for the
word of God, and for the testimony
which they held: 10 And they cried
with a loud voice, saying, How long,
O Lord, holy and true, dost thou not
judge and avenge our blood on them
that dwell on the earth? 11 And
white robes were given unto every
one of them; and it was said unto
them, that they should rest yet for a
little season, until their fellowservants
also and their brethren, that should
be killed as they *were,* should be
fulfilled. 12 And I beheld when he
had opened the sixth seal, and, lo,
there was a great earthquake; and the
sun became black as sackcloth of hair,
and the moon became as blood; 13
And the stars of heaven fell unto the
earth, even as a fig tree casteth her
untimely figs, when she is shaken of
a mighty wind. 14 And the heaven
departed as a scroll when it is rolled
together; and every mountain and
island were moved out of their places.
15 And the kings of the earth, and
the great men, and the rich men, and
the chief captains, and the mighty
men, and every bondman, and every
free man, hid themselves in the dens
and in the rocks of the mountains;
16 And said to the mountains and
rocks, Fall on us, and hide us from
the face of him that sitteth on the
throne, and from the wrath of the
Lamb: 17 For the great day of his
wrath is come; and who shall be able
to stand?

In the remaining part of this chapter we have the opening of the fifth and the sixth seals.

I. The fifth seal. Here is no mention made of any one who called the apostle to make his observation, probably because the decorum of the vision was to be observed, and each of the four living creatures had discharged its duty of a monitor before, or because the events here opened lay out of the sight, and beyond the time, of the present ministers of the church; or because it does not contain a new prophecy of any future events, but rather opens a spring of support and consolation to those who had been and still were under great tribulation for the sake of Christ and the gospel. Here observe,

1. The sight this apostle saw at the opening of the fifth seal; it was a very affecting sight (*v.* 9): *I saw under the altar the souls of those that were slain for the word of God, and for the testimony which they held.* He saw the souls of the martyrs. Here observe, (1.) Where he saw them—*under the altar;* at the foot of the altar of incense, in the most holy place; he saw them in heaven, at the foot of Christ. Hence note, [1.] Persecutors can only kill the body, and after that there is no more that they can do; their souls live. [2.] God has provided a good place in the better world for those who are faithful to death and are not allowed a place any longer on earth. [3.] Holy martyrs are very near to Christ in heaven, they have the highest place there. [4.] It is not their own death, but the sacrifice of Christ, that gives them a reception into heaven and a reward there; they do not wash their robes in their own blood, but in the blood of the Lamb. (2.) What was the cause in which they suffered—*the word of God and the testimony which they held,* for believing the word of God, and attesting or confessing the truth of it; this profession of their faith they held fast without wavering, even though they died for it. A noble cause, the best that any man can lay down his life for—faith in God's word and a confession of that faith.

2. The cry he heard; it was a loud cry, and contained a humble expostulation about the long delay of avenging justice against their enemies: *How long, O Lord, holy and true, dost thou not judge and avenge our blood on those that dwell on the earth? v.* 10. Observe, (1.) Even *the spirits of just men made perfect* retain a proper resentment of the wrong they have sustained by their cruel enemies; and though they die in charity, praying, as Christ did, that God would forgive them, yet they are desirous that, for the honour of God, and Christ, and the gospel, and for the terror and conviction of others, God will take a just revenge upon the sin of persecution, even while he pardons and saves the persecutors. (2.) They commit their cause to him to whom vengeance belongeth, and leave it in his hand; they are not for avenging themselves, but leave all to God. (3.) There will be joy in heaven at the destruction of the implacable enemies of Christ and Christianity, as well as at the conversion of other sinners. When Babylon falls, it will be said, *Rejoice over her, O thou heaven, and you holy apostles and prophets, for God hath avenged you on her, ch.* xviii. 20

3. He observed the kind return that was made to this cry (*v.* 11), both what was given to them and what was said to them. (1.) What was given to them—*white robes,* the robes of victory and of honour; their present happiness was an abundant recompence of their past sufferings. (2.) What was said to them—that they should be satisfied, and easy in themselves, for it would not be long ere the number of their fellow-sufferers *should be fulfilled.* This is a language rather suited to the imperfect state of the saints in this world than to the perfection of their state in heaven; *there* is no impatience, no uneasiness, no need of admonition; but in this world there is great need of patience. Observe, [1.] There is a number of Christians, known to God, who are appointed as *sheep for the slaughter,* set apart to be God's witnesses. [2.] As the measure of the sin of persecutors is filling up, so is the number of the persecuted martyred servants of Christ. [3.] When this number is fulfilled, God will take a just and glorious revenge upon their cruel persecutors; he will recompense tribulation to those who trouble them, and to those that are troubled full and uninterrupted rest.

II. We have here the sixth seal opened, *v.* 12. Some refer this to the great revolutions in the empire at Constantine's time, the downfal of paganism; others, with great probability, to the destruction of Jerusalem, as an emblem of the general judgment, and destruction of the wicked, at the end of the world; and, indeed, the awful characters of this event are so much the same with those signs mentioned by our Saviour as foreboding the destruction of Jerusalem, as hardly to leave any room for doubting but that the same thing is meant in both places, though some think that event was past already. See Matt. xxiv. 29, 30. Here observe,

1. The tremendous events that were hastening; and here are several occurrences that contribute to make that day and dispensation very dreadful:—(1.) *There was a great earthquake.* This may be taken in a political sense; the very foundations of the Jewish church and state would be terribly shaken, though they seemed to be as stable as the earth itself. (2.) *The sun became black as sackcloth of hair,* either naturally, by a total eclipse, or politically, by the fall of the chief rulers and governors of the land. (3.) *The moon* should *become as blood;* the inferior officers, or their military men, should be all wallowing in their own blood. (4.) *The stars of heaven shall fall to the earth* (*v.* 13), and that *as a fig-tree casteth her untimely figs, when she is shaken of a mighty wind.* The stars may signify all the men of note and influence among them, though in lower spheres of activity; there should be a general desolation. (5.) *The heaven* should *depart as a scroll when it is rolled together.* This may signify that their ecclesiastical state should perish and be laid aside for ever. (6.) *Every mountain and island shall be moved out of its place.* The destruction of the Jewish nation should affect and affright all the nations round about, those who were highest in honour and those who seemed to be best secured; it would be a judgment that should astonish all the world. This leads to,

2. The dread and terror that would seize upon all sorts of men in that great and awful day, *v.* 15. No authority, nor grandeur, nor riches, nor valour, nor strength, would be able to support men at that time; yea, the very poor slaves, who, one would think, had nothing to fear, because they had nothing to lose, would be all in amazement at that day. Here observe, (1.) The degree of their terror and astonishment: it should prevail so far as to make them, like distracted desperate men, call *to the mountains to fall upon them, and to the hills to cover them;* they would be glad to be no more seen; yea, to have no longer any being. (2.) The cause of their terror, namely, the angry countenance *of him that sits on the throne, and the wrath of the Lamb.* Observe, [1.] That which is matter of displeasure to Christ is so to God; they are so entirely one that what pleases or displeases the one pleases or displeases the other. [2.] Though God be invisible, he can make the inhabitants of this world sensible of his awful frowns. [3.] Though Christ be a lamb, yet he can be angry, even to wrath, and *the wrath of the Lamb* is exceedingly dreadful; for if the Redeemer, that appeases the wrath of God, himself be our wrathful enemy, where shall we have a friend to plead for us? Those perish without remedy who perish by the wrath of the Redeemer. [4.] As men have their day of opportunity, and their seasons of grace, so God has his day of righteous wrath; and, when that day shall come, the most stout-hearted sinners will not be able to stand before him: all these terrors actually fell upon the sinners in Judea and Jerusalem in the day of their destruction, and they will all, in the utmost degree, fall upon impenitent sinners, at the general judgment of the last day.

CHAP. VII.

The things contained in this chapter came in after the opening of the six seals, which foretold great calamities in the world; and before the sound of the seven trumpets, which gave notice of great corruptions arising in the church: between these comes in this comfortable chapter, which secures the graces and comforts of the people of God in times of common calamity. We have, I. An account of the restraint laid upon the winds, ver. 1—3. II. The sealing of the servants of God, ver. 4—8. III. The songs of angels and saints on this occasion, ver. 9—12. IV. A description of the honour and happiness of those who had faithfully served Christ, and suffered for him, ver. 13, &c.

AND after these things I saw four
angels standing on the four
corners of the earth, holding the four
winds of the earth, that the wind
should not blow on the earth, nor on
the sea, nor on any tree. 2 And I
saw another angel ascending from the
east, having the seal of the living God:

and he cried with a loud voice to the
four angels, to whom it was given to
hurt the earth and the sea, 3 Saying,
Hurt not the earth, neither the sea,
nor the trees, till we have sealed the
servants of our God in their foreheads.
4 And I heard the number of them
which were sealed: *and there were*
sealed a hundred *and* forty *and* four
thousand of all the tribes of the children of Israel. 5 Of the tribe of Juda
were sealed twelve thousand. Of the
tribe of Reuben *were* sealed twelve
thousand. Of the tribe of Gad *were*
sealed twelve thousand. 6 Of the
tribe of Aser *were* sealed twelve
thousand. Of the tribe of Nepthalim
were sealed twelve thousand. Of the
tribe of Manasses *were* sealed twelve
thousand. 7 Of the tribe of Simeon
were sealed twelve thousand. Of the
tribe of Levi *were* sealed twelve thousand. Of the tribe of Issachar *were*
sealed twelve thousand. 8 Of the
tribe of Zabulon *were* sealed twelve
thousand. Of the tribe of Joseph *were*
sealed twelve thousand. Of the tribe of
Benjamin *were* sealed twelve thousand.

9 After this I beheld, and, lo, a
great multitude, which no man could
number, of all nations, and kindreds,
and people, and tongues, stood before
the throne, and before the Lamb,
clothed with white robes, and palms
in their hands; 10 And cried with
a loud voice, saying, Salvation to our
God which sitteth upon the throne,
and unto the Lamb. 11 And all the
angels stood round about the throne,
and *about* the elders and the four
beasts, and fell before the throne on
their faces, and worshipped God, 12
Saying, Amen: Blessing, and glory,
and wisdom, and thanksgiving, and
honour, and power, and might, *be* unto
our God for ever and ever. Amen.

Here we have, I. An account of the restraint laid upon the winds. By these winds we suppose are meant those errors and corruptions in religion which would occasion a great deal of trouble and mischief to the church of God. Sometimes the Holy Spirit is compared to the wind: here the spirits of error are compared to *the four winds,* contrary one to another, but doing much hurt to the church, the garden and vineyard of God, breaking the branches and blasting the fruits of his plantation. The devil is called *the prince of the power of the air;* he, by a great wind, overthrew the house of Job's eldest son. Errors are as wind, by which those who are unstable are shaken, and carried *to and fro,* Eph. iv. 14. Observe, 1. These are called *the winds of the earth,* because they blow only in these lower regions near the earth; heaven is always clear and free from them. 2. They are restrained by the ministry of angels, *standing on the four corners of the earth,* intimating that the spirit of error cannot go forth till God permits it, and that the angels minister to the good of the church by restraining its enemies. 3. Their restraint was only for a season, and that was *till the servants of God were sealed in their foreheads.* God has a particular care and concern for his own servants in times of temptation and corruption, and he has a way to secure them from the common infection; he first establishes them, and then he tries them; he has the timing of their trials in his own hand.

II. An account of the sealing of the servants of God, where observe, 1. To whom this work was committed—to an angel, *another angel.* While some of the angels were employed to restrain Satan and his agents, another angel was employed to mark out and distinguish the faithful servants of God. 2. How they were distinguished—the seal of God was set upon their foreheads, a seal known to him, and as plain as if it appeared in their foreheads; by this mark they were set apart for mercy and safety in the worst of times. 3. The number of those that were sealed, where observe, (1.) A particular account of those that were sealed of the twelve tribes of Israel—twelve thousand out of every tribe, the whole sum amounting to *a hundred and forty-four thousand.* In this list the tribe of Dan is omitted, perhaps because they were greatly addicted to idolatry; and the order of the tribes is altered, perhaps according as they had been more or less faithful to God. Some take these to be a select number of the Jews who were reserved for mercy at the destruction of Jerusalem; others think that time was past, and therefore it is to be more generally applied to God's chosen remnant in the world; but, if the destruction of Jerusalem was not yet over (and I think it is hard to prove that it was), it seems more proper to understand this of the remnant of that people which God had reserved according to the election of grace, only here we have a definite number for an indefinite. (2.) A general account of those who were saved out of other nations (*v.* 9): *A great multitude, which no man could number, of all nations, and kindreds, and people, and tongues.* Though these are not said to be sealed, yet they were selected by God out of all nations, and brought into his church, and there stood before the throne. Observe, [1.] God will have a greater harvest of souls among the Gentiles than he had among the Jews. *More are the children of the desolate than of the married woman.* [2.] The Lord knows who are his, and he will keep them safe in times of dangerous temptation. [3.] Though the church of God is but a little flock, in comparison of the wicked world, yet it is no contemptible society, but really large, and to be still more enlarged.

III. We have the songs of saints and angels on this occasion, *v.* 9—12, where observe,

1. The praises offered up by the saints (and, as it seems to me, by the Gentile believers) for the care of God in reserving so large a remnant of the Jews, and saving them from infidelity and destruction. The Jewish church prayed for the Gentiles before their conversion, and the Gentile churches have reason to bless God for his distinguishing mercy to so many of the Jews, when the rest were cut off. Here observe, (1.) The posture of these praising saints: they *stood before the throne, and before the Lamb,* before the Creator and the Mediator. In acts of religious worship we come nigh to God, and are to conceive ourselves as in his special presence; and we must come to God by Christ. The throne of God would be inaccessible to sinners were it not for a Mediator. (2.) Their habit: they were *clothed with white robes, and had palms in their hands;* they were invested with the robes of justification, holiness, and victory, and had palms in their hands, as conquerors used to appear in their triumphs: such a glorious appearance will the faithful servants of God make at last, when they have *fought the good fight of faith and finished their course.* (3.) Their employment: they *cried with a loud voice, saying, Salvation to our God who sitteth upon the throne, and to the Lamb.* This may be understood either as a *hosannah,* wishing well to the interest of God and Christ in the church and in the world, or as a *hallelujah,* giving to God and the Lamb the praise of the great salvation; both the Father and the Son are joined together in these praises; the Father contrived this salvation, the Son purchased it, and those who enjoy it must and will bless the Lord and the Lamb, and they will do it publicly, and with becoming fervour.

2. Here is the song of the angels (*v.* 11, 12), where observe, (1.) Their station—*before the throne of God,* attending on him, and about the saints, ready to serve them. (2.) Their posture, which is very humble, and expressive of the greatest reverence: *They fell before the throne on their faces, and worshipped God.* Behold the most excellent of all the creatures, who never sinned, who are before him continually, not only covering their faces, but falling down on their faces before the Lord! What humility then, and what profound reverence, become us vile frail creatures, when we come into the presence of God! We should fall down before him; there should be both a reverential frame of spirit and a humble behaviour in all our addresses to God. (3.) Their praises. They consented to the praises of the saints, said their *Amen* thereto; there is in heaven a perfect harmony between the angels and saints; and then they added more of their own, *saying, Blessing, and glory, and wisdom, and thanksgiving, and honour, and power, and might, be unto our God for ever and ever. Amen.* Here, [1.] They acknowledge the glorious attributes of God—his wisdom, his power, and his might. [2.] They declare that for these his divine perfections he ought to be blessed, and praised, and glorified, to all eternity; and they confirm it by their *Amen.* We see what is the work of heaven, and we ought to begin it now, to get our hearts tuned for it, to be much in it, and to long for that world where our praises, as well as happiness, will be perfected.

13 And one of the elders answered,
saying unto me, What are these which
are arrayed in white robes? and
whence came they? 14 And I said
unto him, Sir, thou knowest. And
he said to me, These are they which
came out of great tribulation, and
have washed their robes, and made
them white in the blood of the Lamb.
15 Therefore are they before the
throne of God, and serve him day and
night in his temple: and he that
sitteth on the throne shall dwell
among them. 16 They shall hunger
no more, neither thirst any more;
neither shall the sun light on them,
nor any heat. 17 For the Lamb
which is in the midst of the throne
shall feed them, and shall lead them
unto living fountains of waters: and
God shall wipe away all tears from
their eyes.

Here we have a description of the honour and happiness of those who have faithfully served the Lord Jesus Christ, and suffered for him. Observe,

I. A question asked by one of the elders, not for his own information, but for John's instruction: ministers may learn from the people, especially from aged and experienced Christians; the lowest saint in heaven knows more than the greatest apostle in the world. Now the question has two parts:—1. *What are these that are arrayed in white robes?* 2. *Whence came they?* It seems to be spoken by way of admiration, as Cant. iii. 6, *Who is this that cometh out of the wilderness!* Faithful Christians deserve our notice and respect; we should *mark the upright.*

II. The answer returned by the apostle, in which he tacitly acknowledges his own ignorance, and sues to this elder for information: *Thou knowest.* Those who would gain knowledge must not be ashamed to own their ignorance, nor to desire instruction from any that are able to give it.

III. The account given to the apostle concerning that noble army of martyrs who stood *before the throne of God in white robes,* with palms of victory in their hands: and notice is taken here of, 1. The low and desolate state they had formerly been in; they had been in great tribulation, persecuted by men, tempted by Satan, sometimes troubled in their own spirits; they had suffered the spoiling of their goods, the imprisonment of their persons, yea, the loss of life itself. The way to heaven lies through many tribulations; but tribulation, how great soever, shall not *separate us from the love of God.* Tribulation, when gone through well, will make heaven more welcome and more glorious. 2. The means by which they had been prepared for the great honour and happiness they now enjoyed: they had *washed their robes, and made them white in the blood of the Lamb, v.* 14. It is not the blood of the martyrs themselves, but the blood of the Lamb, that can wash away sin, and make the soul pure and clean in the sight of God. Other blood stains; this is the only blood that makes the robes of the saints white and clean. 3. The blessedness to which they are now advanced, being thus prepared for it. (1.) They are happy in their station, for *they are before the throne of God night and day;* and he *dwells among them;* they are in that presence where there is fulness of joy. (2.) They are happy in their employment, for they serve God continually, and that without weakness, drowsiness, or weariness. Heaven is a state of service, though not of suffering; it is a state of rest, but not of sloth; it is a praising delightful rest. (3.) They are happy in their freedom from all the inconveniences of this present life. [1.] From all want and sense of want: *They hunger and thirst no more;* all their wants are supplied, and all the uneasiness caused thereby is removed. [2.] From all sickness and pain: they shall never be scorched by *the heat of the sun any more.* (4.) They are happy in the love and guidance of the Lord Jesus: *He shall feed them, he shall lead them to living fountains of waters,* he shall put them into the possession of every thing that is pleasant and refreshing to their souls, and therefore *they shall hunger and thirst no more.* (5.) They are happy in being delivered from all sorrow or occasion of it: *God shall wipe away all tears from their eyes.* They have formerly had their sorrows, and shed many tears, both upon the account of sin and affliction; but God himself, with his own gentle and gracious hand, will wipe those tears away, and they shall return no more for ever; and they would not have been without those tears, when God comes to wipe them away. In this he deals with them as a tender father who finds his beloved child in tears, he comforts him, he wipes his eyes, and turns his sorrow into rejoicing. This should moderate the Christian's sorrow in his present state, and support him under all the troubles of it; for *those that sow in tears shall reap in joy; and those that now go forth weeping, bearing precious seed, shall doubtless come again rejoicing, bringing their sheaves with them.*

CHAP. VIII.

We have already seen what occurred upon opening six of the seals; we now come to the opening of the seventh, which introduced the sounding of the seven trumpets; and a direful scene now opens. Most expositors agree that the seven seals represent the interval between the apostle's time and the reign of Constantine, but that the seven trumpets are designed to represent the rise of antichrist, some time after the empire became Christian. In this chapter we have, I. The preface, or prelude, to the sounding of the trumpets, ver. 1—6. II. The sounding of four of the trumpets, ver. 7, &c.

AND when he had opened the
seventh seal, there was silence
in heaven about the space of half an
hour. 2 And I saw the seven angels
which stood before God; and to them
were given seven trumpets. 3 And
another angel came and stood at the
altar, having a golden censer; and
there was given unto him much incense, that he should offer *it* with the
prayers of all saints upon the golden
altar which was before the throne.
4 And the smoke of the incense, *which
came* with the prayers of the saints,
ascended up before God out of the
angel's hand. 5 And the angel took
the censer, and filled it with fire of
the altar, and cast *it* into the earth:
and there were voices, and thunderings, and lightnings, and an earthquake. 6 And the seven angels which
had the seven trumpets prepared
themselves to sound.

In these verses we have the prelude to the sounding of the trumpets in several parts.

I. The opening of the last seal. This was to introduce a new set of prophetical iconisms and events; there is a continued chain of providence, one part linked to another (where one ends another begins), and, though they may differ in nature and in time, they all make up one wise, well-connected, and uniform design in the hand of God.

II. A profound *silence in heaven for the space of half an hour,* which may be understood either, 1. Of the silence of peace, that for this time no complaints were sent up to the ear of the Lord God of sabaoth; all was quiet and well in the church, and therefore all silent in heaven, for whenever the church on earth cries, through oppression, that cry comes up to heaven and resounds there; or,

2. A silence of expectation; great things were upon the wheel of providence, and the church of God, both in heaven and earth, stood silent, as became them, to see what God was doing, according to that of Zech. ii. 13, *Be silent, O all flesh, before the Lord, for he has risen up out of his holy habitation.* And elsewhere, *Be still, and know that I am God.*

III. The trumpets were delivered to the angels who were to sound them. Still the angels are employed as the wise and willing instruments of divine Providence, and they are furnished with all their materials and instructions from God our Saviour. As the angels of the churches are to sound the trumpet of the gospel, the angels of heaven are to sound the trumpet of Providence, and every one has his part given him.

IV. To prepare for this, another angel must first offer incense, *v.* 3. It is very probable that this other angel is the Lord Jesus, the high priest of the church, who is here described in his sacerdotal office, having a golden censer and much incense, a fulness of merit in his own glorious person, and this incense he was to offer up, *with the prayers of all the saints, upon the golden altar* of his divine nature. Observe, 1. All the saints are a praying people; none of the children of God are born dumb, a Spirit of grace is always a Spirit of adoption and supplication, teaching us to cry, *Abba, Father.* Ps. xxxii. 6, *For this shall every one that is godly pray unto thee.* 2. Times of danger should be praying times, and so should times of great expectation; both our fears and our hopes should put us upon prayer, and, where the interest of the church of God is deeply concerned, the hearts of the people of God in prayer should be greatly enlarged. 3. The prayers of the saints themselves stand in need of the incense and intercession of Christ to make them acceptable and effectual, and there is provision made by Christ for that purpose; he has his incense, his censer, and his altar; he is all himself to his people. 4. The prayers of the saints come up before God in a cloud of incense; no prayer, thus recommended, was ever denied audience or acceptance. 5. These prayers that were thus accepted in heaven produced great changes upon earth in return to them; the same angel that in his censer offered up the prayers of the saints in the same censer *took of the fire of the altar, and cast it into the earth,* and this presently caused strange commotions, *voices, and thunderings, and lightnings, and an earthquake;* these were the answers God gave to the prayers of the saints, and tokens of his anger against the world and that he would do great things to avenge himself and his people of their enemies; and now, all things being thus prepared, the angels discharge their duty.

7 The first angel sounded, and
there followed hail and fire mingled
with blood, and they were cast upon
the earth: and the third part of trees
was burnt up, and all green grass was
burnt up. 8 And the second angel
sounded, and as it were a great
mountain burning with fire was cast
into the sea: and the third part of
the sea became blood; 9 And the
third part of the creatures which were
in the sea, and had life, died; and
the third part of the ships were destroyed. 10 And the third angel
sounded, and there fell a great star
from heaven, burning as it were a
lamp, and it fell upon the third part
of the rivers, and upon the fountains
of waters; 11 And the name of the
star is called Wormwood: and the
third part of the waters became
wormwood; and many men died
of the waters, because they were
made bitter. 12 And the fourth
angel sounded, and the third part of
the sun was smitten, and the third
part of the moon, and the third part
of the stars; so as the third part of
them was darkened, and the day
shone not for a third part of it, and
the night likewise. 13 And I beheld,
and heard an angel flying through
the midst of heaven, saying with a
loud voice, Woe, woe, woe, to the
inhabiters of the earth by reason
of the other voices of the trumpet
of the three angels, which are yet to
sound!

Observe, I. *The first angel sounded* the first trumpet, and the events which followed were very dismal: *There followed hail and fire mingled with blood,* &c., *v.* 7. There was a terrible storm; but whether it is to be understood of a storm of heresies, a mixture of monstrous errors falling on the church (for in that age Arianism prevailed), or a storm or tempest of war falling on the civil state, expositors are not agreed. Mr. Mede takes it to be meant of the Gothic inundation that broke in upon the empire in the year 395, the same year that Theodosius died, when the northern nations, under Alaricus, king of the Goths, broke in upon the western parts of the empire. However, here we observe, 1. It was a very terrible storm—fire, and hail, and blood: a strange mixture! 2. The limitation of it: it fell on *the third part of the trees,* and on the third part of *the grass,* and blasted and burnt it up; that is, say some, upon *the third part of the clergy* and *the third part of the laity;* or, as others who take it to fall upon the civil state, upon *the third part of the great men*, and upon *the third part of the common people*, either upon the Roman empire itself, which was a third part of the then known world, or upon a third part of that empire. The most severe calamities have their bounds and limits set them by the great God.

II. *The second angel sounded*, and the alarm was followed, as in the first, with terrible events: *A great mountain burning with fire was cast into the sea; and the third part of the sea became blood*, *v.* 8. By this mountain some understand the leader or leaders of the heretics; others, as Mr. Mede, the city of Rome, which was five times sacked by the Goths and Vandals, within the compass of 137 years; first by Alaricus, in the year 410, with great slaughter and cruelty. In these calamities, a third part of the people (called here the sea or collection of waters) were destroyed: here was still a limitation to the third part, for *in the midst of judgment God remembers mercy*. This storm fell heavy upon the maritime and merchandizing cities and countries of the Roman empire.

III. *The third angel sounded*, and the alarm had the like effects as before: *There fell a great star from heaven*, &c., *v.* 10. Some take this to be a political star, some eminent governor, and they apply it to Augustulus, who was forced to resign the empire to Odoacer, in the year 480. Others take it to be an ecclesiastical star, some eminent person in the church, compared to a *burning lamp*, and they fix it upon Pelagius, who proved about this time a falling star, and greatly corrupted the churches of Christ. Observe, 1. Where this star fell: *Upon a third part of the rivers, and upon the fountains of waters*. 2. What effect it had upon them; it turned those springs and streams into wormwood, made them very bitter, that men were poisoned by them; either the laws, which are springs of civil liberty, and property, and safety, were poisoned by arbitrary power, or the doctrines of the gospel, the springs of spiritual life, refreshment, and vigour to the souls of men, were so corrupted and embittered by a mixture of dangerous errors that the souls of men found their ruin where they sought for their refreshment.

IV. *The fourth angel sounded*, and the alarm was followed with further calamities. Observe, 1. The nature of this calamity; it was darkness; it fell therefore upon the great luminaries of the heaven, that give light to the world—*the sun, and the moon, and the stars*, either the guides and governors of the church, or of the state, who are placed in higher orbs than the people, and are to dispense light and benign influences to them. 2. The limitation: it was confined to a third part of these luminaries; there was some light both of the sun by day, and of the moon and stars by night, but it was only a third part of what they had before. Without determining what is matter of controversy in these points among learned men, we rather choose to make these plain and practical remarks:—(1.) Where the gospel comes to a people, and is but coldly received, and has not its proper effects upon their hearts and lives, it is usually followed with dreadful judgments. (2.) God gives warning to men of his judgments before he sends them; he sounds an alarm by the written word, by ministers, by men's own consciences, and by the signs of the times; so that, if a people be surprised, it is their own fault. (3.) The anger of God against a people makes dreadful work among them; it embitters all their comforts, and makes even life itself bitter and burdensome. (4.) God does not in this world stir up all his wrath, but sets bounds to the most terrible judgments. (5.) Corruptions of doctrine and worship in the church are themselves great judgments, and the usual causes and tokens of other judgments coming on a people.

V. Before the other three trumpets are sounded here is solemn warning given to the world how terrible the calamities would be that should follow them, and how miserable those times and places would be on which they fell, *v.* 13. 1. The messenger was *an angel flying in the midst of heaven*, as in haste, and coming on an awful errand. 2. The message was a denunciation of further and greater woe and misery than the world had hitherto endured. Here are three woes, to show how much the calamities coming should exceed those that had been already, or to hint how every one of the three succeeding trumpets should introduce its particular and distinct calamity. If less judgments do not take effect, but the church and the world grow worse under them, they must expect greater. *God will be known by the judgments that he executes;* and he expects, when he comes to punish the world, the inhabitants thereof should tremble before him.

CHAP. IX.

In this chapter we have an account of the sounding of the fifth and sixth trumpets, the appearances that attended them, and the events that were to follow; the fifth trumpet, ver. 1—12, the sixth, ver. 13, &c.

AND the fifth angel sounded, and
I saw a star fall from heaven unto
the earth: and to him was given the
key of the bottomless pit. 2 And he
opened the bottomless pit; and there
arose a smoke out of the pit, as the
smoke of a great furnace; and the
sun and the air were darkened by
reason of the smoke of the pit. 3
And there came out of the smoke
locusts upon the earth: and unto
them was given power, as the scorpions of the earth have power. 4
And it was commanded them that
they should not hurt the grass of the

earth, neither any green thing, neither
any tree; but only those men which
have not the seal of God in their
foreheads. 5 And to them it was
given that they should not kill them,
but that they should be tormented
five months: and their torment *was*
as the torment of a scorpion, when
he striketh a man. 6 And in those
days shall men seek death, and shall
not find it; and shall desire to die,
and death shall flee from them. 7
And the shapes of the locusts *were*
like unto horses prepared unto battle;
and on their heads *were* as it were
crowns like gold, and their faces *were*
as the faces of men. 8 And they
had hair as the hair of women, and
their teeth were as *the teeth* of lions.
9 And they had breastplates as it
were breastplates of iron; and the
sound of their wings *was* as the
sound of chariots of many horses
running to battle. 10 And they had
tails like unto scorpions, and there
were stings in their tails: and their
power *was* to hurt men five months.
11 And they had a king over them,
which is the angel of the bottomless
pit, whose name in the Hebrew
tongue *is* Abaddon, but in the Greek
tongue hath *his* name Apollyon. 12
One woe is past; *and*, behold, there
come two woes more hereafter.

Upon the sounding of this trumpet, the things to be observed are, 1. *A star falling from heaven to the earth.* Some think this star represents some eminent bishop in the Christian church, some angel of the church; for, in the same way of speaking by which pastors are called stars, the church is called heaven; but who this is expositors do not agree. Some understand it of Boniface the third bishop of Rome, who assumed the title of universal bishop, by the favour of the emperor Phocas, who, being a usurper and tyrant in the state, allowed Boniface to be so in the church, as the reward of his flattery. 2. To this fallen star *was given the key of the bottomless pit.* Having now ceased to be a minister of Christ, he becomes the antichrist, the minister of the devil; and by the permission of Christ, who had taken from him the keys of the church, he becomes the devil's turnkey, to let loose the powers of hell against the churches of Christ. 3. Upon the opening of the bottomless pit *there arose a great smoke,* which darkened the sun and the air. The devils are the powers of darkness; hell is the place of darkness. The devil carries on his designs by blinding the eyes of men, by extinguishing light and knowledge, and promoting ignorance and error. He first deceives men, and then destroys them; wretched souls follow him in the dark, or they durst not follow him. 4. Out of this dark smoke there came a swarm of locusts, one of the plagues of Egypt, the devil's emissaries headed by antichrist, all the rout and rabble of antichristian orders, to promote superstition, idolatry, error, and cruelty; and these had, by the just permission of God, power to hurt those who had not the mark of God in their foreheads. 5. The hurt they were to do them was not a bodily, but a spiritual hurt. They should not in a military way destroy all by fire and sword; the trees and the grass should be untouched, and those they hurt should not be slain; it should not be a persecution, but a secret poison and infection in their souls, which should rob them of their purity, and afterwards of their peace. Heresy is a poison in the soul, working slowly and secretly, but will be bitterness in the end. 6. They had no power so much as to hurt those who had the seal of God in their foreheads. God's electing, effectual, distinguishing grace will preserve his people from total and final apostasy. 7. The power given to these factors for hell is limited in point of time: *five months,* a certain season, and but a short season, though how short we cannot tell. Gospel-seasons have their limits, and times of seduction are limited too. 8. Though it would be short, it would be very sharp, insomuch that those who were made to feel the malignity of this poison in their consciences would be weary of their lives, *v.* 6. *A wounded spirit who can bear?* 9. These locusts were of a monstrous size and shape, *v.* 7, 8, &c. They were equipped for their work like horses prepared to battle. (1.) They pretended to great authority, and seemed to be assured of victory: *They had crowns like gold on their heads;* it was not a true, but a counterfeit authority. (2.) They had the show of wisdom and sagacity, *the faces of men,* though the spirit of devils. (3.) They had all the allurements of seeming beauty, to ensnare and defile the minds of men—*hair like women;* their way of worship was very gaudy and ornamental. (4.) Though they appeared with the tenderness of women, they had *the teeth of lions,* were really cruel creatures. (5.) They had the defence and protection of earthly powers—*breastplates of iron.* (6.) They made a mighty noise in the world; they flew about from one country to another, and the noise of their motion was like that of an army with chariots and horses. (7.) Though at first they soothed and flattered men with a fair appearance, there was a sting in their tails; the cup of their abominations contained that which, though luscious at first, would at length bite like a serpent and sting like an adder. (8.) The king and commander of this hellish squadron is here described, [1.] As an angel; so he was by nature, an angel, once one of the angels of heaven. [2.] *The angel of the bottomless pit;* an angel still, but a fallen angel, fallen into the bottomless pit, vastly large, and out of which there is no recovery. [3.] In these infernal regions he is a sort of prince and governor, and has the powers of darkness under his rule and command. [4.] His true name is *Abaddon, Apollyon—a destroyer,* for that is his business, his design, and employment, to which he diligently attends, in which he is very successful, and takes a horrid hellish pleasure; it is about this destroying work that he sends out his emissaries and armies to destroy the souls of men. And now here we have the end of one woe; and where one ends another begins.

13 And the sixth angel sounded,
and I heard a voice from the four
horns of the golden altar which is before God, 14 Saying to the sixth
angel which had the trumpet, Loose
the four angels which are bound in
the great river Euphrates. 15 And
the four angels were loosed, which
were prepared for an hour, and a day,
and a month, and a year, for to slay
the third part of men. 16 And the
number of the army of the horsemen
were two hundred thousand thousand:
and I heard the number of them.
17 And thus I saw the horses in the
vision, and them that sat on them,
having breastplates of fire, and of
jacinth, and brimstone: and the
heads of the horses *were* as the heads
of lions; and out of their mouths
issued fire and smoke and brimstone,
18 By these three was the third
part of men killed, by the fire, and
by the smoke, and by the brimstone,
which issued out of their mouths,
19 For their power is in their mouth,
and in their tails: for their tails *were*
like unto serpents, and had heads,
and with them they do hurt. 20 And
the rest of the men which were not
killed by these plagues yet repented
not of the works of their hands, that
they should not worship devils, and
idols of gold, and silver, and brass,
and stone, and of wood: which neither
can see, nor hear, nor walk: 21 Neither repented they of their murders,
nor of their sorceries, nor of their
fornication, nor of their thefts.

Here let us consider the preface to this vision, and then the vision itself.

I. The preface to this vision: *A voice was heard from the horns of the golden altar, v.* 13, 14. Here observe, 1. The power of the church's enemies is restrained till God gives the word to have them turned loose. 2. When nations are ripe for punishment, those instruments of God's anger that were before restrained are let loose upon them, *v.* 14. 3. The instruments that God makes use of to punish a people may sometimes lie at a great distance from them, so that no danger may be apprehended from them. These four messengers of divine judgment lay bound in the river Euphrates, a great way from the European nations. Here the Turkish power had its rise, which seems to be the story of this vision.

II. The vision itself: *And the four angels that had been bound in the great river Euphrates were now loosed, v.* 15, 16. And here observe, 1. The time of their military operations and executions is limited to *an hour, and a day, and a month, and a year.* Prophetic characters of time are hardly to be understood by us; but in general the time is fixed to an hour, when it shall begin and when it shall end; and how far the execution shall prevail, even to a third part of the inhabitants of the earth. God will make the wrath of man praise him, and the remainder of wrath he will restrain. 2. The army that was to execute this great commission is mustered, and the number found to be of horsemen *two hundred thousand thousand;* but we are left to guess what the infantry must be. In general, it tells us, the armies of the Mahomedan empire should be vastly great; and so it is certain they were. 3. Their formidable equipage and appearance, *v.* 17. As the horses were fierce, like lions, and eager to rush into the battle, so those who sat upon them were clad in bright and costly armour, with all the ensigns of martial courage, zeal, and resolution. 4. The vast havoc and desolation that they made in the Roman empire, which had now become antichristian: a third part of them were killed; they went as far as their commission suffered them, and they could go no further. 5. Their artillery, by which they made such slaughter, described *by fire, smoke, and brimstone,* issuing out of the mouths of their horses, and the stings that were in their tails. It is Mr. Mede's opinion that this is a prediction of great guns, those instruments of cruelty which make such destruction: he observes, These were first used by the Turks at the siege of Constantinople, and, being new and strange, were very terrible, and did great execution. However, here seems to be an allusion to what is mentioned in the former vision, that, as antichrist had his forces of a spiritual nature, like scorpions poisoning the minds of men with error and idolatry, so the Turks, who were raised up to punish the antichristian apostasy, had their scorpions and their stings too, to hurt and kill the bodies of those who had been the murderers of so many souls. 6. Observe the impenitency of the antichristian generation under these dreadful judgments (*v.* 20); the rest of the men who were not killed repented not, they still persisted in those sins for which God was so severely punishing them, which were, (1.) Their idolatry; they would not cast away their images, though they could do them no good, *could not see, nor hear, nor walk.* (2.) Their murders (*v.* 21), which they had committed upon the saints and servants of Christ. Popery is a bloody religion, and seems resolved to continue such. (3.) Their sorceries; they have their charms, and magic arts, and rites in exorcism and other things. (4.) Their fornication; they allow both spiritual and carnal impurity, and promote it in themselves and others. (5.) Their thefts; they have by unjust means heaped together a vast deal of wealth, to the injury and impoverishing of families, cities, princes, and nations. These are the flagrant crimes of antichrist and his agents; and, though God has revealed his wrath from heaven against them, they are obstinate, hardened, and impenitent, and judicially so, for they must be destroyed.

III. From this sixth trumpet we learn, 1. God can make one enemy of the church to be a scourge and plague to another. 2. He who is the Lord of hosts has vast armies at his command, to serve his own purposes 3. The most formidable powers have limits set them, which they cannot transgress. 4. When God's judgments are in the earth, he expects the inhabitants thereof should repent of sin, and learn righteousness. 5. Impenitency under divine judgments is an iniquity that will be the ruin of sinners; for where God judges he will overcome.

CHAP. X.

This chapter is an introduction to the latter part of the prophecies of this book. Whether what is contained between this and the sounding of the seventh trumpet (ch. xi. 15) be a distinct prophecy from the other, or only a more general account of some of the principal things included in the other, is disputed by our curious enquirers into these abstruse writings. However, here we have, I. A remarkable description of a very glorious angel with an open book in his hand, ver. 1—3. II. An account of seven thunders which the apostle heard, as echoing to the voice of this angel, and communicating some discoveries, which the apostle was not yet allowed to write, ver. 4. III. The solemn oath taken by him who had the book in his hand, ver. 5—7. IV. The charge given to the apostle, and observed by him, ver. 8—11.

AND I saw another mighty angel
come down from heaven, clothed
with a cloud: and a rainbow *was*
upon his head, and his face *was* as it
were the sun, and his feet as pillars
of fire: 2 And he had in his hand a
little book open: and he set his right
foot upon the sea, and *his* left *foot* on
the earth, 3 And cried with a loud
voice, as *when* a lion roareth: and
when he had cried, seven thunders
uttered their voices. 4 And when the
seven thunders had uttered their
voices, I was about to write: and
I heard a voice from heaven saying unto me, Seal up those things
which the seven thunders uttered,
and write them not. 5 And the
angel which I saw stand upon the
sea and upon the earth lifted up his
hand to heaven, 6 And sware by
him that liveth for ever and ever, who
created heaven, and the things that
therein are, and the earth, and the
things that therein are, and the sea,
and the things which are therein,
that there should be time no longer:
7 But in the days of the voice of the
seventh angel, when he shall begin to
sound, the mystery of God should be
finished, as he hath declared to his
servants the prophets.

Here we have an account of another vision the apostle was favoured with, between the sounding of the sixth trumpet and that of the seventh. And we observe,

I. The person who was principally concerned in communicating this discovery to John—an angel from heaven, *another mighty angel,* who is so set forth as would induce one to think it could be no other than our Lord and Saviour Jesus Christ! 1. He was *clothed with a cloud:* he veils his glory, which is too great for mortality to behold; and he throws a veil upon his dispensations. *Clouds and darkness are round about him.* 2. *A rainbow was upon his head;* he is always mindful of his covenant, and, when his conduct is most mysterious, yet it is perfectly just and faithful. 3. *His face was as the sun,* all bright, and full of lustre and majesty, *ch.* i. 16. 4. *His feet were as pillars of fire;* all his ways, both of grace and providence, are pure and steady.

II. His station and posture: *He set his right foot upon the sea and his left foot upon the earth,* to show the absolute power and dominion he had over the world. *And he held in his hand a little book opened,* probably the same that was before sealed, but was now opened, and gradually fulfilled by him.

III. His awful voice: *He cried aloud, as when a lion roareth* (*v.* 3), and his awful voice was echoed by *seven thunders,* seven solemn and terrible ways of discovering the mind of God.

IV. The prohibition given to the apostle, that he should not publish, but conceal what he had learned from the seven thunders, *v.* 4. The apostle was for preserving and publishing every thing he saw and heard in these visions, but the time had not yet come.

V. The solemn oath taken by this mighty angel. 1. The manner of his swearing: *He lifted up his hand to heaven, and swore by him that liveth for ever,* by himself, as God often has done, or by God as God, to whom he, as Lord, Redeemer, and ruler of the world, now appeals. 2. The matter of the oath: that *there shall be time no longer;* either, (1.) That there shall be now no longer delay in fulfilling the predictions of this book than till the last angel should sound; then every thing should be put into speedy execution: *the mystery of God shall be finished, v.* 7. Or, (2.) That when this mystery of God is finished time itself shall be no more, as being the measure of things that are in a mutable changing state; but all things shall be at length for ever fixed, and so time itself swallowed up in eternity.

8 And the voice which I heard
from heaven spake unto me again,
and said, Go *and* take the little book
which is open in the hand of the
angel which standeth upon the sea
and upon the earth. 9 And I went
unto the angel, and said unto him,
Give me the little book. And he
said unto me, Take *it*, and eat it up;
and it shall make thy belly bitter,
but it shall be in thy mouth sweet as
honey. 10 And I took the little
book out of the angel's hand, and ate
it up; and it was in my mouth sweet
as honey: and as soon as I had eaten
it, my belly was bitter. 11 And he
said unto me, Thou must prophesy
again before many peoples, and nations, and tongues, and kings.

Here we have, I. A strict charge given to the apostle, which was, 1. That he should *go and take the little book* out of the hands of that mighty angel mentioned before. This charge was given, not by the angel himself who stood upon the earth, but by the same voice from heaven that in the fourth verse had lain an injunction upon him not to write what he had discerned by the seven thunders. 2. To eat the book; this part of the charge was given by the angel himself, hinting to the apostle that before he should publish what he had discovered he must more thoroughly digest the predictions, and be in himself suitably affected with them.

II. An account of the taste and relish which this little book would have, when the apostle had taken it in; at first, while *in his mouth, sweet.* All persons feel a pleasure in looking into future events, and in having them foretold; and all good men love to receive a word from God, of what import soever it be. But, when this book of prophecy was more thoroughly digested by the apostle, the contents would be bitter; these were things so awful and terrible, such grievous persecutions of the people of God, and such desolation made in the earth, that the foresight and foreknowledge of them would not be pleasant, but painful to the mind of the apostle: thus was Ezekiel's prophecy to him, *ch.* iii. 3.

III. The apostle's discharge of the duty he was called to (*v.* 10): *He took the little book out of the angel's hand, and ate it up,* and he found the relish to be as was told him. 1. It becomes the servants of God to digest in their own souls the messages they bring to others in his name, and to be suitably affected therewith themselves. 2. It becomes them to deliver every message with which they are charged, whether pleasing or unpleasing to men. That which is least pleasing may be most profitable; however, God's messengers must not keep back any part of the counsel of God.

IV. The apostle is made to know that this book of prophecy, which he had now taken in, was not given him merely to gratify his own curiosity, or to affect him with pleasure or pain, but to be communicated by him to the world. Here his prophetical commission seems to be renewed, and he is ordered to prepare for another embassy, to convey those declarations of the mind and will of God which are of great importance to all the world, and to the highest and greatest men in the world, and such should be read and recorded in many languages. This indeed is the case; we have them in our language, and are all obliged to attend to them, humbly to enquire into the meaning of them, and firmly to believe that every thing shall have its accomplishment in the proper time; and, when the prophecies shall be fulfilled, the sense and truth of them will appear, and the omniscience, power, and faithfulness of the great God will be adored.

CHAP. XI.

In this chapter we have an account, I. Of the measuring-reed given to the apostle, to take the dimensions of the temple, ver. 1, 2. II. Of the two witnesses of God, ver. 3—13. III. Of the sounding of the seventh trumpet, and what followed upon it, ver. 14, &c.

AND there was given me a reed
like unto a rod: and the angel
stood, saying, Rise, and measure the
temple of God, and the altar, and
them that worship therein. 2 But
the court which is without the temple
leave out, and measure it not; for it
is given unto the Gentiles: and the
holy city shall they tread under foot
forty *and* two months.

This prophetical passage about measuring the temple is a plain reference to what we find in Ezekiel's vision, Ezek. xl. 3, &c. But how to understand either the one or the other is not so easy. It should seem the design of measuring the temple in the former case was in order to the rebuilding of it, and that with advantage; the design of this measurement seems to be either, 1. For the preservation of it in those times of public danger and calamity that are here foretold;

or, 2. For its trial; that it may be seen how far it agrees with the standard, or pattern, in the mount; or, 3. For its reformation; that what is redundant, deficient, or changed, may be regulated according to the true model. Observe,

I. How much was to be measured. 1. *The temple;* the gospel church in general, whether it be so built, so constituted, as the gospel rule directs, whether it be too narrow or too large, the door too wide or too strait. 2. *The altar.* That which was the place of the most solemn acts of worship may be put for religious worship in general; whether the church has the true altars, both as to substance and situation: as to substance, whether they take Christ for their altar, and lay down all their offerings there; and in situation, whether the altar be in the holiest; that is, whether they worship God in the Spirit and in truth. 3. The worshippers too must be measured, whether they make God's glory their end and his word their rule, in all their acts of worship; and whether they come to God with suitable affections, and whether their *conversation be as becomes the gospel.*

II. What was not to be measured (*v.* 2), and why it should be left out. 1. What was not to be measured: *The court which is without the temple measure it not.* Some say that Herod, in the additions made to the temple, built an outer court, and called it *the court of the Gentiles.* Some tell us that Adrian built the city and an outer court, and called it *Ælia,* and gave it to the Gentiles. 2. Why was not the outer court measured? This was no part of the temple, according to the model either of Solomon or Zerubbabel, and therefore God would have no regard to it. He would not mark it out for preservation; but as it was designed for the Gentiles, to bring pagan ceremonies and customs and to annex them to the gospel churches, so Christ abandoned it to them, to be used as they pleased; and both that and the city were trodden under foot for a certain time—*forty and two months,* which some would have to be the whole time of the reign of antichrist. Those who worship in the outer court are either such as worship in a false manner or with hypocritical hearts; and these are rejected of God, and will be found among his enemies. 3. From the whole observe, (1.) God will have a temple and an altar in the world, till the end of time. (2.) He has a strict regard to this temple, and observes how every thing is managed in it. (3.) Those who worship in the outer court will be rejected, and only those who worship within the veil accepted. (4.) The holy city, the visible church, is very much trampled upon in the world. But, (5.) The desolations of the church are for a limited time, and for a short time, and she shall be delivered out of all her troubles.

3 And I will give *power* unto my
two witnesses, and they shall prophesy a thousand two hundred *and*
threescore days, clothed in sackcloth.
4 These are the two olive trees, and
the two candlesticks standing before
the God of the earth. 5 And if any
man will hurt them, fire proceedeth
out of their mouth, and devoureth
their enemies: and if any man will
hurt them, he must in this manner
be killed. 6. These have power to
shut heaven, that it rain not in the
days of their prophecy: and have
power over waters to turn them to
blood, and to smite the earth with all
plagues, as often as they will. 7 And
when they shall have finished their
testimony, the beast that ascendeth
out of the bottomless pit shall make
war against them, and shall overcome
them, and kill them. 8 And their
dead bodies *shall lie* in the street of
the great city, which spiritually is
called Sodom and Egypt, where also
our Lord was crucified. 9 And they
of the people and kindreds and
tongues and nations shall see their
dead bodies three days and a half,
and shall not suffer their dead bodies
to be put in graves. 10 And they
that dwell upon the earth shall rejoice
over them, and make merry, and shall
send gifts one to another; because
these two prophets tormented them
that dwelt on the earth. 11 And
after three days and a half the
Spirit of life from God entered into
them, and they stood upon their feet;
and great fear fell upon them which
saw them. 12 And they heard a
great voice from heaven saying unto
them, Come up hither. And they
ascended up into heaven in a cloud;
and their enemies beheld them. 13
And the same hour was there a great
earthquake, and the tenth part of the
city fell, and in the earthquake were
slain of men seven thousand: and
the remnant were affrighted, and gave
glory to the God of heaven.

In this time of treading down, God has reserved to himself his faithful witnesses, who will not fail to attest the truth of his word and worship, and the excellency of his ways. Here observe,

I. The number of these witnesses: it is but a small number and yet it is sufficient. 1. It is but small. Many will own and acknowledge Christ in times of prosperity who will desert and deny him in times of persecution; one witness, when the cause is upon trial, is worth many at other times. 2. It is a sufficient number; for in the mouth of two witnesses every cause shall be established. Christ sent out his disciples two by two, to preach the gospel. Some think these two witnesses are Enoch and Elias, who are to return to the earth for a time: others, the church of the believing Jews and that of the Gentiles: it should rather seem that they are God's eminent faithful ministers, who shall not only continue to profess the Christian religion, but to preach it, in the worst of times.

II. The time of their prophesying, or bearing their testimony for Christ. *A thousand two hundred and threescore days;* that is (as many think), to the period of the reign of antichrist; and, if the beginning of that interval could be ascertained, this number of prophetic days, taking a day for a year, would give us a prospect when the end shall be.

III. Their habit, and posture: they prophesy in sackcloth, as those that are deeply affected with the low and distressed state of the churches and interest of Christ in the world.

IV. How they were supported and supplied during the discharge of their great and hard work: they stood before the God of the whole earth, and he gave them power to prophesy. He made them to be like Zerubbabel and Joshua, the two olive-trees and candlestick in the vision of Zechariah, *ch.* iv. 2, &c. God gave them the oil of holy zeal, and courage, and strength, and comfort; he made them olive-trees, and their lamps of profession were kept burning by the oil of inward gracious principles, which they received from God. They had oil not only in their lamps, but in their vessels—habits of spiritual life, light, and zeal.

V. Their security and defence during the time of their prophesying: *If any attempted to hurt them, fire proceeded out of their mouths, and devoured them, v.* 5. Some think this alludes to Elias's calling for fire from heaven, to consume the captains and their companies that came to seize him, 2 Kings i. 12. God promised the prophet Jeremiah (*ch.* v. 14), *Behold, I will make my words in thy mouth fire, and this people shall be wood, and it shall devour them.* By their praying and preaching, and courage in suffering, they shall gall and wound the very hearts and consciences of many of their persecutors, who shall go away self-condemned, and be even terrors to themselves; like Pashur, at the words of the prophet Jeremiah, *ch.* xx. 4. They shall have that free access to God, and that interest in him, that, at their prayers, God will inflict plagues and judgments upon their enemies, as he did on Pharaoh, *turning their rivers into blood,* and restraining the dews of heaven, shutting heaven up, that no rain shall fall for many days, as he did at the prayers of Elias, 1 Kings xvii. 1. God has ordained his arrows for the persecutors, and is often plaguing them while they are persecuting his people; they find it hard work to *kick against the pricks.*

VI. The slaying of the witnesses. To make their testimony more strong, they must seal it with their blood. Here observe, 1. The time when they should be killed: *When they have finished their testimony.* They are immortal, they are invulnerable, till their work be done. Some think it ought to be rendered, *when they were about to finish their testimony.* When they had prophesied in sackcloth the greatest part of the 1260 years, then they should feel the last effect of antichristian malice. 2. The enemy that should overcome and slay them—*the beast that ascendeth out of the bottomless pit.* Antichrist, the great instrument of the devil, should make war against them, not only with the arms of subtle and sophistical learning, but chiefly with open force and violence; and God would permit his enemies to prevail against his witnesses for a time. 3. The barbarous usage of these slain witnesses; the malice of their enemies was not satiated with their blood and death, but pursued even their dead bodies. (1.) They would not allow them a quiet grave; their bodies were cast out in the open street, the high street of Babylon, or in the high road leading to the city. This city is spiritually called Sodom for monstrous wickedness, and Egypt for idolatry and tyranny; and here Christ in his mystical body has suffered more than in any place in the world. (2.) Their dead bodies were insulted by the inhabitants of the earth, and their death was a matter of mirth and joy to the antichristian world, *v.* 10. They were glad to be rid of these witnesses, who by their doctrine and example had teazed, terrified, and tormented the consciences of their enemies; these spiritual weapons cut wicked men to the heart, and fill them with the greatest rage and malice against the faithful.

VII. The resurrection of these witnesses, and the consequences thereof. Observe, 1. The time of their rising again; after they had lain dead *three days and a half* (*v.* 11), a short time in comparison of that in which they had prophesied. Here may be a reference to the resurrection of Christ, who is *the resurrection and the life. Thy dead men shall live, together with my dead body shall they arise.* Or there may be a reference to the resurrection of Lazarus on the fourth day, when they thought it impossible. God's witnesses may be slain, but they shall rise again: not in their persons, till the general resurrection, but in their successors. God will revive his work, when it seems to be dead in the world. 2. The power by which they were raised: *The spirit of life from God entered into them, and they stood upon their feet.* God put not only life, but courage into them. God can make the dry bones to live; it is the Spirit of life from God that quickens dead souls, and shall quicken the dead bodies of his people, and his dying interest in the world. 3. The effect of their resurrection upon their enemies: *Great fear fell upon them.* The reviving of God's work and witnesses will strike terror into the souls of his enemies. Where there is guilt, there is fear; and a persecuting spirit, though cruel, is not a courageous, but a cowardly spirit. Herod feared John the Baptist.

VIII. The ascension of the witnesses into heaven and the consequences thereof, *v.* 12, 13. Observe, 1. Their ascension. By heaven we may understand either some more eminent station in the church, the kingdom of grace in this world, or a high place in the kingdom of glory above. The former seems to be the meaning: *They ascended to heaven in a cloud* (in a figurative, not in a literal sense) *and their enemies saw them.* It will be no small part of the punishment of persecutors, both in this world and at the great day, that they shall see the faithful servants of God greatly honoured and advanced. To this honour they did not attempt to ascend, till God called them, and said, *Come up hither.* The Lord's witnesses must wait for their advancement, both in the church and in heaven, till God calls them; they must not be weary of suffering and service, nor too hastily grasp at the reward; but stay till their Master calls them, and then they may gladly ascend to him. 2. The consequences of their ascension—a mighty shock and convulsion in the antichristian empire and the fall of *a tenth part of the city.* Some refer this to the beginning of the reformation from popery, when many princes and states fell off from their subjection to Rome. This great work met with great opposition; all the western world felt a great concussion, and the antichristian interest received a great blow, and lost a great deal of ground and interest, (1.) By the sword of war, which was then drawn; and many of those who fought under the banner of antichrist were slain by it. (2.) By the sword of the Spirit: *The fear of God fell upon many.* They were convinced of their errors, superstition, and idolatry; and by true repentance, and embracing the truth, *they gave glory to the God of heaven.* Thus, when God's work and witnesses revive, the devil's work and witnesses fall before him.

14 The second woe is past; *and,*
behold, the third woe cometh quickly.
15 And the seventh angel sounded;
and there were great voices in heaven,
saying, The kingdoms of this world
are become *the kingdoms* of our Lord,
and of his Christ; and he shall reign
for ever and ever. 16 And the four
and twenty elders which sat before
God on their seats, fell upon their
faces, and worshipped God, 17 Saying,
We give thee thanks, O Lord God
Almighty, which art, and wast, and
art to come; because thou hast taken
to thee thy great power, and hast
reigned. 18 And the nations were
angry, and thy wrath is come, and
the time of the dead, that they should
be judged, and that thou shouldest
give reward unto thy servants the
prophets, and to the saints, and them
that fear thy name, small and great;
and shouldest destroy them which
destroy the earth. 19 And the temple
of God was opened in heaven, and
there was seen in his temple the ark
of his testament: and there were
lightnings, and voices, and thunderings,
and an earthquake, and great hail.

We have here the sounding of the seventh and last trumpet, which is ushered in by the usual warning and demand of attention: *The second woe is past, and, behold, the third woe cometh quickly. Then the seventh angel sounded.* This had been suspended for some time, till the apostle had been made acquainted with some intervening occurrences of very great moment, and worthy of his notice and observation. But what he before expected he now heard—the seventh angel sounding. Here observe the effects and consequences of this trumpet, thus sounded.

I. Here were loud and joyful acclamations of the saints and angels in heaven. Observe, 1. The manner of their adorations: they rose from their seats, *and fell upon their faces, and worshipped God;* they did it with reverence and humility. 2. The matter of their adorations. (1.) They thankfully recognise the right of our God and Saviour to rule and reign over all the world: *The kingdoms of this world have become the kingdoms of our Lord and of his Christ, v.* 15. They were always so in title, both by creation and purchase. (2.) They thankfully observe his actual possession of them, and reign over them; they give him thanks because he had taken to him his great power, asserted his rights, exerted his power, and so turned title into possession. (3.) They rejoice that this his reign shall never end: *He shall reign for ever and ever,* till all enemies be put under his feet; none shall ever wrest the sceptre out of his hand.

II. Here were angry resentments in the

world at these just appearances and actings of the power of God (*v.* 18): *The nations were angry;* not only had been so, but were so still: their hearts rose up against God; they met his wrath with their own anger. It was a time when God was taking a just revenge upon the enemies of his people, recompensing tribulation to those who had troubled them. It was a time in which he was beginning to reward his people's faithful services and sufferings; and their enemies could not bear it, they fretted against God, and so increased their guilt and hastened their destruction.

III. Another consequence was the opening of the temple of God in heaven. By this may be meant that here is now a more free communication between heaven and earth, prayer and praises more freely and frequently ascending and graces and blessings plentifully descending. But it rather seems to intend the church of God on earth, a heavenly temple. It is an allusion to the various circumstances of things in the time of the first temple. Under idolatrous and wicked princes, it was shut up and neglected; but, under religious and reforming princes, it was opened and frequented. So, during the power of antichrist, the temple of God seemed to be shut up, and was so in a great degree; but now it was opened again. At this opening of it observe, 1. What was seen there: *the ark of God's testament.* This was in the holy of holies; in this ark the tables of the law were kept. As before Josiah's time the law of God had been lost, but was then found, so in the reign of antichrist God's law was laid aside, and made void by their traditions and decrees; the scriptures were locked up from the people, and they must not look into these divine oracles; now they are opened, now they are brought to the view of all. This was an unspeakable and invaluable privilege; and this, like the ark of the testament, was a token of the presence of God returned to his people, and his favour towards them in Jesus Christ the propitiation. 2. What was heard and felt there: *Lightnings, voices, thunderings, an earthquake, and great hail.* The great blessing of the reformation was attended with very awful providences; and by terrible things in righteousness God would answer those prayers that were presented in his holy temple, now opened. All the great revolutions of the world are concerted in heaven, and are the answers of the prayers of the saints.

CHAP. XII.

It is generally agreed by the most learned expositors that the narrative we have in this and the two following chapters, from the sounding of the seventh trumpet to the opening of the vials, is not a prediction of things to come, but rather a recapitulation and representation of things past, which, as God would have the apostle to foresee while future, he would have him to review now that they were past, that he might have a more perfect idea of them in his mind, and might observe the agreement between the prophecy and that Providence that is always fulfilling the scriptures. In this chapter we have an account of the contest between the church and antichrist, the seed of the woman and the seed of the serpent. I. As it was begun in heaven, ver. 1—11. II. As it was carried on in the wilderness, ver. 12, &c.

AND there appeared a great
wonder in heaven; a woman
clothed with the sun, and the moon
under her feet, and upon her head a
crown of twelve stars: 2 And she
being with child cried, travailing in
birth, and pained to be delivered.
3 And there appeared another wonder
in heaven; and behold a great red
dragon, having seven heads and ten
horns, and seven crowns upon his
heads. 4 And his tail drew the
third part of the stars of heaven, and
did cast them to the earth: and the
dragon stood before the woman which
was ready to be delivered, for to devour her child as soon as it was born.
5 And she brought forth a man
child, who was to rule all nations with
a rod of iron: and her child was
caught up unto God, and *to* his
throne. 6 And the woman fled into
the wilderness, where she hath a place
prepared of God, that they should
feed her there a thousand two hundred *and* threescore days. 7 And
there was war in heaven: Michael
and his angels fought against the
dragon; and the dragon fought and
his angels, 8 And prevailed not;
neither was their place found any
more in heaven. 9 And the great
dragon was cast out, that old serpent,
called the Devil, and Satan, which
deceiveth the whole world: he was
cast out into the earth, and his angels
were cast out with him. 10 And I
heard a loud voice saying in heaven,
Now is come salvation, and strength,
and the kingdom of our God, and the
power of his Christ: for the accuser
of our brethren is cast down, which
accused them before our God day and
night. 11 And they overcame him
by the blood of the Lamb, and by
the word of their testimony; and they
loved not their lives unto the death.

Here we see that early prophecy eminently fulfilled in which God said he would *put enmity between the seed of the woman and the seed of the serpent,* Gen. iii. 15. You will observe,

I. The attempts of Satan and his agents to prevent the increase of the church, by devouring her offspring *as soon as it was born:* of this we have a very lively description in the most proper images.

1. We see how the church is represented in this vision. (1.) As a *woman,* the weaker part of the world, but the spouse of Christ, and the mother of the saints. (2.) As *clothed with the sun,* the imputed righteousness of the Lord Jesus Christ. Having put on Christ, who is *the Sun of righteousness,* she, by her relation to Christ, is invested with honourable rights and privileges, and shines in his rays. (3.) As having *the moon under her feet* (that is, the world); she stands upon it, but lives above it; her heart and hope are not set upon sublunary things, but on the things that are in heaven, where her head is. (4.) As having on her head *a crown of twelve stars,* that is, the doctrine of the gospel preached by the twelve apostles, which is a crown of glory to all true believers. (5.) As in travail, crying out, and *pained to be delivered.* She was pregnant, and now in pain to bring forth a holy progeny to Christ, desirous that what was begun in the conviction of sinners might end in their conversion, that when the children were brought to the birth there might be strength to bring forth, and that she might see of the travail of her soul.

2. How the grand enemy of the church is represented. (1.) As a *great red dragon*—a dragon for strength and terror—a red dragon for fierceness and cruelty. (2.) As *having seven heads,* that is, placed on seven hills, as Rome was; and therefore it is probable that pagan Rome is here meant. (3.) As having *ten horns,* divided into ten provinces, as the Roman empire was by Augustus Cæsar. (4.) As having *seven crowns upon his head,* which is afterwards expounded to be seven kings, *ch.* xvii. 10. (5.) As drawing with his tail a *third part of the stars in heaven,* and *casting them down to the earth,* turning the ministers and professors of the Christian religion out of their places and privileges and making them as weak and useless as he could. (6.) As standing *before the woman, to devour her child as soon as it should be born,* very vigilant to crush the Christian religion in its birth and entirely to prevent the growth and continuance of it in the world.

II. The unsuccessfulness of these attempts against the church; for, 1. She was safely delivered of a *man-child* (*v.* 5), by which some understand Christ, others Constantine, but others, with greater propriety, a race of true believers, strong and united, resembling Christ, and designed, under him, *to rule the nations with a rod of iron;* that is, to judge the world by their doctrine and lives now, and as assessors with Christ at the great day. 2. Care was taken of this child: it *was caught up to God, and to his throne;* that is, taken into his special, powerful, and immediate protection. The Christian religion has been from its infancy the special care of *the great God and our Saviour Jesus Christ.* 3. Care was taken of the mother as well as of the child, *v.* 6. She *fled into the wilderness, a place prepared* both for her safety and her sustenance. The church was in an obscure state, dispersed; and this proved her security, through the care of divine Providence. This her obscure and private state was for a limited time, not to continue always.

III. The attempts of the dragon not only proved unsuccessful against the church, but fatal to his own interests; for, upon his endeavour to devour the man-child, he engaged all the powers of heaven against him (*v.* 7): *There was war in heaven. Heaven* will espouse the quarrel of the church. Here observe,

1. The seat of this war—*in heaven,* in the church, which is *the kingdom of heaven* on earth, under the care of heaven and in the same interest.

2. The parties—*Michael and his angels* on one side, and *the dragon and his angels* on the other: Christ, the great Angel of the covenant, and his faithful followers; and Satan and all his instruments. This latter party would be much superior in number and outward strength to the other; but the strength of the church lies in having the Lord Jesus for the captain of their salvation.

3. The success of the battle: *The dragon and his angels fought and prevailed not;* there was a great struggle on both sides, but the victory fell to Christ and his church, and the dragon and his angels were not only conquered, but cast out; the pagan idolatry, which was a worshipping of devils, was extirpated out of the empire in the time of Constantine.

4. The triumphant song that was composed and used on this occasion, *v.* 10, 11. Here observe, (1.) How the conqueror is adored: *Now have come salvation, strength, and the kingdom of our God, and the power of his Christ.* Now God has shown himself to be a mighty God; now Christ has shown himself to be a strong and mighty Saviour; his own arm has brought salvation, and now his kingdom will be greatly enlarged and established. The salvation and strength of the church are all to be ascribed to the king and head of the church. (2.) How the conquered enemy is described. [1.] By his malice; he was *the accuser of the brethren,* and *accused them before their God night and day;* he appeared before God as an adversary to the church, continually bringing in indictments and accusations against them, whether true or false; thus he accused Job, and thus he accused Joshua the high priest, Zech. iii. 1. Though he hates the presence of God, yet he is willing to appear there to accuse the people of God. Let us therefore take heed that we give him no cause of accusation against us; and that, when we have sinned, we presently go in before the Lord, and accuse and condemn ourselves, and commit our cause to Christ as our Advocate. [2.]

By his disappointment and defeat: he and all his accusations are cast out, the indictments quashed, and the accuser turned out of the court with just indignation. (3.) How the victory was gained. The servants of God overcame Satan, [1.] *By the blood of the Lamb,* as the meritorious cause. Christ by dying *destroyed him that hath the power of death, that is, the devil.* [2.] *By the word of their testimony,* as the great instrument of war, *the sword of the Spirit, which is the word of God,*—by a resolute powerful preaching of the everlasting gospel, *which is mighty, through God, to pull down strongholds,*—and by their courage and patience in sufferings; *they loved not their lives unto the death,* when the love of life stood in competition with their loyalty to Christ; they loved not their lives so well but they could give them up *to death,* could lay them down in Christ's cause; their love to their own lives was overcome by stronger affections of another nature; and this their courage and zeal helped to confound their enemies, to convince many of the spectators, to confirm the souls of the faithful, and so contributed greatly to this victory.

12 Therefore rejoice, *ye* heavens,
and ye that dwell in them. Woe to
the inhabiters of the earth and of the
sea! for the devil is come down unto
you, having great wrath, because he
knoweth that he hath but a short
time. 13 And when the dragon saw
that he was cast unto the earth, he
persecuted the woman which brought
forth the man *child.* 14 And to the
woman were given two wings of a
great eagle, that she might fly into
the wilderness, into her place, where
she is nourished for a time, and times,
and half a time, from the face of the
serpent. 15 And the serpent cast
out of his mouth water as a flood
after the woman, that he might cause
her to be carried away of the flood.
16 And the earth helped the woman,
and the earth opened her mouth, and
swallowed up the flood which the
dragon cast out of his mouth. 17
And the dragon was wroth with the
woman, and went to make war with
the remnant of her seed, which keep
the commandments of God, and have
the testimony of Jesus Christ.

We have here an account of this war, so happily finished in heaven, or in the church, as it was again renewed and carried on in the wilderness, the place to which the church had fled, and where she had been for some time secured by the special care of her God and Saviour. Observe,

I. The warning given of the distress and calamity that should fall upon the inhabitants of the world in general, through the wrath and rage of the devil. For, though his malice is chiefly bent against the servants of God, yet he is an enemy and hater of mankind as such; and, being defeated in his designs against the church, he is resolved to give all the disturbance he can to the world in general: *Woe to the inhabitants of the earth, and the sea, v.* 12. The rage of Satan grows so much the greater as he is limited both in place and time; when he was confined to the wilderness, and had but a short time to reign there, he comes with the greater wrath.

II. His second attempt upon the church now in the wilderness: *He persecuted the woman who brought forth the man-child, v.* 13. Observe, 1. The care that God had taken of his church. He had conveyed her as on eagles' wings, into a place of safety provided for her, where she was to continue for a certain space of time, couched in prophetic characters, taken from Dan. vii. 25. 2. The continual malice of the dragon against the church. Her obscurity could not altogether protect her; the old subtle serpent, which at first lurked in paradise, now follows the church into the wilderness, and *casts out a flood of water after her, to carry her away.* This is thought to be meant of a flood of error and heresy, which was breathed by Arius, Nestorius, Pelagius, and many more, by which the church of God was in danger of being overwhelmed and carried away. The church of God is in more danger from heretics than from persecutors; and heresies are as certainly from the devil as open force and violence. 3. The seasonable help provided for the church in this dangerous juncture: *The earth helped the woman, and opened her mouth, and swallowed up the flood, v.* 16. Some think we are to understand the swarms of Goths and Vandals that invaded the Roman empire, and found work for the Arian rulers, who otherwise would have been as furious persecutors as the pagan had been, and had exercised great cruelties already; but God opened a breach of war, and the flood was in a manner swallowed up thereby, and the church enjoyed some respite. God often sends the sword to avenge the quarrel of his covenant; and, when men choose new gods, then there is danger of war in the gates; intestine broils and contentions often end in the invasions of a common enemy. 4. The devil, being thus defeated in his designs upon the universal church, now turns his rage against particular persons and places; his malice against the woman pushes him on to *make war with the remnant of her seed.* Some think hereby are meant the Albigenses, who were first by Dioclesian driven up into barren and mountainous places, and afterwards cruelly murdered by popish rage and power, for several generations; and for no other reason than because *they kept the commandments of God* and *held the testimony of Jesus Christ*. Their fidelity to God and Christ, in doctrine, worship, and practice, was that which exposed them to the rage of Satan and his instruments; and such fidelity will expose men still, less or more, to the end of the world, when *the last enemy shall be destroyed*.

CHAP. XIII.

We have, in this chapter, a further discovery and description of the church's enemies: not other enemies than are mentioned before, but described after another manner, that the methods of their enmity may more fully appear. They are represented as two beasts; the first you have an account of, ver. 1—10, the second, ver. 11, &c. By the first some understand Rome pagan, and by the second Rome papal; but others understand Rome papal to be represented by both these beasts, by the first in its secular power, by the second in its ecclesiastical.

AND I stood upon the sand of the
sea, and saw a beast rise up out
of the sea, having seven heads and
ten horns, and upon his horns ten
crowns, and upon his heads the name
of blasphemy. 2 And the beast
which I saw was like unto a leopard,
and his feet were as *the feet* of a bear,
and his mouth as the mouth of a
lion: and the dragon gave him his
power, and his seat, and great authority. 3 And I saw one of his
heads as it were wounded to death;
and his deadly wound was healed:
and all the world wondered after the
beast. 4 And they worshipped the
dragon which gave power unto the
beast: and they worshipped the beast,
saying, Who *is* like unto the beast?
who *is* able to make war with him?
5 And there was given unto him a
mouth speaking great things and
blasphemies; and power was given
unto him to continue forty *and* two
months. 6 And he opened his
mouth in blasphemy against God, to
blaspheme his name, and his tabernacle, and them that dwell in heaven.
7 And it was given unto him to make
war with the saints, and to overcome
them: and power was given him over
all kindreds, and tongues, and nations. 8 And all that dwell upon
the earth shall worship him, whose
names are not written in the book of
life of the Lamb slain from the foundation of the world. 9 If any man
have an ear, let him hear. 10 He
that leadeth into captivity shall go
into captivity: he that killeth with
the sword must be killed with the
sword. Here is the patience and the
faith of the saints.

We have here an account of the rise, figure, and progress of the first beast; and observe, 1. From what situation the apostle saw this monster. He seemed to himself to stand upon *the sea-shore*, though it is probable he was still in a rapture; but he took himself to be in *the island Patmos*, but whether in the body or out of the body he could not tell. 2. Whence this beast came—*out of the sea;* and yet, by the description of it, it would seem more likely to be a land-monster; but the more monstrous every thing about it was the more proper an emblem it would be to set forth the mystery of iniquity and tyranny. 3. What was the form and shape of this beast. It was for the most part *like a leopard,* but its *feet were like the feet of a bear and its mouth as the mouth of a lion;* it had *seven heads, and ten horns, and upon its heads the name of blasphemy:* a most horrid and hideous monster! In some part of this description here seems to be an allusion to Daniel's vision of the four beasts, which represented the four monarchies, Dan. vii. 1—3, &c. One of these beasts was like a lion, another like a bear, and another like a leopard; this beast was a sort of composition of those three, with the fierceness, strength, and swiftness, of them all; the seven heads and the ten horns seem to design its several powers; the ten crowns, its tributary princes; the word blasphemy on its forehead proclaims its direct enmity and opposition to the glory of God, by promoting idolatry. 4. The source and spring of his authority—*the dragon; he gave him his power, and seat, and great authority.* He was set up by the devil, and supported by him to do his work and promote his interest; and the devil lent him all the assistance he could. 5. A dangerous wound given him, and yet unexpectedly healed, *v.* 3. Some think that by this wounded head we are to understand the abolishing of pagan idolatry; and by the healing of the wound the introducing of the popish idolatry, the same in substance with the former, only in a new dress, and which as effectually answers the devil's design as that did. 6. The honour and worship paid to this infernal monster: *All the world wondered after the beast;* they all admired his power, and policy, and success, and *they worshipped the dragon* that *gave power to the beast,* and *they worshipped the beast;* they paid honour and subjection to the devil and his instruments, and thought there was no power able to withstand them: so great were the darkness, degeneracy, and madness of the world! 7. How he exercised his infernal power and policy: He had *a mouth, speaking great things, and blasphemies; he blasphemed God, the name of God, the tabernacle of God, and all those that dwell in heaven; and he made war with the saints, and overcame them,* and gained a sort of universal empire in the world. His malice was principally levelled at the God of heaven, and his heavenly attendants—at God, in making images of him that is invisible, and in worshipping them;—at the tabernacle of God, that is, say some, at the human nature of the Lord Jesus Christ, in which God dwells as in a tabernacle; this is dishonoured by their doctrine of transubstantiation, which will not suffer his body to be a true body, and will put it into the power of every priest to prepare a body for Christ;—and *against those that dwell in heaven,* the glorified saints, by putting them into the place of the pagan demons, and praying to them, which they are so far from being pleased with that they truly judge themselves wronged and dishonoured by it. Thus the malice of the devil shows itself against heaven and the blessed inhabitants of heaven. These are above the reach of his power. All he can do is to blaspheme them; but the saints on earth are more exposed to his cruelty, and he sometimes is permitted to triumph over them and trample upon them. 8. The limitation of the devil's power and success, and that both as to time and persons. He is limited in point of time; his reign is *to continue forty-and-two months* (*v.* 5), suitable to the other prophetical characters of the reign of antichrist. He is also limited as to the persons and people that he shall entirely subject to his will and power; it will be only those *whose names are not written in the Lamb's book of life.* Christ had a chosen remnant, *redeemed by his blood, recorded in his book, sealed by his Spirit;* and though the devil and antichrist might overcome their bodily strength, and take away their natural life, they could never conquer their souls, nor prevail with them to forsake their Saviour and revolt to his enemies. 9. Here is a demand of attention to what is here discovered of the great sufferings and troubles of the church, and an assurance given that when God has accomplished his work on mount Zion, his refining work, then he will turn his hand against the enemies of his people, and those who have killed with the sword shall themselves fall by the sword (*v.* 10), and those who led the people of God into captivity shall themselves be made captives. Here now is that which will be proper exercise for *the patience and faith of the saints*—patience under the prospect of such great sufferings, and faith in the prospect of so glorious a deliverance.

11 And I beheld another beast
coming up out of the earth; and he
had two horns like a lamb, and he
spake as a dragon. 12 And he ex-
erciseth all the power of the first
beast before him, and causeth the
earth and them which dwell therein
to worship the first beast, whose
deadly wound was healed. 13 And
he doeth great wonders, so that he
maketh fire come down from heaven
on the earth in the sight of men, 14
And deceiveth them that dwell on
the earth by *the means of* those
miracles which he had power to do in
the sight of the beast; saying to
them that dwell on the earth, that
they should make an image to the
beast, which had the wound by a
sword, and did live. 15 And he had
power to give life unto the image of
the beast, that the image of the beast
should both speak, and cause that as
many as would not worship the image
of the beast should be killed. 16
And he caused all, both small and
great, rich and poor, free and bond,
to receive a mark in their right hand,
or in their foreheads: 17 And that
no man might buy or sell, save he
that had the mark, or the name of
the beast, or the number of his name.
18 Here is wisdom. Let him that
hath understanding count the number
of the beast: for it is the number of
a man; and his number *is* Six hundred threescore *and* six.

Those who think the first beast signifies Rome pagan by this second beast would understand Rome papal, which promotes idolatry and tyranny, but in a more soft and lamb-like manner: those that understand the first beast of the secular power of the papacy take the second to intend its spiritual and ecclesiastical powers, which act under the disguise of religion and charity to the souls of men. Here observe,

I. The form and shape of this second beast: *He had two horns like a lamb,* but a mouth that *spoke like the dragon.* All agree that this must be some great impostor, who, under a pretence of religion, shall deceive the souls of men. The papists would have it to be Apollonius Tyanæus; but Dr. More has rejected that opinion, and fixes it upon the ecclesiastical powers of the papacy. The pope shows the horns of a lamb, pretends to be the vicar of Christ upon earth, and so to be vested with his power and authority; but his speech betrays him, for he gives forth those false doctrines and cruel decrees which show him to belong to the dragon, and not to the Lamb.

II. The power which he exercises: *All the power of the former beast* (*v.* 12); he promotes the same interest, pursues the same design in substance, which is, to draw men off from worshipping the true God to worship those who by nature are no gods, and subject the souls and consciences of men to the will and authority of men, in opposition to the will of God. This design is promoted by popery as well as by paganism, and by the crafty arts of popery as well as by the secular arm, both serving the interests of the devil, though in a different manner.

III The methods by which this second beast carried on his interests and designs; they are of three sorts:—1. Lying wonders, pretended miracles, by which they should be deceived, and prevailed with to worship the former beast in this new image or shape that was now made for him; they would pretend to bring down fire from heaven, as Elias did, and God sometimes permits his enemies, as he did the magicians of Egypt, to do things that seem very wonderful, and by which unwary persons may be deluded. It is well known that the papal kingdom has been long supported by pretended miracles. 2. Excommunications, anathemas, severe censures, by which they pretend to cut men off from Christ, and cast them into the power of the devil, but do indeed deliver them over to the secular power, that they may be put to death; and thus, notwithstanding their vile hypocrisy, they are justly charged with killing those whom they cannot corrupt. 3. By disfranchisement, allowing none to enjoy natural, civil, or municipal rights, who will not worship that papal beast, that is, the image of the pagan beast. It is made a qualification for buying and selling the rights of nature, as well as for places of profit and trust, that they have *the mark of the beast in their forehead* and *in their right hand,* and that they have *the name of the beast* and *the number of his name.* It is probable that *the mark, the name,* and *the number of the beast,* may all signify the same thing—that they make an open profession of their subjection and obedience to the papacy, which is receiving the mark in their forehead, and that they oblige themselves to use all their interest, power, and endeavour, to promote the papal authority, which is receiving the mark in their right hands. We are told that pope Martin V. in his bull, added to the council of Constance, prohibits Roman catholics from suffering any heretics to dwell in their countries, or to make any bargains, use any trades, or bear any civil offices, which is a very clear interpretation of this prophecy.

IV. We have here *the number of the beast,* given in such a manner as shows the infinite wisdom of God, and will sufficiently exercise all the wisdom and accuracy of men: *The number* is *the number of a man,* computed after the usual manner among men, and it is 666. Whether this be the number of the errors and heresies that are contained in popery, or rather, as others, the number of the years from its rise to its fall, is not certain, much less what that period is which is described by these prophetic numbers. The most admired dissertation on this intricate subject is that of Dr. Potter, where the curious may find sufficient entertainment. It seems to me to be one of those seasons which God has reserved in his own power; only this we know, God has written *Mene Tekel* upon all his enemies; he has numbered their days, and they shall be finished, but his own kingdom shall endure for ever.

CHAP. XIV.

After an account of the great trials and sufferings which the servants of God had endured, we have now a more pleasant scene opening; the day begins now to dawn, and here we have represented, I. The Lord Jesus at the head of his faithful followers, ver. 1—5. II. Three angels sent successively to proclaim the fall of Babylon and the things antecedent and consequent to so great an event, ver. 6—13. III. The vision of the harvest, ver. 14, &c.

AND I looked, and, lo, a Lamb
stood on the mount Sion, and
with him a hundred forty *and* four
thousand, having his Father's name
written in their foreheads. 2 And I
heard a voice from heaven, as the
voice of many waters, and as the
voice of a great thunder: and I heard
the voice of harpers harping with
their harps: 3 And they sung as it
were a new song before the throne,
and before the four beasts, and the
elders: and no man could learn that
song but the hundred *and* forty *and*
four thousand, which were redeemed
from the earth. 4 These are they
which were not defiled with women;
for they are virgins. These are they
which follow the Lamb whithersoever he goeth. These were redeemed
from among men, *being* the firstfruits
unto God and to the Lamb. 5 And
in their mouth was found no guile:
for they are without fault before the
throne of God.

Here we have one of the most pleasing sights that can be viewed in this world—the Lord Jesus Christ at the head of his faithful adherents and attendants. Here observe, 1. How Christ appears: as a Lamb standing upon *mount Zion.* Mount Zion is the gospel church. Christ is with his church and in the midst of her in all her troubles, and therefore she is not consumed. It is his presence that secures her perseverance; he appears as *a Lamb, a true Lamb, the Lamb of God.* A counterfeit lamb is mentioned as rising out of the earth in the last chapter, which was really a dragon; here Christ appears as the true paschal Lamb, to show that his mediatorial government is the fruit of his sufferings, and the cause of his people's safety and fidelity. 2. How his people appear: very honourably. (1.) As to the numbers, they are many, even all who were sealed; not one of them lost in all the tribulations through which they had gone. (2.) Their distinguishing badge: they had *the name of God written in their foreheads;* they made a bold and open profession of their faith in God and Christ, and, this being followed by suitable actings, they are known and approved. (3.) Their congratulations and songs of praise, which were peculiar to the redeemed (*v.* 3); their praises were loud as the thunder, or *as the voice of many waters;* they were melodious, as *of harpers;* they were heavenly, *before the throne* of God. *The song was new,* suited to the new covenant, and unto that new and gracious dispensation of Providence under which they now were; and their song was a secret to others, *strangers intermeddled not with their joy;* others might repeat the words of the song, but they were strangers to the true sense and spirit of it. (4.) Their character and description. [1.] They are described by their chastity and purity: *They are virgins.* They had not defiled themselves either with corporal or spiritual adultery; they had kept themselves clean from the abominations of the antichristian generation. [2.] By their loyalty and stedfast adherence to Christ: *They follow the Lamb whithersoever he goes;* they follow the conduct of his word, Spirit, and providence, leaving it to him to lead them into what duties and difficulties he pleases. [3.] By their former designation to this honour: *These were redeemed from among men, being the first-fruits to God, and to the Lamb, v.* 4. Here is plain evidence of a special redemption: *They were redeemed from among men.* Some of the children of men are, by redeeming mercy, distinguished from others: *They were the first-fruits to God and to the Lamb,* his choice ones, eminent in every grace, and the earnest of many more who should *be followers of them, as they were of Christ.* [4.] By their universal integrity and conscientiousness: *There was no guile found in them,* and *they were without fault before the throne of God.* They were without any prevailing guile, any allowed fault; their hearts were right with God, and, as for their human infirmities, they were freely pardoned in Christ. This is the happy remnant who attend upon the Lord Jesus as their head and Lord; he is glorified in them, and they are glorified in him.

6 And I saw another angel fly in
the midst of heaven, having the
everlasting gospel to preach unto
them that dwell on the earth, and to
every nation, and kindred, and tongue,
and people, 7 Saying with a loud
voice, Fear God, and give glory to
him; for the hour of his judgment is
come: and worship him that made
heaven, and earth, and the sea, and
the fountains of waters. 8 And
there followed another angel, saying,
Babylon is fallen, is fallen, that great
city, because she made all nations
drink of the wine of the wrath of her
fornication. 9 And the third angel
followed them, saying with a loud
voice, If any man worship the beast
and his image, and receive *his* mark
in his forehead, or in his hand, 10
The same shall drink of the wine of
the wrath of God, which is poured
out without mixture into the cup of
his indignation; and he shall be tormented
with fire and brimstone in the
presence of the holy angels, and in
the presence of the Lamb: 11 And
the smoke of their torment ascendeth
up for ever and ever: and they have
no rest day nor night, who worship
the beast and his image, and whosoever
receiveth the mark of his
name. 12 Here is the patience of
the saints: here *are* they that keep
the commandments of God, and the
faith of Jesus.

In this part of the chapter we have three angels or messengers sent from heaven to give notice of the fall of Babylon, and of those things that were antecedent and consequent to that great event.

I. The first angel was sent on an errand antecedent to it, and that was *to preach the everlasting gospel, v.* 6, 7. Observe, 1. The gospel is an everlasting gospel; it is so in its nature, and it will be so in its consequences. Though all flesh be grass, the word of the Lord endureth for ever. 2. It is a work fit for an angel to preach this everlasting gospel; such is the dignity, and such is the difficulty of that work! And yet we have this treasure in earthen vessels. 3. The everlasting gospel is of great concern to all the world; and, as it is the concern of all, it is very much to be desired that it should be made known to all, even *to every nation, and kindred, and tongue, and people.* 4. The gospel is the great means whereby men are brought to fear God, and to give glory to him. Natural religion is not sufficient to keep up the fear of God, nor to secure to him glory from men; it is the gospel that revives the fear of God, and retrieves his glory in the world. 5. When idolatry creeps into the churches of God, it is by the preaching of the gospel, attended by the power of the Holy Spirit, that men are *turned from idols to serve the living God,* as the Creator of *the heaven, and the earth, and the sea, and the fountains of waters, v.* 7. To worship any God besides him who created the world is idolatry.

II. The second angel follows the other.

and proclaims the actual fall of Babylon. The preaching of the everlasting gospel had shaken the foundations of antichristianism in the world, and hastened its downfal. By Babylon is generally understood Rome, which was before called *Sodom* and *Egypt*, for wickedness and cruelty, and is now first called *Babylon,* for pride and idolatry. Observe, 1. What God has fore-ordained and foretold shall be done as certainly as if it were done already. 2. The greatness of the papal Babylon will not be able to prevent her fall, but will make it more dreadful and remarkable. 3. The wickedness of Babylon, in corrupting, debauching, and intoxicating the nations round about her, will make her fall just and will declare the righteousness of God in her utter ruin, *v.* 8. Her crimes are recited as the just cause of her destruction.

III. A third angel follows the other two, and gives warning to all of that divine vengeance which would overtake all those that obstinately adhered to the anchristian interest after God had thus proclaimed its downfal, *v.* 9, 10. If after this (this threatening denounced against Babylon, and in part already executed) any should persist in their idolatry, professing subjection to the beast and promoting his cause, they must expect *to drink deep of the wine of the wrath of God;* they shall be for ever miserable in soul and body; Jesus Christ will inflict this punishment upon them, and the holy angels will behold it and approve of it. Idolatry, both pagan and papal, is a damning sin in its own nature, and will prove fatal to those who persist in it, after fair warning given by the word of Providence; those who refuse to come out of Babylon, when thus called, and resolve to partake of her sins, must receive of her plagues; and the guilt and ruin of such incorrigible idolaters will serve to set forth the excellency of the patience and obedience of the saints. These graces shall be rewarded with salvation and glory. When the treachery and rebellion of others shall be punished with everlasting destruction, then it will be said, to the honour of the faithful (*v.* 12): *Here is the patience of the saints;* you have before seen their patience exercised, now you see it rewarded.

13 And I heard a voice from heaven
saying unto me, Write, Blessed *are*
the dead which die in the Lord from
henceforth: Yea, saith the Spirit,
that they may rest from their labours;
and their works do follow them. 14
And I looked, and behold a white
cloud, and upon the cloud *one* sat
like unto the Son of man, having on
his head a golden crown, and in his
hand a sharp sickle. 15 And another
angel came out of the temple, crying
with a loud voice to him that sat on the
cloud, Thrust in thy sickle, and reap:
for the time is come for thee to reap;
for the harvest of the earth is ripe. 16
And he that sat on the cloud thrust
in his sickle on the earth; and the
earth was reaped. 17 And another
angel came out of the temple which
is in heaven, he also having a sharp
sickle. 18 And another angel came
out from the altar, which had power
over fire; and cried with a loud cry
to him that had the sharp sickle,
saying, Thrust in thy sharp sickle,
and gather the clusters of the vine of
the earth; for her grapes are fully
ripe. 19 And the angel thrust in his
sickle into the earth, and gathered
the vine of the earth, and cast *it* into
the great winepress of the wrath of
God. 20 And the winepress was
trodden without the city, and blood
came out of the winepress, even unto
the horse bridles, by the space of a
thousand *and* six hundred furlongs.

Here we have the vision of the harvest and vintage, introduced with a solemn preface. Observe,

I. The preface, *v.* 13. Here note, 1. Whence this prophecy about the harvest came: it came down from heaven, and not from men, and therefore it is of certain truth and great authority. 2. How it was to be preserved and published—by writing; it was to be matter of record, that the people of God might have recourse to it for their support and comfort upon all occasions. 3. What it principally intended, and that is, to show the blessedness of all the faithful saints and servants of God, both in death and after death: *Blessed are the dead that die in the Lord from henceforth,* &c. Here observe, (1.) The description of those that are and shall be blessed—such as die in the Lord, either die in the cause of Christ, or rather die in a state of vital union with Christ, such as are found in Christ when death comes. (2.) The demonstration of this blessedness: *They rest from their labours, and their works do follow them.* [1.] They are blessed in their rest; they rest from all sin, temptation, sorrow, and persecution. *There the wicked cease from troubling, there the weary are at rest.* [2.] They are blessed in their recompence: *Their works follow them;* they do not go before them as their title, or price of purchase, but follow them as their evidence of having lived and died in the Lord; and the memory of them will be pleasant, and the reward glorious, far above the merit of all their services and sufferings. [3.] They are happy in the time of their dying, when they have lived to see the cause of God reviving, the peace of the church returning, and the wrath of God falling upon their idolatrous cruel enemies. Such times are good times to die in; they have Simeon's desire: *Now, Lord, let thou thy servant depart in peace, for mine eyes have seen thy salvation.* And all this is ratified and confirmed by the testimony of the Spirit witnessing with their spirits and with the written word.

II. We have the vision itself, represented by a harvest and a vintage.

1. By a harvest (*v.* 14, 15), an emblem that sometimes signifies the cutting down of the wicked, when ripe for ruin, by the judgments of God, and sometimes the gathering in of the righteous, when ripe for heaven, by the mercy of God. This seems rather to represent God's judgments against the wicked: and here observe,

(1.) The Lord of the harvest—one so *like unto the Son of man* that he was the same, even the Lord Jesus, who is described, [1.] By the chariot in which he sat—*a white cloud,* a cloud that had a bright side turned to the church, how dark soever it might be to the wicked. [2.] By the ensign of his power: *On his head was a golden crown,* authority to do all that he did and whatsoever he would do. [3.] By the instrument of his providences: *In his hand a sharp sickle.* [4.] By the solicitations he had from the temple to perform this great work. What he did, he was desired to do by his people; and, though he was resolved to do it, he would for this thing be sought unto by them, and so it should be in return to their prayers.

(2.) The harvest-work, which is, to thrust the sickle into the corn, and reap the field. The sickle is the sword of God's justice; the field is the world; reaping is cutting the inhabitants of the earth down and carrying them off.

(3.) The harvest-time; and that is when the corn is ripe, when the measure of the sin of men is filled up, and they are ripe for destruction. The most inveterate enemies of Christ and his church are not destroyed till by their sin they are ripe for ruin, and then he will spare them no longer; he will thrust in his sickle, and the earth shall be reaped.

2. By a vintage, *v.* 17. Some think that these two are only different emblems of the same judgment; others that they refer to distinct events of providence before the end of all things. Observe, (1.) To whom this vintage-work was committed—to an angel, *another angel that came out from the altar,* that is, from the holiest of all in heaven. (2.) At whose request this vintage-work was undertaken: it was, as before, at the cry of an *angel out of the temple,* the ministers and churches of God on earth. (3.) The work of the vintage, which consists of two parts:—[1.] The cutting off, and *gathering, the clusters of the vine,* which were now ripe and ready, *fully ripe, v.* 18. [2.] Casting these grapes *into the wine-press* (*v.* 19); here we are told, *First,* What was the wine-press: it was *the wrath of God,* the fire of his indignation, some terrible calamity, very probably the sword, shedding the blood of the wicked. *Secondly,* Where was the place of the wine-press—*without the city,* where the army lay that came against Babylon. *Thirdly,* The quantity of the wine, that is, of the blood that was drawn forth by this judgment: it was, for depth, up *to the horses' bridles,* and, for breadth and length, *a thousand and six hundred furlongs* (*v.* 20); that is, say some, 200 Italian miles, which is thought to be the measure of the holy land, and may be meant of the patrimony of the holy see, encompassing the city of Rome. But here we are left to doubtful conjectures. Perhaps this great event has not yet had its accomplishment, but *the vision is for an appointed time;* and therefore, though it may seem to tarry, we are to wait for it. *But who shall live when the Lord does this?*

CHAP. XV.

Hitherto, according to the judgment of very eminent expositors, God had represented to his servant, John, I. The state of the church under the pagan powers, in the six seals opened; and then, II. The state of the church under the papal powers, in the vision of the six trumpets that began to sound upon the opening of the seventh seal: and then is inserted, III. A more general and brief account of the past, present, and future state of the church, in the little book, &c. He now proceeds, IV. To show him how antichrist should be destroyed, by what steps that destruction should be accomplished, in the vision of the seven vials. This chapter contains an awful introduction or preparation for the pouring out of the vials, in which we have, 1. A sight of those angels in heaven who were to have the execution of this great work, and with what acclamations of joy the heavenly hosts applauded the great design, ver. 1—4. 2. A sight of these angels coming out of heaven to receive those vials which they were to pour out, and the great commotions this caused in the world, ver. 5, &c.

AND I saw another sign in heaven,
great and marvellous, seven
angels having the seven last plagues;
for in them is filled up the wrath of
God. 2 And I saw as it were a sea
of glass mingled with fire: and them
that had gotten the victory over the
beast, and over his image, and over
his mark, *and* over the number of his
name, stand on the sea of glass, having the harps of God. 3 And they
sing the song of Moses the servant
of God, and the song of the Lamb,
saying, Great and marvellous *are* thy
works, Lord God Almighty; just and
true *are* thy ways, thou King of saints.
4 Who shall not fear thee, O Lord,
and glorify thy name? for *thou* only
art holy: for all nations shall come
and worship before thee; for thy
judgments are made manifest.

Here we have the preparation of matters for the pouring out of the seven vials, which was committed to seven angels; and observe how these angels appeared to the apostle—*in heaven;* it was in a wonderful manner, and that upon account, 1. Of the work they had to do, which was to finish the destruction of antichrist. God was now about to pour out his seven last plagues upon that interest; and, as the measure of Babylon's sins was filled up, they should now find the full measure of his vindictive wrath. 2. The spectators and witnesses of this their commission: all *that had gotten the victory over the beast,* &c. These stood on a *sea of glass,* representing this world, as some think, a brittle thing, that shall be broken to pieces; or, as others, the gospel covenant, alluding to the brazen sea in the temple, in which the priests were to wash (the faithful servants of God stand upon the foundation of the righteousness of Christ); or, as others, *the Red Sea,* that stood as it were congealed while the Israelites went through; and, the pillar of fire reflecting light upon the waters, they would seem to have fire mingled with them; and this to show that the fire of God's wrath against Pharaoh and his horses should dissolve the congealed waters, and destroy them thereby, to which there seems to be an allusion by their *singing the song of Moses,* in which, (1.) They extol the greatness of God's works, and the justice and truth of his ways, both in delivering his people and destroying their enemies. They rejoiced in hope, and the near prospect they had of this, though it was not yet accomplished. (2.) They call upon all nations to render unto God the fear, glory, and worship, due to such a discovery of his truth and justice: *Who shall not fear thee? v.* 4.

5 And after that I looked, and behold, the temple of the tabernacle of
the testimony in heaven was opened:
6 And the seven angels came out of
the temple, having the seven plagues,
clothed in pure and white linen, and
having their breasts girded with
golden girdles. 7 And one of the
four beasts gave unto the seven angels
seven golden vials full of the wrath of
God, who liveth for ever and ever.
8 And the temple was filled with
smoke from the glory of God, and
from his power; and no man was
able to enter into the temple, till the
seven plagues of the seven angels
were fulfilled.

Observe, I. How these angels appeared—coming out of heaven to execute their commission: *The temple of the tabernacle of the testimony in heaven was opened, v.* 5. Here is an allusion to the holiest of all in the tabernacle and temple, where was *the mercy-seat, covering the ark of the testimony,* where the high priest made intercession, and God communed with his people, and heard their prayers. Now by this, as it is here mentioned, we may understand, 1. That, in the judgments God was now about to execute upon the antichristian interest, he was fulfilling the prophecies and promises of his word and covenant, which were there always before him, and of which he was ever mindful. 2. That in this work he was answering the prayers of the people, which were offered to him by their great high priest. 3. That he was herein avenging the quarrel of his own Son, and our Saviour Jesus Christ, whose offices and authority had been usurped, his name dishonoured, and the great designs of his death opposed, by antichrist and his adherents. 4. That he was opening a wider door of liberty for his people to worship him in numerous solemn assemblies, without the fear of their enemies.

II. How they were equipped and prepared for their work. Observe, 1. Their array: They were *clothed with pure and white linen,* and had *their breasts girded with golden girdles, v.* 6. This was the habit of the high priests when they went in to enquire of God, and came out with an answer from him. This showed that these angels were acting in all things under the divine appointment and direction, and that they were going to prepare a sacrifice to the Lord, *called the supper of the great God, ch.* xix. 17. The angels are the ministers of divine justice, and they do every thing in a pure and holy manner. 2. Their artillery, what it was, and whence they received it; their artillery, by which they were to do this great execution, was *seven vials filled with the wrath of God;* they were armed with the wrath of God against his enemies. The meanest creature, when it comes armed with the anger of God, will be too hard for any man in the world; but much more an angel of God. This wrath of God was not to be poured out all at once, but was divided into seven parts, which should successively fall upon the antichristian party. Now from whom did the angels receive these vials? From one of the four living creatures, one of the ministers of the true church, that is, in answer to the prayers of the ministers and people of God, and to avenge their cause, in which the angels are willingly employed.

III. The impressions these things made upon all who stood near the temple: they were all, as it were, wrapt up in clouds of smoke, which filled the temple, from the glorious and powerful presence of God; so that *no man was able to enter into the temple,* till the work was finished. The interests of antichrist were so interwoven with the civil interests of the nations that he could not be destroyed without giving a great shock to all the world; and the people of God would have but little rest and leisure to assemble themselves before him, while this great work was a doing. For the present, their sabbaths would be interrupted, ordinances of public worship intermitted, and all thrown into a general confusion. God himself was now preaching to the church and to all the world, by terrible things in righteousness; but, when this work was done, then the churches would have rest, the temple would be opened, and the solemn assemblies gathered, edified, and multiplied. The greatest deliverances of the church are brought about by awful and astonishing steps of Providence.

CHAP. XVI.

In this chapter we have an account of the pouring forth of these vials that were filled with the wrath of God. They were poured out upon the whole antichristian empire, and on every thing appertaining to it. I. Upon the earth, ver. 2. II. Upon the sea, ver. 3. III. Upon the rivers and fountains of water, ver. 4. Here the heavenly hosts proclaim and applaud the righteousness of the judgments of God. IV. The fourth vial was poured out on the sun, ver. 8. V. The fifth on the seat of the beast. VI. The sixth on the river Euphrates. VII The seventh in the air, upon which the cities of the nations fell, and great Babylon came in remembrance before God.

AND I heard a great voice out of
the temple saying to the seven
angels, Go your ways, and pour out
the vials of the wrath of God upon
the earth. 2 And the first went, and
poured out his vial upon the earth;
and there fell a noisome and grievous
sore upon the men which had the
mark of the beast, and *upon* them
which worshipped his image. 3 And
the second angel poured out his vial
upon the sea; and it became as the
blood of a dead *man:* and every
living soul died in the sea. 4 And
the third angel poured out his vial
upon the rivers and fountains of
waters; and they became blood. 5
And I heard the angel of the waters
say, Thou art righteous, O Lord,
which art, and wast, and shalt be, because thou hast judged thus. 6 For
they have shed the blood of saints
and prophets, and thou hast given
them blood to drink; for they are
worthy. 7 And I heard another out
of the altar say, Even so, Lord God
Almighty, true and righteous *are* thy
judgments.

We had in the foregoing chapter the great and solemn preparation that was made for the pouring out of the vials; now we have the performance of that work. Here observe,

I. That, though every thing was made ready before, yet nothing was to be put in execution without an immediate positive order from God; and this he gave out of the temple, answering the prayers of his people, and avenging their quarrel.

II. No sooner was the word of command given than it was immediately obeyed; no delay, no objection made. We find that some of the best of men, as Moses and Jeremiah, did not so readily come in and comply with the call of God to their work; but the angels of God excel not only in strength, but in a readiness to do the will of God. God says, *Go your ways, and pour out the vials*, and immediately the work is begun. We are taught to pray that the will of God may be done on earth as it is done in heaven. And now we enter upon a series of very terrible dispensations of Providence, of which it is difficult to give the certain meaning or to make the particular application. But in the general it is worth our observation that,

1. We have here a reference and allusion to several of the plagues of Egypt, such as the turning of their waters into blood, and smiting them with boils and sores. Their sins were alike, and so were their punishments.

2. These vials have a plain reference to the seven trumpets, which represented the rise of antichrist; and we learn hence that the fall of the church's enemies shall bear some resemblance to their rise, and that God can bring them down in such ways as they chose to exalt themselves. And the fall of antichrist shall be gradual; as Rome was not built in one day, so neither shall it fall in one day, but it falls by degrees; it shall fall so as to rise no more.

3. The fall of the antichristian interest shall be universal. Every thing that any ways belonged to them, or could be serviceable to them, the premises and all their appurtenances, are put into the writ for destruction: their earth, their air, their sea, their rivers, their cities, all consigned over to ruin, all accursed for the sake of the wickedness of that people. Thus the creation groans and suffers through the sins of men. Now we proceed to,

(1.) The first angel who poured out his vial, *v.* 2. Observe, [1.] Where it fell—*upon the earth;* that is, say some, upon the common people; others upon the body of the Romish clergy, who were the basis of the papacy, and of an earthly spirit, all carrying on earthly designs. [2.] What it produced—*noisome and grievous sores on all who had the mark of the beast.* They had marked themselves by their sin; now God marks them out by his judgments. This sore, some think, signifies some of the first appearances of Providence against their state and interest, which gave them great uneasiness, as it discovered their inward distemper and was a token of further evil; the plague-tokens appeared.

(2.) *The second angel poured out his vial;* and here we see, [1.] Where it fell—*upon the sea;* that is, say some, upon the jurisdiction and dominion of the papacy; others upon the whole system of their religion, their false doctrines, their corrupt glosses, their superstitious rites, their idolatrous worship, their pardons, indulgences, a great conflux of wicked inventions and institutions, by which they maintain a trade and traffic advantageous to themselves, but injurious to all who deal with them. [2.] What it produced: It turned the sea into blood, *as the blood of a dead man, and every living soul died in the sea.* God discovered not only the vanity and falsehood of their religion, but the pernicious and deadly nature of it—that the souls of men were poisoned by that which was pretended to be the sure means of their salvation.

(3.) The next angel poured out his vial; and we are told, [1.] Where it fell—*upon the rivers, and upon the fountains of waters;* that is, say some very learned men, upon their emissaries, and especially the Jesuits, who, like streams, conveyed the venom and poison of their errors and idolatries from the spring-head through the earth. [2.] What effect it had upon them: *It turned them into blood;* some think it stirred up Christian princes to take a just revenge upon those that had been the great incendiaries of the world, and had occasioned the shedding of the blood of armies and of martyrs. The following doxology (*v.* 5, 6) favours this sense. The instrument that God makes use of in this work is here called *the angel of the waters,* who extols the righteousness of God in this retaliation: *They have shed the blood of thy saints, and thou hast given them blood to drink, for they are worthy,* to which another angel answered by full consent, *v.* 7.

8 And the fourth angel poured out
his vial upon the sun; and power was
given unto him to scorch men with
fire. 9 And men were scorched with
great heat, and blasphemed the name
of God, which hath power over these
plagues: and they repented not to
give him glory. 10 And the fifth
angel poured out his vial upon the
seat of the beast; and his kingdom
was full of darkness; and they gnawed
their tongues for pain, 11 And
blasphemed the God of heaven because of their pains and their sores,
and repented not of their deeds.

In these verses we see the work going on in the appointed order. The fourth angel poured out his vial, and that fell upon the sun; that is, say some, upon some eminent prince of the popish communion, who should renounce their false religion a little while before his utter downfal; and some expect it will be the German emperor. And now what will be the consequence of this? That sun which before cherished them with warm and benign influences shall now grow hot against these idolaters, and shall scorch them. Princes shall use their power and authority to suppress them, which yet will be so far from bringing them to repentance, that it will cause them to curse God and their king, and look upward, throwing out their blasphemous speeches against the God of heaven; they will be hardened to their ruin. The fifth angel poured out his vial, *v.* 10. And observe, 1. Where this fell—*upon the seat of the beast,* upon Rome itself, the mystical Babylon, the head of the antichristian empire. 2. What effect it had there: The whole kingdom of the beast *was full of darkness* and distress. That very city which was the seat of their policy, the source of all their learning, and all their knowledge, and all their pomp and pleasure, now becomes a source of darkness, and pain, and anguish. Darkness was one of the plagues of Egypt, and it is opposed to lustre and honour, and so forebodes the contempt and scorn to which the antichristian interest should be exposed. Darkness is opposed to wisdom and penetration, and forebodes the confusion and folly which the idolaters should discover at that time. It is opposed to pleasure and joy, and so signifies their anguish and vexation of spirit, when their calamities thus came upon them.

12 And the sixth angel poured out
his vial upon the great river Euphrates; and the water thereof was
dried up, that the way of the kings of
the east might be prepared. 13 And
I saw three unclean spirits like frogs
come out of the mouth of the dragon,
and out of the mouth of the beast,
and out of the mouth of the false
prophet. 14 For they are the spirits
of devils, working miracles, *which* go
forth unto the kings of the earth and
of the whole world, to gather them
to the battle of that great day of God
Almighty. 15 Behold, I come as a
thief. Blessed *is* he that watcheth,
and keepeth his garments, lest he
walk naked, and they see his shame.
16 And he gathered them together
into a place called in the Hebrew
tongue Armageddon.

The sixth angel poured out his vial; and observe,

I. Where it fell—*upon the great river Euphrates.* Some take it literally, for the place where the Turkish power and empire began; and they think this is a prophecy of the destruction of the Turkish monarchy and of idolatry, which they suppose will be effected about the same time with that of the papacy, as another antichrist, and that thereby a way shall be made for the conveniency of the Jews, those princes of the east. Others take it for the river Tiber; for, as Rome is mystical Babylon, Tiber is mystical Euphrates And when Rome shall be destroyed her river and merchandise must suffer with her.

II. What did this vial produce? 1. The drying up of the river, which furnished the city with wealth, provisions, and all sorts of accommodations. 2. A way is hereby prepared *for the kings of the east.* The idolatry of the church of Rome had been a great hindrance both to the conversion of the Jews, who have been long cured of their inclination to idols, and of the Gentiles, who are hardened in their idolatry by seeing that which so much symbolizes with it among those called Christians. It is therefore very probable that the downfal of popery, removing these obstructions, will open a way for both the Jews and other eastern nations to come into the church of Christ. And, if we suppose that Mahomedism shall fall at the same time, there will be still a more open communication between the western and eastern nations, which may facilitate the conversion of the Jews, and of *the fulness of the Gentiles.* And when this work of God appears, and is about to be accomplished, no wonder if it occasion another consequence, which is, 3. The last effort of the great dragon; he is resolved to have another push for it, that, if possible, he may retrieve the ruinous posture of his affairs in the world. He is now rallying his forces, recollecting all his spirits, to make one desperate sally before all be lost. This is occasioned by the pouring out of the sixth vial. Here observe, (1.) The instruments he makes use of to engage the powers of the earth in his cause and quarrel: *Three unclean spirits like frogs* come forth, one *out of the mouth of the dragon,* another *out of the mouth of the beast, and* a third *out of the mouth of the false prophet.* Hell, the secular power of antichrist, and the ecclesiastical power, would combine to send their several instruments, furnished with hellish malice, with worldly policy, and with religious falsehood and deceit; and these would muster up the devil's forces for a decisive battle. (2.) The means these instruments would use to engage the powers of earth in this war. They would work pretended miracles, the old stratagem of him *whose coming is after the working of Satan, with all power, and signs, and lying wonders, and with all deceivableness of unrighteousness,* 2 Thess. ii. 9, 10. Some think that a little before the fall of antichrist the popish pretence of power to work miracles will be revived and will very much amuse and deceive the world. (3.) The field of battle—a place called *Armageddon*; that is, say some, the mount of Megiddo, near to which, by a stream issuing thence, Barak overcame Sisera, and all the kings in alliance with him, Judges v. 19. And in the valley of Megiddo Josiah was slain. This place had been famous for two events of a very different nature, the former very happy for the church of God, the latter very unhappy; but it shall now be the field of the last battle in which the church shall be engaged, and she shall be victorious. This battle required time to prepare for it, and therefore the further account of it is suspended till we come to the nineteenth chapter, *v.* 19, 20. (4.) The warning which God gives of this great and decisive trial, to engage his people to prepare for it, *v.* 15. It would be sudden and unexpected, and therefore Christians should be clothed, and armed, and ready for it, that they might not be surprised and ashamed. When God's cause comes to be tried, and his battles to be fought, all his people shall be ready to stand up for his interest and be faithful and valiant in his service.

17 And the seventh angel poured
out his vial into the air; and there
came a great voice out of the temple
of heaven, from the throne, saying,
It is done. 18 And there were
voices, and thunders, and lightnings;
and there was a great earthquake,
such as was not since men were upon
the earth, so mighty an earthquake,
and so great. 19 And the great city
was divided into three parts, and the
cities of the nations fell: and great
Babylon came in remembrance before
God, to give unto her the cup of the
wine of the fierceness of his wrath.
20 And every island fled away, and
the mountains were not found. 21
And there fell upon men a great hail
out of heaven, *every stone* about the
weight of a talent: and men blasphemed God because of the plague
of the hail; for the plague thereof
was exceeding great.

Here we have an account of the seventh and last angel pouring forth his vial, contributing his part towards the accomplishment of the downfal of Babylon, which was the finishing stroke. And here, as before, observe,

I. Where this plague fell—*on the air,* upon the prince of the power of the air, that is, the devil. His powers were restrained, his policies confounded; he was bound in God's chain: the sword of God was upon his eye and upon his arm; for he, as well as the powers of the earth, is subject to the almighty power of God. He had used all possible means to preserve the antichristian interest, and to prevent the fall of Babylon—all the influence that he has upon the minds of men, blinding their judgments and perverting them, hardening their hearts, raising their enmity to the gospel as high as could be. But now here is a vial poured out upon his kingdom, and he is not able to support his tottering cause and interest any longer.

II. What it produced, 1. A thankful voice from heaven, pronouncing that now the work was done. The church triumphant in heaven saw it, and rejoiced; the church militant on earth saw it, and became triumphant. It is finished. 2. A mighty commotion on the earth—an earthquake, so great as never was before, shaking the very centre, and this ushered in by the usual concomitants of thunder and lightnings. 3. The fall of Babylon, which was divided into three parts, *called the cities of the nations* (*v.* 19); having had rule over the nations, and taken in the idolatry of the nations, incorporating into her religion something of the Jewish, something of the pagan, and something of the Christian religion, she was as three cities in one. God now remembered this great and wicked city. Though for some time he seemed to have forgotten her idolatry and cruelty, yet now he gives unto her *the cup of the wine of the fierceness of his wrath.* And this downfal extended further than to the seat of antichrist; it reached from the centre to the circumference; and every island and every mountain, that seemed by nature and situation the most secured, were carried away in the deluge of this ruin.

III. How the antichristian party were affected with it. Though it fell upon them as a dreadful storm, as if the stones of the city, tossed up into the air, came down upon their heads, like hailstones of a talent weight each, yet they were so far from repenting that they blasphemed that God who thus punished them. Here was a dreadful plague of the heart, a spiritual judgment more dreadful and destructive than all the rest. Observe, 1. The greatest calamities that can befal men will not bring them to repentance without the grace of God working with them. 2. Those that are not made better by the judgments of God are always the worse for them. 3. To be hardened in sin and enmity against God by his righteous judgments is a certain token of utter destruction.

CHAP. XVII.

This chapter contains another representation of those things that had been revealed before concerning the wickedness and ruin of antichrist. This antichrist had been before represented as a beast, and is now described as a great whore. And here, I. The apostle is invited to see this vile woman, ver. 1, 2. II. He tells us what an appearance she made, ver. 3—6. III. The mystery of it is explained to him, ver. 7—12. And, IV. Her ruin foretold, ver. 13, &c.

AND there came one of the seven angels which had the seven vials, and talked with me, saying unto me, Come hither; I will show unto thee the judgment of the great whore that sitteth upon many waters:
2 With whom the kings of the earth have committed fornication, and the inhabitants of the earth have been made drunk with the wine of her fornication.
3 So he carried me away in the spirit into the wilderness: and I saw a woman sit upon a scarlet coloured beast, full of names of blasphemy, having seven heads and ten horns.
4 And the woman was arrayed in purple and scarlet colour, and decked with gold and precious stones and pearls, having a golden cup in her hand full of abominations and filthiness of her fornication:
5 And upon her forehead *was* a name written, MYSTERY, BABYLON THE GREAT, THE MOTHER OF HARLOTS AND ABOMINATIONS OF THE EARTH.
6 And I saw the woman drunken with the blood of the saints, and with the blood of the martyrs of Jesus: and when I saw her, I wondered with great admiration.

Here we have a new vision, not as to the matter of it, for that is contemporary with what came under the three last vials; but as to the manner of description, &c. Observe, 1. The invitation given to the apostle to take a view of what was here to be represented: *Come hither, and I will show thee the judgment of the great whore,* &c., *v.* 1. This is a name of great infamy. A whore [in this passage] is one that is married, and has been false to her husband's bed, has forsaken the guide of her youth, and broken the covenant of God. She had been a prostitute to the kings of the earth, whom she had intoxicated *with the wine of her fornication.* 2. The appearance she made: it was gay and gaudy, like such sort of creatures: *She was arrayed in purple, and scarlet colour, and decked with gold, and precious stones, and pearls, v.* 4. Here were all the allurements of worldly honour and riches, pomp and pride, suited to sensual and worldly minds. 3. Her principal seat and residence—*upon the beast that had seven heads and ten horns;* that is to say, Rome, the city on seven hills, infamous for idolatry, tyranny, and blasphemy. 4. Her name, which *was written on her forehead.* It was the custom of impudent harlots to hang out signs, with their names, that all might know what they were. Now in this observe, (1.) She is named from her place of residence —*Babylon the great.* But, that we might not take it for the old Babylon literally so called, we are told there is a mystery in the name; it is some other great city resembling the old Babylon. (2.) She is named from her infamous way and practice; not only a harlot, but a mother of harlots, breeding up harlots, and nursing and training them up to idolatry, and all sorts of lewdness and wickedness—the parent and nurse of all false religion and filthy conversation. 5. Her diet: she satiated herself with *the blood of the saints and martyrs of Jesus.* She drank their blood with such greediness that she intoxicated herself with it; it was so pleasant to her that she could not tell when she had had enough of it: she was satiated, but never satisfied.

7 And the angel said unto me,
Wherefore didst thou marvel? I will
tell thee the mystery of the woman,
and of the beast that carrieth her,
which hath the seven heads and ten
horns. 8 The beast that thou sawest
was and is not; and shall ascend out
of the bottomless pit, and go into
perdition: and they that dwell on the
earth shall wonder, whose names
were not written in the book of life
from the foundation of the world,
when they behold the beast that was,
and is not, and yet is. 9 And here
is the mind which hath wisdom.
The seven heads are seven mountains,
on which the woman sitteth. 10 And
there are seven kings: five are fallen,
and one is, *and* the other is not yet
come; and when he cometh, he must
continue a short space. 11 And the
beast that was, and is not, even he is
the eighth, and is of the seven, and
goeth into perdition. 12 And the
ten horns which thou sawest are ten
kings, which have received no kingdom as yet; but receive power as
kings one hour with the beast. 13
These have one mind, and shall give
their power and strength unto the beast.

Here we have the mystery of this vision explained. The apostle wonders at the sight of this woman: the angel undertakes to open this vision to him, it being the key of the former visions; and he tells the apostle what was meant by the beast on which the woman sat; but it is so explained as still to need further explanation. 1. This beast *was, and is not, and yet is;* that is, it *was* a seat of idolatry and persecution; *and is not,* that is, not in the ancient form, which was pagan; *and yet it is,* it is truly the seat of idolatry and tyranny, though of another sort and form. *It ascends out of the bottomless pit* (idolatry and cruelty are the issue and product of hell), and it shall return thither and go into perdition. 2. *This beast has seven heads,* which have a double signification. (1.) *Seven mountains*—the seven hills on which Rome stands; and, (2.) *Seven kings*—seven sorts of government. Rome was governed by kings, consuls, tribunes, decemviri, dictators, emperors who were pagan, and emperors who were Christian. Five of these were extinct when this prophecy was written; one was then in being, that is, the pagan emperor; and the other, that is, the Christian emperor, was yet to come, *v.* 10. This beast, the papacy, makes an eighth governor, and sets up idolatry again. 3. This beast had ten horns; which are said to be *ten kings which have as yet received no kingdoms; as yet,* that is, as some, shall not rise up till the Roman empire be broken in pieces; or, as others, shall not rise up till near the end of antichrist's reign, and so shall reign but as it were *one hour with her,* but shall for that time be very unanimous and very zealous in that interest, and entirely devoted to it, divesting themselves of their prerogatives and revenues (things so dear to princes), out of an unaccountable fondness for the papacy.

14 These shall make war with the
Lamb, and the Lamb shall overcome
them: for he is Lord of lords, and
King of kings: and they that are
with him *are* called, and chosen, and
faithful. 15 And he saith unto me,
The waters which thou sawest, where
the whore sitteth, are peoples, and
multitudes, and nations, and tongues.
16 And the ten horns which thou
sawest upon the beast, these shall
hate the whore, and shall make her
desolate and naked, and shall eat her
flesh, and burn her with fire. 17 For
God hath put in their hearts to fulfil
his will, and to agree, and give their
kingdom unto the beast, until the
words of God shall be fulfilled. 18
And the woman which thou sawest is
that great city, which reigneth over
the kings of the earth.

Here we have some account of the downfal of Babylon, to be more fully described in the following chapter.

I. Here is a war begun between the beast and his followers, and the Lamb and his followers. The beast and his army, to an eye of sense, appear much stronger than the Lamb and his army: one would think an army with a lamb at the head of them could not stand before *the great red dragon.* But,

II. Here is a victory gained by the Lamb: *The Lamb shall overcome.* Christ must reign till all enemies *be put under his feet;* he will be sure to meet with many enemies, and much opposition, but he will also be sure to gain the victory.

III. Here is the ground or reason of the victory assigned; and this is taken, 1. From the character of the Lamb: *He is King of kings and Lord of lords.* He has, both by nature and by office, supreme dominion and power over all things; all the powers of earth and hell are subject to his check and control. 2. From the character of his followers: *They are called, and chosen, and faithful.* They are called out by commission to this warfare; they are chosen and fitted for it, and they will be faithful in it. Such an army, under such a commander, will at length carry all the world before them.

IV. The victory is justly aggrandised. 1. By the vast multitude who paid obedience and subjection to the beast and to the whore. She sat upon (that is, presided over) many waters; and these waters were so many multitudes of people, and nations, of all languages; yea, she reigned not only over kingdoms, but over the kings, and they were her tributaries and vassals, *v.* 15, 18. 2. By the powerful influence which God hereby showed he had over the minds of great men. Their hearts were in his hand, and he turned them as he pleased; for, (1.) It was of God, and to fulfil his will, that these kings *agreed to give their kingdom unto the beast;* they were judicially blinded and hardened to do so. And, (2.) It was of God that afterwards their hearts were turned against the whore, to hate her, and to *make her desolate and naked, and to eat her flesh, and burn her with fire;* they shall at length see their folly, and how they have been bewitched and enslaved by the papacy, and, out of a just resentment, shall not only fall off from Rome, but shall be made the instruments of God's providence in her destruction.

CHAP. XVIII.

We have here, I. An angel proclaiming the fall of Babylon, ver. 1, 2. II. Assigning the reasons of her fall, ver. 3. III. Giving warning to all who belonged to God to come out of her (ver. 4, 5), and to assist in her destruction, ver. 6—8. IV. The great lamentation made for her by those who had been large sharers in her sinful pleasures and profits, ver. 9—19. V. The great joy that there would be among others at the sight of her irrecoverable ruin, ver. 20, &c.

AND after these things I saw another angel come down from
heaven, having great power; and the
earth was lightened with his glory.
2 And he cried mightily with a strong
voice, saying, Babylon the great is
fallen, is fallen, and is become the
habitation of devils, and the hold of
every foul spirit, and a cage of every
unclean and hateful bird. 3 For all
nations have drunk of the wine of the
wrath of her fornication, and the
kings of the earth have committed
fornication with her, and the merchants of the earth are waxed rich
through the abundance of her delicacies. 4 And I heard another voice
from heaven, saying, Come out of her,
my people, that ye be not partakers
of her sins, and that ye receive not of
her plagues. 5 For her sins have
reached unto heaven, and God hath
remembered her iniquities. 6 Reward her even as she rewarded you,
and double unto her double according
to her works: in the cup which she
hath filled fill to her double. 7 How
much she hath glorified herself, and
lived deliciously, so much torment
and sorrow give her: for she saith in
her heart, I sit a queen, and am no
widow, and shall see no sorrow. 8
Therefore shall her plagues come in
one day, death, and mourning, and
famine; and she shall be utterly
burned with fire: for strong *is* the
Lord God who judgeth her.

The downfal and destruction of Babylon form an event so fully determined in the counsels of God, and of such consequence to his interests and glory, that the visions and predictions concerning it are repeated. 1. Here is another angel sent from heaven, attended with great power and lustre, *v.* 1. He had not only light in himself, to discern the truth of his own prediction, but to inform and enlighten the world about that great event; and not only light to discern it, but power to accomplish it. 2. This angel publishes the fall of Babylon, as a thing already come to pass; and this he does with a mighty strong voice, that all might hear the cry, and might see how well this angel was pleased to be the messenger of such tidings. Here seems to be an allusion to the prediction of the fall of pagan Babylon (Isa. xxi. 9), where the word is repeated as it is here: *has fallen, has fallen.* Some have thought a double fall is hereby intended, first her apostasy, and then her ruin; and they think the words immediately following favour their opinion. *She has become the habitation of devils, and the hold of every foul spirit, and the cage of every unclean and hateful bird, v.* 2. But this is also borrowed from Isa. xxi. 9, and seems to describe not so much her sin of entertaining idols (which are truly called *devils*) as her punishment, it being a common notion that unclean spirits, as well as ominous and hateful birds, used to haunt a city or house that lay in its ruins. 3. The reason of this ruin is declared (*v.* 3); for, though God is not obliged to give any account of his matters, yet he is pleased to do so, especially in those dispensations of providence that are most awful and tremendous. The wickedness of Babylon had been very great; for she had not only forsaken the true God herself, and set up idols, but had with great art and industry drawn all sorts of men into the spiritual adultery, and by her wealth and luxury had retained them in her interest. 4. Fair warning is given to all that expect mercy from God, that they should not only *come out of her,* but be assisting in her destruction, *v.* 4, 5. Here observe, (1.) God may have a people even in Babylon, some who belong to the election of grace. (2.) God's people shall be called out of Babylon, and called effectually. (3.) Those that are resolved to partake with wicked men in their sins must receive of their plagues. (4.) When the sins of a people reach up to heaven, the wrath of God will reach down to the earth. (5.) Though private revenge is forbidden, yet God will have his people act under him, when called to it, in pulling down his and their inveterate and implacable enemies, *v.* 6. (6.) God will proportion the punishment of sinners to the measure of their wickedness, pride, and security, *v.* 7. (7.) When destruction comes on a people suddenly, the surprise is a great aggravation of their misery, *v.* 8.

9 And the kings of the earth, who
have committed fornication and lived
deliciously with her, shall bewail her,
and lament for her, when they shall
see the smoke of her burning, 10
Standing afar off for the fear of her
torment, saying, Alas, alas that great
city Babylon, that mighty city! for
in one hour is thy judgment come.
11 And the merchants of the earth
shall weep and mourn over her; for
no man buyeth their merchandise any
more: 12 The merchandise of gold,
and silver, and precious stones, and
of pearls, and fine linen, and purple,
and silk, and scarlet, and all thyine
wood, and all manner vessels of ivory,
and all manner vessels of most precious wood, and of brass, and iron,
and marble, 13 And cinnamon, and
odours, and ointments, and frankin-
cense, and wine, and oil, and fine
flour, and wheat, and beasts, and
sheep, and horses, and chariots, and
slaves, and souls of men. 14 And
the fruits that thy soul lusted after
are departed from thee, and all things
which were dainty and goodly are
departed from thee, and thou shalt
find them no more at all. 15 The
merchants of these things, which
were made rich by her, shall stand
afar off for the fear of her torment,
weeping and wailing, 16 And saying, Alas, alas that great city, that
was clothed in fine linen, and purple,
and scarlet, and decked with gold,
and precious stones, and pearls! 17
For in one hour so great riches is
come to nought. And every ship-
master, and all the company in ships,
and sailors, and as many as trade by
sea, stood afar off, 18 And cried
when they saw the smoke of her
burning, saying, What *city* is like
unto this great city! 19 And they
cast dust on their heads, and cried,
weeping, and wailing, saying, Alas,
alas that great city, wherein were
made rich all that had ships in the
sea by reason of her costliness! for
in one hour is she made desolate.
20 Rejoice over her, *thou* heaven,
and *ye* holy apostles and prophets;
for God hath avenged you on her.
21 And a mighty angel took up a
stone like a great millstone, and cast
it into the sea, saying, Thus with
violence shall that great city Babylon
be thrown down, and shall be found
no more at all. 22 And the voice
of harpers and musicians, and of
pipers, and trumpeters, shall be heard
no more at all in thee; and no craftsman, of whatsoever craft *he be*, shall
be found any more in thee; and the
sound of a millstone shall be heard
no more at all in thee; 23 And the
light of a candle shall shine no more
at all in thee; and the voice of the
bridegroom and of the bride shall be
heard no more at all in thee: for thy
merchants were the great men of the
earth; for by thy sorceries were all
nations deceived. 24 And in her
was found the blood of prophets, and
of saints, and of all that were slain
upon the earth.

Here we have,

I. A doleful lamentation made by Babylon's friends for her fall; and here observe,

1. Who are the mourners, namely, those who had been bewitched by her fornication, those who had been sharers in her sensual pleasures, and those who had been gainers by her wealth and trade—the kings and the merchants of the earth: *the kings of the earth,* whom she had flattered into idolatry by allowing them to be arbitrary and tyrannical over their subjects, while they were obsequious to her; and *the merchants,* that is, those who trafficked with her for indulgences, pardons, dispensations, and preferments; these will mourn, because by *this craft they got their wealth.*

2. What was the manner of their mourning. (1.) They stood afar off, they durst not come nigh her. Even Babylon's friends will stand at a distance from her fall. Though they had been partakers with her in her sins, and in her sinful pleasures and profits, they were not willing to bear a share in her

plagues. (2.) They made a grievous outcry: *Alas! alas! that great city, Babylon, that mighty city!* (3.) They wept, and *cast dust upon their heads, v.* 19. The pleasures of sin are but for a season, and they will end in dismal sorrow. All those who rejoice in the success of the church's enemies will share with them in their downfal; and those who have most indulged themselves in pride and pleasure are the least able to bear calamities; their sorrows will be as excessive as their pleasure and jollity were before.

3. What was the cause of their mourning; not their sin, but their punishment. They did not lament their fall into idolatry, and luxury, and persecution, but their fall into ruin—the loss of their traffic and of their wealth and power. The spirit of antichrist is a worldly spirit, and their sorrow is a mere worldly sorrow; they did not lament for the anger of God, that had now fallen upon them, but for the loss of their outward comforts. We have a large schedule and inventory of the wealth and merchandise of this city, all which was suddenly lost (*v.* 12, 13), and lost irrecoverably (*v.* 14): *All things which were dainty and goodly have departed from thee, and thou shalt find them no more at all.* The church of God may fall for a time, but she shall rise again; but the fall of Babylon will be an utter overthrow, like that of Sodom and Gomorrah. Godly sorrow is some support under affliction, but mere worldly sorrow adds to the calamity.

II. An account of the joy and triumph there was both in heaven and earth at the irrecoverable fall of Babylon: while her own people were bewailing her, the servants of God were called to *rejoice over her, v.* 20. Here observe, 1. How universal this joy would be: heaven and earth, angels and saints, would join in it; that which is matter of rejoicing to the servants of God in this world is matter of rejoicing to the angels in heaven. 2. How just and reasonable; and that, (1.) Because the fall of Babylon was an act of God's vindictive justice. God was then avenging his people's cause. They had committed their cause to him *to whom vengeance belongs,* and now the year of recompence had come for the controversies of Zion; and, though they did not take pleasure in the miseries of any, yet they had reason to rejoice in the discoveries of the glorious justice of God. (2.) Because it was an irrecoverable ruin. This enemy should never molest them any more, and of this they were assured by a remarkable token (*v.* 21): An *angel* from heaven *took up a stone like a great millstone, and cast it into the sea, saying,* "*Thus shall Babylon be thrown down with violence, and be found no more at all;* the place shall be no longer habitable by man, no work shall be done there, no comfort enjoyed, no light seen there, but utter darkness and desolation, as the reward of her great wickedness, first in *deceiving the nations with her sorceries,* and secondly in destroying and murdering those whom she could not deceive," *v.* 24. Such abominable sins deserved so great a ruin.

CHAP. XIX.

In this chapter we have, I. A further account of the triumphant song of angels and saints for the fall of Babylon, ver. 1–4. II. The marriage between Christ and the church proclaimed and perfected, ver. 5—10. III. Another warlike expedition of the glorious head and husband of the church, with the success of it, ver. 10, &c.

AND after these things I heard a
great voice of much people in
heaven, saying, Alleluia; Salvation,
and glory, and honour, and power,
unto the Lord our God: 2 For true
and righteous *are* his judgments: for
he hath judged the great whore,
which did corrupt the earth with her
fornication, and hath avenged the
blood of his servants at her hand.
3 And again they said, Alleluia.
And her smoke rose up for ever and
ever. 4 And the four and twenty
elders and the four beasts fell down
and worshipped God that sat on the
throne, saying, Amen; Alleluia.

The fall of Babylon being fixed, finished, and declared to be irrecoverable in the foregoing chapter, this begins with a holy triumph over her, in pursuance of the order given forth: *Rejoice over her, thou heaven, and you holy apostles and prophets, ch.* xviii. 20. They now gladly answer the call; and here you have, 1. The form of their thanksgiving, in that heavenly and most comprehensive word, *Alleluia, praise you the Lord:* with this they begin, with this they go on, and with this they end (*v.* 4); their prayers are now turned into praises, their hosannas end in halleluias. 2. The matter of their thanksgiving: they praise him for the truth of his word, and the righteousness of his providential conduct, especially in this great event—the ruin of Babylon, which had been a mother, nurse, and nest of idolatry, lewdness, and cruelty (*v.* 2), for which signal example of divine justice they ascribe *salvation, and glory, and honour, and power, unto our God.* 3. The effect of these their praises: when the angels and saints cried *Alleluia,* her fire burned more fiercely and *her smoke ascended for ever and ever, v.* 3. The surest way to have our deliverances continued and completed is to give God the glory of what he has done for us. Praising God for what we have is praying in the most effectual manner for what is yet further to be done for us; the praises of the saints blow up the fire of God's wrath against the common enemy. 4. The blessed harmony between the angels and the saints in this triumphant song, *v.* 4. The churches and their ministers take the melodious sound from the angels, and repeat it; falling down, and worshipping God, they cry, *Amen, Alleluia.*

5 And a voice came out of the
throne, saying, Praise our God, all
ye his servants, and ye that fear him,
both small and great. 6 And I heard
as it were the voice of a great multitude, and as the voice of many
waters, and as the voice of mighty
thunderings, saying, Alleluia: for the
Lord God omnipotent reigneth. 7
Let us be glad and rejoice, and give
honour to him: for the marriage of
the Lamb is come, and his wife hath
made herself ready. 8 And to her
was granted that she should be
arrayed in fine linen, clean and white:
for the fine linen is the righteousness
of saints. 9 And he saith unto me,
Write, Blessed *are* they which are
called unto the marriage supper of the
Lamb. And he saith unto me, These
are the true sayings of God. 10 And
I fell at his feet to worship him. And
he said unto me, See *thou do it* not:
I am thy fellowservant, and of thy
brethren that have the testimony of
Jesus: worship God: for the testimony of Jesus is the spirit of prophecy.

The triumphant song being ended, an epithalamium, or marriage-song, begins, *v.* 6. Here observe,

I. The concert of heavenly music. The chorus was large and loud, *as the voice of many waters and of mighty thunderings.* God is fearful in praises. There is no discord in heaven; the morning stars sing together; no jarring string, nor key untuned, but pure and perfect melody.

II. The occasion of this song; and that is the reign and dominion of that omnipotent God who has *redeemed his church by his own blood,* and is now in a more public manner betrothing her to himself: *The marriage of the Lamb has come, v.* 7. Some think this refers to the conversion of the Jews, which they suppose will succeed the fall of Babylon; others, to the general resurrection: the former seems more probable. Now, 1. You have here a description of the bride, how she appeared; not in the gay and gaudy dress of the mother of harlots, but *in fine linen, clean and white,* which *is the righteousness of saints;* in the robes of Christ's righteousness, both imputed for justification and imparted for sanctification—the *stola,* the *white robe* of absolution, adoption, and enfranchisement, and the white robe of purity and universal holiness. She had *washed her robes and made them white in the blood of the Lamb;* and these her nuptial ornaments she did not purchase by any price of her own, but received them as the gift and grant of her blessed Lord. 2. The marriage-feast, which, though not particularly described (as Matt. xxii. 4), yet is declared to be such as would make all those happy who were called to it, so called as to accept the invitation, a feast made up of the promises of the gospel, *the true sayings of God, v.* 9. These promises, opened, applied, sealed, and earnested by *the Spirit of God,* in holy eucharistical ordinances, are the marriage-feast; and the whole collective body of all those who partake of this feast is the bride, *the Lamb's wife;* they eat into one body, and drink into one Spirit, and are not mere spectators or guests, but coalesce into the espoused party, the mystical body of Christ. 3. The transport of joy which the apostle felt in himself at this vision. *He fell down at the feet of the angel, to worship him,* supposing him to be more than a creature, or having his thoughts at the present overpowered by the vehemency of his affections. Here observe, (1.) What honour he offered to the angel: *He fell at his feet, to worship him;* this prostration was a part of external worship, it was a posture of proper adoration. (2.) How the angel refused it, and this was with some resentment: "*See thou do it not;* have a care what thou doest, thou art doing a wrong thing." (3.) He gave a very good reason for his refusal: "*I am thy fellow-servant, and of thy brethren which have the testimony of Jesus*—I am a creature, thine equal in office, though not in nature; *I,* as an angel and messenger of God, *have the testimony of Jesus,* a charge to be a witness for him and to testify concerning him, and thou, as an apostle, having *the Spirit of prophecy,* hast the same testimony to give in; and therefore we are in this brethren and fellow-servants." (4.) He directs him to the true and only object of religious worship; namely, God: "*Worship God,* and him alone." This fully condemns both the practice of the papists in worshipping the elements of bread and wine, and saints, and angels, and the practice of those Socinians and Arians who do not believe that Christ is truly and by nature God, and yet pay him religious worship; and this shows what wretched fig-leaves all their evasions and excuses are which they offer in their own vindication: they stand hereby convicted of idolatry by a messenger from heaven.

11 And I saw heaven opened, and
behold a white horse; and he that
sat upon him *was* called Faithful and
True, and in righteousness he doth
judge and make war. 12 His eyes
were as a flame of fire, and on his
head *were* many crowns; and he had
a name written, that no man knew,
but he himself. 13 And he *was*
clothed with a vesture dipped in

blood: and his name is called The
Word of God. 14 And the armies
which were in heaven followed him
upon white horses, clothed in fine
linen, white and clean. 15 And out
of his mouth goeth a sharp sword,
that with it he should smite the nations: and he shall rule them with a
rod of iron: and he treadeth the
winepress of the fierceness and wrath
of Almighty God. 16 And he hath
on *his* vesture and on his thigh a
name written, KING OF KINGS AND
LORD OF LORDS. 17 And I saw an
angel standing in the sun; and he
cried with a loud voice, saying to all
the fowls that fly in the midst of
heaven, Come and gather yourselves
together unto the supper of the great
God; 18 That ye may eat the flesh
of kings, and the flesh of captains,
and the flesh of mighty men, and the
flesh of horses, and of them that sit
on them, and the flesh of all *men*,
both free and bond, both small and
great. 19 And I saw the beast, and
the kings of the earth, and their
armies gathered together to make
war against him that sat on the
horse, and against his army. 20 And
the beast was taken, and with him
the false prophet that wrought miracles before him, with which he deceived them that had received the
mark of the beast, and them that
worshipped his image. These both
were cast alive into a lake of fire
burning with brimstone. 21 And
the remnant were slain with the
sword of him that sat upon the
horse, which *sword* proceeded out of
his mouth: and all the fowls were
filled with their flesh.

No sooner was the marriage solemnized between Christ and his church by the conversion of the Jews than the glorious head and husband of the church is called out to a new expedition, which seems to be the great battle that was to be fought at Armageddon, foretold *ch.* xvi. 16. And here observe,

I. The description of the great Commander, 1. By the seat of his empire; and that is *heaven;* his throne is there, and his power and authority are heavenly and divine. 2. His equipage: he is again described as sitting *on a white horse,* to show the equity of the cause, and certainty of success. 3. His attributes: he is *faithful and true* to his covenant and promise, he is righteous in all his judicial and military proceedings, he has a penetrating insight into all the strength and stratagems of his enemies, he has a large and extensive dominion, many crowns, for he is *King of kings, and Lord of lords.* 4. His armour; and that is *a vesture dipped in blood,* either his own blood, by which he purchased this mediatorial power, or the blood of his enemies, over whom he has always prevailed. 5. His name: *The Word of God,* a name that none fully knows but himself, only this we know, that this *Word was God manifest in the flesh;* but his perfections are incomprehensible by any creature.

II. The army which he commands (*v.* 14), a very large one, made up of many armies; angels and saints followed his conduct, and resembled him in their equipage, and in their armour of purity and righteousness—chosen, and called, and faithful.

III. The weapons of his warfare—*a sharp sword* proceeding from *his mouth* (*v.* 15), with which *he smites the nations,* either the threatenings of the written word, which now he is going to execute, or rather his word of command calling on his followers to take a just revenge on his and their enemies, who are now put into the wine-press of the wrath of God, to be trodden under foot by him.

IV. The ensigns of his authority, his coat of arms—*a name written on his vesture and thigh, King of kings, and Lord of lords,* asserting his authority and power, and the cause of the quarrel, *v.* 16.

V. An invitation given *to the fowls of heaven,* that they should come and see the battle, and share in the spoil and pillage of the field (*v.* 17, 18), intimating that this great decisive engagement should leave the enemies of the church a feast for the birds of prey, and that all the world should have cause to rejoice in the issue of it.

VI. The battle joined. The enemy falls on with great fury, headed by *the beast, and the kings of the earth;* the powers of earth and hell gathered, to make their utmost effort, *v.* 19.

VII. The victory gained by the great and glorious head of the church: *The beast and the false prophet,* the leaders of the army, are taken prisoners, both he who led them by power and he who led them by policy and falsehood; these are taken and *cast into the burning lake,* made incapable of molesting the church of God any more; and their followers, whether officers or common soldiers, are given up to military execution, and made a feast for *the fowls of heaven.* Though the divine vengeance will chiefly fall upon *the beast, and the false prophet,* yet it will be no excuse to those who fight under their banner that they only followed their leaders and obeyed their command; since they would fight for them, they must fall and perish with them. *Be wise now therefore, O you kings, be instructed, you rulers of the earth; kiss the Son, lest he be angry, and you perish from the way,* Ps. ii. 10, 12.

CHAP. XX.

This chapter is thought by some to be the darkest part of all this prophecy: it is very probable that the things contained in it are not yet accomplished; and therefore it is the wiser way to content ourselves with general observations, rather than to be positive and particular in our explications of it. Here we have an account, I. Of the binding of Satan for a thousand years, ver. 1—3. II. The reign of the saints with Christ for the same time, ver. 4—6. III. Of the loosing of Satan, and the conflict of the church with Gog and Magog, ver. 7—10. IV. Of the day of judgment, ver. 11, &c.

AND I saw an angel come down
from heaven, having the key of
the bottomless pit and a great chain
in his hand. 2 And he laid hold on
the dragon, that old serpent, which is
the Devil, and Satan, and bound him
a thousand years, 3 And cast him
into the bottomless pit, and shut him
up, and set a seal upon him, that he
should deceive the nations no more,
till the thousand years should be fulfilled: and after that he must be
loosed a little season. 4 And I saw
thrones, and they sat upon them, and
judgment was given unto them: and
I saw the souls of them that were
beheaded for the witness of Jesus,
and for the word of God, and which
had not worshipped the beast, neither
his image, neither had received *his*
mark upon their foreheads, or in their
hands; and they lived and reigned
with Christ a thousand years. 5 But
the rest of the dead lived not again
until the thousand years were finished.
This *is* the first resurrection. 6
Blessed and holy *is* he that hath part
in the first resurrection: on such the
second death hath no power, but
they shall be priests of God and of
Christ, and shall reign with him a
thousand years. 7 And when the
thousand years are expired, Satan
shall be loosed out of his prison, 8
And shall go out to deceive the nations which are in the four quarters
of the earth, Gog and Magog, to
gather them together to battle: the
number of whom *is* as the sand of
the sea. 9 And they went up on
the breadth of the earth, and compassed the camp of the saints about,
and the beloved city: and fire came
down from God out of heaven, and
devoured them. 10 And the devil
that deceived them was cast into the
lake of fire and brimstone, where the
beast and the false prophet *are*, and
shall be tormented day and night for
ever and ever.

We have here, I. A prophecy of *the binding of Satan* for a certain term of time, in which he should have much less power and the church much more peace than before. The power of Satan was broken in part by the setting up of the gospel kingdom in the world; it was further reduced by the empire's becoming Christian; it was yet further broken by the downfal of the mystical Babylon; but still this serpent had many heads, and, when one is wounded, another has life remaining in it. Here we have a further limitation and diminution of his power. Observe, 1. To whom this work of binding Satan is committed—to *an angel from heaven.* It is very probable that this angel is no other than the Lord Jesus Christ; the description of him will hardly agree with any other. He is one who has power to *bind the strong man armed, to cast him out, and to spoil his goods;* and therefore must be stronger than he. 2. The means he makes use of in this work: he has a *chain* and a *key, a great chain* to bind Satan, and *the key of the* prison in which he was to be confined. Christ never wants proper powers and instruments to break the power of Satan, for he has the powers of heaven and the keys of hell. 3. The execution of this work, *v.* 2, 3. (1.) *He laid hold on the dragon, that old serpent, which is the devil, and Satan.* Neither the strength of the dragon, nor the subtlety of the serpent, was sufficient to rescue him out of the hands of Christ; he caught hold, and kept his hold. And, (2.) He *cast him into the bottomless pit,* cast him down with force, and with a just vengeance, to his own place and prison, from which he had been permitted to break out, and disturb the churches, and deceive the nations; now he is brought back to that prison, and there laid in chains. (3.) He is *shut up, and a seal set upon him.* Christ shuts, and none can open; he shuts by his power, seals by his authority; and his lock and seal even the devils themselves cannot break open. (4.) We have the term of this confinement of Satan—*a thousand years,* after which he was to *be loosed* again for *a little season.* The church should have a considerable time of peace and prosperity, but all her trials were not yet over.

II. An account of the reign of the saints for the same space of time in which Satan continued bound (*v.* 4—6), and here observe,

1. Who those were that received such honour—those who had suffered for Christ, and all who had faithfully adhered to him, not receiving the mark of the beast, nor worshipping his image; all who had kept themselves clear of pagan and papal idolatry.

2. The honour bestowed upon them. (1.) They were raised from the dead, and restored

to life. This may be taken either literally or figuratively; they were in a civil and political sense dead, and had a political resurrection; their liberties and privileges were revived and restored. (2.) *Thrones,* and power of *judgment, were given to them;* they were possessed of great honour, and interest, and authority, I suppose rather of a spiritual than of a secular nature. (3.) *They reigned with Christ a thousand years.* Those who suffer with Christ shall reign with Christ; they shall reign with him in his spiritual and heavenly kingdom, in a glorious conformity to him in wisdom, righteousness, and holiness, beyond what had been known before in the world. This is called *the first resurrection,* which none but those who have served Christ and suffered for him shall be favoured with. As for the wicked, they shall not be raised up and restored to their power again, till Satan be let loose; this may be called a resurrection, as the conversion of the Jews is said to be *life from the dead.*

3. The happiness of these servants of God is declared. (1.) They are *blessed and holy, v.* 6. None can be blessed but those that are holy; and all that are holy shall be blessed. These were holy as a sort of first-fruits to God in this spiritual resurrection, and as such blessed by him. (2.) They are secured from the power of the second death. We know something of what the first death is, and it is awful; but we know not what this second death is. It must be much more dreadful; it is the death of the soul, eternal separation from God. The Lord grant we may never know what it is by experience. Those who have had experience of a spiritual resurrection are saved from the power of the second death.

III. An account of the return of the church's troubles, and another mighty conflict, very sharp, but short and decisive. Observe, 1. The restraints laid for a long time on Satan are at length taken off. While this world lasts, Satan's power in it will not be wholly destroyed; it may be limited and lessened, but he will have something still to do for the disturbance of the people of God. 2. No sooner is Satan let loose than he falls to his old work, *deceiving the nations,* and so stirring them up to make a war with the saints and servants of God, which they would never do if he had not first deceived them. They are deceived both as to the cause they engage in (they believe it to be a good cause when it is indeed a very bad one), and as to the issue: they expect to be successful, but are sure to lose the day. 3. His last efforts seem to be the greatest. The power now permitted to him seems to be more unlimited than before. He had now liberty to beat up for his volunteers in all *the four quarters of the earth,* and he raised a mighty army, the number of which was *as the sand of the sea, v.* 8. 4. We have the names of the principal commanders in this army under the dragon—*Gog and Magog.* We need not be too inquisitive as to what particular powers are meant by these names, since the army was gathered from all parts of the world. These names are found in other parts of scripture. *Magog* we read of in Gen. x. 2. He was one of the sons of Japheth, and peopled the country called *Syria,* from which his descendants spread into many other parts. Of *Gog and Magog* together we only read in Ezek. xxxviii. 2, a prophecy whence this in the Revelation borrows many of its images. 5. We have the march and military disposition of this formidable army (*v.* 9): *They went up on the breadth of the earth, and compassed the camp of the saints about, and the beloved city,* that is, the spiritual Jerusalem, in which the most precious interests of the people of God are lodged, and therefore to them a beloved city. The army of the saints is described as drawn forth out of the city, and lying under the walls of it, to defend it; they were encamped about Jerusalem: but the army of the enemy was so much superior to that of the church that they compassed them and their city about. 6. You have an account of the battle, and the issue of this war: *Fire came down from God out of heaven, and devoured the enemy.* Thus the ruin of *Gog and Magog* is foretold (Ezek. xxxviii. 22), *I will rain upon him and upon his bands an overflowing rain, and great hailstones, and fire and brimstone.* God would, in an extraordinary and more immediate manner, fight this last and decisive battle for his people, that the victory might be complete and the glory redound to himself. 7. The doom and punishment of the grand enemy, *the devil:* he is now cast into hell, with his two great officers, *the beast and the false prophet,* tyranny and idolatry, and that not for any term of time, but to be there *tormented night and day, for ever and ever.*

11 And I saw a great white throne,
and him that sat on it, from whose
face the earth and the heaven fled
away; and there was found no place
for them. 12 And I saw the dead,
small and great, stand before God;
and the books were opened: and
another book was opened, which is
the book of life: and the dead were
judged out of those things which were
written in the books, according to
their works. 13 And the sea gave
up the dead which were in it; and
death and hell delivered up the dead
which were in them: and they were
judged every man according to their
works. 14 And death and hell were
cast into the lake of fire. This is the
second death. 15 And whosoever
was not found written in the book of
life was cast into the lake of fire.

The utter destruction of the devil's kingdom very properly leads to an account of the day of judgment, which will determine every man's everlasting state; and we may be assured there will be a judgment when we see *the prince of this world is judged,* John xvi. 11. This will be a great day, *the great day, when all shall appear before the judgment-seat of Christ.* The Lord help us firmly to believe this doctrine of the judgment to come. It is a doctrine that made Felix tremble. Here we have a description of it, where observe, 1. We behold *the throne,* and tribunal of judgment, *great* and *white,* very glorious and perfectly just and righteous. *The throne of iniquity, that establishes wickedness by a law,* has no fellowship with this righteous throne and tribunal. 2. The appearance of the Judge, and that is the Lord Jesus Christ, who then puts on such majesty and terror that *the earth and the heaven flee from his face, and there is no place found for them;* there is a dissolution of the whole frame of nature, 2 Pet. iii. 10. 3. The persons to be judged (*v.* 12): *The dead, small and great;* that is, young and old, low and high, poor and rich. None are so mean but they have some talents to account for, and none so great as to avoid the jurisdiction of this court; not only those that are found alive at the coming of Christ, but all who have died before; the grave shall surrender the bodies of men, hell shall surrender the souls of the wicked, the sea shall surrender the many who seemed to have been lost in it. All these are the king's prisons, and he will cause them to set forth their prisoners. 4. The rule of judgment settled: *The books were opened.* What books? The book of God's omniscience, who is greater than our consciences, and knows all things (there is a book of remembrance with him both for good and bad); and the book of the sinner's conscience, which, though formerly secret, will now be opened. *And another book* shall be *opened*—the book of the scriptures, the statute-book of heaven, the rule of life. This book is opened as containing the law, the touchstone by which the hearts and lives of men are to be tried. This book determines matter of right; the other books give evidence of matters of fact. Some, by *the other book,* called *the book of life,* understand the book of God's eternal counsels; but that does not seem to belong to the affair of judgment: in eternal election God does not act judicially, but with absolute sovereign freedom. 5. The cause to be tried; and that is, *the works of men,* what they have done and whether it be good or evil. *By their works men shall be justified or condemned;* for though God knows their state and their principles, and looks chiefly at these, yet, being to approve himself to angels and men as a righteous God, he will try their principles by their practices, and so will *be justified when he speaks and clear when he judges.* 6. The issue of the trial and judgment; and this will be according to the evidence of fact, and rule of judgment. All those who have *made a covenant with death,* and an *agreement with hell,* shall then be condemned with their infernal confederates, cast with them into the lake of fire, as not being entitled to eternal life, according to the rules of life laid down in the scripture; but those whose names are written in that book (that is, those that are justified and acquitted by the gospel) shall then be justified and acquitted by the Judge, and shall enter into eternal life, having nothing more to fear from death, or hell, or wicked men; for these are all destroyed together. Let it be our great concern to see on what terms we stand with our Bibles, whether they justify us or condemn us now; for the Judge of all will proceed by that rule. *Christ shall judge the secrets of all men according to the gospel.* Happy are those who have so ordered and stated their cause according to the gospel as to know beforehand that they shall be justified in the great day of the Lord!

CHAP. XXI.

Hitherto the prophecy of this book has presented to us a very remarkable mixture of light and shade, prosperity and adversity, mercy and judgment, in the conduct of divine Providence towards the church in the world: now, at the close of all, the day breaks, and the shadows flee away; a new world now appears, the former having passed away. Some are willing to understand all that is said in these last two chapters of the state of the church even here on earth, in the glory of the latter days; but others, more probably, take it as a representation of the perfect and triumphant state of the church in heaven. Let but the faithful saints and servants of God wait awhile, and they shall not only see, but enjoy, the perfect holiness and happiness of that world. In this chapter you have, I. An introduction to the vision of the new Jerusalem, ver. 1—9. II. The vision itself, ver. 10, &c.

AND I saw a new heaven and a
new earth: for the first heaven
and the first earth were passed away;
and there was no more sea. 2 And
I John saw the holy city, new Jerusalem, coming down from God out of
heaven, prepared as a bride adorned
for her husband. 3 And I heard a
great voice out of heaven saying,
Behold, the tabernacle of God *is*
with men, and he will dwell with
them, and they shall be his people,
and God himself shall be with them,
and be their God. 4 And God shall
wipe away all tears from their eyes;
and there shall be no more death,
neither sorrow, nor crying, neither
shall there be any more pain: for the
former things are passed away. 5
And he that sat upon the throne said,
Behold, I make all things new. And
he said unto me, Write: for these
words are true and faithful. 6 And
he said unto me, It is done. I am
Alpha and Omega, the beginning and
the end. I will give unto him that is
athirst of the fountain of the water

of life freely. 7 He that overcometh
shall inherit all things; and I will be
his God, and he shall be my son. 8
But the fearful and unbelieving, and
the abominable, and murderers, and whoremongers, and sorcerers, and idolaters, and all liars, shall have their part in the lake which burneth with fire and brimstone: which is the second death.

We have here a more general account of the happiness of the church of God in the future state, by which it seems most safe to understand the heavenly state.

I. A new world now opens to our view (*v.* 1): *I saw a new heaven and a new earth;* that is, a new universe; for we suppose the world to be made up of heaven and earth. By the new earth we may understand a new state for the bodies of men, as well as a heaven for their souls. This world is not now newly created, but newly opened, and filled with all those who were the heirs of it. The new heaven and the new earth will not then be distinct; the very earth of the saints, their glorified bodies, will now be spiritual and heavenly, and suited to those pure and bright mansions. To make way for the commencement of this new world, the old world, with all its troubles and commotions, *passed away.*

II. In this new world the apostle *saw the holy city, the new Jerusalem, coming down from heaven,* not locally, but as to its original: this new Jerusalem is the church of God in its new and perfect state, *prepared as a bride adorned for her husband,* beautified with all perfection of wisdom and holiness, meet for the full fruition of the Lord Jesus Christ in glory.

III. The blessed presence of God with his people is here proclaimed and admired: *I heard a great voice out of heaven, saying, Behold, the tabernacle of God is with men,* &c., *v.* 3. Observe, 1. The presence of God with his church is the glory of the church. 2. It is matter of wonder that a holy God should ever dwell with any of the children of men. 3. The presence of God with his people in heaven will not be interrupted as it is on earth, but he will dwell with them continually. 4. The covenant, interest, and relation, that there are now between God and his people, will be filled up and perfected in heaven. *They shall be his people;* their souls shall be assimilated to him, filled with all the love, honour, and delight in God which their relation to him requires, and this will constitute their perfect holiness; and he will be their God: *God himself will be their God;* his immediate presence with them, his love fully manifested to them, and his glory put upon them, will be their perfect happiness; then he will fully answer the character of the relation on his part, as they shall do on their part.

IV. This new and blessed state will be free from all trouble and sorrow; for, 1. All the effects of former trouble shall be done away. They have been often before in tears, by reason of sin, of affliction, of the calamities of the church; but now *all tears shall be wiped away;* no signs, no remembrance of former sorrows shall remain, any further than to make their present felicity the greater. God himself, as their tender Father, with his own kind hand, *shall wipe away the tears* of his children; and they would not have been without those tears when God shall come and wipe them away. 2. All the causes of future sorrow shall be for ever removed: *There shall be neither death nor pain;* and therefore *no sorrow nor crying;* these are things incident to that state in which they were before, but now all *former things have passed away.*

V. The truth and certainty of this blessed state are ratified by the word and promise of God, and ordered to be committed to writing, as matter of perpetual record, *v.* 5, 6. The subject-matter of this vision is so great, and of such great importance to the church and people of God, that they have need of the fullest assurances of it; and God therefore from heaven repeats and ratifies the truth thereof. Besides, many ages must pass between the time when this vision was given forth and the accomplishment of it, and many great trials must intervene; and therefore God would have it committed to writing, for perpetual memory, and continual use to his people. Observe, 1. The certainty of the promise averred: *These words are faithful and true;* and it follows, *It is done,* is as sure as if it were done already. We may and ought to take God's promise as present payment; if he has said that he *makes all things new, it is done.* 2. He gives us his titles of honour as a pledge or surety of the full performance, even those titles of *Alpha and Omega, the beginning and the end.* As it was his glory that he gave the rise and beginning to the world and to his church, it will be his glory to finish the work begun, and not to leave it imperfect. As his power and will were the first cause of all things, his pleasure and glory are the last end, and he will not lose his design; for then he would no longer be the *Alpha and Omega.* Men may begin designs which they can never bring to perfection; but *the counsel of God shall stand,* and he will do all his pleasure. 3. The desires of his people towards this blessed state furnish another evidence of the truth and certainty of it. They thirst after a state of sinless perfection and the uninterrupted enjoyment of God, and God has wrought in them these longing desires, which cannot be satisfied with any thing else, and therefore would be the torment of the soul if they were disappointed; but it would be inconsistent with the goodness of God, and his love to his people, to create in them holy and heavenly desires, and then deny them their proper satisfaction; and therefore they may be assured that, when they have overcome their present difficulties, *he will give them of the fountain of the water of life freely.*

VI. The greatness of this future felicity is declared and illustrated, 1. By the freeness of it—it is the free gift of God: *He gives of the water of life freely;* this will not make it less but more grateful to his people. 2. The fulness of it. The people of God then lie at the fountain-head of all blessedness: they *inherit all things* (*v.* 7); enjoying God, they enjoy all things. He is all in all. 3. By the tenure and title by which they enjoy this blessedness—by right of inheritance, as *the sons of God,* a title of all others the most honourable, as resulting from so near and endeared a relation to God himself, and the most sure and indefeasible, that can no more cease than the relation from which it results. 4. By the vastly different state of the wicked. Their misery helps to illustrate the glory and blessedness of the saints, and the distinguishing goodness of God towards them, *v.* 8. Here observe, (1.) The sins of those who perish, among which are first mentioned their cowardliness and unbelief. *The fearful* lead the van in this black list. They durst not encounter the difficulties of religion, and their slavish fear proceeded from their unbelief; but those who were so dastardly as not to dare to take up the cross of Christ, and discharge their duty to him, were yet so desperate as to run into all manner of abominable wickedness—*murder, adultery, sorcery, idolatry,* and *lying.* (2.) Their punishment: *They have their part in the lake that burns with fire and brimstone, which is the second death.* [1.] They could not burn at a stake for Christ, but they must burn in hell for sin. [2.] They must die another death after their natural death; the agonies and terrors of the first death will consign them over to the far greater terrors and agonies of eternal death, to die and to be always dying. [3.] This misery will be their proper part and portion, what they have justly deserved, what they have in effect chosen, and what they have prepared themselves for by their sins. Thus the misery of the damned will illustrate the blessedness of those that are saved, and the blessedness of the saved will aggravate the misery of those that are damned.

9 And there came unto me one of
the seven angels which had the
seven vials full of the seven last
plagues, and talked with me, saying,
Come hither, I will show thee the
bride, the Lamb's wife. 10 And he
carried me away in the spirit to a
great and high mountain, and showed
me that great city, the holy Jerusalem,
descending out of heaven from
God, 11 Having the glory of God:
and her light *was* like unto a stone
most precious, even like a jasper stone,
clear as crystal; 12 And had a wall
great and high, *and* had twelve gates,
and at the gates twelve angels, and
names written thereon, which are
the names of the twelve tribes of the
children of Israel: 13 On the east
three gates; on the north three gates;
on the south three gates; and on the
west three gates. 14 And the wall
of the city had twelve foundations,
and in them the names of the twelve
apostles of the Lamb. 15 And he
that talked with me had a golden
reed to measure the city, and the
gates thereof, and the walls thereof.
16 And the city lieth foursquare, and
the length is as large as the breadth:
and he measured the city with the
reed, twelve thousand furlongs. The
length and the breadth and the
height of it are equal. 17 And he
measured the wall thereof, a hundred
and forty *and* four cubits, *according
to* the measure of a man, that is, of
the angel. 18 And the building of
the wall of it was *of* jasper: and the
city *was* pure gold, like unto clear
glass. 19 And the foundations of
the wall of the city *were* garnished
with all manner of precious stones.
The first foundation *was* jasper; the
second, sapphire; the third, a chalcedony;
the fourth, an emerald; 20
The fifth, sardonyx; the sixth, sardius;
the seventh, chrysolyte; the
eighth, beryl; the ninth, a topaz; the
tenth, a chrysoprasus; the eleventh,
a jacinth; the twelfth, an amethyst.
21 And the twelve gates *were* twelve
pearls; every several gate was of one
pearl: and the street of the city *was*
pure gold, as it were transparent glass.
22 And I saw no temple therein:
for the Lord God Almighty and the
Lamb are the temple of it. 23 And
the city had no need of the sun,
neither of the moon, to shine in it: for
the glory of God did lighten it, and
the Lamb *is* the light thereof. 24
And the nations of them which are
saved shall walk in the light of it:
and the kings of the earth do bring

their glory and honour into it. 25
And the gates of it shall not be shut
at all by day: for there shall be no
night there. 26 And they shall bring
the glory and honour of the nations
into it. 27 And there shall in no wise
enter into it any thing that defileth,
neither *whatsoever* worketh abomination, or *maketh* a lie: but they which
are written in the Lamb's book of life.

We have already considered the introduction to the vision of the new Jerusalem in a more general idea of the heavenly state; we now come to the vision itself, where observe,

I. The person that opened the vision to the apostle—*one of the seven angels, that had the seven vials full of the seven last plagues, v.* 9. God has a variety of work and employment for his holy angels. Sometimes they are to sound the trumpet of divine Providence, and give fair warning to a careless world; sometimes they are to pour out the vials of God's anger upon impenitent sinners; and sometimes to discover things of a heavenly nature to those that are *the heirs of salvation.* They readily execute every commission they receive from God; and, when this world shall be at an end, yet the angels shall be employed by the great God in proper pleasant work to all eternity.

II. The place from which the apostle had this glorious view and prospect. He was taken, in ecstasy, into *a high mountain.* From such situations men usually have the most distinct views of adjacent cities. Those who would have clear views of heaven must get as near heaven as they can, into the mount of vision, the mount of meditation and faith, whence, as from the top of Pisgah, they may behold the goodly land of the heavenly Canaan.

III. The subject-matter of the vision—*the bride, the Lamb's wife* (*v.* 10); that is, the church of God in her glorious, perfect, triumphant state, under the resemblance of Jerusalem, having the glory of God shining in its lustre, as *uxor splendit radiis mariti—the bride comely through the comeliness put on her by her husband;* glorious in her relation to Christ, in his image now perfected in her, and in his favour shining upon her. And now we have a large description of the church triumphant under the emblem of a city, far exceeding in riches and splendour all the cities of this world; and this new Jerusalem is here represented to us both in the exterior and the interior part of it.

1. The exterior part of the city—*the wall* and *the gates,* the wall for security and the gates for entrance.

(1.) The wall for security. Heaven is a safe state; those that are there are enclosed with a wall, that separates them and secures them from all evils and enemies: now here, in the account of the wall, we observe, [1.] The height of it, which, we are told, is very high, *seventy yards* (*v.* 17), sufficient both for ornament and security. [2.] The matter of it: *It was as jasper;* a wall all built of the most precious stones, for firmness and lustre, *v.* 11. This city has a wall that is impregnable as well as precious. [3.] The form of it was very regular and uniform: *It was four-square, the length as large as the breadth.* In the new Jerusalem all shall be equal in purity and perfection. There shall be an absolute uniformity in the church triumphant, a thing wanted and wished for on earth, but not tô be expected till we come to heaven. [4.] The measure of the wall (*v.* 15, 16): *Twelve thousand furlongs* each way, each side, which is forty-eight thousand furlongs in the whole compass, or fifteen hundred German miles. Here is room sufficient for all the people of God—*many mansions in their Father's house.* [5.] The foundation of the wall, for heaven is a city that hath her foundations (*v.* 19); the promise and power of God, and the purchase of Christ, are the strong foundations of the church's safety and happiness. The foundations are described by their number and by their matter; by their number—*twelve,* alluding to the twelve apostles (*v.* 14), whose gospel doctrines are the foundations upon which the church is built, *Christ himself being the chief corner-stone;* and, as to the matter of these foundations, it was various and precious, set forth by twelve sorts of precious stones, denoting the variety and excellency of the doctrines of the gospel, or of the graces of the Holy Spirit, or the personal excellencies of the Lord Jesus Christ.

(2.) The gates for entrance. Heaven is not inaccessible; there is a way opened into the holiest of all; there is a free admission to all those that are sanctified; they shall not find themselves shut out. Now, as to these gates, observe, [1.] Their number—*twelve gates,* answering to the twelve tribes of Israel. All the true Israel of God shall have entrance into the new Jerusalem, as every tribe had into the earthly Jerusalem. [2.] Their guards which were placed upon them—*twelve angels,* to admit and receive the several tribes of the spiritual Israel and to keep out others. [3.] The inscription on the gates—*the names of the twelve tribes,* to show that they have a right to the tree of life, and to enter through the gates into the city. [4.] The situation of the gates. As the city had four equal sides, answering to the four quarters of the world, east, west, north, and south, so on each side there were three gates, signifying that from all quarters of the earth there shall be some who shall get safely to heaven and be received there, and that there is as free entrance from one part of the world as from the other; *for in Christ there is neither Jew nor Greek, Barbarian, Scythian, bond, nor free.* Men of all nations, and languages, who believe on Christ, have by him access to God in grace here and in glory hereafter. [5.] The materials of these gates—they were all of pearls, and yet with great variety: *Every gate one pearl,* either one single pearl of that vast bigness, or one single sort of pearl. Christ is the pearl of great price, and he is our way to God. There is nothing magnificent enough in this world fully to set forth the glory of heaven. Could we, in the glass of a strong imagination, contemplate such a city as is here described, even as to the exterior part of it, such a wall, and such gates, how amazing, how glorious, would the prospect be! And yet this is but a faint and dim representation of what heaven is in itself.

2. The interior part of the new Jerusalem, *v.* 22—27. We have seen its strong wall, and stately gates, and glorious guards; now we are to be led through the gates into the city itself; and the first thing which we observe there is the street of the city, *which is of pure gold, like transparent glass, v.* 21. The saints in heaven tread upon gold. The new Jerusalem has its several streets. There is the most exact order in heaven: every saint has his proper mansion. There is converse in heaven: the saints are then at rest, but it is not a mere passive rest; it is not a state of sleep and inactivity, but a state of delightful motion: *The nations that are saved walk in the light of it.* They walk with Christ in white. They have communicn not only with God, but with one another; and all their steps are firm and clean. They are pure and clear *as gold and transparent glass.* Observe,

(1.) The temple of the new Jerusalem, which was no material temple, made with men's hands, as that of Solomon and Zerubbabel, but a temple altogether spiritual and divine; *for the Lord God Almighty, and the Lamb, are the temple thereof.* There the saints are above the need of ordinances, which were the means of their preparation for heaven. When the end is attained the means are no longer useful. Perfect and immediate communion with God will more than supply the place of gospel institutions.

(2.) The light of this city. Where there is no light, there can be no lustre nor pleasure. Heaven is *the inheritance of the saints in light.* But what is that light? There is no sun nor moon shining there, *v.* 23. Light is sweet, and a pleasant thing it is to behold the sun. What a dismal world would this be if it were not for the light of the sun! What is there in heaven that supplies the want of it? There is no want of the light of the sun, *for the glory of God lightens that city, and the Lamb is the light thereof.* God in Christ will be an everlasting fountain of knowledge and joy to the saints in heaven; and, if so, there is no need of the sun or moon, any more than we here need to set up candles at noon day, when the sun shineth in its strength.

(3.) The inhabitants of this city. They are described here several ways. [1.] By their numbers—whole nations of saved souls; some out of all nations, and many out of some nations. All those multitudes who were sealed on earth are saved in heaven. [2.] By their dignity—some of the kings and princes of the earth: great kings. God will have some of all ranks and degrees of men to fill the heavenly mansions, high and low; and when the greatest kings come to heaven they will see all their former honour and glory swallowed up of this heavenly glory that so much excels. [3.] Their continual accession and entrance into this city: *The gates shall never be shut.* There is no night, and therefore no need of shutting up the gates. Some one or other is coming in every hour and moment, and those that are sanctified always find the gates open; they have *an abundant entrance into the kingdom.*

(4.) The accommodations of this city: All the *glory and honour of the nations shall be brought into it.* Whatever is excellent and valuable in this world shall be there enjoyed in a more refined kind, and to a far greater degree—brighter crowns, a better and more enduring substance, more sweet and satisfying feasts, a more glorious attendance, a truer sense of honour and far higher posts of honour, a more glorious temper of mind, and a form and a countenance more glorious than ever were known in this world.

(5.) The unmixed purity of all who belong to the new Jerusalem, *v.* 27. [1.] There the saints shall have no impure thing remaining in them. In the article of death they shall be cleansed from every thing that is of a defiling nature. Now they feel a sad mixture of corruption with their graces, which hinders them in the service of God, interrupts their communion with him, and intercepts the light of his countenance; but, at their entrance into the holy of holies, they are washed in the laver of Christ's blood, and presented to the Father without spot. [2.] There the saints shall have no impure persons admitted among them. In the earthly Jerusalem there will be a mixed communion, after all the care that can be taken. Some roots of bitterness will spring up to trouble and defile Christian societies; but in the new Jerusalem there is a society perfectly pure *First,* Free from such as are openly profane. There are none admitted into heaven who work abominations. In the churches on earth sometimes abominable things are done, solemn ordinances profaned and prostituted to men openly vicious, for worldly ends; but no such abominations can have place in heaven. *Secondly,* Free from hypocrites, such as make lies, say they are Jews, and are not, but do lie. These will creep into the churches of Christ on earth, and may lie concealed there a long time, perhaps all their days; but they cannot intrude into the new Jerusalem, which is wholly reserved for those that are called, and chosen, and faithful, who are all written, not only in the register of the visible church, *but in the Lamb's book of life.*

CHAP. XXII.

In this chapter we have, I. A further description of the heavenly state of the church, ver. 1—5. II. A confirmation of this and all the other visions of this book, ver. 6—19. III. The conclusion, ver. 20, 21.

AND he showed me a pure river
of water of life, clear as crystal,
proceeding out of the throne of God
and of the Lamb. 2 In the midst
of the street of it, and on either side
of the river, *was there* the tree of
life, which bare twelve *manner of*
fruits, *and* yielded her fruit every
month: and the leaves of the tree
were for the healing of the nations.
3 And there shall be no more curse:
but the throne of God and of the
Lamb shall be in it; and his servants
shall serve him: 4 And they shall
see his face; and his name *shall be* in
their foreheads. 5 And there shall
be no night there; and they need no
candle, neither light of the sun; for
the Lord God giveth them light: and
they shall reign for ever and ever.

The heavenly state which was before described as a city, and called the new Jerusalem, is here described as a paradise, alluding to the earthly paradise which was lost by the sin of the first Adam; here is another paradise restored by the second Adam. A paradise in a city, or a whole city in a paradise! In the first paradise there were only two persons to behold the beauty and taste the pleasures of it; but in this second paradise whole cities and nations shall find abundant delight and satisfaction. And here observe,

I. The river of paradise. The earthly paradise was well watered: no place can be pleasant or fruitful that is not so. This river is described, 1. By its fountain-head—*the throne of God and the Lamb.* All our springs of grace, comfort, and glory, are in God; and all our streams from him are through the mediation of the Lamb. 2. By its quality—*pure and clear as crystal.* All the streams of earthly comfort are muddy; but these are clear, salutary, and refreshing, giving life, and preserving life, to those who drink of them.

II. The tree of life, in this paradise. Such a tree there was in the earthly paradise, Gen. ii. 9. This far excels it. And now, as to this tree, observe, 1. The situation of it—*in the midst of the street, and on either side the river;* or, as it might have been better rendered, *in the midst between the terrace-walk and the river.* This tree of life is fed by the pure waters of the river that comes from the throne of God. The presence and perfections of God furnish out all the glory and blessedness of heaven. 2. The fruitfulness of this tree. (1.) It brings forth many sorts of fruit—*twelve sorts,* suited to the refined taste of all the saints. (2.) It brings forth fruit at all times—*yields its fruit every month.* This tree is never empty, never barren; there is always fruit upon it. In heaven there is not only a variety of pure and satisfying pleasures, but a continuance of them, and always fresh. (3.) The fruit is not only pleasant, but wholesome. The presence of God in heaven is the health and happiness of the saints; there they find in him a remedy for all their former maladies, and are preserved by him in the most healthful and vigorous state.

III. The perfect freedom of this paradise from every thing that is evil (*v.* 3): *There shall be no more curse; no accursed one—καταναθεμα,* no serpent there, as there was in the earthly paradise. Here is the great excellency of this paradise. The devil has nothing to do there; he cannot draw the saints from serving God to be subject to himself, as he did our first parents, nor can he so much as disturb them in the service of God.

IV. The supreme felicity of this paradisaical state. 1. There the saints shall see the face of God; there they shall enjoy the beatific vision. 2. God will own them, as having his seal and name on their foreheads. 3. *They shall reign with him for ever;* their service shall be not only freedom but honour and dominion. 4. All this shall be with perfect knowledge and joy. They shall be full of wisdom and comfort, continually walking in the light of the Lord; and this not for a time, *but for ever and ever.*

6 And he said unto me, These
sayings *are* faithful and true: and the
Lord God of the holy prophets sent
his angel to show unto his servants
the things which must shortly be
done. 7 Behold, I come quickly:
blessed *is* he that keepeth the sayings
of the prophecy of this book. 8 And
I John saw these things, and heard
them. And when I had heard and
seen, I fell down to worship before
the feet of the angel which showed
me these things. 9 Then saith he
unto me, See *thou do it* not: for I
am thy fellowservant, and of thy
brethren the prophets, and of them
which keep the sayings of this book:
worship God. 10 And he saith unto
me, Seal not the sayings of the prophecy of this book: for the time is at
hand. 11 He that is unjust, let him
be unjust still: and he which is filthy,
let him be filthy still: and he that is

righteous, let him be righteous still:
and he that is holy, let him be holy
still. 12 And, behold, I come quickly;
and my reward *is* with me, to give
every man according as his work shall
be. 13 I am Alpha and Omega, the
beginning and the end, the first and
the last. 14 Blessed *are* they that
do his commandments, that they may
have right to the tree of life, and may
enter in through the gates into the
city. 15 For without *are* dogs, and
sorcerers, and whoremongers, and
murderers, and idolaters, and whosoever loveth and maketh a lie. 16 I
Jesus have sent mine angel to testify
unto you these things in the churches.
I am the root and the offspring of
David, *and* the bright and morning
star. 17 And the Spirit and the
bride say, Come. And let him that
heareth say, Come. And let him
that is athirst come. And whosoever
will, let him take the water of life
freely. 18 For I testify unto every
man that heareth the words of the
prophecy of this book, If any man
shall add unto these things, God shall
add unto him the plagues that are
written in this book: 19 And if any
man shall take away from the words
of the book of this prophecy, God
shall take away his part out of the
book of life, and out of the holy city,
and *from* the things which are written
in this book.

We have here a solemn ratification of the contents of this book, and particularly of this last vision (though some think it may not only refer to the whole book, but to the whole New Testament, yea, to the whole Bible, completing and confirming the canon of scripture); and here, 1. This is confirmed by the name and nature of that God who gave out these discoveries: he is *the Lord God, faithful and true,* and so are all his sayings. 2. By the messengers he chose, to reveal these things to the world; the holy angels showed them to holy men of God; and God would not employ his saints and angels in deceiving the world. 3. They will soon be confirmed by their accomplishment: they are things that must shortly be done; Christ will make haste, *he will come quickly,* and put all things out of doubt; and then those will prove the wise and happy men who have believed and kept his words. 4. By the integrity of that angel who had been the apostle's guide and interpreter in these visions; this integrity was such that he not only refused to accept religious adoration from John, but once and again reproved him for it. He who was so tender of the honour of God, and so displeased with what was a wrong to God, would never come in his name to lead the people of God into mere dreams and delusions; and it is a still further confirmation of the sincerity of this apostle that he confesses his own sin and folly, into which he had now again relapsed, and he leaves this his failing on perpetual record: this shows he was a faithful and an impartial writer. 5. By the order given to leave the book of the prophecy open, to be perused by all, that they might labour to understand it, that they might make their objections against it, and compare the prophecy with the events. God here deals freely and openly with all; he does not speak in secret, but calls every one to witness to the declarations here made, *v.* 10. 6. By the effect this book, thus kept open, will have upon men; those that are filthy and unjust will take occasion thence to be more so, but it will confirm, strengthen, and further sanctify those that are upright with God; it will be a savour of life to some and of death to others, and so will appear to be from God, *v.* 12. 7. It will be Christ's rule of judgment at the great day; he will dispense rewards and punishments to men according as their works agree or disagree with the word of God; and therefore that word itself must needs be faithful and true. 8. It is the word of him who is the author, finisher, and rewarder of the faith and holiness of his people, *v.* 13, 14. He is *the first and the last,* and the same from first to last, and so is his word too; and he will by this word give to his people, who conform themselves to it, *a right to the tree of life,* and an entrance into heaven; and this will be a full confirmation of the truth and authority of his word, since it contains the title and evidence of that confirmed state of holiness and happiness that remains for his people in heaven. 9. It is a book that condemns and excludes from heaven all wicked, unrighteous persons, and particularly *those that love and make lies* (*v.* 15), and therefore can never be itself a lie. 10. It is confirmed by *the testimony of Jesus, which is the Spirit of prophecy.* And this Jesus, as God, is *the root of David,* though, as man, his offspring—a person in whom all uncreated and created excellencies meet, too great and too good to deceive his churches and the world. He is the fountain of all light, the *bright and the morning star,* and as such has given to his churches this morning light of prophecy, to assure them of the light of that perfect day which is approaching. 11. It is confirmed by an open and general invitation to all to come and partake of the promises and privileges of the gospel, those streams of the water of life; these are tendered to all who feel in their souls a thirst which nothing in this world can quench. 12. It is confirmed by the joint testimony of the Spirit of God, and that gracious Spirit that is in all the true members of the church of God; *the Spirit and the bride* join in testifying the truth and excellency of the gospel. 13. It is confirmed by a most solemn sanction, condemning and cursing all who should dare to corrupt or change the word of God, either by adding to it or taking from it, *v.* 18, 19. He that adds to the word of God draws down upon himself *all the plagues written in this book;* and he who takes any thing away from it cuts himself off from all the promises and privileges of it. This sanction is like a flaming sword, to guard the canon of the scripture from profane hands. Such a fence as this God set about the law (Deut. iv. 2), and the whole Old Testament (Mal. iv. 4), and now in the most solemn manner about the whole Bible, assuring us that it is a book of the most sacred nature, divine authority, and of the last importance, and therefore the peculiar care of the great God.

20 He which testifieth these things saith, Surely I come quickly; Amen. Even so, come, Lord Jesus. 21 The grace of our Lord Jesus Christ *be* with you all. Amen.

We have now come to the conclusion of the whole, and that in three things:—

I. Christ's farewell to his church. He seems now, after he has been discovering these things to his people on earth, to take leave of them, and return to heaven; but he parts with them in great kindness, and assures them it shall not be long before he comes again to them: *Behold, I come quickly.* As when he ascended into heaven, after his resurrection, he parted with a promise of his gracious presence, so here he parts with a promise of a speedy return. If any say, "Where is the promise of his coming, when so many ages have passed since this was written?" let them know he is not slack to his people, but long-suffering to his enemies: his coming will be sooner than they are aware, sooner than they are prepared, sooner than they desire; and to his people it will be seasonable. The vision is for an appointed time, and will not tarry. *He will come quickly;* let this word be always sounding in our ear, and let us give all diligence that we may be found of him in peace, *without spot and blameless.*

II. The church's hearty echo to Christ's promise, 1. Declaring her firm belief of it: *Amen, so it is,* so it shall be. 2. Expressing her earnest desire of it: *Even so, come, Lord Jesus; make haste, my beloved, and be thou like a roe, or like a young hart on the mountains of spices.* Thus beats the pulse of the church, thus breathes that gracious Spirit which actuates and informs the mystical body of Christ; and we should never be satisfied till we find such a spirit breathing in us, and causing us to *look for the blessed hope, and glorious appearance of the great God and our Saviour Jesus Christ.* This is the language of the church of the first-born, and we should join with them, often putting ourselves in mind of his promise. What comes from heaven in a promise should be sent back to heaven in a prayer, "*Come, Lord Jesus,* put an end to this state of sin, sorrow, and temptation; gather thy people out of this present evil world, and take them up to heaven, that state of perfect purity, peace, and joy, and so finish thy great design, and fulfil all that word in which thou hast caused thy people to hope."

III. The apostolical benediction, which closes the whole: *The grace of our Lord Jesus Christ be with you all, Amen.* Here observe, 1. The Bible ends with a clear proof of the Godhead of Christ, since the Spirit of God teaches the apostle to bless his people in the name of Christ, and to beg from Christ a blessing for them, which is a proper act of adoration. 2. Nothing should be more desired by us than that the grace of Christ may be with us in this world, to prepare us for the glory of Christ in the other world. It is by his grace that we must be kept in a joyful expectation of his glory, fitted for it, and preserved to it; and his glorious appearance will be welcome and joyful to those that are partakers of his grace and favour here; and therefore to this most comprehensive prayer we should all add our hearty *Amen,* most earnestly thirsting after greater measures of the gracious influences of the blessed Jesus in our souls, and his gracious presence with us, till glory has perfected all his grace towards us, for he is a sun and a shield, *he gives grace and glory, and no good thing will he withhold from those that walk uprightly.*